Variety's
FILM
REVIEWS

Contents

OF THE TWENTY-VOLUME SET

VARIETY'S®
FILM
REVIEWS
1987-1988

VOLUME 20

R.R. Bowker

Volume 20, 1987-1988 of Variety Film Reviews
was prepared by R.R. Bowker's Database Publishing Division

Peter Simon, Vice President, Database Publishing Group
Albert Simmonds, Editorial Director, Bibliographies

Doreen Gravesande, Senior Managing Editor
George Tibbetts, Senior Editor
Gene Gold, Senior Associate Editor

Published by R. R. Bowker, a division of Reed Publishing (USA) Inc.
121 Chanlon Road, New Providence, NJ 07974

Volume Twenty, 1987-1988

PRINTED AND BOUND IN THE UNITED STATES OF AMERICA

Library of Congress Serial Data

Variety Film Reviews, 1987-1988
    Volume 20

ISBN 0-8352-2667-0

Manufactured in the United States of America

ISBN 0 - 8352 - 2667 - 0

90000

9 780835 226677

Preface

The reviews contained in this volume are complete and comprehensive reproductions of the original reviews printed in *Variety*. Only full-length feature films are included. Short subjects and made for television films are not included.

User's Guide

The reviews in this collection are published in chronological order, by the date on which the original review appeared. The date of each issue appears at the top of the column where the reviews for that issue begin. The reviews continue through that column and all following columns, until a new date appears at the top of the page. Where blank spaces occur at the end of a column, this indicates the end of that particular week's reviews. An index to film titles for the years 1987-1988 is published in this volume.

1987

Superfantozzi
(ITALIAN-COLOR)

A Medusa release of a Scena Film production, in association with Reteitalia. Produced by Augusto Caminito. Directed by Neri Parenti. Stars Paolo Villaggio. Screenplay, Leo Benvenuti, Piero De Bernardi, Alessandro Bencivenni, Domenico Saverni, Villaggio Parenti; camera (Eastmancolor by Cinecittà, Cristiano Pogany) music, Fred Bongusto. Reviewed at Reale Cinema, Rome, Jan. 2, 1987. Running time: **85 MINS.**
Ugo Fantozzi . . . . .Paolo Villaggio
Pina . . . . .Liù Bosisio
Mariangela . . . . .Fernando Plinio
Adam, etc. . . . . .Luc Merenda
Eve, etc . . . . .Eva Lena

Rome — Paolo Villaggio is one of Italy's genuinely talented screen comedians. His immortal invention is office clerk Ugo Fantozzi, the underdog's underdog, seen here in his seventh feature. Alas, even great characters run out of steam, and Fantozzi saw his day a while ago. "Superfantozzi," helmed by Villaggio's faithful director Neri Parenti, is a ghost of his best work, with precious few moments of the filmic sophistication and social cutting edge that has made Fantozzi a household word in Italy. Nonetheless, Christmas b.o. has been good around the country.

Pic's gimmick is to show various incarnations of Fantozzi through the ages, from the Garden of Eden to the Space Age. In each skit, naturally, he, homely wife Pina (Liù Bosisio) and their monstrous daughter Mariangela (limned by a boy, Fernando Plinio) get history's short end of the stick.

Opening skit is perhaps the best, pitting Fantozzi and Pina (God's original mistake) against the beautiful couple (Luc Merenda and Eva Lena) that got made on a second try.

On the sacrilegous side, Fantozzi finds himself on the losing end even when he crosses paths with Jesus (when the Lord calls the little children to him, Fantozzi's hard-grown garden gets trampled; Fantozzi thinks he's rich when his uncle dies — but it turns out to be Lazarus, etc.). The Beautiful People reappear as his perennial historical antagonists, French aristocrats who refuse to be guillotined, Jazz Age boozers who get Fantozzi arrested for celebrating his new cold-water flat with a drop of wine, and even the ruling class of the 21st century.

Though pic is jumpy and uneven, there are still some funny bits and Villaggio's humiliated little man is a treat of comic gestuality. His cartoon-like resilience and indestructibility makes him easy for kids to like. Supporting cast is fine, technical credits okay. —*Yung.*

7 Chili in 7 Giorni
(15 Pounds In 7 Days)
(ITALIAN-COLOR)

A Columbia Pictures release of a C.G. Silver Film production. Produced by Mario and Vittorio Cecchi Gori. Directed by Luca Verdone. Stars Carlo Verdone, Renato Pozzetto. Camera (Technicolor), Danilo Desideri; editor, Antonio Siciliano; music, Pino Donaggio. Reviewed at Adriano Cinema, Rome, Jan. 1, 1987. Running time: **112 MINS.**
Alfio Tamburini . . . . .Carlo Verdone
Silvano Barocchi . . . . .Renato Pozzetto
Snob . . . . .Tiziana Pini

Rome — Christmas leader at the Italo b.o. is "15 Pounds In 7 Days," marking the feature debut of young tv helmer Luca Verdone. Director's brother Carlo and costar Renato Pozzetto, a pair of likeable, plump comedians, are the secret of pic's success, as self-styled dietologists who run a shady health farm. Routine and unsophisticated by any standard, pic is strictly local entertainment.

Unemployed med school grads Alfio (Carlo Verdone) and Silvano (Pozzetto) convince Alfio's wife to set them up on a diet farm outside Rome. A tv ad brings the first score of fatties into their clutches, including a boxer, an opera singer, a teenage brat, a shapely snob (Tiziana Pini). The first day's unsuccessful diet leads to a mass stomach pumping operation; thereafter, the heavyweights get nothing but imaginary psycho-dinners and a few olives to eat. Amid Alfio's family crises and Silvano's bedding the pretty blond, the diet farm falls to pieces, but rises again triumphantly at pic's end as "The Two Gluttons" country trattoria.

Thesps don't have much scope in the confines of a story like this, but they are unquestionably the best thing about a pic that strains after gags that are heavier than its cast. Verdone brings some anxious humanity to his character (he thinks he's killed a former patient, and the role of diet quack weighs heavily on him). Pozzetto is likeably cool and collected, whatever his misdeeds. Rest of cast, though undistinguished, will be easily identified with by anyone who's ever struggled to resist a plate of lasagna.

Technical work on this very clean, family comedy is adequate.
— *Yung.*

Thanatos
(MEXICAN-COLOR)

A Peliculas Mexicanas release of a Gecisa Intl. production. Produced by Maria Luisa Medina Pulido, Cristian González, Pla Ana Corti. Directed by Cristian González. Stars Nuria Bages. Screenplay, González, Juan Carlos Martin; camera (color), J.C. Martin; editor, Sigfrido García Muñoz; music, Edgar Sosa Corona. Reviewed at Havana Film Festival, Dec. 9, 1986. Running time: **92 MINS.**
Alejandra . . . . .Nuria Bages
Viches . . . .Ricardo Sánchez de la Barquera
Norma . . . . .Gabriela Araujo
Captain . . . . .Alejandro Rábago

Havana — The Mexican pic "Thanatos" is an unsuccessful effort by director Cristian González to make a low-budget fanciful art film. It was produced for participation in Mexico's III Experimental Film Competition.

Although it strives to be a modern retelling of the Faust legend, it emerges as a pretentious and sometimes kinky tale centering on the mysteries of life and death.

The story, told through a confused jumble of short conflicting scenes, concerns the fate of a tv personality when fired because of a sharp decline in his ratings. His destiny crosses with that of Alejandra (Nuria Bages), a brooding beauty capable of vague supernatural powers.

Eventually our tv personality makes a deal with a moustachioed devil in an effort to regain his lost prestige through a series of awkwardly staged illusions involving Alejandra in various bondage routines in an attempt to harness her and her powers.

Pic's title "Thanatos" refers to the Greek god of death, who comes at the end to claim his due. But a god of death has managed to keep a finger on the entire production and any boxoffice potential will be lost by the film's slow pace and confused narrative time.

The film tries to use atmosphere and visual tone to cover up for the lack of special effects demanded by the script, which comes off awkward and unbelievable. There is an overemphasis placed on the collage of brash and striking images, explained by the fact that the script was coauthored by cameraman Juan Carlos Martin. Yet these images alone fail as a narrative device.

"Thanatos" is an immature work and shows the director's inability to work with abstraction. Perhaps its failures will guide González in future films. —*Lent.*

The Bedroom Window
(COLOR)

Interesting suspense film promises more than it delivers.

A De Laurentiis Entertainment Group release and production. Executive producer, Robert Towne. Produced by Martha Schumacher. Written and directed by Curtis Hanson. Stars Steve Guttenberg, Elizabeth McGovern, Isabelle Huppert. Camera (J-D-C Widescreen, color), Gil Taylor; editor, Scott Conrad; music, Michael Shrieve, Patrick Gleeson; sound, Bill Daly; art direction, Rafael Caro; costume design, Clifford Capone; stunt coordinator, Thomas Rosales. Reviewed at Broadway screening room, N.Y., Dec. 10, 1986. (MPAA Rating: R.) Running time: **112 MINS.**
Terry . . . . .Steve Guttenberg
Denise . . . . .Elizabeth McGovern
Sylvia . . . . .Isabelle Huppert
Colin Wentworth . . . . .Paul Shenar
Det. Jessop . . . . .Frederick Coffin
Det. Quirk . . . . .Carl Lumbly
Defense attorney . . . . .Wallace Shawn
Henderson . . . . .Brad Greenquist

"The Bedroom Window" is a thriller with an interesting premise and competent execution but lacking that pzazz which made its Alfred Hitchcock models such enduring hits. Credit filmmaker Curtis Hanson with avoiding the urge to directly ape the master but overall pic is less than riveting entertainment.

Cast against type, Steve Guttenberg plays a malleable young executive carrying on an affair with his boss' wife, the sexy Sylvia (Isabelle Huppert). During a tryst at Guttenberg's apartment one night after a party, Huppert, looking out his bedroom window, sees a girl (Elizabeth McGovern) being assaulted outside. Fearing complications with her husband, Huppert does not come forward as a witness, but civic-minded Guttenberg agrees to help the police, pretending that he witnessed the assault. He's coached by Huppert on details of what she saw and what the suspect looked like.

Because of inconsistencies in his story and some guilty-seeming behavior, Guttenberg ultimately becomes a suspect in the rash of rape and murder cases, forcing him in the Hitchcock tradition to begin his own investigation in trying to prove who the real killer is. Of course, Guttenberg eventually becomes involved with McGovern, even using her as a willing decoy to trap the killer.

Hanson's screenplay involves several ingenious plot twists, notably a courtroom hearing in which the defense attorney (Wallace Shawn, surprisingly cast in a noncomedy role) totally destroys Guttenberg's credibility as a witness, allowing the killer to go free. Structurally, Huppert carries the first half of the film, replaced by McGovern in importance in the final reels and both actresses are alluring and mysterious in keeping the piece suspenseful. The killer's identity is revealed very early on, but Guttenberg's behavior and too-good-to-be-true image help to keep the viewer guessing concerning his own possible involvement in wrongdoing. Unfortunately, a lot of coincidences and just plain stupid actions by Guttenberg are relied upon to keep the pot boiling.

Tech credits are impressive, though there is one repeated gaffe, as the building name where Guttenberg works is misspelled "Wentworth Developement Corporation" onscreen consistently.—*Lor.*

On a volé Charlie Spencer!
(Charlie Spencer's Been Robbed!)
(FRENCH-COLOR)

An AAA release of a Pacific prod./Sélena Audiovisuel/Films A2 coproduction. Produced by Patricia and Pierre Novat. Written, directed by and starring Francis Huster. Camera (Eastmancolor), Daniel Vogel; editor, Nicole Berckmans; sound, Harrik Maury; art director, Hervé Boutard; costumes, Evelyne Correard; makeup, Eric Muller; technical advisor, Nina Companeez; production manager, Dominique Rigaux. Reviewed at the Gaumont Ambassade cinema, Paris, Dec. 26, 1986. Running time: **96 MINS.**

Bank employee . . . . Francis Huster
Movie star . . . . Béatrice Dalle
Suzette . . . . Isabelle Nanty
  Also with: Jacques Spiesser, Jean-Pierre Aumont, Anne Lasmezas, Emmanuelle Devos, Antoine Dulery, Elisabeth Rodriguez, Eric Wapler, Christian Zanetti, Monique Melinand.

Paris — Filmmaking has become so self-referential that some pictures tend to resemble movie quizzes rather than films — all that's missing is a response buzzer for the audience. In this gratuitous buff mold is "On a volé Charlie Spencer!" writing-helming debut of French legit and screen actor Francis Huster, who also stars.

It's a trite Walter Mitty fantasy so rife with film quotations, winks and nods (beginning with the title, an homage to Charlie Chaplin) that whatever point or poignancy Huster aims for is lost in the crush. In style and content, Huster's film ranges far and wide through movieland myth and lore, with generous borrowings of Hitchcock, Cocteau and other textbook giants.

The actor-director even salutes himself as drama teacher in an over-extended valentine to the claustrophic realm of 1930s French "poetic realism," during which he casts a good part of his Parisian thesping school in paraphrases of scenes from Marcel Carné's "Hotel du Nord" and other such classics. Veteran Jean-Pierre Aumont slums here by replaying his part of the suicidal lover in "Hotel du Nord."

Pic is as short on story and character development as it is long on demonstrating how filmwise Huster is. He has the benefit of working with a first-rate tech crew which furnishes the necessary gloss, but his own style is limited to grabbag mummery. Dialog strains sententiously after epigrammatic pith.

Huster plays a cowered bank clerk who's fallen in love with a banal blond whom he's gotten pregnant but is reluctant to marry. He takes refuge in his imagination casting himself in a movie in which, resuming his real-life social role, he becomes an outlaw in company of a femme fatale who has robbed his bank.

Just to keep reference up to date, the sultry "star" of his mental movie is Béatrice Dalle, hot off the celebrity press of Jean-Jacques Beineix' "Betty Blue."

Huster's own affected performance, which has earned him both praise and criticism locally, is apt here but unempathetic. Dalle pouts and stares at the camera without great effort. Only newcomer Isabelle Nanty, as Huster's drab girl friend, manages at moments to touch a genuine human chord.

— *Len.*

Wisdom
(COLOR)

Dreary tale of a rebel without a cause.

A 20th Century Fox release of a Gladden Entertainment presentation. Executive producer, Robert E. Wise. Producer, Bernard Williams. Written and directed by Emilio Estevez. Stars Estevez, Demi Moore. Camera (Deluxe color), Adam Greenberg; editor, Michael Kahn; music, Danny Elfman; production designer, Dennis Gassner; art director, Dins Danielson; set decorator, Richard Hoover; sound (Dolby), Richard Portman, Thomas Gerard; costumes, Jonathan Kinsey; assistant director, Bernard Williams; casting, Penny Perry. Reviewed at 20th Century Fox studios, L.A., Dec. 30, 1986. (MPAA Rating: R.) Running time: **109 MINS.**

Karen Simmons . . . . Demi Moore
John Wisdom . . . . Emilio Estevez
Lloyd Wisdom . . . . Tom Skerritt
Samantha Wisdom . . . Vernoica Cartwright
Williamson . . . . William Allen Young

Hollywood — "Wisdom" marks 23-year-old actor Emilio Estevez' directorial debut — and it shows. Filmmaker's naiveté is evident from a completely implausible script and unending sophomoric dialog that even the young star's winsomeness can't make bearable. B.o. prospects look dismal.

Estevez plays an essentially good kid named John Wisdom, a misnomer, who took one wrong turn as a youth and ended up with a felony mark on his record.

For the first hour of the film, he drones on and on about how the system has done him wrong and how he's really a good, hardworking guy who just needs a break.

Except for his adoring girlfriend, played by Demi Moore, Estevez has a hard time getting understanding from anyone, including his blank-faced parents (Tom Skerritt, Veronica Cartwright) and potential employers. It appears he has virtually no friends.

Frustrated that he's a "criminal without a crime," he gets it in his head to be an outlaw but one that will help people, not hurt them — sort of a Robin Hood, '80's style.

His idea: save the American Dream for farmers, homeowners and others who are having a hard time preventing foreclosure on their properties, by holding up banks and blowing up all the mortgage records. The goal: "to temporarily screw up the system."

This is hardly the kind of compelling material upon which to build an interesting drama.

Estevez is totally unconvincing playing both a moral citizen and conscience-of-the-country out to do right by the simple man and an Uzi-brandishing, self-styled commando on a rampage through America's heartland.

Not only do he and dutiful Moore elude the FBI through five states, but they manage to win friends and influence the media with nearly every turn on the road.

He becomes the Rebel Without A Cause, the anti-hero with his anti-heroine supporting him all the way, behaving like an obedient puppy fetching for junk food and Tofutti at appropriate intervals.

What is presumably supposed to be an adventure of two innocents out to prove a point, ends up a tedious ride with protagonists who quickly become insufferable instead of sympathetic.

Part of the problem is that it's hard to care for these two since they seem so joyless in their cause. Dialog that consists of drivel about the injustices wrought by our financial institutions interspersed with that about their love for one another makes for very dreary going.

Not suprisingly, story never gets very deep, it just ends — the last few moments proving to be the film's nadir. — *Brit.*

SuperFantaGenio
(Aladdin)
(ITALIAN-COLOR)

An Italian Intl. Film release (Cannon in U.S.) of a Cannon Group presentation. Produced by Ugo Tucci for Compania Generale R.T. Directed by Bruno Corbucci. Stars Bud Spencer. Screenplay, Mario Amendola, Marcello Fondato, Corbucci; camera (Telecolor), Silvano Ippoliti; editor, Daniele Alabiso; music, Fabio Frizzi. Reviewed at Supercinema, Rome, Jan. 3, 1987. Running time: **100 MINS.**

Genie . . . . Bud Spencer
  Also with: Luca Venantini, Janet Agren, Umberto Raho, Julian Voloshin, Daimy Spencer.

Rome — Lensed in Miami, "SuperFantaGenio" is an amiable Cannon kidpic that has friendly giant Bud Spencer working miracles for a poor boy from the wrong side of the tracks. This contemporary update of Aladdin's Lamp has fared less well than other holiday pics on Italo screens.

Alan is a wide-eyed 14-year-old who works in a junk shop after school to pick up a couple bucks. One day, while polishing a rusty old oil lamp, a fabulous genie materializes in front of him and asks to be commanded.

Not long on imagination, pic contents itself with fulfilling some pretty obvious teen wishes — owning a Rolls, flying over a traffic jam, beating up bullies and becoming a basketball champ. The genie is also good at cleaning up the local mafia, terror of Miami shopkeepers who have to make "insurance" payments. Mr. Siracusa, the boss, (who also harasses Alan's pretty mom Janet Agren), gets his in the end.

Pic may be too tame for some kids' taste; its violence is limited to fistfights, flipping baddies into the ocean, and turning them into pigs and mice.

With his powerful physique and squinty eyes, Bud Spencer makes a classic genie right out of Baghdad; young costar is a passable average kid. It's technically okay. — *Yung.*

Yuppies 2
(ITALIAN-COLOR)

A Filmauro release and production. Produced by Luigi and Aurelio De Laurentiis. Directed by Enrico Oldoini. Screenplay, Oldoini, Liliana Betti; camera (Technicolor), Sergio D'Offizi; editor, Raimondo Crociani; music, Manuel De Sica; art direction, Mario Chiari; assistant director, Betti. Reviewed at Garden Cinema, Rome, Jan. 2, 1987. Running time: **99 MINS.**

Lorenzo . . . . Massimo Baldo
Giacomo . . . . Jerry Calà
Sandro . . . . Christian De Sica
Margherita . . . . Federica Moro
Isabella/Gina . . . . Athina Cenci
  Also with: Ezio Greggio, Gioia Scola, Lisa Stothard.

Rome — In this second installment of yuppies Italian style, Filmauro passes the reins from ideators Carlo and Enrico Vanzina to Enrico Oldoini, a veteran scripter recently turned helmer of tired comedies. His recycled quartet of ad execs, dentists, and their consorts is so laid back they don't even strain after laughs, yet the formula is a magic one at local wickets, and pic has done good holiday business around the country.

Only real comics in the cast of teen stars are Massimo Boldi, who plays a staid little hubby unjustly tossed out of the house by his jealous spouse, and Athina Cenci in the double role of an icy femme industrialist and an actress hired to play her. Jerry Calà and Federica Moro are a boring couple who succeed in having a baby by pic's happy ending, Christian De Sica a swaggering, would-be Cassanova in love with a Russian beauty, and Enzo Greggio an obnoxious social climber fated to make it big.

No matter how flat the joke, "Yuppies 2" uses it twice. The gag of lookalikes and mistaken identities is used and replayed when Boldi dresses up as his sister (a nun), there are two jealous wives, and two gorgeous girls who appear out of nowhere. Pic oddly fails to get any comic mileage out of its absurd parade of status symbols, from yachts (two) and Ferraris to polo and golf games, all of which are taken very seriously. All that's missing is the opera: instead, cast goes to a sneak preview of "King Kong" at the opera house, where producers Luigi and Aurelio De Laurentiis have borrowed quite a lot of footage from cousin Dino.

Sergio D'Offizi's quality camera-work is a relief. Manuel De Sica's pop score, which leads off with the original cover of "Spirit In The Sky," is dull. — *Yung.*

Que Me Maten de una Vez
(Let Them Kill Me Once And For All)
(MEXICAN-COLOR)

A Peliculas Mexicanas release of a Circo, Maroma y Teatro production. Produced by Sonia Linar. Directed by Oscar Blancarte. Stars Sonia Linar, José Angel Espinosa (Ferrosquilla). Screenplay, Blancarte, Oscar Torrero; camera (color), Oscar Torrero Salcido; editor, Sigfrido García Muñoz, Sigfrido García Jr.; music, Joaquín López Chapman. Reviewed at Havana Film Festival, Dec. 11, 1986. Running time: **100 MINS.**

Blind Matias . . . . José Angel Espinosa
                  (Ferrosquilla)
Desirée . . . . Sonia Linar
Julio . . . . Humberto Cabañas
El Secretitos . . . . Juan Antonio Llanes
Doctor Fausto . . . . Rubén Calderón
Alberto . . . . Luis Caso
Beatriz . . . . Mar Castro

Havana — The Mexican collection of six short films "Que Me Matan de una Vez" (Let Them Kill Me Once And For All) should find that its wish will come true at the boxoffice. A quick death would be the most merciful.

The six disparate tales of human foibles are strung together loosely by blind story-teller Matías (José Angel Espinoza "Ferrosquilla"), who begins each account by strumming his guitar and crooning the tale's theme.

The stories themselves are set up with an O. Henry-type twist at the end, but they really amount to little more than bad jokes framed by awkward narration, forced dialogs and almost no attention to detail.

Subjects concern a troubador in love with his donkey, an aging actress and her brush with death, a repressed homosexual doctor, a ghost revolutionary warrior, Aztec spirits, etc.

Pic is complicated by its pretensions to high art, trying to present allegories about man's vanity. But, rather than art, we wind up with a pretentious mess that reflects more on the vanity of the filmmaker. The art crowd will find the effort insulting and the general public, interested in a good story, will find this pic sadly disappointing. — *Lent.*

L'Etat de grâce
(State Of Grace)
(FRENCH-COLOR)

An AAA release of a Mod Film/Sélèna Audiovisuel coproduction. Produced by Jacques Kirsner. Directed by Jacques Rouffio. Stars Nicole Garcia, Sami Frey. Screenplay, Kirsner, Rouffio; camera (Fiaji color), Dominique Chapuis; editor, Anna Ruiz; music, Philippe Sarde; end title song lyrics, Pierre Perret; art director, Jean-Jacques Caziot; sound, Dominique Levert; makeup, Judith Gayo; assistant director, Vincent Canaple; production manager, Hugues Nonn.

Reviewed at the Mercury cinema. Paris, Dec. 28, 1986. Running time: **89 MINS.**

Florence Vannier . . . . Nicole Garcia
Antoine Lombard . . . . Sami Frey
Jean-Marc Vannier Buchet . . . Pierre Arditi
Pierre-Julien . . . . Philippe Léotard
Angéle Lombard . . . . Dominique Labourier

Paris — "L'Etat de grâce" is a mild-mannered love story about an affair between a bachelor junior minister in the French socialist government (tale is set in 1983) and a married but freely entreprising rightist businesswoman. Despite a hot and heavy carnal attraction that surmounts ideological obstacles, the lovers have a time of it trying to meet and both finally throw caution, and personal ambition, to the wind before their happy-ever-after final embrace.

Directed by Jacques Rouffio from an original screenplay he penned with Jacques Kirsner (who also produced), "State Of Grace" opts for conventional Gallic bittersweet romantic treatment that demonstrates the general inability of French filmmakers to deal bluntly with politics, despite some meek stabs at satire in story and characterization.

Film is further removed from reality by casting of dreamy, soft-spoken Sami Frey as the leftist secretary of state whose ideals take a beating when his higher education reform bill is sacrificed by political compromise; and Nicole Garcia as the high-society industrialist who runs a factory and a family headed by a priggish Protestant banker husband (Pierre Arditi).

Frey and Garcia give the sugar-coated complications some of the blithe Gallic charm offshore audiences tend to enjoy in their occasional French fare, though Rouffio and Kirsner have passed alongside a piquant comedy of sexual-political manners that could have lifted this above dramatic cliché.—*Len.*

After Pilkington
(BRITISH-COLOR)

A BBC-TV release. Produced by Kenith Trodd. Directed by Christopher Morahan. Screenplay, Simon Gray; camera (color), Andrew Dunn; editor, Dan Rae; music, Stephen Oliver; production design, Graeme Thomson; costumes, Cetriona Tomalin. Reviewed at the London Film Festival, Nov. 16, 1986. Running time: **98 MINS.**

James . . . . Bob Peck
Penny . . . . Miranda Richardson
Boris . . . . Gary Waldhorn
Derek . . . . Barry Foster
Amanda . . . . Reina James
Wilkins . . . . Richard Brenner
Diedre . . . . Mary Miller
Pottsy . . . . John Gill
Doctor . . . . Nigel Nevinson
Young James . . . . Richard Grant
Young Penny . . . . Sarah Butler

London — "After Pilkington" ranges from broad slapstick comedy to outright terror in a story of loyalties forged in childhood forced to be upheld in adult life. It's a per-fectly rounded feature topped by fine leading performances.

Director Christopher Morahan has made a tv feature far different from his recent feature film comedy "Clockwise" though he has stuck to education as the starting point for his characters. Here, though, his combatants are university dons in the purlieued setting of Oxford U.

James (Bob Peck) is a slightly bumbling professor whose life is thrown into turmoil when he meets again his childhood sweetheart Penny (Miranda Richardson), who is now married to a scheming classics don.

In their youth she was "Captain Patch" and he her faithful "Porker," and James still clings to those memories as the happiest days of his life. After a surreptitious assignation it transpires she knows something about the missing archaeologist called Pilkington.

In fact she has killed him, and on the strength of their childhood ties she wants James to help move the body from the woods near her home. James at once says he will help — after all when Captain Patch calls, Porker is always at hand.

The plot thickens as James hilariously drugs Penny's philandering husband Derek (a wonderful performance by Barry Foster) and rushes off to the grim task of moving the body. It slowly dawns on him, though, that Penny may not be the innocent party who killed in self defense as she claims.

After the body has been dumped he cleans up and declares his love to his old sweetheart. Suddenly her schizophrenic character comes to the surface and she tries to kill James.

"After Pilkington," while dealing with loyalties forged in youth, manages to shift from comedy to tragedy so subtly that you hardly see the change coming, and is helped greatly by a wonderfully complex performance from Miranda Richardson (so good in "Dance With A Stranger").

She is well complemented by Bob Peck, whose insecure don is a man of action as well as being a sentimental, easily influenced, character.

Director Morahan has made good, though not overpowering, use of his Oxford locations, and produced a feature that combines charm and chills. —*Adam.*

El Extraño Hijo del Sheriff
(The Sheriff's Strange Son)
(MEXICAN-COLOR)

A Películas Mexicanas release of an ATA (Artistas y Técnicos Asociados)-Conacite Dos-Estudios América production. Executive producer, Armando Duarte. Directed by Fer-nando Durán. Stars Eric del Castillo, Mario Almada. Screenplay, Del Castillo, Barbara Gil; camera (color), Agustín Lara; editor, Angel Camacho; music, Rafael Carrión. Reviewed at Havana Film Festival, Dec. 7, 1986. Running time: **90 MINS.**

Sheriff Frederick Jackson .Eric del Castillo
Dr. Jack Miller . . . . Mario Almada
Rosa . . . . Rosa Gloria Chagoyán
Fred/Erick . . . . Luis Mario Quiroz
Sam . . . . Ramón Menedez
Judge . . . . Alfredo Gutiérrez
Jeremías Santos . . . . Wally Barón
    Also with: Mario Delmar, Guillermo Inclán, Edmundo Barahona, Antonio Aguilar, Julián Abitia, David Montenegro, Blanca Lidia Muñoz.

Havana — "The Sheriff's Strange Son," from the Mexican cinema workers union ATA, shows strong commercial potential as an off-beat entertainment vehicle.

As a species of horse-opera "Exorcist," pic's director Fernando Durán follows the disturbing tale closely keeping the audience wondering what will happen next.

Story, full of ominous symbols, centers on a small-town sheriff (Eric del Castillo), who is the father of a pair of siamese twins, Fred and Erick. He has kept the boys hidden since birth and when they reached childhood, he demands that the local doctor (Mario Almada) separate them. During the operation, Erick dies, but not before passing his consciousness into Fred's body — and the two boys inhabit one body.

Things complicate when Erick demands retribution for his murder. The sheriff is brought to trial and sentenced to the gallows. Even then, Erick does not relinquish his control over Fred.

Pic has the opportunity to use some modest-but-effective special effects and even though the audience is left with some unanswered questions, overall the tale offers some engrossing moments of entertainment.

Acting and production talents are consistantly competent throughout and the film should prove to be a thematic and interesting change of pace for Hispanic viewers. —*Lent.*

Désordre
(Disorder)
(FRENCH-COLOR)

A Forum Distribution release of a Forum Prods. Intl. production. Produced by Claude-Eric Poiroux. Written and directed by Olivier Assayas. Camera (color), Denis Lenoir; editor, Luc Barnier; music, Gabriel Yared; art director, François-Renaud Labarthe; sound, Philippe Sénéchal. Reviewed at the Gaumont Ambassade cinema, Paris, Dec. 9, 1986. Running time: **90 MINS.**

Yvan . . . . Wadeck Stanczak
Anne . . . . Ann-Gisel Glass
Henri . . . . Lucas Belvaux
    Also with: Simon de la Brosse, Remi Martin, Corinne Dacla, Etienne Chicot, Juliette Mailhe, Philippe Demarle, Etienne Daho.

Paris — "Disorder," a somber chronicle of the '80s rock generation, is a fine debut feature by former critic Olivier Assayas, who recently racked up positive credits as screenwriter with director André Techiné, whose influence is apparent in the taut, muted authority of Assayas' direction. Film, produced by local producer-distrib Claude-Eric Poiroux in his recent linkup with Gallic subsidiary of Virgin Records, received the critic's prize at the Venice festival.

Assayas' script explodes the pop movie cliché about the band of youths happily pooling their forces to form a rock group. His protagonists, through promiscuity, selfishness, fear and mendacity, are unable to get their act together, literally and figuratively, and their pop dreams dissolve variously into suicide, mediocrity or loneliness.

Film opens in a nightmare as story's principal characters — two boys and a girl who's involved with both — burgle a music shop to get instruments for their band are forced to kill the proprietor who catches them red-handed.

Though the police never pick up their trail, their crime weighs heavily on their subsequent behavior and leads gradually to the breakup of the trio and their mates, despite attempts to pursue their pop dreams. One of the young men finally hangs himself while the remaining protagonists try to pick up the pieces of their broken illusions.

Despite the Virgin connection, Assayas has avoided making a straight film with musical interludes, but a drama about young people who cannot make music because there is no psychological harmony among them. The occasional rock fragments — including a sequence at London's Gibus club featuring the Woodentops — serve as counterpoint to the action, rather than dramatic relief.

Assayas' brooding direction exacts performances of jagged relief from his leads, Ann-Gisel Glass, Lucas Belvaux and Wadeck Stanczak (revealed by Techiné in his "Rendezvous" and "Scene Of The Crime," on which Assayas worked). Supporting roles are filled with the same precision.

Lensing, editing and other tech credits are all stylishly low-keyed.
—Len.

Square Dance
(COLOR)

Well-acted but mild drama of a young girl's maturation.

An Island Pictures release of a Michael Nesmith presentation, produced in association with NBC Prods. Executive producers, Charles Haid, Jane Alexander. Produced and directed by Daniel Petrie. Stars Jason Robards, Alexander, Winona Ryder, Rob Lowe. Screenplay, Alan Hines, based on his novel; camera (Allied color; Metrocolor prints), Jacek Laskus; editor, Bruce Green; music, Bruce Broughton; production design, Jan Scott; set decoration, Erica Rogalla; costume design, Elizabeth McBride; sound, Bob Wald; assistant director, Katterli Fraunfelder; associate producers, P'nenah Goldstein, Cyris Yavneh; second unit camera, Rick Anderson; casting, Shari Rhodes, Liz Kiegley. Reviewed at Lorimar-Telepictures, Culver City, Calif., Jan. 14, 1987. (MPAA Rating: PG-13.) Running time: **112 MINS.**

Dillard	Jason Robards
Juanelle	Jane Alexander
Gemma	Winona Ryder
Rory	Rob Lowe
Gwen	Deborah Richter
Frank	Guich Koock
Beecham	Elbert Lewis

Hollywood — A very traditional drama about a young girl's search for a home and an identity, "Square Dance" provides a showcase for some fine performances but emotionally never quite flowers as bountifully as it should. Tastefully produced Island release had its world premiere Jan. 16 in Salt Lake City as the opener for the U.S. Film Festival and seems destined for okay, if not remarkable, b.o. results in class situations.

Winona Ryder, first seen onscreen last year in "Lucas," plays a 13-year-old whose normal pubescent awkwardness is compounded by her general unwantedness. Raised by a gruff grandpa (Jason Robards) in rural Texas, she finds solace mainly in church activities, and when her slatternly mother (Jane Alexander) turns up to take her away, the girl refuses to go.

However, a spat with the old man prompts Ryder to hop a bus to Fort Worth and surprise Mom, who lives above a gas station with a man she doesn't deserve and works at a nearby beauty parlor, where Ryder gets a new "do" and is immediately given a job.

The youngster's burgeoning loveliness is all the more apparent in these tawdry surroundings, where the women are all tarts and moneygrubbing is the only ideal. She quickly falls in chaste but intense love with a retarded fellow, played in a drastic change-of-pace by Rob Lowe, which momentarily distracts her from the fact that her mother still has not made room for her in her life and still is basically as selfish as the day she walked out on her father and daughter. As Mama puts it, "You don't belong anywhere, kiddo."

Drama rises to its peak during the climactic mother-daughter confrontations, and while the scenes are strongly acted explorations of an emotionally potent dilemma, they are not as painful or incisive as they might have been. As written, Ryder's character bears up almost unbelievably well under mightily adverse conditions, and quick cutting away from moments of the greatest tension prevents the impact from being total.

Director Daniel Petrie's handling of the material proves very conventional and film overall could have profited from further tightening by 10 minutes or so, but Petrie's work with the actors is exemplary. Ryder's big brown eyes, composed seriousness and budding looks rivet the attention throughout, and she carries off the demanding central role with thorough impressiveness.

Alexander is also right on as the brassy mom who torments her daughter by revealing she has no idea who the child's father is, so numerous were the candidates, and who has obviously always foresaken any sense of responsibility for another night of good times. Robard's embittered crustiness is utterly believable, and Lowe, while never disguising his too-good looks, manages to pull off his role of the pathetic but pure-hearted soulmate of Ryder's.

Guich Koock delivers a strong supporting turn as Alexander's struggling, well-intentioned man, while Deborah Richter is flashy as the number one floozy in town.

Pic is modest technically, with Jacek Laskus' muted lensing and Jan Scott's straightforward production design helping set the mood without overloading the atmosphere. —Cart.

Robot Holocaust
(COLOR)

Low-budget sci-fi for the video market.

A Wizard Video presentation of a Tycin Entertainment production. Produced by Cynthia DePaula. Written and directed by Tim Kincaid. Camera (Precision color; prints by United), Arthur D. Marks; editor, Barry Zetlin; music, courtesy of Richard Band Publishing; sound, Mike Cribben; production design, Medusa; art direction, Marina Zurkow, Ruth Lounsbury; assistant director, Rebecca Rothbaum; production manager, Joe Derrig; costume design, Celeste Hines; special visual effects, Jeremie Frank; robot creature effects design, Ed French; special makeup effects, Tom Lauten; robot masks, Ralph Cordero; robot suits, Valarie McNeill. Reviewed on Wizard Video vidcassette, N.Y., Jan. 8, 1987. (No MPAA Rating.) Running time: **79 MINS.**

Neo	Norris Culf
Deeja	Nadine Hart
Klyton	Joel Von Ornsteiner
Myta	Jennifer Delora
Kai	Andrew Howarth
Valaria	Angelika Jager
Torque	Rick Gianasi
Jorn	Michael Downend

Also with: George Gray, Nicholas Reiner, Michael Azzolina, John Blaylock, Amy Brentano.

"Robot Holocaust" is an okay science fiction adventure made by the New York-based team who did "Breeders" and "Bad Girls Dormitory." Low-budgeter lacks the production values and large-scale setpieces required of a theatrical action pic, but is a suitable entry for homevideo fans.

Set in the future after a rebellion by billions of robots against their human masters has left New Terra devastated (with accompanying radiation spills), story has Neo (Norris Culf) leading a group of human rebels on a trek to the Power Station, where the evil Dark One controls humankind's artificial atmosphere.

The Dark One's sadistic aide Valaria (Angelika Jager) is torturing scientist Jorn (Michael Downend) for the secret of his being able to breathe the poisoned atmosphere, the result of an implant device he has also applied to his daughter Deeja (Nadine Hart), who is with Neo and the rebels. The stalwart heroes and heroines finally overthrow the Dark One and Valaria (whose true identity is a predictable plot twist) gets her comeuppance.

The robot designs are intriguing, with writer-director Tim Kincaid using "Star Wars" as inspiration for a C-3PO styled robot Klyton sidekick to Neo and echo-chamber voices reminiscent of James Earl Jones' Darth Vader. Acting is mainly deadpan, except for the beautiful Angelika Jager, camping it up as the villainess. Monsters are disappointing, including "Hideous giant worms" that turn out to be hand puppets and a Beast Of The Web which looks like the Black Tooth furry paw from Soupy Sales' tv show. —Lor.

Critical Condition
(COLOR)

Unfunny mishmash for Richard Pryor.

A Paramount Pictures release. Produced by Ted Field, Robert Cort. Executive producer, Bob Larson. Directed by Michael Apted. Stars Richard Pryor. Screenplay, Denis Hamill, John Hamill, based on a story by Denis Hamill, John Hamill, Alan Swyer; camera (Technicolor), Ralf D. Bode; editor, Robert K. Lambert; music, Alan Silvestri; production design, John Lloyd; set decorator, George Robert Nelson; costumes, Coleen Atwood; sound, Willie Burton; assistant director, Robert V. Girolami; associate producer, Eric Lerner; casting, Margery Simkin. Reviewed at Paramount screening room, Hollywood, Jan. 14, 1987. (MPAA Rating: R.) Running time: **100 MINS.**

Eddie	Richard Pryor
Rachel	Rachel Ticotin
Louis	Rubén Blades
Chambers	Joe Mantegna
Dr. Foster	Bob Dishy
Maggie	Sylvia Miles
Stucky	Joe Dallesandro
Box	Randall (Tex) Cobb
Dr. Joffe	Bob Saget
Helicopter Junkie	Garrett Morris

Hollywood — Someday someone will come up with the right material for Richard Pryor, but "Critical Condition" isn't it. Pryor barks, growls, walks on all fours and pretends to be a doctor, but misses the mark on almost all counts in this half-baked shaggy dog story. Fans of the comic will find little to cheer about here.

Real culprits are scriptwriters Denis and John Hamill, who have left Pryor stranded in situations even his comic inventiveness can't salvage. Basis of Pryor's appeal has been the believability of his responses. No matter how extreme the setting his feelings always seem correct and based on real life experience.

In "Critical Condition," Pryor is left off the leash in setups too dumb to be real and, without any earned emotion, all his hopping around is meaningless. Director Michael Apted's touch isn't loose enough for madcap comedy or warm enough for light romance and, despite good intentions, tone of the film is blatantly bogus.

As a would-be theater developer, Pryor gets mixed up with the Mafia and to stay out of jail pleads insanity. He lands in a mental ward but escapes and is mistaken for a doctor one stormy night when a hurricane leaves the hospital in chaos. It's a premise with some promise but the script hasn't a clue where to take it.

Peppered with hokey street jargon for effect, all the Hamills can come up with is a loony bin filled with crazies from central casting and characters running around the hospital manically moving helicopters, generators and anything else that's not nailed down.

There's some lip service to what a doctor's responsibility should be and doing the right thing in a pinch, but most of the film is a search for absurd jokes that mostly fall flat. Pryor manually relieves an old lady's constipation; Pryor applies a leg cast; Pryor in the operating room and Pryor delivering a baby.

There's even a little time for romance with hospital administrator Rachel Ticotin. She's quite lovely, but what draws them together is really a mystery. Pryor, too, seems a bit lost in all the commotion as he tries to keep the hospital running. He is clearly not connecting with the dreamer with a heart of gold his character is supposed to be.

At the same time pic has subplots too numerous to mention and any hospital where Sylvia Miles is the head nurse has got to be cracked. Joining Miles as a killer on the loose is her old Andy Warhol partner Joe Dallesandro, but it's anyone's guess what he's up to here.

Making more of an impression is singer/songwriter Rubén Blades as a savvy orderly. In the midst of this storm, he is the one calm, intelligent center. Also likable is Randall Cobb

as Pryor's buddy in the psychiatric ward. Garrett Morris is wasted as an addict waiting for his fair share of methadone.

Production design adds to the artificiality of the story with walls that are obviously cardboard easily giving way to the phony fury of the raging storm. Other tech credits are adequate but can't save the film from drowning. — *Jagr.*

The Stepfather
(COLOR)

Topnotch suspenser.

A New Century/Vista release of an ITC production. Produced by Jay Benson. Directed by Joseph Ruben. Screenplay, Donald E. Westlake, from story by Westlake, Carolyn Lefcourt, Brian Garfield; camera (color), John W. Lindley; editor, George Bowers; music, Patrick Moraz; sound (Ultra-Stereo), Larry Sutton; production design, James Newton Westport; art direction, David Willson; set decoration, Kimberley Richardson; assistant director, Michael Steele; production manager, Warren Carr; casting, Mike Fenton, Jane Feinberg, Judy Taylor, Sid Kozak. Reviewed at Magno Preview 4 screening room, N.Y., Dec. 4, 1986. (MPAA Rating: R.) Running time: **98 MINS.**
Jerry Blake . . . . Terry O'Quinn
Stephanie Maine . . . . Jill Schoelen
Susan Blake . . . . Shelley Hack
Jim Ogilvie . . . . Stephen Shellen
Dr. Bondurant . . . . Charles Lanyer

"The Stepfather" is an engrossing suspense thriller that refreshingly doesn't cheat the audience in terms of valid clues and plot twists. Pic from ITC Prods. represents a marketing opportunity and challenge for newcomer distrib New Century/Vista.

Terry O'Quinn toplines as a mild-looking guy who immediately is revealed to be a psychotic who has murdered his entire family. A year later he has started a new life as Jerry Blake, married to young Susan (Shelley Hack) who has a teenage daughter Stephanie (Jill Schoelen).

Stephanie has a natural resentment of her new dad, but apart from his occasional talking to himself there is no overt evidence of Blake being crazy. His past eventually catches up with him as his previous brother-in-law Jim (Stephen Shellen) is still researching the murder of his sister with the help of a reporter, the police and (independently) Stephanie's psychiatrist Dr. Bondurant (Charles Lanyer).

What makes "The Stepfather" work is its believability, as writer Donald Westlake expertly injects clues which can trip up Blake's new identity (e.g., a photo circulated by Jim). A most ingenious plot peg has Blake carefully planning out his new identity (quitting his job, finding a new home, etc.) each time before he goes completely over the edge and sets out to murder his family. Underlying theme of the picture, a man's desperate need to create a happy, carefree family unit and the

incredible frustration when matters go awry, has resonance lifting the film out of the realm of pure escapism.

O'Quinn gives a measured, effective performance balancing the normalcy and craziness of the character, while Shoelen is powerfully empathetic as the young heroine. Hack also scores in a natural career departure as an older woman than her prior castings.

Helmer Joseph Ruben brings a lot more credibility to the film than his previous "Dreamscape" assignment, toning down somewhat the story's inevitable carnage and emphasizing the type of sunlit horror that gives the picture more impact than a corny gothic approach. Tech credits are fine. — *Lor.*

Sweet Country
(COLOR)

Sprawling, ineffectual drama about political turmoil in Chile.

A Cinema Group release of a Playmovie Prods. production. Executive producer, Yannoulla Wakefield. Produced by Michael Cacoyannis, Costas Alexakis. Written and directed by Cacoyannis, based on a novel by Caroline Richards. Camera (color), Andreas Bellis; editor, Dinos Katsourides, Cacoyannis; music, Stavros Xarhakos; set decorator, Antonis Kyriakoulis; production manager, George Iakovides; sound, Nicos Ahladis; casting, Lois Planco. Reviewed at Broadway Screening Room, N.Y., Jan. 15, 1987. (MPAA Rating: R.) Running time: **147 MINS.**
Anna . . . . Jane Alexander
Ben . . . . John Cullum
Eva . . . . Carole Laure
Paul . . . . Franco Nero
Monica . . . . Joanna Pettet
Juan . . . . Randy Quaid
Mrs. Araya . . . . Irene Papas
Mr. Araya . . . . Jean-Pierre Aumont
Father Venegas . . . . Pierre Vaneck

"Sweet Country" is a sprawling, overly stylized and disappointing film played against the backdrop of totalitarian Chile after the 1973 assassination of Marxist leader Salvador Allende. Tale of two families and what befalls them in a country of political chaos and fear is surprisingly flat considering the subject matter, and b.o. prospects must be considered slim.

Based on the 1979 novel by Caroline Richards, story is a complex web of love, terror and treachery told from the point-of-view of Anna (Jane Alexander), an American who has moved to Chile with her husband Ben (John Cullum).

Perhaps producer/writer/director/editor Michael Cacoyannis was too close to his subject matter, having himself been exiled from his native Greece from 1966-74 after a military takeover. The majority of scenes, in addition to being too long, are overly staged and stylized to the point of pretentiousness. Throughout the film we can see the strings being pulled from behind the camera.

Anna and Ben are friends with a Chilean family headed by Irene Papas that is drawn directly into the political turmoil because daughter Eva (Carole Laure) had worked for the Allende government. The imprisonment and torture of her and thousands of others leads to Anna's involvement in an underground movement, setting the stage for the film's violent conclusion.

The film's hollow quality is no more evident than in the bizarre casting of Randy Quaid as Juan, a sadistic Chilean security officer. Standing a full foot taller than his South American army brethren and speaking in an accent reminiscent of his days on "Saturday Night Live," Quaid terrorizes Eva and her sister Monica (Joanna Pettet) with sneers and leers and generally undermines one of the more crucial plot elements in the story.

Other characters in the film include a Canadian journalist (Franco Nero) who either is or isn't a spy for the Chilean military (not to give away one of the few good twists in the film) and a left-wing priest (Pierre Vaneck), among others.

Alexander notches a credible performance under such trying conditions, but even good acting gets lost in this meandering and ultimately, directionless film.

Cacoyannis obviously wrestled long and hard with this difficult and important subject matter, but unfortunately it got the better of him.

—*Roy.*

Travelling North
(AUSTRALIAN-COLOR)

A CEL release of a View Pictures Ltd. production. Produced by Ben Gannon. Directed by Carl Schultz. Stars Leo McKern. Screenplay, David Williamson, based on his play; camera (Eastmancolor), Julian Penny; editor, Henry Dangar; music coordinator, Alan John; production design, Owen Paterson; sound, Syd Butterworth; production manager, Julia Overton; assistant director, Colin Fletcher; casting, Sandra McKenzie. Reviewed at Academy Twin, Sydney, Dec. 7, 1986. Running time: **96 MINS.**
Frank . . . . Leo McKern
Frances . . . . Julia Blake
Freddy . . . . Graham Kennedy
Saul . . . . Henri Szeps
Also with: Michele Fawdon, Diane Craig, Andrea Moor, Drew Forsythe, John Gregg.

Sydney — It's early days yet, but "Travelling North" already looks set to be a major contender in the 1987 Australian Film Awards, especially in the acting stakes. This superbly crafted adaptation of David Williamson's popular stage play makes few concessions to the youth audience, but as a mature, frequently funny and ultimately most moving story of old age and retirement, it doubtless will be dubbed Australia's "On Golden Pond." With the right handling, it could do solid biz anywhere.

Opening scenes are set in Melbourne. Leo McKern plays Frank, a rather cantankerous ex-Communist and civil engineer who retires from work at age 70. A widower, he has persuaded his close friend, Frances (Julia Blake), a widow but not as old as he, to accompany him north, to subtropical northern Queensland. Marriage doesn't enter into the arrangement, but Frances goes along, and they both say farewell to their families (Frances has two awful, selfish daughters — Michele Fawdon and Diane Craig — married to equally hopeless husbands, while Frank has become estranged from his son though is still quite close to daughter Andrea Moor).

After a nostalgic final visit to Melbourne's art gallery they make the long drive north where Frank has purchased a spectacular clifftop house. Here they meet their over-friendly neighbor (Graham Kennedy), who talks too much to hide his own loneliness and whose political convictions are far removed from Frank's; and a doctor (Henri Szeps) who also becomes a friend.

After many happy days fishing, reading and listening to music (and enjoying the sexual side of the relationship), Frank's health begins to deteriorate. He becomes bad tempered and cranky, and Frances starts to yearn to see her family again. Frank reluctantly accompanies her on a trip back to Melbourne, but it isn't a success. Returning to Queensland, he finds his faculties are failing, he's no longer able to make love, he's often in pain, and his future is circumscribed. He and Frances decide to marry, and fly down to Sydney for a hilarious honeymoon weekend before returning to Queensland for the final stages of Frank's illness and the film's emotional resolution.

Australian-born Leo McKern, in his first Australian film, gives a remarkable performance as the crotchety, yet endearing, Frank. His humanity shines through, and he delivers David Williamson's frequently witty dialog with considerable style. It's a hugely enjoyable portrayal. As Frances, Julia Blake positively glows; she plays a patient, loving woman with a determination of her own, and it's a rich characterization. Michele Fawdon is suitably horrid as Blake's older daughter, while Henri Szeps, as the small-town doctor, also creates a fully rounded character. As the chatty neighbor, Graham Kennedy proves again he's one of Australia's best character actors, with an ability to show the loneliness and pain beneath the apparently brash and shallow exterior.

Credit for the entire production must go to director Carl Schultz, best known for "Careful He Might Hear You" (1983). Schultz came late to "Travelling North" (originally to have been directed by

Michael Blakemore, who handled most of the principal casting), but he has handled his chores with distinction, giving the film a fluidity and pace the belies its stage origins. His use of visual metaphors (such as a strange fern which closes in on itself when touched by humans) is assured.

Producer Ben Gannon has put together a top-class production, with fine lensing by Julian Penny, clever production design by Owen Paterson, very tight editing by Henry Dangar and a fine choice of classical music excerpts. It all makes for a touching film about old age and death that's never heavy, though there will be few dry eyes by the end. It's a good start to the year for Australian cinema. —*Strat.*

Emmanuelle 5
(FRENCH-COLOR)

An AAA release of an AS production. Produced by Alain Siritzky. Directed by Walerian Borowczyk. Screenplay, Borowczyk, Alex Cunningham, based on an original idea by Emmanuelle Arsan; camera (color), Max Montheillet; editor, Franck Mathieu; music, Pierre Bachelet; theme song performed by Sandy Stevenson; sound, Jean-Claude Reboul; art director, Alain Faure. Reviewed at the Marignan-Concorde cinema, Paris, Jan. 10, 1987. Running time: **78 MINS.**
Emmanuelle . . . . Monique Gabrielle
Charles Foster . . . . . . Dana Burns Westberg
Eric . . . . Crofton Hardester
Rajid . . . . Yaseen Khan

Paris — Another yawner like this one and "Emmanuelle" could be ready for boxoffice beddy-bye. The sex symbol who has reaped a commercial bonanza in four previous film installments in the past dozen years, seems now to be coasting lazily on its reputation, the usual repertoire of softcore copulations and the same bored post-synchronized moans of pleasure. "Emmanuelle 5" should still turn a profitable trick in its usual markets, but even the most heavy-breathing followers may start to notice the series is petering out. Still, producer Alain Siritzky has announced a tv miniseries spinoff for 1987.

Emmanuelle is now two actresses removed from her original screen performer, Sylvia Kristel, who was succeeded by Mia Nygren in "Emmanuelle 4." Now it's the turn of 23-year-old Monique Gabrielle, an attractive French-born (but California-raised) lass who's had some dance, film and legit experience, but nothing to prepare her for what is now a walk-through/lie-through role of no personal definition or erotic flavor.

She's as quickly forgettable as everything else in this flabbily perfunctory affair, in which the heroine creates a scandal at the Cannes Film Festival as star of a new sex opus, before she falls into the virile arms of a mysterious billionaire industrialist and the

clutches of an Eastern despot who wants to add her to his harem.

Number Five was written ineptly and directed by none other than Walerian Borowczyk, who once upon a time enjoyed international critical esteem and festival honors for his animation films and live-action erotic features, of which "Emmanuelle 5" seems the ultimate (unconscious) parody.—*Len.*

Return To Horror High
(COLOR)

Silly backstage shrieker.

A New World Pictures release in association with Balcor Film Investors of a Greg H. Sims production. Executive producer, Greg H. Sims. Produced by Mark Lisson. Directed by Bill Froehlich. Screenplay, Froehlich, Lisson, Dana Escalante, Greg H. Sims; camera (color), Roy Wagner; editor, Nancy Forner; music, Stacy Widelitz; production design, Greta Grigorian; costumes, Marcy Grace Froehlich; associate producers, Jason Hoffs, Joan Baribeault; casting, Linda Francis; assistant director, Rachel Talalay. Reviewed at Cineplex Odeon Eaton Center, Toronto, Jan. 9, 1987. (MPAA Rating: R.) Running time: **95 MINS.**
Callie . . . . Lori Lethin
Steven Blake . . . . Brendan Hughes
Barry Sleerik . . . . Alex Rocco
Josh Forbes . . . . Scott Jacoby
Principal Kastleman . . . . Andy Romano
Arthur Lyman . . . . Richard Brestoff
Amos . . . . Al Fann
Chief Deyner . . . . Pepper Martin
Officer Tyler . . . . Maureen McCormick
Richard Birnbaum . . . . Vince Edwards

Toronto — With opening credits that announce "Starring (in pieces)," the laughs come faster than the frights, which makes "Return To Horror High" not quite the slasher pic the target audience might hope for. Its crude special effects and lack of thrills will propel it to a zippy trip to the video shelves.

Producer Mark Lisson and director Bill Froehlich have set up a film within a film. A production crew goes to Crippen High School, where five years earlier a rash of murders occurred. Natch, the killer is still lurking about somewhere.

At top of pic, there is a barrage of police cars at the school, bloodied bodies strewn everywhere, and one survivor — the screenwriter — who relates the debacle of the making of the film.

Seems that during the production, crew members keep disappearing, stage blood gets mixed with real blood, and the white-masked killer stalks the halls again, because of the dropout rate, actors have to triple up on roles. Even real highschool teachers are asked to recreate their roles in the new pic, including Vince Edwards as a lecherous biology teacher and Andy Romano as the depraved principal.

The love interest, police officer Steven Blake (Brendan Hughes) who plays one of the original students, and actress Callie (Lori Lethin), join forces to find the killer

lurking in the basement of the school.

Special effects are less than startling: gushing blood and severed limbs just don't have the cachet they used to. Before pic opened in Toronto, the Ontario Film Review Board made two cuts of a "knife cutting a torso, ripping out of heart, and placing heart in mouth" and one of graphic decapitation. In one scene, Vince Edwards is nailed to the ground through various parts of his body while the killer dissects him, but it's more for laughs.

Pic is more an in-joke for the industry about the making of a low-budget film. An actor with a hatchet through his head asks the harried director (Scott Jacoby) what's his motivation. An ultra-sleazoid producer (Alex Rocco) orders a gofer to get him a pastrami sandwich — but not from the truck.

The confusing technique of first-person recollection, flashbacks to the making of the pic, all cut with real killer scenes is just that — confusing.

Script is slack on the bellylaughs, with much of the humor merely lame and crude. Uninspired camerawork follows the victims as they walk down the hall, against an ominous soundtrack, and meet up with the black-shrouded murderer.

The plot twist at the end is just plain twisted. The decimated crew turns out to be just "playing dead," thanks to the genius of their make-up man. It's a publicity stunt to insure the picture makes b.o. bingo. But it also means the door is wide open for another return to Horror High.—*Devo.*

Hotel Colonial
(U.S.-ITALIAN-COLOR)

A Columbia Pictures release (Orion in U.S.), of a Yarno Cinematografica/Legeis Theatrical coproduction. Produced by Mauro Berardi, William M. Siegel. Executive producer, Ira R. Barmak. Directed by Cinzia Th Torrini. Stars Robert Duvall, John Savage. Screenplay, Enzo Monteleone, with the participation of Torrini, Barmak, consultation by Robert Katz; camera (Technicolor), Giuseppe Rotunno; editor, Nino Baragli; music, Pino Donaggio; art direction, Giantito Burchilliaro. Reviewed at Barberini Cinema, Rome, Jan. 3, 1987. (No MPAA Rating.) Running time: **104 MINS.**
Marco Venieri . . . . John Savage
Carrasco . . . . Robert Duvall
Irene . . . . Rachel Ward
Werner . . . . Massimo Troisi
Also with: Anna Galiena.

Rome — "Hotel Colonial" is another Italian attempt to break into the international marketplace. This American financed coproduction comes closer than most to getting the look right, thanks to colorful lensing in Mexico locates masquerading as Colombia and a top cast of Yank thesps. Unfortunately, the talent goes to waste in a totally inconsequential, and pretty illogical, pastiche of adventure yarns that once more unveils the worst horrors of the jungle, where a mad Mr. Kurtz reigns over his heart of darkness. B.o. looms as a large question mark for this big-budgeter, the third feature of young femme helmer Cinzia Th Torrini.

When Marco Venieri (John Savage) learns brother Luca, an ex-terrorist, has just shot himself in Colombia, he goes to the refrigerator and has a flashback to their childhood on the Venice Lido, when Luca found his first real pistol. Next the improbable Venetian Savage is in Bogotá to identify the body. Friendly embassy aide Irene (Rachel Ward) confirms the fingerprints of the mutilated corpse Marco sees aren't his brother's. Marco's thirst to know the truth about Luca's disappearance takes him through sordid backs streets peopled by ill-intentioned locals, a picturesque cock fight and a filthy jail.

At last he arrives in a remote outpost with a comfy hotel and swimming pool, owned by the mysterious drug trafficker Carrasco (Robert Duvall). Carrasco takes a shine to the boy and tries to teach him to love the ways of the jungle by showing him how to blast cute monkeys out of trees, but to no avail. Not even a displaced Italian ferryman crazy over soccer (great Neapolitan character actor Massimo Troisi is pic's one, true highlight) can coax a sportive spirit out of grave Marco. Then Marco discovers a chest full of little Indios girls' scalps, and takes it upon himself to mete out justice.

At least the action is fast-paced, and ace cameraman Giuseppe Rotunno turns every shot into a picturesque visual delight, thanks also to art director Giantito Burchilliaro's splashy sets, and helmer Torrini's skill at blocking the action. Savage and Duvall do their valiant best to overcome painful dialog and hopelessly clichéd roles, but it's a losing battle. Only Troisi, who seems to have written his own part, gives pic a breather with some honest comic relief. — *Yung.*

Massacre In Dinosaur Valley
(ITALIAN-COLOR)

A Doral Film production. Directed by Michael E. Lemick (Michele Tarantini). Stars Michael Sopkiw, Susane Carvall (Suzanne Carvalho). Screenplay, story, editor, Lemick (Tarantini); camera (Luciano Vittorio color), Edison Batista; music, uncredited; art direction, Mauro Monteiro; production managers, Christopher Riggs, Phidias Barbosa; assistant director, Tania Lamarca, Renato Brazil. Reviewed on Lightning Video vidcassette, N.Y., Jan. 10, 1987. (No MPAA Rating.) Running time: **82 MINS.**
With: Michael Sopkiw (Kevin), Susane Carvall {Suzanne Carvalho} (Ellie), Milton Morris, Martha Anderson, Joffrey Soares, Gloria Cristal, Susie Hahn, Marie Reis, Andy Silas, Leonid Bayer, Carlos Imperial, Samuca, Ney Pen, Albert Silva, Jonas Dalbecchi,

Paul Sky, Paul Pacelli, Norton Kays, Indio Xin, Robert Roney.

———

"Massacre In Dinosaur Valley" is a poor Italian exploitation film, made worse by an intentionally misleading title: there are no dinosaurs or fantasy elements in this potboiler. Pic was lensed in Brazil in 1985 with "Stranded In The Valley Of Dinosaurs" as its working title.

Format is in the corny vein of "Five Came Back:" a bunch of folks are caught in the jungle and swamp when their light plane crashes en route to Manaos. Among the passengers are an archaeologist (Michael Sopkiw), a scientist who's killed in the crash, his pretty daughter (Susane Carvall, usually credited as Suzanne Carvalho) plus several other beauties. They're attacked by indians, fall prey to leeches and quicksand, plus the other tired gimmicks of the genre.

Sopkiw finally frees two girls from the clutches of the indians and an hour into the film finds fossilized dinosaur footprints. Just when the film might be getting interesting, the three survivors are captured by a creep using slave labor for his mining operation. The rest of the picture is devoted to the boring subplot of Sopkiw engineering another escape with Carvalho.

This sexploitationer mixes pratfall comedy, disrobing women and the usual gore carelessly.—*Lor.*

Assassination
(COLOR)

Fun Bronson vehicle.

A Cannon Group release of a Golan-Globus production. Produced by Pancho Kohner. Executive producers, Menahem Golan, Yoram Globus. Directed by Peter Hunt. Stars Charles Bronson. Screenplay, Richard Sale; camera (TVC color), Hanania Baer; editor, James Heckert; music, Robert O. Ragland, Valentine McCallum; production design, William Cruise; art director, Joshua S. Culp; sound, Thomas Brandau; costumes, Shelley Komarov; assistant director, Craig Huston; casting, Perry Bullington. Reviewed at Hollywood Pacific theater, Hollywood, Jan. 9, 1987. (MPAA Rating: PG-13.) Running time: **88 MINS.**
Jay Killian . . . . Charles Bronson
Lara Royce Craig . . . . Jill Ireland
Fitzroy . . . . Stephen Elliott
Charlotte Chang . . . . Jan Gan Boyd
Tyler Loudermilk . . . . Randy Brooks
Reno Bracken . . . . Erik Stern
Senator Bunsen . . . . Michael Ansara
Briggs . . . . James Staley
Polly Simms . . . . Kathryn Leigh Scott

Hollywood — Short on plausibility but diverting enough to while away a Saturday afternoon, "Assassination" is the kind of bare bones entertainment Hollywood used to turn out by the score, usually as the back end of a double bill. Formula filmmaking from the first frame, pic has a good performance by Charles Bronson and enough wit to win over an audience not looking for great art.

Story sandwiches an antagonistic man and woman in danger in a pair with more holes than Swiss cheese. It's sort of a poor man's "To Catch A Thief" with elements of "It Happened One Night" thrown in for good measure. In the film's main section, with White House secret service agent Bronson traveling cross country on the run with the First Lady (Jill Ireland), one hasn't the foggiest idea where they are going or why.

What makes the film watchable anyway is Bronson's self-assured charm. No matter that he's reaching retirement age for a secret service man and has no business chasing young chippies, Bronson has by now mastered a low-key but menacing presence that's simply fun to watch and rarely has he been better.

The fact that a corrupt senator (Michael Ansara) wants Ireland dead and the chase takes them over land, water, rail and air only adds to the silliness of the film, but this kind of entertainment was never meant to be taken seriously and Bronson and director Peter Hunt know it.

Phoniness of the sets, a whiter than white White House and an awful matte job for the Washington backdrop, and inauthenticity of the action only adds to the film's likable comic book mentality. Luckily Richard Sale's script introduces little politics and has a nice sense of tongue-in-cheek humor to boot.

Action scenes are less pleasing and by the end are downright monotonous. Chased by a high-priced terrorist (Erik Stern) who is good enough to somehow survive a fall off a cliff in a burning truck, Bronson and his colleagues fire more bullets than the allied forces in World War II.

As for romance, Bronson scores with one of his colleagues (Jan Gan Boyd) but not surprisingly resists Ireland's charms. Though they spend most of the film bantering, there is not much chemistry between the two. The First Lady, or "One Momma" as she is referred to in the jargon, is really rather a bore and impossible to take seriously, but that seems to be the point here.
—*Jagr.*

———

Il Burbero
(The Grouch)
(ITALIAN-COLOR)

A C.D.I. release of a C. G. Silver Film production. Produced by Mario and Vittorio Cecchi Gori. Associate producer, Luciano Luna for Alexandra Film. Written and directed by Castellano & Pipolo. Stars Adriano Celentano. Camera (Cinecittà color), Alfio Contini; editor, Antonio Siciliano; music, Detto Mariano; art direction, Massimo Corevi. Reviewed at Ariston Cinema, Rome, Jan. 1, 1987. Running time: **113 MINS.**
Tito Torrisi . . . . Adriano Celentano
Mary Cimino Macchiavelli . . . Debra Feuer
Giulio Macchiavelli . . . . Jean Sorel

Also with: Mattia Sbragia, Angela Finocchiaro, Peppe Lanzetta, Percy Hogan.

Rome — Top b.o. attraction Adriano Celentano snarls and grumbles his way through his Christmas pic, "The Grouch," under the direction of vet comic team Castell. & Pipolo. Pic is a light, easy-to-digest mix of Celentano comedy and tongue-in-cheek mystery, as the star grudgingly helps a dumb American blond look for her missing husband. B.o. has been satisfying locally, and should garner the star his usual audiences offshore in related markets.

After N.Y.C. waitress Mary (Debra Feuer) gets a phone call from new hubby Giulio Macchiavelli (Jean Sorel) in Florence, telling her to take the next plane because they've struck it rich, she crosses paths with the obnoxious lawyer Tito Torrisi (Celentano). He reluctantly makes her acquaintance and takes the case when Sorel turns out to be missing — and involved in a big bank robbery. By plain, train and jeep, they search for his treasure, following a Nancy Drew-type coded map that leads them to Siena. Mary does some very dumb things, like falling out windows, and the Grouch withholds affection until the very last scene.

Bereft of singing and dancing for once, pic has more continuity than most, and keeps buoyant spirits for its duration. Pretty newcomer Feuer is a peppy plus and plays well beside Celentano's dead-pan misanthrope. "Grouch" doesn't hang onto reality as much as Yank adventure films, preferring cartoon-style gags like Tito blinding a pilot with a pocket mirror, even though the plane is flying away from him. Plowing through the silliness, you can find a few entertaining gags at the bottom of the hayloft.

It's technically adequate.— *Yung.*

Snowballing
(COLOR)

Lightweight teen comedy.

A Comworld production and presentation. Produced and directed by Charles E. Sellier Jr. Executive producers, Dick Callister, Charles Ison. Coproducer, Toby Martin. Screenplay, Thomas C. Chapman, David O'Malley, from story by Norman Hudis; camera (Alpha-Cine color), Henning Schellerup; editor, Jerry Whittington, Michael Spence, music, Larry Whitley; songs, Toni Bellin, Pat Carpenter; sound, Athan Gigiakos, Rod Sutton; art direction, Charlie Bennett; production manager-assistant director, Leon Dudevoir; stunt coordinator, John Meier; second unit director, Spence. Reviewed on Prism vidcassette, N.Y., Jan. 5, 1987. (MPAA Rating: PG.) Running time: **97 MINS.**
Roy Balaban . . . . Alan Sues
Andy . . . . P.R. Paul
Karen . . . . Mary McDonough
Greg . . . . Adam Mills
Dan . . . . Michael Sharrett
Bonnie . . . . Bonnie Hellman
Cheryl . . . . Jill Carroll
Al . . . . Steven Tash

Also with: Billie Hayes, Bill Zuckert, Tara Buckman, Bob Hastings, Dan Rogers, Holly Roberts.

_____

"Snowballing" is an innocuous teen comedy, sort of a sanitized version of "Hot Dog ... The Movie." Picture was lensed in Park City, Utah, four years ago with various alternate titles such as "Winter Vacation," "Snow Job" and "Smooth Moves," but never received a theatrical release from Comworld Pictures, debuting now on vidcassette instead.

Formula plot has kids from Monroe High School arriving for an annual skiing competition, but cheated on their vacation fees by the corrupt organizer of the event, Tolson (Bob Hastings), who's in cahoots with the local sheriff (Bill Zuckert).

A trio of teens (P.R. Paul, Michael Sharrett and Steven Tash) are trying to get some action going with the local girls as well as their female classmates, leading to the usual gags. Skiing stunts are okay, while the film's humorous content is weak. Best gag has the kids' nerdish chaperone/science teacher Roy Balaban (Alan Sues camping it up) buying an Indiana Jones hat as a fashion statement, and then chased all around the resort by a giant snowball.

Despite feeble attempts at vulgarity, this is intended as wholesome entertainment, made by filmmakers from the Sunn Classics school. Vidcassette packaging tries to make it seem more risqué than it is, with the misleading labeling of "No rating" on the box, while the proper PG rating is indicated only on the cassette inside.—*Lor.*

Kol Ahavotai
(All My Loving)
(ISRAELI-COLOR)

_____

A YNYL presentation of a Doran Eran & Yaud Levanon production. Produced by Dov Keren. Written and directed by Yohanan (Jorge) Weller. Camera (color), Gad Danzig; editor, Era Lapid; art direction, Yaakov Stein. Reviewed at Tamuz Cinema, Tel Aviv, Jan. 2, 1987. Running time: **85 MINS.**
With: Alon Aboutboul (Daniel) Ree Rosenfeld (Sigal), Dov Navon (Oren), Dorit Adi, Dalia Malka, Ran Apfelberg.

_____

Tel Aviv — A half-baked, adolescent attempt by recent Tel Aviv graduate Jorge Weller to unfold an innocent love story in retrospect, this effort lacks both the charm and wit to sustain its feeble plot.

Daniel surveys his affair with Sigal, which ended abruptly after two years of bliss. He sits in front of his typewriter and tries to put down on paper the origins of the relationship and of everything else he has experienced in the romantic domain since he was 10 years old.

However, there is nothing interesting or original in all these memories, direction of actors appears to be almost nonexistent and all technical credits are below average.

Betting on Alon Aboutboul, the rising new star of the local cinema, with five films under his belt in one year and scheduled to play in two new ones soon, and on Ree Rosenfeld, another young talent on her way up, didn't help very much either, since both look entirely disoriented by the proceedings.

The gravest failure is on the script level, since Argentine-born Weller has little knowledge of Israeli background and wrote his script referring to his country of origin. Transposed to an alien background, the plot loses any semblance of credibility and leaves the impression it is located somewhere in limbo.

Film has spent almost a year on the shelves before release and its quick withdrawal does not augur well for Weller's commercial future.
—*Edna.*

Kapax del Amazonas
(Kapax The Man From The Amazon)
(COLOMBIAN-COLOR)

_____

A Pel-Mex release of a Maro Prods. de Colombia-Focine production. Written and directed by Miguel Angel (El Indio) Rincón O. Stars Alberto Rojas Lesmez. Camera (color), Tote Trenas; editor, José Rojo; indigenous music, original music, M.A. Rincón. Reviewed at Havana Film Festival, Dec. 10, 1986. Running time: **92 MINS.**
Kapax . . . . Alberto Rojas Lesmez
Woman . . . . Marla Bauza Max
Man . . . . Aldo Sambrell
Also with: Eva Bravo, Rosa Marla Mora, Flor Marina Rodríguez, Elza Cristina Porras, Alfonso Sanahuria Lozano, Pepe Lozano Vargas, Gabriel de los Rlos.

_____

Havana — Although the storyline of the Colombia feature "Kapax The Man From The Amazon" comes off like a shopworn vehicle, director Miguel Angel (El Indio) Rincón has based the pic on real events.

In 1965, anthropologist Linda Smaely and her husband flew to Colombia in a small plane to study the Yagua Indians. Since he had been drinking heavily on the flight into the Amazon, once he gets behind the wheel, the husband crashes their small plane in the middle of nowhere.

Linda is pulled alive from the wreckage by the Yagua warrior Kapax, who nurses her back to health, woos here and eventually chooses her to be his mate. In the end, she rejects the choice to return to civilization, preferring to remain with her "noble savage" and his people.

The film version of this story is of mixed results. El Indio handles the storyline awkwardly. It is not until almost a quarter into the pic, when we meet Kapax and his people, that the picture comes alive with vivid photography and a depiction of indigenous tribal behavior that calls to mind the best moments of "The Emerald Forest."

Rincón's feelings about the Amazon and its people come out in a

brilliant capturing of the Yagua, their dances, music, rites and tribal complexity. Here he is at home with the material and the heart of the story is revealed.

Instead of making a feature fiction film, Rincón should pare this uneven effort down to its basic focus and intent; the resulting hour would make for a fascinating docu.
—*Lent.*

Flodder
(DUTCH-COLOR)

_____

A Concorde film release of a First Floor Features production. Produced by Laurens Geels, Dick Maas. Written and directed by Maas. Camera (Fuji color; prints by Cineco), Marc Felperlan; editor, Hans van Dongen; music, Maas; sound, Georges Bossaers; art direction, Hubert Pouille; set direction, Hans Voors; stunt coordinator, Marc Boyle. Reviewed at Tuschinski theater, Amsterdam, Dec. 28, 1986. Running time: **111 MINS.**
With: Nelly Frijda, Huub Stapel, Tatjana Simico, Rene van't Hof, Lou Landré, Herbert Flack, Nano Lehnhausen, Jan Willem Hees, Appolonia van Ravenstein.

_____

Amsterdam — Dick Maas, helmer of the 1983 Dutch thriller "The Lift," opted for laughs in his second theatrical outing, "Flodder." Pic uses a tried and tested comic theme: a goodhearted, streetwise family of slum dwellers rehoused in a salubrious uptown area. Set in an unidentifiable Western country, and snappily paced with well-timed gags, this could be one of those rare Dutch films to break out in foreign territories.

Ma Flodder (Nelly Frijda), her three sons and two daughters, and their grandfather live in a slum located on chemically polluted soil. A do-gooding social worker persuades the city housing committee to move them, as an experiment, into a home in a plushy estate.

That's the start of this sitfarce. The Flodders have an underdeveloped sense of property and propriety. They go in for a little bit of thieving here, a little thuggery there, a touch of pimping and a dash of whoring — but, of course, they have hearts of gold.

Their moneyed neighbors, typically arrogant snobs — except for one, (Appolonia van Ravenstein), who is married to a dull tank regiment officer. She leaves him for the elder Flodder son (Huub Stapel) and moves in with the clan. When the family unexpectedly inherits some money, they party to celebrate the event and invite the up market neighbors. Everyone has a ball until the cuckolded husband makes an entrance — in a tank.

The characters speak Dutch, but is this really Holland? The number-plates of the cars do not belong to any identifiable country. Boys deliver newspapers American style, throwing them from their bicycles onto the lawns. This is an imaginary country — multinational movie-

land, for multinational consumption.

Technical credits are above average for local product, especially camerawork and editing. The film looks worth more than its $1,700,000 budget. The characters may be slightly two-dimensional (though the actors make a good shot at trying to add some depth), but essentially this is a film to entertain — and it succeeds admirably on that score. —*Wall.*

Witchboard
(COLOR)

_____

Effective supernatural horror.

_____

A Cinema Group release of a Paragon Arts Intl. production. Produced by Gerald Geoffray. Executive producer, Walter S. Josten. Supervising producer, Ron Mitchell. Written and directed by Kevin S. Tenney. Camera (color), Roy H. Wagner; editor, Steve Waller, Dan Duncan; music, Dennis Michael Tenney; associate producer, Roland Carroll. Reviewed at Northland Cinema 8, Columbus, Ohio, Jan. 10, 1987. (MPAA Rating: R.) Running time: **98 MINS.**
Jim . . . . Todd Allen
Linda . . . . Tawny Kitaen
Brandon . . . . Stephen Nichols
Sarabeth . . . . Kathleen Wilhoite
Dewhurst . . . . Burke Byrnes
Mrs. Moses . . . . Rose Marie

_____

Columbus — Don't mess with a Ouija board. That's the message delivered with a certain flair in the low-budget but often intriguing "Witchboard," being given a test run in three Columbus theaters.

The film tells a somewhat complicated tale in a fairly straightforward manner. Brandon (Stephen Nichols) attends a party at the home of Jim (Todd Allen) and girlfriend Linda (Tawny Kitaen), bringing along his Ouija board. Jim and Brandon had been friends, but fell out when Jim apparently stole Linda away. Jim's working in home construction, having dropped out of medical school. He doesn't believe in the power of the Ouija board, even when Brandon apparently summons the spirit of a 10-year-old, David, who died by drowning some 30 years earlier.

Brandon conveniently forgets to take the board home, and Linda becomes fascinated. She uses the board alone (that's a no-no, Brandon later explains) and "talks" to the spirit. Turns out the spirit is evil (surprise!) and takes a special interest in Linda as a possible parent for reincarnation purposes. The spirit kills one of Jim's fellow workers, then confronts a punk-attired medium (Kathleen Wilhoite), who supplies the film's only comic relief before perishing nastily.

Jim and Brandon finally join forces to try to save Linda from the evil being unleashed through the wicked board. There's a goose-bump-raising climax, followed by a relatively happy ending.

"Witchboard" takes itself seriously. The script is well paced, althought director/writer Kevin S. Tenney likes to make his audience jump through some rather tired devices, such as the heroine confronting her own image in a mirror and jumping in fright, and one person scaring another by approaching silently from behind.

But "Witchboard" also develops tension, especially toward the end. The film spends too much time establishing that Jim and Brandon don't like each other, before finally letting them patch things up.

Technical credits are fine, especially some outstandingly moody photography by Roy H. Wagner. The film was shot around the San Francisco area.

Acting is okay. Kitaen can be somewhat wooden and mechanical, but it's that kind of a role. Burke Byrnes has a good turn as a noisy cop. Rose Marie, the veteran comedienne, is wasted in a 30-second cameo.

Rated R, "Witchboard" keeps its gore to a reasonable minimum. The suspense occurs from an unseen force, which almost always is more frightening than something visible.
— *Pow.*

Un Hombre de Exito
(A Successful Man)
(CUBAN-COLOR)

A ICAIC release of an Instituto Cubano del Artes e Industria Cinematográfico production. Produced by Humberto Hernández. Directed by Humberto Solas. Stars César Evora. Screenplay, Solas; camera (color), Livio Delgado; editor, Nelson Rodríguez; music, Luigi Nono. Reviewed in competition at Havana Film Festival, Dec. 12, 1986. Running time: **110 MINS.**

Javier . . . . César Evora
Raquel . . . . Raquel Revuelta
Rita . . . . Daisy Granados
Dario . . . . Jorge Trinchot
Leana . . . . Mabel Roche
Puig . . . . Carlos Cruz
Also with: Rubens de Falco, Miguel Navarro, Angel Espasande, Omar Valdés and Jorge Alí.

Havana — "Un Hombre de Exito" (A Successful Man), by perhaps Cuba's best directing talent Humberto Solas, is an ambitious venture covering 30 years and contrasting the lives of two brothers separated by ideology and ambition.

The art direction pays meticulous attention to detail with hundreds of costumed extras and reconstructions of Havana from 1932 to the beginning of the Cuban Revolution.

The problem with the film is that it is too ambitious in scope, while dealing with a meager story that gets lost in the panorama and parade of characters.

With so many side characters, we hardly have time for the two protagonists, Javier (César Evora), the successful man, and his revolutionary brother Dario (Jorge Trinchot).

The tale begins with their student days full of promise for the future. Whereas Javier begins to sell out, Dario is out planting bombs and distributing leaflets.

It is the story of corruption versus innocence and purity of rightful action. Once you begin to compromise yourself, where do you stop? Yet the story is simplistic. The sketchy characters are little more than clichés. In fact, we never know much about Dario except that he appears from time to time involved in revolutionary actions. Javier receives the bulk of attention, set within a world of bourgeois opulence.

Some of the supporting actors deserve mention for their performances, notably leading legit star Raquel Revuelta and Daisy Granados.

"A Successful Man" is not a successful film. Perhaps in the future, Solas will devote to the script some of the same care he has given to production.—*Lent.*

Veneno para las Hadas
(Poison For Fairies)
(MEXICAN-COLOR)

A Películas Mexicanas release of an Instituto Mexicano de Cinematografía (Imcine)-Sindicato de Trabajadores de la Producción Cinematográfica production. Written and directed by Carlos Enrique Toboada. Camera (color), Guadalupe García; editor, Carlos Savage; music, Carlos Jiménez Mabarak. Reviewed at Havana Film Festival, Dec. 13, 1986. Running time: **90 MINS.**

Verónica . . . . Ana Patricia Rojo
Flavia . . . . Elsa María

Havana — "Veneno para las Hadas" (Poison For Fairies), winner of five Ariel awards (Mexico's equivalent to the Oscar), is a disturbing look at the dangerous world of childhood fantasies and their repercussions when allowed to be taken seriously.

Produced by the Mexican Film Institute (Imcine) in conjunction with the cinema's workers union, the pic is a strange collection of scenes and tones about imagination run wild.

The storyline concerns two young girls at an expensive private school. New kid at school Verónica (Ana Patricia Rojo) is an orphan and self-proclaimed witch, while her friend Flavia (Elsa María) is both fascinated and dominated by the former.

Everything eventually hinges on the manufacture of some poison for the fairies, historical enemies of the forces of evil. Each child finds her own poison, which brings out her own evil.

The story is kept in the realm of childhood and its all-consuming belief in mystery. Any inclusion of adults is dealt with indirectly. All grownup characters are relegated to either an arm or leg on the side of the screen or shown from the back and never seen full-face.

Director Carlos Enrique Toboada does his best to present this mysterious childhood world. His frequent use of dreams and nightmares continues the mystery evoked in the narrative.

The two young stars carry their parts well. They are always believable and never cute in the Spielberg sense. Tech credits are adequate but at times they are too fanciful and self-conscious of their effects, which distance the viewer rather than wrap him within the tale.

Yet the film is not a commercial venture and would probably find resistance from an Anglo audience, even among the art crowd. The pace is uneven and the techniques a bit too pretentious. Latin boxoffice should also prove limited due to pic's non-Latin themes and focus on precocious evil. —*Lent.*

Le Mal d'aimer
(The Malady Of Love)
(FRENCH-ITALIAN-COLOR)

An AAA release of a Sandor Prods./FR3 Films Prod./Séléna Audiovisuel/AFC/Cinema & Cinema coproduction, with the participation of the French Ministry of Culture, RAI and Radio Televisione Italiana. Executive producers, Lise Fayolle, Paolo Zaccaria. Directed by Giorgio Treves. Screenplay, Vincenzo Cerami, Pierre Dumayet, from an original story by Cerami; camera (Eastmancolor), Giuseppe Ruzzolini; editor, Carla Simoncelli; music, Egisto Macchi; art direction, Lorenzo Baraldi; sound, François Wesldisch; makeup, Claudia Reymond-Shone; costumes, Jost Jakob; production managers, Gérard Gaultier, Angelo Barbagolo; casting, Shula Siegfried; assistant director, Béatrice Banfi. Reviewed at the Gaumont Ambassade theater, Dec. 19, 1986. Running time: **88 MINS.**

Robert Briand . . . . Robin Renucci
Marie-Blanche . . . . Isabelle Pasco
Eleonore . . . . Carole Bouquet
Therese . . . . Piera Degli Esposti
Robert's father . . . . Erland Josephson
Trader . . . . Andrzej Seweryn

Paris — "Le Mal d'aimer," a Franco-Italian coproduction directed by newcomer Giorgio Treves (a one-time assistant to Italian greats like Francesco Rosi, Vittorio de Sica and Luchino Visconti), is a fable of love, death and disease set in a 15th century leper-colony. Treves, working from an original script by himself, Pierre Dumayet and Vincenzo Cerami, succeeds at atmosphere but fails at involving drama.

Robin Renucci is the tormented physician-director of a medieval lazar-house whose inmates include patients afflicted with a mysterious new malady: syphilis. Among his latest arrivals is a beautiful young girl (Isabelle Pasco) who has been picked up by authorities though she exhibits no external symptoms of the disease. Drawn by the girl's apparent purity, Renucci defies his profession, peers and society and possible infection — by choosing to defend and finally run away with Pasco.

Solid tech credits — notably Giuseppe Ruzzolini's lensing, Lorenzo Baraldi's production design and Claudia Reymond-Shone's makeup work — graphically recreate the murk, clamminess and insalubrity of the prison-like lepercolony, but the characters and their oppressions are as distant as the period and its mores. Reading tale in relation to the current AIDS scourge (which the authors claim they never intended) doesn't give the film any greater immediacy or meaning.

Okay international supporting cast include Erland Josephson as Renucci's father, Carole Bouquet as a noblewoman quarantined for having a syphilitic lover, Piera Degli Esposti as Renucci's assistant and sexual comforter and Andrzej Seweryn as a tradesman. —*Len.*

The Kindred
(COLOR)

Imitative sci-fi.

An F/M Entertainment release. Produced by Jeffrey Obrow. Executive producer, Joel Freeman. Coproducer, Stacey Giachino. Directed by Obrow, Stephen Carpenter. Screenplay, Carpenter & Obrow, John Penney & Earl Ghaffari, Joseph Stefano; camera (Technicolor), Carpenter; editor, Penney, Ghaffari; music, David Newman; production design, Chris Hopkins; art director, Becky Block; set decorator, Susan Emshwiller; costumes, Lynne A. Holmes; special creatures created by Michael John McCracken; assistant director, David Householter; associate producer, Diane Nabatoff; casting, Janet Hirshenson, Jane Jenkins; Denise Chamian. Reviewed at the Four Star theater, L.A., January 7, 1986. (MPAA Rating: R.) Running time: **91 MINS.**

John Hollins . . . . David Allen Brooks
Dr. Phillip Lloyd . . . . Rod Steiger
Melissa Leftridge . . . . Amanda Pays
Sharon Raymond . . . . Talia Balsam
Amanda Hollins . . . . Kim Hunter
Hart Phillips . . . . Timothy Gobbs
Brad Baxter . . . . Peter Frechette
Cindy Russell . . . . Julia Montgomery
Nell Valentine . . . . Bunki Z

Hollywood — "The Kindred" is another example of a film that puts its energy in the wrong place. A team of young filmmakers has conspired to turn out what they believe will be commercial instead of using their talents to create something personal or original. Ironically, "The Kindred" is such a poor imitation of "Aliens" and other supernatural sci-fi that an audience will find little reason to see it.

Problem is not that the film doesn't look good. In fact production values are emphasized at the expense of story and character. Codirectors Jeffrey Obrow and Stephen Carpenter, who also take producer and cinematographer credits, respectively, have left little of the fun of '50s sci-fi films and seem to take this nonsense as seriously as if they were directing "Citizen Kane."

No fewer than five writers, including Obrow and Carpenter, have put their heads together to come up with the story of a female scientist

(Kim Hunter) who dies and leaves her son (David Allen Brooks), also a scientist, to destroy her controversial genetic experiments that have created some dangerous semi-human life forms.

Along for the ride are a merry band of nitwits disguised as scientists who try to help Brooks sort out the mess at his mother's country house that looks something like where Norman Bates used to live with his mother.

Wouldn't you know that a mysterious woman (Amanda Pays) and an evil scientist (Rod Steiger) are on the scene to help the monster. Pays turns into an amphibian (really) and Steiger is slimed to death by the creature, which is unfortunate since Pays is far too attractive and intriguing and Steiger too talented to be wasting their time on this fooolishness.

Filmmakers have failed to capture either the playful campiness of films like "Creature From The Black Lagoon" or the suspenseful thrills and chills of "Aliens." In shooting for flashy special effects (creatures were designed by Michael John McCracken), they neglected the human context that gives the horror its edge, as it did in "Aliens."

Acting is too wooden to win any sympathy for these people and dialog is so weak that the most memorable lines are the squealing of the creature. —*Jagr.*

Capablanca
(CUBAN-SOVIET-COLOR)

An ICAIC release of an Instituto Cubano de Artes y Indústrias Cinematográficas production. Produced by Santiago Llapur, Nicolai Velmiski. Directed by Manuel Herrera. Stars César Evora, Galina Belyayeva. Screenplay, Herrera, Eliseo Alberto Diego, Dal Orlov; camera (color), Igor Klebanov; editor, Justo Vega; music, Sergio Vitier. Reviewed at Havana Film Festival, Dec. 11, 1986. Running time: **95 MINS.**

José Raúl Capablanca . . . . . . .César Evora
Sacha Mozhaeva. . . . . . . .Galina Belyayeva
Amelia . . . . .Beatriz Valdés
Vera . . . . .Marina Yakovlieva
José María Picón . . . . . . .Adolfo Llaurado
Gonzalo . . . . .Ramón Veloz
Eremaev . . . . .Boris Nevsorov
Barraque . . . . .Alejandro Lugo
Also with: Javier Avila, Rogelio Meneses, Igor Tarasov, Grigori Liampe, Dimitri Orlovki.

Havana — The Cuban-Soviet coprod "Capablanca" is a biographical look at one period in the life of Cuban World Chess Champion José Raúl Capablanca. The period in question is when he decided to participate in the 1925 Moscow World Chess Championship.

The story finds Capablanca in top form yet at odds with his success. This is still two years before he surrendered his crown to Alexander (Alokhine) Allojin in Buenos Aires in 1927, and much before his rapid decline and early death in New York.

Against the advice of his friends, he goes to the young Soviet Union where he reunites with old flame Amelia (Beatriz Valdés) and meets and woos Soviet dancer Sacha (Galina Belyayeva).

Cuban leading man César Evora is believable in the brooding protrayal of the complex and restless figure of Capablanca, pacing about competitions unable to sit through an entire game, sometimes playing whole groups of contenders at the same time, sometimes losing a game on purpose so he can leave the game early to walk with Sacha.

Considering the pic's theme, dealing with the world of chess and chessmasters, director Manuel Herrera keeps the story moving through Capablanca's romantic and personal involvements.

Lavish attention is paid to details with authentic recreation of the period, and much of the action is confined to studio interiors.

The pic bogs down at times with textual problems related to exposition and social commentary on the problems of Cuba and the sense of hope in the first years of new Soviet state. And, certain background characters, such as the Russian landlord, are portrayed as happy Russian folklore figures without any real personality beyond the cliché. Also, almost every Moscow street scene is full of happy prols dancing around in one parade or other.

Although there are some wonderful moments in the film, there are not enough of these instances to make for a completely satisfying whole. At the end of the film, we still do not really know what makes our chess champion tick. His complications are a little beyond the scope of the story which only hints at a brooding undercurrent of self-destruction that will later be manifested and relegated to history. —*Lent.*

Wanted: Dead Or Alive
(COLOR)

Lowgrade actioner.

A New World Pictures release. Executive producer, Arthur Sarkissian. Produced by Robert C. Peters. Coproduced by Barry Bernardi. Directed by Gary Sherman. Stars Rutger Hauer. Screenplay, Michael Patrick Goodman, Brain Taggert, Sherman; camera (CFI color), Alex Nepomniaschy; editor, Ross Albert; music, Joseph Renzetti; art director, Jon Hutman; production designer, Paul Eads; sound, Peter Bentley; assistant director, Alan Curtiss; casting, Ellen Meyer, Sally Stiner. Reviewed at New World Pictures, L.A., Jan. 8, 1987. (MPAA Rating: R.) Running time: **104 MINS.**

Nick Randall . . . . .Rutger Hauer
Malak Al Rahim . . . . .Gene Simmons
Philmore Walker . . . . . . .Robert Guillaume
Terry . . . . .Mel Harris
Danny Quintz . . . . .William Russ

Hollywood — Last two minutes of "Wanted: Dead Or Alive" save

the film from being a complete bust. Steely demeanor of Rutger Hauer is about the only arresting characteristic of this actioner which, if less violent, easily could be thought of as episodic tv.

Pic should do healthy sales in the vidcassette market after a marginal theatrical run.

Hauer plays a modern-day bounty hunter and fictional great-grandson of the character Steve McQueen played on the tv series of the same name that ran in the late 1950s.

While McQueen brought in outlaws of the Old West, Hauer brings in villains of our modern media world who have a high price on their heads — no matter what their crimes.

As an embittered ex-CIA agent, Hauer gets a certain amount of satisfaction commanding high fees from ex-bosses he mostly despises.

They are dependent on him to bring to society's most rotten and he needs them to pay for his high-tech warehouse loft home/office (complete with what must be an illegal arsenal of weapons) and a boat docked at San Pedro.

Nearly the first hour is one drawn out scenario showing Hauer in his various locales and moods (mostly unsmiling ones) while mapping out a strategy to capture the diabolical Malak Al Rahim (Gene Simmons), who's terrorizing Los Angeles with random bombings.

Plot has more holes in it than Hauer's shooting range (also a feature of his loft) and consequently, story never seems to get beyond the good guy versus bad guy chase level.

Nice performances are turned in by Hauer's two law enforcement buddies, one an old CIA partner (Robert Guillaume) and the other a lieutenant in the L.A.P.D. (William Russ), both of whom have a unique friendship with the bounty hunter that should have been developed more.

Unfortunately, scripters try to move things along by substituting Rahim's dastardly deeds at regular intervals for those that give his works some color by explaining what motivates the man responsible for them.

The squeamish will not find this pic too easy to sit through as it seems that someone gets blown to bits, sliced up or shot every few minutes, not including a couple of group annihilations.

The saving grace is the last scene that is so ludicrous, it's unintentionally riotous but nevertheless a uniquely entertaining payoff for those who can sit through to the end. —*Brit.*

Outrageous Fortune
(COLOR)

Shelley Long-Bette Midler comedy teaming is hilarious.

A Buena Vista release of Touchstone Pictures presentation of an Interscope production. Produced by Ted Field, Robert Cort. Coproduced by Peter V. Herald, Scott Kroopf, Martin Nickelson. Directed by Arthur Hiller. Stars Shelley Long, Bette Midler. Screenplay, Leslie Dixon; camera (Deluxe color), David M. Walsh; editor, Tom Rolf; music, Alan Silvestri; production design, James D. Vance; set decorator, Rick T. Gentz; art direction, Sandy Veneziano; set design, Danile Maltese; sound (Dolby stereo), Gerald Jost; costumes, Gloria Gresham; assistant director, Jim Van Wyck; casting. Lynn Stalmaster, Mally Finn. Reviewed at General Cinema, Sherman Oaks, Calif. Jan. 16, 1987. (MPAA Rating: R.) Running time: **100 MINS.**

Lauren . . . . .Shelley Long
Sandy . . . . .Bette Midler
Michael . . . . .Peter Coyote
Stanislov Korenowski . . . . . .Robert Prosky
Atkins . . . . .John Schuck
Frank . . . . .George Carlin
Weldon . . . . .Anthony Heald
Cab Driver . . . . .Ji-Tu Cumbuka

Hollywood — "Outrageous Fortune" is the third comedy to bear the stamp of the new Disney production team and, like the others, it's all well crafted, old-fashioned entertainment that takes some conventional elements, shines them up and repackages them as something new and contemporary. For the most part, it's a formula that works and with a few curve balls from Leslie Dixon's clever script and winning performances from Bette Midler and Shelley Long, "Outrageous Fortune" should be another hit for the studio.

Although it somehow has picked up an R rating, "Outrageous Fortune" is really a risqué film for a conservative audience. It's a traditional male buddy film but the twist here is that it has substituted women and the main plot device is that the two heroines are sleeping with the same man.

Dixon's script plays off the tried-and-true formula of two disparate personalities thrown together under adverse conditions who must leave to cooperate and wind up liking each other. From the start Midler and Long are like the North and South poles, so different are they in style, background, goals and attitude. Sure enough they learn they share more than they think.

For starters they share the same lover. Michael (Peter Coyote) is the find of the century, a nice eligible elementary school teacher with a heart of gold, or is he?

Midler and Long collide even before their affections do in an acting class given by the eminent Russian director Stanislov Korenowski (Robert Prosky). Long is a wealthy, spoiled dilletante while Midler last starred in "Ninja Vixens."

Director Arthur Hiller makes the most of the conflicting styles of the two women. Long is sleek in silk and speaks in an upper East side purr while Midler wears an electric blue vinyl raincoat and talks like a truck driver. There's no way these two are going to get along and when the audience learns they're sharing the same man before they do, it's a delicious moment complete with one image-shattering sight gag.

Now that Dixon has them in the same bed, she turns up the heat and the film takes off as a chase picture with the girls following Coyote to New Mexico to demand a decision.

They're not the only ones looking for him. It seems the CIA is not on his trail as is the KGB. To top things off, it turns out Korenowski is a Russian agent first and a director second.

Along the way the students get to practice their acting talent and in one marvelous role reversal, Long, playing a cop, barks at some heavies to move against the wall or she'll blow 'em away.

It may be a bit disillusioning to learn Coyote is really an immoral swine, but not improbable since the actor carries a dark side almost like a five o'clock shadow. However, it's really the Midler and Long show and even when Dixon's script sags and becomes a bit repetitious in the long New Mexico chase section, they are never less then fun to watch.

Midler is an accomplished comedienne who has successful blended elements of Mae West and Marilyn Monroe into an audacious style all her own. As for Long, her character is not unlike Diane on ''Cheers,'' but she carries off some rough house action with aplomb and remains charming even when her character is a pain. Together they make an inspired pair.

Supporting cast, unfortunately, has a few rough spots. Prosky never seems to click as the agent/actor and George Carlin, as a spaced out hippie leftover in the New Mexico desert, is a little too bizarre to get a handle on. John Schuck is amusing as the bumbling CIA funtionary. Tech credits are first rate throughout.

Still there is something a bit disturbing in a film where the good guys are the government agents, the Russians are patently evil and Coyote's flamboyant individualism is discredited. No wonder Carlin can't seem to find his way around.

—*Jagr.*

Jocks
(COLOR)

Funny tennis court antics sunk by cornball sex comedy.

A Crown Intl. Pictures release of a Mt.

Olympus Prods. presentation of an Ahmet Yasa production. Produced by Yasa. Directed by Steve Carver. Screenplay, Michael Lanahan, David Oas; camera (Deluxe color), Adam Greenberg; supervising editor, Richard Halsey; editor, Tom Siiter; music, David McHugh; sound, Mark Ulano; production manager-associate producer, John Broderick; art direction, Randy Ser; set decoration, Greg Melton; casting, Mary Ann Barton, Michael Greer. Reviewed at RKO Warner 1 theater, N.Y., Jan. 23, 1987. (MPAA Rating: R.) Running time: **91 MINS.**

The Kid	Scott Strader
Jeff	Perry Lang
Nicole	Mariska Hargitay
Chip Williams	Richard Roundtree
Coach Beetlebom	R.G. Armstrong
Pres. White	Christopher Lee
Andy	Stoney Jackson
Tex	Adam Mills
Chito	Trinidad Silva
Ripper	Don Gibb
Julie	Katherine Kelly Lang
Chris	Tom Shadyac
Tony	Christopher Murphy

''Jocks'' is a formula teen comedy which shows flashes of life in some humorous scens of psyching on the tennis court, but the package is sunk by warmed-over clichés. Pic was filmed at the end of 1984 (and foolishly has onscreen signs throughout tying it in with a 1984 tournament) under the title ''Road Trip'' and finally comes off the shelf after shifting distributors.

Lame premise has the six-man tennis team of L.A. College trekking to Las Vegas for the championships, under the tutelage of Coach Chip Williams (Richard Roundtree). Trying to sabotage their efforts is the school's athletic director (R.G. Armstrong camping it up in a poorly fitting wig) who wants tennis scratched from the roster since it's a ''pansy sport,'' as well as the Dallas team and its girl friends who are up to dirty tricks. The college president (Christopher Lee, in an atypically hammy performance) wants victory to impress the alumni.

Of course, the boys carouse in Vegas, with the same old wet t-shirt contest, assignation with call girls and other corny gags of the teen sex genre. Film finally picks up on the court, where the antics of the team's animal named Ripper (Don Gibb, with a linebacker's physique) are hilarious, and Stoney Jackson is also quite funny pretending to be a gay blade on the court to psyche his opponent. Even here, director Steve Carver (known for his action pictures) goes to the well too often and the tennis hijinks become repetitious.

Lead players Scott Strader and Perry Lang are bland while heroine Mariska Hargitay reveals her resemblance (the eyes) to mom Jayne Mansfield, but is once again stuck with a crummy role. Smaller roles, including the requisite topless girls and a funny transvestite, are uncredited.—*Lor.*

Radio Days
(COLOR)

Warm and funny look-back by Woody Allen.

An Orion Pictures release. Produced by Robert Greenhut. Executive producers, Jack Rollins, Charles H. Joffe. Written and directed by Woody Allen. Camera (Duart color), Carlo Di Palma; editor, Susan E. Morse; musical supervision, Dick Hyman; production design, Santo Loquasto; art director, Speed Hopkins; set decorator, Carol Joffe, Les Bloom; set dresser, Dave Weinman; sound, James Sabat; costumes, Jeffrey Kurland; assistant director, Ezra Swerdlow; narrator, Allen; casting, Juliet Taylor. Reviewed at Orion screening room, Century City, Calif. Jan. 15, 1987. (In U.S. Film Festival in Park City, Utah). (MPAA Rating: PG). Running time: **85 MINS.**

Sally White	Mia Farrow
Joe	Seth Green
Mother	Julie Kavner
Abe	Josh Mostel
Father	Michael Tucker
Bea	Dianne Wiest
Masked Avenger	Wallace Shawn
Latin bandleader	Tito Puente
Rocco	Danny Aiello
Rocco's mother	Gina DeAngelis
Biff Baxter	Jeff Daniels
Radio singer	Kitty Carlisle Hart
''Silver Dollar''	
Emcee	Tony Roberts
Irene	Julie Kurnitz
Roger	David Warrilow
New Year's singer	Diane Keaton

Hollywood — Although lacking the bite and depth of his best work, ''Radio Days'' is one of Woody Allen's most purely entertaining pictures. It's a visual monolog of bits and pieces from the glory days of radio and the people who were tuned in. ''Radio Days'' will undoubtedly be a special treat for those who were listening at the time and despite its very specific setting, film is so sweet and inviting, that Allen fans should have little trouble recognizing the territory. As usual non-converts may be baffled by the fuss.

Territory in question is Rockaway Beach, a thin strip of land on the outskirts of New York City, where young Joe (Seth Green) and his family live in not-so splendid harmony and for entertainment and escape to listen to the radio. Set at the start of World War II, it's a world of aunts and uncles all living on top of each other and the magical events and people, real and imagined, that forever shape one's young imagination.

Expanding the vignette structure of ''Zelig'' and the peek behind the curtain of reality approach of ''The Purple Rose of Cairo,'' ''Radio Days'' is able to penetrate the familial world of Rockaway and the glamorous whirl of New York night life.

Allen is not looking for realism,

but a reality filtered through memory that it glows like a sepia-toned photograph. Not surprisingly, ''Radio Days'' is a splendid visual achievement from Carlo Di Palma's evocative photography to Santo Loquasto's period-perfect production design.

Unlike other New York period comedies, such as ''Brighton Beach Memoirs,'' most recently, ''Radio Days'' is not simply about nostalgia, but the quality of memory and how what one remembers informs one's present life. What could be a more appropriate vehicle than radio since as a medium it is totally dependent on the mind's eye to fill in the spaces?

Although Allen wrote the screenplay and narrates the film, and many of the family incidents must be taken from his own experience, it would be too narrow to interpret ''Radio Days'' as a straight autobiography any more than Alvy Singer in ''Annie Hall'' is Woody Allen.

Allen has always been a literary-minded director and the narrator here, the grownup voice of the young Joe, is omnipotent, taking long, amusing looks at the denizens of Broadway and his own block at the same time.

To keep the narrative whole, he weaves together running commentary on some half-dozen odd characters. Susan E. Morse's editing is a big plus in allowing the film to jump from one character to another without losing momentum or cohesiveness.

As kooky and eccentric here as she was in ''Hannah And Her Sisters,'' Dianne Wiest is delicious as an aunt who is desperate to find a husband but somehow keeps meeting Mr. Wrong. Julie Kavner and Michael Tucker are the mother and father who ponder whether they could have made better choices. This doesn't stop Tucker from coming up with numerous hair-brained schemes to make a quick buck.

Also on hand in the neighborhood is Uncle Abe (Josh Mostel) who is never seen without a fish in hand which he gets from friends at Sheepshead Bay. What would any neighborhood be like without communist sympathizers, a teenage girl dating a black musician (gasp!), provocative women and homely kids who somehow imagine themselves as budding Clark Gables?

Where the film is most successful is in conveying the link between the mundane lives of the ordinary folk and the glamorous doings of New York's hoity-toities, which when examined under such a fine lens are not that very different. Both celebrate New Year's Eve together, although in Rockaway they toast with Hoffman's ginger ale, not champagne as at the Stork Club.

Things are not always what they seem and the robust Masked Avenger is, in real life, the diminutive Wallace Shawn. Mia Farrow is a none-too-bright cigaret girl with a yen for stardom who magically transforms her life. David Warrilow and Julie Kurnitz are a Dorothy and Dick Kilgallen morning team who do more than cover the openings when they're out reporting at night.

One of the joys of "Radio Days" is picking out Allen's stock players in bit parts throughout the picture. Tony Roberts turns up as a quiz show emcee and Danny Aiello as a mafia hit man with a soft spot for Farrow.

A real sentimental treat at the end of the film is Diane Keaton as a lounge singer warbling, appropriately on New Year's Eve, Cole Porter's "You'd Be So Nice To Come Home To." Music, in fact, is a delightful addition to the action and Dick Hyman has assembled a fabulous group of period tunes, some even performed live. Tito Puente does a great turn as an Xavier Cugat-type club act.

Other vignettes played through Joe's adult sensibilities take on absurd proportions such as an extreme working of "The Stratton Story," in which a baseball player continues competing after losing one limb after another.

What Allen sees as he surveys a past "slowly growing dimmer with each new year" is a loving place full of grotesque people who are not always virtuous and admirable but never less than human. —*Jagr.*

84 Charing Cross Road
(COLOR)

Moving drama with a terrific Anne Bancroft turn.

A Columbia Pictures release of a Brooks-films production. Produced by Geoffrey Helman. Executive producer, Mel Brooks. Directed by David Jones. Stars Anne Bancroft, Anthony Hopkins. Screenplay, Hugh Whitemore, based on the book by Helene Hanff, originally adapted for the stage by James Roose-Evans. Camera (Rank & TVC color), Brian West; editor, Chris Wimble; music, George Fenton; production design, Eileen Diss (London), Edward Pisoni (N.Y.); costume design, Jane Greenwood (N.Y.), Lindy Hemming (London); sound, Gary Alper (N.Y.), David John (London); assistant director, Mark McGann (N.Y.), Jake Wright (London); associate producers, Randy Auerbach, Jo Lustig; casting, Judy Courtney, D.L. Newton (N.Y.), Marilyn Johnson (London). Reviewed at the U.S. Film Festival, Park City, Jan. 23, 1987. (MPAA Rating: PG.) Running time: **97 MINS.**

Helene Hanff	Anne Bancroft
Frank Doel	Anthony Hopkins
Nora Doel	Judi Dench
Maxine Bellamy	Jean De Baer
George Martin	Maurice Denham
Cecily Farr	Eleanor David

Kay	Mercedes Ruehl
Brian	Daniel Gerroll
Megan Wells	Wendy Morgan
Bill Humphries	Ian McNeice
Ginny	J. Smith-Cameron
Ed	Tom Isbell

Park City, Utah — An uncommonly and sweetly civilized adult romance between two transatlantic correspondents who never meet, "84 Charing Cross Road" is an appealing film on several counts, one of the most notable being Anne Bancroft's fantastic performance in the leading role. Genuinely moving on numerous occasions, this Brooks-films production does not fit snugly into any of the conventional marketing niches, but cast and quality give Columbia enough to work with to open and build the film intelligently with urban and older audiences.

Helene Hanff's slim volume of letters between herself and a dignified antiquarian bookseller in London would not seem to repre-

Original Play

A Michael Redington presentation of a play in two acts, adapted by James Roose-Evans from a book by Helene Hanff. Staged by James Roose-Evans; setting, Richard Marks; costumes, Barbara Wilson; lighting, Peter Hunter. Opened Nov. 26, 1981, at the Ambassadors Theater, London; $11.65 top.

Helene Hanff	Rosemary Leach
Frank Doel	David Swift
Cecily Farr	Barbara Ward
Megan Wells	Charmian May
Mr. Martin	Charles Kinross
William Humphries	Adrian Hall
Maxine Stuart	Charmian May
John Todd	Susanna Best

sent the most promising material for a popular feature film, although book has already appeared in a BBC-TV adaptation and as a stage play in London and New York.

Dramatist Hugh Whitemore, who penned the BBC version in 1975, has stuck closely to the content of the original letters, which began in 1949 as formal requests by the New Yorker Hanff for old books over a 20-year period into a warm, loving exchange of missives and gifts between her and much of the staff of the bookshop of Marks & Co.

Filling this out visually are scenes from the lives of both Hanff and her principal correspondent, the prim, undemonstrative Frank Doel. With all the efficiency possible, Doel manages to fill the most esoteric and obscure request for old volumes, which are treasured above all else by the spinsterish but vibrant New Yorker.

With food rationing keeping the English on limited diets during the post-war period, Hanff sends her friends all manner of canned foods. Touched by her generosity, the quietly eccentric bookstore staff begin pleading with Hanff, the ultimate Anglophile, to finally come to

England, but one thing and another always prevent it until it is too late.

Built on a basis of mutually held taste, knowledge, interests and consideration, the bond between Hanff and Doel becomes a form of pure love, which is why the film is so touching in spots. Doel has his wife and two girls in London, and Hanff has her increasingly more successful tv writing career in New York, but their relationship is unique and untouchable, so much so that Doel's wife finally admits that she felt jealous of it.

Although well balanced between events on both sides of the pond, story suffers from an imbalance between the active, initiating Hanff, who occasionally addresses the camera directly, and the relatively passive, inexpressive Doel. At the end, the man's humor and high intelligence are described, but these traits are never revealed; agreeable and very recognizable as a type, and quite perfectly embodied by Anthony Hopkins, one never gets beneath his surface to know what he may be thinking.

On the other hand, Anne Bancroft brings Helene Hanff alive in all her dimensions, in the process creating one of her most memorable characterizations. The voluble, opinionated Manhattanite on the one hand, she is also very alone with her books, cigarets and booze. A significant part of her emotional life is tied up with her love of London and literature, which are inextricably linked with Doel. Bancroft has a great deal of fun with the role, but catches the viewer by the throat with it as well.

Director David Jones, who did such a fine job with the screen version of "Betrayal," is both tactful and precise in his work here. With very delicate material, he has managed to plant numerous emotional depth charges that detonate with increasing power along the way. Clearly a firstrate talent, Jones' name would be welcome on films more frequently than has been the case.

Film is loaded with an exceptional number of locations that are used for very brief sequences. Production designers Eileen Diss and Edward Pisoni, as well as costume designers Jane Greenwood and Lindy Hemming, have responded expertly to the challenge of subtly revealing the changes in London and New York over a period of two decades, and of other behind-the-scene craftspeople is thoroughly pro.

A nagging frustration with the story is Hanff's utter inability to just pick herself up and get over to England. An array of excuses is presented, but the bottom line is that it's not prohibitively expensive to

make the trip regardless of economic station, and since she would have had a place to stay, she could have avoided those costly London hotels. But that's the way it was, which makes the tale just that much sadder. —*Cart.*

Beyond Therapy
(COLOR)

Play adaptation misfires.

A New World Pictures release of a Roger Berlind production of a Sandcastle 5 film. Produced by Steven M. Haft. Executive producer, Roger Berlind. Directed by Robert Altman. Stars Julie Hagerty, Jeff Goldblum, Glenda Jackson, Tom Conti, Christopher Guest. Screenplay, Christopher Durang, Altman, based on Durang's play; camera (color), Pierre Mignot; supervising editor, Steve Dunn; editor, Jennifer Augé; music, Gabriel Yared; production design, Stephen Altman; art direction, Annie Sénéchal; costume design, John Hay; sound, Philippe Lioret, Daniel Belanger; assistant director, Yann Gilbert; associate producer, Scott Bushnell. Reviewed at the U.S. Film Festival, Park City, Jan. 24, 1987. (MPAA Rating: R.) Running time: 93 MINS.

Prudence	Julie Hagerty
Bruce	Jeff Goldblum
Charlotte	Glenda Jackson
Stuart	Tom Conti
Bob	Christopher Guest
Zizi	Geneviève Page
Andrew	Cris Campion
Cindy	Sandrine Dumas

Park City, Utah — "Beyond Therapy" is a mediocre film version of Christopher Durang's mediocre play. The difference is that this comedy somehow won a good measure of popular success onstage, whereas the screen version is headed nowhere.

Set in New York but lensed — with distracting obviousness — in Paris, farce about young singles and their shrinks already seems out of date in its attitudes and concerns. Jeff Goldblum plays a bisexual fellow who lives with a man but keeps meeting nervously neurotic Julie Hagerty, no matter what personal ad he places in New York magazine.

The big jokes come when Goldblum brings Hagerty home for dinner while his b.f., Christopher Guest, is still hanging around and when it turns out that the duo's respective psychiatrists, Glenda

Original Play

A Warner Theater Prods., Claire Nichtern, FDM Productions, Francois de Menil & Harris Maslansky presentation of a play in two acts (nine scenes), by Christopher Durang. Staged by John Madden; scenery, Andrew Jackness; costumes, Jennifer von Mayrhauser; lighting, Paul Gallo; musical arrangements, Jack Feldman. Stars John Lithgow, Dianne Wiest; features Peter Michael Goetz, Kate McGregor-Stewart, Jack Gilpin, David Pierce. General management, Tyler Gatchell Jr., Peter Neufeld; publicity, Jeffrey Richards Assoc.; stage managers, Craig Jacobs, Trey Hunt. Opened May 26, 1982, at the Brooks Atkinson Theater, N.Y.; $22.50 weeknights, $25 weekend nights.

Bruce	John Lithgow
Prudence	Dianne Wiest
Stuart	Peter Michael Goetz

Charlotte . . . . Kate McGregor-Stewart
Bob. . . . . Jack Gilpin
Andrew . . . . David Pierce

Jackson and Tom Conti, are themselves involved.

A small handful of Durang's one-liners still get laughs, but director Robert Altman has soured the already threadbare proceedings to such an extent that, with the possible exception of the delightfully dizzy Hagerty, it is not even a pleasure to watch the wonderful actors, assembled here.

This is the comedy of frustration and irritation pushed to an obnoxious and wearying degree.

Paris shooting has resulted in any number of wrong details, and all the foreign accents and French dialog from secondary actors make this a perfect cast for a picture about the Tower of Babel.

In all events, this would seem to be a judicious moment for Altman to move out of his play adaptations phase, or at least to start selecting better works to spend his time on.—*Cart.*

Waiting For The Moon
(COLOR)

Charming view of Gertrude Stein and Alice B. Toklas.

A Skouras Pictures release of New Front Films/Laboratory for Icon and Idiom/A.B. Films production in association with American Playhouse/the Société Française de Production/ARD-Degeto/Channel Four. Produced by Sandra Schulberg. Executive producer, Lindsay Law. Line producers, Jean Achache, Frederic Bourboulon. Directed by Jill Godmilow. Screenplay, Mark Magill, from a story by Godmilow and Magill; camera (color), Andre Neau; editor, Georges Klotz; music, Michael Sahl; production design, Patrice Mercier; costume design, Elisabeth Tavernier; associate producer, Barbara Lucey. Reviewed at the U.S. Film Festival, Park City, Jan. 21, 1987. (MPAA Rating: PG.) Running time: **87 MINS.**
Alice B. Toklas . . . . Linda Hunt
Gertrude Stein . . . . Linda Bassett
Henry Hopper . . . . Andrew McCarthy
Fernande Olivier . . . . Bernadette Lafont
Ernest Hemingway . . . . Bruce McGill
Guillaume Apollinaire . . . . Jacques Boudet

Park City, Utah — A film of considerable loveliness and charm. "Waiting For The Moon" is an imaginary look at episodes in the later lives of literary lioness Gertrude Stein and her longtime companion Alice B. Toklas. Decidedly an art house item that will play best to viewers who are at least familiar with the names of the leading characters, picture is at the same time funny and accessible enough to make some inroads with general audiences, specifically that which embraced "A Room With A View" so warmly.

Known during production as "On The Trail Of The Lonesome Pine" (reportedly Stein's favorite song), film opens on a beautiful

summer's day with the two middle-aged women proof-reading one of Stein's manuscripts at their French country home while also attending to an unexplained baby. Director Jill Godmilow covers the action with a beautifully choreographed to-and-fro tracking shot, and brittle, intelligent dialog here sets the tone on a high plane from which it rarely slips.

Mark Magill's script flips in a fragmentary way back somewhat earlier moments during the mid-1930s when the couple drove through France and also endured a very difficult period in their relationship prompted by Stein's refusal to discuss with Toklas her possibly fatal illness.

Picture is nothing but talk, but Magill has risen to the occasion and provided the two women with conversation worthy of their reputations, and makes one believe that they really could have been like this. Portrait is entirely believable, even if Godmilow and Magill have insisted that what's on view is entirely fictional.

On their motor tour through the countryside, the women pick up a hitchhiking American, Henry Hopper, who is on his way to the Spanish Civil War. They also pick up Fernande Olivier, Picasso's mistress, with whom Toklas enjoys a particularly strong rapport — "What about your genius?," they ask each other, and are joined by the poet Appollinaire, who, around a cmapfire, hauntingly tells of having eaten mushrooms with Jean Cocteau on a mountaintop on a night when they named all the constellations in the sky after people they knew.

Less successful is the portrait of Ernest Hemingway, who is crudely depicted as a drunken, whoring buffoon lacking the sensitivity of the other characters.

The core of the film is the wonderful relationship between the two women, which is alive and resilient even at its worst. Hemingway, among others, calls Toklas a saint for putting up with the tough, demanding Stein, and the two test and spar with each other just as they give comfort and provide constant reminders of their extraordinary mutual knowledge.

Lack of narrative thrust will put off some viewers, as will the juxtoposition of Summer villa scenes with other sequences set at different times. Appeal of the film rests on the relatively superficial levels of epigrams and peeks into the lives of the famous, but pic operates extremely well on that level.

Tale is narrated by Toklas, and Linda Hunt virtually walks away with the picture in the role. Fed up with, hurt and frustrated by her

companion, she nevertheless understands and loves her thoroughly, and Hunt conveys all of this with an exemplary economy of expression. Linda Bassett is similarly fully up to the demands of her role as Stein, never overdoing the arty or bossy sides and getting across a great deal through looks and the authority of her line delivery.

Period feel is seemlessly expressed through Patrice Mercier's production design and Elisabeth Tavernier's costuming, and Andre Neau's lensing is subtly adaptable to the changing moods of the piece.

—*Cart.*

No Picnic
(B&W-16m)

Amateur night on the Lower East Side.

A Gray City presentation of a Great Jones Film Group/Films Charas production. Produced by Doris Kornish. Executive producer, Chris Sievernich. Written and directed by Philip Hartman. Camera (b&w), Peter Hutton; editor, Grace Tankersley; music, Ned Sublette, The Raunch Hands; art direction, Tina Chaden; sound, Frank Kern; assistant director, Kevin O'Brien; second unit camera, Michael Spiller, Jacki Ochs, Jeff Preiss. Reviewed at the U.S. Film Festival, Park City, Jan. 17, 1987. (No MPAA Rating.) Running time: **84 MINS.**
Mac . . . . David Brisbin
Stripe . . . . Myoshin
Anne. . . . . Anne D'Agnillo

Park City, Utah — "No Picnic" is no picnic to sit through. Amateurish in every department, pic plays like a kindergarten imitation of Jim Jarmusch but also feels like it was made at least five years ago due to its mannered punk posturing. Commercial prospects are less than zero.

Cofounder of the New York inspot the Great Jones Cafe, first-time writer-director Philip Hartman attempts to spin an offbeat yarn about a music industry fringe type who encounters no end of colorful Lower East Side characters on his way to his appointment with destiny.

Unfortunately, Hartman keeps any talent he may have for narrative storytelling expertly concealed, and his attempt to impose some wit on the proceeding lays an egg thanks to some particularly lame voiceover narration, which is also there to try to disguise the fact that most of the pic was shot without sound.

Soundtrack is loaded with tunes by such underground musicians as Richard Hell, Raw Youth and The Raunch Hands, but neither can they conceal the lack of originality and inspiration brought to bear here. Overall effect is stultifying. —*Cart.*

The Trouble With Dick
(COLOR)

Bedroom farce meets sci-fi.

A Frolix production in association with Roert Augur. Produced, written and directed by Gary Walkow. Executive producer, Augur. Coproducer, Leslie Robins. Line producer, Albert Barasso. Camera (color), Daryl Studebaker; music. Roger Bourland; production design, Eric Jones, Pui Pui Li; sound design, George Budd; special effects supervisor, James Zarlengo; costume design, Ted Sewell; assistant director, Charlie Mullin; second unit camera, Bill McDonald; casting, Susan Young. Reviewed at the U.S. Film Festival, Park City, Jan. 19, 1987. (No MPAA Rating.) Running time: **86 MINS.**
Dick Kendred . . . . Tom Villard
Diane . . . . Susan Dey
Sheila Dibble . . . . Elaine Giftos
Haley Dibble . . . . Elizabeth Gorcey
Lars . . . . David Clennon
Samsa . . . . Jack Carter
Betty . . . . Marianne Muellerleile

Park City, Utah — While it could have pushed its imagination further and in even bolder ways, "The Trouble With Dick" provides a generally funny look at writer's block brought on by the scribe's increasingly complicated sex life. Despite its limitations, first feature by Gary Walkow shows a sure, professional hand both with actors and the camera, and pic could make a modest showing commercially in major cities and college areas if distributed intelligently.

Tom Villard ably plays the title character, a young sci-fi writer with one novel under his belt who presently can't even get a short story published. Desperately in need of a sale, he takes a cheap room in a nice old Los Angeles house also occupied by former college heartthrob Susan Dey, with whom Dick would finally like to get a romance going.

As Dey, a terribly serious science researcher, proves unreceptive, Dick puts up no resistance when the landlady's Lolita-like daughter, Elizabeth Gorcey, flings herself at him. As if one hot number were not enough, the landlady herself, artsy aerobics nut Elaine Giftos, also puts the make on the confused fellow, and finally succeeds as well.

The bedroom farce aspects are handled with aplomb by the director and thesps, with tone remaining racy without falling into crudeness. Setting these scenes off are dreamlike snippets of the sci-fi tale Dick is writing, a yarn about a convict trying to escape an arid prison planet.

Sci-fi sequences could have been much more imaginative and bizarre, and thereby have added to the amount of incident in the picture, which is basically restricted to two settings and a limited number of characters. Furthermore, Dick's emotional breakdown stemming from all the sexual and creative stress comes on rather too suddenly, as does his recovery.

Nevertheless, the action moves along quite amusingly for the most part, and Walkow's look at artistic frustration is refreshingly unpretentious. Villard is attractive enough to validate the provocative attention he receives from the two women, but also has an edge of naiveté and dorkiness that makes him plausible as a sci-fi nut.

Dey, Giftos and Gorcey are all right on the money in their characterizations, and film's technical aspects, notably Daryl Studebaker's lensing, production design by Eric Jones and Pui Pui Li, and special effects by James Zarlengo, are all outstanding for such a low-budget affair. —*Cart.*

From The Hip
(COLOR)

Slapstick treatment doesn't save dumb study of legal ethics.

A De Laurentiis Entertainment Group release of an Indian Neck production. Produced by Rene Dupont, Bob Clark. Executive producers, Howard Baldwin, Bill Minot, Brian Russell. Directed by Clark. Screenplay, David E. Kelley, Clark, story by Kelley; camera (J-D-C Widescreen, Technicolor), Dante Spinotti; editor, Stan Cole; music, Paul Zaza; production design, Michael Stringer; art direction, Dennis Bradford; set decoration, Edward (Tantar) LeViseur; costume design, Clifford Capone; sound, David Stephenson; associate producer, Ken Heeley-Ray; assistant director, Ken Goch; casting, Mike Fenton, Jane Feinberg. Reviewed at the Directors Guild of America Theater, L.A., Jan. 30, 1987. (MPAA Rating: PG.) Running time: **111 MINS.**

Robin Weathers	Judd Nelson
Jo Ann	Elizabeth Perkins
Douglas Benoit	John Hurt
Craig Duncan	Darren McGavin
Larry	Dan Monahan
Steve Hadley	David Alan Grier
Roberta Winnaker	Nancy Marchand
Phil Amos	Allan Arbus
Raymond Torkenson	Edward Winter
Matt Cowens	Richard Zobel
First Judge	Ray Walston
Scott Murray	Robert Irvin Elliott
Second Judge	Beatrice Winde
Lt. Matt Sosha	Art Hindle
Mrs. Martha Williams	Priscilla Pointer

Hollywood — Bob Clark attempts to bring the spirit of "Porky's" into the courtroom in "From The Hip," but ends up with a neither fish-nor-fowl concoction that veers from raucous comedy on the one hand to ethical attitudinizing on the other. Commercial prospects look modest for this lively but mild entertainment.

Film's first section actually proves surprisingly funny and spirited, as recent law school graduate Judd Nelson, in the employ of an eminent Boston firm, connives his way into getting to argue a case in court, an unheard-of assignment for so young an attorney.

Case looks hopeless going in, as the firm's client openly admits he slugged the plaintiff and is willing to pay the price. Nelson's inexperience proves to be his ace-in-the-hole, however, as he does impressive battle with the prosecuting attorney and wins the jury over by cleverly showing the victim's battery charge to be frivolous.

Now the firm's fair-haired boy instead of its black sheep, Nelson next takes on a much more difficult case. English professor John Hurt is accused of sexually molesting and murdering a young girl. Despite heavy circumstantial evidence of his guilt, Nelson believes he can get the man off, but increasingly comes to loathe his brilliant, repellently arrogant client, finally becoming convinced of his guilt.

So what begins as a pleasantly irreverent social comedy evolves into serious consideration of the moral priorities of attorneys and the legal system as a whole. Nelson is forced to ask himself how far he will go in defending a man he knows is lying, and dramatic crux of the picture demonstrates how he adroitly and honorably deals with his dilemma.

Pic's first half is about virtually nothing at all, but Clark manages to keep the proceedings buoyant by throwing in endless throwaway gags and energizing all the performances in disarming fashion. As soon as the story decides to take up an issue and become concretely about something, pace sags and the sense of inventiveness slackens.

Nelson hits the same aggressive note throughout the entire film, but his gutsiness is convincing and not unappealing. Elizabeth Perkins gets to be warm and, for the most part, supportive as his g.f., and John Hurt is believably odious as the ingenious murder suspect.

Supporting cast is greatly responsible for keeping the picture alive for so long. Darren McGavin, Nancy Marchand and Allan Arbus make a delightful trio at the head of the law firm, fellow young attorneys David Alan Grier and Dan ("Porky's") Monahan amusingly support Nelson in his outrageous ploys, Richard Zobel, as the prosecuting attorney, makes a fine foil for the hero, Ray Walston and Beatrice Winde each have some choice moments as judges, and Edward Winter is hilariously self-satisfied as Nelson's first client.

At 111 minutes, pic is decidedly too long. Tech credits are fine.
—*Cart.*

Warrior Queen
(COLOR)

Silly sword & sandal epic.

A Seymour Borde & Associates release of a Lightning Pictures production. Produced by Harry Alan Towers. Directed by Chuck Vincent. Stars Sybil Danning, Donald Pleasence, Richard Hill. Screenplay, Rick Marx, based on a story by Peter Welbeck (Towers); camera (TVC color), Lorenzo Battaglia; editor, Vincent, Joel Bender, Jim Sanders, Tony Delcampo; music, Ian Shaw, Kai Joffe; production design, Lucio Parise; costumes, Parise; sound, Larry Revene; assistant director, Per Sjostedt; associate producers, Aristide Massaccesi, Donatella Donati. Reviewed at the Hollywood Egyptian theater, Hollywood, Jan. 23, 1987. (MPAA Rating: R.) Running time: **69 MINS.**

Berenice	Sybil Danning
Clodius	Donald Pleasence
Marcus	Richard Hill
Chloe	Josephine Jacqueline Jones
Vespa	Tally Chanel
Philomena/Augusta	Stasia Micula
Veneria	Suzanna Smith
Victo	David Cain Haughton
Roberto	Mario Cruciani
Goliath	Marco Tullio Cau

Hollywood — "Warrior Queen" is a below-average exploitation pic without enough action or flesh to please fans of the genre. In fact, it's rather tame stuff and even the presence of veteran schlock queen Sybil Danning doesn't do much to validate the experience.

One thing is certain, it didn't take long for Danning to memorize her lines since she does little more than grimace and change togas through the film's 69 minutes. She's the mistress of the Roman emperor slumming in Pompeii (film's original title) at the time of the big roast.

City is run by Donald Pleasence who looks more like Mayor Koch than Mayor Clodius. There's some minor depravity in the town but nothing to get too excited about. Nonetheless Danning turns her nose up on the whole affair while trying to save the purity of two young kittens in bondage (Tally Chanel and Suzanna Smith).

Pic has the usual assortment of good guys with big muscles and bad guys with big muscles. Richard Hill is the best of the just and Marco Tullio Cau is worst of the rest.

Story is, of course, besides the point and only real fun to be had is watching the scenery. The non-human kind is patently phony, which, again, is part of the fun. Director Chuck Vincent has cut in a good deal of footage from another film to show the eruption of Mt. Vesuvius and the fleeing mob. Inconsistency in cinematography stands out like a chariot on 42d Street.

Chanel, as the object of Hill's affection, is a Goldie Hawn lookalike who certainly has all the assets to find more work in similar pics. But no one can sneer with the authority of Danning. —*Jagr.*

Black Widow
(COLOR)

Handsomely made suspenser has two great actresses but no thrills.

A 20th Century Fox release of a Laurence Mark production, produced in association with Americent Films and American Entertainment Partners. Produced by Harold Schneider. Executive producer, Mark. Directed by Bob Rafelson. Stars Debra Winger, Theresa Russell. Screenplay, Ronald Bass; camera (Deluxe color), Conrad L. Hall; editor, John Bloom; music, Michael Small; additional music, Peter Rafelson; production design, Gene Callahan; set decoration, Jim Duffy, Buck Henshaw, Rick Simpson; costume design, Patricia Norris; sound (Dolby), David MacMillan; assistant director, Tommy Thompson; casting, Terry Liebling. Reviewed at the 20th Century Fox Studio, L.A., Jan. 28, 1987. (MPAA Rating: R.) Running time: **103 MINS.**

Alexandra Barnes	Debra Winger
Catharine	Theresa Russell
Paul	Sami Frey
Ben	Dennis Hopper
William Macauley	Nicol Williamson
Bruce	Terry O'Quinn
Sara	Lois Smith
Michael	D.W. Moffett
Ricci	Leo Rossi
Shelley	Mary Woronov
Irene	Rutanya Alda
Shin	James Hong
Etta	Diane Ladd

Hollywood — Lacking the snap and sharpness that might have made it a firstrate thriller, "Black Widow" instead plays as a moderately interesting tale of one woman's obsession for another's glamorous and criminal lifestyle. High-gloss production holds the attention in large measure because of Debra Winger and Theresa Russell's presence centerstage at all times, and b.o. action should be decent.

Known primarily to buff audiences for her work in the films of her husband Nicolas Roeg, Russell portrays an icy-hard, beautiful woman who, it quickly becomes clear, makes an exceptionally handsome living by marrying wealthy men, murdering them, then collecting the settlements from the wills.

This female Bluebeard is terrifically discreet and careful when it comes to dispatching her victims and covering her tracks. She neatly poisons items bound to be consumed by the men, then makes sure she is out of town when the deaths actually occur.

Pattern would go unnoticed were it not for conscientious, disheveled Justice Dept. agent Winger, who thinks she smells a rat and begs permission to pursue the case.

Following Russell to Hawaii, where the blond beauty is mourning the passing of her latest spouse, Nicol Williamson, while getting a great tan, Winger befriends her just as Russell is targeting her next victim, international hotel tycoon Sami Frey.

Smart cookie that she is, Russell grows suspicious of Winger's interest in her, and the intrigue grows even thicker as both women become involved with Frey and begin hatching strategies against the other while maintaining a guarded friendship.

Winger first takes off after her prey for purely professional reasons, but the most intriguing aspect of Ronald Bass' screenplay is the barely submerged sexual jealousy the overworked government employee feels for the sexy, utterly confident manipulator of sex and lives.

Although Winger herself is saucy as always, her character is supposed to be a shlumpy, neurotic woman who hasn't had a date in years, and is thus fascinated by, and mightily envious of, this lady who can seduce any rich man she wants and then get away with all his money. Tension from these emotional currents reaches its height during the episodes with dreamboat Frey, who really wants Russell but is willing to settle for Winger when she is placed at his feet.

This angle could have been played up to more powerful effect, because the dramatic progression of the story is fairly straightforward and not especially suspenseful. There is never a moment's doubt in Winger's or the viewer's mind as to Russell's guilt, so it is only a matter of her being caught, and how. While the situation is unusual enough to keep one hooked, the dialog and what's actually happening onscreen are not that lively or stimulating.

In his first feature outing since "The Postman Always Rings Twice" six years ago, Bob Rafelson puts in a very professional but seemingly impersonal effort, getting the essentials up there but not getting the most out of the possibilities present.

Returning after an even longer absence — 11 years — is ace cinematographer Conrad Hall, whose work is characteristically handsome and luminous. Indeed, all the craft contributions, including Gene Callahan's varied production design, John Bloom's responsive editing and, notably, Michael Small's very effective score, are of the highest Hollywood order.

Winger and Russell are both among the most talented and watchable young actresses on the scene today, so the picture has a lot going for it thanks to their casting alone. At the same time, both play very tense, brittle women operating in a zone rather near the breaking point, so there is a nervousness and restraint in both performances that harnesses them slightly.

Frey is a delight, as always, although his character invites considerable incredulity when he announces he wants to build a luxury hotel on top of an active Hawaiian volcano. Other supporting actors, including Williamson and Dennis Hopper, are in very briefly, but James Hong is very effective as a seedy island detective in the employ of both women. —*Cart.*

Allan Quatermain And The Lost City Of Gold

Adventure send-up goes nowhere.

A Cannon Group release of a Golan-Globus production. Executive producer, Avi Lerner. Produced by Menahem Golan, Yoram Globus; line producer, Michael Greenburg. Directed by Gary Nelson. Additional scenes directed by Newt Arnold. Stars Richard Chamberlain, Sharon Stone. Screenplay, Gene Quintano, from novel "Allan Quatermain" by H. Rider Haggard; camera (J-D-C Widescreen, Rank Color), Alex Phillips (Zimbabwe), Frederick Elmes (L.A.); editor, Alain Jakubowicz; music, Michael Linn, and (uncredited) Jerry Goldsmith; sound (Ultra-Stereo), David Jones (Zimbabwe), Mark Ulano (L.A.); production design, Trevor Williams (Zimbabwe), Leslie Dilley (L.A.); set decoration, Patrick Willis (Zimbabwe), Portia Iversen (L.A.); production manager, Michael Games (Zimbabwe), Chris Pearce (L.A.); assistant director, Tony Tarruella (Zimbabwe), Nicholas Batchelor (L.A.); special effects makeup, Colin Arthur; stunt coordinator, Solly Marx (Zimbabwe), Don Pike (L.A.); mechanical effects supervisor, Richard Johnson (Zimbabwe), Germano Natali; special effects supervisor, Eric Allard (L.A.); visual effects supervisor, Ermanno Biamonte; postproduction supervisor, Michael R. Sloan; casting, Robert MacDonald. Reviewed at RKO Warner 2 theater, N.Y., Jan. 30, 1987. (MPAA Rating: PG.) Running time: **99 MINS.**

Allan Quatermain	Richard Chamberlain
Jesse Huston	Sharon Stone
Umslopogaas	James Earl Jones
Agon	Henry Silva
Swarma	Robert Donner
Nasta	Doghmi Larbi
Queen Nyleptha	Aileen Marson
Sorais	Cassandra Peterson
Robeson Quatermain	Martin Rabbett

"Allan Quatermain And The Lost City Of Gold" is Cannon's poor followup to its 1985 remake of "King Solomon's Mines." Pic in fact is a remake of Harry Alan Towers' 1977 film "King Solomon's Treasure," which starred John Colicos as H. Rider Haggard's adventure hero Allan Quatermain (from the book by that name). Towers' version, lensed in Swaziland and featuring rather silly dinosaurs, was never released theatrically, a fate which almost loomed for Cannon's expensive version after numerous postponements of its release last year.

Gene Quintano's embarrassing screenplay jettisons Haggard's enduring fantasy and myth-making in favor of a back-of-the-envelope plotline and anachronistic jokes about Cleveland. Quatermain (Richard Chamberlain reprising his role) receives a gold piece from a dying man that inspires him to trek to East Africa in search of his brother Robeson (Martin Rabbett), who's been hunting for a lost white race. Joining him are his archaeologist girlfriend (Sharon Stone, also in the 1985 film), and African warrior (James Earl Jones), a comic relief mystic (Robert Donner camping it up) and five expendable bearers.

After considerable filler, they find the lost race of Phoenicians, ruled by bland beauty contest queen Nyleptha (Aileen Marson; Britt Ek-land was a lot more fun in the role in Towers' version). In some confusing action, Chamberlain brings the house down and kills the baddies with molten gold.

Film relies frequently on a very phony gimmick of a spear-proof tunic and story completely runs out of gas once the heroes arrive at their destination. Director Gary Nelson has some attractive Zimbabwe locations such as Victoria Falls to work with, but most of the footage is underlit. Additional scenes directed by Newt Arnold back in Hollywood a year after principal photography appear to be on the sets of Cannon's "Journey To The Center Of The Earth" remake, providing irrelevant roller-coaster type footage in a cave, notable for poor blue screen work and obvious models.

Acting is embarrassing, ranging from Chamberlain's unfunny tongue-in-cheek delivery and Stone's hysterical approach, to the villain played by Henry Silva in a fright wig. Donner's routine went out with Gunga Din, while Cassandra Peterson, as the queen's evil sister, has no dialog and will duly be mocked in the way she threw barbs at the performances in the horror films she hosted as tv's Elvira.

Typical of cutting corners, the bulk of the music here is Jerry Goldsmith's rousing theme music from "King Solomon's Mines," played at least a dozen times. —*Lor.*

Death Before Dishonor

Well-made terrorist actioner.

A New World Pictures release, in association with Balcor Film Investors of a Lawrence Kubik/M.P.I./Bima production. Executive producers, Frank Capra Jr., Arthur Maslansky, William Braunstein. Produced by Lawrence Kubik. Directed by Terry J. Leonard. Screenplay and story, Capra, Kubik, John Gatliff; camera (Deluxe color), Don Burgess; editor, Steven Mirkovich; music, Brian May; production design, Kuli Sandor; set decorator, Doron Efrat; costumes, Rochelle Zaltzman; sound, Shabtai Sarig; assistant director, Eli Cohen; associate producer, Nava Levin; casting, Michael McLean, April Webster. Reviewed at the Directors Guild theater, L.A., Jan. 27, 1987. (MPAA Rating: R.) Running time: **95 MINS.**

Sergeant Jack Burns	Fred Dryer
Colonel Halloran	Brian Keith
Ambassador	Paul Winfield
Elli	Joanna Pacula
Maude	Kasey Walker
Jihad	Rockne Tarkington
Ramirez	Joey Gian
James	Peter Parros

Hollywood — "Death Before Dishonor," as suggested by the U.S. Marine credo that is its title, trumpets the macho virtues of a handful of Marines — this time fighting against terrorists in a fictitious Arab country called Jamal.

This new twist on an old plot is surprisingly good, due in no small measure to the fact that it is so time-ly. There is actually a line in the film where the U.S. ambassador to Jamal says: "The U.S. does not, nor will not, negotiate with terrorists," that elicited considerable laughter from the screening audience.

Exploitation pictures filmed in Israel like "Death Before Dishonor" used to be Cannon's domain. Now New World's got one, and it should do well by it; if not in the theaters, then in video.

Heading this corps of troopers is Sgt. Jack Burns (Fred Dwyer), who is transferred with his Camp Pendelton superior, Colonel Halloran (Brian Keith) to Jamal to act as advisers to the Jamali military — bringing lots of American hardware with them.

Keith, a crusty Armed Services lifer, gets kidnapped; the U.S. ambassador (Paul Winfield) won't negotiate, so Dryer has to take things in his own hands.

Dryer's adversaries, a new group that could be described as "designer terrorists" for the snappy get-up they wear, are the stereotypically ruthless Arab bunch who kill innocent people, torture victims and do a Kamakaze number on the U.S. Embassy. They're also, for the most part, very wooden actors, most notably, the butch international terrorist Maude (Kasey Walker) and the photojournalist Elli (Joanna Pacula).

Dryer is very effective as a sort of steely Clint Eastwood type, undaunted by being completely outnumbered by terrorists on most occasions. Never mind the odds, he always gets 'em — by bazooka, grenade, whatever's handy.

Of course, a few of his loyal boys get sacrificed along the way, but it does help to heighten the sympathy when a Marine dies, tears well up in Dryer's eyes and some patriotic American tune can be heard in the background.

Like so many of these films, there's a lot of bloodshed and carnage and a corresponding amount of magnificent stunt work and fancy pyrotechnics to go with them — all quite impressive.

For a nice change from the Phillippines, a favorite spot to shoot Vietnam exploiters, location here is an idyllic, isolated Israeli coastal town. —*Brit.*

Stregati
(Bewitched)
(ITALIAN-COLOR)

A Columbia Pictures release of a Mario and Vittorio Cecchi Gori presentation. Produced by Gianfranco Piccioli for Union P.N. and C. G. Silver Film Prods. Directed by Francesco Nuti. Stars Nuti, Ornella Muti. Screenplay, Vincenzo Cerami, Giovanni Veronesi, Nuti; camera (Luciano Vittori color),

Giuseppe Ruzzolini; editor, Sergio Montanari; music, Giovanni Nuti; art direction, Ugo Chiti. Reviewed at Etoile Cinema, Rome, Jan. 1, 1987. Running time: **95 MINS.**
Lorenzo . . . . Francesco Nuti
Anna . . . . Ornella Muti
    Also with: Novello Novelli, Alex Partexano, Mirta Pepe, Sergio Solli.

Rome — Young comic Francesco Nuti once more pairs himself with Ornella Muti, after last season's hit "Blame It On Paradise." A much more somber and downbeat romance, "Bewitched" has failed to produce the b.o. magic of Nuti's best work. Besides a thin boy-meets-girl, boy-loses-girl storyline, pic has some unpleasant scenes that have put off local holiday audiences. Chances offshore look sparse.

Nuti (who also directs) plays a nocturnal d.j. named Lorenzo. Sporting a boyish grin and one gold earring, Lorenzo is the playboy of Genoa, whose philosophy is "you can love for a single moment." In a distasteful opener, we find him seducing a silly young married woman, then tiptoeing out of the room and letting his buddies take his place in bed. In the dark she's not supposed to notice the difference. The ploy actually succeeds with the first pal, who later turns out to be Lorenzo's father, owner of a porn theater.

This gives us an idea of the boy's intractable character and sets the stage for the appearance of a mysterious beauty, Anna (Muti), one rainy night. Always clowning, Lorenzo pretends to be a cab driver and takes her down to the port, where he overcomes her initial diffidence and eventually beds her. She takes umbrage at his playboy airs, he pursues her, gets his comeuppance, but has to surrender when he discovers she's getting married on the morrow to another man. They part regretfully at the train station.

As brief encounters go, it's a pretty melancholy tale. Nuti deliberately plays up the foggy, moody atmosphere of Genoa by night, via Giuseppe Ruzzolini's soft lensing and Giovanni Nuti's super-mellow musical accompaniment. Even the carousing and horseplay Lorenzo and his pals indulge in has a painfully sad twang to it, but pic doesn't extract much significance out of these plaintive *vitelloni*, just a rather depressing mood.

Stars Nuti and Muti make a pretty pair, but like the film as a whole are so laid-back they don't raise much heat.— *Yung.*

Legacy Of Rage
(HONG KONG-COLOR)

A D&B production and release. Executive producer, Dickson Poon. Directed by Ronnie Yu. Stars Brandon Lee, Michael Wong, Regina Kent, Chan Wai-man, Mang Hoi. (No other credits provided by producer/distributor). Reviewed at Jade theater, Hong Kong, Jan. 4, 1987. Running time: **95 MINS.**
(Cantonese soundtrack with English subtitles)

Hong Kong — It is unfair to compare Bruce Lee's son Brandon Lee in his debut Hong Kong film with his dad, but the comparison is inevitable. Brandon has good presence and physique at 21 years of age but looks very American for Asians to sympathetically fight with him all the way in his big screen troubles.

Brandon has a girlfriend and is framed by good friend Michael Wong, son of a triad kingpin. His suffering in jail while the girlfriend runs off to Brazil, then revenge is a standard format.

"Legacy Of Rage" is a mess and Brandon Lee has been mistreated with a senseless debut.

The best part of the film is the photography of Hong Kong at the beginning. Otherwise, it's a waste of talents in a plot without charm, wit, reason and believability. The boorish villains are caricatures, including the suffering leading lady (Regina Kent). —*Mel.*

Light Of Day
(COLOR)

Misguided rock 'n' roll drama.

A Tri-Star Pictures release of a Taft Entertainment Pictures/Keith Barish Prods. presentation. Produced by Rob Cohen, Keith Barish. Executive producer, Doug Claybourne. Directed by Paul Schrader. Stars Michael J. Fox, Gena Rowlands, Joan Jett. Screenplay, Schrader; camera (Astro color), John Bailey; editor, Jacqueline Cambas; music, Thomas Newman; title song, Bruce Springsteen; production design, Jeannine Claudia Oppewall; set decorator, Lisa Fischer; sound (Dolby), J. Paul Oddo, Bill Pellak; costumes, Jodie Tillen; assistant director, Mark Radcliff; associate producer, Alan Mark Poul; casting, Bonnie Timmermann. Reviewed at Lorimar-Telepictures screening room, Culver City, Calif., Jan. 27, 1987. (MPAA Rating: PG-13.) Running time: **107 MINS.**
Joe Rasnick . . . . Michael J. Fox
Jeanette Rasnick . . . . Gena Rowlands
Patti Rasnick . . . . Joan Jett
Bu Montgomery . . . . Michael McKean
Smittie . . . . Thomas G. Waites
Cindy Montgomery . . . . Cherry Jones
Gene Bodine . . . . Michael Dolan
Billy Tettore . . . . Paul J. Harkins
Benji Rasnick . . . . Billy Sullivan
Benjamin Rasnick . . . . Jason Miller

Hollywood — Directors haven't had much luck in transferring the energy and emotion of rock 'n' roll to film and Paul Schrader is the latest to fail. Visceral power of rock simply doesn't stand up to the literal expression Schrader attempts in "Light Of Day." After much huffing and puffing about the meaning of the music, film finally connects towards the end, but likely will lose most of its audience along the way.

"Light Of Day," like many of Schrader's films, probably looked a lot better on paper than it does on the screen. Director has the tendency to write characters as representations of ideas rather than flesh and blood people. Consequently, action seems schematic and stilted rather than spontaneous.

This time out Schrader has taken his search for redemption to Cleveland, the legendary heartland of rock. At heart, "Light Of Day" is a tortured family melodrama with a rock 'n' roll beat. Renegade daughter Patti Rasnick (Joan Jett) and her younger brother Joe (Michael J. Fox) play in the Barbusters, a talented but routine bar band that performs in taverns around Ohio.

Schrader, who also wrote the screenplay, has spread enough guilt around this family to fill a book. Jett has a four-year-old son (Billy Sullivan), but won't tell anyone who the father is. She hates her mother (Gena Rowlands) despite mom's attempts to show her God's way. With the passive father (Jason Miller) and the dutiful son (Fox), this could be anyfamily U.S.A. as written by Eugene O'Neill.

Everyone wears their emotions on his sleeve, except Jett who wears them on her shoulder. Escape hatch from all this backbiting is supposed to be rock 'n' roll but when one talks too much about the saving grace of music, as Jett does, it tends to come out as childish and silly.

The proof that "music is all that matters" should be in the doing and although Schrader has peppered the soundtrack with lots of good cuts and Jett gets to perform a number of tunes herself, the music is basically dull and lifeless. There is no joy to the sound and with her excursions into petty theft and heavy metal, Jett just becomes a rather distasteful character.

It is only late in the film when Rowlands suffers the mandatory fatal illness that Jett shows her true feelings and brings some life to the character. Deathbed reconciliation between Jett and Rowlands is an exquisitely written and extremely moving scene. If only Schrader had packed the earlier scenes with as much feeling.

Despite the over-the-edge quality of her character, Rowlands makes even the most ludicrous lines seem feasible. It's a fine and controlled performance. Also winning is young Billy Sullivan as Benji, a born crowd pleaser who can even play a toy guitar.

Fox is basically miscast as the good-natured brother who idolizes his sister and tries to cover for her. He's a likable actor but out of his element as a tortured urban rocker and factory worker by day. His lack of intensity punctures the film's attack. Jett looks the part and even manages to hit the mark from time to time, but for every hit there's a miss.

Visually "Light Of Day" is a return to the grittiness of Schrader's first picture "Blue Collar." John Bailey's photography manages to capture the poetry of smokestacks and dinginess of dead-end bars. Title tune by Bruce Springsteen performed over the end credits by Jett and Fox is probably the strongest song in the film but still far from the unifying anthem called for.

Other tech credits are individually fine, but overall the film has an "almost real" look. So much has been written and said about the liberating power of rock and the purity of the working class that it's a thin line between the real and the romanticized. Unfortunately, Schrader has gone the wrong way.—*Jagr.*

Dead Of Winter
(COLOR)

Highly suspenseful impersonation drama.

An MGM/UA Distribution release from MGM Pictures. Produced by John Bloomgarden, Marc Shmuger. Directed by Arthur Penn. Stars Mary Steenburgen. Screenplay, Shmuger, Mark Malone; camera (Metrocolor), Jan Weincke; editor, Rick Shaine; music, Richard Einhorn; production design, Bill Brodie; set decorator, Mark S. Freeborn; costume design, Arthur Rowsell; sound, Lee Dichter; assistant director, Tony Thatcher; associate producer, Michael MacDonald; casting, Maria Armstrong, Ross Clydesdale. Reviewed at MGM, Culver City, Calif., Jan. 26, 1987. (MPAA Rating: R.) Running time: **100 MINS.**
Katie McGovern . . . . Mary Steenburgen
Mr. Murray . . . . Roddy McDowall
Dr. Joseph Lewis . . . . Jan Rubes
Rob Sweeney . . . . William Russ
Roland McGovern . . . . Mark Malone

Hollywood — Even though it's not based on a play, Arthur Penn's "Dead Of Winter" follows in the tradition of such terrific legit-to-screen suspensers as "Sleuth" and "Deathtrap," where most of the intrigue happens in the confines of a couple of rooms.

Dialog may not be as sophisticated or sardonic as the two celebrated Broadway hits that it resembles, but machination is equally riveting.

Without big name stars, film needs a unique campaign to attract an audience and and certainly something better than the trailer currently playing in theaters.

Mary Steenburgen is first-rate as the struggling actress hired by an unusually accommodating casting director (Roddy McDowall) to audition as a double for an actress removed from a film-in-progress because of an alleged nervous breakdown.

She's taken to the isolated country estate of a psychiatrist-turned-producer during a violent snowstorm (hence the title "Dead Of Winter") where she undergoes a complete makeover until she — quite uncannily — resembles the stricken actress.

Little does she know she's become the patsy for a couple of blackmailers who have bumped off the other actress, as revealed in the very first scene of the film.

Suspense is built artfully around her gradual realization that she's trapped with a sly shrink and his obsequious factotum, McDowall, considerably more malevolent than he first appeared.

Unlike the more clever "Deathtrap" and "Sleuth" scripts where the trappers and trapee play word games and second-guess each others' moves, this one pits a very up-front victim (who makes her fears well known to her captors) against villains who are at once nice, then nasty, then nice again.

To compensate for a lack of fascinating-evil characters, Penn weaves in the use of a number of suspense staples — cut phone lines, drugged liquids, two-way mirrors — but doesn't just throw them in at obvious places.

Part of the thrill is watching the three play cat and mouse in the maze of a house to which they are restricted. Production designer Bill Brodie should be credited with creating a setting that is superficially cozy and inviting (fire in the fireplace, lots of antiques, overstuffed furniture and Old Master fakes) while in some of the more unusual places are found all kinds of creepy surprises.

Complicating the tag game is Steenburgen's triple role playing as her own character, the actress she's doubling for and that actress' sister, which would be a challenge for any actress, and one she masterfully handles.

Steenburgen and McDowall are the adversaries to follow, even though it would seem more likely that the wheel-chair bound doctor, Jan Rubes, should be the one to watch. Rubes is simply not sinister enough to be the mastermind behind this scheme.

There are other such flaws in the plot, but none is readily apparent since there's no time to breathe between scenes to give them any thought.

What helps to heighten the staccato tempo is cinematographer Jan Weincke's engrossing camera angles and Richard Einhorn's compelling score. —Brit.

Arquiesta Emilio Varela
(Emilio Varela's Band)
(MEXICAN-COLOR)

A Peliculas Mexicanas release of a Cipsa Films production. Produced by Miguel Angel Barragán. Directed by Ralph Portillo. Stars Mario Almada. Screenplay, José Castro, Portillo; camera (color), Adolfo Martínez Solares; editor, Pedro Velásquez; music, Rafael Carrión, with appearance of group Los Grillos. Reviewed at Big Apple Cine 2, N.Y., Jan. 13, 1987. Running time: **87 MINS.**

Emilio Varela . . . . Mario Almada
Camelia . . . . Silvia Manríquez
   Also with: Jorge Russek, José Castro, Jenny.

It's difficult to know exactly what Mexican filmmaker Ralph Portillo had in mind when he made the genre pic "Arquiesta Emilio Varela."

The confused storyline recounts a tale of revenge: Emilio Varela (Mario Almada) is the middleman in a counterfeit operation run by Camelia (Silvia Manríquez). When he wants out, she shoots him and dumps his body in the middle of nowhere. Coincidentally, a young woman and her uncle happen to be in the middle of nowhere, find his feeble body, nurse him back to health and he returns to wreak vengence.

Various improbable coincidences pop up throughout the pic. Also, several characters — including Camelia — sing commentaries on the plot in a ranchero "corrido" style amost like a parody of a musical. Yet they come off as gratuitous spots thrown into the film out of context. Combined with the routine and predictable storyline, the results are merely confusing. —Lent.

Over The Top
(COLOR)

Likable Stallone tale of filial affection and armwrestling.

A Warner Bros. release of a Cannon Group/Golan-Globus production. Produced by Menahem Golan, Yoram Globus. Executive producer, James D. Brubaker. Directed by Golan. Stars Sylvester Stallone. Screenplay, Stirling Silliphant, Stallone, from story by Gary Conway, David G. Engelbach; camera (Panavision, Metrocolor), David Gurfinkel; editor, Don Zimmerman, James Symons; music, Giorgio Moroder; production design, James Schoppe; art direction, William Skinner; set design, Roland E. Hill Jr., Ross Gallichotte; set decoration, Cloudia; costume design, Tom Bronson; sound (Dolby), Charles M. Wilborn; associate producer, Tony Munafo; assistant director, Tom Davies; casting, Ron Surma. Reviewed at the Warner Hollywood Studios, L.A., Feb. 6, 1987. (MPAA Rating: PG.) Running time: 93 MINS.

Lincoln Hawk . . . . Sylvester Stallone
Jason Cutler . . . . Robert Loggia
Christina Hawk . . . . Susan Blakely
Bob "Bull" Hurley . . . . Rick Zumwalt
Michael Cutler . . . . David Mendenhall
Tim Salanger . . . . Chris McCarty
Ruker . . . . Terry Funk

Hollywood — Having beaten all challengers in the ring and Southeast Asia, among other arenas, Sylvester Stallone muscles his way to the top of the heap in the beefy world of armwrestling in "Over The Top." Routinely made in every respect, melodrama concerns itself as much with a man's effort to win the love of his son as it does with macho athletics, and probably will fall in the middle range of Stallone grossers.

Star and cowriter's plotline is as simple and straightforward as always and, almost as if in counterbalance to the roughness of "Rambo" and "Cobra," seems conspiculously designed to emphasize the lovable, big puppydog side of the actor that came out in "Rocky."

At the outset, Stallone, as a down-on-his-luck trucker named Lincoln Hawk, appears out of the blue to fetch his son when the latter graduates from military academy. Absent from both the kid's and mama Susan Blakely's lives for years, for reasons he repeatedly refers to but never explains (a longer-than-usual stint in 'Nam remains a possibility), Stallone proposes a get-to-know-you truck ride back home to Los Angeles, much to the annoyance of Blakely's possessive, filthy-rich father, Robert Loggia.

Little Michael, played by David Mendenhall, doesn't make things especially easy for his papa, his military rigidity and formality, along with his understandable resentment, providing a formidable barrier. At truckstops along the way, Stallone introduces his son to the thrills of armwrestling, and after taking a spin behind the wheel of a heavy diesel, Michael's transfor-

mation from spoiled intellectual snot to future regular guy is well underway.

Loggia grabs the kid back when Blakely suddenly dies in surgery and, after a term in the slammer for ramming his semi through the front door of Loggia's mansion (recognizable as the one from "The Beverly Hillbillies"), Stallone heads for Las Vegas and the world armwrestling championships.

Just as he has always seemed a bit overmatched physically in his "Rocky" bouts, so does Stallone stack up as a decided underdog here, for his competitors are some of the meanest, ugliest, nastiest Neanderthals assembled since the cast party for "Night Of The Living Dead." Such is the suspense over whether or not Sly will beat his beastly opponent, the 6-ft. 5-inch 360-pound Rick Zumwalt, that it would be unthinkable to give it away, but little Michael proves resourceful enough to slip out of grandpa's clutches and make his way to Vegas for the main event.

Menahem (Where Does He Find The Time?) Golan pushes all the buttons for both sentiment and action payoff, and it is possible that audiences will go for this hokum despite its utter predictability. Stallone is sincere and soulful as a "father who messed up pretty bad" and just wants his kid back, David Mendenhall is a likable tyke, and justice is served in the end. There have been a lot worse films in the last year or two.

Giorgio Moroder's score is subdued by his standards but, just the same, makes sure the film doesn't sag for a moment. —Cart.

Fire And Ice
(COLOR)

For ski nuts.

A Concorde Pictures release. Produced, directed, written and photographed (Panavision, color) by Willy Bogner. American version by George Schlatter, Digby Wolf; editors, Petra Von Oelffeh, Claudia Travnecek; music, Harold Faltermeyer, Gary Wright, Panarama, Alan Parsons, John Denver; second camera, Peter Rohe; sound (Dolby), Manfred Maier; associate producers, Oliver Stahel, Karl-Heinz Faessler, Giovanni Mahler, Hussain Majadi; narrator, John Denver; John's voice, John Cooper. Reviewed at the Bruin Theater, L.A., Feb. 3, 1987. (MPAA Rating: PG.) Running time: **80 MINS.**

John . . . . John Eaves
Suzy . . . . Suzy Chaffee

Hollywood — Willy Bogner's ski extravaganza "Fire And Ice" plays like a feature-length succession of second-unit sequences, which makes sense since Bogner was the mastermind behind the spectacular stunt skiing sequences in four James Bond pictures. Loaded with eye-popping athletic feats accomplished on extraordinary international locales to the accompaniment of a throbbing musical score, film wouldn't seem to represent a domestic b.o. draw for viewers other than skiers, but probably has a decent future as a video attraction.

Storyline, such as it is, has ski bum John Eaves hitchhiking from New York City to Aspen in pursuit of blond ski bunny Suzy Chaffee. Every five minutes, John has a fantasy that sets off a big production number, most of which feature amazingly acrobatic skiing, but a few of which feature ski surfing, hang gliding, wind surfing and related derring-do.

Eaves, a Canadian freestyle champion, appears to be a virtual contortionist on skis, and displays considerable clowning abilities as well as he chases Chaffee over cliffs, into trees, indoors and even without skis, skidding down mountains wearing only boots.

Perhaps inevitably, pic does become repetitious at times, but at 80 minutes doesn't wear out its welcome, and Bogner's often amazing lensing rivets the attention and probably does make this the ultimate ski film for those looking for wild stunts and magnificent backdrops. Viewers in this category will probably prefer having the film on tape and checking out some of the action time and again rather than seeing it once on the big screen.

Bogner, a former Olympic skier from Germany and head of the Bogner fashion line, spent six years on the film, which opened a year ago in Germany in a somewhat different version. Narrated by John Denver, this American edition gives Eaves a somewhat annoyingly thick accent though he speaks with a normal American-Canadian one in real life. —*Cart.*

Mannequin
(COLOR)

Stiff comedy.

A 20th Century Fox release of a Gladden Entertainment picture. Executive producers, Edward Rugoff, Joseph Farrell. Produced by Art Levinson. Directed by Michael Gottlieb. Screenplay, Gottlieb, Rugoff; camera (Duart color, Deluxe prints), Tim Suhrstedt; editor, Richard Halsey; music, Sylvester Levay; art direction, Richard Amend; set decoration, Elise Rowland; costume design, Lisa Jensen; sound, Jan Brodin; assistant director, Michael Haley; casting, Marci Liroff. Reviewed at 20th Fox screening room, Feb. 6, 1987. (MPAA Rating: PG.) Running time: **89 MINS.**

Jonathan Switcher	Andrew McCarthy
Emmy	Kim Cattrall
Claire	Estelle Getty
Felix	G.W. Bailey
Richards	James Spader
Hollywood	Meshach Taylor
Roxie	Carole Davis

Hollywood — "Mannequin" is as stiff and spiritless as its title suggests. The animated performances of the leading characters try to inject life into what fertile ground there is, but under the weight of a wooden script and leaden direction, their efforts suffocate. Boxoffice should prove equally lifeless.

"Mannequin" seems to be made in the mold of "Splash," where the engaging relationship of two hopeless lovers makes us want to suspend our disbelief so that they can be together. (Situation is very similar to the premise of the hit stage musical and feature film, "One Touch Of Venus"—*Ed.*)

Instead of a mermaid, it's a mannequin (Kim Cattrall) as the latest reincarnation of an Egyptian princess who has known Christopher Columbus and Michelangelo in her journey through time. Instead of a food broker, he's an aspiring artist working as a model maker (Andrew McCarthy) and creator of a mannequin which has the likeness of a woman he could easily love — if only she were real.

He dances with her, caresses her, talks to her, and may even have a slightly unnatural attraction to her that is strange, to be sure, but not perverted in any sense.

While McCarthy is a charming ne'er-do-well and ripe with enough personality to venture down any number of quirky, unexpected paths, scripters never let him stray from a most uninvolving course.

After losing his position as a mannequin maker and then a succession of other, more menial jobs — the result of which his girlfriend (Carole Davis) drops him cold — the despondent McCarthy is out in the rain on his motorcycle one night and spots his beloved mannequin in the window of the staid Prince department store.

The next day, he ventures back to visit his mute friend and manages to land a job as a stock clerk after saving the store owner (Estelle Getty) from getting hit in the head as a sign is being hoisted over the store's entrance.

Night work makes strange bedfellows of McCarthy and Hollywood (Meshach Taylor), the flamboyant near-transvestite who dresses the store windows, and of McCarthy and Emmy (Cattrall), his mannequin. She comes alive when they're alone together, but reverts back to her cold self if anyone else appears.

With all the improbability of this setup, scripters Michael Gottlieb, who also makes his debut as a director here, and Edward Rugoff don't make much of this duo's unique arrangement.

McCarthy and Cattrall certainly are an attractive couple — when she's alive — but they don't get to do much more than kiss and dance around the store after hours — playing dress-up in the various departments — before time draws nigh and she has to be back in the window.

What is supposed to liven up the proceedings is the friction between McCarthy and the store's insufferably preppy manager, Richards (James Spader).

McCarthy and Cattrall are creating phenomenal window displays and bringing needed business back to Prince, the old grey lady of department stores.

This really goads Spader, the perfectly unctuous assistant to Getty, because he's also working as a double agent for Illustra, a glitzier store where he's promised a piece of the action if Prince goes belly up.

Material is too thin to carry interest for the length of time it takes to peel way the surface of an interesting story, when there's only more surface material underneath.

Comic development is given over to the secondary characters (Taylor, Spader and the night watchman, G.W. Bailey).

It should be funny to see McCarthy and Cattrall entwined in each other arms when she suddenly turns into a stiff at a third person's unexpected appearance. Maybe if they were outside the store among real people in real situations, the excitement of being exposed would heighten the humor. Unfortunately, the only ones who ever come close to discovering them are Taylor, a little kinky himself, and a moronic nightwatchman (Bailey) on the prowl with his stupid pooch.—*Brit.*

Cara de Acelga
(Spinach Face)
(SPANISH-COLOR)

An Incine, Jet Films, Lince Films production. Executive producer, Alfredo Matas. Written and directed by José Sacristán, based on story by Carlos P. Merinero, Sacristán. Camera (Eastmancolor), Carlos Suárez; editor, Jose Luis Matesanz; sets, Felix Murcia; costumes, Luis Valles; music, Ricardo Miralles; sound, Daniel Goldstein, Ricardo Steinberg. Reviewed at Cine Coliseo, Madrid, Jan. 20, 1987. Running time: **101 MINS.**

Antonio	José Sacristán
Madariaga	Fernando Fernán Gómez
Olga	Marisa Paredes
Eusebio	Emilio Gutiérrez Caba
Paquito	Miguel Rellán

Also with: Amparo Baró, Rafaela Aparicio, Raul Sender, Amparo Soler Leal, Francisco Algora, Alberta Bove, Maria Isbert.

Madrid — This is thesp José Sacristán's second feature as a director-writer (first was "Soldados de Plomo"). Despite some pithy dialog, fine acting throughout and a sincere effort to do a road picture, item falls short in that its plot is paper thin.

Sacristán casts himself as Antonio, a slightly mysterious drifter hitching a ride on a deserted Castilian back road. Being a good-natured loser, he easily makes friends along the way, spontaneously offering his services as a waiter in a busy roadside restaurant, helping out an aging lady who runs a village cinema and who remembers a troupe of actors that played the house long ago (the moppet performer was none other than Antonio).

Later, at a village dentist's, he makes the acquaintance of Madariaga (Fernando Fernán Gómez), a rich eccentric who persuades Antonio to dress up as a priest and steal a painting from a nearby nunnery. Some of the antics are occasionally droll, but Sacristán and Fernán Gómez have long since suffered from overexposure in Spain and by now are over-familiar for those seeking a road pic about thesps, Fernán Gómez himself recently directed and thesped in one which was far more effective.

Even though Sacristán tries to tie up loose ends in the last minutes of the film, "Spinach Face" is too rudderless to hold audience interest.
—*Besa.*

Wheels Of Terror
(U.S.-BRITISH-COLOR)

A Panorama Film Intl. production. World sales, Manley Productions. Produced by Just Betzer, Benni Korzen. Line producers, Korzen, Milos Antic. Directed by Gordon Hessler. Stars David Carradine, Don W. Moffett. Screenplay, Nelson Gidding, based on a novel by Sven Hassel; camera (Eastmancolor), George Nikolic; editor, Bob Gordon; music (Dolby stereo), Ole Hoyer; production design, Vladislav Lasic; production facilities, Avala Film 41 Studios (Belgrade). Reviewed at the Imperial, Copenhagen, Feb. 4, 1987. Running time: **101 MINS.**

Colonel von Weisshagen	David Carradine
Captain von Barring	Don W. Moffett
"Old Man"	Keith Szarabajka
Porta	Bruce Davison
Tiny	Jay O. Sanders
The Legionaire	David Patrick Kelly
Sven	Slavko Stimac
Stege	Andrija Maricic
Bauer	Boris Komnenic
Müller	Bane Vidakovic
The General	Oliver Reed

Also with: Irena Prosen (the Madam), Svetlana, Gordana Les, Lidija Pletl, Annie Korzen.

Copenhagen — "Wheels Of Terror," based on Sven Hassel's internationally bestselling novelizations of his own wartime experiences, is a carefully tooled World War II actioner cum comedy. Devoid of high-minded artistic ambition, it is likely to do fast threatrical playoff business wherever it is picked up before heading for near-immortality as a surefire video item.

"Wheels" is structured as any and all such war pictures from "All Quiet On The Western Front" to (especially) "Kelly's Heroes." We are told the story of a platoon of hard-punching armored division troopers doing their best to win the war by venturing far behind enemy lines to blow up an ammunition train. The twist is that this time the boys are Germans and members of one of Hitler's particular Penal Regiments, made up of hardened criminals as well as of political or religious dissidents.

We can still root for these men since the enemy is, of course, the Russians on the 1943 Eastern Front. Also, these Germans have been disillusioned with the Führer and all Nazi propaganda. Otherwise, it is hail to the old gang of stock characters: the tenderfoot, the clown, the brute, the bitter wisenheimer, the professor type with the literary quotes, all of them getting tougher all the time but also being turned into a fine fighting team.

Run-ins with the officers (the good: Don W. Moffett; the bad: David Carradine; and the ugly: Oliver Reed in a cameo) belong to the story as well as do robust whorehouse fun and a sequence of near-idyll cavorting in a river with much frontal male and female nudity on display.

Screenplay and production occasionally lean towards the crude, but most of the way plot and character delineations as well as the playing in all roles are cleancut and convincing. Bloodshed and brutality and the awful noise of battle (latter complemented by even louder soundtrack music) is kept reasonably in check. Author Hassel's personal period and military knowhow adds many refreshing insights to helmer Gordon Hessler's well-handled genre specimen.

The fun of "Wheels" involves, especially, the oddball characters of huge Tiny (Jay O. Sanders), The Legionaire (David Patrick Kelly) and mildly psychotic Porta (Bruce Davison), a trio sure to endear itself with all audiences (and to be a repeat for the sequel already being prepped by producers Just Betzer and Benni Korzen). Strictly of serious mien, David Carradine adds fine nuance to his playing of mean Col. von Weisshagen. Oliver Reed, however, comes on too late in the picture to make any impact.—*Kell.*

Withnail & I
(BRITISH-COLOR)

A Cineplex Odeon Films release (U.S.) of a Handmade Films production. Produced by Paul M. Heller. Executive producers, George Harrison, Denis O'Brien. Written and directed by Bruce Robinson. Coproducer, David Wimbury. Camera (color), Bob Smith; editor, Alan Strachan; music, David Dundas; production design, Michael Pickwoad; art director, Henry Harris; sound, Clive Winter; costumes, Andrea Galer; assistant director, Peter Kohn; casting, Mary Selway. Reviewed at BAFTA, London, Jan. 8, 1986. Running time: **108 MINS.**
Withnail . . . . Richard E. Grant
Marwood/I . . . . Paul McGann
Monty . . . . Richard Griffiths
Danny . . . . Ralph Brown
Jake . . . . Michael Elphick
Irishman . . . . Daragh O'Mallery
Issac Parkin . . . . Michael Wardle
Mrs. Parkin . . . . Una Brandon-Jones
General . . . . Noel Johnson
Waitress . . . . Irene Sutcliffe

London — "Withnail & I" is about the end of an era. Set in 1969

England, it portrays the last throes of a friendship mirroring the seedy demise of the hippie period, delivering some comic gems along the way.

Pic is uncompromisingly English, though its tale of two city boys stuck in a dilapidated country cottage in the middle of nowhere is familiar enough. The humor is both brutal and clever, and the acting uniformly excellent, though whether pic can appeal to offshore audiences is iffy.

First time writer/director Bruce Robinson (Oscar-nominated for his "The Killing Fields" screenplay) admits the pic is more than a little autobiographical, but he has a writer's eye for quirks and incident, and his characters are both tragic and humorous.

Pic opens with a pan round the disgusting London flat of out-of-work actors Withnail and Marwood (the "I" of the title), and dwelling on the kitchen where the sink is filled with piles of unwashed crockery and green fungus that may just be alive. Marwood (Paul McGann) is the nervous type trying to look John Lennon, while Withnail (Richard E. Grant) is gaunt, acerbic, and never without a drink in his hand.

Life is getting too much for the duo, so Marwood declares the need to "get into the countryside and rejuvenate." A visit to Withnail's Uncle Monty secures them the loan of his country cottage, and the two head off into the night, their battered Jaguar packed with alcohol and cigarets.

They eventually arrive at the remote cottage, only to discover there is no light, no heat, and no water. Withnail's search for wood for the fire and discovering the joys of cooking food that doesn't come out of a can make for some fine screen fun.

Withnail decides the best way to dry out their sodden boots is to leave them in the oven, so the next day they are reduced to heading off in search of food and alcoholic solace with plastic bags tied to their ankles. Along the way they encounter delights such as a romantically inclined bull who takes a shine to Marwood, and a deranged poacher who doesn't take a shine to Withnail.

Uncle Monty (a standout performance by the portly Richard Griffiths) arrives with a fresh supply of wine and a twinkle in his eye when he is sidling up closer to Marwood. Monty's ardor and a telegram from his agent with news of a job are enough to convince Marwood that home is where the heart is, and he and Withnail retreat back to London.

When Marwood finds he has

been offered an acting job elsewhere in the U.K., the two realize their friendship is coming to an end. Marwood leaves the flat, his hair shorn for the acting role, while Withnail is still drunk and clinging to the last vestiges of their era.

The first 20 minutes are a bit raw, but when the pair makes it to the cottage the action gains more class. Robinson's astute direction and clever lines make for a fine first effort, but one that will probably be hard to sell to foreign markets — but then that was probably said about "Letter To Brezhnev" and "My Beautiful Laundrette."

— *Adam.*

Hotshot
(COLOR)

Amateurish 'Rocky' clone.

An Intl. Film Marketing release. Produced by Steve Pappas. Executive producers, Pappas, Herman Meckler. Directed by Rick King. Screenplay, Joe Sauter, King; additional material, Ray Errol Fox, Bill Guttentag; camera (Deluxe color), Greg Andracke, Edgar Moura; editor, Stan Salfas; music, William Orbit; production design, (N.Y.) Ruth Ammon, (Brazil) Berta Segall; set decorator, Betsy Klompus; costumes, Karen Perry; assistant director, Matthew Carlisle; casting, Maureen Fremont. Reviewed at Charles Aidikoff Screening Room, Beverly Hills, Calif., Jan. 21, 1987. (MPAA Rating: PG.) Running time: **91 MINS.**
Jimmy Kristidis . . . . Jim Youngs
Santos . . . . Pelé
Vinnie Fortino . . . . Billy Warlock
Coach . . . . Leon Russom
Jerry Norton . . . . David Groh
Georgia Kristidis . . . . Rutanya Alda
Nick Kristidis . . . . . Peter Henry Schroeder

Hollywood — "Hotshot" is another entry in the seemingly endless pile of "Rocky" clones, this time set in the world of professional soccer. Amateurishly made and acted, pic was probably designed for the huge international soccer audience and features a low-keyed and likeable performance by one-time soccer hero Pelé. However, even fans of the sport are likely to find little to cheer about here.

Screenplay by Joe Sauter and Rick King pulls a switcheroo and instead of a young hero poor as a church mouse, he's rich as a king. In fact, that's his problem. Mommy and Daddy have better things in mind than a career in professional soccer for their son Jimmy (Jim Youngs).

Boys being boys, Jimmy rebels, leaves the safe confines of the family mansion and tries out for the New York Rockers. When things go sour there he heads for Brazil and soccer lessons from the retired master himself, played by Pelé.

After family squabbles, the crippling of his best friend, outcries fist fights, Jimmy scores the winning goal in the championship game, surprise, surprise. Director

Rick King delivers this action with a remarkable lack of drama, helped in no small measure by a screenplay which may not have one good line to its credit.

Cast is uniformly stiff with nearly every scene horrendously blocked and totally false. Music by William Orbit is bombastic, if nothing else.

So with so much going for it does the soccer action save the day? Unfortunately, no. Game footage is, for the most part, dull and uninvolving with camera work by Greg Andracke and Edgar Moura concentrating on the narrow point of view and sacrificing the flow and scope of the game. King breaks into gratuitous slow motion too many times for it to have any purpose or effect.

As silly as "Hotshot" is, it's harmless nonsense. Though he is not a professional actor and doesn't seem to speak very much English, Pelé is a delight to watch for his smile and handling of a soccer ball. Once a champ, always a champ, even in a losing cause. — *Jagr.*

Season Of Dreams
(COLOR)

Dull drama runs the changes again on rural America theme.

A Spectrafilm release of an Embassy Home Entertainment and American Playhouse Prods. presentation of a Nepenthe production. Produced and directed by Martin Rosen. Executive producer, Lindsay Law; Coproducers, Peter Burrell, Patrick Markey. Stars Christine Lahti, Frederic Forrest. Screenplay, Victoria Jenkins; camera (Duart color), Richard Bowen; additional photography, Paul Elliot; editor, Patrick Dodd; music, Patrick Gleeson; production design, David Wasco; art direction, Sharon Seymour; set decoration, Sandy Reynolds Wasco; costume design, Linda Bass; sound, Hans Roland; assistant director, Dick Feury; second unit camera, Ron Scott; casting, Amanda Mackey. Reviewed at the U.S. Film Festival, Park City, Jan. 22, 1987. (No MPAA Rating.) Running time: **109 MINS.**
Kathleen Morgan . . . . Christine Lahti
Buster McGuire . . . . Frederick Forrest
Anna Mae Morgan . . . . Megan Follows
Gary Connaloe . . . . Jason Gedrick
Dan Morgan . . . . Ray Baker
Photographer . . . . Peter Coyote
Clate Connaloe . . . . James Gammon
Connie Van Buskirk . . . . Kaiulani Lee
Mrs. Connaloe . . . . Jacqueline Brookes
Mrs. McGuire . . . . Irene Dailey
Auctioneer . . . . Pat Coggins

Park City, Utah — Two outstanding performances can't save "Season Of Dreams" from a fate of dullness and overfamiliarity. Known until very recently as "Stacking," this is yet another story of perseverance and coming-of-age in rural America, and one without anything new or interesting to say. In the wake of the premiere screenings at the U.S. fest, producer-director Martin Rosen reportedly will be cutting up to 20 minutes from the picture, but film will have to be improved significantly to win the favorable reviews necessary to put this sort of small, low-voltage drama over with a sizable public.

Just when one thought one had seen enough pictures about good, simple folks who are about to lose their land, along comes "Season Of Dreams," set in the Big Sky Country of Montana in the early 1950s. The difference here is that Pa and Ma are so far into bitterness and self-pity that the only one willing to fight to save the farm is their 14-year-old daughter Anna Mae (Megan Follows), an adorable and resilient kid who coaxes layabout farmhand Frederic Forrest to help her rebuild the mechanical haystacker, the only thing that can enable them to make some quick money.

Dramatic situation seems pretty clear at the outset, but Victoria Jenkins' lumpy screenplay then takes off in all sorts of different directions, dilly-dallying over unfocused digressions and never making up its mind where the heart of the film lies.

Much too much time, for instance, is spent with the incapacitated father, hospitalized after a domestic accident and now useless to his wife and daughter. After dwelling upon young Anna Mae for a while, film's attention shifts to her mother (Christine Lahti), a lovely lady who suddenly realizes she easily could spend the rest of her days wasting away as a waitress in the local diner and now feels compelled to do something about it, regardless of the consequences for her husband or daughter.

Pic comes alive in the scenes between Follows and Forrest, the latter in the role of the drunken town good-for-nothing who, years ago, lost Lahti to her future husband and now becomes seized with jealousy when he observes the budding Follows flirting with a good-looking teenaged cowboy.

Forrest brings an enormous supply of unexpected humor to his role, milking every line for all its worth and through amusing looks and gestures creating considerable sympathy for an essentially dumb and foolish soul who has nothing to show for his life.

The Canadian actress Follows, acclaimed for her performance in "Anne Of Green Gables" on television, is a dream of a young thesp, convincing in her most demanding dramatic scenes and fascinating to watch in repose. She's so good that one misses her whenever she is off screen, which is too often, and winces whenever the script takes her character in misguided directions.

Although good as always, Christine Lahti is burdened with a role that is too repressed for the actress

to let out the stops and display her usual wit, intelligence and energy. Peter Coyote rides in on a motorcycle for about five minutes to tempt Lahti and starts her dreaming seriously about taking off.

Martin Rosen, director of the animated features "Watership Down" and "The Plague Dogs" and producer of last year's U.S. Film Festival winner "Smooth Talk," makes his dramatic directorial debut here, and has handled matters in a polite, decorous fashion. He and lenser Richard Bowen have captured many beautiful Western landscapes, but emphasis on pastoralism, along with undue running time, makes for very slow going through much of the picture. —*Cart.*

John And The Missus
(CANADIAN-COLOR)

A PeterO'Brian/Independent Pictures production. Produced by O'Brian, John Hunter. Executive producer, O'Brian. Co-executive producer, S. Howard Rosen. Written and directed by Gordon Pinsent, based on his novel. Stars Pinsent, Jackie Burroughs. Camera (Medallion color), Frank Tidy; editor, Bruce Nyznik; music, Michael Conway Baker; art direction, Earl Preston; set decoration, Jeanie M. Staple; costume design, Olga Dimitrov; sound, Rob Young; assistant director, William Spahic; associate producer, Gabrielle Mrtinelli; casting, Deirdre Bowen. Reviewed at the U.S. Film Festival, Park City, Jan. 21, 1987. (No MPAA Rating.) Running time: **100 MINS.**

John Munn	Gordon Pinsent
Missus	Jackie Burroughs
Matt	Randy Follett
Faith	Jessica Steen
Fred Budgell	Roland Hewgill
Denny Boland	Timothy Webber
Tom Noble	Neil Munro
Sid Peddigrew	Michael Wade
Alf Sheppard	Jerry Doyle

Park City, Utah — Beautifully made and nobly intended, "John And The Missus" is a very decent film about a very decent man whose sense of family and personal heritage pits him against his government and the sweep of history. Leading Canadian actor Gordon Pinsent, working from his own 1973 novel, makes an impressive feature film directorial debut here, even if the pacing ultimately renders the picture too slow to generate much excitement. B.o. prospects are iffy Stateside.

What could have been made into an impassioned political tract about insensitive officials not playing straight with innocent citizens has instead been made into an intensely human closeup look at the effect uprooting has on a small community.

Premise is simple enough. Set in economically depressed Newfoundland in 1962, action sees many copper miners being laid off until finally, after an underground accident, the mine is closed and the locals are asked to resettle in another town.

Most of the seacoast villagers go

along with the plan, which includes some financial compensation, but not so John Munn, as solid responsible and likeable a man as one could want to meet but a stubborn one too. John was born in the town, as was his father, and he simply will not be moved.

Despite the confrontational situation, most of the running time is not occupied with political standoffs. Rather, film closely details the day-to-day progression of the community's deterioration and depopulation, and shows John as he confronts crises big and small, domestic and social.

Film starts very well, but before the mid-way point becomes somewhat becalmed dramatically despite the rising tensions. John's ultimate decision about what to do is dallied over for too long, although his solution, when it comes, is both poetic and satisfying Emotional range is also limited, falling between genial humor and restrained turmoil.

Film's quality is mainly to be found in its precise, loving look at a dying community, but an enormous amount of its appeal comes from Gordon Pinsent's persona. Affable even in distress and always spontaneous to the situation at hand, he's both as soft as a stuffed animal and hard as a rock. A fine actor with a career dating back 20 years, he now becomes a director to watch.

Visually, film is outstanding, and cinematograher Frank Tidy must receive much of the credit for this, along with the spectacular land and seascapes, which resemble Ireland in their rugged beauty. Also notable is the subtle, most effective score by Michael Conway Baker.

As the Missus, Jackie Burroughs is a strong match for Pinsent, and all supporting performances are warmly observed. — *Cart.*

Her Name Is Lisa
(COLOR-16m)

Inept fish-out-of-water comedy.

A Rachid Kerdouche production. Produced and directed by Kerdouche. Executive producer, Arnold Scott. Screenplay, Ron Gott, based on a story by Frank Boccio, Kerdouche; camera (Duart color), Klaus Quinn-Hoch, Wayne McDaniel; music, Richard Sohl; set design, Charles Mission: sound, Stephanie Cote; associate producer, Laumic Co. Reviewed at the U.S. Film Festival, Park City, Jan. 19, 1987. (No MPAA Rating.) Running time: **79 MINS.**

Hargus Beesley	Bill Rice
Julius Marlboro	Rockets Redglare
Lisa	Lisa Wujnovich

Park City, Utah — Once it makes up its mind what it wants to be about, "Her Name Is Lisa" plays like a poor man's "After Hours," a rube's nightmare odyssey through the sexual fringes of New York's nocturnal netherworld. Ineptly

filmed between 1983-1985 under the title "Rendezvous," self-financed second feature by French-born Rachid Kerdouche garners unintentional laughs due to its unsophisticated treatment of a clash between old-fashioned and new-fangled notions of romance and morality. Chances of any b.o. inroads are remote.

In an unnecessarily convoluted manner, pic tells of the single-minded search of an almost unbelievably naive, middle-aged Vermont farmer for a seemingly silly young woman he once romanced.

From what is shown, Lisa had good reason for leaving homely Hargus Beesley, since the embarrassingly earnest fellow could give Norman Bates a run for his money in the mother hangup department. So extreme is his devotion to his ailing mama that he can never bring himself to make love to his more than willing paramour for fear the old lady might climb out of bed and find them in the barn.

With mother now departed, Hargus takes the bus to Gotham to claim his lady love. Problem is, he has no idea where she lives, so with his hotel neighbor, the portly, effete Julius Marlboro as his guide, the hayseed hits the pavement in search of Lisa.

If only because Julius is gay, most of the characters encountered on the quest represent sexual extremes — a campy critic and his fawning black lover, a militant feminist, an obnoxious ladies' man and cabaret singer, a repressed garage mechanic and others.

Through it all, farmboy Hargus plays utterly dumb with attitudes seemingly formed no later than the 1930s. His unblinking naiveté in the face of bizarre lifestyle is supposed to represent a hilarious juxtoposition, but Hargus is such an unappealing jerk that you can just want him to shut up and go back to the boonies where he so clearly belongs. Many successful comedies from "Beverly Hills Cop" on down have effectively made hay out of similar fish-out-of-water formats, but the approach here is both unhip and unfunny.

After a particularly grim first half-hour, pic perks up a bit with the arrival of New York performance artist Rockets Redglare in the role of Julius, an impish, rolly-polly character who, with his beret and light-on-his-feet manner, recalls Dan Seymour in "To Have And Have Not." Other performances are either boring or outright caricatures. A hokey melodramatic climax brings matters to a merciful conclusion.

Tech credits are mediocre, particularly the indistinct sound and murky night photography. —*Cart.*

Sullivan's Pavilion
(COLOR)

Easy to take comic memoir.

A Ritchie/Sullivan/Sweeney production. Produced, directed, written, edited by Fred G. Sullivan. Executive producers, Charles L. Ritchie Jr., William A. Sweeney. Camera (Duart color), Hal Landen; music, Kenneth Higgins. James Calabrese; art direction, Susan Neal; costumes, Carol Gabridge; sound, Rip Allen; associate producers, Daniel P. Reilly, Bill Sweeney. Reviewed at the U.S. Film Festival, Park City, Jan. 20, 1987. (No MPAA Rating.) Running time: **83 MINS.**
Themselves . . . . . . Polly, Tate, Katie, Kirk, Ricky & Fred G. Sullivan
Bear/Narrator . . . . Jon Granik
Conrad P. Drizzle . . . . James R. Hogue
The Temptress . . . . Jan Jalenak
Sister Mary Anthony . . . . Judith Mayes
The Cretin Beer Lover . . . . . Don Samuels
Gillian Solomon, M.D. . . Roberta Schwebel

Park City, Utah — A highly unusual and personal work, "Sullivan's Pavilion" is the whimsical autobiography of an independent filmmaker, a comic memoir about the difficulty of balancing family and professional lives. In effect an extremely elaborate and ambitious home movie starring the director, his wife and four kids, film is disarming in its unpretentiousness, but also limited in potential due to its small scope and specialized concerns. Best commercial route would lie in individually tailored single runs in major cities and film-wise college towns.

Fred G. Sullivan is a bearish, bearded, 40-ish, outdoorsy guy with one feature film, "Cold River," to his credit. Up to his ears in the rigors of parenthood, he lives a chaotic, basically impoverished but not unpleasant life in the Adirondack Mountains, and watches the years slip away as the prospect of making real films grows increasingly elusive.

A self-revelation without self-analysis, pic gives the viewer the contours of Sullivan's life, starting with photos of his parents and 8m movies he made as a kid. Then there are the college years, his stint as a Eugene McCarthy worker, his Army service and his hustling efforts to scrounge together the money for his initial screen foray, all presented to the disparaging remarks of his kids, who can't understand why their dad is such a flake.

A jocular meditation on life's necessary choices and a light-hearted consideration of such weighty questions as, "When do dreams peter out?" film does become a bit silly at times, and Sullivan's mind seems so preoccupied with the details of living, and so unburdened by urgent artistic matters, that one comes out of spending nearly 90 minutes with him uncertain whether or not he has anything beyond this unique one-shot to offer.

Given the self-importance with which so many directors regard themselves, however, Sullivan is to be commended for placing the filmmaking obsession in a humorous perspective, as well as sizing it up in the context of real life instead of some fantasy world. Sullivan certainly knows how to laugh at himself, which makes his film very easy to take.—*Cart.*

Yo, El Ejecutor
(I, The Executioner)
(MEXICAN-COLOR)

A Películas Mexicanas release of a Cinematográfica Sol production. Produced by Gilberto de Anda. Directed by and stars Valentín Trujillo. Screenplay, Trujillo, Ramón Obón; camera (color), Antonio de Anda; editor, Sergio Soto; music, Kiko Campos. Reviewed at Big Apple Cine 1, N.Y., Jan. 27, 1987. Running time: **95 MINS.**
Valente Carrera (Thompson)Valentín Trujillo
Amy Samanta . . . . Patricia María
Captain . . . . Mario Almada
Padrino . . . . Pedro Weber (Chatanuga)
Lupita . . . . Gabriela Ruffo
Also with: Arturo Martínez, Carlos East, René Cardona Sr., Victoria Ruffo.

As a director of his own vehicle, Mexican actor star Valentín Trujillo has developed, knowing how to pace an exciting tale and vary the interest level through strong, well-defined characters.

His latest venture, "Yo, El Ejecutor" (I, The Executioner), begins like a Rambo clone. As a secret agent Valente Carrera, a.k.a. Thompson, Trujillo manages to kill over 20 persons — with knives, darts, pistols, arrows, machineguns and explosions — before the opening credits. After this bloody introduction, the story settles down to develop his character as that of a normal guy, who cares about his family and carries on a Superman-Lois Lane relationship with a reporter at a Spanish-language newspaper in Los Angeles, played by Patricia María.

Although there are some improbable moments in the script, a few holes here and there as well as some corny romantic flashbacks, overall the pic has some exciting action scenes and a high-tech, big-budget feel with locations in Brazil, Washington, D.C., L.A. and Acapulco. This is heightened by a driving disco score by Kiko Campos.

As a commercial director of fast-paced, action-packed films directed at Hispanic audiences, Trujillo has proved once again he has a strong future. —*Lent.*

When The Wind Blows
(BRITISH-ANIMATED-COLOR)

A Recorded Releasing release of a Meltdown production in association with the National Film Finance Corp./Film Four Intl./TVC London/Penguin Books. Produced by John Coates. Executive producer, Iain Harvey. Directed by Jimmy Murakami. Screenplay, Raymond Briggs, based on his book; art director, animation and layout design, Richard Fawdry; background and color design, Errol Bryant; storyboard, Murakami, Fawdry, Joan Ashworth; technical manager, Peter Turner; production coordinator, Anne Goodall; special effects sequences planned and animated, Stephen Weston; music (Dolby stereo), David Bowie, Roger Waters, Genesis, Paul Hardcastle, Squeeze, Hugh Cornwall. Reviewed at British Film Academy, London, Jan. 22, 1986. Running time: **85 MINS.**
Voices Of:
Hilda . . . . Peggy Ashcroft
Jim . . . . John Mills

London — "When The Wind Blows" is a classy animated feature that looks seriously at the horrors of a nuclear holocaust while at the same time poking fun at the British government's "Protect and Survive" campaign.

Film has a tendency to wander, as if the basic storyline of an elderly, stoic British couple coping with nuclear destruction wasn't enough. It would be far stronger if pic lost some 20 minutes of animation experiments and dream sequences. That apart, its strength and impact are undeniable, and the production is given extra gloss with the voiceovers by John Mills and Peggy Ashcroft, plus a title song from David Bowie.

Based on the best selling cartoon book of the same name by Raymond Briggs, film focuses on the lives of happily retired Jim and Hilda Bloggs in their rural cottage. Jim has his finger on the pulse of the international scene because he reads the newspapers at the local library, and has picked up governmental leaflets on how to protect the household in case of nucelar war.

Over dinner, they hear the news on the radio that there could be war in a few days. "They say there may be a pre-emptive strike," says Jim. "Oh not another strike. It's wicked. Blessed Communists," responds Hilda.

The film is punctuated with other charming malapropisms, and as Jim starts building their "inner-core-or-refuge" using doors and cushions according to governmental recommendations, they reminisce about the blitz and the happy days of World War II.

When they finally get a three-minute warning over the radio Hilda is keen to get her washing in, but Jim bundles her into the "inner-core-or-refuge" as the blast blows through their house. Animation has the edge over live-action when it comes to depicting nuclear destruction, and the pictures of the devastation look harrowingly realistic though human death is never focused on.

"Blimey," is Jim's only reaction as the shock of the bomb abates, and from then on the elderly couple are faced with major problems like not being able to brew a cup of tea, and the paper delivery boy being late with his deliveries. The horror of the situation is made all the worse since Jim and Hilda don't really understand what is happening.

Ever optimistic, they put the sores, bleeding gums, and falling hair down to their age, and talk about how they are going to have a "good rest after that blessed bomb."

The makers of the acclaimed animated short film "The Snowman" have produced a remarkable non-political film that is both funny and touching. The animation is generally excellent.

ABC's "The Day After" and BBC-TV's "Threads" have shown that nuclear war makes compulsive viewing, and with the established popularity of Brigg's book, feature version should also have b.o. pull. —*Adam.*

My Dark Lady
(COLOR)

Effective drama with a nod to 'Pygmalion.'

A Film Gallery release of a Frederick King Keller production. Executive producer, Keller. Produced by Carole Terranova, Stratton Rawson. Directed by Keller. Screenplay, Fred A. Keller, Gene Brook and Frederick King Keller, from an original story by Fred A. Keller; camera (color), Thom Marini; editor, Darren Kloomok; music, Ken Kaufman; production design, Stratton Rawson; set decoration, Gary Matwijkow; costumes, Elizabeth Haas Keller; sound, Dan Sack; assistant director, Rick Seeberg. Reviewed at the North Park Theater, Buffalo, N.Y., Feb. 5, 1987. (No MPAA Rating.) Running time: **104 MINS.**
Sam Booth . . . . Fred A. Keller
Lorna Dahomey . . . . Lorna Hill
Malcolm Dahomey . . . . . Raymond Holder
Jonathan Park . . . . John Buscaglia
Samuel T. MacMillan . . . . Evan Perry
Sarah Teasdale . . . . Barbara Cady
Horace Babinski . . . . Stuart Roth
Minnie O'Hara . . . . Tess Spangler
Terry Terranova . . . . Steven Cooper

Buffalo — A fair lady lurks in the heart of "My Dark Lady," the latest product of Buffalo-area filmmaker Frederick King Keller. As in the musical version of the George Bernard Shaw tale, an elegant man of letters endeavors to improve the lifestyle of a lowlife lass through exterior behavior modification.

Fred A. Keller (the director's father) is a Shakespearean actor down to his last aside and on the lam from the law for shoplifting in a Santa Claus suit. He takes refuge as a roomer in the home of Lorna Hill, whose principal income is derived from hospitality on a shorter, one-on-one basis.

Hill's son, Raymond Holder, turns out to possess a natural bent for Shakespeare. Keller teachers him the ropes of the stage and further shows Hill how to move upscale to the higher-income brackets in her bedroom business.

Hill's higher earnings pay Holder's way into prep school but trouble ensues when Headmaster John Buscaglia learns the background of his prize minority pupil and seeks to have him ousted. Hill and Keller invoke everything short of Banquo's ghost to turn the tide in a happy conclusion.

Hill is smashing with her elegant sensuality. Holder has a natural innocence seldom seem in child actors anywhere and seems a better Shakespearean than Keller right from the start. Headmaster Buscaglia secretes slime the way other actors secrete tears. Barbara Cady gleams in a cameo as Holder's prep-school drama coach.

Ken Kaufman's whimsical yet romantic score ranks among the picture's greatest assets and when the dialog stops while the music and pictures take over, "My Dark Lady" flies.

One wonders throughout whether any of the characters would encounter many of these problems in real life, given the current color-blind liberality in education, and some dialog sounds downright rehearsed, scripting and delivery equally at fault.

Scenics are grand, exploiting many Western New York locations. Set details, particularly newspaper pasteups, are sloppy. Most of the comedy works but some of the slapstick seems mechanical. Most of the picture has a good sense of pace and the storyline consistently holds the tone of a modern-day fairytale of a type seldom seen anymore.—*Doug.*

Crystal Heart
(COLOR)

Cornball drama.

A New World Pictures release. Produced by Carlos Vasallo. Directed by Gil Bettman. Screenplay, Linda Shayne, from a story by Alberto Vazquez-Figueroa; camera (Technicolor), Alexander (Alejandro) Ulloa; editor, Nicholas Wentworth; music, Joel Goldsmith; production design, Jose Maria Alarcon; sound (Dolby stereo), Manuel Rincon; costumes, Etta Leff; choreography, Marcea D. Lane; assistant director, Alvaro Forque; casting, Vikkie Vicars. Reviewed at Lions Gate Studios screening room, L.A., Feb. 3, 1987. (MPAA Rating: R.) Running time: **103 MINS.**

Christopher Newley .... Lee Curreri
Alley Daniels .... Tawny Kitaen
Frank Newley .... Lloyd Bochner
Diana Newley .... May Heatherly
Jean-Claude .... Simon Andreu
Justine .... Marina Saura
Jasper .... LaGena Lookabill

Hollywood — Old tv shows don't die; they become bad films. Borrowing heavily from the 1976 Spelling-Goldberg production "The Boy In The Plastic Bubble," "Crystal Heart" resurrects the poor bubble boy, has him fall in love with a

rock star and break out of his hermetically sealed environment only to meet an untimely death in the arms of his beloved. This is one bubble that never should have been broken.

Mining such emotionally-charged material takes a light touch, but "Crystal Heart" has both feet on the scale and a hand on the heartstrings. Feelings aren't allowed to surface and breathe, they're suffocated.

Film takes a wrong turn from the start when it tries to turn a moving and remarkable true story into a rock 'n' roll fairy tale. Script by Linda Shayne based on a story by Alberto-Vazquez Figueroa is looking for some contemporary ground to set down on. Result could have well be called "Flashbubble."

Restricted to his cell since birth because of a faulty immune system, Christopher Newley (Lee Curreri) is an otherwise healthy young man who writes songs and has an unbelievably cheery disposition. Budding rock star Tawny Kitaen and her sleazy manager Simon Andreu are both attracted to Curreri, but for decidedly different reasons.

Even though Kitaen and Curreri have negative charisma together their romance flourishes culminating in a ludicrous love scene with each of them on opposites of the glass. In between Kitaen runs off and does rock videos and shoe commercials, waiting for her big break.

At 103 minutes, pic goes on far longer than it should and director Gil Bettman stuffs in extraneous music sections, mostly so Kitaen can show off her Melrose wardrobe, and scenes that play like nonsequiturs.

Aside from the ridiculous setups, biggest credibility gap is the couple itself. Curreri is a likeable supporting actor but can't begin to carry a film himself. His puppy dog expression only undermines the film's attempt to generate real feelings.

On her own Kitaen is quite lovely, but seems to be off in a different film. Dance numbers would be more fun if there were less of them. As the boy's doting parents, Lloyd Bochner and May Heatherly are cardboard cut-outs, due more to the writing than the acting.

Music is mostly forgetable disco-pop with Kitaen lip-synching a host of tunes. Tech credits are nothing to write home about with photography often over-saturated for no discernible reason.—*Jagr.*

Bullseye
(AUSTRALIAN-COLOR)

A Cinema Group (in U.S.) release of a PBL Prods.-Dumbarton Films production. Produced by Brian Rosen. Directed by Carl

Schultz. Screenplay, Robert Wales; additional dialog, Bob Ellis, camera (System 35 Widescreen, Eastmancolor), Dean Semler; editor, Richard Francis-Bruce; music, Chris Neal; production co-ordinator, Elizabeth Symes; production manager, Carol Hughes; assistant director, Charles Rotherham; casting, Michael Lynch (Forcast). Reviewed at Hoyts Center, Sydney, Oct. 26, 1986. Running time: **95 MINS.**

Harry Walford .... Paul Goddard
Lily Boyd .... Kathryn Walker
Bluey McGurk .... John Wood
Don McKenzie .... Paul Chubb
Dora McKenzie .... Lynette Curran
Purdy .... Bruce Spence
Spence .... David Slingsby
Merritt .... John Meillon
Mrs. Gootch .... Kerry Walker
Judge .... Rhys McConnochie

Sydney — Shot under a variety of different titles, and completed some months before "Travelling North," Carl Schultz' "Bullseye" is an entertaining outdoor adventure film with expansive production values, a strong basic narrative (based on fact) and a relaxed, jokey style. Not a film for the arthouse circuit, it's an Aussie Western played largely for laughs and, with the right handling, possibly could tap into audiences seeking more laconic Down Under humor in the "Crocodile Dundee" tradition, though this one lacks the charismatic lead character that helped make "Dundee" a hit.

The tall, but basically true, tale is set in the last century, not long after the intrepid explorers, Burke and Wills, had perished trying to cross the Australian continent. Opening scenes are set on a remote Queensland cattle ranch managed by blustering Paul Chubb. One of his lowly employees is pic's hero, Paul Goddard, frustrated at being lumbered with all the worst jobs around the place. Goddard is sweet on pretty Kathryn Walker, a demure beauty who works as a maid for Chubb's long-suffering wife, Lynette Curran. When Walker inherits money from a deceased aunt and takes the train to the southern port city of Adelaide to collect her inheritance, Goddard is disconsolate. He and his comic sidekick, John Wood, decide to steal some cattle from Chubb, and wind up rustling 1,000 head of cattle, plus (inadvertently) a priceless pedigreed bull which tags along after the cows.

Accompanied by a couple of engaging comic villains (Bruce Spence, David Slingsby), Goddard and Wood set out with their booty to cross the same inhospitable desert terrain in which Burke and Wills had perished; and miraculously, they make it to Adelaide where they sell the cattle for a vast sum. Meanwhile, Walker has discovered her inheritance amounts only to a few dollars, and has taken a job as a maid at a brothel. On the very day she graduates from maid to prostie, her first customer turns out to be, natch, the newly wealthy Goddard.

Schultz has cast his two lead roles with unknowns (Walker is, in fact, a student with no training as an actor; she acquits herself delightfully), and they play it straight while a fine cast of character actors in support play for laughs. John Wood is fun as Goddard's jocular mate; Paul Chubb is fine as the ill-tempered ranch manager; Lynette Curran (the wife in "Bliss") makes the wife in this film a more than usually interesting character. Bruce Spence and David Slingsby are colorful villains; Kerry Walker is great as the brothel's evil madam; John Meillon (from "Crocodile Dundee") is funny as the hero's drunken lawyer in the climactic trial, while Rhys McConnochie makes an impact as a pompous judge.

Schultz and editor Richard Francis-Bruce keep the pace fast. Just when the narrative threatens to flag (after the heroine's rescue from the brothel) they come up with a funny, brilliantly shot courtroom sequence and a cheerful, upbeat ending. Dean Semler's expansive photography is tops, with dazzling, vast exteriors contrasted with handsomely-designed, low-key interiors. Production designer George Liddle has, once again, done outstanding work, and there's an apt, cheerful music score from Chris Neal.

Occasionally, a joke misfires, but in the main this is a delightful, bawdy entertainment which should have wide appeal in Australia (no local distrib has been set to date) and in other territories too with careful handling. It deserves to overcome the current prejudice against Westerns. Though it has some of the trappings of a western, it's basically a stirring romantic drama that doesn't take itself at all seriously.
—*Strat.*

Tata Mia
(Nursemaid Mine)
(SPANISH-COLOR)

A Profilmar and El Iman presentation. Produced by José Luis Borau for El Iman, in association with Isasi Prods. Cinematográficos, in collaboration with Televisión Espapola, the Diputación General de Aragón and the Madrid Development Institute. Associate producer, Antonio Isasi Jr. Written and directed by José Luis Borau. Camera (Agfa color), Teo Escamilla; editor, Emilio Rodriguez; music, Jacobo Duran-Loriga; sound, José Nogueira; sets, Rafael Richart; costumes, Maiki Marin; production manager, José Luis Tristan. Reviewed at Cine Roxy, Madrid, Jan. 9, 1987. Running time: **100 MINS.**

Tata .... Imperio Argentina
Teo .... Alfredo Landa
Elvira .... Carmen Maura
Peter .... Xabier Elorriaga
Alberto .... Miguel Rellán
Paloma .... Marisa Paredes
Magda .... Julieta Serrano
Also with: Enriqueta Carballeira, Emma Suárez, Paloma Gómez, Alica Moro, Saturno Cerra, Chema Mazo, Matías Maluenda, Felix Dafauce.

Madrid — "Tata Mia" marks the return to Spanish screens of famed singing star and thesp of the 1930s Imperio Argentina, cast now as a matronly companion and former wetnurse from a pueblo. Helmer-scripter José Luis Borau, one of Spain's most prestigious filmmakers, does provide Argentina the chance to sing one song. Rest of pic is a tongue-in-cheek comedy, albeit with critical overtones.

The premise of the story has ample ingredients for humor: the daughter of a deceased rightwing general has been in a convent for 13 years, but now wishes to face the world again. Unsure of herself, and with nymphomaniacal propensities, she seeks out her former wetnurse and entices her to come back to Madrid with her.

In the capital, she meets up with her fascist brother, a spaced-out neighbor who used to be her playmate and a handsome historian trying to ferret out her father's past for a book. Borau amusingly plays these characters off against each other in a vein of light humor, throwing in the cute antics of a sheepdog as well.

Pic is directed well and through most of it pacing is good. Borau's meticulous hand can be seen, as he pokes gentle fun at the old sacred cows of Spain — the aristocracy, the military establishment and the Church. Thesping, however, is often too unrestrained. Even the often ebullient Alfredo Landa is rather tame, and Argentina and Miguel Rellán are weak.

Still, item comes across as a warm and mellow film in which Borau skillfully caricatures some of Spain's stock institutions.—*Besa.*

A Walk On The Moon
(COLOR)

Botched drama of U.S. idealism in the Third World.

A Benenson/Midwest Films production. Produced by Dina Silver. Executive producer, Bill Benenson. Directed by Raphael Silver. Screenplay, William B. Mai; camera (Duart color), Adam Greenberg; editor, Peter Frank; music, Paul Chihara; production design, Holger Gross; sound, Robert Gravenor; casting, Bonnie Timmermann. Reviewed at the U.S. Film Festival, Park City, Jan. 21, 1987. (No MPAA Rating.) Running time: **95 MINS.**
Everett Jones ....Kevin Anderson
Lew Ellis.................Terry Kinney
Marty Ellis ....Laila Robins
India......................Patrice Martinez
Doctor ....Pedro Armendariz
Candy....................Roberto Sosa

Park City, Utah — The full potential of the material has not nearly been achieved in "A Walk On The Moon." Tale of Peace Corps workers trying to cope in Colombia in 1969 had the seeds of a trenchant analysis of American idealism and a glimpse of nascent Third World anti-Americanism, but execution blandly fails to follow through on story's promise. This one will be a tough sell.

Set during a period when the bright optimism of the JFK years, still the inspirational focus of the Peace Corps, clashed with the anger and cynicism bred by the Vietnam War, William B. Mai's interesting script lands young volunteer Kevin Anderson in a drought-stricken village to take over from a married couple. Pair has split up, however, with the husband, Terry Kinney, having gone wacko and the wife having taken up an affair with the local medico.

Shocked by the disinterest with which the natives react to his do-gooder enthusiasm, Anderson nevertheless proceeds with a plan to bring electricity to the impoverished community, and also becomes involved in a rather unlikely romance with India (Patrice Martinez), the foxiest lady in the vincity, a young woman who was probably Kinney's mistress earlier.

Over time, Anderson wises up a bit, but not enough to avoid making the mistake of impregnating and marrying his native sweetie. In a wildly melodramatic sequence, the rains finally come to Afogados, and the American's waterwheel succeeds in lighting up the town, but Anderson and his bride are separately washed away in the flood, with the former going nuts and the latter conveniently never to be heard from again.

Based on personal experiences of both scripter Mai and executive producer Bill Benenson, story provides plenty of opportunities for insights into how the good intentions of Americans abroad can easily achieve results opposite from those intended. It might also have been provocative to show a parallel influence on the natives from the left, by way of comparison of the methods of the communist and capialist power spheres to win favor in underdeveloped nations.

Unfortunately, director Raphael Silver shows little feel for the setting or the characters. The natives are presented indifferently — more should have been made of the resentment felt by the sexy woman's teenage brother over the American's conquering of his sister — and even the leads are not shown in either a sympathetic or, alternatively, a critical light. In short, film lacks a point of view.

Contributions of lenser Adam Greenberg and production designer Holger Gross lend verisimilitude to the effort, which was shot in Mexico. Title refers directly to the technological triumph of landing men on the moon at the same time the characters on view are groveling in the dirt.—*Cart.*

Moa
(SWEDISH-COLOR)

A Sandrews release (international sales, Swedish Film Institute/Lena Enquist) of a Filmstallet production with the Swedish Film Institute, SR/TV-2, Sandrews, ABF and LO. Produced by Anders Birkeland. Written and directed by Anders Wahlgren. Stars Gunilla Nyroos, Reine Brynolfsson. Camera (Eastmancolor), Ronald Sterner; editor, Solveig Nordlund; music, Gunnar Edander; sound, Lasse Ulander, others; lighting, Ted Lindahl; production design, Lasse Westfeldt; costumes, Ingrid Hjelm, others; production management, Elisabeth Lee. Reviewed at Nordic Film Festival, Helsinki, Jan. 22, 1987. Running time: **91 MINS.**
Moa Martinson née
  Helga Johansson ....Gunilla Nyroos
Harry Martinson ......Reine Brynolfsson
Karl, Moa's first
  husband ....Lennart Hjulström
Ottar......................Grethe Ryen
Moa's mother ....Berta Hall
K.O. Bonnier ....Percy Brandt
  Also with: Roland Hedlund, Krister Henriksson, Lars Humble, Mats Bergman, Dan Ekborg, Harald Hamrell, Anders Ekborg, Mikael Segerström, Anita Irene Wall, Elisabeth Lee.

Helsinki — "Moa" looks more like a painter's than a natural film talent's tribute to Moa Martinson, a working class heroine and novelist of Sweden in the 1920s and '30s. Writer-director Anders Wahlgren has done careful research and displays much historical detail. He is also a near-master in his collaboration with cinematographer plus lighting and sound crew, but he is at a loss with dramatic drive and and with having his actors do much beyond posing for individual or group portraits.

Moa Martinson was beloved in Sweden. The feature film devoted to her life and career will not give offshore audiences as much as an inkling of her worth as either a novelist or as a socialist-cum-women's-lib polemicist.

Martinson (Gunilla Nyroos of grim mien, with too little melting into sensual happiness of any kind) came from peasant stock. She married a heavy-drinking mine worker and had five children, lost two of them in an accident, and saw her husband blow himself up with dynamite. She had a young (13 years her junior) seaman-poet (Reine Brynolfsson as a babyfaced, shy Harry Martinson) move in with her in the country. They stayed together for 10 years, both rising to fame as writers. The age difference and the different directions their writing would take (he went on to become a critics' darling and eventually won a Nobel Prize for literature) led to their divorce. Moa found solace in socialist solidarity with the lower classes while at the same time dressing up in mink and sipping champagne with people she tongue-lashes with glee.

The little tableaux through which Wahlgren tells this story rarely if ever come alive. The difficulty of giving a cinematic impression of a writer's (let along two writers') work is never overcome. It does not help that Wahlgren remains very devoted to the idea that less is more, so he pulls any dramatic punch to the point where boredom sets in. Also, he fails utterly to convince us that his two main protagonists were ever exciting enough personalities to produce art beyond meticulous embroidery. The soft tinkling of a piano accompanies the non-action in a respectful way, as at a wake.

—*Kell.*

Le Beauf
(FRENCH-COLOR)

A G.P.F.I./Arturo Prods./TF1 Films coproduction. Executive producer, Jean-Claude Fleury. Produced by Charlotte Fraisse. Stars Gérard Jugnot, Gérard Darmon, Marianne Basler, Zabou. Directed by Yves Amoureux. Screenplay, Amoureux, Guy Beaumont; additional dailog, Boris Bergman; camera (Eastmancolor), Thierry Arbogast; editor, Catherine Renault; music, Alain Bashung; art director, Jean Bauer; sound, Dominique Duchatelle; production manager, Jean-Claude Cartier; assistant director, Dominique Tabuteau. Reviewed at the Pathé Clichy cinema, Paris, Jan. 7, 1987. Running time: **105 MINS.**
Gilbert ....Gérard Jugnot
Gisèle.................Marianne Basler
Serge...................Gérard Darmon
Maryline.......................Zabou
Nicolas ....Nicolas Wostrikoff
Marc ....Didier Sauvegrain
Rocky...................Boris Bergman
Bank supervisor ....Jean-Pol Dubois

Paris — "Le Beauf," an uneven mixture of psychological study and caper thriller, succeeds foremost as a dramatic showcase for popular funnyman Gérard Jugnot, who like fellow café-theater transplant Michel Blanc (costar of Bertrand Blier's "Menage") displays non-comic limning ability in this tale of a bank employee baited into a robbery of his own establishment.

Jugnot etches a persuasive study in mediocrity pushed to its nightmarish limit. Cast as a "beauf," both a slang for brother-in-law and a neologism for a ploddingly unambitious petty bourgeois, he is a homely Gallic everyman who has traded in his youthful dreams for conventional middle-class stability: wife, kid, house and secure job.

The job is monotonous, but unusual: employed at the Banque de France, he operates the furnace that weekly destroys millions of francs in used notes.

Jugnot's daily proximity to all this condemned lucre lures an old comrade (Gérard Darmon) who connives to force his complicity in a heist.

After a kidnap charade that backfires, Darmon wins over Jugnot by playing on his nostalgia and dormant pop dreams (they were part of an amateur rock group). When Jugnot discovers Darmon and his attractive wife (Marianne Basler) are having a fling, he plots to murder his treacherous pal by leaving him in the bank furnace to be incinerated.

Coscripted and directed by newcomer Yves Amoureux (one-time assistant to such helmers as Joseph Losey, Otto Preminger and Blake Edwards) "Le Beauf" is psychologically gripping but melodramatically perfunctory, with the climactic caper putting a strain on the script's realism. The unlikely plot involves Jugnot sabotaging its machinery, then dropping into the furnace at night through the chimney with Darmon to collect the still-unburned bills.

A happy ending in which Jugnot purges his revenge instinct in time and is reunited with his wife (and some of the money) also vitiates an otherwise unsentimental drama of hard-earned domesticity undermined by greed, baseness and betrayal.

Basler is fine as Jugnot's seemingly placid and still attractive wife (their rapport is so subtly tuned that one never doubts that she could marry bald, pudgy Jugnot and be content with him), and Darmon gives an often harsh portrait of cynicism and debased macho self-confidence. Supporting cast is sound.

Good tech credits include a catchy rock score by local pop favorite Alain Bashung. —Len.

Peter von Scholten
(DANISH-COLOR)

A Metronome release of Metronome Film (Bent Fabricius-Bjerre) and Crone Film production with the Danish Film Institute (consultant producer, Claes Kastholm Hansen). Produced by Nina Crone. Directed by Palle Kjärulff-Schmidt. Stars Ole Ernst. Screenplay, Sven Holm; camera (Eastmancolor), Mikael Salomon; editor, Kasper Schyberg; music, Fabricius-Bjerre; production design, Sören Krag Sörensen; sound, Stig Sparre-Ulrich; associate producer (Virgin Islands locations), Jörgen Hinsch, production coordinator (Virgin Islands), Betty Sperber; coproducer (for Metronome), Tivi Magnusson; costumes, Lotte Dandanell; assistant director, Ake Sandgren. Reviewed at the Dagmar Bio-1, Copenhagen, Feb. 1, 1987. Running time: **112 MINS.**
Peter von Scholten . . . . Ole Ernst
Anna Heegaard . . . . Etta Cameron
Frederik von Scholten . . . . Jesper Langberg
Edvard Heilbuth . . . . Preben Kristensen
Organist Pram . . . . Olaf Ussing
Mrs. Holten . . . . Bodil Udsen
Kunzen . . . . Torben Jensen
Buddhoe . . . . Dale Smith
Lt. Irminger . . . . Sören Pilmark
Frederik Oxholm . . . . . . Preben Neergaard
Katka . . . . Leonard Malone
King Frederik VI . . . . . . Henning Moritzen
Mrs. von Scholten . . . . Karen-Lise Mynster
Also with: **Arne Hansen**, Lars Lunöe, Raymond Adjavon, Bodil Lassen, Guido Paevatalu, Dick Kaysöe, Torben Jetsmark, Anna Adair, Hans Henrik Krause, Edwin Donoghue, Birgit Conradi, Hans Chr. Aegidius, Fritze Hedemann, John Larsen, Henning Jensen.

Copenhagen — Add a few aerial shots of the former Danish (now U.S.) Virgin Islands and a few words of text or narration on the general lay-of-the-land of impending freedom for the mid-19th century Caribbean colonies' black slaves under different sovereign rules, and "Peter von Scholten," the story of one white man's fight for black emancipation in the face of his faraway government's commercial maneuverings and lack of local insight, should easily gain access to specialized situation cinema screens worldwide.

Peter von Scholten (played with strength and originality by Ole Ernst) was the real-life Virgin Islands governor who set up for "my children," the slaves' offspring, regular schools to prepare them to handle eventual emancipation so as to forestall such bloodshed as occurred in the surrounding British and French archipelagean colonies when freedom was precipitately sprung on totally illiterate blacks.

Hewing close to historical and biographical fact, film sees von Scholten as a complex man, larger than life among petty political dwarfs, but also as a voluptuary who liked the rich life and lived it by not being above taking his out of local trade and customs duties. He had a loving wife at home in Denmark and a loving black live-in mistress in the Islands. Neither of the women seemed to mind, since the man's charm was considerable.

It was increasing scheming

among local government officials plus either lethargy or electoral strategy on the part of His Majesty's back-home goverment in Copenhagen that forced von Scholten in 1948 to shout his emancipation declaration to a crowd of finally belligerent blacks.

Bloodshed was avoided all right, and the government was forced to uphold the emancipation, but von Scholten was suspended and put in the dock (so we are told in a postscript to the film) and charged with treason. A higher court was to acquit him, but he died soon after, literally of a broken heart — saving, crowed the Danish press, the state a sizable pension.

Helmer Palle Kjärulff-Schmidt has a wondrous cast of fine actors, with glowing little vignette portraits of colonial whites supplied by Jesper Langberg, Torben Jensen and Bodil Udsen and of stay-at-home Danes by Karen-Lise Mynster (as Mrs. von Scholten) and Henning Moritzen (as Denmark's last absolute monarch).

Film has rich cinematography by Mikael Salomon, who has simultaneously lit all interiors (done in Denmark) in beautiful harmony with tropical exteriors. Sven Holm's screenplay might have displayed greater punch and immediacy. Too often it leaves episodes dangling.

Even with such shortcomings, Kjärulff-Schmidt has worked chamber dramatics effectively into his historical meller fabric. He has also avoided drowning out his story's essential psychological finesse in genre thunder. —Kell.

Tenebrae
(Unsane)
(ITALIAN-COLOR)

A Bedford Entertainment/Film Gallery release of a Sigma production. Executive producer, Salvatore Argento. Produced by Claudio Argento. Directed by Dario Argento. Screenplay, Dario Argento, George Kemp, from story by Argento; camera (Technovision, Eastmancolor), Luciano Tovoli; editor, Franco Fraticelli; music, Claudio Simonetti, Fabio Pignatelli, Massimo Morante; art direction, Giuseppe Bassan; set decoration, Maurizio Garrone; production manager, Giuseppe Mangogna; assistant director, Lamberto Bava, Michele Soavi; special effects, Giovanni Corridori. Reviewed at Cine 42, N.Y., Feb. 13, 1987. (MPAA Rating: R.) Running time: **100 MINS.**
Peter Neal . . . . Anthony Franciosa
Bulmer . . . . John Saxon
Anne . . . . Daria Nicolodi
Inspector . . . . Giuliano Gemma
Also with: Mirella D'Angelo, Veronica Lario, John Steiner, Lara Wendel, Christian Borromeo, Ania Pieroni, Eva Robins, Mirella Banti, Isabella Amadeo, Carola Stagnaro.

"Tenebrae" (released Stateside as "Unsane") finds Italian horror maestro Dario Argento returning to the roots of his success (beginning back in 1970 with "The Bird With The Crystal Plumage") in a routine whodunit, albeit saturated with

gore. Lack of fantasy elements and the colorful stylization that denote his best work is a disappointment. Film was a hit release in Italy in 1982.

Tony Franciosa stars as thriller author Peter Neal, whose latest novel is subjected to the usual criticism of being overly violent and sexist. A rash of gory murders occurs, executed in similar fashion to those depicted in his book and soon people around him (and even himself in a failed attempt) are subjected to the violent attacks, resolved with a twist in a Grand Guignol climax.

Argento apparently uses this thin story as a vehicle to vent his own feelings about criticism regarding the violence in his films, featuring extreme, almost laughable bloodletting here as a way of thumbing his nose at his detractors. However, film largely devolves into an uninteresting series of vignettes of beautiful women being stalked and slashed, reducing Argento's craft to the mindless level of his many exploitation-minded imitators.

With most of the setpieces filmed at a modern villa, Argento eschews the fabulous studio creations and pastel lighting that are his trademarks in features such as "Suspiria." Cameraman Luciano Tovoli gets to flex his gyroscopic muscles in the flashy manner of his work on Michelangelo Antonioni's "The Passenger" but to little purpose. Cast is attractive but hurt by some clumsy dubbing. —Lor.

Ormen's väg pa hälleberget
(The Serpent's Way Up The Naked Rock)
(SWEDISH-COLOR)

A Svensk Filmindustri release (foreign sales, Swedish Film Institute/Lena Enquist) of a Crecendo and SF production with the Swedish Film Institute and SR/TV-1. Produced by Göran Lindström. Written, directed and edited by Bo Widerberg, from a novel by Torgny Lindgren. Camera (Eastmancolor), Jörgen Persson, Rolf Lindström; music, Stefan Nilsson; production design, Pelle Johansson; sound, Björn Gunnarsson, Stefan Ljungberg; lighting, Ulf Björck; costumes, Inger Pehrsson; production management, Ann Collenberg. Reviewed at Nordic Film Festival, Helsinki, Jan. 24, 1987. Running time: **112 MINS.**
Tea . . . . Stina Ekberg
Karl Orsa . . . . Stellan Skarsgaard
Jani . . . . Reine Brynolfsson
Eva . . . . Pernilla W. Oestergren
Jakob . . . . Tomas von Brömssen
Ol Karlsa . . . . Ernst Günther
Grandma . . . . Birgitta Ulfsson
Grandpa . . . . Nils Brandt
Jani as child . . . . Johan Widerberg
Eva as child . . . . Melinda Kinnaman
Tilda . . . . Amelia Glas-Drake
Sara . . . . Lisa Tönnerfors
Rakel . . . . Emma Tönnerfors

Helsinki — For tenant farmers in Sweden's northern rural areas in the 19th century it was not unusual for indebted families to pay their dues via woman's sexual submission to the creditor, a landlord or a store owner. When a mother would lose her allure, her oldest daughter took over. On this theme, Torgny Lindgren six years ago created "The Serpent's Way Up The Naked Rock," an instant classic in modern European literature. Now Bo Widerberg has turned Lindgren's sparse prose and stark narrative into a feature film to match: not his most easily accessible work, but one that is sure to reach world audiences even if sales may progress slowly.

Novel's story is told by Tea, whose husband hanged himself when faced with seeing Tea led away for sex with Ol Karlsa, the local trading post owner. Tea never complains, and she does not doubt the rightness of God's way in allowing the poor of the earth to suffer. Ol Karlsa feels justified by the very same bible in which Tea seeks solace. Widerberg is his own mute narrator, never pointing a moralistic finger, leaving instead the luminous and tightly controlled acting of Stina Ekblad to work as a perfect substitute for Lindgren's first person singular prose.

When Ol Karlsa dies, his son Karl Orsa (played as a pale-faced victim of circumstance himself by Stellan Skarsgaard) comes to collect the annual debt. He does not see himself as a brute or a moral criminal either, but as a just representative of society's as well as of God's laws. He would like to be considered a member of Tea's family in some small way (after all, he has fathered most of her children), but on this point Tea never relents.

Tea briefly experiences happiness with Jakob, a vagrant who is soon to be arrested for thefts. All kinds of miseries are inflicted upon Tea and her growing flock of children. Toward the end of the story, Karl Orsa insists Tea is getting too old and that her 16-year-old daughter must start paying the family's annual dues. He ignores Tea's plea that the daughter is actually her own father's child, since the church register reports only an "unknown father."

When Karl Orsa lies down to have the young girl service him, her brother comes forward with a knife and castrates him. This does not lead to criminal action against the brother. Somehow Karl Orsa, as pasty-faced and innocent of guilt as ever, comes back one year later and demands payments of debts in the usual manner, innocent of guilt or anger.

Thus, "The Serpent's Way" is a story without villains, and its victims are denied the martyr's pose at every turn. With fine rewards, Widerberg has relied on his ability to conduct his actors through high drama with the most minimal display of outward emotion.

Trimming by at least 15 minutes would benefit "The Serpent's Way." Some key scenes are left dangling in midair because Widerberg was loath to dispense with them entirely. Elsewhere the action becomes hard to follow or understand since 90% of the picture takes place inside a log cabin with light coming only from a fireplace or through a tiny window. Some clumsy devices unworthy of a major film talent such as "One Year Later" text frames easily could be eliminated.

Bo Widerberg remains a greater director than an editor. Afterwards, however, "The Serpent's Way" will linger in the minds of audiences to haunt them with its particular visions of mankind's common fate.

Film's title is borrowed from the Book of Proverbs: "Three things never cease to amaze me, and a fourth I shall never understand: the eagle's flight across the sky, the serpent's way up the naked rock, the ship's passage over the ocean, and a man's move towards a woman."

—*Kell.*

La Busqueda
(The Search)
(ARGENTINE-COLOR)

A Cine-International (Munich) release of a Grupci c/o Cine-International production. Directed by John C. (Juan Carlos) Desanzo. Screenplay, Lito Espinosa; camera (color), John C. Lenardi; editor, Sergio Zottola; music, Baby Lopez Furts; sound, Carlos Abbate. Reviewed at the India Film Festival (Competition), Delhi, Jan. 13, 1987. Running time: **91 MINS.**

Patricia . . . . Marta Gonzalez
Monica . . . . Luisina Brando
Also with: Rodolfo Ranni, Emilio Disi, Andrea Tenuta.
(English dubbed)

Delhi — "The Search" is a German-released Argentine actioner made up to look passably American. Tale of a daughter's revenge after watching a gang of hoods murder her father is a cross between "A Clockwork Orange" and "Death Wish," on a B-level. Lurid plot and fast pace should find it spots in many markets not picky about horrid English dubbing. It was more than a little out of place in competition at the India Film Festival.

Scene is set in Princeville, Calif., where a normal family of four is having a peaceful breakfast. Suddenly a gang of stocking-masked thugs bursts in and ties them up, sexually abuses them, and kills the father. The rest of the traumatized family soon self-destructs. Young brother stops talking and has to be institutionalized, mother hangs herself, and daughter Patricia (Marta Gonzalez) embarks on a loony vendetta to set herself up as bait in Luisina Brando's massage parlor and lure the gang to their deaths.

After gorily (accidentally) crushing one to death in a garage, she plays hide-and-seek with the others in the family house, which is reduced to a shambles by the end. Particularly hard on the linoleum is when Patricia cra... drives a jeep through the front window, not once but several times, and somehow runs over the baddies in the living room. Ending is upbeat.

Helmer Juan Carlos ("John C.") Desanzo goes for the throat in most scenes and creates a climate of building violence. Cast is encouraged to overàct. As the strung-out daughter, Gonzalez has a south-of-the-border preppie look that makes her swing to mayhem even more perverse. — *Yung.*

La Vie dissolue de Gérard Floque
(The Debauched Life Of Gérard Floque)
(FRENCH-COLOR)

A Gaumont release of a Cathala Prods./Gaumont/Films 21/TF1 Films coproduction. Executive producers, Alain Poiré, Norbert Saada. Directed by Georges Lautner. Screenplay, Lautner, Christian Clavier, Martin Lamotte, based on story by Jean-Jacques Tarbes, Christian Watton; camera (Fujicolor), Yves Rodallec; editor, Michèle David; music, Daily News; art director, Alain Gaudry; sound, Alain Lachassagne; costumes, Maïka Guezel; makeup, Maryse Félix; assistant director, Gérard Pujolar; production manager, Guy Azzi. Reviewed at the Gaumont Ambassade cinema, Paris, Jan. 15, 1987. Running time: **78 MINS.**

Gérard Floque . . . . Roland Giraud
Martine . . . . Marie-Anne Chazel
Cécile . . . . Clémentine Célarié
Mammy . . . . Jacqueline Maillan
Francis . . . . Gérard Rinaldi
Pauline . . . . Mathilda May
Nasal . . . . Michel Galabru
Also with: Christian Clavier, Jacques François, Mireille Darc, Catherine Lachens, Laurent Gendron, Maaike Jansen. Dominique Besnehard, Richard Taxi.

Paris — A facile comedy of middleclass manners, routinely directed by veteran Georges Lautner, "La Vie dissolue de Gérard Floque" throws its smug protagonist, Roland Giraud, into a professional and domestic tizzy, but is content to let him off easy in a script that puts no new wrinkles into a familiar formula.

Giraud is a seemingly hot-shot advertising pro whose life collapses in a single day. Fired for producing a commercial that shocks an agency client, he returns home early to discover his daughter has been arrested for drug dealing and to find his wife (Clémentine Célarié) in bed with a noted tv celebrity (Gérard Rinaldi).

The distraught Giraud finds solace in the arms of his punk secretary (Marie-Anne Chazel) and her initially jealous but no less compliant mate (Mathilda May), who introduce him to their fast and cool lifestyle.

The lazy scripting and commonplace direction are redeemed partially by an energetic cast, notably Giraud (since "Three Men And A Cradle" a much-demanded serio-comic lead), and Jacqueline Maillan, who brushes off the stereotype of the nosy mother-in-law with marvelous timing and delivery.—*Len.*

La Ley del Deseo
(The Law Of Desire)
(SPANISH-COLOR)

A Cinevista (U.S.) release of an El Deseo and Laurenfilm production. Executive producer, Miguel A. Pérez Campos. Written and directed by Pedro Almodóvar. Camera (Eastmancolor), Angel Luis Fernández; editor, José Salcedo; costumes, José M. Cossio; sets, Javier Fernández; sound, James Willis; associate producer, Agustin Almodóvar. Reviewed at Cine Madrid, Feb. 11, 1987. Running time: **101 MINS.**

Pedro Quintero . . . . Eusebio Poncela
Tina Quintero . . . . Carmen Maura
Antonio Benitez . . . . Antonio Banderas
Juan Bermúdez . . . . Miguel Molina
Also with: Manuela Velasco, Bibi Andersen, Fernando Guillén, Nacho Martinez, Helga Liné, Fernando G. Cuervo, Germán Cobos, Maruchi León, Marta Fernández Muro.

Madrid — Spain's master of pop and pastiche, Pedro Almodóvar, turns his talents here to a gay love triangle, with extraneous touches of fantasy farce and camp humor, in a film that will please his fans (especially the gay community) but may turn off wider audiences. In its Madrid release, pic is drawing hefty attendance, because Almodóvar's films are always an "in" event here and arouse considerable curiosity.

More than the thin plot, it is the touches of slangy humor and droll but unlikely situations that Almodóvar comes up with which catch the audience's fancy. Pic also has a certain outrageous look to it which makes the antics more palatable.

Convoluted story concerns a famous film director, Pablo, and his way-out sister, Tina. Pablo is madly in love with Juan, who works in an outdoor bar in Andalucia. The third part of the triangle, Antonio, falls deeply in love with the director, and ultimately decides to get rid of his competitor, Juan, by pushing him off a cliff. Tina, the sister turns out to have changed her sex, and lives with her director-brother as well as a 10-year-old girl, who's a model. The model's mother is played by a well-known Spanish transvestite, Bibi Andersen (no relation to the Swedish actress).

Buoying pic are some of Almodóvar's clowning touches, such as having a kind of ornate chapel in Pablo's apartment to which Tina and the kid offer mocking prayers, or two mock-heroic detectives investigating Miguel's death. However, some audiences may fail to empathize with the many gay sex sequences, an integral part of the film from the first to the last frame. Many a lingering homosexual kiss, interspersed through the length of the film, and the frequent sniffing of cocaine form part of Almodóvar's swinging Madrid scene, and are certainly not for the straitlaced.

Eusebio Poncela puts in a good performance as the putative director. Antonio Banderas is the square-jawed, hulky lover and Carmen Maura provides the zany touch as the unpredictable sister. Technical credits are up to crack.

Pic could generate interest in select international markets where earlier films by Almodóvar such as "What Have I Done To Deserve This!" garnered attention. —*Besa*.

D'Annunzio
(ITALIAN-COLOR)

A Selvaggia Film release. Produced by Franco Casati and Sergio Martinelli for Selvaggia Film Productions. Directed by Sergio Nasca. Stars Robert Powell, Stefania Sandrelli. Screenplay, Piero Chiara, Fabio D'Agostini, Nasca; camera (color); Romano Albani; editor, Nino Baragli; art direction, Giorgio Luppi; music, Sergio Sandrelli. Reviewed at Etoile Cinema, Rome, Feb. 2, 1987. Running time: **109 MINS.**
Gabriele D'Annunzio . . . . . . Robert Powell
Elvira/Barbara Leoni . . . Stefania Sandrelli
Maria Gravina . . . . Sonia Petrovna
First wife . . . . .Teresa Ann Savoy
Also with: Florence Guerin, Paolo Bonacelli, Laurent Terzieff, Stefano Torossi.

Rome — Screen representations of flamboyant turn-of-the-century novelist and poet Gabriele D'Annunzio are usually limited to the poet-novelist's mature years, when he achieved notorious fame and was associated with the Mussolini regime. Sergio Nasca's "D'Annunzio," instead, chooses to depict five years when its subject was passing from journalism to his first success as a novelist with "Pleasure" and "The Innocent." These happen to be the years when he went through two marriages and one important love affair, which film chiefly concentrates on. However, despite the presence of various sex stars (Stefania Sandrelli, Florence Guerin) and numerous bedroom scenes, this biopic has a serious core. Main audience would seem to be Italians of at least middle age, who studied the author at school before he became a symbol of kitsch.

They might disagree, however, with Robert Powell's portrayal of young D'Annunzio as a vain, conceited flatterer and Don Juan, a skillful scribe but a far cry from a genius, a writer who borrowed heavily from French authors like Guy de Maupassant. In the dubbed Italo version, Powell is badly lip-synched and looks mannered in his red goatee and moustache and all those funny clothes. Though D'Annunzio is clearly meant to be a bit foolish and self-deceived, Powell caricatures him as awkwardly transparent and unsympathetic.

In contrast, Sandrelli turns in a remarkable mature performance in one of her rare roles as a sensitive,

intelligent woman; a lover of sensual pleasures, yes, but also a person able to make judgments. After almost two hours of giving her best to the sweet-talking philanderer, she sagely concludes it's better to bid adieu. The ironic epilog to their affair is that D'Annunzio went on to become rich and famous; his lover was left with her memories.

Nasca, who is not a very refined lenser, gets his points across anyway. He takes no small swipes at his hero's hypocrisy, money-grubbing, and bald-faced way of using women who crossed his path. Supporting cast is surprisingly good, from Teresa Ann Savoy as an ugly noblewoman who was his first wife, to Florence Guerin as Sandrelli's friend and an intelligent onlooker, and Laurent Terzieff as D'Annunzio's perplexed country cousin and friend. Pic indulges in its sharpest digs at the aristocracy with Sonia Petrovna in a thankless Princess role.

Costumes, lensing, and music are above average. —*Yung*.

Der Traum Vom Elch
(I Dreamed Of My Elk)
(EAST GERMAN-COLOR)

A DEFA-Studio fur Spielfilme production. Directed by Siegfried Kuhn. Screenplay, Christa Muller, Hasso Hartmann, from a novel by Herbert Otto; camera (color), Peter Brand; editor, Brigitte Krex; music, Hans Jurgen Wenzel; sound, Klaus Tolstorf. Reviewed at the India Film Festival (Competition), Delhi, Jan. 13, 1987. Running time: **88 MINS.**
Anna . . . . Katrin Satz
Stefan . . . . Detlef Heintze
Ludwig . . . . Christian Steyer
Anette . . . . Marie Gruber

Delhi — "I Dreamed Of My Elk" is a modern story of sex and love, so heavily centered on emotions it could be set in almost any European country. This sensitive, non-moralistic portrait of a young woman's feelings by East German helmer Siegfried Kuhn could have a chance in Western art houses with the right handling.

Anna (Katrin Satz) is a nurse around 30, whose passions are consumed in loving an absent man, Marcus. This idealized lover, whom she calls the Elk, comes by once a year if she's lucky, but she thinks of him constantly.

Girlfriend Anette (Marie Gruber) is a fragile divorcee, in love with an egocentric painter named Ludwig (Christian Steyer) who treats her like dirt. Rejecting clinging-vine Anette, he seduces aloof Anna. But Anna impulsively has an affair with Ludwig's friend Stefan (Detlaf Heintze), a married factory manager. Relations become even more contorted when Anette commits suicide, an event that jolts Anna into escaping to the mountains to take stock of her love life.

Acting is firstrate and lensing professional. The settings — a hospital, an artist's spacious loft, the girls' apartments, a mountain cabin — have the slightly unreal look of young singles' habitats in any part of the world. — *Yung*.

The Bikini Shop
(The Malibu Bikini Shop)
(COLOR)

Lameduck sexploitation comedy.

An Intl. Film Marketing release of a Wescom production, in association with Romax Prods. Produced by Gary Mehlman, J. Kenneth Rotcop. Coproducer, Leo Leichter. Executive producers, Charles C. Thieriot, Andrew Bullians, Jean Bullians, Sandy Climan. Written and directed by David Wechter. Camera (CFI color), Tom Richmond; editor, Jean-Marc Vasseur; music supervision, Don Perry; art direction, Dian Perryman; set decoration, Kayla Koeber; costume design, Rita Riggs; sound (Dolby), Dana Gray; associate producer, Ron Bechtel; assistant director, Clifford C. Coleman. Reviewed at the Egyptian Theater, L.A., Feb. 10, 1987. (MPAA Rating: R.) Running time: **99 MINS.**
Alan . . . . Michael David Wright
Todd . . . . Bruce Greenwood
Ronnie . . . . Barbra Horan
Jane . . . . Debra Blee
Ben . . . . Jay Robinson
Cindy . . . . Galyn Gorg
Kathy . . . . Ami Julius
Richard J. Remington . . . . . . Frank Nelson

Hollywood — Made in 1984 and in regional release since last May under its original title, "The Bikini Shop," which name appears in the credits, "The Malibu Bikini Shop," as it is now known, has popped up in Los Angeles before its imminent date with destiny in homevideo shops. Pic could have done nicely in the heyday of cheapo sexploitation comedies, but that was over a decade ago.

Usual dimwitted story, about how two brothers — one a California beach boy, the other an uptight MBA graduate — inherit a Venice (not Malibu) boardwalk bikini store, presents plenty of opportunities for the requisite t&a, what with girls trying on new models behind see-through mirrors and running into the surf sporting dissolving threads.

Frustration factors stem partly from the fact that the three lovely shop assistants — Barbra Horan, Galyn Gorg and Ami Julius — maintain PG levels of decency throughout an R picture, as well as from the screenwriters' insistence upon concocting endless plot complications to keep the film running a good 20 minutes longer than necessary.

Pic looks as cutrate as the budget undoubtedly was, although prevailing tone is amiable enough.
—*Cart*.

The Right Hand Man
(AUSTRALIAN-COLOR)

A New World (in U.S.), Greater Union (in Australia) release of a UAA presentation of a Yarraman Prod. Produced by Steven Grives, Tom Oliver, Basil Appleby. Executive producer, David Thomas. Directed by Di Drew. Stars Rupert Everett, Hugo Weaving. Screenplay, Helen Hodgman, from the book by Kathleen Peyton; camera (Eastmancolor), Peter James; editor, Don Saunders; music, Allan Zavod; sound, Syd Butterworth; production design, Neil Angwin; costumes, Graham Purcell; production manager, Renate Wilson; assistant director, Phil Rich; casting, Liz Mullinar. Reviewed at Mosman screening room, Sydney, Feb. 10, 1987. Running time: **100 MINS.**
Harry Ironminster . . . . Rupert Everett
Ned Rowlands . . . . Hugo Weaving
Sarah Redbridge . . . Catherine McClements
Dr. Redbridge . . . . Arthur Dignam
Lady Ironminster . . . . Jennifer Claire

Sydney — "The Right Hand Man" is an extremely beautiful, but only fitfully engrossing, melodrama of the type Gainsborough Studios used to make Britain in the 1940s; James Mason and Stewart Granger would have been ideal casting for the principal male roles here.

Story concerns the sickly, diabetes-suffering young aristocrat Harry Ironminster (very well played by British thesp Rupert Everett) who's inadvertently the cause of his father's death in a horse-drawn coach accident. Injuries Harry sustains at the time result, eventually, in the amputation of his right arm (an unnecessarily graphic sequence). Unable to ride his beloved horses, Harry becomes morose and even his pretty girlfriend, Sarah (Catherine McClements), scientifically inclined daughter of the local doctor (Arthur Dignam), can't help him.

Harry's temporary salvation turns out to be Ned Rowlands (Hugo Weaving), the dashing driver of the Leviathon, a giant stagecoach that thunders down the rough roads to Sydney every week. Realizing that coaches soon will give way to steamtrains, Ned agrees to come to work for Harry, and even enters into a bizarre relationship with Sarah.

It's at this point that Helen Hodgman's screenplay, adapted from Kathleen Peyton's novel, goes off the rails. It's just beyond the realm of possibility that the sensible Sarah (beautifully played by newcomer McClements) would agree to sleep with Ned, however charmingly Weaving plays him, in the way she does here. Pic suffers a major credibility gap at this point.

Otherwise, it's an impressive effort. Di Drew, directing her first feature after winning prizes for her short films, does a fine job of direction, and works very well indeed with the actors. Cinematographer Peter James provides outstandingly beautiful images, often evoking the delicate lighting of Stanley Kubrick's "Barry Lyndon," which is high praise. Production design of Neil Angwin is also a major plus.

Trouble is, audiences aren't motivated solely by visuals, and, as indicated, the plotting here leaves something to be desired. As compensation, there are a couple of finely staged action scenes, including the initial accident that triggers the plot and a breathtaking sequence in which the fast-moving Leviathon almost collides with another, smaller, coach on the highway. Special tribute should be paid to actor Weaving, who obviously did most of his own driving under clearly difficult conditions. —*Strat.*

True Colors
(HONG KONG-COLOR)

A Cinema City production, released by Golden Princess. Executive producer, Catherine Hun. Associate producer, Herrick Wong. Directed by Kirk Wong. Stars Raymond Wong, Ti Lung, Lin Ching Hsia, Gary Lim. Screenplay, Raymond Wong; camera (color), Henry Chan; editor, Johnson Chow; music, Danny Chung, art direction, Andy Li. Reviewed at President theater, Hong Kong, Jan. 1, 1987. Running time: **95 MINS.**
(Cantonese soundtrack with English subtitles)

Hong Kong — "True Colors" is an example of the corny and predictable gangster flick now in vogue due to the tremendous success of "A Better Tomorrow" of Cinema City. The cinematography is fine. Ti Lung is in excellent macho form while Lin Ching Hsia as decorative heroine maintains her glamorous aura.

Everything is overdone and there is no subtlety. Kirk Wong directs with conviction, but Raymond Wong is all wrong and funny for the part of a juvenile delinquent and then reformed man of the cloth.

The story idea is to have Ti Lung return to Hong Kong after a long period of hiding from fellow gangsters and cops. His friendship with Wong is resumed and his love for Lin Ching Hsia, now married to a nasty gangster kingpin, is rekindled with a disastrous, bloody outcome.

The gang boss mistreats the heroine and that makes hero Ti Lung mad. Revenge is the natural solution to avenge the murder of Lin Ching Hsia while escaping from the baddies. —*Mel.*

Morgan Stewart's Coming Home
(COLOR)

Teen comedy is no fun.

A New Century/Vista release of a Kings Road production. Produced by Stephen Friedman. Directed by Alan Smithee (see note below). Screenplay, Ken Hixon, David Titcher; camera (Deluxe color), Richard Brooks; editor, Bob Letterman; music, Peter Bernstein; production design, Charles Bennett; set decorator, Victor Kempster; sound, Danny Michael; assistant director, Lewis Gould; associate producer, Patrick McCormick; costumes, Molly Maginnis. Reviewed at ABC screening room, Century City, Calif., Feb.

11, 1987. (MPAA Rating: PG-13). Running time: **96 MINS.**
Morgan Stewart ....Jon Cryer
Nancy Stewart ....Lynn Redgrave
Tom Stewart ....Nicholas Pryor
Emily......................Viveka Davis
Jay Sprinsteen ....Paul Gleason
General Fenton.........Andrew Duncan
Ivan ....Savely Kramorov
Garrett..............John David Cullum

Hollywood — Shot in 1985 as "Homefront," with Paul Aaron succeeding the original director Terry Winsor, pic is finally being released as "Morgan Stewart's Coming Home" with the fictitious Alan Smithee receiving directorial credit. Not surprisingly, the wait wasn't worth it.

As it stands, "Morgan Stewart's Coming Home" is a lifeless comedy about a kid brought home from boarding school to be a political ploy in his father's senate campaign. Poor execution and one-dimensional characters make this one a sure loser at the boxoffice.

Possibly the only thing to recommend in the film is the performance by Jon Cryer as the 17-year-old in search of a family, but not quite. Cryer is a likable enough actor but in this case it's too much of a good thing. He is the only remotely interesting person here but scriptwriters Ken Hixon and David Titcher fail him too, as they do all the other collected cartoon characters.

There is absolutely nothing going on except what's on screen and a more contrived, hackneyed treatment would be hard to come up with.

Cryer is a typical teen with a fondness for monster films and junk food. Lynn Redgrave is his no-nonsense mother who doesn't believe parents should be pals with their kids. She has little patience with Morgan and even less understanding. Delivering lines as if she were leading an elocution class, Redgrave is too extreme to laugh at.

Nicholas Pryor as the senator father is a bit more sympathetic, but again too ineffectual to side with. This is a family without soul and no amount of tomfoolery is going to give it to them.

Plot, such as it is, involves a corrupt aide (Paul Gleason) who hatches a scheme to incriminate the politician and allow his opponent to win the election. Since the good guys are so marginally interesting, it's a hollow victory when they foil the fix.

Along the way Cryer picks up a girlfriend (Viveka Davis), a charming kid who also likes horror films, but that's about all there is to their relationship which is so inexplicably chaste that they shower with their underwear on.

Direction fails to develop a consistent tone for the picture, ranging from broad slapstick to sappy. Realism and caricature collide con-

tinually. Production values are undistinguished and all the while there is an insipid score insisting that all this must be great fun.

This is the kind of film that gives families a bad name. —*Jagr.*

Some Kind Of Wonderful
(COLOR)

Thoughtful teen pic.

A Paramount Pictures release of a John Hughes production. Produced and written by John Hughes. Executive producers, Michael Chinich, Ronald Colby. Directed by Howard Deutch. Camera (Technicolor), Jan Kiesser; editor, Bud Smith, Scott Smith; music, Stephen Rague, John Musser; production design, Josan Russo, art director, Greg Pickrell; set decorator, Linda Spheeris; costume designer, Marilyn Vance-Straker; sound (Dolby), David MacMillan; assistant director, Jerry Zissmer; casting, Judith Weiner. Reviewed at Paramount Pictures screening room, L.A., Feb. 18, 1987. (MPAA Rating: PG-13). Running time: **93 MINS.**
Keith Nelson ....Eric Stoltz
Watts ....Mary Stuart Masterson
Amanda Jones ....Lea Thompson
Hardy Johns ....Craig Sheffer
Cliff Nelson ....John Ashton
Skinhead ....Elias Koteas
Shayne ....Molly Hagan
Laura Nelson ....Maddie Corman
Carol Nelson ....Jane Elliot
Cindy Nelson ....Candace Cameron

Hollywood — "Some Kind of Wonderful" is a simple, lovely and thoughtful teenage story that occasionally shines due to fine characterizations and lucid dialog. While plot is largely predictable, there is vitality enough to attract modest business from a youthful audience.

Writer-producer John Hughes and director Howard Deutch, who collaborated on "Pretty In Pink," return here for an empathetic portrait of dilemmas on such weighty matters as individuality, genuine friendship and love. Hughes and Deutch deftly avoid being ponderous via steady and sure pacing, even during slower sequences.

Film is set in L.A.'s San Pedro area and centers on high school senior Eric Stoltz, who is a sensitive young man struggling to develop his artistic talent while juggling school, part-time work as a car mechanic and the distraction of the immensely popular Lea Thompson that he can't quite pick up on the emotions of Mary Stuart Masterson, whom Stoltz dismisses early on as just a tomboy friend.

It seems that the whole world is watching — or at least the entire school — as Thompson fights with her wealthy and arrogant b.f., Craig Sheffer. Stoltz manages to get her to accept a date amidst the furor and stage is set for the inevitable confrontation with Sheffer.

While we may be fairly certain where it's all heading, Hughes-Deutch make the passage so engaging as Stoltz' perspective is accessed through relationships with people closest to him. It's especially satisfying to watch the bond deepen between him and longtime friend Masterson.

She's a bit on the tough side and may be most happy rocking time away on the drums. However, there is here a wise and caring young woman who is sounding board for Stoltz as he plays out his fantasy of taking out Thompson.

Masterson is so adept and appealing in her role that she becomes the most interesting character of all. Fortunately, however, Stoltz has the substance to maintain his lead role.

Further weaving the fabric of Stoltz' life, Hughes-Deutch introduce family and friends of real believability. John Ashton as his father is stern but likeable; Maddie Corman as one of his younger sisters is just precocious enough to avoid being unlikeable; Elias Koteas as the disaffected punk outsider manages to deliver a comical but realistic performance.

Once Thompson and Sheffer are suitably established as unsympathetic characters, Stoltz is ready to actually go out on that date. By now the event has taken on a symbolic grandeur of such consequence that risk is all else yet to unfold may be anticlimactic.

Stoltz and Masterson, however, team up for an inventive way to arrive at anticipated destination of the story. Resolution nicely underscores just how appropriate the casting has been.

Project was a worthy undertaking that reaffirms Hughes' credentials as one of the most insightful writers around on contemporary American youth. —*Tege.*

Hay Que Deshacer La Casa
(We Must Undo The House)
(SPANISH-COLOR)

A Lince Films, Jet Films, Incine production, presented by Luis Sanz. Directed by José Luis García Sánchez. Screenplay, García Sánchez, Rafael Azcona based on novel by Sebastián Junyent; camera (Eastmancolor), José Luis Alcaine; editor, Pablo G. del Amo; music, Miguel Morales; sets, Gerardo Vera. Reviewed at Cine Paz, Jan. 24, 1987. Running time: **93 MINS.**

Ana	Amparo Rivelles
Laura	Amparo Soler Leal
Frutos	Joaquín Kremel
Ramón	José María Pou
Pepe Luis	José Luis López Vázquez
Huete	Agustín González

Also with: Luis Merlo, Luis Ciges, Félix Rotaeta, Guillermo Montesinos, Miguel Romero, Francisco Valladares, Antonio Gamero.

Madrid — Poking fun at Spain's old sacred cows had been one of scripter Rafael Azcona's salient talents since his early stints with directors such as Luis García Berlanga and Marco Ferreri in the 1950s. He and co-writer/director José Luis García Sánchez set their yarn against the background of Holy Week in a provincial Castilian city which, predictably, gives them ample opportunity to set up anachronistic penitents, processions and Catholic images which are made fun of, and to ridicule Old Guard sentiments.

Crux of story revolves around two sisters who, after the death of

their rightwing father, must come to a settlement and "undo" the houses. One of the sisters, Ana, has never dwelt anywhere but in the town, where she is married, has children and lives the boring life of a petite bourgeoise. The other sister, Laura, long ago moved to Paris and has returned for no sentimental reason, but merely to get her financial due.

Main action of pic is the sensitively thesped shifting relationship between two sisters as they alternately delve into their pasts, come to grips with the present and evaluate their lives and the myths they have built them upon. The drama is lightened constantly by touches of wry humor. Two homosexuals are worked into the story for questionable comic relief. One of them, a queen, performs a magnificent *saeta*, sung from a balcony during the religious procession.

Though well done and entertaining, pic is local in scope. The ribbing of traditional values, over a decade after Franco's death, is becoming somewhat tiresome. The part of the diehard Fascist (predictably played by Agustín González) has itself become an overfamiliar stock character at which to aim barbs. —*Besa.*

A Nightmare On Elm Street 3: Dream Warriors
(COLOR)

Special effects dominate poor story; boxoffice outlook still strong.

A New Line Cinema release of a New Line, Heron Communications and Smart Egg Pictures presentation of a Robert Shaye production. Produced by Shaye. Executive producers, Wes Craven, Stephen Diener. Coproduced by Sara Risher; line producer, Rachel Talalay. Directed by Chuck Russell. Screenplay, Craven, Bruce Wagner, Russell, Frank Darabont, from story by Craven, Wagner, based on characters created by Craven; camera (Deluxe color), Roy H. Wagner; editor, Terry Stokes, Chuck Weiss; music, Angelo Badalamenti; song, Dokken group; additional music, Ken Harrison, Don Dokken, also Charles Bernstein (from Part 1); sound, William Fiege; art direction, Mick Strawn, C.J. Strawn; set decoration, James Barrows; special makeup effects, Mark Shostrum, Chris Biggs, Greg Cannom, Mathew Mungel; Freddy makeup, Kevin Yagher; special visual effects, Dreamquest Images — supervisor, Hoyt Yeatman; mechanical effects, Peter Chesney; stopmotion animation, Doug Beswick; stunt coordinator, Rich Barker; second unit director, Dan Perri; postproduction supervisor, Joseph Fineman; casting, Annette Benson; associate producer, Niki Marvin. Reviewed at Magno Preview 4 screening room, N.Y., Feb. 18, 1987. (MPAA Rating: R.) Running time: **96 MINS.**

Nancy Thompson	Heather Langenkamp
Kristen Parker	Patricia Arquette
Max	Larry Fishburne
Dr. Elizabeth Simms	Priscilla Pointer
Dr. Neil Goldman	Craig Wasson
Freddy Krueger	Robert Englund
Elaine Parker	Brooke Bundy
Joey	Rodney Eastman
Phillip	Bradley Gregg
Will	Ira Heiden
Kincaid	Ken Sagoes

Jennifer	Penelope Sudrow
Taryn	Jennifer Rubin

Also with: John Saxon, Clayton Landey, Nan Martin, Stacey Alden, Kristin Clayton, Sally Piper, Rozlyn Sorrell, Dick Cavett, Zsa Zsa Gabor.

"A Nightmare On Elm Street 3: Dream Warriors" is a cannily conceived followup in the hit series which unfortunately tips the balance heavily towards the special effects department, leaving the human side of the equation deficient. Fans will surely turn out in big numbers for this one and merely laugh at the plot and acting gaffes.

With input from the original's creator, Wes Craven, "3" shifts its focus away from the homely neighborhood horror to a sort of Sam Fuller "Shock Corridor" setting of seven nightmare-plagued teens under the care of medicos Priscilla Pointer (instantly hissable) and Craig Wasson (decidedly miscast).

Heather Langenkamp, young heroine of the first film in the series (who didn't show up for Part 2), returns as an intern assigned to the ward who is, natch, plenty simpatico with the teens. She's been using an experimental dream-inhibiting drug to keep her wits about her and proposes using it on the kids. Plot quickly becomes illogical and contradictory, as Langenkamp fights with Wasson to get use of the drug, then encourages group hypnosis and shared-dream activities, all while the teens try strategems to stay awake, with various results.

While everyone is stewing in their juices, pic is mainly focused on the violent special effects outbursts of Freddy Krueger (ably limned under heavy makeup by Robert Englund), the child murderer's demon spirit who seeks revenge on Langenkamp and the other Elm St. kids for the sins of their parents. Freddy's parentage is the subject of an elaborate subplot involving a nun (Nan Martin) who keeps popping up to bug Wasson.

Another subplot which gets in the way of the narrative (and through misguided crosscutting, interrupts the exciting action of the finale) concerns Wasson and Langenkamp's dad (John Saxon, also back from Part 1) searching for Freddy's remains in order to exorcize his spirit. Happy ending is arbitrary and confusing, seeming to wrap up the series until the obligatory groaner of a final twist to make room for Part 4.

Debuting director Chuck Russell elicits poor performances from most of his thesps, making it difficult to differentiate between pic's comic relief and unintended howlers during even the simplest of exposition scenes. Langenkamp, looking stunning but far too cheerful for the role, declares "my mother died in her sleep" and it's all downhill from there to campsville.

Fortunately, the legions of special effects experts working here more than deliver their goods and that component, plus an extraneous but satisfying nude scene by an uncredited actress, should be enough for the target audience. Of special note are Doug Beswick's stopmotion animation (including a skeleton homage to the genius of Ray Harryhausen), and monster makeup by various hands, peaking in a scary sequence where a vast Freddy-headed worm starts eating heroine Patricia Arquette gradually, from the feet up.

Arquette, younger sister of Rosanna, proves to be an excellent screamer, but gets little chance to act. Ditto the rest of the cast. Poor taste screenplay has a monster wheelchair chase down the crippled teen and has Freddy sprout 10 hypodermic needles on his fingers to give a real jolt to the ex-drug addict in the bunch. Ken Sagoes gets the biggest laughs but is saddled with a woefully stereotyped black characterization.

The very real and recognizable nightmares and fears dealt with in this film series could give rise to interesting psychological treatment, but the inspiration of Val Lewton and Jacques Tourneur has now given way to the prevailing attitude: "let the special effects guys take care of it." —*Lor.*

La Famiglia
(The Family)
(ITALIAN-FRENCH-COLOR)

A UIP release of a Massfilm/Cinecittà/RAI-TV Channel 1/ Les Films Ariane Cinemax coproduction. Produced by Franco Committeri. Directed by Ettore Scola. Stars Vittorio Gassman, Fanny Ardant. Screenplay, Ruggero Maccari, Furio Scarpelli, Scola; camera (Cinecittà color), Ricardo Aronovich; editor, Scola; music, Armando Trovajoli; art direction, Luciano Ricceri. Reviewed at Barberini Cinema, Rome, Feb. 1, 1987. Running time: **130 MINS.**

Carlo	Vittorio Gassman
Adriana	Fanny Ardant
Beatrice	Stefania Sandrelli
Young Carlo	Andrea Occhipinti

Also with: Alberto Gimignani, Massimo Dapporto, Carlo Dapporto, Cecilia Dazzi, Jo Champa, Ottavia Piccolo, Athina Cenci, Alessandra Panelli, Monica Scattini, Ricky Tognazzi, Renzo Palmer, Philippe Noiret, Memè Perlini, Sergio Castellitto.

Rome — Ettore Scola's latest effort, "The Family," is a predictable assembly of the minor joys and sorrows that befall a middle-class Roman family, 1906-1986. Even with effervescent thesp Vittorio Gassman around for most of these years to glue the piece together, pic has about as much excitement as watching an old station wagon patiently putt its way homeward. The passengers just grow older as it goes along. It's an example of family entertainment that has taken off at the Italo boxoffice in an exceptionally strong early weeks' showing.

After Scola showed how an entire

film could be shot on a single set in "Le Bal," he continues to impose a rigorous, arbitrary rule of all-studio shooting on himself: "Family" takes place in one rambling apartment, where Carlo is born and lives, until film leaves him celebrating his 80th birthday. The initial menage includes Carlo's mother and father, grandfather, brother, a trio of bickering maiden aunts, and a servant. The atmosphere recalls an Italian version of Norman Rockwell, with the little boys wrestling on the rug and Papa trying to paint Mama's portrait.

Sometime around 1926, Carlo has turned into a handsome youth (Andrea Occhipinti) and is giving lessons at home to juvenile Beatrice (Stefania Sandrelli, the most appealing member of the cast, and the only one able to age convincingly). Though he marries Beatrice, he really loves her wild, artistic sister Adriana (Jo Champa, later Fanny Ardant). Pic takes us through their fervent but inconclusive relationship with as many clichés as it's possible to script into one film, including a single night of adultery when they're 50. Meanwhile, Fascism has come and gone (one fiery pal flees to Paris, dies in Spain; Carlo's brother goes to war and returns a disillusioned man). Carlo abruptly leaps from tender youth to Vittorio Gassman sometime around the end of the war. By then his own kids are growing up; script marches ahead to treat us to Fanny Ardant as a gray-wigged 80-year-old, still fighting with almost doddering Carlo, who now shares the apartment with his grown-up grandson.

Main difference between this and an accelerated daytime drama is there's no drama. Scripters deliberately aim for the low-key and uneventful, apparently in the belief nothing big or interesting happens in the life of a typical family. Pic's breakneck race through a lifetime strikes only the surfaces, with the result that the whole project feels lightweight.

Visually, this is a dark house. Armando Trovajoli's score underscores pic's nostalgic side. — *Yung.*

Les Fous de Bassan
(In The Shadow Of The Wind)
(CANADIAN/FRENCH-COLOR)

A Vivafilms Intl. presentation. Produced by Justine Héroux. Directed by Yves Simoneau. Screenplay, Sheldon Chad, based on the novel by Anne Hébert; camera (color), Alain Dostie; editor, Joelle Van Effenterre; music, Richard Grégoire; director of production, Roger Héroux; art director, Michel Proulx; sound, Paul Dion. Reviewed at Complexe Desjardins Cinema, Montreal, Jan. 2, 1987. (In competition at Berlin Film Festival.) Running time: **107 MINS.**
Stevens Brown . . . . Steve Banner
Olivia Atkins . . . . Charlotte Valandrey
Nora Atkins . . . . Laure Marsac
Pastor Jones . . . Bernard-Pierre Donnadieu
Perceval Brown . . . . Lothaire Bluteau
Irene Jones . . . . Marie Tifo

Montreal — While much has been made of Denys Arcand's acclaimed "The Decline Of The American Empire" in the last year, hotshot young director Yves Simoneau has also been making waves in Quebec film circles, albeit in far more low-key fashion. Simoneau, who dazzled audiences last year with his low-budget, high-tech chiller "Pouvoir Intime," takes on a far more complex subject in "Fous" but is equal to the task.

The film, official Canadian selection for competition at the Berlin Film Festival, is an absolutely stunning, exquisitely crafted study in alienation and repression, set in a primitive, seaside Quebec outpost in the 1930s.

Although the characters in the original Anne Hébert novel were English, the Canadian/French production team opted to shoot in French with francophones in the lead roles. While the Hébert opus took the points of view of several characters, the film's focus is primarily that of Stevens Brown (Steve Banner), both as a young man in 1936 and as an older man (Jean-Louis Millette) in the present.

The younger Brown's return to his quaint Gaspé roots isn't heralded by all in the community. A wild-eyed dreamer and drifter, he stirs the sexual passions of many a lady in the area. Given all the guilt and repression that exists, it doesn't take too much time until fireworks are ignited, resulting ultimately in the rape of two sisters (Charlotte Valandrey and Laure Marsac).

With minimal action and dialog, Simoneau is able to deftly elicit the forboding, medieval-like atmosphere that has plagued many a rural Quebec community, where the Church is a prime force. Again, Simoneau is able to convey his haunting message with some truly breathtaking cinematography. Of course, the handsomely rugged Gaspé provides the perfect setting for Simoneau's striking images.

As is the norm for a Simoneau pic, production values are impeccable. Despite the accent differences between the native Quebec and French players, the acting is strong. Banner, in particular, brings the necesary emotional and physical danger to his role of Brown, while Lothaire Bluteau is very effective as his retarded brother Perceval. Also in line for praise are Bernard-Pierre Donnadieu as the sexually obsessed priest and Valandrey as the sensuous Atkins sister who is able to resist Brown's animal magnetism.

Prospects for pic on international market bode well, if past success of "Decline" and "Les Bons Debarras" is any indication.—*Bro.*

Stella i orlofi
(Stella On Vacation)
(ICELANDIC-COLOR)

An Umbi Film release and production. Produced by Ingi Björg Briem. Directed by Thorhildur Thorleifsdottir. Screenplay, Gudny Halldorsdottir; camera (Eastmancolor), Jan Pehrson; editor, Kristin Palsdottir; music, Valgeir Gudjonsson; production design, Halldor Thorgeirsson. Reviewed at Nordic Film Festival, Helsinki, Jan. 23, 1987. Running time: **86 MINS.**
With: Edda Björgvinsdottir (Stella), Thorhallur Sigurdsson (Salomon), Gestur E. Jonasson (Georg), Eggert Tjorleifsson.

Helsinki — It seems like a female posse of filmmakers is out to take revenge here. "Stella On Vacation" (to be marketed abroad as "The Icelandic Shock Station") is a crudely fashioned farce in which a femme helmer (Thorhildur Thorleifsdottir) and her team of sister professionals (producer, writer, editor, etc.) punish every male within plot sight for such offenses as infidelity, piggish chauvinism, boozing and boasting.

A Swedish alcoholic comes to Iceland for a cure at the AA home, but is mistaken at the airport for a local storeowner's business associate and is, when the storekeeper is hospitalized with two broken arms after a boisterous brithday party, taken by the Icelander's pretty wife Stella to a salmon fishing retreat.

At this remote spot, a gang of Kiwanians, a bunch of illegal salmon breeders led by an airline pilots, assorted children plus the storekeeper's visiting Danish mistress *and* the storekeeper himself (escaped from the hospital) converge to indulge in all kinds of games of mistaken identity and pratfalls of the lowest order.

Everybody overàcts grossly throughout, and out of 10 sight gags, at least eight fail to work because of insecure handling of elementary gag mechanics. Still, the proceedings have a lot of energy and a modicum of disarming, innocent charm. Item has been seen by 50% of Reykjavik's population since its release in November 1986, and a few video and tv deals with offshore territories are reportedly about to be signed. —*Kell.*

Nattseilere
(Night Voyage)
(NORWEGIAN-COLOR)

A Kommunernes Filmsentral release (foreign sales, Norsk Film/Frieda Ohrvik) of a Norsk Film production with NRK/TV. Produced by Svein H. Toreg. Directed by Tor M. Törstad. Screenplay, Ivar Enoksen; camera (Eastmancolor), Svein Krövel; editor, Edith Toreg; music, Geir Böhren, Bent Aserud. No further credits available. Reviewed at Nordic Film Festival, Helsinki, Jan. 24, 1987. Running time: **110 MINS.**
Girl from the Sea . . . . Vera Holte
Borr . . . . Helge Jordal
Olai . . . . Frode Rasmussen
Andrea . . . . Katja Medböe
Wieth . . . . Per Oscarsson

Jeppe . . . . Kalle Oeby
Provincial governor . . . . . Sigmund Säverud

Helsinki — Helge Jordal shines in exuberant swashbuckling style as a philosophy-spouting, tender-hearted, man-of-action vagabond Borr (he brings the early film exploits of Jean-Paul Belmondo to mind) in "Night Voyage," but Tor M. Törstad's adventure thriller for the very young is otherwise mostly a dud of muddled story-telling and poor execution of everything from comedy routines to action sequences.

Story has Borr, the vagabond, busy 100 years ago in remote northern Norway helping a 14-year-old abandoned girl with amnesia get back to whatever folks and land she came from before being shipwrecked. Borr is wanted by the law, but beloved by people in general for his charm and essential good nature. With the girl, he gets in and out of trouble until a vapid happy ending leaves him with nothing to do but lie back and gaze vacantly into the sky.

Each sequence in "Night Voyage" is staged like a piece of amateur theater with professional actors hamming away like crazy (in particular Per Oscarsson), while Vera Holte as the young girl supposed to inspire all the events looks lost and vacantly pretty throughout. Film has been received well by audiences in Norway, where tv fans will share their experience next year when item gets chopped up in four parts for a series to be beamed by coproducer NRK/TV.—*Kell.*

Living On Tokyo Time
(COLOR)

Offbeat ethnic comedy.

A Farallon Films production. Produced by Lynn O'Donnell, Dennis Hayashi. Directed by Steven Okazaki. Stars Minako Ohashi, Ken Nakagawa. Screenplay, John McCormick, Okazaki; camera (Monaco color), Okazaki, Zand Gee; editor, Okazaki; sound, Giovanni Di Simone, Sara Chin; assistant director, Judith Nihei. Reviewed at the U.S. Film Festival, Park City, Jan. 18, 1987. (No MPAA Rating.) Running time: **83 MINS.**
Kyoko . . . . Minako Ohashi
Ken . . . . Ken Nakagawa
Mimi . . . . Mitzie Abe
Carl . . . . Bill Bonham
Michelle . . . . Brenda Aoki
Lana . . . . Kate Connell
Richie . . . . John McCormick
Nina . . . . Sue Matthews
Jimbo . . . . Jim Cranna
Warren . . . . Alex Herschlag
Lambert . . . . Keith Choy
Sheri . . . . Judi Nihei
Lane . . . . Lane Nishikawa

Park City, Utah — A slight but charmingly offbeat look at a culturally mismatched couple, "Living On Tokyo Time" represents another promising regional film by and about a minority culture not often depicted on the big screen. First fictional feature from Bay Area-based Steven Okazaki, an Oscar nominee for his docu "Unfinished Business," displays a droll sensibility at work despite occasional awkwardnesses and slow spots. This could do some business in carefully nurtured specialized situations.

Setting is San Francisco, where an attractive young Japanese woman, Kyoko, has decided to stay on in the U.S. to get over a broken engagement and prove to her family she can make it on her own. With very little English and no particular prospects, she works in a restaurant and lives at the YWCA while writing home that things will be fine.

In desperate need of a green card, Kyoko is set up with a young Japanese-American named Ken, a bland lad who speaks no Japanese and works as a janitor while harboring dreams of becoming a rock star. Latter eventuality is unlikely given his staggering lack of talent, so Ken has little to offer Kyoko except legal status.

That's enough for Kyoko, who enters into marriage on a strictly businesslike basis. Ken accepts this at first, but gradually the dull-witted fool comes alive, falls in love with her and tries to really make her his wife.

Unfortunately, while Ken comes out of his shell, Kyoko remains within hers, instinctively refusing to Americanize herself or to sentimentally fall for Ken's embryonic display of romanticism. Ultimately, she comes to the astute realization that, if she stays much longer, she won't be able to go home again.

As presented by Okazaki, Ken's Japanese ancestry counts for very little where Kyoko is concerned and, in fact, Ken's thoroughly Americanized sister gets along with her Caucasian husband much better than Ken could ever hope to do with Kyoko. Pic is full of brassy, loud Japanese-American women to whom Kyoko represents a sharp contrast.

Okazaki loads film with sardonic comments about cultural differences, but it's all quite light, never trenchant, and he has fun with the brief scenes in which Ken's rock band attempts to get it together under the leadership of John McCormick, cowriter of the pic's screenplay.

Despite the agreeable pleasures offered up, however, film is diminished by the extreme uncommunicativeness of the two leads, as well as a frequent slackness to the storytelling. As colorful as many of the secondary characters may be, there is only so far you can go with obviously amateur performers, and a little more urgency in both the pacing and the important point-making would have helped a lot.

Minako Ohashi makes for a lovely, if thoroughly enigmatic, leading lady, while Ken Nakagawa's klutziness is amusing and frustrating by turns.

Shot by the director, along with Zand Gee, and edited by Okazaki as well, pic looks good on an obviously minimal budget (supplied in part by the American Film Institute and the National Endowment for the Arts). Lively soundtrack is comprised of numerous new wave tunes.—*Cart.*

Pandemonium
(COLOR)

Stillborn spoof.

An MGM/UA release from United Artists of a Krost/Chapin production. Executive producer, Barry Krost. Produced by Doug Chapin. Directed by Alfred Sole. Stars Tom Smothers, Carol Kane. Screenplay, Richard Whitley, Jaime Klein; camera (Panavision, Technicolor), Michel Hugo; editor, Eric Jenkins; music, Dana Kaproff; sound, Keith Wester; production design, Jack De Shields; art direction, James Claytor; set decoration, Chuck Graffeo; production manager-second unit director, Bill Watkins; assistant director, Ed Milkovich; casting, Havens/Rabin Casting; associate producers, Klein, Whitley. Reviewed on MGM/UA Home Video vidassette, N.Y., Feb. 15, 1987. (MPAA Rating: PG.) Running time: **81 MINS.**
Sgt. Cooper . . . . Tom Smothers
Candy Jefferson . . . . Carol Kane
Andy Jackson . . . . Miles Chapin
Sandy . . . . Debralee Scott
Randy . . . . Marc McClure
Glenn . . . . Judge Reinhold
Mandy . . . . Teri Landrum
Bambi . . . . Candy Azzara
    Also with: David L. Lander, Paul Reubens (a.k.a. Pee-wee Herman), John Paragon, Don McLeod, Gary Allen, Eve Arden, Pat Ast, Kaye Ballard, Eileen Brennan, Candi Brough, Randi Brough, Tab Hunter, Sydney Lassick, Edie McClurg, Jim McKrell, Lenny Montana, Donald O'Connor, Richard Romanus, Izabella Telezynska.

"Pandemonium' is an unfunny horror spoof from the MGM/UA vaults (where such unreleased goodies as "O.C. & Stiggs" and "The American Snitch" still reside). Reviewed here for the record, pic, originally titled "Thursday The 12th," had test bookings in 1982, HBO exposure and is now widely available as a homevideo entry. Ironically, an Aussie horror spoof also titled "Pandemonium" has just entered production.

Lamely lampooning the flood of horror films flourishing at the time (1981), pic is set at It Had To Be U., an Indiana college where cheerleaders are murdered at the annual cheerleaders camp. Endless series of gags substituting for the genre's gory deaths comes off as merely juvenile and silly rather than funny.

Director Alfred Sole has experience with straight horror thrillers ("Alice, Sweet Alice" and "Tanya's Island") but demonstrates no feel for comedy. In fact, one elongated scene of a beautiful but dippy girl (Teri Landrum) murdered with a drill while brushing her teeth plays like a gore scene hamstrung by the need to try for laughs instead.

Tom Smothers has a smallish role (but star billing) as a Canadian mountie on the case, oddly teamed

with assistant Paul Reubens, who does a version of his Pee-wee Herman character sans the exaggerated voice. Oodles of guest stars, including an unbilled Eileen Brennan, pad out the running time, with the best bit by twins Candi & Randi Brough as diner waitresses. Film most closely resembles in both intent and execution another flop, Paramount's "Student Bodies."

Though picture was filmed in 1981, it bears a 1980 copyright on the vidcassette. —*Lor.*

Talmae Wa Pomdari
(Talmae And Pomdari)
(NORTH KOREAN-COLOR)

A Korean Feature Film Studio production. Directed by Yun Ryong Gyu. Screenplay, Kim Sung Gu; camera (Widescreen, color), Pak Gyong Won; music, Chon Chang Il. Reviewed at the India Film Festival (Competition), Delhi, Jan. 12, 1987. Running time: **83 MINS.**
Talmae . . . . Kim Yong Suk
Pomdari . . . . Gho Myong Son
Imdon . . . . Choe Chang Su
Gen. Hong . . . . Yu Wom Jun

Delhi — "Talmae And Pomdari" is a sweeping, widescreen historical romance from North Korea, complete with fully orchestrated music and dance sequences·plus blazing colors. Based on a legend from Mt. Taesong, film is an enjoyable enough exercise of its sort. Fresh young hero and heroine are fearless patriots of olden times who defend their country and its magic "rainbow tile" to the death. Corny, sentimental, and probably limited to a few Eastern markets, this is the last film of veteran Yun Ryong Gyu, who died in December.

Plot revolves around a mysterious early-warning device called the rainbow tile, which blazes in a mini-aurora borealis whenever enemies menace the border. In a musical prelude, handome Pomdari (Gho Myong Son) and lovely lass Talmae (Kim Yong Suk) are rejoined after the last war, in which the youth has killed 200 enemies and proved he values military discipline more than his life.

All Talmae wants is a peaceful family life, but when her father (Choe Chang Su) is killed guarding the tile, the pair is launched into a series of misfortunes and adventures. It boils down to Talmae going into a grueling course of solitary training in the martial arts, Rocky-style, in order to compete in a tournament, vindicate her father's honor, and safeguard the country. Her antagonist is a beautiful spy as cruel as she is cunning.

Film makes the most of some spectacular castle sets and breathtaking natural locales. Leads are called on to do more horseback riding and posing than acting, but they're adequate for the task.
—*Yung.*

Madhvacharya
(INDIAN-COLOR)

An Ananthalakshmi Films production. Written and directed by G.V. Iyer. Camera (color), Madhu Ambat; editor V.R.K. Prasad; music, Balamurali Krishna; art direction, P. Krishnamurthy; sound, Kitty Govindaswamy. Reviewed at the India Film Festival, Delhi, Jan. 18, 1987. Running time: **164 MINS.**
Madhvacharya . . . . Poorna Prasad
Achyuta Prajna . . . . . G.M. Krishnamurthy
Pandit Trivikrama . . . . Hayagrivachar
Old monk . . . . G.V. Shivanand
    (Dialog in Kannada)

Delhi — This biopic on the life of 13th century Hindu holyman Madhvacharya is a sprawling, mystic epic with the hypnotic fascination of an endless chant. Enterprising programmers could turn it into the cult movie of the Hare Krishna set: it's a curious item from any point-of-view.

Helmer G.V. Iyer is something of a guru himself, having worked in film since the 1940s and authored the first film in Sanskrit (President's award for best Indian film, 1984). Current pic continues his series on seminal Hindu philosophers.

Running almost three hours, first half is the freshest and most enjoyable. Young Madhvacharya grows up in an orthodox Brahmin household, where he learns his Vedas by heart and studies Monism — the belief that every individual soul is the essence of the Absolute. It isn't long, however, before the boy is posing questions his teachers can't answer. He decides in childhood to become an ascetic and is ordained a monk against his family's wishes.

As a youth, Madhvacharya (Poorna Prasad) studies under the open-minded guru Achyuta Prajna (G.M. Krishnamurthy). Bucking tradition, he rejects the idea of life as illusion, and propounds the philosophy of Duality (body and soul both exist). His pilgrimages throughout the land and debates with leading scholars of the time win him fame and disciples.

Filmmaker has tried to simplify Duality for the layman and ladle it out in small doses. This cheerful philosophy holds life is to be relished and is charmingly debated by smiling, soft-spoken monks in orange-colored robes. A continually moving camera keeps film going at a satisfying pace throughout the first half: pic loses steam later, when Madhvacharya makes too many pilgrimages and vanquishes too many petty enemies. Whereas Iyer seems incapable of taking a false step in pic's early part, viewer awakens from the trance later and starts counting the minutes. Lensing is superior and concentrates on breathtaking mountain scenery and nature, plus folkloristic sets of the monastery. Cast is excellent.
—*Yung.*

Jeg elsker dig
(I Love You)
(DANISH-COLOR)

A Metronome release of Ebbe Preisler Film/TV production with the Danish Film Institute and DR/TV. Produced by Preisler, Finn Clausen. Written and directed by Li Vilstrup. Dialog consultant, Hanne Hostrup Larsen; camera (Eastmancolor), Judy Irola; editor, Camilla Skousen; music, Claus & Svend Agmussen; sound, Iben Haahr Andersen; production design, Per Flink Basse; costumes, Mariann Preisler. Reviewed at Metronome screening room, Copenhagen, Jan. 20, 1987. Running time: **84 MINS.**
Jens . . . . Peter Hesse Overgaard
Janne . . . . Pernille Hansen
Marriage counselor . . . . . Ulla Henningsen
Also with: Sonja Oppenhagen, Egon Stoldt, Jörgen Bing, Sissel Brandi-Hansen, Malene Krogh, Bodil Lassen, Henrik Moltzen, Rolf Munkholm-Jensen.

Copenhagen — It may all be true, but what we see and hear in Li Vilstrup's "I Love You" is a trite rehash of cliché truths brought forward by a marriage counselor-psychologist during therapy sessions with a young couple about to split. *She* does not get the tenderness she has been in need of since childhood; *he* keeps his more tender emotions hidden as has been his habit since early experiences with a mother who regarded sex as obnoxious.

The young couple (puppy play-acting by Pernille Hansen, adroit nuancing by Peter Hesse Overgaard) is seen doing their ritual role dance steps of come-ons and refusals at home and then in session with the psychologist (a warmly persuasive Ulla Henningsen) at whose slightest suggestion the youngsters reel off exactly the childhood experiences needed to prove their present behavioral patterns.

Since the two youngsters are claimed (story reportedly is based on the real-life journals of psychologist Hanne Hostrup Larsen who provided screenplay and dialog aid) to be medical students, it is hard to believe they would seek or need outside help at all at a point where they are so openly aware of their own faults or weaknesses. As delivered in mock fictional & mock documentary retelling by Li Vilstrup, story and film drag narrative feet heavily over cardboard characters and situations.

Although the acting is good and the cinematography (by America's Judy Irola) is expert and fluid, "I Love You" looms to meet a hard time on the theatrical circuit (it has a four-print initial release) before ending up on educational tv or somewhere in the lecture halls of budding, very budding — marriage counselor-psychologists. —*Kell.*

Venner for altid
(Forever Friends)
(DANISH-COLOR)

A Nordisk Film release of Jens Ravn Film production with Nordisk Film and The Danish Film Institute (consulting producer, Ida Zeruneith). Produced by Ravn. Directed by Stefan Christian Henszelman. Screenplay, Henszelman, Alexander Körschen; camera (Eastmancolor), Marcel Berga; editor, Henszelman, Camilla Skousen; music, Morti Vizki, Christian Skeel, Kim Sagild; sound, Iben Haahr Andersen, others; production design, Lars Rune Nilsson; assistant director, Louise Kjär; production management, Gerd Roos, others. Reviewed at the Palads, Copenhagen, Feb. 3, 1987. Running time: **93 MINS.**
Kristian . . . . Claus Bender Mortensen
Patrick . . . . Thomas Sigsgaard
Henrik . . . . Thomas Elholm
Ayoe . . . . Lill Lindfors
Mads . . . . Morten Stig Kristensen
Anette . . . . Christine Skou
High school principal . . . . Rita Angela
Also with: Carsten Mörch, Stefan Henszelman, Jens Ravn, Ulla Nielsen, Lars Kyhlmann Jacobsen, Rasmus Bay Barlby, Trine Torp Hansen, Christian Kamienski, Claus Steenstrup Nielsen, Mourad Slimani, Lone Wassard, Christine Seedorf.

Copenhagen — Stefan Henszelman has won several prizes at home and abroad for a couple of short fiction films. One of these, "Forever Friends," he has now cannibalized and given rebirth as a serious-minded youth feature comedy melodrama. Film, dealing with a high school boy's sexual and other initiations, rushes one through its first half hour with a fleet cinematic style plus dramatic verve and fine psychological insights. Then it goes slack to wind messily, congratulating itself on its own liberal attitudes both in plot's final stages and in a pasted-on musical skit that looks and sounds like a commercial for soda pop or cake mix.

Story has Kristian, age 16, arriving at a new school. He is eager to be accepted as one of the guys but runs afoul of the classmates he likes best, both of them soon disclosed as gay. It is stated after the credits that "Innocence is no excuse," and Kristian must learn to roll with the punches he experiences. Toward the end, having been initiated safely into heterosexual moods and methods by a not so young visiting pop singer (Sweden's husky-voiced Lill Lindfors), he comes out waving the banner of (all kinds of) liberty during a minor school rebellion.

Even though "Forever Friends" soon defeats its own artistic purposes, helmer Henszelman gets to display much cinematic flair and finesse. He coaxes fine performances from his lead actors, notably Claus Bender Mortensen as gentle Kristian, Thomas Elholm as Henrik of the refined lifestyle, and Thomas Sigsgaard as toughguy Patrick who comes out of his closet as a proud gay.

Most of the other young performers are amateurs left to sink or swim by Henszelman and most of them sink. —*Kell.*

Dreamaniac
(COLOR)

Some gore and a snooze.

A Wizard Video presentation of a Taryn production. Produced and directed by David DeCoteau. Screenplay, Helen Robinson; camera (Fotokem color), Howard Wexler; editor, Peter Teschner; music supervision, Tom Milano, Don Great; sound, Rick Pierce; production design, Rozanne Taucher; production manager, Anthony Ferrari; assistant director, Ellen Cabot; stunt coordinator, Jake Ryan; special makeup effects, Tom Schwartz, Linda Nottestad; associate producers, Ronel Huth, Jackie Snider; casting, Rick Paskay. Reviewed on Wizard Video vidcassette, N.Y., Jan. 29, 1987. (No MPAA Rating.) Running time: **82 MINS.**
With: Thomas Bern (Adam), Kim McKamy (Pat), Sylvia Summers (Lily), Lauren Peterson (Jodi), Bob Pelham, Cynthia Crass, Brad Laughlin, Linda Watts, Matthew Phelps, Lisa Emery, Michael Warren, Brent Black.

"Dreamaniac" is a violent horror film in search of a better screenplay. Filmmaker David DeCoteau demonstrates the requisite atmospherics and ability at audience manipulation, but the material is uninvolving.

Thomas Bern portrays Adam, a young writer living in a remote house who conjures up a succubus Lily (Sylvia Summers). When his girlfriend Pat (Kim McKamy) and her sister Jodi (Lauren Peterson) invite over a group of friends for a party, Lily starts killing them and eventually gets Adam under her murderous spell, causing him to go on a rampage as well.

Dotted with shock effects, picture relies on those hoary old melodrama standbys, opening with a nightmare wakeup sequence and disappointingly resolved with a rational explanation that destroys the fantasy element, followed by the corny violent final twist. Cast is competent, but the Lily role required an exotic actress, perhaps in the British school of Caroline Munro or Martine Beswick, to work.

Feature was marketed by distrib Wizard Video in tandem with "The Headless Eyes" as films supposedly too gory for theatrical release. "Eyes" turns out to be an X-rated 1971 feature which did in fact play theatrically; "Dreamaniac" is a film shot in California in 1986 which has debuted on vidcassette. —*Lor.*

Vroeger Is Dood
(What's Past Is Dead)
(DUTCH-COLOR)

The Movies release of a Linden Film production. Produced by Jos van der Linden. Written and directed by Ine Schenkkan, based on the book by Inez van Dulleman; camera (Kodak color; Super 16m; RCM prints), Geert Giltay; editor, Jorge Hoogland; music, Simon Burger; sound, Peter Flamman; art directon, Freek Biesiot; casting, Hans Kemna. Reviewed at The Movies theater, Amsterdam, Jan. 26, 1987. Running time: **90 MINS.**
Inez . . . . Jasperina de Jong
Father . . . . Max Croiset
Mother . . . . Elise Hoomans

Amsterdam — Ine Schenkkan has possible chosen the most difficult subject for a debutant film — old age, senility, death, and the way it affects various members of a family. Yet out of these potentially morbid elements, she has fashioned an astonishingly moving and uplifting film, which could make an impact on tv and possibly the art-house circuit.

Pic is based on an autobiography by Inez van Dulleman about the death of her parents. Her father, a retired attorney-general, becomes increasingly forgetful, incontinent, noisy — in a word, senile — and is packed off to an old people's home.

Her mother, a former belle with artistic pretensions, strong-willed and self-sufficient, refuses to leave her home and her freedom. She also refuses to admit the severity of her husband's condition and declines to visit him in hospital.

Inez (Jasperina de Jong), is the devoted daughter, herself happily married with two children, who looks after both her parents as old age takes its final toll. Her mother succumbs first, falling ill, being moved to a private home, and then to a hospital where she dies. Her father is shunted to another home for the elderly, where he deteriorates and finally fades away.

Schenkkan obviously has affinity for this type of subject; her first picture as director was a 35-minute short about a woman and a dying old man. Here, she has created a tightly structured pic, with every detail taken care of. Camera is constantly on the move, very alive in this tale of death, but operating in an unfussy way.

De Jong, more noted for roles as an exuberant and eccentric dame in musicals and cabarets, gives a wise and sensitive performance as the daughter, wife and mother, while Schenkkan also obtains subtle outings from the rest of the cast. Technical credits are fine all round.
— *Wall.*

Más Buenas que el Pan
(Better Than Bread)
(MEXICAN-COLOR)

A Películas Mexicanas release of a Productores Tollocán production. Produced by Guillermo Herrera. Directed by Alfredo B. Crevenna. Stars Lalo el Mimo, Pedro Weber (Chatanuga). Screenplay, Ramón Obón; camera (color), Juan Manuel Herrera; music, Gustavo Pimentel, with appearances of groups Los Trés Aces, Felipe Arriaga y Su Mariachi, Los Broncos de Reynosa, Carmen Rivero y Su Orquesta. Reviewed at Big Apple Cine 1, Feb. 13, 1987. Running time: **91 MINS.**
Felemón . . . . Lalo el Mimo
Jovita . . . . Lilia Prado
Moyer . . . . Pedro Weber (Chatanuga)
Daughter No. 1 . . . . Arlette Pacheco
Daughter No. 2 . . . . Jacquelín Castro
Also with: Alfonso Dávila, Fernando Ciangherotti, Lupe Pallas, Charlie Valentino, Alejandro Ciangherotti, Mireya Cantú, Jaime Reyes, Paco Muller, Felipe Arriaga.

The title of this low-budget sex comedy "Más Buenas que el Pan" (Better Than Bread), by Mexican filmmaker Alfredo B. Crevenna, refers to two curvaceous gals who have backsides that are more rounded than loaves of bread. The rest of the pic is based on this same type of low-brow humor.

Film deals with Mexico's two most passionate concerns: sex and soccer. Two old friends, Felemón and Moyer (played by Lalo el Mimo and Pedro Weber, respectively), are torn over bets on the soccer pool and sexual yearnings — Felemón for his buddy Moyer's wife Jovita (Lilia Prado), Moyer for his friend Felemón's two pubescent daughters (Arlette Pacheco and Jacquelín Castro), who run around in miniskirts and attract the attention of everyone in the neighborhood.

Somewhere around the middle of the film, after Felemón wins millions of pesos in the soccer pool, the plot gets lost and the pic wanders all over the place and never finds its way back. The filmmaker throws in appearances by lots of musical groups — salsa, ranchero, mariachi — to take up screentime and distract the audience from the gaping holes in the plot and the profusion of minor characters.

Lensing is uneven with shifting light values and the cuts are sometimes awkward. Despite a scattering of amusing scenes, audience interest level tends to wander as the plot does.

A teaser is thrown in at the end hinting that there might be a sequel to this film. Instead, Crevenna should have confined both plots to the first installment and might have come up with enough elements to make one complete film.—*Lent.*

Jäähyväiset Presidentille
(Goodbye, Mr. President)
(FINNISH-COLOR)

A Finnkino release of a Skandia Film (Kaj Holmberg) production. Produced by Holmberg. Directed by Matti Kassila. Screenplay, Kassila, Taavi Kassila, based on novel by Pentti Kirstilän; camera (Eastmancolor), Kari Sara; editor, Irma Taina; music, Heikki Sarmanto; production design, Erkki Saarainen; sound, Ossi Viskari; production management, Milja Salomies. Reviewed at the Bristol-1, Helsinki, Jan. 27, 1987. Running time: **84 MINS.**
Asko Mertanen ....Hannu Lauri
Eeva-Maria Kokkonen ....Laila Räikkä
Hanhivaara....................Antti Litja
Chief Detective Kairamo ......Esa Saario
President ....Tarmo Manni
Also with: Markku Huhtamo, Markko Nieminen, Aake Kalliala, Martti Pennanen, Rauha Puntti, Olavi Ahonen, Tarja Siimes, Pentti Järventie.

Helsinki — "Goodbye, Mr. President" might, apart from Finnish locale and dialog, pass for topnotch Hollywood thriller entertainment and thus would seem assured worldwide video and tv sales plus limited offshore theatrical business.

Basing his plot on a 1979 novel by Pentti Kirstilän, veteran writer-director Matti Kassila puts all genre credentials on display along with a fine storyline and plot development plus technical credits and production dress of the most brilliant order.

"Goodbye, Mr. President" tells about a cool crackpot who is also a crack shot. He works as a waiter in a popular dance restaurant and has an easy way with women, but actually more of a sexual relationship with his guns and with his obsession to shoot the president of the republic. He sees him, rightly or wrongly, as the epitome of corruption and himself as the world's redeemer.

For practice, the man shoots a couple of innocent pedestrians, one of whom, by accident, is the lady he bedded the night before. A methodical manhunt is set up with individual detectives described in sharply etched vignettes. The killer gets run down just as he has the president in his gunsight and does pull the trigger. There is a brief car chase before a witty ending that has the president expressing wonder at how a bottle of beer exploded in his hand.

"Goodbye, Mr. President" may lack what Fred Zinnemann's "Day Of The Jackal" had in way of drawn-out building of suspense and psychological finesse, but as it stands, this Finnish version of the same theme is a direct hit. The acting by Hannu Lauri as the assassin has the cool shine of gun metal.
—*Kell.*

Redondela
(SPANISH-COLOR)

A Pedro Costa presentation. Produced and directed by Costa. Screenplay, Manolo Marinero, Costa; camera (Fujicolor), Juan Amorós; editor, Pablo G. del Amo; music, Jesus Gluck; sets, Eduardo Hidalgo; production manager, Martin Cabañas; sound, Miguel Angel Polo. Reviewed at Cine Roxy A, Madrid, Jan. 31, 1987. Running time: **113 MINS.**
Jose María Gil Ramos ..... Patrick Newell
Padín ....Carlos Velat
José Luis Peña ....Fernando Guillén
Arturo Méndez........Carlos Larrañaga
Also with: Marina Saura, Agustin González, Ricardo Lucia, Blanca Sendino, Francisco Merino, Conrado San Martin, Manuel de Blas, Francisca Gabaldón.

Madrid — Producer-helmer-writer Pedro Costa, whose former credit was the taut "Caso Almería," tackles another political hot potato, this one during the late Franco years. Though the subject matter has plenty of meat, "Redondela" is on the talky side and never builds to its dramatic highpoints. Instead, Costa takes us step by step through a case history involving the theft of 4,000 tons of oil in 1972 which indirectly implicated Franco's brother.

Buoying the film is the performance by British thesp Patrick Newell, cast as "Gil Ramos," thinly disguised version of the liberal politico Gil Robles, who volunteers to undertake the defense of a minor functionary who has been accused of the fraud, and who, in fact, was merely a scapegoat for higherups in the Franco administration. Newell, toting an umbrella, is more reminiscent of Alfred Hitchcock or Dr. Watson than a Spanish lawyer, but manages to add the only touch of color to the film.

Pic leads us through a labyrinth of clues, investigations and suspects, as well as a suicide and an assassination, both to this day unexplained. Often the volume of names bandied about is hard to follow, as scenes shift from Galicia (Redondela is the name of a town there), to Madrid and Seville. The final courtroom scenes, in which the judge seems ot thwart justice by not letting the defense attorney (Newell) fully interrogate those on the stand, fail to generate much dramatic tension. The sentence, to no one's surprise, is in favor of the state prosecutor, and Ramos takes the train back to Madrid. —*Besa.*

Amma Ariyan
(A Report To Mother)
(INDIAN-B&W)

An Odessa Movies production. Written and directed by John Abraham. Camera (b&w), Venu; sound, Krishnanunni; editor, Beena; music, Sunitha, art direction, Ramesh. Reviewed at the India Film Festival, Delhi, Jan. 1987. Running time: **115 MINS.**
Purushan ....Joy Mathew
Paru....................Maji Venkitesh
Also with: Nilamboor Balan (Balettan), Harinarayanam (Hari), Kunhulakshmi Amma (Purushan's mother), Iringal Narayani (Hari's mother), Nazim (Satyajit).
(Dialog in Malayalam)

Delhi — "Amma Ariyan (A Report To Mother)" was made on less than a shoestring — it was financed by minimal contributions from thousands of people, on the understanding that producer Odessa Movies would use a 16m network to reach out-of-the-way Indian towns and show the film free, if necessary. Helmer John Abraham, who won acclaim for "Donkey In A Brahmin Village," habitually shoots in black and white, but this b&w is so high-contrast it obliterates facial features and becomes an aesthetic unto itself. This off-beat road movie about the Kerala region and the fate of its politically committed sons isn't an easy film to watch, but it is one of the more original and thoughtful Indian pics of late. It could spark interest at a gutsy film festival.

Impetus of the story is the suicide of a young drummer named Hari (Harinarayanam). Purushan (Joy Mathew), a student on his way to Delhi, becomes wholly obsessed with his tragic death. First he brings acquaintances to the morgue until they positively identify the body. Then, in an interminable trip across Kerala, from the northern highlands to the coastal town of Cochin, he informs friends about the suicide, and in an ever-growing body they go to tell Hari's mother. The whole story is told as a letter Purushan is writing his own mother (who recites scripture passages about the Mother Goddess).

The intellectual's journey through his poor, tormented land is continually measured against the impotence of his generation to mount effective social change. While a medical students' demonstration is successful, a horrifying scene of police torture shows how long a way there is to go. Abraham has an elegant taste for fixed-frame lensing, and a gift for mixing newsreel-type footage with his fictional story. Pic's uncompromisingly slow pace and maddening repetitions will wear out the patience of some, as it doggedly spirals around the central event until it reaches the heart of a generation's defeat. It's a maverick film that ranges from Marxism to mother worship in its complex portrait of a contradictory, multi-layered society. — *Yung.*

Maldeniye Simion
(Simion Of Maldeniye)
(SRI LANKA-COLOR)

Produced by Vijaya Ramanayake. Directed by D.B. Nihalsingha. Screenplay and camera (color), Nihalsignha; editor, Chandradasa Rubasinghe; music, Premasiri Kemadasa. Reviewed at the India Film Festival (Competition), Delhi, Jan. 20, 1987. Running time: **135 MINS.**
Simion ....Joe Abeywicrema
Jane/Soma ....Anoja Weerasinghe
Karuan ....Swarna Mallawarachchi
Dayaratne ....Ravindra Randeniya
Also with: Vincent Wass (village headman), Dayaratne Jayawardene (police chief).

Delhi — "Simion Of Maldeniye" is a good, old-fashioned tragedy that recalls steamy stories of Southern family woes and their unalterable destinies in 1,000-page novels. In over two hours "Simion" has the chance to unfold at a leisurely pace. It's well-directed, enjoyable entertainment from Sri Lanka's pioneer helmer D.B. Nihalsingha, who's also responsible for script and photography.

Pic was honored at the Indian Film Festival with a Best Actress award to Anoja Weerasinghe for her dual role as mother Jane and daughter Soma, but it could just as well have gone to fiery veteran Joe Abeywicrema in the title role.

Simion is a backwoods bootlegger, rustler and gambler in the 1930s. He's also a man of high principle who refuses to bribe the police chief to look the other way. He virtually forces a country girl named Jane to marry him, then beats her until she runs away with another man, leaving him three kids to bring up. His love for her is such that he never touches another woman in his life.

Jailed for 20 years, Simion comes home lame from police beatings, but his moral fiber is unchanged. His hot-headed, grown up son gets them all arrested again, and daughter Soma (who of course resembles her mother uncannily) sacrifices her virginity to get Simion out of jail. She selfishly goes on sacrificing more of the same to feed and clothe the old man, right up to a *sturm und drang,* burn the house down finale when he learns the truth.

Nihalsingha orchestrates a medley of juicy characters, topped by the King Lear-like moonshiner Simion. Among the more subtly directed scenes is the flashback to how Soma went to visit the police chief when her father was in jail. The hard knocks in this girl's life get a little out of hand, as even her beloved finacé puts her up to entertaining his clients, but pic's overall impact is moving.

Lensing is pro and full exploits the paradisical lushness of its locations. Local music score is a plus. — *Yung.*

Varjoja paratiisissa
(Shadows In Paradise)
(FINNISH-COLOR)

A Finnkino release of a Villealfa Film production. Written and directed by Aki Kaurismäki. Camera (Eastmancolor), Timo Salminen; editor, Raija Talvio; no further credits available. Reviewed at Nordic Film Festival, Helsinki, Jan. 22, 1987. Running time: **73 MINS.**

Nikander	Matti Pellonpää
Ilona	Kati Outinen
Ilona's girlfriend	Kylli Köngäs
Nikander's friend	Sakari Kuosmanen

Also with: Esko Nikkari, Jukka-Pekka Palo.

Helsinki — "Shadows In Paradise" borrows its title from an Erich Maria Remarque novel about wartime refugees. Writer-helmer Aki Kaurismäki has fashioned an ultra-subdued little comedy love story about a couple of society's lower-ladder characters wandering in a lost manner over the coldly indifferent urban landscape of Finland's capital city. It is strictly fluff, but has some funny insights and it transmits the muted anger and pain of its protagonists neatly. Limited offshore tv sales would appear item's likely future.

Nikander of the sad and sallow face is a garbage truck driver with an absolutely empty private life. He gets to know Ilona, the less-than-pretty supermarket cashier, by accident, and neither of the two seems able to follow through on the opportunities offered by their meeting. She is fired and takes revenge by stealing, running away with Nikander to a rural hotel, where they take single rooms. He takes the stolen goods back to the supermarket and Ilona moves in with him without making it an affair.

There are some timid approaches between the two, some hemming and hawing, but both seem unable to cope with anything as imposing as romance, let alone love. Obviously they are to be seen as intimidated by a world not of their own making, but they are shadows longing for light and at long last Nikander pulls himself together and the two are seen off on their "honeymoon to faraway shores" — actually a daytrip by boat to Estonia across the bay from Helsinki.

Matti Pellonpää and Kati Outinen lend quiet sympathy to their roles. Picture has a fine narrative rhythm, and Aki Kaurismäki treats his characters without condescension throughout. — *Kell.*

Australian Dream
(AUSTRALIAN-COLOR)

A Ronin Films (Australia) release of a Filmside production. Executive producer, Ross Matthews. Produced by Susan Wild, Jacki McKimmie. Written and directed by McKimmie. Camera (color), Andrew Lesnie; editor, Sara Bennett; music, Colin Timms; production design, Chris McKimmie; sound, Ian Grant; costumes, Robyn McDonald; production manager, Susan Wild; assistant director, David Munro. Reviewed at Mosman screening room, Sydney, Feb. 4, 1987. Running time: **86 MINS.**

Dorothy Stubbs	Noni Hazlehurst
Geoffrey Stubbs	Graeme Blundell
Todd	John Jarratt
Sir Bruce	Barry Rugless
Tracy	Jenny Mansfield
Jason	Caine O'Connel

Also with: Margaret Lord (Sex-aids demonstrator), Lil Kelman (Sandra), John Kerr (Frank), Alexandra Black (Shirley), Jill Loos (Barbara), James Ricketson ("Baby").

Sydney — Jacki McKimmie, with her first feature film, unfortunately has not lived up to the promise of her prize-winning short film of a few years back, "Stations." She's attempted a comedy about the awfulness of life in the sprawling suburbs of Australia's major cities, but "Australian Dream," set in Brisbane, simply isn't very funny.

Central character is Dorothy, played by the always-reliable Noni Hazlehurst, the long-suffering wife of Geoffrey (Graeme Blundell), a crass butcher and aspiring right-wing politician. Like the Tom Ewell character in "The Seven Year Itch," Dorothy is constantly dreaming erotic daydreams, all of them involving the spunky Todd (John Jarratt) whom she met while attending a demonstration of sex aids. Needless to say, when she finally makes it with her idol, she's disappointed.

Audiences will be, too, because McKimmie misses out on plenty of opportunities for no-holds-barred satire inherent in the subject. There are a few wildly amusing jokes about the sameness of suburban life, but most of them are pretty obvious. The second half of the pic is taken up with a raucous fancy-dress party held at Dorothy's home and attended by a variety of types including a political leader, a pregnant woman, an adulterous couple, a pair of religious fanatics and a rock band led by Todd. Party scene goes on and on without making much sense (it looks as if quite a bit of footage got left on the cutting-room floor, as a subplot involving the theft of electrical equipment from houses in the street is inexplicable in this version).

It's very much to the credit of Noni Hazlehurst that she makes as much of poor Dorothy as she does. For the rest, Graeme Blundell makes her husband almost *too* repulsive and John Jarratt is rather wooden as the love object. Visually, film attempts to capture the poor-taste of these suburban dwellers, but, again, the net result is tedium rather than humor. Main problem seems to be the underwritten screenplay, by McKimmie herself, and the often awkward direction. A theatrical career looks doubtful, but pic could work in video and other ancillary markets. It was obviously made on a low budget. — *Strat.*

Chocolate Inspector
(HONG KONG-COLOR)

A Michael Hui/Golden Harvest coproduction. Executive producers, Michael Hui, Raymond Chow. Directed by Philip Chan. Stars Michael Hui, Anita Miu, Ricky Hui, Michael Chow. Screenplay, Michael Hui, art direction, David Chan. (No other credits provided by producer/distributor). Reviewed at Queen's theater, Hong Kong, Jan. 9, 1987. Running time: **98 MINS.**
(Cantonese soundtrack with English subtitles)

Hong Kong — "Chocolate Inspector" is perfect escapist Cantonese holiday entertainment for all ages. It's the most refined of all the Michael Hui series of slapstick comedies. The old stereotypes are still present (aggressive old maid, drag jokes, retarded partner). The visual humor is natural and its effectiveness is directly related to Hui who plays a police inspector (who loves chocolate candies), searching for a kidnaped kid of a television personality.

The best of the comedy sequences (in a department store, toilet scene, satire on a beauty contest) are all brilliantly staged and timed.

As can be expected, the storyline is simplistic and the film has that look of a collection of funny anecdotes rather than a coherent story. For once, singer/actress Anita Miu plays herself and her vamp beauty contestant image to the hilt which is very refreshing. She has style and good comedic flair, a perfect match to Hui's hysterical facial contortions. Hui is definitely Hong Kong's answer to Mel Brooks and should do more films.

The film is a high grosser for Hui and Golden Harvest as it raked over $HK18,000,000 during the holiday season beating Cinema City, D & B and minor attractions. — *Mel.*

Sidste Akt
(Final Curtain)
(DANISH-COLOR)

A Nordisk Film release of Nordisk Film, Edward Fleming with The Danish Film Institute production. Film Institute consultant producer, Claes Kastholm Hansen. Executive producer, Bo Christensen. Directed by Edward Fleming. Stars Birgitte Federspiel, Mime Fönss. Screenplay, Fleming, from the play "Waiting In The Wings" by Noël Coward; camera (Eastmancolor), Claus Loof; editor, Grete Möldrup; sound, Preben Mortensen; production design, Hanning Bahs; assistant director, Tom Hedegaard; costumes, Annelise Hauberg, Ole Gläsner, Pia Myrdal; production management, Lene Nielsen, Gisela Bergquist. Reviewed at the Imperial, Copenhagen, Jan. 18, 1987. Running time: **101 MINS.**

Lotta	Birgitte Federspiel
May	Mime Fönss
Miss Archie	Kirsten Rolffes
Perry	Holger Juul Hansen
Mr. Osborne	Ebbe Rode
Molly	Lily Broberg
Bonnie	Erni Arneson
Sarita	Else Petersen
Elvira	Elin Reimer
Ester	Tove Mäes
Cora	Jytte Breuning
Board Chairman	Lisbeth Movin
Martha	Berthe Quistgaard

Also with: Axel Ströbye, Lillian Tillegreen, Ove Sprogöe, Anne Marie Helger (the journalist), Vera Gebuhr, Helle Merete Jensen, Gerda Gilboe.

Copenhagen — Edward Fleming, a veteran director of folksy fare with an artistic dash added, has scored his biggest hits with youth comedy-mellers. With "Final Curtain," based on a near-forgotten Noël Coward stage play "Waiting In The Wings," he pays tribute to the other end of the age spectrum, presenting a bevy of elderly actresses now performing mostly to impress (or depress) each other in an institution set up for them by a foundation run by a very authoritative board.

A handful of Denmark's most accomplished veteran actresses perform with gusto as Fleming directs them with zest and sympathy through the skimpiest of plots (the board won't grant the actresses' home a much-hoped for new glass veranda, but a weekly magazine will — at the price of access to the privacy of the faded ladies' current life) that mostly serves as a platform for fireworks displays of dialog and brief sketches of internecine warfare.

Mostly, Fleming follows Coward in seeing these ladies as grand old broads who survive dire straits with the aid of robust vulgarity although always with some degree of pride and sensitivity in evidence, too. A few males appear to court or encourage the female flock and they are seen as truly shining knights albeit with their armor battered.

Helmer as well as performers seem to have had the time of their lives doing this film and their mood illuminates the screen throughout. With no music score to sustain the narrative flow, swift maneuvering of camera in the essentially one-room area of acting serves, along with eye-catching costumes, precise editing and overall handsome production dress, to keep the dust of otherwise too traditional theatrical stage devices out of audiences' eyes.

But to what audiences does "Final Curtain" cater? Offshore sales seem highly improbable for a Noël Coward item transferred into a Danish-language film with the original British names of persons and places retained. Boxoffice at home would appear hampered by picture's particular appeal to age groups above those normally relied upon by the exhibition trade. Still, wit, fine acting and a sense of socko comedy dramatics may well pay off for a production partnership that included Fleming himself. —*Kell.*

Angel Heart
(COLOR)

Powerful and stylish mystery thriller should benefit from ratings publicity.

A Tri-Star Pictures release of a Mario Kassar and Andrew Vajna/Carolco Intl. presentation of a Winkast-Union production. Produced by Alan Marshall, Elliott Kastner. Executive producers, Kassar, Vajna. Directed by Alan Parker. Stars Mickey Rourke. Screenplay, Parker, based on the novel "Falling Angel" by William Hjortsberg; camera (Technicolor), Michael Seresin; editor, Gerry Hambling; music, Trevor Jones; production design, Brian Morris; art direction, Kristi Zea, Armin Ganz; set decoration, Robert J. Franco (N.Y.), Leslie Pope (N.O.); costume design, Aude Bronson-Howard; sound (Dolby), Danny Michael; assistant director, Ric Kidney; casting, Risa Bramon, Billy Hopkins. Reviewed at Lorimar screening room, Culver City, Calif., Feb. 25, 1987. (MPAA Rating: R.) Running time: **113 MINS.**

Harry Angel	Mickey Rourke
Louis Cyphre	Robert De Niro
Epiphany Proudfoot	Lisa Bonet
Margaret Krusemark	Charlotte Rampling
Ethan Krusemark	Stocker Fontelieu
Toots Sweet	Brownie McGhee
Doctor Fowler	Michael Higgins
Connie	Elizabeth Whitcraft
Sterne	Eliott Keener
Spider Simpson	Charles Gordone
Winesap	Dann Florek
Nurse	Kathleen Wilhoite
Izzy	George Buck
Izzy's Wife	Judith Drake
Pastor John	Gerald L. Orange
Mammy Carter	Peggy Severe

Hollywood — Even if it may be a specious work at its core, "Angel Heart" still proves a mightily absorbing mystery that also represents the best sustained filmmaking of director Alan Parker. Highly exotic and heavily elaborated telling of a small-time detective's descent into hell will grab serious viewers with its powerful technique and intricate visual patterns, but Faustian theme, heavy bloodletting and pervasive grimness may represent barriers too great for general audiences to surmount. Controversy over the initial X rating, later reduced to an R, certainly put the picture on the map and won't hurt initial b.o.

It appears to be against Parker's nature to tell a story simply, his tendency being to goose up every sequence with a bath of misty light and a frenzy of nervous editing. While completely recognizable from his previous films, his style here is put to generally excellent use, and sometimes brings to mind the dense layering often associated with Nicolas Roeg.

Based upon William Hjortsberg's novel "Falling Angel," Parker's screenplay, set in 1955, has seedy Gotham gumshoe Mickey Rourke engaged by mysterious businessman Robert De Niro to locate a certain Johnny Favorite, a big band singer from the pre-war days who, De Niro says, failed to live up to the terms of a contract.

Rourke as Harry Angel, quickly discovers that Favorite, a war casualty and reportedly a vegetable, was removed years earlier from the nursing home where he was supposedly under care, and follows his leads to New Orleans, and particularly the jazz and voodoo elements within its black community.

Several people die distinctly unpleasant deaths shortly after being visited by Rourke, who himself is the victim of numerous assaults by people who don't like the sensitive areas he's poking into. Nor do the local authorities appreciate his liaison with the black 17-year-old daughter of a voodoo priestess, played by Lisa Bonet.

Climax reveals the deceptive hocus-pocus that lies at the heart of "Angel Heart," but it is also powerful in its inexorable inevitability, thanks largely to the combinations of imagery Parker has been building over the course of nearly two hours.

As Roman Polanski did with "Rosemary's Baby," Parker here gets the absolute maximum out of somewhat suspect material.

He clearly prepared the project with extraordinary meticulousness; his script is well ordered, the locations in New York and New Orleans all have an evocative lived-in quality, the brown-dominated color scheme is desaturated and bereft of primary hues, and the supporting players are uniformly fresh and engaging.

Rourke is a commanding lead, putting everyone around him (except De Niro) on edge, but unfortunately he looks like he just stepped off the set of "Year Of The Dragon." His constant designer stubble is completely inappropriate for the era in question.

De Niro, who has four major scenes, sports elegant attire, a beautiful cane and ever-growing manicured fingernails to offset his equally anachronistic big beard and long hair left over from "The Mission." His character, which he plays with great precision and economy, and also as if in on a joke of which nobody else in the cast is aware, is so weird, however, that the offbeat look seems acceptable.

Charlotte Rampling is in very briefly as an elegant fortune teller, while Lisa Bonet's striking looks are rather undercut by her Valley Girl accent, not terribly convincing for a poor black girl from bayou country.

Technically, film is superlative in every way, from Michael Seresin's immaculate lensing to Brian Morris' resourceful production design and Trevor Jones' ominous, mostly electronic score.

Pic was caught in Parker's original version, which received a much-publicized X rating from the Classification and Rating Administration of the Motion Picture Assn. of America and ultimately had to be trimmed by 10 seconds to win an R. Controversial lovemaking scene between Rourke and Bonet becomes rather rough but, probably more to the point, involves torrents of blood leaking down on them from the ceiling, all of this being intercut with glimpses of voodoo rituals.

Bed action is quickly spied from overhead angles, but there is no frontal nudity, and sequence has its clear point, or, to twist an old phrase, "redeeming artistic value." The view here is that much, much more than this has slipped into previous R-rated pictures, and that the scene in context is by no means far heavier or more disturbing than the implications that come out in the rest of the film. In short, X rating seems absurd, and indicates the ratings standards are becoming increasingly conservative. — *Cart.*

Alien Predator
(The Falling)
(COLOR)

Boring par excellence.

A Trans World Entertainment release of a Continental Motion Pictures production. Executive producers, Helen Sarlui, Eduard Sarlui. Produced by Deran Sarafian, Carlos Aured. Directed by Sarafian. Screenplay, Sarafian, based on a screenplay "Massacre At R.V. Park" by Noah Blogh; camera (color), Tote Trenas; editor, Dennis Hill; additional editing, Peter Teschner; music, Chase/Rucker Prods.; sound, Anthony Bloch; coproducer-second unit director, Michael Sourapas; production manager, Joe Ochoa; special effects, John Balandin; casting, Lee Payne. Reviewed at 42d St. Cine 1, N.Y., Feb. 22, 1987. (MPAA Rating: R.) Running time: **90 MINS.**

Damon	Dennis Christopher
Michael	Martin Hewitt
Samantha	Lynn-Holly Johnson
Prof. Tracer	Luis Prendes
Capt. Wells	J.O. Bosso

"Alien Predator" (that's what it says on-screen, despite confusing ads which spell it "Alien Predators") is a truly stupid horror film shot in Spain in 1984 as "The Falling." Initially aimed at release along with two other Helen Sarlui productions by Film Ventures Intl., pic went on the shelf when that company experienced financial problems and surfaces instead via homevideo firm turned theatrical distrib TWE. A lawsuit or at least stern warning should be in the offing from 20th Century Fox, since new title not only intones the likes of Fox' "Alien" and "Aliens" hits, but also augurs Fox' upcoming Arnold Schwarzenegger-starrer "Predator." TWE also cut corners by virtually duplicating the poster art here from its 1984 flop "Creature."

It would be difficult to come up with a more obnoxious triumvirate than leading players Dennis Christopher, Martin Hewitt and Lynn-Holly Johnson, smirking, flirting and pouting as three squeaky-clean kids on a vacation in Spain in their massive recreation vehicle and dune buggy. Too bad for them that Skylab crashed nearby in 1979 and five years later Spaniards are being exposed to the result of an experiment conducted on Skylab involving living microbes found on the moon from the Apollo 14 mission. These microbes result in an alien critter (shown only briefly as an imitation of the small, early forms of the monster in "Alien") that inhabits a human host, drives the human crazy and in 48 hours pops out in time-honored chestburster fashion to begin the process again.

Tedious presentation actually apes Michael Crichton's "The Andromeda Strain" (filmed by Robert Wise in 1970) with a NASA scientist Prof. Tracer (Luis Prendes sporting an incongruous Spanish accent) coming up unbelievably with an instant antidote using himself as guinea pig. As in "Strain," there is a multi-leveled, underground complex.

Deran Sarafian's direction is sluggish, relying on pointless car chases to try and drum up excitement. His script is worse, filled with mushy speeches by the three young leads and a series of idiotic references to Rod Serling's "The Twilight Zone." Special effects are weak and audiences will be very angry at the nonappearance of the expected, full-grown title monster.

—*Lor.*

Raising Arizona
(COLOR)

Funny treatment of family rearing from the 'Blood Simple' team.

A 20th Century Fox release of a Circle Films presentation of a Ted and Jim Pedas/Ben Berenholtz production. Produced by Ethan Coen. Executive producer, James Jacks. Coproducer, Mark Silverman. Directed by Joel Coen. Screenplay, Ethan and Joel Coen; camera (Duart color), Barry Sonnenfeld; editor, Michael R. Miller; music, Carter Burwell; production design, Jane Musky; art director, Harold Thrasher; set decorator, Robert Kracik; costumes, Richard Hornung; assistant director, Deborah Reinisch, Kelly Van Horn; sound (Dolby), Allan Byer; associate producer, Deborah Reinisch; casting, Donna Isaacson, John Lyons. Reviewed at 20th Century Fox screening room, L.A., Feb. 23, 1987. (MPAA Rating: (PG-13). Running time: **94 MINS.**
H.I. ....Nicolas Cage
Ed ....Holly Hunter
Nathan Arizona Sr. ....Trey Wilson
Gale....................John Goodman
Evelle ....William Forsythe
Glen ....Sam McMurray
Dot ....Frances McDormand
Leonard Smalls ......Randall (Tex) Cobb
Nathan Jr....................T.J. Kuhn
Florence Arizona .....Lynne Dumin Kitei
Prison Counselor..........Peter Benedek

Hollywood — There are not many films in which a man is blown up by a hand grenade for comic effect, but "Raising Arizona" is just such a film. Pic is the Coen Brothers' twisted view of family rearing in the American heartlands and although different in style and tone from their debut effort, "Blood Simple," it is full of the same quirky humor and off-the-wall situations. "Raising Arizona" may not be everyone's cup of tea, but it's fresh enough to find a faithful following with the right handling.

Quite possibly there has never been another film like "Raising Arizona," with "Repo Man" and "True Stories" perhaps coming closest to its generous look at the denizens of society's underbelly. As written by Joel and Ethan Coen, directed by Joel and produced by Ethan, the film captures the surrealism of everyday life. Characters are so strange here that they seem to have stepped out of late-night television, tabloid newspapers, talk radio and a vivid imagination.

Nicolas Cage and Holly Hunter are the off-center couple at the center of the doings. As H.I. McDonnough, Cage is a well-meaning petty crook with a fondness for knocking off convenience stores. Edwina is the cop who checks him into prison so often that a romance develops.

H.I. and Ed soon learn marriage is "no Ozzie and Harriet Show" and when she learns she can't have kids or adopt them, they do the next logical thing — steal one. Target is furniture magnate Nathan Arizona (Trey Wilson) and his wife (Lynne Dumin Kitei) who have just been blessed with much-publicized quints.

Once H.I. and Ed have the child things don't get any easier as they are confronted by several models of the "family unit." One neighboring couple is intent on wife swapping while H.I.'s crazed prison buddies, Gale (John Goodman) and Evelle (William Forsythe) who beat a path to his door after tunneling out of the joint, are another alternative. And the generically named Arizonas are yet another possible direction for the new family.

Loosely structured around a voice-over narration by Cage, "Raising Arizona" is as leisurely and disconnected as "Blood Simple" was taut and economical. While film is filled with many splendid touches and plenty of yocks, it often doesn't hold together as a coherent story.

Plowing right through the middle of the story is the mad motorcyclist of the apocalypse (Randall [Tex] Cobb), who is the enemy of all families. As the film's central villain, he's a weak and unfocused creation with Cobb's performance lacking the teeth to make the character stick.

While Cage and Hunter are fine as the couple at sea in the desert, "Raising Arizona" sports at least one outstanding performance from John Goodman as the con brother who wants a family too. Here, as in "True Stories," Goodman is a rarity on the screen, an actor who can communicate friendliness and goodwill in spite of his foolishness. Consequently, scenes with the two brothers are the most animated and entertaining in the picture.

As a director Coen demonstrates an assured technical touch (though perhaps a bit too much low-angle framing) and camerawork by Barry Sonnenfeld is richly colored and adds to the texture of Jane Musky's sets. — *Jagr.*

Rage Of Honor
(COLOR)

Padded actioner.

A Trans World Entertainment release of a Rage production. Executive producers, Moshe Diamant, Moshe Barkat, Sunil R. Shah. Produced by Don Van Atta. Directed by Gordon Hessler. Stars Sho Kosugi. Screenplay, Robert Short, Wallace Bennett, from story by Short; camera (Technicolor, Cinecolor), Julio Bragado; editor, Robert Gordon; music (Dolby stereo), Stelvio Cipriani; production design, Adrian Gorton; art direction, Kirk Demusiak (Arizona), Abel Fagellio (Argentina); special effects supervisor, Paul Staples; martial arts choreography-special weapons design, Kosugi; second unit director, Van Atta; postproduction supervisor, Barry Parnell; casting, Barbara Hanley, Kathy Henderson. Reviewed at UA Twin 2 theater, N.Y., Feb. 28, 1987. (MPAA Rating: R.) Running time: **91 MINS.**
With: Sho Kosugi (Shiro Tanaka), Lewis Van Bergen, Robin Evans, Gerry Gibson, Chip Lucia, Richard Wiley, Carlos Estrada, Alan Amiel.

"Rage Of Honor" is a substandard action vehicle for martial arts star Sho Kosugi, who gets the chance to choreograph the fight scenes and introduce gadgety weapons but is otherwise sunk by pointless writing and limp direction.

Kosugi plays Shiro Tanaka, a Phoenix-based U.S. narcotics investigator who gets in a tizzy when his assistant is tortured and murdered. He quits his job, hops a plane to Buenos Aires seeking revenge (improbably taking along his blond girl friend) and there ensues a boring series of fights and double crosses until nearly the entire cast is wiped out.

Besides being at least two reels too long, film doesn't work because Kosugi is never in any real danger and all incidents are merely functional devices to get a fight scene going. The ease with which he dispatches at least 100 adversaries robs the fights of excitement. Nadir occurs in the Argentine jungle, where indians attack and Kosugi, not content with wiping out baddies, massacres dozens of indians in situational self-defense.

Kosugi's difficulty in delivering English dialog is still a hindrance and the supporting cast here is exceedingly bland. The main villain (character roles are not identified in the credits) seems to be auditioning for a career as Harrison Ford's stunt double. Tech credits are acceptable, but Gordon Hessler's direction seems phoned in. —*Lor.*

Street Smart
(COLOR)

Farfetched urban thriller fails to convince.

A Cannon Group release of a Golan-Globus production. Produced by Menahem Golan, Yoram Globus. Directed by Jerry Schatzberg. Stars Christopher Reeve. Screenplay, David Freeman; camera (TVC color), Adam Holender; editor, Priscilla Nedd; music, Robert Irving 3d; production design, Dan Leigh; art direction, Serge Jacques (Canada); set design, Raymond Larose, Katherine Matthewson (Canada); set decoration, Bill Stabile (N.Y.); costume design, Jo Ynocenio; sound (Dolby), Patrick Rousseau (Canada); associate producer, Evzen W. Kolar; assistant directors, Jacques Methe (Canada), Herb Gains (N.Y.); casting, Joy Todd. Reviewed at the Cannon screening room, L.A., Feb. 27, 1987. (MPAA Rating: R.) Running time: **95 MINS.**
Jonathan Fisher ....Christopher Reeve
Fast Black .,...........Morgan Freeman
Punchy....................Kathy Baker
Alison Parker ....Mimi Rogers
Leonard Pike ....Jay Patterson
Ted Avery ....André Gregory
Harriet............Anna Maria Horsford
Joel Davis ....Frederick Rolf
Reggie ....Erik King
Art Sheffield ....Michael J. Reynolds
Darlene...................Shari Hilton
Yvonne ....Donna Bailey

Hollywood — "Street Smart" is a well-made but unpersuasive concoction about an uptown journalist who gets caught up in the downtown world of pimps and prostitutes. Role of a dishonest, unscrupulous reporter represents a change of pace for Christopher Reeve, but gap between the gritty backdrop and farfetched plotting creates a strain the modest production can't bear. B.o. prospects look slim.

Faced with a pressing deadline and a complete lack of material, freelance write Reeve whips up a fabricated story about the private life of a successful pimp that creates a sensation when run as she cover story in the chic New York Journal.

Suddenly the toast of the Big Apple, Reeve is brought aboard an on-the-spot tv news show called "Street Smart" and all looks rosy, except for the fact that the dude described in the fictitious piece bears an uncanny resemblance to one Fast Black, a vicious pimp concurrently up on a murder charge.

Reeve is jailed for contempt after refusing to turn over this "notes" to the D.A.'s office and, under pressure from the pimp, later produces phony notes to show Fast Black was elsewhere when the murder was committed. Yarn proceeds from there to a violent and severely unlikely conclusion.

Despite the famous case a few years back of the Pulitzer Prizewinning newspaper article that turned out to be fiction, the premise of David Freeman's screenplay is rather hard to take, but not as much as the series of coincidences that follow. Furthermore, Reeve's character becomes increasingly unlikeable with each compromise and shady agreement he makes, which would be all right if there seemed to be some notable moral or ethical point being made.

Unfortunately, pic doesn't add up to much at all except as a cynical commentary on journalistic and legal procedures, which seem unfair and unconvincing.

Under the adverse circumstances, director Jerry Schatzberg still manages to come up with some potent scenes, particularly those involving Morgan Freeman, who turns in a strong and disturbing performance as the volatile pimp. Pic suffers from some less than indelible charaterizations in other parts, however.

Production team has done an excellent job in making Montreal pass for New York City (only three weeks of lensing were done in Gotham), and score is notable for some solo work by Miles Davis.—Cart.

Lethal Weapon
(COLOR)

Slickly made paean to revenge and violence.

A Warner Bros. release. Produced by Richard Donner, Joel Silver. Directed by Donner. Stars Mel Gibson, Danny Glover. Screenplay, Shane Black; camera (Technicolor), Stephen Goldblatt; editor, Stuart Baird; music, Michael Kamen, Eric Clapton; production design, J. Michael Riva; set decorator, Marvin March; art director, Eva Bohn, Virginia L. Randolph; sound (Dolby), Bill Nelson; costumes, Mary Malin; assistant director, Benjamin Rosenberg; associate producer, Jennie Lew; casting, Marion Dougherty. Reviewed at Lorimar screening room, Culver City, Calif., Feb. 20, 1987. (MPAA Rating: R.) Running time: **110 MINS.**
Martin Riggs . . . . Mel Gibson
Roger Murtaugh . . . . Danny Glover
Joshua . . . . Gary Busey
The General . . . . Mitchell Ryan
Michael Hunsaker . . . . Tom Atkins
Trish Murtaugh . . . . Darlene Love
Rianne Murtaugh . . . . Traci Wolfe
Amanda Hunsaker . . . . Jackie Swanson
Nick Murtaugh . . . . Damon Hines
Carrie Murtaugh . . . . Ebonie Smith

Hollywood — "Lethal Weapon" is one part "Rambo Comes Home" and one part "48 HRS." It's a film teetering on the brink of absurdity when it gets serious, but thanks to its unrelenting energy and insistent drive, it never quite falls. Picture is slick enough to conceal some disturbing attitudes about heroes and violence in America and satisfy action fans out for a good time.

Screenwriter Shane Black has stacked the deck with bits of Vietnam, the generation gap, male bonding and the joys of family life, and director Richard Donner plays his hand well, but in the end it's a bluff.

Donner wants it both ways. He wants a tough picture but with sensitivity and the two strains simply don't graft well here. First half of the film is devoted to male bonding rituals before it becomes an old-fashioned shootout filled with frontier morality about holding one's ground and fighting fire with fire.

Danny Glover is a family-man detective who gets an unwanted partner in the possibly psychotic Mel Gibson. Story is on the back burner as the two men square off against each other, more as adversaries than partners. Although it's nearly impossible to tell where the story is going, Donner keeps the heat up and the action on the edge through intense closeups and rapid-fire cutting.

Gibson is all live wires and still carries Vietnam with him 20 years after the fact. He's caught in the 1960s. Though he's 15 years his senior and also a Nam vet, Glover is meant to be a sensitive man of the '80s.

Donner tries to supercharge their exchange, but mostly it's fake dynamics. Gibson simmers while Glover worries about his pension.

While the film is trying to establish its emotional underpinnings, a plot slowly unfolds involving a massive drug smuggling operation headed by the lethal Vietnam vet Joshua (Gary Busey).

Ultimately the common-ground for Glover and Gibson is staying alive as the film attempts to shift its buddy story to the battlefields of L.A. Pic tries to humanize the brutality and introduce some all-American values into the battle, going so far as to have Glover's teenage daughter (Traci Wolfe) kidnaped by the bad guys.

Gibson, in one of his better performances, holds the fascination of someone who may truly be dangerous, but it is difficult to swallow the film's premise that he is a true-blue American hero when there is really little heroic or admirable about the man.

He is a trained killer just like the drug smugglers and admits he never has been good at anything else. He is part of a chain of revenge that can only lead to more killing and violence, despite the film's suggestion that once he's completed his mission, he can return to the warmth of Glover's family.

It's a rather cowardly conclusion, since unlike "Taxi Driver," it fails to recognize and accept the volatile violence that's walking the streets and can erupt at any time. "Lethal Weapon" wants it both ways — a killer who can be compassionate, too, but it just doesn't wash.

Even so, as long as the film is bounding along at a brisk pace one can roll with the punches, suspend judgment and ignore holes in the plot and faulty logic that has the two cops launching a seemingly independent and unsupervised war.

As the arch villain, Busey is the kind of character with ice in his veins and, with his unnatural white hair, he's a true angel of death. Gibson is supposed to be a sympathetic character based on his grieving for his dead wife, and here, as in "Mad Max," he can project a certain untarnished virtue.

However, it's a tough character to buy and when the script tries to give him mythic proportions, he looks foolish as often as not.

Glover, too, is likable and so is Darlene Love as his wife, but he and Gibson come from two different worlds the film never really reconciles.

"Lethal Weapon" is a piece of bravado filmmaking and tech credits are first-rate throughout. Stephen Goldblatt's photography manages to be gritty and glamorous at once. Perhaps that's the film's fatal flaw. It's style masquerading as content. — Jagr.

Prick Up Your Ears
(BRITISH-COLOR)

A Samuel Goldwyn Co. release (U.S.) of a Civilhand/Zenith Prod. Produced by Andrew Brown. Directed by Stephen Frears. Screenplay, Alan Bennett, based on the biography by John Lahr; camera (Eastmancolor), Oliver Stapleton; editor, Mick Audsley; music, Stanley Myers; production design, Hugo Luczyc-Wyhowski; art director, Philip Elton; sound, Tony Jackson; costumes, Bob Ringwood; assistant director, Michael Zimbrich; casting, Debbie McWilliams. Reviewed at Bijou Preview theater, London, Feb. 12, 1987. (MPAA Rating: R.) Running time: **108 MINS.**
Joe Orton . . . . Gary Oldman
Kenneth Halliwell . . . . Alfred Molina
Peggy Ramsay . . . . Vanessa Redgrave
John Lahr . . . . Wallace Shawn
Elsie Orton . . . . Julie Walters
William Orton . . . . James Grant
Leonie Orton . . . . Frances Barber
Anthea Lahr . . . . Lindsay Duncan
Mrs. Sugden . . . . Janet Dale
Mr. Sugden . . . . Dave Atkins

London — Though selling itself as a biography of controversial young British playwright Joe Orton, who was murdered in 1967, "Prick Up Your Ears" actually says very little about Orton the author, but deals almost totally with his relationship with Kenneth Halliwell, his lover and bludgeon killer.

Director Stephen Frears, whose last pic, "My Beautiful Laundrette," garnered critical acclaim on both sides of the Atlantic, has made a fine film, but one that gives little insight into the daring comic writing skills of Orton, and thus may leave audiences wondering what made him popular at all. Acting and script are excellent, but a question mark must hang over pic's prospects in foreign markets.

"Prick Up Your Ears" appears to have been a pet subject for Frears, who seems to delight in taking every opportunity of mocking the British Midlands city of Leicester, the hometown of both himself and Orton. Set in the '50s and '60s, pic lacks a sense of the passing of years, and Orton's transition from tongue-tied Leicester youth to confident writer seems too sudden.

Halliwell hammered the sleeping Orton to death in their small London flat, then took an overdose of barbiturates, and it is at that point that the film begins, following biographer John Lahr's attempts to trace the life of the playwright.

Orton and Halliwell met at the Royal Academy of Dramatic Art where both were training to be actors. The inarticulate Orton fell for the seemingly sophisticated Halliwell, and for a while the pic dwells on Orton's promiscuity, mainly in public toilets, at a time when homosexuality was still illegal in the U.K.

The couple write together, Halliwell's hair falls out, and they are jailed for stealing and defacing library books. Suddenly, after years of obscurity, Orton becomes an overnight success, and for the West End opening night of his play "Entertaining Mr. Sloane" he buys Halliwell an illfitting wig.

Halliwell's resentment at Orton's success increases and even a carefree and promiscuous holiday in Tangier cannot ease the tension. When they return to England Orton visits Leicester for his mother's funeral while Halliwell seeks psychiatric help.

When Orton returns to the flat he suggests the couple split — Halliwell's reaction is to kill Orton and himself. At the cremation, the two sets of ashes are mixed together, and Vanessa Redgrave as Orton's agent, Peggy Ramsay, gets the best line of the film when she tells Orton's sister, who is worried about not putting the same amount of ashes into an urn, "It's a gesture, not a recipe."

Frears and screenwriter Alan Bennett, with seven tv collaborations to their credit, display an easy skill. The script is witty, the direction fluid, with one of the homosexual orgy scenes in a public toilet almost balletic, and the depiction of the lovers' life in their flat suitably claustrophobic.

Gary Oldman (so good in "Sid And Nancy") is excellent as Orton, right down to remarkable resemblance, while Alfred Molina creates both an amusing and tormented Halliwell. Redgrave takes top honors, though, as a compassionate and benign agent. Julie Walters appears briefly as Orton's mother, but plays it for high comedy, which doesn't really work.

Technical credits are all fine, though the lack of a feeling of passing of time sometimes grates. "Prick Up Your Ears" is thoughtfully stylized, and as a study of the capricious Orton it succeeds. As an insight into Orton the irreverent playwright, however, it leaves something to be desired.—*Adam.*

Die Wannseekonferenz
(The Wannsee Conference)
(WEST GERMAN-COLOR)

A Rearguard release of an Infafilm GmbH Munich-Manfred Korytowski/Austrian Television-ORF/Bavarian Broadcasting Corp. coproduction. Produced by Korytowski. Executive producer, Siegfried B. Glöker. Directed by Heinz Schirk. Screenplay, Paul Mommertz; camera (color), Horst Schier; editor, Ursula Möllinger; art direction, Robert Hofer-Ach, Barbara Siebner; costumes, Diemut Remy; sound, Sigbert Stark; historical advisor, Shlomo Aronson. Reviewed at the Fine Arts theater, Beverly Hills, Calif., Feb. 20, 1987. (No MPAA Rating.) Running time: **87 MINS.**

Hofmann	Robert Artzorn
Müller	Friedrich Beckhaus
Eichmann	Gerd Böckmann
Leibbrandt	Jochen Busse
Luther	Hans W. Bussinger
Meyer	Harald Dietl
Stuckart	Peter Fitz
Bühler	Reinhard Glemnitz
Neumann	Dieter Groest
Lange	Martin Lüttge
Secretary	Anita Mally
Heydrich	Dietrich Mattausch
Schöngarth	Gerd Rigauer
Kritzinger	Franz Rudnick
Klopfer	Günter Spörrle
Friesler	Rainer Steffen

Hollywood — The little-known Wannsee Conference was one of the momentous occasions of the 20th century, a conclave of 15 leading Nazis at which the decision to proceed with the "Final Solution Of The Jewish Question" was detailed and implemented. This West German film, financed largely by German and Austrian television and relesed there in 1984, represents a fastidious and fascinating reconstruction of the event virtually in real time, as the entire conference lasted a mere 85 minutes. Entering U.S. release on Feb. 25 in Los Angeles, docudrama will probably be pitched primarily to Jewish audiences and others already concerned with the period and issues in question, but would also prove stimulating to anyone interested in history.

Although the rounding up, expulsion and killing of Jews had taken place virtually since Hitler's coming to power, the plan to finally achieve the Führer's longtime goal of ridding the Reich of all Jews had not been formalized and systematized until the meeting at Wannasee, on the outskirts of Berlin, on Jan. 20, 1942.

Convened by Reinhard Heydrich,

Chief of the Security Police and the SS and widely considered to be Hitler's likely successor, conference was attended by representatives of the many competing security arms and bureaucracies within the regime, and detailed notes taken by a secretary and found after the war provided the incredible raw material for Paul Mommertz's dense screenplay.

First 20 minutes are occupied with arrivals of the principals and preliminaries, at which Heydrich, the "ideal Aryan" and in all ways a whirlwind of efficiency, clarity and purpose is briefed by subordinates and confers with such advisors as Adolf Eichmann, the "Jewish specialist."

Evidently with only slight editing from the actual event, and under the constant forward pressing of Heydrich, the meeting moves like wildfire, covering an enormous number of subjects and considerations in a terribly brief period of time. Various Nazis express concern that such concentration on the Jews will divert resources from the war effort, particularly on the Russian front; some forward the notion that mass public executions are messy and make for bad p.r.; others still are concerned with transportation problems, reduction in the armaments work force with the Jews eliminated, et al., ad nauseum.

Climax, such as it is, comes in a heated discussion of the fate of half-Jews, their offspring and any subjects of mixed blood. None of the participants here would have been at the meeting in the first place if they didn't fundamentally agree on the evil represented by the Jewish people, but topic still causes tempers to flare and results in one man's resignation.

Limitations of the approach are a lack of identification of who the participants are and what interests they represent, and a lack of clarity concerning the jurisdictional factions and frictions between them. Although overt, documentary-like labels might have seemed a crude device, they still would have helped.

Nevertheless, director Heinz Schirk's approach to the essentially static and heavily talky material is visually elegant and to the point, and the pace he sets is terrific. Acting by the entire ensemble is utterly believable, with special kudos going to Dietrich Mattausch's commanding portrait of Heydrich.

Such seemingly dry history might not be the stuff normal art house patrons like to feed on, but the drama and fascination inherent in the material and its treatment should give any intelligent audience plenty to chew on.—*Cart.*

Skorbnoe Besčuvstvie
(Heartless Grief)
(SOVIET-COLOR)

A Sovexport release and Lenfilm production. Directed by Aleksandr Sokurov. Screenplay, Jurij Arabov, based on George Bernard Shaw's play "Heartbreak House;" camera (Cinemascope, color), Sergej Jurizdickkij; editor, Leda Seménova; sound, Vladimir Persov; production design-costumes, Elena Amsinskaja; choreography, J. Mjacin. Reviewed at the Berlin Film Festival (Competition), Feb. 22, 1987. Running time: **95 MINS.**

Shotover	Ramaz Cchikvadze
Ariadna	Alla Osipenko
Hesione	Tat'jana Egoreva
Hector	Dimitrij Brjancev
Mazzini	Vladimor Zamanskij
Ellie	Viktorija Amitova
Mangan	Il'ja Rivin
Nurse Guinness	Irina Sokolova
Doctor Knife	Vadim Zuk
Randall	Andrej Resetin

Also with I. Sergeev, V. Dimitriev, P. Pribytko, L. An, J. Simonov.

Berlin — Coming right out of the recent *glasnost* relaxing of the political doctrinaire grip on the Soviet arts, young (born 1951) Aleksandr Sokurov's 1986 doomsday comedy-meller "Heartless Grief," loosely based on a George Bernard Shaw play titled "Heartbreak House," flutters like a glittering hummingbird from the cage unto the world of free cinema and could become the smart thing to see and to talk about for some time to come.

More surprising than the looks and contents of the film itself is the fact that Russian writers and directors are now given opulent budgets to make films that most Western film financiers would shy away from, especially when faced with projects as deliberately obscure as "Heartless Grief."

The obscurity of Sokurov's work, however, only serves to provide bait for analytical minds. Wild boars are peeking out from under tables; a corpse on the autopsy slab comes alive to scold whinnying women; and a stork joins part of what is soon to be seen as a Dance Macabre on the eve of the end of the world.

Seen dancing, eating, philosophizing and indulging in elegant eroticism in and around a curiously ark-shaped mansion is a group of friends and relatives at the time of World War I. The war is seen and heard outside via recurring images and interpolated documentary footage, which is distorted by its forced adaptation to the Cinemascope format

Other interpolations are docu shots of starving African children and of African tribal dancers, and Shaw himself is seen (more docu footage alternating with a Russian

actor behind the famous beard) being interviewed; tucked into bed; being dumped on the front porch, etc. Finally, a Zeppelin hovers over the landscape, obviously a carrier of technological evil.

Everything comes out with fluid grace as a young filmmaker's flip indulgence in cinematic styles and devices. Most of the direct action and plot development (not to say obfuscation) has somnolent acting performed in a late Victorian décor of rooms dimly, but beautifully lit. Everybody is ready with a Shavian quote ("Men are the only beings who tear apart their victims without being in need of their flesh for food") or some literary name-dropping (Prudhomme, Voltaire, Rousseau each get a spin along with sundry icons of the Bible). Mostly the preoccupation of one and all seems to be either covertly lustful or openly murderous.

Although the film is blessedly short, its stylistic fun gets repetitious. The production dress is one of sheer beauty and all technical credits are of the highest order. The cinematography is made to look like a finely handled, latter-day colorization job, and anachronisms abound in visuals as well as in a clever use of bits of recorded music from the Glenn Miller World War II band to updated piano jazz and to "Who's Afraid Of The Big Bad Wolf." Latter tune is heard repeatedly lest audiences should fail to catch film's indictment of the mindless egocentrics at play under gathering clouds.
— *Kell.*

Vera
(BRAZILIAN-COLOR)

An Embrafilme presentation of a Nexus Cinema e Video, São Paolo production, in association with Quanta Centro de Prod. Cinematográficas, Ilia & Ana Maria Warchawchik/Celso Lafer. Coproduced with the Cultural Center of the State of São Paulo. Produced, written and directed by Sergio Toledo. Camera (color), Rodolfo Sanchez; editor, Tercio G. da Mota; music, Arrigo Barnabé; sound, Karin Stuckenschmidt; sets, Naum Alvez de Souza, Simone Raskin. Reviewed at Berlin Film Festival (Competition), Feb. 25, 1987. Running time: **87 MINS.**

Vera	Ana Beatriz Nogueira
Prof. Trauberg	Raul Cortez
Clara	Aida Leiner
Orphanage director	Carlos Kroeber

Also with: Cida Almeida, Adriana Abujamra, Imara Reis, Norma Blum, Abram Faarc, Liana Duval.

Berlin — For his first feature film, Brazilian helmer Sergio Toledo has chosen to tell the story of an ultimate outcast. Not only is his titular heroine, Vera, an orphan, she is also a juvenile delinquent, a tough cookie and desperately unhappy with the female body bestowed upon her. It isn't that she has lesbian tendencies, what she wants most of all is a change of sex which, she feels, will match the body with the soul.

This is a bit too much to unload on one film and Toledo can't help stepping on some shopworn clichés, particularly when dealing with boarding school scenes which fill up practically all the first half.

In the traditional manner, there is one tutor who understands and sympathizes, and becomes the one personal on whom Vera feels she can lean in her hour of need. There is also the classmate who is first repelled and then won over by Vera's advances, but is incapable of fully comprehending her complex personality.

Wisely, Toledo does not attempt to find solutions or supply readymade answers for the girl's plight, but rather assesses the reaction of society around her to her conduct. To wit, the librarians who demand that Vera be dismissed because she appears at work in masculine garb, considered by her colleagues to be utterly immoral, in spite of their perfectly chaste cut. There are also numerous flashbacks to the boarding school period, long after she has graduated, to elaborate on the social pressure made upon the girls to appear more feminine and suitable to society's expectations.

Given the choice of the subject, however, the treatment is pretty tame, as if Toledo preferred not to tread too far on dangerous paths and the characters around Vera, including the sympathetic teacher, are treated as social symptoms, not really developed for their own sake.

Well shot and adequately acted, the film's main interest lies in the choice of the subject, treated in a correct, but not very exciting manner. —*Edna.*

Napló Szerelmeimnek
(Diary For My Loves)
(HUNGARIAN-COLOR/B&W)

A Budapest Studio, Mafilm, production. Directed by Marta Meszáros. Screenplay, Meszáros, Eva Pataki; camera (Eastmancolor), Miklos Jancso Jr.; editor, Eva Karmentö; music, Zsolt Döme; production design, Eva Martin; sound, Istvan Sipos; costumes, Fanni Kemenes. Reviewed at Hungarian Film Week, Budapest, Feb. 18, 1987. (In competition at Berlin Film Festival.) Running time: **135 MINS.**
Juli . . . . Zsuzsa Czinkoczi
Magda . . . . Anna Polony
Janos/Father . . . . Jan Nowicki
Grandfather . . . . Pal Zolnay
Grandmother . . . . Mari Szemes
Erzsi . . . . Erzsi Kutvölgyi
Anna Pavlovna . . . . Irina Kuberskaia
Natasha . . . . Adel Kovats

Budapest — In 1982, Marta Meszáros made "Diary," later known as "Diary For My Children," an autobiographical account of her childhood in the USSR and her return to Hungary after the war following the death of her mother and the imprisonment of her sculptor father during one of Stalin's purges. The film was held up for two years by nervous officials in Hungary (who presumably feared hostile reactions to it from Moscow) but it was eventually shown to foreigners at the 1984 Film Week, where it won the Gene Moskowitz Award (prize of the foreign guests).

Now comes the sequel, "Diary For My Loves," which takes up where the earlier film left off, in 1949, and concludes in 1956, a traumatic year for Hungary. The same actors repeat their roles, and scenes from the first film (which was shot in black and white) are incorporated into the new one, which is repping Hungary at the Berlin festival, and should be a very strong contender.

The 18-year-old Joli (Zsuzsa Czinkoczi) has left the home of the foster mother, Magda (Anna Polony) whom she hates and goes out on her own, but finds life in this period of unrelenting Stalinism extremely hard. She yearns to locate her father, and also to see her friend, Janos, who reminds her of her father (both roles are played by Jan Nowicki), Magda's former lover, who has been imprisoned unjustly along with many other innocent political prisoners of the period.

Eventually, Juli gets a scholarship to study film in Moscow, and commutes between the two cities. The death of Stalin (news broadcast to the students as they bathe in the morning) brings about a thaw, and Janos is released from prison, a broken man. Later, Juli hears that her beloved father's reputation has been rehabilitated, but also that he's been dead since 1944.

Despite the thaw, Juli's first documentary film is heavily criticized for its brutal honesty. In October, 1956, she travels to Moscow to receive her diploma, and while she's there hears about the upheavals at home in Hungary. She's prevented from leaving the USSR; the border has been sealed.

"Diary For My Loves" represents another frank portrait of the 1950s from the Hungarian cinema, but told from a personal viewpoint which makes it riveting as drama. Though long, this beautifully-made film is filled with interesting incidents and characters, and the understated but deeply-felt style is perfectly suited to the theme. Newsreel footage is adroitly incorporated into the drama.

Meszáros is to be congratulated for seeing her dream project through, despite the delays caused by the original shelving of Part I. This new film should win accolades, be sought after by fests, enjoy a modest art house career, and combined with the original "Diary" will make for a formidable document on a 10-year period of recent history as seen through the keenly observant eyes of an intelligent, troubled young woman. A third film in a trilogy is now in the planning stage.
—*Strat.*

Masques
(Masks)
(FRENCH-COLOR)

An MK2 production and release. Coproducer, Films A2. Produced by Marin Karmitz. Directed by Claude Chabrol. Screenplay, Chabrol, Odile Barski; camera (Eastmancolor), Jean Rabier; editor, Monique Fardoulis; music, Matthieu Chabrol; art director, Françoise Benoit-Fresco; sound, Jean-Bernard Thomasson and Maurice Gilbert; assistant director, Alain Wermus; production manager, Catherine Lapoujade. Reviewed at the Gaumont Ambassade cinema, Paris, Feb. 15, 1987. (In competition at Berlin Film Festival.) Running time: **100 MINS.**
Christian Legagneur . . . . . . Philippe Noiret
Roland Wolf . . . . Robin Renucci
Colette . . . . Monique Chaumette
Catherine . . . . Anne Brochet
   Also with: Bernadette Lafont, Roger Dumas, Pierre-François Duménaud.

Paris — "Masques" is more minor league work from director Claude Chabrol, but it's also his best directed effort in a long while, which may reconcile him with erstwhile art house fans turned off by the uninspired pics he has been dong of late. It is Chabrol's third production for leading indie Marin Karmitz and is currently shaping up commercially as one of the New Wave veteran's boxoffice best.

The script doesn't reflect an effort on Chabrol's part to strike out in new directions and depths: he's again rattling skeletons in well-kept bourgeois closets. It would all sound hollowly familiar if it were not for Chabrol's cool, stealthy direction and a fine cast headed by Philippe Noiret.

Story, by Chabrol and Odile Barski, takes the form of an investigation into the life of a popular French tv personality (Noiret), who commands high ratings with a rose-colored show devoted to the elderly.

A young man presenting himself as a journalist (Robin Renucci) proposes to pen a biography of the celebrity, who magnanimously invites him out to his country estate for a few days to tape his oral memoirs.

Renucci is in fact no journalist, but the brother of an obscure actress who had spent some months in Noiret's home where she became a companion to Noiret's convalescing young goddaughter (Anne Brochet) and suddenly disappeared.

Renucci's snooping, and his deepening romantic involvement with the sickly Brochet, bring to light the ugly truth about the reputedly altruistic Noiret, who has appropriated Brochet's rightful inheritance, been keeping his ward in a drugged state and had Renucci's sister murdered when she stumbled on to the facts.

All told, the tale's quotient of suspense and surprise is limited, and the borrowings from and paraphrasings of scenes from Hitchcock are by now par for the course (as are the more Chabrolian dining table set pieces), but the helmer has at lest recovered much of his storytelling mastery, sense of rhythm and feeling for atmosphere.

Noiret, who has shed some weight, brings panache and cunning to the role of beloved public figure who has carefully composed a mask to hide all the greed, baseness and contempt that has nurtured him through life. Renucci is less satisfactory as his prying antagonist.

As members of Noiret's country entourage, Bernadette Lafont, ever faithful to the Chabrol portrait gallery, Monique Chaumette, Roger Dumas and Pierre-François Duménaud lend ambiguity and flavor to the proceedings. Brochet, a screen newcomer, makes a subtly tuned debut as Noiret's desperately doped-out ward, brought back to life by Renucci's solicitous presence.
— *Len.*

Vlci Bouda
(Wolf's Lair)
(CZECHOSLOVAKIAN-COLOR)

A Barrandov Studio, Ceskoslovensky Film production. Produced by Jan Suster. Directed by Vera Chytilová. Screenplay, Chytilová, D. Fischerova; Cjaromir Sofr; camera (color), Sofr; production design, L. Siroky; music, Michael Kocab. Reviewed at Berlin Film Fest (Competition), Feb. 21, 1986. Running time: **92 MINS.**
The "Father" . . . . Miroslav Macháček
Dingo . . . . Tomás Palaty
Babeta . . . . Stepánka Cervenková
   Also with: Stanek, Bidlas, Fiser, Pycha, Horácek, Zelenková, Dudusová, Racková, Slaviková.

Berlin — Vera Chytilová, one of the key figures of the new wave of Czech filmmakers in the 1960s, is back with a strange, contrived allegory about evil authority figures and the need for the oppressed to unite in order to escape their proscribed existence. Setting is an isolated ski resort in winter, known as The Wolves' Lair, site of an endurance course organized by three mysterious group leaders, an old man who calls himsef "Father," a beautiful young woman, and a sinister type called Dingo. Ten teenagers of both sexes have enrolled in the course, but 11 turn up, and no one will admit who is the ringer.

The three in charge are strict disciplinarians, but there's something funny going on (sinister electronic music, strange little moments). For a while it almost seems as if this is going to be a Czech slasher pic — it's the perfect setting and situation

— but it turns into an Aliens From Outer Space film when it's revealed that the three are evil extra-terrestrials. Why they'd bother with these silly Czech teenagers is never made clear, but they want the kids to sacrifice the 11th member of the group, whoever he or she is, and are apparently encouraged by the continual way the youngsters, during arguments, exclaim that they'd like to kill whoever it is that's annoying them. In the end, though, the kids work in unison to defeat the aliens, which they do with very little bother.

Whatever hidden meanings can be extrapolated from all this, and there are quite a few, it remains a basically silly film. Performances are variable (Tomás Palaty, who plays the most sinister alien, looks as if he's rehearsing for a villain's role in small-town rep) and the screenplay is so contrived and full of holes that exasperation sets in.

Compounding this is Chytilova's visual style. In the 1960s, her distinctive use of zoom lens and free-wheeling hand-held camera was felt by many to be innovative, but in this film, as in her last ("The Very Late Afternoon Of A Fawn") the constant use of rapid zooms and zippans is likely to give the average viewer a severe case of vertigo or even nausea. The wild, snowbound settings are a plus, and the music by Michael Kocab is fine until the choral climax which sounds as if it was written for "The Robe." —*Strat.*

Aah, Belinda!
(TURKISH-COLOR)

An Odak Film production. Produced by Cengiz Ergun. Directed by Atif Yilmaz. Screenplay, Paris Pirhasan; camera (Fujicolor), Orhan Oguz; editor, Mevlüt Koçak; music, Omno Tunç; sound, Erkan Aktas; production design, Sahin Kaygun. Reviewed at Berlin Film Fest (Panorama), Feb. 25, 1987. Running time: **100 MINS.**
With: Müjde Ar, Macit Koner, Yilmaz Zafer, Füsun Demirel, Fatos Sezer, Tarik Pabuççuoglu, Güzin Ozipek, Amzi Orses.

Berlin — A bright comedy along the lines of "Peggy Sue Got Married" is not the usual Turkish fare sent to film fests, so "Aah, Belinda!" makes a welcome change. Plotting is ingenious, and, after a rather awkward start, pic has a suitably light touch.

The heroine, Serap (Turkish siren Müjde Ar), is a sophisticated young woman who has a rich boyfriend, a job in the theater, and a swank apartment. She's agreed to do her first tv commercial, for a brand of shampoo called "Belinda." For this she's given an average family: dull, doting husband and two kids. She meets the actors playing these roles on the set the day the shooting starts.

Then something inexplicable happens: during the shooting of the scene where she shampoos her hair under the shower (demurely clad in a one-piece bathing suit), the camera crew suddenly disappears and Serap finds herself in a drab little apartment where she apparently lives with her husband and children. The fiction of the commercial has become reality.

Frantically, she tries to return to her usual life. But her boyfriend and her colleagues at the theater don't know her and someone else is living in her apartment. Very reluctantly, she returns to her husband's apartment and goes to work next day in a bank just as the fictitious housewife did in the commercial.

What follows is skillfully worked out, and the playing and direction are relaxed and full of good humor. Pic should be popular at fests where comedy is usually in very short supply, and it will please those who've always felt there was more to Turkish cinema than the ultra-serious fare that usually travels abroad. Direction and thesping are deft, and there's fine work from production designer Sahin Kaygun.—*Strat.*

Der Tod des Empedokles
(The Death Of Empedocles)
(FRENCH-W. GERMAN-COLOR)

A Dopa Film (Paris) and Hamburger Film-büro release of a Janus Film (Frankfurt) with Les Films du Losange (Paris) production in collaboration with Hessian Television (Hamburg), Dopa Film and the French Center National de la Cinematographie. Produced by Klaus Hellwig, Rosy Gockel. Written, directed, edited and screenplay by Jean-Marie Straub and Danièle Huillet, based on Friedrich Hölderlin's 1798 verse play. Camera (Eastmancolor), Renato Berta, Jean-Paul Toraille, Giovanni Canfarelli; sound, Louis Hochet, Georges Vaglio, Allessandro Zanon; costumes, Huillet. Reviewed at Berlin Film Festival (Competition), Feb. 26, 1987. Running time: **132 MINS.**
Empedocles . . . . Andreas von Rauch
Hermocrates . . . . Howard Vernon
Pausanias . . . . Vladimir Baratta
Panthea . . . . Martina Baratta
Delia . . . . Ute Cremer
Also with: Federico Hecker, Peter Boom, Giorgio Baratta, Manfred Esser, Georg Brinstrup, Achille Brunini, Peter Kammerer.

Berlin — "The Death Of Empedocles" is quite willfully made to look and sound like a non-film by Alsacian writer-helmer Jean-Marie Straub and his collaborator Danièle Huillet who earlier on and together have defied the normal groundrules of cinematic art by insisting on stage rhetoric spouted by actors whose feet seem nailed to the ground inside frames of minimal, if any, movement.

With the exception of devoted followers, most everybody will feel that Straub and Huillet have carried their devices to a silly extreme with their filmed (in a patch of a clearing in the woods near Agrigent, Sicily) rendition of the late 18th Century German poet Friedrich Hölderlin's verse tragedy about the Fifth Century Greek poet-visionary-politician-philosopher Empedocles, who killed himself by jumping into the crater of volcano Etna.

The 132 minute-long film is a series of dialogs on the value of life and death and the exercise of free will in the face in disasters imposed upon mankind and the Earth by evil men: priests and/or politicians. Good citizens of Agrigent implore Empedocles to let them give him a king's crown, but he turns them away as he has the priest-politicians, and he talks to a young boy and girl (disciples) about the strength to save the world belonging to the young while he himself considers it fit for his age to return to the realms out of which new life grows.

The words spoken are actually quite poetic, but they are all mouthed so as to sound like environmental tract texts, and even if it is never quite clear what evil threatens the 5th Century world, it is obvious tha a bad case of word pollution is at hand. As Empedocles, white-maned Andreas von Rauch looks either deadly bored or irritated, and hectoring anger is his sole tonal inflection throughout. Most of the other actors follow suit with monotonous spouting of words and somber miens, while a few try to liven things up with a bit of mimic hamming. They are soon called to order again, so that the only things really stirring within the frames are leaves and the skies behind the actors.

"The Death Of Empedocles" is consistent in its voluntary stylistic barrenness and in its self-righteous renditions of Hölderlin's lauding of the Earth's natural beauty and values. It is a film for True Believer audiences only. Anybody else who sits through this one to the end will feel cruelly cheated by not even getting to see the Great Man take the fatal jump. Like any other phony, he just talks about it endlessly.
—*Kell.*

Kronika wypadków milosnych
(A Chronicle Of Amorous Accidents)
(POLISH-COLOR)

A Zespoly Filmowe/Film Group Perspektyva production. International sales, Galeszka Moravioff/Films Sans Frontières (Paris). Directed by Andrzej Wajda. Screenplay, Wajda, Tadeusz Konwicki, based on Konwicki's novel; camera (Orwocolor), Edward Klosinski; editor, Halina Prugar-Ketling; music, Wojciech Kilar; sound, Danuta Zankowska; production design, Janusz Sosnowski, Barbara Nowak; production management, Barbara Pec-Slesicka. Reviewed at Berlin Film Festival (Competition), Feb. 24, 1987. Running time: **120 MINS.**
Alina . . . . Paulina Mlynarska
Witek . . . . Piotr Wawrzynczak
Greta . . . . Bernadetta Machala
Engel . . . . Dariusz Bobkowski
Lowa . . . . Jaroslaw Gruda
Cecylia . . . . Johanna Szczepkowska
Olimpia . . . . Gabriela Kownacka
Witek's mother . . Krystyna Zachawatowicz
The Stranger . . . . Tadeusz Konwicki

Berlin — After his excursions into poignantly realistic political drama ("Man Of Iron," "Danton"), Poland's Andrzej Wajda is back in his own classical style of the real and the surreal mixed evocatively and with superior craft in "A Chronicle Of Amorous Accidents," a work of beauty but also, alas one of occasional boredom.

The time of the story is the summer months preceding the September 1939 outbreak of World War II. The place is the then-Polish part of Lithuania, where German girls were vacationing with well-to-do Poles, while passing Catholic processions and orthodox Jews diligent at work in their shops and schools were bowed to respectfully by one and all.

It was a time, too, when young Witek, hoping to pass his final exams to enter a university, could brave an irate father's attempts to fire a shotgun directly at his behind when the prize was that of the man's pretty high school daughter Alina.

It also was a time for all the young to fight and frolic romantically and to talk sententiously of death while bursting with a rage to live. It was ultimately a time when troop movements, especially those of Poland's famous Ulan Cavalry, were all around everything and everybody.

Basing his film on parts of a novel by Tadeusz Konwicki, who co-scripted and who appears now and again as The Stranger to make young Witek take peeks into his own future, Andrzej Wajda indulges in soft-focus nostalgia a bit more than all the little incidents and encounters will sustain.

When the flashes of cavalry occur, they seem to come as a relief as much to the director as they do to his audience. They may signal impending doom, but they are hard to really see as anything but full of happy colors, speed, rhythm, light and, in general, cinematographic wizardry.

At the end, Wajda pulls all stops on his poetic visions and comes through with as lovely a sexual encounter in the grass as anything on that order in cinema history. He then has the two youngsters (Piotr Wawrzynczak and Paulina Mlynarska in fine, subdued performances), clad in white, wade into the river to act out, all alone, their own wedding ceremony.

This is where "A Chronicle" will bring forth choked sobs around the globe. Unfortunately the bombs start falling and everything becomes just the tiniest shade too obvious.
—*Kell.*

Le Miraculé
(The Miracle Healing)
(FRENCH-COLOR)

A Cannon France release of an Initial Groupe/Koala Films/FR3 Films coproduction. Executive producers, Jean Cazes, Denis Freyd. Directed by Jean-Pierre Mocky. Stars Michel Serrault, Jean Poiret, Jeanne Moreau. Screenplay, Mocky, Jean-Claude Romer, Patrick Granier; camera (Fujicolor), Marcel Combes; editor, Mocky; music, Jorge Arriagada; art directors, Patrice Renault, Jean-Claude Sevenet, Etienne Mery; sound, Philippe Combes; production manager, Bernard Bourgade. Reviewed at the UGC Biarritz cinema, Paris, Feb. 15, 1987. (In competition at Berlin Film Festival). Running time: **85 MINS.**

Papu	Jean Poiret
Ronald Fox Terrier	Michel Serrault
Sabine	Jeanne Moreau
Angelica	Sophie Moyse
Monseigneur	Jean Rougerie
Mme. Fox Terrier	Sylvie Joly
Plombie	Roland Blanche
Abbe Humus	Marc Maury

Paris — "Le Miraculé," competing at the Berlin fest, is a botched one-joke comedy about a phony invalid en route to Lourdes pursued by an observant but mute insurance inspector. Dunked into the healing pond of the holy grotto, the shammer finds himself genuinely handicapped, while in insurance man miraculously recovers his voice, albeit in a foreign tongue.

Returning to the mainstream fold after a number of offbeat, ill-made personal films, director Jean-Pierre Mocky belabors obvious satiric targets in the slapdash production salvaged at moments by its starring trio of Jean Poiret, Michel Serrault and Jeanne Moreau. Pic's irreverent bad taste humor may boost commercial prospects, especially if official Catholic outrage helps it along with unwanted publicity, as happened with Jean-Luc Godard's "Hail, Mary."

Domestically, one of the film's main attractions should be reteaming of Serrault and Poiret, a one-time top comedy duo whose careers peaked in the Paris production of Poiret's "La Cage aux folles." Their reunion here under Mocky (who directed both in several of his 1960s commercial comedies) is not exploited to the fullest, however.

Poiret in particular, who excels in sophisticated comic parts, doesn't shine in the principal role of seedy low-life who claims disability insurance after being knocked down by a car, and is subsequently carted off by wheelchair to a Lourdes pilgramage by his (platonic) girlfriend (Moreau), a secular sister of mercy on the fringes of Paris.

Serrault, a farceur with a broader low comedy range, is more at home in the vulgar antics imagined by Mocky and his cowriters Jean-Claude Romer and Patrick Granier. As the devout but speechless insurance agent bent on exposing Poiret's charade, Serrault revives a gesticulating form of Harpo Marxist shenanigans, which often seem more improvised than planned in Mocky's overly casual (and often downright inept) stagings.

More dependent on script and only fitfully pungent dialog, Moreau manages to make a few scenes memorable, notably when she lends a literal helpful hand to alleviating Serrault's sexual frustration from his marriage to even more bigoted Sylvie Joly.

Otherwise, "Le Miraculé" is a good spoof idea sloppily executed, constantly failing back on the most obvious barbs and particularly weak in integrating its gallery of secondary characters into the main story line. Apart from its principals, acting suffers from a lack of firm directorial harmonizing. Tech credits are mediocre. —*Len.*

Die Verliebten
(Days To Remember)
(W. GERMAN-YUGOSLAVIAN-COLOR)

A Von Vietinghoff Filmproduktion-Art Film 80 (Belgrade) coproduction. (Metropolis Film, world sales.) Produced by Joachim von Vietinghoff. Aleksander Stojanovic. Executive producers, Udo Heiland, Nikola Popovic. Directed by Jeanine Meerapfel. Stars Barbara Sukowa. Screenplay, Meerapfel; camera (Agfacolor), Predrag Popovic; editor, Ursula West; music, Jürgen Knieper; sound, Marko Rodic; production design, Rainer Schaper; assistant director, Eva Ebner; production manager, Alexander Juncker. Reviewed at Berlin Film Festival (Competition), Feb. 27, 1987. Running time: **94 MINS.**

Katharina	Barbara Sukowa
Peter	Horst-Günter Marx
Uncle Savo	Bata Zivojinovic
Dusan	Rade Serbedzija
Mother	Liljana Kontic
Danica	Stela Cetkovic

Berlin — Jeanine Meerapfel came up with a charming first feature in "Malou" (1981), which played at several fests. She's made documentaries and worked in tv since then, but her second feature, "Days To Remember," sadly must be counted a major disappointment. It's nothing more than a sappy love story that takes itself far too seriously.

Pic is set in Montenegro, the mountainous part of Yugoslavia. Katharina (Barbara Sukowa) is a German tv reporter of Yugoslav origins. She's a workaholic, about to head for the big time in New York, and her timetable is well organized in advance. However, after doing a story on the German-born children of Yugoslav guest workers, she takes time off to visit her family. Along the way she meets Peter (Horst-Günter Marx), a surly young German plodding around the mountains searching for evidence of his father's guilt or innocence during the war.

For reasons that will remain incomprehensible to many viewers this intelligent, beautiful young career woman sets her sights on this unappealing youth. Just as incomprehensibly, he rejects her advances, but tags along with her. Maybe Meerapfel wanted to explore a situation where the woman takes the lead and the man holds back, but it comes across in the film as tiresome, and the man's behavior seems incredibly silly.

He's taken home to meet the family, and then they continue on, though he insists they stay in separate rooms when they stay in a small hotel (Sukowa relieves her evident frustration by going for a midnight swim in a lake).

Finally they make love, in a singularly cheerless scene, but the young man still has to fulfill his ambition to discover his father's past, and unwisely enters an area of unexploded mines, with predictable results.

It's sad when a seriously intended film fails as badly as this one does, but it must be said this seems to have been a completely misconceived project. Sukowa brings authority and beauty to her role, but newcomer Marx is inadequate as the dreary young German, and it's the conception and playing of his role that sinks the picture. Predrag Popovic's crisp photography of some magnificent lakes, mountains and sunsets is the film's chief asset.
—*Strat.*

Heat
(COLOR)

Lackluster Burt Reynolds vehicle.

A New Century/Vista Film Co. release, presented by Elliott Kastner and New Century Entertainment, of a Cassian Elwes production for Escalante Prods. Produced by Keith Rotman, George Pappas. Directed by R.M. (Dick) Richards. Stars Burt Reynolds. Screenplay, William Goldman, based on his novel; camera (Technicolor), James Contner; editor, Jeffrey Wolf; music, Michael Gibbs; art director, Jerry Wunderlich; sound, Rusty Coppleman; costumes, Norman Salling; assistant director, Jerry Sobul; associate producers, John Vane, Vicki Taft; second unit director, Stan Barrett; casting, Rich Pagano (L.A.), Paula Herald (N.Y.). Reviewed at ABC Entertainment Center, (L.A.), Feb. 25, 1987. (MPAA Rating: R.) Running time: **101 MINS.**

Mex	Burt Reynolds
Holly	Karen Young
Cyrus Kinnick	Peter MacNicol
Pinchus Zion	Howard Hesseman
Danny DeMarco	Neill Barry
Cassie	Diana Scarwid

Hollywood — Whatever spark of an absorbing story pitting Burt Reynolds in his trademark toughie-with-a-heart role against slimy Las Vegas types is never allowed to come to full flame in the lukewarm actioner, "Heat."

Under R.M. (Dick) Richards' plodding direction, William Goldman's script (adapted from his book) becomes a muddled, violent, and sadly, humorless experience. (Three other directors besides Richards worked on this film during a much-publicized, troubled shoot. —*Ed.*)

Pic will find an audience in those who like gritty, seamy productions, but "Heat" is sure to get a cold reception from women who've always been attracted to Reynolds' suave, witty ways.

Role of a down-on-his-luck gambler and sometime bodyguard suits Reynolds just fine. He's known as "Mex," a nickname for his real name Nick Escalante, a heavy known on the streets of Sin City as an occasionally brutal but principled man.

Reynolds' persona is established early on in a series of scattered sequences that show him drunk, hung over and generally depressed that he will ever get his act, or enough money, together to realize his dream of leaving Vegas forever and visiting Venice.

In-between shots of him popping another four aspirin, he finds himself grudgingly tracking down the perverted punk mobster's son (Neill Barry) who brutally attacked his former neighbor (Karen Young) and taking on an assignment to be the bodyguard at the casinos for a teetotaling, lowrolling millionaire (Peter MacNichol).

Tone of the pic alternates between a sad portrayal of a lonely, bitter man and a slice-'em-up crime story involving the underbelly of Vegas where police never figure in.

Reynolds has two interesting relationships, with Young and with MacNichol, and just when the dialog starts to get beyond the immediate and Reynolds seems about to open up, Richards cuts to the next scene.

It's never quite clear how these two people's lives have impacted Reynolds' character. He seems to be affected by their vulnerability, but you never see it in his face — resulting in a cold and somewhat detached drama.

The sight of Young's severely bruised face should elicit some deeper reaction from Reynolds than his physical drive to avenge her assailants. Even if the actress plays her role a little too much on the hard side (she never cries), she is still a pathetic figure.

Not enough is made of Reynolds' relationship to MacNicol, either — the more complex and interesting of the two supporting roles.

There was a kernel of an intriguing friendship that could have been better developed between them, but is it squelched time and again in favor of the less involving scenes like those focusing on Reynolds' night playing blackjack (he wins $100,000 and still can't crack a smile) or facing off against Barry and his oversized thugs.

Pic races to its conclusion after lumbering along for over an hour as Reynolds, rather masterfully, manages to spear, set afire and suffocate three of Barry's henchmen in a matter of minutes.

Lawless feeling of this suspenser from beginning to end results in a lackluster ending, even if the good guys do win out.

Best minor performance is turned in by Diana Scarwid, who exhibits as much emotion in her three speechless minutes on film as the blackjack dealer than any other actors with speaking parts.

Tech credits are uneven. Richards resorts to slo-mo shots when Reynolds is doing his karate number, usually a low-budget feature staple, but the jazzy score adds mood where little exists. —*Brit.*

Hunk
(COLOR)

Timid adolescent fantasy.

A Crown Intl. Pictures release. Produced by Marilyn J. Tenser. Written and directed by Lawrence Bassoff. Camera (Fotokem color), Bryan England; editor, Richard E. Westover; music, David Kurtz; art direction, Catherine Hardwicke; costume design, Bernadette O'Brien; sound (Dolby), Bernie Kriegel; assistant director, R.B. Graham; casting, Paul Bengston, David Cohn. Reviewed at the Pacific Metro theater, L.A., March 6, 1987. (MPAA Rating: PG.) Running time: **102 MINS.**
Hunk Golden . . . . John Allen Nelson

Bradley Brinkman . . . . Steve Levitt
O'Brien . . . . Deborah Shelton
Sunny . . . . Rebeccah Bush
Dr. D . . . . James Coco
Garrison Gaylord . . . . Robert Morse
Constantine Constapopolis Avery Schreiber

Hollywood — "Hunk" is the perfect film for lonely beach bunnies to see on a wintry day, a time when their favorite golden boys have retreated to the tanning salons. With no sex, no violence and only a handful of salacious lines, pic is easily adolescent fare.

As beach stories go, "Hunk" isn't exactly junk. And it does have a new twist that distinguishes it from other fun-in-the-sun schlock films — the blond, blue-eyed main character doesn't surf. He does, however, drive a snazzy convertible, flex his pecs a lot and turn all the pretty girls' heads.

Here, the hunk is actually named Hunk. Hunk Golden (John Allen Nelson), formerly the computer nerd Bradley Brinkman (Steve Levitt) who trades his soul for the summer in exchange for hardbody and instant popularity.

The she devil who made him do it comes in the form of a gorgeous brunet (Deborah Shelton of "Dallas" fame). Trouble is, she's going to turn him back into a wimp by Labor Day if he doesn't consent to live in Hell for all eternity and help her do Satan's work on earth.

The late James Coco turns up as Dr. D, the he devil and mastermind of this scheme. He's about the only one in this silliness interested in Allen's soul, and not his body. At one time or another, he shows up as a Nazi, a pirate and a ghoulish caveman — looking about as sinister as a cream puff. If he's having fun, and he appears to be, what does it matter? This isn't Dante's "Inferno."

Dialog is above par most of the time, sinking below the surf when it tries to be serious. Screenwriter Lawrence Bassoff has a psychologist with the unlikely professional moniker of Dr. Sunny Graves (Rebeccah Bush) fall all over the golden boy, lecturing him on how beauty is only skin deep.

If the filmmakers really believed this, there wouldn't be much of a point to this pic. —*Brit.*

Swimming To Cambodia
(COLOR)

Free association monolog suffers on the big screen.

A Cinecom Pictures release of a Jonathan Demme picture. Produced by R.A. Shafransky. Executive producers, Lewis Allen, Peter Newman; co-executive producers, Amir Malin, Ira Deutchman. Directed by Demme. Stars Spalding Gray. Screenplay, Gray; camera (color), John Bailey; editor, Carol Littleton; music, Laurie Anderson; production designer, Sandy McLeod; associate producer, Edward Saxon; Reviewed at Mag-

no Preview 4 screening room, N.Y., March 5, 1987. (No MPAA Rating.) Running time: **87 MINS.**
With: Spalding Gray; also Sam Waterston, Ira Wheeler.

Witnessed in its original incarnation as a staged monolog, Spalding Gray's free-associating recollection of his experiences in Thailand during the making of "The Killing Fields" had an exhilarating immediacy which is mostly absent in this compressed filmed performance of "Swimming To Cambodia."

Director Jonathan Demme obviously was limited in cinematically expanding the anecdotal soliloquy performed at the Performance Garage in the SoHo district of Manhattan. In spite of incendiary flashes of biting comedic insight, the loopy impact of Gray's freewheeling narrative is diminished on the big screen and does not figure to generate the word-of-mouth necessary for sustained boxoffice. It could find a following as a small-screen video item, however.

Addressing a live audience from a seat at a bare table, the emotionally expansive, anti-heroic raconteur skillfully fosters an illusion of spontaneous, confessional intimacy, but in spite of zooming closeups this bond is irretrievably diminished on the screen. Nevertheless, there's a compelling originality in Gray's breathless rhetorical four-walling, as this self-effacing, self-styled "perceiver" drolly seeks to divine a grand connective design in the absurd fabric of life experience.

Gray can leap effortlessly from contemplating the assassination of a noisy SoHo neighbor, to an Amtrak encounter with a sex-addicted Navy warhead operator, to an uncomprehending elegiac reflection on the horrific "auto-genocide" wrought upon the Cambodian people by the Khmer Rouge armies in the mid-'70s. That terrible mass murder was documented in "The Killing Fields," for which Gray was cast in a small part by director Ronald Joffé ("a combination of Zorro, Jesus and Rasputin"), and haunted the actor long after his few scenes, amusingly recalled here, were over.

Recreating a dislocating culture-shocked odyssey that takes him from the surreal fleshpots of Bangkok to a nearly suicidal quest for a "perfect moment" at a spectacularly paradisical Thai beach, Gray elicits compassion and universal recognition for his serio-comic search for self. Although the sheer inventiveness of Gray's monolog shines through, its raving passion is kept at a fatal remove on the screen. This is hardly mitigated by a grab-bag of camera angles, brief outtakes from "The Killing Fields" and tropico-Oriental minimalist musical flourishes by Gray's fellow downtown performance artist Laurie Anderson.—*Rich.*

Tin Men
(COLOR)

Funny version of the tit-for-tat comedy feud format.

A Buena Vista release of a Touchstone Pictures presentation in association with Silver Screen Partners II. Produced by Mark Johnson. Written and directed by Barry Levinson. Stars Richard Dreyfuss, Danny DeVito, Barbara Hershey. Camera (Nuart color, Deluxe prints), Peter Sova; editor, Stu Linder; music, Fine Young Cannibals, David Steele, Andy Cox; production design, Peter Jamison; set decoration, Philip Abramson; costume design, Gloria Gresham; sound (Dolby), Bill Phillips; assistant director, Albert Shapiro; associate producer, Kim Kurumada; casting, Louis DiGiaimo, Lisa Clarkson. Reviewed at Avco Cinema Center, L.A., March 2, 1987. (MPAA Rating: R.) Running time: **112 MINS.**
BB . . . . Richard Dreyfuss
Tilley . . . . Danny DeVito
Nora . . . . Barbara Hershey
Moe . . . . John Mahoney
Sam . . . . Jackie Gayle
Gil . . . . Stanley Brock
Cheese . . . . Seymour Cassel
Mouse . . . . Bruno Kirby
Wing . . . . J.T. Walsh
Carly . . . . Richard Portnow
Looney . . . . Matt Craven
Stanley . . . . Alan Blumenfeld
Masters . . . . Brad Sullivan
Bagel . . . . Michael Tucker

Hollywood — The improbable tale of a pair of feuding aluminum siding salesmen, i.e. "Tin Men," winds up as bountiful comedy material in the skillful hands of writer-director Barry Levinson. Returning to the hometown well of Baltimore as he did for "Diner," Levinson has transformed the early 1960s into a pic that should easily keep Disney's Touchstone Pictures on its 1986-87 b.o. roll.

Film is packed with laughs, thanks to taut scripting and superb character depictions by Richard Dreyfuss, Danny DeVito and a fascinating troupe of sidekicks. These fast-buck hustlers collectively fashion a portrait of superficial greed so pathetic it soars to a level of black humor notable in the works of author Kurt Vonnegut.

Additional element of considerable consequence is casting of some 40 local residents for location shooting in Baltimore. Resulting framework is so credible that audience is readily drawn into the milieu of this tacky business of pushing the aluminum siding fad onto gullible homeowners. Levinson manages to make these unsavory con men into a nearly likeable bunch of scammates.

Central storyline finds Dreyfuss and DeVito tangling from the start after an accident damages both of their Cadillacs — a brand visible throughout as the quintessential sign of success. Conflict between the two strangers — who don't find out until later they're both tin men — escalates to the point where Dreyfuss seeks to get even by wooing DeVito's unhappy wife into bed.

Barbara Hershey falls for the ploy by the dapper and slick Dreyfuss character, who cranks out some well-honed sales bull to lure her quickly. When Dreyfuss brazenly phones DeVito to taunt him with the development, latter cavalierly claims he doesn't really want her anyway.

DeVito is nonetheless so enraged he hurls his wife's personal effects into the street in a hilarious sequence. His character's mumblings and blatterings throughout the pic are enhanced terrifically by DeVito's masterful adoption of a city of "Ball-mer" accent.

As the conflict between the men grows, Levinson illuminates the world of tin men via montages of sales pitches, periodic coffee shop gabfests and intimate shots of patrons at a neighborhood bar. They're most effective in establishing the feel of time and place.

While each of the tin men is revealed as a compelling, off-center type in his own right, the one played by Jackie Gayle especially shines. Previously cast as one of Woody Allen's deli-roundtable comedians for "Broadway Danny Rose," Gayle's ribald lines reflecting on the then-popular "Bonanza" tv series are side-splitting.

In latter stages of the film, proceedings begin to take on a more serious tenor as a state investigation of tin men begins; Dreyfuss and Hershey develop a relationship and DeVito's life falls further apart as the IRS dogs him.

Plot by now seems only important as a vehicle for determining just how the Dreyfuss-DeVito feud and film itself will fare. Necessity of dramatic resolution prevails over initial and mid-point strength of the comedy.

By pic's end Hershey is left well in the background after a callous bit of wheeling and dealing by the tin men in her life. It turns out she's been along mostly as a foil anyway, with scant development of her role.

Peter Sova's camerawork is tops here and costuming by designer Gloria Gresham captures the period nicely.

Film overall clearly contains seeds of a tv series — such as the one developed from Touchstone's successful "Down And Out In Beverly Hills" theatrical. —Tege.

Cross
(FRENCH-COLOR)

An AAA release of a Cinémax/Cinéma 5 coproduction. Produced by André Djaoui. Written and directed by Philippe Setbon. Stars Michel Sardou, Roland Giraud. Camera (color), Jacques Steyn; editor, Nicole Lubtchansky; music, Michel Goglat; theme song, Philippe Setbon, Jean-Pierre Rourttayre; sound, Jean-François Auger; art director, Juvenal; assistant director, Philippe Rony; production manager, Antonia Seabra. Reviewed at the Georges V cinema, Paris, March 2, 1987. Running time: **85 MINS.**
Thomas Crosky ("Cross") . Michel Sardou
Eli Cantor . . . . Roland Giraud
Simon Lenhardt . . . . Patrick Bauchau
Catherine Crosky . . . . . Marie-Anne Chazel
Jacques Kester . . . . Stéphane Jobert
Sandro . . . . Maxime Leroux
Also with: Arnold Boiseau, Gérard Zalcberg, Philippe Polet, Andrea Ferraz, Anny Mirande, Louba Guertchikoff, Jean Barney.

Paris — "Cross" is a routine thriller and an unsuitable star vehicle for Gallic pop singer Michel Sardou, in his first starring film role as a lone wolf cop who recruits a professional killer to save his ex-wife and daughter from a band of psychotic kidnapers holed up in an abandoned hotel.

The simplistic, predictable script is by screenwriter Philippe Setbon, who makes an undistinguished debut as director, claiming inspiration from the quickie thrillers of Roger Corman.

Film's only interesting oddity is the casting-against-type of comedy thesp Roland Giraud (one of the "Three Men And A Cradle") as the hired assassin. Not a convincing portrayal though the fault lay more with deficiencies of script and direction than with the capacities of the actor.—Len.

Ratas de la Ciudad
(City Rats)
(MEXICAN-COLOR)

A Películas Mexicanas release of a Cinematográfica Sol-Cinematográfica Jalisco production. Produced by Rodolfo de Anda. Directed by and stars Valentin Trujillo. Screenplay, Trujillo, Gilberto de Anda; camera (color), Antonio de Anda; editor, Sergio Soto; music, Marco Flores, with appearance of group Los Caminantes. Reviewed at Cinema Hollywood 1, N.Y., Feb. 21, 1987. Running time: **93 MINS.**
Pedro Macías . . . . Valentin Trujillo
Zúñiga . . . . Rodolfo de Anda
Rita González . . . . Angélica Chaín
Pachuco . . . . Enrique (Flaco) Guzmán
El Flaco . . . . Humberto Elizondo
Also with: Isaura Espinoza, Joaquín Cordero, Lyn May, Lalo el Mimo, Alberto Rojas (Caballo), Lourdes Mungula.

The violent Mexican melodrama "Ratas de la Ciudad" (City Rats) somehow managed to garner five Diosa de Plata (Silver Goddess) awards from the cinema writers group Pecime in 1986, including best director for pic's helmer-star Valentin Trujillo.

What could have been a sizzling indictment of Mexican urban society fizzles out as a shopworn potboiler aimed at sensationalizing society's shortcomings and hypocricies.

Wandering storyline concerns out-of-work physical therapist Pedro Macías (Trujillo) who arrives in the capital with his young son in search of a better life. All goes well until one day, while the two are at an amusement park, a speeding car goes out of control and runs over Pedro's son.

While the son goes to the hospital, Pedro is taken to the police station to make a statement. There he discovers the driver (Humberto Elizondo) is a secret policeman and more than likely will escape punishment. Pedro loses his cool and ends up in the slammer while his son, thinking he has been abandoned, takes to the streets where he joins hordes of urchins who prey on the defenseless. The story goes downhill from there.

The weak script, cowritten by Trujillo, fails in a variety of ways: at the slightest provocation, Pedro comes out fighting, then wonders at the injustice of reprisals. After a while the viewer tends to lose both sympathy and patience with him. The romance that develops between Pedro and social worker Rita González (Angélica Chaín) makes no sense and seems to have been inserted only because someone though the script needed a love interest.

Lensing by Antonio de Anda is uneven. At times it is imaginative in setting mood and tone, yet it falters when dealing with the more mundane nature of the narrative.

The pic's overuse of violence is out of keeping with the social message Trujillo wishes to get across and it alienates the audience from the central story.

Although the film is clearly designed to give the audience a few cheap thrills, it is a mystery why it received any prizes. —Lent.

Berlin Film Reviews

Rita, Sue And Bob Too
(BRITISH-COLOR)

An Orion Classics release (U.S.) of a Film Four Intl.-Umbrella Entertainment production, in association with British Screen. Executive producer, Oscar Lewenstein. Produced by Sandy Lieberson. Directed by Alan Clarke. Screenplay, Andrea Dunbar, based on her plays "The Arbor" and "Rita, Sue And Bob Too;" camera (Eastmancolor), Ivan Strasburg; editor, Stephen Singleton; music, Michael Kamen; sound, Mike McDuffie; production supervisor, Garth Thomas; coproducer, Patsy Pollock. Reviewed at Berlin Film Festival (Market), March 1, 1987. Running time: **95 MINS.**
Sue . . . . Michelle Holmes
Rita . . . . Siobhan Finneran
Bob . . . . George Costigan
Michelle . . . . Lesley Sharp
Sue's father . . . . Willie Ross
Sue's mother . . . . Patti Nicholls
Aslam . . . . Ghir Kulvindar

Berlin — Britain's Film Four has come up with another winner in the "Letter To Brezhnev," "My Beautiful Laundrette" tradition with "Rita, Sue And Bob Too," a sad-funny comedy about sex and life in the Yorkshire city of Bradford. Orion Classics should have another hit with this gem, if they can avoid an X rating.

Rita and Sue are two schoolgirls who sometimes babysit for a well-off couple, Bob and Michelle. In the film's opening sequence, the odious yet somehow charming Bob, a real-estate agent, gives the girls a lift home, but stops off first on the moors above the city and without preliminaries, proposes sex with them. The girls are agreeable, with Sue taking the first turn on the reclining seat in Bob's Rover.

Immediately screenwriter Andrea Dunbar injects a completely convincing mixture of raunchy comedy and sadness. The girls, with their dry Yorkshire humor, exchange cheerful wisecracks about the situation, describing Bob's member as being comparable to "a frozen sausage," and showing concern for each other's welfare ("Is that all she's getting?" asks Rita when Bob and Sue have finished). Bob is supremely self-confident, but sadly the girls seem to find this joyless, uncomfortable illicit sex perfectly acceptable.

They continue to meet secretly with Bob until Michelle gets suspicious after finding a packet of condoms in her husband's trousers. Bob denies any wrongdoing, and the girls express innocence, but when one of Michelle's friends spots the three dancing together at a local disco, Michelle's patience is at an end (the ensuing row amusingly involves the entire neighborhood).

Meanwhile Rita has been complaining that, in their sessions with Bob, Sue always gets to go first, leaving Bob without as much stamina for her. Eventually she starts seeing Bob without her friend, and gets pregnant. Michelle leaves her husband, and Rita moves in with Bob, to the annoyance of Sue, who rejects Bob's suggestion that he can still keep seeing her. She moves in with Aslam, a Pakistani, but it's none too satisfactory, since his sister speaks no English and won't let them share the same bed. After Rita miscarries, the girls decide to get together again, with Bob joining them in a cheerful *ménage à trois*.

It comes as a surprise to discover that Dunbar's marvelous screenplay, with its rich vein of North Country humor, is based on two stage plays; there's nothing in the least stagey about the film. Dunbar herself comes from the same Bradford housing estate where the story is set, and the film obviously is derived from firsthand observation, filtered with a great sense of humor.

Even while audiences will laugh at the hilarious situations and dialog (spoken in easily understood Yorkshire dialect), they'll be moved by the plight of these people.

The girls both live in terrible conditions. Sue's drunken father (a painfully real performance from Willie Ross) hasn't worked in years, and can hardly communicate any more, while her bitter, aggressive mother can only abuse him. Rita lives in a filthy building on what obviously was once a prestige post-war housing estate. The Pakistanis live in even worse conditions, and are subjected to daily racism, especially from the generation of the girls' parents. The school is overcrowded and undisciplined, unemployment is rampant, and there's little to do except to have "a good time" via sex with married men.

Rita and Sue, splendidly played by Siobhan Finneran and Michelle Holmes, are pathetic figures as they trip along in their tight miniskirts, but they're lively and funny. George Costigan makes Bob a charming character, despite his ingrained seediness.

Director Alan Clarke, who made "Scum" some years ago, directs with skill, and cameraman Ivan Strasburg ensures the film is fluidly shot with fine use of Steadicam. The music score's another asset, and technically pic is fine.

The dialog is relentlessly raunchy, with constant use of four-letter words and a completely uninhibited attitude to all things sexual, though nudity is almost nonexistent (Bob's bottom is the only exception). Though at first audiences may find the occasional use of slang a problem, it soon will become obvious what 'having a jump'' means.

This one's in the finest tradition of British realist cinema, and is a credit to all concerned. It won't be a film for everyone, but it should pack in discriminating audiences, given the right handling and promotion. —Strat.

Uni To Dokuyaku
(The Sea And Poison)
(JAPANESE-B&W)

A Nippon Herald release of a Sea and Poison Committee production. Produced by Kanou Otsuka, Takayoshi Miyagawa. Executive producer, Keiichiro Takishima. Directed by Kei Kumai. Screenplay, Simsako Endo, from his novel; camera (b&w), Masao Tochizawa; editor, Osamu Inoue; music, Teizo Matsumura; production design, Takeo Kimura; sound, Yakio Kubota; assistant director, Yoshihiro Takane. Reviewed at Berlin Film Festival (Competition), Feb. 23, 1987. Running time: **121 MINS.**
Suguro ....Hiji Oknda
Toda ....Ken Watanabe
Shibata ....Mikio Narita
Asai.......................Ken Nishida
Gondo...............Shigeru Kamiyama
Hattori (Investigator) .....Masumi Okada
Also with: Kyoko Kishida (Old woman), Kie Nigishi (Ueda), Hiroshi Kusano (Tanaka), Rancho Tsuji (Mural), Masatane Tsugayama

(Miyasaki), Yuimi Kuroki (Mrs. Tabe), Akiko Togawa (Her mother), Mariko Oishi (Her sister), Maria Watanabe (Hilda), Eagle Galley (American prisoner).

Berlin — One of the most harrowing films in memory, Kei Kumai's "The Sea And Poison" is a searing account of one of the great horror stories of World War II. Based on a novel written in 1948, the film is set in 1945 in the University Hospital at Kyushu. Here two rival surgical teams are carrying out operations under difficult conditions, lacking research facilities they consider vital. Quite early in the film, one team decides to operate on the lungs of the niece of an influential figure within the University. It's the first of two agonizingly real operating sequences.

When the patient dies on the operating table, the surgeon's team agrees to cover up the death and to pretend the patient died post-operatively. It's a decision that sets the stage for a later, and far more devastating decision: to operate on eight healthy Americans, captured B-29 crewmen, in a deliberate surgical experiment which results in the deaths of all the victims.

Director Kei Kumai, who has always been interested in making films about social issues, has wanted to film this grim tale since 1960. The resulting film will leave no viewer unaffected. Though stately in pace, and lacking the visual elan of the greatest Japanese films, "The Sea And Poison" is tremendously powerful.

The operating scenes, especially the first one, are presented with utmost realism; visually and, just as important, aurally, nothing is left to the imagination. Despite a warning before the screening in Berlin, quite a few members of the audience ankled during this sequence.

Obviously this is not a film for the faint-hearted, and it's interesting to find a Japanese film which unflinchingly presents hospital staff and senior military officers as monsters who partake in the heinous crime of vivisection: in the second operation scene, on a fresh-faced young airman from California, military staff are present, ghoulishly taking photographs. After the young man's death, they order the surgeons to remove his liver which they propose to eat at a drunken, celebratory dinner.

Audiences for this horror story will be limited, but there's no denying the honesty or the skill of the film, and Kumei is to be commended for his lengthy battle to tell this terrible story on film. Acting is fine down the line, and technical credits are well up to the usual high Japanese standards. —Strat.

So viele Träume
(So Many Dreams)
(EAST GERMAN-COLOR)

A Defa Aussenhandel release of a Defa-Studio with Gruppe Babelsberg production. Directed by Heiner Carow. Screenplay, Carow, Wolfram Witt, based on documentary material collected by Imma Lüning; dramaturgic collaboration, Erika Richter; camera (Orwocolor), Peter Ziesche; editor, Evelyn Carow; music, Stefan Carow; production design, Christopher Schneider; costumes, Regina Viertel; production management, Ralph Retzlaff; assistant director, Hanna Seydel. Reviewed at Berlin Film Festival (Competition), Feb. 28, 1987. Running time: **82 MINS.**
Christine Klüver ....Jutta Wachowiak
Ludwig Grabner ......Peter René Lüdicke
Claudia Seydel ....Dagmar Manzel
Gunnar Klüver ....Heiko Hehlman
Also with: Thomas Hinrich, Gudron Okras, Christine Harbort.

Berlin — "So Many Dreams" is the third (but independent) feature in East German writer-director Heiner Carow's trilogy of portraits of women who achieve independence in the present-day world. It is also a tawdry, old-fashioned melodrama with sylistic and narrative cliches brought down from sundry cinematic attics. Filming in lusterless Orwocolor blows away no dust from the proceedings either.

Jutta Wachowiak, whose strong and intelligent face and acting makes her a solitary standout in an otherwise dull cast, plays Christine, a midwife about to receive a medal for having brought 6,400 babies into the world when her own, carefully built world starts collapsing.

Christine lives in harmony with a deaf-mute son and a young musician-lover and has completely put behind her the facts of a divorce in which she let a no-good husband get custody of their daughter Claudia. On the day of the party for the medal, Claudia turns up and immediately starts accusing Christine of being the cause for the wayward life she herself has led.

What follows are long and dry sequences of talking-into-their-wine monologs by the two women, who proceed alternately to scream at each other, fall into each other's arms, scream again, then do a wild whirl of dancing together, while people around them mostly mope or gape.

A long dream sequence at film's beginning is film school aping of Fellini and later flashback bits have Christine looking exactly as she does today only wearing yesteryear's fashions. As Claudia, Dagmar Manzel is either shrill or looking deadly bored. —Kell.

Du Mich Auch
(So What?)
(W. GERMAN-SWISS-B&W)

A Känguruh Filmproduktion (Berlin)-Filmkollektiv (Zurich) coproduction. (World

sales, Metropolis Film.) Executive producer, Ingrid Winkler. Directed by Helmut Berger. Screenplay, Berger, Anja Franke, Dani Levy; camera (b&w), Carl Friedrich Koschnick; music, Nicki Reiser, production design, Marion Strohschein; sound, Andreas Klein, Slavko Hitrov; production manager, Priska Forter. Reviewed at Berlin Film Festival (Out of Competition), Feb. 21, 1987. Running time: **90 MINS.**
Julia ....Anja Franke
Romeo ....Dani Levy
Gigolo ....Jens Naumann
Romeo's father ....Mathias Gnädinger
Romeo's mother ....Regine Lutz
Madame ....Helma Fehrmann
Sunshine ....Karleen Rutherford
Also with: Michael Kesting (Small bodyguard), Hans-Eckart Eckhardt (Big bodyguard), Gerd Jessat (Senator), Ruth Fahlke (Woman in bath).

Berlin — Here's a lively, entertaining feature which has something of the feel of "Diva" about it, but without the smooth visuals of the Jean-Jacques Beineix film. This modest black & whiter is technically a bit rough round the edges, but full of charm despite that.

It's a first feature for Helmut Berger (not the actor), who wrote it together with his engaging leads, Anja Franke and Dani Levy. The team exudes youthful elan and brio, and communicates to the audience a sense of fun and eccentricity, allied to a bizarre thriller plot which takes its characters all over Berlin in summer.

Julia, a sax player, met Romeo, a Swiss guitarist, when they were playing on the same street corner. It was love at first sight, and they moved in together, but now the quarrels have begun and one morning Romeo ankles leaving behind a disconsolate Julia. He heads for a very seedy brothel, and has an unsuccessful session with a statuesque black prostie, but returns to play one last gig with Julia — at a golden wedding party for the smart set.

During the party, where Julia insists on telling a funny off-color joke, to the alarm of the guests, Romeo spots a man he'd seen hand in a large sum of money at the brothel; seems the man is a member of the Berlin Senate. Then the lights go out, and when they go on again there's a body at Romeo's feet with a knife in it. From then on the chase begins with the couple on the run from the cops and from the killers.

Along the way they meet some wonderfully eccentric characters, such as an old woman having a bath who conceals her presence at first when they go to a toilet for a talk; or a strange man in an elevator who keeps whistling tunelessly, or another character who's locked himself in his own apartment and can't get out.

They take time off for a dinner at the home of Romeo's stuffy parents, where Julia has an hilarious laughing fit with her mouth full, but later danger reasserts itself when the bddies catch up with them and Julia is kidnaped and taken to the brothel where Romeo has to effect a rescue. There's a strange, poetic ending.

Anja Franke is a charming young actress with a pouting style and eccentric ways. She's well partnered by the droll Dani Levy, a sad-sack hero of resourcefulness and wit. They make an offbeat romantic team, but they obviously had fun making the film, and the fun is communicated to the audience. Director Berger makes sure the action never flags, that the laughs (and, to a degree, the thrills) keep coming. Probably the film's commercial chances will be limited by its black & white camerawork, but fests looking for original, light-hearted fare, from a talented new team, should grab the pic and art house chances should follow as a result. —*Strat.*

Meier
(WEST GERMAN-COLOR)

A production of Pro-ject Filmproduction im Filmverlag der Autoren, Munich, in coproduction with Popular Film, Hans H. Kaden and Maran Film, Stuttgart. Written and directed by Peter Timm. Camera (color), Klaus Eichhammer; editor, Corinna Dietz, sound, Jochen Schwarzat; art direction, Martin Dostal, costumes, Petra Kranz. Reviewed at the Berlin Film Festival (Market), Feb. 22, 1987. Running time: **95 MINS.**

Meier . . . . Rainer Grenkowitz
Lore . . . . Nadja Engelbrecht
Kalle . . . . Alexander Hauff
Erwin . . . . Thomas Bestvater
Klausi . . . . René Grams
Escape Organizer . . . . Joachim Kemmer
Waiter . . . . Dieter Hildebrandt

Berlin — "Meier" is an amusing well-done comedy that probably won't travel well. Much of the humor depends on the irony of the two Germanies, especially East and West Berlin.

Meier (Rainer Grenkowitz) is an East Berlin wallpaper hanger who with a small inheritance from a Western relative dreams of a world tour. To do this he must defect and through an illegal organization arranges to get all the false I.D. and tickets he needs. Comic complications arise when he tries to return only to discover that with his new passport he can only make daily visits to his old life and must leave East Berlin every evening with the other day tourists.

Much of the humor hinges on Meier's trips back and forth between East and West. His girlfriend (Nadga Engelbrecht) suspects a rival and the border crossing guards start to give him a hard time. To make matters worse the communists plan to honor him as a "working class hero" for his increased productivity at work.

This amiable film has a good supporting cast and for those who are up on relations between the two halves of the divided city there are gem-like moments capturing the in-

anity and frustration fostered by the infamous wall. Professional work by all concerned. —*Owl.*

Francesca
(WEST GERMAN-COLOR-16m)

A Heide Breitel Films production in conjunction with Verena Rudolph and ZDF TV. Executive producers, Heide Breitel, Renee Gundelach. Produced by Elke Peters. Written and directed by Verena Rudolph. Camera (color, 16m), Eberhard Geick; editor, Susann Lahaye; music, Fulvio Di Stafano, Leopoldo Sanfelice; sound, Nana Gravesen, Petra Buda; art direction, Mario-Angela Capuano, Hans Thiemann; set direction, Nazzareno Scolacchia; assistant director, Juliane Geick. Reviewed at Berlin Film Festival (Market), Feb. 27, 1987. Running time: **93 MINS.**

Countess . . . . Eva Lissa
Cook . . . . Dorothea Neff
Grujinski . . . . Bernhard Wosien
Dolly . . . . Dolly Worzbach
Olga . . . . Olga von Togni
Matisti . . . . Karl Dönch
Anita Meyer . . . . Ruth Drexel
   Also with: Pietro Tordi (Giacomo), Gina Rovere (Elena), Tito Le Duc (transvestite), Barbara Herrera (Mamma Lupa), Alessandra Vazzoler (silent film star), Arnaldo Colombaioni (clown), Fulvio Di Stafano (accordion player), the Big Vanity Sisters, Marianne Hoppe, Bernhard Minetti and the Sisters of St. Mary's Convent in Niederviehbach, Bavaria, with Mother Superior Roswitha Schneider.

Berlin — "Francesca," a tongue-in-cheek, lyrical look at how myths are made, is an impressive first feature by 35-year-old Verena Rudolph. Film, which took top honors in Max Ophüls competition in January, is a very hot item, as is Rudolph. Commercial prospects for this pair are unlimited.

Rudolph's film takes on almost a documentary quality by observing 80th birthday commemorations in Germany and Italy for Francesca Aramonte, legendary star of German stage and screen in the 1920s and 1930s, later leading lady in Federico Fellini's "Francesca degli Angeli" (sic). Raised by nuns in Bavaria, she ran off with a traveling circus. A mystic who converses with angels, Francesca is the patron saint of a small mountain village in rocky, Southern Italy, where villagers pray to her for rain and protection from earthquakes.

Rudolph produces an array of aging German and Italian thesps, plus impromptu appearances by people with no acting experience, to give witness to the sometimes mundane, sometimes extraordinary accomplishments of Francesca, whom they loved, worshipped — or hated.

Of course, there is no Francesca Aramonte and never was. She is only a legend. The point Rudolph is making is that legend-building and myth-making are essential to human nature, and that myths say more about the people who made them up than they do about the figures behind the myths.

Personal highlight of film comes early on, at a Bavarian convent,

where ancient nuns (all of them genuine) recall the young orphan Francesca. In an endearing scene, the elderly sisters busily iron and fold linens while arguing about a miracle involving Francesca, a tree and a bolt of lightning. Those not involved in the squabble giggle knowingly to each other, enjoying the scene their sisters are putting on.

There's the interview with a countess (with stately Eva Lissa perfectly cast in the role), who tells of seeking to conceal the infant Francesca from the count, then giving her up to the convent. Countess holds a birthday celebration for Francesca, attended by such German stars of yesteryear as Marianne Hoppe and Bernhard Minetti. Fact is intertwined with fantasy as, for example, Hoppe speaks of her years on the stage with Francesca. Hoppe, real-life second wife of Gustaf Gründgens (model for the central figure in novel and film "Mephisto"), is very convincing.

Dreamlike quality of film reaches its peak in Italy, where Rudolph engaged Cinecittà character actors from Fellini films, gave them a script outline and turned them loose to improvise on the theme of a mock birthday celebration for their supposed former coworker Francesca. Separating fact from fancy becomes impossible as these eccentric old hands swap tales about Francesca, Fellini and life in general.

Film ends on mystical note with black-garbed peasant women in a remote Italian village relating wondrous legends about their own "Francesca degli angeli," and chanting her praises.

Technical credits are more than adequate, despite limitations of 16m format. Excellent camerawork under direction of Eberhard Geick holds audience interest even during extended talky sections.

Film is sure of b.o. success in Germany, with excellent export prospects, especially because of Fellini link. —*Gill.*

Quiet Days In Sommières
(WEST GERMAN-DOCU-COLOR)

An Aspekt/Telefilm-Prod. (Hamburg) production. Written and directed by Peter Leippe; camera (Eastmancolor, 16m) René Perraudin, Rainer Borgman, Werner Nitschke; editor, Leippe; music, Maurice Ravel excerpts; sound, Erich Lutz. Reviewed at Berlin Film Festival (Panorama), Feb. 27, 1987. Running time: **80 MINS.**

With: Lawrence Durrell, Chili Hawes.

Berlin — West German film documentarist Peter Leippe has made fine tv marks for himself with "Isak Dinesen's African Dream" (1985) and "The Civil War" (1987). Some limited, but worldwide cinema exposure plus tv sales may be predicted for his "Quiet Days In

Sommières," in which he has a striking-looking young American gallery owner (Chili Hawes as herself) go to the French Provençal city of the title to spend a couple of weeks in early summer of 1986 eating, drinking, strolling, browsing through old photos, talking and going to bloodless bullfights with British novelist Lawrence Durrell, who wrote "The Alexandria Quartet."

Durrell, who turned 75 the day of this film's world preem at the Berlin fest, is wary at first of his visitor's intentions. It seems she wanted to do a show of what he calls his "Sunday Paintings" (done under the pseudonym Oscar Epf, who employs deft and color-happy Impressionistic strokes), but then she found out about his identity and, knowing and admiring his literary oeuvre, she enlisted Leippe to turn her visit into this docu-interview film.

Film is without great literary pretense on the part of the interviewer. Soon accepted as Durrell's friend, the rather small man with the twinkling blue eyes and the grey hair takes her by the hand and shows her the pleasures of landscapes, cityscapes and friendships of his chosen widower's retirement terrain. He also takes her back to his days as a Foreign Office press officer-cum-author in Greece, Egypt and Yugoslavia.

He comments loyally yet lucidly and candidly on his two wives and on his father, mother and brother Gerald as well as on fellow writers and good friends Dylan Thomas and Henry Miller (it is latter's "Quiet Days In Clichy" that has inspired this docu's title). Durrell is mellow throughout, keeping his comments to the point while quite obviously enjoying his company and having fun remembering and musing aloud on matters small and big.

Often, "Quiet Days In Sommières" has the look and feel of very private persons being observed without their knowledge, but still there is no inkling of prying and, however candid, Durrell always keep discreet about essentials. Hemingway once said that "it is always a mistake to know an author" (personally). Maybe so, but then Lawrence Durrell comes through here as a happy exception.—*Kell.*

Konbu Finze
(The Terrorizers)
(TAIWANESE-COLOR)

A Central Motion Picture Corp. production. Produced by Hsu Kuo-Liang. Directed by Edward Yang. Screenplay, Yang, Sheau Yee; camera (color), Chang Yian; editor, Liao Ching Sung; art director, Lai Ming-Tang. Reviewed at Berlin Film Festival (Market), Feb. 26, 1987. Running time: **112 MINS.**

With: Miaw Chian-Ren, Lee Lih-Chuyn, Jin Shyh-Jye, Wang Ann.

Berlin — Withdrawn at the last moment from the Berlin Forum program and due to unspool later this year, in Cannes' Un Certain Regard section, Edward Yang's third feature film is a complex and intricate drama, running on three parallel lines which finally converge through accidental circumstances, affecting the lives of all the people involved, complete strangers to each other.

First, there is a couple, a physician and a writer whose marriage is on the rocks. On a second level, there is a young amateur photographer who witnesses by chance a police raid on the hideout of several young hoodlums, in which one of the hoodlums is shot to death, another one is captured while a third member, a teenage girl, manages to escape with a sprained ankle.

There is nothing in common among all these people, each concerned exclusively with his very private world. The doctor is trying to manipulate himself into a promotion at the hospital after the sudden death of his immediate superior. His wife goes through an acute creativity crisis, feels her world shrinking around her, thinks of going back to work and renews an affair with a former lover. The photographer is entranced by the face of the mysterious girl he has photographed. He blows up her pictures and spreads them all over his flat, to the despair of his girl friend, and finally he even moves into the place in which the gang was trapped. As for the injured girl, her mother picks her up from the hospital, brings her back home, and locks her in her room. Out of boredom, she calls people at random on the phone, among them the doctor's home. She talks with his wife, implies she might have an affair with her husband and hangs up, leaving at the other end of the line a woman whose previous doubts about her marriage have been confirmed, in a way, by the anonymous conversation.

The plot develops into that of thriller, as the audience is kept wondering how the three separate stories are going to meet, with definite threats of violence implied in the later part.

Yang is in complete control of his material at every stage. The city, and life within its confines, is kept constantly in the background, glanced at through windows, or supplying the location for many of the scenes. Very stylized direction often uses sound to introduce a scene, long before it materializes visually on the screen, and there is subtle use of camera angles and color to create specific climates for every scene. Dialog is kept at a functional minimum.

This is by no means a film for a lazy audience. Empty frames, sounds that aren't always connected to the image, separate plots whose coexistence on the screen takes some time to make sense, constitute the kind of puzzle film buffs are sure to enjoy. The interdependence of characters who believe they are in absolute control of their destinies is remarkably well profiled, and Taipei is revealed both in its modern, shining new structures, and the underbelly of its slums.
—*Edna*.

Um Filme 100% Brazileiro
(A 100% Brazilian Film)
(BRAZILIAN-COLOR)

An Embrafilme-Grupo Novo de Cinema production. Produced by Tarcisio Vidigal. Directed by José Sette. Screenplay, Sette based on a work by Blaise Cendrars; camera (color), José de Barros; editor. José Tavares de Barros, Amauri Alves; music, Luiz Eça; production design, Mario Drummond, Fernando Tavares; sound, Licio Marcos. Reviewed at Berlin Film Festival (Forum), Feb. 28, 1987. Running time: **80 MINS.**
With: Paulo Cesar Pereiro, Odete Lara, Maria Gladys, Guara Rodrigues, Savero Roppa, Luiza Clotilde, Wilson Grey, Kimura Schettino, Jesus Pingo.

Berlin — This wild, chaotic film aptly expresses the mood of Rio during carnival time, though it will be too rich and strange for the taste of most audiences. Director José Sette combines the visits of two foreigners to Brazil, visits made more than 60 years apart.

In 1924, during the Modernist period of art, Frenchman Blaise Cendrars arrived during the carnival. His impressions are intertwined with those of a contemporary poet, who views the city and the carnival from the perspective of the mid-'80s.

What follows is barely coherent, but a series of set-pieces, sexual encounters, moments of comedy and violence, all swamped in color and music. It will be exhilarating, or infuriating, according to the point of view of the individual.

There are relatively frank sex scenes in which the poets shack up in a hotel room with beautiful Brazilian girls. There's a satanic figure, given to making dramatic speeches. There are anecdotes from Brazil's past, such as the story of a man who ordered the castration of his rival, or a romantic story of a landowner who fell for a pretty girl, or a sad tale of a young homosexual, imprisoned under a turn-of-the-century law.

Sette plunges the viewer from one exotic scene into the next, filling his film with visual and literary references which will be lost on many. There's no denying the brash energy and anarchic glee with which this strange, slapdash pic has been made, and it could have cult appeal if properly handled. —*Strat*.

Leptomeria Styn Kypro
(A Detail In Cyprus)
(CYPRIOT-COLOR)

A Tanion production. Produced by Symvoulion Paragogis. Written and directed by Panikkos Chrysanthou. Camera (color), Andras Gerö; editor, Antonis Tempos; music, Michael Christodoulides; sound, Antonakis Christoforides, Dinos Kittou. Reviewed at Berlin Film Festival (Panorama), Feb. 26, 1987. Running time: **67 MINS.**
With: Marina Kittou (Mother), Electra Chrysanthou (Daughter) Michael Stavri, Chrystalla Loizou, Mahan Halil, Nicolas Paphitis, Cristina Nichola, Loizos Koukoufkiaos.

Berlin — More documentary than fiction, this modest film is a poetic lament for the destruction of a way of life on the island of Cyprus, a world destroyed in 1964 when Greeks and Turks fought out longstanding enmities and the island was divided by a so-called "Green Line."

First-time director Panikkos Chrysanthou, a Greek-Cypriot, takes his camera back to the village where his family and friends once lived, and which is now deserted and ruined. The camera lingers over once-beautiful Byzantine and Venetian frescoes in the ruined church, and the remains of houses, shops and cafes, while former villagers describe how their way of life was abruptly ended.

A poetic commentary adds a further touch of pathos to this sad little pic, which is more likely to find an outlet on tv than in theaters. It's a quietly effective item, despite its tiny scale. The print caught in Berlin was barely adequate, however.
—*Strat*.

Konzert für die Rechte Hand
(Concerto For The Right Hand)
(WEST GERMAN-COLOR-16m)

An Igelfilm release of a Michael Bartlett Films production. Produced by Albrecht Gmelin, Heinz Deddens. Written and directed by Bartlett; camera (color, 16m), Gerhard Friedrich, Peter Kramm, Klaus Krieger; editor, Gaby Bartels, Bartlett; music, Lothar Mankewitz, Fernando Lafferriere; sound, Hans Martin; orchestra direction, Jens Holzkamp and members of the Berlin Radio Symphony Orchestra. Reviewed at Berlin Film Festival (New German Film series), March 1, 1987. Running time: **79 MINS.**
Sanitation worker . . . . Miklós Königer
Boutique owner . . . . Henry Akina
The Hand and waitress . . . . . Sushila Day
Accordionist . . . . Ivo Kviring
"Lady" in shop . . . . Kio
Pastor and bartender . . . Calvin Mackerron

Berlin — American-born Michael Bartlett has produced a bizarre and highly imaginative look at masculine and feminine human characteristics in "Konzert für die Rechte Hand" (Concert For The Right Hand). Film is well suited for fest circuit and special outlets. Skimpy dialog reduces the German lingo hassle.

Film's dreamlike (some might say nightmarish) plot centers on the lonely lives of two West Berlin men. One, a sanitation worker in a park full of nude sunbathers, stumbles onto a female mannequin, which he stashes in a trash bag and scuttles off with to his dreary basement apartment. On the way, mannequin's right arm falls out of the bag and is retrieved by an effeminate boutique owner who has no right arm. He scuttles off, too and once back in his swell pad, puts on the feminine arm, which comes to life.

The park worker (with forlorn-looking Miklós Königer well cast in role) traces the missing arm of his fiberglass fiancée to the boutique owner (Henry Akina). Ensuing struggle results in the park worker losing his own right arm to the boutique owner, who, now fully masculine, marries the mannequin.

Bartlett, who plays viola with the Berlin Philharmonic and the Berlin Radio Symphony, incorporates musical metaphors into the film to underscore his point about masculine and feminine expression.

Tongue planted firmly in cheek, Bartlett intrigues his audience with ambisexual symbolism. Hardly a scene goes by that does not include a hand (billboards, statues, etc.) or some erotic element.

Technical credits are above average, though 16m print used in Berlin screenings was much the worse for wear.

Classical chamber music, primarily by Mozart, dominates bulk of film, which has virtually no dialog.
—*Gill*.

Crazy Love
(BELGIAN-COLOR)

A Multimedia production in cooperation with the Ministries of Culture of the Flemish and French Communities. Produced by Erwin Provoost, Alain Keytsman. Directed by Dominique Deruddere. Screenplay, Marc Didden, Deruddere based on "The Copulating Mermaids Of Venice, California" and other material by Charles Bukowski; camera (Eastmancolor), Willy Stassen; editor, Ludo Troch, Guido Henderickx; music, Raymond Van Het Groenewoud; sound, Peter Flamman; art directors, Hubert Pouille, Erik Van Belleghem. Reviewed at the Berlin Film Festival (Panorama), March 3, 1987. Running time: **90 MINS.**
Harry Voss . . . . Josse De Pauw
Harry Voss (age 12) . . . . . . Geert Hunaerts
Stan . . . . Michael Pas
Jeff . . . . Gene Bervoerts
Bill . . . . Amid Chakir
Also with: Florence Béliard, Karen Vanparys, Carmela Locantore, An Van Essche, Doriane Moretus.

Berlin — A Charles Bukowski adaptation naturally suggests an orgy of perversions brought up from the dark recesses of the human mind out into broad daylight, but it is also a tremendous challenge that very few would dare to tackle.

If Dominique Deruddere hasn't entirely succeeded in his endeavor, he has certainly gone about it in a clever way, sticking to Bukowski's spirit rather than to the letter of the text, and building up an introduction which prepares, explains and to a certain extent justifies the extreme acts of necrophilia, in the last episode. The film consists of three such episodes, in which the degree of freakishness is gradually increased, from what could be considered average adolescent sexual pranks and rites of initiation, in the first episode, to high-school sexual confusion in the second one, and finally to desperate ghoulishness, in the last one, the only one indebted directly to Bukowski.

Deruddere takes his hero, Harry Voss, through a period of 21 years, from 1955 to 1962 and then to 1976. First, he is an innocent 12-year-old, dreaming of romantic love, convinced his father has eloped with his mother after vanquishing his competitors for her hand in fair fight. He is initiated by an older pal into the secrets of physical love, the desire involved which he abhors and adores at the same time, and he learns there is no impulse stronger in human nature than the sexual one.

Next, he is 19, suffering from the most horrific case of acne ever displayed on screen, in love desperately with the queen of the class, and terrified of approaching her or indeed, of leaving his home. His appearance throws off even the most determined nympho who had been set up for him by a friend, and only when he covers his face with toilet paper, does the object of his desires consent to grant him a dance, but not more.

The third episode, and the first to be shot, has the look of a typical horror movie, in the lighting, the sets and the makeup of the two leading characters. The boils are gone from Harry's face, but he is still far from handsome, and drink is the only medicine capable to lift his spirits. After a drunken bout with a friend, they steal a corpse on its way from the hospital to the mortuary, and when they unwrap it, they discover the dead body of a young girl. After copulating with it, they both reach the conclusion she was the greatest woman they ever had. At this stage there is no evading the Bukowski excessiveness, but Deruddere's preparatory work has made it clear that it is not lust, but real passion, which causes them to act this way.

This is not an easy subject to take. Deruddere managers to put some soul in his portrayal of necrophiliacs, and even if they remain unacceptable, at least they can be considered victims less than criminals. Thus, significantly, the corpse is played by the same actress incorporating romantic live in the first episode.

The first episode may be a little too familiar, after so many films on adolescents discovering sex, but the second episode is already less so, and the third touches new territory.—*Edna.*

A Cor Do Seu Destino
(The Color Of Destiny)
(BRAZILIAN-COLOR)

An Embrafilme presentation of Nativa Filmes production. Produced and directed by Jorge Durán. Screenplay, Nelson Natotti, Durán, Jose Joffily based on story by Durán; camera (Eastmancolor), José Tadeu Ribeiro; editor, Dominique Paris; sets, Clóvis Bueno; music, David Tygel. Reviewed in the Berlin Film Festival (Panorama), Feb. 20, 1987. Running time: **104 MINS.**
Paulo . . . . Guilherme Fontes
Laura . . . . Norma Bengel
Victor . . . . Franklin Caicedo
Patricia . . . . Julia Lemmertz
Helena . . . . Andréa Beltrão
Also with: Chico Diaz, Antonio Grassi, Anderson Schereiber, Antonio Ameijeiras, Marcos Palmeira, Paulinho Mosca, Anderson Müller, Duda Monteiro.

Berlin — A scriptwriter who has worked with some of the top talents in Brazilian cinema, Jorge Durán has chosen for his first solo flight as writer-producer-director a subject that is particularly close to his heart, about Chilean refugees forced by political circumstances out of their own country, after the Pinochet takeover, and now living in Brazil.

A refugee himself and close to their problems, this is obviously a personal statement as seen from within, which could find its echoes, however, in all other communities of expatriates, wherever they may be. Duran tries to deal with the problems of these people on several levels and manages to do it quite convincingly.

The central character is Paulo, the 18 year-old son of a refugee family, pursued constantly by the remembered image of his older brother arrested back in Chile in the most brutal manner. It's the kind of memory he cannot deal with and which he tries to sublimate through his intense fascination with plastic arts, with forms and colors, closely connected to the nightmares visiting him constantly.

This young man is not only at odds with his parents who have their own problems dealing with the past, but also with other young persons of his own age, all of them Brazilians who were never forced to face the circumstances he was in, and are as indifferent to politics and as concerned with trifles as any youth in the West can be expected to be.

The personal crisis of the young man is increased even more by the arrival of a female cousin, his own age, just released from Chilean jail and its own brand of treatment, after taking part in demonstrations against the regime. Paulo is torn between the emotional involvement but also the political one, offered by the character of his cousin, and the easy-going insouciance of his regular pals.

All these aspects, combined with memories from the past, flights of fantasy and a lot of visual inventions keep the story going.

Acting is on the whole convincing, especially that of Guilherme Fontes, as Paulo, the introvert teenager looking for answers, Norma Bengel as his mother, Chilean actor Franklin Caicedo as his father, as well as Julia Lemmertz as the young cousin arrived from Santiago. Cameraman José Tadeu Ribeiro does credit to the many shape and color experiments in which the film indulges, to good effect.—*Edna.*

Sashshennyi Fonar
(The Lit Lantern)
(RUSSIAN-COLOR)

A Mosfilm presentation of an Armenfilm, Studio A, Bek-Nasarian production. Written and directed by Agassi Aivasian. Camera (color), Levon Atoyanz; editor, I. Mikaelian; music, Tigran Mansurian; sound, Eduard Vanunz; art direction, Grigor Torosian, W. Panosian; costumes, S. Tonoian. Reviewed at the Berlin Film Festival (Forum), Feb. 26, 1987. Running time: **88 MINS.**
Vano . . . . Vladimir Kotscharian
Vera . . . . Violetta Geworkian
Merktum . . . . Absalom Loria
Gasparelli . . . . Leonid Sarkisov
Also with: Genrich Alaverdían, Karlos Martirosian, Manvel Dawlabetkian, Aschot Chudaverdian, J. Jasulowitsch, T. Semina, J. Grabbe, A. Belliawski, M. Gluski, V. Ferapontov.

Berlin — The Armenian cinema is showcased well in this charming, lyrical film.

A painter who at the age of 62 is signing only his second feature film, Agassi Aivasian has the keen eye of naive artists marveling at every aspect of the world and transmits his awe and enthusiasm in images of rare beauty infused with deep love for man and nature. From the opening shots showing first one flute player, then more and more filling up the narrow cobbled streets of Tiflis with the sound of their instruments, the nature of the film is evident, and Aivasian keeps it at a consistently high level.

Vano Chodshabekov is a naive painter who tends shop for a rich man, Merktum, but his mind is only on drawing everything he sees around him, with a keen, observing eye, to the despair of his wife who has to keep the household going on her own. Loved and admired by the simple people, he is told by one of them, a lantern lighter who is also a poet, that he has been given the magic ladder and it is his duty to climb up for only very few have been blessed with such a gift.

Merktum, however, is less impressed with art, and fires Vano for mismanaging the shop, and the shamed artist is afraid to go home to face his wife's anger and disappointment. Finally he decides, with some help from his friends, to appease Merktum's wrath by presenting him with a painting, the first he has ever done in color.

The presentation of the gift is one of the most delightful scenes in the entire film, as each member of the two families breathlessly waits to see how the gift will be accepted. Vano does get his shop back for a short while, but it is taken from him again, poverty being somehow the natural condition for a dedicated artist, whose compensation is that his soul is free, the greatest treasure of them all.

Aivasian's simple, poetic film statements are a pleasure to watch, whether he presents the townfolk in brief inserts, or draws a beautiful allegory of the artist's soul escaping from its chains. The closeness of man to nature, the respect of elementary individual rights, the joy of living and the hymn to life glow from every frame of this picture and from every actor's face.

Music plays a major role at every stage of this film, the blending of folk sounds with sweeping romanticism supplying solid support for the visuals. As for the cameraman, he must have a true artist's eye both for color and construction of frames. Produced in 1983, but reaching the West for the first time, it should be able to generate interest in spite of the fact that it has very little to do with politics, the one topic everybody seems to be looking for, lately, in Soviet production.—*Edna.*

Unfinished Business...
(U.S.-COLOR)

An American Film Institute (Directing Workshop) production. Produced by Annie Wells, Walter Hart, Gwendolyn Howard. Written and directed by Viveca Lindfors. Stars Lindfors. Camera (color), Sean McLin; editor, Dale Ann Stieber; music, Patricia Lee Stotter; sound, Davoud Ismaili; production design, Johanna Leovey; costumes, Marty Rodenbush; assistant director, Paul Small. Reviewed at Berlin Film Fest (Panorama), Feb. 21, 1987. Running time: **65 MINS.**
Helena . . . . Viveca Lindfors
Ferenzy . . . . Peter Donat
Vickie . . . . Gina Hecht
Jonathan . . . . James Morrison
Anna . . . . Anna Devere Smith
Kristina . . . . Haley Taylor-Block
Also with: Herriett Guiar (Cynthia), James Ward (Chauffeur), Chuck Cochran (Manager).

Berlin — Actress Viveca Lindfors turns to direction with this modestly-made but penetrating drama of family relationships. Clearly a personal film about people she knows intimately, the writer-director seems to be exorcising some personal demons via the film.

She plays Helena, a theater director (specializing in Brecht) who lives alone after her Hungarian-born husband, Ferenzy (Peter Donat) left her 15 years earlier. Now he returns for a theater festival and the couple, together with Helena's son and his wife, reopen the past and still-festering old wounds.

It's a drama filled with talk, but it's well written ("Im so sick and tired of theatrical moments in my own life," says James Morrison, as the son, Jonathan, at one point) and ultimately very tender. Conversations reveal that Helena and Ferenzy had first met the very day Jonathan was born, and also that Jonathan had met his German wife (Gina Hecht) when she was his step-father's mistress.

Film opens with Helena rehearsing the role of The Jewish Wife from "Brecht On Brecht," while Ferenzy arrives during the rehearsal. Apart from this first scene, action takes place entirely within Helena's spacious home.

Film was shot on video and transferred to film; result makes for murky lighting and wobbly soundtrack (affecting the music especially), but despite these technical shortcomings, Lindfors is to be commended on producing a moving and abrasive little drama which should find its way around fests and even possibly play small theatrical situations if double-billed with a similar pic.

It's a pity, though, that she couldn't have found a more original title: "Unfinished Business" is also the title of a 1985 film by Steven Okazaki and a 1984 film by Australia's Bob Ellis. —Strat.

Lien Lien Fung Chen
(Dust In The Wind)
(TAIWANESE-COLOR)

A Central Motion Picture production. Produced by Ling Deng Fei. Directed by Hou Hsiao Hsien. Screenplay, Wu Nien Jen, Chu Tien Wen; camera (color), Lee Ping Bin; editor, Liao Ching Sung; sound, Chi Chiang Sing; art director, Liu Ji Hwa. Reviewed at the Berlin Film Festival (Forum), Feb. 24, 1987. Running time: **109 MINS.**
With: Sin Shu-Fen, Wang Tsin-Wen, Lee Tien-Mu, Mei Fang.

Berlin — This new film by one of Taiwan's top young filmmakers, Hou Hsiao Hsien, confirms the qualities and the motives he has established in his previous work, which has already acquired him a solid following on the festival circuit.

While leaving the world of childhood and of the personal memories which have been the concern of his earlier films, Hsiao Hsien doesn't wander too far off, his protagonists being a young man who leaves his native village for the big city, to make some money and send home, and eventually to put aside the necessary sum in order to marry the girl he has considered his future wife since childhood.

As usual in his films, there isn't

much of a plot, the script seeming more like a diary registering the small, insignificant events of everyday life, but doing it with so much sensitivity and care that it becomes a highly affecting experience. The supreme quality of the picture, however, is its profound sympathy and understanding for characters, good and bad alike, and its interest for the smallest details.

Not that there is anything lacking, visually. A stylist at heart who keeps his camera movements and close-ups as spare as possible, Hsiao Hsien constructs every frame with the utmost care and exploits every corner of it. Editing is unhurried and deliberate, leisure being an absolute requisite in order to create the right atmosphere. While never forcing the note, the helmer sneaks in his remarks about the generation gap and political situation in Taiwan, but it is done with a lot of understanding and feeling for the characters.

One moving moment occurs when the grandfather accompanies his grandson to the railway station, as he is on his way to join the army; another is the silent gaze of the family upon the son's promised bride, who has in the meantime married someone else, and comes to visit her family back home. Then, of course, there is the gap between the village and the city, where all the young people reprofile their lives in a different fashion.

Possibly less compact than his earlier films, but just as touching, featuring solid technical credits and very natural and unforced acting, this is a worthy addition to the new Taiwanese cinema, and probably bound for a long list of festivals this year. —Edna.

Das Tribunal — Mord am Bullenhuser Damm
(The Tribunal — The Murders On Bullenhuser Street)
(WEST GERMAN-COLOR-16m)

A Sender Freies Berlin (SFB) production and release. Directed by Lea Rosh. Screenplay, Günther Schwarberg; camera (color, 16m), Wolfram Seibt, Werner Schulz; editor, Ursula Bleckmann; sound, Klaus Vogler. Reviewed at Berlin Film Festival (New German Film series). March 2, 1987. Running time: **148 MINS.**

Berlin — "Das Tribunal" (The Tribunal) is the latest in a series of documentary films by tv journalist Lea Rosh to goad West Germans into confronting Nazi atrocities. Film records a mock trial last April involving judges from four countries to delve into the gruesome murders of 20 children and 28 adults at a school on Bullenhuser Damm, a street in Hamburg.

As such, prospects abroad for this lengthy, exceedingly talky production are slim indeed.

Rosh is Jewish and is noted for her hard-hitting interviews in a land where people with titles in front of their names are still given considerable deference. Previous films have dealt with acquittals of alleged war criminals, as well as German industry's willing use of slave labor during the Nazi regime and persecution of gypsies.

Latest film trial concerns a stormtrooper accused of ordering the hanging deaths of the children and adults in the cellar of the school after medical experiments had been carried out on them. Genuine legal proceedings were never held. Film is a valuable piece of German journalism. —Gill.

Yuki Yukite Shingun
(Forward, God's Army)
(JAPANESE-DOCU-COLOR-16m)

A Shisso-Films production, Imamura Prods., Zanzo-sha. Produced by Sachiko Kobayashi. Directed by and camera (color), Kazuo Hara, based on idea by Shohei Imamura. Editor, Atsushi Nabeshima; music, Shigeru Yamakawa; sound, Toyohiko Yukimura. Reviewed at the Berlin Film Festival (Forum), Feb. 21, 1987. Running time: **134 MINS.**

Berlin — This is an amazing, one-of-a-kind documentary, both in its form and its content. Based on an idea suggested by Shohei Imamura, whose own company helped with the production, the film focuses on one person's fanatical search for justice and truth, in which the end justifies all the means.

Kenzo Okuzaki, a WW II veteran with a criminal record, is a violent, determined character, a kind of holy innocent who will not let anything stand in his way. For years before director Kazuo Hara's cameras pick him up, he has been physically attacking the Emperor, Hirohito, and his "accomplices" who have betrayed the Japanese people by sending them into the war. His actions were intended not to cause bodily harm but express his attitude to these false gods, and every time he was sent to court, he would spit on the judges and insult them, leading his own private war to re-establish God's true gospels on earth.

It is out of this same concern that he decides to unveil the truth about the fate of his comrades, with whom he fought in New Guinea, and who never returned home. Riding in his van, equipped with loud-speakers, he crisscrosses the country baiting the policemen who try to stop him advertising his opinions out loud, and looks for survivors who might shed some light on a particular event, the execution of two soldiers by their officer, 23 days after the end of the war.

Every time he reaches one of the potential witnesses, he pulls out the

pictures of the two victims, states his intentions straight away, and refuses to leave until he gets what he considers satisfying answers to his questions. Whenever there is an attempt to hide evidence, he starts by browbeating the witness and often ends with his jumping all over him and beating him up, in holy wrath.

At a certain point he has relatives of the victim joining him in his search, and in one very moving scene, when a sergeant who had served in that unit tearfully refuses to go back to those horrible events, Okuzaki's violent temper gives way to the sorrow, which he shares with the relatives of the departed.

As he stubbornly proceeds on his way, Okuzaki's quest gradually leads to a horrifying picture, for with every new bit of evidence it becomes clearer the soldiers had been executed at the time for no particular crime, after their names had been drawn in lots, to feed their starving comrades. None of those questioned is willing to come out and say as much in the open, until the last sequence when Okuzaki goes back to a sick old man who provides final details of the terrible truth.

Hara's role in the proceedings is that of an observer who sticks to Okuzaki's every move and word, the presence of the camera not only being acknowledged at all times, but also exploited as an additional instrument to intimidate the witnesses into submitting to the literal third degrees they are put through. Every time one of them protests, Okuzaki is the first to suggest the possibility of calling the cops and having his arrest put on film.

Unfolding in the manner of a thriller built around a most unusual character, this is a frighteningly powerful indictment of Japan's leaders, who are ultimately responsible for the terrifying tragedy, even more than the person who pulled the trigger at the time. The background, slums and lower middle-class quarters, are a far cry from the exoticism one usually expects in a Japanese film, and all the more convincing for that.

Given the poor lighting conditions, Hara has done a commendable job, and if length might seem a bit excessive, it is absolutely necessary in order to introduce all the elements involved in this all too gruesome real-life drama. —Edna.

Der Kleine Staatsanwalt
(The Little Prosecutor)
(WEST GERMAN-COLOR)

A Filmverlag der Autoren release of a Hamburg Kino-Kompanie Hark Bohm Films production, in conjunction with NDR Tv. Produced by Jürgen Böttcher. Written and directed by Bohm. Camera (color), Klaus Brix; editor, Inge Bohmann; music, Jean

(Toots) Thielemans, Herb Geller; sound, Wolfgang Schröter; art direction, Jochen Krumpeter; assistant director, Peter Carpentier. Reviewed at Berlin Film Festival (Panorama), Feb. 28, 1987. Running time: **91 MINS.**

König	Hark Bohm
Kaiser	Martin Lüttge
Frau Meffert	Corinna Harfouch
Wuttke	Michael Gwisdek
Siegmann	Alexander Radszun
Frau Keile	Ute Christensen

Also with: Ulrich von Dobschütz (Dr. Kleinsteuber), Klaus Pohl (Scepanek), Tilo Prückner (von Knörringen), Rainer Hunold (Rademacher), Marquard Bohm (trumpeter).

Berlin — West German veteran character actor Hark Bohm directed, wrote and stars in "Der Kleine Staatsanwalt" (The Little Prosecutor), which provides a showcase for talents his previous supporting roles never did. Result is a fast-paced satire on West German bureaucracy and chamber of commerce-oriented politics. Film is Bohm's best yet.

Plot involves an upwardly striving but exceedingly cautious state prosecutor (Bohm). His hopes of advancement are jeopardized when he is forced to confront a seemingly smalltime construction firm bankruptcy scam that turns out to have major political implications. Backed into a legal corner, the bungling, absent-minded little prosecutor opts for personal and professional integrity, at the expense of his career and an innocent man's future.

Bohm is best known outside Germany for his numerous roles as mousy, bespectacled accountants, pianists or smalltime crooks in such R.W. Fassbinder films as "The Marriage Of Maria Braun," "Berlin Alexanderplatz" and "Lili Marleen."

Taking full advantage of his gaunt plainness, Bohm shines as the stammering, befuddled prosecutor forced grudgingly to choose between expediency and justice.

His screenplay is written tightly, preventing film from itself becoming a victim of the byzantine bureaucracy it portrays. Bohm's character is genuinely human and full of understated humor seldom seen in thesp's previous roles.

Kudos to Martin Lüttge, who plays a naive executive set up to be the fall guy in the bankruptcy scam, and to Alexander Radszun, appropriately oily as the scam's mastermind.

Also notable is Corinna Harfouch as the prosecutor's assistant who eagerly bends the law in her idealistic pursuit of bringing the guilty to justice. —*Gill.*

Igry Dlja Detej Skol'nogo Vozrasta
(Games For Schoolchildren)
(SOVIET-COLOR)

A Sovexportfilm release of a Tallinfilm production. Directed by Lejda Lajus and Arvo Icho. Screenplay, Marija Septunova, adapted from the novel "The Adoptive Mother" by S. Rannamaa; camera (color), Icho; sound, Enn Siade, Olga Alp; music, Lepo Sumera; set decoration, Tynu Virve. Reviewed at the Berlin Film Festival (Kinderfilmfest), Feb. 25, 1987. Running time: **88 MINS.**

Marie	Monika Jarv
Robby	Hendrik Toompere
Tauri	Tauri Tellermaa
Kerttu	Kerttu Aaving
Melita	Edit-Hellen Kuusk
Sijri	Sijri Sisask
Anne	Jaanika Kalleus
Erzieherin	Helle Kuningas
Robby's mother	Marie Lill
Marie's father	Evald Hermanjuns
Tauri's father	Eduard Tinn

Berlin — This sympathetic portrait of youngsters confined to a foster care facility in the Soviet Union should be of interest to young people the world over. No softsell or mawkish sentimentality piece, it is a straightforward look at life for young people who no longer can live with their families.

Marie, 16, played with haunting simplicity by Monika Jarv, is returned to foster care after running away to see her abusive, widowed father. Through incidents and impressions we glimpse the unsettled daily life of the youngsters at the facility. There are visits by unstable parents, squabbles that turn vicious and clashes with authority.

More and more Marie is isolated from her peers until two very different boys vie for her affections. The rougher, Robby (Hendrik Toompere), seems the least suitable for her gentle nature, but she comes to favor him. When she is forced to identify him as a participant in an earlier disruptive incident, he is sent to a more secure facility.

Pic demonstrates that even in the East Bloc children can be the helpless victims of family breakups, and could be a step in humanizing our view of complicated Soviet society.

— *Owl.*

Die Chinesen Kommen
(The Chinese Are Coming)
(WEST GERMAN-COLOR)

A Delta release of a Journal Film-Maran Film coproduction. Executive producer, Elke Peters. Produced by Klaus Volkenborn. Directed by Manfred Stelzer. Screenplay, Stelzer, Ulrich Enzensberger; camera (color), David Slama; editor, Thorsten Näter; music, Rio Reiser; sound, Michael Eller; production design, Mathias Faulmüller, Henry Kobierski; assistant director, Thorsten Näter. Reviewed at Berlin Film Festival (New German Cinema Section), March 2, 1987. Running time: **99 MINS.**

Hansi Pfnurr	Jorg Hube
Schorsch Schmierer	Hans Brenner
Ralth	Martin Sperr
Rose	Monika Baumgartner
Junior	Rolf Zacher
Li	Hu Bo
Wang	Lu Chuhlian

Also with: Alfons Biber (Dachs), Hans Schuler (Ritzer), Bembe Bowakow (Chiang), Zenghua Su (Gua).

Berlin — Bearing some similarities to Ron Howard's "Gung Ho," "The Chinese Are Coming" is a comedy about a group of Chinese who acquire a disused factory somewhere in Bavaria. They don't mean to get it going again, but plan to take all the machinery back to China with them. It's a film inspired by real events.

The factory had always been the lifeblood of the picturesque Alpine village, but it closed down two years earlier after the owner's son, Junior, took over and found it impossible to deal with the union and its intractable shop steward, Hansi Pfnürr (Jörg Hube). When Hansi learns Junior has sold the factory to the Chinese, he's horrified at first, but then decides to supervise the Chinese workers as they disassemble the equipment ready for shipment.

Complicating matters is the fact that Hansi's friend, Schorsch Schmierer (Hans Brenner), who's also the father of his girl, Rose (Monika Baumgartner), has his eye on one machine in the factory; if he can smuggle this particular machine, the one he always worked himself, out of the place before the Chinese take it, he can set himself up in a modest way.

Meanwhile, the frustrated Rose is making her own approaches to the Chinese on a more personal level, unknown to her father or her boyfriend.

The film aims most of its satire at the conservative Bavarians, and the way they react to the presence of Chinese in their midst. There are some funny moments, and the film is consistently mildly amusing if never hilarious. Hube and Brenner steal the show as the two lumbering, rather stupid, Bavarians who gradually come to respect the polite, hardworking Chinese. —*Strat.*

Siekierezada
(Axiliad)
(POLISH-COLOR)

A Film Polski release of a Zespoly Filmowe, "Perspektiva" Unit, production. Directed by Witold Leszczynski. Screenplay, Leszczynski, based on novel by Edward Stachura; camera (color), Jerzy Lukaszewicz; editor, Lucja Osko; music, Jerzy Satanowski, Antonio Vivaldi; sound, Jerzy Szawlowski; art director, Maciej Putowski; production manager, Tadeusz Drewno. Reviewed at the Berlin Film Festival (Forum), Feb. 27, 1987. Running time: **82 MINS.**

Pradera	Edward Zentara
Katny	Daniel Olbrychski
Peresada	Ludwig Pak

Berlin — Jan Pradera, a young and idealistic poet, turns his back on civilization and decides to return to the sources. In the middle of winter, he goes to a small village, surrounded by forests, rents a bed in the house of an old woman, and sets out to make his living as a lumberjack.

Soon he realizes the world around him is still far from perfect or happy. Nightmares of a past love story visit him constantly and he never really establishes any intimate relations with the villagers. Only when another man just like him (the resemblance is physical as well) reaches the village and rents the bed next to him, is there a real contact, based on past dreams and hopes shattered.

It is evidently no accident that many details are left unspecified in the film. Whenever asked about his hometown, Pradera will say only he comes from up north, the entire village seems to be removed from any exact reference in time and space, and the general tone is one of an allegory about disappointment and despair. The title itself (an exact translation), indicates the metaphorical intentions, since it is a combination of the word Axe, a lumberjack's tool, and of Scheherazade, the Oriental fairytale spinner. Naturally, the parable can be interpreted politically as well, given the recent history of Poland.

If on a realistic level the film might be found somewhat inconclusive and abrupt, director Witold Leszczynski makes up for it with evocative images, powerful use of countryside landscape and particularly of the night forest and its giant trees being felled constantly by human hands. The dialog is spare, but more than compensated for by the expressive faces of the village people, while Jerzy Satanowski's soundtrack, using extensively Vivaldi church music, lends even better support to the allegorical level.

The script is based on a very personal novel by Edward Stachura, a writer who has committed suicide some years ago just like his hero, which adds considerable poignancy in the context of this film.

Edward Zentara, who plays the lead, is thoroughly convincing as a person desperately wishing to believe he can enjoy a new life. Daniel Olbrychski takes a secondary but highly significant role as the latecomer in the village, Pradera's soul brother in a way, who triggers the final and fatal crisis.

At a brief 82 minutes, this picture that already won the critics' prize here offers a highly relevant glimpse into the less-than-happy subconscious of Poland today, and does it with much force and originality.

—*Edna.*

Rattis
(Ratty)
(SWEDISH-ANIMATED-COLOR)

A Swedish Film Institute release (international sales, SFI/Lena Enquist), Kanalfilm with the Swedish Film Institute production.

Produced by Lisbet Gabrielsson. Written, animated and directed by Lennart Gustafsson. Co-animators, Ylva-Li Björk, Jonas Adner; camera (color), Mikael Gerdin, Anders Holt; editor, uncredited; music, Markus Wikström, Bie Carlsson, Johan Stern, Ylva-Li Björk, Stefan Axelsson, Urban Wrethagen; sound, Leif Westerlund. Reviewed at Children's Film Festival (Competition) in Berlin Film Festival, Feb. 23, 1987. Running time: **82 MINS.**
Voices: Leif Westerlund, Ylva-Li Björk, Jonas Adner, Lennart Gustafsson, Angela Sogrell, Mikael Gerdin.
(International soundtrack available)

Berlin — "Ratty" is a first-time feature-length animation effort for writer-director-animator Lennart Gustafsson who is clearly indebted to such diverse talents as Ted Avery, Ralph Bakshi and Walt Disney, but who still comes through as an original artist in his own right.

The title figure looks like a loosely drawn sketch for Bugs Bunny, but this Ratty is the teenaged son of a rat family with a mother addicted to house-cleaning, a father with a Leonardo da Vincian inventor's dreams, a dotting but ever so sly Grandpa and an army of kid sisters and brothers who peer through Ratty's keyhole when he brings home pink Rosetta, the rat girl, and tells the parents that Ratty and Rosetta are ..., well, the inevitable four-letter word is used repeatedly as language that is spoken by present-day teenagers everywhere is unabashedly used throughout.

Innocent charm and some rather diffuse suspense in Ratty's rivalry with a motorcycle tough for Rosetta's favor constitute the essence of an animation film that is also a musical with a jazzy score plus some lyrical moments. Dancing and singing by various groups of animals and rat soloists plus the Moon above has verve and wit.

Creator Lennart Gustafsson addresses himself via "Ratty" to kids as if they were full-fledged adults, but there is also a sense of fun and games for all ages throughout, and item is sure to sell widely. Some foreign territories' dubbers may want to dilute the language. This should not detrack noticeably from this little outing into baroque animation.
— *Kell.*

Vermischte Nachrichten
(Odds And Ends)
(WEST GERMAN-COLOR)

A Filmverlag der Autoren release of a Kairos Film production. Produced and directed by Alexander Kluge. Screenplay, Kluge; camera (color), Werner Lüring, Thomas Mauch; editor, Beate Mainka-Jellinghaus, Jane Seitz; sound, Joe Dillinger, Georg Otto. Olav Reinke; art direction, Jürgen Schell; assistant director, Kay Drath, Matthias Keuthen, Bernd Schlehsak, Dagmar Steurer; production manager, Daniel Zuta, Karin Petraschke. Reviewed at Berlin Film Festival, Feb. 22, 1987. Running time: **103 MINS.**
Restless woman ....Marita Breuer
Successful man ....Rosel Zech
African female ....Sabine Wegner

Waiter Max................André Jung
Announcer ....Sabina Trooger

Berlin — Alexander Kluge's latest foray into the German psyche is a handsomely edited series of often documentary-style vignettes that strike deep emotional chords among German audiences, infuriating some viewers and delighting others. Unfortunately, non-Germans tend to come away shaking their heads and wondering what happened. Hence, prospects are limited to the fest circuit and special outlets.

Film is supposed to be like the "Miscellaneous News" column of a daily newspaper — the hodgepodge of little two-paragraph news shorts along the lines of "Son Shoots Pop For Battering Mom" or "Study Finds Most Waiters Carry Trays With Left Hand."

Those are, in fact, two of film's vignettes, taken, as it were, from everyday life in West Germany. There are loads of others. Film opens with shots of a boy crossing his eyes as a clock strikes 12, defying the old European wives' tale that they'll get stuck that way. One vignette consists entirely of a newborn child lolling on a bed.

All are well lensed by cameramen Werner Lüring, and Thomas Mauch. Editing is superb, as is to be expected of the team of Beate Mainka-Jellinghaus ("Nosferatu," "Fitzcarraldo") and Jane Seitz ("Das Boot").

While some vignettes stand well on their own, it is hard not to escape the suspicion that some were included merely to show off the editing team's talents. An unidentified Marlene Dietrich silent film shows up in one vignette. It is beautifully framed and edited, but does not fit film's journalistic, semi-documentary style.

Three vignettes are supposed to hit home at German attitudes toward blacks, toward the terminally ill and toward monstrous memories of a war their country started. Unfortunately, Kluge's screenplay is flat and the acting is too wooden to make any of it seem real. Whatever his reasons for it might have been, making white actress Sabine Wegner put on blackface and a cheap afro-style wig to play the part of the black refugee just doesn't cut it.

Best part is a segment contributed (with fleeting credit mention) by Volker Schlöndorff. Piece accompanies ex-Chancellor Helmut Schmidt on a December 1981 trip to hobnob with East German leader Erich Honecker. Schlöndorff's eye for the absurd produces some prize scenes, such as an entourage of black Mercedes limos barreling through grim, wintry East German streets. Closing sequence of Schmidt and Honecker awkwardly dragging out their good-byes while

waiting for Schmidt's train to leave is priceless. It puts the rest of film in the shade. —*Gill.*

Hungarian Film Reviews

Szamárköhögés
(Whooping Cough)
(HUNGARIAN-COLOR)

A Hunnia Studio, Mafilm, production. Executive producer, Andras Elek. Directed by Peter Gardos. Screenplay, Andras Osvat, Gardos; camera (Eastmancolor), Tibor Mathé; editor, Maria Rigo; music, Janos Novak; production design, Jozef Romvari; sound, Janos Réti, Istvan Sipos; costumes, Agnes Gyarmathy; consultant, Sandor Simo. Reviewed at Hungarian Film Week, Budapest, Feb. 15, 1987. Running time: **87 MINS.**
Grandmother ....Mari Töröcsik
Father....................Dezsö Garas
Mother..................Judit Hernadi
Tomi ....Marcell Toth
Annamari ....Ezter Kárász
Akos ....Karoly Eperjes
The Maid ....Anna Feher

Budapest — More and more Hungarian films are tackling the traumatic theme of the so-called counter-revolution of 1956 and the subsequent Soviet invasion of Hungary. "Whooping Cough" sees the events entirely through the eyes of one ordinary family, especially two young children.

Brief newsreel footage is all we get to see of the terrible fighting and killing that went on during October and November of that year. For this family, which rarely ventures outside their apartment, the events are more frightening for being unseen: grandmother returns home with bullet-riddled bread; gunfire is heard in the night; but otherwise there's an unreal feeling of living in limbo while unknown dramas take place not far away.

The children have to stay home from school, but the self-confident Tomi makes a couple of forays back to the empty school. On the first occasion, he's accosted by a caretaker, on the second he and his friends find the caretaker's body in a stairwell. Another frightening experience comes when the children, together with some others, are playing on the railway line when there's gunfire from unseen soldiers and one of their friends is killed.

Father, a wonderful performance from Dezsö Garas, stays home from work and spends his time wondering if he'll flee to America and become a tap dancer like Fred Astaire. His younger wife has a secret lover, and is also in a quandary. Her mother, beautifully played by Mari Töröcsik, remains a calm center during the terrifying ordeal. They listen to English-language news broadcasts (actually about the Suez Crisis and not the Hungarian situation), but they can't understand what's being

said. There's a phone call in the middle of the night from relatives in America, but how can the true situation be revealed when the phone may be tapped?

Mother and son take a trip into the snowbound countryside to get chickens to eat, and witness hundreds of refugees fleeing across a field to board a train bound for Vienna. All these scenes evoke a bizarre and frightening period with precision, though more conventional coming-of-age scenes involving the boy's sexual obsessions, are a bit familiar. Still there's a lovely moment when Tomi comes across the family's young maid taking a bath.

Peter Gardos also injects some humor into the film, such as a scene where the boy's uncle decides to emigrate to wherever he sticks a pin into an atlas and is discomfited when he comes up with Tirana, capital of unfriendly Albania. Film ends as school resumes after the mostly unseen events have subsided, and a teacher calls the roll (several kids have emigrated and one is dead) before resuming lessons.

Beautifully acted by the entire cast, "Whooping Cough" is marred only by the director's penchant for shooting through out-of-focus foreground objects (such as trees) which is ugly and irritating. This stylistic flaw aside, the film is a fascinating look at a terrible period as seen through naive and childish eyes.
— *Strat.*

Zuhanas Közben
(The Fall)
(HUNGARIAN-COLOR)

A Dialog Studio, Mafilm, production. Written and directed by Tamas Tolmar. Camera (Eastmancolor), Emil Novak; editor, Peter Timar; music, György Selmeczy, Peter Petardi; production design, Laszlo Gardonyi; sound, Karoly Peller, Istvan Wolf; costumes, Zsuzsa Partenyi. Reviewed at Hungarian Film Week, Budapest, Feb. 16, 1987. Running time: **112 MINS.**
Wolf ....Attila Kaszas
Nora ....Judit Pogany
Gyuri ....Peter Rudolf
Zsuzsa ....Hilda Harsing
Ildiko ....Adel Kovats
Nora's husband ....Tamas Vegvari
Kovacsics ....Frigyes Hollosi
Török ....Geza Balkay
The Englishman .....Zbigniew Zapasiewicz

Budapest — A first feature by Tamas Tolmar, "The Fall" is a romantic *film noir* about a young racketeer on the run from the mob and the people who cross his path.
Wolf (Attila Kaszas) is in love

with a beautiful ballerina, Ildiko. He's involved in illegal distribution of VCRs and vidcassettes and is trying to make a fast forint because he suspects, rightly, that his girl is having an affair with a smooth English choreographer (an odd role for Polish actor Zbigniew Zapasiewicz).

Paralleled with Wolf's story is that of Gyuri (Peter Rudolf), a taxi driver who also has woman trouble. His girl works in a cafe and is tired of their rather hopeless relationship.

Wolf hires Nora (Judit Pogany), an English teacher, to do a Hungarian voice-over dub on an illegal cassette of "The Texas Chainsaw Massacre" and she senses the plight he's in and tags along with him, half mothering him (she's distinctly middle-aged), half wanting him. When he runs afoul of local Mafia types and gets badly beaten, she tends his wounds, and later makes love with him in his car before deciding to end it all by driving them both into the Danube.

At this point, fate steps in. Gyuri, the taxi driver, sees the car go into the river and dives in to help. He rescues Nora and Wolf, but at the cost of his own life.

Where all too many Hungarian films tend to be incoherently structured, "The Fall" is a model of clarity. It's well paced, tells an intriguing story, is handsomely, stylishly shot (by Emil Novak) and contains a gem of a performance from Judit Pogany as the slightly over-the-hill woman who clings to the young racketeer out of her own lonely desperation.

Tolmar also brings off one unusual stylistic device. At a key point in the story, after Wolf has been beaten badly and tended by Nora, he replays the same scene three times: first with Nora tearfully telling Wolf about their alcoholism; then with Wolf talking about his problems; and finally with them both sitting in embarrassed silence. It's an unusual device which works, and indicates a director not afraid to take chances, despite the conventional (by Hungarian standards) plotline.
— *Strat.*

Magic-Queen In Hungary
(HUNGARIAN-BRITISH-DOCU-COLOR)

A Hungarofilm presentation of a Queen Films, Multimedia Europe Films, London, Mafilm/Dialog Studio, Budapest coproduction. Directed by János Zsombolyai. Camera (Eastmancolor), Elemér Ragályi. Reviewed at the Budapest Congress Center, Feb. 17, 1987. Running time: **90 MINS.**
With: Queen group — John Deacon, Brian May, Freddie Mercury, Roger Taylor.

Budapest — A straightforward record of the first tour by the rock group Queen in Eastern Europe, the picture concentrates on their July 27, 1986 concert at the Budapest People Stadium, with very little

frills around it.

Except for the opening sequence, showing their triumphant reception by enthusiastic local fans, there is only the group performing some of their greatest hits, execedingly well shot by a team that obviously was familiar with every line and movement of the foursome. For a live performance film, it is of the highest quality, including sound, as far as could be assessed from the playback system in Budapest.

The obligatory interviews usually adorning this kind of film are happily missing, the flow of the concert being interrupted only briefly by flashes of each of the four going around town. For Queen fans this is a must. —*Edna.*

Szörnyek Evadja
(Season Of Monsters)
(HUNGARIAN-COLOR)

A Dialog Studio, Mafilm, production. Executive producer, Istvan Fogarsi. Directed by Miklos Jancso. Screenplay, Jancso, Gyula Hernadi; camera (Eastmancolor), Janos Kende; music, Zoltan Simon; editor, Zsuzsa Osakany; sound, György Pinter; art direction and costumes, Tamas Banovich; saxophone soloist, Laszlo Dog. Reviewed at Hungarian Film Week, Budapest, Feb. 13, 1987. Running time: **88 MINS.**

Dr. Bardocz	Gyorgy Cserhalmi
Kovacs	Ferenc Kallai
Komondi	Jozsef Madaras
Kato	Juli Nyako
Annabella	Katarzyna Figura
The Girl in Leather	Erzsi Cserhalmi
Zoltai	Andras Balint

Also with: Bela Tarr (The Disciple In White), Andras Kozak (Colonel Antal), Lajos Balazsovitz (Zimmermann), Miklos B. Szekely (Deaf-mute).

Budapest — One of the most imposing figures of Hungarian cinema of the 1960s and early 1970s, Miklos Jancso has, of late, been working on documentaries and television specials. He also made an ill-starred feature, "Dawn," last year in Israel. Now he's back with his first Hungarian cinema feature since "The Tyrant's Heart" in 1981, and though on this occasion he's tackled a modern theme, he hasn't changed his familiar, and increasingly sterile, style.

"Season Of Monsters" starts out interestingly enough with an expatriate academic returning to Hungary from the U.S. and giving a tv interview. Soon after, he commits suicide, leaving a note for a former school friend, now a successful doctor (György Cserhalmi). So far, so good, but then Jancso shifts the action from the city to a lakeside setting where a gathering is taking place involving a couple of teachers and a handful of nubile young women who spend as much time undressed (in traditional Jancso style) as they do dressed.

From here on the plot becomes hard to unravel. The group is joined by the doctor and the policeman in-

vestigating the suicide. A helicopter circles overhead. The lake erupts in (marvelously staged) pyrotechnics; Janos Kende's camera sweeps and spins around the characters to dazzling, dizzying effect. Jancso seems to be studying a clash between the elitist physician and the egalitarian yet sinister, teacher (Jozsef Madaras), but instead of clarifying his debate he seems to have become overwhelmed with the desire to stun his audience with visual coups. It *is* magnificent to look at, but it's also a bit hollow and chintzy.

The girls are more beautiful even than those who populated earlier Jancso films, and the actors are all fine, given the limitations the director imposes on them. Andras Balint, as the suicide, makes the strongest impression in his brief appearance. Music is also important as an element in ths strange, surreal drama.

For all its splendors, "Season Of Monsters," is, in the end, so irritatingly obscure that audiences are likely to be turned off. Commercial chances look doubtful, though if the film goes the fest route and picks up some learnedly favorable reviews it could attract a cult following. Technically, it's firstclass.
—*Strat.*

Malom a Pokolban
(Mills Of Hell)
(HUNGARIAN-COLOR)

A Hunnia Studio, Mafilm, production. Directed by Gyula Maar. Screenplay, Maar, György Moldova, from Moldova's novel; camera (Eastmancolor), Ivan Mark; editor, Julia Sivo; production design, Tamas Banovich; sound, Karoly Peller; costumes, Judit Schäffer. Reviewed at Hungarian Film Week, Budapest, Feb. 17, 1987. Running time: **100 MINS.**

Janos Flandera	Frigyes Funtek
Altschuler	Dezső Garas
Nadezhda	Anna Rackevei
Erzsi Bona	Edit Vlahovics
Ildiko Demjen	Marianna Moor

Budapest — Another film in which the injustices of the Stalinist 1950s are dissected and reviled, "Mills Of Hell" is a grim item about an ambitious, rather surly young student (Frigyes Funtek) whose career is defined as much by his romantic indiscretions as by the machinations of intolerant university committees.

Opening in 1950, pic establishes Funtek as a talented student being kept by a woman journalist older than he. He applies for a scholarship to study in Moscow, and she jealously denounces him, revealing to the university board that he is, in effect, a gigolo ("Communists are special people," he's sternly told, and special people don't have older women as mistresses). Not only does he not get the scholarship, but he's sentenced to a year's hard labor.

During this period, he befriends

the son of a former aristocrat who had been a member of left-wing movements for 20 years and yet is being punished simply because of his background. Funtek sticks up for his friend, and gets into more trouble.

Having abandoned his jealous mistress, he takes up with a pretty, young, naive tram conductor (Edit Vlahovics) and gets her pregnant before moving on to the crippled daughter (Anna Rackevei) of a party high official, an indiscretion that brings fatal consequences.

Working from a novel by co-screenwriter György Moldova, director Gyula Maar has made an academic but often engrossing film. Maar always has been a rather literary director, and "Mills Of Hell" is no exception; but the story is interesting and the gloomy images of Ivan Mark perfectly match the theme of life under a stultifyingly rigid regime. Pic could get attention from fests this summer, on its lucid depiction of a grim era and on its trappings of doomed romanticism. Technical credits are all very good.
— *Strat.*

Csók, Anyu
(Love, Mother)
(HUNGARIAN-COLOR)

An Objektiv Studio, Mafilm, production. Directed by Janos Rozsa. Screenplay, Miklos Vamos; camera (Eastmancolor), Elemér Ragalyi; editor, Zsuzsa Csakany; music, Janos Brody; production design, Jozsef Romvari; sound, György Fek; costumes, Fanni Kemenes; production manager, Lajos Ovari. Reviewed at Hungarian Film Week, Budapest, Feb. 16, 1987. Running time: **102 MINS.**

Juli Kalmar	Dorottya Udvaros
Geza Kalmar	Robert Koltai
Mari Kalmar	Kati Lajtai
Peti Kalmar	Simon G. Gevai
Doctor	Sandor Gaspar
Schoolmistress	Ildiko Bansagi
Neighbor	Erika Bodnar
Geza's mistress	Zsuzsa Töreky
Comrade Csezmiczey	Peter Andorai

Budapest — "Love, Mother" tells a sad little story with universal application: that in these hectic times, parents all too often spend so little time with their children and each other that families inevitably break up as a result. The theme is taken to extremes here in a harsh satire on modern living, but the idea is not quite strong enough to sustain a feature length film.

The Kalmar family lives in a luxurious home to which presumably few Hungarians aspire. Father, a businessman, is off to work in the morning early; mother, a tour guide, gets up later and is often home very late at night; teenage daughter goes to high school, and her young brother, left alone to get himself to school, regularly plays truant. The family leaves messages for each other on a large notice board in the kitchen, and these hastily scrawled instructions pass for communication in the household.

Peti, the boy, has constructed an elaborate telescopic spying system by which he can observe everything in the house and neighborhood from a closet in his bedroom (on a realistic level, it's quite impossible that someone in the family wouldn't have noticed what he's doing, but if they had, there'd be no story). On this particular morning, he spies his father when he returns home for a quick fling with his mistress on the living room couch. He also has discovered his sister has a crush on the family doctor, and suspects his mother and the doctor are having an affair.

Meanwhile, grandmother is in the hospital, and only Mari, the daughter, seems to care. When news comes that grandmother has died, the disconsolate and unloved girl attempts suicide. She's saved, and the family rallies round, determined to make amends. They take a whole day off from work and school and try to behave like a real family, but the following day the pressures are on again and it's back to the old routine.

Janos Rozsa, best known for "Sunday Daughters," handles his theme with fluidity and satirizes his characters with surprising gentleness, laying the blame for what's happening to these children equally on husband and wife, both of whom are too self-centered to realize what's happening. There's a good deal of humor in the film, but it's basically a minor tragedy of our age. Outstanding production design by Jozsef Romvari and camerawork by Elemér Ragalyi ensure the film is visually pristine.

For all its qualities, though, it's a predictable and overstated affair which would have needed more depth to make it outside its home territory. Pic won the main prize of both local juries during the Hungarian Film Week. —*Strat.*

Szépleánok
(Pretty Girls)
(HUNGARIAN-DOCU-COLOR)

A Hungarofilm release of a Béla Balázs Studio, Movie Innovation Assn., Budapest production. Written, directed and camera (Eastmancolor) by András Dér, László Hartai. Editor, Dér, Hartai, Mariann Miklós; sound, Peter Laczkovics. Reviewed at the Budapest Congresss Center, Feb. 16, 1987. Running time: **95 MINS.**

Budapest — Documentaries about beauty pageants are a dime a dozen, but this one, about the Budapest Pageant of 1985, has a distinction in its favor, taking place in a Socialist country which has never had one. There is one additional catch to the story, a tragic and unexpected twist, for the win-

ner, 16-year-old girl, Csilla Andrea Molnar, committed suicide before her year-long reign ended.

The film goes behind the scenes to unveil some pretty unsavory details. There were pressures put on the participants, commercial commitments were thrust upon them with which they were completely unfamiliar, and for which they were paid only token wages.

Attempts to force them into signing exclusive contracts with a national agency, Magyar Media, which behaved in the best (worst?) capitalist manner, selling them to nude publications without any warning, as well as other indications of corruption are significant in these circumstances and the local public was delighted when the man presented as the villain is said to have a Moscow education.

The two young filmmakers, who started putting material on video long before they suspected the fatal outcome, transferred it to 35m with satisfactory results. The picture lacks any direct explanation of the girl's desperate act, but supplies sufficient circumstantial evidence of solitude, dehumanization and stress, to push a high school girl over the edge.

Additional interviews with pageant organizers and Csilla's parents she more light on a tragedy that obviously didn't teach anybody except those who were victims, the right lesson. —*Edna.*

Laura
(HUNGARIAN-COLOR)

A Hungarofilm release of a Mafilm-Objektiv Studios Budapest production. Written and directed by Géza Böszörményi; camera (Eastmancolor), Ferenc Pap; editor, Éva Kármentö; music, György Selmeczi, Ferenc Balázs; sound, György Fek; art director, József Romvári. Reviewed at the Budapest Congress Center, Feb. 15, 1987. (In Berlin Film Festival). Running time: **98 MINS.**

Laura . . . . Juli Básti
Ferenc, her husband . . . . . . Gábor Reviczky
Mother-in-Law . . . . Hédi Temessy
Giraffe . . . . György Dörner
Matyus . . . . Tamás Puskás
Dr. Varga . . . . Zbigniew Zapasiewicz

Budapest — Laura is a young woman married to the son of a deceased national hero, and living with her husband and his mother in the family house. Thanks to mother-in-law's relations, she has been promoted from typist to chief of personnel in a big hospital. She has a little daughter, but is unsatisfied with her life.

She lives it on several levels, a tragi-comic one at home, coping with her good-for-nothing husband and his doting mother, a dramatic one in the office finding out unintentionally about the flagrant injustices of the recent past. An almost caricatural level is introduced with the presentation of an

old friend who wants her back with his band and is preparing a music video to promote it, and a romantically mysterious one is used to portray her fling with a young man who keeps following her around. While each of these levels contains fascinating material, blending them together forces writer-director Géza Böszörményi to spread himself rather thin and resort sometimes to hackneyed patterns.

The most relevant aspect of the film is revealed in Laura's professional contact with 60-year-old doctor whom she has to retire from the staff, in her new capacity. The man refuses however, saying the regime has robbed him in the past of some of his best years, when he was interned in a work camp, never prosecuted, never condemned and never told the reasons for his being there. One particular visit to the site of the infamous camp shows how all traces have been thoroughly erased, but the doctor supplies a grim and detailed description which leaves no doubt about the inhumanity of the place.

The least successful sequences are those concerned with the possibility of Laura going back to a singing career and showing her old group preparing a music video in a purposely tasteless but also pretty clumsy manner.

By pulling the audience in too many directions, the film loses some of its impact, a pity since it is very nicely shot. Some of its barbs at present corruption are well-taken in a minor, matter-of-fact sort of way and there are some effective performances, particularly by Juli Básti and Polish actor Zbigniew Zapasiewicz, as the doctor who figures out society owes him the time he spent in prison, but goes the wrong way trying to secure his rights.

—*Edna.*

Keresztuton
(On The Crossroad)
(HUNGARIAN-DOCU-B&W)

A Hungarofilm release of a Mafilm-Objektiv Studio Budapest production. Written and directed by Sándor Sára. Camera (b&w), Sándor Kurucz; editor, Mihály Morell; sound, György Pék. Reviewed at the Budapest Congress Center, Feb. 15, 1987. Running time: 75 **MINS.**

Budapest — If anyone thought talking heads is a derogatory definition for unimaginative documentaries, they will have to contend now with Sándor Sára, one of Hungary's most respected filmmakers who specializes in the area.

Sára's new film consists entirely of identical closeups of heads, all carefully framed to look like talking passport photos. The entire film is dedicated to a community of Hungarian peasants who fled from the wrath of the Austro-Hungarian im-

perial court in the 18th century to the northeastern part of Rumania, and repatriated, which was supposed to be to their advantage, back into the Hungarian hinterland, during World War II in the region next to the Yugoslav border. They were torn away from their own homes and made to appear the invaders of other people's lands, after these have been deported cruelly beforehand.

The film is one long tale of woe by the survivors, mostly women, who went through that grim period in which 42 of their men were lost without a trace. It bears uncomfortable testimony to the reaction of the Yugoslav partisans to the new presence of the innocent peasants who had been resettled next to them.

While the decision to stick to heads only may be justified, theoretically, and the choice of faces, many highly expressive, is quite remarkable, extending the technique for the entire length of a documentary tends to be rather tedious, particularly for someone who does not speak the language.

—*Edna.*

Akli Miklos
(Miklos Akli)
(HUNGARIAN-COLOR)

A Budapest Studio, Mafilm, production. Written and directed by György Revesz, from a novel by Kalman Mikszath. Camera (Eastmancolor), Ferenc Szecsenyi; editor, Klari Majoros; music, Levente Szörenyi, Istvan Marta; production design, Lorant Kezdy; sound, Janos Arato; costumes, Judit Scháffer. Reviewed at Hungarian Film Week, Budapest, Feb. 17, 1987. Running time: **90 MINS.**

Miklos Akli . . . . Istvan Hirtling
Emperor Francis . . . . Laszlo Helyey
Baron Szepessy . . . . György Cserhalmi
Colonel Kovacs . . . . Istvan Kovacs
Ilonka Kovacs . . . . Eva Vejmelkova
Gyuri Kovacs . . . . Laszlo Görög
Count Stadion . . . . Kornel Gelley

Budapest — "Miklos Akli" is a lavish, tongue-in-cheek romantic period pic about the adventures of the court jester to Emperor Francis of Austria during the turbulent Napoleonic period. Pic is visually splendid, thanks to fine use of sets and costumes, but it lacks the dash needed to make it an audience pleaser outside its native Hungary.

Helmer György Revesz (best known for "Land Of Angels" in 1962) seems to be striving for an irreverent approach to history along the lines of Richard Lester's "The Three Musketeers," but he lacks the invention and fails to sustain the humor, which comes in fits and starts.

Istvan Hirtling is charming as the jester who saves the emperor from an assassination attempt and thus becomes his favorite, sparking envy on the part of the monarch's counsellor (Kornel Gelley). The jester is imprisoned on trumped-up charges that he supports Napoleon, but later is cleared. Meanwhile a raffish count, played by the ubiquitous György Cserhalmi, is lusting after the jester's pretty ward (Eva Vejmelkova) who in turn loves only the jester. On the wedding day, the bridegroom is shot and nearly killed by Cserhalmi, but recovers in time for a happy fadeout.

Along the way there are mild jokes about making money from bottling fresh air in smart packaging, and the way the wily Austrians trick Napoleon into a questionable marriage of convenience. It all plays well, but sans the dash and vigor it really needs. Best performance comes from Laszlo Helyey as the quizzical emperor.
—*Strat.*

Golyó a szivbe
(The Dead Ball)
(HUNGARIAN-FRENCH-COLOR)

A Hungarofilm presentation of a Hungarian TV, Budapest, Hamster, Paris, coproduction. Directed by György Gát. Screenplay, Gát, Didier Cohen; camera (color), Sándor Kurucz; editor, Mariann Miklós; music, György Vukán; sound, Gábor Rozgonyi; art director, Tamás Vayer; costumes, Emőke Csengey. Reviewed at the Budapest Congress Center, Feb. 16, 1987. Running time: **90 MINS.**
With: István Bubik, Patricia Barzyk, Phillipe Nicaud, Géza Kaszás, Tibor Szilágyi, Nóra Görbe, György Bárdi, Tamás Végvári.

Budapest — "The Dead Ball" is a nasty and often vicious little thriller about the kidnaping of a soccer star. This French-Hungarian coproduction made for tv and screened here in its French version, has very few redeeming features.

The story is clumsy, its characters unbelievable and the acting poor. In spite of the fact that the hero, a former soccer star who quit at the peak of his career, is constantly on the move, there is no excitement at all generated by this motion. Humor is heavy, whatever there is of it, and it is only as a travelog for the city of Pecz, where the story takes place, that this film has some justification. —*Edna.*

Evil Dead 2
(COLOR)

Zany horror epic will please genre fans.

A Rosebud Releasing release of a Renaissance Pictures presentation. Produced by Robert G. Tapert. Directed by Sam Raimi. Stars Bruce Campbell. Screenplay, Raimi, Scott Spiegel; camera (Technicolor), Peter Deming; night photography, Eugene Shlugleit; art direction, Philip Duffin, Randy Bennett; set decoration, Elizabeth Moore; set dresser, Wayne Leonard; sound, Tom Morrison; assistant director, Joseph Winogradoff; special makeup, Mark Shostrom. Reviewed at UCLA Melnitz Theater, L.A., March 10, 1987. (No MPAA Rating.) Running time: **85 MINS.**
Ash . . . . Bruce Campbell
Annie . . . . Sarah Berry
Jake . . . . Dan Hicks
Bobby Joe . . . . Kassie Wesley
Possessed Henrietta . . . . . . Theodore Raimi
Linda . . . . Denise Bixler
Ed . . . . Richard Domeier
Professor . . . . John Peaks
Henrietta . . . . Lou Hancock

Hollywood — More an absurdist comedy than a horror film, "Evil Dead 2" is a flashy good-natured display of special effects and scare tactics so extreme they can only be taken for laughs. Financed by the De Laurentiis Entertainment Group, which retains foreign and ancillary rights, pic is being released domestically unrated by Rosebud Releasing, which should find solid support among fans of the genre.

(According to Walter Josiah Jr., executive v.p. and general counsel of the Motion Picture Assn. of America, DEG told the MPAA that when they saw the finished film, it was judged to be "unreleasable" by DEG and returned to the producers, who laid off domestic release through Rosebud (though DEG retained all other rights). A DEG spokesman clarified the term "unreleasable" to mean there was no way the film could avoid getting an X rating unless severely edited, and therefore could not be released unrated by DEG, which is a signatoree to the MPAA. Both DEG and the MPAA maintain that Rosebud is completely independent of DEG, although using the apparatus, contacts and support agencies already set in place by DEG in anticipation of the film's release.—*Ed.*)

Story here is merely an excuse for director Sam Raimi to explore new ways to shock an audience and usually he keeps his sense of humor about it. It's as if every scene tries to outdo the one that went before it with Raimi winking at the audience all the while. The result is the kind of camp fest an audience can shout back at.

Action, and there's plenty, is centered around a remote cabin where Ash (Bruce Campbell) and girlfriend Linda (Denise Bixler) run into some unexpected influences. It isn't long before the forces of the

Evil Dead have got ahold of Linda and her head winds up in a vise.

It seems Prof. Knowby (John Peaks) has unleashed the spirits of the dead and they want to escape limbo by claiming possession of the living. They're a remarkably protean lot and take on all sorts of imaginative and grotesque forms almost instantaneously.

While Campbell battles the unknown with chainsaws, sawed-off shotguns, spikes and whatever he can get his hand on (his other hand has been sawed off), four other visitors make their way to the happening place. The professor's daughter, Sarah Berry, tries to clear the air with some hocus-pocus from the Egyptian Book Of The Dead.

From the looks of things, this must be the spirit capital of the universe with all the activity going on at once. Production uses more red water than the Red Sea and it flows about as freely. Other assorted bits include floating eyeballs, disembodied hands, engulfing trees and one creature beyond description.

Although it all becomes a bit monotonous after a while and is basically a one-note picture, Raimi is able to maintain the level of interest with some innovative camera angles and good-looking photography by Peter Deming and Eugene Shlugleit.

Production values are surprisingly high for this type of pic. Mark Shostrom's makeup effects enhance the comic thrust of the action and Campbell cuts a suitable figure as Rambo of the gore world.

After escalating the horror for some 75 minutes when it comes time to end the romp, Raimi is hard pressed to come up with a finale. Though the one he tries is not to be believed it falls a bit flat after what has preceded it.—*Jagr.*

Stadtrand
(WEST GERMAN-COLOR)

A North Rhine-Westphalla Filmbüro production. Produced and directed by Volker Führer. Screenplay, Führer; camera (color), Arthur Ahrweiler; editor, Wolfgang Gessat; music, Bernhard Voss; sound, Regina Wragge; voice dubbing, Sigrid Halvensleben-Kaul; art direction, Ralph Eue, Joe Liebetanz; assistant director, Heniz Dietz; production manager, Pimes Dörfler. Reviewed at Berlin Film Festival, Feb. 23, 1987. Running time: **100 MINS.**
Franz . . . . Leon Boden
Father . . . . Bruno Peters
Insurance detective . . . . Rudolf W. Marnitz
Also with: Herman Brood, Axel Schulz, Susanne Kieselstein.

Berlin — "Stadtrand" (roughly translated "On The Outskirts") is an ambitious first feature-length film by 28-year-old West German filmmaker Volker Führer that starts out promisingly, but works itself into some pretty inextricable corners about halfway through. All market prospects are dim.

Set in the bleak Ruhr Valley industrial region, film cashes in on West Germany's socalled "new poverty" — well-educated, but jobless victims of a post-industrial society.

Unemployed but amibitious young Franz (Leon Boden) lives in a wretched little apartment with alcoholic dad (Bruno Peters). His only solace is his girlfriend, and they are dirt poor but happy.

Franz lands a job as night shift man at a 24-hour gas station. In steps fate. Franz finds a wounded supermarket holdup man hiding in the station garage. Bandit forces him to provide medical attention and food, but later flees and is shot by police. Franz hears that the booty of some 100,000 marks is still missing. Poking around the gas station, he finds the loot and is instantly rich.

Führer wryly allows Franz to act out his small-time dreams of wealth — an evening out with his girlfriend (Susanne Kieselstein) at a pricey Chinese restaurant, flying lessons and new wallpaper for the kitchen. Führer then introduces a shady insurance detective and loses control of his plot. Franz ends up shooting the guy with a gun pulled from nowhere and returning home to find that the apartment building — and the money in a cardboard box — has all gone up in flames.

Leon Boden, an accomplished Austrian-German stage actor, handles the leading role well, doing what he can to make several implausible plot turns almost believable. Rest of cast is fairly weak.

Cameraman Arthur Ahrweiler makes the grimy industrial town setting seem downright homey and, at times, almost attractive.

Film has virtually no commercial appeal outside Germany, but doubtless will catch the eye of German tv producers who will see Führer's promise as a director. —*Gill.*

Terminus
(FRENCH-GERMAN-COLOR)

An AAA release, Hemdale Releasing (U.S.)/of a CAT Production/Films du Cheval de Fer/Initial Groupe/CLB Films/Films A2 coproduction. Executive producers, Anne François, Pierre-William Glenn. Produced by François. Directed by Glenn. Screenplay, Glenn, Patrice Duvic, from an original story by Alain Gillot; camera (Fujicolor), Jean-Claude Vicquery; sound, Michel Desrois; editor, Thierry Derocles; music, David Cunningham; songs, Stan Ridgway; artistic director, Alain Challier; special effects, Jacques and Frédéric Gastineau; costumes, Jacqueline Moreau; makeup, Muriel Baurens; stunt coordinator, Michel Norman; assistant director, Patrick Halpine; second unit director, Patrick Taulère. Reviewed at the UGC Normandie cinema, Paris, Feb. 10, 1987. Running time: **115 MINS.**
Gus . . . . Karen Allen
Stump (Manchot) . . . . Johnny Hallyday
Doctor/Monsieur/"Little
Brother" driver . . . . . . Jürgen Prochnow
Mati . . . . Gabriel Damon
Princess . . . . Julie Glenn
Voice of "Monster" . . . . . . Louise Vincent

Also with: Dieter Schidor, Janos Kulka, Dominique Valera, Jean-Luc Montama, Ray Montama, Bruno Ciarrochi, David Jalil, André Nocquet.

(French-track version)

Paris — There's no tiger in the tank of "Terminus," a low-octane, $6,00,000-plus sci-fi road actioner starring America's Karen Allen, French pop idol Johnny Hallyday and Germany's Jürgen Prochnow. Actors are routed by an unimaginative script over-loaded with videogame plotting and hi-tech clichés, and potholded direction by Pierre-William Glenn, formerly one of France's topflight cinematographers.

Shot in both English and French-track versions, this poor cousin of Mad Max and other road-burning boxoffice antiheros was presold for Stateside theatrical release by Hemdale Releasing and is due for distribution in the U.K., Australia and Scandinavia by 20th Century Fox Intl. Despite Hallyday's popularity on home turf, pic hit a stone wall at wickets here, and seems fated to limited mileage beyond European markets.

Screenplay by Glenn and Patrice Duvic imagines a futuristic international sport that is something of a cross between American football and European motor rally.

Karen Allen is the unlikely contender at the wheel of a computer-guided truck, called Monster, which has been programmed at the terminal point by a super-intelligent boy (Gabriel Damon). Allen's challenge is to reach the terminus while dodging a series of small vehicles bent on intercepting Monster.

When an apparent computer malfunction leads Monster astray into uncharted territory peopled by leather hoods who do not recognize the games, Allen is taken prisoner and tortured.

Allen expires in a local infirmary, but not before bequeathing her mission to Hallyday, a one-time truck driver himself tortured and imprisoned, with whom Allen had spent night in jail. Though he makes a move to come to the woman's aid, Hallyday nonetheless accepts the relay in the company of an intuitive local youngster (played by Julie Glenn, the helmer's daughter).

Making the fatal mistake of killing off one of its stars some 40 minutes into the picture, film compounds its errors with a convoluted plot in which Hallyday's sole interlocutor is the computer, a distant relation of Stanley Kubrick's HAL, further humanized here by a speaker system in form of a human mouth. Awful as the laconic exchanges between Allen and Hallyday are, the subsequent dialogs between man and machine as the pursuing vehicles close in on them, are hilariously inane.

Even worse are the goings-on at "Terminus," a subterannean mountain conclave where the wonder-boy's monitoring of the games is controlled by a mysterious 'Doctor" (Jürgen Prochnow) and an even stranger mad scientist who is using the sport as a decoy for illegal fetus traffic.

Though steeped in Anglo-Saxon movie conventions, "Terminus" is overloaded with pretentious philosophical baggage and mythical allusions that betray the discomfort of the filmmakers with a straightforward lowbrow narrative and slow story's pace to a soporific crawl.

In Glenn, the cinema has lost a lenser but has not gained a filmmaker. He handles the straight action sequences with no more vigor than he does the frequent static scenes and like many a buff helmer, is overly fond of quotes and references to other films.

Sporting white hair and an artificial hand (that serves no dramatic purpose), Hallyday is still a promising screen presence in search of a role and a director. Prochnow is bland in multiple roles, including that of the driver of the fetus-smuggling truck who has a climactic showdown with Hallyday.

Production design and special effects are mostly derivative but are professionally polished. Other credits are adequate. —*Len.*

Burglar
(COLOR)

Comic misfire wastes Whoopi.

A Warner Bros. release of a Nelvana Entertainment production. Produced by Kevin McCormick, Michael Hirsh. Executive producer, Tom Jacobson. Directed by Hugh Wilson. Stars Whoopi Goldberg. Screenplay, Joseph Loeb 3d, Matthew Weisman, Wilson; based on books by Lawrence Block; camera (Technicolor), William A. Fraker; editor, Fredric Steinkamp, William Steinkamp; music, Sylvester Levay; production designer, Todd Hallowell; art director, Michael Corenblith; set decorator, Daniel Loren May; costume designer, Susan Becker; sound (Dolby), Darin Knight; assistant director-associate producer, Michael Green; casting, Marsha Kleinman. Reviewed at Universal Studios, Universal City, Calif., March 11, 1987. (MPAA Rating: R.) Running time: **102 MINS.**

Bernice Rhodenbarr .... Whoopi Goldberg
Carl Hefler .... Bobcat Goldthwait
Ray Kirschman .... G.W. Bailey
Dr. Cynthia Sheldrake . Lesley Ann Warren
Carson Verrill .... James Handy
Detective Todras .... Anne DeSalvo
Detective Nyswander ..... John Goodman
Frankie .... Elizabeth Ruscio
Graybow .... Vyto Ruginis
Knobby .... Larry Mintz

Hollywood — "Burglar" is one of those limited pictures which could easily suffice as a trailer. That's about all the time needed to capture the humor and suspense here. Anything more than a few bucks at the b.o. should be considered a steal.

Whoopi Goldberg handles a couple of funny scenes early on with enough skill to suggest that the laughs can be sustained as mystery unfolds. However, story fizzles almost as quickly as the other characters are introed.

As a shrew ex-con adept at diverse talents from boxing to electrical wiring, Goldberg strains believability as a wonder-woman. This self-described cat burglar is still on the prowl due to the blackmail demands of a former cop who has gone bad (G.W. Bailey).

When a second and more serious crime is committed during one of her jobs, Goldberg is forced to become her own private eye to avoid being tagged with the greater offense.

On screen as her best buddy is Bobcat Goldthwait (credited on-screen with his real name Bob). His presence is superfluous and the daffy schtick he practices is a complete dud.

Lesley Ann Warren turns in a ludicrous performance as a successful dentist who has scammed cash out of her practice for jewelry. This screechy dimwit is purportedly so airheaded that she doesn't know how many days there are in 72 hours.

Some of the others on hand include Anne DeSalvo and John Goodman as police detective partners in pursuit of Goldberg. They're party to a dumb chase sequence through S.F. Absurd attempt to replicate the legendary "Bullitt" action was the work of cinematographer William A. Fraker, who has the camera credit for the original.

What seems most regrettable here is the loss of what may have been a satisfactory mystery story. Those elements alone may well have worked if comedic idiocies had been avoided. —*Tege.*

Hollywood Shuffle
(COLOR)

Scattershot comedy attacks blaxploitation roles, with mixed results.

A Samuel Goldwyn Co. release of a Conquering Unicorn production. Produced by Robert Townsend. Executive producer-production manager, Carl Craig. Directed by, stars Townsend. Screenplay, Townsend, Keenen Ivory Wayans; camera (color), Peter Deming; editor, W.O. Garrett; music, Patrice Rushen, Udi Harpaz; art direction, Melba Katzman Farquhar; sound, William Shaffer; assistant director, Alix Townsend; choreographer, Donald Douglass; stunt coordinator, Steve W. James; casting, Brown & Livingston. Reviewed at Lorimar screening room, March 11, 1987. (MPAA Rating R.) Running time: **82 MINS.**

Bobby Taylor .... Robert Townsend
Lydia .... Anne-Marie Johnson
Bobby's mother .... Starletta Dupois
Bobby's grandmother .... Helen Martin
Stevie .... Craigus R. Johnson
Manvacum .... Domenick Irrera
NAACP president .... Paul Mooney
Producer .... Lisa Mende
Commercial director .... Robert Shafer
Mr. Jones .... John Witherspoon
Tiny .... Ludie Washington
Donald/Jerry Curl .. Keenen Ivory Wayans

Hollywood — Brimming with imagination and energy, "Hollywood Shuffle" is the kind of shoestring effort more appealing in theory than execution. Produced, directed and cowritten by actor Robert Townsend, pic is a freeform look at the trials and tribulations of black actors trying to make it in today's Hollywood. Scattershot humor misses as much as it hits, but film is entertaining enough to lure an audience looking for something a little different.

Based on what must be his personal experience looking for work, Townsend uses this as his starting point for a running series of exaggerated vignettes. Unfortunately, many of the bits simply go on too long and overall tone of the film is too casual and off-handed to bring home some serious points with much impact.

Target of Townsend's musings is the stereotyped roles blacks often are forced to play and their desire to do something better. At a cattle call for a blaxploitation pic to be made by a white production company, Townsend starts to feel guilty and questions if what he's doing is right after he gets the part.

Examination of Townsend's inner workings gives the film an excuse for numerous disgressions. Scenes in the actor's subconscious are dramatized on screen. Most amusing of these is a school for black actors, run by whites, of course, where the students are trained to shuffle, jive and generally fit the preconceived notion of what blacks are like.

Another brilliantly conceived bit is "Sneakin Into The Movies," a takeoff of the Siskel And Ebert film reviewing tv show, this time critiqued by some real soul brothers who have marketedly different taste than their models. Several clips are created for the pair to review, but the scenes drag and are not really very funny in themselves.

In addition, the segment seems to reinforce the very stereotyping of black sensibilities the film is trying to dispel. While the point that "we'll never start playing Rambos until we stop playing Sambos" is well taken, Townsend is not above resorting to skin-deep characterizations and cheap shots to serve his own purpose.

Performances of the ensemble cast, many of whom play more than one role, are likable but without much that sticks to the ribs. Production values are predictably crude given the film's $100,000 budget, but film creates enough good will to allow one to overlook many of its shortcomings. —*Jagr.*

Momo
(ITALIAN-W. GERMAN-COLOR)

A Cinecittà-Sacis (Italy) and Rialto-Iduna (West Germany) production. Produced by Horst Wendlandt. Executive producer, Claudio Mancini. Directed by Johannes Schaaf. Screenplay, Rosemarie Fendel, Schaaf and Marcello Coscia; camera (color), Xaver Schwarzenberger; music, Angelo Branduardi; assistant director, Eugenio Cappuccio; production designer, Danilo Donati; sound, Gaetano Testa; art director, Gianni Giovagnoni, set decorator, Emanuela Alteri; supervisor of special effects, Dario Piana; children's casting director, Ofelia Garcia. Reviewed at Beverly Cineplex, L.A. (American Film Market), March 4, 1987. (No MPAA Rating). Running time: **100 MINS.**

Momo	Radost Bokel
Hora	John Huston
Gigi	Bruno Stori
Beppo	Leopoldo Trieste
Nicola	Mario Adorf
Fusi	Francesco De Rosa
Chief Grey Man	Armin Müller-Stahl
Daria	Elida Melli
Leo	Francesco Perzulli
Nino	Ninetto Davoli
Liliana	Concetta Russina
Mr. Ende	Michael Ende
Grey Man BLW 533/C	Silvester Groth

(English-language soundtrack)

Los Angeles — Arguably an example of the highest of European production values, "Momo" nevertheless is rendered forgettable by the uninvolving direction responsible for a languid pace and one-dimensional performances.

Adapted from another widely read children's story by Michael Ende ("The Neverending Story"), "Momo" raises the question, how're you going to keep kids interested in something this laborious and inert after they've seen "Star Wars?"

Remindful but less entertaining than another European children-oriented pic, the British "Time Bandits," "Momo" focuses on the time-related adventure of a 10-year-old girl, an orphan, as is easily discerned by her curly red hair and the fact that she is introduced in a crevice of a crumbling amphitheater.

Little Orphan Momo sets out to help the villagers who befriended her after they're convinced to give up their leisure time to an icy gang of bald executive types called the Grey Men, headed by Armin Müller-Stahl, the iciest and baldest.

As Momo wends her way through the ominous, monumental sets of ace production designer Danilo Donati, strikingly caught by cinematographer Xaver Schwarzenberger, "Momo" the movie resembles a moppet's version of Kafka's "The Trial."

Headquartered in a rococo palace, John Huston plays the guardian of time and quarry of the Grey Men, who try in vain to induce Momo to betray the old man's hideaway. Huston, in slightly more than a cameo role, gives the film a warmth that is otherwise elusive.

As the young heroine, Radost Bokel seems miscast and as for the supporting actors, director Johannes Schaaf should have told them "less is more."

Shot at Cinecittà in Italy, Italo-German coproduction harbors some well-executed, but low-key, special effects, such as the dissolving one-by-one of the Grey Men when they run out of their life-giving cigars. Only the least demanding young or young-at-heart viewers will be totally absorbed by "Momo." —*Binn.*

The Beat Generation — An American Dream
(U.S.-DOCU-COLOR)

A Renaissance Motion Pictures release. Produced and directed by Janet Forman. Camera (TVC color), Tom Houghton; editor, Peter Odabashian; music, David Amram. Narrated by Steve Allen. Reviewed at the Berlin Film Festival (market), Feb. 21, 1987. Running time: **90 MINS.**

With: David Amram, Amiri Baraka, Ray Bremser, William Burroughs, Carolyn Cassidy, Clark Coolidge, Gregory Corso, Robert Creeley, Diane diPrima, Larry Fagin, Lawrence Ferlinghetti, Allen Ginsberg, Abbie Hoffman, Herbert Huncke, Hettie Jones, Jan Kerouac, Timothy Leary, Peter Orlovsky, Carl Solomon, Anne Waldman, Jack Kerouac, Neal Cassidy, Thelonious Monk.

Berlin — Here's another docu about the 1950s Beat Generation. Producer-director Janet Forman has assembled an absorbing collage of narration, talking heads and vintage 1950s news and home movie footage. For those who know the era and for those just discovering it, the pic is an informative nod back.

All the living principal players are interviewed including Allen Ginsberg, Amiri Baraka (then known as Leroi Jones) and William Burroughs. Era legends Jack Kerouac, Neal Cassidy and Thelonious Monk are represented on archival footage. Steve Allen narrates, reminding us he once cut a record accompanying Kerouac reading his work.

Pic rehashes the era's meaning, how the Beats inspired the liberated 1960s and maybe even the punk crowd. While the film makes a strong case for the legitimization of beatniks by the mass media, especially Life magazine and the publication of Kerouac's "On The Road," there are few new insights.

What's nice to see is how well and articulate the survivors remain. By letting us hear the cultural inheritors of the next generation like Timothy Leary and Abbie Hoffman, we get a sense of the era's pervasiveness.

The most interesting new interview comes from Hettie Jones, Baraka's first wife, who offers a realistic look at the era's meaning. One disturbing note is Jan Kerou-ac's brief appearance describing how she had never read her father until a doctor gave her one of his books to read when she was recovering from a drug overdose in a Bronx hospital.

David Amram provides the musical score and recreates an improvisational performance that captures the spirit of the time.

This docu will do well wherever there is interest in the alienated anti-heroes that emerged in post-war America. —*Owl.*

Death Stone
(WEST GERMAN-COLOR)

An NRF, Tarprobane, CCC coproduction. Produced by Theo M. Werner and Chandran Rutnam. Directed by Franz Josef Gottlieb. Screenplay, H.W. John, John Ferguson; music, Luigi Ceccarelli. (Further credits not listed.) Reviewed at Berlin Film Festival (Market), Feb. 23, 1987. Running time: **95 MINS.**

Kumar	Albert Fortell
Jane Lindström	Birte Berg
Wrickremapala	Ravindra
Brian	Brad Harris
Hemingway	Siegfried Rauch
Merryl Davis	Heather Thomas
Kris Patterson	Elke Sommer
Miguel Gomez	Tony Kendall
Frank	Serge Falck

(English language soundtrack)

Berlin — "Death Stone," shot in tropical Sri Lanka, is an adventure thriller that never comes off. Prospects for this low budgeter shot in English with an eye on the overseas market are best for video rentals, others dim.

(Production was backed by James Aubrey's U.S. company Entermark, which also planned to release it Stateside but company went out of business last year. —*Ed.*)

Plot involves a young architect whose fiancée becomes a victim of drug dealers. He then declares war on the pushers. After opening with a police raid on a jungle drug camp, the action alternates between scenes of violent karate fighting and colorful local celebrations with all the trappings of elephants, dancing, music, and pageantry.

Pic gets its title from a curio found on the beach by Jane, Kumar's ill-fated girl friend. According to Ceylonese legend, the stone means death to anyone possessing it, a belief dismissed by the Europeans as superstition. Predictably, as the story unfolds and the stone passes from one victim to another, all eventually die. Clichés ranging from the obligatory cobra, to the chase and the final clinch, and dialog from B pics of the past, are ever-present.

Even pros like Elke Sommer and Heather Thomas cannot rescue the stilted script, with such gems as "all right sugar, you got yours, now I'll get mine" or "you must have loved her very much."

Technical credits are good, but cannot rescue this turkey. —*Kind.*

Dutch Treat
(COLOR)

Weak vehicle for a Dutch singing group.

A Cannon Group release of a Golan-Globus production. Produced by Menahem Golan, Yoram Globus. Directed by Boaz Davidson. Screenplay, Lorin Dreyfuss, David Landsberg; editor, Bruria Davidson; music, Steve Bates; art direction, Phil Dagort; assistant director, Donald J. Newman; casting, Bonnie Pietila. Reviewed at Cinema Intl., Amsterdam, Feb. 17, 1987. (MPAA Rating: R). Running time: **84 MINS.**

Jerry	David Landsberg
Norm	Lorin Dreyfuss
The Dolly Dots	Themselves

Also with: Terry Camilleri, Linda Lutz, Robbie Sella.

Amsterdam — "Dutch Treat" is an aimless romp, groaning with gags. Helmer Boaz Davidson and editor Bruria Davidson play this at a rip-roaring pace that neatly masks the lack of credible plot. Any impulse to look for one is quickly corrected with a dollop of slapstick.

David Landsberg and Lorin Dreyfuss wrote the story of "Dutch Treat," as they did for their first effort, "Dumb Dicks." In addition to two fat parts for themselves, they also wrote in a juicy part for a group of Dutch warblers, the Dolly Dots, who are popular in Europe and Japan.

Film shows Landsberg and Dreyfuss as knifethrowing entertainers on a cruise ship. A hitch in the act results in two of the ship's officers with knife holes in their bodies and the two heroes landing in a Dutch jail. They are freed on bail, discover the Dolly Dots, pass themselves off as leading Yank music execs and flee back to the States. It's a plot that turns in and out of itself ad infinitum.

Except for the leads, there's not much call for acting. Most characters are gags on legs, and locations are just background for gags. The Dolly Dots are easy to look at and to listen to. Pic is light entertainment, so light it's nearly weightless. A treat for the Dutch, maybe, but not for anyone else.—*Wall.*

The Fourth Protocol
(BRITISH-COLOR)

A Rank production. Produced by Timothy Burrill. Executive producers, Frederick Forsyth, Michael Caine and Wafic Said. Directed by John Mackenzie. Stars Caine, Pierce Brosnan. Screenplay, Forsyth, from his novel, with additional material by Richard Burridge; camera (Rank color), Phil Meheux; editor, Graham Walker; music, Lalo Schifrin; production design, Alan Cameron; art director, Tim Hutchinson; sound, Chris Munro; costumes, Tiny Nicholls; casting, Priscilla John, Lynn Stalmaster. Reviewed at Century Preview Theater, London, Feb. 25, 1987. Running time: **119 MINS.**

John Preston	Michael Caine
Major Petrofsky	Pierce Brosnan
Irina Vassilieva	Joanna Cassidy
General Borisov	Ned Beatty
Eileen MacWhirter	Betsy Brantley

Jan Marais	Peter Cartright
Burnam	David Conville
Tom MacWhirter	Matt Frewer
General Karpov	Ray McAnally
Sir Nigel Irvine	Ian Richardson
George Berenson	Anton Rodgers

London — "The Fourth Protocol" is an expertly crafted thriller with a grim sense of realism that raises it above similar films of the genre. It should have fine b.o. prospects internationally.

A large international cast performs adequately in rather one-dimensional roles, but Michael Caine as a maverick counterespionage expert gives a thorough performance in a part that doesn't really stretch his abilities.

"The Fourth Protocol" is a decidedly contempo thriller, a tale of vying masterspies and a chase to head off a nuclear disaster. Its edge is a fine aura of realism.

Novelist Frederick Forsyth, who also was an executive producer, adapted the pic from his book. Previous films of Forsyth novels like "The Day Of The Jackal," "The Odessa File" and "The Dogs Of War," were moderate successes, but somehow lacked the narrative edge of their sources, which this version comes closer to capturing.

The story is pretty straightforward. A ruthless KGB head plans to detonate a nuclear bomb close to a U.S. airbase in England so the Brits blame the Yanks and the NATO alliance will collapse.

What follows is a good old-fashioned race against time as Caine tracks down his Russian alter ego Major Petrofsky (Pierce Brosnan finally getting to play a spy, albeit a baddie) and after a hand-to-hand scuffle manages to defuse the bomb.

Director John Mackenzie has constructed a well-made piece of hokum, but there is a sense that he has stuck a bit too closely to Forsyth's original version, when new life happily could have been breathed into some sections.

Pic is certainly tense enough, and all actors perform well, especially Ian Richardson as spymaster Sir Nigel Irvine, though the Russian accents of Ray McAnally and Ned Beatty are a bit dubious.

Technical credits are all fine, with Phil Meheux' photography especially good. Despite one of Caine's drunk routines early on, the pic lacks a sense of humor and takes itself a little too seriously.

"The Fourth Protocol" holds attention thanks to its realistic manner rather than falling back on the easy option of glitzy spy routines à la Bond. A strong musical score by Lalo Schifrin helps things along, though there is an uneasy feeling the whole affair could have been better made into an excellent miniseries, explaining all of the book's nu-

ances, rather than a solid, well-made film.—*Adam.*

Down Twisted
(COLOR)

Misguided thriller.

A Cannon Group release of a Golan-Globus production. Produced by Menahem Golan, Yoram Globus. Directed by Albert Pyun. Screenplay, Gene O'Neill, Noreen Tobin, from a story by Pyun; camera (TVC color), Walt Lloyd; editor, Dennis O'Connor; music, Berlin Game; production design, Chester Kaczenski; art director, Richard Hummel, Douglas H. Leonard; sound (Ultra-Stereo), Drew Kunin; costumes, Renee Johnston; assistant director, Ramiro G. Jaloma; associate producers, Karen Koch, Tom Karnowski; casting, Perry Bullington. Reviewed at Mann Westwood theater, L.A., March 13, 1987. (MPAA Rating: R.) Running time: **97 MINS.**
Maxine	Carey Lowell
Reno	Charles Rocket
Michelle	Trudi Dochtermann
Damalas	Thom Mathews
Deltoid	Norbert Weisser
Soames	Linda Kerridge
Brady	Nicholas Guest
Blake	Gaylyn Gorg

Hollywood — "Down Twisted" is a film in search of a style. Part "Maltese Falcon" goes to Central America and part "Romancing The Stone" with hip design and a new wave soundtrack, pic never quite finds the tongue-in-cheek tone it's looking for or a voice of its own. Result is considerably less fun than it pretends to be, and with a no star cast and almost zero awareness it has little chance at the boxoffice.

Charm of classic suspensers has always been their quirky characters rather than plot and in cases like "The Big Sleep" it was nearly impossible to tell exactly what was going on, but with Bogart and company it hardly mattered. One simply gave in to the thrill of being in their presence.

"Down Twisted" probably wanted to do the same thing but as written by Gene O'Neill and Noreen Tobin and directed by Albert Pyun, the characters are too thin to carry a perfectly preposterous story. Somewhere along the line the clues that give a character substance were sacrificed for a more cosmetic look.

Plot centers around an ornate religious relic ripped off from the tiny banana republic of San Lucas. Trail of double-crossings leads to the unsuspecting Maxine (Carey Lowell) who before she knows what hit her is fending off soldiers, terrorists and armed criminals all hunting for the holy grail.

Lowell is thrown together with soldier-of-fortune Charles Rocket and while the two snipe at each other throughout they fail to generate much warmth, let alone heat. Lowell is indeed lovely but her constant whining marks her more as a UCLA coed than a heroine to entice an audience.

For his part, Rocket wisecracks his way through various attacks but shows little aplomb. For heroes these people are simply too ordinary to stir the imagination.

Main villain is Norbert Weisser as a slick businessman who is obsessed with capturing the gold, but there is no passion or glee to his obsession. Consequently, the object of value has too little importance to give a darn about.

Assorted scoundrels along the way include the white-haired Thom Mathews and blond and beautiful Trudi Dochtermann, each out to cut their own deal and their partner's throat. They too are lifeless in their evilness. It's all too much like a game for them.

Plot is severely lacking in credibility with glaring gaps in continuity which allow the heroes to escape several close calls without explaining how. Dialog doesn't help much either.

Production values are adequate but overall look and staging of the film is often stiff and contrived, if not downright laughable.—*Jagr.*

Queen City Rocker
(NEW ZEALAND-COLOR)

A Spectrafilm release (U.S.) of a Mirage Films presentation. Produced by Larry Parr. Directed by Bruce Morrison. Screenplay, Bill Baer; camera (color), Kevin Hayward; editor, Michael Hacking; music, Dave McCartney; production design, Mike Becroft; sound, George Lyle. Reviewed at Westend cinema, Auckland, Feb. 24, 1987. (NZ Rating: RP16.) Running time: **89 MINS.**
Ska	Matthew Hunter
Andrew	Mark Pilisi
Sniper	Ricky Bribiesca
Stacy	Kim Willoughby
Fran	Rebecca Saunders
Ryder	Peter Bland

Auckland — "Queen City Rocker" is an unabashed Kiwi attempt to genre grab in that category of Hollywood adolescent-angst movies made popular by Emilio Estevez and friends in the early 1980s.

It cuts some corners, for plus and minus points, gets close to real drama only to back away, and finally emerges as just a hint of that distinctive slice-of-life street kids' film it might have been.

Marvelously shot in and around Auckland city (camera, Kevin Hayward), the story centers on gang leader Ska (Matthew Hunter) and his growing disillusionment with the life of violence and petty larceny in which he is enmeshed. It takes the death of his best friend Andrew (Mark Pilisi), in gangland retribution for the kids' destruction of a sleazy nightclub where Ska's sister Fran (Rebecca Saunders) reluctantly works, and the love of Stacy (Kim Willoughby) from the moneyed side of town, to impel a breakthrough.

While the script evokes the S.E. Hinton novels adapted to film ("The Outsiders," "That Was Then

... This Is Now"), it lacks their credibility and gift in creating teenagers that ring true.

Too often action for the sake of action displaces scenes necessary to build audience understanding and involvement with the main protagonists. Director Bruce Morrison captures well the three-steps-back explosive expression of street kid life, but cannot seem to handle the close-ups that would reveal individual motivation for the behavior and which are crucial for the human drama taking place.

As a result, the largely inexperienced young cast is given little to breathe life into. Their uncertainties show. Only Pilisi, who had a notable debut opposite Lisa Harrow in John Laing's "Other Halves," has the natural ability to break through the ineptness of much of the dialog.

The minor gangland figures fare better, but even an able trouper like Peter Bland (as the nightclub owner Ryder) falls into some disarray during a confused denouement.

Throughout, there are moments in "Queen City Rocker" which suggest something rather more. The opening sequences placing Ska and Andrew in their close-to-the-edge-of-crime environment are achieved immaculately. The suggested responsibilities of Ska and Fran in bringing up their younger siblings are tantalizing, if undeveloped. Dave McCartney's rock music is a bonus, with the city of Auckland (as it did in "Other Halves") again emerging as a superb natural urban location for filmmaking. —*Nic.*

Lévy et Goliath
. (Levy And Goliath)
(FRENCH-COLOR)

A Gaumont release of a Gaumont Intl./G. Films coproduction. Produced by Alain Poiré. Directed by Gérard Oury. Screenplay, Oury, Danièle Thompson; camera (Panavision, Eastmancolor), Wladimir Ivanov; editor, Albert Jurgenson; music, Vladimir Cosma; sound, Alain Sempé, Jacques Maumont; art director, Théo Meurisse; assistant director, Michel Cheyko; second unit director, Marc Monnet; second unit camera, André Domage; motor stunt coordinator, Rémy Julienne; production managers, Marc Goldstaub, Bernard Bouix. Reviewed at the Gaumont Ambassade cinema, Paris, Feb. 21, 1987. Running time: **97 MINS.**
Moses Levy	Richard Anconina
Albert Levy	Michel Boujenah
Bijou	Jean-Claude Brialy
Malika	Saouad Amidou
Goliath	Maxime Leroux
Brigitte	Sophie Barjac
Drug mogul	Robert Hossein

Paris — Ace commercial comedy director Gérard Oury and his scripter-daughter Danièle Thompson, who had one of their top-grossing successes with the 1973 Louis de Funès topliner "The Adventures of 'Rabbi' Jacob," return to the ethnic vein in "Levy And Goliath," a frantically unfunny effort that spends too much screen time trying to curry audience favor with preachy sentimentalities about tolerance.

Plot might be described as a gefilte fish-out-of-water farce with Richard Anconina playing a typically cloistered young Hassidic Jew from Antwerp who finds himself being pursued by a gang of coke smugglers in Paris, where he is delivering white diamond powder to a local car assembly line plant. Anconina unwittingly unloads several packages of cocaine, slipped into his bag by one of the smugglers on the train to avoid customs inspectors.

Lost in the modern Sodom of Paris ('round Pigalle way) and apparently abandoned by the Almighty — who used to appear to him at home in the steam of a boiling tea-kettle! — Anconina desperately calls for help to his long estranged brother (Michel Boujenah), who lives an assimilated middle-class life with his blond, blue-eyed gentile wife (Sophie Barjac) and their kids.

Rather than develop the action organically from the Anconina-Boujenah confrontations, Oury and Thompson mechanically fall back on the overblown contrivances of chase comedies they've exploited before, and with greater comic imagination. They even resort to the facilities of "Cages aux folles" humor in a series of scenes set at a transvestite club (where Jean-Claude Brialy is a detective working undercover as a screaming drag queen).

Film is finally most unpleasant when it pounds out its messages on tolerance (racial and sexual), love and blood ties. Anconina and Boujenah, both appealing young talents, do their best to make it palatable but Oury's clumsy hand prevails.

The Gaumont production has clicked at home temples, but offshore markets may find this a most unkosher commercial mishmash.
—*Len.*

Cry Wilderness
(COLOR)

Amateur night with Yeti.

A Visto Intl. release and production. Produced by Philip Yordan, Jay Schlossberg-Cohen. Executive producer, William F. Messerli; coproducer, Gene S. Ruggiero; associate producer, James E. Davis. Directed by Schlossberg-Cohen. Screenplay, Yordan; camera (color), Joseph D. Urbanczyk; music, Fritz Heede; music supervisor, Ralph Ives; sound design, Bruce Bell. Reviewed at Aurora Cinema, Seattle, March 6, 1987. (MPAA Rating: PG.) Running time: **95 MINS.**
Paul Cooper . . . . Eric Foster
Will Cooper . . . . Maurice Grandmaison
Morgan . . . . Griffin Casey
Jim . . . . John Tallman
Dr. Helen Foster . . . . Faith Clift

Seattle — "Cry Wilderness"

must be one of the worst films ever made. It's strictly amateur hour with bad acting, poor production values, atrocious dialog and improbable storyline. It's hard to believe it will even recoup its obviously scanty investment in the vid market, let along on the bigscreen.

It's the story of a young boy, Paul, who had befriended Bigfoot while visiting his forest-ranger father in the northern part of California the previous summer.

One night, an apparition of Bigfoot visits Paul at his private L.A. school and tells him his father is in trouble, so Paul dashes away from school and hitchhikes north to come to his father's aid.

From there, the "adventure" begins as Paul realizes Bigfoot is terrorizing the forest, but tries to prevent his father, accompanied by an Indian and a Rambo-like big-game hunter, from killing him. The trio of adults, however, think they're just tracking a Bengal tiger (of all things) that has escaped from the circus.

Bigfoot, when he appears, is so obviously an actor in an apesuit that it's pathetic.

The pic is filled with awful clichés, like the sexpot in the bikini who walks on for about three seconds and contributes nothing to the plot.

But worse, "Cry Wilderness" is just plain boring, with nothing much happening for long stretches, when the photography is frequently and blatantly out of focus.
—*Magg.*

Noi Cei Din Linia Intii
(The Last Assault)
(RUMANIAN-COLOR)

A Romania Film release of a Fifth Film Unit production (Bucharest Studios). Directed by Sergiu Nicolaescu. Screenplay, Titus Popovici; camera (color), Nicolae Girardi; editor, Gabriela Nasta; music, Adrian Enescu; art direction, Radu Corciova. Reviewed at the India Film Festival (Competition), Delhi, Jan. 11, 1987. Running time: **160 MINS.**
With: George Alexandru, Anda Onessa, Valentin Uritescu, Ion Besoiu, Sergiu Nicolaescu, Stefan Iordache.

Delhi — "The Last Assault" is a two-part, 160-minute, all-action World War II battle pic, so cunningly lensed by Rumanian veteran Sergiu Nicolaescu it seems to naturally dispense with any scene that doesn't include machinegun fire. Its young hero starts out wet behind the ears, but soon turns into a fighting machine of such prowess that Rambo would be envious. Strictly for fans of the battle genre, "Assault" is a professional contribution to an overworked genre.

Lt. Horia Lazar (George Alexandru) reports for active duty just in time to take over the platoon of an heroic young casualty. In spite of

being totally inexperienced, Lazar brilliantly carries out his first mission (disobeying orders in the process) and wins the respect of his men and commanding officers alike. Since the town he liberates just happens to be his own village, he gets hero treatment from Mom, Pop and the townsfolk.

Lazar isn't the only over-achiever in the film. This is a picture where every grenade thrown by a Rumanian stops a tank, and every bullet seems to down two Germans. Scripter Titus Popovici keeps the action coming and the quickly sketched G.I.s sympathetic. Touches of humor are mixed in ably when there's a rare lull in the fighting. The handsome young lieutenant gets the only actress in the film, Anda Onessa, who happens to be the general's daughter. Other thesps are touching, comic, eccentric or ruthless, according to genre types.

Pic is divided into two parts of 90 and 70 minutes. The second spans the Battle of Budapest and the final assault of the title. This takes place at a castle in the woods where an S.S. group operating a radio station refuses to surrender after the war is officially over. Technical work is tops, especially Nicolae Girardi's atmospheric photography. —*Yung.*

Proshal Zelen Leta
(Farewell Green Summer)
(SOVIET-COLOR/B&W)

An Uzbekfilmstudio production. Directed by Elior Ishmukhamedov. Screenplay, Jazur Iskhakov, Ishmukhamodov; camera (color, b&w), Yuri Liubshin; music, Edouard Artemiev; art direction, Igor Gulenko. Reviewed at India Film Festival, Delhi, Jan. 11, 1987. Running time: 92 MINS.
Timur . . . . .Fakhretdin Manafarov
Ulphat . . . . .Larisa Belogurova
Also with: Rustam Sagdullaev, Borislav Brondukov.

Delhi — Winner of the India Film Festival, "Farewell Green Summer" is a bittersweet tale of star-crossed young love that gradually steers its way into an indictment of corruption in its native Uzbekistan. This typical product of the Gorbachev years is permeated by a gentle wistfulness and longing that harks back to director Elior Ishmukhamedov's early Tashkent tales ("Tenderness," 1967). It is muted by a creeping sentimentality, but this should be more of a help than a hindrance in getting pic to markets that take popular Soviet product.

The rise and fall of a simple young man named Timur (Fakhretdin Manafarov) begins when Timur is born, and leaves the hospital at the same time as the baby girl fated to be his true love, Ulphat. Opening black and white sequences charmingly recreate the Tashkent of yore, underlined by pretty, nostalgic music and some sequences from an ear-

ly Indian talkie that is wildly popular at the local bijou.

Ishmukhamedov is good at blending the most disparate material into the film. Color arrives when Timur and Ulphat (Larisa Belogurova) are in their teens, supplemented by b&w newsreels of the terrible earthquake of the Sixties. Love blossoms while the city is under repair, but Ulphat's ferocious father and brothers reject her marriage to a poor boy, and beat Timur up. Ulphat is whisked away and forced to marry someone else.

Only years later do they meet again, briefly, on a train — but by then Timur has turned down the path of corruption, and Ulphat has a son. Timur reassesses his life. Heroically trying to blow the whistle on a local boss, he gets killed, but the autoworkers in his factory press for justice. The rest is history.

Pic doesn't mince its reproaches of party favoritism that gets people jobs and saves their skins when they're caught with their hand in the cookie jar. None of this is a secret, as the recent avalanche of arrests in the republic demonstrates. Lensing is professional throughout. —*Yung.*

City On Fire
(HONG KONG-COLOR)

A Cinema City production, released by Golden Princess. Executive producer, Karl Maka. Produced and directed by Ringo Lam. Stars Chow Yun Fat, Sun Yueh, Lee Sau Yin. Screenplay, Tommy Sham, from a story by Ringo Lam; editor, Sone Ming Lam; camera (color), Andrew Lam; music, Teddy Robin; action coordinator, Joseph Chi; art direction, Luk Tze Fung; associate producer, Catherine S.K. Chang; production manager, Catherine Lau. Reviewed at President theater, Causeway Bay, Hong Kong, Feb. 7, 1987. Running time: **98 MINS.**
(Cantonese soundtrack with English subtitles)

Hong Kong — The bloody death of an undercover policeman gets the Royal Hong Kong Police in a complex situation. It temporarily blocks the source of secret information to track down a well-known syndicate specializing in jewel robberies.

Inspector Lau, now past his prime (Sun Yueh) is in charge of the case. Besides the politics in the Force of being replaced by a younger officer, Lau must find someone immediately to take the place of the deceased.

The man he has in mind is Ko Chow (Chow Yun Fat with a new haircut is perfect for the serio-comic role) and is recruited for the mission of penetrating the gangsters. Ko poses as a sly wheeler-dealer of guns for hire. Ko is introduced to Ah Foo (Lee Sau Yin), sort of lieutenant of the syndicate.

Foo is a cautious man and puts Ko to various character tests to assure that security is maintained. In the process, a male bonding is developed between the two supposedly gutter-type characters.

A jewel robbery is set up and implemented with disastrous results both from the gangsters who panic, and police force who can be faulted for lack of coordination. The tragic finale gives the film more dramatic power.

"City On Fire" is Cinema City's answer to "The French Connection." It is highly animated, fast-moving entertainment. The street photography is highly realistic while the dramatic conflicts are well-controled to avoid the usual soap opera ingredients. The off-beat Canto-jazz/soul musical score (performed by Maria of Canton) complements the well-balanced acting.—*Mel.*

My Will, I Will
(HONG KONG-COLOR)

A Molesworth production and release. Directed by Luk Kim Ming. Screenplay, Luk Kim Ming. Stars Chow Yun Fat, Do Do Cheng. (No other credits provided by producer/distributor). Reviewed at Park theater, Hong Kong, Jan. 1, 1987. Running time: **98 MINS.**
(Cantonese soundtrack with English subtitles)

Hong Kong — Chow Yun Fat and Do Do Cheng make a lovely, charming couple with that special man vs. woman screen charisma that truly works. The storyline about a woman trying to get impregnated for a legal heir to her U.S. fortune in oil is corny, but nonetheless amusing when done unpretentiously and beguilingly as a light-hearted romantic comedy.

Chow is in fine natural comedic form while Do Do looks deliciously fashionable for her first class status in hotels and airlines. With her flirty movements, teasing eyes and superstar wardrobe, she looks every inch a super-yuppie, unsuitable for the economy section of life.

There is some forced and over-blown acting in the supporting roles, but overall it's a sprightly Cantonese comedy.

The debut film of new film company Molesworth Prod. paid off well as the boxoffice was over $HK13,000,000, a clear indication that a sequel will be in the offing. —*Mel.*

The Journey
(SWEDISH-DOCU-COLOR/-B&W-16m)

A Peter Watkins, Svenska Freds-och Skiljedomsforeningen (Film for Fred, the Swedish Peace and Arbitration Society), Stockholm, production, with assistance of Cinergy Films and Sky Works Charitable Foundation, Montreal. Post-production services, National Film Board, Canada; many international peace groups, city and national film commissions credited for contributions of materials, services, funding. (World rights, Films Transit, Montreal). Written and directed by Peter Watkins. Production coordinator, Catharina Bragee; post-production coordinator, Peter Wintonick; many cinematographers and crews credited in U.S., USSR, Mexico, Japan, Norway, Mozambique, West Germany, Great Britain, France, Australia, Denmark, New Zealand, Italy, Sweden, Finland, Canada; graphics and animation coordinators, Joan and Jane Churchill; editor, Watkins, Petra Valier, Manfred Becker, Wintonick; sound editors, Watkins, Becker, Tony Reed, Raymond Vermette, Vida Urbonavicius. Reviewed at Berlin Film Festival (Forum), Feb. 24, 25, 26, 1987. Running time: **873 MINS.**
(In English, and with English subtitles to various languages)

Berlin — At 14½ hours, "The Journey" is the longest and strongest of the many films to date that examine the arms race and the threat of nuclear holocaust. It is uncompromising and must show it all, say it all, thus its great length.

"The Journey" is a tour de force for producer-writer-director Peter Watkins, who has labored for years on the film, fundraising and directing the work of film crews in 16 nations. In 1965, Watkins had created a great controversy with "The War Game," a docudrama simulating nuclear war in England. Banned by the BBC for two decades, "The War Game" finally was telecast in 1985. Earlier, it was released theatrically and won an Oscar.

Many sequences within "The Journey" use stock footage or are shot to order, occasionally reinforced with stills and other graphic materials. Superficially, these many sequences may seem discursive, but they meld thematically into a single momentous statement. Among them: the atomic bombings of Nagasaki and Hiroshima illustrate man's willingness to use nuclear annihilation against an enemy. Witnesses and survivors of those bombings describe what it was like, in dignified, painful, ironic understatement. German survivors of Allied fire-bombings against Hamburg discuss today the new technology of warfare that makes child's playthings of the weaponry used against Hamburg. The camera visits Hamburg's underground bunker of World War II, beneath the railway station, still designated as a refuge center for 1,500 people in the next war; they will have supplies for two weeks, a half-liter of warm liquid per day. And then?

We also visit Polynesia, where over 100 nuclear test-explosions have occurred. In the U.S., we see protestors throw themselves on railroad tracks to prevent the passage of trains with nuclear arms. We see Norwegian families evacuated hysterically in drills, alerted that an attack is imminent. We watch African women in remote villages, surrounded by naked children, describe their feelings of solidarity with peace movements abroad, expressing themselves with remarkable sophistication. We examine the arms industry of Sweden, big export business for a neutral, benign peace-loving nation. Soviet adults describe their being orphaned as children during the Great Patriotic War against Germany — the ache for lost parents is never assuaged. Several sequences deal with the triviality of tv news, those "photo opportunities," and other superficial events pretending to be responsible journalism.

As a leitmotif, Watkins emphasizes the universal fear of nuclear warfare among families around the world. Watkins shows video images and still photographs to mothers, fathers and their children, then asks — what do you think? These may seem like typical families but their testimony reveals them to be special, as they are often peace activists. Sometimes it is a scientist who drops out of military work, is scorned by his co-workers, suspected by his neighbors, who with difficulty must find other employment. Ethics and religious faith prevent such people from compromising their standards. Through these families in "The Journey," we see their common idealism, their simple hope, a worldwide sentiment for brotherhood, expressed as a global forum in many languages, at many kitchen tables.

Because of its great length, "The Journey" connects with "Shoah," a hit at Berlin's forum last year, and "Heimat" at Venice in 1985. Theatrical screenings are feasible under special circumstances only, with long intensive screenings for dedicated filmgoers prepared to concentrate. Necessarily, that is a minority audience. Video and 16m sales and rentals to universities, and to peace groups and churches, are a natural, especially as "The Journey" can be structured and paced for discussion purposes. Public tv seems the largest and most logical target audience for the film. For that audience, viewing the entire film will be an unusual experience, even difficult, but ultimately very rewarding. —*Hitch.*

Dal Polo al l'Equatore
(From Pole To Equator)
(GERMAN-ITALIAN-

COMPILATION-B&W-16m)

Produced by Yervant Gianikian, Angela Ricci Lucchi, ZDF-TV. Directed by Gianikian, Ricci Lucchi. Editor, D.A. Pennebaker; music, Keith Ullrich, Charles Anderson. Reviewed at Lumiere theater, Rotterdam, Feb. 5, 1987. Running time: **96 MINS.**

Rotterdam — This is a fascinating and thoroughly engrossing result of three years' work by Yervant Gianikian and Angela Ricci Lucchi, who have been making offbeat films since 1976. Now they have exploited the newly discovered film archives of Luca Comerio (1874-1940), a pioneering figure of Italo docucinema.

Comerio was a court photographer, allowed to film the landing of Italian marines in Libya in 1911, and was the only official film reporter with the Italian army in World War I. His archives also contain work by other filmmakers.

Gianikian and Ricci Lucchi have photographed more than 500,000 frames of archive material from the positive and from the original negative. There is no dialog, and the music is a "minimalist" score, written by two Americans.

Pic shows hunting and shooting of animals at the South Pole, Caucasia, Russia and India. In Africa, the hunt is led by Mussolini's secret political agent. In 1914 in the Dolomites human soldiers (Austrians, Germans, Italians) become the prey.

Sequences are shown at a slowed down pace — not slow motion, but enough to give every movement, every angle, more weight. The synthesized soundtrack, cleverly used, adds to the effect.

Pic grips the viewer throughout and is a natural for fests, universities, and film clubs. Coproducer ZDF will air it in Germany in April, and Italian tv will follow shortly afterwards. It is booked for the Edinburgh and Chicago film festivals. —*Wall.*

The Hanoi Hilton
(COLOR)

Misguided attempt to tell the story of U.S. prisoners during Vietnam War emerges as a right-wing tract.

A Cannon Group release of a Golan-Globus production. Produced and directed by Menahem Golan, Yoram Globus. Written and directed by Lionel Chetwynd. Camera (TVC color), Mark Irwin; editor, Penelope Shaw; music, Jimmy Webb; sound (Ultra-Stereo), Gary Cunningham; production design, R. Clifford Searcy; art direction, Carol Bosselman; set decoration, Ian Cramer; production manager, Joel Glickman; assistant director, Bob Bender; costume design, Richard LaMotte; casting, Perry Bullington. Reviewed at Broadway screening room, N.Y., March 16, 1987. (MPAA rating: R.) Running time: **123 MINS.**
Williamson . . . . Michael Moriarty
Fischer . . . . Jeffrey Jones
Hubman . . . . Paul Le Mat
Miles . . . . Stephen Davies

Cathcart . . . . Lawrence Pressman
Cat . . . . Aki Aleong
Paula . . . . Gloria Carlin
Murphy . . . . John Diehl
Turner . . . . Rick Fitts
Oldham . . . . David Soul
Gregory . . . . David Anthony Smith
Kennedy . . . . Ken Wright
Ashby . . . . Doug Savant
Oliviera . . . . John Vargas
Fidel the Cuban . . . . Michael Russo

———

"The Hanoi Hilton" is a lame attempt by writer-director Lionel Chetwynd to tell the story of U.S. prisoners in Hoa Lo Prison, in Hanoi during the Vietnam War. Special pleading aside (pic's end credits 16 P.O.W.s for their assistance, listing on-screen the extent of their incarceration), pic is a slanted view of traditional prison camp sagas, injecting lots of hindsight and taking right-wing potshots that do a disservice to the very human drama of the subject.

Chetwynd missteps very early on in this overlong (exceeding two hours running time) picture, with the characterization of Aki Aleong as the cultured but sadistic martinet of a prison commandant. Aleong's performance is technically okay, but film fans will immediately recognize the verbal cadence and sinister styling as right out of Richard Loo's memorably hissable (and often-quoted) performance in "The Purple Heart" in 1944. What worked during World War II as propaganda won't wash in a 1987 feature film.

Michael Moriarty heads a curiously bland cast portraying P.O.W.s on a set the conjures up "Hogan's Heroes" rather than the gritty realism intended (pic was lensed in California with unconvincing jungle location scenes and stock footage for action material). He's thrust into a position of authority when the ranking officer played by Lawrence Pressman is taken off to be tortured. Episodic structure introduces new prisoners as more pilots are shot down over a roughly 10-year span (including some comic relief such as one prisoner who says he fell off his ship accidentally and was captured).

Pic is desperately lacking side issues or subplots of interest (such as the fun black humor or interpersonal rivalries of such forerunners as Bryan Forbes' film of James Clavell's "King Rat") with Chetwynd monotonously hammering away at the main issue of survival in the face of inhuman treatment. Main thematic point which carries the narrative was done far better in "The Bridge On The River Kwai;" namely, that the prisoners must maintain military discipline and lines of authority by rank at all costs, lest their captors isolate and break them down.

There is an intrinsic interest in watching the ensemble cast overcome their travails, but unbelieva-bility intrudes, especially in later reels when characters start mouthing statements about the war that benefit from years of hindsight. Worse yet, in attempting to present the P.O.W.'s p.o.v., Chetwynd moves deep into poor-taste territory with verbal potshots at Bertrand Russell and Sen. William Fulbright, an embarrassing pastiche of Jane Fonda (an actress wearing a "Klute" wig sitting next to a guy with a bad complexion is supposed to represent the star, renamed Paula, visiting North Vietnam), and a purely right-wing portrait of a British journalist who covers up a P.O.W.'s bloody, torture-induced wounds so his newsreel camera won't show them and disturb his pro-North Vietnam interview. This is propaganda pure and simple and sounds particularly loathsome (relative to the right's pronouncements lately regarding the Iran/contra affair) when characters blame the news media back home reporting on the war for exacerbating the prisoners' problems.

Cast struggles with this intractable material, with the more familiar faces, such as Jeffrey Jones, Paul Le Mat and David Soul, emerging far too laidback for their roles. At the other extreme, Michael Russo overdoes it as the heinous interrogation officer named (no kidding) Fidel the Cuban. That presumably rules out the film being invited to next year's Havana Film Festival.

Pic was once on track by Chetwynd as a telefilm, and given a network's standards & practices office, which would have removed the scurrilous material, it would undoubtedly have worked better than as a low-budget theatrical feature.
—*Lor.*

———

Lenz
(HUNGARIAN-COLOR)

———

A Hungarofilm release of Béla Balázs Studio Budapest production. Directed by András Szirtes. Screenplay, Szirtes, Mátyás Büki, Tamás Pap (inspired by Georg Büchner's novel); camera (Eastmancolor), András Dávid, Barna Mihók; editor, Eszter Kovács; music, Gustav Mahler; sound, Eszter Matolcsy, Gyula Traub; sets and costumes, Lujza Gecser, László Rajk. Reviewed at the Budapest Congress Center, Feb. 15, 1987. (In Berlin Film Festival — Forum.) Running time: **99 MINS.** With: András Szirtes (Lenz).

———

Budapest — "Lenz" is an experimental film about a scientist exposed to an overdose of atomic radiation which affects his perception of the world around him. Dimensions of time, color and shape change drastically, sensory world is changed and he is plunged into a dream world he cannot comprehend.

Once he comes out of it, he tries to build a machine that will explain these strange visions. When he realizes no machine can explain dreams he opts for a bomb that will destroy all, but at the last moment, when his son walks in on him, he gives up the idea.

As expected in this kind of film, there is a lot of trick photography, a lot of speeded-up sequences and magnifying of infinitely small details, and there are numerous reflections about dream versus reality, the relations between the creative spirit and the spirit created, and of course, about the impenetrability and magnificence of nature, eventually experienced through art but never fully penetrated by science. Mahler's music is used to strong effect, mostly Symphony No. 1 and the song cycle which inspired it.

Strictly limited to selected audiences interested in the avant garde, the film was also screened for the Berlin Forum. —*Edna.*

Making Mr. Right
(COLOR)

———

Comedy misfire about a publicist-android love affair.

———

An Orion Pictures release of a Barry & Enright production. Executive producers, Susan Seidelman, Dan Enright. Produced by Mike Wise, Joel Tuber. Directed by Seidelman. Screenplay, Floyd Byars, Laurie Frank; camera (Deluxe color), Edward Lachman; editor-associate producer, Andrew Mondshein; music, Chaz Jankel; art direction, Jack Blackman; set decoration, Scott Jacobson, Jimmy Robinson 2d; special visual effects, Bran Ferren, costume design, Rudy Dillon, Adelle Lutz; casting, Risa Bramon, Billy Hopkins. Reviewed at Orion Pictures screening room, March 17, 1987 (MPAA Rating: PG-13.) Running time: **95 MINS.**

Jeff Peters/Ulysses . . . . . . John Malkovich
Frankie Stone . . . . Ann Magnuson
Trish . . . . Glenne Headly
Steve Marcus . . . . Ben Masters
Sandy . . . . Laurie Metcalf
Estelle Stone . . . . Polly Bergen
Dr. Ramdas . . . . Harsh Nayyar

———

Hollywood — Susan Seidelman has taken nearly every wrong turn in "Making Mr. Right," a desperately unfunny romance between an android and a New Wave "image consultant."

Orion shouldn't expect to land much coin with this one.

The director must like the mistaken identity theme, which she so charmingly employed in "Desperately Seeking Susan," but handled pretty ineptly here.

Instead of getting animated performances in a funny, screwball comedy, "Mr. Right" is just screwy. The actors nearly suffocate delivering stiff dialog, with jokes that are bad or vulgar (or both) in scenes that reek of contrivance.

Sharing in the blame should be scripters Floyd Byars and Laurie Frank, who have taken Frankenstein and turned him into Frankie Stone (Ann Magnuson).

Her world is Melrose Avenue Miami style, where she's a very unlike-ly whiz-bang publicist with a punk 'do and very ordinary sensibilities who practically moves in with an android and his creator (John Malkovich in both roles) to get the best handle on how to sell the invention to the American public before he's launched into space.

She's supposed to be teaching the android, Ulysses, social graces, but he ends up learning emotions instead — thereby negating much of the sophisticated programming his alter ego, Dr. Jeff Peters, worked so hard in perfecting.

Malkovich takes to his role of Ulysses very earnestly, considering he has to utter such gooey lines as "Why do people fall in love?" and suffer mutterings from Magnuson and her horny girlfriend (Glenne Headly) whether he's anatomically correct.

As Dr. Peters, the actor doesn't have to stretch much playing the role to type as the nerdy, bumbling indignant scientist pushed out of shape that he has to suffer the commercialization of Ulysses at the hands of a disorganized dame.

Whatever women's lib theme ran through "Desperately Seeking Susan" is totally wiped away in this confused effort.

Magnuson portrays a totally dingly girl concerned more with making sure she has lipstick on than whether she's violating every professional ethic publicists have worked to create.

The action follows her while she races around at a frenetic pace between the Chemtech lab and her apartment (both miraculously decorated in terribly trendy '50s style), trying to corral Ulysses.

About the only two bright spots in the film are outside this context, with Ulysses caught buying expensive jewelry for a lovesick coworker, Sandy (Laurie Metcalf), and chasing after Magnuson at her sister's tacky wedding.

These scenes are supposed to build sexual tension between the android and his "image creator," but it isn't until nearly the last five minutes of the film where Magnuson shows even a twinge of desire for the robot.

Why, just minutes before she was totally disgusted at the idea that her girlfriend found him very well endowed indeed and a fantastic lover (even if he short circuited afterwards).

Then, at the wedding, she seemed all but about ready to agree marrying her congressman — that is, after he shaved his mustache off to please her.

Finally, film ends in a ridiculous climax stretching the story's incredulity even further.

Filmmakers seem a little confused on the technical side also. Continuity is often off (a tie knotted one second and loosened the next) and the overall look seems very low-budget, even if this was probably the highest budgeted pic Seidelman ever made. —*Brit.*

Personal Services
(BRITISH-COLOR)

A UIP release, Vestron Pictures (U.S.), of a Zenith production. Produced by Tim Bevan. Directed by Terry Jones. Screenplay, David Leland; camera (Eastmancolor), Roger Deakins; editor, George Akers; production design, Hugo Luczyc-Wyhowski; art director, Jane Coleman; sound, Garth Marshall; costumes, Shuna Harwood; casting, Debbie McWilliams. Reviewed at Curzon Shaftesbury Ave., London, March 8, 1987. (MPAA Rating: R.) Running time: 105 MINS.
Christine Painter . . . . Julie Walters
Wing Commander Morton . Alec McCowen
Shirley . . . . Shirley Stelfox
Dolly . . . . Danny Schiller
Rose . . . . Victoria Hardcastle
Timms . . . . Tim Woodward
Sydney . . . . Dave Atkins
Mr. Popozogolou . . . . Leon Lissek

London — For a pic about sex, "Personal Services" is remarkably unerotic. It deals with society's two-faced attitude to sex-for-sale in a humorous but essentially sad way, and is excellently acted and directed. Offshore prospects could prove sharp (Vestron Pictures has U.S. rights).

Pic received substantial U.K. publicity thanks to a recent court case involving a madam on whom the film is based and who became a household name as a result of the trial. Pic is also very much about English sexual hangups, though most characters come across as affestionate and genial types, albeit kinky as well.

Film's director, Terry Jones, made his name as one of the anarchic Monty Python comedy team, and went on to helm "Monty Python And The Holy Grail," "The Life Of Brian," and "The Meaning Of Life." In this, his first non-Python pic, he keeps the plot bubbling along with a fine eye for detail and a sense of irony.

Pic tells the story of the transition of Christine Painter (a dominating performance by Julie Walters) from waitress to madam of Britain's most pleasant brothel, where the perversions are served up with a cooked breakfast and a cup of tea to follow. She looks after the aged and infirm along with eminent clients, none of whom has a kink her girls can't cater to.

Julie Walters plays Christine as a charmingly vulgar yet benign madam, whose brothel-keeping career seemingly comes to an end when the police raid her London house during a Christmas party. At her trial she recognizes the judge as one of her regular clients.

Writer David Leland (who co-wrote "Mona Lisa") has crafted a script that pokes fun at sexual manners, but also cleverly examines British attitudes while instilling the whole affair with deep-rooted romanticism. Jones directs adroitly, never allowing the pic to become vulgar.

Technical credits are strong, with production design by Hugo Luczyc-Wyhowski especially good. The cast members are all fine, with Julie Walters in fine "Educating Rita" form after two so-so films. Alex McCowan is excellent as her friend and business partner, a former pilot who proudly boasts of a World War II record of 207 missions over enemy territory in "bra and panties." —*Adam.*

Capriccio
(Letters From Capri)
(ITALIAN-COLOR)

A Filmauro release, De Laurentiis Entertainment Group (U.S.), of a San Francisco Film production. Produced by Giovanni Bertolucci. Written and directed by Giovanni Tinto Brass. Camera (Technicolor), Silvano Ippoliti; editor, Brass; music, Riz Ortolani; art director, Paolo Biagetti. Reviewed at Quirinale Cinema, Rome, March 16, 1987. Running time: 100 MINS.
Jennifer . . . . Nicola Warren
Fred . . . . Andy J. Forest
Rosalba . . . . Francesca Dellera
Ciro . . . . Luigi Laezza

Also with: Vittorio Caprioli (Don Vincenzo).

Rome — "Letters From Capri" is cool, classy softcore from Italy's premier erotic director, Giovanni Tinto Brass. Concentrating on technique and atmosphere more than graphic closeups, for a change, Brass succeeds in deliverying a velvet-touch film for the Playboy set. Already picked up by DEG for the U.S., pic should have no trouble entering the world's eroticism markets.

Story is set in the late 1940s, in Rome and Capri, when a handsome Yank couple returns to the place where they spent the last years of the war. Though they're now married and with a child, their unspoken intentions go far beyond a pleasant work-vacation (he's an art restorer). In fact, both lose no time in looking up their old acquaintances, Rosalba (Francesca Dellera), a delectable prostitute who still has a crush on Fred (Andy J. Forest), and Ciro (Luigi Laezza), curly haired hunk who has become a pimp. Jennifer, the cool blond American wife (Nicola Warren), goes all the way to Capri to see "the only man who ever made her feel like a woman;" Fred takes off on a trip through the beautiful Tuscan countryside to romp in the woods with Rosalba.

In the end the legit couple unites, sadder that the past relived is never as good as in memory, but with a new sensual attraction to each other.

Silvano Ippoliti's camera and Riz Ortolani's score create a convincing 1940s feel, all soft-focus and jitterbug. Thesps are quite up to their parts, and despite some explicit female nudity, pic steers clear of the vulgarity that has dimmed the glow of Brass' last few films. Technically, pic is far beyond its subject matter, and makes one long for the day when the director will reach for a weightier argument. —*Yung.*

L'Inchiesta
(The Investigation)
(ITALIAN-COLOR)

An Italian Intl. Film release of an IIF/Clesi Cinematografica/RAI-TV Channel 1/Sacis coproduction. Produced by Fulvio Lucisano, Silvio and Anna Maria Clementelli. Directed by Damiano Damiani. Stars Keith Carradine, Harvey Keitel, Phyllis Logan. Screenplay, Vittorio Bonicelli, Damiani; camera (Cinecittà colori), Franco Di Giacomo; editor, Enzo Meniconi; music, Riz Ortolani; art direction. Reviewed at Capranica Cinema, Rome, Feb. 13, 1987. Running time: 107 MINS.
Tauro . . . . Keith Carradine
Pontius Pilate . . . . Harvey Keitel
Claudia Procula . . . . Phyllis Logan

Also with: Angelo Infanti, Lina Sastri (Mary Magdelene), Paolo Molina, Sylvan, Frencesco Carneluti, Laura De Marchi, Luciano Bartoli, Giorgio Stowe, Lorenzo Piani.

Rome — "The Investigation" is a classic age-of-Christ costumer with a clever premise — that Roman emperor Tiberius sends a special envoy a few years A.D. to investigate the disappearance of Christ's body.

Vet helmer Damiano Damiani casts an unlikely crew of Anglo-Saxon leads and handles the tale in the old-fashioned style of Roman epics of the 1950s, with creaky dialog and horse opera lensing. Local b.o. has been fair. This curiosity item could have a chance for limited offshore play if slanted toward religious audiences with a bent for imaginative early Christian history.

Though pic's look may be old hat, its investigating magistrate Titus Valerius Tauro (Keith Carradine) is a character straight out of today's newspapers. He arrives in Jerusalem in the wake of bloody (read guerrilla/terrorists) attacks against the Roman occupiers. His mission is to find the missing body of a rebel, Jesus of Nazareth. The rumor of his resurrection from the dead is, in Tiberius' view, a story hatched with the aim of inciting the populace to rebel.

Tauro's belief that the Christian cult is a mere case of religious fanaticism is shared by Harvey Keitel in the guise of Pontius Pilate, made insecure and a little neurotic by imperial criticism of his failure to repacify Judea. Of a different opinion is his wife (Phyllis Logan), a closet believer in Jesus. Eventually Tauro's investigations lead him to Mary Magdelene (Lina Sastri), now a saintly nurse in a leper colony. Much in the fashion of present-day judges, he reaches no real conclusion, but sinks into a morass of unsolvable riddles that defeat his Roman-empire rationality.

Shot on location in Tunisia, "Investigation" recreates a standard Biblical world without fanfare. It requires some imagination to accept Carradine, Keitel, and Logan as ancient Romans, though performances are serviceable. Keitel piles on the intensity; Carradine relies on screen appeal more than period believability. — *Yung.*

Salvation! Have You Said Your Prayers Today?
(U.S.-COLOR)

Zany satire of electronic evangelism.

A B movies production. Executive producer, Ned Richardson. Produced by Beth B. Michael H. Shomberg. Directed by Beth B. Screenplay, Beth B, Tom Robinson; camera (color), Francis Kenny; editor, Elizabeth Kling; music, New Order, Cabaret Voltaire, The Hood, Arthur Baker; production design, Lester Cohen; sound, Lee Orloff. Reviewed at Berlin Film Festival, Feb. 24, 1987. (No MPAA Rating.) Running time: 85 MINS.
Rev. Edward Randall . . . Stephen McHattie
Lenore . . . . Dominique Davalos
Rhonda . . . . Exene Cervenka
Jerome Stample . . . . Viggo Mortensen

Also with: Billy Bastiani, Rockets Redglare.

Berlin — Rev. Randall (Stephen McHattie) is an electronic evangelist with a successful tv program — half-charlatan, half-sincere. One dark night the stunning young blond Lenore (Dominique Davalos) raps upon his chamber door, pretending to be having a car emergency, intent on seducing him. Fearful of blackmail, Randall admits Lenore reluctantly. Is she an emissary of Satan? Ranting religious rhetoric, Randall beats and rapes Lenore — but he needn't have, she was willing.

At that moment Jerome, Lenore's brother-in-law, breaks into the house. He beats Randall and drags him to the nearby surf to drown him. Lenore regains consciousness and races to the rescue. Much of this is directed and acted with considerable skill, although far from the intended comedy. Jerome's two thugs, Stan and Ollie, also terrorize Randall.

Almost immediately, Randall agrees to co-host a bigger religious show, with Rhonda, Jerome's wife and sister of Lenore. Randall and Rhonda become big-business cynics, warning the nation against the poison of secular humanism. They share an enormous income, their lawyers negotiating the details of their hustle, including who has what rights to recording sales and T-shirts.

Stephen McHattie as Randall captures the right Southern accent and cadence and evangelical fervor, mixing jingoistic patriotism and Biblical allusions, laced with home-spun charm.

Even at its best, satire is cold and can rarely cut deep, but "Salvation" manages some amusing jabs at hypocrisy, born-again but cash in advance. The easy shifting of gears from violence to sexuality is a recurrent theme.

"Salvation" ends in a music video equivalent of a revivalist orgy, the "Destroy All Evil" finale, with lots of fast cuts of bare flesh, elaborately costumed dancers, gyrating, singing and shouting. Dramatic logic you don't get in "Salvation." Non-stop action, yes, but strong plot and motivation are lacking. Characterizations are shallow, featuring types, not personages.

"Salvation" satisfies as a fast series of comic set-pieces much of the time. It is rather like music video, at which producer-director Beth B has excelled — it's flashy but lacks substance. —Hitch.

Triumph Der Gerechten
(Triumph Of The Just)
(WEST GERMAN-COLOR)

A Bierbichler Films production. Directed by Josef Bierbichler. Screenplay, Bierbichler, from short story by Oskar Maria Graf; camera (color), Jorg Schmidt-Reitwein; editor, Christian Virmond; music, Rudolf Gregor Knabl; sound, Brian Greenman; set decoration, Hans Reindl; costumes, Ann Poppel, Vroni Reindl; assistant director, Virmond; production manager, Robert Spitz. Reviewed at the Berlin Film Festival, Feb. 25, 1987. Running time: **81 MINS.**
The Ape . . . . .Josef Bierbichler
Emperor Maximilian .Felix von Manteuffel
The Intellectual . . . . .Edgar Liegl

Berlin — Though sincerely meant, "Triumph Of The Just," a time-tripping statement about war and history, probably will prove too esoteric for viewers without strong powers of concentration.

The film, which focuses on the atrocities of the Thirty Years' War between Catholics and Protestants, begins with a modern-style bombing raid and ends with humanity back to the stone age. In between, the German peasants suffer and the symbolism lies thick on the landscape.

Director Josef Bierbichler may have made a film only he can understand. Ann Poppel and Vroni Reindl's costumes, however, deserve acclaim, as do Poppel's masks. —Xau.

La Gran Fiesta
(PUERTO RICAN-COLOR)

A Zaga Films production. Executive producer, Roberto Gandara. Produced by Gandara, Marcos Zurinaga. Directed by Zurinaga. Screenplay, Ana Lydia Vega, Zurinaga. camera (color), Zurinaga; editor, Gandara;

music, Angel (Cucco) Pena; set design, Maria Teresa Pecanins; costumes, Gloria Saez, Federico Castillo. Reviewed at the Miami Film Festival, Feb. 13, 1987. Running time: **101 MINS.**
With: Daniel Lugo, Miguelangelo Suarez, Luis Prendes, Cordelia Gonzalez, Laura Delano, Raul Julia, E.G. Marshall, Julian Pastor.

Miami — Don't let the title, "La Gran Fiesta," deceive. This is not a bit-o-mamba/bit-o-samba "musical romp," but Hollywood-handsome moviemaking, full of craft. It doesn't quite have it all, but it's got most of what audiences want — romance, intrigue, betrayal and a "Casablanca" fadeout.

Producers are billing this as Puerto Rico's entry into world cinema, and there is certainly something going on here — enough to attract E.G. Marshall to a supporting role (a low-dialog cakewalk, admittedly) and Raul Julia to a hilarious cameo (as a foppish dipso poet-at-large). Promoter's boast does not seem far from the mark.

Much as the Australians did before them when re-inventing their cinema, the Puerto Rican production team turned to local history for their story. It is 1942, the island is bubbling with fear of the outer conflict and more direct involvement with an inner one, and there is about to be a grand, farewell ball to attract the key players.

In much of the rest of the world there is war, and a sizable faction of leading Puerto Ricans fret about being invaded by the Germans, whose submarines are on patrol throughout the Caribbean. Meanwhile, back at the island, a struggle between liberals led by the colonial governor (a Roosevelt appointee) and conservative grandees (many of them supporters of Franco's fascist Spain), has made life all too interesting even for the rich, who if caught without powerful friends or at least U.S. citizenship can be dealt with summarily.

Typical of these is Don Manolo, a proud Spanish expatriate and once-successful businessman who has fallen on hard times. His last best hope is the impending marriage of his son, a liberal bureaucrat, to the daughter of one of the island's wealthiest and most influential families.

Unbeknownest to Don Manolo, the local district attorney, Vazquez, is assembling a bogus but dangerous case against him in an effort to ingratiate himself with the ruling liberals. Don Manolo's son, Jose Manuel, has fallen in love with a sultry fellow red-taper and has decided to break off his engagement. There is a manner of other activity, some related and some not but all great fun, on the fringes (most notably the attempts of Jose Manuel's ripening younger sister to elude her mother long enough to

flirt), but Don Manolo's troubles are the key.

Half the film goes to establishing the players and their stakes in the affair, which director Marcos Zurinaga gets done with a great deal more grace than is suggested here. The second half, titled "La Gran Culminacion," takes place in the Casino de Puerto Rico, a private club about to be closed and handed over to the U.S. Navy for the duration. Naturally, everyone who is anyone — and that means all the principals — is there.

Zurinaga's work is fine throughout — this is remarkably good-looking for a first feature — but the second half truly shines. As the ball goes on, and the protagonists wheel, deal and maneuver, Zurinaga begins to cut at a steadily swifter pace, until in the film's last few minutes the story is told in a dizzying series of reaction shots.

The performances are first-rate, production values top-line. Picture should have healthy life on art circuit, and should do well as a crossover entry in markets with a substantial Latin population. —Cos.

Iron Warrior
(ITALIAN-COLOR)

A Trans World Entertainment release. Produced by Sam Sill (Ovidio G. Assonitis). Directed by Al Bradley (Alfonso Brescia). Screenplay, Steven Luotto, Brescia; camera (Fujicolor, Technicolor), Wally Gentleman; editor, Tom Kezner; music, Charles Scott; special effects supervisor, Mario Cassar; costume design, Dana Kwitney; casting, Joanna Lester. Reviewed at UA Twin 2 theater, N.Y., March 21, 1987. (MPAA Rating: PG-13.) Running time: **82 MINS.**
Ator . . . . .Miles O'Keeffe
Janna . . . . .Savina Gersak
Deeva . . . . .Iris Peynado
Phoedra . . . . .Elisabeth Kaza
King. . . . . .Tim Lane

"Iron Warrior" pretends to be a fantasy adventure, but it's really just an ad for the Malta tourist board. Beautiful locations filmed on the islands of Malta and Gozo provide the backdrop for incoherent filler, shot in 1985 under the title "Echoes Of Wizardry" by producer Ovido G. Assonitis, whose name is understandably missing from the credits crawl.

Miles O'Keeffe returns for the third time as Ator, mythical warrior given a new history here: his twin brother was kidnaped in childhood by evil witch Phoedra (Elisabeth Kaza in a red fright wig). Some 18 years later Ator is tapped by the nice sorceress Deeva (Iris Peynado) to protect Princess Janna (Savina Gersak) against evil, in the form of his brother who wears a silver skullmask, red bandana and breathes like Darth Vader.

Ator and Janna trek around the rugged Malta rockfaces on various missions for Deeva with absolutely

no continuity to the narrative and some of the worst editing ever used in a feature film. Every couple of minutes Ator gets involved in boring swordplay with baddies and, to pad the running time, footage of another actor (who doesn't resemble O'Keeffe at all) wearing a babushka over his mouth is inserted fighting men on horseback with his sword. A dragon-style monster is shown on poster and ads but fails to show up during the film.

Italian potboiler director Alfonso Brescia ("you can call me Al Bradley") imitates numerous George Lucas films here, lifting equal amounts from both the "Star Wars" sagas and "Indiana Jones" films. Out-theme is a poor imitation of "Star Trek: The Wrath Of Kahn" music.

O'Keeffe is embarrassing, posing instead of acting and, like the rest of the cast, stuck with a funny-looking punk-influenced hairdo. Deborah Raffin-lookalike heroine Savina Gersak at least wears see-through gowns throughout the picture, but the editor nastily deletes her several wet T-shirt scenes. Best thing in the pic is the exotic, blue-eyed black actress Iris Peynado, previously seen in Lamberto Bava's "Monster Shark."

Pic was obviously made for homevideo and undemanding foreign markets, but if another reason from distrib TWE to Stateside theatrical B-picture fans. Oh for the days when Lippert and other second-feature labels gave us engrossing little films starring Dane Clark or Cesar Romero, with interesting storylines and talented supporting casts.—Lor.

Pretty Smart
(COLOR)

Tame sexploiter.

A New World Pictures release, presented by Balcor Film Investors in association with Chroma III and First American Film Capital. Produced by Ken Solomon, Jeff Begun. Co-produced by Melanie J. Alschuler. Directed by Dimitri Logothetis. Screenplay, Dan Hoskins, from an original story by Begun, Alschuler; camera (color), Dimitri Papacostantis; editor, Daniel Gross; music, Jay Levy, Eddie Arkin; production design, Beau Peterson; costume coordinator, Gaelle Allen; casting, F. Daniel Somrack (L.A.), Kostantinos Tzoumas (Athens); second unit director, Solomon. Reviewed at Broward Mall Cinema, Fort Lauderdale, Fla., March 19, 1987. (MPAA Rating: R.) Running time: **84 MINS.**
Daphne Ziegler . . . . . . .Tricia Leigh Fisher
Jennifer Ziegler . . . . .Lisa Lorient
Richard Crawley . . . . .Dennis Cole
Zero . . . . .Patricia Arquette
Torch . . . . .Paris Vaughan
Yuko . . . . .Kimberly B. Delfin
Alexis . . . . .Brad Zutaut
Sara .Kim Waltrip

Fort Lauderdale — Somewhere behind its up-front titillation, "Pretty Smart" (originally titled "The Bentley Academy") aspires to be more than just a peekaboo sexploiter — but not by much.

Dan Hoskins' screenplay dabbles with a clever coverup for a drug middleman and an interesting ruse for the creation of black market vidporn. Execution of the plot elements, however, is routine voyeurism for tamer markets.

Production values are okay and the Athens, Greece, location adds a touch of class to the exteriors, but direction, camerawork and cutting all bear the trademarks of a low-budget item for fast playoff.

Pic's South Florida release went flat in a week; prospects don't look any better for other urban areas. "Pretty Smart" is a likely candidate as a fill for the outdoor market and after hours for tv's mainstream cablers.

The story revolves around competing cliques at a private school in the Mediterranean. Group rivalries keep the girls from realizing the headmaster (Dennis Cole) is using the campus as a cover for his drug activities. He also coyly looks the other way when the coeds couple with students from a nearby boys' school, but is secretly taping their encounters in the dorm for sale to European porn distributors. The girls eventually discover the headmaster's game and turn the tables, resulting in the appointment of a big-sister type to headmistress (Kim Waltrip), less likely to peek while they cavort.

The come-on is the presence of several celebrity kin, including Patricia Arquette (Rosanna's sister) and Paris Vaughan (Sarah's daughter) in featured roles. Tricia Leigh Fisher (Connie Stevens/Eddie Fisher's offspring) takes the lead as a rebellious young woman who eventually learns to bury the hatchet with her rivals in order to focus all their energy on the plot to dump the headmaster. The group effectively garners tyro screen credit while leaving the nudity to the supporting cast, thus averting possible embarrassment in their future careers. A few scenes may be worthy of demo material for casting agents. —*Zink*

De Mujer a Mujer
(Woman To Woman)
(VENEZUELAN-COLOMBIAN-COLOR)

A Pel-Mex release of an E.M. Films (Venezuela)-Prods. Cinematográficas Uno (Colombia) production. Produced by Luis Felipe Betancourt, Bella Ventura. Directed by Mauricio Walerstein. Stars Humberto Zurita. Screenplay, David Suárez, Mario Mitrotti, Walerstein; camera (color), José Alcalde; music, Alejandro Blanco Uribe. Reviewed at Big Apple Cine 1, N.Y. March 15, 1987. Running time: **109 MINS.**

Sergio . . . . Humberto Zurita
Elsa . . . . Elba Escobar
Eloy . . . . Daniel Alvarado
Miranda . . . . Amparo Grisales

The Venezuelan-Colombian coproduction "Woman To Woman" is directed by Mauricio Walerstein, on expatriate Mexican who was a fringe member of the early '70s "New Mexican Cinema" group and also son of producer Gregorio Walerstein.

Story concerns the violence that ruptures the friendship between two women, Elsa (Elba Escobar) and Miranda (Amparo Grisales), when confronted with an unpredictable and erratic sexual force in Sergio, played by Mexican actor Humberto Zurita.

As in Walerstein's 1984 Venezuelan venture "Macho y Hembra," the sexual roles of the characters break down. It is a matter of dominance and submission. Although Sergio originally pairs with Elsa, he later chooses the more psychologically complex and beautiful Miranda. When they run off together, Elsa naturally falls in with Miranda's former bed partner and spouse Eloy (Daniel Alvarado).

It is this sexual energy, whether functional or violent, that pervades the entire pic and eventually leads to everyone's destruction.

José Alcalde's brooding camera knows how to capture tone and detail, which is set off by Alejandro Blanco Uribe's sultry jazz score.

Acting by the principals is strong. When Zurita first appears, with his beard and longish hair, he has the savage sexual magnetism and inherent danger of a Charles Manson.

In his works, Walerstein continues to explore this impulsive and dangerous aspect of sexuality, especially when confronted with the quotidian nature of society and its inherent threat to bourgeois status quo and the family unit. Also, pic delves nto the threat of real-life passion confronting a society that harbors vicarious desires instilled by melodramatic and tawdry soap operas and romantic movies.

"Woman To Woman" is as challenging as it is absorbing in its portrait of life confronted by desire and its ever-consuming sense of destruction as opposed to the procreative nature of sexuality. Its force and compelling characters are as savage as the tropical terrain.
—*Lent.*

Drehort Berlin
(Set In Berlin)
(W. GERMAN-DOCU-COLOR)

A Journal Film production. Directed by Helga Reidemeister. Camera (color), Lars-Peter Barthel; editor Dörte Volk; music, Andi Brauer; sound, Katharina Rosa. Reviewed at the Berlin Film Festival, March 1, 1987. Running time: **110 MINS.**

Berlin — "Drehort Berlin" is a well-made and original docu on the walled city, but its negative approach and the anti-Americanism of many of the interviewees is bound to turn off some viewers.

The film combines attractive scenery shots with monologs by residents of both East and West Berlin, including an East Berlin hairdresser, a West Berlin cemetery visitor, and one woman who fled from East to West and wishes she hadn't. All come off as thoughtful and honest about the fate of Berlin.

Director Helga Reidemeister has constructed a novel and entertaining, if slightly misbalanced, portrait of a complex city.—*Xan.*

Bach And Broccoli
(CANADIAN-COLOR)

A Cinema Plus release of a Prods. La Fête production. Produced by Rock Demers; line producer, Ann Burke. Directed by Andre Melançon. Screenplay. Bernadette Renaud, Melançon; camera (color), Guy Dufaux; art director, Violette Daneau; music, Pierick Houdy; production manager, Josette Perotta; costumes, Huguette Gagne; assistant director, Mireille Goulet. Reviewed at Cineplex Odeon screening room, Toronto, Feb. 26, 1987. Running time: **90 MINS.**

Fanny . . . . Mahee Paiement
Jonathan . . . . Raymond Legault
Sean . . . . Harry Marciano
Bernice . . . . Andrée Pelletier
Grandmother . . . . France Arbour

Toronto — For a pic that has a button-cute orphaned girl, a domesticated skunk and an eccentric uncle, "Bach And Broccoli" is considerably lacking in charm. The third of producer Rock Demers' "Tales For All" series is posed to be solid family fun. It could fare better as a homevideo entry, but it has broken b.o. records in Quebec since its release last month.

The major obstacle to appreciating any spontaneity in the story is the dreadful dubbing from French to English. Not only do the words not match the lip movements, but the voices and laughter are off, and a large element of fun is zapped. Maybe the kids won't mind it and will be enraptured with the sweet tale, but adults will squirm during the extreme closeups of the young tyke.

Melançon, who fared so well in "The Dog Who Stopped The War," is limited here by a well-intentioned but predictable script. It's a more grownup version of "Three Men And A Cradle," in which an 11-year-old girl (Mahee Paiement), whose parents were killed in a car accident when she was a child, is carted off to her sole uncle's house by her ailing grandmother, who's going to a nursing home.

Uncle Jonathan (Raymond Legault) is less than elated at seeing Fanny and hasn't a clue about child rearing. He's taking a leave from his accountancy job so he can concentrate on entering a Bach organ competition. His apartment is a shrine to the composer, and he hums and whistles the music all day.

His first aim is to arrange a proper family for Fanny. He's self-sufficient, stuck in his ways, but vulnerable, and ultimately succumbs to the charms of his new charge, who even prompts him to be more aggressive with a love interest from work (Andrée Pelletier).

Fanny is a wise child, precocious, sensitive, and a lover of animals. Her pet skunk Broccoli is only the first of a menagerie she and downstairs neighbor Sean collect in a renovated shed. Before the end of the pic, roosters, dogs, birds, hamsters and bunnies are cohabitating in the city zoo *chez* Fanny.

Natch, when it comes time for Fanny to be placed in a foster home, Uncle J. is finally able to verbalize the love he's bottled up all these years.

Melançon's able to get fresh performances from the kids and he's coached Legault to give his Jonathan more depth and character than a cardboard kook. There's a goodwill and cheer here and a tidy, happy ending, and maybe that's all kids need for a cinema outing.—*Devo.*

La Rumba
(The Rumba)
(FRENCH-COLOR)

A Hachette Première/UIP release of a Progrefi/TF-1 Films/Hachette Première coproduction. Executive producer, Christine Gouze-Renal. Directed by Roger Hanin. Screenplay, Hanin, Jean Curtelin; camera (color), Jean Penzer; editor, Youcef Tobni; music, Claude Bolling; production designer, Bernard Evein; sound, Daniel Brisseau; makeup, Monique Huylebroeck; costumes, Laurence Brignon; assistant director, Michel Picard; production manager, Philippe Verro; casting, Shula Siegfried. Reviewed at the UGC Normandie cinema, Paris, Feb. 20, 1987. Running time: **92 MINS.**

Beppo Manzoni . . . . Roger Hanin
Malleville . . . . Michel Piccoli
Xavier Detaix . . . . Niels Arestrup
Ma Pomme . . . . Guy Marchand
Madam Meyrals . . . . Patachou
Regina . . . . Corinne Touzet
Valentine . . . . Sophie Michaud
Puppie Ziegler . . . . Stéphane Jobert
Gino Motta . . . . Karim Allaoui
Josephine Baker . . . . Vivian Reed
Nono Gozlan . . . . Lino Ventura

Paris — "La Rumba," a '30s thriller set against the backdrop of encroaching European facism, oozes production gloss with some of the swankiest sets, costumes and model cars in local memory since the Jean-Paul Belmondo pics "Borsalino" and "Stavisky."

Imposing wallflower however is the script by Jean Curtelin and director-star Roger Hanin, a studied and uninspired assembly of genre clichés and stereotypes, heavily dosed with "Cabaret"-style decadence and irony.

Hanin is the protagonist, Beppo Manzoni, one of the kingpins of 1938 Parisian night life with a string of classy cabarets, gambling dens and restaurants and close ties to the underworld. He's also a secret crusader against facism, saving Italian refugees, plotting the assassinations of facist bigwigs and foiling the villainies of a corrupt police inspector in cahoots with extreme right-wing factions.

There's no complexity of nuance in this confrontation between noble patriotic gangsters and dastardly blackshirts and Nazis who clash in a familiar choreography of bullets, broads and booze. Hanin's direction lacks flamboyance and excitement and he guides himself and his prestigious cast through the proceedings with overly self-concious and tight-lipped gravity.

The heavies are played heavily by Niels Arestrup, as the treacherous cop, and Michel Piccoli, as a fascist ringleader, both of whom get their comeuppance from Hanin, his taxi boy-gigolo accomplices and the Paris underworld led by cameo guest star Lino Ventura at his most monolithically authoritative.

Only thesp to exude the breeziness and style the filmmaking lacks is Guy Marchand, who, as the top attraction of Hanin's glitzy cabaret, gives a standout rendition of an old '30s standard à la Maurice Chevalier.

Vivian Reed also stops in to impersonate Josephine Baker out on the town warbling a few bars of "Mes deux amours," while veteran chanteuse Patachou hangs about on the sidelines in a non-singing supporting silhouette.

The real stars of "La Rumba" are art director Bernard Evein (who last year designed the austerely beautiful "Thérèse"), lenser Jean Penzer, costume designer Laurence Brignon and composer-arranger Claude Bolling, who have been given the means●o make the production a sumptous feast for eyes and ears. Unfortunately "La Rumba" doesn't rumble with melodramatic tension or surprises.—*Len.*

Blind Date
(COLOR)

Funny slapstick from Blake Edwards.

A Tri-Star Pictures release. Executive producers, Gary Hendler, Jonathan D. Krane. Co-executive producer, David Permut. Produced by Tony Adams. Directed by Blake Edwards. Stars Kim Basinger, Bruce Willis. Screenplay, Dale Launer; camera (Metrocolor, prints by Technicolor), Harry Stradling; editor, Robert Pergament; music, Henry Mancini; production design, Rodger Maus; art direction, Peter Lansdown Smith; set decoration, Carl Biddiscombe; costume design, Tracy Tynan; sound (Dolby), William M. Randall; assistant director, Mickey McCardle; second unit director, Joe Dunne; casting, Nancy Klopper. Reviewed at the Samuel Goldwyn theater, L.A., March 24, 1987. Running time: **93 MINS.**

Nadia Gates . . . . Kim Basinger
Walter Davis . . . . Bruce Willis
David Bedford . . . . John Larroquette
Judge Harold Bedford . . . . William Daniels
Ted Davis . . . . Phil Hartman
Muriel Bedford . . . . Alice Hirson

Hollywood — Blake Edwards' "Blind Date" is one setup that's a crackup. Madcap adventures with Bruce Willis and Kim Basinger coupled with a PG-13 rating are sure to engage lots of b.o. business for Tri-Star.

Edwards has made a name for himself as a master of slapstick comedy and this is his best effort of late.

It doesn't hurt that he has a deliciously funny script to work with, one by "Ruthless People" screenwriter Dale Launer. Certainly less venal than the Disney b.o. smash, pic nevertheless makes up for lack of biting black humor with raucous silliness.

As in "Back To School," plotline for this film is kind of thin, but strong enough on which to hang some heavy talents.

Bruce Willis, fortunately, has abandoned his mugging tv personality in favor of playing an animated, amiable, hard-working, ambitious financial analyst.

Stuck without a date for a company function, he reluctantly agrees to ask his brother's wife's cousin (Kim Basinger) to accompany him. His first impression: she's darling. His first mistake: he's not supposed to let her drink and ignores the advice. Two sips of champagne later, she's out of control.

Theme of pure mayhem works well because of chemistry between the main trio of actors, Willis Basinger and her spurned ex-beau, John Larroquette.

Basinger is cool when sober and wacky when drunk. Actress is usually a sexy blond, but for some reason is dyed a brunet here — and still sexy. Her part is really secondary to Willis,' who starts out a befuddled date with the manners of a gentleman and ends up not only befuddled, but crazy for the woman.

It's really the psychotic Larroquette who drives this romp. While Willis tries to control his date (or at least figure her out), Larroquette is hot on his tail trying to get her back. Their skirmishes are hilarious.

Pic is essentially a running string of gags with snippets of catchy dialog in-between.

Edwards employs nearly every comedic trick that's ever been used in slapstick —short of a pie fight. Instead, it's paté that's thrown, cars driven through store windows, hallway skirmishes, and lots of drunk jokes (heaving in a car, walking the line). Most work, while a few fall flat. Scenes where a house is driven away or when Willis is held up by female leather types are stupid.

The frenetic pacing punctuated with the character's non-stop bantering may grow wearisome for some viewers hoping for a little social satire or something more meaningful than innocuous nonsense.

Filmmakers plainly wanted to entertain on the most elemental level. Opportunities to take jabs at wealth, the legal system and the single life are passed over in favor of the slick joke.

It all takes place in L.A., locale where the kind of freeway fast, upwardly mobile lifestyle these characters live, fits in.

Along to add yocks is Bill Daniels as Larroquette's bombastic judge father and Phil Hartman as Willis' oily car salesman brother.

Production credits are fine. Music credits run the gamut from Henry Mancini's scoring to Stanley Jordan's guitar solo. In short, hokey and hip — which in this case is a foolproof formula.—*Brit.*

Rawhead Rex
(BRITISH-COLOR)

An Empire Pictures release of an Alpine Pictures-Paradise Pictures-Green Man production. Executive producers, Al Burgess, Paul Gwynn. Produced by Kevin Attew, Don Hawkins. Directed by George Pavlou. Screenplay, Clive Barker; camera (Rank color), John Metcalfe; editor, Andy Horvitch; art direction, Len Huntingford; creature effects, Peter Litten; sound, Pat Hayes; assistant director, Martin O'Malley; casting, Michael McLean/Diane Dimeo and Associates. Reviewed at Empire Pictures, L.A., March 26, 1987. Los Angeles, California. (MPAA Rating: R.) Running time: **89 MINS.**

Howard Hallenbeck . . . . David Dukes
Elaine Hallenbeck . . . . Kelly Piper
Declan O'Brien . . . . Ronan Wilmot
Reverend Coot . . . . Niall Toibin
Rawhead Rex . . Heinrich Von Schellendorf
Det. Insp. Gissing . . . . Niall O'Brian

Hollywood — "Rawhead Rex" is as gooey as an open sore and about as painful to look at. For such an ugly monster, he sure is boring. Ennui is a sure bet at the b.o. too.

It's derivative of every bad low-budget creature film ever made.

Out of nowhere, the monster materializes to wreck havoc on a tiny, Irish town. It turns out, he's the devil incarnate with the local vicar's assistant (Ronan Wilmot) his mortal assistant.

Along come an American historian (David Dukes) and his family to do a little ancestral digging in the parish records. Dukes has timed it just right to be a party to Rawhead Rex' rampage.

It takes practically forever for Rawhead to bite into his first victim, a poor country farmer. It's when he hits on Dukes' snot-nosed son, that their paths cross and the blood begins to flow freely.

Screenwriter Clive Barker strings out the monster's attacks with some very dreary dialog between Dukes and his oversexed wife (Kelly Piper), and with the deranged Wilmot character.

Bad acting abounds, if it isn't Dukes telling his wife she has "dirty eyes" (pant, pant) it's Wilmot with his best Marty Feldman imitation trying to appear real evil without being laughable.

Even the monster has zero personality. He's big and lumbering and constantly dripping red liquid from his gorilla mouth, but looks too fake to be really threatening.

Being that this is a U.K. production, pic does have a few saving graces, like the rolling green hills that is the setting and the lilting Irish brogue of the cast members.

This is the first of five films Barker is scripting from his "Books Of Blood," a collection of horror fiction stories. Hopefully, the rest will be better.

Tech credits are average for this genre. The sound doesn't synch sometimes, but John Metcalfe's camerawork is above par.—*Brit.*

Prettykill
(COLOR)

Substandard exploitation thriller not redeemed by campy elements.

A Spectrafilm release of a Sandy Howard presentation of a Dax Avant production. Executive producer, Howard. Produced by John R. Bowey, Martin Walters. Directed by George Kaczender. Screenplay, Sandra K. Bailey; camera (color), Joao Fernandes; editor, Tom Merchant; music, Robert O. Ragland; sound, Daniel Latour; art direction, Andris Hausmanis; set decoration, Jeff Cutler; assistant director, Richard Flower; second unit camera, Yuri Neyman; additional photography, Peter Lyons Collister; associate producers, David Witz, Michael Masciarelli; casting, Paul Bengston, David Cohn; additional casting, Anne Tait, Diane Polley. Reviewed at Magno Preview 9 screening room, N.Y., March 25, 1987. (MPAA Rating: R.) Running time: **95 MINS.**

Sgt. Larry Turner . . . . David Birney
Heather Todd . . . . Season Hubley
Toni . . . . Susannah York
Harris . . . . Yaphet Kotto
Francie . . . . Suzanne Snyder
Jacques Mercier . . . . Germaine Houde
Carrie . . . . Lenore Zann

Also with: Marsha Moreau, Sarah Polley, O.L. Duke, Heather Smith, Erik King. Richard Fitzpatrick, Ron White, Gary Majchrizak, Louis Turenne, Philip Akin.

"Prettykill," originally titled "Tomorrow's A Killer," is a tame exploitation film from Sandy Howard, revisiting once again the thematic territory of his 1982 pic "Vice Squad." Pic is notable mainly as the vehicle by which former Canadian-U.S. art film distrib Spectrafilm gets its feet wet with grindhouse product.

Three parallel stories intertwine unconvincingly in Sandra K. Bailey's far-fetched script: David Birney is a cop tortured with guilt for killing a guy in the line of duty, whose problems keep mounting as he gets in hot water with his superior, Yaphet Kotto; his girlfriend Season Hubley (star of "Vice Squad") is a $500-a-pop callgirl fed up with her life but unwilling to wed Birney; and Suzanne Snyder is a pretty blond dancer who Hubley takes under her wing to show her the ropes of prostitution.

A key subplot involves Hubley's mentor, an older prostie now working as a madam (Susannah York), who is having problems as her young daughters (raised in the same house where her group of prostitutes work) find out about her line of work and are ostracized at school. This material is played sentimentally and doesn't work.

The drug bust case Birney's working on curiously links up with an investigation of a serial killer of prostitutes, with Birney's conflict of interests leading him to protect York and foolishly punch out Kotto, spelling the end of the line for him as a New York City policeman. Hubley becomes fed up with hooking and decides to quit. Main plot element, however, is revelation (already given away by the film's attractive one-sheet of Snyder in lingerie holding a knife) that Snyder is a schizo, taking on her incestuous father's personality and killing hookers.

Main entertainment value of this plodding film comes in some of the campiest scenes since "Mommie Dearest" as Snyder changes voices and behavior back and forth between her lip-smacking, southern-fried daddy and her own ever smiling (replete with Raggedy Ann doll plaything) little girl personality. Pic climaxes with her made up and styled as a doppelganger for Hubley, taking on daddy's voice and trying to kill her. Sudden happy ending is preposterous.

Birney is miscast as a *film noir* antihero while Hubley is far too cool (one almost starts sympathizing with her sleazy johns when she is so unfriendly to them) for the role. Both Kotto and York maintain their professional standards and

Snyder is a hoot — her performance is ready-made for midnight screenings. Supporting cast is stuck with stereotypes.

Film is professionally lensed, but low on action for a *policier.* One can infer from the end credits (which list gallery credits under "additional photography unit") that a sleazy sequence set in an art gallery, including the film's only nude footage, was shot and added as an afterthought, typical of exploitation features. Though set in New York, film was made primarily in Toronto.—*Lor.*

Mosca Addio
(Moscow Farewell)
(ITALIAN-COLOR)

An Istituto Luce-Italnoleggio release of a Rosco film production, in cooperation with RAI-TV Channel 1. Directed by Mauro Bolognini. Stars Liv Ullmann. Screenplay, Enrico Roseo, Marcello Andrei; camera (Cinecittà color), Ennio Guarnieri; editor, Nino Baragli; music, Ennio Morricone. Reviewed at Rialto Cinema, Rome, March 14, 1987. Running time: 102 MINS.
Ida Nudel . . . . Liv Ullmann
Yuli . . . . Daniel Olbrychski
Elena . . . . Aurore Clément
Also with: Francesca Ciardi, Carmen Scarpitta, Nino Fuscagni, Saverio Vallone.

Rome — Vet helmer Mauro Bolognini tackles the anguishing problem of Jewish dissidents in the Soviet Union in "Moscow Farewell." With the fervor of crusaders (pic's plea of "Don't forget us" reechoes from first frame to last) Bolognini and star Liv Ullmann create a powerful and moving condemnation of anti-Semitism-Soviet immigration policy, and the labor camps. "Moscow handles its subject with more passion than sensitivity, painting the non-Jewish characters (who are all police and officials) in such black colors it leaves itself open to charges of being an anti-Russian caricature. Had the same theme been treated in a Soviet picture (and that day hasn't arrived yet), it would be the toast of festivals and a victory of *glasnost;* in an Italian film, full of inaccurate details and stolen super-8m footage of Moscow exteriors, the political overtones take away from pic's genuine protest. Nevertheless, "Moscow" should find markets in the West, thanks to Ullmann's emotionally charged performance.

Story must qualify as one of the most chilling of our time, all the more depressing because it's based on the unhappy life of a real person, Ida Nudel, a Jewish dissident still living in the USSR. As the curtain rises she is a respected astronomer in Moscow, looking forward to the day when her lover Yuli (Daniel Olbrychski) will be released from a work camp. Return he does, but after police break up a peaceful candlelight vigil during a Jewish holi-

day, Yuli, Ida and her sister Elena (Aurore Clément) decide to immigrate. The papers are granted to Yuli and Elena, but — for no apparent reason — not to Ida. With an act of great self-sacrifice and love, she pretends all is okay and accompanies the pair on the train to Vienna, leaping out just as they near the border.

Back in Moscow, Ida begins taking part in demonstrations (the time is 1980) and is incarcerated in a mental asylum for her trouble. This is only a mild warning, however, compared to what happens after her "second offensive:" a long trip to the icy regions of Siberia. Bolognini transcribes the most horrifying scenes of Alexander Solzhenitsyn's "A Day In The Life Of Ivan Denisovich" to the screen, adding to it the unbelievable twist that a sadistic bureaucrat has assigned Ida to an all-male camp, where she has to fend off hourly rape attempts.

Finally transferred to a lighter woman's camp in the Arctic, Ida is released at last and joyfully returns to Moscow, only to find: 1) another family lives in her apartment; 2) Yuli has gotten married abroad, and 3) she has been banished from the city. Wandering desolately from town to town in internal exile, she at last finds a rudimentary living situation amid non-judgmental villagers, and recounts her story in a moving final monolog to an English reporter.

Film is shot well but badly edited in its theatrical release version (the seven-hour tv miniseries will probably fill in a lot of gaps). Beginning is so jumpy that pic has a hard time establishing its characters, and it takes Ullmann another hour of screen time to emerge from bouts of above-the-lines emoting as a 3-D person worth caring about. Polish star Olbrychski is the only convincing Russian of the lot.— *Yung.*

Quatre Aventures de Reinette et Mirabelle
(Four Adventures Of Reinette And Mirabelle)
(FRENCH-COLOR)

A Les Films du Losange production and release. Coproducer, La Compagnie Eric Rohmer. Written and directed by Eric Rohmer. Camera (color), Sophie Maintigneux; editor, Maria-Luisa Garcia; music, Ronan Girre and Jean-Louis Valero; sound, Pierre Camus, Pascal Ribier; production manager, Françoise Etchegaray. Reviewed at the Balzac cinema, Paris, March 20, 1987. Running time: 97 MINS.
Mirabelle . . . . Jessica Forde
Reinette . . . . Joëlle Miquel
Waiter . . . . Philippe Laudenbach
Gallery owner . . . . Fabrice Luchini
The cheat . . . . Marie Rivière

Paris — Still devoted to the vagaries of fatuous young demoiselles, writer-director Eric Rohmer now aimed his camera at two sweet young things in "Four Adventures Of Reinette And Mirabelle" — a

city girl and a country lass who become friends and share some minor experiences in Paris.

Like "Le rayon vert" (Summer), film was shot in 16m, but Rohmer happily has made less use of improvisation. Though there's still less here than meets the ear, the dialog has enough humor and irony to make this an agreeable addition to the Rohmer opus that should find its audience in the usual art precincts.

Pic is conceived as four sketches of varying lengths and qualities. First (and the dullest) is the "L'Houre bleue," in which Mirabelle (Jessica Forde), a Parisian, makes the acquaintance of Reinette (Joëlle Miquel) when her bike blows a flat near latter's isolated farmhouse.

Though dissimilar, the girls take a liking to one another and seal their friendship one early morning when they catch the "Blue Hour," a brief moment between night and dawn when all natural noises subside.

After this mostly tedious exposition, film perks up with Reinette coming to Paris to share her friend's apartment and attend an arts academy.

Sketch 2 introduces the country girl to the neurotic vicissitudes of city life when she wrangles with a cafe waiter (played with professional comic verve by Philippe Laudenbach) who refuses to accept Reinette's large bill to pay off a coffee.

In the third part, dealing with the girls' conflicting attitudes on charity and altruism, Mirabelle saves a shoplifter from arrest in a supermarket, while Reinette confronts a cheat (Marie Rivière, the wandering drip of "Summer") in a train station.

In the final story, Reinette, while keeping a bet that she can spend an entire day without speaking, tries to sell one of her paintings to an art dealer (Fabrice Luchini) who finally ends up paying her the price she wants.

Though there are two protagonists, main interest is in the chatty country girl, who in the course of her city adventures loses much of the ethical integrity and innocence she constantly sounds off about. As refreshingly played by newcomer Joëlle Miquel, character is one of the more charming of Rohmer's spacey females. Forde, on the other hand, is bland as the more reserved urbanite.

Lensing and other tech credits are unexceptional. —*Len.*

Heaven
(DOCU-COLOR)

Unsuccessful gimmick film by Diane Keaton.

An Island Pictures release of a Perpetual production for RVF prods. Produced by Joe Kelly. Executive producers, Tom Kuhn, Charles Mitchell, Arlyne Rothberg. Directed by Diane Keaton. Camera (color), Frederick Elmes, Joe Kelly; editor, Paul Barnes; music, Howard Shore; art direction, Barbara Ling; sound, Peter F. Chaikin, John E. Kaufer, Tom Moore; associate producer, Tom Stovall; associate editor, Bruce Shaw. Reviewed at the Raleigh Studios screening room, L.A., March 25, 1987. (MPAA Rating: PG-13.) Running time: **80 MINS.**

Hollywood — "Heaven" represents an exercise in frivolous metaphysics, an engagingly light-hearted but ultimately light-headed inquiry into the nature of paradise. Diane Keaton's feature directorial debut is a small-scale, non-narrative work using trendily shot interviews, snazzy optical effects and loads of film clips and songs to illustrate fanciful notions of the hereafter. Keaton's name will provide a draw in limited, specialized theatrical release, but it's no coincidence that a video company, RVP Prods. (formerly RCA Video Prods.) produced the picture, since it probably will perform better in the home arena.

Keaton neither appears nor speaks from behind the camera in this oddity, which has a measure of quirky charm, but little substance despite the potential weightiness of the subject.

Close to 100 individuals, all unknown except for boxing promoter Don King, are quizzed on such matters as, "What is Heaven?" "Is there sex in Heaven?" and "How do you get to Heaven?" The people are interviewed in a variety of distorted, high-tech, expressionistic settings, and lit and shot in such a way that portions of their faces are often obscured by heavy grid shadows and frame edges.

Peppering all these speculations are often goofy clips from old films and tv shows. Excerpts, none of which is identified, range from extravagant depictions of the afterlife, Hollywood-style, to the hilarioius expostulations of early broadcast ministers and evangelists.

Most of the clips verge on the campy in their emphasis on straight, squaresville Americana of the 1950s and before, and while this tendency provides much of the film's amusement, it also erodes any sense of significance. Keaton has a lot of fun with her raw materials, repeating images and sentences, creating funny, jazzy rhythms with the editing and music, cutting quickly and abruptly, and generally tapdancing madly in the postproduction end to keep the show moving.

Unfortunately, film really doesn't build to anything and, with only a handful of the dozens of interview subjects proving memorable, one is left with a picture about which one can legitimately ask, "Where's the beef?"

Undoubtedly with the ultimate video destination in mind, pic has been framed in the old 1.33x1 Academy format. Technically, it's a dream, and Keaton clearly has a feel for image manipulation and the joy of playing with the medium's tools. However, 80 minutes is too long to spend on an illustrated amusement park tour of wacky notions of what might lie in the great beyond.

— *Cart.*

Le Solitaire
(The Loner)
(FRENCH-COLOR)

An AMLF/Cerito release of a Sara Films/Cerito coproduction. Executive producer, Alain Sarde. Produced by Alain Belmondo. Directed by Jacques Deray. Stars Jean-Paul Belmondo. Screenplay, Deray, Alphonse Boudard, Simon Michael, Daniel Saint-Hamont; camera (Fujicolor), Jean-François Robin; editor, Henri Lanoe; songs, Andy Caine, performed by Carlos Sottomayor; art director, Jean-Claude Galloin; car stunts, Rémy Julienne; assistant director, Bernard Bolzinger. Reviewed at the Gaumont Ambassade cinema, Paris, March 20, 1987. Running time: **94 MINS.**

With: Jean-Paul Belmondo (Commissioner Stan Jalard), Jean-Pierre Malo (Charly Schneider), Michel Creton (Simon), Pierre Vernier, Michel Beaune, Patricia Malvoisin, Catherine Rouvel, François Dunoyer.

Paris — With his legit return in "Kean" now playing to SRO houses, screen star Jean-Paul Belmondo is back on cinema marquees concurrently in a new police actioner, "Le Solitaire," his first picture since the 1985 caper comedy, "Hold-Up."

Mechanically directed by veteran Jacques Deray (who helmed his record-breaking 1983 vehicle "Le Marginal"), it's another routinely contrived tale of a lone wolf cop seeking revenge for the murder of a fellow policeman by a vicious mad dog gangster. Strictly for Belmondo fans and undemanding thriller aficionados, it has opened to good business though it looks unlikely to set any new b.o. track records.

Script by Deray and three other writers is so tired that even Belmondo seems somewhat weary as he goes through the motions of a role he (and countless others) have filled before with more energy and humor. There is no romance, just some banal sentimentality in scenes between the actor and his godson, offspring of his murdered colleague, who he decides to bring up himself.

Also missing is the Belmondo trademark of daredevil stunting, here limited to a (faked) jump from a first-story ledge. The hero's fatigue peaks when he finally catches up with his nemesis, but instead of shooting him, decides to send him up the river to rot in prison. "I'm for legality," says the somewhat extralegal Belmondo. More likely he's just too tired to squeeze the trigger.

— *Len.*

Rimini Rimini
(ITALIAN-COLOR)

A Medusa release of Scena Film production. Produced by Augusto Caminito. Directed by Sergio Corbucci. Screenplay, Bernardino Zapponi, Sergio Corbucci, Bruno Corbucci, Mario Amendola, Marco Risi, Gianni Romoli, Massimo Franciosa; camera (Eastmancolor), Danilo Desideri; editor, Tatiana Casini Morigi, art director, Marco Dentici. Reviewed at Adriano Cinema, Rome, March 25, 1987. Running time: **116 MINS.**

Gildo . . . . Paolo Villaggio
Lola . . . . Serena Grandi
Liliana . . . . Eleonora Brigliadori
Rich woman . . . . Laura Antonelli
Gianni . . . . Jerry Calà

Also with: Gigi and Andrea, Paolo Bonacelli, Maurizio Micheli, Sylva Koscina, Elvire Audray.

Rome — A down-market vacation on the Adriatic is spending your holidays on the over-crowded, over-developed beaches of Rimini, a haven for German tourists which has been nobilized accidentally in being Fellini's hometown. If for Fellini the symbol of the place is its gaudy Grand Hotel, helmer Sergio Corbucci finds its quintessence in a squallid merry-go-round of singles on the make. This open-air bedroom farce has opened well domestically, thanks to the appeal of its comedy-star cast.

In the style of the genre, a number of stories overlap without intertwining, the only thing that links them is they all take place in Rimini and they share a tone of lascivious vulgarity. Paolo Villaggio lends his talents to portraying Gildo, a prurient magistrate famous for closing down red-light shows. His sexual hang ups are forced into the open by the aggressive attentions lavished on him by extra-large sex symbol Serena Grandi, who frequently appears in the nude. In a pitiful send up of "Nine ½ Weeks," complete with the Joe Cocker song, she forces Gildo to go to a disco in drag while a paparazzi-accomplice lies in wait to ruin his career.

Laura Antonelli cameos in a garbled tale of a rich woman who thinks her lover has drowned. Her three fat brothers try to console her with violins and a stand-up comic, until her Ulysses staggers out of the sea and proceeds to make up for lost time.

Milanese comic Jerry Calà appears in a trite tale of an aspiring wheeler-dealer who hires a prostitute to pose as his wife and seduce an Agnelli-type millionaire. TV star Eleanora Brigliadori turns up as a recently separated beauty. Her would-be lovers include 1) a bodybuilder afraid of AIDS, 2) an impotent gigolo, 3) a rapacious 10-year-old boy. Only No. 3 is consummated.

For good measure, Andrea Roncati is a priest in shorts who is forced to suck the jellyfish stings on the body of a nun who is topless. Technically unexceptional. — *Yung.*

Anjuman
(INDIAN-COLOR)

A Collective Film production. Produced by Muzaffar Ali, Shabha Doctor. Directed by Ali. Stars Shabana Azmi. Screenplay, Rahi Masoom Reza; camera (color), Ishan Arya; music, Khayyam. Reviewed at the India Film Festival, Delhi, Jan. 13, 1987. Running time: **133 MINS.**

Anjuman . . . . Shabana Azmi
Sajjid . . . . Farouque Shaikh

Also with: Rahini Hattangady (eye-doctor), Shankat Kaifi (Chidiya Khala), Mushtaq Khan (Banke Nawab).

(Hindi dialog)

Delhi — "Anjuman" is a lyrical celebration of the decaying old city of Lucknow and an earnest social protest against the conditions in which the city's *chikan* embroiderers work. Holding these two elements in precarious balance is luminous Shabana Azmi in the title role. Though not a perfect film, "Anjuman" communicates a strong feeling of authenticity for the people of the region. It is lensed sensitively by Muzaffar Ali, a young director with long experience in making features and documentaries with social themes.

Anjuman and her impoverished family live on the reluctant charity of relatives. The girl, a romantic writer of poetry, contributes to the family income weaving delicate *chikan* motifs with the other poor women of the town. Eventually, spurred on by a militant woman eye-doctor, she leads the exploited *chikan* workers in a strike for better rates from the greedy wholesalers who commission the work.

In the tradition of Hindi films, "Anjuman" contains a number of unnecessary characters and scenes, notably a rich young man who comically courts the heroine and almost marries her (she refuses at the altar, to the general scandal of Lucknow). Even more extraneous are the regular interruptions for sentimental singing in the woods, as Anjuman and her star-crossed aristocratic suitor Sajjid dream of happier tomorrows. It is a half-hearted attempt to throw in something for the Hindi market and it shows.

Azmi steals the show from a supporting cast with little presence and pulls pic up several notches. Ishan Arya's camerawork captures the fading grandeur of the old city with feeling.— *Yung.*

The Zero Boys
(COLOR)

Cornball horror pic masquerading as war actioner.

An Omega Entertainment presentation of an Omega Pictures/Forminx production. Executive producer, Isabel Mastorakis. Produced and directed by Nico Mastorakis. Screenplay, Nico Mastorakis, Fred C. Perry, from story by Nico Mastorakis; camera (United color; prints by Technicolor), Steve Shaw; editor, George Rosenberg; music, Stanley Myers, Hans Zimmer; sound (Dolby stereo), Clark Will; art direction, Gregory Melton; assistant director, Betsy Pollock; stunt coordinator, Vince Deadrick Jr.; associate producer, Bob Manning. Reviewed on Lightning Video vidcassette, N.Y., Jan. 12, 1987. (No MPAA Rating.) Running time: **89 MINS.**

Steve . . . . Daniel Hirsch
Jamie . . . . Kelli Maroney
Larry . . . . Tom Shell
Sue . . . . Nicole Rio
Rip . . . . Jared Moses
Trish . . . . Crystal Carson
Killer . . . . Joe Phelan
Also with: Gary Jochimsen, John Michaels, Elise Turner, Steve Shaw, T.K. Webb.

"The Zero Boys" begins promisingly as a he-man picture about young survivalists who yearn to be "Rambo" warriors, but quickly devolves into yet another formula horror film about teens getting slashed in the woods. Unrated feature went directly to the homevideo stores.

Title trio are guys who used to be wimps but now regularly win the weekend competition of war games at a local California park. They go camping for a weekend with two girlfriends and a girl (Kelli Maroney) who they "won" at the latest competition from the leader of the losing team. Staying at an empty house (uninvited), they find snuff tapes and camera setup in the house and then are systematically knifed by unseen killers.

Though the script knowingly makes comical references to "Jason," pic is ultimately just a pale imitation of the "Friday The 13th" series. Gimmick of the teens being armed to the teeth with machine guns and other sophisticated weaponry doesn't pay off, since they are just as vulnerable to the stealthy killers. Cast and technical credits are acceptable. —*Lor.*

Pa liv och död
(A Matter Of Life And Death)
(SWEDISH-COLOR)

A Swedish Film Institute release and production with Filmfotograferne, SR/TV-2, Ariane Film. Produced by Stefan Hencz. Directed and edited by Marianne Ahrne. Stars Lena Olin, Svante Martin. Screenplay, Ahrne, Bertrand Hurault; camera (Eastmancolor), Hans Welin, Lisa Hagstrand; music, Ilja Cmiral; sound, Lasse Lundberg, Asa Lindgren; production design, Anna Brown; production management, Nils Johansson. Reviewed at Nordic Film Festival, Helsinki, Jan. 25, 1987. Running time: **89 MINS.**

Nadja . . . . Lena Olin

Stefan . . . . Svante Martin
Also with: Leif Ahrle, Ann Zacharias, Cecilia Walton, Tin-Tin Andersson, Helge Skoog, Sara Key, Lena Pia Bernahardsson, Lasse Pöysti, Mimi Pollak, Christina Indrenius-Zalewski, Eva von Hanno.

Helsinki — "A Matter Of Life And Death" is a talk-you-to-death picture about a young (she looks 20 at the most) reporter who chooses an assignment at a maternity ward in favor of one taking her to Japan. Why? Because Stefan, a doctor in the ward, left her 15 (!) years ago without ever telling her why he picked another woman to marry and live with happily.

Today, Stefan remains prey to seduction, but still will not commit himself with words and will not renege on his love for his wife. This drives Lena, the reporter, to occasional hysterics (displayed while taking notes and photographs during difficult births) and endless torrents of words about the meaning of love and — of words. Maternity ward cases and personalities are interwoven in Lena's (and writer-director-editor Marianne Ahrne's) orgy of self-indulgence.

Lena Olin puts in a pretty performance, while Svante Martin as the doctor is ludicrously wooden. Film's technical credits have merit, but with all its words, "A Matter of Life And Death" remains lifeless all the way.—*Kell.*

Yerba Sangriente
(Bloody Weed)
(MEXICAN-COLOR)

A Peliculas Mexicanas release of a Peliculas Rodríguez production. Executive producer, Tonatiuh Rodríguez. Produced by Ismael Rodríguez Jr. Directed by Ismael Rodríguez. Stars Alvaro Zermeño, Juan Valentín. Screenplay, Jorge Manriquez, Ismael Rodríguez; camera (color), Fernando Alvarez Colín; editor, Rogelio Zúñiga; music, Ernesto Cortázar. Reviewed at Big Apple Cine 1, N.Y., Jan. 12, 1987. Running time: **97 MINS.**

Meletón García (Norteño) . . . Alvaro Zermeño
Salvador . . . . Juan Valentín
Alegría . . . . Rosenda Bernal
El Diablo . . . . Noe Murayama
Giovanni Rosetti . . . . Rubén Rojo
Pepe . . . . Cuitlahuac Cui
Also with: Arturo Martínez, Gerardo Zepeda, Rubi Ree, Queta Carrasco, Manuel Támez, Marta Elena Cervantes.

Based on a real-life incident, "Yerba Sangriente" (Bloody Weed) is a low-budget exploitation pic out to grab a few bucks at the expense of the suffering of others.

The film concerns a large marijuana plantation that was discovered in 1984 in the north of Mexico. This farm was run by organized crime and used thousands of slave laborers lured there by the promise of good wages for picking cotton. The workers who harvested the illegal crop were held forcibly and brutalized by sadistic guards toting machineguns.

Whereas the U.S. film industry operates on the notion of bigger and grander, this pic is impoverished and instead of thousands of extras, most of the time we only see 25-50. Instead of a Mexican crime syndicate, there is a lone Italian drug kingpin and his five goons.

Story begins with a narrator discribing Mexico's lucrative drug trade. It then centers around two men, Meletón García (Alvaro Zermeño), a friendly, outgoing type who is duped into gathering workers, and Salvador (Juan Valentín), a newspaper reporter whose work is responsible for bringing the operation into the open. We also meet a lot of other people en route, mainly poor folk who, in an effort to escape poverty, end up victims of tyranny and a bad script.

Pic shows a lack of attention to detail: one extra who gets killed mid-film is clearly visible in a later crowd scene. Also, for poor campesinos, the workers are always dressed in brand-new clean clothes.

The exposition is awkward, characterizations clichéd with hilarious overacting by guards high on pot and the tech credits are merely functional. Overall, "Bloody Weed" is a bloody bore.—*Lent.*

El Mofles y los Mecánicos
(Mofles And The Mechanics)
(MEXICAN-COLOR)

A Peliculas Mexicanas release of a Prod. Tijuana production. Produced by Juan Abusaid, Pedro Martínez Garrido. Directed by Víctor Manuel (Güero) Castro. Stars Rafael Inclán. Screenplay, Jorge Patiño, Marco E. Contreras M.; camera (color), José Antonio Ruiz; editor, Sergio Soto; music, Gustavo Pimentel, with appearance of the groups Generación 2000, Los Chicanos, Grupo Centenario. Reviewed at Big Apple Cine 1, N.Y., Jan. 19, 1987. Running time: **85 MINS.**

Luis (El Mofles) . . . . Rafael Inclán
Lupita . . . Maribel Fernández (Pelongocha)
Pepe (El Jefe) . . Pedro Weber (Chatanuga)
Abrelatas . . . . Manuel (Flaco) Ibañez
Doña Chole . . . . Susana Cabrera
Don Gastón . . . . Víctor Manuel Castro
Chocorro . . . . Polo Ortín
Also with: Roxana Chávez, Arturo Martínez, Rasalba Brambila, Alfredo Solares.

"El Mofles y los Mecánicos" (Mofles And The Mechanics) is yet another vehicle for Mexican comedian Rafael Inclán, who plays the title role of a poor, fun-but-good-hearted auto mechanic nicknamed Mofles (Muffler).

Story revolves around Mofles and his friends at a garage called Los Pits, where they all work, and a tenement, where they all live.

At one point in the pic, Mofles crosses paths with a group of bad-guy robbers who have just held up a bottling plant. He ends up with all the loot and the misadventure continues from here.

The plot, replete with sexual puns, is a bit too thin to carry any audience interest beyond that of the

characters. Story is padded by the appearance of three popular musical groups and an overlong birthday party where characters dance and get drunk.

Tech credits are only functional in this cheaply made, throwaway entertainment. Producers are banking on the notion that the mere presence of Inclán will be enough to bring in Hispanic audiences. —*Lent.*

Pandavapuram
(INDIAN-COLOR)

Produced and directed by G.S. Panicker. Screenplay, Sethu, Panicker, from novel by Sethu; camera (color), Divakara Menon; editor, Suresh Babu; music, Mohan. Reviewed at the India Film Festival, Delhi, Jan. 17, 1987. Running time: **90 MINS.**

Devi . . . . Jamila
Jaran . . . . Appu
Unni . . . . James
The son . . . . Master Deepak
(Dialog in Malayalam)

Delhi — "Pandavapuram," name of a town that may or may not exist, attempts to transpose a Malayam novel by Sethu (credited as coscripter) to the screen, but the half-realistic, half-magical tale proves too much for director G. S. Paniker. Prosaic lensing and thesps' lack of magnetism undercut pic's ambitions to blur the line between fantasy and reality. Results are muddy and amateurish.

Devi (played by actress Jamila) is a schoolteacher in a remote village who has been abandoned by her dissolute, good-for-nothing husband. Every day she waits for him to come on the one train, while the townsfolk look on pityingly. One day, however, a young man actually gets off the train and asks for her. Jaran (actor Appu) causes a scandal just by giving his name, since it means "lover." As talkative as Devi is silent, he reminds her they were once together in Pandavapuram. Devi denies it, and a series of glossy flashbacks don't clear up the matter for the viewer, either.

Jaran hangs on at Devi's house for days (the presence of two other women and her son do nothing to stop tongues from wagging). Finally, after some threats from a village elder and a nasty nightmare, he decides he'd better be off. Now it's Devi who imprisons him magically and makes love to him against his will.

When she wakes up the next morning, Jaran is gone. None of the villagers can recall having heard of him or Pandavapuram. Devi goes back to the railway station to resume her vigil.

It's the kind of tale that needs perfect technical control and strong casting to keep the shifting fantasy-reality game engrossing. Pandavapuram is unfortunately no Marienbad, Panicker no Alain Resnais, and intention outstrips results in this one. —*Yung.*

Areias Escaldantes
(Burning Sands)
(BRAZILIAN-COLOR)

A Naive Producoes Aristicas production. Directed by Francisco de Paula. No further credits supplied. Reviewed at Berlin Film Festival (Market), March 1, 1987. Running time: **105 MINS.**
With: Regina Casé, Christina Aché, Diogo Vilela.

Berlin — A comic fantasy about terrorists in a mythical country in the near future (1990), ''Burning Sands'' seems consciously to be aiming at cult status.

Shot in garish colors, with equally vibrant decors, and with actors in bizarre makeup, pic is a bit heavy-handed, but has some good jokes along the way. These urban guerrillas spend most of their time watching tv as they're too scared to go outside for fear of being caught.

A scene in a taxi features back-projection on a studio mock-up the cab, but the film is run backwards and even the leader is shown, while the cab driver spends all his time talking to his fares and never watches the road. A more conventional gag has an ardent swain never able to finish telling a female terrorist he loves her, being interrupted in one way or another every time he gets going.

Another crazy idea, though something of a sick joke, has a bomb planted in a car: the victim gets in carrying a large case, the car explodes, leaving the case intact and undamaged, but no sign of the unfortunate man.

So it goes, with slapdash jokes, fast pacing and stylized images. It's fun sometimes, but drags too, though youth audiences may plug into its zany approach to the theme.
—*Strat.*

Lumikuningatar
(The Snow Queen)
(FINNISH-COLOR)

A Finnkino release of Neofilmi production. Produced, written and directed by Päivi Hartzell. Camera (color), Henrik Paersch; editor, Anne Lakanen, Olli Soinio; music, Jukka Linkola; sound, Paul Jyrälä; production design, Reija Hirvikoski; assistant director, Nadja Pyykkö; special effects, Jukka Ruohomäki, Antti Kari, Lauri Pitkänen; production managers, Heikki Takkinen, Alf Hemming. Reviewed at the Forum, Helsinki, Jan. 23, 1987. Running time: **90 MINS.**
Greta . . . . Outi Vainionkulma
Kaj . . . . Sebastian Kaatrasalo
The Snow Queen . . . . Satu Silvo
Also with: Tuula Nyman, Esko Hukkanen, Pirjo Bergström, Saara Pakkasvirta, Ismo Alanko, Markko Huhtamo, Antti Litja, Elina Salo.

Helsinki — Producer-writer-director Päivi Hartzell fittingly has turned Hans Christian Andersen's most intricate and longest fairytale ''The Snow Queen' into a fantasy feature film of many layers of meaning and finesse. She has fashioned what inevitably will be labeled

a kiddie entertainment, but she will quite obviously thrill and intrigue children and adults alike and may well reach foreign audiences via specialized theatrical situations. Video business can be predicted, too.

Hartzell has added a variety of twists and visions to Andersen's story of the two innocent children, Kaj and Greta, who cruelly get separated when the Snow Queen abducts Kaj, having first had a glass splinter of evil wisdom inserted in his eye so his heart has turned to ice. Greta starts out to look for Kaj, and after travels and travails finds the boy and sees to it that the warmth of her love melts his heart again while the Snow Queen's power is broken for keeps.

Too often, Hartzell's narrative flow is broken because her budget obviously has not matched her special effects ambitions. But never mind, a few loose ends should not hurt a picture that is otherwise beautifully in control of those same special effects plus all kinds of cinematic and optical effects as well.

Item futhermore has some of Jim Henson's brusque humor to help it overcome moments of looming syrupy sentiment. There also is an impressive, semi-symphonic music score to lift the general mood where suspense might otherwise be lagging. The amateur child actors are sweet without being cute, and as the Snow Queen, dressed and made up like a Parisian haute couture icicle, Satu Silvo radiates sexy danger and is glamorous enough to put a whole dynasty of television Evil Ladies to shame. —*Kell.*

Panchagni
(Five Fires)
(INDIAN-COLOR)

A G.P. Vijay Kumar/M.G. Gopinath production. Directed by Hariharan. Screenplay, M.T. Vasudevan Nair; camera (color), Shaji; editor, M.S. Mani; music, Ravi; art direction, S.Vonnanadu. Reviewed at the Indian Film Festival, Delhi, Jan. 20, 1987. Running time: **140 MINS.**
Indira . . . . Geeta
Rashid . . . . Mohanlal
Savitri . . . . Nadia Moidu
Ramettan . . . . Tilakan

Delhi — ''Five Fires'' tells of the tough choices of a high-principled young woman whose idealism leads her to prison. Though it may not sound like the stuff hits are made of, director Hariharan is a veteran with a knack for strong, simple emotions that get across to audiences. This is also just what undercuts all subtlety in the pic. Unlikely to go far abroad, ''Fires'' at least made a good showing in its local region of Kerala.

Background of the story is Kerala's extremist movement of the

1960s and '70s, when a number of tyrannical landowners were assassinated by revolutionary groups. Heroine Indira (actress Geeta) is serving a life sentence for the murder of one such man. His execution is more than justified by an extended, extremely gory flashback showing how he let his watchdogs tear a pregnant woman to pieces.

In India, life imprisonment lasts 14 years. After serving eight of them, Indira comes out on temporary parole in time to see her mother die. Treated as a pariah by townsfolk and most of her relatives, Indira ends up in the consoling arms of a kind-hearted journalist (Mohanlal in an appealing low-key performance). The romance, which includes some tedious songs under the moonlight, ends abruptly when Indira's sense of justice again asserts itself, and she does away with another over-the-top villain, this time with a shotgun. It's back to jail for another 14 years.

Pic is best in presenting a wide variety of credible characters, from the dying old lady who marched with Gandhi to Indira's well-meaning but venal sister and embittered brothers. Only Geeta in the central role seems too self-righteous and trigger-happy to be true. Pic is professionally lensed.— *Yung.*

Las Traigo ... Muertas
(I Do 'Em In)
(MEXICAN-COLOR)

A Peliculas Mexicanas release of a Cinematográfica Filmex production. Produced by J. Fernando Pérez Gabilán. Directed by Rafael Baledón. Stars Otto Sirgo. Screenplay, Fernando Galindo; camera (color), Alberto Arellanos Bustamantes; editor, Francisco Chiu; music, Gustavo C. Carreón. Reviewed at Big Apple Cine 1, N.Y., Jan. 20, 1987. Running time: **85 MINS.**
Francisco (Paco) Gavilán . . . . . . Otto Sirgo
Angélica Vidal de
Cienfuegos . . . . Sasha Montenegro
Marsha . . . . Maribel Guardia
Also with: Lalo (El Mimo), Polo Ortln, César Bono, Oscar Fentanes.

Mexican filmmaker Rafael Baledón's pic ''Las Traigo ... Muertas'' (I Do 'Em In) is an unfunny sex comedy that tries too hard and misses the mark. Chief problem is a self-conscious script, which is compounded by a director and lead actor who lack a sense of comic timing.

Storyline concerns unlucky compulsive gambler Paco (Otto Sirgo), who is up to his ears in debt. Everyone including gang leaders and thugs, are after him for money. When his attractive widowed neighbor Angélica (Sasha Montenegro) tells him how much money she raked in from an insurance settlement on her husband's death, she plants an ace in his deck. Fancying himself a modern Bluebeard, Paco plans to marry women, insure them

heavily, knock them off ... and presto! an easy exit from financial woes.

Of course, like his bad luck at gambling, he ends up victim of his bungled murder attempts. Story continues in this slapstick fashion.

Sirgo's giggling and buffooning for the camera are distancing and the plethora of double-entendres in the dialog come off as forced. Cinematographer Alberto Arellanos Bustamantes' deft camerawork looks out of place in this pic where everything else seems thrown together.

This twisted tale of a blotched Bluebeard should leave director Baledón red-faced. —*Lent.*

La Fuga de Carrasco
(Carrasco's Escape)
(MEXICAN-COLOR)

A Peliculas Mexicanas release of a Filmadora Dal production. Produced by David Agrasánchez. Directed by Alfredo B. Crevenna. Stars José Alonso. Screenplay, Ramón Obón; camera (color), José Antonio Ruiz; editor, Jorge Rivera; music, Chilo Morán. Reviewed at Big Apple Cine 2, N.Y., Jan. 20, 1987. Running time: **80 MINS.**
Juan Carrasco . . . . José Alonso
Leticia . . . . Blanca Guerra
Danielo Rojas . . . . Wolf Ruvinskis
Rosalia . . . . Cristina Molina
Also with: Guillermo Herrera, Héctor Saez, Narciso Busquet, Milton Rodrlguez, Ricardo Carrión.

Revenge is the motive behind Juan Carrasco's return to his homeland in the Mexican genre pic ''La Fuga de Carrasco'' (Carrasco's Escape) by filmmaker Alfredo B. Crevenna.

Action begins 20 years earlier when young Juan accompanies his father and compadre Danielo Rojas (Wolf Ruvinskis) on a run smuggling countraband across the U.S.-Mexico border. Even more importantly, he witnesses his father's death at the hands of the police in compliance with Rojas.

We now cut to present day, where Juan (José Alonso) is a hot-shot maverick gun runner based in Texas. Things go well, until one day he hears of Rojas' countraband empire in Durango and he returns to even old scores. En route he helps an old-friend smuggler, who is being driven out of the market by Rojas, and he also takes the time to woo the friend's sister Leticia (Blanca Guerra).

Things complicate and at one point Carrasco is thrown in jail. His unconvincing escape provokes the pic's title. While there are a few exciting car chases and lots of realistic violence, the plot is forced and doesn't make a whole lot of sense.

Leads Alonso and Guerra, who teamed up in the 1983 thriller ''Motel,'' put in some good moments. Yet they alone are not enough to set this film apart from so many other pics of the same ilk. —*Lent*.

El Muerto del Palomo
(The Death Of Palomo)
(MEXICAN-COLOR)

A Películas Mexicanas release of an Intl. Films-Cinematográfica Sol production. Produced by Jesús Galindo. Directed by Pedro Galindo 3d. Stars Valentín Trujillo. Screenplay, Ramón Obón, Adolfo Torres Portillo; camera (color), Luis Medina; music, Ricardo Carrión, with appearance of group Carlos y José. Reviewed at Big Apple Ciné 2, N.Y., Jan. 26, 1987. Running time: **82 MINS.**
Valente Treviño . . . . Valentín Trujillo
Don Julio . . . . Mario Almada
Julia . . . . Carmen Montejo
Roberto Robles . . . . Pedro Infante Jr.
Gilberto Domínguez . . Humberto Elizondo
Nana . . . . Lourdes Munguía
Luis Robles . . . . Carlos Agosti

Moving along at a fast clip is the Mexican low-budget melodrama "El Muerto del Palomo" (The Death Of Palomo), only functionally helmed by Pedro Galindo 3d.

Pic features action-star Valentín Trujillo as a brooding, small town jockey who suffers a streak of bad luck which, besides losing everything in a race, includes being framed for the murder of his best friend. After several years in prison, shot in one take full of superimposed flashbacks, he returns to win back his girl and the respect of the community. The title refers to the horse the wronged hero uses to ride to victory.

One of the biggest problems with the film is the narrative. The authors and director feel they must include everything in strict chronological sequence, which leaves little room for detail. The story falls flat and seems more like an outline for a feature than a finished film. For example, rather than develop the love story, the director is content to throw in a few sappy flashbacks shot in slow motion, accompanied by corny music.

There are absolutely no surprises in this potboiler. The clumsy exposition prepares the viewer for what is to come so one is never fooled.
—*Lent*.

Versteckte Liebe
(Secret Love)
(WEST GERMAN-B&W)

A coproduction of Gottfried Junker with Pro-ject Filmproduktion in Filmverlag der Autoren and Bayerischer Rundfunk. Written and directed by Junker. Camera (b&w), Egon Werdin; editor, Peter R. Adam; music, Chris Heyne; lyre and singing, Jorgos Skoulas; sound, Matthias Golkowsky. Reviewed at the Berlin Film Festival (Market), Feb. 26, 1987. Running time: **80 MINS.**
Stranger . . . . Peter Cieslinki
The Girl . . . . Dimitra Spanou
Two Boys . . . Jorgos Balasis, Nikos Pekidou
Little Waitress . . . . . . Nektaria Nikolakakis
Priest . . . . Michaelis Georgulakis

Berlin — The storyline might suggest a "Lolita"-type situation, but this modest pic is light years away from that classic. Even so, it might travel well because what little dialog there is proves immaterial to understanding the story.

A blocked writer holed up on a Greek island becomes fascinated with the 11-year-old daughter of a neighbor. Young newcomer Dimitra Spanou has very expressive eyes and mouth, and is the best thing about this otherwise unremarkable pic. The story traces the growing acquaintance between the 30-ish writer and the girl. Her ambivalent behavior to his advances sometimes suggests more woman than child.

The situation grows tedious, however, and the film ends without any clear resolution. Too bad the beauty of the Greek landscape is so muted by the decision to shoot in b&w.—*Owl*.

Instant Justice
(Marine Issue)
(GIBRALTAR-COLOR)

A Warner Bros. presentation of a Mulloway Ltd./Craig T. Rumar production. Executive producer, Ian Charles Serra. Produced and written by Rumar. Directed by Denis Amar (uncredited). Stars Michael Paré, Tawny Kitaen. Camera (Fotofilm color), Douglas F. O'Neons; editor-associate producer, Pieter Bergema; music, David Kurtz; sound (Dolby), George Stephenson; art direction-set design, Luis Vazquez; assistant director, Yousaf Bokhari; production manager, Francisco Ariza; second unit car action, Alain Petit; casting, Ross Brown and Mary Webb (U.S.), Ellen Van Den Beld (Europe). Reviewed on Warner Home Video vidcassette, N.Y., March 1, 1987. (MPAA Rating: R.) Running time: **101 MINS.**
Scott Youngblood . . . . Michael Paré
Virginia . . . . Tawny Kitaen
Jake . . . . Peter Crook
Major Davis . . . . Charles Napier
Silke . . . . Eddie Avoth
Dutch . . . . Scott Del Amo
Kim . . . . Lynda Bridges
Ambassador Gordon . Lionel A. Ephraim
Shelton . . . . Maurice E. Aronow
Lt. Juan Munoz . . . . Aldo Sanbrell

"Instant Justice" is among that new breed of feature films — competently made but not quite ready for theatrical release. Bearing a Gibraltar copyright, filmed in Spain in 1985 and backed financially by Warner Bros. Intl., the actioner has been sent directly to homevideo stores by WB on the domestic front, a decision that will only displease rabid Michael Paré fans.

Pic's director credit is garbled: on screen a fictitious "Christopher Bentley" is listed, while the press kit and cassette packaging give the nod to writer-producer Craig T. Rumar. Pic actually was directed, under the better title "Marine Issue," by French helmer Denis Amar (whose prison thriller "L'Addition" was released Stateside by New World), whose name has been removed for unspecified reasons.

Film opens with Paré receiving a "Colt 45 marine issue" gun as a present for saving the life of the U.S. Ambassador in Paris while jogging one morning. That also describes his character, a standard, loyal, gung ho grunt who whips into one-man revenge action when his sister (played by Lynda Bridges) is murdered in Madrid.

To the cops there (led by Italian Western vet Aldo Sanbrell), it's a closed case, but Paré resigns his Marine post and sets out to clear his sister's name. Some good two-fisted action and car chases ensue.

Though well-made, pic lacks the spark to lift it from the rut of a million B-actioners. Paré is physically right though a bit too laidback for the role, functioning sort of in the manly but passive mode of Joe Dallesandro during his European sojourn. Heroine Tawny Kitaen, as a sort-of-prostitute who teams up reluctantly with Paré (in a fashion right out of a "Man From Uncle" tv episode), looks great but has a nothing role. Charles Napier gets to be a nice guy Marine officer while sidekick Peter Crook makes a good impression as a B-movie version of John Malkovich. —*Lor*.

Ursula
(FINNISH-COLOR)

A Filminor production (and international sales). Produced by Heikki Takkinen. Written and directed by Jakko Pyhälä, based on novel "Puuluola" by Kim Weckström; camera (Eastmancolor), Pertti Mutanen; editor, uncredited; music, Antti Hytti, Raine Salo, selection from Verdi; paintings displayed by Chris of Enehielm; sound, Matti Kuorti; assistant director, Nadja Pykkö; production management, Orvokki Taivalsaari. Reviewed at Berlin Film Festival (Market), Feb. 21, 1987. Running time: **100 MINS.**
Marten . . . . Ville Virtanen
Ursula . . . . Heidi Kilpeläinen
Harri . . . . Petri Aalto
Also with: Tomi Salmela, Ahmed Riza, Chris af Enehielm, Pekka Uotila, Eija Vilpas, Johan Donner, Sauli Poljakoff, Resika Nordin, Raine Salo.

Berlin — "Ursula," written and helmed by Jaakko Pyhälä, is an innocuous meller about two guys and a girl trying half-heartedly to wriggle loose from their life as dope peddlers on the fringe of a metropolitan milieu.

Looking darkly striking, Ursula (Heidi Kilpeläinen) is really an underwritten role although her very presence as the object of the tentative love of hopelessly muddled Marten (Ville Virtanen) is supposed to be pivotal in a belated plot development. This has the two youngsters trying to bid fellow dope carrier Harri (Petri Aalto) and the higher echelon dealers goodbye in a pretty tame attempt at a thriller ending.

Otherwise, Jaakko Pyhälä seems content to do milieu sketches, and he displays some wit and much sense of artistic framing in doing so, while he is at a total loss at basic dramatics.

Ultimately, "Ursula" suffers from over-length. It never reflects any real interest in its characters except as dumb (though loud) figures in a slightly moronic cityscape. Film takes preposterous turns at times as if what it really wants to be is a glittering specimen of state-of-the-art Kitsch.—*Kell*.

Monte Napoleone
(ITALIAN-COLOR)

A Columbia Pictures Italia release of a C.G. Silver Film/Video 80/Reteitalia coproduction. Produced by Mario and Vittorio Cecchi Gori. Directed by Carlo Vanzina. Screenplay, Carlo Vanzina, Enrico Vanzina, Jaja Fiastri; camera (Cinecittà color), Luigi Kuveiller; editor Ruggero Mastroianni; music, Beppe Cantarelli; art director, Mario Chiari. Reviewed at Etoile Cinema, Rome, March 19, 1987. Running time: **92 MINS.**
Elena . . . . Renée Simonsen
Margherita . . . . Carol Alt
Guido . . . . Luca Barbareschi
Roberto . . . . Fabrizio Bentivoglio
Also with: Corinne Cléry (Chiara), Marisa Berenson (Fabrizio's mother), Valentina Cortese (Guido's mother).

Rome — The supposedly glamorous, rich, amoral world of the Milan fashion scene provides the backdrop for this painless piece of froth from Carlo Vanzina, the young helmer who has never made a secret of the fact his sights are set on the boxoffice. His batting average has been good and "Monte Napoleone" should be a successful pic locally. Elsewhere, a cast that includes Marisa Berenson, Valentina Cortese, and several gorgeous fashion models could attract some business.

Pic takes its title from the Fashion Avenue of Milan, virtually a synonym for designer elegance and dizzying prices. It's the nearest thing Italy has to an oil well, so it should come as no surprise film is modeled after a "Dallas"-type tv series, with multiple characters and stories on a dramatic-romantic note. Renée Simonsen (who previously starred in Vanzina's "Nothing Underneath") is a plucky photographer whose veneer of career-girl independence momentarily cracks when one of her overnight lovers gets her pregnant. Her father, a likeable old gent who plays the ponies, also dies.

Carol Alt is Margherita, an ordinary wife and mother (with a million-dollar face) who decides life would be less boring if she got a job. Her first night running a fashion show she meets charming heel Fabrizio Bentivoglio and almost wrecks her marriage. Luca Barbareschi plays the familiar role of a shy gay guy whose mother (Cortese) temporarily doesn't comprehend. Berenson and Corinne Cléry turn up in yet another story, in which Berenson is a hyper-possessive mother whose son is seduced by best friend Cléry.

Sets are classy, lensing is pretty, and top models Simonsen and Alt are so photogenic it doesn't matter whether they're acting or not. Beppe Cantarelli's mocking songs about Milan are, like rest of pic, easy listening. — *Yung.*

Three By Three
(U.S.-COLOR)

A Cross Cut production. Directed by Calogero Salvo. Screenplay, Salvo. No further credits supplied. Reviewed at Berlin Film Festival (Forum), Feb. 28, 1987. Running time: **82 MINS.**
With: Wes Smith, Sharon Sodeil, Ricardo Isidro.

Berlin — This low-budget item, mostly filmed on video, appeared in the Forum section of the Berlin fest as part of a section of new cinema from Venezuela, though it appears to be wholly American produced, albeit by a Venezuelan helmer, Calogero Salvo.

To complicate matters further, pic deals with Cubans who left their homes in 1980. There are 125,000 refugees at the time, most of whom settled in Florida, but a significant number settled in the San Francisco Bay area, among them the homosexual Ricardo (Ricardo Isidro), who was at first amazed at the irony that gays tend to congregate in the "Castro" neighborhood.

Like most of his compatriots, Ricardo is earnest and hardworking he gets a job as a waiter. He also meets a neighbor, an impressionable young American (Wes Smith) who lives with his attractive, but lonely, mother (Sharon Sodeil).

Salvo mixes front-on interviews, using a multiple bank of video screens, as well as enacted scenes, and the result is a very modest, but sincere and well-handled, exploration of both the Cuban community and the world of gays. The semi-experimental nature of the pic will limit it to specialized release.
— *Strat.*

El Socio De Dios
(The Partner Of God)
(CUBAN-PERUVIAN-COLOR)

A presentation of Mercado Del Cine Latinoamericano (Mecla), Havana. Produced by ICAIC, Cuba, and Kuntar, Peru. Directed by Federico Garcia. Camera (color), Rodolfo Lopez; editor, Roberto Bravo; music, Juan Marquez. Reviewed at Berlin Film Festival (Market), Feb. 24, 1987. Running time: **129 MINS.**
With: Adolfo Llaurado; Ricardo Tosco; Rene de la Cruz, Delicia Zalazar; Enrique Almirante; Eslinda Nunez.

Berlin — The partner or equal of god of the title is a power-mad entrepreneur envied for his vast holdings and wealth in Peru in the early 1900s. He is a ruthless promoter and megalomaniac who colonizes and exploits the Amazonian jungles.

Not inappropriately, he is named Julio Cesar, last name Arana. His character is based in part, as are other characters in the film, on real-life historical personages. Rubber for tires is the goal, the obsession. To gratify his scenario, and the scenario of this film, this jungle Caesar must ruthlessly subjugate the Amazonian Indian tribes as rubber-plantation slaves to supply international markets.

Thus the scene is set for a Cuban historial parable-film about the abuse of Third World innocents by those "civilized" decadents who lust obscenely for riches. The contemporary applications of the film are obvious — this is another didactic film giving moral instruction about the evils of capitalism.

The convoluted intrigues and power struggles of the film include the rival imperialisms of "Tio Sam" (Uncle Sam) as embodied by a big jovial American diplomat, a charming cynic, versus a sly, scholarly British foreign service officer who refers with breathless adoration to the then-reigning Queen Victoria back home. These two are among the film's stock company of villains. Their hands remain clean at the top, but they are linked below to violent psychopaths and mercenaries who grin hideously while slaying Indian villagers.

There comes a reckoning. A stealthy puma glides through the night, a force of nature, his recurrent image in the jungle and his growl representing retribution to come. Predictably, the Indians organize a rebellion and strike at night, like the puma. Their righteous arrows prevail against the white man's firearms. In that locale and at that time, the Indians historically did win a limited victory.

At the film's end, we flash-forward to the present, to huge oil rigs and drilling-stations in the Amazon of today. The actor playing the Julio Cesar Arana of a century ago now alights from a helicopter. He is capitalist colonization personified, unchanged. The film's moral is underlined: there are now modern Julius Caesars that compel ever-renewed vigilance and righteous arrows. — *Hitch.*

Macskafogo
(Cat City)
(HUNGARIAN-CANADIAN-W. GERMAN-ANIMATED-COLOR)

A Pannonia Film Studios (Budapest)-Sefel Pictures Intl. (Calgary)-Infafilm (Munich) co-production. Directed by Bela Ternovszky. Screenplay, József Nepp; editor, Magda Hap; music, Tamás Deák; sound, Andras Imre Nyerges; animation, Jozsef Gémes, Zoltan Maros; character design, Maros, Ternovszky; animation camera (Eastmancolor), Maria Neményi, Csaba Nagy, György Varga. Reviewed at Hungarian Film Week, Budapest, Feb. 14, 1987. Running time: **93 MINS.**

Budapest — "Cat City" is an animated feature about the age-old struggle between cats and mice, although this one pales a bit alongside the best American animated features both in script and design. Still, it has some lively characters and amusing situations, despite an extended running time and an over-reliance on dialog.

After some "Star Wars"-style introductory titles, pic establishes a world where evil cats and rats are terrorizing the mice community. A heroic mouse, Grabowski, is sent on a mission to Japan to obtain a method of controlling cats which has been developed by a Japanese mouse. The chief villain, a horrid, blue-colored cat with one eye and a claw in place of one paw, sends a quartet of rats to stop our hero's brave mission.

There are some funny jokes along the way: a mouse entering a security area has his tail checked instead of his fingerprints, and the supermouse hero is able to take photos just by winking his eye. There are also some colorful characters, including a gang of vampire bats who look like Mexican bandits. Some aspects of the film are questionable given the target family audience. For instance, a sequence in which terrorists try to hijack an airliner which results in the aircraft crashing into a jungle with only one survivor is hardly the stuff to entrance youngsters.

Character animation is fine, though backgrounds are rather flat and uninteresting. There's far too much talk, which will necessitate dubbing for non-Hungarian territories. Pic is also about 20 minutes too long. Yet there's plenty of enjoyment here and, with a few modifications, an engaging animation feature could result which could have a long and useful international career. — *Strat.*

Als In Een Roes
(Intoxicated)
(DUTCH-COLOR)

An Altamira Films production. Produced by Lea Wongsoredjo, Ruud Den Drijver. Directed by Pim de la Parra. Screenplay, de la Parra, Judy Doorman, Natasa Hanusova; camera (color), Frans Bromet; editor, Lea Wongsoredjo; music, Lodewijk de Boer, Adriaan van Noord, Jose Leal. Reviewed at the Berlin Film Festival (Panorama), Feb. 26, 1987. Running time: **85 MINS.**
With: Herbert Flack, Liz Snoyink, Thom Hoffman, Devika Strooker, Ellen Vogel.

Berlin — This modest effort from director Pim de la Parra doesn't really come together. The characters and situations are not very credible.

An egocentric playwright is directing his live-in girlfriend in the role of a prostitute in his new play. Dissatisfied with her performance, on a whim he picks up a real hook-

er to demonstrate the tricks of the trade. There are minor subplots, one involving a feuding lesbian couple. All this happens around the imminent opening of the production.

The performers work hard, but they've been given nothing admirable to do. The idea had potential and better scripting might have saved an otherwise undistinguished exercise. — *Owl.*

AFI Film Reviews

'68
(COLOR)

Overly ambitious effort to recreate the hippie era.

A Sixty-Eight Ltd. production. Produced by Dale Djerassi, Isabel Maxwell, Steven Kovacs. Written and directed by Kovacs. Camera (Monaco color), Daniel Lacambre; editor, Cari Coughlin; music, John Cipollina, Shony Alex Braun; art direction, Joshua Koral; set decoration, Kris Boxell; sound, Anne Evans; associate producer, Eli Zaffaroni; assistant director, Karen McCabe. Reviewed at the American Film Institute (AFI Fest), L.A., Feb. 13, 1987. (No MPAA Rating.) Running time: **97 MINS.**

Peter Szabo	Eric Larson
Sandy Szabo	Robert Locke
Zoltan Szabo	Sandor Tecsi
Zsuzsa Szabo	Anna Dukasz
Alana Chan	Miran Kwun
Vera Kardos	Terra Vandergaw
Tibor Kardos	Shony Alex Braun
Piroska Kardos	Donna Pecora
Gizi Horvath	Jan Nemec
Bela Csontos	Rusdi Lane
Beatrice	Nike Doukas
Westy	Neil Young

Hollywood — " '68" is like an ambitious first novel, a work in which the young author tries to cram everything he can think of to say into the framework of a single story. The year 1968 was a momentous one, to be sure, and writer-director Steven Kovacs sympathetically overrreaches himself in trying to explain why in his first feature. With retrospective looks at the Vietnam era now seemingly back in fashion, this could have some possibilities in the commercial arena, notably with student audiences.

Kovacs wants to cover everything — the generation gap, hippies, bikers, gays, the immigrant experience, draft dodging, minority rights, rock music, free love, LBJ, RFK, McCarthy, Martin Luther King, Prague, Chicago, you name it. He tackles this through a presumably autobiographical portrait of a Hungarian family, one that has fled the Old World in 1956 and is still struggling to make a breakthrough in the land of opportunity.

The bull-headed patriarch, a virulent anti-communist, struggles to make a success of a Hungarian restaurant in San Francisco, and can't begin to understand why his son Peter and the rest of the new generation want to protest against the country where "anything is possible."

Peter is kicked out of school, begins working at a biker shop owned by a redneck (rock star Neil Young in a cameo), flirts with political activism and is progressively walloped by the historical events of the spring and summer.

What actually hurts the film more than the cramming in of too much sociology is the suddeness and extremity of the personal drama. Right after Peter's younger brother beds and becomes engaged to a young girl, the kid (oy vay!) discovers he's gay. Then it turns out old pa (mama mia!) wants to elope with the restaurant's young waitress, the kid brother is drafted, the restaurant fails, pa gets sick, and on and on.

Enough incident is packed in here to satisfy a soap opera for a month, and lacking proper preparation matters become a bit silly after awhile. All the events, emotions and reactions are legitimate in their way, but piled one on top of another become more like a litany of cataclysm than convincing drama.

To his credit, Kovacs has managed, to a great degree on a low budget, to recreate the look and feel of San Francisco in the late 1960s. Even more successfully, he accurately conveys modes of behavior, the social casualness, the political and moral openess, the idealism under stress, of the period.

Although lighting is occasionally overly bright, Daniel Lacambre's lensing makes the indie production look richer than it undoubtedly was. A graduate of the Roger Corman school, Kovacs seems to have something to offer, and much of what he is saying here is appealing. However, only a cinematic Tolstoy could have succeeded with the task he set for himself with his first film.
— *Cart.*

Street Trash
(COLOR)

Noxious exploitation pic.

A Chaos production. Produced by Roy Frumkes. Executive producers, James Muro Sr., Edward Muro Sr. Directed by Jim Muro. Screenplay, Frumkes; camera (Technicolor), David Sperling; editor, Dennis Werner; music, Rick Ulfik; production design, Robert Marcucci; art direction, Denise Labelle, Tom Molinelli; special makeup effects, Jennifer Aspinall; special makeup artist, Mike Lackey; sound, Alex Giraldo; costumes, Michele Leifer; assistant director, Bob Hurrie; associate producer, Frank Farel. Reviewed at the American Film Institute (AFI Fest), L.A., March 12, 1987. (No MPAA Rating.) Running time: **91 MINS.**

Fred . . . . Mike Lackey
Bronson . . . . Vic Noto
Bill the Cop . . . . Bill Chepil
Kevin . . . . Mark Sferrazza
Wendy . . . . Jane Arakawa
Winette . . . . Nicole Potter

Frank Schnizer . . . . R.L. Ryan
Also with: Clarenze Jarmon (Burt), Bernard Perlman (Wizzy), Miriam Zucker (Drunken wench), M. D'Jango Krunch (Ed), James Corinz (Doorman), Morty Storm (Black Suit), Tony Darrow (Nick Duran).

Hollywood — "Street Trash" has but one thing on its mind — to be the grossest film yet in the gore exploitation cycle. Much of the meager budget must have been expended on all manner of slime, goop, prosthetics, blood and entrails, but all for naught, since the context in which they are used is so preposterously silly that the special effects have virtually no impact other than as bad jokes. Indie effort had its world premiere at the AFI Fest, although what it's doing in an international film festival is a question for the ages. This has some commercial potential as a midnight show, although best results will probably be found in homevid.

Allegedly inspired by Akira Kurosawa's 1970 study of slum life, "Dodes'ka-den," "Street Trash" entered the world as a 10-minute, 16m film by Jim Muro at the School of Visual Arts in New York. His instructor, Roy Frumkes, not only encouraged the 20-year-old to expand it into a 35m feature, but offered to write and produce.

Unfortunately, it should have remained a short. After a spritely opening chase sequence, in which an assortment of New Yorkers try to apprehend a bum for ripping off their stuff, pic descends quickly into irredeemable idiocy. A motley crew of derelicts, perverts, cretins, winos and terminally deranged Vietnam vets live marginal existences on the streets of New York, occasionally assaulting society but mostly doing damage to each other.

Far from aspiring to the mantle of Kurosawa or the Hector Babenco of "Pixote," Muro clearly dreams of joining the ranks of Cronenberg, Romero, Craven and Hooper. One by one, as skid row denizens get their mitts on bottles of some very bad booze, they self-destruct by bubbling, boiling, bursting and decomposing to death. Flowing ooze comes in every primary color, and is so obviously phoney that effects are only laughably gruesome.

But the highlight — and the scene that virtually cleared the room at the press screening — comes when one of the derelicts takes a leak and has his member sliced off by a mischievous bum. Junkyard residents then proceed to play a game of keep-away with the severed organ, which is photographed in slow-motion closeup flying through the air à la the bone in "2001" as the victim desperately races about trying to retrieve it from his fun-loving pals.

Muro makes ample use of the Steadicam to push the filth in the

audience's face, but he's miscalculated by not even establishing a nominal protagonist among the scum on view and by not funneling the outlandish goings-on into a coherent storyline. This will please only the most easily amused exploitation fans, those who, like Muro, as one learns in the end credits, were taken to see "I Drink Your Blood" when they were six. —*Cart.*

Amazing Grace And Chuck
(COLOR)

**No Nukes Nanette.
Embarrassing misfire.**

A Tri-Star Pictures release of a Tri-Star and Rastar presentation of a Turnstar/David Field production from Tri-Star-ML Delphi Premier Prods. Written and produced by David Field. Executive producer, Roger M. Rothstein. Directed by Mike Newell. Executive consultant, Ted Turner. Camera (Metrocolor; Technicolor prints), Robert Elswit; editor, Peter Hollywood; music, Elmer Bernstein; production design, Dena Roth; art direction, John Myhre; set design, Dawn Snyder; set decoration, Michael J. Taylor; costume design, Jack Buehler; sound (Dolby), Jonathan Stein; assistant director, John T. Kretchmer; casting, Lynn Stalmaster & Associates, Mali Finn. Reviewed at the Chinese Theater (AFI Fest), L.A., March 26, 1987. (MPAA Rating: PG.) Running time: **115 MINS.**

Lynn Taylor . . . . Jamie Lee Curtis
Amazing Grace Smith . . . . Alex English
President . . . . Gregory Peck
Russell . . . . William L. Petersen
Chuck Murdock . . . . Joshua Zuehlke
Johnny B. Goode . . . . Dennis Lipscomb
Jeffries . . . . Lee Richardson

Hollywood — "Amazing Grace And Chuck" is destined to go down in history as the camp classic of the anti-nuke genre. As amazingly bad as it is audacious, pic harks back to such political fantasies of the 1930s as "Gabriel Over The White House" and "Stand Up And Cheer" in its good-hearted naïveté, but the storytelling, if it can be called that, is so inept as to leave one gaping in wonderment that this could have gotten through the usual corporate production barriers. Film has little commercial chance, but it will live forever in the hearts of connoisseurs of Hollywood's most memorably outrageous moments.

Concoction of writer-producer David Field, former production executive at Fox and United Artists, features not so much a plot as an attitude, one fancifully suggesting total nuclear disarmament could be achieved immediately and pacifistically if the correct forces were brought to bear upon the powers-that-be.

At the outset, Little League baseball pitcher Chuck Murdock, having been shown a Minuteman missile under the Montana prairie, announces from the mound before an important game, "I can't play because of nuclear weapons." The coach and other players don't dig this too much because they are

forced to forfeit the game, but who should read a news report of the incident but Boston Celtics star Amazing Grace Smith (played by Denver Nuggets great Alex English), who promptly gives up his $1,000,000-per-year salary to join Chuck in protest of nukes.

Pretty soon, two Miami Dolphin players show their solidarity with the cause, and in no time, hundreds of athletes on both sides of the Iron Curtain are refusing to play until the ultimate weapon is eliminated.

When it looks as though the upcoming baseball season will have to be cancelled due to lack of players, the President of the United States (an impressive Gregory Peck) summons young Chuck to the White House to drum some sense into him. Chuckie won't budge, and when conspiratorial big businessmen rub out Amazing Grace, the kid adopts a vow of silence which, in turn, is picked up on by millions of children around the world.

Rather than being relieved that the little troublemakers have shut up, the President and the Soviet general secretary are so alarmed that their grandchildren won't speak to them that they instantly convene a secret summit meeting, at which it is decided that nuclear weapons will be eliminated over the course of seven years.

This isn't good enough for Chuck, who holds out for, and gets, a commitment to total nuclear disarmament, now! Then, and only then, with the Prez and Russian leader in attendance and Cable News Network broadcasting the event, Chuck dons his Little League uniform and heads out to the mound to make his baseball comeback.

Presence of the CNN microphones and initially mysterious credit for Ted Turner as executive consultant are tipoffs as to who the true auteur of "Amazing Grace" might be. Turner's recent sports and broadcasting initiatives with the Soviets link perfectly with the film's themes.

Even so, it takes a reel or two to get any bearing on what's going on here. Field's dialog is unlike any conversation ever heard on earth, and director Mike Newell ("Dance With A Stranger') can impose no shape or rhythm on the proceedings, and allows most of the actors to flail about in unbecoming ways. Amazing's the word.—*Cart.*

Heroic Pioneers
(TAIWANESE-COLOR)

A Taiwan Film Studio production. Produced by Li Chi-tse. Directed by Lee Shing. Screenplay, Chung Lai; camera (Panavision, color), Chow Yuan-Xing. No other credits available. Reviewed at the American Film Institute (AFI Fest), L.A., Feb. 23,

1987. Running time: **110 MINS.**
With: Ko-Chin-hsiung, Chen Li Li, Ma Jafung, Chiu Su-yi, Chang Yuan-ting.

Hollywood — The title of this expansive Taiwanese historical piece pretty much defines the film's artistic approach, which is both ennobling and simplistic in its description of the first settlement of the island's inland territory in the late 1700s. Colorful and rambunctious, pic is also as hokey as the standard-issue Hollywood Westerns that obviously served as its model, and is not nearly sophisticated enough to appeal to art house or international festival crowds.

In preliminaries that last far too long, nearly half the film, a small group of Chinese decide to break away from their community and head for Kawalan, an undeveloped area that holds great potential for cultivation and is nominally controlled by an aboriginal chieftain.

Main twist from a Western point of view is that the settlers, who set up shop with amazing efficiency and industriousness, are determined to get along with the local natives, not to conquer them. The chief is a pushover due to his weakness for the bottle, but his daughter is a real hellcat and haughtily resistant to the idea of making peace by marrying the most eligible bachelor among the newcomers.

Unfortunately, every appearance by the wild-eyed sexpot marks the occasion for raucous laughter since her wardrobe looks to have been bought at a Chinatown curio shop. In addition, anachronistic modern musical numbers and sporadic jumps into martial arts sequences tend to disrupt the historical verisimilitude.

Eventually, the Chinese win the natives over by curing plague victims with their up-to-date medicine, and even Miss Bauble in her mini-skirt comes around in the end, the future unity of Taiwan thus being assured.

Director Lee Shing and lenser Chow Yuan-ting show some good, bold moves with their widescreen camera, and the performances are generally entertaining, even if exceedingly broad. As history, however, it undoubtedly ranks somewhere in there with "Parnell" and "How The West Was Won." —*Cart.*

Saturday Night At The Palace
(SOUTH AFRICAN-COLOR)

A Davnic production. Produced, directed and camera (Irene color) by Robert Davies. Stars Bill Flynn, John Kani, Paul Slabolepszy. Screenplay, Slabolepszy, Flynn, based on Slabolepszy's play; editor, Lena Farugia, Carla Sandrock; music, Johnny Cleff; art direction, Wayne Attrill, Sandy Attrill; sound, Humphrey Weale; associate producer, Lena Farugia. Reviewed at the Los Feliz Theater (AFI Fest), L.A., March 26, 1987. Running time: **88 MINS.**
Forsie . . . . Bill Flynn
September . . . . John Kani
Vince . . . . Paul Slabolepszy

Hollywood — Adapted from Paul Slabolepszy's stage play that has had successful runs in its native South Africa as well as London and other European cities, "Saturday Night At The Palace" is a symbolic representation of racial tensions in the home of apartheid that probably seems more controversial than it actually is. Often effectively dramatic but also rather predictable in its plot trajectory, pic is of interest as an example of the sort of political material that actually can be produced in South Africa, but undoubtedly would run into trouble in commercial situations from censorious types who believe nothing from that country should be heard or seen regardless of its point-of-view.

Drama is highly reminiscent of the numerous American theater pieces of the 1960s, from "Dutchman" to "When You Comin' Back, Red Ryder?" in which class and racial conflicts were displayed in microcosm through a handful of sociologically opposed characters. Invariably in such works, it's only a matter of time (and enough booze) until the more hateful and explosive of these characters show their true colors and betray the oppressive nature of the dominant ruling class through bigoted and violent behavior.

Situation here opposes Vince, a white, out-of-work, roughneck former soccer player, and September, a hard-working, proper black man who has saved up enough money to return to see his wife and family in the Zulu homeland for the first time in two years.

For the initial half-hour, first-time director Robert Davies intercuts between September and Vince as the latter displays his wildman tendencies and racial prejudice. As he tells his chubby, inexperienced pal Forsie, with whom he attends a late-night drunken party, he refuses to work with or for blacks. "I'd rather maintain my dignity. Stay unemployed," he snaps.

On the way home from the party, Vince and Forsie stop at Rocco's Burger Palace, where September is about to close up. Stage origins show vividly from here on, as Vince launches a one-man terrorist attack upon both the dignified black man and the establishment. September is humiliated and victimized, the mild-mannered Forsie is brought to the breaking point, and all ends tragically in a manner designed to illustrate the self-destructiveness of the South African government's official policy toward blacks.

Schematic approach of the play grows tiresome after awhile, but potent performances, particularly that of playwright Slabolepszy as the possessed firecracker, Vince, hold the attention. On-location lensing in the Johannesburg area lends a strong sense of time and place, although sometimes thick accents require strict concentration to make it through much of the dialog.—*Cart.*

The Secret Of My Success
(COLOR)

Leaden comedy of Fox on the make.

A Universal Pictures release of a Rastar production. Produced and directed by Herbert Ross. Stars Michael J. Fox. Screenplay, Jim Cash, Jack Epps, A.J. Carothers, from a story by Carothers; camera (color), Carlo Di Palma; editor, Paul Hirsch; music, David Foster; production design, Edward Pisoni, Peter Larkin; set decorator, Susan Bode; sound (Dolby), Jim Sabat; costumes, Joseph G. Aulisi; assistant director, Robert G. Girolami; associate producer, Nora Kaye; casting, Mark Colquhoun, Hank McCann. Reviewed at Universal Studios screening room, L.A., April 2, 1987. (MPAA Rating: PG-13.) Running time: **110 MINS.**

Brantley Foster . . . . Michael J. Fox
Christy Wills . . . . Helen Slater
Howard Prescott . . . . Richard Jordan
Vera Prescott . . . . Margaret Whitton
Fred Melrose . . . . John Pankow
Barney Rattigan . . . . . Christopher Murney
Art Thomas . . . . Gerry Bamman
Donald Davenport . . . . Fred Gwynne
Jean . . . . Carol-Ann Susi

Hollywood — "The Secret Of My Success" is a bedroom farce with a leaden touch, a corporate comedy without teeth. What it does have is Michael J. Fox in a winning performance as a likable hick out to hit the big time in New York. Even he can't carry this turkey on his shoulders, although his presence should generate some interest at the boxoffice.

Fresh off the bus from Kansas, Brantley Foster (Fox) doesn't want to return until he has a penthouse, jacuzzi, a beautiful girlfriend and a private jet he can go home in. While his ideals are a yuppie's dream, Fox is sweet and unassuming enough to dilute the boorishness of his goals.

Where the script by Jim Cash, Jack Epps and A.J. Carothers (from a story by Carothers) could have gone for a good screwball social comedy with an edge, it settles for a cliché-ridden ride down easy street.

Fox encounters the predictable crime-infested corners of New York and his squalid apartment is furnished with roaches and rats. When he meets his dream girl (Helen Slater), he is literally thunderstruck and visualizes her in an evening gown parading down the lobby of a Madison Avenue office building.

After young Brantley lands a job in the mailroom of an anonymous N.Y. corporation with the reluctant help of a distant relative (Richard Jordan), he soon proves that "I can do anything if I get a chance." His big chance comes when he takes over an abandoned office and sets himself up as a young exec.

His double life becomes even more complicated when his uncle's neglected wife (Margaret Whitton) seduces him about the same time he's getting started with Slater, an exec at the company, who turns out to be Jordan's mistress.

None of it is terribly convincing and director Herbert Ross pushes it all along with surprising heavy-handedness. Instead of establishing real emotional connections he resorts to cheap montages that jump over the rough spots.

Soundtrack by David Foster is also used as filler and adds some hideous basso profundo moans and overstated music to signal deep emotion.

Jordan and Slater, fine in some scenes, are encouraged to sacrifice a personal and specific voice for broad caricatures. Even Fox, in spite of his inherent charm, lacks a genuine personality and is neither country bumpkin nor city sharpie. Consequently, the film lacks a consistent tone or style.

John Pankow and Christopher Murney as Fox' mailroom buddy and boss, respectively, are fine in supporting roles but overall the corporate types and hangers-on are rendered without much imagination.

Cinematography by Carlo Di Palma impressively captures a city of steel and concrete, but too often the people seem to be made of the same stuff. —*Jagr.*

Dolghyie Provod
(The Long Goodbye)
(SOVIET-B&W)

A Odessa Cinematography production. Written and directed by Kira Muratova. Camera (b&w), Ghenadi Kariuk; editor, V. Oleinik; music, O. Karabanchiuk; art director, E. Rodrigues. Reviewed at the Berlin Film Festival (Forum), March 3, 1987. Running time: **95 MINS.**

Mother . . . . Zenaida Sharko
Son . . . . Oleg Vladimirski

Also with: Yuri Kayourov, Svetlana Kabanova, Tatiana Tetchko, Lydia Vasilevska.

Berlin — It is anybody's guess why this intriguing and quite exceptional little film has been blacklisted for the last 16 years, since it has no direct political references at all.

"The Long Goodbye" is an intimate family picture, beautifully shot in black and white in Odessa, and featuring some intricate and fascinating editing techniques, certainly ahead of their time for 1971, and refreshing even by today's standards. The light satirical drama is about a teenage boy who lives with his mother, a professional translator, in Odessa, but dreams of leaving her to join his father in Novosibirsk, at the other end of the country.

The mother, a marvelous combination of a nagging parent who won't give her son one moment of respite, and a flirt who likes to be courted by men around her, offers an unusually perceptive and accurate study of character. Her self-pitying bouts, her over-excited emotional condition quite close to hysteria, her professional problems as a woman being passed over for promotion, her fear of solitude, are rendered sensitively through intelligent but never exaggerated direction, and a remarkable performance by Zenaida Sharko. The son, as moody and discontented as a teenager can be, tries to cope with the natural problems of adolescence, such as his contact with the opposite sex, his rebellion against adults and his realization that they are dependent on him no less than he on them.

Much of the restlessness in the relations between the two characters is reflected through director Kira Muratova's often intentionally disjointed editing, while the smartly sharp black and white photography is essential for its eloquence and the musical score, mostly piano solos, stresses the humorous side which is never neglected. All this does not detract from Muratova's talent as a consummate actors' director, one particularly adept at establishing moods on the screen, as she does for instance in an early sequence showing a reunion of friends in a country house. She is also blessed with that rare quality of seeing the human dimension even in the most infuriat-

ing acts, which make them acceptable, if not agreeable.

If indeed this film, her second (the first has never been released) will start circulating, as it well might if present winds persist in their direction, Muratova's name soon will become familiar with film buffs the world over. —*Edna.*

Anna
(COLOR)

Terrific theatrical drama spotlighting Sally Kirkland.

A Magnus Films production. Executive producers, Deirdre Ganor, Julianne Gilliam. Produced by Yurek Bogayevicz, Zanne Devine. Directed by Bogayevicz. Screenplay, Agnieszka Holland, from a story by Bogayevicz and Holland; camera (color), Bobby Bukowski; editor, Julie Sloane; sound, Tim Squyres; production design, Lester Cohen; art direction, Danny Talpers; set decoration, John Tatlock; production manager, Brenda Goodman; assistant directors, Lisa Zimble, Ellen Dennis, Amy Herzig; costume design, Hali Breindel; casting, Caroline Thomas. Reviewed at Kabuki theater, San Francisco, April 4, 1987. (No MPAA Rating.) Running time: **95 MINS.**

Anna . . . . Sally Kirkland
Daniel . . . . Robert Fields
Krystyna . . . . Paulina Porizkova
Director #1 . . . . Gibby Brand
Director #2 . . . . John Robert Tillotson
Stage manager . . . . Joe Aufiery
Agent . . . . Charles Randall
Agent's secretary . . . . Mimi Wedell
Baskin . . . . Larry Pine
Producer . . . . Lola Pashalinksi
Professor . . . . Stefan Schnabel
Tonda . . . . Steven Gilborn

San Francisco — In its publicity, Magnus Films is said to be "dedicated to the production of features based on extraordinary scripts with modest budgets." Off MF's first feature, "Anna," which world-preemed at the S.F. Film Festival, this hype is accurate. "Anna," which should do quite well in art venues and has crossover potential, offers a brilliant performance in the title role by legit vet Sally Kirkland, an engaging screen debut by international fashion model Paulina Porizkova, seamless technical credits, exemplary casting by Caroline Thomas, a wry, intelligent, compassionate screenplay by Agnieszka Holland and the wonderfully revelatory direction of rookie filmmaker, and established legit stager, Yurek Bogayevicz.

The storyline is, in its way, a blend of "All About Eve," "Sunset Boulevard" and "The Turning Point," yet in its own way a unique, absorbing yarn.

Kirkland so remarkably shades the character of an expatriate Czech movie queen groping and sometimes groveling for thesp bits in Manhattan that she's like an ensemble; the breadth of her performance is living text, lensed with distinction by Bobby Bukowski. Kirkland takes in a beautiful young Czech refugee, Porizkova, who, in

the great American way, becomes an overnight screen leading lady, assumes Kirkland's trauma-filled past as her own bio and walks off with Kirkland's b.f., a wimpy writer essayed meticulously by Robert Fields.

Yet the Porizkova character is more ingenuous than malicious. She seizes the day, because the day beckons to her. Kirkland's day is entrapped in the past; she is locked into dues-paying, clearly capable but non-glitzy. In one bruising moment — the burning of one of her old films in the projector while she watches it in a grindhouse, her ex-husband-director seated, unknowingly, a few rows behind — Anna's condition-status is exposed, as much to her as the viewer.

Holland's screenplay is not without humor early on. There's a delicious legit audition scene for a play about seven women in which "directors" Gibby Brand and John Robert Tillotson fuss at each other in a fey, running exchange. Pic is filled with charming cameos, including Stefan Schnabel as Anna's old drama prof who urges her to return to Prague so that "you can act. You'll die if you cannot act."

The story works on a number of levels, all spinning off Kirkland and all relevant, universal, cleanly stated. Pic was shot over five weeks at producer-reported cost of "just under $1,000,000." "Anna" should be able to call its own shots for it's an on-target piece of moviemaking in all respects. —*Herb.*

Police Academy 4: Citizens On Patrol
(COLOR)

Low comedy series has run out of gas.

A Warner Bros. release. Produced by Paul Maslansky. Directed by Jim Drake. Screenplay, Gene Quintano, based on characters created by Neal Israel, Pat Proft; camera (Medallion color), Robert Saad; editor, David Rawlins; music, Robert Folk; production design, Trevor Williams; art director, Rhiley Fuller; set decorator, Steve Shewchuk; sound, Ingrid M. Cusiel; costumes, Aleida MacDonald; assistant director, Michael Zenon; associate producer, Donald West; casting, Fern Champion, Pamela Basker. Reviewed at Mann's Chinese theater, Hollywood, April 3, 1987. (MPAA Rating: PG.) Running time: **87 MINS.**

Mahoney . . . . Steve Guttenberg
Hightower . . . . Bubba Smith
Jones . . . . Michael Winslow
Tackleberry . . . . David Graf
Sweetchuck . . . . Tim Kazurinsky
Claire Mattson . . . . Sharon Stone
Callahan . . . . Leslie Easterbrook
Hooks . . . . Marion Ramsey
Proctor . . . . Lance Kinsey
Captain Harris . . . . G.W. Bailey
Zed . . . . Bobcat Goldthwait
Commandant Lassard . . . . . George Gaynes
Mrs. Feldman . . . . Billie Bird

Hollywood — The boobs in blue are back and "Police Academy 4:

Citizens On Patrol" carries the banner of tasteless humor raised in the first three installments to new heights of insipidness. As the films have got worse since their raunchy origins in 1984, the boxoffice has declined and "4" should continue the trend.

Although there is the usual assortment of food jokes, farts, and pratfalls, this is basically material that has run out of steam. The humor is simply perfunctory now and one laughs at what the characters might be rather than what they are. What they have become is a safe bunch of cuddly cops an audience can root for and make fun of at the same time.

As usual, Steve Guttenberg leads the proceedings as Mahoney, the cute cop. By now his act has become so mannered that instead of just resembling a puppy dog, he actually imitates one at one point.

Most of the regulars are back with Bobcat Goldthwait assuming a larger role as the moronic cop Zed, who spends most of his time chasing birdlike Officer Sweetchuck (Tim Kazurinsky). Bubba Smith growls his way through a few scenes and Leslie Easterbrook as the statuesque Officer Callahan gets to show off her talents as well.

Plot, such as it is, has something to do with Commandant Lassard's (George Gaynes) Citizens On Patrol program and attempts by archrival Captain Harris (G.W. Bailey) to make him look bad, a truly difficult task since collectively this police force barely has a triple digit I.Q.

Gene Quintano's script is merely a collection of gags tied together by the slightest suggestion of a story. Unfortunately, most of the bits fall flat as director Jim Drake has failed to find the inherent humor in any of the setups.

Attempt to pump new life into the pic at the end with a chase in hot air balloons and vintage aircraft is too little too late. By then most of the audience will have dozed off.
—*Jagr.*

The Night Stalker
(COLOR)

Cop B-film is too predictable.

An Almi Pictures release of an Almi-Chrystie Prods. presentation of a Striker production. Executive producers, Stephen Chrystie, Michael Landes, Albert Schwartz. Produced by Don Edmonds. Directed by Max Kleven. Stars Charles Napier. Screenplay, John Goff, Edmonds; camera (Alpha Cine color), Don Burgess; editor, Stanford C. Allen; music supervision, Steve Tyrell; music, David Kitay, others; sound, Craig Felburg; production design, Allen Terry; production manager, Sanford Hampton; assistant director, Tom Irving; special effects Paul Stapley; stunt coordinator, James Winburn; co-producers, Jef Richard, Buck Flower; associate producer, Jack Lorenz; casting, Patti Kirkpatrick. Reviewed at Cine 2, N.Y., April 4, 1987. (MPAA Rating: R.) Running time: **89 MINS.**

Sgt. J.J. Striker	Charles Napier
Rene	Michelle Reese
Denise	Katherine Kelly Lang
Charlie Garrett	Robert Viharo
Buddy Brown	Joey Gian
Sommers	Robert Zdar
Terry	Leila Carlin
Vic Gallegher	Gary Crosby
Julius	James Louis Watkins
Captain	John Goff
Lannie	Diane Sommerfield
Brenda	Tally Chanel
Sable Fox	Ola Ray
Mai Wing	Joan Chen
Cook	Roy Jenson
Tramp	Buck Flower

"The Night Stalker" is a 1985 cop picture that is executed in satisfactory fashion but telegraphs each incident and plot twist with depressing regularity. Only thing here apart from standard chases and shootouts to keep the fans awake is a succession of familiar faces to identify in the supporting cast. Pic has gone through innumerable title changes, including "Painted Dolls," "Striker," "The Slayman" and "The Man Who Could Not Be Killed" before final release using the monicker from Darren McGavin's well-remembered supernatural tv series of 15 years ago.

Rugged Charles Napier is well-cast as J.J. Striker, a world-weary L.A. cop, gone over to the bottle, who is working on the case of a serial murderer who kills prostitutes and then paints their bodies with Chinese characters. Since Striker's girl friend is a prostitute (Michelle Reese) and the two of them have been caring for a young woman (Katherine Kelly Lang) who was raised in the prosties' milieu, he has a vested interest in flushing out the killer.

Script by John Goff and Don Edmonds is so routine one easily can pick out each victim of the killer and when it will happen, plus all the hapless misadventures of the cops. The killer, played by oversized Robert Zdar, turns out to be impervious to bullets, a supernatural subplot not adequately justified by a quickie exposition scene involving a psychiatrist inserted in the final reel. Napier destroys him anyway with an exploding shell pistol in a slam-bang finale.

Director Max Kleven, better known as a top second unit director (responsible for the excellent second unit action of Andrei Konchalovsky's "Runaway Train"), delivers solid action and stuntwork, but allows some very hammy performances, particularly by Robert Viharo as Napier's partner and James Louis Watkins as a laughably stereotyped pimp.

Main fun here is spotting so many super starlets in supporting roles as hooker/victims: Ola (Michael Jackson's "Thriller") Ray; beautiful Chuck Vincent discovery Tally Chanel (of "Warrior Queen" and "Sex Appeal"), and Chinese star Joan Chen, lead of "Tai-Pan" and Bertolucci's upcoming "The Last Emperor." Gary Crosby is on hand in the embarrassing role of a cop nobody likes, who has an assignation with a transvestite hooker.

Many of the filmmakers hail from a softcore sexploitation background, where Napier got his start as the square-jawed lead in several Russ Meyer epics before becoming a Jonathan Demme regular and co-starring in "Rambo: First Blood Part II." Producer-cowriter Don Edmonds helmed sexpo epics such as "Wild Honey" and the first two "Ilsa" pics before an ill-fated tenure as production exec at PSO in 1985. — *Lor.*

Radium City
(DOCU-COLOR)

A Carole Langer production. Produced and directed by Langer. Camera (color), Luke Sacher; editor, Langer; music, Tim Cappello. Reviewed at Kabuki theater, San Francisco Film Festival, March 28, 1987. (No MPAA Rating.) Running time: **120 MINS.**

San Francisco — All the ingredients for documentation of a remarkable story, a seminal study of the effects of radium on one American city, Ottawa, Ill., are implicit in "Radium City." Unfortunately, this overlong, rampantly repetitive pic is so poorly sourced and reported it comes off as pure polemic.

Two versions were screened at the Friscofest; the media unspooling ran 100 minutes; version reviewed here and shown publicly is 120 endless minutes. Yarn could have been told effectively, and intelligently, in 90 and been fit fodder for commercial booking at selected venues.

The powerhouse nub of the tale is that a good number of women who worked painting numbers in radium onto clock dials in Ottawa from 1922 on died in untimely fashion, and that the intrusion of radium into the community via two plant sites lingers still. This is strong stuff which must be documented with clarity, precision and reliable attribution if it is to be compelling and convincing.

Producer-director-editor Carole Langer ignores reportage for knee-jerk, frequently mawkish and numbingly undistilled footage of interviews with survivors and contemporary victims. Many interviews play far too long, several are digressive. There is no real attempt at seeking balance — even if it's just an on-film "no comment" from the manufacturers and feds.

It's clear there's a preponderance of evidence on the side of the victims and on behalf of the environmentalists in Ottawa today, but their, and Langer's, case is not argued properly.

The lack of narration tends to make truths and facts inaccessible as Langer tries to have the people of Ottawa guide us through the history of the tragedy. The people tend to be vague, redundant and uninformative.

One of them says the county in which Ottawa sits has the highest per capita incidence of cancer in the U.S. True? Who knows? There's no secondary sourcing.

A story title card tells us "over 40" women died from the effects of wetting radium-tipped brushes with their tongues. This is as specific as the pic gets about the death toll. A little investigative browsing through medical records and death reports would have been helpful and to the point.

Langer, in comments after the screening, said she "worked through" the Harvard School of Public Health in researching the material. Whatever the case, docu leaves one with far more questions than answers — questions one suspects are answerable.

Pic played at the 1986 Cork filmfest. —*Herb.*

Three For The Road
(COLOR)

Uninspired road picture, with Charlie Sheen taking two career steps backward.

A New Century/Vista release of a Vista Organization production. Produced by Herb Jaffe, Mort Engelberg. Directed by B.W.L. Norton. Screenplay, Richard Martini, Tim Metcalfe, Miguel Tejada-Flores, from a story by Martini; camera (DeLuxe color), Steve Posey; editor, Christopher Greenbury; music, Barry Goldberg; production design, Linda Allen; art direction, William Buck; set decoration, Linda Allen; sound, Glenn Berkovitz; costumes, Hillary Wright; associate producer, Greenbury, Jay Cassidy; assistant director, Dennis Maguire; casting, Nina Axelrod. Reviewed at the Preview House, Hollywood, April 3, 1987. (MPAA Rating: PG.) Running time: **88 MINS.**

Paul	Charlie Sheen
Robin	Kerri Green
T.S.	Alan Ruck
Blanche	Sally Kellerman
Missy	Blair Tefkin
Senator Kitteridge	Raymond J. Berry
Virginia	Alexa Hamilton

Hollywood — "Three For The Road" would more aptly be titled "Three Strikes For The Road," so totally does the film fail to connect on all counts. A statically staged and poorly played road pic, unrelieved by an occasional bright performance, story is so slight and execution so uninspired that one can only wonder what the filmmakers had in mind.

It is equally difficult to believe that the script took the talents of three writers, Richard Martini, Tim Metcalfe and Miguel Tejada-Flores, to concoct. Perhaps with a stronger lead and some spark to the romance, pic could have had a sweet charm, but Charlie Sheen's performance as a would-be politician escorting a senator's problem daughter (Kerri Green) to boarding school is so lifeless and flat that it sinks any chance the film had.

As the senator battling to control his daughter, Raymond J. Berry is a caricature of the unfeeling father and gives no dimension to the role. Green is a bit better as the poor little rich girl but seems a mere child next to Sheen. Taking her cross state lines could well be a violation of the Mann Act.

Tagging along for the ride and the only character with any spontaneity is Alan Ruck as Sheen's literary-minded buddy. Ruck is at once likable and mischievous and surely would have turned in a more convincing job as the uptight young pol. Blair Tefkin is likable, if somewhat improbable, as Ruck's love interest.

It's a paint-by-numbers plot with the girl's mother (Sally Kellerman) and boyfriend waiting in the wings to rescue the poor kid. Unfortunately, director B.W.L. Norton can't generate an ounce of real feeling behind any of this nonsense.

Instead, he shoots every imaginable scenic vista he can find and puts and overbearing soundtrack by Barry Goldberg behind it all to indicate what emotion he's calling for. The result is a travelog of places no one wants to visit. —*Jagr.*

Empire State
(BRITISH-COLOR)

A Virgin/Miracle release of a Team Pictures production. Produced by Norma Heyman. Executive producer, Mark Ayres. Directed by Ron Peck. Screenplay, Peck, Ayres; camera (Eastmancolor), Tony Imi; editor, Chris Kelly; music, various artists; production design, Adrian Smith; art director, Val Wolstenholme; sound, Ken Weston; costumes, William Peirce; casting, Sheila Trezise. Reviewed at Century Preview theater, London, March 16, 1987. Running time: **104 MINS.**

Marion	Cathryn Harrison
Pete	Jason Hoganson
Cheryl	Elizabeth Hickling
Danny	Jamie Foreman
Susan	Emily Bolton
Paul	Ian Sears
Chuck	Martin Landau
Richard	Lorcan Cranitch
Frank	Ray McAnally
Rent-boy	Lee Drysdale

London — "Empire State" is a London-set thriller full of good ideas, some that work but more that don't. It will need to be handled with care for impact offshore. Astute direction and strong soundtrack are saving graces.

Pic is low-budget affair but shot to look as glitzy and stylish as possible. Main problem lies with the script by helmer Ron Peck and executive producer Mark Ayres, which could have used polishing and perhaps a firmer hand, and overly intense performances by some youngblood British actors.

Peck has tried to update the U.S. *film noir* gangster pic with a transplant to London's East End, bringing together vying villains, fixed boxing matches, big deals, night clubs, crusading reporters, beautiful molls and naive outsiders. Unfortunately the canvas is too big for the tools Peck has at hand.

Story is complex with plenty of subplots, but the majority of the action is at the Empire State, a nightclub owned by Frank (Ray McAnally) but which young male prostitute-turned-gangster Paul (Ian Sears) wants to take over.

The takeover bid depends on a Yank realtor (a bemused performance by Martin Landau) buying into a massive property development scheme. He pulls out of the deal and a lot of people get upset, but since none of the characters are particularly likable audiences aren't going to care very much.

"Empire State" is shot pop-promo style with plenty of nods to the Yank influences (the Sears character drives a 1950 Pontiac) and works best inside the claustrophobic club where much of the trite dialog is drowned out by the music.

Lensing by Tony Imi is firstrate, and production designer Adrian Smith has made good use of limited resources to create the nightclub set.

Of the acting, Lee Drysdale is impressive as a genial "rent-boy" (homosexual prostitute) whose only ambition is to raise enough money to escape to the U.S., while Ray McAnally is excellent, as usual, as the club owner.

"Empire State" is almost a yuppy gangster film. A little short on action, perhaps a bit too strong on the language, and with plenty of homosexual undertones. —*Adam.*

Ya Tebya Pomnyu
(I Remember You)
(SOVIET-COLOR)

A Uzbekfilm Studio production. Written and directed by Ali Khamrayev. Camera (color), Rifkat Ibragimov; art direction, Rustam Khamdamov. Reviewed at Kabuki theater, San Francisco Film Festival, March 26, 1987. Running time: **93 MINS.**
With: Vyacheslav Bogachev, Gulya Tashbayeva, Zinaida Sharko.

San Francisco — "I Remember You," made in 1985, reportedly held out of release for a time based on politics and then, after Gorbachev's *glasnost,* unspooled at the fest in Nantes, France, is simply a visual stunner.

The framing and cutting is so lushly crafted that one doesn't even

need subtitles to be drawn into the unfamiliar civilization of Samarkand. In a way, this story of a man looking for his father's burial site is a travelog, a round-trip train ride across the Soviet. There's no "evil empire" ambience here; some of the snow-packed gray landscape looks, in fact, like patches of our own Midwest.

The father died in the fighting near Leningrad in World War II. The son, in a not unfamiliar plotline, is trying to find himself by finding the grave. This section of the screenplay is the pic's strength, particularly in brilliantly lensed and cut shots at a military burial records office-warehouse.

There's a wedding scene so painterly that the beauty of the image is emotionally touching; reminiscent of, but so much lovelier than, the "The Godfather" and "The Deer Hunter" ethnic wedding moments.

The find-the-grave seg is too short, for the balance of the pic focuses on a budding train trip romance and flashbacks of the central figure's youth. The story process gets a bit remote at times, but the visuals keep carrying the pic. Print source is Goskino. —*Herb.*

Hour Of The Assassin
(COLOR)

Okay political thriller.

A Concorde Pictures release. Executive producer, Roger Corman. Produced and directed by Luis Llosa. Screenplay-production supervisor, Matt Leipzig; camera (color), Cusi Barrio; editor, William Flicker; music, Fred Myrow; additional music, Richard Emmett; sound, Edgar Lostanau; art direction, Martha Mendez; stunt coordinator, Patrick Statham; second unit camera, Enrique Masias; postproduction supervisor, Deborah Brock; associate producers, Fernando Vasquez de Velasco, Rolando Ore T.; special effects, de Velasco; casting, Daniel Camino, Juan Manuel Ochoa. Reviewed on MGM/UA Home Video vidcassette, N.Y., March 25, 1987. (MPAA Rating: R.) Running time: **93 MINS.**
Martin Fierro . . . . Erik Estrada
Sam Merrick . . . . Robert Vaughn
Ortiz . . . . Alfredo Alvarez Calderon
Folco . . . . Orlando Sacha
Paladoro . . . . Reynaldo Arenas
Adriana . . . . Lourdes Berninzon
Navarro . . . . Ramon Garcia
Casals . . . . Oswaldo Fernandez
Villaverde . . . . Francisco Giraldo

"Hour Of The Assassin," originally titled "License To Kill," is an unusual thriller to come from Roger Corman, filmed in Peru and dealing with a plot to cancel out dramatic reforms in the mythical South American country of San Pedro. Producer-director Luis Llosa starts out like a housafire, with the opening reel playing like "Z," but pic falls back on standard ploys including numerous car chases (so beloved by executive producer Corman) and peters out with an inconclusive end-

ing. Pic opened in Pittsburgh in January and is a May homevideo release.

Erik Estrada portrays a guy whose dad was a San Pedro communist killed by the group whose leader, Roberto Villaverde (Francisco Giraldo), has just won the election and promises democratic reform. Playing on this history, Estrada is recruited in Los Angeles where he currently resides and brought home to assassinate Villaverde to settle the score. Unbeknownst to Estrada, the people hiring him are not leftists but in fact another key faction, the right-wing generals who oppose both the left and Villaverde's democratic party.

Robert Vaughn has a large role here, as the CIA man from the U.S. Embassy who is trying to head off any assassination at all costs. He ultimately goes to the leftists, led by Casals (Oswaldo Fernandez) for help, and though they don't like the CIA, they unite with him against a common enemy, pinpointing Estrada as the likely hitman. Finale unconvincingly has Vaughn saving Estrada's life, with none of the issues at stake resolved.

Up until the finish, pic works well enough, with both Estrada and Vaughn performing adequately and providing lure to tv fans. Leading lady Lourdes Berninzon, as well as other supporting players, is uncomfortable with the English language dialog. Pic benefits from an excellent musical score by Fred Myrow, whose infrequent film assignments include "Leo The Last," "Soylent Green" and the plaintive "Lolly-Madonna XXX" music.—*Lor.*

Hei Pao Shi Jian
(The Black Cannon Incident)
(CHINESE-COLOR)

A Xi'an Film Studio production. Directed by Huang Jianxin. Screenplay, Li Wei; camera (color), Wang Xinsheng, Feng Wei. Reviewed at China Film Import/Export screening room, Peking, Jan. 5, 1987. Running time: **94 MINS.**
Zhao Shuxin . . . . Liu Zifeng
Li Renzhong . . . . Gao Ming
Hans Schmidt . . . . Gerhard Olschewsky

Peking — Produced by the progressive Xi'an Film Studio in 1985, shown in a limited way in China last year and now touring the U.S. as part of the "Discovering The New Chinese Film" package, "The Black Cannon Incident" is a fascinating film to be representing China at this critical political moment, even if its artistic merit is only modest. Very much a product of the liberal, outward-looking policies promoted by Premier Deng Xiaoping, film stands as an attack on petty bureaucrats, narrow-minded xenophobes and the kind of hardline Communist Party thinking that has begun to reassert itself since the

student demonstrations around the New Year. Although not a potential prize-winner, pic would be of interest to festival and specialized audiences.

A seriocomic shaggy dog story that would be funnier if its implications were not so depressing, "Cannon" tells of the colossal waste that stems from ridiculous misunderstanding on the part of the authorities.

Titles refers to a Chinese chess piece, one which business translator Zhao Shuxin loses and about which he sends a telegram in order to replace it. Noting the reference to the mysterious "black cannon," his bosses immediately suspect him of being some sort of spy and remove him from his key position as translator for a visiting German industrialist, in China to supervise a construction job.

Zhao is mortified by his dismissal and, although his replacement, a travel service employee with no technical expertise, makes several horrendous blunders in translation that result in disaster for the project, party officials refuse to reinstate Zhao.

In fact, they hold five meetings to discuss the issue, and it is in these scenes where the political dynamics currently at work in China are most clearly illustrated. Some, of course, value ideology and adherence to the party above all, while others argue the party's interference in business matters hinders progress and does a disservice to the nation. To hear these issues discussed so openly is something new to Chinese films, and farcical treatment leaves no doubt what side the filmmakers are on.

Unfortunately, director Huang Jianxin's approach is quite pedestrian visually, and a lighter touch could have been brought to the many scenes that are clearly intended to be comic, even if their intent is to expose the "leftist lie" about the evil of all foreigners and to critique bureaucratic foolishness.

In putting its cards so forthrightly out on the table, "The Black Cannon Incident" feels like the healthy start of something, a bold, if staggering, step in the right direction. Sadly, there is some danger of it representing the furthest extreme to which a Chinese film might go for some time to come. —*Cart.*

Por Los Caminos Verdes
(On The Green Path)
(VENEZUELAN-COLOR)

Produced and directed by Marilda Vera. Executive producers, Macuto Antonio Llerandi, Luis Rosales. Screenplay, Milagros Rodriguez, Vera; camera (color), Carlos Tovar, Miquel Curiel; editor, Armando Valero; music, Rubén Blades; sound, Josué Saavedra; set decoration, Maria Adelina Vera. Reviewed at the Berlin Film Festival (Forum), Feb. 23, 1987. Running time: **93 MINS.**

With: Jorge Canelón, Joel Escala, Alberto Acevedo, Yulay Sánchez, Pablo Masabet, Ricardo Salazar, Carlos J. González, Carlos Julio Ramírez, Lucila d'Avanzo.

Berlin — An impressive debut by British-born South American woman filmmaker Marilda Vera, "On The Green Path" deals with one of the Latin continent's many political and economic problems. Whether the film can find a wider audience beyond those interested in the subject is unclear. Though made with sensitivity and without heavy political messages, the characters and storyline break no new ground.

A group of Colombian refugees enter Venezuela illegally looking for a better life. They soon establish themselves, some remain in touch, two become lovers. There are the expected adjustment problems, a romantic triangle, and the illegal drug dealing that ends in needless death.

The film is beautifully photographed but at times the pacing is a bit sluggish. Characters are well cast and rendered, and life in exile honestly represented. Rubén Blades' score captures the film's lush, tawdry atomosphere. —*Owl.*

La Sposa Era Bellissima
(The Bride Was Radiant)
(ITALIAN-HUNGARIAN-COLOR)

A Titanus release (Italy) of an AMA Film (Rome)/Mafilm (Budapest) coproduction. Produced by Gianni Minervini. Directed by Pál Gábor. Stars Angela Molina. Screenplay, Lucio Manlio Battistrada, Enzo Lauretta, Stefano Milioto, Gábor, from a novel by Lauretta; camera (Eastmancolor), János Kende; editor, Katalin Kabdebó; art direction, Enzo Eusepl; costumes, Danda Ortona; music, Nicola Piovani. Reviewed at the Hungarian Film Days, Budapest, Feb. 16, 1987. Running time: **90 MINS.**
Maria . . . . Angela Molina
Giuseppe . . . . Marco Leonardi
Sergio . . . . Massimo Ghini
Carmela . . . . Stefania Sandrelli
Also with: Simona Cavallari, Gaetano Scradato, Turi Scalia, Miko Magistro, Mimmo Mignemi.

Budapest — Hungarian helmer Pál Gábor ("Angi Vera") crosses the border almost too well in this Italo coproduction. Not only is "The Bride Was Radiant" set in Sicily with an Italo cast (exception made for star Angela Molina) and script, it has the pace and look typical of Italo art product. Also the same humdrum, no surprises storytelling that never takes off, despite melodramatic turns of plot. Prospects seem limited to local audiences.

Molina plays Maria, a beautiful and still young "white widow" whose husband left her after their son was born to work in Germany and never came back. Her case is typical of many women in the small village. Its breathtaking scenery is small recompense for a lonely life spent being faithful to a ghost, as local custom demands.

One day love appears in the form of a handsome young doctor from Milan (Massimo Ghini). On the advice of less inhibited friend Carmela (Stefania Sandrelli), also a white widow, Maria conquers her doubts and the resistance of her teenage son, Giuseppe (Marco Leonardi), to enjoy male companionship for the first time. For some reason the missing husband keeps threatening to return, but doesn't, casting a pall over the period. To separate the lovers forever, Gábor has Maria die of a mysterious illness. Pic then definitively switches over to the son's p.o.v., as the "white orphan" makes a trip to Munich with the intention of killing his father.

Thesps are good, but their story is too predictable to become involving. Pic can't make up its mind between being a straightforward condemnation of the inhuman social conditions resulting from forced emigration, or a grand tragedy *alla siciliana*. In this compromise, the emotional backdrop remains uncompelling.

Lensing is pro all the way, and Nicola Piovani's melodic score a plus. — *Yung.*

Blond Dolly
(DUTCH-COLOR)

A Holland Film Releasing release of a Gijs Versluys/Riverside Pictures production. Produced by Versluys. Supervising director, Jonne Severijn. Directed by Gerrit van Elst. Camera (Moviecam, Eastmancolor), Theo Bierkens; editor; Ton Ruys; music, Lucas Asselbergs; sound, Mark Glynne; art direction, Jan Roelofs, Ben Van Os; production manager, Remmelt Remmelts; casting, Hans Kemna. Reviewed at Cinema Intl., Amsterdam, Feb. 13, 1987. Running time: **102 MINS.**
Dolly, Sylvia, Kitty . . . Hilde van Mieghem
Eddy Cremer . . . . Peter Tuinman
Also with: Celia Nufaar, Fred Vaassen, Adrian Brine, Herbert Flack.

Amsterdam — "Blond Dolly" is based on the mysterious death of a 32-year-old hooker strangled in her flat in The Hague's red-light district in 1959. It was learned later that she had led several semi-respectable lives. Despite a promising premise, pic lacks excitement and never kicks into life.

The hooker's first identiy is as a greedy whore, often turning more than 30 tricks a day at a basic rate of one dollar per. Identity number two is as an extremely well-dressed lady, speaking several languages, with impeccable manners, regularly seen at galleries, concerts and first nights. Life number three is as a divorced woman available as travelling companion for businessmen with large accounts.

The addresses of some important industrialists and politicians were found in her belongings. It turned out she owned eight houses, an elegant and costly wardrobe and a very fat bank account due to astute investments. Who killed her, and why, remains a mystery. Police files remain closed.

There are many mysteries about the pic, too. The script was originally in the hands of two writers, helped by promising young docudirector Gerrit van Elst, who dropped out of the writing team. Director Jonne Severijn ankled after a few days of shooting, replaced by Van Elst. The press sheet lists no writers, only a script supervisor.

Dialog is stilted and some scenes of middle-class Hague society are plain embarrassing. The actors battle valiantly, but trip over all the loose ends in the script. Belgian actress Hilde van Mieghem, in her first lead role, registers seductiveness, posturing and pouting s directed; it would be unfair to judge her acting potential by this film. Peter Tuinman looks like he would love to be acting elsewhere. —*Wall.*

Laoniang Gou Sao
(Soul)
(HONG KONG-COLOR)

A Moleson/Tomson/Maverick production. Produced by Sally Wu, Hsu Feng, John Sham. Executive producer, Woo Shee Yuen. Directed by Shu Kei. Screenplay, Kei, Manfred Wong; camera (color), Cristopher Doyle; editor, Fong Po Wah; music, Danny Chung; art director, Tony Au. Reviewed at the Berlin Film Festival (Forum), March 1, 1987. Running time: **94 MINS.**
With: Deanie Ip, Elaine Jin, Jacky Cheng, Hou Hsiao Hsien, Ko I-Chen, Sandy Lamb, Dennis Chan.

Berlin — This film spreads itself too thin. It starts with a police inspector apparently committing suicide by jumping off the station roof. His wife, who until then leads the sheltered life of a wealthy lady in a fancy apartment, discovers all kinds of things she never suspected, like her husband having had a Taiwanese mistress who gave him a son four years earlier. She also finds out her husband's death is not the end of the story; somebody tries to kill her as well, and in the process kills the mistress, leaving the wife to take care of the son.

The script just skims the surface of the many possibilities open to it, often opts for the easiest solutions, on top of which it has the tendency to mix gore and slapstick in a strange way. One minute a woman is killed naturalistically in front of the camera, the next another woman picks up a salami and hits the killer over the head with it so forcefully that later he will die.

The clumsiness of the villains is almost endearing at times, except there is no dramatic reason to condone any of their acts.

The best things about the film are the atmosphere, the camerawork as well as some very professional acting from the two female leads, Deanie Ip and Elaine Jin. —*Edna.*

★★★★★★★★★★★★★★★★★★★★★★★★★

AFI Fest Film Reviews

★★★★★★★★★★★★★★★★★★★★★★★★★

Someone To Love
(COLOR)

Moving swan song by Orson Welles. Needs pruning for commercial chances.

An Intl. Rainbow picture. Produced by M.H. Simonsons. Executive producer, Michael Jaglom. Written and directed by Henry Jaglom. Camera (Deluxe color), Hanania Baer; sound, Sunny Meyer; associate producer, Judith Wolinsky. Reviewed at the Los Feliz Theater (AFI Fest), L.A., March 28, 1987. (No MPAA Rating.) Running time: **109 MINS.**
Danny's friend . . . . Orson Welles
Danny Sapir . . . . Henry Jaglom
Helen Eugene . . . . Andrea Marcovicci
Mickey Sapir . . . . Michael Emil
Edith Helm . . . . Sally Kellerman
Yelena . . . . Oja Kodar
Blue . . . . Stephen Bishop
Harry . . . . Dave Frishberg
Also with: Geraldine Baron, Ronee Blakley, Barbara Flood, Pamela Goldblum, Robert Hallak, Kathryn Harrold, Monte Hellman, Jeremy Paul Kagan, Michael Kaye, Miles Kreuger, Amnon Meskin, Sunny Meyer, Peter Rafelson, Ora Rubens, Katherine Wallach.

Hollywood — "Someone To Love" represents Henry Jaglom's alternately engaging and chaotic rumination on loneliness and aloneness in the 1980s. A seriocomic psychodrama in which the filmmaker calls upon his friends to explore why he and they have problems with commitment or finding the right mate, pic is blessed with an almost overwhelming final screen appearance by Orson Welles, but also proves maddening when the nonstop chatter loses its focus and precision. Some additional cutting could be helpful. As with Jaglom's previous efforts, this is a specialty item that will need astute handling if it is to reach its maximum audience in the upscale market.

As before, Jaglom plays himself, a director so frustrated at his girlfriend Andrea Marcovicci's unwillingness to settle down he decides to devote an entire feature to what he perceives as a general malaise of his generation.

Without revealing his intentions, Jaglom invites many friends to a St. Valentine's Day party at a beautiful old legit theater that his brother Michael Emil owns and shortly will demolish (standing in is the still-extant Mayfair Music Hall in Santa Monica). Guests, most of whom are outgoing showbiz types, are somewhat taken aback by their host's desire to scrutinize their innermost feelings and insecurities with a camera, and some bow out.

Others respond glibly to Jaglom's query, "Why are you alone?" some become defensive, others are more matter-of-fact. Similarly, some people prove more interesting on the subject than others, and finally the unrestricted flow of words, words and more words becomes too much.

Dramatically, in fact, story comes to naught, but that doesn't prevent the climax from being dynamite. Orson Welles, who appeared in Jaglom's first feature, "A Safe Place," in 1971, returns here to act as the younger man's mentor and provocateur as he sits in the back of the theater smoking a cigar and delivering stunningly perceptive and intellectually far-ranging comments on aloneness, women's liberation, slavery in world history and the nature of social revolutions.

Glimpsed briefly at the beginning, Welles carries the entire last section of the picture and almost singlehandedly makes the film moving and mandatory viewing for buffs. He is sensationally responsive, inquisitive, impudent and alive playing himself and reacting to the situation in which Jaglom placed him. The very end, where he calls, "Cut," and breaks into his inimitable laugh, stands as one of the warmest screen moments in recent memory.

Also notable is Welles' longtime companion Oja Kodar, who does not appear with her friend but, rather, portrays a visiting Yugoslavian woman with particularly sensitive and personal things to say about being a woman alone. Marcovicci gets to sing impressively and aggravate Jaglom, Sally Kellerman gives a vidid account of what one imagines Sally Kellerman to be like, and Michael Emil here gets his usual humorous philosophical ramblings thrown back in his face for a change.

Technically, this marks something of an improvement on Jaglom's previous films, and the premise, and his way of approaching it, were daring and worth pursuing. A little more intellectual rigor and stylistic control would have helped enormously, but there are more ideas here than in most films. And there is Welles, his personality in full flavor, dominating everything, giving his viewers one last chance to relish his great mind and conversation. —*Cart.*

Bell Diamond
(COLOR-16m)

Produced, written, directed, edited and camera (color) by Jon Jost. Dialog improvised by cast; music, Jon English. Reviewed at the American Film Institute (AFI Fest), L.A., March 2, 1987. (No MPAA Rating.) Running time: **96 MINS.**
With: Marshall Gaddis (Jeff), Sarah Wyss (Kathy), Terrilyn Williams, Scott Andersen, Pat O'Connor, Kristi Jean Hager, Hal Waldrop, Dan Cornell.

Hollywood — "Bell Diamond" is a stillborn effort from maverick San Francisco filmmaker Jon Jost. Painfully slow and uneventful, this study of a fizzled marriage in the boondocks yields few rewards for the effort of sitting through it, and even Jost's small band of admirers no doubt will be disappointed with this outing. Made completely outside the commercial arena on a National Endowment for the Arts grant, pic has no perceivable markets.

After seven years together, Kathy announces to Jeff that she's leaving him while he sits in front of the tv watching a baseball game. They argue, Kathy visits a vulgar friend, she moves out, Jeff drinks and pines over his loss, much of this in real time without the benefit of dramatic devices and expediency.

Jost seems to be building throughout to an emotional epiphany derived from utterly banal circumstances, working on the theory that even the most lowly and inarticulate of people can be deserving of transcendent experiences. Unfortunately, it just doesn't take, so the film just wallows in the mediocrity of the characters' poor Montana surroundings and frittered-away lives.

Nor are there any formal artistic qualities to tide one over. Jost's penchant for placing people and objects in the extreme foreground with infinity stretching behind them becomes tiresome after a while, and impoverished production values don't emerge as a negative virtue either. — *Cart.*

The Puppetoon Movie
(ANIMATED-COLOR)

A Leibovit production. Produced, written and edited by Arnold Leibovit. Associate producer, Fantasy II. Prolog, new animation sequences: animated by Peter Kleinow; animation director, Gene Warren Jr.; voice director, Leibovit; camera (United color), Warren; music, Buddy Baker; art direction, Warren, Michael Minor; sound (Ultra-Stereo), John (Doc) Wilkinson; additional camera, John Huneck. Reviewed at the American Film Institute (AFI Fest), L.A., Feb. 9, 1987. (No MPAA Rating.) Running time: **80 MINS.**

Hollywood — "The Puppetoon Movie" is a straight compilation of 10 George Pal Puppetoon shorts, accompanied by clips from 10 of the late filmmaker's other animated efforts and all framed by some new work featuring Gumby, Pokey and Arnie the Dinosaur. While it's nice to know the Pal's work has been preserved so brilliantly, trying to digest it all in one sitting is akin to overstaying a visit to the candy store. These films were never meant to be consumed all at once, so it's hard to figure out what audiences will have the patience for this even at its relatively brief 80-minute running time.

Arnold Leibovit last year made "The Fantasy Film Worlds Of George Pal," a documentary feature about the Oscar-winning animator and director, and in the opening sequence here has his contemporary puppets explain why Pal was so important.

The glimpse of Pal's initial Dutch work proves instructive, but pic quickly becomes just one short laid end-to-end with another. With prolonged exposure, the early-era roundish wooden figures with painted features begin to look ugly and unappealing, and after a half-dozen featurettes, the bucolic, gingerbread-house world repeatedly on view gets very tiresome, as do the square renditions of Latin and Hawaiian melodies. Overall effect is that of a vast overdose.

On the other hand, jazzman Charlie Barnet is heard in "Jasper In A Jam," which also features Peggy Lee warbling "Old Man Mose." Print, color and sound quality throughout is impeccable.

Other shorts presented in their entirety are "Hoola, Boola," "John Henry And The Inky Poo," "Together In The Weather," "Tubby The Tuba," "Tulips Shall Grow," "The Sleeping Beauty," "Philips Cavalcade," "Philips Broadcast of 1938" and "South Sea Sweethearts," all spanning the 1937-1947 era. —*Cart.*

Dr. Sun Yatsen
(CHINESE-COLOR)

A Pearl River Film Studio production. Directed by Sing Yinnan. Screenplay, He Mengfan, Zhang Lei; camera (Widescreen, color), Wang Hengli, Hou Yong. No other credits available. Reviewed at the Los Feliz Theater (AFI Fest), L.A., March 18, 1987. Running time: **109 MINS.**
Dr. Sun Yatsen . . . . Liu Wenzhi

Hollywood — "Dr. Sun Yatsen" is an ultra-polite, whitewashed biopic of the grandfather of the Chinese revolution. As decorous as a wax museum and photographed as if the subjects were posing for official portraits, film is a superproduction of massive proportion and would have cost tens of millions if made in the West. There is little real history to be learned here and result will only please those satisfied by spectacle and handsome landscapes.

Script's structure becomes both laughable and monotonous after awhile, as the storytelling alternates between important formal occasions, such as the signing of documents, establishment of political parties, foundation of the Chinese Republic and the like, and stupendous battles, in which hordes of soldiers sweep across the screen to no impact, since it's impossible to know who's who.

The dignified politician's tale begins before the turn of the century, follows his assorted failed efforts to overthrow the Manchus, his exile in Japan and establishment of the Chinese Alliance Party, which brought together the various revolutionary factions, the formation of the tenuous Republic in 1912 and his bowing out of the scene in the 1920s, shortly before his death, because he is "tired."

Dr. Sun Yatsen is almost invariably shown striding purposefully through the chaotic proceedings wearing expensive formal Western clothes, and never is there a mention of anything that, from the communist perspective, would be considered controversial, such as his alliance, made stronger through marriage, to Chiang Kai-shek.

Extensive use of the People's Army and superior, unfamiliar locations do provide a feast for the eye, and director Sing Yinnan manages some fine compositions and camera moves. This is children's book history, and hardly sophisticated enough for the international market. —*Cart.*

D.U.I.
(DOCU-COLOR-16m)

A Throne Video and Film production. Produced by Cathleen Doyle, Spike Stewart. Directed by Stewart. Camera (color), Doyle, Stewart, Patrick Stewart, David Vaught, Karl Marderian; editor, Linda Henry. Reviewed at the American Film Institute (AFI Fest), L.A., March 3, 1987. (No MPAA Rating.) Running time: **80 MINS.**
With: Severed Head In A Bag, Tequila Mockingbird, Jon Wayne, Three Day Stubble, Ugly Janitors Of America, Debt Of Nature, John Trubee, Thra's Dumbos, Krew Kuts Klan, Lopex Beatles, Whitehouse, The Free Base Ensemble, Wurm.

Hollywood — "D.U.I." represents a trip to musical nerdsville, a walk on the staggeringly marginal side of the Los Angeles punk/performance art scene. Lensed on video at various local clubs between 1982-1985 and now transfered to film for fest and highly specialized bookings, pic features a baker's dozen of bands that are almost totally unknown, for reasons that readily became apparent upon listening to them. This perhaps has a certain value as documentation of a particular fringe phenomenon, but will anyone who wasn't into it at the time care? Quite certainly not.

D.U.I. stands for Driving Under the Influence, and filmmakers Cathleen Doyle and Spike Stewart have obviously been influenced by Penelope Spheeris' 1981 docu on the L.A. punk scene, "The Decline Of Western Civilization." Whereas Spheeris had some powerful musical acts to give her pic considerable punch and caught the punk movement at its apex, present film spotlights groups that are either utterly talentless or are bent on deconstructing music to a meaningless degree, so far that it is rendered neither funny nor instructive.

Many of the band members seem to have passed through punk on their way to ultimate nebbishhood, notably musicians in such memorably-named groups as Severed Head In A Bag and Three Day Stubble. Latter band takes the cake for bad taste, using the old tune "Mamma's Little Baby Loves Shortnin,' Shortnin,' " and substituting the lyrics, "Little Nigerian Children With Their Bellybuttons Sticking Outward." It's that kind of pic. —*Cart.*

Jane And The Lost City
(BRITISH-COLOR)

A Marcel/Robertson production in association with Glen Films Prods. Produced by Harry Robertson. Directed by Terry Marcel. Screenplay, Mervyn Haisman, based on the comic strip by Norman Pett; camera (Rank color), Paul Beeson; editor, Alan Jones; music, Robertson; production design, Mick Pickwoad; sound, Alan Gerhardt; assistant director, Graham Hickson. Reviewed at the Los Feliz theater (AFI Fest), L.A., March 27, 1987. Running time: **93 MINS.**
Jungle Jack Buck . . . . .Sam Jones
Lola Pagola . . . . .Maud Adams
Jane .Kirsten Hughes
Heinrich . . . . .Jasper Carrott
The Colonel . . . . .Robin Bailey
Carl . . . ./. . . . . .Ian Roberts
Leopard Queen . . . . .Elsa O'Toole
Also with: Graham Stark, John Rapley.

Hollywood — Based upon a racy British comic strip that ran from 1932-63 and was particularly popular during World War II and which inspired a previous film, "The Adventures Of Jane," in 1949, "Jane And The Lost City" is a negligible adventure romp that plays like a high school production of "Raiders Of The Lost Ark." Lack of action and genuine spectacle will disappoint kids, while adults will yawn at the 1940s standard of bawdiness, defined by the heroine being reduced to her lingerie at regular intervals. There is therefore no conceivable audience for this anachronism, least of all a festival audience, as no more than a couple of dozen people turned out for its world premiere as a last-minute substitution at the AFI Fest.

Ho-hum plot finds some Brits and Nazis racing each other to the

Lost City in deepest Africa, where a huge stash of diamonds supposedly awaits the victor. Germans are led by villainous Maud Adams, who occasionally sports Grace Jones drag, while the English have the pert blond trouper Jane as their mascot and along the way enlist the services of old Africa hand Sam Jones.

Although a few laughs poke through, most of the humor is forced, and all the traipsing through the jungle grows tedious when not punctuated by any real action. Best line is deliverd by a veddy proper English colonel who, upon entering a musty underground tomb, proclaims, "Reminds me of my club."

Cast is game, but can hardly overcome the threadbare circumstances. The Mauritius islands stood in here for mainland Africa.—*Cart.*

Means And Ends
(COLOR)

Meandering film with a conscience is headed nowhere.

A Progressive Film production. Produced by Mark Israel. Coproducer, Chuck Duncombe. Directed by Gerald Michenaud. Written, edited by Israel, Michenaud; camera (United color), Israel; art direction, Dave Dann; music, Michenaud; costume design, Karen Keech; sound, Bernie Kriegel; associate producer, Michael Mahler; assistant director, Beth Palmier. Reviewed at the American Film Institute (AFI Fest), L.A., March 5, 1987. (No MPAA Rating.) Running time: **105 MINS.**
Jeff .Cyril O'Reilly
Paul . . . . .Ken Michelman
Ryan . . . . .Reed Birney
Burt . . . . .William Windom
Kelly .Lori Lethin
Tommy Watkins . . . . .Doyle Baker
Bill Henderson . . . . .John Randolph
Mr. Taylor . . . . .Michael Greene
Stewart . . . . .Jack Fletcher

Hollywood — Although earnestly intended and beautifully shot, "Means And Ends" is a mostly laborious commentary on the lack of social consciences among commercial filmmakers. Points made here about young cinema hustlers' utter self-absorption and unscrupulousness are well taken, but pic meanders in all sorts of directions and could have said all it has on its mind in half the time. B.o. prospects for the pic, lensed in 1984, are gloomy.

Premise is promising, as an aspiring producer, director and screenwriter arrive in a sleepy Illinois town to shoot a teen sexploitation pic. All for the production because of the loot it will bring in, civic leaders have actually been bamboozled as to the true content of the feature and hit the ceiling when they discover that the promised "Charlie Chaplin-like comedy" is actually a t&a spectacular.

City fathers insist that the team clean up the script, and the tension over what to do tears the three

friends apart. The writer is inclined to act in a honest, responsible manner, the director is only concerned about the ramifications for his career, and the producer, natch, simply seeks the most expedient solutions and doesn't give a hoot about what the locals think.

Elements are here for a good comedy, but debuting producer-director-writer-lenser-editing-music team of Mark Israel and Gerald Michenaud take themselves rather too seriously and don't know how to structure the story for effective dramatic impact. Points are hammered home in redundant and far too explicit fashion, and none of the true pressure and excitement of on-location filmmaking is put across.

Israel's cinematography is truly elegant, although the long, languid takes further slow down the pace and make it difficult, if not impossible, to cut to move things along. Many shots are held for far too long, and filmmakers' failure to bring things to a head more quickly becomes terribly exasperating.

Technically, Israel and Michenaud have put together an impressive production on $400,000, shooting mostly in California and doing post-production in Paris. Thesps are uniformly good.—*Cart.*

The Violins Came With The Americans
(COLOR)

Naive drama on U.S.-Puerto Rican relations.

A Sun and Moon production. Produced by David Greene. Directed by Kevin Conway. Screenplay, M. Quiros (Mila Burnette); camera (Technicolor), Benjamin Davis; editor, John Tintori; music, Fred Weinberg; set design, Sue Raney; sound, Felipe Borrero; associate producer, Dean Silvers; second unit director, Maria Norman. Reviewed at the American Film Institute (AFI Fest), L.A., Feb. 25, 1987. (No MPAA Rating.) Running time: **94 MINS.**
Annie Adams . . . . .Mila Burnette
David Garcia . . . . . . .Joaquim de Almeida
Don Fulhencio . . . . .José Ferrer
Also with: Maria Norman, Kevin Conway, Norma Candal, Iris Martinez, Paula Trueman, Alba Oms.

Hollywood — The worthwhile intentions of "The Violins Came With The Americans" (originally titled "The Sun & The Moon") enormously outweigh the artistic and political results on view. Independently produced effort to explore the fruits of the United States' long domination of Puerto Rico is aggravatingly simplistic and naive, and doesn't begin to dramatize the situation in in any meaningful way. Commercial prospects are meager.

Mila Burnette wrote the script (as M. Quiros) and plays the lead, a woman of early middle age who splits with her midtown Manhattan husband and returns to relatives in

economically devastated South Bronx, where she grew up.

With considerable difficulty, she motivates and organizes the reclusive tenants to fix up their shabby building and defy the slum landlord. At the same time, she enters into what passes for a romance with a handsome young attorney who argues for Puerto Rican independence at the United Nations.

All this is fine, except that it's done completely unconvincingly and sheds no light either on poverty in the U.S. or the Puerto Rican cause. Leading lady is laughably simple-minded and naïve, and all of her activities are presented without complexity or irony.

Worse, her boyfriend is, for all his alleged education and erudition, a brooding silent type who never even gives her, or the audience, a lesson on the history of Puerto Rico, American involvement there and what's bad about it. Point of the entire picture is clearly the rediscovery of one woman's roots, but writer and director Kevin Conway fails completely to elucidate the situation, or even to state the different sides of the argument.

On a more human level, relationship of the pair is presented as if it was supposed to be a passionate, overwhelming involvement for both parties, but for 90 minutes, nothing exciting or intimate is seen to pass between them. Myth of the Latin lover takes a beating here.

Actor Conway's directorial debut is not overly promising, and characters, from the leads down to the "charming" eccentrics who populate the tenement building, wear out their welcome long before fade-out.
— *Cart.*

Weapons Of The Spirit
(U.S.-FRENCH-DOCU-COLOR-16m)

A Friends of Le Chambon/Pierre Sauvage production, in association with FR3. Produced, directed, written and narrated by Sauvage. Coproducer, Barbara M. Rubin. Camera (color), Yves Dahan; editor, Matthew Harrison; sound, Patrick Baroz. Reviewed at the American Film Institute (AFI Fest), L.A., Feb. 23, 1987. (No MPAA Rating.) Running time: **91 MINS.**
(In English and French; English subtitles)

Hollywood — "Weapons Of The Spirit" breaks remarkable new ground where treatment of the Nazi holocaust is concerned, being a portrait of how 5,000 French villagers saved 5,000 Jews from delivery to concentration camps and, in the process, a rare glimpse of the true spirit of Christianity in action. Subject matter alone would guarantee interest from specialized ethnic audiences, but eye-opening evidence about the extent of Vichy France's cooperation with the Germans and power of the story should make this marketable internationally wherever documentaries are welcome.

Located 40 miles from Vichy and 75 miles from Lyon, Le Chambon-sur-Lignon was inhabited at the start of World War II almost exclusively by Protestants who, as descendants of the Huguenots, represented a religious minority themselves in the overwhelmingly Catholic country.

Out of a tradition of helping "guests in need," the local citizenry began sheltering Jews, two of whom were the parents of present filmmaker Pierre Sauvage, who narrates and shows himself at the outset returning to place where he was born and visiting with some of the people who made his life possible.

The context Sauvage quickly sketches in is startling; vintage newsreel footage reveals virulent anti-Semitic displays in Paris, and Petain and his deputies are shown making the rounds to drum up support for their collaborationist regime. In all, the film underlines, France handed 75,000 Jews over to the Germans.

Body of the picture explores how and why the villagers doubled the population of their community right under the Nazis' noses. Interviews show the locals (many of whom have died since the filming) to be honest, simple folk who believe that it was "a normal thing to do" to behave as they did, and who are embodiments of the basic Christian credo, "Love thy neighbor as thyself."

Pic has extra power because of the intensely peronal meaning it obviously had for its maker, but Sauvage never loses sight of the bigger story and doesn't become maudlin or sentimental. With the grimmest possible backdrop, filmmaker has still been able to tell an upbeat tale, and to make his own subjective experience universally accessible.

—Cart.

Project X
(COLOR)

Manipulative monkey-shines aimed at chimp fanciers.

A 20th Century Fox release of a Parkes/-Lasker production in association with American Films and American Entertainment Partners. Produced by Walter F. Parkes, Lawrence Lasker. Executive producer, C.O. Erickson. Directed by Jonthan Kaplan. Stars Matthew Broderick. Screenplay, Stanley Weiser, from story by Weiser, Lasker; camera (Deluxe color), Dean Cundey; editor, O. Nicholas Brown; film editor, Brent Schoenfeld; music, James Horner; production design, Lawrence G. Paull; set design, Joseph Pacelli, Lynn Christopher; set decoration, Rick Simpson; costume design, Mary Vogt; sound (Dolby), Petur Hliddal; visual effects supervisor, Michael Fink; animal coordinator, Hubert Wells; assistant director, Albert Shapiro; casting, Jackie Burch. Reviewed at the 20th Century Fox Studios, L.A., April 8, 1987. (MPAA Rating: PG.) Running time: **108 MINS.**

Jimmy Garrett . . . . Matthew Broderick
Teri . . . . Helen Hunt
Dr. Carroll . . . . Bill Sadler
Robertson . . . . Johnny Ray McGhee
Sgt. Krieger . . . . Jonathan Stark
Col. Niles . . . . Robin Gammell
Watts . . . . Stephen Lang
Dr. Criswell . . . . Jean Smart
General Claybourne . . . . Chuck Bennett
  Chimps: Willie (Virgil), Okko (Goofy), Karanja (Goliath), Luke (Bluebeard).

Hollywood — If nothing else, "Project X" is the ultimate film for monkey lovers. Some quite endearing chimpanzees share center stage with Matthew Broderick for nearly two hours here, and while they, and he, are engaging enough to watch, picture lets its manipulative strings show too clearly. Commercial prospects depend entirely upon how receptive the public is to accepting chimps in the roles normally played in recent years by cuddly aliens.

Broderick plays a wayward Air Force pilot who, as punishment, is sent to play zookeeper at the Strategic Weapons Research Center, where intelligent chimps are trained for top secret and, it transpires, fatal experiments involving the effects of radiation.

Brightest of the little hairy ones is Virgil, an orphan who was taught sign language under a university program before being recruited by the armed services. Willie, the chimp who plays Virgil, is extremely appealing and intelligent-looking, and with a costar like this, film guarantees itself a certain entertainment value no matter what course the story might take.

In the event, it's a mixed bag, as some passable interest and suspense is generated as Virgil and other chimps are put through flight simulation, then faced with certain death when they are exposed to radiation in the interests of finding out how long pilots might be able to fly after nuclear explosions.

When Virgil is put on the line, Broderick feels compelled to act and end the seemingly needless experiments. This leads to an utterly farfetched climax that will warm the hearts of animal rights proponents everywhere and, despite its ludicrousness, proves amusing as fantasy.

Film makes sympathetic points about the intelligence of chimps and the abuse they suffer in lab confinement, but beyond this, pic doesn't seem to be about anything. Done with a measure of taste and talent, it still doesn't transcend the relatively mundane limits of its story and characters.

Director Jonathan Kaplan keeps the proceedings amiable enough, and has covered the monkeys' actions with loving care and skillful attention, which cannot have been easy. Broderick is rightly more subdued here than in some recent performances, and supporting cast is discreetly effective. Some colorful, impressive computer animation for the flight simulations highlights the generally first-rate technical contributions.

But it's mostly the monkeys' show, and major credit should go to animal coordinator Hubert Wells, who replaced the late Ron Oxley just before shooting commenced.

—Cart.

Rumpelstiltskin
(COLOR)

Minor version of fairy tale is headed for homevideo.

A Cannon Group release of a Golan-Globus production. Executive producer, Itzik Kol. Produced by Menahem Golan, Yoram Globus. Written and directed by David Irving, from a fairy tale by The Brothers Grimm; Camera (Rank color), David Gurfinkel; editor, Tova Neeman; music, Max Robert; production design, Marek Dobrowolski; set decoration, Albert Segal; costume design, Debbie Leon; sound, Elli Yarkoni; associate producer, Patricia Ruben; casting, Wendy Murray, London, Hadassa Degani, Israel. Reviewed at Mann Westwood theater, L.A., April 10, 1987. (MPAA Rating: G.) Running time: **84 MINS.**

Katie . . . . Amy Irving
Rumpelstiltskin . . . . Billy Barty
King Mezzer . . . . Clive Revill
Queen Grizelda . . . . Priscilla Pointer
Prince . . . . John Moulder-Brown
Emily . . . . Yael Uziely
Victor . . . . Robert Symonds

Hollywood — Rumpelstiltskin, the fairy tale, is now "Rumpelstiltskin" the motion picture, the first of Cannon's Movie Tales to be released. The Cannon folks must believe any coin to be made is in video, because this effort is skedded to be in the stores by June. Apparently their hunch is right, since it's unlikely any child much over five is going to find this spellbinding entertainment.

Kids probably won't notice that a dusty grove of eucalyptus trees isn't exactly the Black Forest (pic was shot in Israel) or that this mythical land's inhabitants speak English with a variety of accents.

The King (Clive Revill) has a British accent, his Queen (Priscilla Pointer) an American one, their son the prince (John Moulder-Brown) a British one and the loyal subjects are Israelis.

The important thing is, Amy Irving is innocent enough as the miller's daughter and Billy Barty nasty enough as Rumpelstiltskin.

Film isn't terribly inventive nor is it just a retelling of an oft-told tale. Competently directed and scripted by Irving's brother, David, the overall work generally is an above-par dramatization of a Brothers Grimm favorite.

To stretch a simple story of a poor maiden's success of spinning straw into gold so she can marry her handsome prince, filmmakers inserted a few songs and embellished upon the characters.

While it's not surprising that Irving and Barty take to their parts with ease, it is surprising to find out how good they are warbling silly little ditties. The songs were dubbed, but those are their voices.

Quality of the dialog fluctuates from the very clever to the truly awful. Barty gets to speak all of his in rhymes, which is fun. Mostly, though, it's on the level of "See Sally Spin."

Show's highlight is Irving's musical numbers where she desperately tries to guess Rumpelstiltskin's name. Scenes with Revill and Pointer, both of whom greatly overact, really drag.

Production values are satisfactory for low-budget children's fare, but Cannon could have saved a lot of money and shot the interiors at Disneyland. Sets look like rooms in Sleeping Beauty's Castle washed in pink and purple and having windows with animatronic birds perched on the sills. —Brit.

Les Patterson Saves The World
(AUSTRALIAN-COLOR)

A Hoyts (Australian) release of a Humpstead (Barry Humphries-Diane Millstead) production. Executive producer, Diane Millstead. Produced by Sue Milliken. Directed by George Miller. Stars Barry Humphries, Pamela Stephenson. Screenplay, Humphries, Millstead; camera (Panavision, Eastmancolor), David Connell; editor, Tim Wellburn; music, Tim Finn; production design, Graham (Grace) Walker; costumes, Anna Senior; sound, Syd Butterworth; production manager, Tony Winley; assistant director, Brian Giddens; special effects makeup, Bob McCarron; special effects coordinator, Brian Cox; casting, Liz Mullinar. Reviewed at Hoyts Center, Sydney, April 6, 1987. Running time: **95 MINS.**

Sir Les Patterson . . . . Barry Humphries
Dame Edna Everage . . . . Barry Humphries
Veronique Crudite . . . Pamela Stephenson
Col. Richard Godowni . . . . Thaao Penghlis
Neville Thonge . . . . Andrew Clarke
Dr. Herpes/Desiree . . . . Henri Szeps
Inspector Farouk . . . . . . Hugh Keays-Byrne
Nancy Borovansky . . . . . . Elizabeth Melvor
Mustafa Toul . . . . Garth Meade
General Evans . . . . Arthur Sherman
Mossolov . . . . Josef Drewniak
U.S. President . . . . Joan Rivers
  Also with: Esben Storm (Russian Scientist), Joy Westmore (Lady Gwen Patterson), Connie Hobbs (Madge Allsop), Paul Jennings (Australian Prime Minister), Graham Kennedy (Brian Lannigan), John Clarke (Mike Rooke), David Whitney (Barry Mollison), Sally Tayler (Rhonda), Peter Collingwood (Jeremy Williams).

Sydney — Barry Humphries is an immensely gifted entertainer with a malicious style of comedy who has entertained audiences in Australia and Britain for over 20 years with his one-man stage performances and tv shows. In the early 1970s, he also starred in two films, both directed by Bruce Beresford, based around his characters of Barry Mackenzie and Dame Edna Everage. Now he's back with a lavishly produced slapstick feature with its eye firmly on the international market so successfully tapped by

"Crocodile Dundee," though this time the focus of attention is on one of Humphries' less appealing creations, Sir Les Patterson, a grossly crude and overweight member of Australia's diplomatic corps.

Pic opens with Sir Les disgracing himself at the United Nations where he's making a speech: as a result of drinking too much vodka and eating too many baked beans, he has an extreme attack of flatulence just at the moment that a fellow diplomat is lighting his pipe: the result is a fiery conflagration that incinerates the robes of an Arab oil sheik. As punishment, the disgraced Sir Les is sent to run Australia's diplomatic mission in Abu Niveah, arriving just at the moment when the Sheik is overthrown in a military coup by Col. Godowni, who saves Sir Les from a fate worse than death.

Ensuing plot involves the corpulent Ambassador, whose need for liquor exceeds even that of the late W.C. Fields, attempting to find booze in a country where booze is banned, and also on the lookout for a meaningful extramarital experience. Matters are complicated by the fact that Godowni is intent on destabilizing the West via a horrendous sexual disease, HELP, and is exporting contaminated toilet seats to the U.S. for this purpose. (Cue for some gruesome, "Evil Dead"-style special effects makeup by Bob McCarron.) His tame French scientist, Dr. Herpes, has invented an antidote to HELP which will be worth billions once the disease has taken hold.

From the above it will be seen that "Les Patterson Saves The World" is not a charming, old-style entertainment like "Crocodile Dundee;" Humphries has always confronted audiences with his often outrageously Rabelaisian sense of humor, and lavatory jokes, jokes involving defecating camels, sexual encounters, gays and lesbians abound. The film is cheerfully racist and sexist, with puns based on the fact that one character is called "Herpes," repeated ad infinitum.

Halfway through, Dame Edna — also played by Humphries of course — makes a welcome appearance, ostensibly leading a group of Australian women ("Possums For Peace") on a tour of Abu Niveah, but actually a CIA agent. "She" steals the film, and scenes in which Edna and Sir Les appear together are fun.

Screenplay by Humphries and his wife, Diane Millstead, has some good jokes and some bad ones. It suffers from repetition and a determination to put the crude before the subtle at all costs.

Director George ("Man From Snowy River," "The Aviator") Miller carries out his chores in a functional manner, showing modest aptitude for comedy pacing. As a result, pic seems longer than its 95 minutes. Graham (Grace) Walker's production design is outstanding, with an Arab town convincingly recreated on a Sydney backlot, and a magnificent set of a revolving New York skyscraper restaurant providing the film's climax (when, inevitably, it goes out of control after a koala jams the works). Other technical credits are pro, and producer Sue Milliken has done a top-notch job.

Commercial chances are hard to predict. Critics are likely to be down on the film, but they were down on the Barry Mackenzie films, too, and that didn't stop them doing great business in Australia and Britain. Same may happen again, though Sir Les is not an easy character to like; yet he may appeal to younger audiences. Safe to predict, though, that Paul Hogan's boxoffice crown remains secure.—*Strat.*

Sweet Lorraine
(COLOR)

**Charming, slowpaced
Catskills nostalgia.**

An Angelika Films release of an Autumn Pictures production. Executive producers, Angelika Saleh, Joseph Saleh. Line producer, Iain Paterson. Produced and directed by Steve Gomer. Stars Maureen Stapleton, Lee Richardson, Trini Alvarado, John Bedford Lloyd, Freddie Roman. Screenplay, Michael Zettler, Shelly Altman from a story by Zettler, Altman, George Malko. Camera (color), Rene Ohashi; editor, Laurence Solomon; music, Richard Robbins; production design, David Gropman; art direction, Karen Schulz; set decorator, Richard Hoover; assistant director, Gary Marcus; associate producers, Jerry Lott, Rob Stoller; casting, Barbara Shapiro; costume design, Cynthia Flynt; production manager, Amy Kaufman. Reviewed at the Mercede Cinema 4, Fort Lauderdale, Fla., April 11, 1987. (MPAA Rating: PG-13.) Running time: **91 MINS.**
Lillian . . . . Maureen Stapleton
Molly . . . . Trini Alvarado
Sam . . . . Lee Richardson
Jack . . . . John Bedford Lloyd
Phil Allen . . . . Freddie Roman

Fort Lauderdale — "Sweet Lorraine" is a subdued charmer about the close of an era for the family-run Catskill Mountain Borscht Belt retreats.

The presence of Maureen Stapleton as topliner should give the film a pleasant sendoff in mainstream houses, but staying power isn't likely. Presented softly, like a musical comedy, its ballad style requires careful handling to achieve crossover appeal outside specialty houses and ethnic neighborhoods where it can generate topical interest.

Pic is a realistic, nostalgic story of an 80-year-old Catskills retreat whose matron (Stapleton) realizes she must sell because business is headed toward the newer, more fashionable addresses. Though still mostly fresh outside, the Lorraine is rotting from the inside and renovations are too costly.

Though not presented as a sweeping generalization, the portrait comes off as a typical commemorative. The screenplay tries to focus somewhat on Stapleton's relationships with her longtime salad chef (Lee Richardson) and her granddaughter (Trini Alvarado), but sentiment clearly lies with the hotel.

"Sweet Lorraine" may have been designed around 100-105 minutes to flesh out the human aspects of the story, with cuts made to quicken an even deadlier pace. If so, it hasn't been an entirely happy tradeoff. Despite the camera's affection the story still drags; the ensemble can't develop serious interest in their retrospective performances.

Story covers the hotel's last summer, beginning with the employees' arrivals and a gradual return to life. The matron expresses worry the season will be even tougher than usual, and frets over whether she should drop her attachment to the old place and accept the first buyout offer she's received in 15 years.

Complicating the decision is the chef, who also loves the old place, and the granddaughter, who shows up unexpectedly looking for a job and eventually decides she'd like to help keep the hotel running. The girl also mixes with an appealing corps of seasonal help and has a cute, peripheral summer romance with the local handyman (John Bedford Lloyd).

Performances are good, including Freddie Roman in a warm stereotype as the Lorraine's omnipresent social director. The camera also pans the public rooms regularly for effective scene-setters with the guests. Adding to the sense of realism is predominantly natural lighting, though murky on some interiors.

Uncertainty of focus is a common first-effort problem, one producer-director Steve Gomer hasn't overcome. Still, "Sweet Lorraine's" quietude has an appeal of its own that should result in a modest payoff. —*Zink.*

Campus Man
(COLOR)

Mediocre teen comedy.

A Paramount Pictures release of an RKO Pictures presentation. Executive producers, Barbara D. Boule, Marc E. Platt. Produced by Peggy Fowler, Jon Landau. Directed by Ron Casden. Screenplay, Matt Dorff, Alex Horvat, Geoffrey Baere from a story by Dorff, Horvat; camera (Metrocolor, prints by Technicolor), Francis Kenny; editor, Steven Polivka; music, James Newton Howard; production design, David Gropman; art direction, Karen Schulz; set decoration, J. Allen Highfill; sound, Bruce Litecky; costume design, Elisabetta Rogiani; associate producer, Todd Headlee; casting, Linda Francis. Reviewed at Paramount Pictures, L.A., April 7, 1987. (MPAA Rating: PG.) Running time: **94 MINS.**
Todd Barrett . . . . John Dye
Brett Wilson . . . . Steve Lyon
Dayna Thomas . . . . Kim Delaney
Molly Gibson . . . . Kathleen Wilhoite
Cactus Jack . . . . Miles O'Keeffe
Katherine Van Buren . . . . Morgan Fairchild
Professor Jarman . . . . John Welsh

Hollywood — "Campus Man" gets a D for premise and a B for delivery, which averages out to a C on the entertainment scale. That's not to say mediocrity has never sold well in the theaters, but this entry most likely will just pass on through.

It appears the idea here is to build a fairly tame story (no sex, no swearing, a few long kisses), for a target audience of teenage girls, around likeable beefcakes — Arizona State U. athletes who pose seminude for a campus calendar.

The calendar is the idea of an obnoxious enterprising business education major named Todd Barrett (John Dye), who bamboozles his best buddy, a stunning blond diver (Steve Lyon) to pose for the $5 item, sit through tedious autograph signing sessions to promote it and then agree — reluctantly — to become a slick magazine's "Man of the Eighties." All this because Dye needs to raise a quick $10,000 to pay his tuition.

Unfortunately, they both end up in hot water when Lyon gets yanked off the diving team by the NCAA.

Script was built around the real-life experience of Todd Headlee, the former ASU student given associate producer credit and whose name is the same as the main character.

Scripters took too many liberties with Headlee's undergrad escapades in an effort to give style and depth to a juvenile tale.

For an impoverished student, Dye gets a change of clothing with every scene, high-tech digs and a seemingly unending supply of computers and log time to organize his entrepreneurial venture. In addition, he has nothing but time to run Barrett Enterprises, which calls into question why he's so desperate to meet tuition costs when he doesn't bother attending classes.

To balance out his sleazoid role is Lyon's squeaky clean one — a committed teammate, a serious student and a decent all-around American guy. Whoever doubled for his diving scenes is also excellent.

Actually, for such a jerk, Dye runs in an interesting circle. There's the modish and moralistic school newspaper editor (Kathleen Wilhoite), his loan shark (Miles O'Keeffe) and the brittle and sassy magazine editor (Morgan Fairchild).

Tone wavers from the hip, slick and trendy (as college students like to think of themselves) to the cheesy. This has something to do with the filmmakers making maximum use of the ASU campus and environs. Scenes alternate between nouveau academia (mostly the pool area) to the middle of nowhere

where O'Keeffe as Cactus Jack does his best virile Clint Eastwood imitation.—*Brit.*

Fat Guy Goes Nutzoid
(COLOR)

Unfunny, amateur comedy.

A Troma release of a Golden Boys production. Executive producer, Robert Shinerock. Produced by Emily Dillon. Directed by John Golden. Stars Tibor Feldman, Peter Linari. Screenplay, John Golden, Roger Golden; camera (color), John Drake; editor, Jeff Wolf; music, Leo Kottke; sound, Felipe Borrero; production design, Martin de Maat; production manager-associate producer, Brooke Kennedy; assistant director, Aaron Barsky; executive in charge of production, Robert A. Mitchell; costume design, Lindsay Davis; casting, Susan Shopmaker. Reviewed at 42d St. Liberty theater, N.Y., April 11, 1987. (No MPAA Rating.) Running time: **78 MINS.**

Roger Morloche	Tibor Feldman
The Mouka	Peter Linari
Ronald	John Mackay
Doogle Morloche	Douglas Stone
Harold	Max Alexander

Troma pickup "Fat Guy Goes Nutzoid" is a dud. Filmed in New York in 1983 under the title "Zeisters" (a meaningless exclamation), pic is a tasteless effort that looks like a backyard home movie shot in 35m.

Slim premise has ne'er-do-well Roger Morloche (Tibor Feldman) becoming involved with pathetic, 350-pound Dave (Peter Linari), nicknamed "The Mouka," when he crashes at a camp for retards where his goofy brother Doogle (Douglas Stone) works. The brothers are tossed out after causing the retards to riot and Dave is a stowaway in their truck, getting involved in misadventures back in New York City.

Film takes a sentimental view of the big fellow, who cannot speak but is basically nice and pitiful. However, it uses his predicament as a steady source of cheap, vulgar gags which are neither entertaining nor sympathetic to his plight. Cast overacts to boot and film displays zero production values.

Troma released the film regionally starting last September, but did not even bother to get an MPAA rating.—*Lor.*

The Morning Man
(CANADIAN-COLOR)

An SDA Prods.-3 Themes production, with the assistance of Telefilm Canada, Société Générale du Cinéma du Quebec and CBC. Produced by Gaston Cousineau, Danièle J. Suissa. Executive producer, François Champagne. Directed by Suissa. Screenplay, Clarke Wallace; camera (color), René Verzier; editor, Yves Langlois, Jean Lepage; music, Diane Juster; sound, Serge Beauchemin; production design, Ch. Dunlop; assistant director, Mireille Goulet; production manager, Daniel Lewis; casting, Elite Prods. Reviewed at Berlin Film Festival (Market), Feb. 25, 1987. Running time: **97 MINS.**

Paul Nadeau	Bruno Doyon
Dr. Kate Johnson	Kerrie Keane
Roger	Alan Fawcett
Detective Mailer	Marc Strange

Gerry	Rob Roy
Estelle	Linda Smith
Also with: Marc Blutman, Walter Massey, Vlasta Vrana, Damir Andrei.

Berlin — This tale of an escaped con trying to go straight would be completely implausible were it not for the fact that it's based on a true story. The central character, Paul Nadeau, played by newcomer Bruno Doyon, had robbed 22 banks, just for kicks, and was serving a 20-year prison sentence when he and a companion effected a daring escape. Escape sequence, with the cons clambering over high fences topped with barbed wire and Nadeau getting one hand badly hurt in the process, is effectively staged, but the subsequent escape away from the prison area looks all too easy.

Nadeau's old friends find him an attractive woman doctor (Kerrie Keane), who takes him to live in her swank apartment and cares for his wounds. Again, it doesn't ring true, but it happened. There's even love between escaped con and respectable medico. Nadeau's determined to go straight, and gets a job operating the radio for a taxi company. He manages to foil a robbery planned by his old buddies. After a while, he gets a job as early morning radio announcer in a provincial town, and makes a success of it. After five months he decides to give himself up and return to prison.

It's a good, strong story, but Clarke Wallace's screenplay is at fault for some corny dialog and for an inability to make it all convincing. An overemphatic music score by Diane Juster is no help either. On the plus side, director Danièle J. Suissa handles the material capably and economically, and there are good performances (despite the script) from Doyon as the con and Keane as the doctor.

Publicity for the film will have to stress the true story aspects, otherwise this will come across as just another crime film, indistinguishable from hundreds of others. Outside Canada theatrical will be difficult, but video sales should bring in some coin.

Pic is technically slick. —*Strat.*

Silent Night, Deadly Night Part II
(COLOR)

Cheapo sequel to 1984 splatter scandal. Dumber than original.

A Silent Night Releasing Corp.-Ascot Entertainment Group release of a Lawrence Appelbaum production. Produced by Appelbaum. Directed and edited by Lee Harry. Screenplay, Harry, Joseph H. Earle, from a story by Harry, Earle, Dennis Paterson, Appelbaum, based on a character created by Michael Hickey, Paul Caimi; camera (United color), Harvey Genkins; music, Michael Armstrong; associate producers, Eric Gage, Joseph Earle. Reviewed at the Woods theater, Chicago, April 10, 1987. (MPAA Rating: R.) Running time: **88 MINS.**

With: Eric Freeman, James L. Newman, Elizabeth Clayton, Jean Miller.

Chicago — This low-budget grinder is the sequel to a below-average splatter item released three years ago that obtained notoriety by turning Santa Claus into an axe-wielding psycho.

The sequel is conceptually nowhere near as daring. Its execution is substandard overall, dimming its b.o. prospects considerably.

Ironically, "Silent Night, Deadly Night Part II" could well outgross the relatively superior original. Latter is a case study of how quickly a major studio can drop a property once public outcry reaches sufficient proportion.

Tri-Star released "Silent Night, Deadly Night" in the late fall 1984, not anticipating the clamor from parents' groups put out by its sanguinary depiction of Santa as a demented killer. Once protests grabbed headlines — the outcry was particularly strong in the Milwaukee and Chicago markets — Tri-Star pulled the picture from release, and later unloaded the pic entirely. It was eventually consigned to the netherworld of indie distribution where playdates and grosses proved modest at best.

"Part II" is unlikely to engender much attention largely because it's being dumped onto the market well outside the Christmas season with almost no ad-pub support from Ascot Entertainment Group, the L.A.-based indie that's parent to the pic's releasing company. This is strictly a case of grabbing the money and running.

One indication of that is the fact that at least a third of the sequel, its opening plot exposition, consists of excerpts from the original. Credits of the "Silent Night, Deadly Night" roll in toto on "II's" final crawl, although none of the creative principals nor cast members are involved in the sequel.

Plot simulates that of the original with a familial twist. "Silent Night, Deadly Night" thematically equated Christmas and terror by introing Billy, a psychotic young man whose parents were shot and bludgeoned to death by a sadist dressed as Santa. "Night II" repeats the scenario with younger brother Ricky, who like Billy is consigned to an orphanage run by a hard-hearted Mother Superior before emerging a violent nut case.

Most of the bloodshed of "II" belongs to those excerpts from the original, quite bloody indeed. The mayhem of the sequel once Ricky links Santa Claus and gore is largely uninspired, lacking the blasphemy and violent brio of the original. There is occasional inventiveness when, for example, Ricky impales a mob hitman by jamming an umbrella through his midsection and

then opening it. Another scene has Ricky blowing up the head of an adversary by jamming live battery chargers down his mouth.

In general, special effects, particularly decapitations, are strictly low-budget. So too is the cast. Under director-coscripter-editor Lee Harry's direction, "Deadly Night II" is hambone heaven. Ricky is played for unintentional laughs by Eric Freeman, a Nautilus-sculpted actor who telegraphs states of mind via facial contortions — he crosses his eyes during strangulation scenes. Production values are minimally adequate at best.—*Sege.*

Sale destin!
(Rotten Fate!)
(FRENCH-COLOR)

An AAA release of Solus Prods./Flach Films/Séléna Audiovisuel/Films A2 coproduction. Executive producer, Jean-Marie Duprez. Produced by Duprez, Pascal Hommais, Jean-François Lepetit. Directed by Sylvain Madigan. Screenplay, Madigan, Michel Wichegrod; additional dialog, Jean-Paul Lilienfeld; camera (Eastmancolor), Patrick Blossier; editor, Dominique B. Martin; music, Pascal Arroyo; art director, Robert Nardone; sound, Gérard Lecas, Jean-Paul Loublier; assistant director, Anne Le Monnier; production manager, Frank Le Wita. Reviewed at the UGC Ermitage cinema, Paris, Feb. 3, 1987. Running time: **95 MINS.**

With Victor Lanoux (François Marboni), Pauline Lafont (Rache), Marie Laforêt (Marthe Marboni), Jacques Penot (Alexandre Ragueneau), Michel Aumont (Inspector Marchandon), Martin Lamotte (Denis), Jean-François Stevenin (Djebel Zanera), Aurelle Doazan (Estelle Marboni), Jean-Paul Lillienfeld, Claude Chabrol, Charlotte de Turckheim.

Paris — Prize-winning short film director Sylvain Madigan dabbles in the demanding vein of black comedy for his feature debut, but comes up short on point and punch. Casting is solid and there are some moments of caustic exhiliration, but strain of running time shows through the casually structured plot.

Victor Lanoux is center of this rogue's gallery of mediocrity. He's a lovesick butcher with successful business and screwy family trying to foil blackmailers who are making him pay dearly for his affair with a prostitute (Pauline Lafont). He hires a professional hitman to dispose of the lowlifes, but then finds himself being victimized by the killer.

Technically smooth, film scores its best moments from the supporting actors, notably Marie Laforêt as Lanoux' bored, spacy wife, Jean-François Stevenin as the flaky killer and Michel Aumont as a cop also smitten with the lusciously mercenary Lafont. —*Len.*

I Kekarmeni
(Shaved Heads)
(GREEK-COLOR)

A D.M. Film production. Produced and directed by Dimitris Makris. Screenplay, Makris, N. Kasdaglis, from a novel by Kasdaglis; camera (Eastmancolor), Christos Triandafilou; editor, K. Iordanidis; music, N. Mavroudis; production design, D. Moretti; sound, Theo Giorgiadis. Reviewed at Berlin Film Festival (Market), Feb. 23, 1987. Running time: **107 MINS.**
Lakidis . . . . Spiros Ioannou
The M.P. . . . . K. Markopoulos
Mary . . . . Dora Chatzijanni
The Tall Soldier . . . . M. Donadoni
The Young Girl . . . . Cristina Gentile
The Cook . . . . Christos Zarkadas
Also with: Kali Feri (Vaia), Iulia Vatichioti (Elena), N. Tsakiridis (Camp Commandant), T. Tessarin (Sergeant).

Berlin — An intriguing, neatly structured pic about life in a military barracks in 1953, "Shaved Heads" starts out as a kind of Greek "Heartbreak Ridge," then goes off in some unexpected directions. Theme is a familiar one (a man who is brutalized may himself become a brute), but is done with invention and style.

Early scenes seem quite conventional as the new recruits are shorn of their hair and subjected to harsh discipline. Gradually a series of interlocking stories unfold as five characters come to the fore, each with a story to tell that involves one of the other five. A prostie who works at the local brothel is the focus of the first story and, via her perspective, we see a strange romance between a pretty young whore and a tough, tall soldier. Next, we see the same story from the soldier's perspective, in which gaps from the previous story are filled in. Scenes we've already seen are rerun from a different angle and viewpoint. The film goes on in this vein, the point rammed home with considerable force at the bleak finale.

It's not exactly a variation of "Rashomon," because the stories told aren't conflicting; it's just that motivations change when the viewer is identifying with different characters, so the guy we rooted for in one sequence becomes, via a new angle, the villain of another sequence.

It's to writer-producer-director Dimitris Makris' credit that he makes this complicated plot quite clear, though the film demands a lot from its audience. There's plenty of nudity in the brothel scenes and the brutality of army life isn't glossed over.

Technically, pic is fine, with solid performances down the line. It's ultimately a downer, but should be checked out by fests looking for a new variation on an old theme.
—*Strat.*

Sorority House Massacre
(COLOR)

Same old song.

A Concorde Pictures release. Produced by Ron Diamond. Written and directed by Carol Frank. Camera (Fotokem color; prints by The Filmhouse Group), Marc Reshovsky; editor, Jeff Wishengrad; music, Michael Wetherwax; sound design, David Lewis Yewdall; art direction, Susan Emshwiller; set decoration, Gene Serdena; assistant director, David B. Householter; production manager, Diamond; second unit camera, Ken Wiatrak; postproduction supervisor, Deborah Brock; additional editor, Mike Miller. Reviewed at Cosmo theater, N.Y., April 11, 1987. (MPAA Rating: R.) Running time: **73 MINS.**
Beth . . . . Angela O'Neill
Linda . . . . Wendy Martel
Sara . . . . Pamela Ross
Tracy . . . . Nicole Rio
Bobby . . . . John C. Russell
Andy . . . . Marcus Vaughter
John . . . . Vincent Bilancio
Craig . . . . Joe Nassi
Dr. Lindsay . . . . Gillian Frank

With "Sorority House Massacre," Roger Corman via his Concorde Pictures revisits the genre he seemingly kissed off five years ago with Amy Jones' spoof "Slumber Party Massacre." This time, filmmaker Carol Frank plays it straight and, though technically well crafted, resulting pic has nothing new to offer in a moribund genre.

Pic gets off to a wobbly start, with needlessly complicated crosscutting during the first two reels of three separate narrative strains, all embedded within a film-long flashback related by heroine Beth (Angela O'Neill) from her hospital bed. We gradually learn (though key plot points are immediately obvious and trite) that Beth has survived a massacre that felled many girls and their boyfriends at a sorority house where she was staying for the weekend. The house 13 years earlier was her home (traumatically forgotten except for tingles of *déjà vu*), where her brother killed the whole family, while she escaped.

Bro, unidentified, is shown in a state mental institution in periodic intercuts, while also intercut are nightmare flashbacks of the bloody incident that took her parents and sisters. Further complicating matters are Beth's hallucinations of her brother, his knife, etc., which extend her nightmares into wide-awake scenes.

Director Carol Frank is careful to avoid the much-criticized hallmarks of the slasher film by making sure victims are not just pretty girls but male bystanders as well, while keeping the gore content minimal. Her script also discusses the psychological and paranormal underpinnings of the heroine's plight, almost elevating the picture from terror status to supernatural horror or science fiction categories. Unfortunately, the basic premise has been done a hundred times before and target audience has sat through most of the forebears.

Angela O'Neill as the heroine physically resembles and is styled (only femme on-screen with short hair) to look like the genre's reigning leading lady of 15 years ago, Pamela Franklin. She does a nice job, while the other cast members execute nothing roles.

Pic's brief running time (73 minutes) suggests B-movies of old, but with its only Manhattan playdate in Harlem, one wonders about the viability of such a format. Like the bulk of recent Concorde Pictures product, it is targeted squarely at homevideo — theatrical release a mere anachronism from headier days when drive-ins were in flower.
—*Lor.*

Killer Workout
(Aerobicide)
(COLOR)

Pretty girls in standard slasher epic.

The Winters Group presentation of a Maverick Films production. (World sales, Shapiro Entertainment.) Executive producers, David Winters, Marc Winters. Produced by Peter Yuval. Written, coproduced and directed by David A. Prior. Camera (United color), Peter Bonilla; editor, Prior; music, Todd Hayen; sound, John Hays; production manager, Yuval; assistant director-second unit director-associate producer, Thomas Baldwin; additional photography-second unit camera, Stephen Ashley Blake; choreography, Sheila Howard; additional choreography, Dianne Copeland. Reviewed on Academy Home Entertainment vidcassette, N.Y., March 14, 1987. (MPAA Rating: R.) Running time: **86 MINS.**
Rhonda . . . . Marcia Karr
Lt. Morgan . . . . . . David James Campbell
Jimmy . . . . Fritz Matthews
Chuck . . . . Ted Prior
Jaimy . . . . Teresa Vander Woude
Tom . . . . Richard Bravo
Debbie . . . . Dianne Copeland
Diane . . . . Laurel Mock
Cathy . . . . Lynn Meighan
Rachael . . . . Teresa Truesdale
Martha . . . . Denise Martell
Curtis . . . . Michael Beck

As the title implies, "Killer Workout" is a natural for homevideo fans, combining the popular slasher horror format with lots of footage of pretty girls in aerobics workouts (pic's original title and foreign moniker is the catchy "Aerobicide"). Unreleased theatrically in the U.S., it's unexciting.

Marcia Karr toplines as Rhonda, owner and operator of "Rhonda's Workout," a health spa catering to very well-built young women (plus a few guys), which is suddenly hit with a rash of fatal stabbings. Lt. Morgan (David James Campbell) is the slow-witted cop on the case, finally figuring out after many reels that Rhonda is actually the killer, taking out her anger and jealousy after her budding modeling career was snuffed out five years ago when she received massive burns in a defective tanning box. Final reel boasts a couple of nice twists and an amoral ending.

Pic is too sparing in dishing out nude scenes to satisfy the voyeur trade; it obeys the prudish rule of the better the body, the less skin shown. Best figure belongs to the amazingly statuesque Dianne Copeland (all she strips down to is a bikini), who also contributed to the aerobics choreography. Male cast (previously seen in filmmaker David A. Prior's "Kill Zone") is hunkish, but hardly equal time.—*Lor.*

Shelley
(CANADIAN-COLOR-16m)

A presentation of Films Transit, Montreal, Face to Face Films, Vancouver. Produced, written and directed by Christian Bruyere. Camera (color), Tom Turnbull; editor, Jane Morrison, Doris Dyck; music, Michael Conway Baker. Reviewed at Berlin Film Festival (Market), Feb. 24, 1987. Running time: **80 MINS.**
With: Robyn Stevan, Ian Tracey, Diana Stevan, Christine Hirt.

Berlin — "Shelley" of the title is a runaway 15-year-old, sexually abused by her stepfather. She is drawn reluctantly into a street life of drugs and prostitution where she meets other teenagers similarly victimized. In time, after suffering and humiliation, Shelley achieves awareness and courage. Helped by a social worker, Shelley at last brings charges against her molesting stepfather. At the end of the film, she is cleansed, and so are we, as the film leaves us morally fortified.

Thus "Shelley" is a kind of how-to film for teen audiences — how to resist the sexual exploitation of their elders, whom they are trained to obey, also how to assert and defend themselves.

Production values are perhaps overdone, as there is little feel for the gritty, nasty street life of teen runaways. Ugliness and despair are lacking. The sets are too clean and overlit, action is slow and predictable, and performances are conceived and directed in terms of types. Nevertheless, for teen audiences, "Shelley" can serve as a warning and a lesson. —*Hitch.*

Der Junge Mit Dem Grossen Schwarzen Hund
(The Boy With The Big Black Dog)
(EAST GERMAN-COLOR)

A DEFA-Studio fur Speilfilme production. Executive producer, Ralph Retzlaff. Directed by Hannelore Unterberg. Screenplay, Margot Bleicher; based on the book by Hildegard and Siegfried Schumacher; camera (Orwocolor), Michael Göthe, Norbert Kuhröber; editor; Elsa Krause; music, Gerhard Schöne, Dieter Beckert; sound, Werner Schulze; sets, Joachim Keller; makeup, Karin Menzel; costumes, Isolde Warcyzek; assistant director, Mathias Luther. Reviewed at Berlin Film Festival (Children's Competition), Feb. 27, 1987. Running time: **78 MINS.**
Ulf Kahleberg . . . . Niels Anschütz
Mother Kahleberg . . . . Dagmar Manzel
Father Kahleberg . . . . Hort Hiemer
Oscar . . . . Kurt Böwe
Sabine Schönerstedt . . . . . . Miriam Knabe

Berlin — This pic had all the elements of a good romp. Too bad the direction is flat and the storyline only intermittently rousing. Niels Anschütz and Miriam Knabe are engaging young performers and almost carry the pic.

Plot is old "dog finds boy, boy takes dog home, parents say dog must go" chestnut. Of course, the boy subverts their wishes and with the help of a retired carney man is able to secretly keep the dog. The boy must earn money to pay for the pet's upkeep — life is not a free ride, his new friend counsels. The incidents and resolution are routine.
—*Owl.*

Peng! Du bist tot!
(Bang! You're Dead!)
(WEST GERMAN-COLOR)

A WDR/Delta coproduction. Produced by Richard Claus, Alexander Wesemann. Directed by Adolf Winkelmann. Screenplay, Walter Kempley, Mathias Seelig; camera (color), David Slama; editor, Margot Löhlein; music, Piet Klocke; sound, Gernot Bürger, Karl-Heinz Jansen; set direction, Klaus von Schilling; production manager, Dieter Adenacker. Reviewed at Berlin Film Festival, Feb. 21, 1987. Running time: **96 MINS.**
Kai Westerburg . . . . Ingolf Lück
Andrea Flanagan . . . . Rebecca Pauly
Peters . . . . Hermann Lause
Soviet agent . . . . Volker Spengler
  Also with: Rolf Zacher (the major), Pascale Jean-Louis (Luna), Ulrich Wilduruber (vagrant).

Berlin — After the success last year of Doris Dörrie's "Manner" (Men), there was considerable talk about a new breed of West German film comedy. "Peng! Du bist tot!" (Bang! You're Dead!) levels both barrels to blow away any speculation along those lines as being appallingly premature.

Film dies shortly after opening titles when a New England school marm named Miss Flanagan (Rebecca Pauly) on a trans-Atlantic flight to Germany for a convention of teachers of German gets hooked up with a mad computer scientist named Peters (Hermann Lause) who fakes a heart attack at the Frankfurt airport, but slips out of the ambulance on the way to the hospital. Meanwhile, the good-hearted schoolteacher from Marblehead, Mass. bumps into (literally and repeatedly) Peters' computer-whiz assistant, Kai (Ingolf Lück), and the pair sets off to find Peters and stop his fiendish plan to tap into anybody's and everybody's computers so that people get killed and things generally run amok.

Along the way they encounter a Soviet spy and a robot that opens bottles of a certain leading export brand of German beer, which gets a hefty plug in film, and they wind up in bed before not too long. Lück tries his best at clowning, but is at his funniest taking off his clothes — male nudity has pretty much taken over from the old-fashioned female kind in this new breed of German comedies.

Anglo-American Pauly dons cat's-eye specs and slathers on a thick American accent to her otherwise flawless German in an apparent bid by producers to make her appeal to American audiences. At times it looks as though she's trying to rise above a back-of-envelope screenplay and confused direction by Adolf Winkelmann, but she doesn't stand a chance.

Lause is totally miscast as the alcoholic mad scientist who mutely guzzles whiskey and smirkingly taps away at his computer terminal. Lause is one of the most versatile actors on the West German legit stage, and most recently proved his talent for comedy by breathing life into a wheezing Hamburg legit production of Molière's "The Miser." Film role is a waste of his talents.

Film is billed as "a murderous comedy," appropriately enough.
—*Gill.*

Én is jartam Isonzónál
(I Too Was At The Isonzo Battle)
(HUNGARIAN-DOCU-B&W)

A Hungarofilm release of a Béla Balász Studio, Mafilm-Tarsulas Studio, Hungarian TV, Mafilm-Budapest Studios production. Written and directed by Gyula Gulás, János Gulyás; editor, Eva Farkas; sound, Béla Prohászka. Reviewed at the Budapest Congress Center, Feb. 14, 1987. Running time: **96 MINS.**

Budapest — This full-length documentary takes some time before it clarifies its intentions, but once it does, it carries some effective anti-war punches. The Gulyás brothers start in the conventional manner, by interviewing survivors of the Isonzo battle, one of the key confrontations of World War I, in which Hungarians fought with the Austrian army against the Italians.

As these interviews unfold, one has the impression that the main point is to put historical facts in the right perspective and explain the proceedings of that battle in a correct manner, for somebody says, history often distorts facts for its own convenience, quoting state reasons as a justification.

As the film unfolds, however, the absurdity of that battle clearly becomes more relevant, the tragedy being stressed tenfold by the fact that while the Hungarians were fighting in Italy an enemy they didn't have anything against, for reasons they couldn't comprehend, their homes back in Hungary were ravaged by the Rumanian army, which took possession of considerable chunks of their country. The point is driven home in the final scene, when the survivors, all octogenarians, are taken back to the site of the battle, encounter for the first time some of the Italians who fought against them and, in the final ceremony which takes place in an Italian village, they embrace each other next to the fields where many of them, from both nations, were buried.

The first part could stand some pruning, and many details require a considerable knowledge of Hungarian history to be grasped fully, but there is a healthy degree of humor, both in the interviewees and in the filmmakers, to carry it over.
—*Edna.*

Fonte Da Saudate
(Deep Illusion)
(BRAZILIAN-COLOR)

A presentation of Embrafilme, Empresa Brasileiro de Filmes, Rio de Janeiro. Produced by Diadema Producoes. Directed by Marcos Altberg. Screenplay, Julia Altberg; camera (color), Pedro Farkas; art director, Carlos Prieto; music, Antonio Carlos Jobim; editor, Carlos Brajsblat. Reviewed at Berlin Film Festival (Market), Feb. 23, 1987. Running time: **80 MINS.**

  With: Lucelia Santos, Norma Bengell, Claudio Marzo, Jose Wilker, Paulo Betti, Xuxa Lopes, Thales Pan Chacon, Chico Diaz.

Berlin — Although sentimental and overlong, even at the comparatively brief 80 minutes, "Deep Illusion" can be saluted for its unusual format and the tour-de-force performance of Lucelia Santos, enacting three characters.

Her three women are Barbara, Guida and Alba, and they live in Ipanema, in Rio, on the same plaza. Although unaware of one another, the three have in common their psychological maladjustment per childhood abandonment by their fathers. Now adults, the three attractive young women have been crippled emotionally by the lack of paternal love and guidance. An end-title puts it this way — "Having three names, none of them was hers."

Although Lucelia Santos plays each role with the similarities mentioned, she manages to keep the three characters different and interesting: one is a nagging, super-jealous wife of a nice-guy psychiatrist who can't seem to cure or cope with his wife's possessiveness. Another is a near-catatonic zombie, dominated by an over-protective predator-mother. The third is a restless wife who cheats and sleeps around without purpose or pleasure.

Each woman is played differently, yet each in a sense comes from the same origin, the same child growing up as three different adults. Each is incomplete damaged goods due to the absence of her father — that first man in every daughter's life. Perhaps this is a macho concept and too mechanically applied in this film; nevertheless it provides the unifying premise for a satisfying melodrama. —*Hitch.*

Miss Mona
(FRENCH-COLOR)

AKG Distribution/AAA release of a KG production. Produced by Michèle Ray-Gavras. Written and directed by Mehdi Charef. Stars Jean Carmet, Ben Smail. Camera (Eastmancolor), Patrick Blossier; editor, Kenout Peltier; music, Bernard Lubat; sound, Jean-Paul Mugel, Joel Beldent; costumes, Edith Vesperini, Maika Guezel. Reviewed at the Trois Balzac cinema, Paris, Feb. 25, 1987. (At Berlin Film Festival.) Running time: **98 MINS.**
Miss Mona . . . . Jean Carmet
Samir . . . . Ben Smail
Jean, subway conductor . . . . . Albert Delpy
Manu . . . . Daniel Schad
Club organizer . . . . Francis Frappat
Gilbert . . . . André Chaumeau
Father . . . . Albert Klein
  Also with: Philippe de Brugada, Yvette Petit, Michel Peyleron, Maximilien Decroux, Kader Boukhanef, Remi Martin.

Paris — Mehdi Charef, the young Algerian-born factory worker who traded in tools for a camera and won kudos and prizes with "Le Thé au harem d'Archimède" (Tea In The Harem), returns with "Miss Mona," another bleak, dispassionate study of social survival. Like "Tea," it was made under the aegis of filmmaker Constantin Costa-Gavras and his wife, Michèle Ray-Gavras, who produced.

Moving beyond the autobiographical realm of his first film (based on his own novel), Charef proves even more unsparing and pessimistic in "Miss Mona" in which he describes the desperate relationship between an aging transvestite and a young illegal immigrant he picks up and corrupts.

In a performance of restraint and subtlety, Jean Carmet steers clear of the bathos and facile parody that usually hang over drag parts, making of Miss Mona, the pathetic gay streetwalker who dreams of becoming a real woman, a moving portrait of frustration and bitterness.

Fellow survivor Samir (Ben Smail), a clandestine laborer who has lost his job in a sweatshop and passively allows Carmet to exploit him as a gay hooker since the transvestite is getting too old to turn a regular trick, represents another vision of degradation and despair on the fringes of society.

Though at times overwrought in its dark brush strokes of abjection, and marred by some moments of pretentious surrealism, "Miss Mona" confirms Charef's deft hand with naturalistic, episodic narrative and a tacit sense of characterization.

His script — which also describes the loneliness of a homosexual subway engineer, symbolizing the socially integrated outcast — builds skillfully to a harrowing climax in which Carmet and Smail beat and rob a former transvestite (who has gypped Carmet of his earnings for his own sex-change operation).

When Carmet realizes he had been recognized, Smail returns

alone to the scene of the crime to murder the victim. Ironically the murder crystallizes the only moment of mutual concern between the pair. Carmet uses the stolen lucre to buy the identity card Smail needs to survive, but the Arab is in the meantime nabbed by police — before the eyes of the subway conductor who has unwittingly abetted in his capture.

Drama's unsparing gloom — barring one outright comic scene in which Carmet in Marilyn Monroe wig and white dress spoofs the air vent scene in "Seven Year Itch" — makes this even less commercially marketable than "Tea" though right for the art circuits and festival scene. Tech credits are solid. —Len.

Crazy Boys
(WEST GERMAN-COLOR)

An Export Film Bischoff & Co. release of a Horizont Film production. Executive producer, Albert Heins. Produced by Heinz Diego Leers. Written and directed by Peter Kern. Camera (color), Erberhard Geick; editor, Ina Rasche; music, Franz Plasa; sound, Slavco Hitrov; art direction, Detlef Theune; assistant director, Juliane Geick; production manager, Marie Luise Voggenberger. Reviewed at Berlin Film Festival, Feb. 26, 1987. Running time: **89 MINS.**

Sigrid . . . . Barbara Fenner
Theo. . . . . Albert Heins
Hans . . . . Udo Schenk
Erich . . . . Zacharias Preen
Abdul . . . . Mehmed Yandirer
Fräulein Hermann . . . Marianne Sägebrecht

Berlin — In German slang the English word "crazy" does not mean "insane," but rather something along the lines of "hot to trot." Actor-filmmaker Peter Kern's "Crazy Boys," which is neither insane nor hot, looks likely to die in Germany and anywhere else it might accidentally crop up.

Film attempts to capitalize on a waterfront club of the same name in Hamburg that bills itself as Germany's only male strip joint. Clumsy handling of the fictional account of life behind the beaded curtain and the stage fog kills viewer interest from the start.

Ham-fisted attempts at comedy backfire, and Kern relies all too often on the mere presence on screen of fat ladies and heavily madeup transsexuals for laughs.

Genuine funny moments — too few of them — come from Marianne Sägebrecht, the full-figured thesp who co-starred in the comedy hit "Zuckerbaby" (Sugarbaby) in 1985. She earns her laughs with acting ability, though, not her girth.

Subplot of women ogling men and buying their services is far from novel and goes nowhere.

Kudos to camerawork by Eberhard Geick, who gives film some visual life it lacks otherwise. —Gill.

Plastposen
(Andersen's Run)
(NORWEGIAN-COLOR)

A KF release (international sales: Norsk Film/Frieda Ohrvik), Filminvest with Norsk Film production. Produced by Wenche Solum. Directed by Hans Otto Nicolayssen. Stars Jon Skolmen. Screenplay, Kerry Crabbe, based on an idea by Skolen; camera (Eastmancolor), Halvor Nass; editor, Margit Nordquist; music, Geir Böhren, Bent Aserud; production design, Frode Krogh; sound, Jacob Trier; assistant director, Jan-Robert Jore; production management, Arve Figenschow. Reviewed at Berlin Film Festival (market), Feb. 21, 1987. Running time: **90 MINS.**
Andersen . . . . Jon Skolmen
Patrolwoman Eva . . . . Hilde Grythe
Bank robber . . . . Sverre Anker Ousdal
Patrolman Osvald . . . . . Ingar Helge Gimle
Kiosk lady . . . . Elsa Lysted
    Also with: Per Schaanning, Reidar Sörensen, Anne-Marie Ottersen, Ragnhild Nygaard, Marianne Ustvedt, Mette Tank, Jan Harstadt.

Berlin — "Andersen's Run" (original's title means "The Plastic Bag") is good-natured comedy-cum-farce with Norway's favorite comedy actor Jon Skolmen as the 40-ish bachelor who one morning descends to the street from his suburban apartment house to get rid of a plastic bag full of yesterday's garbage that the over-flowing communal chute won't accommodate.

Wearing only his bathrobe, Andersen tries in vain to unload his garbage on other people's premises until desperately he heaves it over a hedge. Alas, the wind catches most of the bag and its contents and drops it onto the windshield of a trio of bank robbers' getaway car with some of it spilling over and hitting a pursuing motorcycle cop in his face. After that, Andersen gets suspected for complicity and goes through endless, more or less madcap complications, always maintaining the special Jon Skolmen brand of nice-guy cool.

Apart from Hilde Grythe as a police patrolwoman, few of helmer Hans Otto Nicolayssen's other actors match Skolmen in wit or performance, but chuckles are to be had all along. Film's pacing and editing would contribute to limited offshore prospects of sales, especially to television and homevideo in territories already familiar with Skolmen via his co-starring with Sweden's Lasse Aberg in latter's trans-Scandinavian b.o. hits "The Package Tour," 1 and 2.—Kell.

Budawanny
(IRISH-B&W/COLOR)

A Cinegael production, with the assistance of the Irish Film Board, the Arts Council and Channel 4. Executive producer, Miriam Allen. Produced, written and directed by Bob Quinn. Camera (color, b&w), Seamus Deasy; editor, Martin Duffy; music, Roger Doyle; production design, Tom Conroy. Reviewed at Berlin Film Festival (Market), Feb. 22, 1987. Running time: **79 MINS.**
The Priest . . . . Donal McCann
The Woman . . . . Maggie Fegan
The Sacristan . . . . Tomas O'Flatharta
The Bishop . . . . Peadar Lamb
The Garden Woman. . . . . Freda Gillen
The Publican . . . . Sean O'Colsdealbha

Berlin — The bulk of this unusual and often quite beautiful film is made like a silent pic; luminous black and white photography, a music track, and inter-titles to fill in the dialog. It tells a sad little story of a young woman who travels to an island off the coast of Ireland and, on the way there, falls into the sea, in a presumed attempt at suicide. She's rescued, and recovers in the home of the island's priest, eventually becoming his housekeeper and, later still, his mistress ("So much for celibacy," he says, wryly, the morning after they first make love). Inevitably, she becomes pregnant, and then he has to tell his parishoners from the pulpit what they've long suspected ("You'll soon have another reason to call me Father").

Framing this story, and occasionally interrupting it, are scenes in color and with sound in which the Bishop writes a letter to the errant priest in response to a book, "Budawanny," he's written about his story ("Now a Major Film" says a flyer on the book's cover).

Quinn's decision to make the film in this way is interesting but will undoubtedly limit audience appeal, making it a very tough sell. He does create a superb atmosphere in the island scenes (filmed on Clare Island, County Mayo), where the priest occupies a crucial social, as well as religious, role for these isolated people. Many islanders appear in the film, their faces illuminating the story.

Scenes with the pompous Bishop are less successful (and not only because lip synch at the screening caught was very wayward), but overall "Budawanny" succeeds artistically on its chosen level, and there are fine performances from Donal McCann as the all-too-human priest and Maggie Fegan as the troubled, warm hearted woman. —Strat.

Anjos do Arrabalde
(Suburban Angels)
(BRAZILIAN-COLOR)

An A.P. Galante-Embrafilme production. Produced by Antonio Polo Galante. Directed by Carlos Reichenbach. Screenplay, Reichenbach; camera (Eastmancolor), Conrado Sanchez; editor, Eder Mazini; music, Manoel Paiva, Luis Chagas; production design, Sebastião de Souza; production manager, Sara Silveira. Reviewed at Berlin Film Festival (Market), Feb. 28, 1987. Running time: **104 MINS.**
    With: Betty Faria, Clarisse Abujamra, Irene Stefania, Vanessa Elves, Enio Gonçalves, Emilio Di Biasi, Nicole Puzzi.

Berlin — "Suburban Angels" is a well-made drama, set in the crowded suburbs of São Paulo, dealing with four schoolteachers and their efforts to cope with their pupils and themselves in a dangerous and frequently hostile situation.

Director Carlos Reichenbach creates a violent urban world, where a young schoolgirl can be raped and beaten, and yet is too afraid to name her attacker to the authorities. In this grim, sad environment, the teachers mostly find themselves in a no-win situation, where education is a secondary factor.

It's well acted and directed with feeling. —Strat.

Forever, Lulu
(COLOR)

Campy vanity production.

A Tri-Star Pictures release of a Lulu production. Executive producer, Michael Steinhardt. Written, produced and directed by Amos Kollek. Stars Hanna Schygulla. Camera (color), Lisa Rinzler; editor, Jay Freund; music, uncredited; sound, Felipe Borrero; production design, Stephen McCabe; set decoration, Victor Zolfo; production manager, Sarah Green; assistant director, Gary Marcus; costume design, Candace Clements; editing consultant, Ralph Rosenblum; casting, Marcia Schulman. Reviewed at Columbia screening room, N.Y., April 14, 1987. (MPAA Rating: R.) Running time: **85 MINS.**
Elaine Hines . . . . Hanna Schygulla
Lulu . . . . Deborah Harry
Buck . . . . Alec Baldwin
Diana . . . . Annie Golden
Robert . . . . Paul Gleason
Also with: Dr. Ruth Westheimer, Raymond Serra, George Kyle, Harold Guskin, Bill Corsair, Jonathan Freeman, Amos Kollek, Charles Ludlam, Cathy Gati, Beatrice Pons, Sally Jane Heit.

"Forever, Lulu" is an amateurish effort desperately seeking laughs but getting mainly unintentional ones. Fortunately not the clone of "Desperately Seeking Susan" its plot summary suggests, picture is still wide of the mark as entertainment and will be mainly of interest to midnight movie followers of high camp. Mystery is why Tri-Star acquired the indie production, presumably of interest to undemanding homevideo and paycable users but hardly a theatrical entry.

Hanna Schygulla toplines as Elaine Hines, a European transplant living in New York who is working at temporary jobs while writing her novel. Film comically depicts her growing list of misfortunes: fired from her job; stuck with the check on a big date; stuck in the rain; evicted from her apartment, etc. Things pick up when she contemplates suicide: wielding her gun creates confusion and results in a well-dressed couple depositing their coats in her arms out of fright.

Elaine becomes involved in a goofy adventure when she finds a package in the man's coat pocket, which leads her to an apartment where she becomes involved in a gun battle between gangsters and the police. Only Elaine survives, making off with two cases containing drugs and $500,000 in big bills.

Pic's resemblance to Susan Seidelman's hit "Susan" pic peaks when Elaine finds a photo (signed "forever, Lulu") of the eponymous heroine (played by rock star Deborah Harry) and starts searching for her, after earlier placing a personals ad in the paper to find the owners of the coats. Unfortunately for the film and Harry's fans, lured perhaps by her billing over the title with Schygulla, she doesn't find Lulu until the very end, with Harry getting perhaps one line of dialog in what amounts to an extended cameo, popping up on the outskirts of the action as a bystander from time to time. En route to this underwhelming conclusion, Elaine becomes a hit novelist due to the media attention she receives after she turns in the money to the police.

Filmmaker Amos Kollek, who in addition to his behind the camera credits delivers a poor performance as Elaine's cynical literary agent Larry, directs ineptly, with most of his would-be funny lines falling flat. Gimmick of Schygulla, talented dramatic star from the R.W. Fassbinder troupe, giving odd, heavily accented readings to "hip" expressions is more embarrassing than funny. Pic's camp value is finally realized in an over-the-top climax staged at the Fulton St. fish market.

Cast tries hard, with sympathetic readings by Annie Golden and Paul Gleason as Elaine's best pal and ex-lover, respectively. Schygulla has her moments, but is at the mercy of very weak material. Not to be faulted is some extremely colorful pastel lighting by cinematographer Lisa Rinzler, which brightens up the low-budget production.—*Lor.*

Summer Camp Nightmare
(COLOR)

Parable for teens is an uneasy mix of hijinks and lecture.

A Concorde Pictures release of a Crow Prods. presentation of a Butterfly production. Produced by Robert T. Crow, Emilia Lesniak-Crow. Directed by Bert L. Dragin. Screenplay, Dragin, Penelope Spheeris, from William Butler's novel "The Butterfly Revolution;" camera (United color), Don Burgess; editor, Michael Spence; music, Ted Neeley, Gary Chase; sound, Stephan von Hase; production design, Richard McGuire; art direction, Barry Franenberg; set decoration, Jennifer Pray; stunt coordinator, John Branagan; coproducer-production manager, Andy Howard; casting, Bengston & Cohn. Reviewed at Mark Goodson theater, N.Y., April 15, 1987 (MPAA Rating: PG-13). Running time: **87 MINS.**
Mr. Warren . . . . Chuck Connors
Franklin . . . . Charles Stratton
Donald . . . . Adam Carl
Chris . . . . Harold P. Pruett
Heather . . . . Melissa Brennan
John Mason . . . . Tom Fridley
Stanley . . . . Stuart Rogers
Hammond . . . . Shawn McLemore
Debbie . . . . Samantha Newark
Trixie . . . . Nancy Calabrese
Jerome Blackridge . . . . Michael Cramer
Ed Heinz . . . . Rick Fitts

Beneath the intentionally misleading release title "Summer Camp Nightmare" rests an uneasy mixture of teen hijinks pic and cautionary lecture for youngsters. In adapting William Butler's novel "The Butterfly Revolution" (film's original title during its 1985 lensing), filmmaker Bert. L. Dragin and cowriter Penelope Spheeris have created an all-too-obvious anti-fascist parable which is simply not entertaining in the manner of the S. E. Hinton pics or even the John Hughes comedies.

First few reels play like "Meatballs" without the laughs (not for lack of trying, but the gags here fall flat), with the young boys at Camp North Pines dreaming of the slightly older girls at nearby Camp South Pines. Fly in the ointment is new camp director Chuck Connors, styled as a strict disciplinarian who only allows an all-religious channel to play on the camp tv and locks misbehaving boys or counselors up in a detention cabin.

Pic takes a dark turn after 35 minutes when a counselor, played by Charles Stratton, organizes an instant revolution, locking up Connors and his adult staff and having the kids and student counselors run the camp in military fashion. He quickly extends his control to the girls' camp, locking up all the adults there, too.

With teens and kids running the show, film gradually tries for "Lord Of The Flies" commentary, as Stratton's fascist behavior leads to several deaths and the kids descend into barbarism. Unfortunately, Dragin's direction is very soft, denying the film the tough-minded points and power of such forerunners as Harold Becker's "Taps." Instead, we get an alternation of comedy and seriousness which represents a candy-coated lecture few kids will swallow.

Acting is passable, with Stratton very good indeed at suggesting a likable (on the surface) yet megalomaniacal character.—*Lor.*

Walk Like A Man
(COLOR)

Incredibly stupid 'comedy.'

An MGM/UA Distribution release from MGM Pictures. Produced by Leonard Kroll. Executive producer, Robert Klane. Directed by Melvin Frank. Stars Howie Mandel. Screenplay, Klane; camera (Metrocolor), Victor J. Kemper; editor, Bill Butler, Steve Butler; music, Lee Holdridge; production design, Bill Malley; set design, Richard J. Lawrence; sound, Gary Bourgeois, Chris Carpenter, Dean Okrand; assistant director, Roger Joseph Pugliese; casting, Jane Jenkins, Janet Hirshenson, Denise Chamian. Reviewed at MGM/UA screening room, Culver City, Calif., April 15, 1987. (MPAA Rating: PG.) Running time: **86 MINS.**
Bobo Shand . . . . Howie Mandel
Reggie Henry . . . . Christopher Lloyd
Margaret Shand . . . . Cloris Leachman
Rhonda Shand . . . . Colleen Camp
Penny . . . . Amy Steel

Hollywood — "Walk Like A Man" can easily take its place on anyone's list of the 10 stupidest films ever made in Hollywood. The story is ludicrous, the script hollow, the acting wooden, and on and on. Laughs are zilch, about what this stinker should deliver at the box-office.

Originally named "Bobo" for Howie Mandel's lead character, film is an excruciatingly boring attempt to create comic plausibility from an empty premise.

Mandel is lost in the woods as a youngster and is not found for 28 years — during which time he has been raised by a pack of wolves. Returned to the city by animal behaviorist Amy Steel, this man-beast scurries around on all fours and acts like an untrained canine.

Mandel's non-speaking antics early on surely lose anyone over four-years-old or with an IQ above 58. Purported plot has him under the tutelage of Steel, with his evil brother (Christopher Lloyd) trying to trick Bobo out of his share of the family fortune.

Steel's patience and thoughtfulness, of course, inevitably evolves into a half-baked romance while the hapless Lloyd connives to cop his sibling's millions.

Most embarrassing of all amidst the idiotic proceedings is the presence of Cloris Leachman as the guys' crackpot mother. Role is an insult to her skills and past credits.

Other family femme, Colleen Camp as Lloyd's wife, is left with a dimwit part as a greedy alcoholic who resorts to the tiresome reprise of drinking everywhere and anywhere.

All told, pic is one of those instances where the whole is less than the sum of its parts.—*Tege.*

Johnny Flash
(WEST GERMAN-COLOR)

A Werner Nekes (Mullheim) production. Directed by Nekes. Stars Andreas Kunze, Helge Schneider. Screenplay, Nekes, Peter Ritz; camera (color), Bernd Upnmoor, Serge Roman; editor, Astrid Nicklaus; music, Helge Schneider; sound, Andreas Wölki, Wolfgang Wirtz, sets, Dore O. Reviewed at the Berlin Film Festival, Feb. 24, 1987. Running time: **81 MINS.**
Johnny Flash . . . . Helge Schneider
His mother/manager . . . . . . Andreas Kunze
Producer . . . . Heike Melba-Fendel

Berlin — Billed as a "musical grotesquerie," "Johnny Flash" is the first commercial film from avant-garde director Werner Nekes. Though it has its funny moments, the plot is uninvolving and the humor frequently strays off into corniness.

Johnny Flash (Helge Schneider) is the stage name of a nerdy electrician who hits the big time with a two-finger organ piece called "Liebe ist Nicht Peinlich" (Love's Not Embarrassing). The new star is trapped quickly in a power struggle between his mother (actor Andreas Kunze, with a wig), his manager (Kunze, without the wig), and a bosomy tv producer (Heike Melba-Fendel).

The two lead actors, who also play a variety of cameo roles, aren't nearly as funny as they think they are, and the entire production, especially the sets (a crowd scene of a dozen people), smacks strongly of amateurism. Still, the film's subject and kitschy humor may appeal to college audiences.—*Xan.*

Dolls
(COLOR)

Middle-of-the-road comedy-horror film.

An Empire Pictures release. Produced by Brian Yuzna. Executive producer, Charles Band. Directed by Stuart Gordon. Screenplay, Ed Naha; camera (color), Mac Ahlberg, Doll effects by John and Vivian Brunnee, Giancarlo Del Brocco, David Allen. Reviewed at Houston Intl. Film Festival, April 18, 1986. (MPAA Rating: R.) Running time: **77 MINS.**

David Bower . . . . Ian Patrick Williams
Rosemary Bower . . Carolyn Purdy-Gordon
Judy Bower . . . . Carrie Lorraine
Gabriel Hartwicke . . . . Guy Rolfe
Hilary Hartwicke . . . . Hilary Mason
Isabel Prange . . . . Bunty Bailey
Enid Tilley . . . . Cassie Stuart
Ralph Morris . . . . Stephen Lee

Houston — "Dolls," one of Stuart Gordon's latest efforts since "Re-Animator," preemed at the Houston Intl. Film Festival representing a toned-down version of the child-horror genre with only marginal use of the hardcore, on-camera violence many teens seek from their boxoffice faves.

Carrie Lorraine plays little Judy Bower, the undeniable star of the film, whose childish innocence is the only key to survival when her father and stepmother become victims of torrential storm and take shelter in a nearby mansion. Rosemary Bower, portrayed nicely as the more-than-wicked stepmother by Carolyn Purdy-Gordon, almost runs over a pair of rain-sopped teenage hitchhikers and verbally abuses stepdaughter Judy at every opportunity. The instinct to hate becomes automatic, particularly when the gigilo-style father gives in continually to the aging but rich partner on the couple's vacation. Caught in one of London's perpetual rainstorms, the couple seek shelter at a house of a kindly but quirky white-haired couple whose greatest joy in life is children and unique dollmaking.

The trio is later joined by an unassuming businessman who retrieved a pair of teenage punkers from the storm and together they all find temporary shelter.

Little Judy witnesses the first sign of horror and attempts to alert the others but finds only one believer, the bumbling businessman Ralph Morris. In one gory scene after another, the dolls fiercely attack almost everyone sparing Ralph only when Judy intervenes. The cruel father is attended to personally by the Hartwicke couple in a scene that borrows heavily in special effects from "An American Werewolf In London." In the end only Judy and Ralph are allowed to leave while the remaining guests become permanent residents on the dollmakers, shelf. Another storm, another stranded couple take their place in the end and the wheel of misfortune continues.

While there is nothing strikingly new about "Dolls," a working combination of all the classic and contemporary horror flicks should make this a reasonable boxoffice success. —*Pank.*

Wild Thing
(COLOR)

Dated fairy tale is preachy, not funny.

An Atlantic Releasing release of an Atlantic Entertainment Group production, in association with Filmline Intl. Produced by David Calloway, Nicolas Clermont. Executive producers, Thomas Coleman, Michael Rosenblatt. Directed by Max Reid. Screenplay, John Sayles, based on a story by Sayles, Larry Stamper; camera (Sona color), René Verzier; editor, Battle Davis, Steven Rosenblum; music, George S. Clinton; production design, John Meighen, Jocelyn Joli; costumes, Paul-Andre Guerin; sound, Henri Blondeau; assistant director, Pedro Gandol; coproducer, Pieter Kroonenburg; casting, Paul Ventura. Reviewed at Atlantic screening room, L.A., April 15, 1987. (MPAA Rating: PG-13.) Running time: **92 MINS.**

Wild Thing . . . . Rob Knepper
Jane . . . . Kathleen Quinlan
Chopper . . . . Robert Davi
Trask . . . . Maury Chaykin
Leah . . . . Betty Buckley
Wild Thing (age 10) . . . . Guillaume
Lemay-Thivierge
Wild Thing (age 3) . . . . . . Robert Bedarski
Winston . . . . Clark Johnson
Father Quinn . . . . Sean Hewitt

Hollywood — "Wild Thing" is one of those film oddities that is impossible to categorize. Story of an urban Tarzan is by turns sanctimonious and silly with detours for street philosophizing, '60s idealism, gang uprisings and exhortations for non-violence from the neighborhood priest. One can only watch with a curious fascination and wonder what in the world is going on here.

As originally conceived by John Sayles and Larry Stamper film must have had a good deal of quirky humor to offset the '60s sermonizing about the corrupting forces of society, but as delivered by director Max Reid from Sayles' script this is deadly serious business. It's a film with its head in the clouds and it never really comes back down to earth.

Picture opens with the brutal killing of two peace-loving hippies inadvertently mixed up in a botched drug deal as their young son flees for his life only to grow up to become the savior of the ghetto — the legendary Wild Thing.

It's a rather dated fairy tale, but could have been fun in the right hands. Unfortunately, staging by Reid is consistently clumsy without establishing a groove of its own. With Kathleen Quinlan as a naive socialworker who falls in love with the Wild Thing and archvillain Chopper (Robert Davi) trying to hide his crime of years earlier, picture is like a stew that hasn't been stirred enough.

Performances come in all sizes and shapes here and Betty Buckley as the shopping bag woman who raises the young Wild Thing gets to recite lines like "the blue coats work for the company and the white coats scramble your eggs." This is definitely not one of Sayles' better efforts as a screenwriter.

As Wild Thing himself, Rob Knepper is indeed adept at scaling buildings and is a gifted primitive artist to boot, but he doesn't speak much and as attractive as he may be, there is hardly a character hidden behind his warpaint.

Although the villains often take on the tone of cartoon cut-outs to Wild Thing's pseudo-Superman, Davi is a powerful and menacing presence and by far the most intriguing character here.

René Verzier's cinematography is city-slick and stylish but reminiscent of dozens of other hard-edged urban actioners. Although the Troggs' rock anthem "Wild Thing" is used freely, it has little to do with the character it's meant to describe.—*Jagr.*

Buddha's Lock
(HONG KONG-CHINA-COLOR)

A Highland Films Enterprise (Hong Kong), Shen Zhen Film Enterprise (China) coproduction. Directed by Yim Ho. Screenplay, Kong Liang; camera (color), Lu Yue, Wang Ziao Lie; music, Zhao Ji Ping. Reviewed at the Berlin Film Festival (Market), March 2, 1987. Running time: **90 MINS.**

With: John X. Heart, Zhang Lu-tong, Yan Bi De, Suen Fei Hu, Wei Zong Wan, Steve Horowitz.

Berlin — Yim Ho has established quite a reputation after "Homecoming," in which he confronted the lifestyle and concepts of a Chinese woman living most of her adult life in Hong Kong to that of her former friends, left in a small Chinese village. In his new film, sneaked into the Berlin market at the last minute, he uses a real-life incident to elaborate on a different and much clearer clash between East and West.

The script is based on the story of an American officer, James Wood, kidnaped by wild tribes in northern China in 1945 and kept there as a slave for 10 years. During that time he suffered the most abject miseries, often was treated as an animal, once almost was executed for touching the daughter of the chief and reprieved at the last moment. With abolition of slavery and the takeover of the Revolutionary Forces, he was allowed a certain degree of cautious freedom, but new rulers suspected him of being a potential spy. During this period, however, he got close to a widowed former slave woman, with whom he had once shared chains, and with her little girl, and life almost settled down into a kind of simple idyll, when orders arrived to send him back home to Texas, at which stage he was torn between his affection for the woman living with him and his yearning to go back.

Needless to say, the tale itself holds an immense potential, as it offers a direct juxtaposition between two civilizations separated by time and space, a theme which is quite fashionable lately in films like "The Emerald Forest" or "The Mission." Here, however, very little is done with it, Ho staying on a modest level and sticking to flat storytelling which stresses mostly the ethnographic aspects.

The landscape is breathtaking in majesty and beauty and is the film's main asset by far. Shot in China, thanks to Ho's excellent connections, and co-produced by a local company, it offers some striking sights probably never before unveiled in front of the camera. The film's main problem is John X. Heart who plays Wood and has trouble putting any sort of expression on his face. Since he is on the screen constantly, his performance certainly will affect the film's impact.

It seems destined mainly for audiences with a preference for exotic places and ethnographic research. —*Edna.*

Baixo Gavea
(Gavea Girls)
(BRAZILIAN-COLOR)

A presentation of Embrafilme, Empresa Brasileiro de Filmes, Rio de Janeiro. Produced by H.M. Barbosa Producoes Cinematograficos. Written and directed by Haroldo Marinho Barbosa. Camera (color), Antonio Penido; editor, Gilberto Santeiro; music, Sergio G. Saraceni; art direction, Paulo Dubois; costumes, Mila Ashcar. Reviewed at Berlin Film Festival (Market), Feb. 25, 1987. Running time: **116 MINS.**

Dora . . . . Lucelia Santos
Ana . . . . Louise Cardosa

Berlin — In a sense, "Gavea Girls" is a dishonest film, in that it sets up a certain expectations and dramatic logic, then cops out at the end, probably for purposes of boxoffice and popular prejudice.

Given the main characters of this film — a beautifully characterized lesbian, Ana, played by Louise Cardoso, and her straight roommate Dora (Lucelia Santos) — we have a right to expect that life's processes will prevail, that the two ladies inevitably will end up where they belong, in bed together, as star-destined lovers.

Instead, in the irrational final scene, which takes place in a Gavea District bar, the writer-director has Dora, the straight girl, reject the lesbian who truly loves her and go instead for a quickie with a big, ugly and presumably smelly Hells Angel biker.

The lesbian shrugs sadly and philosophically. Her integrity is intact, but the film suffers, as does the audience, because the filmmaker has lacked the courage to face up to his own characters and the challenges of a more adult theme.

Dora, the straight girl, is director of a play about real-life Portuguese poet Fernando Pessoa. When not working at the theater, Dora sleeps around restlessly. Indeed, as the film begins she wakes up in bed with a strange man. In the two hours that follow, covering several weeks, Dora repeatedly has bungled and pleasureless affairs with pickups, philanderers and errant husbands. Some of this is meant as commentary on the characters and events of the Pessoa play, which we watch during rehearsals and which needlessly consumes perhaps a third of the screentime.

Meanwhile, Dora's lesbian roommate, Ana, stands by patiently, as do we, awaiting Dora's self-realization, which never comes. —Hitch.

Sommer
(Summer)
(WEST GERMAN-B&W-16m)

An Anderer Blick release of a Philip Gröning Films production, in cooperation with Munich TV and Film Academy. Produced and directed by Gröning. Screenplay, Gröning, Ralf Zöller, Nicolas Humbert; camera, (b&w, 16m), Ernst Kubiza; editor, Gröning; sound, Humbert, Ludwig Mahacec; art direction, Pavel Pitner. Reviewed at Berlin Film Festival (Market), Feb. 27, 1987. Running time: **105 MINS.**
Father .Michael Schech
Sebastian . . . . .Philipp Rankl
Woman . . . . .Barbara vom Baur
Maid . . . . .Lene Beyer

Berlin — In "Summer," a recently divorced father takes his autistic young son out of a clinical institution and brings him to an Alpine resort in hopes of teaching the boy to speak. Film is sensitively done and well-acted, but heavy-going subject matter limits it to fest circuit and special education interest groups.

Film provides a classic study in autism — as manifested in children and as frustratingly confronted by parents who must cope with an offspring who does not seem to know they exist.

Gröning uses autism as a metaphor for lack of communication. Father, well played by Michael Schech, is brought by his tedious drills with his son to a gradual understanding of his own failure to communicate with women. A fellow resort guest (Barbara vom Baur) takes a romantic interest in the man, but is little enough prepared for his emotional problems, let alone his son's condition.

Much of the film is seen through the eyes of young Sebastian (Philipp Rankl), who spends hours observing marbles or watching passing trains while his father futilely attempts to attract his attention and teach him to speak. Light entertainment it is not. —Gill.

Landscape Suicide
(U.S.-COLOR-16m)

Produced, written, directed, camera (color, 16m) and edited by James Benning. Reviewed at Berlin Film Festival (Intl. Forum of Young Cinema), Feb. 23, 1987. (No MPAA Rating.) Running time: **95 MINS.**
Bernadette Protti . . . . .Rhonda Bell
Edward Gein . . . . .Elion Sucher

Berlin — In form a docudrama, "Landscape Suicide" reconstructs two bizarre murders: 15-year-old Bernadette Protti was a seemingly normal teenager who inexplicably stabbed to death her high school chum, a popular cheerleader. Ed Gein was a reclusive Wisconsin farmer with a secret passion for murdering and stuffing his victims. The latter case variously inspired "The Texas Chain Saw Massacre" and Hitchcock's "Psycho."

Two performers in the present recite unemotionally from the actual testimony of the killers, a recitation supported by stills, related footage and trial discourse.

Two killers have in common a curious dull affect or emotionless delivery, although detailed. The film's impact and its main value as a learning experience is our dawning awareness — if we didn't know it before — that the human animal is strange, mysterious and unknowable.

Thus "Landscape Suicide" is more than a sensationalized morbid look-back at two lunatic killers. It serves a larger purpose, in that the film makes us doubt our placidity and smugness about claiming to know ourselves and our species.

The "landscape" of the title is the physical background of the killings. These two contexts are conformist, monotonous and oppressive, affording little communication. The high school cheerleader and her killer Bernadette Protti lived in an upper-middle-class San Francisco suburb, burdened with all those clichés of respectability. The Wisconsin farmer lived in a grey dreary backwoods, another isolated and antisocial environment conducive to a sudden outburst of violence. The landscape compels self-destructive behavior.

One can predict that "Landscape Suicide" will not play major theaters, but may find its audience on public tv and in specialized theatrical situations. —Hitch.

Quatre Mains
(DUTCH-W. GERMAN-COLOR)

An Added Films, Holland production and release in conjunction with Die Nieuwe Unie of Amsterdam and Provobis Film of West Berlin. Produced by Dirk Schreiner. Directed by Hans Fels. Screenplay, Fels; camera (color), Tony Kuhn; editor, Hans Dunnewijk; music, Paul Prenen; sound, Olaf Liebegall; art direction, Dick Schillemans. Reviewed at Berlin Film Festival (Panorama), March 1, 1987. Running time: **90 MINS.**
Alexander .Peter Fitz
Marte . . . . .Renée Fokker
German friend . . . . .Reinhard von Bauer

Berlin — Hans Fels' first feature-length film, "Quatre Mains," is a slow moving and at times incomprehensible film about a Nazi concentration camp survivor's slow reconciliation with his past, with his rebellious niece and with himself.

Despite brief moments of originality, as when a European Jew (Peter Fitz) visits his boyhood home in Germany, most of the film is just too stilted to hold audience interest.

Screenplay has Fitz playing a moody concert pianist who expresses himself beautifully via the keyboard, but finds it difficult to exchange even simple pleasantries with other human beings. Early on there are hints of an enormous secret between him and his attractive young niece (Rennée Fokker).

Again, the pair communicate beautifully as long as they are playing four-hand pieces for the piano (hence, film's French title). The second the keyboard lid bangs down — which it does more than once in various fits of rebellion by the niece, all communication stops.

Enter German combat photographer boyfriend (Reinhard von Bauer), to rub salt into the open wounds of this sad Dutch family.

Niece follows boyfriend home to Hamburg, with weird old uncle Alexander inexplicably in pursuit. Alex, who was born there, must confront his agonizing past.

Fitz and Fokker have little to do in much of the film except to look sullen and cast knowing glances at each other. Uncle's pursuit quickly becomes ludicrous since audience has no idea what is going on and why. All this is meant to build suspense, but tedious scenes of trenchcoat-clad uncle standing in a parking lot watching his niece's apartment window elicit chortles from the audience.

Sometimes dialog is in Dutch, sometimes in German. Subtitles at the Berlin Film Fest premiere were in English, meaning Berliners who couldn't speak Dutch or English were left guessing much of the time. Technical credits are more than adequate. —Gill.

Romanca Final
(Last Romance)
(SPANISH-COLOR)

Coproduced by Orfeo, Euskal Telebista; TV3 Televisio de Catalunya, Spain. Produced and directed by Jose Maria Forque. Screenplay, Forque, Hermongenes Sainz; camera (color), Alejandro Ulloa; musical direction, Anton Garcia Abril; editor, Mercedes Alonso; orchestra and chorus of the Teatre Del Liceu, directed by Romano Gandolfi; production manager, Mario Morales; costume design, Juan Antonio Cidron; set design, Wolfgang Burman; consultant, opera scenes, Jose Luis Alonso. Reviewed at Berlin Film Festival (Market), Feb. 24, 1987. Running time: **130 MINS.**
Julian Gayarre . . . . .Jose Carreras
Alicia .Sydne Rome
The diva . . . . .Montserrat Caballe

Berlin — Jose Carreras, star of the recently re-recorded "West Side Story" of Leonard Bernstein, enacts in "Last Romance" the career of Julian Gayarre, a real-life historical personage, a famous Spanish opera tenor who died in 1890 at age 45.

Gayarre's life is notable for having brought Spanish musical talent into the opera mainstream. His career illustrates the democracy of talent, as he was the son of a peasant. Gayarre himself was merely a blacksmith, sweating at his forge, while singing Spanish folksongs, when discovered by accident by a traveling priest with a musical ear and access to patrons who loved music.

Gayarre received scholarships, but he had to serve a long, difficult apprenticeship as a minor singer in opera choruses and at funerals and weddings. "Last Romance" traces all this, Gayarre's professional career, while dramatizing his secret romance with a married lady, Alicia, wife of a Spanish aristocrat. Alicia conceives Gayarre's child, a daughter, but her letter of confession is misdirected and burned unread in the fireplace. Certain secrets must be left unknown and so it is with "Last Romance."

In the film's single philosophical scene, Gayarre realizes he wrongly has sacrificed love for career, that love matters more, that a performance is transient and lives only briefly, only as long as those who have heard his song, that performing is a secondary skill, not primary like that of the originating creative artist. Therefore, for such secondary performers, love is better.

Though overlong and melodramatic, "Last Romance" works and should find its place within U.S. distribution. Jose Carreras reveals himself as a skillful and attractive performer. He handles well the excerpts from a dozen opera — principally by Mozart, Verdi and Wagner. —Hitch.

Jim & Piraterna Blom
(Jim & The Pirates)
(SWEDISH-COLOR)

An SF (Svensk Filmindustri) release and production with Stugan. Produced by Waldemar Bergendal. Directed by Hans Alfredson. Screenplay, Alfredson, Stellan Skarsgard; camera (Eastmancolor), Ralph Evers, Bertil Rosengren; editor, Jan Persson; music, Stefan Nilsson; sound, Christer Furubrand; production design, Stig Boquist; costumes, Cecilia Lagergren, Gunilla Alfredson; assistant director, Daniel Alfredson; production management, Ann Collenberg, Eva Ivarsson. Reviewed (Competition) in Berlin Children's Film Festival, Berlin Film Festival, Feb. 21, 1987. Running time: **91 MINS.**

Jim ....Johan Akerblom
His mother................Ewa Fröling
His late father.........Stellan Skarsgard
Mother's suitor ....Jan Malmsjö
Mr. Kick-The-Bucket .....Hans Alfredson
Potato Al ....Stig Olin
The teacher ....Carl Billquist
Inez ....Lena T. Hansson
Bruno................Kenneth Milldorf
Eskil Blom ....Jesper Danielsson/-
Sten Hellström
Adam Blom ......Christina Schultzberg/-
Rolf Adolfsson
Also with: My Skarsgard, Sam Skarsgard, Licka Sjöman, Dora Söderberg, Börje Norrman, Mats Bergman, Vanja Rodefeldt, Jim Hughes.

Berlin — Writer-helmer-actor Hans Alfredson, always a humorist of serious mien and intent, has switched this time around from thriller-mellers to kiddie entertainment with strong appeal to adults, too. With "Jim & The Pirates" (actually "Jim & The Family Blom Pirates" in an allusion to Steve Canyon's Terry cartoon strip which had the name substituted with Jim in Europe), Alfredson plunges daringly, and successfully, into a combination Hans Christian Andersen, Astrid Lindgren and Lewis Carroll territory. His film would seem destined to find all kinds of venues worldwide.

For its running time and intended audience, "Jim & The Pirates" may be a bit too episodic, but the errant storyline still has plenty of sly wit, good old-fashioned pratfalls plus food for thought to redeem it, along with vigorous acting.

Death is actually what it is all about. Physical suspense eludes him and so does gut appeal to anybody's emotions when he tells about a sub-teenage boy's making up in Walter Mitty-ish dreams of glory for the loss of his father, a small-town restaurateur-cum-chef who comes back to encourage his son by teaching him how to chop onions; how to conquer his jealousy when faced with his mother's new suitor; and how to turn a rather dreary birthday party into a dream of a pirates' adventures at high seas.

Here again, quaint inventions of scenery and makeup do the trick where dramatic substance fails. The "Alice In Wonderland" touch is yielding rich results in the Blom Family of Pirates with two actors combining for rich comical effect behind

each mask. Elsewhere, a provincial town street parade has kids taking over as adults while adults are clowning rather pitifully around made up as children.

Alfredson himself turns up now and again as a kind of Death's messenger riding a delivery tricycle and whispering wisdom about stones falling from your heart to split and to have inner diamonds of survival power emerge. For each such turn and twist, comic relief is provided by having some other adult getting his feet — or much more — wet.

Screenplay cowriter Stellan Skarsgard (lead player in Alfredson's very adult thrillers "False As Water" and "The Simple-Minded Murderer") puts a mute on his acting as befits a ghost, while Ewa Fröling as the young vivacious widow and Johan Akerblom as her son Jim are all sweetness and light without a single digression into the cute.
—*Kell.*

Djadde Haye Sard
(Frosty Roads)
(IRANIAN-COLOR)

A Farabi Cinema Foundation production. Produced by Syamak Taghi Poor. Directed by Massoud Jafari Jozani. Screenplay, Poor, from the story "If Daddy Dies," by Reza Sarshar; camera (color), Toraj Mansoori; editor, Davood Yooseffian; music, Kambiz Roshan Ravan; production design, Vahij Ollah Fariborzi; sound, Mohsen Roshan; assistant director, Ali Reza Raeesian; production manager, Chasem Taghi Poor. Reviewed at Berlin Film Festival (Panorama), Feb. 24, 1987. Running time: **93 MINS.**

Esmaeil ....Majid Nasiri
Moosavi ....Ali Nassirian
Rahman ....Hamid Jebeli
Darvish Gorgali .....Esmaeil Mohammadi
Moosavi's wife Farzaneh Neshat Akhavan

Berlin — A well-made tale of a determined schoolboy's efforts to bring medication to his sick father in mid-winter, "Frosty Roads" is not up to the high standard of the best Iranian films seen at fests in recent years, but it's still an item worth catching within a festival context.

Set in a small village, it establishes a dogged youngster, Esmaeil, who's anguished at the decline of his beloved father, who has jaundice. The boy decides to trek through the snowbound countryside to the nearest town to get medication, and his mother reluctantly agrees to the pilgrimage with the village's crippled schoolteacher going along too. The village simpleton, a kindly, gentle young man, also tags along.

The teacher gets left behind along the way and is menaced by a pack of wolves, but the boy and his friend make it to the town (where they're intrigued by posters for Steve McQueen in "Nevada Smith" at the local cinema) and, after some problems, manage to get the vital medicine. Health-conscious viewers may note, here, that both the doctor and

the druggist who help the boy are smoking cigarets on duty.

Camerawork, usually an impressive feature in Iranian films, is a major asset here too, though the film lacks the poetry to be found in the best pics from this country. Acting is acceptable, and the dialog (spoken in Farsi) is obviously funnier than the poor English subtitles would indicate, judging by the reactions of members of the audience at the screening caught, who evidently appreciated a degree of humor not evident to the uninitiated.
—*Strat.*

Zischke
(WEST GERMAN-B&W)

An Ingefilm Medienvertrieb release. Produced by Backhaus/Krieger Filmproduction, Berlin. Written and directed by Martin Theo Krieger, dramaturgy, Reinhard Muenster; camera (b&w), Claus Deubel; sound, Wolfgang Schukrafft; editor, Raimund Maria Barthelmes. Reviewed at Berlin Film Festival (New German Films), Feb. 20, 1987. Running time: **91 MINS.**

With: David Strempel, Amira Ghazalla, Michael Altmann, Heinz Kraehkamp; Dominik Bender, Youssef el Sidani, Amado Meaini.

Berlin — This low-budget b&w production has a good feel and could do well at specialized cinemas outside Germany. The all too familiar story of a teen's misadventures is given new credibility set against Berlin's current problems with illegal aliens and asylum-seekers.

A divorced mother takes off with her American G.I. boyfriend, leaving a teenaged son behind to fend for himself. A budding cartoonist nicknamed Zischke (David Strempel), he decides he's had enough neglect and wants to take a trip. While figuring out a way to raise trainfare, he stumbles upon a couple of forged passports and immediately recognizes their potential resale value.

A pretty Lebanese actress, nicely played by Amira Ghazalla, has arranged the phony documents to secure the safety of her fugitive brothers who have managed to slip illegally into West Germany through East Berlin. A couple of immigration cops hot on the trail prove easily corruptible — one for love and the other for money.

Sixteen-year-old non-pro Strempel turns in a credible performance as a sensitive, troubled teen, and the other players are all firstrate, including the cops played by Michael Altmann and Heinz Kraehkamp, a popular acting duo from Berlin's legit stage.

No new territory here but some imaginative scripting and direction by Martin Theo Krieger. Contemporary West Berlin is seen beyond the usual touristy post-war attractions as a gritty urban center coping

with petty corruption, aliens and alienated youth. —*Owl.*

Pasos Largos: El Ultimo Bandido Andaluz
(Long Strider)
(SPANISH-COLOR)

A Berango Internacional Films production. Written and directed by Rafael Moreno Alba. Camera (color), José Garcia Galisteo; editor, Pedro del Rey; music, Emilio de Diego; production design, Javier Artiñano, Eduardo Hildago. Reviewed at Berlin Film Festival (Panorama), Feb. 26, 1987. Running time: **109 MINS.**

Juan Gallardo (Pasos Largos) ..Tony Isbert
Maria ....Marina Saura
Lieutenant ....Eusebio Lazaro
Juan ....Felipe Velez
Juan's wife ....Covadonqa Guijar
Father................Raul Fraire
Don Esteban ....Francisco Guijar

Berlin — The theme of the noble outsider driven by poverty and the brutality of law enforcers to become an outlaw has been a staple of the cinema from Jesse James to Ned Kelly. Here's a tale about the last Andalusian bandit, known as Long Strider, whose career ended not long before the Spanish Civil War. According to the film, he was a poor man whose poaching activities caused him to fall foul of a local landowner and a sadistic boss of the regional Civil Guard.

Despite attempts to make a hero out of the bandit, he remains in the film a totally unappealing character, thanks to a screenplay that has him commit ugly, cold-blooded murders and even shoot his faithful dog when it starts to follow him. Tony Isbert plays the character as a brute without charm.

Since the landowners and the pursuing Civil Guard aren't presented sympathetically either, and even the heroine is far from appealing, the audience really has nobody with whom to identify. The result is a handsomely produced but dull film, with repetitive scenes of the bandit being hunted in savage mountain scenery.

The numerous scenes in which birds and animals are shot to pieces won't endear the film to viewers who care about wildlife.—*Strat.*

Zacharias
(W. GERMAN-DOCU-COLOR-16m)

An Irene Dische production in conjunction with ZDF Tv. Written and directed by Dische. Camera (color, 16m), Horst Zeidler; editor. Meir Süssmann; music, Nan Marks. Reviewed at Berlin Film Fetival (New German Film), Feb. 28, 1987. Running time: **90 MINS.**

Narrator ....Jutta Lampe

Berlin — German-American author-filmmaker Irene Dische has made a very intimate portrait of her father, a Viennese Jew who fled to France and was interned during the Nazi occupation, and who at age 90 now lives in a small apartment on Manhattan's west side.

With an eye for both American and European audiences, Dische has turned out a film that appeals to both. It's a natural for the fest circuit and specialty outlets looking for the out of the ordinary.

Ancient pop, Zacharias Dische, talks about his long, sometimes perilous life in talking head interviews and voiceovers. He speaks for the most part in German, sometimes mixing Viennese expressions and the English of the land that has been his home since he arrived in New York some 40 years ago with a dollar bill in his pocket.

He talks about his most profound memories, blending a touch of the poetic with generous amounts of humorous self-effacement.

In the most endearing segment, he reminisces about Viennese literary coffee house of the 1920s, then mentions his favorite "Kaffeehaus-restaurant" in Manhattan. Cut to him entering a McDonald's as he continues to extoll the establishment's virtues.

Horst Zeidler's camera homes in on New York streetscape details that Europeans find exotic as the white-haired nonagenarian shuffles through streets of Spanish Harlem wearing running shoes. Cutaway shots of dad's chaotic desk, mementos and modest furnishings turn such everyday items as light switches and the Manhattan phone book into exotica, even for American eyes.

During talky sections film tends to drag, then is saved by such observations as: "I spent 75 years waiting for the return of my old friend Halley's comet. What a disappointment." And, "There's hardly a woman over 80 who's even the least bit attractive. That's the bad thing about being 90." —*Gill.*

Adios, Pequena
(Goodbye, Little Girl)
(SPANISH-COLOR)

A production of Travelling Films, in association with the Ministry of Culture, Spain, and Television Espanola. Produced by Javier Inchaustegui. Directed by Imanol Uribe. Screenplay, Uribe, Ricardo Franco; camera (color), Angel Luis Fernandez; editor, Eduardo Biurrun; music, Alberto Iglesias; art director, Ferran Sanchez. Reviewed at Berlin Film Festival (Market), Feb. 25, 1987. Running time: **74 MINS.**
Beatriz . . . . Ana Belen
Lucas . . . . Fabio Testi
Fidel . . . . Marcel Bozzuffi
Also with: Jose M. Cervino, Juan Echanove, Nacho Martinez, Antonio V. Valero, Miguel Ortiz, Marisa Tejada; Juan Antonio Bardem.

Berlin — Rape, murder, drug smuggling, double-cross, crooked cops, car smashups — these are the obligatory elements that make up the modern crime thriller. "Goodbye, Little Girl" uses all these ba-nalities, but has the virtue of its brevity (74 minutes), thus the sex and mayhem move fast and generate a certain excitement if one is not too demanding.

Lucas (Fabio Testi) is busted again for drugs and visited in prison by court-appointed lawyer Beatriz (Ana Belen). Both are young and attractive. He is working-class poor, she upper-class rich. Naturally they fall in love instantaneously, but the mob lurks nearby and rape and murders ensue. Lucas on bail is forced to reveal the whereabouts of a stash of cocaine. After his rubout, Beatriz stalks and neatly executes each of his killers — surely beyond the professional ethics of even the most dutiful attorney.

Beatriz' trail of investigation leads her at last to her father, a respected tycoon leading a double life as a drug kingpin. Fidel (Marcel Bozzuffi) reveres his daughter, but senses she is troubled. He approaches to embrace her, to comfort his beloved "little girl" of the title, unaware of the pistol beneath her fashionable coat. A shot rings out. Has she killed him? — or is it her own suicide, unable to endure the cruel knowledge of his duplicity? We'll never know, as the end credits roll.

Spain's Ministry of Culture coproduced this crime-meller, but one looks in vain for any Spanish culture. —*Hitch.*

Hotet/Uhkkádus
(The Threat)
(SWEDISH-DOCU-COLOR)

A Stefan Jarl/Filmfotograferne production. (Intl. sales, Svensk Filmindustri (Catherina Stackelberg.) Conceived and directed by Stefan Jarl. Camera (Eastmancolor), Per Källberg; editor, Anette Lycke-Lundberg; music, Ulf Dageby. Reviewed at Berlin Film Festival (Market), Feb. 27, 1987. Running time: **72 MINS.**

Berlin — With this hard-hitting docu bearing the double Swedish-Sami (Lap) title of "Hotet/Uhkkádus," meaning "The Threat," Stefan Jarl engages in a bit of emotional blackmail by saying a whole nation of Last European Wilderness people, the Laps or Samis of Sweden's Northernmost Lapland province, is having its way of life doomed to extinction as a consequence of a government decree of last summer, when large herds of reindeer were killed for fear they'd suffered contamination via the Chernobyl accident.

Jarl studiously avoids burdening his docu with facts and figures such as these: no more than the 75,000 head out of a reindeer population of 300,000 were killed, which means the same number that would have been killed for normal profit to Laps and Sweden's supermarkets anyway, and the government paid the set price of the season for each animal killed.

More unmentioned facts: no scientific claims have been made for slaughtering reindeer since it was admitted, a short time after the government-imposed killings, the fallout contamination of the region has never been near the danger point.

Nevertheless, Jarl was morally indignant enough to dash through the making of a scare docu that mixes very gory shots of ordinary for-profit reindeer slaughter indiscriminately with the government-decreed killings, latter mostly visualized via shots of helicopters lifting into the air and carrying away untidy bundles of animals with their antlers sticking out.

A couple of clean-looking young Sami are seen in lingering closeups as endlessly bemoaning the end of their world as they knew it. An elderly tribal head is heard singing a native chant while his son cuts an ornament into a piece of wood. A lone reindeer is seen in profile on a mountain ridge in the sunset, and large herds are seen like massed army columns moving up and down grey-white slopes. —*Kell.*

Caspar David Friedrich
(WEST GERMAN-COLOR)

An Allianz Filmproduktion-Peter Schamoni Filmproduktion. (World sales; Filmverlag der Autoren.) Executive producers, Lilo Pleimes, Horst Hartwig. Directed by Peter Schamoni. Screenplay, Schamoni, Hans A. Neunzig; camera (Eastmancolor), Gerard Vandenberg; editor, Katja Dringenberg; music, Hans Posegga, Franz Schubert; sound, Rolf Spielmann; production design, Alfred Hirschmeier; costumes, Christiane Dorst; assistant director, Thomas Nennstiel; production manager, Wolfgang Lange. Reviewed at Berlin Film Festival (German Section), Feb. 22, 1987. Running time: **84 MINS.**
Carl Gustav Carus . . . . Helmut Griem
Caroline Friedrich . . . . Sabine Sinjen
V.A. Schukowski . . . Hans Peter Hallwachs
Ramdohr . . . . Walter Schmidinger
Ernst Moritz . . . . Hans Quest
Also with: Lothar Blumhagen, Udo Samel, Otto Sander, Eric Vaessen, Friedrich Schönfelder.

Berlin — Casper David Friedrich (1774-1840) was one of Germany's most celebrated landscape painters. In his work, which was revolutionary in its day, the landscape dominates the people in the picture, who are usually seen as tiny figures in the foreground, facing the awesome vistas. Peter Schamoni has attempted to make a film about Friedrich in the style of his paintings; we see the artist only twice: once as a small child at the funeral of his brother (who died rescuing him from an icy river) and again in a portrait (self-portrait?) at the very end.

Indeed, the film tells us next to nothing about Friedrich's life. We see a great many of the surviving paintings (only half of his work survives today) and, as breathtakingly photographed by Gerard Vandenberg, we see the landscapes that inspired them: the mist-shrouded mountains, the Baltic sea, the frozen Elbe river; the sunsets and snow-covered trees.

All of this is very beautiful but pretty academic. Dramatic scenes consist mostly of arguments about the artist's worth, with Helmut Griem appearing as his friend and champion and Sabine Sinjen as his rather woebegone wife. The film certainly makes the viewer want to see more of Friedrich's classical works, but as a film about an artist and his work it is inferior to the classics of this genre. — *Strat.*

Nae-shi
(Eunuchs)
(S. KOREAN-COLOR)

An Action Bros. release (U.S.) of a Doo Sung Cinema production. A Seoul coproduction. Produced and directed by Lee Dooyong. Screenplay, Kwak Il-lo, based on a treatment by Yoon Sam-Yook; camera (color), Sohn Hyon-chae; editor, Lee Kyong-ja; music, Chong Yon-joo; sound, Kim Kyong-il; set decoration, Park Hyo-jin; costumes, Lee Hye-yoon; planning, Lee Soon-yong. Reviewed at Berlin Film Festival (Panorama), March 3, 1987. Running time: **108 MINS.**
With: Ahn Song-ki, Lee Mee-sok, Nam Koong-won, Kim Jin-ah, Kil Yong-woo, Tae Hyon-sil, Tae Il, Pyon Hee-bong.

Berlin — "Eunuchs" is a violent tale of 16th-century Korea involving a king, concubines, eunuchs and warriors. The colorful outing might be well received on art-house screens and other special venues.

The daughter of a court counsellor loves the son of a petty official. The outraged father hoped his daughter would gain the king's favor. To ensure the end of the romance, the father has the lover castrated and forced into the ranks of the court eunuchs.

The king, aware of the counsellor's ambitions, passes over the daughter and spitefully makes her a servant to one of his courtesans. The star-crossed lovers try to flee together, but the attempt is foiled and the boyfriend is forced to stand guard while the king has his way with the counsellor's daughter. Events at the palace come to a head with an abortion, miscarriage, executions, murder and suicide.

Though a bit overlong and bloody, the pic is a fascinating glimpse at a barbaric time set amidst exquisite period decor and costumes.—*Owl.*

Trinajstata Godenica Na Princa
(The Thirteenth Bride Of The Prince)
(BULGARIAN-COLOR)

A production of Bulgariafilm, Sofia. Directed by Ivanka Grubcheva. Screenplay, the Mormarev Bros.; camera (color), Grisha Wegenstein; music, Georgi Genkov; art director, Valentina Mladenova. Reviewed at Berlin Film Festival (Kinderfest), Feb. 25, 1987. 1987. Running time: **88 MINS.**

With: Georgi Partsalev, Tatyana Lolova, Nickolai Tsankov, Petya Milaoinonov, Georgi Mamalev.

Berlin — The short dumpling Prince Alfonso of the mythical kingdom Calenby has long been shopping for a bride, but the new wife Rosalia proposed by neighboring kingdom Dalenby is even more ugly than he. Therefore the kings, who don't want repulsive granchildren, kidnap Elena, the beautiful daughter of a peasant, as Alfonso's subsititute bride, but Elena is in love with the gallant, handsome dairy farmer Boyan who, to rescue Elena, must befriend Pero, itinerant Robin Hood type.

All this occurs in the film's first few minutes. Thereafter, everybody swaps clothes, double and triple identities take place, further complicated by the arrival of aliens from another planet in a strange spaceship. They enable the filmmakers to use electronic special effects, creating sudden appearances and disappearances.

Finally, the characters drink a magic potion that kicks off a comic medieval soccer game. While the king is being blackmailed for ransom, Boyan rescues Elena from the castle dungeon, complete with daring fencing gymnastics. Finally, love triumphs.

Director Ivanka Grubcheva further postulates that Bulgarian kids today — and maybe all kids — like their national fairy tales and folklore enriched with new sci-fi special effects and plenty of innovative technical tricks.

At the Kinderfilmfest screening of "Thirteenth Bride," the audience of 2,000 West Berlin children in the Urania Theater went bonkers.
— *Hitch.*

Die Dreckschleuder
(The Muckrakers)
(AUSTRIAN-COLOR-16m)

An Austrian Film Commission release of a Teamfilm Production for ORF TV. Executive producers, Thomas Konrad, Wolfgang Rest. Written and directed by Niki List. Camera (color, 16m), Hans Selikovsky; editor, Ingrid Koller, Brigitte Tauchner; music, Ernie Seuberth; art direction, Rudolf Czettel. Reviewed at Berlin Film Festival (Market), Feb. 27, 1987. Running time: **60 MINS.**
Mario Übermorgen . . . . . . Andreas Vitasek
Assistant . . . . Christian Schmidt

Berlin — Niki List wrote the screenplay to "Die Dreckschleuder" (The Muckrakers) for Austrian tv last year before the release of his enormously successful comedy feature film "Müllers Büro" (Muller's Office), which topped the 1986 b.o. chart in Austria and became the first state-subsidized film there ever to make good on its subsidy. The tv production is in some ways better than the theatrical release, and has possibilities for the video market.

In "Müllers Büro" List spoofed 1950s detective films. This time around it is European tv's penchant for mounting gaudy variety shows with singers who lip-sync to their own titles.

Comic team of Andreas Vitasek and Christian Schmidt is back again. Vitasek, who bears a slight physical resemblance to Bill Murray, plays a down-and-out show host reduced to emceeing a local variety show in a village with a name longer than its main street. Schmidt is a fair-haired, pretty boy type along European Top-40 music scene lines.

Bulk of the film is devoted to parody stage acts in front of a beer-guzzling, pretzel-chomping audience of locals decked out in Alpine regalia.

Vitasek, who played Schmidt's assistant in "Müllers Büro," has a chance to step literally into the spotlight. His monologs, taken together with the zany stage acts and antics by the yokels, make for good comedy and biting satire.

As an accompaniment to other List outings, this film is a must-see, despite its minimal length.—*Gill.*

Dixia Ging
(Love Unto Waste)
(HONG KONG-COLOR)

A D&B release of a Pearl City production. Produced by Dickson Poon. Executive producer, Vicky Lee Leung. Directed by Stanley Kwan. Screenplay, Lai Kit; camera (color), Johnny Koo; editor, Chow Chueng-Kan; music, Violet Lam. Reviewed at the Berlin Film Festival (Forum), Feb. 1, 1987. Running time: **97 MINS.**
Billie . . . . Irene Wan
Jade Screen . . . . Elaine Jin
Jane . . . . Tsai Chin
Tony . . . . Tony Leung
Sgt. Lau . . . . Chow Yun Fat

Berlin — Three young women, Billie, a model, Jade Screen, a starlet, and Jane, a singer, are the central figures in a film that treats subjects like incommunicability, death of feelings and emptiness of modern life and ideals.

The plot appears first to be the portrait of a dissipated playboy, bored with his father, a rice merchant, whom he helps enthusiastically during the day, while at night he gets drunk in fashionable bars. In one of these he meets the three girls and falls hard for Billie, the one who always plays cool and

wears sunglasses, as if to keep the world at a distance.

Soon, the nature of the film changes when the starlet, who shares an apartment with the singer, comes back one night to discover that her roommate has been brutally murdered. At this stage one more leading character is introduced, that of a plainclothes policeman, who investigates the case in the style of Peter Falk's Columbo. The thriller element stays with the script down to the end, but its importance wanes, as the characters' background becomes more important, their relations more complicated, and a trip to Taiwan, where both the singer and the starlet were born, offers a glimpse of what they left behind. By the end, it seems less important to find a solution for the whodunit and far more relevant to see what the different characters are doing with their lives.

High quality technical credits, extremely intriguing faces of all three actresses and the suggestion of pain dissimulated behind the flashy, composed personalities, are more than ample justification to give this film a try. —*Edna.*

Cain
(SPANISH-COLOR)

A Manuel Iborra production with Brezal Videoplaning (Seville). Executive producer, Rafael Diaz-Salgado. Written and directed by Iborra. Camera (Eastmancolor), Carlos Gusi; editor Teresa Font; music, Santi Arisa; sound, Goldstein & Steimberg; set decoration, Miguel Chicharro. Reviewed at the Berlin Film Festival (Children's Competition), Feb. 25, 1987. Running time: **100 MINS.**

With: Jose A. Romero, Carlos Velat, Antonio Resines, Veronica Forque, Santi Arisa, Ramon Reparaz, Paul Riba, Lali Ramon, Cuco Sierra, Ricardo Solfa, Amparo Valle, Marta Angelat Jaume Sorribas, Luisa Quinones, Agustin Velazquez.

Berlin — There should be a warning on the print of this pic in the form of a skull and crossbones. If the makers of this exploitative outing consider it suitable for children, perhaps life in sunny Spain is grimmer than imagined.

An elementary school class is disrupted constantly by the students themselves as well as violent intruders. The teacher is hopelessly unable to cope and the one authority figure, the school principal, conducts himself like a parody of a gangster.

There are episodic incidents that never amount to much of a storyline. The title character Cain (Jose A. Romero) is a bright, curious youngster who yearns to imitate the older boys. In the course of events he gets his first taste of puppy love. There are gratuitous scenes of knife and gunplay that seem inappropriate for youngsters "from age six" as the Children's Festival program suggests.

This is a scattered effort by a young filmmaker with a flair for characterization who should've worked a little more on his script.
— *Owl.*

La Rubia Del Bar
(The Blond At The Bar)
(SPANISH-COLOR)

An Els Films de la Rambla, Lauren Films presentation, in association with the Ministerio de Cultura and with the Departamento de Cultura de la Generalitat de Catalunya. Executive producer, J.A. Gonzalez Serret. Directed by Ventura Pons. Screenplay, Pons, Raul Nunez; camera (color), Tomas Pladevall; editor, Amat Carreras; music, Gato Perez; art director, Isabel Torras; sound, Licio Marcos de Oliveira. Reviewed at Berlin Film Festival (Market), March 2, 1987. Running time: **94 MINS.**
Mario . . . . Enric Majo
Ortega . . . . Ramoncin
Marta . . . . Nuria Hosta
Also with: Pepe Martin, Carme Sansa.

Berlin — The blond at the bar is a cheap pickup plying her trade, a nice girl gone wrong, dressed tantalizingly, but essentially commonplace. That also describes the movie.

Marta the blond is in the bar when Mario first sees her. She contemptuously throws her earnings at her pimp Ortega, then stalks out. Ortega buys Mario a drink and explains — he and Marta live together, he's her pimp, but he prefers males, especially North Africans who frequent certain bars in Barcelona. This is the first of perhaps a dozen scenes that take place in bars, as characters, sit, talk, smoke and drink, half-bored with one another, half-boring us. Context is lower-class Barcelona, the night-people, dreamers, hustlers, petty criminals, pushers, porno producers, who use drugs casually. Franco would have disapproved.

Mario — a frustrated novelist, henpecked at home — becomes obsessed with Marta and visits her on duty at the brothel. In time, Mario deserts his shrewish wife, and he and Marta live together in frugality and love. She becomes a softcore porn star, then a cover girl, then leaves him for bigger stakes. Mario is crushed and sinks to the bottom, then pulls himself together. In his hovel he writes his novel, that long-submerged epic that expresses the heartbreak of life in Barcelona's lower depths. The satisfaction of his work enables him to forgive Marta, himself, overcome his writer's block and reorient his life.

In form and content, "Blond" is ordinary Spanish melodrama, with predictable sin, suffering and redemption. Nuria Hosta as Marta acquits herself well in her film debut. —*Hitch.*

A Weave Of Time
(U.S.-DOCU-COLOR/B&W)

Produced by Susan Fanshel with Deborah Gordon, John Adair. Directed by Fanshel. Camera (color), Robert Achs, Jack Parsons; editor, Fanshel, Gordon; music, Jim Pepper, Ken Werner; sound, Michael Penland, Jack Loeffler. Produced in association with the N.Y. Foundation for the Arts and Wheelwright Museum of the American Indian. Reviewed at the Berlin Film Festival (Forum), Feb. 25, 1987. Running time: **60 MINS.**

Berlin — "A Weave Of Time" is a docu portrait of the Navajos of the American Southwest. It avoids an outright condemnation of U.S. government policies which are partly responsible for destroying their traditional ways of life. The inclusion of b&w footage shot by anthropologist John Adair in 1938 carries the docu a bit above average.

Filmmaker Susan Fanshel uses the Adair footage as a point of reference to tell the story of the Burnside family. We see the day-to-day life of an earlier generation and learn about problems facing their descendants today. The film emphasizes the growing loss of native language and crafts like rug weaving. There are no references to the catastrophic land grab by greedy coal interests threatening Navajos in the nearby Four Corners region.

A film made with commitment, but little substantive new information, it might do well going the special screenings route.—*Owl.*

Eau/Ganga
(Water/Ganges)
(INDIAN-FRENCH-DOCU-COLOR)

A Viswanadhan-Musée National d'Art Moderne coproduction. Produced and directed by Viswanadhan. Screenplay, Viswanadhan; camera (color, 16m), Adoor Gopalakrishnan; editor, Philippe Puicouyoul; sound, Jacques Guillot. Reviewed at Berlin Film Festival (Forum), March 2, 1987. Running time: **135 MINS.**

Berlin — Made over a two-year period (1984-85), Viswanadhan's lengthy, poetic docu about the River Ganges was commissioned by France's National Museum of Modern Art. Shot in 16m by the celebrated director Adoor Gopalakrishnan, the film is an extended mood piece, evoking the sights and sounds of India's holy river.

The camera lingers on the water and the people who use it; on the fishermen and the holy men; on the children swimming and the women washing clothes. There are the cattle, wallowing in the water to keep cool, and the men working antiquated irrigation equipment.

There are the towns and villages on the river's bank, the palaces, old forts and shrines. There are the myths and legends surrounding the river, the beauty and the poverty.

All of this is told purely in visuals, sans commentary, but with haunting music, mostly of a local religious nature. It's a film that requires patience from a sympathetic audience, but it weaves its spell, though is probably better seen out of the crowded context of a major international film festival. It's a delicate, gentle experience.—*Strat.*

Pesti Ve Tme
(Fists In The Dark)
(CZECH-COLOR)

A Barrandov Studios, Ceskoslovensky Film, production. Executive producer, Milan Futera. Directed by Jaroslav Soukup. Screenplay, Soukup, Jaroslav Vokral; camera (color), Richard Valenta; editor, Jiri Brosek; music, Zdenek Bartak Jr.; production design, Jiri Hlupy; sound, A. Vrbata; assistant director, Vaclav Kristek. Reviewed at Berlin Film Festival (Market), Feb. 25, 1987. Running time: **99 MINS.**

Jakub Vilda . . . . Marek Vasut
Ema Gabrielova . . . . Eliska Balzerova
Blanka Adamova . . . . Jana Krauzova
Kurt Schaller . . . . Josef Nedorost
Also with: F. Kruta, J. Vinklar, P. Novy, K. Hermanek, Jiri Tomek.

Berlin — "Fists In The Dark" is a well made, true-life drama, set in 1936, about a champion Czech boxer, Jakub Vilda, and his two boxing bouts with German champ Kurt Schaller.

The "Rocky" influence is much in evidence, but "Fists In The Dark" has additional resonance because it really happened.

Pic opens in Berlin with Vilda beating his rival, until his manager throws in the towel. The disgusted Czech returns home to Prague and finds himself a new manger to prepare him for a re-match. (He later learns the first manager was pressured by Nazis to throw the fight.)

Against a background of increasing German influence on Czechoslovakia, Vilda discovers his girl, a nurse, has left him for a doctor; at first he doesn't realize she's helping Jewish refugees escape Germany. He himself becomes involved with a German actress, older than he, popular in Czech films being made at the time (some fascinating scenes on the set). When the rematch comes, in a packed Prague venue, it's a bitter affair which is won by the Czech, with fatal results for his actress friend who has been under Nazi pressure to make sure Germany doesn't lose.

Despite some conventional trappings, the political background and the old-fashioned skill with which the film has been made make "Fists In The Dark" worth seeing. Production design is first class, camerawork is of a h igh standard, and a mournful trumpet score is very apealing. Marek Vasut is convincing in the lead, and the boxing scenes are staged expertly.

A final title tells us Vilda was killed in 1943 when flying as a pilot in the Czech unit of the RAF.
—*Strat.*

Bar-cel-ona
(SPANISH-COLOR)

A presentation of the Cinematografia de la Generalitat de Catalunya, Barcelona. Produced by Center Promotor de la Image, Betania, Spain. Executive producer, Jordi Tusell. Directed by Ferran Llagostera i Colli. Screenplay, Josep Albanelli; camera (color), Antonio Ono. Reviewed at Berlin Film Festival (Market), Feb. 22, 1987. Running time: **90 MINS.**

Manolo . . . . Alfred Luchetti
Ona . . . . Ovidi Montllor

Berlin — "Bar-cel-ona" is hyphenated because nice girl Ona is part of the title. Ona is a vivacious teenager, and she represents the romantic, infectious spirit of Barcelona, which we are to love.

Barcelona is the capital and chief port of Catalunya, a province within Spain long esteemed for its independent spirit, having its own language, culture and tradition. "Barcel-ona" connects with all that, as a popular entertainment.

Ona, as an attractive "Miss Fixit" character, personifies the charm of the city. She is the lure that keeps young restless guitarist Manolo there, despite the steamer ticket in his pocket. In one long day together, they endure various comic adventures until at last, at night, Manolo realizes Barcelona and Ona are alike, as one. He must love them and stay with them. They are nice clean kids, but curiously among their young friends one sees lots of casual drugs and sex, about which the film expresses no moral disapproval.—*Hitch.*

Heartstrings: Peter, Paul & Mary In Central America
(DOCU-COLOR)

A First Run Features release of a New Tomorrow/The American Council production. Executive producer, Margery Tabaukin. Associate producer, Brenda Goodman. Produced, written and directed by Ana Carrigan. Stars Peter Yarrow, Noel Paul Stookey, Mary Travers. Camera (color), Foster Wylie; editor, Juliet Weber; location sound, Jack Krieger. Reviewed as part of Global Village Docu Festival, Global Village, N.Y., April 20, 1987. Running time: **60 MINS.**

As an accessible mass-market vehicle to raise uninformed American consciousness about the damage caused by U.S. involvement in Central America, the docu "Heartstrings: Peter, Paul & Mary In Central America" is effective. It more than makes up in earnestness and good intentions for what it lacks in giving any real insights into this problematic region. Rather, this film is a testimony by the trio to inform the U.S. public that despite its political feelings in the matter, the continued warfare is exacting a heavy toll on the civilian population.

After completing a 60-concert national tour in 1985-86, the seasoned folk music trio Peter, Paul & Mary put up $85,000 of their own money to coproduce this docu of a factfinding visit to El Salvador and Nicaragua, highlighted by a few goodwill concerts. What emerged is a personal account of the group and their emotional encounters with civilians and also officials from both sides in each country visited. Pic begins in El Salvador, engaged in a seven-year civil war, before moving on to Nicaragua, whose socialist government is under seige by the U.S.-backed Contras.

The tone of the film can best be summed up by Mary Travers, who noted before the opening credits that as an American, she wasn't prepared for what she saw and heard on the trip. And as Americans, their responses to what they see and hear is often compassion and naive amazement.

For anyone acquainted with the area, the group's innocence is astounding. While talking to displaced persons living in wretched conditions in a Salvadoran refugee camp, they ask: "Why won't your president do something?" "Do you feel like a brave person?" they ask a woman concerned with mere survival.

The most striking images from this section comes from the drawings of young children. These drawings depict homes being bombed by helicopters while tiny villagers are threatened by mammoth soldiers carting gigantic rifles.

In Nicaragua, the trio visits hospitals, orphanages, missionaries, refugees and even President Daniel Ortega. At one point, they talk with the Contras hoping to establish dialog and basic understanding.

The main difference between the two countries, they discover, is that in Nicaragua they find hope and excitement, compared to the fear and abandon that marks El Salvador. Yet in both countries it is the civilian population that must bear the brunt of war. A touching encounter with a mother whose daughter was killed by a Contra raid leaves the group comforting their tearful translator, who we later discover was widowed in the same raid.

The images are interspersed with some of the trio's most famous tunes to good results. They sing "Puff The Magic Dragon" to a group of Nicaraguan youngsters; "All My Trials" as their bus rides through the countryside. Tin Managua, they are joined on stage in "If I Had A Hammer" by national singer Luis Enrique Mejía Godoy and the group Mancotal. Other songs include "Blowin' In The Wind," "Day Is Done," "Salvador," "Weave Me The Sunshine" and "Canción Urgente para Nicaragua." Sound level is consistently good.

The photography, both concert footage and on-the-road shots, is varied. Selective editing attempts a montage of impressions much like a travel diary.

The docu is an attempt to reach middle-America through a personal and almost simplistic approach to basic questions: "What is happening in Central America?" "Who are the real losers in these wars?" "How are U.S. tax dollars used to extend suffering in no-win situations?" The answer is blowing in the wind. —Lent.

The Messenger
(U.S.-ITALIAN-COLOR)

Poor Fred Williamson actioner.

A Snizzlefritz release of a Realta Cinematografica-Po' Boy production. Produced by Fred Williamson, Pier Luigi Ciriaci. Directed by Williamson. Screenplay, Brian Johnson, Conchita Lee, Anthony Wisdom, based on a story by Williamson; camera (Fujicolor), Giancarlo Ferrando, Craig Greene; editor, Meuller; music, William Stuckey; casting, Jaki Baskow; no other credits provided. Reviewed at the Woods theater, Chicago, April 23, 1987. (MPAA Rating: R.) Running time: **92 MINS.**
Jake Sebastian Turner . . . . Fred Williamson
Sabrina . . . . Sandy Cummings
Clark . . . . Val Avery
Emerson . . . . Michael Dante
FBI Agent Parker . . . . Chris Connelly
Police Capt. Carter . . . . . Cameron Mitchell
Harris . . . . Peter Turner
Rico . . . . Joe Spinell

Chicago — Fred Williamson, that aging blaxploitation smoothie, is

back again with this muddled actioner, the only interesting point of which is how the money was packaged to get the thing made. B.o. prospects are poor in all but the most product-hungry overseas markets.

Incoherently told plot has Williamson toplining as a former Green Beret, musical prodigy from Chicago who spends three years in an Italian slammer as a gentleman cat burglar. That's touching all bases.

Williamson is reunited with his svelte wife (Sandy Cummings), who's bumped off eight minutes into the picture — not before appearing in a nude love scene showing more of Williamson — because she's involved in an international drug ring. Williamson becomes the "messenger of death" avenging the wife by knocking off white dudes and mobsters in Italy (where much of the pic was lensed), Chicago, Las Vegas and Los Angeles.

Williamson, pushing 50, is getting a bit long in the tooth for this stuff. He appears out of shape trying to resuscitate the bad black stud of his blaxploitation heyday nearly two decades ago. Fight scenes are listless, and briefly staged with Williamson showing signs of fatigue. He still strokes an ample mustache, however, and smokes a mean cigar.

As a director, Williamson is strictly laissez faire, permitting the cast to what it pleases. Results are sporadically amusing.

Cameron Mitchell as a cigar-chomping police captain appears to ad lib much of his dialog and seems to be acting in another movie. Newcomer Sandy Cummings as the wife looks good. Joe Spinell puts in another pleasant turn as an unctuous mobster although his tries at fear and desperation provoke unintended laughs.

Technical credits are generally poor. Pic is an Italo-American coproduction involving Williamson's Po' Boy concern and Italy's Realta Cinematografica.

Even given a severely limited budget, cinematography and sound recording are unusually uneven. Italian footage looks good, while U.S. footage is severely underlit. Sound recording is sub-par throughout. —Sege.

Extreme Prejudice
(COLOR)

Tongue-in-cheek homage to 'The Wild Bunch.'

A Tri-Star Pictures release of a Carolco Pictures production. Produced by Buzz Feitshans. Executive producers, Mario Kassar, Andrew Vajna. Directed by Walter Hill. Stars Nick Nolte. Screenplay, Deric Washburn, Harry Kleiner, from a story by John Milius, Fred Rexer; camera (Technicolor), Matthew F. Leonetti; editor, Freeman Davis; music,

Jerry Goldsmith; production design, Albert Heschong; art direction, Joseph C. Nemec 3d; set designer, Beverli Eagan; costumes, Dan Moore; sound (Dolby), Richard Bryce Goodman; special effects, Tom Fisher; assistant director, Dirk Petersmann; associate producer, Mae Woods; second unit director-stunt coordinator, Bennie Dobbins; casting, Judith Holstra, Marcia Ross. Reviewed at Mann's Chinese theater, Hollywood, April 22, 1987. (MPAA Rating: R). Running time: **104 MINS.**
Jack Benteen . . . . Nick Nolte
Cash Bailey . . . . Powers Boothe
Major Paul Hackett . . . . . Michael Ironside
Sarita Cisneros . . . . Maria Conchita Alonso
Sheriff Hank Pearson . . . . Rip Torn
Sgt. Larry McRose . . . . Clancy Brown
Sgt. Buck Atwater . . . . Wiliam Forsythe
Sgt. Declan Patrick Coker . . Matt Mulhern
Sgt. Charles Briddle . . . . Larry B. Scott
Sgt. Luther Fry . . . . Dan Tullis Jr.

Hollywood — "Extreme Prejudice" is an amusing concoction that is frequently offbeat and at times compelling. Taut direction and editing prevail despite overstaged hyper-violence that is so gratuitous to be farcical. Actioner should strike a chord with a certain crowd domestically and offshore, with some decent payback at the boxoffice.

Story pivots on the adversarial relationship between small town Texas Ranger Nick Nolte and drug kingpin Powers Boothe. Originally childhood friends, they are now on opposite sides of the law and the U.S.-Mexican border.

Presented as a severe and humorless straight arrow, Nolte's character is not easy to like but his acting nonetheless intrigues. Freewheeling and provocative, Boothe is the film's wild card as director Walter Hill signals right off that he's going to have some fun here.

Intro of Boothe shows this cocaine smuggling bad guy attired in pure white suit and brim as he fondles a scorpion before squeezing it to death. Thunderous score by Jerry Goldsmith, whose work is apropos throughout, heightens the whimsical touch.

Best aspect of the plot is involvement of a commando unit of U.S. military men operating under deep cover. Led by Michael Ironside, this squad employs the latest high tech gadgetry and weapons as they slip into town on a mission involving Boothe's drug-related cash and records. Their activity and connections are deftly revealed in a way that keeps one fascinated regardless of the parallel Nolte-Boothe conflict.

Presence early on of Rip Torn as the local sheriff adds a colorful touch since portrayal is of such full dimension. His swift dispatch surely stands as the film's greatest lost opportunity.

As Nolte, Boothe and the commandos move toward the ultimate showdown, violence escalates and the fetish in some quarters for stylized violence takes hold. Hill seems

to relish the explosives more than just about any other aspect of the pic as semi-automatics blaze away.

In any case, story proceeds through some interesting twists on the commando front while Nolte and Boothe try to reconcile their friendship and separate paths.

Noisy windup gets out of hand with some grotesque gunplay, but Boothe gets a chance to play his role to the hilt.

Through it all, pic is suspenseful enough to maintain audience interest. Production values are tops.
—Tege.

The Princess Academy
(U.S.-YUGOSLAV-FRENCH-COLOR)

An Empire Pictures release of a Cloverleaf-Jadran-Sofracima production. Executive producer, Fred Weintraub. Produced by Sandra Weintraub. Directed by Bruce Block. Screenplay, Sandra Weintraub, from an idea by Fred Weintraub; camera (color), Kent Wakeford; editor, Martin Cohen; music, Roger Bellon; sound, M. Curtis Price, Gregory H. Watkins, Leonard Peterson; Eva Gabor's wardrobe, Nolan Miller; casting, Myrna Meth (U.S.), Paul Defreitas (Yugoslavia). Reviewed at Empire Pictures, L.A., April 24, 1987. (MPAA rating: R.) Running time: **90 MINS.**
Countess . . . . Eva Gabor
Cindy . . . . Lar Park Lincoln
Fraulein Stickenschmidt . . . . . . Lu Leonard
Drago . . . . Richard Paul
Sonia . . . . Carole Davis
Sarah . . . . Badar Howar
Izzie . . . . Barbara Rovsek
Pamela . . . . Yolande Palfrey
Lulu . . . . Britt Helfer

Hollywood — It would be more fun to kiss a frog than to sit through "The Princess Academy." Film has no redeeming social values and it's not even rated X — even though filmmakers tried very hard to insert as many lines as possible about virginity, reaching sexual ecstasy and how to fake "it" (and mostly when the pretty young things are parading around in lacy Frederick's of Hollywood-like corsets).

Each of the teenage lovlies in this picture represent a different nationality with a couple of things in common — they want to meet a rich guy (hopefully titled) and have sex. Only holdout is Cindy (Lar Park Lincoln), a winner of the first scholarship to the prestigious Swiss Von Pupsin Academy who is a really sweet but easily influenced juvenile delinquent.

Lincoln become the fall gal when the other girls' antics get out of hand at the local brothel. That's where they've arranged a secret rendezvous for two lovesick virgins, one from the girls' school and one from the boys' school. The Von Pupsin Academy's taskmaster Fraulein Stickenschmidt (Lu Leonard in her classic butch character) busts in and breaks up the festivities. The girls then blackmail her for her lascivious ways with the school's spineless administrator (Richard Paul).

One wonders who the target audience is for such drivel, except maybe pre-teenage boys who don't care a whit about dialog and just want to see girls' bodies in any shape, way or form. Adult men would rent a porno film instead and girls of all ages would — or should — be insulted and the actresses ashamed.

In one scene, four of the girls prepping a virgin for her big night try their best to instruct her how to moan in the most convincing way to fake a climax.

Executive producer Fred Weintraub ("Enter the Dragon," "Outlaw Blues") would be wise to rethink what direction he intends to follow as an indie filmmaker if he wants to salvage his reputation. Ditto his daughter, Sandra Weintraub, who is pic's producer and screenwriter. — *Brit.*

Nice Girls Don't Explode
(COLOR)

Mixing explosions with romance doesn't make a fired-up film.

A New World Pictures release of the Nice Girls production. Produced by Doug Curtis, John Wells. Directed by Chuck Martinez. Stars Barbara Harris, Michelle Meyrink. Screenplay, Paul Harris; camera (color), Steven Katz; editor, Wende Phifer Mate; music, Brian Banks, Anthony Marinelli; production designer, Sarina Rotstein; costumes, Belinda Wells; executive in charge of production, Bob Stein; associate producers, Jim Moores, Belinda Wells, Paul Harris; makeup, Margaret Sunshine. Reviewed at the Bannister Square theater, Kansas City, Mo., April 16, 1987. (MPAA Rating: PG.) Running time: **92 MINS.**
Mom . . . . Barbara Harris
April . . . . Michelle Meyrink
Andy . . . . William O'Leary
Ellen . . . . Wallace Shawn
Ken . . . . James Nardini
Little April . . . . Margot Gray
Little Andy . . . . Jonas Baugham
Dr. Stewart . . . . William Kuhlke

Kansas City — Nice girls don't explode, but the nice girl, Michelle Meyrink, in this tight-budgeter can cause explosions and set fires. That's because of a quirky metabolism which causes a nearby plant, or tree, or car, or other item to go up in flames, or burst apart when she gets near a young man, especially if there is any romantic inclination. The curse is involuntary, a legacy given to her while still in the womb by her mother who swallowed a toxic substance. Mom (Barbara Harris), carries on the legacy with a magnified possessive instinct, setting some fires and explosions on her own, if daughter's syndrome doesn't function.

Much of this fiery outburst focuses on William O'Leary as the childhood sweetheart grown up,

who perserveres through losing his car, his clothes blown to tatters and his face blackened. He doesn't buy Mom's story about the metabolism, suspects Mom is the perpetrator and suggests to Michelle that they can prove it by bedding together when Mom isn't around. So it is, and Mom is forced to lay down her explosives and permit romance to have its way.

While the story idea is farout, it is no more so than a score of other current releases that go in for si-fi and/or special effects. This one doesn't make the front burner, as director Chuck Martinez fails to get the most out of his players and scripter Paul Harris leaves too many episodes unlaced. Her role gives Harris little chance to be assertive and she comes off as a limpid little mother. Meyrink is adequate as the romance-thwarted daughter. Young O'Leary puts some spirit into his assignment and probably is the best of the lead roles. Wallace Shawn is wasted as the escaped pyromaniac.

Some special interest attaches to the film as much of it was produced in and around nearby Lawrence, Kan., on a shoestring of $1,000,000. It preemed in Lawrence, and was pre-released in the K.C., Colorado Springs and Austin, Texas, markets.

Costuming is neatly contemporary, and some camerawork is first-rate. Some of the sets ring true, but on too many the cardboard shows through. The direction fails to set up the comedy lines, and a flow of would-be laughs — such as about the ping pong scholarship to China — draw nary a snicker. Pyrotechnics are plentiful and effective. Up against the general flow of big screen features today, the entertainment glow from this one is little more than that from a pilot-light.
— *Quin.*

My Demon Lover
(COLOR)

Minor horror comedy.

A New Line Cinema release of a Robert Shaye production. Executive producers, Pierre David, Larry Thompson. Produced by Shaye. Directed by Charles Loventhal. Screenplay, Leslie Ray; camera (color), Jacques Haitkin; editor, Ronald Roose; music, David Newman; production design, Brent Swift; art direction, Douglas Dick; coproducer, Sara Risher; special makeup effects, Carl Fullerton, John Caglione Jr., Neal Martz, Doug Drexler. Reviewed at Embassy 2 theater, N.Y., April 24, 1987 (MPAA Rating: PG-13.) Running time: **86 MINS.**
Kaz. . . . . Scott Valentine
Denny . . . . Michelle Little
Fixer . . . . Arnold Johnson
Charles . . . . Robert Trebor
Capt. Phil Janus . . . . Alan Fudge
Sonia . . . . Gina Gallego

Horror fans going to see "My Demon Lover" will hardly be on the

edge of their seats and the laughs aren't as abundant as they could be, but the pic's personable Scott Valentine (of the tv sitcom "Family Ties") and offbeat premise combine for a mildly diverting movie.

The film opens on the well-cast Michelle Little as Denny — a meek girl whose long string of bad relationships continues as she watches her current boyfriend rob her Manhattan apartment and leave her.

Kaz (Scott Valentine) is a girl-crazed streetperson who chases any woman in sight, and, when sexually aroused, transforms into a variety of demonic beings. When Kaz wakes up one day in a pile of garbage and spots Denny dining at an outdoor eatery, he talks with her till he must (literally) turn tail and run.

Women are getting killed in the city by something dubbed "the Mangler," although there is little onscreen depiction of the beast's violent crimes. One of the victims who survives is the sister of Denny's

friend Sonia, a psychic who owns an antique knife store (two plot elements that figure heavily into the pic's climax).

A street psychic looks into Kaz' past and reveals that Kaz has been "pazzassed," and that the only way to rid himself of the curse is to do something noble. The funniest scenes in the film center on Kaz' developing relationship with the relationship-hungry Denny, as he gradually makes her believe the seriousness of his sexual problems.

Unfortunately, only occasionally does "My Demon Lover" manage to capitalize on the fine line between real horror and comedy, and that unique tension is all but lost as the film barrels its way toward a convenient conclusion.

Gina Gallego as Sonia and Robert Trebor as Charles are strong in their supporting roles, and the special effects range from nifty to poor.
— *Roy.*

Films At Cannes Fest

Cronaca di una Morte Annunciata
(Chronicle Of A Death Foretold)
(ITALIAN-FRENCH-COLOR)

An Istituto Luce/Italnoleggio Cinematografico release of an Italmedia Film (Rome)/Soprofilms/Les Films Ariane/FR 3 Films Production (Paris) coproduction, in association with RAI-2. Produced by Yves Gasser, Francis Von Büren. Directed by Francesco Rosi. Stars Rupert Everett, Ornella Muti. Screenplay, Rosi, Tonino Guerra, from the novel by Gabriel Garcia Marquez; camera (Super Techniscope, Eastmancolor), Pasqualino De Santis; editor, Ruggero Mastroianni; music, Piero Piccioni; art director, Andrea Crisanti; costumes, Enrico Sabbatini. Reviewed at Fonoroma, Rome, April 23, 1987. (In Competition at Cannes Film Festival.) Running time: **109 MINS.**
Bayardo San Roman . . . . . . Rupert Everett
Angela Vicario . . . . Ornella Muti
Cristo Bedoya . . . . Gian Maria Volonté
Angela's mother . . . . Irene Papas
Santiago's mother . . . . Lucia Bosè
Santiago Nasar . . . . Anthony Delon
Also with: Alain Cuny (widower), Sergi Mateu (young Cristo Bedoya), Carolina Rosi (Flora Miguel), Caroline Lang (Margot), Silverio Blasi, Carlos Miranda, Rogerio Miranda, Leonor Gonzales, Vicky Hernandez, Edgardo Roman.

Rome — The combination of Francesco Rosi's intelligent moral gaze on the violence and constricting traditions of Southern society, and writer Gabriel Garcia Marquez' fantasy and emotion, proves a powerful duo in "Chronicle Of A Death Foretold." Love and death are the intertwining vines of the tale, set in the torbid atmosphere of a sleepy Colombian river town in the 1950s. With an international cast headlining attractive young players Rupert Everett, Ornella

Muti and Anthony Delon, pic promises to generate the chronicle of a happy boxoffice foretold.

Essentially faithful to the book, film opens in the present day, when Cristo Bedoya (Gian Maria Volontè) returns to the town he grew up in and relives the tragic death of his best friend, Santiago Nasar. Anthony Delon plays Santiago as a sensual young rake, only child of the patrician Lucia Bosè. His carefree life is terminated abruptly one sunny day by twin brothers forced by society's antiquated code of honor to revenge the loss of their sister's virginity, presumably (but not unquestionably) at Santiago's hands.

Skipping back and forth in time, Rosi and editor Ruggero Mastroianni cinematically underline the inevitability of the tragedy, while rather contradictorily pointing an accusing finger at those who did nothing to avoid it. The guilty are not so much the reluctant pair of killers as the townsfolk, who seem to enjoy the atmosphere of scandal. They stand around and watch events leading up to the murder like spectators at a sports match they hope won't be canceled.

The stranger who arrives in town to set events in motion is Bayardo San Roman (Rupert Everett), a rich drifter who courts the sultry Angela Vicario (Ornella Muti) and finally marries her. Everett is a curious casting choice for a Latin character, particularly in pic's "original language" version where he speaks English in the heart of Colombia for no good reason. Certainly credible as an eccentric, he is harder to swallow as a champion of manly honor when he packs his bride back to her family on the wedding night, precipitating the tragedy. Despite some slippages, however, Marquez' story has a magic resonance that sweeps everything along before it in an irresistibly romantic ending, with the unexpected triumph of love between the gray-haired protagonists. Santiago's senseless death is, for the moment, shelved.

Lenser Pasqualino De Santis makes superb use of a new Super-Techniscope camera to bring out the grandeur of the landscape, much of it shot on location and parts beautifully reconstructed by art director Andrea Crisanti. Biggest technical credit, though, goes to composer Piero Piccioni's moving, melodic score, relied on heavily throughout pic to up the emotion.—*Yung.*

Pokayaniye
(Repentance)
(SOVIET-COLOR)

A Studio Gruzia Film (Tblisi) production. World sales: Sovexport. Screenplay by Tengiz Abuladze, Rezo Kveselava, Nana Dzhanelidze. Directed by Abuladze; camera (Orwo-color) Mikhail Agranovitj, editor, uncredited; production design, Georgi Mikeladze; music score selector, Dzhanelidze. Reviewed at private screening, Malmö, Sweden, April 26, 1987. (In competition at the Cannes Film Festival.) Running time: **145 MINS.**
Varlam Aravidze (father) and Abel Aravidze
(son) .... Avtandil Makharadze
Guliko .... Ija Ninidze
Tornike .... Merab Ninidze
Ketevan Barateli .... Zejnab Botsvadze
Nino Barateli .... Ketevan Abuladze
Sandro Barateli ...... Edisher Giorgobiani
Mikhail Korisheli .... Kahki Kavsadze
Elena Korisheli ...... Nino Zakariadze
Ketevan (child) .... Nato Otjigava
Abel (child) .... Dato Kemkhadze

Malmö — As an unexpected export item, Tengiz Abuladze's Georgian-language feature film "Repentance" is the fairest child yet (its production year is 1984) of the current *glasnost* policy of artistic freedom and is sure to be received with huzzahs everywhere. Picture is, however, hardly a shoo-in beyond the art exhibition circuit.

"Repentance" is on continuous tragedy-cum-farce, constantly unsettling in its effects, some of which are special indeed, highly entertaining, too, even if slightly overburdened with dialog (in Georgian, the production coming out of Stalin's home state) and engrossingly dramatic and striking in its visual values. Kafkaesque moods and Buñuel imagery are obvious inspirations throughout.

A late dictator's grave is being violated repeatedly by a woman with a grievance, and she now stands before the judges of a state that is never pinpointed in time or fashion: the judges wear wigs like in a British court, the prisoners,

dressed in modern clothes, are taken away in Medieval horse-drawn wagons, etc. What makes the woman's acts especially alarming is that the dead man now keeps popping up to give trouble like Hitchcock's "Harry."

The dictator's son, himself a high official with vested interests, would like his father to remain buried and one day slaps his own son for being too inquisitive about the old man's deeds. The result is that the youngster literally shoulders the burdens of his grandfather's sins and commits suicide.

The sins in question include the old tyrant's dealings with a friend, a painter. He woos the painter to win him over for his cause, but the painter refuses him and is then exiled to Siberia. Later he is tortured and crucified upside down in an old church, now converted into a science lab. Symbolism and allegory need no learned keys to deciphering anywhere in Abuladze's film, yet the club of sanctimonious propaganda is never yielded.

The gist of picture's moral is that art and individual freedom will prevail. When the painter is crucified, the walls of the church instantly catch fire. The artist's wife, not knowing about his destiny, goes down to the river in the hope of finding his name or a message from him carved in the timber coming from the north. She finds nothing, but another woman on a similar errand does and is seen embracing the dead wood, talking to it and finally kissing it like it was truly the mouth of her loved one.

All acting (with Avtandil Makharadze doing a cunning job of playing both the grotesque dictator figure and the dictator's son struggling with his conscience) is subjugated neatly to story's natural flow, but Makharadze is likely to strike everybody as their own heart's Mr. Everyman when, towards film's end, he makes sure the dictator stays dead by exhuming him once more this time throwing him down the mountain slope to be eaten by the crows. A more Christian message comes through in picture's final frames where the painter's daughter is in her kitchen decorating a cake with small crosses. Through the window, an old woman asks about the way or road to the church. There is no church, she is told. Why then, she persists, is the road still there?

It would appear relevant to add that Tengiz Abuladze is no flash-in-the-pan. He was born in 1924, is a graduate of the Moscow Film School and has done at least eight feature films. Even to Cannes, he is no newcomer. He won a prize there in 1956 for his short film "Magdan's Donkey." —*Kell.*

The Surfer
(AUSTRALIAN-COLOR)

A Hemdale release (in U.S.) of a Frontier Films production, in association with The Producers Circle. (foreign sales: Overview Films.) Produced by James M. Vernon, Frank Shields. Executive producer, Grahame Jennings. Directed by Shields. Screenplay, David Marsh; camera (Eastmancolor), Michael Edols; editor, Greg Bell; music, Davood Tabrizi; production design, Martin O'Neill; sound, Max Bowring; production manager, Penny Wall; assistant director, John Warren. Reviewed at Chauvel, Sydney, Aug. 1, 1986. (In Directors Fortnight at Cannes Festival.) Running time: **96 MINS.**
Sam Barlow .... Gary Day
Gina .... Gosia Dobrowolska
Hagan .... Rod Mullinar
Calhoun .... Tony Barry
Jack .... Gerard MacGuire
Trish .... Kris McQuade
Slaney .... Stephen Leeder
Murph .... David Glendenning

Sydney — "The Surfer" is a romantic chase thriller, set in Australia's sub-tropical north. Its selection for the Directors Fortnight in Cannes took the local industry by surprise, partly because the Australian film community has usually felt its numerous prestige "serious" films were more likely fest prospects, and partly because this particular pic was greeted without enthusiasm when it competed in last year's Australian Film Awards: it received no nominations.

The basic plot is classical enough. Sam Barlow (Gary Day) is a Vietnam vet who lives in the beach resort of Surfers' Paradise, where he operates a rundown stall hiring out surfing equipment (he's never actually seen to do any surfing in the film). When his best friend is murdered, apparently by a couple of Vietnamese hitmen, Barlow becomes involved.

He discovers a blackmail plot involving a government minister caught in bed with a Vietnamese girl, wife and another vet. Determined to avenge his friend, Barlow comes up against a crooked cop (Tony Barry) and a ruthless mercenary (Rod Mullinar). He also becomes involved with a beautiful, cool blond (Gosia Dobrowolska) who accompanies him on a trip to followup his only real clue: the pending arrival of a ship at one of Queensland's northern ports.

This is the second feature of director Frank Shields, who previously made another thriller, "Hostage' (1983), based on a true story. He also made a prize-winning docu, "The Breaker," some time before Bruce Beresford's fictionalized film about the same character, "Breaker Morant." Working on a low budget, Shields demonstrates a vivid flair for handling action scenes; the first part of the film neatly establishes the plot and principal characters, the central section keeps the protagonists on the move, while allowing time for the inevitable love

affair between the hero and heroine (Dobrowolska is a beauty very much in the Hitchcock tradition of cool blonds), and the climax contains an unexpected twist, revealing the "Macguffin" hasn't been drug smuggling, as we've assumed all along it was.

The pace sags occasionally, and Shields is not yet in the Samuel Fuller league, though this is the area in which he's working. Having this film picked as the only Aussie pic in an official section in Cannes is a bit akin to, say, Fuller's "House Of Bamboo" being selected over Delbert Mann's "Marty" in 1955: in hindsight, maybe not such a bad choice, either.

There certainly will be pros and cons about this one, but it should play off well in action markets no matter what the critics think. And there certainly will be reviewers (though maybe not in Australia) willing to recognize Shields' rough-hewn talens. There's a solid central performance from Day, top-notch support from Tony Barry, as the cop, and the invaluable Kris McQuade, as the murdered man's widow. Given the tightness of the budget, the technical credits are good, with Michael Edols' location lensing deserving special mention. —*Strat.*

Hol Volt, Hol Nem Volt
(A Hungarian Fairy Tale)
(HUNGARIAN-COLOR/B&W)

A Hungarofilm presentation of a Mafilm-Objektiv Studio Budapest production. Directed by Gyula Gazdag. Screenplay, Gazdag, Miklós Györffy; camera (Eastmancolor, b&w), Elemér Ragályi; editor, Júlia Sivó; musical arrangements, István Mártha; sound, György Fék; art direction, József Romvári; costumes, Andrea Flesch. Reviewed at the Budapest Congress Center, Feb. 14, 1987. (In Directors Fortnight at Cannes Film Festival.) Running time: **97 MINS.**
Andris, the boy .... Árpád Vermes
Mária, his mother .... Mária Varga
Orbán, the clerk .... Frantisek Husák
The Girl .... Ezster Csákányi
Also with: Szilvia Tóth, Judit Pógany, Géza Balkay, Gábor Reviczky.

Budapest — One of the more distinguished members of Hungary's younger generation of filmmakers, Gyula Gazdag's new picture is an allegorical fairytale whose references are planted solidly on home ground, but its meaning is valid for the rest of the world as well.

It seems a local law, still in existence, provides that if the name of a child's father hasn't been registered with the authorities by the time he is three, a fictitious one has to be entered in his documents, whether of an existing person or an imaginary one.

A boy born out of one night of magic love, inspired by Mozart's "Magic Flute" which is heard throughout the film, is being raised by his mother. Once the three years are up, she is asked by an officious clerk to invent a name for the boy's father, and she uses the clerk's own family name. Some years later she dies in an accident and, left all alone, the boy sets out to find his father, not knowing the name on the birth certificate is fictitious.

The clerk goes berserk and throws all the paternity files he has compiled so carefully through the years into a fire. Later there is also a nurse who has given up on the system which doesn't allow her to do her job properly, who joins these two, and the trio escapes, in the last sequence, from the grim, unsympathetic realities of life, its moronic bureaucracy and its silly conformism, to an unspecified land. The scene itself is intended by Gazdag as a kind of tribute to Vittorio de Sica's "Mirale In Milan."

Shot in luminous black and white, the presentation and the montage have the brisk pace of a short film, in its brief sequences, telescoped events, economy of dialog and quick characterizations. It was one of the few entries in the Hungarian Week attempting to establish a personal and original film language and bravely tackling challenges all along the way. Characters from a dream sequence all suddenly reappear in real life, and the final shot, showing the three protagonists being borne away on the wings of a stone eagle, is entirely divorced from reality.

Arguing a point which is diametrically opposed to the classical position of modern drama, Gazdag starts by sending his young hero in search for his identity, but concludes by maintaining that only when you are rid of this cumbersome burden can you hope to take off into a better world.

Sophisticated and well directed, the film was awarded the Gene Moskowitz prize by the foreign press here. —*Edna.*

Da Yue Bing
(The Big Parade)
(CHINESE-COLOR)

A China Film release of Xi'an Film Studio production. Directed by Chen Kaige. Screenplay, Gao Lili; camera (Widescreen, color), Zhang Yimou; editor, Zhou Xinxia; music, Qu Xiaosong, Zhao Quiping; production design, He Qun. Reviewed at Hong Kong Film Festival, April 14, 1987. (In Intl. Critics Week at Cannes Film Festival.) Running time: **94 MINS.**

With: Huang Xueqi, Sun Chun, Lu Lei, Wu Ruofu.

Hong Kong — Chen Kaige's 1984 pic "Yellow Earth" was not only a critical breakthrough for Chinese cinema: it has already performed commercially beyond expectations in key territories (Britain and Australia), suggesting that the art house market is ready for quality Chinese films at last. Thus Kaige's second

feature, "The Big Parade," made in 1985 but held up for several months, has been eagerly awaited.

However, the new film is unlikely to find audiences in the West in the same way the first one did. Though superbly made (with magnificent 'Scope photography by Zhang Yimou), pic has a familiar ring to it. The theme involves the training of an airborne squadron to prepare them for the "big parade" — the October, 1984 celebrations of the 35th anniversary of (communist) China in Peking's central square.

A group of men, under a tough veteran, Sergeant Sun, are licked into shape over a period of several weeks. Sun, a character not far removed from the one Clint Eastwood played in "Heartbreak Ridge," but without the love life, is a tough disciplinarian and, as we discover with a shock of surprise, a Vietnam vet. (He was wounded in a later war against the Vietnamese.)

His men are the usual mix of the tough and the more sensitive, the weak and the strong. In the great tradition of this kind of training film, they come to respect the no-nonsense Sun by fadeout. The training scenes are very well handled, with one sequence in which the men stand for three hours in blazing heat in full uniform shot with shimmering images that make the viewer almost as affected as the men themselves. One soldier tries to quit in protest against being treated "like a robot," but sees the error of his ways.

In interviews, Kaige has suggested that the film should be seen as a metaphor for modern China, and that his concern was really "the problems that arise between the individual and the group." The fact that the film has been on the shelf for almost two years suggests the authorities found it, to a degree, subversive in its approach to the subject. These nuances may be lost on the western viewer, who may become confused by the fact that there's first-person narration by not just one, but several characters in the film, and by the fact that, with shaven heads and wearing helmets, it's sometimes difficult to distinguish between the soldiers. Appalling subtitles in the print under review don't help.

Even if, on first viewing, "The Big Parade" is a more conventional film than "Yellow Earth," it's still clearly the work of an accomplished filmmaker, aided by a fine cameraman. The opening helicopter shots of men marching across a seemingly endless parade ground take the breath away.

Based on Kaige's formidable reputation, "The Big Parade" will be in demand at fests where pros and cons may decide its commercial chances in the West.—*Strat.*

L'Eté dernier à Tanger
(Last Summer In Tangiers)
(FRENCH-COLOR)

An ÄAA release of an Ariane Films/Alexandre Films/Films A2 coproduction. Produced and directed by Alexandre Arcady. Screenplay, Arcady, Alain Le Henry, Tito Topin, based on the novel, "The Devil His Due" by William O'Farrell; camera (Agfa-Gevaert color), Robert Alazraki; editor, Luce Grunenvaldt; music, Philippe Sarde; art director, Jean-Louis Poveda; sound, Alain Sempé; costumes, Mic Cheminal; second unit director, Marc Angelo; assistant director, François Charlent; second unit camera, Elso Roque; production managers, Henri Brichetti, Mohammed Lofti. Reviewed at the AMLF screening room, Paris, April 5, 1987. (In Market at Cannes Film Festival.) Running time: **123 MINS.**

Carla/Claudia	Valéria Golino
Corrigan	Thierry Lhermitte
Barrès	Roger Hanin
Roland Barrès	Vincent Lindon
Max Pasquier	Jean Bouise
Gomez	Julien Guiomar
Marcus	Jacques Villeret
Myrrha	Anna Karina
Karim	Saïd Amadis

Paris — "Last Summer In Tangiers" is sunlit *film noir,* being a transposition of a Yank print thriller in a Mediterranean setting. Alexandre Arcady's relocation of a revenge tale by William O'Farrell is otherwise conventional in its display of worldweary private eyes, venal policeman, pompous gangsters and sultry gun-toting beauties. One longs for the chiaroscuro and dark alleys.

Arcady tried a similar genre revamp in his 1981 pic, "The Big Pardon," a sort of Algerian Jewish Godfather saga, in which the corpses were piled as high as the bar mitzvah smorgasbord table. It didn't work, but there was a certain gall and ardeur to the enterprise that's entirely missing here.

Pic opens with a gangland-style massacre in a Tangiers villa, then shoots ahead several years to 1956, when the port city is going through the throes of annexation by Morocco. Arcady and his coscripters bank ineffectually on the socio-historical background enriching the familiar thriller formula.

Italo actress Valéria Golino has the lead role of the massacre victim's daughter returning home to exact revenge on local underworld kingpin Roger Hanin (who was the gottfather of "Big Pardon"). Golino hires local dick Thierry Lhermitte and seduces Hanin's ne'er-do-well son (Vincent Lindon) as she cold-bloodedly proceeds to execute all the thugs involved in her father's murder.

There is much ironic and parodic intent in the scripting, especially in Lhermitte's detective, who dreams of leaving for New York with his cabaret singer-girlfriend (Anna Karina), but Arcady's prosaic, often sentimental direction misses the mark.

Production is glossy.—*Len.*

Le Grand chemin
(The Big Road)
(FRENCH-COLOR)

An AAA release of a Flach Film/Séléna Audiovisuel (AAA)/TF-1 Films coproduction. Produced by Pascal Hommais, Jean-François Lepetit. Written and directed by Jean-Loup Hubert. Camera (Eastmancolor), Claude Lecomte; editor. Raymonde Guyot; music, Georges Granier; art director, Thierry Flamand; sound, Bernard Aubouy; assistant director, Olivier Horlait, Martine Durand; production manager, Farid Chaouche; casting, Marie-Christine Lafosse. Reviewed at Gaumont Ambassade cinema, Paris, April 1, 1987. (In Market at Cannes Film Festival.) Running time: **107 MINS.**

Marcelle	Anémone
Pello	Richard Bohringer
Louis	Antoine Hubert
Martine	Vanessa Guedj
Claire	Christine Pascal
Priest	Raoul Billery
Yvonne	Pascale Roberts
Solange	Marie Matheron
Simon	Daniel Rialet

Paris — "Le Grand chemin" is a bittersweet heartwarmer about a city boy's near-traumatic stay in the country with a childless couple. Scripted from personal memories and directed with warm restraint by Jean-Loup Hubert, this Flach Films ("Three Men And A Cradle") production offers a good blend of pathos and humor, and excellent performances from adult and child thesps alike.

Hubert cast his own son, Antoine, in the pivotal role of a sensitive nine-year-old Parisian packed off by his pregnant mother (Christine Pascal) to spend the summer with an old girlfriend (Anémone) and her husband (Richard Bohringer) in their isolated village.

Disconcerted by the unfamiliar environment, the boy befriends a slightly older local girl who initiates him into the mysteries of rural life. The youngster, troubled by the unexplained separation of his parents, finds himself the object of a tug-of-war between Anémone and Bohringer, who vie for his affections to replace the child they lost at birth years ago.

Hubert's script has conscious echos of René Clément's "Forbidden Games" and other classics about children, but there is freshness and poignancy in his dialog and direction of actors.

The kids, both new to acting, are fetching — Vanessa Guedj, 11, is particularly winning as the savvy, precocious little village girl.

Real acting honors go to Anémone and Bohringer as the embittered rubes whose conjugal life died with their child and who now are wrenched from their repressed states by the presence of the boy.

Tech credits are fine.—*Len.*

Epidemic
(DANISH-B&W/COLOR)

An Obel Film release of Element Film production with the Danish Film Institute. Produced by Jacob Eriksen. Film Institute producer-consultant, Claes Kastholm Hansen. Directed by Lars von Trier. Screenplay, von Trier, Niels Vörsel. Camera, (Eastmancolor), Henning Bendtsen, (b&w, 16m), Kristoffer Nyholm, others; editor, von Trier, Thomas Krag; sound, Peter Engleson; music, Peter Bach, Wagner, J.S. Bach and composite; special effects, Sören Gam Henriksen; production manager, Per Arman. Reviewed at IFT screening room, Copenhagen, April 27, 1987. (In the Un Certain Regard section of Cannes Film Festival.) Running time: **106 MINS.**

16m sequences:
The Film Director . . . . Lars von Trier
The Screenwriter . . . . Niels Vörsel
Udo Kier . . . . Udo Kier
Writer's wife . . . . Susanne Ottesen
Film Institute
producer . . . . Claes Kastholm Hansen
Hypnotist . . . . Svend Ali Hamann
His Medium . . . . Gitte Lind
Oenologist . . . . Jörgen Christian Krüff
Customs' officer . . . . . Jan Kornum Larsen
35m color sequences:
Nurse . . . . Caecilia Holbek
Pathologist . . . . Olaf Ussing
Neurologist . . . . Ib Hansen
Orthopedist . . . . Ole Ernst
Epidemiologist . . . . Lars von Trier
Priest . . . . Michael Simpson
Librarian . . . . Michael Gelting
Also with: Allan de Waal, Colin Gilder, Anja Hemmingsen, Kirsten Hemmingsen, Gert Holbek, Leif Magnusson, Gunner Ottesen, Lennart Pasborg, Tony Shine, others.

Copenhagen — Lars von Trier, undoubtedly Scandinavia's most experimentally daring and technically most dazzling filmmaker, now at work (his "The Element Of Crime" was a Prix Technique winner at Cannes in 1984), has done "Epidemic" on a dare at a subminimal budget and sees it as an intermission Part 2 of a trilogy begun with "Crime."

"Epidemic," filmed mostly in black & white, features primarily the director himself, his screenwriter and their private cohorts, while a handful of professional actors are seen in sharply etched cameos. A story of a kind is told about helmer and writer devoting 18 months to thinking about a horror film, which has been promised a government production grant, and coming up at the end with only a few visualized sequences and a 12-page plot outline.

This may sound like self-indulgence — and it is. Outside of highly specialized situations, "Epidemic" will find the going tough. Still, such is von Trier's cinematic wizardry that his once acknowledged mastery of technique and dramatics should have at least the international fest circuit clamoring to see what he has been doing as an encore after his previous opus, which was an English-language futuristic shocker.

The greater part of "Epidemic" is filmed in 16m and constitutes a tongue-in-cheek rendition of von Trier's and writer Niels Vörsel's kicking ideas around during researching and side trips to secret library vaults; hospital pathology departments; labs specializing in rat behavior; sessions with an oenologist describing the "noble rot" that precedes the harvesting of great white grapes; and to Germany to travel among atomic energy plant towers and to listen to actor Udo Kier telling about his pre-natal experiences during a World War II bombing raid on Cologne.

Bits of Wagnerian music and allusions to Wagnerian lore are dropped along this grainy, but always beautifully framed and moving excursion into non-action, and there is plenty of sly wit and farcical sleight-of-hand to go with it. In between, we get the 35m parts (color film, but subdued to match the b&w sequences). Here, we have the late Carl Dreyer's favorite cinematographer Henning Bendtsen gloriously at work again after years of retirement.

The 35m bits come as jolts of astonishing, slightly surrealistic imagery combining to indicate what the two young filmmakers really had in mind if only they might get a right angle on things. It would be the story of an idealist epidemologist (played by von Trier in a neatly non-committing performance) who, with his doctor's bag of needles and antidotes, ventures outside the big city that has been sealed off in anticipation of the arrival of a rumored plague.

What the young doctor does not know is that somebody has planted the plague virus in his bag and that there will be no plague victims anywhere until that bag is once opened. Scenes of classical horror follow, but they are all restricted to fantasy flashes with suitably obscure dialog to go with them.

There is really some great horror stuff budding here, and audiences may well wish that von Trier had scrapped the filmmaker-at-work parts in favor of going all out on the real McGhoul. They will have to wait until von Trier scares up the international financing he needs for his trilogy's Part 3, existing already in screenplay form under the title "The Grand Mal." However, just as the mood and immediacy of the toils, troubles and fun of the two auteurs tend to flag, von Trier comes up with a surprise ending that is, in any sense of the word, a true scream. —*Kell.*

Smrt Krásných Srncu
(Death Of A Beautiful Dream)
(CZECH-COLOR)

A Ceskoslovenský Filmexport release of a Barrandov Film Studios production. Directed by Karel Kachyňa. Stars Karel Heřmánek. Screenplay, Kachyňa, based on the novel by Ota Pavel; camera (color), Vladimír Smutný; music, Luboš Fišer; art direction, Karel Lier. Reviewed at Dag Hammarskjöld Library, United Nations, N.Y., April 3, 1987. (In Market at Cannes Film Festival.) Running time: **90 MINS.**
Leo Popper . . . . Karel Heřmánek
Herma Popper . . . . Marta Vančurová
Little Ars . . . . Mirek Valter
Hugo . . . . Jan Jiránek
Jenda Hermansky . . . . Jiří Krampol
Irma Korálková . . . . Dana Vlková
Jirka . . . . Jiří Stach
Karel Prosek . . . . Rudolf Hrusínský
Horalek . . . . Ladislav Potmesil

The feature "Death Of A Beautiful Dream," by Czechoslovak filmmaker Karel Kachyňa, is another attempt to define the turbulent years of World War II. Yet, its personal and often comic approach will give it the appeal needed to compete in the international arena.

With a screenplay by Kachyňa, film is adapted from the popular short autobiographical novel of the same name by journalist and author Ota Pavel, based on memories of his father. Like Pavel, Kachyňa knows how to change horses gracefully in mid-stream by charming the audience to enter into the narrative through use of light comedy and then, suddenly presenting them with something infinitely richer — a moral tale of human proportions.

The film revolves around the character and exploits of Leo Popper (Karel Heřmánek), an ardent fisherman and enterprising vacuum-cleaner salesman for Elektrolux during the years preceding the Nazi invasion of Czechoslovakia. Leo is a vibrant, inventive man full of joie de vivre, who is happily married and has three sons he loves dearly. Like any good traveling salesman, he is also prone to a few capricious adventures on the road, including amorous attempts on the boss' curvacious wife.

The first part of the film is episodic and rollicking as we follow the freewheeling and hilarious hijinks of our quixotic hero. It is not until past the pic's halfway point, when the Nazis come into control, that the film shows its serious side. The top salesman is dismissed from his job as the audience suddenly discovers that Leo is Jewish.

The film's title "Smrt Krásných Srncu" translates literally as "The Death Of The Beautiful Roebucks," and refers to the pic's central metaphor: the deer that inhabit the forest where Leo goes to fish. Leo regards the deer as sacred and creatures of innocence, beauty and grace. When Leo's two eldest sons receive notice that they will be sent to a concentration camp, Leo is forced to kill the deer in order to give the boys sufficient food.

Acting talents by the entire cast rate high, but kudos must be lauded to Heřmánek who goes believably from a sympathetic comic character to the serious dramatic role of a man at odds with what he believes in defense of his family's survival.

Photography by Vladimír Smutný is lush and imaginative in capturing pic's fragile tone through movement and close cropping of images. The editor too knows exactly when to pick up the pace and when to let the audience dwell on different scenes. Karel Lier's able art direction has lovingly recreated the time period with close attention to detail.

Pic's uncertain ending leaves the audience stunned and yet with a feeling of optimism by the appearance of a narrator, who tells us that someone has survived to present this train of memories and impressions that live on.

"Death Of A Beautiful Dream" is one of those rare films that rides a fine line successfully and glides smoothly from one genre to another with such grace that the audience suddenly finds itself caught up in a human tragedy and is defenseless to resist its pathos. —*Lent.*

L'Association des malfaiteurs
(Association Of Wrongdoers)
(FRENCH-COLOR)

An AMLF release of a Films 7/FR3 Films coproduction. Produced and directed by Claude Zidi. Screenplay, Zidi, Simon Mickael, Michel Fabre, Didier Kaminka; camera (Eastmancolor), Jean-Jacques Tarbes; editor, Nicole Saunier; music, Francis Lai; sound, Jean-Louis Ughetto; Olivier Mauffroy; art director, Françoise Deleu; costumes, Olga Pelletier; assistant director, Stéphane Clavier; casting, Mammade; production manager, Pierre Gauchet. Reviewed at Marignan-Concorde cinema, Paris, March 20, 1987. (In Market at Cannes Film Festival.) Running time: **108 MINS.**
Gérard . . . . Christophe Malavoy
Thierry . . . . François Cluzet
Francis . . . . Gérard Lecaillon
Daniel . . . . Jean-Claude Leguay
Claire . . . . Claire Nebout
Bernard Hassler . . . . Jean-Pierre Bisson
Tonton Gadin . . . . Hubert Deschamps
Monique . . . . Véronique Genest

Paris — "Association des malfaiteurs" is sporadically successful entertainment with much of its energy generated by screen gagsmith Claude Zidi's brisk direction and the vigorously appealing performances by Christophe Malavoy and François Cluzet.

Zidi displayed unusual flair for dramatic comedy in his smash 1984 "Les Ripoux" (My New Partner). After a failed return to his old stamping grounds of low comedy ("Les Rois du gag" in 1985), the helmer is back with another psychologically toned situation comedy, coscripted by "Ripoux" collaborators Didier Kaminka and Simon Mickael.

Sags come in the screenplay, which lacks the tart coherent flavor of "Les Ripoux" and takes too long and too many detours before getting to the dramatic payoff. There are enough cleverly turned situations and bright interplay between the main characters to confirm this vein of comedy as one Zidi will hopefully persevere in.

Malavoy and Cluzet play two hot-shot young business execs on the run from police after being accused of stealing a large sum of money from the safe of an unscrupulous tycoon (Jean-Pierre Bisson), a former business school classmate who has become their principal bugbear.

The bizarre predicament is the result of a practical joke Malavoy and Cluzet play on a luckless colleague (Jean-Claude Leguay), whose utopian business speculations have led him nowhere. The prank of making Leguay think he has won big in a national lottery backfires when he buys a worthless piece of land from Bisson, putting his mother's shop up as security.

When Bisson brutally refuses to refund the check, Malavoy and Cluzet stoop to underworld methods by stealing his safe, which also contains several million dollars Bisson is holding for certain shady political transactions.

Retrieving the check, the friends return the safe and its contents, but Bisson nonetheless presses charges, accusing them of having also kept the money. Malavoy and Cluzet, unable to prove Bisson is lying, escape from the police and hole up in a suburban garage, from which they plot to again rob their nemesis in order to "return" the allegedly purloined cash.

Subsidiary plot developments, sometimes belatedly woven into the main action, include Cluzet's girl friend (Claire Nebout), who uses Bisson's attraction to her to help the fugitives, and a former flame of Malavoy's (Véronique Genest) who has since become a police commissioner and is assigned to the case.

Tech credits are solid. —*Len.*

Xiangnu Xiao-xiao
(Xiao-xiao — A Girl From Hunan)
(CHINESE-COLOR)

A China Film release of a Beijing Youth Film Studio production. Directed by Xie Fei. Screenplay, Zhang Xian, from the novel by Shen Congwen; camera (Widescreen, color), Fu Jingsheng; editor, Zhang Lanfang; production design, Xing Zheng. Reviewed at Hong Kong Film Festival, April 21, 1987. (In the Un Certain Regard section, Cannes Film Festival.) Running time: **99 MINS.**

With: Na Renhua, Liu Qing, Deng Xiaoquang, Ni Meling.

Hong Kong — It seems a bit early for Chinese filmmakers to be remaking their modern classics, but this item is a virtual remake of Huang Jianzhong's 1984 pic, "A Girl Of Good Family." Tale is set earlier this century and tells the sad story of Xiao-xiao, a 12-year-old peas-

ant girl forced to enter into an arranged marriage: her husband, a baby of two, is still being suckled by his mother at the time of the nuptials.

Story unfolds predictably. Four years on, Xiao-xiao catches the lustful eye of a farmhand; the inevitable happens in the hayloft during a convenient rainstorm from which both are sheltering. Xiao-xiao seems to enjoy the experience, because she comes back for more, and before long she's pregnant. Only then does she realize the rigid clan laws of the village call for the death by drowning of a woman caught committing adultery.

Abandoned by her lover, the 16-year-old seeks religious consolation in a temple, but finally runs off, though she returns to face the music. Ultimately, the cycle will repeat itself; Xiao-xiao will herself agree to an arranged marriage for her son.

Source of the screenplay is a famous novel by Shen Congwon, set in the 1920s. For audiences who haven't seen "A Girl Of Good Family," "Xiao-xiao" will be a fascinating experience; but those who know the earlier film will find themselves in overly familiar territory. Pic is very well made, with lush photography of the village and its environs. It has been selected for the Un Certain Regard section of the Cannes Film Festival. —*Strat.*

Sofía
(Sophia)
(ARGENTINE-COLOR)

A Rosafrey release of a Rosafrey y Susy Surany y Asociados production. Produced by Diana Frey. Directed by Alejandro Doria. Stars Dora Baret, Héctor Alterio, Graciela Dufau. Screenplay, Doria, Jacobo Langsner, based on story idea by Miguel Rodríguez; camera (color), Rodríguez; music, Luis María Serra, based on a Grieg theme. Reviewed at the Broadway cinema, Buenos Aires, April 16, 1987. (Rating in Argentina: forbidden for under 16s). (In the Un Certain Regard section of Cannes Film Festival.) Running time: **100 MINS.**

Sofía . . . . Dora Baret
Pedro . . . . Alejandro Milrud
Pedro's mother . . . . Graciela Dufau
Pedro's father . . . . Héctor Alterio
Also with: Lito Cruz, Mónica Villa.

Buenos Aires — Notch up another qualitative success for the new Argentine cinema. "Sophia" is a craftily handled, mature tale of the love affair between a 17-year-old lad and a woman more than twice his age, against the backdrop of constant and ruthless dragnets during the government of the recent Argentine military juntas. It has been invited to the Cannes and Valladolid fests.

When Pedro first gets involved with her, Sofía, suspected as a subversive because her previous lover was a Communist, is on the verge of collapse after 23 days of hardly eat-

ing or sleeping while keeping permanently on the move to try to avoid arrest.

Pedro hides her and love develops by fits and starts while his schooling suffers and his parents become more and more alarmed at his strange behavior. Meanwhile the climate of fear coagulates in the city around them as brutal raids are shown taking place at any time by gun-waving men both in uniform and in civvies.

The film is sustained by a succession of powerful, true-ringing sequences. A hilarious assignation between a group of schoolboys, a prostitute — and her husband. A hair-raising speech by a school official who demands that every pupil become an informer: "We know how to root out the evil (of subversion)!" A high-charged mutual seduction carried out by the book — which is to say à la "Kama Sutra." A funny conversation between the clearly proud father and the son regarding the latter's mistress.

Above all, two potent scenes between Pedro and his mother, scenes which are admirable and moving without a hint of mawkishness.

A couple of minor objections, ranging from the conventionality of the final freeze shot to the unlikelihood of a fireplace functioning as merrily as is shown here after the person looking after it has left, don't seriously mar the overall effect. — *Olas.*

Bohater Roku
Hero Of The Year)
(POLISH-COLOR)

A Zespoly Filmowe production, Film Unit Perspektywa. Written and directed by Feliks Falk. Stars Jerzy Stuhr. Dialog, Falk, Stuhr; camera (color), Witold Adamek; editor, Lucja Ośko; music, Jan Kanty Pawuluśkiewicz; art director, Halina Dobrowolska; sound, Krzysztof Grabowski; production manager, Dorota Ostrowska-Orlińska. Reviewed at Film Polski, Warsaw, March 13, 1987. (In Market at Cannes Film Festival.) Running time: **115 MINS.**

Ludwik Danielak . . . . Jerzy Stuhr
Zbigniew Tataj . . . . . Mieczyslaw Franaszek
Maja . . . . . . Katarzyna Kozak-Paszkowska
Also with: Piotr Machalica, Marian Opania, Mirosława Marchekluk, Byszard Kotys, Bogusław Sobczuk, Michal Tarkowski.

Warsaw — "Hero Of The Year" is an impressive look at the compromises and squalor of certain post-Solidarity conformists; here, a tv host funnels pic's critique of a whole way of thinking. Director Feliks Falk lenses this sequel to his hit "Top Dog" in fast-paced, widescreen closeups that make for raw-edged realism. Style and theme should make it a natural pickup for fests and Western art houses able to handle Polish product.

Jerzy Stuhr, who headlined in "Top Dog" and who has a dialog credit, reappears as Ludwik Danie-

lak, smooth-talking hustler with a spreading waistline. In the previous installment, he got sacked from his tv job in '81; now he's ready for a comeback. His idea is a program called "Hero Of The Year," and his first star is to be Zbigniew Tataj (Mieczyslaw Franaszek), a quiet storekeeper who saved an apartment building by alerting people there was a gas leak.

Backed by the tv heads, Danielak arranges to take his hero on a nationwide tour. Gradually, however, it becomes clear Tataj won't be allowed to talk frankly to the people but will be forced to read a prepared speech. At a hyped-up concert resembling something out of "Nashville," he walks off stage in disgust, leaving Danielak wide-eyed and empty handed.

Though the time is now, the days of Solidarity are not far around the corner — it's Danielak's repressed past, popping up to frighten him every time victory seems within reach. Pic paints him as a traitor to the just cause, but also as a victim of manipulation himself by higher-ups who imagine threatening "metaphors" in a simple warning against gas leaks. Stuhr is totally convincing as the brash mover; Franaszek a noble everyman as the humble, honest Tataj. Witold Adamek's camerawork has the realistic immediacy of a John Cassavetes film. — *Yung.*

Gondoviseléš
(Tolerance)
(HUNGARIAN-COLOR)

A Hungarofilm release of a Mafilm Budapest Studio and Hungarian TV Budapest coproduction. Directed by Pál Erdöss. Screenplay, István Kardos; camera (Eastmancolor), Ferenc Pap, Tamás Sas; editor, Klára Majoros; music, Ferenc Balázs; sound, Péter Laczkovich; art director, Ferenc Jeli. Reviewed at the Budapest Congress Center, Feb. 16, 1987. (In Market at Cannes Film Festival.) Running time: **97 MINS.**

András . . . . Dénes Döbrei
Eva . . . . Erika Ozsda

Budapest — Director Pál Erdöss is becoming a specialist at portraying the underbelly of Hungarian society, usually using actress Erika Ozsda, in the lead role.

In his third such film, a man who comes out of prison after two-and-half years, finds authorities have put his children into foster homes, since neither he nor his wife, jailed for defending herself in too drastic a manner in an attempted rape, could provide an adequate home for their offspring. Determined to get them back, the couple sets out to find its own home, bribe the social worker into writing a favorable report which would permit them to regain control of the two daughters and, when one of the foster parents tries to resist forcibly returning the child, the man asks his friends to help him secure his rights.

Once again, Erdöss focuses on marginals, and displays profound sympathy for the vicious circles of poverty and crime in which they find themselves, records the petty bureaucratic miseries they encounter, and lashes out at the corruption that simmers under the respectable surface of socialist society.

He does not allow himself too many generalizations and the condemnation is not total however. On the other hand, he certainly does not idealize the couple or appeal to the audience's pity for them.

Remarkable performances by Ozsda and Dénes Döbrei, plus solid camerawork, provide good support for the story. This is Erdöss' first film in color, but he manages to avoid the temptations of glamor. The music sounds particularly unimaginative.—*Edna.*

Erzékeny Bucsu A Fejedelemtöl
(A Fond Farewell To The Prince)
(HUNGARIAN-COLOR)

A Dialog Studio, Mafilm, production. Directed by Laszlo Vitezy. Screenplay, Agnes Hankiss; camera (Eastmancolor), Peter Jankura; editor, Teréz Losonci; music, Istvan Martha; production design, Tamas Banovich; sound, György Kovacs; costumes, Erzsebet Mialkovszky; assistant director, Gyula Kormos; production manager, Sandor Ducsay. Reviewed at Hungarian Film Week, Budapest, Feb. 15, 1987. (In Market at Cannes Film Festival.) Running time: **96 MINS.**

Prince Gabor Bethlen . . . . Ferenc Bessenyei
Don Diego . . . . Krzysztof Wakulinski
Catherine . . . . Hanna Mikuc
Gabor Bathory . . . . György Cserhalmi
Lady-in-waiting . . . . Vera Papp

Budapest — During the 17th century, Hungary was divided between the Austrian Empire in the west and Turkey in the east, with only the province of Transylvania (which, ironically, today is no longer part of Hungary but part of Rumania) given autonomy under Prince Gabor Bethlen. This rather stodgy period piece deals with the dying days of Bethlen's rule, and his relationship with a Spanish dancer-poet brought from Venice to write a favorable history of the Prince.

As historical drama, pic is inadequate. Actors mostly look awkward in their roles, and sets and costumes are below par. Also, there's not much to the drama itself; the prince's young wife falls for the bisexual Spaniard, who finds himself in an awkward situation as a result. Flashbacks are a bit more lively, containing a strong performance from rugged György Cserhalmi as a man of action who's murdered to prevent him rocking the boat and making Transylvania's delicate situation between Eastern and Western influences more volatile.

This East-West theme gives a clue to a possible allegory, which makes an otherwise undistinguished film more interesting. If we substitute the Soviet Union for the Eastern country, which exerts maximum power over the tiny nation, then we can, perhaps, see the prince as the current Hungarian leader Kadar, who has pursued a similar policy of slow progress without wanting to antagonize friendly neighbors.

Allegory or not, the film won't spark much international interest. It's a disappointment coming from helmer Laszlo Vitezy whose 1982 feature "Red Earth," was one of the best Hungarian films of recent years. —*Strat.*

Gardens Of Stone
(COLOR)

___

Disappointing Vietnam home front drama.

___

A Tri-Star Pictures release from Tri-Star-ML Delphi Premier Prods. Produced by Michael I. Levy, Francis Coppola. Executive producers, Stan Weston, Jay Emmett, Fred Roos. Co-executive producer, David Valdes. Directed by Coppola. Screenplay, Ronald Bass, based on novel by Nicholas Proffitt; camera (Deluxe color), Jordan Cronenweth; editor, Barry Malkin; music, Carmine Coppola; production design, Dean Tavoularis; art direction, Alex Tavoularis; set decoration, Gary Fettis; sound (Dolby stereo), Thomas Causey; costumes, Willa Kim, Judianna Makovsky; assistant director, David Valdes; casting, Janet Hirshenson, Jane Jenkins, Bonnie Timmermann. Reviewed at Lorimar screening room, L.A., April 24, 1987. (MPAA Rating: R.) Running time: **111 MINS.**

Clell Hazard . . . . James Caan
Samantha Davis . . . . Anjelica Huston
"Goody" Nelson . . . . James Earl Jones
Jackie Willow . . . . D.B. Sweeney
Homer Thomas . . . . Dean Stockwell
Rachel Field . . . . . Mary Stuart Masterson
Slasher Williams . . Dick Anthony Williams
Betty Rae . . . . Lonette McKee
Lt. Weber . . . . Sam Bottoms
Pete Deveber . . . . Elias Koteas
Flanagan . . . . Larry Fishburne
Wildman . . . . Casey Siemaszko
 Also with: Peter Masterson, Carlin Glynn, Erik Holland, Bill Graham.

___

Hollywood — "Gardens Of Stone," Francis Coppola's muddled meditation on the Vietnam War, seems to take its name not so much from the Arlington Memorial Cemetery, where much of the action takes place, but from the stiffness of the characters it portrays. As story telling, it is a seriously flawed film. As a political tract, it is shamelessly incomplete. And as filmmaking, it is a major disappointment.

Coppola's name above the title will ensure some interest at the box-office, but somber tone and turgid pace are sure to keep the lines short.

Structured around the small details and formal rituals of military life, pic opens and closes with a funeral and in between is supposed to be the emotional stuff that makes an audience care about the death of a soldier. But it is a case of form substituting for feeling and although there is unlikely to be a dry eye in the house at the finale, there is a hollowness at the film's core.

As a two-time combat vet biding his time training young recruits for the Old Guard, the Army's ceremonial unit at Fort Myer, Va., Clell Hazard (James Caan) knows the war is wrong but cannot oppose it. Rather than protest, he feels it is his responsibility to prepare the young soldiers as best he can, especialy young Private Willow (D.B. Sweeney), the son of an old Korean war buddy.

Script by Ronald Bass, from Nicholas Proffitt's novel, attempts to create sympathetic soldiers whose first loyalty is to their brothers in arms. It's a point of view, however, that totally begs the issue of moral responsibility and seals the soldiers off from the rest of the world.

Indeed it is a world unto itself as Caan swaps tales of horrors and heroism with his buddy "Goody" Nelson (James Earl Jones). It is hard to grasp the affection and values of these men although they are given numerous opportunities to hold forth. Since there is little or no organic flow to the action, scenes are often merely set-ups for awkward exposition.

Most contrived of the relationships is Caan's affair with Anjelica Huston who plays a Washington Post reporter vehemently opposed to the war. For starters the attraction is assumed rather than demonstrated and Huston seems far too intelligent to make the choice she does. Basically the supportive woman waiting in the wings, she also has enough stilted dialog to destroy her character.

At the heart of the film is Caan's connection to the youngster, but Sweeney's character is such a gung-ho soldier that even the explanations offered here can't condone his actions. On a more visceral level, he's simply not an engaging presence.

Staging is surprisingly static and Coppola's view of army life lacks the emotional underpinnings to allow an audience to embrace its apologist politics. It is not enough to simply feel strongly about a position to make it dramatically convincing.

More to the point and Coppola's proven strengths are some lovely ensemble scenes such as when Sweeney courts his wife-to-be (Mary Stuart Masterson) and gets a decidedly mixed reception from her family (played by her real-life parents, Peter Masterson and Carlin Glynn). Here the cross-fire and play of conflicting values creates a tension that says more about the era than the puffed up posturing of the rest of the film.

Given the material they have to work with, performances fail to ignite the characters with Caan having his moments but overall remaining mostly an enigma. Huston is often stiff and stagey while Jones is in another universe all together.

As in most Coppola films, production values are first-rate with longtime collaborator Dean Tavoularis' production design evoking the mood of the times. Jordan Cronenweth's cinematography is dark and suggestive, if only the film had more to say. —*Jagr.*

Regina
(ITALIAN-B&W)

___

An Istituto Luce-Italnoleggio release of a Falco Film production. Produced by Carla Apuzzo. Directed by Salvatore Piscicelli. Stars Ida Di Benedetto. Screenplay, Piscicelli, Apuzzo; camera (b&w), Tonino Nardi; editor, Domenico Varone, Piscicelli; music, Helmut Laberer, art direction, Luciano Vedonilli-

Levi. Reviewed at Rialto Cinema, Rome, April 25, 1987. Running time: **83 MINS.**

Regina . . . . Ida Di Benedetto
Lorenzo . . . . Fabrizio Bentivoglio
Lalla . . . . Giuliana Calandra

Rome — Director Salvatore Piscicelli and scripter-producer Carla Apuzzo continue to make very particular films quite different from each other and anomalous for the Italo market. After their much-praised Neapolitan melodrama "Immacolata And Concetta" and a fast-moving rock film, "Metropolitan Blues," the team opts for a profoundly depressing, black & white drama of an actress who discovers her own masochism during a love affair with a young man. Hardly a film for all tastes, "Regina" has made a few waves locally, and indeed seems too austere and intellectualized an experiment even for most art houses.

Regina is a rich and famous actress of 40 (Ida Di Benedetto), recuperating in the mountains after collapsing onstage performing Lady Macbeth. Describing herself as the perfectly emancipated woman — no husband, no kids, no restrictions on her freedom — Regina is pretty clearly headed for a nervous breakdown.

At a party her eyes fall on the pretty face of Lorenzo (Fabrizio Bentivoglio), an aspiring actor who poses in hardcore magazines. As Lorenzo falls in love, Regina torments him with her punish-me whims, such as forcing him to make love to her aging, bitchy agent (Giuliana Calandra) while she watches. Piscicelli's straightforward attitude to the seamier realities of human sexuality, and equally frank use of obscene language, makes this an adults-only picture without pornography.

In contrast to its sexual modernity, Tonino Nardi's shadowy, b&w camerawork and attentive lensing beautifully hard back to a past epoch and style. Dialog is deliberately theatrical, particularly the way Di Benedetto enunciates here in her Neapolitan accent. Add Helmut Laberer's brooding, banging piano score and the most innocent line ("Do you prefer tea — *or cognac?*") takes on a load of arch, Fassbinder-like irony.

What keeps "Regina" from being a cousin to Fassbinder's b&w "Veronica Voss," another tormented actress story, is its lack of emotion that might make the viewer feel more than a cerebral sympathy for pic's technical bravura and its unhappy heroine. —*Yung.*

Debajo del mundo
(Beneath The World)
(ARGENTINE-CZECH-COLOR)

An Argentina Sono Film presentation. Produced by Jorge Estrada Mora, Leo Mehl. Written and directed and by Beda Docampo Feijóo, Juan Bautista Stagnaro. Camera (col-

or), Frantisek Uldrich; editor, Pablo Mari; music, José Luis Castiñeira de Dios; sets, Miguel Angel Lumaldo, Boris Moravec; costumes, Helena Vondruskova. Reviewed at the Metropolitan cinema, Buenos Aires, April 16, 1987. (Rating in Argentina: forbidden for under 13s.) Running time: **100 MINS.**

With: Sergio Renán, Bárbara Mugica, Víctor Laplace, Oscar Ferrigno Jr., Gabriel Gibot, Paula Canals, Bruno Stagnaro, Gabriela Toscano.

Buenos Aires — With this film the Argentine cinema breaks new ground literally and figuratively, the latter both in the matter of coproductions and thematically. Czechoslovakia, where this wartime drama was filmed, stands in for Poland where, in this true story, a family of Jews spent the Nazi years in a shallow, covered hole dug in the ground and later other similarly improvised and crude shelters, in permanent fear for their lives and suffering several murders along the way. Local anti-Semitic bands were no less against them than the German occupiers.

The fact that the actors speak Spanish takes some adjusting to, in the case of audiences who understand it or are at least familiar with its sound — until they realize that in the many war films in which Mittel-Europeans were shown speaking English, this was also no more than a storytelling convention. At film's end there emerges a connection between this wrenching wartime Polish story and Argentina. This led to the interest in the case by first-time directors Beda Docampo Feijóo and Juan Bautista Stagnaro, whose main prior credit was the script of 1985 foreign-language Oscar nominee "Camila."

Their earnestly conceived and executed picture will find interest as a record of fortitude and ingenuity in the face of atrocious conditions and dangers. Its tone isn't consistently sustained — at some points it seems to communicate the practical problems of survival better than the anguish, and some of the dialog is too declamatory, — but the overall balance is positive.

The film chronicles all the fronts on which this family had to struggle: the claustrophobia, the shame of having to submit to existing like moles in the first place, the deluges of slime when it rained, the lice, the rotting away of their clothes, and also the help received from a few acquaintances amid the horror of constant fear and intermittently immediate peril.

The family is shown to have been not only resourceful but also daring, one of the their hiding places being right under the noses of the Germans for the advantage of not having to worry about their tracks in the snow during their night-time forays for food — the tracks mingled with those of the Germans themselves.

"Worthy" is an adjective that

suggests itself not only for the film's sentiments but also for its achievements, without being essential Holocaust viewing. —*Olas.*

Robert Wilson And The Civil Wars
(U.S.-W. GERMAN DOCU-COLOR)

A Unisphere release of an Aspekt Telefilm, Hamburg/Unisphere Pictures, N.Y. production. Produced by Markas Trebitsch, Orin Wechsberg, Howard Brookner. Directed and narration written by Brookner. Camera (color), Ira Brenner, Bob Chappell, Tom Di Cillo; editor, Michelle Bahlke. Reviewed as part of Global Village (N.Y.) Docu Festival, April 20, 1987. Running time: **90 MINS.**

The title of Howard Brookner's docu "Robert Wilson And The Civil Wars," explains everything. First part of the film is an attempt to delve into the life and work of one of the world's most controversial theatrical artists, Robert Wilson, while the second half concerns his fight to create and mount the monumental project "the Civil Wars," with production set for the 1984 Olympic Games.

Known for the unconventional stagings of his operas, the creator of "Einstein On The Beach" and "The Life And Times Of Sigmund Freud" had a unique and epic concept for this projected overall new work. The piece, based on the theme of the U.S. Civil War, would be created simultaneously in six countries using six different composers. Each participating country developed segments of the work which were first performed separately in the country of origin. The resulting complete nine-hour version, slated for the L.A. Olympics, was to have united and interrelated all the casts and crews into a multi-disciplined masterpiece of staging and world theater. Unfortunately the dream which began in 1979, was never realized and the film only documents Wilson's personal battles concerning "The Wars."

The major problem is financing. The Olympics Committee would put up matching funds, but Wilson and his supporters needed first to raise around $1,500,000, which they tried to do through pledges and a series of exhibits selling the artist's designs and drawings from the work.

In a race against time to prepare the piece and raise needed capital, Wilson is seen traveling around the world working with casts beginning in Rotterdam, Cologne, Tokyo, Minneapolis, Marseilles, and finally Rome, where an unexpected electricians' strike threatens to shut down the entire operation.

Although Wilson's work tends to be static, there is high drama behind the scenes. The mounting of this piece, so dependent on the precise coordination of its disparate parts, builds in tension as the final cutoff

day approaches. Wilson tears himself the twin tasks of director to six separate productions around the globe and chief fundraiser, trying to drum up support.

The 90-minute theatrical release of this docu re-edited in West Germany by Michelle Bahlke, differs greatly from the two-part two-hour version of the film prepared for British tv.

The first section, concerning the man and his work, uses minimum narration and relies on a series of talking head comments about the artist by collaborators (Phillip Glass, Gavin Bryers, Heiner Müller, et al.), family and friends. Their statements are cut with scenes from Wilson's past work — "Deafman Glance," "Letter For Queen Victoria," "Einstein On The Beach," etc. — and also to an exploration of his early years growing up in Waco, Texas, and his first New York job working with brain-damaged children. Editing tends to be circular, showing the man through a multisided approach, all clues to help us understand Wilson's fascinating and dense work.

The second part, which concentrates on "The Wars," only offers the audience a hint of what promised to be an impressive monumental major work. Its sense of urgency as impending failure looms on the horizon carries the audience along to an anti-climax.

The poignancy of Howard Brookner's docu is that this film is the closest record that remains of "The Wars." Through it, various glimpses of the overall work are shown and we can only imagine what might have been. —*Lent.*

Yige He Bage
(One And The Eight)
(CHINESE-COLOR)

A China Film release of a Guangxi Film Studio production. Directed by Zhang Junzhao. Screenplay, Zhang Ziliang, from a poem by Guo Xiaochuan; camera (color), Zhang Yimou, Xiao Feng; editor, Ci Minghe; production design, He Qun. Reviewed at Hong Kong Film Festival, April 15, 1987. Running time: **90 MINS.**

With: Tao Ziru, Cheng Daoming, Lu Xiaoyan.

Hong Kong — Released at last after a three-year ban, "One And The Eight" proves to be another major film from the emerging Chinese cinema. In fact, it predates the trailblazing "Yellow Earth," since it was the first film made at the new Guangxi Film Studio in Nanning (near the border with Vietnam), established in April 1983 for "youth productions;" "Yellow Earth" was the unit's second production.

The film is based on a long poem set in 1939 during the Sino-Japanese war. A frontline unit of Chinese infantry is burdened by nine prisoners: three are thieves, three deserters, one's a spy and one a poisoner. The ninth, Wang, who strenuously protests his innocence, is the sole survivor of a unit that was wiped out, and he's accused of collaboration with the Japanese.

The enemy closes in, and there's a terrible massacre of the regular soldiers: only their commander, Xu, survives, and he's badly wounded. Wang rallies the prisoners around and they fight valiantly against the Japanese. In the end, three, including Wang, survive to carry on the fight.

Unfortunately, the authorities in Peking strongly objected to the film when it was completed. Apparently they felt it showed disrespect to regular soldiers in its depiction of the courage of these scrungy criminals (a theme identical to that of "The Dirty Dozen" of course). The filmmakers were ordered to make about 70 changes, and re-shooting and re-dubbing have apparently watered-down the original quite considerably.

Despite this, "One And The Eight" is still a very gripping film. Once again, the photography of Zhang Yimou (who also shot "Yellow Earth" and "The Big Parade") is a major asset: he uses the barren desert landscape of pock-marked cliffs and bluffs to great effect, and the film is filled with striking images. Director Zhang Junzhao stages both the claustrophobic scenes involving the prisoners in makeshift cells, and the brief, brutal battle scenes, with great flair, and even manages to get over the problem of the presence of a pretty female nurse (often a cliché of Western platoon-under-fire pics).

The film begins and ends very abruptly, though, with opening titles (over black and white photos) sketchily filling in the story so far and the final resolution left, frustratingly, up in the air. Despite this, the film is very accessible, very impressive and sufficiently stylish to enable it to make its mark internationally. —Strat.

Programmed To Kill
(COLOR)

Inept gender switch on 'The Terminator.'

A Trans World Entertainment release of a Retaliator production. Produced by Don Stern, Allan Holzman. Directed by Allan Holzman, with additional scenes directed by Robert Short. Screenplay, Short; camera (color), Nitcho Lion Nissim, Ernest Holzman; editor, Michael Kelly; music, Jerry Immel, Craig Huxley; sets, Michael Parker, Pola Schreiber; sound, Pat Moriarty, Eli Yarkoni; makeup, Maria Haro; special effects, Vern Hyde, John Carter; costumes, Vicki Graff, Lennie Barin. Reviewed at UA Egyptian theater, L.A., April 23, 1987. (MPAA Rating: R.) Running time: **92 MINS.**
Eric . . . . Robert Ginty
Samira . . . . Sandahl Bergman
Broxk . . . . James Booth
Blake . . . . Alex Courtney
Jason . . . . Paul W. Walker
Sharon . . . . Louise Caire Clark
Donovan . . . . Peter Bromilow
Mike . . . . George Fisher
Chris . . . . Jim Turner
Hassim . . . . Arnon Tzador

———

Hollywood — "Programmed To Kill" (original title: "The Retaliator") is a tired rewrite of "The Terminator," with a female cyborg responsible for most of the destruction this time around. This film doesn't have any of the crackle or inventiveness of James Cameron's thriller, and quickly reveals itself to be a third-rate action flick with no tension at all. Leads Robert Ginty and Sandahl Bergman are okay, but never get a chance to distinguish themselves because of a poor screenplay that seems to consist entirely of clichés. Boxoffice prospects are dismal.

Weak story begins with Samira (Bergman), a member of "a PLO splinter group" (can we get any more vague than that?), joining internationally-known terrorist Hassim (Arnon Tzador) and his buddies in blowing away a market full of innocent shoppers in Greece. Two American children, evidently too dumb or panicked to notice that she's carrying a machine gun, run right into her arms and are kidnaped.

This heist is "a big one," so CIA can't trust their regular operatives with the rescue mission. They instead call on weary mercenary Eric Mathews (Ginty) and he accepts. Mathews' band overruns the headquarters of terrorists, who promptly become the gang that can't shoot straight. He rescues the children and captures Samira, but Hassim gets away.

Back in the States, Mathews wants to question Samira, but finds that the CIA has taken the nearly brain-dead terrorist away. Their evil plan: perform complex neural surgery that programs her into a fighting machine for the U.S. They perform the operation, with a team of surgeons that look like they just left the frat house, and then send her back to the Middle East where she slaughters Hassim and his group.

Then this pre-programmed Rambette starts having some serious flashbacks, realizes she's just laid waste to all her loved ones, and decides to get revenge on everyone involved with her capture. She heads back to America and goes on a killing spree whose sole purpose seems to be proving that even a half-human killing machine can still look good in a leather miniskirt.

Ultimate showdown takes place on a military airfield, with Mathews just lucky enough to stumble on to a revved-up bulldozer at the critical moment.

Besides lame script and mostly bad acting, production credits range from mediocre to atrocious, with fluttery soundtrack (occasionally out of sync with lip movements) and muddy photography a frequent distraction. —Camb.

Ngati
(NEW ZEALAND - COLOR)

———

A Pacific Films presentation. Produced by John O'Shea. Directed by Barry Barclay. Screenplay, Tama Poata; camera (color), Rory O'Shea; editor, Dell King; music, Dalvanius; art director, Mathew Murphy; sound, Robert Allen. Reviewed at National Film Unit theater, Auckland, April 8, 1987. Running time: **88 MINS.**
Iwi . . . . Wi Kuki Kaa
Jenny Bennett . . . . Judy McIntosh
Greg Shaw . . . . Ross Girven
Sally . . . . Connie Pewhairangi
Tione . . . . Michael Tibble
Ropata . . . . Oliver Jones
Sam Bennett . . . . Alice Fraser
Dr. Paul Bennett . . . . Norman Fletcher

———

Auckland — Barry Barclay's "Ngati" is a deceptively simple low-budget feature that releases the miraculous essence of community strength and joy.

The film signals the gathering strength of Maori New Zealanders in the industry, and the kind of insight and skill they can bring to human themes that too often emerge jaded and unpalatable.

In its measured form and style, "Ngati" — the Maori word for tribe — reflects Barclay's background in documentary film making ("The Neglected Miracle," "Tangata Whenua") and something of the early Satyajit Ray films ("Pather Panchali," "The World Of Apu"). But in this, his first dramatic feature, he clearly is his own directorial master.

Set in a tiny New Zealand coastal town, circa 1948, "Ngati" has as a pivot the homecoming of a young man Greg Shaw (Ross Girven). Unaware of his exact cultural heritage and roots, he becomes absorbed in the heartbeat of the predominantly Maori community, which has time for its youngest and oldest inhabitant even as the forces of economic progress beat at the door.

In this interregnum, both Maori and European medicines are used in the attempt to save the life of a young boy, Ropata (Oliver Jones) while his friend Tione (Michael Tibble) keeps loyal watch. Sally (Connie Pewhairangi), fresh from the city, urges the local men to run the local meatworks themselves when the owners threaten to pull out. Iwi (Wi Kuki Kaa), Ropata's father, is given the chance to hold back the closure when he assumes management of a big sheep and cattle station.

Greg's hosts, the local European doctor Paul Bennett (Norman Fletcher), his wife Sam (Alice Fraser) and their daughter and local schoolteacher Jenny (Judy McIntosh) show their ease in crossing cultural boundaries as a "minority" in the community.

Barclay's character focus settles most on Greg and young Tione, the one in the process of finding his identity, the other about to lose his closest friend.

It is the community — the sum of the parts — that predominates, and which is the catalyst for a thumpingly powerful ending which Barclay glides you towards and through almost before you realize it. This evocation of the ever-recurring surge of life and death is profound and resonant.

This achievement is not gained without cost. The strands of the plot (screenplay, Tama Poata) are elusive at times, while the dialog contains its share of non sequiturs.

The cast is a mix of professional and very amateur. Best acting moments come from Fraser, McIntosh and Kaa, and in a scene between Girven and Tibble towards film's end that ties the main strands.

The photography of Rory O'Shea is impeccable, while the soundtrack of Dalvanius should have spinoff hits in its blend of contemporary and traditional Maori songs.

A slow opening to the film will not ensure easy marketing of the pic. But the emotional force Barclay can generate through his technique of puritanical restraint in dramatically realizing life and action in "Ngati" should help sell it on art house circuits, and in festivals in many countries outside New Zealand. —Nic.

———

Los dueños del silencio
(The Owners Of Silence)
(ARGENTINE-SWEDISH-COLOR)

———

An Argentine Sono Film release of a GC Prods. (Argentina), Crescendo Film (Sweden) coproduction. Produced by Guillermo Calligari (Argentina), Göran Lindstrom (Sweden). Directed by Carlos Lemos. Screenplay, Lemos; camera (color), Juan Carlos Lenardi; editor, Luis Mutti; music, Luis de Matteo; sets, Miguel Angel Lumaldo; costumes, Angélica Fuentes. Reviewed at the Vigo screening room, Buenos Aires, March 31, 1987. (Rating in Argentina: forbidden for under-16.) Running time: **95 MINS.**
Swedish ambassador . . . . . . Bibi Andersson
Swedish journalist . . . . . . Thomas Hellberg
Argentine captain . . . . Peder Falk
Argentine lieutenant . . . . . . Oscar Martinez
Kidnapee's father . . . . Arturo Bonin
Also with: Per Myrberg, Grynet Molveig, Sara Kay, Soledad Silveyra, Maria Valenzuela, Selva Alemán, Victor Laplace, Gabriel Rovito, Julio de Grazia, Maria Vaner.

———

Buenos Aires — One of the human rights cases which gained widest international notoriety during the years of the Argentine military juntas was the disappearance (case never fully cleared up) of Dagmar Hagelin, a girl of dual Argentine-Swedish nationality. This film, built as a political thriller in the Costa-Gavras mold, gives a gripping version of events under a light fictional mantle, i.e., names and a military rank or two are changed. This, and the presence of Bibi Andersson in the cast, are its strong suits on the international stage.

Last year, in one of the human rights trials being carried out under the current, democratic Argentine government, a Navy officer was found guilty of Hagelin's kidnaping — though not of her presumed murder — but was not imprisoned for the crime because the statute of limitations for kidnaping had run out. He is nevertheless in jail under other accusations. "The Owners Of Silence" ends with an image of the filmic culprit enjoying untrammeled freedom, giving an erroneous impression of the real-life legalities.

In the initial sequences, it also exaggerates, presumably for visual impact, the number of armed men which the military government actually needed to deploy in public places. Otherwise, it seeks a palpable correlation with the feel of the country in those times.

In actual fact, the ploy barely delves into the case of the kidnaped girl and centers, in time-honored filmic fashion, on the investigation of a Swedish journalist who seeks information on her case, and also attempts to blow the lid off the entire human rights violations situation. The military intelligence services, meanwhile, are on the trail, leading to situations of increasing suspense.

This is achieved without harping on torture scenes, though glimpses of the horror are included.

The film is spoken in Spanish, Swedish and English according to the situation, and Swedish actor Peder Falk is believable as the smooth Argentine heavy. Most of the filming was done in Buenos Aires. This drama, even while growing out of a true episode, is quite traditional in its thriller structure, solidly put together by director Carlos Lemos (an Argentine living and working in the film industry in Sweden since the late 1960s), and gut-wrenching.—*Olas.*

Miracles
(COLOR)

Energetic screwball comedy suffers from strained premise.

An Orion Pictures release of a Steve Roth presentation. Executive producer, David Greenwalt. Produced by Roth, Bernard Williams. Written and directed by Jim Kouf. Stars Tom Conti, Teri Garr. Camera (Super Techniscope, Technicolor; prints by Deluxe), John Alcott; editor, Susan E. Morse, Dennis Virkler; music, Peter Bernstein; sound (Dolby), Kirk Francis; production design, Terence Marsh; set decoration, Michael Seirton; special effects supervisor, John Stears; production managers, G. Mac Brown, Vicente Escriva — Mexico, Donna Smith — L.A.; stunt coordinator, Bud Davis; costume design, Cynthia Bales; mattes, Dream Quest Images; associate producer, Lynn Bigelow; casting, Melissa Skoff — U.S., Claudia Becker — Mexico. Reviewed on HBO/Cannon Video vidcassette, N.Y., April 11, 1987. (MPAA Rating: PG.) Running time: **87 MINS.**
Roger Briggs . . . . Tom Conti
Jean Briggs . . . . Teri Garr
Juan . . . . Paul Rodriguez
Harry . . . . Christopher Lloyd
    Also with: Adalberto Martinez "Resortes" (Witch doctor), Jorge Russek (the Judge), Jorge Reynoso (K'In), Charles Rocket (Michael), Barbara Whinnery (Hooker), Ken Hixon (Missionary).

"Miracles" is another casualty of the video revolution. A top-of-the-line production shot in Mexico in 1984 by Orion (with a reported $10,-000,000 budget), pic received a negligible regional release in July 1986 ahead of its current homevideo availability. Without the simple (and remunerative) vidcassette option, Orion might have given this one a little push theatrically.

Pic in fact is fitfully entertaining, but hampered severely by writer-director Jim Kouf's antiquated premise, which unwittingly recalls the Cecil B. de Mille approach of the late silent era. As implied by its title, all events in the film are connected, ever so tenuously and always unconvincingly, by divine intervention. At first it's cute, with lightning bolts and falling rocks setting into motion slapstick occurrences which literally mean life or death for the hapless protagonists. Eventually, the conceit becomes annoying.

Screwball farce is set into motion when an Indian witch doctor in some unidentified Latin American country prays to the heavens for assistance in saving his chief's daughter who is dying. North of the border, the first few of many lightning bolts cause disruptions which bring together inept bank robbers Paul Rodriguez and Christopher Lloyd with just-divorced surgeon Tom Conti and his lawyer wife Teri Garr. Rodriguez kidnaps the duo and Lloyd flies the four of them to that Latin country to escape police.

Predictably Conti ends up at the Latin village after numerous misadventures and saves the little girl, who had an appendicitis attack. By film's end the bickering couple is back together, remarried in a Spanish ceremony.

Way overreaching (his early credits include the script for the horrendously static 1982 comedy "Pink Motel"), filmmaker Kouf evidently was aiming for the 1930s romantic farce, replete with stars Conti and Garr dressed in formal evening clothes throughout, plus the expansive "Romancing The Stone" adventure grafted on. Alas, they are hardly William Powell and Carole Lombard, and though it is fun to watch Garr's patented, fast-talking explosions, Conti is seriously miscast. Attempting a neutral, American accent, he is not believable; in any event, the pic calls for a superstar personality, not a talented character actor. Conti's other 1984 starring assignment, "Saving Grace," similarly was given only a token release via Columbia.

"Miracles" has outstanding technical credits, including the late John Alcott's crystal-sharp lensing, Terence Marsh's large-scale and wide-ranging production design and impressive stuntwork and special effects. A series of fun setpieces do not a movie make. —*Lor.*

Steele Justice
(COLOR)

Silly actioner.

An Atlantic release of a John Strong production. Executive producers, Thomas Coleman, Michael Rosenblatt. Produced by Strong. Written and directed by Robert Boris. Camera (United color), John M. Stephens; editor, John O'Connor, Steve Rosenblum; music, Misha Segal; sound, Clifford Gynn; production manager-assistant director, Thomas A. Irvine; production design, Richard N. McGuire; set decorator, John Nelson Tichler; costume design, Leslie Wilshire; choreography, Jeff Kutash Dancin' Machine; associate producer, John O'Connor; casting, Paul Ventura. Reviewed at Magno Preview 9 screening room, N.Y., April 23, 1987. (MPAA Rating: R.) Running time: **95 MINS.**
John Steele . . . . Martin Kove
Tracy . . . . Sela Ward
Bennett . . . . Ronny Cox
Reese . . . . Bernie Casey
Harry . . . . Joseph Campanella
Gen. Kwan . . . . Soon-Teck Oh
Cami . . . . Jan Gan Boyd
Lee Van Minh . . . . Robert Kim
Pham . . . . Peter Kwong
Angela . . . . Shannon Tweed
Kay . . . . Sarah Douglas
    Also with: David Froman, Irene Tsu, Asher Brauner, Chris Hillman & the Desert Rose Band, Astrid Plane.

It's rather difficult to tell whether writer-director Robert Boris is playing it straight with "Steele Justice," a cornball actioner in which the unintentional laughs come fast and furious. Grindhouse fans are likely to be confused.

Martin Kove toplines as John Steele, the umpteenth Vietnam vet back home in L.A. with a problem. South Vietnamese General Kwan (Soon-Teck Oh) betrayed his unit back in 1975 and is now a California bigshot posing as a philanthropist but actually heading up a drug ring, assisted by his sadistic son Pham (Peter Kwong).

Things come to a head when Steele's best pal from Vietnam, Lee Van Minh (Robert Kim) and his family are murdered by Pham, with the cute daughter Cami (Jan Gan Boyd) surviving. Steele whips into action and bodies pile up

Format might have made for an acceptable, routine *film noir,* but Boris includes a wealth of silly material that causes the film's credibility to evaporate. Most obvious gaffe is a largescale central sequence of guest star Astrid Plane warbling in a musicvideo shoot (replete with Jeff Kutash choreography) directed by Steele's beautiful ex-wife (Sela Ward). The oriental gangsters and a squad of good guys show up, and it is the hapless *chorus line* that gets mowed down in machinegun fire. Producer John Strong likewise emphasized a hard rock score in a previous effort, "Savage Streets," but it doesn't help matters this time.

Kove's acting is one-note, a surly sneer and more bare-chested scenes than William Shatner or Charlton Heston in the '60s.

Bernie Casey lends strength and wry humor as a cop pal of Steele's while poor Ronny Cox as the police chief looks like he strayed in from the set of "Beverly Hills Cop II," even wearing the same sports jacket. Oddball casting has soap stars popping in, Sarah Douglas as a district attorney, and cast against type, Shannon Tweed as a beautiful gangster and Joseph Campanella as another bad guy. Worst decision was to have Jan Gan Boyd, recently impressive as an adult in "Assassination" (replete with a tasteful sex scene with Charles Bronson) and "A Chorus Line," fitted out here with pigtails as a whiny little girl.

Tech credits are good.—*Lor.*

Psychos In Love
(COLOR)

Gory homage to 'Eating Raoul' strains for yocks.

An ICN Bleecker release of a Wizard Video presentation of a Generic Films production. Executive producer, Gary Bechard. Produced, directed, edited and camera (Precision color) by Gorman Bechard. Screenplay, Carmine Capobianco, Gorman Bechard; music, Capobianco; additional music, Gorman Bechard; sound-associate producer, Shaun Cashman; production manager-assistant director-associate producer, H. Shep Pamplin; costumes, Debi Thibeault; special effects, Pamplin, Matt Brooks, Jan Radder, Jan Pedis, Nina Port, Capobianco; special effects props, Jennifer Aspinall, Tom Molinelli; makeup/hair, Frank Stewart. Reviewed on Wizard Video vidcassette, N.Y., March 10, 1987. (No MPAA Rating.) Running time: **87 MINS.**
Joe . . . . Carmine Capobianco
Kate . . . . Debi Thibeault
Herman . . . . Frank Stewart
Nikki . . . . Cecilia Wilde
Heather . . . . Donna Davidge
    Also with: Shawn Light, LeeAnn Baker, Tressa Zannino, Kate McCamy.

"Psychos In Love" is an underground film which tries so hard to become a cult favorite it self-destructs. Shamelessly emulating the premise and several details of Paul Bartel's hit "Eating Raoul," filmmakers Gorman Bechard and Carmine Capobianco mix gore and yocks to occasionally funny results but far more care, rewriting and taste were required to fashion a complete feature. Released on vidcassette in February, pic has been booked theatrically in New York by the filmmakers to open in May, reversing the usual release pattern. (Review is of the videocassette version; film has subsequently been re-edited for theatrical use.)

Capobianco and Debi Thibeault topline as a bartender and manicurist who each get their kicks killing people (in extremely bloody fashion to gross out the fans). After a sympatico date, Thibeault moves in with him, each retaining the autonomy to go out with (and kill) dates of their own choosing. In their world, murder is the new form of "safe sex" (safe for the murderer, that is).

Ultimately they decide to "do one together," i.e., murder Cecilia Wilde, the topless dancer at Capobianco's bar. Despite endless stabbing and gouts of blood everywhere, she will not die, until Capobianco beans her with a trusty frying pan — it is at this point that the film's homage to "Eating Raoul" becomes plagiarism. Like "Raoul," a black comedy cannibalism theme is introduced, as the couple's sink becomes stopped up (due to becoming full of human body parts) and the plumber, Frank Stewart, turns out to be another psycho who eats his victims. He offers them a scheme whereby he'll take the bodies to be used as food. Film quickly runs out of steam and finishes with an amateurish (sound synch is way off) nonending.

Technically, "Psychos In Love" is a step down from Bechard's debut feature "Disconnected," which was also a horror thriller but played straight. "In Love" overdoes everything, running gags into the ground and not seeming aware that gore films, dating back to the original one, "Blood Feast" in 1963, have always been tongue-in-cheek and do not need an overlay of satire. Overuse of tight closeups and exterior shots that look like a backyard movie also mar the picture.

Balding Capobianco is pleasant enough but hardly star material, while costar Thibeault seems uncomfortable in her role, especially when called upon to do comedy with her face and body covered in fake blood. Talky script has some funny lines, but a repetitious gag of the leads launching into a rote lecture on how they hate grapes is way overdone. Bechard's attempted shot-for-shot imitation of Hitchcock's "Psycho" shower scene is embarrassing film school filler. Typical of microbudgeted filming, cast triples up on behind-the-camera chores as well.

These Connecticut filmmakers obviously have some talent, but they will have to do the woodshedding and careful preparation it takes to make a full-fledged feature in order to escape the current cycle of merely cranking out quickies to feed the insatiable homevideo maw. —*Lor.*

Angustia
(Anguish)
(SPANISH-COLOR)

A Pepón Cormina production, for Samba P.C. and Luna Films. Executive producer,

Pepón Coromina. Written and directed by Bigas Luna. Camera (Eastmancolor, Agfa color), Josep Maria Civit; editor, Tom Sabin; music, J.M. Pagan; sets, Felipe de Paco; casting-costumes, Consol Tura; makeup, Matilde Fabregat; special effects, Paco Teres; direct sound, Barbara Becker; associate producers, Xavier Visa, George Ayoub; production managers, Paco Poch, Joan Porcar; production designer, Andreu Coromina. Reviewed at Real Cinema, Madrid, April 11, 1987. Running time: **89 MINS.**
With: Zelda Rubinstein, Michael Lerner, Talia Paul, Angel José, Clara Pastor, Isabel Garcia Lorca. et al.
(English soundtrack available)

Madrid — Catalan helmer Bigas Luna has come up with what must be the best thriller-horror pic ever made in Spain, a gripping, tightly scripted and acted item which could spell big bucks in any territory in the world. Since part of pic was shot in New York and California, using Yank as well as Spanish thesps, pic has an international look to it.

Bigas Luna has long titillated horror buffs here with films such as "Bilbao" and "Caniche" in which his almost morbid obsession with gore and detail yielded films which were brilliantly compulsive, but not altogether balanced. With "Angustia" he succeeds in combining dementia and repulsiveness with madmen-run-loose action.

First half of pic concerns an obese lab technician who works in an eye clinic and lives in a cluttered old-time house with his domineering mother. In the clinic, he is the keeper of a huge collection of eyeballs kept in alcohol. One day his clumsy behavior towards a patient causes a complaint to be lodged against him, triggering his dismissal. Upon returning home, his squat, unsightly mother urges him to seek revenge.

After a gory scene in which he not only cuts the throat of the woman and her fey husband with a scalpel but also gouges out her eyes for his collection, pic veers upon a startling new tack, as Bigas Luna shows us the action thus far has been a film within a film. As the camera pulls back, we see we are sitting in an old ramshackle cinema, located in a modern American site in Los Angeles.

Action now centers on two young girls who have been watching the film. One of them turns queasy, goes out to the rest room, only to encounter a man with a silencer-gun, also with a mother obsession, who has shot two of the attendants and has dragged their bodies into the toilet. Thereupon ensues a strange but fascinating mix of the two killers stalking members of the audience as they are watching the very film with the eye doctor, who sneaks up behind people seated in the audience and dispatches them. A clever plot twist at the end perfectly rounds out this 90-minute, taut film.

Fine thesping, especially by the two killers, Michael Lerner and Angel José, excellent production

values, good special effects, and compulsive editing and Dolby music track make item a winner. —*Besa.*

Lo Negro del Negro
(The Black Side Of Blackie)
(MEXICAN-COLOR)

A Peliculas Mexicanas release of a Cinematográfica Escamilla-Gonzalez production. Executive producer, Alberto Escamilla Espinosa. Directed by Angel Rodriguez Vazquez, Benjamin Escamilla Espinosa. Stars Rodolfo de Anda, Ricardo Deloera. Screenplay, Angel Rodriguez, based on the book of the same name of José González González; camera (color), Fernando Alvarez Colin; editor, Francisco Chiu; music, Carlos Torres Marin. Reviewed at Big Apple Cine 2, N.Y., March 5, 1987. Running time: **109 MINS.**
Flaco . . . . Rodolfo de Anda
Negro . . . . Ricardo Deloera
Elvia . . . . Ivon Govea
El General . . . . Rafael Buendia
Zenón . . . . Eric del Castillo
Also with: Juan Pelaez, Arturo Martinez Jr., Bruno Rey, Fabián, Rubi Re, César Sobrevals, Sergio Bustamante, Norma Lee, Roberto Cañedo, Don Arturo Martinez, Consuelo Veronica, Ramón Blanco, Marta Elena Cervantes, Jorge Fegán.

"Lo Negro del Negro" (The Black Side Of Blackie) is a cheap and dishonest attempt to make some quick cash from the scandals of Mexico's former political administration (1976-82). Pic is based on the national best-selling book of the same name chronicling the corrupt rule and alleged crimes of former Mexico City Police Chief Arturo (Negro — "Blackie") Durazo Moreno, at present on trial in Mexico for tax fraud, possession of illegal firearms and contraband and extortion of money from the police department.

The exposé was written by former body guard José González González, called "El Flaco" in the film and played by Rodolfo de Anda.

All other real-life names have been altered slightly, the country left unnamed. A cowardly and dishonest warning appears at both the beginning and end of the film to acknowledge it is based on the book and unconnected with anyone living or dead. To avoid further political problems, the pic coddles the current administration while carefully avoiding direct mention of former president José López Portillo.

The book was poorly penned and its big-screen adaptation is even worse. There is little sense of narrative, not even a psychological glimpse into the corruptive nature of power. Instead, there is merely a tedious chronicle of abuses that, when piled one atop the other, dull the senses.

While "Blackie" (Ricardo Deloera) wallows in his black deeds, "El Flaco" is depicted as the only sensitive, hard-working honest family man working in the fox' lair.

Production values are inconsistent depending on the light source used. A few of the daytime exteriors tend to be washed out. The thesping is completely flat and lifeless, adher-

ing too closely to the two-dimensional script.

"The Black Side Of Blackie"is no south-of-the-border "Scarface." What could have been a probing study of evil and the corruption of power ends up merely a titillating parade of heinous abuses. Here the filmmakers are as guilty of abuse and self-indulgence as the subject they try to expose.—*Lent.*

Zabou
(WEST GERMAN-COLOR/B&W)

A Neue Constantin Film (Munich) release of a Bavaria Atelier (Munich) production in coproduction with Neue Constantin Filmproduktion and WDR (Cologne). Executive producer, Michael Rohrig. Produced by Günter Rohrbach. Directed by Hajo Gies. Stars Götz George. Screenplay, Martin Gies, in association with Axel Götz; camera (color, b&w), Axel Block; editor, Hannes Nikel; music, Klaus Lage; title song "Now That You're Gone," sung by Joe Cocker; sound, Thomas Meyer; art direction, Jan Kott; assistant director, Stefan Schieder; production managers, Rolf M. Degener, Friedhelm Schatz; stunt coordinator, François Doge; special effects, Heinz Ludwig; action scenes, Robert Menegoz; costumes, Rosemarie Hettmann; associate producer, Heidi Steinhaus. Reviewed at Esplanade cinema, Hauptwache, Frankfurt, W. Germany, March 26, 1987. Running time: **102 MINS.**
Schimanski . . . . Götz George
Conny/Zabou . . . . Claudia Messner
Thanner . . . . Eberhard Feik
Also with: Wolfram Berger (Hocks), Hannes Jaenicke (Melting), Dieter Pfaff (Schäfer), Ralf Richter (Sandrowski), Klaus Lage (cook), Annette Kreft (hostess).

Frankfurt — Seldom has film p.r. been more accurate than in the line "Götz George Is Schimanski." During a long and varied career in theater, film and tv, the rugged, attractive George (born in 1938 as the son of the famous actor and actress Heinrich George and Berta Drews) consistently has been one of Germany's most popular and identifiable stars despite the third-rate commercial productions in which he almost always has worked. His greatest success to date has been the role of the anarchic, emotional, none too scrupulous police commissioner Schimanski, which he originally created for German tv's long-lived, popular crime thriller series "Tatort" and which he has also portrayed in the two made-for-cinema Schimanski flics, "Zahn um Zahn" and the current "Zabou," both directed by Hajo Gies, one of the creators of the tv character.

"Zabou's" plot is simple to the point of simple-mindedness, though related in a manner that is at times as confusing as it is unbelievable. In this episode Schimanski tackles the drug world that has taken root in his rainy, gray native city of Duisburg in Germany's Rühr district. Together with his friend and sidekick Thanner (Eberhard Feik, as always) he moves in on the ultrachic new disco club Sunflash run by the shady former peepshow proprietor Hocks (Wolfram Berger). There, while roughing up clientele and employees in his typical ersatz-Rambo style, Schimanski recognizes in a beautiful nightclub dancer/hostess the daughter of a long since forgotten love, a girl named Conny (promising newcomer Claudia Messner in her second film role) whom he had loved as if she had been his own daughter, but who in the bloom of adolescence had been completely infatuated with him.

Schimanski decides to rescue her from the evils of drugs. However, Conny is no longer the girl he once knew, the flirtatious blond child the audience witnesses in nostalgic black & white flashbacks as the credits start to roll. Conny now calls herself Zabou — and she hasn't the slightest intention of being rescued.

The rest of the story fails to explore at any depth the love-hate relationship of Conny/Zabou to her neglectful father-figure/lover, but rather loses itself in frantic chases, deceits, conflicts between fellow cops and among the drug bosses.

Although Axel Block's camera gives the film a polished look, it is directed without inspiration and written sloppily. It fails to flow and never reaches the height of *film noir* melodrama. Perhaps "Zabou's" very mediocrity accounts in part for its relatively good commercial success, and it is not unlikely that the vulnerable toughness of its hero and the crude fascination of some of its action scenes will assure the film a certain amount of b.o. popularity beyond Germany's borders. —*Loc.*

Stewardess School
(COLOR)

Comedy aims low; strictly for ancillary markets.

A Columbia Pictures release from Columbia-Delphi V Prods. of a Summa Entertainment Group-Triton Ltd. production. Produced by Phil Feldman. Written and directed by Ken Blancato. Camera (Deluxe color), Fred J. Koenekamp; editor, Kenneth C. Paonessa, Lou Lombardo; music, Robert Folk; sound, Dick Raguse; production design, Daniel A. Lomino; set design, Sue Lomino; set decoration, Robert Zilliox; production manager-coproducer, Jerry A. Baerwitz; coproducer, Michael Kane; assistant director, Bill Scott; associate producers, Don McFarlane, Elizabeth A. Bardsley; casting, Melissa Skoff. Reviewed on RCA/Columbia Home Video vidcassette, N.Y., March 21, 1987. (MPAA Rating: R.) Running time: **93 MINS.**
Philo .Brett Cullen
Kelly . . . . .Mary Cadorette
George . . . . .Donald Most
Wanda . . . . .Sandahl Bergman
Miss Grummett . . . . .Vicki Frederick
Sugar Dubois . . . . .Judy Landers
Jolean . . . . .Wendie Jo Sperber
Pimmy . . . . .Julia Montgomery
Snake . . . . .Dennis Burkley
Cindy . . . . .Corinne Bohrer
  Also with: Rob Paulsen, Vito Scotti, Rod McCary, William Bogert, Alan Rosenberg, Sherman Hemsley, Yuliis Ruvál, Richard Erdman, Brooke Bundy, Gloria Leroy, Joe Dorsey, Leslie Huntly, Fran Ryan.

It doesn't take a lot of hindsight to see the problem Columbia had

with its "high concept," "can't miss" project "Stewardess School." Unabashed attempt to capitalize on the success of WB's "Police Academy" and Par's "Airplane" features contains some effective yocks but is extremely vulgar, suited for drive-in audiences. Drive-ins are not exactly a primary market for Col, so the pic played briefly in Detroit last August, ahead of its April vidcassette release.

Working with a substantial budget ($8,000,000) for this type of sexploitation comedy, debuting writer-director Ken Blancato has a good cast and impressive production scale. What's lacking is cast chemistry and a fresh storyline.

Heroes Brett Cullen and his sidekick Donald Most try stewardess school when their budding careers as airplane pilots crash with Cullen's poor eyesight, causing them to be kicked out of pilot school. The stewardess academy is lorded over by martinet Vicki Frederick, intent on washing out the misfits, who happen to include our heroes plus a motley crew of attractive young women. Chief among these is accident-prone Mary Cadorette, the voluptuous Judy Landers (whose sister Audrey similarly costarred with Frederick in Col's "A Chorus Line") as an ex-hooker with always-alluring décolletage, butt of fat jokes Wendie Jo Sperber and in solid casting, statuesque Sandahl Bergman as an ex-wrestler.

Misfits are literally sold to poverty row airline owner Vito Scotti to get him past an inspection run and of course Cullen's bad eyes (plus a guest appearance by Sherman Hemsley as a blind passenger) figure prominently in the climax.

Blancato's humor is several notches below the gross-out approach of a "Porky's" pic, with toilet gags and sexual material (Landers "relaxing" an agitated passenger during the big flight) abounding. Principals keep their clothes on, with requisite nudity left to such alluring femmes as Lesli Huntly and Playboy model Yuliis Ruvál (a.k.a. Lillian Müller).

It's highly unlikely that David Puttnam's regime at Col will followup on this watershed film.
—*Lor.*

Anayurt Oteli
(Motherland Hotel)
(TURKISH-COLOR)

An Odak Film production and release. Produced by Cengiz Ergun. Written and directed by Omer Kavur. Camera (color, 16m), Orhan Oguz; music, Atilla Ozdomiroglu; editor, Mevlud Kogak; art director, Sahin Kaygijn. Reviewed at the Istanbul Film Days, April 17, 1987. Running time: **110 MINS.**
Zebercet . . . . .Macid Koper
  Also with: Serra Yilmaz, Orhan Cagman.

Istanbul — Local standout at the Istanbul Film Days was

"Motherland Hotel," a sophisticated tale of pathological loneliness with nods to Freud by Omer Kavur, a young director who has already made seven features. A surprising, stimulating work with nothing of the conventionally "Turkish" about it, "Motherland Hotel" is already on its way to international fests and is an excellent pick-up for adventurous art circuits.

Setting is a sprawling old hotel in a small provincial town, which a quiet young man named Zebercet (Macid Koper) has inherited from his parents. Pic's low-key start sets the stage but hardly prepares the viewer for the shift in register that occurs after a pretty girl spends a night in the hotel. She promises to return in a week, and Zebercet begins an impatient vigil. When she doesn't come back, he starts falling to pieces in a most preoccupying way, revealing a psychopathic, Norman Bates personality below his melancholy, reserved exterior. First he sends prospective clients away, and passes his time sleeping in "her" room. After meeting a youth at a cockfight, Zebercet hesitantly turns down his homosexual overtures, only to rape the hotel maid and strangle her to death. He leaves the body where it is, kills her cat, and nonchalantly helps police get on the trail of an old client. Only at pic's end, after Zebercet has quietly done away with himself, does camera move in on an old photo of his mother, who has the same face as the girl he waited for in vain.

Apart from its psychological intrigue, "Hotel" is splendidly shot and edited. Stage thesp Koper puts on a one-man show of perturbing fascination. —*Yung.*

De Tal Pedro, Tal Astilla
(Like Father, Like Daughter)
(CUBAN-COLOR)

An ICAIC production and release. Produced by Ricardo Avila. Written and directed by Luis Felipe Bernaza. Camera (color), Jorge Haydu; editor, Mirita Lores; music, Tony Tano, Aneiro Tano. Reviewed at Berlin Film Festival (Market), Feb. 24, 1987. Running time: **90 MINS.**
With: Reynaldo Miravilles, Ana Viña, Nancy Gonzalez, Gilberto Reyes, Thais Valdes, Nestor Rivero, Hilario Peña, Tito Junco, Tania Perez James, Orlando Casin.

Berlin — "Like Father, Like Daughter" is a routine comedy-with-songs about rival cattle ranchers. The opening credits admit inspiration from Shakespeare, and there are elements of "Romeo And Juliet," "The Taming Of The Shrew" and "A Comedy Of Errors" in this predictable affair.

Two former friends, cattle ranchers, have been rivals for years and are forever in competition as to who's better at his job. Then the son of one falls for the daughter of another and a cowboy working for one also falls for a daughter of his boss'

rival. The ensuing complications are entirely predictable, and the film is in every way undistinguished, though the locations are attractive.

This is a Cuban production which appears to have been produced purely as entertainment, with no thought whatever for any kind of social message. —*Strat.*

Le Foto di Gioia
(Photos Of Joy)
(ITALIAN-COLOR)

A Medusa release of a Devon Film/Dania Film/Medusa Distribuzione/Filmes Intl./Natl. Cinematografica coproduction. Presented by Medusa, Dania and Reteitalia. Directed by Lamberto Bava. Stars Serena Grandi. Screenplay, Gianfranco Clerici, Daniele Stoppa; camera (Technicolor), Gianlorenzo Battaglia; art direction, Antonello Geleng; music, Simon Boswell. Reviewed at Quirinale Cinema, Rome, April 26, 1987. Running time: **93 MINS.**
Gioia .Serena Grandi
Evelyn . . . . .Dari Nicolodi
Kim . . . . .Katrine Michelsen
Flora . . . . .Capucine
Sabrina . . . . .Sabrina Salerno
Roberto . . . . .David Brandon
  Also with: Vanni Corbellini (Tony), George Eastman, Karl Zinny (Mark).

Rome — Misleadingly advertised as an erotic topliner buxom star of the moment Serena Grandi and several lesser lights, "Photos Of Joy" falls more comfortably into the thriller category beloved of director Lamberto Bava. Though setting revolves around the editorial offices of Pussycat, a men's magazine, the one female nude is there strictly to be better stung to death by bees, and Grandi, to the disappointment of her fans, has nary a real nude in the picture. To the disappointment of Bava's fans, "Photos" isn't much of a chiller, either. It has produced little joy at the local boxoffice.

Grandi plays the rich widow Gioia, heiress to a softcore mag in which she once appeared as a model. Now a respectable porn publisher, she watches while her brother Tony (Vanni Corbellini) reshoots one of her most famous layouts with model Katrine Michelsen. That evening, a crazed murderer, who breathes noisily and sees the world in shades of red and violet, puts a pitchfork through Michelsen.

Another model, Sabrina Salerno, meets the beekeeper's death not long after, and Pussycat sales shoot up. The killer's sadistic trademark is making a photo of his disfigured victims in front of a blow-up of Gioia, much to the latter's distress. Adding to her problems are a few other pesky characters: Capucine in the role of a high-strung competitor who wants to buy her out, and Karl Zinny as a crippled neighbor with a spy telescope. Daria Nicolodi, a favorite villainess in Dario Argento chillers, appears in a supporting role as Gioia's editor and friend.

Everyone is a suspect, and the killer seems to be selected at random, making the denouement of this mystery quite uninteresting. Able craftsman that he is, Bava keeps camera and action on the move, but without much result. Antonello Geleng's imaginative sets give pic an above-average look.

— *Yung.*

Yama — Yararetara Yarikaese
(Yama — Attack To Attack)
(JAPANESE-DOCU-COLOR)

A 'Yama' Production Committee production. Produced and directed by Mitsuo Sato, Kyoichi Yamaoka. Camera (color), Sato, Yamaoka. No further credits supplied. Reviewed at Hong Kong Film Festival, April 18, 1987. Running time: **109 MINS.**

Hong Kong — This docu about labor unrest in Japan must be unique in that both the directors who worked on it were murdered. Apparently they were killed because they dared to expose the way *yakuza,* or gangsters, use standover tactics and extortion in the labor area.

Pic was started in December 1984 by Mitsuo Sato; just over two weeks into filming, he was stabbed to death. Kyoichi Yamaoka took over as cameraman/director, and completed the film in December 1985, but was himself shot to death two weeks later. Both murders were blamed on the *yakuza.*

Given these dual tragedies, it's sad to say the film that cost the lives of two crusading men isn't better, or at least more accessible, than it is. It's a rambling, often incoherent, exposé which sets out to reveal the plight of day laborers in the construction industry, most of whom live in the Sanya slum area of Tokyo. Gangster families run a protection racket and a "mutual aid society," creaming off money from the workers, and adding to their misery, according to the film.

Not content with this theme, which is powerful enough, the docu then goes off to explore the plight of Korean coalminers and the appalling way they're treated. This sidetracking only adds running time.

Still, the self-styled "fighting film" has some strong scenes of confrontations and demonstrations, and is well shot, under often taxing conditions. The music score is no asset. —*Strat.*

SES
(The Voice)
(TURKISH-COLOR)

A Serif Oür production. Directed by Zeki Okten. Screenplay, Fehmi Yasar; camera (color), Orhan Oguz; music, Tarik Ocal. Reviewed at the Istanbul Film Days, April 16, 1987. Running time: **87 MINS.**
Young man . . . . Tarik Akan
Girl . . . . Nur Sürer
Also with: Kamuran Usluer.

Istanbul — Zeki Okten, one of Yilmaz Güney's most talented co-

directors ("The Herd" with Güney; "The Wrestler" on his own), unfolds a tale of a former political prisoner's repressed rage in "The Voice." On the quiet side, with nothing flashy about it (except a knockout setting on the Aegean coast), pic takes its time building to a tense final showdown.

Okten clearly had his hands tied to a certain degree, and "Voice" lacks the emotional payoff that seems to be coming. An up-in-the-air ending may discourage offshore viewers unused to filling in the blanks, but festplay is indicated.

A young man (Tarik Akan) with a haunted, unhappy look arrives in a small fishing village, after spending six years behind bars. Fitting in neither with the kindly fishermen, nor the summer vacationers, the man leads an aimless existence. A girl on vacation (Nur Sürer) befriends him and a romantic relationship begins to develop between them. Then one night he thinks he recognizes the voice of one of his prison torturers. He kidnaps the suspected torturer and ties him up in an abandoned church, but the girl discourages him from taking revenge, saying simply that "it isn't his voice."

Acting is low-key but effective, and Okten is a master at sensitively rendering the nuances of the delicate man-girl relationship, establishing their intimacy in the very few words they exchange. The stranger's friendship with the fishermen is equally laconic, and in fact most of the talking is left to the cruel, swaggering "suspect" whose hated voice brings memories of the past flowing back to the man.

"Voice" is a subtle, sensitive film that tackles the painful political situation in Turkey not directly but from behind, and gains much in resonance from this roundabout approach. Only the ambiguity of the ending leaves something to be desired, something more to be said.

Orhan Oguz's clear, bright lensing is quite dazzling. —*Yung.*

Degirmen
(The Mill)
(TURKISH-COLOR)

An Odak Film production and release. Produced by Cengiz Ergun. Directed by Atif Yilmaz. Screenplay, Baris Pirhasan; camera (color), Orhan Oguz; music, Arif Erkin. Reviewed at the Istanbul Film Days, April 16, 1987. Running time: **100 MINS.**
Halil Hilmi . . . . Sener Sen
Naciye . . . . Serap Aksoy
Also with: Levent Yilmaz.

Istanbul — Versatile veteran filmmaker Atif Yilmaz has already had three features in release this year, including last year's top b.o. grosser "Aah...Belinda." "The Mill" is a delightful historical farce with serious underpinnings, set in a small town near Istanbul in 1914.

In addition to poking fun at gullible bureaucrats during the Ottoman Empire, "Mill" points an accusing finger at the hidden poverty of the land and state indifference to same. Off-beat and fun, it should slip into some foreign fests.

Talk of the sleepy town is an exciting new Bulgarian belly dancer named Naciye, who has the menfolk in a tizzy. The local rich landowner invites the new district officer, Halil Hilmi (Sener Sen), to see her perform in an all-male dinner. A mild earthquake disjoints several limbs in the middle of the evening, as the cowardly officials run for their lives. The next day, news of the "earthquake" nobody else felt gets into the Istanbul papers, and one thing leads to another.

A special disaster commission stages a visit with money and food for the victims; then higher and higher officials are announced, until the prince himself appears on the scene. The good-hearted but ineffectual Halil Hilmi, who has been demoted, is reappointed to deal with the crisis by faking a natural catastrophe. As Hilmi sadly remarks, the collapsing buildings and inhuman living conditions of the inhabitants have no need of being faked, and poverty is the real earthquake of the region.

Yilmaz' point is clear, even though dressed up as light entertainment. Bumbling Civil Service gags may not make for belly laughs offshore, but there are many smiles in this mild comedy, well-acted, well-paced and well-lensed. —*Yung.*

El Placer de la Venganza
(The Pleasure Of Vengeance)
(MEXICAN-COLOR)

A Peliculas Mexicanas release of a Prod. Esme-Alianza Cinematográfica Mexicana production. Produced by Carlos Vasallo. Directed by Hernando Name. Stars Susana Dosamantes. Screenplay, Carlos Valdemar, Roberto Schlosser; camera (color), Xavier Cruz; editor, Rogelio Zúñiga; music, Carlos Torres Marín. Reviewed at Big Apple Cine 1, N.Y., March 1, 1987. Running time: **89 MINS.**
Cristina Ruiz . . . . Susana Dosamantes
Adrián Parra . . . . Hugo Stiglitz
Commandante
Gallardo . . . . Pedro Armendáriz
Omar Mendoza . . . . : Andres García Jr.
Julius . . . . Eleazar García Jr.
Also with: Diana Ferreti, Ricardo Carrión, Raúl Araiza Jr.

"El Placer de la Venganza" (The Pleasure Of Vengeance) is a technically well-made Mexican psychological thriller with some built-in stumbling blocks.

Where the pic falls the hardest is in its pandering to the cheap and bloody violence expected from the title, which is neither effective nor convincing.

Actress Susana Dosamantes plays a psychiatrist whose husband and two children are slaughtered when

they accidentally chance upon the remote robbery of an armored car by a motorcycle gang of young toughs. Rather than seek mental help, we find her in church thanking God for sending her one of the assassins (Andres García Jr.), who inadvertently comes to her for consultations when he suffers a pang of conscience. She kills the gang one by one until they get wise to her.

Script is muddled by the inclusion of a contrived rivalry between secondary characters Comandante Gallardo (Pedro Armendáriz), a hard-boiled cop two steps and no leads behind whatever is happening, and Adrián Parra (Hugo Stiglitz), an investigative reporter with an uncanny sense of timing.

Tech credits hold up and the acting talents, especially Dosamantes, are strong, despite the incongruities of the script.—*Lent.*

Sventlyachki
(Fireflies)
(SOVIET-COLOR)

A Goskino release of a Gruziafilm production. Directed by David Dzanelidze. Screenplay, Revaz Ivanishvili; camera (color), Leri Macaidze. Reviewed at Kabuki theater, San Francisco Film Festival, April 5, 1987. Running time: **60 MINS.**
With: Marech Likokeli, Becyk Odishelishvili.

San Francisco — "Fireflies" is a slow-moving mood piece, a character study of the loneliness of a 10-year-old girl. In Georgian, and subtitled, pic is first feature of young director David Dzanelidze and technically okay.

Pic never reaches the "poetry" level hyped in Friscofest program notes, but it's often touching. Child lives only with the father, who's out working most of the day. She has contact, just for one day, with an orphan boy he brings home and tries to extend that emotional contact after the boy leaves.

The girl plays with a cat, plays bingo solo, and visits — in a marvelously moving moment, the snow-covered grave of her mother. Not much happens, or should. —*Herb.*

Sworn Brothers
(HONG KONG-COLOR)

A Bo Ho Film & Movie Impact coproduction, released by Golden Harvest. Executive Producer, Sammo Hung. Directed by David Lai. Screenplay, David Lai, from story by Manfred Wong; music, Chris Babida; art direction, Tony Au; asssociate producer, Peter Chan. Reviewed at Park theater, Hong Kong, April 3, 1987. Running time: **98 MINS.**
With: Lau Tak Wah, Cheung Kowk Keung, Vivien Siu, Tung Biu.
(Cantonese soundtrack with English subtitles)

Hong Kong — "Sworn Brothers' is another pic structured in the mode of cops and robbers films with the indispensible gun-shooting and blood-splashing scenes. It's a melodrama centering on the theme of loyalty to the crime synidcate and love towards the paternal guardian.

Lau Tak Wah portrays a hit man, an orphan raised under the paternal custody of Tung Biu who also has a son played by Cheung Kwok Keung. Both father and son are servicemen in the police force though the father has retired.

Cheung is a graduate of the Scotland Yard, and as soon as he reports to duty at the police headquarters, he is assigned to the case which involves Lau's syndicate. Despite his undoubted fraternal love for Lau, he is determined to have Lau brought to justice.

The eventual shoot-out is marvelously filmed. It ends when Lau, wounded and bleeding, walks down the crowded streets of the Hong Kong city; gun still in one hand, passes the gangster, and turns, facing him and shooting at him point-blank.

The director has a good dramatic set pieces but they come off as overly sentimental. The portrayal of Cheung as a law enforcer is sadly forced and unconvincing. —Mel.

Noi Uomini Duri
(Us Real Men)
(ITALIAN-COLOR)

A CDI release of a C.G. Silver Film production. Produced by Mario and Vittorio Cecchi Gori. Directed by Maurizio Ponzi. Stars Renato Pozzetto, Enrico Montesano. Screenplay, Leo Benvenuti, Piero De Bernardi, Ponzi; camera (Eastmancolor), Alessandro D'Eva; editor, Sergio Montanari; music, Beppe Cantarelli. Reviewed at Eden Cinema, Rome, March 25, 1987. Running time: **90 MINS.**
Silvio . . . . Renato Pozzetto
Mario . . . . Enrico Montesano
    Also with: Isabel Russinova, Antonella Vitale, Alessandra Mussolini, Maria Angela Giordano, Ovidio Martucci, Novello Novelli.

Rome — Producers Mario and Vittorio Cecchi Gori fall back on the old trick of putting Northern and Southern audiences together via stars Renato Pozzetto (Milan) and Enrico Montesano (Rome), in an above-average comedy set in a survival camp. Local boxoffice has been excellent, and its genteel humor and human characters should play well in related markets.

The survival camp in question features a two-week course on how to make out in the midst of an Amazonian rain forest when your equipment has been washed down river in a flash flood. The dozen participants are a diversified lot, whose interest in taking the course ranges from preparing for their next trip to the Amazon (a sporty dentist and his wife) to finding a partner of the opposite sex (a schoolteacher and girl from Perugia quickly find each other and forget the course). There is also a father and son, a middle-aged grocer and his jolly frau, plus a pair of fun-loving girls.

The heroes have come to prove to themselves they are "real men:" Pozzetto because his shrink has advised him to get in touch with his body to combat impotency problems, Montesano because his wife left him and he suffers from feelings of insecurity. Though he is only a tram conductor, Montesano arrives posing as an airline pilot. Pozzetto the banker tries to escape all difficulties by waving his checkbook. Equally incompetent on the trail, the two inevitably pair up and, after misadventures and a big quarrel, finish the course with flying colors, the best of friends.

Director Maurizio Ponzi, whose recent credits include the Sophia Loren tv film "Aurora," injects a fairly subtle character study of mid-age crisis into a routine story, without spoiling any of the comedy. Pic is entirely lensed in simple, natural surroundings.—Yung.

Water Also Burns
(TURKISH-COLOR)

A Toei Co. release of a Young Cinema 85 production. Directed by Ali Ozgentürk; camera (color), Ertunc Senkay; editor, Peter Presgodard; music, Sarper Ozhan. Reviewed at the Istanbul Film Days, April 18, 1987. Running time: **115 MINS.**
The director . . . . Tarik Akan
Wife . . . . Sahika Tekand
Girlfriend . . . . Nathalie Douverné

Istanbul — Ali Ozgentürk has made a courageous outcry for freedom of speech in "Water Also Burns," a film with little chance of getting past the Turkish censors and into general release nationally. The tale of a film director who wants to make a film but is tormented by the political-psychological difficulties of such an endeavor, quickly becomes repetitive and tiresome, reducing its chances for fest and art house play abroad as well.

Tarik Akan toplines as the nameless director, who has just been released from prison after serving a long sentence. He lives in a modern flat with his wife, a nurse (Sahika Tekand), and their daughter, but his love affair with a soul-scraching French woman (Nathalie Douverné) who "fought in Paris in '68" breaks up the marriage. Of the three main characters, the wife emerges as the most sensible and sympathetic of the lot, while the egotistical husband (who looks a lot like a Turkish Nikita Mikhalkov) loses points by the minute. Naturally, he loses both women in the end.

His film, however, gets made, or at least begun in the last sequence. Surviving another harrowing, unwarranted arrest, the director somehow gets the go-ahead to shoot — though with what chances of release, Ozengtürk himself could ruefully recount.

Best thing in "Water" is Ertunc Senkay's poetic images of dawn, wind, sea, and many striking compositions, like women in mourning bearing giant pictures of their loved ones, presumably missing victims of the regime. Too bad storyline is not more tightly scripted. Film was produced with the help of Ozgentürk's share of the Tokyo Film Festival cash prize for best first film. Toei Co. is billed as distributor. — Yung.

Magino-Mura Monogatari
(Tales From The Magino Village)
(JAPANESE-COLOR-16m)

An Ogawa production. Produced by Hiro Fuseya. Written and directed by Shinsuke Ogawa. Camera (color), (16m), Masaki Tamura, editor, Ogawa, Toshio Iizuka, Yoko Shirashi; music, Masahiko Togashi; sound, Yukio Kobota, Noboyuki Kikuchi; sets, Shiro Tatsumi, Sadatoshi Mikado. Reviewed at the Berlin Film Festival (Forum), Feb..22, 1987. Running time: **222 MINS.**
    With: Tatsumi Hijikata, Junko Miyashita, Masao Kikuchi, Cho Kimura (first tale), Takahiro Tamura, Choichiro Kawarazaki, Renji Ishibashi, Shogo Shimada, Masio Igarashi, Kichiemon Inoue, Masaki Kimura, Masuo Igarashi, Toshiro Takahashi, Toshio Takemura, Hideaki Yoshida (second tale).

Berlin — Shinsuke Ogawa is nothing if not a thorough artist. To make this film, about life in a small Japanese village, he spent some 13 years there, trying to go one more step into the rural existence of his country, already amply expanded upon in his previous marathon documentary about the Furuyashiki village. Typically, it is once again the Berlin Forum, as usual extremely keen on ethnographical items of this kind, that unspools the new picture, after having shown the previous one three years ago.

Ogawa, who wants to reach the roots and the essence of living in a village, with all the worries, preoccupations, but also all the myths, customs and local legends which still influence the villagers to a great extent, starts in a very methodical manner. For the first 40 minutes, one has the impression of watching a very detailed documentary about planting rice, the kind one would expect to find on instructional tv. Only then does Ogawa move into the legends and their relation to dailylife, legends first told by one of the villagers, than commented upon by history teachers, and finally re-enacted for the benefit of the camera. He dwells upon myths and rites and enlarges the scope, while returning from time to time to the scientific aspects of agriculture, as applied today in the village.

The different levels employed here blend together quite effectively, since Ogawa shares with his audience his interest for the different aspects, and leads naturally from one to another, keeping all of them, including the dramatized scenes, in a subdued, natural form.

Breathtaking photography offers some glorious landscapes from Japan's countryside, the only serious obstacle the film has, being its excessive length. At close to four hours, this is an item bound to interest primarily students of either ethnography or cinema, for whom this is a must. —Edna.

El Hombre de la Deuda Externa
(The Man Of The Foreign Debt)
(ARGENTINE-COLOR)

An Irondel release of a Kane production. Executive producer, Mario Vitali. Directed by Pablo Olivo. Screenplay, Olivo, Carlos Brandi; camera, Juan Carlos Lenardi; editor, Sergio Zotola; music, Carlos Fradkin, Daniel Berardi; production design, Jorge Marchegiani; sound, J. Stavropoulos; assistant director, Gumersindo Rama. Reviewed at Berlin Film Festival (Market), March 1, 1987. Running time: **95 MINS.**
Pedro . . . . Hector. Alterio
Alicia . . . . Luisina Brando
Marcelo . . . . Jorge Mayorano
Ines . . . . Adriana Gardiazabal
    Also with Carlos Caceres, Carola Reyna, Raul Rossi, Elida Gay Palmer, Rosa Rosen, Perla Santalla.

Berlin — This is a rather labored comedy about an adman who inherits a gigantic fortune — enough to pay off Argentina's crippling foreign debt.

Hector Alterio, a gifted actor, can't make much of the poorly written character of Pedro a dreamy fellow given to Walter Mitty-type fantasies (he sees his imposing woman boss in various threatening guises). His life changes once he becomes a multibillionaire and agrees to pay off his country's borrowings although his wife leaves him and goes off to Europe and he's eventually assassinated.

Needless to say, it was all a dream, and when a call comes which indicates the dream may be coming true, he refuses to take it.

This shapes up as a pic strictly for home consumption where the jokes and references will mean something. Level of humor is low, and Alterio is called upon to act more broadly than is his usual style.

Technically, film is adequate.
                            —Strat.

Der Bärenhäuter
(Bear-Skinned Man)
(EAST GERMAN-COLOR)

A DEFA production. Produced by Siegfried Kabitzke. Written and directed by Walter Beck, from a fairy tale by the Brothers Grimm; camera (color), Günter Heimann; editor, Ilse Peters; music, Günther Fischer; sound, Werner Dibowski; art direction, Paul Lehmann; assistant director, Hanna Seydel; animation effects, Erich Günther, Heiko Ebert, Tony Loeser, Frank Wittstock, Wolfgang Chevallier. Reviewed at Berlin Film Festival (Children's Film Fest), Feb. 26, 1987. Running time: **81 MINS.**
Christoffel . . . . Jens-Uwe Bogadtke
Katarina . . . . Janina Hartwig
Satan . . . . Manfred Heine

Berlin — An East German medieval costume drama for kiddies, "Der Bärenhäuter" (Bear-Skinned Man) is nicely shot and acted, but much too talky.

Film retells ye olde yarne by the Grimm Bros. about a penniless youth who makes a pact with the devil. Hapless knave agrees not to bathe or cut his hair for seven years in return for a coat with magic pockets ever full of gold. Handsome as he is, young Christoffel (creditably played by Jens-Uwe Bogadtke) soon becomes repulsive to all — nay, save yon faire maid Katarina (Janina Hartwig), who spies inner beauty beneath the funk.

Fortified by her innocent love, he holds out and gets both coat and girl after the seven years are over.

Alas and alack, film's drawn-out handling makes unspooling time seen about that long, too. By Year Two Teutonic tykes at this Berlin Film Fest screening have got mighty squirmy. By Year Four a spitball fight has broken out across one of the aisles.

Truce is declared and the air clears briefly during an adequate animation sequence in which Satan (Manfred Heine) magically propels soap, a straight razor and shears through the air to put Christoffel back in shape.

Some cutting room devil should have taken the shears and trimmed this film down to the half-hour format its story treatment can carry.
—*Gill.*

Das Treibhaus
(The Hothouse)
(W. GERMAN-COLOR/-B&W-16m)

A Peter Goedel Films production, in conjunciton with WDR, NDR, BR, HR and SWF Tv stations and Cult Film Tv Filmproduktion. Written and directed by Goedel, from the novel by Wolfgang Koeppen. Camera (color, b&w, 16m), David Slama; editor, Christiane Jahn, Goedel; sound, Michael Loeken; art direction, Bohdan Wozniak. Reviewed at Berlin Film Festival (Panorama), Feb. 28, 1987. Running time: **98 MINS.**
With: Christian Doermer, Jörg Hube, Hanns Zischler, O.A. Buck, Leila-Florentine Freer.

Berlin — The English title for Peter Goedel's seemingly interminable "Das Treibhaus" is very appropriately "The Hothouse." Claustrophobic film is a talky, heavy-handed yawner which resembles a German radio play more than a film. Prospects are bleak.

Film dies with a talking-head opening interview with Wolfgang Koeppen, whose 1953 novel "Das Treibhaus" portrayed Bonn of the early 1950s as a hothouse for cultivating the same socioeconomic interests that had prevailed before the fall of Nazi Germany. Koeppen rambles on for several minutes about his intentions of nearly 35 years ago.

Interview is followed by a "dramatization" of the novel consisting primarily of a narrator reading lengthy extracts from the book while thesp Christian Doermer goes through the motions of portraying an idealistic parliamentarian who scowls a lot and says little. Most of film is shot in b&w, which only succeeds intensifying its stuffiness.
—*Gill.*

Duma Vez Por Todas
(Play ... Boy)
(PORTUGUESE-COLOR)

A Rosi Burguete production for Producoes Off. Executive producer, Joao Pinto Nogueira. Written and directed by Joaquim Leitao. Camera (color), Daniel Del Negro; editor, Leonor Guterres; music, António Emiliano; art direction, Nuno Carinhas; sound, Pedro Caldas. Reviewed at the Berlin Film Festival (Market), Feb. 24, 1987. Running time: **105 MINS.**
With: Pedro Ayres Magalhaes, Vicky, Filipe Ferrer, Jasmin de Matos, Julian Maynard, Vitor Norte, Madalena Pinto Leite, Henrique Viana, Natalina José.

Berlin — This overlong film had a slow start and when it finally got going it was over. With cutting, the film might do business in the U.S. and other world markets. The female lead, Vicky, proves a sensuous delight and whenever she's on screen the interest quotient shoots up.

A peeping tom (Pedro Ayres Magalhaes) grows fascinated with the life of a beautiful neighbor (Vicky). She's some kind of a call girl, but he can't figure out exactly what's going on until she brings a john to the hotel where he works as a desk clerk. Meeting her gets him gradually caught up in a drug deal double-cross and several murders.

Heavily influenced by French and American filmmakers, this is director Joaquim Leitao's debut and shows lots of promise. He has a nice feel for framing shots and character revelation, but the storyline needs tighter focusing. —*Owl.*

De Ratelrat
(The Rattlerat)
(DUTCH-COLOR)

A Concorde Film release of a Spiegel Filmproductiemaatschappij/Avro-tv production. Produced by Frans Rasker. Directed by Wim Verstappen. Screenplay, Verstappen, Janwillem van de Wetering, Rogier Proper, from the novel by de Wetering; camera (Agfa color), Frans Bromet; editor, Rob van Steensel; music, Ruud Bos; sound, Kees Linthorst; art direction, Dorus van der Linden; production manager, Remmelt Remmelts. Reviewed at City 7 theater, Amsterdam, Feb. 12, 1987. Running time: **88 MINS.**
Captain Grijpstra . . . . Rijk de Gooyer
Lieutenant De Gier . . . . Peter Faber
Also with: Bernard Droog, Hidde Maas, Pieter Lutz, Tetske Ossewaarde, Femke Boersma.

Amsterdam — "De Ratelrat" is helmer Wim Verstappen's second stab at Janwillem van de Wetering's thriller novels about two Amsterdam detectives. Rijk de Gooyer continues to portray the elder cop, Captain Grijpstra, but Peter Faber takes over from Rutger Hauer as Lieutenant De Gier.

Producers have played it safe for Dutch audiences. Pic isn't too fast, there isn't much violence and the sex and nudity are well within limits. The numerous deaths, multiple car crashes and assorted catastrophes are cushioned with horseplay and comic relief. Chances for theatrical release overseas are limited.

Plot is convoluted, with rival gangs of Chinese drug smugglers mixing with bent cops and straight cops, with a few tax evasions and marriage problems thrown in for good measure. Naturally, all ends well, including the matrimonial hardships.

The acting is creditable, with de Gooyer and Hidde Maas (the rural officer) standing out, while Frans Bromet's photography accords well with Verstappen's laid-back style of storytelling. —*Wall.*

Idegenlégiosok
(Mercenaries)
(HUNGARIAN-DOCU-COLOR)

A Magyar Television production. Directed by Gabor Koltai. Screenplay, Koltai, Geza Risko; camera (color), Tamás Andor; editor, Margit Galamb; sound, György Kovacs. Reviewed at Hungarian Film Week, Budapest, Feb. 15, 1987. Running time: 132 MINS.

Budapest — "Mercenaries" is actually the eighth and final episode of a series made for tv called "Szep volt, fiuk..." ("That was Great, Boys!"). Series investigates the state of Hungarian soccer and this final segment was shown as an integral docu feature during the annual Hungarian film week.

Film explores the careers of Hungarian football players who've left the country to play for foreign teams, often at hugely inflated salaries. There are interviews with players, team managers and other officials, plus footage of various matches.

There are some expected problems faced by these expatriate sportsmen who are often ill-equipped to live outside their home country. One sportsman playing with a French team complains bitterly about the undercooked food in France.

Mostly talking heads, film is basically for tv in countries where soccer is played. —*Strat.*

The Legend Of Wisely
(HONG KONG-COLOR)

A Cinema City production, released by Golden Princess. Executive producers, Cinema City/Sam Hui. Directed by Teddy Robin. Stars Sam Hui, Teddy Robin, Ti Lung, Bruce Baron, Wong Joe-Yin. Screenplay, based on the sci-fi novels of I Kwan; camera (color), Peter Bao; costume design, Shirley Chan Ku Fang; art direction, Kenneth Yee Chung Man. Reviewed at President theater, Causeway Bay, Hong Kong. Feb. 6, 1987. Running time: 98 MINS.
(Cantonese soundtrack with English subtitles)

Hong Kong — "Legend Of The Wisely" is Cinema City's big-budget (over $HK20,000,000) science fiction film, based loosely on I Kwan's popular characters from a series of domestic novels. Filmed on exotic locations including Nepal, Taiwan and Cairo, picture works well as high adventure with topnotch production values, but falters as comedy.

Wisely (played by producer Sam Hui, miscast) is a scholar-adventurer goes to Nepal looking dor old friend Prof. Kwan (Teddy Robin), who was chasing after clues to a legendary cult in the Himalayas. He rescues the prof, not realizing that Kwan has stolen a holy object from a five-year-old child monk with extraordinary powers, who is the cult's spiritual leader.

After Kwan dies in a plane crash, Wisely returns to Katmandu only to find the child monk waiting for him. Hero agrees to help the child retrieve the object for the sake of his people. Picture has obvious imitative similarities to Paramount's "Indiana Jones" films and even "The Golden Child," but the I Kwan novels were published long before the "Indiana Jones" character was conceived.

Hui's acting in the lead role is wooden, while Ti Lung in a minor part gives a stronger impression.

Having grossed over $HK18,-000,000 so far, film is reportedly being re-edited and dubbed in English for foreign sales to be made at the Cannes Market, accompanied by a Cinema City promotional contingent.—*Mel.*

Die Papierene Brücke
(The Paper Bridge)
(AUSTRIAN-COLOR-16m)

A Filmladen 1987 (Vienna) production. Executive producer, Josef Aichholzer. Directed by Ruth Beckermann. Camera (color, 16m), Nurith Aviv, Claire Bailly Du Bois; music, Arvo Pärt. Reviewed at the Berlin Film Festival, March 1, 1987. Running time: 95 MINS.

Berlin — "The Paper Bridge" is director Ruth Beckermann's very personal view of the surviving Jewish community in Eastern Europe. Though the subject is important and some of the interviewees are warm and funny, the film never really rises to its theme, and Beckermann's scattered, static directing style is difficult to follow.

Beckermann's cameras trace her relatives' migration around several small towns in the area of Theresienstadt, a concentration camp in which thousands of Jews died. By choosing to focus almost entirely on the current Jewish community there as opposed to the past, Beckermann has left us with little more than a collection of elderly subjects getting dressed, patting their dogs, and waving at the camera.

Nurith Aviv and Claire Bailly Du Bois' camerawork also contains an impressive number of incredibly clichéd shot, from the five-minute focus out a bus window to an endless shot out a moving car's windshield. The sound, however, is sharp and excellent, and Beckermann herself does a good job with the narration. —*Xan.*

Valet Girls
(COLOR)

Weak party comedy.

An Empire Pictures release of a Lexyn production. Produced by Dennis Murphy. Directed by Rafal Zielinski. Screenplay, Clark Carlton; camera (United color), Nicholas von Sternberg; editor, Akiko B. Metz; music, Robert Parr; sound, Ed White; art direction, Dins Danielsen; production manager, Bill Berry; assistant director, Scott White; costume design, Kathie Clark; stunt coordinator, Dan Bradley; special effects makeup, John Buechler. Reviewed on Vestron Video vidcassette, N.Y., April 21, 1987. (No MPAA Rating.) Running time: **82 MINS.**

Lucy . . . . Meri D. Marshall
Rosalind . . . . April Stewart
Carnation . . . . Mary Kohnert
Dirk Zebra . . . . Christopher Weeks
Tina Zebra . . . . Patricia Scott Michel
Lindsay . . . . Jon Sharp
Alvin Sunday . . . . Michael Karm
Ike . . . . Steve Lyon
Ramon . . . . Randy Gallion
Also with: Stuart Fratkin, John Terlesky, Jeane Byron, Charles Cooper, Kenny Sacha, Richard Erdman, Rick Lieberman, Bridget Sienna, Matt Landers, Ron Jeremy.

"Valet Girls" is a meek edition in the party-styled comedies that have emerged endlessly since "Animal House" was a hit nearly a decade ago. Rafal Zielinski-helmed film most closely resembles Crown Intl. Pictures product, such as "My Chauffeur," and was accorded a test-release by Empire Pictures in January, followed by current home-video availability.

Meri D. Marshall and April Stewart topline as young women in Hollywood working as car parking attendants. Problems ensue when they're assigned to work at the mansion of Dirk Zebra (Christopher Weeks) who holds an endless series of parties for movie and record biz folk. Joined by a third girl named Carnation (Mary Kohnert), fresh off the farm, their hiring displaces a trio of guys who attempt to create practical jokes disrupting the parties and trying to get the girls fired.

Gags here are old hat and the whole format, while recalling Blake Edwards' adventurous Peter Sellers film "The Party," is cornball as well. Meri D. Marshall performs several rock songs well, while costar April Stewart is pretty, sports an alluring British accent, but is given nothing interesting to do. Vet character actor Richard Erdman

pops up as a drunken waiter.
Tech credits are adequate.—*Lor.*

Zygfryd
(Siegfried)
(POLISH-COLOR)

A Zespoly Filmowe, Film Unit TOR production. Directed by Andrzej Domalik. Stars Gustaw Holoubek. Screenplay, Domalik, from a short story by J. Iwaszkiewicz; camera (Agfacolor), Grzegorz Kedzierski; editor, Malgorzata Domalik; music, Jerzy Satanowski; art direction, Jerzy Sajko; production manager, Henryk Romanowski. Reviewed at Film Polski, Warsaw, March 13, 1987. Running time: **93 MINS.**

Zygfryd . . . . Gustaw Holoubek
Stefan Drawicz . . . . Tomasz Hudziec
Maria . . . . Maria Pakulnis
Waldo . . . . Jan Nowicki

Warsaw — First feature by Andrzej Domalik is an extraordinarily poetic and moving parable on what it means to be an artist; it is also the account of the tragic collision between a world of culture and a world without. This new release should have excellent prospects for foreign fest pickup.

The artist in question is Zygfryd (Gustaw Holoubek), a handsome young circus acrobat with a withdrawn, introspective temperament. An orphan, he is under the protection of circus owner Waldo (Jan Nowicki) and his wife Maria (Maria Pakulnis), a blond bareback rider of irresistible sensuality. In fact, Zygfryd is irresistibly drawn to her.

A rich intellectual recluse, Stefan Drawicz (Tomasz Hudziec), patron of the arts (and of young artists, like an architect restoring a church), stumbles onto Zygfryd's heart-stopping act under the big top, and offers the boy his friendship. He also opens up cultural horizons, and teaches Zygfryd to consciously reflect on life, something he never did before. It is a heady sensation, but ends in tragedy when the boy finds circus life (that is, physical life) "no longer enough," and falls from the top of a ladder, locus of his performance, his art.

Story is set in 1936 Poland, but its unworldly atmosphere is really timeless and countryless. Helmer Domalik captures the microcosm of the circus with as much love as he does the rich man's book-lined study. Cast and technical work are top-flight down the line. —*Yung.*

Una Pura y Dos Con Sal
(One Straight And Two With Salt)
(MEXICAN-COLOR)

A Peliculas Mexicanas release of a Cima Films production. Produced by and starring Vicente Fernández. Directed by Rafael Villaseñor Kuri. Screenplay, Adolfo Torres Portillo; camera (color), Javier Cruz; editor, Max Sánchez; music, Carlos Torres. Reviewed at Big Apple Cine 2, N.Y., Feb. 13, 1987. Running time: **87 MINS.**

Don Rogelio Andrade . . Vicente Fernández
Aurelia Reyes . . . . Blanca Guerra
Celayo . . . . Lalo el Mimo

Diana . . . . Irma Porter
Also with: Victor Junco, Oscar Traven.

Popular Mexican ranchero singer-actor Vicente Fernández again has teamed with director Rafael Villaseñor Kuri to produce this shaky vehicle about an aging philanderer's attempt to make peace with himself.

"Una Pura y Dos Con Sal" (One Straight And Two With Salt) begins with Diana (Irma Porter) visiting her father Don Rogelio (Fernández) after a hiatus of 15 years. Since his wife left him, Don Rogelio has been jumping from woman to woman in his efforts at happiness. With his daughter's appearance, Don Rogelio launches into an extended flashback depicting his meeting, marriage and subsequent separation from his feisty wife Aurelia (Blanca Guerra). From time to time, flashback is broken by comic scenes of daughter Diana chasing Don Rogelio's current girlfriends out of the house. She has plans to reunite her parents.

Fernández fans probably will delight at seeing their hero once again in the role of a good-hearted rogue who sings ranchero songs whenever the mood strikes him. Following the storyline tends to get a bit confusing, however.

No clear definition or care is given to the flashback sequences. Although Fernández' hair is dyed black in his youthful scenes, nothing else is changed to delineate differences between past and present. A bit of care given to the photography and props could have remedied this easily.

While the film seriously pretends to contrast Mexico's macho attitudes with those of the modern independent woman, we end up with the notion that a woman only needs to be put in her place, which is at her husband's side.

Sound quality changes completely every time that Fernández decides to belt out one of his tunes. Also, cameraman Javier Cruz decides to throw in some of his own hokey lensing devices to embellish the songs.

"Una Pura y Dos Con Sal" is recommended only for the most hardcore Fernández fans. —*Lent.*

Robinson No Niwa
(Robinson's Garden)
(JAPANESE-COLOR)

A Lay Line production. Produced by Aya Shinohara. Directed by Masashi Yamamoto. Screenplay, Yamamoto, Mikio Yamazaki; camera (color), Tom Dicillo, Noboru Asano; editor, Chiaki Tohyama; music, Jagatara, Hamza El Din, Yoichirou Yoshikawa; sound Simpei Kikuchi; art directors, Minoru Osawa, Yuji Hayashida, Akira Ishige; makeup, Mako Kato. Reviewed at the Berlin Film Festval (Forum), Feb. 26, 1987. Running time: **123 MINS.**

With: Kumiko Ota, Tshiibo, Matschida Machizo, Yuko Uneo, Mitsuwa Sakamoto,

Izaba, Oto.

Berlin — After the dark, gritty and nightmarish "Carnival Of The Night" which introduced him four years ago to the forum audiences in Berlin, experimental Japanese filmmaker Masashi Yamamoto returns with another visual poem of remarkable beaty. It's about self-destructing modern society and about nature, which will recoup its own rights, in spite of all the efforts invested by human hands to pollute and destroy this planet.

The picture also has a plot of sorts, concerning a young Japanese dropout who decides to leave her middleclass, nondescript lodging and move into a ruined factory, which she revamps for her own use. She always tries to tame the wild vegetation surrounding the crumbling building, in the middle of town, goes through nightmares and yearns for her departed grandfather. She tries all kinds of trendy fads, trying somehow to make some sense of her life, Yamamoto's comment about modern confusion.

At the end, all the wall paintings are washed away by the rain, the grass invades and covers every vestige of civilization, and the thick roots of the trees penetrate the solid cement walls. In the final, symbolic shot, a little girl flies a toy airplane which goes round and round in the air, without any point or destination.

Yamamoto makes his point less through story or dialog, mostly through strong images, exquisitely photographed. Some sequences, like the interminable night ride on a bicycle, taken in one shot, are reminiscent of his previous film and are virtuoso pieces in their own right. The best moments, however, are the close looks at the marvels of nature, showing the keen eye of both helmer and cameraman. The music, a combination of modern Japanese beat performed by Jagatara, with Indian and Arab sounds, gives the picture its blend of cultural influences popular with the young generation today. —*Edna.*

Zeit der Stille
(Time Of Silence)
(WEST GERMAN-B&W-16m)

A Thorsten Näter Films production for ZDF television. Produced and directed by Thorsten Näter. Screenplay, Näter, from a story by Nino Jacusso; camera (b&w, 16m), Peter von der Reed; editor, Näter; sound, Stefan Guntl; art direction, Andreas M. Velten; assistant director, Dieter Funk; casting, Manfred Stelzer. Reviewed at Berlin Film Festival (Forum), Feb. 25, 1987. Running time: **82 MINS.**

Johanna . . . . Irina Hoppe
Stefan . . . . Pavel Sacher

Berlin — West Berlin serves not only as backdrop for "Zeit der stille" (Time Of Silence), but also in a way as a supporting actor upstaging two thesps who amble through town without saying a word during most of the film. As a glimpse of the real Berlin tourists seldom see, film is a natural for specialty outlets and the fest circuit, despite its 16m, b&w format. Minimum of dialog lowers the German lingo barrier a bit.

Grayness of this divided city at yuletide is used to good advantage in tracing a day in the gray lives of lackadaisical kitchen worker Stefan (Pavel Sacher) and flaky nursing home aide Johanna (Irina Hoppe). Pair do not know each other, and it is only through a wrong number in final minutes of last reel that the duo finally come into contact and dialog begins.

Until then they lurch through a drizzly day toward each other. Soundtrack is the city itself — traffic noises, Christmas carols and kitchen clatter all eloquently boost story along. Knowledge of German lingo and society is helpful, but not necessary to understanding the comic-tragic events that befall the pair during the course of a rather eventful day.

Lack of dialog is scarcely noticed during scenes of a food fight in the kitchen, an erotic encounter in a department store changing room and an armed assault in a garage.

Hoppe and Sacher carry off their essentially pantomime roles well, and transition to dialog comes naturally. Their comic abilities keep grayness at bay. —Gill.

W Starym Dworku
(In An Old Manor House)
(POLISH-COLOR)

A Zespoly Filmowe production. Written and directed by Andrzej Kotkowski, based on the play by Stanislaw Ignacy Witkiewicz. Stars Beata Tyszkiewicz. Camera (color), Witold Adamek; editor, Jaroslaw Wolejko; music, Zbigniew Raj; art director, Malgorzata Zaleska; sound, Stanislaw Piotrowski; production manager, Wojciech Nowicki. Reviewed at Film Polski, Warsaw, March 12, 1987. Running time: **99 MINS.**
Anastasia . . . . Beata Tyszkiewicz
Annette Nevermore . Grazyna Szapotowska
Tadzeus . . . . Gustaw Holubek
   Also with: Jerzy Bonczak.

Warsaw — Andrzej Kotkowski's film version of "In An Old Manor House," based on a play by painter-playwright Stanislaw Witkiewicz, is an occasionally amusing, but mostly confusing, farce that launches a political message of puzzling import. A good-humored cast and the bandying-about of a lot of high-sounding ideas about art and commerce, truth and falsehood, love, beauty and revolution, have gotten pic some limited fest play.

The black humor of the piece manages to come through even pedestrian direction. In a country house at the turn of the century live a family of eccentrics. Anastasia (Beata Tyszkiewicz), the beautiful

mistress of the manor, enjoys the amorous attentions of her stepson Blarney so openly that her husband Diapanasius takes out his shotgun and shoots her.

The family accepts her end as matter-of-factly as, soon afterwards, they accept her return as a voyeuristic ghost intent on interfering with their love lives. Anastasia's two adorable daughters poison themselves to join their mother as ghostlings.

Story gets stranger still when Anastasia has a posthumous son, Tadzeus (Gustaw Holoubek), who is "born" by clambering out of a tree trunk. She seduces him, too, and drives the other menfolk so crazy they kill her another couple of times.

Climax has Tadzeus, the arch-rebel, demagogically leading a mob on a raid of the old manor house, shouting "Down with wishy-washy democracy, long live the gray, undifferentiated masses!" Much is the pity that film's p.o.v. is too submerged to make the play comprehensible, at least to viewers unfamiliar with it beforehand.

Thesps are almost all stage hands, and stay ably in tune with the deliberately exaggerated romantic look of this fragile relic of the early Polish avant garde.— Yung.

Ha'Instalator
(The Plumber)
(ISRAELI-COLOR)

A Trinity Film presentation of a Rosenfilm production. Produced by Mel Rosen. Executive producer, Rafi Riebenbach. Directed by Micky Bahagan. Stars Tuvia Tzafir. Screenplay, Hanan Peled; camera (color), Gad Danzig; editor, Nissim Musak; music, Micky Gavrielov; costumes, Obbie Ossi; assistant director, Mark Rosenbaum; associate producers, Nathan Hakeini, Zwi Grossman. Reviewed at the Sivan Cinema, Tel Aviv, April 11, 1987. Running time: **100 MINS.**
Pinkhas . . . . Tuvia Tzafir
Mimi . . . . Clara Ron
Striker . . . . Assi Hanegbi
   Also with: Rami Baruch, Avner Hizkiahu, Avi Kushnir, Shimon Finkel, Avraham Asseo, Ophelia Strahl.

Tel Aviv — A comedy restricted to local consumption, "The Plumber"'s main asset is star Tuvia Tzafir, a highly rated tv entertainer. His name is bound to attract early crowds, but it is doubtful whether word-of-mouth will help it in the long run.

This political satire about a plumber who by accident becomes Minister of Finance and makes a real attempt to grapple with the job, unlike all the crooked politicians before him, is neither funny nor edifying. Frank Capra's populist comedies may have been the inspiration, but the script is completely botched, plot doesn't even try to make sense, the story could have been told in five minutes, but drags on for another hour and a half and cast seems completely lost in the pro-

ceedings.

Tzafir, who can be a riot when given the right material, has nothing to sink his teeth into, while the rest of the cast hams it up any old way.

Technical credits are less than impressive and, in spite of the very long time it has taken to finish the picture, it looks very much like a clumsy overnight job. —Edna.

The Final Test
(HONG KONG-COLOR/B&W)

A Bo Ho Films (a member of Golden Harvest Group) release. Presented by Leonard Ho. Executive producer, Sammo Hung. Written and directed by Lo Kin. Stars Wai Tin Chi, Chin Siu Ho, Debra Sim. (No other credits provided by producer/distributor.) Reviewed at State theater, Hong Kong, April 7, 1987. Running time: **98 MINS.**
(Cantonese soundtrack with English subtitles)

Hong Kong — The time of "The Final Test" is the 21st century. The place is a plant where a certain kind of metal for military purpose is produced.

The opening sequence of the film is the best part. Filmed in black and white, there is no dialog except for the announcement that a certain worker has caused severe damage to the plant's productivity and has to be eliminated. The problem involves a worker who had an argument with a man who occupies an office equipped with the latest high-tech computer systems. The identity of the man is not known to the audience until the very end of the film.

Sadly, it disintegrates rapidly to a low level, with lots of dialog and meaningless jokes. The fight scenes every five or 10 minutes reveal this effort is just a showcase for Wai Tin Chi's beefcake and kung-fu.

Ben, played by Wai Tin Chi, has just been employed as the security chief of the plant. It doesn't take long for Ben to find out the evil deeds of the plant foreman, played by Chin Siu Ho. The creepy fellow goes about injecting addictive drugs into the workers who then have to depend on the management to stay alive. For these addicted workers to obtain the drugs, they have to give the foreman their wages.

Ben later gains the confidence of the female doctor of the plant, played by Debra Sim (totally wrong for the role), and falls in love with her. As the secret of the plant is revealed, Ben has to be exterminated. In sequence after sequence of chasing and fighting the couple try to escape.

The film tries to evoke the mysterious and alienated mood of a sci-fi movie and fails dismally. All the fighting has taken up most of the running time. There is simply no room for any intimate development of the characters and scenario.
               —Mel.

Le Cœur musicien
(The Musical Heart)
(FRENCH-DOCU-COLOR)

A Les Films Singuliers release of a Midas/Antenne-2/CNC coproduction. Produced by Marie-François Mascaro. Directed by Frédéric Rossif. Commentary, Frédéric H. Fajardie, narrated by Pierre Vaneck; camera (color), Daniel Barrau; second unit camera, Richard Andry, Dominique Chapuis, Jean Boffety, Jacques Dorot, Jean Jacques Flori, Jacques Loiseleux, Gérard Simon; editor, Dominique Caseneuve; sound, Gérard Lecas, Jean Umansky; assistant director, Christian Fournie; production manager, Nicole Philibert. Reviewed at the Empire theater, Paris, Jan. 13, 1987. Running time: **84 MINS.**

Paris — This Frédéric Rossif docu began with a commission from former Culture Minister Jack Lang to celebrate his national music fêtes on the first day of summer. Coproduced by the Antenne-2 network (and not its cinema affiliate Films A2), film had a commitment to theatrical release, though it's much too lightweight for other than home-screen audiences.

A montage ode to the international musical spirit, film is composed of pre-existent and freshly shot footage (notably during the 1985 Fête de la Musique) documenting the variety and range of music and its performers, both famous and obscure, from traditional Breton chorists and Latin American folk groups to modern street musicians and jazz stars.

There's a grabbag feel to the assembly of clips, and a rhetorical commentary underlines the vague sense of purpose that makes the feature length excessive. —Len.

Cernite Lebedi
(Black Swans)
(BULGARIAN-COLOR)

A Bulgarian Cinematography production. Directed by Ivan Nitchev. Screenplay, Nitchev, from the novel by Bogumil Raynov; camera (color), Richard Lentchevski; music, Bojidar Petkov. No further credits supplied. Reviewed at Mosman screening room, Sydney, March 10, 1987. Running time: **104 MINS.**
Violetta . . . . Diana Raynova
Mimi . . . . Dorothea Tontcheva
Young Violetta . . . . . . Zornitsa Mladenova
   Also with: Todor Kolev, Donka Shishmanova, Maris Liepa, Leda Tasseva, Yassen Vultchanov, Irina Stoyanova.

Sydney — This behind-the-scenes story of a prima ballerina severely deglamorizes the world of the ballet. Its thesis is that to strive for success in such an art form is mostly a painful experience, but that pain can bring achievement and with it, delight.

Focus of attention is Violetta (Diana Raynova), who wanted to be a prima ballerina since childhood. Through arduous years of training, her ambitions solidified, but after her graduation in 1969 she often found her personal life severely affected by her professional ambitions. There were a series of unhappy relationships, one with a married photographer, and an abortion. There was love for a man who wanted her to give up her career, but she refuses and the film ends with her in the spotlight, dancing a leading role, but lonely and somewhat embittered.

"You cannot always avoid defeat, but you can avoid surrender" says a closing title, and that's the theme of this well-made but downbeat pic. Director Ivan Nitchev, who made a charming film about the theater a few years back ("Stars In The Hair, Tears In The Eyes") is obviously fascinated by this backstage world, and his adaptation of Bogumil Raynor's novel has the ring of truth about it.

For ballet enthusiasts there are numerous dance sequences in the film, but the emphasis here is on a sad, tough, demanding way of life that only the very strong and very dedicated can survive.

Pic, made in 1984, has somehow been overlooked by fests, but is worth catching. —*Strat.*

Son Urfali
(The Last Man Of Urfa)
(TURKISH-COLOR)

A Candemir Film Ltd. (CFL) production. Directed by Omer Ugur. Screenplay, Ugur, Cemal Gözütük; camera (color), Umit Ardabak; music, Haluk Ozkan. Reviewed at the Istanbul Film Days, April 17, 1987. Running time: **95 MINS.**
Sehmus . . . . Talat Bulut
Girlfriend . . . . Nur Sürer
  Also with: Savas Yurttas.

Istanbul — The broken dreams of a group of poor Turkish construction workers make for a mad, depressing tale in "The Last Man Of Urfa." Director Omer Ugur, a scriptwriter on his first turn behind the camera, has a feeling for character and great empathy for his subject, but pic is a bit too obvious and simplistic to make it far abroad. Ugur's sincerity is apparent, however, making him a director to watch.

Sehmus (Talat Bulut) is a nice young man from backwoods Anatolia. He comes to Istanbul to work as a laborer on a construction site, but his dream is to become a famous singer, like another boy from Urfa did. He is aided and abetted by his jolly foreman, also from his village.

The austere life of the workers, who live together camp-style inside the unfinished building they're putting up, makes German films' portrayal of *gastarbeiter* living conditions look attractive in comparison. Nevertheless, there is a spirit of camaraderie among the men and even time for outings with the occasional girlfriend. Nur Sürer plays Sehmus' love interest; a primary school teacher with a head on her shoulders and the strength to resist her mother's disapproval for "debasing" herself with a workman, Sürer is a sympathetic friend to the whole group.

The crisis comes when Sehmus and the foreman let their illusions get away with them and enter an obviously rigging singing contest. The results are all to easy to foresee, and pic rather drags through to a tragic finale. Spending the group's money on the entry fee instead of sending a sick co-worker to the hospital, they lose everything, including their own self-respect.

Technical work squeaks through. Thesps are fine.— *Yung.*

Seven Years Itch
(HONG KONG-COLOR)

A Cinema City presentation, released by Golden Princess theater circuit. Produced and written by Raymond Wong. Directed by Johnny To. Executive producer, Catherine Hun; associate producer, Kenneth Ng. Stars Raymond Wong, Sylvia Chang, Li Chi, Eric Tsang. Camera (color), Paul Chan; editor, David Wu; music, Anders G. Nelson; art direction, Raymond Chan. Reviewed at President theater, Hong Kong, April 10, 1987. Running time: **98 MINS.**
(Cantonese soundtrack with English subtitles)

Hong Kong — "Seven Years Itch," the latest film by Raymond Wong, is about the insatiable desire of men for one night stands with women.

The movie centers on the durability of a couple's marriage. They have been living together for seven years, but not legally registered as a married couple. The wife has always been faithful and caring, a perfect housewife. Though Wong has been abstaining from flirting with other women, he's not the least unmoved by the sexy ladies around him.

His adulterous adventure begins on a business trip to Singapore. At the airport, a female thief, played by Li Chi, slips her stolen jewelery into Wong's luggage while being tailed by the police. On board the plane, Li Chi attempts to retain the jewelry by pretending to be coquettish to the unknowing Wong who mistakes it for a real treat. Back in the hotel room, Li Chi gets what she is after, that is, the gems, and leaves Wong a note of love. A sufficient amount of gags are built around these incidents though they come-off as pretentious and forced.

Besides popular comedians Raymond Wong and Eric Tsang, another promotional gag is the visual attraction of the big chester sex symbol Li Chi. In the film, she is costumed in low-necklined blouses and tight mini-skirts, with the movements of a true Hollywood-type sex symbol. —*Mel.*

Cuo Wei
(The Stand-In)
(CHINESE-COLOR)

A China Film release of a Xi'an Film Studio production. Directed by Huang Jianxin. Screenplay, Huang Xin, Zhang Min; camera (color), Wang Xinsheng; production design, Qian Yunxuan; music, Han Yong. Reviewed at Hong Kong Film Festival, April 16, 1987. Running time: **88 MINS.**
Zhao Shuxin . . . . Liu Zifeng
  Also with: Mou Hong, Yang Kun, Sun Kihu.

Hong Kong — "The Stand-In" is an ill-advised sequel to "The Black Cannon Incident," in which the engaging Liu Zifeng repeats his role as the dedicated Zhao Shuxin. Where the earlier (1985) production had the loyal Zhao suspected, wrongly, of illicit deals with foreigners, and exposed paranoia among middle-level Chinese bureaucrats, the new pic attempts something quite different: it's a sci-fi comedy.

Zhao is no longer a modest engineer: now he's a boss, head of a large corporation, and forced to attend so many boring meetings he no longer has time to work on the things he cares about. So, he invents a robot which looks exactly like him, and sends it off to attend the meetings and handle the dull side of the job. Trouble is, the robot develops a mind of its own; it decides it wants some love life, and also starts smoking, though Zhao's a confirmed non-smoker.

Unfortunately, director Huang Jianxin, who also made "The Black Cannon Incident," does little with this promising premise. The film has a glossy, hard, high-tech look that comes as something of a surprise in a Chinese film, but the emphasis on reds and whites and blacks, inventive in the earlier film, gets dull here. Nor can Huang inject much humor into the plot. There are a couple of good moments, one being when the robot plugs itself into an electric power point during a conference and causes a blackout, but generally the slow pacing and predictable gags work against the comedy. The denouement (it was all a dream!) makes for a very flat ending to a disappointing sequel to one of the contemporary Chinese cinema's most original and exciting productions.—*Strat.*

Sapporo Story
(HONG KONG-COLOR)

A D&B Films and Loong Hsiang coproduction. Released by D&B Films. Executive producer, Dickson Poon. Produced by Wang Hing Hsiang, John Sham, Wong Wah Kay. Associate producer, John Chan. Directed by Wong Wah Kay. Stars Su Ming Ming, Olivia Cheng. (No other credits provided by producers.) Reviewed at Jade theater, Hong Kong, April 1, 1987. Running time: **98 MINS.**
(Cantonese and Japanese soundtrack with English and Chinese subtitles)

Hong Kong — The film, shot on location in Tokyo, is about the pitiful experiences of two women tricked into prostitution in Japan. One is from Hong Kong (Olivia Cheng), the other from Taiwan (Su Ming Ming).

Cheng becomes a prostitute because of her belief that gambling is the ultimate salvation, Su Ming Ming because of her innocent love for a pimp disguised as a gentleman.

The story follows the relationship between the two victims who share the same dream of returning to their respective homelands as soon as they have paid back their debts to the pimp by working as hostesses in nightclubs. But they become detached from their dream as their degradation increases. First they work in high-class metropolitan clubs, but as trouble deepens, they are transported to a dingy, remote brothel in the northern tip of Hokaido.

Unnecessary erotic scenes are altogether restrained except for a brief strip-show. The success of the film lies in its compulsive rhythm. The crisp, coherent editing keeps the story intact. Also passable are the acting skills of the two attractive lead actresses, who provide dramatic tension. —*Mel.*

Arriva Frank Capra
(Here Comes Frank Capra)
(ITALIAN-COLOR)

An Electra Film release of a Radiotelevisione Italiano-RAI-1 production. Produced by Dino Di Dionisio. Directed by Gianfranco Mingozzi, Camera (color), Safai Tehrani. Reviewed at Kabuki theater, San Francisco Film Festival, April 2, 1987. Running time: **80 MINS.**

San Francisco — This docu was orginally part of a seven-hour Italian version series called "Stories of Cinema And Migrants" and tries, a bit too hard considering the tenuous linkage (in Capra's mind), to pump a plotline that might read: " Sicilian makes it big in Hollywood."

Capra was born in Sicily, in 1897, but moved to the U.S. at the age of six and admits he has no recollections of his roots. In footage on a visit to his birthplace, he says, "I was too young to remember" any of the sights he's being shown.

The documakers are forced to ask Capra about his work with Italian actors, and he speaks of directing Frank Sinatra. Then there's a seg about financing of pics by Bank of America founder A.P. Giannini. Talk about reaching for an angle.

Most of the docu has Capra, on camera, tracing his career through silents and Oscars and World War II production.

There are interviews with Donna Reed, Lionel Stander, Hope Lange and Colleen Gray, plus intercut scenes from the helmer's major, and some minor, features.

Intros to the clips are not always smooth, and several of the pics are used more than once.

Capra notes, "I'm proud of all the films I made ... Once you're a director, you tell everybody what to do. You think you can do everything better than they can. Lots of people don't like it. And I don't see why they should like it."

In the genre of docus about filmmakers, "Here Comes Frank Capra" is back in the pack. It's best fit for classrooms. —Herb.

Bejalai
(To Go On A Journey)
(MALAYSIAN-COLOR)

An Action Films production. Produced by Stephen Teo, Zarul Albakri. Directed by Teo. Screenplay, Teo; camera (color), Jim Shum; editor, Zhang Jiande, Shen Shengde; sound, Carrie Wong. Reviewed at Hong Kong Film Festival April 20, 1987. Running time: 95 MINS.
Rentap . . . . Dickie Isaac
The Girl . . . . Saloma Kumpeing
The Old Man . . . . Chiling Nyanggai

Hong Kong — Said to be the first feature film made in the Iban language and shot in Sarawak, one of the 13 states of the Federation of Malaysia, "Bejalai" is, in many ways, an archetypal Third World film. The first third depicts a way of life that's being threatened; in the central section the changes occur; and the film ends in the soullessness of a modern city (albeit a very small one).

Early scenes are very detailed and exhaustive as they show an ageless village lifestyle culminating in a harvest festival. The region is threatened by a hydroelectric scheme, and the inhabitants are forced to scatter. Rentap, the film's young protagonist, finds a job working for a timber company that's decimating the beautiful forests of the region. An old farmer is disoriented without his land. A young girl wanders through, winding up in the city, probably fated for life as a call girl.

Stephen Teo, a native of Sarawak now living in Hong Kong, has overcome most of the problems occasioned by shooting on such remote locations. His nonprofessional actors acquit themselves well in classical roles. It's not a very original piece of work, but it's adequately made and should be of interest to students of Asian or Third World Cinema. The modest credits are all fine, and the film has been proficiently subtitled in English. —Strat.

Yi Lou Yi
(Reunion)
(HONG KONG-COLOR)

A Films Creative Studio production. Executive producer, Chan Ho-pang. Directed by Kwan Park-huen. Screenplay, Thomas Pang, Kwan Park-huen; camera (color), Herman Yau; editor, Kwan; music, Herman Yau, Roland Morales; production design, Mango Kwan; sound, Choi Kam-chuen; production manager, Leung Shin-chong; assistant director, Thomas Pong. Reviewed at Hong Kong Film Festival, April 16, 1987. Running time: 81 MINS.

With: Pau Wai-leung (Chak), Yiu Hin-shui, Cheng Hon-ki, Joanna Lai, Bo Bo, Sze Ku, Lui Tak.

Hong Kong — This low-budget indie item charts a day in the life of Chak (Pau Wai-leung), unemployed and separated from his wife. A surly fellow, given to rape fantasies, Chak starts the day by visiting a prostie friend who's setting up a new apartment which is being painted bright pink. Later he visits his sister, who's about to leave home to live with her boyfriend, and his widowed mother, who plans to remarry.

Finally, accompanied by his small son, he visits his estranged wife, seeking a reconciliation. She'll have none of him, and a row ensues which escalates until Chak starts a fire in the apartment. In the ensuing fray, the wife accidentally kills the little boy, Chak stabs her to death and is sent to prison.

It's a bleak little tale of a hopeless existence, but director Kwan Park-huen leaves out rather too much vital information (such as why Chak can't get a job and why he and his wife split in the first place). An unexplained sequence set in a swamp, where Chak is bitten by a snake, could be a flashback or, more likely, a nightmare, but the viewer is kept in the dark.

The pic's too anecdotal and tentative to make much impact, but the climactic sequence, in the wife's apartment, pulls it all together for a chilling finale. No doubt Kwan has talent, and it remains to be seen if his future work will be more cohesive. —Strat.

El Hijo de Pedro Navajas
(The Son Of Pedro Navajas)
(MEXICAN-COLOR)

A Películas Mexicanas release of a Producciones Rosas Priego-Producciones Ega-Gazcón Films-Cineproducciones Intl. production. Produced and directed by Alfonso Rosas Priego R. Stars Guillermo Capetillo. Screenplay, Ramón Obón, Rosas Priego, based on the song "Pedro Navajas" by Rubén Blades; camera (color), Antonio de Anda; music, Arturo Castro, with appearance of groups Los João, Pepe Arevalo y Sus Mulatos. Reviewed at Cinema Hollywood 2, N.Y., Feb. 22, 1987. Running time: 91 MINS.
Pedro Navajas Jr. . . . . Guillermo Capetillo
Tismany . . . . Sasha Montenegro
Mickey . . . . Adalberto Martínez (Resortes)
Sandra . . . . Gabriela Goldsmied
Burth . . . . Jorge Luke
Filos . . . . Rodolfo de Anda
Roja . . . . Ana Luisa Peluffo
Susana . . . . Diana Ferreti
Also with: Pepe Romey, Socorro Bonilla, Isaura Espinoza, Carmelina Encinas, Marcia Bell, Humberto Elizondo, Bruno Rey, Lucy Tovar, Griselda Mejía, Mari Carmen Resendes, Paco Sañudo.

In 1984, Mexican director Alfonso Rosas Priego R. made a big-screen venture of the song "Pedro Navajas," a Latino version of "Mack The Knife," by Panamanian actor-salsa singer-songwriter Rubén Blades. The cheapo pic

starred leading man Andrés Garcia and former Miss Costa Rica Maribel Guardia as a pimp and prostitute who kill each other.

The pic raked in lots of money due to the popularity of the song and an accompanying media blitz. To capitalize on the success of the first pic, Rosas Priego produced an equally boring sequel that concerns the adventures of Navajas' son Pedro Jr. (Manuel Capetillo). If the first venture was a shoddy exploitation of Blades' theme song, the second is an even bigger insult. Like the first film, the soundtrack includes the title track performed by Pepe Arevalo y Sus Mulatos.

Whereas dad lived by exploiting women, junior defends the ladies. He grew up in the U.S. and only when his mom is killed by her lover does sonny boy travel to Mexico. To his horror, he discovers dad also has been killed. Like dad, Pedro Jr. learns he lives up to his name "Navajas" (Blades) and becomes quite handy with the switchblade.

The pic continues with some sex, some violence and a bit of humor, supplied by veteran Mexican comedian Adalberto Martinez (Resortes). But overall, it is a big bore. Blades fans should stand warned. —Lent.

Toda la Vida
(All Life Long)
(MEXICAN-COLOR)

A Películas Mexicanas release of a Producciones Esme-Hermes Internacional-Alianza Cinematográfica Mexicana production. Executive producer, Abraham Cherem. Produced by Carlos Vasallo. Directed by Víctor Manuel (Güero) Castro. Screenplay, Fernando Galiana; camera (color), Raúl Domínguez; editor, Max Sánchez; music, Carlos Torres Marín, with title song sung by Franco. Reviewed at Big Apple Cine 1, N.Y., Feb. 15, 1987. Running time: 91 MINS.
Poncho . . . . Roberto (Flaco) Guzmán
Jorge . . . . Jorge Luke
Lola . . . . Rebeca Silva
Lalo . . . . Manuel (Flaco) Ibáñez
Leticia . . . . Diana Ferreti
Also with: Charlie Valentino, José Magana, Alfonso Dávila, Polo Ortín, Víctor Manuel Castro, Maricarmen Resendess, Carlos Yustis, Alejandro Peniche, Yirah Aparicio.

This low-budget pic, by Mexican director Víctor Manuel (Güero) Castro, was tossed together to cash in on the popularity of the Latin hit "Toda la Vida" (All Life Long), released simultaneously by pop singers Franco and Emmanuel.

Uneven comedy revolves around a group of guys who spend all their time between a bar, booze, bowling and beauties. Their women eventually get fed up with them arriving home late and drunk every night, reeking of strange perfume. Thus, the gals also start frequenting the bar to give the men a taste of their own medicine.

Tucked in somewhere between a lot of worn-out sexually oriented one-liners and visual gags is the seri-

ous message: to be merely a macho is not necessarily the same as being a real man.

Tech credits are up to par but plot meanders so much that director Castro tries to fill up the gaps with superfluous sideplots that only make matters worse. Whenever things get totally out of hand, the title track is played again and the characters dance to show that all personal problems have been resolved. Yet, the script problems keep the pic bogged down in limbo. The film needs more than an upbeat pop song to bring its diffuse elements into a cohesive and satisfying whole. —Lent.

Uhoho Tankentai
(The Hours Of Wedlock)
(JAPANESE-COLOR)

A Toho release of a New Century Producers & Directors production. Produced by Yutaka Okada. Directed by Kichitaro Negishi. Screenplay, Yoshimitsu Morita, from a book by Agata Hikari; camera (color), Osamu Maruike; editor, Akimasa Kawashima; music, Saeko Suzuki. Reviewed at Hong Kong Film Festival, April 14, 1987. Running time: 100 MINS.
Tokiko . . . . Yukiyo Toake
Kazuya . . . . Kunie Tanaka
Also with: Mariko Fuji.

Hong Kong — Yoshimitsu Morita, whose films "The Family Game" and "Sorekara" have been playing the fest circuit of late, penned the screenplay for this pic about a crumbling marriage. It's basically familiar stuff, though given a lift thanks to strong performances and some amusing touches.

Kazuya works as a scientist and has to reside at the laboratory, which is some distance from the city where his wife, Tokiko, a journalist, and his two sons live. On one of his rare visits home, the tension in the air is unnoticed by the kids, who simply have a good time, especially the little one. Kazuya reveals to his wife that he has a mistress at his workplace, telling her he could easily have said nothing and deceived her, but that he didn't want to cheat her.

The children react badly to the news, with the elder boy going off to inspect his father's new woman and the younger taking refuge with his grandmother. Tokiko, meanwhile, starts to consider an affair of her own. Pic ends with a repentant Kazuya returning to tell his family that his affair is over.

Director Kichitaro Negishi ("The Far Thunder") is excellent with his actors, and the small-fry are particularly good. Basically this is rather slim and familiar material, which tricky photography can't really lift. Performers can, and do.

There are some sharply handled scenes, such as the elder boy trying on his father's suits, or the reluctant wife paying a visit to her husband's new home to meet the mistress, who promptly gets drunk and passes out. There's the occasional imposing image, such as that of a giant ferris wheel dwarfing an adjacent graveyard. The freeze-frame ending, though, is a bit clichéd. —*Strat.*

Escuadrón de la Muerte
(Death Squad)
(MEXICAN-COLOR)

A Películas Mexicanas release of a Producciones Metropolitana production. Executive producer, Ignacio García. Produced by Ebe Glazer. Directed by Alfredo Gurrola. Screenplay, Armando Armendáriz; camera (color), Agustín Lara; editor, Francisco Chiu. Reviewed at Hollywood Twin Cinema, N.Y. April 6, 1987. Running time: **99 MINS.**
Captain Balbuena . . . . Mario Almada
Sergio Enríquez . . . . Hugo Stiglitz
Ramón Cabrera . . . . Sergio Goyri
Fabian Ordoñez . . Miguel Angel Rodríguez
"El Loco" Ordoñez . . . . Jorge Luke
Also with: Gerardo Vigil, Rojo Grau, Alexandro Parodi, Humberto Luna, Rube Ré.

Mexican filmmaker Alfredo Gurrola has assembled a group of action pic leads for his latest venture "Escuadrón de la Muerte" with an agreeable script that allows for both humor and fast-paced violence.

Plot centers on ex-police Capatain Balbuena (Mario Almada), relieved from a case because he has gotten too close to the truth: the police are in collusion with a large dope-smuggling ring. Acting as maverick, he assembles a group of five professional outlaws, each with a different skill, which the press subsequently labels "the death squad." Living up to the moniker, the gang uses bombs and bullets to wreak havoc with the underworld. Gang includes Sergio Goyri, Miguel Angel Rodríguez and Hugo Stiglitz.

When the captain and his family are gunned down, the group adds munitions expert "El Loco" Ordoñez (Jorge Luke) and using their combined forces and wit, this dirty half-dozen manages to bring down the entire operation.

What makes this film work is the strong ensemble acting by the principals with a script that stresses camaraderie and humourous interaction. Although no star emerges to grab the spotlight, each character has individual scenes in which his role is established and defined.

Agustín Lara's sharp lensing and Francisco Chiu's imaginative editing keep the action well-focused with attention to detail. On the other hand, the music is only sometimes appropriate to the tone of the pic.

"Escuadrón de la Muerte" is one of the rare Mexican action films that manages to transcend the genre and deliver what the audience expects: entertainment in a starstudded vehicle. —*Lent.*

Cartucha Cortada
(Cocked Gun)
(MEXICAN-COLOR)

A Películas Mexicanas release of a Producciones Tollocán production. Produced by Guillermo Herrera. Directed by Rafael Villaseñor Kuri. Stars Fernando Almada. Screenplay, Jorge Patiño; camera (color), Antonio Ruiz Juárez; editor, Max Sánchez; music, Carlos Torres. Reviewed at Hollywood Twin Cinema 2, N.Y., April 5, 1987. Running time: **89 MINS.**
Dr. César Fuentes . . . . . Fernando Almada
El Comandante . . . . Mario Almada
Ana Fuentes . . . . Marta Ortiz
Don Queaga . . . . Víctor Junco
Also with: Humberto Herrera, Oscar Traven, Ernesto Bog, María Bardhai, Gina Leal, Luis Elías Villaseñor Kuri, Pancho Muller, Lupita Bustamantes.

"Cocked Gun," by Mexican director Rafael Villaseñor Kuri, is a revenge pic that hasn't been developed fully.

Although the film features both of the Almada brothers — top national action stars — the lead goes to younger brother Fernando, who plays a kind-hearted surgeon and concerned family man named Dr. César Fuentes.

The doctor is a happy man until one day his former gardener, along with the son of a top drug smuggler, kidnap Dr. Fuentes' young son for a $20,000 ransom. Unfortunately, the snotty kid never survives the kidnaping. The sight of his battered body makes the doctor forget his Hippocratic oath and become obsessed with revenge.

Tension builds when the doctor captures the son of the drug smuggler and holds him hostage while daddy sends out his goons. A few badly plotted car chases ensue and the son manages to whine about his terrible childhood growing up with a drug smuggler, etc.

Even though the good doctor is spared actually killing anyone, the bloodbath ending is absurd and excessive. Tech credits are functional and thesping talents have little more than clichéd characters with which to work.

With a little bit of thought, the film might have been tense and effective. As it stands, it barely maintains interest level. —*Lent.*

Esta Noche Cena Pancho
(Despedida de Soltero)
(Tonight Pancho Dines Out — Bachelor Party)
(MEXICAN-COLOR)

A Películas Mexicanas release of a Film Exito production. Executive producer, Mario Cris. Produced by Guillermo Calderón S. Directed by Víctor Manuel (Güero) Castro. Stars Alfonso Zayas. Screenplay, Francisco Cavazos, Alfonso Anuya, Castro; camera (color), Raúl Domínguez; editor, José Liho; music, Marcos Lifshitz, with appearance of the group Chico Che y La Crisis. Reviewed at Hollywood Twin Cinema 2, N.Y., April 13, 1987. Running time: **86 MINS.**
Pancho Medrano . . . . Alfonso Zayas
Sra. Medrana . . . . Carmen Salinas
Marcelo Granadas . . . . . Armando Silvestre
Sergio . . . . Alberto (Caballo) Rojas

Oscar . . . . Alfredo (Pelón) Solares
Also with: Rebeca Silva, Diana Ferreti, Elsa Montes, Griselda Mojía, Rosalba Brambile, Leandro Espinosa, Patricia Castro, Morris Grey.

Mexican filmmaker Víctor Manuel (Güero) Castro, known for churning out over a half-dozen quickie low-budget sex comedies annually, has followed his shopworn formula in "Tonight Pancho Dines Out."

Pic stars comedian Alfonso Zayas (on loan from Frontera Films), who plays title character Pancho, a lawyer unhappily wed to a plump termagant (Carmen Salinas) and surrounded by a tribe of kids.

Subtitled "Bachelor Party," film takes off when friend Marcelo (Armando Silvestre) announces she is eloping with the daughter of a wealthy businessman. Zayas and two buddies, played by Alberto (Caballo) Rojas and Alfredo (Pelón) Solares, decide to throw an old-fashioned bachelor party with lots of "babes and booze."

Such is the weak grab-bag premise that director Castro has set up to toss in all sorts of sexual double-entendres, sexist comments, tasteless jokes about cripples and lots of wornout sight gags. Popular salsa singer Chico Che and his group La Crisis manage to add filler.

Lensing is below par and haphazard editing makes some of the sequences difficult to follow. —*Lent.*

Albures Mexicanos
(Mexican Double-Entendres)
(MEXICAN-COLOR)

A Películas Mexicanas release of a Filmadora Dal production. Produced by David Agrasánchez. Directed by Alfredo B. Crevenna. Stars Alfonso Zayas, Carmen Salinas. Screenplay, Ramón Obón; camera (color), Antonio de Anda; editor, Jorge Rivera; music, Pedro Placenicia. Reviewed at Big Apple Cine 2, N.Y., Feb. 16, 1987. Running time: **90 MINS.**
Chief Jr. . . . . Alfonso Zayas
Susana . . . . Carmen Salinas
Rita . . . . Grace Renate
Ruperto Colorado . . . . Sergio Ramos
Also with: Chaff y Quelli, Carmelita González, Joaquín García, Cristián Crishan.

"Albures Mexicanos" takes its name from a type of slang or fast wordplay popular among Mexico's working class and best translated as locker-room humor peppered with sexual puns. As the title promises, pic is nearly bursting with these picaresque double-entrendres.

Known for his quickie low-budget sex comedies, filmmaker Alfredo B. Crevenna has put together a bunch of short skits punctuated by scantily clad beauties and tucked them within a threadbare plot.

Story concerns a traveling tent show called the "Carpa Colonial." Having been run out of several towns for risqué material and lack of permits, the troupe sets up camp illegally on land belonging to Chief

Jr. (Alfonso Zayas), a cold-hearted developer planning to use the land for a housing complex.

The rest of the pic alternates between his efforts to evict the troupe while the company, led by Susana (Carmen Salinas), tries to stall him. Film cuts back and forth between the storyline and troupe's routines, vaudeville-type entertainment full of comic asides from comedians Chaff & Quelli.

Most of the characters, except for comedienne Salinas, are too sketchy to be either believable or involving. Tech credits are strictly bargain basement.

"Albures Mexicanos" fulfills its promise of lots of double-entendre jokes. Unfortunately, a bunch of jokes is not enough to make a satisfying feature. —*Lent.*

Policías de Narcoticos
(Narcotics Police)
(MEXICAN-COLOR)

A Películas Mexicanas release of a Cinematográfica Sol production. Produced by Rodolfo de Anda. Directed by Gilberto de Anda. Stars Valentín Trujillo, Sergio Goyri. Screenplay, X. Randa; camera (color), Antonio de Anda; editor, Sergio Soto; music, Gustavo Pimentel. Reviewed at Cinema Hollywood 1, N.Y., Feb. 21, 1987. Running time: **87 MINS.**
Julián Carrera . . . . Valentín Trujillo
Roberto Rojas . . . . Sergio Goyri
Antonio Farkas . . . . Rodolfo de Anda
Albina . . . . Angélica Chaín
El Licenciado . . . . Julio Alemán
Also with: Bruno Rey, Isaura Espinoza, Arturo Alegro, Edgardo Gazcón, Edna Bolkan.

Although not mentioned in the title, the Mexican action pic "Policías de Narcoticos" (Narcotics Police) is a sequel to the earlier Valentín Trujillo-Gilberto de Anda production "Un Hombre Violento" (A Violent Man).

Having settled his accounts in the first film, Julián Carrera (Trujillo) decides to join the Mexican police force in an attempt to channel his violent urges. In this sequel, other characters show Trujillo he doesn't hold a corner on violence, and the screen is virtually splattered with fake blood.

Carrera teams up with agent Roberto Rojas (played by fellow action star Sergio Goyri) and the two try to break a vicious narcotics smuggling ring run by Antonio Farkas (pic's producer Rodolfo de Anda) and his partner-in-crime, Albina (Angélica Chaín).

Among the myriad realistic atrocities detailed in this excessive pic are multiple stabbings, one machine-gun massacre, the kidnapping and disemboweling of a child, two slit throats, one beheading, lots of shootings and human entrails fed to dogs.

Unlike "Un Hombre Violento," emphasis here is on violence and special effects rather than storyline.

Characters are little more than cartoons.

Shell-shocked Trujillo fans, accustomed to excessive violence, may find their hero has gone too far.
—*Lent.*

Cidade Oculta
(Hidden City)
(BRAZILIAN-COLOR)

A presentation of Embrafilme, Empresa Brasileiro de Filmes, Rio de Janeiro. A production of Orion Cinema e video. Executive producer, Wagner Carvalho. Directed by Chico Botelho. Screenplay, Botelho, Arrigo Barnabe; Walter Rogerio; camera (color), Jose Roberto Eliezar; editor, Danilo Tadeu; music, Barnabe; art direction-costumes, Ana Maria Abreu. Reviewed at Berlin Film Festival (Market), Feb. 24, 1987. Running time: **74 MINS.**
Shirley . . . . Carla Camurati
Anjo . . . . Arrigo Barnabe
Ratao . . . . Claudio Mamberti
Japa . . . . Celso Saiki

Berlin — "The "hidden city" of the title is the underground criminal subculture of São Paulo. At night these citizens of São Paulo are busy in nonstop rapes and murders, heists, drug capers and shootouts.

This is, of course, the familiar landscape and setting for the standard crime thriller. "Hidden City" is somewhat different in that it uses a flashback or envelope format à la Brecht, with a nightclub oral-historian at the film's start, throughout and at the end, singing and remembering the true sad story of Shirley (Carla Camurati) and her lover Anjo (Arrigo Barnabe).

Shirley and Anjo both are deep in the criminal life of São Paulo, but we sense they are worthy of better destinies. She's a whore and fence of stolen jewelry. He's a drug-hijacker and ex-con. Of course, life has short-changed them so, accordingly, they betray one another, themselves and everyone else in the film. Yet, in our naive optimism, we feel they are salvageable, misdirected nice kids. Chief nemesis is Ratty or Ratao (Claudio Mamberti), obese crooked police chief who shoots up heroin at his desk while watching himself on a tv news program about a drug bust. An exotic touch of this otherwise standard crime meller is the character Japa (Celso Saiki), a Brazilian Japanese, a clever gangleader who gets his in the film's final (at last) shootout. Japa has a lively personality and is seen sympathetically in the semi-documentary atmosphere of São Paulo's "Liberdade" or "Japan-town." —*Hitch.*

- -
Cannes Film Reviews
- -

The Belly Of An Architect
(BRITISH-COLOR)

A Hemdale Releasing release (U.S.) of a Callender production. Produced by Colin Callender, Walter Donohue. Written and directed by Peter Greenaway. Camera (Technicolor), Sacha Vierny; editor, John Wilson; music, Wim Mertens, Glenn Branca; sound, Peter Glossop; art director, Luciana Vedovelli; set dresser, Giorgio Desideri; costumes, Maurizio Millenotti; assistant director, Fabio Jephrott; associate producers, Conchita Airoldi, Dino di Dionisio. Reviewed at Metro Cinema, London, April 26, 1987. (In competition at Cannes Film Festival.) (No MPAA Rating.) Running time: **118 MINS.**
Stourley Kracklite . . . . Brian Dennehy
Louisa Kracklite . . . . Chloe Webb
Caspasian Speckler . . . . . . Lambert Wilson
Frederico . . . . Vanni Corbellini
Io Speckler . . . . Sergio Fantoni
Flavia Speckler . . . . Stefania Casini
Julio Ficcone . . . . Alfredo Varelli
Caspetti . . . . Geoffrey Coppleston
Pastarri . . . . Francesco Carnelutti

London — "The Belly Of An Architect" is a visual treat, almost an homage to the style of Rome's architecture, lensed with skill and packed with esoteric nuances, but doubts about the story and the skill of the acting linger.

Pic will probably pack the art-houses, and Peter Greenaway admirers will surely be excited and impressed by the director's third theatrical effort, which offers a more accessible plot and bigger name actors than his first two. Greenaway falls in the "love-him-or-hate-him" category; reaction will be very split on this pic. Commercial prospects may be hampered by the running time (118 minutes) and Greenaway's arty reputation.

Greenaway helms with precision, almost clinically detached. With the aid of experienced and talented cinematographer Sacha Vierny his shots are always beautifully framed, though sometimes allowed to linger too long as if trying to convince the audience he has created a masterpiece.

The main problem with "The Belly Of An Architect" lies with Greenaway the screenwriter. His story is simply not gripping or convincing enough as a contempo psychological drama, and the characters are not well rounded or at all sympathetic.

The belly in question is the stomach of a U.S. architect, played by a suitably paunchy Brian Dennehy, who arrives in Rome with his fickle wife to set up an exhibition celebrating French architect Boullee. He becomes convinced he is being slowly poisoned by his wife, who is having an affair with a rival Italian architect (Lambert Wilson).

The Dennehy character becomes obsessed both with his pain and the exhibition, and also gets over-fond of photocopying pictures of the stomachs of the Roman Augustus (who was poisoned by his wife) and that of Boullee. Greenaway throws in plenty of mirrors for the Yank's many obsessions with the architecture of Rome, and his stomach pains with those of his pregnant wife.

Dennehy, usually spotted in Yank actioners, makes an adirable effort as the troubled architect, but the rest of the cast — mostly European — turn in generally poor efforts. Chloe Webb as his wife looks okay, but her voice (apt in "Sid And Nancy") just seems irritating, while Lambert Wilson as the rival architect/lover is little more than a clotheshorse.

Technical credits are all excellent, especially Vierny's lensing and the set dressing by Giorgio Desideri. Music by Wim Mertens and Glenn Branca helps the dramatic atmosphere.

"The Belly Of An Architect" looks wonderful, but beneath all the sheen and trappings, Greenaway gives an impression that he's not much interested in acting and character. Towards the end of the pic one yearns for a frame that isn't perfectly structured and is, just once, off center. —*Adam.*

Cudzoziemka
(The Stranger)
(POLISH-COLOR)

A Zespoly Filmowe production, Film Unit OKO. Directed by Ryszard Ber. Stars Ewa Wiśniewska. Screenplay, Maria Kuncewiczowa, based on her novel; camera (color), Jerzy Stawicki; editor, Alina Faflik; music, Anna Izykowska-Mironowicz; art director, Andrzej Borecki; sound, Leszek Wronko; production manager, Jerzy K. Frykowski. Reviewed at Film Polski, Warsaw, March 13, 1987. (In Market at Cannes Film Festival.) Running time: **115 MINS.**
Róza . . . . Ewa Wiśniewska
Marta . . . . Joanna Szczepkowska
Alan . . . . Jerzy Kamas
Also with: Andrzej Precigs, Katarzyna Chrzanowska, Miroslaw Konarowski, Malgotzata Lorentowicz.

Warsaw — Based on the true story of an unhappy woman violinist, "The Stranger" is a sensitively lensed mood piece by veteran helmer Ryszard Ber. The subject is a difficult one: a bitter old lady who makes life hell for herself and those around her. After a few fest outings, pic will most probably be left to the appreciation of patient local audiences.

We meet Róza (artificially aged actress Ewa Wiśniewska) when she's already nearing death. Judging from the cowed expressions of her separated husband (Jerzy Kamas) and children, she has been on the warpath for years — in fact, since the day she was married. Problem stems from when her first love broke off their engagement without an explanation. The other bitter pill in Róza's life is her unfulfilled ambitions as a violinist. Though her husband, successfully opposed her career, he is powerless to stop her from trying to live vicariously through her poor daughter Marta (Joanna Szczepkowska), a not-bad singer. Everyone suffers terribly.

The mystery is why the family doesn't poison the old lady, who is treated instead with enormous respect no matter what tantrums she throws. Yet only evidence we have of her lost genius are some beautifully lensed shots of Róza in the Leningrad Conservatory playing violin as a young girl. (Her family's mized Russian-Polish background is another source of torment for her — pic's title is alternately translated "The Alien.") A mysterious, unmotivated happy ending arrives on her death-bed, when she realizes she's been wrong and dies reconciled to life.

Cast is top-drawer. If Wiśniewska is a little one-note in the title role, she has enough venomous intensity to put Joan Collins in the shade.
—*Yung.*

Schloss & Siegel
(Lock & Seal)
(WEST GERMAN-COLOR)

An Export Film release of a Frankfurt Filmwerkstatt production in cooperation with ZDF. Executive producer, Ute Tuers. Produced by Michael Smeaton. Directed by Heidi Ulmke. Screenplay, Geraldine Blecker, Ulmke; camera (color), Jorg Jeshel; editor, Susanne Hartmann; music, Peter W. Schmitt; sound, Jürgen Edelmeyer; art direction, Klaus Wischmann. Reviewed at Berlin Film Festival, Feb. 23, 1987. (In Market at Cannes Film Festival.) Running time: **80 MINS.**
Michael . . . . Karl-Heinz Maslo
Babsi . . . . Christiane Carstens
Andy . . . . Susanne Bredehoft
Susan . . . . Geraldine Blecker
Klaus . . . . Gerd Knebel
Gerd . . . . Karl Heuer

Berlin — A West German film that can make audiences laugh while tugging at the heartstrings is a rarity. Heidi Ulmke's first feature film "Schloss & Siegel" (Lock & Seal) does both. Film, being released with little fanfare, does not deserve to be kept under lock and key, and has potential outside the German-language market.

Using actual prison locations, film traces the pen pal love affair between a lonely pair of inmates incarcerated at separate penitentiaries. Action culminates with eventual momentary meeting between mouse Babsi (Christiane Carstens) and worse-for wear Michael (Karl-Heinz Maslo) after months of bureaucratic red tape.

Intelligent, witty screenplay by Geraldine Blecker (British singer-actress who served time in a German prison and has a supporting role in film) prevents things from getting maudlin. Maslo, as a con who cites legal chapter and verse to his warders, and Carstens, as an imp who knows more than her prayers, are convincing as the love struck pair determined to see each other at least once.

Backing them up and keeping the action from becoming too confining is a fine crew of supporting actors.

Especially effective are scenes in which the lovebird-jailbirds wrangle with Teutonic bureaucrats for permission to visit each other. When permission comes through, they make frantic preparations for a two-hour rendezvous with uniformed chaperones.

Technical credits are adequate for a film blown up from 16m.—*Gill.*

Babette's gästebud
(Babette's Feast)
(DANISH-COLOR)

A Just Betzer/Panorama Film Intl. production with Nordisk Film and The Danish Film Institute. (World sales, Walter Manley.) Produced by Just Betzer, Bo Christensen. DFI consultant-producer, Claes Kastholm Hansen. Directed by Gabriel Axel. Screenplay, based on Isak Dinesen's novella, Axel; camera (Eastmancolor), Henning Kristiansen; editor, Finn Henriksen; music, Per Nörgaard; sound, Michael Dela, John Nielsen; production design, Sven Wichman; costumes for Stephane Audran, Karl Lagerfeld, for others, Annelise Hauberg; assistant director, Tom Hedegaard; production management, Lene Nielsen. Reviewed at the Palladium-2, Copenhagen, April 25, 1987. (In the Un Certain Regard section, Cannes Film Festival.) Running time: **102 MINS.**

Babette . . . . Stéphane Audran
Achille Papin . . . . Jean-Philippe Lafont
Lorenz Löwenhielm
  (young) . . . . Gudmar Wivesson
Lorenz Löwenhielm
  (old) . . . . Jarl Kulle
Swedish Court Lady-
  in-Waiting . . . . Bibi Andersson
Filippa (young) . . . . Hanne Stensgaard
Martine (young) . . . . Vibeke Hastrup
Filippa (old) . . . . Bodil Kjer
Martine (old) . . . . Birgitte Federspiel
Old Nielsen . . . . Bendt Rothe
Christopher . . . . Ebbe Rode
The Widow . . . . Lisbeth Movin
The Captain . . . . Preben Leerdorff Rye
The Vicar . . . . Pouel Kern
Narrator's voice (international
  version) . . . . Michel Bouquet
Narrator's voice (Danish
  version) . . . . Ghita Nörby
Filippa's singing voice . . . . Tina Kiberg
Also with: Axel Ströbye, Ebba With, Else Petersen, Thérèse Höjgaard, Asta Esper Andersen, Finn Nielsen, Holger Perfort, Erik Petersen, Lars Lohmann, Tine Miche-Renard.

Copenhagen — Isak Dinesen's most widely read work, next to "Out Of Africa," is the short novel "Babette's Feast," a rousing yarn of delicate philosophical overtones about a French female *chef de cuisine* of five-star repute, exiled after the Paris uprisings of 1871, who survives as a maid and cook to a couple of elderly puritan and devout spinster daughters of a strict sectarian vicar-prophet, now passed away, on a remote and rugged Scandinavian North Sea coast.

Gabriel Axel, a veteran of Danish filmmaking (his "The Red Mantle" was a Prix Technique winner at the 1967 Cannes fest) and lately more active as a helmer of several major French tv series, may well come across to the great writer's global audiences with his workmanlike motion picture version of one of her loveliest and funniest stories.

Story has its title character given a fling at preparing and serving up one final great dinner by blowing on it her entire 10,000 Golden Francs winnings from a lottery ticket. At the table are the villagers, sect members lately fallen to bickering among themselves, innocent and even averse to any food beyond brown bread soup and dried cod with water on the side. A visiting Swedish general and diplomat, once a suitor to one of the vicar's daughters, has happened by, too. Now, they are all momentarily propelled spiritually heavenwards by what they eat and drink.

After a somewhat lingering start, helmer Axel succeeds where it really counts. On the screen he serves up the famous dinner with vigor and in enough juicy detail to send audiences away longing to partake in similar *haute cuisine* and happy to have watched France's Stéphane Audran in a warm and witty performance well beyond her established image of cool sophistication. She is even heard speaking broken Danish neatly (a babble of tongues are employed throughout, the meanings of the words being generally obvious enough to make the need for subtitling minimal).

Axel's style may be a bit too folksy for the more discriminating Isak Dinesen cognoscenti and arthouse patrons. He aims to reach wider audiences and in this he is greatly helped by a roster of veteran actors. Buffs will recognize many of them as stars of Carl Th. Dreyer's later films. Along with cameo players Bibi Andersson and French opera star Jean-Philippe Lafont, they now and again succeed in adding substance to the cardboard character vignettes they have been given to work with.

What bogs "Babette" down a bit at the outset is Axel's resorting to voice-over narration technique in supplying story background and motivations for later plot and character development. His pictures lacks narrative subtlety and cinematographic flash to parallel the particular Isak Dinesen genius for sketching in essential subplots and character delineations in a line-and-a-half asides.

Still, the overall mood of the original story is faithfully retained, and Sweden's Jarl Kulle, one of Ingmar Bergman's favorite actors, matches Audran in wit and depth although the two are never seen together. Kulle gives a moving portrayal of a man who has won the riches and glories of the world but who does not see the true meaning of life until plunged into this one holy moment of a gourmet's career.

That moment occurs when the general places upon his tongue what he instantly recognizes from his Parisian youth to be the very same *caille-en-sarcophage* that once created the renown of the Café Anglais' lady chef. Now, eating this course in the company of villagers sworn to culinary celibacy, he sees their spirits exalted by it and finds himself, at last, on the side of the angels. Art has truly triumphed over matter.—*Kell.*

Club de rencontres
(Lonelyhearts Club)
(FRENCH-COLOR)

An AMLF release of a T. Films/Films A2 coproduction. Produced by Alain Terzian. Directed by Michel Lang. Screenplay, Lang, Guy Lionel; camera (Afga-Gevaert color), Daniel Gaudry; editor, Hélène Plemiannikov; music, Michel Legrand; art director, Jean-Pierre Bazerolle; sound, André Hervéc; assistant director, Jean-Claude Marchant; production manager, Philippe Lièvre; casting, Marie-Christine Lafosse. Reviewed at the Triomphe cinema, Paris, March 22, 1987. (In Market at Cannes Film Festival.) Running time: **98 MINS.**

With: Francis Perrin (Nicolas), Jean-Paul Comart (Bernard), Valérie Allain (Cricri), Isabelle Mergault (Bunny), Herma Vos, Blanche Ravalec, Caroline Jacquin, Léon Spiegelman, Louba Guertchikoff, Jean Rougerie, Charles Gérard, Katia Tchenko, Henri Guybet, Mike Marshall, Annie Jouzier.

Paris — "Club de rencontres" casts funnyman Francis Perrin as frantically quick-witted director of a Parisian singles club evading family responsibilities as he uses his establishment to facilitate his sexual conquests, while offering self-serving help to a timid, wallflower friend.

This latest sex comedy by specialist Michel Lang goes through the predictable farcical motions before arriving at a typically moral conclusion in which the libido is vanquished by the comforts of monogamy and the right match.

Pic is thoroughly routine material for domestic use, but executed with a certain amount of *savoir-faire* by Lang, who knows a thing or two more than many of his loftier auteur colleagues about filmmaking basics. Perrin is often funny as the marathon philanderer, and the other players provide amusing silhouettes as ill-assorted club members.—*Len.*

Grand Guignol
(FRENCH-COLOR)

A UGC release of a Films du Chantier/Monthyon Prods./UGC/Top 1/Films Aramis coproduction. Produced, written and directed by Jean Marboeuf. Camera (Eastmancolor), Gérard Simon; editor, Anne-France Lebrun; art director, Jérome Clément; sound, Alix Comte; makeup-costumes, Danielle Vuarin, Pascale Bouquière; production manager, Marie-Annick Jarlegan. Reviewed at the Triomphe cinema, Paris, March 9, 1987. (In Market at Cannes Film Festival.) Running time: **87 MINS.**

Baptiste . . . . Guy Marchand
Sarah . . . . Caroline Cellier
Mr. Albert . . . . Jean-Claude Brialy
Charlie . . . . Michel Galabru
Germaine . . . . Marie Dubois
Coco . . . . Olivia Brunaux
The proprietor . . . . Denis Manuel
Paolo . . . . Jacques Chailleux
Adelaide . . . . Claire Nadeau
The Creature . . . . Catherine d'At
Clients . . . Serge Marquand, Violetta Ferrer

Paris — Jean Marboeuf follows his critically appreciated 1985 feature, "Vaudeville," with "Grand Guignol," which also uses theatrical metaphor in a serio-comic drama of human relationships. It's a drab, awkwardly made, tentatively acted art item that probably will disappoint admirers of the indie writer-director.

Story is set in the theater milieu and follows a second-rate troupe trying to revive the antiquated chills of Grand Guignol in a provincial tour.

Amidst rehearsals in a dreary suburban dance hall, the disparate members of the company try to cope with, or forget, their personal problems and frustrations. The troupe's very existence is menaced by the impending split between the blocked dramatist-director (Guy Marchand) and his weary actress wife (Caroline Cellier), who befriends an apparently jolly local with a joke and novelty shop (Michel Galbru).

The difficulties of the theatrical couple pale alongside the marital misery of the impotent Galabru and his wretched wife (Marie Dubois), who cracks up and takes a hatchet to her mate before slitting her wrists.

Marboeuf strives for macabre poignancy in contrasting the risible artificial gore of the Grand Guignol with the more subverted horrors and violence of failed lives, but for all the stage hemoglobin flowing, his personages remain quite bloodless and unconvincing.

Helmer does manage a memorable final scene in which the dead couple is apotheosized morbidly in the troupe's premiere before a local audience, represented by two tapered coffins which form a graveyard valentine when joined together. —*Len.*

Spalt-Prozesse
(Nuclear Split)
(W. GERMAN-COLOR-16m)

A Filmverlag der Autoren release of a Project Films production. Written and directed by Bertram Verhaag and Claus Strigel. Camera (color, 16m), Strigel, Waldemar Hausschild, Thomas Schwan, Christoph Boekel; editor, Draha Cizek; music, Ulrich Bassenge, Wolfgane Neumann; sound, Peter Bergmann, Lothar Kreutzer; assistant director, Liane Grimm; production manager, Friedrich Klütsch. Reviewd at the Berlin Film Festival (New German Film series), March 1, 1987. (In Market at Cannes Film Festival.) Running time: **100 MINS.**

Berlin — "Spalt-Prozesse" (Nuclear Split) is a documentary that purports to examine the societal split that has occurred in West Germany over plans to build the country's first nuclear fuel reprocessing plant in a rural Bavarian community. Film actually focuses entirely on anti-nuke protestors at often violent clashes at the construction site.

Total lack of objectivity weakens legitimate environmental concerns the film is trying to get across. Prospects outside a few specialty houses in Germany are severely limited.

Film offers spectacular shots of protestors setting up a squatters village inside the site as well as dramatic sequences showing riot police equipped with armored vehicles and helicopters going up against the squatters. There are also good impromptu remarks from conservative local residents who join the protestors. However, sequences lack continuity and quickly become repetitious. You always know when police are approaching because film's music turns threatening. —Gill.

The Story Of
Dr. Sun Yat-Sen
(TAIWANESE-HONG KONG)

A Taiwan/Hong Kong/First Films coproduction, released by Golden Princess Executive producer, Ernie Hoi Wong. Directed by Ting Shang-zi. Stars Lam Wei-sung, Alex Man, Wang Hsiao-feng, Hui Ying-Hung, Leung Ka-yen. (No other credits provided by First Films and coproducers.) Reviewed at President theater, Hong Kong, April 1, 1987. Running time: **200 MINS.** (commercial release). Edited version for Cannes Film Market: approximately **120 MINS.**
(Mandarin/Cantonese soundtracks available with English subtitles)

Hong Kong — Here's a $HK30,000 biopic on Dr. Sun Yat-Sen, the founding father of China. The Taiwanese film involves more than 90 scenes, 30,000 men, 3,000 horses and army uniforms. Filming took more than three months. It also includes brief appearances by more than a dozen well-known actors and actresses from Hong Kong and Taiwan.

The film follows in criss-cross style the revolutionary activities of Dr. Sun and his comrades in Canton from 1894 until he dies in 1925. In the course of this historical era, the bravery and sacrifices of the revolutionaries, the emotional outbursts of their wives and lovers, and the slyness of the Ching officials are handled in ways which resemble more a soap opera melodrama than a biography with psychological or political depth.

All its characters are stereotyped as "good guys" and "bad guys." They walk, talk and heroically pose according to their assigned categories. In the scene where Dr. Sun is held captive in the Ching legation in London, the diplomat and his adviser are depicted as men who lack mental capacity and diplomacy. The villains are often shown as coward caricatures.

At the other end of the scale, manipulation of the emotions of the heroic ones for the sake of dramatization is overwhelming. It's so overworked it loses the intended impact. The noisy musical accompaniment is maneuvered in a similar way.

The portrayal of Dr. Sun by newcomer Lam Wei-sung is questionable. In dignified moments, he often is filmed from a low angle while assuming the pose of classical sculpture. His facial expressions range from vacant stare of the eyes to slight curve of the lips. Even his eyebrows hardly move as statued heroes are meant to be idolized.

The soldiers and horses are employed to no avail. There's confusion and clutter in the presentation. The Taiwanese film version is definitely more commercially oriented than a recent production from China.

Per First Films, which will market this project to commemorate the 120th birthday of Dr. Sun Yat-Sen, the Cannes Film Market version will be shorter and re-dubbed. —Mel.

C.K. Dezerterzy
(The Deserters)
(POLISH-HUNGARIAN-COLOR)

A Zodiak Unit, Film Polski-Hunnia Studio, Mafilm, coproduction. Directed by Janusz Majewski. Screenplay, Majewski, Pavel Hajny, from the novel by Kazimierz Sejda; camera (color), Witold Adamek; editor, Elzbieta Kurkowska; music, György Selmeczy; production design, Andrzej Halinski; sound, Stanislaw Piotrowski; production managers, Zygmunt Krol, Istvan Fogarasi. Reviewed at Berlin Film Fest (Market), Feb. 22, 1987. (In Market at Cannes Film Festival.) Running time: **166 MINS.**
Kania . . . . Marek Kondrat
Benedek . . . . Zoltan Bezeredy
Chudej . . . . Wiktor Zborowski
Haber . . . . Jacek Sas-Uhrynowski
Captain . . . . Zbigniew Zapasiewicz
Also with: Robert Koltai, Josef Abraham.

Berlin — The setting for this elaborate, lengthy comedy of army life is a military barracks in a small Hungarian town during World War I. The soldiers are "politically suspect" characters from within the mighty Austro-Hungarian empire; there are Czechs and Jews and even Italians, though the officers in charge are German. The men spend most of their time in the local brothel, or fleecing the civilians of their cash.

Things are going well until a new lieutenant arrives, a German martinet who sets about bringing discipline to the unit. He's a sadist who delights in humiliating the men, and he also beats his Italian batman. After a while, the men close ranks to avenge themselves against this unpleasant character; they kidnap him one night and string him up in a public toilet; later, during a surprise inspection of the barracks by a high-ranking general, they make sure the German falls afoul of his superior.

The five ring leaders almost make up a cross section of the empire: a Pole, a Hungarian, a Czech, an Austrian Jew and an Italian. After a while, they're imprisoned and decide to desert, eventually winding up in Budapest where they have all manner of adventures, posing as guards or veterinary surgeons (a funny scene when a colonel instructs them to treat his horse) before they're caught and sent back to face their old tormentor in a court-martial.

It's a familiar tale in which the prevailing mood is light hearted and anti-authoritarian. Treatment is altogether too leisurely, though, and, at 166 minutes, pic is way too long. Still, there are good performances from the polyglot cast, some funny scenes, and fine visuals and production dress. It's probably too mainstream a film for the fest route. —Strat.

Hajnali Háztetök
(Roofs At Dawn)
(HUNGARIAN-COLOR)

A Budapest Studio, Mafilm, Magyar Television coproduction. Executive producer, Gabor Hanak. Directed by Janos Dömölky. Screenplay, Dömölky, Géza Ottlik; camera (Eastmancolor), Lajos Koltai; editor, Maria Nagy; music, Zdenko Tamassy; production design, Laszlo Zsoter; sound, Istvan Sipos; costumes, Marta Janoskuti; assistant director, Andras Sipos. Reviewed at Hungarian Film Week, Budapest, Feb. 16, 1987. (In Market at Cannes Film Festival.) Running time: **85 MINS.**
Benedek Both . . . . György Cserhalmi
Peter Halasz . . . . Peter Andorai
Marta . . . . Katalin Takacs
Lili . . . . Dorottya Udvaros
Alice . . . . Denise Dér
Jozsi . . . . Peter Haumann
Writer . . . . Andras Balint

Budapest — "Roofs At Dawn" is an unnecessarily convoluted drama about the influence of politics on art (among other things) which should have been a lot more gripping than it is. Unfortunately, the clumsy and overly complicated use of flashbacks detracts from the viewer's enjoyment.

Pic opens in August 1956; a painter, Benedek Both, known to his friends as B.B., learns of the death of his lifelong friend, Peter Halasz, in Paris. The flashbacks begin, but this tale of a friendship since childhood isn't easy to follow because the flashbacks aren't shown in any particular order, individual scenes are enacted without an overall sense of style and rhythm and, despite Lajos Koltai's luminous photography and some excellent actors, the film comes across as a muddle. Nor are the characters themselves terribly interesting or sympathetic as presented here; Halasz is an unpleasant type who treats women badly while B.B. mopes around with painter's block.

The film comes alive briefly in scenes involving the heavy-handed Stalinist period, and there's one marvelous moment in which a group of Hungarian artists try to get their message across to an uncomprehending Soviet army officer; a young woman interpreter is unable to keep up with the stream of passionate supplications coming from the Hungarians and collapses in tears as the Russian simply walks away.

A couple of good scenes do not a good picture make, and "Roofs At Dawn" (title refers to the title of a painting) is a lost opportunity, lacking clarity, precision and, above all, style. —Strat.

Ishtar
(COLOR)

Beatty-Hoffman-May creation a big dud; b.o doubtful.

A Columbia Pictures release of a Columbia-Delphi V production. Produced by Warren Beatty. Written and directed by Elaine May. Camera (Technicolor), Vittorio Storaro; editors, Stephen A. Rotter, William Reynolds, Richard Cirincione; sound and music coordinator, John Strauss; original songs, Paul Williams, Elaine May; production design, Paul Sylbert; art directors, Bill Groom, Vicki Paul; set decorators, Steve Jordan, Alan Hicks; costumes, Anthony Powell; sound mixer, Ivan Sharrock; assistant director, Don French; associate producers, David L. MacLeod, Nigel Wooll; casting, Howard Feuer. Reviewed at Century Plaza theater, L.A., May 9, 1987. (MPAA Rating: PG-13.) Running time: **107 MINS.**

Lyle Rogers	Warren Beatty
Chuck Clarke	Dustin Hoffman
Shirra Assel	Isabelle Adjani
Jim Harrison	Charles Grodin
Marty Freed	Jack Weston
Willa	Tess Harper
Carol	Carol Kane
Emir Yousef	Aharon Ipale

Hollywood — "This is unbelievable," says one on-screen character of the Warren Beatty-Dustin Hoffman singing duo. Comment might readily have been addressed not only to their warblings but to the entire "Ishtar" venture, which never gets beyond a lame concept propped up by two name talents. Despite their draw and audience curiosity, release will have a tough time making back its large nut at the box-office.

It's inconceivable, really, that this picture ever would have been made without the packaging of writer-director Elaine May, producer-lead Warren Beatty and Dustin Hoffman. In what amounts to a massive leveraging of their clout, trio managed to convince Columbia to ante up lots of coin to capture this farce on film. Were they really just putting everyone on to see how far they could stretch the studio system and hold one group of execs hostage to the threats of taking the project elsewhere?

Right from the start such flip arrogance is suggested as Beatty-Hoffman work out some awful lyrics not just over the opening credits but the preceding Col logo. By the time they're involved much later on with a blind camel in the African desert, one can't help but wonder if the camel was the only blind creature who had something to do with this picture.

Here's how the story goes: Beatty and Hoffman are struggling and mightily untalented songwriters-singers in New York. They hook up with talent agent Jack Weston (who delivers a fine character performance) and wind up getting booked into the Chez Casablanca in Morocco.

Before leaving town, Beatty's wife (Tess Harper) splits after a short screen time in an odd little throwaway part. She's out of the pic for good by the time the guys hit the "road" — yes, there's the obvious parallels to the Hope-Crosby films.

Arrival in Africa finds Beatty-Hoffman stopping in the mythical kingdom of Ishtar, where most implausible development of all occurs. Hoffman yields his passport to Isabelle Adjani moments after she makes an impassioned appeal during a random encounter at the airport. Sure!

Swirl of events leads Beatty-Hoffman into vortex of Middle East political turmoil, with Adjani functioning as a left-wing rebel trying to overthrow the U.S.-backed Emir of Ishtar.

By this point, audience has been asked to believe Beatty's casting against type. He's the kind of guy here who stuffs a wad of ballpoint pens into the pocket of his white tee-shirt. He's also a bit of a bumpkin from Texas and doesn't quite know how to deal with the ladies. Right!

Hoffman, meantime, is the stronger of the two, with more street smarts and a bit of a personal flair. His nickname is The Hawk and he can be shrewd. Hoffman can also be quite funny but certainly neither he nor Beatty should sing anywhere but in the shower.

Enter Charles Grodin, who upstages all involved via his savagely comical portrayal of a CIA agent. He provides the connecting link as a series of zigzag plot points unfold because of an important map.

Grodin recruits Hoffman for the agency. Adjani supposedly wins over Beatty. Beatty-Hoffman wind up on everybody's hit list and stumble around the desert on their sightless camel.

Desert sequences provide some of the film's high points as Beatty and Hoffman finally develop some genuine rapport under adverse conditions. There are also a few hilarious scenes as vultures circle an exhausted Hoffman and later as he's thrust into role as a translator for gunrunners and their Arab buyers.

Slapdash developments lead Beatty-Hoffman back to the stage for a final, painful exercise of performing. When they bellow "I Look To Mecca," almost anyone who's stayed this long will be looking to the exits.

Pic features 26 original or standard tunes, most of them "sung" by Beatty-Hoffman. No selection is more satisfying than Maurice Williams' own recording of "Little Darlin,' " which mercifully plays over the closing credits. — *Tege.*

Nail Gun Massacre
(COLOR)

Amateur horror for video.

A Reel Movies Intl. release of a Terry Lofton and Futuristic Films presentation. Executive producer, Linda Bass. Produced by Lofton; line producer, Joanne Hazelbarth. Directed by Lofton, Bill Leslie. Screenplay, Lofton; camera (Ultracolor), Leslie; editor, Lynn Leneau Calmes; music, Whitey Thomas; sound, Roy Cherryhomes; production manager, Ginger Lewis; special effects, Lofton; casting, Lofton. Reviewed on Magnum Entertainment vidcassette, N.Y., May 2, 1987. (No MPAA Rating.) Running time: **84 MINS.**

Doc	Rocky Patterson
Linda	Michelle Meyer
Sheriff	Ron Queen
Bubba	Beau Leland

Also with: Sebrina Lawless, Monica Lawless, Mike Coady, Staci Gordon, Randy Hayes, Joanne Hazelbarth, Roger Payne, Kit Mitchell.

"Nail Gun Massacre" is an amateurish horror feature trading on the commercial value of a name in the vein of successes also emphasizing the tools of killing. It's a shot-in-Texas yawner for a clearly circumscribed video audience (no domestic theatrical release has occurred).

Pic opens with a girl being gang-raped by construction workers. Episodic structure that follows has an unidentifiable avenger dressed in khaki military gear and black helmet killing people gorily with a nail gun. It turns out to be the rape victim's brother, though all clues point towards the girl herself (with cheating by the filmmakers who use two women from the cast in the killer's outfit before the final unveiling).

Acting and technical credits are poor, typical of regional horror filmmaking. Premise of the killer (with distorted voice) making silly jokes while killing folks proves to be funny. Realistic blood effects are the pic's raison d'être.—*Lor.*

Malone
(COLOR)

Well-acted 'Shane' clone.

An Orion Pictures released. Produced by Leo L. Fuchs. Directed Harley Cokliss. Stars Burt Reynolds. Screenplay, Christopher Frank, from the novel "Shotgun" by William Wingate; camera (Deluxe color), Gerald Hirschfeld; editor, Todd Ramsay; music, David Newman; production designer, Graeme Murray; casting, Joseph D'Agosta, Carole Kenneally; stunt coordinator, Bud Davis; assistant director, Brad Turner; sound, Richard Van Dyke; set decoration, Barry Brolly; costume design, Norman Salling; casting (Vancouver), Trish Robinson; associate producers, Gerard Croce, Mary Eilts. Reviewed at the Hollywood Pacific theater, L.A., May 1, 1987. (MPAA Rating: R.) Running time: **93 MINS.**

Malone	Burt Reynolds
Delaney	Cliff Robertson
Hawkins	Kenneth McMillan
Jo Barlow	Cynthia Gibb
Paul Barlow	Scott Wilson
Jamie	Lauren Hutton
Harvey	Philip Anglim
Calvin Bollard	Tracey Walter
Dan Bollard	Dennis Burkley

Hollywood — "Malone" is a surprisingly well-acted thriller, with Burt Reynolds giving a magnetic, likeable performance as a disillusioned CIA hit man who thinks his killing days are behind him. Director Harley Cokliss has toned down some of the excesses from his "Black Moon Rising," showing a bit more control in his direction while setting the table for some above-average action sequences. Prospects at boxoffice seem only so-so.

Film starts off unconvincingly; unless, that is, you think CIA is ordering assassinations in broad daylight in major U.S. cities. Man assigned to pull the trigger, alias Richard Malone (Reynolds), can't come across this time and tells love interest and fellow deep-cover agent Jamie (Lauren Hutton, in a nicely played small part) that he wants out.

Malone seeks refuge in the Pacific Northwest, stopping in a small Oregon town when his beloved '69 Mustang breaks down. He pushes it to small gas station, owned and operated by Vietnam vet Paul Barlow (Scott Wilson) and his teenage daughter Jo (Cynthia Gibb).

At this point, plot turns start borrowing so much from Clint Eastwood's "Shane"-rewrite "Pale Rider" as to become almost obnoxious. Throw in Carrie Snodgress and a little more religious imagery and you could have a sequel, a century later.

It turns out the tiny town of Comstock is being systematically taken over by millionaire Charles Delaney (Cliff Robertson), who is buying land at 10 times its value, running people out of town and building the h.q. for a reactionary paramilitary empire that is slowly spreading its influence throughout the country.

Several incidents show Malone protecting Barlow, who has rejected land offers, and his increasingly lovestruck daughter from repeated harassment by Delaney's goons. One of them, obligatory big ugly guy (Dennis Burkley) makes some pointed sexual remarks at Jo in presence of Malone, who dutifully pounds him into submission.

Big ugly guy's drunk brother (played with about as much depth as the description) then seeks revenge, but is blown away himself in a murder attempt.

This puts Malone in trouble with the Comstock sheriff (Kenneth McMillan), who is owned lock, stock and rifle by the paranoid Delaney, who thinks Malone has been sent up to kill him. They face off for the first time in wonderfully taut scene at the police station, which leaves Delaney with an almost obsessive respect for his new enemy.

Police department's request for more information about "Richard Malone" pricks ears of CIA headquarters in Langley, whence Jamie is sent back to Oregon to kill her man. She's almost too late, though, since Delaney has already dispatched two hired hands from New York to do him in. Malone is injured while killing the first two gunners but recovers in time to seduce Jamie, who can't bring herself to poison him.

Delaney's local hoods get to Jamie, though, while Malone is out retrieving his car and the final confrontation is thus set. This, also, plays just like "Pale Rider," with seemingly invincible (and invisible) Malone wiping out all of Delaney's hired hands before facing off with the leader himself.

Cokliss has a knack for good angles and builds well to some nice action scenes, but he has no subtlety when it comes to music. The too-obvious, too-loud scoring detracts from a few quieter scenes (the worse has violins competing with tender heart-to-heart between Malone and the smitten Jo, obscuring a nicely controlled performance from Gibb).

Overall effect is positive, however, with Reynolds, in his 43d film, constructing a serious character with a believable story, and playing it straight and true throughout.

—*Camb.*

The Allnighter
(COLOR)

Surf's up in lame teen comedy.

A Universal Pictures release. Written, produced and directed by Tamar Simon Hoffs. Co-produced by Nancy Israel. Executive producer James L. Stewart. Stars Susanna Hoffs; camera (CFI color), Joseph Urbanczyk; editor, Dan M. Rich; music, Charles Bernstein; production design, Cynthia Sowder; set decoration, Debra Combs; costume design, Isis Mussenden; sound, Rick Alexander, Andrew MacDonald, Daniel Leahy; special surf cinematographer, George Fillinger 3d; assistant director, H. Gordon Boos; casting, Carrie Frazier. Reviewed at the Avco Cinema, L.A., May 2, 1987. (MPAA Rating: PG-13.) Running time: **108 MINS.**
Molly	Susanna Hoffs
Val	Dedee Pfeiffer
Gina	Joan Cusack
C.J.	John Terlesky
Killer	James Anthony Shanta
Mickey Leroi	Michael Ontkean
Sgt. MacLeish	Pam Grier

Hollywood — "The Allnighter" lasts 108 interminable minutes and is distinguishable only in that every other line of dialog seems to end in the word dude, as in "Hey, dude," "Surf's up, dude" and "Totally, dude."

Bangles band member Susanna Hoffs gets to say a good portion of the other half of the dialog in her first starring role, but she never sings. She should have.

Perhaps her mother, making her debut as a feature director here (as well as writing and producing) wanted to launch both their film careers. If so, this isn't going to do it, since pic insults even a bored teenager's

intelligence. Evidently, the Hoffses have been more successful making rock videos together.

Pic's title refers to the all-night partying on the eve of commencement from a ficticious SoCal college of three roomies who share a beach house (Hoffs, Dedee Pfeiffer, Joan Cusack) and their surfing buddies who live next door (John Terlesky, James Anthony Shanta).

Hoffs is the brainy one. She plays a valedictorian student who must have had a C average. Seems neither she, nor her girlfriends, can find much more to talk about than boys who say "dude" a lot and surf.

Hoffs desperately wants to tell her bronzed blond neighbor, C.J. (Terlesky) that she's mad about him and always has been before they all moved away after graduation. He doesn't know what to make of her.

Until that climactic moment near the end of the picture when they finally "get together," it's scenes with Hoffs and her girlfriends doing what girls do (paint their toes, stuff the top of their bathing suits, have innocuous adventures) and boys being surfers (beers for breakfast after surfing, and calling each other "dude").

At least two of the actors, Shanta as the philosophizing surfer ("I came, I saw, I surfed") and Cusack as the aspiring video artist, have two of the more moronic characters ever to grace this genre.

Shanta talks as if he'd been hit in the head too many times by a surfboard. In one of his better lines, he pokes his buddy Terlesky in the chest and says, "You is you ... dude."

Cusack, the college's only new wave artist and the only student without a golden tan, talks in code.

Then there's Terlesky, allegedly bound for law school, but finding it not the last bit inconsistent that he writes term papers for friends so they can graduate. At least one unintentional laugh comes when Shanta thanks him for writing an A paper for him on Spinoza.

Production values are about average for a low-budget beach pic. Continuity is poor but George Fillinger's surf cinematography compensates — sort of. —*Brit.*

Creepshow 2
(COLOR)

Boring followup lacks thrills.

A New World Pictures release of a Laurel Entertainment production. Produced by David Ball. Executive producer, Richard P. Rubinstein. Directed by Michael Gornick. Screenplay, George A. Romero, based on stories by Stephen King; camera (Technicolor), Dick Hart, Tom Hurwitz; editor, Peter Weatherly; music, Les Reed; additional music, Rick Wakeman; production design, Bruce

Miller; costume design, Eileen Sieff; sound, Felipe Borrero; animation supervisor, Rick Catizone; make-up effects, Howard Berger, Ed French; associate producer, Mitchell Galin; assistant directors, Joe Winogradoff, Katarina Wittich; casting, Leonard Finger. Reviewed at New World screening room, L.A., April 30, 1987. (MPAA Rating: R.) Running time: **89 MINS.**
Annie Lansing	Lois Chiles
Ray Spruce	George Kennedy
Martha Spruce	Dorothy Lamour
The Creep	Tom Savini
Boy Billy	Domenick John
Ben Whitemoon	Frank S. Salsedo
Sam Whitemoon	Holt McCallany
Fatso Gribbens	David Holbrook
Andy Cavenaugh	Don Harvey
Deke	Paul Satterfield
Laverne	Jeremy Green
Randy	Daniel Beer
Rachel	Page Hannah
Annie's Lover	David Beecroft
The Hitchhiker	Tom Wright
George Lansing	Richard Parks
Truck Driver	Stephen King
Voice of the Creep	Joe Silver

Hollywood — The type of junk that can be turned out just because a couple of major names attach themselves to a project can be observed in full flower in "Creepshow 2." The names in question are George A. Romero and Stephen King, with the former having adapted three of the latter's stories for this omnibus snoozefest which is utterly lacking in chills or thrills. Concept, names and film's status as a sequel to the 1982 "Creepshow," on which Warner Bros. earned $10,000,000 in domestic rentals, forecast a certain level of opening biz, but this will be in video stores before too long.

Tied together with some humdrum animated sequences, three vignettes on offer obviously were produced on the absolute cheap, mostly in the wilderness with a minimal number of actors. All are so deficient in imagination and scare quotient they wouldn't pass as even satisfactory episodes on a tv show like "Amazing Stories" or "The Twilight Zone."

Whatever interest some might have in seeing George Kennedy and Dorothy Lamour is undercut by their roles as helpless victims of a smalltown robbery and double murder in the first tale, "Old Chief Wood'nhead," a lifeless and listless yarn about a storefront Indian who comes to life to avenge the crimes.

"The Raft" concerns four good-time teens trapped on a platform in the middle of a small lake, then eaten alive by what looks like tarpaulin covered with black goo. Climax of this sequence features the one nice little jolt in the entire picture.

Just when one is feeling that two episodes of this stuff would be more than enough, along comes "The Hitchhiker," a painfully protracted telling of how rich gal Lois Chiles hits and runs from a hitchhiker on the highway at night and is then haunted by the bloodied but far-from-dead fellow.

Nature of the comic book-inspired material is most suited for kids in their early and mid-teens, so it's a mystery why two of the three installments concern characters in mid-age or older. R rating, which seemingly stems from some rather gratuitously foul language and brief thrown-in nudity, might also limit attendance by those most interested in getting in. —*Cart.*

American Ninja 2:
The Confrontation
(COLOR)

Satisfying action pic.

A Cannon Group release of a Golan-Globus production. Produced by Menahem Golan, Yoram Globus. Executive producer, Avi Lerner. Directed by Sam Firstenberg. Stars Michael Dudikoff. Screenplay, Gary Conway, James Booth, story by Conway, based on characters created by Avi Kleinberger, Gideon Amir; camera (TVC color), Gideon Porath; editor, Michael J. Duthie; music, George S. Clinton; production design, Holger Gross; art direction, Robert Jenkinson; costume design, Audrey M. Bansmer; sound (Ultra-Stereo), Phillip Key; associate producer, Mati Raz; assistant director, Richard Green; martial arts choreographer, Michael Stone; second unit director, B.J. Davis; second unit camera, Rod Stewart. Reviewed at the Hollywood Pacific Theater, L.A., May 1, 1987. (MPAA Rating: R.) Running time: **89 MINS.**
Joe Armstrong	Michael Dudikoff
Curtis Jackson	Steve James
Sgt. Charlie McDonald	Larry Poindexter
Leo (The Lion) Burke	Gary Conway
Col. (Wild Bill) Woodward	Jeff Weston
Alicia Sanborn	Michelle Botes
Tojo Ken	Michael Stone
Pat McCarthy	Len Sparrowhawk
Taylor	Jonathan Pienaar

Hollywood — Third teaming, after "American Ninja" and "Avenging Force," of stars Michael Dudikoff and Steve James and director Sam Firstenberg is a rollicking actioner that will satisfy targeted martial arts fans. Chock-full of casual good humor and an offhand sense of make-believe, "American Ninja 2: The Confrontation" never transcends its genre, but delivers the desired goods for an okay b.o. outlook.

This time out, globetrotting Army hardbodies Dudikoff and James arrive on a small Caribbean island to investigate the disappearance of four U.S. Marines. It turns out that a local drug kingpin is kidnaping soldiers and others to turn them into genetically reengineered ninja assassins who will do his bidding worldwide.

All this merely provides an excuse for an ample number of martial arts showdowns between the heroes and the black-robed baddies who swarm from all directions only to be dispatched in tidy fashion by the good guys. Script by actors Gary Conway (who plays the narcotics overlord) and James Booth trades heavily upon the notion of Americans' inherent mental and physical superiority to native warriors, who are a dime a dozen, but in such a comic way that the viewer can laugh with it rather than at it.

Other quaint sidelights have the U.S. military populated almost exclusively by guys sporting "Miami Vice"-style clothes and coiffures, and American soldiers going after government officials of a nation hosting the U.S. Armed Forces.

Pic was lensed in South Africa, and is extremely picturesque despite the modest means. All hands in front of, and behind, the camera keep things jumping at a snappy clip, resulting in good dumb fun.
— *Cart.*

Number One With A Bullet
(COLOR)

Solid lead performances don't save thin actioner.

A Cannon Films release of a Golan-Globus production of a Jack Smight film. Produced by Menahem Golan and Yoram Globus. Directed by Jack Smight. Screenplay, Gail Morgan Hickman, Andrew Kurtzman, Rob Riley, James Belushi, from a story by Hickman; camera (color), Alex Phillips; editor, Michael J. Duthie; music, Alf Clausen; production design, Norm Baron; production supervisor, Rony Yacov; casting, Robert Mac-Donald, Perry Bullington; stunt coordinator, Fred Lerner; aerial coordinator, James Gavin; assistant director, Gerald Walsh; associate producer, Hickman. Reviewed at Cine Harris theater, N.Y., May 7, 1987. (MPAA Rating: R.) Running time: **101 MINS.**
Berzak . . . . .Robert Carradine
Hazeltine . . . . .Billy Dee Williams
Teresa Berzak . . . . Valerie Bertinelli
Capt. Ferris. . . . . .Peter Graves
Mrs. Berzak . . . . .Doris Roberts
Malcolm . . . . .Bobby Di Cicco
Lt. Kaminski . . . . .Ray Girardin
Dacosta . . . . .Barry Sattels
Casey. . . . . .Mykel T. Williamson

"Number One With A Bullet" is a character-heavy, but story-light film. Though the chemistry between the suave Billy Dee Williams and intense Robert Carradine, paired as L.A. detectives, is at times humorous, the hackneyed plot keeps the film from ever getting off the ground.

Carradine is Det. Berzak, nicknamed "Berserk" because of his unorthodox police tactics. He is obsessed with busting the Mr. Big of L.A. drug dealers, the problem being the bigtime dealer, Dacosta, is a wealthy, respectable pillar of the community.

Billy Dee Williams is the opposite of his partner — smooth, lucky with the ladies, expressive and a great musician on the side.

In place of original plot turns we get exotic locations for stylized action sequences. Occasional nice touches, such as Carradine using a kid to keep tabs on his ex-wife, are all but lost in the overwhelming predictability of the script.

The overall effect is a lack of tension, a malaise that increases as the

film chugs to its tired conclusion. Director Jack Smight does his best with the weak material — keeping the deflated ball rolling with some nifty camera work and getting good performances from his two leads — but it too is not enough.

The act of slapping a snappy title on a dull piece of merchandise is symptomatic of this film's problems. Shame is that Carradine and Williams could have been a delight in a well-tuned vehicle. —*Roy.*

Hot Pursuit
(COLOR)

Teen comedy entertains without patronizing.

A Paramount Pictures release of an RKO Pictures production. Executive producer, Tom Mankiewicz, Jerry Offsay. Produced by Pierre David, Theodore R. Parvin. Directed by Steven Lisberger. Screenplay, Lisberger, Steven Carabatsos from story by Lisberger; camera (Metrocolor), Frank Tidy; editor Mitchell Sinoway; sound, Manuel Topete, Eric Batut; art direction, Fernando Ramirez, Chris Dorrington; production design, William J. Creber; music, Rareview; assistant director, Max Kleven; casting, Amanda Mackey. Reviewed at Paramount studio screening room, L.A., May 8, 1987. (MPAA Rating: PG-13.) Running time: **93 MINS.**
Dan Bartlett . . . . .John Cusack
Mac MacClaren . . . . .Robert Loggia
Victor Honeywell . . . . .Jerry Stiller
Lori Cronenberg . . . . .Wendy Gazelle
Bill Cronenberg . . . . .Monte Markham

Hollywood — "Hot Pursuit" is the kind of terrific teen adventure comedy fast becoming a rarity in Hollywood. It doesn't pander to or insult its audience or alienate anyone over 13.

What it does do is entertain, with hearty laughs, likable characters and enough roadblocks to make matters interesting. Mostly, though, it's the altogether winning performance of John Cusack that distinguishes this effort from most others. Word of mouth could generate some heat at the b.o.

Cusack is supposed to join his girlfriend (Wendy Gazelle) and family on vacation, but misses the plane and has one heck of a time trying to catch up. He lands on the Caribbean island okay, but gets sidetracked by three pot-smoking natives, and is shanghaied by a buccaneer (Robert Loggia), finding himself at wits end when he lands in jail on trumped-up charges.

He gets a break, and finally is within earshot of Gazelle and her family — now on a yacht that is soon to be hijacked by a crook — when things to go awry again.

This is the sort of romp that is predictable in its storyline but original in its delivery.

Cusack has the kind of gawky, quasi-naive personality almost everyone can identify with their teenage years.

Under some fairly adversarial conditions (also some pretty unrealistic ones), he manages to mumble, bumble and tumble his way through the jungles of paradise with a certain clumsy finesse that's hard not to chuckle at.

He is certainly one of the most appealing disheveled tourists to grace the screen recently. He's neither an Ugly American, a spoiled rich kid, sex-crazed jock nor yuppie preppie. Rather, he's a regular guy who becomes "Mr. Determined" in his quest to find his gal, with whom he has a real, healthy, affectionate friendship.

It certainly helps that the characters he encounters, even the evil ones, are benign. Towards the end when he tries to be a teenage Rambo against a bunch of gun-brandishing thugs, there's never a hint anyone's going to die. This is safe and sane comedy where the good guys and the bad guys play tag until the bad guys are had.

Loggia acts as if he's having a good time playing a rogue living on a none-too-seaworthy sloop and Gazelle is at first self-conscious, but

later seems quite comfortable with her role as Cusack's adoring sweetheart.

There are, however, numerous holes in the plot and some questionable typecasting of secondary characters. Action starts out on an island where the natives turn out to be friendly, though thoroughly preoccupied with getting stoned. Next land mass is a banana republic inhabited by Spanish-speaking greasy types who are corrupt and/or stupid.

Director Steven Lisberger handles it all with real warmth, for which he can be forgiven for a few trespasses. At one point, Cusack poses as a Latino to get on a flight, where he then exposes a hijacker with a fake bomb, takes command of the plane — and demands a piña colada.

Another surprise of this film is to realize, after a space of time, the absence of a throbbing rock score in the background.

Frank Tidy's beautiful cinematography makes this frenetic adventure with a hapless high schooler a real pleasure to watch.—*Brit.*

Official Cannes Entries

Wish You Were Here
(BRITISH-COLOR)

A Film Four Intl. release of a Zenith production (an Atlantic Releasing release, U.S.), in association with Working Title. Produced by Sara Radclyffe. Directed by David Leland. Screenplay, Leland; camera (color), Ian Wilson; music, Stanley Myers; sound, Billy McCarthy; production design, Caroline Amies; assistant director, Steve Finn; costumes, Shuna Harwood; casting, Susie Figgis. Reviewed at Metro Cinema, London, April 28, 1987. (In the Directors Fortnight section at Cannes Film Festival.) (No MPAA rating.) Running time: **91 MINS.**
Lynda . . . . .Emily Lloyd
Eric. . . . . .Tom Bell
Mrs. Parfitt . . . . .Clare Clifford
Valerie . . . . .Barbara Durkin
Hubert . . . . .Geoffrey Hutchings
Gillian. . . . . .Charlotte Barker
Margaret . . . . .Chloe Leland
Tap Dancing Lady . . . . . .Trudy Cavanagh

London — Set in a thoroughly uptight, provincial British seaside resort in the '50s, this touching account of a girl's growing pains marks the directorial debut of rising young talent, director-scripter David Leland.

While best known for his bitter look at modern British society via a four-parter he scripted for the small screen several years ago, Leland shows he has more arrows to his bow than social satire. He can be compassionate and funny about human foibles as well as disgusted; and his eye for the telling visual detail shows promise of becoming as

practiced as his facility for sharp-edged dialog.

But pic hardly charts any new territory. Audience always knows exactly where its sympathies are supposed to lie: the indictment of provincial hypocrisy and small-mindedness is hardly original. What makes it interesting is the character of the heroine; her refreshing rudeness disconcerts those around her but also wins over the audience.

By focusing on a spunky but troubled 16-year-old girl named Lynda (played with exasperating charm by newcomer Emily Lloyd), Leland also squeezes out more poignancy than would have been possible had the central character been the typical gawky male youth of most films about sexual awakening.

What makes the girl troubled is the fact that her mother died when she was 11; the wistful triteness of the title is in keeping with the atmosphere of the film — and no one has replaced that essential loss.

Because she is spunky, Lynda's reaction to her plight is to shock people with her rudeness and to taunt the opposite sex. This makes for some verbally sharp and occasionally visually eloquent scenes, especially those in which Lynda jeopardizes one job after another because she can't hold her tongue nor stop trying to entice boys.

Lynda's rebelliousness eventually leads to a potentially sinister liaison with a seedy older man (played with taciturn intensity by Tom Bell), as much a misfit as she is. Their scenes together, though quite limited, are highly charged.

Inevitably Lynda gets pregnant for her pains, but refuses to get a back-street abortion. In the last scene she returns triumphantly to town, strutting in a bright yellow dress and pushing a baby carriage, complete with yellow whirl-a-gig down the boardwalk past former beaux.

Despite the exhilaration, the sense is that her triumph will be brief: the film in fact opens and closes with a Fellini-like scene of an aging, dolled-up tapdancer performing her routine on the boardwalk to a wistful, crackling victrola.

Like so many of the new batch of small-budget British films, most of them made with money from the U.K.'s Channel 4, "Wish" will need proper handling to break it out into a larger market. Though pic focuses on teenagers, most likely audience would be those 30-ish and older who relish what is touching and literate rather than mentally taxing or just titillating. They won't be disappointed: despite a few awkward scenes, this is an enjoyable, well acted, technically sound production.—*Guid.*

Cartoline Italiane
(Italian Postcards)
(ITALIAN-COLOR)

An Istituto Luce/Italnoleggio release of a Mean Cinematografica production, in association with RAI-TV Channel 2. Directed by Memè Perlini. Star Genevieve Page, Lindsay Kemp. Screenplay, Perlini, Gianni Romoli; camera (color), Carlo Carlini; editor, Carlo Fontana; art direction and costumes, Antonello Agliotti; music, Stefano Mainotti. Reviewed at Studio 23, Rome, May 4, (In the Un Certain Regard section at Cannes Film Festival.) Running time: **93 MINS.**

Silvana . . . . Genevieve Page
Vinicio Secchi . . . . Lindsay Kemp
Lidia . . . . Cristiana Borghi
Also with: David Brandon (Vittorio), Stefano Davanzati, Antonello Fassari, Rosa Fumetto, Alessandro Genesi, Franco Piacentini, Ines Carmona, Maria Marchi, Giovanna Bardi, Isabella Martelli.

Rome — As an often clever, sometimes touching record of his seminal work on the Italian avant-garde stage, Memè Perlini's "Italian Postcards" should find ample appreciation among a restricted circle of theater enthusiasts. This rule-breaking treatise on the actor's craft is hardly meant for mass consumption, and like many creative marriages of stage and screen will have a tough time scaring up an audience, despite fine performances from Genevieve Page and likable clown Lindsay Kemp.

Freewheeling story has young woman named Lidia (Cristiana Bor-

ghi) pass herself off as an actress to gain admittance to a boarding house run by Pola Mareschi, a legendary stage star now well on her way down Sunset Boulevard. Object of the deception is to get a stolen "interview" with the unapproachable diva for Lidia's boyfriend David Brandon.

The boarding house, where most of the film takes place, is a slightly disguised theater peopled by thesps of every stripe. Leading lights are the former leading lady, limned by a charismatic Page, and her aging "dresser"prompter, Vinicio (Kemp).

Before the ever-more-enchanted eyes of the intruder Lidia, landlady and renters act out scenes from Shakespeare to Pirandello, with "real life" mixed in.

Lidia finds herself caught up in the theatrical rites, and even after her hidden mirophone is discovered, after she's been robbed in the middle of the living room by a motor-cycle gang, and after her boyfriend catches her in bed with a young actor, she can't bring herself to leave the apartment, where she is both spectator and player.

Though it gets repetitive, actors putting on a show for each other can be surprisingly entertaining when Perlini's sophisticated sense of humor clicks. There is a naked girl with a razor blade, a Buster Keaton-faced mime who talks in sign language, and imaginative use of cutting and sound. —*Yung.*

The Whales Of August
(U.S.-COLOR/B&W)

An Alive Films release produced with Circle Associates in association with Nelson Entertainment. Produced by Carolyn Pfeiffer, Mike Kaplan. Executive producer, Shep Gordon. Directed by Lindsay Anderson. Stars Bette Davis, Lillian Gish, Vincent Price, Ann Sothern. Screenplay, David Berry, based on his play; camera (TVC Labs processing; CFI color prints), Mike Fash; editor, Nicolas Gaster; music, Alan Price; production design, Jocelyn Herbert; art direction, K.C. Fox, Bob Fox; set decoration, Sosie Hublitz; costume design, Rudy Dillon; Bette Davis' costumes, Julie Weiss; sound, Donald Summer; associate producer, Stuart Besser; assistant director, Broderick Miller. Reviewed at Lorimar Telepictures screening room, Culver City, Calif., April 24, 1987. (No MPAA rating.) (Out-of-competition offical entry at Cannes Film Festival.) Running time: **90 MINS.**

Libby Strong . . . . Bette Davis
Sarah Webber . . . . Lillian Gish
Mr. Maranov . . . . Vincent Price
Tisha Doughty . . . . Ann Sothern
Joshua Brackett . . . . Harry Carey Jr.
Mr. Beckwith . . . . Frank Grimes
Old Randall . . . . Frank Pitkin
Young Randall . . . . Mike Bush
Young Libby . . . . Margaret Ladd
Young Tisha . . . . Tisha Sterling
Young Sarah . . . . Mary Steenburgen

Hollywood — Several remarkable artists, each representing different significant traditions and eras in film history, have joined forces for "The Whales Of August," and the

result is lovely on all counts. Muted but engrossing tale about the balance of power between two elderly sisters boasts superior lead performances from two of the screen's most legendary actresses, Bette Davis and Lillian Gish, and interest in seeing these two ladies in a quality film will assure strong business in arthouses and possibly beyond its theatrical openings this fall. World premiere takes place May 15 at the Cannes Film Festival.

Occasion also marks the first American outing for director Lindsay Anderson, who has bounced back from the boundless absurdism of "Brittania Hospital" with a precise, rigorously controlled work that gets the most out of modest material. Completely without pretention or a false sense of self-importance, pic is scaled just right to let the drama take hold and the performers take off.

Adapted by David Berry from his 1981 play, story has two sisters living alone in a comfortable but basic home they have occupied for decades on the striking coast of Maine. Sarah (Gish) is a doting busybody who is obliged to care for her sister Libby (Davis), because the latter is blind.

As she putters around the house tidying up and doing her sister's bidding, Gish continually refers to Davis as "dear," although she is anything but. Irascible, cranky and stubborn, with only occasional pleasant streaks, Davis clearly would have been a handful even in the best of times, but in her dotage is a burden her sister cannot shake off.

Trouble rears its head in the form of Vincent Price, a White Russian of considerable charm and gentlemanliness who for decades has lived as a "houseguest" of numerous ladies. Having had yet another woman die on him, Price clearly is casting about for a new situation and sets his sights on the eager Gish. Davis, however, will have none of it, and does all within her limited powers to interfere with this potentially dramatic change in her living conditions.

Such are the simple dramatic contours of the piece. Lacking in explosive fireworks or even startling confrontations, it makes its points quietly, with understatement that resonates with time.

Creating much of this resonance, of course, are the two actresses. Gish's career dates virtually to the beginnings of narrative cinema in the U.S., and despite much fine work in the intervening years, she still is most often thought of as having set the standards for acting on the silent screen.

Davis, of course, was queen bee during the golden studio era, and is

as famous for her forthrightness and frequent treachery in her roles as Gish is for her resilient innocence. In "Whales," Gish looks older but essentially little changed from former appearances, while Davis, in her first bigscreen part since a stroke and major surgery, is not instantly recognizable. Wearing long, pure white hair, which Gish carefully brushes in one of the film's magical moments, Davis looks gaunt, grim and disturbed, but her performance is restrained in such a way that may even increase its power.

Gish is a delight throughout, and has one beautiful scene all to herself late in the picture when she celebrates her wedding anniversary by dressing up, putting on the gramophone, pouring a glass of port and reminiscing with her long-departed mate.

Ann Sothern is winning as the ladies' jocular neighbor, and Price, in his first non-horror film in 25 years, brings a warm sophistication to his gentleman caller, even if his light Russian accent slips in and out. As a local handyman, Harry Carey Jr. contributes enormous pep to his brief scenes.

Material is low-key, but picture casts a quiet, special spell and has a number of privileged moments film lovers will cherish. Further, it has none of the cloying cuteness and sentimentality of the last major feature about old people, "On Golden Pond." Contributing heavily to the delicate mood is Alan Price's outstanding score, as well as the wind-blown Maine seashore, which is nicely caught by Mike Fash's camera and abetted by Jocelyn Herbert's discreet production design. A black & white prolog, in which Mary Steenburgen, Tisha Sterling and Margaret Ladd appear as the women in their youth, gets the film off to a nice start.—*Cart.*

Good Morning Babilonia
(Good Morning Babylon)
(ITALIAN-FRENCH-
U.S.-COLOR)

A Vestron Pictures release (U.S.) of a Filmtre/MK2 Prods./Pressman Film Corp./RAI-1/Films A2 coproduction. Produced by Giuliani G. De Negri. Directed by Paolo and Vittorio Taviani. Screenplay, the Tavianis, based on an idea by Lloyd Fonvielle; script collaborator, Tonino Guerra; camera (color), Giuseppe Lanci; music, Nicola Piovani; art director, Gianni Sharra; costumes, Lina Nerli Taviani; editor, Roberto Perpignani; sound, Carlo Palmieri; assistant director, Mimmola Cirosi; production manager, Tommaso Calevi; associate producers, Lloyd Fonvielle, Caldecot Chubb, Milena Canonero, Marina Gefter Cervi. Reviewed at the Club del'Etoile, Paris, April 30, 1987. (Out-Of-Competition at Cannes Film Festival.) Running time: **115 MINS.**

Nicola . . . . Vincent Spano
Andrea . . . . Joaquim de Almeida
Edna . . . . Greta Scacchi
Mabel . . . . Désirée Becker

Bonnanno ....Omero Antonutti
D.W. Griffith ....Charles Dance
Mrs. Griffith ....Bérangère Bonvoisin
The Venetian ....Margarita Lozano
Massimo Venturiello .....David Brandon
Andrea Prodan............Brian Freilino

Paris — Italo filmmaking brothers Paolo and Vittorio Taviani go west in their first English-language film, which chronicles the adventures of two Tuscan mason brothers who emigrate to America before World War I and become set designers on D.W. Griffith's motion picture spectacular, "Intolerance."

The premise is exciting, but the Tavianis, working with a budget large by Italian standards but inadequate for the needs of their script, have made a molehill of a picture out of a mountain of an idea. Running out-of-competition at Cannes (with several other films set in the movie world), "Good Morning Babylon" will need strong play on the Tavianis' arthouse reputation to get by, though admirers may admit the directors are out of their element with material that removes them from their cultural and geographic roots.

Buff expectations of a recreation of the production of the Griffith masterpiece will be sorely disappointed by the Tavianis' fanciful, coyly schematic view of early Hollywood (in fact filmed largely in Italy), and sticklers of historical accuracy will let out a howl of indignation at their preposterous approximation of filmmaking in its pioneer days, before the mecca of cinema became a Babylon of legendary immorality and excess.

Lacking the material means to evoke a physical reality (with glaringly second-rate model work and glass shot special effects by art director Gianni Sbarra), the Tavianis try to compensate by treating their story as an intimate pastoral epic. Hollywood indeed may have looked like a sprawling bungalow colony, but the image of the film industry as a glorified day camp for adults is often risible.

The liberties taken with the realities of Hollywood on the eve of the war might have gone down better had the Tavianis succeeded in their characterizations. But there is little depth or psychological insight in the twin protagonists: inseparable brothers (in the image of the Tavianis themselves) who set out for America to make the fortune that will save the family's venerable church restoration business from bankruptcy.

After a transatlantic crossing that's charmingly treated like a Chaplin vignette, the brothers work their way painfully across America until they happen upon a group of other Latin immigrants who've been hired to build the Italian Pavilion at the San Francisco Exposition of 1914.

Deeply impressed by a screening of the Italian movie blockbuster "Cabiria," D.W. Griffith is further excited by the expo pavilion and orders its architects to be hired for his planned superproduction.

Though mere laborers, the brothers brazenly impersonate the master masons, but are exposed and relegated to menial labors. When they learn Griffith is seeking an elephant motif for his film's massive Babylonian settings, they fabricate a large paper-maché model that bowls the filmmaker over. They share the acclaim heaped on Griffith at the film's premiere, though the outbreak of war compromises pic's career.

In the meantime the brothers wed two aspiring actress-dancers in the studios, but the death of one of them in childbirth destroys the siblings' mystical equilibrium. Finally both go off to war in Europe and meet their end on the battlefield, filming each other's final moments with a motion picture camera.

Since the Tavianis' salute to the pioneers of cinema (likened by Griffith in one scene to the cathedral builders of history) can only be suggested, film's exaltation of the collective artisanal spirit is merely an empty gesture.

Acting too leaves something to be desired with the inseparable brothers blandly portrayed by Vincent Spano and Joaquim de Almeida, and Griffith impersonated by Charles Dance as a smug artiste who seems to anticipate his place in future film history tomes. Désirée Becker and Greta Scacchi (so fine in Diane Kurys' movieland romance, "A Man In Love") founder as love interest for the protagonists.

Attractively lensed by Giuseppe Lanci and scored by Nicola Piovani, film could have benefited from some tighter editing, especially for Stateside playoffs. —*Len.*

Un Zoo la Nuit
(Night Zoo)
(CANADIAN-COLOR)

A Cinéma Plus release (in Canada) of a Les Productions Oz Inc. production in association with the National Film Board. Produced by Roger Frappier, Pierre Gendron. Written and directed by Jean-Claude Lauzon. Camera (color), Guy Dufaux; editor, Michel Arcand; sound, Yvon Benoit; art direction, Jean-Baptiste Tard; set designer, Michèle Forest; costumes, Andrée Morin; music, Jean Corriveau; associate producer, Suzanne Dussault. Reviewed at Cannes Film Festival (in Directors Fortnight section), May 8, 1987. Running time: **115 MINS.**
Albert ....Roger Le Bel
Marcel ....Gilles Maheu
Julie ....Lynne Adams
Georges ....Lorne Brass
Charlie ....Germain Houde

Cannes — "Un Zoo la Nuit" is an astonishingly mature first feature from Quebec's Jean-Claude Lauzon. Pic is a continuously gripping effort that alternates between overt toughness and tenderness — scenes of brutal sex, homo and hetero, and murder that are played off almost surrealistically and are balanced by at times whimsical yet powerful reconciliation between a son and his aging and dying father. Because of the violence (though no blood is shown) and depiction of homosexual rape, the pic is for demanding situations and not predicted for wide release. It's still a major debut and bound to draw positive attention.

Lauzon, in full command of his complex story and the many layers of filmic requirements it makes, is aided by Guy Dufaux' superb camera work and Jean-Baptiste Tard's excellent, artistic but never overwhelming art direction.

Pic begins with a homosexual scene in jail; the young man raped, while a guard watches, is freed after two years and is pursued by violent cops for whom he had been running dope. They want their cut; within the pic's first 10 minutes there is another homosexual scene, aborted between a cop and the young man who punches his way out of a seedy restaurant washroom.

Meanwhile, the man's father is shown living at the rear of another restaurant, owned by friends, but undergoing renovations that force him to squeeze further onto smaller quarters.

Pushed around by the cops and knifed by one of them on the cheek, the young man turns to brutal sex with his former girlfriend who works at a sex peep club. And he slowly comes to terms with his father, who, it turns out, has hidden both cocaine and a pile of cash for his return from jail.

Tv sets seen in various scenes all show news coverage of violent events; buildings are under renovation; the young man's mother has left his father; there is rough sex (no vital parts shown), but love only between the father and his cronies and between father and son that's crystallized on a fishing trip.

With help from a homosexual former jail mate, the young man gets revenge on the cops murdering them in a sleazy hotel. Without missing a beat, Lauzon then turns full attention on the dying father who just wants to go on a hunting trip with his son.

But the father is hospitalized with heart trouble and his days are numbered. So, the son sneaks into his bedside a movie projector, shows him a film about moose and then whisks him to a zoo at night where there is no moose but an elephant whom the father thinks he has killed with a gun the son has bought him.

The pic, which begins savagely, ends with a slightly protracted soft-focus recall of the fishing trip shot from a misty distance.

Gilles Maheu as the son and Roger Le Bel as his father are outstanding, and all other actors ably assist. Production values, notably sound, are tops. —*Adil.*

A Month In The Country
(BRITISH-COLOR)

An Orion Classics release (U.S.) of a Euston Films production. Produced by Kenith Trodd. Executive producers, Johnny Goodman, John Hambley. Directed by Pat O'Connor. Screenplay, Simon Gray, from the novel by J.L. Carr; camera (color) Kenneth Macmillian; music, Howard Blake; sound, Tony Dawe; production design, Leo Austin; assistant director, Bill Craske; costumes, Judy Moorcroft; casting, Michelle Guish; associate producer, Dominic Fulford. Reviewed at Metro Cinema, London, April 27, 1987. (In the Un Certain Regard section, Cannes Film Festival.) (MPAA Rating: PG.) Running time: **96 MINS.**
Birkin ....Colin Firth
Moon ....Kenneth Branagh
Mrs. Keach ....Natasha Richardson
Rev. Keach ....Patrick Malahide
Douthwaite ....Tony Haygarth
Ellerback ....Jim Carter
Col. Hebron ....Richard Vernon

London — "A Month In The Country" is a gentle but moving pic about two men recovering from the horrors of World War I during an idyllic summer in remote rolling English countryside.

Pic has the feel of plush period drama done so well by the British. Articulate writing, deft acting and talented direction place it apart from similar tales of the genre, and offshore b.o. potential could be good if handled properly.

Helmer Pat O'Connor (whose last pic was Warner's "Cal") shows considerable sensitivity handling dilemmas of the two troubled soldiers. He also shoots with great dexterity, showing off the English countryside in summertime to its best advantage.

Pic opens with the Colin Firth character arriving at the remote Yorkshire village of Oxgodby to uncover a medieval wall painting in the local church. There he meets Kenneth Branagh as Moon, who is excavating a grave outside the churchyard.

Both are tormented by their war experiences, but during a beautiful summer month they experience the tranquility of the idyllic community that gradually helps them come to terms with their problems.

Firth falls in love with the wife (Natasha Richardson) of an unfriendly local vicar, but never lets on to her about his passion, while the Branagh character turns out to be a homosexual. When their work is done, Firth returns to his wayward wife, and Branagh goes excavating in faraway Baghdad.

"A Month In The Country" is beautifully filmed, and praise should go to cinematographer Kenneth Macmillan for stunning work, and to Simon Gray for a sensitive adaptation of J.L. Carr's book. Other technical credits are excellent.

Colin Firth and Kenneth Branagh are talented young actors to watch for — especially Branagh who has great screen presence. Natasha Richardson looks slightly uncomfortable in a very understated role, while Richard Vernon as a doddery old colonel is a joy in his few scenes, bringing welcome comic relief.

The restrained love affair, and the tribulations of the two men are elegantly handled, and alongside the picturesque Yorkshire countryside make for a gently rounded pic.
—*Adam.*

Dilan
(TURKISH-SWISS-WEST GERMAN-COLOR)

A Hakan Film (Istanbul)/Limbo Film (Zurich)/ZDF (Mainz) coproduction. (World Sales, Metropolis Films, Zurich). Produced by Luciano Gloor, Hakan Balamir. Directed by Erden Kiral. Screenplay, Kiral, Omer Polat; camera (Agfacolor), Martin Gressmann; editor, Roswitha Henze; music, Nizamettin; sound, Michael Hemmerling; assistant director, Konstantin Schmidt. Reviewed at Cannes Film Festival (Directors Fortnight), May 10, 1987. Running time: **92 MINS.**

Dilan	Derya Arbas
Kerim	Hakan Balamir
Paso Bey	Yilmaz Zafer
Mirkan	Mehmet Erikci
Dilan's mother	Güler Okten
Dilan's father	Dilaver Uyanik
Paso's mother	Keriman Ulusoy

Cannes — A painfully slow drama about sweethearts separated by cruel fate, "Dilan" is a disap-

pointing new film from Erden Kiral, who previously scored fest plaudits with "A Season In Hakkari" and "The Mirror."

Filmed in Eastern Anatolia, near the border with Iran, where the peasants eke out a slim existence on barren land, pic starts out establishing the fact that Dilan (Derya Arbas) loves Mirkan (Mehmet Erikci), a poor shepherd, and is in turn loved by Paso (Yilmaz Zafer), son of a comparatively wealthy landowner. Dilan's father demands a dowry of sheep, which Mirkin can't afford; but he decides to try to raise money across the border. Paso bribes his stableman, Kerim (Hakan Balamir) to make sure Mirkan doesn't return.

Though unquestionably well intentioned, "Dilan" sometimes seems almost a parody of Turkish films. The leading actress, who was born in Los Angeles and resides there, looks far too beautiful and elegant to be a poor peasant only just surviving. And the static, heavy pacing makes the film seem interminable.

It doesn't even have the visual qualities that made "Hakkari" a pleasure to watch: Martin Gressmann's camerawork is flat and gloomy, and there are abundance of images of vast, arid plains on which tiny figures can barely be glimpsed, which won't look good on television.

Erden Kiral has lived in Berlin for four years now, and maybe feels that "Dilan" is the kind of arthouse Turkish film West European audiences want to see. There's the strong impression of an academic exercise up there on the screen, not a deeply, personally felt drama.
—*Strat.*

✱✱✱✱✱✱✱✱✱✱✱✱✱✱✱✱✱✱✱✱✱✱
Competing At Cannes
✱✱✱✱✱✱✱✱✱✱✱✱✱✱✱✱✱✱✱✱✱✱

Barfly
(U.S.-COLOR)

A Cannon release of a Francis Ford Coppola presentation of a Golan-Globus production. Produced by Barbet Schroeder, Fred Roos, Tom Luddy. Executive producers, Menahem Golan, Yoram Globus. Directed by Barbet Schroeder. Stars Mickey Rourke, Faye Dunaway. Screenplay, Charles Bukowski; camera (TVC color), Robby Müller; editor, Eva Gardos; production design, Bob Ziembicki; set decoration, Lisa Dean; visual consultant-costume designer, Milena Canonero; sound (Ultra-Stereo), Petur Hliddal; associate producer-assistant director, Jack Baran; casting, Robert MacDonald, Pat Orseth, Nancy Lara. Reviewed at the Cannon screening room, L.A., May 7, 1987. (In Competition at Cannes Film Festival). Running time: **99 MINS.**

Henry Chinaski	Mickey Rourke
Wanda Wilcox	Faye Dunaway
Tully Sorenson	Alice Krige
Detective	Jack Nance
Jim	J.C. Quinn
Eddie	Frank Stallone

Hollywood — "Barfly" is a lowlife fairytale, an ethereal seriocomedy about gutter existence from the pen of one who's been there, Charles Bukowski. First American fictional feature from Swiss-French director Barbet Schroeder is spiked with unexpected doses of humor, much of it due to Mickey Rourke' quirky, unpredictable, most engaging performance as the boozy hero. Grungy, squalid characters and settings probably will limit domestic audiences to the arthouse circuit, but overseas take should be stronger due to heavy foreign interest in Bukowski, not to mention the director and stars, and inter-

national appeal of pics showing the underside of American life.

Much as in a Bukowski short story, a bar is the center of the universe here. Populating the dive in a seedy section of Los Angeles are a floating assortment of winos and derelicts, of which one of the youngest and most volatile is Henry, a self-styled poet of the bottle who maintains, "It takes a special talent to be a drunk."

Played by Rourke, Henry takes a nearly nightly pleasure in picking a fight with the beefy barkeep, and is in every respect a total mess. Nevertheless, it shortly becomes clear Henry, in his drunkenness, lives a charmed, privileged existence of a sort. For one thing, he meets a terribly attractive fellow alcoholic, Wanda (Faye Dunaway), who immediately takes him in and keeps him well plied with drink and sex, to the extent they are both interested in and capable of the latter.

For another, he is pursued by Tully Sorenson (Alice Krige), a beautiful, upscale magazine publisher who has taken a fancy to Henry's down-to-earth prose and wants to shower him with money. Henry has no objections either to the cash or Tully's body, but quickly blows his earnings by buying too many rounds for his fellow barflies, and ends up back where he started on the drunken merry-go-round.

Story doesn't amount to that much and is pitched at a rather modest level of artistic ambition. But on its own terms, pic succeeds strongly in capturing a mood, character and state of mind, and projects a timeless quality that exists alongside, but apart from, everyday reality as most people experience it. In the barfly's world, conventional notions of time, relativity and responsibility become warped and finally irrelevent, and Schroeder has captured this admirably.

At the same time, humor comes brimming to the surface even at the most unlikely moments. Bukowski's dialog is punctuated with wry philosophical comments on life, and Rourke, who usually is so intense and sometimes overwrought on-screen, relaxes here to deliver what is probably his most appealing and successful characterization since his pre-star turn in "Diner."

Virtually unrecognizable at first with his dangling, dark, long-unwashed hair and unglamorous stubble, Rourke affects a Walter Brennan-ish gimpy walk, pitches his voice high and sets an offbeat rhythm to his talk that amusingly illuminates both the man's lucidity and self-willed handicaps. Performance is the centerpiece of the film, and keeps it bouyantly alive throughout.

Faye Dunaway also is on the right

wavelength as the "distressed goddess" who grows dependent upon and loyal to the wildly unreliable Rourke. One would like to know something more about her background, however, and her appearance, while rundown, still seems too sharp for the bottom-of-the-barrel milieu in question.

Alice Krige more than adequately fills her one-dimensional role, and remainder of the cast, most of whom play barroom habitués, look like the real thing.

Clearly done on a limited budget, production still looks first class thanks to Robby Müller's top lensing and contributions of production designer Bob Ziembicki and visual consultant-costume designer Milena Canonero. Storytelling is tight, not languid as in some of Schroeder's previous features, and what could have been an overly depressing tale about hopeless losers has been leavened by considerable, unforced comedy. —*Cart.*

Champ d'Honneur
(Field Of Honor)
(FRENCH-COLOR)

An AAA release of a Baccara/Palmyre/Selena Audiovisuel La SEPT production. Produced by Antoine Gannage, Eric Dussart. Directed by Jean-Pierre Denis. Screenplay, Denis, Hubert au Petit with Christian Faure, Françoise Dudognong; camera (color), François Catonne; editor, Genevieve Winding; sound, Alain Curvellier; music, Michel Portal; production design, Marc Petitjean; costumes, Anne Le Moal; production management, Jacques Lacour; associate producer, Thierry Brissaud. Reviewed at Cannes Film Festival (In Competition), May 9, 1987. Running time: **87 MINS.**

Pierre	Cris Campion
Henriette	Pascale Rocard
Arnaud	Eric Wapler
The Child	Frederic Mayer

Also with: Marcelles Dessalles, André Wilms, Vincent Martin, Marion Audier, Robert Sandrey, Lilly Genny, Louis-Marie Taillefer, Francois Segura, Gisele Boubou, others.

Cannes — Writer-helmer Jean-Pierre Denis has won minor honors at earlier Cannes fests for minor works. He is back with this big-budget production and small-scale epic war meller titled "Field Of Honor," the field being the Alsace terrain where the Prussians overan the French armies in 1870. If one can imagine a film as a tender and warmhearted report from a battlefront strewn with dead bodies, "Field Of Honor" is it, and on its very special merits it may reach numerous foreign markets with some careful nursing.

Casual killing and graphically described military action are as much in evidence here as in "Platoon," but director-coscripter Jean-Pierre Denis is out to prove the ultimate triumph of the better basic human response, and does so in a story that denies neither the occurence of wanton cruelty nor of honorable striving to do the right thing.

This story has a poor young peasant and a rich man's son as winner and loser, respectively, in a pre-war conscription officer's lottery to decide who is inducted and who goes free. To pay his family's debts, the poor youngster takes the rich boy's place in the army and goes off to what soon proves to be real war. At home, the rich boy suffers pangs of conscience; on the field of honor the poor farmer-in-uniform sees his comrades slain, while he somehow escapes.

In his flight, the soldier is joined by a small Alsacian boy. Gradually, they learn to love and respect one another across their language barrier. They get separated. The boy goes south and finds refuge in the soldier's village after being rescued from an arsonist's forest fire by the well-to-do youth who escaped army service.

There is high drama in the subdued telling of all this. There are fine production values to admire, and there is honest and natural acting supplied by everybody in the cast, including Cris Campion (Walter Matthau's sidekick from Polanski's ''Pirates'') as the farmer-soldier, Eric Wapler as the rich youngster and Frederic Mayer as the little boy, looking sweet, but never falling into the cutesipoo trap. Film shies away from the maudlin and the gratuitously cruel. —*Kell.*

Un Homme amoureux
(A Man In Love)
(FRENCH-COLOR)

A Gaumont release of a Camera One/Alexandre Films/J.M.S. coproduction. Executive producer, Michel Seydoux. Produced by Marjorie Israel, Armand Barbault, Roberto Guissani (Italy). Directed by Diane Kurys. Screenplay, Kurys, Olivier Schatzky; camera (Eastmancolor), Bernard Zitzermann; art direction, Dean Tavoularis; editor, Joëlle Van Effenterre; sound, Bernard Bats; Gérard Lamps; costumes, Brigitte Nierhaus; makeup, Joël Lavau; music, Georges Delerue; assistant director, Paolo Barzman; production manager, Bertrand Van Effenterre. Reviewed at the Gaumont Colisée cinema, Paris, May 8, 1987. (In Competition at Cannes Film Festival.) Running time: **117 MINS.**
Jane Steiner . . . . Greta Scacchi
Steve Elliot . . . . Peter Coyote
Michael Pozner . . . . Peter Riegert
Julia Steiner . . . . Claudia Cardinale
Harry Steiner . . . . John Berry
Bruno Schlosser . . . . Vincent Lindon
Susan Elliot . . . . Jamie Lee Curtis
Pizani . . . . Jean Pigozzi
Sam . . . . Elia Katz
De Vitta . . . . Constantin Alexandrov
Paolo . . . . Michele Melega
Dr. Sandro . . . . Jean-Claude de Goros

Paris — Diane Kurys scored both critically and commercially at home and abroad with her 1983 film ''Coup de foudre'' (Entre Nous), a moving, well observed drama inspired by her own family history. ''A Man In Love,'' her fourth feature and first English-lingo effort, operates in more conventional territory, the Movieland Romance, but Kurys by now is skilled and thoughtful enough a commercial filmmaker to give the material a winning facelift. Pic's running in the Cannes competition alongside more highbrow contenders probably is an error, but one that shouldn't damage its chances at the pay windows, despite the lack of marquee names.

The story, imagined by Kurys and developed with coscripter Olivier Schatzky, is dime novel syrup with a filip of culture: an American movie star (Peter Coyote) who has come to Rome to make a film about the Italian poet Cesar Pavese falls in love with a supporting player (Greta Scacchi) and carries on with her openly during the production.

Naturally, the actor imperils the entire film with his moody liaison as well as his marriage to a neurotic but supportive ex-actress (Jamie Lee Curtis); while Scacchi has not only a jealous boyfriend in Paris but a mother (Claudia Cardinale) who is dying of cancer in the background.

A plot like this is a potential minefield of clichés, but one of the film's pleasures is the way Kurys maneuvers with finesse around obvious soap operatics and fulfills her unabashedly romantic design without bathos.

Kurys' other considerable triumphs are her confident handling of a complex production abroad — much of the film was shot at Cinecittà studios — and her seamless direction of a multinational cast. Unlike many European filmmakers who direct American actors with a crippling sense of awe, Kurys gets authentic, uncaricatured performances from Coyote and the other shrewdly chosen actors.

There's no condescension in Coyote's portrayal of a Yank film celebrity who has the talent, idealism and arrogance to pass up a chunky Hollywood contract to act in an arty European biopic, but is shown up as indecisive in his personal relationships. Scacchi is radiant as the aspiring thesp who blithely lands her first important movie role, takes her dead-end affair with Coyote in stride, and inherits the life-loving moral force of her mother in the end.

Cardinale embodies quintessential fortitude and grace in the small but important role of the doomed mother. Scacchi's father, an alcoholic journalist desperately attached to wife and daughter, is appealingly acted by Paris-based Yank filmmaker John Berry.

In other colorful supporting parts, Peter Riegert is Coyote's faithful Brooklyn-born personal assistant and Jamie Lee Curtis is the star's complaining but devoted spouse. Vincent Lindon is funny and forlorn as Scacchi's Parisian legit helmer boyfriend.

With the aid of Dean Tavoularis' art direction, Kurys divests the film-within-a-film business of the starry-eyed self-indulgence that nags most movies about filmmaking, while retaining the aura of make-believe and fascination. Helmer no doubt will come in for some knocks for her evocation of Cesar Pavese, a Communist author and poet who committed suicide in 1950, as the subject of the film Coyote is making. The biopic is something of a thematic MacGuffin for Kurys, though she makes a nervy association between Pavese and Cardinale (who commits suicide to end her own and her family's pain).

Bernard Zitzermann's rich color photography and the unmistakable Georges Delerue score are other assets in this civilized, sincerely felt entertainment.—*Len.*

Shinran: Shiroi Michi
(Shinran: Path To Purity)
(JAPANESE-COLOR)

A Schochiku release of a Shochiku/Nichiei/Kinoma Tokyo coproduction. Produced by Kiyoshi Fujimoto. Executive producers, Nabuyoshi Otani, Hiroski Kato and Matsuo Takahashi. Directed by Rentare Mikuni. Screenplay, Don Fujita, Rentaro Mikuni, based on a book by Mikuni; camera (color), Yoshi Yamazaki; editor, Osamu Inoue; music, YAS-KAZ; (Canyon Records Inc., Japan); art direction, Takee Kimura; lighting, Shosaku Kato; recording, Fumio Hashimoto; Hisayuki Miyamoto; assistant director, Hisao Maur; production manager, Kazuhiko Furuya. Reviewed at Cannes Film Festival (In Competition), May 9, 1987. Running time: **127 MINS.**
Shinran (Zenshin) . . . . . . Junkyu Moriyama
Asa . . . . Michio Ogusu
Ijika . . . . Shigeru Izumiya
Atota . . . . Guto Ishimatsu
Renshe Utsunemiya . . . . . . Hosei Komatau
Shi-ina . . . . Ako
Ogure . . . . Masayo Asada
Woman from Inada . . . . Miki Odagiri
Lady-in-waiting . . . . Senas Nakahara
Ayai . . . . Izumi Hara
Chiyo . . . . Mako Mideri
Fusshi . . . . Junko Miyashita
Itto . . . . Kazuo Ando

Cannes — This last-minute entry in the Cannes fest's main competition shapes up as a curious blend of spiritual uplift in intent and narrative chaos in execution. The latter renders the pic almost thoroughly incomprehensible, making ''Shinran'' an extremely tough sell to Western markets.

''Shinran'' would pose formidable challenges under the best of circumstances.

Its chief concern is the title character, also known as Kenshin-Daishi, who founded the Shin-shu sect of Buddhism. The period is the late 12th century when the samurai were taking control of much of Japan and visiting barbarically cruel retribution on the enemy often by indiscriminate decapitation.

By combining the story of Shinran with the tangled socio-political history of the Japan of 800 years ago, first-time director Rentaro Mikuni has bitten off a lot more than he can chew. It's hard enough to pull an understandable, empathetic plot out of factional infighting among 12th century Buddhist sects. To add the additional complexities of the period's social-political upheaval makes things much worse. The audience is left scratching its collective head trying to figure out who's doing what to whom and why.

The emphasis of the pic, of course, is religious. Shinran (Junkyu Moriyama) is presented as a tenacious, stoical, highly sensitive man who recoils from the violence of his period. He enters the priesthood at 13, and eventually becomes the disciple of Priest Honon, founder of a Buddhism sect.

Shinran inaugurates marriage into the priesthood, and works doggedly to spread Buddhism as a religion of the masses, especially the poor. His heightened spirituality gives him the strength to weather a series of reversals and asserted horrors with grim-faced determination.

Shinran witnesses village burnings, several decapitations, a rape and incineration of a female admirer and, in one of the pic's more moving scenes, the death of his youngest child in an epidemic. The priest chooses to have the child's body cremated on a funeral pyre, a decision that alienates his wife and eventually ends his marriage.

The pic is physically impressive. It cost some $7,000,000 to produce, an unusually high sum for a Japanese pic. It was lensed in eight separate locations in Japan including the always photogenic old capitol of Kyoto.

Director Mikuni and editor Osamu Inoue move things along via short scenes and frequent cuts. While that approach may be an admirably economical in telling simpler plots, it tends to reinforce ''Shinran's'' air of confusion. Characters aren't given even minimal development. Dialog is reduced to homilies.

Worse yet, the abruptness of scene shifts plus the complexity of the material — refugees wander up a mountain in winter, come down the other side seconds later in late spring — undercut the universal elements of ''Shinran's'' spirituality. It fails to fully communicate its larger religious perspective.

Director Mikuni generally gets

solid performances from a large cast. Moriyama performs with praiseworthy restraint as Shinran while Michiyu Ogusu gives strength to the role of his wife. Only occasionally does the pull-out-the-emotional-stops sort of melodramatic acting, often found on Japanese tv dramas, mar the proceedings. —*Sege.*

Yeelen
(Brightness)
(MALI-COLOR)

A Les Films Cissé production in association with Government of Mali Minister of Information and Culture/Direction of Cinematography Prod. (Burkina Faso), Minister of Culture/Minister of Foreign Affairs/Minister of Cooperation/CNC/UTA (France), WDR Television (Cologne) and Fuji (Tokyo). Written and directed by Souleymane Cissé. Camera (Fujicolor), Jean-Noel Ferragut, Jean-Michel Humeau; editor, Dounamba Coulibaly, Andree Davanture, Marie-Catherine Mique; music, Michel Portal; art direction and costumes, Kossa Mody Keita. Reviewed at the Cannes Film Festival (In Competition), May 7, 1987. Running time: **105 MINS.**

Son . . . . Issiaka Kane
Young wife . . . . Aoua Sangare
Father . . . . Niamanto Sanogo
Peul king . . . . Balla Moussa Keita
Also with: Soumba Traore (mother), Ismaila Sarr (uncle), Youssouf Tenin Cissé (young boy), Koke Sangare (Komo chief).

Cannes — Long in the making, Souleymane Cissé's ''Brightness'' survived a troubled production history (the list of funders is longer than the credits) to bow in competition at Cannes. It is a meticulously crafted and beautifully lensed piece of filmmaking the very sophistication of which puts it out of reach for many unacquainted with African culture and unused to its unhurried pacing and interests.

On the other hand, film's complex interweaving of ancient tribal magic, the primordial conflict between fathers and sons, and political parable lend it a special fascination for viewers willing to take a chance on a difficult film. On the strength of Cissé's reputation alone (his two previous features, ''Baara'' and ''The Wind,'' both have been blue-ribboned at African fests), ''Brightness'' is bound to get a hearing at other fests and special venues.

Set in the past, story tells of the young hero's journey on a search for knowledge and resolution of a conflict with his father. He is about to be initiated into the secrets of ''Komo,'' the ancestral teaching of the Bambara tribe, covering all the life sciences and based on a knowledge of signs referring to time and space. Film's brief introduction doesn't take the unversed viewer very far into this obviously complicated sphere, and one is left to make what one can out of the two sacred symbols: a huge magic pylon carried by two men, used to seek out criminals, and a carved ''wing,'' also with magic powers.

As film opens, the evil magician-father (played by Niananto Sanogo, an actual religious eader) is intent on killing his son Nianankoro (Issiaka Kane) to prevent him from getting access to knowledge of how to master the forces of the universe, and so become his equal. The boy's mother sends him away to save his life, but the father chases him with the magic pylon. In film's powerful final sequence, father and son confront each other in a showdown on the desert sands, pitting pylon against wing, and destroy each other in an apocalyptic explosion.

If the rituals are sometimes hard to fathom, pic's authenticity is irresistible. Cast is mostly made up of non-actors, who perform without a hitch. Apart from a few overly long sequences, film is eminently watchable, with high technical standards.
— *Yung.*

Pierre et Djemila
(Pierre And Djemila)
(FRENCH-COLOR)

AAA Classic release of a Films Plain-Chant/Prods. du Cercle Bleu/Séléna Audiovisual/AAA/Films A2/Xanadu Films coproduction. Produced by Philippe Diaz. Directed by Gérard Blain. Screenplay, Blain, Michel Marmin, Mohamed Bouchibi; camera (color), Emmanuel Machuel; sound, Christophe Heaulme, Alain Contreault, Luc Yersin; art direction, Michel Vandestien, Pierre Gattoni; editor, Catherine Deiller; music, Olivier Kowalski, Gabor Kristof; lyrics, Maurice Rollot; song performed by Fabienne Guyot; production manager, Nicole Flipo. Reviewed at the Ponthieu screening room, Paris, April 25, 1987. (In Competition at Cannes Film Festival.) Running time: **86 MINS.**

Pierre . . . . Jean-Pierre André
Djemila . . . . Nadja Reski
Djaffar . . . . Abdelkader
Djemila's father . . . . Salah Teskouk
Djemila's mother . . . . . . Fathia Cheriguene
Lakhdar . . . . Lakhdar Kasri
Alicha . . . . Djedjigue Ait-Hamouda
Pierre's father . . . . Jacques Brunet
Pierre's mother . . . . . Francine Debaisieux

Paris — One-time New Wave actor Gérard Blain, who began directing in 1970, is at Cannes for the third time with ''Pierre And Djemila,'' his sixth feature. A Romeo and Juliet-style tragedy in a northern French city, pic is an austere but compelling drama of racially star-crossed romance that should find specialized exposure at home and abroad.

Blain is an uncompromising disciple of filmmaker Robert Bresson and his minimalist theories on acting and dramatization. In his earlier films, this borrowed manner of neutral, non-emotive storytelling often seemed mere stylistic attitudinizing. But the reductive tone seems right in ''Pierre And Djemila'' and Blain succeeds in some dramatic moments of pathetic intensity.

Blain's young lovers are Pierre, a shy 16-year-old French boy, and Djemila, the 14-year-old daughter of Algerian immigrants. Both their families live in the same lower income housing project of an industrial northern town, where the melting pot atmosphere often seethes with barely suppressed intolerance.

The two teens nonetheless manage to fall in love and see one another on the sly, though their folks soon get wind of the affair. Pierre's father, an Algerian War veteran, advocates a separate-but-equal policy of racial coexistence, but accepts his son's actions. Djemila's older brother, who cannot contain his hatred of France and the French, tries to separate the couple.

When they continue to go out together, the brother knifes Pierre to death. Djemila, whose grief is aggravated by her family's plans for a traditional arranged marriage, drowns herself.

Treated in a conventional mode, story might have seemed simplistic hokum, but Blain's doggedly spare direction distills a powerful sense of oppression and social fatality, and his presentation of immigrant mores and contradictions enriches the authenticity.

Nonprofessionals Jean-Pierre André and Nadja Reski are cast as Pierre and Djemila and exude candor and innocence despite the unnatural deadpan expressions they must adopt.

Emmanuel Machuel's clean neutral photography avoids the visual clichés of most grim social dramas. Other tech credits are fine.

Film's bookending theme song, sung by Fabienne Guyot, is hauntingly lovely and could find independent play as a single. —*Len.*

The Glass Menagerie
(U.S.-COLOR)

A Cineplex Odeon Films release. Produced by Burtt Harris. Directed by Paul Newman. From the play by Tennessee Williams. Camera (Du Art color), Michael Ballhaus; editor, David Ray; music, Henry Mancini; production design, Tony Walton; art director, John Kasarda; set decorator, Susan Bode; sound, Andrew McKee; costumes, Walton; assistant director, Burtt Harris; associate producer, Joe Caracciolo. Reviewed at the Cannes Film Festival (In Competition) May 11, 1987. (No MPAA Rating). Running time: **130 MINS.**

Amanda . . . . Joanne Woodward
Tom . . . . John Malkovich
Laura . . . . Karen Allen
Gentleman Caller . . . . James Naughton

Cannes — Paul Newman's adaptation of ''The Glass Menagerie'' is a reverent record of Tennessee Williams' dream play and one watches with a kind of distant dreaminess rather than an intense emotional involvement. It's a play of stunning language and brilliant performances creating living nightmares well served by Newman's direction. Like a literary classic, everyone will know about it but relatively few will actually see it.

Williams' characters are like a textbook of the tortured family, not because everyone has read the play in high school, but because he wrote them to be examples of lives eating away at each other. His accomplishment was to blend realism and symbolism into a kind of demonstration of how parents and children emotionally betray each other.

In this dreamscape Amanda (Joanne Woodward) is the center of a universe of her own making and her children are satellites. But she is every overbearing mother more than a specific character, and she and her children are drawn in broad strokes and dark colors that keep them at a distance and contain their emotional impact.

Newman has heightened this impression by framing the action at the beginning and the end with Tom (John Malkovich) returning years later to look back at the wreck of his life. Smack in the middle of Depression America, he, too, is any son who longs to escape the banality of his life and demands of his mother.

With his sleepy sweet voice and slightly fey body movements, Malkovich is able to suggest the feelings he is carrying inside as the casualty of a woman who has fed him illusions all his life.

But the greater victim in this world is his crippled sister Laura (Karen Allen) who is doomed to live in perpetual waiting for a gentleman caller who will never come, and whose life is worthless because of it. While Amanda's sexual attitudes are even more antiquated today than when the play was written in 1954, it is the psychology that still rings true.

In this darkened deadend, Allen's wide open face shines with an unbearable sadness. When her gentleman caller finally does come, the clash between her reticence and James Naughton's hollow optimism is heartbreaking in its failure to hold out any promise.

But as in any great production of ''The Glass Menagerie,'' all of the performances must reflect off of Amanda, and Woodward is a constantly moving center of nervous neurotic energy with her active hands and darting eyes always seeming to be reaching out for something to grab on to. Her frenzy when the gentleman caller is due to arrive and when he's gone is heated without being exaggerated.

Credit on this count must go to Newman who has his hand on the emotional pulse of the piece and seems always to have the camera there too. Kudos also to cinematographer Michael Ballhaus who virtually keeps the whole film bathed in a haunting dark glow suitable to a dream.

Henry Mancini's music is uncharacteristically subtle while Tony Walton's production design and costumes add to the half real, half imagined atmosphere.

Ultimately this may not be the definitive production of "The Glass Menagerie," but it may be the definitive film, and as the only screen version of the play it's good to have it on the shelf. —*Jagr.*

Zegen
(The Pimp)
(JAPANESE-COLOR)

A Toei Co. release and coproduction with Imamura Prods. Produced by Yoshiniko Sugiyama, Kunio Tokoshige and Jire Ooba. Exec producers, Atsushi Mihori and Goro Takita. Directed by Shohei Imamura. Stars Ken Ogata and Mitauke Boishe. Screenplay, Imamura, Kote Okabe; camera (color), Masao Techizawa; score, Shinichiro Ikaba; sound, Kenichi Benitani; lighting, Yasuo Iwaki; art direction, Yoshimaga Yokeo. Reviewed at the Cannes Film Festival (In Competition), May 10, 1987. Running time: **124 MINS.**

Iheiji Muraoka ("Zegen") . . . . . Ken Ogata
Shiho . . . . Mitsuko Baisho
Tomenaga (Bizenya) . . . . Norihei Miki
Shimada (The Barber) . . . . Taiji Tonsyama
Iheiji's last wife, Kino . . . Mami Kumagaya
"Boss" Wang . . . . Ko Chun-Hsiung

Cannes — Constructing a two hours-plus period drama on an ironic conceit linking Japanese economic and military expansionism to the fortunes of a pimp is both an appealing and dangerous excercise. "Zegen" does exactly that and peradoxically emerges as a boldly conceived historical yarn and a bore.

However, thanks to director Shohei Imamura's international reputation, the pic looms reasonably well as a foreign sales attraction. It bows in Japan Sept. 5, a prestige item of Japanese major Toei Co. and the one which distributed Imamura's "Narayamabushi-ko" (The Ballad Of Narayama). That pic four years ago copped the top competitive prize at Cannes, the Palme d'OR.

"Zegen" is based on the actual adventures of one Iheiji Muraska, a likable and intensely patriotic scoundrel who begins the pic as a Hong Kong castaway shortly after the turn of the century. As Japan's military adventurism reaches throughout Southeast Asia, Muraska engages in low-level sabotage in Manchuria before hitting upon the notion of setting up a chain of brothels throughout Asia.

As Imamaura presents him, Muraoka (Ken Ogata) is charming, a bit of a dolt but blessed with energy, a sense of fairness, a respect for money and with an unbridled patriotism. He becomes a pimp-entrepreneur on behalf of Emperor Maiji. This is no ordinary flesh peddler. He even wound up owning a rubber plantation in Malaya.

Director-coscripter Imamura obviously is taken with his chief character who reigned as self-styled "Big Boss of the South Seas" for the first 20 years of this century. He just as obviously is ambivalent about him, regarding Muraoka as both a likable sort and a bit of a bum.

This ambivalence comes through in the film putting a distance between the audiences and the pic itself. This zegen may provide amusement throughout but he's presented an unnerving distance dafying much audience sympathy or empathy.

The director imbues the outing with the naturalistic, sweaty carnality and feel for life at low levels. As a brothel keeper whose fortunes waxed and waned with those of Japan itself, Muraoka is surrounded by sex. "Zegen" doesn't stint in the couplings, some of which may have to be trimmed for Western exposure.

"Zegen" belongs to Ogata, a superb 50-year-old character actor who emerged as an international star two years ago in director Paul Schrader's "Mishima." Ogata plays Muraoka with energy, strength and subtlety. It's a first class performance.

Production values are topnotch. Yoshimaga Yokeo's period set designs are especially good. —*Sege.*

erotic, item is a spoof on a handful of persons and risqué situations in the city, loosely linked to the deejay's increasingly frantic adventures throughout the night.

Amadeu, the d.j., gets a call from the German ambassador's young daughter, left alone for the evening with her kid brother; their relationship grows over the wee hours — first to sex on the phone, ultimately culminating in a visit by the girl to the station, where they proceed for real. Mixed in are Amadeu's flirtations with a neighbor, a Hell's Angels motorcyclist and his moll who make love on a chopper before crashing, two bakers working the night shift who are turned on by the program, a taxi driver, husband of the languid neighbor, also caught up in a bit of sex and other sundry characters.

Tone of pic is clownish, and the thin, tasteless humor occasionally spills into mock melodrama. Laughs from the occasional zany skits are not enough to keep interest from flagging. English subtitles are riddled with mistakes and misspellings. —*Besa.*

Gor
(U.S.-COLOR)

A Cannon Intl. release. Produced by Harry Alan Towers, Avi Lerner. Directed by Fritz Kiersch. Screenplay, Rick Marx, Peter Welbeck, based on the novel "Tarnsman Of Gor" by John Norman; camera, (Rank color), Hans Khule; editor, Max Lemon, Ken Bornstein; production supervisor, John Stode; stunt coordinator, Reo Ruiters; sound mixer, Peter Poole. Reviewed at Cannes Film Festival (market), May 9, 1987. Running time: **94 MINS.**

Cabot . . . . Urbano Barberini
Talena . . . . Rebecca Ferratti
Surbus . . . . Paul L. Smith
Sarm . . . . Oliver Reed
Xenos . . . . Jack Palance
Also with: Larry Taylor, Graham Clarke, Janine Denison, Donna Denton, Jennifer Oltmann.

Cannes — With dialog the depth of comic book jargon and action scenes that are choreographed to avoid realism, "Gor" is a sword and sorcery vehicle that seems geared to under 16 audiences, despite some pastiche erotica. That comes mainly in the form of the well endowed Rebecca Ferratti, who saunters through the film in a two-piece costume designed to emphasize her charms.

Most of the action transpires in a never-never desert land where evil "barbarians," whose wicked, articulate high priest is played by Oliver Reed, snatch away the "lifestone" from a virtuous, freedom-loving group whose catchiest leader is Talena. Coming to the rescue is a nerdy prof from 20th century America, who is conveniently transported to this land of mock cruelty and conflict after wrapping his car around a tree in humdrum modernity.

Producers throw in a helpful dwarf, a distaff sword duel, a dissipated tavern scene, a bit of torture and fisticuffs, as a handful of heroes escape through catacomb tunnels; there are occasional touches of would-be humor. Talena and Cabot bloodlessly run innumerable heavies through with their swords, kicking and fighting their way to ultimate victory to recover what looks like a glowing piece of plastic. An arrow through the chief villain's neck is about the only convincing effect in the film; then Cabot, by now a muscular sword slasher, returns to his college campus, awakening from his vacation in the land of Gor.

There's also a cameo by Jack Palance at the end of the film, introducing him as the new villain, thereby cuing him for the second part of this silly fantasy. Item should be limited to homevid and tv outlets as a filler.—*Besa.*

The Kitchen Toto
(BRITISH-COLOR)

A Cannon Group release of a British Screen-Film Four Intl. presentation of a Skreba film. Executive Producers, Menaheim Golan, Yoram Globus. Produced by Ann Skinner. Written and directed by Harry Hook. Camera (color), Roger Deakins; editor, Tom Priestley; music, John Keane; production design, Jamie Leonard; costumes, Barbara Kidd; sound, Christien Wangler; production manager, Ted Morley; assistant director, Guy Travers; casting, Anne Henderson. Reviewed at Cannes Film Festival (market), May 9, 1987. (No MPAA Rating.) Running time: **95 MINS.**

John Graham . . . . Bob Peck
Janet Graham . . . . Phyllis Logan
Mwangi . . . . Edwin Mahinda
Mary . . . . Kirsten Hughes
D.C. . . . . Robert Urquhart
Mugo . . . . Nicholas Chase
Also with: Job Seda, Leo Wringer.

Cannes — Handsomely filmed on location in Kenya and inherited by Cannon from Screen Entetainment Ltd., "The Kitchen Toto" is an intriguing, well mounted pic with an awkward title and lethargic pacing. It could go the arthouse route and, with thoughtful handling, find modest returns.

Pic unfolds in 1950 when the British were facing attacks from a Kikuyu terrorist group known as Mau Mau. Bob Peck plays a regional police officer in charge of a small force of native Africans who lives with his frustrated wife (Phyllis Logan) and son; he's having a secret affair with the niece (Kirsten Hughes) of a neighbor. When Mau Mau murder a black priest who's condemned them from his pulpit, Peck agrees to take in the dead man's young son (Edwin Mahinda) as his "kitchen toto," or houseboy.

Story unfolds from the perspective of this alert, intelligent young-

---

•••

Cannes Market Selections

La Radio Folla
(Radio Speed)
(SPANISH-COLOR)

An Opal films production. Executive producer, J.A. Pérez Giner. Directed by Franceso Bellmunt. Screenplay, Quim Casas, Carlos Benpar, Santiago Lapeira, Bellmunt; camera (color), Hans Burmann; editor, Teresa Alcocer; music, Joan Enric Garde, sets, Jordi Artigau; production manager, Joan Pros; sound, Joan Quilis. Reviewed at Cannes Film Festival (market), May 8, 1987. Running time: **95 MINS.**

Amadeu . . . . Sergi Mateu
Cervantes . . . . Pep Munné
Canguro . . . . Silvia Sabaté
Also with: Carme Conesa, Susana Sentis, José María Cañete, Xus Estruch, Cristian Dios, Carles Canus, Rosa María Sardà, Pere Ponce.

(Original soundtrack in Catalan; Castilian version available)

Cannes — This inane sex comedy concerns a hot summer night's adventures of a d.j. who peppers his music with intimate chats with listeners of a small radio station in Barcelona. Rather than being itself

ster who's torn between his tribal feelings on the one hand and the loyalties he has both to his murdered father and to the British who, despite their unthinking and ingrained racism, have been kind to him.

After a strong opening, establishing the patronizing ways the white settlers behave, and the murder, tension is allowed to slacken in the lengthy scenes establishing the young black's experiences in the policeman's home. Depiction of the daily routine is well handled, but audiences are likely to fidget after a while. The climax, when it comes, is strong stuff, with Mau Mau invading the house one day while Peck is off with his mistress and attempting to kidnap the wife: trying to rescue his mother, her son accidentally shoots and kills her.

During the '50s, two pics dealt with the Mau Mau emergency to good effect (the British "Simba" and Richard Brooks' "Something Of Value"); writer-director Harry Hook returns to the subject matter from a different perspective, but fails to establish the frightening vulnerability of a handful of whites lording it in a black country.

This is not a pic for action marts, but for quality situations. Peck is solid as the cop, Logan suitably tight-lipped as his repressed wife, and young Edwin Mahinda excellent as the troubled, tragic hero, torn between two sides in an ugly conflict. Roger Deakins' location photography is extremely beautiful, and there's a subtle music score by John Keane. —Strat.

To Market, To Market
(AUSTRALIAN-COLOR)

A Goosey Ltd. production, in association with Film Victoria. Produced, written and directed by Virginia Rouse. Camera (Fuji color), Jaems Grant; editor, Tony Paterson; sound, Laurie Robinson; music, Ben Fitzgerald, Kate Reid, Fincina Hopgood, Mahler, Brahms (music consultant, Erwin Rado); art direction, Rouse; production manager, associate producer, Trish Carney; assistant director, Katherine Hayden. Reviewed at Cannes Film Festival (market), May 10, 1987. Running time: **85 MINS.**
Edward Riat . . . . Philip Quast
Edward Riat (aged 13) . . . Marcus Gollings
William Riat Sr. . . . . Noel Trevarthan
Jackie . . . . Kate Reid
Mother . . . . Maureen Edwards
Richard . . . . Tony Llewellyn-Jones
Susanna . . . . Genevieve Picot
William Riat Jr. . . . . Wayne Cull

Cannes — This is an offbeat first feature by a former stills photographer and assistant to director Paul Cox; Virginia Rouse has come up with a strikingly original yet overly elliptical effort which will need very careful handling and strong critical support if it's to find an audience.

The theme is the emotional deprivation of a child from an Estab-

lishment background, a child who becomes no more than a puppet manipulated by his family and close friends. It's a striking look at class structures within Australia's supposedly classless society, and centers around an uppercrust Melbourne family.

First part of the pic unfolds in 1965 when 13-year-old Edward Riat (Marcus Gollings) is attending an awful boarding school run along British lines. His best friend is an Asian boy who hangs himself when he can stand the racism of his classmates no longer.

Years later, in the present, Edward, now played by Philip Quast, is a strange young man torn between loyalty to his family and his natural, decent instincts. Loyalty wins out when he reluctantly agrees to help his older brother in a scheme to launder money which, unknown to Edward, is drug related; the brother winds up squeaky clean, but Edward is exposed as a criminal, disgraced and humiliated.

Rouse contends that a man such as Edward, though basically decent, has been conditioned since birth to the extent he no longer is able to think for himself. She has devised some excellent sequences, notably one involving mealtime at the school, and another of a bitter family conference, but overall her approach is too distant; her characters remain merely ciphers, and the audience is unlikely to be very concerned about Edward's plight. Awkward acting in the school sequences doesn't help.

Despite an obviously modest budget, it looks superb, thanks to the camerawork of Jaems Grant and Rouse's own art direction. Erwin Rado acted as consultant for the music score, which is another plus.

Responses to the film will vary: it's certainly a very different kind of Aussie pic and merits attention, though its overly academic style will limit its chances. It should be of interest to fests looking for unusual fare, especially by new directors, and find its way into specialized theatrical outlets. —Strat.

Eu
(Me, Myself And I)
(BRAZILIAN-COLOR)

An Embrafilme-Cinearte production. Produced by Anibal Massaini Neto. Directed by Walter Hugo Khouri. Screenplay, Khouri; camera (color), Antonio Mellande; editor, Luiz Elias; music, Juilio Medaglia; production design, José Duarte de Aguiar; costumes, Marineida M.C. Massaini. Reviewed at Cannes Film Festival (market), May 8, 1987. Running time: **120 MINS.**
With: Tarcisio Meira (Marcelo Rondi), Bia Seidl, Nicole Puzzi, Monique Lafond, Christiane Torloni, Walter Forster.

Cannes — The central character of "Me, Myself And I" (the original

title means, simply, "I") is a self-centered, wealthy businessman in his 50s whose voracious appetite for beautiful young women masks the fact that he lusts after his own daughter. Writer-director Walter Hugo Khouri takes far too long to get to the point where father and daughter finally get to bed, padding out the film with plenty of nudity and softcore sex in exotic settings along the way.

It's all quite easy on the eye, but basically trite and predictable. The numerous women, including the businessman's two regular live-in mistresses, his latest acquisition, the daughter and the daughter's enigmatic best friend, are all played by attractive actresses, and it's hard to work out why they all fall for Tarcisio Meira's jaded charm; probably it's because the character is supposed to be rich.

Softcore video is about the only place where this one will find an audience outside Brazil. It's technically well made, though the color is unevenly graded. Some fine old standard songs on the soundtrack help smooth over the many dull spots.
—Strat.

La Bamba
(COLOR)

Good prospects for solid biopic of teen rocker.

A Columbia release of a New Visions production. Produced by Taylor Hackford, Bill Borden. Executive producer, Stuart Benjamin. Written and directed by Luis Valdez. Camera (Deluxe color), Adam Greenberg; editors, Sheldon Kahn, Don Brochu; original music, Carlos Santana, Miles Goodman; Ritchie Valens' music performed by Los Lobos; executive music producer, Joel Sill; production design, Vince Cresciman; set decoration, Rosemary Brandenburg; costume design, Sylvia Vega-Vasquez; sound (Dolby), Susumu Tokunow; associate producer, Daniel Valdez; assistant director, Stephen J. Fisher; second unit camera, Chuck Colwell; casting, Junie Lowry. Reviewed at the Egyptian theater, Seattle Film Festival, May 14, 1987. (MPAA Rating: PG-13.) Running time: **108 MINS.**
Ritchie Valens . . . . . Lou Diamond Phillips
Bob Morales . . . . Esai Morales
Connie Valenzuela . . . . . . Rosana De Soto
Rosie Morales . . . . Elizabeth Pena
Donna Ludwig . . . . . . Danielle von Zerneck
Bob Keene . . . . Joe Pantoliano
Ted Quillin . . . . Rick Dees
Buddy Holly . . . . Marshall Crenshaw
Jackie Wilson . . . . Howard Huntsberry
Eddie Cochran . . . . Brian Setzer
Lelo . . . . Daniel Valdez

Seattle — There haven't been too many people who died at age 17 who have warranted the biopic treatment, but 1950s rock 'n' roller Ritchie Valens proves a worthy exception in "La Bamba." World premiered (two months ahead of its national release) as the opening-night attraction at the 12th Seattle Intl. Film Festival, pic is esthetically conventional but inspires substantial interest due to Valens' extreme youth and unusual cultural background. If given a good push with youthful audiences heretofore unfamiliar with the singer, summer b.o. should be solid.

Known primarily for his three top-10 tunes, "Come On Let's Go," "Donna" and the title cut, Valens was killed — just eight months after signing his first recording contract — in the 1959 private plane crash that also took the lives of Buddy Holly and The Big Bopper, and thus attained instant legendhood.

For anyone to achieve his dreams by 17 is close to miraculous. It was even more so for Valens who, less than two years before his death, was a Mexican-American fruitpicker named Ricardo Valenzuela living in a tent with his family in Northern California.

As shown here, the teenager's great love for his mother, brother and sisters possibly was surpassed only by his passion for rock 'n' roll. He carried his guitar everywhere, even to the school classes he attended with decreasing frequency, and it wasn't long before smalltime gigs, and then ultra-cheap recording sessions were coming his way.

Backgrounding this, however, was tremendous emotional turbulence created mostly by Ritchie's half-brother Bob. An ex-con who rides a motorcycle, deals drugs and makes his entrance here by returning after a long absence and blithely deflowering Ritchie's teen sweetheart, Bob embodies everything negative about stereotypical Latin machismo and causes no end of pain for those around him, even ruining Ritchie's headliner debut by leading his biker buddies in a drunken brawl.

Nevertheless, Ritchie continues his rapid rise to stardom with tv appearances, a slot in one of disk jockey Alan Freed's rock 'n' roll extravaganzas and, finally, his fateful tour with Holly and The Big Bopper.

In fact, compared with many of the tales of struggle and hardship that have been told about aspiring artists, Valens' brief life story seems remarkably free of obstacles and setbacks. The only difficulty he encounters outside his family is the opposition to him expressed by the WASPy father of Donna, the blond he fell for who inspired his famous teen lament.

In the teenpics of the 1950s, even the most cleancut rockers were subject to the outraged moralizing of their elders, but here, even the biker riot at an American Legion hall provokes no repercussions.

Culturally, film is somewhat provocative for its presentation of Ritchie's denial of his roots and total buy-in to the American dream, especially given writer-director Luis Valdez' background with "Zoot Suit" and as a grapeworkers' strike activist. The song "La Bamba" notwithstanding, Valens says several times in the picture that he doesn't speak Spanish, and his idols clearly are Elvis Presley and other white performers. His mother is a hard-driving work-ethic type who would have been completely at home in an MGM film of the 1930s.

Although many of the plot developments are pro forma for the genre, "La Bamba" is engrossing throughout and boasts numerous fine performances. In Lou Diamond Phillips' sympathetic turn, Valens comes across as a very fine young man, caring for those important to him and not overawed by his success. Rosana De Soto scores as his tireless mother, and Elizabeth Pena has numerous dramatic moments as Bob's distraught mate.

Most of the fireworks are Bob's, and Esai Morales makes the most of the opportunities. Remembered as Sean Penn's opponent in "Bad Boys," thesp commands the screen whenever he's around, and makes the tormented brother a genuinely complex figure.

Musically, Valens' tunes have been covered outstandingly by the contempo band Los Lobos. Lots of other period music fills out the soundtrack, and concert highlight is provided by Howard Huntsberry's electrifying impersonation of Jackie Wilson singing "Lonely Teardrops."

Film could have benefited from increased attention to Ritchie's subjective view of things, showing his excitement at being included in the Freed show and the like. But Valdez has done a good, workmanlike job of getting the kid's story onto the screen sympathetically.—*Cart.*

Terug naar Oegstgeest
(Return To Oegstgeest)
(DUTCH-COLOR)

A Meteor Film/The Movies release of a Movies Film Prods. production. Produced by Chris Brouwer, Haig Balian. Executive producer, Anna Brouwer. Written and directed by Theo van Gogh, based on novel by Jan Wolkers; camera (Fuji AX, Cineco color prints), Marc Felperlaan; editor, Willem Hoogenboom; music, Rainer Hensel; sound, Arno Hagers; art direction, Harry Ammerlaan; assistant director, Jan de Haan; production manager, Arnold Heslenfeld; casting, Frank Krom. Reviewed at Alfa theater, Amsterdam, April 21, 1987. Running time: **95 MINS.**

Father	Tom Jansen
Mother	Geert de Jong
Jan	Cas Enklaar
Uncle Louis	Leen Jongewaard
Mother as old woman	Elise Hoomans

Amsterdam — Theo van Gogh's latest pic confirms him as one of Holland's most talented young directors. He makes film appear the most natural way of telling a story, has a sophisticated touch with the camera, and appears able to get the best out of his actors at just the right moment.

It's a pity, then, that all these assets notwithstanding, "Return To Oegstgeest" winds up as no more than a specialty dish for gourmets, who will be able to savor the rich mix of ingredients and cinematographic skills.

Main reason for this is that Van Gogh has attempted to film an unfilmable book. Jan Wolkers' evergreen bestseller (28 printings in 22 years) uses typically literary skills to build an autobiography. The narrator speaks both from the standpoint of a middle-aged man in the 1960s and as a youth in the 1930s, and the story is carefully built from small, random pieces of information.

Pic is about a family balancing on the edge of lower middle class, and dominated by a fire and brimstone Protestantism. Using a series of flashbacks at the father's deathbed, pic explores the love-hate relationship between father and son, the beginning of World War II, and the death of a brother (not to mention cruelty to animals, a recurring theme for Wolkers and one which

also seems to fascinate Van Gogh). Technical credits are above average (the imaginative treatment of sound and silence is especially fascinating) and acting honors are shared by all the leading actors. Pic is pure festival fare, with negligible theatrical chances abroad. — *Wall.*

Beverly Hills Cop II
(COLOR)

Noisy, sloppy remake. B.o. gold assured.

A Paramount Pictures release of a Don Simpson/Jerry Bruckheimer production, in association with Eddie Murphy Prods. Produced by Simpson, Bruckheimer. Executive producers, Robert D. Wachs, Richard Tienken. Directed by Tony Scott. Stars Eddie Murphy. Screenplay, Larry Ferguson, Warren Skaaren, story by Murphy, Wachs; based on characters created by Danilo Bach, Daniel Petrie Jr.; camera (Panavision, Technicolor), Jeffrey L. Kimball; editor, Billy Weber, Chris Lebenson, Michael Tronick; music, Harold Faltermeyer; production design, Ken Davis; art direction, James J. Murakami; set decoration, John Anderson; sound (Dolby), William B. Kaplan; assistant director, Peter Bogart; casting, Bonnie Timmermann; L.A. casting, Vickie Thomas. Reviewed at the National theater, L.A., May 17, 1987. (MPAA Rating: R.) Running time: **102 MINS.**

Axel Foley	Eddie Murphy
Billy Rosewood	Judge Reinhold
Maxwell Dent	Jürgen Prochnow
Andrew Bogomil	Ronny Cox
John Taggart	John Ashton
Karla Fry	Brigitte Nielsen
Harold Lutz	Allen Garfield
Chip Cain	Dean Stockwell
Jeffrey Friedman	Paul Reiser
Inspector Todd	Gil Hill
Nikos Thomopolis	Paul Guilfoyle
Mayor Egan	Robert Ridgley
Biddle	Brian O'Connor
Jan Bogomil	Alice Adair
May	Eugene Butler
Willie	Glenn Withrow
Chauffeur	Stephen Liska
Sidney Bernstein	Gilbert Gottfried

Hollywood — "Beverly Hills Cop II" is a noisy, numbing, unimaginative, heartless remake of the original film. Everything that was funny and appealing the first time has been attempted again here, but it's all gone sour and cold. This won't impede a b.o. stampede, however, as most of those who made the initial 1984 outing a smash to the tune of $108,000,000 in domestic rentals will want to return to partake of Axel Foley's latest adventures. But after "The Golden Child" and this one, Eddie Murphy had better pay closer attention to the scripts he approves, as they are getting increasingly sloppy.

Distinction between the first and second editions very closely parallels the difference between "Raiders Of The Lost Ark" and "Indiana Jones And The Temple Of Doom." In both series, the flair, offhanded charm and breezy humor of the original lapsed into a deadening heaviness that pounds the viewer into helpless submission in the follow-up, even though many of the

key artistic contributors remained the same in both instances.

Of course, the key to successful sequels over the years has rested in maintaining continuity of cast members and not meddling too much with the winning formula. In the present case, however, the latter provision has been observed to an absurd degree, so that a redo of nearly every memorable scene from the original can be found here, resulting in a picture of overpowering familiarity and predictability.

Getting Murphy back to Beverly Hills from his native Detroit turf is the critical wounding of police captain Ronny Cox by a group of rich baddies committing the "Alphabet Crimes," a series of violent robberies at heavily guarded locations. Once again, he goads reluctant cops Judge Reinhold and John Ashton into straying from the straight and narrow, once again the group visits a strip joint that looks like a "Flashdance" spinoff, and finally shoot it out with the villains.

Complicating matters for everyone is new city police chief Allen Garfield, a disagreeable sort looking for any excuse to fire those who were around before him. But in dramatic terms, he's just being set up for the big fall, which inevitably comes.

Criminal element is represented by enforcer Dean Stockwell, towering hitwoman Brigitte Nielsen, who looks like Max Headroom's sister, and kingpin Jürgen Prochnow, barely visible in his initial scene because of ludicrously heavy backlighting that obscures his face.

On the most elementary level, script doesn't work because it has the gangsters committing major crimes on consecutive days and Murphy, working on no substantial evidence, somehow guessing where and when they will occur and racing to the scene. Just as annoying, virtually every clever phrase in the dialog is repeated more than once just to make sure the audience will hear it. Screenwriting 101 teaches the error of this ploy as a fundamental.

But then there's Eddie Murphy, who, as he has done before, keeps things entertainingly afloat with his sassiness, raunchy one-liners, take-charge brazenness and innate irreverence. Murphy's a hoot in numerous scenes, but less so than on other occasions because of the frosty context for his shenanigans.

Blame for the shortcomings must be put on both the screenwriters and director Tony Scott, who, for some reason, felt the need to unnecessarily hype up the proceedings with pointless car chases (screeching tires is the dominant motif of the picture) and a soundtrack designed to outdecibel the one for his "Top Gun."

In the press notes, Scott said, "I want the audience to leave the theater exhausted," and in that dubious ambition he has depressingly succeeded.

Furthermore, the visual style he and lenser Jeffrey L. Kimball have applied is totally inappropriate, as the nice hard edge of "Beverly Hills Cop" and so many other Paramount films of recent years has been replaced by lighting that atomizes the characters so much that they barely seem to exist, not an effective technique for a comedy.

Insiders will note that much of the action takes place outside the confines of Beverly Hills, notably in Pasadena, at a racetrack and in the oilfields of Baldwin Hills. Also, it is becoming increasingly irritating that Murphy, no matter what he's playing, makes himself out to be such a stud but is never seen displaying the slightest inclination to prove it. For him to remain appealing to the general public, it appears, Murphy must seem sexually unthreatening. But none of this will matter at the boxoffice, as Murphy, Simpson, Bruckheimer, et al., will once again laugh all the way to the bank.

—*Cart.*

Meatballs III
(COLOR)

Dull-witted comedy of sexual initiation.

A TMS Pictures (The Movie Store) release of a Dunning/Link/Carmody production. Executive producers, Andre Link, Laurence Nesis. Produced by Don Carmody and John Dunning. Directed by George Mendeluk. Screenplay, Michael Paseornek, Bradley Kesden; camera (color), Peter Benison; music, Paul Zaza; editor, Debra Karen; sound, David Lee; casting, Barbara Claman, Lucinda Sill, Michael Wener, Ginette D'Amico, Chantal Condor. Reviewed at the Fox Theater, Hollywood, Calif., May 15, 1987. (MPAA Rating: R.) Running time: **94 MINS.**

Roxy Du Jour	Sally Kellerman
Rudy	Patrick Dempsey
Saint Peter	Al Waxman
Wendy	Isabelle Mejias
The Love Goddess	Shannon Tweed
Rita	Jan Taylor
Mean Gene	George Buza

Hollywood — Number one among the myriad problems with this mindless sexploitation flick is that the people who wrote, produced and directed it evidently have forgotten what teenagers — specifically teenagers in heat — are like.

Film unintentionally insults the intelligence of anyone who's ever been young and in lust: none of the characters' speech, actions, reactions, sexual behavior, humor, attitudes, relationships or thought processes is even remotely believable. Combine the blatantly unfunny handling of the subject with less-than-adroit direction — about half

the closeups are of breasts — and what emerges is a terrible movie with lousy boxoffice prospects.

Struggling valiantly against the confines of this disaster is Sally Kellerman, who gives an affecting turn as aging porn queen Roxy Du Jour, who dies while filming a particularly heated scene. She is denied passage through the gates of heaven because she's never done a good deed, but is given a reprieve: she's got two weeks to become somebody's good samaritan.

Her project turns out to be hopeless class nerd Rudy (Patrick Dempsey) who goes to summer camp determined to lose his virginity. She must play the Patron Saint of Sexual Conquest and help Rudy achieve his simple goal.

Roxy's counseling (when it comes to women, "no means yes") and supernatural powers alternately get Rudy into and out of trouble as she follows him through a series of sexual near-misses. She finally gets him to change his clothes and image, and in doing so, she changes his character; he goes from being unbelievably dorky to unbelievably stupid and insensitive.

Throughout the film, he rejects the amorous advances of Wendy (Isabelle Mejias), whose Cyndi-Lauper-on-hallucinogens wardrobe turns him off. While the existence of her character telegraphs the film's happily-ever-after ending, credibility once again is strained by her behavior. The only thing more unfathomable than this pretty girl being attracted to Rudy the Nerd is his character's constant denial of her interest. Mejias plays the small and thankless part well, while wearing hideous white and black lipstick.

Film's finish, involving a woman named "The Love Goddess," a bull, a band of boaters who look like Hell's Angels on water and two brain-dead teens trying to make a quick buck is stupid and complicated, but no one could possibly still be interested by the time director George Mendeluk brings things to a screeching yet boring conclusion.

Ultimately, one is left wondering what could have happened if Kellerman's character was given a story with wit and cleverness.—*Camb.*

Official Cannes Entries

Oci Ciornie
(Black Eyes)
(ITALIAN-COLOR)

A UGC release of an Excelsior Film-TV/RAI 1 coproduction. Produced by Silvia D'Amico Bendico and Carlo Cucchi. Directed by Nikita Mikhalkov. Stars Marcello Mastroianni. Screenplay, Alexander Adabakhian, Mikhalkov, with the collaboration of Suso Cecchi D'Amico, based on short stories by Anton Chekhov; camera (Eastmancolor by Cinecittà), Franco Di Giacomo; art direction, Mario Garbuglia, Adabakhian; editor, Enzo Meniconi; music, Francis Lai; associate producer, Gilbert Marouani. Reviewed at Cannes Film Festival (In Competition), May 10, 1987. Running time: **117 MINS.**

Romano	Marcello Mastroianni
Elisa	Silvana Mangano
Tina	Marthe Keller
Anna	Elena Sofonova
Pavel	Vsevolod Larionov
Governor	Innokenti Smoktunovsky

Also with: Pina Cei (Elisa's mother), Roberto Herlitzka, Paolo Baroni, Oleg Tabakov, Yuri Bogatiriov, Dimitri Zolothukin (Konstantin).

Cannes — "Black Eyes," a freely adapted amalgamation of some short stories by Anton Chekhov, is a joyful sleighride through the turn of the century with director Nikita Mikhalkov once more demonstrating his prowess at cracking the whip on this type of period piece. Carried along on the sheer energy of Marcello Mastroianni's sterling performance, film effortlessly swings from farce to tenderness, love to betrayal, and exuberance to poignancy without missing a beat.

Those who think of Chekhov as a serious, gloomy writer may find this version out on a limb, adaptationwise, and deem pic's literary source to be no more than the cultural trappings for a pretty, agreeable Italian production that owes more to Fellini than Soviet cinema. Whatever the case, Mikhalkov and scripter Alexander Adabakhian have served up a winning piece of entertainment with verve and conviction that should further expand their audience for "Slave Of Love." It is also a character study in its own right of no little merit.

Story is told by an aged, down-at-the-heels Mastroianni, whom we meet on board a ship at the turn of the century. He introduces himself to a kindly Russian passenger, Pavel (Vsevolod Larionov) and begins ironically recounting his life.

Once Romano was the idle husband of a rich aristocrat, Elisa (Silvana Mangano). She had married him for love when he was a poor student, and still defends him against her hostile family. His clowning is endearing, but his habit of running away from problems to some health spa a cross to bear.

It is to one such place that Romano retreats when Elisa tells him the family bank is about to close, and it is there he meets Anna (Elena Sofonova). This shy Russian lady with a lapdog is different from the other women in the spa ready to succumb to his charming buffoonery. Anna, too, succumbs, but it is the beginning of a deeply felt love that so upsets her she flees back to Russia. Romano determines to travel to her small village to see her again.

The Russian part of the film is prefaced by a lengthy interlude showing Romano's farcical efforts to get traveling papers by passing himself off as a manufacturer of unbreakable glass. Eventually he bluffs his way to the town and finds Anna married to the ridiculous Governor of Sisoiev (Innokenti Smoktunovsky). Anna and Romano's fleeting reunion takes place in the midst of broad comedy vodka toasts, gypsy bands and mistaken identity. He leaves, promising to come back soon and marry her. But once back in Italy, all his fine intentions vanish before the sight of Elisa, who has really gone bankrupt and is selling the house. It is the easy excuse he needs to betray Anna. He never returns to Russia, and his last glimpse of her occurs in a long-prepared "surprise" ending, which is no surprise but at least is gracefully handled.

Apart from the fact that "Black Eyes" is beautifully photgraphed by Franco Di Giacomo and scored by Francis Lai, and art direction — credited to both Mario Garbuglia and scripter Adabakhian — some of the most atmospheric of the period, film is buoyed up by a splendid international cast (including Marthe Keller in the role of Romano's alter ego and friend, Tina). Young Russian actress Sofonova is a timid, awkward, very moving Anna; Mangano and Larionov so perfect the parts seem written for them. Actually, script was written for Mastroianni, heart and soul of the picture, who turns in one of the most outgoing, enjoyable performances of his long and illustrious career.

— *Yung.*

La Casa de Bernarda Alba
(The House Of Bernarda Alba)
(SPANISH-COLOR)

A Paraiso production. Executive producers, Jaime Borrell, José Miguel Juarez and Antonio Oliver. Directed by Mario Camus. Screenplay, Camus, Antonio Larreta, based on play by Federico Garcia Lorca; production manager, Ricardo Garcia Arrojo;

camera (Eastmancolor), Fernando Arribas; editor, José Maria Biurrun; sets, Rafael Palmero; costumes, José Rubio. Reviewed at Cine Palafox, Madrid, April 24, 1987. (In the Un Certain Regard section at Cannes Film Festival.) Running time: **99 MINS.**

Bernarda Alba .... Irene Gutiérrez Caba
Adela .... Ana Belén
Poncia .... Florinda Chico
Angustias .... Enriqueta Carballeira
Martino .... Vicky Peña
Magdalena .... Aurora Pastor
Amelia .... Mercedes Lezcano

Madrid — Garcia Lorca's famous play about a dominating Andalusian mother and her six daughters, who are forced to go into mourning after their father's death, has been faithfully transferred to film by Mario Camus, using an excellent cast of Spanish femme thesps.

Camus succeeds in capturing the somber, oppressive mood as it was written by Garcia Lorca but adds little of his own invention to give a new dimension or insight into the work. The film, with the exception of a badly edited scene in a church, is shot entirely within the walls of the house, and some of it is pretty slow going. The climax, when Adela (Ana Belén) hangs herself after realizing she will never marry or escape the matriarchal tyranny, never builds up dramatically.

Though a literal adaptation of the play, pic's major attraction is its acting. Especially fine performances are turned in by Irene Gutiérrez Caba as the dour Bernarda, Florinda Chico as the sympathetic maid and Aurora Pastor, Enriqueta Carballeira and Belén as the daughters. Sets have been well designed to simulate the 1920s, but Camus never, for example, manages to convey the heat of an Andalusian summer, notwithstanding the occasional fan toted by the women.

Item is more apt to find exposure on PBS and in educational circuits than in theatrical release. Only musical score is a few minutes of strident *cante jondo* during opening and closing titles. Other production credits okay. — *Besa.*

Matewan
(U.S.-COLOR)

A Cinecom Intl. production. Produced by Peggy Rajski, Maggie Renzi. Executive producers, Amir Jacob Malin, Jerry Silva. Directed by John Sayles. Screenplay, Sayles; camera (DuArt color), Haskell Wexler; editor, Sonya Polonsky; music, Mason Daring; production design, Nora Chavooshian; art director, Dan Bishop; set decorator, Anamarie Michnevich, Leslie Pope; associate producer, Ira Deutchman, James Dudelson, Ned Kandel; assistant director, Matia Karrell; casting, Barbara Shapiro; costumes, Cynthia Flint. Reviewed at Cannes Film Festival (in Directors Fortnight), May 18, 1987. (No MPAA rating.) Running time **130 MINS.**

Joe .... Chris Cooper
Danny .... Will Oldham
Elma Radnor .... Mary McDonnell
C.E. Lively .... Bob Gunton
"Few Clothes" Johnson ... James Earl Jones
Hickey .... Kevin Tighe
Griggs .... Gordon Clapp

Mayor Testerman .... Josh Mostel
Sephus Purcell .... Ken Jenkins
Hillard .... Jace Alexander
Bridey Mae .... Nancy Motto
Ludie .... Gary McCleery
Sid .... David Strathairn
Fausto .... Joe Grifasi
Tolbert .... James Kizar
Ellix .... Michael Preston

Cannes — The history of the American labor movement with its built-in conflicts has proved a fertile territory for filmmakers, and now John Sayles has turned the ground once more. "Matewan" is a heartfelt, straight-ahead tale of labor organizing in the coal mines of West Virginia in 1920 that runs its course like a train coming down the track. It's a beautifully mounted, if overlong, piece of work that surely will find an audience among more sophisticated filmgoers.

It's one of the ironies of the film that it probably will not be seen by the working class it champions. It's a case of preaching to the converted without much of a possibility of reaching the uninitiated.

As a screenwriter, Sayles has not escaped the trap into which most American political pictures fall, i.e., polarizing the sides right from the start with the bad guys lacking subtlety or depth. They make forceful characters, but they don't have much dimension as people.

On the other side are the decent folk who share a common spirit. Sayles makes his point eloquent and it is his commitment to the worth of these people that gives the film its power.

Among the memorable characters is Joe Kenehan (Chris Cooper), a young union organizer who comes to Matewan to buck the bosses. With his strong face and Harrison Ford good-looks, Cooper gives the film its heartbeat.

Of the townfolk, 16-year-old Danny (Will Oldham) is already a righteous preacher and a seasoned union man who passionately takes up the working man's struggle. Sayles adds some texture to the mix by throwing in Italian immigrants and black migrant workers who become converted to the union side.

Most notable of the black workers is "Few Clothes" Johnson (James Earl Jones), a burly good-natured man with a powerful presence and a quick smile. Jones' performance practically glows in the dark. Also a standout is Sayles veteran David Strathairn as the sheriff with quiet integrity who puts his life on the line.

Management goons are headed by Hickey (Kevin Tighe) and Griggs (Gordon Clapp), two men whose mothers probably even despised them. Once Sayles has set the conflict in motion and set up the battle lines, he introduces the factions within the union. One of the lead-

ers, C.E. Lively (Bob Gunton), it turns out is a stooge for the bosses and tries to frame Kenehan. It's a familiar tactic in this type of picture, but Sayles cleverly diffuses it with an impassioned sermon from Oldham.

As always, Sayles has written some stunning dialog, completely in character, that sounds as if it actually could have been uttered by these people. He is still less adept at keeping up a film's momentum as a director and the action tends to come in spurts with the climactic scene a bit long in arriving.

Sayles has developed considerably as a filmmaker however, and "Matewan" has a keener sense of visual imagery than his earlier pictures. Many of the scenes pack a considerable wallop. Undoubtedly adding to the power of the story, which is based on the real-life Matewan massacre, is Haskell Wexler's stunning camerawork, Wexler creates a dusty, dried-out and faded look, similar to what he achieved on "Bound For Glory," stamping the town with an authentic quality.

"Matewan" is certainly Sayles' best-looking, most professional film to date with period-perfect production design from Nora Chavooshian and well-worn costumes by Cynthia Flint. "Matewan" is as rich in atmosphere as any Hollywood film, and with a lot more heart.
—*Jagr.*

I've Heard The Mermaids Singing
(CANADIAN-COLOR)

A Cinephile release (in Canada) of a Vos production. Produced by Patricia Rozema. Alexandra Raffé. Executive producer, Don Haig. Written and directed by Rozema. Stars Sheila McCarthy, Paule Baillargeon. Camera (color), Douglas Koch; editor, Rozema; music, Mark Korven; set design, Valanne Ridgeway; sound editor, Steven Munro. Reviewed at Cineplex Odeon screening room, Toronto, April 30, 1987. (In Directors Fortnight at Cannes Film Festival.) Running time: **81 MINS.**

Polly Vandersma .... Sheila McCarthy
Gabrielle St-Peres ..... Paule Baillargeon
Mary Joseph .... Ann-Marie McDonald
Warren .... John Evans
Japanese Waitress .... Brenda Kamino
Critic .... Richard Monette

Toronto — "I've Heard The Mermaids Singing," a low-budget seriocomedy, is an offbeat, power-packed first feature for Toronto-based director-coproducer-scripter-editor Patricia Rozema. It's bursting with confidence, with Rozema in full control in all capacities nearly every step of the way. Camerawork by Douglas Koch is excellent as are all other production values. Pic neatly blends film and video and comedy with serious undertones. It has an obvious active life in the art market, on the fest circuit and in subsequent tv and video playoff.

Plot centers on a klutzy and innocent temporary secretary who is jobbed in at an art gallery run by an older femme, whom it is established quickly on takes a flagged fancy to her without the secretary cottoning on.

Living alone in cramped quarters, the secretary lives a fantasy life via deliberately grainy black & white scenes in which she flies through the air, walks on water and actually hears mermaids singing. Those sequences are soaringly portrayed with accompanying classical music. In other off times, she observes daily life by taking photographs.

Meanwhile back at work, the gallery owner's girlfriend returns, resumes their previous love affair, with a kissing scene observed on video by the shocked secretary. Narrating the entire plot on video, the secretary recalls a line about half lives half lived — the pic's theme.

The secretary later discovers what appears to be the owner's own thrill-making canvases. Taking one of them, cleverly just a blaze of framed white light, the secretary hangs it in the gallery; it's heralded by the press, and the gallery owner attains fame. But the secretary is dejected because of the growing love affair between the two other women and rejection of her photos.

The secretary discovers the "perfect" art actually was created by the gallery owner's girlfriend who, out of love, has allowed the deception. A final resolution is somewhat clumsy and forced, but apparently happy for the three central characters.

Sheila McCarthy, a waif-faced Canadian stage thesp in her first lead film role, gives a dynamic, strongly believable and constantly assured performance as the secretary. She is captivating. And she is ably assisted by Paule Baillargeon (the gallery owner) and to a lesser degree by Ann-Marie McDonald, whose role is limited. The pic's two male performers are just cameos but done effectively.—*Adil.*

Federico Fellini's Intervista
(Interview)
(ITALIAN-COLOR)

An Aljosha Prods./RAI-TV Channel 1/Cinecittà coproduction. Produced by Ibrahim Moussa. Written and directed by Federico Fellini. Camera (Eastmancolor), Tonino Delli Coli; editor, Nino Baragli; music, Nicola Piovani, with a tribute to Nino Rota; screenplay collaborator, Gianfranco Angelucci; art direction, Danilo Donati; line producer, Pietro Notarianni; English version, Paul Mazursky, Leon Capetanos. Reviewed at Cannes Film Festival (out of competition), May 18, 1987. Running time: **105 MINS.**

Federico Fellini .... Federico Fellini
Mandrake .... Marcello Mastroianni
Anita Ekberg .... Anita Ekberg
Reporter .... Sergio Rubini

Asst. director ....Maurizio Mein
Bride ....Lara Wendel
Star.....................Paola Liguori
Vestal virgin ....Nadia Ottaviani
Young girl ....Antonella Ponziani

Cannes — Begun as a tv special, "Federico Fellini's Intervista" (or more simply, "Interview") has wound up on the big screen, where it will delight Fellini fans worldwide as a trip down the Maestro's personal memory lane. Really a scrapbook on Cinecittà, the Roman studios that have always been identified with the director, it is at the same time a recap of his most famous trademarks, whether they be actors, places, images or tone. "Interview" is more like an anniversary party than a film (and in fact, it was made on Cinecittà's 40th anni). Light but entertaining, it should have no trouble finding wide audiences.

By its very nature, "Interview" can't be called on unforgettable work, since it's constructed entirely out of bits and pieces of previous creative labors. A Japanese tv crew arrives at Cinecittà one night to shoot a docu on Fellini, and they find the master at work with his usual crew. Over the next few days, we see him doing screen tests and location scouting for a new film based of Kafka's "Amerika" (a real project).

With the help of faithful assistant director Maurizio Mein, cameraman Tonino Delli Coll, art director Danilo Donati and his crew, Fellini takes us on a backstage tour of the world of filmmaking, with lots of fun along the way. There is also a Fellini alter ego, played by Sergio Rubini, who fancifully tells the story of how the Maestro first visited the studios as a young reporter, assigned to interview the Star (Paola Liguori), how he saw director Alessandro Blasetti at work, and fell in love with the cinema.

This Fellini documentary is full of elephants and elephantine women, spectacular sets and petty humanity hurling four-letter words at each other, usually with affection. Its one truly enchanting sequence is when Fellini takes Marcello Mastroianni (outfitted as Mandrake the Magician for an ad) to visit Anita Ekberg. With a flick of his baton, Mandrake brings to life some famous scenes from "La Dolce Vita," when both thesps were young and unspeakably beautiful; the contrast with them 27 years later brings tears to Ekberg's eyes.

Not just a sentimental tour of Fellini mannerisms, "Interview" suggests the long-gone past can be recaptured only on film stock — maybe not a very new idea, but entertainingly expressed. Fans can test their own memories to see how many films get homage here (not forgetting the recent attacks on television, rapped again in a genial finale). — *Yung.*

Sous Le Soleil De Satan
(Under The Sun Of Satan)
(FRENCH-COLOR)

A Gaumont release of an Erato Films/Films A2/Flach Films/Action Films/CNC/SOFICA coproduction. Executive producer, Daniel Toscan du Plantier. Produced by Claude Abeille. Directed by Maurice Pialat. Stars Gérard Depardieu, Sandrine Bonnaire. Screenplay, Sylvie Danton, Pialat, from the novel by Georges Bernanos; camera (Fuji-Agfacolor), Willy Kurant; editor, Yann Dedet; music, Henri Dutilleux; production design, Katia Vischkof; sound, Louis Gimel; costumes, Gil Noir; production managers, Jean-Claude Bourlat, Edith Colnel; assistant director, Didier Creste. Reviewed at Cannes Film Festival (In Competition) May 13, 1987. Running time: **98 MINS.**
Father Donissan ....Gérard Depardieu
Mouchette ....Sandrine Bonnaire
Menou-Segrais ....Maurice Pialat
Marquis de Cadignan ....Alain Artur
Gallet.....................Yann Dedet
Mouchette's mother.....Brigitte Legendre
Malorthy ....Jean-Claude Bourlat

Cannes — Maurice Pialat's latest, "Under The Sun Of Satan," is very different from his last few pics ("Loulou," "To Our Loves," "Police"); it's a demanding adaptation of a 1926 novel by the celebrated Catholic author Georges Bernanos and deals with a country priest's confrontation with evil. Filled with powerful scenes and very well acted, it will create controversy and may only be fully appreciated by Catholics. Careful handling in art house situations is indicated.

The film initially intros two separate characters and themes. Father Donissan (Gérard Depardieu) is a dedicated priest who makes up for his lack of intelligence by an almost fanatical dedication. He flagellates himself with a chain, believes in his own inner strength, and despises his superior (played by Pialat himself) whom he sees as a dilettante.

The other character is Mouchette (Sandrine Bonnaire), a precocious 16-year-old, pregnant by an impoverished nobleman and also mistress of a wealthy, married politician. She shoots and kills the nobleman when he refuses to go away with her (whether by accident or design we're never certain) and later loses her baby; the killing is accepted as suicide.

These two characters meet during a long night when the priest has been sent to another parish. Exhausted and lost, he encounters a horse-trader who first helps him, then plants a passionate kiss on his lips; the priest believes he's encountered Satan himself. Later, he encounters Mouchette and has an instant vision in which he knows all about her: he confronts her with her crime intending, as he later says "to restore her to God," but she kills herself, instead.

Pialat manages to stage scenes of immense power, such as Depardieu carrying Bonnaire's body to the church altar, or later, a magical sequence in which he miraculously restores a dead child to life. Catholic audiences may be more able to tackle the themes raised here, but everyone will experience the extraordinary thrall of this demanding, rigorous film.

Depardieu has always worked well with Pialat (he won best actor at Venice two years ago for "Police"), and he's exceptional again here as the rigidly doctrinaire priest who ultimately believes Satan has conquered the world. Bonnaire, discovered by Pialat for "To Our Loves," also impresses as the lying, promiscuous teenager who thinks it's fun just to be beautiful. Pialat himself gives an authoritative performance as Depardieu's concerned superior.

The pic needs an attentive audience, ready to go along with its long dialog scenes, its sudden shifts forward in time, and its complex, contradictory characters. Fine camerawork by Willy Kurant, telling use of music and sound, provocative editing and precise direction all help.

Not everyone will go for this discourse on good and evil, but there's no denying the quality of Pialat's work. Despite pros and cons, this was head and shoulders above the other French films competing in Cannes.—*Strat.*

Accroche-coeur
(Lovelock)
(FRENCH-COLOR)

An Extension Films/Europimages production. Produced by Lionel Bellina. Written and directed by Chantal Picault, based on the novel "Les Platanes" by Monique Lange. Camera (Fujicolor), Gilberto Azevedo; sound, Yves Osmu; editor, Frédéric de Chateaubriant; music, Luc Le Masne. Reviewed at the Centre National du Cinéma, Paris, April 27, 1987. (In Perspectives on French Cinema at Cannes Film Festival.) Running time: **90 MINS.**
Leo ....Patrick Bauchau
Sara ....Sandrine Dumas
Also with: Laslo Szabo, Elisabeth Kaza.

Paris — "Accroche-coeur" is a two-for-the-road movie about a man's unsuccessful attempts to ditch his obstinate young mistress on a trip to the south of France. Adapting a novel by Monique Lange, newcomer Chantal Picault makes a promising but dramatically unsatisfying feature debut that suffers from the monotony and repetition inherent in the material.

Sandrine Dumas is the voluble motor of the story, a young girl madly in love with a handsome, but laconic middle-aged architect (Patrick Bauchau) who is looking for solitude to recover from a breakup with his actress wife.

Unwilling to let him out of her sight, Dumas begs him to let her accompany him for the first stretch of his trip, then keeps finding ways to stick with him all the way south.

Picault displays low-keyed skill in the intimate mode and is at ease with her two players though has difficulty spinning the action out to a feature's length. Despite the good performances, the characters don't gain in density or appeal once it's clear Dumas will have her way.

Tech credits are okay. — *Len.*

Der Himmel Uber Berlin
(The Sky Over Berlin)
(Wings Of Desire)
(WEST GERMAN-FRENCH-B&W/COLOR)

A Road Movies (Berlin), Argos Films (Paris) coproduction, with WDR. Produced by Wim Wenders, Anatole Dauman. Executive producer, Ingrid Windisch. Directed by Wenders. Stars Bruno Ganz, Solveig Dommartin, Peter Falk. Screenplay, Wenders, in collaboration with Peter Handke; camera (b&w/color), Henri Alékan; editor, Peter Przygodda; music, Jürgen Knieper; production design, Heidi Ludi; costumes, Monika Jacobs; sound, Lothar Mankiewicz; assistant director, Claire Denis; associate producer, Joachim von Mengershausen. Reviewed at Cannes Film Festival (In Competition), May 17, 1987. Running time: **130 MINS.**
Damiel ....Bruno Ganz
Marion ....Solveig Dommartin
Cassiel...................Otto Sander
Homer.....................Curt Bois
Peter Falk ....Peter Falk

Cannes — Wim Wenders returns to Germany with a sublimely beautiful, deeply romantic film for our times; this tale of angels watching over the citizens of Berlin springs from the great tradition of pics about angels involved in human affairs ("It's A Wonderful Life," "Here Comes Mr. Jordan," etc.), but is a quintessential Wenders film. It should find appreciative audiences in art houses around the world.

Bruno Ganz and Otto Sander are angels who spend their time watching over the humans of the divided city. Sometimes in flight (we never see them actually fly, though) and sometimes perched in high places, they come down to Earth to listen to the thoughts of the sad or lonely or needy. First part of the film establishes this mysterious world, with the whispering thoughts of humans filling the soundtrack.

Three humans are singled out. One's an old man, played by veteran Curt Bois, with memories of Berlin's shattered past. Another is Peter Falk, American movie actor in Berlin to make a pic about the Nazi era. The third is a beautiful trapeze artist, Solveig Dommartin. One of the angels, the one played by Ganz, begins to feel mortal when he watches the girl, and the film, which hitherto has been in black & white, has moments of color as humanity begins to encroach on the world of this angel.

There's a magical moment when Sander, the other angel, notices Ganz is leaving footprints; it means he's almost completely human. Last quarter of the film, all in color, has a humanized Ganz walking the streets, meeting with Falk — who reveals he was once an angel himself! — and, finally, meeting the girl who made him mortal.

Wenders invests this potentially risible material with such serenity and beauty that audiences will go along willingly with the fable. Above all, pic does for the city of Berlin what "Kings Of The Road" and "Alice In The Cities" did for the German countryside and "Paris, Texas" did for the Lone Star State. The film is a valentine to the city, with Henri Alékan's camera gliding and prowling around familiar landmarks as well as unknown backstreets. Visually, the film is a joy.

Peter Przygodda's editing is typically loose; Wenders has never hurried things, and he doesn't here, delivering a 130-minute film that doesn't overstay its welcome. Jürgen Knieper's music beautifully enhances the moods the director is seeking.

Bruno Ganz makes the angel who becomes human a very warm character; Otto Sander is memorable as his watchful partner; Solveig Dommartin is lovely as the girl on the flying trapeze; and Peter Falk has some amusing moments as one human who can feel the presence of an angel because he was once one himself.

Wenders' affection of rock music is here, too; the climactic meeting between Ganz and Dommartin takes place at a bar alongside a concert hall where Nick Cave and the Bad Seeds are performing. Typically, this scene is not at all shmaltzy; when the couple finally meet, they talk seriously about the future.

Wenders is on top form with this lovely effort, dedicated to "all former angels" — they include Yasujiro Ozu and François Truffaut. —Strat.

Slam Dance
(U.S.-BRITISH-COLOR)

An Island Pictures and Zenith Prods. presentation of a Sho Films production. Produced by Rupert Harvey, Barry Opper. Executive producer, Cary Brokaw. Directed by Wayne Wang. Screenplay, Don Opper; camera (DeLuxe color), Amir Mokri; editor, Lee Percy; music, Mitchell Froom; production design, Eugenio Zanetti; art director, Philip Dean Foreman; assistant director, John R. Woodward; casting, Lora Kennedy. Reviewed at Cannes Film Festival (Images du Cinema), May 13, 1987. (MPAA Rating: R.) Running time: **99 MINS.**

C.C. Drood ....Tom Hulce
Helen ......Mary Elizabeth Mastrantonio
Yolanda ....Virginia Madsen
Bobby Nye ....Millie Perkins
Jim ....:....Adam Ant
Buddy ....Don Opper
Smiley..............Harry Dean Stanton
Mrs. Raines ....Herta Ware
Gilbert ....John Doe
Frank ....Robert Beltran
Bean ....Judith Barsi

Cannes — "Slam Dance" is like junk food. It's brightly packaged, looks good and satisfies the hunger for entertainment, but it isn't terribly nourishing or well-made. Pic is self-consciously hip for a young urban crowd who probably will turn out in fairly good numbers for select engagements.

Latest in a growing line of films that sell style over substance, "Slam Dance" doesn't really make much sense as a mystery story, but keeps up its high spirits with visual flash and a likable performance by Tom Hulce.

Hulce is underground cartoonist C.C. Drood, a man whose life has come apart cheerfully at the seams. He's separated from his wife (Mary Elizabeth Mastrantonio) and daughter (Judith Barsi), though he still imagines them back together as a family.

Drood's the kind of man who never lets a little thing like marriage stand in the way of a good time or a hot romance with the beautiful and mysterious Yolanda (Virginia Madsen). Only one day Yolanda turns up dead and Drood's the prime suspect.

Script by Don Opper has a short attention span and introduces threads, follows one for a bit, then drops it for a new one. Finally he winds up with some kind of political sex scandal involving a top cop (John Doe) and a retiring detective (Harry Dean Stanton), for whom Drood is poised to be the scapegoat.

Except for Drood, characters are never given the opportunity to take hold and much of the acting talent is wasted. Mastrantonio is lovely as always, but without direction. Madsen fares even worse and has virtually nothing to do but look glamorous in a few scenes. Connection between Drood and Yolanda is tenuous at best.

Adam Ant decorates the screen as Drood's two-timing buddy, but basically he's just along for the ride. What really holds the film together is Hulce's loosey-goosey performance which sets the tempo for the action.

Director Wayne Wang tries to find a visual style to match the loose-limbed story and hits the mark about half the time. Since Drood is a visual artist, Wang has the opportunity to look at the world through his eyes and comes up with some original images. At other times he resorts to hackneyed visu-

al tricks and fancy cutting.

Production design is predictably current with an array of the latest fashion inventions. Drood's studio is a particularly nice piece of minimalist design, but then minimal is the operative word here.—*Jagr.*

Tough Guys Don't Dance
(U.S.-COLOR)

A Cannon Films release of a Golan-Globus production in association with Zoetrope Studios. Produced by Menahem Golan and Yoram Globus. Executive producers, Francis Coopola, Tom Luddy. Written and directed by Norman Mailer. Camera (credited as visual consultant) (TVC color), John Bailey; editor, Debra McDermott; music, Angelo Badalamenti; production design, Armin Ganz; set decorator, Gretchen Rau; sound, Drew Kunin; casting, Robert MacDonald, Bonnie Pietillia, Bonnie Timmerman. Reviewed at Cannes Film Festival (Out Of Competition), May 16, 1987. (No MPAA Rating.) Running time: **108 MINS.**

Tim Madden...............Ryan O'Neal
Madeline..............Isabella Rossellini
Patty Lareine ....Debra Sandlund
Regency..................Wings Hauser
Wardley Meeks ......John Bedford Lloyd
Bolo...............Clarence Williams 3d
Doug Maggen ....Lawrence Tierney
Big Stoop..................Penn Jillette
Jessica Pond ....Frances Fisher
Lonny Pangborn ......R. Patrick Sullivan
Stoodie ....Stephen Morrow
Spider ....John Snyder

Cannes — Norman Mailer's "Tough Guys Don't Dance" is like a film school assignment to create a *film noir* thriller turned in by a very gifted student. He knows all the moves, but it just doesn't have any heart. "Tough Guys" is part parody and part serious with a nasty streak running right down the middle. Picture may generate some interest as a curiosity item but as a filmgoing experience it's certain to leave audiences cold.

Mailer violates the cardinal rule for this kind of genre fare, he fails to create characters that can make up for the absurdities of the plot. As a scriptwriter working from his novel, he offers a convoluted story that goes on far too long and runs out of steam before its over, making the resolution of little interest when it finally does come.

What the film does do well is create a sense of time and place for the story to unfold. Set in a small coastal town in Massachusetts, cinematographer John Bailey (listed in the credits as visual consultant) gives the picture a mournful look right from the opening credit montage.

It's the sort of place where everyone knows everyone else's business and for Tim Madden (Ryan O'Neal), business is bad. Story has something to do with a botched drug deal, men who love the wrong women and women who love the wrong men. In the course of playing its hand, Madden's wealthy wife (Debra Sandlund), a washed up porno star (Frances Fisher), a suicidal

southerner (John Bedford Lloyd), a gay sugar daddy (R. Patrick Sullivan) and a corrupt police chief (Wings Hauser) all get blown away.

Things just seem to happen to Madden that he can't do anything about so he just lives with it, gritting his teeth along the way. It's a typical dry, flat, nothing-ruffles-my-feathers performance from O'Neal, effective only as long as what's happening to him holds some mystery.

Film is at its best when it's tongue-in-cheek and it's fun to listen to the guys talk tough and throw out such lines as, "People just don't know how tough it is out there." And the biggest, baddest, nastiest one of them all is Lawrence Tierney as O'Neal's father, a man who won't dance for anyone.

At its worst "Tough Guys" has a rather dismal view of human nature with women, perhaps, even more vicious and predatory than the men. So at the end when Madden gets back with his true love Madeline (Isabella Rossellini) one can only wonder if Mailer is a closet romantic masquerading as a tough guy.

—*Jagr.*

Jenatsch
(SWISS-FRENCH-COLOR)

A Metropolis Films Presentation of a Limbo Films (Zurich), Bleu Prods. (Paris), Beat Curti (Zurich), Société de Banque Suisse, Fernsehen DRS (Zurich), ZDF (Mainz), production. Executive producers, Theres Scherer, Luciano Gloor. Directed by Daniel Schmid. Screenplay, Martin Suter, Schmid; camera (Kodak color), Renato Berta; editor, Daniela Roderer; music, Pino Donaggio; sound, Luc Yersin; art director, Raul Gimenez; assistant director, Martha Galvin; costumes, Marianne Milani; Reviewed at Cannes Film Festival (in Un Certain Regard section), May 14, 1987. Running time: **97 MINS.**

Cristophe ....Michel Voita
Nina ....Christine Boisson
Jenatsch ....Vittorio Mezzogiorno
Tobler ....Jean Bouise
Miss von Planta ....Laura Betti
Lucrezia ....•......Carole Bouquet
Also with: Raul Gimenez, Roland Bertin, Jean-Paul Muel, Lucrezia Giovannini, Rolf Lyssy, Fredi Murer.

Cannes — In one of the most ambitious Swiss productions of the year, Daniel Schmid attempts to wipe out the barriers between past and present, but doesn't quite manage to pull it off.

Known for his frequent explorations of the thin line separating reality and imagination, Schmid seems to be more cautious than usual this time in choosing his film language, and takes very few chances, precisely when daring and imagination were indicated.

The result is a film lacking the adventurous experiments Schmid indulged in the past and which made him famous, but not sufficiently classical in form to make its points the old-fashioned way.

A reporter is assigned the task of interviewing an archeologist investigating the murder of a 16th century folk figure. First rather skeptical and detached, the journalist becomes gradually involved in the investigation and even imagines being a witness to the events that happened 400 years ago. He suffers hallucinations, which he believes to be real experiences, disrupting his present state of affairs, his peace of mind and his relationship with his girlfriend, who can't understand his strange behavior.

Schmid has lots of trouble incorporating historical events and current ones on an equal level of consciousness. The transitions from past to present to past are often arbitrary and the characters lack consistency, since they are only instruments manipulated to fit into a certain theoretical pattern. No wonder acting is somewhat unfocused and the Voita-Boisson couple don't look too comfortable together.

Brief but incisive performances are given by Jean Bouise as the weird scientist looking for a 400-year old murderer and Laura Betti, as a direct descendant of a noblewoman suspected of engineering Jenatsch's murder. Former Bond girl Carole Bouquet lends her striking beauty to a mysterious, speechless walkon. Two well-known Swiss directors, Rolf Lyssy and Fredi Murer, do bit parts as well.

Cameraman Renato Berta tried hard to give the film two separate visual styles, and he succeeds as long as one is not expected to dissolve smoothly into the other, for the transition is seldom smooth.

Schmid's films have never been easy, specialized as they were for select audiences, who probably will remain faithful to him after this one as well, even if it is not quite on a par with earlier efforts. —*Edna.*

Angelus Novus
(ITALIAN-COLOR)

An Istituto Luce release of a Libra Film production. Produced by Francesca Noe. Written and directed by Pasquale Misuraca. Camera (Fujicolor, Orwo b&w, by Cinecittà), Bruno Di Virgillo, Paolo Carnera; editor, Roberto Perpignani; art direction and costumes, Alexandra Zampa; music, Vittorio Gelmetti; sound, Fabio Felici. Reviewed at Cannes Film Festival (in Intl. Critics Week section), May 13, 1987. Running time: **80 MINS.**
The poet . . . . Domenico Pesce
Also with: Tomaso Ricordy, Stefano Valoppi, Eliana Cifa, Ignazio Fenu.

Cannes — Pier Paolo Pasolini, Italian filmmaker, poet and intellectual, was and continues to be a central figure for the contemporary Left. His scandalous life (as a homosexual), films (the last was "Salò") and thought (unorthodox and original), as well as his tragic death, would seem to lend themselves especially well to a biofilm. The first attempt, however, is a gray, stuffy academics' revelry, whose few moments of genuine insight don't go very far to redeeming the tedium of the whole. Its audience is hard to fathom.

Written and directed by Pasquale Misuraca, an assistant prof in the Sociology of Conscience taking his first turn behind the camera, "Angelus Novus" suffers visibly from trying to impose very abstract ideas about film form and structure on the bones of what might have been an interesting bio-essay. Thus we have a lengthy, wordless opening of someone in a car driving around nighttime Rome recalling something out of a Straub film. First spark of interest comes some way into the film, when the Poet (played by Domenico Pesce, a lookalike in shadow and in profile) ruminates on the hated faces of four powerful Christian Democrat politicians, and considers how they should be put on trial for crimes against the people, as the basis of a new national conscience.

Another sequence of architectural tours of Rome follows, again with nothing to put it in context. Better are the shots of the poet watching young boys swim at Ostia, if only because it recalls a recognizable Pasolini logo. A scene with "Salò" glimpsed on the editing table contributes, in its awkward way, to showing the gap between Pasolini's radical thinking and that of the average rank and file Communist. His final interview adds another piece of his thinking, namely, that conspiracy theories serve to hide a less tolerable truth about society's degradation. See last sequence.

This is the one inspired scene, a poetic-expressionistic recreation of Pasolini's motiveless murder by a group of young boys on the Ostia beach. The nervous b&w camera and Roberto Perpignani's cutting give it a power not present in what has gone before, and hopefully point to the direction Misuraca's future work might take. — *Yung.*

Shy People
(U.S.-COLOR)

A Cannon Films release of a Golan-Globus production. Produced by Menahem Golan, Yoram Globus. Directed by Andrei Konchalovsky. Screenplay, Gerard Brach, Konchalovsky, Marjorie David, from a story by Konchalovsky; camera (Rank color), Chris Menges; editor, Alain Jakubowicz; music, Tangerine Dream; production design, Steve Marsh; art director, Leslie McDonald; set decorator, Leslie Morales; sound, Mark Ulano; assistant director, Michael Schroeder; casting, Bob MacDonald. Reviewed at Cannes Film Festival (In Competition), May 14, 1987. (No MPAA Rating.) Running time: **118 MINS.**
Diana . . . . Jill Clayburgh
Ruth . . . . Barbara Hershey
Grace . . . . Martha Plimpton
Mike . . . . Merritt Butrick
Tommy . . . . John Philbin
Paul . . . . Pruitt Taylor Vince
Mark . . . . Don Swayze
Louie . . . . Michael Audley
Larry . . . . Brad Leland
Jake . . . . Paul Landry

Cannes — Don't be fooled by the title: "Shy People" is not about people who stand in the corner at a party but people who stand in the corner of the world where life is still wild and mythical. Director Andrei Konchalovsky explores again the struggle for survival in a hostile environment, this time in the dense backcountry swamps of the Louisiana bayou.

For most of the way it's a compelling journey, but one to which filmgoers will have to be cleverly coaxed. Bets here are for satisfactory but not sensational b.o.

Film opens with a sweeping aerial view of New York where Cosmopolitan writer Diana Sullivan (Jill Clayburgh) lives in splendid disharmony with her teenage daughter Grace (Martha Plimpton). Clayburgh is totally in her element as a spoiled middle-age woman trying to cope with her too-hip daughter.

They are soon out of their element, though, when they travel to Louisiana for a story Clayburgh is writing about a long-lost branch of her family. It is not simply a case of invaders from civilization soiling a pure culture, though there are elements of that. Story is deepened by the exploration of family ties.

Konchalovsky and cinematographer Chris Menges offer a slow and seductive descent into this world of alligators and primordial beauty. Wearing a shiny red coat and a bright yellow New York sweater, the two visitors are like queens of the Nile on a runaway boat.

What they find when they arrive is Ruth Sullivan (Barbara Hershey), the matriarch of a family of three sons, one of whom is kept in a cage and another retarded, plus a pregnant daughter (Marc Winningham). Also very much present is Hershey's husband Joe, Clayburgh's great-uncle, who has been dead 15 years but is believed by the family to still lurk in the swamps to protect them.

Although they don't recognize what they are seeing, mother and daughter have gone from a world of abstractions in New York to a world of absolutes where "you're either for us or against us" and people's dispositions run hot and cold, but never lukewarm.

In the Sullivan clan, Ruth rules with an iron will and there is no question of individual freedom, only survival against a nature that also runs hot and cold. It is adherence to the family and age-old beliefs that keep life whole here. What the newcomers bring is chaos and anarchy because they disturb the order of things.

Grace introduces Tommy (John Philbin), the caged brother, to drugs and sex. In the climactic scene, with the mother out of the house, everything collapses. Paul (Pruitt Taylor Vince) lets the goats out and Mark (Don Swayze) gets stoned for the first time and tries to rape Grace.

As a result, both Grace and Diana become stranded in the swamp, order is restored, when they are saved by what seems to be Uncle Joe. Ruth explains it by saying that in the swamps sometimes you see what you want to see.

There is plenty to see. Konchalovsky has a keen eye for detail and has loaded the film with images that say more than long-winded exposition ever could. White egrets soar low over the swamps and moss shuffles in the breeze as if it were alive. Here as he did in "The Killing Fields," Menges' photography is able to suggest that more is going on than meets the eye.

On a story level, "Shy People" is a bit less successful with Gerard Brach, Konchalovsky and Majorie David's screenplay sagging a bit in the middle section before all hell finally breaks loose. Generally they have created a memorable collection of faces, however.

Clayburgh gives one of her best performances and seems right at home with the ticks and self-centered mannerisms of a modern woman. Plimpton nearly steals the show with her mixture of girlish brashness and suggestive sexuality.

In undoubtedly the strangest role of her career, Hershey presents a bit of a problem and not for her acting, which is quite solid. At times she just seems wrong for the part of the young matriarch and comes off more like Mammy Yokum than a forceful presence. Part of the difficulty is in the script which, where Ruth is concerned strains the limits of credibility.

Music by Tangerine Dream helps to heighten the tension and suggest unseen mysteries. Technical credits throughout are impressive, especially with Steve Marsh's production design packing the corners of the screen with subliminal images. Fortunately "Shy People" does not sink under the weight of its material. It's a dense film without being ponderous.—*Jagr.*

Falsch
(BELGIAN-FRENCH-COLOR)

A Dérives Prod./RTBF (Liege)/Arcanal/-Théâtre de la Place coproduction, with the participation of the Belgian Ministry for the French Community. Executive producer, Dérive Prods. Written and directed by Jean-Pierre and Luc Dardenne, from the play by Rene Kalisky. Camera (Eastmancolor), Walther Vanden Ende; sound, Dominique Warnier; editor, Denise Vindevogel; art director, Wim Vermeylen; music, Jean-Marie Billy, Jan Franssen; assistant director, Anne-Levy Morelle; production manager, Geneviève Robillard. Reviewed at the Centre National du Cinéma, Paris, April 27, 1987. (In Perspectives on French Cinema at Cannes Film Festival.) Running time: **82 MINS.**

With: Bruno Cremer (Joe), Jacqueline Bollen (Lilli), Nicole Colchat (Mina), Christian Crahay (Gustav), Millie Dardenne (Bela), Bérangère Dautun (Rachel), John Dobrynine (Georg), André Lenaerts (Ruben), Christian Maillet (Jacob), Jean Mallamaci (Benjamin), Gisèle Oudart (Natalia), Marie-Rose Roland (Daniella), François Sikivie (Oscar).

Paris — Belgian brothers Luc and Jean-Pierre Dardenne, known at home for their video documentaries, make their theatrical fiction feature debut with "Falsch," a technically slick, well performed but pretentious adaptation of a play by René Kalisky, about a German Jewish family's reunion.

Gimmick of the piece was that all its members are dead, coming together only to welcome its last deceased member, Joe (Bruno Cremer), who with two other brothers escaped the Nazi Holocaust and began a new life in the U.S.

The clan's Otherworldly get-together — family name is Falsch, German for "false" — begins with sentimental abandon but soon degenerates into a tormented series of breast-beating guilt trips, and mutual accusations as the members explore the reasons most refused to leave Germany while there was still time and allowed themselves to be led to their deaths.

The Dardennes' cinematic concept was to reset the fantasy piece in a small deserted airport, symbolizing a place of transit between life and death. Helmers move the action with dreamlike fluidity (courtesy of excellent camerawork by Walther Vanden Ende) from the main hall into the nooks and crannies of its hallways, duty free counters and toilets.

Despite the clever filmic solutions to stage-to-screen transfer, Kalisky's rather rhetorical inquiry into the identity crisis of Diaspora Jews and the guilt of the survivors remains superficial and mannered, though the fine cast members — notably Cremer — coax some sparks of emotion out of their material.

With world attention once again focused on Nazi war crimes and the Holocaust, via the trial of Klaus Barbie, et al., film could benefit with specialized exposure.—*Len.*

Rigoletto
(WEST GERMAN-COLOR)

A Beta Film presentation of a Unitel production. Executive producer, Horant H. Hohlfeld. Directed by Jean-Pierre Ponnelle. Stars Luciano Pavarotti, Edita Gruberova. Libretto, Francesco Maria Piave based on Victor Hugo's play "Le roi s'amuse;" camera (color), Pasqualino de Santis; music, Giuseppe Verdi; set designer, Gianni Quaranta; costumes, Martin Schlumpf; performed by the Vienna Philharmonic and the State-Opera Chorus, conducted by Riccardo Chailly. Reviewed at the Cannes Film Festival (Cinema & Opera Panorama), May 8, 1987. Running time: **117 MINS.**
Rigoletto . . . . Ingvar Wixell
Duke . . . . Luciano Pavarotti
Gilda . . . . Edita Gruberova
Sparafucile . . . . Ferruccio Furlanetto
Maddelena . . . . Victoria Vergaga
Also with: Bernd Weikl, Louis Otey, Remy Corazza, Kathleen Kuhlmann, Roland Bracht, Fedora Barbieri.

Cannes — Made for television in 1983, this production of the Verdi classic doesn't stand the test of being blown up on a full-scale screen. While musically there is much to enjoy here, it is difficult to be satisfied with Jean-Pierre Ponnelle's obvious and stagebound visualization after the imaginative efforts of film directors such as Losey, Rosi and Zeffirelli. At best, what Ponnelle does is imitate classical paintings with still pictures in Felliniesque fashion, but films are supposed to be more than stills. Granted that opera is one of the most difficult things to do on film, there are certainly far richer ways to do it than Ponnelle is prepared to explore here.

Victor Hugo's play about a philandering monarch who seduces the daughter of his buffoon, was turned by Verdi into a true hit parade of arias, not his most sophisticated work but certainly among his most popular. Interpreters such as Pavarotti and Gruberova, whose tremendous voices are impressive on stage, thanks to the distance between them and the audience, overcome the small screen test, because of its size, but are massacred once they are put into huge closeups that reveal their minimal acting capability as well as their very approximate physical capacity to handle their roles.

Ponnelle's staging does nothing to help them, with scenes like Pavarotti supposedly perched on a fence, and resting there comfortably in spite of his bulk, being an example of moments when charitable smiles are bound to come out.

The entire conception is totally theatrical, whether in the way the chorus is spread out in front of the camera, or the singers perform for it as a substitute for the live audience.

While famed Italian cameraman Pasqualino de Santis does a beautiful lighting job, most camera movements and cutting follow basic tv standards, and at least one set, that

of the palace, looks embarrassingly fake, with the fresh boards supposed to blend into medieval architecture.

Opera purists may argue that Ponnelle treats Verdi with more respect than Zeffirelli did in "Otello" and they may be quite right, but visually it's a far cry from it.

Since this Beta production originally was intended for television, and indeed it has been extensively shown all over the world with very few complaints, it is quite possible the error in this case was not with the producers but rather with the programmers in Cannes who chose this specific item to kick off their "film and opera" section. Opera, it is; film, the jury's still out. — *Edna.*

Terre étrangère/Das Weite Land
(Unknown Country) (FRENCH-AUSTRIAN-COLOR)

A Beta Films (Munich) presentation of a Progefi (Paris)/Arabella Film (Vienna)/Almaro Film (Munich)/Antenne 2/RAI 2/-ORF/WDR coproduction. Produced by Christine Gouze-Renal, Michael Wolkenstein. Directed by Luc Bondy. Screenplay, Bondy, Lubor Meir Dohnal, based on the play, "Das Weite Land" by Arthur Schnitzler; camera (color), Thomas Mauch; art director, Ina Peichl; editor, Ingrid Koller, sound, Johannes Paiha, Michael Wunderl; costumes, Beatrice Stein-Lepert and Birgit Hutter; music, Heinz Leonardsberger. Reviewed at the Centre National du Cinema, Paris, April 23, 1987. (In Un Certain Regard section at Cannes Film Festival.) Running time: **103 MINS.**
With: Michel Piccoli (Friedrich Hofreiter), Bulle Ogier (Genia), Wolfgang Hübsch (Dr. Mauer), Barbara Robeochini (Erna), Milena Vukotic (Frau Wahl), Dominique Blanc (Adèle Natter), Paul Burian (Natter), Jutta Lampe, Gabriel Barylli, Friedrich Hammel, Jeff Layton, Paul Manker.
(French-track version)

Paris — This multinationally produced film, made for tv, but premiered at Cannes in the Un Certain Regard program, is a feeble adaptation of a play by Austrian dramatist Arthur Schnitzler (staged in English in a version by Tom Stoppard entitled "Undiscovered Country").

Zurich-born director Luc Bondy staged the piece here in 1984 with Michel Piccoli and Bulle Ogier, and has recast them in the film, which was shot on Austrian locations. The picturesque opening-up of the play doesn't add any resonance to the work, though helps alleviate the boredom of this ponderously handled period piece, which may have some theatrical expectations in limited arthouse playoff.

Tale is a typical Schnitzlerian dramatic X-ray of decadent Austrian society in the years before World War I and has the familiar quota of romantic and sexual roundelays, idle country outings and climactic duels of honor. Bondy even throws in a scene in which the main charac-

ters attend a performance of Schnitzler's controversial sex comedy, "Reigen" (La Ronde).

Piccoli plays a philandering Viennese industrialist who is vexed by the inexplicably icy fidelity of his much-courted wife (Ogier) but plays his role of dishonored husband by killing in a duel a young officer who has been wooing her.

Like Chekhov (another doctor-turned-author), Schnitzler performed his scalpel-sharp dissection of a dying world with tragicomic finesse and mordant irony, but these qualities are lost in Bondy's callously inelegant direction.

And where smooth ensemble performances are crucial, film is further disabled by mediocre-to-poor acting, not excluding Piccoli and Ogier, both at their attitudinizing worst in difficult, fundmentally unsympathetic roles.

Most of the supporting cast, German or Austrian, were dubbed for French-langue version. Tech credits are passable. — *Len.*

Diary Of A Mad Old Man
(DUTCH-BELGIAN-FRENCH-COLOR)

A Cannon Group release of a Fons Rademakers Productie (Amsterdam)/Iblis Films (Brussels)/Dedalus Films (Paris) coproduction. Produced by Henry Lange, Pierre Drouot, Fons Rademakers. Directed by Lili Rademakers. Screenplay, Hugo Claus, Claudine Bouvier, from the novel by Junichiro Tanizaki; camera (Fujicolor), Paul van den Bos; editor, Ton de Graaff; music, Egisto Macchi; production design, Philippe Graff; sound, Victor Dekker; production managers, Jean-Marie Bertrand, Daniel Geys; assistant director, Gerda Diddens. Reviewed at Cannes Film Festival (in Directors Fortnight), May 12, 1987. Running time: **91 MINS.**
Marcel Hamelinck . . . . Ralph Michael
Simone . . . . Beatie Edney
Denise Hamelinck . . . . Suzanne Flon
Philippe . . . . Derek de Lint
Sister Alma . . . . Dora van der Groen
Karin . . . . Ina van der Molen
(In English)

Cannes — This second feature of Lili Rademakers (following "Minuet" in 1982) is a beautifully made adaptation of a Japanese novel by Junichiro Tanizaki about an old man's erotic obsession with his daughter-in-law. Cannon will need to go the specialist route with this low-key English-track entry which plays down the kinkier aspects inherent in the subject.

The old man (Ralph Michael) is a rich businessman living with his wife and family in a large house outside Brussels (though the exact location is never specified, and every member of the cast speaks very upper-class English). His daughter-in-law (Beatie Edney, current on Broadway in "Les Liaisons Dangereuses," whose last film was "Highlander") is vivacious and attractive, and the old man gradually falls under her spell.

While pretending to be shocked when he wants to watch her shower or fondle her feet, she actually encourages him, though never letting him go very far. He even agrees to build a swimming pool so he can see her in a bathing suit. His obsession seems to keep him alive after the death of his wife.

It may sound kinkier than it actually is, but this is more a discreet mood piece, elegantly handled, but possibly too tame for many tastes. The two British leads carry the film, with Ralph Michael very good as the pathetically obsessed old man. Supporting cast of Dutch, Belgian and French thesps have all been dubbed, but for once the dubbing looks convincing.

Production credits are all pro, and Rademakers indicates again her talents as a director. She's married to Fons Rademakers, winner of the 1986 foreign language Academy Award for "The Assault." —*Strat.*

Um Trem Para as Estrelas
(A Train For The Stars)
(BRAZILIAN-COLOR)

An Embrafilme Presentation of a CDK Prods. (Rio), Chrysalide Films (Paris) production. Executive producer, Rodolfo Brandao. Directed by Carlos Diegues. Screenplay, Diegues, Carlos Lombardi; camera (color), Edgar Moura; editor, Gilberto Santeiro (Brazil), Dominique Boischot (France); music, Gilberto Gil; sound, Jorge Saldanha (Brazil), Rene Levert (France); art director, Lia Renha; production manager, Rene Bittencourt. Reviewed at Cannes Film Festival (In Competition), May 15, 1987. Running time: **103 MINS.**
Vinicius . . . . .Guilherme Fontes
Freitas . . . . .Milton Goncalves
Drimi . . . . .Taumaturgo Ferreira
Nicinha . . . . .Ana Beatriz Wiltgen
　Also with: Ze Trindade, Miriam Pires, Tania Boscoli, Flavio Santiago, Betty Prado, Paulao, Cristiana Lavigne, and guest performances by Jose Wilker, Betty Faria, Daniel Filho, Cazuza.

Cannes — After the peripatetic "Bye Bye Brazil" and the vast dimensions of "Quilombo," leading Brazilian director Carlos Diegues returns to the modest dimensions of an intimate film in this story about the bleak horizons in store for his country's youth. The grimness of the picture is, however, toned down by a good-humored sense of ridicule and a considerable amount of music, typical of Diegues' films.

Vinicius, a young saxophonist who tries to make a living out of his music, looks all over Rio for his girlfriend, who disappears without leaving a trace. He contacts the police who immediately suspect the girl of prostitution and crime. He goes to her parents, but they are both lost in private in an unreal world of illusions. He tries the press

without much luck and even asks for the help of his mother, who runs a cheap strip joint.

Diegues keeps his film strictly away from the glamorous touristic sites, going deep into the poverty-stricken shantytowns around town and in its rundown suburbs. Poverty, ignorance and brutality are common denominators for this side of society, in which everyone is motivated by a desperate need to escape one way or another, at any cost. If real physical escape is impossible, at least the dreams are free.

While critical of everything he shows, Diegues has kept intact his humanistic approach which allows him to see both sides of every character, be it a rough cop, a hardened stripper, a street punk, or even a drug dealer, all at least partly justified in their actions in spite of all their crimes, being themselves victims in a system which offers no way out of the misery.

The trouble with the film is that Diegues doesn't care very much for script construction, the search for the disappearing girl never really advancing, plotwise. At one point there is even the suspicion of an inspiration from Antonioni's "L'Aventura" when a similar disappearance was the excuse to trigger another story altogether. Here, however, the film is never more than a long line of episodic observations, some managing to achieve poetic dimensions while others are correct at best, but their lyrical efforts are too visible for comfort.

Guilherme Fontes, the new heart-throb of Brazilian cinema, shows lots of sympathy for the character of Vinicius, displaying the kind of exalted temper one expects an artist to have, and the rest of the satisfactory cast displays a kind of natural spontaneity which in this case is an asset. Two well-established stars of the Brazilian cinema, Betty Faria and Jose Wilker, contribute cameos bound to delight local audiences. Camerawork faithfully deglamorizes the sights to fit in with Diegues' conception.

Veteran musician Gilberto Gil wrote the soundtrack, not his most original effort, but a solidly functional one, particularly in the instance of one sax solo which truly reflects the despair of the player after the death of his closest friend.

Among Diegues pictures this should figure together with "Chuvas de Verao" as far as ambience is concerned, but unlike the earlier movie, the social comment in the new one comes out stronger than the emotional one.—*Edna.*

Hotel de France
(FRENCH-COLOR)

A Claude Berri presentation of a Les Film du Volcan release of a Renn Prods./Camera One Nanterre-Amandiers production, with participation of Canal Plus and the French Communications Ministry/PTT. Executive producer, Helene Vager. Directed by Patrice Chereau. Screenplay, Chereau, Jean-François Goyet, based on Anton Chekhov's "Platanov Chronicles;" camera (Agfacolor), Pascal Marti; editor, Albert Jurgenson; sound, Michel Vionnet; production design, Sylvain Chauvelot; costumes, Caroline de Vivaise. Reviewed at Cannes Film Festival (in Un Certain Regard section), May 17, 1987. Running time: **98 MINS.**
Michel . . . . .Laurent Grevil
Sonia . . . . Valeria Bruni-Tedeschi
Serge .Vincent Perez
Anna . . . . .Laura Benson
Nicolas . . . . .Thibault de Montalembert
Philippe Galtier . . . . .Marc Citti
Richard Veninger . . . . .Bernard Nisille
Catherine . . . . .Marianne Cuau
Marie . . . . .Isabelle Renaud
　Also with: Bruno Todeschini, Agnès Jaoui, Helene Saint-Père, Jean-Louis Richard, Ivan Desny, Thierry Ravel (Manu).

Cannes — An awesome lot of cinematic flash, flair and energy and perfectly instrumentalized improvisational acting wind up going down a dark drain in French theater's wunderkind Patrice Chereau's second major feature film, "Hotel de France," set to be beamed via pay-channel Canal Plus three days ahead of its theatrical release immediately after the Cannes fest closes. On the home screen, viewers will see mostly darkness in pic's last third. Some theatrical pickups abroad loom as a brighter future for Chereau's present-day version of Chekhov story-cum-play.

"Hotel de France" is another ostensibly typical French tour de force of family communal eating, drinking, talking, yelling, screaming, goading each other on, all in the course of one afternoon and evening in and around the restaurant of the title. The generation gap, an unexpected meeting between erstwhile lovers, financial and erotic interdependencies, yearnings, social barriers — these are among the topics explored in dialog and much physical élan .

Most of the day passes as one long bawl with intermissions of kicking a ball on the highway or cavorting in a nearby river, while high drama is whipped up, only to end in suffocating defeat for everybody involved. Director Chereau switches from noisy scenes with everybody talking at once to sudden near-silences with the rest of the party listening to individual monologs or couples' quarrels.

Although some individuals are etched more sharply than others, Chereau sees his characters as one homogeneous whole, held together by their differences. The entire large cast has been recruited mostly from the drama school of Nanterre-Am-

andiers, and they all perform as if they had been in films all along. Without exception, they excel in being convincing until they disappear in the chiaroscuro of an open ending of common misery. Pascal Marti's camera is all over the place without ever turning somersaults, and film's production dress is snappy and just right for the occasion.
　　　　　　　　　　　　　　　—*Kell.*

Yer Demir, Gok Bakir
(Iron Earth, Copper Sky)
(TURKISH-WEST GERMAN-COLOR)

An Interfilm (Istanbul)/Road Movies (Berlin)/WDR (Cologne) coproduction. Produced by Ülker Livaneli, Wim Wenders. Directed by Ömer Zülfü Livaneli. Screenplay, O. Z. Livaneli, from the novel by Yashmar Kemal; camera (color) Jürgen Jürges; editor, Bettina Böhler; music, O. Z. Livaneli; production design, Gürel Yontan; costumes, Yudum Yontan; production manager, Peter Schulze. Reviewed at Cannes Film Festival (in Un Certain Regard), May 13, 1987. Running time: **104 MINS.**
　With: Rutkay Aziz, Macide Tanir, Yavuzer Cetinkaya, Eray Özbal, Serap Aksoy, Tuncay Akca, Melih Cardak, Dilek Damlacik, Yasemin Alkaya, Gürel Yontan, Peter Schulze, Ingeborg Carstens, Ugur Esen, Hülya Güler.

Cannes — A lyrical, hauntingly beautiful drama set in a remote, snowbound village, "Iron Earth, Copper Sky" marks the debut as director of Ömer Zülfü Livaneli, best known thus far as composer of the music for Yilmaz Güney's "The Herd" and Helma Sanders-Brahms' "Shirin's Wedding."

Bearing the imprimatur of coproducer Wim Wenders, pic has a mythic quality to it. Villagers in an Anatolian hamlet await with dread the arrival of their landlord, since there's little money to pay the rent. The local headman, acolyte of the landlord, is hated by all, but they have no one else to turn to.

The only dissenter is Tashbash, a rakish character with a criminal past, who hates the headman. When one villager purports to see a vision in which a famous mountain saint appears in the form of Tashbash, the villagers seize on him as their salvation. Though he strenuously denies he's a saint, they persist in treating him like one until even he comes to believe it.

Pic is a bit too long, and could stand some pruning in the middle to make it even more accessible. Nonetheless, it's a film of distinction, with its exotic tale handled beautifully by the tyro director who's aided immeasurably by the glorious camerawork of Jürgen Jürges. Expectedly, there's an imposing score by the director to accompany the beautiful images.

This could possibly be the first Turkish film since "Yol" to attract the attention of braver distribs in English-speaking territories, as it could find an audience on its majestic beauty and exotic theme. The Wenders name will help some.

—*Strat.*

Przypadek
(Blind Chance)
(POLISH-COLOR)

A Film Polski presentation of a Polish Corp. For Film Prod. Zespoly Filmowe, Unit TOR, production. Written and directed by Krzysztof Kieslowski. Camera (color) Krzysztof Pakulski; editor, Elzbieta Kurowska; music, Wojciech Kilar; production design, Rafal Waltenberger; sound, Michal Zarnechi; production manager, Jacek Szeligowski. Reviewed at the Cannes Film Festival, (In Un Certain Regard section), May 8, 1987. Running time: **122 MINS.**

Witek Dlugosz	Boguslaw Linda
Werner	Tadeusz Lomnicki
Adam	Zbigniew Zapa Siewicz
Czuszka	Boguslawa Pawelec
Werka	Marzena Trybala
Marck	Jacek Borowski
Olga	Monika Godzdzik

Also with: Zygmunt Hübner (faculty dean), others.

Cannes — In his seventh feature film, "Blind Chance," writer-director Krzysztof Kieslowski has the same young man, Witek, a medical student, subjected to three different "fates," each equally likely to decide the life of an intelligent young Pole in search of truth and happiness. Three stories, then, and three different fates, and you have what sounds like rather bookish stuff, but Kieslowski employs solid cinematic narrative techniques and keeps up a modicum of suspense even when indulging in dialectics and discursive dialog. With careful nursing, "Blind Chance" should reach at least a limited international arthouse exposure.

There's quite a bit of Polish *glasnost* on display here, too. The three episodes all begin with Witek running to catch a train. In the first, he just makes it and, having broken off his medical studies in spite of his late father's wishes, gets half-heartedly involved in Communist youth politics; has an affair with a girl of very independent mind; and is about to go abroad for a Catholic conference when strikes break out at home.

In the second segment, Witek misses the train, behaves uncivilly to a station guard and must serve time with a work brigade. Here, he gets involved with the underground anti-Communist movement; has an affair with a Jewish girl, and turns to religion to such a degree that he is about to leave Poland yet again for an international Catholic conference when authorities confiscate his passport — but only after he has been reluctant to take up their offer to do some spying for them abroad.

In the third vignette, the young man's career and life goes up in flames, literally, after he finally really gets airborne to appear at a

surgeons conference in Libya.

It's understood that having again missed the train, Witek decided to follow his father's wishes when he saw a fine career open to him. This time, he even married the girl he had casually slept with.

The acting in "Blind Chance" is of the subdued realism school. The production design is of the same order and highly professional, too. The political, ethical, religious and other philosophizing is usually so open-ended that audiences are left free to form their own conclusions, one of which film would suggest all Poles have been tied in a no-win situation since 1945. —*Kell.*

Camera Arabe
(The Young Arab Cinema)
(TUNISIAN-DOCU-COLOR)

A Satpec (Tunis) and M3M (Paris) release. Produced by Ferid Boughedir with the participation of Satpec (Tunis), Institut du Monde Arabe (Paris), Channel 4 (London), FR3 Nord-Pas-Calais, Tunisian Ministry of Cultural Affairs, French Ministry of Culture, and others. Written and directed by Boughedir. Camera (color), Ahmed Zaaf; editor, Moufida Tlatli; sound, Faouzi Thabet. Reviewed at Cannes Film Festival (in Images du Cinema section), May 16, 1987. Running time: **60 MINS.**

Cannes — Following the successful formula of his well known docu on black African cinema, "Camera Afrique," Ferid Boughedir has put together a fast-moving, enlightening hour of clips from key Arab films of the last 20 years. An hour format is too brief to do much more than touch base on the top pictures and directors, but it provides a solid introduction for those interested in an overview. It will be aired on England's Channel 4, which stepped in to save the project in extremis, and "Camera Arabe" should find similar forums.

Egyptian production was long the only cinema made in the Arab countries, with its popular genres and entertainment pictures. Since the late '20s, it has commercially dominated the Arab world. Only in the 1960s, when the North African countries gained independence, did other films emerge with new themes and aims. "Camera Arabe" presents highlights from a number of them, including works by Mohamed Lakhdar-Hamina, Mahmoud Ben Mahmoud, Abdellatif Ben Ammar, Merzak Allouache, Souheil Ben Barka, Mohamed Malass and Nouri Bouzid. A special place is reserved for Egyptian helmer Youssef Chahine. Chahine's intelligent, anguished battle to describe Arabs' shaken sense of their own identity in a world rocked by dramatic political events rather sums up the film.

Boughedir suggests the 1967 war with Israel, President Sadat's visit to Jerusalem in '77, and the war in

Lebanon are events that have unmanned the Arab intellectual as film traces the political themes in recent film production. At the same time, capsule interviews with the major directors show a broad range of thinking on the possibility of putting political messages into films.

Boughedir takes up the cause of Bouzid's controversial "Man Of Ashes," described as the first film to show friendship between an Arab youth and an old Jew. Bouzid himself touches on another sensitive issue when he says each film should push back censorship a bit more.

The thorny problem of financing and distributing an essentially non-commercial cinema is broached, but not delved into at any length. The fact that many of the films presented in "Camera Arabe" have received only limited release in their countries of origin is a difficulty that only shows signs of getting worse, as state money for production tightens and piracy rages.

—*Yung.*

Nuit Docile
(Docile Night)
(FRENCH-COLOR/B&W)

A Sinfonia (Paris) release of Tracol Film production. Written and directed by Guy Gilles. Camera (Eastmancolor, b&w), Jacques Boumendil; editor, Marie-Hélène Quinton; music, Vincent Marie; sound, Michel Flour. Reviewed at Cannes Film Festival (in French Perspectives), May 12, 1987. Running time: **90 MINS.**

Jean	Patrick Jouane
Stella	Claire Nebout
Jeannot	Pascal Kelaf
Madeleine	Françoise Arnoul

Cannes — The "Docile Night" of Guy Gilles' highly artistic, technically brilliant, not very easily accessible new feature film is one of self-realization and quiet learning for a trio of people. It deals with life, love and art. It has endless strings of highfaluting dialog, but also flashes of humor and brilliant imagery. It will hardly travel far beyond the narrowest of art circuits.

Jean, a well-to-do painter, leaves his model/mistress for good, but he criss-crosses Paris from phone booth to phone booth, calling her to talk about his motive for leaving. Sometimes she hangs up on him or she goes to the apartment of a mutual friend, a filmmaker. Jean calls her there, too. The filmmaker also was Jean's lover at one time. All the time, Jean is being stalked by a 16-year-old male prostitute. A kind of philosopher-pupil relationship, and briefly a homosexual one, develops during the nocturnal wanderings between Jean and the boy.

The present is presented in black & white, past events or mental associations in color. The narrative is split up, twisted and turned but eventually hits a more normal main-

stream, where it might have been better off all the time. As a film medium experimenter, Guy Gilles has nothing new to offer, but he works quiet magic with his cinematographer as well as with his actors.

Most of the abundant talk is delivered in a softspoken fashion, stressing its sincerity neatly. There is an awesome amount of literary and artistic name-dropping going on and many a "quote" in cinematic imagery from famous paintings. The gist of the picture's psychological contents seems to be that the painter cannot really love people, since his heart always lies with his art.

In an extended cameo, Françoise Arnoul, a leading lady of French films of the early '50s, displays wit, charm and well-preserved good looks. In the lead, Patrick Jouane has both the blond handsomeness and the famous jawline in common with Jean Marais, and the casting may not be accidental at all. His role is a true Jean Marais role of doomed beauty. — *Kell.*

Hotel du Paradis
(BRITISH-FRENCH-COLOR)

An Umbrella Films-Portman Films production, in association with Film Four Intl., London Trust Prods., Antenne-2. (World sales: Global Distribution, London.) Produced by Simon Perry. Executive producer, Dominique Antoine. Directed by Jana Bokova. Stars Fernando Rey. Screenplay, Bokova; camera (color), Gerard de Battista; editor, Bill Shapter, Yves Deschamps; music, Rodolfo Mederos; artistic advisor, Gualberto Ferrari; production design, Patrick Webel; sound, Bruno Charier; production manager, Dominique Antoine; assistant director, Jean-Luc Oliver. Reviewed at Cannes Film Festival (Information Section), May 11, 1987. Running time: **113 MINS.**

Joseph Goldman	Fernando Rey
Arthur	Fabrice Luchini
Frederique	Berangere Bonvoisin
Maurice	Hugues Quester
Marika	Marika Rivera
Sarah Goldman	Carola Regnier
British producer	Michael Medwin

Also with: Raul Gimenez (Emilio), Georges Geret (Dr. Jacob), Sheila Kotkin (Sheila), Aurelle Doazan (dream girl), Max Berto (Max), Juliet Berto (whore), Sacha Briquet (Georges), Lou Castel (tramp), Pascal Aubier (head waiter).

Cannes — Once in a while along comes a film made with the best of intentions but with no discernible audience; such a film is "Hotel du Paradis," feature debut of Czech emigré Jana Bokova, who carved out a reputation in tv documentaries in Britain before being backed by producer Simon Perry to make this irritatingly self-absorbed exercise.

Pic was shot in Paris in 1985, back-to-back with another Perry production, "Nanou," and has had a troubled postproduction history. It's far more French than British, and seems an odd project for a British producer; doubtless Bokova's reputation was the main motive.

Setting is a small Paris hotel away

from the tourist areas. Like the classic "Grand Hotel"-type pics of the '30s, this one takes a cross-section of characters and explores their lives. They include Fernando Rey as a Jewish actor from Eastern Europe who's trying his luck in a small cafe theater after his Hollywood career has ended; Fabrice Luchini as a wheeler-dealer Frenchman trying to break into films; Berangere Bonvoisin as a woman hiding from the lover she's left; Carola Regnier as Rey's wife; and so on.

Trouble is, none of these are very interesting charcters. They talk a lot, but never say much that's interesting; the dialog is filled with filmic anecdotes, most of them well worn ("Did you know Samuel Goldwyn's name was really Goldfish?"), and none of the characters resolve much during the course of the film. Rey's final line of dialog, the obscene equivalent of "Get lost!" sums it up. —*Strat.*

Un Amour à Paris
(A Romance In Paris)
(FRENCH-COLOR)

A Prods. de la Lune production. Written and directed by Merzak Allouache. Camera (Fujicolor), Jean-Claude Larrieu; sound, Philippe Lioret; art director, Bruno Held; editor, Marie Josée Audiard; music, Jean Marie Senia; production manager, Brigitte Haegeli. Reviewed at the Centre National du Cinéma, Paris, April 28, 1987. (In Perspectives on French Cinema at Cannes Film Festival.) Running time: **83 MINS.**
Ali . . . . Karim Allaoui
Marie . . . . Catherine Wilkening
Benoit . . . . Daniel Cohn Bendit
Justine . . . . Sophie Vigneaud
Monika . . . . Juliet Berto
Also with: Isabelle Weingarten, Xavier Maly, Jim Adhi Lima, Zaira Ben Badis, Attica Guedj, Michel Such, Mostefa Djadjam, Marie de Poncheville, Jean Perimony, Etienne Draber, Muriel Combeau.

Paris — A sympathetic, disarmingly simple Paris love story, "Un Amour à Paris" is the first local picture by Algerian filmmaker Merzak Allouache, who attracted attention with his 1976 debut feature "Omar Gatlato."

Subtitled "Marie Of Algiers, Ali Of Clichy," Allouache's script tells of an Algerian Jewish girl (Catherine Wilkening) who comes to Paris hoping to make a career as a model but takes a romantic detour when she meets Karim Allaoui, a French-born Arab who's just served a prison term for robbery and is making firm plans to get his share of the loot and head for Houston, Texas. He dreams of becoming a "cosmonaut" for NASA.

Tone is romantically seriocomic, with Allouache carefully preparing a downbeat conclusion in which Allaoui is gunned down by police when he arrives at a meeting with a former crony to get his cut of holdup money. Ironically, he is killed as he watches a live tv newscast of the tragic Challenger space launch.

Story's often quirky charm owes much to the personable appeal of newcomer leads Wilkening and Allaoui, who stood out (he's 6-ft., 2-inches) in Roger Hanin's recent thriller "La Rumba." Pair's physical incongruity nicely underlines their out-of-reach dreams.

Supporting performances include a funny cameo from Daniel Cohn Bendit, onetime firebrand ringleader of the May 1968 student uprisings in Paris. Here he plays a friend of Wilkening's who bemoans his resemblance to Daniel Cohn Bendit! —*Len.*

Lucky Ravi
(FRENCH-COLOR)

A Pari-Films release (foreign sales, Films du Volcan) of an Out-One (Paris) production. Directed by Vincent Lombard. Screenplay, Lombard, Richard Matas; camera (color), Pascal Lebegue; sound, Olivier Schwob; editor, Jean-François Naudon; music, Laurent Grangier. Reviewed at Cannes Film Festival (in Perspectives On French Cinema section), May 16, 1987. Running time: **84 MINS.**
Lucky Ravi . . . . Michel Didym
Miss Cote d'Azur . . . . Assumpta Serna
Gino . . . . Rüdiger Vogler
Hotel manager . . . . Jean-Pierre Bisson
Plantation owner . . . . Alain Cuny

Cannes — "Lucky Ravi," a feature film bow for writer-helmer Vincent Lombard, takes itself far more seriously than any audience anywhere is likely to, but some foreign tv sales may come in as a consolation prize.

Picture comes near to having the looks and sounds of a *serie noir* parody, but is delivered too sedately to work as anything but a morose meller with maybe a social significance thematic overtone. Everybody looks and acts in a correspondingly morose way.

In sun-drenched southern Provence, fruitpickers work and sulk. A grim old plantation owner (Alain Cuny) tells his foreman to hire drifters to set fire to a nearby hotel that threatens the old look and way of life of the region.

At the hotel, which has a management staff of mobsters, a clean-cut, lissome beauty queen and her lover are drifting apart, so the woman drinks a lot. She also keeps her elegant cool, while she takes Ravi to bed with her.

Ravi is a handsome but dimwitted young man who would like to please everybody and who gets knocked about for his trouble. He stares while the woman wakes from her sleep to sit up and go into a heavy-breathing masturbation scene.

The hotel fire comes off badly. Ravi shoots the woman's former lover by accident. She then dumps him on the street in Marseilles. Everything is told in badly connected and poorly written sequences, and a lot of clichéd dialog is rendered in sonorous declarations as if it were Greek tragedy performed by present-day thugs. The overall production look is insecure, and the color print has a muddy tone. Young Lucky Ravi's surname indicates he is ravishing, but the dish he (Michel Didym looking lost most of the time) is served up in is yesterday's ravioli. —*Kell.*

Andjeo Cuvar
(Guardian Angel)
(YUGOSLAVIAN-COLOR)

A Singidinum-Jugoart/Morava Film presentation (foreign sales, Jugoslavlia Films.) Produced, written and directed by Goran Paskaljevic. Camera (color), Milan Spasic; editor, Olga Skrigin, Olga Obradov; music, Zoran Simjanovic. Reviewed at Cannes Film Festival (in Directors Fortnight section), May 14, 1987. Running time: **88 MINS.**
Dragan . . . . Ljubisa Samardzic
Mila . . . . Neda Arneric
Chayine . . . . Jakup Amzic
Chayine's father . . . . Saban Bajramovic
Also with: Esmeralda Ametovic (child prostitute), Mejaz-Majo Pasic (cigaret boy), Trajko Demirovic (Moussa), Rade Dervisevic, Trajko Saitovic, Gordana Jovanovic.

Cannes — The traffic in gypsy children between Yugoslavia and Italy (and other European countries) is a little-publicized scandal that Goran Paskaljevic's "Guardian Angel" seeks to tackle directly. Though it sometimes veers perilously close to becoming an exposé-type docu, in the end film finds a moving, poetic tone that keeps it firmly on this side of fiction. The drama — unfortunately all too true of kidnaped, battered, exploited kids — makes for a gripping tale without an easy, happy ending. It's a natural pickup for art house trade.

The racket of gypsy bosses selling children to be beggars and thieves in Europe is being investigated by Dragan (Ljubisa Samardzic), a kindly reporter fond of both kids and gypsies. He tries talking to a group of youngsters who have run away from their bosses in Italy, but they're reticent and scared, especially Chayine (Jakup Amzic), who has whip marks on his back. Social worker Neda Arneric puts them on a train for their home villages, but they're caught by the racketeers before they finish the trip.

Next Dragan visits a poor gypsy village, where he picks up Chayine's trail. He finds the boy in Venice, under the heel of a vicious gangster. It takes a while for Dragan to win the boy's confidence, but eventually — after a horrifying torture sequence — he convinces him to go back to Yugoslavia. Here, good intentions aren't enough, however. When Chayine learns his mother is dead, he voluntarily sells himself to the local child merchant, to help feed his sisters and crippled brother. Dragan realizes too late he's gone too far, and is killed in the middle of a village celebration.

The child cast is top-flight, while Samardzic adds just the right note as the well-meaning outsider who imagines he's invincible and doesn't heed the social worker's warning that one man alone can do nothing. Film's viewpoint on gypsy life and culture is more tolerant than most, though the way the kids are treated can only be called sickening, and the squalor and filth of the camps is equally offputting.

Lensing is finely expressive, with high points of true visual poetry. Zoran Simjanovic's score is a melancholy refrain. —*Yung.*

Az otlsó kézirat
(The Last Manuscript)
(HUNGARIAN-COLOR)

A Hungarofilm presentation of a Mafilm-Studio Dialog Budapest production. Directed by Károly Makk. Screenplay, Makk, Zoltán Kámody, based on "A Funny Funeral" by Tibor Déry; camera (Eastmancolor), János Tóth; editor, György Sivó; music, László Vidovsky; sound, János Réti; art director, Tamás Vayer; costumes, Emöke Csengey. Reviewed at Cannes Film Festival (In competition), May 15, 1987. Running time: **110 MINS.**
The writer . . . . Jozef Kroner
Relli . . . . Alexander Barbini
Vica . . . . Irén Psota
Emilia . . . . Hédi Váradi
Franz . . . . Béla Both
Flora . . . . Flóra Nagy-Kálózi

Cannes — Veteran Hungarian filmmaker Károly Makk should have concluded this film with his opening scene, for it is certainly the most impressive achievement here: a brilliantly sarcastic sequence of a grand national funeral which reaches grotesque proportions when the corpse walks out of his coffin and steps into his own grave, while everybody else is in a state of complete panic. This kind of opening is indeed very hard to top, and the rest of the picture, much more staid and conventional, is a letdown.

The story, based on a popular Hungarian novel, concerns the last days in the life of a famous writer. He is fully conscious of his terminal condition, and so are his friends and family, each interested only in those specific aspects of the impending tragedy that will concern him personally. The one subject which worries them all is the rumor that a certain manuscript, written by the dying man in secret, reveals unknown details from his past which he has never told anyone.

Nobody likes the idea of such a document reaching a wide audience, for in his long life, the writer has witnessed and suffered from political and social injustices aplenty. Since some of those responsible for his miseries still are close to him, the idea of being crucified by the posthumous document doesn't appeal to them.

The satirical aspects of the script are combined with the tragic progress of the disease and with a last romantic fling, when a young and pretty violinist cancels all her previous commitments in order to return to Hungary to visit him. The literary origins of the material are obvious in the abundant dialogs, which Makk treats in a straightforward, conventional and often repetitive manner.

Alexander Barbini, as the friend of the writer who desperately tries to keep up appearances of friendship while trying to lay his hands on the mysterious manuscript, offers the best performance of the movie, but Jozef Kroner, as the writer, Irén Psota as his wife and Flóra Nagy-Kálózi as the young violinist offer valuable contributions. The film however, could stand some extensive pruning to give it more of an impact.

Camera, sets, costumes and editing are all brilliantly employed in the first sequence and while there is no complaint about their standards later on, there is no similar challenge they have to meet for the rest of the picture. And that, of course, is the wrong way to reach a dramatic climax. —*Edna.*

Yam Daabo
(The Choice)
(BURKINA FASO-COLOR)

A Les Films de l'Avenir production. Written and directed by Idrissa Quedraogo. Camera (16m, color), Jean Monsigny, Sekou Quedraogo, Issaka Thiombiano; editor, Arnaud Blin; music, Francis Bebey; sound, Issa Traore. Reviewed at Cannes Film Festival (Intl. Critics Week), May 11, 1987. Running time: **80 MINS.**
With: Aoua Guiraud, Moussa Bologo, Assita Quedraogo, Fatimata Quedraogo, Oumarou Quedraogo, Rasmané Quedraogo,
Salif Quedraogo, Màdi Sana, Ousmane Sawadogo.

Cannes — Feature film debut by Idrissa Quedraogo, a multi-prized documentarist ("Issa The Weaver") from Burkina Faso, is a gentle, sensitive protrait of life in the bush. It is still too close to ethnographic documentary to have much power as fictional storytelling, and one waits for the director's talents to expand with a more intriguing tale.

In the parched brown landscape of the drought-ridden north, a family of farmers (old mother and father, youthful daughter Bintou and her beau Salam, and little Ali) decides to migrate to the more verdant south. Passing through a city, where they sell their donkey, Ali is hit by a car and killed in an eloquently understated scene.

But life goes on. In their new location, the family meets old friends and makes an enemy of a malicious, half-crazy layabout, who sets his sights on Bintou. She repulses him and gets pregnant by Salam, causing problems with her father. A boy who left for the city comes back, to the joy of all, especially the girl he left behind. Love triumphs for both couples, and Bintou and Salam's baby is born.

This simple story of love, pain and joy begins in an arid wasteland of skeletal dead trees and ends in a green, earthly paradise. It is illuminated by its optimism and tenderness for the life it depicts. The technical handicaps that plague African cinema (film was shot in 16m and blown up to 35m; actors are non-pros) are incorporated into Quedraogo's documentary approach and present less of a problem than in more scripted films. All is given a seductive rhythm with Francis Bebey's score. —*Yung.*

Cannes Market Selections

Five Corners
(U.K.-BRITISH-COLOR)

A Cineplex Odeon Films release (U.S.-Canada) of a Handmade Films presentation. Produced by Forrest Murray, Tony Bill. Executive producers, George Harrison, Denis O'Brien. Directed by Bill. Screenplay, John Patrick Shanley; camera (color), Fred Murphy; editor, Andy Blumenthal; music, James Newton Howard; production design, Adrianne Lobel; sound, Bill Daly; costumes, Peggy Farrell; assistant director, Joel Segal; associate producers, Michael McDonnell, Shanely; casting, Doug Aibel. Reviewed at Cannes Film Festival (market), May 13, 1987. (MPAA Rating: R.) Running time: **92 MINS.**
Linda ....Jodie Foster
Harry.....................Tim Robbins
James....................Todd Graff
Heinz ....John Turturro
Melanie ....Elizabeth Berridge
Mrs. Sabantino ....Rose Gregorio
Mazola ....Gregory Rozakis
Sullivan ....John Seitz
Mrs. Fitzgerald ....Kathleen Chalfant

Cannes — "Five Corners" starts out as an affectionate look back at a Bronx neighborhood circa 1964 and then about halfway through takes a darker turn into urban violence. But the script has such a strong hold on its characters and the ensemble cast realizes them so effectively that the film never totally loses its way. Pic is an above average piece of work that could find its way to a selective audience.

Although the ethnic flavors of urban life have been covered extensively in film in recent years, "Five
Corners" proves it's still fertile ground for the right writer. In his first produced script, Shanley clearly has drawn from his experience to create the variety of personalities and swirl of influences that make life in the boroughs of New York City so distinctive.

And it is no accident that Shanley chose 1964 for his story for it was then that the social upheaval known as the '60s was about to touch even the five corners of the Bronx. When Harry (Tim Robbins), a would-be freedom fighter in Mississippi, listens to "The Times They Are A Changin'" on his tinny mono phonograph, one can almost feel the rush of excitement that song once brought with it.

But before he goes off to save the world, there is business for him to take care of in the old neighborhood. Local no-goodnik Heinz (John Turturro) is out of jail and looking to renew his old battle with Harry and his old longing for Linda (Jodie Foster).

Also drawn into this tangled urban web is Linda's boyfriend James (Todd Graff) who now limps for life thanks to his latest encounter with Heinz. Other residents of the neighborhood, first seemingly unrelated, gradually touch on the central action like ripples in a pond.

Revenge and retribution story takes its sweet time to unfold and almost seems a contrivance to allow the characters to play out their parts. But they are marvelously drawn parts and Robbins as the Irish working class kid with a social conscience gets into the heart and soul of the character. Turturro is downright scary but also sympathetic as the schoolyard psychotic.

Also excellent is Graff as the wounded lover who delivers many of the film's best lines with a manic glee. Foster is serviceable, but a little out of her element as a tough Catholic kid. Supporting players add to the neighborhood flavor with Kathleen Chalfant especially impressive as Harry's mother, in a role that for once makes a parent an actual thinking and feeling person.

Credit must also go to director Tony Bill for assembling his cast of relative unknowns and keeping the characters honest even when the story starts to fudge.

Tech credits are first rate and Adrianne Lobel's production design and Fred Murphy's camerawork contribute to the neighborhood atmosphere without making it feel like it was store-bought. —*Jagr.*

Les Exploits d'un jeune Don Juan
(The Exploits Of A Young Don Juan)
(FRENCH-ITALIAN-COLOR)

AAA release of an Orphée Arts/Séléna Audiovisual/Films Ariane/Lagonda Films/Antea (Rome) coproduction. Executive producer, Nicolas Duval. Produced by Claire Duval. Directed by Gianfranco Mingozzi. Screenplay, Jean-Claude Carrière, Peter Fleischmann, from the novel by Guillaume Apollinaire; camera (Agfa-Gevaert color), Luigi Verga; art director, Jacques Saulnier; editor, Alfredo Muschietto; sound, Jean-Pierre Delorme, Lucien Yvonnet; music, Nicola Piovani; costumes, Yvonne Sassinot de Nesle; makeup, Marc Blanchard; assistant director, Jean Léon. Reviewed at the Georges V cinema, Paris, April 14, 1987. (In market at Cannes Film Festival.) Running time: **95 MINS.**
The Mother ....Claudine Auger
Ursule ....Serena Grandi
Madam Muller ....Marina Vlady
Roger ....Fabrice Josso
The Father ....François Perrot
Aunt Marguerite.....Bérangère Bonvoisin
The monk ....Rufus
Mr. Frank ....Laurent Spielvogel
Hélène ....Rosette
Elisa ....Alexandra Vandernoot
Kate.................Marion Peterson
Berthe ....Virginie Ledoyen
Roland ....Yves Lambrecht
Adolphe ....Aurélien Recoing

Paris — Less of a snooze than most softcore erotic items, "Exploits Of A Young Don Juan" brings some finesse and humor to this adaptation, by screenwriter Jean-Claude Carrière and Peter Fleischmann, of a libertine novel by the poet Guillaume Apollinaire.

Tale is classic one of a young boy's sexual initiation, which Apollinaire set in a country chateau during the summer of 1914, when Europe was strolling nonchalantly towards war.

Roger (Fabrice Josso) is the 16-year-old son of a maimed and impotent arms industrialist (François Perrot) and a stuffy but still attractive Claudine Auger, who stoically takes part in her mate's vicarious sexual fantasies.

Still a virgin but anxious to do something about it that summer in the family's country home, Roger is tantalized by the abundance of alluring female flesh lolling about in the sensuous atmosphere. His initial attempts to get up his first skirt are clumsy and unfruitful.

War is declared however, and the menfolk march off to the slaughter, leaving young Josse every opportunity to prove his sexual prowess. He beds, and impregnates, not only the buxom maid (Italy's Serena Grandi), but his aunt and even his sister. Expending his desires, Josso busies himself trying to marry the women off to cover up his deeds and preserve social appearances.

Italo director Gianfranco Mingozzi treats the amoral hanky-panky with a good-humored zest and a modicum of style, though more demanding fans of erotica probably will be dissappointed by film's well-behaved suggestiveness.

This Franco-Italian coprod has assembled a reputable cast that doesn't give the impression of marking time while waiting for the paycheck, and high-caliber tech collaborators such as composer Nicola Piovani, art director Jacques Saulnier and costume designer Yvonne Sassinot de Nesle. —Len.

Enemy Territory
(U.S.-COLOR)

An Empire Pictures release of a Millennial production. Produced by Cynthia DePaula, Tim Kincaid. Executive producer, Charles Band. Directed by Peter Manoogian. Screenplay, Stuart M. Kaminsky, Bobby Liddell, from Kaminsky's story; camera (Precision color), Ernest Dickerson; editor, Peter Teschner; music, Sam Winans, Richard Koz Kosinaki; sound (Ultra-Stereo), Mik Cribben; visual consultant, Ruth Lounsbury; production design, Medusa Studios, Marina Zurkow; art direction, Joanne Besinger; assistant director, Michael Speero; production manager, Joe Derrig; special makeup effects supervisor, John Bisson; stunt coordinator, Dave Copeland, pyrotechnic special effects, Matt Vogel; second unit camera, Robert Ebinger; casting, Judy Henderson, Alycia Amuller, Anthony Barnao; associate producer, Hope Perello. Reviewed at Cannes Film Festival (market), May 14, 1987. (MPAA Rating: R.) Running time: **90 MINS.**
Barry . . . . .Gary Frank
Jackson . . . . Ray Parker Jr.
Parker . . . . .Jan-Michael Vincent
Elva Briggs . . . . .Frances Foster
The Count . . . . .Tony Todd
Toni Briggs . . . . .Stacey Dash
Chet . . . . .Deon Richmond
Barton. . . . . .Tiger Haynes
Mr. Beckhorne . . . . .Charles Randall

Cannes — Though it deals in the down-to-Earth subject of urban violence, Empire's "Enemy Territory" is a very commercial picture which is far-fetched enough to almost qualify for the fantasy genre with which Charles Band's company is normally associated. Violent pic benefits considerably from a very effective film starring Ray Parker Jr.

As its title suggests, pic's plotline is another variant on the surefire "behind enemy lines" structure previously used for Walter Hill's gang trailblazer "The Warriors." Gary Frank portrays a meek young insurance agent sent after hours by his unscrupulous superior (Charles Randall) to a ghetto project apartment house to get Frances Foster to sign and pay for her $100,000 insurance policy. Alimony-ridden and not closing many clients lately, Frank is desperate for the commission and even agrees to giving Randall a big kickback on the deal.

A young white man and naive in the extreme, Frank immediately incurs the wrath of a young black in the project hallway. While Frank is getting Foster to sign and receiving her $6,000 premium in cold cash, the youth fetches his building gang,

the Vampires, and all hell breaks loose. After the Vampires shoot down the black security guard who tries to protect the helpless Frank, a good samaritan telephone company workman (Ray Parker Jr.) takes Frank under his wing. The rest of the picture is their extremely tense attempt to survive until daybreak as the entire building is under siege by the Vampires.

Director Peter Manoogian executes many a vivid action scene, utilizing the claustrophobic premise to harrowing advantage. Pic's main drawback is that despite the physical realism of the production, lensed in New York City, the script relies upon far too many lucky breaks and narrow escapes for the heroes to be believable. Target audience has to suspend all disbelief and then wallow in the carefully justified ultraviolence.

Gary Frank is terrific as the white man placed in an untenable situation and thoroughly unprepared to cope; his transition to bloodthirsty survivalist is very well-handled. Ray Parker Jr. exudes personality, acts well, and wins and maintains audience sympathy with ease; after this baptism he is clearly ready for the big time on screen (already having scored a bullseye as the "Ghostbusters" theme singer).

In support, Jan-Michael Vincent has a brief but showy role as an embittered Vietnam War vet in a wheelchair waging his own war in the building, while Tony Todd is frightening as the nihilistic leader of the gang. As the old lady who definitely needs that big insurance policy, Frances Foster is solid, getting big laughs when she takes over Vincent's machinegun post. Stacey Dash is very sexy (resembling Rae Dawn Chong) and adept at physical action as Foster's resourceful niece. Tech credits are proficient.—Lor.

Vincent — The Life And Death Of Vincent Van Gogh
(AUSTRALIAN-DUTCH-COLOR)

A Roadshow (Australian) release of an Illumination Films/Look Films/Ozfilms (Australia)/Dasha Films (Netherlands) coproduction. (Foreign sales: Seawell Films, Paris). Produced by Tony Llewellyn-Jones. Directed by Paul Cox. Screenplay, Cox, based on the letters of Vincent Van Gogh; camera (Fujicolor), editor, Cox; music, Vivaldi, Rossini, Norman Kaye; production design, Neil Angwin; costumes, Jennie Tate, Beverly Boyd; sound, Jim Currie; additional paintings and drawings, Asher Bilou, Bill Kelly; coproducer, Will Davies. Reviewed at Cannes Film Festival (market), May 11, 1987. Running time: **103 MINS.**
Voice of Vincent . . . . .John Hurt

Cannes — This very special art film is neither documentary nor fiction. Paul Cox, one of Australia's foremost directors, was born in Holland and has made an exquisite,

timeless tribute to Vincent Van Gogh using as his text simply the letters Vincent wrote to his brother Theo, letters beautifully read by John Hurt.

Van Gogh worked as a painter for only 10 years, and during that period produced about 1,800 works, but when he killed himself at 37 in 1890 he had only sold one of them, and was unknown and impoverished. Cox' film covers those last 10 years, but "Vincent" is in no way comparable to Vincente Minnelli's Van Gogh film, "Lust For Life," in which Kirk Douglas portrayed the artist. Save for one brief moment at the end, when Van Gogh's funeral is depicted, the central character of the drama is never seen, but his thoughts and philosophies are enunciated superbly on the soundtrack.

The letters begin when Van Gogh is studying for the priesthood, but describe his gradual obsession to work as an artist.

With these wonderful letters as a starting point, Cox traveled to the places Van Gogh knew, lived and worked; to the meadows of Holland, the Borinage, the Midi, Arles and so on. The images accompanying the text are of trees and fields and birds in flight, and the inevitable sunflowers. And, of course, there are the paintings themselves.

More controversial is Cox' characteristic use of hand-held, grainy footage (shot on 8m) which crops up from time to time, and his decision to recreate some scenes with actors. These are sometimes charming, but sometimes (notably in a scene in a Paris bar involving a voluminous chanteuse) redundant. The depiction of the painter's suicide, via a first-person camera, is chillingly effective.

As always in a Cox film, there's an intelligent use of music (by Vivaldi, Rossini and others) and an intelligent sensibility at work. One feels Cox identifies strongly with his subject's uncompromising philosophies.

There will be debates about the director's handling of the subject, but "Vincent" will be a film with a long life, and though theatrical possibilities will be limited, it will be much in demand by schools, colleges and art lovers in years to come.—Strat.

Warm Nights On A Slow Moving Train
(AUSTRALIAN-COLOR)

A Filmpac Holdings release (in Australia) of a Western Pacific Films presentation of a Ross Dimsey production. Executive producers, William T. Marshall, Peter Sherman, Robert Ward. Produced by Dimsey, Patric Juillet. Directed by Bob Ellis. Stars Wendy Hughes. Screenplay, Ellis, Denny Lawrence;

camera (color), Yuri Sokol; editor, Tim Lewis; music, Peter Sullivan; production design, Tracy Watt; costumes, Alexandra Tynan; sound, Gary Wilkins; production manager, Darryl Sheen; assistant director, Robert Kewley; casting, Liz Mullinar. Reviewed at Cannes Film Festival (market), May 10, 1987. Running time: **91 MINS.**
The Girl . . . . .Wendy Hughes
The Man . . . . .Colin Friels
The Salesman . . . . .Norman Kaye
The Football Coach . . . . .John Clayton
The Soldier . . . . .Rod Zuanic
The Brother . . . . .Lewis Fitz-gerald
The Singer . . . . .Steve J. Spears
The Politician . . . . .Grant Tilly
The Steward . . . . .Peter Whitford
Also with: Chris Haywood (stationmaster), John Flaus (taxi driver), Peter Carmody (second-class passenger).

Cannes — This upperclass drama, toplining Wendy Hughes as a prostie who solicits for high-class trade weekends on an overnight train plying between Sydney and Melbourne, has an intriguing premise, frequently witting script, adroit direction and a gallery of excellent actors. Despite its theme, it's not an erotic film (there's no nudity), but the intelligent viewer should be intrigued by the situation and the way it develops. Also, it showcases Hughes in one of her best screen performances.

She plays the unnamed protagonist who, via a special deal with gay train steward Peter Whitford, has access to the July Garland Suite reserved for visiting celebrities who don't like flying. Each Saturday, she travels to Syndey, returning home next day. A chameleon-type character, she changes her appearance and style according to her prospective clients, not telling them she'll want money from them until it's too late for them to change their minds.

Among her clients are a football coach (John Clayton) planning to write a Dostoevskian novel; a retired salesman (Norman Kaye) who's found God; a lonely young soldier (Rod Zuanic); and a burly amateur singer (Steve J. Spears). For each, Hughes comes up with a different story: to the coach, she's a schoolteacher, to the soldier, a private secretary, to the salesman, a nurse; and she wears different wigs and dresses each time.

The truth, as we gradually discover, is that she is all these things; she teaches art at a Catholic school and cares for her brother (Lewis Fitz-gerald), a former Olympic sprinter crippled from a car crash and hooked on morphine; her weekend work pays for his habit.

The pattern changes when she meets a handsome stranger (Colin Friels) who takes her without paying. She falls heavily in love, and reluctantly agrees to assist him in the assassination of a politician scheduled to travel on the train. This takes a bit of believing, given what we know about the Hughes character thus far, but it just about works. Fact that the politician is played by New Zealand actor Grant Tilly, who looks somewhat like the current N.Z. prime minister, will have audiences pondering.

Director Bob Ellis, helming his second pic after the successful low-budget item "Unfinished Business," originally planned a much longer version of the film: 35-40 minutes have been cut from the version he wanted. Those who've seen both versions assert the longer one, which allowed more time for each character to be established, had more humor. In any event, the release version moves very briskly.

On the basis of this version, at least, pic should do good business in Australia thanks to its strong cast and classy look. It's worth a look by overseas distribs, too. Pic is technically up to the usual high standard, with fine photography from Yuri Sokol, intelligent production design by Tracy Watt, and lively music from Peter Sullivan. Editor Tom Lewis has done a commendable job under the circumstances.
—*Strat.*

China Girl
(U.S.-COLOR)

A Vestron Pictures release in association with Great American Films of a Street Lite production. (World sales, Interaccess Film Distribution.) Executive producers, Mitchell Cannold, Steven Reuther. Produced by Michael Nozik. Directed by Abel Ferrara. Screenplay, Nicholas St. John; camera (Du-art color), Bojan Bazelli; editor, Anthony Redman; music, Joe Delia; sound (Dolby), Petur Hliddal; production design, Dan Leigh; set decoration, Leslie Rollins; costume design, Richard Hornung; assistant director, Louis D'Esposito; production manager, Mary Kane; casting, Marcia Shulman; associate producer, Kane. Reviewed at Cannes Film Festival (market), May 14, 1987. (MPAA Rating: R.) Running time: **88 MINS.**
Alby . . . . James Russo
Tye . . . . Sari Chang
Tony . . . . Richard Panebianco
Mercury . . . . David Caruso
Yung . . . . Russell Wong
Su Shin . . . . Joey Chin
Gung Tu . . . . James Hong
Mother . . . . Judith Melina

Cannes — "China Girl" is a masterfully directed, uncompromising drama and romance centering on gang rumbles (imaginary) between the neighboring Chinatown and Little Italy communities in New York City. Unspooled in the Cannes market but obviously worthy of official or sidebar slotting in the fest, extremely violent picture will need and stands a good chance of receiving critical approval to attract discerning audiences.

Nicholas St. John's screenplay hypothesizes an outbreak of a gang war when a Chinese restaurant opens in Italian territory (in reality, the current gang wars are strictly internecine between Chinese factions). In the midst of the battling,

a beautiful Chinese teenager (Sari Chang) falls in love with a pizza parlor gofer (Richard Panebianco). A la "West Side Story" and its source "Romeo And Juliet," the adults oppose the relationship and, more to the point, the Mafia dons and Chinese elder gangsters are in cahoots to maintain peace in their bordered territory, waiting to clamp down violently on both sets of youth gangs.

Director Abel Ferrara adopts a *film noir* visual style (lots of back-lighting, wet streets at night and looming shadowplay) and it comes as no surprise that the pic builds to a tragic (and currently unfashionable) ending. He exacts potent thesping from the entire cast (several of the supporting players previously seen in Michael Cimino's "Year Of The Dragon"), with showy turns by James Russo as the hero's older brother and David Caruso as a hothead (given some of the film's funniest lines).

Russell Wong (as handsome as a shirt ad model) and sidekick Joey Chin dominate their scenes as the young Chinese gang leaders, while newcomer Panebianco is a forceful and charismatic young find. Title roler Sari Chang is called upon merely to be an idealized porcelain beauty and she fills the bill.

Ferrara, recently gaining notice as helmer of the pilot show for tv's "Crime Story" after such features as "Ms. 45" and "Fear City," creates remarkably vivid violent scenes, yet some of the picture's best work is in romantic interludes on the dancefloor of downtown clubs or a classic setpiece of grief and rage set in a funeral parlor. Joe Delia's musical score plus some vibrant rock songs punch along the action insidiously. —*Lor.*

Hellraiser
(BRITISH-COLOR)

A New World Pictures release, in association with Cinemarque Entertainment of a Film Futuras production. Executive producers, Christopher Webster, Mark Armstrong, David Saunders. Produced by Christopher Figg. Written and directed by Clive Barker, based on his novel "The Hellbound Heart." Camera (Technicolor), David Worley; music, Christopher Young; sound (Dolby), John Midgely; assistant director, Selwyn Roberts; art direction, Jocelyn James; stunt arranger, Jim Dowdall. Reviewed at Cannes Film Festival (market), May 13, 1987, (No MPAA Rating). Running time: **90 MINS.**
Larry Cotton . . . . Andrew Robinson
Julia Cotton . . . . Clare Higgins
Kirsty . . . . Ashley Laurence
Frank Cotton . . . . Sean Chapman
Frank the monster . . . . Oliver Smith
Steve . . . . Robert Hines
Also with: Antony Allen, Leon Davis, Michael Cassidy, Frank Baker, Kenneth Nelson, Gay Barnes, Niall Buggy.

Cannes — "Hellraiser" is a well-paced sci-fi cum horror fantasy which should appeal to a wide youth

audience around the globe. Though there's little new here within the horror genre and the makeup effects occasionally look rather rubbery, item has several twists for the devotees of gore to delight in. Pic is well made, well acted, and the visual effects are generally handled with skill.

Film concerns a dissipated adventurer who somewhere in the Orient buys a sort of magic music box which is capable of providing its owner hitherto undreamt of pains and pleasures, and which ultimately causes him to be torn to shreds in a temple which transforms itself into a torture chamber.

Back home, his brother has just moved into a rickety old house with his new wife or girlfriend; digs had formerly been the dwelling of the ill-fated adventurer. Latter returns, by rising through the floorboards, partly decomposed, seeking human flesh and blood which, when devoured, will enable him to regain his human form. To attain this, he uses his sister-in-law, who also happens to have been his ex-lover. She lures men up to an empty room and dispatches them with a hammer. After a while, the brother's daughter gets wind of the queer goings-on, and she nearly becomes the new victim of the terror, as she grapples with the skinless uncle, the magic box, and the city never looked less attractive. The monsters and the uncle (who has meantime killed her father) pursue her, but she manages to make her escape at the end, after countless gallons of blood and ooze have been spilled.

The horror and violence should be a come-on in most theatrical markets, but could prove a handicap where such fare is prohibited. Pic is also rather strong for tv including, as it does, beside the anatomical horror effects, several fornication scenes. On the whole, red-blooded youth and audiences with a taste for horror pics should lap up this item with relish.—*Besa.*

Shadows Of The Peacock
(AUSTRALIAN-COLOR)

A Laughing Kookaburra production, in association with Australian European Finance Corp. Executive producer, Jan Sharp. Produced by Jane Scott. Directed by Phillip Noyce. Stars Wendy Hughes, John Lone. Screenplay, Jan Sharp (additional material, Anne Brooksbank); camera (color), Peter James; editor, Franz Vandenburg; music, William Motzing; production design, Judith Russell; costumes, Clarissa Patterson; sound, Tim Lloyd; production manager, Antonia Barnard; assistant director, Chris Webb; casting, Liz Mullinar. Reviewed at Cannes Film Festival (market), May 11, 1987. Running time: **90 MINS.**
Maria McEvoy . . . . Wendy Hughes
Raka . . . . John Lone
George McEvoy . . . . Steven Jacobs
Judy . . . . Peta Toppano
Terry . . . . Rod Mullinar

Mitty . . . . Gillian Jones
Julia McEvoy . . . . Claudia Karvan
Also with: Rebecca Smart (Tessa), Matthew Taylor (Simon), Vithawat Bunnag (Sali), Prasert (Kasem), Lynda Stoner (Beth Mason), Ray Harding (Paul Mason), Penny Stehli (Mrs. Evans), Dibbs Mather (Rev. Whitely), Don Pascoe (Senator Blayney), Jan Boreham (Nun), Ruth Caro (Nurse), Marjorie Child (Maria's mother).

Cannes — After a six-year absence from feature films, director Phillip Noyce ("Newsfront," "Heatwave") returns with a well made, high-toned soaper about a Australian wife who has a love affair with a Balinese dancer she meets while holidaying in Thailand. Toplining one of Australia's finest actresses, Wendy Hughes, and John Lone (pic was made just before the latter started work on Bertolucci's "The Last Emperor"), pic should spark lots of interest and do wonders for tourism in Thailand.

Ironically, pic was originally, and far more logically, to have been set in Bali, but just four days before production commenced, the Indonesian government, miffed by an article in a Sydney newspaper, canceled all visas for Australians; pic was hurriedly relocated, and it's much to the credit of the production team that the resulting pic shows few signs of the troubles it encountered.

Opening and closing scenes are set in Sydney in winter, lashed by rain and wind, and the city never looked less attractive. Hughes plays Maria, married to philandering lawyer Steven Jacobs, and distressed by the death of her beloved father. When she discovers her husband's infidelities, her anguish mounts. A woman friend suggests she come along on a holiday to a Thai beach resort run by a sexually ambiguous Aussie expatriate (neatly played by Rod Mullinar), and there she meets Raka (Lone), himself an exile from his native Bali. Before long, Maria is in love with the handsome, esthetic dancer.

Pic can best be compared to David Lean's "Summertime," also about a frustrated woman holidaying in an exotic place who falls for a handsome local. As per usual, Wendy Hughes gives a performance of great sensitivity and depth; opening scenes, of her father's death in the hospital, his funeral, and her discovery of her husband's secret girlfriend, are beautifully handled by all concerned. The Thai scenes, shot in Phuket and adroitly interpolated with studio sets in Australia (top marks to production designer Judith Russell) also look good, thanks to Peter James' camerawork.

Pic is not totally satisfactory, however. Jan Sharp's screenplay, with additional material by Anne Brooksbank, tends towards the predictable but, more crucially, John Lone never really convinces as a passionate lover. He certainly looks the part, and scenes in which he performs a traditional Balinese dance are delightful, but the sparks, which should be there in the love scenes, aren't. In contrast, Steven Jacobs is convincingly sleazy as Hughes' wayward spouse. There are also some curious ambiguities, especially in the Rod Mullinar character, which are hinted but never spelt out, let alone resolved.

Technically, pic is fine, with tight editing (Franz Vandenburg) and a charming music score (William Motzing). In the old days, this would have been dubbed "a womans's pic" and, with skillful marketing, should find an audience on its names and its exotic locale. Production was hitherto known as both "Promises To Keep" and "Love On A Tourist Visa."—*Strat.*

Body Slam
(U.S.-COLOR)

A De Laurentiis Entertainment Group release of a Hemdale presentation of a Musifilm production. Produced by Shel Lytton, Mike Curb. Directed by Hal Needham. Stars Dirk Benedict, Tanya Roberts. Screenplay, Lytton, Steve Burkow, from story by Lytton; camera (CFI color), Mike Shea; editor, Randy Thornton; music, Michael Lloyd, John D'Andrea; sound (Ultra-Stereo), Michael Evje, James McCann; art direction, Pamela Warner; production manager, Mary Eilts; assistant director, Tom Connolly; rock & wrestling consultant, David Wolff; coproducer, Graham Henderson. Reviewed at Cannes Film Festival (market), May 10, 1987. (No MPAA Rating.) Running time: **89 MINS.**

Harry Smilac	Dirk Benedict
Candace Van Der Vegen	Tanya Roberts
Rick Roberts	Roddy Piper
Capt. Lou Milano	Capt. Lou Albano
Sheldon	Barry Gordon
Vic Carson	Charles Nelson Reilly
Tim McClusky	Billy Barty
Scotty	John Astin
Mrs. Van Der Vegen	Dani Janssen
Tonga Tom	Sam (Tama) Fatu
Elmo	Dennis Fimple

Cannes — "Body Slam" is a pleasant surprise, a genuinely funny film that pokes fun at a scheming record industry manager while utilizing popular wrestlers to capture the spirit of the current pro wrestling renaissance.

Dirk Benedict is terrific as a glad-handing promotor, always one step ahead of the repo man. His music career failing, he lucks into managing a wrestler, Quick Rick Roberts (played by popular pro Rowdy Roddy Piper), and though creating a war with traditional managers quickly achieves success in this new field. Forced to book his rock group set in tandem with the wrestlers, he accidently creates the rock 'n' wrestling craze.

Simple premise works because there is a load of humorous situations and slapstick, while the emphasis upon wrestling is not over-powering. As a result, pic's entertainment quotient is not limited to wrestling freaks. Conversely, the presence of an ecumenical grouping of wrestlers drawn from the various pro leagues is a treat for enthusiasts.

Besides Benedict, who exudes charm as the unscrupulous guy you can't resist, cast benefits from solid support turns by various comedians. In addition, Piper, who has retired from wrestling to pursue an acting career full time, is very sympathetic in a large role. Virtually parodying his larger-than-life manager persona, Capt. Lou Albano is very funny as Piper's irate former mentor. Sam Fatu, who wrestles under the name Tama, makes a good impression as Piper's tag team partner, while there are numerous other grapplers on display, including cameos by Ric Flair, Bruno Sammartino, the Samoans Afa & Sika, Freddie Blassie and Sheik Adnan Al Kaissy.

As Benedict's rock group, Kick shares the spotlight performing several okay musical numbers. David Wolff, who with Albano and his client Cyndi Lauper launched the rock 'n' wrestling connection three years ago, served as a consultant on the picture.

"Body Slam" marks a solid comeback for director Hal Needham, who gets the comedy timing down right and provides some effective stunts which keep the wrestling footage from merely regurgitating what is shown constantly on tv. Tech credits are pro. —*Lor.*

White Of The Eye
(BRITISH-COLOR)

A Cannon Group release of an Elliott Kastner presentation in association with Cannon Screen Entertainment of a Mrs. Whites production. Produced by Cassian Elwes, Brad Wyman. Directed by Donald Cammell. Stars David Keith, Cathy Moriarty. Screenplay, Donald Cammell, China Cammell, from novel "Mrs. White" by Margaret Tracy; camera (Consolidated color; Technicolor prints), Alan Jones, Larry McConkey; editor, Terry Rawlings; music, Nick Mason, Rick Fenn; music supervision, George Fenton; sound, Bruce Litecky; production manager, Sue Baden-Powell; assistant director, Andrew Z. Davis; special effects, Thomas Ford; stunt coordinator, Dan Bradley; associate producers, Baden-Powell, Vicki Taft; casting, Pamela Rack. Reviewed at Cannes Film Festival (market), May 9, 1987. (MPAA Rating: R.) Running time: **110 MINS.**

Paul White	David Keith
Joan White	Cathy Moriarty
Charles Mendoza	Art Evans
Mike	Alan Rosenberg
Ann Mason	Alberta Watson
Phil	Michael Greene

Also with: Mark Hayashi, William Schilling, David Chow, Danielle Smith, China Cammell.

Cannes — Notable for marking the screen return of filmmaker Donald Cammell (a decade after "Demon Seed") and actress Cathy Moriarty, "White Of The Eye" is an intriguing thriller that almost qualifies as a sleeper. Unfortunately, Cammell piles on the fancy editing and ostentatious camerawork to a fare-thee-well, ultimately sinking the pic.

Beneath the layers of flashbacks and at times almost subliminal imagery is a conventional storyline, sound expert David Keith, living in a small Arizona town, is having marital problems with frau Cathy Moriarty. Circumstantial evidence points strongly at Keith, with cop Art Evans in from Phoenix to hound him in the case of a serial murder who mutilates the corpses of his wealthy housewife victims.

With lots of clues and red herrings introduced in the early reels (including a heavy emphasis on 10 years-earlier 16m blowup flashbacks of Moriarty first meeting Keith while trekking westward with her boyfriend Alan Rosenberg), picture maintains considerable suspense heightened by Cammell's edgy camera and fractured editing.

After 75 minutes, Cammell has David Keith matter-of-factly reveal that he *is* the killer, proceeding to terrorize Moriarty and their young daughter for the rest of the anticlimatic picture. Reintroduction of Rosenberg, now living nearby as a brain-damaged garage helper, to figure in the windup is awkward and unconvincing.

Though the flashbacks are set in 1976, this footage and film's psychedelic style (plus pithy, zonked-out dialog for Keith) harken back to the fabulous 1960s. It's certainly fun much of the way to sort out through the stylish tricks, but they're eventually self-defeating.

Moriarty is quite forceful here and her distinctive screen presence deserves more frequent vehicles. Keith likewise creates a powerful figure, but character becomes a stock psychotic (painted face and all) once the mystery is fully out of the bag. Other than Rosenberg, supporting cast has little to do.

Location-lensed feature reeks of atmosphere, with obviously low-budget production values fitting Cammell's treatment. British-financed, it has been inherited by Cannon as part of the Screen Entertainment Ltd. library purchased last year (and among titles still retained post-sale of bulk of the features to Weintraub Entertainment Group).
—*Lor.*

Burnin' Love
(U.S.-COLOR)

A De Laurentiis Entertainment Group release of a Hemdale production. Produced by Michael Gruskoff. Executive producers, John Daly, Derek Gibson. Directed by John Moffitt. Screenplay, Terrence Sweeney, Lanier Laney; camera (CFI color), Mark Irwin; editor, Danford B. Greene; music, Charles Fox; additional music, Tom Rizzo; sound, Peter Shewchuk; production design, Roy Forge Smith; art direction, Gordon White; set decoration, Brendan Smith; assistant director, Jerry A. Swartz; costume design, Linda Matheson; postproduction supervisor, Randy Thornton; coproducer, Armand Speca; associate producer, Donald C. Klune. Reviewed at Cannes Film Festival (market), May 13, 1987. (No MPAA Rating.) Running time: **83 MINS.**

Miles	Patrick Cassidy
Sara Lee	Kelly Preston
Parson Babcock	Bud Cort
Nathaniel	David Graf
Judge Samuel John	Stuart Pankin
Mayor Upton	Dave Thomas
Faith	Barbara Carrera
Widow Chastity	Georgia Brown

Also with: Annie Golden, Audrie Neenan, Jayne Eastwood, Dr. Joyce Brothers.

Cannes — "Burnin' Love" is a far-out, irreverent sendup of the Salem Witch trials that packs plenty of laughs for its targeted Mel Brooks audience.

Producer Michael Gruskoff has worked with Brooks on several features and the influence shows. Besides the patented "Blazing Saddles" brand of flatulence humor there is a healthy respect for slapstick and vulgarity here, sometimes missing the mark but often scoring. John Moffitt, a tv grad, pilots with aplomb and Terrence Sweeney and Lanier Laney's screenplay is chock full of clever anachronis-mims.

Patrick Cassidy and Kelly Preston are well cast as idealized young lovers in 1692 Salem, caught up in the witchhunt hysteria created by the unscrupulous town judge (Stuart Pankin) and mayor (Dave Thomas, using just a trace of his patented Bob Hope impression) who are burning landowners as witches in order to confiscate their property as part of a real estate development scheme.

A real witch (Barbara Carrera, deliciously sexy) shows up and accuses Preston of the crime in order to take Cassidy for herself. In the manner of "Tom Jones," which remains the template for these period tales (right down to Carrera's plunging decolletage), Georgia Brown as a local tavern owner shows up in court to reveal Preston's actual parentage and save the day.

Cast excels in this romp, with many outstanding turns. Bud Cort gets some big laughs as the local parson who is struck blind by Carrera (similar to Elizabeth Montgomery's tv witch on "Bewitched," she just has to squint to work magic), while Audrie Neenan as his crusty old mama steals many a scene using a voice like Margaret Hamilton's. Pankin and Thomas make a comfortable team of bumbling villains in powdered wigs while Cassidy and Preston are effective butts of many physical gags as the too-good leads.

Period feel is captured well on Canadian locations, with a satirical music score by Charles Fox ramming home the jokes (plus some outlandish touches such as The Kingsmen's hit "Louie, Louie" playing at Thanksgiving Dinner after the Indians pass around the peace pipe).—*Lor.*

Starlight Hotel
(NEW ZEALAND-COLOR)

A Challenge Film Corp. presentation, in association with the New Zealand Film Commission. Produced by Finola Dwyer, Larry Parr. Directed by Sam Pillsbury. Stars Peter Phelps, Greer Robson. Screenplay, Grant Hinden Miller, based on his novel "The Dream Monger;" camera (color), Warrick Attewell; editor, Mike Horton; production design, Mike Becroft; costumes, Barbara Darragh; sound, Mike Westgate; production manager, Hammond Peck; assistant director, Chris Graves. Reviewed at Cannes Film Festival (market), May 11, 1987. Running time: **93 MINS.**

Patrick . . . . Peter Phelps
Kate . . . . Greer Robson
Detective Wallace . . . . Marshall Napier
Spooner . . . . The Wizard
Aunt . . . . Alice Fraser
Uncle . . . . Patrick Smyth
Dave Marshall . . . . Bruce Phillips

Also with: Donogh Rees (Helen), Timothy Lee (Maxwell), Peter Dennet (Des), Teresa Bonney (Melissa), Elrich Hooper (Principal), John Watson (Mr. Curtis), Mervyn Glue (Skip).

Cannes — A road movie centering on the friendship between a man on the run from the law and a 13-year-old girl looking for her father may not sound original, but this Kiwi offering is likely to be a winner, especially on its home turf.

Setting is the central South Island in 1930, with farmers forced to leave their land as the Depression bites. Kate, whose mother is dead, hates living with an aunt and uncle and runs away to try to find her father, who's looking for work in Wellington on the North Island.

She soon encounters Patrick, a man whose life was shattered by his experiences in the world war and later, when his wife left him. He's wanted by the police for beating a repo-man who was taking advantage during the Depression, and is trying to get to a port and then passage to Australia.

All the classic elements of this kind of film are here: jumping on trains, hiding out in barns, making friends and enemies along the way. Above all there's the relationship between the lonely child and the taciturn outlaw, and the film benefits enormously from the charismatic performances in the leads. Peter Phelps is an Aussie actor whose cinema career to date ("Undercover") hasn't been significant: his rugged, charming performance as Patrick looks likely to set him on the road to international stardom (he's upcoming in "The Lighthorsemen"). Greer Robson, remembered as the little girl in "Smash Palace,"

is growing up to be a real beauty, and has the required toughness and sensitivity for this role.

Sam Pillsbury, helming his second pic (after "The Scarecrow") has put together all the elements with style. Pic is well paced, builds to an exciting climax as the police move in on the fugitives, and has an ending that will send audiences away happy. Warrick Attewell's camerawork of magnificent New Zealand scenery is tops, with the little farms and small towns forming an integral element in the drama.

Title refers to the "hotel" where the runaways sleep: under the stars. It's a catchy handle to a very appealing pic which could well be another winner for the Kiwis.—*Strat.*

High Tide
(AUSTRALIAN-COLOR)

A Hemdale release (Filmpac in Australia) of an FGH/SJL production. Executive producers, Antony I. Ginnane, Joseph Skrzynski. Produced by Sandra Levy. Directed by Gillian Armstrong. Stars Judy Davis. Screenplay, Laura Jones; camera (color), Russell Boyd; editor, Nicholas Beauman; music, Mark Moffiatt, Ricky Fataar; production design, Sally Campbell; sound, Ben Osmo; production manager, Julie Forster; assistant director, Mark Turnbull; casting, Liz Mullinar; associate producer, Greg Ricketson. Reviewed at Cannes Film Festival (market), May 14, 1987. Running time: **104 MINS.**

Lilli . . . . Judy Davis
Bet . . . . Jan Adele
Ally . . . . Claudia Karvan
Mick . . . . Colin Friels
Col . . . . John Clayton
Lester . . . . Frankie J. Holden
Tracey . . . . Monica Trapaga
Mechanic . . . . Mark Hembrow

Cannes — Director Gillian Armstrong teams with Judy Davis again for the first time since "My Brilliant Career" and the result is a powerful emotional, beautifully made film which will touch the hearts of all but the very cynical. It should perform solidly worldwide in quality situations.

Setting is the small New South Wales coastal town of Eden. Davis plays a member of a trio of blond-wigged backup singers to Elvis Presley imitator Frankie J. Holden (opening sequence, featuring their acts, looks like a moment from Armstrong's second feature, "Starstruck"). Fired by Holden because of her bitchy attitude, and stranded when her car breaks down, Davis rents a cheap trailer by the sea while she awaits completion of the auto repairs.

One night, when hopelessly drunk in a toilet block, she's helped by an adolescent girl (Claudia Karvan) who lives with her grandmother (Jan Adele) in another trailer. Davis befriends the child, who spends much of her time in the surf on a board that belonged to her long-dead father; only when Davis meets the grandmother does she

realize Karvan is her own daughter who she'd left years before in the aftermath of her husband's death.

The grandmother wrongly believes Davis has tracked down the child deliberately intending to take her away; but Davis isn't looking to be tied down, though she's drawn to the wide-eyed child who is so obviously lonely and troubled. The stage is set for an emotionally wrenching climax.

If the above sounds perilously like soap opera, it doesn't play that way at all, thanks to the well written screenplay by Laura Jones, the fine direction of Armstrong and the powerful performances. Jan Adele makes the grandmother, who still enjoys a sexual fling even though she has a regular lover, a wonderfully warm character. Claudia Karvan sharply etches the pain and insecurity hiding beneath the tough, tomboyish exterior of the child; and Judy Davis, always a consummate actress, provides great depth and subtlety, making her character come vividly alive. She even extends her range in this role, and few will forget the scene where her daughter finally asks if she's her mother.

Davis' real-life husband, Colin Friels, has a small but crucial role as a local fisherman with whom she has an affair and to whom she tells the truth about her daughter. When Davis walks out on him, he spills the beans, provoking the climax. Support roles are all well-etched.

Russell Boyd's camerawork is outstanding, and editor Nicholas Beauman did a good job in keeping the pacing tight. Opening scenes are seemingly disconnected, but it all comes together quickly. Special mention should be made of the beautiful, classy credit titles.

"High Tide" seems set for good runs in Australia and major cities round the world. It's basic story may be deceptively simple, but thanks to Armstrong's assured handling it becomes a memorable emotional experience. — *Strat.*

The Love Child
(BRITISH-COLOR)

A British Film Institute-Channel 4 presentation of a Frontroom Film. Produced by Angela Topping. Directed by Robert Smith. Stars Sheila Hancock, Peter Capaldi. Screenplay, Gordon Hann; camera (color), Thaddeus O'Sullivan; editor, John Davies; production design, Caroline Hanania; sound, Davies; costumes, Katharine Naylor; assistant director, Andy Powell. Reviewed at Cannes Film Festival (market), May 8, 1987. Running time: **102 MINS.**

Edith . . . . Sheila Hancock
Dillon . . . . Peter Capaldi
Maurice . . . . Percy Herbert
Bernadette . . . . Lesley Sharp
The voices . . . . Alexei Sayle
Stan . . . . Arthur Hewlett

Also with: Cleo Sylvestre (Celia), Stephen Lind (Colin), Ajay Kumar (Majid), Andrew Seear (Tony), Kevin Allen (Cliff), Robert

Blythe (Elvis), Cathy Murphy (Linda), Stephen Frost (tough policeman), Steven O'-Donnell (young policeman).

Cannes — A low-budget British comedy, "The Love Child," in its quietly humorous way, says a lot about the current state of Britain. Its quirky approach won't appeal to everyone, and one or two things don't work, but overall this is a very enjoyable affair which lingers in the memory.

Dillon, the "love child" of the title, is orphaned as a child when his unmarried hippie parents die in an auto accident; raised by his unmarried grandmother, he works in an accounts office, and has few friends.

He then meets a cheerful girl who's moved in to squat in a rundown house nearby, and he's shyly attracted to her. His gran, meanwhile, is surprised when the man who made her pregnant 40 years earlier, and then disappeared, returns from Australia wanting to marry her.

Around this simple plot are some carefully observed and often sweetly funny scenes depicting life for Dillon and his grandmother in the southern London suburb of Brixton, where the cops are mindlessly, cheerfully violent and the whole place seems to be in a permanent state of decay. Dillon, neatly played by Peter Capaldi (from "Local Hero") is very straight, and disapproves of his parents and grandmother (he says that, with his family background, he always thought "role models" were pickled herrings), but he's thrilled when he meets a couple of aging layabouts who remember his father was lead singer for a rock band called The Pink Frogs.

The grandmother, beautifully played by vet actress Sheila Hancock, is unsure what the future holds and is amazed when her old flame (Percy Herbert) returns to marry her. And Dillon's girl, Bernadette (Lesley Sharp from "Rita, Sue And Bob Too") is far from a conventional heroine, who asks the shy Dillon why he thinks men are frightened of women just as they're about to go to bed for the first time.

Scenes on the streets, in the office where Dillon works and in the local pub, are etched sharply, but less successful are scenes in which inanimate objects "talk" to Dillon (voiced by Alexei Sayle).

The humor throughout (and the accents) are very English, and this may be too modest a film to find the same kind of theatrical success that other recent indie British pics have enjoyed. Nonetheless, it should please a lot of people. —*Strat.*

The Place At The Coast
(AUSTRALIAN-COLOR)

A Daedalus II Film, in association with the New South Wales Film Corp. Produced by Hilary Furlong. Directed by George Ogilvie. Screenplay, Furlong, based on the novel "The Bee Eater" by Jane Hyde; camera (color), Jeff Darling; editor, Nicholas Beauman; production design, Owen Paterson; music, Chris Neal; sound, Phil Stirling; production manager, Fiona McConaghy; assistant director, Chris Webb; production supervisor, Lynn Gailey; costumes, Anna French. Reviewed at Cannes Film Festival (market), May 11, 1987. Running time: 92 MINS.

Neil McAdam . . . . John Hargreaves
Margot Ryan . . . . Heather Mitchell
Ellie McAdam . . . . Tushka Bergen
May Ryan . . . . Margo Lee
Fred Ryan . . . . Willie Fennell
Dan Burroughs . . . . Garry McDonald
Also with: Julie Hamilton (Enid Burroughs), Ray Meagher (Uncle Doug), Michele Fawdon (Aunt Helen), Sue Ingleton (Nan Montgomery), Aileen Britton (Gran), Brendon Lunney (Seymour Steele), Rod Zuanic ("King"), Emily Crook (Julie Montgomery), Alexander Broun (Bob Montgomery), Lillian Crombie (Mrs. Lundy), Beverley Bergen (Mum), Kate Beattie (Ellie 8 years), Dora Batt (Marnie).

Cannes — Filmed as "The Bee Eater," title of the Jane Hyde novel on which producer Hilary Furlong based her screenplay, "The Place At The Coast" is a slight, modest little drama along the lines of "The Member Of The Wedding" or Claude Miller's French pic "L'Effrontée." It could be a tough sell.

Pic marks sharp change of pace for director George Ogilvie, whose first solo feature (after codirecting "Mad Max Beyond Thunderdome") was the tough-minded urban custody drama, "Short Changed."

Central character here is a pubescent girl played by Tushka Bergen. Years before, her mother was killed in a car accident for which she was partly responsible. Now she and her doctor father (John Hargreaves) arrive at their "place at the coast," the seaside holiday home where they've spent summers for years. But this summer, she's bored when her father spends his time fishing. She chats with neighbors, or paints wildflowers and birds, until the arrival of a 25-year-old woman (Heather Mitchell), daughter of neighbors. Mitchell has just returned from Europe and the young girl forms a close friendship with her.

That friendship is disrupted, however, when Hargreaves and Mitchell fall in love. The child is devastated at no longer having either exclusive access to her father or to her new-found friend. Her world is also disturbed by a proposed commercial development of the hitherto unspoiled coastline, which will destroy the environment and endanger the birds she loves so much.

Ogilvie seems to have realized his material here was rather slight, and has tried to jazz it up with some very self-concious photograpy. Cinematographer Jeff Darling's camera is almost always on the move, and the simplest scene is embellished with elaborate tracking. It catches the eye for a while, but then one longs for a little stillness.

Acting is okay. The reliable John Hargreaves is the father; Heather Mitchell is fine as the woman; but young Tushka Bergen, a pretty newcomer, unfortunately has a tendency to shriek unintelligibly in moments of crisis. Australian audiences will be puzzled to see that popular comedian Garry McDonald has a minuscule part, as the husband of the local shopkeeper, and does nothing whatsoever with it.

Technically, pic is as pristine as most Aussie films, though Chris Neal's music isn't up to par.

— Strat.

Hammerhead Jones
(U.S.-COLOR)

A Vernon Films presentation of a Michael Charles Preger/Ted Vernon production. (World sales, Shapiro Entertainment.) Produced by Preger. Executive producer, Vernon. Directed by Robert Michael Ingria. Screenplay, Manny Diez, from story by Vernon; camera (Continental color), Henry Lynk, Orson Ochoa; editor, Angelo Ross; music, Joe Galdo, Larry Dermer; music direction, Ron Albert, Howard Albert, Steve Alaimo; music consultant, Allen L. Jacobs; assistant director-production manager, Benny Waldman; art direction, Cary Roberts, Cliff Guest; sound (Dolby), Dick Bomser; second unit director, Waldman; wrestling choreography, Joe Mascaro, Rusty Brooks. Reviewed at Cannes Film Festival (market), May 16, 1987. (No MPAA Rating.) Running time: 82 MINS.

Ted (Hammerhead) Jones . . . . Ted Vernon
Numbers Cooper . . . . Anthony Albarino
Also with: R.S. King, Marilyn Downey, Joe Mascaro, Rusty Brooks, Joe Mirto, Fred (Bubba) Uttman.

Cannes — After a group of wrestling comedies, including "Grunt" "Bad Guys" and "Body Slam," comes a picture on the subject that takes itself (and the pro grapplers' show) ever-so-seriously, "Hammerhead Jones." Actually a vanity production masterminded by title-roler Ted Vernon, pic is an absurd and mawkish clunker that fails even as camp.

With most of the key story elements spoofed in the form of voiceover by a ring announcer, pic opens with heavyweight champ Hammerhead Jones (Vernon) angrily lecturing a young journalist that wrestling is real and very dangerous. This sets the tone for a cloud-cuckoo land excursion into the parallel world of the American Council of Professional Wrestling, a mythical league where opponents never rehearse their moves with each other, a suplex can almost knock one unconscious (even in the gym) and the center of the wrestling universe is Miami.

Plot catalyst is the death of a top promoter, with his utterly unscrupulous son Numbers Cooper (Anthony Albarino overacting as if cast in the role of a 19th century mustachioed villain) deciding to exploit the bevy of top wrestlers under contract to him by demanding they appear in "death matches:" contests sans referee or time limit and continued until one grappler is physically injured and cannot continue.

Self-righteous screenplay at this point assures as current, loyal wrestling fans will not partake of these gladiatorial travesties, with thrill-seekers substituting in the audience, but this premise is contradicted later. In any event, Hammerhead as champ refuses to take part but ultimately is strongarmed and goaded into The Big Match in corny fashion.

Before the underwhelming climax in the ring (which relies on the standard hokum viewable on any tv wrestling show, not some ultraviolent-to-the-death variation), pic indulges in ridiculously sentimental drivel, such as Hammerhead visiting the Catholic Orphange he single-handedly supports, playing with and lecturing a cute kid there on bullies and sportsmanship and a subplot of his pal Joe Mascaro (who was a wrestling consultant on the shoot) getting put in a wheelchair because of death match injuries. Even small fry will see through the old-fashioned, goody-two-shoes tone.

Another major problem is that pic makes the fatal mistake (as did the other films in the genre except "Body Slam") of not utilizing onscreen top name wrestlers for the fans' delectation. The most familiar wrestler here is chubby Rusty Brooks, hardly a headliner. As for star Vernon (a new car dealer in real life), he is bald, bearded, given to wearing flashy shirts, but nondescript. He looks and plays like a ham & egger (i.e., journeyman wrestler), doesn't have an arresting interview rap routine and seems too nice even in tough guy confrontations. The rest of the cast, including an actress playing a nun who prays for Hammerhead's victories, is weak.

Tech credits are good but in a losing cause. Only a handful of extras are employed for the arena audiences.— Lor.

The Rosary Murders
(U.S.-COLOR)

A Samuel Goldwyn Co. presentation. Executive producers, Robert G. Laurel, Michael Mihalich. Directed by Fred Walton. Screenplay, Elmore Leonard, Walton; camera (color), David Golia; editor, Sam Vitale; music, Bobby Laurel, Don Sebesky; associate producer, Chris Coles. Reviewed at Cannes Film Festival (market), May 9, 1987. (No MPAA Rating.) Running time: 105 MINS.

Father Koesler . . . . Donald Sutherland
Father Nabors . . . . Charles Durning
Lt. Koznicki . . . . Josef Sommer
Pat Lennon . . . . Belinda Bauer
Also with: James Murtaugh, John Danelle, Addison Powell, Kathleen Tolan, Tom Mardirosian, Anita Barone.

Cannes — Neither as a thriller nor as a psychological drama concerning the dilemmas of a Catholic priest's confessional secrets does this film make the grade. A string of a half dozen murders committed by someone with a grudge against the Catholic Church, his victims being nuns and priests in a Detroit parish, are lacking suspense or dramatic buildup, and what should have been the final climactic sequences are as flat as a holy wafer.

Pic revolves mostly around a priest, Father Koesler, who sets about trying to solve the murders while the police seem to be twiddling their thumbs. The priest turns sleuth after the murderer drops a few clues to him during a confessional box session. As a man of the cloth, latter can't tip off the police or probable victims because of his secrecy vows.

Little by little the priest unveils the story of a girl in the parochial school attached to his church who committed suicide three years earlier. But with each step of his investigation, and with each murder committed, the suspense seems to decrease instead of build. Even a fleeting face-to-face encounter in the girl's home between priest and the girl's killer is anticlimactic and over in a matter of seconds.

When the priest, with a little help from the police, finally catches the assassin, the criminal's motivations for the multi-killings are rather weak and unconvincing.

Yarn is rather lamely padded out with a subplot about a femme reporter from one of the local papers, who falls in love with the priest during the early part of the investigation. The romance comes to nothing, and about halfway through the film the girl drops out of the story, though she returns to stand in a doorway of the priest's office when the crime is solved. To say "hello" to Father Koesler, or to lure him away from the priesthood maybe? We're never told.

Sutherland puts in a good performance as the liberal-minded investigating priest, and Charles Durning is fine as the hard-line father superior. Production has a handsome look to it and technical credits are good, as are dialog and direction. Pic might do okay in initial playoffs using a splash release on basis of advertising of murder and church theme, with Sutherland as an additional drawing card, but is unlikely to have durable legs.

— Besa.

Mascara
(BELGIAN-DUTCH-FRENCH-U.S.-COLOR)

A Cannon Group release of an Iblis Films (Brussels), Praxino Pictures (Amsterdam), Dedalus (Paris) and Atlantic Consolidated Enterprises (New York) coproduction. Produced by Pierre Drouot, Rene Solleveld, Henry Lange. Directed by Patrick Conrad. Stars Charlotte Rampling, Michael Sarrazin. Screenplay, Hugo Claus, Drouot, Conrad, in collaboration with Frank Daniel, Malia Scotch Marmo; camera (color), Gilberto Azavedo; editor, Susana Roseberg; music, Egisto Macchi; sound, Henri Morelle; set design, Misjel Vermieren, Dirk Debou; costumes, Yan Tax; production directors, Jean-Marie Bertrand, Daniel Gaye. Reviewed at Cannes Film Festival (market), May 16, 1987. (No MPAA rating.) Running time: **98 MINS.**

Gaby Hart .... Charlotte Rampling
Bert Sanders .... Michael Sarrazin
Chris Brine .... Derek de Lint
Lana .... Romy Haag
Pepper .... Eva Robins
David Hyde .... Herbert Flack
Harry Wellman .... Serge-Henri Valcke
Colonel March .... Jappe Claes
Minister Weinberger .... John van Dreslen
P.C. .... Harry Cleven

Cannes — This English-language mishmash is notable only for being atmospheric and kinky while at the same time being insufferably witless and boring. Don't blame Cannon for this pretentious mess since it was acquired as part of that company's Screen Entertainment buy of a year ago.

Whatever its murky origination, pic looms as an unredeemable b.o. loser. Belgian-born director-coscripter Patrick Conrad has come up with a yarn about a big city police commissioner (Michael Sarrazin) with an interesting nightlife. He spends most evenings patronizing a literally subterranean night spot frequented by opera-singing homosexuals, transvestites and transsexuals.

Commissioner's devoted sister (Charlotte Rampling) knows nothing of her brother's pastime, and couldn't care less until she falls for the tiresome costume designer of the local opera company. Designer and commissioner cross paths when former loans a Bob Mackie-type gown to the latter. He in turn, has the designer dress the cop's, innamorata of the moment, usually a transsexual, who lip-synchs snippets of Richard Strauss and "Ave Maria" before being killed.

Enough said that the plot makes no sense whatsoever. Conrad occasionally adds some evocative touches to "Mascara" but the nightclub goings-on are for those with stout stomachs.

Rampling, seen in Claude Montana outfits, looks good and does her best. Sarrazin isn't terrible but the rest of the cast is. —*Sege.*

Goofballs
(U.S.-COLOR)

A Shapiro Entertainment release of a Filmcap Corp. presentation of a Dale Falconer production. Produced by Dale Falconer. Directed by Brad Turner. Screenplay, Skip West; music, Robert Rettberg. (No other credits supplied.) Reviewed at Cannes Film Festival (market), May 16, 1987. (No MPAA rating.) Running time: **87 MINS.**

With: Ben Gordon, Ron James, John Kozak, Wayne Robson, Cynthia Belliveau, Laura Robinson, Ilana Linden, Wayne Flemming, John Hemphill.

Cannes — "Goofballs" must be one of the weakest, lame-brained socalled comedies to appear for some time. With laughs that can be counted on one hand and a plot that's microscopic in dimension, pic seems a surefire tv, homevideo or cable item, as theatrical release would surely be a mistake in most territories.

Antics, or lack of them, take place at a golf resort in the Bahamas, where vacuous Josh Wheeler, played by Ben Gordon, is entertainment director. Seemingly his only friend is a wise-mouthed parrot; why filmmakers continue to put birds with atrocious human voiceovers in films remains a high mystery, but the tortuous dialog between bird and man in this pic is more excruciatingly banal than usual.

Out of the blue Gordon receives a call from a former criminal friend who took the rap for a heist in which Gordon was the getaway driver and bungled; Gordon is told to make amends by accommodating some thugs at the resort.

Gordon tells the resort owner the thugs are members of a golf confederation assessing the resort's course; he consequently has to stage a golf tournament and bring in a completely talentless cousin who does impersonations of Flipper the dolphin to fill in for the various celebs the owner somehow thinks will flock to the tournament.

Mixed up with this are various encounters with some Arabs, who are stashing gold under a rock in the resort's gardens; they're trying to corner Gordon because he stole some moolah, while the criminals insist on making him rig the tournament and then getting a slice of the action with the Arabs. Meanwhile, one of the thug's companions, for no reason at all, falls hopelessly in love with Gordon's dull cousin.

About the only laughs come from the crims' laconic appraisal of the ritzy resort; pic's roundabout, thin storyline quickly becomes tedious, and the acting, is, on the whole, hardly inspired and certainly not the stuff of comedy. Neither is there the schoolboy sex of other minor comedies to attract an audience who aren't that fussy about the laughs.

Tech credits are passable. — *Doch.*

The Farm
(U.S.-COLOR)

A Trans World Entertainment release and production. Produced by Ovidio G. Assonitis. Executive producer, Moshe Diamant. Directed by David Keith. Stars Will Wheaton. Screenplay, David Chaskin; camera (Widescreen, Fujicolor & Technicolor), Robert D. Forges; editor, Claudio M. Cutry; music, Franco Micalizzi; sound (Dolby), John Lawrence; production design, Frank Vanorio; visual effects, Kevin Erham; makeup, Frank Russell; models, Mark Moller; casting, David Kingsley; associate producer, Lucio Fulci. Reviewed at Cannes Film Festival (market), May 15, 1987. (No MPAA Rating.) Running time: **90 MINS.**

Zachary Hayes .... Will Wheaton
Nathan Hayes .... Claude Akins
Cyrus .... Malcolm Danare
Dr. Alan Forbes .... Cooper Huckabee
Carl Willis .... John Schneider
Alice Hayes .... Amy Wheaton
Charley Davidson .... Steve Carlisle
Frances Hayes ... Kathleen Jordan Gregory
Esther Forbes .... Hope North
Mike .... Steve Davis

Cannes — Actor David Keith makes an auspicious film directing debut with "The Farm," a well-made and well-acted horror opus that is distrib TWE's best picture to date by a wide margin.

Similar to the H.P. Lovecraft story "The Color Out Of Space" (previously filmed in England as a Nick Adams-Boris Karloff starrer), tale concerns a meteorite that lands on a small farm in Tellico Plains, Tenn. Dismissed as merely a frozen block of waste presumably dropped by a passing airplane, the glowing ball melts down and contaminates the farm's water supply, altering the flora and fauna while disfiguring the Hayes family members and driving them nuts.

Exceptions are the young kids (played by Will Wheaton and in her debut, younger sister Amy Wheaton). They avoid the food and water, against the objections of tyrannical and religiously fanatic stepfather Claude Akins. With the aid of local doctor Cooper Huckabee and visiting TVA official John Schneider, the kids finally escape as the homestead literally crumbles like the House of Usher. Of course, true to the genre, an open ending is tacked on that is anything but happy.

Keith, who appears only in a cameo, leavens the horror narrative with interesting and often funny details and fine manipulation of various subplots, particularly the sexual frustration of Akins' homely wife Kathleen Jordan Gregory, plus the in-joke shock of Huckabee's prim wife turning out to be a sexpot played by Hope North. He directs the cast very well, all conforming to good ole boy roles, of which Steve Carlisle's slick and unscrupulous real estate speculator is a highlight.

Special effects are acceptable,

---

though some of the modelwork looks really teeny. Much of the crew (including associate producer and noted horror helmer himself Lucio Fulci) are credited with anglicized names instead of their Italian monikers, but they have nothing to be ashamed about. —*Lor.*

House II: The Second Story
(U.S.-COLOR)

A New World Pictures releases of a Sean S. Cunningham production. Produced by Sean S. Cunningham. Written and directed by Ethan Wiley. Camera (Metrocolor), Mac Ahlberg; editor, Marty Nicholson; music, Henry Manfredini; production design, Gregg Fonseca; sound, Kim Ornitz; associate producer, Andrew Z. Davis; casting, Melissa Shott; assistant director, Betsy Magruder. Reviewed at Cannes Film Festival (market), May 15, 1987. Running time: **85 MINS.**

Jesse McLaughlin .... Arye Gross
Charlie .... Jonathan Stark
Gramps .... Royal Dano
John .... Bill Maher
Bill Towner .... John Ratzenberger
Kate .... Lar Park Lincoln
Lana .... Amy Yasbeck
Also with: Gregory Walcott (Sheriff), Dwier Brown (Clarence), Lenora May (Judith), Devin Devasquez (Virgin).

Cannes — The original "House" had some suspense and quirky humor; the sequel has neither. This house isn't worth a visit.

What passes for a plot in director Ethan Wiley's throwaway screenplay has Arye Gross move into the house in which his parents were murdered 25 years earlier. He hears about the existence of a skull filled with jewelry, supposedly buried with the body of one of his ancestors, so he and entrepreneur pal Jonathan Stark exhume the 170-year-old corpse, played by Royal Dano, unrecognizable under disfiguring makeup.

The oldtimer wants to have fun now that he's alive again, but an evil spirit wants that skull, and soon the trio is transported through the walls of the house into another world — a primeval jungle — to do battle.

Wiley is determined to be cute rather than scary. He intros some cuddly creatures — a baby pterodactyl, plus a critter who's a cross between a dog and a caterpillar — but they don't add anything to the pic's charm. Action scenes aren't very thrilling or suspenseful, and the pic's uncertain tone will prevent much audience involvement.

It may open strong if marketed imaginatively, but word of mouth is likely to be murder. Don't expect a third story in the "House" series.
— *Strat.*

Made In U.S.A.
(U.S.-COLOR)

A De Laurentiis Entertainment Group release of a Hemdale presentation. Produced by Charles Roven. Executive producers, John Daly, Derek Gibson. Written and directed by Ken Friedman. Camera (CFI color), Curtis Clark; editor, uncredited; music, Sonic Youth; production design, James Newport; art director, Tom Southwind; set design, Cynthia Redman; sound, David Brownlow; assistant director, Bill Corcoran; casting, Dennison/Seltzer. Reviewed at Cannes Film Festival (market), May 15, 1987. (MPAA Rating: R.) Running time: **87 MINS.**

Dar . . . . Adrian Pasdar
Tuck . . . . Christopher Penn
Annie . . . . Lori Singer
Cora . . . . Jackie Murphy
Dorie . . . . Judy Baldwin
Cowboy . . . . Dean Paul Martin

Cannes — "Made In U.S.A." is an offensive, self-righteous look at what's wrong with America today in the form of a free-wheeling road picture in which three unlikable characters steal their way across the country. It's meant to be a gritty, hard-edged view of the country, but comes across as an empty-headed blast by people out of touch with life outside L.A. Hemdale is releasing its own cut over the objections of writer-director Ken Friedman, but it's unlikely either version would have a chance at the boxoffice.

Modeled after Bertrand Blier's mid-'70s biting social comedy, "Going Places," in which Gérard Depardieu and Patrick Dewaere traveled across France wreaking havoc in their path, "Made In U.S.A." has added a political explanation for its characters' misbehavior which trivializes the anarchistic spirit driving it.

Film tries to blend a '60s feeling of carefree spontaneity with today's social concerns, and in the process never seems quite contemporary. "Made In U.S.A." is quick to point its finger at the bad guys, the polluters and exploiters of the environment, but its heroes have only destructive and negative solutions.

Dar (Adrian Pasdar) and Tuck (Christopher Penn) are on the run from the gas spills and unemployment of Centralia, Pa. They steal a car and head west where they soon meet up with Annie (Lori Singer), the kind of beautiful improbable character that one can only meet in films.

She, too, has a tale of woe about deadly dioxyns killing her father and a score to settle with anyone in her way. Screenplay by Friedman has her mouthing pop pablum such as "we're all dyin', it's the ride that counts," as a justification for her willingness to do whatever pops into her head.

Penn and Pasdar, who are more than a little in love with her, do anything she says for a while but finally draw the line at robbing a bank, supposedly suggesting that they really are moral people at heart. It's this pretense at morality that sinks the picture because if they were truly concerned they could never be so callous to so many people. They have neither the abandonment nor charm of true nihilists or the humanity of concerned citizens.

What they do have is a self-serving romp through the heartland that goes nowhere fast. Stealing a Mack truck from a couple of grotesque and obese rednecks and tormenting them is what they do for fun. Characters display a distasteful superiority towards the unwashed masses and then blame them for their own emptiness.

In this us-against-them setup there really isn't anyone to root for. Film soon becomes repetitious and tedious despite Friedman's technical proficiency in staging a variety of scenes in well-chosen scenic locations.

But it's basically the characters that sink this one. As the brooding member of the trio, Penn displays some of his older brother's intensity and sensitivity but squanders any sympathy he wins. Pasdar is well cast as the other heavy and does a credible job within the limitations of his character.

Singer's character, however, lacks any credibility though she gives it a good college try and spends plenty of time in the sack. As an actress she is indeed beautiful, but it's a fragile beauty that doesn't translate to a hard-nosed, stop-at-nothing hellraiser.

Score includes a selection of ersatz Springsteen and Mellencamp tunes that aim for working class soul but miss the target. Other tech credits are commendable, particularly Britisher Curtis Clark's heavily saturated camerawork that seems a good deal more real than the rest of the film. —*Jagr.*

Sommarkvällar pa jorden
(Summer Nights)
(SWEDISH-COLOR)

A Swedish Film Institute release (world sales, SFI) of a Spice Film/SFI/Swedish Television/SVT-2 production. Produced by Peter Hald. Directed by Gunnel Lindblom. Screenplay by Lindblom, based on Agneta Pleijel's play; camera (Eastmancolor), Lasse Björne; editor, Helene Berlin; music, Göran Klintberg, Thirteen Moons; sound, Adel Kjellström; production design, Kaj Larsen; production manager, Marianne Persson. Reviewed at Cannes Film Festival (market), May 9, 1987. Running time: **104 MINS.**

Karna . . . . Sif Ruud
Ulrika . . . . Margaretha Byström
Tomas . . . . Per Mattsson
Magda . . . . Harriet Andersson
Bror . . . . Leif Ahrle
Gertrud . . . . Mona Malm
Fredrik . . . . Ulf Johanson
Tanja . . . . Inga-Lill Andersson

Cannes — One of Sweden's pubcaster tv channels has a bit of production coin in "Summer Nights," so that's one venue still left open for a feature film that has failed badly at the boxoffice at home, and deservedly so, since it is a safe bet for a place on anybody's list of all-time worst films.

Ex-Ingmar Bergman actress Gunnell Lindblom bowed as a director some years ago with "Paradise Place," a family reunion story of wit, warmth and charm. Basing her new film on a stage play, Lindblom once more uses the family reunion framework, but what she puts into it is poor dramatic structuring of a non-plot, contrived character confrontation, trite and shrill dialog, plus good actors (for the most part) losing themselves in expressions of bravura and self-pity.

The gathering has a grandmother, her three daughters and their husbands/lovers plus a teenage granddaughter celebrating the old lady's birthday on an islet in the Stockholm archipelago. Everybody brings complaints of wasted opportunities rather than gifts. One daughter, an actress, screams at her lover for not being ready to become a father. He would, actually, rather sit down at his typewriter and fashion a Strindbergian drama about the whole sorry ménage.

None of the problems sketched in for the rest of the family appear, however, to be one cut above or below the small everyday experiences of humdrum people everywhere. Worse, the writer-director is fishing out of the biggest barrel ever of clichéd dialog morsels so tired as to match perfectly the slackness of her dealing with her actors. Even the hazy-days-of-summer cinematography is one prolonged cliché, crowding for as much attention as the corny jazz trumpet of the musical score.—*Kell.*

Deranged
(U.S.-COLOR)

A Platinum Pictures release. (International sales, Skouras Pictures.) Produced and directed by Chuck Vincent. Line producer, Bill Tasgal. Screenplay, Craig Horrall; camera (color), Larry Revene; editor, James Davalos; music, Bill Heller; sound, Peter Penguin; art direction, Marc Ubell; special effects, Vincent Guastini; assistant director, Chip Lambert; associate producer, Bill Slobodian. Reviewed at Cannes Film Festival (market), May 10, 1987. (No MPAA Rating.) Running time: **81 MINS.**

Joyce . . . . Jane Hamilton
Frank . . . . Paul Siederman
Mary Ann . . . . Jennifer Delora
Mother . . . . Jill Cumer
Father . . . . James Gillis
Nick . . . . Gary Goldman

Cannes — The team of filmmaker Chuck Vincent and actress Veronica Hart (credited here under her real name, Jane Hamilton) score respective tour de force stints in "Deranged," an innovative thriller simply not suited to today's market. Duo achieved something of a breakthrough six years ago with the crossover porn film "Roommates," but "Deranged" is neither the expected exploitation film nor a pedigreed art picture and thus is unlikely to reach either extreme of the audience spectrum.

Taking the unpromising premise of a woman going crazy and suffering escalating hallucinations (most similar forerunner being Robert Altman's "Images"), Vincent draws upon his legit theatrical background in creating a claustrophobic atmosphere for his story. After brief opening scenes in which Hamilton's husband goes off to London and her resentments of her sister (Jennifer Delora) and patrician mother (Jill Cumer) become evident, virtually the rest of the film is played out in Hamilton's New York City apartment.

Accosted by a burglar clad head to toe in black, she kills the intruder in self-defense à la "Dial M For Murder" with a scissors. This traumatic incident causes her hallucinations to multiply rapidly until the viewer is not sure what is real and what is merely a projection of the heroine's fears and memories.

Vincent audaciously uses lengthy takes (recalling Alfred Hitchcock's experiment with "Rope") and a dollying camera that prowls past walls into every room of the apartment, while characters constantly enter or disappear just out of camera range. Even elements of kabuki theater are integrated into the format, as the black-clad intruder reappears and skulks around the apartment, dodging Hamilton's real visitors yet visible to her and the audience. This elaborate technique provides several elegant transitions within a shot to move between various periods of the heroine's life as well as spatially, as in the recurring surprise appearances of her psychoanalyst interrogating her in the living room she imagines to be his office.

Though there are some weak segments, film overall holds one's interest and builds suspensefully to a violent conclusion. Hamilton, on screen almost constantly, handles her lengthy monologs very well and really shines in the eventual transition from tormented heroine to unhinged avenger with a strange look in her eye. Rest of the cast, which includes porno vets Jerry Butler and Jamie Gillis as her husband and father (billed under different names), is okay in functional capacities.

—*Lor.*

The Marsupials: The Howling III
(AUSTRALIAN-COLOR)

A Bacannia Entertainment presentation. Produced by Charles Waterstreet, Philippe Mora. Executive producers, Edward Simons, Steve Lane, Robert Pringle. Directed by Mora. Screenplay, Mora, based on the book "Howling III" by Gary Brander; camera (color), Louis Irving; editor, Lee Smith; music, Allan Zavod; special effects, Bob McCarron; production and costume design, Ross Major; co-producer, Gilda Baracchi; sound, Bob Clayton; assistant director, Stuart Wood; production manager, Rosslyn Abernethy; casting, Forcast. Reviewed at Cannes Film Festival (market), May 15, 1987. Running time: **94 MINS.**

Prof. Harry Beckmeyer	Barry Otto
Jerboa	Imogen Annesley
Olga Gorki	Dasha Blahova
Thylo	Max Fairchild
Professor Sharp	Ralph Cotterill
Donny Martin	Leigh Biolos
Jack Citron	Frank Thring
U.S. President	Michael Pate
Dame Edna Everage	Barry Humphries

Also with: Carole Skinner (Yara), Brian Adams (General Miller), Bill Collins (Doctor), Christopher Pate (Security agent).

Cannes — The third "Howling" film has little in common with the first two, except for the werewolf transformations; it's a tongue-in-cheek parody of the genre, handled with lots of verve and affection by Philippe Mora, who made rather heavy weather of a straight approach to the same subject in "Howling II." The new pic, made entirely in Australia, will have a career on video, but should also please the buffs in theaters, where average-to-good biz can be expected, especially Down Under.

Barry Otto (who played the lead in "Bliss") lends the pic distinction via his role as a scientist obsessed with finding out about a species of uniquely Australian werewolves, marsupials who, like kangaroos and kaolas, carry their newborn in a bouch and suckle them there. With Ralph Cotterill as his skeptical sidekick, Otto discovers a tribe of marsupial werewolves living in the Australian bush, though one of them, the beautiful Jerboa (Imogen Annesley) wanders into Sydney and gets a job as extra on a horror film, "Shape Shifters Part 8," being directed by Frank Thring.

She falls for assistant director Donny Martin (Leigh Biolos), who takes her to see a horror flick ("It Came From Uranus") which doesn't impress her. Meanwhile, three female members of her tribe come to the city dressed as nuns looking for her; when they turn into werewolves during the film's wrap party, there's consternation.

There's another werewolf in Sydney, however: Olga, a Russian ballerina (played by Czech actress Dasha Blahova who once starred in Vera Chytilova's "The Apple Game"). Olga is a traditional, European werewolf, come to Australia to mate with the leader of the marsupial werewolves (Max Fairchild). Her transformation, during a pas de deux on the stage of the Sydney Opera House, is one of the film's comic highlights.

Mora knows his horror films, and has fun sending them up. Audience willing to go along will have great fun with the jokes and excesses. Aussie audiences, especially, will enjoy the on-screen presence of tv personality Bill Collins, playing a doctor who becomes a victim of the werewolves, and Barry Humphries, in his Dame Edna Everage disguise, who makes a last-moment appearance as the presenter at an Academy Awards-type ceremony who's horrified when the best actress winner transforms into a werewolf before his eyes.

Michael Pate does a good turn as the U.S. President ("I'm as anticommunist as the next man!") who isn't surprised to hear of a rare species of werewolf in Australia ("There are all sorts of natural freaks down there"). Frank Thring is outrageously campy as the director of the film within the film, justifying its excesses as "a study of pop culture."

Special effects tend towards the bizarre and comic rather than horrific, such as a surprisingly touching scene in which Annesley gives birth to a tiny creature which, as marsupial infants do, crawls up her stomach and into her pouch. Use of music is fun, too, for example the introduction of a song, "All Fall Down," as one character plummets from a high building.

Joe Dante's original "The Howling" was a landmark horror pic, done straight. Mora's sequel was a flat reworking of the werewolf genre. Now he's sent it all up with relish, and it works. Those who want to know where Mora gets the best Eggs Benedict should sit through the end credits. — *Strat.*

Lust For Freedom
(U.S.-COLOR)

A Troma release of a Mesa Films/Troma production. Executive producers, Lloyd Kaufman, Michael Herz. Produced and directed by Eric Louzil. Coproducer, Laurel A. Koernig. Screenplay, Craig Kusaba, Duke Howard; camera (TVC color), Ron Chapman; editor, Steve Mann, David Khachatorian; music, John Messari; sound, Mann, Anna Krupa; assistant director-production manager, Rob Rosen; stunt coordinator, William J. Kulzer; second unit camera, John Sprung; postproduction supervisor, Khachatorian. Reviewed at Cannes Film Festival (market), May 14, 1987. (MPAA Rating: R.) Running time: **91 MINS.**

Jillian Cates	Melanie Coll
Sheriff Cole	William J. Kulzer
Pusker	Judi Trevor
Big Eddie	Deana Booher
Warden Maxwell	Howard Knight
Vicky	Elizabeth Carlisle

Also with: Shea Porter, Michelle Bauer, Crystal Breeze.

Cannes — "Lust For Freedom" is a sexploitation mishmash, the result of Troma acquiring an unreleased feature entitled "Georgia County Lock-Up" and fiddling with it, somewhat in the manner (though less extreme) of Woody Allen's Japanese dub job "What's Up, Tiger Lily?" Result is difficult to endure, though probably better than a straight version would have been.

Reason for this is that producer-director Eric Louzil delivered utterly listless footage, a mechanical and boring run-through of women's prison films clichés. At least the Troma dubbed-in asides, grunts, wisecracks and dumb narration fill in a few of the dead spots.

Melanie Coll portrays an undercover agent for the government who is aimlessly driving through Georgia County (supposedly located near the California border with Mexico and filmed in Ely, Nevada), when she is detained by the sheriff (William J. Kulzer), who escorts her to the women's correctional facility. It turns out this lawless county, under the auspices of dirty old man Warden Maxwell (Howard Knight), grabs women passing through, incarcerates them and sells them as part of a white slavery scam.

Premise is simply an excuse for softcore sex scenes, ranging from 1960s soft porn-style whipping scenes and rape to a sensual lesbo coupling featuring familiar sex stars Crystal Breeze and Michelle Bauer. Deana Booher, known for her tv appearances on Roller Derby and the female wrestling show "Glow," plays a huge thug who wrestles uppity prisoners to their death.

Drab, ugly visuals make the picture appear to be 20 years older than it is, as does the content. Acting is so bad it's funny at times without the soundtrack prompting. —*Lor.*

From A Whisper To A Scream
(U.S.-COLOR)

A Conquest Entertainment presentation of a Darin Scott/William Burr production. (World sales, Manson Intl.) Produced by Scott, William Burr. Executive producer, David Shaheen. Directed by Jeff Burr. Screenplay, C. Courtney Joiner, Jeff Burr, Darin Scott; camera (United color), Craig Greene; editor, W.O. Garrett; music, Jim Manzie; additional music, Pat Regan, sound, Jerry Wolfe; assistant director, Mark Hannah; special makeup effects, Rob Burman. Reviewed at Cannes Film Festival (market), May 13, 1987. (No MPAA Rating.) Running time: **96 MINS.**

Julian White	Vincent Price
Stanley Burnside	Clu Gulager
Jesse Hardwick	Terry Kiser
Felder Evans	Harry Caesar
Sideshow owner	Rosalind Cash
Sergeant	Cameron Mitchell
Bess Chandler	Susan Tyrrell
Stephen	Ron Brooke
Amaryllis	Didi Lanier
Katherine White	Martine Beswick
Carny barker	Angelo Rossitte
Official at execution	Lawrence Tierney

Cannes — "From A Whisper To A Scream" unwittingly solves the problem facing anthology horror films in the "Tales From The Crypt" mold: how do you order the various segments to achieve balance and proper pacing? In this case, all four segments are mediocre so there's no problem — just string 'em together with a boring cover story added.

Vincent Price is the mellow host, telling boring tales of terror to inquiring reporter Susan Tyrrell (as calm and dull as one would never expect of her), on the occasion of the execution of his niece Martine Beswick (that's one for genre buffs to ponder) for a string of murders. Price maintains that the evil influence of the small town of Oldfield, Tenn., has corrupted its denizens, cueing acts of greed and horrific ruthlessness. Tyrrell listens to his guff before predictably socking it to him in the finale.

Lengthy opening tale has Clu Gulager convincingly made up as a horny old man whose girl of his dreams won't give him a tumble, so he chokes her and has a necrophiliac fling with her corpse in the funeral chapel. The title card reads "9 Months Later," so it's utterly predictable that a Rick Baker-styled monster baby comes out of the grave to confront him.

Terry Kiser is the victim of even more extreme irony as a greedy creep who flees into the bayou with a severe chest wound dealt by some enemies. Black hermit Harry Caesar nurses him back to health, but when Kiser tries to steal the secret of Caesar's mystical longevity (he's over 200 years old), Caesar chops him and burns him with Kiser doomed to live on another 70 years in agony.

A very silly nod to Tod Browning's "Freaks" (featuring dwarf actor Angelo Rossitto who appeared in "Freaks" 55 years earlier) has pro Glass Eater (Ron Brooks) falling in love with a young blond (Didi Lanier) and incurring the wrath of carny owner Rosalind Cash when he runs off with her. Cash invokes some voodoo and Brooks erupts with yucky makeup effects. Happy ending, for Cash, has Lanier involuntarily joining the carnival as a human pin cushion.

Final seg is frankly disgusting, reviving that old saw about Civil War revenge with a new twist. Cameron Mitchell (sporting a bit of a drawl) plays a sadistic Union Army sergeant who gets his comeuppance at the hands of a group of Rebel kids (none of whom have southern accents) who obviously grew up watching "Night Of The Living Dead" rather than "Forbidden Games." Point-of-view here is crass and nauseating.

Though pic makes many references to H.P. Lovecraft, it's strictly shlock, with weak production values. Cast members are on their own.

—*Lor.*

The Barbarians
(U.S.-COLOR)

A Cannon Group release of a Golan-Globus production. Produced by John Thompson. Directed by Ruggero Deodato. Stars The Barbarian Bros. (David Paul, Peter Paul), Richard Lynch. Screenplay, James R. Silke; camera (Telecolor), Gianlorenzo Battaglia; editor, Eugenio Alabiso; music, Pino Donaggio; sound (Dolby), Massimo Loffredi; production design, Giuseppe Mangano; production manager, Luciano Balducci; assistant director, Roberto Palmerini; stunt coordinator, Benito Stefanelli; makeup and visual effects. Francesco Paolocci, Gaetano Paolocci; costumes, Francesca Panicali, Michela Gisotti. Reviewed at Mann's National theater, L.A., May 15, 1987 (In market at Cannes Film Festival.) (MPAA Rating: R.) Running time: **88 MINS.**

Kutchek . . . . David Paul
Goro . . . . Peter Paul
Kadar . . . . Richard Lynch
Ismena . . . . Eva La Rue
Canary . . . . Virginia Bryant
China . . . . Sheeba Alahani
Dirtmaster . . . . Michael Berryman
Kara . . . . Tiziana Di Gennaro

Hollywood — Far, far away in the mythical land of the Ragnicks lived twin bodybuilders who called each other "bonehead" and tried to pass themselves off as actors in a cheesy Italian sword and sorcerer epic called "The Barbarians."

They were pretty comfortable grunting and groaning, lifting boulders and such, but when it came to the speaking part, they appeared nervous — until they heard the other actors.

So then they relaxed and had a good time with their scantily clad friends mouthing dimwitted dialog and slaying plastic dragons and "The Barbarians" turned out to be so bad it was good.

With a little magic, pic could stay in theaters for a week.

The Barbarians actually are David Paul and Peter Paul, two grotesquely overdeveloped weightlifters with a lot of charm and screen presence considering how ridiculous a situation they find themselves in.

Action begins when they are children and their band of itinerant artists and entertainers, the Ragnicks, led by the beautiful queen Canary (Virginia Bryant), are captured by the evil Kadar (Richard Lynch) and his sadistic sorceress, China (Sheeba Alahani).

The cute little boys grow up into big bad slaves, their lives spared because of a promise Lynch kept to Bryant that he would never harm them as long as she remained his captor and pledged him her total allegiance. The whole time, he never seduces her and she doesn't age a

day. They both have amazing power.

One day, Lynch orders the Paul Bros., gladiator-style, to fight to the death. But they wise up, escape rather handily, team up with a pretty cave girl (Eva La Rue), then regroup with their old buddies the Ragnicks and overthrow Kadar to try and recapture the Queen.

Not one second goes by when any of the actors seem to make even a passable attempt at trying to be credible medieval characters, except perhaps for Lynch who has made a career out of playing bad guys of yore.

Opening dialog is spoken by Bryant whose nasal, grating voice is like listening to fingernails on a chalkboard. Nearly everyone else follows suit. La Rue says her lines in Valspeak.

If the sound was turned down, better yet off, it would still be easy to figure out what was happening.

Film is actually quite interesting to watch; the scenery is beautiful, especially in those scenes in the expansive green valley, and the sets by Giuseppe Mangano and costumes by Francesca Panicali truly imaginative and colorful.

There is a little dismemberment, some fire breathing, dragons in dungeons and vice versa, misty lagoons with creatures lurking beneath the surface of the water and and lots of comely young girls with most of their flesh exposed.

There virtually is no suspense as the story unfolds, but it is fascinating to watch to the closing credits one filmmaker's unabashed shameless production that is so laughable as to be entertaining. —*Brit.*

The Beat
(U.S.-COLOR)

A Vestron Pictures release of a Ruthless/Klik/Wachsler production. (World sales, Interaccess Film Distribution.) Executive producers, Ruth Vitale, Lawrence Kasanoff. Produced by Julia Phillips, Jon Klik, Nick Wechsler. Camera (color), Tom DiCillo; editor, Elizabeth Kling; music, Carter Burwell; sound (Dolby), Lee Orloff; production manager, Kevin Dowd; assistant director, Steve Love; production design, George Stoll; casting, Marcia Shulman. Reviewed at Cannes Film Festival (market), May 13, 1987. (No MPAA Rating.) Running time: **98 MINS.**

Mr. Ellsworth . . . . John Savage
Rex Voorhaus Ormine . . . . David Jacobson
Billy Kane . . . . William McNamara
Kate Kane . . . . Kara Glover
Dr. Waxman . . . . Jeffrey Horowitz

Cannes — "The Beat," originally titled "Conjurer," is a fatuous treatment of the problems of ghetto youth in New York City, leaving no cliché unturned in its search for synthetic drama. Playing like a vulgarized tv movie of "Dungeons And Dragons," pic stands little chance of attracting a theatrical audience.

John Savage toplines (with many a meaningful gesture) as stereotyped sympathetic English teacher Mr. Ellsworth, trying to get through to his school-hating class in "Hellesbay" New York. The kids, underprivileged but nearly all white, belong to two warring street gangs, the Marathon Boulevard group including brother-sister team Billy & Kate Kane (William McNamara and Kara Glover).

Catalyst for the story is new kid in class, nerd Rex Voorhaus Ormine (David Jacobson overacting considerably), a disturbed youth who spouts inane poetry. Reviled by the kids at first, he eventually wins them over to his nutty philosophy and mind games, a variant upon "Dungeons And Dragons" in which he imagines the adult world already is dead via nuclear holocaust, with himself as the mythic hero Voorhaus, Billy as The Beggar and Kate as the Priestess/Princess ready to start a new civilization, chanting nonsense rhymes and marching to The Beat.

Since poetry is teach's pet project, soon the recalcitrant class is indulging in all sorts of idiotic self-expression and the leads form a musical group, Mutants Of Sound, whose rap routine to The Beat brings the house down at the school talent show. Hounded by the nasty school shrink, Voorhaus barely escapes the men in the white coats coming to take him away, and commits suicide in the ocean instead. His pals believe he's gone off to a better place and carry on his nutty mysticism, presumably worshiping the coat he left behind.

With adult figures (particularly the shrink and school principal) portrayed as laughable caricatures, "The Beat" is one of those well meaning films that sets up many a straw man to knock down. Writer-director Paul Mones uses Voorhaus as the mouthpiece for many inane explanations of young people's rebellious behavior, none of which ring true. Pic is as dated as its slam dancing centerpiece.

Coming off better than leads Savage and Jacobson are the brother-sister act, with McNamara sympathetic as a young Ricky Nelson type and Kara Glover's Wilhelmina model beauty shining out through the plain, feisty wrapping. Film's tech contributions are acceptable, but its misguided attempt at realism ends up looking smaller than life (particularly a scene at the siblings' home that looks like early Salvation Army).—*Lor.*

Dirty Dancing
(U.S.-COLOR)

A Vestron Pictures release. Produced by Linda Gottlieb. Executive producers, Mitchell Cannold, Steven Reuther. Directed by Emile Ardolino. Screenplay, Eleanor Bergstein; camera (color), Jeff Jur; editor, Peter C. Frank; music, John Morris; production design, David Chapman; art director, Mark Haack, Stephen Lineweaver; sound (Dolby stereo), Miranda John Pritchett; costumes, Hilary Rosenfield; choreography, Kenny Ortega; coproducer, Bergstein; assistant director, Herb Gains; associate producer, Doro Bachrach; casting, Bonnie Timmermann. Reviewed at Cannes Film Festival (market), May 12, 1987. (MPAA Rating: PG-13.) Running time: **97 MINS.**

Baby Houseman . . . . Jennifer Grey
Johnny Castle . . . . Patrick Swayze
Jake Houseman . . . . Jerry Orbach
Penny Johnson . . . . Cynthia Rhodes
Max Kellerman . . . . Jack Weston
Lisa Houseman . . . . Jane Brucker
Marjorie Houseman . . . . Kelly Bishop
Neil Kellerman . . . . Lonny Price
Robbie Gould . . . . Max Cantor
Tito Suarez . . . . Charles Honi Coles
Billy Kostecki . . . . Neal Jones

Cannes — It's summer 1963 and college kids carry copies of "The Fountainhead" in their back pocket and condoms in their wallet. It's also a time for "Dirty Dancing" and in her 17th summer, at a Borscht Belt resort, Baby Houseman (Jennifer Grey) learns how to do it in this skin-deep but inoffensive teen-throb pic designed to titillate teenage girls. Beyond that b.o. prospects are fairly limited.

"Dirty Dancing" is a coming of age film cut from the same mold as "The Flamingo Kid" but with a bit less insight and period flavor. Too often the story takes a conventional turn rather than a true one.

Good production values, some nice dance sequences and a likable performance by Grey make the film more than watchable, especially for those acquainted with the Jewish tribal mating rituals that go on in the Catskill Mountain resorts.

A headstrong girl bucking for a career in the Peace Corps, Baby gets an education in life and loses her innocence when she befriends a young dancer (Cynthia Rhodes) in need of an abortion. She also gets involved with the hotel's maverick dance instructor Johnny Castle (Patrick Swayze) who teaches her to dance and a few other steps besides.

Although there are several crises along the way it's basically a pretty easy coming-of-age with all the rough edges smoothed off. Daddy (Jerry Orbach) is a doctor and probably more forgiving and permissive than any father was in real life, especially in 1963. Hyped up drama and lack of real conflicts give the film a fairytale-like quality.

Period flavor is simulated through a selection of well chosen pop tunes and several of the dance numbers are fun, particularly one to "Love Is Strange" as Baby and Johnny lip synch the words. Appalling, however, is the spectacle of the great tap dancer Honi Coles doing a disco shuffle.

Some of the other supporting characters are well drawn in screenplay by Eleanor Bergstein, who obviously knows this territory first-hand.

What really keeps the film moving over its numerous credibility gaps and glaring inconsistencies is Grey's energetic performance. Swayze's character is played too soft to be convincing but much of that seems to come from the writing and the direction by Emile Ardolino. But then they probably came out with exactly the film they wanted to make.—*Jagr.*

Straight To Hell
(BRITISH-COLOR)

A J&M presentation of an Island Pictures release of an Initial Pictures production of a Commies from Mars film. Produced by Eric Fellner. Directed by Alex Cox. Screenplay, Cox, Dick Rude; camera (color), Tom Richmond; music, The Pogues; production design, Andrew McAlpine; sound, Ian Voight; assistant director, Joe Ochaha. Reviewed at Cannes Film Festival (market), May 14, 1987. Running time: 86 MINS.
Norwood . . . . Sy Richardson
Simms . . . . Joe Strummer
Willy . . . . Dick Rude
Velma . . . . Courtney Love
Farber . . . . Dennis Hopper
Hives . . . . Elvis Costello
Sonya . . . . Grace Jones
Mr. Dade . . . . Jim Jarmusch
Also with: Biff Yeager, Zander Schloss, Sara Sugarman, The Pogues, Juan Torres.

Cannes — Audiences looking forward to the new Alex Cox pic, after "Repo Man" and "Sid and Nancy," will be sorely disappointed with "Straight To Hell," a strenuously unfunny comic-strip Western. It's going straight to nowhere.

Shot quickly in Almeria, Spain, but deliberately in view of a highway so traffic is seen frequently on the horizon, pic starts promisingly by introing three scrungy outlaws (Sy Richardson, Joe Strummer, Dick Rude) and their moll (Courtney Love) who wake up too late one morning to fulfill an assassination contract. After a desultory bank robbery, they head for the hills, and when their car breaks down, bury the loot and go on into a small town in which the rest of the action is set.

What follows is a labored parody of westerns, especially those of Leone and Peckinpah. It looks as though the cast and crew had fun, but only the most easily amused audience will raise a smile. Pic seems to be striving for cult status, but even this is iffy. It gets pretty dull as the tired jokes are dragged out; John Landis covered similar territory far more amusingly in "Three Amigos."

The cast has a variety of accents, and each does his or her own thing. Dennis Hopper makes a brief appearance, Elvis Costello has a running joke as a waiter always ready with a tray of coffee, even during the shootouts, and Jim Jarmusch makes a belated appearance as a villain. The prolonged gun battle that climaxes the film is nothing to write home about, but at least has some action to watch as opposed to the dreary first two-thirds of the pic. Most apt line of dialog comes from a girl who says: "Can I please go now? It's really boring for me." Many in the audience will feel sympathy.

There are joke credits for "Sex and Murder Consultant" and "Unnatural Acts Researcher," but funny credits do not a picture make. Final credit promises a sequel, "Back To Hell," a most unlikely event in the circumstances. —*Strat.*

The Gate
(CANADIAN-COLOR)

A New Century Entertainment/Vista Organization release of an Alliance Entertainment production. Produced by John Kemeny. Directed by Tibor Takacs. Screenplay, Michael Nankin; camera, (Medallion Film Labs color), Thomas Vamos; editor, Rit Wallis; music, Michael Hoenig, J. Peter Robinson; production design, William Beeton; sound (Dolby), Doug Ganton; special effects, Randall William Cook; makeup, Craig Reardon; coproduced by Andras Hamori; assistant directors, Michael Zenon, Bill Bannerman, Kathleen Meade; casting, Mary Gail Artz, Clare Walker. Reviewed at Cannes Film Festival (market), May 15, 1987 (MPAA Rating: PG-13). Running time: 92 MINS.
Glen . . . . Stephen Dorff
Al . . . . Christa Denton
Terry . . . . Louis Tripp
Lori Lee . . . . Kelly Rowan
Linda Lee . . . . Jennifer Irwin
Mom . . . . Deborah Grover
Dad . . . . Scot Denton

Cannes — Well written and directed, with excellent special effects and sympathetic performances, "The Gate" is a winner in the horror genre. What it lacks in plot and originality, pic more than makes up for in scary monsters and good fun, while keeping violence within bounds to hold on to PG-13 status. B.o. prospects are good.

The gate of the title is an innocent seeming hole in the backyard of a typical suburban home through which the Demon Lord and his gruesome minions emerge to try to take possession of the earth. Lead character Glen, a sensitive little boy plausibly limned by Stephen Dorff — vet of commercials and Disney's "Still The Beaver" — and his imaginative best friend (Louis Tripp) dig open the hole to get neat rocks, inadvertently unloosing all the stored-up evil, though baddies don't strike till mom and dad go away for the weekend, leaving Glen's older sister (Christie Denton) in charge.

After a series of dark omens including death of the family dog and a bout of levitation, the boys realize something supernatural is going on. Amusingly, they find out that the Demon Lord is behind it thanks to the liner notes of an LP by a heavy metal group. Attack by the evil forces, consisting mainly of waves of slimy pint-sized trolls, takes up last third of the pic, building to a suitably chilling climax, with happy-ending denouncement.

Realistic movement and expressions of the little monsters highlight Randall Cook's fine effects. But unlike most others in the genre, pic doesn't depend exclusively on the gory trappings of horror technology for its appeal. Script — maiden effort by Michael Nankin — and knowing touch of Canadian helmer Tibor Takacs (producer John Kemeny is also Canadian) create and sustain interest in what becomes of the characters, though they remain stereotypes. If any of the more recent horror titles can be deemed suitable for kids, this one shouldn't scare parents off, precisely because credible human elements predominate over ooze. —*Jay.*

I Love N.Y.
(U.S.-COLOR)

A Manhattan Films production (world sales, Manley Prods.). Produced by Andrew Garroni, Gianni Bozzacchi. Executive producer, Edward Meadow. Written and directed by Bozzacchi. Stars Scott Baio, Christopher Plummer, Kelly Van Der Velden. Camera (color), Armando Nannuzzi; music, Bill Conti. Reviewed at Cannes Film Festival (market), May 14, 1987. (No MPAA rating.) Running time: 110 MINS.
Mario Cotone . . . . Scott Baio
John R. Yeats . . . . Christopher Plummer
Nicole Yeats . . . . Kelly Van Der Velden
Irene . . . . Jennifer O'Neill
Leo . . . . Jerry Orbach
Anna Cotone . . . . Virna Lisi

Cannes — A glossy production veneer and personable topliners are not enough to breathe life into "I Love N.Y.," a predictable youth romance set against equally predictable Big Apple settings.

(Pic, which combined N.Y. locations with interior work at Rome's Cinecittà, surfaced in the Cannes market for international sales after a bumpy financial ride during production.)

Theme is a routine uptown girl-downtown guy affair, setting rising photographer Scott Baio in pursuit of well-heeled Kelly Van Der Velden, daughter of irascible stage star Christopher Plummer.

Result is a painting-by-numbers excursion through much too obvious terrain: young love, parental opposition, anguish, triumph, etc. New York, the love object of the title, has never looked more familiar.

Performances are all fine, and technically pic's adequate, but businesswise, it has little to offer.

— *Rant.*

Three Kinds Of Heat
(U.S.-COLOR)

A Cannon Intl. release. Produced by Michael J. Kagan. Written and directed by Leslie Stevens. Stars Robert Ginty, Victoria Barrett, Shakti. Camera (Rank color), Terry Cole; editor, Bob Dearberg; music, Michael Bishop, with Scott Page; sound, Stan Phillips; production design, Duncan Cameron; art direction, Alan Hunter Craig; set decoration, Robyn Hamilton-Doney; assistant director, Steve Bernstein; special effects supervision, John Gant; stunt coordinator, Peter Diamond; postproduction supervision, Michael Hartman; casting, Noel Davis, Jeremy Zimmerman, Bob McDonald; associate producer, Michael Hartman. Reviewed at Cannes Film Festival (market), May 17, 1987. (MPAA Rating: R.) Running time: 87 MINS.
Elliot Cromwell . . . . Robert Ginty
Sgt. Terry O'Shea . . . . Victoria Barrett
Major Shan . . . . Shakti
Harry Pimm . . . . Sylvester McCoy
George Norris . . . . Barry Foster
Angelica . . . . Jeannie Brown
Also with: Paul Gee, Malcolm Connell, Trevor Martin, Mary Tamm, Keith Edwards, Jack Hedley, Bridget Khan.

Cannes — "Three Kinds Of Heat" is a negligible action picture that plays rather like a busted tv pilot than a feature film. Admirers of writer-director Leslie Stevens will be bewildered by this shoddy production.

Burdened with an utterly wooden trio of contrasting lead players, Robert Ginty as a state department agent, 6-ft.-tall blond Victoria Barrett as a N.Y.C. cop and 6-ft.-tall oriental Shakti as a Hong Kong policewoman, pic throws them together on a chatty mission for Interpol. They're tracking down Sylvester McCoy, using the beautiful (and she looks to be 6-ft.-tall as well) Jeannie Brown as their surveillance target to get to him. Trail leads from New York (poorly faked since pic was shot in London) to London and back again, with a fiery finale in a warehouse that explains the film's original title, "Fireworks."

Mechanical action scenes dot the laborious running time en route to a boring explanation of the plot's twists, as well as an underwhelming unveiling of who the criminal mastermind is. Production is so threadbare and direction limp enough to make an action fan scream.

Ginty walks through his part drowsily, delivering lines with evident boredom. Barrett has little personality and is very unflatteringly photographed in her closeups. Shakti is odd-looking rather than pretty, and all Stevens does is make fun of her character's inability to pronounce the latter L. There is no heat whatsoever between them, no sex, no nudity and nothing to keep one from dozing off.

Credits list top British sex symbol/singing star Samantha Fox in a small role but she didn't show up in the print screened. She probably wasn't tall enough.—*Lor.*

Dear Cardholder
(AUSTRALIAN-COLOR)

A Mermaid Beach production, in association with Multifilms. Produced, written and directed by Bill Bennett. Camera (color), Tony Wilson; editor, Denise Hunter; music, Michael Atkinson; sound, Danny Cooper; production coordinator, Debbie Samuels; assistant director, Philip Rich; associate producer, Jenny Day. Reviewed at Cannes Film Festival (market), May 14, 1987. Running time: **90 MINS.**

Hec Harris . . . . Robin Ramsay
Aggie Smith . . . . Jennifer Cluff
Jo Harris . . . . Marion Chirgwin
Alfred Block . . . . Russell Newman
Hart . . . . John Ewart
Ardent . . . . : . . . . Patrick Cook
Terence . . . . Bob Ellis
Antoinette . . . . Arianthe Galani

Cannes — Bill Bennett's third feature, after his dramatized docu, "A Street To Die" and his improvisational thriller, "Backlash," is another change of pace: it's a comedy with serious undertones and a universal message about the madness of living beyond your means, on credit.

The pic's hapless hero is Hec Harris, a widower with a smart 12-year-old daughter; he's a humble clerk in the tax office, and dreams of devising a computer program to help the average Joe complete his tax form. He decides to buy a computer on credit, though since he's previously paid for everything in cash, he has no credit rating. Once this problem is solved (he borrows $500 from the bank and immediately returns it, incurring a hefty bill for interest in the process), he obtains a platinum credit card and starts spending.

After spending $10,000 in less than a week, he finds his credit cut off, but now that he knows the ropes he simply acquires other credit cards to pay off the first one. His debt eventually catches up with him, and the light mood of the film turns very dark when he loses his job, his apartment and his daughter, placed in a foster home by the welfare people. His one consolation is that he's fallen for an impoverished chicken farmer, sweetly played by Jennifer Cluff (the director's wife).

Indeed, the film has an abundance of charming supporting performances, including Marion Chirgwin as the feisty little daughter; John Ewart as the hero's kinky landlord; Patrick Cook as Hec's boss; Russell Newman as his avuncular bank manager; and writer-director Bob Ellis as a bum who was once a university lecturer.

But despite all these qualities, "Dear Cardholder" doesn't spark the way it should, and part of the problem is Robin Ramsay's lackluster performance in the lead; Ramsay plays Hec in a one-dimensional, unemotional fashion, and loses audience empathy as a result. Bennett's surprisingly detached direction is at fault, too; he seems uncomfortable with comedy, and is more confident in the film's more dramatic scenes.

Much of the humor is derivative (the inane announcements in the tax office, a joke that worked better in "Mash") or simply too slight. Buffs will smile at a Bennett in-joke, though, featuring a couple of cops who seem to have strayed in from "Backlash."

With its contrived happy ending (our hero gets a job with Apple) the serious points Bennett is making about the crazy way Australians (and, indeed, people all over the Western world) are getting deep into debt as a result of all-too-easy credit, tend to get lost along the way. Chalk this one down as a disappointment from one of Australia's most interesting talents, but the prodigious Bennett is already in postproduction on his fourth feature, a drama titled "Jilted."—*Strat.*

The Chipmunk Adventure
(U.S.-ANIMATED-COLOR)

A Samuel Goldwyn Co. presentation of a Bagdasarian Film production. Produced by Ross Bagasarian. Executive producer, Hope London. Directed by Janice Karman. Screenplay, Karman, Bagdasarian; music, Randy Edelman, others; Chipmunk and Chipettes design, Sandra; character design, Louise Zingarelli; production design, Carol Holman Grosvenor; directing animators, Skip Jones, Don Spencer, Andrew Gaskill, Mitch Rochon, Becky Bristow; associate producer, Gwendolyn Sue Shakespeare. Reviewed at Cannes Film Festival (market), May 9, 1987. (MPAA Rating: G.) Running time: **90 MINS.**
Voices: Ross Bagdasarian, Janice Karman, Dody Goodman, Susan Tyrrell, Anthony DeLongis, Frank Welker, others.

Cannes — After an on-again, off-again career in records and tv, Ross Bagdasarian Sr.'s creation of "The Chipmunk's," the bright-and-busy brothers Alvin, Simon and Theodore, are back again in their first animated feature, produced by Ross Jr. and directed by Janice Karman.

Pic is a friendly and, of course, tuneful little adventure story that has the three Chipmunks challenging the newly invented girl trio of The Chipettes to a real live round of their favorite videogame, "Around The World In 80 Days." Result is animated family entertainment with no hint of horror to scare censors anywhere, and "The Chipmunk Adventure," while never venturing into any new vistas or conceptions of animation, would seem sure to find its place on the holiday repertoire of the international cinema circuit.

The two threesomes kick off with a hilarious hot air balloon race, not knowing they actually are decoys for a couple of big-time diamond smugglers, Claudia (a blond witch for a change) and Klaus Furstein (a Klaus Kinski takeoff likely to enthuse adults as well). The race takes them into dangerous situations in high seas, even higher Alps and among Fiji Island natives.

All action is interspersed with smooth sequences of song and dance, the singing, of course, of the speeded-up, high-pitched Chipmunks variety matched, rather too shrilly, by the vocalizing of the Chipettes. The musical style is neatly polished pop/rock by score composer Randy Edelman, Terry Shaddick (of "Let's Get Physical" fame), Donna Weiss and Randy Goodrum. —*Kell.*

Broken Noses
(U.S.-DOCU-COLOR/B&W-16m)

A Steven Cohen and Kira Films production in association with Nan Bush. Executive producer, Cohen. Directed by Bruce Weber. Camera (color/b&w), Jeff Priess; editor, Phyllis Famiglietti; music coordinator, Cherry Vanilla; music, Julie London, Chet Baker Robert Mitchum, Danny Small, Gerry Mulligan, Joni James, Ken Nordine; sound, John Boisseau; production manager, Emie Amemiya; sound editing, Constance Rodgers, art director, Sam Shahid; associate producer, Bush. Reviewed at Cannes Film Festival (market), May 13, 1987. (No MPAA Rating.) Running time: **75 MINS.**

Cannes — "Broken Noses," the directorial bow of still photographer Bruce Weber, is an effective, affectionate subculture docu centered on off-the-wall personality of former National Golden Gloves boxing champ Andy Minsker.

Deftly avoiding most pug pic clichés — this is no "Kid Galahad" or "Golden Boy" — Weber, using a mixture of color and monochrome, concentrates less on Minsker the pro fighter than on Minsker the dynamo of the Mt. Scott boys boxing club near Portland, Ore.

A complex picture emerges of young narcissists whose violent pastime is submerged in a culture of camaraderie and self-discipline, animated by Minsker's unfailing determination to see his boys compete and succeed.

Revealing interviews with both boys and Minsker's family (plus lengthy contributions from the boxer himself) suggest the psychological depths behind what on the surface is just another smalltown story.

Helmer Weber applies a deceptively naive fly-on-the-wall technique, which in fact makes a carefully crafted, closely studied portrait of an unusual character and his surroundings.

"Noses" is hardly mass market fare, but has the qualities to build both cultish and crossover audiences in metropolitan sites in the U.S. and offshore, plus tv playoff. —*Rant.*

Backfire
(U.S.-COLOR)

An ITC Productions presentation. Produced by Danton Rissner. Directed by Gilbert Cates. Screenplay by Larry Brand, Rebecca Reynolds; camera (color), Tak Fujimoto; editor, Melvin Shapiro; music, David Shire; production design, Dan Lonino; sound, Larry Sutton; assistant director, Don Hauser; casting, Mike Fenton, Jane Feinberg. Reviewed at Cannes Film Festival (market), May 13, 1987. (No MPAA rating.) Running time: **91 MINS.**
Maura . . . . Karen Allen
Reed . . . . Keith Carradine
Donnie . . . . Jeff Fahey
Clint . . . . Bernie Casey
Jake . . . . Dean Paul Martin
Jill . . . . Dinah Manoff

Cannes — "Backfire" is an aptly named non-thriller since it never finds the spark to ignite it. Despite a few isolated thrills, pic mostly plods through a murky marital murder plot. Name cast may draw some interest but commercial outlook is decidedly downbeat for this clunker.

Story is constructed around the psychological scars of a Vietnam veteran (Jeff Fahey) who has a recurring nightmare of combat. Luckily he's rich enough not to have to do much in life and he has his wife (Karen Allen), who he brought over from the wrong side of the tracks, to take care of him. Or does he?

Something is clearly rotten in Denmark as Fahey's worst fears have a way of becoming reality. Of course there's an ex-lover (the late Dean Paul Martin) lurking in the background and once he mysteriously disappears Keith Carradine shows up on the scene to take his place.

Several disasters later, after Fahey has been reduced to a catatonic state, the story finally stumbles to its conclusion, but it still doesn't make a whole lot of sense. Screenplay by Larry Brand and Rebecca Reynolds is just a lot of plot for plot's sake without creating characters interesting enough to leap the credibility gap.

Peformances, as well, leave the characters up in the air and surely don't win any sympathy where needed. It is almost impossible to become involved in a psychological thriller if one doesn't know what the characters are thinking and why.

Director Gilbert Cates stages several dream scenes and one in the shower which are truly chilling, but lack of empathy fails to sustain the mood. Film is sorely lacking in pacing and rhythm and again misfires at the climax.

It's rather a shame, too, since considerable talent seems to be on hand and tech credits, especially Tak Fujimoto's deep green photography on the west coast of Canada, provide a moody setting for what could have been. —*Jagr.*

Levsha
(Left-Hander)
(SOVIET-COLOR)

A Lenfilm Studio production. Written and directed by Sergei Ovcharov. Camera (color), Valery Fedosov; art direction, Natalia Vasilieva; music, Igor Matsievski. Reviewed at the Cannes Film Festival (market), May 8, 1987. Running time: **91 MINS.**

With: Nikolai Stotski (Lefty), Vladimir Gostyukhin, Leonid Kuravliov, Yuri Yakovlev.

Cannes — "Lefty" is the film version of an old Russian folktale by Leskov, shot by Leningrad helmer Sergei Ovcharov with consummate skill and an acrobatic imagination. This top-quality kidpic lays on the comedy with everything from slapstick to camera tricks, backed by a topnotch cast.

Historical setting takes us back to the time of the emperor Alexander Pavlovich, who travels around Europe in search of novelties. The most amazing thing he finds is a steel flea made in England, so minute it has to be viewed through a microscope. It even performs a little dance when wound up with a tiny key.

Years later his successor, the emperor Nikolai Pavlovich, has the wonder shown to Russian craftsmen to se if they can improve on the British invention. After several days a trio of poor, roughly dressed craftsmen (including young Lefty) give back the flea. They have put microscopic shoes on it, with their names engraved on them.

Rest of this tall tale, enacted by comically outfitted characters, recounts how Lefty takes a trip to England to be introduced to the king, and his catastrophic return with a drunk old sailor.

Ovcharov's sense of humor is literate and witty, his editing snappy, and Natalia Vasilieva's sets a treat.

Pic captures the spirit of the Russian folktale quite convincingly, with a winning performance from Nikolai Stotski as the sympathetic, exploited young genius who remains a patriot to the end. Unmistakably Russian, too, is the last shot of an army of tattered workmen, praised as history's anonymous heroes in a voiceover. —*Yung.*

Dirigentarna
(A Woman Is A Risky Bet: Six Orchestra Conductors)
(SWEDISH-DOCU-COLOR)

A Swedish Film Institute release and world sales (Lena Enquist), Haga Film with Swedish Film Institute production. Conceived and directed by Christina Olofson. Camera (Eastmancolor), Lisa Hagstrand; editor, Johanna Hald; sound, Wille Peterson-Berger; production management, Inger Antonsson. Reviewed at Cannes Film Festival (market), May 14, 1987. Running time: **80 MINS.**

Cannes — Toscanini is quoted as having said that "conductors have to be geniuses ... and women are not creative genuises." Nevertheless, America's JoAnn Faletta is one conductor who won the Toscanini prize. Faletta, currently in charge of the Queens, N.Y. Philharmonic, is one of the symphony conductors of high international standing documentarist Christina Olofson has sought out to talk to privately and watch at work for her "A Woman Is A Risky Bet: Six Orchestra Conductors."

Result is a sinewy docu with particular flash in its capturing of the conductors' work processes, but also with a keen and alert ear for the sometimes assertive, at other times tentative statements these women make about the whys, wherefores and hows of their profession.

"A Woman is A Risky Bet" most likely will be wooed by many tv outlets around the world, and already here in Cannes a number of bids were made.

Conductors presented are Faletta; the Roanoke, Va., Symphony's Victoria Bond; The Stockholm People's Opera's Kerstin Nerbe; freelancer Ortrud Mann of Sweden; Norway's Camilla Kolchinsky, Russian-born and formerly working with the Israel Symphony; and the Moscow State Symphony's Veronika Dudarova. Caught at work, either with their backs to the camera or with their hands and faces in closeups (including private sounds of cajoling or swearing), Dudarova and Faletta are especially expressive of the very physical/psychological heart of all great music.

These women avoid feminist whimpers, but they do stress the particular hazards of baton-wielding womanhood: people, including musicians, tend to expect conductors to ooze physical strength ("their problem, not mine," says Bond, who certainly does not want her femininity, mental or physical, played under wraps in favor of brusque play-acting), and managers are loath to take on female talent, although there is an international shortage of conductors.

Documentarist Olofson also avoids feminist hectoring. She does great work when showing the world what women have to offer in a field where they rarely have excelled in the past. She however loses her way in some fantasy imagery about Elfrida Andrée (1841-1929) who tried but never really made it as a conductress.

She also verges on the maudlin in some obviously staged sequences about Nerbe finding the career-going tough, and film is structured too loosely and has too much landscape and cityscape footage of no true relevance. None of this, however, keeps "A Woman Is A Risky Bet" from being a sure-fire winner in its genre. —*Kell.*

Surf Nazis Must Die
(U.S.-COLOR)

A Troma presentation of an Institute production. Produced by Robert Tinnell. Executive producer, director, Peter George. Screenplay, Jon Ayre; camera (color), Rolf Kesterman; editor, Craig Colton; music, Jon McCallum; art director, Byrnadette diSanto; associate producer, Antonyia Verna. (No other credits supplied.) Reviewed at Cannes Film Festival (market), April 14, 1987. (MPAA Rating: R.) Running time: **80 MINS.**

With: Barry Brenner, Gail Neely, Michael Sonye, Dawn Wildsmith, Tom Shell, Dawne Ellison, Bobbie Bresee.

Cannes — It can't be denied there's a significant base of shlock underpinning any Cannes market; to rise above the swag of offerings, what better way could there be than to call a pic "Surf Nazis Must Die." That's a once-only moniker which surely has made this offbeat offering one of the most talked about, but not necessarily viewed, titles at this year's Cannes mart.

Coming from a company whose stable of titles includes "The Curse Of The Cannibal Confederates," "Demented Death Farm Massacre" and "I Was A Teenage TV Terrorist," there's no way "Surf Nazis Must Die" can or should be taken seriously. A sort of "Clockwork Orange" meets "Mad Max" on the beach, pic hasn't one redeeming feature, but as a wacko, tongue-in-cheek concept it could well profit from some sort of cult fixture status.

Time is the near future and California's social fabric has been torn apart by a devastating earthquake. Law and order have disappeared and it's hell out there on the beaches where gangs such as the "Samurai Surfers" rule the waves.

Striving for supremacy are the Surf Nazis, who live in a beach bunker, own beweaponed surf boards, bristle with knives and swastika tattoos, and are fueled by a surfing Führer — he has of course changed his name to Adolf — who has a dream of owning the "new beach."

Not much else is clear until a revenge-seeking mother takes on the Nazis after they kill her son; prior to this there are various and often bloody fights between the Nazis and the other gangs, and there's even regular surf footage interspersed throughout although how it fits in the rest of the film is anybody's guess.

The hulking mother, played by Bobbie Bresee, turns out to be quite a handful and wreaks gory retribution on each of the nasty Nazis.

Much of "Surf Nazis Must Die" is incoherent, the rest gratuitous.

Pic looks like most of its budget went on its titles, a not unlikable score, and a surprisingly punchy and facetious trailer, but there's a market out there for this sort of aberration, made up of those who thrive on such oddities, and, of course, the plain curious. —*Doch.*

The Caller
(U.S.-COLOR)

An Empire Pictures release of a Frank Yablans/Michael Sloan production. Executive producer, Charles Band. Produced by Yablans. Directed by Arthur Allan Seidelman. Screenplay, Sloan; camera (Technicolor), Armando Nannuzzi; editor, Bert Glatstein; music, Richard Band; sound, Beth Bergeron; production design, Giovanni Natalucci; special effects John Buechler; associate producer, Debra Dion; casting, Anthony Barnao. Reviewed at the Cannes Film Festival (market), May 13, 1987. (No MPAA Rating). Running time: **98 MINS.**
The Caller . . . . Malcolm McDowell
The Girl . . . . Madolyn Smith

Cannes — "The Caller" is a two-character suspense meller that has its moments of tension, but is handicapped by a script that strains credibility. The costars strive to rise above the plot, and their performances could help to stimulate some b.o. potential.

The setting is a cabin in an isolated forest, where a young widow lives alone. Her young daughter is with friends, and she's expecting her lover for dinner. Instead, comes the title character — his car has broken down, may he use the phone, please. Trembling, she reluctantly lets him in, then inexplicably offers him a drink, then a cigaret. He neither drinks nor smokes. Eventually, he waits outside for the tow truck. But the next morning he reappears in the village, and even more inexplicably she agrees to take a ride with him up a mountain road.

That evening, he's back at the cabin and, still trembling, (but for a different reason) she invites him to stay the night. There's heavy panting, but he fails to consummate. All the time, each is scoring points off the other. She illustrates how she could murder him, as he accuses her of having murdered her husband and lover. Having rescued her from a burning garage, she attacks him with a crossbow, and as he stumbles, he grabs a live wire and the sparks literally fly. At that point, the mystery of the caller is solved — as his face dissolves into a glutinous and gruesome mess, and the flesh rolls off his hand. He is, believe it or not, just a robot. There's more to come: before the fade, the caller, Mark 11 (a perfect clone), is back, this time flashing a sheriff's card for the young woman.

Most of the action takes place within the confines of the cabin, which seems singularly well equipped for sinister goings on with, in addition to the crossbow, a large axe with which she threatens her uninvited guest, and an array of murderous knives and daggers. Apart from her stupidity in encouraging the caller, it is hard to believe any young woman would choose to live in such a lonely and isolated home, virtually cut off from civilization.

As he wanders around the cabin, looking for hidden secrets, he opens a cupboard in the child's room, to reveal a lifesize doll hanging — for a moment given the impression it's her daughter given with the noose around her neck. It's that sort of picture, with artificial thrills to heighten the atmosphere.

Both Malcolm McDowell and Madolyn Smith to their credit give the impression they believe in what's happening. It is no easy task for them to sustain interest for more than an hour and a half, and they largely succeed. Arthur Allan Seidelman's direction keeps the two-hander on the move, and the Technicolor lensing by Armando Nannuzzi is fine. —*Myro.*

The Method
(U.S.-COLOR)

A Pacific Star Prods. presentation. Produced and directed by Joseph Destein. Screenplay, Rob Nilsson, Joel Adelman, Destein; camera (Monaco color), Steven Lighthill; editor, Jay Boekelheide, Victoria Lewis; music, Ray Obiedo; art direction, Gary Frutkoff; sound, Ann Evans; associate producer, Franklin Simone. Reviewed at Cannes Film Festival (market), May 10, 1987. (No MPAA Rating.) Running time: **105 MINS.**

Anna Beringer . . . . Melanie Dreisbach
Nick . . . . Richard Arnold
Monique . . . . Deborah Swisher
Tony . . . . Anthony Cistaro
Vincenzo . . . . Robert Elross
Greg . . . . Jack Rikesa
Deni . . . . Kathryn Knotts
Michael . . . . Rob Reece

Cannes — "The Method" is a well meaning indie effort from San Francisco that displays a lot of talent without coming up with a totally successful film. Story of a married woman who leaves her family to pursue her dream of being an actress is loaded with clichés, but still manages to cut through to some emotional truths. Pic is still a hard sell and will have its best shot in specialty venues and on the festival circuit.

Best thing going for this film is the knockout performance by Melanie Dreisbach as the 40-year-old beginner in a profession that worships youth and beauty. Her transformation from retiring housewife to uninhibited actress often takes easy street and skips a few stops along the way, but the sense of struggle always seems real.

Arriving in San Francisco and finding a cool reception from her roommate (Kathryn Knotts), Dreis-

bach sets out to learn her craft and has a series of predictable adventures in the process. The James Dean of the acting class (Anthony Cistaro) tries to seduce her, and then her acting teacher (Robert Elross) tells her if the going's too tough, then get out. Not exactly what she wanted to hear, but good advice.

In fact the strongest writing in the screenplay by Rob Nilsson, Joel Adelman and Joseph Destein is in the teacher-student sections. Elross contributes a good deal here too as he plays the crafty old mentor with just the right blend of gruffness and sympathy to make it believable.

First-time director Destein, who also produces, occasionally shows his inexperience but clearly has an affection and talent for working with actors, perhaps too much so.

Montages of actors working in class are repeated at least three times while exterior scenes often seem artificial. Destein is too concerned with filling the frame and frequently chooses locations for their scenic beauty rather than their function in the story.

Music is overused and overly sentimental, especially the title tune, as in the end credit return of the abandoned husband.

On the plus side, tech credits are professional and Steven Lighthill's camerawork captures the grittiness of the struggling actors world. But it's Dreisbach's show and she covers a great deal of emotional ground from a naive newcomer to a would-be prostitute researching a role.

Other performances also have their moments including Richard Arnold as a friend with possible romantic intentions and Knotts as a woman who has had too many hard knocks. —*Jagr.*

Testet
(The Test)
(SWEDISH-COLOR)

A Sandrews release of an AZ production with the Swedish Film Institute, Sandrews Films, FilmTeknik. Executive producer, Ann-Marie Harms. Produced, written and directed by Ann Zacharias. Camera (Eastmancolor), Hans Schött; sound and editor, Jean-Paul Vauban; music, Eva Dahlgren, Andres Glenmark; production design, Ann Zacharias. Reviewed at Cannes Film Festival (market), May 16, 1987. Running time: **92 MINS.**
The Woman . . . . Ann Zacharias
The Man . . . . Jean-François Garreaud

Cannes — "The Test," a Swedish feature shot with French dialog, has a young couple talking the subject of the woman's pregnancy, just discovered, to virtual cinematic abortion.

It's a woman's film in that the female viewpoints are presented poignantly (discussions are about facing reality and responsibility), the man being presented in whining, insecure, dilly-dallying ways.

It's also a woman's film in that Sweden's Ann Zacharias (born in 1956 and with a career in French films by Jacques Doillon, Alain Corneau, Claude Zidi, et al., behind her) produced, wrote, directed, did the production design and plays the female lead.

France's Jean-François Garreaud plays The Man. As a couple, the two actors look handsome and give credible performances, but their dialog zigzags between empty rhetoric and clichéd statements about the general human condition in a time of nuclear threats, pollution, etc.

Camerawork has professionalism, but here again no consistency is evidenced. Some framings are direct and natural, others contrived and pointless. Tempers flare, sweetness takes over, to be replaced by wry irony, while the two dress, undress, dress, undress, ad infinitum, within the near-naked walls of an apartment enlivened only by flower arrangements.

"The Test" is a non-film, but it has a certain feeble auteur stamp about it, and since it is French-speaking throughout, a French art circuit pickup would appear its only obvious offshore pickup chance. —*Kell.*

Sleep Well, My Love
(BRITISH-SWEDISH-COLOR)

A Bell Prods. presentation of a Planborg Film production. Executive producer, Paul Lichtman. Producer (and world sales), Conny Planborg. Directed by Arne Mattson. Screenplay, Jonathan Rumbold, based on story by Ernest Hotch; camera (Eastmancolor), Tomislav Pinter; casting, Maude Spector; production design, Zeljko Senecic; music, Alfi Kabiljo; sound, Jan Brodin; editor, Derek Trigg; production management, Gisela Bergquist. Reviewed at Cannes Film Festival (market), May 14, 1987. Running time: **97 MINS.**
Siska Torot . . . . Debra Beaumont
Her father . . . . Mark Burns
Her mother . . . . Fiona Curzon
Tom Berto . . . . Norman Bowler
The Hitman . . . . Michael Gothard
  Also with: Philip Bond, Carl Duering, Pedrag Bjelac (The Stud), Lidija Jenko, others.

Cannes — Incest is obviously great grist for the meller mill of today. In "Sleep Well, My Love," a self-styled drama-thriller of British-Swedish origin, treatment of the subject verges on the ludicrous, to the extent that director Arne Mattsson might better have shot his picture as tongue-in-cheek comedy.

"Sleep Well" may keep homevideo viewers sitting up when the end credits of "Dallas" and "Dynasty" have faded away. We move once again among the very rich, this time on Yugoslavian luxury hotel locations, where a divorced couple either hire a hitman or browbeat a lover into wiping the other out. The reason: Dad has a prolonged incestuous affair with his 16-year-old

daughter Siska, and Mom uses her knowledge of this to blackmail Dad. Only both of them are outsmarted (and killed) at the instigation of Siska who has designs on Mom's lover (at least on one of them).

Mattson, who won fame about 60 feature films ago with "One Summer Of Happiness," is now a journeyman helmer who turns in a credible job of thriller mush. Here, however, he works with a screenplay so silly and so badly structured it defeats him. Film's production dress is neat.

The acting, by British and Yugoslav professionals, has, well, professionalism. Only brunet Debra Beaumont, even when teary-eyed, fails to deliver anything beyond Barbie Doll posturing and a shrill voice. There is much more vicious punch of the Joan Collins "Alexis" variety to Fiona Curzon's glamorous blond Mom. To weigh it down rather than lift it up, "Sleep Well" has several sequences of trite softcore porn. —*Kell.*

Red Riding Hood
(U.S.-COLOR)

A Cannon Group release of a Golan-Globus production. Executive producer, Itzik Kol. Produced by Menahem Golan, Yoram Globus. Directed by Adam Brooks. Screenplay, Carole Lucia Satrina, from fairytale by The Brothers Grimm; camera (Rank color), Danny Shnegur, Ye'ehi Neyman; editor, David Tour, music, Stephen Lawrence; lyrics, Michael Korie; production manager, Asher Gat; costume design, Mirra Steinmatz; associate producer, Patricia Ruben; casting, Wendy Murray, Dalilah Hovers; in Dolby stereo. Reviewed at Cannes Film Festival (market), May 14, 1987. (No MPAA Rating.) Running time: **80 MINS.**
Godfrey Percival . . . . Craig T. Nelson
Lady Jeanne . . . . Isabella Rossellini
Red Riding Hood . . . . Amelia Shankley
Dagger The Wolf . . . . Rocco Sisto
Badger Kate . . . . Linda Kaye
Nanny Bess . . . . Helen Glazary
Allen Owen . . . . Julian Joy-Chagrin

Cannes — Cannon's Movietale version of "Red Riding Hood" is a desultory effort lacking imagination and inspiration. Though made as a theatrical film, it is as disposable as the recurring canned tv specials reviving public domain material at regular intervals in a form of planned obsolescence.

Carole Lucia Satrina's script pads out the modest storyline with a tale of a kingdom ruled by evil Godfrey (Craig T. Nelson) for seven years after his nice twin Percival (Nelson again) is missing in the wars. Godfrey leches after his bro's wife Lady Jeanne (Isabella Rossellini) and uses his magic powers to change his righthand man Dagger (Rocco Sisto) back and forth between man and wolf to act as his spy. Final reel has Sisto giving little Red Riding Hood (Amelia Shankley), so named because of the magical protective garment given her by her granny (Helen

Glazary), a hard time, even eating her up before a happy ending.

As the evil brother, Nelson hams embarrassingly, acting as if auditioning for a Richard III role. Sisto, supposedly in for comic relief, is also overwrought and unappealing. The female characters are wafer-thin but are given attractive and personable readings, especially by a radiant Rossellini and cute Shankley. Sappy songs that serve as necessary feature-length filler are sung indifferently, though Shankley's voice is fine.

Instead of horrific, low-budgeter looks merely pleasant, with nondescript forest settings, underdressed interior sets and poverty row attempts at musical numbers.
—*Lor.*

Outtakes
(U.S.-COLOR)

A Marketechnics release of a Sell Pictures production. (World sales, Noble Prods.) Produced by Jack M. Sell, Adrianne Richmond. Executive producers, Warren Dominick, Edward Sweeney. Directed by Sell. Screenplay, Sell, Richmond, Jim Fay; camera (color), Ron Bell, Sell; editor, Sell; theme music, Sell; music, Rich Daniels, Chris Lay; production manager, Kerry Lenovich; assistant director, Richmond; associate producers, Lenovich, Rob Meiresonne, Eric Pudil, Bruce Richmond; art direction, Marianne Heidecke. Reviewed at Cannes Film Festival (market), May 10, 1987. (No MPAA Rating.) Running time: **71 MINS.**
With: Forrest Tucker, Bobbi Wexler, Joleen Lutz, Curt Colbert, Marilyn Adams, Warren Davis, Coleen Downey, Jim Fay, Jack M. Sell.

Cannes — Its title something of a misnomer, "Outtakes" is a lame-duck entry in the comedy sketch film genre which numbered such hits as "The Groove Tube" and "Tunnelvision" over a decade ago. There are a few laughs, lots of vulgarity and long stretches of boredom.

Pic is dedicated upfront to the late Forrest Tucker, who acts as irreverent host to the mélange of skits on view. Clapperboards indicate the Tucker scenes were filmed in 1983, though the pic itself was completed in 1985.

Extremely long segments are devoted to an often funny spoof of the Phil Donahue tv show, and a lampoon of latenight tv newscasts which has its moments but is a pale imitation of so much funnier material on "Saturday Night Live" or in "Tunnelvision." A satire of a Santa Claus as slasher in horror pics is stupid and amateurish, while the interstitial sketches are brief but unfunny. Actual outtakes do not appear until the end credits which drag on in order to pad out the feature's abbreviated running time.

Filmmaker Jack M. Sell obviously is having fun, even poking barbs at himself, but his frequent onscreen appearances as the sleazy director ultimately seem like an ego trip (he even warbles the title song he wrote in an opening poverty-row budget attempt at a music video about a starlet's travails in Hollywood). Rest of repertory cast is pretty weak, the unidentified Donahue imitator doing the best job. Tucker seems uncomfortable, even beyond the put-on "fed up" routine he is called upon to enact. —*Lor.*

Belinda
(AUSTRALIAN-COLOR)

A Fontana production. Produced by Bedrich Kabriel. Written and directed by Pamela Gibbons. Camera (color), Malcolm McCullogh; editor, David Huggett; production design, Herbert Pinter; sound, Tim Lloyd; choreography, Robyn Moase; production manager, Sue Wild; assistant director, Adrian Pickersgill; casting, Alison Barrett. Reviewed at Cannes Film Festival (market), May 11, 1987. Running time: **97 MINS.**
Belinda .... Deanne Jeffs
Crystal .... Mary Regan
Sandra .... Kaarin Fairfax
Benny .... Nicos Lathouris
Doreen .... Hazel Phillips
Graeme..................... John Jarratt
Mandy .... Elizabeth Lord
Belinda's mother .... Gerda Nicholson
Belinda's father .... Alan Cassell
Jamie .... Tim Burns
Also with: Caz Lederman (Rhonda), John Haddon (Jeremy Shaw), Joy Smithers (Liz), Jeff Rhoe (Tim), Armando Hurley (Billy James).

Cannes — "Belinda" is light on narrative but very strong on atmosphere and character. Former dancer and actress Pamela Gibbons apparently was inspired by her own experiences to make "Belinda," a first feature which vividly evokes the world of a naive 16-year-old ballet dancer who gets a job in the chorus at a seedy Sydney nightclub in 1968. In the leading role, newcomer Deanne Jeffs, herself only 16 during the pic's production, gives an immensely appealing performance, and can dance, too. She has a future.

Belinda comes from a strait-laced, conservative family, and continues to live at home even though working in the sleaziest district of Australia, Sydney's King's Cross. Yet she retains her innocence, despite coming into contact with some very shady characters.

Best scenes involve Belinda's relationships with the other girls in the chorus line, led by Crystal, an older woman who yearns to be with her son, who's been sent off to school overseas. As Crystal, New Zealand actress Mary Regan ("Heart Of The Stag") steals the film with a glowing performance as a woman near the end of her emotional tether. Her fate, when it comes, provides the film with a chilling climax.

"Belinda" also charts the dying days of an era, since by the late 1960s many clubs, like the one in which Belinda works, were closing down to make way for discos. Closure of this particular club is abruptly announced by the sinister club manager (Nicos Lathouris) in another of the film's best scenes.

Deanne Jeffs manages to encapsulate a tough, dogged determination as well as all-pervading naiveté, and copes well with the film's big dramatic scene, where she's viciously assaulted by a jealous woman (Caz Lederman) in an alley behind the club. Scenes in which she attends ballet school under teacher John Jarratt add a further dimension to her character.

Gibbons fills the picture with interesting cameos, obviously culled from personal reminiscence: the club's transvestite cleaning woman, the gay guy in charge of wardrobe, the sinister types who come and go, carrying out their unknown, doubtless nefarious dealings behind the scenes, the motherly woman (Hazel Phillips) who's in charge of the girls and is never without a dog in her arms, the small, wide-eyed boy, deaf and crippled, son of one of the girls, whose playground is the women's dressing room.

Technically, "Belinda" is good, with solid camerawork by Gibbons' husband, Malcolm McCullogh, and a very sharp soundtrack. it was mostly shot in the Fontana Film Studios in Sydney. — *Strat.*

Sotto Il Ristorante Cinese
(Below The Chinese Restaurant)
(ITALIAN-COLOR)

A D.M.V. release of a Reteitalia/Bozzetto Intl. coproduction. Directed by Bruno Bozzetto. Screenplay, Bozzetto, Fabio Conara; camera (color), Agostino Castiglioni; editor, Roberto Frattini; music, Ugo Rossi; art direction, Carmelo Patrono. Reviewed at Cannes Film Festival (market), May 9, 1987. Running time: **89 MINS.**
Ivan Rosco .... Claudio Botosso
Eva .... Amanda Sandrelli
Ursula Bridge .... Nancy Brilli
Father .... Bernard Blier
Mother .... Claudia Lawrence

Cannes — "Below The Chinese Restaurant" is well made Italo entertainment for young teens who like their sci-fi mixed with comedy and a little romance. Bruno Bozzetto, helmer of several animated features, directs a likable, low-key cast in adventures ranging from bank robbery to time travel. There is some make-believe violence in which nobody gets hurt, but pic's erotic candor sometimes seem precocious for kids who'd go for such an innocent tale.

Ivan (Claudio Botosso) is a nice, ordinary young man about to get married to his boss (Nancy Brilli), a blond, harsh and domineering exec. His eccentric mother (Claudia Lawrence), an aged ballerina, doesn't care for her.

One morning Ivan gets mixed up in a bank holdup. While trying to escape from the robbers, he stumbles onto a secret door in the basement under a Chinese restaurant. He opens it onto a golden sand beach — actually another world with strange E.T.-like creatures and twin suns, inhabited only by young Eva (Amanda Sandrelli) and her eccentric inventor-father Bernard Blier.

For Eva it's love at first sight, and she impulsively follows Ivan back to his world. Ivan stodgily rejects her advances, until another adventure with criminals on his wedding day convinces him Eva's his match. He leaves his bossy fiancée in the arms of a barbarian in another dimension, leaves Mom dancing with Blier under the twin suns, and takes Eva back to live with him in his smoggy city.

Special effects are limited, though the occasional animated monster appears to make one smile. The chase scenes are played more for comedy than chills. Well filmed on the whole. — *Yung.*

Kidnapped
(U.S.-COLOR)

A Hickmar production. (World sales, Fries Entertainment.) Produced by Marlene Schmidt. Written and directed by Howard Avedis. Stars David Naughton. Camera (Deluxe color), Tom De Nove; editor, Michael Luciano, Lloyd Nelson; music, Ron Jones; sound, Bayard Carey; assistant director, John Woodward. Reviewed at Cannes Film Festival (market), May 11, 1986. (No MPAA Rating.) Running time: **98 MINS.**
Det. Vince McCarthy .... David Naughton
Bonnie .... Barbara Crampton
Victor Nardi .... Lance LeGault
Tony .... Chick Vennera
Debbie .... Kim Evenson
Porno shop clerk .... Jimmie Walker
Buster .... Kin Shriner
Marsha .... Michelle Rossi
Carl .... Robert Dryer
Frank Nardi .... Gary Wood
Police lieutenant .... Charles Napier

Cannes — Boasting a solid cast, "Kidnapped" is a routine action thriller done well. It's not special enough to make any noise theatrically, but is good programming fodder for other media.

Barbara Crampton and Kim Evenson are blond sisters on the town in L.A. who get mixed up with a photographer (Chick Vennera) trying to pick them up on the street. He has Evenson kidnaped and delivered to gangster Lance LeGault who drugs her in preparation for starring her in a porn film.

Crampton teams with sympatico cop David Naughton to track Evenson down and their rather klutzy approach (which causes many a headache to his police superior Charles Napier) hits a funny nadir when the duo pose as porno thesps and are mighty embarrassed when Gary Wood (as the gangster's brother) has them audition for a porn flick.

A happy ending ensues but not before Evenson gets manhandled considerably.

With an effective sense of humor, pic gets by with some seamy material, covering the same ground as Paul Schrader's "Hardcore" but with a different point-of-view. Film's softcore exploitation scenes are suitable exploitative, and writer-director Avedis makes a sharp distinction that it is underground "teenage" porn, not the mainstream porn industry, that constitutes the heavies of this story.

Naughton and Crampton are attractive leads, Evenson a stunning pinup (a mite old to be playing sweet 16) and LeGault a cool heavy. Wood is excellent as the self-righteous pornographer and remaining cast is fine. Tech credits are good, though Avedis largely substitutes cheapo foot chases for more elaborate action stagings.—*Lor.*

Om Kärlek
(About Love)
(SWEDISH-COLOR)

A Sandrews (Stockholm) release of an Omega Film production with Swedish Television/SVT-1 and The Swedish Film Institute. Produced by Peter Kropenin. Directed by Mats Arehn. Screenplay, Arehn, Thomas Samuelson, Anette Kullenberg; camera (Fujicolor), Mischa Gavrjusjov; editor, Thomas Samuelson; music, Ulf Wahlberg, Wlodek Gulgowski, main title theme sung by Susanne Alfvengren, Mikael Rickfors; production design, Cian Bornebusch; sound, Samuelson; production management, Raili Salmi. Reviewed at Cannes Film Festival (market), May 11, 1987. Running time: **97 MINS.**
Peter . . . . Sven Wollter
Helene . . . . Linn Stokke
Christian . . . . Sverre Anker Ousdal
Eva . . . . Pia Green
Also with: Kalle Wollter, Maria Koblanck, Emma Samuelson, Ruth Stevens.

Cannes — Totally undaunted and with almost total failure, Swedish director and cowriter Mats Arehn tries to turn the old "A Man & A Woman" trick into magic again with "About Love."

A divorced father with two live-in kids meets a girl, recently married to a businessman with one live-in kid by a former marriage. When everybody has met at a school graduation, they all go off on vacation only to meet again (no accident) on Majorca. The businessman is absent, or absentminded, some of the time, while the new love blooms.

Everybody returns to Sweden where the would-be lovers finally bed down dismally in a cheap motel and wake up and split with a bad taste in their mouths. Soon a reunion is contrived and at least two of the kids join in a happy ending as phony as three-kroner bill. Romantic music that is pure swill accompanies each tentative approach between the man and the woman, and some trite scenic cinematography and shots of Majorcan folklore are

thrown in for bad measure.

Worst of all is the combination of a totally insipid screenplay and slack direction of actors who (Sweden's Sven Wollter at his usual vigorously inventive best) strain to install Arehn's flat-out candy-floss romancing with a minimum of redeeming, lifelike absurdity. Unfortunately, Norway's Linn Stokke, although pretty as a picture in the female lead, displays about as much personality as a supermarket shampoo bottle, but raises no foam at all.
—*Kell.*

The Woo Woo Kid
(In The Mood)
(U.S.-COLOR)

A Lorimar Motion Pictures release of a Gary Adelson/Karen Mack Prods. production. Produced by Adelson, Mack. Written and directed by Phil Alden Robinson. Stars Patrick Dempsey, Talia Balsam, Beverly D'Angelo. Camera (color), John Lindley; editor, Patrick Kennedy; music, Ralph Burns; costumes, Linda Burns. Reviewed at Cannes Film Festival (market), May 9, 1987. (No MPAA Rating.) Running time: **99 MINS.**
Sonny Wisecarver . . . . Patrick Dempsey
Judy Cusimano . . . . Talia Balsam
Francine Glatt . . . . Beverly D'Angelo
Mr. Wisecarver . . . . . Michael Constantine
Mrs. Wisecarver . . . . Betty Jinett

Cannes — "The Woo Woo Kid" is a daffy comedy allegedly based on a real story set in 1944 of a California 15-year-old who took up with two women in their 20s, married one of them, and made headlines in hero style and was dubbed "the woo woo kid."

Pic begins in high spirits with the teener skipping school regularly, aching to grow up and have sex with the lady across the street. They both run away from home, are married, get caught. He's sentenced in court to leave town for the summer and keep away from her. The marriage is annulled.

He finds another lonely lady but, caught again, is up against the same stern judge, is jailed, escapes and in a sweet ending finds a girl his own age whom he marries off camera.

Director Phil Alden Robinson loses much of the fun near the halfway mark and only partly recovers. Pic is kept in period, except for a jarring and extraneous courtroom sequence where the teen's mother says he's big for her age. Teen spectators applaud the double entendre and the judge has the bailiff go out and measure the youth who is pronounced normal size.

Teener Patrick Dempsey is fine and innocent looking, Talia Balsam just as fine and Beverly D'Angelo a perky knockout and properly brassy to boot. No sex scenes are shown.

Production values are good and the story, told via voiceover, is bouncy enough for reasonable theatrical playoff and afterlife in all ancillaries. It's a quiet comedy that

should have been better done, but is okay as is. —*Adil.*

La Vida Alegre
(A Life Of Pleasure)
(SPANISH-COLOR)

An El Catalejo production, in collaboration with Spanish Television. Executive producer, Ana Huete. Written and directed by Fernando Colomo. Camera (color), Javier Salmones; sound, Miguel Angel Polo; production manager, Esther Garcia; costumes, Lala Huete. Reviewed at Cannes Film Festival (market), May 9, 1987. Running time: **98 MINS.**
Ana . . . . Veronica Forqué
Antonio . . . . Antonio Resines
Carolina . . . . Ana Obregón
Rosi . . . . Massiel
Also with: Miguel A. Rellán, Guillermo Montesinos, Itziar Alvarez, José A. Navarro, Gloria Muñoz, Alicia Sánchez, Chus Lampreave, Rafaela Aparicio, Gran Wyoming and Javier Gurruchaga.

Cannes — Probably the year's top comedy from Spain, "La Vida Alegre" is a well paced and scripted romp set in modern Madrid. Pic has been doing boffo biz in its own country and could tickle the funny bones of spectators in other territories as well.

Action and laughs revolve mostly around the wife of the assistant minister of health who sets up a small office to fight venereal disease. To attract clients she goes out with her workmate to canvass business in the red light district and in gay bars, while her bumbling husband tries to clean up the dust she raises with his boss, the health minister. The minister, together with his wife and his paramour, gets drawn into the shenanigans. Tone of pic sometimes brushes the farcical, but never degenerates into slapstick. Many of the situations are truly hilarious; dialog is perky and clever.

Contributing greatly is alternately deadpan and agitated performance on Antonio Resines, who is here at his best in many years. Buoying up pic is delightful performance of comedienne Veronica Forqué and a motley set of characters who enliven this comedy of modern Madrid manners.

Tightly scripted, using lotsa modern Spanish slang, pic is the best film Colomo has done and confirms his claim to being the leader of the new Madrid comedy. His humor here is always honed to a fine point and never slips into the gratuitous or vulgar. — *Besa.*

Prison Ship
(Star Slammer)
(U.S.-COLOR)

A Worldwide Entertainment release of a Jack H. Harris presentation of a Viking Films Intl. production. (International sales, Films Around The World.) Produced by Harris, Fred Olen Ray. Directed by Ray. Stars Ross Hagen, Sandy Brooke, Susan Stokey. Screen-

play, Michael D. Sonye; camera (Fujicolor), Paul Elliott; editor, Miriam L. Preissel; music, Anthony Harris; sound (Ultra-Stereo), Robert Janiger; production design, Michael Novotny, Wayne Springfield; art direction, Maxine Shepard; assistant director, Tony Brewster; production manager, Robert Tinnell; special makeup effects, Matt Rose, Mark Williams; special effects design, Bret Mixon; stunt coordinator, John Stewart; production assistant, Peter George. Reviewed at Cannes Film Festival (market), May 11, 1987. (No MPAA Rating.) Running time: **86 MINS.**
Bantor . . . . Ross Hagen
Taura . . . . Sandy Brooke
Mike . . . . Susan Stokey
The Justice . . . . John Carradine
Torturer . . . . Aldo Ray
Muffin . . . . Dawn Wildsmith
Warden Exene . . . . Marya Gant
Krago . . . . Michael D. Sonye
Also with: Richard Hench, Lindy Skyles, Johnny Legend, Bobbie Bresee, Jade Barrett.

Cannes — A thorough knowlege of sci-fi B-movies pervades "Prison Ship" (alternately titled "Star Slammer" and subtitled "The Adventures Of Taura Part I"), an affectionate camp effort made in 1984 by prolific indie helmer Fred Olen Ray. Target audience is buffs who will catch the various in-jokes and elements of spoof.

Pic is styled as a serial with four chapters. First seg is set on Planet Arous (a nod to the John Agar '50s classic) and has the look of a B-Western shot in some canyon. Sandy Brooke is Taura, a tough gal miner who runs afoul of Magistrate Bantor (Ross Hagen), who represents the hated Sovereign. She brutally burns Bantor's hand in a fight and is framed and sent to Star Slammer (that's Chapter 2's title), the prison ship Vehemence.

Remainder of pic, recycling used sets from such flms as "2010," "Galaxy Of Terror" and "Android," takes place in this Outer Space women's prison, with spirited mocking of the clichés of women-in-chains features. Brooke is thrown in with some very tough babes, but quickly establishes her own fighting prowess and trustworthiness. Teaming up with the gal's leader Mike (Susan Stokey) and a beautiful doctor who is working for the underground (Jade Barrett), she helps engineer a successful jailbreak, setting up a promised sequel titled "Chain Gang Planet."

On a miniscule budget, "Prison Ship" provides okay modelwork for space battles, cute little monsters called Jagger Rats and lots of assorted silliness. Acting is way over the top, with Marya Gant as the grotesque Rubensesque warden and Dawn Wildsmith as her right hand momma taking home hambone honors. Director Ray has gone on to bigger projects since making this one so the sequel is anything but certain. Film's cheapo production values are part of its charm but certainly will limit its marketability.
————————————— *Lor.*

Frenchman's Farm
(AUSTRALIAN-COLOR)

A Goldfarb (U.S.), CEL (Australia) release of a Mavis Branston production. Produced by James Fishburn. Executive producer, Colson Worner. Directed by Ron Way. Screenplay, Way, Fishburn, Matt White, based on a screenplay by William Russell; camera (Eastmancolor), Malcolm McCulloch; editor, Pippa Anderson; music, Tommy Tycho; art direction, Richard Rooker; sound, Max Bowring; production manager, Penny Wall; assistant director, Dorian Newstead; associate producer, Matt White. Reviewed at Greater Union screening room, Sydney, April 28, 1987 (in market at Cannes Film Festival.) Running time: **102 MINS.**

Jackie Grenville	Tracey Tainsh
Barry Norton	David Reyne
Benson	Ray Barrett
Rev. Aldershot	Norman Kaye
Bill Dolan	John Meillon
Det. Mainsbridge	Andrew Blackman
John Hatcher	Phil Brock

Also with: Tui Bow (Old Lady), Kym Lynch (George Slater), Andrew Johnston (William Morris), Lynne Schofield (Mme. Cheveraux).

Sydney — A supernatural melodrama about a ghostly executioner guarding a treasure left over from the French Revolution, "Frenchman's Farm" is a bland programmer. Theatrical possibilities will be limited to undemanding venues, but there may be a career ahead for easygoing video fans.

Heroine Tracey Tainsh, supposedly atop her law class at college, though you'd never guess it from the way she behaves, is driving through the Queensland countryside when she takes a detour off the main road to avoid a bush fire and stumbles on lonely Frenchman's Farm where she witnesses a murder: a tall man with a pale face and funny boots beheads a World War II soldier. Seems the killing actually took place in 1944, and was reported in the press at the time: Tainsh sees a photo of the man arrested for the crime, but knows the killer she saw wasn't him.

Accompanied by boyfriend David Reyne, another unlikely law student, who moonlights as a rock singer, she returns to the farm where she meets the current owner (Ray Barrett), a drunk. The local priest (Norman Kaye), an amateur historian, is more helpful, and meanwhile a veteran cop (John Meillon) is on the trail. The ghostly killer keeps killing, and there's no happy ending.

The screenplay, by first-time director Ron Way (from tv), producer James Fishburn and associate producer Matt White, is a mass of clichés, compounded by the wooden acting of the leads and the obvious direction. The music, which employs a heavenly choir at key moments, doesn't help, and Way has an annoying habit of repeating significant moments when they're referred to again later in the film, just to nudge those members of the audience too dumb to be following the plot.

Actually, the plot's pretty incomprehensible, except for the fact that the ghostly killer, whose fixed stare gives the impression he's been watching too much daytime tv, finds plenty of victims. An uncredited clip from an ancient French Revolution pic ("Orphans Of The Storm" perhaps?) shapes up as the most vivid footage in the film.

Such normally reliable thesps as Norman Kaye, John Meillon and Ray Barrett can do little with their material and technical credits are average. The heroine's obligatory nude swim (shot form behind) takes place in some very stagnant-looking water. Best hope for this item is quick playoff, and then onto the video shelves pronto. —*Strat.*

It's Alive III: Island Of The Alive
(U.S.-COLOR)

A Warner Bros. presentation of a Larco production. Executive producer, Larry Cohen. Produced by Paul Stader. Written and directed by Cohen. Camera (Technicolor prints), Daniel Pearl; editor, David Kern; music, Laurie Johnson; "It's Alive" theme music, Bernard Herrmann; sound (Ultra-Stereo), Kim Ornitz; production manager-supervising producer, Paul Kurta; special makeup effects, Steve Neill; original baby design, Rick Baker; model effects, William Hedge. Reviewed at Cannes Film Festival (market), May 12, 1987. (No MPAA Rating.) Running time: **91 MINS.**

Steve Jarvis	Michael Moriarty
Ellen Jarvis	Karen Black
Sally	Laurene Landon
Ralston	Gerrit Graham
Dr. Perkins	James Dixon
Dr. Brewster	Neal Israel
Swenson	Art Lund
Miss Morrell	Ann Dane
Judge Watson	Macdonald Carey

Cannes — Various types of satire blend satisfyingly in "It's Alive III: Island Of The Alive," a belated followup to Larry Cohen's 1970s tales of monster babies. The first pic was a sleeper hit for WB (thanks to a clever "Rosemary's Baby"-styled campaign) while "It Lives Again" flopped. Latest entry is geared towards homevideo where it is a safe bet to please genre fans.

Michael Moriarty has a lot of fun (and is on a long leash) in the lead role of Steve Jarvis, father of a monster child who is in court to prevent the state from executing the kid as a threat to the community. Opening scene and clever dialog that follows establish the premise of mutated monster children as raising issues closely akin to the current hot topics of abortion and even the AIDS epidemic (a prostie who sleeps with Jarvis is horrified he didn't warn her of his status as father to a monster), allowing Cohen to mock attitudes without hitting such hot potatoes head on.

Sympathetic Judge Watson (Macdonald Carey) sides with Jarvis and the monster babies (four in all) are sent to a remote island to be quarantined. Five years later (no new babes have been born in civilized society) Jarvis is summoned to be part of a scientific expedition to the island. By this time the kids have grown up already and even have an infant of their own on the island.

The monsters wipe out the scientists, but capture Jarvis to pilot their ship to Florida in order to meet with Jarvis' ex-wife Ellen (Karen Black), mother of their informal leader. Jarvis is set adrift by them, lands in Cuba and in one of the film's typically playful scenes is escorted by some firendly Cubans to Florida after they believe his outrageous story.

The monsters, who look like midgets with grotesquely large heads, have fights with bikers, save Ellen from a would-be masher and conk out due to a measles-type rash just before the police close in on them. Wild happy ending has the Jarvises and grandchild forming a literal nuclear family, penniless but cheerful and carefree.

Cohen pours on the black humor and though film is too talky for an actioner. it remains interesting throughout. The monsters are an effective combo of stopmotion animation, puppets and little guys in costumes. Laurie Johnson's score captures a nice 1940s *film noir* feel.
— *Lor.*

Munchies
(COLOR)

A Concorde Pictures release. Produced by Roger Corman. Coproducer, Ginny Nugent. Directed by Bettina Hirsch. Screenplay, Lance Smith; Munchies created by Robert Short; production manager, Jamie Beardsley; art director, John Ballowe; costumes, Katie Sparks; casting, Rosemary Welden. Reviewed at Brywood theater, Kansas City, April 15, 1987 (in market at Cannes Film Festival.) (MPAA Rating: PG.) Running time: **85 MINS.**

Cecil/Simon	Harvey Korman
Paul	Charles Stratton
Cindy	Nadine Van Der Velde
Melvis	Alix Elias
Eddie	Charlie Phillips
Big Ed	Hardy Rawls
Dude	Jon Stafford
Bob Marvelle	Robert Picardo
Marge Marvelle	Wendy Schaal
Buddy Holly	Scott Sherk

Also with: Lori Birdsong, Traci Huber-Sheridan, Paul Bartel.

Kansas City — "Munchies" is an unabashed attempt to capitalize on the "Gremlins" genre by low-budgeteer Roger Corman, who tries with this production to follow in the footsteps of Joe Dante, a Corman protégé and the actual maker of "Gremlins." Corman has the framework of a decent script idea, but it is poorly crafted with the budget limitations showing through. There's not much a creature fan could sink his teeth into.

Harvey Korman has a dual role, first as an anthropologist who discovers the cute little creature in a cave high in the Peruvian mountains. He brings it home to his small Texas town and puts it in the care of his son (Charles Stratton) and his girlfriend (Nadine Van Der Velde). The name "Munchies" becomes a natural for the critter as it munches on tidbits fed to it in its leather carrying pouch.

The other Korman is a dimwitted brother of the scientist, neither are in any scenes with the other. The brother tries to steal the Munchie, discovering in the process that the cute little creature can become a mean little cuss under pressure, and worse, when cut in two it can fully regenerate and become two Munchies. Dimwit doesn't get the idea, continues to have them slashed apart until there is a flock. They cut a trail of violence, steal Stratton's car to begin a car chase, disrupt a motorcycle gang and leave a path of destruction in their wake.

Fortunately, Stratton finds the cure to be "God power" (lightning) of the Incas, or electricity by his interpretation. A Munchie can be turned to clay by an electric shock, and in one of the better scenes Stratton electrocutes them all as they come off a production line inadvertently set up by the dimwit. The proceedings generally are muddled, however, because of loose-gaited script and direction.

Korman is adequate as the scientist father, but almost a slapstick as the brother. Stratton and Van Der Velde are adequate in the boy-girl roles, but rest of the cast is called upon for little more than being present. Laughs come where they should not and incongruities abound — such as a 2-ft. Munchie driving a car, even with help from another Munchie on the accelerator.—*Quin.*

Blood Hook
(U.S.-COLOR)

A Troma release of a Golden Chargers production for Spider Lake Films. Produced by David Herbert. Executive producers, Lloyd Kaufman, Michael Herz. Directed by James Mallon. Screenplay, Larry Edgerton, John Galligan; camera (Duart color), Marsha Kahm; editor, Kahm; music, Thomas A. Naunas; sound, Naunas; assistant director, Jo Anne Garrett. Reviewed at Cannes Film Festival (market), May 10, 1987. (MPAA rating: R.) Running time: **95 MINS.**

Peter	Mark Jacobs
Ann	Lisa Todd
Rodney	Patrick Dana
Kirsten	Sara Hauser
Wayne Durst	Paul Drake
Luedke	Don Winters

Cannes — "Blood Hook" is an entertaining horror feature that manages to singlemindedly milk suspense and honest yocks out of its overdone and intentionally fishy premise. It's a minor discovery in a decadent genre.

Peter (Mark Jacobs) and his teen friends are obvious prey for a maniacal fisherman when they go to the Wisconsin backwoods house of his granddad, killed 17 years ago in mysterious fashion. There are many goofball locals to qualify as suspects, with the killer turning out to be a war vet whose metal plate in his head picks up radio music and cicadas' chirping vibrations that drive him crazy and force him to kill. He uses a huge three-hooked gadget to gorily snag and reel in his victims.

A Muskie Madness fishing competition is in full swing thereabouts, causing the local sheriff, in time-honored "Jaws" fashion, to ignore the evidence of foul play so as not to jeopardize the tourist trade.

Such conventional material is made palatable by film's incessant stress upon all things having to do with fish, loading the script with puns and an entertaining sense of the ridiculous. The absence of outright spoof is refreshing, so the pic plays straight but is still funny. Cast is okay (and hammy where called for) and lakeside locations attractive and atmospheric.—*Lor.*

China Run
(U.S.-DOCU-COLOR)

A Reel Movies Intl. release of Great Friendship Run/Mickey Grant production in collaboration with Beijing Film Studios. Producer, Grant. Executive producer, Stan Cottrell. Directed by Grant. Stars Cottrell. Conceived by Cottrell, Grant; camera (color) Du Yuzhuang; editor, Douglas St. Clair Smith; music, Brian Mendelsohn. Reviewed at Cannes Film Festival (market), May 11, 1987. Running time: **92 MINS.**

Cannes — "China Run" is a documentary sure to gain access to tv screens just about everywhere in the world, while some special-situation theatrical exposure would seem likely, too. With the central character, long-distance runner Stan Cottrell, radiating star quality and being instrumental in all aspects of the production, producer-director Mickey Grant deserves his share of the praise sure to come the way of an extraordinary work that records Cottrell's 1985 run over 2,125 miles in 53 days from atop the Great Wall north of Peking to the South China city of Canton.

Cottrell is seen and heard throughout as a man pursuing a fantasy and making true a dream while he defies dust, cold, heat, stony paths, loss of weight, lack of potable water and many other hazards including the constant invasion of his privacy by film crews and interviewers. All of this is, of course, self-imposed but Cottrell comes out of it no less the hero and conqueror.

En route, he often turns interviewer himself, as he meets the just-folks of rural China. He also does some honest political philosophizing, naive at first, later on ripe with canny observations on the post-Cultural Revolution openness that nevertheless has not put basic Marxism as the state religion on the shelf or made for more than token personal freedom for individuals.

It took Cottrell five years to set up his Great Friendship run. It took him another 18 months to get the Beijing Studios footage out of China. There is glorious friendship between the American and the film crew and the common people of China on display here, but a certain wariness shows through on both sides, too.

Cottrell staked his family's very existence on this run. What he gained is more than an athletic achievement, and, in spite of occasion graininess nd lopsided framings, "China Run" shines with wit, wisdom, sweat and genuine suspense. — *Kell.*

Maschenka
(BRITISH-GERMAN-COLOR)

A Goldcrest Pictures release of a Clasart production. Produced by Herbert G. Kloiber, Fritz Buddenstedt. Executive producer, Manfred Heid. Directed by John Goldschmidt. Screenplay, John Mortimer, based on the novel "Mary" by Vladimir Nabokov; camera (Geyer Berlin color), Wolgang Treu; editor, Tanja Schmidbauer; music, Nick Glowna; production design, Jan Schlubach; art director, Albrect Conrad; sound, Dieter Schwarz; costumes, Barbara Baum; assistant director, Marijan Vajda. Reviewed at Cannes Film Festival (market), May 9, 1987 (No MPAA Rating). Running time: **103 MINS.**

Ganin	Cary Elwes
Maschenka	Irina Brook
Lilli	Sunnyi Melles
Alfyrov	Jonathan Coy
Podtyagin	Freddie Jones
Vater	Michael Gough
Kolin	Jean-Claude Brialy
Klara	Lena Stolze

Cannes — "Maschenka" is an overripe, over-sentimentalized translation of a Vladimir Nabokov novel without any sense of the writer's irony or control. Pic aims for the most obvious features in a tale of lost love among Russian emigres in 1924 Berlin. Despite some lovely scenery, "Room With A View" audience likely will find this slow going.

Main problem here is overproduction as even turmoil in prerevolutionary Russia looks as if it were airbrushed onto the screen. Production design is so meticulous as to rob the story, slight as it is, of any impact.

Contrived plot is simply a setup to examine the power of memory to create a reality of its own. Ganin (Cary Elwes) is a refugee from Russia whose family fortune and youthful love affair with the beautiful Maschenka (Irina Brook) is recalled in sun-drenched soft-focus reveries.

Hook for the story that sends his mind roaming across his back pages is the discovery that the girl has married a boorish boarder (Jonathan Coy) at Ganin's rooming house and is now coming to join him. This sets off his longing for the glorious old days, further heightened by the pre-revolutionary mutterings of boarder Freddie Jones.

John Mortimer's screenplay is a bit too literal in illustrating the connections between personal and political history while John Goldschmidt's direction hammers home the message with unrelenting heavy-handedness.

Performances are fine but fail to bring much subtlety to the characters, although as Maschenka Brook is so radiant her presence almost fills the gap.

Despite all of its excesses, film does manage to stir the emotions on occasion, largely because the leads make such a pretty couple it's impossible not to share some of their longing. It's a heady dose of old-fashioned romanticism with a filmmaking style to match.—*Jagr.*

Summer Heat
(U.S.-COLOR)

An Atlantic Entertainment Group release and production. Produced by William Tennant. Executive producers, Thomas Coleman, Michael Rosenblatt. Directed by Michie Gleason. Screenplay, Gleason, based on the novel "Here To Get My Baby Out Of Jail" by Louise Shivers; camera (CFI color), Elliot Davis; editor, Mary Bauer; music, Richard Stone; sound, E. Lee Haxall; production design, Marsha Hinds; art direction, Bo Johnson; set decorator, Jan K. Bergstrom; assistant director, Elliot Lewis Rosenblatt; casting, Junie Lowry. Reviewed at Cannes Film Festival (market), May 15, 1987. (MPAA Rating: R.) Running time: **90 MINS.**

Roxy	Lori Singer
Aaron	Anthony Edwards
Jack	Bruce Abbott
Also with: Kathy Bates, Clu Gulager.	

Cannes — "Summer Heat" is a well-made low-key period piece set in North Carolina in the 1930s. It's a time when tobacco is king and life goes its uneventful way until a star-crossed love affair shakes the foundations. Subject matter and scope limit the pic to specialty venues where it could find a modest following.

Lori Singer's a local girl whose beauty doesn't make life any bed of roses for her. When her grandmother dies, the only option is to marry and in a few years she's tired of her husband (Bruce Abbott) and ready for something to happen. That something is Anthony Edwards who arrives in town one hot and dusty day and soon lights a fire in Singer.

Edwards gets in good with Abbott to be near Singer and soon is living in their spare rooms. From the first time she spots Edwards at her Daddy's funeral parlor, there it little doubt where this story is headed. The pair exchange meaningful glances while Abbott goes about the everyday business of harvesting the tobacco crop, unitl the inevitable erupts.

One day when her husband's gone, Edwards jumps her in the fields and now there's no stopping them as their affair heats up. But even in the throes of desire there isn't enough intensity to suggest the crime of passion that Edwards finally commits. It's an act too violent for this lazy corner of the world and the town moves rapidly to regain its equilibrium.

Narrated by Singer as an older woman looking back at her life, story tries to be a character study and a crime story in one and is only partially successful. Script by Michie Gleason, who also directed, doesn't reveal any surprising truths about the Singer character and hers is truly an unremarkable life by today's standards. She really only becomes interesting after the murder as she attempts to rebuild her life.

Singer is well suited to the passive, diminutive role and gives the character a likable sweetness. As the lover she can't say no to, Edwards looks like a young Robert De Niro and conveys his desire without overdoing it. Abbott delivers the most textured performance as he suggests a decent man who has his limitations but is not the right man for his wife. Clu Gulager is almost recognizable in a likeable turn as the girl's father.

As a director, Gleason doesn't pull any tricks and allows the material to speak for itself, which it does in a rather quiet, contained voice. Tech credits are first-rate with Elliot Davis' cinematography creating an atmosphere bathed in a yellow light perhaps too soft to allow any violence to disrupt it. —*Jagr.*

Harry And The Hendersons
(COLOR)

Unappealing, derivative creature feature.

A Universal Pictures release of a Universal/Amblin Entertainment production. Produced by Richard Vane, William Dear. Directed by Dear. Screenplay, Dear, William E. Martin, Ezra D. Rappaport; camera (Deluxe Color), Allen Daviau; editor, Donn Cambern; music, Bruce Broughton; sound (Dolby), Willie Burton; production design, James Bissell; art direction, Don Woodruff; set design, Wiliam James Teegarden; set decoration, Linda DeScenna; ''Harry'' designer, Rick Baker; assistant director, L. Andrew Stone; second unit director, Bissell; casting, Mike Fenton, Jane Feinberg, Judy Taylor (L.A.), Patti Kalles (Seattle). Reviewed at Universal Pictures, Universal City, Calif., May 21, 1987. (MPAA Rating: PG.) Running time: **110 MINS.**

George Henderson . . . . John Lithgow
Nancy Henderson . . . . Melinda Dillon
Sarah Henderson . . . . . . Margaret Langrick
Ernie Henderson . . . . Joshua Rudoy
Harry . . . . Kevin Peter Hall
Jacques Lafleur . . . . David Suchet
Irene Moffitt . . . . Lainie Kazan
Dr. Wrightwood . . . . Don Ameche

Hollywood — ''Harry And The Hendersons'' is proof that the folks at Amblin Entertainment, a.k.a. Steven Spielberg's production company, can't keep using the same ''E.T.'' formula for every kiddie pic.

Here, they've taken Big Foot, put him in Chewbacca's leftover ''Star Wars'' costume and given him E.T.'s sweet disposition — resulting in a lobotomized hairy animal who is so wimpy, it's painful.

What was once original, clever and appealing in previous Spielberg fare has become so predictable to be boring. Still, attachment of the filmmaker's name and a PG rating should generate a healthy b.o., but adults would be wise to bring a dose of insulin if they intend to sit through to the end.

Film could be titled, ''Big Foot Meets A Happy, Loving Suburban Family In The Woods Camping And Goes Home With Them To Become Docile When Bathed And Fed.''

The excitement and suspense of running into Big Foot, later named Harry (Kevin Peter Hall), is wrapped up in the first few minutes of the film when Dad (John Lithgow) runs over the beast in the family stationwagon, figures him for dead, straps him on the roof and takes him home to Seattle with the rest of the family sort of agreeing to it.

Theirs is a typical Spielberg house in the 'burbs — decorated in yuppie coziness that's soon turned topsy-turvy when Harry revives and scares the living daylights out of the Hendersons.

To complicate matters, while he's wreaking havoc (but acting more like the Cowardly Lion), nettlesome neighbor Irene (Lainie Kazan) is being a pest while nearby lifelong Big Foot stalker Jacques Lafleur (David Suchet) is hot on his nemesis' trail.

Maybe if Harry were ferocious a little while longer, or didn't understand English so well or acted a little funny or quirky, there might have been some spark to his character. About the only gags that work come from when he bumps his head on the door.

Family is a little too perfect also. Mom (Melinda Dillon) is genuinely good-natured, with a bratty son (Joshua Rudoy) and a very obedient teenage daughter (Margaret Langrick) to complement Dad's growing hysteria as Harry is sighted around town and quickly becomes a misunderstood beast in the eyes of the terrified public.

Lithgow, who started out a hunter working in his father's gun store, finally discovers that maybe shooting animals isn't a worthwhile form of recreation.

That's about it for message, but enough for screenwriters to milk it for all its worth.

At 110 minutes, outing really drags towards the end with a seemingly endless chase scene where Harry is pursued in a garbage truck by a zillion cops and several crazy rifle-brandishing zealots.

Filmmakers tried hard for a three-hanky ending when Harry is ordered back to the wild to escape getting killed. Indeed, watching his soulful blue eyes tear up with the thought of leaving his pals, the Hendersons, is bathos to the max — and sickeningly so.

Children want to be surprised and delighted by creatures they see on the screen, not wishing they would get lost. —*Brit.*

Necropolis
(COLOR)

Embarrassingly poor Big Apple supernatural flick.

An Empire Pictures release of a Tycin Entertainment production. Produced by Cynthia DePaula, Tim Kincaid. Written and directed by Bruce Hickey. Camera (Precision color), Arthur D. Marks; editor, Barry Zetlin, Tom Mesherski; music, excerpted from Empire releases ''Eliminators,'' ''Trancers,'' ''The Alchemist;'' additional music, Don Great, Tom Milano; sound, Russell Fager; art direction, Ruth Lounsbury, Marina Zurkow; set design, David Morong; assistant director, Rebecca Rothbaum; production manager, Michael Spero; special makeup effects, Ed French; special effects second unit director, Matt Vogel; choreography, Taunie Vrenon. Reviewed at 42d St. Liberty theater, N.Y., May 23, 1987. (MPAA Rating: R.) Running time: **76 MINS.**

Eva . . . . LeeAnne Baker
Dawn . . . . Jacquie Fitz
Billy . . . . Michael Conte
Rev. Henry James . . . . . . William K. Reed
  Also with: George Anthony, Jett Julian, Nadine Hart, Anthony Gioia, Gy Mirano, Jennifer Stall, Paul Ruben, Adrianne Lee.

''Necropolis'' poses the thorny question: how does Empire Pictures' brass decide which of their films will be released theatrically. This meager, N.Y.-lensed effort is far below the level of quality of several of Empire's recent direct-to-video releases, yet it popped up unannounced on 42d Street on a triple bill to bore the pants off a horror-hungry audience. Home viewers at least will have the fast forward option.

By an unfortunate application of the Peter Principle, erstwhile bit player LeeAnne Baker graduates to a leading role here, sashaying trashily through ''Necropolis'' as a 300-plus-year-old devil worshiper, preying upon New Yorkers to suck out their lifeforce. It seems, per a ludicrously cheap prolog set in New Amsterdam in 1686, that she was interrupted in a satanic ritual and must now complete it in order to obtain eternal life for herself and a grisly bunch of ghouls. Most interesting gimmick is an Ed French makeup effect giving Baker three sets of breasts with which to suckle the ghouls with the genre's requisite (ever since ''Alien'') daily requirement of KY jelly.

Al Pacino-lookalike Michael Conte unconvincingly plays the cop on the case, while British-accented Jacquie Fitz is a bland heroine and William K. Reed the neighborhood black reverend, ever ready with a set of wooden crosses to stake Baker and her ghouls.

Campiest material has Baker, looking hideous with short-cropped platinum blond hairdo, eyelids covered in black, garbed in trashy black outfits emulating Vanity and Madonna, doing exotic dances by herself without warning. Under Bruce Hickey's limp and static direction, even this isn't funny on a camp level.—*Lor.*

A Dança dos Bonecos
(Dance Of The Dolls)
(BRAZILIAN-COLOR)

An Embrafilme release of a Grupo Novo de Cinema e TV production. Executive producer, Tarcisio Vidigal. Directed by Helvecio Ratton. Screenplay, Ratton, Tairone Feitosa, Angela Santoro; camera (Eastmancolor), Fernando Duarte; editor, Vera Freire; music, Nivaldo Ornelas; dolls created by Alvaro Apocalypse, Teatro Giramundo de Bonecos; art design and costumes, Paulo Henrique Pessoa, Juliana Junqueira, Anisio Medeiros; production direction, Marcus Lage, Helena da Rocha; associate producers, Embrafilme, Sky Light, Bernardo Nadaud, Secretary of Culture of the State of Minas Gerais. Reviewed at Gramado Film Festival, Embaixador theater, April 29, 1987. Running time: **90 MINS.**

Mr. Kapa . . . . Wilson Grey
Geléia . . . . Kimura Schettino
Ritinha . . . . Cinthia Vieira
Jack Domina . . . . Ezequias Marques
Iara . . . . Divana Brandao
Destino . . . . Rui Pollanah
Almerinda . . . . Claudia Gimenez
Vitorino . . . . Rogerio Fallabela
Rua . . . . Derly De'Cea

Gramado — Children's films are not exactly part of the tradition of the Brazilian cinema. Biggest exception is the Troublemakers films which, for almost 20 years, have been leading the local b.o.

''A Dança dos Bonecos,'' directed by Minas Gerais-born Helvecio Ratton, subverts some established tendencies of local movies made for children. First, it is not a comedy. Second, it does not treat children as mentally retarded. Story has a doll craftsman in an inland city facing bankruptcy when a couple of street performers arrive in the village. They sell a ''magic water'' which even they didn't know is really enchanted. The liquid brings life to the dolls belonging to the craftsman's granddaughter. A chain of greed and robberies immediately starts.

Ratton's camera is vivid and brings movement and often emotion to the story. His dolls are technically perfect, performing with no visible human aid.

All technical credits, including music by Nivaldo Ornelas, are excellent in this odd magic story coming from the Minas' cinema. ''A Dança dos Bonecos'' certainly will enchant most children under 10. Best of all, it by no way is likely to bore an adult.—*Hoin.*

Qingchun Nuchao
(Grow Up In Anger)
(HONG KONG-COLOR)

A Golden Harvest production and release. Produced by Anthony Chow. Directed by Clifford Choi. Screenplay, Choi, Terence Cheung; camera (color), Wan Man-kit; editor, Cheung Yiu-chung; sound, Chow Siu-lung; production design, Colette Koo. Reviewed at Hong Kong Film Festival, April 22, 1987. Running time: **92 MINS.**

With: Thomas Wong, Chan Ngor-lun, Stephen Ho, So Chi-wei.

Hong Kong — This teenage pic starts off like a Hong Kong version of a John Hughes film, but early promise isn't sustained.

The young hero, Joe, who comes from a happy but dull family, attends a private church school where his best friends are the rebellious Ben and the poor but studious Man-kit, who has earned a scholarship. Their teacher is a strict disciplinarian, with a fondness for teenage girls.

When Ben is expelled for cheating during an exam, his place is taken by the lissome Gigi, on whom Joe quickly develops a crush.

This is when the film starts to get silly, and the seemingly accurate depiction of teenage life in the first couple of reels is junked in favor of some melodramatic nonsense.

Man-kit attempts suicide by throwing himself from an upper-story window after a dressing-down from the teacher; but both he and

Ben have no trouble getting good jobs. The moral seems to be: you don't need to finish school, because jobs are there for the asking. Joe, meanwhile, crashes Gigi's mother's expensive sports car and simply leaves it on a country road.

The disappointing climax has Joe and Gigi consummating their love after a romantic midnight swim during which they're fully clothed. It looks too uncomfortable to be very passionate. Clifford Choi starts off in a realist mood, but quickly opts for the slick and glossy treatment. Result is disappointingly dumb. —*Strat.*

Anjos da Noite
(Night Angels)
(BRAZILIAN-COLOR)

An Embrafilme release of a Superfilmes production. Executive producers, Andre Klotzel, Zita Carvalhosa. Directed by Wilson Barros. Screenplay, Barros; camera (color), Jose Roberto Eliezer; editor, Renato Neiva Moreira; music, Servulo Augusto; art direction, Cristiano Amaral, Francisco de Andrade; costumes, Marisa Guimaraes; production director, Alvaro Pedreirsa. Produced by Superfilmes. Reviewed at Cine Embaixador, Gramado Film Festival, May 1, 1987. Running time: **98 MINS.**

Malu	Zeze Motta
Jorge	Antonio Fagundes
Marta	Marilia Pera
Guto	Marco Nanini
Mauro	Chiquinho Brandao
Bimbo	Aldo Bueno
Fofo	Claudio Mamberti
Maria Clara	Ana Ramalho
Teddy	Guilherme Leme
Milene	Aida Lerner
Cissa	Be Valerio

Gramado — A new tendency can be detected easily in the current São Paulo cinema. It is somehow a return to the idea of a realistic cinema, a cinema made on the streets and focusing on the social question in general, and São Paulo itself as the stage for the social and human conflicts, in particular. Less than one year ago, "Cidade Oculta," by Chico Botelho, appeared as a trademark for this new cinema. Now, "Anjos da Noite," which was written almost at the same time as "Cidade Oculta" and got the screenplay approval at the same contest, appears with great similarities with the film by Botelho. In both, the action takes place over one night; both have the city of São Paulo as the main character, both deal with the marginality in the big city. But their marginals are somehow different. In "Cidade Oculta," they are the bandits, the small smugglers living like rats in the undergrounds. Here, the marginals are taxi-boys, high class prostitutes, cocaine dealers.

Director Wilson Barros (a graduate at the Cinema Studies Department of NYU) made several shorts since 1978 but this is his feature film debut. He wrote the story about several crimes that are found to be to

be part of any average night in São Paulo. A black model, a young sociology student, a taxi-boy, a wealthy homosexual, a theater director, all are interconnected parts of the author's universe, which is not described through a linear narrative.

Barros deals with a good cast — especially Marilja Pera, Zeze Motta and Marco Nanini — which is not always optimized, and with an outstanding technical crew, which guarantees to the film a brilliant technical standard. It is impossible, however, not to regret the author does not go deeper into his fascinating universe. Moralistic background is somehow disappointing, as the excessive appeal to self-references. Yet, "Anjos da Noite" is an intriguing film that is immediately involving. It has the smell of a hit (including for foreign audiences).

—*Hoin.*

Hidden City
(BRITISH-COLOR)

A Hidden City production. Produced by Irving Teitelbaum. Written and directed by Stephen Poliakoff. Camera (color), Witold Stok; editor, Peter Coulson, music, Michael Storey; sound, Malcolm Hirst; production design, Martin Johnson; assistant director, Peter Jacques; art director, Alastair Paton; costumes, Daphne Dare; casting, Gail Stevens; associate producer, Ron Purdis. Reviewed at the Metro Cinema, London, April 27, 1987. Running time: **107 MINS.**

James Richards	Charles Dance
Sharon Newton	Cassie Stuart
Anthony	Bill Paterson
Brewster	Richard E. Grant
Hillcombe	Alex Horton
Barbara	Tusse Silberg
Jodie	Laura Welch

London — Firsttime writer-director Stephen Poliakoff tries very hard with "Hidden City." Unfortunately he tries too hard, and the result is an overlong film with too many storylines and not enough good acting that rambles along with an air of self-importance.

It is unfortunate the basic premise of the film doesn't stand up, because Poliakoff, an established legit playwright, displays a good directorial eye, and at times the pic is quite fascinating. Poliakoff the writer, however, has simply gone overboard. Offshore prospects look dim.

"Hidden City" takes an alternative look at London, peeking beyond the tourist facade and into the city's darker corners, but the novelty of interesting locations is not enough to sustain a flaccid storyline.

Poliakoff is fond of the conspiracy-style story. For British tv he wrote plays like "Stronger Than The Sun" and "Caught On A Train," which had a sinister edge to them. "Hidden City," though, is too extended and uneven to really grip.

Charles Dance plays a statistician whose well-ordered and smug life is shattered when he gets involved with Cassie Stuart, who is obsessed with finding a mysterious piece of film that appears to have been hidden by the government.

The search for fragments of the lost film takes them into a maze of tunnels underneath London packed with official government archive film and discarded classified material, and into brushes with the police.

At this point the action loses its way, with characters appearing and disappearing for no good reason, and with too many questions left unanswered. The climax is okay, but not gripping, with the fragments of the film turning out to be footage of a secret government experiment that went wrong.

Dance is in good form as the sexy statistician, though he looks a bit bemused at some of the situations the storyline pushes him into. The casting of Stuart as the impetuous woman is a problem. She has an appealing waif-like quality, but her acting here amounts to looking intense, running about, and shouting "quick, hurry up" to Dance a great deal.

The acting — and comic — abilities of Bill Paterson and Richard E. Grant are wasted. Both are excellent in their few scenes and add some much needed brevity to the proceedings. All technical credits are fine, with lensing by Witold Stok especially strong.

"Hidden City" is full of good ideas, but the format would have worked so much better as a miniseries where a few more of the questions could have been answered and characters sketched out more fully.

—*Adam.*

A Guerra do Brazil
(War of Brazil)
(BRAZILIAN-COLOR)

An Embrafilme release of a Sylvio Back production. Produced by Sylvio Back Produções Cinematográficas, Embrafilme, and National Fund of Educational Development. Directed by Back. Research and screenplay, Back. Iconographic research, Ana Maria Belluzzo, Mariana Ochs, Mary Montes de Lopez Moreira, Leon Pomer; camera (Eastmancolor), Jose Medeiros, Jose Francisco dos Anjos; editor, Laercio Silva; animation, Marcello G. Tassara; sound, Miguel Sagatio, Juarez Dagoberto; narration, Hermano Henning; production direction, Eliane Bandeira, Sylvio Back. Reviewed at Cine Embaixador, Gramado Film Festival, April 29, 1987. Running time: **88 MINS.**

Gramado — From 1864-70, a bloody conflict took place in South America, known as the Paraguay War (or Big War, as it is known in Paraguay) and involved Paraguayan troops against an alliance formed by Brazil, Argentina and Uruguay. In fact, Brazil and

Paraguay were the main protagonists of the episode that killed 1,000,000 people and yet is almost unknown in Brazil, covered by official versions and omitted from the school texts.

Filmaker Sylvio Back has been, over the last years, involved in a deep research on southern Brazilian civilization. Since 1975 he brought out important documentaries on the revolution of 1930, the so-called Farrapos War, the Nazism in south Brazil, the Polish influence in the state of Parana and so forth.

For "A Guerra do Brasil," Back developed patient research in Brazil, Argentina, Uruguay and Paraguay. He talked to historians, scholars and even direct descendants of soldiers. The result is an informative report, but not necessarily an attractive film. Back lacked sufficient images for the information he collected, so what is seen often on screen is poor material drawn from a couple of films made in Argentina and Brazil.

His attempt to overcome such deficiencies by making an unconventional documentary does not succeed. "A Guerra do Brasil" is a film perfectly conventional in structure, full of information about a forgotten episode of the Latin American story, but much more useful for historians than cinema audiences.—*Hoin.*

Ernest Goes To Camp
(COLOR)

Lame comedy vehicle for tv pitchman.

A Buena Vista release of a Touchstone Pictures production, in association with Silver Screen Partners III. Produced by Stacy Williams. Executive producers, Elmo Williams, Martin Erlichman. Directed by John R. Cherry 3d. Stars Jim Varney. Screenplay, Cherry, Coke Sams; camera (Deluxe color), Harry Mathias, Jim May; editor, Marshall Harvey; music, Shane Keister; art director, Kathy Emily Cherry; casting, Hank McCann, Rich Schirmer. Reviewed at the Pacific Paramount theater, Hollywood, May 22, 1987. (MPAA Rating: PG.) Running time: **93 MINS.**

Ernest P. Worrell	Jim Varney
Nurse St. Cloud	Victoria Racimo
Sherman Krader	John Vernon
Indian Chief	Iron Eyes Cody
Bronk Stinson	Lyle Alzado
Jake	Gailard Sartain
Eddy	Daniel Butler
Moustafa	
Hakeem-Jones	Hakeem Abdul-Samad
Bobby Wayne	Patrick Day
Crutchfield	Scott Menville
Bubba Vargas	Jacob Vargas

Hollywood — Jim Varney's creation of Ernest P. Worrell, honed through years of tv commercials, has become a sort of poor man's Pee-wee Herman: a living cartoon of an obnoxious, know-it-all simpleton that people either find funny, or don't. Unfortunately, in his second film after "Dr. Otto & The Riddle Of The Gloom Beam," Varney's Ernest loses his edge and spends most of the time being merely a simpleton. Bad dialog and unimaginative scripting (with the exception of turtle paratroopers in the climactic scene), along with too-liberal doses of comic-book violence, quickly drag the film down. Bottom-line prospects are up in the air, but film has a shot at bringing in a significant prepubescent audience.

Ernest's lifelong goal has been to become counselor at Kamp Kikakee, but he's relegated to janitorial duties, where his frequent mishaps are documented in several unfunny physical humor gags.

Camp has religious, historical significance for Indian chief (Iron Eyes Cody) who owns the land and granddaughter (Victoria Racimo, doing a lot with a little), who works as camp nurse. Whitebread camp atmosphere is violated by the presence of six kids from reform school (who collectively look about as sinister as "Our Gang") who are brought to the camp as part of a second chance program.

An accident to one of the counselors leaves crew short-handed, so they assign Ernest to counsel the misfits. He and the little hoods never get a chance to show any on-screen chemistry, because of the weak dialog (how many 10-year-old delinquents use the term "lead-pipe cinch" these days?).

Only Hakeem Abdul-Samad, as Moustafa, the one kid who likes Ernest, gets to show any personality. The rest must lamely read dumb lines and act like certain adults think kids act.

Things come to a head when a greedy land developer dupes Ernest into convincing the Indian chief to sign away rights to the land, forcing the camp to close. This brings on the deciding fight and underscores one of the film's implicit messages (hey kids, the best way to solve a disagreement is arson).

While tech credits are mostly okay and Shane Keister's score particularly appropriate, film never recaptures the persistent wackiness of Ernest's tv commercials. Fault is not Varney's. Even Ernest is no match for a bad screenplay.—Camb.

Happy Hour
(COLOR)

Lamebrained 'comedy' about beer.

A TMS Pictures (The Movie Store) release of a Four Square production. Executive producer, J. Stephen Peace. Produced by Peace, John De Bello. Directed by De Bello. Screenplay, De Bello, Constantine Dillon, Peace; camera (CFI color), Kevin Morrisey; editor, De Bello; music, Rick Patterson, Neal Fox; song, Devo; sound (Ultra-Stereo), Joe Thompson Jr.; production design, Dillon; stunt coordinator, Monty Jordan; production supervisor, Robert Matzenauer; casting, Samuel Warren & Associates. Reviewed at UA Twin 2 theater, N.Y., May 22, 1987. (MPAA Rating: R.) Running time: **86 MINS.**
Blake Teegarden . . . . Richard Gilliland
Fred . . . . Jamie Farr
Misty Roberts . . . . Tawny Kitaen
Bill . . . . Ty Henderson
Mr. X . . . . Rich Little
Hancock . . . . Eddie Deezen
Cathy Teegarden . . . . Kathi Diamant
Meredith Casey . . . . Debbie Gates
Also with: James Newell, Beverly Todd, Debi Fares, Eric Christmas.

The filmmakers of the intentionally bad 1977 release "Attack Of The Killer Tomatoes" have not progressed one iota in a decade, judging by the singularly unfunny "Happy Hour," a purported comedy about beer. Poor writing and inept technique will have the viewer claiming "Sour Grapes," pic's original title when shot back in 1985.

Richard Gilliland blandly portrays a scientist working for Marshall Beer who accidentally invents an ingredient which makes the product irresistible and addictive. Unfortunately, he cannot reproduce his formula, so only one bottle of the stuff exists, half of which is stolen by rival Lakeside Beer.

Picture consists of poorly staged and ill-timed slapstick as a bunch of zanies try to capture both breweries' vials of the ingredient. Charmless overacting is encouraged by director John De Bello, except for the casting of mimic Rich Little as a James Bond type of suave spy, given a very laidback, boring reading by Little. Film is so dated that Little has a running gag vocally doing an impression of Cary Grant to fool security guards.

Despite its R rating, pic has no nudity or sex. Technical quality is disgraceful, with poorly synched dialog (done intentionally as a gag in "Killer Tomatoes" but just a boner here), and no color correcting. Latter caused most of the print screened to be very reddish, virtually making lovely costar Tawny Kitaen look as garish as a circus clown; some shots are greenish with no matching. The only pro credit is an effective music score. Pic ends with a bimbette addressing the audience directly, informing us we probably are too stupid to understand the film's message. Supposedly a satire of society's crassness as epitomized in beer advertising, film's shoddy attempt to make a fast buck is transparently clear to any movie fan.—Lor.

Hunter's Blood
(COLOR)

Silly 'Deliverance' imitation.

A Concorde Pictures release of a Cineventure presentation. Produced by Myrl A. Schreibman. Executive producer, Judith F. Schuman. Directed by Robert C. Hughes. Screenplay, Emmett Alston, based on a novel by Jere Cunningham; camera (Deluxe color), Tom DeNobe; editor, Barry Zetlin; music, John D'Andrea; casting, Al Onorato, Jerold Franks; production manager, Andrew LaMarca; stunt coordinator, Rawn Hutchinson; art director, Douglas Forsmith; costume designer, Jacqueline Johnson; associate producer, George Springmeyer; co-associate producer, Alexander Beck. Reviewed at the USA Cinemas Pi Alley theater, Boston, May 15, 1987. (MPAA Rating: R.) Running time: **102 MINS.**
David Rand . . . . Sam Bottoms
Melanie . . . . Kim Delaney
Mason Rand . . . . Clu Gulager
Al . . . . Ken Swofford
Marty Adler . . . . Joey Travolta
Ralph . . . . Mayf Nutter
Red Beard . . . . Lee DeBroux
One Eye . . . . Bruce Glover
Snake . . . . Billy Drago

Boston — "Hunter's Blood" is a low-rent version of "Deliverance," with some "Texas Chainsaw Massacre" thrown in for good measure. A bunch of guys decide to go deer-hunting in the Arkansas backwoods to prove to themselves they're still real men even though they live in the city.

Mason (Clu Gulager) and his son David (Sam Bottoms) can handle themselves, but the other three are just Yankee trash looking to be picked off by the crazed poachers and rednecks who live in the woods. For the first 45 minutes we get an unending stream of hints about the danger in store.

"I've seen a man's chest blasted open by another hunter," says Uncle Ralph (Mayf Nutter), letting us know this will be one of the sights we'll get to see later on in the film. Marty (Joey Travolta) takes pictures of the locals as if he were on safari, fascinated that they're going to be stopping at a "redneck beer joint."

Indeed, the film probably will play differently in the cities than in the country. For urban audiences, this is obviously intended as some sort of horror story/cautionary tale about crazy cannibals and murderers running through the wilderness.

In the sticks, this could be sold as a comedy, for both the city slickers and the good ole boys are among the stupidest people to walk across a movie screen. The poachers, out to capture the hunters before they can summon help, allow two of them to escape within minutes of each other through their inability to tie a knot.

Meanwhile, having just seen some of the rednecks pass by, Ralph and Marty decide to have a heart to heart about the danger they face. Apparently the killers are not only vicious, but hard of hearing as well.

The film sinks to new depths when David's wife Melanie (Kim Delaney) appears and is captured by the hillbillies. At this point audiences are unlikely to care what happens to any of them.

Bottoms and Gulager struggle mightily to bring some feeling to their roles, but the material defeats them. At times they look so noble one expects them to turn on the other members of their hunting party for not measuring up.

A silly punchline to the film suggests the heroes have escaped from the frying pan only to land in the fire. —Kimm.

Where The Heart Roams
(DOCU-COLOR)

A Film Arts Foundation release. Produced, written and directed by George Paul Csicsery. Camera (color), John Knoop. Reviewed at Winifred Moore Auditorium, St. Louis, May 14, 1987. (No MPAA Rating.) Running time: **83 MINS.**
Participants include: Barbara Cartland, Janet and Bill Dailey, Chelley, Ted and Gina Kitzmiller, Kathryn Falk, Jude Deveraux, Rebecca Brandewyne, John Gfeller, Hilari Cohen, Vivian Stephens, Diane Dunaway, Lori and Jerry Herter, Brenda Trent, Kathryn Davis, Lida Lunt, Chamisa James, Maralys Wills, E. Jean Carroll, Linda Wisdom, Robert Pearson.

St. Louis — The American zany and the American documentary filmmaker have walked hand-in-hand through garlic festivals, pet cemeteries, gumbo cookoffs and a variety of other celebrations.

Now, filmmaker George Csicsery rides the love train, a week-long celebration of historical romance fiction, its readers and its writers.

Romance fiction is big business: writers like Barbara Cartland, the English grand doyenne of the genre, and Americans Rosemary Rogers and Janet Dailey are multimillionaires, and their readers number in the millions.

A fan and would-be writer (all the fans seem to be would-be writers) named Chelley Kitzmiller had the idea of the rolling convention, via Amtrak from Los Angeles to New York, in 1983, and Csicsery went along, with everyone then spending a few days in New York at the Romantic Booklovers' Conference, an orgy of autographed copies and admiring squeals.

Csicsery is more observer than participant; he turns on the camera and lets it go as readers and writers talk about their heroes and heroines, the writing styles and the unabashed love that the fans hold for the authors.

Editors, and reporter E. Jean Carroll, are far more cynical as they discuss the formulas and the marketing techniques, and Carroll points out that the romance is the perfect solution for a woman who wants to be seduced by a different man every night while never leaving the solitary confines of her living room.

Romance novels are big business — 120-150 titles every month, readership over 20,000,000, a Barbara Cartland with 370 novels and some 400,000,000 copies sold.

The mix is good by the filmmaker; he does not sit in judgment, but allows the participants full rein. Both readers and writers show their hopes and dreams, with writers and editors adding the touch of commercialism, fans displaying their limitless adoration.

Cinematographer John Knoop has a sure touch with the camera, and Csicsery, who worked with Errol Morris on "Gates Of Heaven," and who is an experienced documentarian on his own, tells a smooth story, heightened by the presence of Cartland as a singer on the track.

The sad conclusion is to learn that the readers of romances all think they can easily become writers, something that never occurs to those who read, say, John Updike or William Faulkner, or even Stephen King.

The film is a fascinating look at an American subculture, and should be a winner on the fest and college circuits. — *Jopo.*

Asignatura Aprobada
(Passing The Course)
(SPANISH-COLOR)

A Nickel Odeon Dos production. Produced and directed by José Luis Garci. Executive producer, Mario Morales. Screenplay, Garci, Horacio Valcárcel; camera (Eastmancolor and Fujicolor), Manuel Rojas; production manager, José Luis Merino; editor, Miguel G. Sinde; sets, Jesús Quirós, Luis Vázquez; music, Jesús Gluck; costumes, Maiki Marln. Reviewed at Cine Conde Duque, Madrid, April 29, 1987. Running time: **95 MINS.**
José Manuel Alcántara . . . . . . Jesús Puente
Elena . . . . Victoria Vera
Lola . . . . Teresa Gimpera
Edi . . . . Eduardo Hoyo
Also with: Pastor Serrador, Manuel Lorenzo, Pablo Hoyo, Juan Cueto, Santiago Amón, Pedro Lazaga, José Manuel Fernández, Silverio Cañada, Pedro Infanzón.

Madrid — When José Luis Garci made his first film, "Asignatura Pendiente" (Flunking Out), in 1977 it marked a whole new era in Spanish cinema; pic was in turn witty, incisive and sentimental and aptly summed up the lost opportunities of a whole generation of Spaniards who had grown up under Franco.

Now, 10 years later, Spain's only Oscar-winning director has limned what presumably is a second part to the story, although the thesps are different and no reference, other than the similarity in the title, is made to the original. Those 10 years seem to have brought only sorrow and disenchantment, at least as far as this introspective and maudlin story is concerned.

Script is a mixture of poetic lucubrations and snappy monologs and dialogs as Garci delves into the personal problems of a playwright who has withdrawn to a northern coastal town and whose artistic and personal lives are burnt out. Intelligent, sensitive, now in his late 40s or early 50s, José (Jesús Puente) dwells on the human condition and the impossibility of retrieving isolated moments of happiness from his past.

To help the story along a bit, Garci brings in a former actress flame of his, who is doing a play in the provincial town; José also has an ill-defined relationship with a rich woman who paints, drives a Porsche and maintains a 20-year-old lover. At one point, pic seems to take a new tack when José's dropout son pays him a visit and claims to have contracted AIDS. But these are mere diversions, and the central theme of pic certainly is the solitude and seeming hopelessness of the protagonist.

Despite a topnotch performance by Puente and good production values, supporting cast and intelligent script, pic is too downbeat to augur well for success with audiences. The "life ends at 50" message is bound not to appeal either to youth audiences or to those who have reached that age. One can understand despair and ennui, but one would at least like to see an attempt made to overcome them. — *Besa.*

Iris
(DUTCH-COLOR)

A Concorde Film release of an Iris Film production. Produced by Frans Raskers. Directed by Mady Saks. Screenplay, Felix Thijssen, based on an idea by Saks; camera (Agfa color), Frans Bromet; editor, Jutta M. Brandstaedter; music, Loek Dikker, sound, Kees Linthorst; art direction, Dorus van de Linden; set decoration, Wilem de Leeus; assistant director, Pieter Walther Boer; production manager, Arnold Heslenfeld; casting, Hans Kemma. Reviewed at Cinema Intl., Amsterdam, March 23, 1987. Running time: **90 MINS.**
Iris . . . . Monique van de Ven
Versteeg . . . . John Kraaykamp
Also with: Roger van Hool, Titus Tiel Groenestege, Elsje Scherjon, Marja Habraken.

Amsterdam — Mady Saks, a documaker who previously tracked feminist/Third World issues, debuted in the fiction stakes in '83 with "Breathless." Pic, which focused on a young woman's postnatal depression, grabbed critics' attention, but still had a noticeable docu feel.

With "Iris," Saks attempts to steer clear from documentary influences, which should spell better local b.o. chances. Possibilities also are enhanced via an outstanding performance from Monique van de Ven, who limns eponymous heroine's triumph over prejudice with remarkable conviction.

On her 18th birthday Iris runs away from her small-town home and after a few days in the big city moves in with Paul, a successful and sophisticated architect. For a while she acts the good housewife. Against the trend, however, she decides to train as a vet, and uses an inheritance to buy a practice in a backward region of the Netherlands.

Iris meets with open disapproval from the villagers. The women distrust her because she's pretty, unmarried and wears jeans, while the men lech and leer. She becomes a victim of gossip, practical jokes and finally violence.

A potentially muddled screenplay is saved by Van de Ven, who transforms Iris into a rounded human being and a convincing vet. But pic has basic scenario problems, with director Saks seemingly straining to escape possible documentary pollution and cramming in too many plotlines.

Overseas options seem low, but pic could fit into an early afternoon tv slot for women. — *Wall.*

Cannes Festival Reviews

Aria
(U.S.-BRITISH-COLOR)

An RVP Prods. and Virgin Vision presentation. Produced by Don Boyd. Executive producers, Jim Mervis, RVP Prods., Tom Kuhn, Charles Mitchell; coproducer, Al Clark, Mike Wahs; associate producers, David Barvar, Michael Hamlyn; coordinating editors, Marie-Therese Boiche, Mike Cragg. Reviewed at Cannes Film Festival (In Competition), May 15, 1987. (No MPAA Rating.) Running time: **98 MINS.**
Sequence 1 — Director, Nicolas Roeg; camera, Harvey Harrison; artistic director, Diana Johnson; editor, Tony Lawson; opera "Un Ballo in Maschera;" composer, Verdi; voice, Leontyne Price, Carlo Bergonzi, Robert Merrill, Shirley Verrett, Reri Grist; cast, Theresa Russell.
Sequence 2 — Director, Charles Sturridge; camera, Gale Tattersall; artistic director, Andrew McAlpine; editor, Matthew Longfellow; opera, "La Forza del Destino;" composer, Verdi; aria, "La Vergine degli Angeli;" voice, Leontyne Price, Giorgio Tozzi, Ezio Flagello; cast, Nicola Swain, Jack Kyle, Marianne McLoughlin.
Sequence 3 — Director, Jean-Luc Godard; camera, Carolyn Champetier; editor, Godard; opera, "Armide;" composer, Lully; aria, "Enfin il est en ma puissance;" voice, Rachel Yakar; cast, Marion Peterson, Valerie Allain.
Sequence 4 — Director, Julien Temple; camera, Oliver Stapleton; artistic director, Piers Plowden; editor, Neil Abrahamson; opera, "'Rigoletto;'" composer, Verdi; aria, "La Donna è Mobile;" voice, Alfredo Kraus, Anna Moffo, Annadi Stasio; cast, Buck Henry, Anita Morris, Beverly D'Angelo, Gary Kasper.
Sequence 5 — Director, Bruce Beresford; camera, Dante Spinotti; artistic director, Andrew McAlpine; editor, Marie-Therese Boiche; opera, "Die Tote Stadt;" composer, Korngold; aria, "Gluck, das mir Verblieb;" voice, Carol Neblett, Rene Kollo; cast, Elizabeth Hurley, Peter Birch.
Sequence 6 — Director, Robert Altman; camera, Pierre Mignot; artistic director, Stephen Altman; editor, Robert Altman; opera, "Les Boreades," composer, Jean-Philippe Rameau; voice, Jennifer Smith, Anne-Marie Rodde, Philip Langridge; cast, Julie Hagerty, Genevieve Page, Cris Campion, Sandrine Dumas.
Sequence 7 — Director, Franc Roddam; camera, Frederick Elmes; artistic director, Mathew Jacobs; editor, Rick Elgood; opera, "Tristan und Isolde;" composer, Wagner; aria, "Liebestod;" voice, Leontyne Price; cast, Bridget Fonda, James Mathers.
Sequence 8 — Director, Ken Russell; camera, Gabriel Beristain; artistic director, Paul Dufficey; editor, Michael Bradsell; opera, "Turandot;" composer, Puccini; aria, "Nessun Dorma;" voice, Jussi Bjoerling; cast, Linzi Drew.
Sequence 9 — Director, Derek Jarman; camera, Mike Southon; artistic director, Christopher Hobbs; editor, Peter Cartwright, Angus Cook; opera, "Louise;" composer, Gustave Charpentier; aria, "Despuis le Jour;" voice, Leontyne Price; cast, Tilda Swinton, Spencer Leigh, Amy Johnson.
Sequence 10 and linking scenario — Director, Bill Bryden; camera, Gabriel Beristain; editor, Marie-Therese Boiche; opera, "I Pagliacci;" aria, "Vesti La Giubba;" composer, Leoncavallo; voice, Enrico Caruso; cast, John Hurt, Sophie Ward.

Cannes — "Aria" is a film that could not have happened without the advent of music videos. A string of selections from 10 operas illustrated by 10 directors, it's the kind of sensory overload, albeit of a more sophisticated nature, that today's viewing audience has become accustomed to. Paradox of this picture is that opera purists will probably be turned off by the visual flash and film buffs might be turned off by the opera. Heavyweight talent involved and unique nature of the project should ensure respectable returns at specialty outlets.

Style of the "Aria" segments has little in common with the rapid-fire editing of music videos, but they are nonetheless renderings of visual images designed to accompany songs or music. Producer Don Boyd, who orchestrated the project, instructed the directors not to depict what was happening to the characters in the operas but to create something new out of the emotion and content expressed in the music. The arias were the starting point for the films.

Result is both exhilaratingly successful and distractingly fragmented. Individual segments are stunning but they come in such speedy succession that overall it is not a fully satisfying film experience. One watches with detached fascination as the duelling directors try to top each other.

Action rises and falls without really working up a head of steam or building to a climax. Along the way one or two segments fall totally flat and conclusion offers no real payoff. But it is still a ride with strikingly original sights and sounds along the way.

Selections also represent a variety of filmmaking styles from Bruce Beresford's rather pedestrian working of a love theme from Korngold's "Die Tote Stadt" to Ken Russell's characteristically excessive treatment of an idea distilled from Puccini's "Turandot."

Using the "Nessun Dorma" aria as his starting point, Russell suggests a state of limbo in which a woman is surrounded by the rings of Saturn and tattooed with jewels. This segment may be the most purely visual of the bunch with a twist ending providing a jolt.

Structurally, the most ambitious of the selections is Jean-Luc Godard's working of Lully's "Armide" which he transposes to a body building gym where two naked women try unsuccessfully to attract the attention of the men. Insinuating aria accompanies images of the cleaning women before the royalty of the gym.

On a more whimsical note, Nicolas Roeg offers an interpretation of Verdi's "Un Bello in maschera." Set in Vienna in 1931, piece preserves most of the elements of the original opera about a King Zog of Alhenia who is visiting his girlfriend but is concerned by assassination rumors. Melodrama is played almost tongue-in-cheek, a feeling further heightened by Theresa Russell, who plays the good king.

If opera was the soundtrack of a mainstream film it might look something like Julien Temple's version of Verdi's "Rigoletto" in which a producer chooses to cheat on his wife at the same place she's cheating on him. Buck Henry and Beverly D'Angelo as the not so happy couple enhance the Hollywood parody of the piece.

The most striking clash of images is achieved by Franc Roddam who moves Wagner's "Tristan Und Isolde" to Las Vegas. As the lush strains of the music blare, the neon sea of the casinos has never looked more strange. But even in the crassest place on earth, a loving couple can achieve the most delicate and intimate exchange.

Robert Altman turns the table on Jean-Philippe Rameau's "Les Boreades" by focusing not on the stage but an 18th century Hogarthian audience full of whores and lunatics in commedia dell'arte make-up. It's a scene out of "Marat/Sade" as Julie Hagerty and Genevieve Page, among others, listen with mock seriousness to the exaggerated marital problems of Queen Alphise.

Other scenes with less zip are Charles Sturridge's elegiac theme from Verdi's "La Forze del Destino" and Derek Jarman's nostalgic "Louise" by Gustave Charpentier.

Individual segments are loosely woven together by pieces from Leoncavallo's "I Pagliacci." Paralelling some of the real life drama of Enrico Caruso who sings the aria, John Hurt plays a troubled opera star on his way to the theater. Once arrived, he encounters his elusive muse (Sophie Ward). Finally the aria concludes with Hurt performing before an empty house and then collapsing, demonstrating the agony and ecstasy of being a performer.

Like rock videos, the selections collected here feature plenty of sex with no fewer than five including love scenes and some nudity. Viewers unfamiliar with opera might get the idea that sex goes with the territory.

Each short film was produced independently of the others but what they share are uniformly lush production values. Costumes, staging and locations are worthy of any great opera production and sound quality is loud and clear and crisp.

But what these small films actually add to the music of the operas is questionable. They seem more like separate and unrelated works that now stand on their own. Luckily the film is rich enough to allow for viewers to find their own vantage point. —*Jagr.*

Testament d'un poète juif assassiné
(Testament Of A Murdered Jewish Poet)
(FRENCH-COLOR)

Feeling Prods./La SEPT/Images des Anges/TF 1/Swan Prod. coproduction, with the participation of the Centre National du Cinéma and YNYL Prod. (Tel Aviv). Produced by Hubert Niogret. Directed by Franck Cassenti. Stars Michel Jonasz and Erland Josephson. Screenplay, Cassenti, Annie Mercier, from the novel by Elie Wiesel; camera (Eastmancolor). Patrick Blossier; sound, Michel Guiffan, Paul Bertault; art director, Yves Brover; music, Gabriel Yared; editor, Annie Mercier. Reviewed at Centre National du Cinema. Paris, April 28, 1987. (In Perspectives on French Cinema at Cannes Film Festival.) Running time: **87 MINS.**
Paltiel Kossover . . . . Michel Jonasz
Zupanev . . . . Erland Josephson
The judge . . . . Wojtek Bertault
Bernard Hauptmann . . . . . Philippe Léotard
Grisha Kossover . . . . Vincent David
Inge . . . . Anne Zacharias
Raissa Kossover . . . . Anne Wiazemsky
Paltiel's father . . . . Moscu Alcalay
Paul Hamburger . . . . Laszlo Szabo

Paris — "Testament Of A Murdered Jewish Poet" is the second screen adaptation of an Elie Wiesel novel and was virtually shot back-to-back with Miklos Jancso's film of the author's "Dawn" (screened at the Berlin festival in 1986). Bankruptcy of original producer Evelyne July prevented "Testament" from being completed until a new banner, headed by director Franck Cassenti and indie producer Hubert Niogret, found the financing to finish the picture early this year.

Devotion to the project is evident in the film's solemnly respectful tone, but pious reverence to Wiesel and his heavyweight themes is among the factors that make it a demonstrative, dramatically unpersuasive affair.

Also committed to the film was its star, Michel Jonasz, a top French pop singer who turns down his high voltage stage energy for a low-keyed but stolid perfomance as the poet of the title, a Rumanian Jew who ends a grim historical calvary in a Stalinist prison in the early 1950s.

His "testament" is in fact the confession he is forced to write by an examining magistrate (Wojtek Pszoniak) and which contains his own personal history. A humane court registrar (Erland Josephson) purloins the document and years later transmits it to the poet's young son. Reading of the testament in the now abandoned prison building (where wrecking balls are moving in to erase the traces of Stalinist evil) sets up film's flashback structure.

Unfortunately, like many an ambitious project that lacks the means, "Testament" provides only a schematic production in retracing Jonasz' tragic journey from the pogrom-besieged ghetto of his native Rumania, to the idealistic Communist circles of Berlin in 1933 and Paris during the Popular Front (with a Zionist interlude in Palestine, thanks to some location shooting in Israel).

Cassenti's bland direction adds to the telefilm feeling of the whole, and the home screen probably is where pic will have its best chances. —*Len.*

American Gothic
(BRITISH-COLOR)

A Brent Walker, in association with Pinetalk Ltd. presentation of a Manor Ground production. Produced by John Quested, Chris Harrop. Executive producers, George Walker, Mike Manley, Ray Homer. Directed by John Hough. Screenplay, Hough, Terry Lens; camera (color), Harvey Harrison; editor, John Victor Smith; line producer, Lens. Reviewed at Cannes Film Festival (market), May 13, 1987. Running time: **90 MINS.**
Pa . . . . Rod Steiger
Ma . . . . Yvonne De Carlo
Cynthia . . . . Sarah Torgov
Also with: Michael J. Pollard, Fiona Hutchinson, William Hootkins.

Cannes — "American Gothic" is a standard, low-budget chiller whose plot can pretty well be guessed from title and tagline: "We'll keep them down on the farm." Rod Steiger and Yvonne De Carlo are featured as a pair of deranged backwoods murderers with a brood of monstrous assassins for kids; six normal teenagers are their victims. For the drive-in set.

Forced to land their plane on a remote island off the coast, the six weekend campers stumble across a house decorated more or less in the style of the 1920s. They find this far more eerie than it appears to the viewer; the same might be said for their shock on seeing the old-fashioned owners of the house arrive.

Instead of tossing the intruders out, Ma and Pa courteously offer them a meal and a bed for the night, when mayhem might be expected to occur. Instead, nothing out of the way happens until the next morning, when the first victim meets his fate at the hands of two of the monstrous, over-age "kids." His corpse creates an emergency situation in the group, but before proper suspense can be built, the other campers begin meeting horrible deaths, strangled with jump-ropes, punctured with knitting needles, necks broken and the like. Killing takes place offscreen but the cadavers are gruesome enough, especially seen hanging in the basement with previous victims.

Finally only Cynthia (Sarah Torgov) is left. The sight of the monstrous daughter's mummified baby pushes her over the edge, and she briefly becomes one of the family, before wreaking revenge on all. Film leaves her alone on the island, waiting for the next visitor.

Director John Hough gets good performances out of the Gothic side of his cast, which includes Michael J. Pollard as a son. Younger thesps are generic teen cyphers. Atmosphere isn't terribly terrifying. —*Yung.*

A Return To Salem's Lot
(U.S.-COLOR)

A Warner Bros. presentation of a Larco production. Produced by Paul Kurta. Executive producer, Larry Cohen. Directed by Cohen. Screenplay, Cohen, James Dixon; camera (color), Daniel Pearl; editor, Armond Leibowitz; music, Michael Minard; art direction, Richard Frisch; costumes, Catherine Zuber; associate producer, Barry Shils, Janette Cohen; assistant director, Tim Lonsdale; creative consultant, Stephen King. Reviewed at Cannes Film Festival (market), May 13, 1987. (No MPAA Rating.) Running time: **95 MINS.**
Dad . . . . Michael Moriarty
Jeremy . . . . Richard Addison Reed
The Judge . . . . Andrew Duggan
Van Meer . . . . Sam Fuller
Aunt Clara . . . . June Havoc
Sally . . . . Ronee Blakley
Also with: Evelyn Keyes.

Cannes — Tongue-in-cheek horror entry about a little New England town ruled by vampires succeeds because it doesn't take itself at all seriously and yet also manages not to overdo the camp. Performances are fine from solid pro cast (plus cult director Sam Fuller), funny lines abound and special effects convince. Though not really scary, film also has its share of chilling moments.

Only real resemblance with

Stephen King's best-selling "Salem's Lot" and 1979 made-for is in the basic premise of smalltown New England vampires. King figures in the credits as creative consultant.

Story follows an anthropologist (Michael Moriarty) who's summoned back from studying savages in the wilds by his ex-spouse and saddled with looking after his resentful, dirty-mouthed young teen son (Richard Addison Reed). Opening scene in obviously fake jungle sets the tone with Moriarty photographing a gruesome ritual with an assistant, who gasps, "But they're killing they guy. I thought you said this was a fertility rite." "It is," deadpans Moriarity as the victim's heart is cut out. "He knocked up the chief's favorite wife."

Father and son move to the former's old hometown of Jerusalem's Lot (Salem's Lot for short) in Maine — pic was shot mostly in Vermont — and install themselves in a broken-down bungalow inherited from an aunt. When locals attack a vanful of kids who stray into town, a girl takes refuge with the newcomers, tipping them off that there's something odd going on, in case they hadn't noticed that the locals only come out at night. The village patriarch (Andrew Duggan) makes no bones about telling them they're all vampires, and, in a ridiculous twist, persuades Moriarty to stay and use his anthropologist's skills to chronicle local history.

They have their faults, but these vampires are sort of likeable compared to the run-of-the-mill variety. They don't drink much human blood because it's unhealthy, what with all the chemicals and risk of hepatitis or AIDS. Before climbing into their coffins to snooze, they don pajamas and say, "Good day, dear." The local school play is "Dracula (Our Version)."

Father-son relationship is also developed with cynical humor, as hopelessly irresponsible Moriarty goes off with a vampiress and gets her pregant while the boy gets hooked on a little crush of his own (occasioning a kinky bout of pre-pubescent necking). Action picks up with the arrival of rambunctious old Mr. Van Meer (Fuller), in town on the trail of a Nazi war criminal. He quickly forms an alliance with Moriarty, teaches how to gain his son's respect — grabbing the kid by the ear and shouting at him — and they drive the inevitable stakes through hearts and so on, with Salem's Lot going up in flames at the finish.

Pic is about 10 minutes too long and gets a little draggy toward the end. Quantity of violence and gore is average for the genre, but it's never shocking or gross in quality. Technical aspects are in synch with the subject in a generally fun, spoofy entertainment. —Jay.

City Of Blood
(SOUTH AFRICAN-COLOR)

A Distant Horizon release of a Blood City Film Ltd. production. Produced by Anant Singh. Directed by Darrell Roodt. Camera (Technicolor), Paul White; editor, Dave Heitner; associate producer, Les Volpe. Reviewed at the Cannes Film Festival (market), May 12, 1987. Running time: **96 MINS.**
Joseph . . . . Joe Stewardson
Inspector . . . . Ian Yule
Abigail . . . . Liz Dick
Also with: Susan Coetzer, Ken Gampu.

Cannes — "City Of Blood" is a fairly well-lensed thriller from South Africa dealing directly with racial tension and violence. The most interesting thing about it, however, is the suspense of figuring out film's point-of-view on apartheid, which would appear to be a key element for audiences. In the end, pic hedges its bets, indicting black violence along with police murders, and concluding the whole situation is an endless nightmare with innocent victims on both sides. Not itself excessively gory, but containing a number of well-built suspense sequences, film could be a pickup for specialized thriller markets offshore.

Story is told through the eyes of a middle-aged white coroner, Joseph Anderson (Joe Stewardson), whose job brings him into contact with horrible homicides every day. The one he mentions first is a nun found with her limbs cut off. His wife has divorced him and taken the kids to live in a saner country, but he has moodily stayed behind.

A series of murders involving hookers with their skulls bashed in by some strange instrument sends him roaming the streets at night. Though pal Ian Yule on the police force warns Joseph against amateur sleuthing, Joe can't resist the pull of the nighttime streets. One of the girls, Liz Dick, becomes his lover — it doesn't do much for his peace of mind to know she's out on the deserted streets in the middle of night.

Worst of all, a charismatic black leader whose name is a variation of Nelson Mandela's has been accidentally tortured to death in prison by the police, and the P.M. himself is after coroner Joseph, a known liberal, to sign a death certificate saying he died of natural causes. Put through a moral wringer by friends and foes, Joseph sticks to his guns and refuses to sign the certificate, but as pic's ironic finale shows, one man's courage makes little difference.

Film's most effectively chilling — and ambiguous — characters are ghosts — club-carrying spirit warriors in terrifying African tribal dress and masks, who can materialize anywhere to murder whites. The past taking its revenge? Figments of whites' guilty imaginations? Black power killers? Pic leaves it unclear.

Helmer Darrell Roodt does a decent job of lensing, handicapped by lousy acting from principals. At times unnecessarily slow, "City" redeems itself as an actioner with its shock effects. Four-letter words abound, apparently to give the wishy-washy cast a veneer of toughness. —Yung.

Macbeth
(FRENCH-COLOR)

A Dedalus production. Directed by Claude d'Anna. Screenplay, Francesco Maria Piave, based on the play by William Shakespeare; camera (color), Pierre Dupouey; editor, Reine Wekstein; music, Giuseppe Verdi; production design, Eric Simon. Reviewed at Cannes Film Festival (Cinema & Opera Panorama), May 18, 1987. Running time: **135 MINS.**
Macbeth . . . . Léo Nucci
Lady Macbeth . . . . Shirley Verrett
Banquo . . . . Johan Leysen
(voice: Samuel Ramey)
Macduff . . . . Philippe Volter
(voice: Veriano Lucchetti)

Cannes — To the burgeoning list of filmed operas, add Claude d'Anna's "Macbeth," a production of one of Giuseppe Verdi's best, if not most famous, efforts. It's a film for opera buffs, not for the film crowd, and will have a longer life on video and the small screen than it will theatrically.

Claude d'Anna, bouncing back from last year's best-forgotten "Salomé," made for Cannon, has done a straightforward job, filming most of the opera inside a real Belgian castle; result is a rather gloomy look, with blue the dominant color. It makes for claustrophobia after more than two hours, and there's relief when a battle scene, modestly staged, takes place outside.

Léo Nucci, an Italian baritone, is an effective Macbeth; black warbler Shirley Verrett is a most imposing Lady Macbeth. Key support roles are mimed by actors having been pre-recorded.

This will be a timeless item for opera buffs, a useful addition to anyone's collection, but it's cinematically unmemorable. —Strat.

Devil's Paradise
(WEST GERMAN-COLOR)

A Concorde release (in Germany) of an Atossa Film production. (Foreign sales: Overview Films, London.) Executive producer, Renée Gundelach. Produced by Vera Tschechowa, Vadim Glowna. Directed by Glowna. Stars Jürgen Prochnow, Sam Waterston, Suzanna Hamilton. Screenplay, Leonard Tuck, Glowna, Joe Hembus, Chris Doherty; camera (Agfacolor), Martin Schäfer; editor, Heidi Handof; production design, Nicos Perakis; music, Jürgen Knieper; sound, Christopher Price; costumes, Regine Batz; production manager, Kirsten Hager; casting, Leo Davis, Marc Holt. Reviewed at Cannes Film Festival (market), May 9, 1987. Running time: **91 MINS.**
Escher . . . . Jürgen Prochnow
Mr. Jones . . . . Sam Waterston
Julie . . . . Suzanna Hamilton
Schomberg . . . . Mario Adorf
Gato . . . . Dominique Pilon
Madame . . . . Ingrid Caven
Wong . . . . Wong Chun-man
Captain Davidson . . . . Vadim Glowna
Quinn . . . . Tony Doyle
(English language soundtrack)

Cannes — Though the credits don't say so, "Devil's Paradise" is adapted from Joseph Conrad's "Victory," about a strange, lonely man (Jürgen Prochnow) who's spent much of his life wandering around some distant islands. Pic was shot on spectacular locations in Thailand with a top German crew (including cinematographer Martin Schäfer and production designer Nicos Perakis) and looks magnificient even though the post-synched English dialog is often distracting.

Escher, the Prochnow character, is in partnership in a coal mining venture on a small island with a disreputable Irishman (Tony Doyle) who, early on, is murdered by natives. Escher travels to the mainland town of Soerabaya and checks in at the inaptly named Grand Pacific Hotel, run by an arrogant German (Mario Adorf) and his native wife.

Here Escher meets the sinister Mr. Jones (Sam Waterston), a pervert, who "likes to be entertained" and who travels together with his quietly ruthless companion, Gato (Dominique Pilon). Escher also meets a lovely half-English girl, Julie (Suzanna Hamilton), who plays sax in an all-girl band, and who has just discovered that Adorf intends to have her for himself. Escher helps her escape to his island, where they fall in love, but they're followed by Waterston and Pilon who precipitate the film's action climax.

Given the project's literary antecedents, it's no surprise the characters are prone to philosophize from time to time, and since the film is set in the 1930s, there are further resonances to be found in the subtext.

Best performances come from Waterston and Pilon as the villains; Prochnow is a rather stolid hero, and Hamilton is called upon to change character dramatically at one point (possibly because some scenes have been cut).

Director Vadim Glowna is in for a small part as the captain of a vessel that operates among the islands, and Ingrid Caven is there, briefly, and sings a song as the leader of the band, though the credits bill her as a "Madame."

Apart from the dubbing, the pic is first-rate in every department. In English-speaking territories, it will play better on video than theatrically, which is a pity as the visual splendors will be lost as a result. —Strat.

Hansel And Gretel
(U.S.-COLOR)

A Cannon Group presentation of Golan-Globus production. Produced by Menahem Golan, Yoram Globus. Executive producer, Itzik Kol. Directed by Len Talan. Screenplay, Nancy Weems, Talan, from fairy tale by the Brothers Grimm; camera (color), Ilan Rosenberg; editor, Irit Raz; music (based on Engelbert Humperdinck score), Michael Cohen; lyrics, Enid Futterman, Nancy Weems; production design, Marek Dobrowolski; Nancy Weems; production design, Marek Dobrowolski; costumes, Meira Steinmatz; casting & associate producer, Patricia Ruben; production manager, Zion Haen. Reviewed at Cannes Film Festival (market), May 9, 1987. (No MPAA Rating.) Running time: **86 MINS.**

Hansel . . . . Hugh Pollard
Gretel . . . . Nicola Stapleton
The Mother . . . . Emily Richard
The Father . . . . David Warner
The Witch . . . . Cloris Leachman
Also with: Eugene Kline, Warren M. Feigin, Josh Buland, Lutuf Nouasser, Beatrice Shimshoni.

––––––

Cannes — Will Cannon's Movietales sell tickets? Maybe, but only if the kiddies and their parents want to watch thoroughly unsophisticated but very straightforward storytelling with only the slightest inkling of modern technical production values.

In essence, the Brothers Grimm's "Hansel And Gretel," from which associate producer/casting director Patricia Ruben and director Len Talan have fashioned this family entertainment, is the straight goods as a horribly fascinating tale of innocence's triumph over the horror of poverty, as well as over witchcraft and any other power beyond the grasp of common folks.

With fragile though neat production dress (pic was lensed largely in an Israeli studio) and an economy budget, the film version emerges a rather flatfooted rendition with stodgy acting and rather tame special effects. In the story of the poor woodcutter's kids imprisoned in the witch's gingerbread house, the initial suspense suffers from being drawn out way beyond the filmmakers' skills.

True horror is on display only briefly and not convincingly to any alarming degree. Cloris Leachman does add a twist and a slightly Marty Feldman-esque turn to run-of-the-mill witch portraiture. As the kids' father, David Warner generates some sympathy, but in the title roles Hugh Pollard and Nicola Stapleton appear nice enough but terribly bland.

The original 19th century opera score by Engelbert Humperdinck has very little added to its insipid musical contents by its present-day adapters. Plot's happy ending wrapup clearly is a dud. —*Kell.*

Mirage
(CHINESE-HONG KONG-COLOR)

––––––

A Golden Principal Organization/China Film Coproduction Corp. coproduction. Executive producers, Hon Pou Chou, Lee Chi Ming. Written and directed by Siu-Ming Tsui. Camera (Widescreen, color), Li Wan Jie; music, Joseph Koo. Reviewed at the Cannes Film Festival (market), May 17, 1987. Running time: **95 MINS.**
Tant Ting Xuan . . . . Yu Yung Kang
Fatty . . . . Siu-Ming Tsui
Gazanova . . . . Pasha Romani
Nice girl . . . . Connie Khan
Also with: Fang Dong Yu, Wang Hwa.

(English-dubbed soundtrack)

Cannes — China Film Corp. makes three or four martial arts pics each year, many in coproduction with Hong Kong. Last year's "Shaolin Temple" was a hit that made the charts in Eastern Europe as well as in Asia. This year's big offering is "Mirage," a widescreen, all-action spectacular by Hong Kong helmer Siu-Ming Tsui, who is also costar, martial instructor and stunt coordinator. As violent and fast-paced as any kung fu pic, "Mirage" has the added advantage of breathtaking natural landscapes and an enormous cast of extras and stuntmen who keep the fights coming.

Pic opens with a young photographer, Tang Ting Xuan (Peking actor Yu Yung Kang) following a trade caravan along China's Silk Route in the 1930s. In the middle of the desert, the caravaneers sight a miraculous mirage of a beautiful girl galloping on her horse. Tang is smitten and determines to find her at all costs, with the help of some pictures he takes of the mirage. His travels lead him through innumerable brawls, until he finally stumbles across a sultry bandit queen, Gazanova (Pasha Romani), the girl from the mirage. She happens to be the fiercest fighter of all, and she becomes his greatest nemesis, before falling in love with him.

Naturally, story takes a backseat to giant-scale, choreographed martial arts fights, which turn pic into a battleground, every 10 minutes or so. Siu-Ming Tsui has the best of all worlds with car chases, horse chases, motorcycle chases and enough explosions and collapsing buildings to make a good war film. The hero always comes out unscathed, except when the fearsome Gazanova takes a good bite out of his neck, spits it out, and drinks his horse's blood. After viciously trying to kill Tang in every way imaginable, Gazanova begins to like the chap, but by then it's Tang who rejects her. "I'm disappointed in you," he explains, gingerly feeling the missing part of his throat.

This is not a film for viewers fussy about dialog; dubbed English print has characters speaking inane American slang. Judged on their karate skills, thesps are game enough, and leads are attractive. Widescreen lensing is well-done, the cutting brisk. Enjoyable of its kind. —*Yung.*

Coeurs croisés
(Crossed Hearts)
(FRENCH-COLOR)

––––––

A Forum Distribution release of an Incite/SEPT coproduction. Produced by Joel Santoni, Daniel Messère. Written and directed by Stéphanie de Mareuil. Camera (color), Hélène Louvart; editor, Anne-Marie Hardouin; music, Vladimir Cosma; song, Caroline Loeb; sound, Pierre Donnadieu, Alain Villeval; assistant director, Anne-Isabelle Estrada; associate producers, Laurence Bachman, Jacques Tronel. Reviewed at the Centre National du Cinéma, Paris, April 27, 1987. (In French Perspectives section at Cannes Film Festival.) Running time: **87 MINS.**
With: Caroline Loeb (Paulette), Roger Mirmont (Ferdinand), Julie Jezequel (Tina), Laure Tran (Marylou), Bernard Farcy (Fano), Cécile Corre (Lucie), Hammou Graia (Hads), Anton Nicoglou (Thomas), Tonie Marshall, Eric Do.

––––––

Paris — "Coeurs croisés" interweaves sentimental vignettes among the inhabitants of an apartment house on the Rue Saint Denis, Paris' notorious red light district. This featherweight item, a sort of poor man's Eric Rohmer moral tale, is the neophyte work of Stéphanie de Mareuil, a young French journalist who has notably written for Cosmopolitan.

Pic's basic problem is that it was originally made as a medium-length film and only later padded out to a full 87 minutes, which the material doesn't justify. De Mareuil shows some flair and humor in her depiction of flirts, couplings, uncouplings and mismatches but the characterizations remain superficial and the film's brittle charm dissipates before long.

Cast is mostly young and appealing, especially rising local pop singer Caroline Loeb, whose recent hit single, "C'est la ouate," closes pic. —*Len.*

Distant Lights
(ITALIAN-COLOR)

––––––

An Intersound Film production, in cooperation with Reteitalia. Produced by Claudio Argento. Directed by Aurelio Chiesa. Screenplay, Chiesa, Roberto Lerici, Roberto Leoni; camera (color), Renato Tafuri; editor, Anna Napoli; music, Angelo Branduardi. Reviewed at the Cannes Film Festval (market), May 13, 1987. Running time: **89 MINS.**
Bernardo . . . . Tomas Milian
Renata . . . . Laura Morante
Also with: William Berger, Giacomo Piperno.

(English-dubbed soundtrack)

Cannes — Screened in an unconvincingly dubbed English-language version in the Cannes market, "Distant Lights" is passable Italo sci-fi from young helmer Aurelio Chiesa. Extraterrestrials who come to Earth and assume the bodies of the dead have nothing of the horrific about them, but a soothing tone that coaxes the viewer into rooting for the aliens. The bad dubbing will relegate it to B-circuits worldwide, which is a pity, because cast and camerawork are better-grade.

Pic begins on a mawkish note: a little boy whose mother has just died insists he sees his dead mom every day in a deserted park. Dad Tomas Milian investigates with the help of the boy's schoolteacher, Renata (Laura Morante), and sure enough, he too sights his dead wife. When the mayor and police chief open the woman's coffin, they find it empty.

Soon other corpses start coming to life in the small Italian town, until resuscitation becomes a local epidemic. The authorities round up all suspected living dead and lock them in a room where the alien spirits — nice guys just looking for a little physical presence — give up and project themselves into outer space, leaving the dead bodies behind.

Complicating the story is Milian's love affair with the spirit who first inhabits his wife's body, then transfers to the more cinematic one of Morante when the schoolteacher is killed in a car crash. The couple shacks up togther and film temporarily wanders off into a weak, learning-to-live-in-this-body farce (the new Renata hangs out the laundry wrong, while Milian warns her the neighbors will start gossiping). Human lovemaking comes as a pleasant surprise to her, and she soon gets pregnant. Ending is upbeat.

Technical work is quality level, particularly Renato Tafuri's masterful lensing. —*Yung.*

The Tale Of Ruby Rose
(AUSTRALIAN-COLOR)

––––––

A Hemdale release, in association with Antony I. Ginnane and F.G.H. A Seon Film production. Executive producer, Basia Puszka. Produced by Bryce Menzies, Andrew Wiseman. Written and directed by Roger Scholes. Camera (Eastmancolor), Steve Mason (second unit camera, Scholes); editor, uncredited; music, Paul Schutze; art director, Bryce Perrin; sound, Bob Cutcher; associate producer, Ian Pringle; production manager, Christine Gallagher; assistant director, James Legge; casting, Liz Mullinar. Reviewed at Cannes Film Festival (market), May 11, 1987. (No MPAA Rating.) Running time: **101 MINS.**
Ruby Rose . . . . Melita Jurisic
Henry Rose . . . . Chris Haywood
Gem . . . . Rod Zuanic
Bennett . . . . Martyn Sanderson
Grandma . . . . Sheila Florance

––––––

Cannes — Visually magnificent, though dramatically sometimes muddled, "The Tale Of Ruby Rose" has the look of a labor of love. It will need to be lovingly handled to find an audience, because it's essentially a mood piece in which some towering mountain scenery dwarfs the human characters.

Tale is set in the southern island state of Tasmania in 1933. Ruby Rose (Melita Jurisic) lives with her husband Henry (Chris Haywood) and their adopted son Gem (Rod Zuanic) in a remote mountain hut; Henry and Gem trap and skin opossums and wallabies, though the youth hates the killing. Ruby is terrified of the dark as the result of a childhood trauma, but her self-absorbed husband offers her little comfort, and she has retreated into a world of illusion and fantasy.

Climax comes when she treks down the mountain into the valley to seek a solution to her problems and there, in the film's best scenes, meets the elderly grandmother she never knew. A sequence in which she shares a bath with the old lady, delightfully played by Sheila Florance, is a joy.

Jurisic has a difficult role as the deprived Ruby, who can barely read and lives an incredibly hard life during the bitterly cold winters; she gives a rather stilted performance, but it fits the character. Haywood is, as usual, in good form as her unfeeling husband, while Zuanic acquits himself well as the youth. The star attraction is the camerawork of Steve Mason with second unit work by writer-director Roger Scholes himself. Even when the narrative bogs down, the viewer can derive considerable pleasure from the way the spectacular scenery has been captured on film.

Paul Schutze's score is a plus, in evoking needed atmosphere. Editing is ragged at times (no credit for editor on the print), but otherwise pic is technically perfect. Scholes evidently put his heart into this one, but his intentions are somewhat obscure. An abrupt opening title serves no purpose, and could be deleted with no ill effect.

Hemdale will have to nurse this one, but it will be worth it if an audience can be found for this strange, hauntingly beautiful mood piece.
—*Strat.*

Dragonard
(U.S.-COLOR)

A Cannon Intl. release of a Cannon Films production. Produced by Harry Alan Towers. Executive producer, Avi Lerner. Directed by Gérard Kikoïne. Screenplay, Peter Welbeck (H.A. Towers), Rick Marx, based on the novel by Rupert Gilchrist, camera (color), Gérard Loubeau; editor, Allan Morrison; designer, Leonardo Coen Cagli; associate producer, John Stodel; assistant directors, Dominique Combe, K.C. Jones; casting, Don Pemrick. Reviewed at Cannes Film Festival (market), May 13, 1987. (No MPAA Rating.) Running time: **90 MINS.**

Capt. Shanks	Oliver Reed
Naomi	Eartha Kitt
Honore	Annabel Schofield
Arabella	Claudia Udy
Richard Abdee	Patrick Warburton
Pierre	Drummond Marais
Governor	Dennis Folbigge
Manroot	Winston Gamma

Cannes — "Dragonard" purports to be a costume drama about slavery and colonial oppression during the 18th century in the Caribbean, but rarely rises above being the standard gratuitous flesh and violence peek-a-boo. It hasn't the scope or the acting — despite Oliver Reed's questionable presence — to sustain more than minimum b.o. success, if that.

Pic puts forward the rather tired plot of a slave, handsome Richard Abdee (Patrick Warburton), exiled from the U.K. for treason, who falls lustily in love, after some encouragement, with Honore (Annabel Schofield), sister of a cruel plantation owner.

Turns out Warburton is wrongly convicted and accordingly pardoned as well as coming into a hefty inheritance, but not before an interlude with Schofield, subsequent escape, flogging, and a slave uprising. Much of the plot is set in a brothel run by the crafty Naomi (Eartha Kitt), with corset-clad girls dallying with the colonialists.

Continual reference is made to the dragonard, a whipping post, which ultimately becomes the film's symbol and focus of colonial oppression.

Certainly attempts are made in "Dragonard" to portray the cruelty and injustice of those times, but so much emphasis is put on the titillation of the gentry by Naomi's girls, the passion between Warburton and Schofield, and the lustings of Arabella, the local governor's spoilt daughter (Claudia Udy) who schemes to win Warburton for herself, that slavery and notions of freedom become more of a backdrop than anything else.

Weak scenario is hardly helped by some indifferent acting from Oliver Reed, as a captain of the local garrison, who blusters and shouts in an outrageous Scottish accent but does little else; and Patrick Warburton, who may have the looks but not the enthusiasm in this debut feature appearance to make his character in any way believable (and is hardly helped by his out of place U.S. accent).

Only noteworthy performance is put in by Drummond Marais as Schofield's tyrannical brother, although Schofield, also making her debut here, acquits herself nicely, backed up by her super looks.

Ending sees a half-hearted uprising coupled with Warburton dashing around dressed as a Roman (because of a prior costume party). Final scene, with the burning of the dragonard and Warburton's torrid address about liberty, is totally nonsensical, stemming either from bad editing or a desperate attempt to wind the film up somehow. Only high score for this pic is its fine costumes, but that's not about to make up for the rest of "Dragonard's" shortcomings. A sequel, "Master of Dragonard Hill," has recently been filmed. —*Doch.*

The Care Bears Adventure In Wonderland!
(CANADIAN-ANIMATED-COLOR)

Cineplex Odeon Films release of a Nelvana production. Produced by Michael Hirsh, Patrick Loubert, Clive A. Smith. Directed by Raymond Jafelice. Screenplay, Susi Snooks, John Deklein from a story by Loubert, Peter Sauder; songs written and performed by John Sebastian; score composed and performed by Trish Cullen. With the voice of Colin Fox, others not credited. Reviewed at Cannes Film Festival (market), May 14, 1987. (No MPAA Rating.) Running time: **75 MINS.**

Cannes — Grumpy and his Care Bears pals are back for a third adventure, this time with Alice in Wonderland, and exhibs and home-vid retailers should be pleased with the results. Small fry, top age about six, will consider this a must-see.

Action, none violent and all kind of sweet, is nonstop. John Sebastian's music, as in the previous two, rocks and animation by Toronto-based Nelvana is polished enough for a good time.

Script drags the Care Bears through the looking glass along with a reluctant Alice for her to pose as the princess of Wonderland who has been abducted by the Evil Wizard. A lot more than Wonderland is thrown in, such as pointed references to "The Wizard Of Oz," "Treasure Island," "Androcles And The Lion" and a heap of skill-testing quests from Grimm fairytales.

Wonderland characters, the white rabbit, the Queen of Hearts, the Cheshire Cat, the Jabberwocky, Tweedle dum and Tweedle dee, and the Mad Hatter are here, too, some in different form than in the Alice books.

Moral messages also are delivered: Don't take a ride from strangers; You're special if you think you are.

Voicing is also bouncy, notably by Colin Fox as the Evil Wizard. Exhibs, get the popcorn ready and the staff to clean it up off the floor. —*Adil.*

Rolling Vengeance
(U.S.-COLOR)

An Apollo Pictures release and production. (World sales, Mansion Intl.) Produced by Jack E. Freedman, Steven H. Stern. Directed by Stern. Stars Ned Beatty. Screenplay, Michael Montgomery; camera (color), Laszlo George; Ron Wiseman; art direction, H.E. Thrasher; music, Phil Marshall. Reviewed at Cannes Film Festival (market), May 15, 1987. (No MPAA Rating.) Running time: **90 MINS.**

Joey Rosso	Don Michael Paul
Big Joe	Lawrence Dane
Tiny Doyle	Ned Beatty
Big Joe's wife	Susan Hogan
Misty	Lisa Howard
Steve	Barclay Hope
Vic Doyle	Todd Duckworth
Lt. Sly	Michael J. Reynolds

Cannes — This not-bad actioner offers a reasonable selection of worthy attributes — a compelling situation, echoes of "Rocky" and "Death Wish," an appealing character performance from lead Ned Beatty — to put the pic head-and-shoulders above most market fare here. Manson Intl.'s sales prospects should be favorable.

Title refers to a giant, fire-spitting vehicle built by the truck-driving young hero (Don Michael Paul) to demolish various smalltown meanies who kill off his family and rape his girlfriend. The machine is a monster, weighing some eight tons, that scripter Michael Montgomery asks the audience to believe was built in the young man's backyard garage in his spare time.

The hero lives in what appears to be southern redneck country. The pic is in a muddle about geography; although the villains are bad ole boys, the license plates place the locale in Ohio. Pic actually was shot in Canada outside Toronto.

Producer-director Steven H. Stern milks the obvious situations actually getting some subtle performances from a mostly unknown cast. Stern even lends a gentle dignity to the hero's relationships with his trucker father (Lawrence Dane) and pleasant-looking girlfriend (Lisa Howard), providing a strong emotional foundation for the action.

Ned Beatty obviously relishes his role as the villain, a keeper of a highway topless joint who sends out his dimwitted and often inebriated sons to menace the locals. Beatty spits out his lines with physical abandon, providing his most credible character sketch in a film in some time.

Laszlo George's photography is evocative, adding spice and credibility to the action. It is also obvious that "Rolling Vengeance" spent more than a pittance on special effects. That fire-spitting vehicle is nicely designed by Michael Welch.

Overall it's a pleasant surprise. — *Sege.*

The Haunting Of Hamilton High
(CANADIAN-COLOR)

A Norstar Releasing release (in Canada) of a Simcom production. Produced by Peter Simpson. Executive producers, Simpson, Peter Haley. Directed by Bruce Pittman. Screenplay, Ron Oliver; camera (color), John Herzog; editor, Nick Rotundo; production design, Sandy Kybartas; music, Paul Zaza; special effects, Jim Doyle; associate producer, Ilana Frank; coproducer, Ray Sager. Reviewed at Cannes Film Festival (market), May 11, 1987. Running time: **96 MINS.**

Mary Lou Maloney	Lisa Schrage
Vicki Carpenter	Wendy Lyon
Principal Bill Sr.	Michael Ironside
Bill Jr.	Justin Louis
Father	Richard Monette

Cannes — It's the demon-in-the-high-school unleashed after 30 years in "The Haunting Of Hamilton High," an effective sequel to the 1980-81 exploitation chiller, "Prom Night."

Director Bruce Pittman and special effects devised by Jim Doyle recreate the climax of the first pic, in which a jilted boyfriend, heaving a stick of dynamite, burns his girlfriend to death seconds before she's crowned prom queen.

Cut, and it's 30 years later. Same high school where the jilted boyfriend is now principal and it's days before yet another prom dance. This time, school girl Wendy Lyon, though ordinary in every other way, sweet but not innocent, is possessed by the girl who was burned and now seeks revenge.

One high school girl is choked in a frenzied scene; a priest prays at a shrine to the dead girl whom he tried to seduce but gets a cross in the heart; a computer student gets rayed to death by his computer, and two more teen bodies pop up. Action scenes are fast-paced and technically diverting.

Heroine Lyon is sucked into a blackboard that turns into a swirling water inferno. One student remarks it's "Linda Blairsville." Accurate all right, but in this pic there is no exorcist, only the principal who shoots the possessed girl just as she's being crowned prom queen.

As a capper, and after a properly grotesque lifelike shape unfolds from the dead girl's body, it's made sharply clear the demon lives on in the principal for maybe another sequel.

Acting's okay, special effects are better than average and Pittman's work is just fine. Smart theatrical and especially long life on homevid seem assured.—*Adil.*

Feel The Heat
(U.S.-COLOR)

A Trans World Entertainment release of a Negocios Cinematograficos production, in association with M'Amsel Tea Entertainment. Produced by Don Van Atta. Executive producers, Moshe Diamant, Stirling Silliphant. Directed by Joel Silberg. Screenplay, Silliphant; camera (Cinecolor), Nissim Nitcho (Argentina), Frank Harris (U.S.); editor, Christopher Holmes, Darren Holmes; music, Thomas Chase, Steve Rucker; sound (Dolby), Enrique Sansalvador Viale; production design, Jorge Marchegiani; production manager, Jorge Velasco; stunt coordinator-martial arts coordinator, Alan Amiel; casting, Caro Jones. Reviewed at Cannes Film Festival (market), May 13, 1987. (No MPAA Rating.) Running time: **87 MINS.**

Waldo	David Dukes
Checkers Goldberg	Tiana Alexandra
Jason Hannibal	Rod Steiger
Danny	Brian Thompson
Raul	Jorge Martinez
Ike	John Hancock
Brody	Brian Libby
Maria	Jessica Schultz
Dozu	Prof. Toru Tanaka

Cannes — "Feel The Heat" is an unabashed action showcase for oriental actress Tiana Alexandra, wife of film's scripter Stirling Silliphant. Previously seen in TWE's exercise vidtape "Karatix," Alexandra is a real looker, solid martial arts practioner and the only reason to sit through this weak programmer.

With apologies to Whoopi, Alexandra stars as Checkers Goldberg, a government narcotics agent working for David Dukes, who is sent undercover to Buenos Aires to infiltrate Rod Steiger's drug ring. She poses in outrageous Suzie Wong slit dresses as a bubbleheaded dancer, immediately turns Steiger on and stumbles upon the secret of the smuggling operation. It turns out (believe it or not) that Steiger has $500,000 of heroin surgically implanted in his dancers' breasts unbeknownst to them, and sends them to America where silicone is substituted for the smack. Alexandra dutifully goes along with the gag in hopes that boss Dukes will arrive in the nick of time before her cover is blown, i.e., before Steiger and his doctor discover she already has a massive chest hidden under those tight-fitting gowns.

This nonsense is just an excuse for all-purpose chase scenes and shootouts, plus Alexandra kicking into submission various thugs, even felling the massive former wrestler Prof. Toru Tanaka. She's alluring and sports a perky personality, but hubby Silliphant's klutzy script sinks the outing. It's hard to believe the writer of "Narcissus On A Red Fire Engine" for tv's "Route 66" series and a horde of other interesting shows and pics penned the dumb puns and vulgarities here.

Dukes, Steiger and the supporting cast have little to do.—*Lor.*

Cassandra
(AUSTRALIAN-COLOR)

A Parrallel Films production. (World sales outside North America: OP Entertainment.) Produced by Trevor Lucas. Executive producers, Philip Gerlach, Mikael Borglund. Directed by Colin Eggleston. Screenplay, Eggleston, John Ruane, Chris Fitchett; camera (Agfa color), Gary Wapshott; editor, Josephine Cooke; music, Trevor Lucas, Ian Mason; production design, Stewart Burnside; sound, Robert Clayton; associate producer/production manager, Steve Amezdroz; assistant director, Michael Faranda. Reviewed at Cannes Film Festival (market), May 12, 1987. Running time: **93 MINS.**

Cassandra	Tessa Humphries
Steven Roberts	Shane Briant
Helen Roberts	Briony Behets
Libby	Susan Barling
Graham	Tim Burns
Also with: Kit Taylor, Lee James, Jeff Trueman.	

Cannes — A routine whodunit with slim theatrical chances but a career in video if enticingly packaged, "Cassandra" doesn't make much sense.

The eponymous heroine, played by newcomer Tessa Humphries, is plagued with horrifying nightmares in which she sees a small boy drive a woman to suicide. Her parents deny there's any basis for the nightmares, but when her photographer father's mistress, a model, is stabbed to death, Cassandra discovers her parents are really brother and sister and that her twin brother was responsible for her mother's death when the children were only three. The twin has been in a mental home but, in the great tradition of this sort of film, now he's out and ready to kill. Question is, which of the men around of the right age group is he?

All this would be a perfectly good basis for a suspense thriller, and for a while it all looks promising, with director Colin Eggleston handling the murder of the model with aplomb. A later scene, where Cassandra's mother is terrorized, also works. But in the end the film gets overloaded with improbabilities and downright contradictions, and the heroine's motives, even though she's supposed to be under the influence of her murderous twin, become obscure.

Audiences who eventually catch the film on video won't mind, because they can hang on for the next attack of the killer. On that level, pic is tame when compared to most Hollywood pics in this genre.

No acting awards likely for this one, but it's technically fine.

—*Strat.*

Treasure Of The Moon Goddess
(U.S.-COLOR)

An Ascot Entertainment release of a Patsa production. (World sales, Manson Intl.) Produced by Gerald Green. Executive producer, Joseph Wolf. Co-executive producer, Peter Miller. Directed by Joseph Louis Agraz. Screenplay, Eric Weston, Asher Brauner, from story by J.P. Dutilleu; camera (United color), Timothy Ross; editor, Chic Ciccolini, Gabrielle Gilbert; music, Victor Hall, Stephen Metz; sound, Robert Dreeben; production design, Bruno Rubeo; assistant director, Sean Ferrer; production manager, Alexandra Hernandez; special effects, Yves De Bono; executive in charge of production, Weston; casting, Claudia Becker. Reviewed at Cannes Film Festival (market), May 11, 1987. (No MPAA Rating.) Running time: **89 MINS.**

Sam Kidd	Asher Brauner
Harold	Don Calfa
Lu De Belle	Linnea Quigley
Brandy	Jo-Ann Ayres

Cannes — They hardly come as chintzy as "Treasure Of The Moon Goddess," a talkative "adventure" film that recalls those listless 1940s thrillers made on poverty row in Hollywood. This pic was started in Manila in 1984 and finished up in Mexico in 1986, but for all its absent production values it might as well have been shot on the back lot.

Pic is yet another opus in the vein of "Romancing The Stone:" Don Calfa dictates his autobiographical novel to a shapely oriental secretary while the viewer is treated to illustrated footage of his purported adventures. As sleazy manager to a smalltime songstress played by Linnea Quigley, Calfa buckles under to a gangster's wishes and arranges to have boat captain Asher Brauner deliver Quigley to a South American town called Quintana. En route, local natives and the gangsters vie to capture her, to exploit her resemblance to the local idol of the moon goddess.

Amidst stock footage of flora and fauna, lifelessly static action scenes and Calfa's hyper attempts at comic relief, pic plods along with the heroes repeatedly getting captured, escaping and captured once again. It turns out that Quigley really is the hoped-for goddess, but the natives illogically let her and everyone go at the end to set up several contradictory happy endings.

The two sets of basic footage do not match up well and lots of transition material is missing. Lack of a big action setpiece undoubtedly will disappoint adventure fans.

Calfa is the best part of the pic, looking in his white suit like a latter-day Peter Lorre and twice as untrustworthy. Oddly enough, the other characters are also ringers: Quigley is styled to look and act like Goldie Hawn (whom she normally resembles not one whit); lead Asher Brauner seems an older relative of Michael Dudikoff and his romantic partner, Jo-Ann Ayres, is a dead ringer for Theresa Russell. It's not an assignment that advances any of their careers.—*Lor.*

Distortions
(U.S.-COLOR)

A Jackelyn Giroux production. (World sales, Cori Films.) Executive producer, Marie Hoy; coproducer, Daniel Kuhn; Directed by Armand Mastroianni. Screenplay, John Goff; camera (color), John Dirlam; editor, Jack Tucker; music, David Morgan; technical supervisor, Gary Graver; associate producer, Richard Bennett Warsk. Reviewed at Cannes Film Festival (market), May 10, 1987. (No MPAA Rating.) Running time: **96 MINS.**

Amy	Olivia Hussey
Margot	Piper Laurie
Scott	Steve Railsback
Mildred	Rita Gam
Kelly	June Chadwick
Also with: Terence Knox, Edward Albert, Tom J. Castronova, Leon Smith.	

Cannes — About every thread-bare and overworn cliché in the suspense genre has been written into this supremely predictable and humdrum drama about a conspiracy to declare an ostensibly widowed woman insane to cash in on an insurance policy. The false leads and would-be suspense trappings are so unimaginatively handled that there is never any real doubt created. The "surprise" ending will hardly come as such to most audiences.

In what seems like a gay lover's quarrel, a young man is killed and pushed over a cliff in his car. When his wife Amy (Olivia Hussey) identifies him in the morgue, his face is almost unrecognizable due to the burns. Hussey is then drawn into a society of women with lesbian overtones, each of whom tries to help or control her.

Her aunt Margot (Piper Laurie) convinces Hussey to move into her mansion, where she proceeds to play tricks on her and feeds her drugs to convince Hussey she is going mad (there has been a history of madness in the family, we are shown in a flashback). Mysterious men appear and disappear in windows and doorways, some made up to look like the burned-to-a-char husband.

The hide-and-seek histrionics ultimately lead to the "surprise" revelation that the husband is really not dead at all, and that a simpatico admirer, the only one apparently believing she's not mad, is a cop on the trail of those who would defraud Hussey of her future wealth.

As the not-so-bereaved housewife, Hussey does the best she can with the script, and Piper Laurie is good as the domineering, threatening Aunt Margot. Presumably shot on a modest budget, pic seems more apt for tv and video than theatrical release.—*Besa.*

La Vie est Belle
(Life Is Rosy)
(ZAIRE-BELGIAN-FRENCH-COLOR)

A Lamy Films (Brussels)/Stephan Films (Paris)/Sol'oeil Films (Kinshasa) coproduction, in cooperation with Belgian Radio-TV, Zaire Office of Radio and TV, and others. Executive producer, Kabasele K. Munga. Directed by Benoit Lamy and Ngangura Mweze. Stars Papa Wemba. Screenplay, Mweze, Maryse Leon, Lamy; camera (Fuji color), Michel Baudour; editor, Martine Giordano; art direction, Mutoke Wa Mputu, Barly Baruti; music, Papa Wemba, with additional music by Klody, Zaiko Langa Langa, Tshala Muana; associate producers, Vera Belmont, Mweze. Reviewed at the Cannes Film Festival (market), May 15, 1987. Running time: **85 MINS.**
Kourou .... Papa Wemba
Kabibi .... Krukwa Bibi
Mamou .... Landu Nzunzimbu
Nvouandou .... Kanku Kasongo
Also with: Lonkinda Mengi Feza, Kalimazi Lombume, Mazaza Mukoko, Maitre Nono.

Cannes — Zaire singing star Papa Wemba is the heart of this light, joyful entertainment, coproduced and codirected by Belgium (producer-director Benoit Lamy) and Zaire (feature film debut of helmer Ngangura Mweze). This African musical comedy has been sold to many territories and should have no trouble working at special venues.

Papa Wemba plays Kourou, a ragged country boy who comes to the city in hopes of becoming a singer. In the end he succeeds, of course, but first he passes through a traumatic love affair with beautiful Kabibi (Krukwa Bibi), a poor girl whose mother marries her off as second wife to a childless businessman. A medium warns the businessman to wait a month before consumating the marriage, if he wants to have children, and that gives the young lovers just enough time to get together again, before a rocking finale in the disco, where Kourou performs pic's theme song "La vie est Belle" before the tv cameras. The businessman is forgiven by his first wife, and all ends happily.

All hands are sympathetic and script is genuinely funny. Papa Wemba has the shy appeal of a young Harry Belafonte, and his music is a treat, no matter how many times film repeats one song. It's technically adequate, too.
— *Yung.*

The Women's Club
(U.S.-COLOR)

An Inter-Ocean Film Sales release. Produced by Fred Weintraub in association with Scorsese Prods. Written and directed by Sandra Weintraub. Camera (United color), Kent Wakeford; editor, Martin Cohen; music, David Wheatley, Paul F. Antonelli; art director, Tim Duffey; sound, Bob Abbott; coproducer, Martin Hornstein. Reviewed at Cannes Film Festival (market), May 12, 1987. (No MPAA Rating.) Running time: **89 MINS.**
Patrick .... Michael Paré
Angie .... Maud Adams
Carlos .... Eddie Velez

Cannes — "The Women's Club" is a witless sex romp in which the man becomes the object of desire. Even though it may be a women's club, it's still a man's world as the fantasy is seen from a male perspective, even more surprising since a woman wrote and directed the picture. Despite the suggestion of more serious concerns, "The Women's Club" is really just a slightly better than average exploitation film.

"The Women's Club" is of the breed of film that is hatched in Los Angeles and draws from the filmmakers' experience in the business. In other words it's about itself.

Patrick (Michael Paré) is a struggling screenwriter who can't get a break until he uses his other talents to land a job as a male stud. Independent businesswoman Maud Adams gives him a tryout and then installs him in a Hollywood Hills house with an Armani wardrobe and a sleek sports car.

The plan is to write by day and entertain clients by night. At first it's a dream job as an array of L.A.'s lonely and lovely come by for some tea and sympathy. But Paré soon tires of the work, loses his girlfriend and, worst of all, has writer's block.

Finally Paré, who has been making tapes of his encounters along the way, decides to use his experience to write a script which the women try to block. Direction by Sandra Weintraub has added a slapstick comedy going on simultaneously as a buffoon journalist tries to uncover the story. Unfortunately, the two threads fail to come together in anything resembling a consistent tone.

Pic, in fact, is full of inconsistencies and clichés. Paré objects to being treated as a sex object, but he's still in control. He abandons the trappings of success on the one hand and strives for them on the other.

At heart the film is little more than a setup to introduce various sexual encounters and expose different appetites, although the action is overall surprisingly tame.

Saving grace of the pic is Michael Paré, who displays a real touch for light comedy and remains likable in spite of his character's shortcomings. Also very good is Eddie Velez as his fast-talking sidekick. Adams is photographed rather unflatteringly and looks a bit worn and drawn in a number of scenes.

Tech credits are professional but the music is an embarrassment.
—*Jagr.*

Initiation
(AUSTRALIAN-COLOR)

A Goldfarb Distributors (outside Australasia) and Intl. Film Management release of a Filmbar production. Executive producer, Antony I. Ginnane. Producer, Jane Ballantyne. Directed by Michael Pearce. Screenplay, James Barton; camera (Eastmancolor), Geoffrey Simpson; editor, Denise Haratzis; designer, Jon Dowding; sound, Toivo Lember. Reviewed at Cannes Film Festival (market), May 11, 1987. Running time: **100 MINS.**
Nat Molloy .... Bruno Lawrence
Danny Molloy .... Rodney Harvey
Sal .... Arna-Maria Winchester
Stevie .... Miranda Otto
Kulu .... Bobby Smith

Cannes — A lightweight offering that attempts to combine an action-adventure yarn with a rites of passage undertone, "Initiation" is a well-made and visually handsome film, but over-saturated by too many of the ingredients that rightly or wrongly are perceived to be attractive to the U.S. market.

Premise is that a streetwise, sassy teenager from Brooklyn, Danny Molloy, played by youthful U.S. actor Rodney Harvey, travels to the Aussie outback in search of his father following the death of his mother. He finds his tough-as-leather father, played by well-known Kiwi actor Bruno Lawrence, as well as a stepmother (Arna-Maria Winchester) and her daughter Stevie, played by Miranda Otto, and sets up residence, at first none-too-welcome, at their back of beyond homestead.

Out of place, and a born troublemaker, Harvey, after various entanglements with his estranged family and the locals, is told by Kulu, an aboriginal with occult powers portrayed by Bobby Smith, that he's in for more trouble. Turns out that Lawrence has started running drugs in his light plane; Harvey accompanies him on a drop and the plane crashes in the wilderness. Lawrence is injured.

Harvey's trek out of the bush is of course his "initiation;" his trials and tribulations, however, are coupled with semi-supernatural events arising from his link with Smith, who has determined to help guide Harvey spiritually through his "walkabout."

Thus, with such a stranger in a strange land setting, stage is set for a corollary of ingredients deemed quintessentially Australian from their exposure through other tv and film offerings over the years, even down to the cutaway shots of a dozing koala or bounding wallaby.

Problem is that so much time is spent emphasizing that scenario the characters tend to take second place and have little dimension. Then again, the mid-to-older teen audiences "Initiation" seems best suited to would probably be more interested in the thrills and spills, and how the characters come to grips with them throughout the pic.

Whether or not international fascination in all things Australian is as strong as "Initiation's" makers seem to think, Geoffrey Simpson's camerawork skillfully captures the light and colors of native Aussie bushland and desert, topped off by some excellent aerial work.

That, the basic level of action underlining the plot, and a score largely made up of songs from well-known Aussie rock bands could see "Initiation" garner an adolescent audience abroad. — *Doch.*

Business As Usual
(BRITISH-COLOR)

A Cannon Group presentation in association with Film Four Intl. Produced by Sara Geater. Executive producers, Menahem Golan, Yoram Globus. Written and directed by

Lezli-An Barrett. Camera (Rank color), Ernie Vincze; music, Paul Weller, Andrew Scott; art director, Hildegard Bitchler; sound, Ken Weston; casting, Dorothy Andrew. Reviewed at Cannes Film Festival (market), May 14, 1987. (No MPAA Rating.) Running time: **88 MINS.**

Babs Flynn . . . . Glenda Jackson
Kieran Flynn . . . . John Thaw
Josie Patterson . . . . Cathy Tyson
Stevie Flynn . . . . Mark McGann
Mr. Barry . . . . Eammon Boland
Mark . . . . James Hazeldine
Paula Douglas . . . . Buki Armstrong
Terry Flynn . . . . Steve McGann
Tim Flynn . . . . Philip Foster
Rosa . . . . Natalie Duffy

———

Cannes — "Business As Usual" is a British working-class drama which takes an updated look at the entrenched caste system in the marketplace. The action centers on the issue of sexual discrimination, but it could stand as a symbol for racial and religious battles of earlier years. It's a wellmade, conventional piece of work, and presence of Glenda Jackson in the lead role adds a touch of class. Picture should enjoy some success in select engagements Stateside.

Framework for the story takes a bit long to set in place as first-time director Lezli-An Barrett, working from her own screenplay, sketches the social conditions in England where unemployment is rampant and the labor union movement is crippled by in-fighting and ineffectiveness.

Jackson is assistant manager of a Liverpool dress shop, recently acquired by a chain that supplies a bit of glamor to working class girls in the form of affordable designer duds. Overseeing the shop and taking full liberties with the shop girls, especially lovely Cathy Tyson, is company rep Eammon Boland.

Barrett draws the sides early, with Boland and the bosses representing exploitive self-serving attitudes. For most of the way, "Business As Usual" is an examination of tactics for overcoming such social injustice.

On one side is Jackson's husband (John Thaw), a former factory worker now unemployed after a long battle to keep the business open. On the other side are Jackson's two pro-union sons who urge an all-out fight against management. A woman without much worldly experience, Jackson is caught in the middle and doesn't know which way to turn.

Gradually Jackson shreds her mousey demeanor and demands her rights in a world that threatens to trample her. Unlike her husband, she decides not to stand by passively and watch her life be destroyed and in the process of staging a nation-wide strike becomes a voice for all disenfranchised women.

Conclusions are rather one-sided and price paid for the victory is not given much consideration, but it is difficult not to root for the underdogs even if it is perfectly clear they are bound to win. Subtlety is beside the point here and the bad guys are truly evil and the workers are just, even as they experience bouts of self-doubt.

Strong performances keep the film from becoming sheer polemic with Jackson not afraid to show her age and famous face in a less glamorous light. Thaw is fine as the disillusioned counter-point and Boland is fittingly loathesome as the lecherous executive. Although her role offers little range, it is impossible not to stare at Tyson while she is on the screen. — *Jagr.*

Kurier
(Messenger Boy)
(SOVIET-COLOR)

———

A Mosfilm production. Directed by Karen Shakhnazarov. Screenplay, Alexander Borodyansky; camera (color), Nikolai Nemolyayev; music, Eduard Artemyev; art direction, Konstantin Forostenko. Reviewed at the Cannes Film Festival (market), May 16, 1987. Running time: **89 MINS.**

Ivan . . . . Fyodor Dunayevsky
Katya . . . . Anastasia Nemolyayeva
Mother . . . . Inna Churikova
Also with: Oleg Basilashvili (Professor), Svetlana Kryuchkova.

———

Cannes — Youth's disaffection with the society they live in and the distance they take from traditional values are familiar complaints all over the world, such givens nobody makes films about them anymore. In "Messenger Boy," directed by Karen Shakhnazarov from his short story, all this seems like a brand new discovery. Film's frank treatment of its young dropout hero is sympathetic and not condescending, making it seem tailor-made for local teen audiences. For Westeners, it offers a curious glimpse on growing up in Moscow today.

Opening scene shows Ivan's parents splitting up in a divorce courtroom. Ivan (Fyodor Dunayevsky) makes a show of solidarity with his father, an engineer with a young lover. Towards his wronged mother (Inna Churikova), instead, the boy displays only hostility and scorn. He even tries to set the apartment on fire. It doesn't take a psychologist to find the roots of his rebellion.

Rejected by the university as unfit for the subject his mother has chosen for him, Ivan passively lets her get him a job as a messenger boy for a publishing company. He blows his first delivery to a professor, but makes the acquaintance of the prof's very lovely daughter Katya (Anastasia Nemolyayeva). It takes some suspension of disbelief to accept that homely, brash Ivan wins the girl over with his originality and bad manners, but apparently he does. Repeatedly tossed out by Katya's father, he eventually wins the prof over, too.

Film is very natural in portraying the things young people do in Moscow: guitars, discos, somewhat stilted parties for Katya's set (they belong to the capital's rich élite, and are markedly more privileged than Ivan's friends from the housing development). When asked what he wants from life, Ivan says: an easy job and money. Sexual mores are also treated frankly, without moralizing. In a disturbing last scene, Ivan seems to think more deeply about his life for the first time when he stars at a passing soldier, young, somber, with a scar across his face.

Shakhnazarov's touch is light and sure throughout. Lensing is no-frills and efficient. — *Yung.*

———

Berserker
(U.S.-COLOR)

———

A Shapiro Entertainment release of an American Video Group and Paradise Filmworks production. Executive producers, Robert A. Foti, Robert Seibert. Produced by Jules Rivera. Written and directed by Jef Richard. Camera (color), Henning Schellerup; editor, Marcus Manton; music, Chuck Francour, Gary Griffin; production manager, Joan Weidman. Reviewed at Cannes Film Festival (market), May 10, 1987. (No MPAA rating.) Running time: **85 MINS.**

With: Joseph Alan Johnson, Valerie Sheldon, Greg Dawson.

———

Cannes — As the number of splatter horror pics continues to swell, so do the variations on a theme. "Berserker" goes to a new silly extreme, offering the standard group of winsome students camping in the woods, terrorized this time by a risen-from-the-dead Viking warrior who rends his victims apart grizzly bear style.

Just why an undead Viking is stalking the woods isn't made quite clear, apart from a Nordic legend espoused by the students, who for some reason have a fascination about the topic, which tells that "berserkers," ferocious drug-induced fighters, were cursed by the Norse gods to be reincarnated in their blood kin because they ate human flesh.

The local camping ground manager hails from the "old country" and has fallen under this curse. He proceeds to pick off the happy-go-lucky youngsters as they effortlessly and repeatedly lose themselves in the woods.

Students eventually win through, ranks depleted, but there's the inevitable twist ending.

Young cast is good looking but makes little headway with their stereotyped characters. Local police officer, who shares some unexplained ancestral link with the berserker, not to mention a saunter that rivals John Wayne, barely rises above mediocrity.

Tech credits are okay, but the effects aren't that special; a man wearing a bear snout and claws, as berserkers apparently were wont to do, is hardly enough to scare hardened horror fans these days. There's an obligatory sex scene (juxtaposed with much slashing and screaming going on not too far away) but the limited gory effects, umpteen shots of sneaker-shod feet running through the same section of forest again and again, and the overall silly premise behind the plot, make it likely "Berserker" will join the homevideo ranks with barely a struggle. — *Doch.*

The Great Land Of Small
(CANADIAN-COLOR)

———

A New World Pictures (U.S.), Cinema Plus release (in Canada) of a Les Prods. La Fête production. Produced by Rock Demers. Directed by Vojtech Jasny. Screenplay, David Sigmund; camera (color), Michel Brault; editor, Hélène Girard; music, Guy Trépanier, Normand Dube; art direction, Violette Daneau; costumes, Michèle Hamel; special effects, Louis Craig, Les Productions, Pascal Blais. Reviewed at Cannes Film Festival (market), May 10, 1987. (No MPAA Rating.) Running time: **94 MINS.**

Jenny . . . . Karen Elkin
David . . . . Michael Blouin
Fritz . . . . Michael J. Anderson
Flannigan . . . . Ken Roberts
Mother . . . . Lorraine Desmarais
Grandpa . . . . Gilles Pelletier
Grandma . . . . Françoise Graton
Sarah . . . . Michelle Elaine Turmel

———

Cannes — Visually attractive, charming and whimsical, "The Great Land Of Small" makes for a compelling and winning family feature that should have wide appeal.

Pic focuses on two city kids who visit their grandparents in the countryside and become involved with a midget from the inner space world of The Great Land of Small. He comes to earth with a bag of magic gold dust and gets into the wrong hands. Led by the midget, who can be seen only by those who believe in magic, the kids are transported to his world, which is vividly created.

Matters get resolved happily after neat scenes of jeopardy played off without violence but just enough action to lock in the small fry.

Michel Brault's camera work is lush and Vojtech Jasny's direction is competent if a bit slow-paced. Special effects are kept within bounds of a low budget but with some style. English dialog is strained in parts but the pic overcomes.

The fifth family pic — the first one in English — in a steady output from Montreal producer Rock Demers definitely has theatrical life in all locales and bright chances for tv and homevid, too. — *Adil.*

———

Mace
(U.S.-COLOR)

A Double Helix Films presentation of an RMC Films production. Produced by Michael A. Simpson, William VanDerKloot. Executive producers, Jerry Silva, Stan Wakefield, Kirk K. Smith, Mike Malloy. Directed by VanDerKloot. Screenplay, Simpson; camera (color), John Davis; editor, VanDerKloot; music, James Oliverio; second unit camera, VanDerKloot; stunt coordinator, Victoria VanDerKloot; casting, Joan D'Incesso. Reviewed at Cannes Film Festival (market), May 15, 1987. (No MPAA Rating.) Running time: **88 MINS.**

Malcolm (Mace) Douglas	Ed Marinaro
Mark Cain	Darrell Larson
Amber	Cassandra Gava
Jamal	Isaac Hayes
Talbot	John Hancock
Brennan	William Sanderson
Webster	Corbin Bernsen
McWhorter	William Windom
Androsov	Harry Goz
Johnson	Terry Beaver
Sheila Freeman	Lynn Whitfield

Also with: Sandi Brannon, Diana Brittain, Carol Chambers, Shirlene Foss, Marisu Wehrenberg, Donna Biscoe.

Cannes — Television star Ed Marinaro makes an unsuccessful transition to a leading role in a feature film via "Mace," an impoverished police thriller. Stillborn pic doesn't even play as exploitation fodder, despite its down and dirty theme.

Marinaro is an Atlanta cop nicknamed Mace, because he sprayed mace down a suspect's throat a while back, causing him to be demoted from homicide lieutenant to the vice squad. He's assigned to a case with partner Darrell Larson, involving the suspicious drug overdose deaths of a series of topless dancers (pic is so wimpy they rarely are topless despite endless strip sequences as filler).

Convoluted plotline (delivered mainly in gobs of verbal exposition) has the strippers connected somehow with security leaks, KGB agents, Bulgarian diplomats (pic's original title was "The Sofia Conspiracy") and blackmail. The FBI finally steps in and Mace is bounced off the case. He loses his badge when he continues anyway in order to help protect a stripper he has fallen for (Cassandra Gava a.k.a. Gaviola) and protracted windup is a sick variant on Dirty Harry behavior.

This nonsense might have been diverting with an adequate budget, to deliver the globehopping thriller narrative replete with dateline/city i.d. superimpositions. Instead, painfully underlit cheapie takes place entirely in Atlanta, with cast endlessly discussing the international implications.

Marinaro is grumpy and unappealing, not an antihero, but a nonstarter here. Rest of the principals are merely adequate and the strippers are not sexy enough by a country mile. Tech credits are weak.
— *Lor.*

Over grensen
(The Feldmann Case)
(NORWEGIAN-COLOR)

A Syncron Film release (world sales: Norsk Film) of a Marcus Film production with Norsk Film, Esselte Video, Sunnmørsbanken, Kodak Norge, Johan Ankerstjerne. Produced by Jeanette Sundby. Coproduced and directed by Bente Erichsen. Screenplay, Erichsen, based on novel by Sigurd Senje; camera (Eastmancolor), Rolv Haan; editor, Björn Breigutu; music, Nissa Nyberget; sound, Svein Hovde; costumes, Alain Touzinaud. Reviewed at Cannes Film Festival (market), May 11, 1987. Running time: **94 MINS.**

Arnfinn Madsen	Björn Sundquist
Mikkel Arness	Sverre Anker Ousdal
Holly	Inger Lise Rypdal
Rakel Feldmann	Ingerid Vardund
Jacob Feldmann	Finn Kvalem
Harald Sagstuen	Oivind Berven
Paul Plassen	Trond Braerne
Ole Sagstuen	Terje Dahl

Cannes — Based on a real-life World War II incident and postwar court case, "The Feldmann Case" by veteran producer and debuting writer-director Bente Erichsen is a tight little meller of combined documentary flavor and a lively, Raymond Chandleresque sense of the sodid yet colorful detail that harks of detective work in a murder mystery.

"The Feldmann Case" (titled the tamer "Over The Border" at home where the case remains controversial to this day) deals with a journalist's and a police detective's combined, but not always united, efforts to reopen the case of Rakel and Jacob Feldmann, a middle-aged Jewish couple, who were killed, robbed, weighted down with stones and drowned while being aided in their 1942 flight from Norway's occupying Nazis.

The killers were members of the Norwegian resistance, who were to claim the Feldmanns had to die to save the escape route for many others. The case was suppressed by local authorities, and the mountain village population knew how to keep mum and stand together against any outside attempt to find the truth.

With the case reopened, old animosities and guilts are brought back to life. After a series of confrontations, some violent, the case reaches Norway's highest court. The guilt of the accused men seems solidly established via the dogged work of the journalist (Bob Hoskins lookalike Björn Sundquist) and the detective (a marvelous portrayal of passion-within-woodenness by Sverre Anker Ousdal), but once again the men in the dock are acquitted.

Sales to international tv seem assured, and even some theatrical exposure abroad looms to provoke discussion about the skeleton in Justice's closet in a showcase democracy like Norway. Even without any such debate assets, Bente Erichsen's picture constitutes a straight, albeit grim, piece of crime fare entertainment. — *Kell.*

Le Moustachu
(The Field Agent)
(FRENCH-COLOR)

An AAA release of a CAPAC/Agepro Cinéma/Séléna Audiovisuel (AAA)/TF-1 Films corproduction. Produced by Marie-Christine de Montbrial, Paul Claudon. Written and directed by Dominique Chaussois. Stars Jean Rochefort, Grace de Capitani, Jean-Claude Brialy. Camera (Fuji, Eastmancolor), Claude Agostini; editor, Georges Klotz; music, Vladimir Cosma; art direction, Didier Naert; artistic advisor, Alexandre Trauner; sound, Dominique Levert; assistant director, Olivier Peray; production manager, Hubert Merial; casting, Romain Bremond. Reviewed at the Marignan-Concorde cinema, Paris, May 17, 1987. (In Cannes Film Festival Market.) Running time: **86 MINS.**

Duroc	Jean Rochefort
The girl	Grace de Capitani
Leroy	Jean-Claude Brialy
The General	Jean-Louis Trintignant
Young motorist	Jean-Claude Leguay
Staub	Maxime Leroux
Sully	Jacques Mathou

Paris — "Le Moustachu" is a tongue-in-cheek espionage spoof with Jean Rochefort as a veteran field agent involved in a mission in which everything goes wrong. Newcomer writer-director Dominique Chaussois has some good gag ideas and fair technical skill, though the whole feels like a string of individual scenes without a sense of organic unity.

A good part of the action is set in a deserted rest stop zone off a French highway where Rochefort must deliver a boobytrapped car destined for a gang of terrorists. Plan backfires because the terrorists have been tipped off and set an ambush for Rochefort instead. In the meantime, the agent must deal with a series of human nuisances who happen on the scene. When Rochefort finally falls into the hands of his antagonists, he is roughed up but succeeds in outwitting them.

Rochefort is as always a winning phlegmatic farceur and finds some amusingly tight-lipped support from Jean-Louis Trintignant, as a no-nonsense general and newly appointed secret service exec, and Jean-Claude Brialy as Rochefort's civilian superior. — *Len.*

Angel Of Vengeance
(U.S.-COLOR)

A Reel Movies Intl. release of an Odyssey Pictures II production. Produced by Jeffrey C. Hogue. Directed by Ted V. Mikels. Screenplay, Mikels, Gary Thompson, Hogue; camera (color), Pat Kerby; editor, Mikels; music, Chuck Dodson; sound, Maria De La Rosa, Jim Mungo; production manager, Carl Irwin; associate producer, T. Craig Heller. Reviewed at Cannes Film Festival (market), May 9, 1987. (No MPAA Rating.) Running time: **76 MINS.**

Tina Davenport	Jannina Poynter
The Major	David O'Hara
Manny	Macka Foley

Also with: Carl Irwin, Jeffrey C. Hogue, Jason Holt, Ed Walters, Linda Eden.

Cannes — "Angel Of Vengeance" doesn't make much of its premise: gung ho survivalists killing folks in a remote mountain spot as practice for the war they believe is imminent. Pic is relentlessly dull.

Jannina Poynter toplines as a young woman researching a book about her late father, a military man, who has several runins with the survivalists led by single-minded David O'Hara. About to be summarily executed as were the rest of the group's unlucky prisoners (including members of a local biker gang, called Thrill Killers), she talks O'Hara into letting her act as human prey for the troops, and then proceeds to skillfully kill all of them.

Until Poynter goes on the rampage in the final reel, picture unfolds listlessly with aloof camerawork, weak acting and mundane action scenes. A parallel subplot of a couple of thrill-seeking guys also on the rampage makes for filler leading to a predictable final twist.—*Lor.*

My African Adventure
(U.S.-COLOR)

A Cannon Group release of a Golan-Globus production. Executive producer, Avi Lerner. Produced by Menahem Golan, Yoram Globus. Directed by Boaz Davidson. Screenplay, Golan; camera (color), Joseph Wain; editor, Natan Zahavi, Bruria Davidson. Reviewed at Cannes Film Festival (market), May 14, 1987. (MPAA Rating: PG.) Running time: **93 MINS.**

Big Bad Joe	Dom DeLuise
Mozambo	Jimmie Walker
Ben	David Mendenhall
Bonzo	Deep Roy
Palermo	Warren Berlinger
Mackintosh	Herbert Lom
Ship's Captain	Len Sparrowhawk

Also with: Peter Elliott, Fats Dibeco, Graham Armitage, Mike Westcott.

Cannes — Cannon's family-oriented adventure comedy has all the ingredients whose passing the cinema wiseacres lament — action without violence, comedy without grossness and a storyline any parent would approve their kids seeing. Trouble is, the wiseacres don't buy the tickets these days.

"My African Adventure" is an amiably innocent piece of nonsense involving an American boy in the Dark Continent with his hysterical custodian (Dom DeLuise), a local tour guide (Jimmie Walker) and a chimp named Bonzo. (The last may ring bells among the politically inclined.)

Plot involves saving Bonzo, who can talk, from a corrupt local police chief (Herbert Lom reprising his Pink Panther roles) and an acquisitive circus owner (Warren Berlinger).

It's slapsticky and rough, and there are more chuckles than yocks, but it's not short of appeal for an undemanding junior. Kids, though, seem to demand more, and "Adventure's" closing hint of a sequel seems optimistic in the extreme. Innocence and gentle whimsy probably aren't enough.—*Rant.*

Magnificent Warriors
(HONG KONG-COLOR)

A D&B Films presentation and release, Executive producer, Dickson Poon. Produced by John Sham, Linda Kuk. Associate producer, Yank Wong. Directed by David Chung. Stars Richard Ng, Michelle Khan, Matsui Tetsuya, Yee Tung Shing, Lowell Lo. Screenplay, Tsang Kan Cheong; camera (color), Ma Chun Wah; art direction, Oliver Wong; editor, Chiang Kowk Kuon; original music, Chan Wing Leong. Reviewed at Cannes Film Festival (market), May 10, 1987. Running time: **95 MINS.**
(Cantonese soundtrack with English subtitles)
English soundtrack, Mandarin versions also available.

Cannes — In terms of Hong Kong pics, this savvy movie has a high budget (rumored around $HK30,000,000, just like Cinema City's "Legend Of Wisely"). On the positive side, the set design, art direction and cinematography are in good order, but as an action drama, pic has no vitality, no vigor to entertain, no vim to amuse the lowest Cantonese taste in the mass market it was geared to attract.

Inept story is set in Bhutan in the 1930s and revolves around three men and two women who vow to chase the Japanese out of the city Kaal where they plan to build an experimental center for a poisonous gas chamber.

The plot is simplistic, yet there is much confusion in telling the tale. The storyline is but a framework for the stars to carry out their physical stunts. Director David Chung tries to make an action pic but fails dismally in an aborted attempt at agitated suspense that never materializes.

Pic is too much in the "Indiana Jones," "Jewel Of The Nile" vein. Michelle Khan, an ex-beauty queen from Malaysia doing work for the D & B stable, is topcast. She is supposedly the hottest female action star, per publicity blurb.

Film obviously was made and conceived to showcase her swift and lethal martial arts (yet one can easily detect many doubles). What spoils this project is the lack of imagination in utilizing the attractive production design to advantage, making the male stars prominent instead of concentrating on the femme lead.

Richard Ng, a capable comedian, and singer Lowell Lo are useless sub-characters and there is no room for handsome Yee Tung Shing to be a foil (like Michael Douglas) for Khan. Sadly, the lady has little chance to be an international star via the Cannes market. However, she can still make it as a Chinatown action queen abroad. —*Mel.*

The Darkside
(CANADIAN-COLOR)

A Magnatta production. (World sales, Shapiro Entertainment.) Produced by Constantino Magnatta, Phillip M. Good. Directed by Magnatta. Screenplay, Allan Magee, Matt Black; camera (Film House color), Gilles Corbail; editor, Claudio DeGrano; music, Greg Diakun; sound, Gord Thompson; stunt coordinator, Ken Quinn; associate producer, DeGrano. Reviewed at Cannes Film Festival (market), May 17, 1987. Running time: **98 MINS.**
Tony . . . . Tony Galati
Laura . . . . Cyndy Preston
Lou . . . . Peter Reed
Sully . . . . John Tench
Roscoe . . . . Charles Loriot
Chuckie . . . . Davie Hewlett

Cannes — "The Darkside" is an obnoxious Canadian exploitation film, wallowing in the same demeaning areas it simultaneously moralizes about.

Tony Galati toplines as a Toronto cabbie working the night shift who reluctantly saves a half-clad beautiful blond (Cyndy Preston) from the clutches of a Cockney creep in a dinner jacket (John Tench). She's running away from a gangster (Charles Loriot) who got her drunk and made a porno tape of her, which she hides in Tony's cab.

Corny story of everyone trying to get their hands on the tape unfolds at a leisurely pace, with filmmaker Constantino Magnatta pouring on the sleaze while taking potshots at the dastardly porno types. Pic is generally too tame for its subject matter and the only fun scene is a goofy sequence of some bikers (including a topless girl) chasing Tony through a rundown apartment. Elsewhere, he stupidly crosscuts between fast-forward footage of the dreaded porno tape and strictly tease footage of Galati and Preston in bed making love. The equation is mindless.

Despite the title and potential for *film noir* action, most of the pic takes place in the daytime and little Sin City atmosphere is generated. Tech credits are merely adequate. Acting by the lead couple is fine, but Loriot and Tench ham it up as comic strip villains.—*Lor.*

White Whales
(ICELANDIC-COLOR)

An Icelandic Film Corp. release and coproduction with the Icelandic Film Fund. Produced and directed by Fridrik Thor Fridriksson. Screenplay, Fridriksson, Einar Karason; camera (Agfacolor), Ari Kristinsson; editor, Tomas Gislason; music, Hilmar Oern Hilmarsson, Bubbi Morthens, Sykurmolarnir; sound, Thorbjörn Erlingsson. Reviewed at Cannes Film Festival (market), May 11, 1987. Running time: **80 MINS.**
Grimur . . . . Thorarinn Thorarinsson
Bubbi . . . . Eggert Gudmundsson
Also with: Hrönn Steingrimsdottir, Karl Gudmundsson, Eggert Thorleifsson, Balduin Halldorsson, Helgi Björnsson, Harald G. Haraldsson, Guddbjörg Thoroddsen.

Cannes — "White Whales" has spectacular introductory footage of the ocean's giant mammals, but the story of Fridrik Thor Fridriksson's first feature deals more with the stranded human variety, in this case a couple of laid-off whale-boat sailors on a binge with a tragic ending. Pic will represent the emerging Icelandic film production neatly via offshore television, but the picture lacks the firm structuring needed to bring foreign audiences into theaters.

Fridriksson, who has based his story on real events, has a nice sense of pacing and framing, and his cinematographer (Ari Kristinsson) is a wiz with lighting.

Fridriksson's weaker points are character delineations and general handling of his actors, who remain rather undefined and vacant. Of the two leads, one is shown to have a grudge because his girlfriend of long standing has suddenly slammed her door in his face. She has shipped his belongings over to his mother, who is not too happy to see her son, either, since both he and his sweet simpleton buddy reek of liquor.

Soon, the two men are to both reek and reel even more, but nothing really happens during their wanderings through the saloons and discos of Reykjavik to explain why they end up breaking into a sporting goods store to steal shotguns and engage in a murderous gunbattle with the police. Inevitable final chase sequence has speed and urgency, however, and film's production dress is handsome. Also, a country-rock music score of local origin has originality and punch. —*Kell.*

Snow White
(U.S.-COLOR)

A Cannon Group presentation of a Golan-Globus production. Produced by Menahem Golan and Yoram Globus. Executive producer, Itzik Kol. Written and directed by Michael Berz. Art director, Etan Levy; production manager, Chaim Sharir. Reviewed at Cannes Film Festival (market), May 14, 1987. (No MPAA Rating.) Running time: **83 MINS.**
Mean Queen . . . . Diana Rigg
Iddy . . . . Billy Barty
Show White at 16 . . . . Sarah Patterson
Snow White at 7 . . . . Nicola Stapleton
Biddy . . . . Mike Edmunds
Kiddy . . . . Ricardo Gil
Diddy . . . . Malcolm Dixon
Fiddy . . . . Gary Friedkin
Liddy . . . . Tony Cooper
King . . . . Douglas Sheldon
Also with: Dorit Adi, Ian James Wright, Annon Meskin.

Cannes — Some delicious comic villainy from Diana Rigg apart, Cannon's excursion into familiar fairytale terrain is likely to elicit less a Heigh Ho than a heave ho from paying spectators.

"Snow White" stays alive whenever Rigg's present with her relish, heavy hamming, but tends to founder when she's offscreen. Rest is nice enough, but not sufficiently so to come near supplanting the Disney animated version.

Under director Berz, the pace is kept up (though his screenplay is written Ivanhoe-style, in an English dialect one might call "costumer-antique").

Overall feel, particularly whenever anyone sings, is of a pic 20 years out of date. Nevertheless, production values are good, and the story is strong, so "Snow White" can be expected to play. Probably not theatrically, though: look to foreign tv and homevid for main exploitation of this item. —*Rant.*

Mr. Nice Guy
(CANADIAN-COLOR)

Shapiro Entertainment release of a Wolf Film Corp. production. Produced by Henry Wolfond, Constantino Magnatta. Directed by Wolfond. Screenplay, Wolfond, Mark Breslin, based on story by Mark Breslin, Wolfond, Leonard Smofsky, Mike MacDonald; camera (color), Smofsky; editor, Ion Webster; music, Paul Hoffert. Reviewed at Cannes Film Festival (market), May 16, 1987. (MPAA Rating: PG-13.) Running time: **92 MINS.**
Curt Murdoch . . . . Mike MacDonald
Dr. Lisa Rayon . . . . Jan Smithers
Lazer Fish . . . . Joe Silver
Jerry Reemer . . . . Harvey Atkin
The Don . . . . Howard Jerome
Mrs. Romano . . . . Maxine Miller

Cannes — A mildly likeable comedy script and an okay cast of character actors are steamrolled by overly broad and untutored direction in "Mr. Nice Guy." Unrealized potential is evident throughout.

Plot centers on an efficient retail store guard who joins a company that advertises killings for hire and takes all major credit cards. It competes with a boardroom-convened Mafia, which is not pleased with the rival operation.

The guard-turned-expert assassin falls in love with a psychiatrist who promotes her nut-cases service on tv. Turns out her father is the Mafia don and he's especially angered to discover her husband-to-be is the rival company's top gun. All is resolved at the end, but flatly.

Toronto standup comic Mike MacDonald, in his pic lead debut, shows promise and Jan Smithers, who is called on to be pert, is that and nothing more. Rival company bosses Harvey Atkin and Howard Jerome also can do better.

Leonard Smofsky's camerawork, Paul Hoffert's music, performed by Canadian rock group Lighthouse, and all production values, are slight.

Outlook: tv in undiscriminating locales, Canadian paycable and limited homevid.—*Adil.*

Geek
(U.S.-COLOR)

A Norstar Releasing release (in Canada) of an Overlook Films/Dean Crow Prods. production. (World sales, Shapiro Entertainment.) Produced by Maureen Sweeney. Directed by Crow. Screenplay, Charles Joseph; camera (color), Jon Gerard; editor, Chris Hodapp; art direction; Jacque Workman; music, Skeet Bushor. Reviewed at Cannes Film Festival (market), May 12, 1987. (No MPAA Rating.) Running time: **90 MINS.**

Jamie	Brad Armacost
Karen	Christina Noonan
Eben	Dick Kreusser
William	Jack O'Hara

Cannes — Yuppie couple, he a doctor and she a hardy trekker, go camping in the woods. A forest ranger tells them to go this way because that way they may not be safe.

They go that way, meet up with backwoods man, his young and silent daughter and his mentally deranged and violent grown son. The son rips the heads off chickens, goes after the trekker and everyone, except the couple and the young daughter, is killed. Even the forest ranger. Direction and production values are slow, always telegraphed and subpar. The only point seems to be: Listen to the forest ranger, he knows best. No one else involved did.

Outlook, even in homevid, seems as dim as the makeup on the imbecile dubbed "the geek." —*Adil.*

Krugovorot
(Succession Of Events)
(SOVIET-COLOR)

A Gruziafilm Studios production. Directed by Lana Gogoberidze. Screenplay, Zaira Arsenishvili, Gogoberidze; camera (color), Nugzar Erkomaishvili, art direction, Georgi Mikeladze. Reviewed at the Cannes Film Festival (market), May 14, 1987. Running time: **101 MINS.**

Manana	Leila Abashidze

Also with: Liya Eliava, Guram Pirtskhalava, Otar Megvinetukhusesi.

Cannes — "Succession of Events" has all the hallmarks of the new Georgian cinema — a jumpy, discontinuous story, a score of eccentric characters only casually related to each other, sophisticated lensing — without being an engrossing picture. The various intertwined stories are basically uninvolving, and it's hard to imagine an audience for them outside a small local market.

The character who reappears most is Manana (Leila Abashidze), a former actress now well past her prime and prone to dressing in ridiculous leopard-print coats and hats with veils. The few souls who still recognize her get touched for a loan.

There is a young woman dying in a hospital; the father of her daughter Anne has never married her; and it's a pretty anguished end. After her death, the lonely woman from the next bed, Rusudan, decides to adopt the little girl, but then the father seems grimly determined to have her. Film's distance is such that it doesn't make much difference, one way or the other.

Director Lana Gogoberidze gives pic a stylish look, and actors are convincing pros. As Manana, Leila Abashidze offers a fine comic performance. Background is modern Tbilisi. —*Yung.*

Indian Summer
(BRITISH-COLOR)

A Metro Film Corp. presentation of a Bevanfield film. (World sales, Cori Films.) Executive producers, Dayanand Mandre, Pamela Mandre, Sunanda Murali Manohar. Produced by Laurie Hardie Brown, Mary Swindale. Written and directed by Timothy Forder. Camera (Metrocolor), Walter Lassally; editor, Mike Murray; music, Barrie Guard, Ilaya Raja; sound, Tony Dawe, Shep Dawe; production design, Manzoor Amrohi; costumes, Christine Staszewska; associate producer, Christopher Sutton; production manager, Jagdish; assistant director, A. Rao; casting, Michael Barnes. Reviewed at Cannes Film Fest (market), May 13, 1987. Running time: **95 MINS.**

Oliver Sutherland	Peter Chelsom
Caroline Sutherland	Shelagh McLeod
Marie	Michelle Evans
Patrick	Trevor Baxter
Spencer	Derek Waring
Fiona	Rosalind Bailey

Also with: Bridget McConnel (Victoria), Farida (Maharanee), Asha (housekeeper), Charu Hassan (Ray), Roshan Ara (Meera).

Cannes — An insipid romance drama that wastes its Indian locations, this one's heading nowhere. Television soaps have stronger screenplays and are usually better acted.

Oliver Sutherland is a British film director making a pic in India; his lonely wife Caroline spends bored days in the lavish home they've rented. With nothing to do, she imagines her husband is having an affair with the French actress playing the lead role in the film.

All the characters are dull, including the film's breezy producer and his snobbish wife. If the director had simply talked to his wife in reel one, or she'd asked him if he was involved with his leading lady straight out, there'd have been no picture.

For all the use of the pic makes of authentic Indian locations, it might as well have employed Pinewood's sound stages. On every level, it's a listless effort, with half-hearted sex scenes, pallid drama, and much talk about very little. —*Strat.*

Graveyard Shift
(U.S.-COLOR)

A Shapiro Entertainment release of a Cinema Ventures production of a Lightshow Co. picture. Produced by Michael Bockner. Executive producers, Arnold H. Bruck, Stephen Flaks. Written and directed by Gerard Ciccoritti. Camera (color), Robert Bergman; editors, Bergman, N. Smith; music, Nicholas Pike; production design, Lester Berman; production manager, Peter Bobras; assistant director, Allan Levine. Reviewed at Cannes Film Festival (market), May 16, 1987. (MPAA Rating: R.) Running time: **88 MINS.**

Stephen Tsepes	Silvio Oliviero
Michelle	Helen Papas
Eric Hayden	Cliff Stoker
Gilda	Dorin Ferber

Also with: Dan Rose, Don Jones.

Cannes — Lensed in Canada, this is an above-average entry in the minor horror stakes. Central character is a taxi driver/vampire, who brings new meaning to the term "graveyard shift;" as well essayed by Silvio Oliviero, he's genuinely scary.

Helen Papas plays a tv director who discovers she has only a short time to live; she goes with the sinister taxi driver for a sexual experience, and becomes vampirized.

It's basically familiar stuff, but writer-director Gerard Ciccoritti shows flair, and the urban nighttime setting is neatly evoked. That, plus the unusually strong leads, make it a watchable outing.

There's not an excess of gore, but plenty of femme nudity. It should have a video career after a modest theatrical release. Ciccoritti and Oliviero should be heard from in the future. —*Strat.*

The Emperor's New Clothes
(U.S.-COLOR)

A Cannon Films release of a Golan-Globus production. Produced by Menahem Golan, Yoram Globus. Executive producer, Itzik Kol. Directed by David Irving. Stars Sid Caesar, Clive Revill, Robert Morse. Screenplay, Anna Mathias, Len Talan, David Irving from a story by Hans Christian Andersen; camera (color), David Gurfinkel; editor, Tova Neeman; music, David Krivoshei; production design, Marek Dobrowlski; art director, Avi Avivi; costumes, Buki Shieff; sound, Eli Yarkoni; associate producer, Patricia Ruben, second unit camera, Nicho Leon. Reviewed at Cannes Film Festival (market), May 9, 1987. (No MPAA Rating.) Running time: **80 MINS.**

Henry	Robert Morse
Nicholas	Jason Carter
Gilda	Lysette Anthony
Prime Minister	Clive Revill
Duke	Julian Joy-Chagrin
Sergeant	Eli Gorenstein
Wenceslas	Israel Gurion
Christine	Susan Berlin-Irving

Cannes — Sid Caesar, embroidering on material similar to that of his early-days tv series "Your Show Of Shows," is the only tailored turn in "The Emperor's New Clothes."

His Emperor, spouting Caesar's trademark foreign language jibberish and nervous delivery, gives the only spark. Even that's all too brief in an otherwise lifeless, costumed pic intended for kiddies. They're too smart to fall for this one.

Castle sets look as if they're made of cheap cardboard; a trunk of jewels looks as if it's crammed with stale egg salad topped by pimiento, and the voices of many performers throughout and of some native English speakers, especially at the beginning, are obviously and poorly dubbed.

Pic appears to be a musical; a few original but derivative songs are sung and then abandoned quickly. David Gurfinkel's camera work is flat, as is the script. Costumes are lackluster and also look cheap.

David Irving's direction is dull. Like the emperor's new clothes themselves, there isn't anything here. Theatrical possibilities, except in very undemanding locales, seem nil as does much life on cable or video. Kids 10 years and up are unlikely and those from three to nine have better things to do. Like stay home and read the original story. —*Adil.*

Bloody New Year
(BRITISH-COLOR)

A Lazer Entertainments production in association with Cinema & Theater Seating. (World sales, Smart Egg Pictures.) Produced by Hayden Pearce. Executive producer, Maxine Julius. Directed by Norman J. Warren. Screenplay, Frazer Pearce, in association with Warren, Hayden Pearce; camera (Fujicolor by Rank), John Shann; editor, Carl Thomson; music, Nick Magnus; sound, Doug Turner; production design, Hayden Pearce. Reviewed at Cannes Film Festival (market), May 11, 1987. Running time: **90 MINS.**

Lesley	Suzy Aitchison
Janet	Nikki Brooks
Spud	Colin Heywood
Rick	Mark Powley
Carol	Catherine Roman
Tom	Julian Ronnie

Cannes — "Bloody New Year" is a negligible horror film rehashing the corniest format available. Its sights are set squarely on the undiscriminating homevideo market.

With several nods to Stanley Kubrick's 'The Shining," British helmer Norman J. Warren rounds up six teens who play at an amusement park and then go boating, unhappily ending up on an island with a spooky old hotel. It appears that ghosts of a 1960 New Year's party are haunting them there until a preposterous scientific explanation states that an experimental invisibility plane crashed, upsetting laws of time and matter in the vicinity.

Warren uses this as an excuse to have any odd thing happen to the kids, including attacks by the undead and various poorly executed monsters. It's strictly filler, as are the nostalgia references in clothing and music to the 1960 milieu. Acting by the colorless thesps is poor and the Fujicolor visuals (especially the bright daylight exteriors) are far too pretty and cheerful to create the desired horror atmosphere. —*Lor.*

What's Love
(U.S.-COLOR)

A Hollywood Intl. Film Corp. of America release. No producer credit. Directed by Carlos Tobalina. Screenplay, Bill Cable, Tobalina; camera (color), Tobalina; editor, Elizabeth McCormick, Anita Jefferson; music, Bulleto; sound, Douglas Meyers; special effects, Sam Nelson, Albert Foley, Patricia Buchanan; special effects editor, Phil Bergandi. Reviewed at the Cannes Film Festival (market), May 9, 1987. (No MPAA Rating.) Running time: **105 MINS.**
With: Bill Cable, Donna Lee Drake, Troy Walker, Sharon Kelly, Ginger Lynn, Tom Byron, John Regis, Diana St. Cyr, Carlos Tobalina, Karen Maria Stage, Jake Munroy, Lisa Marie.

Cannes — Watching an "R-rated" version of a pic originally designed as hardcore is like taking a shower with your clothes on. The full effect isn't achieved.

"What's Love" is more or less a standard Hollywood-originated X-rater with such familiar prono hands as Ginger Lynn, Tom Byron and Sharon Kelly (a.k.a. Colleen Brennan). Under director-coscripter Carlos Tobalina, pic is divided into three separate but linked stories of equal stupidity.

Porno performers, whatever their athletic skills, are most often atrocious actors. "What's Love" underscores the point. Physical action in current version (the hard X and an even softer version were being sold via cassette) is uninspired and heavily skewed to lesbian encounters.

Plot has something to do with lovers expiring after sex and meeting again in some friendlier celestial context. Production values are minimal. "Special effects" are decidedly unpro. —*Sege.*

The Legend Of Wolf Lodge
(CANADIAN-COLOR)

An SC Entertainment Corp. production. Produced by Nicolas Stiliadis. Executive producer, Syd Cappe. Directed by Graeme Campbell. Stars Susan Anspach, Olivia d'Abo, Art Hindle, Lee Montgomery. Screenplay, Jessie Ballard; camera (color), Rhett Morita; editor, Harvey Zlatarits; art direction, John Dondertman; music, Andy Thompson; sound, David Jolliat; special effects, Ted Ross; prosthetics, Gianico Pretto. Reviewed at Cannes Film Festival (market), May 12, 1987. Running time: **92 MINS.**

Rosalind Winfield . . . . Susan Anspach
Dirk Winfield . . . . Art Hindle
Liette . . . . Olivia d'Abo
Wade Burnett . . . . Lee Montgomery
Vivian . . . . Maureen McRae
Policeman . . . . Steve Pirnie
Jimmy . . . . John Dondertman

Cannes — Deep in "The Legend Of Wolf Lodge," there's a possibility of a tight double-doublecross thriller, but it comes far too late in the pic. Director Graeme Campbell and scripter Jessie Ballard don't know how to make it happen quicker, then don't seem to know what to do when they get there.

Susan Anspach, looking as though she's on an enforced snowy winter stay in Canadian cottage country where the pic is set, is a deranged lodge owner. She loves to shoot, sets up a male handyman into believing her husband is a brute. The handyman also takes up with a local waitress who it turns out also is in league with the husband.

Husband Art Hindle, it's discovered, plans to dynamite the handyman, take his identity and flee to Rio with $500,000 insurance money. The wife thinks she'll join him, so does the waitress. They all get killed in the end.

Instead of making that the focus, the pic aimlessly and far too slowly drags in much else. Waitress Olivia d'Abo shows off her ample breasts and her diction is dreadful. Production values are less than routine.

Pic is destined for Canadian pay-cable because of Canadian content regulations and that's about it. —*Adil.*

The Stabilizer
(INDONESIAN-COLOR)

A Parkit Films (Jakarta) release of a Punjabi Bros. production. Directed by Arizal. Screenplay, John Rust, Deddy Armand; camera (Eastmancolor), Bambang Trimakno; editor, Benny Ms; music, GSD'Arto; title song, Wayne O'Holmes, Elliot Solomen. Reviewed at Cannes Film Festival (market), May 10, 1987. Running time: **90 MINS.**

Peter Goldson . . . . Peter O'Brian
Silvia Nash . . . . Gillie Beanz
Gregg Rainmaker . . . . Craig Gavin
Captain Johnny . . . . Barry Capry
Christina Provost . . . . Dana Christina

Cannes — Unashamedly aimed at the action market, "The Stabilizer" is virtually a nonstop series of pun-chups, shootouts and hand-to-hand fighting, karate style. There is an occasional and welcome change of pace with non-erotic sexual encounters of a familiar kind.

Villians are an international gang of drug dealers determined to obtain the formula of a drug detector from a professor who chooses torture rather than surrender his secret. The FBI is on their trail, led by the title character, but the baddies don't give in easily, and there are endless corpses, exploding buildings and smashed vehicles before they eventually are brought to justice.

An intriguing element in the action sequences is the inclusion of a couple of females on the side of law and order, and they are no mean hands at wielding machine guns or delivering well aimed karate kicks. Intriguing in a different (and not particularly edifying) way is the inclusion of a short sequence in which characters eat live lizards, are unscathed by flames around the body, roll about on broken glass and even slit their tongues. It's not exactly in the "Mondo Cane" class, but could be a talking point.

Certainly Arizal knows how to manipulate the action, and keeps the cast on the go right to the final credits. Peter O'Brian plays the title character with determination and vigor, assisted with breathless enthusiasm by Barry Capry, Dana Christina as the professor's daughter and Gillie Beanz as O'Brian's partner. Masterminding the drug dealing operation, Craig Gavin is free and easy with the torture and a totally ruthless villain. Technical credits are up to par, and the film is in English.—*Myro.*

Scared Stiff
(U.S.-COLOR)

A Daniel F. Bacaner presentation of a Fremont Group production. Produced by Daniel F. Bacaner. Directed by Richard Friedman. Screenplay, Mark Frost, Richard Friedman, Bacaner; camera (color), Yuri Denysenko; editor, Nick G. Stagliano; music, The Barber Brothers; production design, Wynn P. Thomas; prosthetic effects, Tyler K. Smith; associate producer, Charles S. Carroll. Reviewed at Cannes Film Festival (market), May 15, 1987. (No MPAA rating.) Running time: **80 MINS.**

Masterson . . . . David Ramsey
Elizabeth . . . . Nicole Fortier
David Young . . . . Andrew Stevens
Kate Kristopher . . . . Mary Page Keller
Jason . . . . Josh Segal
Detective Whitcomb . . . . Jackie David
Dr. Brightman . . . . . . William M. Hindman

Cannes — The ghost of a cruel slavedriver from the 1850s comes back to haunt the modern occupants of a southern mansion, but this pic never generates enough horror or suspense to keep audience interest alive. The makeup and special effects are pretty standard and unspectacular, and the creaky trappings do anything but scare the audience stiff.

In opening flashbacks to Charlesberg and the Ivory Coast in 1857 we see the slavetrader mistreating blacks and also his own wife and child, after which a curse is put upon him. In modern times, a woman with a history of mental disorders, her young child and her new husband-psychiatrist move into the house.

It plods along rather ponderously and occasionally we are treated to a dream sequence either by the girl or through the eyes of her child. These gradually become more elaborate, until the slaver virtually possesses the husband, first only sporting a twisted, cruel visage, later his burned-flesh guise. There's also a bit of mummery about an old broken talisman which works magic and finally destroys the monster when the principals find themselves transported back to 1857.

David Ramsey is a convincing villain as the ruthless slave driver, but unfortunately is given less screen time than other, weaker cast members. Technical credits are okay, though most of the makeup is old hat.

Violence will be too tame for gore buffs, too explicit near end of pic for the squeamish. Item might rack up some biz in homevid, but isn't likely to generate much interest theatrically. — *Besa.*

Spettri
(Specters)
(ITALIAN-COLOR)

A DMV Distribuzione release of a Reteitalia/Trio Cinema & TV production. (World sales, Intra Films.) Produced by Maurizio Tedesco. Directed by Marcello Avallone. Screenplay, Avallone, Tedesco, Andrea Purgatori, Dardano Sarchetti, from story by Avallone, Tedesco, Purgatori; camera (Luciano Vittori color), Silvano Ippoliti; editor, Andriano Tagliano; music, Lele Marchitelli, Daniele Rea; special effects, Sergio Stivaletti; makeup, Dante Trani; art direction, Carmelo Agate; production manager, Marco Donati; in Dolby stereo. Reviewed at Cannes Film Festival (market), May 12, 1987. Running time: **90 MINS.**

Marcus . . . . John Pepper
Alex . . . . Katrine Michelsen
Prof. Lasky . . . . Donald Pleasence
Also with: Massimo de Rossi, Riccardo De Torrebruna, Lavinia Grizi, Riccardo Parisio Perrotti, Giovanni Bilancia, Erna Schurer.

Cannes — "Specters" is a disappointing shaggy-dog Italian horror film, technically okay but not delivering any scares and hardly any action until the finale. Helmer Marcello Avallone gets the technical side right but has a lot of stylistic (and pacing/construction) lessons to learn from the maestros of horror.

Story is similar to Nigel Kneale's classic "Quatermass & The Pit" (a.k.a. "5,000,000 Years To Earth"): work on the subways in Rome disrupts an archaeological dig nearby run by Prof. Lasky (who else but Donald Pleasence), opening an ancient vault. It takes a full hour of red herrings until the monster shows up, a barely shown imitation of the tacked-on critter in Jacques Tourneur's "Night Of The Demon."

Topnotch lenser Silvano Ippoliti provides some nice travelling shots through the catacombs but pic is all buildup and no delivery. Pleasence hams it up as the only cast member whose English language voice fits his mug. —*Lor.*

Funland
(U.S.-COLOR)

A Double Helix Films presentation of a Hyacinth/RMC production. Producers, William VanDerKoot, Michael A. Simpson. Directed by Simpson. Screenplay, Simpson, Bonnie Turner, Terry Turner; camera (Eastmancolor) VanDerKloot; editors, VanDerKloot, Wade Watkins; music, James Oliverio. No further credits available. Reviewed at Cannes Film Festival (market), May 13, 1987. (MPAA Rating: PG-13.) Running time: **84 MINS.**

With: William Windom (Funland owner), David L. Lander (the old clown), Bruce Mahler, Clark Brandon, Robert Sacchi, Terry Beaver, Jill Carroll, Lane Davies, Mary McDonough.

Cannes — Theatrical exhibition of "Funland" seems highly unlikely for this family-aimed comedy thriller done as what looks like enthusiastic homework by all-chores handymen William VanDerKloot (primarily producing) and Michael A. Simpson (mostly helming).

Picture and its story constitute a bazaar of the bizarre, a silly fantasy served up messily, but moments of genuine fun do occur. A bankrupt amusement park is threatened with takeover by the Mafia. The Mafia gets its comeuppance from the park's pizza parlor franchise clown, who shoots his designated, child-hating successor while latter is riding the rollercoaster.

"Funland" has several deaths, but none to be taken seriously. One of the dead turns up again, with a hole in the head to be sure, to join forces with the clown and with Humphrey Bogart (yes, Robert Sacchi of "The Man With Bogart's Face" doing it again) in the wax museum.

The mishmash, in which no episode is tied up before it is thrown away, also has some sweaty "Porky's"-style pratfalls. William Windom and David Lander strive mightily to make their talents shine through the muddiness of their roles. The production dress is shabby, the color gaudy to gruesome.
— *Kell.*

Higher Education
(CANADIAN-COLOR)

A Norstar Releasing release (in Canada) of a Simcom production. Produced by Peter Simpson. Executive producers, Simpson, Peter Haley. Directed by John Sheppard. Screenplay, Sheppard, Dan Nathanson; camera (color), Brenton Spencer; editor, Stephan Fanfara; art direction, Andrew Deskin; music, Paul Zaza; coproducers, Ilana Frank, Ray Sager. Reviewed at Cannes Film Festival (market), May 12, 1987. Running time: **92 MINS.**
Andy Cooper . . . . Kevin Hicks
Carrie Hansen . . . . Isabelle Mejias
Nicole Hubert . . . . Lori Hallier
Dean Roberts . . . . Stephen Black
Guido . . . . Maury Chaykin
Robert Bley . . . . Richard Monette

Cannes — "Higher Education," an intended college comedy, begins on a bus and goes nowhere.

Canadian actor-singer Kevin Hicks, in his film debut, enrolls in a fine art course, has a Mafia son for a roommate, beds down quickly with both a fellow student and a similarly curvaceous art teacher, wins a sculpture prize, loses the student and gets her back.

That description is tighter than the pic. The script wanders, so does direction. Overall, there's a what's-this-all-about reaction. Even alter-

nating sex scenes, topless show only, play off without fire.

The sole spark comes from Maury Chaykin as a squeeky-mouthed Mafia bodyguard who protects the roommate and keeps Hicks away from the student lover.

Pic's only possibilities are for five indie Canadian tv outlets that helped finance it and Canadian paycable which must meet Canadian content regulations. Otherwise, it's a failed grade. —*Adil.*

One Way Out
(U.S.-COLOR)

A Reel Movies Intl. presentation of a Cobra Prods. film. Written and produced by Ivan Rogers. Directed by Paul Kyriazi. Camera (color), Jan Van Tassell; editor, Joseph Anderson; music, Vincent Smith; special effects, Dieter Strum; karate choreographer, Eric Lee. Reviewed at Cannes Film Festival (market), May 11, 1987. (No MPAA Rating.) Running time: **85 MINS.**
With: Ivan Rogers, Sandy Brooke, Rick Sutherlin, Doug Irk, Norman Matthews, Mike Rizk.

Cannes — Thin in story but virtually nonstop with action, "One Way Out" is about a black cop with a grudge, tracking down drug traffickers in Indianapolis. Presumably filmed on a low budget with unknown thesps, actioner seems suited mostly for tv and homevid, but could garner some bucks in less demanding overseas markets.

The cop, whose wife has been raped and slashed by a drug ring, is loose with his fists and feet and itchy with his trigger finger as he lays flat menacing miscreants. Though there's lotsa action, real graphic violence is avoided as the cop and his blond lady partner are captured, break away, shoot and fight their way out of innumerable tight spots (usually using the same karate swing kick). Final scene has the moody cop riding on the top of a car going at full speed, somehow holding on, and jumping just in time before the car crashes.

Ivan Rogers is convincing as the steely-eyed officer, but supporting cast is rather weak. Technical credits are at times wobbly, especially sound and some of the lensing. —*Besa.*

High Stakes
(CANADIAN-COLOR/B&W)

A Norstar Releasing release (in Canada) of a Simcom production. Produced by Peter Simpson. Executive producers, Simpson, Peter Haley. Directed by Larry Kent. Screenplay, Bryan McCann, John Sheppard; camera (color), Doug McKay; editor, Frank Irvine; music, Paul Zaza. Reviewed at Cannes Film Festival (market), May 10, 1987. Running time: **82 MINS.**
Bo Baker . . . . David Foley
Terri Carson . . . . Roberta Weiss
Dorian Kruger . . . . Winston Rekert
Bill . . . . Jackson Davies
Eric Roberts . . . . Jack Webster

Frank Valenta . . . . Alex Diakun
Nicholas Von Reich . . . . Anthony Holland

Cannes — Reviewed for the record, "High Stakes" is an incompetent low-budget comedy that even the consortium of five Canadian indie tv outlets which helped finance it should be unhappy to expose.

It's something about a nerd whose relatives hate him, who dreams in black & white sequences about being a Bogart-type star newspaper reporter, something about criminals and something about a hidden treasure of the Third Reich and other nasties. None of the somethings are explained, explored or even seem worth the time.

Acting, except for vet Vancouver news commentator Jack Webster in his film debut, is over the top and feeble. Direction and other production values are substandard and the only mystery left by the unattentive script is why anyone bothered. —*Adil.*

Concrete Angels
(CANADIAN-COLOR)

Shapiro Entertainment release of a Brightstar-Leader Media Film production. Produced by Anthony Kramreither, Carlo Liconti. Directed by Liconti. Screenplay, Jim Purdy; camera (color), Karol Ike; editor, John Harding; art director, Tom Doherty. Reviewed at the Cannes Film Festival (market), May 13, 1987. Running time: **97 MINS.**
Bello . . . . Joseph Dimambro
Sean . . . . Luke McKeehan
Ira . . . . Omie Craden
Jessie . . . . Dean Bosacki

Cannes — Teen drama "Concrete Angels" is a series of missed opportunities.

Pic focuses on slow learner, immigrant teens, some of whom pull off a heist and all of whom form a rock band to win the radio station contest and be onstage when The Beatles play Toronto's Maple Leaf Gardens in 1964.

They lose in a preliminary round, so do the aimless script, lackluster direction by Carlo Liconti, dullish performances by teens recruited from Toronto high schools and overall insubstantial production values.

Some sequences give notice of what might have been: an Italian family at home; a Jewish family happily inspecting a home in a suburban community under construction and a school class in which the teacher tells the kids they are slow and unable to cope because of their backgrounds.

Handsome newcomer Omie Craden shows promise and the camera likes him very much.

Use of Beatles music and Chuck Berry's "Johnny B. Goode" is about all that comes across strongly in denoting the period.

Slight homevid and Canadian paycable are the most obvious chances. —*Adil.*

The Survivalist
(U.S.-COLOR)

A Skouras Pictures release of a Lodestar Prods. production. Produced by Steven Shore, David Greene. Directed by Sig Shore. Stars Steve Railsback, Susan Blakely, Marjoe Gortner. Screenplay, John V. Kraft; camera (Precision color), Benjamin Davis. No other credits provided. Reviewed at Cannes Film Festival (market), May 11, 1987. (No MPAA Rating.) Running time: **97 MINS.**
Jack Tillman . . . . Steve Railsback
Danny . . . . Jason Healey
Kurt Youngman . . . . Marjoe Gortner
Vincent . . . . Cliff DeYoung
Linda . . . . Susan Blakely
Dub Daniels . . . . David Wayne

Cannes — This inept, cheapo meller tries to mine the post-nuclear-explosion scenario treated in many films ranging from "Road Warrior" to last year's Cannes hit, "The Sacrifice." "The Survivalist" can't come close to these pics by any measure, and seems destined for homevideo sale only.

Premise has a nuclear explosion in Siberia being blamed by the Russians on the U.S., with retaliation threatened. Yank authorities prepare for the worst by declaring martial law.

This in turn prompts bikers, rapists and assorted other meanies to go berserk in the U.S., taking virtual control of this pic's locale, Texas (actually Utah's Moab desert). Chief character, played by Steve Railsback, fights back since he's trying to retrieve his son in a remote summer camp area.

Enough said that the premise is almost as threadbare as John V. Kraft's script, which has a reasonably talented cast mouthing one inanity after another. To make matters worse, director Sig Shore (he of producing "Superfly" fame) stages action scenes with enough incompetence to make the audience long for additional dialog.

Railsback, Susan Blakely, Cliff DeYoung and David Wayne are aboard; they deserve better. Perfectly in tune with the material is Marjoe Gortner as a nasty National Guardsman intent on doing in the hero. Gortner, to put it charitably, is inadequate.

Pic was produced by Shore's son, Steven. —*Sege.*

Hangmen
(U.S.-COLOR)

A Shapiro Entertainment release of a Cinema Sciences Corp. production. Produced by J. Christian Ingvordsen, Steven W. Kaman, Richard R. Washburn. Executive producers, C. Steven Duncker, Robert Anderson. Directed by Ingvordsen. Screenplay, Ingvordsen, Kaman; camera (Precision color), Kaman; editor, Ingvordsen; music, Michael Montes; art direction/costumes, Beth Rubino; associate producers, Marc L. Bailin, Peggy Jacobson; assistant director, Jacobson. Reviewed at Cannes Film Festival (market), May 17, 1987. (No MPAA Rating.) Running time; **90 MINS.**
Bob Green . . . . Richard R. Washburn

Moe Boone	Jake LaMotta
Dog Thompson	Dog Thomas
Kosmo	Kosmo Vinyl
Danny Green	Keith Bogart

Cannes — This Gotham-lensed action tale, slickly directed and full of flashy camerawork, boils down to an empty series of shootouts with machine guns. Scripting is predictable to the point of utterly eliminating any hope of suspense. Characters are so cardboard it's impossible to care who survives.

Slim plot involves efforts of a college kid (Richard R. Washburn) to save his father (Keith Bogart), a former Green Beret turned spy, targeted for death by a rival within the CIA, which supplies an endless stream of dummies to get shot up. Son recruits veterans of dad's unit in Vietnam to come to his aid and they get the necessary firepower from a Mafia gunrunner (ex-boxing champ Jake LaMotta) before taking on the bad guys in a marathon shootout in a power station. Final confrontation with NYPD outside the plant is gratuitously tacked on, ending proceedings on an amateurish note.

Throughout, closeups abound — of clips being loaded, empty shells pouring forth, mouths talking into telephones, fingers dialing telephones. There are no surprises. There is not the slightest trace of humor. Soundtrack adds a pulsing Pink Floydy rhythm to the rat-tat-tat-tat. Sound is poor in some sequences, but tech credits generally deserve better material. — *Jay.*

Sleeping Beauty
(U.S.-COLOR)

A Cannon Group release of a Golan-Globus production. Produced by Menahem Golan, Yoram Globus. Executive producer, Itzik Kol. Directed by David Irving. Stars Morgan Fairchild, Tahnee Welch, Nicholas Clay, Sylvia Miles. Screenplay, Michael Berz, from a story by Charles Perrault; camera (color), David Gurfinkel; editor, Tova Neeman; production design, Marek Dobrowlski; costumes, Debbie Leon; associate producer, Patricia Ruben. Reviewed at Cannes Film Festival (market), May 12, 1987. (No MPAA Rating.) Running time: **90 MINS.**

Queen	Morgan Fairchild
King	David Holliday
Rosebud	Tahnee Welch
Prince	Nicholas Clay
Red Fairy	Sylvia Miles
Elf	Kenny Baker
White Fairy	Jane Weidlin
Court Advisor	Julian Chagrin

Cannes — Acting is bland to poor and direction distracted, but there's just enough action and color in "Sleeping Beauty" to keep small kiddies awake.

Script follows the original story fairly closely and with some exceptions editing maintains a steady clip. Musical numbers are extraneous and derivative. Kenny Baker manages a vigorous, mischievous elf,

and costumes and sets rate good marks. Morgan Fairchild's gowns are always allowed to display a generous and heaving bosom for fathers, uncles and granddads accompanying the small fry.

Best outlook seems in homevid.
—*Adil.*

Beauty And The Beast
(U.S.-COLOR)

A Cannon Films release of a Golan-Globus production. Produced by Menaham Golan and Yoram Globus. Executive producer, Itzik Kol. Directed by Eugene Marner. Stars Rebecca DeMornay, John Savage. Screenplay, Carole Lucia Satrina, based on the story by Madame De Villeneuve; camera (color), Avi Karpick; editor, Tova Ascher; production designer, Marek Dobrowolski; costumes, Buki Shiff; music, Lori McKelvey; associate producer, Patricia Ruben. Reviewed at Cannes Film Festival (market), May 17, 1987. (MPAA Rating: G.) Running time: **93 MINS.**

Beauty	Rebecca DeMornay
Beast/Prince	John Savage
Father	Yossi Graber
Kuppel	Michael Schneider
Bettina	Carmela Marner
Isabella	Ruth Harlap
Oliver	Joseph Bee

Cannes — Rebecca DeMornay is Beauty and John Savage her beast-prince.

She has cameo-brooch looks and his beast makeup closely resembles every "Wolf Man" pic.

The pair sings together and, per end credits, in their own voices. The result will not make the pop charts.

Acting overall, including DeMornay and Savage, is so flat and direction so weak that the pic might be presumed to be an intended spoof. It's all passed off seriously, however, with overstaged and overlong scenes, hardly any action, a harsh mix of accents and a castle that looks snapped together far too quickly. Songs also go nowhere.

Film buffs with a taste for dumb pics may find some fun. Kiddies, for whom the pic is intended, won't.—*AdH.*

The Untouchables
(COLOR)

Handsomely made gangster epic delivers the goods.

A Paramount Pictures release of an Art Linson production. Produced by Linson. Directed by Brian DePalma. Screenplay, David Mamet; camera (Technicolor), Stephen H. Burum; editor, Jerry Greenberg, Bill Pankow; music, Ennio Morricone; art direction, William A. Elliott; visual consultant, Patrizia Von Brandenstein; set decoration, Hal Gausman; set design, E.C. Chen, Steven P. Sardanis, Gil Clayton, Nicholas Laborczy; costume design, Marilyn Vance-Straker; wardrobe, Giorgio Armani; sound (Dolby), Jim Tanenbaum; stunt coordinator, Gary Hymes; assistant director, Joe Napolitano; associate producer, Ray Hartwick; casting, Lynn Stalmaster & Associates, Mali Finn. Reviewed at Paramount Pictures Studio theater, May 28, 1987. (MPAA Rating: R.) Running time: **119 MINS.**

Eliot Ness	Kevin Costner
Jim Malone	Sean Connery
Oscar Wallace	Charles Martin Smith
George Stone	Andy Garcia
Al Capone	Robert De Niro
Mike	Richard Bradford
Payne	Jack Kehoe
George	Brad Sullivan
Nitti	Billy Drago
Ness' Wife	Patricia Clarkson

Hollywood — "The Untouchables" is a beautifully crafted portrait of Prohibition-era Chicago. Film's elements enhance one another as script, directing, characterization, wardrobe, art direction and score jointly evoke the celebrated conflict between gangster bootleggers and federal agents. Visually reminiscent of "The Sting" as much as several other underworld sagas, this picture should deliver the goods for Paramount at the summer box-office.

Director Brian DePalma sets the tone in a lavish overhead opening shot in which Robert De Niro's Al Capone professes to be just "a businessman" giving people the product they want. That such business often required violent methods is immediately depicted as prelude to arrival of idealistic law enforcer Eliot Ness (Kevin Costner).

While the dichotomy of values is thus established between these two adversaries, it is the introduction of street cop Jim Malone (Sean Connery) that truly gives the film its momentum. A wily veteran who tutors Ness on "the Chicago way" of success and survival, Connery commands one's attention during every moment of his screen presence.

Propelled by scripter David Mamet's rich dialog, Connery delivers one of his finest performances ever. It is filled with nuance, humor and abundant self-confidence. Connery's depth strongly complements the youthful Costner, who does grow appreciably as Ness overcomes early naivete to become just hard-bitten enough without relinquishing the innocence of his

personal life. Costner solidifies his acting credentials here.

Rounding out the quartet of "Untouchables" are Charles Martin Smith and Andy Garcia, who offer distinctly different portrayals. The diminutive Smith is completely plausible — and at times quite comical — as a government accountant who now wields a shotgun. Garcia's South Side police recruit is as likeable as he is tough.

These lawmen are pitted against Capone's corrupt infrastructure that reaches up through top police ranks, to the courts and to Mayor (Big Bill) Thompson over at city hall. Depicting the man at the center of it all, De Niro is a compelling figure who stops just short of caricature.

With the addition of 30 lbs. and the legendary facial scar, De Niro is quite convincing — perhaps never more so than during one powerful scene in which he wields a baseball bat while philosophizing about business with his lieutenants. It is one of those instances that will be synonymous with "The Untouchables."

As fine as De Niro is here, limited screen time is the pic's most notable shortcoming. His number five billing suggests as much but could still disappoint. It also must be noted that there are several loose ends in the sequence involving a raid conducted outside the city.

In directing the proceedings, De-Palma has brought his sure and skilled hand to a worthy enterprise. His signature for this film may well be an intense scene involving a baby carriage. Filmmakers liken it to the Odessa Steps montage from 1925's "The Battleship Potemkin" by Sergei Eisenstein.

No stranger to filmic violence, De-Palma employs it appropriately throughout and benefits from excellent camerawork by Stephen Burum.

Overall texture of the film — from exteriors on La Salle Street near Chicago's Board of Trade building to cop shop interiors — is a tribute to the work of art director William A. Elliott, costume designer Marilyn Vance-Straker, wardrober Giorgio Armani and visual consultant Patrizia Von Brandenstein. Kudos also to Ennio Morricone for the music.

Giving the story some final perspective, writer Mamet concludes with a short exchange that not only further humanizes Ness but neatly questions the whole foolhardy national exercise of trying to eliminate alcohol. However it may have failed, Prohibition did wind up providing superb dramatic material for these skilled collaborators a half century later. — *Tege.*

Athens, Ga. - Inside Out
(DOCU-16m)

A ASA Communications release of a David Mazor presentation of a Subterranean Prods. and Spotlight production. Produced by Bill Cody. Written and directed by Tony Gayton. Camera (color, 16m), Jim Herbert; editor; Adam Wolfe; assistant producers, Clark Hunter, Lisa Mae Wells; assistant camera, Lance Wyatt; sound, Jim Hawkins assistant editor, Amy Tomkins; music mix, John Keane, Bryan Cook. Reviewed at Preview Nine screening room, N.Y., May 12, 1987. (No MPAA Rating). Running time: **82 MINS.**

With: The B-52s, Bar-B-Q Killers, Dreams So Real, Flat Duo Jets, Kilkenny Cats, Limbo District, Love Tractor, Pylon, R.E.M., The Squalls, Time Toy, Jeremy Ayers, William Orten Carlton, Rev. Howard Finster, Jim Herbert, Rev. John D. Ruth, John Seawright, Chris Slay.

How did a small southern town become the locus for a cottage industry of idiosyncratic rock 'n' roll bands? A nearby university, a network of small clubs and the commercial success of two local groups, R.E.M. and the B-52s, apparently convinced most of the marginally talented bands featured in this casually made documentary that there are few better ways to pass the time.

Left by filmmaker Tony Gayton to speak for themselves, most of the denizens of the Athens, Ga., rock scene do not come across as exciting musicians or particularly interesting individuals. Consequently, the audience for this docu should be limited to dedicated aficionados of contemporary rock and after a perfunctory theatrical release, it should be relegated to its proper place in the backwaters of cable and public access tv and, with good luck, to the dusty corners of music video shelves.

In an era in which urban careerism, conspicuous materialism and ambitious self-aggrandizement have achieved trendy legitimacy "Athens, Ga. — Inside Out" does provide a healthy corrective affirmation of individualistic creativity as an alternative lifestyle. As one musician says, Athens has plenty of cheap places to live and lots of part-time restaurant jobs. The pace of the place, as captured in the docu, is certainly not stressed-for-success.

Endearingly, the Athens rockers care much more about the personal fulfillment of musical self-expression than in achieving show business success. The former lead singer of Pylon, a manic and original Athens group which gained a small national following before it disbanded several years ago, says she never intended to become a rock star and therefore doesn't mind trading life in the rock 'n' roll spotlight for her present job in a photocopy shop.

Most of the Athens rockers, however, are inclined to credit themselves with more originality than they possess. The Athens "sound," if there is one, is based largely on recycled punk and pop styles of the U.K. and New York new music scenes in the mid and late '70s. The B-52s, who did eventually take their act to New York, are worlds more sophisticated musically and far more smug personally than their parochial stay-at-home townsmen.

Gayton attempts to add a sense of local color and cultural depth by including characters such as the Rev. Howard Finster, a banjo-playing, refuse-collecting eccentric whose neighbors had to revise their opinion of him when his bizarre paintings began to turn up in exhibitions and on the cover of the Talking Heads' LP "Little Creatures," which he proudly notes was "album cover of the year." Too much of the documentary, however, is aimless, and the music, in spite of flashes of raw exuberance, more often than not commits the ultimate rock 'n' roll sin of being boring.
—*Rich.*

Opposing Force
(COLOR)

Engrossing combat training drama stumbles at the finish line.

An Orion Pictures release of a Glaser & Berk production, in association with Eros Intl. Film Prods., Jeff Wald & Associates. Produced by Daniel Jay Berk, Tamar E. Glaser. Executive producers, Jeff Wald, Peter Nevile. Directed by Eric Karson. Screenplay, Gil Cowan; camera (Deluxe color), Michael A. Jones; editor, Mark Conte; music, Marc Donohue; sound, Carey Lindley (Philippines), Barry Thomas (Miami); production design, Art Dicdao; art direction, Janice Flating; production manager, Ted Adams Swanson; Jean Higgins (L.A.); assistant director, Jerry O'Hara (Philippines), Jerry Grandy (Miami); stunt coordinator, Ray Lykins (Philippines), Ricou Browning (Miami); associate producers, Hugh Corcoran, Brad Smart; casting, Al Onorato, Jerold Franks; Maria Metcalfe (Philippines). Reviewed on HBO/Cannon vidcassette, N.Y., May 25, 1987. (MPAA Rating: R.) Running time: **97 MINS.**

Major Logan	Tom Skerritt
Lt. Casey	Lisa Eichhorn
Becker	Anthony Zerbe
Sgt. Stafford	Richard Roundtree
Betts	Robert Wightman
Gen. McGowan	John Considine
Tuan	George Kee Cheung

Also with: Dan Hamilton, Paul Joynt, Jay Lauden, Ken Wright, Michael James, Warren MacLean, John Melcher, Scott Sanders, Jerald Williams, Steven Rogers.

"Opposing Force" is a strong, fascinating film about overzealous military training techniques which unfortunately lacks a third act, concluding most unsatisfactorily. As a result, pic, previously titled "Clay Pigeons" and "Hell Camp," received only a test booking by Orion last August in San Antonio, ahead of its current homevideo availability.

Tom Skerritt toplines as a major who enrolls in a special escape & evasive training program in order to prepare for a return to active duty as a pilot after years on a desk job. The training is run by Anthony Zerbe, who has become sadistic in his post, meting out both physical and psychological torture to the mainly young soldiers, as administered by his basically good-guy aide Richard Roundtree.

The catalyst to a showdown is the presence of Lisa Eichhorn as a femme lieutenant, the first of her sex to be accepted into the program, even though women have yet to be authorized for combat. When she arrives, Zerbe goes off the deep end and in addition to the usual physical abuse (which the soldiers accept begrudgingly as part of their expected rigorous training) he rapes her, in order to "prepare her for what the enemy would do." Finding out that Eichhorn has been raped by the commandant, Skerritt drops his cool demeanor and goes on the warpath, organizing an escape and setting up a violent showdown with the authorities.

For most of its length, picture doesn't pull any punches, depicting a gruelling, war games-style environment to test and weed out the soldiers. Gil Cowan's script, forcefully directed by Eric Karson, raises many serious issues, including the limits to which training can or should simulate actual combat, the danger of adopting the enemy's inhuman tactics in order to compete and the difficulties in attempting to treat women as equals in a military situation. Final reel, however, degenerates into melodramatics and shootouts, with a terrible, abrupt freeze frame/voiceover ending that unsuccessfully shifts from an objective presentation to the Eichhorn character's subjective, wishy-washy point-of-view.

Cast cannot be faulted, punching home the drama forcefully. Zerbe offers a finely shaded performance to what might have been a monster role, even delivering somewhat convincing arguments to justify his brutal behavior. Skerritt is solid as the hero forced to take action, while Roundtree brings out the duality of his pivotal role, the enforcer who nevertheless has a moral code. Eichhorn is outstanding in handling an unglamorized, both physically and emotionally demanding assignment.

Tech credits, including atmospheric lensing on Filipino and Miami locations are top-notch. Too bad an organic ending synthesizing the material did not round off this sleeper.—*Lor.*

High Season
(BRITISH-COLOR)

A Hemdale release, presented by British Screen and Hemdale, Film Four Intl., Curzon Film Distributors and Michael White Film. Produced by Clare Downs. Executive producer, Michael White. Directed by Clare Peploe. Stars Jacqueline Bisset, James Fox. Screenplay, Mark Peploe, Clare Peploe; camera (color), Chris Menges; editor, Gabriella Cristianti; music, Jason Osborn; production design, Andrew McAlpine; costumes, Louise Stjernsward; associate producer, Mary Clow. Reviewed at Bijou Preview theater, London, May 26, 1987. Running time: **92 MINS.**

Katherine	Jacqueline Bisset
Patrick	James Fox
Penelope	Irene Papas
Sharp	Sebastian Shaw
Rick	Kenneth Branagh
Carol	Lesley Manville
Konstantinis	Robert Stephens
Yanni	Paris Tselios

London — "High Season" is one of those picture-postcard films; it looks marvelous but has very little else to offer other than the view. Pic may have some success in the summer U.K. market, but offshore prospects must be limited.

Someone should have told helmer Clare Peploe that shots of beautiful scenery do not a boffo film make, and since she co-wrote the screenplay (with Mark Peploe), she has to shoulder some of the blame for a weak and generally unfunny script.

The publicity material describes it as a "comedy about the absurdities of life," but the comedy — what there is — is too gentle to raise little more than a smile. In its favor the pic has very few pretensions, and the scenery is easy on the eye.

"High Season" has a weaving plot with lead characters meandering in and out, but it pivots around Jacqueline Bisset as a photographer and the folk she meets up with in a tiny village in Rhodes.

As well as poking fun at the tourists, also thrown in are subplots about a valuable Grecian urn, an elderly Russian spy — an art-historian friend of Bisset, with overtones of Anthony Blunt — and a rebellious Greek national.

Everything gets rounded off to a relatively happy ending with Bisset and her estranged hubby (James Fox) reunited, a tacky statue to the "unknown tourist" destroyed, and Sharp (Sebastian Shaw), the elderly spy, off to Russia via Turkey.

Best of the cast are Kenneth Branagh and Lesley Manville as a seemingly archetypal English tourist couple, but in fact he is a bungling British agent while she falls in love with Yanni, the local hunky Greek shopowner. Irene Papas seems to enjoy herself overacting madly, while James Fox looks unsure about what sort of film he is appearing in.

Chris Menges' photography makes you want to book the next flight to Greece, and in fact gives the pic a look of quality and style that belies the script. It is staggering to believe it took two people to produce such a weak story.

Other technical credits are fine.—*Adam.*

The Sentimental Bloke (1918)
(AUSTRALIAN-B&W)

A Southern Cross Feature Film Co. production. Produced and directed by Raymond Longford. Stars Arthur Tauchert, Lottie Lyell. Screenplay, Longford, from the poem "The Songs Of The Sentimental Bloke," by C.J. Dennis; camera (b&w), Arthur Higgins; assistant directors, Arthur Cross, Clyde Marsh. Reviewed at Cannes Film Festival (Informative section), May 13, 1987. Running time: **75 MINS.**

Bill, The Bloke . . . . Arthur Tauchert
Doreen . . . . Lottie Lyell
Ginger Mick . . . . Gilbert Emery
The Bloke's mate . . . . Stanley Robinson
The Stror 'at Coot . . . . Harry Young
Doreen's Mother . . . . Margaret Reid
The Parson . . . . Charles Keegan
Uncle Jim . . . . William Coulter
Nurse . . . . Helen Fergus

Cannes — Australia's contribution to the Information Section at Cannes this year was the country's great silent film classic, Raymond Longford's "The Sentimental Bloke," made in 1918 but not released until a year later.

For nearly 20 years, from 1905, Australia was a major film producing country, though few pics from this era have survived. The leading director of the period was undoubtedly Longford, and "The Sentimental Bloke" was his most popular achievement. Pic was adapted from a poem by C.J. Dennis (author is seen, briefly, sitting at his desk in the film's opening shot).

It's a very simple story about a "larrikin" — a rough-and-tumble, hard-drinking, working-class type — who's softened by his love for Doreen, a sweet girl he meets and marries. There's not much more to it, except that Longford and his cameraman, Arthur Higgins, filmed on locations in the Sydney dockside area of Wooloomooloo — and captured that famous area as it was nearly 70 years ago with great affection. Pic is historically fascinating, not only because of the location work, but because of the way it captures the manners and mores of a bygone era.

Lead actor Arthur Tauchert was a vaudevillian, here seen in his first film. He's perfect as The Bloke. Lottie Lyell, 25 at the time, was Longford's collaborator behind the camera as well as his favorite actress. Her tragically early death seven years later (of tuberculosis) robbed the Australian cinema of a great figure and, apparently, devastated Longford, who was about to marry her.

Pic is filled with lengthy intertitles, taken from the text of the poem. They're written in a quaint — and long obsolete — form of slang which isn't easy for Australians today to follow, let alone foreign audiences; but they add to the authentic period feeling.

The character listed in the credits as "The Stror 'at Coot" is a "coot" (fellow) who wears a straw hat.

"Bloke" was a perennial popular success in Australia, and is still greatly loved for its authentic, naïve depiction of a lost era. A 1932 talkie remake by F.W. Thring (father of actor Frank Thring) made little impact.

Longford's career declined after Lyell's death; he made occasional appearances as an actor, but lived his final days in near poverty. He died in 1959. A year earlier, he gave an interview to a tv reporter, and that 4-minute film accompanied the Cannes screening of his greatest triumph.

Acknowledgement in Cannes of a virtually unknown (outside Australia) silent classic was a great experience for the enthusiastic buffs who attended the single screening. Print was supplied by Australia's National Film And Sound Archive.
— *Strat.*

Amazons
(COLOR)

Mundane actioner for sci-fi buffs.

A Concorde Pictures presentation of a Concorde/Aries Films production. Produced by Hector Olivera. Directed by Alex Sessa. Screenplay, Charles Saunders; camera (color), Leonard Solis; editor, Edward Lowe; music, Oscar Camp; art direction, Julie Bertotto; coproducer, Frank K. Isaac Jr.; associate producer, Roger Corman. Reviewed on MGM/-UA Home Video vidcassette, N.Y., May 20, 1987. (No MPAA Rating.) Running time: **76 MINS.**
With: Windsor Taylor Randolph (Diala), Penelope Reed (Tashi), Joseph Whipp (Kalungo), Danitza Kingsley (Tashinge).

Filmed in Argentina, "Amazons" is a lightweight entry in the science fiction/fantasy sweepstakes, offering some statuesque beauties doing hand and sword battle, and little else. Pic has bypassed theatrical release, going straight to video.

Servicable plotline, in the manner of sf comic magazines, offers a collection of tribes at war with each other, and thinly drawn character types. Kalungo (Joseph Whipp) is the evil leader of a group called the Pegash; he has the ability to summon lightning bolts with his fingertips (and via some chitzy special effects) and uses his powers to lord it over the surrounding villages, among them the peaceful women-dominant village of Shinar.

The Queen of Shinar appoints her two best warriors Diala (Windsor Taylor Randolph) and Tashi (Penelope Reed) to, firstly, remove for safekeeping the Spirit Stone, which will give Kalungo even more power should he acquire it; and secondly, seek out and bring back the Sword of Azundati, a mystical Excalibur-type weapon that also gives its owner world-beating power. Subplots include the infighting between Diala and another Amazon, Tashinge (Danitza Kingsley), whose feud stretches back to when Diala's mother fought Tashinge over a man, to wit Tashi's father. In addition, Tashinge is a traitor to her tribe, conspiring with Kalungo to bring him the sword.

Story is harder to follow than it should be, with not much dramatic impetus to maintain viewer interest. Filmmakers, while intent on lining up the most attractive actresses they can, strain credibility by casting two thesps of same approximate age as mother and daughter. Besides the unconvincing lightning bolts, a montage in which a lion transforms into a naked young woman is clumsily handled; they did it better in "The Wolf Man" 46 years ago.

A broad-daylight nude swim break, and a firelit lovemaking scene effectively break up the monotony of the rest of the goings on. The three female warriors are portrayed with more enthusiasm than the material deserves, and Whipp hams it up as best he can. Sets, mostly cave and rock dwellings, are well done, and most other tech credits are fine. Majority of the lead actors speak English; some are dubbed rather obviously. —*Gerz.*

Killer's Nocturne
(HONG KONG-COLOR)

A Bo Ho Film production, released by Golden Harvest (HK). Presented by Leonard Ho. Executive producers, Samo Hung, Choi Lan. Directed by Nam Lai-Choi. Stars Alex Man, Chin Siu-ho, Patricia Ha, Tsen Yin. Screenplay, Man Chun, from story by Wong Ching; camera (color), Nam Nai Choi. (No other credits provided by producer/distributor.) Reviewed at Golden Harvest preview theater, Hammer Hill Road, Hong Kong, May 5, 1987. Running time: **98 MINS.**
(Cantonese soundtrack; with English subtitles.)

Hong Kong — Shanghai, the fabled "sin" city, an exciting place for the adventurous in the early '30s, is brought back to life in "Killer Nocturne" and is the best that can be said of this commercial crowdpleaser. "Nocturne" is an exploitative wedding of gore, violence and male bonding in love/hate conflicts, along with tragic heroes coping with villains in white suits.

The story is revenge, a son trying to regain the lost reputation of his murdered, rich, retired father in a game of mahjong. Chin Siu-ho has to suffer considerably before he finally kills headman Alex Man, now typecast as the hateful gang boss. Chin has to deal with sadistic murderers while training in the game of mahjong, and even fight a kangaroo just to raise the stakes to encounter the hateful Man who owns a club and its resident singer (Patricia Ha), lovely in her period gowns.

The film is excessively flamboyant in the fighting sequences, set pieces of blood-letting and assorted decapitations that border on absurdity.

Chin is sympathetic to the underdog turned champion in the end who mysteriously survives a sword thrust in his chest. Alex Man overacts again his standard baddie portrayal. Added plus is the appropriate soundtrack song interpreted in the style of the era, the costumes and high quality, soft-focus lensing of smoke-filled rooms, with two erotic side attractions. —*Mel.*

Flicks
(COLOR)

Unfunny movie spoof.

A United Film Distribution Co. presentation of a Flicks Films production. Executive producers, Salah M. Hassanein, Edward R. Pressman. Produced by Bert Kamerman, David Axelrod. Directed by Peter Winograd. Screenplay, Larry Arnstein, David Hurwitz, Lane Sarasohn, Winograd; camera (Movielab color), Scott Miller; editor, Barbara Pokras; music, John Morgan; sound, Kirk Francis; production design, Jack McAnelly; art direction, Philip Thomas; set decoration, Linda Burbank; animation director and design, Kirk Henderson; special visual effects, The Magic Lantern; special visual effects supervisor, Anthony Doublin; additional special visual effects, Private Stock Effects; costume design, Pat Tonnema; production manager, Patrick Crowley; assistant director, Dennis White; laser effects, Robert Greenberg; masks, Stephen Chiodo, Charles Chiodo, Jeff Kennamore, Cary Howe, Scott Dearborn; stunt coordinator, David Cass; associate producers, Edward Glass, Barry Schoor, Penn Sicre; casting, Barbara S. Claman, Eleanor Ross. Reviewed on Media Home Entertainment vidcassette, N.Y., May 23, 1987. (MPAA Rating: R.) Running time: **78 MINS.**
Liz . . . . Pamela Sue Martin
Capt. Grace . . . . Joan Hackett
Arthur/Tang . . . . Martin Mull
Beth Lyle . . . . Betty Kennedy
Also with: Richard Belzer, Barry Pearl, Lincoln Kilpatrick, Paula Victor, Danny Dayton, George (Buck) Flower; voices of Harry Shearer, Sandra Kearns, Gregory Mark Lewis.

A lot of effort from divers hands went into "Flicks," a.k.a. "Loose Joints" and "Hollyweird," a homage to various film genres which fails the crucial test: is it funny? Contributors include the late Joan Hackett and production consultant Clark Paylow plus numerous folks who have gone on to bigger things: mask makers Stephen and Charles Chiodo, currently making their own pic "Killer Klowns;" a set dresser Bill Paxton who has since got meaty acting roles in "Aliens" and other films. Picture was shot in 1981, but was never released theatrically, surfacing finally in video stores.

Director Peter Winograd's format tries to re-create the old-fashioned cinema program: coming attractions, a cartoon, a serial and main feature. If the writing and execution had been amusing the pic might have attracted an audience; instead, it is merely pastiche, emulating in very ordinary fashion the film prototypes.

Animation director Kirk Henderson captures the style of a "Tom & Jerry" cartoon in various "Cat And Mouse" segments, but the material is boring, concerning the twosome at a cartoon characters' retirement home alternately brawling and reminiscing about the good old days of non-limited animation.

Coming attractions satires are puerile: "No Way José," an all-star film that is too expensive to be made, and "Whodunit," a flat, boring mystery pic. "News R Us" uses old newsreel footage to spoof the "March Of Time" format for the nth time. The main feature (a padded half-hour segment) stars Martin Mull and Betty Kennedy in "House Of The Living Corpse," playing like a clichéd horror pic rather than commenting on same.

Two segments starring Joan Hackett from an Outer Space serial feature cute special effects, mocking "2001," the original "Flash Gordon" serials and other space epics.

Ironically, if "Flicks" had been released, it might have changed film history a bit, in that its second feature segment "Philip Alien Space Detective" commits in bold relief exactly the same errors which sank "Howard The Duck" years later. As voiced by Harry Shearer and Sandra Kearns, humanoid moths (guys wearing elaborate masks) come to Earth on a tough-guy detective case, with Philip Alien styled as a Bogey-type moth gumshoe. The seduction scene with human Pamela Sue Martin plays just like Lea Thompson's similar assignment in "Howard The Duck," and the belaboring of the premise (of treating an invader in a weird mask as normal) is identical. —Lor.

Let's Get Harry
(COLOR)

Routine actioner buoyed by Robert Duvall & Gary Busey.

A Tri-Star Pictures release from Tri-Star-Delphi IV & V Prods. Produced by Daniel H. Blatt, Robert Singer. Directed by "Alan Smithee" (Stuart Rosenberg). Screenplay, Charles Robert Carner, from story by Mark Feldberg, Samuel Fuller; camera (Metrocolor), James A. Contner; editor, Ralph E. Winters, Rick R. Sparr; music, Brad Fiedel; sound (Dolby), Don Johnson; art direction, Mort Rabinowitz, Agustin Ituarte (Mexico); costume supervisor, Gilda Texter; stunt coordinator, Bobby Bass; special effects coordinator, Eddie Surkin; production manager, David S. Hamburger; assistant director, Benjamin Rosenberg; casting, Judith Holstra, Marcia Ross; associate producers, Feldberg, Hamburger. Reviewed on HBO/Cannon vidcassette, N.Y., May 24, 1987. (MPAA Rating: R.) Running time: **107 MINS.**

Corey Burke	Michael Schoeffling
Pachowski	Tom Wilson
Spence	Glenn Frey
Jack Abernathy	Gary Busey
Norman Shrike	Robert Duvall
Curt	Rick Rossovich
Harry Burke Sr.	Ben Johnson
Clayton	Matt Clark
Alphonso	Gregory Sierra
Veronica	Elpidia Carrillo
Harry	Mark Harmon
Amb. Douglas	Bruce Gray
Ochobar	Guillermo Rios

"Let's Get Harry" is a well made, but utterly routine action picture released by Tri-Star last October ahead of its current home-video status. Pic is worth catching for two excellent (as usual) support performances by Robert Duvall and Gary Busey. Director Stuart Rosenberg took his name off the credits, reportedly due to a contretemps during postproduction (pic was lensed in Mexico and Illinois in 1985).

Project originally was planned as a film by Samuel Fuller, writing and directing, in 1981; he is credited with cowriting the story. It's the trite concept (almost identical to another current release, Vestron's "Nightforce") of a group of young guys, led by Michael Schoeffling, deciding to take matters into their own hands to go to Colombia to rescue Schoeffling's brother Harry (Mark Harmon), kidnaped along with the U.S. ambassador (Bruce Gray) by terrorists. These "terrorists" are actually drug dealers, holding the twosome hostage until their fellow dealers are released from prison.

Picture follows rigidly the clichés of this mini-genre: the old hand mercenary (Robert Duvall) who takes the youngsters under his wing; the hands-are-tied government officials ("we don't negotiate with terrorists under any circumstances" is the policy line) and stereotyped bad guys. There's even a totally illogical female role written in, played by Elpidia Carrillo, who is cast in virtually every south-of-the-border Hollywood opus.

Fortunately, film is redeemed somewhat by Duvall, with shaved head and authoritative thesping, as a gung ho medal-of-honor winner shaded differently than his similar roles in "Apocalypse Now" and "The Great Santini." Busey is also delightful as a smooth-talking car dealer who agrees to bankroll the mission if he can come along for a "hunting trip." Unfortunately both Duvall and Busey eventually are written out of the scenario, and film dies without them around.

Lead roles are colorless, with Schoeffling doing any okay job but singing star Glenn Frey making little impression as one of his pals. Rugged he-man Rick Rossovich is cast against type as the wimp of the group. —Lor.

They Still Call Me Bruce
(COLOR)

Poorly made sequel.

A Shapiro Entertainment release of Jihee production. Produced, written and directed by Johnny Yune and James Orr. Stars Yune. Camera (color), R. Michael Delahoussaye; editor, Roy Watts; music, Morton Stevens; art direction, Jeff McManus; casting, Gary Chasen. Reviewed at the Hollywood Egyptian theater, May 29, 1987. (MPAA Rating: PG.) Running time: **91 MINS.**
With: Johnny Yune, David Mendenhall, Bethany Wright, Don Gibb, Robert Guillaume, Pat Paulsen, Joey Travolta, Carl Bensen.

Hollywood — "They Still Call Me Bruce" rips off every film that ever ripped off "Rocky," from "Rocky II" to "The Karate Kid Part II." It's a sequel itself, of 1982's "They Call Me Bruce" (or "A Fistful Of Chopsticks") which inexplicably got good business worldwide. As lame as the underpinnings for this plot are — there's this Oriental guy, see, named Bruce (as in Lee), only he's no good at martial arts — this might be where the streak ends. Domestic boxoffice will probably be limited to relatives of the participants.

Story follows Bruce Won (Johnny Yune), who arrives in America looking for G.I. Ernie Brown, who saved his life during the Korean War. He goes to the V.A. office in Houston where he's given a list of possible "E. Browns."

After a series of utterly stupid instances of mistaken identity and contrived communication difficulties, a bruised Bruce goes to a martial arts studio, hoping to learn some tactics of self-defense. Instead, he winds up getting a job as a figurehead black belt, since the white owner is losing business to Oriental studios in the city.

While faking his way through his first class, he meets a young orphan boy (David Mendenhall) and ... well, you know the rest. Both young and old learn valuable lessons about trust and commitment along the way, both have championship fights in which they beat bigger opponents thanks to the force imparted them by a special sock ("Michael Jackson has just one glove, you have one sock," says Bruce).

Bruce's romantic interest (Bethany Wright) is a prostitute who works for Mr. B (Carl Bensen), an organized crime boss who Bruce fears might be the man who saved his life gone bad. She is a believable bimbo.

Closing scene, in which little Billy comes out of a one-day coma, sneaks out of a hospital and heroically staggers to the coliseum to give Bruce the inspirational sock is inadvertently hilarious.

While Yune certainly means well, he has no gift for a screenplay, little feel for direction and no discernible acting ability. Too often here, what is presumably supposed to pass for deadpan humor emerges as nothing more than bad timing.

Cameos by Robert Guillaume (as V.A. officer) and Pat Paulsen (as psychiatrist) are pathetic.

In addition to a disturbing overload of comic-book violence, racial stereotypes abound. Besides Pimps #1, #2 and #3, there's another jive-talking character listed in closing credits simply as "Black Dude."

Technical credits are poor, with R. Michael Delahoussaye's photography constantly looking drab and washed out, and the dated disco soundtrack simply gruesome.

—Camb.

The Witches Of Eastwick
(COLOR)

Uneven adaptation boasts bravura Jack Nicholson turn.

A Warner Bros. release of a Guber-Peters Co. production of a Kennedy Miller film. Produced by Neil Canton, Peter Guber, Jon Peters. Executive producers, Rob Cohen, Don Devlin. Directed by George Miller. Stars Jack Nicholson. Screenplay, Michael Cristofer, based on novel by John Updike; camera (Panavision, Technicolor), Vilmos Zsigmond; editor, Richard Francis-Bruce, Hubert C. De La Bouillerie; music, John William; production design, Polly Platt; art director, Mark Mansbridge; set design, Robert Sessa, Stan Tropp; set decoration, Joe D. Mitchell; sound (Dolby), Art Rochester; visual effects (ILM) supervisor, Michael Owens; special effects supervisor, Mike Lanteri; special makeup effects, Rob Bottin; animation supervisor, Ellen Lichtwardt; stunt coordinator, Alan Gibbs; costumes, Aggie Guerard Rodgers; assistant director, Chris Soldo; production manager, Michael Glick; casting, Wally Nicita. Reviewed at The Burbank Studios, Burbank, Calif. June 2, 1987. (MPAA Rating: R). Running time: **118 MINS.**
Daryl Van Horne . . . . Jack Nicholson
Alexandra Medford . . . . Cher
Jane Spofford . . . . Susan Sarandon
Suki Ridgemont . . . . Michelle Pfeiffer
Felicia Alden . . . . . . Veronica Cartwright
Clyde Alden . . . . Richard Jenkins
Walter Neff . . . . Keith Jochim
Fidel . . . . Carel Struycken

Hollywood — "The Witches Of Eastwick" is a brilliantly conceived metaphor for the battle between the sexes that literally poses the question must a woman sell her soul to the devil to have a good relationship? It's an intriguing question as three beautiful witches and a glorious devil play out their passions in the birthplace of America.

Unfortunately, the film never really solves the riddle or sheds a great deal of light on the age-old mystery, but with a no-holds-barred performance by Jack Nicholson as the horny Satan, it's still a very funny and irresistible set-up for anyone who has ever been baffled by the opposite sex.

Based on the novel by John Updike, "The Witches Of Eastwick" presents archetypes of the male and female spirit. Updike and scripter Michael Cristofer are in awe of the creative power of women represented here by three sides of the gender.

Sukie Ridgemont (Michele Pfeiffer), a writer for the local newspaper, is the intellectual; Jane Spofford (Susan Sarandon), a high school music teacher, is the woman of feeling and Alexandra Medford (Cher), a sculptress, represents the sensuous side. They're all divorced and they're all looking for a Mr. Right.

Enter Daryl Van Horn (Jack Nicholson), the answer to their collective longing for a man of wit, charm and intelligence. For Nicholson it's the role of a lifetime, the chance to seduce these women and be cock of the roost.

The seduction is a spectacle to behold with Nicholson prancing, strutting, cajoling the three witch women with just the right blend of bravado and promises. The secret of his power is that he knows what they need and with it can tap the source of their creative energy. All he wants in return is everything.

It's not the traditional struggle between good and evil the devil usually engages in, but a battle of wills that leaves Nicholson braying at the moon that ancient complaint: Women — can't live with 'em and can't live without 'em.

"Witches" covers the main events of a relationship including the seduction, initial fulfillment followed by disillusionment, Nicholson's desperation to hold on, the messy break-up, childbirth and life after coupling.

Yet the film fails to get under the skin of how men and women relate on an everyday basis and sounds only a single high-pitched note. At times it makes for grand entertainment. Individual scenes, among them a world class tantrum for the devil, soar with an inspired lunacy, but overall action remains on one level of intensity and consequently falls a bit flat.

Director George Miller seems to become a bit impatient with the material as well and tries to hike it up a notch towards the end with some inappropriate special effects apparently designed to wake up the older audience and lure in the younger crowd.

Spectacle of the film is really Nicholson. Dressed in eccentric flowing robes, odd hats and installed in a lush mansion, he is larger than life, as indeed the devil should be. The witches, lovely though they are, are a good deal less imaginative and exist more as types than distinct personalities.

Performances by Cher, Sarandon and Pfeiffer have their charm but without Nicholson's ferocious magnetism. In fact, it's a bit unbalanced since it is the women who dominate in the end.

Veronica Cartwright as a townie who figures out what's happening to Eastwick and hysterically tries to fight it is suitably shrill, but she's no match for the life force unleashed by her foes.

Miller keeps the film in constant motion, continually moving his camera, complemented well by Richard Francis-Bruce and Hubert C. De La Bouillerie's pregnant editing. Polly Platt's production design is totally contemporary while suggesting the historical roots of the town and the struggle going on there.

Vilmos Zsigmond's photography creates a deeply saturated, supra-real environment where anything can happen and does. —*Jagr.*

Rosa de la Frontera
(Rose Of The Border)
(MEXICAN-COLOR)

A Peliculas Mexicanas release of a Producciones Esme-Alianza Cinematográfica Mexicana production. Produced by Carlos Vasallo. Directed by Hernando Name. Stars Susana Dosamantes. Screenplay, Name, Roberto Schlosser; camera (color), Xavier Cruz; editor, Sigfredo García, Enrique Murillo; music, Ricardo Carrión, with appearance of group Los Broncos de Reynosa. Reviewed at Hollywood Twin theater 1, N.Y., April 13, 1987. Running time: **89 MINS.**
Rosa Guerra . . . . Susana Dosamantes
Tomás . . . . Humberto Herrera
Gabión . . . . Eleazar García
Sheriff . . . . Hugo Stiglitz
Emilio Guerra . . . . Jorge Vargas
  Also with: Eric del Castillo, Diana Ferreti, Carlos Fast, Paulino Vargas

The Mexican pic "Rosa de la Frontera" (Rose Of The Border), directed by Hernando Name, is a convoluted drama with enough complications to make several movies. The film is so full of plot, there seems little room for anything else.

Story focuses on the character of Rosa Guerra (Susana Dosamantes) who, with her younger brother, flees to the U.S. after a friendly horserace turns to murder. When her husband is tossed in jail, Rosa discovers that she must somehow raise the money both to free him and save the farm. Also, Mexican bad guys are hot on her trail.

Well, if Rosa had problems in Mexico, things only get worse in the U.S. One by one, she takes on an armed bank robber, a sadistic motorcycle gang, a bunch of crooks who wear funny neckties and finally, the police led by a Mexican-hating sheriff (Hugo Stiglitz).

Tech credits are functional and Dosamantes does what she can to overcome the excesses of the script. Yet, the film is a perfect example that too much is sometimes not enough. —*Lent.*

Roxanne
(COLOR)

Wild and crazy guy in sappy version of 'Cyrano.'

A Columbia Pictures release. Produced by Michael Rachmil, Daniel Melnick. Executive producer, Steve Martin. Directed by Fred Schepisi. Stars Martin, Daryl Hannah. Screenplay, Martin, from the play "Cyrano de Bergerac" by Edmond Rostand; camera (Deluxe color), Ian Baker; editor, John Scott; music, Bruce Smeaton; sound (Dolby stereo), Rob Young; production design, Jack DeGovia; art direction, David Fischer; set decoration, Kimberly Richardson; assistant director, Michael Steele; casting, Pennie du Pont. Reviewed at Samuel Goldwyn theater, Beverly Hills, Calif., June 4, 1987. (MPAA Rating: PG.) Running time: **107 MINS.**
C.D. Bales . . . . Steve Martin
Roxanne . . . . Daryl Hannah
Chris . . . . Rick Rossovich
Dixie . . . . Shelley Duvall
Chuck . . . . John Kapelos
Mayor Deebs . . . . Fred Willard
Dean . . . . Max Alexander
Andy . . . . Michael J. Pollard

Hollywood — "Roxanne" has enough laughs for a 5-minute standup routine and that way audiences would be spared the inconvenience of sitting through the other 102 minutes. As a reworking of Rostand's "Cyrano de Bergerac," the only reason to see the film is for a few bits of inspired nonsense by Steve Martin as the nosey lover. This, however, may not be a big enough draw and boxoffice outlook is limited.

Written by Martin to suit his special talent for sight gags, he sacrifices much of the poetry and poignancy of the original. This Cyrano, called C.B. here, is just a wild and crazy guy with a big nose and a gift for gab.

Of course, the central plot device of the play, in which a true love writes letters to help another suitor with the same woman he doesn't love as much, has been used in numerous setups and here it's adapted to a small ski community in Washington State where Martin is fire chief.

The film is barely underway when Roxanne (Daryl Hannah) is out of her clothes and locked out of her house. When C.B. comes to the rescue it's love at first sight, but his enlarged proboscis disqualifies him as a serious suitor, or so he thinks.

Instead, Roxanne turns her attentions to Chris (Rick Rossovich), a new recruit on the fire department who is all but rendered dumb in front of women. Eventually, Roxanne learns Rossovich is only after her body and realizes Martin loves her truly. This being Hollywood, the lovers are united in a happy ending, unlike the play where Roxanne learns the truth too late.

Although Martin makes good use of the opportunity to duel with tennis rackets and verbally joust with buffoons in the local watering hole and is generally likable, Hannah is a wimpy and unconvincing Roxanne. As an astronomy student searching the skies for an as yet undiscovered comet she is indeed beautiful but lacks the spirit to make Martin's passion believable.

One can sympathize with C.B.'s longing, but since the object of his desire is such an airhead, the whole force of the film floats away. For anyone who has been moved by the Rostand play this lack of depth will indeed be disappointing. Even for a general audience that has never heard of Cyrano, there is not much to get excited about here.

Action away from the romance is often amusing with inept fire fighters supplying most of it. Headed by Michael J. Pollard, crew of volunteers are really the gang that couldn't squirt straight.

As the would-be lover who finds greener pastures with a local waitress, Rossovich is a likable hulk without much personality. Shelley Duvall handles the thankless role of C.B.'s friend and confessor with as much élan as the hapless part will allow.

Aussie director Fred Schepisi, who has elsewhere handled much rougher material, does a professional job of creating a breezy atmosphere, but in the end it's hopelessly sappy stuff.

Tech credits are commendable with Jack DeGovia's production design and Ian Baker's cinematography creating a smalltown wonderland suitable for a fairy tale like "Roxanne."—*Jagr.*

Commando Squad
(COLOR)

Stillborn action film.

A Trans World Entertainment release and production. Produced by Alan Amiel. Executive producer, Yoram Pelman. Coproduced and directed by Fred Olen Ray. Stars Brian Thompson, Kathy Shower. Screenplay, Michael D. Sonye; camera (Foto-Kem color), Gary Graver; editor, Kathie Weaver; sound, David Waelder; art direction, Corey Kaplan; special effects coordinators, Kevin McCarthy, Sandy McCarthy; second unit director, Michael Kelly; assistant director, Gary M. Bettmann; associate producer, Herb Linsey. Reviewed at Cine 42 #1 theater, N.Y., June 6, 1987. (MPAA Rating: R.) Running time: **89 MINS.**

Clint	Brian Thompson
Cat	Kathy Shower
Morgan	William Smith
Iggy	Sid Haig
Milo	Robert Quarry
Long John	Ross Hagen
Casey	Marie Windsor
Quintano	Mel Welles
Anita	Benita Martinez

Also with: Dawn Wildsmith, Russ Tamblyn, Lane McClure, Michael D. Sonye.

Prolific action director Fred Olen Ray operates on automatic pilot with "Commando Squad," a deadly dull picture that tries to be a destitute man's "Extreme Prejudice." Outlook not so good, quoth the Magic Eight Ball.

In her film starring debut, former Playboy magazine Playmate of the Year Kathy Shower keeps her apparel firmly on her bod at all times, essaying the role of a government drug enforcement agent sent to Mexico by her boss Robert Quarry (the screen's "Count Yorga" with many pounds added) to wipe out a cocaine factory operated by an agent turned bad, William Smith. She teams up south of the border with fellow agent Brian Thompson and they withstand torture at the hands of B-movie vet Sid Haig in a boring series of encounters with the baddies en route to a fiery conclusion.

Pic starts out promisingly with a nicely staged and arrestingly lit (in various pastel tones) shootout in a power station, but falls apart in the second reel, never to recover its momentum. Donned almost through-

out the film in an unbecoming black wig, Shower is unimpressive, her beauty hidden and characterization embarrassingly relegated to nonstop voiceover narration. Costar Brian Thompson is an unappealing leading man, delivering lines in bored fashion and looking more like Klaus Kinski than a heartthrob.

Of the typically Olen Ray-roundup of vet actors (he's replaced A.C. Lyles in this regard), William Smith and Ross Hagen are forceful, Mel Welles has a funny turn and Marie Windsor is hilarious operating the Hollywood Book & Poster store as a front for gunrunning. Russ Tamblyn pops up uncredited, just as he was in Ray's concurrent release "Cyclone."

Most of the listless action takes place where many old Hollywood Westerns and serials were shot, not convincingly doubling for Mexico. Best tech credits are explosions.

—*Lor.*

Private Investigations
(COLOR)

Routine tv-style action.

An MGM/UA Communications release from MGM Pictures of a Polygram Movies production. Produced by Steven Golin, Sigurjon Sighvatsson. Executive producers, Michael Kuhn, David Hockman. Directed by Nigel Dick. Screenplay, John Dahl, David Warfield; camera (color), David Bridges; editor, Scott Chestnut; music, Murray Munro; production design, Piers Plowden; art direction, Nick Rafter; sound (Dolby), Bob Dreebin; assistant director-associate producer, David Warfield; casting, Jeff Gerrard. Reviewed at MGM/UA screening room, Culver City, Calif., June 4, 1987. (MPAA Rating: R.) Running time: **91 MINS.**

Joey Bradley	Clayton Rohner
Ryan	Ray Sharkey
Lt. Wexler	Paul LeMat
Jenny Fox	Talia Balsam
Eddie Gordon	Phil Morris
Cliff Dowling	Martin Balsam
Charles Bradley	Anthony Zerbe
Kim	Robert Ito
Detective North	Vernon Wells
Larry	Anthony Geary

Hollywood — "Private Investigations" is little more than a serviceable, tightly packaged cops-as-crooks actioner. Its furious intensity cannot overcome the mostly sterile and empty characters. Since one can see just about the same material on "Miami Vice" for free, it's unlikely limited openings will generate enough interest to justify a wide roll-out.

Yarn opens in San Francisco as newspaper editor Anthony Zerbe plans a meeting with an informant who will unload on an L.A.-based police ring that is selling drugs confiscated during their busts. A phone call is tapped; details of a rendezvous are passed on to the bad guys; and Zerbe's son in L.A. (Clayton Rohner) is unwittingly sucked into the turmoil.

Events catapult at a stupendous

pace as a private investigator is murdered at Rohner's apartment. Simplistically enough, it turns out that the homicide cops are the same ones who may be ratted on by Zerbe's contact. The detective (Ray Sharkey) supposedly assigned to protect Rohner instead tries to kill him.

Gratuitous violence escalates as Sharkey's pursuit moves to the streets. Plot jerks in a new direction when Rohner is hit by a car. Driver Talia Balsam takes him to her place where early signs of a future coupling surface.

Film's low point follows as events lead Rohner to the Baldwin Hills oil fields, which become the site of some especially pointless brutality.

While an album-for-sale soundtrack pulsates on and on, Rohner winds up back in town — only to be chased some more by Sharkey. Rohner sure covers a lot of ground in L.A. without a car and somehow manages to make his way back to Balsam's apartment.

Lovers at last on their second encounter, Rohner-Balsam's morning afterglow becomes the crucible for figuring out crucial details just in time to show up for the secret session between Zerbe and the informer. It's held at a visually clever location — an abandoned Western town film set. Confrontation there with the cops, however, leads to a predictable conclusion that only reminds how much the whole outing is like a tv show.

Zerbe's involvement at the end and in earlier scenes lacks spark while Talia's real-life dad Martin Balsam is flat during his couple of scenes.

Production values and tech credits are up to par.—*Tege.*

The Believers
(COLOR)

Realistically staged occult thriller.

An Orion Pictures release. Produced by John Schlesinger, Michael Childers, Beverly Camhe. Executive producer, Edward Teets. Directed by Schlesinger. Stars Martin Sheen, Helen Shaver. Screenplay, Mark Frost from novel, "The Religion" by Nicholas Conde; camera (Deluxe color), Robby Müller; editor, Peter Honess; music, J. Peter Robinson; production design, Simon Holland; art direction, John Kasarda (N.Y.), Carol Spier (Canada); set decoration, Susan Bode (N.Y.), Elinor Rose Galbraith (Canada); costume design, Shay Cunliffe; sound (Dolby), Nicholas Stevenson; second unit directors, Michael Childers, Patrick Crowley; second unit directors, Michael Childers, Patrick Crowley; second unit camera, Peter Norman; casting, Donna Isaacson, John Lyons (U.S.), Maria Armstrong, Ross Clydesdale (Canada). Reviewed at the Samuel Goldwyn theater, Beverly Hills, Calif., June 3, 1987. (MPAA Rating: R.) Running time: **114 MINS.**

Cal Jamison	Martin Sheen
Jessica Halliday	Helen Shaver
Chris Jamison	Harley Cross
Lieutenant Sean McTaggert	Robert Loggia
Kate Maslow	Elizabeth Wilson
Donald Calder	Harris Yulin
Dennis Maslow	Lee Richardson
Marty Wertheimer	Richard Masur
Mrs. Ruiz	Carla Pinza
Tom Lopez	Jimmy Smits

Hollywood — John Schlesinger's "The Believers" is not unlike his previous pic, "Marathon Man," which builds on some pretty strange goings-on in New York, grows increasingly complicated and obtuse, finally falling back to center for an unsettling wrapup. This meticulously violent occult thriller is more fascinating then frightening; its theme just at the edge of reality to pass off as fiction. For those who enjoy intense rides, this is the E ticket.

Opening scenes, while seemingly unrelated, would get anyone's heart going; the first an electrocution of psychotherapist Cal Jamison's (Martin Sheen) wife, the second a tribal stabbing of a young boy.

How these two horrors are related, and what takes scripter Mark Frost almost too long to explain, is the connection between the practice of Santeria (a strange sacrificial faith based on Catholic saints) and its effect on nearly everyone Sheen comes to know upon moving to Manhattan.

In his capacity of counseling members of the New York City police force, Sheen soon connects the crazy behavior of one cop (Jimmy Smits) to a series of ritualistic (and very gory) stabbings. Being the good PhD that he is, Sheen uses what meager clues he has, does a little research and comes upon the rationale for the brutal murders — one of the tenets of Santeria is the belief that if the firstborn son is sacrificed, his parents will realize success beyond their wildest imaginings.

With production designer Simon Holland's perfect eye for the strange and the most ordinary of urban settings, Schlesinger is crafty enough to walk a fine line between using too many pat scary tricks (rainstorms, blackouts, drugged liquids) and milking the voodoo bit to the point where the sight of entrails, amulets, totems and blood loses its visual impact.

It isn't difficult to accept that the things that happen in "The Believers" could happen in real life, which is why the picture is so riveting.

Consider the weird goings on of other cults that have flourished in the United States recently, notably attempted murders by the followers of Synanon and the Bagwan Shree Rajneesh to name just two.

What Schlesinger does is take it one step further, into the realm of horror. Incantations in the basement of a Spanish Harlem store whose owner practices Santeria is one thing; spiders crawling out of a hole in a woman's cheek is another.

Central characters, including Sheen, make it somehow believable. Naturally, Sheen has only one child, a son (Harley Cross) whose housekeeper (perfect casting in Carla Pinza) just happens to practice Santeria (the good kind, though).

In his adaptation of Nicholas Conde's book, Frost expects us to take more than a few leaps in plot development and swallow a number of coincidences.

The action moves along too fast to notice, however, finding time for Sheen to fall in love with his landlady (Helen Shaver) across the street and all the complications that arise from that.

In addition to Shaver's nice ladyfriend act are good turns by Smits (from the tv series, "L.A. Law") as the crazed Tom Lopez and Robert Loggia at his crusty best as Lt. Sean McTaggert.

If nothing else, Schlesinger knows how to produce a film where pain and horror are beautiful to watch, a sick thought, but one that has its believers. —*Brit.*

Under Cover
(COLOR)

Boring drug bust caper.

A Cannon Group release of a Golan-Globus production. Produced by Menahem Golan, Yoram Globus. Directed by John Stockwell. Screenplay, Stockwell, Scott Fields; camera (color), Alexander Gruszynski; editor, Sharyn L. Ross; music, Todd Rundgren; sound (Ultra-Stereo), Glenn Berkovitz; production design, Becky Block; production manager, Neil Rapp; assistant director, Allan Nicholls; stunt coordinator, Greg Walker; postproduction supervisor, Michael R. Sloan; casting, Pat Orseth; associate producers, Susan Hoffman, Fields. Reviewed at Cine 42 No. 2 theater, N.Y., June 6, 1987. (MPAA Rating: R.) Running time: **94 MINS.**
Sheffield . . . . David Neidorf
La Rue . . . . Jennifer Jason Leigh
Sgt. Irwin Lee . . . . Barry Corbin
Lucas . . . . David Harris
Corrinne . . . . Kathleen Wilhoite
Also with: David Denney, Brent Hadaway, John Philbin, Brad Leland, Mark Holton, Carmen Argenziano.

"Under Cover" is a lethargic, uninteresting melodrama about cops busting kids using drugs at a southern high school. Young actor (from "Top Gun," "Radioactive Dreams" and many other pics) turned director John Stockwell directs with little energy and like several other Cannon releases of late, pic opened in N.Y. sans advertising at a 42d St. grindhouse.

David Neidorf (who physically resembles auteur Stockwell somewhat) plays a Baltimore cop who goes to Port Allen, South Carolina (pic was actually lensed in Louisiana) to join local narcs operating under cover at a high school. His fellow cop and pal (John Philbin)

was recently murdered down there and Neidorf is out to bring the killers to justice. He is teamed up with pretty narc Jennifer Jason Leigh but runs into resistance from his local, southern-fried boss (and obvious heavy) Barry Corbin.

Though Neidorf and Leigh below their covers halfway through the film in order to finger the school kids in a mass bust, pic continues in its listless narrative towards a wishy-washy ending in which even the bad guy is left alive and described as not really all bad.

Neidorf unwisely tries to imitate Mickey Rourke here with constant smirk and throwaway readings, creating a vacuum at film's center. He's way too old for the role, but script merely mentions that and goes on full-speed ahead. Leigh looks sexy but has little to do and supporting cast is weak. Tech credits and score by Todd Rundgren are unimpressive. —*Lor.*

Cyclone
(COLOR)

Limp action pic with veteran cast.

A Cinetel Films release. Produced by Paul Hertzberg. Directed by Fred Olen Ray. Stars Heather Thomas. Screenplay, Paul Garson, from a story by Ray; additional material written by T.L. Lankford; camera (color), Paul Elliot; editor, Robert A. Ferretti; music, David A. Jackson; additional music; James Saad; art direction, Maxine Shepard; sound, Rob Janiger, David Waelder; stunt coordinator, John Stewart; assistant director, Gary M. Bettman; production manager-coproducer, Neil Lundell; special effects coordinator, Kevin McCarthy; Cyclone design and creation, Tracy Design Inc. Reviewed at Hollywood Pacific theater, June 5, 1987. (MPAA Rating: R.) Running time: **83 MINS.**
Teri Marshall . . . . Heather Thomas
Rick Davenport . . . . Jeffrey Combs
Carla Hastings . . . . Ashley Ferrare
Rolf . . . . Dar Robinson
Waters . . . . Martine Beswicke
Knowles . . . . Robert Quarry
Bosarian . . . . Martin Landau
Long John . . . . Huntz Hall
Bob Jenkins . . . . Troy Donahue
Henna . . . . Dawn Wildsmith
Also with: Michael Reagan, Tim Conway Jr., Bruce Fairbairn, Sam Hiona, Michael D. Sonye, Russ Tamblyn.

Hollywood — "Cyclone" is a perfectly routine exploitation pic elevated slightly by a sense of humor about itself. Story of a super-charged motorcycle designed for the government and sought by double agents generates little excitement on the screen and should do about as well at the boxoffice.

Although film is under 90 minutes and takes forever to get into gear, it still seems overlong as it builds to a limp climax. All the fuss is about a super weapon, the Cyclone, designed for the feds by crack scientist Rick Davenport (Jeffrey Combs) and powered by a high-tech hydrogen energy source.

Of course, anything that good

everyone wants a piece of and the bad guys led by Rolf (the late stunt ace Dar Robinson) murder Combs and go after the machine but his girlfriend (Heather Thomas) stands in their way.

Most of the rest of the film involves sorting out the good guys from the bad buys. Brains behind the heist is Martin Landau as a James Bondish villain.

Screenplay by Paul Garson shows little originality in the set-ups but allows Thomas a few goods lines and some tongue-in-cheek humor. It would be impossible to take this stuff seriously in any case.

Director Fred Olen Ray stages several chases in conventional fashion that seems almost slow motion by today's standards. Performances are marginally competent with Landau supplying an element of glee to his sinister characterization.

Tech credits feature some so-so stunts and grainy photography. The violence is mostly of the comic book variety. —*Jagr.*

The Perfect Match
(COLOR)

Winning low-budget romantic comedy.

An Airtight production. Produced and directed by Mark Deimel. Coproducer, Bob Torrance. Screenplay, Nick Duretta, David Burr, Deimel; camera (color), Torrance; editor, Craig Colton; music, Tim Torrance; production design, Maxine Shepard; sound, Rob Janiger; associate producers, Daniel Carlson, George Vaughan. Reviewed at Seattle Intl. Film Festival, Egyptian theater, June 1, 1987. (No MPAA Rating.) Running time: **92 MINS.**
Tim Wainwright . . . . Marc McClure
Nancy Bryant . . . . Jennifer Edwards
Vicki . . . . Diane Stilwell
John Wainwright . . . . Rob Paulsen

Seattle — "The Perfect Match" is the first film from Airtight Prods. and also marks the theatrical feature debut of producer-director Mark Deimel. Despite its highly predictable outcome, this romantic comedy has genuinely funny material and two lead characters who often take the opportunity to go beyond formula to deliver solid performances.

The love story revolves around two insecure 29-year-olds who lack the necessary skills to be single in the city and are searching for the perfect companion in order to avoid a lifetime alone. They meet through a newspaper ad placed by Tim, a classic nerd who drinks Coke, watches basketball and who lies in the ad about his various athletic and cultural interests. He meets Nancy Bryant, a career student, vegetarian and classic wallflower — his exact opposite in personal interests. She, however, also lies about herself. She says she's a college professor with natural athletic abilities.

Their first date ends in near-disaster, but they somehow find themselves going back for more. Their next venture, a weekend in the mountains, ends in true disaster as each tries to impress the other with their outdoorsiness.

It could all end there except for her growing attraction to him and his mother talking to him about how different she and his father were, but how happy they were together. Naturally, in the end, the pair decide they're not such a horrendous mismatch after all.

Like many independent productions, this is a low-budget affair. However, strong performances by Marc McClure, best known for his recurring role as Jimmy Olsen in the "Superman" films and Jennifer Edwards, daughter of Blake Edwards who has appeared in several of her dad's pictures, coupled with Deimel's apparent talent as a director overcome any inadequacies in production.

One of the nicest touches is a restrained scene in which she catches him clothed in outrageous shorts, sipping Coke, and enthusiastically rooting on a basketball game on television. He doesn't know she's watching, and she doesn't say anything, but it's clear the lies are beginning to unravel. — *Magg.*

Hard Ticket To Hawaii
(COLOR)

Campy action pic.

A Malibu Bay Films release. Produced by Arlene Sidaris. Written and directed by Andy Sidaris. Camera (United color), Howard Wexler; editor, Michael Haight; music, Gary Stockdale; assistant director, M.M. Freedman; production design, Sal Grasso, Peter Munneke; costume design, Fionn; martial arts choreography, Harold Diamond; skateboard stunts, Russell Howell; second unit camera, Harmon Lougher; associate producer, Tina Scott. Reviewed at Broadway screening room, N.Y., June 4, 1987. (MPAA Rating: R.) Running time: **96 MINS.**
Rowdy Abilene . . . . Ronn Moss
Donna . . . . Dona Speir
Taryn . . . . Hope Marie Carlton
Jade . . . . Harold Diamond
Seth Romero . . . . Rodrigo Obregon
Edy . . . . Cynthia Brimhall
Pattycakes . . . . Patty Duffek
Jimmy-John Jackson . . . . Wolf Larson
Rosie . . . . Lory Green
Kimo . . . . Rustam Branaman
Ashley . . . . David DeShay
Michelle/Michael . . . . . . Michael Andrews
Whitey . . . . Andy Sidaris
Also with: Kwan Hi Lim, Joseph Hieu, Peter Bromilow, Glen Chin, Russell Howell, Richard LePore, Joey Meran, Shawne Zarubica.

Currently in regional release, "Hard Ticket To Hawaii" is a very campy action picture that fondly recalls the bosomy Russ Meyer epics of the 1970s. Filmmaker Andy Sidaris, better known as a sports director for ABC-TV, shares Meyer's obsession with extremely well-built young women and is more than willing to share same with escapist audiences.

Former Playboy magazine models Dona Speir and Hope Marie Carlton topline as women running an air freight service in Hawaii who become entangled unwittingly with diamond smugglers. Rowdy Abilene (Ronn Moss) is called in to help, bringing along his martial arts sidekick Jade (Harold Diamond), with extraneous subplots involving an international drug ring and a large snake on the loose which, per the risible dialog, "has been infected by deadly toxins from cancer-infested rats."

To quote the film's memorable coming attractions' tag line: "This ain't no hula!" Rather, Sidaris treats his disposable plotline and array of groaner one-liners as a thinly veiled excuse to have numerous beauties strip for the camera. Voyeurs will be delighted, camp followers will have a field day with the bad acting and action fans should be contented with particularly outré setpieces. Strangest action scenes include a skateboarder henchman (Russell Howell) shooting at the heroes while carrying a full-size inflatable lovedoll; Moss simply whips out a bazooka and explodes the guy. Hilarious climax has the deadly snake popping out of the toilet to confront Speir (and, of course, yielding a wet t-shirt shot in the process), with Moss crashing in through a wall on his motorcycle in the nick of time to blast the beastie with his trusty bazooka.

As noted, cast is an eyeful, backed up by some lovely Hawaiian locations. Acting is a hoot while tech credits are acceptable. Some of the in-jokes are a bit obscure, but Sidaris fans will recognize the auteur in a lengthy, self-mocking cameo role and appreciate endless plugola for his previous pics, particularly "Malibu Express," to which "Hard Ticket" is a sequel. —Lor.

Captive Hearts
(COLOR)

Old-fashioned, dull wartime romance.

An MGM/UA Communications release from MGM Pictures. Produced by John A. Kuri. Executive producer, Milton Goldstein. Directed by Paul Almond. Stars Pat Morita. Screenplay, Morita, Kuri from a work by Sargon Tamimi; camera (Metrocolor), Thomas Vamos; editor, Yurij Luhovy; music, Osamu Kitajima; costumes, Nicoletta Massone; production design, Steve Sardanis, Francois DeLucy; set decoration, Claudine Charbonneau, Anne Galea; sound, Patrick Rousseau; second unit director, Kuri; second unit camera, Daniel Vincelette. Reviewed at MGM, Culver City, Calif., June 5, 1987. (MPAA Rating: PG.) Running time: **97 MINS.**
Fukushima .... Noriyuki (Pat) Morita
Robert .... Chris Makepeace
Miyoko .... Mari Sato
Sergeant McManus ...... Michael Sarrazin

Takayama .... Seth Sakai
Masato .... Denis Akiyama

Hollywood — "Captive Hearts" is a sentimental love story between a fresh-faced Army Air Corps lieutenant and a vulnerable young Japanese woman during World War II. As far as old-fashioned melodramas go, it has its moments. As far as captivating large audiences, chances are slim.

Soldiers, from time immemorial, have fallen for the enemy's women — and it has been a theme used in many a film.

Here, it happens after two U.S. airmen, Robert, a young lieutenant (Chris Makepeace) and his nemesis, Sergeant McManus (Michael Sarrazin) are shot down in a remote village behind enemy lines in northern Japan.

Sarrazin, laying on a thick Brooklynese, hates Japs and not only won't cooperate with his captors, he will do anything to antagonize them. Not so, the gentle Makepeace, who practically signs up for hard labor if it means saving his skin. (Presumably the Marine credo, "Death before dishonor" doesn't apply to the U.S. Army Air Corps.)

In any event, it's the beginning of winter and while Sarrazin goes off and gets his (bleep) frozen, Makepeace makes friends with the villagers.

Pat Morita plays the town's elder statesman, bringing along Makepeace for walks in the countryside and showing him how his hawk deftly kills little animals on command. As it turns out, the hawk has the most interesting role.

As the traditional Japanese woman, Miyoko (Japanese tv star Mari Sato) is always two steps behind them — to cook, draw the bath, instruct Makepeace on the Japanese way to do things, etc.

Makepeace and Sato have a very innocent romance — also one which is very s-l-o-w to develop.

There are a couple of screws thrown into the works to thwart their being alone together, mostly in the presence of a wizened old man determined to make her his wife. But overall, this is an uncomplicated — and uninvolving story.

Also, pic doesn't really explain any mysteries of the Japanese culture not explored in other works or draw on the differences between these gentle types and those of other civilizations.

Perhaps the biggest flaw in the story is the lack of urgency. Except for one brief, unsuspenseful scene where a couple of Japanese soldiers come looking for the downed airman, there is little evidence that a war is even going on. We know differently. —Brit.

Predator
(COLOR)

Schwarzenegger is the most dangerous game in okay actioner.

A 20th Century Fox release of a Gordon-Silver-Davis production, in association with Amercent Films and American Entertainment Partners. Produced by Lawrence Gordon, Joel Silver, John Davis. Executive producers, Laurence P. Pereira, Jim Thomas. Directed by John McTiernan. Stars Arnold Schwarzenegger. Screenplay, Jim Thomas, John Thoma; camera (Deluxe color), Donald McAlpine, Leon Sanchez (Mexico); editor, John F. Link, Mark Helfrich; music, Alan Silvestri; sound (Dolby), Manuel Topete; production design, John Vallone; art direction, Frank Richwood, Jorge Saenz; John K. Reinhart Jr. (Mexico); set decoration, Enrique Estevez; creature created by Stan Winston; stunt coordintor, Craig Baxley; special visual effects, R/Greenberg — supervisor, Joel Hynek; Thermal Vision effects supervisor, Stuart Robertson; additional visual effects, Dream Quest Images; assistant director, Beau E. L. Marks; Jose Luis Ortega (Mexico); production managers, Art Seidel, Marks; special effects supervisors, Al Di Sarro, Laurencio (Choby) Cordero; second unit director, Baxley; second unit camera, Frank E. Johnson; casting, Jackie Burch; associate producers, Marks, Vallone. Reviewed at Darryl F. Zanuck Theater, Century City, June 8, 1987. (MPAA Rating: R.) Running time: **107 MINS.**
Dutch .... Arnold Schwarzenegger
Dillon .... Carl Weathers
Anna .... Elpidia Carrillo
Mac .... Bill Duke
Blain .... Jesse Ventura
Billy .... Sonny Landham
Poncho .... Richard Chaves
Gen. Phillips .... R.G. Armstrong
Hawkins .... Shane Black
Predator .... Kevin Peter Hall

Hollywood — The Terminator's on the other foot this time, with Arnold Schwarzenegger playing the prey rather than the hunter. "Predator" is a slightly above-average actioner that tries to compensate for tissue-thin-plot with ever-more-grisly death sequences and impressive special effects. Telegraphed story line slows the pace, though, as audience spends most of the film waiting for the inevitable ultimate confrontation. Schwarzenegger's reliable appeal, plus word-of-mouth from genre fans, should make this a boxoffice success.

Schwarzenegger plays Dutch, the leader of a vaguely defined military rescue team that works for allied governments. Called into a U.S. hot spot somewhere in South America, he encounters old bubby Dillon (Carl Weathers), who now works for the CIA.

It is made clear early on that Dutch is not just your everyday mindless killer, but one with a conscience. When Dillon asks him why he didn't take part in the U.S. raid on Libya, he says, "We're a rescue team, not assassins." Minutes later, he sheds a tear moments before slaughtering a guerrilla unit in an unsuccessful rescue attempt.

On the way out of the jungle, the

unit starts to get decimated in increasingly garish fashion by an otherworldly Predator. Enemy is a nasty, formidable foe with laser powers, but his creation was obviously a committee decision: at various times, the alien creature resembles a wild boar turned inside out, a camouflaged FTD florist, Reddi Kilowatt and Road Warrior From Hell.

While some of the action sequences are imaginative, the film moves slowly to its conclusion, as the Predator wastes the band of warriors one by one. By the time the showdown does begin, pic has lost whatever momentum it had, and the battle between Dutch and the Predator carries none of the emotional baggage of what has gone on before.

Schwarzenegger, while undeniably appealing, still has a character who's not quite real. He plays the film's first half looking and acting like Clint Eastwood's Tom Highway in "Heartbreak Ridge." While the painted face, cigar, vertical hair and horizontal eyes are all there, none of the humanity gets on the screen, partly because of the sparse dialog. Last section of the film has Schwarzenegger covered in mud and blood, resorting to use of bow-and-arrow, à la Rambo.

Supporting cast is mostly adequate but hardly great. Weathers can't breathe any life into the cardboard character of Dillon, who goes from being unbelievably cynical to being unbelievably heroic in about five minutes. Among the rest, Sonny Landham goes beyond his stereotyped character, which amounts to a modern-day Tonto, and Bill Duke plays the over-the-edge soldier Mac with a delicious sense of doom.

McTiernan tries to lay a thin sheen of moral righteousness on the proceedings (Dutch fights fair), but the unreal situation and the almost nonexistent script detract.

While Donald McAlpine's lensing is mostly sharp, some of the jungle greenery is obviously artificial and McTiernan relies a bit too much on special effects "thermal vision" photography, in looking through the Predator's eyes, while trying to build tension before the blood starts to fly. —Camb.

Matar o Morir
(Kill Or Die)
(MEXICAN-COLOR)

A Peliculas Mexicanas release of a Cumbre Films production. Produced by Luis Berlos. Directed by Rafael Villasenor Kuri. Stars Vicente Fernández. Screenplay, Fernando Galiana; camera (color), Javier Cruz; editor, Max Sánchez; music, Carlos Torres. Reviewed at Hollywood Twin theater, N.Y., May 12, 1987. Running time: **99 MINS.**
Arturo Mendoza .... Vicente Fernández
Lt. Anthony Collins ...... Pedro Armendariz
Vicente Mendoza .... Humberto Herrera

Daniela .... Gabriela Leon
 Also with: Maria Montaño, Julieta Rosen,
Rafael Fernández, Lena Jiménez, Alma Thelma, Alejandra Vidal, Tito Guillen, Raul Guerrero, Manolo Cárdenas.

"Matar o Morir" (Kill Or Die) is
an interesting yet uneven vehicle for
popular Mexican ranchero singer
Vicente Fernández. Directed by veteran Fernández helmer Rafael Villaseñor Kuri, film is an unhappy
marriage of two distinct genres: a
ranch comedy and a psychological
murder mystery. Sadly, the filmmaker is unable to do justice to
either form.

The film opens briskly. The audience is introduced to the good-
hearted rogue don Arturo Mendoza
(Fernández) and his son Vicente
(Humberto Herrera). The two enjoy
competing, not only in the rodeo
but also for the affections of the
same woman. The father drinks and
sings ranchero tunes and the son is
unlucky at cards. Turning point
comes when dad discovers sonny
boy has stolen from his own father
to pay off his gambling debts. There
is a fight and the son is sent away in
disgrace.

Pic changes directions when don
Arturo receives a phone call from
the U.S. police, informing him of
his son's death. The boy had
received seven bullets, five in the
back. Don Arturo speeds to the
scene to join Lt. Tony Collins
(Pedro Armendáriz), a Mexican-
hating cop, in the investigation.

Although the film does contain a
few tense and effective scenes, the
narrative line is confused and choppy. Tech credits are functional.
Fernández gets to sing a few songs,
but the background incidental music by Carlos Torres is badly matched
to later action and tends to distract.

Fans will find the theme interesting within the body of Fernández'
films, but as successful entertainment, the pic doesn't quite cut it.
—Lent.

Million Dollar Mystery
(COLOR)

Crass gimmick pic.

A De Laurentiis Entertainment Group release. Produced by Stephen F. Kesten. Direct-
ed by Richard Fleischer. Screenplay, Tim Met-
calfe, Miguel Tejada-Flores, Rudy De Luca;
camera (Technicolor), Jack Cardiff; editor,
John W. Wheeler; music, Al Gorgoni; sec-
ond unit director, Vic Armstrong; stunt coor-
dinator, George Fisher; associate producer,
Kuki Lopez Rodero; production design, Jack
G. Taylor, Jr.; casting, Marily Black.
Reviewed at Cary Grant theater, Culver City,
Calif., June 5, 1987. (MPAA Rating: PG).
Running time: 95 MINS.
Rollie .... Eddie Deezen
Lollie .... Wendy Sherman
Stuart Briggs .... Rick Overton
Barbara Briggs .... Mona Lyden
Howie Briggs .... Douglas Emerson
Tugger .... Royce D. Applegate
Dotty .... Pam Matteson
Crush .... Daniel McDonald
Charity .... Penny Baker

Faith .... Tawny Feré
Hope .... LaGena Hart
Sidney Preston .... Tom Bosley
Fred .... Mack Dryden
Bob .... Jamie Alcroft
Slaughter .... Rich Hall
Officer Gretchen .... Gail Neely
Officer Quinn .... Kevin Pollak
Awful Abdul .... H.B. Hagerty
Bad Boris .... Bob Schott

Hollywood — As a promotional
gimmick, "Million Dollar Mystery"
is cynically inspired: offer people
enough money and they'll do a lot
of things, including watch a bad
film over and over again. Storyline
is so loose that this is less of a film
than a series of unrelated physical
humor sketches. The krazy komedy
hijinks of "Mystery" wear thin real
fast.

Hunt starts when on-the-lam con
man Sydney Preston (Tom Bosley)
takes a fatal bowl of chili at side-of-
the-road diner somewhere in Arizona. During one of the longest,
worst-acted, least believable dying
scenes in recent memory, Preston
utters the first clue to finding four
different stashes of $1,000,000
each, "Start at the City of the
Bridge ..."

Over the next 90 minutes, the
band of cardboard characters assembled at the diner goes in madcap
search for the lost loot, picking up
another full batch of treasure hunters along the way. This could have
been handled cleverly, but it's all
lame stuff here, as the group pursues
clues that are alternately obvious
and far-fetched, with everybody
fanning out for the search, then all
arriving at each critical spot at the
same time.

Consistent with the low-level intelligence of the characters herein is
the fate of the first $3,000,000,
which accidentally gets dropped off
a bridge, sucked into a paper shred-
der and dropped out of a hot-air
balloon in million-dollar incre-
ments. Some lucky member of the
audience, of course, will get to find
the other million, with clues supplied in the film and in accompanying literature.

While making a million bucks has
rarely been this dull, a few of the
young comedians used to flesh out
the cast provide a bit of levity. The
best is Rich Hall, as Slaughter, a
bumbling Vietnam vet who's "worn
out his Rambo tape."

Hall has a nice sense of timing,
provides the film's best physical humor and has the funniest line (when
told he's on the trail of $4,000,000,
he ponders, wide-eyed, "You know
how many lottery tickets that would
buy?").

Siblings Tugger (Royce D. Applegate) and Dotty (Pam Matteson)
are the only pair that seems believably connected, and they team with
each other and Hall for some of the
film's better scenes. Impresisonist

Kevin Pollak, who does a good
Dudley Moore, so-so Woody Allen
and too much Peter Falk, also
breathes life into a couple of bits.

Some of the action sequences here
are terrific — especially the landing
of a twin-prop Beechcraft on a
street in heavy traffic. But none of
the events or stunts are particularly
connected; film has no momentum,
no thrust, no continuity and, ultimately, nothing to recommend it
other than the possible payoff.
— Camb.

Winners Take All
(COLOR)

Overlong bike racing pic.

An Apollo Pictures release, produced in association with Embassy Home Entertainment. Produced by Christopher W. Knight,
Tom Tatum. Executive producer, David R.
Axelrod. Directed by Fritz Kiersch. Screen-
play, Ed Turner, from story by Tatum,
Knight; camera (Deluxe color), Fred V. Mur-
phy 2d; editor, Lorenzo De Stefano; music,
Doug Timm; production design, Steve P. Sar-
danis; set decoration, Tom Talbert; costume
design, Darryl Levine; sound, Gerald B.
Wolfe; assistant director, John W. Wood-
ward; action unit camera, Leo Napolitano;
casting, Caro Jones. Reviewed at the Raleigh
Studios screening room, L.A., June 2, 1987.
(MPAA Rating: PG-13). Running time: 102
MINS.
Rick Melon .... Don Michael Paul
Judy McCormick .... Kathleen York
(Bad) Billy Robinson ...... Robert Krantz
Cindy Wickes .... Deborah Richter
Wally Briskin .... Peter DeLuise
Goose Trammel .... Courtney Gains
Frank Bushing .... Paul Hampton
Johnny Rivera .... Gerardo Mejia
Bear Nolan .... Tony Longo
Peggy Nolan .... Isabel Grandin

Hollywood — "Winners Take
All" is a passable teenpic set in the
world of Supercross motorcycle racing that actually could have been a
lot worse. A few mildly surprising
plot turns of a sort one never expects in such cut-from-the-mold
products help perk the attention,
and femme lead Kathleen York
would seem to be an actress to
watch. Unfortunately, pic's running
time, too long by 20 minutes, dilutes
virtually all the goodwill the other
elements generate, and heavy concentration on racing footage will
dull the interest of all but hardcore
biker fans. Theatrical b.o. outlook
for Apollo's first release is dim.

Most of the action is assembly
line stuff about smalltown racer
Don Michael Paul who can win local events but has always run
second-best to boyhood friend
Robert Krantz, who's not a national champion and returns to town
and casually takes his old g.f. away
from Paul.

After quitting the sport in despair, Paul recharges himself and
predictably decides to take on his
buddy in a big deal Supercross race
in Dallas, which ends in very unusual fashion. Then there's yet another race, which takes forever to

end.

Paul and Krantz are abnormally
tormented for the usual bland
sports picture heroes, with Paul
suffering from an inferiority complex and Krantz suspecting that he's
on the way out at the ripe old age of
25. Deborah Richter's trampy bimbo who shuttles between the two
guys and Paul Hampton's smarmy
personal manager are viewed with a
more acutely critical eye than is the
custom in such fare.

Despite all the elaborately staged
and filmed motorbike footage,
which will do little to promote interest in the specialized sport among
the uninitiated, pic most comes to
life when Kathleen York is onscreen. As a highly intelligent and
practical racer who rides almost as
well as the men, actress displays an
appealing directness and sense of
self that puts the strutting, posing
guys to shame.

Film looks and sounds okay, but
is padded with far too much second
unit action footage for general consumption. —Cart.

Benji The Hunted
(COLOR)

Anthropomorphic saga for youngsters.

A Buena Vista release of a Walt Disney Pictures presentation, in association with Silver
Screen Partners III, of an Embark production,
in association with Mulberry Square Prods.
Produced by Ben Vaughn. Executive producer, Ed Vanston. Supervising producer, Carolyn H. Camp. Written and directed by Joe
Camp. Camera (CFI color), Don Reddy; editor, Karen Thorndike; music, Euel Box, Betty
Box; sound (Dolby), Bob Sonnamaker; art
direction, Bob Riggs, Ray Brown; Benji
trained by Bryan L. Renfro, Frank Inn, Ju-
anita Inn; cougar work, Sled Reynolds,
Gideon; wild animal trainers, Steve Martin,
Bobi Gaddy, Madeleine Cowie Klein, Rey-
nolds; assistant director-producer manager,
Carolyn Camp; associate producer, Erwin
Hearne. Reviewed at Disney screening room,
L.A., June 9, 1987. (MPAA Rating: G.) Run-
ning time: 88 MINS.
Benji .... Himself
Hunter .... Red Steagall
Newscaster .... Nancy Francis
TV cameraman .... Mike Francis
Frank Inn .... Himself

Hollywood — What actor wears
a gold chain with his name on it, has
a hairy chest and mugs shamelessly
for the camera? It's Benji the wonder dog and he's back in "Benji The
Hunted," a curious piece of work in
which animals are endowed with
human characteristics. Youngsters
under 10 may get caught up in the
story of survival in the wilds while
parents get a good snooze.

Although the film raises issues
important to kids such as the
responsibility of friendship, it is
strange to see animals making moral
choices. Even more startling is the
sight of the dog going through human thought patterns complete with
flashbacks.

Furthermore, nature is portrayed as a playground where animals have human values and live almost like people. While films have long anthropomorphized animal behavior, one can't help wondering if pictures like "Benji The Hunted" don't give kids a distorted view of nature.

Shipwrecked after a storm, Benji is like a little person finding his way in unfamiliar territory. Not only can he emote like crazy, Benji can reason. He is a philosophical pooch who can see beyond his next meal and deal with questions of the higher good.

When he discovers a brood of cougar cubs orphaned by a hunter's handywork, Benji takes them under his wing and spends most of the film finding a new home for them. He understands of course, that he must complete his mission before he can answer the call of his trainer (Frank Inn) who has come searching for him in a helicopter.

Along the way Benji and the cubs meet a big bad wolf, but Benji is able to outsmart him since it is well known that dogs have higher I.Q.'s than wolves. Besides, Benji is no ordinary household pet, but a dog who can adapt easily to the rigors of life in the great outdoors. Benji is not just another pretty face, he can really act and is trained superbly with many of his stunts truly remarkable.

Everyday logic and common sense are suspended to the point where film seems almost condescending to its target audience. Main accomplishment of writer/director Joe Camp is his ability to tell a story almost entirely without people or dialog. Music, then, becomes doubly important but will likely seem overly sweet to older ears.

Don Reddy's camerawork presents the mountains of Washington and Oregon at their pristine best, adding to the film's sanitized view of the world. It may be a dog's life, but not for Benji. —*Jagr.*

Made In Argentina
(ARGENTINE-COLOR)

A Juan José Jusid Cine production, distributed in Argentina by Mundial Films and worldwide by Progress Communications (U.S.). Directed by Jusid. Stars Luis Brandoni, Marta Bianchi, Leonor Manso, Patricio Contreras. Screenplay, Nelly Fernández Tiscornia, based on her play "Made In Lanús," based in turn on her tv play "Pals" ("Country"); camera (color), Hugo Colace; editor, Juan Carlos Macías; music, Emilio Kauderer; art direction, Luis Pedreira; costumes, Pepe Uría. Reviewed at the Vigo screening room, Buenos Aires, May 5, 1987. (Rating in Argentina: forbidden for under 13.) Running time: **86 MINS.**
Osvaldo...................Luis Brandoni
Mabel...................Marta Bianchi
Yoli....................Leonor Manso
Negro...................Patricio Contreras
Also with: Alberto Busaid, Hugo Arana, Jorge Rivera López, Mario Luciani, Gabriela Flores, Alejo García Pintos, Paula Natalicio, Debbie Better, Frank Vincent.

Buenos Aires — Already committed to festival presentations in Montreal and Moscow, this drama plays out situations familiar to many Argentines, and which undoubtedly find echos in other parts of the world. Plot concerns various questions related to the abandonment of one's country to seek a better or at least safer life abroad.

Osvaldo and Mabel, one of the two couples forming the principal foursome in this story, have left Argentina as victims of political persecution under the military juntas, and have lived in New York for 10 years. After a scene-setter filmed in Gotham, they return to Buenos Aires for the first time, under the current democracy, to meet their family, specifically Yoli and El Negro. Though Osvaldo and Mabel's exile has been political, several of the points raised in their temporary homecoming also apply to economic exile. Film could find an echo all over the Americas, where many are immigrants or descendants of recent immigrants, and in other situations worldwide where exile, emigration and immigration are topical.

Story advances mainly through a series of conversations in which bitterness wells up to varying extents, not only between the two couples, but also within each of them.

In this fictional situation with many real-life counterparts, when Osvaldo and Mabel ran into the political trouble (for opposing the military government) which forced their exile, many of their acquaintances and even relatives refused their help and pretended not to know them. A decade later, Osvaldo is tempted to forgive and return to his country for good; for his wife, "they are all dead," as far as she is concerned, and she was opposed to event returning to Argentina for a visit.

In the other couple, while El Negro dreams of leaving for the U.S. to improve the lot which has fallen to him in the Buenos Aires blue-collar suburb of Lanús, his wife Yoli favors struggling right there where their roots are.

Main characteristic of the film is a highly emotional tone, handled well. Analysis of the subject matter is good as far as it goes. The filmmakers were particularly interested in showing the potential for reconciliation in Argentine society. At some points in the development of the story, the latter appears to verge on a more vitriolic series of accusations and counter-accusations, particularly vis-a-vis third parties, but the deeper delving is avoided.

Only a line or two of dialog, for instance, deals with the once widespread feeling here that those who were persecuted were indeed ipso facto subversives. Also, not only do many who left the country accuse those who stayed of lack of support during their last days here, but many who stayed accuse those who left of having had an easy life abroad while they remained to face the hard times at home. More about this could have been aired in the present work to make its overview more complete. Still, film offers a very effective treatment of the area into which it delves: the pangs of separation, the mixed emotions of some reunions, the whys and wherefores of leaving and of returning.

The soundtrack offers some nifty blending of tango and pop music. However, it might profitably do without an end-song which unsubtly drums in the moral of the story after it has already been made quite clear. —*Olas.*

Herencia de Valientes
(Legacy Of The Brave)
(MEXICAN-COLOR)

A Películas Mexicanas release of a Producciones Hermanos Tamez production. Executive producer, Hugo Tamez. Produced by Orlando Tamez, Guadalupe Viuda de Tamez. Directed by Fernando Durán. Stars Sergio Goyri, Edgardo Gazcón. Screenplay, Carlos Valdemar, based on an idea by Arnulfo Benavides; camera (color), Agustín Lara; editor, Enrique Murillo; music, Diego Herrera, with appearance of the group Los Montaneses de Monterrey. Reviewed at Hollywood Twin theater 2, N.Y., June 5, 1987. Running time: **85 MINS.**
Marcos...................Sergio Goyri
Sosteras................Edgardo Gazcón
Daniela......................Patsy
Don Imperio...........Roberto Cañedo
Also with: Fernando Almada, Gregorio Casal, Antonio Zubiaga, Carlos Cardán, Jorge Victoria, Guillermo Lagunes, Clarissa Ahuet, Jorge Noble, Sergio Sánchez, Javier García, Jorge Fegán, Nena Delgado, Chelelo, Isaura Espinoza.

Fernando Durán's "Herencia de Valientes" (Legacy Of The Brave) is a tenuous sequel to the Mexican genre pic "Todos Eran Valientes" (They Were All Brave), starring Fernando Almada and Gregorio Casal. A few moments from the earlier film are shown in slow motion and on b&w stock during the opening credits to give reference and show passage of time. These scenes also explains screen credits given to Almada and Casal.

A few grudges from the first revenge pic are carried over to clutter up the plot here. The characters give them lip service and then find new grievances.

Plot concerns a robbery where the daughter of an important politician is taken hostage. She (Patsy) is also the cousin of pic's heroes, Marcos (Sergio Goyri) and Sosteras (Edgardo Gazcón), who work independently of the police to free her.

Film follows a strict 1-2-3 chronology with few surprises; even the violent shoot-outs lack excitement. Tech credits and acting are routine. —*Lent.*

Mi General
(My General)
(SPANISH-COLOR)

A Figaro Films production. Executive producer, Antoni Maria C. Baquer. Directed by Jaime de Armiñán. Screenplay, Armiñán, Fernando Fernán-Gómez; camera (Agfa color), Teo Escamilla; editor, José Luis Matesanz; music, Vainica Doble; sound, Joan Quilis; sets, Félix Murcia. Features Fernando Rey, Fernando Fernán-Gómez, Héctor Alterio, José Luis López Vázquez, Mónica Randall Rafael Alonso, Amparo Baró, Alvaro de Luna, Alfredo Luchetti, Joaquin Kremel, Juanjo Puigcorbé. Reviewed at Cine Palacio de la Música, Madrid, May 27, 1987. Running time: **107 MINS.**

Madrid — A group of Spanish generals, up for a special training course to initiate them into the secrets of modern warfare, comes in for plenty of good-natured ribbing in this comedy by Jaime Armiñán. (Item will be officially repping Spain at the upcoming Montreal fest.) The jesting and droll situations generate a good many laughs, but a third of the way through, pic loses its steam and seems uncertain which tack to take. At the end it doesn't take any, and the ribbing turns into monotony.

Armiñán has thrown virtually every well-known male actor in Spain into this film, all of them doing stints as armed forces generals, none of them really believable as such. This aging cluster of top brass is sent to a training course held in a comfortable army camp, in which the instructors are of lower rank, but superior knowledge.

The old-time military men, suddenly forced to return to school, try to rebel against the profs as for the most part they fail to understand the new techniques being taught them. They carry on at times like schoolchildren; their pampered existence and presumed superiority are undermined when junior officers show them their ignorance from spelling to nuclear missiles.

Two rather lame subplots concern a confrontation between one of the generals (Fernando Fernán-Gómez) with one of the instructors, since former had tyrannized latter many years earlier at a military academy; second sublot concerns another general (Héctor Alterio), who suddenly falls madly in love with a saleslady in a pharmacy.

Throughout most of pic Armiñán treads softly in his depiction of the bumbling generals. Only once, near the end, are we momentarily jolted during a ballroom scene when someone says, "The only mistake Hitler made was losing the war." Are these men, underneath, vicious Fascists? Well, for Armiñán they seem rather to be endearing anachronisms with their seemingly harmless foibles and dithering ineptitudes.

Item is well directed and thesped.

Technical credits are up to crack except but blurry direct sound. Much of the dialog, and there's plenty of it, is geared to local audiences. Offshore commercial prospects seem dim. —Besa.

Nightmare At Shadow Woods
(COLOR)

Trite slasher flick.

An FCG (Film Concept Group) release of a Marianne Kanter production. Executive producer J. W. Stanley. Produced by Kanter. Directed by John W. Grissmer. Screenplay, Richard Lamden; camera (CFI color), Richard E. Brooks; editor, Michael R. Miller; music, Richard Einhorn; production design, Jim Rule; special effects coordinator, Ed French; casting, Amanda Mackey. Reviewed at Metro Norwest theater, Detroit, June 1, 1987. (MPAA Rating: R). Running time: **84 MINS.**
Maddy . . . . Louise Lasser
Todd/Terry . . . . Mark Soper
Dr. Berman . . . . Marianne Kanter
Karen . . . . Julie Gordon
Julie . . . . Jayne Bentzen
Brad . . . . William Fuller

Detroit — A hackneyed script, wooden acting and trite plot all conspire to turn "Nightmare At Shadow Woods" into just another jiggling teen slasher movie whose box-office life likely will be as short-lived as its cast.

But some heavy-handed humor — particularly a campy performance by Louise Lasser — mixed with buckets of blood may provide this three-year-old slash-and-splash movie only now getting a theatrical run with a healthy afterlife in the undiscriminating homevid market. It was previously titled "Complex," "Slasher" and "Blood Rage."

As plots go, we've all been here before.

Terry Simmons is the evil twin who sneaks out of his mother's car at a Jacksonville, Fla., drive-in with shy brother Todd and slits someone's throat. Before anyone can find him, Terry wipes blood on his brother's face and thrusts a hatchet in his hand.

Incredulous at the gory scene, Todd remains mute and is carted off to a hospital for the criminally insane.

Ten years pass, and at a Thanksgiving dinner during which Lasser announces she and her boyfriend plan to wed, she gets a phone call that Todd has escaped.

That's cheery news to Terry, who's been a model son. Todd's escape means he can start killing again, which he does with great dispatch. No sooner has everyone finished dessert and Terry grabs a machete and gets cracking, slicing his way through his mother's boyfriend, his school chums, his

Florida neighbors and his own girlfriend.

The audience is always three scenes ahead of the picture.

Todd/Terry's homicidal maniac listlessly walks around his Jacksonville apartment complex. Of course we know he's sick because at one point he licks his blood-spattered shirt and mutters: "Boy, that's not cranberry sauce."

No one seems to notice he's off, however. Indeed, everyone is slow on the uptake in this film.

For example, Lasser's boyfriend's last words as he turns to see Todd standing before him with a machete are, "Well, look what the cat dragged in."

Only Lasser, experienced enough to realize the anemic script can only be played for laughs, has any screen presence as the mother who, despite being surrounded by murder and mayhem, remembers to tell her son to wear a sweater outside — "The blue one."

By the the time Todd and Terry meet for an anticlimactic face-off, Lasser has realized Todd's no sweetie. Only now it's too late. Just about everyone in the movie is dead, and the audience is too bored to care.—Advo.

Trein naar Holland
(Train To Holland)
(DUTCH-HUNGARIAN-DOCU-COLOR-16m)

A Nederlands Filminstituut release of a Bubofilm (Amsterdam), Mafilm (Budapest) coproduction. Executive producer, Bubo Damen. Directed by Hilde van Oostrum. Screenplay, Katalin Mészáros, Van Oostrum; camera (Eastman color), János Kende; editor, Margit Galamb; music, György Vukan; sound, György Fék; production manager, András Ozorai, Joost Schipper. Reviewed at Amsterdam Filmhuis, May 11, 1987. Running time: **75 MINS.**

Amsterdam — After both World Wars I & II Holland launched an appeal to help Hungarian children, and thousands were welcomed into Dutch families. Quite a number stayed in the Netherlands. Following the '56 Hungary uprising, Holland gave asylum to another 5,000 refugees.

Of those who stayed, a handful never assimilated, while some second-generation children even considered themselves outsiders. Of those who returned to Hungary, many felt dislocated by an adolescence spent in a different culture.

These feelings and situations appear to make ideal material for a docu, filmed under the auspices of an intergovernmental cultural treaty between Hungary and the Netherlands. However, director Hilde van Oostrum seems to mistrust chronological storytelling, and replaces it with a sketchy screenplay which mostly consists of stick-and-paste interviews. Many of these are shot

in trains, presumably on the way to Holland. As for other locations, it is often not clear whether they are in Hungary or Holland. Few of the interviewees emerge with identifiable personalities.

Van Oostrum's earlier sensitive docus on Catholic girlhood were real eye-openers for local audiences. In "Train To Holland" she builds up an intimate relationship with the people appearing in her film, but this time doesn't manage to involve the viewer, mainly because of the capricious style of storytelling. The cinematography of János Kende is excellent; the other, chiefly Hungarian, technical credits are above average. —Wall.

Nightforce
(COLOR)

Low octane rescue flick.

A Vestron Pictures presentation of a Star Cinema production. Produced by Victoria Paige Meyerink. Executive producers, Lawrence D. Foldes, Russell W. Colgin, Meyerink. Coproducers, Foldes, Colgin, William S. Weiner. Directed by Foldes. Stars Linda Blair, James Van Patten, Chad McQueen, Richard Lynch. Screenplay, Foldes, from his story; additional screenplay material, Colgin, Michael Engel, Don O'Melveny; camera (Fotokem color), Roy H. Wagner, Billy Dickson; editor, Ed Hansen; music, Nigel Harrison, Bob Rose; sound, Anson Forge, Scott A. Smith; production design, Curtis A. Schnell; production manager, Eric Barrett; stunt coordinator, Terrance James; stunt choreography, Eddy Donino; special effects coordinator, Paul Staples; second unit director, Colgin; executive in charge of production, Joe Tornatore; associate producer, Marc Dodell; casting, Brad Waisbren. Reviewed on Lightning Video vidcassette, N.Y., May 24, 1987. (MPAA Rating: R.) Running time: **82 MINS.**
Carla . . . . Linda Blair
Steve Worthington . . . . . James Van Patten
Bishop . . . . Richard Lynch
Henry . . . . Chad McQueen
Eddie . . . . Dean R. Miller
Mack . . . . James Marcel
Christy Hanson . . . . Claudia Udy
Estoban . . . . Bruce Fisher
Sen. Hanson . . . . Cameron Mitchell
Raoul . . . . Cork Hubbert
Mrs. Hanson . . . . Jeanne Baird
Bob Worthington . . . . Casey King

"Nightforce," also known during lensing as "Night Fighters," is a desultory action picture covering the corny territory of youngsters going south of the border on a mission to save their friend. Plotline was handled better in previous films "Toy Soldiers" and "Let's Get Harry."

Linda Blair is cast once again as a tough young babe, who insists on going on a commando raid with her male buddies when her best pal Christy (Claudia Udy) is kidnaped by terrorists. Her father, a U.S. senator (Cameron Mitchell), has opposed any negotiation with terrorists in his legislation and similarly, the government's "hands are tied." Led by Christy's boyfriend Steve (James Van Patten), the youngsters head for Central America.

They're getting nowhere fast when a good samaritan Vietnam vet Richard Lynch protects them against Mexican baddies and volunteers to help out. Pic sags miserably during an uneventful middle section, followed by a corny climax (Christy has become militant and picks up a gun to shoot one of her tormentors).

Okay stuntwork and Udy's randomly inserted nude scenes are the main diversions here, while Blair capably sings a theme song over the opening and closing credits. —Lor.

---

5 Nacos Asaltan a Las Vegas
(5 Nerds Take Las Vegas)
(MEXICAN-COLOR)

A Películas Mexicanas release of a Víctor Films production. Executive producer, Víctor Herrera Z. Produced by Salvador Barrajas. Directed by Alfredo B. Crevenna. Screenplay, Eduardo de la Peña, J.A. Rodríguez; camera (color), Juan Manuel Herrera, Pedro Ramírez; editor, Roberto Benet Portillo; music, Luis Alcaraz. Reviewed at Hollywood Twin theater 2, N.Y., May 14, 1987. Running time: **87 MINS.**
Pelonchas . . . . Eduardo de la Peña
(Lalo el Mimo)
Chaquetas . . Sergio Ramos (El Comanche)
Babas . . . . Luis de Alba
Perrote . . . . Sergio Corona
Borras . . . . . . Guillermo Rivas (El Borras)
Peter McCabe . . . . Al Alvarez
Also with: Carmelita González, Alejandra Meyer, Queta Lavat, Carmen Araujo, Aurora Alonso.

Mexican filmmaker Alfredo B. Crevenna's latest low-budget comedy "5 Nerds Take Las Vegas" brings together a team of character actors and comedians much in the old Bowery Boys tradition, but with less ensemble success.

Storyline concerns a group of five friends who go to the U.S. illegally to rob a casino in order to escape both poverty and their wives. En route, the loose tale meanders through lots of cornball gags and one-liners.

The main joke behind all the shenanigans and hijinks is that five Mexican nerds, through their ineptitude, are capable of taking on not only Las Vegas but also the U.S. government.

Bulk of the budget appears to have gone for the location shooting at the Dunes rather than proper care of tech credits, which are barely visible.

Scripter and lead comedian Eduardo de la Peña, better known as Lalo el Mimo, has stated this pic is the first of a series of "Naco" (Nerd) comedies. Although the films may have national appeal, the humor is too local to find much international interest.—Lent.

Happy Bigamist
(HONG KONG-COLOR)

A Bo Ho Film production, released by Golden Harvest (H.K.). Presented by

Ho. Executive producers, Samo Hung, Alfred Cheung. Directed by Chan Friend. Stars Friend, Kenny Bee, Anita Miu, Patricia Ha. Camera (color), Cheung Shing-tung; art direction, Szeto Wai-hong. Reviewed at State theater, Hong Kong. May 5, 1987. Running time: **98 MINS.**
(Cantonese soundtrack with English subtitles)

Hong Kong — Chan Friend directs and stars in the title role of this compassionate and sympathetic modern Cantonese comedy. He is married to Anita Miu. One day his ex-wife (Patricia Ha) returns to Chan, then decides to stay in his house due to financial problems. There's naturally the love/hate relationship all around, not to mention the intense jealousy between the two women. To get rid of the ex-wife, Anita does some hasty matchmaking.

During the second half of the film, the role of the insecure wife is reversed. Chan instead gets irritated because of the successful matching of Kenny Bee with Patricia.

Chan's talent to amuse shines in this project. Reasonable and effective dosage of subplots keeps the audience interested, smiling and then laughing heartily with mostly colloquial verbal humor. The Chinese opera sequence where Chan confronts Bee in front of the audience is the highlight. It is apparent the duo are friends and work well together.

The warm, low-key cinematography successfully generates the desired effect of frustrations projected by the trio, then quartet of lead actors. The film grossed over $HK20,000,000. —*Mel.*

Blood Sisters
(COLOR)

Horror by-the-numbers.

A Reeltime Distributing production. Produced by Walter E. Sear. Written and directed by Roberta Findlay. Camera (Studio Film color), Findlay; editor, Sear, Findlay; music, Sear, Michael Litovsky; sound, Russell G. Fager, Felipe Borrero; art direction-costume design, Jeffrey Wallach; production manager, Sear; assistant director, John Fasano. Reviewed on Sony Video Software vidcassette, N.Y., June 6, 1987. (MPAA Rating: R.) Running time: **86 MINS.**

Linda	Amy Brentano
Alice	Shannon McMahon
Russ	Dan Erickson
Marnie	Maria Machart
Bonnie	Elizabeth Rose
Cara	Cjerste Thor
Diana	Patricia Finneran
Ellen	Gretchen Kingsley
Laurie	Brigette Cossu

Also with: Randall Walden, Brian Charlton Wrye, John Fasano.

"Blood Sisters" is a relatively new horror film (lensed last year under the generic title "Slash"), but relies upon an old-hat format that genre fans tired of at least five years ago. Pic bypassed theatrical distribution for homevideo use instead.

Filmmaker Roberta Findlay's script mixes one part "The Nesting" and one part "Hell Night:" seven pledges to the Kappa Gamma Tau sorority are escorted to a spooky old mansion by sorority sister Linda (Amy Brentano), where they have to spend the night without getting scared while searching for objects (a la scavenger hunt) as their initiation assignment. Of course, frat boys have rigged up the place with practical joke tricks.

Per a helpful prolog sequence, site was a brothel 13 years ago where a prostitute and her customer were killed by shotgun blasts. Sure enough, the traumatized little boy (locked in a room by his prostie mother during childhood) has grown up and is killing the pledges one by one. Adding a supernatural element, the girls, to varying degrees, see hallucinations in the mansion (especially in mirrors) of the ghosts of the dead prosties and their customers.

Pic consists mainly of the girls wandering around the house searching with flashlights, picked off in gory fashion. There is plenty of nudity and softcore sex (including the requisite lesbian scene) but no scares and little of interest. As a snooty pledge, Maria Machart is the prettiest actress in the cast, but none of them have challenging roles. Special effects are minor. —*Lor.*

✳✳✳✳✳✳✳✳✳✳✳✳✳✳✳✳✳✳✳✳✳✳✳
Sydney Fest Reviews
✳✳✳✳✳✳✳✳✳✳✳✳✳✳✳✳✳✳✳✳✳✳✳

Friends And Enemies
(AUSTRALIAN-DOCU-COLOR)

A Jotz production, with the assistance of the Documentary Fellowship Scheme of the Australian Film Commission. Written, produced and directed by Tom Zubrycki. Camera (color), Fabio Cavadini, Larry Zetlin; editor, Les McLaren; sound, Kieran Knox; music, Paul Charlier. Reviewed at Sydney Film Festival, June 6, 1987. Running time: **89 MINS.**

Sydney — Three years ago, Tom Zubrycki made a remarkable feature docu, "Kemira - Diary Of A Strike," which covered a coal miners' strike in a provincial Australian city, and the ultimate defeat of the miners. Now, working with a Film Commission Documentary Fellowship grant, he's back with "Friends And Enemies," which deals with another strike, this time by electricity workers in the state of Queensland, that ended in defeat for the strikers.

Setting the scene via tv news programs and interviews, Zubrycki lucidly establishes the conflict. The electricity workers waged a fight against the ultra-conservative Queensland government when, in the wake of the 1984 recession, the authorities tried to cut costs by employing private contractors in the industry. Battle lines are drawn between the strikers and their supportive families on the one hand, and Queensland Labor Minister Vince Lester on the other. Lester, who looks remarkably like evangelist Jerry Falwell, apparently thought Zubrycki and his crew were shooting a favorable pic about him, because he shamelessly hogs the camera whenever possible, especially in a bizarre scene where he visits a school and tells some tiny children it doesn't matter if they're not brainy ("I wasn't!") as long as they work hard, or again when he attends an incredibly old-fashioned debs' ball in a small country town and cheerfully dances the night away.

As for the strikers, they're a feisty lot who are gradually betrayed by their own union (which seeks inevitable compromises) and by the Labor Party machine. Its their wives and families who react most strongly to the final defeat, with at least two of the women emerging as stars of the film with their infectiously grim humor and sensible, forthright approach to the increasingly difficult situation.

End titles remind Australians that the defeat of the electrical unions in Queensland led to the resurgence of the so-called New Right, and Zubrycki's film will be much appreciated by unionists and their supporters though not, perhaps, by the Labor Party, which is supposedly pro-union. The complex issues are spelled out clearly, and the pic should be received well at overseas fests, especially those highlighting docus.

Only quibble is that, on a couple of occasions, Zubrycki's camera obviously missed catching a key moment though sound tapes kept running. These gaps are covered with rather obvious reaction shots. Also, the superb opening sequence, in which, during an annual parade of war vets, an elderly man solemnly removes his medals and tries to hand them to the Governor as a protest "against tryanny" (he's promptly arrested by police), is never referred to again; we'd like to have heard more about what happened to this particular character.

Nonetheless, these are minor quibbles. "Friends And Enemies" is a strong, gutsy, uncompromising film, like the strikers whose struggle it celebrates.—*Strat.*

Wielki Bieg
(The Big Race)
(POLISH-COLOR)

A Film Unit X-Poltel-Perspektywa Unit production. Directed by Jerzy Domaradzki. Screenplay, Feliks Falk; camera (color), Ryszard Lenczewski; editor, M. Garlicka; music, Jerzy Matula. Reviewed at Sydney Film Festival, June 7, 1987. Running time: **102 MINS.**

Stefan Budny	Tadeusz Bradecki
Radek Stolar	Jaroslaw Kopaczewski
Party Chairman	Leon Niemczyk
Wrzesien	Krzysztof Pieczynski
Janek Druciarek	Tadeusz Chudecki
Kazimierz Sosna	Tomasz Dedek
Fastyn	Cesary Harasimowicz

Sydney — The Sydney fest scored a coup in obtaining permission to screen this long-shelved (since 1981) Polish pic. "The Big Race" is a very powerful attack on Polish Communist Party officials during the Stalinist era (film is set in 1952), but also works very effectively as a suspense drama, thanks to Feliks Falk's superb screenplay and the taut direction of Jerzy Domaradzki.

Film is structured around a "Peace Run," staged as a shameless piece of anti-U.S. propaganda. Idea is that a couple of hundred loyal Party members take off on a 3-day marathon for peace, the winner to be presented with a shiny new motorbike by the country's president. Chief organizer of the run is a ruthless manipulator who'll stop at nothing to ensure the right man wins: he's the archetypal party fanatic of the period, though still a young man (and chillingly played by Krzysztof Pieczynski).

Pic focuses attention on two of the runners. Budny (Tadeusz Bradecki) wants to win because his father has been imprisoned by the regime, though innocent: Budny has written a letter he wants to hand to the President during the prize-giving. Stolar (Jaroslaw Kopaczewski), on the other hand, is a shameless opportunist: he's not a Party member, and is first seen hopping aboard a train without buying a ticket, then puffing a cigaret in a nonsmoking compartment. He's cheerfully ignorant as to Communist beliefs (he hardly knows who Karl Marx is) and bluffs his way into the race seeking the prize — and perhaps a little sex from one of the eager young Party members.

Stolar very quickly sabotages the guy who's been handpicked to win, by the simple process of stealing one of his special running shoes. Though he and Budny quarrel, he lets the latter win, not because he believes in his cause, but more as a cheerful gesture of defiance to the authorities. Ultimate irony is that Budny, the race-winner, isn't allowed anywhere near the President: his background has been discovered, and Pieczynski shamelessly and instantly rewrites history, allowing the amazed runnerup to collect the winner's prize.

Strong stuff, and no wonder the film's been under wraps for six years. It's beautifully made, with excellent performances (especially Pieczynski and Kopaczewski as the devil-may-care Stolar) and very strong direction from Domaradzki, who adds nothing extraneous and never allows the tension to drop. Indeed, the film could work with audiences not at all attuned to the riveting behind-the-scenes political drama being played out.

Now that it's finally available, "The Big Race" will be much in demand by fests, but could also attract art house attention since its theme of winners and losers and the rigging of a race — and, by extension — the rigging of a whole country — will be of universal interest. Indeed, much more can be read into the film if the "Peace Run" is seen as a political contest during the immediate post-war period.—*Strat.*

Susman
(The Essence)
(INDIAN-COLOR)

An Assn. of Corps.-Apex Societies of Handloom-Sahyadri Films production. Produced and directed by Shyam Benegal. Screenplay, Shama Zaidi; camera (color), Ashok Mehta; editor, Bhanudas Divkar; sound, S.W. Deshpande; music, Sharang Dev, Vanraj Bhatia; production design, Nitish Roy; costumes, Sushama; assistant director, Joy Roy; executive producer, S.K. Misra. Reviewed at Sydney Film Festival, June 8, 1987. Running time: **126 MINS.**

Ramulu . . . . Om Puri
Gauramma . . . . Shabana Azmi
Mandira . . . . Neena Gupta
   Also with: Kulbhushan Kharbanda, Mohan Agashe, K.K. Raina, Annu Kapoor, Harish Patel, Ila Arun.

Sydney — Ten years ago, Shyam Benegal made "Manthan," a film about a milk cooperative, financed by members of the co-op. Now he's made a similar film with "Susman," financed by handloom weavers in Andra Pradesh state. Once again, Benegal seems to be able to take an objective view of the problems faced by his financial backers, and the result is another fine film from this consistently interesting director.

Central character is Ramulu (Om Puri), a master weaver, whose silk designs are superlative works of art: it's much to the credit of this fine actor that he handles the loom as if he'd spent a lifetime working at the job. As a result of an intricate (and sometimes confusing) power play within the co-op, Ramulu is now working for the ex-secretary of the society, who has set himself up on his own. When a pushy government woman comes to the village looking for the best designs to use in an exhibition to be staged in Paris, she's

struck by Ramulu's work, and commissions his new employer to produce the silk she needs. The decision sparks off jealousies among co-op members.

Matters are further complicated when Ramulu's wife persuades him, against his better judgment, to set aside some of the valuable silk with which he's been provided to make a special wedding sari for their daughter. The deception is discovered, and Ramulu disgraced. The daughter marries and moves to a nearby town where her unfeeling husband works on a modern, mechanized, loom: but conditions there are frightful, the married couple having to share a room in a tin shed with other workers, and labor unrest provoking street riots.

Despite the bribery, cheating and stealing that is almost taken for granted in the handweaving industry, according to the film, Ramulu continues in his traditional way, eventually winding up in Paris trying to answer questions put to him by a French journalist. Benegal's theme is that the traditional artisan must not only be allowed to survive, but must live decently: for it's the master craftsman who puts "the essence of his soul" into his weaving.

"The Essence" is at its most beautiful in the sequences where we simply watch the protagonist at work, but Benegal's exposé of the behind-the-scenes maneuvers in the handloom industry will fascinate western audiences. Film is a bit long, but shot in fine, clear color, and boasting strong performances. —*Strat.*

Full Metal Jacket
(COLOR)

Powerful though familiar war & training drama.

A Warner Bros. release. Produced and directed by Stanley Kubrick. Executive producer, Jan Harlan. Coproducer, Philip Hobbs. Screenplay, Kubrick, Michael Herr, Gustav Hasford, based on the novel "The Short-Timers" by Hasford; camera (Rank color), Douglas Milsome; editor, Martin Hunter; music, Abigail Mead; production design, Anton Furst; art direction, Rod Stratford, Les Tomkins, Keith Pain; costume design, Keith Denny; sound, Edward Tise; special effects supervisor, John Evans; technical adviser, Lee Ermey; associate producer, Michael Herr; assistant director, Terry Needham; casting, Leon Vitali. Reviewed at The Burbank Studios, Burbank, June 16, 1987. (MPAA Rating: R.) Running time: **116 MINS.**

Pvt. Joker . . . . Matthew Modine
Animal Mother . . . . Adam Baldwin
Pvt. Pyle . . . . Vincent D'Onofrio
Gny. Sgt. Hartman . . . . Lee Ermey
Eightball . . . . Dorian Harewood
Cowboy . . . . Arliss Howard
Rafterman . . . . Kevyn Major Howard
Lt. Touchdown . . . . Ed O'Ross
   Also with: John Terry, Kirk Taylor, Ian Tyler, Papillon Soo Soo, Tan Hung Francione, Costas Dino Chimino, Peter Merrill, Kierson Jecchinis, John Stafford, Gary Landon Mills, Ngoc Lee, Leanne Hong, Gil Kopel, Herbert Norville, Bruce Boa, Tim Colceri, Sal Lopez, Peter Edmund, Marcus D'Amico, Keith Hodiak, Nguyen Phong.

Hollywood — After a 7-year silence and amidst the usual atmosphere of secrecy, speculation and high expectations, Stanley Kubrick has delivered "Full Metal Jacket," an intense, schematic, superbly made Vietnam War drama that will impress some and confound others.

Previewed in more than 100 theaters June 19, Warner Bros. release should open well due to advance interest, but ultimate b.o. will depend upon whether "Platoon" has created a deep new market for Vietnam War stories or, in fact, has stolen the new film's thunder.

As has been the case with all of the director's films since "2001: A Space Odyssey," initial reaction will be strongly divided; anyone anticipating the ultimate Vietnam trip, a Southeast Asian "Dr. Strangelove" or a topper to "Platoon" will surely be let down. As always with Kubrick, it is best to throw all preconceived ideas to the wind.

Kubrick has dealt with the futility and horrors of war on numerous occasions in the past, notably in "Fear And Desire" (his little-seen first film), "Paths Of Glory" and "Dr. Strangelove," and if there is a way in which "Full Metal Jacket" does disappoint, it is in the familiarity of the basic combat genre material. Most of what's on view here has been seen before in some way or another, and pic is perhaps lacking that extra philosophical dimension that has marked Kubrick's greatest films.

But this graphic portrait of two levels of hell on earth generates considerable power via many riveting sequences, extraordinary dialog and first-rate performances.

Like the source material, Gustav Hasford's ultra-violent novel "The Short-Timers," Kubrick's picture is strikingly divided into two parts. First 44 minutes are set exclusively in a Marine Corps basic training camp, while remaining 72 minutes (including end credits) embrace events surrounding the 1968 Tet Offensive and skirmishing in the devastated city of Hue.

Always a great screen subject, basic training has surely never had its essential mechanics and motivations stripped so bare as they are here. Boldly and with considerable dark humor, entire section illustrates how young men are systematically dehumanized and refashioned as killing machines, and reminds somewhat of "A Clockwork Orange" in its portrait of the reprogramming of young men.

Gradually emerging through it all are the irreverent Pvt. Joker (Matthew Modine) and the earnest Cowboy (Arliss Howard), but engaging the D.I.'s special interest is the overweight simpleton Pvt. Pyle (Vincent D'Onofrio), whom the sergeant bullies and ridicules mercilessly until the kid goes over the edge. Kubrick acidly demonstrates how successfully the Marine machine transforms boys into killers, and first act ends with a stunning act of violence that exposes the potential for a trained soldier to warp into an assassin.

Director's other point as he makes the jump over to Vietnam is that not even the contorted rigors of camp can prepare one for the realities of warfare; the demands of the former are a known quantity and can be fulfilled to the letter, whereas the latter is ruled by chance and uncertainty.

Film softens a bit in the midsection as Joker and Rafterman (Kevyn Major Howard), both working for Stars and Stripes, check the lay of the land. But the screws soon tighten again as Cowboy's men, joined by the journalists, slowly move through the bombed-out city and begin being picked off by sniper fire. Pic concludes with a dramatic confrontation that echoes the climax of the first section.

Brilliantly staged and time, protracted finale recalls "Paths Of Glory" in its searing delineation of war's awful essentials, but Kubrick's dispassionate calculation also gives the sequence the dimensions of a fateful chess game in which all are disposable pawns. The director's assessment of human beings and the world they have wrought remains low.

Much wonderment was devoted to how Kubrick, who won't fly and supposedly hasn't left the British Isles in some 20 years, would recreate the Vietnam War in the environs of London. He has done so with precise details but on a limited scale, with just a few soldiers running and hiding among the ruins in an urban conflict.

In this regard, production designer Anton Furst has amazingly fashioned a cohesive alien world, while lenser Douglas Milsome, moving up from second unit cameraman, has helped his boss obtain a subdued, slightly desaturated look dominated by greens, blues and gray skies. Film is, unsurprisingly, technically impeccable.

While it doesn't develop a particularly strong narrative line, script by Kubrick, Michael ("Dispatches") Herr and novelist Hasford is loaded with vivid, outrageously vulgar military vernacular that contributes heavily to the film's power.

Performances by the all-male cast (save for a couple of Vietnamese hookers) are also exceptional. Surrounded on one side by humorously macho types such as Adam Baldwin's Animal Mother and Dorian Harewood's Eightball, and on the other by less secure soldiers such as Cowboy and Rafterman, Modine holds the center effectively by embodying both what it takes to survive in the war and a certain omniscience.

But most memorable of all, from the opening section, are Vincent D'Onofrio as the blubbery recruit who snaps from sweet dummy to madman, and Lee Ermey, a former Marine and Vietnam vet who doubles as technical adviser here (a role he filled on "Apocalypse Now," "The Boys In Company C" and "Purple Hearts") and is mesmerizing as the D.I. who never speaks beneath a shout. One shudders to think of Kubrick making him do 50 takes of all his scenes.—Cart.

Spaceballs
(COLOR)

Unfunny 'Star Wars' parody arrives way too late.

An MGM/UA Communications release from MGM Pictures of a Brooksfilms presentation. Produced by Mel Brooks. Co-producer Ezra Swerdlow. Directed by Brooks. Screenplay, Brooks, Thomas Meehan, Ronny Graham; camera (Metrocolor), Nick McLean; editor, Conrad Buff 4th; additonal editing, Nicholas C. Smith; music, John Morris; production design, Terence Marsh; art direction, Harold Michelson; Diane Wager; set design, Peter Kelly, Richard McKenzie, Jacques Valin; set decoration, John Franco, Jr.; sound (Dolby), Randy Thom, Gary Rydstrom; special visual effects, Apogee; visual effects supervisor, Peter Donen; costumes, Donfeld; assistant director, Dan Kolsrud; production manager, Robert Latham Brown; stunt coordinator, Richard Warlock; casting, Bill Shepard, Lynn Stalmaster & Associates, David Rubin. Reviewed at Filmland screening room, Culver City, Calif., June 18, 1987.

(MPAA Rating: PG.) Running time: **96 MINS.**
President Skroob .... Mel Brooks
Yogurt .... Mel Brooks
Barf .... John Candy
Dark Helmet .... Rick Moranis
Lone Starr .... Bill Pullman
Princess Vespa .... Daphne Zuniga
King Roland .... Dick Van Patten
Colonel Sandurz .... George Wyner
Radar Technician ..... Michael Winslow
Voice of Dot Matrix .... Joan Rivers
Dot Matrix .... Lorene Yarnell
John Hurt .... Himself
    Also with: Sal Viscuso, Ronny Graham, Jm J. Bullock, Leslie Bevis, Jim Jackman, Denise Gallup, Dian Gallup, Sandy Helberg, Jack Riley, Tom Dreesen, Rudy DeLuca, Deanna Booher, voice of Dom DeLuise.

Hollywood — Mel Brooks will do anything for a laugh. Unfortunately, what he does in "Spaceballs," a misguided parody of the "Star Wars" adventures, isn't very funny. Brooks, the quintessential ethnic joker, gears his humor here for a young crowd and misses the mark by light years. Older folks probably won't be amused either.

While the film misfires on all cylinders, it may have been irrevocably wrong from its very conception. Whereas Western and horror films were ripe for parody in "Blazing Saddles" and "Young Frankenstein," the charm of "Star Wars" was that it never took itself too seriously and existed as almost a self-parody to begin with.

In addition, many of the obvious "Star Wars" jokes already have been exploited elsewhere and writers Brooks, Thomas Meehan and Ronny Graham fail to come up with much that is original or innovative. One expects silliness from Brooks, but "Spaceballs" beats the gags into the ground with a rubber chicken.

On a story level, film is also dismal and barely keeps going as it interupts itself with constant asides and non sequiturs.

After every joke pic practically winks at the audience. Brooks also has peppered the script with industry in-jokes about videocassettes and merchandising that are sure to be wasted on the "Star Wars" audience and only add to the film's self-consciousness. At its worst "Spaceballs" displays a colossal ego at work and humor better left to home movies.

Picture also suffers from the absence of the Brooks stock company although Dom DeLuise does the voice for a giant pizza-like creature. As suitably moronic as Rick Moranis is as Dark Helmet, no one quite approaches the satiric edge of Madeline Kahn or the lovable dumbness of Gene Wilder.

Instead there is Bill Pullman as Lone Starr and Daphne Zuniga as Princess Vespa, former a composite of Harrison Ford and Mark Hamill, latter a Carrie Fisher clone. Pullman's partner is John Candy as Barf, a half-man, half-dog creature who is his own best friend. Equipped with a constantly wagging tale and furry sneakers, Barf is one of the better comic creations here.

The plot about the ruthless race of Spaceballs out to steal the air supply from the planet Druidia is more clichéd than the original. Brooks turns up in the dual role of President Skroob of Spaceballs and the all-knowing, all-powerful Yogurt, who passes on the power of the Schwartz to young Lone Starr.

Production does offer some amusing sight gags including the first look at the ridiculously enormous Spaceball spacecraft and Lone Starr's flying Winnebago, but other special effects are inferior to the original and provide little fireworks. Brooks' direction is far too static to suggest the sweeping style of the "Star Wars" epics and pic more closely resembles Flash Gordon programmers.

Other tech credits are well done, highlighted by Terence Marsh's daffy production design and Donfeld's ridiculous costumes, but aside from a few isolated laughs "Spaceballs" is strictly not kosher. — Jagr.

Stripped To Kill
(COLOR)

Low-budget thriller delivers.

A Concorde Pictures release. Produced by Andy Ruben, Mark Byers, Matt Leipzig. Executive producer, Roger Corman. Directed by Katt Shea Ruben. Screenplay, Katt Shea Ruben, Andy Ruben; camera (Film House Group color), John Leblanc; editor, Zach Staenberg; music, John O'Kennedy; sound, Ann Krupa, Jan Brodin; sound design, David Yewdall; art direction, Paul Raubertas; choreography, Ted Lin; production manager, Clif Gordon; assistant director, Byers; special effects makeup, Michael Westmore; special effects, Roger George; stunt coordinator, John Stewart. Reviewed at Cine 2 theater, N.Y. June 19, 1987. (MPAA Rating: R.) Running time: **84 MINS.**
Cody/Sunny .... Kay Lenz
Sgt. Heineman .... Greg Evigan
Ray .... Norman Fell
Fanny .... Tracy Crowder
Zeena .... Athena Worthey
Cinnamon .... Carlye Byron
Dazzle .... Debbie Nassar
Brandy .... Lucia Nagy Lexington
Angel .... Michelle Foreman
Eric/Roxanne .... Pia Kamakahi
Mobile entrepreneur .... Tom Ruben
Shirl .... Diana Bellamy
Pocket .... Peter Scranton
    Also with: Brad David, J. Bartell, Andy Ruben, Debra Lamb.

"Stripped To Kill" is a solid little thriller set in the world of topless dancing. Nearing the end of its regional theatrical run, pic is likely to do well in the homevid market on the basis of its exploitation angles.

Kay Lenz stars as a policewoman in L.A. assigned by her partner Greg Evigan to go undercover, posing as a stripper to catch a serial killer of dancers at a local club. She gets a dancing job from club owner Norman Fell after winning an amateur striptease contest there, with help from an audience stacked with off-duty cops.

Scripters Katt Shea Ruben (former actress who also makes her helming debut here) and Andy Ruben play fair with the audience, offering legitimate clues and red herrings regarding the killer's identity. Solution to the whodunit is ingenious; though very difficult to guess even by the alert viewer it is satisfying.

Lenz, firmly established as a sexy screen persona 15 years ago in her debut in Clint Eastwood's "Breezy," is extremely effective here, faking several stripteases which substitute acting for professional dancing. Director Ruben stylizes the frequent strip sequences, using stylish pastel lighting effects and elaborate, acrobatic choreography by Ted Lin to create more traditional burlesque routines than the strictly sex approach. A cast of mainly pro dancers perform well; ditto support roles by Evigan and Fell plus a funny turn by Diana Bellamy as a taciturn lady at police headquarters. —Lor.

Equalizer 2000
(COLOR)

Tame futuristic Western shot in the Philippines.

A Concorde Pictures production and release. Produced by Leonard Hermes. Directed by Cirio H. Santiago. Screenplay, Frederick Bailey, from story by Bailey, Joe Mari Avellana; camera (color), Johnny Araojo; editor, Pacifico Sanchez Jr.; musical director, Edward Achacoso; sound, Roly Ruta; production design, Avellana; art direction, Ronnie Cruz; production manager, Aurelio Navarro; assistant director, Jose Torres; set design, Boyet Camaya; makeup, Tersa Mercader; production consultant, Matt Leipzig. Reviewed on MGM/UA Home Video vidcassette, N.Y., June 10, 1987. (MPAA Rating: R.) Running time: **79 MINS.**
    With: Richard Norton, Corinne Wahl, William Steis, Robert Patrick, Frederick Bailey, Rex Cutter, Warren McLean, Peter Shilton, Dan Gordon, Ramon D'Salva, Vic Diaz, Bobbie Greenwood.

The Equalizer 2000 of the title of this Philippines-shot actioner appears to be the quick-firing automatic weapon that all those in the picture seem to want to get hold of, since it is far more effective than the conventional pistols and such that are in adequate supply. Guns and gasoline are the motivating factors in this dull Western set in a sun-scorched Alaska "100 years after the nuclear winter," as the narrator ominously explains at the outset. Unoriginal pic wouldn't exist had there never been a "Mad Max," and it's only showing up now on vidcassette, having skipped the theatrical scene.

Prolific director Cirio H. Santiago gets right into the action, which offers a "rebel wind" of speed demon desperados trying for the umpteenth time to overthrow The Ownership, group that controls (hordes) the supply of gasoline and other things needed to gain upward mobility in this harsh landscape. Pic is a laugher from the start, since viewer will be more interested in where the protagonists got those muscular physiques, chic black leather garb and blow-dry hairdos.

Richard Norton shows up as a maverick, softspoken loner out for his own survival, and before long he's hooked up with Corinne Wahl (née Alphen, Penthouse model and actress now married to actor Ken Wahl). She's on the run after having swindled some rebels in a gas-for-fresh water trade. The pair (who don't quite make it as hero types) hole up in Wahl's cave lair, where she shows Norton (who has the macho name Slade) her weapon, the titular device. Norton fondles it and slowly repairs and streamlines it utilizing the myriad lathes and drill presses with which the cave is equipped. Scene is shot in loving montage style to hilarious effect.

Norton, an Aussie with a Chuck Norris beard, and Wahl, looking mighty good in tight leather slacks and halter top, have a coyly shot lovemaking scene that had it been the least bit explicit would have been this pic's lone highlight.

Norton and Wahl, two of the actors who aren't dubbed into English (but post-synched anyway) give competent performances, though Norton is too sullen throughout. Pic has an overall clean look, due to its being shot mainly outdoors and in bright sunshine. — Gerz.

Innerspace
(COLOR)

Smashing miniaturization comedy headed for a huge b.o.

A Warner Bros. release of a Steven Spielberg presentation from Amblin Entertainment of a Guber-Peters production. Produced by Michael Finnell. Coproducer, Chip Proser. Executive producers, Spielberg, Peter Guber, Jon Peters. Coexecutive producers, Frank Marshall, Kathleen Kennedy. Directed by Joe Dante. Screenplay, Jeffrey Boam, Proser, from story by Proser; camera (Technicolor), Andrew Laszlo; editor, Kent Beyda; music, Jerry Goldsmith; production design, James H. Spencer; art direction, William Matthews; set design, Judy Cammer, Gene Nollman; set decoration, Richard C. Goddard; costume design, Rosanna Norton; sound (Dolby), Ken King; visual effects supervisor, Dennis Muren; special makeup effects, Rob Bottin; assistant director, Pat Kehoe; second unit action director, Glenn Randall Jr.; second unit camera, David Worth; casting, Mike Fenton, Jane Feinberg, Judy Taylor. Reviewed at the Avco Cinema, L.A., June 20, 1987. (MPAA Rating: PG.) Running time: **120 MINS.**
Lt. Tuck Pendelton . . . . Dennis Quaid
Jack Putter . . . . Martin Short
Lydia Maxwell . . . . Meg Ryan
Victor Scrimshaw . . . . Kevin McCarthy
Dr. Margaret Canker . . . . Fiona Lewis
Mr. Igoe . . . . Vernon Wells
The Cowboy . . . . Robert Picardo
Wendy . . . . Wendy Schaal
Pete Blanchard . . . . Harold Sylvester
Dr. Greenbush . . . . William Schallert
Mr. Wormwood . . . . Henry Gibson
Ozzie Wexler . . . . John Hora
Dr. Niles . . . . Mark L. Taylor
Lydia's Editor . . . . Orson Bean
Duane . . . . Kevin Hooks
Dream Lady . . . . Kathleen Freeman
Messenger . . . . Archie Hahn
Cab Driver . . . . Dick Miller
Man In Restroom . . . . Kenneth Tobey

Hollywood — "Innerspace" has b.o. smash written all over it. An archetypal Steven Spielberg summer entertainment directed by Joe Dante with his own special brand of fun, visual roller coaster serves up the right blend of comedy, adventure and the fantastic to keep packing audiences in at least through Labor Day.

Using the same premise as the 1966 sci-fier "Fantastic Voyage," pic has a miniaturized Dennis Quaid injected into the body of Martin Short, but does entirely different things with the situation, as both Quaid and Short are subjected to equal amounts of outrageous danger.

Hot dog Air Force flyer Quaid is prepared at the outset to be shrunken and pilot a tiny craft through the bloodstream of a laboratory rabbit. Evildoers are on to the unprecedented experiment and, after a hectic chase around Silicon Valley, the syringe bearing the fearless voyager finally implants itself in the behind of Short, a hapless grocery clerk.

Filmmakers' ingenuity quickly begins asserting itself. As Quaid travels through different parts of the unsuspecting shnook's body and speaks to him over his radio, Short believes he's going crazy. "Somebody help me, I'm possessed!" he cries, before finally accepting what's happened to him.

In the meantime, the baddies, representing amoral multinational interests willing to sell the miniaturization technique to the highest bidder, are in hot pursuit of Short, since Quaid carries with him the missing piece of device's mechanism. As Quaid can see the outside world through Short's eyes on a video monitor, he directs his meek host on how to cope with physical threats in a macho way.

At the same time, Short enlists the help of Quaid's girlfriend, reporter Meg Ryan, to whom he quickly takes a shine and, to the growing annoyance of the helpless Quaid, he starts to romance. In all respects, pic's plot twists and turns managed with great cleverness and ultimately dovetail smoothly.

Some major comic adventure and special effects set pieces are particularly successful, notably Short's escape from a speeding refrigerated truck into a car alongside, his computerized plastic surgery that amazingly transforms him into a villain and back again, the partial minia-turization of arch-fiends Kevin McCarthy and Fiona Lewis to the size of midgets (or gremlins), and a battle to the death between Quaid and an assassin conducted above a cauldron of acid in Short's stomach.

Quaid is engagingly reckless and gung-ho as the pioneer into a new dimension, although he is physically constrained in his little capsule for most of the running time. Short has infinitely more possibilities and makes the most of them, coming into his own as a screen personality as a mild-mannered little guy who rises to an extraordinary situation. Meg Ryan is game as the spirited doll both men hanker for, and supporting cast is filled out with a good assortment of familiar faces.

Director Dante keeps the action moving at a dynamic by not exhausting clip, and never lets an opportunity for comedy slip by. The one major sequence in Jeffrey Boam and Chip Proser's script that doesn't work at all has Quaid temporarily transferred through the flimsiest of devices, into Ryan's body and discovering she's pregnant, but otherwise, writers and director have honed the material expertly for maximum entertainment value.

Technical aspects all have the expected Spielberg-ILM expertise.
—Cart.

Sakura Killers
(U.S.-TAIWANESE-COLOR)

A Bonaire Films production. (World sales, Overseas Filmgroup.) Produced by K.L. Lim (Taiwan), Roy McAree (U.S.). Directed by Richard Ward. (U.S. sequences written and directed by Dusty Nelson.) Screenplay, David Marks; camera (United color), Alan Brennecke (U.S.), Taiwan footage uncredited; editor, uncredited; music, William Scott; assistant director, Rosemary Brennecke (U.S.), Nimmo Gasrarri (Taiwan); sound, Tom Galt (U.S.). Reviewed on Key Video vidcassette, N.Y., May 3, 1987. (No MPAA Rating.) Running time: **87 MINS.**
The Colonel . . . . Chuck Connors
Sonny . . . . Mike Kelly
Dennis . . . . George Nichols
Karen . . . . Cara Casey
Manji . . . . Manji Otsuki
  Also with: John Ladalski, Brian Wong, Thomas Lung.

An okay martial arts picture, "Sakura Killers" is a bit schizophrenic in that it consists of two separate sets of footage, shot by different filmmakers in Taiwan and the U.S., joined together in a convincing whole.

Chuck Connors is featured in the U.S. shoot (written and directed by Dusty Nelson), wearing his old Brooklyn Dodgers warmup jacket while fiddling with a modern version of his rifle (not the trademark flip-cocking model of his "The Rifleman" tv series). He sends Mike Kelly and George Nichols on a mission to Taiwan to retrieve a stolen videotape of genetic engineering experiments, lifted from a secret scientific installation by ninjas.

Athletic team of Kelly & Nichols discover that a Japanese organization of Sakura killers is behind the action and planning to sell the U.S. secrets to the Soviets. Fortunately, the Yanks get intensive training from a martial arts master.

Action scenes are well done, though the usual exaggeration of sound effects detracts. William Scott's energetic musical score is a plus, as are several attractive women in the cast. Sound recording for the U.S. footage is fine, but the post-synching of the Taiwan segments is crude.—Lor.

Adventures In Babysitting
(COLOR)

Strained teen comedy should score with target audience.

A Buena Vista release from Touchstone Pictures, in association with Silver Screen Partners III, of a Hill/Obst production. Produced by Debra Hill, Lynda Obst. Directed by Chris Columbus. Screenplay, David Simkins; camera (DeLuxe color), Ric Waite; editor, Fredric Steinkamp, William Steinkamp; music, Michael Kamen; production design, Todd Hallowell; casting, Janet Hirshenson, Jane Jenkins; art direction, Gregory Keen; set decoration, Dan May; sound (Dolby), David Lee. Reviewed at Westwood Egyptian theater, L.A., June 19, 1987. (MPAA Rating: PG-13.) Running time: **99 MINS.**
Chris . . . . Elisabeth Shue
Sara . . . . Maia Brewton
Brad . . . . Keith Coogan
Daryl . . . . Anthony Rapp
Joe Gipp . . . . Calvin Levels
Dawson . . . . Vincent Phillip D'Onofrio
Brenda . . . . Penelope Ann Miller
Dan . . . . George Newburn
Pruitt . . . . John Ford Noonan
Mike . . . . Bradley Whitford
Gangster . . . . John Chandler

Hollywood — "Ferris Bueller" meets "Risky Business" in this teen-dream set in (where else?) the suburbs of Chicago. Chris Columbus weighs in adequately in his directorial debut, thanks to a fresh, solid lead performance from Elisabeth Shue. Yet the film can never rise above the leaden script of David Simkins and, despite some nice flashes of humor, winds up only a cut above the usual adults-chase-kids formula. Nevertheless, this is a sure bet at the boxoffice, where it will be necessary viewing for every self-respecting suburbanite under 18.

An apparently average day in the life of 17-year-old Chris Parker (Shue, much more comfortable in front of the camera than in her feature-film bow in "The Karate Kid"), starts with the mid-afternoon discovery that her dream date with main squeeze Mike (Bradley Whitford) has been cancelled. With nothing else to do, she takes an assignment babysitting for the two Anderson kids, the 15-year-old

Brad (Keith Coogan), who has a crush on her, and Sara (Maia Brewton), a little brat who idolizes comicbook hero Thor.

Trouble starts when Chris gets a call from her best friend Brenda (Penelope Ann Miller), who had decided to run away from home but then thought better of it upon reaching the bus station in downtown Chicago.

Chris heads down to the city with Keith, his best friend Daryl (Anthony Rapp) and Sara in tow and, in short order, blows out a tire, realizes she's left her purse back in the 'burbs, gets a tow from a one-armed man who drives by his house to find his wife cheating on him, sneaks into the car that's being hotwired by professional car thief Joe Gipp (Calvin Levels), and winds up in the headquarters of a national car-theft ring. The kids escape, but only after Keith's best friend Daryl steals a copy of Playboy with vital financial information in it, belonging to gangster John Chandler.

Thus the chase begins, with the action reaching the sublimely ridiculous level when the kids stumble through a back door onto the stage of a blues club. Chicago bluesman Albert Collins won't let them leave until they sing the blues, so Chris leads them through a spontaneously-composed "Babysitting Blues," that steers perilously close to being a blatantly racist stereotype. Columbus and crew pull the scene off, although Shue's high fives to the black patrons on her way out are a bit much.

There's lots more chasing, with credibility straining and straining until it completely snaps in a scene at a garage where the kids pick up the car and, eventually, race the parents home. Guess who wins that one?

While Columbus keeps the action moving, he undercuts a few scenes with a poor choice of angle sequences — a great sight gag with a 2½-pound rat mistaken for a cat gets blunted because the audience never gets a good look at the industrial-strength rodent — and he lets (or makes) his young cast overact badly in a few scenes. The only party not guilty of that is Levels, who gives a sweetly controlled performance in his bit as the young thief with a conscience.

Tech credits are mostly okay, with the film's bluesy soundtrack contrasting nicely with the WASPs' long journey into the Chicago night. —*Camb.*

Banzai Runner
(COLOR)

Routine action fare.

A Montage Film production. Produced and directed by John G. Thomas. Screenplay, Phillip I.. Harnage; camera (United color), Howard A. Wexler; editor, Drake Silliman; music, Joel Goldsmith; sound, Neil Wolfson; production manager, Bob Gibson; associate producer, Kenneth L. Hulbert; casting, Danny Travis. Reviewed on Vidmark Entertainment vidcassette, N.Y., June 12, 1987. (No MPAA Rating.) Running time: **86 MINS.**

Bill Baxter	Dean Stockwell
Beck Baxter	John Shepherd
Traven	Charles Dierkop
Shelley	Dawn Schneider
Maysie	Ann Cooper
Osborne	Barry Sattles
Syszek	Billy Drago

Also with: Rick Fitts, Mary Lou Kenworthy, John Wheeler, Eric Mason, Kim Knode.

"Banzai Runner" is an utterly conventional action picture, symptomatic of the new breed of production which reflects limited aspirations. Good performance by name actor in the cast, Dean Stockwell, is the drawing card and homevideo shelves the destination.

With the film vaguely resembling confrere Dennis Hopper's forgettable 1981 pic "King Of The Mountain," Stockwell toplines as a California state trooper frustrated by local rich guys, dubbed "runners," who drive their costly, souped-up cars at night at speeds approaching 200 mph in informal races. Stockwell's brother was killed, run off the road by one of these dudes, and he's frustrated by official opposition which prevents him from souping up the cop cars to pursue the offenders.

Rather, his new boss Eric Mason wants him to concentrate on drunk drivers. After a speeding incident and another run-in construed as harrassment of a "runner," Stockwell is fired and gets a new job working undercover to bust drug dealers for the federal government. Unconvincing plot contrivance has him getting into a race with two runners who also are the local drug kingpins and one of whom, Billy Drago (Frank Nitti in "The Untouchables" feature), killed his brother.

There's some good, high-speed chasing en route to the predictable finish, but filmmaker John G. Thomas fails to introduce interesting variations on the timeworn theme of a cop's problems. Stockwell is convincing both behind the wheel and in dramatic scenes, but the supporting cast is generally too low-key. Tech credits are standard. Unrated pic is extremely tame, devoid of nudity or other exploitation elements. — *Lor.*

Keeping Track
(CANADIAN-COLOR)

A Shapiro Entertainment release of a Telescene (Keeping Track) Prods. production, with the participation of Telefilm Canada. Executive producer, Neil Léger. Produced by Robin Spry, Jamie Brown; line producer, Bob Presner. Directed by Spry. Stars Michael Sarrazin, Margot Kidder. Screenplay, Brown, from story by Spry, Brown; camera (Sonolab color), Ron Stannett; editor, Diann Ilnicki; music, Ben Low; sound, Don Cohen; production design, Michel Proulx; production manager, Peter Bray; stunt coordinator, Dave Rigby; casting, Elite Prods., Nadia Rona. Reviewed on Charter Entertainment vidcassette, N.Y., June 11, 1987. (MPAA Rating: R.) Running time: **102 MINS.**

Daniel Hawkins	Michael Sarrazin
Claire Tremayne	Margot Kidder
Royle Wishert	Alan Scarfe
Capt. McCullough	Ken Pogue
Double Agent	John Boylan
Chuck	Vlasta Vrana
Covington	Donald Pilon
Shanks	James D. Morris

Robin Spry's "Keeping Track" is a fast-paced, engrossing little thriller, head and shoulders above comparable pictures being made recently. Benefitting from the comfortable teaming of Margot Kidder and Michael Sarrazin, pic is a treat, though relegated to the now-standard limited theatrical release ahead of homevideo distribution.

Sarrazin portrays a cocksure Montreal tv anchorman thrust into an adventure straight out of "The 39 Steps" when he and banking analyst Kidder witness a murder on a train headed for New York. Soon not only the killers are after them but also the bank, police and government. Sarrazin is determined to get to the bottom of the matter but it is being covered up due to national security implications, as the KGB is involved with stealing U.S. technology. Film's McGuffin is a computer chip that will create a cyborg with artificial intelligence and possibly upset the balance of power depending upon who gets possession of it.

Spry and his writer-coproducer Jamie Brown maintain a breathless pace, with the usual mechanical transition footage and extraneous filler left out of an action picture for a change. The stars, particularly Kidder in a followup to her Disney "Trenchcoat" sort of role, are bright and breezy and tech credits are solid down the line. —*Lor.*

T. Dan Smith
(BRITISH-COLOR)

An Amber Film in association with the British Film Institute and Channel 4 Television. Produced, written and crewed by members of Amber Films: Elaine Drainville, Vivienne Dawson, Dave Eadington, Richard Gras, Ellin Hare, Sirkka-Liisa Konnttinen, Pat McCarthy, Murray Martin, Jane Neatrour, Lorna Powell, Peter Roberts, Ray Stubbs, Judith Tomlinson, Steve Trafford; music, Ray Stubbs. Reviewed at New Crown preview theater, London, May 20, 1987. Running time: **85 MINS.**

T. Dan Smith	Himself
Jack Johnston	Himself
Ken Sketheway	Himself
Dennis Skinner	Himself
George Vickers	Himself
Alan Deal	Art Davies
Jack Cross	Dave Hill
Jeremy Haudsley-Long	Christopher Northey

London — In the '60s, T. Dan Smith was a major political figure in the northern British city of Newcastle, but in 1974 he was sentenced to six years in jail for corruption. "T. Dan Smith," which looks at both the man and the myth, figures to have little b.o. impact anywhere.

Amber Films is a filmmaking collective based in the north of England whose mandate is to produce "documents" of working class life in the north of England. "T. Dan Smith" links a documentary aspect with interviews with Smith and some of his contemporaries, and a fictional element which reflects Smith's downfall.

The complicated structure of interweaving strands proves a bit too much for the filmmakers, who are also impaired by some rther wooden acting and a script that unconvincingly tries to imply a devious and shadowy world.

The documentary aspect of the film is far more interesting that its political thriller side, and T. Dan Smith himself comes across as a slightly sad figure who refuses to accept he did wrong.

Smith claims political coverups and Intelligence collusion, but interesting though they are, they remain just claims as no attempt is made to make this a rounded film taking in the other side of the argument.

Technical credits are okay, though some of the camerawork and writing occasionally lapses into pretension. There is no denying "T. Dan Smith" was made by a group of people passionately committed to what they believe in. —*Adam.*

En el Nobre de Dios
(In The Name Of God)
(SPANISH-CHILEAN-DOCU-COLOR-16m)

A Television Española (Spanish Television) presentation of a Santiago Cinematográfica and Patricio Guzmán production. Produced by Arturo Feliú. Written and directed by Guzmán. Camera (color, 16m), Jaime Reyes, José Cobos, Germán Maliz; second unit camera, Hernán Castro; editor, Luciano Beriatria; music, José Antonio Quintano; sound, Mario Diaz. Reviewed at private screening room, Santiago, Chile, June 5, 1987. Running time: **97 MINS.**

Santiago — Well known for his "Battle Of Chile" trilogy, which received considerable international exposure and press coverage during the 1970s, Patricio Guzmán returned to his native country in 1986 to shoot this docu for Spanish tv. Although arrested shortly after the 1973 coup and interned for some weeks at the National Stadium, Guzmán did not leave the country via asylum at a foreign embassy, but rather emigrated on his own. This technicality probably explains why, unlike Miguel Littin and other filmmakers, Guzmán was never black-listed among the exiles who were forbidden to reenter the country.

"In The Name Of God" deals with the role of the Roman Catholic Church in Chile during the years following the coup, with special emphasis on its human rights stance. In this field the Church, mainly through its Vicarage of Solidarity, has been extremely active over the years, which obviously did not make it popular with the government. In fact, the young doctor and lawyer who, in the docu's early part, explain the vicarage's workings, are later arrested and jailed.

To structure his film, Guzmán continuously alternates certain basic elements: police repression with truncheons, tear gas and water cannons; testimonials by relatives of missing persons, both about their own plight and the assistance they receive from the Church; priests at the grassroots level and their work, including Pierre Dubois, a French clergyman, who was later expelled from the country. Slum dwellers talk about their way of life and their relationship with the Church and contrast is provided through official ceremonies with military chaplains officiating, and closeup views of General Pinochet attending mass. Furthermore, half a dozen bishops and Cardinal Silva Henríquez (though not the more conservative Cardinal Primate Francisco Fresno) are questioned on the human rights situation, the Church's relations with the Government and other touchy subjects on which these ecclesiastical authorities speak out firmly.

Guzmán provides a lively and technically solid view of a complex subject that is up to the standard of his earlier work. "In The Name Of God" should obtain festival exposure and also become of interest on the nontheatrical market.
—*Amig.*

Juana la Cantinera
(Juana The Saloon Keeper)
(MEXICAN-COLOR)

A Películas Mexicanas release of a Producciones Fílmicas Rolo production. Executive producer, Pedro Rodríguez Garay. Produced, written and directed by Pepe Loza. Camera (color), Antonio Ruiz; editor, Enrique Murillo; music, Javier del Río, with appearance of the groups Los Caminantes, Los Hermanos Banda de Salamanca, Javier Lozano, Los Clásicos Norteños and Casino Shanghai with Ulalume. Reviewed at Hollywood Twin theater 2, N.Y., May 29, 1987. Running time: **91 MINS.**
Juana . . . . Rossy Mendoza
Pancho . . . . Alvaro Zermeno
Also with: Ana Luisa Peluffo, Federico Villa, Ivonne Govea, Pedro Rodríguez (Fufurufu), Yolanda Ciani, Jaime Reyes, Fernando Loza, Viviane Salazar, Ireida Márquez, Cari Conesa.

The Mexican pic "Juana la Cantinera" (Juana The Saloon Keeper),

produced, written and directed by Pepe Loza, is a curious grabbag of diverse scenes spotlighting, with confused intentions, some of the ills of contemporary society.

Despite the title, the film is not about Juana (Rossy Mendoza) and her saloon. She and her story are only one small part of a larger scheme that includes approximately 20 separate main characters enmeshed within seven different storylines of which only a couple overlap. These tales are shuffled together haphazardly and are introduced, picked up, developed and dropped in random fashion with all loose ends tied up by pic's end.

These stories include: an illegitimate juvenile delinquent who is brought closer to his mother after he is arrested for manslaughter; a young woman who had been raped later gets revenge on her attackers; an infertile macho's wife is forced into infidelity when her husband demands she have a child as proof of his manhood, etc.

While most of these tales are realistically presented, there are some quirks. The love story of an ex-con played by Pedro Rodríguez (Fufurufu) and a widow (Ana Luisa Peluffo) is handled like a musical comedy with Fufurufu singing and dancing. Also, somehow figuring into this is a ghost story about a macho who abandons a woman when she becomes pregnant. He meets her a year later and they set up a date, only to be informed by her parents that the girl had died during an illegal abortion.

Tech credits are strictly bargain basement throughout with various scenes using only a one camera setup. The lighting is irregular and sound quality generally poor.

As an entertainment, "Juana The Saloon Keeper" doesn't work. The separate sections do not flow and the individual stories are too sketchy. Characterization never goes beyond cliché and, overall, the structure is too confusing to be effective. — *Lent.*

Thunder Warrior 2
(ITALIAN-COLOR)

A Trans World Entertainment presentation of a Fulvia Films Intl. production. Directed by "Larry Ludman" (Fabrizio De Angelis). Screenplay, David Parker Jr., "Ludman" (De Angelis); camera (Technicolor), Sergio D'Offizi; editor, Albert Moryalty; music, Walter Ritz; assistant director, Mary Keller; art direction, Alexander M. Colby; production manager, Marina De Tiberiis; stunt coordinator, Alain Petit; dialog director, Arne Elsholtz. Reviewed on TWE vidcassette, N.Y., June 9, 1987. (No MPAA Rating.) Running time: **93 MINS.**
Thunder . . . . Mark Gregory
Sheriff Roger . . . . Bo Svenson
Rusty . . . . Raimund Harmstorf
Sheena . . . . Karen Reel
Also with: William Rice, Vic Roych, Clayton Tevis, Bill Rossly, Mike Bower, Rex Blackwell, Dennis O'Reilly.

Thunder is back and Bo Svenson's got him in "Thunder Warrior 2," a photogenic if uneventful sequel to the Italian made-in-U.S.A. action pic of several years back.

Indian hero Thunder (Italian thesp Mark Gregory) returns home in the sequel, appointed by the governor as a deputy sheriff to Sheriff Roger (Bo Svenson), who had him sent to prison in part one. His adversary once again is the corrupt deputy (Raimund Harmstorf), running a profitable drug trade. An Indian chief is murdered by the drug ring and Thunder is out to get to the bottom of this when Harmstorf frames him for murder and it's back to Arizona's state pen.

Thunder escapes on cue and there's plenty of chases and helicopter stunts in Monument Valley until the hero puts on his war paint to go after Harmstorf. Finale is disappointing and confusing with Svenson sending the hero (with wife Karen Reel) away and cryptically taking aim at their car with his rifle in final shot. Never fear, a third installment is in the works.

Monument Valley is a lovely backdrop for this nonsense, rendered a bit hard to take by the pidgin English dialog. Filmmaker Fabrizio De Angelis evidently gets away with minimal efforts like these, but even a lowkey hero like Thunder will need more interesting challenges to keep an audience coming back for more.—*Lor.*

Sinvergüenza ... Pero Honrado
(Shameless ... But Honorable)
(MEXICAN-COLOR)

A Películas Mexicanas release of a Cumbre Films production. Directed by Rafael Villaseñor Kuri. Stars Vicente Fernández. Screenplay, Adolfo Torres Portillo; camera (color), Javier Cruz; editor, Max Sánchez; music, Carlos Torres; musical director, Fernando Méndez; associate producer, Fernández. Reviewed at Hollywood Twin Theater 2, N.Y., June 7, 1987. Running time: **96 MINS.**
Alberto . . . . Vicente Fernández
Carmen . . . . Blanca Guerra
Cecilia . . . . Cecilia Camacho
Flavio . . . . Manuel Capetillo
Don Pepe . . . . . Pedro Weber (Chatanooga)
Dona Carmen . . . . Carmelita González
Ramón . . . . Guillermo Murray
Also with: Alicia Encines, Carmelina Encines, Raúl Araiza Jr., Aurora Alonso, Roberto Cardona, Gabriel Cardona, Eugenia Avendaño, Antonio Miguel, Xerardo Moscoso, Irma Infante, Tito Guillén.

Although not mentioned in the title or on the accompanying poster, the comedy "Sinvergüenza ... Pero Honrado" (Shameless ... But Honorable) starring popular Mexican ranchero singer Vicente Fernández is a sequel to his earlier film "El Sinvergüenza" (The Shameless Guy). Like the first pic, the sequel is directed by perennial Fernández helmer Rafael Villaseñor Kuri.

As "the shameless guy," Fernán-

dez played a likeable rogue and gambler named Alberto, who is down on his luck. His married friend Ramón (Guillermo Murray) offers to give him some ready cash if he will pose as husband to his mistress (Blanca Guerra) while her parents are in town.

Despite his propensity to have a good time, Alberto takes this new role to heart, wins over the woman and her four children and ends up usurping the position of breadwinner from Ramón.

In the second installment, Alberto learns the meaning of commitment. Having been a long-time bachelor, suddenly he finds himself with a wife and four children whose respect he must earn.

The script, written by Adolfo Torres Portillo, offers many comic moments and is a strong vehicle for Fernández. It takes good-natured swipes at Alberto's old-fashioned macho attitudes and ranchero pretentions, and it spotlights Fernández' strongest assets: his singing and his comic acting. Four tunes make their way into this pic.

Fans will find that although tech credits are on the weak side, here is the Fernández character that they best wish to see and hear.—*Lent.*

Corrupción
(Corruption)
(MEXICAN-COLOR)

A Películas Mexicanas release of a Prod. Rodríguez production. Directed by Ismael Rodríguez. Screenplay, Rodríguez, Ricardo Gariby; camera (color), Fernando Colín; music, Ernesto Cortázar. Reviewed at Hollywood Twin Theater 1, N.Y., May 18, 1987. Running time: **87 MINS.**
Dr. Antonio Arenas . . . . Eduardo Loys
Virginia Arenas . . . . Abril Campillo
Jesusa . . . . Carmen Salinas
Valentín Bravo . . . . Pedro Infante Jr.
Uncle René . . . . . . Alberto (Caballo) Rojas
Also with: Rafael Inclán, Rosita Bonchot, Charito Granados, Emilia Guiú, Lucy Gallardo, Ana Luisa Peluffo, Gustavo Rojo.

Mexican scriptwriter Ricardo Gariby, who penned the two top-grossing national "Miluso" (Jack-of-All-Trade) films, also authored this pic "Corrupción" (Corruption), a potboiler whose title tells all.

Like the "Miluso" films, "Corrupción" is little more than a propaganda vehicle made to deter poor-but-honest country folk from moving to Mexico City in search of a better life.

Helmed by veteran director and co-scripter Ismael Rodríguez, the film has all the sincerity and subtlety of a "Reefer Madness," but with too many local references to achieve international cult attention.

Pic concerns the fate of a dedicated country doctor when he receives an important position at a large Mexico City hospital. The doctor was widowed years earlier and lives with his innocent daughter Virginia

(Abril Campillo) and foppish brother-in-law René (Alberto Rojas). When the three travel to the capital, Virginia leaves behind her fiance Valentin Bravo (Pedro Infante Jr.), a fiercely honest rancher and crusading journalist who cannot be bought off.

The doctor can't be bought off either, until he arrives in the capital. He and his family soon discover Mexico City is the great corruptor with influences that are impossible to resist.

Eventually the doctor is paid to endorse fradulent antibiotics while his daughter gets an illegal abortion when she is abandoned by her new boyfriend. An infection leaves her in the hospital where she dies as a result of the worthless antibiotics and the circle is complete.

Tech credits are uneven. The barebones lensing is flat and lacks imagination. Although the actors try hard, they are bogged down by clichéd characters.

The film is little more than an illustrated sermon with a comic book approach to story and characterization. Gariby and Rodríguez' inept prescription here hits the audience as merely bad medicine.—*Lent.*

Murder Lust
(COLOR)

Monotone saga of a serial killer.

An Easy Street Filmworks production. (Foreign sales, Film Ventures Intl.) Produced by James Lane. Directed by Donald Jones. Screenplay, Lane; camera (color), James Mattison; editor, Jones; music, Lane; sound, Stefan Hawk; assistant director, Dennis Gannon; stunt coordinator, William J. Kulzer. Reviewed on Prism Entertainment vidcassette, N.Y., June 10, 1987. (No MPAA Rating.) Running time: **90 MINS.**
Steve . . . . Eli Rich
Cheryl . . . . Rochelle Taylor
Neil . . . . Dennis Gannon
Marene . . . . Bonnie Schneider
Debbie . . . . Lisa Nichols
Joe . . . . H. Burton Leary
Lyman . . . . Bill Walsh
    Also with: George J. Engelson, Dayna Quinn, Martha Lane, Ashley St. Jon, Linda Tucker-Smith, James Lane.

"Murder Lust," a B-feature originally titled "Mass Murderer" during production two years ago, takes a rather interesting premise (i.e., treating a deranged serial killer sympathetically) and wastes it via poor production values and execrable acting. Filmmaker Donald Jones codirected (with Mikel Angel) the more successful black comedy version of this theme, "The Love Butcher," a decade ago.

Eli Rich, a stone-faced thesp, portrays Steve Belmont, a seemingly okay guy who works as a security guard and does Sunday School volunteer work as a teacher. Twist is he covers up his impotency with women by picking up prostitutes, strangling them and throwing the bodies down a ravine out in the desert.

Besides his psychosis, Steve is burdened with numerous other problems: falling behind in his rent, losing his job when he's nasty to a woman, harrassed by his mean cousin (Dennis Gannon) who hires him as a janitor in his store, etc. He's also trying to get away with faking his nonexistent college degrees to land a cushy job running an adolescent crisis unit at the Sunday School, which his girlfriend (Rochelle Taylor) rightly figures could be a focal point for the serial killer to seek out victims.

He's pushed over the edge when she gets the crisis unit's funding delayed until the killer is apprehended, putting Steve into a Catch-22 situation since he's the killer.

Painting such a monster as an outwardly kindly, community service-oriented chap is an effective story ploy, most tellingly essayed by Richard Attenborough in "10 Rillington Place." Here, topliner Rich is woefully inadequate, reading most of his lines as if reciting the phone book. Supporting cast, including several of the crew members in dual assignments, is nondescript. Tech credits are threadbare, not helped by a shrill synthesized musical score by writer-producer James Lane.—*Lor.*

✳✳✳✳✳✳✳✳✳✳✳✳✳✳✳✳✳✳✳✳✳✳✳✳✳✳✳✳✳✳✳✳
Film Fest Reviews
✳✳✳✳✳✳✳✳✳✳✳✳✳✳✳✳✳✳✳✳✳✳✳✳✳✳✳✳✳✳✳✳

Landslides
(AUSTRALIAN-COLOR)

An Australian Film Institute Distribution release (in Australia and New Zealand) of a Red Heart Pictures-Film Australia coproduction, in association with the Australian Broadcasting Corp. Produced and directed by Sarah Gibson, Susan Lambert. Screenplay, Gibson, Lambert; camera (color), Michael Ewers, Jack Lambert, Mick Bornemann; editor, Ray Thomas; music, Cameron Allan; sound, Denise Haslam, Howard Spry; animation, Pam Lofts. Reviewed at Mosman screening room, Sydney, June 16, 1987. Running time: **75 MINS.**

Sydney — "Landslides" is a very striking, very original, and often quite baffling, film. Sarah Gibson and Susan Lambert have been collaborating on short films since 1977 (they've made "Ladies' Rooms," "Size 10," "Behind Closed Doors," "Age Before Beauty" and "On Guard"), but this is their most ambitious effort. It will be in demand from specialized fests and women's film events.

Film is an exploration of The Body, on a variety of levels. We see babies, toddlers, adult women bathing naked; via images of surgical operations (some very graphic footage) we move inside the body. Then there are "heavenly bodies" — stock footage of NASA space exploration — the moon, the stars, and astronauts floating in space.

The images on screen are almost always counterpointed by the soundtrack. For example, when we see a spaceflight, what we hear is women arguing about the ageing process; again, while we see the strange rock formations of the Australian outback, we hear a discussion on bodily functions. The most visceral footage of surgery in progress is accompanied by a discussion of possible life on other planets.

Sometimes, pic smacks of home movie as Gibson and Lambert literally are seen at home, or on an aircraft, or on a tour of some famous underground caves near Sydney. The unusual structure devised by the filmmakers always raises the film a notch or two above expectations.

"Landslides" has been playing a commercial run in the Australian Film Institute's Chauvel theater in Sydney, and its original 10-day season has been extended because of audience demand. So on its modest level, commercial chances look bright locally for this challenging, provocative effort. —*Strat.*

Ibunda
(Mother)
(INDONESIAN-COLOR)

A PT Satrya Perkasa Esthetika Film-PT Suptan Film production. Produced by Sudwakitmono, R. Soenarso. Directed by Teguh Karya. Screenplay, Karya; camera (Widescreen, color), George Kamarullah; editor, B. Benny; music, Idris Sardi; sound, Zakaria Rasyim. Reviewed at Melbourne Film Festival, June 12, 1987. Running time: **103 MINS.**
    With: Tuti Indra Malaon, Alex Komang, Niniek L. Karim, Ria Irawan, Galeb Husin.

Melbourne — Latest pic from Indonesia's best-known director, Teguh Karya ("November 1828," "Bitter Coffee") is a family saga written and directed along familiar lines. Film apparently has been praised much at home, but to most foreign audiences it will be seen as a conventional work, although the last 10 minutes or so are very well staged.

Tuti Indra Malaon plays the eponymous mother, a widow who finds herself facing problems on two fronts. Her youngest daughter has fallen in love with a student from Irianjaya (formerly known as West Irian), and other members of the family object to her liaison with a non-Javanese.

Further, her oldest son (Alex Komang), an actor, has left his wife

and child and is having an affair with an actress. Karya attempts to parallel the main story via a revolutionary opera being filmed with Komang as the star. Opera is, to put it mildly, undistinguished, and we got to see slabs of it on three lengthy occasions.

Mostly, though, "Mother" is a simple family saga which could be taking place just as easily anywhere in the world, even on daytime tv. Production credits are good, and thesping is also fine, with Komang much more restrained than usual.
— *Strat.*

Witch Hunt
(AUSTRALIAN-COLOR)

A Documentary Films production. Produced and directed by Barbara A. Chobocky. Screenplay, Chobocky, Jeffrey Bruer; camera (color), editor, Bruer; sound, Steve Best; music, Thomas Mexis. Reviewed at Sydney Film Festival, June 14, 1987. Running time: **92 MINS.**
Chris Nakis . . . . Jaye Paul
Inspector Thomas . . . . Bill Brady
George Theodorakis . . . . Danny Carett
Matthew Argias . . . . . . Stavros Economidis
Angela Argias . . . . Nancy Carvana
David Rofe, Q.C. . . . . Leslie Dayman
Presenter . . . . George Donikian

Sydney — On April 1, 1978, Australian federal police swooped down on the homes of Greek-Australians in Sydney and arrested 1,000, plus a number of doctors serving the Greek community. Police claimed a conspiracy was underway to defraud the government's welfare agency, but when the last prosecutions were finally dropped eight years later, not one offense had been proved.

Barbara A. Chobocky's startling dramatized docu is a frontal attack on the Aussie police force for its mishandling of the so-called "Greek Conspiracy" case. Chobocky uses interviews with victims of the arrests, including a couple of doctors who were apprehended in their surgeries; and she's also talked to the man who instigated the raids, former Inspector Thomas, who, amazingly, seems to feel still that he did no wrong (he left the police force in 1981).

The facts of the case are a bit complicated, and the film demands concentration from an audience. Also, it's a bit disconcerting at first when actors take over to reenact scenes involving real-life people we've already met in interview scenes. Gradually, the threads come together, and the appalling injustice of it all overpowers the viewer. Australians who believe they're living in a democracy will be appalled at this grim tale, which resulted in the suicide of one wrongly accused victim, and many shattered lives. That racism was the root cause of the whole sorry affair is ultimately not in doubt.

Chobocky melds the reenacted scenes with the docu footage to good effect, and has done a fine piece of reportage. Narrator-presenter George Donikian is a smooth, if not always essential, front man. Pic premiered at the Sydney fest, to a capacity house consisting of vociferously enthusiastic patrons, and goes to air almost immediately on the Special Broadcasting Service network.

—*Strat*.

Macbeth
(FINNISH-COLOR)

A Finnkino release of Villealfa production. Produced by Aki Kaurismäki. Directed by Pauli Pentti. Screenplay, Pentti, based on Shakespeare's play; camera (Eastmancolor), Olli Varja; editor, Timmo Linnasalo; music, excerpts from Verdi's "Aïda," Mikko Mattila, Tapio Siitonen; production management, Jaakko Talaskivi. Reviewed at Midnight Sun Film Festival, Sodenkylä, Finland, June 12, 1987. Running time: **70 MINS**.

Macbeth . . . . Mato Valtonen
Lady . . . . Pirkko Hämäläinen
Duncan . . . . Antti Litja
Banquo . . . . Partti Sveholm
Duncan's son . . . . Turo Pajala
Napoleon . . . . Sakke Järvenpää
Also with: Saku Kuosmanen, Vesa Vierikko, Sanna-Kaisa Palo, Esko Nikkari, Mari Rantasila.

Sodenkylä, Finland — Forget about the Shakespearean title and plot conceit of this "Macbeth," a second feature effort by Pauli Pentti. Instead, this picture should be seen as a *film noir* parody-cum-tribute. In selective situations, some audiences will cheer, others jeer.

Writer-helmer Pentti throws Shakespearean quotes and name-droppings in a wildly swinging story about present-day Finnish gangsters and their molls, who bump off each other and themselves while their paranoia escalates and their reactions grow in violence. Macbeth's blond girlfriend Lady who egged him on to murder(s) in the first place, swims to her death after having seen what she takes to be a severed head placed on her dinner plate.

Most of the multifaceted action takes place in blue-hued darkness, making continuity obscure and obscuring, too, such silliness as goes beyond the point-of-no-return of good satire. The genre tribute aspects of Pentti's "Macbeth" are tongue-in-cheek all the way and so is the acting. Film looks good and is never boring.—*Kell*.

Älä itkė, Iines
(Gone With The Mind)
(FINNISH-COLOR)

A Finnkino release of Tuotanto/RT production. Written and directed by Janne Kuusi. Camera (Eastmancolor), Tahvo Hirvonen; editor, Anne Lakanen; production design, Pertti Hilkamo; sound, Mikael Sievers. Reviewed at Midnight Sun Film Festival, Sodenkylä, Finland, June 14, 1987. Running time: **96 MINS**.

Iines . . . . Eija Vilpas
Sylvestri . . . . Karl Väänänen
Tipi . . . . Sari Mällinen
Also with: Pirkka-Pekka Petelius, Vesa Vierikko, Pertti Sveholm, Sanna Fransman, Kari Heiskanen, Maija Leino.

Sodenkylä, Finland — The original title of writer-director Janne Kuusi's second feature film translates as "Don't Cry, Iines," but item is to be marketed offshore as "Gone With The Mind." Both titles are appropriate, since Iines, the young woman of many tears, tends to overdo everything, and since the whole thing aims at blowing anybody's mind.

"Gone With The Mind" will be tough to sell outside Finland, and even at home it has endeared itself only to aficionados of a certain off-center Helsinki theater tradition of improvised farcical acting. Transferring latter to film, Kuusi has come up with a messy, exuberant, noisy and ultimately self-defeating comedy with shrill overtones of social satire, featuring a cast allowed to cavort to their hearts' delight.

Result has bad directorial timing and expert cinematography and is a mix of silent film and Dario Fo stage acting techniques with a lot of gross circus clown romping and raw vulgarity in words and visuals. The story indicated (told is hardly the word) has to do with the survival struggle of a slum area commune of grotesques who live some of the time in an attic and otherwise in a garbage container in the yard.

The characters dream and scheme and work their way in zigzag patterns towards what are never really going to become careers in either fashion modelling (Iines, a buxom blond was once a runnerup in a beauty contest) or petty crime or extortion of the welfare agencies. They spend a lot of time eating what they have just stolen in supermarkets, and as guests at their dinners they have a waif who just saved Iines from committing suicide in the subway; a shipping magnate in hiding after a financial swindle; and a rent-collector who has taken up permanent residence in the communal bathtub.

Iines has a lover, a brute who keeps his cigaret in his mouth, a bowler on his head and his dress-shirt front and cuffs on while raping women left and right, one of them supplying the film's minimal musical score by sitting around, scantily clad, on rooftops playing the bagpipes. Rather than music, the soundtrack otherwise offers mostly animal noises emitting from invisible bullfrogs and sundry rodents. Pratfalls and everything else work repetitiously via near-total chaos towards an ending of utter confusion.—*Kell*.

Link-Up Diary
(AUSTRALIAN-DOCU-COLOR)

A Ronin Films release of an Australian Institute of Aboriginal Studies Film Unit production. Produced and directed by David MacDougall. Camera (color), editor, sound, MacDougall. Reviewed at Sydney Film Festival, June 10, 1987. Running time: **87 MINS**.

Sydney — A fascinating theme is to be found in this amateurish docu. From 1900-1969, the government of New South Wales regularly took aboriginal children away from their families. The reasons were humanitarian, to give these impoverished children better lives, but the results were broken homes and tragic families.

Link-up is an organization of social workers set up to try to help with the reunification of displaced families. Filmmaker David MacDougall has made a kind of diary consisting of a week in the activities of Link-up officers Coral Edwards, Peter Read and Robynne Vincent. During this period they travel from Canberra to Sydney and introduce a pregnant woman to her long-lost father, a reunion that's joyful at first, but about which the woman later has second thoughts.

If the theme is fascinating, MacDougall's treatment of it isn't. Maybe he was forced to make the film single-handedly because of budgetary restraints, but his attempt to combine the roles of director-cameraman-soundman simply doesn't work. The sound recording is mostly terrible, making a lot of the dialog virtually inaudible. The camerawork is clumsy — which isn't surprising given the fact that MacDougall must have been carrying around an awful lot of equipment.

To make matters worse, in his role as editor MacDougall has remained true to his diary concept, leaving in an awful lot of extraneous material. His own voice-over narration is sometimes useful, often intrusive, and sometimes manipulative.

This is a good subject for a docu, spoiled by indulgent treatment. The audience is prevented from experiencing the pain of these family reunions, or approaching the work of the Link-up team. A more objective approach was needed.—*Strat*.

House
(THAI-COLOR)

A Phol Siam Films production, Bangkok. Produced by Manae Limpipholpiboon. Directed by Chart Kopjitti. Screenplay, Kopjitti, from his novel "Deadend," camera (color), Boonyong Monkonmung. Reviewed at Asian American Intl. Film Festival, N.Y., June 14, 1987. Running time: **110 MINS**.

Winner as Best Screenplay of the Thai Oscars, 1987, "House" is based upon the first novel, called "Deadend," by director Chart Kopjitti. It concerns a young family — parents, a daughter and a son — who leave the wretched poverty of the countryside to join the multitudes of Bangkok who toil in equally wretched conditions of the indifferent big city.

As the film begins, the family arrives in Bangkok. Searching frantically, the father finally finds work, hard labor at little pay. The wife sews, the daughter sells flowers at a traffic light, the little boy peddles newspapers. Soon there is another child. The grandfather arrives from the country, having lost the family farm. He makes his rounds, sharpening knives and scissors. They long for a house of their own and save their pennies. Finally, the family builds a tiny shack on a fetid swamp.

Then troubles accumulate. The young father is laid off during the general economic slump. He is cheated and in debt for the house. He becomes a fisherman, is gone for long periods. The boat is interned and its crew imprisoned for violating fishing rights. The family begins to crumble. Now crippled after being assaulted by muggers, the grandfather struggles to care for the children. His is a fully realized character, even down to the little nods and hums of satisfaction as he watches his grandchildren taste Pepsi for the first time. Their little pleasure is made all the more sad as we realize they are doomed.

At the end of the film, the house that was meant to be the center of the family now stands empty.

—*Hitch*.

Damortis
(FILIPINO-COLOR-16m)

Produced by Maria Branca Filmworks, Manila. Directed by Briccio Santos. Screenplay, Santos, Jorge Arago; camera (color), Ricky Ligon; music, Winston. Reviewed at Asian American Intl. Film Festival, N.Y., June 14, 1987. Running time: **93 MINS**.

Anna . . . . Madeleine Nicolas
Miguel . . . . Lito Carating
Lando . . . . Roberto Villanueva

Produced in 1984, as the Marcos regime was in decline, "Damortis" is a psychological drama, almost an occult allegory, about the abuse of power of a demagog-faithhealer. Lando's power derives from the ignorance and trust of villagers who turn to him for cure of their physical and psychic ailments. Lando abuses that innocent dependence but eventually is undone by his own excesses.

"Damortis" is the work of a Filipino director, Briccio Santos, educated in psychology in London.

Miguel (Lito Carating), young seminarian, returns to his village and falls by chance into the faith-healing racket, combining pagan ritual and Christianity, performing his medical miracles in a clinic cum chapel. As his practice becomes lucrative, his bride Anna (Madeleine Nicolas) becomes obsessed with materialism — furniture, jewelry, electronic fixtures. As his clientele increases, Miguel takes on an apprentice, Lando (Roberto Villanueva), whose skills soon exceed those of his master. Miguel becomes apathetic, a drunk, accidentally killing a child, and is jailed. Lando now has the business all to himself, but he wants to include Anna. After he rapes her, she plots revenge.

The film has several documentary scenes, e.g., of fishing and farming, as background versimilitude. It is notable for stylized experimental interludes, but they seem more like self-conscious insertions into the film rather than part of an overall conception. Roberto Villanueva as Lando is outstanding, an actor with a striking head and figure, a sinister charmer. As the film ends, he loses that head, quite literally. —*Hitch.*

The Living Daylights
(BRITISH-COLOR)

An MGM/UA Distribution release from United Artists of an Eon production. Produced by Albert R. Broccoli, Michael G. Wilson. Directed by John Glen. Stars Timothy Dalton. Screenplay, Richard Maibaum, Wilson, from story by Ian Fleming; camera (Panavision, Technicolor), Alec Mills; editor, John Grover, Peter Davies; music, John Barry; James Bond theme, Monty Norman; songs; "The Living Daylights" by a-ha, composed by Pal Waaktaar, Barry, "Where Has Every Body Gone," and "If There Was A Man," by The Pretenders, music by Barry, lyrics by Chrissie Hynde; production design, Peter Lamont; supervising art direction, Terry Ackland-Snow; set decoration, Michael Ford; costume design, Emma Porteous; sound, Colin Miller; special effects supervisor, John Richardson; second unit director, Arthur Wooster; assistant director, Gerry Gavigan; stunts arranger, Paul Weston; driving stunts arranger, Rémy Julienne; aerial stunts arranger, B.J. Worth; production supervisor, Anthony Waye; associate producers, Tom Pevsner, Barbara Broccoli; casting, Debbie McWilliams. Reviewed at the Odeon Leicester Square, London, June 29, 1987. (MPAA Rating: PG.) Running time: **130 MINS.**
James Bond............Timothy Dalton
Kara Milovy.............Maryam d'Abo
Gen. Georgi Koskov.......Jeroen Krabbé
Brad Whitaker..........Joe Don Baker
Gen. Leonid Pushkin...John Rhys-Davies
Kamran Shah................Art Malik
Necros............Andreas Wisniewski
Saunders.............Thomas Wheatley
Q...................Desmond Llewelyn
M.....................Robert Brown
Minister of Defence.......Geoffrey Keen
General Anatol Gogol......Walter Gotell
Miss Moneypenny........Caroline Bliss
Felix Leiter................John Terry
Also with: John Bowe, Julie T. Wallace, Kell Tyler, Catherine Rabett, Dulice Liecier, Nadim Sawalha, Alan Talbot, Carl Rigg, Tony Cyrus, Atik Mohamed.

London — "The Living Daylights" is just the ticket to mark James Bond's 25 years on the screen. The mesh of above-par story, action spectacle and virile new star gives the series a solid uplift that bodes big worldwide returns atop the near-$750,000,000 global rentals already bagged. This one will be tough to top.

Timothy Dalton's a class act, be it in Shakespeare on the London stage or as the new 007. The fourth Bond registers beautifully on all key counts of charm, machismo, sensitivity and technique. He's an actor, not just a pretty face with a dimpled chin, and in "Daylights" he's abetted by material that's a healthy cut above the series norm of super hero fantasy. If the new boy poses a marketing challenge going in, not for long.

Pic isn't just a high-tech action replay with the usual ravishing vistas and ditto dames. Everyone seems to have tried a little harder this time. The Richard Maibaum-Michael Wilson scripting partnership came up not just with sustained clever excitement but with a human dimension for Bond not hitherto plumbed. There are even some relatively touching moments of romantic contact between Dalton and lead femme Maryam d'Abo as Czech concert cellist. Belatedly, the Bond characterization has achieved appealing maturity.

There's a more mature story of its kind, too, this one about a phony KGB defector involved in gunrunning and a fraternal assassination plot. Early apprehensions of yet more unshaded, ho-hum Cold War shenanigans become tempered. By the conclusion there's even a strong hint of the new *glasnost* spirit — in both directions, with more than one Soviet honcho sporting a decidedly human face. It's a welcome change.

Though lengthy, pic has a good, well-utilized pace, with a nice balance of human and high-tech action. Repeat helmer John Glen handles it all smoothly, at a guess himself refreshed by the various refresher elements.

Reassuringly, though, the meatier narrative is at no sacrifice to expected .spectacle, on which count "Daylights" is a bonanza even for hardened fans. Two daredevil sequences stand out: one the pursuit of Bond's Aston-Martin across snow-covered mountain terrain, and a climactic escape by flying transport from a shootout in the Afghanistan outback. Both are sustained corkers.

The most comically clever touch is the gizmo whereby the fake "defector" is spirited out to the West in a capsule via the trans-Siberian natural gas pipeline.

As ever with this series, pic is a stunning paean to stunting (arranged by Paul Weston) and the arts of modelmaking and playful special effects. The craft tricks are as socko as any coproducer Albert Broccoli has presided over since his personal annuity got started with "Dr. No."

D'Abo, in a part meant to be something more than that of window-dressed mannikin, handles her chores acceptably. Able support is turned in by Joe Don Baker as a nutcase arms seller, Jeroen Krabbé and John Rhys-Davies as respective KGB bad and good types (a little less arch than the usual types), and Art Malik as an Oxford-educated (this is fantasy) Afghan freedom fighter. Also, Robert Brown as M and Caroline Bliss (vice Lois Maxwell) as the new Miss Moneypenny. Hers is the usual quickie, but she makes it a good one and warrants the role's lease.

As a typical exercise in megabuck travelog, the 25th anni Bond locationed in Gibraltar, Austria, Morocco, the U.S. and Italy, as well as homebase England and the Pinewood lot.

The usual massive Eon Prods. credit list is justified by way of spreading merited honors, not least the second unit crews, yeoman editing, John Barry's basic score (unassertively enhancing), and the inimitable main titles of Maurice Binder. Everyone seemed up for this one, and it shows. —*Pit.*

She Must Be Seeing Things
(COLOR)

Lame lesbian drama.

Produced, written and directed by Sheila McLaughlin. Camera (color), Mark Daniels; supplementary footage, Heinz Emigholz; editor, Ila Von Hasperg; music, John Zorn; art director, Leigh Kyle; sound, Margie Crimmins; associate producer, Christine LeGoff. Reviewed at Castro theater, San Francisco, June 19, 1987. (No MPAA Rating.) Running time: **90 MINS.**
With: Sheila Dabney, Lois Weaver, Kyle DeCamp, John Erdman.

San Francisco — The 11th S.F. Intl. Lesbian and Gay Film Festival, a 10-day affair with fetures and vidpics in three venues, had a festive getaway — until the feature unspooled.

"She Must Be Seeing Things," which drew more than 1,000 to the Castro, is a technically uneven, lamely written and directed exposition of a lesbian relationship between a filmmaker (Lois Weaver) and lawyer (Sheila Dabney). Both actresses hold Obie awards, but their talent is not evident in this yarn.

The lighting is skimpy, the sound often distorted. Frameline, the fest sponsoring organization, presented McLaughlin with a $2,000 "completion" award before the pic unspooled.

Dabney portrays a jealous lover and often drifts into fantasy when contemplating the flirtations of girlfriend Weaver, who's busy directing a film within the film, an equally dismal pic at that. There is no explicit sex in the pic or, for that matter, an explicit pic. — *Herb.*

Dragnet
(COLOR)

Disappointing parody.

A Universal Pictures release of an Applied Action/Bernie Brillstein production. Produced by David Permut, Robert K. Weiss. Executive producer, Brillstein. Directed by Tom Mankiewicz. Stars Dan Aykroyd, Tom Hanks. Screenplay, Aykroyd, Alan Zweibel, Tom Mankiewicz; camera (Deluxe color), Matthew F. Leonetti; editor, Richard Halsey, William D. Gordean; music, Ira Newborn; production design, Robert F. Boyle; art direction, Frank Richwood; set decoration, Arthur Jeph Parker; costume design, Taryn DeChellis; sound (Dolby), Willie Burton; assistant director, David Sosna; associate producer, Don Zepfel; casting, Lynn Stalmaster & Assoc., David Rubin; Reviewed at the Directors Guild theater, L.A., June 22, 1987. (MPAA Rating: PG-13. Running time: **106 MINS.**
Joe Friday...............Dan Aykroyd
Pep Streebek...............Tom Hanks
Reverend Whirley...Christopher Plummer
Capt. Bill Gannon........Harry Morgan

Connie Swail . . . . .Alexandra Paul
Emil Muzz . . . . .Jack O'Halloran
Jane Kirkpatrick . . . . .Elizabeth Ashley
Jerry Caesar . . . . .Dabney Coleman

Hollywood — "Dragnet" tries very hard to parody its 1950s tv series progenitor but winds up more innocuous than inventive. Dan Aykroyd as Jack Webb as Sgt. Joe Friday gives the role his best but confines of the ultra-straight cop make humor difficult to sustain. Unfettered by such limits, Tom Hanks becomes the pic's winning wildcard as Friday's zany sidekick. However disappointing the whole package may be, film probably has a decent shot at some okay summer business.

Many of the funniest moments are right up front as homage to the tv original is set up via such voice-overs as "This is the city ... Los Angeles, California." Aykroyd's staccato patter takes the audience swiftly inside the p.d., where we learn he's the nephew and namesake of the Webb character.

Dressed in a drab off-the-rack suit with tie snug to the collar, the crew-cut Aykroyd hilariously establishes his stern and no-nonsense persona. Since his partner has exited the force to begin operating a goat farm, Friday is teamed with a new and unlikely colleague — one Pep Streebek (Tom Hanks).

Streebek's freewheeling style — ranging from hip clothes to health food to after-hours socializing choices — offends every rock-ribbed precept of Friday's. Pairing does give the film a vitality that is lacking in the storyline.

Inevitably, Friday and Streebek must pursue a case. It is here that the pic starts unraveling rapidly — largely due to exaggerated caricatures that recall tv's "Batman" series and the feature film "Superman" outings. Christopher Plummer is the kinkiest of the lot as televangelist Reverend Whirley. He considers L.A. the "current capital of depravity," heads up MAMA (Moral Advanced Movement of America) but secretly leads a cultist outfit called the PAGANs (People Against Goodness and Normalcy).

Whirley is somehow allied with Police Commissioner Jane Kirkpatrick (Elizabeth Ashley) and is purportedly at odds with Bait sex magazine kingpin Jerry Caesar (Dabney Coleman). Relying primarily on a speech impediment for his comic device, Coleman falls short of his usual topnotch performance. Role largely becomes the excuse for gratuitous t & a as Caesar's "Baitmates" populate his secluded mansion.

Friday and Streebek plunge into the bizarre goings-on by posing undercover as street freaks. This desperate bid to get really wacky leads duo to a Pagans' ritual where they manage to free "the virgin Connie Swail of Orange County" (Alexandra Paul) just in the nick of time. Grandiose setting for the rescue contains elements of "Ghostbusters," but is so ludicrous that it actually ends up as the film's low point.

Even as pic is bottoming out, love blossoms for Friday and Ms. Swail in story's biggest break with the no-woman-on-the-scene Dragnet lore. Following events do humanize and loosen up the Aykroyd-Webb character somewhat. Nonetheless it is still possible for Streebek to refer to his partner as "generally less fun to be around than anyone I've ever met."

Challenge overall is to allow Friday to be just that way without making him so tragically sincere that he is just plain boring. To liven him up with outlandish costuming, mindless car chases and explosive confrontations isn't the answer.

Script doesn't make enough of the opportunities for interplay that used to be a mainstay between Webb and Harry Morgan, who reprises the part here in a nice touch than finds him elevated to captain.

With a 1980s perspective, the Webb-Morgan exchanges look very campy — as perhaps they did somewhat at the time. More of that here between Aykroyd and Hanks — and less concern for stupefying action — could have provided the vital connecting links between past and present. In any case, one hopes the two comedic actors will get to combine talents theatrically again.
— *Tege.*

To Hurt And To Heal
(CANADIAN-DOCU-COLOR-16m)

A film by Sky Work Charitable Foundation, Toronto, Ontario. Produced, written and directed by Laura Sky. Camera (color), Jim Aquila; music, Patrick Godfrey. Reviewed at American Film Video Festival, N.Y., June 20, 1987. Running time: **105 MINS.**

Winner of the Blue Ribbon in the Health Issues, Features, category, "To Hurt And To Heal" is a penetrating examination of modern high-tech medical care of newborn and infants who suffer from radical birth defects. The film is serious, intelligent and compassionate. It is commendably frank and unsentimental while other films often become maudlin or wallow in phony optimism.

Filmed in Toronto hospitals and in private homes, "Hurt" gives viewers a behind-the-scenes look at the extraordinary facilities available for the care of damaged children. It's often not enough — the childen die. Emphasis is on the parents, for whom the cliché "heroic" is far from adequate. They suffer, as does the child. Their anguish is especially poignant because they can do nothing to relieve the physical pain being endured by the helpless blob of precarious flesh they call their child. Such infants do feel pain, their nurses attest, despite the casual claims of some, not all, doctors, who in self-defense hide behind an armor of stoicism.

One nurse, although a veteran of pediatrics, weeps when describing the futility she feels, unable to relieve the child's ordeal. Similarly, the parents discuss with the camera their indecision, whether to turn off the life-sustaining machines when further efforts become hopeless. Theirs is a heart-breaking choice.

Several doctors, specialists devoting their careers to this field, describe its progress, but without illusions. The film might well have been entitled — "To Hurt And To Try To Heal." Theirs is a noble attempt, but not always successful.
— *Hitch.*

Ira, You'll Get Into Trouble
(DOCU-B&W-16m)

A New Line Cinema release. Produced, directed, camera (b&w, 16m) by Stephen A. Sbarge; editor, Mark Rappaport. Reviewed at American Film Video Festival, N.Y., June 22, 1987. (No MPAA Rating.) Running time: **85 MINS.**

Produced during 1968-70, "Ira" was released briefly in 1971, then withdrawn. It has languished forgotten until this courageous — one does not say foolhardy — reissue by New Line in 1987. Their faith in thus raising the dead inspires respect, but will the corpse walk?

Background of "Ira" includes the troubled campuses and streets, acrid with tear gas, of the late 1960s, of the Democratic Convention in Chicago. In New York City, Black activists sought to gain community control of schools from the white hierarchy downtown; 200,000 high-schoolers stayed out in sympathy, also protesting Vietnam, the draft, on-campus military recruitment, the lack of integration in U.S. society. Legitimate grievances escalated, things turned nasty, the United Federation of Teachers struck, Mayor John Lindsay waffled, students marched. Then New York's finest moved in fast and hard, some mounted, swinging truncheons, using tear gas, filling up the paddywagons. "Get in there — that's what you wanted anyhow," growls a husky middle-aged cop as he bounces a kid into the wagon.

Most of "Ira" sticks closely to one small group of highschoolers, primarily white males, one of them the "Ira" of them all. We see them watching then discussing Black Panther films from (Third World) Newsreel; writing, printing, hand-delivering radical student newspapers; putting on make-up, giggling, then taking part in a tv talk-show; horseplay at the beach, rolling in the sand, as a prelude to heavy political strategy; and endlessly rapping about overthrowing the oppressive system, a collective overthrow, i.e., "we won't have a revolution unless we get all the groups together." Perhaps their affectations will become, in time, their nature.

It would be easy to label these kids punks. One longs to spank them. They are so obviously showing-off, sounding-off, playing to the camera, playing with themselves, mouthing revolutionary rhetoric that would bring a quiet smile to the lips of, say, Che Guevara, an authentic.

Yet the "punks" label would miss the point. Although the student discord of two decades ago is now ancient history, of interest only to Studs Terkel and three or four sociologists, there is a sub-text in "Ira" that redeems the self-conscious posing and the half-baked sloganizing of the teenagers. "Ira" shows their eager faith in reformist politics is naive but touching. They're trying to grow up. Clumsily, this is democracy at work.

Where are these student revolutionaries today? Somewhere, they are nearing 40. The film's 1987 epilog asks but doesn't know and wishes them good luck. They may now be parents themselves, with teenagers in highschool, both appalled by and proud of them. Perhaps that is why New Line is taking a risk with an old b&w documentary on obsolete New York politics — because the film's spirit and its depiction of a process are not old. —*Hitch.*

Miss...Or Myth?
(DOCU-COLOR)

A Gold Mountain production. Produced by Geoffrey Dunn, Mark Schwartz, Claire Rubach. Directed by Dunn, Schwartz. Camera (color), editor, Schwartz; written by Dunn; assistant director, Rubach; music, Liz Story. Reviewed at Roxie theater, San Francisco, June 20, 1987. (No MPAA Rating.) Running time: **60 MINS.**

San Francisco — This pic has played at six festivals and had a brief commercial run at the quasi-artsy Roxie in tandem with a delightful 30-minute Les Blank look at "Gap-Toothed Women."

It's a perfect pairing, for "Miss...Or Myth?" examines a 1985 feminist protest against the staging of the Miss California contest in Santa Cruz. In straightforward, reasonably balanced fashion, "Miss" offers arguments on both sides of the ongoing American ethic extolling slim-pretty. (That the contest has been shifted to San Diego indicates the impact of the Santa Cruz demonstration.)

The docu never postures. There are strident, reasoned arguments from both pageant directors and participants and demonstrators. A most fascinating figure among the protestors is ex-model Ann Simonton, victim of a gang rape and, off her emotional narrative here, worthy of a complete docu of her own.

Whatever the viewer's position, she or he is bound to be caught up in the contention "Miss" purveys, and therein lies the basic strength of this work: audience involvement. Throughout the reportage, there's a lack of middle ground testimony, even though the producers believe they plumbed that from actress and ex-Miss America Lee Ann Meriwether.

The downside of this project may be that beauty contests are not, considering the contemporary advertising emphasis as sex-provocative as once perceived. The feminists of Santa Cruz are entitled to their position, to be sure, but as a national issue, and thus potential b.o. for this docu, "Miss" events are strictly back-burner.

Still, for selected venues, the combo of "Miss" and "Gap-Toothed" might be a rewarding booking. Blank's half-hour delight, which has Lauren Hutton cheerfully chatting about the space in her mouth, proves that beauty is in the eye, if not the dentures, of the beholder. —*Herb.*

Sentimientos: Mirta de Liniers a Estambul
(Feelings: Mirta From Liniers To Istanbul)
(ARGENTINE-COLOR)

A Magia Films release of a Clip S.C.I. production. Produced by José Luis Rey Lago. Directed by Jorge Coscia, Guillermo Saura. Stars Norberto Díaz, Emilia Mazer, Víctor Laplace, Marla Vaner. Screenplay, Jorge Coscia; camera (color), Diego Bonacinn; editor, Darío Tedesco, Susana Nadal; music, Leo Sujatovich; sets and costumes, Guillermo Palacios. Reviewed at the Vigo screening room, Buenos Aires, April 27, 1987. (Rating in Argentina: forbidden for under 16s.) Running time: **100 MINS.**
Mirta.................Emilia Mazer
Enrique................Norberto Díaz
    Also with: Arturo Bonín, Víctor Laplace, Marla Vaner, Guillermo Battaglia, Saim Urgay, Elvia Andreoli, Cristina Banegas, Marcelo Alfaro, Ricardo Bartis.

Buenos Aires — Winner of the special prize of the jury to the best *opera prima* and of the prize of the jury of international critics, at Huelva, and of the Radio Havana prize as well as participating in Toronto, Málaga, Madrid and the American Film Market, this is a sensitive 2-part study rolled into one film.

First it is an edgy portrait of student life in an Argentine university at a time when an increasingly ruth-less police state is being set up under the recent military governments. It centers on the romance between an initially apolitical student, Mirta, and an activist, Enrique.

As the noose of repression tightens around him, they flee to exile in Sweden, and the nature of their life, and of the film, suddenly alters. It becomes a ruminative, rueful examination of life in exile, with the longings and tensions which can corrode lifestyles. "Exile isn't a neurosis but it bugs you," a character says. Mirta, an unassuming girl from a working class neighborhood of Buenos Aires (the Liniers of the picture's subtitle), finds herself in Stockholm falling in love with an also exiled Turk — with whom she can only communicate in halting Swedish.

The film has a disjointed feel to it, caused by a sudden hinge in the middle. The disjunction, however, only mirrors that of going into exile. The viewer is led to reflect that if the film isn't wholly of one piece, neither is life itself. Codirector Guillermo Saura says the work is based "about 40%" on a real-life case.

This is Saura's and Jorge Coscia's first directorial venture. Emilia Mazer, 22, who plays the lead, is shaping up as one of Argentina's most perceptive and accomplished actresses.

Second part of the film was shot on location in Stockholm and Athens, which stood in for Istanbul.
—*Olas.*

Näkeminn, hyvästi
(Farewell, Goodbye)
(FINNISH-COLOR)

A Finnkino release of Reppufilmi production. Produced by Petra Tarjanne. Written and directed by Anssi Mänttäri. Camera (Eastmancolor), Heikki Katajisto; editor, Marjo Valve (no further credits provided). Reviewed at Midnight Sun Film Festival, Sodenkylä, Finland, June 14, 1987. Running time: **99 MINS.**
Tuula.................Aino Seppo
Ellu.................Elisa Partanen
Jorma.............Juuso Hirvikangas
Mononen................Eero Saarinen
Juho.................Harri Nikkonen
Elisa.................Ritva Arvelo
Lauri Valve...............Lasse Pöysti
    Also with: Tiina Nyström, Mikko Hänninen, Liisa Halonen, Alina.

Sodenkylä, Finland — Prolific filmmaker Anssi Mänttärri's new comedy feature "Farewell, Goodbye" carries its burden of philosophizing on life and death and the meaning of both blessedly lightly, while yet another typical Mänttäri story is told in a rambling way about people who cannot make up their minds, and when they do, they usually have instant regrets.

Foreign sales prospects beyond the minor fest circuit for this picture about modern urban Finns in their (possibly) natural habitat of much heavy drinking and brooding are dim, although "Farewell, Goodbye" develops its skimpy storyline neatly and has neat acting jobs set in an equally neat production dress.

Tuula, a newly divorced mother with a small daughter, cannot make up her mind about taking her lovers or suitors seriously. Jorma, her ex-husband, now re-married, keeps returning to Tuula. Lauri Valve, Tuula's father and a noted cancer surgeon, is dissatisfied with hospital politics and intrigue. He unburdens his troubles while strolling in the park with a terminally ill woman patient but is rather late in letting his wife of 25 years know that he is off to Africa on a job for the Red Cross.

In spite of a faint dramatic pulse, "Farewell, Goodbye" has a softly convincing heartbeat all its own and a ring of truth, too. While it lacks a sense of narrative direction, it has fine guitar-strumming to help it on its way to an open ending. —*Kell.*

Neptune's Holiday
(SOVIET-COLOR)

A Lenfilm Studio production, financed by Mosfilm's Debut Unit. Directed by Yuri Mamin. Screenplay, Vladimir Vardunas; camera (color), Anatoli Lapshov; art direction, Georgi Kropachev; sound, A. Gavrichenko. Reviewed at Domkino, Leningrad, May 30, 1987. Running time: **60 MINS.**
Khokhlov.............Viktor Mikhailov
Klavdia Vasilievna . Violetta Zhukhimovich
Dubinkin...........Robert Kurliandchik

Leningrad — Though it's received only limited release at home, "Neptune's Holiday," a short satire on bureaucracy by newcomer Yuri Mamin, already has won top laurels at foreign fest outings (Mannheim and Gabrovo). Satire is not a common genre in the snowy Russian north, and Mamin is a worthy, if solitary, practitioner with a sense of humor that could travel.

In "Small Hills," an idyllic village nestled under a mantle of snow, bureaucratic bragging has created an embarrassing situation for the city fathers. The town's "Walrus Club" for enthusiasts of winter swimming was disbanded years ago, but in a report someone has made the five remaining swimmers swell to 150. Result is a delegation of Swedish walruses being dispatched to look at all these hardy Russians.

Officials scramble to find citizens willing to strip and jump into a hole in the ice, and concoct a supposedly traditional Neptune's Holiday for the visitors. Freezing with cold, costumed villagers wait for the Swedish bus to arrive, as Prokoviev's "Battle on the Ice" from "Alexander Nevsky" is heard. A bare-chested band plays a hearty welcome, but no one seems willing to make the first plunge. Then, unpredictably, people begin jumping in the water not for the Swedes but for fun, and have a real holiday.

Lensing is serviceable on this low-budgeter; characters are a fast-talking chorus.—*Yung.*

Blind
(DOCU-COLOR-16m)

A production of Zipporah Films, Cambridge, Mass. Produced, directed, sound, editor, Frederick Wiseman. Camera (color, 16m), John Davey. Reviewed at American Film Video Festival, N.Y., June 20, 1987. (No MPAA Rating.) Running time: **133 MINS.**

Frederick Wiseman's "Deaf And Blind" series of four films was funded by a MacArthur grant several years ago. Each film was shot at a different school or training program within the Alabama Institute for The Deaf And Blind. The four titles are "Blind," "Deaf," "Multi-Handicapped," and "Adjustment And Work."

"Blind" shows the teaching and daily routine of blind students, from about five to 18. Emphasis of the school is on self-sufficiency to the extent possible, to be in charge of their own lives. "Blind" shows, for example, very small children who are able to navigate the corridors of the schools, use the stairs, move about in classrooms, etc., with an uncanny sense of place. We don't feel pity for them but rather admiration.

"Blind" begins with teenagers in red jackets, a school band, playing at the local racing-car track. They are greeted by a church deacon who says that Christ gives us abundance despite apparent lacks, that through the love of Christ we can find a rich world around us. We realize that the young band-players are blind. An armless war veteran introduces them to the bleachers crowd before they are bussed away to the Institute. As always with Wiseman, there is no explanatory narration; he prefers his usual ironic ambiguity. It is a method that keeps his viewers working with him, filling in and speculating, and it reflects his faith in our participation.

Of course, the Institute is integrated and the blind children are both black and white. In the playgrounds and in their sleeping dorms, the blacks and whites are side by side and oblivious of color, chattering and helping one another for all the world as if bigotry in this nation didn't exist.

Classes teach how to make change with coins, and also with bills, folding them just so, as a code to each denomination. Others learn to bake. Also, all formal academic subjects are taught. In the gym, blind boys test their strength in wrestling with sighted boys from local schools. Blind girls bounce on the trampoline and learn rhythmic dancing. The film intercuts meetings and reports — of course, the

Institute has its bureaucracy, and committees discuss policy and what to do with a disturbed blind boy who breaks windows — shall we spank him? At the dance in the cafeteria, the children put on make-up and funny hats although they can't see one another. A teenage girl weeps and a boy pats her head and shyly embraces her. Who needs narration. —*Hitch.*

Fieras en Brama
(Savage Creatures In Heat)
(MEXICAN-COLOR)

A Películas Mexicanas release of a Cinematográfica Intercontinental-Cinematográfica Jalisco production. Produced by Edgardo Gazcón, Raúl de Anda. Directed by Gilberto de Anda. Stars Valentín Trujillo. Screenplay, T. Serranda, adapted by Dean St. Gilbert; camera (color), Antonio de Anda; editor, Francisco Chiu; music, Ernesto Cortázar. Reviewed at Hollywood Twin theater 2, N.Y., June 3, 1987. Running time: **97 MINS.**
Pedro . . . . Valentín Trujillo
Elisa . . . . Sasha Montenegro
Don Rodrigo . . . . Eric del Castillo
María . . . . Mónica Sánchez Navarro
Don Porfirio . . . . Don Raúl de Anda
Juan . . . . Gilberto de Anda
    Also with: Gilberto Trujillo, Ada Carrasco, Edgardo Gazcón.

Despite the corny title, "Fieras en Brama" (Savage Creatures In Heat) is not à sex comedy. Rather, the pic, directed by Gilberto de Anda, is yet another vehicle for popular Mexican action star Valentín Trujillo, this time with a twist.

In this movie, Trujillo plays a young man named Pedro, on the eve of taking Holy Orders. Instead of taking his final vows, he is sent home for a year to make up his mind.

Right away he meets with temptations of the flesh in the person of the boss' new wife Elisa (Sasha Montenegro), a fierce cold-blooded vixen who doesn't give a damn who she hurts in her selfish pursuits.

The man of the cloth is also enticed by the boss' daughter María (Mónica Sánchez Navarro), his former childhood playmate now blossomed into a beautiful, sensitive woman.

Rather than turn the other cheek, local bullies provoke the novitiate to fisticuffs. In short, his vocation takes a vacation.

Further plot entanglements include jealousy, betrayal, revenge, misunderstandings, etc. The camerawork is imaginative and varied, while the plot is absorbing.

The movie offers a new twist to an old theme and also presents a new characterization for Trujillo. His fans may find their hero's role a bit too subdued, especially after "Yo, el Ejecutor" and "Un Hombre Violento." His acting is reduced mostly to puppy-dog looks and guilty stammerings. Yet, the character is likeable and always convincing.
—*Lent.*

Psycho Girls
(CANADIAN-COLOR)

A Cannon Intl. release of a Lightshow Communications production. Produced by Michael Bockner. Directed by Gerard Ciccoritti. Screenplay, Bockner, Ciccoritti; camera (Film House color), Robert Bergman; editor, Bergman; music, Joel Rosenbaum; sound-associate producer, Peter Boboras; art direction, Craig Richards; assistant director, Leo Faragalli; production manager, Salvatore Greco. Reviewed on MGM/UA Home Video vidcassette, N.Y., June 17, 1987. (MPAA Rating: R.) Running time: **92 MINS.**
Richard Foster . . . . John Haslett Cuff
Sarah . . . . Darlene Mignacco
Victoria . . . . Agi Gallus
    Also with: Rose Graham, Silvio Oliviero, Pier Giorgio Dicicco, Michael Hoole, Dan Rose, Kim Cayer, Dorin Ferber, Frank Procopio, Fernn Kane, Michael Bockner, Maria Cortese, Nikki Pezaro, Gerard Ciccoritti.

"Psycho Girls" is a Toronto-made horror thriller that self-destructs. Shot at the end of 1984, it was released marginally last summer by Cannon and is now a home-video title.

Pic begins quite promisingly with pulp detective story writer Richard Foster (John Haslett Cuff) pounding away at his typewriter and narrating a tale with colorful quips like "What is money anyway, but paper with germs on it?" Unfortunately, the tall tale he relates soon switches from suspense to sadistic Grand Guignol horror of little interest.

Tale begins in 1966 when young parents are murdered by their daughter Sarah with a poisoned meal on their anniversary. Fifteen years later Sarah's an inmate of Lakeview Asylum who escapes to revenge herself on older sister Victoria, who predictably was the real murderer though Sarah took the rap.

Victoria is working as Foster's cook, and Sarah shows up as her replacement after offing her sister. She drugs the food at an anniversary dinner party thrown by Foster and his wife Diana, and then, aided by two crazy henchmen, proceeds to torture and murder them one by one. Punchline of how the humble narrator/writer is mixed up in this mayhem is lifted from Billy Wilder's "Sunset Boulevard."

With the promised gore mainly occurring off-screen, resulting film is neither fish nor fowl, with little to recommend it to the target gross-out audience. Pity that filmmaker Gerard Ciccoritti (who shows up on screen in a cameo looking a lot like Judd Nelson as a pizza delivery boy) couldn't have stuck to hard-boiled fiction with dialog to match.

Cast is weak, hampered by very artificial post-synched dialog (with other folks' voices in some cases, per the end credits). —*Lor.*

Robachicos
(Childstealers)
(MEXICAN-COLOR)

A Películas Mexicanas release of an Instituto Mexicano de Cinematografía (Imcine)-Conacine production. Written and directed by Alberto Bojórquez. Camera (color), Guadalupe García; editor, Reynaldo Portillo; music, Leonardo Valázquez; sound, Cruz Carrasco; art direction, Enrique Domínquez. Reviewed at Hollywood Twin theater 1, N.Y., June 14, 1987. Running time: **101 MINS.**
Juanito Aguilar . . . . Gerardo Vigil
Julián . . . . José Carlos Ruiz
Victoria . . . . Alma Muriel
El Comandante . . . . Narciso Busquets
    Also with: María Rojo, Elsa Maya, Sergio Bustamante, Noe Murayama.

Before the opening crdits for the picture "Robachicos" (Childstealers), Mexican filmmaker Alberto Bojórquez states his intention: to raise public awareness concerning the ugly truth about the trafficking of children. He then goes on to make a very routine low-budget detective film weighted down by a clumsy storyline inhabited by one-dimensional characters.

Script, also by Bojórquez, has all the sensitivity and depth of a banner headline from one of the many scandal sheets found at a supermarket checkout counter. Everything from child abuse to sexual misconduct makes its way into the pic.

Plot details are structured around the adventures of private detective Juanito Aguilar (Gerardo Vigil) and his blunders in tracing down a child trafficking ring led by Julián (José Carlos Ruiz).

For a government-sponsored production, the tech credits are surprisingly weak. Camera is limited to the most unimaginative and functional set-ups, using very few cut-aways or reaction shots. Interiors, especially those showing the children in their prisons, are dark and badly lit. Sync sound levels are also uneven.

Such noted Mexican actors as Ruiz and María Rojo are given very little in the way of characterization. Child actors are allowed to mug for the camera and the overall blocking of the action is confused.

"Robachicos" sensationalizes a serious problem. It works neither as an exposé nor fictional adventure film. In its recent efforts to raise the quality of national cinema, the Mexican Film Institute Imcine failed entirely with this project.—*Lent.*

Rembulan Dan Matahari
(Moon And Sun)
(INDONESIAN-COLOR)

A P.T. Darma Putra Jaya Film Corp., Intl. Cine and Studio Center, Garuda Film, Jakarta, production. Executive procucer, Bob Harijanto. Produced by A. Sugijanto, Nyoo-HanSiang, Hendrick Gozali. Directed by Slamet Rahardjo. Screenplay, Rahardjo; camera (Widescreen, color), Tantra Suryadi; editor, Suryo Susanto; music, Franki Raden. Reviewed at Asian American Intl. Film Festival, N.Y., June 14, 1987. Running time: **105 MINS.**

Director Slamet Rahardjo, formerly a stage actor, has written and directed "Moon And Sun" as his debut film and as an expression of his belief that youthful excesses must be forgiven and allowed to work themselves out. Like the moon and sun, youth and maturity are opposites but need each other and circle each other. First released in 1980, "Moon And Sun" dramatizes the balance and harmony.

Pic begins in the red-light district of the big city. Wong Bagus (Djago Sasongko) is disenchanted with his career as a producer. He bids farewell to the attractive, cheerful prostitute (Christine Sukandar), vowing to return to his remote native village, hoping to atone for his former misdeeds by serving the villagers.

Once in the village, Wong encounters his mother, old friends, and his childhood sweetheart (Nungki Kusumastuti). She has given birth out of wedlock to his son, now seven, who has been adopted by her ineffectual nice-guy husband.

Complications ensue as the good-hearted prostitute arrives in the village. Wearing high heels, she falls into a mudhole while pursuing virile local hero, Wong. Meanwhile, an itinerant health team arrives to introduce condoms and to lecture the village woman on family planning, proffering the argument that love with their husbands will improve if they plan together to space their babies. The village women giggle, but remain unpersuaded. Finally, as his childhood love dies in childbirth, Wong realizes the strange logic of life, the alternating moon and sun, the succession of joy and sadness.—*Hitch.*

Space Rage
(COLOR)

Meek 22d Century Western.

A Vestron Pictures release from Vestron Entertainment of a Morton Reed production. Produced by Reed; reshoots produced by Eric Barrett. Directed by Conrad E. Palmisano. Reshoots directed by Peter McCarthy. Stars Richard Farnsworth, Michael Paré, Lee Purcell, William Windom, John Laughlin. Screenplay, Jim Lenahan, from story by Reed; camera (Deluxe color), Timothy Suhrstedt, reshoots, Tom Richmond; editor, W. Peter Miller; additional editing, Arthur Bressan Jr., Amy Sumner; music, Billy Ferrick, Zander Schloss; sound, Nolan Roberts, reshoots, Calvin Allison; art direction, Cliff Cunningham, William Pomeroy, reshoots, Richard Rollison; set decoration, Diana Allen Williams; stunt coordinator, Bruce Paul Barbour, reshoots, Rick Barker; production manager, Charles Skouras 3d; assistant director, Leon Dudevoir; special effects, Roger George, Frank DeMarco; associate producers, Damian Lee, Patrick Wells. Reviewed on Lightning Video vidcassette, N.Y., June 20,

1987. (MPAA Rating: R.) Running time: **77 MINS.**

The Colonel	Richard Farnsworth
Grange	Michael Paré
Walker	John Laughlin
Maggie	Lee Purcell
Gov. Tovah	William Windom
Drago	Lewis Van Bergen
Quinn	Dennis Redfield
Bryson	Harold Sylvester
Old codger	Hank Worden

"Space Rage," subtitled "Breakout On Prison Planet," represents an abortive early effort by video giant Vestron to enter the ranks of motion picture producers. Project went through innumerable title changes, including "A Dollar A Day," "Trackers: 2180," "Trackers" and "The Last Frontier" and was test-booked at home in Stamford, Conn., for Christmas 1985 before further bookings a year later and current homevideo availability.

Numerous credits for "reshoots" and the tacking on of a very inappropriate soundtrack of hard rock songs indicate a lot of second thoughts went into the film, final version of which is a brief 77 minutes long.

Concept is to update, cheaply, prison film and Western formats to appeal to the public's fascination with sci-fi. Unreconstructed in look from his various Western roles, Richard Farnsworth portrays an ex-LAPD cop now living in New Botany Bay, actually the planet Proxima Centauri 3 in the 22d century. He is mentor to various young guys including tracker (bounty hunter) John Laughlin, who drives a modified dune buggy and ruthlessly captures or kills escapees from the local penal colony.

Michael Paré, in a switch on his usually heroic casting, is an utterly evil prisoner who engineers an escape and kills people (including the warden/governor of the colony William Windom) in cold-blooded fashion until the underwhelming Wild West shootout with Farnsworth.

Special effects are meager and there is almost no futurism to the picture's design, an instant disappointment for sci-fi fans. A good cast is wasted, particularly Lee Purcell as token femme on view. Westerns are dead and enough clunkers like this one will kill off the space opera as well. —*Lor.*

Odd Jobs
(COLOR)

Comedy tries too hard.

A Tri-Star Pictures release of an HBO Pictures presentation, in association with Silver Screen Partners. Produced by Keith Fox Rubinstein. Directed by Mark Story. Screenplay, Robert Conte, Peter Martin Wortmann; camera (Metrocolor), Arthur Albert; editor, Dennis M. Hill; music, Robert Folk; sound, Ed White; production design, Robert R. Benton; set decoration, Sydney Ann Smith-Kee; production manager, Bob Manning; postproduction supervisor, James L. Honoré; additional photography, Peter Lyons Collister; associate producer, Patricia Whitcher; casting, Paul Bengston, David Cohn. Reviewed on HBO, June 22, 1987. (MPAA Rating: PG-13.) Running time: **88 MINS.**

Max	Paul Reiser
Dwight	Robert Townsend
Woody	Scott McGinnis
Byron	Paul Provenza
Roy	Rick Overton
Wylie	Leo Burmeister
Sally	Julianne Phillips

Also with: Thomas Quinn, Savannah Smith Boucher, Richard Dean Anderson, Richard Foronjy, Jake Steinfeld, Leon Askin, Andra Akers, Don Imus.

"Odd Jobs" is the last of seven unsuccessful features made about three years ago by HBO and Silver Screen Partners to see the light of day, barely. Lensed in 1984, overwrought attempt at comedy wastes the talents of several young performers soon to achieve prominence.

Paul Reiser (currently scoring in "Beverly Hills Cop II") toplines as a college kid working for the Cabrizzi Bros. moving firm for the summer (pic originally was titled alternately "Summer Jobs" and "This End Up"). First half of the film disjointedly crosscuts back and forth between his misadventures and those of four of his classmates: Robert Townsend (pre-"Hollywood Shuffle") and Paul Provenza working as caddies; Rick Overton selling vacuum cleaners door-to-door and Scott McGinnis as a waiter.

Each one loses his job, teaming up to form a moving company in deadly competition with the Cabrizzis. Pranks and physical humor are moderately funny in the second half, but pic is way too talky, overloaded with pointless and endless voiceover narration by Reiser and others trying to create the structure of the story being related to a femme journalist.

Director Mark Story smothers the potential comedy with overly broad performances and heavy-handed direction. Reiser emerges as a pleasant lead, but includes Jerry Lewis-style mannerisms which clash with his character. Rest of the cast, particularly Jake Steinfeld (of Body by Jake training fame) as a goonish mover, tend to ham it up, while Townsend is quite bland compared to his "Shuffle" persona. Julianne Phillips (future Mrs. Bruce Springsteen) is totally wasted as the female lead, and radio star Don Imus performs his evangelist impression briefly to no effect. —*Lor.*

Vzlomshik
(Burglar)
(SOVIET-COLOR)

A Lenfilm Studio production. Directed by Viktor Ogorodnikov. Screenplay, Viktor Priyomikhov; camera (color), G. Mironov; art director, Viktor Ivanov; music, V. Kisin; artistic producer, Irakli Kwirikadze. Reviewed at Domkino, Leningrad, May 29, 1987. Running time: **83 MINS.**

With: Oleg Yelikomov, Konstantin Kinchev, Y. Teapnik, S. Gaitan, P. Petrenko.

Leningrad — "Burglar," a much talked-about first feature from Lenfilm Studio by helmer Viktor Ogorodnikov, is the fictionalized equivalent of outspoken documentaries on the Soviet teen fringe like "Is It Easy To Be Young?" Its echoes of French and American film style, and imaginative use of sounds and camera, make for a lively, watchable film by a promising young talent.

Pic opens with a scene of kids breakdancing and boogie-woogieing, Russian-style. Its hero is a boy of 12, a hip kid who lives with an always-absent father (the mother is dead) and who worships his older brother Kosta, a rock guitarist. In casual, almost candid camera style, "Burglar" shows the boys walking around town, talking to their friends on the street and going to concerts (Kosta plays while little brother listens, enraptured).

The film displays a fresh realism in describing the tacky interior of a multi-family apartment, or a punk party where a girl gets beaten up without anybody taking notice. Equally realistic is the family drama — the ineffectual, weak father feels compelled to ask his sons' blessing to marry a lonely, well-meaning girlfriend. The little hero is a silent observer who absorbs more than we realize, until he steals a synthesizer from a disco to prevent his beloved brother (who is being blackmailed for money) from doing it. Pic's ending is a surrealistic motorcycle scene, in which Kosta fights with his nemesis-blackmailer, nicknamed The Joker.

To its credit is film's direct, sympathetic approach to its outsider characters, from the rebel Kosta and his loser father, to the "metalists" (Russian punks) who make their own studded leather outfits and tattoo hammers and sickles on their arms.—*Yung.*

Prizemyavane
(Return To Earth)
(BULGARIAN-COLOR)

A Bulgariafilm production. Directed by Roumyana Petrova. Screenplay, Névélina Popova; camera (color), Svetla Ganeéa; art direction, Yuliana Bozhkova; music, Raicho Lyubenov. Reviewed at Pesaro Film Festival, June 17, 1987. Running time: **113 MINS.**

Christina Daneva	Plaména Gétova

Also with: Vassil Mihailov, Detelina Lazarova, Georgi Kishkilov, Yuri Yakovlev, Bogdana Voulpé, Zhana Karaivanova, Georgi Mamalev.

Pesaro — A sophisticated, very accessible second feature by Romana Petrova, "Return To Earth" traces the existential crisis of a liberated Bulgarian woman. Made by an all-woman équipe (director, scripter Névélina Popova, camera-woman Svetla Ganeéa), and dealing perceptively with a feminine world, film could make a popular pickup for enterprising programmers of women's film retros and fests.

Christina (Plaména Gétova) is a successful radio exec and a prize-winning writer of children's books. Her busy professional life tends to squeeze out personal commitments — to husband, son, and lover who have to take what they can get of her free time.

This well-juggled but basically superficial existence is suddenly called into question by the death of her son's playmate, a death he was partially responsible for.

Shocked by her son's pain, Christina begins to withdraw from her hectic life and analyze her own responsibilities. Her husband doubts her sincerity; a woman friend is supportive. All is handled with great sensitivity and naturalness. Thesp Plaména Gétova leads a strong cast in a convincing and very sympathetic performance. Pic's only fault is a bit of excess padding that draws running time out more than necessary.

Though story could take place anywhere in the west, and Christina's dilemma is a modern universal, film's setting is very specifically the new high-rises of today's Sofia.
—*Yung.*

Australian Made
(AUSTRALIAN-DOCU-COLOR)

A Hoyts release of a Captured Live production. Executive producer, Ian Gow. Produced by John McLean. Directed by Richard Lowenstein. Camera (color), Andrew De Groot; editor, Jill Bilcock; music production, Mark Optiz; sound, Roger Savage; second unit director, Ray Argall. Reviewed at the Hoyts Entertainment Center, Sydney, June 24, 1987. Running time: **90 MINS.**

Sydney — Technically, this chronicle of Australia's biggest ever tour of Aussie bands — Australian Made — is topnotch, but as a record of the atmosphere, personalities, and behind-the-scenes goings-on "Australian Made" only partially succeeds.

Hailed as a coming of age for the Aussie music industry, the Australian Made tour — running through January this year, attracting some 139,000 people across the country's cities — made it clear Australian bands and concert prodution values were on an equal footing with the world.

"Australian Made" likewise reflects state-of-the-art tech ability; it claims to be the first fully digitally recorded and post-produced Aussie feature, and certainly sound quality is exceptional.

Camerawork is fine and performances well captured, but overall effect tends towards repetitiveness since the bulk of the film is taken up with stage performance, usually shot at the same venue.

What's missing is atmosphere, the behind-the-scenes life, the build-up, the dramas. Some of it's there, cannily shown by providing band members with their own portable Video-8m cameras, and there's some crowd interaction, yet it doesn't seem to give a complete picture for a tour that would surely have seen much go on that the audience never saw.

Without that, "Australian Made" becomes little more than a highly classy longform musicvideo, which is surprising given the creative flair director Richard Lowenstein has shown in other features ("Dogs In Space," "Strikebound") and the musicvid medium.

One obvious omission from the pic is the complete absence, due to legal reasons, of any footage relating to Mental As Anything, a major name on the 9-band bill and a lively, humorous outfit. Four songs were said to have been filmed, and there must've been some painstaking editing to erase the band's presence from the video sequences; it's as if they never existed.

Given the popularity here and abroad of other featured bands such as INXS and Jimmy Barnes, "Australian Made" could comfortably find a widespread audience. Pic's makers would seem to think likewise as those two bands take up half of the song footage. "Australian Made," however, despite its great big screen look, is best suited for homevideo. —*Doch.*

Robocop
(COLOR)

Comic book violence shapes up as a summer smash hit.

An Orion Pictures release of a Jon Davison production. Produced by Arne Schmidt. Directed by Paul Verhoeven. Executive producer, Davison. Screenplay, Edward Neumeier, Michael Miner; Camera (Duart color; Deluxe prints), Jost Vacano; editor, Frank J. Urioste; music, Basil Poledouris; production design, William Sandell; art direction, Gayle Simon; set decoration, Robert Gould; set design, James Tocci; Robocop designed, created by Rob Bottin; special makeup effects, Bottin; ED-209 designed, created by Craig Davies, Peter Ronzani; ED-209 sequences by Phil Tippett; special photographic effects, Peter Kuran; special effects, Dale Martin; optical supervision, Robert Blalack; costume design, Erica Edell Phillips; sound (Dolby), Robert Wald; assistant director, Michele A. Panelli; second unit director, Mark Goldblatt; second unit camera, Rick Anderson; associate producers, Stephen Lim, Tippett; casting, Sally Dennison, Julie Selzer. Reviewed at the Samuel Goldwyn theater, Beverly Hills, June 30, 1987. (MPAA Rating: R.) Running time: **103 MINS.**

Robocop/Wagner	Peter Weller
Lewis	Nancy Allen
Jones	Ronny Cox
Clarence	Kurtwood Smith
Morton	Miguel Ferrer
Sgt. Reed	Robert DoQui
The Old Man	Daniel O'Herlihy

Hollywood — "Robocop" is a comic book movie that's definitely not for kids. Even so, the welding of extreme violence with 4-letter words is tempered with enough gut-level humor and technical wizardry to create the kind of talked-about film that is sure to forge a wide swath at the summer b.o. for Orion.

Pic was originally rated X, then cut to an R, but there is enough spilling of guts, raw firepower and visually assaulting scenes remaining to jolt even the most hardened viewer.

If there is anything that says this is the work of Dutch director Paul Verhoeven, it is the theme he has employed in his other films like "A Soldier Of Orange" and "Spetters" — that life is expendable. Otherwise, there is nothing that suggests this is Verhoeven's first American Film. "Robocop" is as much a Hollywood picture as "Rambo," "Dawn Of The Dead," "The Terminator" and "Blade Runner," from which screenwriters Michael Miner and Edward Neumeier have derived several of their ideas, with a nod to the Aussie production "Mad Max" as well.

Verhoeven has deftly managed to incorporate the best elements of these films and still create a fantasy that has an identity all its own.

Roller coaster ride begins with the near-dismemberment of recently transferred police officer Murphy (Peter Weller), to the southern precinct of the Detroit Police Dept. in the not-too-distant future.

As could be said today, in the words of the pic's old line corporate establishment, "Detroit has a cancer, and the cancer is crime."

Except for a couple of 1-liners referring to the Henry Ford Memorial Hospital and Lee Iacocca Elementary School, setting could be any decayed city overrun by corruption. Backdrops are largely futuristic matte paintings where the figures are superimposed, interior shots on the highest floors of any skyscraper and exterior shots of rusted-out factories.

There are three organizations inextricably wound into Detroit's anarchical society — the police, a band of sadistic hoodlums and a multinational conglomerate which has a contract with the city to run the police force.

It's a bleak world they inhabit, one where there's a thin line between lawfulness and lawlessness. Nearly everyone depicted here, anyway, exhibits a certain out-for-number-one mentality, be he cop or crook.

Weller is blown to bits just at the time an ambitious junior exec at the multinational is ready to develop a prototype cyborg — half man, half machine programmed to be an indestructable cop. Thus Weller becomes Robocop, unleashed to fell the human scum he encounters, not the least among them his killers.

It is hard to tell from among the 100-plus names listed in the credits who is to be lauded the most in creating this very original piece of filmmaking, cold-blooded though it is.

Work is so compelling technically, the sight of watching human lives being wasted becomes almost secondary. Nearly every scene contains some amazing stunts or camerawork.

Robocop himself is a fascinating character. How he works and analyzes things and what he is capable of doing is what keeps this adventure at full throttle from the time he walks on screen to the last brutal moment.

True to form for the other cartoon characters come-to-life, those he interacts with are largely 1-dimensional. As sicko sadists go, Kurtwood Smith is a well-cast adversary. Nancy Allen as Weller's partner (before he died) provides the only warmth in the film, wanting and encouraging Robocop to listen to some of the human spirit that survived inside him.

Inventiveness shows up in other ways, too. Screenwriters Neumeier and Miner keep things going at a frenetic pace, yet allowing for a certain amount of silliness and dumb jokes to give the audience a breather and remind them not to take it all too seriously.

"Robocop" is as tightly worked as a film can be, not a moment or line wasted. Even Leeza Gibbons and Mario Machado's co-anchor spot announcing the news, usually throw-away expository stuff, was worked out down to the letter.

Robocop designer and creator Rob Bottin deserves special mention. How he worked out that Weller's human face could be attached to an all-metal exposed brain is completely mesmerizing.

Jost Vacano's photographic eye has also managed the amazing — giving a clean look to chaos. —*Brit.*

Midnight
(HONG KONG — COLOR)

A Make Hero Film production, distributed by Lui Ming Film. Presented by Yeung Ka Wah, Anthony Au. Executive producers, Lui Ming, Wong Ka Hee. Directed by Yeung Ka On. Stars Chan Pui Kee, Ngan Lai Yu, Yu Chi Wei, Lee Wan Kwong, Charles Tao, Chan Yuen Lai, Chan Shuk Yee. Screenplay, Yeung Ka On; camera (color), Ma Kam Cheung; art direction, Hua Wing Choi. Reviewed at Supreme preview room, Hong Kong, June 24, 1987. Running time: **98 MINS.**

(Cantonese soundtrack with English subtitles)

Hong Kong — "Midnight" is another exploitative film about the plight of prostitutes working under the dominant power of the male sex aggressor. With praises and greetings from the audience and reviewers, "Midnight" extended its midnight shows before moving on to the regular screening slots.

The plot follows the conventional story of the prostitute who has to 'work' hard to pay back the pimp and the sister who volunteers to take her sister's place selling body and soul.

The flow of subplots is fluent enough to enhance dramatic tension throughout the doomed destiny of the girls. Except for the role of the master pimp played by Charles Tao, the rest of the characters including the two sisters can't act, but have a lot of flesh to show. —*Mel.*

Mon bel amour, ma déchirure
(My True Love, My Wound)
(FRENCH-COLOR)

A Bac Films release of an Odessa Films/Canal Plus Prods./Générale d'Images coproduction, with the participation of Images Investissements and the Ministry of Culture. Produced by Yannick Bernard. Directed by José Pinheiro. Stars Stephane Ferrara, Catherine Wilkening. Screenplay, Louis Calaferte, Sotha, Pinheiro; camera (color), Richard Andry; music and songs, Romano Musumarra; sound, Jean-Marcel Milan, Vincent Arnardi; editor, Claire Pinheiro-L'Itévévder; art director, Théo Meurisse; costumes, Delphine Bernard, Karlien Nel, Frédérique Menichetti; makeup and special effects, Reiko Kruk, Dominique Colladant; assistant director, Bernard Bourdeix; production manager, Ilya Claisse. Reviewed at the Marignan-Concorde cinema, Paris, June 25, 1987. Running time: **107 MINS.**

Patrick	Stéphane Ferrara
Catherine	Catherine Wilkening
The director	Véra Gregh

Clémentine . . . . Véronique Barrault
Jean-Ba . . . . Jacques Castaldo
Julien . . . . Philippe Manesse
Jacky . . . . Jacky Sigaux
Mouss . . . . Mouss

Paris — "Mon bel amour, ma déchirure" choreographs a new tango in Paris in this hot and heavy tale of sexual passion between a ruffian and an actress. Co-writer and director José Pinheiro doesn't shy away from full frontal male and female nudity, and flash graphic closeups of erections in his coarse depiction of carnal clashes, though pic has only been banned to kids under 13 here. With sexy European pics enjoying something of a popular revival, Stateside especially, this could bully its way abroad, though it fails on deeper emotional and artistic levels.

Former French middleweight boxing champ Stéphane Ferrara (seen in Jean-Luc Godard's "Détective") leads with his crotch in his first starring role as a street tough who arrives at a small café-theater to collect a debt from the troupe manager and catches sight of Catherine Wilkening, a petite, attractive, dark-eyed thesp who seems both disturbed by and attracted to the strapping brute.

After the show Ferrara accosts Wilkening in the street and unceremoniously rapes her against a car, then comes back later for a return engagement on the stage of the empty theater.

Wilkening is stunned and shaken — but she likes it, and soon can't get enough of Ferrara's animalistic lovemaking. Their ensuing clandestine couplings — Wilkening tries to keep the liaison a secret from her fellow actors, which include her live-in boyfriend — take them out to Britanny where the troupe is touring, and back to Paris, where Wilkening lands a leading role in a major dramatic production.

The girl's deepening involvement in rehearsals leads to a predictable cooling of her sexual desires, but by now Ferrara is more than superficially hooked on her. When Wilkening tells him it's over between them, the jock throws her into his car and stages a spectacular Grand Guignolesque suicide on the highway. Wilkening miraculously survives and returns to the theater where she enjoys a personal triumph.

Wilkening and Ferrara (in his best moments a cross between Joe Dallesandro and Gérard Depardieu) generate a good deal of uninhibited intensity, though the screenplay lacks the insight and complexity to make their tragic tryst genuinely affecting. Pic's theme of initiation and sexuality was handled with more style and finesse in André Techiné's Cannes-laureled film "Rendezvous," in which Juliette Binoche also was an aspiring actress

steeped in morbid sexual excess.

Supporting players make do with roles that seem often to have been sacrificed in the cutting room. Véra Gregh gives a vivid performance as the directorial writer-director in whose pretentious piece Wilkening stars, a personage ostensibly inspired by local celebrity director Ariane Mnouchkine. —*Len.*

The Squeeze
(COLOR)

Nonsensical comedy is a bore.

A Tri-Star Pictures release of a Tannen-Hitzig production. Produced by Rupert Hitzig, Michael Tannen. Executive producers, Harry Colomby, David Shamroy Hamburger. Directed by Roger Young. Stars Michael Keaton. Screenplay, Daniel Taplitz; camera (Duart color, Technicolor prints), Arthur Albert; editor, Harry Keramidas; music, Miles Goodman; production design, Simon Waters; art direction, Christopher Nowak; set decoration, Ted Glass; sound (Dolby), Milton C. Burrow; costume design, Jane Greenwood; assistant director, James Chory; casting, Lynn Kressel. Reviewed at the Coronet theater, L.A., July 1, 1987. (MPAA Rating: PG-13.) Running time: **101 MINS.**
Harry Berg . . . . Michael Keaton
Rachel Dobs . . . . Rae Dawn Chong
Hilda Berg . . . . Liane Langland
Gem Vigo . . . . Leslie Bevis
Honest Tom T. Murray . . . John Davidson
Titus . . . . Meat Loaf
Rigaud . . . . Ronald Guttman

Hollywood — Not much life can be wrung out of "The Squeeze," a hapless comedy that runs dry fast. B.o. should be equally barren.

Michael Keaton and Rae Dawn Chong try to do their bit to pump some energy into an essentially nonsensical story about a corrupt Lotto controller named Honest Tom T. Murray (John Davidson in a classic parody of his real-life tv pitchman self), and his unctuous accomplices lead by Monsieur Rigaud (Ronald Guttman).

Keaton's sort of an artist and a con man. Chong first meets up with him trying to serve him papers in her silly role as a bill collector and would-be detective. At about the same time, Keaton goes to retreive a package at his soon-to-be-exwife's apartment and finds a dead man in the closet. He doesn't call the police.

Story by Daniel Taplitz has about two laughs, but in total, the script fails on nearly every level, not the least of which because it is simply unbelievable.

With some great leaps in plot, Taplitz involves the dead body with lottery fixing with Chong working as a detective for both Keaton and Guttman.

Director Roger Young, even while working with a script full of holes, doesn't know where to take his characters with the material he's got.

Keaton and Chong's romance springs from nowhere and has no

spark. Their adversarial relationships to the bad guys is almost cartoonish since it seems their run-ins with them are totally contrived and without fear or fun.

Meat Loaf takes a turn as the lead thug who is constantly sweating and fanning himself. He doesn't emote much, but even so, still comes off like a reject from a bad Mafia movie.

The other nasty characters (Guttman, Leslie Bevis) play their roles as if told to "act heavy." Heavy in this case is wooden.

All told, the bottom line is these folks aren't worth caring about and a thrown Lotto game isn't exactly the most compelling topic. Combination of dull personalities and a leaden script adds up to boredom.

Sad to say, considering that Keaton and Chong can be very funny, "The Squeeze" would make even a bad vidpic. —*Brit.*

Attention bandits
(Warning, bandits)
(FRENCH-COLOR)

An AAA release of a Films 13/TF1 Films coproduction. Produced and directed by Claude Lelouch. Stars Jean Yanne, Patrick Bruel, Marie-Sophie L. Screenplay, Lelouch, Pierre Uytterhoeven; camera (Fujicolor), Jean-Yves Le Mener; editor, Hugues Darmois; music, Francis Lai; art director, Jacques Bufnoir; sound, Harold Maury; production manager, Tania Zazulinsky. Reviewed at the Marignan-Concorde cinema, Paris, June 20, 1987. Running time: **108 MINS.**
Simon Verini . . . . Jean Yanne
Marie-Sophie . . . . Marie-Sophie L.
Mozart . . . . Patrick Bruel
Tonton . . . . Charles Gérard
Manouchka . . . . Corinne Marchand
Mme. Verini . . . . Christine Barbelivien
Also with: Hélène Surgère, Hervé Favre.

Paris — Nothing new from Claude Lelouch other than his leading lady, Marie-Sophie Pochat, a 26-year-old legit actress whom the director promptly married after putting this film in the can. Lelouch's infatuation with Pochat (coyly billed as Marie Sophie L.) is such that the pic is bloated with long, innumerable closeups that tend to turn her role, as the daughter of an unjustly imprisoned outlaw played by Jean Yanne, into little more than a glorified screen test.

Otherwise "Attention bandits" is a weak throwback to the romantic thrillers Lelouch used to make on occasion before embarking on his over-ambitious sentimental-historical epics. Helmer has said that he did some heavy thinking after the failure of his "A Man And A Woman" sequel last year, but to judge from this soggy retread of the Noble Gangster cliché, his thinking cap wasn't plugged in to the right commercial socket. Pic is doing fair business locally, but hasn't much to commend it for other markets.

Pochat is asked to give some substance to role of a young girl

brought up in a classy Swiss pension who in the course of long correspondence with her absent father, whom she believes to be away in South America, learns he is really a professional fence doing a 10-year jail term for a robbery committed by others.

Grown into a conventionally proper young woman with a conventionally proper (and conveniently dull) fiancé, Pochat falls adoringly into Yanne's arms upon his release from prison, but her romantic impressions of daddy as a modern-day Robin Hood get brutally shaken up when Yanne tracks down and cold-bloodedly executes (with Pochat on the scene) the hoods who stole the booty he was fencing and murdered his wife.

Pochat's revulsion doesn't last long because Yanne is soon again nabbed by police. A young bandit (Patrick Bruel) in love with Pochat finally wins her heart and hand by springing Yanne with an audacious (and totally implausible) phony bomb threat.

Yanne is at his most stolid as an old-style bandit openly modelled on Jean Gabin, to whom Lelouch pays tribute by beginning the action in 1976 at the moment of the celebrated actor's death.

Lelouch's direction has rarely been duller — even his usually galloping camera seems afflicted by the script's creeping inertia. Pic could easily be trimmed for export, especially by shearing away all those useless closeups as well as some excruciatingly long and static sequence shots. —*Len.*

Perelet Vorobiev
(Migration Of Sparrows)
(SOVIET-B&W)

A Gruziafilm production. Written and diected by Teimuraz Babluani. Camera (Widescreen, b&w), Viktor Andrievski; art direction, Yuri Kvakadze; music, Babluani. Reviewed at Pesaro Film Festival. June 18, 1987. Running time: **60 MINS.**
With: Gudza Burduli, Teimur Bichiashvili, Rezo Esadze, Amiran Amiransvili, Z. Bakradze, S. Nozadze, G. Salaridze, K. Batukasvili, L. Alibapasvili, S. Schirtladze.

Pesaro — Teimuraz Babluani's first film, "Migration Of Sparrows," was made in 1980 but has just been put into circulation, after the release of his second feature "Brother." It is a short, swift, rollicking ride on a second class night train to Georgia, where drama and laughs tumble over each other in a dazzling tour de force of succinct scripting. It's highly indicated for fest exposure and bold art houses, where it might be coupled with another short feature.

Astonishingly enough, though most of the action takes place in the claustrophobic quarters of a train compartment, film is shot in stretched b&w widescreen, masterfully lensed by Viktor Andrievski. A motley crew of characters is squeezed into benches and sleeping bunks overhead — ingenuous hicks, a pretty girl, a pair of monstrous-looking travelers. The central figure is a blond Southern-type gentleman who passes himself off for an actor and learnedly holds forth on his world travels.

The only passenger who doesn't hang on his every word is an unshaven, burly man in front of him with a tame sparrow under his jacket. This criminal-type finally calls his bluff and the two have a knockdown fistfight until the guards come and chase the unsavory bird owner down the length of the sleeping train.

Next morning gentleman and criminal get off at the same stop — the middle of nowhere, but breathtaking — and continue their ferocious quarrel, while a boy on a bicycle leisurely robs them. They end up almost friends.

Free-wheeling structure and unpredictable characters leave never a dull minute in this fast-moving piece of filmic bravura. — *Yung.*

Korotkie Vstrechi
(Brief Encounters)
(SOVIET-B&W)

An Odessa Film Studio production. Directed by Kira Muratova. Screenplay, Muratova, Leonid Zhukovitski; camera (b&w), Gennadi Kariuk; art direction, Alexandra Kanardova, Oleg Peredeti; music, Oleg Karavaichuk, Vladimir Visotski; editor, Olga Charkova. Reviewed at the Pesaro Film Festival, June 20, 1987. Running time: **95 MINS.**
Nidia . . . . Nina Ruslanova
Maxim . . . . Vladimir Visotski
Valentina Ivanovna . . . . . . Kira Muratova
Also with: L. Bazilskaia, O. Vikland, A. Glazyrin, V. Isakov, T. Midnaia, K. Marinchenko.

Pesaro — Kira Muratova acts as well as directs in "Brief Encounters," a film from 1967 put into release this year. In many ways a companion piece to "Long Farewells" (both films have the same clear b&w camerawork of Gennadi Kariuk), "Encounters" shows the originality, experiment and unpredictable qualities that are Muratova's hallmarks. Story concerns the intersecting love of a city official (Muratova) and her housemaid for the same man, played by Vladimir Visotski. Film was lensed before Visotski became a famous folk singing idol, later to be ostracized officially, before his current posthumous rehabilitation as a tragic counterculture figure.

All three characters have their say in turn. Though scenes are shuffled artily, story really begins when Nidia (Nina Ruslanova), a robust country girl and very young, leaves her village for the city. On the way she meets a lanky geologist named Maxim (Visotski) and ingenuously falls for him. He slips away; she goes searching for him in the city. By chance, she finds employment with Maxim's wife, Valentina (Muratova). Gradually realizing how much they love each other, the maid nobly takes her leave.

Rapid editing jumps back and forth in time from one scene to another, and keeps pic moving at a fast clip. Valentina gets most of the sympathy as the sweet-tempered, rather spacy commissioner who worries about water shortages and shoddy building construction. Her relations with Nidia are friendly and casual; if the girl doesn't want to keep house, Valentina offers to find her a job in a factory instead(!) Maxim is always absent and together the two women share their memories, dreams, jokes. More than a husband, Visotski portrays a romantic vagabond with a guitar who always has to be movin' on.

Film is as unusual and charming as its cast, and has the same offhanded naturalness. — *Yung.*

Gunpowder
(BRITISH-COLOR)

A Lazer Entertainments production. Produced by Maxine Julius. Directed by Norman J. Warren. Stars David Gilliam, Martin Potter. Screenplay, Rory H. MacLean; camera (Rank color), Alistair Cameron; editor, Julius; music, Jeffrey Wood; sound, Patrick Graham; production design, Hayden Pearce; assistant director, Howard Arundel; fight coordinator, Gilliam; fight arranger, Steve Powell; special effects supervisor, Ben Trumble; second unit director, MacLean; second unit camera, Derek Little; associate producers, MacLean, David C. Ball. Reviewed on Vestron Video vidcassette, N.Y., July 4, 1987. (No MPAA Rating.) Running time: **85 MINS.**
Gunn . . . . David Gilliam
Powder . . . . Martin Potter
Sir Anthony Phelps . . . . . . Gordon Jackson
Lovell . . . . Anthony Schaeffer
Dr. Vache . . . . David Miller
Coffee Carradine . . . . Debra Burton
Penny Keynes . . . . Susan Rutherford
Miss Belt . . . . Rachel Laurence

"Gunpowder" is a destitute man's answer to James Bond. Actually, this low-budget British entry for the homevideo trade plays like a cheap version of Lindsay Shonteff's Bond spoofs and is made palatable by the efforts of a game cast.

Alarmingly implausible plot has Gordon Jackson tearing his hair out as a U.K. government official faced with news that lots of gold is being sold, undermining Western currencies and economics. He calls for Gunpowder, the special agent team of Gunn (David Gilliam, with American accent) and his partner Powder (Martin Potter, swishily entertaining as an effete sidekick).

A mad scientist Dr. Vacho (David Miller, wearing a gold bow tie and belt) is in France, scheming to take over by virtue of his invention of causing gold to stay in liquid form without heating. He has British scientist Penny Keynes (Susan Rutherford) kidnaped to help him, but the heroes rescue her and save the day. A subplot involving a pretty double agent improbably named Coffee Carradine (Debra Burton) is typically tongue-in-cheek.

Apart from a helicopter/speedboat chase, film is hurt by its inadequate budget, much of which appears to be in the form of donations or extensive product plugola such as shameless hawking of a dairy (that serves as a front for the baddies' gold-smuggling operations). Rachel Laurence portrays the Miss Moneypenny-styled character of this series, with the switch that she joins in the action in the final reel, commando-style. —*Lor.*

Omega Syndrome
(COLOR)

Wimpy action pic.

A New World Pictures release, in association with Prey Presentations and Smart Egg Pictures. Executive producer, George Zecevic. Produced by Luigi G. Cingolani. Directed by Joseph Manduke. Stars Ken Wahl, George DiCenzo. Screenplay, John Sharkey; camera (United color), Harvey Genkins; editor, Stephen A. Isaacs; music, Nicholas Carras, Jack Cookerly; sound, Kim Ornitz; art direction, Nancy Arnold; assistant director, James M. Freitag; production manager, John Curran; second unit director-stunt coordinator, Spiro Razatos; second unit camera, Mike Shea; postproduction supervisor, Bud S. Isaacs; associate producer, Paul DiSalvo; casting, Barbara Remsen & Associates, Ann Remsen. Reviewed on New World vidcassette, N.Y., July 1, 1987. (MPAA Rating: R.) Running time: **88 MINS.**
Jack Corbett . . . . Ken Wahl
Phil . . . . George DiCenzo
Jessie . . . . Nicole Eggert
Det. Milnor . . . . Doug McClure
Also with: Xander Berkeley, Ron Kuhlman, Bill Morey, Robert Gray, Colm Meaney, Bob Tzudiker, Al White, Patti Tippo, Robert Kim, George Fisher, Christopher Doyle.

"Omega Syndrome" is a low-effort example of an action film backed by European producers to be sold on the world market as an American product. Pic is U.S.-made but lacks the energy and diverting elements to be a credible theatrical release. New World has had several bookings this year but has rushed it out on its video label soon after.

Ken Wahl is a journalist down on his luck, hitting the booze. He whips into action when his 13-year-old daughter (cute Nicole Eggert) is kidnaped during a liquor store robbery. The L.A. police led by Doug McClure, are portrayed as particularly lame here, so Wahl teams up with his ex-Vietnam buddy George DiCenzo to find the kidnapers and rescue Eggert. It turns out she's in the hands of a group of neo-Nazi terrorists, identifiable by their omega symbol wrist tattoos.

Boring film consists mainly of Wahl and DiCenzo interviewing people for clues, punctuated by perfunctory action scenes and explosions. In very cornball fashion, a one-night stand with Patti Tippo is written in for Wahl — that went out with Screenwriting 101. Elsewhere, John Sharkey's clutzy dialog is ridiculous, right down to the imitation James Bond/Schwarzenegger throwaway quip, as DiCenzo exclaims: "Say Goodnight, Gracie" before wasting a heavy. —*Lor.*

Tandem
(Duo)
(FRENCH-COLOR)

An AMLF Release of a Cinéa/Hachette Première/Films A2 coproduction. Produced by Philippe Carcassonne, René Cleitman. Directed by Patrice Leconte. Stars Gérard Jugnot, Jean Rochefort. Screenplay, Leconte, Patrick Dewolf; camera (Eastmancolor), Denis Lenoir; editor, Joëlle Hache; music, François Bernheim; sound, Alain Curvelier, Dominique Hennequin; art director, Ivan Maussion; assistant director, Etienne Dhaene; production manager, Frédéric Sauvagnac. Reviewed at the Marignan-Concorde cinema, Paris, June 28, 1987. Running time: **92 MINS.**
Rivetot . . . . Gérard Jugnot
Mortez . . . . Jean Rochefort
Bookseller . . . . Sylvie Granotier
Waitress . . . . Julie Jezequel
Councillor . . . . Jean-Claude Dreyfus

Paris — Patrice Leconte, who has directed a number of mostly indifferent commercial comedies with actors usually recruited from the café-theater milieu, breaks away from his routine anonymity with "Tandem," a male-bonding road comedy starring Gérard Jugnot and Jean Rochefort.

Rochefort plays the veteran producer-host of a long-running itinerant radio quiz show which he broadcasts daily from a different provincial town. On the road with him is his faithful sidekick Gérard Jugnot who serves as chauffeur, secretary, sound man, confidant and male nurse.

The script by Leconte and Patrick Dewolf describes their last lap together, during which Jugnot intercepts a message from the home station that the show is being cancelled because of diminishing ratings. Terrified that the news will be a fatal blow to his boss, Jugnot tries to keep him in the dark as long as possible.

Despite some inevitable platitudes about loneliness and camaraderie and a happy ending that strikes a false note, "Tandem" is often fresh, funny-sad and maliciously ironic in its look at the mediocrity of success and its ignominious side-effects. Leconte directs with an alertness and feeling for tone and atmosphere that weren't evident in previous pictures.

The Rochefort-Jugnot tandem of course is pic's main trump, with former, looking like an aging gigolo, limning a pathetically funny portrait of a straw man personality trying to hold on to his tinsel dignity and backwater renown. Jugnot, who has donned a wig and shaved his mustache to look a bit younger, confirms the nuanced dramatic skill he displayed in his previous roles as Rochefort's bedeviled drudge and alter ego.

Tech credits are fine. —*Len.*

Masterblaster
(COLOR)

Uneventful survival games opus.

An Artist Entertainment Group release from Radiance Films Intl. of a First American Entertainment production. (Intl. sales, Overseas Filmgroup.) Executive producer, William Grefe. Produced by Randy Grinter. Directed by Glenn R. Wilder. Screenplay, Grinter, Wilder, Jeff Moldovan, from story by Grinter; camera (color), Frank Pershing Flynn; editor, Angelo Ross; music, Alain Salvati; sound, Henry Lopez; stunt coordinator, Scott Wilder; second unit director-camera, Grinter; assistant directors, Don Moody, Marty Swartz; production manager, Jon Williams; associate producers, Chuck Greenfield, Angela Greenfield, Jeanna Plafsky, Richard Pitt. Reviewed on Prism Entertainment vidcassette, N.Y., July 3, 1987. (MPAA Rating: R.) Running time: **84 MINS.**

Jeremy Hawk ....Jeff Moldovan
Samantha ....Donna Rosae
DeAngelo ....Joe Hess
Lewis ....Peter Lundblad
Mike ....Robert Goodman
Also with: Richard St. George, George Gill, Earleen Carey, Jim Reynolds, Julian Byrd, Ron Burgs, Tracy Hutchinson, Bill Whorman, Ray Forchion, Lou Ann Carroll, Kari Whitman.

Currently in regional release ahead of its homevideo destiny, "Masterblaster" is another entry in the stillborn genre of mock-killing games that get out of hand (e.g., "TAG: The Assassination Game," "Gotcha" or "The Zero Boys").

Jeff Moldovan (who also coscripted) plays Jeremy Hawk, a Vietnam vet involved in a tournament to decide who is masterblaster, the best at a survival/fortune hunt course in which losers are shot with red paint rather than bullets. Of course, a madman is on the loose, killing the participants for real. Despite numorous red herrings, including Hawk's rumored background of war atrocities, killer's identity is fairly easy to guess, though his motives are unbelievable when finally revealed.

Low-budget actioner shot in Florida is heavy on talk. Typical of recent pictures in which stunt persons figure prominently both behind and in front of the camera, pic's acting is flat, particularly that of taciturn lead Moldovan. Several false endings in which characters thought to be dead turn out to be still kicking come off as extremely hokey.—*Lor.*

I Was A Teenage Zombie
(COLOR-16m)

A Horizon Releasing release of a Periclean Motion Picture production. Produced by Richard Hirsh, John Elias Michalakias. Directed by Michalakias. Screenplay, James Martin; additional scenes and dialog, George Seminara, Steve McCoy; camera (color, 16m), Peter Lownes; editor, Michalakias; music, Jonathan Roberts, Craig Seaman; sound, Hirsh, Sal Lumetta; special makeup effects, Carl Sorenson, Mike Lacky. Reviewed at Magno Preview 4 screening room, N.Y., June 24, 1987. (No MPAA Rating.) Running time: **92 MINS.**

Dan Wake ....Michael Ruben
Gordy ....George Seminara
Mussolini ....Steve McCoy
Rosencrantz ....Peter Bush
Cindy Faithful ....Cassie Madden
Miss Lugae ....Cindy Keiter
Margo ....Gwyn Drischell
Lieberman ....Allen L. Rickman
Hilda ....Lynnea Benson
Lenny ....Ray Stough

The best thing about "I Was A Teenage Zombie," unfortunately, is its title, harking back to the Herman Cohen hits of the 1950s that launched the acting careers of Michael Landon and Gary Conway. New pic is a low-budgeter that is amateurish in every department and a very long shot to curry favor in midnight bookings.

Thin plot has a drug pusher named Mussolini (hambone Steve McCoy) selling toxic marijuana to high school students, causing one of them (George Seminara) to go through special makeup convulsions that are a hint of the poorly executed, grossout makeup effects to come. Mussolini ends up dead and dumped in the river, but comes back to life (face painted green) as a zombie caused by a leak into the river from a nearby nuclear power plant.

When the hero (Michael Ruben) is killed, his pals dump him into the river to create a good guy zombie to do battle with Mussolini. Pic climaxes with extreme gore at the high school dance.

Besides the phony, done better many times before makeup effects, pic suffers from idiotic dialog, amateur acting and direction worthy of a home movie. A nonstop score of rock songs functions as droning muzak in the background.—*Lor.*

Laka
(The Stain)
(SOVIET-B&W)

A Grusiatelefilm production. Written and directed by Aleko Tsabadze. Camera (b&w), Nodar Namgaladze; art direction, Gogi Tatishvili. Reviewed at Domkino, Tbilisi, June 1, 1987. Running time: **90 MINS.**

Kiesha ....Kishward Glunchadze
Mother ....Rusudan Kvlividze
Amiran ....Z. Begalishvili
Also with: O. Bazgadze (father), G. Mgaloblishvili (Truti), D. Khurtsilova, V. Chumburidze, G. Shanidze.

Tbilisi—"The Stain" is a much talked-about debut feature by Aleko Tsabadze, made in black & white for Georgian tv. The offhanded glimpse it offers of the seamier side of young people's lives stirred a good deal of interest when it was nationally aired in May, and Western fests are already after it.

Story is told so casually it isn't clear there is a story till a long way into the film. Kiesha (Kishward Glunchadze), a fairly typical teen, is a college student never seen cracking a book. He spends his time rehearsing with a band, cutting up, loping around town. At one point he bets 1,000,000 cigars on the toss of a coin — and loses. The easy-going winner says 3,000 rubles will do, and he means it. Kiesha realizes he's come up against a gangster. He has no choice but to pay up, and his idleness turns into a desperate search for money.

"Stain" 's rough, amateur lensing, full of zooms and hand-held camerawork, contributes to create a primitive New Wave look that underlines the shagginess of its characters. It's the kind of atmosphere where you're not surprised to see a girl shooting heroin in a cheap hotel room, non-actors cheerfully pulling their pants down for the camera, and the kind of casual violence usually associated with urban life in the West. It comes as no surprise Kiesha and his pals don't dream of turning to the police. In this Georgian home-movie version of "Breathless," there is even a gratuitous dramatic finale.

Interesting if flawed, "Stain" reveals a helmer to watch. — *Yung.*

Mi Nombre Es Gatillo
(My Name Is Gatillo)
(MEXICAN-COLOR)

A Peliculas Mexicanas release of a Galmex Films-Telefilms Corp. (Televicine) production. Executive producers, Jesús Galindo, Eduardo Galindo. Produced by Pedro Galindo Jr. Directed by Pedro Galindo 3d. Stars Alvaro Zermeno. Screenplay, Galindo Jr., Carlos Valdemar, adapted by Galindo 3d; camera (color), Miguel Arana; editor, Carlos Savage; music, Manuel Esperón; special effects, Pepe Parra; stunts, Alberto Vázquez. Reviewed at Hollywood Twin theater II, N.Y., June 24, 1987. Running time: **89 MINS.**

Pablo Moncada (Gatillo) .Alvaro Zermeño
Andrea Orsina ....Ana Luisa Peluffo
Lucio Contreras
(Ruso).............Eleazar Garcia Jr.
Chato ....Julio Ahuet
Captain Nichols ....Juan Gallardo
Rebeca ....Roxanna Chávez
Also with: Javier García, Christopher Lago, Reynaldo Martínez (El Gallero), Manuel Benítez, Carlos González, Manuel Rodero Jr., Jorge Guerra, Regino Herrera, George Samano Jr., Rodolfo Lago, Armando Galván, Martín Quintana, Antonio López, Baltazar Guzmán.

The latest offering from Mexico's Galindo family, "Mi Nombre Es Gatillo" (My Name Is Gatillo), is an overly complicated and confusing action picture, directed by Pedro Galindo 3d.

Action revolves around the character of U.S. special narc agent Pablo Moncada (Alvaro Zermeño), a free-wheeling two-gun hero who wears a cowboy hat and is known by the moniker "Gatillo" (trigger). Accompanied by his faithful sidekick Chato (Julio Ahuet), Gatillo hunts down his arch nemesis Andrea Orsina (Ana Luisa Peluffo), a cocaine and heroin smuggler, and her partner in crime "Ruso" Contreras (Eleazar Garcia Jr.), an international terrorist.

The film has a comic-book approach to narration. Villians are bad because they're supposed to be. They live and work in an underground Texas-based fortress with Swastikas decorating the walls for no reason and they control an army of loyal followers. They continue to live and work there even after the place has been discovered and raided by the cops.

Although the villains are extremely dangerous and boast an army of machinegun-toting bad guys, Gatillo and Chato go after them single-handedly with only the minimum reinforcements for the final showdown.

The audience is asked time and again to stretch its imagination. We discover that the reason the cold-blooded Andrea hates Gatillo is that she's the mother of his son. She is now a former housewife turned international arch thug.

Fight sequences are often too exaggerated to be effective, while Miguel Arana's imaginative lensing tries to cover up for what's lacking in production costs.

Overall, "Mi Nombre Es Gatillo" doesn't make a whole lot of sense. It's an illustrated comic book with none of the camp fun and larger-than-life characters that usually accompany such a simplistic view of life.—*Lent.*

Der Nachbar
(The Neighbor)
(SWISS-GERMAN-COLOR)

A Rex Film Zollikon (Zurich) release of a Boa Filmproduktion, Zurich-ZDF (Second German tv network) coproduction. Directed by Markus Fischer. Screenplay, Fischer, Alex Gfeller; camera (color), Jorg Schmidt-Reitwein; editor, Fischer; music, Pi-Rats; art direction, Hans Gloor; costumes, Ann Poppel; sound, Hanspeter Fischer; lighting, Michael Stöger; production manager, Tosho Martin Pfeifer. Reviewed at the Studio Commercio, Zurich, June 26, 1987. Running time: **96 MINS.**

Georg Walz ....Rolf Hoppe
Rita Romani ....Eva Scheurer
Ali ....Larbi Tahiri
Renato ....Marco Morelli
Barmaid ....Vera Schweiger
Eva ....Erika Eberhard
Hassan/Peter ....David Höner
Susanne ....Eva Scheurer

Taxi driver . . . . Ales Urbanczik
Civil official . . . . Peter Fischli
Policeman . . . . Jodoc Seidel
Old man . . . . Erwin Parker

Zurich — Swiss helmer Markus Fischer, whose last effort, the 1985-made "Kaiser und eine Nacht" (Kaiser And One Night), was a critically panned boxoffice disaster, picks up with "Der Nachbar" (The Neighbor). The new film is a neat little psychological meller with a *film noir* quality, but without the special touch which would lift it out of the ordinary.

The original story, written by Fischer together with Alex Gfeller, concerns an ex-cop who cannot come to grips with his past. In pursuing an Arab, he accidentally shot an innocent passerby, causing the woman irreparable mental damage. Prematurely retired, the guilt-ridden, elderly policeman now lives isolated and anonymous in the old part of Zurich.

He spends his time watching his neighbor, a young woman whose flat he has tapped with bugs and video. She resembles the woman he shot and has an Arab boyfriend who might serve as a lead to the man he missed in the pursuit. He gets in touch with the woman and they become friends in a sort of father-daughter relationship.

When she is threatened repeatedly by her jealous ex-lover, he comes to her rescue, and the violent dispute ends with the lover's accidental death. They remove the body in panic and are now accomplices. The older man's fear of discovery reaches almost paranoid dimensions.

East German character actor Rolf Hoppe, who gave a memorable performance as General Göring in István Szábo's Oscar-winning "Mephisto," again offers an impressive characterization, managing even to rise above script deficiencies and loopholes. Screen newcomer Eva Scheurer as the pretty neighbor involuntarily involved in a crime, has an expressive face, but limited possibilities, also due to the uneven script. The same must be said of Fischer's direction.

The camerawork by Jörg Schmidt-Reitwein (who lensed some Werner Herzog films) prefers dark and toned-down colors benefiting the picture's somber atmosphere. Other technical credits are routine.
—*Mezo.*

Ladies Of The Lotus
(CANADIAN-COLOR)

A North American Pictures presentation, in association with Columbia Western Management. Produced by John A. Curtis, Lloyd A. Simandl. Directed by Simandl, Douglas C. Nicolle. Screenplay, Jane Mengering Hausen; camera (Alpha Cine color), Victor Nicolle; editor, Simandl, Douglas C. Nicolle; music & sound, Greg Ray; songs,

Collin Weinmaster, Michael Rheault, Greg Ray; production design-production manager, Lyne J. Grantham; art direction, George Pantages; costume design, Christopher Knox, Gwen Bottomley; associate producers, Sharon Christensen, Ken Sherk, Frank Trebell; casting, Evalon K. Shandler. Reviewed on Magnum Entertainment videcassette, N.Y., June 30, 1987. (No MPAA Rating.) Running time: **88 MINS.**
Phillip . . . . Richard Dale
Dominique . . . . Angela Read
Sean . . . . Patrick Bermel
Tara . . . . Darcia Carnie
Also with: Martin Evans, Nathan Andrews, Lisanne Burk, April Alkins, Nikki Murdock Marloe, Marney McGiver, Hay Hay Jotie.

"Ladies Of The Lotus" is an oddball exploitation film that suffers from the pernicious influence of music videos. Shot on film but with postproduction done on video it is in any case too boring for theatrical use.

Confusing and slapdash storyline concerns warring gangsters in the Vancouver area. Lotus Inc. is involved in drugs and white slavery, while rival thugs are mowing down the Lotus personnel and fashioning scams of their own involving a modeling studio run by Lotus villainesses Angela Read and Darcia Carnie.

Lead palyer Richard Dale begins as a clichéd character, a musclebuilding nut who installs a secret camera that photographs the models in their dressing room; then he stalks them and kills them. He goes through this routine with Carnie and then unbelievably turns into her instant savior when the gangsters also try to kill her. Most of the loose ends in the final reel are settled rather simply by gunfire.

Tiresome film is just an excuse to show pretty models in lingerie at every opportunity. Cast is either watching music videos or daydreaming in the form of music videos; action scenes are poorly executed.

An undertone of light bondage links the film to codirector Lloyd Simandl's previous effort, the 1979 picture "Autumn Born" starring the late Dorothy Stratten, a softcore bondage opus that was unflatteringly represented in Bob Fosse's "Star 80." — *Lor.*

Heartbeat 100
(HONG KONG-COLOR)

A Cinema City production, released by Golden Princess theater circuit. Produced by Raymond Wong. Executive producer, Wan Ka Man. Directed by Kent Cheng, Lo Kin. Stars Lui Fong, Maggie Cheung, Bonnie Law, Mark Cheng. Screenplay, Raymond Wong, Philip Chong, Ng Man Fai; camera (color), James Chan; music, David Wu; art direction, Andy Li; associate producer, Parkman Wong. Reviewed at President theater, Hong Kong, June 19, 1987. Running time: **98 MINS.**

(Cantonese soundtrack with English subtitles)

Hong Kong — "Heartbeat 100" is a thriller about a female writer (Maggie Cheung) going off to an old village to dig up some inspiration for her upcoming story. She is accompanied by her sister (Bonnie Law) and "weeny eyes" (Lui Fong).

In the old village they are involved in a series of murder cases mainly because of Maggie's curiosity. Her quest for sources for her stories eventually leads to the murderers attempting to kill the trio who have revealed their crime.

As a cliffhanger, it fails due to plot. Combination of irrelevant gags and childish comedy takes a lot of time which could have been used to establish tension.

None of the roles is played properly by any of the leads. For instance, viewers wouldn't know that Maggie is a writer, if she hadn't kept repeating it. Is the police sergeant (Mark Cheng) supposed to be a dutiful and brave guy? There's no way of telling as the characters remain underdeveloped.

Wu Fung, who plays the conspirator of the murders, is the only actor whose character creates the kind of atmosphere required

This one won't go far outside Chinatowns abroad.—*Mel.*

Mutant Hunt
(COLOR)

Okay for B-movie fans.

A Wizard Video presentation of an Entertainment Concepts (Tycin Entertainment) production. Produced by Cynthia DePaula. Written and directed by Tim Kincaid. Camera (Precision color), Thomas Murphy; editor, Barry Zetlin; music supervisor, Tom Milano; production design, Ruth Lounsbury; set decoration, Marina Zurkow; costume design, Jeffrey Wallach; special effects, Matt Vogel; special makeup effects, Ed French; cyborg mechanical design, Tom Lauten; combat sequences stager, Ron Reynaldi; production manager, Tina Kacanides; assistant director, Budd Rich; second unit camera, Arthur D. Marks. Reviewed on Wizard Video vidcassette, N.Y. July 1, 1987. (No MPAA Rating.) Running time: **77 MINS.**
Matt Riker . . . . Rick Gianasi
Darla Haynes . . . . Mary Fahey
Johhny Felix . . . . Ron Reynaldi
Elaine Eliot . . . . Taunie Vrenon
Z . . . . Bill Peterson
Paul Haynes . . . . Mark Umile
Domina . . . . Stormy Spill
Also with: Doug De Vos, Leeanne Baker, Adriane Lee, Eliza Little.

"Mutant Hunt" (originally titled "Matt Riker: Mutant Hunt") is another in the series of low-budget "New York" science fiction features kicked off by the cult success of "Liquid Sky." Pic is a dead-pan homage to 1950s monster pics from the team that made "Breeders" and "Robot Holocaust" (it was actually filmed as the first of the trio) and like them is debuting on vidcassette, bypassing domestic theatrical release. Soundtrack repeats much of the music from "Breeders."

Rick Gianisi toplines as rugged mercenary of the future Matt Riker, called in to hunt down wild, mutant cyborgs of the Delta 7 model, designed by scientist Paul Haynes (Mark Umile), but being used for evil by megalomaniac Z (Bill Peterson). With Haynes' sister Darla (Mary Fahey), Riker recruits a team including comic relief martial arts expert Felix (Ron Reynaldi, also the film's combat stager) and pretty government agent Elaine (Taunie Vrenon), who doubles as exotic dancer at Manhattan's Club Inferno.

Another evildoer in the heroes' way is Domina (played by the memorably named actress Stormy Spill), who is jealous of Z and out to get the drug Euphoron which he is using on the mutants (and to which she is addicted). Finale has Domina unveiling her own creation, a beefy Delta 8 cyborg.

Suffering from some continuity errors and a very weak ending, "Mutant Hunt" if fun on the level of those monotone second features of 30 years ago which no-name casts pondered World War III or responded to alien invasions. As usual, filmmaker Tim Kincaid livens things up with a villainess sporting a funny accent; this time Stormy Spill gets the laughs talking like Anjelica Huston in "Prizzi's Honor." Amidst some rather gory scenes, film's highlight is a lifesize puppet of a half-destroyed cyborg, with kudos going to Ed French and Tom Lauten for creating an effect that's as impressive as many expensive animatronics creatures. —*Lor.*

The Edge Of Hell
(Rock 'n' Roll Nightmare)
(CANADIAN-COLOR)

A Shapiro Entertainment presentation of a Thunder Films production. Executive producers, Jerry Landesman, Cynthia Sorrell. Produced and written by Jon-Mikl Thor. Directed by John Fasano. Camera (Medallion color), Mark MacKay; editor, Robert Williams; music, The Tritonz; sound, Ray van Doorn; art direction, Wolfgang Siebert; production manager-postproduction supervisor, Robert Connelly; assistant director, Cindy Sorrell; special makeup effects, Arnold Gargiulo 2d, Fascination Film Effects; creatures, Gargiulo, Fasano, John Gibson, Jim Cirile, Anthony Bua, Frank Dietz, Vincent Modica; associate producer, Mike Dolgy. Reviewed on Academy Home Entertainment vidcassette, N.Y., July 3, 1987. (MPAA Rating: R.) Running time: **83 MINS.**
John Triton . . . . Jon-Mikl Thor
Lou Anne . . . . Jillian Peri
Roger Eburt . . . . Frank Dietz
Max . . . . Dave Lane
Randy . . . . Teresa Simpson
Also with: Adam Fried, Denise Dicandia, Liane Abel, Jim Cirile, Gene Kroth, Jesse D'Angelo, Rusty Hamilton.

"The Edge Of Hell" (known in homevideo circles as "Rock 'n' Roll Nightmare") is a low-budget supernatural hörror film of interest strictly for its varied hand puppet monsters.

Canadian-made opus is the umpteenth attempt of late to marry horror films with heavy metal music. Premise, almost identical with a foreign opus "Blood Tracks," has the band The Tritonz holing up in a remote farmhouse for five weeks to rehearse and create material for their new album. Neaby barn has a modern recording studio, with film padded out unconvincingly by lengthy musical numbers, replete with concert lighting, supposedly taking place in the barn.

Monsters from hell, typically masquerading as band members or groupies, kill off the cast one by one. Ridiculous payoff has band singer Jon-Mikl Thor (who also wrote and produced the film) facing off against Satan and revealing that he (Thor) is the only real character, the rest of the cast having been phantoms he conjured up to lure Satan out in the open. Thor is supposedly the archangel Triton and he defeats Satan with a choke hold. Garbed at finish in jeweled loin cloth, heavy eye makeup and teased blond hair, Thor is fairly embarrassing. Rest of the cast has little to do.

Makeup effects and puppetry is childish but fun, with the main contribution (including the skeletal Satan figure) made by Arnold Gargiulo 2d, whose varied credits range from "The Deadly Spawn" and "Spookies" to "The Devil In Miss Jones Part 2." Insistent musical score is a drag. —Lor.

Mujeres Salvajes
(Savage Women)
(MEXICAN-COLOR)

A Peliculas Mexicanas release of a Cooperativa Rio Mixcoac production. Executive producer, Jorge Santoyo. Produced, written and directed by Gabriel Retes. Stars Tina Romero, Santoyo. Camera (color), Genaro Hurtado; editor, Edgardo Pavàn; music, Juan José Çalayud. Reviewed at Hollywood Twin theater I, N.Y., June 20, 1987. Running time: 82 MINS.
Gaviota . . . . Tina Romero
Pablo. . . . . Jorge Santoyo
Arturo . . . . Abel Woolrich
Lucha . . . . Patricia Mayers
Also with: Vicky Vàzquez, Gonzalo Lora, Isabel Quintanar, Tomás Leal, Alejandro Tamayo.

The motivation behind the 1984 Mexican film "Mujeres Salvajes" (Savage Women) seems pretty obvious: to show a lot of women running around naked. As kinky as this film is, there are simply not enough excesses to attract any international cult interest.

Produced by Mexico's film cooperative Rio Mixcoac, pic was written, produced and directed by Gabriel Retes, who received national critical attention for such socially realistic films as "Chin Chin el Teporocho," "Nuevo Mundo" and "Bandera Rota." "Savage Women" marks a low point in his

oeuvre.

Storyline deals with a group of six women in prison who discover the whereabouts of a buried treasure. Pledging eternal loyalty, they manage an easy escape. Then it's off to a deserted beach where they can take off their clothes and look for the treasure. First, they chance upon six guys camping in the vacinity.

Retes spends a lot of time contrasting the two groups, showing the cold selfish men and the gentle affectionate women at work and play. Sexual messages are confusing. Most of the women are men-haters, but they go absolutely crazy when they discover that two of the men are homosexual. Whereas they forgive the man who brutally rapes one of them, the gays must be executed. Then it is survival of the fittest as both their ranks diminish.

Lensing tends to focus a lot on location with a travelog approach to palm trees and white sand beaches. Editing and sound levels are uneven and jerky throughout.

"Savage Women" is impoverished, lacking ideas, talent and satisfactory tech credits. Above all, it isn't savage enough. Although there is lots of nudity, male and female homosexuality, masturbration and other such goings on, none of it seems to be any fun for either the audience or particpants. —Lent.

Hope And Glory
(BRITISH-COLOR)

A Columbia Pictures release, in association with Nelson Entertainment and Goldcrest. Executive producers, Jake Eberts, Edgar F. Gross. Produced, written and directed by John Boorman. Camera (Technicolor), Philippe Rousselot; music, Peter Martin; production design, Anthony Pratt; art direction, Don Dossett; set decoration, Joan Woollard; costume design, Shirley Russell; sound, Peter Handford; special effects coordinator, Phil Stokes; assistant director, Andy Armstrong; second unit director-coproducer, Michael Dryhurst; additional photography, John Harris; casting, Mary Selway. Reviewed at The Burbank Studios, Burbank, July 9, 1987. (MPAA Rating: PG-13.) Running time: 113 MINS.
Grace Rohan . . . . Sarah Miles
Clive Rohan . . . . David Hayman
Mac . . . . Derrick O'Connor
Molly . . . . Susan Wooldridge
Dawn Rohan . . . . Sammi Davis
Grandfather . . . . Ian Bannen
Bill Rohan . . . . . . Sebastian Rice-Edwards
Bruce . . . . Jean-Marc Barr
Grandmother . . . . Annie Leon
Hope . . . . Amelda Brown
Faith . . . . Jill Baker
Charity . . . . Katrine Boorman
Sue Rohan . . . . Geraldine Muir
Roger . . . . Nicky Taylor
Headmaster . . . . Gerald James
Pauline . . . . Sara Langton
Teacher . . . . Barbara Pierson
Luftwaffe Pilot . . . . Charley Boorman

Hollywood — John Boorman makes a real change of pace from his adventures through the realms of legend and the mystical in "Hope And Glory." Essentially a collection of sweetly autobiographical anecdotes of English family life during World War II, richly made pic boasts numerous piquant sequences, but hits mostly familiar notes and never develops a strong dramatic line. British homefront war stories have been few and far between in recent times, and those that have gotten made, such as "Hanover Street" and "Yanks," were duds, so it will be difficult for Columbia to carve out a domestic commercial niche for this one beyond the specialized houses where the director's name will mean something.

In creating by far the most conventional film of his highly individual career, Boorman often evokes memories of such stately, even sappily sentimental oldies as "This Happy Breed" and "Mrs. Miniver" while trying to convey how special his childhood was during the blitz. After all the years, some of the emotional traps are still easy for the viewer to fall into, but material feels like slice-of-life vignettes rather than inspired fiction that has been properly reshaped for dramatic purposes.

Tale is narrated from an adult perspective by Billy, an exquisite-looking nine-year-old who finds great excitement in the details of warfare but also has the air of a detached observer and, therefore, possible future writer. With war

declared in 1939, Dad goes off to serve king and country (by becoming a typist), while Billy, his sexually precocious teenage sister and his other (younger) sister almost get shipped off to Australia. At the last minute the children are held back to endure the incessant air raids and generally experience everyday life under extraordinary conditions.

Best scenes are those with Billy centerstage, and particularly those showing the unthinking callousness kids can display in the face of others' misfortune and tragedy. As soon as a raid is finished, the boys can be counted upon to run out into the rubble of the devastated suburban houses and loot them. The greater the destruction, the greater their excitement, and Boorman hits a very true note when some of the lads boast and fight over having been the first to learn about the death of a neighbor girl's mother.

After well over an hour, film has only briefly left the middle-class street, and one suspects that the design of the work is meant to reveal the war from this oblique vantage point. Then the Rohan family's home is destroyed, and Mom Sarah Miles takes the kids out to Grandpa's idyllic home by a river in the country, where the raging conflict becomes an afterthought.

Certain visual flourishes involving the water and lush greenery strikingly conjure up memories of other, more exotic Boorman films, and it appears that the writer-director might be entering more subjective territory as a way of charting his own flight from mundane reality to the world of imagination and creativity. Alas, this proves not to be the case, and the last half-hour of the picture, which is dominated by Ian Bannen's broad portrayal of the old patriarch, meanders way off the subject, never to return.

The melodrama normally found in such a setting has been largely avoided — Dad isn't injured or killed, Mom doesn't have an affair in his absence, there are no particularly painful separations, although Dawn, the adolescent daughter, predictably becomes pregnant thanks to her affair with a Canadian serviceman.

Unfortunately, Boorman has found little to serve in its stead except for some rosily remembered moments that made childhood for his generation in its own way unique.

Happily, young Sebastian Rice-Edwards is a marvelous camera subject and holds the center well. His younger sister, played by Geraldine Muir, is even cuter, as is Sara Langton as the girl whose mother is killed. The adults, however, come off rather less well, with Sarah Miles overdoing things and projecting little inner feeling and no one else making much of an impression.

Physically, film is outstanding, as lensing, production design and costumes are all aces. Peter Martin's score, however, is annoyingly intrusive, and soundtrack in general seems much too loud and cluttered. —Cart.

Rich And Famous
(HONG KONG-COLOR)

A Johnny Mak production, released on the Golden Harvest theater circuit. Presented by Johnny Mak. Directed by Wong Tai Lo. Stars Chow Yun Fat, Alex Man, Man Chi Leung, Andy Lau, Alan Tam, Carina Liu, Li Sau Yin. (No other credits provided by producer and distributor.) Reviewed at State theater, Hong Kong, June 22, 1987. Running time: 98 MINS.
(Cantonese soundtrack with English subtitles)

Hong Kong — The cast in this prequel to the hit "The Tragic Hero" are all familiar faces in the prevailing gangster genre. Aside from the omnipresent Chow Yun Fat, there are current marquee attractions and Li Sau Yin, the actor who is typecast as a cop. The most popular singer in Hong Kong, Alan Tam, also has a part, as a coward-turns-hero small con man. The producer is Johnny Mak who started the "realistic action" trend.

The gunfights, fistfights and car chases are professionally executed, but have all been done before with variations.

The movie deals with the relationships, comradeship feelings between brothers, friends, father and son, and husband and wife. Mainly it's about Man Chi Leung who betrays his brother (Andy Lau) and gangster boss (Chow) and turns to work for the rival gang who conspires to kill Chow.

As traitor, Man drives the tension of the film forward and eventually comes to taste the consequences of his own gangster deeds. —Mel.

Nadine
(COLOR)

Disappointing romantic thriller-comedy trifle.

A Tri-Star Pictures release from Tri-Star-ML Delphi Premier Prods. Produced by Arlene Donovan. Executive producer, Wolfgang Glattes. Written and directed by Robert Benton. Stars Jeff Bridges, Kim Basinger. Camera (Metrocolor, Technicolor prints), Nestor Almendros; editor, Sam O'Steen, music, Howard Shore; production design, Paul Sylbert; art direction, Peter Lansdown Smith, Cary White; set decoration, Lee Poll; costumes, Albert Wolsky; sound, David Ronne; assistant director, Ron Bozman; casting, Howard Feuer. Reviewed at the Coronet theater, L.A., July 10, 1987. (MPAA Rating: PG.) Running time: 83 MINS.
Vernon Hightower .... Jeff Bridges
Nadine Hightower .... Kim Basinger
Buford Pope .... Rip Torn
Vera .... Gwen Verdon
Renee Lomax .... Glenne Headly
Raymond Escobar .... Jerry Stiller

Dwight Estes .... Jay Patterson
Boyd .... William Youmans
Floyd .... Mickey Jones

Hollywood — "Nadine" is an innocuous soufflé from writer-director Robert Benton so lightweight that in the end one can't help wondering where the film is. Set in Austin in 1954, Benton tries to get by on Texas charm but the recipe of screwball comedy and small-town thriller fails to jell. Result is pleasant but forgettable and a distinct disappointment from a major director.

"Nadine" is a return to the genre-bending territory Benton explored with more success in "The Late Show" 10 years ago. Instead of Art Carney and Lily Tomlin as battling allies trying to solve a murder-mystery, Jeff Bridges and Kim Basinger are husband and wife on the verge of divorce drawn together again by a suspicious killing.

Both characters are likeable if unexceptional. As Vernon Hightower, proprietor of the unsuccessful Bluebonnet saloon, Bridges has a smile and an excuse for every mishandled situation. As Nadine, Basinger is a kvetch with a twang, who gives manicures in the local beauty parlor.

Benton is obviously shooting for a quaint slice of American pie, but these people are too precious and stylized as if they were in a museum display of life in the '50s in Texas; lots of texture but not enough soul.

"Nadine" is a character piece too shallow to pull the murder plot. Despite some bull's-eye one-liners, story is too clever and neat to be believable or compelling. Every twist is convenient without being dangerous.

Things get going when Basinger witnesses the murder of two-bit photographer Raymond Escobar (Jerry Stiller) who happens to have in his possession some "art" shots of Nadine, thereby giving her a motive for the killing. The real meat of the matter are some photos for a proposed highway that Escobar has gotten his hands on and local mobster Buford Pope (Rip Torn) wants back at any cost.

Pope is the only truly interesting character here and the film comes alive when he's on the screen. What he has that the others don't is a complex personality and Torn is skillful in showing it. Pope is a working crook, if there is such a thing. By turns ornery, dangerous and almost courtly, he is never as mean as he means to be.

Bridges turns in his usual winning performance and Basinger, reminiscent of any number of Texas heroines, including her own from "Fool For Love," has got a Texas squeal down pat. Gwen Verdon turns up as Nadine's mother confessor at the beauty shop while Mick-

ey Jones creates an unmistakable presence as Pope's heavy.

While it is amusing to watch a car chase in vintage automobiles, letter perfect period detail (except for a reference to 7-11 which was not yet discovered) almost seems painted on as the characters and story are too thin to hold the colors.

Cinematography by Nestor Almendros is up to his usual high standards. Score by Howard Shore is low-key and appropriate and several relaxed moments, when Vernon and Nadine ride in a car to pleading guitar strains communicate the love that is being restored. If only it meant more. —Jagr.

Slammer Girls
(COLOR)

Gals' prison parody misfires.

A Lightning Pictures release of a Vestron Entertainment presentation of a Platinum Pictures production. Produced and directed by Chuck Vincent. Screenplay, Craig Horrall, Vincent, Rick Marx; additional dialog, Larue Watts; camera (color), Larry Revene; editor, Marc Ubell (Vincent); music, Ian Shaw, Kai Joffe; sound, Peter Penguin; assistant director, Bill Slobodian; production manager, Philip Goetz; costumes, Eddie Heath; associate producer, Jeanne O'Grady; casting, John Weidner. Reviewed on vidcassette, N.Y., July 9, 1987. (MPAA Rating: R.) Running time: 80 MINS.
Melody .... Devon Jenkin
Harry .... Jeff Eagle
Crabapples .... Jane Hamilton
Gov. Caldwell .... Ron Sullivan
 Also with: Tally Brittany, Darcy Nychols, Stasia Micula, Sharon Cain, Beth Broderick, Sharon Kelly, Kim Kafkaloff, Philip Campanaro, Michael Hentzman, Louie Bonanno, Janice Doskey, Jane Kreisel, Captain Haggerty.

"Slammer Girls," a.k.a. "The Big Slammer," is a frenetic, all-out spoof of the durable women's prison genre, that comes off as silly rather than funny. Made in 1985, pic has been quietly slipped into regional release by Vestron subsidiary Lightning Pictures.

Heavyhanded source of black humor is watching the cast manhandle (and womanhandle) pretty, blond, virginal heroine Melody (Devon Jenkin), convicted of a murder attempt against the governor (Ron Sullivan, better known as porn director Henri Pachard), which results in the loss of his family jewels. While he and pretty assistant Candy (Tally Brittany, a.k.a. Tally Chanel) are working on getting him a transplant, Melody is put through the wringer by sadistic prison matron Miss Crabapples (Jane Hamilton, a.k.a. Veronica Hart) and various touch cellmates. Reporter Harry Wiener (Jeff Eagle) disguises himself as a woman to go undercover and get her true story which, in lame "Tom Jones" imitation, has Melody being the illegitimate daughter of the governor and Crabapples.

Filmmaker Chuck Vincent makes a similar mistake as the unsuccessful New World spoof in the same vein, "Reform School Girls," in thinking that exaggeration and hambone "acting" is funny or campy. In fact, the original women's prison films, whether from the '50s or '70s, definitively provide the drama and/or laughs without need of highlighting.

Cast, including numerous porno stars on holiday, is embarrassing, with even the reliable Veronica Hart overdoing her prison matron stint to a fare-thee-well. Lead actress Devon Jenkin looks pretty but proves to be an overly bland central presence. —Lor.

O.C. And Stiggs
(COLOR)

Silly Altman comedy escapes from the vaults.

An MGM/UA Distribution release from MGM. Produced by Robert Altman, Peter Newman. Executive producer, Lewis Allen. Directed by Altman. Screenplay, Donald Cantrell, Ted Mann, from a story by Tod Carroll, Mann, based on a story from National Lampoon magazine; camera (Metrocolor), Pierre Mignot; editor, Elizabeth Kling; special music, King Sunny Adé and his African Beats; production design, Scott Bushnell; art direction, David Gropman; set decoration, John Hay; sound, John Pritchett; assistant director, Stephen P. Dunn, Paula Mazur; associate producer, Scott Bushnell. Reviewed at Filmland screening room, Culver City, Calif., July 10, 1987. (MPAA Rating: R.) Running time: 109 MINS.
O.C. .... Daniel H. Jenkins
Stiggs .... Neill Barry
Randall Schwab .... Paul Dooley
Elinore Schwab .... Jane Curtin
Randall Schwab Jr. .... Jon Cryer
Gramps .... Ray Walston
Garth Sloan .... Louis Nye
Florence Beaugereaux .... Tina Louise
Pat Coletti .... Martin Mull
Sponson .... Dennis Hopper
Wino Bob .... Melvin Van Peebles
Jack Stiggs .... Donald May
Stella Stiggs .... Carla Borelli
Michelle .... Cynthia Nixon

Hollywood — After over three years on the shelf, MGM has decided to clean house and give Robert Altman's "O.C. And Stiggs" a test run in several cities. While the film is no worse than many of the mindless youth romps foisted on the public, and offers a few vintage Altman touches, most of the director's techniques now seem half-hearted and dated. Audience should be limited to fans of the director and the unsuspecting.

Loosely based on a story in the National Lampoon, pic is an anarchistic jab at the insurance business and any other American institution that happens to be handy. In his best work such as "Nashville" and "Mash," Altman was able to weave together an array of sights and sounds into a distinctive social commentary. In "O.C. And Stiggs" the structure comes apart and what's left is mostly random silliness.

Plot, such as it is, has something to do with O.C. (Daniel H. Jenkins) and Stiggs' (Neil Barry) efforts to extract a pound of flesh from Arizona insurance magnate Randall Schwab (Paul Dooley) in revenge for cancelling the old age insurance of O.C.'s grandfather (Ray Walston). Screenplay by Donald Cantrell and Ted Mann is mostly a scattershot attack on middle American hypocrisies and foibles.

Along for the ride through the desert heartland is Schwab's drunken wife (Jane Curtin), Stiggs' leacherous father (Donald May) and bird-brained mother (Carla Borelli), a shell-shocked Vietnam vet (Dennis Hopper) and a horny high school nurse (Tina Louise), to name just a few.

Instead of creating a revealing portrait of American life through peripheral people, action is too broad to hit its mark and deteriorates into overblown set pieces and incoherent asides including a visit from the African juju band King Sonny Adé and his African Beats.

In spite of the shortcomings and tedium of the production, there are moments when it becomes evident there is a vision and talent behind all the nonsense. Performances are uniformly good, with Dennis Hopper once again excelling as a madman. Production design by Scott Bushnell is rich, creating a sort of suburban Disneyland for the Schwab house. Tech credits, too, are better than average.

Unlike most contemporary comedies, "O.C. And Stiggs" fails not from too little ambition, but too much. —*Jagr.*

The Brave Little Toaster
(ANIMATED-COLOR)

Brilliant animation but plodding plotline.

A Hyperion-Kushner-Locke production. Produced by Donald Kushner, Thomas L. Wilhite. Directed by Jerry Rees. Screenplay, Jerry Rees, Joe Ranft; screen story, Rees, Ranft, Brian McEntee, based on the novella by Thomas M. Disch; art director, McEntee; color stylist, A. Kendall O'Connor; music, David Newman; songs, Van Dyke Parks. Reviewed at the L.A. Intl. Animation Celebration, Wadsworth theater, Westwood, July 10, 1987. (No MPAA Rating.) Running time: **80 MINS.**
Voices of:
Radio....................Jon Lovitz
Lampy....................Tim Stack
Blanky..............Timothy E. Day
Kirby..............Thurl Ravencroft
Toaster............Deanna Oliver
Air Conditioner, Hanging
  Lamp..............Phil Hartman
B&W TV............Jonathon Benair
Elmo St. Peters............Joe Ranft

Hollywood — This full-length animated feature, while ultimately enjoyable, is slowed by too-plodding and too-predictable plot progres-

sions, a group of utterly forgettable songs from Van Dyke Parks and an absence of any real tension in climactic scene. The animation, though, is superb, but the five main characters (all inanimate objects) may not be cuddly enough for kids, who will regardless miss much of the humor that lies just beneath the surface here. As with any animated feature that isn't tied directly to toys or well-known children stories, this pic's domestic financial future is anybody's guess.

Story centers on five household objects — a toaster, radio, vacuum cleaner, lamp and electric blanket — that come to life in a summer cabin, where they've waited for years for their master (a boy named Rob) to return and put them to good use.

Each character is fully realized, but three stand out. Kirby the vacuum cleaner, possessor of a dour stare, comes on like a cranky John Wayne with Thurl Ravencroft's voice. Jon Lovitz turns his characterization of a blabby radio back to the golden days of *that* medium, calling out bits of baseball games and news headlines. While his voice is pure '30s, his character also conjures up Tom Waits' spunky emcee in "The Cotton Club."

Stealing the show, however, is the crybaby blanket (voice by Timothy E. Day), a cross between Casper the Friendly Ghost and the Snuggles Bear from the fabric softener commercials. Blanket also gets some of the best visual humor, playing a flying carpet in one scene, a camp tent in another.

After a showdown with an air conditioner (played in the voice of Jack Nicholson by Phil Hartman, who turns around and does Peter Lorre as a sinister hanging lamp in another scene), the quintet decides to brave the wilds of the country hills in search of their master, whom they presume to be living in a nearby city.

Most of the film involves a calamitous search for Rob, with group encountering rainstorms, wild animals, a nefarious electric repairman, hypermodernized home appliances and, finally, a huge electromagnet in a silly conclusion at a junkyard.

Pic has a decidedly Disneyish feel to it, and for good reason. It was originally purchased by that studio five years ago. When producer Tom Wilhite left in 1984, he took the project with him, employing a group of Disney vets to work on it.

Jerry Rees, who directed the computer animation sequences in "Tron," keeps things moving most of the time here, but what stands out is the animation, brilliantly supervised by art director Brian McEntee and color stylist A. Kendall O'Connor, whose work har-

kens back to Disney's glory days of animation. Unfortunately, the story just isn't compelling enough to keep up with the pictures. —*Camb.*

Revenge Of The Nerds II: Nerds In Paradise
(COLOR)

Simple hijinks in minor sequel.

A 20th Century Fox release of an Interscope Communications production, in association with Amercent Films and American Entertainment Partners. Produced by Ted Field, Robert Cort, Peter Bart. Executive producer, Joe Roth. Directed by Roth. Screenplay, Dan Guntzelman, Steve Marshall, based on characters created by Tim Metcalfe, Miguel Tejada-Flores, Steve Zacharias, Jeff Buhai; camera (Deluxe color), Charles Correll; editor, Richard Chew; music, Mark Mothersbaugh, Gerald V. Casale, performed by Devo; production design, Trevor Williams; costume design, Jeffrey Kurland; sound (Dolby), Jack Dalton; assistant director, Jim Chory; associate producers, Richard Chew, Paul Schiff; casting, Pam Dixon. Reviewed at Zanuck theater, 20th Century Fox, L.A., July 9, 1987. (MPAA Rating: PG-13.) Running time: **92 MINS.**
Lewis.................Robert Carradine
Booger...............Curtis Armstrong
Lamar..................Larry B. Scott
Poindexter....:........Timothy Busfield
Sunny...........Courtney Thorne-Smith
Wormser..............Andrew Cassese
Ogre....................Donald Gibb
Roger.............Bradley Whitford
Buzz....................Ed Lauter
Stewart..................Barry Sobel

Hollywood — The Nerds are back on the big screen with some goofy hijinks that aren't worth the price of admission. Even the summer escapist urge may barely be satisfied here since there are too few laughs. As a sequel, however, pic may tap its presold audience and do modest business.

Setting is Fort Lauderdale at a supposed national fraternity conference, where the nerds' contingent is repping its college after prevailing over mainstream frat brothers in the initial film. Once again on the outside looking in, the nerds fight back when ostracized by the unlikeable, archetypal Greeks.

However outlandishly the nerds are portrayed in their struggle for individual identity amidst conformist pressures, they are seen so sympathetically that only a curmudgeon would root for those nasty fraternity types. Alas, latter are doomed to suffer a justified comeuppance the end of the proceedings.

In winding his way through this simple yarn, director Joe Roth relies heavily on the ongoing sight gag of the Nerds, their attire and quirky mannerisms. Back for the sequel are: Lewis Skolnick (Robert Carradine), Arnold Poindexter (Timothy Busfield), Wormser (Andrew Cassese), Dudley "Booger" Dawson (Curtis Armstrong) and Lamar Latrelle (Larry B. Scott). They go together like charter members of the nation's first college computer club.

Joining the group is the newest

nerd, Stewart Lipsey (ably portrayed by Barry Sobel). Also on hand is hotel desk clerk Sunny Carstairs (Courtney Thorne-Smith), who counters the cinematic stereotype of a beautiful woman and sides with the Nerds.

A high point of the antics comes midway with a nerd rap tune — "No On Fifteen" — which denounces a fraternity conference resolution requiring physical prowess as a condition for membership. Tune itself and staging of the number are tops.

Pic's theme "Back To Paradise" by 38 Special has all the earmarks of a top 40 winner — especially if this sequel stirs the cult-like following of "Nerds I." —*Tege.*

Overkill
(COLOR)

Weak L.A. Yakuza actioner with ridiculous payoff.

A Movie Factory presentation of a United Independent Films production. (Sales, Manson Intl.) Produced and directed by Ulli Lommel. Line producer, Sholto von Douglas. Screenplay, David Scott Kroes; camera (color), James Takashi; editor, Ron Norman; music supervision, Bill Roebuck; production design, Manuel Riva; set decoration, Bob McElvin; assistant director, Mick Verraux; stunt coordinator, Frank Disanto; associate producers, Jochen Breitenstein, Cookie Amerson; casting, Brown-Livingston. Reviewed on Vista Org. Home Video vidcassette, N.Y., July 8, 1987. (No MPAA Rating.) Running time: **81 MINS.**
Mickey Delano..............Steve Rally
Akashi.....................John Nishio
Jamie....................Laura Burkett
Collins...................Allen Wisch
Steiner.................Roy Summersett
Police chief............Antonio Caprio
Neighbor..............Michelle Bauer

"Overkill" is one of German helmer Ulli Lommel's weakest films since he relocated to the U.S. a decade ago. Actioner plods along listlessly until the final three minutes when several impossible plot twists make the film memorably bad.

L.A. cop Mickey Delano (Steve Rally) is convinced that Japanese Yakuza gangsters are a major organized crime threat to the U.S., but his superiors on the force don't agree. With tons of verbal exposition, he tries to root out the Nipponese heavies, but his partner Steiner (Roy Summersett) is killed in the second reel, causing Delano to team up with visiting Tokyo cop Akashi (John Nishio). Pic climaxes with Delano killing his corrupt police chief in cold blood, and then the nonsense starts.

In short order, Delano quits the force ostensibly to enact personal revenge, but ends up being a sushi chef. He kills one gangster and the other Yakuza big shots meekly offer a truce — cut to him teaching a paralyzed young boy (victim of the gangsters) to ride a horse — The

End.

Lommel has had some success Stateside with horror films, particularly "The Boogeyman," and "Overkill" contains lots of blood and extraneous gore. Nondescript cast is unexciting, with hero Steve Rally looking far more comfortable in a scene where he poses as a male stripper than as the tough-guy cop.
— *Lor.*

Sufre Mamón
(Suffer Mammon)
(SPANISH-COLOR)

A "G" P.C., Paco Lara Polop, Manuel Summers production. Executive producer, Paco Lara Polop. Directed by Summers. Screenplay, Francisco Tomás, Summers; camera (color), Tote Tenas; editor, Elena Sainz de Rozas; music, David Summer; sets, Gumersindo Andrés. Reviewed at Cine Jovellanos, Gijón, Spain, July 5, 1987. Running time: **97 MINS.**

David . . . . David Summers
Javi. . . . . Javier Molina
Dani. . . . . Daniel Mezquita
Rafa. . . . . Rafael Gutiérrez
Patty. . . . . Marta Madruga
Riky . . . . Gerardo Ortega
    Also with: Curro M. Summers, Antonio Gamero, Tomás Zori, Luis Escobar.

Gijón — Los Hombres G (The G-Men) is one of the hottest rock groups in Spain and its leader, David Summers, is the son of veteran helmer Manuel Summers, so what should be more natural than that both should want to filmically capitalize on their fame?

Manuel Summers being a skillful helmer and writer, "Sufre Mamón" (name of one of the hit songs) is a well-paced, amusing pic with the right amount of clowning and song recitals to make it popular in Spain. Although there is a rather pointless love story thrown in, it is the snappy, slangly, wisecracking dialog that is one of the main attractions of the film, and which will be lost on all but the most "in" crowd in Spain.

That still leaves the half-dozen or so musical numbers from the foreign standpoint, and these could carry the film provided Los Hombres G are well enough known via record releases in offshore territories. Story is built loosely around four *macarra* pals who decide to form a rock group. Their adversaries in school are a group of *pijos* (rightwing swells). The leader, David, falls for a pretty co-ed, but she two-times him during a wavering romance, until he discovers the truth and sends her packing.

David Summers has lotsa charm, and puts in a good performance, but the scene is usually stolen by Javi, the drummer, a kind of Spanish John Belushi who's by far the most amusing of the group. Lively camerawork and good direction help keep the pacing lively. Some of the musical numbers are shot in a studio, others are lensed before a large live audience. —*Besa.*

The Oracle
(COLOR)

Revenge from beyond the grave.

A Reeltime Distributing release of a Laurel Films production. (Sales, JER Pictures.) Produced by Walter E. Sear. Directed by Roberta Findlay. Screenplay, R. Allen Leider; camera (Cineffects color), Findlay; editor, Findlay; music, Sear, Michael Litovsky; sound, Steven Rogers; assistant director, Rafael Guadalupe; production manager, Sear; special effects, Horrorefx; makeup, Jean Carballo; set decoration, Cecilla Holzman; stunt coordination, Webster Whinery; second unit camera, Steve Kaman. Reviewed on U.S.A. Home Video vidcassette, N.Y., July 11, 1987. (MPAA Rating: R.) Running time: **94 MINS.**

Jennifer . . . . Caroline Capers Powers
Ray . . . . Roger Neil
Farkas. . . . . Pam LaTesta
Dorothy Graham . . . . Victoria Dryden
Pappas . . . . Chris Maria DeKoron
Tom Varney . . . . Dan Lutzky
Cindy . . . . Stacey Graves
Ben . . . . G. Gordon Cronce

"The Oracle" covers familiar horror ground with a supernatural tale of a dead spirit contacting the living to enact posthumous revenge. Pic was made in New York in 1984, released regionally last year and now in video stores.

Plotline is similar to the subsequent hit "Witchboard:" heroine Jennifer (Caroline Capers Powers) finds an old crate containing a planchette (generic form of a Ouija board, made of a sculpted hand and quill pen). At a Christmas dinner party she and husband Ray (Roger Neil) plus another couple try out the instruments, but no one except Jennifer believes the resulting spirit messages it traces.

Ghost is businessman William Graham, murdered but covered up by his wife Dorothy (Victoria Dryden) as a suicide. Jennifer starts "seeing" the actual murder and when she contacts Dorothy she is targeted as the next hushup victim.

Though the monster and gore effects are unsatisfactory in this low-budgeter, it sports one neat twist: Dorothy's chief henchman turns out to be a large, chubby woman. As portrayed by Pam LaTesta, this thug is filmmaker Roberta Findlay's main point of interest, styled mannishly (an updated version of the late Madame Spivy), she is androgynous for the first few reels, picking up a prostitute whom she bloodily slashes when mocked for being unable (natch) to "perform." It turns out to be a fresh approach to the slasher cliché and the horror genre's fondness for transvestite villains. Rest of the cast is unimpressive.—*Lor.*

Leif
(SWEDISH-COLOR)

An SF (Svensk Filmindustri) release of an SF and Kulturtuben production. Produced by Waldemar Bergendahl. Written and directed by Claes Eriksson. Camera (Eastmancolor), Dan Myhrman; editor, Jan Persson; music, Claes Eriksson, Charles Falk; production design, Rolf Allan Hakansson; costumes, Gunilla Henkler; sound, Christian Persson; assistant director, Michael Sevholt; production management, Thomas Allercrantz; stunts, Johan Torén and Svenska Stuntgruppen. Reviewed at the Palladium, Malmö, Sweden, July 8, 1987. Running time: **103 MINS.**

Gunnar Volt . . . . Anders Eriksson
Doris Volt, others . . . . . . Kerstin Granlund
Max Koger,
    Councilman Hylén . . . . . . Claes Eriksson
"Rambo" Larsson,
    others . . . . Knut Agnred
Niklas Kortnoj,
    others . . . . Per Fritzell
Inspector Mard,
    others . . . . Peter Rangmar
Lars E.I. Fred,
    others . . . . Jan Rippe
    Also with: Per Westman, Laila Westersund, Bengt Hernvall, Pierre Jonsson, Kimmo Rajala.

Malmö — The burlesque-cum-barbership quartet After Shave and the Monty Pythonesque musical review team Galenskaberne (The Madcaps) worked their acts into one and won the hearts of all Swedes with their tv series "Mackan" (The Gas Station), a kind of New Swedish Gothic-style portraiture of rural & provincial folks' foibles & follies, generally done without much satirical social or political spice.

Svensk Filmindustri producer Waldemar Bergendahl lured the "Mackan" troupe away from the thematically narrow path of tv fun and set their writer-director Claes Eriksson to do "Leif," a large-scale farce feature meant, literally, to torpedo the double moral standards exercised by government big and small wigs and of munitions and arms manufacturers everywhere.

"Leif" has brought otherwise sluggish Swedish boxoffice to an instant sizzle. Whether its shots will be heard around the world remains doubtful however. It has hardly hurt business that secret sales scandals to nations not on the print media's current honor lists broke almost to coincide with picture's release. Still, Claes Eriksson depends very heavily on the deadpan, square-jawed, but determinedly befuddled persona of Anders Eriksson, well-established and beloved with the Swedes, but bound to appear rather bland and nondescript to offshore audiences.

Otherwise, the story of a small town's big-time arms plant's sudden need to explain itself to the anonymous signer of an indignant letter-to-the-editor, and thus to the government and to the nation, is developed mostly as a mix of sight gags, slapstick, bits of double-talk dialog and two-faced plotting with some song & dance routines plus a Mack Sennett chase sequence thrown in (in lieu of pies). Sometimes it works, sometimes it winds up as ineffectual as a beetle turned over on its back.

Most of the acting in "Leif" has the actors similarly positioned, shadow-boxing and generally overdoing it.

There is a vigor to their performances, however, and between all the misses, the hits are there to be observed with guffawing pleasure. There is a sweet vaudeville lilt to film's music score, and its production dress has been crafted with a precision that often steals the show.
—*Kell.*

Summer School
(COLOR)

Teen comedy misses a chance for substance.

A Paramount Pictures release of a George Shapiro-Howard West production. Executive producer, Marc Trabulus. Directed by Carl Reiner. Screenplay, Jeff Franklin, story by Stuart Birnbaum, David Dashev, Franklin; camera (Panavision, color), David M. Walsh; editor, Bud Molin; music, Danny Elfman; production design, David L. Snyder; art direction, Joe Wood; set design, John Warnke; costume supervisor, Ray Summers; sound mixer, Joe Kenworthy; first assistant director, Marty Ewing; second assistant director, James Dillon; associate producer, Jeff Franklin; casting, Penny Perry. Reviewed at the Mann Chinese theater, Hollywood, July 18, 1987. (MPAA Rating: PG-13.) Running time: **98 MINS.**

Freddy Shoop . . . . Mark Harmon
Robin Bishop . . . . Kirstie Alley
Phil Gills . . . . Robin Thomas
Kevin . . . . Patrick Laborteaux
Pam . . . . Courtney Thorne-Smith
Chainsaw . . . . Dean Cameron
Dave . . . . Gary Riley
Denise . . . . Kelly Minter
Larry . . . . Ken Olandt
Rhonda . . . . Shawnee Smith

Hollywood — "Summer School" is a well-meaning but shallow film that attempts to confront such weighty topics as alcoholism, juvenile delinquency, teacher-student affairs, dyslexia and teen pregnancy while remaining primarily a laugh-a-minute teen comedy. Director Carl Reiner's quick pacing and scripter Jeff Franklin's scatter-shot storytelling render much of the dramatic action superficial and much of the comedy stilted. Given Mark Harmon's appeal and the subject matter, none of the above should prevent this from being a summer hit.

Harmon plays Freddie Shoop, a gym teacher who lives for fun and games and summer vacation. Moments before taking off for Hawaii with his girlfriend, he is blackmailed by a vice-principal (Robin Thomas) into teaching a summer school remedial English class to a band of misfits and malcontents.

Shoop quickly meets a straitlaced yet miniskirted honors history teacher Robin Bishop (Kirstie Alley, whose gravelly voice will remind many of Debra Winger), with whom he immediately falls in love. She naturally thinks he's sort of cute, but has no respect for him as a teacher and is in any case already dating the vice-principal.

While Shoop's pursuit and eventual (and inevitable) conquest of Bishop keeps popping up throughout, most of this film concerns the cast of unruly students that he must make proficient at English (or else be denied his tenure).

Almost every one has a special "problem" to overcome, and in most cases these are brought up so casually and solved in such short order later on as to be laughable. There's a kid with a drinking problem, a student who sleeps through classes because he's a professional stripper by night, an unwed pregnant girl, a perpetual nerd, and another girl who can't pass her driver's test.

While underachieving horror movie buffs Chainsaw (Dean Cameron) and Dave (Gary Riley) have the biggest student parts — and are responsible for much of the comedy herein — both are ultimately overshadowed by Courtney Thorne-Smith's relatively small but subtly played role of Pam, a surfer student with a crush on teacher.

Her pursuit of Shoop — she's full of innuendo early and then tries to seduce him in his bedroom at a party — is so convincing that it injects some much needed tension into the smooth and superficial ride to the requisite happy ending.

Reiner undercuts the crucial scene, following a couple of the unwritten rules of youth-oriented comedy — never let things get too heavy, and always let the protagonist take the moral high ground — and quickly moves merrily on to the next problem.

While Harmon is appealing in his first feature film lead, he never is able to generate much chemistry with Alley, and his character is little more than a cousin of his beer commercial persona. Still, he has enough charisma and acting chops to keep this film going through the rough spots, of which there's many.

Tech credits are fine, with Danny Elfman's unobtrusive score a rarity for teen movies.—*Camb.*

Macho Que Ladra No Muerde II (Nos Reimos de la Mafia)
(Macho That Barks Doesn't Bite — We Laugh At The Mafia) (MEXICAN-COLOR)

A Películas Mexicanas release of a Cinematográfica Calderón production. Executive producer, Mario Gris. Produced by Guillermo Calderón Stell. Directed by José Luis Urquieta. Stars Alfonso Zayas, Sasha Montenegro. Screenplay, Francisco Cavazos; camera (color), Raúl Domínguez; music, Marcos Lifshitz. Reviewed at Hollywood Twin theater II, N.Y., July 5, 1987. Running time: **94 MINS.**

Constancio Salvatierras . . . . Alfonso Zayas
Silvia Gabrioni . . . . Sasha Montenegro
Luigi Gabrioni . . . . Rafael Inclán
Petito . . . . Javier López (Chabelo)
   Also with: Evita Muñoz, María Cardinal, Polo Ortín, Susana Cabrara, Alfredo (Pelón) Solares, Lizbeth Chris, Sonia Piña, Víctor Manuel (Güero) Castro, Leandro Espinoza, Leonardo Trebole, Adriana Muñoz, Mayte Gerard, Colocho.

Despite its awkward title and perhaps even more awkward presentation of plot details, "Macho Que Ladra No Muerde II (Nos Reimos de la Mafia)" (Macho That Barks Doesn't Bite — We Laugh At The Mafia) has enough genuine chuckles to raise it above the profusion of low-budget Mexican sex comedies.

Both pictures were penned by Francisco Cavazos. That Part II is better than its 1985 predecessor of the same name, helmed by Víctor Manuel (Güero) Castro, is owned by sequel director José Luis Urquieta.

Actor Alfonso Zayas plays an unlikely gigolo who attracts the attentions of Silvia (Sasha Montenegro), wife of Italian gangster Luigi Gabrioni (Rafael Inclán), better known as "King Of The Scalpers." The rest of the film concerns the couple's flight all around Mexico City with the mafia hot on their trail. Things are further complicated by the repeated appearance of Zayas' 6'4" infant son (Javier López), who makes dad's life hell.

Humor comes from development of comic characters rather than through the convoluted plot situations. Over the years, comedian Zayas has honed a whole spectrum of comic looks and gestures, which he puts to use to good effect. On the other hand, Inclán is restrained as the jealous mafia boss, who speaks fake Italian throughout. While he shows more control than usual over his character, Inclán also finds less latitude to develop particular comic bits.

Mexican sex star Montenegro manages to keep her clothes on most of the time. Although she is adequate as a heavy, she has little feel for comedy and her role here is stiff and lifeless.

Tech credits are handled effectively, especially the lensing by Raúl Domínguez, which tries to parody "The Godfather" and other films.

As a low-budget genre pic, it is obvious that everyone here has worked just a little harder to milk entertainment from such mediocre material.—*Lent.*

Jaws — The Revenge
(COLOR)

Preposterous No. 4 in horror series.

A Universal Pictures release of a Joseph Sargent production. Directed by Sargent. Screenplay, Michael de Guzman, based on character created by Peter Benchley; camera (color), John McPherson; editor, Michael Brown; music, Michael Small (theme from "Jaws," John Williams); production manager, Frank Baur; art direction, Don Woodruff; set design, Carl Aldana; costume supervision, Marla Denise Schlom, Hugo Pena; sound, Willie Burton; special effects supervisor, Henry Millar; assistant director, Wes McAfee, Stephen Southard; associate producer, Baur; casting coordinator, Valerie McCaffrey. Reviewed at Hollywood Pacific theater, L.A., July 17, 1987. (MPAA Rating: PG-13.) Running time: **100 MINS.**

Ellen Brody . . . . Lorraine Gary
Michael . . . . Lance Guest
Jake . . . . Mario Van Peebles
Carla . . . . Karen Young
Hoagie . . . . Michael Caine
Thea . . . . Judith Barsi
Louisa . . . . Lynn Whitfield

Hollywood — In search of yet another chapter to the "Jaws" saga, the makers of this installment have chosen to waste some good performances on an implausible, poorly paced story with one of the more preposterous conclusions of the genre. Director Joseph Sargent politely telegraphs all of the attack scenes, so much of the suspense for the audience rests with guessing just what part of the victim's anatomy and/or accompanying boat is going to get chomped in the next ambush. Film may come out of the box strong, but word of mouth should prevent it from being too long of a runner.

Story for part 4 picks up after the Roy Scheider character of "Jaws" and "Jaws 2" has died of a heart attack. Lorraine Gary nicely reprises her role as the now-widowed Ellen Brody, living a peaceful life in the New England resort town of Amity. One of her sons has taken over his dad's job as deputy sheriff and is killed by a shark while out in the channel on a routine complaint.

Ellen heads down to the Bahamas to be with other oher son, marine biologist Michael (Lance Guest), and his family (Karen Young makes the most out of the small role of Michael's wife; 9-year-old Judith Barsi, more than just cute, gives a nice performance), and tries to convince him to quit his job because she's sure "it" is out to get the family. The filmmakers never make clear whether the entire shark population is after the Brodys or, as they hint, one obsessed shark made the long swim from Amity to the Bahamas to further terrorize them.

Guest's well-controlled Michael, a man obsessed with and haunted by sharks, is the pivotal character in the film and his scenes with both Gary and Young are compelling.

Less successful are sequences with research partner Jake (Mario Van Peebles). Van Peebles is better here than in "Heartbreak Ridge," but his characterization is pretty much limited to wearing dredlocks and saying "mon" a lot.

Oscar-winner Michael Caine, the '80s hardest-working man in show business, is Ellen's delightfully irresponsible suitor, but doesn't get enough screen time to really develop the character, and the romance is dropped to make way for the silly turn of events that lead to the conclusion.

After the shark practically walks up to the beach to get a bite out of the third generation Brody (Barsi), Ellen goes out after "it" by herself. Things quickly get ridiculous, with Caine, Guest and Van Peebles landing a plane a few feet away from the boat just in time for the ludicrous conclusion which, in one theater on opening day, earned derisive catcalls from audience members.

Sargent's pacing leaves a lot to be desired and the moment-of-attack sequences, full of jagged cuts and a great deal of noise, more closely resemble the view from inside a washing machine. While several scenes are appropriately grisly, story's lack of credibility stunts the cumulative effect (in one scene, the shark draws blood from a boat).

Screenplay aside, some of the performances stand out. This installment didn't need Roy Scheider so much as original "Jaws" scripters Peter Benchley and Carl Gottleib. —*Camb.*

The Lost Boys
(COLOR)

Dumb vampire epic for dim-witted youngsters.

A Warner Bros. release of a Richard Donner production. Produced by Harvey Bernhard. Executive producer, Donner. Co-executive producers, Mark Damon, John Hyde. Directed by Joel Schumacher. Screenplay, Janice Fischer, James Jeremias, Jeffrey Boam, story by Fischer, Jeremias; camera (Panavision, Technicolor), Michael Chapman; editor, Robert Brown; music, Thomas Newman; production design, Bo Welch; art direction, Tom Duffield; set design, John Warnke; set decoration, Chris Westlund; costume design, Susan Becker; sound (Dolby), David Ronne; vampire prosthetics & effects, Greg Cannom; assistant director, William S. Beasley; casting, Marion Dougherty; second unit director, James Arnett; second unit camera, Paul Goldsmith. Reviewed at the Warner Hollywood Studios, L.A., July 7, 1987. (MPAA Rating: R.) Running time: **92 MINS.**
Michael . . . . Jason Patric
Sam . . . . Corey Haim
Lucy . . . . Dianne Wiest
Grandpa . . . . Barnard Hughes
Max . . . . Ed Herrmann
David . . . . Kiefer Sutherland
Star . . . . Jami Gertz
Edgar Frog . . . . Corey Feldman
Alan Frog . . . . Jamison Newlander
Paul . . . . Brooke McCarter
Dwayne . . . . Billy Wirth
Marko . . . . Alexander Winter
Laddie . . . . Chance Michael Corbitt

Hollywood — "The Lost Boys" is a horrifically dreadful vampire teensploitation entry that daringly advances the theory that all those missing children pictured on garbage bags and milk cartons are actually the victims of bloodsucking bikers. Blatantly pitched at the lowest common denominator of the adolescent audience, unholy brew qualifies as undoubtedly the dumbest summer release to date, but may have enough salable "elements" to rack up good grosses for a few weeks.

Arriving in a Santa Cruz-like community that is dominated by a huge amusement park and is described as the "murder capital of the world," Dianne Wiest and her sons check in at grandpa's creepy house, and the boys quickly fall in with the wrong crowd.

Latter includes some unhealthy looking punks, led by Kiefer Sutherland, who take older brother Jason Patric back to their lair and, through the foxy but wasted Jami Gertz, tempt him into the ways of the undead.

Getting wind of the vampire problem, little brother Corey Haim teams up with two pint-sized Rambos to combat the plague on their houses, and it all ends in a colossal battle with bats, punks, froth, spears and blood flying through the air in a frenzy of nonsensical action.

Pic could go over with undiscriminating audiences due to its combination of wild effects, hip kids, rock music and gruesome prosthetics, but film panders to the basest instincts and is hokey even on its own ludicrous terms. At 92 minutes, it still seems to last all night long.—*Cart.*

Slate, Wyn & Me
(AUSTRALIAN-COLOR)

A Hemdale Releasing (U.S.), Filmpac (Australia), Palace Pictures (U.K.) release of a Hemdale-Intl. Film Management-Ukiyo Films production. Executive producers, Antony I. Ginnane, William Fayman. Produced by Tom Burstall. Directed by Don McLennan. Stars Sigrid Thornton, Simon Burke, Martin Sacks. Screenplay, McLennan, from the novel "Slate and Wyn and Blanche McBride," by Georgia Savage; camera (Panavision, Eastmancolor), David Connell; editor, Peter Friedrich; music, Peter Sullivan; sound, Andrew Ramage; production design, Paddy Reardon; costumes, Jeanie Cameron; line producer, Brian D. Burgess; production manager, Rosslyn Abernethy; assistant director, Brett Popplewell; casting, Jo Larner. Reviewed at Film Australia screening room, Lindfield, Sydney, July 19, 1987. Running time: **90 MINS.**
Blanche McBride . . . . Sigrid Thornton
Wyn Jackson . . . . Simon Burke
Slate Jackson . . . . Martin Sacks
Morgan . . . . Tommy Lewis
Molly . . . . Lesley Baker
Sammy . . . . Harold Baigent
Daphne . . . . Michelle Torres
Martin . . . . Murray Fahey
Pippa . . . . Taya Straton
Del Downer . . . . Julia MacDougall
Old Man Downer . . . . Peter Cummins
Sgt. Wilkinson . . . . Reg Gorman

Sydney — It's been seven years since Don McLennan's previous film, the well received, prize-winning low-budgeter "Hard Knocks" which dealt with a young woman living a precarious existence on the edge of the Melbourne underworld. Now he's back with an adaptation of an interesting book by Georgia Savage about two brothers, one a Vietnam vet, who kidnap a schoolteacher who's a witness when one of them guns down a policeman.

Martin Sacks is the vet and Simon Burke the younger brother who actually does the shooting in a moment of panic when they're caught robbing a small-town bank. Sigrid Thornton plays the witness who's uncermoniously bundled into the trunk of their battered car as the brothers make a getaway across country. They plan to kill her, too, but before long they're both attracted to her. She, in turn, plays off one against the other, though ultimately seems to enjoy living on the run more than life back home.

One of the main problems with the film is that the character of Blanche, though well played by Thornton, is never well defined; her motivations remain obscure, right to the end. As a result, the viewer looses interest in the drama, which doesn't contain enough action scenes for the youth audience and which is too flawed to appeal to more sophisticated customers.

It's a pity, because the film is handsomely produced, with magnificent location photography and a potentially interesting situation. An early suspense sequence, in which the trio cross a very rickety bridge, is excellent, and an indication of what the rest of the film could have been like. McLennan seems to be under the influence of Terrence Malick's "Badlands" (which was itself, and more productively, influenced by James Dean pics) and there are rather too many self-concious scenes here in which the bare-chested brothers strut around with rifles — there's even a repeat of a scene from "Giant." There are also too many elements that lack conviction: especially the final scene, which fails to ring true on any level.

As noted, the film looks great, and is a classy production, but its uncertainty of direction, its aimlessness and lack of conviction will make it a tough sell indeed. —*Strat.*

Firehouse
(COLOR)

Three gals and their hoses.

A Shapiro Entertainment presentation of a Too Hot production. Executive producer, C. Steven Duncker. Produced by J. Christian Ingvordsen, Steven Kaman. Directed by Ingvordsen. Screenplay, Ingvordsen, Kaman, from story by Rick Marx, Ingvordsen, Kaman; camera (color), Kaman; editor, Kaman; music, Michael Montes; additional music, David Biglin; sound, Dennis Green; production design, Debbie Devilla; art direction, Beth Rubino; production manager-assistant director, Daniel Lupi; special effects supervisor, Scott Gagnon; associate producers, Marc L. Bailin; Peggy Jacobson; casting, Jacobson. Reviewed on Academy Home Entertainment vidcassette, N.Y., July 18, 1987. (MPAA Rating: R.) Running time: **90 MINS.**
Barrett Hopkins . . . . Gianna Rains
Shannon Murphy . . . . . . Martha Peterson
Violet Brown . . . . Renee Raiford
John Anderson . . . . Gideon Fountain
Dickson Willoughby . . . . . Peter MacKenzie
Lt. Wally . . . . Joe Viviani
Timmy Ryan . . . . Jonathan Mandel
Warren Frump . . . . Henry David Keller
Also with: Susan Van Deven, Elizabeth Richardson, Donna Davidge, Jennifer Stahl, Ruth Collins.

"Firehouse," a feature film being released domestically on vidcassette, is a throwback to the scores of exploitation films that flourished in the early 1970s for the drive-in market, featuring three young, beautiful women in various professions (e.g., stewardesses, models, nurses, cops). Television shows like "Charlie's Angels" co-opted the format.

Gianna Rains, Martha Peterson and Renee Raiford are the lovelies in question, first female firefighters assigned to Hose One, a fire station that has been criticized for insensitivity to community problems. Warren Frump (Henry David Keller) is a political candidate whose secret agenda for revitalizing the city is to remove the city's Northend slum area by arson, to make way for a development project involving condominiums. The gals save the day and Frump (rhymes with ...) is arrested.

Shot-in-New Jersey pic is strong on topless scenes and unsuccessful in generating laughs, despite its obvious intent to join the parade of "Police Academy" imitations. Tech credits are fine.

Cassette packaging erroneously credits the cast members with their characters' names, rather than professional monikers.—*Lor.*

El dueño del sol
(The Owner Of The Sun)
(ARGENTINE-COLOR)

A Luz Comunicaciones production. Written and directed by Rodolfo Mórtola. Stars Alfredo Alcón. Camera (color) and art direction, Aníbal Di Salvor; editor, Jorge Pappalardo; music, Mario Ferré; sets, Miguel Angel Lumaldo, Enrique Bordolin. Reviewed at the Vigo screening room, Buenos Aires, April 21, 1987. (Rating in Argentina: forbidden for under 18s.) Running time: **101 MINS.**
Father . . . . Alfredo Alcón
Juan . . . . Luis Luque
Ana . . . . Noemi Frenkel
Maria . . . . Emilia Mazer
Martín . . . . Gustavo Belatti

Buenos Aires — This is a serious and well-crafted but overloaded allegory by first-time director Rodolfo Mórtola, who nevertheless has been working in the Argentine cinema since 1969, including scriptwork and assistant direction for top helmers like Leopoldo Torre Nilsson and Leonardo Favio.

Plot is a hothouse overgrowth of theatrical tragedy themes. Two sons and two daughters compete for the favor of a dying landowner who gets his kicks by playing each one off against the others, drawing forth an overextended catalog of lusts and cupidities.

The title refers to a type of bogeyman found in regional folklore. The father figure acts as such, but one of the characters wisely warns that overthrowing one bogeyman only risks replacing him with another, because there is one of them lurking inside each person — a statement with obvious political implications in dictator-prone lands.

The father may represent Argentina and his children — dreamers, graspers, overly stubborn workhorses, agitators, victims — may stand for the inhabitants of a country which toys with them and repays their efforts (some sincere, some not) with cruel hoaxes, empty words, real promises, fake promises, repression liberation.

It is a well-intentioned film by someone who clearly knows his way around a set, but who on this occasion turned that set into too much of a pressure cooker. Whirling around in the overheated atmosphere are conscious or unconscious echoes of Greek and Freudian themes, of the father-son rivalry over the use of farmland, found in "Hud," of the currying of favor with a dying man, found in the play "Volpone," etc.

Still, there is undeniable, though morbid, fascination in the spectacle of this power play — and of a generation destroying itself by fire.

By the time of release, the "El dueño del sol" team was able to announce the film had been selected for screening by the British Film Institute and at the Figueira da Foz festival in Portugal.—*Olas.*

Brotherhood
(HONG KONG-COLOR)

A D&B production and release. Executive producer, Dickson Poon. Produced by Linda Kuk. Directed by Stephen Shin. Stars Danny Lee, Alex Man, Vincent Lam, Ho Chuen Hung, Lam Wai. (No other credits provided by producer.) Reviewed at D&B Preview theater, Hong Kong, June 15, 1987. Running time: **98 MINS.**

Hong Kong — Since the box-office magic of "A Better Tomorrow," the local cinema is flooded with a stream of cops and robbers films. Almost all place emphasis on gangsters' ethics as a vehicle for story development.

Ethics is also the frequently mentioned word in "Brotherhood." The protagonist is a gang chieftain (played by Ho Chuen Hung). He can be likened to a corporation executive, and he treats his followers with filial devotion thus gaining respect from them. When three of his high ranking men are in danger of being sentenced to severe prison terms, they conspire to turn against Ho.

Meanwhile Hon (played by Lam Wai), who once saved Ho's life and has been given favors by him ever since, sets out to kill all three of the traitors for loyalty's sake.

The distinction between this film and the prevailing comradeship gangster genre is that it tells of the betrayal of the mafia-like serecy in-

stead of glorifying it. The stylized funeral scene in memory of the loyal servant of Ho who dies in defense of his master is in fact a farewell to the long-respected gangster bond.

Picture is also tightly packed with emotional conflicts involving father and son, master and servant, brothers and friends.

A weaker sub-plot concerns Hon's wife who would do anything to stay in Hong Kong as she is an illegal immigrant. Also exploited is a rape scene where the wife is molested.

The action segments are executed with extreme brutality for commercial mass appeal. —*Mel.*

Más Vale Pájaro en Mano ...
(A Bird In The Hand Is Worth ...)
(MEXICAN-COLOR)

A Peliculas Mexicans release of a Cinematográfica Filmex production. Produced by J. Fernando Pérez Gavilán. Directed by Jesús Fragoso Montoya. Screenplay, Fragoso Montoya, De la Peña; camera (color), Alberto Arellanos Bustamante; editor, Rogelio Zúñiga; music, Gustavo C. Carrión, with appearance by the group Conjunto Africa. Reviewed at Hollywood Twin theater II, July 4, 1987. Running time: **86 MINS.**
Rafael Lara (Rafa) ...Eduardo de la Peña
                (Lalo el Mimo)
Tropico .....Sergio Ramos (El Comanche)
Kalimán ....Julio Alvarado
El Borras ....Guillermo Rivas
Lucero ....Leticia Perdigón
Mecánico ....Oscar Fentanes
Eva ....Maricarmen Reséndez
Anabel ....Merle Uribe
Nancy ....Jacqueline Castro
Lawyer ....Humberto Elizondo
Sr. Mariscal ....Otto Sirgo
    Also with: Queta Lavat, Alfredo Guitiérrez, Pancho Muller, José Zambrano, Ariadne Welter, César Bono.

"Más Vale Pájaro en Mano ..." (A Bird In The Hand ...) is an unfunny comedy vehicle for Mexican comedian Eduardo de la Peña, better known to fans as Lalo el Mimo.

Film focuses on the schemes of mechanic Rafael Lara (De la Peña), whose winning lottery ticket allows him to fulfill his desires. He buys a series of auto repair shops that he leaves in the hands of four friends. He also maintains a series of separate households that he entrusts to four separate wives. It seems the mechanic cannot say no to either his friends or his girlfriends.

Of course everything comes to light and Lara is sent to prison where his lifestyle makes him the envy of other prisoners and guards alike.

The script tries to develop its humor in two ways. First, the movie tries to function as a buddy film with lots of salty interaction between the five pals, featuring well-known comedians Sergio Ramos (El Comanche) and Guillermo Rivas. Second, picaresque humor is developed from the various courtships of the different wives.

Director Jesús Fragoso Montoya

has a few idiosyncrasies such as throwing in two musical numbers with actor Julio Alvarado backed by a trio of mechanics.

Overall, the cheapo production functions as an illustrated party napkin with an artificial and forced notion of humor. —*Lent.*

Viaje al Paraiso
(Trip To Paradise)
(MEXICAN-COLOR)

A Peliculas Mexicanas release of an Instituto Mexicano de Cinematografla (Imcine) production. Directed by Ignacio Retes. Stars Ernesto Gómez Cruz, Maria Rojo. Screenplay, Retes, camera (color), Guadalupe Garcia; editor, Jesús Paredes; music, Leonardo Velázquez. Reviewed at Hollywood Twin theater I, N.Y., June 20, 1987. Running time: **89 MINS.**
Victor ....Ernesto Gómez Cruz
Pajaro ....José Carlos Ruiz
Queta ....Marla Rojo
Ramiro ....Alejandro Parodi
Felipe ....Jorge Zepeda
Julia ....:...........Gina Morett
    Also with: Jorge Balzaretti, Lolo Navarro, Zaide Silva Gutiérrez, Gabriela Roel, Yirah Aparicio, Salvador Sánchez, Demián Bichir, Juan Pelaez, Rodrigo Puebla.

The film "Viaje al Paraiso" (Trip To Paradise), written and directed by Mexican filmmaker Ignacio Retes, intends to be a biting satire on the Mexican bourgeoisie in the tradition of Luis Alcoriza's 1971 pic "Mecánica Nacional." Instead, the confused narrative provides little more than a collage of disparate scenes featuring corrupt, selfish and insensitive people in their efforts to get ahead in a corrupt, selfish and insensitive society.

Script won the 1983 screenplay competition sponsored annually by the writers society Sogem, although the Mexican Film Institute Imcine delayed production for almost three years.

Story finds impetus when eight family and extended-family members of "Chilangos" (Mexico City residents) go on vacation in the provinces. They are loud, obnoxious and constantly squabbling about everything. A comparison here would be unsophisticated New Yorkers on the loose in small-town America.

When they are robbed by revolutionaries, they become involved with cops, politicians and entertainment personalities, each using his position or ideology to attain his individual notion of the good life.

This could be material for an excellent study of Latino mores and quirks, but the trouble here is that the themes have not been well plotted. Individual sequences are too self-conscious and lack both impact and humor.

Also, the technical aspects of the pic are sparce with lean visual attention paid to the narrative. Retes passes up too many opportunities with almost no attention to details.

Acting is merely functional with more cliché than characterization.

"Viaje al Paraiso" passes up all opportunities to be a biting, savage comedy aimed at the rising middle-class in Latin America. There is so little vitality to this film that it is surprising that it should attempt so ambitious a theme. —*Lent.*

The Wrong Couples
(HONG KONG-COLOR)

A D&B Films presentation and release. Executive producer, Dickson Poon. Produced by John Sham. Directed by John Chiang. Stars Richard Ng, Josephine Siu Fong Fong, Paul Chiang, Pauline Kwan, Maggie Li, Dennis Li. Screenplay, John Chan; camera (color), Yee Tung Lung; associate producers, John Chan, Dennis Chan; art direction; Fong Ying. Reviewed at Jade theater, Hong Kong, July 9, 1987. Running time: **98 MINS.**
(Cantonese soundtrack with English subtitles)

Hong Kong — Josephine Siu Fong Fong, the lovely teen-idol of the '60s, makes a charming matured comeback in this family comedy-drama with shades of "The Goodbye Girl" and "The Odd Couple." Her charm and aura intact, Fong Fong makes her Marsha Mason-esque character lovable, believable and touching with subtle shades of humor, executed in an Asian environment.

Richard Ng is a sailor who returns home to discover that his wife Chiao Chiao has left him and rented the apartment to old maidish Fong Fong. The two are forced to stay together initially through the intervention of young daughter Pauline Kwan. The three have their idiosyncrasies, but living together has a way of transforming hate to affection and possibly to love.

Ng is determined to fight for the custody of his daughter but all his efforts fail even in court. Meanwhile, Fong Fong gathers enough courage to express her love to Ng as she turns 36. After a series of slapstick complications and misunderstandings, the power of love wins in the end.

The acting is well balanced and the film is only flawed with a corny finale and Ng's effort to be a melodramatic actor. Fong Fong excels in a solo sequence as she eats her noodles alone, feeling dejected, rejected on her birthday as an unmarried woman. "The Wrong Couples" may not go far outside the Asian circuit but it is surely one of the better efforts of D&B in 1987.
—*Mel.*

The Delos Adventure
(COLOR)

Mild actioner about a covert operation.

An American Cinema Marketing presentation of a Delos Ltd. Partnership production.

Executive producers, A.W. Bud Morrison, Jack F. Murphy. Produced and directed by Joseph Purcell. Screenplay, Purcell, Roger Kern; camera (United color), William Meurer; editor, Robert Ferretti; music, Richard DeLabio, Kenny Kotwitz; sound (Ultra-Stereo), Margaret Duke; art direction, Tony Stabley; production manager, Russ Brandt; stunt coordinator, Steve Frohardt; special effects, Paul Staples; associate producer, Rachel Purcell; casting, Roger Kern. Reviewed on TWE vidcassette, N.Y., July 16, 1987. (MPAA Rating: R.) Running time: **98 MINS.**

Bard Clemens . . . . Roger Kern
Deni . . . . Jenny Neumann
Arthur McNeil . . . . Kurtwood Smith
Luis . . . . E.J. Castillo
Greg . . . . Kevin Brophy
Koutsavaki . . . . Al Mancini
Jim . . . . Charles Lanyer
Darrensborg . . . . James Higgins
Stacy . . . . Kathryn Noble
Tana . . . . Sands Hall
Alfonso . . . . David Vallalpando
Commando . . . . Steve Frohardt

"The Delos Adventure," filmed in 1985 and debuting domestically on vidcassette, has a storyline that promisingly seems torn from today's headlines: a covert operation by the U.S. military in South America using a scientific project to front for surveilliance of Russian submarines. Unfortunately, this relatively low-key film resembles the rather lightweight action films of the 1950s rather than a hardhitting contemporary thriller.

Roger Kern, who also had a hand in scripting and casting of the feature, toplines as Bard, an earth scientist into prospecting, who is hired by old pal and fellow scientist (Charles Lanyer) to work on a project for Stafford Research. Project involves accompanying beautiful blond environmentalist Deni (Jenny Neumann) to the tiny island of San Crispin off the coast of Chile to install seismic sensors underwater that will broadcast back (via satellite link on the island) to California on earthquakes, etc. Deni is there to do a survey for her ailing father on environmental concerns.

It turns out that all this actually is a front for a secret Cold War operation run by the U.S. military, which has bribed Stafford Research scientist McNeil (Kurtwood Smith) into running the show in return for appropriation of government funding. Scheme is to neutralize Soviet subs off the Chilean coast by installing secret sensors, but the fly in the ointment is the presence of Soviet commandos on the island, who proceed to kill several of the scientists and hunt down the rest.

Pic is too slowly paced (action doesn't really get going until the second half) to be exciting, preferring to emphasize a scenic approach to showcasing some lovely locations and beautiful leading lady Neumann. It should have been a nailbiting, brink of disaster, eyeball to eyeball tale of superpowers' confrontation.

Acting is competent, with star Kern okay as a Kurt Russell-ish type of reluctant hero while Kurtwood Smith, currently on screen as heavy in "Robocop," turns out quite surprisingly to be a straight shooter when the chips are down. An abrupt and too convenient ending comes as a letdown.

Tech credits are fine. —*Lor.*

Superman IV: The Quest For Peace (COLOR)

Second-rate outing for the Man of Steel.

A Warner Bros. release of a Cannon Group/Golan-Globus production. Produced by Menahem Golan, Yoram Globus. Executive producer, Michael Kagan. Directed by Sidney J. Furie. Stars Christopher Reeve, Gene Hackman. Screenplay, Lawrence Konner, Mark Rosenthal, story by Reeve, Konner, Rosenthal; camera (J-D-C Widescreen, Rank color), Ernest Day; editor, John Shirley; music, John Williams; music adapted, conducted by Alexander Courage; production design, John Graysmark; art direction, Leslie Tomkins; set decoration, Peter Young; costume design, John Bloomfield; sound (Dolby), Danny Daniel; visual effects supervisor, Harrison Ellenshaw; special effects supervisor, John Evans; model effects supervisor, Richard Conway; flying unit director, David Lane; flying/second unit directors, Lane, Ellenshaw, Reeve; second unit camera, Godfrey Godar; associate producer, Graham Easton; assistant director, Gino Marotta; casting, Noel Davis, Jeremy Zimmermann. Reviewed at the Paramount Theater, L.A., July 24, 1987. (MPAA Rating: PG.) Running time: **89 MINS.**
Superman/Clark Kent . . Christopher Reeve
Lex Luthor . . . . Gene Hackman
Perry White . . . . Jackie Cooper
Jimmy Olsen . . . . Marc McClure
Lenny . . . . Jon Cryer
David Warfield . . . . Sam Wanamaker
Nuclear Man #2 . . . . Mark Pillow
Lacy Warfield . . . . Mariel Hemingway
Lois Lane . . . . Margot Kidder

Hollywood — At one point in this fourth installment of the lucrative "Superman" series, Gene Hackman's villainous Lex Luthor says, "When I escaped from prison, I had one thing on my mind — the end of Superman." Despite his failure to dispatch the caped hero on the screen, it would appear that Luthor's wish has finally come true, for Superman has finally been done in — by the makers of this film. Unlike the case for numerous other recent successful series, b.o. for the "Superman" pics has dropped rather precipitously with each entry — the second earned 21% less in rentals than the first, and the third was off 43% from the second. That factor, plus the new film's second-rate look, certainly will reduce revenues to the point where continuing the expensive series would no longer be profitable.

For this chapter, the Salkinds passed the producing baton to Cannon's Menahem Golan and Yoram Globus, while Sidney J. Furie has taken over from Richard Lester behind the camera. Neither change has been for the good, as this production has a chintzy appearance one does not associate with the earlier entries, and Furie lacks the light touch Lester applied with particular success in "Superman II."

Another credit of note is star Christopher Reeve's as coauthor of the story, which sees Superman taking up where "Amazing Grace And Chuck" left off in singlehandedly forcing the world to junk its nuclear arms.

Opening sequence shows Superman has picked up the spirit of *glasnost* as he flies into space to rescue an imperiled cosmonaut and utters his first lines of the picture in Russian. Film then becomes earthbound for a long stretch, as the Daily Planet goes tabloid after being bought by tycoon Sam Wanamaker as a plaything for his daughter, Mariel Hemingway.

Mariel takes a fancy to Clark Kent, and there is mild comedy attendant to a double date she and Margot Kidder's Lois Lane are supposed to have with Kent and Superman. This is all fluff next to Superman's newly assumed mission, however, which sees him addressing the United Nations to tell the world he personally is going to remove all nuclear weapons from the face of the earth.

Niftiest sequence in the film has the Man of Steel intercepting launched missiles, stuffing them in a giant net in outer space, then flinging them, hammer-throw-style, smack into the sun.

At this point, relatively early in the picture, it would seen everyone's troubles are over, except that Lex Luthor has created an evil clone of Superman called Nuclear Man, who wreaks havoc with famous landmarks around the world and does savage battle with the hero on the face of the moon until Superman discovers his nemesis' single flaw.

The earlier films in the series were far from perfect, but at their best they had some flair and agreeable humor, qualities this one sorely lacks. Hackman gets a few laughs, but has less to work with than before, and everyone else seems as if he's just going through the motions and having less fun doing so. Major new cast addition, Hemingway, looks great and seems game, but hasn't been given the special sock scene she needs to try to score with either Kent or Superman.

Flying effects look notably cheesier than in the earlier installments, but that's in keeping with the more threadbare look of the entire production.

From the evidence here, it seems clear even Superman needs a rest once in a while, and that the time has arrived.—*Cart.*

Poule et frites (Chicken And Chips) (FRENCH-COLOR)

A Gaumont release of a French Prod./Intl. Prods./Planetes et Compagnie/C.K. Music coproduction, in association with Sofinergie and Stone Prod. Executive producer, Emmanuel Schlumberger. Produced by Pierre Sayag. Directed by Luis Rego. Screenplay, Rego, Michel Ehlers, Jackie Berroyer; cam-

era (color), Gérard de Battista; editor, Catherine Kelber; music, Rego, Scott Allen, Vincent Palmer, Miguel Castagnos; sound, Harald Maury; art direction, Olivier Paultre; production manager, Gérard Gaultier; associate producer, Dick Hamel. Reviewed at the George V cinema, Paris, July 7, 1987. Running time: **87 MINS.**
With: Luis Rego (Roger), Anémone (Bébé), Michel Galabru (Martinez), Claire Nadeau (Minou), Carole Jacquinot (Vera), Claude Gensac (Françoise), Laurent Romor (Jimmy), Eva Darlan, Marc Jolivet.

Paris — "Poule et frites" is a rancid sex farce from Luis Rego, erstwhile funnyman with the once-popular Les Charlots team, here making his writing-directing debut — without promise on either count.

Rego also acts the main role of a philanderer who operates an unlicensed french fries and ice cream concession with his family at a Riviera resort. He has been living a harmoniously two-timing existence for years between wife and mistress, but overreaches himself when he tries to add a luscious but sado-masochistic cabaret singer to his daily menu.

He rushes the plot into rusty gear without much concern for making any of the characters charming or palatable, with the result that everybody becomes quickly obnoxious, especially the frenzied Rego. Anémone, as the mistress, and Michel Galabru, as Rego's uncle and accomplice, bring little relief to the distasteful antics. — Len.

Maid To Order
(COLOR)

**Cinderella in reverse comedy
is sanitized and predictable.**

A New Century/Vista Film Co. release of a Vista Organization production. Produced by Herb Jaffe, Mort Engelberg. Directed by Amy Jones. Stars Ally Sheedy. Screenplay, Jones, Perry Howze, Randy Howze; camera (Deluxe color), Shelly Johson; editor, Sidney Wolinski; music, Georges Delerue; sound (Ultra-Stereo), Rick Waddell; production design, Jeffrey Townsend; costume design, Lisa Jensen; assistant director, Kristine Peterson; second unit director, Jeffrey Townsend; casting, Nina Axelrod. Reviewed at New Century/Vista screening room, L.A., July 21, 1987. (MPAA Rating: PG.) Running time: **96 MINS.**
Jessie Montgomery . . . . Ally Sheedy
Stella . . . . Beverly D'Angelo
Nick McGuire . . . . Michael Ontkean
Georgette Starkey . . . . Valerie Perrine
Stan Starkey . . . . Dick Shawn
Charles Montgomery . . . . Tom Skerritt
Audrey James . . . . Merry Clayton
Maria . . . . Begoña Plaza

Hollywood — "Maid To Order" is a fantasy, actually Cinderella in reverse. This skewed fairy tale adaptation finds Ally Sheedy as a poor little rich girl forced to work as a maid and in the process learning humility, sensitivity and diligence. There's a fairy godmother to guide her and a prince to adore her. Occasionally funny and sometimes clever, mostly it's cute — just the sort of

pic a reader of "Tiger Beat" would love.

Ally Sheedy doesn't know how not to be cute, even when she's supposed to be an insufferable brat. She's a party girl from Beverly Hills who grew up without a mother but has a decent, if indulgent father (Tom Skerritt).

Cuteness only goes so far and even "Daddy" has a threshold, that being when Sheedy parties a little too hearty and lands in jail for speeding and cocaine possession. In exasperation, Skerritt wishes upon a star his girl had never been born and voila, his wish is granted. Enter Beverly D'Angelo as the '80s fairy godmother encountering the now homeless Sheedy out on the streets swilling cheap liquor with a park bench resident.

At first she dismisses D'Angelo as a raving nut, but comes to learn, as the audience does with her intermittent appearances, that she's her conscience.

Meanwhile, Sheedy's desperate for food after a whole one night on her own and lands a job with a too-hip Malibu couple (the late Dick Shawn plus Valerie Perrine) who want a white maid (as in Anglo) since they already have a Latino (Begoña Plaza), a black (Merry Clayton) and a scruffy mechanic cum chauffeur (Michael Ontkean).

Unlike the heroine of Charles Perrault's classic tale, Sheedy's character, Jessie, totally lacks any domestic talents and doesn't have any particular desire to learn them either. That doesn't sit too well with the resentful Salvadoran maid played with authority by Plaza, or with the cook, a good role for the earthy Clayton.

Likability aside, subtlety is not the operative word here since most folks surrounding Sheedy are drawn without shading or complexity. Plaza gleefully sends money back home, Clayton can sing with gusto, cook and ooze love for her family and Ontkean is an all-around decent guy.

The watered-down evil roles go to Shawn and Perrine, whose Hollywood shtick is milked to the nth degree. What is initially mildy amusing obnoxious behavior runs thin after a while.

Shawn's a dealmaker looking for a charity gig to hype his latest star, in this case the real life Starlight Foundation that gets more plugs than are used in his character's hair transplant. She recycles tin foil and newspapers, uses hotel soap for guests and generally is a good voluptuous housewife with horse sense and no taste.

Sight gags of malfunctioning vacuums, backfiring limos and burnt clothes work only once and fortunately, they are kept to a minimum. That leaves the personalities

to carry the comedy, but after a few times on screen, we know all about them and the fun is gone. Essentially, the "downstairs" folks have more talent than the "upstairs" folks in the talent business.

As soon as Sheedy gets a handle on how to clean and who she's dealing with, pic falls into the realm of sappy predictability. She transforms from a sourpuss to a sweety pie, gets her prince and her Daddy back and everyone lives happily ever after.

With no sex, little nudity, no profanity, a PG rating and morals to boot, "Maid To Order" might well have been written by a subversive couple for their wayward kids.
—*Brit.*

An Autumn's Tale
(HONG KONG-COLOR)

A D&B Films production and release. Executive producer, Dickson Poon. Produced by John Sham. Directed by Yuen Ting (Mabel) Cheung. Stars Chow Yun Fat, Cheri Chung, Danny Chan, Gigi Wong, Wong Man, Brenda Lo, Joyce Houseknecht, Cindy Ou, Chan Yiu Yin, Tom Hsiung. Screenplay, Alex Law; camera (color), James Hayman, David Chung; music, Lowell Lo; associate producer, Winnie Yu; art direction, Christy Addis, Yank Wong. Reviewed at Jade theater, Hong Kong, July 17, 1987. Running time: **98 MINS.**
(Cantonese soundtrack with English subtitles)

Hong Kong — Young and middle-class bred Cheri Chung goes to college in New York City to study acting, also to re-unite with rich boyfriend Danny Chan.

Chung discovers spoiled beau Chan has a new live-in Americanized girlfriend. She is very disappointed and in her sadness begins to be a loner. With distant relative Boat Head's care (played by Chow Yun Fat), sympathy and guidance, Chung gradually forgets her adolescent romantic notions and adapts to her new surroundings. She builds up her confidence in both study and work.

Boat Head falls in love with his charming ward, but since he spent most of his life at sea, he is very inept in expressing his feelings, especially to a girl he fancies. He also feels inferior, but she understands his limitations. Chung is mature enough to realize the man she likes does not necessarily mean the man one should marry as they are from two extreme worlds.

As winter approaches, Chung accepts a job in Long Island and must leave the apartment building where Boat Head resides. As they say goodbye, neither makes explicit his inner feelings, but they know they will always remember that particular autumn in Manhattan. She gives him an old pocket watch and he gives her an antique bracelet for her watch.

This is the second feature of Mabel Cheung, who made an impact

with her debut work at Shaw Brothers two years ago called "The Illegal Immigrant." Her "tale" is supposedly autobiographical which explains the inherent sensitivity and warmth throughout the presentation. It is, however, deeply flawed with too many coincidences. Some of the main characters seem to be cued to appear at the right time and the right place when the heroine needs them most.

Cheri Chung is lovely to watch and shows some signs of dramatic presence. —*Mel.*

Messalina, Messalina
(ITALIAN-COLOR)

A Medusa Distribuzione production. Executive producer, Renato Jaboni. Produced by Franco Rossellini. Directed by Bruno Corbucci. Screenplay, Mario Amendola, Corbucci; camera (color), Marcello Masciocchi; editor, Daniele Alabiso; music, Maurizio De Angelis, Guido De Angelis; art director (uncredited), Danilo Donati; set adaptation, Claudio Cinini; costumes, Alberto Verso; makeup, Franco Di Girolamo; sound, Gianfranco De Mattheis, Massimo Jaboni. Reviewed on Video City Prods. vidcassette, N.Y., July 16, 1987. (No MPAA Rating.) Running time: **81 MINS.**
Messalina . . . . Anneka Di Lorenzo
Claudius . . . . Vittorio Caprioli
Caius Silius . . . . Giancarlo Prete
Baba . . . . Tomas Milian
Julius Nelius . . . . Lino Toffolo
Also with: Lory Kay Wagner, Raf Luca, Bombolo, Pino Ferrara, Sal Borgese, Alessandra Cardini, Luca Sportelli, Ombretta di Carlo, Primo Marcotulli, Sandra Cadini, Viviana Larice.

Shot about 10 years ago on the sets of "Caligula," "Messalina, Messalina," is a would-be comedy, set during the reign of the Emperor Claudius, that is less sexually explicit than its predecessor but far cruder. Mainly incomprehensible pic appears to have been cut considerably to bring it down to its current 81-minute running time, but it's hard to imagine anything meaningful being excised. Pic has never been theatrically released in the U.S. and is now on vidcassette, packaged as "Messalina, Empress Of Rome."

Anneka Di Lorenzo, who appeared in "Caligula," stars here in the role of the emperor's lusty wife. Main plotline follows her various attempts (almost always successful) to bed men and women of all stripes, from senators to a Venetian tourist (Lino Toffolo). She's naked most of the time, and is certainly eye-pleasing, but the numerous softcore sex scenes are hammed up for laughs, thus unerotic.

Di Lorenzo also is given to Mae West-isms, while Tomas Milian, who plays a drunken philosopher, seems to be aping Edward G. Robinson (at least that's how he comes across in this atrociously dubbed version). Among many pointless excursions on view, Di Lorenzo has Milian doped, brought to her palace, and dressed as the emperor so that when he comes to he's treated to the high life, only to be doped again and deposited in a slum haystack.

The empress also gets it on with g.f. Lory Kay Wagner. The pair in-interfaced memorably in "Caligula;" their encounter here is less spectacular, and it's been intercut with quick shots of some decidedly more explicit sexual activity involving two unidentified women. More disturbing is the film's climax, an orgy of violence wherein arms, legs and heads are lopped off in large numbers and blood shoots out like water from a garden hose. It's not funny, though it's meant to be.

Dialog, when it can be understood, is strictly single entendre. When someone rips off an effeminate male prostitute, he screams "Stop, thief! He's stolen all my vaseline!" And a centurion whose job it is to procure men for Messalina wanders throughout the film babbling about penis size.

Noteworthy disclaimer at the start of pic explains, "Certain elements of the sets and decorations created for the film 'Caligula' by Danilo Donati have been used in the production of this film without his consent."—*Gerz.*

L'Eté en pente douce
(Summer On A Soft Slope)
(FRENCH-COLOR)

An AAA release of a Solus Prods./Flach Film/Séléna Audiovisual (AAA)/Films A2 coproduction, with the participation of the Ministry of Culture. Produced by Jean-Marie Duprez, Pascal Hommais, Jean-François Lepetit. Directed by Gérard Krawczyk. Screenplay, Krawczyk, Jean-Paul Lilienfeld, from Pierre Pelot's novel; camera (color), Michel Cenet; editor, Marie-Josephe Yoyotte; music, Roland Vincent; sound, Pierre Befve, Jean-Paul Loublier; art direction, Jacques Dugied; assistant director, Evelyne Ragot; production manager, Bernard Grenet. Reviewed at the 7 Parnassiens cinema, Paris, July 13, 1987. Running time: **98 MINS.**
With: Jean-Pierre Bacri (Fane), Pauline Lafont (Lilas), Jacques Villeret (Mo), Guy Marchand (André Voke), Jean Bouise (Olivier Voke), Jean-Paul Lilienfeld (Shawenhick), Jacques Mathou (Jeannot), Dominique Besnehard (Mr. Leval), Claude Chabrol (priest).

Paris — A stodgy, synthetic tale of three misfits struggling for dignity and love in a southern French burg, "L'Eté en pente douce" looks like a clumsily gallicized version of some sub-Faulknerian or ersatz Tennessee Williams potboiler, complete with village idiot, loose-hipped sexpot, envious, small-minded local yokels, and egregiously Southern-styled musical scoring.

Ironically this second feature by Gérard Krawczyk, who struck out last year with his senseless Frenchlingo adaptation of Ben Hecht's "I Hate Actors," is based on a local novel by Pierre Pelot, a prolific young author of more than 100 books, mostly sci-fi and thriller quickies, often inspired by Yank

models. His typed characters and situations, thus twice-removed from their apparent source, lose whatever veracity they might have had on the page in Krawczyk's dramatically pale film.

Story concerns a young ne'er-do-well with vague dreams of being a novelist (Jean-Pierre Bacri) who returns to his hometown after his mother's death to take over the family house and look after his dim-witted brother (Jacques Villeret). He brings with him a pea-brained, but luscious blond (Pauline Lafont) whom he saved from a brutal boyfriend by swapping a rabbit for her.

The couple's arrival in town sparks local animosity and lust as a nearby garagist (Guy Marchand) schemes to force Bacri to sell his property so he can enlarge his business. Marchand tries to come on to Lafont and when that fails he rallies the bigoted townspeople against the odd threesome, who nonetheless succeed in giving their antagonists a just comeuppance before heading out for more hospitable climes.

Krawczyk is a little more at ease in the realistic register than in the broad lampooning of "I Hate Actors," but his script (written with Jean-Paul Lilienfeld) and direction betray a weakness for colorful characters rather than truthful characterization. The acting of the principals is earnest but self-conscious, notably Lafont's sentimental baby doll on a hot tin roof.
— *Len.*

Return To Departure
(CANADIAN-DOCU-
COLOR-16m)

A film by K. Tougas Film Prods., Vancouver, Canada. Produced and directed by Kirk Tougas. Written by Chi O'Farrell; camera (color, 16m), Tougar; editor, uncredited; sound, Paul Sharpe. Produced in association with the National Film Board and the Canada Council. Reviewed at the American Film Video Festival, N.Y., June 22, 1987. Running time: **83 MINS.**

The full title of the film is: "Return To Departure — Biography Of A Painting, Or Watching Pigment Drying, And Other Realisms." The film's preamble states that for a few years now new creative artists have been creeping out of the crawl spaces, gulags, displaced-persons camps, and other unlikely places, and they are invigorating Canadian art.

"Return To Departure" is both the name of the film and the name of a painting being painted within the film, condensed from several months of work. The painter, Chi O'Farrell, informally describes his methodology in voiceover as we watch his brushes at work in closeup. Sometimes his hands are seen; such images account for 90% of the run-

ning time. Because his are the only words heard in the film, O'Farrell is credited as screenwriter. He is never seen except in quick fragmentary glimpses, a dark and rather handsome young man with glasses.

As we watch the painting take shape, O'Farrell unseen chats casually with the filmmaker, also unseen, about light and shadows, warm and cool colors, perspective, texture, the aging process of a canvas, the superiority of egg tempura technique over oil, and, more personally, the subliminal values of his own work.

O'Farrell's ruminations on his painting technique are intercut with his semi-audible mumbles, humming, singalong with the radio and occasional expletives. Once or twice an off-screen phone rings and is answered by a child.

"Return To Departure" is not a portrait of an artist but is perhaps a portrait of a painting. To the extent that we learn anything more, we may say that the film humanizes the artist behind the canvas, shows us his working ambience and suggest his creative processes. This film can prove of interest to serious practitioners of painting. —*Hitch.*

Madrid
(SPANISH-COLOR)

A Linterna Mágica production, in coproduction with RTV. Produced by Luis Gutiérrez, José Luis Garcia Sánchez. Written and directed by Basilio Martin Patino. Camera (color), Augusto G. Fernandez Balbuena; editor, Pablo Martin Pascual; music, Carmelo Bernaola; sets, Polo i Bombin; research, Elbia Alvarez López. Reviewed at Cine Alcázar, Barcelona, July 18, 1987. Running time: **98 MINS.**
Hans . . . . Rüdiger Vogler
Lucia . . . . Verónica Forqué
Pancho . . . . Ricardo Contalapiedra
Also with: José Prat, Luis Ciges, Ana Duato, María Luisa Ponte, Félix Defauce.

Barcelona — The 50th anniversary of the outbreak of the Spanish Civil War was commemorated last year by a spate of programs, tv shows and documentaries in and out of Spain which pretty well exhausted the subject, at least as far as laymen were concerned. Now, helmer Basilio Martin Patino has come up with his own, personal lucubrations on the subject. Now only does he fail to add anything new to the subject, already skillfully covered by his own earlier films, "Caudillo" and "Cancoines," but he comes up with a dull, aimless and pretentious pic, the point of which gets lost in high-falutin' verbiage.

The shaky peg upon which the anemic story dangles is an assignment given to a German tv director, sent down to Madrid to do a documentary on the Civil War. Instead of getting on with the job, the helmer dawdles, takes walks, philosophizes, has a fleeting romance and, mostly, watches old footage,

almost all of it supremely well known (even Robert Capa's super-famous shots are included).

Moreover, the Teutonic tv director clearly knows nothing of Spain, not even what a zarzuela is (although he speaks passable Spanish). Notwithstanding, he tries to come up with something profound to say, some eternal verity, which, of course, eludes him. His producer tells him again to get on with the assignment, but he continues to search for the inscrutable "truth."

Much of the pic consists of familiar docu footage. German actor Rüdiger Vogler is expressionless, brooding and boring. Not even the presence of lively Spanish thesp Verónica Forqué can buoy up this heavyhanded slab of a film. —*Besa.*

The Thirty Million Rush
(HONG KONG-COLOR)

A Cinema City Co. Ltd. presentation, released by Golden Princess theater circuit. Executive producer, Karl Maka. Produced by Wellington Fung. Directed by Maka. Stars Maka, Lin Ching Hsia, Paula Tsui, Eric Tsang, Mark Cheng, Anglie Leung, Wong Ching, Lau Kar Leung. Camera (color), Bob Thompson, Andrew Lau, editor, Tony Chow, Wong Ming Lam; music, Alvin Kwok; art direction, Vincent Wai. Reviewed at President theater, Hong Kong, July 9, 1987. Running time: **98 MINS.**
(Cantonese soundtrack with English subtitles)

Hong Kong — Some 30,000,000 old Hong Kong bank notes are left undestroyed over the weekend and are locked up in the cremation stations for overused paper currency. Eric Tsang who works in the bank gets the notion to get rich quick and organizes his old friends Mark Cheng and Anglie Leung to a conspiracy of burglary. They also seek ex-convict Karl Maka for consultation but the secret leaks out to hardworking nun Lin Ching Hsia who wants to stop crime and save souls.

From this simplistic plot emerges a lively collection of popvisual razzmatazz and snippets in a Mad magazine format. Presentation is high on energy, creativity, movement and exuberance, with lots of humorous split-screen visual effects.

Like pop music, the movie is easy listening, easy watching and easy thinking. Cantonese kids will love this cartoonish film. —*Mel.*

Pula Film Festival Reviews

Uvek spremne zene
(Woman's Day)
(YUGOSLAV-COLOR)

A Film Danas (Belgrade)/Croatia Film (Zagreb)/Smart Egg Pictures (London) coproduction. Directed by Branko Baletic. Screenplay, Milan Secerovic, Baletic; camera (color), Zivko Zalar; music, Zoran Simjanovic; art direction, Nemanja Petrovic. Reviewed at the Pula Film Festival, July 20, 1987. Running time: **107 MINS.**
With: Mirjana Karanovic, Radmila Zivkovic, Tanja Boskovic, Dara Dokic, Gordana Gadzic, Cvijeta Mesic, Ksenija Pajic.

Pula — "Woman's Day" is an offbeat entry on the Yugoslav scene: a fast-moving, ribald comedy about unemployment with seven femme protagonists. This third feature by Branko Baletic (new head of CFS/Avala Film) doesn't go in for subtlety but has vitality to spare and is generally a lot of fun.

Film gets rolling with a bunch of rowdy women farmhands who, revolting against the manager who won't pay their wages, shanghai a tractor, and hightail it to someplace like a town.

Objective is to get a shady operator named Jura to find them jobs in Munich. After he takes their passports and money, he gets arrested for employing women illegally, apparently a local racket. Undaunted, the spunky gals go through a humorously recounted gynecological exam to get a health certificate — all pass, including an alcoholic one who's pregnant.

They hunt down temporary work, everything from factory labor to smuggling and casual prostitution. They get beat up, raped, drowned and abused, but keep swinging. A hard-hitting finale shows them at last fixed up with permanent employment in a new factory — only to discover the raw materials are lacking and the plant won't be able to open.

Punctuated with gags, pic keeps up a lively pace. Whole femme cast is game, willing to dress like hicks and swagger around like construction workers. Lensing is serviceable.— *Yung.*

U ime naroda
(In The Name Of The People)
(YUGOSLAV-COLOR)

A Cannon Group release of a Zeta Film (Budva)/Avala Pro-Film (Belgrade)/Centar Film (Belgrade)/Montex (Niksic) coproduction. Directed by Zivko Nikolic. Screenplay, Nikolic, Dragan Nikolic; camera (color), Savo Jovanovic; music, Vuk Kulenovic; art direction, Bosko Odalovic. Reviewed at the Pula Film Festival, July 23, 1987. Running time: **121 MINS.**

Milutin . . . . Miodrag Krivokapic
Marinka . . . . Savina Gersak
Also with: Petar Bozovic, Vesna Pecanac.

Pula — Zivko Nikolic's "In The Name Of The People" is a disappointingly bland social drama from a director who usually shows more flair for out-of-the-way storytelling and striking visuals ("Unseen Wonder," "The Beauty Of Vice"). Here, a somber yarn about official abuse of power lacks all surprise, while Nikolic's characteristic touches of grotesque comedy remain in the background. Acquired by Cannon, pic will need very special handling to get before audiences.

Theme bears a superficial resemblance to the Stalinist finger-pointing of the Soviet film "Repentance:" (also acquired by Cannon) in the mid-'60s, a number of factory and municipal authorities misused their powers of office, arbitrarily firing workers, imprisoning their enemies, sleeping with their wives. Set in one of the poorest sections of Montenegro, where the populace lives in a muddy shantytown, tale describes the arrest of a well-liked factory boss, Todor, by a jealous group of plotters.

The wronged man's one defender is an honest supervisor, Milutin (Miodrag Krivokapic), who is first demoted, then fired, for taking the director's wife and kids under his protection.

People are painted strictly in terms of black and white, evil (like Milutin's unscrupulous wife) and good (Todor's wife, played with helpless feminity by Savina Gersak). Then the twist comes: a government cleanup turns the world right side up again; the baddies are arrested, Todor reinstated. To keep the peace Todor pretends he was away on business all this time, and honest Milutin stays out on the street for wanting the whole truth told.

Pic is professionally lensed and Krivokapic's performance in the main role is a strong point, though not enough to overcome the meandering, obvious script.— *Yung.*

Usodni Telefon
(The Fatal Telephone)
(YUGOSLAV-BLACK & WHITE)

A E-Motion Film/Skuc/TDS SKD Brut (Ljubljana)/Filmoteka 16 (Zagreb) coproduction. Written and directed by Damjan Kozole. Camera (b&w), Andrej Lupinc; editor, Vesna Lazeta; music, Otroci Socializma; art direction, Roman Bahovec. Reviewed at the Pula Film Festival, July 25, 1987. Running time: **74 MINS.**
With: Miran Sustersic, Vinoi Vogue-Anzlovar.

Pula — This b&w, grainy experimental first feature by 22-year-old helmer Damjan Kozole is notable chiefly for being one of the only known professional feature films made outside Yugoslavia's traditional studio system. Coming out of Ljubljana, where Viba Film has a de facto monopoly on all Slovenian filmmaking, the youthful co-op E-Motion Film managed to complete this indie project on a shoestring with help from the Cultural Assn. and Brut Film. Result certainly has the look of an alternative production, chock full of freshness and vitality, low on structure and story. It could play in youth fests.

The Slovenian New Wave esthetic visually resembles the grainy b&w lensing and nervous editing of many other youth productions. Backdrop alternates between street traffic and apartment interiors decorated with James Dean posters. Story is minimal: two buddies are casually making a film anyway they can; their main preoccupation is to stretch the running time out to 90 minutes and find some sound to go with the image. They tape New Wave bands and old ladies at the open market. One tapes a private phone call of the other, who is in love with an unknown girl who keeps calling. They will use the mysterious voice to end the film.

A plot like this doesn't make for a very involving picture, and pic's brief running time seems to last much longer than it does. It is enlivened with small gags and hijinks. Filmer Kozole has no ax to grind and pic is devoid of anger or any other strong emotion, though his infatuation for cinema comes through loud and clear. The two main actors, Miran Sustersic and Vinoi Vogue-Anzlovar, are hip, sympathetic non-pros.— *Yung.*

Hi-Fi
(YUGOSLAV-COLOR)

A Vardar Film (Skopje) production. Directed by Vladimir Blazevski. Screenplay, Goran Stefanovski, from his play; camera (color), Miso Samoilovski; editor, Petar Markovic; music, Ljupco Konstantinov; art direction, Nikola Lazarevski. Reviewed at Pula Film Festival, July 22, 1987. Running time: **106 MINS.**
Matthew . . . . Danco Cevrevski
Boris . . . . Fabijan Sovagovic
Also with: Elizabeta Dorevska, Meto Jovanovski, Vukosava Doneva, Pepi Lakovic, Aco Jovanovski, Dusko Kostovski.

Pula — A first feature by Vladimir Blazevski, "Hi-Fi" is a professionally lensed character study with a classic touch, but not much excitement. Theatrical origins in a well-known play by Goran Stefanovski are both virtue and fault, as pic does little to open itself up spatially, concentrating instead on the interaction between the two central characters, a father and son, superbly limned by Fabijan Sovagovic (père) and Danco Cevrevski (fils). Film won the Best Direction award at the national film fest. Offshore, this Macedonian entry would need an audience of rare patience to be appreciated.

Boris Bojanovski (Sovagovic) is a cantankerous, tough old man who has just spent five years in jail for undisclosed reasons. He comes home to find his long-haired, laidback son Matthew (Cevrevski) living with a girlfriend (Elizabeta Dorevska) and an American hitchhiker. Unable to find a job, the son has transformed the apartment into a mini-recording studio where he and band make not-bad music.

Boris, an authoritarian old Leninist, is scandalized by the "disorder" and sets about turning his shaggy offspring into a man. The confrontation between the dispirited youth with hound dog eyes and eccentric father, bent on typing up his totally uninteresting prison memoirs, unfolds with too little energy to be engrossing, though its offbeat comic tone (even when Boris handcuffs Matthew to keep him typing) helps. Thesps work together extremely well, arousing sympathy for the unhappy duo despite their shortcomings. Camerawork by Miso Samoilovski, fluid and fast, helps lighten the claustrophobia of the apartment where most of the action takes place.
— *Yung.*

Veo Videno
(Déjà Vu)
(YUGOSLAV-COLOR)

An Art Film 80/DFS Avala Film (Belgrade)/Croatia Film (Zagreb)/Smart Egg Pictures (London) coproduction. Written and directed by Goran Markovic. Camera (color), Zivko Zalar; music, Zoran Simjanovic; art direction, Slobodan Rundo. Reviewed at the Pula Film Festival, July 24, 1987. Running time: **104 MINS.**
Mihailo . . . . Mustafa Nadarevic
Olga . . . . Anica Dobra
Zoran . . . . Miroslav Mandic

Pula — Winner of this year's national film prize, Goran Markovic's "Déjà Vu" is a rare and intriguing transplant of the Western psychological thriller à la Hitchcock and DePalma to Yugoslav cinema. A sure fest pick, it has the kind of international appeal that could transfer well to art house audiences abroad with careful handling.

This is Markovic's fifth feature and shows the director continuing to push at filmic frontiers as few of his compatriots do. Story centers around Mihailo (Mustafa Nadarevic), misfit and loner in a continuing education school, where he teaches piano. As a youth he was predicted to turn into a brilliant pianist, but family traumas, which pic gradually unveils, have blocked him from touching the keyboard for 25 years.

One day his lonely existence is overturned in the most unexpected manner: a sexy blond in a miniskirt (time is 1971) turns up to teach a modeling course. Pursued by every male in sight, Olga (Anica Dobra) chooses to become the lover of the homely, shy piano teacher. Actually she's desperately unhappy living with an alcoholic father and sick brother, and she uses sex as a means of escape. Mihailo figures obscurely in her plan to climb the social ladder.

Though gratified by his unexpected fortune, Mihailo finds himself having strange flashbacks to terrible scenes of his childhood, with Olga a stand-in for his beloved, aristocratic mother. Mother attempts suicide, father is condemned to death by a revolutionary tribunal after the war ... Though déjà vu may not exactly describe Mihailo's ills, it serves to advance the plot to a climatic Youth Night Olga organizes at the school. Mihailo is supposed to play Chopin, but runs off stage in panic. The humiliation and loss of Olga is so great his mind snaps, and he wreaks havoc on Olga's pitiful family before being carted off to the asylum.

There is also a postscript that shows the trauma being passed on to the next generation.

Stylishly lensed with atmosphere to spare by Zivko Zalar and aided by a spooky score by Zoran Simjanovic, "Déjà Vu" manages to combine offbeat characters with hidden perversions and historical problems into a resonant, classy picture. Thesps turn in believable, quality performances despite their characters' obvious eccentricities. — *Yung*.

Kraljeva zavrsnica
(King Of Endings)
(YUGOSLAV-COLOR)

A Marjan Film (Split)/Centar Film (Belgrade) coproduction. Directed by Zivorad Tomic. Screenplay, Tomic, Nebojsa Pajkic; camera (color), Boris Turkovic; editor, Zoltan Wagner; music, Vuk Kulenovic; art direction, Mario Ivezic. Reviewed at the Pula Film Festival, July 19, 1987. Running time: **98 MINS.**
Branko Krajl . . . . Irfan Mensur
Visnja . . . . Ena Begovic
Irene . . . . Vladica Milosavljevic
Also with: Milan Strljic.

Pula — "King Of Endings" is a confused first feature by Zivorad Tomic. Pic starts out detailing the tensions of a love triangle (husband, wife, mistress), then uncomfortably segues into a mystery (who killed the wife?) and finally concludes with a protracted homicidal rampage by the over-wrought husband. Director shows an aptitude for elegant lensing and understated performances from his actors (mostly stage

thesps), but these classic virtues are not what is needed to pull together such diverse material. Result is quite uninvolving.

Irfan Mensur plays hero Branko Krajl, a successful young lawyer who prefers chess to his dazzling wife Visnja (Ena Begovic). Why he should be straying into the arms of relatively plain Vladica Milosavljevic is explained in the wife's accusing one-liner: "You always liked blonds." What either lady sees in the boring, strait-laced and unerotic Krajl is never explained at all.

Marital tensions come to a head when couple takes an overnight train to Split to see their ailing son. To keep from talking to each other, they separate, Krajl following a chess match in one carriage, Visnja alone in another. When she is raped by three men who work on the train, no one hears her screams. Krajl turns up just as she jumps out the door to her death.

The rest of the pic is spent with Krajl trying to overcome partial amnesia, which prevents him from piecing the tape together for the police. Finally he takes another night train where it all comes back to him, and one after the other he brutally murders Visnja's attackers. Unfortunately, his robot-like killing has as little emotional resonance as his chess playing, especially when interrupted tv-thriller style by anxious confabs between concerned mistress and police back at headquarters. Somehow they know everything (how?) and are waiting with handcuffs at the station when he arrives.

Pic's title, for those interested, comes from a chess move: Krajl-king in Serbocroatian.— *Yung*.

Stakeout
(COLOR)

Commercial but synthetic combo of comedy & cop thriller.

A Buena Vista Pictures release of a Touchstone Pictures presentation, in association with Silver Screen Partners II. Produced by Jim Kouf, Cathleen Summers. Supervising producer, Gregg Champion. Executive producer, John Badham. Directed by Badham. Stars Richard Dreyfuss, Emilio Estevez. Screenplay, Kouf; camera (Deluxe color), John Seale; editor, Tom Rolf, Michael Ripps; music, Arthur B. Rubinstein; production design, Philip Harrison; art direction, Richard Hudolin, Michael Ritter; set decoration, Rose Marie McSherry, Leslie Beale; sound (Dolby), Larry Sutton; assistant director, Rob Cowan; associate producer, Dana Salter; casting, Mike Fenton/Jane Feinberg; Judy Taylor, Sidney Kozak. Reviewed at Avco Cinema, Westwood, Calif., July 27, 1987. (MPAA Rating: R.) Running time: **115 MINS.**
Chris Lecce . . . . Richard Dreyfuss
Bill Reimers . . . . Emilio Estevez
Maria McGuire . . . . Madeleine Stowe
Richard Montgomery . . . . Aidan Quinn
Phil Coldshank . . . . Dan Lauria
Jack Pismo . . . . Forest Whitaker
Caylor Reese . . . . Ian Tracey
Captain Giles . . . . Earl Billings
FBI Agent Lusk . . . . Jackson Davies

Hollywood — "Stakeout" is a slick, sure-footed entertainment that has enough wit and speed to sidestep gaping holes in credibility, character development and simple human behavior. One part buddy comedy and one part police actioner stitched together with a dash of romance, film is another phony, formula picture executed well enough to make big money if people find out what it's about.

Characters in "Stakeout" are pure film creations without much relation to reality. They are built on a few quick hooks and 1-liners by scripter Jim Kouf and that's it. They can't be trusted or believed but they're fun.

Particularly problematic is Richard Dreyfuss as a reckless cop whose life is unraveling slowly. While he's on familiar ground talking his way out of tight spots and jousting with partner Emilio Estevez, when the plot calls for rough stuff, it's a stretch he doesn't make.

As the more stable, but still mischievous anchor of the pair, Estevez is likable, if a bit flat. He's not an actor with a great gift for comedy, and many of his exchanges with Dreyfuss lack chemistry.

As Seattle cops (the film as shot in Vancouver), the wisecracking duo is assigned to a routine stakeout where they are supposed to wait for an escaped con (Aidan Quinn) to contact his ex-girlfriend (Madeleine Stowe). Dreyfuss is not a man to wait around for something to happen and as he barrels into the case, he falls in love with Stowe.

For the long middle section, director John Badham plays the pic as another problematic love story with Quinn's impending arrival the heat under the pan. Quinn is a time

bomb waiting to explode as Badham intercuts his roundabout journey to Seattle to collect money he has stashed at Stowe's house.

As an actor, Quinn seems to have inherited Dennis Hopper's mantle as the pyschopath in the crowd. With eyes like laser beams, Quinn is so close to the edge that occasionally he tips over into a cartoonish crazy.

Where the film really sags is in the love story and especially Stowe's character. In this kind of film, love comes cheap and almost overnight. Lovely though she is, it is hard to get a handle on her character, let alone her attraction to Dreyfuss. It's just another skin-deep affair passed off as true love.

Kouf has opted for clever rather than deep, and fortunately Badham is able to whip it all into a fast-paced, pleasing package. Pic tries to satisfy light romance fans and action-mongers and consequently the shifts into intense violence may come as too much of jolt. Chase scenes are also too numerous to be interesting.

Arthur B. Rubinstein's pop score synthesizes the action even more by pouring on a tinny layer of sound. John Seale's camerawork, however, fixes the film in a Northwest earthiness otherwise lacking in the story.— *Jagr*.

Une Flamme dans mon coeur
(A Flame In My Heart)
(FRENCH-SWISS-COLOR)

A Bac Films release of a Garance/La Sept/Filmograph coproduction, with the participation of the Ministry of Culture, the PTT, Télévision Suisse Romand, Cab Production and Filmorgen. Executive producer, Dominique Vignet. Produced by Paolo Branco. Directed by Alain Tanner. Screenplay, Myriam Mézières, Tanner; camera (color), Acacio de Almeida; editor, Laurent Uhler; music, Bach, performed by Nell Gotkovsky; sound, Joaquim Pinto; assitant director, Claire Lusseyran. Reviewed at the UGC Biarritz cinema, July 10, 1987, Running time: **112 MINS.**
Mercedes . . . . Myriam Mézières
Johnny . . . . Aziz Kabouche
Pierre . . . . Benoit Régent
Also with: Biana, Jean-Yves Berthelot, André Marcon, Anne Rucki, Jean-Gabriel Nordmann.

Paris — Peripatetic Swiss filmmaker Alain Tanner shot this low-budget quickie as a vehicle for its lead, Myriam Mézières, who lets it all hang out in an original story of her own psychodramatic confection. It's more her picture than Tanner's, whose direction is largely undistinguished, and art audience response will depend on whether one finds Mézières of sufficient dramatic mettle to carry the overlong tale.

Mézières and Tanner compose an uninhibited portrait of an actress whose romantic absolutism tries the patience of two widely contrasting lovers. First part of the film finds her struggling to break up with her current boyfriend, an unsympathetic, bullying lowlife who keeps coming back, despite her weak-willed attempts to convince him it's irremediably over between them.

She finally ditches him, only to shack up soon after with a respectable journalist, whom she brazenly picks up in a subway. He's more stable and appealing, but his frequent professional absences drive the increasingly obsessed girl to neurotic distraction. When her lover finally takes her along on an assignment in Egypt, she wanders off into the Cairo night, apparently lost to the journalist and perhaps to herself.

The screenplay is not especially probing, but Mézières throws herself body and soul — mostly body — into her performance of a single woman consumed by her own amorous demands. In a couple of sexually frank sequences, Tanner impassively records an unfaked session of masturbation and her provocative striptease in a sleazy urban fairground, a job she takes after quitting the legit production she had been rehearsing.

Ironically, for all of Mézières' investment in her role, one is more touched by Benoit Régent's quietly effective performance as the sincere, emotionally straight journalist lover, at first seduced then gradually bemused and forlorn by the girl's eccentric behavior. — *Len.*

L'Ami de mon amie
(My Girl Friend's Boy Friend)
(FRENCH-COLOR)

An AAA/Films du Losange release (Orion Classics in U.S.) of a Films du Losange production. Produced by Margaret Menegoz. Written and directed by Eric Rohmer. Camera (color), Bernard Lutic; editor, Maria Luisa Garcia; music, Jean-Louis Valero; sound, Georges Prat, Dominique Hennequin; production manager, Françoise Etchegaray. Reviewed at the Publicis screening room, Paris, July 30, 1987. Running time: **103 MINS.**

Blanche . . . . Emmanuelle Chaulet
Léa . . . . Sophie Renoir
Fabien . . . . Eric Veillard
Alexandre . . . . François-Eric Gendron
Adrienne. . . . . Anne-Laure Meury

Paris — Eric Rohmer's latest is the sixth in his Comedies and Proverbs cycle (his preceding film, "4 Adventures Of Reinette And Mirabelle," strangely is not considered part of the series), and provides a gently ironic illustration of the saying: "A friend of my friend's is a friend of mine." By extension one can say that an admirer of Rohmer's previous '80s films is an admirer of this one as well.

Rohmer reportedly wrote the script and dialog alone, without any help from his young players (as was the case in "Le Rayon vert" and "Reinette And Mirabelle"). Story thus has the carefully planned structure and fluidly natural conversational tone of his best work. One, however, guesses quite early in the story Rohmer's design and outcome, so that a certain amount of

boredom creeps in on occasion, especially when the talk is at its most droningly banal and shallow.

Story is a romantic quadrille involving two gals and two guys, who in the end form two new couples. The girls, Sophie Renoir, a student, and Emmanuelle Chaulet, newly arrived in town with a job at the city hall, meet in the opening scenes and become friends, with all the attendant exchanges of views and confidences.

Renoir has a boy friend, Eric Veillard, with whom she's currently shacked up but apparently unsatisfied. Chaulet hasn't found a fellow yet, but has an admiring eye on a young engineer, François-Eric Gendron, though she becomes flustered and tongue-tied in his presence.

When Renoir suddenly decides to take some vacation alone, Chaulet finds herself becoming friends with Veillard, but their platonic relationship takes an unexpectedly romantic turn, from which she backs off, guilt-ridden at having betrayed her girl friend and still mooning after Gendron.

Renoir returns home but shortly after announces to Chaulet that she's split up with Veillard. Disappointed her girl friend still hasn't made a connection with Gendron, Renoir tries to help her out, only to herself fall for the handsome engineer when he comes on to her. Chaulet in the meantime realizes her infatuation with Gendron has run its course, and renews her relationship with her girl friend's ex-boy friend.

In a final scene of misunderstandings, the two girls, both ignorant of what's happened on the other end and each feeling she's done the other wrong, patch up their illusory differences and part with their respective new mates.

It's middling Rohmer, but pleasant because the quartet of attractive players is better company than the scatterbrains, pests and bores Rohmer has shoved on us in the past.

Rohmer shot his film in and around Cergy-Pontoise, a modern suburb of Paris, whose malls, parks and commercial centers acquire a warm, friendly air via Bernard Lutic's fine lensing.

Pic opens (non-competitively) the Venice Film Festival, where "Rayon vert" won last year's Golden Lion trophy.—*Len.*

Ele, o Boto
(He, The Dolphin)
(BRAZILIAN-COLOR)

An Embrafilme release of a L.C. Barreto production. Executive producer, Flavio R. Tambellini. Produced by L.C. Barreto, in association with Lorentzen Empreendimentos, Embrafilme, Cine de Tempo and Transvideo. Directed by Walter Lima Jr. Screenplay, Lima Jr., Tirone Feitosa, based on the argument of Lima Barreto inspired by an idea of Vanja Orico; camera (Eastmancolor), Pedro

Farkas; underwater sequences by Roberto Faissal Jr.; editor, Mair Tavares; music, Wagner Tiso; art direction, Paulo Flaksman; sets, Ana Schlee; costumes, Sergio Silveira; sound, Marc Van der Willingen; special effects, Sergio Farjallo, Marco Antonio Franca, Persio Freire. Reviewed at Cine Veneza, Rio de Janeiro, July 16, 1987. Running time: **100 MINS.**

The Dolphin . . . . . . Carlos Alberto Riccelli
Tereza .Cassia Kiss
Rufino . . . . .Ney Latorraca
Corina .Dira Paes
Luciano . . . . .Paulo Vinicius
Ze Amaro . . . . Ruy Polanah
Aunt . . . . Maria Silvia
  Also with: Tonico Pereira, Lutero Luiz, Bebeto Bahia, Airton Vieia, Marcos Palmeira, Sandro Solviati (fishermen) and the voice of Rolando Boldrin, reading a text by Affonso Romano de Sant'Anna.

Rio de Janeiro — The legend of the dolphin, common in Brazil's northern region of Para, tells of dolphins that late at night become men and come to the land to conquer the local women. They are irresistible to any woman, so fishermen-husbands are afraid of them. The dolphin-man can make himself invisible to ordinary men and his offspring with women are, like the father, man and dolphin. Popularly, every child of an unknown father is seen in some northern regions as "son of the dolphin."

A treatise on the dolphins legend was written in 1964 by filmmaker Lima Barreto, based on a story by Walter Lima Jr., the director of "Inocencia" and "Lira do Delirio," who stresses the universality of the myth and developed several characters. Lima's filmography, highly influenced by classic Brazilian filmmaker Humberto Mauro, is centered in the romanticism and ideological interpretation of local values.

In his interpretation, Walter Lima develops the tragedy of the ambiguous nature of the dolphin as well as the permanent danger surrounding the fishermen and their wives, within the context of the instinctive creation of a very particular culture. In doing so, he explores the latent sensuality of the plot, in which no woman is safe but all their dreams are inhabited by the strange creature, who, the legend says, is the strange, handsome man.

Production relies on special effects, the strong music composed by Wagner Tiso and the cinematography, deliberately hyper-realistic, of Pedro Farkas, bringing different levels of reality to the village in which the action takes place. Lima avoids picturesque approaches to cultural values, helping the action to flow naturally.

The rejection of such stereotypes also helps "Ele, o Boto" to be more genuinely a product of Brazilian culture, while universal in its comprehension. It was a difficult film to make, but the result is a work of high integrity and interest to most audiences. Cassia Kiss, as the "dolphin's woman," is the strongest

presence in the cast, and all technical credits are fine.—*Hoin.*

Juntos
(Together)
(MEXICAN-COLOR)

A Peliculas Mexicanas release of a Producciones Rosales Durán production. Produced by Roberto Rosales Durán, Enrique Rosales Durán. Directed by Rafael Rosales Durán. Associate director, Javier Durán. Stars Oscar Athie. Screenplay, Rafael Rosales Durán, Reynaldo Díaz; camera (Eastman color), Manuel Tejada; editor, Enrique Murillo; music, Marcos Flores. Reviewed at Hollywood Twin theater I, N.Y., June 29, 1987. Running time: **91 MINS.**

Himself . . . . .Oscar Athie
Laura .Laura Flores
Martin . . . . Héctor Kiev (Tacho)
Diana . . . . .Elvira Lodi
Rafael . . . . .Rafael Amador
  Also with: Eduardo Noriega, Jorge Fegán, Alejandra Vidal, Poly, Carla Rodriguez, Bruno Rey, Pedro Vaquier, Ernesto Juarez, Jorge Abaunza, Gerardo Flores.

"Juntos" (Together) is a semi-autobiographical entertainment vehicle for popular Mexican romantic ballad singer Oscar Athie, produced by the Rosales Durán family and helmed by Rafael Rosales Durán.

This low-budget picture is almost entirely devoid of tension or at times, even interest. In A-B-C fashion, young Oscar rises rapidly from a singer at a sleazy Mexico City nightspot to become a top-selling media idol, if we are to believe what others say about him. The audience sees very little of this.

Athie's unfettered ascent is paralleled by the concurrently successful career of love interest Laura, played by real-life partner Laura Flores.

The blond-haired, blue-eyed crooner and his girlfriend share a screen relationship here that is sweet enough to pour over a stack of pancakes. They deserve to be successful because they are both so nice and earnest. While music plays, they hold hands, gaze fawningly into each other's eyes and exchange tons of toothy grins. They also perform a duet on the pic's title tune before announcing their oncoming marriage. The only flaw to all this happiness and success is the appearance of former flame Diana (Elvira Lodi), who goes absolutely crazy because of Oscar's good fortune.

Supporting actor Héctor Kiev (Tacho) puts in some good moments as Athie's manager Martin, but overall, characterizations are strictly 1-dimensional.

Lensing by Manuel Tejada is mediocre, especially the performance footage where a bit of vitality and imagination are called for.

Fans will be pleased to find Athie's music. Besides his duet with Laura, Athie has four solo spots, Laura sings two solo numbers and guest artist Rafael Amador has one song.

On the whole, the film has the texture and appeal of a fanzine. Non-Athie devotés will find his self-portrayal flat and unconvincing.

—*Lent.*

The Girl
(BRITISH-COLOR)

A Shapiro Entertainment (U.S.) release of Lux Film Prods. (U.K.) production. Produced and directed by Arne Mattson. Screenplay, Ernest Hotch; camera (Panavision, color), Tomislav Pinter; editor, Derek Trigg; music, Alfi Kabiljo; sound (Dolby), Lasse Lundberg, Asa Lindgren; production design, Anders Barreus; production manager, Björn Ulfung; costumes, Mago; makeup, Eva Helene Wiktorson, Jan Kindahl. Reviewed at Magno Review 1 screening room, N.Y., Aug. 3, 1987. (No MPAA Rating.) Running time: **104 MINS.**

John Berg	Franco Nero
Eva Berg	Bernice Stegers
Pat - The Girl	Clare Powney
Lindberg, reporter	Frank Brennan
Hans	Mark Robinson
The General	Clifford Rose
The General's wife	Rosy Jauckens
The Janitor	Derek Benfield
Zilenski	Mark Dowling
Viveca	Lenore Zann
Peter Storm	Christopher Lee
A Journalist	Tim Earle
Antonio	Sam Cook
David	Heinz Hopf
Grandez	Ragnar Ulfung

"The Girl," new feature from Swedish director Arne Mattson, is billed as an erotic thriller. Erotic it is, as newcomer Clare Powney fills the frame with an innocent yet eerily detached sensuality. It fulfills its promise as a thriller, too, though the onscreen magic between Powney and Franco Nero relegates the bizarre plot to a supporting role.

"The Girl" opens with a jolt as Pat (Powney), a blond 14-year-old schoolgirl, approaches John Berg (Nero), a successful 40ish attorney, and offers to sleep with him for 300 crowns. Berg takes Pat back to his apartment and pays her the 300 crowns, but instead of accepting Pat's offer, Berg gives her lunch with a glass of milk.

Undeterred, Pat shows up the next day. In the kind of scene one would expect from director Mattson, pioneer of art film erotica, Pat slowly raises her dress and suddenly Berg's life is turned upside down.

The idea of a successful middle-aged man falling into a romantic tryst with a very young girl is certainly not a new one. The "Lolita" type character has often surfaced, most notably in Woody Allen's "Manhattan" and more recently in "Blame It On Rio" toplining Michael Caine. Yet both Allen and Caine portrayed tortured souls, harboring a puritanical guilt that was ultimately the undoing of their May-December relationship.

Not Franco Nero. Playing Berg to cool perfection, Nero exhibits no perceptible signs of remorse. In fact, he immediately whisks Pat away to a private island paradise where the pair set up housekeeping.

Luckily for Berg, his wife Eva (Bernice Stegers) is having an affair with taxi driver Hans (Mark Robinson), so she doesn't question Berg's

extended "business trip" alibi.

Once on the island, Pat and Berg make love against a backdrop of sweeping ocean vistas and craggy shoreline. Powney is photographed in various stages of undress, often nude, yet the footage never appears exploitative.

The utopia is short-lived, however, as Berg and Pat are followed to the island by a ruthless reporter, Lindberg (Frank Brennan).

Lindberg is investigating the smuggling of 25,000,000 in Swedish currency out of the country by one of Berg's clients, Grandez (Ragnar Ulfung). What Lindberg doesn't realize is that Berg is aiding Grandenz in the crime.

Lindberg steps onto the island to find Berg and Pat in an embrace. The scandal-scrounging Lindberg is in his element, threatening to expose Berg's indiscretion unless Berg provides information pertaining to Grandenz and the 25,000,000.

The small island and its three inhabitants set the stage for the film's startling conclusion. A conclusion that is perhaps too startling, however, considering the otherwise surreal quality of the movie.

From the moment Lindberg sets foot on the island, the storyline seems to run contrary to believability as it thrusts the characters into a mire of murder and coverup.

Ernest Hotch's screenplay, too, takes a verbose turn at the end, no longer allowing the visual language of film to speak for itself. Fortunately, the unraveling of the script does little to damage the lasting imprint "The Girl" leaves upon the emotions.

Soft, impressionistic cinematography by Tomislav Pinter and Mattson's taut direction ultimately prevail. It is a beautiful film to look at, a rich collection of images combining to create a melancholy composite that is impervious to the last-minute ravages of dialog and plot.

— *Chuk.*

The Big Bang
(BELGIAN-FRENCH-ANIMATED-COLOR)

A 20th Century Fox France release of a Zwanz/Comedia coproduction, with the participation of the French Ministry of Culture and the Ministry of the French Community of Belgium. Produced by Boris Szulzinger. Directed by Jean-Marc Picha. Screenplay, Picha, Tony Hendra; animation, Stout Studio (Paris); technical director, Francis Nielsen; editor, Nicole Garnier-Klippel; music, Roy Budd; sound, Peter Hearn. Reviewed at the Annecy Animation Film Festival, June 2, 1987. Running time: **77 MINS.**

Voices (English-language track): David Lander, Carol Androfsky, Marshall Efron, Alice Playten.

Paris — Picha, the irreverent Belgian cartoonist who skewered the Tarzan myth and Darwinism in his previous adult animation features, "Shame Of The Jungle" and "The

Missing Link," sets his randy sights on the apocalyptic future in "The Big Bang." Again scripted by British lampoonist Tony Hendra, it's typically lewd and leering in its punning (English) dialog and satiric graphics, but imagination often flags, leaving film to coast on its aggressive bad taste and vulgarity.

The Big Bang is the Fourth World War that menaces the planet Earth after the previous nuclear conflict, which has left the globe divided into two super-state continents: the male mutant-populated USSSR, a fusion of the U.S. and the Soviet Union (capital: Washingrad), and Vaginia, manned by what remains of the earth's female population. A new holocaust is brewing with each side threatening to unleash its ultimate secret weapons.

The new war could spell the end of the rest of the universe, so an intergalactic council summons Fred, a washed-out, henpecked superhero (employed alongside Darth Vader and some other has-beens as interplanetary garbage collectors), back into service to zip down to Earth and avert the impending cataclysm. He bungles the job and all hell breaks loose in the end, though Fred literally is blown to Seventh Heaven in the arms of the luscious virgin he saves from the USSSR tyrant and lusts after vainly throughout his mission.

Picha dreams up a large gallery of priapic grotesques, including Hitler clones, Walkyrie-shaped tanks, deadly ballerina warriors, an anal ectoplasmic warlord, and his multibreasted Amazonian counterpart. It's a non-stop onslaught of ultimate sexual warfare, but the satiric broadsides only sporadically explode with genuine hilarity, and the animation is frequently inferior to Picha's previous work. —*Len.*

Mujeres de la Frontera
(Women Of The Frontier)
(NICARAGUAN-CUBAN-COLOR)

An Empresa Nicaragüense de Distribución y Exhibición Cinematográfica (Enidiec) release of an Instituto Nicaragüense de Cine (Incine) — Instituto Cubano del Arte e Indústria Cinematográfica (Icaic) production. Executive producer, Julio Torres. Produced by Carlos Alvarez. Directed by Iván Argüello. Screenplay, Argüello, Ramiro Lacayo, Gioconda Belli, Antonio Conte; camera (color), Rafael Rulz, Luis Garcla Mesa; editor, Eduardo Guadamuz, Justo Vega; music, Cedrick d'Ila Torre; sound, José León, Guillermo Granera; assistant director, Clarissa Hernández. Reviewed at N.Y. Latino Fest, Public theater, July 23, 1987. Running time: **60 MINS.**

With: Chana Rivera, Luisa Jiménez.

Bearing the distinction as Nicaragua's first feature, the 60-minute film "Mujeres de la Frontera" (Women Of The Frontier) brings to light some of the problems affecting the country, based around real-life persons living in Jalapa, the border region between Nicaragua and Hon-

duras, in 1982-83. It also establishes the solidarity of the civilian population confronting these problems and its efforts to solve them. It also shows how the war and revolution are working to change the entire structure of society.

The film is a coproduction between the newly formed Incine (Instituto Nicaragüense de Cine) and Cuba's film institute Icaic, and it is helmed by Ivan Argüello. As a piece of positive propaganda, pic is meant to reinforce faith in collective efforts for domestic audiences, and at the same time, bolster international sympathy for those trying to live in a country under siege.

The form of the film is that of a war diary, narrated by villager Paulina Rivera (Chana Rivera). And as a diary, it is open to a whole gamut of observations, comments, confrontations, ideas, complaints, etc. As Paulina develops and learns, so does the audience. At times, the form slips and we learn things Paulina has no access to.

Film begins with the initial attack and death of Paulina's father. When all the menfolk go off to the front, the relocated women do what they can to get by with limited rations and keep their families together.

The government does what it can to help, but for Paulina this is not enough. She is fiercely independent and takes matters into her own hands: with no thought of personal safety, she sneaks back to the village to harvest corn. She also leads the other women out of the refugee camp and to their new homes. As time goes by, the women become more and more self-sufficient. The whole order of the previous macho society changes. When the men do return home, they find out quickly that these are not the same women they left behind. It's all part of the revolutionary process.

The camerawork and cropping of images is influenced by cinéma vérité, as if the camera were merely documenting the incidents we see. Acting talents are competent, especially Rivera as the determined Paulina.

Owing to the situation in Nicaragua, this debut film touches on the politics without hysteria or pointing any fingers. It is merely saying this is who we are and this is what we are doing. Local interests with Nicaragua should guarantee boxoffice internationally and pic would work well at sympathetic fund-raisers because of its low-key appeal for understanding and acceptance.

—*Lent.*

The Danger Zone
(COLOR)

Fun throwback to '60s biker epics.

A Danger Zone production. (Sales. Skouras Pictures.) Produced by Jason Williams, Tom Friedman. Directed by Henry Vernon. Stars Robert Canada, Jason Williams. Screenplay, Williams, Friedman, Karen Levitt; camera (United color); Daniel Yarussi; editor, Louis George, Susan Medaglia; music, Robert Etoll; sound, Mike Clark; art direction, Marty Cusack; assistant director, Mike Kehoe; second unit director, Louis George. Reviewed on Charter Entertainment videcassette, N.Y., July 26, 1987. (MPAA Rating: R.) Running time: **89 MINS.**

Reaper	Robert Canada
Wade	Jason Williams
Judy	Kris Braxton
Simon	G. Cervi
Kim	Dana Dowell
Reptile	Mickey Elders
Jamie	Jamie Ferreira
Needles	Daniel Friedman
Linda	Cynthia Gray
Munch	R.A. Mihailoff
Jake	Rick Nightingale
Skin	Juanita Ranney
Ronnie	Axel Roberts
P.J.	Joe Sabatino
Heather	Suzanne Tara
Summer	Theresa Trousdale
Nose	Michael Wayne
Curtis	Mike Wiles

"The Danger Zone" is an unpretentious actioner that conjures up the delights of the nonsensical biker pics that filled drive-ins nationwide two decades ago. Alas, most drive-ins are gone and those remaining play the same films as indoors, so this serviceable entry becomes merely homevideo fodder domestically.

Functional plotline pits a band of ornery bikers led by Reaper (Robert Canada) against a stranded group of six pretty femme singers, whose car has broken down en route to a "Celebrity Exposure" tv talent show competition being held in Las Vegas. The bikers and their molls terrorize the gals until they are saved by a combination of their own wits, a friendly prospector (Rick Nightingale) and an undercover narc who has infiltrated the gang (Jason Williams).

Blessed with a flavorful songs score, low-budgeter plays off smoothly with solid acting, especially a chilling psycho turn by Robert Canada as Reaper which recalls the youthful nasties essayed long ago by John Davis Chandler and Arch Hall Jr. Filmmaker/costar Williams, best-known for his title role in "Flesh Gordon," is fun adopting the tough guy readings of a Clint Eastwood. The girls, especially wet T-shirt prone Suzanne Tara, are easy on the eye. —*Lor.*

Jeux d'artifices
(Games Of Artifice)
(FRENCH-COLOR)

A Forum production and release, with the participation of Virgin France, the Ministry of Culture, Investimage and Sofinergie. Produced by Claude-Eric Poiroux. Written and directed by Virginie Thévenet. Camera (color), Pascal Marti; editor, Jacqueline Mariani; music, André Demay; costumes, Friquette Thévenet; art direction, David Rochline; sound, Pierre Donnadieu, François Groult; makeup, Geneviève Peyrelade; assistant director, Manuel Fleche. Reviewed at the Studio 28, Paris, June 23, 1987. Running time: **98 MINS.**

With: Myriam David (Elisa), Gaël Seguin (Eric), Ludovic Henry (Jacques), Dominic Gould (Stan), Friquette Thévenet, Andrée Putman, Eva Ionesco, Arielle Dombasle, Claude Chabrol, Etienne Daho, Virginie Thévenet, Farida Khelfa, Philippe Collin, Marc Prince.

Paris — Second feautre by Virginie Thévenet, who had an enviable art house success with her shoestring-budgeted "La Nuit porte jaretelles" in 1985, "Jeux d'artifices" is freely inspired by Jean Cocteau's novel, "Les Enfants terribles" (filmed by Jean-Pierre Melville in 1950), but drowns Cocteau's themes of incest and illusion-vs.-reality in a bath of playful Parisian chic.

Thévenet's script concerns an orphaned and homeless brother and sister (newcomers Gaël Seguin and Myriam David) who are lent a baroque duplex apartment where they create a photo studio and compose a series of "tableaux vivants," with a variety of amateur models recruited haphazardly from outside.

The parade of strangers through their personal guarded universe sparks inevitable jealousies and tensions between the ambiguously inseparable siblings, but events take a dramatic turn when sis gets romantically involved with a fellow who in the end takes off with her brother.

More visually alert than the raggedly made "Porte Jaretelles," "Jeux d'artifices" extracts some initial fascination from the androgynous resemblance of Seguin and David, but as in her debut pic, Thévenet again shows herself unable to spin her initial premise out for a feature-length running time. Thévenet has fun (in which the audience shares) with the mod tableaux vivants, but when the games start to go stale, the film follows suit.

Still, film shows that with a comfortable budget and solid technical support, Thévenet can manage some impertinent cinematic flair. She could certainly do with an outside hand in her scripting phase. —*Len.*

Screwball Academy
(CANADIAN-COLOR)

An American Cinema Marketing presentation from Rose & Ruby of a Loose Ends production. Produced by David Mitchell, Damian Lee. Directed by "Reuben Rose" (John Blanchard). Screenplay, Mitchell, Charles Dennis, Michael Pascornek; camera (Medallion color), Ludvik Bogner; editor, Gary Zubeck, Mairin Wilkinson, Mike Robison; music, Charles Barnett; additional music, Brian Bell; sound, Nolan Roberts; art direction, Roy Smith; production manager, Sean Ryerson; second unit director, Mitchell; second unit camera, Curtis Peterson; stunt coordinator, Dwayne McLean. Reviewed on TWE videcassette, N.Y., July 20, 1987. (MPAA Rating: R.) Running time: **87 MINS.**

Liberty Jean	Colleen Camp
Elder Seth	Ken Welsh
Lita Lota	Christine Cattell
Lodz Kukoff	Charles Dennis
Urjak Kukoff	Angus MacInnes
Bishop Wally	Damian Lee

Also with: Peter Spence, Wendy Bushell, Henry Ramer, Sonja Smits, Shirley Douglas, George Buza, Janet Good, Sean Ryerson.

"Screwball Academy," its title having nothing to do with the film, is a weak example of the string of similarly monikered Canadian comedies vainly attempting to duplicate the success of the Bill Murray hit "Meatballs." Picture entered production in summer 1983 as "Loose Ends," with director John Blanchard credited at that time, though final credits attribute the direction to fictional "Reuben Rose" (presumably a play on words on the production entity Rose & Ruby).

Colleen Camp perks matters up a bit portraying a director fed up with advertising (which she finds exploitative) who ventures to Wagatno Beach to do a feminist low-budget feature film. Her efforts interfere with the plans of pop culture evangelist Bishop Wally (played by pic's coproducer Damian Lee with an intentionally phony-looking mustache) to flee to the island just ahead of federal investigators.

Requisite nerd for this attempted beach party film is Pete Spence as a 17-year-old brought up in Wally's Divine Light church.

Pic's satirical elements are weak and much of the material has become dated as in references to 3-D filming (still cooking back in '83). Some extraneous nude footage (not involving any of the principal thesps) seems tacked on. —*Lor.*

Les Mois d'avril
sont meurtriers
(April Is A Deadly Month)
(FRENCH-COLOR)

A Sara/CDF release of a Sara Films/Canal Plus Prods./Little Bear coproduction, with the participation of Images Investissements. Executive producer, Alain Sarde. Produced by Louis Grau. Directed by Laurent Heynemann. Screenplay, Heynemann, Bertrand Tavernier, Philippe Boucher, from the Robin Cook novel "The Devil's Home On Leave," camera (Fuji color), Jean-François Gondre; editor, Armand Psenny; music, Philippe Sarde; art direction, Valérie Grall; costumes, Olga Berluti; sound, Guillaume Sciama, Claude Villand, Bernard Leroux; assistant director, Frédérique Noiret. Reviewed at the 3 Parnassiens cinema, Paris, May 26, 1987. Running time: **88 MINS.**

Fred	Jean-Pierre Marielle
Gravier	Jean-Pierre Bisson
Baumann	François Berleand
Clara	Brigitte Rouan
Christine	Guylaine Pean

Paris — Familiar cat-and-mouse thriller material in a lugubrious Gallic vein, "Les Mois d'avril sont meurtriers" is slickly executed and well acted, but leaves little room for suspense and audience involvement.

Script by director Laurent Heynemann and Bertrand Tavernier (who originally planned to helm himself) is in fact another French recycling of an Anglo-Saxon print mystery (by Robin Cook), with the accent on talky psychological show-

down rather than action. Another Cook novel was the source of Jacques Deray's equally moody and overly literary "On ne meurt que deux fois" (1985).

Story falls into the "Crime And Punishment" mold with devious professional killer Jean-Pierre Bisson being harassed by equally sly *flic* Jean-Pierre Marielle, who knows he is the author of a particularly gruesome gangland killing but hasn't any proof to nail him.

Despite fine performances, the Marielle-Bisson confrontations lack tension and the ironic showdown is both predictable and overdue. When Marielle is not stalking his prey he engages in long interior monologs that reveal his chronically morbid state, a consequence of his daughter's recent death and spouse's plunge into madness.

Heynemann's clinical direction is perfect in establishing the macabre tone of the police procedural scenes, but otherwise never lets any heat into a story that needs sparks to keep intrigue going. —*Len.*

Les Oreilles entre les dents
(Ears Between The Teeth)
(FRENCH-COLOR)

A UGC release of a Madeleine Films/Hachette Première et Cie coproduction. Produced by Gilbert de Goldschmidt. Directed by Patrick Schulmann. Screenplay, Schulmann, Didier Dolna, michel Zemer; camera (Fuji color), Jacques Assuerus; editor, Aline Asseo; music, Patrick Schulmann; sound, Philippe Sénechal, Gérard Lamps; costumes, Olga Pelletier; art direction, Michel Modai; assistant director, Henri Grimault; production manager, Michel Zemer. Reviewed at the UGC Biarritz cinema, Paris, July 8, 1987. Running time: **98 MINS.**

Jean-Paul Blido	Jean-Luc Bideau
Luc Fabri	Fabrice Luchini
Max	Laurent Gamelon
Léa Stagnari	Jeanne Marine
Dancourt	Féodor Atkine
Gayat	Guy Montagné
Korg	Philippe Khorsand
Boris	Gérard Manzetti
Atilla	Kevin Burgos

Also with: Jeanne Herviale, Alain Boismery, Gabriel Cattand, Claude Melki, Christophe Salengro, Michèle Brousse, Rosette.

Paris — "Ears Between The Teeth" is a lame mystery spoof about a series of gruesome murders in which the victims are found with their ears cut off and stuffed into their mouths. Basic gag, revealed from the start, is that there is no one murderer, but several unrelated perpetrators using the modus operandi of the initial crime — in fact an isolated underworld slaying -- to throw the police off their trail.

It's a promising idea for a sendup of police procedural whodunits, but the script expends its satiric points quickly and with little narrative cleverness, while Patrick Schulmann's direction is limp. Schulmann, who's career has been mostly downhill since his sleeper debut smash "Et la tendresse? ... Bordel!" in 1979, recovered boxoffice favor two years ago with his classroom comedy, "P.R.O.F.S.," but "Ears" is showing less legs locally.

Film's major comic energy comes from Jean-Luc Bideau as a pretentious criminal psychologist who is called in by the government to sketch the mental makeup of the supposed maniac and winds up persecuting an entirely innocent martial arts buff who corresponds to his composite police portrait.

Schulmann and his coscripters stitch in a number of feeble subplots, including a parallel investigation led by the daughter of the initial victim with the aid of a journalist, and the efforts of a hapless government functionary seeking some renown by claiming to be the hunted psychopath. —Len.

Poussière d'ange
(Angel Dust)
(FRENCH-COLOR)

A UGC release of a Président Films/-UGC/Top 1/Films de la Saga/FR3 Films Prod./La Sofica coproduction. Executive producer, Jacques-Eric Strauss. Directed by Edouard Niermans. Screenplay, Niermans, Jacques Audiard, Alain Le Henry; camera (Eastman color), Bernard Lutic; editor, Yves Deschamps, Jacques Witta; music, Léon Senza, Vincent-Marie Bouvot; art direction, Dominique Maleret; sound, Jean-Pierre Ruh, Paul Bertault; assistant director, Philippe Leriche; production manager, Pierre Tati; casting, Mamade. Reviewed at the Ermitage cinema, Paris, June 26, 1987. Running time: **94 MINS.**

Simon Blount . . . . Bernard Giraudeau
Violetta Reverdy . . . . Fanny Bastien
Martine Blount . . . . Fanny Cottençon
Landry . . . . Jean-Pierre Sentier
Florimont . . . . Michel Aumont
Broz . . . . Gérard Blain
Gabriel . . . . Luc Lavandier

Also with: Véronique Silver, Daniel Laloux, Yveline Ailhaud, Patrick Bonnel, Bertie Cortez, Henri Marteau, Daniel Russo.

Paris — "Angel Dust" is another Gallic *film noir*, yet a stylish cut or two above the rest, and confirmation of the talent of director Edouard Niermans. Niermans, 44, debuted in theatrical features wit the unusual "Anthracite" (1980), a drama about life in a Jesuit school, obviously enriched by personal experience, but apart from a couple of tv films, had to wait over five years for his second cinema feature, which began as an assignment from producer Jacques-Eric Strauss, who wanted a thriller.

Vigorously abetted by coscripters Alain Le Henry and Jacques Audiard (son of the late screenwriter Michel Audiard), Niermans delivers the goods. Though on the surface of it just another tale about a world-weary cop getting involved with a strange girl who drags him into a mire of murder and deceit, "Angel Dust" is shot through with a bristling cinematic energy and vivid performances by Bernard Giraudeau and Fanny Bastien.

Ironically Giraudeau gives one of his best screen performances in a hand-me-down role of the seedy,

boozing detective who hits the skids when his wife leaves him for another man, then recharges his batteries when he meets Bastien, a mysterious waiflike creature, who strikes him as a bit of "angel dust." She in fact has a demonic side, ruthlessly organizing the murders of several pimps, lawyers and police officials linked with the slaying years earlier of her prostitute mother. Bastien gives the term *femme fatale* a disturbingly fresh interpretation.

Niermans and his writers invest the obvious dramatic scheme with imaginative twists and turns and an abiding sense of humor. Example of the latter is the way they withhold at first Giraudeau's profession: picked up one night for drunken vagrancy, Giraudeau wakes up next morning in a police station cell, shares a cigaret with a fellow prisoner, then before latter's amazement, pulls out his key ring and lets himself out.

Niermans and his first-rate lenser Bernard Lutic create a composite urban landscape of menacing unfamiliarity by mixing locations (often within a single sequence) shot in different French cities, notably Paris, Marseille and Lyons.

Supporting cast and other tech credits are all sharp.

Film unspools at the Venice fest in the Critics Week section. *Len.*

Dirty Laundry
(COLOR)

Screwball comedy has plenty of laughs but runs out of gas.

A Seymour Borde & Associates presentation of a Westwind/480 and The DeYoung Co. production. (Intl. sales, Skouras Pictures.) Produced by William Webb, Monica Webb. Executive producers, Kent Snyder, Roger DeYoung. Directed by William Webb. Screenplay, Brad Munson, from story by William Webb; camera (color), John Huneck; editor Richard Casey; music, Sam Winans; additional music, Elliot Solomon; sound Glen Berkowitz; art direction, John Javonillo; assistant director, Matt Hinkley; stunt coordinator, Jeff Smolek; associate producer, Mei Ling Andreen; casting, Al Onorato, Jerry Francis. Reviewed on Sony Video Software vidcassette, N.Y., July 19, 1987. (MPAA Rating: PG-13.) Running time: **79 MINS.**

Jay . . . . Leigh McCloskey
Trish . . . . Jeanne O'Brien
Marty . . . . Frankie Valli
Maurice . . . . Sonny Bono
Vito . . . . Nicholas Worth
Oscar . . . . Robbie Rist
Also with: Donald May, Herta Ware, Edy Williams, Carl Lewis, Greg Louganis, Johnny B. Frank, Judith Goldstein, Hope North, Jill Terashita, John Moschitta Jr., Sean Coulter, Jeff Smolek, Deanna Booher.

Spurred on by a goofball cast, "Dirty Laundry" is a crazy comedy that provides lots of fun before sputtering to a sentimental, unsatisfying conclusion. Picture is headed for a homevideo release in fall via Sony.

Leigh McCloskey toplines as a rock concert sound man working for corrupt manager Sonny Bono. Bono's involved in a drug deal that goes awry in a drop at a laundry,

with McCloskey accidentally walking off with a laundry bag filled with money. Hero is soon on the run, accompanied by dizzy journalist Jeanne O'Brien, with Bono's gangster boss Frankie Valli ordering his henchmen to get them and the money, or else!

Among the numerous casting oddities of this feature are, in addition to Valli and Bono at odds with their singer images, Olympic stars Greg Louganis and Carl Lewis who show up respectively as McCloskey's party animal roommate and a spoof of Phillip Michael Thomas' "Miami Vice" character Tubbs. Edy Williams also is on board shaking her moneymakers and wrestler Deanna Booher is typecast as a dominatrix. Stars McCloskey and O'Brien make a pleasant, romantic sparring team and Robbie Rist is fun as their nerdish helper.—*Lor.*

La Ruletera
(The Female Cabbie)
(MEXICAN-COLOR)

A Películas Mexicanas release of a Prods. Tijuana production. Produced by Juan Abusaid Ríos, Pedro Martínez Garrido. Written and directed by Víctor Manuel (Güero) Castro. Stars Rafael Inclán, Maribel Fernández (La Pelangocha). Camera (color), Antonio Ruiz; editor, Sergio Soto; music, Gustavo Pimentel, with appearance of the group Los Tremendos Sepultureros. Reviewed at Hollywood Twin theater 2, N.Y., July 22, 1987. Running time: **87 MINS.**

Officer Ramón . . . . Rafael Inclán
Perla . . . . Maribel Fernández
. . . . (La Pelangocha)
Sergeant . . . . Raúl (Chato) Padilla
Lieutenant . . . . Manuel (Flaco) Ibañez

Client . . . . Polo Ortín
Commandante . . . . Ricardo de Loera
Also with: Don Miguel Manzano, Joaquín García (Borolas), Jackeline Castro, Griselda Mejía, Pancho Muller, Humberto Dupeyrón, José Magaña, Orietta Aguilar, Alfredo (Pelón) Solares, Sonia Piña, María Bardhal, Leo Villanueva, Verónica Hortensia Martínez, Juliana Aguilar F.

"La Ruletera" (The Female Cabbie) is a low-budget comedy written and directed by Víctor Manuel (Güero) Castro, Mexico's most prolific cheapo filmmaker. Castro churns out approximately a half-dozen uninspired formula features annually using a core of comedians including Rafael Inclán, Polo Ortín, Manuel (Flaco) Ibañez, etc. "La Ruletera" is no different.

Pic is an open-form product revolving around the leads: Inclán, who plays an incompetent traffic cop, and Maribel Fernández (La Pelangocha), who plays a dizzy Mexico City taxi driver.

The film is made up of too many separate scenes that never come together. There are scenes with Inclán, scenes with Fernández and sequences of the two of them, but no overriding plotline that holds the whole mess together.

Rushed production is evident throughout with sloppy lensing and editing. Sound levels are uneven.

Inclán and Fernández make an agreeable team and there are moments of interaction that make one wonder what the two of them would be like if they were given more challenging material. —*Lent.*

****
* **Moscow Festival Reviews** *
****

Komissar
(Commissar)
(SOVIET-B&W)

A Gorky Studio production. Directed by Alexander Askoldov. Screenplay Askoldov, based on "The City Of Berdish" by Vasily Grossman; camera (Widescreen, b&w), Valeri Ginzberg; editor, Askoldov; music, Alfred Schnitke. Reviewed at Domkino, Moscow Film Festival, July 11, 1987. Running time: **110 MINS.**

Klavdia . . . . Nonna Mordukova
Efrain . . . . Rolan Bykov
Maria . . . . Raisa Niedashkovskaya
Commander . . . . Vasili Shukshin

Moscow — One of the revelations of the Moscow Film Festival, and surely one of the most important Soviet films to be resuscitated after a long period of lying on the shelf (in this case, 20 years — pic was lensed in 1967), is Alexander Askoldov's "Commissar." Askoldov made this, his first and only film, at Gorky Studio for children's films, which rejected the finished product as its "greatest political and esthetic failure."

Screened at the fest on the request of the director and some guests, it immediatley was proclaimed a re-

discovered masterpiece and officially designated the last banned pic to get Goskino's greenlight for release. Version shown in Moscow may be integrated with additional cut footage by the director before it goes into general release. It is already much in demand by fests, notably San Francisco, which invited it at the time it was made and never got a print.

What all the controversy was about can only be guessed at now. Story is set in the 1920s, when the Red Army was still fighting for control of some outlying areas. The hard-boiled leader of one of these fighting units is a woman commissar, Klavdia, a masculine blond built like a tank and totally dedicated to the cause. One of our first glimpses of her is a harrowing scene where she orders a young man to be shot.

Next, the *coup de théâtre:* the commissar emotionlessly tells her second-in-command (played by the young Vasili Shukshin) she's leaving because she's pregnant. She finds lodging in the humble, actually destitute, house of a large Jewish family. Father Rolan Bykov initially grumbles over giving his room up to the stranger, but the pretty young mother (Raisa Niedashkovskaya) welcomes her, particularly when she learns the commissar is expecting. In a *tour de force* birth sequence, Klavdia struggles through labor, feverishly imagining horses pulling a cannon through the desert. Film's astonishing technical bravura — most dazzling in these expressionistic scenes, but evident in every shot — owes much to its brilliant cameraman Valeri Ginzberg, and in conception to classic Soviet silent cinema, Eisenstein, Pudovkin, Dovzhenko, Trauberg.

Once the baby is born, Klavdia is a new woman — tender, feminine, protective of her little one. Above all a mental revolution comes over her, and she — along with Bykov and his populous family, huddled in a shack while bombs fall outside — begins to question whether any aim is worth killing and war. Yet her final decision is to leave her infant behind and go back to fight, joining a line of young soldiers marching through the mud to the strains of the Internationale.

One of the things that most disturbed the censors was probably film's absolute originality on the esthetic plane, still its most striking aspect. Ginzberg's piercingly clear, black and white widescreen lensing finds its match in the avant garde soundtrack by composer Alfred Schnitke.

Thesps also make top class contributions, from Shukshin in a small role to Bykov hamming it up in the comically moving part of the poverty-stricken little Jewish père who dances with his kids while the bombs drop. Nonna Mordukova is solidly convincing both as commissar in hip boots and Army pants and as a human mother, whose final choice comes as a surprise but not an impossibility. — *Yung.*

Oktoberfest
(YUGOSLAV-COLOR)

An Inex Film production. Directed by Dragan Kresoja. Screenplay, Goran Radovanovic, Kresoja; camera (color), Predrag Popovic; editor, Andrija Zafranovic; music, Vranesevic brothers; art direction, Vladislav Lasic. Reviewed at the Moscow Film Festival (competition), July 8, 1987. Running time: **120 MINS.**
Luka Benjamin ....Svetislav Goncic
Also with: Zeljka Cvijetan, Zoran Cvijanovic, Tatjana Pujin, Zarko Lausevic, Vesna Trivalic, Vladica Milosavljevic, Velimir-Bata Zivojinovic.

Moscow — Broken dreams and crushed spirits follow a whirlwind tour of Belgrade by night seen through the eyes of its young denizens, in "Oktoberfest." In his third feature, helmer Dragan Kresoja makes a touching contrast between the harsh social reality of a jobless present and uncertain future with the hero's daydreams of non-stop

fun and beer in Munich. Pic manages to paint a bitter picture in a fascinating way, thanks to a well-written script by Goran Radovanovic and a fine cast of believable young thesps. In some ways their similarity to Western youth is striking, and pic could have art house interest with special handling.

Avoiding a gloomy approach, film concentrates on the misadventures of resilient hero Luka Benjamin, limned by sympathetic Svetislav Goncic. Returning with a bunch of chums from a trip abroad, he gets into a scrape with the police over drugs and has his passport confiscated. An unemployed college grad, Luka has nothing better to do than hang out in bars and cafes with his pals, and live life on the wild side.

Boozing and riding around town all night in an old Chevy, the heroes meet up with a tough punk gang (led by a policeman's kid), get into fights and have run-ins with the cops. Sex is easy, but Luka fantasizes about a rich dream girl he never gets. He gets badly beaten up by cops and punks alike, but takes it all in stride fatalistically. All he wants is to get his passport back and go to the Oktoberfest, which he imagines as a kind of carnival-fairyland. Through the good offices of his mother he succeeds, but by that time he's so embittered and demoralized it seems tragically doubtful he'll make it to Munich.

Pic's one fault is a series of anti-climatic endings that don't add to the final punch. There's also a subplot involving the mean cop's unfaithful wife, who leaves him, and punk son, who kills himself, that lays on the melodrama when the point — that everybody is desperate — has already been made. In spite of minor flaws, pic is lively, watchable, and remarkably open in describing the violence and frustration of everyday life.

Lensing by Predrag Popovic makes excellent use of color and nocturnal shades. — *Yung.*

Perlyotniye Ptit
(Migrating Birds)
(AFGHAN-COLOR)

An Afghan Film production and release. Directed by Latif Abdul Latif. Screenplay, Latif, Sarwar Anwari; camera (color), Kader Tahiri; music, Mohamed Shah Hakparast; sound effects, Abdul Rachman Sefati. Reviewed at the Moscow Film Festival (competition). July 13, 1987. Running time: **103 MINS.**
Nawob.....................Nasser Aziz
Noor Goul ....Asadullah Aram
Girl.....................Odella Adim

Moscow — A violent, primitively put together entry from Afghanistan, "Migrating Birds" probably will entertain mostly local audiences with its tale of infighting rebel groups that do each other in. Offshore interest will center around

scattered docu footage of refugee camps and some ethnic pageantry.

Though film obviously takes a position backing the government, its presentation of the rebels avoids the worst villainizing clichés. Bad continuity makes it hard to distinguish between the two conflicting groups at first: one a bunch of outlaws bent on robbing caravans on their way across the mountains, the other sincere but increasingly demoralized "freedom fighters." The bandit leader Noor Goul (played with glowering evil by Asadullah Aram) is a blackguard who shoots his own wounded men, but the fighters' leader Nawob (Nasser Aziz) has a human heart that softens even too much when a girl enters the picture.

Action kicks off on a fast note: a colorful wedding turns to tragedy when an unsuccessful suitor shoots the bridegroom to death. Beautiful Odella Adim, the widow, must marry her husband's brother as a matter of honor — but that happens to be the rebel leader. The sorrowful old father packs up the family and sets off across the border to Pakistan to find his other son and deliver the girl. Nawob accepts her as his wife, but she distracts him from concentrating on the Holy War and his men lose faith in him.

Multiple conflicts provide plenty of opportunity for dramatic bloodshed. Constant music sometimes adds to the atmosphere and sometimes seems to work at cross-purposes with the scene, while sound effects are positively eccentric and often more interesting than the hard-to-follow story.

Helmer Latif Abdul Latif has made five features, several screened at fests. — *Yung.*

Mirch Masala
(A Touch Of Spice)
(INDIAN-COLOR)

A National Film Development Corp. presentation and production. Directed by Ketan Mehta. Stars Naseeruddin Shah, Smita Patil. Screenplay, Hriday Lani, Trijawani Sharma; camera (color), Jahangir Choudhury; editor, Sanjiv Shah; music, Rajat Dholakia. Reviewed at Moscow Film Festival (in competition), July 7, 1987. Running time: **125 MINS.**
Sudebar ....Naseeruddin Shah
Sonbai ....Smita Patil
Mukhi ....Suresh Oberoi
Mukhi's wife ....Deepti Naval
Guard ....Om Puri

Moscow — The most surprising feature of this Indian drama of unrequited lust and revenge is that it is set in the 1940s, just before India attained its independence from Britain, whereas an onlooker might be forgiven for believing it was all happening a century or two back.

The annual celebration of the festival of the goddess is marred for the villagers of an isolated outpost by the arrival of the tax collector and his band of soldiers. That in itself would be seen as bad news. Matters are made far worse when he casts his lustful eye on a young married woman Sonbai, who not only rejects his advances, but slaps his face for good measure.

The tax collector, known as the Sudebar, sets his soldiers to capture the woman, but she takes refuge in a spice factory, where the old guard barricades her — and the other women toilers — and obstinately refuses to open the gates, finally choosing death rather than surrender. When the gates are finally rammed open, the women who had been begging Sonbai to give in, take the offensive and blind the Sudebar with the factory's hot spices.

Apart from a sluggish opening, which readily could be trimmed, this is a well-crafted film which merits festival attention, and possibly limited art house exposure. The story is revealing for illustrating the power of the revenue man and the fear he instills in ignorant villagers, and also for the way in which most of the men treat their women. Also revealing is the outrage felt by the mukhi (village headman) when he discovers his daughter is attending the local school. Learning is not for girls!

Although there is a little too much mustache twirling by the Sudebar and the mukhi, the acting is not unduly exaggerated; indeed, by the standard of many films from India it is remarkably restrained. The direction is conscientious rather than inspired, but there is some good lensing, and generally okay technical credits. — *Myro.*

★★★★★★★★★★★★★★★★★★★★★★★★★★★
★ **Pula Festival Reviews** ★
★★★★★★★★★★★★★★★★★★★★★★★★★★★

Na puta za Katangu
(On The Road To Katanga)
(YUGOSLAV - COLOR)

A Film Danas (Belgrade) Baker Film (Bor) coproduction. Directed by Zivojin Pavlovic. Screenplay, Rados Bajic; camera (color), Radoslav Vladic; music, Baronijan Vartkes; art direction, Miodrag Miric. Reviewed at the Pula Film Festival, July 25, 1987. Running time: **107 MINS.**
Palve Bezuha ....Svetozar Cvetkovic
Zhana ....Mirjana Karanovic
Also with: Rados Bajic.

Pula — "On The Road To Katanga" is a Yugoslav man's movie, combining the workers' theme with adventure-drama in the mines. There's more than one echo of the Far West in this tale of a restless drifter passing through his hometown, on his way to Africa and riches. Filmed with consummate professionalism by veteran helmer Zivojin Pavlovic and slanted for easy emotion, "Katanga" should be popular on shore. It is probably too much a crossbreed between the social and commercial for Western markets.

Hero is Pavle Bezuha, played by Svetozar Cvetkovic as a kind of Marlboro man. He has been living in France, but some scrapes with the police (smuggling, money) got him thrown out of the country. He plans to head down to the diamond mines in Katanga, where a video he carries around with him shows how easy it is to get rich quick. First he has to sell his dead father's house.

The trip home begins with meeting a saloon girl, Zhana (Mirjana Karanovic), a flighty chanteuse who travels with a pillow up her dress to simulate pregnancy and keep those lusty, brawling miners at bay. In addition there's an old flame, now wedded with kids who Pavle makes another play for.

Meeting his old buddies again, Pavle gets swept up in an emergency in the mine and watches his best friend get seriously injured. A helicopter flies them into Belgrade, aboard which the old flame (a nurse) performs an urgent blood transfusion between Pavle and buddy. The pal dies, Pavle loses both girls, gets drunk, and hops on the first train out of town. His manly conscience tells him he's running away, and at the last minute he hops off again to work shoulder to shoulder with his own people. Zhana walks with him.

Thesps throw themselves wholeheartedly into limning these familiar types, and inject them with enough human warmth to make them passably believable. Lensing is pro.— *Yung.*

Strategija svrake
(The Magpie's Strategy)
(YUGOSLAV-COLOR)

A Forum production (Sarajevo). Directed by Zlatko Lavanic. Screenplay, Mladen Materic; camera (color), Danijal Sukalo; editor, Zoltan Wagner; music, Braca Vranesevic; art direction, Predrag Lukovac. Reviewed at the Pula Film Festival, July 19, 1987. Running time: **113 MINS.**
Budimir Sarenac . . . . Predrag-Pepi Lakovic
Grandson . . . . Zvonko Lepetic
Slavica . . . . Radmila Zivkovic
Also with: Boro Stjepanovic, Branko Cvejic, Nada Durevska, Davor Dujmovic, Sukrana Gusani.

Pula — Documaker Zlatko Lavanic's first feature, "The Magpie's Strategy," is a low-key comedy set in the period just before and after Tito's death. Cowritten by Mladen Materic and Emir Kusturica, it is laced with Kusturica's ironic, mocking humor even if it doesn't achieve the cohesion and poignancy it strives for. A nearly 2-hour running time slows it down considerably, and the concluding tragedy, which should have given film its punch, remains ambiguous.

Hero of the tale is old Buda (Predrag-Pepi Lakovic), a retired standard bearer and sincere Communist. A few drunken revelry scenes with his buddies establishes him as an okay guy. He kindly invites a caravan of gypsies into his backyard to watch Tito's funeral on tv with the family — then invites the gypsies to move into the backyard, over family protests.

It's the kind of happy family where no tragedy seems able to occur because everyone is so well adjusted and accepts life as it comes. When a gypsy tyke throws a stray grenade, grandson Budimir (Zvonko Lepetic), the story's other hero, is struck dumb, but grandpa learns sign language and that's that.

The worst thing is that grandpa's gold watch with its inscription praising him for 40 years of fighting for a better future gets stolen by a magpie, and he gives himself no rest hunting for it. At the same time, he raises funds in town to send his grown daughter Slavica (Radmila Zivkovic) to a Swiss hospital, not realizing she's faking her illness. When he learns the truth, the old man loses faith in his ideals and apparently shoots himself, though ending is poorly done and leaves a note of doubt.

Tone is light, and with a more tightly woven yarn could have worked even better. As it is, we have a little too much of charming country life and its eccentric inhabitants (played by a fine cast, from grandpa to grandson). — *Yung.*

Zivot Radnika
(A Worker's Life)
(YUGOSLAV-COLOR)

Produced by Mirza Pasic for Forum Prods. (Sarajevo) and Sarajevo Television. Directed by Miroslav Mandic. Screenplay, Haris Kulenovic, Mandic, in collaboration with Emir Kusturica; camera (color), Vilko Filac; art direction, Kemal Hrustanovic; editor, Andrija Zafranovic; music, Zoran Simjanovic. Reviewed at the Pula Film Festival, July 21, 1987. Running time: **97 MINS.**
Musa Sokolovic . . . . Istref Begoli
Zilha . . . . Mira Banjac
Sead . . . . Emir Hadzihafizbegovic
Mira . . . . Anica Dobra
Also with: Boro Stjepanovic, Dragan Maksimovic, Zvonko Lepetic, Mladen Nelevic, Jelena Covic, Zeljko Nincic.

Pula — Feature debut by Miroslav Mandic tackles the tough life of working folk in Yugoslavia, showing how unemployment can lead to crime and the breakup of family life. This gloomy theme is brightened a little by the indefatigable spirit of the younger generation, who add a lighter touch to what is basically a pretty tragic story. Pic looks hard to place offshore.

Center of the story is elusive. Musa (Istref Begoli) is nearing retirement age, but following a strike at the saw mill over bad working conditions and low salaries, he decides not to go back. Though Musa is a thread that leads through the film, he's played as such an introverted, dour character that attention wanders to his son.

Sead (Emir Hadzihafizbegovic), the son, is jobless, wants to be a soccer player, and loves pretty Anica Dobra, who runs a newsstand at the station. He merrily robs the supermarket to feed his family. Musa fights with son and wife Mira Banjac, and throws both out of the house one rainy night. The mother goes crazy and dies. The son is arrested — not for theft, but for a rape he didn't commit. Happily, the young people know how to take knocks in their stride, and get married in prison. Unhappily, the father is left alone, a brooding, broken man.

Lensing is professional, as are thesps. The curious mixture of light and dark shades may come partly from Emir Kusturica, given a screenplay mention.— *Yung.*

Oficir s ruzom
(Officer With A Rose)
(YUGOSLAV-COLOR)

A Jadran Film (Zagreb)/Centar Film (Belgrade) coproduction. Produced by Suleymane Kapic, Djordje Milojevic. Written and directed by Dejan Sorak. Camera (Eastmancolor), Goran Trbuljak; editor, Vesna Lazeta; art direction, Stanko Dobrina. Reviewed at Pula Film Festival, July 21, 1987. Running time: **106 MINS.**
Matilda . . . . Ksenija Pajic
Petar Horvat . . . . Zarko Lausevic
Ljiljana . . . . Dragana Mrkic
Also with: Vicko Ruic, Boris Buzancic, Vida Jermank, Andrea Bakovic, Lena Politeo, Zvonko Torijanac.

Pula — "Officer With A Rose" is a professionally lensed, post-war love story that puts a curious trio of characters through some rather predictable developments. This one looks less like an art house item than respectable tv fare.

In liberated Zagreb, 1945, delicate, refined young Matilda (Ksenija Pajic) quietly slips into peacetime existence as the rich widow of a war hero. An attractive, Communist lieutenant, Peter Horvat (Zarko Lausevic), assigns a room in her spacious apartment to his fiancee, Ljiljana (Dragana Mrkic), a revolutionary firebrand in army fatigues who hides her finer feelings behind militant slogans and swaggering. All three are endearing.

Ljiljana rejects Matilda's bourgeois style of living, but can't help admire her femininity; the older woman's rounded body and creamy skin are superior to her flat chest and bullet-holed thigh (bath scene). Lt. Horvat thinks so, too, and here comes the crunch.

Matilda loves her impetuous revolutionary renter, but she loves the dashing young lieutenant even more. When Ljiljana is transfered to another town, pregnant, their love blooms unimpeded, until Horvat's narrow-minded commanding officer makes him choose between Matilda and the revolution. The dilemma is resolved romantically by his tragic death, chasing a last covey of outlaws in the forest.

Helmer Dejan Sorak, on his second feature, demonstrates plenty of ability at developing interesting characters and elegant lensing. Pic could have done with a dose of irony to raise its sophistication quotient, but should be an audience pleaser the way it is, melodramatic ending and all. All hands fill their roles adequately. — *Yung.*

Hamburger Hill
(COLOR)

Well-made but conventional Vietnam War drama.

A Paramount release of an RKO picture. A Marcia Nasatir and Jim Carabatsos production in association with Interaccess Film Distribution. Executive producers, Jerry Offsay, David Korda. Directed by John Irvin. Screenplay, Carabatsos; camera (Rank color, Technicolor prints), Peter MacDonald; editor, Peter Tanner; music, Philip Glass; production design, Austen Spriggs; art direction (Philippines), Toto Castillo; sound (Dolby), David Hildyard; special effects coordinator, Joe Lombardi; assistant directors, Steve Harding, Soc Jose (Philippines); coproducer, Larry De Waay; casting, Mary Colquhoun, Ken Metcalfe (Philippines). Reviewed at Paramount Studios, L.A., Aug. 4, 1987. (MPAA Rating: R.) Running time: **110 MINS.**

Languilli .... Anthony Barrile
Motown .... Michael Patrick Boatman
Washburn .... Don Cheadle
Murphy .... Michael Dolan
McDaniel .... Don James
Frantz .... Dylan McDermott
Galvin .... M.A. Nickles
Duffy .... Harry O'Reilly
Gaigin .... Daniel O'Shea
Beletsky .... Tim Quill
Bienstock .... Tommy Swerdlow
Doc .... Courtney Vance
Worcester .... Steven Weber
Lt. Eden .... Tegan West
Mama San .... Kieu Chinh
Lagunas .... Doug Goodman
Healy .... J.C. Palmore
Newsman .... J.D. Van Sickle

Hollywood — "Hamburger Hill" is the third and least entry in the current cycle of Vietnam War dramas. Well produced and directed with an eye to documentary-like realism and authenticity, pic centers upon a military undertaking of familiar futility and, crucially, never cements intense audience identification with its diverse dogfaces. Abundance of tough action should be enough to satisfy mainstream audiences, and approach is sufficiently serious to warrant a respectful reception for decent b.o. results.

Most of the Vietnam films released to date, going all the way back to "The Green Berets," have etched strong points of view, either political or artistic, and so have registered vividly in the mind and memory. "Hamburger Hill" is probably the most straightforward of the bunch, as it follows a squad of 14 recruits from initial R&R through 10 days' worth of hell, as the men make 11 agonizing assaults on a heavily fortified hill.

First 40 minutes attempt to show the developing relationships among the guys, and screenwriter-coproducer Jim Carabatsos has been particularly attentive to delineating the tensions between the blacks and whites in the group. They're all on the same side in the same mess, but the blacks feel they have had no choice but to come, whereas somehow it's different for the white boys.

The joke here, however, is on the whites, since the majority of them are very thinly differentiated from one another. Few of the characters are supplied with recognizable backgrounds and personal stories, even if some have — à la "A Chorus Line" — little scenes all to themselves. Compounding the problem is that the actors seem rather similar to one another, more like New York stage actors than authentic rednecks.

The net result is that, by the time the squad is helicoptered in to begin its attempt to take the hill, the viewer feels something for only one or two of the men. By and large, these could be any guys from anywhere, which might be part of the point but doesn't help the interests of storytelling.

More than an hour is devoted to the protected effort to scale the indistinguished piece of Vietnamese real estate of the title. As physically impressive as some of it is, the acting also proves dispiriting and depressing, as the soldiers slide helplessly down the muddy slopes in the rain and are inevitably picked off by enemy gunfire.

With an empty, Pyrrhic victory as its conclusion, film is clearly commenting upon the senselessness of war, but also seeks to pay tribute to the grunts who had to do the dirty work, both by way of intercutting shots of the Vietnam War Memorial into the opening credits, and via a concluding poem.

On another level, pic implicitly endorses the view of many conservatives that the United States made its biggest mistake by agreeing to fight the war on the enemy's terms on its own turf, rather than blowing the communists to smithereens.

Carabatsos' dialog is rife with colorful Army slang, and most interesting quiet scenes have the G.I.s expressing their bitterness about the longhaired peaceniks back home who are dumping on them and, they imagine, making out with their girlfriends as well.

Director John Irvin, who shot a documentary in Vietnam in 1969, the year the action takes place, makes fine use of the Philippines locations and the verisimilitude supplied by the production team.

After underscoring the opening titles, original music by Philip Glass doesn't reappear again for 90 minutes, and even then only briefly. Most of the score is comprised of recognizable period rock tunes. Very welcome indeed is the RKO antenna logo, which appears just after the Paramount mountain at the outset. —*Cart.*

En Retirada
(In Retirement)
(ARGENTINE-COLOR)

An Instituto Nacional de Cinematografía Argentina release of an Arte Diez production. Produced by H.L.Y. Asociados. Directed by Juan Carlos de Sanzo. Stars Rodolfo Ranni. Screenplay, De Sanzo, based on an original work by De Sanzo, Feinmann, Oves; camera (color), Juan Carlos Lenardi; editor, Sergio Zottla; music, Baby López Furst; art direction, Pablo Olivo. Reviewed at N.Y. Latino Festival, Public Theater, July 30, 1987. Running time: **87 MINS.**
Ricardo (Oso) .... Rodolfo Ranni
Julio .... Julio de Grazia
Also with: Osvaldo Terranova, Lidia Lamaisón, Villanueva Cosse, Edda Bustamante, Osvaldo Tesser, Jorge Sassi, María Vaner, Gerardo Sofovich.

The Argentine feature "En Retirada" (In Retirement, a.k.a. Beating A Retreat) is a brutal study of those for whom violence and power is a way of life, such as were allowed to exist during the so-called "dirty war" of Argentina's military rule (1976-83). The film also delves into what happens to such people when a political system that has validated this way of life changes and they no longer have a place within the existing order.

"En Retirada" is a powerful indictment against the former military regime, scripted and helmed by Juan Carlos de Sanzo during the 1984 transition period while the country was still recovering from the shock of what had taken place.

The film raises many questions. How fragile is Argentina's civilian democracy? What is the possibility such a situation will recur? How are the different military governments linked throughout Latin America? How did multi-national companies work with the military government to benefit from official repression?

In an effort to contrast those who can assimilate into the new order and those who can't, the film follows one of the latter: Ricardo (Rodolfo Ranni), better known as "Oso" (Bear), a thug who has kidnaped and tortured under the military regime.

Rather than command fear and respect as in the past, Oso is suddenly being followed in the streets by the father (Julio de Grazia) of one of the many "disappeared" to have passed through his hands. He beats a retreat by visiting his mother in the provinces, first such visit in five years. He tries to take up again with a former lover, but everything falls to pieces around him.

Oso returns to the capital only to discover that the whole organization has gone underground. He is alone and feels deserted and betrayed. He wants revenge.

De Sanzo structures the film as a tense thriller. Oso becomes both a danger to society and also to the system that produced him.

Acting is strong, lensing tight and the editing keeps the story gripping.

The film is not without its loose ends as sloppy details mar pic's full effectiveness and impact. Overall the picture should find an international market on interest sparked by such features as "The Official Story." — *Lent.*

The Monster Squad
(COLOR)

Summit meeting of monsters aimed at smallfry.

A Tri-Star Pictures release of a Taft Entertainment Pictures/Keith Barish Prods. film, in association with Home Box Office. Produced by Jonathan A. Zimbert. Directed by Fred Dekker. Executive producers, Peter Hyams, Rob Cohen, Keith Barish. Screenplay, Shane Black, Dekker; camera (Panavision, Metrocolor), Bradford May; editor, James Mitchell; music, Bruce Broughton; production design, Albert Brenner; coproducer, Neil A. Machlis; visual effects, Richard Edlund; monster design, Stan Winston; casting, Penny Perry; art direction, David M. Haber; assistant director, Richard Luke Rothschild; sound (Dolby), Richard Church; stunt coordinator, John Moio; costume supervisors, Michael Hoffman, Aggie Lyon. Reviewed at Tri-Star screening room, Century City, Aug. 3, 1987. (MPAA Rating: PG-13.) Running time: **81 MINS.**
Sean .... Andre Gower
Patrick .... Robby Kiger
Del .... Stephen Macht
Dracula .... Duncan Regehr
Frankenstein .... Tom Noonan
Horace .... Brent Chalem
Rudy .... Ryan Lambert
Phoebe .... Ashley Bank
Eugene .... Michael Faustino
Emily .... Mary Ellen Trainor

Hollywood — Can that venerable old quartet of baddies — Count Dracula, the Wolfman, Frankenstein and the Mummy — still strike fear into the heart of America's youth? That's the key question for makers of this brightly written, mostly well-acted kiddie thriller. While serious problems with pacing blunt its effectiveness, pic is still clever and satisfying. It's anybody's guess, though, whether video-age kids will turn out to see these vintage villains.

Film takes place in the present with Count Dracula resurrected to round up the usual nefarious characters — plus one, "Gill Man," whose sole purpose in the movie seems to be as a special effect; he's totally out of place with the other "classic" monsters. The group heads for Small Town, U.S.A. to retrieve an ancient amulet that controls the balance between good and evil.

This very same small town contains a group of pre- and edge-of-adolescent kids who have formed a club devoted to monsters, and they stumble onto the amulet's secret also. Because this self-appointed "Monster Squad" is the only group that believes monsters *might* be real, they're the only ones who can do what's necessary to save the world.

Group is led by the terrific Andre Gower, as Sean, giving a performance that belies his age of 14. His main cohorts are Patrick (the likeable, low-key Robby Kiger, who will remind many of "E.T.'s" Henry Thomas), and the obligatory fat kid who gets scared easily, Horace (Brent Chalem).

Director Fred Dekker and Shane Black co-wrote the screenplay, and they give the young actors dialog that is usually credible and a lot sharper than the norm for children's films.

Screenplay's incongruity comes with the kids themselves, who are forced to play younger characters than their speech, actions and personas would indicate. Thus they still harbor a belief in monsters and, except for the slightly older Rudy (Ryan Lambert), virtually ignore the female of the species.

Other major problem is pacing, with most of the action occurring in the last five minutes, as Black and Dekker set up a showdown at a predetermined crucial moment in history, much like "Back To The Future."

While the trip to that climax seems overlong, it is for the most part pleasant, with the ensemble of childhood actors showing real chemistry, while the largely unidimensional adults (subplot about marital friction between Sean's parents goes nowhere) are relegated to limited screen time.

It's not likely that many teen viewers will be scared by the goings-on. Only Duncan Regehr's Count Dracula generates any real venom, with Tom Noonan's Frankenstein playing as an oversized buffoon with an artificial heart of gold, befriending a little girl and eventually helping to do in the other monsters.

Still, for all of its muted horror elements and lagging storyline, this film does have the crisp dialog and Gower's magnetic performance going for it, and anyone under the age of 13 is liable to enjoy the film immensely. Unfortunately film is rated PG-13, so this picture might not find its audience until it hits the homevid racks.—*Camb.*

No Way Out
(COLOR)

Topnotch remake with sure-fire thriller formula and controversial windup.

An Orion Pictures release of a Neufeld/-Ziskin/Garland production. Executive producer, Mace Neufeld. Produced by Laura Ziskin, Robert Garland. Directed by Roger Donaldson. Stars Kevin Costner, Gene Hackman. Screenplay and screen story, Garland, based on Kenneth Fearing's novel "The Big Clock;" camera (Metrocolor, Deluxe prints), John Alcott; editor, Neil Travis; music, Maurice Jarre; songs, "No Way Out," Paul Anka, Michael McDonald, sung by Julia Migenes, Anka, "Say It," Anka, Richard Marx, sung by Anka; sound (Dolby), Jack Solomon; production design, Dennis Washington; art direction, Anthony Brockliss; set design, Dick McKenzie, Henry Alberti, Gerald Sigmon; set decoration, Bruce Gibeson; assistant director, Herb Adelman, Tim Coddington (New Zealand); production manager, Mel Dellar, William Grieve (N.Z.); stunt coordinator, Richard Diamond Farnsworth, Peter Bell (N.Z.); postproduction supervisor, Tony Di Marco; camera (N.Z.), Alun Bollinger; associate producer, Glenn Neufeld; casting, Ilene Starger. Reviewed at Orion screening room, N.Y., July 15, 1987.

(MPAA Rating: R.) Running time: **116 MINS.**

Tom Farrell	Kevin Costner
David Brice	Gene Hackman
Susan Atwell	Sean Young
Scott Pritchard	Will Patton
Sen. Duvall	Howard Duff
Sam Hesselman	George Dzundza
Major Donovan	Jason Bernard
Nina Beka	Iman
Marshall	Fred Dalton Thompson

Also with: Leon Russom, Dennis Burkley, Marshall Bell, Chris D., Michael Shillo, Nicholas Worth, Leo Geter, Matthew Barry.

Orion's "No Way Out" is an effective updating and revamping of the 1948 *film noir* classic "The Big Clock," also based on Kenneth Fearing's novel of that name. The sure-fire plot devices and twists still work well, though Robert Garland's adaptation introduces a surprise ending (presskit asks reviewers not to reveal the final twist) which departs radically from Fearing's concept and is hard to swallow. Boxoffice prospects loom as good, especially riding on the coattails of star Kevin Costner's much-publicized Eliot Ness role recently in the hit "The Untouchables."

Fearing's book, stylishly filmed for Paramount by John Farrow in 1948, revolved around a magazine empire (reputedly based on Henry Luce's Time Inc.) tyrannically run by Charles Laughton, the headquarters of which (including a symbolic clock tower) served as the setting for a climactic chase. "No Way Out" is set primarily in the Pentagon, with heroic Costner cast as a Lt. Commander assigned to the Secretary of Defense (Gene Hackman), acting as liaison to the CIA under Hackman's righthand man Will Patton.

Costner has a torrid love affair with good-time girl Sean Young, ended when she is murdered by her other lover, Hackman. Key plot gimmick unravels as follows: Young has Costner rush out of her apartment when she sees Hackman arriving outside; Costner recognizes his boss in the shadows but Hackman sees only an unidentified figure leaving; after killing Young in a jealous rage, Hackman is convinced by Patton to cover up the scandalous event by launching a hurry-up investigation to find the unidentified man he saw leaving the apartment, thought to be the Soviet agent, Yuri, they're already searching for; Costner is put in charge of the top-security investigation to catch himself.

Film's pace and suspense pick up at this point, especially as an eyewitness who saw Costner and Young on a weekend outing spots Costner in the Pentagon, leading to the climax of the entire Pentagon thoroughly searched room by room to have two witnesses finger the spy and "killer" Yuri. Costner races to escape detection while nominally in charge of the search, a perfect nail-biter. One excellent touch in this update has a computer simulation pro-gram, run by Costner's buddy George Dzundza, displayed on tv terminals everywhere, gradually forming Costner's distinctive facial features as the search continues.

Main changes from the original "Big Clock" come in streamlining: Costner has no wife in this version (no Maureen O'Sullivan role), he is not the crime-solving investigative whiz Ray Milland was, and colorful minor characters such as Elsa Lanchester are omitted. With helmer Roger Donaldson tightening the screws, new version is far more explicit in sexual and violent matters, with Patton in George Macready's role verbally identified as homosexual in place of the ambiguity regarding such types in '40s thrillers. Final two twists are surprising but wildly implausible.

As in "The Untouchables," Costner is extremely low key in his acting, even in most pressure-packed scenes, thus conforming to the '40s heroes model (e.g., Robert Mitchum, Mark Stevens). Hackman glides through his role, avoiding the delightful but tipoff malignancy of Charles Laughton in the original, while Patton dominates his scenes, overplaying his villainous hand. Young is extremely alluring, replete with nude scene, as the heroine, and former model Iman rebounds after her disastrous starring debut in Otto Preminger's "The Human Factor" to turn in a sympathetic performance as Young's roommate.

Technical credits are top-flight, with razor-sharp, fluid lensing by the late John Alcott in his final feature assignment. Two Paul Anka songs are satisfying in their own right, but are injected for romantic interludes that interrupt and unnecessarily distend the action.

—*Lor.*

Who's That Girl
(COLOR)

Derivative comedy vehicle for the Material one.

A Warner Bros. release. Executive producers, Peter Guber, Jon Peters, Roger Birnbaum. Produced by Rosilyn Heller, Bernard Williams. Directed by James Foley. Stars Madonna, Griffin Dunne. Screenplay, Andrew Smith, Ken Finkleman from a story by Smith; camera (Technicolor), Jan DeBont; editor, Pembroke Herring; art direction, Don Woodruff; set decoration, Cloudia; costume design, Deborah Lynn Scott; stunt coordinator, Bud Davis; sound (Dolby), Ed White; assistant director, Ric Kidney; casting, Glenn Daniels. Reviewed at the Mann Chinese theater, L.A., Aug. 7, 1987. (MPAA Rating: PG.) Running time: **94 MINS.**

Nikki Finn	Madonna
Loudon Trutt	Griffin Dunne
Wendy Worthington	Haviland Morris
Simon Worthington	John McMartin
Det. Bellson	Robert Swan
Det. Doyle	Drew Pillsbury
Raoul	Coato Mundi
Benny	Dennis Burkley
Montgomery Bell	John Mills

Hollywood — In "Who's That Girl," Griffin Dunne reprises his role as the crazed, overwrought straight man while Madonna lays on a thick New Yawk bimbette act in this frenetic and ridiculously reworked "After Hours"-"Arthur" combination. All three pictures, not incidentally, are Warner Bros. releases.

If not for Dunne's charm and the pop singer's strangely fascinating persona, this alleged comedy would earn no coin.

The Material Girl, who fits the bleached-blond starlet role perfectly, plays a just-out-of-jail back-talking petty thief who's bent on avenging the thugs who made her take the rap for a murder she didn't commit.

As she's released, weak-kneed lawyer type Dunne is sent by his megabucks soon-to-be father-in-law (John McMartin) to pick her up and make sure she's on the next bus home. Dunne accepts McMartin's incredible explanation for the task and also dutifully stops by the docks on the way there and picks up a rare cougar. All this occurs on the eve of his wedding to McMartin's ice princess daughter (Haviland Morris).

Madonna wastes no time stomping her way through the early scenes, her voice like fingers on a chalkboard and her movements more like a streetwalker than a wrongly treated, misunderstood good girl at heart.

She bamboozles Dunne into doing what she wants to do, turning him into a near nut case bashing up his future mother-in-law's Corniche, losing the rare cat, buying stolen goods in Harlem, stealing right and left, and so on.

Fortunately, Dunne's playful personality eventually counterbalances Madonna's shrillness and their adventures together, while completely farfetched, finally become involving.

In "After Hours," action takes place in the space of a few hours where Dunne is trapped due to circumstances beyond his control and his own urban paranoia, whereas here it's because of sheer ineptness.

Like "Arthur," Dunne's an uppercrust boy marrying great wealth and having to deal with stuffy in-laws, which turns his interest to a femme from across the tracks.

What's lacking is pure and simple good humor.

Andrew Smith and Ken Finkleman rush things so much to leave little time for comedic development. Scenes come and go in a flash and many of the secondary characters are wasted in lackluster roles, notably the detective duo (Robert Swan, Drew Pillsbury) and the captured bridesmaids.

None of their ideas is particularly original, except perhaps getting a cougar to protect Madonna as she commands.

The wild cat is neither ferocious

nor totally tame and is actually somewhat non-threatening considering its potential for mauling people.

Title sequence by Broadcast Arts is terrific as is Madonna's title track.—*Brit.*

Can't Buy Me Love
(COLOR)

Underachieving, low-budget teen comedy.

A Buena Vista release of Touchstone Pictures presentation in association with Silver Screen Partners III, of an Apollo Pictures production. Executive producer, Jere Henshaw, Ron Beckman. Produced by Thom Mount. Directed by Steve Rash. Coproduced by Mark Burg. Screenplay, Michael Swerdlick; camera (Foto-Kem color, Deluxe prints), Peter Lyons Collister; editor, Jeff Gourson; music, Robert Folk; production design, Donald L. Harris; set decoration, Christian W. Russhon, Andrew Bernard; costume design, Gregory Poe; choreographer, Paula Abdul; sound (Dolby), Peter Bentley; assistant director, Jerram Swartz; casting, Caro Jones. Reviewed at the Samuel Goldwyn Theater, Beverly Hills, Aug. 6, 1987. (MPAA Rating: PG-13.) Running time: **94 MINS.**
Ronald Miller . . . . Patrick Dempsey
Cindy Mancini . . . . Amanda Peterson
Kenneth Wurman . . . . Courtney Gains
Chuckie Miller . . . . Seth Green
Barbara . . . . Tina Caspary
Iris . . . . Devin Devasquez
Patty . . . . Darcy de Moss
John . . . . Eric Bruskotter

Hollywood — It will be interesting to see if securing the expensive rights to use the original Beatles tune for the title song and having mainline Touchstone Pictures release "Can't Buy Me Love" will earn this lackluster, low-budget youth comedy any coin at the b.o.

Originally titled "Boy Rents Girl," this first effort under Apollo Pictures banner had a promising premise that went flat upon execution.

High School nerd Ronald (Patrick Dempsey) is so desperate to be a part of the "cool" crowd, he "rents" neighbor and Miss Popularity, Cindi (Amanda Peterson), at $1,000 for a month. Their contract stipulates they charade as boyfriend and girlfriend, as long as there's no physical contact.

In no short time, Dempsey undergoes a makeover — new duds, new doo and no more Friday night poker games with the nerd patrol. He's now in Miss Popularity's inner circle.

Dempsey has a charm about him, not unlike John Cusack and even in certain moments, Woody Allen.

The only inspired moments on screen, and there are too few, come after he and Peterson "break-up" and before she exposes him at a party when drunk.

It's amateur hour for most of the rest of the cast, who are mostly hopeful would-be actors with generally pleasing looks and little presence not unexpected for this level production.

Scripter Michael Swerdlick has

tried to build a non-exploitative, sensitive light comedy about the often cruel and crucial experiences that shape teenagers as their personalities develop.

Result, however, is something again. This hasn't the polish of a John Hughes picture, nor the originality of many other singular works about youth like "American Graffitti" and "Lucas."

There is a cohesive theme — be yourself — but it isn't just acted out in a number of scenes where Dempsey purposefully alienates his old buddies, it comes up in some fairly dreary dialog that could easily have been rewritten or excised entirely.

Swerdlick has potential as a writer, as evidenced by a handful of inventive set-ups, notably when Dempsey thinks he's watching "American Bandstand" and masters instead an African tribal number in an effort to fit in at the school dance.

Giving some shading to secondary characters would have elevated this from the mundane. The jocks are all meatheads, the nerds geeks from top to toe and the cheerleaders horny and fickle. Dempsey has a little brother, and not surprisingly, he's a brat whose nosing around part goes nowhere. —*Brit.*

Coda
(AUSTRALIAN-COLOR)

A Premiere Film Marketing presentation of a Genesis Films production. Executive producer, Tom Broadbridge. Produced by Terry Jennings. Directed by Craig Lahiff. Stars Penny Cook, Arna-Maria Winchester, Liddy Clark. Screenplay, Craig Lahiff, Terry Jennings; camera (color), David Foreman; editor, Catherine Murphy; music, Frank Strangio; sound, Robert Cutcher; production design, Anni Browning; production manager, Elspeth Baird; assistant director, Gus Howard; stunts, Glen Boswell; casting, Jan Killen. Reviewed on Palace Home Video vidcassette, Sydney, July 31, 1987. Running time: **99 MINS.**
Kate Martin . . . . Penny Cook
Dr. Steiner . . . . Arna-Maria Winchester
Sally Reid . . . . Liddy Clark
Det.-Sgt. Turner . . . . Olivia Hamnett
Mike Martin . . . . Patrick Frost
Anna . . . . Vivienne Graves

Sydney — Latest in the seemingly endless series of "Psycho" rip-offs is "Coda," an Aussie thriller lensed in Adelaide which has one additional gimmick; all the principal characters are women. Bypassed for theatrical release, it's gone straight to the vidcassette market, where it may please undemanding thriller buffs.

Setting is a university, where a music student is attacked in her room and falls from a high window: miraculously she survives, but an intruder creeps into the hospital where she's in intensive care and finishes the job. Prime suspect is the ex-husband of the dead woman's best friend, Kate, though he claims he's innocent.

Kate (Penny Cook) and her ebul-

lient new chum Sally (Liddy Clark, providing welcome comic relief) now find themselves threatened by a mystery man, though there's never much doubt that the killer is the sinister Dr. Steiner (Arna-Maria Winchester), the dead woman's tutor and lover, who dresses up as the brother she'd murdered years earlier to do her killings. Next to die, in time-honored tradition, is the cop in charge of the case, who's also a woman (Olivia Hamnett): this is "Coda's" equivalent to the Martin Balsam murder in "Psycho" and also takes place on stairs. There's also a stabbing scene modelled precisely on the murder-by-scissors sequence in "Dial M For Murder."

This kind of film can only enthrall an audience if it's convincing, and credulity is stretched beyond breaking point time and again during "Coda." Thesping is not at all bad, with both Penny Cook and Liddy Clark providing pleasing characters as the frightened ladies. The protracted climax, consisting of endless chases down college corridors and then yet another fall from a high window (again, miraculously non-fatal) is merely dullsville.

Pic is technically competent, though Frank Strangio's music is boringly repetitive. — *Strat.*

Masters Of The Universe
(COLOR)

Tedious, imitative fantasy epic.

A Cannon Group release of a Golan-Globus production, in association with Edward R. Pressman Film Corp. Produced by Menahem Golan, Yoram Globus, Executive producer, Pressman. Directed by Gary Goddard. Stars Dolph Lundgren, Frank Langella. Screenplay, David Odell; camera (Metro color), Hanania Baer; editor, Anne V. Coates; music, Bill Conti; production design, William Stout; art direction, Robert Howland; set design, Daniel Gluck; Michael Johnson; costume design, Julie Weiss; make-up conceptual design, Michael Westmore; sound (Dolby), John Larson, Robert A. Rutledge; special visual effects, Richard Edlund; stunt coordinator, Walter Scott; co-producer, Elliot Schick; casting, Vicki Thomas. Reviewed at UA Egyptian theater, Hollywood, Aug. 7, 1987. (MPAA Rating: PG.) Running time: **106 MINS.**
He-Man . . . . Dolph Lundgren
Skeletor . . . . Frank Langella
Evil-Lyn . . . . Meg Foster
Gwildor . . . . Billy Barty
Julie Winston . . . . Courteney Cox
Detective Lubic . . . . James Tolkan
Sorceress . . . . Christina Pickles
Kevin . . . . Robert Duncan McNeil
Man-At-Arms . . . . Jon Cypher
Teela . . . . Chelsea Field

Hollywood — All elements are of epic proportions in this "Conan"—"Star Wars" hybrid ripoff, based on the best-selling line of children's toys. Epitome of Good takes on Epitome of Evil for nothing less than the future of the universe, and the result is a colossal bore. The tedium will be lost on 5-9-year-old "Masters" fans, who will flock to see this anyway.

Dolph Lundgren's He-Man is an impressive physical specimen, the ultimate warrior epitomizing all that is good and defending the honor of inhabitants of the planet Eternia, especially the Sorceress of Greyskull Castle, whose power keeps the forces of light in charge.

On the dark side is the hideously made up Frank Langella, as Skeletor, on quite a power trip ("I must possess all... or possess nothing"). He has captured the Sorceress, locking her in a tubular energy field and absorbing her power, which evidently comes from Eternian moonbeams.

Skeletor's minions include the four grossest-looking creatures the Cannon makeup department could create, and they are uniformly grotesque. His infantry is made up of a thousand Darth Vader clones, none of whom seem to have eyes. This would explain why their laser aim isn't worth a damn. Typical battle scene has Lundgren taking on two or three dozen of these bad guys, deflecting or dodging all their shots, then gunning down the whole regiment within a minute or two.

Turns out the battle to control the future of universal power takes place at a used music store in a small town in California. Circumstances that bring main characters into this setting are too ridiculous to recount, but suffice to say He-Man and his allies are searching for a cosmic key (it resembles, more than anything, one of those cylindrical outdoor bug zappers) that will unlock the Sorceress from her nasty gravity field, help He-Man do in Skeletor and save the peace-loving Eternians until its time for a sequel.

Cosmic key is lost when He-Man and his buddies accidentally zap themselves to Earth, and is discovered by Julie Winston (Courteney Cox, she of Bruce Springsteen's "Dancing In The Dark" video fame) and her musician boyfriend, Kevin (Robert Duncan McNeil).

Julie is getting ready to move back east to live with her aunt, since her parents have been killed in a plane crash. After paying respects at the cemetery, she and Kevin stumble upon the key, which the less-than-bright boyfriend mistakes for "one of those new Japanese synthesizers."

For the rest of the film, forces of good and evil take turns imitating the Keystone Kops, getting control of the key and then losing it again. Finally the whole cast zaps themselves back to Skeletor's big living room for the ultimate showdown and liberation of the Sorceress.

While Lundgren is appealing and certainly imposing, he doesn't have enough of a character to carry the film, and the story's trite imagery ("the dark can embrace the light, but never eclipse it," says the Sorceress at one point) only highlights the lack of character development.

Billy Barty turns in his typical cuddly performance as the dwarf inventor Gwildor and Cox shows more skill than on her "Misfits Of Science" tv stint. Unfortunately, director Goddard doesn't spend enough time showing the stakes of the battle itself, or the goodness of He-Man's Eternian sidekicks, the wily veteran Man-At-War (Jon Cypher) and his jealous daughter Teela (Chelsea Field).

Instead, audience gets transported around the galaxies by the cosmic key, watches a tedious series of laser fights and listens to Langella's rantings as the embodiment of evil. It all gets old quickly.

Makeup and costuming is universally good, special effects uninspiring. Bill Conti's soundtrack is such an obvious imitation of John Williams' "Star Wars" scores as to be laughable. —Camb.

Happy New Year
(COLOR)

Amiable, lightweight buddy comedy.

A Columbia Pictures release from Columbia-Delphi IV Prods. Produced by Jerry Weintraub. Executive producer-production manager, Allan Ruban. Directed by John G. Avildsen. Stars Peter Falk. Screenplay, "Warren Lane" (Nancy Dowd), based on Claude Lelouch's film "La Bonne Année;" camera (Continental color, Deluxe prints), James Crabe; editor, Jane Kurson; music, Bill Conti; sound, Jane Sabat; production design-associate producer, William J. Cassidy; art direction, William F. Matthews; set decoration, Don Ivey; assistant director, Clifford Coleman; second unit director, Bruce Malmuth; special prosthesis makeup, Robert Laden. Reviewed at Columbia 5th Avenue screening room, N.Y., Aug. 5, 1987. (MPAA Rating: PG.) Running time: **85 MINS.**

Nick . . . . Peter Falk
Charlie . . . . Charles Durning
Carolyn Benedict . . . . Wendy Hughes
Edward Sanders . . . . Tom Courtenay
Sunny . . . . Joan Copeland
Nina . . . . Tracy Brooks Swope
Curator . . . . Daniel Gerroll
Police Lt. . . . . Bruce Malmuth
Also with: The Temptations, Peter Sellars, Anthony Heald, Claude Lelouch.

Crime pays off in this unpretentious buddy picture about two middle-aged jewel thieves going for the big score in Palm Beach. Columbia, releasing "Happy New Year" without much fanfare, may have calculated a modest boxoffice payoff, but topliners Peter Falk and Charles Durning team with an easygoing charm that will play amiably on the tv screen when this film makes its way to video, feevee and broadcast outlets.

Nick (Peter Falk) and Charlie (Charles Durning) are career criminal partners who've never been scared straight by time in the slammer. According to Durning's retrospective voiceover narrative — a device which neuters the film of suspense but tilts viewer sympathy toward the protagonists — these heist-meisters are a couple of old fashioned guys whose values were

shaped in the 1940s when "dames" and "broads" could always be counted on to fall for a bauble.

Film is funniest and most engrossing in the first hour or so when Falk and Durning are casing the Palm Beach branch of Harry Winston jewelers. Falk's modus operandi is to masquerade alternately as a doddering, rich octogenarian and his sister who, driven in a hot Rolls Royce chauffered by Durning, are shopping for 5- and 6-figure trinkets. This leads to a series of amusing encounters with the fey and smarmy jewelry store manager Edward Sanders (expertly rendered by Tom Courtenay), who from Falk's hardboiled honor-among-thieves perspective is a soulless money-grubber deserving the worst.

Along the way Falk meets and falls for a beautiful, high-toned antiques dealer, Carolyn Benedict (Wendy Hughes) who moves in a circle of insufferably smug and wealthy pseudo-sophisticates. After some initial resistance Hughes improbably falls for this charming conniver because he's a man "who knows who he is," although she does not know just who Falk really is. She finds out when the heist goes awry and Falk is extradited back home to New York while Durning gets away.

Even more improbably, Hughes stands by her man, although she does so in ample Manhattan luxury and with one slight breach of faithfulness. This sets up some clumsy sermonizing on sexual mores in changing times by Durning, whom the cops are hoping to catch by springing Falk on early parole. The police, however, underestimate this master of disguise, the power of love and the allure of Rio de Janeiro.

Although the film sags towards its resolution, director John G. Avildsen handles the story with a light touch, including a gentle soundtrack of pre-rock 'n' roll standards that would be at home in a Woody Allen film and a cameo by Claude Lelouch, who directed the original French film.—Rich.

Hot Child In The City
(COLOR)

Familiar cautionary tale.

A Mediacom Filmworks production, in association with Fairfield Prods. and MVA-1. Produced by Giovanna Nigro-Chacon. Executive producers, Ronald Altbach, A.J. Cervantes. Directed by John Florea. Screenplay, George Goldsmith; camera (Foto-Kem color), Richard C. Glouner; editor, Marcy Hamilton; music, W. Michael Lewis; music supervision, Rick E. Ambrose; sound, George Hauser; production design, Anthony Sabatino, William H. Harris; set decoration, George Peterson; assistant director, Norm Stevens; production manager-associate producer, Patricia Sonsini; postproduction supervisor, Strathford Hamilton; casting, Joy Dolce. Reviewed on Prism Entertainment videcassette,

N.Y., July 31, 1987. (No MPAA Rating.) Running time: **85 MINS.**
Rachel . . . . Leah Ayres Hendrix
Abby . . . . Shari Shattuck
Det. Osborne . . . . Geof Prysirr
Charon . . . . Antony Alda
Tim . . . . Will Bledsoe
Tony . . . . Ronn Moss

"Hot Child In The City" fits comfortably in the new wave of high-concept homevideo: a feature-length film built around a familiar pop song title (by Nick Gilder and James McCulloch) which approximates a B-movie of old and goes directly to homevideo stores. Competent direction by John Florea and an attractive cast make for okay, nothing-special entertainment.

Leah Ayres Hendrix plays a beautiful blond visiting her sister, similarly beautiful blond Shari Shattuck, in Los Angeles, where Shattuck works as a high-powered recording company executive. Hendrix is a bit shocked at sis' life style, partying all night and hanging out with her androgynous client Antony Alda, a 1970s singing star attempting a comeback.

Shattuck is murdered in the second reel and most of the male cast is suspect. Hendrix, who has already started dressing up in sis' clothes, is attracted to the cop on the case (Geof Prysirr) and more or less fills sis' shoes in her circle of friends and nightclub hoppers. Predictably, the murderer goes after Hendrix.

Pic resembles a telefilm but with brief nudity and harsh language. Acting is competent (Alda the standout) and the rock songs score (particularly two Billy Idol tunes) brightens things up considerably. Casting, perhaps intentionally, is a bit disconcerting in that the two heroines could have flipped a coin over who plays which role. —Lor.

Otto — Der Neue Film
(Otto — The New Movie)
(WEST GERMAN-COLOR)

A Tobis release of a Rialto Filmproduktion production. Produced by Horst Wendlandt. Executive producer, Hans Otto Mertens. Directed by Xaver Schwarzenberger, Otto Waalkes. Stars Waalkes. Screenplay, Waalkes, Bernd Eilert, Robert Gernhardt, Peter Knorr; camera (color), Schwarzenberger; editor, Jutta Hering; music, Thomas Kukuck, Christoph Leis Hendorff; art and set direction, Ulrich Schröder, Albrecht Konrad; sound, Detlev Fichtner; associate producer, Willy Egger. Reviewed at Kino-Center, Hamburg, Aug. 4, 1987. Running time: **90 MINS.**
With: Otto Waalkes, Anja Jaenicke, Ute Sander, Georg Blumensaat, Dirk Dauzenberg Joachim Kemmer, Friedrich Schoenfelder.

Hamburg — Otto Waalkes, a gangly, blue-eyed, beak-nosed, straw-haired yokel from the North Frisian windmill country, is West Germany's leading standup comic. His long-awaited second film promises to do even better, already breaking another record with 1,720,000 admissions in the first seven days.

Waalkes' style most closely ap-

proaches the manic delivery of Robin Williams, supplemented by zany acrobatics reminiscent of the young Groucho Marx. His monolog — his films consist primarily of 1-liners bounced off of supporting actors — are heavily dependent on German puns and West German society's eccentricities.

That makes this film's prospects outside the German market limited, but that's not to say there is no future for this gifted comic elsewhere. Delivering English lines with a "Chermann" accent would make him only funnier.

There's not much plot to "Otto." Hayseed can't make it in the big city, but can't go home until he repays his landlord for three months' overdue rent. His job as an all thumbs handyman brings Otto into contact with shapely new tenant who has a crush on a brawny film star bearing an uncanny resemblance to Arnold Schwarzenegger. Otto's attempts to woo her end predictably.

Through it all, Waalkes pokes good-natured fun at the Teutonic need for conformity and propriety, and especially at the German reverence for uniforms and titles. In one attempt to seduce his voluptuous neighbor, Otto dons a white smock and passes himself off as a veterinary psychiatrist. Impressed, the young lady addresses him as "Herr Professor" until he interrupts her with, "Let's dispense with the "Herr Professor, my dear. Just call me 'Herr Doktor.' "

Many of the lines, though, are disappointing, as, for example, when Waalkes delivers a weak opening monolog about how poor he is. "I even lost my one and only book: The telephone book. Lousy plot, but what a cast of characters!"

Waalkes is capable of much better than that. It is as though he knew that funny faces and periodic pratfalls would be enough to get him through this pic without trying.

Helping to tide over film's weak spots is handsome camera work by Xaver Schwarzenberger, who co-directed with Waalkes.

Schwarzenberger provides some fine moments in "Otto," most notably a hilarious "Psycho" spoof in a scene with Waalkes as an addle-pated babysitter. —Gill.

Back To The Beach
(COLOR)

Fun lampoon of beach party genre.

A Paramount Pictures release. Produced by Frank Mancuso Jr. Directed by Lyndall Hobbs. Stars-coexecutive producers, Frankie Avalon, Annette Funicello. Screenplay by Peter Krikes, Steve Meerson, Christopher Thompson, from a story by James Komack, based on characters created by Lou Rusoff; camera (color), Bruce Surtees; editor, David Finfer; music (Ultra-Stereo), Steve Dorff; production design, Michael Helmy; costume designer, Marlene Steward. No further technical credits available. Reviewed at Paramount Studio Theater, L.A., Aug. 7, 1987. (MPAA Rating: PG.) Running time: **92 MINS.**

Annette	Annette Funicello
The Big Kahuna	Frankie Avalon
Connie	Connie Stevens
Sandi	Lori Loughlin
Michael	Tommy Hinkley
Bobby	Demian Slade
Troy	John Calvin
Zed	Joe Holland
Mountain	David Bowe

Also with: Pee-wee Herman, Don Adams, Bob Denver, Alan Hale, Tony Dow, Jerry Mathers, Dick Dale, Stevie Ray Vaughan.

Hollywood — "Back To The Beach" is a wonderfully campy trip down pop culture's trash-filled memory lane. Starring Frankie Avalon and Annette Funicello as larger-than-life versions of themselves, the feature film debut of director Lyndall Hobbs pokes fun at the entire beach movie genre while at the same time remaining true to its central tenets. Boxoffice prospects look good, with enough familiar faces for children of the '70s and '80s to make this more than a '60s nostalgia trip.

Five different people are credited with working on the script's skewed perspective, which takes Frankie and Annette as we remember them — as the stars of several '60s beach parties — and builds a storyline from there.

Avalon, known here as "The Big Kahuna," and Annette have married and moved out of Tinseltown to settle down in Ohio, where he sells cars and she drives her 14-year-old son Bobby to the brink of matricide by serving up a numbing series of peanut butter sandwiches.

Family decides it's time for a vacation and stops over in L.A. to visit daughter Sandi (Lori Loughlin, who gives a nice turn with a limited character), only to discover she's living on a pier with her boyfriend Michael (Tommy Hinkley, graduate of the Bill Murray School of the Perpetual Smirk).

Conflict over the parents' arrival spells the end of domestic bliss for Michael and Sandi and shortly thereafter, Frankie and Annette are on the outs when they run into perpetual "bad girl" barowner Connie (Connie Stevens), who revives The Big Kahuna's studly self-image and sets up the rift between the Happy Couple.

Thus there are two relationships to be repaired, plus the future of the wayward youth Bobby to be decided. He takes up with a gang of leather-clad punk surfers who are threatening to take over the beach.

Hobbs plays out the story in reverent lowbrow style, with Funicello leading the girls through a pajama party number, Avalon going on an all-night bender and Nearly Every Washed-Up TV Star of the last 20 years making an appearance along the way. Included is Bob Denver's Gilliganish bartender, who

wants to tell everyone about his "long trip;" Don Adams, reprising the best-known lines from the "Get Smart" years; and about half the cast of "Leave It To Beaver," including Tony Dow and Jerry Mathers doing the best sendup yet of Siskel and Ebert.

There's even an appearance from that '80s icon of anti-hip, Pee-wee Herman, fairly destroying the cover of "Surfin' Bird" that serves as prelude to the great reconciliation and wholesale smooching at the inevitable beach bonfire.

Scripters have perhaps gone to the well once too often by stretching the film out 15 more minutes for the anti-climactic surfing showdown between Avalon and one of the surf-punk leaders.

Performances are surprisingly good, with Funicello and Stevens playing their celluloid stereotypes with real glee and Avalon giving a nice showing also, once he is brought back to his beach boy past. Audience also gets some real chemistry between secondary characters Loughlin and Hinkley.

Hobbs' gossip-page journalism pays off, with film never more than a moment away from another pop cultural reference, whether it be an old tv show, Funicello's Skippy commercials or an appearance by a contemporary rock star (Stevie Ray Vaughan, working with surf music relic Dick Dale on "Pipeline").

It's a fine line between stupid-funny and just plain stupid, but more often than not Hobbs and company wind up on the right side of the beach. —*Camb.*

Un Sábado Más
(One More Saturday)
(MEXICAN-COLOR)

A Películas Mexicanas release of Cinematográfica Tabasco production. Produced by Daniel Galindo. Directed by Sergio Vejar. Stars Pedrito Fernández. Screenplay, Kiki Galindo Ripoll; camera (color), Luis Medina; editor, José Li-Ho; music, Jorge Zarzosa. Reviewed at Hollywood Twin theater I, N.Y., July 31, 1987. Running time: **96 MINS.**

Martín	Pedrito Fernández
Tania	Tatiana
Isauro (Grande)	José Elias Moreno
Diego	Gilberto Trujillo
Lucía	Adela Noriega

Also with: Jorge Pais, Jaime Santos, Mauricio Méndez, Gabriela Hassel, Alfredo García Márquez.

Former Mexican child singer-actor Pedrito Fernández is getting older. No longer is he playing abandoned street urchin-thieves á la "Oliver Twist," who hang out in Garibaldi Square singing mariachi songs while thwarting bad guys. He is now a respectable teen and has undergone an image change.

As a rock singer, he is currently under contract with CBS/Columbia Intl. in Mexico, backed by an exclusive contract with Cinematográfica Tabasco, which began with the 1986

teen pic "Delincuente" costarring Lucerito. This was followed by "Un Sábado Más" (One More Saturday), costarring Tatiana, young costar of the Mexico City legit musical "Kumán."

"One More Saturday" tells the story of smalltown dirt-bike enthusiastic Martín (Fernández), who wishes to win a race against rich-kid rival Diego, played by Gilberto Trujillo, younger brother of popular action star Valentín Trujillo. He also wants to win the love of Diego's girl Tania (Tatiana), because Diego doesn't appreciate or deserve her.

The rest of the plot is fairly predictable. There are a few story details such as Martín's relationship with his alcoholic father or his friendship with a crippled motorcycle repairman, played by José Elias Moreno. Overall, there are very few surprises.

Both Fernández and Tatiana get to sing a few songs, there is an exciting motorcycle race and all ends happily. For kids, it is good, clean entertainment.

Fernández' new audience won't be as broad as his previous one, but judging from the film, it will be a loyal one.—*Lent.*

Ground Zero
(AUSTRALIAN-COLOR)

A Hoyts (Australia) release of a Michael Pattinson-Burrowes Film (Australia) release of a Michael Pattinson-Burrowes Film Group presentation of a BDB production. Produced by Pattinson. Directed by Pattinson, Bruce Myles. Stars Colin Friels, Jack Thompson, Donald Pleasence. Screenplay, Jan Sardi, Mac Gudgeon; camera (Panavision, Eastmancolor), Steve Dobson; editor, David Pulbrook; music, Chris Neal; sound, Gary Wilkins; production design, Brian Thomson; line producer, assistant director, Stuart Freeman; production manager, Narelle Barsby; casting, Bruce Myles, second unit director-camera, David Eggby. Reviewed at Harts screening room, Sydney, Aug. 11, 1987. Running time: **109 MINS.**

Harvey Denton	Colin Friels
Trebilcock	Jack Thompson
Prosper Gaffney	Donald Pleasence
Pat Denton	Natalie Bate
Commission President	Simon Chilvers
Hooking	Neil Fitzpatrick
Wallemare	Bob Maza
Ballantyne	Peter Cummins

Sydney — The pic with most nominations (9) in the 1987 Australian film awards is a crackerjack contemporary thriller with a powerful political theme. It should do great business Down Under, and perform solidly elsewhere. The Michael Pattinson-Bruce Myles film looms as one of the brightest Aussie productions.

Theme is a classic one: a man searches for the truth about his father's death over 30 years ago, and in doing so stumbles on a secret that places him, and those close to him, in danger. The man is Harvey Denton (Colin Friels), a cinematographer first seen shooting a hot dog commercial in downtown Melbourne. His father was also a cameraman, and Denton is in the

process of transferring his old 16m home movies to video when unexpected things start happening. His apartment is burgled, and film is stolen; at the same time, his sister's house is also robbed. Also, he starts getting anonymous phone calls from a man with a strange voice urging him to watch the television news: Denton's ex-wife (Natalie Bate), a Tv news-reporter, is currently covering an Australian Commission of Enquiry into British nuclear testing which took place in South Australia in the late '40s and early '50s.

Denton meets a mysterious type from ASIO (Aussie equivalent of the CIA) and learns that his father hadn't accidentally drowned in 1953, as his family had been told, but had been shot at the British test site. The ASIO man is played, with icy intensity, by Jack Thompson, giving another strong, but, for him, very different, performance.

Denton's life is threatened, and he seeks the solution to the mystery at the former test site in the desert, where he meets an old cripple who has to communicate via an artificial voice-box; this old man had come from England to select the best sites for testing, but had stayed on, an obsessed hermit. Donald Pleasence gives a characteristically strong performance in this role.

Plot comes down to some missing film, shot by Denton's father, which will apparently give the lie to British assertions that no aborigines were killed during the tests; apparently Denton Sr. had filmed aboriginal bodies at the site. The villains turn out to be British secret service agents, trying to cover up what happened all those years ago.

All this will ring true to Australian audiences, because the Commission of Enquiry actually did take place (the film apparently uses actual testimony in some scenes) and the British have shown recently that they don't take kindly to guilty secrets of the recent past being exposed (as evidenced by the Thatcher government's attempts to suppress the book, "Spycatcher").

All this has been packed into a suspenseful thriller, which only falters slightly about two-thirds of the way in, to pick up for an edge-of-the-seat climax, and then an effectively unexpected epilog. The production is handsome in every department, with superior photography (Steve Dobson), interesting production design (Brian Thomson) and a solid music score (Chris Neal). Colin Friels makes an impressive hero, and the supporting cast is tops down the line. For Michael Pattinson, who produced and co-directed, this is a big step forward after his last film, the disappointing youth pic, "Street Hero."

Television footage of President Reagan and Aussie Prime Minister

Bob Hawke discussing nuclear issues, plus old newsreel footage of then-P.M. Robert Menzies at the South Australian atom test site, add to the authenticity. The film ends with a long list of service personnel known to have been at the test site, who have died since from cancer.

Titles also note that no statistics were ever kept for aborigines who may have perished as a result of tests: they were counted in with the kangaroos and emus who died in the nuclear blasts. —*Strat.*

```
*************************************
*                                   *
* Moscow Festival Reviews           *
*                                   *
*************************************
```

Odinokaya Zhenchina Zhelaet Poznakomitaya
(Lonely Woman Seeks Life Companion)
(SOVIET-COLOR)

A Kiev Film Studio production. Directed by Viacheslav Krishtofovich. Stars Irina Kupchenko. Screenplay, Viktor Merezhko; camera (color), Vasili Trutkovsky; music, Vadim Khrapachev; art direction, Alexei Levchenko. Reviewed at the Moscow Film Festival (market), July 9, 1987. Running time: **91 MINS.**
Klavdia . . . . Irina Kupchenko
Neighbor . . . . Elena Solovei
Valentin . . . . Alexander Zbruyev
Also with: Mariann Vertinskaya.

Moscow — "Lonely Woman Seeks Life Companion," an unpretentious entertainment entry from Kiev Studios, is a small gem, delightful in its simplicity and never banal. Thanks to the wonderfully controlled performance of Irina Kupchenko as a lonely 40-year-old who advertises for a mate, pic meshes comedy and drama into a smooth yarn. Dignified and eminently watchable, it could please offshore audiences willing to give Russian pics a try.

Kupchenko plays Klavdia, an attractive single with a boring but steady job, a nice apartment — and no man. Klavdia has a notable streak of the unpredictable in her, and she impulsively tacks up a note with her name and phone number. By the time the men start streaming to her door she's already tired of the idea, but too late. Valentin (Alexander Zbruyev), a down-and-out, crazy alcoholic, has already insinuated himself into her life, and Klavdia can't dislodge him without having second thoughts and calling him back.

Actually Zbruyev plays the character so sympathetically it's clear the two are meant for each other. The lonely woman's ambivalent feelings are examined realistically (the last thing she wants is a penniless drunk for a husband; on the other hand, there are extenuating circumstances, and Valentin's ex-wife is despicable).

The merry-go-round of together-apart keeps turning, mostly in a comic vein, as plump next-door neighbor Elena Solovei grabs one of the men from Klavdia's ad. Ending is realistic and melancholy, both for the two lonely women and the good-hearted bum Valentin.

Viktor Merezhko's screenplay skillfully sidesteps the clichés story would tend to, aided by an excellent cast. Lensing is professional, like the decor and music. —*Yung.*

Kreutzerova Sonata
(The Kreutzer Sonata)
(SOVIET-COLOR)

A Cannon Group release of Mosfilm Studio production. Directed by Mikhail Schweitzer, Sofia Milkina, Stars Oleg Yankovsky. Screenplay, Schweitzer, based on the novel by Leo Tolstoy; camera (color), Mikhail Agranovich; music, Sofia Gubaidulina; art direction, Igor Lemeshev, Vladimir Fabrikov. Reviewed at the Moscow Film Festival (market), July 15, 1987. Running time: **158 MINS.**
Vasili Pozdnyshev . . . . Oleg Yankovsky
Lisa . . . . Irina Selezneva
Also with: Alexander Trofimov, Alla Demidova, Alexander Kalyagin.

Moscow — And now for a classic screen adaptation of a classic book, Tolstoy's "The Kreutzer Sonata," previously filmed in Italy in 1985. This team effort (directed by Mikhail Schweitzer and Sofia Milkina) doesn't skimp on the master's work, running 158 minutes and distributing a lavish budget on rich period sets and costumes. Though the approach is tried and true, film is a satisfying viewing experience that would translate perfectly to tv segmenting offshore.

"Kreutzer" is held together, and kept engrossing, by a strong performance from Oleg Yankovsky as the tormented hero Vasili Pozdnyshev. He tells his tale of married hell as a flashback while he sits awake all night on a train, sipping tea and compulsively confessing to a compassionate stranger the feelings that led to murdering his wife.

In his youth, Pozdnyshev reports, he was a gay blade who had a way with women. At the appropriate moment, he courted a nice girl from a good family, Lisa (Irina Selezneva), married her properly, even fell in love with her. Things begin to go wrong on their honeymoon in Italy. Gradually, misunderstandings and spats grow into nagging, indifference, boredom, hatred. Pozdnyshev treats his wife like a possession, but Lisa isn't much more sympathetic as a shrewish 19th century hysteric subject to fainting fits.

Tragedy comes when a gypsy musician starts giving Lisa piano lessons. The sonata they play together

is a great success, but Pozdnyshev is overcome with irrational jealousy. He fights it off for several scenes, but in the end succumbs, tries to kill the musician, but kills Lisa instead. The court apparently acquits him for this crime of passion, but he loses the right to see his children, and wanders over the face of the earth, smitten with remorse.

Thesps, decor, lighting and music are all high quality. Selezneva makes a pretty but ambivalent wife; supporting cast is fine. — *Yung.*

Alshazhia
(Shrapnel)
(LIBYAN-B&W)

A General Cinema Organization (KHAYALA) production and release. Directed by Mohamed Ali Alfarjani. Screenplay, Alfarjani, Abdul Salam Almadani. (No other credits available). Reviewed at the Moscow Film Festival, July 11, 1987. Running time: **100 MINS.**
With: Ali Aliresi, Altaher Alquabaili, Kariman Gabr.

Moscow — "Shrapnel" is a surprisingly forceful parable from Libya about good, evil, and the inscrutable ways of the Lord. Film has technical weaknesses, yet sincerity of the simple, sobering tale largely redeems it. This curiosity item from a little-heard-from country is worth more fest exposure.

Director Mohamed Ali Alfarjani constructs virtually the whole film around two men, Bahlool the bad and Salim the good, one camel and a desert. When the two men meet, both have tragedies behind them they've faced in different ways. Gentle, God-fearing Salim was once a happy young nomad with an enticing wife and three small kids. In the midst of their desert idyll, the wife runs over a dune and gets blown up, along with their sheep, by an old mine. The horrible thing about this part of the desert is that it is littered with World War II mines, and Salim is one of the few who knows how to negotiate his way across the dunes in relative safety. Now all he has left is a camel to gather firewood and feed his kids.

Bahlool is a hot-tempered murderer fleeing from justice, having taken vengeance when the girl he wanted was married off to another man. He steals the camel but Salim, "because he fears God," offers to guide him through the mine fields. The flashbacks are too lengthy, but Alfarjani is skillful at building tension, and even stages a heart-stopping nighttime wolf attack without any special effects, or particular help from the pair of stiff-jointed thesps.

The real surprise is the disquieting ending, when the two part almost buddies, and Salim — having saved Bahlool's life a few times — puts his foot on a mine. He knows the second he lifts it that it's cur-

tains, and has Bahlool dig a grave behind him. With a backward flip the good soul jumps into his final resting place as the mine explodes. A chastised Bahlool piously buries him, resolving to return the camel to Salim's orphans.

Film turns a mini-budget to its advantage by keeping things essential. The lethal desert is used effectively as both histroical reproach to the Italian, German and British armies who left the mines behind, and as a larger symbol. —*Yung.*

Zawgat Ragol Mohim
(Wife Of An Important Man)
(EGYPTIAN-COLOR)

An El-Alamia for TV & Cinema production and release. Produced by Hussein Kalla. Executive producer, Fathi Yussri. Directed by Mohammed Khan. Stars Ahmed Zaki, Mervet Amin. Screenplay, Raouf Tawfik; camera (color), Moheen Ahmed; editor, Nadia Chukri; music, George Kazazian; art direction, Onsy Abuseif. Reviewed at the Moscow Film Festival (competition), July 8, 1987. Running time: **114 MINS.**
Hisham . . . . Ahmed Zaki
Mona . . . . Mervet Amin
Samiha . . . . Zizi Mustafa
Ismail . . . . Ali Ghandour
Also with: Hassan Houssny, Ahmed Mokhtar, Khairy Beshara (Safwat), Nahid Samir.

Moscow — Though it may look like a standard family melodrama at first glance, "Wife Of An Important Man" contains a pointed message against fascist police tactics and their frequent use in recent Egyptian history. Helmer Mohammed Khan is a skilled veteran lenser able to target liberal politics in films for mass audience consumption. Local nature of the problem limits pic to Arabic markets, without detracting from its value.

Story begins in 1975 in a small town, where Mona (Mervet Amin), a shy, romantic girl mad about folk singer Abdel-Halim is being courted by a good-looking young police chief. Hisham (played by boxoffice star Ahmed Zaki, a fine actor) is ambitious and ruthless, hardly the match for Mona's gentle soul.

He gets promoted to the Secret Police and they move to a fancy apartment in Cairo. Mona plays the meek, subservient, happy housewife for a time, but rebels against having to socialize with corrupt VIPs. She ends up neglected and starts gambling with the next door neighbor. In 1977 two important events occur: Abdel-Halim dies, mourned by millions (including Mona, shaken to the core), and serious civil disorders are repressed ruthlessly by the police (naturally Hisham is one of the worst).

He may be a wife-beating authoritarian, who imagines himself above the law, but Hisham is also depicted as sincerely believing he's serving his country and protecting its security. When he's kicked off the police force for all those trumped-up arrests and beatings,

Hisham is stunned. He loses his mind and shoots at his wife (killing her father, which is worse), then kills himself.

Khan keeps the action moving at an entertaining pace. Both Zaki and Mervet Amin are effective players able to round out characters with a lot of negative personality points. Zaki, known as the "Tanned Knight" of Egyptian cinema for his dark complexion, makes a good contrast with pale-faced Amin.
— *Yung.*

Viragaya
(The Way Of The Lotus)
(SRI LANKAN-COLOR)

A Dilini Films production. Produced by Chandra Mallawarachchi. Written and directed by Tissa Abeysekara, based on a novel by Martin Wickramasinghe. Stars Sanath Gunatilaka. Camera (color), Lal Wickremarachchi; editor, Lal Piyasena; music, Sarath Fernando; art direction, K.A. Milton Perera. Reviewed at the Moscow Film Festival, July 17, 1987. Running time: **180 MINS.**

Aravinda	Sanath Gunatilaka
Sarojini	Sriyani Amarasena
Siridasa	Douglas Ranasinghe
Bathee	Sabita Perera

Also with: Asoka Peiris, Daya Alwis, Joe Abeywickrema, Somalatha Subasingha (mother), Sunethra Sarachchandra.

Moscow — Based on a classic of Sri Lankan literature, Martin Wickramasinghe's novel "Viragaya," "The Way Of The Lotus" provides one more example of how literature doesn't translate into film. Helmer Tissa Abeysekara, formerly a scripter and short story writer, adopts a pious, get-it-all-in approach that draws a modest story out to a full three hours running time — when half that would have sufficed. In lands where the book's hero Aravinda is not a household word, film will have a hard time finding audiences.

As played by Sri Lankan star Sanath Gunatilaka, Aravinda is enigmatic, but more pathetic than captivating. As a young man he falls quietly in love with clever Sarojini (Sriyani Amarasena), but gives her up to his best friend. Gentle, self-effacing, unmaterialistic, he's a hard guy to admire from the egocentric Western p.o.v.

After he lets the girl get away, he allows his greedy sister to kick Mom out of the house after his father dies; then he himself is made to feel unwelcome, and moves. He lives with a beautiful adopted daughter, which sets tongues wagging, but again he doesn't have the gumption to turn his longings into action and marry the girl. Working as a humble civil servant in a job we're given to understand is far beneath his capacities, Aravinda plods through a wasted life until he gets sick and dies.

For no good reason, story is told as a posthumous flashback by an old friend who reads Aravinda's diary.

Lensing is pedestrian and colors are too often whited out. — *Yung.*

Zavtra Bila Voina
(Tomorrow There Was War)
(SOVIET-COLOR/B&W)

A Gorky Film Studio production. Directed by Yuri Kara. Screenplay, Boris Vasiliev; camera (color, b&w), Vadim Semenovykh; art direction, Anatoli Kochurov. Reviewed at the Moscow Film Festival (market), July 9, 1987. Running time: **91 MINS.**

With: Sergei Nikonenko, Nina Ruslanova, Vladimir Zamansky, Irina Chernichenko, Yuliya Tarkhova, Natalia Negoda.

Moscow — Glasnost filters down into all sorts of pictures these days, including this conventionally lensed, the-way-we-were look at growing up just before World War II. Aided by a game cast of youngsters, "Tomorrow There Was War" shows the people's resistance to Stalinist repression, within the hackneyed genre of high school memory films. A professionally lensed effort by helmer Yuri Kara, film will probably find most of its offshore playdates within Soviet film weeks.

Friendship, homeroom camaraderie and first love mix with betrayal, nighttime arrests and Young Communist League meetings here. Iskra Pekikova, the young heroine, lives with a severe mother too busy poring over Party literature to fix her supper. Iskra, head of the school's Young Communists, has absorbed mom's political ideals but not her rigidity. When the liberal father of her rich classmate Vika is arrested, she finds it hard to condemn him blindly. He was a friend of Mayakovsky's and introduced her to Yesenin's poetry, officially frowned on at the time. Vika commits suicide to keep from having to testify against her father, and Iskra bravely defies her mother and teacher to make a heartfelt speech at his funeral.

Next year, we're reminded, isn't going to be much of an improvement: our young friends don't know it yet, but they'll be marching off to the front to fight the Naxis. Pat ending gives a rundown on the heroic deaths this and that character will meet — Iskra and her mother will be hung as partisans, etc. In this context, the tragedy of the war appears to sanitize the whole Stalinist epoch and turn everyone into heroes.

Pic is raised several notches by Vadim Semenovykh's highly atmospheric camerawork, which simulates lensing in films like "My Friend Ivan Lapshin" by switching back and forth from black & white to sepia to color, in this case all too predictably. It's pretty to watch, anyway. — *Yung.*

Those Dear Departed
(AUSTRALIAN-COLOR)

A Village-Roadshow (Australia) release of a Phillip Emanuel production. Produced by Emanuel. Directed by Ted Robinson. Stars Garry McDonald, Pamela Stephenson. Screenplay, Steve J. Spears; camera (Eastmancolor), David Burr; editor, Robert Gibson; music, Phil Scott; sound, Phil Keros; production design, Roger Ford; associate producer, Barbara Gibbs; production manager, Rosanne Andrews-Baxter; assistant director, Steve Andrews; casting, Liz Mullinar. Reviewed at Village theater, Sydney, Aug. 10, 1987. Running time: **90 MINS.**

Max Falcon	Garry McDonald
Marilyn Falcon	Pamela Stephenson
Norda Thompson	Su Cruickshank
Richard Kowalski	Marian Dworakowski
Inspector Jerry	John Clarke
Phil Rene	Ignatius Jones
Phoebe Furlong	Antonia Murphy
Dr. Howie	Graeme Blundell
The Producer	Arthur Dignam
Sgt. Steve	Jonathon Biggins
Tristan	Patrick Cook
Bronwyn	Maureen O'Shaughnessy

Sydney — Garry McDonald, one of Australia's most popular tv comics, has been given a raw deal in films until now, but he gets a starring role in "Those Dear Departed" and that will please his many fans Down Under. First-time director Ted Robinson (also from tv) strains too hard for comic effects, though, and his over-the-top style often threatens to swamp his material.

Basic plot is a very British affair, harking back to those comedies about murder and haunting (especially Noël Coward's "Blythe Spirit"). McDonald is an egotistical Aussie stage star (so celebrated he's made the cover of Time magazine), currently starring in a musical about Freud. His sensual wife (Pamela Stephenson) is having an affair with their Polish chauffeur (Marian Dworakowski), a frustrated poet on the side (his most recent work: "Gomorrah Tomorrow — Poems Of Pain,") and together they plot to kill McDonald. Early attempts — crushed glass in his pasta, an assassination in the park — come to nothing, and on the third attempt it's McDonald's manager (Su Cruickshank) who's the victim when she imbibes a poisoned drink intended for her client.

Eventually the lovers do manage to kill the actor, who finds himself in a half-way station where the dead with unfinished business back on earth are consigned. It's a pleasant plot conceit that this never-never world is a theater, where an imperious Producer (Arthur Dignam) holds sway, following instructions from Higher Authority. Here, McDonald meets up with his vengeful manager and his father, whom he'd accidentally killed years before. The trio returns to earth as ghosts to haunt the murderers.

Much of this is quite funny, but the approach lacks subtlety. McDonald is a comedian whose style is broad, but the abundance of unnecessary special effects used in the

---

haunting scenes tend to swamp even him. These effects were probably inserted to appeal to the young crowd, but the film's ideas are on a more sophisticated level and they come across as gratuitous.

Early scenes, intercutting between the plotting lovers and McDonald performing on stage in "Freud The Musical," (which features a chorus of topless femmes) are frenetic in the style of '60s comedies, complete with fancy editing wipes, but once the pic settles down it's quite enjoyable. Thesping is good, given the overly broad style often chosen by director Robinson, with the formidably large Su Cruickshank seizing all her opportunities as the manager and making with lots of showbiz in-jokes. John Clarke steals his scenes as the cop in charge of the case, while cartoonist Patrick Cook has some good moments as the stage manager in the ghostly theater.

Overall, "Those Dear Departed" doesn't live up to its possibilities; probably a less hysterical approach to the material would have provided more satisfactory comedy. Garry McDonald's name should spark initial interest in Australia and word of mouth will have to take it from there. Overseas propects look uncertain. — *Strat.*

North Shore
(COLOR)

Effective surfing escapism.

A Universal Pictures release of a Randal Kleiser production, in association with the Finnegan Pinchuk Co. Produced by William Finnegan. Executive producer, Kleiser. Directed by William Phelps. Screenplay, Tim McCanlies, Phelps, from a story by Phelps, Kleiser; camera (Duart color), Peter Smokler; editor, Robert Gordon; music, Richard Stone; production design, Mark Balet; set decoration, Wally White; sound (Dolby), Tim Himes; costumes, Kathe James; assistant director, Bruce Shurley; second unit director, Gregory Harrison; associate producer, McCanlies, Gregory Hinton; casting, Lisa Clarkson. Reviewed at Universal Studios screening room, Universal City, Calif., Aug. 11, 1987. (MPAA Rating: PG.) Running time: **96 MINS.**

Rick	Matt Adler
Chandler	Gregory Harrison
Kiani	Nia Peeples
Turtle	John Philbin
Vince	Gerry Lopez
Lance Burkhart	Laird Hamilton
Alex Rogers	Robbie Page
Occy	Mark Occhilupo
Professor	John Parragon
Rick's mother	Cristina Raines
Contest director	Lord James Blears

Hollywood — "North Shore" is an entertaining, lighthearted bit of hokum set amidst the surfing scene in Hawaii. It's a fantasyland of waves, videos and girls where hardly anyone over 20 soils the pristine beaches. Clearly geared for a young teen audience, pic is everything summer escapism should be and could win some fans before the school bells sound.

Unlike many surfing pics "North Shore" treats its subject seriously without playing for camp value. In fact, film attempts a kind of documentary rendering of the surfing life along Oahu's north shore. It's an adolescent's view of the world to be sure, but not without its charm.

Story is sort of a surfing variation on "The Karate Kid" in which an innocent from the mainland comes to the island to surf and is confronted with a strange culture. Script by Tim McCanlies and director William Phelps is pretty tame stuff but its very simplicity backed by swell action footage make it unthreatening, painless fun.

Young Rick Kane (Matt Adler) is the Candide in question who journeys to the north shore on his winnings from a surf tank competition in his native Arizona. In Hawaii the waves are bigger and the people tougher than anything he has encountered before.

Rick learns the ways of this world from surfboard designer Chandler (Gregory Harrison) and comes to understand the value of native culture. He even gets a local girlfriend (Nia Peeples) as his reward. The choices and conflicts are obvious but not without some power.

What keeps the film from sinking are the lightweight and unassuming characters, particularly Adler's wide-eyed performance. As silly as the romance is, Adler and Peeples make an attractive couple and Harrison does a good job suggesting his affection for his young protege.

Then there's the ever-present wall of water, impressively photographed from a variety of angles by Peter Smokler. Phelps gives the film a nice breezy tone and other tech credits, especially Tim Himes' sound mix, add to the realism of the milieu.

Soundtrack, pandering to the teen audience, features a collection of nondescript rock tunes, seemingly all the same, that trivialize the action, a burden that the film can ill afford. —*Jagr.*

Reto a la Vida
(Challenge To Life)
(MEXICAN-COLOR)

A Películas Mexicanas release of a Cinematográfica Filmex production. Produced by J. Fernando Gavilán. Directed by Rafael Baledón. Stars Julio Alvarado. Screenplay, Fernando Galiana; camera (color), Alberto Arellanos Bustamante; editor, Francisco Chiu; music, Armando Manzanero, with appearance of groups Alfonso Duran y Grupo Eslabón, José Zambrano y Los Galleros; musical arranger, Rogelio Vergara; art direction, Ana María Martínez. Reviewed at Hollywood Twin theater II, N.Y., Aug. 1, 1987. Running time: **91 MINS.**
Carlos Muñoz . . . . Julio Alvarado
Elena Sandoval . . . . Helena Rojo
Yolanda Sánchez (Yolis) . . . . Olivia Collins
Inspector . . . . Jorge Luke
Tijuana . . . . Manuel Ojeda
Doctor . . . . José Carlos Ruis
Don José . . . . Jaime Garza
Also with: Luis Manuel Pelayo, Oscar Fentanez, Ademar Arau I., Jorge González H., Rubén Conoray, Queta Carrasco, Pablo Márquez, Efren Martínez G., Eduardo Muñoz, Raúl Antonio Palacio, Mónica Muñoz.

The Mexican feature "Reto a la Vida" (Challenge To Life), helmed by Rafael Baledón, is an inspirational potboiler that is little more than a propaganda tool to fight drug abuse, starting with abandoned street urchin-thieves using drugs to escape their wretched lives.

Pic is a mixed bag of film styles that attempts with uneven results to blend such diverse genres as social realism, corny message manipulation, fast action-adventure, a love story and even elements of a musical.

Story concerns ex-con Carlos Muñoz (Julio Alvarado), recently released from four years behind bars for drug peddling. His homecoming is marred by the discovery that his younger brother has followed in his footsteps, but became hooked and eventually locked up in a mental institution.

Vowing to put his life back on the right track, Carlos opens a small electronics fix-it shop and becomes involved with helping homeless street kids. He also takes on his former drug-dealer cronies, led by Tijuana (Manuel Ojeda), and becomes involved romantically with teacher Elena Sandoval (Helena Rojo).

In the tradition of Mexican melodramas, the hero can also sing. Alvarado manages to croon five numbers, for which Baledón tries to give some sort of context. The most imaginative comes about while Carlos is checking the reception of a tv set where a mariachi band plays.

Overall, the film is too full of messages to be taken seriously as entertainment. —*Lent.*

Lo Sam Zayin
(Don't Give A Damn)
(ISRAELI-COLOR)

A Gelfand Films presentation of Roll Films production. Produced by Yair Pradelsky, Israel Ringel. Executive producer, Nissim Levy. Directed by Shmuel Imberman. Screenplay, Hanan Peled, based on novel by Dan Ben Amotz; camera (color), Nissim (Nitcho) Leon; editor, Atara Horenstein; music, Benny Nagari. Reviewed at Pe'er Cinema, Tel Aviv, July 4, 1987. Running time: **102 MINS.**
Rafi . . . . Ikka Zohar
Nira . . . . Anath Waxman
Maya . . . . Liora Grossman
Eli . . . . Shmuel Vilojni
Amnon . . . . Shlomo Tarshish
Also with: Dudu Ben Ze'ev, Idith Tzur, Shmuel Shilo, Motz Matalon, Dr. Avraham Ori.

Tel Aviv — Based on a best seller published almost 20 years ago about a young soldier wounded in battle who is paralyzed from the waist down, this is the kind of subject that almost begs to be made in a country which has known as many wars, as Israel.

While the opening sequence shows a group of high school graduates arguing about the draft, this is the last time political aspects are discussed. The necessity of joining the Army is taken for granted

and the importance of serving in a combat unit as well. The drama is a very personal one, focusing on the trauma of the main character, who tries to adjust psychologically, sexually and socially.

Script purposely ignores any reference to the specific period mentioned by the novel, since sadly enough, Israelis always have been only too familiar with such cases. The background indicates the story takes place in the present.

There is little doubt, judging by the enthusiastic reception at home, that domestic audiences identify with the plot and find much in it that is close to their own experiences. They are not bothered by Hanan Peled's uneven script, nor by the exclusive attention focused on one character, the rest never really coming through convincingly in spite of some valiant efforts by Shlomo Tarshish, playing an older invalid who has learned to live with his handicap and tries to offer some helpful advice, and Liora Grossman, as the sister-in-law who shows more understanding than the rest. Best performances are given by non-actors, such as doctors, nurses or real invalids, playing themselves in the film.

Ikka Zohar, in the lead, works very hard, trying to stay faithful to the image of a person in a constant state of extreme stress, who has to explode once every few minutes. Director Shmuel Imberman manages to deliver the dramatic climaxes, but has problems handling the more introspective parts and the quieter moments. Story is told, however, in an efficient manner and the moral attitude is similar to last year's "Ricochets:" the war is an unpleasant, tragic, unavoidable fact of life here, young men are its blameless victims, but the issue is not the war itself, but how to survive its effects.

Production is unusually polished, by local standards, and the picture is already the top moneymaker of this summer.—*Edna.*

Disorderlies
(COLOR)

Embarrassing vehicle for Fat Boys.

A Warner Bros. release. Executive producers, Charles Stettler, Joseph E. Zynczak. Produced by Michael Schultz, George Jackson, Michael Jaffe. Directed by Schultz. Screenplay, Mark Feldberg, Mitchell Kelbanoff; camera (color), Rolf Kesterman; editor, Ned Humphreys; art direction, George Costello; sound, William Stevenson; costumes, Susie deSanto; second unit director, Hubie Kerns Jr. Reviewed at the Mann Hollywood Fox, L.A., Aug. 14, 1987. (MPAA Rating: PG.) Running time: **96 MINS.**
Kool . . . . : . . Damon Wimbley
Buffy . . . . Darren Robinson
Markie . . . . Mark Morales
Albert Dennis . . . . Ralph Bellamy
Miguel . . . . Tony Plana
Winslow Lowry . . . . Anthony Geary
Luis Montana . . . . Marco Rodriguez
Carla . . . . Troy Beyer

Hollywood — Everything about "Disorderlies" is gross. Obese rap singers ("The Fat Boys") playing inept orderlies (as in "Disorderlies") might have seemed an appealing idea on paper, but the result is something else again.

Warner Bros. would neither screen the film nor provide a complete product kit, by press time. Thus it wasn't until the last excruciating moment of the film that one found out the Beach Boys had a cameo appearance that either ended up on the cutting room floor or was completely obscured from the cameras.

Fat jokes form the basis for this "comedy" vehicle for Fat Boys Damon Wimbly, Darren Robinson and Mark Morales, three grossly overweight rappers who get one chance to shine in 96 minutes of (literally) embarrassing filmmaking, when they sing "Baby You're A Rich Man," their current release.

Pic opens with singers gorging themselves on cake at America's most rundown convalescent hospital, where they work as orderlies.

Enter Anthony Geary on the scene to hire the most incompetent threesome he can find to care for his ailing millionaire uncle (Ralph Bellamy) in hopes they'll do something stupid to cause the old man to die so that nearest relative Geary inherits the whole pot.

Instead Bellamy revives as the orderlies take him out to the roller derby so he can paw a young chick, inadvertently destroy his medication and other such inanities. In fact, he and the Fat Boys become chums.

In a succession of pathetic scenes, the Fat Boys suffer one humiliation after another — if they're not flailing around in the pool, they're panting after Bellamy as he jogs or worse, unable to play polo because excess poundage prevents them from staying in the saddle.

If only the Fat Boys sang more, even if they're not a pretty sight, at least there's some evidence of (well hidden) talent.

Curious why director Michael Schultz ("Krush Groove," "Car Wash") chose to completely downplay rap and the Fat Boys' particularly unique style of it.

It is clear these boys are not actors and the dialog should have been written around them not for them. Curiously, the lyrics to their song are clearer than anything they say.

As for Bellamy's role, it is undistinguished and he plays it as if catatonic. Geary and his band of thugs are cardboard characters.

Tech credits are poor. Even without studio-supplied production notes, it's evident from watching "Disorderlies" it was not shot anywhere resembling Palm Beach.
—*Brit.*

Talking Walls
(COLOR)

Dated exercise in voyeurism.

A Jacob Y. Terner and Drummond Prods. presentation of a Philip A. Waxman production. Produced by Waxman. Directed by Stephen Verona. Screenplay, Verona, from Mike McGrady's novel "The Motel Tapes;" camera (color), Scott Miller; editor-creative consultant, Jonathan Lawton; music, Richard Glasser; songs, Glasser (music), Sam Kunin (lyrics); sound, Richard Van Dike; art direction, Rick Carter; production manager-assistant director, John Romeyn; costumes, Irene Tsu; casting, Barbara Claman, Mark Schwartz, Don Pemrick. Reviewed on New World videocassette, N.Y., Aug. 12, 1987. (No MPAA Rating.) Running time: **83 MINS.**
Paul Barton .... Stephen Shellen
Jeanne .... Marie Laurin
Prof. Hirsh .... Barry Primus
Luna .... Karen Lee Hopkins

Also with: June Wilkinson, Sally Kirkland, Sybil Danning, Don Davis, Rae Davis, Hector Elias, Bobby Ettienne, Marshall Efron, Don Calfa, Donna Ponterotto, Marty Brill, Eileen Barnett, John Moschitta Jr., Jill Choder.

"Talking Walls" is a feature that can't make up its mind whether to be sexploitation or serious-minded about human relationships; comedy or suspenser. Resulting mishmash was lensed nearly five years ago, alternately titled "Motel Vacancy," and, hopelessly dated, gone to homevideo in lieu of a theatrical release.

Filmmaker Stephen Verona delivers an opening reel emphasizing first-person camerawork that is pure sex tease: student Stephen Shellen setting up video equipment and 2-way mirrors at Don Davis' Total Media Motel in order to photograph couples for his master's thesis on intimacy and human relationships.

After this cute opening, featuring plenty of nudity, attempted jokes and spoofing of the outlandish motel decor (with its sheep room, shoe room, etc.), pic bogs down in endlessly boring soul searching about whether his project is ethical (his sociology prof Barry Primus doubts this) or productive. Extremely corny romantic interludes with his girl friend Marie Laurin (who's also carrying on with Primus, it turns out) pad the film as well. Ultimately, Shellen rejects technology and after a recap filler montage concludes that "the answer is love — live life, don't record it." On this pithy note, pic launches one of its vulgar theme songs "Better In The Backseat."

Pic is so dated that it includes a joke about herpes. Of course, the constant bedhopping theme has been rendered archaic by the AIDS epidemic. —*Lor.*

Candy Mountain
(SWISS-CANADIAN-FRENCH-COLOR)

A Metropolis Film presentation of a Xanadu Films, Zurich production, coproduced with Les Films du Plain-Chant, Les Films Vision 4 Inc., George Reinhart, Zurich, TS Prods., Milena Poylo, Paris, Swiss TV (SSR), Film A2. Produced by Ruth Waldburger. Executive producer, Gerald Dearing. Directed by Robert Frank, Rudy Wurlitzer. Stars Kevin J. O'Connor. Screenplay, Wurlitzer; camera (color), Pio Corradi; editor, Jennifer Auge; music, Dr. John, David Johansen, Leon Redbone, Rita MacNeil, Tom Waits; music supervision, Hal Wilner; sound, David Joliat; art direction, Brad Ricker (N.Y.), Keith Currie (Canada); costumes, Carol Wood; casting, Risa Bramon, Billy Hopkins, Heidi Lewitt (U.S.), Gail Carr (Canada). Reviewed at the Locarno Film Festival (non-competing), Aug. 10, 1987. Running time: **91 MINS.**
Julius .... Kevin J. O'Connor
Elmore .... Harris Yulin
Al Silk .... Tom Waits
Cornelia .... Bulle Ogier

Also with: Roberts Blossom (Archie), Leon Redbone (Huey), Dr. John (Henry), Rita MacNeil (Winnie), Joe Strummer (Mario), Laurie Metcalf (Alice), Jayne Eastwood (Lucille), Kazuko Oshima (Koko).

Locarno — A road movie which definitely improves in the second half, "Candy Mountain" is an outsider's vision of America, critical and disenchanted.

Julius Booke is a failed rock star who dreams of rekindling his sagging career. He pretends to know intimately a famous guitar builder. Elmore Silk, and to be able to bring him out of his seclusion. A $2,000 advance and the promise of a substantial bonus send Julius wandering from New York to the north, into Canada, on the tracks of the elusive Elmore whom in reality he has never met.

The plot is built on a series of brief encounters along the road, short sketches reflecting a certain image of America's underbelly. Julius is outsmarted at every turn, each new step in his search leaving him a little poorer. He is even thrown into a strange sort of improvised jail in Canada, before he reaches his goal.

The American sketches south of the border, including that of Tom Waits who plays Elmore's brother, are closer to caricature than they are to human observation, but once the border is crossed, Robert Frank and Rudy Wurlitzer seem to be more inclined to take their time and learn to like their characters better. Harris Yulin, as the drop-out guitar building genius running away from civilization and trying to achieve perfect freedom, offers a nice cameo as the object of the film is to show a selfish innocent discovering what life is really all about.

The glamorless scenery of Julius' trip pretends at no time towards esthetic values, for that too would have been against the grain of the picture, as visualized by Frank and Wurlitzer, both of them familiar with the genre and not willing to compromise. If neither one equals their originality in past achievements and do not produce another cult movie (Frank had directed "Pull My Daisy" and Wurlitzer wrote "Two-Lane Blacktop"), they still manage to deliver a personal, if limited, portrait of the American continent.

Kevin J. O'Connor has the right forlorn quality in the lead even if a whole picture is a bit too much of a load on his shoulders. The score offers several memorable moments, thanks to Waits, Rita MacNeil and David Johansen, and there are some good performances by Roberts Blossom as a self-appointed Canadian justice of the peace and Bulle Ogier as a French woman lost in the barren Canadian landscape.

As road movies go, this may not be at the top of the list, but is certainly a respectable contender.

—*Edna.*

Zjoek
(DUTCH-COLOR-16m)

An Allart Enterprises presentation of an Allart Enterprises, Haagse Filmstichting VPRO-Cinema production. Produced by Kees Kasander, Denis Wigman. Directed by Eric van Zuylen. Screenplay, Marietta de Vries, based on "The Mind Of A Mnemonist" and "The Man With The Shattered World" by Alexander R. Luria; camera (color, 16m), Witold and Piotr Sobocinski; editor, Jan Dop; music, Henk Hofstede; sound, Hugo de Vries; art direction, Jan Roelfs, Ben van Os. Reviewed at the Locarno Film Festival (competing), Aug. 11, 1987. Running time: **90 MINS.**
Solomon .... Hans Dagelet
Ljova .... Felix-Jan Kuypers
Olga .... Guusje van Tilborgh
Luria .... Rudolf Lucieer

Locarno — Basic material for this film undoubtedly is fascinating, for it attempts to deal with the mechanism of human memory by confronting two opposite cases: an officer who has lost his memory to the point he can't even remember the meaning of words as the result of an injury in battle, and a showman who has made a living out of his amazing capacity to remember everything.

In fact, these are two separate books by Russian scientist Alexander Luria, combined into one script hoping each case will become clearer when juxtaposed against the other.

The trouble is that as riveting as the subject is, trying to visualize it in a film turns out to be too much of a challenge. The script doesn't quite find a satisfactory solution to bringing the separate cases into one plot, and the images selected to portray the recesses of the human mind seem flat and arbitrary, almost accidentally accompanying the overflowing text, without adding to its substance.

It is certainly interesting to follow the process of associations used by the virtuoso mnemonist to keep in order the amazing amount of data accumulating in his mind and the treatment of the soldier who again learns the use of language, through hesitant and faltering steps. In neither case is the visual aspect truly functional, the potential behind the words seeming much greater than anything materializing on screen.

The film is supposed to take place in 1943, on the Russian front, and describe the fashion in which Luria treated the officer with the help of the showman, but there is no real storyline to hang all the long monologs on, and acting is by necessity declamatory. The presence of Luria's female assistant helps define the state of the patient as that of pure emotion which has no verbal outlet, and that of the showman as pure intellect frightened by the simple idea of an emotion that might disturb the delicate system of memory on which he functions.

Technical credits are above average, in spite of the 16m print screened here, and music is functional, but insufficiently imaginative to put life into the 90 minutes this picture runs. —*Edna.*

Poisons
(SWISS-FRENCH-COLOR)

A Light Night presentation of a Light Night, Switzerland, Maison de la Culture du Havre, France, Television Suisse Romande coproduction. Written and directed by Pierre Maillard. Camera (color), Patrice Cologne; editor, Rodolfo Wedeles; music, Jacques Robellaz; sound, Pierre-Alain Besse; art direction and costumes, Laurence Bruley. Reviewed at the Locarno Film Festival, Aug. 8, 1987. Running time: **105 MINS.**
Northrup .... Maurice Garrel
Ann .... Mimsy Farmer
Loiseau .... Pierre Dubillard
Marc .... François Berthet
Lewis .... Rufus

Locarno — A handsomely shot allegory which never manages to function on a realistic level, Pierre Maillard's second feature film confirms his visual talents, but again faces serious narrative problems.

Bob Northrup, a famous painter, is kept prisoner in a secluded villa by three brothers, Jacques, Lewis and Marc Loiseau, with whom he obviously has been associated for a long time. The oldest, Jacques, an unctuous, oily crook, who is the leader of the trio, used to be the painter's agent. Lewis looks like a retarded goon relating only to his dogs and acting as a guard, while Marc, also known as Spirit, is an emotionally underdeveloped and childish character.

All three try to persuade Northrop to go back to his work, which is their only means of subsistence, but the artist, while putting up no physical opposition to his confinement, simply refuses to produce any more paintings.

The arrival in the middle of the night of a strange woman looking for him complicates matters, as there is no evident explanation for her presence in the villa or insistence on meeting the painter in person.

All this is highly metaphorical, referring to the relations between art and society, but the conclusions aren't very relevant, the plot goes around in circles, none of the characters comes alive and none of their actions is even lightly credible. Whether one accepts or rejects the theoretical point of view that an artist would rather have the dubious security of a jailed existence (like the symbolic goldfish in a bowl introduced twice in the film), as long as it saves him the trouble of facing reality himself, the argument put by Maillard is not sufficiently convincing.

Actors can't help overdoing their parts as they are given rather thin material, with Maurice Garrel, playing the withdrawn and enigmatic painter, coming out best for he is required to do the least. Camerawork is much more rewarding, successfully establishing a strange and moody atmosphere while drawing references to the world of painting. The musical score helps consistently all along, but without a stronger script these qualities are sadly wasted.
—*Edna.*

Three Bewildered People
In The Night
(U.S.-B&W-16m)

A Desparate Pictures production. Written, directed and edited by Gregg Araki; camera (b&w; 16m,) Araki. Revewed at the Locarno Film Festival (completing), Aug. 11, 1987. Running time: **92 MINS.**

Alicia .Darcy Marta
David . . . . .Mark Howell
Craig . . . . .John Lacques

Locarno — A juvenile soul-searching item long out of fashion, this 1-man operation which filmmaker Gregg Araki says cost only $3,000 to producer, has little to-recommend it.

The title fits it well enough, as it is about three rather uninteresting young persons, two men and a woman, all supposed to be over 25 but acting very adolescent in their despondent attempts to come to terms with life, art and sexuality.

Alicia is a video artist whose specialty is confessing in front of a camera, then watching the confessions. She lives with Craig, supposedly a journalist who wishes to go back to acting, and her best friend is David, a homosexual performance artist.

Professional life, however seems to be immaterial in their relationship, which goes on only at night, involves countless phone calls and revelatory conversations in which the vocabulary consists mostly of 4-letter words, and even those are limited in variety.

Running around in circles, Araki tries to show the dissolution of a heterosexual relationship, the establishment of a homosexual one and an ending in which both relationships are reconciled. The anguish which is supposed to trigger this drama is not quite clear, the plot has trouble doing anything except repeating itself, the characters are superficial at best and the actors are incapable of adding any personal dimension to their parts.

Wandering around coffeeshops, empty streets and galleries, the three protagonists are shot in grainy black and white, not very original but very difficult to take for a whole picture, without a moment of relief. There are several references to other filmmakers, such as Jean-Luc Godard and Jim Jarmusch, while the black patch covering David's eye brings to mind any number of famous directors who wore one before, from John Ford and Fritz Lang on.

It seems gay groups are pledging their support to this item, but outside these circles, the going may prove very tough. —*Edna.*

O Bobo
(The Jester)
(PORTUGUESE-COLOR)

An Animatografo Film production. Produced by Henrique Espirito Santo. Directed by José Alvaro Morais. Screenplay, Morais, from a play by Alexandre Herculano, adapted with Rafael Godinho; camera (color), 16m), Mário de Carvalho; editor, José Nascimento; music, Carlos Azevedo, Carlos Zingaro, Pedro Caldeira Cabral; sound, Vasco Pimentel; art direction, Jasmim. Reviewed at the Locarno Film Festival (competing), Aug. 15, 1987. Running time: **127 MINS.**

With: Fernando Heitor, Paula Guedes, Luis Lucas, Luisa Marques, Victor Ramos, Glicinia Quartim, Isabel Ruth, João Guedes, Maria Amélia Motta, Luis Miguel Cintra, Raúl Solnado.

Locarno — "The Jester" is a remarkably creative and fiendishly difficult to follow first film, whose production took years to complete and even then was rushed at the last moment to meet the Locarno Festival deadline.

The plot, evolving on several levels which reflect on each other, refers to Portuguese history, ancient and modern, to artistic expression and at some points even makes some tentative attempts at developing a thriller. The unifying basis of its all is a love affair going through an acute crisis.

The leading character is a theater director, rehearsing a 19th century historical play entitled "O Bobo" (The Jester), by Alexandre Herculano, about the foundation of 12th century monarchy in Portugal. The director also plays the Jester, mostly in modern dress while all other participants are in costume.

The person producing the play is an old friend of the director, once a dedicated member of the leftist resistance, now stuck with a package

of arms he tries to sell for profit to criminals, as his ideals have faded away.

Story is told in flashback, as the theater director and his girlfriend, a tv actress disenchanted with her career, are sitting in a bar after the body of the murdered producer has been found accidentally behind the sets in an old film studio used for rehearsals.

If that wasn't already sufficiently complicated, there is also the fact that some of the actors in the play are friends in real life, that there are relationships overlapping from one level to another, and there is constant use of voice-over, which means the audience is supposed to follow the story and a commentary on it at the same time. This approach may have been induced by the fact the film was shot silent, its sound added in postproduction.

In spite of the fact that it was shot in 16m, this is a stimulating visual experience, rich in imagination and in its use of color and movement. The distinction made by actors between over-stylized stage performance and loose conduct in modern dress may sometimes be a bit too forced, but the intentions are absolutely clear. The Locarno jury awarded it first prize. —*Edna.*

Aurelia
(ITALIAN-COLOR)

A Bim Distribution presentation of an Antea Film, Telecentauro production. Written and directed by Giorgio Molteni. Camera (color), Raffaele Mertes; editor, Carlo Fontana; music and songs, Paolo Conte; sound, Marco Grillo. Reviewed at the Locarno Film Festival, (competing), Aug. 12, 1987. Running time: **86 MINS.**

Guiditta . . . . .Maddalena Crippa
Tommaso . . . . .Fabio Sartor
Car driver . . . . .Nicola Pistoia
Truck driver . . . . .Carlo Monni
Bicyclist . . . . .Vittorio Crippa

Locarno — A road movie by definition, since the title refers to the name of a certain road in north Italy, this picture could have been much nicer if not for its predictability and pretensions.

Tommaso is a scientist hitchhiking on a beautiful summer day to his wedding. No car stops to pick him up until he is joined by Giudditta, a blond lady with short cropped hair. Together, this couple will spend two days on the way to the wedding, start a tentative romance which culminates in a torrid night of lovemaking, just as they reach their destination.

The film fails on two main counts. First, the brief affair between the two protagonists follows the oldest and most hackneyed rules of the genre. Second, the dialog between them is preposterously pretentious, a kind of tiresome philosophizing.

The camera is kept pretty close to the actors throughout, the scenery becoming almost irrevelant, more so since print looks very much like a mediocre blowup. Characters

joining in for a bit, on the road, and then disappearing, are never developed beyond the limits of a tentative joke, and the visual imagination of the director is sadly limited.

The only outlandish element is Paolo Conte's music, lending a certain ironic dimension.

Fabio Sartor as the timid scientist yearning for a last fling before his final commitment, and Maddalena Crippa, who could be interpreted as the incarnation of his sensual dreams, are not required to overstretch themselves in their roles.

Altogether, this eventually could serve as a latenight filler feature, but is hardly up to the standards of a fest competition. —*Edna.*

Odinokij Golos Celoveka
(Man's Solitary Voice)
(SOVIET-B&W/COLOR)

A Sovexportfilm presentation of a Lenfilm production. Directed by Aleksandr Sokurov. Screenplay, Jury Arabov, based on tales by Andrei Platonov; camera (b&w, color), Sergei Yourizditzky; editor, Sokurov; art direction, Vladimir Lebedev. Reviewed at the Locarno Film Festival (competition), Aug. 7, 1987. Running time: **90 MINS.**

With: Andrei Gradov, Tatiana Coriatcheva.

Locarno — Those who were mystified by Aleksandr Sokurov's outlandish adaptation of George Bernard Shaw's play "Heartbreak House," shown this year in Berlin, won't find much solace here, in an item made in 1978 but never unveiled until now.

A protégé of the late Andrei Tarkovsky, to whom this film is dedicated, Sokurov obviously tries to follow his master's steps in creating a kind of visual equivalent to verbal poetry, but he is much less coherent and quite often drifts into an obscurity whose necessity seems doubtful.

Based on stories by Andrei Platonov, the writer who inspired Andrei Konchalovsky's "Maria's Lovers," the film attempts to transmit the lyrical sense of the prose more than its narrative value. It deals with the emotional drainage of young people at the outset of the Russian revolution. A young man of evidently proletarian background returns to his village after "killing all the bourgeois" as his father ironically remarks, and marries a young girl whose parents obviously once belonged to the middle class. There is no way this couple can really work out, and this is substantiated in a series of images evoking their respective pasts.

Visually, the picture is very carefully fashioned, and in spite of mediocre quality of the print screened, it is often visually striking. It is difficult, however, to follow the pattern which determined his choice of images, or for that matter, the alternate use of black & white and color. Actors are asked to convey moods more than characters, the use of symphonic music, conducted by one of the foremost Russian musicians, Gennadi Rozhdestvensky, is remarkably effective, and so is the restless, tormented country landscape. —*Edna.*

Les Mendiants
(The Beggars)
(FRENCH-SWISS-COLOR)

A Marion's Films presentation of a Marion's Films, Les Prods. J.M.H., La Television Suisse Romande (TRS), La Sept production. Produced by Jean-Marc Henchoz, Sylvette Frydman. Directed by Benoit Jacquot. Screenplay, Jacquot, Pascal Bonitzer, based on novel by Louis-René de Forets; camera (color), Acacio de Almeida, José Antonio Loureiro, Karim Youkana, Denis Jutzeler; editor, Dominique Auvray, Isabelle Lorente, Marielle Babinet; music, Jorge Arriagada; sound, Laurent Barbey, Dominique Hennequin, Gita Cerveira; costumes, Renée Renard. Reviewed at the Locarno Film Festival (noncompeting), Aug. 13, 1987. Running time: **95 MINS.**
With: Dominique Sanda (Helene), Jean-Philippe Escoffey (Fred), Anne Rousel (Annabelle), Assane Fall (Gregoire), Pierre Forget (grandfather), Steve Baes (the Catalan), Judith Godreche (Catherine), Camille Clavel, Renaud Bernadet, Philippe Levy, François Nelias, Yann Marquand.

Locarno — Benoit Jacquot's reputation as a controversial director will remain intact after "The Beggars." Adapted from an existing novel with leading French critic Pascal Bonitzer, it draws parallel patterns of power and possession, betrayal and reprisals among criminals, for people in a love affair, and among children aping adults. The begging, implied by the film's title, refers obviously to the desperate need for affection which all the characters seem to have.

The adults smuggle drugs, the children just steal lemons for the fun of it, women take away men from other women. Two actors playing Othello and Desdemona on stage have an affair in real life which is just the opposite of the Shakespeare premise, culminating in her shooting him during a fit of jealousy after he has taunted her by flirting with another girl.

This could be made interesting had a real plot, with real characters, been supplied, but Jacquot's dramatic situations are barely sketched, plot is manipulative throughout, while acting and direction are on the hysterical side. This film offers little of the emotional or affective dimension needed to hold an audience.

Dominique Sanda, in her third film with Jacquot, seems to have acquired a certain detached style. This appears true of the other adult actors as well, while the children, who are supposed to carry an important part of the film, are not sufficiently secure in front of the camera.

Most likely destined for the festival circuit, the picture is bound to divide critical as well as audience opinion everywhere. The mixed reaction of the public on Locarno's Piazza Grande seems a fair indication of things to come.—*Edna.*

Avril Brisé
(Broken April)
(FRENCH-COLOR)

A JM Prods. presentation of a JM, Telema Smepa, La Franco American Films, La Sept, Icav. coproduction. Produced by Frédéric Mitterrand, Charles Gassot, Jacques Arnaud, Jacques Tronel, Denys Pleutot. Directed by Liria Begeja. Screenplay, Begeja, Olivier Assayas, Vassilis Vassilikos, based on novel by Ismail Kadaré; camera (color), Patrick Blossier; editor, Luc Barnier; music, Steve Beresford; sound, Eric Vaucher; production design, Michel Lagrange; costumes, Judy Shewsbury. Reviewed at the Locarno Film Festival (competing), Aug. 9, 1987. Running time: **100 MINS.**
Gjerg . . . . Jean-Claude Audelin
Diane Vorpsi . . . . Violeta Sanchez
Bessian Vorpsi . . . . Alexandre Arbatt
Also with: Sadri Sheta, Hasan Zhubi, Xhémil Vraniqi, Hajrédim Islamaj.

Locarno — On paper, this story must have seemed like a timely thing to do, what with the constant references nowadays to primitive societies, like Iran or in this instance Albania, and their bloodthirsty traditions, which the West is desperately trying to understand and cope with. In spite of a top writing team, including French critic and filmmaker Olivier Assayas, Greek writer Vassilis Vassilikos who wrote "Z," not to mention the novel by Ismail Kadaré, probably the best known Albanian author, the result is not much more than a flat, esoteric curiosity.

Undecided whether to take the ethnographic way and focus mainly on customs and stress authenticity, or develop the plot and the characters in depth, director Liria Begeja falls short on both counts, for her picture, shot in Corsica, can't pretend to deliver the real scenic sights, and the story, as presented by her, is wooden and schematic.

Action takes place on a remote and desolate plateau, in 1933, among mountain people ruled by the Kanun, a fierce and pitiless code of honor. Gjerg Berisha is a young man who has just tried to avenge the death of his brother by killing the murderer, in a family feud which has been going on for 100 years and already has taken 44 lives. Now that he has done it, he is in line as the next victim for the members of the family to take revenge upon.

The central Albanian government, only recently installed after centuries of Turkish occupation, is trying to put a stop to this barbarous custom and sends an emissary, trained abroad, to bring Gjerg to the capital to stand trial. The emissary, Vorpsi, brings along his new French wife, who feels lost and forlorn in the strange country and among the strange people she does not understand, but who develops a keen affection for the doomed Gjerg.

Vorpsi's modern ideas clash with the old iron laws of the mountain, which nobody dares challenge, and what's more, nobody wishes to, since this is an integral part of their national heritage.

This point is insufficiently made, the absolute necessity of the Kanun for this society is not evident and therefore, instead of understanding the fascination its majesty might have on a foreigner encountering them for the first time, as it happens in the film, one is rather annoyed by the stubborn primitive customs and can't help feeling there isn't a reason in the world to respect the people who stick by them.

The trouble is more serious because characters are sketched only tentatively, lack depth or interest and therefore leave the audience quite indifferent to their problems. Acting is no help either, the professionals looking amateurish and the amateurs, in the smaller parts, lacking that authenticity which would compensate for the inevitable clumsiness.

Editing can't improve on a rhythm missing from script and direction, and camerawork makes great efforts to impose a dark mood by making even daylight look murky and ominous.

In Locarno, the filmmaker, who is of Albanian origins, said she hopes her picture will improve relations between France and Albania. It is difficult to see how. — *Edna.*

Checkpoint
(U.S.-COLOR)

A New Film Group, MTA production. Executive producer, Mary Apick. Written, produced and directed by Parviz Sayyad. Camera (color), Michael Davis; editor, Sayyad; music, Ahmad Pejman; sound, Youssef Shahab, Andrew Herbert; assistant director, Bob Yari. Reviewed at the Locarno Film Festival (competing), Aug. 14, 1987. Running time: **91 MINS.**
With: Mary Apick (Firouzeh), Houshang Touzie (Kazem), Peter Spreague (Mike), Mark Nichols (Bob), Buck Kartalian (Frank), Michael Zand (Farhad), Mayeva Martin (Kate), Ali Poutash (Hatam), Ali F. Dean (Ali), Masha Manesh (Abe), Zohreh Ramsey (Zari), Keyvan Nekoui (Iraj), Parviz Sayyad (Younesi).

Locarno — Based on a real incident, evidently adapted to suit the requirements of filmmaker Parviz Sayyad, this story concerns a busload of Iranian students who were not allowed to come back into the United States after a vacation day in Canada, victims of the improvised reprisals devised in 1980 by President Carter as a response to the hostage situation in Teheran.

Sayyad is obviously anti-Khomeini, rejecting everything taking place in his home country lately. This was evident in his previous film "The Mission," also shown in Locarno. Now he goes a step further, expressing his disgust with the Iranian revolution.

The situation lends itself perfectly to this purpose. The bus is stuck a whole night in no man's land, between the U.S. and Canada, and the eight Iranian students on it, together with three Americans who refuse to leave them on their own, have ample time to discuss their differences of opinions.

Sayyad states his position quite clearly. For him, everybody connected with the revolution, whether the religious or the political one, is immediately labeled a villain, a definition further stressed as the characters slip into revelatory speeches.

Needless to say, fanatics remain fanatics, more repellent the louder they get, and Sayyad, who uses one of the girls, Firouzeh (played by exec producer Mary Apick), as his spokeswoman most of the time, can't resist the temptation to step in himself, as an Iranian electronics engineer who has made it in America and has all the right answers to explain the Iranian tragedy.

The message the film tries to convey is a bit too simplistic for its own good. It rejects outright any justification for what happened in Iran and avoids dealing with it, by showing only the reflections of the events on young Iranians abroad, identified by their political creeds. Not much is said about their social and personal background, or who's paying their tuition.

Many of the things said in the heated exchange of opinions are relevant, but it is akin to attending a symposium on Iranian problems consisting of a series of speeches given by intelligent and logical pro-Western speakers and opposed by strident, incoherent fanatics.

Acting, on the whole, may not be very sophisticated but is committed and determined, the performers obviously intimately familiar with the types they play. Characters lack personal depth, being mostly concerned with delivering their soliloquies in the director's biased spirit.

As much as one feels like agreeing with Sayyad, it is a pity he didn't make a better case for himself and his positions, by giving some credit to his characters and his audience that they are able to perceive the truth even if it is not stated in black and white notions.—*Edna.*

A Dos Aguas
(The Entire Life)
(ARGENTINE-COLOR)

A Metropolis World Sales presentation of a Jorge Estrada Mora & Avica production. Executive producer, Sabine Sigler. Directed by Carlos Olguin. Screenplay, Olguin, Martha Gavensky; camera (color), Rodolfo Denevi; editor, Armando Blanco, Jorge Valencia; music, Rodolfo Mederos; sound, Mario Antognini; art direction, Julio Lavallen; producer delegate, Jorge Sabate. Reviewed at the Locarno Film Festival (competition), Aug. 10, 1987. Running time: **74 MINS.**
Rey . . . . Miguel Angel Sola
Isabel . . . . Barbara Mugica
Maria . . . . Cipe Lincovsky
Also with: Aldo Braga (Patricio/Weintraub), Jorge Sassi (Rey's alter ego), Osvaldo Tesser, Monica Lacoste, Mario Sanchez Rivera, Antonio Ugo.

Locarno — "The Entire Life" is one more Argentine picture dealing with the trauma of the country's fascist past, the heavy guilt complex carried by its survivors and the efforts to adapt again to a normal existence.

The plot concerns two characters heavily marked by this period, who had tried to get away and are now back in the country. The man, Rey, escaped an authoritarian father and returned only for his funeral, but the parent's heavy influence is present constantly in the son's mind to such an extent he is shown physically (he has one leg in a cast for most of the picture) as well as emotionally impaired. The woman, Isabel, had to leave the country after her lover disappeared, leaving behind her husband and her son whom she comes to help recuperate many years later.

The message director Carlos Olguin appears to convey here is that the load of the past cannot be divested in five minutes, a phrase repeated several times, that the departure of the fascist regime has caused an over-relaxation of moral standards, and that only time, understanding and true commitment can heal the old wounds.

Since Rey, who studied law under his father's pressure but always wanted to be a film director, is preparing to shoot his picture, this can also be interpreted as both the real story of Isabel and Rey, who were close to each other 15 years earlier, at the university, but this can also be the result of Rey's first efforts, as it is clearly indicated the script he intends to shoot is autobiographical.

Olguin however, lays his symbolic messages with such a heavy hand, with painted sets and trumpeted intentions possibly because he has to hide the lack of a real script or the development of real characters. If anything, the film is more a statement than a dramatic experience, and even at 74 minutes it still seems too long.

A Gardel tango used often in the score compensates for emotional impact otherwise lacking.—*Edna.*

With Love To The Person Next To Me
(AUSTRALIAN-COLOR)

A Standard Films Ltd. production. Produced by John Cruthers. Directed by Brian McKenzie. Screenplay, McKenzie; camera (Fujicolor), Ray Argall; editor, Argall, David Greig; sound, Mark Tarpey; production design, Kerith Holmes; production manager, Daniel Scharf; assistant director, Deborah Hoare; casting, Liz Mullinar. Reviewed at Dendy theater, Sydney, Aug. 6, 1987. (In Locarno and Edinburgh Film Festivals.) Running time: **98 MINS.**

Wallace	Kim Gyngell
Sid	Paul Chubb
Bodger	Barry Dickins
Gail	Sally McKenzie
Irene	Beverley Gardiner
Drunken passenger	Phil Motherwell

Sydney — An almost Germanic exercise in urban alienation, this low-budget drama belongs to the same school of cinema as other Melbourne-based pics such as "The Plains Of Heaven" and "Wrong World;" as such, it will attract critical attention, and some fest exposure, but will be a very, very tough sell in the commercial market.

Setting is a sleazy suburb near the waterfront where Wallace (Kim Gyngell), a taxi-driver, lives a lonely, solitary life; his only hobby is making apple cider, which he does continually. His neighbor, Gail (Sally McKenzie) is an outgoing shoe-factory worker frustrated by her relationship with the oafish Sid (Paul Chubb), her live-in lover who, together with his mate, Bodger (Barry Dickins) is forever bringing home stolen electrical goods.

Before long, the police catch up with Sid and Bodger, but not before Gail has moved away. Wallace, meanwhile, has taken to secretly taping the conversations of his passengers and playing them back at home later. They're mostly the usual cross-section of drunks and loudmouths, but Wallace is especially moved by one woman (Beverley Gardiner) who pours out to him a long monolog about her unhappy childhood (her father had sold her into prostitution) and how it's affecting her as an adult.

This is the first dramatic feature of Brian McKenzie, who previously scored with an award-winning short docu, "Winter Harvest," and two feature docus, "I'll Be Home For Christmas" (about city down-and-outs) and "The Last Day's Work" (about the daily grind of workers). It's not surprising, then, that there's a strong documentary feel to his new film, with Ray Argall's outstanding photography capturing in minute detail the events and places where the story unfolds, especially Wallace's shabby, ant-infested apartment.

As with McKenzie's docus, however, "With Love To The Person Next To Me" is ultimately too slowly paced, and too remote, to grab a wide audience. The viewer can admire McKenzie's rigorous approach to his material, while feeling alienated from it, despite the good performances involved (with Paul Chubb, as the awful Sid, a standout).

Ultimately, the film goes nowhere. It climaxes with another long monolog in which Wallace himself pours out his troubles into the tape recorder — the only way, it seems, he can cope with his miserable existence. It's an unsatisfactory ending to a tantalizing film — tantalizing because there's imagination and talent on display here, but never satisfactorily resolved.

Pic should play the fest circuit, where its true audience lies; this month, it's to unspool in Locarno and Edinburgh. Finding a paying audience will be another matter altogether.—*Strat.*

● ●
Moscow Fest Reviews
● ●

Severny Anekdot
(A Bad Joke)
(SOVIET-COLOR)

A Mosfilm production. Written and directed by Alexander Alov, Vladimir Naumov. Camera (color), Anatoli Kuznetsov; music, Nikolai Karetnikov. Reviewed at the Moscow Film Festival, July 16, 1987. Running time: **98 MINS.**

Pseudonimov	Evstigneev Sergachev

Moscow — The well-known directing team of Alexander Alov and Vladimir Naumov, makers of many respectable films with patriotic themes ("Pavel Korchagin"), passed through a troubled period with the authorities after they made "the "the wrong version of Dostoevsky" "A Bad Joke." It isn't hard to guess what bothered the stodgy censors about this 1965 film, recently okayed for release. It really is a wild, off-the-wall farce, bursting with grotesque characters, sets that look like outtakes from "The Cabinet Of Dr. Caligari," and music deliberately unconnected to the visuals. Pic is nothing if not bold and ambitious, but unfortunately Alov and Naumov often overreach themselves and the attempt to pull it all off isn't entirely successful. Though certainly of historical interest, "A Bad Joke" is tiresomely hard to follow and numbingly repetitive. After once being censored as too avant garde, film paradoxically suffers from a dated, academic look today.

Hero of the yarn is Pseudonimov (Evstigneev Sergachev), a nervous young bridegroom; like all the other poor folk in the film, he looks like he was sketched by Daumier, bulbous nose and all. His bride is a real horror and the raucous, rowdy guests a motley crew. Suddenly, a sinister figure appears out of nowhere to cast a pall on the merrymaking: His Excellency, a man of unlimited power and malevolent whimsy. He terrorizes the company, until they all get so drunk they forget to be afraid of him, and the soused demagog himself slips under the table and starts talking to people's shoes. Though intermittently funny, wedding is a long, drawn-out affair, lensed with camera tricks like a fish-eye lens, extra-low ceiling, etc.

Finally the scene changes and exhausted Pseudonimov has a chance to introduce his wife to the bridal chamber. They fight and he ends up sleeping with a drunken stranger. His Excellency also spends the night. Luckily there are no serious repercussions from the uninvited guest; in fact, by pic's end the tables are turned, and His Excellency is inexplicably out on the street in front of Pseudonimov's lopsided house, begging.

Technical work is top class, notably Anatoli Kuznetsov's lensing and Nikolai Karetnikov's score.—*Yung.*

Interventsia
(Intervention)
(SOVIET-COLOR)

A Lenfilm production. Directed by Gennady Poloka. Screenplay, Lev Slavine; camera (color), Vladimir Bourykine; music lyrics, Vladimir Vysotsky. Reviewed at the Moscow Film Festival, July 15, 1987. Running time: **94 MINS.**

Michel Voronov	Vladimir Vysotsky
Also with: Y. Bouriguine.	

Moscow — Gennady Poloka, a popular director who is still active, had a run-in with the censors over his single experimental picture "Intervention," produced by Lenfilm in 1968 and released this year. Commissioned to make a film commemorating the 50th anni of the October revolution, Poloka managed to get a complete version shown on the eve of the 70th. The director's idea was to "avoid canonizing the image of the revolution" while making a hit film; result looks like what might happen if, for example, Godard and Fellini joined forces in '68 to co-direct a cabaret show with the Red Army. Bizarre by any account, "Intervention" is an astonishing way to approach a patriotic film.

Though of mainly historical interest today, pic is bright, fast moving and certainly a rare enough species to merit some festival exposure.

Pic was lensed entirely in the studio, using colorful theatrical sets that aim to be a cross between Meyerhold and Brecht. Setting is Odessa, where bourgeois capitalists made up like clowns, police and the Army are hunting revolutionaries. Opening scene has a row of fat chorus girls poured into band uniforms, while in the background a dress parade dances as it marches, and a general makes calculations about military spending on an abacus.

Film sets a frantic pace of nonstop talk and madcap antics from the beginning. Dialog is said to be in racy Odessa argot spiced with underworld slang and swearing. Hero is the uncatchable Communist agitator named Brodsky or Voronov; he's cooly limned by Vladimir Vysotsky, who at the time wasn't yet an underground singing idol, but whose screen charisma is obvious. Zhena, son of a rich woman who tries to ship out before the revolution overtakes Odessa, is attracted to the Communists and particularly to pretty Sasha, but he sells out to gangsters, businessmen and the cops to pay his gambling debts, and dies an Enemy of the Working

Class. Brodsky dies a hero's death in prison.

Running from surrealism to broad farce and slapstick, "Intervention" boasts sophisticated sets (a brothel, a Jewish pharmacy), music recalling the '20s (plus some lyrics by Vysotsky), top-class thesps, and rapid-fire editing. — Yung.

Pesaro Festival Reviews

Rodnik Dlia Zhazhdushchikh
(A Fountain For The Thirsty)
(SOVIET-B&W)

A Dovzhenko Studio production. Directed by Yuri Ilienko. Screenplay, Dratch; camera (b&w), Ilienko. (No other credits available.) Reviewed at the Pesaro Film Festival, June 20, 1987. Running time: **70 MINS.**
With: Miliutenko, Alisova, Kadochnikova, Majouga, Erchov.

Pesaro — This 1965 work by Yuri Ilienko, Ukranian director best known for "The White Bird With Black Markings" made five years later, is one of the more important shelved films now being released in the USSR. Subtitled "a film parable," "A Fountain For The Thirsty" offers an austere impression of the life of an old man and some members of his family on the edge of a desert. Spendidly lensed by the director-cameraman in black and white, it is visually experimental to the point of abstraction, a film for connoisseurs rather than the general public, but unquestionably top of its class.

It's hard to extract a story from this overexposed landscape of memory, even with the help of occasional titles like "A Coffin Is Needed." Dialog is minimal. Life revolves around a well, where the occasional passerby comes to drink. A montage of faces shows all the people whose thirst has been slaked. During the war, a soldier is shot at the well. Later, a grim war memorial is erected, while an old woman cries. Film conveys an overwhelming impression of sadness; besides a house and the well, the only piece of scenery in this desolate wasteland is a sandy graveyard.

Ilienko's expressive images sometimes veer towards surrealism, at other times take on an almost documentary realism. Viewer is left to interpret two brides observing a coffin, or the old man imprisoned in his well. Then, when you're least expecting it, a jet flies overhead and a family arrives by car for a visit, bringing a tape recorder as a present.

Lensing and editing are masterful and always foregrounded. Though practically a silent film, "Fountain" uses sound inventively in contrast to the image — falling trees, for example, or kids shouting in the middle of the desert. Actors are icon-like. — Yung.

Prosti
(Forgive Me)
(SOVIET-COLOR)

A Lenfilm production. Directed by Ernest Jassan. Screenplay, Viktor Merezhko; camera (Widescreen, color), Ivan Bagaev; editor, C. Tanaeva; music, Vadim Bibergan; art direction, Stanislav Romanovski. Reviewed at the Pesaro Film Festival, June 22, 1987. Running time: **82 MINS.**
Masha . . . . Natalia Andreichenko
Kiril . . . . Igor Kostolevski
Vladimir . . . . Viktor Merezhko
Also with: Alexandra Yakovleva (Natasha), Alisa Friendlich (Elisaveta Andreevna), Vladimir Menshov, Alexi Zarkov, Tatiana Mikhailova.

Pesaro — A hard-hitting commercial entry from Lenfilm director Ernest Jassan, "Forgive Me" is a modern comedy-drama centered on a young wife who discovers her husband has a mistress. Scripted by Viktor Merezhko and starring Natalia Andreichenko, who have both worked with Nikita Mikhalkov, film has made waves in the USSR, and could be aimed at foreign audiences interested in Russian films.

Masha (Andreichenko) is a modern woman who has a nice apartment, a job in a research lab and a daughter she mostly neglects. The revelation that her loving husband is having an affair takes her completely by surprise. Though not a moralist like some of the women in her lab, Masha is shattered (most of this part of film is played in a comic vein) and furiously throws the errant husband out of the house.

Her friends invite her to parties to meet men. A taxi driver who knows the story tries to taker her home, but his own wife turns up unexpectedly. Masha stumbles out the door into the night, and pic takes a tragic turn: she gets raped by a gang of toughs. She wanders home in a terrible state and probably makes up with her husband, who says he'll leave his girlfriend.

A fine cast is dominated by Andreichenko's tough and not always likable heroine. Though the final rape is above-the-lines as a plot device, story as a whole unfolds convincingly at a steady pace. Technically it's pro. — Yung.

Fala
(Wave)
(POLISH-DOCU-COLOR)

A Karol Irzykowski Studio (Warsaw) production. Written and directed by Piotr Lazarkiewicz. Camera (color), Julian Szczerkowski, Andrzej Wolf, Walderma Kolosicki; sound,

Magdalena Sliwa. Reviewed at Pesaro Film Festival, June 19, 1987. Running time: **82 MINS.**

Pesaro — The new generation of Polish teens is the subject of this feature docu by young documaker Piotr Lazarkiewicz, embedded into a Woodstock-like account of the 1985 rock festival in Jarocin. Here the main thing's not the music but the lyrics, and the right-on response of some 20,000 kids camped out for the concert.

"Wave" offers a rare glimpse of young Poles today, whose profoundly apolitical, live-for-the-moment attitude may strike some Westerners as surprisingly Western and jaded. Had Lazarkiewicz edited it with a few more surprises, pic could have gone beyond its current fest run.

The scenario can be imagined: thousands of teens stripped to shorts and bikinis swarm into a fenced-off site on the outskirts of a picturesque little town. Filmer asks the kids questions like, what do you think the future will bring? They have no idea and nothing to say. A procession of groups onstage sing songs full of post-punk nihilism with religious overtones. In tv interviews, the mayor, police chief and local organizers show some nervousness, but they offer smiling reassurances law and order will be maintained and affirm rock is beautiful. Incredibly, one authority even claims the kids "somehow express a consensus for our national goals," but the image hardly bears him out.

There is a beauty pageant, a nude rock group, and two young priests hearing confessions. There is a collection taken for starving kids in Ethiopia, and a club of picketing "squares" opposed to decadent rock lyrics. Mostly there is a strong current of empathy between musicians and listeners, united in their rebellion against the world they've been handed; a generalized, not especially political discontent that appears largely contained within the limits of the police cordon. — Yung.

Lionheart
(COLOR)

Limp medieval tale.

An Orion Pictures release of a Taliafilm II production. Produced by Stanley O'Toole, Talia Shire. Executive producers, Francis Coppola, Jack Schwartzman. Directed by Franklin J. Schaffner. Screenplay, Menno Meyjes, Richard Outten; story by Meyjes; camera (color), Alec Mills; editor, David Bretherton, Richard Haines; music, Jerry Goldsmith; production design, Gil Parrondo; costumes, Nana Cecchi; production supervisor, Scott Wodehouse; assistant director, Gary Daigler. Reviewed at Cineplex Odeon Canada Square theater, Toronto, Aug. 18, 1987. (MPAA Rating: PG.) Running time: **104 MINS.**
Robert Nerra . . . . Eric Stoltz
The Black Prince . . . . Gabriel Byrne
Blanche . . . . Nicola Cowper
Michael . . . . Dexter Fletcher
Mathilda . . . . Deborah Barrymore
Charles de Montfort . . . . Nicholas Clay
Simon Nerra . . . . Bruce Purchase
King Richard . . . . Neil Dickson
Odo . . . . Chris Pitt

Toronto — The Children's Crusades of the 12th century is the subject of Franklin J. Schaffner's "Lionheart," a flaccid, limp kiddie adventure yarn with little of its intended grand epic sweep realized. Based partly on myth, partly on historical accounts, the story concerns bands of medieval tykes who set out to search for the elusive King Richard II on his quest to recapture the Holy Land from the Moslems.

This pic should have set out on a campaign for a credible screenplay. It'll be quite iffy at the boxoffice and should head straight for the homevideo shelves.

Young knight Robert Nerra (Eric Stoltz) rides off disillusioned from his first battle and meets up with mystical Blanche (pretty Nicola Cowper) and her brother Michael (Dexter Fletcher), two teen circus performers who convince him to travel to Paris and join King Richard's crusade. Along the way the trio enlists a limping con artist tyke Odo, a blond thief Baptista, and King R.'s falconer, Hugo.

The dark threat of the Black Prince looms overhead in all corners of the misty forest. Gabriel Byrne plays him like an ennui-stricken Darth Vader. His goal is to recruit all the kids and sell them into slavery. The youngsters also have adventures in the secret underground world of orphans in 12th century Paris.

The whole ragtag band, under Stoltz' disjointed leadership, has the ultimate confrontation with the Black Prince at an impressively recreated medieval castle by the sea at the pic's finale.

Menno Meyjes' ("The Color Purple") and Richard Outten's script is full of high ideals that never gel. It's very nice to protect the downtrodden and innocent, but these kids just don't seem to have what it takes.

There's unintentional hilarity in the lines, too. When the group meets up with Mathilda (Roger

Moore's daughter Deborah Barrymore), who reveals her female identity after winning a tough jousting contest, her Lord/Dad pouts, "I don't want you to bring me honor. I want you to bring me a son-in-law."

Schaffner shot the pic in Hungary and Portugal and recruited hundreds of Slavic kids to play the orphans. They do about as well as the leads. Stoltz sleepwalks through his role and Cowper is all pouty and teary-eyed at life's injustices, but there's spirit in Dexter Fletcher's dreamy Michael and Chris Pitt's sneaky Odo.

Locations in medieval fortresses and scenes of Middle Ages entertainment and large feasts (including 4 and 20 doves flying out of a pie) recreate the period well, in spite of the choppy editing and surfeit of solid dialog.—*Devo.*

The Year My Voice Broke
(AUSTRALIAN-COLOR)

A Kennedy-Miller production. Produced by George Miller, Doug Mitchell, Terry Hayes. Directed by John Duigan. Screenplay, Duigan; camera (color), Geoff Burton; editor, Neil Thumpston; music coordinator, Christine Woodruff; production design, Roger Ford; sound, Ross Linton; production manager, Dixie Betts; assistant director, Charles Rotherham; associate producer, Barbara Gibbs; casting Alison Barrett. Reviewed at Chauvel theater, Sydney July 23, 1987. Running time: **103 MINS.**
Danny Embling . . . . Noah Taylor
Freya Olson . . . . Loene Carmen
Trevor . . . . Ben Mendelsohn
Nils Olson . . . . Graeme Blundell
Anne Olson . . . . Lynette Curran
Bruce Embling . . . . . . Malcolm Robertson
Sheila Embling . . . . Judi Farr
Bob Leishman . . . . Tim Robertson
Jonah . . . . Bruce Spence
Tom Alcock . . . . Harold Hopkins
Sgt. Pierce . . . . Nick Tate
Headmaster . . . . Vincent Ball
   Also with: Anja Coleby (Gail Olson), Kylie Ostara (Alison), Kelly Dingwall (Barry), Dorothy St. Heaps (Mrs. Beal), Coleen Clifford (Gran Olson), Kevin Manser (Mr. Keith), Mary Regan (Miss McColl), Queenie Ashton (Mrs. O'Neil), Helen Lomas (Sally), Emma Lyle (Lisa), Louise Birgan (Lyn), Matthew Ross (Malseed), Allan Penney (Martin), Robert Carlton (Pierdon).

Sydney — The difference between the Australian (and British) approach to teenage films as opposed to the usual treatment of teens in Yank pics is once again demonstrated in John Duigan's "The Year My Voice Broke," an outstanding new low-budget feature from Kennedy-Miller which has been nominated in several key categories for the upcoming Australian film awards.

Duigan's approach to his characters is realistic and humanistic: he tells a familiar tale of kids struggling with their emotions and feelings as they find themselves approaching adulthood, but doesn't sensationalize or condescend. These are real characters in real, sometimes painful, situations.

Setting is a small country town (pic was shot in Braidwood, N.S.W.) in 1962. Danny (Noah Taylor) and Freya (Loene Carmen) have been friends from childhood: his parents run the local pub, hers the local cafe. They've spent so much time together when they were growing up that there's even a kind of telepathy between them.

Now Danny is confused and troubled because Freya, though she's the same age he is, is maturing far more rapidly. She starts, as she tells him, to "move in different circles," and she falls heavily for Trev (Ben Mendelsohn), an older, hyperactive, football coach. Poor Danny can only hang around on the sidelines as his girl passes him by, and a trip to the local cinema with her younger sister is no compensation.

Things turn out badly: Freya gets pregnant, Trev gets in trouble with the law. Danny tries to help his friends, but an old scandal involving Freya's mother, who died giving birth to her, surfaces causing more distress. Ultimately, Freya leaves town for the city, and Danny knows he'll never see her again.

All of this is handled by John Duigan, who penned the original screenplay, with insight and understatement. The characters are memorable ones, and beautifully played by the three young newcomers, with Noah Taylor especially effective as the lovesick Danny. Supporting roles are played by a fine roster of familiar Aussie thesps, including Bruce Spence as an eccentric writer who befriends the youngsters (he lives in an abandoned railway carriage and is busily writing what he hopes will be the first "truly erotic" Australian novel), Graeme Blundell and Lynette Curran as Freya's adoptive parents and Malcolm Robertson and Judi Farr as Danny's parents. Even small roles, such as the local police sergeant and the headmaster, are played by such seasoned performers as Nick Tate and Vincent Ball.

Geoff Burton's attractive camerawork makes the most of the smalltown setting, with its pub, cafe, school, church hall, swimming hole and even haunted house on the edge of town. Setting and characters are completely convincing. Film ends on a very touching note, with Duigan and his actors evoking a genuinely sad moment without resorting to sentimentality.

Duigan, whose previous films include such stand-outs as "Mouth to Mouth" and "Winter Of Our Dreams" has been working in television lately. His excellent work on this new feature ranks as his best. It should be snagged by fests in coming months, and in Australia will play theatrically in October before appearing on the Ten network during 1988.—*Strat.*

Born In East L.A.
(COLOR)

Good-natured solo vehicle for Cheech.

A Universal Picture release of a Clear Type production. Produced by Peter Macgregor-Scott. Executive producer, Stan Coleman. Written and directed by Richard (Cheech) Marin. Stars Marin. Camera (CFI color, Deluxe prints), Alex Phillips; editor, Don Brochu; music, Lee Holdridge; art direction, J. Rae Fox, Lynda Burbank, Hector Rodriguez; set decoration, Steven Karatzas, Enrique Estevez; costume design, Isabella Van Soest; sound, William B. Kaplan; assistant director, Javier Carreno; casting, Junie Lowry. Reviewed at the Hollywood Pacific, L.A., Aug. 21, 1987. (MPAA Rating: R.) Running time: **84 MINS.**
Rudy . . . . Cheech Marin
Javier . . . . Paul Rodriguez
Jimmy . . . . Daniel Stern
Dolores . . . . Kamala Lopez
McCalister . . . . Jan-Michael Vincent
Marcie . . . . Neith Hunter
Gloria . . . . Alma Martinez
Feo . . . . Tony Plana

Hollywood — "Born In East L.A.," Cheech Marin's first solo outing after years of partnership with Tommy Chong, proves to be an amiable, moderately amusing cross-cultural comedy. Unscreened in advance by Universal, shaggy pic generated quite a few laughs among the largely Hispanic crowd on hand opening day on Hollywood Boulevard and could collect some okay late summer coin in urban and Southwestern situations.

A simple tale of a misunderstanding resulting in no end of comic woe for the hero, film has L.A. native Cheech inadvertently picked up in an immigration service raid and unceremoniously dumped, along with a bunch of illegals, south of the border.

Without identification or cash, Cheech, who is useless at speaking Spanish, is forced to live by his wits while figuring out a way to get back to the U.S. While wit may not be the most exact definition of Cheech's brand of humor, the man is quick on his feet and has a keen ear for jokes, musical or otherwise, based on pop culture.

Forced to take what he can get, Cheech goes to work in Tijuana for smalltime gringo operator Daniel Stern and makes quite a success as a barker for a sleazy club. He also draws tattoos, sells oranges, sings on streetcorners, gets thrown in the clink a couple of times and attracts the attention of a lovely young lady from El Salvador who herself is working to make the trip north.

When he gets fed up with waiting to go home, Cheech tries to outsmart the border guards, and one of the funniest and most irreverent moments has him leading hundreds of Latinos streaming down a hillside to the strains of Neil Diamond's "America." He also gets good mileage out of a routine in which he teaches a bunch of dimwitted Chinese and Indians the right "atti-

tude" and street smarts in preparation for their inevitable arrival in the land of cool.

Pic stands or falls on a moment-by-moment basis, but actually gets stronger as it goes along and even works up a little unabashed sentiment toward the end. A running gag involving Cheech's moronic cousin played by comedian Paul Rodriguez, is pretty embarrassing, and technical credits are quite rudimentary, but there are more laughs than in the last few Cheech & Chong efforts and the film seems good hearted, so it could have been a lot worse.
—*Cart.*

Trespasses
(COLOR)

Unconvincing melodrama.

A Shapiro Entertainment release of an XIT production. Executive producer, Robert J. Kuhn. Produced by Loren Bivens, Richard Rosetta. Directed by Bivens, Adam Roarke. Screenplay, Bivens, Lou Diamond Phillips, Jo Carol Pierce; camera (Allied/WBS color), Monte Dhooge, Phil Curry; editor, Sherri Galloway; music, Wayne Bell, Chuck Pennell; sound, Bell, Brian Hansen; art direction, Becky Block, Lisa Kight; associate director, John Woodward; associate producers, Dede Clark, JuaNita Mullins. Reviewed on Academy Home Entertainment vidcassette, N.Y., Aug. 15, 1987. (MPAA Rating: R.) Running time: **100 MINS.**
Franklin . . . . Robert Kuhn
Richard . . . . Van Brooks
Sharon Rae . . . . Mary Pillot
Drifters . . . . Adam Roarke,
                              Lou Diamond Phillips
August Klein . . . . Ben Johnson
Catherine . . . . Deborah Neumann
Johnny . . . . Thom Meyer
Johnny's girlfriend . . . . Marina Rice
Robin . . . . KaRan Reed
Gibby . . . . George Sledge
   Also with: Lou Perry, John Henry Faulk.

"Trespasses" is a Texas-made melodrama that proves that the lightning that made "Blood Simple" a sleeper hit doesn't necessarily strike twice. Filmmaker Loren Bivens is working from similar hothouse material but fails to come up with the style and thrills of the earlier Coen Bros. effort. Pic was shot in 1983 under the moniker "Forgive Us Our Trespasses."

Executive producer Robert Kuhn toplines as Franklin Ramsey, a simple cattle farmer who, in a poorly integrated prolog, learns the perils of being a good samaritan, when he and his son Johnny (Thom Meyer) fight with two thugs (codirector Adam Roarke and cowriter Lou Diamond Phillips) who are raping neighbor Mary Pillot at her farm. Phillips kills Johnny and the thugs escape.

Six months later, the killers are still on the loose. Pillot's dad (Ben Johnson), who runs the local bank, dies, leaving her Yankee husband (Van Brooks) in charge.

Melodramatic gimmick that makes the plot tick is that Pillot and Kuhn feel a bond from the traumatic rape incident and fall in love. Hubbie Brooks actually witnessed the rape but was too gutless to help out. When he finds out about the adulterous affair he seeks revenge. Totally improbable twist has Roarke and Phillips, fresh from a police lineup, hired by Brooks to poison Kuhn's cattle. Kuhn catches the thugs in the act, kills them in self-defense and plot unravels as Brooks spirals to suicide.

Acting is way too lowkey by the leads, especially comatose Kuhn and Brooks. With a mournful musical score, picture is sleep-inducing rather than suspenseful. Only point of interest is the presence of Phillips, currently the hot star as Ritchie Valens in "La Bamba," very convincing with moustache as an evil young heavy. —*Lor.*

A Fior di Pelle
(Skin Deep)
(ITALIAN-COLOR)

A Fiordifilm Milano production. Directed by Gianluca Fumagalli. Screenplay, Edoardo Erba, Roberto Traverso, Fumagalli; camera (color), Fabio Cianchetti; editor, Osvaldo Bargero; music, Roberto Cacciapaglia. Reviewed at the Locarno Film Festival (competing), Aug. 9, 1987. Running time: **85 MINS.**
With: Mariella Valentini, Claudio Bisio, John Murphy, Athina Cenci.

Locarno — The practically untranslatable title refers to an acutely sensitive state of mind, akin to that of an open wound.

In this case, it refers to two characters, a man and a woman, each one of them alone after an abortive love affair, and trying to re-establish a sort of equilibrium in their emotional life. Most of the action focuses on these two persons only, as they alternatively support, hurt and test each other.

The most promising sequence comes at the very beginning, when the young woman, enrolled in a drama course, is forced by her instructor (during rehearsals of improvised scenes) to face her own sensuality in its darker and uncontrollable aspects.

Later, after she discovers her boyfriend has fallen in love with another woman, she allows herself to be picked up by a biker, she is made love to brutally by a strange man in front of his wife, then goes back to the biker for a series of tentative trysts through which they try to establish a relationship, without being too sure they really want it as the memory of the previous affairs still looms heavy over them.

If the opening theater rehearsal sequences hold a lot of promise, this is soon dispelled by a script which seems to have serious difficulties making up its mind which way to go, and by direction which doesn't help the thin narrative much.

Most of the physical sensuality, for that is the film's main concern, far more than emotions, stems from the personality of Mariella Valenti-

ni, helped by John Murphy's shrewdly controlled cameo as the drama instructor. Claudio Bisio has trouble conveying the brittleness of his character.

While sex and passion are constantly in the forefront, the film is relatively tame. Still, feminists may be easily inclined to protest some statements that female sexuality requires a strong and firm male hand in order to be satisfied. —*Edna.*

John Huston & The
Dubliners
(DOCU-COLOR-16m)

A Liffey Films presentation. (Sales, Gray City Inc.) Executive producers, Chris Sievernich, Wieland Schulz-Keil. Produced and directed by Lilyan Sievernich. Camera (Foto-Kem color, 16m), Lisa Rinzler; editor, Miroslav Janek; music, Alex North; sound, Don Sanders, Walt Martin, Margaret Duke. Reviewed at Broadway screening room, N.Y., Aug. 21, 1987. (No MPAA Rating.) Running time: **60 MINS.**
With: John Huston, Anjelica Huston, Tony Huston, Roberto Silvi, Tom Shaw, Donal McCann, Rachael Dowling, Helena Carroll, Cathleen Delany, Ingrid Craigie, Dan O'Herlihy, Marie Kean, Donal Donnelly, Katherine O'Toole, Sean McClory, Frank Patterson.

"John Huston & The Dubliners" is a perceptive documentary on legendary director John Huston and his working methods, shot on the set of his latest film "The Dead" early this year.

Documaker Lilyan Sievernich (whose husband Chris Sievernich is an executive producer of "The Dead") succeeds in revealing, by interviews with Huston, his cast and crew members, plus vérité footage of scenes being filmed and rehearsed, how Huston gets exactly what he wants by gentle suggestions, cajoling and simply doing things till they come out right. As one of the Irish actresses comments: "I've heard he's a tough director. When you're pleasing him, he's lovely."

At first looking frail and tired, fitted with tubes to a respirator throughout the filming, Huston is shown by Sievernich to be in absolute control of his set and material. He knows the James Joyce story and screenplay by his son (Tony Huston) backwards and forwards and watches his tv monitor like a hawk looking for improvements on the blocking, timing and readings of each take that's filmed. An actress notes: "He expects you to come prepared. You're allowed to contribute. Obviously he's getting exactly what he wants, but you feel you're doing it." Huston comments, "I don't do storyboards. I very often let a scene develop. Each scene, within the emotional frame of the picture, is allowed to breathe."

When Sievernich presses Huston with a leading question or threatens to become overly analytical towards his work, he smoothly scoffs at such notions and sets the discussion back

on track in self-effacing fashion. As his film editor Roberto Silvi says: "He's one of the last gentlemen in this industry."

Docu give glimpses of some moving scenes from "The Dead," including 78-year-old actress Cathleen Delany singing a song, coached by Irish tenor Frank Patterson, who's also in the cast. Huston and others joke that the breaking of a wishbone after the film's centerpiece dinner constitutes the most action that occurs in "The Dead," but Huston points out: "My idea of action isn't the conventional car chase. Action can be in people's minds and thoughts — as long as they race, that constitutes action."

Pic would have benefitted from superimposed titles identifying the interviewees. As is, it is an effective portrait of Huston at work, with nontheatrical and tv use indicated, as well as in conjunction with retrospectives of Huston's films.
—*Lor.*

The Last Of England
(BRITISH-COLOR)

A Tartan Films release. A British Screen/Channel 4/ZDF presentation of an Anglo-International film. Produced by James Mackay, Don Boyd. Directed by Derek Jarman. (No screening credit). Camera (color), Derek Jarman, Christopher Hughes, Cerith Wyn Evans, Richard Heslop; editor, Peter Cartwright, Angus Cook, Sally Yeadon, John Maybury; music, Simon Turner, Andy Gill, Mayo Thompson, Albert Oehlen, Barry Adamson, El Tito; production design, Christopher Hobbs; lighting design, Christopher Hughes; sound architect, Simon Turner; costumes, Sandy Powell; associate producers, Yvonne Little, Mayo Thompson. Reviewed at Warner West End, London, July 30, 1987. Running time: **87 MINS.**
With: Tilda Swinton, Spencer Leigh, Spring, Gay Gaynor, Matthew Hawkins, Gerrard McArthur, John Phillips, and the voice of Nigel Terry.

London — "The Last Of England" has the rare ability to envelop one in its swirling images and bleak comedy one moment, and send a viewer off to sleep the next. Derek Jarman's pic is a boxoffice no-no, though it will likely have some arthouse draw.

Following the avant garde helmer's most accessible film to date, the 1986 "Caravaggio," he has returned with a blatantly personal vision which combines documentary-style footage of ruined streets, home movies, and a segment with glimpses of a screen story. All is filmed and linked abstractly, but without the glimmer of plot or narrative line.

As usual with this sort of pic, a fast flick through the production notes provides most of the answers, in this case that Jarman shot the film in Super 8m, and that the home movies are of Jarman, his parents and grandparents.

"The Last Of England" is a self-indulgent number, opening with an actor (Spring) kicking and abusing a Caravaggio painting. Profane

Love, and proceeding with a tirade of images of urban destruction and deprived youth. Interspersed are extracts from the Jarman family's home movies, which make an interesting contrast to the abrasive images with their views of colonial and RAF (Royal Air Force) life.

Towards the end of pic Tilda Swinton and Spencer Leigh (both Jarman regulars) act out what could almost be taken to be a story, with Leigh getting shot and Swinton getting married.

Jarman directs in pop-promo style with some sections working a great deal better than others — especially an impressive scene with a twirling Swinton, her swirling wedding dress illuminated by a blazing fire.

Technical kudos should go to Simon Turner, credited with the grand title of Sound Architect, whose sound effects and editing complements and often enhances the images. Other technical credits are okay, though editing is a shade manic.

"The Last Of England" will excite a few viewers and bore a great many others, but Jarman's innovative skills should not be dismissed even if this number is too smug and preachy. —*Adam.*

The Garbage Pail Kids Movie
(COLOR)

Kiddie pic is not for kids.

An Atlantic Entertainment Group release of a Topps Chewing Gum production. Executive producers, Thomas Coleman, Michael Rosenblatt. Produced and directed by Rod Amateau. Coproduced by Michael Lloyd, Melinda Palmer. Screenplay, Palmer, Amateau; camera (Image Transform & United color), Harvey Genkins; editor, Leon Carrere; music, Lloyd; production design, Robert I. Jillson; set decoration, Hug Braden; costume design, Judie Champion; sound, Clifford Gynn; Garbage Pail Kids animatronics, John Buechler, Mechanical Make-up Imageries Inc.; assistant director, Thomas A. Irvine; casting, Pam Rack. Reviewed at Atlantic Entertainment screening room, W. Hollywood, Aug. 19, 1987. (MPAA Rating: PG.) Running time: **100 MINS.**
Capt. Manzini . . . . Anthony Newley
Dodger . . . . Mackenzie Astin
Tangerine . . . . Katie Barberi
Juice . . . . Ron MacLachlan
Ali Gator . . . . Kevin Thompson
Greaser Greg . . . . Phil Fondacaro
Foul Phil . . . . Robert Bell
Nat Nerd . . . . Larry Green
Windy Winston . . . . Arturo Gil
Messy Tessie . . . . Sue Rossitto
Valerie Vomit . . . . . Debbie Lee Carrington

Hollywood — Vile, smelly, rude, ugly — that's what characterizes "The Garbage Pail Kids Movie," a far cry from wholesome children's entertainment. Topps Chewing Gum sold the little creatures first as bubble gum characters and now it brings thm to life via this production. Better they should have been left inanimate.

"The Garbage Pail Kids" is at the opposite end of the kid film spectrum from saccharine stuff like the "Care Bears" series. Each kid is distinguished by a revolting bodily function alluded to in his name: Windy Winston (flatulence is a specialty), Foul Phil (killer breath), Messy Tessie (gooey, running nose), Ali Gator (likes to eat toes) and Valerie Vomit.

They are germinated out of green slime in a garbage can heavily guarded by an eccentric magician cum antique dealer (Anthony Newley).

Mackenzie Astin, playing the shopkeeper's helper, inadvertently lets the midget monsters loose. At first he's revolted, then he warms to them as they help him become popular with the girl of his fancy, Tangerine (Karie Barberi), a punky neophyte fashion designer.

It is hard to tell what niche filmmakers intended for this pic. Astin's an innocent and Newley's likeable, if conspicuously absent much of the time, but presence of a trashy manipulative femme as an object of the boy's desires and the sadistic circle she runs in is clearly not geared to adolescents.

There appears to be little distinction between what's good behavior and what's bad behavior and The Garbage Pail Kids are about one notch higher on the discipline scale than the baddies who like to beat up on poor, defenseless Astin.

Usually children's film fare has some moral colorfully woven in with the adventure. This one comes off as a total free-for-all for the Kids, whose antics go unchecked, while Astin learns at an early age that women can be manipulative.

Granted, the Garbage Pail Kids seem to be having a lot of fun. The question is, can anyone stand watching them?

There is one glorious moment in the film — when The Garbage Pail Kids get locked away in the State Home for the Ugly. —Brit.

You Talkin' To Me?
(U.S.-COLOR)

An MGM/UA Entertainment release from United Artists of a Second Generation Films production. Produced by Michael Polaire. Written and directed by Charles Winkler. Camera (color), Paul Ryan; editor, David Handman; music, Joel McNeely. Reviewed at Montreal World Film Festival (competing), Aug. 22, 1987. (MPAA Rating: R.) Running time: **97 MINS.**

Bronson Green	Jim Youngs
Peter Archer	James Noble
Thatcher Marks	Mykel T. Williamson
Dana Archer	Faith Ford
Judith Margolis	Bess Motta
Kevin	Rex Ryon
James	Brian Thompson
Alan King	Alan King

Montreal — A winsome performance by Jim Youngs as a desperate New York actor doing the Hollywood shuffle with a psycho right-wing tv producer centers this uneven but combative cautionary satire. Showbiz scion Charles Winkler's debut feature depicts Tinseltown as a mirror of modern America's egocentric indifference to the corruption of its decent basic values, but the filmmaker's skewer is sometimes blunted by obviousness. Aggressive promotion, stressing the production's independent genesis, could help the picture's fortunes if it's played off in big cities as an exclusive release.

The unifying conceit of "You Talkin' To Me?" is the worshipful identification of marginal actor Bronson Green (Youngs) with actor's actor Robert De Niro, particularly the character of Travis Bickle, on-the-edge protagonist of Martin Scorsese's urban fable "Taxi Driver." Bronson's very best buddy is a black man, Thatcher Marks (appealingly played by Mykel T. Williamson), who's also ambitious to make it in Manhattan but cannot find work as a model. Together they head for Hollywood where Thatcher hits paydirt with print ads and billboards promoting cow-juice for the "American Milk Council." Bronson, however, finds only a cabbie's gig and endless rejection as the "wrong type" for contempo Hollywood hunk heaven.

In an amusing sequence (that parallels scenes in Robert Townsend's "Hollywood Shuffle") Bronson makes the rounds of grotesque agents who revel in disdaining the actor for his raven-haired ethnicity and seething energy, traits deemed "too New York" and out of fashion in Winkler's late-'80s Hollywood. When an airhead messenger with surf-god looks walks into one casting call and gets Bronson's role without even asking for it, the New Yorker has a California epiphany. He bleaches his hair, dons a flower-print shirt, gets real laid-back and overnight becomes a righteous So-Cal dude.

Bronson breaks up with his opportunistic actress girlfriend Judith (Bess Motta), but his new blond look soon catches the eye of Dana Archer (Faith Ford), a real blond Hollywood rich kid. She watches admiringly as Bronson emulates Travis Bickle by standing up when a pricey surfer boutique is held up by a yuppie with a cap pistol. Dana's father is a wealthy, sanctimonious racist who produces syndicated tv shows that preach the gospel of "the pure truth, the white truth" to "real Americans." James Noble, as Peter Archer, lends an edge of disturbing plausibility to the stereotypical character of the rich right-wing nut, replete with guns and Aryan goons (in one of the many L.A. in-jokes here, one bodyguard is an Arnold Schwarzenegger lookalike). Archer has been searching in vain for a convincing new tv spokesman and credits divine intervention with sending him the hungry and pliable bottle-blond actor.

Mesmerized by the opportunity, Bronson is inexorably corrupted by money and success. Inevitably, he loses his old "stand up guy" values as well as the respect of Thatcher, his old and new girl friends and finally himself. Ultimately, his big chance for self-redemption plays as a major role in a minor morality play about the deadly dangers of self-delusion.

Youngs' self-assured screen presence (the kid brother of John Savage also recalls a young Christopher Walken) and obvious relish for the character of the De Niro-fixated Bronson pump some vitality into the screenplay's clichéd milieu of life on the fringes of Hollywood. Downtown L.A. locations stand in adequately for New York, abetted by grainy and flat cinematography that obscures the very real differences between the two cities.

—Rich.

Noce en galilée
(A Wedding In Galilee)
(BELGIAN-FRENCH-COLOR)

A Lasa Films (Paris) release of a Marisa Films (Brussels)/LPA (Paris) coproduction, with the participation of the French Ministry of Culture, the French Community Ministry of Belgium and ZDF. Produced by Michel Khleifi, Bernard Lorain. Written and directed by Khleifi. Camera (color), Walther van den Ende; editor, Marie Castro Vasquez; music, Jean-Marie Senia; sound, Ricardo Castro; art direction, Yves Brover; assistant director, Alain Tasma; production manager, Jacqueline Louis. Reviewed at the Cinémathèque Française, Paris, June 4, 1987. (In Montreal Film Festival.) Running time: **113 MINS.**

With: Ali Mohammed Akili (The Moktar), Nazih Akly (the groom), Mabram Khouri (the military governor), Anna Achdian (bride), Sonia Amar (the young sister), Emtiaz Diab, Georges Khleifi, Hassan Diab, Abkas Himas.

Paris — Though provocatively billed (in press materials) as a Belgian-French-Palestinian coproduction, "Noce en galilée" transcends propaganda and dramatic facility to present a complex and affecting picture of an Arab village on the occupied Left Bank.

Michel Khleifi, 36, wrote and directed with deep understanding and a lucid eye. Born and raised in Nazareth, he has pursued a career in theater, tv, radio and film in Belgium, where he also teaches directing at the INSAS film school. He devoted a first (docu) feature to Palestine in his 1980 production, "La Mémoire fertile."

The dramatic premise of Khleifi's script is a traditional Arab wedding in a village where a curfew has been imposed by Israeli authorities following violent demonstrations and incidents.

The village elder, the moktar, who is marrying his son off, wants a ceremony in grand style, but the curfew is the major obstacle to the festivities. Appealing to the Israeli military governor, he is dealt a daunting condition: the governor and his staff must be official guests, to insure the peace.

The moktar accepts the arrangement, though immediately gets flak from the radical elements in the village, who begin plotting a terrorist action during the celebrations.

Working skillfully with an ostensibly non-professional cast and filming on location in a Palestinian village, Khleifi fills his dramatic canvas with vivid vignettes of Arab culture that are often schematized or neglected in propaganda pieces.

Preparations for the wedding and its tense long-day's-journey-into-night consummation occupy most of the screen time as the village elder attempts to harness local energies and prevent threatened violence. Internal problems and the groom's inability to perform his conjugal duties (without which the fête cannot be considered ended) prolong an atmosphere of compromised tradition and forced gaiety.

Though the Israeli guests are treated with cool distance and some irony — asked if he's enjoying himself, the military governor tactlessly responds that he wishes he could stay a hundred years — Khleifi keeps the Palestinian locals and their often contradictory problems as the film's dramatically humane mainstay.

Walther van den Ende's lensing caps pic's first-rate technical credits, which never betray any feeling of travelog or tourist superficiality.

Film, unspooling at the Montreal film fest, stands a good chance for specialized playoff, in addition to offering rich ethnographic detail for non-commercial and educational use. In any case, it promotes Khleifi to vanguard position among Belgium's exportable filmmakers.

—Len.

Les Noces barbares
(The Barbarous Wedding)
(BELGIAN-FRENCH-COLOR)

A Man's Film (Brussels)/Flach Film (Paris)/RF-1 Film/RTL-TV1 coproduction, with the participation of the French and Flemish Communities Ministries of Belgium. Produced, written and directed by Marion Hansel, based on the novel by Yann Quéffelec. Camera (Agfa-Gevaert color), Walther van den Ende; editor, Susana Rossberg; music, Frédéric Devrees; artistic adviser, Henri Colpi; art direction, Véronique Melery; sound, Henri Morelle, Jacques Julian; production managers, Josef van de Water, Gérard Vercruysse. Reviewed at GTC, Joinville-le-Pont, April 28, 1987. Running time: **99 MINS.**

Nicole	Marianne Basler
Ludo (child)	Yves Cotton
Ludo (teen)	Thierry Frémont
Micho	André Penvern
Mlle Rakoff	Marie-Ange Dutheil
Tatav	Frédéric Sorel

Paris — Based on the 1985 winner of the prestigious Goncourt literary prize, "Les Noces barbares" is another harrowing journey beyond the pathological fringe from Belgium's Marion Hansel, courageously pursuing a career devoted to downbeat, intimate themes.

Like "Dust," her previous film (which won the Silver Lion at Venice in 1985), it is an unrelenting closeup study of frustrated filial love climaxing in madness and (real or imagined) parricide. Unlike "Dust," which didn't betray its literary origins, "Noces" is frequently uneasy in its page-to-screen transfer, reflecting Hansel's difficulty in imposing a harmonious style on material that shifts abruptly from pathetic naturalism to the grotesque and the caricatural.

"Noces barbares" is the tragedy of an unloved, slightly retarded child born to an attractive provincial girl who has been raped by American GIs in the years after the war. The secret shame of a petit boureois household, the boy, Ludo, is kept locked away in the attic, before being let out when his mother contracts a loveless marriage with an older but tolerant man, who is willing to adopt him.

Ludo's craving for the love of his traumatized mother, slowly sinking into abject alcoholism and sloth, finally leads to his being packed off to a mental institution. Exposed to other sicknesses, the boy one day flees and takes refuge on a beached and rusting tanker, from which he contacts his mother, whom he murders (or thinks he murders) in a climactic fit of despair and rage. In film's final shot, he ships out to sea with her body on a raft for the title's "barbarous" alliance.

Hansel is powerfully in command when dealing with the respective and interlocked solitudes of mother (movingly portrayed by the sensual and sensitive Marianne Basler) and son (embodied with vivid pathos first by 10-year-old Yves Cotton, then by 24-year-old Thierry Fremont, who looks much younger).

Her control slips in the description of the often monstrous secondary characters, including Ludo's slimy, good-for-nothing stepbrother, and the matron of the mental home, whose heavily satirized maternalism hides another warped and affection-starved mind. In transposing characters created by novelist Yann Quéffelec, Hansel misjudges the nuances between literary and cinematic caricature.

Hansel also has trouble with the novel's wide timespan. In "Dust" and her first film, "The Bed," she was working in depth with temporally condensed "No Exit" situations. Though here she has skillfully recast the novel's linear narrative in a flashback structure, Hansel is obliged to skim and skip in order to cram the essential setpieces into her film, with a loss of density and dramatic rhythm.

Still, in its best sequences, Hansel impresses with her urgent sincerity and cinematic skill, a risk-taking filmmaker with a sense of deep commitment to her material. Her faithful technical crew, headed by ace lenser Walther van den Ende, are an evident part of that commitment.

Pic's grimness obviously limits it to art house and festival exposure, though in France, where the book was a bestseller, chances may be better. It won the grand prize at the Barcelona film fest and is unspooling currently at Montreal.—*Len.*

A Tiger's Tale
(U.S.-COLOR)

An Atlantic Entertainment release of a Vincent Pictures production. Produced and Directed by Peter Douglas. Stars Ann-Margret, C. Thomas Howell, Charles Durning. Screenplay, Douglas from a book by Allen Hannoy 3d; camera (CFI color), Tony Pierce-Roberts; editor, David Campling; music, Lee Holdridge; production design, Shay Austin; production manager, Donald Goldman; assistant director, Alan B. Curtiss; casting, Patricia Mock. Reviewed at World Film Fest, Montreal, Aug. 22, 1987. (MPAA Rating: R.) Running time: **97 MINS.**

Rose	Ann-Margret
Bubber	C. Thomas Howell
Charlie	Charles Durning
Shirley	Kelly Preston
Claudine	Ann Wedgeworth
Randy	William Zabka
Sinclair	James Noble

Also with: Tim Thomerson, Steven Kampmann, Traci Lin, Angel Tompkins.

Montreal — First feature directed by Peter Douglas, son of Kirk, is an amiable, lightweight reworking on the theme of love between a middle-aged woman and a teenager. The picture is handled adroitly and has several engaging characters, but makes no lasting impact, and Atlantic may have a tough sell finding a substantial audience for it. Names of C. Thomas Howell and especially Ann-Margret will help.

Setting is a small Texas town where 19-year-old Bubber (Howell) is dating spoiled Kelly Preston until he decides her mother (Ann-Margret) is an altogether more desirable woman. She's willing to go along at least once, and love blossoms so that before long the jealous and embarrassed Preston is calling for her father (long divorced and with a young girl friend of his own in tow) to come and take her away. "This has destroyed my whole adolescence," she complains.

A subplot involves Bubber's genial father (Charles Durning), a retired veterinarian with a houseful of animals, mostly huge snakes, including a handsome tiger raised from birth but starting to get too big for Howell to wrestle. Eventually, Howell comes to accept that "you can't hold on to things too long," meaning the woman as well as the tiger.

Though looking older than 19, Howell proves once again he's an adept light comedian and handles his chores effectively. Durning has little to do, but Ann-Margret positively glows as the woman in love. An odd aspect of the film is the clinical way female contraception is discussed: the jealous Preston punctures her mother's diaphragm, leading to her pregnancy, and the film includes scenes where the damaged item is examined and inspected almost as if this were a sex education pic.

Good production dress and tight running time are assets to a generally pleasant, but unremarkable pic which will occupy that commercially tricky middle-of-the-road area: it lacks the big laughs or the big emotions which might make it stand out from the crowded field of indie product jostling for the audience dollar. —*Strat.*

Travelling avant
(Dolly In)
(FRENCH-COLOR)

A UGC release of an Erato Films/JCT Prods./Sept coproduuction, with the participation of Sofinergie et Sofica Créations. Executive producer, Daniel Toscan du Plantier. Produced by Claude Abeille. Written and directed by Jean-Charles Tacchella. Camera (Fujicolor), Jacques Assuerus; editor, Marie-Aimée Debril; music, Raymond Allessandrini; sound, Pierre Lenoir, Alain Lachassagne, Jean-Paul Loublier; art direction, Georges Levy; assistant director, Patrick Poubel; casting, Ginette Tachella. Reviewed at the UGC Champs-Elysées cinema, Paris, Aug. 20, 1987. (In Montreal Film Festival.) Running time: **114 MINS.**

Nino	Thierry Fremont
Donald	Simon de la Brosse
Barbara	Ann-Gisel Glass
Angèle	Sophie Minet
Janine	Laurence Cote
Gilles	Luc Lavandier
Vicky	Nathalie Mann
Uncle Roger	Jacques Serre
Wanda	Alix de Konopka

Paris — Jean-Charles Tacchella takes a gentle stroll down memory lane in this chronicle about the film buff generation of the late '40s. Sincere and straightforward, it has some quiet charm but fails to distill the passion of the post-war movie nuts, many of whom went on to forge the New Wave movement of criticism and cinematic language.

Tacchella, one of those silver-screen-struck youths, attempts to recreate the period in a tale of two buff pals — one a penniless provincial (Thierry Fremont), the other Parisian of bourgeois stock (Simon de la Brosse) — who pool their energies in an attempt to create a ciné-club (film society) in a suburban commercial hardtop.

The failure of their venture only deepens the rift between friends: though Fremont wants to continue with the ciné-club experiement, De la Brosse is already trying to weasel his way into the studios and become a filmmaker.

Also standing between them is Ann-Gisel Glass, a more realistic buff, who seeks romance in the arms of the handsome but opportunistic De la Brosse, before finding her true love match in Fremont, who finally sees the light of the real world as balancing that reflected off the movie screen.

Tacchella generally passes up the temptation of using film technique to exteriorize inner feelings or simply to set the tone of fantasy obsession, though the talk and vicarious manner of his protagonists call for exactly that kind of film reference, show-off direction, so irritatingly superfluous in many of the now-classic films of the New Wave.

Most of what we perceive of his heroes comes from what they say, not from what they do or from what the director communicates in a purely visual manner, though Tacchella does make some half-hearted attempts at illustration when one or the other of the buffs tries to recast a moment as a film director might. (When De la Brosse watches a sexual conquest come out of the bathroom the next morning stark naked, he imagines her first as a femme fatale in a Hollywood movie — exiting fully dressed — then as a Gallic counterpart — walking in wearing her slip.)

Tacchella takes nearly two hours with his story, far too much time for personages finally too shallow and not sufficiently unusual to warrant the attention. Ironically, he shows that movie buffs aren't really worth a movie.

Technically routine, "Travelling avant" will be a hard picture to dolly abroad. —*Len.*

Tel Aviv-Berlin
(ISRAELI-COLOR)

A Tel Aviv-Berlin Ltd. production. Produced by Smadar Azriely. Directed by Tzipi Trope. Screenplay, Trope; camera (color), Gadi Danzig; editor, Rachel Yaguil; music, Shalom Weinstein; production design, Eli Landau; sound, Daniel Matalon; costumes, Dafna Hendly. Reviewed at World Film Fest, Montreal, Aug. 23, 1987. Running time: **96 MINS.**

Benjamin	Shmuel Vilozny
Leah	Rivka Noiman
Gusti	Anat Harpazy
Jacob Miller	Joseph Carmon

Montreal — An intriguing drama about the difficulties some European Jews experienced when they first settled in Israel, "Tel Aviv-Berlin," while basically a low-key affair, could generate specialized b.o. interest, especially in cities with large Jewish communities.

Film opens in 1943 in Tel Aviv with a brief prolog in which Benjamin (Shmuel Vilozny), who recently escaped from Germany, meets Leah (Rivka Noiman), a nurse: they fall in love. Five years later they have a child they adore, but Benjamin, who lived an intellectually rewarding life in Berlin's cafe society before the war, finds life in Israel dull, whereas Leah, who comes from a small Polish village, is content. When Benjamin meets the beautiful Gusti (Anat Harpazy), also from Berlin, he's attracted and begins to neglect his wife.

A subplot has Benjamin trying to pluck up enough courage to confront a man he recognizes as a former *kapo* who made life miserable for inmates of the camp in which he was interned; the man now works as a blacksmith.

Shmuel Vilozny is very dour as Benjamin, and gives a rather monotonous performance, but the two women are excellent, with Rivka Noiman radiating warmth as the troubled Leah and Anat Harpazy giving Gusti, who says she survived her incarceration simply because she was pretty, just the right degree of sophistication and vulnerability. Story and setting are intriguing, and writer-director Tzipi Trope, helming her second feature, handles the material with delicacy and confidence.

Pic should make the fest rounds, and do modest business in special situations.—*Strat.*

Dixieland Daimyo
(Jazz Daimyo)
(JAPANESE-COLOR)

A Daiei production. Produced by Yo Yamamoto, Masa Kobayashi. Directed by Kihachi Okamoto. Screenplay, Toshiro Ishido, Okamoto, based on a novel by Yasutaka Tsutsui; camera (color), Yudai Kato; editor, Yoshitami Kuroiwa; sound, Nobuyuki Tanaka; design, Kazuo Takenaka. Reviewed at Montreal World Film Festival (Japanese Cinema Of Today), Aug. 22, 1987. Running time: **85 MINS.**
With: Ikko Furuya, Ai Kanzaki, Mami Okomoto, Taiji Tinoyama, Ron Nelson, Pharez Whitted, Lenny Marsh, George Sparky Smith.

Montreal — It's 1865 in the American South, and four emancipated slaves who also happen to be crack Dixieland musicians are determined to sail back to Africa. Instead, they wash ashore with their instruments in Shogunate Japan smack in the middle of a nasty conflict between neighboring *daimyo,* samurai warlords. That's the wacky premise of this freewheeling absurdist parable about the discombobulating influence of Western culture on an insular Japanese civilization. Given the recent U.S. breakthrough of Japanese new wave comedies such as "Comic Magazine" and "Tampopo," this occasionally hilarious romp could work as an arthouse curiosity item. There's also an outside possibility that a segment of the black mainstream audience that's supported "She's Gotta Have It" and "Hollywood Shuffle" might take a chance on this film if it's promoted properly.

Anachronistic and cross-cultural incongruities are a big part of the fun in "Dixieland Daimyo." The four-ex slaves, when not speaking in overdubbed Japanese, talk and act much more like contemporary black men than refugees from "Uncle Tom's Cabin." Director Kihachi Okamoto makes sport of Westerns — spaghetti and otherwise — during the New Orleans-bound musicians' misdirected odyssey to the Pacific. Japanese-English subtitles such as "Sierra Madre mountains: aproach with caution" set and sustain a tone of inspired foolishness.

Three of the four musicians survive Indian attacks and stormy seas to reach an isolated part of Japan populated by feuding, bumbling samurai clans and their respective *daimyo.* Fortunately for the former slaves, they are discovered by the clan of an enlightened warlord, Uminogo, who would rather play nerve-shattering music on his flute than fight for more territory. Uminogo's best warrior is his princess daughter, who's fond of skateboarding on an abacus. The court is populated by other bizarre characters, including one who communicates with the shipwrecked expatriates in effective pidgin English.

Naturally, Uminogo becomes intrigued with the foreigners' strange new music, and appropriates their dead comrade's clarinet — and the swinging Dixieland sound — for himself. Okamoto has a ball turning the conventions of traditional samurai dramas upside down and inside out, culminating in an hallucinatory big band production number that's delightfully ridiculous. —*Rich.*

Blues LaHofesh HaGadol
(Late Summer Blues)
(ISRAELI-COLOR)

A Nachshon Films presentation of a Blues Ltd. production. Produced by Ilan de Fries, Renen Schorr, Doron Nesher. Executive producer, de Fries. Directed by Schorr. Screenplay, Nesher; camera (color, 16m), Ethan Harris; editor, Shlomo Hazan; music, Rafi Kadishsohn. Reviewed at the Jerusalem Film Festival, June 27, 1987. (In Montreal Film Festival — competing.) Running time: **101 MINS.**
With: Dor Zweigenbaum (Arale), Yoav Tzafir (Mossi), Noa Goldenberg (Naomi), Vered Cohen (Shosh). Shahar Segal (Margo), Sharon Bar-Ziv (Kobi), Ada Ben Nahum, Edna Fliedel, Miki Kam, Moshe Havatzeleth, Amith Gazith.

Jerusalem — Enthusiastically received by most local reviewers, Renen Schorr's first feature film obviously benefits from a combination of nostalgia and wistfulness on the part of its audience. It was produced with the help of the Ramat Can Film Academy, in which Schorr teaches, which supplied most of the crew, and with additional assistance from the Fund for the Promotion of Quality Films.

A group of 18-year-olds about to be drafted into the army are shown spending their last summer holidays outside uniforms. The question they grapple with and the arguments which divide them are typical for the period in which the story takes place, the summer of 1970, but are as relevant today, since many of the questions raised then, such as the moral justification of occupying the West Bank or sacrificing three of the best years of their lives to the Army, have still to find unequivocal answers.

Schorr and scriptwriter Doron Nesher split the story into four separate parts, each bearing the name of one lead character, not a necessary measure since there is no basic difference in approach or point of view between the episodes. The plot focuses on two major points, the attitude and the arguments around the imminent draft, and the graduation show prepared by the high school students, pretty innocent to begin with, but growing angry and critical of the government's policies, as represented by parents and teachers, after the first youngster to be drafted is killed in uniform. More spice is added by adolescent love leading in one case to an early marriage, and a certain degree of corruption which allows talented youngsters to avoid being drafted to combat units and join instead military entertainment groups.

Local audiences have been affected strongly by the memories triggered by the film, even when Schorr and Nesher were a bit hesitant, both in writing and direction. Some of the stronger statements are made in the graduation show, staged by scripter Nesher himself.

Maurice
(BRITISH-COLOR)

A Cinecom Pictures release of a Merchant Ivory production, in association with Cinecom Pictures and Film Four Intl. Produced by Ismail Merchant. Directed by James Ivory. Screenplay, Kit Hesketh-Harvey, Ivory, from E.M. Forster's novel; camera (Technicolor), Pierre Lhomme; editor, Katherine Wenning; music, Richard Robbins; sound (Dolby), Mike Shoring; production design, Brian Ackland-Snow; art direction, Peter James; costume design, Jenny Beavan, John Bright, William Pierce; production supervisor, Raymond Day; assistant director, Michael Zimbrich; casting, Celestia Fox; associate producer, Paul Bradley. Reviewed at Magno Review 1 screening room, N.Y., July 28, 1987. (In Venice Film Festival — competing; also in Montreal Film Festival.) (No MPAA Rating.) Running time: **140 MINS.**

Maurice Hall	James Wilby
Clive Durham	Hugh Grant
Alec Scudder	Rupert Graves
Dr. Barry	Denholm Elliott
Mr. Ducie	Simon Callow
Mrs. Hall	Billie Whitelaw
Lasker-Jones	Ben Kingsley
Mrs. Durham	Judy Parfitt
Anne Durham	Phoebe Nicholls
Risley	Mark Tandy
Ada Hall	Helena Michell
Kitty Hall	Kitty Aldridge
Simcox	Patrick Godfrey
Archie	Michael Jenn
Dean Cornwallis	Barry Foster
Mr. Borenius	Peter Eyre
Pippa Durham	Kate Rabett
Young Maurice	Orlando Wells
Lady at cricket match	Helena Bonham Carter

Cast consists mostly of relatively inexperienced newcomers, some undoubtedly destined to become familiar faces on local screens after this opus, supported by a handful of veterans in secondary adult parts.

The film's limited budget is inevitably visible, but in this case it may be an advantage as it adds a touch of stark, unadorned realism to the proceedings. As one of the characters is an amateur 8m movie freak shooting his friends at all times, there is also an element of film within a film, which intervenes several times, but again, the dramatic potential of the situation is not exploited fully.

Foreign audiences might have some problems relating correctly to the picture to its end, if they are not familiar with the atmosphere and the moods in this country, and could misconstrue the final decision of the anti-draft protester who joins the army in spite of all, as a sort of political statement by the filmmakers, when, in reality, it portrays a state of things, which, with very rare exceptions was generally true. The film has been accepted in Montreal fest competiton and it will be interesting to see reaction of an audience away from home. — *Edna.*

"Maurice," based on a posthumously published novel by E.M. Forster, is a well-crafted, worthy successor by the team that scored a critical and commercial hit with Forster's "A Room With A View" last year. Theme of homosexuality, handled tastefully but with explicitness, will prove no barrier to the pic's arthouse acceptance in the wake of "My Beautiful Laundrette" and "Prick Up Your Ears," but presents a formidable marketing challenge for distributor Cinecom's quest for crossover audiences.

Penned in 1914 but not allowed to be published until 1971 (a year after Forster's death) because of its subject matter, "Maurice" is not ranked among Forster's best work. Thematically it fits very comfortably in D.H. Lawrence territory, with many echoes of such works as "Women In Love" and the class-conscious "The Virgin And The Gypsy" and "Lady Chatterley's Lover."

Director James Ivory, who co-scripted with Kit Hesketh-Harvey, carefully uses abruptly edited vignettes to set the stage for developing the titular hero's crisis of sexual identity. Key opening scene has Maurice (pronounced Morris, British-style) as a schoolboy on a beachside outing being lectured by his teacher (Simon Callow), in comically fastidious fashion, on the changes that will soon occur in his body with the onset of puberty. Maurice Hall (James Wilby) is next seen grown up and attending Cambridge where, through contact with uppity aristocrat Risley (Mark Tandy) he meets handsome Clive Durham (Hugh Grant). Durham falls in love with him and though resisting at first Maurice later reciprocates, all on a platonic level.

Duo's lengthy affair is interrupted when Maurice is expelled from Cambridge and later strained due to a highly publicized trial for seducing a guardsman that sends Risley to prison, with Durham feeling guilty for not having given character testimony on his former school chum's behalf.

Durham, under pressure from his mother (Judy Parfitt), gets married to a naive girl (Phoebe Nicholls) while Maurice finally physically consummates his homosexual inclination with Durham's young gamekeeper Alec Scudder (Rupert Graves). Despite blackmail attempts by Scudder, Maurice eventually commits himself to the gamekeeper while Durham literally closes the door on his earlier phase of sexual experimentation.

With melodramatic elements taking hold in later reels, "Maurice" nonetheless conforms to the urbane, literate approach typical of Ismail Merchant/James Ivory films and is technically immaculate. Pierre Lhomme's visuals are sharp, with hard-edged lighting and none of the soft-focus nonsense engendered in many period pieces.

Wilby as Maurice gives a workmanlike performance, adequate to the role but never soaring. He is far outshadowed by a superlative supporting cast. Notable is Grant's shaded turn as Durham (thesp played a similar aristocrat in the Oxford-set film "Privileged" and is currently appearing as Lord Byron in the feature "Rowing With The Wind") and "Room With A View" alumnus Graves' earthy portrayal of the gamekeeper.

High comedy is provided (with very witty lines to match) by Ben Kingsley as a goofy hypnotist with a hilarious American accent who tries to help Maurice; Callow as the dense, supercilious teacher; Nicholls (a memorable child star, then named Sarah Nicholls, in Ken Russell's film of "Women In Love") as Durham's gullible wife; Billie Whitelaw as Maurice's equally naive mother; plummy-voiced Helena Mitchell as Maurice's lookalike sister and Denholm Elliott as Maurice's no-nonsense doctor. "Room With A View" star Helena Bonham Carter pops up uncredited and costumed as if she just stepped out of the previous film as a lady watching the principals eagerly at a cricket match.

A beautifully handled final scene virtually mirrors the finale of Lawrence's "Women In Love" and the film of same, the main difference being the state of awareness by the protagonist's wife. For the record, Forster wrote "Maurice" in 1914, Lawrence did his first draft of "Women In Love" in 1913, completing it in 1917 and publishing it in 1920. —*Lor.*

tic coast. If all those bad guys couldn't get rid of the stubborn man that way, they could at least get him accused of murdering the woman, who had once been his lover.

The story has the doctor running off in several directions almost at once: to console the mother of two boys who die after having been exposed to the radiation; to descend a ladder from a helicopter to the doomed ship, whose crew we understand to have been "removed;" to hide another victim, the old man from the lighthouse, from the local police chief, who is in cahoots with the military; to dash back and forth in a cabin cruiser between his coastal town hospital and a rocky promontory where he kills an English soldier who has chased him down; etc.

Red herrings and loose ends are hanging around all over a picture that has too many beginnings left undeveloped and an open ending of both hope and no hope. Things are not made any clearer by having a lot of the action run off in darkness without proper camera lighting. The acting has good performers interchanging stoic heroics with subdued villainy.

Wherever it appears, Arctic nature is photographed to fine effect, but claustrophobic fumbling has the camera stymied in most interiors. —*Kell.*

Mio In The Land Of Faraway
(SWEDISH-SOVIET-NORWEGIAN-COLOR)

A Sandrews release (Sweden) of Nordisk Tonefilm Intl. (Sweden) and Gorky Film Studio production, in association with V/O Sovinfilm, the Swedish Film Institute and the Norway Film Development Co. Produced by Ingemar Ejve. Executive producers, Klas Olofsson, Terje Kristiansen. Associate producers, William Aldridge, Göran Lindström. Directed by Vladimir Grammatikov. Stars Nicholas Pickard, Christopher Lee. Screenplay, William Aldridge, based on novel "Mio, My Son" (Mio, min Mio) by Astrid Lindgren; camera (Technicolor), Kjell Vassdal; editor, Darek Hodor; music, Anders Eljas, Benny Andersson, Björn Ulväus, others; sound, Bengt Löthner; costumes, Jevgenia Zagorsky; production design, Konstantin Zagorsky; production management, Hans Lönnerheden, Mikhail Zilberman, Robert Simmons; production coordinator, Lennart Norbäck. Reviewed at Norwegian Film Festival, Haugesund, Aug. 18, 1987. Running time: **104 MINS.**

Mio	Nicholas Pickard
Jum-Jum	Christian Bale
The Wicked Knight	Christopher Lee
The King	Timothy Bottoms
The Weaver Woman	Susannah York
Aunt Edna	Gunilla Nyroos
The Sword-Maker	Sverre Anker Ousdal

Also with: Linn Stokke, Stig Enström, Geoffrey Staines.

Haugesund, Norway — A Russian-language version of "Mio In The Land Of Faraway" came and went, largely unnoticed, as a Children's Films competition entry in the recent Moscow festival. The English-language version of this large-scale kiddie adventure is likely to work its way slowly into world markets where solid entertainment

fare for small fry and subteens is a rare commodity.

The name of Astrid Lindgren, on whose novel the team led by Swedish producer Ingemar Ejve and Russian director Vladimir Grammatikov have based their film, should add to its international market appeal, even though Grammatikov's exploration of a basic Lindgren theme, a child's strength in applying his imagination to his predicament of loneliness, is rather heavy-handedly disposed of in an introductory sequence showing orphan Mio being bullied by a foster aunt and backyard playmates at home in Stockholm.

A dream vision of a bearded messenger from The Land of Faraway sweeps Mio off the ground and takes him to meet his father, a Medieval king (Timothy Bottoms). The boy is rejoined on Green Meadow Island by a friend, Jum-Jum, from back home. Together, the boys mount a white horse and ride off to find the Black Knight (Christopher Lee) with The Heart of Stone and The Iron Claw, who has taken hundreds of children prisoners and turned them into birds, eternally circling his castle on The Highest Mountain over The Deepest Lake.

Finding a Magic Sword and receiving the gift from The Weaver Woman (Susannah York) of a coat that, when reversed, turns him invisible, allows Mio to fight and defeat The Black Knight, and also to see all the dizzy birds turned back into carefree children. This is the stuff of the Brothers Grimm and largely told without Astrid Lindgren's touches of wry, tough humor. Helmer Grammatikov indulges in no flights of artistic fancy but sticks to a workmanlike reading of the original text as transferred into a screenplay by England's William Aldridge.

Grammatikov is not very subtle in his handling of actors either. The two boys, Britishers Nicholas Pickard and Christian Bale (latter subsequently the star of Steven Spielberg's "Empire Of The Sun"), speak their lines woodenly and are generally made to stand still and face the camera while speaking them. The roles of The King and The Weaver Lady are too undeveloped for Timothy Bottoms and Susannah York to do much about them except look vaguely romantic. Only Christopher Lee remains good at playing evil without becoming a caricature.

Filmed on locations in the Crimea and in Scotland as well as in Moscow studios, "Mio" has good looks and high production values. All sequences of action and suspense are executed with speed and precision, and special effects are handled expertly. Sequences of lyrical idyll tend towards the vapid, which again is hardly the way Astrid Lindgren would have wanted it, but her basic message comes

●●●●●●●●●●●●●●●●●●●●●●●●●●●●●●●●●●●●●●
●
Film Reviews
●
●●●●●●●●●●●●●●●●●●●●●●●●●●●●●●●●●●●●●●

Etter Rubicon
(After Rubicon)
(NORWEGIAN-COLOR)

A VCM Film release of Filmeffekt (Dag Alveberg) and Norsk Film production for Norsk Film, The Credit Service Group and Viking Film. Produced by Dag Alveberg. Directed by Leidulv Risan. Screenplay, Arthur Johansen, Harald Paalgard, Leidulv Risan; camera (Eastmancolor, Fuji color), Harald Paalgaard; editor, Russell Lloyd, Yngve Refseth; costumes, Wenche Petersen, Anne Siri Bryhni; music, Geir Böhren, Bent Aserud; singer, Arve Moen Bergset; sound, Jan Lindvik; special effects director, Petter Borgli; production design, Frode Krogh; production management, Aage Aaberge. Reviewed at the Norwegian Film Festival, Haugesund, Aug. 18, 1987. Running time: **92 MINS.**

Jon Hoff	Sverre Anker Ousdal
Mona Axen	Ewa Carlsson
Maria Hamaröy	Ellen Horn
Carl Berntsen	Toralv Maurstad
Thorvald Hoff	Jack Fjeldstad

Also with: Alf Malland, Jan Harstad, Björn Sundquist, Christin Sampson, Stein Erik Skattum, John Ausland.

Haugesund, Norway — "After Rubicon" is a nuclear radiation

scare exploitation thriller done with some limited technical skill by the same producer (Dag Alveberg) and special effects wiz Petter Borgli who turned "Orion's Belt" into a minor international hit. Set to be given a sizable publicity launch by coproducer Viking Film via its London marketing affiliates, offshore attention seems assured once more, but a changing of helmer guard from "Orion's" Ola Solum to ex-docu director Leidulv Risan plus a muddy and highly improbable story may give some buyers pause.

To "buy" this thriller of ragged political overtones, you have to believe NATO forces, along with the High Command of the Norwegian armed forces, would burn to death an innocent woman in hopes of disposing at the same time of a doctor who was chasing evidence that a nuclear radiation leak had taken place on board a ship off Norway's Arc-through clear and proper; that Evil always gets its comeuppance if you dare to dream. Then the dream will take substance and emerge as Real Life. —*Kell.*

Blood Diner
(COLOR)

Horror send-up goes kaput.

A Vestron release of a Lightning Pictures presentation of a PMS Filmworks production. Executive producers, Lawrence Kasanoff, Ellen Steloff. Produced by Jimmy Maslon; creative consultant, Bill Osco. Directed and coproduced by Jackie Kong. Screenplay, Michael Sonye; camera (color), Jurg Walther; editor, Thomas Meshelski; music, Don Preston; sound effects, Bob Biggart; production design, Ron Petersen; costume design, Shiz Herrera; production manager, Jay Koiwai; art direction, Keith Barrett; assistant director, Bill Laxson, Paul LeCalir, Val Norwood; special effects, Bruce Zahlava; makeup artist, Loraina Drucker. Reviewed at Strand Theater, San Francisco, Aug. 22, 1987. (MPAA Rating: R.) Running time: **90 MINS.**
Michael Tutman ....Rick Burks
George Tutman..............Carl Crew
Mark Shepard..............Roger Dauer
LaNette La France ....Sheba Jackson
Connie Stanton ....Lisa Guggenheim

San Francisco — Helmer Jackie Kong, whose previous pics were "The Being" and "Night Patrol," has more gore bore lore in store with "Blood Diner," a self-cancelling cannibalism caper which shoots down its send-up style. Despite a socko windup, the parody of bloodlust is a pathetic bust, the sound uneven, the dialog uninspired.

Premise has a pair of wacko moppets inspired by a certifiable uncle whose brain, and eyeballs, they have exhumed. As adults, and diner managers, their mission is to assemble body parts from an assortment of virgins and bad girls so that Sheetar, a goddess about 5,000,000 years old, or thereabouts, can be restored to life.

The brothers, portrayed with some measure of bug-eyed broadness by Rick Burks and Carl Crew, hack, chop, slice, dice, puree and disect with verve, but without any inherent humor. Even a mass murder at a nude aerobics class fails to generate the presumably hoped-for giggles.

The only way "Blood Diner" could possibly reach its high camp intentions is if it had been filmed in a lean-to on Mt. Everest. —*Herb.*

Forajidos en la Mira
(Outlaws In The Viewfinder)
(MEXICAN-COLOR)

A Películas Mexicanas release of a Producciones Latinas Americanas-Producciones P.L.A.C. II production. Produced by Orlando R. Mendoza. Directed by Alberto Mariscal. Stars Sergio Goyri. Screenplay, Mariscal, based on a story by Mendoza, Gilberto de Anda; camera (color), Manuel Tejeda Monreal; editor, Angel Camacho Leppe; music, Gustavo César Carrión. Reviewed at Hollywood Twin theater II, N.Y., Aug. 16, 1987. Running time: **106 MINS.**
Julián Morieta ....Sergio Goyri
Rosa ....Silvia Manríquez
Marshal ....Fernando Casanova
Lucio Alvarez ....Eric del Castillo
Pistola Taylor ....Juan Gallardo
Flaco ....Alejandro Camacho
Also with: Carlos Rotzinga, Priscila, Antonio Raxel, Ramón Menéndez. Benjamin Islas, Regino Herrera, José Luis Avendaño, Jaime Pizano, Inés Murillo, Rafael Fernández, Raymundo Gómez, Alejandro de la Peña, José Luis Salgado, Manuel Anaya, Fidel Abrego.

Suffering has always been a theme in post-conquest Mexico, seen in its literature, songs and of course, its cinema. One of the major differences between American and Mexican melodramas is that while U.S. films tend to have a "happy ending," their Mexican counterparts often end tragically.

"Forajidos en la Mira" (Outlaws In The Viewfinder), directed by Alberto Mariscal, follows the Mexican formula. Film is a *vaquero* (cowboy) genre pic much like a standard Western, based on the tragic life of gunslinger Julián Morieta, played by action star and soap opera heartthrob Sergio Goyri.

When he revenges his parents' brutal murder, Moreita gains a reputation as a fast gun. He wanders the west until a small-town lawman (Fernando Casanova) recognizes Morieta's worth and hires him as town sheriff. His first official act is to stop a gang in the process of robbing the local bank. The outlaws, headed by Lucio Alvarez (Eric del Castillo), are eventually caught and sent to prison.

Sheriff Morieta finds happiness for the first time in his life: he marries the marshal's daughter and they settle down to begin a family. Everyone is happy except the former bank robbers, who seek revenge. Bodies stack up as in an Elizabethan tragedy.

Script is credible, albeit single-minded. Characters are either good or bad and most happy moments are immediately followed by conflict, as if to remind the audience that fate is the final victor. All warning signs are ignored.

In general, production values are good, except for superimposed images used to evoke memories. These scenes are sloppily executed and visually confusing. Careful art direction captures the period well. At times the music by Gustavo César Carrión becomes obtrusive rather than serving to underscore the mood.

Overall, the pic should fare well at Hispanic boxoffices due in part to the fast action, clearly defined drama and the likable persona of Goyri in the lead. —*Lent.*

A Chinese Ghost Story
(HONG KONG-COLOR)

A Cinema City presentation, released by Golden Princess Distribution network. Executive producer, Tsui Hark. Produced by Claudie Chung. Directed by Ching Siu Tung. Stars Leslie Cheung, Wong Tsu Hsien, Wo Ma. Screenplay, Yuen Kai Chi; camera (color), Poon Hang Seng, Sander Lee, Tom Lau, Wong Wing Hang; music, Romeo Diaz, James Wong; art direction, Yee Chung Man; costume design, Chan Ku Fong; production manager, Won Kar Man. Reviewed at President theater, Hong Kong, Aug. 2, 1987. Running time: **98 MINS.**
(Cantonese soundtrack with English subtitles)

Hong Kong — A heavy rainstorm compelled an intellectual and gentle young man Ling Choi Sin (Leslie Cheung) to trespass the supposedly haunted Lan Ro Temple for a night on his way to Kwok Pak Village to collect debts.

In the middle of the night, Ling awakens to haunting music played on an ancient Chinese instrument by a lovely, mysterious woman called Lit Siu Seen (Wong Tsu Hsien). Ling is unaware that resident Taoist Monk Yin Chek Hsia (Wo Ma) has impeded Lit's murder attempt. Despite Yin's objection, the young couple fall madly in love and decides to run away from the monastery.

The escape is Lit's betrayal of Lau Lau, her captor and now master in the spirit world. Lau is an androgynous, bisexual creature/monster who talks like a man/woman and can manipulate purchased spirits to kill strong men to sustain his longevity like a vampire. Lau's strength increases every time a man is trapped and his protruding tongue elongates to collect bodies like a hungry venus flytrap. Yin comes to their rescue, but Ling finally realizes his lady love is but a body without a soul.

Adapted from a series of popular classic literary ghost stories, Cinema City is to be congratulated for searching original Chinese material. The art direction, costumes, cinematography and soundtrack music are all exceptional.

The storyline portrays the beauty and fragility of life on earth: End result is an entertaining love story with a tantalizing horror background, mixed with fantasy escapism that won't insult adult viewers. —*Mel.*

Coming Up Roses
(BRITISH-COLOR)

Skouras Pictures is releasing Stephen Bayly's Welsh-language film "Coming Up Roses" Sept. 4 at N.Y.'s 57th St. Playhouse. Pic was reviewed as "Rhosyn a Rhith" from the Cannes Film Festival (Un Certain Regard section) in the May 21, '86 issue of *Variety.*

Strat. stated in his notice: "It's a gentle, sweet little item about the effect on various characters of the closure of a smalltown cinema ... There's a touch of the old Ealing comedies in this rather quaint tale of little people pulling together in time of adversity."

Esperando la Carroza
(Waiting For The Pallbearers)
(ARGENTINA-COLOR)

An Instituto Nacional de Cinematográfica Argentina release of a Rosafrey production. Produced by Diana Frey. Directed by Alejandro Doria. Screenplay, Doria, Jacobo Langsner; camera (color), Juan Carlos Lenardi;

editor, Silvia Ripoll; music, Feliciano Brunelli. Reviewed as part of Latino Festival, Public Theater, N.Y., Aug. 23, 1987. Running time: **103 MINS.**

With: Luis Brandoni, China Zorrilla, Antonio Gasalla, Julio de Grazia, Betiana Blum, Andrea Tenuta, Cecilia Rosetto, Mónica Villa.

———

There is a popular saying that whenever two Argentines get together, you already have three different opinions. When a large family complete with in-laws gets together — especially one plagued with infighting and family intrigues — the result here is uproarious chaos à la Argentine.

Number two national boxoffice grosser for 1986, the gaucho feature "Esperando la Carroza" (Waiting For The Pallbearers, a.k.a. Waiting For The Float) is a rollicking black comedy satirizing traditional Latino domestic dramas.

Directed by Alejandro Doria, the movie penetrates into the core of Argentine society by examining the attitudes of the various members of one family, each having settled into a different economic stratum and consequently each having nothing to do with the one poorer than itself. Add to this a mutual family conflict, bring all members of the family together and stand back. At times, decibel levels rise to near rock-concert levels.

Storyline concerns senile octogenarian Mama Cora and her four children (Jorge, Sergio, Antonio and Emilia). Mama Cora has been living with her eldest son Jorge and his wife Susana, making their life a living hell. Unable to take it any longer, they appeal to the rest of the family to share in the responsibility — something everyone avoids. While Jorge and Susana are making their appeal, Mama wanders over to a neighbor's where she is asked to babysit for a couple of hours.

When Jorge and Susana return to find the house empty, a manhunt begins, ending at the Buenos Aires morgue, where all four children mistakenly recognize their mother as the corpse of a woman who has thrown herself in front of a train. The wake that follows shows there's nothing like tragedy to bring out the hidden soap opera talents in most Latinos.

The situation proves a superb vehicle for bringing the disparate family members together. The film also exposes such clichéd notions about Hispanic family structure as reverence for the mother, Latino family bonds, respect for the elderly, and also the practice where younger Latino family members care for their elderly by inviting them to live and participate actively in their homes. The bourgeois pretentions of an evolving middle class also are brought up to scrutiny.

Doria has a good sense of timing coupled with a scathing eye cast toward the petty details and foibles of human nature. He seldom passes up the opportunity for surprise and is able to reverse all situations at a moment's notice with either a simple phrase or a major coup de théâtre.

Leads all are portrayed excellently, although a few secondary characters such as a drunk cousin, a deaf aunt and daughter Emilia, poorest of the lot, unfortunately are underdeveloped and their inclusion distracts from the strong ensemble core.

"Waiting For The Pallbearers" should fare well on the international market and at the same time show today's audience another side to Argentine cinema than has been seen through recent international hits like "The Official Story," "Camla" or "Man Facing Southeast."

—Lent.

———

Besame Mucho
(Kiss Me Tight)
(BRAZILIAN-COLOR)

An Embrafilme release of a H.B. Filmes production. Executive producer, Angelo Gastal. Produced by Hector Babenco, Francisco Ramalho Jr. Directed by Ramalho. Screenplay, Ramalho, Mario Prata, based on a play by Prata; camera (Eastmancolor), Jose Tadeu Ribeiro; editor, Mauro Alice; music, Wagner Tiso; sound, Romeu Quinto; art direction, Marcus Weinstock; sets, Nordana Benetazzo; costumes, Domingos Fuschini. Reviewed at Museum of Modern Art screening room, Rio de Janeiro, Aug. 10, 1987. Running time: **95 MINS.**

Tuca . . . . Antonio Fagundes
Dina . . . . Christane Torloni
Xico . . . . Jose Wilker
Olga . . . . Gloria Pires
Soror Encarnacion . . . . Isabel Ribeiro
Cesar . . . . Paulo Betti
Also with: Giulia Gam, Sylvio Mazzucca, Jessie James, Marthus Mathias, Iara Janra, Vera Zimmermann, Linda Gay, Wilma de Aguiar.

———

Rio de Janeiro — The title of this pic refers to the famous bolero that enchanted young couples during the 1960s. "Besame Mucho" tells the story of two of these couples, focusing on their lives over the '60s, '70s and '80s. It actually progresses in reverse, starting in the '80s.

That was precisely the gimmick that made the play by Mario Prata so popular on Brazilian stages. Prata himself adapted it with director Francisco Ramalho Jr., who debuts in a full-length film after making some fine short films.

Both couples are very symbolic products of their age: they have dealt with political movements, ingenuous romances and college disputes. But the first information we get from them is how everything has affected their lives. Later on, the film reveals the causes.

When that happens, most audiences over 40 will have sympathy for the characters. The music — ranging from the Beatles to punk groups — is well known, and so is the ambience, carefully reproduced by art director Marcos Weinstock. That does not however, necessarily provide much relevance to today's times. The sin of becoming only a nostalgic reference can be detected in this otherwise well-detailed work.

Main cast — all top stars of Brazilian novelas — are convincing though not warm. Director Ramalho is determined to keep to the original gimmick, yet he achieves a very careful production, up to international standards in most components, especially music and cinematography. Pic has unquestionable universal appeal, while based in elements of Brazilian culture.—*Hoin.*

———

Narco Terror
(Narcotics Terror)
(MEXICAN-COLOR)

A Peliculas Mexicanas release of a Prods. Galubi, Prods. Torrente-Dinamic Film production. Executive producer, Raúl Galindo Ubierna. Produced by Rubén Galindo Ubierna. Directed by Rubén Galindo. Stars Eduardo Yáñez. Screenplay, Galindo, Carlos Valdemar; camera (color), Antonio de Anda; editor, Carlos Savage; music, Jesús (Chucho) Zarzosa. Reviewed at Hollywood Twin Theater I, N.Y., Aug. 19, 1987. Running time: **86 MINS.**

Roca Durán . . . . Eduardo Yáñez
Arturo Durán . . . . Alfredo Leal
Bernardo Treviño . . . . Juan Gallardo
Maura Treviño . . . . Felicia Mercado
Morris Serur . . . . Juan Verduzco
Also with: Raúl Meraz, Claudio Baez, Leo Villanueva, Gabriela Goldshmied, Alfredo Gutiérrez, Roberto Montiel, Fabián Aranza, Vicky Conti, Carlos González.

———

After about a half dozen features, Mexican action star Eduardo Yáñez has been typecast firmly as an innocent victim forced by circumstances to seek revenge for injustice. "Narco Terror," directed by Rubén Galindo, is no different.

Whereas most Yáñez-Galindo collaborations have been well made and entertaining, this latest venture is poorly scripted, portraying 2-dimensional characters caught in improbable situations.

Tale begins ironically on the wedding day of Roca Durán (Yáñez) and Maura Treviño (Felicia Mercado). When Roca goes home to make prenuptial arrangements, he discovers his father (Alfredo Leal) in a panic. It seems that as a bank executive, dad has been working with the Mafia for years. Although he often looked the other way during the clan's activities, he drew the line at drug trafficking. He wants out and since he knows too much, both father and son go into hiding.

There are multiple unimaginative shootouts, car chases and bloody special effects before father and son finally are shot down. Yáñez of course survives to get revenge and then the bullets really fly. One of the most improbable coincidences is that Yáñez' fiancée Maura just happens to be the daughter of the Mafia boss. Yáñez also singlehandedly takes on and shoots down whole armies of hoods from a seemingly endless supply of bullets.

Acting tends to be flat and lifeless to accompany the under-developed formula-ridden script. Tech credits look rushed and uninspired.

For all its car chases, shootouts and fast action, there is not enough substance, care or entertainment value in "Narco Terror" to make an audience wonder how its hero will get out of his latest scrape.

—*Lent.*

———

Pa stigende kurs
(Rising Stock)
(NORWEGIAN-COLOR)

A KF release of a Flöifilm with Norsk Film production. Produced by Stein Roger Bull. Directed by Bo Hermansson. Screenplay, Andreas Markusson, Hermansson, based on novel by Kare Prytz; camera (Eastmancolor), Svein Krövel; editor, Hermansson; music, Egil Monn-Iversen; production design, Sven Wickman; costumes, Anne Hamre, Runa Fönne; production management, Bitte Monn-Iversen; location manager (Miami), Nora Cooper Denslow. Reviewed at the Saga 1, Oslo, Aug. 20, 1987. (In Norwegian Film Festival — Haugesund.) Running time: **96 MINS.**

Roger . . . . Dag Fröland
Treasury Agent . . . . Anders Hatlo
Roger's wife . . . . Mari Maurstad
His mother-in-law . . . . Wenche Foss
His Miami flirt . . . . Kjersti Holmen
Police Chief . . . . Arve Opsahl
Also with: Kristian Guldbrandsen, Christine Larsen, Sven Wickström, Knut M. Hansson, Karl Sundby, Rolf Söder.

———

Oslo — "Rising Stock" introduces Dag Fröland, who has the potential to be an international, Keatonesque comedy star, but who hardly will reach foreign shores via Bo Hermansson's thoroughly inept farcical satire.

In the story about an innocent tax-evader (he paints a friend's house on the grey market in his spare time from a lowly job), Dag Fröland, popular in Norway as a standup comedian and elegant performer in stage skits and sketches, is surrounded by overacting established film thesps. Only by the valiant artistic effort of high carat shine does he get his head and talent raised above the morass of a screenplay that never knows whether or where it is coming or going (a moralistic satire, a goofy farce, a sitcom-ish entertainment for the bigger screen?), and a directorial effort that either pulls its punches to the point of somnolence or goes brash, shrill and, ultimately, as flat as fallen arches.

There is a good idea behind this mess: the hero is a true innocent who somehow learns to move gracefully to the rhythms of the phony morals of officialdom. When he suddenly finds himself a millionaire, he sees everybody around him, including the authorities, turning into all kinds of cheats. He turns, sadder but wiser, to his small son who used to cuddle up to him while listening to his reading aloud of fairytales, but by now the kid has found a walkman to replace him.

Looking like a mix between Little Orphan Annie and Dagwood, but always with his own personal deadpan style holding back while exuding worlds of mute wisdom, Dag Fröland holds one's attention throughout, making one wish to see him in worthier surroundings. If there was an international festival for Great Performances from Terrible Films, Fröland would be an established comedy star just from any snippet with him at the center chosen from "Rising Stock."—*Kell.*

Deadline
(WEST GERMAN-COLOR)

A Skouras Pictures release of a Virgin Vision presentation of a Creative Film/Caro Film/Norddeutcher Rundfunk production, in association with GPHS Intl. Produced by Elisabeth Wolters-Alfs. Line producer, Michael Scharfstein. Directed by Nathaniel Gutman. Stars Christopher Walken. Screenplay, Hanan Peled; camera (Geyer-Werhe color), Amnon Salomon, Thomas Mauch; editor, Peter Przygodda; music, Jacques Zwart, Hans Jansen; art direction, Yoram Barzily; assistant director, Ricky Shelach; special effects coordinator, Yoram Polack. Reviewed at Magno Review 1 screening room, N.Y., July 24, 1987. (MPAA Rating: R.) Running time: **100 MINS.**

Don Stevens	Christopher Walken
Mike Jessop	Hywel Bennett
Linda Larson	Marita Marschall
Hamdi Abu-Yussuf	Arnon Zadok
Yessin Abu-Riadd	Amos Lavie
Samira	Ette Ankri
Bernard	Martin Umbach
Abdul	Moshe Ivgi
Bassam	Sason Gabay
Habib	Shahar Cohen
Micha	Shlomo Bar-Aba

Also with: Gaby Shoshan, Igal Naor, Jerry Weinstock, Reuven Dayan, Nader Masraawi, David Menachem, Shlomo Tarshish, Moni Mushonov.

"Deadline" is a stilted topical thriller about Middle East politics and violence. Told in the already overused format of a cynical journalist caught in a hotbed of conflicting factions ("Under Fire," "Salvador," Volker Schlöndorff's "Circle Of Deceit"), subject matter is intrinsically interesting but deadened by the lackluster direction of Israeli helmer Nathaniel Gutman.

Christopher Walken has almost a 1-man show as a cavalier correspondent for fictitious ABS news, dispatched to Beirut in 1983, fresh from covering a European fashion show. Though scoffed at by the longtime hands on the scene, especially even more cynical Brit reporter Hywel Bennett, Walken quickly scores a coup by getting an exclusive interview with PLO moderate Yessin, who declares on audiotape that the PLO should have renounced terrorism as a policy long ago. Coming on the eve of Arafat and other PLO leaders leaving Beirut, story is a worldwide bombshell.

Unfortunately, it is soon revealed that Walken has been duped, having interviewed an imposter. As he scurries to unravel the mess, both the imposter (Bassam) and Yessin are murdered. Walken becomes a reluctant hero, caught between warring parties and trying to warn everyone before the Christian Phalangists carry out the massacre of folks in the Palestinian refugee camps. Nobody trusts or believes this Cassan-

dra and in a phony conclusion Walken walks away unscathed from the melee replete with exclusive footage of the massacre.

Walken tries to pep up the surprisingly bland proceedings with an exercise in method acting, an understandable solution to the problem of playing scenes with a monotone, sleepwalking supporting cast. His acting comes off merely as forced, with Hywel Bennett getting a few laughs as his foil. Local Israeli cast is dullsville.

Gutman directs limply, conjuring up a couple of arresting images, such as an array of corpses laid out neatly when Walken goes to identify Bassam, but generally using bright, even lighting that conveys no atmosphere at all. The concept of sudden violence breaking out in an otherwise placid scene was done with far better effect in "Under Fire."

Tech credits are competent at a B-movie level. Picture was filmed under the title "War Zone," with British-based Yank Mark Forstater listed as producer, though his name has disappeared from the final screen credits. — *Lor.*

Eastern Condors
(HONG KONG-COLOR)

A Golden Harvest production and release. Presented by Raymond Chow. Produced by Leonard Ho. Executive producer, Wong Ping Yiu. Directed by Samo Hung. Stars Hung, Yuen Biao, Joyce Mina Godenzi, Lam Ching, Ying, Kiki Cheung, Y. Karata, Dr. Haing S. Ngor. Camera (color), Wong Yau Tai; art direction, Lee King Man. Production services by Kicking Horse Prods. (Canada), PMP Motion Picture Prods. (Philippines). Reviewed at State theater, Hong Kong, Aug. 10, 1987. Running time: **96 MINS.**
(Cantonese soundtrack with English subtitles)

Hong Kong — An action adventure movie about Vietnam shot on location in the Philippines with the assistance of the Dept. of National Defense was meant to be a boxoffice sensation during the summer season of '87. It was not.

It grossed over $HK20,000,000 and cost over $HK30,000,000 to make. Samo Hung directs as well as stars as the leader of a group of convicts (mercenary) recruited to carry out a highly dangerous mission for the American military in Vietnam. They also are to destroy an ammo base hidden in one of the jungles. Once the mission is completed, all the convicts will be freed from prison.

The storyline was lifted from many sources. Soon after the first 15-20 minutes of intro is over, the movie plunges into a series of fistfights and gunfights between the Vietcong and the bravados.

Main problem with the film lies in the fact that there are too many characters for the director to handle effectively. They are mere signatures of their respective roles. Except for the mission, there isn't anything that carries enough weight and

interest to keep the audience attuned to the whole effort.

Samo attempts to be a Cantonese Rambo and even tries to use slow motion to dramatize some sequences He can't capture the timing essential to an action pic. The unkindest cut of all is the presence of Oscarwinner Dr. Haing S. Ngor of "The Killing Fields" seen moonlighting in this ludicrous, embarrassing Hong Kong project that drags his international prestige to the make-believe Vietnamese mud in the Philipines, supposedly set during the fall of Saigon in 1975. —*Mel.*

Asi Como Habían Sido
(The Way They Were)
(SPANISH-COLOR)

A Multivideo ALPC production. Directed by Andrés Linares. Screenplay, Linares, Joaquín Jordá; camera (Eastmancolor), Federico Ribes; editor, Guillermo S. Maldonado; sets, Fernando Verdugo; costumes, María José Iglesias. Reviewed at Cinearte screening room, Madrid, Aug. 27, 1987. Running time: **88 MINS.**

Tomás	Massimo Ghini
Alberto	Juan Diego
Damián	Antonio Banderas
Elena	Nina Van Pallandt
Carol	Ana Vasoni

Also with: Eufemia Román, Amparo Climent, Cristina Juan, Miki Moreno, Javier Ayala.

Madrid — This first feature by Andrés Linares is a well-directed, sensitive effort which has its touching, even moving moments but is not likely to appeal to a wide audience. The story of three college friends who break up and are then brought together 10 years later is perhaps too familiar, and the twists Linares gives are only partially convincing, though he does keep the pacing lively and prevents interest from flagging.

Much of yarn is told as a long flashback. A successful concert pianist, Tomás, returns to Spain from the States with his American wife planning to seek out two of his old buddies in order to set to music an epic poem by Juan Ramón Jiménez written while the poet lived in exile in New York.

One of his old friends now works in a recording studio and has settled down to a life of quiet resignation. The third of the original trio of musicians has gone off to live in a pueblo after making a mess of his life; he has been in prison, has attempted suicide, and has lost the use of his left arm.

As Tomás delves into their past, he comes to discover various facts he was unaware of, sacrifices made by his friends and his ailing mother, that had enabled him to win a scholarship to Juilliard and make a success of his life and career. The three old friends are reconciled at the end, after Tomás tracks down the third of the group, Damián, playing a virtuoso trumpet piece with one hand in the fiesta of a little village.

Italo thesp Massimo Ghini puts

in a restrained but convincing performance as Tomás, while Juan Diego and Antonio Banderas are excellent as the friends who could not "give their all" for music. Voices are all dubbed into Spanish, which detracts from naturalness, especially in the case of Tomás' supposedly Yank wife, who speaks a rather too impeccable Spanish.

Production values otherwise are good, though makeup fails to convince that the group has aged over a period well beyond 10 years. Commercial outlook is decidedly weak. —*Besa.*

Eulalia
(COSTA RICAN-COLOR)

A Cinematográfica del Istmo production. Produced and directed by Oscar Castillo. Screenplay, Samuel Rovinski; camera (color), Víctor Vega; editor, Sigfrido Bacyne; music, Alvaro Esquivel, with appearance of singers Sandra Solano, Jorge de Castillo and the group Train Latino. Reviewed at Latino Festival, Metro Cinema 2, N.Y., Aug. 11, 1987. Running time: **90 MINS.**

Eulalia	Maureen Jiménez
Don José	Alfredo (Pato) Catania
Rafael	Miguel Calacci
Gustavo	Rubén Pagura
Yami	Rosita Zúñiga

Also with: Bernal García, Olga Marta Barranto, Luis Herrera.

Machismo is a problem prevalent in all parts of Latin America. In Costa Rica, which has always been singularly democratic and progressive, things are no different, evident in the new feature "Eulalia." Pic is helmed by Oscar Castillo, who made the 1985 comedy "La Segua" as a coprod with Mexico.

"Eulalia," penned by national playwright Samuel Rovinski, is a portrait of Latin machismo, deceit and class distinctions set within a satire of Latin American soap opera conventions. In this, the script is only partially successful. Rather than play up the soap opera style, what emerges is a picaresque, meandering sex comedy with a bittersweet ending. The heroine comes out on top but at the price of a friendless, family-less and loveless future.

Storyline is straight cliché. One of six daughters living with her family in the countryside, Eulalia (Maureen Jiménez) is forced by economic difficulties to work as a maid in the capital. The blossoming beauty lives with her hot-to-trot cousin and spends most of her time fighting off the amorous attentions of both her boss and his pubescent son. The wife's discovery of the situation leads to the young woman's immediate dismissal and a new job at a San José Pizza Hut.

The fortunes of our heroine zigzag like a stock market chart on a bad day on Wall Street. Following soap conventions, she is seduced and subsequently dropped when she becomes pregnant. A marriage of convenience with an impotent old gentleman lead to exhaustion when her pulchritude awakens him with renewed vigor.

Overall the film is uninspired and there is little new to set it apart for other Latino sex farces. There are a few ingenious touches, but they get lost within the genre. It should be noted that Costa Rica boasts limited feature production but technically this picture stands up to its Latin counterparts. Acting is also competent.

The film is an obvious commercial venture and should pick up coin both nationally and internationally at Hispanic boxoffices due to lots of exposed flesh, picaresque characters and focus on the music featuring popular national singers and groups. A soundtrack album has been released to accompany the pic.

—*Lent.*

Entre Ficheras Anda el Diablo
(The Devil Lurks Among Bar-Girls)
(MEXICAN-COLOR)

A Peliculas Mexicanas release of a Filmadora Exito production. Produced by Guillermo Calderón Stell. Directed by Miguel M. Delgado. Screenplay, Francisco Cavazos, Víctor Manuel (Güero) Castro; camera (color), Fernando Colín; editor, Jorge Bustos; music, Gustavo C. Carrión; choreography & sets, Juan Alonso, Enrique Sánchez. Reviewed at Hollywood Twin theater II, N.Y., Aug. 15, 1987. Running time: **100 MINS.**

MINS.
Gerardo . . . . Jorge Rivero
Gerardo's wife . . . . Sasha Montenegro
Cochola . . . . Carmen Salinas
Rafael . . . . Rafael Inclán
Satan . . . . Alfonso Zayas
Don Cacama . . . . . . Manuel (Loco) Valdez
The Devil . . . . Luis de Alba
Doñanita . . . . Ana Luisa Peluffo
Perla . . . . Angélica Chaín
Butler . . . . Lalo (El Mimo)
Dr. Judo . . . . Héctor Suárez
Dr. Barrientos . . . . Jaime Moreno
Also with: Cristina Molina, Wanda Seux, Armando Silvestre, Polo Ortín, Francisco Muller, Alfredo (Pelón) Solares, Raúl Padilla, César Escalero, Mary Montiel, Leandro Espinoza.

The Mexican sex comedy "Entre Ficheras Anda el Diablo" (The Devil Lurks Among Bar-Girls) features an all-star lineup in a silly script that goes nowhere. Pic was penned by Francisco Cavazos and veteran gag-writer-director Víctor Manuel (Güero) Castro.

Directed by Miguel M. Delgado, the film is composed of three separate bare-bones sketches that are intercut and only vaguely linked through two cross characters, played by Carmen Salinas and Rafael Inclán.

The first tale concerns artist Sasaha Montenegro, who uses her muscle-bound husband Gerardo (Jorge Rivero) as a model for her painting of Atlas. She begins the nude starting at the head and finishes it while he is off on a business trip. The painting captures him perfectly except for one part of the anatomy, so Gerardo suspects infidelity. The second story deals with a veterinary surgeon (Héctor Suárez) who is crazy about a showgirl (Angélica Chaín). This trio is rounded out with a senseless tale of a red-

suited Satan (Alfonso Zayas); who decides to abandon hell to enjoy some earthly pleasures. Since the boss, i.e. the Devil (Luis de Alba) is hot on his trail, he and accomplice Inclán disguise themselves as bar-girls, etc.

These pithy and improbable sketches are juggled together for lack of a real story and the result is an unsatisfactory mess.

Tech credits are adequate at best with little imagination given to details, especially the nightclub scenes where choreography is cramped within a small area. Acting is flat throughout.

Despite its drawbacks, the film will pick up coin as a result of interest in such a large group of well-known actors and comedians assembled here. Too bad such talent is brought together for nought.—*Lent.*

Elvis-Kissan Jäljillä
(On The Trail Of Elvis The Cat)
(FINNISH-COLOR)

A Kinotuotanto release and production. (Intl. Sales, Finnish Film Foundation). Produced, written and directed by Claes Olsson. Camera (color), Sakari Rimmenen; editor, Alvaro Pardo; music, Yari; sound, Tero Malmberg, Heikki T. Partanen; costumes, Johanna Hänninen, Sirkku Katila; assistant director, Nadja Pyykkö. Reviewed at the Finnish Film Foundation cinema, Helsinki, Aug. 7, 1987. Running time: **80 MINS.**
Tom . . . . Claes Olsson
Sirpa, Pirjo, Vaimo . . . . Satu Silvo
Taxi driver . . . . Markus Weckström
Marilyn Monroe . . . . Marita Siirtola
Striptease dancer . . . . Eboni
Also with: Heidi Siljander, Sisko Ramsay, Raimu Hiltunen, Jussi Tuominen, Heikki T. Partanen, Vera Olsson.

Helsinki — "On The Trail Of Elvis The Cat" is an amicable little semi-surrealistic fable about a bewildered film director named Tom (played by writer-producer-helmer Claes Olsson himself) who, at his wit's end with financial worry, wife and mistress trouble, sets out to look for his lost youth, symbolized by a female cat that once was his cuddliest friend.

Olsson has patched early 8m 1969-73 home movies, clips from some of his own animated shorts, plus snippets from the original "King Kong" together with the bulk of his present-day footage, which retains some of the shot-from-the-hip attributes. The total impression is one of smooth, satirical self-portrayal worked to self-indulgence and over-length. If a fest circuit for the better do-it-yourself-via-your-garage film exists, that's where this one will shine.

After much stumbling and foolin' around, Tom (Olsson, otherwise balding at 39, wears a wig and a real moustache) finds his cat dead in the apartment of a former girl friend who has just been moved to an insane asylum. Tom shaves his head, dresses in white rags, digs a grave, buries the cat, and is forgiven for everything by his wife (Satu Silvo, who also plays two other roles with quiet conviction).

"On The Trail Of Elvis The Cat" displays good cinematic rhythms. —*Kell.*

★★★★★★★★★★★★★★★★★★★★★★★★★★★★
★ Venice Festival Reviews ★
★★★★★★★★★★★★★★★★★★★★★★★★★★★★

The Dead
(U.S.-COLOR)

A Vestron release of a Vestron and Zenith Prods. presentation of a Wieland Schulz-Keil and Chris Sievernich production for Liffey Films. Executive producer, William J. Quigley. Produced by Schulz-Keil, Sievernich. Directed by John Huston. Stars Anjelica Huston, Donal McCann. Screenplay, Tony Huston, camera (Foto-Kem color), Fred Murphy; editor, Roberto Silvi; music, Alex North; production design, Stephen Grimes, in collaboration with Dennis Washington; set decoration, Josie McAvin; costume design, Dorothy Jeakins; sound (Dolby), Bill Randall; assistant director, Tom Shaw. Reviewed at the Raleigh Studios, L.A., Aug. 25, 1987. (at Venice Film Festival-out of competition.) (No MPAA Rating.) Running time: **83 MINS.**
Gretta . . . . Anjelica Huston
Gabriel . . . . Donal McCann
Lily . . . . Rachael Dowling
Aunt Julia . . . . Cathleen Delany
Aunt Kate . . . . Helena Carroll
Mary Jane . . . . Ingrid Craigie
Mr. Browne . . . . Dan O'Herlihy
Bartell D'Arcy . . . . Frank Patterson
Freddy . . . . Donal Donnelly
Mrs. Malins . . . . Marie Kean
Molly Ivors . . . . Maria McDernottroe
Mr. Grace . . . . Sean McClory
Also with: Kate O'Toole (Miss Furlong), Maria Hayden (Miss O'Callaghan), Bairbre Dowling (Miss Higgins), Lyda Anderson (Miss Daly), Dara Clarke (Miss Power), Colm Meany (Mr. Bergin), Cormac O'Herlihy (Mr. Kerrigan), Paul Grant (Mr. Duffy), Patrick Gallagher (Mr. Egan), Amanda Baird (Young Lady), Paul Carroll (Young Gentleman), Redmond M. Gleason (Nightporter), Brendon Dillon (Cabman).

Hollywood — With poetic irony, "The Dead" will come before audiences posthumously as John Huston's last film, and as such will represent a delicate coda in a minor key to his illustrious 46-year directorial career.

Film especially will appeal to connoisseurs of James Joyce, Huston and things Irish, although its modest scale and scope will limit commercial potential to upscale arthouse audiences. World premiere is at the Venice Film Festival, with theatrical bow set for Nov. 20 in New York and Los Angeles.

A well-crafted miniature, the cardinal virtues of which have to do with the relishing of performance and the English language, this dramatization of the Joyce story directly addresses the theme of how the "shades" from "that other world" can still live in those who still walk the earth, and so it will be for Huston and the public on this occasion.

Huston was on record to the effect that Joyce had a greater influence on him than any other writer, and paid homage to his hero with an adaption that is, with one perplexing exception, scrupulously faithful to both the letter and the spirit of the 50-page tale, the con-

cluding story in Joyce's youthful "Dubliners" collection.

Set in Dublin in 1904, Tony Huston's screenplay is a discreet elaboration upon the original text. Opening hour is set exclusively in the warm town house of two spinster sisters, who every winter holiday season throw a festive party and dinner for their relatives and friends.

Opening reels mainly consist of mild revelry, with various of the formally dressed characters singing, playing piano, dancing and reciting before sitting down to a lengthy dinner accompanied by lively conversation and capped by a moving speech in honor of Irish hospitality and generosity.

For readers of the story, this section represents a remarkable physicalization of the details noted by Joyce, from the richly burnished browns of the home to the polite dancing, barbed political talk and the characters themselves, who seem unerringly true. The uninitiated, however, may experience some trouble getting a fix on things, as no plot asserts itself and no characters assume particularly more importance than any others.

By evening's end, the focus clearly has been placed upon the handsome couple of Gretta and Gabriel, played by Anjelica Huston and Donal McCann. Back at their hotel, Gabriel attempts some rare intimacy with his distracted wife, who, prompted by a haunting song, "The Lass Of Aughrim," she has heard sung at the party, throws him into deep melancholy by telling him a secret of a youthful love.

Learning to his distress how his wife still broods about her teenage lover, who died, she believes, because of her, Gabriel sets upon a profound discourse about the living and the dead to the visual accompaniment of snow falling on bleak Irish landscapes. Although shot by a second unit, this climactic sequence represents a moving finale to both the film and Huston's career, and is marked in particular by the words, "Better to pass boldly into that other world, in the full glory of some passion, than fade and wither dismally with age."

Brought in for the California shoot, the virtually all-Irish cast brings the story to life completely and believably, with Helena Carroll's big-hearted Aunt Kate and Donal Donnelly's drunken Freddy Malins being special delights.

Anjelica Huston proves fully up to the demands of her emotionally draining monolog, and Donal

McCann simply is ideal as the thoughtful husband who has never felt true love and knows he can't inspire it in his wife.

The one instance in which the script curiously deviates from the story has to do with the lust Gabriel is supposed to feel for Gretta on the way back to the hotel. The build-up of his emotions is important so that his letdown at his wife's revelations will be all the more severe, but the Hustons completely ignore it except for a glancing remark after the fact.

Dedicated to Huston's longtime companion, Marciela (Hernandez), film looks fine, thanks to Fred Murphy's sharp lensing, Stephen Grimes' production design, done in collaboration with Dennis Washington, and Dorothy Jeakins' costumes.

Time will put "The Dead" in perspective within the context of Huston's other achievements, but from a personal and thematic point of view, it could hardly be more apt as parting gesture from a lively, very smart old artist.—*Cart.*

Lunga Vita alla Signora!
(Long Live The Lady!)
(ITALIAN-COLOR)

A Sacis Intl. (in Italy Istituto Luce/Italnoleggio) release of a RAI-1/Cinemaundici coproduction, in association with the Istituto Luce. Written and directed by Ermanno Olmi. Camera (Eastman Kodak, color by Cinecittà), Olmi, Maurizio Zaccaro; editor, Olmi, Giulia Ciniselli; music, Georg Philip Teleman; coordination, Bianca Giordano; production director, Giampietro Bonamigo; costumes, Francesca Sartori. Reviewed at Cinecittà, Rome, Aug. 25, 1987. (In competition at Venice Film Festival.) Running time: **115 MINS.**
Libenzio . . . . Marco Esposito
Corinna . . . . Simona Brandalise
Mao . . . . Simone Dalla Rosa
Anna . . . . Stefania Busarello
Ciccio . . . . Lorenzo Paolini
Pigi . . . . Tarcisio Tosi
The Signora . . . . Marisa Abbate

Rome — After a 4-year layoff from film work due to illness, Ermanno Olmi returns to the screen with one of his most original thought-provoking pictures, "Long Live The Lady!" This quintessential Olmi film (written, directed, lensed, edited, etc.) recounts a bizarre dinner part in a castle-hotel, where 15-year-old waiters are initiated into their profession at a surrealistic gathering of VIPs.

Combining the director's penchant for documentary with an atmosphere of heavy Lombard Gothic, and even some comedy thrown in, "Long Live The Lady!" is as spellbinding as a gothic novel and fresh as the unblemished faces of its teen heroes. A film as offbeat as this is bound to get fest play and industry prizes; with careful handling, it could find a niche among film lovers of any land.

Pic opens with six youngsters, top grads of a hotel school, being picked up in a jeep and introduced into an isolated medieval castle, now a luxury hotel for rich snobs. Wide-eyed

and timid, they watch a huge staff prepare an elaborate banquet, where they are to help wait on tables. The first-job theme recalls one of Olmi's early films, "The Job," so does his affectionate portrait of the kids, excited to be part of what appears to them a magic, extraordinary occasion.

Minimal dialog gives maximum weight to faces and the admittedly fascinating visual interiors. The kids are put through a series of dead-serious rehearsals, including filmed instructions for correctly setting a table, while in the background a security man tests the bulletproof stained glass windows.

Only when the tastelessly overdressed guests begin arriving does the magic atmosphere start chipping away. Especially in the eyes of Libenzio (Marco Esposito), dreamiest of the new recruits, the scene becomes as grotesque as a Fellini film. He associates a charming girl with freckles and the picture of a guardian angel that fascinated him as a child; but girl and her father (most normal of the guests) are forced to leave mid-party on account of some subtle political intrigue at the table. The dinner is lengthy but quite funny, presided over by a mummified "Lady" of infinite power.

At dawn Libenzio (who has seen his father downstairs in a touching scene, and escaped the seduction attempt of a plump socialite) succumbs to an irrepressible urge to escape while his companions are still asleep — a conclusion left open to several interpretations. — *Yung.*

Un Ragazzo di Calabria
(A Boy From Calabria)
(ITALIAN-FRENCH-COLOR)

A Sacis Intl. release of an Italian Intl. Film (Rome)/U.P. Schermo Video (Rome)/Carthage Film (Paris)/Canal Plus Prods.-General Image (Paris) coproduction, in association with RAI-1. Produced by Fulvio Lucisano. Associate producer, Tarak Ben Ammar. Directed by Luigi Comencini. Screenplay, Comencini, Ugo Pirro, Francesca Comencini, based on a screenplay by Demetrio Casile; camera (Eastman Kodak, color by Telecolor), Franco Di Giacomo; editor, Nino Baragli; art direction, Ranieri Cochetti; music, Antonio Vivaldi. Reviewed at Cinecittà, Rome, Aug. 26, 1987. (In competition at Venice Film Festival.) Running time: **106 MINS.**
Mimi . . . . Santo Polimeno
Nicola . . . . Diego Abatatuono
Felice . . . . Gian Maria Volonté
Mariuccia . . . . Therese Liotard
Also with: Giada Faggioli (Crisolinda), Jacques Peyrac, Enzo Ruoti, Jean Masrevery.

Rome — Poor boy with a passion for running overcomes family opposition to win the race in "A Boy From Calabria," latest offering from veteran helmer Luigi Comencini. The story is tried and true, and there are few surprises in what looks mostly like quality tv fare, made with a family audience in mind. Good cast helps enliven the predictable unfolding of yarn, particularly its boy hero, a nonpro.

Mimi (Santo Polimeno) is 13; set-

ting is the southern countryside in the 1960s when life is still relatively simple and fathers like Nicola (Diego Abatatuono) can dispose of their offspring as they wish. Nicola wants his son to have a brighter future than he has as a strong-arm caretaker at a mental insitution. He insists Mimi devote his free time to study, but all the boy wants to do is take off his heavy shoes and run barefoot, like his hero Abebe Bikila, whom he sees win the Olympic marathon on a neighbor's tv.

Mimi's ally is Felice (Gian Maria Volonté), a lame bus driver kept at arm's length by the community for his presumed communist sympathies. As Mimi's long-suffering mother, Therese Liotard protects her son as best she can from the father's ire, beatings and punishment (once he's locked up overnight in the asylum; when that doesn't work, Nicola turns him over to be worked to death by some ropemakers).

Naturally, there are a number of races interlacing the father-son conflict, near wins, scenes of Felice training the boy, and so on. Wiry little Polimeno is a likable, spunky underdog and his ultimate triumph in a big race in Rome makes an obvious but satisfying conclusion for a film without any rough edges or disagreeable psychological ambiguity. Technical work is pro.
— *Yung.*

Hip, Hip, Hurra!
(Hip, Hip, Hooray!)
(SWEDISH-DANISH-
NORWEGIAN-COLOR)

A Sandrews (Sweden), Kärne Film (Denmark) and KF (Norway) release of a Swedish Film Institute, Sandrew Film 86 KB, Danish Film Institute, Palle Foghtdal and Norsk Film production. (Intl. sales, the Swedish Film Institute — Lena Enquist.) Produced by Katinka Farago. Danish Film Institute producer-consultant, Peter Poulsen. Executive producers, Klas Olofsson, Palle Fogtdal. Written and directed by Kjell Grede. Stars Stellan Skarsgard, Helge Jordal, Morten Grunwald. Camera (Eastmancolor), Sten Holmberg; editor, Sigurd Hallman; music, Fuzzy, Brahms, Mahler; production design, Peter Höimark; costumes, Jette Termann, Kerstin Lokrantz; sound, Lasse Summanen, Lars Ulander; production manager, Thomas Nilsson; assistant director, Gert Fredholm. Reviewed at Norwegian Film Festival (non-competing), Haugesund, Norway, Aug. 15, 1987. (In the Venice Film Festival — competing. Also in Montreal Film Festival.) Running time: **110 MINS.**

Sören Kröyer . . . . Stellan Skarsgard
Lille . . . . Lene Brondum
Marie Kröyer . . . . Pia Wieth
Christian Krogh . . . . Helge Jordal
Michael Ancher . . . . Morten Grunwald
Martha Johansen . . . . . Karen Lise Mynster
Viggo Johansen . . . . Jesper Christensen
Elsie . . . . Lene Tiemroth
Hugo Alfvén . . . . Stefan Sauk
Bonatzie . . . . Ove Sprogöe
Also with: Ghita Nörby, Preben Lerdorff Rye, Holger Boland, Sten Kalö, Benny Poulsen, Tove Maës, Henning Jensen, Tor Stokke, Linn Stokke, Rose Marie Tillisch, Jens Arentzen, Björn Kjellmann, Johan Hison Kjellgren, Percy Brandt, Erik Paaske.

Haugesund, Norway — The sheer visual beauty, poetic sym-

bolism and discreet *angst* psychology of Swedish writer-director Kjell Grede's large-canvassed feature "Hip, Hip, Hooray!" may persuade some esthetically-minded audiences to forgive this portrait of life among end-of-the-19th-century artists and writers at work, at play and in love on the Danish Skaw peninsula for being boring to the point of deadliness. Devoid of any but the most obscure narrative structuring, it features a cast of Nordic actors (item is a Swedish-Danish-Norwegian joint effort in all respects, artistic as well as financial) who speak their lines at cross purposes in a cruel crashing of thesping styles.

The members of the socalled Skaw (or Skagen) Colony of painters are currently enjoying high prices in international markets for works done in a style that refused to be influenced by the Impressionism emerging elsewhere in Europe. Mostly, their pictures radiated either their own joy of living or their superficial preoccupation with the poor and austere local population of fishermen. A Prince of Lightness among them all was P.S. (Sören) Kröyer, whose painting of an al fresco champagne dinner has lent its title also to Grede's film.

It is Grede's conceit that Kröyer, remembered by most everybody else as a whole and happy man, was hiding deep and secret sorrows while posing as more or less The Eternal Child. In the film, he is seen hospitalized with a nervous breakdown, and we are told that his mother, who gave birth to him in an asylum for the insane, haunted him as a vigilante shadow outside his home.

Constantly underscoring the danger of Kröyer's insistent flirt with happiness are the appearances of an old village God's Fool woman who exhorts him to "paint dark, Sören, paint black!" Further symbolism is introduced via a Norwegian painter, Christian Krogh, who makes attempts at having a tame falcon fly, and via an old German vagabond's finding his end of the road at the peninsula's sea-swept tip. There is also the mute friendship seen struck up between Kröyer and a small, blissfully imbecilic little boy.

Also used to illustrate the alleged shallowness of Kröyer's claim to happiness are his brief affair with an undersize, naive church organist, who bore him a child without letting him know about his fatherhood, and his marriage to a woman generally acknowledged to be the most beautiful of the era, but who was to run off with a Swedish composer.

Film's ending has Kröyer seeing himself damning the unworthiness of the flesh as he crawls away from his one carnal embrace with the tiny organist. Whether eating, drinking or making love, they are all very gloomy about their pleasures in "Hooray!" and their famous dinner parties are seen more like wakes.

Sweden's Stellan Skarsgard has a fine free-spirit air about him, and his blond, slightly pudgy good looks radiate true innocence convincingly. Up there with him in the ranks of superior modern acting are Denmark's Karin Lise Mynster as another painter's wife of strength and wry humor and Norway's Helge Jordal as Christian Krogh, another painter.

The Skaw school of painting was famous for its light. This light — plus many emulations of the original paintings — make "Hooray!" a pleasure to look at. Film's music exploits Brahms' Opus 45 and Mahler's First Symphony predictably but neatly. All production credits are of the highest order, serving to earn the multi-national filmmakers at least some small cheers. —*Kell.*

Au revoir, les enfants
(Goodbye, Children)
(FRENCH-WEST GERMAN-COLOR)

An MK2 release of a Nouvelles Editions de Films/MK2 Prods./Stella Film, Munich/-NEF, Munich, coproduction. Produced, written and directed by Louis Malle. Camera (Eastmancolor), Renato Berta; editor, Emmanuelle Castro; art direction, Willy Holt; sound, Jean-Claude Larreux, Claude Villand; costumes, Corinne Jorry; makeup, Susan Robertson; music, Schubert, Saint-Saens; production manager, Gerald Molto; assistant director, Yann Gilbert; casting, Jeanne Biras, Iris Carrière, Sylvie Meyer. Reviewed at the Ponthieu screening room, Paris, Aug. 24, 1987. (In Venice Film Festival — competing.) Running time: **104 MINS.**
With: Gaspard Manesse (Julien), Raphaël Fejtö (Bonnet), Francine Racette (Mme. Quentin), Stanislas Carré de Malberg (François Quentin), Philippe Morier-Genoud (Father Jean), François Berleand (Father Michel), François Negret (Joseph), Peter Fitz (Muller), Pascal Rivet, Benoit Henriet, Richard Leboeuf, Xavier Legrand, Arnaud Henriet.

Paris — Louis Malle returns to France in fine style with this moving quasi-autobiographical drama set in a provincial Catholic boarding school in the last months of World War II. The finely rendered chronicle about youth, a Malle specialty, assumes the dimensions of tragedy when the Gestapo disrupts the cloistered routine to arrest the school fathers and three Jewish children they are hiding there under false names.

Basis of the film is a true incident that has haunted Malle ever since his schoolboy days in a similar religious establishment near Fontainebleau. A nascent friendship with a new boy in class ended brutally when the latter, son of Jews who had been carted off to the death camps in the infamous Vel d'Hiver roundup of 1942, was arrested and sent to his death with two other youths and the school director, a clandestine resistant.

Malle says this is the film he has wanted to make since the beginning of his career, and he has not betrayed his subject matter. Applying skillful dramatic license to his memories, the writer-director has extracted one of the best films, an elegy to a friendship nipped in the bud by war and hate.

He directs with clarity and understatement, setting the mainstage of the drama with detailed recall of lulling rhythms of boarding school life, its secret collective pleasures (a screening of Chaplin's "The Immigrant" in a 9.5m format, with the music instructors providing piano and violin accompaniment), and the intrusions of the real world, banal at first, finally erupting in all their horror.

Most of the youthful cast are nonprofessional, directed with a sure hand by Malle. Gaspard Manesse is his alter ego, Julien, a boy (like Malle) of upper middle class background, who is intrigued by a new arrival after the Christmas holiday in the early days of 1944.

Bonnet (Raphaël Fejtö), the new boy, is reserved, different and cultivated, and a threat to Julien's academic superiority in class. Julien's initial distrust and jealousy slowly evolve towards more positive sentiments as the two boys discreetly find common interests in books and music, and share some extramural adventures (lost in the woods after a treasure hunt with the other classmates, Julien and Bonnet are brought back by some patrolling German soldiers).

The friendship follows its natural course despite, or because of, Julien's gradual awareness that Bonnet is Jewish. Secretly poking about latter's closet, he comes across a book with Bonnet's real name still legible; later he awakens in the night to watch him upright next to his dormitory bed, whispering a Sabbath prayer in front of two lit candles.

The full meaning of his new friend's origins only hit him, however, when the Gestapo enter the classroom and demand the Jewish boy by his real name.

The vivid depiction of life under the German Occupation also forms a pendant to Malle's 1974 film "Lacombe Lucien," though without that controversial picture's ambiguous portraiture. Still, the character of a lame scullery boy who is dismissed by the school director for black market activities, an action that triggers the final tragedy, can be seen as a distant cousin to Malle's protagonist in "Lacombe."

Some of the film's most powerful scenes dramatize the irony and contradictions of the period. Most striking is a sequence in a village restaurant where Julien's mother has taken him, his brother and Bonnet during a Sunday visit. An elderly Jewish gentleman (who has managed to avoid the racist dragnet until now) suddenly is confronted by some members of the Vichy militia, but latter are promptly ejected from the premises by a Wehrmacht officer enjoying a convivial meal, which the barkings of the French collaborators have disturbed.

Among adult players, Philippe Morier-Genoud, a stage actor, is excellent as Father Jean, the head of the school, giving the role sharp, subtle definition despite its episodic nature. Francine Racette, as Julien's starchy bourgeois mother, and Peter Fitz, as a Gestapo agent who carries out the climactic raid, also are vivid.

Renato Berta's lensing and Emmanuelle Castro's editing contribute to the film's fluid movement and lucid direction.

"Au Revoir, les enfants" is competing at Venice and has the right qualities to travel, despite the downbeat ending. For the ailing domestic film scene, Malle's homecoming is, in any case, one of the best things to have happened to the French this year. —*Len.*

Gli Occhiali d'Oro
(The Gold-Rimmed Glasses)
(ITALIAN-FRENCH-YUGO-SLAV-COLOR)

A D.M.V.-Reteitalia release of a L.P. Film (Rome)/Paradis Film (Paris)/Avala Profilm (Belgrade) coproduction in association with Reteitalia. Produced by Leo Pescarolo. Directed by Giuliano Montaldo. Stars Philippe Noiret, Rupert Everett. Screenplay, Nicola Badalucco, Antonella Grassi, Montaldo, based on Giorgio Bassani's novel; camera (Agfa-Gevaert, color by Telecolor), Armando Nannuzzi; editor, Alfredo Muschietti; art direction, Luciano Ricceri; costumes, Nanà Cecchi; music, Ennio Morricone; associate producers, Eric Heumann, Stephane Sorlat; executive producer, Guido De Laurentiis. Reviewed at Telecolor, Rome, Aug. 24, 1987. (In competition at Venice Film Festival.) Running time: **110 MINS.**
Dr. Fadigati . . . . Philippe Noiret
Davide Lattes . . . . Rupert Everett
Nora Treves . . . . Valeria Golino
Eraldo . . . . Nicola Farron
Mrs. Lavezzoli . . . . Stefania Sandrelli
Also with: Roberto Herlitzka, Riccardo Diana, Anna Lezzi, Giovanni Rubin De Cervin, Lavinia Segurini, Luca Zingaretti, Ivana Despotovic (Carlotta), Rade Markovic (Bruno Lattes).

Rome — Giuliano Montaldo's screen adaptation of Giorgio Bassani's modern classic "The Gold-Rimmed Glasses" (forming part of a trilogy on the rich northern town of Ferrara in the prewar period, along with "The Garden Of The Finzi-Continis") is a respectable, straightforward rendition that should be most appealing to adult viewers on the small screen. Ably lensed by a quality team (Rupert Everett and Philippe Noiret are standouts in a deft cast), "Glasses" unfolds its twin themes of intolerance — middle-class ostracism of a homosexual doctor, growing Jewish prejudice — with typical television rhythms and discretion. Same qualities make it a little tiresome as a big-screen experience.

Nonetheless, Montaldo brings a range of often fascinating characters to life. Everett offers an amiable, sensitive portrayal of college student Davide Lattes, scion of a well-to-do Jewish family and increasingly involved in the burgeoning resistance movement as Mussolini's racial laws take root (time is 1938). He loves Nora Treves (Valeria Golino), a rich Jewish girl, but fearful of the future, she converts to Catholicism and marries a Fascist officer.

Sidestepping pathos by inches, Philippe Noiret imparts a sentimental dignity to Dr. Fadigati, an esteemed doctor ruined by provincial mores when he imprudently falls for a handsome young boxer (Nicola Farron employs his haunting features in the ambiguous role). A good part of film takes place at a swanky seaside resort, frequented by Ferrara's high society. At a climactic evening ball, Davide loses Nora and the young boxer betrays, beats up and robs his lover Fadigati.

After this double drama, followup in Ferrara is a bit stretched. Cut off from work and society, abandoned even by a stray dog he has adopted, Fadigati makes a pitiful trip to the river to commit suicide. Davide holds on. A trite bulletin at pic's end tells of their destinies, all obvious.

In a cameo Stefania Sandrelli shines as a malicious, gossiping socialite. Ennio Morricone's retro score is romantic to the point of exasperation, while cameraman Armando Nannuzzi's gray hues add a dreaminess to the visuals. The single nude love scene (Davide and Nora) takes place before a cozy fire. —*Yung.*

La Vallée fantôme
(The Ghost Valley)
(FRENCH-SWISS-COLOR)

An MK2 release of a Filmograph (Geneva)/MK2 (Paris) coproduction, in association with Westdeutscher Rundfunk (Cologne), Télévision Suisse Romande (Geneva), La Sept, and CAB Prods. Executive producers, Alain Tanner and Marin Karmitz. Produced by Jean-Louis Porchet. Written and directed by Tanner. Camera (Eastmancolor), Patrick Blossier; sound, Jean-Paul Mugel; editor, Laurent Uhler; music, Arié Dzierlatka; production manager, Gérard Ruey. Reviewed at the Ponthieu screening room, Paris, Aug. 25, 1987. (At Venice Film Festival — competing.) Running time: **102 MINS.**

Paul . . . . Jean-Louis Trintignant
Jean . . . . Jacob Berger
Dara . . . . Laura Morante
Madeleine . . . . Caroline Cartier
Dara's father . . . . Ray Serra
Jane . . . . Jane Holzer
Casting director . . . . Françoise Michaud

Paris — Alain Tanner is again wandering in the desert of congenial subject matter. In "The Ghost Valley," his second coproduction with France's Marin Karmitz, the restless Swiss helmer strays from the tranquil affluence of Geneva to the wilds of Brooklyn via the sleepy Italian town of Chioggia (just across the lagoon from Venice, where this film is competing at the festival).

Tanner's script begins as yet another bit of navel-contemplation about a filmmaker's difficulty in making a film. Here Jean-Louis Trintignant is a Swiss auteur, given to long soul-searching musings in a valley near his home outside Geneva (hence the title, which has only the slightest rhetorical bearing on the story), who cannot find the right actress for a film idea he has been nurturing and finally throws the script out in a movement of ill humor.

Enter an easygoing penniless film student (Jacob Berger, son of Tanner's erstwhile script collaborator John Berger, in his acting debut) who lands a job as Trintignant's assistant and is soon dispatched to Italy to track down a young actress, who has abandoned the metier and returned to her hometown.

After some initial difficulties, Berger finds the girl (Laura Morante), working as a waitress in her uncle's restaurant, and firmly set against returning to the cinema. Trintignant, just as firmly set on having the girl for his film, prods Berger on. The assistant persists and finally wrings an agreement from her on the condition that he take her to New York to visit her father, who emigrated some 10 years before. In the meantime, Berger also succeeds in falling in love with the secretive girl.

Until this point Tanner manages to hold our interest in the situation and characters, but story and purpose quickly blur as the three protagonists meet up in a seamy melting pot neighborhood in Brooklyn, where Morante's dad runs a diner. Berger throws a fit of jealousy when Trintignant monopolizes Morante for work sessions, while the Italo-American papa chafes at the sight of two men he firmly believes are only interested in getting under his dear daughter's skirt.

Tanner does little with these ill-motivated complications and all too hastily packs his trio back to Chioggia for some sort of reconciliation, of which the viewer is left to draw his own conclusions, if not much satisfaction.

Tanner directs in a seductively furtive manner, but never transcends the flimsiness of his script. Technically fine, "The Ghost Valley" seems geared to specialized audiences with a knowledge of Tanner's previous work and the willingness to connect the thematic dots.
—Len.

Montreal Festival Reviews

King Lear
(U.S.-SWISS-COLOR)

A Cannon Films production. Produced by Menahem Golan, Yoram Globus. Written and directed by Jean-Luc Godard. Camera (color), Sophie Maintigneux; sound, François Musy. Reviewed at World Film Festival, Montreal (hors concours), Aug. 30, 1987. Running time: **90 MINS.**
Lear . . . . Burgess Meredith
Shakespeare . . . . Peter Sellars
Cordelia . . . . Molly Ringwald
Professor . . . . Jean-Luc Godard
Mr. Alien . . . . Woody Allen
Also with: Norman Mailer, Kate Miller.

Montreal — In the wake of the Chernobyl disaster "movies and art no longer exist and must be reinvented," muses William Shakespeare the fifth, a development veep for the "Cannon Cultural Division," who's traveling in Europe in search of bankable projects. He's come to Nyons, France, looking for a reclusive filmmaker who can help him rediscover "meaning" in reality as well as art. While dining at a luxury seaside hotel he becomes fixated upon a mad old American and his devoted, introspective daughter. Shakespeare endeavors to put Mr. Lear and his daughter Cordelia in a film, but it isn't easy.

So much for the story synopsis of Jean-Luc Godard's fascinating first feature in English, a lyrical and purposely provocative "approach" to "King Lear." If Godard has not totally succeeded in challenging conventional assumptions about illusion and reality, this is a noble failure that restores meaning to the bankrupt term "art film." As such it deserves a carefully handled specialty release aimed at audiences who are prepared to accept and possibly enjoy this surreal meditation on its own terms.

Following the pattern of his recent films, "Détective" and "Hail Mary," Godard freely employs disconnected imagery and relooped soundtrack effects to strip images and words of surface meanings in favor of an anarchic sensory bombardment. This, the filmmaker suggests, is how the consciousness perceives the world behind the mask of sanity. Burgess Meredith as Lear does a fine job of imparting the erratic lucidity of mental disintegration as conveyed by Godard's rambling, fragmentary script. Beauty in Godard's "Lear" is akin to salvation, and the filmmaker's eye alights upon the china-like loveliness of Molly Ringwald's features with lingering closeups not likely to be found in a John Hughes flick. Her deadpan, emotionless line readings stand in cool relief to the overboiled ramblings of Lear, Shakespeare V and the filmmaking "Professor" (Godard), whose deadlocks

of wires and cables testify to the insanity-inducing potential of chasing pure images.

The scenario is loosely connected with wordplay intertitles along the lines of "Nothing — No-Thing," as it shifts points-of-view with dreamlike illogic. Always industry-minded, Godard opens "Lear" with the distorted but distinct accents of Cannon topper Menahem Golan pledging his loyalty to the project. There's also a prolog using brief footage shot of Norman Mailer and his daughter before they dropped out of Godard's "Lear."

Walkouts are inevitable at this sort of film, but it almost seems as if Godard anticipated the pitter-patter of early exits as a counterpoint to his "message." Those who stick around until the end (as did most at a Montreal World Film Festival public screening) are rewarded with a cameo by Woody Allen (Mr. Alien) as a film editor tangled up in runaway celluloid.—Rich.

The Kid Brother
(CANADIAN-JAPANESE-U.S.-COLOR)

A Kinema Amerika-Yoshimura/Gagnon-Toho coproduction. Executive producers, Matsuo Takashani, Makoto Yamashina. Produced by Kiyoshi Fujiimoto. Coproduced by Hirohiko Sueyoshi. Written and directed by Claude Gagnon. Camera (Fujicolor), Yudai Kato; editor, André Corriveau; music, François Dompierre; production design, Bill Bilowit; costumes, Maureen Hogan; sound, Russell Fager, production manager, Kathleen Caton; line producer, Dennis Bishop; assistant director, Eduardo Rossoff. Reviewed at World Film Festival, Montreal (competing), Aug. 28, 1987. Running time: **95 MINS.**
Kenny . . . . Kenny Easterday
Sharon . . . . Caitlin Clarke
Sharon Kay . . . . Liane Curtis
Jesse . . . . Zack Grenier
Eddy . . . . Jesse Easterday Jr.
Billy . . . . Tom Reddy
Philippe . . . . Alain St-Alix
Grandfather . . . . John Carpenter

Montreal — A film that's likely to become a talking point wherever it's shown, "The Kid Brother" is built entirely around its 13-year-old star, the severely handicapped Pennsylvania boy.Kenny Easterday, who has no legs or lower torso. French-Canadian director Claude Gagnon has made a presumably fictionalized film about Kenny and his family, financed with Japanese coin. Result is heartwarming and disturbing in about equal proportions.

Without young Kenny, there'd be simply no film. He proves to be a relaxed and charming young actor, who is amazingly agile in getting around, via his long, strong arms. His dramatic range is impressive, more so, in fact, than that of some of his costars. His real-life brother, Jesse Jr., also is effective as his

brother, though the character is called Eddy in the film. Caitlin Clarke and Zack Grenier play the boy's loving parents with strength and sympathy, but Liane Curtis seems a bit out of her depth in the crucial role of Kenny's 18-year-old sister, who has left home because she finds it hard to be around her kid brother whom she accuses of taking advantage of other members of his family.

Curtis has a regular jock for a boyfriend, whom Kenny hero-worships. But she craves her independence, and spends a night with a member of a French television crew that's come to make a documentary about Kenny and his family. This rebellion spurs her eventual departure from the family's small home, and Kenny's daring trip to Pittsburgh to find her, sparking the film's climactic confrontation as she pours out to her brother her feelings about him.

The early part of the film is given over to satirizing the French film crew, and especially the bland director (Alain St-Alix) who ostensibly has come to make a record of the way the family lives, but who actually manipulates them into his own vision of how they should be living. Gagnon himself is equally open to the charge of manipulation, and there will be controversy, when "The Kid Brother" goes into wide release. A scene where young Kenny is threatened by a Doberman belonging to a bad-tempered neighbor, smacks as a contrived bit of drama, unnecessary in the context of the film.

Handouts for the pic were amazingly coy about what makes Kenny different from other kids: his first appearance comes as quite a jolt, but he's obviously reconciled to what he is, and the film's most telling scenes are those in which he rebels against having to use artificial legs and lower torso, pointing out they only slow him down and are intended not for him, but so that his condition won't shock people who see him. The plucky, endearing youngster came on stage after the competing screening at the Montreal fest and took a well-deserved bow.

The fact that there'll be audiences the world over who will want to be inspired by Kenny Easterday's pluck should give "The Kid Brother" wide international release. Critical debates may add to public interest, so the offbeat item looks to have a useful career ahead of it.
—Strat.

Pociag Do Hollywood
(Train For Hollywood)
(POLISH-COLOR)

A Zespoly Filmowe, Rondo Unit, producton. Written and directed by Radoslaw Piwowarski. Camera (color), Witold Adamek; editor, Irena Chorynska; music, Jerzy Matula; production design, Tadeusz Kosarewicz; sound, Aleksander Golebiowski. Reviewed at World Film Festival, Montreal (competing), Aug. 26, 1987. Running time: 97 MINS.

"Marilyn" . . . . Katarzyna Figura
Piotr . . . . Piotr Siwkiewicz
Rafal . . . . Rafal Wegrzyniak
Sandra . . . . Grazyna Kruk
The Director . . . . Jerzy Stuhr
   Also with: Eugeniusz Priwiezncew, Krystyna Feldman.

Montreal — Poland's competing entry in Montreal's World Film Festival is a frenetic, patchy comedy about a comely young woman who thinks she's another Marilyn Monroe. Katarzyna Figura is certainly a looker, but is far from being a Monroe type. She gives a game performance in an overdone, sometimes silly pic.

She's finished acting school but doesn't want to work in the theater and has been turned down for film and tv roles because of uneven teeth. She writes constantly to Billy Wilder in Hollywood, because she saw "Some Like It Hot" when she was a child and wants to play that kind of role.

Until a call from Wilder comes, she sells beer on a train and shares a converted rail coach with a girlfriend who's forever having unhappy love affairs, mostly with foreigners. Then she meets a nice young man (Piotr Siwkiewicz) who wants to be a film cameraman, only he's color blind. Meanwhile, he works (and apparently lives) in the studio props department.

Marilyn gets the occasional bit role (she's burned at the stake in a period epic) and she's a hustler and won't take No lying down. The trouble is that, having created a potentially interesting character, writer-director Radoslaw Piwowarski does little with her. He encourages the actress to overplay and to rely heavily on her spectacular good looks and figure, but it's not enough. Even a promising scene where she goes for an audition to the hotel room of a tearful, mother-fixated film director (Jerzy Stuhr) goes for little.

Eventually, pic retreats into fantasy, with Marilyn scoring three wishes when she finds a goldfish in a beer bottle; unselfishly, she makes her wishes on behalf of others and they come true; but just as she's made love to her boyfriend for the first time (he can see colors at last) that call from Billy Wilder comes.

During a period when there have been many excellent Polish films, this is a disappointingly bland item. It may catch the attention of Polish audiences abroad for its in-jokes about the film industry, or for its appealing lead actress, but it's a minor and only intermittently successful effort. —*Strat.*

Three O'Clock High
(U.S. COLOR)

A Universal Pictures production and release. Executive producers, Aaron Spelling, Alan Greisman. Produced by David E. Vogel. Directed by Phil Joanou. Screenplay, Richard Christian Matheson, Thomas Szollosi; camera (color), Barry Sonnenfeld; editor, Joe Anne Fogle; production design, Bill Matthews, Tom Bugenhaven; music, Tangerine Dream. Reviewed at World Film Festival, Montreal (out of competition), Aug. 27, 1987. (No MPAA Rating.) Running time: 97 MINS.

Jerry Mitchell . . . . Casey Siemaszko
Franny . . . . Anne Ryan
Brie . . . . Stacey Glick
Vincent Costello . . . . Jonathan Wise
Buddy Revell . . . . Richard Tyson
Mr. Rice . . . . Jeffrey Tambor
   Also with: Liza Morrow, Phillip Baker Hall, John P. Ryan.

Montreal — Tyro director Phil Joanou brings a gimmicky, cartoonish film school sensibility to bear upon the familiar teen-in-trouble genre, but compromises obvious promise here in a bargain with the story formula requirements of the Hollywood studios. "Three O'Clock High" gives the teen situation story an interesting twist of paranoid dark humor but cops out to conventionality in the end. Nevertheless it shows more imagination that overrated confections such as "Pretty In Pink" and "Ferris Bueller's Day Off" and certainly deserves a national release in which its fate might depend upon word-of-mouth.

By the time Jerry Mitchell (Casey Siemaszko) arrives for his job as student store manager at his all-American (but virtually all-white) southern California high school, his day already has gotten off to a bad start. He oversleeps, is awakened by his needling kid sister, dries his wet laundry in the microwave while heating a pop-tart and nearly totals his mom's auto while eyeballing a pretty blond student in the adjacent lane. Then things get progressively worse.

The entire student body is talking about one thing: the arrival on campus of a legendary incorrigible bully, Buddy Revell, whose reputation for awesomely violent outbursts at the slightest provocation has preceded him. Believing the premise that this Terminator-type thug would still be in school instead of prison is necessary for accepting the scenario's subsequent hallucinatory bent.

Jerry's best friend, the editor of the school newspaper, assigns the hapless hero to do a "welcome aboard" piece on the fearsome Buddy, who especially doesn't like to be touched. Naturally that's one of the first things Jerry does in a pathetic attempt to get acquainted.

The oversized brute challenges Jerry to an after-school fight in the parking lot, a 3 o'clock rendezvous from which he promises there will be no escape. The normal goings on at school, as seen from Jerry's perspective of mounting terror and dread, are overlaid with grotesque humor. Joanou's depiction of the faculty as cruel, thoughtless autocrats and borderline nut cases is not going to win him any friends at the American Federation of Teachers. One exception is the bookstore supervisor (perfectly cast with Jeffrey Tambor of "Hill Street Blues" and "Max Headroom") who's the only adult around who senses that something is bothering the usually ultra-normal Jerry.

In leading up to Jerry's moment of truth, Joanou shows off an assortment of high-speed/slow-mo camera tricks, skewered angles and sight gags. In one brief but funny sequence, a football pep rally is modeled after the "2-minute hates" of George Orwell's "1984." The film also makes sport of stereotyped teen pic characters: jocks, nerds, punks, hustlers, self-centered girls and even obnoxious would-be filmmakers.

The deceptively bland Siemaszko displays sure control over his character's steady disintegration and makes Jerry a likable and sympathetic victim of this walking nightmare. The picture's resolution, however, is disappointingly standard and at odds with the nose-thumbing, off-center tone of the narrative. Techno-pop music by Tangerine Dream is effective, if under-utilized. —*Rich.*

Verne Miller
(U.S.-COLOR/B&W)

An Alive Films release of a Three Aces production. Produced by Ann Broke Ashley. Written and directed by Rod Hewitt. Camera (color/black & white), Misha Suslov; editor, John O'Connor; production design, Victoria Paul; music, Tom Chase, Steve Rucker; sound, Larry Loewinger; costumes, Leslie Ballard; special effects, Vern Hyde. Reviewed at World Film Festival, Montreal (competing), Aug. 30, 1987. (No MPAA Rating.) Running time: 95 MINS.

Verne Miller . . . . Scott Glenn
Vi . . . . Barbara Stock
Al Capone . . . . Thomas G. Waites
   Also with: Ed O'Ross, Andrew Robinson.

Montreal — There's about as much action — but as little excitement — in "Verne Miller" as in any period gangster pic that has been or is soon likely to be made. The promising "true story" premise of a legendary South Dakota sheriff who crossed the fine line between law and crime to enlist as Al Capone's top enforcer is fatally undermined here by major flaws in conception and execution. These include an embarrassingly coy narrative voiceover by the female lead, garbled line readings that almost beg for subtitles, a script that fails to develop its hero's potentially fascinating transformation, dialog ridden with genre clichés, and direction that substitutes episodic hopscotching for pacing and suspense.

Alive's best shot here is to hope audiences have not been satiated this summer by the Capone-era banquet served up in "The Untouchables," and to promote this mobsters & molls meller to an unsuspecting marketplace as another helping of Prohibition-period pie.

The story opens in 1925, when ex-lawman and notorious fast gun Verne Miller has been sprung from prison where he somehow learned that cops and crooks essentially are "in the same business." Filmmaker Rod Hewitt would have been wise to cut subsequent footage in order to devote some time to Miller's metamorphosis from sheriff to jailbird to mercenary killer. Instead, he is sprung upon the screen a full-blown criminal, invincibly self confident and malevolently defiant of all who would stand in his way.

Verne is rendered dependably by Scott Glenn with requisite vulpine understatement. Not only is he a prince among murderers, but a natty dresser possessed of irresistible sexual charisma as well. His main moll is nightclub singer Vi, played by Barbara Stock, who delivers her voiceover and on-camera lines with all the mesmerizing force of a soap commercial. If Verne takes a couple of years to look her up after being sprung from the joint it could be because her singing and the period torch music soundtrack score here are execrable. Verne has more than women on his mind, however. His aim is to work "with, not for" the king of Chicago crime, Al Capone.

Maybe because they both have a soft spot for children, both have syphilis and both enjoy a good kill, Capone takes an immediate shine to Verne, who quickly proves his mettle by handling several nasty jobs for Scarface. Although Robert De Niro's "Untouchables" Capone will stand as the definitive portrait for a long time to come, Thomas G. Waites tackles the role of the egomaniacal sociopath with seething gusto. Capone eventually dispatches Verne to be sort of a mob viceroy in Kansas City, where the cool and courtly ex-cop and his moll live in a country club mansion with nubile maids and seek entree to the town's social and power elite.

Meanwhile, the Windy City gang wars heat up and the feds begin to crack down — sequences shown in a newsreel-style black & white that might have been used a little more liberally. When Verne decides to no longer play the mob game by Capone's rules he must choose between the slow doom of syphilis or the quick death of the gunman.

There are numerous murder scenes in "Verne Miller" meant to show off the superior ingenuity of the hero. Although intended to reflect Verne's dispassionate attitude toward his work, the action sequences are perfunctory and devoid of the thrills audiences crave and demand from gaudy crime pics. The one brief, outstanding exception is the depiction of the socalled Kansas City massacre in which Verne and friends violently try and fail to rescue a mobster from the feds.

The production and design here are first-rate, particularly in light of the picture's reported $2,500,000 budget, but add no more life to

"Verne Miller" than do fancy outfits to a mannequin.—*Rich.*

Hotarugawa
(River Of Fireflies)
(JAPANESE-COLOR)

A Shochiku release of a Kinema Tokyo/Nichiei production. Executive producers, Matsuo Takahashi, Hiroaki Kato. Produced by Kiyoshi Fujimoto. Directed by Eizo Sugawa. Screenplay, Sugawa, Kyohei Nakaoka, from a novel by Teru Miyamoto; camera (color), Masahisa Himeda; editor, Jun Nabeshima; music, Masatsugu Shinozaki; production design, Iwao Akune; sound, fujio Sato; costumes, Satoyoshi Kubo, Tomio Okubo; special effects, Koichi Kitakawa. Reviewed at World Film Festival, Montreal (competing), Aug. 27, 1987. Running time: **114 MINS.**

Tatsuo . . . . Takayuki Sakazume
Shigetatsu . . . . Rentaro Mikune
Chiyo . . . . Yukiyo Toake
Eiko . . . . Tamae Sawada
Harue . . . . Tomoko Naraoka
Ginzo . . . . Taiji Tonoyama

Montreal — A well-made, though basically familiar tale about the growing pains of an alert 14-year-old in a provincial city over the period of a few months during 1962, "River Of Fireflies" is modest fare, but nevertheless an entertaining example of current Japanese cinema.

Young Tatsuo has a crush on Eiko, a girl in his class, and fights his friend over her. Meanwhile, his businessman father (finely played by vet Rentaro Mikune) has money troubles and is suffering regrets over the fact that, years earlier, he'd left his loyal wife, Harue, when his mistress, Chiyo, Tatsuo's mother, got pregnant. Father and son have a heart-to-heart just before Mikune suffers a severe heart attack as a result of which he eventually expires in hospital, triggering a reunion between the former wife, now a successful innkeeper, and the impoverished second wife and son.

Tatsuo suffers another loss: his best friend drowns in the river while on a fishing trip. The boy grows up quickly when he has to borrow money on his father's behalf to keep himself and his mother going. Pic's climax comes when the father's old buddy guides Tatsuo, his mother and Eiko to a secret place where once in a while, fireflies congregate to mate by the river. It's said that if a couple sees the fireflies together, they'll eventually marry; but the short-lived insects, who mate then die, also are a symbol of change.

Final magical scenes of the fireflies bring Eizo Sugawa's film to a fine conclusion, making up for some of the over-familiar aspects of screenplay and direction earlier in the film. Certainly pic treads no new ground, but it's well acted and lovingly made, with outstanding camerawork of the winter and spring seasons in the little northern town. Not a world-beater for the competition, but nevertheless a film that, with its traditional values and format, will doubtless charm many.—*Strat.*

Padureanca
(The Maiden Of The Woods)
(RUMANIAN-COLOR)

A Film Company 4-Rumaniafilm production. Directed by Nicolae Margineanu. Screenplay, Augustin Buzura, Margineanu, from a short story by Ioan Slavici; camera (color), Doru Mitran; editor, Nita Chivulescu; production design, Magdalena Marasescu; music, Cornel Taranu; sound, Silviu Camil; costumes, Mioara Trandafira; production manager, M. Patu. Reviewed at World Film Festival, Montreal (competing), Aug. 26, 1987. Running time: **125 MINS.**

With: Victor Rebengiuc, Adrian Pintea, Serban Ionescu, Manuela Harabor, Melania Ursu, Dorel Visan, Nicolae Toma, Mihai Constantin.

Montreal — An overlong and predictable saga set in 19th century Transylvania (then part of the Austro-Hungarian Empire), pic covers famliar territory in its tale of a rich man and a peasant vying for the love of a beautiful independent girl, and proves a routine competing entry in the Montreal World Film Festival.

Pic actually opens with a striking nightmare sequence which could have emerged from a vintage Ingmar Bergman film. Birds gather ominously in a lowering sky; a lone horseman arrives at an apparently deserted and abandoned house; out in the streets, bodies are collected and removed. Seems there's a cholera epidemic, and Iorgovan, son of a rich landowner who's been studying in the city, decides to return home to his father's farm.

Here he falls heavily for a beautiful girl, Simina, daughter of a woodsman; but he has a rival in Sofron, one of his father's servants. What follows is strictly familiar, with the age-old struggle between workers and bosses and the lovely maiden as the prize to be fought over.

Pic was adapted from a short story, but its 2-hour-plus running time serves as a detriment. Technical credits are passable, and acting serviceable. —*Strat.*

Tuesday Wednesday
(CANADIAN-COLOR)

A Pickwauket Films production. Produced and directed by John Pedersen. Screenplay, Pedersen, David Adams Richards; camera (color), John Clement; editor, Pedersen; music, Mark Carmody; production design, costumes, Ilkay Silk; sound, Arthur Makasinki; production manager, Louise Newman; casting, Talent Showcase. Reviewed at World Film Festival, Montreal, Aug. 24, 1987. Running time: **82 MINS.**

Phillip Blayney . . . . Jon Alexander
Evelyn . . . . Liz Dufresne
Tina . . . . Penny Belmont

Montreal — A grimly serious first feature and a rare instance of a Canadian feature film produced in New Brunswick, "Tuesday Wednesday" is about lives ruined as a result of alcohol. Phillip (Jon Alexander), an ex-teacher, is a reformed alcoholic who hitches back to the town where he'd accidentally killed a child when he was drunk.

The child's mother, Evelyn (Liz Dufresne) still grieves, with only her daughter and religion for comfort.

It's a bleak, ultra-slow-moving drama which just stays on the right side of boredom. Pluses are the understated performances, the moody photography and Mark Carmody's excellent score. Director John Pedersen believes in detachment and understatement, and in some scenes — e.g., a confrontation between Phillip and a disillusioned woman cop who used to be his student — his approach works.

The combination of minimal techniques and a downbeat theme will make this one a tough sell indeed, and television seems to be its best bet for exposure. —*Strat.*

Saraba Itoshiki Hito Yo
(The Heartbreak Yakuza)
(JAPAN-COLOR)

A Shochiku-Fuji/Burning Prods. production. Produced by Yoshinori Moniwa. Executive producers, Kazuyoshi Okuyama, Ikuo Suho. Written and directed by Masato Harada. Camera (color), Junichi Fujisawa; editor, Tomoyo Oshima; art direction, Yuji Maruyama; music, Toshihiro Nakanishi; lighting, Sei Takaya; sound, Makio Iké. Reviewed at World Film Festival, Montreal (Japanese Cinema Of Today), Aug. 23, 1987. Running time: **102 MINS.**

Shuji . . . . Hiromi Go
Hitomi . . . . Mariko Ishihara
Tetsuo . . . . Kazuya Kimura
Yoshimasa . . . . Koichi Sato
Yumiko . . . . Reiko Nanjo
Mashiba . . . . Daisuke Shima
Nitta . . . . Kaku Takashina
Kato . . . . Akira Emoto
Kiuchi . . . . Rikiya Yasuoka
Restaurant manager . . . . Chin Naito
Officer Yamamura . . . . Yuya Uchida

Montreal — Films about yakuza mobsters are a popular mainstay genre of Japanese cinema, but this luridly violent and overtly sentimental tale of a Tokyo hitman in search of lost innocence is distinguished by technical flare and solidly convincing performances. Although reportedly intended as a tribute to Samuel Fuller's 1950s crime melodramas, "The Heartbreak Yakuza" is distinctly Japanese in character and consequently best suited for U.S. playoff in locked-run series devoted to Japanese film.

Japanese pop music idol Hiromi Go is cast as Shuji, a rising young star in the Daito mob. In a tingling opening scene (that reveals director Masato Harada's debt to Sam Peckinpah) Shuji carries out a contract hit on several thugs from the rival Toryu gang. His career as a killer, however, hasn't totally erased wistful memories of a pastoral riverside childhood, playing Tom Sawyer and Becky Thatcher with Hitomi, his best friend's kid sister. Shuji tries to deny this residual "softness" in his hardened character, but it leads him to spare the life of Kiuchi (Japanese new wave heavy Rikiya Yasuoka).

This show of mercy leads to trouble for Shuji, as the spared gunfight survivor plots revenge even while the bosses of the two gangs begin negotiations for a treaty to merge their operations. Director Harada uses the hierarchical posturings and codified conduct of the mobsters to lampoon the "gentlemen's agreements" that grease the wheelworks of modern Japanese society.

Shuji has an erotic relationship with a stunning mob prostitute, Yoshimasa (Koichi Sato), but at a gaudy hotel wedding for his boss' daughter the handsome gunman spots his long-lost Hitomi, who's working as a hotel waitress. He tries to reject her, but Hitomi (Mariko Ishihara) is beautiful, tenderly innocent and an incurable romantic devotee of a radio show with a uniquely Japanese concept. It's called "Midnight Tom Sawyer," and presents interviews with successful men who recall the golden days of their childhood, a hallowed time for all Japanese.

Inevitably, Shuji and Hitomi fall in love. Although he's supposed to be hiding out from his pursuers, the self-confident hero takes his new girlfriend disco dancing at a popular yakuza watering hole. The couple dance into a hail of bullets from a vengeful hitman and, although both survive, Hitomi is saddled with the lachrymose handicap of blindness. As a gesture of love, Shuji speaks on the "Midnight Tom Sawyer" program (the station owner is a suitor of Yoshimasa) and declares his intention to turn over a new leaf. This eventually is accomplished over many dead bodies.

Harada and cinematographer Junichi Fujisawa give this story a seductive glossy sheen and spice the narrative flow with a dazzling grab-bag of cuts, dissolves and vertiginous camera angles. There's also a very amusing musical score that blatantly mimics the grandiose meanderings of Sergio Leone's collaborator Ennio Morricone.—*Rich.*

Gozaresh-e Yek Ghati
(Report On A Murder)
(IRANIAN-COLOR)

A Hedayat Film production. Directed by Mohammedali Nagafi. Screenplay, Nagafi, Ali Reza Raiesian; camera (color), Mohammed Aladpoush; editor, S. Tavazoie; production design, F. Haghighi; costumes, A. Radgabi. Reviewed at World Film Festival, Montreal, Aug. 26, 1987. Running time: **87 MINS.**

With: Akbar Zanganpour, Homa Rousta, Nasser Hashemi, Mahnaz Afzali.

Montreal — There have been some interesting Iranian films at fests in recent years, but "Report On A Murder" isn't one of them. It's a confused, amateurish effort poorly acted and staged, about the savagery of the Shah's regime.

Pic opens with the release from prison after a 20-year sentence of a former communist unjustly arrested after the 1953 coup against Prime Minister Moussadegh: he tracks down and murders the man he holds responsible for his incarceration.

The authorities assign a young lawyer, Kaveh, to investigate the killing. It happens that the lawyer is friendly with the ex-convict's family. Matters come to a climax with bloody (but very unconvincingly staged) riots in which the secret police (Savak) attack innocent people demonstrating against injustice.

It's often hard to tell whether a given scene is taking place in the past or the present. Pic is raggedly edited, and despite a potentially interesting theme, has little impact.

A final title notes that the film was made under the supervision of the Institute for Islamic Orientation.—*Strat.*

Eiga Joyu
(Actress)
(JAPANESE-COLOR)

A Toho Eiga release of a Toho production. Produced by Tomoyuki Tanaka, Kon Ichikawa. Directed by Ichikawa. Screenplay, Kaneto Shindo, Shinya Hidaka, Ichikawa; camera (color), Yukio Isohata; editor, Chizuko Osada; music, Kensaku Tanigawa; production design, Shinobu Muraki; sound, Tetsuya Ohashi. Reviewed at World Film Festival, Montreal, Aug. 26, 1987. Running time: **130 MINS.**

Kinuyo Tanaka . . . . Sayuri Yoshinaga
Mother . . . . Mitsuko Mori
Kenji Mizoguchi . . . . Bunta Sugawara
Shiro Kido . . . . Koji Ishizaka
Heinosuke Gosho . . . . Kiichi Nakai
Seiko . . . . Yasuko Sawaguchi

Montreal — A biography of Kinuyo Tanaka (1910-77), one of the great female stars of Japanese cinema, "Actress" is a fascinating film for buffs in that it depicts the pioneering work of Japanese filmmakers, such as Heinosuke Gosho, during the silent era, and recreates scenes of the great Kenji Mizoguchi at work on his masterpiece, "The Life Of Oharu." Apart from those interested in Japanese cinema, the film is perhaps a bit too uneventful to find much of an audience outside Japan.

It starts with a scratchy clip from a 1922 silent film, "Hototogisu," then intros the young Tanaka, convincingly played by lookalike Sayuri Yoshinaga, as she's accepted into the Shochiku studios in 1926 and brings her entire family to live with her. Unfortunately, the long opening sequence, in which the family background is established, is written and directed laboriously, and gets the film off to a shaky start.

Though promoted by up-and-coming director Hiroshi Shimizu, whom she marries, Tanaka's best work in the silent period is with Gosho, for whom she made "Embarrassing Dream" and "The Izu Dancer." She also stars in Japan's first talkie, "A Madame And A Wife" (1931). Soon, she divorces Shimizu and, after the death of her protective mother, lives only with a

"bodyguard." The film makes it clear the policy at Shochiku was much influenced by D. W. Griffith, especially "Broken Blossoms," and the aim was to make films depicting "pathos in daily family life."

In 1940, Tanaka works with Mizoguchi for the first time ("Naniwa Woman") and, according to the film, she forms a strong affection for this demanding, enormously gifted director who, according to this film, coined the expression "You're paid to act, so act. I'm paid to direct," when the actress requests guidance from him. When they collaborated on their greatest film together, "The Life Of Oharu," the film suggests the actress and director were having an affair — but all this is implied rather than shown.

Screenplay by director Kon Ichikawa and Kaneto Shindo, also a distinguished director, as well as Shinya Hidaka, concentrates on Tanaka's film work; scenes away from the studio tend to be talky and dull, because away from her work the actress seems to have lived a very ordinary life. As one character notes, however, she combined passion with naiveté, which is why she was so good on screen.

Ichikawa and company also provide a kind of potted history of Japanese cinema, via lots of stills and occasional clips, noting Sternberg's "Morocco" was the first talkie shown in Japan with subtitles, that "Carmen Comes Home" (1951) was the country's first color film, and that Kurosawa's "Rashomon" was the international breakthrough for Japanese cinema. Some of the stills are unidentified in the English subtitles, which is regrettable.

Film ends very abruptly as Mizoguchi (played by Bunta Sugawara) is seen directing the aging Tanaka in "The Life Of Oharu," an ending so abrupt it may leave audiences wanting more. Like last year's "Final Take," this is a fascinating insider film about the Japanese film industry, and like that film it should play the fest route with success. It's technically superb, but a certain awkwardness in scripting and direction makes it a relatively minor effort from director Ichikawa.—*Strat.*

Personal Foul
(U.S.-COLOR)

A Personal Foul Ltd. production. Produced by Ted Lichtenheld, Kathleen Long. Written and directed by Lichtenheld. Camera (color), J. Leblanc; editor, Steve Mullenix; production design, Bill Jones; music, Greg Brown; sound, Michael Hoffman; costumes, Elizabeth Palmer. Reviewed at World Film Festival, Montreal, Aug. 29, 1987. Running time: **92 MINS.**

Jeremy . . . . Adam Arkin
Ben . . . . David Morse
Lisa . . . . Susan Wheeler Duff
Principal . . . . F. William Parker

Montreal — This character study of friendship and bonding between

three attractive but lonely young adults in the Midwest demonstrates sensitivity towards complex relationships, but moves too slowly along the right track to justify all but the most limited theatrical release. In a picture entirely dependent upon character and dialog, the personal portraits are too sketchy and the exchanges too elliptical to rivet viewer concern on the collective fate of a dedicated schoolteacher, a decent drifter whom he befriends and the pretty but insecure woman they're both drawn to.

Jeremy (Adam Arkin) loves teaching his rambunctious grade schoolers and shooting hoops alone. Although he's supposed to be from the Illinois country (the home territory of director-writer Ted Lichtenheld) he's played by Arkin with jittery urban bluntness. Jeremy doesn't love paperwork, the bureaucratic school principal or the company of the other teachers very much, with the possible exception of Lisa, a new schoolmarm from Texas. He's basically an introspective guy, just like Ben (David Morse), who lives in a beat up van and sells paper flowers to support himself.

One morning after washing up in the playground restroom, Ben meets Jeremy shooting baskets and is reluctantly drawn into a game of "H-O-R-S-E." These two quietly macho types gradually become friends. A key plot point (that's not altogether credible) comes when Jeremy loans Ben a white shirt and tie and recruits him to teach his class the art of making paper flowers.

Impressed by this act is Lisa (Susan Wheeler Duff), who looks like a beauty queen, with a vivacious personality to match, but somehow doesn't have a steady guy. Resentful of brusque treatment from the emotionally erratic Jeremy she makes a calculating play for Ben, whose self-confidence meter is so low he can hardly cope with Lisa's attentions. Ben, it seems, is an excon, but his entire personal history is left off-screen. "I did my time," is all the information the screenplay imparts.

From there the plot thickens, but not too deeply. An inherent flaw in homiletic scenarios is fatiguing predictability. It gives away nothing worth hiding to reveal that Jeremy ultimately learns to love a little himself, Lisa, Ben and even the principal, in an obvious ceremony of mutual implicit understanding.

The three principal performers are appealing, but "Personal Foul" is directed too blandly to make the characters compelling. Some good folk songs by Greg Brown do their best to suggest a mood of existential searching.—*Rich.*

Shuto Shoshitsu
(Tokyo Blackout)
(JAPANESE-COLOR)

A Daiei release of a Daiei-Kansai Telecasting-Tokuma Shoten Publishing Coproduction. Executive producers, Yasuyoshi Takuma, Shichirah Murakami. Produced by Katsumi Mizoguchi, Motoki Kasahara. Directed by Toshio Masuda. Screenplay, Masuda, Hiroyasu Yamaura, from the book "Disappearance Of The Capital," by Sakyo Komatsu; camera (color), Masahiko Imura; editor, Toshio Taniguchi; music, Maurice Jarre; production design, Juichi Ikuno; special effects, Teruyoshi Nakano; sound, Tetsuo Segawa. Reviewed at World Film Festival, Montreal, Aug. 29, 1987. Running time: **120 MINS.**

Tatsuya Asakura . . . . . . Tsunehiko Watase
Mariko Koide . . . . Yuko Natori
Yoshuke Tamiya . . . . Shinji Yamashita
Mieko Matsunaga . . . . Yoko Ishino
Seiichiroh Ohtawara . . . . Shuji Ohtaki

Montreal — Back in the '50s, various monsters threatened the destruction of Tokyo, with the Americans often pitching in to help their Japanese friends. In a new world of hi-tech, depicted in the large-scale "Tokyo Blackout," the threat is a mysterious cloud which, without warning, descends on Tokyo's metropolitan area, cutting off all power and access. This time the Americans are as much a threat to Japanese independence as they are a help.

Pic is adapted from a bestseller, and original title translates literally as "Disappearance Of The Capital." Once the massive cloud covers the area, no one can get in or out; an invisible force field prevents passage. Focus of attention comes to rest on two journalists, one a tv newshen, Mariko, whose daughter is inside the cloud area, the other the go-getting Tamiya; and a scientist, Asakura, who leads the fight to destroy the menace. The film contains lots of impressively obscure scientific jargon, and some passable special effects, seen at their best in a sequence in which a U.S. plane tries to fly into the cloud, losing engine power as it does so.

Reason for the cloud is never explained, but what comes over loud and clear here is the mixed feelings Japan currently has towards the U.S. With the Japanese government incapacitated along with the 20,-000,000 others inside the cloud, officials on the outside, including ambassadors in Washington and London, want to form a provisional government; but the U.S. presses the U.N. to be given trusteeship of Japan, a policy that brings horror to every patriotic character in the film. Prevention of Yank control of their country becomes as important an issue as the destruction of the mystery cloud.

Director Toshio Masuda (co-director, back in 1970, of "Tora! Tora! Tora!") does a good logistical job, and stages some suspenseful sequences, but he tries to pack too much in, and a sequence involving a blind rock singer is just one instance of trying to please too many people in the film. Ending, in which the journalist, Tamiya, succeeds in destroying the cloud after the scientists have failed, is a bit hard to take, and the images of a cute puppy, blooming flowers and sunrise that accompany the lifting of the cloud are strictly cornball.

Music by Maurice Jarre whips the suspense effectively, and crowd scenes are very well handled. Some of the dialog, as translated via the English subtitles, is terrible, and acting is merely functional. At base, this is a fun pic, a throwback to filmmaking of 30 years ago.—*Strat.*

The First Killing Frost
(U.S.-COLOR)

A Unique Film Prods. production. Produced and directed by Rolland Halle. Screenplay, Halle, J. Peter Kelley, Loren S. Miller, John G. Tucker; camera (color), Charles Lew; production design, Allen Randall; music, Don Wilkens, Michael Rendish; sound, Steve Bores; costumes, Jennifer Greenberg. Reviewed at World Film Festival, Montreal, Aug. 24, 1987. Running time: **92 MINS.**
Jim Bradley .... Sidney Friedman
Suzanne Bradley .... Reegan Ray
Bradley daughter .... Lisa Christie
Bradley son .... Joshua Leblanc

Montreal — This leaden, conventional drama about a successful computer engineer traumatized by sudden unemployment would be boxoffice poison for a theatrical distributor, but cable and public tv outlets hungry for well-intentioned, platitudinous product could perhaps use it to fill 90-minute programming vacuums.

Jim Bradley is a research & development whiz who designs computer hardware, drives a BMW, has a picture-book family and enjoys the respect and affection of his colleagues. Jim is still trying to reconcile himself to the death of his father, whom he remembers in voiceover as a loving but emotionally remote man whose passion for woodworking and manual labor this upwardly mobile tech-type never shared. In one of the many clichés that litter the group-written screenplay, Jim senses he can arrive at an understanding of his own true nature only by coming to terms with all that went unspoken between him and his dead father.

Jim avoids confronting these deeper problems by working overtime on a design meant to better a rival company's far superior computer. His corporate bosses panic at the competition, however, and sell out to a coarse, autocratic businessman who promptly fires Jim and his coworkers. At first, Jim's ideal suburban wife, whip-smart daughter and loving son are happy to have dad around the house, confident the talented and experienced engineer will find another job in no time.

The family takes a vacation at Jim's father's lakeside land in the country, where a good-guy sheriff recalls the father fondly and a good neighbor with a nasty teenage son inquires about buying some of the property. Jim's wife insists on keeping the land, but the engineer, subconsciously wanting to distance himself from his father's memory, is tempted to sell the parcel on which stands the old man's toolshed and workshop.

Back in town, Jim's job-hunting, like the stultifyingly predictable plot, goes in circles. Nerves become short, and his relationship with his wife and kids begins to deteriorate along with his self-image. Finally, Jim exiles himself to his father's toolshed while his family, now nearly broke, improbably starts up a home-based meal delivery business.

As played by the lanky, ultra-sincere Sidney Friedman, Jim is presented as a basically decent chap whose eventual triumph over his life-crises is never left in doubt by the homiletic scenario. Supporting performances are adequate as are the technical credits.—*Rich.*

Blindside
(CANADIAN-COLOR)

A Norstar Entertainment release of a Simcom production. Produced by Peter Simpson. Directed by Paul Lynch. Stars Harvey Keitel. Screenplay, Richard Beattie; camera (color), Rene Ohashi; editors, Nick Rotundo, Stephen Lawrence; music, Paul Zaza; production design, Rick Roberts; costumes, Nada Healy; production manager, Robert Wertheimer. Reviewed at World Film Festival, Montreal, Aug. 28, 1987. Running time: **103 MINS.**
Penfield Gruber .... Harvey Keitel
Julie .... Lori Hallier
Adele .... Lolita David
William Freelong .... Michael Rudder
Dolman .... Cordelia Strube
Borden .... Durango Coy
Gilchrist .... Alan Fawcett
Sandy .... James Kidnie
Collinson .... Kenneth McGregor
Peters .... Sam Malkin
Hawk .... Marc Strange

Montreal — "Blindside" rates as one of the most convoluted and confusing thrillers seen in many a moon, needlessly so because the basic idea is straightforward enough. Harvey Keitel toplines as a former behavioral scientist and surveillance expert reduced, since the suicide of his wife (whom he captured on video and watches obsessively), to running a sleazy motel, inaptly named The Sunburst. What follows is a low-life cross between "Rear Window" and "The Conversation," with plenty of violence, some sex, but almost no clarity. It looms as a better bet on video than theatrical.

At the outset, Keitel is hired by a couple of no-goods to spy on one of his tenants, Freelong (Michael Rudder), whom they suspect (rightly) of pulling a double-cross in a drug deal. At the same time, Keitel also bugs the room of another tenant, Gilchrist (Alan Fawcett), who's having a secret affair with a married woman; during the course of his surveillance, Keitel discovers that Gilchrist and the woman's husband are plotting to kill her. He alerts the potential victim, a cool blond played by Lori Hallier, and is soon in the cot with her. What he doesn't know, yet, is that she's linked to the Freelong character as well, though indirectly.

Richard Beattie's screenplay has some ideas, but it's a muddle, and director Paul Lynch doesn't make it lucid. He has fun with a shootout in a parking station, and extracts ghoulish humor from a scene in which a carload of dead bodies is passed off to a suspicious traffic cop as drunks, but he fails on the most basic level of telling a cohesive story. Long after the film is over, audiences are likely to be wondering who really was doing what to whom, and why.

Harvey Keitel is fine as the brooding protagonist, but deserves better material than this. Lolita David, introduced here, is lively as a spunky stripper he unaccountably rejects in favor of the manifestly untrustworthy Lori Hallier.

Pic is technically slick, with the motel setting suitably scrungy, but the editing does nothing to make all the goings on more comprehensible. Word of mouth is likely to be grim, so fast playoff is indicated before a second life on vidcassette.—*Strat.*

Magic Sticks
(W. GERMAN-AUSTRALIAN-COLOR)

A Wolfgang Odenthal Filmproduktion (Munich)-Tale Film (Vienna) production. Produced by Odenthal. Directed by Peter Keglevic. Screenplay, Keglevic, Chris Ragazzo, George Kranz; camera (color), Edward Klosinski; editor, Darren Kloomok; music, Kranz; production design, Stephen McCabe, Sid Bartholomew; sound, Jochen Schwarzat; costumes, Ulrike Schutte; line producer, George Hofmann; casting, Leo Finger. Reviewed at World Film Fest, Montreal, Aug. 23, 1987. Running time: **91 MINS.**
Felix .... George Kranz
Shirley .... Kelly Curtis
Pawnbroker .... Joe Silver
Also with: Chico Hamilton, Ted Lambert, Reginald Vel Johnson, John Gallagher, Jack McGee, David Margulies, Mike Hodge.
(In English)

Montreal — An English-track German production, handsomely shot on New York locations by Polish cinematographer Edward Klosinski, "Magic Sticks" is a cutesy affair about an impoverished young drummer who obtains a pair of magic drumsticks from a street peddler. When he plays with them, he discovers native New Yorkers, but not newcomers to the Big Apple, respond with weird, jerky dancing — they become temporarily in some kind of magic state.

With the sticks, the hero is able to charm music student Kelly Curtis, but finds himself in strife with a couple of smalltime hoods who want some of the magic for themselves. It's a rather precious concept for a film, likely to appeal only to those with a keen sense of fantasy.

Lead actor George Kranz, who also coscripted and composed the music score, displays a rueful charm throughout but standout performance is Joe Silver as a kindly pawnbroker. Pic's major asset, though, is Klosinski's splendid work behind the camera, as a result of which the big city positively shines.
—*Strat.*

Itazu
(Forest Of Little Bear)
(JAPANESE-COLOR)

A Toei release of a Kobushi production. Produced by Hisashi Yabe. Directed by Toshio Goto. Screenplay, Ryunosuke Ono, from a story by Goto; camera (color), Takaya Yamazaki; editor, Atsushi Nabeshima; music, Masaru Sato; production design, Akira Haruki; sound, Hirofumi Miyata; costumes, Kyoto Isho. Reviewed at World Film Festival, Montreal, Aug. 27, 1987. Running time: **117 MINS.**
Ginzo .... Takahiro Tamura
Ippei .... Hiroshi Miyata
Kimi .... Junko Sakurada
Grandmother .... Nijiko Kiyokawa
Heisaku .... Toru Yuri
Tashiro .... B-Sako Sato
Takahara .... Ryutaro Tatsumi

Montreal — An outstanding family pic, "Forest Of Little Bear" is an outdoor saga about a little boy, his wise grandfather and an exceptionally cute bear cub. It should please kids and their parents worldwide.

Set in a mountainous district in 1928, film begins with the return home of an old hunter who discovers his son was killed in the Siberian war. He takes his grandson in hand, teaching him hunting lore. That the old man is a crack shot is demonstrated when he guns down a killer bear (in an exciting sequence), though a dog he's borrowed to help him in the hunt is killed by the huge animal. Only later does the hunter discover he's killed a mother bear, something that goes against his code.

The surviving bear cub now occupies center stage, and in scenes reminiscent of American animal pictures, the cute little creature gets into mischief with swans, snakes, goats, and also tries to get into a beehive, with predictable results.

All of this is charmingly handled, with glowing camerawork of the beautiful mountain locations, and natural performances. Human characters aren't ignored, and all ring true. Few who see the film won't be delighted with it.—*Strat.*

Dao Mazei
(Horse Thief)
(CHINESE-COLOR)

A China Film presentation of a Xi'an Film Studio production. Directed by Tian Zhuang-zhuang. Screenplay, Zhang Rui; camera (cinemascope, color), Hou Yong, Zhao Fei; production manager, Li Changqing. No additional credits supplied. Reviewed at World Film Festival, Montreal, Aug. 25, 1987. Running time: **86 MINS.**
With: Cexiang Rigzin, Dan Zhiji, Daiba.

Montreal — Made at the Xi'an Film Studio in northern China, same studio that produced such key Chinese films as "Yellow Earth," "The Black Cannon Incident" and "The One And The Eight," "Horse Thief" is an immensely impressive production set in the mountains of Tibet in 1923. Arthouse audiences in the West may well be intrigued by this evocation of a remote, timeless world with its strange customs and cruelties.

Story is told almost entirely without dialog. Norbu is a poor shepherd struggling to survive along with his wife and small son. He turns to petty crime, including stealing horses, but when he steals gifts belonging to the officials of the local temple, he's driven away from the village, as a result of which his child dies. His wife gives birth again and the cycle of poverty and death will continue.

With commanding use of the wide screen, cinematographers Hou Yong and Zhao Fei fill the film with unforgettable images: flocks of vultures picking at carcasses outside the village walls; strange religious ceremonies in which thousands of pieces of white paper are scattered to the winds, or prayer wheels are slowly turned; a ceremony in which the villagers wear grotesque masks as they dance. There's also extreme cruelty, and a scene where sickly goats are herded into a pit and buried alive is a bit rugged, as is the ritual slaughter of a sacred lamb.

It says much for the talents of director Tian Zhuangzhuang that he's able to tell his story with lucidity while resorting to only a few snatches of dialog (in Tibetan, with Chinese and English subtitles). Pic was made in 1985 and has proved controversial presumably because of its depiction of Tibetan religious customs. It's a must for the fest circuit, and could well score at arthouses where other Chinese films, like "Yellow Earth," are starting to find appreciative audiences; it's already bringing crowds to London's ICA cinema.

Film is technically good, with a fascinating score. —*Strat.*

The Last Song
(THAI-COLOR)

Directed by Pisarn Akarasainee. In color. Running time: **90 MINS.**

Montreal — This last-minute entry in Montreal's World Film Festival didn't feature in the catalog, and fest officials were unable to provide any credits save the name of the director.

Garish item concerns a handsome youth from the countryside who comes to Bangkok to try his luck as a singer, and becomes involved with gays and transvestites who congregate around a lavish nightclub. Sappy plotline and over-the-top acting make this one strictly for native

consumption. Almost illegible subtitles, misspelled and often hilariously ungrammatical, are additional problems. —*Strat.*

The Suicide Club
(U.S.-COLOR)

A Suicide Prods. production. Produced by James Bruce, Steve Crisman. Coproducers, Sam Waksal, Paula Herold, Mariel Hemingway. Directed by Bruce. Stars Mariel Hemingway. Screenplay, Matthew Gaddis, Suzan Kouguell, Carl Caportoto, from a story by Robert Louis Stevenson; camera (Du Art color), Frank Prizzi; editor, Bruce, Keith Rouse; music, Joel Diamond; production design, Steven McCabe; sound, Paul Cote; costumes, Natasha Landau; production manager, Keith Rouse; assistant director, Mary Beth Hagner; casting, Bonnie Finnegan Reviewed at World Film Festival, Montreal, Aug. 27, 1987. Running time: **90 MINS.**
Sasha Michaels . . . . Mariel Hemingway
Michael Collins . . . . Robert Joy
Cam . . . . Lenny Henry
Nancy . . . . Madeleine Potter
Mervin . . . . Michael O'Donaghue
Catherine . . . . Anne Carlisle
Brian . . . . Sullivan Brown
Cowgirl . . . . Leta McCarty

Montreal — Early scenes in this indie first feature from James Bruce, a former assistant to Louis Malle, establish interesting characters and an intriguing situation, but about a third of the way in, the picture takes off in a whole new direction, which leads nowhere. End result is frustrating and, as a result, commercial prospects, even if a cult audience can be found, look dubious.

Sasha Michaels, alluringly played by Mariel Hemingway, is a world-weary heiress whose brother committed suicide some months earlier. She and her current boyfriend, Michael (Robert Joy), have an edgy relationship, but decide to go out for dinner to a smart restaurant with a girlfriend of Sasha's she hasn't seen in a while and the gf's mate. Restaurant scene is the best in the film, with sharp dialog and fine thesping creating an intriguingly unexplained situation.

Then things start to go off the rails. Cam (Lenny Henry), a handsome and apparently wealthy character, arrives at the restaurant and abruptly invites Sasha to a party; to Michael's anger, she goes. It's a costume ball for the idle rich and terminally fey, at which seemingly lethal games are played when things get dull. Incredibly, Sasha returns again the next day for more, even though she suspects a guest who lost the game the previous night has since been killed. Michael follows her, and there's a tragedy at fadeout.

But by this time, most audiences will have ceased to care, because the characters in the film are so empty and so obnoxious they've become supremely dull. It's a pity, because Bruce shows considerable promise as a director; it's the screenplay, based on a Robert Louis Stevenson story, that lets him down.

Though presumably made on a low budget, the film is technically first-rate, with Natasha Landau's costumes rating a special nod. Hemingway, one of the pic's coproducers, is as good as her sappy character will allow. —*Strat.*

To Mend The World
(CANADIAN-DOCU-COLOR)

A Canadian Broadcasting Corp. production. Produced and directed by Harry Rasky. Screenplay, Rasky; camera (color), Kenneth W. Gregg; editor, Paul Nikolich. Reviewed at World Film Fest, Montreal, Aug. 23, 1987. Running time: **90 MINS.**

Montreal — A new approach to the horrors of the Holocaust is to be found in Canadian docu director Harry Rasky's latest, an evident labor of love which matches the inevitable comments of eye-witness survivors of the camps, plus input from philosopher Emile Fackenham, with a look at hitherto unseen works of art painted by camp inmates.

The paintings are disturbing, affecting and powerful, and add a great deal to this latest sad reminder of man's inhumanity to man. Alongside the expected horrific reminiscences are potent reminders the Allies didn't do as much as they might have to alleviate the suffering of the Jews struggling to survive in the 800 camps, most situated outside Germany. It's noted that though Allied bombing destroyed many rail links, the trains to Auschwitz always ran on time.

Film's title is derived from the idea of some ancient scholars that when God made the world he dropped it and it's up to mankind to mend it. Rasky's quietly effective film, handsomely made, is another must-see to add to our sum of knowledge about those dark, awful times. —*Strat.*

Train Of Dreams
(CANADIAN-COLOR)

A National Film Board of Canada production. Produced by Sam Grana. Associate producer, Sally Bochner. Directed by John N. Smith. Screenplay, Smith, Bochner, Grana; camera (color), David de Volpi; editor, Smith; music, Malcolm MacKenzi Jr.; sound, Jacques Drouin; production manager, Marie Tonto-Donati; assistant director, François Gingras; casting, Lois Siegel. Reviewed at World Film Festival, Montreal Aug. 25, 1987. Running time: **89 MINS.**
Tony Abruzzi . . . . Jason St. Amour
Mrs. Abruzzi . . . . Marcella Santa Maria
The Teacher . . . . Fred Ward
Nicky Abruzzi . . . . Christopher Neil
Tony's lawyer . . . . David Linesky
Crown attorney . . . . Milton Hartman
Judge . . . . Basil Danchyshyn
Girl at party . . . . Sarah Casey

Montreal — A tough-as-nails study of an antisocial 17-year-old Montreal hood who's heading for a life of crime and violence, "Train Of Dreams" is an effective, hard-hitting pic that is so well acted and directed that it has the feel of a

documentary; the viewer has to keep reminding himself this is not for real. John N. Smith's low-budget film should nab critical kudos and perform in arthouses in Canada and, possibly, abroad.

Central character is Tony Abruzzi, played with sullen intensity by Jason St. Amour. He lives with his 10-year old brother and his often distraught mother; his father ankled years before, and it's quite obvious the mother can't cope with a son who's left school, refuses to find work, sleeps all day, and hangs around with street gangs at night, coming home (often drunk or stoned) in the early hours of the morning. Tony has drifted into crime via robberies and soft drugs, and is out on parole when he gets into an argument with his mother (who's been nagging him constantly to shape up) and beats her; she calls the police.

As a result, Tony gets two years in an Ontario correctional institute for young offenders. Some of his fellow inmates are painfully young. At first his attitude is that of sullen noncooperation and there's the feeling he'll never lead a normal life but will be forever in and out of prisons until, maybe, he commits a capital crime.

In the film's wonderful central scene, a teacher (strongly portrayed by Fred Ward) gets through to him via music. He's the only boy in his group to understand and appreciate the words of Billie Holiday's standard "Don't Worry 'Bout Me," and his breakthrough into cooperation is wonderful to behold. On a weekend pass, he's even mature enough to help his mother straighten out his kid brother, who looks to be heading down the same road he did.

Director Smith, who made last year's "Sitting In Limbo," has done a fine job here in finding hope out of a seemingly bleak existence, and gets wonderful performances from his mostly nonpro cast. His editing is a bit confusing at times, and the sound recording is muffled in some early scenes, but despite these relatively minor flaws, the film should find an appreciative audience via fests and arthouses. —*Strat.*

Deaf
(U.S.-DOCU-16m-COLOR)

A Zipporah Films production. Produced and directed by Frederick Wiseman. Camera (color), John Davey; editor, sound, Wiseman. Reviewed at World Film Festival, Montreal, Aug. 24, 1987. Running time: **163 MINS.**

Montreal — A companion piece to "Blind" (*Variety*, July 1), this Frederick Wiseman docu was filmed at the School for the Deaf at the Alabama Institute and it's an immensely long and detailed study of the techniques used to teach deaf children. As with other Wiseman films, its length will be a limiting factor, but Wiseman edits his films himself, so presumably wants it that way.

There's a fascination in watching deaf children patiently taught to speak (theme also effectively tackled, in a far more mainstream fashion, in "Children Of A Lesser God"). We also see the tutors themselves undergoing training, the visits of parents to their children, and the various ways these handicapped youngsters are prepared for the outside world.

There are times when emotion springs from what we're watching, but mostly Wiseman stays detached, content to observe what's happening. In some of his early, famous docus the director implicitly criticized certain U.S. institutions, but here he seems to admire the dedicated work done at the school, as well he might.

As is often the case with Wiseman films, the viewer is often impatient and there's time to speculate that, with more rigorous editing and shaping of the excellent basic material, the films could attract a far wider audience. —*Strat.*

En Dernier Recours
(In The Last Resort)
(CANADIAN-DOCU-COLOR-16m)

A National Film Board of Canada production. Produced by Eric Michel. Directed by Jean Godbout. Screenplay, Godbout; camera (color), Jean-Pierre Lachapelle; music, François Dompierre; sound, Richard Besse. Reviewed at World Film Fest, Montreal, Aug. 24, 1987. Running time: **71 MINS.**

Montreal — A docu made to remind Canadians that terrorism exists in their own country, this is strictly a local item aimed at tv transmission.

Director Jacques Godbout includes interviews with experts, plus video and film footage of such terrorist incidents as a bomb blast at Montreal Central Station, the danger facing Turkish diplomats in Ottawa, the attempt to place a bomb in the path of the Pope, and, worst of all, the planting of a bomb on the Air India jumbo jet.

In all, a sobering reminder for Canadians that terrorism isn't to be found only in the Middle East and Europe. —*Strat.*

Boran — Zeit Zum Zielen
(Boran — Time To Aim)
(W. GERMAN-BELGIUM-COLOR)

A Daniel Zuta Filmproduktion (Hamburg)-Alain Keytsman Prod. (Brussels) coproduction (World Sales: Cine-Intl., Munich). Produced by Zuta, Keytsman. Directed by Zuta. Screenplay, Zuta, Bernard Rud; camera (color), Walther Van Den Ende; editor, Uta Ajoub; music, Okko Berger, Jan Kruger, Lonzo Westphal; production design, Jürgen Schnell; sound, Frank Struys; special effects, Günther Schaidt; production manager, Elvira Bolz; assistant director, Frank Van Melhelen; casting, Gerda Diddens. Reviewed at World Film Festival, Montreal, Aug. 29, 1987. Running time: **100 MINS.**

Philip Boran	Bernard Rud
Linda Mars	Renée Soutendijk
Maconnet	Julien Schoenaerts
His deputy	Jean-Pierre Léaud

Montreal — Billed as the first West German-Belgian coproduction, this first feature by Daniel Zuta takes full advantage of moody Brussels locations to bolster a familiar tale of modern-day film noir. He shows some directorial skills, but pic, despite intriguing aspects, is too slow and uneventful to win wide acceptance, and too locked into its thriller format to make the arthouse circuit.

Bernard Rud, who coscripted, plays Boran, a reformed criminal now movie star. On the night his latest, "No Way Out," preems, his younger brother is killed by police following a bank robbery. An obsessive cop (Julien Schoenaerts) is certain Boran also was involved in the crime, and Boran is just as certain his brother was unjustly killed. He sets an elaborate trap for the overzealous lawman, aided by a glamorous journalist, played with bored elegance by Renée Soutendijk.

Pic's main attraction is not the rather labored plot, but the intriguing atmosphere created. Backstreets of Brussels, lovingly shot by Walther Van Den Ende, are a major plus. Rud is a stolid hero, and Schoenaerts steals the film as his somewhat kinky adversary. Jean-Pierre Léaud is on hand, and less manic than usual, as the cop's dedicated deputy.

Zuta might have tightened his screenplay and direction, both of which have far too many slow spots. Film reeks of atmosphere to the detriment of storyline. Nonetheless, this is a creditable first effort.
—*Strat.*

Love Letter
(JAPANESE-COLOR)

A Nikkatsu Films release of a Gentosha production. Produced by Katsuhiro Maeda. Directed by Yoichi Higashi. Screenplay, Yozoo Tanaka, from the book by Mitsuharu Kanekoi; camera (Cinemascope, color), Koichi Kawakami; editor, Keiko Ichihara; music, Michi Tanaka; production design, Toshiro Ayabe; sound, Yukio Kubota. Reviewed at World Film Festival, Montreal, Aug. 28, 1987. Running time: **85 MINS.**

Yuko Kano	Keiko Sekine
Toshiharu Oda	Katsuo Nakamura
Toyo	Mariko Kaga
Murai	Noboru Nakaya

Montreal — Apparently based on a real-life relationship between a famous poet and his mistress, "Love Letter" (that's the original Japanese title) is a surprisingly touching love story with beaucoup nudity on display. Thanks to a sweet performance in the leading role from Keiko Sekine, this tale of a basically 1-sided relationship has an emotional charge.

Oda, the poet, is a man of the world, married and only looking for a compliant young mistress. He meets Yuko when she's still a schoolgirl, and before long has set her up in a small apartment where she spends long, lonely hours waiting for him to come to spend time with her. Their love scenes together, while strictly softcore, are sufficiently erotic to become the centerpiece of the drama.

Yuko is so charming that the selfish, dreadful Oda comes across as even more of a monster. He won't let her have other friends, but has a fling with her next-door neighbor, a divorced woman. Yuko becomes almost suicidal, especially after Oda forces her into an abortion she never wanted. Eventually, he dies, and the film ends as she's an unwanted mourner at his funeral.

While by no means a major work, this is a deft study of a very unequal relationship, though it's likely to annoy many women viewers because of the famous poet's extreme chauvinism. Production dress is excellent, with fine scope camerawork in mostly cramped interiors.
—*Strat.*

Sheere Sanggy
(Stony Lion)
(IRANIAN-COLOR)

A Farabi Cinema Foundation production. Produced by Ali R. Shoja Noori. Written and directed by Massoud Jafari Jozani. Camera (color), Mahmood Kalari; editor, R. Imami; music, Fareidoun Shahbazian; sound, Izac Khanzadi; costumes, Mahmoody. Reviewed at World Film Festival, Montreal, Aug. 27, 1987. Running time: **94 MINS.**
With: Ali Nassarian, Ezzatollah Entezami, Ali R. Shoja Noori, Hamid Jebeli.

Montreal — This is the second film by director Massoud Jafari Jozani to crop up on the fest circuit this year; his earlier "Frosty Roads" unspooled in Berlin, and was far superior to his latest, "Stony Lion," a slow-moving drama of tribal warfare set during the period when the British were administering Persian oil wells.

Kouhyawr, a tribal shepherd, discovers the body of a murdered British engineer in the desert. He buries the corpse and gives the dead man's boots to a passing wanderer. But the British want to punish the killer, and send an emissary to the region to investigate. Although Kouhyawr swears on the Koran that he didn't kill the Britisher, the authorities don't believe him, and when he's imprisoned, tribal warfare breaks out.

An interesting idea is given mundane treatment here. Pic is repetitive and takes far too long to get to the predictable climax in which the tribes go to battle over custody of the wrongly accused man. Even then, the fighting scenes are awkwardly staged, with unconvincing effects.

On the plus side, the spectacular desert locations are lovingly photographed, and there's a rousing music score to accompany the frequent punctuating shots of horsemen galloping across an arid skyline. But, apart from some fest interest, this is unlikely to arouse much attention.—*Strat.*

Yoshiwara Enjo
(Tokyo Bordello)
(JAPANESE-COLOR)

A Toei production. Produced by Shigeru Okada. Directed by Hideo Gosha. Screenplay, Sadao Nakajima, based on the book "Yoshiwara Conflagration" by Shinichi Saito; camera (color), Fujio Morita; editor, Isamu Ichida; music, Masaru Sato; production design, Yoshinobu Nishioka; sound, Kiyoshige Hirai. Reviewed at World Film Festival, Montreal (Japanese Cinema of Today), Aug. 28, 1987. Running time: **133 MINS.**
With: Yuko Natori, Jinpachi Nezu, Rino Katase, Sayoko Ninomiya, Mariko Fuji, Mineko Nishikawa.

Montreal — The Yoshiwara district of Tokyo was, for 330 years, famous because brothels were legal there (they were outlawed by the Americans in 1946). This saga spans the years 1907-11, and centers on a young girl, Hisano, sold into prostitution to pay off her father's debts. Handsome production, with some softcore sex sequences, climaxes with the big fire of 1911 which destroyed most of the brothels; tighter editing could make it a possible attraction internationally.

At first, young Hisano can't bring herself to work as a prostie, and flees from her first customer. She's brought back and initiated into sex by an older, more experienced woman; resulting sequence is the film's most explicit and erotic. From then on, Hisano plays the game by the rules and rituals of the very traditional brothel, eventually becoming the most sought-after prostie of all.

Some of her colleagues also feature in the overlong saga, including Yoshisato, who goes berserk with a razor and kills herself; Obana, who contracts a fatal disease; and Kokonoe, who finds true love and eventually leaves the brothel. Hisano herself passes up the chance to leave, opting to stay and feature in the annual procession of callgirls through the streets of the district.

Colorful, exotic pic covers too much ground, and could be considerably snipped for greater impact. It gets a bit repetitive in the 2¼-hour version unspooled in Montreal. Production design of Yoshinobu Nishioka is impressive, with the large sets destroyed in the fire which provides the film's climax (in the great tradition of such climactic scenes in Hollywood pics as "In Old Chicago"). —*Strat.*

Man On Fire
(ITALIAN-FRENCH-COLOR)

An AAA (France) release (Tri-Star in U.S.) of a 7 Films Cinema/Cima Produzioni/FR3 Films coproduction. Produced by Arnon Milchan. Directed by Elie Chouraqui. Stars Scott Glenn. Screenplay, Chouraqui, Sergio Donati, based on the novel by A.J. Quinnell; camera (Eastmancolor), Gerry Fisher; editor, Noëlle Boisson; sound, Guillaume Sciama, Claude Villand; art direction, Giantito Burchiellaro; music, John Scott; production managers, Claudio Mancini, Steven Hirsch; assistant director, Inigo Lezzi; associate producer, Robert Benmussa; casting, Barbara Clayman, Daniele Luchetti. Reviewed at Club 13, Paris, Sept. 2, 1987. (MPAA Rating: R.) Running time: 93 MINS.
Creasy ....Scott Glenn
Samantha Belletto ....Jade Malle
David ....Joe Pesci
Ettore Belletto ....Paul Shenar
Jane Belletto ....Brooke Adams
Michael ....Jonathan Pryce
Conti ....Danny Aiello
Julia ....Laura Morante
Sandri ....Alessandro Haber
Rabbia ....Franco Trevisi
(English-language track)

Paris — Poorly contrived, predictable and mawkish, "Man On Fire" never rises above the level of a routine vigilante justice melodrama, with much higher-budget blood and thunder but little genuine excitement or emotion, despite a thick overlay of sentimentality. First English-lingo feature by France's Elie Chouraqui, produced by the multinational Arnon Milchan under Franco-Italian auspices and shot on location in Italy, pic gets its Stateside release next month via Tri-Star. With no star names to carry its cliché-ridden plot, however, it will be an uphill battle at the wickets.

Chouraqui, 37, who has directed four features at home, landed a contract with Milchan when latter saw his 1985 film "Words And Music," a marshmallow romance with Catherine Deneuve and Christophe Lambert. Milchan threw him the script for "Man On Fire," a revenge actioner which, if one believes everything one reads, was written for Marlon Brando, who (understandably) refused. Chouraqui rewrote it (with Sergio Donati), eliminating the downbeat aspects of its familiar framework.

Story breaks down simply — and simple-mindedly — into two distinct parts. In the first section, zombie-like ex-CIA operative Scott Glenn lands a job as bodyguard for a Poor Little Rich Girl (newcomer Jane Malle, daughter of Louis Malle and actress Claude Jade), and slowly becomes attached to the kid, who is suddenly kidnapped by a band of nasty, perverted Italian terrorists and held for ransom.

In part two, Glenn, renouncing his decision never again to resort to violence, suddenly becomes Bronson, Stallone and Eastwood — choose one — and goes gunning for the villains, whom he wipes out one by one with ruthless perseverance, nearly losing his life in the process.

Chouraqui tries to mix European intimacy with American spectacle and botches both. Though he spends some 45 minutes setting up the Glenn-Malle relationship, what we learn of them could have been expedited in one reel. That both underact in a deadpan style doesn't prevent the sap from flowing.

Things don't improve when the bullets start to fly. The plotting and staging become increasingly shabby. The terrorists are so pathetically inept they neglect to execute Glenn when they kidnap the girl (as any self-respecting, cold-blooded terrorist would have done), then later are reduced to sniveling cowards when the hero catches up with them.

In one of the most outlandish sequences, Glenn confronts one hood in a deserted warehouse and extorts info by starting the timing device on a near-at-hand bomb. When some of his cohorts arrive, Glenn flees, pursued soon enough by the gang — who have conveniently forgotten to defuse the bomb!

Film begins at the end of the action with a seriously wounded Glenn apparently dying in a hospital while the Italian press clamor for the story outside. (Why an obscure ex-CIA man should suddenly become a media sensation is never clarified.) Then a voice-over narrative by the supposedly dead protagonist recounts the story, "Sunset Boulevard"-style. Chouraqui, who has enough technical fluency to know better, indulges in such facile outmoded gimmickry as slow-motion camerawork and portentous sound effects.

Glenn, in a role of shallow substance, offers the audience nothing to grab hold of. Malle is pretty and likeable, despite some appalling dialog, but she's virtually out of the picture at half-time. A supporting cast including Brooke Adams, Danny Aiello, Paul Shenar, Laura Morante and Joe Pesci are introduced hurriedly in peripheral parts, then just as quickly disappear. There probably were more victims in the editing room than there are on the screen.

Studio work and special effects, with rain-drenched urban streets constructed at Rome's Cinecittà and De Paolis studios are elaborate. Gerry Fisher's lensing, notably for the first half of the story, is atmospherically superb.

"Man On Fire" opened the Deauville American film fest, coincidental with its French release by AAA. *—Len.*

Penitentiary III
(COLOR)

Latest prison pic is fast and fun.

A Cannon Group release of a Jamaa-Leon production. Produced by Jamaa Fanaka, Leon Isaac Kennedy. Written and directed by Fanaka. Camera (color), Marty Ollstein; editor, Ed Harker; music, Garry Schyman; production design, Marshall Toomey; art direction, Craig Freitag; sound, Oliver Moss; costume design, Maria Burrell Fanaka; stunts, John Sherrod; assistant director, Brent Sellstrom, Pat Kirck. Reviewed at Movieland Broadway, N.Y., Sept. 4, 1987. (MPAA Rating: R.) Running time: 91 MINS.
Too Sweet ....Leon Isaac Kennedy
Serenghetti ....Anthony Geary
Roscoe ....Steve Antin
Warden ....Ric Mancini
Midnight Thud Jessup...Kessler Raymond
Cleopatra ....Jim Bailey
Hugo ....Magic Schwarz
Sugar ....Windsor Taylor Randolph
Also with: Rick Zumwalt, Janet Rotblatt, Madison Campudoni, Bert Williams, Mark Kemble, Jack Rader.

Is "Penitentiary III" fun? Are cartoons and professional wrestling matches fun? If you answer yes to the second question then this movie definitely is for you. The third pic in the "Penitentiary" series zips along with enough action and humor to satisfy the kid in just about everyone.

As the film opens, Too Sweet, a boxer portrayed by Leon Isaac Kennedy with a Sugar Ray Leonard-esque demeanor, is drugged by his trainer during a fight. In the subsequent chemical-induced rage, Too Sweet bludgeons his opponent, El Cid (Madison Campudoni), to death. As a result, Too Sweet lands in the pen.

Too Sweet, upon arriving in the brought up growling and spewing. The mini-monster is thrust into Too Sweet's cell and goes about his main function — the rape of prisoners who displease the sadistic Serenghetti.

As is usually the case in professional wrestling, good conquers evil and Too Sweet clobbers the ferocious Thud. For his efforts, Too Sweet is relegated to a room with no view next to Thud.

A series of events lead to Too Sweet — still refusing to fight — training another pugilist on the warden's team who gets battered by one of Serenghetti's henchmen who has taken the same drug Too Sweet was given in the first scene.

This infuriates Too Sweet. Consequently, he agrees to battle it out with Hugo (Magic Schwarz), a giant Incredible Hulk act-alike, in a free-style match.

Suddenly, Thud speaks. He is not the animal he is perceived to be, but actually is a sort of West Indian mystic who winds up training Too Sweet in what can only be described as some other version of "The Force."

The climactic warfare between Hugo and Too Sweet, replete with body slams, eye-gouging, flying scissor clinches and submission holds, is wonderful. The only thing missing is the broadcast team from the World Wrestling Federation.

Too Sweet — you knew this, didn't you? — triumphs. But not before he is almost clubbed into defeat on countless occasions. The payoff is that Serenghetti is disgraced — not to mention his loss of a huge wager to the warden — and prison life is better for all.

"From now on," the warden says to Too Sweet, "this place will be run like it should be. No more gambling with institution funds."

"Penitentiary III" is by no means a shining example of filmmaking. The looping, for example, sometimes looks like dubbing from a Japanese horror flick.

Despite its technical shortcomings, the film is a rollicking roller-coaster of entertainment. It floats like a butterfly and stings like a bee. It's the "thrilla in the cinema." It's better than a ringside seat. And a lot cheaper. —*Chuk.*

Nowhere To Hide
(CANADIAN-COLOR)

A New Century/Vista Film Company release of an Alliance Entertainment production. Executive producer, John Kemeny. Produced by Andras Hamori. Directed by Mario Azzopardi. Screenplay, Alex Rebar, George Goldsmith, based on a story by Rebar; camera (Film House color), Vic Sarin; editor, Rit Wallis; music, Brad Fiedel; production executive, Susan Cavan; costumes, Renee April; stunt coordinator, Buddy Joe Hooker; associate producer, Stephane Reichel; sound, Joe Grimaldi, Don White, Michael Liotta; casting, Amanda Mackey, Maria Armstrong, Ross Clydesdale. Reviewed at Hollywood Pacific, L.A., Sept. 4, 1987. (MPAA Rating: R.) Running time 90 MINS.
Barbara Cutter............Amy Madigan
Rob Cutter ....Daniel Hugh Kelly
Johnny Cutter ....Robin MacEachern
Ben ....Michael Ironside
General Howard ....John Colicos
Mike Watson ....Chuck Shamata
Mark Halstead ....Clark Johnson

Hollywood — There's always been a bit of a hard edge to Amy Madigan's femininity and it's put to good use in "Nowhere To Hide" as she plays a strong, physical heroine in this competent actioner. Screenplay and direction let her down, though, as promising storyline is ruined by a connect-the-dots plot progression that telegraphs every development while heavy-handed lenser Mario Azzopardi doesn't examine Madigan's character closely enough. Boxoffice chances are iffy, but word-of-mouth will be mostly good.

Madigan is retired Marine Barbara Cutter, the brainy, artistic wife of USMC officer Rob Cutter (Daniel Hugh Kelly, whose hair is a bit too blow-dried for Corps believability). After two Marine helicopters go down on maneuvers, Rob investigates the wreckage to find out if the cause was something other than human error.

He finds the clue quicker than you can say "crooked defense contractors," and when he brings the faulty rotor part, the key to the military-industrial coverup, home with him, he's gunned down brutally in his son's bedroom.

Story begins to strain under the weight of its incredibility when 6-year-old son Johnny (Robin MacEachern), who has witnessed the murder, keeps the rotor part snapped onto his robot toy, then suffers a case of elective mutism, not talking again until late in the film.

Baddies need to rub out Barbara before she finds the piece — and puts the pieces together — and so middle section has them chasing her all over the Montreal landscape (masquerading, evidently, as the Pacific Northwest).

When Madigan finally gets a clue as to what's up, she finds almost everyone she trusted (save her husband) was implicated and everyone who tries to help her seems to get murdered.

So she heads for refuge to the mountains and Rob's reclusive best buddy Ben (Michael Ironside), whom, the script hints, has been holed up since losing his Vietnamese wife in friendly fire.

By the time the showdown occurs, causing Barbara to finally take rifle in hand again (she spends most of the film unarmed while she flees would-be assassins; go figure), there's little mystery as to how things will turn out. Sting operation that nails villains in the end is just too pat, and reactions of particulars at the moment-of-truth lacks credibility.

Occasionally subpar editing (including some violently bad jump-cuts early on) and sound further hamper the overall presentation.

Madigan usually rises above the story and technical glitches, however, carrying the pic on her sturdy shoulders. —Camb.

Venice Festival Reviews

House of Games
(U.S.-COLOR)

An Orion Pictures release of a Filmhaus production. Produced by Michael Hausman. Written and directed by David Mamet. Story, Jonathan Katz, Mamet; camera (Panavision, color), Juan Ruiz Anchia; editor, Trudy Ship; art direction, Michael Merritt; costumes, Nan Cibula; music, Alaric Jans; special effects, Robert Willard; sound, Anthony John Ciccolini 3d. Reviewed at the Venice Film Festival (competing), Sept. 3, 1987. (MPAA Rating: R.) Running time: **102 MINS.**
Margaret Ford . . . . Lindsay Crouse
Mike . . . . Joe Mantegna
Joey . . . . Mike Nussbaum
Dr. Littauer . . . . Lilia Skala
Businessman . . . . J.T. Walsh
Also with: Willo Hausman, Karen Kohlhaas, Steve Goldstein, Jack Wallace, Ricky Jay, G. Roy Levin, Bob Lumbra, Andy Potok, Allen Soule.

Venice — Writer David Mamet's first trip behind the camera as a director is entertaining good fun, an American film noir with Hitchcockian touches and a few dead bodies along the way. The action unfolds at a steady pace, highlighted by a series of con games which are explained like good card tricks. Not overly sophisticated as a thriller, (Mamet doesn't hesitate to explain his tricks an extra time to be sure they're understood, and anybody who's read a mystery should guess the final hoax 20 minutes before the heroine does), "House Of Games" shows a woman giving in to hidden desires that endanger her safe world. Film should find an audience without difficulty.

Any story that pairs a psychiatrist and a con man has possibilities. Here the famous Dr. Margaret Ford (Lindsay Crouse) finds her patients' lives more interesting than her own, and with the unwitting encouragement of her mentor (Lilia Skala), allows herself to be drawn into a nest of confidence sharks. In the tense atmosphere of a smoky backroom cardtable, the irresistible heel Mike (Joe Mantegna) sets her up for a $6,000 drubbing. The good doctor gets out of that one by comic chance, but drawn to Mike and his dangerous life, she comes back the next night for more.

As a debutant lenser, Mamet devotes more energy to getting through scenes than developing characters, and pic could have done with a hint more work in this department. Why, for example, is Lindsay Crouse decked out in masculine garb and haircut? In the absence of a compelling reason, the part cries out for a cool Hitchcock blond with more fragility, all the better to stun in the last-scene turnaround.

Mantegna, on the other hand, is right on target as one of the screen's most likable baddies, obviously a better psychologist as far as human nature goes than the professional shrink. His big con involves an elaborate setup to convince a conventioneer, picked up by partner Mike Nussbaum, to offer "security" for a suitcase full of money found on the street. Understanding the mechanism is half the fun, and "House Of Games" cleverly selects its cons, explains their workings, then twists them around again, all without boring or losing the viewer.

Where the film shows at the seams is in Dr. Margaret Ford's apparently unlimited gullibility, equaled only by her fatal flaw of making Freudian slips at the wrong moment. Pic opts for a fashionably cynical ending that washes its hands of two potentially deep characters and settles for a cute twist.

Alaric Jans' edgy score and Michael Merritt's classic noirish sets keep film firmly rooted in the thriller genre. Juan Ruiz Anchia's camerawork is simple and effective.
— Yung.

Julia & Julia
(ITALIAN-COLOR)

An Artist Associati (in U.S., Cinecom) release of a RAI-TV production. Directed by Peter Del Monte. Screenplay, Del Monte, Silvia Napolitano, Sandro Petraglia; camera, (high definition video HDVS, color by Technicolor), Giuseppe Rotunno; editor, Michael Chandler; art direction, Mario Garbuglia; music, Maurice Jarre; English dialog, Joseph Minion. Reviewed at C.D.S., Rome, Aug. 26, 1987. (At Venice Film Festival — out of competition.) Running time: **97 MINS.**
Julia . . . . Kathleen Turner
Daniel . . . . Sting
Paolo . . . . Gabriel Byrne
Paolo's Father . . . . Gabriele Ferzetti
Paolo's Mother . . . . Angela Goodwin
Also with: Lidia Broccolino (Carla), Norman Mozzato, Yorgo Voyagis, Mirella Falco, Alexander Van Wyk (Marco), Francesca Muzio, John Steiner, Renato Scarpa (Commissioner).

Venice — "Julia & Julia" weds high tech and the Italo art film in hopes of coming up with international entertainment. Results are mixed. Superficial resemblance to Kathleen Turner's "Peggy Sue Got Married" could be a plus abroad, though this is a colder, European version with sexual morbidity and adult scenes in the place of humor. Convoluted plot also has a tendency to confuse viewers halfway through.

But one of distrib's main headaches will be getting a watchable 35m transfer into theaters. Italy's RAI-TV has been experimenting with high-definition television (HDTV), or video with 1125 lines an image instead of the usual 600-odd, since 1983. "Julia & Julia" was born as a pioneer effort at using the new advances in electronic technology for feature filmmaking, put into artistic hands, budgeted beyond $10,000,000, with a cast headed by starnames Turner and Sting.

Prints screened for press in Rome and Venice showed there were still technical bugs to work out in transfering HDTV to film stock.

Yet despite these problems, director-cowriter Peter Del Monte and his cameraman Giuseppe Rotunno, with the help of art director Mario Garbuglia, manage to turn film's visual into a major asset, creating an eerie atmosphere that recalls De Chirico's metaphysical paintings. It helps, particularly when the going gets rough in the script department.

Viewers meet Julia (Turner) on the day of her wedding to Paolo (Gabriel Byrne). Setting, the Adriatic coast near Trieste, is breathtaking, the couple radiant.

Six years later, Julia is a lonely travel agent still obsessed with her lost love. One night, after driving through a foggy tunnel, she is surprised to find herself in another dimension: in the midst of the life she would have had if the fatal car accident hadn't occurred.

In this other world, she lives in material bliss with Paolo and their little boy. But soon she discovers there's a threat to her happiness, a demonic photographer named Daniel (Sting), who is her secret lover. All her efforts to shake off this violent man prove useless, and after he rapes her practically in the middle of the town square, Julia decides to get rid of him.

The other threat to Julia is that film begins casually shifting her back and forth between this world and reality.

Turner is not at her subtle best acting-wise, tending toward loud overreactions, but if film sticks together at all it's thanks to the force of her star persona, convincing us Julia is sane. Sting handles his small double role with modest understatement, and as the sensitive, comprehensive husband, Byrne makes one of his most successful screen appearances.

The English-language version makes use of the unpleasant convention whereby everyone in Trieste speaks pidgin English, on the flimsy excuse of Julia's American background.

Maurice Jarre's score is right in tune with pic's abstract spookiness.
—Yung.

Made In Heaven
(U.S.-COLOR)

A Lorimar Motion Pictures presentation of a Rudolph, Blocker production. Produced by Raynold Gideon, Bruce A. Evans, David Blocker. Directed by Alan Rudolph. Screenplay, Evans, Gideon; camera (color), Jan Kiesser; editor, Tom Walls; music, Mark Isham; sound, Ron Judkins, Robert Jackson; art direction, Steve Legler; sets, Paul Peters; costumes, April Ferry; special effects, Max W. Anderson. Reviewed at the Venice Film Festival (competing), Sept. 6, 1987. (MPAA Rating: PG.) Running time: **103 MINS.**
Mike Shea/Elmo Barnet . . Timothy Hutton
Annie Packert/
Ally Chandler . . . . Kelly McGillis
Aunt Lisa . . . . Maureen Stapleton
Ben Chandler . . . . Don Murray
Mrs. Packert . . . . Marj Dusay
Mr. Packert . . . . Ray Gideon
Billy Packert . . . . Zack Finch
Annette Shea . . . . Ann Wedgeworth
Steve Shea . . . . James Gammon
Brenda Carlucci . . . . . . Mare Winningham
Also with: Neil Young, Tom Robbins, James Tolkan, Ric Ocasek, Vyto Ruginis, Gailard Sartain, Leon Martell, Matraca Berg, Tom Petty, John Considine, Rob Kneeper, Robert Gould, Debra Dusay and uncredited Ellen Barkin, Debra Winger.

Venice — The differences of opinion between producers and director on this project, some of which were clearly hinted at in the Venice press conferences held by Alan Rudolph, are obviously the source of many of this film's flaws. A gentle comedy which could have been integrated in the romantic fantasy genre along with classics such as "Angel On My Shoulder" and "Here Comes Mr. Jordan," the script obviously held material that was too abundant for one single feature film. Cutting it to reach a playable running time, in this instance, is counterproductive, for it stresses the episodic nature of the story, most episodes lacking necessary substance as they are rushed into the next one.

Mike Shea is a nice smalltown boy who dies and goes to heaven. There he is introduced to eternal life by his long deceased aunt Lisa, he meets the solicitious Annie, a beautiful guide with whom he falls in love, and finally encounters Emmett, the strange person who is not God but is in charge of seeing that everything proceeds smoothly, as ordained.

Mike falls in love with Annie, who was born in Heaven, but before they can establish a valid union, she is sent to do her stint on Earth. He begs Emmett to let him go back as well and is granted 30 years to find his love again down below.

At this point, the script leaves Heaven and comes back to flesh and blood reality, as it telescopes the 30 years at the end of which the couple is inevitably to meet, just before deadline.

Except for one episode, in which Elmo meets a tough cookie and is led by her, through his innocence, to participate in a gang fight, the script displays the kind of trust in human nature and its finer qualities that is rare these days, and Rudolph packages it all in a kind of rosy cheerful light, both Heaven and Earth being shown as places were nothing really bad can happen, even death being only a transitory stage from one place to another.

The nature of the story invites obviously all sorts of religious and philosophical speculations, which are pretty much ignored here, even on the narrative level. For instance, one wonders about the possibility of being born in Heaven or having sex and children there, a premise which obviously would be shocking to traditional faith still discussing the sexual identity of angels.

Rudolph appears to have opted for a purely romantic approach, that is showing a love so perfect and strong that it can survive any obstacles, and inferring that there are such things as being paired in Heaven and that searching for the perfect mate on Earth is indeed justified.

If Timothy Hutton and Kelly McGillis are likeable, it is mostly through their own personalities that this quality comes out, the script pushing them around too much to allow any leisurely character building. Which, one could add, is exactly the opposite of what usually happens in a Rudolph movie.

Some cameos in the film, like Maureen Stapleton's luminous Aunt Lisa, and Ann Wedgeworth as Mike's original mother who meets him again on his second stint on Earth and has a hand in his completing his destiny, are quite engaging.

The film has a good chance of becoming something of a cult item thanks to numerous guest performances, some of them uncredited, of show business personalities such

as Neil Young, who besides writing the film's theme, plays a truck driver, or Tom Petty who pops up as a mechanic. Ellen Barkin plays the hellcat who almost deprives Hutton's character of his pure innocence, but she refused a credit, while Emmett, the great supervisor in the sky, a youngish looking redhead credited as "playing himself," is none other than Debra Winger, Hutton's spouse, who assumed the part on condition that it be kept a secret, by now revealed to all.

Musical score can also be expected to help, Rudolph relying once again, as he did many times before, on songs to support the story and convey its meanings. The attempt to separate between periods by changing color patterns, is less successful, and art direction seems to be hesitant as to the right way of telling apart fantasy and reality.

That a certain quality of gentleness and warmth is still there, in spite of the many problems, is definitely a credit to Rudolph and his cast, but it is not quite sufficient to compensate for the rest. —*Edna.*

Sibaji
(Contract Mother)
(SOUTH KOREAN-COLOR)

A Shin Han Motion Pictures production. Produced by Jung Do-hwan. Directed by Im Kwon-t'eak. Screenplay, Song Gil-han; camera (color), Goo Joong-mo; editor, Park Sunduk; art direction, Won Ki-su; music, Shin Byung-ha. Reviewed at the Venice Film Festival (competing), Sept. 2, 1987. Running time: **95 MINS.**
Onyia . . . . Kang Soo-yeon
Sangkyu . . . . Lee Goo-soon
Old lady . . . . Han Eun-jin
   Also with: Bang Hee (Yoon Ssi), Yoon Yang-Ha (Chi-ho).

Venice — The lengths to which childless couples will go to have an heir, and consequent dramas and suffering of everyone involved, are often told in South Korean films. In "Contract Mother," the practice under fire — distanced in a historical setting, however — is that of renting poor women to have "contract babies" for a sterile pair of nobles; the secret mother is forced to surrender her infant at birth and agree never to see it again.

However exotic the setting, theme seems lifted from today's newspapers, a coincidence that might give this chicly lensed film a leg up on art circuits. A number of kinky scenes of torture, sex and childbirth also won't hurt. Helmer Im Kwon-t'aek, veteran maker of 86 films in 25 years, has an astute sense of dramatic pacing and doesn't shy away from exploiting the more sensational sides of the tale, although a social message manages to get through.

After 12 years of marriage, Sangkyu's (Lee Goo-soon) wife is still childless (pic opens with her trying an agonizing remedy, boiling oil on the belly, to be repeated for 300 days). Though Sangkyu is a goodhearted guy who loves his wife, fa-

mily pressures forces him to accept a "sibaji," a penurious country girl willing to have his child in exchange for a few acres of land. The wife urges him to go through with it, fearing she'll be repudiated if an heir isn't produced fast.

A sassy, carefree 17-year-old virgin is picked (Kang Soo-yeon, a newcomer whose career was launched by this film). Since we're far from the days of scientific fecundation, film makes the most of the girl's painful tattooing and deflowering, while the legitimate wife waits outside, calling out instructions in the manner of Masters and Johnson.

Onyia, the rented mother, soon falls in love with her master-lover; he returns the feeling. Their too-frequent couplings in house and garden are the subject of reproach for the husband, flogging for the girl. A wide assortment of corporal punishment is inflicted on the female cast (bodily functions also are noted), culminating in a horrifying childbirth sequence that combines natural and unnatural torture. No sooner is the baby born than the girl and her mother are thrown off the estate. A year later, we're told, Onyia hangs herself.

Elegantly lensed, with curious period costumes and essential decor, "Contract Mother" is a visual pleasure. — *Yung.*

Comédie!
(Comedy!)
(FRENCH-COLOR)

A Sara Distribution-CDF release of a Sara Films produciton. Produced by Alain Sarde. Directed by Jacques Doillon. Screenplay, Doillon, Jean-François Goyet, Denis Ferraris; camera (Eastmancolor), William Lubtchansky; editor, Catherine Quesemand; sound, Jean-Claude Laureux, Claude Villand; music, Philippe Sarde; end credits song by Alain Souchon, performed by Souchon and Jane Birkin; production manager, Christine Gozlan. Reviewed at the Publicis screening room. Paris, Sept. 3, 1987. (At Venice Film Festival-competing.) Running time: **82 MINS.**
   With: Jane Birkin, Alain Souchon.

Paris — "Comedy!" in competition at the Venice festival, is a romantic 2-hander from Jacques Doillon, who has abraded many with his totured dramas of people in a permanent state of crisis. Superbly photographed by William Lubtchansky, pic offers a change to a lighter ironic tone, though Doillon's characteristic obsessions remain the motor of the film. Neither especially charming nor particularly irritating, it should do its thing in art circuits and fests without altering one's opinion of the auteur one way or another.

Alain Souchon, cuddly local pop idol, and British actress Jane Birkin are the only characters, playing lovers who wrap up the first year of their relationship with a trip to former's isolated country house.

The high-strung Birkin, who has never been there before, immediately becomes jealous of the hilltop

abode, with its souvenirs and ghosts of Souchon's past love life. No sooner are the wraps off the furniture and swimming pool then the two are locked in Games People Play psychodramatics, with the more reserved Souchon parrying as best he can Birkin's neurotic blows.

Things do turn out well, as this is supposed to be a serious romantic comedy. He finally utters the magic words, "I love you," and the couple melt into each other's arms. This is a French film, remember.

Despite Birkin's hysterical behavior (a lighter replay of her performance in Doillon's controversial "La Pirate"), "Comedy" is inoffensive, though one may detect a faint air of narcissism hanging over the film — Birkin is Doillon's real-life mate and the setting of the film is the director's own provincial retreat. The feeling that Doillon is playing open house with his private life could rub some viewers the wrong way.—*Len.*

Toronto Festival Reviews

A Prayer For The Dying
(BRITISH-COLOR)

A Samuel Goldwyn Co. release of a Peter Snell production. Produced by Snell. Directed by Mike Hodges. Stars Mickey Rourke, Bob Hoskins, Alan Bates. Screenplay, Edmund Ward, Martin Lynch, from Jack Higgins' novel; camera (Kay/Metrocolor), Mike Garfath; editor, Peter Boyle; music, Bill Conti; sound (Dolby), Chris Munro, Sandy McRae; production design, Evan Hercules; assistant director, Terry Needham; stunt arranger, Colin Skeaping; costume design, Evangeline Harrison; special effects, Ian Scoones; associate producer, Christabel Albery; casting, Mary Selway, Debbie McWilliams. Reviewed at Magno Review 1 screening room, N.Y., Aug. 12, 1987. (In Toronto Film Festival.) (MPAA Rating: R.) Running time: **107 MINS.**

Martin Fallon . . . . Mickey Rourke
Father Da Costa . . . . Bob Hoskins
Jach Meehan . . . . Alan Bates
Anna . . . . : . . . . . Sammi Davis
Billy . . . . Christopher Fulford
Liam Docherty . . . . Liam Neeson
Siobhan Donovan . . . . Alison Doody
Jenny . . . . Camille Coduri
Also with: Ian Bartholomew, Mark Lambert, Cliff Burnett, Anthony Head, David Lumsden, Lenny Termo.

"A Prayer For The Dying" is a disappointing thriller adapted from Jack Higgins' novel. Impressive list of topliners is a guarantee to get the public's attention, but release version of the film already has been disowned by its director Mike Hodges, who joined the project on short notice, succeeding the original project's helmer Franc Roddam before shooting commenced last year.

Originally planned to be filmed a decade ago by a different production team, with Edward Dmytryk to direct and Robert Mitchum to star, film finally got made by producer Peter Snell, representing U.S. distributor Samuel Goldwyn Co.'s biggest production investment to date.

Mickey Rourke, styled with red hair and Irish brogue, portrays Martin Fallon, an IRA hitman who sees the light in the opening scene when a bomb aimed at British soldiers blows up a busload of school kids instead. Without permission from his IRA superiors, he flees to London. To get out of the country he reluctantly agrees to carry out a mob hit for gangster Jack Meehan (Alan Bates), but the killing, staged at a cemetery, is witnessed by priest Father Da Costa (Bob Hoskins).

Fallon cannot bring himself to kill the priest to silence him, even when Meehan orders it. Instead, and this constitutes the picture's key plot device, he confesses the murder to the priest. Though outraged at this misuse of religion, Da Costa feels dutybound by the sanctity of the confessional and refuses to identify Fallon to the police.

Film becomes rather conventional at this point, with Fallon outwitting the gangsters, police and IRA hitmen (Liam Neeson, Alison Doody) hot on his case, aided by the sympathetic, blind niece of the priest, Anna (Sammi Davis). Director Hodges conjures up some of the tough, ruthless style of his Michael Caine-starrer "Get Carter" in detailing Rourke's run-ins with his adversaries. Finale, set in the church, ironically develops imagery that recalls Edward Dmytryk's little-seen 1949 classic "Christ In Concrete," though Dmytryk ultimately was not involved in "A Prayer For The Dying."

Whoever is to blame for the final result, "Dying" emerges as a cold, unexciting affair, lightened up only by Bates' funny overplaying of the villain. Casting is a bit perverse, since Hoskins is tailor-made for Bates' gangster role, and a bit hemmed-in playing the priest (though he gets some violent outbursts, ascribed to his previous war hero exploits prior to his taking the cloth). Bates, conversely, is looking more and more like the late Robert Preston and could have handled the priest-on-the-spot assignment more credibly.

Though his accent gets a bit overdone (as in his repeated references to the priest as "Fa'r"), Rourke is convincing as the antihero and ably supported by Davis, an angular-featured young actress who is also quite striking in John Boorman's "Hope And Glory." As an IRA hit-lady, Alison Doody looks more like a fashion model.

Tech credits are acceptable, though pic lacks the atmosphere and large-scale logistics audiences have come to expect in thrillers.

—Lor.

Too Outrageous!
(CANADIAN-COLOR)

A Spectrafilm release of a Roy Krost production. Produced by Krost. Written and directed by Richard Benner. Camera (color), Fred Guthe; editor, George Appleby; music, Russ Little; costumes, Alisa Alexander; art direction, Andris Hausmanis; production manager, Dan Nyberg; makeup, Inge Klaudi; assistant director, Tony Thatcher. Reviewed at Cineplex Odeon screening room, Toronto, Aug. 31, 1987. (At Toronto Festival of Festivals.) Running time: **100 MINS.**

Robin Turner . . . . Craig Russell
Liza Connors . . . . Hollis McLaren
Bob . . . . David McIlwraith
Luke . . . . Ron White
Betty Treisman . . . . Lynne Cormack
Lee Sturges . . . . Michael J. Reynolds
Rothchild . . . . Timothy Jenkins
Tony Sparks . . . . Paul Eves
Manuel . . . . Frank Pellegrino
Phil Kennedy . . . . Barry Flatman

Toronto — Craig Russell turns in a spanking performance in Dick Benner's sequel to his 1977 hit "Outrageous," but the saga of the female impersonator and his schizophrenic girlfriend is diluted by a transparent script. Audience will be polymorphously diverse, with a large curiosity factor making initial boxoffice brisk, but it should fall off after that.

"Too Outrageous!" takes place 10 years later and Robin Turner (Russell), now a drag queen making it big on the New York gay club circuit, has been living in a cozy friendship with Liza Connors (Hollis McLaren), a former mental patient Robin has nurtured and saved a number of times. This time, Robin is becoming a major hit, wowing his leather-clad friends with his polished transformations into Mae West, Peggy Lee, Ella, Barbra, et al., helped along by a laudatory magazine article by Liza.

He is courted by two high-powered caricatures of New York agents, Betty (Lynne Cormack) and Lee (Michael J. Reynolds), who want to finetune and temper Robin's outrageousness for a mainstream audience. (One agent asks the other, "Do you want to sign him?" "No," she answers, "I want to own him.")

The more successful Robin gets, the more isolated he feels. Betty decides to move him from the New York scene back up to hometown Toronto with his entourage to work out new MOR material.

Liza, who has been haunted by personal demons she calls "the others," meets a Latino bartender, Manuel (Frank Pellegrino), who seduces and ingratiates himself to her, leaving Robin très depressed. Robin's manager Bob (David McIlwraith) has linked up with musical arranger Luke (Ron White). In the decade since "Outrageous" appeared, AIDS headlines are all-pervasive, and of course one of the characters in the pic contracts the disease.

Robin meets Tony (Paul Eves), a stunning hustler who's also a chanteuse, and becomes his lover. he wants to be part of a duet with Robin, but agent Betty nixes the idea. It turns out to be a real slap in the face for Robin, when he finds Tony was hired to service him by his agent.

The vitality falls in "Too Outrageous!" with a trite storyline and a sappy finale. Liza's crazies don't seem as menacing, and her relationship with Manuel is barely credible. The happy ending, after Liza is hospitalized and once again rescued by Robin (this time impersonating her mother), and his "I gotta be me" attitude is too sentimental.

It's Russell's show here and when he's on screen he perks up even the most innocuous dialog.

Benner extracts fine turns from Russell's associates, notably McIlwraith and White and handmaiden Timothy Jenkins. Hollis McLaren re-inhabits Liza, but she just doesn't seem convincing this time out. The director also uses New York City and Toronto locales well, grabbing the night flavor and especially nabbing the frenzy of the Christopher Street Halloween gay parade.

—Devo.

Gondola
(JAPANESE-COLOR)

An OM production. Produced by Mayato Sadasue. Directed by Chisho Itoh. Screenplay, Itoh, Yashi Natsume; camera (color), Toshihiko Uriu; editor, Shuichi Kakesu; sond, Harehisa Otsuka; music, Satoru Yoshida. Reviewed at Bloor Cinema, Toronto, Sept. 1, 1987. (At Toronto Festival of Festivals.) Running time: **112 MINS.**

Kagari . . . . Keiko Uemura
Ryo . . . . Kenta Kai
Also with: Midori Kiuchi, Sumie Sasaki, Hideo Satoh, Hide Demon.

Toronto — Slick, assured camerawork marks the directorial debut of Chisho Itoh in "Gondola," but the slow and lumbering storyline of two lonely souls undermines the pic's mainstream appeal. Domestic audiences probably will be limited to the arthouse circuit, but recent film school graduates can use "Gondola" as a rich resource in technique.

Almost spartan in its script, film's narrative is sustained by its telling images.

Kagari is a young, ennui-laden 5th-grade girl, living alone with her glamorpuss mother in a Tokyo highrise. She's isolated and scorned by her schoolmates and amuses herself with her attachment to her pet birds and by playing her tuning fork.

Ryo, a recent arrival in Tokyo from a northern fishing village, is a window washer on the skyscrapers in the city. He lives in a squalid apartment and is overcome by lyrical memories of his fishing town. Ryo meets Kagari on the street after one of her birds is seriously attacked by the other. Ryo befriends her and takes the young girl to the vet.

The two strike up an amiable bond. She's the first person he's ever talked to behind the window. They exchange a minimum of words, but do more to support each other's lives than their friends or family. He takes her to his village to visit with his parents and to give her bird, who ultimately dies, a proper funeral.

Direction is highly stylized, with polished, inventive camera angles, dramatic use of black & white memory shots, and with sound and silence given equal weight in the drama.

Itoh fixes on many powerful images — a suspended metronome, the dead bird Kagari places in a lunch box in the fridge, the dizzying view of downtown Tokyo from the 50th floor of an office tower — but they often translate into contrivances.

The actors Keiko Uemura and Kenta Kai use a minimal style to communicate their disjunction and their relationship doesn't translate as pretentious. It's just that the flashy, surreal photography outweighs the tale of the somber duo, who have very few moments of joy. —*Devo.*

Life Classes
(CANADIAN-COLOR)

A Cinephile release in Canada of a Picture Plant production. Executive producer, William D. MacGillivray. Produced by Stephen Reynolds. Camera (color), Lionel Simmons; editor, MacGillivray; art direction, Mary Steckle; sound, Jim Rillie; music, Alexandra Tilley; production manager, Terry Greenlaw; assistant director, Gordon Parsons. Reviewed at Bloor Cinema, Toronto, Sept. 2, 1987. (At Toronto Festival of Festivals.) Running time: **117 MINS.**

Mary Cameron	Jacinta Cormier
Earl	Leon Dubinsky
Nanny	Evelyn Garbary
Mrs. Miller	Mary Izzard
Gloria	Francis Knickle
Marie	Jill Chatt
Mr. Cameron	Leo Jessome
Mrs. Sitwell	Caitlyn Colquhoun

Toronto — "Life Classes" is a disarming, moving and funny feature by Nova Scotia helmer Bill MacGillivray. There are many levels of enjoyment in this quiet, modest pic about a young woman's journey to becoming a self-sufficient artist, and it deserves special handling to reach the right audiences.

MacGillivray's tale centers on Mary Cameron (Jacinta Cormier), a young Cape Breton woman who wiles away the time in her rural town with paint-by-numbers projects, working in her dad's pharmacy and seeking out her Gaelic past with her beloved, ailing Nanny. When Mary discovers she's pregnant by her laid-back boyfriend Earl, the local bootlegger (Leon Dubinsky), she decides to go to Halifax — the big city — to have the baby.

While working in a department store she is befriended by Gloria, a punky college art student who convinces Mary to model nude for life drawing classes. Mary gradually takes the road to self-fulfillment by starting to sketch her daughter Marie and then herself, developing her own latent talents and becoming an acknowledged artist.

She returns to Cape Breton at the end to start work on the lovely house her nanny bequeathed her when she died, and decides to go it alone despite Earl's offer of support.

The leisurely pace and character development all are part of the personal style of MacGillivray, who in the past has directed docus and a feature, "Stations." There's deadpan, lowkey humor in most of the vignettes, especially in a primal therapy art "happening" in which Mary sings nude and confesses her feelings about her family and Earl, while it is being picked up by Earl's illegal satellite dish.

MacGillivray also pops the balloon of self-conscious, pretentious art historians. His sense of place of Nova Scotia is right on target and with cinematogapher Lionel Simmons, translates the measured motion and down-home, proud nature of the province.

The cast is almost uniformly solid. Cormier brings vulnerability, anger and self-confidence to Mary, who has a beautiful voice for her Gaelic tunes, too. The real find here is Leon Dubinsky; his Earl is natural, lively, above-board and sweet. Jill Chatt's Marie is button-cute, while the only weak link is Leo Jessome as Mary's stilted father.

Subtext of finding cultural roots and taking responsibility for one's life — and creation — is woven into the fabric of his pic without seeming heavyhanded. Maritime Canada is well served by this production, shot for \$C622,000. —*Devo.*

Fatal Attraction
(COLOR)

Extramarital thriller is a surefire crowd-pleaser.

A Paramount Pictures release of a Jaffe/Lansing production. Produced by Stanley R. Jaffe, Sherry Lansing. Directed by Adrian Lyne. Stars Michael Douglas, Glenn Close, Anne Archer. Screenplay, James Dearden, based on his original screenplay; camera (Technicolor), Howard Atherton; editor, Michael Kahn, Peter E. Berger; music, Maurice Jarre; production design, Mel Bourne; art direction, Jack Blackman; set decoration, George DeTitta; costume design, Ellen Mirojnick; sound (Dolby), Les Lazarowitz; assistant director, Robert Girolami; casting, Risa Bramon, Billy Hopkins. Reviewed at the Bruin Theater, L.A., Sept. 8, 1987. (MPAA Rating: R.) Running time: **119 MINS.**

Dan Gallagher	Michael Douglas
Alex Forrest	Glenn Close
Beth Gallagher	Anne Archer
Ellen Gallagher	Ellen Hamilton Latzen
Jimmy	Stuart Pankin
Hildy	Ellen Foley
Arthur	Fred Gwynne
Joan Rogerson	Meg Mundy
Howad Rogerson	Tom Brennan
Martha	Lois Smith

Hollywood — As if there weren't already enough warning signs posted about the hazards of promiscuity these days, now "Fatal Attraction" comes along to serve as an additional cautionary tale to those who might dare to fancy a weekend fling once in awhile. The screws are tightened expertly in this suspenseful meller about a flipped-out femme who make life hell for the married man who scorns her, and audience delight in being chilled by the cat-and-mouse game should make this a strong fall performer for Paramount.

Voluptuously filmed by Adrian Lyne, this tale of a vengeful lover going off the deep end to become an emotional terrorist possesses a number of disturbing elements. Traditional women may not care for the adulterous protagonist, feminists may blanch at the portrait of a sick lady who allows a man to exert so much power over her, and many men will become antsy at the idea of a casual date quickly becoming a mortal enemy.

All of these discomforting emotional elements contribute significantly to the unsettling mood developed after the first half-hour, which is devoted to a quickie affair between New York attorney Michael Douglas and publishing exec Glenn Close. Douglas is happily married to the gorgeous Anne Archer and has a lovely daughter, but succumbs to Close's provocative flirtations while his wife is out of town.

It appears that these two sophisticated adults are in it just for fun and sport, but when Close slits her wrists in despair over the end of the affair, Douglas knows he's taken on more of a burden than he bargained for. Regretful over having cheated on his wife, he tries to put Close off, but the more he insists that it's over, the harder she pushes, following him around, bombarding him with phone calls, claiming to be pregnant and eventually physically endangering him and his family.

To non-fans of his previous work, Lyne's rigor in sticking to plot propulsion and solid characterization will come as a pleasant surprise. For once, his staging is coherent, done without mannered frills, and the imagination and energy pumped into nearly every scene results in a genuinely suspenseful tale of psychological disturbance and peril.

Pic does go over the top at times notably when Close makes predictable use of the child's cute pet rabbit, even moreso in the wrenching climax, which dares to resurrect the hackneyed device of the dead rising from the grave one last time, a gambit seemingly used and abused in 90% of the late 1970s-early 1980s horror entries but, from the evidence of preview audience reaction, still wildly effective.

Cast topliners acquit themselves in fine fashion. Michael Douglas, in a family man role, seems warmer and more sympathetic than before, and well conveys the evasiveness and anguish of his cornered character. Glenn Close throws herself into the physical abandon of the early reels with surprising relish, and become genuinely frightening when it comes clear she is capable of anything. Although denied as many dramatic opportunities as her costars, Anne Archer at long last has a role of substance in a film of merit and comes out shining; she is most appreciatively photographed and helps make the quieter domestic scenes interesting.

Film becomes somewhat repetitive as Close dogs Douglas' tracks and two full hours is a bit too much of a good thing, but Lyne very adeptly jangles the viewer's nervous system on his way to the big payoff scene, which will produce plenty of screaming, screeching and armgrabbing, just the ticket for an audience pleaser.

Technical contributions are absolutely first-class, from Howard Atherton's rich lensing and Mel Bourne's lush production design to Maurice Jarre's helpful scoring and Michael Kahn and Peter E. Berger's razor-sharp cutting.

Unusual credit to James Dearden for his (very good) screenplay "based on his original screenplay" stems from the fact that pic is based on Dearden's 45-minute film "Diversion," which he wrote and directed in 1979. — *Cart.*

The Big Town
(U.S.-COLOR)

A Columbia Pictures release of a Martin Ransohoff production. Executive producer, Gene Craft. Produced by Martin Ransohoff. Co-producer, Don Carmody. Directed by Ben Bolt. Screenplay, Robert Roy Pool, based on the novel "The Arm" by Clark Howard; camera (color), Ralf D. Bode; editor, Stuart Pappe; music, Michael Melvoin; production design, Bill Kenney; costumes, Wendy Partridge; production manager, Joyce Kozy King; art direction, Dan Yarhi; assistant director, Don French; associate producer, Jon Turtle; casting, Nancy Klopper. Reviewed at Leicester Square Theater, London, Sept. 8, 1987 (MPAA Rating: R.) Running time: **109 MINS.**

J.C. Cullen	Matt Dillon
Lorry Dane	Diane Lane
George Cole	Tommy Lee Jones
Mr. Edwards	Bruce Dern
Ferguson Edwards	Lee Grant
Phil Carpenter	Tom Skerritt
Aggie Donaldson	Suzy Amis
Sonny Binkley	David Marshall Grant

London — Despite its veneer of glamour 'n gambling, and gangsters 'n gals, "The Big Town" is essentially a very moral period pic that promises more than it actually delivers. Despite a host of name actors and a slick '50s sound-track, b.o. success will probably be limited.

A question mark must still be put against Matt Dillon's ability to carry a larger-budget pic, and though actors of the stature of Tommy Lee Jones, Bruce Dern, Tom Skerritt and Lee Grant were undoubtedly brought in to bolster the film, they end up putting Dillon somewhat in the shade.

Producer Martin Ransohoff made his name with pics like "The Cincinnati Kid," and to an extent "The Big Town" — a tale about craps shooting — could be seen to be trying to fit into the same genre as numbers like "The Cincinnati Kid," and "The Hustler." Unfortunately dice rolling lacks the cinematic appeal of pool or poker, and while the other two involved skill craps seems to be mainly about luck.

Apparently country-boy J.C. "Cully" Collen (Dillon) has got the "cool" according to his gambling mentor — meaning he is a dice player who always seems to win — so he packs his bags and heads off to the Windy City to make his fame and fortune.

He is hired as a crapshooting "arm" by a blind Bruce Dern, and Lee Grant, and sets about breaking into all of the big money games in town. Along the way he is attracted to the nice girl (Suzy Amis) but falls for the floozie (Diane Lane) to the chagrin of her gangster husband Tommy Lee Jones.

The complex storyline has about one plot too many, but though Dillon momentarily loses his "cool" he soon gets it back, and ends up breaking the gangster, helping the floozie but being deceived by her, and eventually realizing what he really wants is the nice girl. And everyone lives happily ever after — apart from Tommy Lee Jones who is arrested for murder, but that is another subplot.

First-time theatrical director, Briton Ben Bolt lenses with confidence, and is greatly helped by cinematographer Ralf D. Bode's use of

vivid colors, but would have been advised to tighten up the story and inject slightly more dramatic tension. Everything looks perfect — from the plentiful neon signs to the costumes — but "The Big Town" never really shifts up that extra gear to make it a winner.

Diane Lane as stripper Lorry Dane makes the perfect floozie, and her sexy fan dance adds a much needed bit of sleaze to the story, while Suzy Amis (who looks uncomfortably like June Allyson at times) is spot-on as down to earth single parent Aggie.

Dern, Skerritt and Grant all perform well, but it is Tommy Lee Jones as the malevolent gangster with slicked-back hair, silk shirt and dollar-sign tie clip, who scowls and sneers his way through the scenes, easily stealing most he is in.

The ethics and morals of "The Big Town" are such that it could easily have been made in the '50s, and beneath all the gloss and glitz a simple tale is struggling to get out. Similarly beneath Dillon's macho bravura there lurks a better actor than this role, or his leading man mantle, seems to allow. —*Adam.*

Too Much
(COLOR)

Stillborn kidpic with robot.

A Cannon Group release of a Golan-Globus production. Produced by Menahem Golan, Yoram Globus. Line producer, Yosuke Mizuno. Directed by Eric Rochat. Screenplay, Rochat; narration, Joan Laine; camera (Imagica color; TVC prints), Daisaku Kimura; editor, Alain Jakubowicz; music, George S. Clinton; sound, Shyotaro Yoshida; assistant director, Toshiaki Arai; art direction, Tsuneo Kantake; special effects coordinator, Osamu Kung; robot supervisor, Masaharu Ogawa; postproduction supervisor, Michael R. Sloan; casting, Kazuki Manabe; associate producer, Dov Maoz. Reviewed at Movies at Town Center 2, Boca Raton, Fla., Sept. 6, 1987. (MPAA Rating: PG.) Running time: **89 MINS.**

Suzy	Bridgette Andersen
Too Much	Masato Fukazama
Tetsuro	Hiroyuki Watanabe
Prof. Finkel	Char Fontana
Bernie	Uganda

Boca Raton — "Too Much" is a feeble comedy for kids about a little girl and her playmate robot's adventures in Japan. Modest Cannon offering is a summertime territorial release.

French writer-director Eric Rochat (who previously helmed "The Story Of O, Part II" at the other end of the audience spectrum) has concocted a very flimsy storyline in which cute Bridgette Andersen is in Tokyo with her parents (dad's on a business trip) when "Uncle" Tetsuro (Hiroyuki Watanabe) gives her a prototype robot as a gift. She exclaims: "You're too much," so it's named Too Much, or TM for short.

There follows a series of slapstick misadventures as the robot refuses to leave her when she's due to fly home to America with her family. On the run, the twosome are helped

out by a young Japanese boy in avoiding the grasp of evil scientist Prof. Finkel (Char Fontana) and his goonish henchman Bernie (Uganda).

Silly windup is right out of a Gammera monster film: heroes are holed up in a department store with lots of toy robots for a confrontation with riot police, only to be saved by hundreds of Japanese kids showing solidarity with Too Much.

Title amply describes Rochat's treatment of cute heroine Andersen; a pleasant moppet, she becomes grating with sweetness by film's end. Clutzy dialog is not enhanced by Joan Laine's puerile narration voiced by the heroine. Scenic Japanese locales are photographed in documentary fashion, with music video-style editing to a peppy score by George S. Clinton. Gags are frequent but unfunny. —*Lor.*

Project A (Part II)
(HONG KONG-COLOR)

A Golden Harvest/Golden Ways production, presentation and release. Executive producer, Raymond Chow. Produced by Leonard Ho. Directed by Jackie Chan. Coordinator, Willie Chan. Stars Jackie Chan, Maggie Cheung, Rosamund Kwan, Carina Lau. (No other credits provided by producer and distributor. Reviewed at State theater, Sept. 1, 1987, Hong Kong. Running time: **98 MINS.**

(Cantonese soundtrack with English subtitles).

Hong Kong — The first Jackie Chan "Project A" was such a box-office sensation a sequel was mandated. Production is for the Hong Kong mass audience, and Chan knows his market well to combine his exquisite martial arts skills with high comedy, colloquial Cantonese and pure corny slapstick, resulting in blockbuster magic that is unequalled in the Hong Kong film industry today.

In "Project A," Chan was at the turn of the century Hong Kong as Dragon Ma and his exploits as a marine man protected the meek and eradicated the evil. In Part II, he returns to the same setting with some Sun Yat Sen revolutionaries to contend with. He's inducted into the Edwardian Hong Kong police then promoted to superintendent to stop the corruption that emanates from high-powered politicians in a place called Sai Wan.

The plot is immaterial as action is the main objective. There are giggling damsels in distress costumed to act as decorative pieces. Chan athletically performs many marvelous, eye-filling stunts.

There are many chases à la Keystone Cops. The antique sets look all too new to be believable. The only glimpse of style is when Chan hides in a dark study of the Governor and blends into a huge painting with Victorian characters.

Since children are supposedly the people who fill theaters, Chan's

dream of recognition in the U.S. may materialize, despite provincial mentality of the production. End credits feature some very interesting outtakes that are better than the selected segments featured in the main film. —*Mel.*

Amazon Women On The Moon
(COLOR/B&W)

Bawdy parody anthology.

A Universal Pictures release. Produced by Robert K. Weiss. Directed by Joe Dante, Carl Gottlieb, Peter Horton, John Landis, Robert K. Weiss. Executive producers, Landis, George Folsey, Jr. Associate producer, Robb Idels. Screenplay, Michael Barrie, Jim Mulholland; camera (Technicolor), Daniel Pearl; editor, Bert Lovitt, Marshall Harvey, Malcolm Campbell; art direction, Alex Hajdu; set decoration, Julie Kaye Towery; sound, Susmu Tokunow; assistant directors, Deborah Love, Daniel Schneider, David Sosna; casting, Sally Dennison, Julie Selzer. Reviewed at Universal Pictures screening room, Universal City, Calif., Sept. 11, 1987. (MPAA Rating: R.) Running time: **85 MINS.**

With: Rosanna Arquette, Ralph Bellamy, Carrie Fisher, Griffin Dunne, Steve Guttenberg, Sybil Danning, Monique Gabrielle, Kelly Preston, Russ Meyer, Steve Forrest, Joey Travolta, Ed Begley Jr., Henny Youngman, Steve Allen, Paul Bartel, Arsenio Hall, Howard Hesseman, Lou Jacobi, B.B. King.

Hollywood — "Amazon Women On The Moon" is as irreverent, vulgar and silly as its predecessor, "The Kentucky Fried Movie," and similarly has some hilarious moments and some real groaners too. In the 10 intervening years between releases, John Landis & Co. have found some '80s things to satirize — like yuppies, the vidcassette biz, dating, condoms — done up in a way that's not particularly shocking anymore. Entire work is amusing enough to earn return visits from those who enjoy anthology comedies and probably some crossovers from the Russ Meyer camp as well. Universal should do just fine.

Besides Landis, directors Joe Dante, Carl Gottlieb, Peter Horton and Robert K. Weiss take turns doing sketches — Weiss' "Amazon Women On The Moon" '50s parody of bad sci-fi pics being the one that was stretched piecemeal throughout the film in a semi-successful attempt to hold this anthology together as one comedic work. As the featured piece it is also the least original. Sight gags like ones where the wire which holds the planets and spaceships in space is purposefully illuminated work only once or twice, as do the mock play-offs between macho astronaut Steve Forrest and his goofy crewmen Joey Travolta and Robert Colbert. Casting Sybil Danning as Queen Lara will make the industry crowd chuckle, considering how many B movies she's been in, but the joke sure will be lost on the general public.

Eighteen other segs fill up the pic's 85 minutes, some mercifully short like Weiss' "Silly Paté" while

Landis' "Hospital" is one of those slow-building, totally zany bits where the chuckles grow as the situation gets more ridiculous and you wish there was more. Griffin Dunne's wacko doctor role is the best thing about "Amazon Women On The Moon."

While "Kentucky Fried Movie," created by the "Airplane" team of Jim Abrahams, David and Jerry Zucker, spoofed tv, "Amazon" spoofs many other media, mostly with a rightfully cynical eye. However, take-off of a swashbuckler called "Video Pirates," which shamefully plugs MCA Home Video, is as crass as many of the subjects that are derided here.

Nudity and sex, not surprisingly, are the basis for a number of routines. Filmmakers have engaged the expertise of none other than the King of the Naked Femme Torso himself — Russ Meyer — to play a role in the most outrageous skit, "Video Date," a salacious few minutes with a lonely guy and his VCR. Meyer probably had a hand in casting a couple of other titillating segs as well that feature well-endowed women.

Women get a turn too — watching a nude man run around, Ed Begley Jr. as the "Son Of The Invisible Man" who isn't invisible.

Scripters Michael Barrie and Jim Mulholland have targeted their audience to the hip "Saturday Night Live" crowd that is amused, not offended, when American values and its culture is satirized, and less to juvenile audiences who are supposedly too young for this sort of thing (pic's rated R). Since audiences are pretty jaded these days, in no small part because of the success of "Saturday Night Live," "SCTV" and their clones, filmmakers seemed to find the need to do those things they can't do on tv namely lots of nudity and profanity.

The numbing of American sensibilities lessens the entertainmen value of a lot of previously sacred subjects, meaning vignettes like "Roast Your Loved One" where an Irish wake is conducted in the style of a bad Vegas act or "First Lady Of The Evening," about a President's wife with a past, cause only faint smiles since it seems we've seen them before.

Tech credits are great — appropriately tacky where they should be and top-rate at all other times.
— Brit.

He's My Girl
(COLOR)

Funny comedy in drag.

A Scotti Bros. Entertainment release. Executive producers, Tony Scotti, Fred Scotti, Ben Scotti. Produced by Lawrence Taylor Mortorff, Angela Schapiro. Directed by Gabrielle Beaumont. Screenplay, Taylor Ames, Charles F. Bohl; camera (Guffanti color), Peter Lyons Collister; editor, Roy Watts; sound, Ed Somers; art direction, Cynthia Kay Charette; set decoration, Gary D. Randall; costume design, Patricia Field; assistant director, Xavier H. Reyes; casting, Meryl O'Laughlin. Reviewed at Scotti Bros. screening room, Santa Monica, Calif., Sept. 10, 1987. (MPAA Rating: PG-13.) Running time: **104 MINS.**
Reggie/Regina . . . . .T.K. Carter
Bryan . . . . .David Hallyday
Tasha . . . . .Misha McK
Lisa . . . . .Jennifer Tilly
Simon Sledge . . . . .Warwick Sims
Mason Morgan . . . . .David Clennon
Sally .Monica Parker

———

Hollywood — "He's My Girl" is a funny sex farce from Scotti Bros. Entertainment that rises well above its low-budget rock 'n' roll genre by the sheer exuberance of its cast working from a snappy script. Unknown talent and indie distributor might limit b.o., but creative marketing and lead song tie-in may help ticket sales.

French singer David Hallyday gets star billing as a hungry rock musician from Missouri, but his black gas station attendant/manager T.K. Carter steals this show.

The duo win a contest from Video Lala, an MTV-type Los Angeles station, to be limoed around Hollywood for a week at the end of which they get a splashy, media-hyped debut on national tv.

The hitch is Hallyday is told he must bring a girl with him and for every reason like loyalty, friendship and plain old obligation (Carter was the one who entered the contest), the rocker gives in to Carter's persuasive powers and agrees to allow him to dress like a femme and parade as his *objet d'amour.*

Under Gabrielle Beaumont's lively direction, working with Taylor Ames and Charles F. Bohl's often-clever script and aided tremendously by Roy Watts' crisp editing, this youth comedy surfaces with a certain amount of freshness as it falls somewhere between a parody of rockers and transvestites and the silliness that sometimes characterizes their lives and sentimental love-at-first-sight story.

Fortunately, filmmakers have also managed to keep the rock score down to a few, unobtrusive numbers at the beginning and at the end — but to be able to sell the picture to that crucial youth market.

Mistaken identity theme, thankfully, has a much wider appeal, which distinguishes this from the blatantly commercial pop that's released ad nauseam today

Carter is a considerable talent and, whether it's unintentional or not, plays a better slightly-less-than-trampy transvestite than he does hetero music manager. His character undergoes a number of humiliations that would make even Jim Bailey blanch, but none too salacious to offend. Equally good, if less intriguing a persona, is David Clennon as Video LaLa's huckster Mason Morgan. He's got a thing for black women, whom he refers to by any number of diminutives — all very funny.

Secondary characters are considerably more 1-dimensional, including Hallyday, who has managed to lose any trace of his French accent and unfortunately has allowed a certain blandness into his performance as well. Also, both his and Carter's love interests could have used some different personality traits. Misha McK, the gorgeous assistant at Video LaLa, is sweet, but otherwise it's hard to see what Carter's fussing about. Jennifer Tilly tries too hard to be both an ardent sculptor and ditzy cocktail waitress. Warwick Sims, as the has-been acid rocker Simon Sledge, has some choice moments on screen — the best when he accidentally gets his gum caught in his long tresses and decides that rather than discarding it, to stick it back in his mouth.

There are some problems with continuity and sound mixing which aren't particularly egregious, but are noticeable.

Pic ends with a where-are-they-now seg that is totally unnecessary and actually detracts from the niceness of the finale. — Brit.

———

Rio Quarenta Graus
(Rio 100°)
(BRAZILIAN-B&W)

A New Yorker Films release. Produced, written and directed by Nelson Pereira dos Santos. Camera (color), Helio Silva; editor, Rafael Justo Valverde; set design, Julio Romito, Adrian Samailoff; music, Radames Gnatalli, with songs by Zeaketi, Tau Silva, Moacir Soares Pereira; assistant director, Jece Valadao. Reviewed at Public theater, N.Y., Aug. 18, 1987. Running time: **90 MINS.**
Maid .Glauce Rocha
Marine . . . . .Roberto Batalin
Girl on the beach . . . . .Ana Beatriz
Miro (hoodlum) . . . . .Jece Valadao
Daniel (soccer player) . . . . .Al Ghiu
Bookmaker . . . . .Sady Cabral
The kid . . . . .Haroldo de Oliveira

———

Nelson Pereira dos Santos, considered the "pope" of Brazil's Cinema Novo movement, made his directorial debut with the 1955 pic "Rio Quarenta Graus" (Rio 40°C/-Rio 100°F). With this film, he was able to define some of the theories he had developed at national film conferences held in 1952 and '53, and set a path for what would become the movement that dominated the domestic industry for almost two decades. Now, after 32 years, the film has been picked up for U.S. release by New Yorker Films and is reviewed here for the record.

The movie offers a multifaceted portrait of Rio and is structured around five young peanut vendors who live in one of the city's sprawling "favelas," or slums. The action all takes place on one hot Sunday as the quintet divide up in the morning, each to peddle his wares in a different section of the city: Copacabana Beach, Sugar Loaf Mountain, Quinta da Boa Vista, Corcovado Mountain and the soccer stadium. At each of these sites, the audience is introduced to different inhabitants of Rio involved in fragmentary scenes, allowing us a glimpse into the different aspects of a cross-section of cariocan life. The film continually cuts back and forth between these different stories. We meet a maid who has been seduced by a marine, a-bourgeois family on the beach, a popular soccer player at the end of his career, the jealous confrontation of two men over the same woman, etc. Each of these scenes present the audience with a different segment of cariocan society and are linked only tenuously by the presence of the boys, who occupy society's bottom rung.

The film's texture owes much to the Italian neorealism school, especially through use of non-professional actors and employing the real unromanticised favela as backdrop to the harsher realities of life. Its structure most resembles Roberto Rossellini's 1946 classic "Paisan," where the city of Rio de Janeiro is the real subject of the film as Italy was in the former pic. Through a collage effect the larger mosaic patterns emerge.

Although the film has a dated feel, the themes belong to contemporary Latin America: the extreme differences between rich and poor; currying political favor; passion and betrayal; etc.

The film ends as night falls bringing with it joy and pain, life and death, and a return to the favela. It is merely a day in the life of the city.

Originally, the film was to be the first of a trilogy about Rio de Janeiro. The second pic, "Rio Zona Norte" was filmed in 1957, and the final section of the triptych, "Rio Zona Sur," had to be abandoned because of financial difficulties.
— Lent.

Marusa No Onna
(A Taxing Woman)
(JAPANESE-COLOR)

A Japanese Films presentation of a Itami Prods., New Century Producers production. Produced by Yasushi Tamaoki, Seigo Hosogoe. Written and directed by Juzo Itami. Camera (color), Yonezo Maeda; editor, Akira Suzuki; music, Toshiyuki Honda; sound, Osamu Onodera; art direction, Shuji Nakamura. Reviewed at the Venice Film Festival (competing), Sept. 5, 1987. Running time: **127 MINS.**
Ryoko . . . . Nobuko Miyamoto
Gondo . . . . Tsutomu Yamazaki
Also with: Masahiko Tsugawa (assistant chief inspector Hanamura), Hideo Murato (motel president), Shuji Otaki (tax office manager), Daisuke Yamshita, Shinsuke Ashida, Keiju Kobayashi, Mariko Okada, Kiriko Shimizu, Kazuyo Matsui, Yasuo Daichi, Kinzo Sakura, Hajimeh Asoh, Shiro Ito, Eitaro Ozawa.

Venice — This is the third and best organized film by Juzo Itami, who has traded his acting career for a new one behind the camera. A tremendous commercial success in Japan, Itami applies his sardonic sense of humor in this picture to what he considers to be a highly sensitive point with his fellow co-nationals, their wallets.

The taxing woman of the title is that in two respects. First of all, she is a tax inspector, and a most dedicated one, but she is also taxing, since she never tires or lets go of her prey, once she has set her sights on him.

The victim, in this case, is a hood operating adult motels and crooked real estate deals, who doesn't even dream that a fragile, defenseless woman can do him any harm. However, he doesn't count on the lady's tenacity and the full support of her colleagues on the tax police squad, who are sufficiently stubborn not to knuckle under any of the pressures exerted on them.

Itami, who has already displayed his fierce satirical vein when he dealt with funeral rites and with eating habits, paints the portrait of a nation whose favorite pastime is to beat the income tax in each and every possible way. Not only the big sharks do it, but every shop keeper and professional person is searching for ways to evade taxes.

In the tradition of the American thriller, but far more humorously put, the heroine is single, exclusively dedicated to her job, a tough cookie in a remarkably feminine wrapping. Nobuko Miyamoto, who plays the part, happens to be Itami's wife, and she fits the role to perfection, with her big innocent eyes fooling the subjects of her investigations into believing she is a pushover, at which point she turns on them with all the fierce determination of a predatory feline. Entirely committed to her career with the Tax Office, she pursues relentlessly her goal, way beyond the call of duty, and her running duel with Tsutomu Yamazaki, as the limping gangster she chases, holds plenty of twists and surprises, as new plots and tricks for beating the tax rap are introduced and one by one unveiled by the law.

Tighter than his first film, "The Funeral," and better constructed than "Tampopo," "Taxing Woman" drives relentlessly forward, mixing social satire with action and sex, if anything piling it a bit too much for one film, and that in spite of the fact Itami says he used barely one-tenth of the material he collected in his extensive research of the subject.

Strong cast feels entirely at home with the spirit of the satire even if subtlety is not the name of the game here, with Miyamoto and Yamazaki exceedingly effective as the two unlikely rivals, the beauty and the beast. Solid technical credits and tongue-in-cheek use of traditional film genres are professionally handled all through. Since subject is sufficiently international to appeal to practically anyone who has to pay taxes, this is bound to find receptive audiences most anywhere. All of them hoping their own tax collectors are less taxing than Itami's heroine. —*Edna*.

Le Sourd dans la Ville
(Deaf To The City)
(CANADIAN-COLOR)

A Maison des Quatres Arts production, with Telefilm Canada, Société du Cinéma du Québec. SuperEcran, Radio Québec. Executive producer, Louise Carré. Directed by Mireille Dansereau. Screenplay, Dansereau, Michèle Mailhot, Jean-Joseph Tremblay, from story by Thérèse Berube, based on novel by Marie-Claire Blaise; camera (color), Michel Caron; editor, Louise Coté; music Ginette Bellavance; sound, Dominique Chartrand, Serge Beauchemin, Philippe Scultety; art direction, Gaudeline Sauriol; sets, Pierre Gelinas; costumes, Denis Sperdouklis. Reviewed at the Venice Film Festival (competing), Sept. 8, 1987. Running time: **97 MINS.**
Florence . . . . Béatrice Picard
Mike . . : . . . . . . Guillaume Lemay-Thivierge
Gloria . . . . Angéle Coutu
Tim . . . . Pierre Thériaut
Judith . . . . Han Masson
Charlie . . . . Claude Renart
Lucia . . . . Sophie Léger

Venice — A deliberately slow, downbeat drama about extreme loneliness in the big city, each character being enclosed in his own misery which he cannot transmit to anybody else, not even those closest to him, and each trying in his own way to escape his predicament.

The entire plot takes place in a dilapidated hotel run by Gloria, a lively stripper, who lives on the premises with her two daughters, baby Jojo and teenage Lucia who suffocates in her present environment but obviously has no better prospects elsewhere, and her son, Mike, sweetlooking kid suffering from a mysterious but possibly fatal brain tumor.

The hotel is the meeting place for all kinds of lost causes, like Florence, the wife of a rich doctor who has been abandoned by her husband, and comes in seeking to put an end to her existence; Charlie the jailbird, who is Gloria's lover, when he can perform his duties, and Tim, the old alcoholic who has only a dog for a companion. The only ray of hope is supplied by Judith, a school teacher who volunteers to help people in distress but even she can't help any of them.

Mostly static and brooding, Mireille Dansereau's direction offers a grim outlook of human existence, even when it is cheerfully accepted, as in the case of Gloria, a big, handsome, vibrant woman who refuses to give in to all the tragedies around her. She seems as doomed as the others, energetically basking in all kinds of illusions like the trip she promises to undertake with her ailing son to San Francisco, an empty promise with no real chance of ever coming true.

Dansereau allows Florence, the neglected wife, some flashbacks suggesting that she was miserable in her marriage long before she was abandoned. Mike's acute attacks of migraine are accompanied by visions of desolate empty spaces whether of mountain tops or deserts, Lucia and Tim find no solace in the brief escapes outside the hotel, which is evidently the end of the road for most of them.

This unpromising vision of the world lacks a script which would lift these sketches of human suffering into full-blown characters. More than anything they look like representative types left unfocused on purpose to they can fit a large variety of cases. Dansereau's cast either underplays, in the case of Béatrice Picard or overplays, like Angéle Coutu, but is rarely strong enough to really affect and draw the audience into the profound sadness common to them all.

The film is remarkably well shot, has an effective soundtrack and looks very much like a labor of love carefully fashioned in its every detail, rejecting any compromise that would relieve the gloomy atmosphere. An admirable decision, to be sure, even if it may not always help sales.—*Edna*

Orphans
(U.S.-COLOR)

A Lorimar Motion Pictures release. Produced and directed by Alan J. Pakula. Coproducer, Susan Solt. Screenplay, Lyle Kessler, based on his play; camera (color), Donald McAlpine; editor, Evan Lottman; music, Michael Small; design, George Jenkins; costumes, John Boxer; associate producer, John H. Starke. Reviewed at the Toronto Festival of Festivals, Sept. 11, 1987. (MPAA Rating: R.) Running time: **120 MINS.**
Harold . . . . Albert Finney
Treat . . . . Matthew Modine
Phillip . . . . Kevin Anderson
Barney . . . . John Kellogg
Man In Park . . . . Anthony Heald
Also with: Novella Nelson, Elizabeth Parrish, B. Constance Barry, Frank Ferrara, Clifford Fearl.

Toronto — From a collective actors' tour de force trisected by Albert Finney, Matthew Modine and Kevin Anderson, director Alan J. Pakula has fashioned a peculiar and demanding film that will have to be sold to audiences on the strength of its performances. The inherent dramatic insularity of Lyle Kessler's play about two urban outcast brothers and the Mephistophelian gangster who transforms their hermetic world is magnified on the big screen, but the film is driven by the inspired energies of its principal cast.

Treat (Matthew Modine) and Phillip (Kevin Anderson) live in isolated squalor in a ramshackle house on a vacant lot in Newark. Treat is a violent sociopath who ventures in to New York to steal and scavenge. Phillip is a recluse terrified of the world outside the house and the physically dominant older brother who keeps him there, a virtual prisoner of fear. The dynamics of their curious relationship with its shifting bonds of emotional and pragmatic interdependence are simultaneously mesmerizing and repelling. These feral, young, orphans inhabit a nether-world of urban noble savagery in which a state of grace coexists with pitiful despair.

Like the drifters in "Stranger Than Paradise," the brothers speak in a fractured "New Joisy" argot, a cartoonish device that exaggerates their bittersweet, fragmented communication. An apparent simpleton, Phillip is actually hungry for knowledge of the world, particularly the meanings of strange words in the books and magazines Treat has forbidden him to read. Treat, who revels in his role as unfettered predator, is actually terrified of the rampaging emotions that control his frenetic and aimless existence.

Control of self and one's destiny is the gospel of Harold (Albert Finney), a hard-drinking mobster whom Treat lures from a saloon to the house one night with the intention of holding the prosperous looking older man hostage for ransom.

The tables are quickly turned, however, when the mysterious but expansive gunman offers these destitute marginals an opportunity for big money and a spiffy new life. Seems that the old guy was an orphan himself, and sees in these "dead-end kids" a reflection of his own troubled youth.

The transmogrification of Treat and Phillip into well-fed, well-dressed young men and the renovation of their home into something out of House Beautiful, gives the picture a needed shot of plot-point adrenalin precisely halfway to its conclusion. Kessler has a definite talent for writing quirky dialog, but the "message" of the story — the universal power of love to redeem lost lives — is laid out with the obviousness of a fable. The author also has a fondness for precious philosophical aphorisms along the line of "the universe is in flux" which convey less than they are intended to. Fortunately, the script does not entirely abandon its skepticism about the mutability of the human condition in a resolution in which a possibility of hope coexists with the prospect of infinite anomie.

Matthew Modine does all he can to dominate the picture in a tangibly physical performance that seems to use madness as its method and to succeed on those terms more often than not. Pakula's guiding hand is evident, however, in orchestrating a counterbalance to Modine's wild excursions into the turmoil of Treat's psyche. Kevin Anderson portrays Phillip with great sensitivity and an aching pathos that's free of mannered affectation. Finney permits himself to anchor the center between these two extremes in a performance that's deceptively textured beneath a surface of gruff avuncularity. —Rich.

Sammy And Rosie Get Laid
(BRITISH-COLOR)

A Cinecom Pictures release (in the U.S.) of a Cinecom Intl. and Film Four Intl. presentation. Produced by Tim Bevan and Sarah Radclyffe. Directed by Stephen Frears. Screenplay, Hahif Kureishi; camera (color), Oliver Stapleton; sound, Albert Bailey; design, Hugo Lyczyc Wyhowski; editor, Mick Audsley; music, Stanley Myers; costumes, Barbara Kidd; assistant director, Guy Travers. Reviewed at the Toronto Festival Of Festivals, Sept. 12, 1987. Running time: **100 MINS.**
Rafi . . . . Shashi Kapoor
Alice . . . . Claire Bloom
Sammy . . . . Ayub Khan Din
Rosie . . . . Frances Barber
Danny . . . . Roland Gift
Anna . . . . Wendy Gazelle
Vivia . . . . Suzette Llewellyn
Rani . . . . Meera Syal
Ghost . . . . Badi Uzzaman

Toronto — Director Stephen Frears and screenwriter Hanif Kureishi return here with a superheated vengeance to the combustible urban landscape of a present-day England wracked by jarring social flux that they previously dissect-ed in "My Beautiful Laundrette." Cynical and brutally unsentimental in outlook, "Sammy And Rosie Get Laid," brings the force of an accelerated cinematic attack to bear upon its complex thematic juxtaposition of sexual warfare, cross-cultural dislocation, racism and the ruthlessness of power. Compelling independent filmmaking of the highest order, "Sammy And Rosie Get Laid" possesses the superior coherence of performance, writing and vision that should make it a substantial boxoffice attraction in specialty release.

With relentless momentum Frears unfolds the story of Sammy (Ayub Khan Din), the hedonistic, thoroughly English son of a prominent Pakistani politician who abandoned the young man and his mother in London years before to seek wealth and power in his homeland. Sammy, who scrapes out a living as an accountant, lives in a dangerous and decaying black neighborhood with his wife Rosie (Frances Barber), a sexually adventurous feminist journalist specializing in fashionable radical issues. Theirs is an open marriage based, as Rosie puts it, on "freedom plus commitment."

Change enters their lives with the arrival of Rafi (Shashi Kapoor), Sammy's long-lost father who, with considerable funds, has been forced to flee his political enemies in Pakistan. Rafi embodies the predicament of the Anglicised Indo-Pakistani ruling classes who eagerly embraced the British ideal of enlightened democratic order but were unable to control it when unleashed to mutate in the politically chaotic East. Now London itself, "is out of control," muses the dazed Rafi as he contemplates once-peaceful inner-city streets burning and devastated by riots over the police killing of a middle-aged black woman.

Struggling to maintain his self-dignity and command, the elegant Rafi is rapidly discombobulated by Sammy and Rosie's unanchored world and its existential tolerance of sexual liberty, drugs and revolutionary violence. One night as Sammy and Rafi stagger through garishly fire-lit streets, the son points to his burnt-out automobile and comments — with the bitter ironic humor pervading the film — that Rosie views the rioting as an "affirmation of the human spirit."

It is the human spirit's insatiable hunger for love and acceptance in a harsh and uncertain world which unites Frears & Kureishi's gallery of passionate, insecure and self-contradictory characters. Everyone in the film carries deep and unhealed emotional bruises from childhood and later life. Sammy and Rosie seek relief in a roundelay of extra-marital liaisons. Rafi attempts to buy his way back into the affection of his son and that of a beautiful and sensitive Englishwoman, Alice (Claire Bloom) whom he also cruelly abandoned in his self-centered quest for power in the East. Everyone is trying to cope with the ephemeral nature of love and, by extension, life itself. Sammy has an affair with a New York photographer Anna (Wendy Gazelle) whose affection for him is unrequited. Rosie takes up with a charismatic young black man Danny (Roland Gift of the U.K. pop group Fine Young Cannibals) who lives in a colony of nomadic squatters beneath a highway overpass.

Rosie's radicalized affinity for the underclass leads her to turn against Rafi when she discovers that the old man was responsible for the torture and murder of political opponents. With a pragmatic eye on the old man's money and some residual filial loyalty, Sammy assumes a posture of moral indifference to his father's reprehensible past actions. Shashi Kapoor plumbs the tragic dimensions of Rafi's capacity for self-deception as his defense — on the grounds of expediency disintegrates along with his sanity in the terrifying environment of the city he no longer knows.

Frears levitates the film's harsh realism with a fantastical counterpoint in touches like the ghost of a tortured labor leader who haunts Rafi from the outset, and a band of gypsy buskers who serenade the on-going anarchy. Stacatto editing and dialog, bleakly evocative cinematography and most of all the impressively calibrated ensemble acting make this film an indelible experience. —Rich.

The Princess Bride
(COLOR)

Unsuccessful fairy tale sendup.

A 20th Century Fox release of an Act III Communications presentation. Produced by Andrew Scheinman, Rob Reiner. Executive producer, Norman Lear. Directed by Reiner. Screenplay, William Goldman, based on his novel; camera (Deluxe color), Adrian Biddle; editor, Robert Leighton; music, Mark Knopfler; production design, Norman Garwood; art direction, Keith Pain, Richard Holland; set decoration, Maggie Gray; costumes, Phyllis Dalton; sound (Dolby), David John; assistant director, Ken Baker, Peter Bennett; associate producer, Jeffrey Scott, Steven Nicolaides; casting, Jane Jenkins, Janet Hirshenson. Reviewed at Regency Theater, Westwood, Calif., Sept. 11, 1987. (MPAA Rating: PG.) (In Toronto Film Festival.) Running time: **98 MINS.**
Westley . . . . Cary Elwes
Inigo Montoya . . . . Mandy Patinkin
Prince Humperdinck . . . . . Chris Sarandon
Count Rugen . . . . Christopher Guest
Vizzini . . . . Wallace Shawn
Fezzik . . . . Andre The Giant
The Grandson . . . . Fred Savage
The Princess Bride . . . . Robin Wright
The Grandfather . . . . Peter Falk
The Impressive Clergyman . . . . Peter Cook
Valerie . . . . Carol Kane
Miracle Max . . . . Billy Crystal
The Albino . . . . Mel Smith

Hollywood — With "The Princess Bride" director Rob Reiner takes a leap of faith — and falls. Based on William Goldman's novel, it's a post-modern fairy tale that challenges and affirms the conventions of a genre that may not be flexible enough to support such horseplay. Result is a tedious tale almost totally lacking in momentum and magic.

At heart, "Princess Bride" celebrates the power of true love to triumph over adversity but along the way undermines the sentiment with a weak imitation of Monty Python antics. It also doesn't help that Cary Elwes and Robin Wright as the loving couple are nearly comatose and inspire little passion from each other, or the audience.

Also weakening the impact is a storytelling device better suited to the printed page in which grandfather Peter Falk recites the tale to his bedridden grandson Fred Savage. At first it's a clever way to comment on the contemporary appeal of an old fashioned "kissing book," but after several intrusions it becomes a distraction from an already sagging story.

Bound together by their love at a tender age, young Westley (Elwes), then stableboy, falls in love with his beautiful mistress (Wright), but they're separated when he goes off to sea on a mission. After years of grieving for him she becomes bethroned to the evil Prince Humperdinck (Chris Sarandon) who masterminds her kidnaping to strengthen his own position in the kingdom.

As in all good fairy tales, the hero returns to overcome a series of obstacles and regain the hand of his beloved. Unfortunately the hurdles are not particularly imaginative or believable. First off, Westley must defeat a trio of kidnapers headed by the diminutive, but slimy, Wallace Shawn. His accomplices are the kind-hearted giant Fezzik (Andre The Giant) and Inigo Montoya, a Spanish warrior (Mandy Patinkin) out to avenge the murder of his father.

Both the giant and Montoya join young Westley in his fight to rescue the princess and it is their scenes together that are the most delightful in the film and begin to suggest the sweet playfulness Reiner was probably looking for. Patinkin especially is a joy to watch and the film comes to life when his longhaired, scruffy cavalier is on screen.

Not only does Patinkin have great charm, but he has a mission he is passionate about. Chris Sarandon and Christopher Guest are also amusing as the villians, but the leads, alas, are a bore.

Visually, "The Princess Bride" is fairly dull as well. Special effects are unremarkable and the landscape, while unusual, is more stagey than miraculous. It's never really possible to get a fix on where any of this action is supposed to be taking place. Production fails to tap the mythical source that has always given fairy tales their fascination and power.

Instead Reiner seems more eager to exploit the story for moments of comic relief and Goldman's script contributes a number of witty, if inappropriate, one-liners. The cumulative effect of all the nonsense is to leave this fairy tale without anything to believe in, even true love.

—*Jagr.*

The Romance Of Book And Sword
(HONG KONG-COLOR)

A Yeung Tse Kong Movie Enterprise/SIL-Metropole Organization production. Written and directed by Ann Hui, adapted from the novel by Jin Yung. Editor, Chow Muk-leung. Reviewed at the Toronto Festival of Festivals (Eastern Horizons), Sept. 11, 1987. **Running time: 180 MINS.**
With: Zhang Duo Fu, Da Shi Chang, Ai Nuo, Liu Jia.

Toronto — Hong Kong helmer Ann Hui, who scored high on crossover pics "Woo Viet" and "Boat People," might make it a hat trick with "The Romance Of Book And Sword." The two-parter is a solid three hours, but it has the historical vista and character development that often click with audiences outside its home territory.

Almost 3½ years in the making, "The Romance Of Book And Sword" is the eighth film version of Jin Yung's novel, according to director Hui. Its subject matter lends itself to the grand sweep, and in that respect Hui delivers. Drawbacks are the lengthy running time and the sometimes unintentionally ingenuous dialog.

The period is recreated well. It's the time of the overthrow of the Ming dynasty, long the seat of Han rule, by the northern Ching tribe. In a twist of fate that would warm Shakespeare's heart, two Han brothers are separated in infancy. One is sent to the Emperor's to be groomed as a warrior and the other is sent north. The latter, Chen Jalo, is now the leader of the Red Flower Society, which wants to return Han rule to China, while brother Quian Long is leader of the opposition (but his subjects think he's a Manchurian, not a Han).

Chen Jalo helps Chief Mu's tribe retrieve the Koran from the Wei tribe, and during that time meets his daughter Chongking. In the second part, Chen Jalo, disguised as a camel trader, meets Chief Mu's other daughter, Hesili, the fragrant princess, and falls in love with her. It is ordained that they will be married. Chen Jalo has come to help Chief Mu fight the Qing dynasty and ultimately confront his brother.

Hui incorporates sumptuous location settings, period costumes, and a large cast for her swashbuckling battles. There are polished martial arts demonstrations and graphic violence. Above all there are characters that merit attention and care, whose stories lure us in.

That's where Hui's real skill likes, in incorporating human drama, albeit naive and proud, into the panorama of history. It's a winning combination. —*Devo.*

Sister, Sister
(U.S.-COLOR)

A New World Pictures release of a Walter Coblenz production, presented in association with Odyssey Film Partners Ltd. Produced by Coblenz. Executive producers, Gabe Sumner, J. David Marks. Directed by Bill Condon. Stars Eric Stoltz, Jennifer Jason Leigh, Judith Ivey, Dennis Lipscomb, Anne Pitoniak. Screenplay, Condon, Joel Cohen, Ginny Cerrella; camera (color), Stephen M. Katz; editor, Marion Rothman; music, Richard Einhorn; production executive, Cohen; costumes, Bruce Finlayson; design, Richard Sherman; associate producers, Pegi Brotman, Ira Trattner, Yvonne Ramond; special effects, Wayne Beauchamp, Paul Hickerson. Reviewed at Toronto Festival of Festivals, Sept. 11, 1987. (MPAA Rating: R.) Running time: **91 MINS.**
Matt Rutledge . . . . Eric Stoltz
Lucy Bonnard . . . . Jennifer Jason Leigh
Charlotte Bonnard . . . . Judith Ivey
Cleve Doucet . . . . Dennis Lipscomb
Mrs. Bettleheim . . . . Anne Pitoniak
Etienne LeViolette . . . . . Benjamin Mouton
Also with: Natalia Nogulich, Richard Minchenberg, Bobby Pickett, Jason Saucier, Jerry Leggio, Fay Cohn, Ashley McMurray, Ben Book, Casey Levron and Aggie.

Toronto — This dreary, neo-Gothic psychological mystery set in Louisiana bayou contry faces box-office prospects as murky as its rain-soaked, swampy milieu. Some respectable performances in "Sister, Sister" are ultimately compromised by direction that substitutes histrionics for narrative tension and a screenplay whose overcooked red herrings fall to nurture genuine suspense.

Director/co-writer Bill Condon exploits the tired convention of Southern eccentricity in the characters of the nubile, emotionally fragile Lucy (Jennifer Jason Leigh) and her repressed older sister Charlotte (Judith Ivey) who live together in an ante bellum mansion, aptly named "The Willows," bequeathed to them by their dead parents. The Bonnard sisters have turned the estate into a failing guest house which they operate with the aid of a solitary and slightly looney handyman Etienne (Benjamin Mouton).

Etienne knows the sisters almost as well as he knows the bayou which, he tells vacationing Matt Rutledge (Eric Stoltz), is mostly populated by "trappers, shrimpers and psychos like me," as well as a few ghosts it seems. Former mental patient Lucy has apparently communed with the spirits but also devotes her creative imagination to sexual fantasies about the handyman. When the handsome homeboy Matt arrives on holiday from his job as a Congressional staffer in Washington, Lucy quickly refocuses her desires. The real and imagined love-making scenes, lubricated by rainwater leaking through the mansion's sieve-like roof, are easily the most compelling feature of the film.

Charlotte remains unmarried by choice, having repeatedly rebuffed the proposal of earnest and upright town sheriff Cleve Doucet (Dennis Lipscomb), ostensibly because she's devoted her life to caring for Lucy. The sisters, however, share a dark secret concerning a long-ago attempted rape and murder that also involves Cleve, Etienne and Matt, whose face begins to look familiar to the sisters just before the lugubrious scenario's penultimate scene.

Along the way sisters are visited by a chi-chi trio from Beverly Hills, a plot device that stiffs badly as comic relief. They also find their beloved old pet hound dog brutally murdered, one of several plot ploys that fail to whiten the viewer's knuckles. Persistently gloomy lighting and cinematography and a ponderous soundtrack aim to evoke a sense of other-worldly fantasy but like a gator snapping up fresh prey, only drag this ill-conceived project deeper into its own mire.—*Rich.*

Best Seller
(COLOR)

Woods & Dennehy make top thriller team, despite plot holes.

An Orion Pictures release of a Hemdale Film Corp. production. Executive producer, John Daly, Derek Gibson. Produced by Carter De Haven. Stars James Woods, Brian Dennehy. Directed by John Flynn. Screenplay, Larry Cohen. Camera (CFI color), Fred Murphy; editor, David Rosenbloom; music, Jay Ferguson; production design, Gene Rudolf; art direction, Robert Howland; set direction, Chris Butler; sound, Donald O. Mitchell, Rick Kline. Kevin O'Connell; stunt coordinator, Steve Lambert; assistant directors, David Anderson, Leonid Zisman; casting, Michael McLean, Diane Dimeo. Reviewed at Samuel Goldwyn Theater, L.A., Sept. 16, 1987. (MPAA Rating: R.) Running time: **110 MINS.**
Cleve . . . . James Woods
Dennis Meechum . . . . Brian Dennehy
Roberta Gillian . . . . Victoria Tennant
Holly Meechum . . . . Allison Balson
David Madlock . . . . Paul Shenar
Graham . . . . George Coe
Mrs. Foster . . . . Anne Pitoniak
Cleve's Mother . . . . Mary Carver
Monks . . . . Sully Boyar
Annie . . . . Kathleen Lloyd
Cleve's Father . . . . Harold Tyner

Hollywood — "Best Seller" (a.k.a. "Hard Cover") combines the sinister appeal of James Woods at his cold-blooded best with the gruffly lovable persona of Brian Dennehy as a literary cop; on the level of detective thriller, it's a real page-turner. Snappy direction by John Flynn and good lead performances overcome the fact that you could throw Dennehy through some of the plot holes in the script. This pairing may lack sex appeal, but the chemistry is good and word of mouth should make boxoffice results reasonably successful.

Dennehy is Dennis Meechum, a cop who writes a book based on a famous unsolved case, during which he was wounded and three other policeman were killed.

Seventeen years after the incident, he is a lonely burn-out case. His wife has died of cancer and he lives at home with his meek teenage daughter (Allison Balson), trying to crank out another book that just won't come.

Into the picture comes mystery man Woods, full of unctuous charm and foreboding stares. After following Meechum around and saving his life in a dockside shootout, he presents himself as Cleve, a former hit man who worked for "modern robber baron" David Madlock, a pillar of L.A. society who, Cleve claims, ordered murders on everyone from business associates to tax auditors.

The body of the film has Cleve bringing Meechum around the country, providing different details in his story in an attempt to prove its authenticity, while Meechum takes it all down in a book whose ending is written during the closing moments of the film.

These scenes work with varying degrees of success, ranging from the splendid (a darkly humorous scene in which Cleve returns to the scene of a crime) to the stupid (the first evidence of Cleve's still-murderous ways leaves so many plot questions unanswered that it is best ignored completely).

Flynn, keeps things moving through action scenes but is at his best during the psychological cat-and-mouse games in which the two leads find out about one another. Highlight shows Meechum becoming the last one in the theater to figure out that Cleve is the man who wounded him years ago.

Conclusion is seen from a mile away, with one of the main characters changing his ways and partially proving Cleve's contention that he and Meechum have more in common than the cop would care to admit.

While the conclusion is pat, pic is ultimately carried by two lead performances. And here it succeeds: Woods plays the baddie with Jack Nicholsonian glee and Dennehy is warm and dignified in one of the very best roles he's ever had.

Supporting roles are examined deeply enough to be more than perfunctory (Paul Shenar is appropriately despicable as Madlock). Tech credits are pretty good, with Jay Ferguson's score and Fred Murphy's camerawork both impressive. Editing of David Rosenbloom (especially during the early car explosion scene) leaves something to be desired. —Camb.

P.K. And The Kid
(COLOR)

Runaway meets arm wrestle with mild results.

A Castle Hill Prods. release from Sunn Classic Pictures of a Joe Roth production. Produced by Roth. Directed by Lou Lombardo. Stars Paul Le Mat, Molly Ringwald. Screenplay, Neal Barbera; camera (CFI color), Ed Koons; editor, Tony Lombardo; music, James Horner; sound, John Mason; production design, Chet Allen; art direction, Bill Cornford; set decoration, Dian Perryman; assistant director, Scott Maitland; production manager, James Margellos; stunt director, Walter Scott; second unit camera, Paul Hipp. Reviewed on Lorimar Home Video vidcassette, N.Y., Sept. 9, 1987. (MPAA Rating: PG-13). Running time: 89 MINS.
Kid Kane . . . . .Paul Le Mat
P.K. Bayette . . . . .Molly Ringwald
Lester . . . . .Alex Rocco
Bazooka . . . . .Charles Hallahan
Benny . . . . .John De Santi
Flo . . . . .Fionnula Flanagan
Al . . . . .Bert Remsen
Louise . . . . .Leigh Hamilton
Mim . . . . .Esther Rolle
Also with: John Madden, John Matuszak.

"P.K. And The Kid," filmed in 1982 but unreleased until this year, is a modest road movie notable chiefly as Molly Ringwald's first starring feature role, after tv credits and Paul Mazursky's "Tempest." Pic is mild entertainment in the vein of the "little people" rustic dramas of the 1970s.

Ringwald portrays a 15-year-old,

P.K., who runs away from home when her mom (Fionnula Flanagan) fails to protect her against the abusive advances of mom's boyfriend Lester (Alex Rocco). She's befriended on the road by working class hero The Kid (Paul Le Mat, driving a pickup straight out of his "Melvin And Howard" role), who's headed from Colorado to the annual arm wrestling championship at Petaluma, Calif.

Lester keeps popping up to tormet P.K. and accuse The Kid of being the molester. Predictably, The Kid proves himself as a wrist wrestler and P.K., following a beating that puts her in the hospital, finally gets free of her nemesis.

Predating Sylvester Stallone's "Over The Top" flop, pic once again demonstrates that arm (or wrist) wrestling is hardly cinematic fodder, lacking the action and visual appeal of other sports. Le Mat and Ringwald made an attractive, comfortable team in search of an interesting story. Supporting cast is fine, particularly Leigh Hamilton who makes a solid impression as a one-night stand who picks The Kid up at a motel. —Lor.

The Pick-Up Artist
(COLOR)

Skirt-chaser comedy rings false.

A 20th Century Fox release produced in association with Amercent Films and American Entertainment Partners L.P. Produced by David L. MacLeod. Written and directed by James Toback. Stars Molly Ringwald, Robert Downey. Camera (Deluxe color), Gordon Willis; editor, David Bretherton, Angelo Corrao; music, Georges Delerue; production design, Paul Sylbert; art direction, Bill Groom; set decoration, John Alan Hicks; costume design, Colleen Atwood; sound (Dolby), Les Lazarowitz; assistant director, Tom Reilly; casting, Howard Feuer. Reviewed at 20th Century Fox Studios, L.A., Sept. 14, 1987. (MPAA Rating: PG-13.) Running time: 81 MINS.
Randy Jensen . . . . .Molly Ringwald
Jack Jericho . . . . .Robert Downey
Flash .Dennis Hopper
Phil . . . . .Danny Aiello
Nellie . . . . .Mildred Dunnock
Alonzo . . . . .Harvey Keitel
Also with: Brian Hamill (Mike), Tamara Bruno (Karen), Vanessa Williams (Rae), Angie Kempf (Jack's student), Polly Draper (Pat), Frederick Koehler (Richie), Robert Towne (Stan), Victoria Jackson (Lulu), Lorraine Bracco (Carla), Bob Gunton (Portacarrero), Clemenze Caserta (Clem), Christine Baranski (Harriet), Joe Spinell (Eddie), Tony Conforti (Tony), Jilly Rizzo (Floor Manager), Tom Signorelli (Marty), Reni Santoni.

Hollywood — As long as this film sticks to what its title suggests, "The Pick-Up Artist" is a tolerably amusing comedy. But as soon as the compulsive skirt-chaser gets hooked on one girl, James Toback's long-gestating portrait of a 1-track mind beomes bogged down in unconvincing plot mechanics. Molly Ringwald name and a bright sell stressing the comic elements can get this off to a decent start, but b.o. prospects look moderate overall.

Compared to the harsh, raw quality of Toback's previous films, this

is a mild work, one that seems curiously sanitized and lightened in tone from anything he has done before. As "Fingers," "Love And Money" and "Exposed" were notably uncommercial, this softening can't help but create a wider audience for him, but result seems less urgently felt and freshly conceived.

Opening reels possess considerable buoyancy and zip, as makeout king Robert Downey cruises the streets of New York by foot and by car trying out his shtick on every pretty woman who crosses his path.

Playing the percentages with decent success and utterly unfazed by rejection, Downey hits on Ringwald and quickly scores in his convertible, but predictably becomes intrigued by her apparent lack of interest in seeing him again. Suddenly, he's got blinders on and finds himself assuming personal responsibility for some enormous gambling debts the mob expects delivered by high noon.

Dennis Hopper once again plays a drunken, washed-up shell of his former self as Ringwald's irresponsible father, and Harvey Keitel, in an extension of his "Fingers" character, is the threatening collector. The gambling world context into which Toback unnaturally forces the climax of the picture only weakly evokes the power of his script for "The Gambler," and the finale is bogus anyway because Ringwald, who states her age as 19, is two years too young to sit at the tables in Atlantic City.

More responsible for the picture's deterioration than the unnecessary melodrama is Ringwald's thinly conceived character. Her evasiveness with Downey is legitimate because she initially conceals her difficulties from her suitor, but Toback never lets the viewer in on what she really thinks and feels. The character, who unbelievably flits between the disco world of drugs and high rollers and her father's Coney Island apartment, with time out to give guided tours at a museum, is just a cipher, and too serious for the actress to save it with her characteristic offbeat charm.

In that the ending, which has everyone dropping their bad habits of a lifetime after one purgative night, doesn't ring true either, it is surprising how engagingly the picture plays for much of its brief running time. A lion's share of the credit for this goes to Downey who, in his first starring role, is brashly likeable, if perhaps too young, as the indefatiguable but sincere ladies' man.

Even here, however, Toback could have worked harder to further individualize his protagonist. Without asking for a psychological analysis of why he is so compulsive, one could still use a little coloring in of Downey's specific tastes and preferences, some private appreciation of different women's traits and attrib-

utes of the sort to be found in many of François Truffaut's films. All women seem the same (except for Ringwald, for unknown reasons) in Downey's book.

Led by Gordon Willis' lovely lensing of Manhattan in full bloom of summer, production credits are tops. Supporting cast is filled with curious cameos, by everyone from writer Robert Towne and former Miss America Vanessa Williams to longtime Sinatra crony Jilly Rizzo and Mustang Ranch proprietor Tony Conforti.

Warren Beatty developed the project and was listed as producer during shooting, but producer-of-record credit goes to Beatty's cousin, David L. MacLeod. —Cart.

La Brute
(The Brute)
(FRENCH-COLOR)

A Prods. du Daunou/Marifilms release of a Prods. du Daunou/Artistique Caumartin/Capricorne Prod./Gilmi coproduction. Executive producer, Denise Petitdidier. Directed by Claude Guillemot, Screenplay, Guillemot, from the novel by Guy des Cars; camera (Fujicolor), Denys Clerval; editor, Agnès Guillemot; music, Jean-Marie Senia; theme song, Magali Llorca; sound, Gita Gerveira; art direction; Frédéric Astich-Barre; sign language advisor, Didier Flory. Reviewed at the Georges V cinema, Paris. Aug. 18, 1987. Running time: 103 MINS.
Jacques Vauthier . . . . .Xavier Deluc
Solange Vauthier . . . . .Assumpta Serna
Defense attorney Deliot . . . . . .Jean Carmet
Danièlle Geny . . . . .Rosette
Yves Rodallec . . . . .Paul Crauchet
Phylis . . . . .Magali Llorca
John Bell . . . . .Alexandre Sousa

Paris — A neatly contrived but conventional whodunit in the Perry Mason mold (crime, investigation, courtroom climax), "La Brute" is the first French screen adaptation of a book by bestselling novelist Guy de Cars. Adapted and directed by Claude Guillemot, a tv and short subjects helmer, it is solid homescreen fare, but probably not hefty enough for theatrical play offshore.

The crime in question is the murder of an oceanliner of an American lounge lizard, apparently done in by a jealous husband. Mindbender however is that the latter is congenitally deaf, dumb and blind, and thus was not likely to have suspected that his beautiful and heretofore devoted wife (Assumpta Serna) had been having a fling she had regretted immediately.

Rising young actor Xavier Deluc displays quiet technical bravura as the handicapped suspect, who pleads guilty and walls himself up in his silent world. Jean Carmet does a late entry as his defense attorney, using intuition and perseverance to unravel the mystery and nab the real culprit during the trial sequence. Acting is good all around.

Guillemot, who made one previous theatrical feature 20 years ago, handles the material with craftsmanly ease, and deserves a crack at more ambitious projects. —Len.

Like Father Like Son
(COLOR)

Unamusing role-reversal sitcom.

A Tri-Star Pictures release of an Imagine Entertainment production. Produced by Brian Grazer, David Valdes. Directed by Rod Daniel. Stars Dudley Moore, Kirk Cameron. Screenplay, Lorne Cameron, Steven L. Bloom; Camera (Technicolor), Jack N. Green; editor, Lois Freeman-Fox; music Miles Goodman; production design, Dennis Gassner; set decoration, John T. Walker; costume design, Robert Turturice; sound (Dolby), C. Darin Knight; assistant director, Dan Kolsrud; casting, Judith Weiner. Reviewed at Mann's Chinese Theater, Los Angeles, Sept. 17, 1987. (MPAA Rating: PG-13.) Running time: **98 MINS.**

Dr. Jack Hammond . . . . Dudley Moore
Chris Hammond . . . . Kirk Cameron
Trigger . . . . Sean Astin
Dr. Armbruster . . . . Patrick O'Neal
Ginnie Armbruster . . . . Margaret Colin
Dr. Amy Larkin . . . . Catherine Hicks

Hollywood — One wonders after watching "Like Father Like Son" why Dudley Moore has stopped sitting down at the piano in his films, for it seems that every successive nonmusical character he's played since "Arthur" has been increasingly charmless and unamusing. Both he and co-star Kirk Cameron suffer from a bad case of flap jaw in this messy, repetitive role reversal comedy, that really reaches for laughs. Pic will be on the tube soon enough, via homevid.

Underlying Lorne Cameron and Steven L. Bloom's overly talkative script is a premise that defies logic.

Moore plays a stuffy British-born surgeon and Cameron his motor-mouthed teenage son who find themselves in each others bodies' when Moore unknowingly takes a dose of brain transference serum. They manage to switch intelligence and personality but somehow lose the memory chips in the process. Therein lies the comedic potential from which little humor is derived.

When Cameron now goes to school, he acts like his father, which means boring his class with a lengthy discourse on the human respiratory system while out on the track, he blows relay race.

Cameron's from tv's "Growing Pains" and he successfully transfers that talent to screen, instead here it's 98 instead of 30 minutes of benign drivel to regurgitate. He's cute and his teen heart throb persona survives intact.

As Cameron, Moore eats Cocoa Puffs and calls out to his hospital buddies, "Que Pasa?" and "What's Happening?" He plays acid rock air guitar to MTV and tools around in a new, $12,000 Jeep.

It's strictly sitcom stuff, except for smatterings of four-letter words. Sloppy directing and choppy editing also contribute to pic's overall episodic feel.

Unbelievably, neither father or son seems to be in a particular hurry about getting out of their predicament by leaning on the kid responsible (Sean Astin). It just sort of gets worked out in the desert in the last few minutes of the film.

For whatever reason, filmmakers didn't seem to want to convey a sense of panic and without that urgency, the joke's less fun.—*Brit.*

The Principal
(COLOR)

High school drama is risible and unoriginal.

A Tri-Star Pictures release, from Tri-Star/ML Delphi Premier Prods. of a Doric production, Produced by Thomas H. Brodek. Directed by Christopher Cain. Stars James Belushi, Louis Gossett Jr., Rae Dawn Chong. Screenplay, Frank Deese, camera (Technicolor), Arthur Albert; editor, Jack Hofstra; music supervisor; Jellybean Benitez; music, Jay Gruska; production manager, James T. Davis; art direction, Mark Billerman; set decoration, Rick Brown; sound (Dolby), Andy Wiskes; special effects, David Pier; assistant director, Charles D. Myers; stunt coordinator, Everett Creach; casting, Penny Perry. Reviewed at UA Coronet Theater, Westwood Calif., Sept. 15, 1987. (MPAA Rating: R.) Running time: **109 MINS.**

Rick Latimer . . . . James Belushi
Jake Phillips . . . . Louis Gossett Jr.
Hilary Orozco . . . . Rae Dawn Chong
Victor Duncan . . . . Michael Wright
White Zac . . . . J.J. Cohen
Raymi Rojas . . . . Esai Morales
Baby Emile . . . . Troy Winbush
Arturo Diego . . . . Jacob Vargas
Robert Darcy . . . . Thomas Ryan
Jojo . . . . Reggie Johnson
Treena Lester . . . . Kelly Minter

Hollywood — "The Principal" is a well-meaning high school drama that can't decide whether it wants to be "Blackboard Jungle" or "Welcome Back, Kotter." Every scene of ultra-realistic urban conflict is undercut with a wink of the eye and an irreverent — and often inappropriate — comic line. Writer Frank Deese seems to be admitting that he has nothing new to add to the subject. Boxoffice prospects are up in the air, depending on how pic plays in urban locales.

James Belushi is Rick Latimer, a hard-luck teacher at a preppy high school who gets drunk one night and bashes in the windows of his ex-wife's boyfriend's car.

Repercussions are immediate, with Latimer getting "promoted" to principal of the district's worst school, Brandel, the magnet for the city's dead-end, dope-dealing delinquents.

Latimer walks into a war zone, where physical intimidation is a constant factor in every student's life and the risks involved with personal protection making the significance of education pale by comparison. Latimer predictably goes on a mission to straighten things out, teaming up with head of security Jake Phillips (Louis Gossett, Jr. in a promising role that's nothing but cliché).

Key to story is Latimer's attempt to bust down the de facto school principal, gangleader Victor Duncan (Michael Wright, looking lika a young Cleavon Little), who is a model of sinister cool up until a well-played crucial scene.

While the plot progressions are drawn without much subtlety, Belushi gives an assured, charming lead performance. Main problem is his tendency to play virtually every scene for comic effect, testing believability in some scenes and making too quick of a switch to seriousness in others (he splits the difference in the two scenes he plays dramatically).

While the breezy irreverence looks mostly good on Belushi, it doesn't do much for the film. All of this still might haved worked if Deese's script set-up and director Christopher Cain's lensing execution were more sure-footed, but both are found wanting.

For every scene that is brutally effective (a scarifying attempted rape) there are a couple that are ridiculous (Latimer's lecture to the student body that turns into a gang riot, the break-up of a drug deal by Latimer on a cycle). Continuity is a problem too, with Cain almost giving up the storyline halfway through to focus on a series of loosely related vignettes which all lead to approximately the same place.

Supporting performers are uniformly good. Rae Dawn Chong continues her string of competent work as a teacher still trying to teach education in the demilitarized zones of the classrooms, Esai Morales' nicely drawn Raymi Rojas, showing more modulation and control than his larger past roles and the meek, loyal Arturo (well done by Jacob Vargas).

Most impressive is the stocky and sneaky smart "Baby" Emile, sharply rendered by Troy Winbush, who begins as a Duncan disciple before trying to break with the gang — at a terrible price. Winbush displays uncommon sensitivity for a young actor, and the dramatic shadings in his performance stand out against the backdrop of this broadly drawn picture.

Cain is responsible for that flaw, showing the same kind of jackhammer subtlety that characterized his previous "That Was Then, This Is Now." Cain seems to know how urban youths act, but his films show no evidence of his knowing why.

Arthur Albert's photography is sharp, especially against the dingy backdrop of Brandel and costume designer Marianna Aström-DeFina's eye is keenly accurate. Music supervision by Jellybean (formerly Benitez) is mostly obtrusive.
—*Camb.*

Sweet Revenge
(COLOR)

Routine white slavery actioner.

A Concorde Pictures release of a Motion Picture Corp. of America production. Executive producers, Roger Corman, Brad Krevoy. Produced by Steve Stabler. Directed by Mark Sobel. Stars Nancy Allen, Ted Shackelford, Martin Landau. Screenplay, Steven Krauzer, Tim McCoy; camera (Eastmancolor, Film House prints), Shane Kelly; editor, Michael S. Murphy; music, Ernest Troost; sound (Ultra-Stereo), George Mahlberg; production design, Vic Dabao; pyrotechnic effects, Chagar; postproduction coordinator, Eric Brooks. Reviewed at Cineplex Odeon Coliseum 2 theater; N.Y., Sept. 12, 1987. (MPAA Rating: R.) Running time: **78 MINS.**

Jillian Grey . . . . Nancy Allen
Boone . . . . Ted Shackelford
Cicero . . . . Martin Landau
Gil . . . . Sal Landi
Lee . . . . Michele Little
K.C. Gina Gershon
Sonya . . . . Lotis Key
Tina . . . . Stacey Adams
Buddha . . . . Leo Martinez

"Sweet Revenge" is an utterly routine action picture from the Roger Corman stable, reminiscent of the Filipino-lensed films he cranked out for the old New World in the early 1970s.

Nancy Allen (pre-"Robocop") toplines as an L.A. tv reporter doing an undercover story on a white slavery ring, who is abducted by the ring's henchpersons Lotis Key and Sal Landi and taken with three young would-be models to the Far East lair of Cicero (Martin Landau, playing the sort of smug baddie he used to foil weekly on "Mission: Impossible").

In the midst of numerous escapes and chases they are befriended by Boone (Ted Shackelford), a soldier of fortune involved in smuggling counterfeit Chanel No. 5 to the U.S. Pic sags considerably midway through as the leads take time out to help a pirate friend of Boone's.

Direction by Mark Sobel is by-the-numbers, with numerous explosions proving to be the action highlight. A hurried climax kills off each villain one-by-one, leading to a soggy, sentimental coda of Allen reunited with her missing daughter at the airport back home. Acting is okay, with tv star Shackelford physically right as the reluctant hero.—*Lor.*

Lady Beware
(COLOR)

Glum thriller is strictly window dressing.

A Scotti Bros. release, produced in association with Intl. Video Entertainment. Produced by Tony Scotti, Lawrence Taylor Mortorff. Executive producers, Ben Scotti, Fred Scotti. Directed by Karen Arthur. Stars Diane Lane. Screenplay, Susan Miller, Charles Zev Cohen; camera (United color), Tom Neuwirth; editor, Roy Watts; music, Craig Safan; set decoration, Tom Wells; costumes, Patricia Fields; sound (Dolby), Larry Loewinger; associate producer assistant director, Paula Marcus; casting, Diane Dimeo, Joy todd Inc., Sharon & Clayton Hill. Reviewed at the Scotti Bros. screening room, Santa Monica, Calif., Sept. 11, 1987. (MPAA Rating: R) Running time: **108 MINS.**

Katya Yarno . . . . Diane Lane
Jack Price . . . . Michael Woods
Mac Odell . . . . Cotter Smith
Lionel . . . . Peter Nevargic
Thayer . . . . Edward Penn
Nan . . . . Tyra Ferrell

Hollywood — Beware of "Lady Beware," an unthrilling thriller in which the central psychopath has more success boring the audience to death than knocking off the heroine. Too "serious" to work as an exploitationer but too dramatically inept to measure up to its own aspirations to thematic importance, dreary meller will make a quick pitstop in theaters on the way to it rendezvous with homevid destiny.

Above-the-title star Diane Lane plays a fashionable young lady come to Pittsburgh to make her name as the most radical department store windowdresser on the Monongahela. Her punky, avant garde displays attract plenty of attention, including that of Michael Woods, a goodlooking lab technician who clearly jumped off the deep end a long time ago.

Most of the action, such as it is, consists of Woods hounding Lane, leaving sinister messages on her answering machine, breaking into her loft apartment in her absence, and so on. She finally decides to fight back, but not in the traditional film manner of getting a gun and blowing her nemesis away, but by turning the tables.

This appears to be the vaguely feminist point of Karen Arthur's picture, that a woman can retaliate without fleeing or reducing herself to the man's levels. The characters are so uninteresting, however, the pacing so sluggish and the mood so glum, that one's fast-forward finger becomes quickly itchy.

Lane is pleasant enough to watch, but her range is too limited for her to carry such a thinly conceived drama single-handedly. Male fans will be gratified by her big nude scene, parts of which are repeated later on as memory flashbacks of her voyeuristic tormentor.

Michael Woods, star of television's new "Private Eye" series, is obvious hunk material but won't turn anyone on here with his thoroughly repulsive character, and Cotter Smith comes and goes as Lane's aspiring boyfriend.

Finally, there's no excuse for pic of this nature with so little action running 108 minutes when 90 would have been more than enough.
—*Cart.*

Le Jupon rouge
(The Red Skirt)
(FRENCH-COLOR)

An AAA Classic release of an Antares/-Séléna Audiovisual AAA/Bullock Prods. coproduction. Executive producer, Geneviève Lefebvre. Produced by Michèle Dimitri. Directed by Lefebvre. Screenplay, Lefebvre, Nicole Berckmans; camera (color), Ramon Suarez; editor, Josie Miljevic; music, Joanna Bruzdowicz; sound, Pierre Lorain, Gérard Lamps; art direction, Danka Semenowicz; makeup, Chantal Houdoy; costumes, Christina Olhson; technical advisor, Claude Luquet. Reviewed at the 7 Parnassiens cinema, Paris, Aug. 25, 1987. (In Montreal Film Festival and Toronto Film Festival.) Running time: **90 MINS.**

Manuela . . . . Marie-Christine Barrault
Bacha . . . . Alida Valli
Claude . . . . Guillemette Grobon

Paris — A women's film in the best sense, "Le Jupon rouge" is an emotionally gripping drama about three ladies of different generations and social background. Passionate performances by Alida Valli and Marie-Christine Barrault and fine close-quarters direction by newcomer Geneviève Lefebvre (who also produced and coscripted) place this prominently among the year's best debut features, with good chances on the foreign art house circuit.

Barrault is the pivot of the story as a costume designer whose close friendship with Valli, an aging human rights militant who still bears the physical and psychic scars of the Nazi concentration camps, is menaced when former begins a lesbian relationship with a younger protegé of Valli's.

The affair shocks and disturbs the possessive Valli, whose equilibrium is further disrupted by news of an old colleague's death. Barrault struggles to save her friendship with Valli and her liaison with the girl (well played by beautiful screen newcomer Guillemette Grobon), but sacrifices the latter when the older woman, who shows increasing signs of mental distress, suddenly disappears after weeks of self-isolation.

Lefebvre draws her character studies with deep feeling and sound filmmaking skill, to which Barrault and Valli respond full-bloodedly. The scenes between Barrault and her lover have a strong emotional and erotic charge obtained without pandering overstatement.

Film's title refers to one of Barrault's designs, in which Grobon poses, otherwise nude. When Valli sees Barrault's sensual painting, the truth of the relationship dawns on her.

Ramon Suarez' densely textured lensing effectively cloisters the torn trio of women. Other credits are fine.

Film's more banal English title is "Manuela's Loves." —*Len.*

Relação fiel e verdadeira
(A True And Accurate Report)
(PORTUGUESE-COLOR-16m)

A Margarida Gil/Instituto Portugues de Cinema Rado-tevisão Portuguesa production. Executive producer, Henrique Espirito Santo. Directed by Margarida Gil. Screenplay, Gil, João César Monteiro, based on the autobography of Antónia Margarida de Castelo Branco; camera (color, 16m), Manuel Costa e Silva; editor, Leonor Guterres; music, José Alberto Gil; sound, Joaquim Pinto, Vasco Pimentel; art direction, Juan Sotullo. Reviewed at the Venice Film Festival (Critics' Week), Sept. 1, 1987. Running time: **85 MINS.**

With: Catarina Alves Costa, António Manuel Sequeira, Jorge Rola, Laura Soveral, Cremilde Gil, Sonia Guimaraes, Aurora Gaia, Adelaide Teixeira, Philip Spinelli, Luis Cunha.

Venice — Based on the autobiography of a 17th century nun and transferred into the present, Margarida Gil's first feature film effort has troubles both in updating the story and telling it in an interesting fashion.

A young woman is married off by her mother to a moody gambler and womanizer of good family but no means. The marriage turns into disaster, the wife's devotion to the husband being returned by fits of jealousy, which, combined with the man's evident self-destructive tendencies leave the wife no other alternative, after the death of her child, than the convent.

While as a historical piece this might have held several interesting aspects, particularly on the emotional level, brought up to date it tooks outdated and archaic. As all acting is wooden without exception, the emotional aspects are completely lost. The feelings of the husband and wife for each other, a combination of fidelity and wishing to belong, on one hand, and of extreme macho possessiveness on the other, are never sufficiently convincing to explain their conduct, certainly not in a modern context.

Pretentious soundtrack using German opera excerpts and murky 16m photography of landscapes that could have been far more dramatic don't help very much either.

Protesting the condition of women in a society which both through its religion and tradition is a male-oriented one seems to have been the intention here, but there are more persuasive ways of putting it.
—*Edna.*

The Lighthorsemen
(AUSTRALIAN-COLOR)

A Cinecom release (Hoyts in Australia) of an RKO Pictures presentation of a Picture Show production. Executive producer, Antony I. Ginnane. Produced by Ian Jones, Simon Wincer. Directed by Wincer. Screenplay, Jones; camera (Panavision, Eastmancolor), Dean Semler; editor, Adrian Carr; music, Mario Millo; production design, Bernard Hides; sound, Lloyd Carrick; stunt coordinator, Grant Page; costumes, David Rowe; production supervisor, Phillip Corr; special effects, Steve Courtley; assistant director, Bob Donaldson; horse masters, Gerald Egan, Bill Willoughby, Jim Willoughby, Ray Winslade; production consultant, Gil Brealey. Reviewed at Hoyts screening room, Sydney, July 28, 1987. Running time: **128 MINS.**
Scotty . . . . Jon Blake
Dave Mitchell . . . . Peter Phelps
Lt. Col (Swagman Bill)
Bourchier . . . . Tony Bonner
Lt. Gen. Sir Harry Chauvel . . . . . Bill Kerr
Tas . . . . John Walton
Frank . . . . Gary Sweet
Chiller . . . . Tim McKenzie
Anne . . . . Sigrid Thornton
Major Meinertzhagen . . . Anthony Andrews
Gen. Sir Edmund
Allenby . . . . Anthony Hawkins
Ismet Bey . . . . Gerard Kennedy
Reichert . . . . Shane Briant
Rankin . . . . Serge Lazareff
Von Kressenstein . . . . Ralph Cotterill
Also with: John Heywood (Mr. Mitchell), Di O'Connor (Mrs. Mitchell), Grant Piro (Charlie), Patrick Frost (Sgt. Ted Scager), Adrian Wright (Lawson), Anne Scott-Pendle-

bury (Nursing sister), Brenton Whittle (Padre), Jon Sidney (Grant), Graham Dow (Hodgson), James Wright (Fitzgerald), Gary Stalker (Nobby), Scott Bradley (Lt. Burton), Peter Merrill (young German officer), Peter Browne (Arch).

Sydney — Toward the end of this 2-hour 8-minute epic about Aussie cavalry fighting in the Middle East in 1917, there's a tremendously exciting and spectacular 14-minute sequence in which soldiers of the Light Horse charge on German/-Turkish-occupied Beersheba. Sequence is a magnificent piece of filmcraft, impeccably shot, edited, staged and stunted, and for many this scene alone will be worth the price of admission to "The Lighthorsemen." It's as much a show-stopper as the climax to Michael Curtiz' "The Charge Of The Light Brigade."

It's a pity writer and coproducer Ian Jones couldn't come up with a more substantial storyline to build around his terrific climax, because the 104 minutes of footage before the charge is much less enthralling and compares unfavorably to Peter Weir's "Gallipoli," which it often resembles (both films were shot principally in the same area of South Australia, both are set during World War I, and there are even a couple of actors common to both).

Focus of attention is on Dave Mitchell, very well played by Peter Phelps. Opening sequence, which is breathtakingly beautiful, is set in Australia and involves young Dave deciding to enlist in the Light Horse after seeing wild horses being mustered for shipment to the Middle East. Action then shifts to Gaza for the first of several miscalculated scenes involving German or Turkish officers: these poorly written and awkwardly acted segments should be pruned, as they add little to the basic story, and destroy much of the authenticity the film creates in other scenes.

Main story involves four friends (Jon Blake, John Walton, Tim McKenzie, Gary Sweet) who are members of the Australian cavalry, chafing because the British, who have overall command of allied troops in the area, misuse the cavalry time and again, forcing the Australians to dismount before going into battle. Sweet is wounded in one encounter with the enemy, and he dies after learning his fiancée has married another man. His place is taken by Phelps, who's at first resented by the other three until he proves his courage and loyalty. But Phelps finds himself unable to shoot at the enemy, and eventually is relegated to being a stretcher bearer (cue for romance with pretty nurse Sigrid Thornton) before courageously going to the help of his friends in the final battle.

Or every conceivable technical level, "The Lighthorsemen" is a super production. It was expensive to make, but the money's up there on the screen. Dean Semler's Panavision photography gloriously captures the spectacle of desert warfare; Bernard Hides' production design authentically recreates Palestine in South Australia; Adrian Carr's editing, especially in the action scenes, is very precise. As long as the film concentrates on the young Australian cavalrymen, it's entertaining, although the Phelps-Thornton romance is very familiar territory.

Scenes, however, involving the officers, and especially the enemy officers, just don't work, and usually reliable actors such as Gerard Kennedy and Ralph Cotterill are unconvincing. Nor does imported British actor Anthony Andrews add anything in his role as Gen. Allenby's aide: he overplays the stiff-upperlip Britisher to the point of caricature.

Despite these flaws, "The Lighthorsemen" should perform very well at the Australian boxoffice; word of mouth about the tremendous climactic charge sequence should ensure the public comes to see the flag-waving spectacle. Overseas prospects look good, too, especially if the more awkward scenes are eliminated. The principal leads are very well played, with Peter Phelps a standout as the most interesting of the young soldiers. John Walton scores as the quick-tempered leader of the group, while Tim McKenzie creates a character out of very little material. Topbilled Jon Blake is thoroughly charming as Scotty, and it's sad to note this promising young actor is still hospitalized as a result of an auto accident in which he was involved when driving home from the final day's shooting of the film several months ago.

Back in 1941, Australian director Charles Chauvel used the charge of the Light Horse at Beersheba for the climax of his popular film "Forty Thousand Horsemen." The expertise with which the heroic battle has been staged here will ensure the popularity of Simon Wincer's film on which, a final title assures us, no horses were killed or injured. —*Strat.*

De Orionnevel
(Orion Nebula)
(DUTCH-COLOR)

A Cor Koppies Filmdistribution release of a Horizon Filmproductions production. Produced by Frans Rasker. Written and directed by Jurriën Rood. Camera (Kodacolor, Super 16m, Cineco prints), Goert Giltay; editor, Hans von Dongen; music, Rood, Arjen Hogendorp; sound, Jan Musch; art direction, Gert Brinkers; casting, Hans Kemna. Reviewed at Cinecenter Amsterdam, Sept. 4, 1987. Running time: **81 MINS.**
Gerdo . . . . Bert Kuizenga
Bril . . . . Han Kerckhoffs
Baard . . . . Michiel Romeyn

Amsterdam — Jurriën Rood's feature debut is a pleasant surprise — imaginative, intelligent, warm and humorous. There are these three men, all in their thirties, all with their fare share of quirks, one of them downright pixilated. Gerdo started lots of careers, was good at most of them, but he always stopped. They gave him no real satisfaction. He's mad at life because it does not give him what he wants. He does not know what he wants, except one thing, the return of his girl, who left him for a civil servant. She haunts him: he sees her floating in front of his window, emerging out of the wall, everywhere.

Then there's Foureyes with his prim little glasses. He's a science teacher, who can't keep order in class, gets not enough respect from his pupils and from the girls who occasionally enter his existence. He finds peace and quiet on his roof, looking through his telescope, photographing the stars.

Finally there's Beard. He used to be a social worker. Then he sold things on street corners. Then his wife left him. Now he collects old newspapers, drinks a bit and talks with people. His youth was unhappy. It all fits quite logically together, thinks Beard.

The three met by accident, forming a brittle friendship. The film is a tale about a generation which lost its direction. They were too young to play a part in the revolt of youth versus established authority in '68, but their formative years were deeply influenced by the resulting "democratization." Everyone had to have a say (literally) in every decision which might influence his life. Committees sprouted everywhere. Schoolchildren codecided about their education; technical staff had a voice in reshaping university science departments.

Words and rhetoric, squabbles and feuds took lots of time; resolutions did not resolve anything. People lost their footing and their sense of direction under the onslaught of tidal waves of verbiage. It happened in many countries, but the substitution of hard thinking by soft patter went specially far in the Netherlands.

The actors are practically unknowns, their acting surprisingly expert, helped by the camera in the mostly short sequences. The direction is cinematic while keeping tv in mind. Technical credits are very good.

Rood's debut is not blockbuster, neither is it a film for an elite. It's entertainment for people who enjoy an unusual fable, often hilarious, sometimes subdued. Pic needs further tightening before going abroad, because it sags somewhat after the first hour. Then it will be fare for festivals, art houses, and television in the later evening hours. It has been made on a budget of less than $325,000, and that sometimes shows. —*Wall.*

Si le soleil ne revenait pas
(If The Sun Never Returns)
(SWISS-FRENCH-COLOR)

A Sara-CDF release of a JMH Prod./Télévision Suisse Romande/Marion's Films/Sara Films/Canal Plus Prods. coproduction. Executive producer, Jean-Marc Henchoz. Produced by Henchoz, Sylvette Frydman. Written and directed by Claude Goretta, from the novel by Charles Ferdinand Ramuz. Stars Charles Vanel, Philippe Léotard, Catherine Mouchet. Camera (Eastmancolor), Bernard Zitzermann; editor, Eliane Guignet; sound, Etienne Metrailler, Dominique Dalmasso; music, Antoine Auberson; makeup, Valérie de Buck; production manager, François Roch. Reviewed at the Gaumont Colisée cinema, Paris, Aug. 31 1987. (At Venice Film Festival — competing.) Running time: **116 MINS.**
Anzevui . . . . Charles Vanel
Isabelle Antide . . . . Catherine Mouchet
Arlettaz . . . . Philippe Léotard
Denis Revaz . . . . Raoul Billery
Follonier . . . . Claude Evrard

Paris — An isolated village high in the Swiss mountains anxiously waits out a long dark winter in "Si le soleil ne revenait pas," Claude Goretta's parable of despair and hope in the face of impending apocalypse. Despite Goretta's typical care with character and atmosphere and the universality of theme, drama remains as remote as the alpine peaks that hem in its principals. Competing at Venice, film will need careful handling outside home territory for specialized playoff.

Adapted from a novel by Charles Ferdinand Ramuz, a Swiss literary glory, film recounts the reactions of villagers to a prophecy by a local patriarch and self-styled oracle about the death of the sun, which the tiny hamlet is deprived of during a 6-month winter. The sun, announces the ancient, will not keep its usual spring rendezvous, plunging the world into permanent night.

Film (like the book) is set in 1937, when the radio — one of the mountaineers' few links with the outside world during these misty, snowbound months — issues distressing reports from distant Spain, where bloody civil war rages. By maintaining the historical specificity, and not framing the story in an intemporal zone where anything might happen, Goretta robs the story of any genuine suspense. One watches dispassionately as the superstitious mountaineers react variously to the portent of Doomsday, which we know will never take place.

A carefully selected cast brings professional conscience, but little interior illumination to their roles. Catherine Mouchet falls from the state of grace of "Thérèse" to the part of a young girl, disappointed from her recent marriage to a local yokel, but tenaciously optimistic about the future and the return of the sun.

At the antipodes is Philippe Léotard as the local lush, miserable and lonely since the departure of his daughter, who upon hearing the prediction sells his coveted fields to subsidize his future descent into alcoholic stupor.

The old sorcerer is played by the doyen of French screen actors, Charles Vanel, who turned 95 last month, and has not been seen since Francesco Rosi's 1980 "Three Brothers." Avoiding the hokey effects such a part might inspire in lesser actors, Vanel brings a calm wizened dignity to the awe-inspiring sage, who in announcing the death of the sun in fact only predicts his own demise.

Shot on location in an isolated hamlet in the Valais region, film has superb pictorial qualities (courtesy of lenser Bernard Zitzermann), a feeling of place out of time, a sense of concern with ordinary people confronting realities beyond their grasp. But the deeper emotion of audience empathy gets lost in the snow.—*Len.*

Michelangelo, Self-Portrait
(U.S.-DOCU-COLOR)

A Snyder-Sonnabend production. Produced and directed by Robert Snyder. Written by Michael Sonnabend. Camera (Eastmancolor), Umberto Galeassi; editor, Robert A. Fitzgerald; music, Claudio Monteverdi; conducted by Michel Corboz. Reviewed at invitational showing during Venice Film Festival, Sept. 4, 1987. Running time: **85 MINS.**

Venice — Robert Snyder, an Academy Award-winning filmmaker, has preserved on celluloid prominent shakers and do-ers of our times, among them Igor Stravinsky, Pablo Casals, Willen de Kooning, Henry Miller, Caresse Crosby, Buckminster Fuller and Anais Nin. He has spent the last nine years on his screen biography of Michelangelo.

His inspiration for this project was Robert Flaherty's 1950 "The Titan," a 67-minute, black-and-white documentary about the colossus that won rave reviews and an Academy Award. A classic of its genre, it has served as the model for this fine new film.

Snyder's version opens with Michelangelo at 89 when he sculpted his last work, another Pieta in St. Peter's. As he conjures up thoughts of his past flashbacks carry the spectator to his beginning and his life, filled with strife and miseries, his monumental achievements and his spiritual evolution are outlined against the scene of the high noon of the turbulent Renaissance.

A forceful, informative commentary, written by Michael Sonnabend and spoken by Snyder (uncredited) accompanies the tour of the magnificent art treasures. Its text is drawn from Michelangelo's letters, diaries, poems and from his own words as recorded by Vaseri and other of his contemporaries. This brings him into vivid focus as an extraordinary character, forever meditating on the battle of the sacred and the profane.

There is a stunning photography

of his giant David statue and his mighty marble of Moses. Snyder was granted special permission by the Vatican to film St. Peter's Pieta inside the bullet-proof glass partition installed since an act of vandalism. The Sistine Chapel frecoes of the Day of Judgment are revealed in detail.

This "Titan II" profits, too, by the inclusion of Michelangelo works that have been unearthed in the last 30 years, notably the wooden crucifix, his wall drawings in the Sotteraneo and the original head of Christ of the Pieta Rondanini.

The film has been invited by Ambassador Maxwell Rapp to a showing in the US embassy in Rome. It is a natural for universities and art school projections and for tv. As with Kenneth Clark's TV series on art history it is an item for video libraries. —*Curt.*

Agent Trouble
(Trouble Agent)
(FRENCH-COLOR)

A Bac Films release of an AFC/Koala Film/Canal Plus Prods./ FR3 Films Prod. coproduction. Produced by Maurice Bernart. Written and directed by Jean-Pierre Mocky, based on the novel, "The Man Who Liked Zoos" by Malcolm Bosse. Camera (Eastmancolor), William Lubtchansky; editor, Mocky; music, Gabriel Yared; sound, Jean-Bernard Thomasson, Jacques Julian, art direction, Michèle Abbé; production managers, Gérard Gaultier, Louis Wipf. Reviewed at the Gaumont Colisée cinema, Paris, Sept. 10, 1987. Running time: **88 MINS.**

Amanda Weber	Catherine Deneuve
Alex	Richard Bohringer
Victorien	Tom Novembre
Karen	Dominique Lavanant
Stanislas	Pierre Arditi
Edna	Sylvie Joly
Julie	Kristin Scott Thomas
Delphine	Sophie Moyse
Tony	Hervé Manson
Museum director	Héléna Manson
Government man	Jean-Pierre Mocky

Paris — "Trouble Agent" is a thriller without thrills, and a star vehicle without a motor. Jean-Pierre Mocky's film, drawn from a Yank novel by Malcolm Bosse, has Catherine Deneuve in a dark wig and wire-rim specs wandering lost in a sub-Hitchockian intrigue, while Richard Bohringer, as a world-weary contract killer, gives indifferent chase.

Film nonetheless begins with macabre promise as Tom Novembre, a bohemian animal lover, comes upon a tourist bus in the mountains full up with dead passengers. He relieves the corpses of their valuables and passports and returns to Paris, waiting for official word of the bizarre mass murder. Days later the tv reports in busload of tourists had died when their transport plunged into a lake.

Novembre, as sole witness to the incident, seeks to draw profit from his knowledge by blackmail, but when he confronts Bohringer for a shakedown, he's unceremoniously plugged by the killer — this a mere half-hour into the story. So much

for the film's most interesting character and original performance (November is a professional pop singer with screen presence and a rich speaking voice).

Over to Deneuve, Novembre's museum employee auntie, who's in on the secret and determined to avenge her nephew's murder. She decides to retrace the mortal tourist route and signs up for a motorized Alsatian tour, which includes Bohringer, who has orders from on high to eliminate her too. Deneuve finally gets whiff of a chemical wastes accident for which a government coverup meant sacrificing a bunch of tourists, but is foiled in a final twist that has served innumerable second-rate Reasons of State thrillers.

Mocky puts his signature on the story by dotting the action with offbeat details and supporting characters, but otherwise his writing and direction are pedestrian. Mocky is more at home in idiosyncratic, low-budget thrillers than he is in mainstream genre fare.

Deneuve's role offers her little to do, while Bohringer's hit man is only a competent carbon copy of his character in Michel Deville's "Péril." Some bit parts, notably by veteran Héléna Manson as Deneuve's museum boss, and Dominique Lavanant as a man-hungry tourist, are juicier. Mocky also has a cameo as Bohringer's government contact.

Tech credits are above par for a Mocky picture, with moody photography from William Lubtchansky. —*Len.*

Een maand later
(A Month Later)
(DUTCH-COLOR)

A Warner Bros. release of a Sigma Film-productions production. Produced by Matthijs van Heijningen. Production supervisor Guurtje Buddenberg. Directed by Nouchka van Brakel. Stars Renée Soutendijk, Monique van de Ven, Edwin de Vries. Screenplay, Van Brakel, Jan Conkers, Ate de Jong, based on Jan Donkers' play; camera (Agfacolor Cineco prints,) Peter de Bont; editor, Edgar Burcksen; music, Rob van Donselaar; sound, Georges Bossaers; art direction, Hadassah Kann; production manager, Simon Jansen; casting, Hans Kemna. Reviewed at Cinema Intl., Amsterdam, Sept. 8, 1987. Running time: **98 MINS.**

Liesbeth	Renée Soutendijk
Monika	Monique van de Ven
Constant	Edwin de Vries

Also with: Sunny Bergman, Tijmen Bergman, Jeroen Oostenbrink, Jean Yves Berteloot, Bas Voets.

Amsterdam — "A Month Later" is the first Dutch film bought by an American major during production for international distribution, including the Netherlands. The film was shot in two versions, Dutch and English, with the same actors speaking their parts in both versions. It opened the Dutch Film days in Utrecht Sept. 16th and the English version will be ready in October. This is a friendly comedy (no

baddies, some sillies), nice, naughty and nutty. It all started with an ad in The Village Voice in 1985, offering an exchange of lives. Two women were to take over each other's lives, professional and private, during one month. Jan Donkers saw the ad, wrote a short play for two actresses, one set, which was successfully produced in Amsterdam in '86. The screenplay opened it up and brought in a host of additional characters.

Liesbeth (Renée Soutendijk) is the wife of psychiatrist Constant (Edwin de Vries), and mother of a teenage girl and two younger boys. They're a contented family. Constant, using his professional skills, is the undisputed master of the household. Liesbeth, the perfect wife and mother, arranges her days following a roster of duties, according to the needs and wishes of husband and children.

Liesbeth, however, is not quite happy. She thinks she's missing something, perhaps her identity. Constant is full of understanding. Liesbeth should break out and experience different aspects of life. It is he who thinks up the ad. The children are informed and agree. Constant is upset, however, when Liesbeth makes a deal with an applicant without consulting him. Has she made the right choice? Who is this Monika woman?

Monika (Monique van de Ven) is a free-lance, not only as a journalist. She has a kind of apartment in a big building shared by a colorful collection of tenants. She runs a bric-a-brac shop with two other girls. She sings in a very feminine chorus. She writes the occasional article for a feminist magazine. He love life is equally multifaceted. She answers the ad following a dare of friends and for potential story material.

Constant gets one shock after another from this gaudily dressed and made up woman. The kids complain because all pampering has stopped. Then — although we are in Holland we're also very much in Hollywood — everyone develops soft spots. Affection and love break triumphantly through the clouds, and even Monika and Constant fall for each other.

Comedy is a break with Van Brakel's previous three films. She sets the pace well, the zaniness of characters and story is properly, that is to say quite seriously, treated. The timing of jokes and gags now and then shows her lack of exerience with manipulated laughter. The three main characters are perfectly cast. Van de Ven has the most rewarding part as the hard cookie which may crumble but never crumple. Soutendijk shows her acting prowess in scenes where tragedy is on the brink of smashing the lightweight structure of the comedy. De Vries limns the change

from masterful mind explorer and top banana to ordinary lovestricken John Doe without floundering.

Van Brakel is very good showing the changes in each of the trio during the few weeks of the experiment, also when directing larger groups of people. She was less successful in casting and directing the smaller parts, especially the men.

The film could do with a little tightening towards the end when the screenplay tries too hard to bring too many possible solutions into play, and the fun starts to get strained. Technical credits are good, the art direction is excellent.

On the whole Van Brakel and Van Heijningen succeeded very well in their effort to produce a Dutch comedy which is entertainment with a capital E. Warner Bros. seems to have made a useful investment.
— *Wall.*

Balada Da Praia Dos Cães
(The Ballad Of Dogs' Beach)
(PORTUGUESE-SPANISH-COLOR)

An Animatógrafo/Andrea Film//Filmform production. Directed by José Fonseca e Costa. Screenplay, Fonseca e Costa. António Larreta, Pedro Bandiera Freire; based on an original story by José Cardoso Pires; camera (color), Acácio de Almeida; editor, Pablo del Almo; music, Alberto Iglesias; sound, Gita Cerveira. Reviewed at World Film Festival, Montreal, Aug. 28, 1987. Running time: **90 MINS.**

Inspector Elias	Raul Solnado
Mena	Assumpta Serna
Capt. Luis Dantas	Patrick Bauchau

Also with: Sergei Mateu, Carmen Dolores, Henrique Viana, Mário Pardo, Pedro Efe.

Montreal — This slightly surreal police procedural film with political overtone is maddeningly slow until Spanish actress Assumpta Serna shows up and ignites the screen with incendiary sensuality. As in Pedro Almodóvar's "Matador" (yet to be released in the U.S.), Serna plays a woman who is both a victim of her unbridled sexuality and a victimizer of a macho man who attempts to bend her but is broken instead. Limited but fiery sequences of sexual explicitness could help this arty but mostly static exercise pick up a domestic distributor.

It's 1960 in Portugal, which is under a military dictatorship not entirely to the liking of some soldiers who have served in Angola. The body of one rebel, Capt. Luis Dantas, is found brutally murdered on a beach outside of Lisbon months after his escape from a military prison. The film's narrative, through the perspective of a solitary and repressed police inspector, explains whodunit and why.

Inspector Elias (Raul Solnado) is a middle-aged man who lives alone and keeps an altar to the memory of his mother. His probe into the murder of the escaped Capt. Dantas (Patrick Bauchau), leads him to a wealthy countess whose daughter

Mena (Serna) was the soldier's lover.

Through flashbacks elicited under the inspector's interrogation, the aristocratic and beautiful Mena expresses a liberated sexual ethic particularly shocking for Portugal circa 1960. She was introduced to the captain by her officer father and it was love at first sight, Mena recalls. "Did he take you for his lover then," asks the fascinated inspector. "No, I took him," she replies.

Mena recounts her 4-year affair with Dantas and its culmination with her life on the lam with him following his escape. Mena and two of the captain's former soldiers, who are totally dominated by the powerfully charismatic officer, hole up in a country house as the pursuing police close in. Emotional and sexual tensions among the small group rise until they culminate in an inevitable act of violence.

Director José Fonseca e Costa and actor Solnado do a good job of depicting the interior turmoil unleashed in the policeman as he probes into this tale of ruptured passions. Bauchau has the requisite physical appearance to make the uptight and egomanical captain believable. Nevertheless, the film's pacing is seriously crippled by disjointed narrative backtracking, a device that saps viewer patience before things start to get interesting.
—*Rich.*

El Hombre Desnudo
(The Naked Man)
(MEXICAN-COLOR)

A Películas Mexicanas release of a Uranio Films, S.A.-Uranio Films Intl. production. Produced by José Lorenzo Zakani. Directed by Rogelio A. González Jr. Stars Barry Coe, José Alonso. Screenplay, Myriam S. Price, González Jr.; camera (color), Francisco Colin; editor, Carlos Savage; music, Javier Castro, Francisco Rodríguez; special effects, Dan Logan, Jim Nielson. Reviewed at Hollywood Twin theater I, N.Y., Sept. 15, 1987. Running time: **89 MINS.**
Moe . . . . .Barry Coe
Nameless drifter . . . . .José Alonso
Lisa Hastings . . . . .Irma Lozano
Virginia . . . . .Celene La Freniere
Also with: Katy Payne, Terry Kelly, Barney O'Sullivan, Dan Logan, John Scott, Ivor Harries, Wanda Wallenson.

As its title implies, the Mexican Western "El Hombre Desnudo" (The Naked Man), helmed by Rogelio A. González Jr., borders on the kinky, both in sex and excessive violence.

Filmed on location in British Columbia, pic features two twisted, concurrent plots. The first uses an old horse-opera convention: a group of bad guys attempt to drive villagers from their homes to take control of the region. Led by Moe (Barry Coe), the band savagely and repeatedly rapes and kills townfolk. The other story concerns a good-guy fast-gun drifter (José Alonso), who is obsessed with making bad guys undress so he can inspect their backsides. Although this may ap-

pear rather odd and our drifter-cowboy may seem of the "midnight" variety, all confusion is cleared up by the movie's end. It seems the drifter's parents were killed by someone with a brand scar on his tusch.

Dramatic tension is diluted as audience is bombarded with images of bloodied bare-breasted women and callipygous men as Moe and the proctological drifter head for the inevitable showdown, which is long in coming. All violent scenes are lingered upon in slow motion with lavish attention paid to realistic special effects. The fake blood virtually pours as characters go through extended rictus throwing scarlet stains upon the snowy landscape.

Lensing is competent yet constant use of slow motion and repeated images to represent memories halt the rhythm and jar the viewer with a morbid fascination for violence. Pic has also been awkwardly dubbed giving both dialog and voice-overs an artificial feel. Acting is strictly 1-dimensional.

The naked truth is that "El Hombre Desnudo" is a piece of sensationalism with kinky overtones that doesn't quite make it as entertainment. No butts about it.—*Lent.*

Pliumbum, ili Opasnaia Igia
(Plumbum, Or A Dangerous Game)
(SOVIET-COLOR)

A Mosfilm Studio production. Directed by Vadim Abdrashitov. Screenplay, Alexander Mindadze; camera (color), George Rerberg; music, Vladimir Dashkevich; art direction, Alexander Tolkachev. Reviewed at the Venice Film Festival (competing), Sept. 6, 1987. Running time: **96 MINS.**
Ruslan Chutro . . . . Anton Androsov
Sonia . . . . .Elena Dmitrieva
Maria . . . . Elena Yakovleva
Also with: Alexander Foklistov ("Grey"), Alexander Pashutin (father), Vladimir Sieklov (Lopatov), Soia Lirova (mother), Alexeit Saitsev (Kolia-Oleg).

Venice — One of the hardest-hitting Soviet pictures yet to appear in the *glasnost* generation, Vadim Abdrashitov's "Plumbum, Or A Dangerous Game" has as its hero a pint-sized monster, a 15-year-old police informer whose twisted ideas about cleaning up crime are portrayed with scary clarity. Even more chilling is the generalization the director and his scriptwriter Alexander Mindadze strive to make about dangerous tendencies at work in society — that exercising power without moral maturity is dangerous business.

Child thesp Anton Androsov emanates a sinister fascination as Ruslan, or Plumbum as he prefers to call himself. In a telling exchange, the boy explains his nickname comes from the Latin word for lead, as Stalin came from steel, "today we live in the age of soft metals." With a child's body and aged face (he likes to give his age as 40), Plumbum totters on the brink of

adulthood, trying to insinuate himself into a group of volunteer vigilantes who help the police round up gamblers, black marketeers and the like. Though they repulse him several times, his information is good and they willingly follow his leads.

Whether motivated by a thirst for justice, need for self-assertion, or the fun of playing cops and robbers, Plumbum ruthlessly pursues "state criminals," most of whom look pretty harmless (like a band of bums toting bags at the train station without a license). The boy tests his power, playing cat and mouse with his victims before turning them in to the authorities. A model (Elena Yakovleva) lets herself abe humiliated and seduced (suggested but not shown) in a futile attempt to protect her boyfriend. Plumbum even arrests his own father, caught fishing out-of-season.

Film's weak point is that Plumbum makes a better malevolent dwarf than a real little boy. The attempt to have him live in both the real world of school and a happy family (parents are ignorant of his secret life) and a symbolic dimension, where he represents a social tendency, doesn't meld well, and pic's tragic ending in particular has little dramatic impact. Nonetheless, the main character is so curious, film is watchable up to the end, and ought to stir interest among offshore programmers of Soviet films.

Technically "Plumbum" is neatly lensed and staged, with a pulsating thriller score from Vladimir Dashkevich. — *Yung.*

Sorobanzuku
(All For Business' Sake)
(JAPANESE-COLOR)

A Toho release of a Fuji Television production. Produced by Masaru Kakutani. Directed by Yoshimitsu Morita. Screenplay, Morita; camera (color), Yonezo Maeda; editor, Akira Svzuki. Reviewed at World Film Festival, Montreal, Sept. 1, 1987. Running time: **108 MINS.**
With: Takaaki Ishibashi, Noritake Mori, Shigemi Yasuda, Kaoru Kobayashi.

Montreal — Yoshimitsu Morita, best known for "The Family Game" and "And Then . . . ," has come up with a strident new satire on Japanese ad agencies, constructing his film like an extended tv commercial. Though it has moments of frenzied invention, pic quickly overstays its welcome.

Focus of attention is on two ambitious young employees of the No ad agency, who are friends and rivals. The head of a rival agency, Ra, is head-hunting, and the whizbang narrative winds up a comedy about industrial espionage.

The film opens with a bang as a naked girl screams abuse from a balcony high above the city. Sex being a major ingredient of the ad world, the film has plenty of jokes about Japanese obsession for, and

coyness about, nudity, and in one scene little black circles obscure the genitals of a group of men in a shower.

There are disco, barroom and bedroom scenes, but the brightest moments satirize the production of the tv ads themselves. There are good ideas here, but it's a very hit and miss affair, with pointlessly rapid cutting within scenes, ripe overacting, and much very broad comedy. Film seems aimed at a young and easily pleased audience.
—*Strat.*

The Leading Edge
(NEW ZEALAND-COLOR)

A Southern Light Pictures and Everard Films presentation. Produced by Barrie Everard. Directed by Michael Firth. Screenplay, Firth, Grant Morris; camera (color), Stuart Dryburgh; editor, Pat Monaghan; music, Mike Farrell; art direction, Greg Taylor; sound, Mike Westgate. Reviewed at Regent Theater, Palmerston North, New Zealand, Aug. 26, 1987. Running time: **78 MINS.**
With: Mathurin Molgat, Bruce Grant, Evan Bloomfield, Mark Whetu, Christine Grant, Melanie Forbes, Billy T. James.

Palmerston North, N.Z. — Michael Firth's ski movie "Off The Edge" won fans and an Academy Award nomination in the documentary section in 1977.

A decade later "The Leading Edge" schusses in, just as amiable and just as likely to arouse interest and enthusiasm among armchair ski adventurers and fans of the real thing.

A cobbled plot takes Matt (Mathurin Molgat), a ski-patroller at Telluride, Colorado, to the uncrowded virgin powder snow slopes of New Zealand. He meets up with a bunch of Kiwi ski bums and is initiated into such native customs as skiing active volcanos, mountain pinnacles and glacial formations.

At feature's end, Canadian-born Molgat, actor and real-life world-class skier, joins the lineup in an Iron Man-type contest that pits skiing alongside mountain climbing, kayak racing and a final race to the tape.

"The Leading Edge" is gung-ho in the manner of a Down Under "Boy's Own" tale. The characters are tirelessly enthusiastic and alert to every possible physical challenge in the great outdoors.

More closely confined in a unisex outdoor spa pool, the impulse is to disappear (in fade out) underwater with a bottle of tequila.

Firth's ski adventure II does not pretend to be a study of individual character and motivation. It is mostly clean and totally wholesome entertainment in the healtheries wonderland of clean air, nuclear-free New Zealand.

While this injects little tension and sense of danger to Matt's exploits, there are, nonetheless, some great action sequences and impeccable photography (by Stuart Dryburgh). A pounding music track does more than the dialog to move the semblance of a story along.

It will be surprising if "The Leading Edge" does not market well in North America and further afield — and not just among hot-doggers in the après ski lodges of Aspen, Breckenridge, Taos and Telluride.

—*Nic.*

Drachenfutter
(Dragon Food)
(W. GERMAN-SWISS-B&W)

A Novoskop Film/Jan Schütte, Hamburg/Probst Film, Bern production, with the Kuratorium Junger Deutscher Film, Hamburger Filmbüro Filmförderung. Executive producer, Eric Nellessen. Directed by Schütte. Screenplay, Schütte, Thomas Strittmatter; camera (b&w), Lutz Konermann; editor, Renate Merck; music, Claus Bantzer; sound, Ernst Hermann Marell, Richard Borowski; art direction, Katharina Mayer-Woppermann. Reviewed at the Venice Film Festival (Critics' Week), Sept. 2, 1987. Running time: **70 MINS.**

Shezad................Bhasker
Xiao.................Ric Young
Rashid...........Buddy Uzzaman
Also with: Ulrich Wildgruber (cook), Wolf-Dieter Sprenger (Herder), Frank Oladeinde (Dale), Louis Blaise (Louis), Su Zeng Hua (Wang), Young Me Song (Herder's wife).

Venice — A modest enterprise of surprising impact, Jan Schütte's first feature film may remind veterans of the refugee stories by Erich Maria Remarque. The difference being that Remarque was writing about exiles escaping Nazi Germany before World War II, while Schütte deals with the floating population of the 1980s, coming from the Third World and trying to find shelter in the West. In this case, it is Pakistanis entering West Germany with false papers, asking for political asylum and trying to establish a livelihood, while waiting for the courts to review their case.

Schütte does his best to adopt an observer's point of view, never pretending to speak for the characters themselves. He even refrains from translating the conversations they have in their own language, which, as a Westerner, he is not supposed to understand, but he obviously is entirely sympathetic to their tragedy.

Film starts with one Pakistani, Shezad, being kicked out of a Chinese restaurant when he attempts to sell flowers to the customers. It ends with the same maitre d' who did the kicking, a Chinese and an alien in a foreign land as well, now Shezad's partner in a Pakistani restaurant they have mounted with their own hands, watching their common venture go down the drain when Shezad is deported from West German after his asylum plea has been rejected.

In between these two points, Schütte gives a pretty succinct and sensitive picture of this constantly growing community of these homeless people, from different nations, without any means of existence, their impotence and their despair in a world which finally — even when

smiling upon them — wouldn't lift a finger to improve their lot.

Shot entirely in a decidedly unglamorous Hamburg, in black and white (except for the credits, in flaming red), Schütte's film doesn't preach and doesn't point accusing fingers in any specific direction, except to the vultures who make money out of the misfortune of others. In spite of the grim subject and unflattering scenery in which it evolves, both direction and performances, particularly those of Bhasker and Ric Young as the unlikely partners, preserve a human, at times humorous dimension that works to the picture's advantage.

At 70 minutes (the film runs shorter than the timing mentioned in the Venice catalog), this may have some problems theatrically, but is bound to get lots of tv and festival exposure. — *Edna.*

Chechechela — Una Chica del Barrio
(Hey, Hey, Chela)
(ARGENTINE-COLOR)

An Instituto Nacional de Cinematográfica Argentina release. Produced by Rolando Gardelin. Directed by Bebe Kamin. Screenplay, Kamin, Mirko Buchin, based on the novel by Buchin; camera (color), Rodolfo Denevi; music, José Luis Castiñeiras de Dios; art direction, Alfredo Iglesias; makeup, Mirta Blanco. Reviewed at Latino Festival, Public Theater, N.Y., Aug. 16, 1987. Running time: **90 MINS.**

Celia (Chechechela)....Ana María Picchio
Julio, Titti, Alberto.......Victor Laplace
Also with: Tina Serrana, Alejandra Da Passano, Juan Manuel Tenuta, Ana María Giunta, Julio López, Silvana Silveri, Noemi Morelli, Renée Roxana.

The 1986 Argentine domestic b.o. hit "Chechechela," subtitled "A Girl From The Neighborhood," is a satirical and charming comedy starring Ana María Picchio in the title role. Picchio was featured in the earlier Oscar-nominated 1974 gaucho drama "La Tregua" (The Truce).

Helmed by Bebe Kamin "Chechechela" finds its narrative form through use of extended flashbacks interrupting the process of the aging heroine (approaching 30) into a church on her wedding day as she ponders the men in her life and wonders whether she made the right choice. Victor Laplace, through varying use of facial hair, admirably plays the three men in question.

First, there is wild and mysterious Julio, whom she meets on a Buenos Aires street looking like a young unshaven Marcello Mastroianni. Although he comes by to visit her almost every night, he tells here nothing of his life and work, not even his address, but, since she met him first, she gives him first dibs. Yet, that doesn't stop her from flirting with mustachioed Titti, a secret police agent she meets at a neighborhood fiesta. Also, an overnight trip to the provinces allows her a romp with clean-shaven countryboy Al-

berto. And, as the wedding party nears the altar, the audience is made to wonder which of the three she finally has chosen.

The movie uses voice-over commentary by Picchio full of bourgeois pretentions and romantic notions garnered from television soap operas. Chechechela eagerly awaits her white-knight to rescue her from her drab life in a tenement house and work at a downtown haberdashery. Her life and the lives of her neighbors is that of mundane expectations — an endless stream of kids and domestic squabbles.

Kamin brings a great deal of wit and invention to the film in a burlesque of the soap opera form. Although she is no great beauty or sparkling conversationalist, Chechechela lives in a world where men throw themselves at her. In one confrontation scene between all three rivals, she expects them to fight it out among themselves with herself as prize. After her marriage, she already is plotting her intrigues.

Acting tends toward character types, something demanded by the form, with good ensemble interaction. For his part, Laplace delineates the roles well in subdued fashion, since the three gentlemen callers must remain only romantic notions. Dialog sparkles with humor and insight.

With the international appeal of romantic novels and soaps, "Chechechela" easily could demonstrate that its boxoffice appeal is not just dependent on the domestic market.

—*Lent.*

Mer om oss barn i Bullerby
(More About The Children Of Bullerby Village)
(SWEDISH-COLOR)

An SF (Svensk Filmindustri) release and production. Produced by Waldemar Bergendahl. Directed by Lasse Hallström. Screenplay (based on her books), by Astrid Lindgren; camera (Eastmancolor), Jens Fischer; editor, Susanne Linnman; music, George Riedel; sound, Göran Carmback, Eddie Axberg; costumes, Inger Pehrsson, Susanne Falck; production design, Lasse Westfelt; production management, Anita Tesler; assistant director, Catti Edfeldt. Reviewed at the Scannia, Malmö (Sweden), Sept. 13, 1987. Running time: **86 MINS.**

Lisa................Linda Bergström
Lasse........Crispin Dickson Wendenius
Bosse.............Henrik Larsson
Britta............Ellen Demerus
Anna.............Anna Sahlin
Olle.............Harald Lönnbro
Kerstin..................Tove Edfeldt
The shoemaker............Olof Sjögren
Also with: Sören Pettersson, Ann-Sofie Knape, Ingwar Svensson, Elizabeth Nordquist, Bill Jonsson, Catti Edfeldt, Louise Raeder, Ewa Carlsson.

Malmö — "More About The Children Of Bullerby Village" was shot back-to-back with "The Children Of Bullerby Village" (*Variety,* Dec. 17, 1986) by helmer Lasse Hallström and based on Astrid Lindgren's tiny tots Bullerby novels and her own screenplay. The outcome is, of course, more of the

same, i.e., 1920 rural idylls in which the tots cavort happily and with nary a threat to their joy plus practically always out of reach (or any other real contact) with adults. Both films will soon be available worldwide in English-dubbed versions and will please aunts and uncles and their youngest relations but hardly anybody in ages in-between.

A bit more of the typical Astrid Lindgren salt and Lassie Hallström ("My Life As A Dog") spice has been sprinkled over the Bullerby sequel, in which the tinies go back to school; see a lamb die; experience toothaches but nothing worse. Everything is seen through a golden haze, latter beautifully recorded by Jens Fischer's camera, and there is not much to make you remember any of the young non-actors as individuals. They certainly come on with natural ease and never a touch of the phony or contrived. The adult professionals, however, have been left badly in a lurch by Hallström. Technical credits are top-notch. —*Kell.*

Odyssée d'amour
(Love Odyssey)
(DUTCH-COLOR)

A Concorde Film release of an Altamira Films production. Produced by Lea Wongsoredjo, Ruud den Drijver. Directed by Pim de la Parra. Screenplay, De la Parra, Rudi F. Kross, Dorna van Rouveroy; camera (Fujicolor, prints by Haghe Film), Frans Bromet; editor, Kees Linthorst; music, Adriaan van Noord, Eddy Bennett; sound, Georges Bossaers; production design, Rebecca Gieskus; assistant director, Leonard Retel Helmrich; production manager, Sherman de Jesus. Reviewed at City 2 theater, Amsterdam, Aug. 27, 1987. Running time: **107 MINS.**

Paul Henkes..............Herbert Flack
Elizabeth................Sarah Brackett
Valerie..................Patty Brard
Zippy....................Liz Snoyink
Ramon...............Eddy Marchena
Nicholas.........Ramon Todd Dandare
Bart Buisman..........Thom Hoffman
Ramona................Devika Strooker
Alexander de Winter....John van Dreelen

Amsterdam — Pim de la Parra has an immense natural talent for telling stories through film, but he stubbornly refuses to pay enough attention to screenplays. His latest picture, "Love Odyssey," was shot in Bonaire, part of the Dutch Antilles. It is a story of love (meaning sex with stray emotional ties), interlarded with some Greek mythology, poetry and miscellaneous symbolism.

A Dutch engineer (Herbert Flack) lives more or less with middle-aged English sculptress Elizabeth (Sarah Brackett), a mother-lover-confidante figure. He has innumerable mistresses, many concurrently. A young son of his dies unexpectedly after a routine operation. Paul is stunned. His friends, male and female, can't help him. The males have women trouble of their own, the females find themselves pregnant or otherwise disturbed. The arrival from Holland of his half sister, with whom he has a half-incestuous relationship of long standing, brings things to a climax after Paul nearly dies diving in a grotto where he experienced mythological apparitions.

The film is very easy to look at. Frans Bromet's photography is very good, as are all technical credits. There are some unintentionally humorous facets to this love odyssey: bring a male and female inhabitant of Bonaire together and they will be at it before you can say De la Parra; and the pic's natural macho stance finds all these luscious lovelies lusting after and quarreling over their men. English Elizabeth is the exception.

Pic could do with a severe trimming, especially in the second half. At present, it slowly fizzles out. Before that, Bromet's photography and the amorous perils of Paul and his friends keep one entertained and mildly intrigued.

Acting is generally good, but outstanding are Herbert Flack and Sarah Brackett, plus Thom Hoffman as a novice from Holland, unaccustomed to the furious pace of love on the island. Liz Snoyink was remarkably pregnant during the shooting which diminished her credibility as the odyssey's incestuous siren.

"Odyssée d'amour" should have chances abroad (especially in a shortened version) wherever softcore sex and sensuous nudity are more important than narrative tension and sense. — *Wall.*

Born Again: Life In A Fundamentalist Baptist Church
(DOCU-COLOR-16m)

A presentation of the South Carolina Educational Television Network, Columbia, S.C. Produced and directed by James Ault, Michael Camerini; associate director, Adrienne Miesmer. Camera (color, 16m), Camerini; editor, Sarah Stein; music, Paul Moravec; sound, Carol Ramsey; narrator, Norman Rose; assistant director, Miesmer. Produced with funding from New England Foundation for The Humanities, the Corporation for Public Broadcasting and the Massachusetts Foundation for The Humanities and Public Policy. Reviewed at the American Museum of Natural History, N.Y., in Margaret Mead Film Festival, Sept. 1, 1987. Running time: **87 MINS.**

By focusing solely on a single fundamentalist Baptist church in a small town of central Massachusetts, "Born Again" debunks the popular misconception that fundamentalism is essentially a Southern movement. Fundamentalism began at the turn of the century in Boston, New York and Chicago. Nationally, the movement numbers 25,000,000 adherents and is growing rapidly, especially in the Northeast.

Fundamentalism is characterized by the belief that salvation hinges solely on being "born again" spiritually through acceptance of Jesus Christ as one's personal saviour. The film deals with these individual believers, not with the familiar superstar tv evangelists Jerry Falwell, Oral Roberts, Jimmy Swaggart, and Tammy and Jim Bakker. We see no holy rollers, speaking-in-tongues, faithhealing or snake-handling.

Co-directed by Michael Camerini, a documentary professional, and James Ault, latter a trained sociologist, professor at the University of California/San Diego, "Born Again" was carefully researched and produced with restraint and respect for this close-knit Baptist community. Thirty-five hours of footage in modified cinema-vérité style were shot over a period of seven months. We find here no cheap tricks of editing and narration to satirize and deflate the sublime confidence of these fundamentalists that each one has a direct personal rapport with God. They have total faith in their righteousness, despite their admitted fallibilities.

From young Pastor John, a convert from Catholicism, his flock receives a passionate admonition to practice marital harmony. Husbands are instructed to respect their wives, whom God has given them as "helpmates." Wives must focus on their families. Pastor John condemns "that Devil television" that corrupts us through sex.

Because they believe "the garbage" taught in public schools is the work of Satan, the church in self-protection has founded its own Christian academy, from kindergarten through high school. The school day begins with prayers, the pledge of allegiance to the Bible and to the Christian and American flags. "The first priority is the Bible, the second is the Constitution." The curriculum is structured so that "all subjects point to God." Classes discuss carnality versus the spiritual while some students snicker and squirm. They learn that "creationism makes sense over evolution, it's more accurate, because the Earth is only 10,000 years old." Attitudes toward society are rigidly conservative — "We born again have a special mission to get rid of the unrighteous," and "Christians are meant to be a moral disinfectant in a world where moral standards are nonexistent."

Some students of the Academy are restless: "I go through the motions, but I don't feel anything" and "I get sick of the 'can't' all the time" (this from Pastor John's daughter). Rock music, commercial tv, even ice skating are forbidden.

"Born Again" chooses four or five families, closely bound to their church, for special emphasis. Despite the constant surveillance of Pastor John, some of these fundamentalist families have the same troubles that beset the rest of us — stale marriages, infidelity, desertion, alcoholism, vengeful custody squabbles and threats of violence, so damaging to the children who watch.

"Born Again" ends with an epilog describing the church's expansion and optimism, also the changes that have occurred within the few families emphasized. — *Hitch.*

★★★★★★★★★★★★★★
★ Tokyo Fest Review ★
★★★★★★★★★★★★★★
Taketori Monogatari (Princess From The Moon) (JAPANESE-COLOR)

A Toho Intl. release of a Toho/Fuji Television coproduction. Executive producers, Tomoyuki Tanaka, Shigeaki Hazama. Production supervisor Yasushi Mitsui. Produced by Masaru Kakutani, Hiroaki Fujii, Junichi Shinsaka. Directed by Kon Ichikawa. Screenplay, Ryuzou Kikushima, Mitsutoshi Ishigami, Shinya Hidaka, Kon Ichikawa; camera (color), Setsuo Kobayashi; editor, Chizuko Osada; music supervisor, Kensaku Tanigawa; special effects, Shokei Nakano; costume supervisor, Hiroshi Saito; costume design, Emi Wada; sets, Shinobu Muraki; production consultant, Kazuo Baba; sound, Tetsuya Ohashi; recordist, Teiichi Saito, assistant director, Kazuo Yoshida, production manager, Shigekazu Hirama. Reviewed at Museum of Modern Art, N.Y., Sept. 14, 1987. (In Tokyo Film Festival, non competing.) Running time: **120 MINS.**
Taketori-no-Miyatsuko . . . Toshiro Mifune
Tayoshime, his wife . . . . Ayako Wakao
Kaya (Princess Kaguya) Yasuko Sawaguchi
Mikado (Emperor) . . . . Koji Ishizaka
Otomo-no-Dainagon
  (Minister of Military) . . . . . Kiichi Nakai
Kuramochi-no-Miko
  (Minister of Culture) . . Koasa Shumputei
Abe-no-Udaijin
  (Minister of Finance) . Takatoshi Takeda
Akeno . . . . Megumi Odaka
  Also with: Katsuo Nakamura, Shiro Itoh, Fujio Tokita, Takeshi Kato, Kyoto Kishida, Hirokazu Yamaguchi, Jun Hamamura, Gen Idemitsu, Michiyo Yokoyama, Hirokazu Inoue, Miho Nakano.

Kon Ichikawa's "Taketori Monogatari" ("Princess From The Moon") opens like an art film and closes like a science fiction extravaganza. In between there is an extraordinary display of costuming, with seemingly enough flowing kimono cloth to stretch from Times Square to Tokyo.

"Princess From The Moon" is not the kind of film that conforms easily to description.

The story is based on a 9th century Japanese legend about a young moon woman temporarily marooned on earth. The main characters — Taketori-no-Miyatsuko (Toshiro Mifune) is a bamboo cutter and Kaya (Yasuko Sawaguchi) is a moon child — are hardly the type with which one can easily identify.

Yet "Princess" possesses a sort of magical charm that acts to suspend reality in adults much the same way fairytales do with children. The combination of a millennium-old Oriental parable enmeshed with futuristic space travel underpinnings awakens the kid in all but the chronically jaded.

"Princess" begins as Taketori-no-Miyatsuko and his wife Tayo-shime (Ayako Wakao) are mourning the death of their young daughter, Kaya. Later, when Taketori-no-Miyatsuko is walking in a bamboo forest, he discovers a golden capsule that contains a baby girl.

Wondrously, the infant grows instantly into a five year old child (Miho Nakano) with eerily glowing blue eyes. The shocked bamboo cutter brings the girl home and his wife decides the child is Kaya reincarnate.

Before Taketori-no-Miyatsuko has a chance to recover from his extraterrestrial encounter, little Kaya suddenly transforms into a princess of rare beauty. A beauty that makes her irresistible to any male.

Taketori-no-Miyatsuko, fearing Kaya will be discovered, sells the gold cradle that carried her to Earth and builds a lavish residence in the country in an attempt to shield his newfound daughter from the curious.

Three noblemen, however, cast eyes upon Kaya/Princess Kaguya and fall hopelessly in love with her. She gives them each a task — thought for centuries to be impossible — and promises to marry whomever brings her what she asks.

The ensuing pursuit of these unattainable goals by the noblemen, the shedding of innocence by Kaya and an ultimate acceptance of the inevitability of personal loss by Kara's parents provide the often melancholy, yet constantly uplifting tone of "Princess From The Moon."

Befitting an ancient allegory born of a still older culture, the treatment of these universal phases of the human condition is at once pragmatic and poetic. Characters accept their fate with dignity rather than ignoble resignation. The irreversible change wrought by the passage of time is portrayed as an opportunity for understanding, not a reason for remorse.

Kon Ichikawa's direction efficiently captures this sentiment, delivered via a myriad of masterful performances. Kudos really must go to Emi Wada's collection of brilliantly colorful costumes and Setsuo Kobayashi's indelible photography.

The highlight of the costuming — including 9th century men's dress, no-shi and kari-ginu — is the spectacular juni-hitoe. Juni-hitoe, ladies' formal wear, consists of six kimonos; kara-ginu, mo, uchigi, itsutsu-ginu, hitoe and kosode.

The images lensed by Kobayashi are sometimes so remarkable, frames resemble silk screens in motion.

Also worthy of note are the special effects fashioned by Shokei Nakano. A bamboo forest, where much early action takes place, actually is a miniature set. A mammoth spaceship, an important element in the climactic final scene, is as convincing as any on film.

"Princess From The Moon" was premiered in front of a predominately American audience at the Museum of Modern Art. The attendees appeared to receive the film well but, considering the eclectic tastes of the constituents at such gatherings, the event may not have been a true test.

Whether "Taketori Monogatari," with all its visual elegance, can capture the imagination of U.S. moviegoers remains to be seen. In a market that seems to place a high premium on car chases, body counts and explicit trysts, that may prove a difficult task. — *Chuk*.

Toronto Festival Reviews

Near Dark
(COLOR)

Slick vampire pic.

A De Laurentiis Entertainment Group release of a Feldman/Meeker production. Produced by Steven-Charles Jaffe. Executive producers, Edward S. Feldman, Charles R. Meeker. Coproducer, Eric Red. Directed by Kathryn Bigelow. Screenplay, Red, Bigelow; camera (CFI color), Adam Greenberg; editor, Howard Smith; music, Tangerine Dream; sound (Ultra-Stereo), Donald Summer; production design, Stephen Altman; art direction, Dian Perryman; costume design, Joseph Porro; special effects makeup, Gordon Smith; assistant director, Guy Louthan; second unit camera, Chuck Colwell; associate producers, Diane Nabatoff, Mark Allan; casting, Karen Rea. Reviewed at the DEG screening room, Beverly Hills, Aug. 27, 1987. (In Toronto Film Festival.) (MPAA Rating: R.) Running time: **95 MINS.**

Caleb	Adrian Pasdar
Mae	Jenny Wright
Jesse	Lance Henriksen
Severen	Bill Paxton
Diamondback	Jenette Goldstein
Loy	Tim Thomerson
Homer	Joshua Miller
Sarah	Marcie Leeds

Hollywood — "Near Dark" achieves a new look in vampire films. High-powered but pared down, slick but spare, this is something akin to a "Badlands" of the supernatural, a tale that introduces the unearthly into the banality of rural American existence. Second feature, but first mainstream effort, by director Kathryn Bigelow is intense and extremely well made, and target audience of DEG's marketing effort for this violent pickup should be the hip action crowd that went for "The Road Warrior" and "The Terminator." Pic had its world premiere at the Toronto Festival of Festivals.

Nervous, edgy opening has sharp young cowboy Adrian Pasdar hooking up with Jenny Wright, a good-looking new girl in town not averse to some nocturnal roistering as long as she gets home by dawn.

Wright soon welcomes Pasdar into her "family," a bunch of real low-down boys and girls that would have done Charles Manson proud. Led by the spidery Lance Henriksen, the gang hibernates by day, but at night scours the vacant landscapes in search of prey.

Rules of vampirism as set forth here have the newcomer in a kind of halfway state once he's bitten by his girlfriend. He won't become a full-

fledged prince of darkness, however, until he's killed for himself, and he's put to the test in an agonizingly frightful roadhouse scene in which the bloodsuckers systematically dispatch the unfortunate habitues one by one.

Pasdar seems fully headed for a life on the wild side when the gang makes the mistake of licking their chops over the prospect of dining on his dad and little sister. Still human enough to find this idea distasteful, he begins plotting against his colleagues. Killing a vampire has never been easy, and climax consists of some prolonged and rather spectacular assaults on the creatures who believe they will never die.

Script by Bigelow and Eric Red ("The Hitcher") is cool and laconic, and the evildoers essentially come off as some very nasty bikers who kill for sport as well as necessity. Group is a particularly colorful one, as it reunites three veterans of "Aliens" — Henriksen, the exhuberant scene-stealer Bill Paxton and the formidable Jenette Goldstein — and throws in Joshua Miller, the superbly ghastly little kid from "River's Edge," for good measure.

Main point of interest will be the work of Bigelow, who has undoubtedly created the most hard-edged, violent actioner ever directed by an American woman. Her debut film, "The Loveless," made in 1981 in collaboration with Monty Montgomery, was an intriguingly arty biker pic with a stylistic debt to Douglas Sirk via Rainer Werner Fassbinder.

"Near Dark" sees her working much more in the tough, highly visual Hollywood mode of Brian DePalma, Walter Hill and Jim Cameron, with a nod to Sam Peckinpah on one side and Terrence Malick on the other. Pic is a stylistic and generic hybrid, to be sure, but strongly and gutsily made on its own terms.

Leads are appealing enough, but don't quite generate the heat together that convinces one that this healthy young man would throw over his entire life for such a dubious alternative. In addition, with all the transferring of blood going on, both through imbibing and transfusion, it will undoubtedly occur to viewers to ask whether or not vampires are susceptible to AIDS. An-

swer isn't revealed here.

Behind-the-scenes contributions on this modestly budgeted production are excellent, notably Adam Greenberg's evocative lensing, Howard Smith's very tight editing, Tangerine Dream's appropriate score and Gordon Smith's makeup effects, which make the vampires burn very realistically when they are struck by sunlight. —*Curt*.

Baby Boom
(U.S.-COLOR)

An MGM/UA Distribution release of a United Artists Pictures presentation of a Nancy Meyers/Charles Shyer production. Produced by Meyers. Directed by Shyer. Stars Diane Keaton, Harold Ramis, Sam Wanamaker. Screenplay, Meyers, Shyer; camera (color) William A. Fraker; editor, Lynzee Klingman; song, Burt Bacharach, Carole Bayer Sager, Conti, music, Bill Conti; production design, Jeffrey Howard; associate producer, Bruce A. Block; costumes, Susan Becker; casting, Pam Dixon; production manager, Michele Ader; assistant director, John Kretchmer; art direction, Beala Neel; set decoration, Lisa Fischer. Reviewed at the Toronto Festival Of Festivals, Sept. 17, 1987. (MPAA Rating: PG.) Running time: **103 MINS.**

J.C. Wiatt	Diane Keaton
Steven Buchner	Harold Ramis
Fritz Curtis	Sam Wanamaker
Ken Arrenberg	James Spader
Hughes Larrabee	Pat Hingle
Vern Boone	Britt Leach
Elizabeth Wiatt	Kristina and Michelle Kennedy
Dr. Jeff Cooper	Sam Shepard

Also with: Linda Ellerbee, Kim Sebastian, Mary Gross, Patricia Estrin, Elizabeth Bennett, Peter Elbing, Shera Danese.

Toronto — The makers of "Baby Boom" are clearly gambling that ticket-buyers will be suckered in by the goo-goo precocousness of its button-cute twin baby stars and the marquee pull of its lead performer, Diane Keaton. There's little else to recommend this transparent and 1-dimensional parable about a power-devouring female careerist and the unwanted bundle of joy that turns her obsessive fast-track life in Gotham upside down. Constructed almost entirely upon facile and familiar media clichés about "parenting" and the super-yuppie set, "Baby Boom" has the superficiality of a project inspired by a lame New York Magazine cover story and sketched out on a cocktail napkin at Spago's.

J.C. Wiatt (Diane Keaton) is a dressed-for-success management consultant with an Ivy League pedigree whose steamroller ambition has earned this workaholic the proudly flaunted nickname, "Tiger Lady." She lives in trendy high-rise splendor with bland investment banker Steven Buchner (Harold Ramis), to whom she reluctantly allots a 4-minute slot for lovemaking before returning to late-night paperwork. J.C. has just been offered a partnership position by her boss Fritz Curtis (Sam Wanamaker) and with the prospect of a corner office just ahead things have never looked better. Suddenly, J.C. learns that a cousin whom she hasn't seen since

childhood has died together with her husband in an accident in England. The compulsively acquisitive J.C. is intrigued to learn that she's inherited something from this misfortune but, to her considerable shock, this turns out to be a precious apple-cheeked 12-month old girl, Elizabeth (Kristina and Michelle Kennedy).

Initially, selfish J.C. resists this intrusion with characteristic steely callousness. She slings the infant around like a shopping bag and deposits her at the coat-check during a crucial power lunch. Boyfriend Steven is even less enthusiastic about the new addition to their household and strongly urges J.C. to put their adorable little charge up for adoption. J.C. tries to do so, but appalled at the ghastly American Gothic couple who plan to raise the little girl in a trailer in Dubuque — one of many insultingly silly touches typical of the picture's flip disregard for narrative believability — the aggressive and beautiful executive holds on to her new daughter.

In the meantime all kinds of cute things are going on as J.C. learns to diaper and otherwise care for her food-throwing, gurgling ward who has the adorable buff rosiness of a born Gerber baby. All of this Dr. Spock-ing, however, proves too much for Steven who moves out, avoiding a potentially interesting conflict that the script might have developed to the movie's advantage. One of the egregious flaws of "Baby Boom" is its story-conferenced tendency to rush events along in a glossy, predictable progression. Naturally, J.C.'s suppressed maternal instincts begin to flower, she loses her edge in the corporate boardroom and finally decides to chuck it all and move with Elizabeth to a charming house in a charming village in charming Vermont, far from the madding Manhattan rat-race, and the absurdly competitive yuppie parents and their pre-educated super-babies.

J.C. goes through some character-building experiences in rustic Vermont, but naturally emerges as a better person and, of course, a better mother as well. The entrepreneurial, M.B.A. aspect of her personality devotes itself to making and marketing home-made "Country Baby" applesauce with you-know-who on its label. All that's missing is Mr. Right, who turns up at the appropriate time in the person of laconic veterinarian Jeff Cooper, portrayed by Sam Shepard who shambles through the role with palpable embarrassment. When her old company wants to buy "Country Baby" in a multi-million dollar deal, J.C. must choose between her former life and her happy new situation, a dilemma she resolves in unsurprising fashion.

"Baby Boom" tries to be a lot funnier than it actually is, and handsome production design and cinematography do little to compensate for its annoying over-reliance on cornball action montages and a dreadfully saccharine soundtrack score. —*Rich*.

Gaby — A True Story
(U.S.-COLOR)

A Tri-Star Pictures release of a Pinchas Perry-Luis Mandoki production. Produced by Pinchas Perry. Directed by Luis Mandoki. Screenplay, Martin Salinas, Michael James Love; camera (color), Lajos Koltai; editor, Garth Craven; music, Maurice Jarre; art direction, Alejandro Luna; sound, Robert Grieve; associate producers, Jacobo Feldman, Marcos Salame, Rafael Jauregui, Marc A. Solomon. Reviewed at Toronto Festival of Festivals, Sept. 14, 1987. (MPAA Rating: R.) Running time: **110 MINS.**
Sari . . . . Liv Ullmann
Florencia . . . . Norma Aleandro
Gaby . . . . Rachel Levin
Michel . . . . Robert Loggia
Fernando . . . . Lawrence Monoson
Luis . . . . Robert Beltran

Toronto — There's an ebullient spirit permeating "Gaby," the true story of a Mexican Jewish girl born with severe cerebral palsy who, against all odds, went on to become an accomplished poet and writer.

Luis Mandoki's feature is a true labor of love, with total cooperation and blessings from the real Gaby Brimmer, and the unsentimental feel-good attitude should easily lead to boxoffice sparks.

Mandoki succeeds in recreating Gaby's spirit. She was born with a disease that left her unable to move any part of her body except her left leg. Her parents, Sari (Liv Ullmann) and Michel (Robert Loggia) settle in Mexico in 1938 to escape Jewish persecution in Austria. Pic focuses on Gaby's intellectual development — for that part of her was unimpaired — through the nurturing relationship with her devoted nanny, Florencia (Norma Aleandro).

Florencia teaches Gaby to talk through the use of an alphabet board and typewriter. Gaby attends a handicapped school straight-A classmate, Fernando, with whom she falls in love. Mandoki directs a love scene between them that is both poignant and painfully touching.

Gaby fights to attend a normal junior high school and, ultimately, university, but this results in a falling out with Fernando, due to his parents' displeasure at Gaby's pressure on him to try to overcome his handicaps and be integrated into a regular classroom.

Most luminous is Gaby's relationship with her nanny, who devotes her life to caring for her beloved charge. Norma Aleandro is radiant in her depiction, never patronizing and always supportive. With one glance or gesture she communicates all her love and good intentions.

Stage actress Rachel Levin, who has recently recovered from her own near-total paralysis due to Guillain-

Barre syndrome, is multifacetedly adept at inhabiting Gaby's every thought and body movement. Her keen intelligence, positive faith, and incredible network of support allow her to succeed. Her journey for expression as a sexual woman is also depicted with grace.

Liv Ullmann and Robert Loggia, in encouraging Gaby to express herself fully, are always commanding presences, but they're both a bit too restrained and cool in their parental roles.

Mandoki must be complimented for not falling into all the "handicapped are just like you and me" traps and for making "Gaby" a singularly special project. — *Devo*.

Chuck Berry: Hail! Hail! Rock 'n' Roll!
(U.S.-DOCU-COLOR)

A Universal Pictures release of a Delilah Films production. Produced by Stephanie Bennett. Directed by Taylor Hackford. Camera (color), Oliver Stapleton; editor, Lisa Day; music producer, Keith Richards; music recorded by Michael Frondelli; concert production design, Kim Colefax; associate producers, Albert Spevak, Jane Rose. Reviewed at Toronto Festival of Festivals, Sept. 18, 1987. (MPAA Rating: PG) Running time: **120 MINS.**
With: Chuck Berry, Eric Clapton, Robert Cray, Etta James, Julian Lennon, Keith Richards, Linda Ronstadt, Phil Everly, Don Everly, Jerry Lee Lewis, Bo Diddley, Little Richard, Roy Orbison, Bruce Springsteen.

Toronto — "If you had tried to give rock 'n' roll another name, you might call it Chuck Berry," pronounces John Lennon in an old interview at the outset of Taylor Hackford's glowing 2-hour love letter to the kingpin of rock 'n' roll.

"Chuck Berry: Hail! Hail! Rock 'n' Roll!" is a joyous docu that effortlessly weaves luminary rock interviews with performance footage, mostly shot at Berry's 60th birthday bash concert at the Fox Theater in St. Louis.

It's a must for rock aficionados, but will cross over to old fans, new converts, and general audiences who want a look at the plucky Berry as well as an overview of the history of blacks in r 'n' r.

Talking heads interviews with such rockers as Phil and Don Everly, Jerry Lee Lewis, Bo Diddley, Little Richard, Keith Richards, Roy Orbison and Bruce Springsteen testify to the fact that Berry's influence is all-pervasive in rock. As a singer, songwriter, guitarist, and bop-till-you-drop performer, Berry was a real "troubadour."

Springsteen notes that all rock stars owe a debt of gratitude to Berry's style of writing lyrics the way people talk and his eye for detail. A fairly articulate Keith Richards questions if Berry even knows what he did. (He lovingly adds, "He's given me more headaches than Mick Jagger, but I love him.") Eric Clapton admits there's not a whole lot of ways to play rock 'n' roll except the way Chuck plays it.

Berry's ruminations cover everything from his love of cars, to breaking the color code, payola, his 40-year marriage, and how he chose to adapt his lyrics and subjects to cross over to white audiences.

Hackford doesn't press Berry on discussing his "brushes with the law" or his rumored bitterness at having people rip him off. Berry comes across as powerful, insightful, charismatic, intelligent and warm.

Although Hackford has Berry recreate some early concert gigs, the birthday performance footage is what shines here. In rehearsals music producer Keith Richards works on specific chords and setups with Berry, but on stage Berry encourages him to wing it — change keys, change tempos, anything.

All-star backup and singers at the gig include Eric Clapton, Robert Cray, Etta James, Julian Lennon (singing "Johnny B. Goode") and Linda Ronstadt, rocking to "Living in the U.S.A."

It's not surprising that Robbie Robertson is credited as creative consultant, for pic is quite reminiscent of "The Last Waltz." Interviews are seamlessly geared up with performances, and in most cases the last anecdotes about Berry's style are then realized in song. Hackford uses the same creative camera closeups, long shots, and audience takes, too.

Either Hackford had a magical trust going with the interviewees, or they're all blessed with skills at sparkling repartee. Little Richard steals the day with his infectious screams and his scathing overview of what white audiences wanted.

Hackford catches Berry walking onstage during his never-ending performing sked of 1-nighters, guitar in hand, without an entourage, and going out there to rock the socks off the audience. Docu could be pruned a bit, but even in its length nabs the spirit of Berry the man and performer. Roll over, Beethoven, and watch the crowds line up for this one. — *Devo*.

South Of Reno
(COLOR)

Promising indie melodrama.

An Open Road production in association with Pendulum Prods. Produced by Robert Tinnell. Coproducer, Joanna Stainton. Executive producers, Victor Markowicz, Stainton. Directed by Mark Rezyka. Stars Jeffrey Osterhage, Lisa Blount. Screenplay, Rezyka, T.L. Lankford; camera (CFI color), Bernard Auroux; editor, Marc Grossman; music, Nigel Holton, Clive Wright; production design, Phillip Duffin; art direction, Elizabeth Moore; sound, Rob Janiger; associate producer, Eric Liekefet; second unit director, Tinnell; casting, Barbara Remsen & Assoc./Anne Remsen. Reviewed at CFI Labs, L.A., Sept. 10, 1987. (In Toronto Film Festival.) (No MPAA Rating.) Running time: **94 MINS.**
Martin . . . . Jeffrey Osterhage
Anette . . . . Lisa Blount

Hector . . . . Joe Phelan
Willard . . . . Lewis Van Bergen
Susan . . . . Julia Montgomery
Brenda . . . . Brandis Kemp
Louise . . . . Danitza Kingsley
Manager of Motel . . . Mary Grace Canfield
Howard Stone . . . . Bert Remsen

Hollywood — A quirky tale of a loser who tries to escape the hand fate has dealt him, "South Of Reno" is a gorgeously filmed independent picture that reveals promising talent in several departments. Shot last fall in the Mojave Desert under the title "Darkness, Darkness," first feature by Mark Rezyka is too stark and uneventful for mass consumption, but is a natural for the festival circuit and could develop a following on the art house circuit with crafty promotion. World premiere took place at the Toronto Festival of Festivals.

Opening sequence is enough to draw in anyone attracted to the offbeat, as desert dweller Jeffrey Osterhage is observed tossing broken glass and nails across the highway. One suspects a devious scheme afoot, but in fact the poor guy just wants tires to blow out so he can talk to the drivers for awhile and have a little company.

The rest of the time, he sits in his barber's chair in his shack watching through fuzzy reception at the only tv broadcast he can even remotely receive. His wife, Lisa Blount, has long since given up on him and spends most of her time making time with scuzzy auto mechanic Lewis Van Bergen.

With such layabouts as protagonists, it is difficult for awhile to figure out where to place one's sympathies or interest, but melodrama soon rears its head when Osterhage catches his wife cheating on him and decides to do something about it. At the same time, the man's pathetic dreams of starting up anew in Reno is revealed to have sprouted a private, magical world of lights and spinning windmills, and sequence devoted to this is like something out of Fellini in its wondrous imagery.

The specter of "Paris, Texas" is conjured up, not only through the figure of the isolated, lonely man set against monumental scenery, but by the spectacularly fine cinematography of Bernard Auroux. Outdoor shots are dominated by high blue skies and stark mountains and flats, while interiors are photographed with exquisite luminosity.

On the other hand, some viewers will undoubtedly think of "Blood Simple" when the rival men start thinking of how to do the other in, and the ironic ending immediately reminds of John Huston, with its laughter prompted by the cruel but appropriate twist that befalls the survivor.

A native of Poland who grew up in Montreal and has made some 70 music videos, Rezyka clearly has a strong visual sense and a taste for strange humor. Pacing and story-telling are uneven, and performances, particularly that of Osterhage, who resembles Paul Le Mat, seem to lack confidence at first, but gain over time.

Pic is thoroughly professional on all counts despite an obviously very low budget, and score by Nigel Holton and Clive Wright is an excellent patch on Ry Cooder. —Cart.

Big Shots
(U.S.-COLOR)

A 20th Century Fox release of a Lorimar Pictures production. Produced by Joe Medjuck, Michael C. Gross. Executive producer, Ivan Reitman. Directed by Robert Mandel. Screenplay, Joe Eszterhas; camera (color), Miroslav Ondricek; editor, Bill Anderson, Sheldon Kahn, Dennis Virkler; music, Bruce Broughton; production design, Bill Malley; sound, Bill Randall. Reviewed at Toronto festival of Festivals, Sept. 19, 1987. (MPAA Rating: PG-13.) Running time: **90 MINS.**

With: Rucky Busker, Darius McCrary, Robert Joy, Robert Prosky, Jerzy Skolimowski, Paul Winfield.

Toronto — The unlikely friendship between a white suburban boy and an inner-city black boy is the fulcrum for the action in "Big Shots," latest feature from Robert Mandel ("F/X"). There's plenty of energy, plot twists, and sentimental sidebars to make it appealing to both kids and their parents, but the script is often too contrived to make it credible.

Joe Eszterhas has the right high-spirited commercial touch here to please the youth market, with a swift soundtrack as well. A young white boy, Obadiah, whose father has just died suddenly, gets lost on his bike in the black ghetto of Chicago. When a gang of rednecks steal the watch his father gave him, he is befriended by a sharp black kid Jeremy.

Jeremy is a funny, street-smart wisecracker, who lives alone in the basement of a local dive hotel. He drinks beer, hangs out in bars, and considers himself a shrewd businessman.

The duo's daring adventures begin when Jeremy jump-starts a Mercedes and drives off. Unfortunately for them, there's a dead body in the trunk, and the two thugs who did the contract killing are now on the path to nab the kids.

The naive Obadiah learns fast from his buddy and withdraws funds from his bank account to retrieve his dad's watch, which he and Jeremy saw for sale in the display case of the local pawn shop.

The loan shark pockets the money without delivering the goods and kicks the kids out. They return, hold up the pawnbroker with cap guns, and drive off in their stolen car.

Meanwhile their friendship grows and they discover their links to their fathers. Obadiah mourns the loss of his, and Jeremy bemoans the fact that his dad left him when he was little.

The boys find out where Jeremy's father is living and then are off to Louisiana to meet him. Along the way they're chased by the Mercedes owners and fall victim to a Bible salesman scam. Obadiah is transformed to a street kid, who dons black shades, felt hat, and talks jive, and can suddenly maneuver a car like Mario Andretti.

Car chases and crashes plus a pulsing rock beat speed things along as the boys become partners in crime. There's a mushy reconciliation between Jeremy and his pa.

Most surprising casting coup comes in the form of Robert Joy and Jerzy Skolimowski as the hired killers, who bring snap to their roles. Paul Winfield does a smart turn as a street smart dude.

Mandel can direct fast action scenes well, but in this case he's more successful in developing the humorous acting talents of the two unknown leads, Ricky Busker and Darius McCrary. Because they're not self-consciously cute acting school grads, they inject an innocence and camaraderie in their parts. Too bad Eszterhas' script supports the kids' lack of responsiblity for their madcap criminal adventures and condones it because it leads to a family reunion. — Devo.

Dudes
(COLOR)

Silly Survival opus.

A New Century/Vista Film release of a Vista Organization production. Produced by Herb Jaffe. Executive producer, Mort Engelberg. Line producer, Gordon Wolf. Directed by Penelope Spheeris. Screenplay, J. Randal Johnson; camera (color), Robert Richardson; editor, Andy Horvitch; sound (Ultra-Stereo), Walter Martin; production design, Robert Ziembicki; assistant director, Guy Louthan; casting, Nina Axelrod. Reviewed at Magno Preview 9 screening room, N.Y. Aug. 10, 1987. (In Toronto Film Festival.) (MPAA Rating: R.) Running time: **90 MINS.**

Grant . . . . Jon Cryer
Biscuit . . . . Daniel Roebuck
Milo . . . . Flea
Missoula . . . . : . . . . Lee Ving
Jessie . . . . Catherine Mary Stewart
Also with: Billy Ray Sharkey, Glenn Withrow, Michael Melvin, Axxel G. Reese, Marc Rude, Calvin Bartlett, Pete Willcox, Vance Colvig, Pamela Gidley.

How can a film that brings punk rockers from Queens, cowboys, indians and crazed homicidal villains together in Utah be taken seriously? The answer, of course, is that it can't. Even on a superficial level, "Dudes" fails to round up a good time.

"Dudes" tells the story of three punked-out New Yorkers — Milo, Grant and Biscuit — who set out for Hollywood in a Volkswagen and get attacked while camping out in Big Sky country by characters who seem to have walked over from the set of "Deliverance" or "The Hills Have Eyes."

Milo is murdered by Missoula, leader of a wild-eyed gang that roams the west killing Mexicans.

Grant and Biscuit vow to avenge Milo's death.

Even if one were inclined to overlook the derivative story line, "Dudes" still manages to throw itself from the saddle so many times it bruises the sensibilities. The humor, when intentional, is slapstick. The dialog is hopelessly adolescent, the music incredibly loud and the plot is dependent on a bizarre sequence of coincidences.

For instance, when Grant and Biscuit start out on their road to revenge, they are in the middle of nowhere with absolutely no idea how to find Missoula. As they are driving along in their Volkswagen, they just happen to come across a dying member of Missoula's crew who has been wounded fatally by the maniacal Missoula himself. Of course, he manages to stay alive long enough to give Grant and Biscuit a clue to Missoula's whereabouts.

The element of chance plays such an important role in several subsequent scenes that it gets silly. Grant and Biscuit happen to be standing in the exact creek where Missoula chooses to dump a dead deer.

Grant and Biscuit stay on Missoula's trail by stumbling across a ripped jacket on a desolate stretch of Wyoming road.

Grant and Biscuit career off the highway into a ravine and are rescued immediately from the wreckage by Jesse, a female tow-truck driver they met at a gas station who — you guessed it — just happened to be driving by.

The way everyone keeps bumping into each other, one gets the impression Utah and Wyoming are the size of a parking lot.

As "Dudes" spirals to its conclusion, things get pretty bizarre. Grant begins to see an apparition of a cowboy which no one else sees and Biscuit starts believing he's an indian. As this is going on, Jesse spends free time shooting beer bottles off a fence rail with a sixgun.

Director Penelope Spheeris obviously opted for the outrageous in making "Dudes." Yet movies of this genre are more effective with tongue-in-cheek dialog delivered by spunky, likeable characters. "Dudes' " characters — Grant is a brooding youth looking for a purpose in life while Biscuit is an overweight over-eater who keeps stuffing food in his mouth — are cliches.

There is a very thin line between wonderfully zany and pointlessly strange, between suburbia and Wyoming. In the case of "Dudes," it was a line that was crossed in the wrong direction. —Chuk.

Alfred Laliberte, Sculpteur
(CANADIAN-DOCU-COLOR)

A Les Films François Brault/Les Prod. Dix-Huit production. Produced by Claude Sylvestre. Written and directed by Jean-Pierre Lefebvre. Camera (color), François Brault; editor, Barbara Easto; music, Dominique Tremblay. sound, Joseph Champagne, Daniel Masse, Philippe Hochard. Reviewed at Toronto Festival of Festivals, Sept. 14, 1987. Running time: **80 MINS.**

With: Paul Hebert, Odette Legendre, Albert Millaire, Marcel Sabourin, Nicole Filion, Francine Ruel.

Toronto — Prolific Quebecois writer-director Jean-Pierre Lefebvre, winner of the 1982 Intl. Critics' Prize at Cannes for his feature "Les fleurs sauvages," takes on a biography of the equally prolific Quebecois sculptor Alfred Laliberte.

Already aired on Radio Canada, French-track CBC-TV web, the film, while interesting, is of obviously limited appeal.

Laliberte's work is familiar to anyone who has ever visited Montreal, where the sculptor died in 1953. His statues grace parks, churches, government buildings and well-known squares of the city and of the province. As beautiful as his work may be, Laliberte is not an artist well known outside Quebec.

It's unfortunate that the audience at the Toronto Festival of Festivals, obviously enthusiastic about the documentary, were subjected to a flawed soundtrack and often laughable subtitles that did not do justice to the script.

What's special, however, about this documentary, Lefebvre's first, is the highly original style in which Laliberte's life is chronicled. The past is superimposed on the present, drama is blended with documentary and a story is told in an unusual form that the producer Claude Sylvestre calls "documented dramatic film." —Zerb.

La Moine et La Sorcière
(Sorceress)
(FRENCH-U.S.-COLOR)

A European Classics release of a Lara Classics production, in association with Bleu Prods., George Reinhart Prods., La Cecilia, Selena Audiovisual, Sofinergie S.A. Executive producers, Vincent Malle, Martine Marignac. Produced by Pamela Berger, Annie Leibovici, George Reinhart. Directed by Suzanne Schiffman. Screenplay, Pamela Berger, Schiffman; camera (color), Patrick Blossier; art direction, Bernard Vezat; editor, Martine Barraque; music, Michel Portal; costumes, Mouchi Houblinne, Françoise Autran, production managers, Martine Marignac, Michelle Cretel; associate producer, Barbara Lucey. Reviewed at Toronto Festival of Festivals, Sept. 13, 1987. Running time: **90 MINS.**

Etienne de Bourbon . . . . Tcheky Karyo
Elda . . . . Christine Boisson
The Cure . . . . Jean Carmet
Simeon . . . . Raoul Billery
Cecile . . . . Catherine Frot
The Count . . . . Feodor Atkine
Agnes . . . . Maria de Medeiros

Toronto — François Truffaut's longtime screenwriter and assistant director Suzanne Schiffman turns director with an absorbing period drama about a 13th century Dominican friar on a mission to hunt heretics. While it's pristine in its historical accuracy, based on the treatise of Etienne de Bourbon, and lovingly photographed, it will probably be a hard sell for mainstream audiences, although medieval-philes will relish the care that was graced upon the screenplay.

Pic was the brainchild of Boston art historian Pamela Berger, who was researching the writings of Etienne de Bourbon, a friar who tried to stop villagers in a small rural town in France from worshipping a saint named Guinefort. The twist is that the saint was a greyhound who once saved a lord's baby hundreds of years before, and is now revered as the saint of sick children.

In the film Etienne arrives in a stone-walled town that is reproduced so accurately by art director Bernard Vezat that it could be mistaken for a page in an illuminated manuscript. The costumes are spot on, too, but these peasants are rather clean.

Seeking out heretics, Etienne is intrigues by a local woman, Elda, who is a faith healer living in the woods, a true heroine to the superstitious villagers. He feels that her mysterious potions from leaves and plants may be against the grain of God. One night he follows a woman with a very ill child to Elda's territory.

When her potions to cure the baby's fever fail, Elda reluctantly takes the child to the "grove," where the friar witnesses a ritual that he deems demonic, an abomination to the Lord, and the work of a sorceress. Etienne rants that Elda and the townspeople mock the Christian saints when he learns that the women are praying at the grave of Guinefort, the dog saint, who is called upon to return the lady's healthy son. Etienne sentences Elda to be burnt at the stake.

In private conversation with him Elda enlightens him of her past, how she was raped on her wedding night by a lord, sent to this small village to have the baby that she conceived. The truth about Etienne's regretful past is unearthed after years of repression, and it is he who must confess his sins to the benevolent cure.

Schiffman's approach to the subject matter is factually correct, although open to interpretation. She touches on religious fervor, witchhunting, and women's precarious roles in medieval times.

She gets well-developed performances from Tcheky Karyo, who chooses to play the friar not as intractable but with vulnerability. Christine Boisson is confident, proud and centered as Ella.

The script is clever and the pic handsomely photographed, with long shots of the village evoking the medieval flabor. Its audience will have to connect with the time frame and the subject matter. —Devo.

And Then You Die
(CANADIAN-COLOR)

A Canadian Broadcasting Corp. production. Executive producer, Bernard Zukerman. Produced by Brian McKenna. Directed by Francis Mankiewicz. Screenplay, Wayne Grigsby, Alun Hibbert; camera (color), Richard Leiterman; editor, Gordon McClellan, Alfonsio Peccia; sound, Gerry King; music, Marty Simons; art direction, Marian Wihak; associate producer, Harris Verge. Reviewed at Toronto Festival of Festivals, Sept. 16, 1987. Running time: **90 MINS.**
Eddie Griffin . . . . Kenneth Welsh
Det. Sgt. James McGrath . . R.H. Thomson
Wally Degan . . . . Wayne Robson
Liz Griffin . . . . Maggie Huculak
Garou . . . . Pierre Chagnon
Scarecrow . . . . Guy Thauvette
Mikey . . . . Graeme Campbell
Pieter Vanderkeist . . . . Tom Harvey
Prego . . . . George Bloomfield

Toronto — "And Then You Die" invades the bowels of Montreal's criminal underworld and doesn't surface until the last contract murder is efficiently completed.

Francis Mankiewicz' ("Les Bons Debbarras," 'Le Temps d'une Chasse") made-for-tv pic is decorated with Richard Leiterman's inspired, moody cinematography and topnotch performances from leads Ken Welsh, R.H. Thomson, and Wayne Robson. The screenplay by Wyne Grigsby and Alun Hibbert is rooted in real, recent gangland events in the city.

Story focuses on big-time cocaine dealer Eddie Griffin (Welsh), whose middleman position in a high-profile drug ring has made life quite comfy. His wife and child live well in their spiffy suburban home, but lately the wife is threatening to leave because of the harrowing, dangerous lifestyle with Eddie.

When the local Mafia chieftain is murdered, there's a power struggle for new leadership. Eddie fashions a deal with Prego (George Bloomfield), the heir apparent, but when he demands a better cut Eddie calls upon his biker contacts to eliminate him. These guys, with leader Garou, want a big stake in Eddie's territory.

Always on his case is the gnawing presence of Det. Sgt. McGrath (Thomson), who relentlessly puts the pressure on Eddie to give himself up. McGrath finds the most vulnerable link in Eddie's gang in Wally (Robson), who he blackmails with a damaging videotape, to inform him about a huge coke deal that's going down.

Mankiewicz maneuvers his players with the authenticity of a docu. The seaminess and power plays of the Mafia ring true. The quiet moments of family peace in the midst of extreme violence in Eddie's life are forceful.

This is really "Montreal Vice," with the city itself a key player, acquiring a gritty, dangerous sheen. No pastel palettes and designer plainclothes linen suits here, though. Even the drug raid looks like it came right off the 11 o'clock news footage.

Mankiewicz orchestrates a nimble game of double dealings and misplaced loyalties. The cast shines here. Welsh is a tough, plucky dealer, with a flipside familial compassion. The always-charismatic R.H. Thomson is witty, cruel, and doggedly professional in his search.

Leiterman's camerawork caresses the darkness of this Hollywood North noir and transmits the director's jittery tension throughout.
—Devo.

Rachel River
(U.S.-COLOR)

An American Playhouse Theatrical Films presentation of a Marx/Smolan production. Produced by Timothy Marx. Executive producer, Lindsay Law. Directed by Sandy Smolan. Screenplay, Judith Guest, based on the stories of Carol Bly; camera (color), Paul Elliott; editor, Susan Crutcher; music, Arvo Part; production design, David Wasco; associate producer, Nan Simons; costumes, Linda Fisher. Reviewed at the Toronto Festival Of Festivals, Sept. 16, 1987. Running time: **90 MINS.**
Momo . . . . Zeljko Ivanek
Mary . . . . Pamela Reed
Marlyn . . . . Craig T. Nelson
Jack . . . . James Olson
Beske . . . . Alan North
Harriet . . . . Viveca Lindfors
Estona . . . . Jo Henderson
Baker . . . . Jon De Vries
Also with: Ailene Cole, Courtney Kjos, Ollie Osterberg, Wellington Nelson, Richard Jenkins, Michael Gallagher, Richard Riehle, Ron Duffy, Don Cosgrove, Stephen Yoakum, Cliff Rakerd, Patricia Mary Van Oss.

Toronto — "Rachel River" possesses the very characteristics of American Playhouse productions that some jaundiced observers find fashionably safe to knock. Indeed, this is a pretty to look at film that celebrates the rock-ribbed American virtues of community spirit and individual perseverance in the face of trouble, and does so in steady, unspectacular fashion. "Rachel River," however, is graced by performances that are as sturdy as the American-Scandinavian north Minnesota milieu it's set in. Depending on how it's handled, the picture could have modest boxoffice prospects before its journey to public television and the section of video shelves perused by those in quest of thoughtful, non-clamorous entertainment.

Focus of the story is Mary (Pamela Reed), an attactive and intellectually aware mother of three who's separated from her thoughtless husband. Mary is a community radio correspondent for a station in a larger town, and has resisted offers to move up in the broadcasting world in order to remain with her kids in the cold and cozy countryside. When an eccentric old widow dies alone at her dilapidated farm one day, Mary begins research into the woman's life that intensifies her awareness of her own suppressed loneliness.

The film's narrative is pegged to the various denizens of the titular town who touch Mary's life one weekend while the kids are with their father. Among them are Marlyn (Craig T. Nelson), a hard-drinking, locally colorful but not very bright deputy sheriff and Jack (James Olson), a sincere fellow who's considered something of a failure by the gossipy townspeople for doing nothing with a college degree but working in a funeral home. Marlyn is the dead woman's nephew, and most of the neighbors are convinced that this worthless fellow stands to inherit a fortune that his aunt was rumored to have stashed away. Closer to Mary than anyone is Harriet (Viveca Lindfors), a beautiful and next-to-saintly older woman who still speaks with a strong accent and who has moved into a hospital to be beside her dying husband. There's also a poor town simpleton named Momo, who serves as a sort of silent witness to all that goes on in Rachel River.

Nothing very much does go on, however, as these hardy folk wait for the first snow to fall. The action revolves around various life crises and their resolution. Will Mary sleep with the funky but masculine Marlyn or the upright milquetost Jack? Will Marlyn or his meanspirited sister inherit auntie's money or will it be someone else? Will Harriet be okay when she wanders off into the woods after learning that her son has sold the farm she can no longer manage on her own? Fortunately, these plot points are rescued from soap-operatic mawkishness by a nicely controlled balance of dialog and characterizations that make "Rachel River" a small but respectable drama. —Rich.

A Winter Tan
(CANADIAN-COLOR)

Produced by Louise Clark with the participation of The Ontario Film Development Corp. and Telefilm Canada, and the assistance of The Canada Council and The Ontario Arts Council. Directed by Clark, Jackie Burroughs. John Frizzell, John Walker and Aerlyn Weissman. Screenplay, Burroughs, based on the book "Give Sorrow Words," by Maryse Holder; camera (color), Walker; editor, Alan Lee; supervising editor, Susan Martin; music, Ahmend Hassan, John Lang; sound, Weissman; associate producer, Dulce Kuri. Reviewed at the Toronto Festival of Festivals Sept. 17, 1987. Running time: **91 MINS.**
Maryse Holder . . . . Jackie Burroughs
Miguel Novaro . . . . Erando Gonzalez
Lucio Salvador . . . . Javier Torres
Pam . . . . Anita Olanick
Edith . . . . Diane D'Aquila
Also with: Fernando Perez de Leon, Dulce Kuri, Ruben Dario Hernandez, Abraham Hernandez Castillo, Maricarmen Dominguez, Reyna Lobato Mariche, John Frizzell, John Walker, Jorge Galcedo, Luis Lobato, Servando Gaja, Alberta Chalulas, Librado Jiminez.

Toronto — In a virtual one-woman show, Jackie Burroughs makes a brave effort to recreate the sorrowful final months in the life of Maryse Holder, a New York feminist whose dissolute and ultimately fatal sexual hegira in Mexico she chronicled in posthumously published letters upon which the Canadian actress based her screenplay. Holder is portrayed as a wild and life-loving soul who unfortunately could not cope with the reversals she endured in a tormented quest for emotional and and creative self-fulfillment. Unfortunate as well were the expectations of the filmmakers that the inchoate prose ramblings and hedonistic vagabondings of this dubious heroine would make an absorbing film. Over-long and portentous, "A Winter Tan" is yet another independent project that might find a niche at specialty festivals but has little chance to make an impact in the theatrical marketplace.

Holder's frenetic Mexican blow-out is narrated in epistolary flashback through the eyes of the heroine who addresses the audience directly in a frontal assault on the camera. Mysterious Mexico's tropical sensuality unleashes a flood of disordered impressions in the apostate feminist intellectual as she boozes and drugs her way through an indiscriminate sexual conquest of the all-too-willing lads of Acapulco. For a film with ostensible radical sensibilities, "A Winter Tan" displays an astonishingly callous attitude of cultural-racial condescension towards Mexican men, whom the hypocritically imperialist heroine regards as brutish and disposable phallic studs. Holder's endless binge of beach-bumming, disco-cruising and intoxicated one-night stands unfolds in a fevered stream of free-associating, self-fixated letters in which her disquieting inner turmoil is exposed like a festering infection.

Eventually, Holder does have one transcendent and all-consuming affair with Miguel (Ernando Gonzalez), whose macho contempt for the licentious *gringa* proves fatally attractive to the pathetically self-destructive Maryse. Burroughs displays more than competent acting skill in depicting the anorexic heroine's contradictory struggle between the self-loathing and self-loving aspects of her personality. Holder's darkly humorous arrogance (she compares herself favorably as a writer to Malcolm Lowry and proclaims the need for "a new kind of feminism — sluttish and heterosexual") and remorseless renunciation of her unhappy past in New York are rendered by Burroughs with an abrasive believability. The burden of Holder's sad story, however, can only be comfortably borne by viewers prepared to identify closely with it. —Rich.

Aquabat Jaber: Vie de Passage
(Aquabat Jaber: Passing Through) (FRENCH-DOCU-COLOR)

A Dune Vision production. Produced by Thibaut de Corday. Written and directed by Eyal Sivan. Camera (color), Nurith Aviv; editor, Ruth Schell; sound, Remy Attal. Reviewed at Toronto Festival of Festivals, Sept. 18, 1987. Running time: **80 MINS.**

Toronto — As parched and spare as the landscape it chronicles, "Aqabat Jaber: Passing Through" is a coarsely realistic and depressing look at one of the largest Palestinian refugee camps. Strictly for specialty houses, pic would fare better as a public broadcasting spec than a theatrical feature.

Aqabat Jaber was set up on the occupied West Bank in 1948 for 65,000 Palestinians who were uprooted from 116 villages. Today there are only 3,000 refugees left. First-time director Eyal Sivan takes his camera on-site to the remaining inhabitants, most of whom are convinced that they will one day, through political or divine inervention, return to their homeland.

They all express similar sentiment — their land is the very source, they are homesick for their villages and orchards, and feel that Aqabat Jaber is a "temporary situation," although they've been there for 38 years (pic was shot in 1986).

Some refugees welcome the chance to introduce themselves, air their grievances and bemoan their fates; others scorn the filmmakers. Sivan, ever sympathetic to their conditions, extracts detailed life stories from these displaced persons as he pans the daily life at the camps — women baking bread, men sitting around smoking from a hookah, children playing in abandoned baked earth houses.

The United Nations Relief and Works Act, which set up the camp now provides it with a minimal of sustenance every two months. In the summer there's no water.

It's all hopeless and full of despair. Being and nothingness are the watchwords at the camp as well as this docu. Sivan should have established the details of the camp's politics and history at the outset to make the individual stories more accessible to the viewer, instead of saving a paragraph of description for the end. There's no narration or music either.

These people's plights are poignant, but there are too many unanswered questions as to why they're still here, why neighboring Arab countries didn't take them in, and why their embitterment paralyzes them.—Devo.

The Last Straw
(CANADIAN-COLOR)

A Cinema Intl. Canada release of a National Film Board of Canada production. Produced by David Wilson, Giles Walker. Directed by Walker. Screenplay, Walker, Wilson; camera (color), Andrew Kitzanuk; editor, David Wilson; sound, Yves Gendron; music, Robert Lauzon, Fernand Martel; production manager, Maurice Pion; costumes, Janet Campbell; associate producer, Denise Beaudoin; assistant director, François Cingras. Reviewed at National Film Board, Toronto, Sept. 4, 1987. (At Toronto Festival of Festivals.) Running time: **98 MINS.**
Alex . . . . .Salverio (Sam) Grana
Laura . . . . .Fernanda Tavares
Dr. Cameron . . . . .Maurice Podbrey
Nurse Thompson . . . . . . .Beverley Murray
Blue . . . . .Stefan Wodoslawsky
Hyang-Sook . . . . .Christine Pak
Manager . . . . .Wally Martin

Toronto — Giles Walker takes the two leads of his 1985 National Film Board comedy "90 Days" on an even droller, more surreal journey in his clever, exuberant sequel, "The Last Straw." Its humor is for mature, informed audiences and it taps into some of the major concerns in adult contempo society — infertility, feminism and conspicuous consumption.

Pic focuses primarily on Alex (Sam Grana), who is now the most potent man in the world. In "90 Days" he was asked to be a sperm donor for sleek businesswoman Laura's (Fernanda Tavares) friend. Now Laura has opened an infertility clinic and has Alex' potency tested. In hilarious scenes with the wacky, impossibly restrained Nurse Thompson (Beverley Murray), who clinically provides background mood music for his sperm donor duties, Alex has discovered he has an extraordinary 99.5% sperm motility.

Dr. Cameron, who works on artificial insemination with bulls, wants to put Alex into production on the spot. He's as much a prize bull as the doc's barnyard varieties.

The infertility clinic (not too much in the future, it seems) now features a catalog with head shots of sperm donors. Couples can select the potential father of their baby from the book. Natch, Alex becomes the number one choice with his high percentage of impregnation rate.

His fame attracts the most opportunistic leeches, from a huckster manager who uses a megaphone on a busy Montreal street to feature Alex to the crowds on a platter like a circus sideshow freak, to an American businesswoman who wants to pay him millions to service women in her nuclear-proof clinic.

Plot gets a bit loopy, though, when Australian agents attempt to abduct Alex to recruit him as a stud to solve Australia's infertility problem and revive the image of the potent Aussie male. The Aussies tell him things went potty around the time of Germaine Greer.

A companion storyline follows Blue (Stefan Wodoslawsky), who in "90 Days" married a Korean mail-order bride, Hyang-Sook (Christine Pak). They're living in wedded bliss but are having trouble conceiving. After temperature charts and an exotic water cooling device to lower Blue's scrotum temperature, they, too, resort to Laura's clinic and want to receive Alex' sperm.

The film is unapologetically Canadian, with Alex touting his product as Canadian-made and newscasters announcing that artificial insemination is sure to be a hot topic in the Canadian-U.S. free trade talks. A Canadian task force is set up when Alex is kidnaped, and charts Canadian, Russian, and American sperm production since 1965.

Walker loves his characters and gets a very appealing, deadpan performance from his lead. Sam Grana gives Alex credibililty and irony in a delicate and humorous situation. Beverley Murray's nurse is a loony professional, who wears gloves when she's anywhere near Alex ("I don't want children myself," she says).

Wodoslawsky and Pak are a surprisingly believable, compassionate couple, despite their unusual history. The script glistens and shines throughout with comic gems and, while the story goes off the wall, the basic premise and subtext of designer donors and high-tech babies is topical and on the mark.

The accessibility of this low-budgeter should be the key for a careful, wide release. —Devo.

Family Viewing
(CANADIAN-COLOR-16m)

A Cinephile release (in Canada) of Ego Film Arts production with the participation of the Ontario Film Development Corp., The Canada Council and The Ontario Arts Council. Written and directed by Atom Egoyan. Camera (color, 16m), Robert Macdonald, Peter Mettler; editor, Egoyan, Bruce Macdonald; music, Michael Danna; production manager, Camelia Frieberg; art direction, Linda Del Rosario; design, Ian Greig; sound, Ross Redfern, Steven Munro. Reviewed at the Toronto Festival Of Festivals, Sept. 15, 1987. Running time: **86 MINS.**
time: 86 MINS.
Stan . . . . .David Hemblen
Van . . . . .Aidan Tierney
Sandra . . . . .Gabrielle Rose
Aline . . . . .Arsinée Khanjian
Armen . . . . .Selma Keklikian
Aline's Mother . . . . .Jeanne Sabourin
Van's Mother . . . . .Rose Sarkisyan
Young Van . . . . .Vasag Baghboudarian
Also with: David Mackay, Hrant Alianak, John Shafer, Garfield Andrews, Edwin Stephenson, Aino Pirskanen, Souren Chekijian, Johnnie Eisen, and John Pellatt.

Toronto — He's something of a darling to the Canadian new wave cinema, but Atom Egoyan's second feature is particularly exasperating precisely because there are streaks of filmmaking talent visible through the pretentious murk of this disjointed story about a single-minded young man and his emotionally pulverized family life. U.S. specialty distributors are unlikely to touch "Family Viewing" with the proverbial 10-foot pole, but it will probably become a staple at indie-oriented cinephile festivals.

Egoyan's film stands shakily upon a glib foundation of familiar themes. These include ruptured familial communication is an impersonal urban society, the displacement of human feelings in an age of instant sensual gratification and the subsuming of modern lif to the omnipresent value systems of the video tube. At the center of all this is college graduate Van (Aidan Tierney), who lives in a high-rise co-op with his slightly kinky father Stan (David Hemblen) and dad's provocatively flirtatious mistress Sandra (Gabrielle Rose).

Van's mother has abandoned the home fires out of apparent disgust for her selfish husband who, in her absence, has stashed his mother-in-law Armen in a low-budget nursing home where grandson Van is her only visitor and source of solace. Conveniently located in the next bed is the mother of Aline (Arsinée Khanjian), a beauty from Montreal who works for a telephone sex-call service that numbers old stan as one of its regular clients. Aline's mother dies while she's out of town on an "escort" assignment, but Van the video buff (his dad sells video hardware with which he records his boudoir heroics) gets the whole funeral on tape. There is plenty of such dubious dark humor in "Family Viewing" and more follows as Van and Aline conspire to rescue Armen from the nursing home.

Herky-jerky narrative pacing, vertiginous camera work and editing and a frenetic percussive soundtrack are meant to emphasize the emotional disorientation of this not very appealing lineup of characters, but also prove taxing to the viewer in that Egoyan is showing off without paying off on these artistic indulgences. The devices of home movies (in which the family lives on in its happier nuclear past) and the tiresome use of b&w tv static patterns between scenes are clever mostly in the sophomoric sense. By the time Egoyan moves to bring this affair to a hopeful resolution the actors don't seem to care very much and neither should the audience.
—*Rich.*

Taking Care
(CANADIAN-COLOR)

A Norstar Entertainment release (in Canada) of a Telltales Ltd. production. Produced by Pasia Schonberg. Executive producer director, Clarke Mackey. Screenplay, Rebecca Schechter. Camera (color), Keith Hlady; editor, Terese Hannigan; production designer, Carol Holland; sound, Brian Avery; music, Jane Fair. Reviewed at Toronto Festival of Festivals, Sept. 14, 1987. Running time: **90 MINS.**
Angie . . . . Kate Lynch
Marie . . . . • . . . Janet Amos
Carl . . . . Saul Rubinek
Dr. Barton . . . . Allan Royal
Ed . . . . Sean McCann
Dr. O'Donnell . . . . Bernard Behrens

Toronto — Inspired by the headline-making investigation into mysterious baby deaths at Toronto's Hospital for Sick Children, "Taking Care" is a hospital chiller about the arrest of a nurse charged with murdering her patients — in this case, healthy laboring mothers — and the consequent unveiling of a coverup.

Director Clarke Mackey's first feature since his 1971 pic "The Only Thing You Know" has a polished screenplay and a roster of top Canadian acting talent. This low-budgeter has the look, feel, and pace of a slick made-for-tv film and will probably have more success on the small screen than as a theatrical release.

In a downtown hospital, three healthy mothers have died within two weeks in suspicious circumstances after giving birth. When the police are called in to investigate they discover that one nurse, Marie (Janet Amos) was on duty for all three patients, all of whom were administered injections. The other nurses are naturally distressed, especially Angie (Kate Lynch), who isn't at all sure that Marie is at fault.

There is a coroner's inquest and more questions. Angie starts her own clandestine investigation. Her father, a retired obstetrician (Bernhard Behrens) supports her enthusiasm but is simultaneously reticent. Her husband, Carl (real-life husband Saul Rubinek), who works in the hospital pharmacy, has a funny, negative bent, and dismisses the deaths as typical for the hospital.

Angie alone is confronted with the corruption of the hospital and the patronizing attitudes of the male doctors toward the nurses. She feels it's the nursing staff who are scapegoats for the hospital 's negligence. Through her research and personal conversations with her friend, Ed (Sean McCann), a pharmacy worker, she finds out that one of the mothers died from an injection of a mislabeled drug.

Most unsettling is Angie's discovery that the smug chief of obstetrics knew about the mislabelling and agreed with the hospital administration to cover it up. She also has to deal with her father's knowledge of the incident as well.

Rebecca Schechter's script has the right blend of alliances unturned, red herrings, and well-researched courtroom scenes. She makes the plight of an individual searching for truth to be entirely credible, and has sketched out well-rounded familial relationships.

Clarke Mackey keeps the pic well-paced. While some of the characters are written and acted one-dimensionally, bulk of cast is strong. Kate Lynch is solid, determined, and vulnerable as the questioning nurse. As her husband, the ever-engaging Saul Rubinek can take even a supporting role and dress it up with humor and emotional depth. Janet Amos makes Marie into a sympathetic victim of the hospital's politics.

Mackey, who's done many docus and tv dramas, is able to weave layers of themes into a tidy framework. Tech credits are okay.—*Devo.*

Zoeken naar Eileen
(Looking For Eileen)
(DUTCH-COLOR)

An Eerste Amsterdamse Filmassociatie production. Produced by Leon de Winter, Eddy Wijngaarde. Directed by Rudolph van den Berg. Screenplay, Van den Berg, De Winter, based on latter's novel, "Zoeken naar Eileen W." camera (color), Theo van de Sande, editor, Wim Louwrier; music, Boudewijn Tarenskeen, Pim Kops; sound, Piotr van Dijk, Lucas Beoke. Reviewed at Toronto Festival of Festivals, Sept. 19, 1987. Running time: **98 MINS.**
With: Thom Hoffman, Lysette Anthony, Kenneth Herdigein, Hans Kemna, John van Dreelen.

Toronto — "Looking For Eileen" is a "Vertigo"-inspired romantic thriller that self-destructs at midpoint. Rudolph van den Berg kicks off the action in a slick and seductive manner, and then, led by a quickly deteriorating script, succumbs to hackneyed directorial tricks.

Audiences are too smart to buy this sudden turn, and Toronto fest fans were howling at the reversal. Boxoffice prospects outside the home turf are iffy, save for those who admired van den Berg's other collaboration with Leon de Winter, "Bastille."

At the outset, Philip and Marjan have a beautiful marriage. She's a bookshop owner, going to London for an auction, but dies in an automobile accident en route. Philip, an architect, is devastated, tries suicide, but gradually recovers.

One year later, on a dark and rainy night, a dead ringer for Marjan appears in the bookshop with her young baby, looking for "Tristan and Isolde." Philip can't believe what's happening, follows her to a decaying warehouse to return her baby's pacifier. They go out for a meal, she says she's Eileen W. from Belfast and can't tell him any other details about why she's here. She disappears.

This is followed by the sudden arrival of her husband, Mark, who at gunpoint screams at Philip that he must get his wife. The two men take off for seedy Amsterdam, where they track her down to a brothel. She's staying with her best friend and her boyfriend, who's the true father of her baby. One murder later and the case is closed.

Cut to two years later, Philip meets Eileen again. This time she's changed her name to Karen and works as a nanny at a mansion that Philip's architectural firm is renovating. This is where the director and screenwriter must have gone on to other projects. Eileen's bio about her past is ludicrous. They agree they shouldn't see each other, but then have second thoughts and reunite in a slo-mo exchange that looks like a commercial for a feminine hygiene product.

The photography and pacing of the first half is enticing, aided by an emotionally charged soundtrack. There are real moments of suspense, and Amsterdam never looked so menacing. Thom Hoffman and Lysette Anthony do the most with their ill-conceived roles. Maybe their grand smiles of reconciliation at the pic's finale were really relief that the film was over. —*Devo.*

Lihko Li Bit Mladjim
(Is It Easy To Be Young?)
(SOVIET-DOCU-COLOR)

A Riga Film Studio production. Directed by Yuris Podnieks. Screenplay, Abram Kliotskin, Evgeny Margolin, Podnieks; camera (color), Kalvis Zaltsmanis; music, Martin Brauns. Reviewed in Leningrad, May 28, 1987. (In Montreal Film Festival and Toronto Film Festival.) Running time: **84 MINS.**

Leningrad — In this devastating docu from Latvia, "Is It Easy To Be Young?," youngsters tell it like it is to helmer Yuris Podnieks' free-wheeling camera. The result is an eye-opening and extremely frank glimpse of what Soviet teens really think of their society. Film has been a smash hit domestically in its opening months, and has clear potential for foreign release in special situations.

Organized in topics ranging from teenage vandalism to boys coming back from the war in Afghanistan, "Is It Easy" steers a course through once unpublicized fringes of youth culture, interviewing 16-to-20-year-old rockers, drug addicts, and dropouts of every sort. There is a girl who attempted suicide and a boy who dissects corpses for a living — actually, for 80 rubles a month, Hare Krishnas and punk musicians with home-made spiked jewelry and eye makeup: in short, not your standard Youth Organization material.

Just how representative the film's subjects are isn't clear, but their message has a very familiar ring to it for the Western viewer. "We just want to have fun, adventure," says one of six minors put on trial for destroying two railway cars (but 150 youngsters participated in the vandalism). "I don't know a single ideal that would be worth going crazy or fighting for," says another. "You might have had ideals in your day, but we don't care about anything at all." "All I want out of life is money."

This is strong stuff even for *glasnost* days, and Podnieks skillfully draws out his interviewees, who generally express total cynicism and uninterest in the adult world. Most sobering of all is the long final sequence of interviews with Afghanistan veterans, whose shock at trying to reinsert themselves into civilian life is strikingly like experiences reported by Vietnam vets.

Film unfolds without commentary from its makers, Podnieks, Abram Kliotskin and Evgeny Margolin. It is punctuated by a home movie by a 20-year-old named Igor, an existential nightmare that illustrates the film's attitude to the hornet's nest of problems it has raised.
— *Yung.*

Kyeoul Nagune
(The Winter Wayfarers)
(SOUTH KOREAN-COLOR)

A Don-A Exports Co. production. Produced by Lee Woo-suk. Directed by Kwak Chi-gyoon. Screenplay, Choi In-ho; camera (color), Chung Kwang-suk; editor, Kim Hee-su; music, Kim Nam-yoon. Reviewed at Toronto Festival of Festivals, Sept. 11, 1987. Running time: **116 MINS.**
With Ahn Sung-ki, Kang Suk-woo, Lee Mee-sook, Lee Heh-young, Kim Chung-chul, Lee Hee-sung, Cho Roo-mee.

Toronto — Students of florid screen tearjerkers of the 1940s might appreciate this tepid carbon.

Cóllege pair have a cute meet, but after watching his father about to die and learning that his real mother might have been part of the demimonde the hero turns abruptly to a life of crime.

The girl still pines for him. He returns briefly only to walk out. She and his best friend find that he's married to a former prostitute who bore his child. Girlfriend and best friend marry and the hero finds it too late to make amends and is killed by police.

Main cast is handsome, but director Kwak Chi-gyoon in his feature debut rushes too fast in key expository scenes and languishes on minor ones. Commercial potential on this side of the Pacific is very doubtful.
—*Adil.*

En El Humo De Esta Epoca
(The Houses Are Full Of Smoke)
(U.S.-DOCU-COLOR-B&W-16m)

An FOC Inc. production. Produced, written and directed by Allan Francovich. Camera (color, 16m), Juan Bigley, Peter Chapel, Frank Piñeda; editor, Francovich, Manuel Sorto; music, Marimba Ixtateca, Nana Vasconcelos, Marimba Tecum Uman, Banda Tepuani, Luis Lopez y Crupo Anastacio Aquinto. Reviewed at the Toronto Festival of Festivals. Sept. 17, 1987. Running time: **180 MINS.**

Toronto —Exhaustive,stark and seamlessly developed, this documentary on the history of U.S. involvement in Guatemala, El Salvador and Nicaragua, presents without didactics a powerfully relevant overview of the region's violent political struggle between the haves and have-nots.

Scrupulously careful to present the viewpoints of virtually all the warring, intractable social forces, director Allan Francovich presents a heavy accumulation of testimony pointing to official American connivance with the morally reprehensible actions of putative Central American leaders.

Indispensable programming for documentary and more eclectic festivals, "The Houses Are Full Of Smoke'" is neatly partitioned into three 1-hour segments ideally tailored for episodic broadcasting on public tv and cable outlets.

Utilizing archival news footage, original talking heads interviews and on-scene documentary footage gathered himself, Francovich opens with a riveting explication of the situation in Guatemala dating back to the Eisenhower era. A former CIA agent recalls running a young Che Guevara out of the country and muses that the course of the region's history might have taken another direction if the Cuban revolutionary had been allowed to stay.

Interviews with the country's indigenous population, the Quiche Indians, indicate clearly that grinding poverty and hopelessness, not abstract imported ideologies, have led them to take up arms against a violently repressive military government almost wholly controlled by white Hispanics and trained by the U.S.

Right-wing politicians and military commanders are allowed to develop their argument that the Indian revolt has not true popular support, but their words seem shallow and unconvincing in the context of evidence to the contrary.

The role of the Roman Catholic Church in the region is examined through interviews with activist and conservative clergy in Guatemala. Likewise, in El Salvador — where Archbishop Romero was martyred for siding with those in favor of social change — the clergy are confronted with their temporal powerlessness to combat the Death Squads, whose very existence is brushed aside by Salvadoran and U.S. officials.

Gruesome and harrowing accounts of kidnapping, torture and murder are provided, however, in interviews with remorseful former Death Squad members. One recalls it as "good money for little work," and notes that the alternative would have been forced conscription into the Salvadoran army or worse.

Many viewers will be pushed to the limit by the graphic accounts and visual representations of torture in Guatemala and El Salvador. As Francovich obviously intended, they lend a compelling moral urgency to the case against right-wing autocrats such as Robert D'Aubisson, who is given ample opportunity for his transparent rebuttals.

Francovich brings the docu full circle in its third hour to Nicaragua, where he develops a case for an interlocking conspiracy of revanchist forces in the region. Former CIA operatives tell of recruiting Argentine mercenaries to fight the Sandinista government which, in spite of its own serious transgresssions against human rights, is depicted as having the most popular support of any governing body in the region.

Ultimately, "The Houses Are Full Of Smoke" succeeds in casting a coherent light on the dark and painful tangle of comtemporary Central American power politics.
—*Rich.*

Dann Ist Nichts Mehr Wie Vorher
(Then Nothing Was The Same Anymore)
(WEST GERMAN-COLOR)

An Olga-Film production. Coproduced by Bayerischen Rundfunk with the Berliner Filmförderung and the Bayern Filmföderung. Directed by Gerd Roman Forsch. Screenplay, Edeltraud Rabitzer, Forsch; camera (color), Jürgen Jürges; music, Lutz Köhler; sound, Gunter Kortwich. Reviewed at the Toronto Festival of Festivals, Sept. 15, 1987. Running time: **87 MINS.**
Norbert Kalka . . . . .Zacharias Preen
Gabriele Matern . . . . .Barbara Rudnik
Hilde Kalka . . . . .Karin Baal
Also with: Heinz Hönig, Christoph M. Ohrt, Bernd Vollbrecht, Gerhard Theisen, Shaun Lawton.

Toronto — Gerd Roman Forsch's first feature is a listless look at the familiar theme of individual anomie in the conformist sterility of contemporary West German society. This derivative piece of new wave filmmaking is unlikely to be picked up for distribution in the U.S., but could make the rounds of various festivals that feed on international low-budget fare.

Norbert (Zacharias Preen) has a fondness for movies and the 1950s, but little else. He works at a mind-numbing job as a bank trainee and lives with his mother, a remote woman whom he resents for breaking off with the father he never knew. Norbert has baby-faced pop idol looks, but he's deeply alienated from "the same old crowd" of friends who do nothing much but hang out at a roller rink. Norbert spends most of his free time wandering alone through the nearly deserted streets, parks and train stations of an anonymous, frozen-over city (Berlin). As is usually the case with this type of protagonist, he's searching for something, but knows not for what.

Norbert's longing for a father figure attracts him to an accused murderer and a cab driver, men in their late thirties, who look as if they could possibly have sired him. One day he meets a mysterious and beautiful young woman who's slightly older then him. She's run away from something and is living in a hotel room which becomes the base for a love affair. Inevitably, this brief interlude of happiness in Norbert's life comes to an end, and his mind becomes unglued, with tragic consequences.

The elliptical dialog in which Norbert and Gabriele (Barbara Rudnik) communicate is intended to underscore the characters' common emotional isolation, but estranges the viewer's interest in the process. Cute little references by the hero to the contemptible similarity between his life situation and the clichés of the movies are as barren as the film's shadowy, urban winter landscapes. —*Rich.*

Seven Women, Seven Sins
(W. GERMAN-FRENCH-U.S.-AUSTRIAN-BELGIAN-COLOR)

A ZDF Television production. Produced by Brigitte Kramer, Maya Constantine, Maxi Cohen. Directed by Helke Sander, Bette Gordon, Maxi Cohen, Chantal Akerman, Valie Export, Laurence Gavronn and Ulrike Ottinger. Screenplay by directors and Doerte Haak; camera (color), Nurif Aviv, Frank Prinzi, Luc Benhamou, Joel Gold, Edgar Osterberger, Ottinger, Martin Schäfer; editors, Elizabeth Kling, Bettina Baehler, Ewa Fichtel, Monique Prim. Reviewed at Bloor Cinema, Toronto, Sept. 4, 1987. (At Toronto Festival of Festivals.) Running time: **120 MINS.**

With: Evelyne Didi, Gariela Herz, Delphine Seyrig, Kate Valk, Roberta Wallach, Susanne Widl, Irm Hermann.

Toronto — "Seven Women, Seven Sins" is another rendering on the theme of the Seven Deadly Sins, pride, lust, envy, sloth, greed, anger and gluttony. Seven femme directors from five countries each tackle a sin in an overlong omnibus effort that's certain not to fill seats, even in most demanding situations. Low-budget pic, apparently shot on video, is amateurish, uneven and relatively incomprehensible despite subtitles.

Ulrike Ottinger's statement on "pride" is made repeatedly, as old news footage of Chairman Mao, Juan Peron, Idi Amin and an assortment of other totalitarian types is intercut with lengthy and most bizarre processions of pigs and freaks.

Chantal Akerman's "sloth" has the director turning the camera on her lazy self unable to get out of bed to make her vignette. Eve's victimization of Adam (or might be the other way), first in the Garden of Eden and then on the German autobahn, is related in Helke Sander's "gluttony."

Aside from Maxi Cohen's mini docu on "anger," pic leaves the overall impression that the producers unintentionally articulate the 8th Deadly Sin — self indulgence, surely the deadliest of them all.
—*Zerb.*

Johnny Monroe
(FRENCH-COLOR)

A Benjamin Simon/ATC 3000/FR3 Cinema 16 production. Produced by Benjamin Simon, Jacques Portet. Directed by Renaud Saint-Pierre. Screenplay, Louis Bellanti, Virginie Kirsch; camera (color), Serge Marcheux; editor, Alain Caron; music, Jean Musy. Reviewed at Toronto Festival of Festivals (Contemporary World Cinema), Sept. 11, 1987. Running time: **80 MINS.**
Johnny Monroe . . . . .Jean-Luc Orofino
Ben . . . . .Philippe Caroit
Also with: Jean-Pierre Aumont, Marisa Pavan, Gerard Guillaumat, Patrick Depeyrat, Jacqueline Danno, Clementine Celarié, Brigitte Lahaie.

Toronto — An oddball buddy picture, "Johnny Monroe" marks the feature debut from tv docu helmer Renaud Saint-Pierre. There's a nervous rhythm to this occasionally wry and touching effort, but save for Jean-Luc Orofino's confident performance, pic is a tough sell commercially, except as a curiosity item.

Johnny Monroe, as he calls himself, is a 26-year-old jean-clad midget, who constantly takes a beating for the criminal ring he's hooked up with. One night a handsome mute boy, Ben, who's been roaming the streets trying to make contact with a pretty girl he saw on the bus, saves Johnny from a shakedown by two guys who accuse him of blowing their dough.

The two become fast friends. Johnny takes Ben, who lost his voice in a childhood harpoon accident, on a tour of the underworld, of sorts — he gets him his first prostitute, steals a book from an antiques shop with him, and dines in an elegant restaurant.

Johnny has created a rich fantasy world for himself, as he's obsessed with Marilyn Monroe and tells Ben that his wife is a movie star.

Their camaraderie develops from their mutual outcast position, but Johnny has a deep joie de vivre. As played by the wonderful Orofino, he's full of feistiness, buoyant hopes, and a sharp sense of humor. He's processed the pain of being one of society's fringe members as well. Before he leaves on his travels he tells Ben (Philippe Caroit as a pretty boy without much to do) to keep telling himself he's different.

Saint-Pierre films at night, outside Paris, and his camerawork has a raw vitality. Script has a naive adventurous nature, but the pic takes a violent turn before it becomes a touch too sentimental. —*Devo.*

Someone To Watch Over Me
(COLOR)

Stylish thriller overcomes script implausibilities.

A Columbia Pictures release of a Thierry de Ganay production. Produced by De Ganay, Harold Schneider. Executive producer and directed by Ridley Scott. Screenplay, Howard Franklin; camera (Deluxe color), Steven Poster; editor, Claire Simpson; music, Michael Kamen; sound (Dolby), Gene Cantamessa; production design, Jim Bissell; set decoration, Linda de Scenna; assistant director, Joseph P. Reidy; production manager, Max Stein, N.Y. — Bill Gerrity; costume design, Colleen Atwood; stunt coordinators, Glenn Wilder, Ronnie Rondell; associate producer, Mimi Polk; casting, Joy Todd. Reviewed at Columbia 5th Avenue screening room, N.Y., Sept. 23, 1987. (MPAA Rating: R.) Running time: **106 MINS.**

Mike Keegan	Tom Berenger
Claire Gregory	Mimi Rogers
Ellie Keegan	Lorraine Bracco
Lt. Garber	Jerry Orbach
Neil Steinhart	John Rubinstein
Joey Venza	Andreas Katsulas
T.J.	Tony DiBenedetto
Koontz	James Moriarty
Win Hockings	Mark Moses
Scotty	Daniel Hugh Kelly
Tommy	Harley Cross

"Someone To Watch Over Me" is a stylish and romantic police thriller which manages, through the sleek direction of Ridley Scott and persuasive ensemble performances, to triumph over several hard-to-swallow plot developments. Benefitting from topliner Tom Berenger's post-"Platoon" prominence, pic stands to do well at the fall box-office in a year totally dominated by police and crime films.

Berenger portrays Mike Keegan, a happily married N.Y. cop from the Bronx who has just been promoted to detective and finds himself assigned on the night shift to protect socialite Claire Gregory (Mimi Rogers), witness to a brutal murder. The heinous killer, Joey Venza, played with economical nuance and menace by Andreas Katsulas, tracks Gregory down at the Guggenheim Museum and terrorizes her in the ladies' room while Keegan is distracted. Though he subsequently chases Venza down and effects the collar, failure to read the goon his rights results in Venza back on the street and Gregory marked for death.

Though wife Lorraine Bracco and son Harley Cross are loveable and supportive, plot dictates that Berenger fall in love and bed down with the at first chilly Rogers. As with the current hit "Fatal Attraction," this infidelity is a key story element but a hurdle for the audience to believe. Even more difficult to swallow is a highly contrived climax: after his wife finds out about the affair and Berenger moves out, the killer kidnaps his wife and child, leading Berenger to bring Rogers to the scene in a hostage exchange ruse. Though suspenseful and well-staged, the violation of police procedure is incredible and unconvincing.

Papering over these holes in Howard Franklin's screenplay, director Scott consistently commands attention with his trademark visual style, which frequently turns the otherwise gritty, New York thriller into something out of his sci-fi epic "Blade Runner" (opening aerial shot of Manhattan, '40s music, smoked sets and backlit, fogged street scenes often evoke the prior film). Tech credits are all topnotch, though overuse of the title standard, whether warbled by Sting, Roberta Flack or played as an instrumental, proves counterproductive.

Berenger carries the film handily, utterly convincing as the working class stiff out of his element accompanying Rogers through her elegant apartment or posh parties. Rogers is alluring as the romantic interest, recalling the sharpness and beauty of Laraine Day, while wife Bracco is fully sympathetic and easily has the viewer siding against the two leads during their hanky-panky segments. James Moriarty provides welcome comic relief as an uppity fellow cop while John Rubinstein is saddled with the thankless role of Rogers' creepy, rich boy friend.
—*Lor.*

Slave Girls From Beyond Infinity
(COLOR)

'Most Dangerous Game' in Outer Space.

An Urban Classics release of a Titan production. Produced and directed by Ken Dixon. Coproduced by John Eng, Mark Wolf. Screenplay, Dixon; camera (Foto-Kem color), Ken Wiatrak, Thomas Callaway; editor, Bruce Stubblefield, James A. Stewart; music, Carl Dante; music supervision, Jonathan Scott Bogner; sound, Rick Fine, Paul Bacca; art direction, Escott Norton; assistant director-production manager, Don Daniels, Devorah Hardberger; special effects supervisor, Wolf; special visual effects, Eng; androids & Phantazoid warrior by John Buechler; zombie & mutant by Joe Reader; special effects makeup, David Cohen; stunt coordinators, Mike Cooper, Greg Cooper; second unit camera, Bryan Cooke; postproduction coordinator, Juliet Avola. Reviewed at 42d St. Liberty theater, N.Y., Sept. 26, 1987. (MPAA Rating: R.) Running time: **72 MINS.**

Daria	Elizabeth Cayton
Tisa	Cindy Beal
Shela	Brinke Stevens
Zed	Don Scribner
Rik	Carl Horner
Vak	Kirk Graves
Krel	Randolph Roehbling

"Slave Girls From Beyond Infinity" is definitely a B-picture, low in budget, heavy in atmosphere and easily digested as dumb escapism. Mainly a skin show spotlighting three pretty women in distress, pic has opened in tandem with another new feature, "Creepozoids," reviving the firstrun doublebill package hardly used since the mid-1970s.

Statuesque blonds Elizabeth Cayton and Cindy Beal topline as beautiful prisoners who escape in a space shuttle from their chains and crashland on a verdant planet. Don

Scribner is the evil Zed, given to hunting down humans (or humanoids) and having his two androids Vak and Krel mount the victims' heads on his trophy wall.

The two blonds are joined by sexy-voiced brunet Brinke Stevens, another crash survivor, in the ultimate hunt, and manage to outwit Zed with the aid of some silly Rambo-styled weaponry (Zed uses a laser beam crossbow). Pic is mainly concerned with watching the three heroines topless or in an array of skimpy lingerie, traipsing through the jungle.

Various monsters plus the androids are okay, but filmmaker Ken Dixon (who previously helmed the video compilation "Famous T&A") delivers utterly corny dialog, indifferently recited by the cast. There's a nice set provided for Zed's trophies, a too-often repeated matte shot to suggest scale and other visual niceties, but pic is strictly aimed at voyeurs, not fantasy fans.—*Lor.*

Heat And Sunlight
(U.S.-B&W)

A Snowball Prods./New Front Alliance Films production. Produced by Steve Burns, Hildy Burns. Written and directed by Rob Nilsson. Camera (video, b&w), Tomas Tucker; editor, Henk van Eaghen; music, David Byrne, Brian Eno, from "My Life In The Bush Of Ghosts;" production design, Hildy Burns, Steve Burns; sound, Dan Gleich. Reviewed at the Toronto Festival of Festivals, Sept. 17, 1987. Running time: **92 MINS.**

Mel	Rob Nilsson
Carmen	Consuelo Faust
Mitch	Don Bajema
Also with: Raven de la Croix.	

Toronto — Every once in a while a little film comes along that breaks new ground. "Heat And Sunlight" is that kind of effort.

Shot for $90,000 on ½" Beta video in a mere 60 hours, "Heat And Sunlight" is a manic look at modern relationships that marries the feel of a John Cassavetes film with the immediacy of the six o'clock news. There's even a bit of Woody Allen.

Writer-director Rob Nilsson calls his style "direct action cinema," first developed with his "Signal 7." It's a technique that makes a rather mundane story come to life.

The action takes place over a 24-hour period. A fortyish photographer (Nilsson), obsessed with a beautiful dancer named Carmen (Faust) and the starving Biafrans he encountered in Nigeria 17 years earlier, is celebrating his birthday alone. He's depressed. He's hurt. He thinks nobody loves him.

It doesn't sound like much and, in fact, it really isn't but it still makes for an entertaining 92 minutes.

Nilsson's script, only 30 pages long, was just a starting point for the cast. All the dialog was improvised during the shoot. The results are sometimes silly but, more often than not, they're screamingly funny. A lovemaking scene is electrifying. A jealous tantrum by the protagonist is hysterical. The charactrs feel real. They have depth — right down to the stand-up comic whose shtick is not being funny at all ("She was so fat she was obese").

The lighting, while rather flat and uninteresting, allowed the camera to move freely. The unfettered lens whips around 360° to where the action is. Editing, done on a ¼-inch U-matic, adds excitement to the story. Transferred from tape to 35m, the images are kind of grainy but somehow seem like they're pictures from the front lines of a far-off war. In this case, the simple form contributes significantly to the content.
— Zerb.

Creepozoids
(COLOR)

Dreary monster thriller.

An Urban Classics release of a Titan production. Produced by David DeCoteau, John Schouweiler. Directed by DeCoteau. Screenplay, Burford Hauser, DeCoteau; camera (Foto-Kem color), Thomas Callaway; editor, Miriam L. Preissel; music, Guy Moon; music supervision, Jonathan Scott Bogner; sound, Marty Kasparia; production design, Royce Mathew; production manager, Ellen Cabot; assistant director, Nigel Parker; special makeup & creature effects, Next Generation Effects, Thom Floutz, Peter Carsillo; special mechanical effects, John Criswell; stunt coordinator, John Stewart; second unit director, Callaway; postproduction supervisor, Juliet Avola; casting, Stan Shaffer. Reviewed at 42d St. Liberty theater, N.Y., Sept. 26, 1987. (MPAA Rating: R.) Running time: 71 MINS.
Bianca . . . . Linnea Quigley
Butch . . . . Ken Abraham
Jesse . . . . Michael Aranda
Jake . . . . Richard Hawkins
Kate . . . . Kim McKamy
Scientist . . . . Joi Wilson

"Creepozoids" is a lame attempt at a monster thriller, suffering from meager inspiration, budget and execution. Glum cheapie, which revives the old complaint that "it looks like it was filmed in a coalpit," has little to offer to fantasy aficionados.

Set in 1998, six years after a nuclear holocaust, slim plotline concerns five deserters from the army who hole up in an empty scientific installation to hide out from the acid rain outdoors. A monster lurks inside (it looks like the creature from "Alien" only with tusks) and attacks them one by one, while large rat hand puppets also grab at the good guys.

With exceedingly dim lighting (to hide the poor creature effects from view), pic unfolds at a snail's pace with no personality provided for the cast. Linnea Quigley fills her t-shirt well and takes a nude shower with her boyfriend but that's about it in the way of entertainment. Idiotic, distended finale has a monster baby (an imitation of Rick Baker's "It's Alive" creations) crawling out of the monster's body to do battle with the last surviving human before a corny freezeframe finish.—Lor.

Hoxsey: The Quack Who Cured Cancer
(DOCU-COLOR/B&W-16m)

A film by Realidad Prods., Santa Fe, New Mexico. Produced by Ken Ausubel, Catherine Salveston. Written and directed by Ausubel; additional direction by Salveston. Camera (color, 16m), Alton Walpole; editor, Ernest T. Shinagawa; music, Peter Rowan, Jeff Nelson; narrator, Max Gail. Produced with funding from the National Endowment for The Arts, New Mexico Arts Division and other sources. Reviewed at American Museum of Natural History, N.Y., Sept. 3, 1987. (In Margaret Mead Film Festival.) Running time: 100 MINS.

The subject of this documentary, Harry M. Hoxsey, was not a medical doctor with formal education and a fancy certificate. An ex-coal miner, Hoxsey had inherited a family herbal formula for curing, or for alleviating, cancer.

By 1924, Hoxsey had founded his first clinic. For the next third of a century, Hoxsey warred with organized medicine, which branded him a charlatan, the worst cancer quack in the country. Hoxsey supporters claim he was arrested more times than any other man in medical history, an outrageous "quackdown" that denied Hoxsey's alternative medicine to the American public.

By the 1950s, Hoxsey clinics were busy in 17 states. Several federal courts had upheld the value of Hoxsey's tonic, despite prolonged opposition by the American Medical Assn. and the Food and Drug Administration.

Today, the Hoxsey treatment, non-surgical and non-radiation, has retreated south of the border. The clinic in Tijuana, Mexico, claims a cancer-cure rate of 80%, but medical officers still maintain the Hoxsey formula is worthless.

This film is in form a reconstruction using old b&w stock footage, stills, posters and other surviving artifacts, combined with recent color interviews of Hoxsey partisans and others, including former patients who proffer fervent testimonials.

The premise of the film, its accusation, is that institutional medicine suppresses unorthodox cancer cures, such as Hoxsey's, fearing a threat to their income and their traditional authority. Thus cancer has become enmeshed in politics and power struggles, and the public pays the price. Final images of the film show Americans in the Hoxsey bus being shuttled through the U.S. border station at Tijuana, en route to the Hoxsey clinic. The Hoxsey war with establishment medicine continues.
—Hitch.

Thou Shalt Not Kill...Except
(COLOR)

Charles Manson meets Rambo.

A Filmworld Distributors release of an Action Pictures production. Executive producers, Shirley Becker, Arnold Becker. Produced by Scott Spiegel. Directed by Josh Becker. Stars Brian Schulz, Sam Raimi. Screenplay, Josh Becker, Scott Spiegel, from story by Josh Becker, Sheldon Lettich, Bruce Campbell; music, Joseph Lo Duca. Reviewed at Americana Theater, Southfield, Mich., Sept. 12, 1987. (No MPAA Rating.) Running time: 94 MINS.
Stryker . . . . Brian Schulz
Miller . . . . John Manfredi
Jackson . . . . Robert Rickman
Tyler . . . . Tim Quill
Cult leader . . . . Sam Raimi
Sally . . . . Cheryl Hanson
Otis . . . . Perry Mallette
Also with: Rick Hudson (kennel owner), Connie Craig (cult girl 1), Ivih Fraser (cult girl 2), Terry Brumfield (cult girl 3), Ted Raimi (Rubber Mask), Al Johnson (huge biker 1), Kirk Haas (Leather Vest), Glen Barr (Archer), Gary O'Conner (Green), Sayle Jackunas (Eddie Munster), Dave Gerney (Van Crazy), Scott Mitchell (Philo Crazy).

Detroit — From the same bunch who produced "Evil Dead" and "Evil Dead II" comes "Thou Shalt Not Kill ... Except," an ambitious, albeit low budget, slice and dice number that asks the question: what would happen if Charles Manson met Rambo?

Despite its youthful sense of humor and good intentions to make a slasher film that's a cut above the norm, "Thou ..." will likely find limited appeal on the theatrical circuit, itself chopped up by the plethora of mainstream movies coming out this fall.

Its liberal use of Kayro syrup blood, inventive direction and rousing finale could warrant the film a zestful homevideo life and will appeal not only to slasher devotees but also to those looking for a fun party tape.

The film opens in Vietnam (not altogether successfully recreated in and around Detroit) in 1969, where Sgt. Jack Stryker and his Marine comrades Jackson, Tyler and Miller are trapped outside a small village controlled by the Viet Cong.

Because of his bullheaded C.O., Stryker is wounded and sent home, where he shyly begins where he left off with his old girlfriend, Sally.

They are about to meet for a date when Sally is suddenly kidnapped by a Charles Manson-like band that is terrorizing the community.

Meanwhile, Stryker's old army buddies blow into town, and after a night of heavy carousing, decide to look up their old buddy.

More drinking ensues, but by next morning, they realize Stryker's dog, Whiskey, is gone. When they find the hound skinned and strung up, they begin to think there's trouble ahead. Soon realizing Sally has been kidnapped, this Dirty Foursome decides to "go and clean them up!"

The ending is predictable, and no amount of mayhem is enough to stop our boys. (One of Stryker's buddies pulls a 6-inch knife from his stomach, stomps his adversary, rubs some grass over the wound and is ready for more fun.)

Becker has infected this Kayro syrup-drenched slice-and-dicer with enough humor and high energy direction to carry the audience through to the final drive into the sunset. —Advo.

Nightstick
(COLOR)

Routine police actioner.

A Production Distribution Co. release of a Sandy Howard presentation. Produced by Martin Walters. Directed by Joseph L. Scanlan. Screenplay, James J. Docherty; camera (color), Robert Fresco; editor, Richard Wells, Daniel Radford, music, Robert O. Ragland; art direction, Reuben Freed; set decoration, Tony Duggan-Smith; costume design, Eva Gord; special effects, Carere Special Effects; associate producer, Risa Gertner; assistant director, Ken Girotti; casting, Paul Bengston, David Cohn, Ann Tait. Reviewed at Showcase Allston Cinemas, Boston, Sept. 12, 1987. (MPAA Rating: R.) Running time: 92 MINS.
Jack Calhoun . . . . Bruce Fairbairn
Robin Malone . . . . Kerrie Keane
Ray Melton . . . . Robert Vaughn
Adam Beardsley . . . . John Vernon
Evans . . . . Leslie Nielsen
Roger Bantam . . . . Walker Boone
Jerry Bantam . . . . Tony De Santis
Pat Bantam . . . . David Mucci

Boston — This Sandy Howard production, originally filmed as "Calhoun," is a strictly routine formula picture with lone wolf cop Jack Calhoun (Bruce Fairbairn) on the track of three supposed terrorists. They are threatening to blow up Manhattan unless banker Adam Beardsley (John Vernon) comes up with $5,000,000 in cash.

At the start the Bantam brothers (Walker Boone, Tony De Santis and David Mucci) have been knocking over chemical companies to get the component parts for nitroglycerin. Only pretending to be terrorists, they plan to get banker Beardsley to fork over a ransom to prevent his banks from being blown up.

Enter Calhoun, who's no Dirty Harry. According to formula we must meet the hero when he defuses a dangerous situation that otherwise has nothing to do with the story. Here a psycho with a shotgun is holding hostages in the hospital. Atypically, the psycho looks like a businessman having a nervous breakdown and Calhoun, after disarming him, promises the man that he will receive proper treatment. Chuck Norris or Charles Bronson, of course, would have blown him away.

Calhoun's two superiors, Melton (Robert Vaughn) and Evans (Leslie Nielsen), disagree as to Calhoun's value to the police department. Evans decides to put Calhoun on the case, and Melton objects. We never find out why, and ultimately it proves to be as irrelevant to the story as the psycho.

The proceedings are strictly by the numbers. When Calhoun's girlfriend Robin (Kerrie Keane) inexplicably becomes involved as a hostage — so that the matter is now personal — he meets the bad guys in a climatic shootout in (where else?) a deserted warehouse.

Director Joseph L. Scanlan fails to make much of the material, frequently defusing the suspense by tipping us off to what will happen next. Rated R for the violence, it is a soft R, with most of the action taking place off camera or in long shot. In one scene, Robin is kidnaped off the street in front of the hospital where she works. It happens behind the Bantams' truck so that the audience only *hears* the scuffle.

While veteran actors Vaughn, Nielsen and Vernon do what is expected of them, leads Fairbairn and Keane show real possibilities given a better script and direction. Fairbairn, who must carry the movie, attempts to inject some life into the proceedings, and shows a welcome sense of humor.

Lensed in Ontario, the film has been padded out with New York location footage in an attempt to give it some atmosphere. —*Kimm.*

```
******************************************
*                                        *
* Boston Fest Reviews                    *
*                                        *
******************************************
```

Rampage
(COLOR)

Forceful Friedkin drama about the insanity plea.

A De Laurentiis Entertainment Group presentation. Produced by David Salven. Directed by William Friedkin. Screenplay, Friedkin, based on the novel by William P. Wood; camera (Technicolor), Robert D. Yeoman; editor, Jere Huggins; music, Ennio Morricone; production design, Buddy Cone; art direction, Carol Clements; set decoration, Nancy Nye; sound (Dolby), David MacMillan; casting, Rick Montgomery; assistant directors, Michael Daves, Regina Gordon. Reviewed at USA Cinemas Copley Place, Sept. 14, 1987. (In the Boston Film Festival.) (MPAA Rating: R.) Running time: **97 MINS.**
Anthony Fraser . . . . Michael Biehn
Charles Reece . . . . Alex McArthur
Albert Morse . . . . Nicholas Campbell
Kate Fraser . . . . Deborah Van Valkenburgh
Dr. Keddie . . . . John Harkins
Mel Sanderson . . . . Art Lafleur
Judge McKinsey . . . . Billy Greenbush
Gene Tippetts . . . . Royce D. Applegate
Naomi Reece . . . . Grace Zabriskie
   Also with: Roy London, Donald Hotton, Andy Romano.

Boston. — Anthony Fraser (Michael Biehn) is the assistant district attorney in charge of the major crimes division and is handed a grisly murder case by his boss with orders to go for the death penalty. The case involves a psychopath named Charles Reece (Alex McArthur) who has killed five people, mutilating four of them and drinking their blood. Fraser doesn't want the case because he's against the death penalty.

In other hands this would turn into some sort of vigilante film in which the psycho escapes and menaces the hero and his family. Writer-director William Friedkin instead elects to explore the frustration of the legal system's insanity defense.

Mental illness is divorced from the legal definition of insanity, where the defendant's ability to distinguish right from wrong determines whether he's fit to stand trial. The problem is that, from the layman's viewpoint, anyone who would commit a crime like Reece's must be insane, leading a jury to consider him "not guilty by reason of insanity."

Friedkin refuses to present an easy out to the dilemma. Even Dr. Keddie (John Harkins) who, as the defense's chief psychiatrist, is presented as the chief perpetrator of obfuscating psychobabble, is given his moment to defend his position. Likewise Reece's public defender (Nicholas Campbell) is forceful without being painted as a bleeding heart eager to send Reece back to the streets.

"Rampage" follows Reece's case from the commission of the gruesome crimes (handled with admirable restraint by Friedkin) to the verdict by the jury and its aftermath. To underscore the general confusion over the insanity defense, we even get a glimpse of the jury struggling to understand what it means before they render their verdict. An escape sequence seems tacked on to provide some action in the latter half of the film, and ultimately proves irrelevant.

In contrast to the typical courtroom melodrama which emphasizes the reactions from the spectators, the court scenes feature backgrounds largely in shadow. Although a few odd shots call attention to themselves (including Reece's fantasy of drenching himself in blood) cinematographer Robert D. Yeoman's tone overall is somber and subdued, striving for realism as Friedkin depicts the system's struggle to deal with an aberration like Reece.

The cast is top-notch all around with Biehn (once cast as a crazed killer in "The Fan") suggesting the anguish beneath the cool exterior of his prosecutor. Deborah Van Valkenburgh brings some depth to the supporting role of Biehn's wife. We learn that the death of their daughter (and Biehn's guilt about it) have strained their marriage to the breaking point. Her objection to his arguing a death penalty case now threatens to push it over the brink.

As Reece, McArthur appears dangerous and unstable, but remains opaque, so we — like the lawyers and the doctors — can never be completely sure if he knew what he was doing when he committed the murders. Among the supporting cast, Royce D. Applegate is particularly notable as the husband and father of two of the victims, who must somehow pick up the pieces of his life after the tragedy.

"Rampage" is a deadly serious inquiry into how our legal system dles those who commit truly heinous crimes. Currently scheduled for a November release, it is ideally suited for the fall season's tradition of serious movies for adult audiences.—*Kimm.*

Patti Rocks
(COLOR)

Frank, funny battle of the sexes needs special handling.

A Film Dallas Pictures release. Produced by Gwen Field, Gregory M. Cummins. Executive producer, Sam Grogg. Directed by David Burton Morris. Screenplay & story by Morris, Chris Mulkey, John Jenkins, Karen Landry, based on characters created by Victoria Wozniak in the film "Loose Ends;" camera (Foto-Kem color), Cummins; editor, Cummins; music, Doug Maynard; art direction, Charlotte Whitaker; sound, Matthew Quast; associate producer, Brian John Dilorenzo; assistant director, Kirby Dick; casting, Laurie Grossman. Reviewed at the New World Pictures screening room, L.A., Sept. 10, 1987. (In Boston Film Festival.) (No MPAA Rating.) Running time: **87 MINS.**
Billy . . . . Chris Mulkey
Eddie . . . . John Jenkins
Patti . . . . Karen Landry

Hollywood — An often bitingly humorous expose of the male ego accomplished dramatically in one night, "Patti Rocks" is a quintessential American independent production, and a very good one. Scabrously sexual dialog will no doubt put off some viewers (producers claim they received, then rejected, an X rating from the MPAA on the basis of the obscenities' "cumulative impact"), but this raw look at the ways in which the sexes both do and do not understand one another should create enough of an impression with sophisticated audiences to gain a following. Pic had its world premiere at the Boston Film Festival.

Film opens with the phrase "Twelve years later...," a cute reference to David Burton Morris' first feature, "Loose Ends," which involved the same leading characters but is in no way mandatory viewing for appreciating the follow-up.

"Patti Rocks" picks up Billy (Chris Mulkey), a working stiff who seems to be refusing to grow up even though he's into his thirties with a wife and two kids. During the cold Christmas season in Minnesota, Billy shanghais his old buddy Eddie (John Jenkins), a garage foreman, to drive with him to a distant town to help him tell a woman he's "knocked up" that he's hitched and that she ought to have an abortion.

Eddie is understandably unenthusiastic about this errand, but ends up sitting in the passenger seat for hours as Billy delivers a torrential monolog of ever-escalating sexual boasts and fantasies, which consists of what he claims he has done, will do or would do if he could, to women. Long nocturnal sequence, which is hilariously punctuated by an episode in which a lady demands that Billy put up or shut up, probably represents women's worst nightmares of how men talk about them, and highly concentrated dose of vulgarity will certainly disturb those with delicate sensibilities.

The tone changes dramatically, however, once the boys reach the home of Patti Rocks. Too chickenhearted to break the news to her himself, Billy sends Eddie into her bedroom to do the job, and that's when the twists are added. Resolution does not prove that surprising, but is quite satisfactory and believable on human terms.

Developed and written by Morris in conjunction with the three principal actors, film simultaneously takes on greater gravity and humor as it progresses. From the brittle cold of the men's conversation in the car, the climate instantly becomes warmer and more intimate the moment they enter the warmth of Patti's apartment, so that the braggadocio of the man-to-man talk stands in stark contrast to the emotional directness of the male-female encounters.

Quite reserved about his own sentiments with Billy, the taciturn Eddie opens up with Patti, and the latter's ability to cope with the basic things of life, despite her obvious difficulties, puts the men in their place and even to shame.

Made on a frugal $350,000 budget, film is totally dialog and performance oriented, and stands up well on both counts. Unknown thesps are not charismatic, but are vividly believable as regular folk who are both evasive and brutally frank about sex and life.

Limitations of scale and production will restrict this to the domestic specialized circuit, but pic deserves as strong a push as Film Dallas can give it. Commercial openings, after fest exposure, will come after the first of the year.

—*Cart.*

Eat The Rich
(BRITISH-COLOR)

A New Line Cinema release of a Comic Strip film in association with British Screen, Film Four Intl., Recorded Releasing and Smart Egg Pictures. Executive producer, Michael White. Produced by Tim Van Rellim. Directed by Peter Richardson. Screenplay, Pete Richens, Richardson; associate director, Richens; camera (color), Witold Stok; editor, Chris Ridsdale; music, Motorhead; sound, John Hayes; costumes, Frances Haggett;

makeup, Gordon Kay; assistant directors, Glynn Purcell, Sean Dromgoole, Marwan Al-Khafaji. Reviewed at the Boston Film Festival, Sept. 20, 1987. (No MPAA Rating.) Running time: **88 MINS.**

Alex	Lanah Pellay
Nosher	Nosher Powell
Fiona	Fiona Richmond
Commander Fortune	Ronald Allen
Sandra	Sandra Dorne
Ron	Ron Tarr
Jimmy	Jimmy Fagg
Spider	Lemmy

Also with: Robbie Coltrane, Angie Bowie, Linda McCartney, Paul McCartney, Rik Mayall, Peter Richardson, Koo Stark, Ade Edmonson, Nigel Planer, Dawn French, Jennifer Saunders, Bill Wyman, Miranda Richardson.

Boston — With the right handling "Eat The Rich" has all the makings of a cult success like "Repo Man" or "Eating Raoul." Set in modern Britain, it charts the course of a gang of revolutionaries, headed by the sexually ambiguous Alex (Lanah Pellay), in their fight against Nosher, the "Fascist cockney" who serves as Home Secretary (stuntman Nosher Powell).

Pic tips us that comedy will be broad and dark right from the opening scene set in a restaurant for the obnoxiously rich called "Bastards." There the wealthy can dine on endangered species and make their business deals. Alex, employed there as a waiter, soon finds himself out of a job and with dim prospects.

Attempting to go on the dole, he finds welfare bureaucrats who relax and sip cocktails while they torment their poverty stricken-applicants. Alex can take no more and joins forces with Ron (Ron Tarr), who has also come looking for a government handout. After Alex shoots up the place, they take to the hills. "Isn't it funny," he muses, "how a few seconds with a gun can change your life?"

This doesn't set well with Nosher, a cabinet officer who conducts public policy with his bare knuckles. Told that terrorists are holding hostages at the Israeli embassy, he breaks in, beats up both the terrorists and the ambassador, and declares the Middle East crisis resolved. Meanwhile his wife (Sandra Dorne) is outside taking snapshots of her husband in action.

Alex and Ron subsequently meet up with two more misfits (Jimmy Fagg, Fiona Richmond). Aided by Commander Fortune (Ronald Allen), a British intelligence officer actually in the pay of the Russians, Alex leads them on a raid on "Bastards." They rename the place "Eat The Rich," a nitery that intends, literally, to serve its wealthy clientele.

The revolutionaries are not always clear what they are fighting for, and a supply raid includes picking up a board game to help while away the time between atrocities. Alex's call to arms ("We're starting a people's uprising — do you fancy joining us?") is hardly one to inspire the masses.

The real scene stealer here is Nosher, whether he is attending a diplomatic dinner carrying a six pack of beer, or making a television address where he tells the poor that they're "lazy bastards." He wears his boorishness as a badge of pride, and seems to know how to twist every potentially embarrassing situation to his advantage, even after it appears that he's dined on his prime minister.

Peter Richardson, helming his second feature after "The Supergrass," keeps the bizarre and often hilarious proceedings moving along at a steady clip. There are brief cameos along the way by Paul McCartney, Robbie Coltrane and many others, most of which will be lost on American audiences. (Many are from the British comedy team, the Comic Strip, of whom director Richardson is one of the founding members.) The brisk pace works to the film's advantage.

This is hardly the sort of film likely to obtain a royal command performance, but the young and cynical on both sides of the Atlantic should find it a hoot.—*Kimm.*

The Secret Policeman's Third Ball
(BRITISH-COLOR)

A Virgin Films release of an Elephant House production for Amnesty Intl. Produced by Neville Bolt, Tony Hollingsworth. Executive producers, Pat Duffy, John Gau. Production executives for Virgin Vision Mike Watts, Angus Margerison. Directed by Jen O'Neill. Camera (color), Stephen Foster; editor, John Hackney; music coordinator, Paul Gambaccini; theme written and performed, Bill Wyman, Terry Taylor; comedy stage director, Paul Jackson; production manager, Rebecca Perkins; art direction, Dennis de Groot. Reviewed at Rank Preview theater, Sept. 14, 1989. Running time: **92 MINS.**

The secret policeman's voice by Bob Hoskins. Also with: Joan Armatrading, Jackson Browne, Paul Brady, Kate Bush, David Gilmour and Nick Mason, John Cleese, Robbie Coltrane, Phil Cool, Duran Duran, Stephen Fry and Hugh Laurie, Ben Elton, Peter Gabriel, Youssou N'Dour, Bob Geldof, Lenny Henry, Nik Kershaw, Mark Knopfler and Chet Atkins, Emo Philips, Lou Reed, Spitting Image, Ruby Wax.

London — Despite its title "The Secret Policeman's Third Ball" is in fact the fifth in a series of Amnesty Intl. fundraising revues though only the third to be filmed for theatrical release.

Though there is some input of Yank talent — musicians Lou Reed and Jackson Browne, and comedian Emo Philips — the show (filmed over four nights at the London Palladium) was mainly British in humor and style. Acts are linked by commentary by Yank comedienne (now U.K.-based) Ruby Wax. Box office is likely to be healthy in Britain, and pic is amusing enough for specialized dates abroad.

The fundraising series began in 1976 when U.K. comic John Cleese rounded up a few friends for "A Poke In The Eye (With A Sharp Stick)". Following year's "The Mermaid Prolics" was directed by Terry Jones. In 1979 there was "The Secret Policeman's Ball," with "The Secret Policeman's Other Ball" staged in '81, the former a tv, record, and video release, the latter released theatrically along with video and disk (two were combined for U.S. release).

The problem with a 92-minute truncated version of a stage show is that one is constantly conscious that bits of the action are missing. Entire cast and production team, along with many technical suppliers, gave their services free for an obviously worthy cause.

Pic opens with an animated segment of the secret policeman with voiceover by Bob Hoskins, and from there moves to a series of comic, sketches and music turns.

The musical acts include duos by Lou Reed and Peter Gabriel, Kate Bush and Dave Gilmour, and Mark Knopfler and Chet Atkins, plus rock from Duran Duran and a superior solo by Joan Armatrading.

The comedy seemed to lack the polish and precision of the musical spots, though a standout was Lenny Henry's routine of a black U.S. blues singer. A strong line in sexual jokes was supplied by Ben Elton, while Cleese makes only a cameo appearance.—*Adam.*

Adjustment And Work
(U.S.-DOCU-COLOR-16m)

A Zipporah Films production. Produced and directed by Frederick Wiseman. Camera (color, 16m), John Davey; editor and sound, Wiseman. Reviewed at World Film Festival, Montreal, Aug. 25, 1987. Running time: **120 MINS.**

With: staff and students of the E.H. Gentry Technical Facility and staff and workers at the Alabama Industries For The Blind.

Montreal — One of four films in a 9-hour documentary on the life of the disabled, "Adjustment And Work" examines the training of blind people in employable skills. Frederick Wiseman's skillful use of cinema verité technique is demanding but succeeds in deeply involving the viewer with the documentary's subjects. Public and cable tv as well as special theatrical and nontheatrical venues seem to be natural outlets.

Wiseman's camera captures the human face of the disabled and the sympathetic but matter-of-fact attitude of the rehabilitation professionals who seek to help them. It's safe to say that blindness and the prospect of the helplessness it engenders is one of the handicaps most feared by sighted people, yet Wiseman's subjects, most of whom have been blind for a long time, show no self pity. Instead, the problems presented here are of the practical variety. "I want to get back to doing something productive, I'm tired of just dragging around," says a middle-aged man whose inherited poor vision has deteriorated to near-blindness.

He hopes to start a vending machine business. Another student, who has shown academic promise in college is anxious to become a sewing machine operator in order to feel useful. Another wants to become an auto mechanic, but is discouraged from doing so by a supervisor who criticizes his skills and poor attitude.

If life is not easy in general, it's doubly hard for the blind. Perhaps the most moving sequence shows a student learning how to approach intersections and cross the street. Wiseman's unblinking camera eye registers the painful uncertainty of the experience which transcends itself to become a noble struggle for basic self-sufficiency. —*Rich.*

The Climb
(CANADIAN-COLOR)

A Cinetel Films (U.S.) and Cineplex Odeon (in Canada) release of a Wacko production. Produced by Wendy Wacko. Written and directed by Don Shebib. Stars Bruce Greenwood, James Hurdle, Ken Pogue, Kenneth Walsh. Story editor, Claude Harz; editor,

Ron Wisman; camera (color) Richard Leiterman; music, Peter Jermyn; associate producer, Curtis Petersen. Reviewed at the Toronto Festival of Festivals, Sept. 19, 1987. (MPAA Rating: PG.) Running time: **90 MINS.**

Herman Buhl . . . . Bruce Greenwood
Dr. Karl Herrligkoffer . . . . . James Hurdle
Walter Frauenberger . . . . . . Kenneth Walsh
Peter Aschenbrenner . . . . Ken Pogue
Also with: Thomas Hauff, Guy Bannerman, Denis Forest, David Elliott, Jeremy Wilkin, Tom Butler.

Toronto — When a group of German mountain climbers took on the 26,000-ft. Nanga Parbat Himlayan peak in 1953 the endeavor was undoubtedly exciting, but Canadian writer/director Don Shebib has somehow transformed their story into a tedious exercise in genre filmmaking. Wooden acting, dialog and direction combined with the monotony of its snow-blown mise en scène will make it an uphill trek at the boxoffice for "The Climb," in regional release since May.

"Because it's there," went Sir Edmund Hilary's famous reply to a query on why he challenged Mt. Everest. While the British climber and his team were scaling the heights of glory a team of German and Austrian mountaineers were assaulting the reputedly more difficult Nanga Parbat. As the film tells it, the Germans were driven by an obsession similar to Hilary's but compounded by a post-War need for national redemption plus the fact that a previous expedition in 1932 had claimed the life of their obdurate leader's half-brother.

The leader, Dr. Herrligkoffer (James Hurdle) is pitted in a contest of wills against the team's star climber, Herman Buhl (Bruce Greenwood) who writes embarrassingly sappy letters to his faithful frau back home begging her forbearance with his "madness to climb mountains at whatever cost." The picture's predictable plot revolves around whether or not the team will subjugate this "mountain of destiny for the German people" and, in a horn-lock of stubborn Teutonic egos, whether they will do it the leader's way or the star climber's way.

Due credit must be given to the production team for making the film in difficult terrain and weather and for capturing the mountainous landscape's austere and terrifying beauty with impressive camera accents, stiff character conflicts and inevitable conclusion is as numbing as a walk without boots through a mile-high snowdrift.—*Rich.*

Blue Monkey
(COLOR)

Preposterous horror effort.

A Spectrafilm release. Produced by Martin Walters. Executive producer, Tom Fox. Directed by William Fruet. Screenplay, George Goldsmith; camera (Medallion color), Brenton Spencer; editor, Michael Fruet; music,

Patrick Coleman, Paul Novotny; production manager, John Ryan; art direction, Reuben Freed; set direction, Brendon Smith; costume design, Gina Kiellerman; sound, Urmas Rosin; stunt coordinator, Shane Cardwell; associate producer, Risa Gertner; casting, Paul Bengsten, David Cohn, Anne Tait. Reviewed at Hollywood Pacific theater, Sept. 30, 1987. (MPAA Rating: R.) Running time: **98 MINS.**
Detective Jim Bishop . . . . . Steve Railsback
Dr. Rachel Carson . . . . . Gwynyth Walsh
Dr. Judith Glass . . . . Susan Anspach
Roger Levering . . . . John Vernon
George Baker . . . . Joe Flaherty
Sandra Baker . . . . Robin Duke
Elliot Jacobs . . . . Don Lake
Fred Adams . . . . Sandy Webster
Marwella . . . . Helen Hughes
Dede Wilkens . . . . Joy Coghill

Hollywood — Keeping up with the story progressions of "Blue Monkey" is like trying to discern movement in the minute hand of a clock. This slow-slower-slowest moving horror film, originally titled "Green Monkey," plods along for the first hour and then outdoes itself by getting slower, thanks to a mind-numbing strobe-light effect achieved by a lamely conceived power outage in a hospital that has all the characters seeming to move in slow motion. Boxoffice action should be even slower.

In the lifetime of 98 minutes it takes for this pic to unspool, director William Fruet and scripter George Goldsmith conspire to make a lot that happens seem like very little.

Story would have some promise if it received a lethal reality injection, but instead: a man gets cut by a strange plant and then 20 minutes later spits out a foot-long caterpillar. Rather than immediately quarantining the e.r. and calling in the world's most renowned scientists, the staff at Mill Valley hospital — not wearing surgical gloves at the time — puts the larva-stage monster into a bedpan, leaves him in an examining room and lets a bunch of little kids sneak in so they can feed him steroids and allow him to grow into a slime monster of serious proportions.

Watching all this take place is Detective Jim Bishop (Steve Railsback) and the doctor he has his eye on, Rachel Carson (Gwynyth Walsh). The two characters spend most of the picture walking around the hospital, asking stupid questions and looking more and more worried, perhaps from slowly reaching the realization that they are in one awful horror film.

By the time this thing plays itself out, filmmakers have aped just about every film in the genre, with little kids doing brave things while in mortal danger, couples making out before getting eaten alive and even protagonist Railsback staring the beast in the eye (eyes?) and calling it a "son of a bitch."

Redeeming performances come from Susan Anspach as nononsense Dr. Judith Glass and Joy Coghill as Dede Wilkens, a harddrinking, elderly blind woman who wears Wayfarers and sneaks bour-

bon into her ailing friend Marwella (Helen Hughes). Coghill brings the film what intentional humor it possesses, but silly behavior by the authorities is good for a few laughs, if you're still awake for it.

Slime monster in question is no great shakes and sound is woefully inconsistent. Someone should have stepped in during a story meeting, rather than asking the audience to believe that a quiet, smalltown hospital, which resembles an early Norman Rockwell painting, has a world-class wing for laser research connected to it.—*Camb.*

No Dead Heroes
(COLOR)

Ordinary war pic.

A Cineventures presentation, in association with Maharaj-Miller Film. (International sales, Manson Intl.) Executive producer, Marciano Jao. Produced and directed by J.C. Miller. Screenplay, Miller, Arthur N. Gelfield; camera (color), Freddie C. Grant; editor, Edgar Vine; music, Marita M. Wellman; assistant director, Joel Freeman; special effects, Jun Rambell; stunt coordinator, Val Morris; casting, Paul Vance, Daniel Zale. Reviewed on Sony Video Software videassette, N.Y., Aug. 23, 1987. (No MPAA Rating.) Running time: **86 MINS.**
Ric Sanders . . . . Max Thayer
Harry Cotter . . . . John Dresden
Barbara Perez . . . . Toni Nero
Ivan . . . . Nick Nicholson
Frank Baylor . . . . Mike Monty
Gen. Craig . . . . Dave Anderson

Unveiled at last year's Mifed market, "No Dead Heroes" is a perfunctory war film released directly to homevideo stores Stateside.

Lengthy prolog takes place during the Vietnam War, with G.I.'s played by Max Thayer and John Dresden on a rescue mission, the enemy including a nasty Russian played by Nick Nicholson.

Ten years after, Dresden, who was captured, is now an agent programmed to kill by a special computer chip put into his head by Russian scientists. Nicholson is controlling him in a "Manchurian Candidate" plot. Thayer is summoned by the CIA to put Dresden out of commission and sent to Latin America where Dresden is trying to disrupt the Pope's visit.

Hampered by clutzy post-synching of the English dialog, pic is unconvincing, especially in a dumb finale when Dresden, hit on the head, suddenly resists the microchip and becomes his old good guy self. Toni Nero as a busty double agent livens things up a bit, brandishing a machine gun while wearing an evening gown.—*Lor.*

Running From The Guns
(AUSTRALIAN-COLOR)

A Hoyts (Australia) release of a Burrowes Film Group production. Produced by Geoff Burrowes. Executive producer, Dennis Wright. Directed by John Dixon. Stars Jon Blake, Mark Hembrow. Screenplay, Dixon;

camera (color), Keith Wagstaff; editor, Ray Daley; music, Bruce Rowland; production design, Leslie Binns; sound, John Schiefelbein; stunts, Chris Anderson; special effects, Brian Pearce; assistant director, Bob Donaldson; production manager, Bill Regan; casting, Suzie Maizels. Reviewed at Hoyts center 6, Sydney, Sept. 16, 1987. Running time: **87 MINS.**
Dave Williams . . . . Jon Blake
Peter . . . . Mark Hembrow
Jill . . . . Nikki Coghill
Bangles . . . . Terence Donovan
Gilman . . . . Bill Kerr
Terence . . . . Peter Whitford
Martin . . . . Warwick Sims
Big Jim . . . . Gerard Kennedy
Dave's Mum . . . . Toni Lamond
Mallard . . . . Greg Ross
Chazza . . . . Gus Mercurio
Ocker . . . . Ken Snodgrass
Sir Julian . . . . Barry Hill
Also with: Patrick Ward (Mulcahy), Delilah (Marathon Mandy), Nick Waters (Raeburn), David Bickerstaff (Cranston), Ray Rivamonte (Muppet), James Wright (The Chairman), Susie Masterton (The Madame), Ben Michael (The Apprentice).

Sydney — Lensed about 18 months ago as "Free Enterprise," "Running From The Guns" emerges as a very lean, energetic comedy-thriller made along familiar lines. Thanks to engaging performances from Jon Blake and Mark Hembrow in the leads, and some efficient stuntwork, pic is mostly fun, but boxoffice prospects both at home and abroad must be considered questionable.

With the notable exception of the "Mad Max" films, Aussie-made genre pics of this sort have never clicked at the local boxoffice or made a mark in major overseas markets. Writer-director John Dixon's maiden effort has more going for it that most, but it's still unlikely to reverse the existing pattern.

Premise involves two friends, Dave (Blake) and Peter (Hembrow), who pick up a container of Taiwanese-made toys from a warehouse near the Melbourne docks. There's been a switch, and what they've got is a container of great value to some highly-placed businessmen operating on the wrong side of the law. The fun starts when a quartet of accident-prone nerds set out in their jeep after the friends, and succeed in wrecking their vehicle and causing a multiple pile-up on the freeway without their intended victims ever realizing they've been in danger.

Seems the containers were switched by Bangles (Terence Donovan), a middle-level crook who wants to sell the illegal merchandise (which turns out to be laundered cash) back to its owners. Bangles soon finds himself out of his depth, and is sadistically murdered by Martin (Warwick Sims), chief hatchet man for crime boss Bill Kerr. Meanwhile, Dave is romancing Jill (Nikki Coghill), a cool blond investigator for a crime commission.

When Blake and Hembrow are on the screen, "Running From The Guns" is pretty enjoyable; the two actors make an appealing team, their laconic Australian humor being one of the film's more appealing factors. Nikki Coghill makes a charming heroine, too. The villains are stock figures, though, and corny rather than menacing. The film gets rather silly towards the end, as members of a dock-workers union — hitherto mocked by the film when they carry ancient banners from the Korean and Vietnam wars into a strike rally — come to the rescue with an amazing arsenal of automatic weaponry.

Pic has obviously been subjected to a great deal of post-production work, with editing to bring it down to a very economical 87 minutes. There are still scenes that seem out of place, such as a ludicrous episode in a brothel/gym in which Bangles is humiliated by a formidable black dominatrix (Delilah). Also, the regular addition of deafening and invariably inappropriate rock songs onto the soundtrack sometimes makes the film an aural endurance test: do kids really respond to such a blatantly out-of-context use of music?

Nonetheless, on the film's chosen level, there's enough slick entertainment value — comedy and thrills — to keep undemanding audiences happy. Technically pic is okay, though print previewed was grainy in spots. —Strat.

Distant Harmony
(U.S.-DOCU-COLOR)

A Luchina Ltd. Partnership production. Produced by John Goberman, DeWitt Sage, Daniel Wigutow. Executive producer, R. Scott Asen. Directed by Sage. Camera (color), Miroslav Ondricek, Richard Gordon; editor, Victor Kanefsky, Oreet Rees, Coco Houwer, Sam Pollard; sound, Andrew Wiskes, Daniel Gleich; production manager, Eva Fyer. Reviewed at the Toronto Festival of Festivals, Sept. 19, 1987. Running time: **85 MINS.**
With: Luciano Pavarotti, Kallen Esperian, Madelyn Renee, and the cast of "La Boheme" with members of the Genoa Opera Company Orchestra and Chorus.

Toronto — This celebrity travelog documentary about Luciano Pavarotti's 2-week trip to China in the summer of 1986 will be of particular interest to the many fans of the preeminent Italian tenor. Although it is not memorable documentary making, "Distant Harmony" is congenial viewing that could reasonably be programmed at docu festivals and on public tv.

Prior to a public screening at the Toronto Festival of Festivals, filmmaker DeWitt Sage indicated he was somewhat constrained by the Chinese authorities in his lensing and therefore had to shoot what he could get. This results in a good deal of predictable footage: Pavarotti getting the red carpet treatment at the airport, in convivial conversation with various musicians and officials, bicycling through Beijing, applauding a gymnastics exhibition, conducting clinics for promising

Chinese students of Western opera, performing recitals and appearing in rehearsals and full-scale performances of "La Boheme."

As a mark of the high esteem in which he was held by the Chinese, Pavarotti, according to the docu, was the first Westerner to perform in the Great Hall of the People. Naturally, there were logistical hassles to be ironed out, and Sage duly documents the routine backstage difficulties that inevitably result when Westerners are confronted in a working situation with "the different culture and mentality" (as one of the tenor's aides put it) of the Chinese.

"Distant Harmony" provides yet more affirmation of contemporary China's desire for contact with the West, although it confines itself mostly to that elite segment of Chinese society fortunate enough to be involved with the visit of a foreign celebrity. Ultimately, the documentary is held together by the exuberant charisma of its subject, whose comportment is at once grandly noble and broadly democratic. Pavarotti's unbounded good humor is evident throughout, but particularly in a short but amusing sequence in which he dons full Chinese operatic regalia and gamely joins in with local performers, true to his role as trouper and cultural ambassador whose like had not been seen in China before. —Rich.

Marauders
(AUSTRALIAN-COLOR)

A Magic Men production. Produced and directed by Mark Savage. Screenplay, Savage; camera (color), Savage; editor, Paul Harrington, Colin Savage, Mark Savage; music, John Merakovsky, Mark Horpinitch; sound, Harrington; special effects makeup, Colin Savage; stunts, Shaun Sullivan; casting, The Magic Men; associate producers, Richard Wolstencroft, Colin Savage, Harrington. Reviewed at Mosman screening room, Sydney, Sept. 19, 1987. Running time: **76 MINS.**
Emilio East .... Colin Savage
Jamie (JD) Kruger .... Zero Montana
Becky Howard .... Megan Napier
David Fraser .... Paul Harrington
Also with: Janie Fearon, Sam Davies, Michael Deflorid, Audrey Davies, Kerry Harrington, James Cain, Richard Wolstencroft, Anthony Artman.

Sydney — On one level, 24-year-old writer-producer-cinematographer-director Mark Savage is to be praised for turning out a fine technical job with this ultra-low budget ($A150,000) exploitation thriller, which is aimed at the video market. It's a pity that the obviously talented young helmer couldn't have raised h is sights above the wretched story and vile characters presented in "Marauders."

Protagonists Emilio (Colin Savage) and Jamie (Zero Montana) are ugly low-lifes, mindless thugs who bring violence and terror in their wake. In the opening scenes, Emilio beats up his wife and then shoots her in the head because she won't give him the keys to the car; then he

discovers they were in his pocket all along. Jamie, meanwhile, gets upset because his mother has called the cops about the bodies he's been bringing home to "play with." He stabs Mom to death.

Meanwhile schoolgirl Becky (Megan Napier) has an assignation to meet womanizing David (Paul Harrington), first seen in bed with two other girls. Driving to meet Becky, David nearly runs down Jamie; so Jamie and Emilio pursue the couple out of the city into the countryside. Stopping occasionally to steal petrol and booze, and to rape and murder an innocent girl walking down the road (a particularly ugly scene), Emilio and Jamie track down Becky and David to the house in the woods where Becky has discovered David's true nature. Meanwhile, a posse of vigilantes from the nearby town, consisting of women and children as well as men, is hunting the two rapist-murderers.

Climax of the film is bloody, with several children getting killed before Jamie is hanged and Emilio shoots himself to avoid capture. Pic ends when Becky guns down David. It's all depressing, meaningless violence, with no point of relevance, unless the photos, which precede the end credits, of the four leading characters when they were a few years younger, are supposed to mean something.

As noted, film is technically fine, given the minuscule budget and the fact that the actors seem to have pitched in to help behind the scenes as well. They should have paid more attention to their acting chores, because only Colin Savage as the manic Emilio gives a completely convincing performance.

Dialog is consistently crude, with verbal descriptions of sexual activity stated repeatedly in the crudest terms. Despite the fact that a woman, the schoolgirl Becky, turns the tables at the end, the film's attitude to women in general is horrific.

Undemanding video fans may conceivably go for this stuff, which is a depressing thought in itself. The filmmakers should, perhaps, ponder on where their careers can go from here. —Strat.

Warriors Of The Apocalypse
(COLOR)

Crude fantasy pic.

A Film Concept Group release. Executive producer, Just Betzer. Produced and directed by Bobby A. Suarez. Screenplay, Ken Metcalfe, from story by Suarez; camera (Rank color), Jun Pereira; editor, uncredited; music, Ole Hoyer; production design, Ruben Arthur Nicdao; action coordinator, Franco Guerrero; postproduction coordinator, Edward J. Francis; casting, Maria Ezpeleta. Reviewed on Lightning Video videcassette, N.Y., Sept. 9, 1987. (MPAA Rating: R.) Running time: **95 MINS.**
Trapper .... Michael James
Sheba .... Debrah Moore
Anouk .... Franco Guerrero
Goruk .... Ken Metcalfe

Also with: Robert Marius, Charlotte Cain, David Light, Mike Cohen, David Brass, Steven Rogers.

"Warriors Of The Apocalypse" is a subpar, Filipino-lensed fantasy film trying to fit into the "Road Warrior" mold. In regional release for over a year, with alternate titles "Searchers Of The Voodoo Mountain" and "Time Raiders," it is now a homevideo entry.

Set after a nuclear war 150 years in Earth's future, pic stars Michael James as Trapper, leader of a nomadic group who encounter a young guy (Franco Guerrero) who claims to be 100 years old. Together they search for the Voodoo Mountain and film shifts from desert desolation to a verdant jungle setting.

Amidst numerous battles with indians, they reach their destination, lorded over by Ken Metcalfe (who also scripted), attended by a sexy queen (Debrah Moore) and numerous scantily clad women. The heroes free the mutant slaves who are tending to Metcalfe's ancient nuclear power plant inside a cave. Finale has baddies dispatched, but with them the immortality secret is gone, James left to rebuild a new civilization from scratch.

Pic has weak English dubbing and an orchestral score that oddly evokes "The Godfather." It's a programmer with ultimately more in common with the Filipino fantasy films of the 1960s then the current "Mad Max" craze.—Lor.

Evil Spawn
(COLOR)

Campy horror film for diehards.

A Camp Motion Pictures and American-Independent Prods. presentation. Produced by Anthony Brewster. Coproduced by Frank Bresee. Written and directed by Kenneth J. Hall. Camera (color), Christopher Condon; editor, William Shaffer; music, Paul Natzke; sound, David Wilder; art direction, Roger McCoin; creature design, Ralph Miller 3d; special makeup effects, Cleve Hall; transformation makeup, Thom Floutz; additional makeup effects, John Criswell, Joe Dolinich; special effects, Dan Bordona, Christopher Ray; second unit camera, Scott Ressler, Frank Isaacs; postproduction supervisor, Skip Malanowski; associate producers, Condon, Gary J. Levinson; casting, Mei-Ling Andreen. Reviewed on Camp Video videcassette, N.Y., Sept. 25, 1987. (No MPAA Rating.) Running time: **73 MINS.**
Lynn Roman .... Bobbie Bresee
Ross Anderson .... Drew Godderis
Brent Price .... John Terrence
Evelyn ...Donna Shock (Dawn Wildsmith)
Harry Fox .... Jerry Fox
Elaine Talbot .... Pamela Gilbert
Dr. Zeitman .... John Carradine
Mark Randall .... Mark Anthony
Tracy .... Leslie Eve
Will .... Chris Kobin
Betty .... Sue Mashaw
Dr. Leibowitz .... Gary J. Levinson
Symanski .... Michael S. Deak
Bordona .... Roger McCoin
Pool Man .... Forrest J. Ackerman

"Evil Spawn," previously titled "Alive By Night" and "Deadly

Sting," is a tolerable, poverty row variation on Roger Corman's 1959 Susan Cabot-starrer "The Wasp Woman." Topliner Bobbie Bresee provides enough flesh and ham acting to please camp followers (pic appropriately is released by Camp Video, from Fred Olen Ray's new AIP production banner).

In a script far too overloaded with in-jokes on the world of low-budget filmmaking, Bresee toplines as Lynn Roman, a fading superstar actress who jumps at the chance to look younger via a formula given her by unscrupulous scientist Evelyn Avery (played by Donna Shock, a pseudonym for Dawn Wildsmith). Side effects turn her, werewolf style, into an insect-like monster.

Though some of the monsters on view are rubbery, pic's gore is impressive and combines with enough nudity to keep the hardcore horror fans alert, however, pic's jokes are unfunny and storyline is a drag. Besides Bresee, a cult figure from "Mausoleum," Wildsmith, from "Surf Nazis Must Die" is an elegant villainess. John Carradine appears in one scene of "generic footage," a lengthy dialog opposite Wildsmith in which both thesps speak entirely in euphemisms, suitable for splicing into any thriller film.—*Lor.*

Julia's geheim
(Juliet's Secret)
(DUTCH-COLOR-16m)

A Cinemien release of a Topaz Pictures production. Produced by Tom Burghard. Written and directed by Hans Hylkema. Camera (Eastmancolor, Haghefilm prints), Fred Mckenkamp; editor, Hetty Konink; sound, Lukas Boeke; art direction, Anne Marie van Beverwijk; assistant director, José Ruigrok; production manager, Niek Koppen. Reviewed at Cinepressclub, Amsterdam, Sept. 18, 1987. Running time: **105 MINS.**
Arzu . . . . Funda Müjde
Ibrahim . . . . Nahit Güvendi

Amsterdam — This sympathetic and unpretentious film is about the problems of the substantial Turkish minority in the Netherlands. Ibrahim came originally to work in the Ford automobile plant, lost his job through reorganization, then started his own business: repairing and altering clothes, and making dresses for wholesalers.

His daughter, Arzy has been betrothed as a little girl to the son of grandpa's neighbor in Ibrahim's native village, where the family goes every year for its vacation. There's no hurry, the marriage may be years away.

It's a jubilee year at Arzu's high school. They'll stage "Romeo And Juliet" with Arzu as Juliet. Ibrahim will never allow it — theater, embracing Romeo, is quite impossible for a nice Turkish girl. So Arzu, with the help of her brother Erdal, lies. Evening rehearsals are called an embroidery course. Truth will out, and an enraged pa keeps her at home, working at her sewing ma-

chine. The teachers intervene and Ibrahim relents. She's allowed to act. Arzu hopes that pa will come to see the performance and will notice the resemblance between her situation and Juliet's fate.

Dialog is in Turkish (subtitled) and Dutch. Scenes are kept short and to the point. Hylkema worked mainly with amateurs, which was actually an asset while filming the school Shakespeare shenanigans, although not in some other sequences. There's humor and the viewer's attention is held at all times, not least by the very expressive face of the talented Funda Müjde as Arzu.

"Juliet's Secret," which was chosen as the closing performance of the Dutch Filmdays, was cofinanced by Dutch tv. The movie should be of interest in Germany with its large Turkish immigrant population, and wherever a minority culture has difficulties assimilating, or where women's rights are largely ignored.
—*Wall.*

Magdalena Viraga
(U.S.-COLOR)

A Menkes Film Production. Produced and directed by Nina Menkes. Screenplay, Menkes, including poetry by Gertrude Stein, Ann Sexton, Mary Daly; camera (color), Menkes; editor, Menkes; Music Grupo Travieso; sound, Duane Dell'amico. Reviewed at the Toronto Festival of Festivals, Sept. 17, 1987. Running time: **90 MINS.**
Ida . . . . Trinka Menkes
Claire . . . . Claire Aguilar
Also with: Victor Flores, Paul Shuler, Nora Bendich.

Toronto — Entire minutes tick by without a single movement — either by cast or camera — in "Magdalena Viraga." Nothing happens. Nobody speaks. Finally, the silence is broken. An enigmatic line is repeated over and over and over again by the wooden actors. The effect is numbing.

"Magdalena Viraga" focuses on an L.A. prostitute named Ida. She lives in an ugly hotel. She works an ugly bar. She wears ugly clothes. She services an endless stream of customers. Throughout, she is mostly silent, staring into space. She doesn't want to be there. She hates her life. She hates her work. She hates the Johns. She is trapped. She can't escape. She finally murders a customer. She goes to prison.

Director Nina Menkes, a film teacher at California State University, also produced, wrote, shot and edited this film which has a largely Hispanic cast. The script is silly (Gertrude Stein, whose poetry makes up a good part of the dialog, would be mortified). Photography is uninspired. The soundtrack sounds like it was taped in a crowded steam room. The editing is boring. Pic is cheap and looks it.
—*Zerb.*

God Rides A Harley
(CANADIAN-DOCU-COLOR-16m)

An Arto-Pelli Motion Pictures production. Produced by Andreas Erne, Stavros C. Stavrides. Directed by Stavrides. Screenplay, Michael Wainwright; camera (color), James Crowe; editor, Steve Stephenson; sound, Peter Sawade. Reviewed at World Film Festival, Montreal, Aug. 31, 1987. Running time: **81 MINS.**

Montreal — Motorbike gangs were threats to society in such films as "The Wild One" and "The Wild Angels," but bikers became doomed heroes in "Easy Rider." In "God Rides A Harley," director Stavros C. Stavrides introduces a clutch of born-again bikers who've found religion; they're members of the Christian Riders Motor Cycle Club and Righteous Riders. Film takes these new Fundamentalists at face value, sans a hint of irony, so best placement for the docu is on religious tv networks, where it could be a hit.

Film intros John, on probation with the Christian Riders; he used to be into weapons, but is now a reformed character. Rocky has a violent temper and was a dirty fighter; Brian, a self-styled "grizzly bear," was a member of the violent Outlaw Biker gang for 10 years; Paul hated the world and lived in sin with a woman; Les once partied in a funeral home (maybe emulating the party Peter Fonda and friends held in a church in "The Wild Angels"). All are now reformed characters, who have roadside prayer meetings, proclaim themselves and their bikes "Property Of Jesus" and sing hymns.

Technically, Stavrides efficiently captures on film the odd world of these leather-jacketed Christians, though lip synch is way off in a prayer meeting sequence late in the film. Outside of the converted, the film's chances are negligible.
—*Strat.*

N.Y. Film Fest Review

Anita — Tänze des Lasters
(Anita — Dances Of Vice)
(WEST GERMANY-COLOR/B&W)

A Rosa von Praunheim/Road Movies production, in collaboration with ZDF. Directed by Von Praunheim. Screenplay, Von Praunheim, Hannelene Limpach; camera (color, b&w), Elfi Mikesch; sound and editing, Mike Shephard; music, Konrad Elfers, with Rainer Rubbert, Alan Marks, Ed Lieber; costumes, Anne Jud; sets, Inge Stiborski; makeup, Uschi Menzel, Willi P. Konze, Oliver Ziem; titles, Volker Marz. Reviewed at N.Y. Film Festival, Sept. 30, 1987. Running time: **85 MINS.**
With: Lotti Huber (Anita Berber), Ina Blum, Mikael Honesseau.

Anita Berber was something of a scandalous figure in post-World War I Berlin with a propensity for

exotic dancing that gave her an excuse to strip and expose herself in cafe society. An amoral woman in immoral times, she was bisexual and a heavy cocaine user. Apparently she was all the rage of 1920s Berlin until imitators came along and made her act pretty routine. She died of tuberculosis at age 29.

Rather than a straightforward biopic, Berlin filmmaker Rosa von Praunheim gives an expressionistic view of moments from her life filtered through the fantasies of an elderly woman (Lotti Huber) who as the film opens is stripping on a contemporary Berlin street claiming to be the long dead Berber.

She's hustled off to a mental institution and the realities of her confinement, shot in black and white with sound, are contrasted with recreations of Berber's shenanigans, photographed in silent color, with dialog and descriptions on title cards drawn to suggest the art of the period.

The filmmaker is less concerned with narrative threads than the overall impact of disjointed scenes and set pieces from the dancer's life than have inspired him. Huber, as the deluded old woman, is a great discovery. The 75-year-old actress has an impressive screen presence and attacks the role with voluptuous zest. She is a wholly engaging film personality.

The other performers, a superb collection of unforgettable faces, are peripheral in that they function more as instruments of the director's collective vision rather than recreating full-blown characterizations. They are immediately recognizable but have no life beyond the visual image assigned them.

The film is paced like a piece of music: a visual fugue. Cleverly edited (Mike Shephard) and beautifully photographed (Elfi Mikesch), this is a resourceful film made on a low budget. Von Praunheim, a contemporary of the late Rainer Werner Fassbinder, has made over 35 films, including "It's Not The Homosexual Who Is Perverse, Rather The Situation In Which He Lives" (1970) and "A Virus Has No Morals" (1985), a satire of the AIDS crisis.

This tribute to Anita Berber is certain to be well-received at festivals and in art house bookings.
— *Owl..*

Tokyo Fest Reviews

The Last Emperor
(ITALIAN-HONG KONG-COLOR)

A Columbia Pictures (U.S.) release of a Jeremy Thomas presentation. Produced by Thomas. Directed by Bernardo Bertolucci. Stars John Lone, Joan Chen, Peter O'Toole. Screenplay, Mark Peploe, with Bertolucci; intial screenplay collaboration, Enzo Ungari. Camera (Technovision, Technicolor), Vittorio Storaro; editor, Gabriella Cristiani; music, Ryuichi Sakamoto, David Byrne, Cong Su; production design, Ferdinando Scarfiotti; art direction, Gianni Giovagnoni, Gianni Silvestri, Maria Teresa Barbasso; costume design, James Acheson; sound (Dolby), Ivan Sharrock; associate producers, Franco Giovale, Joyce Herlihy; assistant director, Gabriele Polverosi; casting, Joanna Merlin, Patricia Pao (Hong Kong), Ulrike Koch (China). Reviewed at the Tokyo Intl. Film Festival (closing night, non-competing), Oct. 4, 1987. Running time: 160 MINS.

Pu Yi	John Lone
Wan Jung	Joan Chen
Reginald Johnson (R.J.)	Peter O'Toole
The Governor	Ying Ruocheng
Chen Pao Shen	Victor Wong
Big Li	Dennis Dun
Amakasu	Ryuichi Sakamoto
Eastern Jewel	Maggie Han
Interrogator	Ric Young
Won Hsiu	Wu Jun Mei
Chang	Cary Hiroyuki Tagawa
Ar Mo	Jade Go
Yoshioka	Fumihiko Ikeda

Also with: Richard Vuu (Pu Yi — 3 years), Tijger Tsou (Pu Yi — 8 years), Wu Tao (Pu Yi — 15 years), Fan Guang (Pu Chieh — adult), Henry Kyi (Pu Chieh — 7 years), Alvin Riley 3d (Pu Chieh — 14 years).

Tokyo — A film of unique, quite unsurpassed visual splendor, "The Last Emperor" makes for a fascinating trip to another world, but for the most part also proves as remote and untouchable as its subject, the last imperial ruler of China. A prodigious production in every respect, Bernardo Bertolucci's first film in six years is an exquisitely painted mural of 20th century Chinese history as seen from the point of view of a hereditary leader who never knew his people. Shown in its world premiere as the closing night attraction at the second Tokyo Intl. Film Festival, picture will deservedly receive serious attention upon its release next month. Performance in debut engagements should be strong, but key to recoupment of its $25,000,000 cost will lie in whether domestic audiences are seduced by its exotic qualities, or put off by its cold virtuosity.

The life story recounted here is an utterly singular one without possible equal. In 1908, the 3-year-old Pu Yi is installed as Lord of Ten Thousand Years, master of the most populous nation on earth. Shortly, he is forced to abdicate, but is kept on as a symbolic figure, educated by his English tutor and tended to by a court that includes 1,500 eunuchs and countless other manipulative advisers.

Technically considered a god, little Pu Yi can do anything he wishes except leave the great Forbidden City in Peking. Except for hearsay and what he learns in magazines, he is ignorant of the convulsions being experienced by his country; a prisoner in the most glorious gilded cage ever created.

Finally booted out by the new government, Pu Yi, by now in his late 20s, moves with his two wives to Tientsin and lives like a Western playboy, wearing tuxedos at elegant dances while gradually coming under the influence of the Japanese, who eventually install him as puppet emperor of Manchuria, home of his ancestors.

After World War II, he is imprisoned for 10 years by the communists, during which time he writes his memoirs, and ends his life as a gardener and simple citizen in Mao's China.

This is a lot of ground to cover in a feature film, and doubly difficult to traverse since even the most basic facts of the history involved are unfamiliar to most Westerners. Unfortunately, screenwriter Mark Peploe, working with Bertolucci from initial work prepared by Enzo Ungari, has not entirely cracked the problem of how to seamlessly integrate necessary documentary data with personal dramatic material.

Script is full of dry dialog included merely to establish dates and events, as well as identifying exclamations such as, "The Japanese!" "The Russians!" "The Red Guard!" and so on.

While effective in presenting the stark contrasts between the decadent imperial court and the severity of communist times, the scenario's structure is quite conventional. The framing device of Pu Yi's detention in 1950 and subsequent memories and confessions to prison interrogators provides an easy jumping-off point for flashbacks to key points over the previous 42 years.

Given the extreme historical breadth of the story and the exceptionally lofty central character — and being a Westerner to boot — Bertolucci probably had little choice but to approach the subject from the outside. Film is an incredibly rich tapestry of events that in the foreground always features a figurehead, not a 3-dimensional person.

This does not at all prevent the picture from being constantly absorbing and tremendously interesting, but it will stand in the way of strong involvement for many mainstream viewers. The progression Bertolucci follows is that of a man who is always a prisoner — first of the imperial court, then of the Japanese and finally of the communists — but ultimately achieves his greatest freedom in normal life. One can sympathize with the little boy's desire to escape the ancient walls that describe his world, but that's as far as one's feelings for him can go.

Nevertheless, at every moment, the extraordinary aspects of both the story and the physical realization of it are astonishing to witness. For virtually the first 90 minutes, Bertolucci makes full use of the red-dominated splendor of the Forbidden City, which has never before been opened up for use in a Western film.

Many vivid images emerge, including little Pu Yi making eunuchs and a camel chase him through a courtyard, his attempted escape over the roof, and the adult emperor and his wives, dressed just right for a Southampton summer afternoon, playing tennis on a specially built court.

Middle section reverberates with strong echoes of the director's "The Conformist," as the emperor works out of an art deco office while his beautiful wife lethargically slips into opium addiction and a lesbian affair. The red flag waving in the concluding section will also remind viewers of "1900," but politically, Bertolucci is playing no favorites here, presenting everything, including Japanese treachery, in a straight-forward manner.

Star of the production, other than China itself, is cinematographer Vittorio Storaro, whose widescreen lens goes gliding through the decades and innumerable settings with breathtaking grace and beauty. Opening prison scenes are drained of almost all color, while initial sequences at court are burnished with a golden sepia before rich, full colors are allowed to take hold.

On the same ultra-refined level of accomplishment are Ferdinando Scarfiotti's amazing production design, James Acheson's no-expenses-spared costumes and the extremely resonant musical score of Ryuichi Sakamoto, David Byrne and Cong Su.

Actors all do good jobs within the somewhat confining nature of the conception of the roles, which does not allow for psychological or emotional exploration. John Lone, who plays Pu Yi from age 18 to 62, naturally dominates the picture with his carefully judged, unshowy delineation of a sometimes arrogant, often weak man. Joan Chen is exquisite and sad as his principal wife who almost literally fades away, and Peter O'Toole doesn't really have that much to do but act intelligently concerned for the emperor's well-being.

Finally, acknowledgement must be made of the enormously impressive job pulled off by Jeremy Thomas in organizing such an ambitious production. The independent British producer had to secure total Chinese cooperation with many unprecedented requirements, and then finance such an expensive undertaking without the upfront involvement of any major company.

In Tokyo, Thomas revealed that a 4-hour cut of the picture exists and will be made available for tv showing in either two or four installments if the feature proves successful.

—Cart.

Dancers
(U.S.-COLOR)

A Cannon Group release of a Golan-Globus production, in association with Hera/Baryshnikov Prods. Produced by Menahem Golan, Yoram Globus. Executive producers, Nora Kaye, Jack Brodsky. Directed by Herbert Ross. Stars Mikhail Baryshnikov. Screenplay, Sarah Kernochan; camera (Cinecittà color), Ennio Guarnieri; editor, William Reynolds; "Giselle" ballet music. Adolphe Adam; original music, Pino Donaggio; production design, Gianni Quaranta; art direction, Luigi Marchione; set decoration, Ello Altamura; contemporary clothes, Adriana Spadaro; ballet costumes, Anna Anni, Enrico Serafini; sound (Dolby), Clive Winter; ballet sequences staged by Baryshnikov; associate producers, Charles France, John Thompson; assistant director, Gianni Arduini Piaisant; casting, Francesco Cenieri. Reviewed at the Tokyo Intl. Film Festival (competing), Sept. 27, 1987. (MPAA Rating: PG.) Running time: 99 MINS.

Anton Sergoyev	Mikhail Baryshnikov
Francesca	Alessandra Ferri
Nadine	Leslie Browne
Patrick	Thomas Rall
Muriel	Lynn Seymour
Wade	Victor Barbee
Lisa	Julie Kent
Contessa	Mariangela Melato
Paolo	Leandro Amato

Also with: Gianmarco Tognazzi (Guido), Desmond Kelly (Duke of Courland), Chrisa Keramidas (Bathilde), Amy Werba (Interviewer), Jack Brodsky (Jack), Robert Argand (Impresario), Amanda McKerrow (Moyna), Bonnie Moore (Zulma), and the artists of the American Ballet Theater.

Tokyo — With "Dancers," Herbert Ross, Mikhail Baryshnikov and Leslie Browne return to the backstage-at-the-ballet world of their 1977 hit, "The Turning Point," but with markedly less success. Less than compelling both as drama and dance, film sets itself up as a potentially intriguing study of the callous Don Juanism of a superstar, but then succumbs to unedifying mawkishness. Boxoffice chances look slim.

Picture's first half is devoted to a mild account of the behind-the-scenes doings as Baryshnikov, playing himself is everything but name, prepares to shoot a film version of the 19th century ballet "Giselle" (which was this film's working title) in an Italian coastal town.

Rehearsals are presented in a perfunctory manner, with little of the backstage madness normally associated with ballet pics or inside looks at filmmaking. The only intrigue, in fact, stems from the star's simultaneous involvement with four women, three as the action commences, with another added as he becomes intrigued by a teenaged American newcomer to the company.

Not only is Baryshnikov, quite plausibly, a notorious womanizer, but he's a fatigued one. He himself admits that he can't feel anything and can't show passion, and his best friend, nicely played by veteran musical comedy performer and classical dancer Thomas Rall, tells him, "All these years have gone by and you haven't gotten mature, somehow."

This represents interesting self-analytical territory for a film with which Baryshnikov was involved on every level, but it all goes soft, very quickly, as the jaded, aging little boy becomes goo-goo-eyed over the new girl who barely looks old enough to drive, much less hold her own with the ballet world's greatest Lothario. The script's willingness to allow the lech to prey upon young Lisa's extreme innocence and vulnerability creates additional disturbing possibilities, but again the ball is dropped, and the film ends without informing the viewer what really might have happened between the two, other than for both to say that it was really meaningful and memorable and, for him, revivifying.

The reason much of this falls by the wayside is that the film-within-a-film staging of "Giselle" occupies most of the second half. Ross, who certainly knows how to photograph dance by this time, attempts to relate the dance story and the real-life entanglement through intercutting, but the ballet does not begin to address the troubling material Sarah Kernochan's screenplay has unearthed, so it all unravels to disappointing results.

Only test given to the women in the cast is to convincingly express jealousy, which they all pass, and newcomer Julie Kent appealingly resembles an adolescent Jane Seymour. Tech contributions are pro, except that Ennio Guarnieri's lensing has suffused everything in heavy filters and so much blue that the troupe sometimes appears to be dancing underwater. Film is dedicated to Ross' late wife, Nora Kaye, who was coexecutive producer.
—*Cart.*

The Man With Three Coffins
(SOUTH KOREAN-COLOR)

Produced by Myung-won Lee. Directed by Chang-ho Lee. Screenplay, Jacha Lee, based on his novel; camera (color), Seung-bae Park; music, Jong-gu Lee. (No other credits provided.) Reviewed at the Tokyo Intl. Film Festival (competing), Sept. 29, 1987. Running time: **105 MINS.**
Soon-suk Yank . . . . Myung-kon Kim
Yang's wife, a nurse,
    a prostitute . . . . Bo-hee Lee

Tokyo — This derivatively experimental pic is another from director Chang-ho Lee, who seemed to employ his entire family for its behind-the-camera chores. For a number of impenetrable reasons, "Man" comes across as preciously

stylized as it is dull.

The story, based on a short novel ("The Wanderer Never Rests Even On The Road") by the pic's scripter, is never coherent. A young widower (Myung-kon Kim) heads for Korea's Kang-won area to rediscover the origins and to scatter the ashes of his dead wife.

His adventures include encounters with a prostitute, a nurse and even the spirit of his dead wife, all played by Bo-hee Lee. Much of the action, if that's the term, is pushed forward by corny voiceover narration accompanies by various precious but none-too-clear photographic effects.

Almost all of the picture is shot in sepia tones for no apparent reason. The effect can give the viewer a headache. Acting generally is sufficient although production values are mainly subpar. Shots of Korea's mountain areas in snow are attractive. —*Sege.*

Housekeeping
(U.S.-COLOR)

A Columbia Pictures release. Produced by Robert L. Colesberry. Written and directed by Bill Forsyth, based on the novel by Marilynne Robinson. Camera (Rank color), Michael Coulter; editor, Michael Ellis; music, Michael Gibbs; production design, Adrienne Atkinson; costume design, Mary-Jane Reyner; sound (Dolby), Ralph Parker. Reviewed at the Tokyo Intl. Film Festival (competing), Sept. 27, 1987. (MPAA Rating: PG.) Running time: **116 MINS.**
Sylvie . . . . Christine Lahti
Ruth . . . . Sara Walker
Lucille . . . . Andrea Burchill
Lily . . . . Anne Pitoniak
Nona . . . . Barbara Reese
Sheriff . . . . Bill Smillie
Mr. French . . . . Wayne Robson
Helen . . . . Margot Pinvidic

Tokyo — Both enervating and exhilarating, "Housekeeping" is a very composed film about eccentric behavior. Beautifully observed in many of its details, particularly in its very close examination of the relationship between sisters, picture does lag at times and gets carried away with some of its tangents. Scottish director Bill Forsyth, in his first North American effort, strikes out in some bold new directions here and shows increased range and muscle in the face of the challenge of material not his own. Modest scale and quirky material makes for a tricky sell, and whether this can make any kind of run commercially depends largely upon the critical reception.

Based upon Marilynne Robinson's well-regarded novel, Forsyth's screenplay is structured around the impulsive arrivals and departures of characters fundamental to the lives of two sisters in Washington State after World War II. Men never enter the picture, as the girls successively live with their mother, grandmother, great-aunts and mother's sister in the splendid isolation of a small mountain town.

Margot Pinvidic appears as the mother. It is also in these initial scenes that Forsyth's instantly recognizable brand of deadpan humor and charm asserts itself for the only time. The way it's left behind after the first reel virtually amounts to a statement by the director that he can still easily do what's expected of him, but he's not interested in that anymore.

Six years after their abandonment, when the girls are on the brink of adolescence, into their lives steps their long-lost aunt Sylvie, played by Christine Lahti. Tale then becomes that of the proverbial crazy ladies in the old house on the edge of town, but played rigorously without sentimentality or cuteness.

Lahti inevitably becomes close to her motherless charges, but by this time the girls have become understandably wary of new parental figures and can view their aunt with a certain justifiable skepticism. Bracingly, the film is neither a sweet character study of a lovable spinster auntie nor an ennobling look at how two youngsters make a go of it on their own.

What it actually is will probably perplex some viewers, most likely the members of the great public, but it has much to do with the arbitrariness of life, how it can change so utterly from one moment to the next, and yet one goes on.

On the downside, the sameness of tone and prolonged exposure to the same three voices fosters a monotony in the second half, and some of the household events and discussions are less than compelling as they unfold. Strong impact tends to come here in jabs, rather than sustained performance, and premise and plot are too fragile to carry the audience effortlessly through some of the tedious scenes.

There are questions, too, about Lahti's work. Having stolen nearly every film in which she has appeared as a supporting actress by being both more ballsy and saucy than the star, she is getting leads herself now and seems just a tad too eager to please. Then, just as she begins doing interesting things with the character, along comes a line reading that sounds uncannily like Diane Keaton, and since Keaton was long slated to play this part, one begins to wonder what's going on.

Newcomers Sara Walker and Andrea Burchill are splendid as the girls, as they manage to suggest the lifelong and quite particular bond between the sisters as much through body language and looks as through dialog.

Behind-the-scenes contributions are also first-rate. All hands have collaborated to fashion a discreet period portrait, Michael Coulter's lensing on Nelson, B.C., locations is exquisite, and Michael Gibbs' score comes across as unusually rich and supportive of mood.—*Cart.*

The Last Day Of Winter
(CHINESE-COLOR)

A China Film Export & Import Corp. release of a Xiaoxiang Film Studio production. Directed by Wu Ziniu. Screenplay, Qiao Xuezhu; camera (color), Yang Wei; music, Wang Xilin. (No other credits provided.) Reviewed at Tokyo Intl. Film Festival (Young Cinema Competition), Sept. 27, 1987. Running time: **94 MINS.**
With: Li Ling, Tao Zeru, Yu Meng, Hong Yuzhou, Zhang Xiaomin.

Tokyo — If you're at all curious about the range of deficencies in contempo Chinese films, an extended look at Wu Ziniu's banal meller should cover just about all the bases. The 1986 pic, the director's latest after "The Candidate" and "Secret Decree," is overlong, talky, overacted, didactic and dull. Export potential is virtually zilch.

The pic's slender premise has three strangers, a young man, young woman and a prepubescent girl (not a boy, as is stated in Tokyo Fest's program note) separately visiting a "labor reform" prison camp in China's northwestern desert. They are individually intent on visiting wayward brothers or sisters who ran afoul of the authorities for various infractions.

Qiao Xuezhu's script has the three meeting accidentally to set up an interplay between each character and his or her imprisoned relative. Relationships are interwoven via flashbacks and clumsy voiceover narration. Actors onscreen are allowed to emote excessively as the visitors confront wayward relatives and engage in not-very-interesting emotional exchanges.

Script's message — and that's meant literally since closing credits are accompanied by a homily about filial devotion generated by preceding action — is that although one person commits a crime, the victims are many. The "crimes" are apparently mild stuff; a sister's brush with prostitution, a brother's bout of shiftlessness, etc. Keep in mind that the setting is China.

Technical aspects of the production are subpar, especially muddled sound recording. Wang Xilin's bombastic musical score (performed by China's Central Orchestra) is almost as preachy in its prodding way as director Wu's handling of the material. This is the 34-year-old helmer's fourth pic, and it's been entered into the Tokyo Fest's young cinema competiton. —*Sege.*

The Outing
(COLOR)

Not even a genie could rescue silly horror pic.

A TMS Picture release of a Warren Chaney production, in association with HIT Films. Executive producers, Fred T. Kuehnert, M.N. Sanousi, Produced by Warren Chaney. Directed by Tom Daley. Screenplay, Chaney; camera (color), Herbert Raditschnig; editor, Claudio Cutry; music, Joel Rosenbaum,

Bruce Miller; sound, Tim Himes; production design, Robert Burns; assistant director, Stanford Hampton; special effects, Martin Becker's Reel EFX Inc. — supervisor, Frank Inez; associate producer, Deborah Winters. Reviewed at the KB Foundry, Washington, D.C., Sept. 17, 1987. (In Tokyo Film Festival — fantastic film section.) (MPAA Rating: R.) Running time: **85 MINS.**

Eve Farrell	Deborah Winters
Dr. Al Wallace	James Huston
Alex Wallace	Andra St. Ivanyi
Ted Pinson	Scott Bankston
Mike Daley	Mark Mitchell
Tony Greco	Andre Chimene
Babe	Damon Merrill
Ross	Barry Coffing
Gwen	Tracye Walker
Terry	Raan Lewis
Harley	Hank Amigo
Max	Brian Floores
Faylene	Michelle Watkins

Washington — The enduring fable bout the genie in the lamp is lifted with goulish variations for this puny horror number (originally titled "The Lamp"), that is inept in every department. Its future would have to be considered bleak.

Unlike the accommodating spirit from mystical lore, the fellow unleashed in this escapade has grown downright cranky after 5,000 years of confinement. Discovered by thugs who rob an old woman's home, he exacts immediate revenge, then ends up in a local museum where he lays waste to everything in his path, reveling in creative ways to eliminate some amorous adolescents.

Much of the dialog appears to have been improvised on the spot by a cast that plays roles in comic book fashion. Some token suspense might have been offered had the film not been so predictable, but the lamp's inhabitant probably has audiences laughing too hard to squirm in their seats. Several scenes were not color corrected. — *Paul.*

Once We Were Dreamers
(ISRAELI-COLOR)

A Hemdale release of a Belbo film. Produced by Ben Elkerbout, Ludi Boeken, Katriel Schory. Directed by Uri Barbash. Screenplay, Benny Barbash; camera (United color), Amnon Salomon; editor, Tova Asher; music, Misha Segal; production design, Eilon Levy; U.S. casting, Paula Herold. Reviewed at the Tokyo Intl. Film Festival (competing), Sept. 26, 1987. Running time: **110 MINS.**

Anda	Kelly McGillis
Marcus	John Shea
Sima	Christine Boisson

Also with: Arnon Zadok, Chad Schahar, Robert Pollak, Sinai Peter, Yaskov Amall, Zareh Vertanian.

Tokyo — If nobility and high-minded earnestness were all that counted, "Once We Were Dreamers" would be a masterpiece. Unfortunately, those are about the only strong traits that mark this English-language Israeli production. Dramatically obvious and drearily verbose, this tale of pioneer Jewish settlers in Palestine after World War I has widely been referred to simply as "Dreamers," but bears the longer title onscreen. Domestic commercial outlook is slight.

Entire action is placed within the immediate vicinity of a commune established in craggy Galliee by a dozen or so idealistic Jews either driven out of, or fed up with, the Old World. Dedicated to principles of absolute equality, they have nearly as much trouble negotiating arguments among themselves as they do fighting off the occasional ambushes of the Arabs whose territory they've occupied, but they are soon able to celebrate the successful cultivation of the arid land, and their desired foothold has been gained.

Of course, the presence of a beautiful woman, Kelly McGillis, at the center of things breeds great divisiveness among the hot-blooded men at this isolated encampment, and brings the three leaders to grief. It appears that, under their general agreement, traditional couples are frowned upon, but it is still obvious that McGillis and dashing violinist John Shea are meant for each other. Zev, the ideological chief of the group, doesn't see it that way, and events slowly but ultimately conspire to sour the Utopia the group has envisaged for itself.

Nevertheless, this is a symbolic tale about the formation of Israel, and thus remains essentially dedicated to notions of optimism and hope in the face of adversity on all fronts. Both the dramatic events and political attitudes are thoroughly predictable, making this a long trek through the desert to an inevitable destination.

Characters are given to a lot of unedited speechifying and director Uri Barbash, whose 1984 prison drama "Beyond The Walls" was nominated for a best foreign film Oscar, betrays a marked tendency toward stagy, composed groupings of characters, circling them around or staggering them behind the speaker as they listen to yet another impassioned oration.

Performances are uniformly intense and purposeful, with no room given over to humor or behavioral detail. Technical aspects are quite acceptable. — *Cart.*

Soigne ta droite
(Keep Up Your Right)
(FRENCH-SWISS-COLOR)

A Gaumont/JLG Film/Xanadu Film production. Written, directed and edited by Jean-Luc Godard. Camera (Eastmancolor), Coroline Champetier de Ribes; music, Rita Mitsouko; sound, François Musy. Reviewed at the Tokyo Intl. Film Festival (competing), Oct. 2, 1987. Running time: **82 MINS.**

The Idiot and the Prince	Jean-Luc Godard
The Individual	Jacques Villeret
The Man	François Périer
The Cricket	Jane Birkin
The Admiral	Michel Galabru
The Admiral's Wife	Dominique Lavanant
The Policeman	Jacques Rufus
The Golfer	Pauline Lafont
Musician	Catherine Ringer
Musician	Frederic Chichin

Tokyo — Those whose patience has been tried by most of Jean-Luc Godard's recent "commercial" films will find no relief in "Keep Up Your Right." A generally facetious contemplation of life on this planet and the journey towards death, film occasionally verges on the poetic, but plays for the most part like a metaphysical cartoon. Announced for, then abruptly withdrawn from, at least a couple of recent film festivals, Godard's latest was shot after "King Lear" (which debuted last month in Toronto) and had its world premiere at the Tokyo Fest. Commercial chances are even less than usual for the director due to lack of any sex angle.

For a short time, the film's goofy playfulness sustains a certain interest, as Godard, appearing again as an actor as he frequently does these days, bumps and lurches around through some crude slapstick, tipping his hat to strangers like a latter-day Jacques Tati and spilling cans of film on his way to a screening.

In his usual disconnected manner, Godard intercuts among three principal continuities, which involve some musicians in a recording session (in an echo of his "Sympathy For The Devil" with the Rolling Stones), a chubby worker who tries to connect with various couples, and a group of travelers, Godard among them, taking a chaotic plane trip under the care of a pilot who is reading a how-to book on suicide.

All of the essentially nonsensical scenes are overlaid with high-flown philosophical narration and, at times, the combination of the director's musings, editing patterns and striking recurring imagery (a sky with a jetstream, a little girl getting a glass door slammed in her face, a corpse with a big knife in its belly, a man dancing with the same woman in various stages of undress) achieve an undeniable poetic effect.

It's not enough. Godard betrays certain timorous tendencies towards meditative and transcendent cinema, but seems afraid to follow up on them seriously, feeling more comfortable with his mocking, offhand attitude. Result is artistic doodling, not a coherent, fully developed work.

Jokiness extends to the credits, which refer to a film "de Monsieur Godard," photography "de Monsieur Eastman et Mademoiselle Champetier de Ribes," etc. — *Cart.*

Hikaru Anna
(Luminous Woman)
(JAPANESE-COLOR)

A Toho Co. release. Directed by Shinji Somai. Screenplay, Yozo Tanaka, based on novel by Hiroshi Koshiyama; camera (Agfa Color, Imagica processing), Mutsuo Naganuma; music, Shigeaki Saegusa. (No other credits provided.) Reviewed at Tokyo Intl. Film Festival (competing), Sept. 28, 1987. Running time: **110 MINS.**

Sensaku Matsunami	Keiji Mutoh
Kuriko Sakura	Narumi Nasuda
Yoshino Koyama	Michiru Akiyoshi
Cabaret owner	Suma Kei

Tokyo — With his first film since sharing the remunerative first prize in the young cinema competition in the Tokyo Intl. Film Festival two years ago, director Shinji Somai shows a sure hand with uneven material. Although this pic has its share of weaknesses, it demonstrates the Japanese helmer's self-assured style that marks him as a figure to watch.

Based on a novel by Hiroshi Koshiyama, "Hikaru Anna" has a plot that's difficult to recount — even to completely make sense of. In a loosely sequential way, it tells the story of a hulking country bumpkin (Keiji Mutoh) from Japan's northern island of Hokkaido who pursues his betrothed (Narumi Nasuda) in the fleshpots of Tokyo.

He discovers that she is enthralled with and abused by a sleazy cabaret owner (Suma Kei). The hulk also meets a young singer (Michiru Akiyoshi) who works at the night club. She has operatic aspirations and talent but is reduced to playing the chirpy Japanese teen idol.

Somai and scripter Yozo Tanaka tell this tale in a highly elliptical fashion, layering rather than connecting specific scenes. The loss of narrative tension is compensated by sharply etched characters and agreeably quirky dialog that alternates between incisive patter and poetic abstraction.

Overall, the mood set here lingers and the characters aren't easily forgotten. A professional wrestler, Mutoh in his film debut is right for the hulk part. The singer is portrayed by the daughter of jazz pianist-bandleader Toshiko Akiyoshi.

Pic is being handled by Toho. It was financed by the director's winnings in the initial edition of the Festival in 1985. His cited pic, "Typhoon Club," took a look at a group of Japanese junior high school students. This pic couldn't be more different. Overall it's a lot better.—*Sege.*

Old Well
(CHINESE-COLOR)

A Xi'an Studio production. Directed by Wu Tianming. Screenplay, Zheng Yi. Camera (color), Chen Wancai, Zhang Yimou; editor, Chen Dali; music, Xu Youfu; art direction, Yang Gang; sound, Li Lashna. Reviewed at the Tokyo Intl. Film Festival (competing), Sept. 26, 1987. Running time: **140 MINS.**

Sun Wangquan	Zhang Yimou
Zhao Qiaoying	Liang Yujin
Duan Zifeng	Lu Liping

Tokyo — Mildly interesting as an example of current Chinese cinema, "Old Well" proves just too slow-moving and tedious to warrant the attention of anyone other than specialists. Wu Tianming's third film, after "Flow Of The River Without Any Signs" and "Life," ploddingly illustrates how new methods must be found to replace the old ways that don't work anymore in today's China. Few are likely to get too excited about this news.

Of course, in China at this moment, the "old ways" can be interpreted to mean two different things, how things were in prerevolutionary times, or how they became during the excesses of the Cultural Revolution.

However, the inhabitants of the film's setting, remote Sansei-Shu Province, have barely entered the 20th century in any regard, so the distinction is moot. What these people need is just the barest technology to pull them out of the depths of the primitivism that chains them to the past.

After having lived and studied in the city, Sun Wangquan, who must be pushing 40, comes to the small mountain community to try to apply his learning to real life. Two women pursue him and, after marrying the more obnoxious of the two for her dowry, he still keeps the other as a mistress.

Central dilemma here is the punishing lack of water. Since time began, the villagers have been digging wells in hopes of discovering a reliable supply, and everyone has

relatives and ancestors who have died in the effort.

With time out for his sexual escapades (fairly explicit by Chinese standards, but still PG stuff in Western terms), entire picture is devoted to the attempt, reenergized by Sun Wangquan, to dig a successful well. It is fair to say that there have sometimes been more exciting ideas for motion pictures than this.

Wu Tianming is most successful with the two big action setpieces, a vicious fight between the peasants with a village faction that has been hoarding water from a secret well, and the collapse of a well, which kills a major character and traps others down below. If he had included more impressively physical scenes such as these, pic would have held considerably more impact.

As it is, one has to make due with the depiction of the highly restricted and rustic conditions under which some rural Chinese still live, the stark landscapes, which remind somewhat of southern Utah, and the presence in the leading role of Zhang Yimou, brilliant cinematographer of "Yellow Earth" who also cophotographed this picture.

—Cart.

****

Gdansk Fest Reviews

****

Niedzieine Pgraszki
(Sunday Pranks)
(POLISH-B&W)

A Karol Irzykowski Film Studio production. Directed by Robert Glinski. Screenplay, Glinski, Grzegorz Torzecki; camera (b&w), Jerzy Rekas, Torzecki; editor, Lucja Osko; music, Lech Branski; art direction, Andrzej Nowacki. Reviewed at the Gdansk Film Festival, Sept. 13, 1987. Running time: 60 MINS.
Half-wit . . . . Miroslawa Marcheluk
Caretaker . . . . Stefan Szmidt
Caretaker's wife . . . . Emilia Krakowska
 Also with: Daria Trafankowska, Halina Romanowska, Wojciech Skibinski, Jerzy Zass.

Gydnia — A standout in the Polish Feature Festival, "Sunday Pranks" is a chilling little tale about kids playing in a bombed-out Warsaw courtyard on the day of Stalin's death, while their elders are away at church or a memorial procession. Turning his street urchins into a microcosm of society, Robert Glinski's hourlong debut has been held up for release since 1983. In spite of an awkward length, it should make fest rounds and would be a prestige offering for tv and special situations offshore.

Shot in stunning black and white by cameramen Jerzy Rekas and Grzegorz Torzecki, the mockingly titled "Sunday Pranks" seems to recount the innocent adventures of Our Gang, left unattended on a very special day. The tone quickly turns

to macabre surrealism. A pudgy boy, disliked as a snob and a bully, appears decked out in a black suit covered with his father's medals. He is to go to the train station, but first steals some other pre-war medals form the porter's ragged son. It's the second group of decorations that outrages the party members who come to pick him up, and get his parents arrested. The terrible ironies and senselessness of the adult world pass over the heads of the kids, who go on playing games like "Uprising" and "Shoot The Jews."

In their childish cruelty — not all imitation of adults, but also partly natural — the kids torment a half-wit woman, then try to make the porter's son strangle the courtyard kitten. Maryska, a girl who always sticks to herself, is chased up and down the precarious scaffolding and finally buried in the sandbox along with the dead kitten. The games go on.

"Sunday Pranks" is a highly cinematic work, underlining its casual courtyard of horrors with black and white lensing, framing and pace. Glinski, who has since made a tv film, is a talent to watch.

—Yung.

Matka Krolow
(The Mother Of Kings)
(POLISH-B&W)

A Filmpolski release of an "X" Unit and Rondo Film Unit coproduction. Written and directed by Janusz Zaorski, based on the novel by Kazimierz Brandys. Camera (b&w), Edward Klosinski; editor, Jozef Bartczak; music, Przemyslaw Gintrowski; art direction, Teresa Barska; production manager, Andrzej Smulski. Reviewed at the Gdansk Film Festival, Sept. 13, 1987. Running time: 127 MINS.
Lucja Krol . . . . Magda Teresa Wojcik
Klemens . . . . Bougslaw Linda
Wiktor Lewen . . . . . . Zbigniew Zapasiewicz
Cyga . . . . Franciszek Pieczka
Stas . . . . Michael Juszczakiewicz
 Also with: Adam Ferency (Zenon), Krzysztof Zaleski (Roman).

Gdynia — This stark black and white drama, on the shelf since 1982 for its intimate questioning of political events in Poland, took the Gold Lion of Gdansk with its moving story of a brave Mother Courage who raises four sons before and after the war. Real interest is the skill with which helmer Janusz Zaorski weaves recent history (1933-1956) into what could have been just a list of sufferings and sacrifices. A natural fest choice, "Mother Of Kings" could do well with specialized audiences abroad, where its off-limits' seal from the martial law period will be an added attraction.

Yet seen today film's indictment of Stalinism rings more distant and obvious than it might have before, and theme can be called contemporary only by an effort of extrapolation. Film opens with the death of Lucja Krol's husband under a tram. She gives birth to her fourth son on the floor of a new apartment. Neighbor Wiktor, a Communist intellectual, befriends the poverty-stricken family but is soon arrested and sent to jail.

The war passes amid bombs, cold and hardship; Lucja (the fine Magda Teresa Wojcik, who won Best Actress laurels for this part) narrowly escapes a Nazi roundup at the black market. Her son Klemens (Boguslaw Linda) and Wiktor hold ardent Communist meetings in their flat, with Lucja's blessing. She unselfishly works her fingers to the bone without a murmur. (Last line of film: "So many others had it worse.") After the war, a new nightmare arrives: Klemens is inexplicably arrested, accused by the new regime of being a collaborator. In trying to defend him, Wiktor, now a high-ranking Party leader, himself falls into disgrace.

Klemens is tortured into a "confession," but true son of a mother of marble, retracts in 1953 and dies in jail, a Communist to the end. They never tell Lucja her son is dead, and 1956 finds her writing a letter to the Party chief, asking to keep her large apartment because she's waiting for her sons to return.

There is some strong stuff in "Mother Of Kings" (title puns the

family name Krolow), probably more significant to local audiences, but more of a revelation to Western ones. Classically lensed, with support from Przemyslaw Gintrowski's warm musical score, film has a strong emotional appeal, even if it winds with some didactic illustration of Party politics in the 1950s.

—Yung.

Magnat
(The Magnate)
(POLISH-COLOR)

A Poltel release of a Tor Film Unit production. Written and directed by Filip Bajon. Camera (color), Piotr Sobocinski; editor, Wanda Zeman; music, Jerzy Satanowski; art direction, Andrzej Kowalczyk; production manager, Anna Gryczynska. Reviewed at the Gdansk Film Festival, Sept. 14, 1987. Running time: 165 MINS.
Prince Hans von Teuss . . . . . . Jan Nowicki
Franzel . . . . Olgierd Lukaszewicz
Conrad . . . . Jan Englert
Bolko . . . . Boguslaw Linda
Marisca . . . . Grazyna Szapolowska
 Also with: Maria Gladkowska (Daisy), Rolf Hoppe (Heinberg).

Gdynia — Unabashed soap opera at its classiest, "The Magnate" traces the fascinating saga of an almost-real princely Polish dynasty 1900-1935. Theatrical version is only a sample of six tv hours made with German television. Though a shorter version is in preparation, one would prefer to see more rather than less of this superbly acted and expensively filmed drama, one of the most costly Polish productions ever made. Helmer Filip Bajon immerses the action in its historical setting so skillfully it's part of the drama instead of superfluous overlay.

Though editing cuts back and forth in time, in an intelligent and intelligible way, main events can be listed chronologically. In 1900 Prince Hans von Teuss (Jan Nowicki) entertains Emperor Wilhelm II with a bison hunt at his palatial residence. He finds out many years later his wife has been the emperor's lover, and divorces her.

In the '20s, there are uprisings in Silesia, and the Prince's son Conrad (Jan Englert) has relations with a foreman's son.

In 1932, the Prince, now married to younger Marisca (Grazyna Szapolowska), becomes paralyzed and confined to a wheelchair. His diabolical elder son Franzel (Olgierd Lukaszewicz) assumes control of the ruined estate, and unknown to his father becomes associated with Hitler supporters, like his German partner Heinberg. In one of the film's memorable set pieces, Marisca and youngest son Bolko (Boguslaw Linda) tryst in the palace bakery on a bed of poppy seeds, while the old Prince slides down a bannister to catch them. He divorces Marisca and forces her and Bolko to marry at a bitter wedding party.

Following strikes in the mines, the estate is taken over by Polish authorities in 1935. Bolko, sent to Munich, is arrested and undergoes a horrifying medical treatment in prison. He dies in front of his father in another wild scene. Franzel, too, is arrested by the Nazis; and the old Prince dies. Only Conrad is left to see the family palace transformed into a tourist attraction after the war.

Based on a real family of Prussian nobility, the von Pleuss, "Magnate" covers a lot of familiar Visconti-type territory without turning it into cliché. Whole cast shines, lead by the sympathetic patriarch Nowicki. Scenery and sets are breathtaking, and period recreation excellent. — *Yung.*

Prywatne sledztwo
(Private Investigation)
(POLISH-COLOR)

A Zespol "Zodiak" Film Unit production. Written and directed by Wojciech Wojcik. Camera (color), Jacek Mieroslawski; editor, Marek Denys; music, Zbigniew Gorny; art direction, Malgorzata Wloch; production manager, Joanna Kopczynska. Reviewed at the Gdansk Film Festival, Sept. 12, 1987. Running time: **99 MINS.**
Rafal Skonecki . . . . Roman Wilhelmi
Friend . . . . Jan Peszek
Major . . . . Janusz Bukowski
Also with: Piotr Dejmek, Jan Jankowski (detectives), Miroslawa Marcheluk (drunk), Andrzej Pieczynski, Jerzy Trela.

Gdynia — A solid commercial offering from the Polish cinema, Wojciech Wojcik's "Private Investigation" shows a good grasp of Western-style storytelling with only a few lapses to damage its credibility. Tale of a citizen-avenger could interest tv buyers out for action product.

Film opens with a car accident in which Rafal's (Roman Wilhelmi) wife and kids are killed. It's the fault of a drunken truck driver, but Rafal can only dimly remember him. Police shelve the hit and run case, spurring the distraught husband to launch an investigation of his own.

Most of the action takes place on motorbike, as the helmeted avenger seeks his man from one side of Poland to the other. A series of brutal slayings of reckless truck drivers (here credibility cedes) get police on his trail, but few will doubt a turnaround ending is in the works. Finale has police closing in ineptly as Rafal and pal Jan Peszek round up their prey.

It's technically okay. — *Yung.*

Zycie wewnetrzne
(Inner Life)
(POLISH-COLOR)

A Filmpolski release of a Karol Irzykowski Film Studio production. Written and directed by Marek Koterski. Camera (color), Jacek Blawut; editor, Miroslawa Garlicka; art direction, Wojciech Saloni-Marczewski; production manager, Jerzy K. Frykowski. Re-

viewed at the Gdansk Film Festival, Sept. 15, 1987. Running time: **89 MINS.**
Mikhail . . . . Wojciech Wysocki
Wife . . . . Joanna Sienkiewicz
Also with: Maria Probosz, Jolanta Nowak, Antonina Gordon-Gorecka, Henryk Bista.

Gdynia — The most contemporary of this year's Polish film crop, both in setting and mood, is "Inner Life," second feature by Marek Koterski ("Madhouse," 1984). "Inner Life" is also set in a type of madhouse, a high-rise apartment building where the hero of the tale unwillingly comes into contact with family and neighbors. A film with more to it than first meets the eye, this black comedy could be screened in special situations with a Polish accent.

Wojciech Wysocki plays Mikhail, as grumpy, thoroughly dislikable neurotic who can stand almost nothing about the people and things that surround him. He scowls back at leering neighbors who ride the elevator with attack dogs, but at night indulges in erotic dreams about women. Most of all he hates his wife.

Joanna Sienkiewicz, sympathetically limning his long-suffering spouse, is a mousy, harmless thing, totally frigid, good-hearted but maddeningly monotonous. Every night they eat cold cuts in front of the tv, while he torments her. "You have to be attractive to have attractive things happen to you." Neither is attractive.

Basically a 2-actor show, "Inner Life" has a low-key cynicism that becomes almost charming as it wears on. Wysocki looks like a young Jack Nicholson and acts like a hysterical hot-head. He's utterly unfair to everybody but then, so is life. A scene where he's comically harassed by three policemen for taking a walk is just part of his misery. Another part is the safety pin on his broken zipper, keeping his pants closed. There is a child, but no one seems to remember him much. He already looks as depressed as Daddy. — *Yung.*

Przyjaciel wesolego diabla
(The Friend Of A Jolly Devil)
(POLISH-COLOR)

A Se-Ma-For Film Studio production. Directed by Jerzy Lukaszewicz. Screenplay, Lukaszewicz, based on the novel by Kornel Makuszynski; camera (color), Lukaszewicz; editor, Miroslawa Garlicka; music, Marek Bilinski; art direction, Piotr Dumala; production manager, Andrzej Zielonka. Reviewed at the Gdansk Film Festival, Sept. 12, 1987. Running time: **87 MINS.**
Janek . . . . Waldemar Kalisz
Piszczalka . . . . Piotr Dziamarski
Witalis . . . . Franciszek Pieczka
Also with: Zbigniew Grabski, Janusz Sterninski, Marcin Zdenicki, Krystyna Lech-Maczka.

Gdynia — "The Friend Of A Jolly Devil" is designed for kids who like their fairy tales spiked with adventure. This Polish production doffs its cap more than once to American blockbusters like "Raid-

ers Of The Lost Ark" and "Star Wars"/"Star Trek," creating some passable thrills on obviously a far more modest budget. Set in pure fantasyland, film ought to have wide market potential. It makes a dignified entry for Poland into the field of live action children's films.

Story is a blend of bits and pieces from many familiar tales. A kindly woodsman (Franciszek Pieczka) finds an infant in a misty, King Arthur-style forest. He raises him as his own son, but when the boy is 10 or 12, the mysterious forces that deposited him in the forest seem to call him back.

Forsaking the woodsman (who has suddenly lost his sight), little Janek (Waldemar Kalisz) sets off on a journey through a strange land inhabited by strange creatures. A lovable monster with long fur and a wrinkled face, Piszczalka (Piotr Dziamarski under the costume), becomes his friend and traveling companion. With Janek's magic crystal, which gives him strength, and Piszczalka's giant dinner fork, which has various powers, the duo brave dwarves and huge spiders, swamps, rolling boulders, mazelike caverns, and a final tussle with the Lord of Darkness. Janek's return home to the woodsman he loves gives the old man his sight back. Moral: there's no place like home.

Special effects are so-so, but atmospheric lensing counts for a lot. Camera credit goes to director Jerzy Lukaszewicz, making his feature film directing bow. Thesps fit nicely into roles having — like the rest of film — no pretense to being deep or original. — *Yung.*

W zawieszeniu
(Suspended)
(POLISH-COLOR)

A Filmpolski release of a Zodiak Film Unit production. Directed by Waldemar Krzystek. Screenplay, Malgorzata Kopernik, Krzystek; camera (color), Dariusz Kuc; editor, Krzysztof Osiecki; music, Jerzy Satanowski; art direction, Tadeusz Kosarewicz; production manager, Michal Zablocki. Reviewed at the Gdansk Film Festival, Sept. 17, 1987. Running time: **93 MINS.**
Anna . . . . Krystyna Janda
Marcel . . . . Jerzy Radziwilowicz
Mother . . . . Slawa Kwasniewska
Also with: Andrzej Lapicki (Ruczynski), Boguslaw Linda (the lieutenant), Bozena Dykiel (Fela).

Gdynia — Feature film debut by Waldemar Krzystek is a tightly made mix of thriller, romance and politics. Wanting to be all things doesn't make for a great film, but pic has the kind of classic plotting that makes it eminently watchable (helmer's tv background shows). With its happy ending (boy gets girl as Stalinism ends), "Suspended" should have audience appeal particularly locally where memories of the grim '50s are still alive.

Krystyna Janda, the hyper-active heroine of "Man Of Marble," is toned down here as Anna, a nurse

who meets her wartime lover Marcel ("Man Of Marble's" Jerzy Radziwilowicz) again in 1951. Learning he's been sentenced to death for the part he played in the Home Army, she hides him in the cellar for something like five years.

Suspense is built through close calls, Anna's lame mother discovering the fugitive, the need to bring in a doctor when Marcel catches pneumonia. Anna passes up a chance to marry a doctor, gets pregnant by Marcel, and has the baby out of wedlock. Despite the hardships and gossip, she's a tough woman and holds up far better than the fugitive. It takes all her morale boosting skill to pull him out of despondency, though the child, whom he peeks at through the cellar window, cheers him up.

When 1956 rolls around the political climate improves. Marcel makes a dramatic reentry into the upper world, and is arrested, but at his rehabilitation trial he's aquitted on grounds of "previous mistakes of the court."

All this is a bit facile and wrung for quick emotion. — *Yung.*

San Sebastian Fest Reviews

El Bosque Animado
(The Enchanted Forest)
(SPANISH-COLOR)

A Classic Film production. Produced by Eduardo Ducay. Directed by Jose Luis Cuerda. Screenplay, Rafael Azcona, based on Wenceslao Fernández Flórez' novel; camera (color), Xavier Aguirresarobe; editor, Juan Ignacio San Mateo; music, Pepe Nieto; production manager, Emiliano Otegui Piedra; sets, Felix Murcia; sound, Bernardo Menz. Reviewed at the San Sebastian Film Festival, Sept. 25, 1987. Running time: **109 MINS.**

Malvis . . . . Alfredo Landa
Geraldo . . . . Fernando Valverde
Hermelinda . . . . Alejandra Grepi
Also with: Encarna Paso, Miguel Rellán, Amparo Baró, Alicia Hermida, Maria Isbert, Luma Gómez, Fernando Rey.

San Sebastian — Based on a series of alternately fantastic and humorous tales published in 1943, and brilliantly adapted for the screen by Rafael Azcona, "The Enchanted Forest" promises to be the hit of the fall season in Spain. Filled with touches of black humor and oddball twists, pic had audience in stitches at the festival, but much of the zany humor is probably too local to generate interest in other parts of the world.

Set in a rural village and forest in the remote region of Galicia sometime in the 1920s, story revolves around some of the local characters who at various points must traverse a forest inhabited by a bumbling, would-be bandit, played brilliantly by Alfredo Landa, and a perambulating ghost. Other personages include a well-digger with an artificial leg, in love with one of the pretty village girls, two spinsters who have sought out what they hope would be the peace and quiet of a farmhouse, a finicky aunt, two children, the local madman, and the members of a wealthy family.

Azcona and director José Luis Cuerda skillfully link all these personages together, as the 1-legged well-digger pursues the little girl, the inept bandit tries to hold up travelers and the ghost mourns his never having gone to America while still alive. Even a burial scene is cause for hilarity as each of the crones watching it pleads with the deceased to deliver messages to relatives in the hereafter.

Pic is crisply lensed and well acted all around, but it is the scintillating script that enables it to come across so amusingly. —*Besa.*

Barbablu Barbablu
(Bluebeard Bluebeard)
(ITALIAN-COLOR)

A RAI-2, Beta Film and Pont Royal Film TV production. Produced by Carlo and Roberto Tuzzi. Written and directed by Fabio Carpi. Camera (Eastmancolor), José Luis Alcaine; editor, Alfredo Muschietti; sound, Luciano Fiorentini; costumes, Alberto Verso. Reviewed at San Sebastian Film Festival, Sept. 24, 1987. Running time: **118 MINS.**
With: Susannah York, John Gielgud, Angelica Boeck, Niels Arestrup, Héctor Alterio, Silvia Mocci.

San Sebastian — The "Bluebeard" of the title is in fact an aged, wealthy and famous psychiatrist, played by John Gielgud, who, claiming to be on his deathbed, gathers to his mansion on Lake Como his offspring from five different marriages.

This assorted and not very interesting group then proceeds to jabber among themselves for nearly two hours, expressing their personal problems and occasionally uttering some reflections on life, love and death. Meanwhile, upstairs, the ailing patriarch is being interviewed before a tv camera.

Pic is a lamentable exercise of verbose monotony, worsened by static camerawork and a pretentious script. There is virtually no action in the film, as the personages bemoan their own fates and shuffle about like zombies before the camera. Theatrical prospects are seemingly nil, and tv ones similarly dim.
—*Besa.*

El Lute — Camina O Revienta
(El Lute — Forge On Or Die)
(SPANISH-COLOR)

An M.G.C.-Multivideo production. Produced by Isabel Mulà, José Marìa Cunilles. Directed by Vicente Aranda. Screenplay, Aranda, Joaquin Jordá, based on Eleuterio Sánchez' autobiography; camera (Fuji color), José Luis Alcaine; editor, Teresa Font; music, José Nieto; sets, Josep Rosell; direct sound, Jim Willis; production manager, José Marìa Rodriguez. Reviewed at San Sebastian Film Festival, Sept. 19, 1987. Running time: **120 MINS.**
El Lute . . . . Imanol Arias
Consuelo . . . . Victoria Abril
Medrano . . . . Antonio Valero
Also with: Carlos Tristancho, Diana Peñalver, Margarita Calahorra, Raul Fraire, Manuel de Blas, Luis Marin, Manolo Zarzo.

San Sebastian — This film version of the early criminal years of Spain's most famous delinquent and escape-artist of the 1960s, El Lute, is sometimes grim but always gripping as helmer Vicente Aranda takes us from El Lute's humble gypsy origins as a chicken thief in Extremadura to his first holdups, prison experiences and escapes. Despite its length, it never flags in interest, both in respect to the human adventures being lived, and in its reflection of the final years of Franco Spain.

Thesp Imanol Arias, already established as one of Spain's most talented actors with such pics as "The Death Of Mikel," "Camila" and "Time Of Silence," puts in a riveting performance as the hunted petty thief who, on occasion at least, gets the better of the Civil Guards.

Pic covers only the first part of El Lute's adventures. (Second part is skedded to go into production in November, with the same producers, lead thesp, and helmer.) Starting as an itinerant peddler of pots and pans and living in a gypsy shantytown, El Lute gradually embarks upon his life of petty criminality, eventually participating in the theft of a jewelry store during which a bystander is killed. The Civil Guards catch up with him pretty fast, but even though under torture he refuses to reveal the identity of his two cohorts, they are caught and all three sentenced to death. A last-minute reprieve signed by General Franco saves them.

Later, while being escorted by two Civil Guards in a train, El Lute manages to escape. For nearly a week he is tracked by police, managing to survive and elude them despite a broken arm, but, somewhat anticlimactically, the Civil Guards track him down and return him to prison.

Producers have tried to reconstruct as much as possible the scenes and sites where the action took place, lensing on location in prisons and towns. Though pic ends on a downbeat note, Spanish audiences, of course, know that El Lute eventually was paroled and is now living in considerable comfort as a minor celebrity in Spain.

Film was well received by audiences at the fest and probably will make a bundle in its fall release in Spain. Some offshore interest is possible, despite local theme of pic and the rather difficult-to-understand jargon and slang spoken by the delinquents.

Though Aranda is not a director experienced in action sequences, he nonetheless handles the escape and persecution scenes well. José Luis Alcaine's lensing is superb, and Victoria Abril puts in a fine supporting performance as El Lute's bedraggled wife. —*Besa.*

El Amor Es Una Mujer Gorda
(Love Is A Fat Woman)
(ARGENTINE-B&W)

A Movimiento Falso and Allart's Enterprises production. Executive producers, Liliana Cascante, César Maidana. Written and directed by Alejandro Agresti. Camera (b&w), Nestor Sanz; editor, René Wiegmans; music, Paul Michael Van Brugge; post-production in Holland, Kees Kasander, Marietta de Vries. Reviewed at San Sebastian Film Festival, Sept. 23, 1987. Running time: **80 MINS.**
José . . . . Elio Marchi
Caferata . . . . Sergio Poves Campos
Also with: Carlos Roffe, Theo McNabny, Mario Luciani, Humberto Tito Haas, Enrique Morales, Harry Havilio, Sergio Lerer.

San Sebastian — A sincere, well-limned filmic cry in the wilderness, this provocative and poignant pic nevertheless is doomed to oblivion due to its downbeat story, local orientation, short running time and black & white format.

Young helmer Alejandro Agresti has an Orson Wellesian taste for odd-angle shots, but also an eye for irony and humor which make palatable his story of a social misfit and loser who cannot come to grips with the complacency in his country and in the world.

José is a kind of drifter and sometime journalist who can never simply draw the line at his assignments. When his editor asks him to cover a documentary on Argentina being filmed by some Yanks, José's ire bursts forth at what he considers to be the filmic exploitation of the poor. He tries to stop the lensing.

Subsequently finding himself out of a job, out of his boarding house and penniless, he seeks out old friends while ranting at the world's apathy. He still is pining for a former flame, still "missing" from the days of the dictatorship.

Agresti softens José's vitriolic vision of the world by adding incisive touches of humor. Even these, however, serve to heighten the denunciatory tone of the film. The sense of futility and disillusionment spills over in every frame, but pic also has a winning, heroic dimension which is wonderfully caught.

Thesping throughout, especially by Elio Marchi, is superb, and camerawork and technical credits are handled with the expertise one has become accustomed to expect from good Argentine cinema.
— *Besa.*

Mientras Haya Luz
(While There Is Light)
(SPANISH-B&W)

A Vienna Films production. Executive producer, Gerardo Herrero. Written and directed by Felipe Vega. Camera (b&w), José Luis López Linares; editor, Miguel A. Santamaria, Ivan Aledo; music, Bernardo Bonezzi, sound, Ricardo Steinberg, Daniel Goldstein; associate producer, Paulo Branco (Filmargem). Reviewed at San Sebastian Film Festival, Sept. 26, 1987. Running time: **102 MINS.**
Jaime . . . . Rafael Diaz
Jorge . . . . Jorge de Juan
Teresa . . . . Teresa Madruga
Marisa . . . . Marisa Paredes
Also with: Joaquin Hinojosa, Patricia Bellinger, Iciar Bollain, José Segura García.

San Sebastian — "While There Is Light" is an amateurish pic with so many flaws it had audiences snickering. Novice filmmaker Felipe Vega throws so many convolutions into his film that little is comprehensible, as he either jumps abruptly from one scene to the next, or has the camera pointlessly lingering over shots. He also likes to fade to black for no obvious reason.

Yarn loosely concerns an anthropologist who is on the lam, persecuted in a pueblo by two gunmen, and a friend, recently returned to Spain from the States with a black girlfriend, who seeks him out in Spain and Portugal. All sorts of extraneous encounters are woven in, most so clumsily handled as to be ludicrous. When the two gunmen shoot a girl (off-screen), or for a few seconds supposedly torture their prey by starting to cut off his ear with a razor, they are about as convincing as moppets doing a school play.

Terribly edited, lensed and directed, pic nonetheless, inexplicably, shared a cash prize given here by the CIGA hotel chain. As if the film weren't bad enough already, its black & white format will make its distribution well-nigh impossible.—*Besa.*

Surrender
(COLOR)

Sitcom runs out of gas.

A Warner Bros. release of a Cannon Group production. Executive producers, Menahem Golan, Yoram Globus. Produced by Aaron Spelling, Alan Greisman. Directed by Jerry Belson. Stars Sally Field, Michael Caine. Screenplay, Belson; camera (TVC color), Juan Ruiz Anchia; editor, Wendy Greene Bricmont; music, Michel Colombier; production design, Lilly Kilvert; art direction, Jon Hutman; set design, Richard Mays; sound (Ultra-Stereo), Steve Nelson; assistant director, Jim Van Wyck; associate producers, Van Wyck, Bricmont; casting, Bonnie Pietila. Reviewed at Warner Bros. screening room, Burbank, Sept. 21, 1987. (MPAA Rating: PG.) Running time: **95 MINS.**

Daisy	Sally Field
Sean	Michael Caine
Marty	Steve Guttenberg
Jay	Peter Boyle
Ace	Jackie Cooper
Ronnie	Julie Kavner
Joyce	Louise Lasser
Hedy	Iman

Hollywood — "Surrender" is a '50s sitcom dressed up in modern clothes. The issues are somewhat updated but the characters still think like Doris Day and Rock Hudson. As the confused lovers, Michael Caine and Sally Field are good for a couple of laughs along the way, but production runs out of steam early and probably will ditto at the boxoffice.

Caine is a casualty of too many marriages and too much success as a pop novelist. Field is a would-be artist who takes the easy way out in the form of a rich and indulgent but unchallenging boy friend (Steve Guttenberg). Together they are so battered that neither of them can tell what they want.

Opening skirmish is love at first fight. But once they've coupled, the series of complications concocted by writer/director Jerry Belson can only lead to an inevitable happy ending. Bone of contention is ostensibly money — Caine is over his head in alimony payments and Field is dependent on her boyfriend to make ends meet — but it's really just a smoke screen for the old she-loves-me, she-loves-me-not.

Caine is likable as the aging womanizer who has sworn off the opposite sex until he is captivated by Field. Although there is never really any reason for the attraction, part of it can be attributed to his impulsive personality.

Things at least move fast and Belson does have an ear for modern courtship and the silly things people say to each other. But once the groundwork is laid, the action just goes back and forth with the same set of shifting circumstances.

Wearing a mustache over his smarmy grin, Guttenberg is an unctuous attorney who conveniently disappears when the romance flowers and returns when a complication is needed. Belson also tries to pick up the sagging action by moving the couple to Vegas where Field hits the jackpot and adds an unnecessary twist to the ties that bind.

Basically it's still the old question — will they or won't they find everlasting happiness together — with little more regard for the external world than people showed in '50s fluff. Belson simply hasn't cut deep enough or injected enough wit to make this kind of thing stand up for today's audience.

Although their acting styles don't quite mesh and there isn't a great deal of chemistry between them, both Caine and Field are strong enough presences to make them entertaining to observe. Also fun, and perhaps the one truly modern character in the stew, is Peter Boyle as Caine's opportunistic attorney with a heart of gold, or some other precious metal.

Tech credits are firstrate, with Juan Ruiz Anchia's camerawork and Lilly Kilvert's production design capturing the pastel colors and airy environs of Los Angeles. Randy Newman is just right bellowing "It's Money That I Love" over the opening credits with more than a hint of "I Love L.A." in the hot breeze.—*Jagr.*

Retribution
(COLOR)

Overdone, overly familiar horror opus.

A United Film Distribution Co. release, in association with Unicorn Motion Pictures of a Renegade Films production. Executive producers, Scott Lavin, Brian Christian. Produced and directed by Guy Magar. Screenplay, Magar, Lee Wasserman; camera (Fuji color by United), camera, Gary Thieltges; editor, Magar, Alan Shetland; music, Alan Howarth; sound (Dolby), Peter Bentley; production design, Robb Wilson King; production manager, Jeanne N. van Cott; assistant director, Doublas F. Dean 3d; special makeup effects, Kevin Yagher; special effects, Court Wizard; stunt coordinator, Bob Yerkes; postproduction supervisor, Jeffrey Reiner; associate producer, Wasserman; casting, Carol Dudley. Reviewed at Magno Review 2 screening room, N.Y., Oct. 8, 1987. (MPAA Rating: R.) Running time: **107 MINS.**

George Miller	Dennis Lipscomb
Jennifer Curtis	Leslie Wing
Angel	Suzanne Snyder
Alan Falconer	Jeff Pomerantz
Dr. Talbot	George Murdock
Sally Benson	Pamela Dunlap
Mrs. Stroller	Susan Peretz
Carla Minelli	Clare Peck
Dylan	Chris Caputo
Lt. Ashley	Hoyt Axton
Amos	Ralph Manza

"Retribution" is a hyped-up supernatural horror film, substituting a noisy soundtrack, gore and a fidgety camera for any substance. It stands an okay chance at attracting less discriminating horror audiences during the Halloween season.

As implied by the title, pic concerns the standard revenge from beyond the grave plot, Dennis Lipscomb plays George Miller, who commits suicide, almost dying, jumping from his hotel roof in the pic's protracted (8-minute) prolog. A man who is brutally murdered at the same time (and who shares Miller's April 1 birthdate) seemingly possesses Miller's body, meting out sadistic, gory deaths to his killers while Miller sleeps. Pic's protagonists, including Miller, his kindly and beautiful shrink (Leslie Wing) and stone-faced cop on the case (Hoyt Axton in a bored walk-through) are much slower than the audience in picking up on the obvious clues.

Padded film runs at least two reels too long for its own good, as feature-debuting filmmaker (after tv experience) Guy Magar dwells unwisely on boring plot recap scenes, a silly excursion to a rastaman witch doctor and overly cutesy filler involving Miller's neighbors at the hotel. Film's biggest fault is that despite Lipscomb's technically okay, twitchy performance, the central character is thoroughly unsympathetic and it remains unbelievable that he has so many friends looking out for his welfare.

Explicit gore and blood is laid on to delight the fans, but pic is needlessly ugly, with Fuji color (by United Lab) that is garish, grainy and with a greenish tint even in "normal" scenes (plus ugly color filters and lighting for effect). Alan Howarth's score is way overdone in a vain attempt to supercharge the visuals, which consist of familiar horror effects. Acting is tolerable, though Suzanne Snyder, playing Miller's prostitute girl friend, is shrill and campy for the second time in a row, following her "Prettykill" shriekathon role. Finale and some of the effects are overly reminiscent of "The Exorcist," with a very corny final twist. —*Lor.*

Ofelas
(Pathfinder)
(NORWEGIAN-COLOR-70M)

A Syncron Film release of a Filmkammeraterne production. (World Sales outside Scandinavia, Carolco Film Intl.) Produced by John M. Jacobsen. Written and directed by Nils Gaup. Camera (Panavision 70, Eastmancolor), Erling Thurmann-Andersen; editor, Niels Pagh Andersen; music, Nils-Aslak Valkeapää, Marlus Müller, Kjetil Bjerkestrand; sound, (Dolby), Sturla Einarson; costumes, Eva Schölberg, Marit Sofie Holmestrand; production management, Arve Figenschou; 2d unit director, Sölve Skagen; 2d unit camera, Erick Arguillere; stunt director, Martin Grace. Reviewed at Colosseum theater, Oslo, Oct. 8, 1987. Running time: **90 MINS.**

Aigin	Mikkel Gaup
Raste	Nils Utsi
Tchude Chief	Svein Scharffenberg
Tchude With Scar	Helgi Skulason
Sierge	Sverre Porsanger
Diemis	Svein Birger Olsen
Orbes	Ailu Gaup
Sahve	Sara Marit Gaup
Varia	Anne-Marja Blind

Also with: Henrik H. Buljo, Ingvald Guttorm, Amund Johnskareng, Nils-Aslak Valkeapää, John S. Kristensen, Knut Walle, Ellen Anne Buljo, Inger Utsi.

Oslo — "Pathfinder," already a world rights pickup by Carolco, is the world's first Lapp-language feature film. It is also a job of epic actioner filmmaking to rank with the best of any country. Its artistic pulse may be weaker than its big, booming technical heartbeat and narrative wizardry, but its beauty and suspense are sustained sufficiently to leave one clamoring for more after its surprisingly short 90 minutes.

Everything else is big in Norwegian producer John Jacobsen and Norwegian-Lapp writer-helmer Nils Gaup's retelling of a Lapp legend of 800 years ago in the Artic North where a very young man, with the aid of guts, brains and some shaman magic, leads a gang of marauding Tchude warriors from the East into a mountain divide to be buried under an avalanche, thus freeing his tribe of Lapp nomads to pursue their peaceful way of life as hunters.

This is truly the stuff of legend, and no great nuancing in portraiture has been deemed necessary by Nils Gaup. He has his Tchudes black-clad and coolly menacing and his Lapps white-clad and rather jolly-looking even in adversity. They fight bears as well as Tchudes by enlisting human wiles along with traditional sorcery and take omens from the appearance of their holy Bull Reindeer as naturally as any piece of common sense advice.

The young man forced to become a pathfinder for the Tchudes is played with subdued boyish charm by Mikkel Gaup. The Tchudes are played with laudable restraint by Norwegian and Icelandic professional actors, the Lapps mostly by amateurs of the Beaivvaza theater group and they, too, pass muster as just right for their roles. Inevitably, the action, stunts, vivid narration and gorgeous cinematography win the day.

Working in temperatures down to minus 40°, cinematographer Erling Thurmann-Andersen has used a 70m format Panavision camera with new high-speed Kodak 5297 film to capture the silent majesty of the Arctic landscapes in frames and nuances of subtlety combined with an almost physical impact that goes well with the Dolby Stereo recording of sounds such as footstep squeaking in the frozen snow and arrows hitting birch trees or human flesh and bone.

Fight scenes have fine choreography and the stunts have been directed with such expertise as is to be expected by England's Martin Grace, who handled similar chores for "The Living Daylights."

"Pathfinder" has a lilting musical score wtih a slight bluesy tint by Nils-Aslak Valkeapää. Somewhere under the surface of the film lurk hints of deeper dramatic insights and shadings. Nils Gaup impresses as a filmmaker of truly international scope, plunged into a wilderness assignment and brought out if it with honors by John M. Jacobsen, a producer of matching ambition, skill and daring. —Kell.

El año del conejo
(The Year Of The Rabbit)
(ARGENTINE-COLOR)

An Aries Cinematográfica Argentina production and release. Produced by Héctor Olivera. Directed by Fernando Ayala. Stars Federico Luppi, Luisina Brando. Screenplay, Oscar Viale, based on a plot idea by Olivera; camera (color), Leonardo Rodriguez Solís; editor, Eduardo López; music, Leo Sujatovich; sets, Emilio Basaldúa; costumes, Patricia Pernía. Reviewed at the Aries screening room, Buenos Aires, Aug. 11, 1987. (Rating in Argentina: forbidden for under 18s.) Running time: **103 MINS.**

Pepe	Federico Luppi
Norma	Luisina Brando
Sergio	Juan Carlos Dual
Karina	Katja Alemann
Milo	Ulises Dumont
Marcelo	Gerardo Romano

Also with Raúl Rizzo, Felisa Rocha, Andrea Barbieri, Daniel Galarza.

Buenos Aires — This is a caustic comedy-drama about financial speculation, scoring several bullseyes along the way.

Subject already has given rise in recent years to a number of other Argentine films, satires with varying amounts of bite, including some by the same team of Fernando Ayala and Héctor Olivera that was responsible for the present work. In times of very high inflation, many people have taken to searching feverishly for the highest-yielding investments and financial schemes.

In tune with increasing freedom and uninhibitedness in sexual matters, the films in this as in other Argentine genres include more and more nudity and sexual activity.

In "Year Of The Rabbit" — an astrological reference which in the case of the story's hero is held to be auspicious — a relatively well-off bank official (Federico Luppi) decides at age 55 that money worries are one reason why, in his view, he hasn't been getting anywhere in life. His wife (Luisina Brando) won't go along with his plans, so he ditches her. He gives up the safe, but unexciting job, sells his lovely town house, and uses the boodle to buy a share of highly speculative financial investments firm.

The fact that his partner (Gerardo Romano) is courting a heart attack and snorting coke to withstand the pace should tell him something, but he doesn't notice much since he is doing all right with an attractive young employee (Katja Alemann), who happens to be very efficient — and extremely ambitious.

Meanwhile, being on her own has freed the potentialities in the wife, who begins to pile up successes with a catering venture.

Despite a question mark left hanging over the last frames of the film, by and large one can see the outcome of the lateblooming speculator a mile off. Yet this motion picture does not attempt to ran through any facile moral, and anyway, it provides good entertainment while getting to that outcome.

A major strength of the plot is the figure of the older man (Juan Carlos Dual) in the life of the hero's daughter, an outrageous, fast-talking wolf who, like the other characters, evolves in interesting ways in the course of the film.
—Olas.

Zombie High
(COLOR)

Underachieving thriller.

A Cinema Group Pictures release of an Elliott Kastner presentation. Executive producer, Cassian Elwes. Produced by Marc Toberoff, Aziz Ghazal. Directed by Ron Link. Screenplay, Tim Doyle, Elizabeth Passerelli, Ghazal; camera (Film House color), David Lux, Brian Coyne; editor, Shawn Hardin; James Whitney; music, Daniel May; production design, Matthew Kozinets; art direction, Hisham Abed; set direction, Martin Jones, Todd Stevens; special effects, Chris Biggs, Mark Messenger; sound, Jon Oh; casting, Kimba Hills. Reviewed at Hollywood Egyptian theater, Oct. 7, 1987. (MPAA Rating: R.) Running time: **91 MINS.**

Andrea	Virginia Madsen
Philo	Richard Cox
Dean Eisner	Kay Kuter
Barry	James Wilder
Suzi	Sherilynn Fenn
Emerson	Paul Feig
Felner	T. Scott Coffey
Ignatius	Paul Williams
Bell	Henry Sutton
Mary Beth	Clare Carey

Hollywood — This decidedly low-budget thriller marks the screen debut of theatrical director Ron Link, who should have held out for more money, or better scripting, or both. Decent horror/thriller premise — boarding school profs are gaining everlasting life by practically lobotomizing students — is rendered idiotic by mediocre acting, horrid story line, awful dialog and perhaps the most abysmal sound of any domestic release this year. Not even Virginia Madsen's growing appeal can save this one.

Madsen turns in a credible performance as the lead, Andrea Miller, a schoolgirl who becomes a member of the first coed class of stately Ettinger Academy.

Leaving her jealous boyfriend Barry (James Wilder) behind, she encounters several narrowly drawn, spoiled types that highlight the contempt with which scripters hold the teenagers of today.

Roomate Suzi (Sherilyn Fenn) and dorm neighbor Mary Beth (Clare Carey) both receive thankless roles as mindless would-be sluts who are attending the school only because of the 10-to-1 male-to-female ratio.

To the girls' dismay, most of the male students are humorless automatons who study endlessly, read the Wall Street Journal, and seem to have undergone some kind of charisma bypass surgery.

Truth turns out to be something like that, as Andrea slowly realizes that every student at Ettinger secretly undergoes an operation in which vital brain tissue is removed and replaced by a quartz crystal. Tissue then goes to create a serum that gives faculty everlasting life while piped-in classical music stimulates quartz crystals that turn students into zombies of the title, devoid of personality or conscience.

Key to exposing this unlikely series of events is Professor Philo (Richard Cox, who seems to be constantly posing for an album cover), a doctor with the hots for Andrea and thus a desire to save her from her cruel fate.

Film is at its nadir when it tries to inject a values dilemma into the storyline: "So that's the tradeoff," says Madsen belaboring the point, "you live forever and the students get lobotomized."

Film's conclusion dares to be stupid — and succeeds on that level — but only the gamest of individuals will still care by that point.

Link's style occasionally comes through (although most of his shots and angles are trite) and photography by David Lux and Brian Coyne is sometimes commendable.

All is overshadowed by the terrible sound (Jon Oh is listed as guilty party in credits, but this disaster had to start at the top), which at certain points is so bad that characters' lines seem to have been dubbed over actors who might be speaking another language.

Madsen's fresh performance is accompanied by Wilder's nice turn as her boyfriend. At the other end of the spectrum is character of Emerson, played by Paul Feig, who has evidently been watching far too many Jon Cryer films.—Camb.

Quartiere
(Neighborhood)
(ITALIAN-COLOR)

An Istituto Luce/Italnoleggio release of a Marzo Cinematografica production. Produced, written and directed by Silvano Agosti. Camera (Luciano Vittori color), Agosti; editor, Agosti; music, Ennio Morricone. Reviewed at the Venice Film Festival (competing), Sept. 7, 1987. Running time: **124 MINS.**

Mother	Vittoria Zinny
The two sisters	Alessandra Corsale, Paola Agosti
Rich boy	Lorenzo Negri
His friend	Ivano Errera
Nino	Sergio Bini
Old bum	Nino Manzone
The doorkeeper	Giorgetta Ranucci

Also with: Dario Ghirardi, Valeria Sable, Lino Salemme, Francesca Trevisannelo, Elisabetta Pellgrini, Elena Donnici, Benedetto Simonelli.

Venice — Silvano Agosti's artisanal approach to filmmaking, strongly influenced by his documentary past, comes out clearly in "Neighborhood." Shot with mostly non-pros over a 3-year period, written, directed, lensed, edited and produced by Agosti (in whose Roman repertory cinema it will surely be shown), "Neighborhood" is a not overly involving hybrid between fiction and documentary, detailing four bizarre "love stories." Audience for this curiosity item looks limited.

Though it recounts some pretty harsh realities, overall impact of pic is gentle and optimistic. First tale shows two sisters (Alessandra Corsale and Paola Agosti) accepting a ride home on New Year's Eve from a bunch of boys, who end up repeatedly raping one of them. Strangely, the younger, prettier sister is spared, and allowed to be traumatized from watching. The elder, instead, recovers, and begins meeting one of her rapists, who repents to the point of marrying her. The family knows but pretends not to. For those who can stomach the painfully protracted rape sequence (shot in dark close-ups, but anguishing), ending is a letdown.

Second yarn brings two pals together, one a very rich young man, one a very handsome one. Love blooms while the rich parents are out of town (but it seems to be just lust or friendliness on the part of the good-looking lad, who keeps explaining he's getting married soon). He leaves the rich boy broken-hearted, listening to "Tosca."

Third episode: a man whose woman has left him becomes obsessed with a tiger, and finally refuses to taker her back.

Fourth tale is an old tramp's, a character seen throughout the film. He lives in an abandoned car, in front of a building whose doorkeeper (Giorgetta Ranucci) takes pity on him. One night she sleeps with him in the car — his first night of love.

An inconclusive quality is common to all the stories, which choose the anecdote over deep character exploration. They also don't hang together too well as the portrait of a neighborhood. Visually film is sensitively lensed, with great attention to framing and a preference for honest, wrinkle-and-blemish close-ups. Thesping has little importance here. —Yung.

Va de Nuez
(Once Again)
(MEXICAN-COLOR)

A Peliculas Nacionales release of a Diplaf-Producciones Chimalistac production. Executive producer, Pablo Boy. Produced by Hugo Scherer, Gonzalo Infante. Directed by Alfredo Gurrola. Stars Rafael Sánchez Navarro, Patricia Reyes Spindola. Screenplay, Jorge Patiño; camera (color), Miguel Garzón; editor, Sergio Soto; music, Amparo Rubín;

sound, Abel Flores. Reviewed at Sala 4, Cineteca Nacional, Mexico City, Sept. 20, 1987. Running time: **95 MINS.**
Pepe Reyes ..... Rafael Sánchez Navarro
Manuela Reyes ... Patricia Reyes Spindola
Also with: Alejandro Parodi, Salvador Sánchez, Socorro Bonilla, Jorge Zepeda.

Mexico City — The Mexican feature "Va de Nuez" (Once Again) is a bold venture to delve into a particularly modern theme — one especially important to Mexico — with both a personal and experimental approach. Helmed by veteran filmmaker Alfredo Gurrola, pic deals with the importance of population control and was coproduced by the state family planning organization Diplaf (Desarrollo de Investigación para la Planeación Familiar).

Film attacks the problem of raising national consciousness by approaching the argument from reverse. The storyline ironically concerns an infertile couple, unable to have a child while living in a country where the inhabitants apparently spawn like salmon. Their anguish leads to mutual incriminations and spills over into their professional lives.

Characters are both involved with film: Pepe (Ramón Sánchez Navarro) directs tv commercials while his wife Manuela (Patricia Reyes Spindola) studies film theory. Gurrola takes judicious advantage of this to vary the texture of images through inserts of video, commercials, film commentaries and even a tribute to his own 1979 experimental *film noir* "Llámanme Mike" (Call Me Mike). Pic's title, a slangy way of saying "va de nuevo," is Mexican film nomenclature for "retake."

Besides the principal theme, which forms the core of the drama, we find a much more personal argument that Gurrola, through the character of Pepe, defends his own ventures into commercial filmmaking, as Pepe must defend his work against the high standards of Manuela's art-film friends. Besides "Llámanme Mike," Gurrola has directed many Mexican action pics including "Escuadrón de la Muerte" (Death Squad) and "Contrato con la Muerte" (Contract With Death).

Jorge Patiño's tight script is well developed dealing with real people involved in a real problem, yet it is balanced by many instances of humor and insight. Both Sánchez Navarro and Reyes Spindola offer multifaceted characterizations. Photography detail, is rich and varied with attention to detail, albeit a bit too dark at times.

"Va de Nuez" is an interesting and experimental approach to dealing with a modern Mexican theme in an accessible and entertaining way. Gurrola uses his film vocabulary well and instead of a heavy-handed statement, he emerges with a small personal project that fits well into what is deemed *cine de autor*. —Lent.

Nights In White Satin
(COLOR)

Never reaching the end.

A Fox/Lorber release of a Mediacom Industries presentation, in association with MVA-1. Produced by Giovanna Nigro-Chacon. Executive producers, A.J. Cervantes, Ronald Altbach. Directed and edited by Michael Barnard. Screenplay, William Kronick; camera (Foto-Kem color), Tom Fraser; music, Paul Farerro; music supervision, Rick E. Ambrose; sound, George Hause; production design, Anthony Sabatino, William H. Harris; art direction, George Petersen; set decoration, Rob Sagrillo; costumes, Candace Walters; makeup/hair, Dina Ousley Carone; production manager-associate producer, Patricia Sonsini; assistant director, John Raymond; choreography, Marla Blakey; casting, Joy Dolce. Reviewed on HBO, Sept. 15, 1987. (No MPAA Rating.) Running time: **96 MINS.**
Walker Jordan .... Kenneth David Gilman
Lisa .... Priscilla Harris
Stevie Hughes .... Kim Waltrip
Marty Fiore .... Michael Laskin
Jacques .... Pierre Manasse
Bag lady .... Connie Sawyer
Tracy .... Diane Manzo
Angela .... Dina Ousley Carone
Howie .... Howard Rosenberg
Candace .... Candace Walters
Gingee .... Nadja von Lowenstein

"Nights In White Satin" is a tedious romantic trifle, which if it were released theatrically would have the fans chanting "More plot!" As is, it preemed late-late night on HBO, ahead of its destined homevideo release.

Meager storyline has fashion photographer Walker Jordan (Kenneth David Gilman) becoming obsessed with street waif Lisa (Priscilla Harris, who looks like a plain Jane version of Cyndi Lauper). He has her move into his apartment, becoming one of his assistants. They fall in love, she becomes a hit model, they part and happy ending reunites them.

Cornball material is merely an excuse for director-editor Michael Barnard to pour on technique that smacks of music videos and "Miami Vice." Beneath the flashy visuals and hit songs soundtrack is nothing. Even the film's ostensible theme, that of Gilman torn between his crass but lucrative glamor shoots and his real desire to do realistic photo studies of street people, is identical to the plot tag of earlier film-to-paycable effort (though a comedy) "Perfect Timing."

The Moody Blues theme song by Justin Hayward finally plays late in the picture to accompany rooftop jazz ballet turn by Harris, but most viewers will have nodded off by then. Cast is extremely bland, nudity minimal and other hits by the Thompson Twins, the Knack and Pat Benatar thrown in arbitrarily. —Lor.

Caught In A Web: L'Impasse
(BRITISH-DOCU-COLOR-16m)

A Malachite Programmes on Film and Video, Lincolnshire, and Channel Four, London production. Produced by Charles Mapleston. Directed and narrated by Toni de Bromhead. Camera (color), De Bromhead; additional camera, Belinda Parsons, David Scott; editor, Susan Manning; music, Mike Wesbrook; sound, David Goodale, Peter Hodges. Reviewed at the Margaret Mead Film Festival, American Museum of Natural History, N.Y., Sept. 7, 1987. Running time: **150 MINS.**
(Partly in French, with English subtitles)

Director Toni de Bromhead opens the film on camera by explaining its format, an alternation of sequences, shot in two different cultures: a small town in West Dorset, England, and a Provencal village in France.

By contrasting and comparing these two societies, she claims, we deepen our understanding of ourselves, whatever our own village. She fulfills her claim, as "Caught In A Web" reveals the essential humanity and the common needs of these two British and French villages, despite their national, historical, geographical, linguistic and religious differences.

However, non-anthropologists attending this anthropological Mead Festival may complain that 2½ hours running time is perhaps an hour too long to make these admittedly important points. One can expect to see the film on public tv here, but discreetly timed.

What is more British than a cricket match, riding to hounds and a pint in a pub? What is more French than a grape harvest, pretty girls and old men sweating and smiling in the vineyards?

These are more than stereotypes. They reveal national characteristics and attitudes and values. The British and French are contrasted in terms of their differing attitudes toward class, individualism, church authority, ties to the land.

By means of this format, the moral codes, social laws, unspoken obligations and privileges of the two societies become visible. The British are quieter than the French, are closer to their women, more decorous, more socially obedient, have well-organized games, government and work. The French are more individualistic, noisier, enjoying male fraternity, are misogynistic although married (one man speculates because married). The French are fatalistic, and pessimistic, laced with black humor. The British are politely subservient to the local manor, relying on fairness.

Late in the film, scenes show the British looking at the French footage and making comments, while the French similarly watch their British counterparts and make ironic observations. Each village in an odd way sees itself "objectively" as an object of study by another village, being scrutinized and judged by strangers. It's a clever format that works, especially as De Bromhead in voiceover narration clarifies

connections and comparisons.
—*Hitch.*

Lo del César
(What Is Caesar's)
(MEXICAN-COLOR)

A Casablanca Films and Televisión Española production. Produced by Carlos Resendi. Directed by Felipe Cazals. Screenplay, Tomás Pérez Turrent; camera (color), Angel Goded; editor, Sigfrido Garcia; music, Amparo Rubin; sound, Fernando Terol. Reviewed at San Sebastian Film Festival, Sept. 21, 1987. Running time: **105 MINS.**

Claudio O'Riley	Humberto Zurita
Cecilia	Assumpta Serna
Leonor	Angelica Aragón
Quijano	Manuel Ojeda

Also with: José Carlos Ruiz, Alejandro Aragón, Alfredo Sevilla.

San Sebastian — This brooding, talky and pretentious takeoff on the Caesar theme seems at times to be taking pot shots at the power structure in Mexico, but whatever the point is supposed to be, it never comes across to the audience. Instead we are served up an indigestible stream of self-conscious monologs and non sequiturs as soporific as they are gauche.

Story about a young, ruthless magnate suffering philosophical angst who lords over the leading fishing cooperative of the country never gets off the ground as the foul-tempered, saturnine "Caesar" drives his sports car around the docks, plays solos on his cello, insults his underlings and peers distractedly into the distance while cuddling with beautiful women. The mood of seething violence fails to break forth into any action, except for the expected, unspectacular death scene at the end.

Badly written and directed, sloppily edited and dreadfully lensed, it is hard to see why this tedium should have been selected for an "A" category film festival.—*Besa.*

Multi-Handicapped
(DOCU-COLOR-16m)

A Zipporah Films production. Produced and directed by Frederick Wiseman. Camera (color, 16m), John Davey; editor-sound, Wiseman. Reviewed at USA Cinemas Copley Place, Boston, Sept. 14, 1987. (In the Boston Film Festival.) Running time: **126 MINS.**

Boston — "Multi-Handicapped" is the third in documentary maker Frederick Wiseman's four film series called "Blind And Deaf." Although somewhat shorter than "Blind" (*Variety,* July 1) and "Deaf" (*Variety,* Sept. 2) it covers much the same ground, this time dealing with students at the Helen Keller School in Alabama who are not only blind or deaf, but who have other impairments as well.

Wiseman's style is to dispense with interviews and narration, instead letting what he observed with his camera and microphone speak for itself. We first see students learning simple functions like sorting different shapes or how to tell time. They are followed by students who are mastering more complex tasks including social skills and reading and writing. Wiseman refuses to go for the maudlin approach of having the audience "root" for a particular student, instead stressing the monotony and small victories of day-to-day life at the school.

Concluding segments show some children who are apparently too young or too ill to train, and a church service involving the entire school. Although it would violate Wiseman's style, some context for this material would be useful. Watching children run around or rock back and forth for several minutes with no explanation requires as much patience as that exhibited by the school's teachers.

Although the "Blind And Deaf" series is appearing over two days at the Boston Film Festival, commercial prospects for the films seem nil, with the primary audience consisting of professionals and others concerned with the education and care of the handicapped. — *Kimm.*

Signed, Lino Brocka
(U.S.-DOCU-COLOR-16m)

A Christian Blackwood production. Produced and directed by Blackwood. Camera (color, 16m), Blackwood; editor, Monika Abspacher; sound, John Murphy. Reviewed at the Toronto Film Festival of Festivals, Sept. 18, 1987. Running time: **90 MINS.**

Toronto — Sardonic and rebellious Filipino filmmaker Lino Brocka and the tribulations of his impoverished but bustling homeland are the intertwined subjects of this engrossing, informative and entertaining documentary by N.Y.-based Christian Blackwood.

Through interviews with the portly, self-effacing Brocka, clips from his films, documentary footage shot in and around Manila, and segments featuring Brocka at work on a new film, Blackwood draws a portrait of a complex man whose life in many ways personifies the recent history of the Philippines.

Evincing a personality at once slyly humorous and gravely serious, Brocka speaks frankly but unpretentiously about the triumphs and compromises in his movie making career, his political activism and homosexuality, his bitterness towards the deposed dictator Ferdinand Marcos and spouse Imelda (whom he expresses a fervent desire to execute) and the terrible cycle of poverty, despair and violence from which his nation is still trying to break free.

Blackwood and Brocka examine such bizarrely compelling subjects as the National Film Center in which workers were entombed in order to meet construction dead-lines for the first Philippine Film Festival, leper colonies, vigilantes, the police-operated "sex underworld" of the capital and the colonies of squatters who live on and from the garbage dumps of Manila.

Brocka's wry commentary on his own films offers illuminating insights into the Filipino romance/action genres which he mastered. Openly conceding his failure to make money as an independent producer of his own projects, Brocka readily admits to making commercial shlock for producers who bailed him out after he was imprisoned for siding with striking jitney drivers.

These rags-to-riches fantasy films, Brocka acknowledges, provide temporary escape from the grinding reality of Philippine slum life. At the same time, Blackwood's portrait makes it abundantly clear that the sympathies of the "frustrated actor" who early on felt "the driving desire to touch the world through film," are wholly on the side of the disenfranchised oppressed. —*Rich.*

Spirale
(Spiral)
(FRENCH-COLOR)

A UGC release of a T. Films/TF1 Films coproduction. Executive producer, Alain Terzian. Written and directed by Christopher Frank. Stars Richard Berry, Claire Nebout. Camera (Eastmancolor), Robert Fraisse; editor, Nathalie Lafaurie; music, Michel Legrand; sound, Bernard Aubouy, Claude Villand; art direction, Dominique André; production managers, Philippe Lièvre, Françoise Galfré; assistant director, Michel Thibaud. Reviewed at the Marignan-Concorde cinema, Paris, Sept. 23, 1987. Running time: **90 MINS.**

Jérôme	Richard Berry
Simorre	Claire Nebout
Kino	Tcheky Karyo
Jean-François	Jean Bouise
Fabienne	Béatrice Camurat
Falconetti	Judith Magre
Stadler	Alexandre Mnouchkine
Valérie	Vanessa Lhoste
Gordon	Peter Hudson

Paris — Fourth feature film written and directed by Franco-British screenwriter-novelist Christopher Frank is a tale of morbid obsession in which Richard Berry falls in with strange company. More style-minded than stylish, "Spirale" is heavy on atmosphere and ambiguous characterization, but proves frustratingly thin on drama.

Berry plays the director of a photo lab who meets mysterious Claire Nebout while vacationing in the south of France. He's soon visiting her on her yacht, where he also makes the acquaintance of her sinister entourage, which includes sleazy ex-hubbie Tcheky Karyo, a sententious homosexual architect (Jean Bouise), and a washed-up sculptor (played by veteran film producer Alexandre Mnouchkine).

Berry's leap into a sexual liaison with Nebout both fascinates and repels him, but he cannot fathom the thick air of mystery that hangs like a shroud over the bizarre peripatetic household, lost in a vortex of despair and inertia.

Constructed like a suspense drama with Hitchcockian overtones, film turns out to be devoid of narrative tension since it becomes clear that Berry, an intrigued observer, is in no physical or even psychological danger. Berry's final comprehension of the Dark Secret is anticlimactic.

Frank works hard to drum up some cinematic excitement with a busy display of enigmatic cross-cutting, oblique dialog, prowling camerawork, and baroque symbolism (notably a statue of a sword-wielding woman submerged in a park lake) but the story's ambiguities evaporate long before Frank is ready to elucidate them.

Performances are otherwise serviceable and tech credits are sound.
—*Len.*

Xochimilco
(MEXICAN-DOCU-COLOR-16m)

A film by El Instituto Nacional Indigenistá, La Secretaria de Agricultura, and Recursos Hidraulicos, Mexico City. Executive producer, Francisco Urrusti. Directed and edited by Eduardo Maldonado. Camera (color), Santiago Nararette; sound, Jesus Sanchez, Ed Herrera. Reviewed at Margaret Mead Film Festival, American Museum of Natural History, N.Y., Sept. 7, 1987. Running time: **90 MINS.**

(In Spanish, with English subtitles)

Sponsored by the government of Mexico, "Xochimilco" is a benign public-relations documentary promoting the village and floating gardens of Xochimilco, popular tourist location in suburban Mexico City. Because the film contains images and information relating to Mexican culture and society, it qualifies for inclusion within the Mead Festival's anthropological mandate. As cinema, it is naive, overlong and repetitious.

Xochimilco is a picturesque neighborhood with an elaborate canal system used for transporting and delighting wedding and baptismal parties, foreign tourists, Mexican vacationers, and others. The area connects with ancient Indian traditions and prehistoric myths that survive as altered customs. Some 400 fiestas per year are serviced there by a professional corps of concessionaires, craftsmen, entertainers, food and drink vendors, and the gondoliers who pole the flat-bottomed canal-boats, which are colorfully painted and bear women's names.

The canals are now contaminated with sewage and industrial waste. Tourism is suffering because of the stink. Some gondoliers are being forced to return to farming. The film assures us that the government is working on the problem.

The film emphasizes the religious

activities at the big Xochimilco church. It's a Catholicism with considerable Indian admixture. Huge crowds of poorly dressed peons press close as the Virgin's statue is paraded by. There are displays of horsemanship, brilliantly costumed dances, a "goddess of flowers" tribute, fireworks, and a visit to the vast cemetery. Food, drink and wine are left for the dead beside their tombstones. We learn that during the night the spirits of the dead take away the aroma. An old man stands in the family crypt and introduces the camera to his deceased grandparents, brothers, aunts and uncles. He will soon join them and be happy here, he says with a smile.

A thriving industry — the manufacture and sale of religious relics and bric-a-brac — is part of the Xochimilco experience. Tiny dolls, miniature cardinals and nuns and saints, minutely costumed and painted, are sold to the public, especially the Indians. A Christ-Child puppet is a particularly popular item. Leading a religious procession, the Bishop passes along, elaborately accoutred, wearing dark glasses. Pretty Indian girls weep with happiness, as the poetic narration explains about the joys of pure faith. —Hitch.

White Phantom
(COLOR)

Okay martial arts item.

A Spectrum Entertainment presentation of a Bonaire Films production. (Sales, Overseas Filmgroup.) Executive producer, Michael Scording. Producer by Roy McAree, K.L. Lim. Directed by Dusty Nelson. Screenplay, David Hamilton, Chris Gallagher, from story by Nelson; camera (color), Alan Brennecke; editor, Carole A. Kenneally; music, Robert J. Resetar; additional music, Kevin Klingler, Bob Mamet; sound, William F. Fiege; fight director, Jimmy Lee; stunts, T.H. Lai; choreography, Page Leong; associate producer, Kathy McClure. Reviewed on Vidmark Entertainment vidcassette, N,Y., Oct. 2 1987. (No MPAA Rating.) Running time: **89 MINS.**
Willi...................Jay Roberts Jr.
Mai Lin....................Page Leong
Hanzo.......................Jimmy Lee
Col. Slater..................Bo Svenson
Bookstore owner ..........H.F. Chiang
Daughter...............Kathy McClure

"White Phantom" is an okay followup to the action film "Sakura Killers." Pic is well-lensed, boasts an evocative, varied musical score and better acting (with well-recorded English dialog) than the usual martial arts fare, but an almost nonexistent plotline keeps it routine (it debuted on vidcassette with no U.S. theatrical exposure).

As with "Sakura Killers," pic opens with a raid by ninjas of a U.S. scientific installation, with five megatons worth of plutonium stolen. Military colonel Bo Svenson's mission is to retrieve it. Action shifts to Taiwan where scruffy young hero (in a N.Y. Yankee cap)

Jay Roberts Jr. is eventually put on the case. Again it's the Sakura family of Japanese gangsters running a local protection racket who are the villians. Dancer Page Leong is an undercover agent who also is fighting the Sakura family.

Roberts, dressing in a white ninja outfit, displays good martial arts skills, but film's premise of retrieving the plutonium gets lost in the shuffle. Similarly, Leong, alluring in her dance routines, is pointlessly written out of the script before the finish. Pic's highlight is a very impressive strobe-light sequence integrating Leong's flashdance routine with an outburst of violence.
—Lor.

Notte Italiana
(Italian Night)
(ITALIAN-COLOR)

A Sacher Film/RAI-TV Channel 1/So.-Fin.A. coproduction. Produced by Nanni Moretti, Angelo Barbagallo. Directed by Carlo Mazzacurati. Screenplay, Mazzacurati, Franco Bernini; camera (color), Agostino Castiglioni; editor, Miro Garrone; music, Fiorenzo Carpi; art direction, Giancarlo Basili, Leonardo Scarpa. Reviewed at the Venice Film Festival (Critics' Week), Aug. 30, 1987. Running time: **92 MINS.**
Otello ....Marco Messeri
Daria...................Giulia Boschi
Tornova ....Mario Adorf
Cecco ....Memé Perlini
Also with: Tino Carraro (Melandri), Ruggeri brothers (surveyors), Antonio Petrocelli, Remo Remotti (Italo), Silvana De Santis (innkeeper).

Venice — An unpretentious little picture that manages to draw the viewer into its down-home characters and plot, "Italian Night" is a first feature by helmer Carlo Mazzacurati and a notable first production effort by popular young director Nanni Moretti and partner Angelo Barbagallo. Tale of a lawyer making property assessments starts low-key, but swings into a full-blown thriller by the end. Most of the intrigue lies in character relationships and pic's stark, empty-frame sketch of the Po Delta region where it is set. A tough film to place outside fests, it's more than worth a look from those who wonder what's happened to young Italian cinema.

Otello (played with shaggy dog appeal by Marco Messeri) is that rara avis, an honest lawyer. He accepts a job sizing up land for a big natural park, and temporarily transfers to a tiny inn in the Po valley. Soon he begins receiving every type of proposition for corruption Italian-style — changing borders, overvaluing pieces of land, and so on. He rebuffs all bribes and faithfully carries on, until on the eve of his departure he uncovers a hidden scandal that has led to the murder of an inspector years ago. Dramatic finale takes place on a long, rainy night.

A film based on nuance, "Italian

Night" makes the most of a minimal number of charaters (there is also Giulia Boschi as Daria, once involved in radical politics and now pumping gas for her old codger of a father Remo Remotti, who provide the pleasantest part of Otello's social life in the country). Though film doesn't chase after realism (example is thesps' mixture of non-regional accents, or the way story evolves into a predictable *noir* thriller), it creates its own unmistakable atmosphere. Especially strong is use of the desolate landscapes of the area that do indeed seem to have secrets to hide (as story will show). Thesps emerge through their faces: Boschi's very Italian waiflike beauty, Messeri's nice guy grin, his pal Memé Perlini's exaggerated buffoonery tinged with profiteering. If nothing else, pic singles out Mazzacurati as a newcomer to watch.
—Yung.

Wierna rzeka
(The Faithful River)
(POLISH-COLOR)

A Filmpolski release of an "X" Film Unit production. Directed by Tadeusz Chmielewski. Screenplay, Halina Chmielewska, Tadeusz Chmielewski, based on a novel by Stefan Zeromski; camera (color), Jerzy Stawicki; editor, Miroslawa Garlicka; music, Jerzy Matuszkiewicz; art direction, Bogdan Solle; production manager, Michal Szczerbic. Reviewed at the Gdansk Film Festival, Sept. 16, 1987. Running time: **140 MINS.**
Salomea ....Malgorzata Pieczynska
Odrowaz ....Olgierd Lukaszewiez
Szczepan ....Franciszek Pieczka
Also with: Maria Homerska (Duchess), Henryk Bista (doctor), Henry Machalica (major), Jerzy Turek, Wojoiech Wysocki (Wiesnicyn).

Gdynia — Why "The Faithful River," said to be the faithful adaptation of a schoolroom classic by Stefan Zeromski, should have been on the shelf since it was made in 1983 has to be guessed at. This historical tale set during the insurgent natonalist movement of 1863 paints a black picture of the Russian Cossacks, and shows both Cossacks and rebels generally shunned and feared by the local populace. Film's main thrust is a tragic romance between a poor gentlewoman and a rebel noble. Veteran director Tadeusz Chmielewski's well-made period piece seems unlikely to travel far outside Polish film weeks.

Action take place in the snowbound countryside and opens after a bloody battle has wiped out a band of nationalist insurgents. Only one escapes, so gruesomely wounded it's painful to watch. It is handsome Duke Odrowaz, who eventually finds shelter and care beyond the call of duty from a land-steward's daughter, Salomea (Malgorzata Pieczynska), holed up in a burned-out manor with an old servant (Franciszek Pieczka).

The Duke's slow recovery takes place as Cossacks ravage the coun-

tryside, though the nationalists don't enjoy much more trust from the peasants. When spring finally comes, the artist's mother turns up to snatch her son away from the poor but faithful Salomea.

Pic has quality lensing and period feel. —Yung.

Scuola di Ladri,
Seconda Parte
(School Of Thieves, Part II)
(ITALIAN-COLOR)

A C.G. Silver Film and Maura Intl. Film production. Directed by Neri Parenti. Stars Paolo Villaggio, Massimo Boldi, Enrico Maria Salerno, Florence Guerin. Screenplay, Laura Toscano, Franco Marotta, Parenti; camera (color), Alessandro D'Eva; editor, Sergio Montanari. Reviewed at Cine Royale, Rome, Oct. 1, 1987. Running time: **95 MINS.**
Dalmazio ....Paolo Villaggio
Egisto..................Massimo Boldi
The Uncle.........Enrico Maria Salerno
Susanna ....Florence Guerin

Rome — The original "School Of Thieves" must have ended badly for clumsy crooks Dalmazio and Egisto because this sequel opens with their release from, respectively, prison and an asylum for the criminally insane. They reunite while trying unsuccessfully to rob the same house. They soon team up with their uncle (played with slippery class by Enrico Maria Salerno) and, in lieu of their old partner Amalio, the beautiful Susanna (Florence Guerin), claiming to be Amalio's daughter.

Egisto (Massimo Boldi) and Dalmazio (Paolo Villaggio, well-known on Italian screens as the comic shlemeil Fantozzi) are the bumbling hoods while uncle and Susanna call all the shots and keep the loot.

After a failed attempt at an armored-car heist, the gang artlessly steals gold bars from a train to finance the bigger scheme — stealing jewels from an ocean liner. Dalmazio and Egisto stow away and then, posing as sailors and waiters, overcome some funny obstacles (such as losing a vital key in a vat of soup), and make their way to the vault to steal the jewels. In the end, the uncle and Susanna steal the jewels from our heroes and scene is set for a possible Part III.

The crimes themselves are simplistic and not much fun to watch, except when the four repeatedly try and fail to double-cross each other. Our heroes are first-class bumblers, though, and with their uncle (whose feigned blindness precipitates all the predictable sight gags, along with some unpredictable ones, like a diagram of the ocean liner in braille) make an enjoyable team. Florence Guerin lacks comic timing and her Susanna only manages to hold the audience's attention by appearing naked or semi-naked, for no apparent reason, in almost every scene.

Lensing is flat and colorless and misses plenty of opportunities for great location shots. Yet pic's do-pey, good-natured fun will appeal to pre-teens — though Guerin's top-lessness might exclude it from a young American audience.

—*Newm.*

The Outsiders
(TAIWANESE-COLOR)

An Oriental Films presentation of a Dragon's Group Film Co. production. Produced by Hu Chi-chung, Wu Gon, Lin Lang. Directed by Yu Kang-ping. Screenplay, Suen Jeung Gwo, from the novel by Kenneth Pai; camera (color), Heh Yong Jeng; editor, Laiw Ching Song. Reviewed at the Toronto Festival of Festivals, Sept. 15, 1987. Running time: **90 MINS.**
With: Suen Yueh, Su Ming Ming, Sheo Hsin, Lee Tai Ling, Kuang-Kuang, Chau Jan, Chiang Ho-jen, Mao Chao-chun, Tsai Peng-tao, David Suen, Tien Wei-wei.

Toronto — ''The Outsiders,'' said to be Taiwan's first gay-oriented movie, follows the exploits of a young homosexual who tries to fit into society after his father kicks him out. The youth succeeds and finds a place for himself, but whether the film finds an audience is not at all sure.

There's no nudity and sex is only suggested, not shown. It's not very campy either. Those expecting an Oriental ''La Cage aux Folles'' or ''Too Outrageous!'' will be disappointed.

There's not much of a plot, the story basically drifts from one event to another in young Ah-Ching's life. While the script may be limp, the performances are not. Suen Yueh as an old queen is a delight. Su Ming Ming charms in her role as an aging chanteuse who acts as den mother to gay street kids. Shao Hsin is convincing as a shy, insecure young gay in a world where there's no room for men like him.

Visually, the film is stunning. The camera floats through a world few people get a chance to visit. The film offers a slice-of-life that tourist guides never describe.

Yet good acting and photography plus a risqué subject are not enough to sustain boxoffice. It's hard to sell this film in the West: there are no stars, no chop-socky. Whether or not Asian audiences will be drawn is iffy considering the taboo focus of the film. After the curiosity factor wears off, there really isn't much left to pack them in.—*Zerb.*

Ryoma o Kitta Otoko
(The Man Who Assassinated Ryoma)
(JAPANESE-COLOR)

A Shochiku-Fuji production. Produced by Yoshinobu Nishioka, Kinuko Kon. Directed by Kosaku Yamashita. Screenplay, Tsutomu Nakamura, based on the novel by Mitsugu Saotome; camera (color), Fujiro Morita; music, Shuichi Chino; production design, Yoshinobu Nishioka. Reviewed at the Tokyo Intl. Film Festival, Oct. 1, 1987. Running time: **109 MINS.**
Tedasaburo Sasaki .... Kenichi Hagiwara
Ryoma Sakamoto .... Jinpachi Nezu
Yae .... Miwako Fujitani
Nei .... Reiko Nakamura

Tokyo — Despite its exceptional visual qualities and dramatic historical setting, ''The Man Who Assassinated Ryoma'' increasingly disappoints the longer it runs. A potent tale of the deadly opposition between men loyal to the Shogunate and those supporting a restoration can't be overcome by the terrific craftsmanship in all departments. Outlook for export is slim.

In its odd, painstaking way, pic builds more sympathy for Sasaki, the imperious, charismatic commander of the Shogun's Kyoto Guard, than it does for the intellectually liberal, but in this context too trendy, Ryoma. The latter has become seriously westernized, as he smokes cigarets while spouting reasons to throw out the old and bring in the new.

A master swordsman, Sasaki (the impressive Kenichi Hagiwara) spends much of his time successfully fending off ambushes, but as these increase in number he begins to lose his mind and grow melancholy over the number of young men whose blood he is forced to spill. Sasaki's brooding and death-filled nightmares are infinitely less interesting than the political intrigue stirred up in the early going.

Finally, Sasaki develops from honorable defender of the establishment to mad butcher, as he carries out the deed indicated in the title, then leads his men into a hopeless, insane battle, a progression that becomes obvious and wearisome long before it is played out.

For quite some time, the exquisite compositions, color schemes and camera moves orchestrated by director Kosaku Yamashita are sufficient to command one's attention. During the first hour in particular, every shot appears so carefully composed, every scene so surely judged, that it seems a shame when the story goes awry and loses its grip. Fujiro Morita's beauteous camera-work is a constant joy, but Shuichi Chino's score proves a major detriment, as it is filled with distractingly modern orchestrations featuring saxophone, piano and synthesizer.

—*Cart.*

Divinas Palabras
(Divine Words)
(SPANISH-COLOR)

An Ion Producciones production. Produced by Victor Manuel San José Sánchez. Directed by José Luis García Sánchez. Screenplay, Enrique Llovet, Abad de Santillan, García Sanchez, based on the play by Ramón del Valle-Inclán; camera (Cinemascope, color), Fernando Arribas; editor, Pablo G. Del Amo; music, Milladoiro; art direction and costumes, Gerardo Vera. Reviewed at the Venice Film Festival (competing), Sept. 6, 1987. Running time: **105 MINS.**
Mari Gaila .... Ana Belen
Pedro Gailo .... Francisco Rabal
Septimo Miau .... Imanol Arias
Rosa ''La Tatula'' .... Esperanza Roy
Also with: Aurora Bautista (Marcia Del Reino), Juan Echanove (Miguelin ''El Padrones'').

Venice — A grotesquely reverberant stage work by Ramón del Valle-Inclán suggesting the early films of Luis Buñuel, ''Divine Words'' has been cleanly filmed with a top-flight cast by director José Luis García Sánchez. Lacking the touch of brilliance or cruel genius that might have made it a classic, film deflects the story's cynical irony into a compassionate, but always distanced, hymn to the poor and the downtrodden. Most audiences will balk at the rougher scenes and coarser sentiments, leaving film's destiny in the hands of art house programmers and fest directors. Yet it contains a moving force sure to win supportive fans.

Though the condemnation isn't final, ''Divine Words'' focuses on human monstrosity. In a rainy, poverty-stricken village of Galizia, an old beggar woman dies, leaving behind a treasure: her hydrocephalic son (played by a dwarf), with whom she went begging. Every relative dives for this golden goose in a pitiful hand-drawn cart. In the end the orphan is split between the sacristan's pretty young wife Mari Gaila (Ana Belen) and her sister-in-law.

At the prompting of a sharp friend, Rosa La Tatula (Esperanza Roy), Mari Gaila begins taking her nephew to county fairs, where he brings in a lot of money along with other unfortunates. Her initial motivation is simple greed, but gradually Mari Gaila uses her new-found freedom to meet Séptimo Miau, a roguish gypsy (Imanol Arias).

Divine vengeance strikes when she leaves the boy unattended in a tavern and he is given so much liquor he dies. The sacrestan (with the ever-haunting face of Francisco Rabal) tries to make a little more money by exhibiting the dead body. The jealous townsfolk catch Mari Gaila trysting with her gypsy and try to stone her to death. Cuckolded husband Rabal shames them in a moving last-scene turnaround by pronouncing, in the midst of all the squalor and inhumanity, the ''divine words.''

If Rabal finishes a saint, Belen is almost noble in the part of the adultress. All the dirty, scheming villagers have a twisted dignity as oppressed folk trapped in a claustrophic universe. The period is moodily recreated in Gerardo Vera's decor and costumes. — *Yung.*

L'Homme Voilé
(The Veiled Man)
(LEBANESE-FRENCH-COLOR)

A UGC release of an Intage (Beirut)/Paris Classics/Hachette-Première + Cie/UGC/-Les Films de la Saga (Paris) coproduction. Produced by Humbert Balsan. Written and directed by Maroun Bagdadi. Dialog, Didier Decoin; camera (Kodak, color by LTC), Patric Blossier; editor, Luc Barnier; music, Gabriel Yared; art direction, Richard Peduzzi. Reviewed at the Venice Film Festival, Sept. 9, 1987. Running time: **93 MINS.**
Pierre .... Bernard Giraudeau
Kassar .... Michel Piccoli
Claire .... Laure Marsac
Also with: Michal Albertini (Kamal), Sandrine Dumas (Julie), Fouad Naim, Sonia Ichti, Jonathan Layna, Kamal Kassar.

Venice — Third film by Lebanese helmer Maroun Bagdadi (''Little Wars'') is set in Paris with French thesps, but pulls viewer back to the ''Mirage City'' or Beirut with every scene. This curious way of talking about the anguishing war in Lebanon, through the eyes of those who have left it or never seen it (including a young French girl who can only fantasize about it), pays off with an original, but distanced, viewpoint. At the same time filmer injects elements of the classic thriller, set against the colorful backdrop of Paris's Arab quarter. Offbeat theme may put some off, attract others, but hopefully attractive packaging (technical credits are first-rate) and engaging thesps will help.

One of pic's perverse gags is casting Michel Piccoli as an Arab, Kassar, a clan chieftan in exile, translated into French as a suave gentleman-manipulator. Bernard Giraudeau (Pierre) starts the ball rolling when he returns to Paris after several years' absence, bearer of a guilty secret. His 16-year-old daughter Claire (played by the ever-hypnotic Laure Marsac) thinks he's been just a doctor helping people, idolizes him and fantasizes about going to the East together (at one point she dons Oriental clothes for a disturbingly sensual dance, audience being her father).

The action of ''Veiled Man'' is not always as crystal clear as the splendid lensing. Pierre has given up the war (we know he killed people as well as healed them), yet he stalks the streets as a cold-blooded murderer, on the trail of two terrorists who have done unspeakable things. Moral boundaries blur quickly, and Pierre would probably prefer not to kill them, especially young Kamal (Michel Albertini), a fugitive who distinctly enjoys exile and the good life in Paris. When Claire learns, thanks to an improbable videotape, that her father has anything but a pacifist past, she rejects him and goes to bed with Kamal. It is Kamal's abandoned wife who finally exacts justice, backed up by her clan.

Many points of view add up to the same condemnation of a senseless war, and pity for all sides who got involved in it.—*Yung.*

Crónica de un Niño Solo
(Chronicle of a Lonely Child)
(ARGENTINE-B&W)

An Instituto Nacional de Cinematográfica Argentina release. Produced by Luis Di Stéfano. Written and directed by Leonardo Favio. Stars Diego Puente. Camera (b&w), Ignacio Souto; editor, Roberto Maccari; music, Cimarosa and B. Marito. Reviewed at Latino Festival, Public Theater, N.Y. Aug. 13, 1987. Running time: **80 MINS.**
With: Diego Puente (Polín), Beto Gianola, Leonardo Favio, María Vaner.

Argentine director Leonardo Favio's 1964 debut effort "Crónica de un Niño Solo" is a fine example of the gaucho nuevo cine movement of the '60s and '70s, and also picked up international and domestic distinctions at Florence, Mar de Plata, Acapulco and from the Asociación de Crónistas Cinematográficas de la Argentina. It is reviewed here for the record.

Pic takes its cue from the Italian neorealist movement and also borrows heavily from Truffaut's "The 400 Blows," although it is closer in structure to fellow countryman Héctor Babenco's 1980 Brazilian feature "Pixote."

Focusing on the life of a young street kid nicknamed Polín (Diego Puente), the movie begins in a juvenile corrections center, later following the boy after escape through the city streets to his home in a Buenos Aires slum and finally back again to detention.

Although the narrative is presented chronologically, the story is developed through a series of short impressionistic scenes beautifully captured in black & white by Ignacio Souto. Shots at the reformatory are tight and almost claustrophobic, contrasted with later shots in the labyrinth of slum dwellings. The only break is a bucolic section at a river where Polín goes to swim, but even this serenity is soon broken when he and a friend are threatened by some local toughs, who make fun of his institution-shaved head.

There is not much future for kids such as Polín, Favio says through this film. They spend their entire lives in and out of institutions. When they are out, poverty drives them back again.

Even though the film has a dated look to it, it still makes a powerful statement.—*Lent.*

Witness To A Killing
(SRI LANKAN-COLOR)

A Taprobane Pictures presentation. Produced by Jayantha Jayatilaka. Executive producer, Asoka Perera. Written and directed by Chandran Rutnam. Camera (Yangtze color), Daryn Okada; editor, Cladwin Fernando; music, Sarath Fernando; art direction, Errol Kelly; assistant director, Salinda Perera. Reviewed at the Tokyo Intl. Film Festival, Sept. 27, 1987. Running time: **71 MINS.**
Salinda . . . . Razi Anwer
Father . . . . Tony Ranasinghe
Mother . . . . Swineetha Weerasinghe

Killer . . . . Ravindra Randeniya
Killer's wife . . . . Anoja Weerasinghe

Tokyo — "Witness To A Killing" is, of all things, a Sri Lankan ripoff of the vintage American thriller "The Window," about a little boy who observes a murder and must then elude the perpetrator, who is out to get him. Awkwardly acted in English and technically abysmal, pic has no potential outside of Third World markets.

Writer-director Chandran Rutnam, who made the previous international festival entry "Adara Kathawa," plays it absolutely straight in trying to build suspense. It's a "boy who cried wolf" story, as neither his parents nor the police will believe the kid when he insists the couple across the street actually knifed a man to death and dragged him down to the beach.

Most of the mercifully brief action consists of the killer trying to dispatch the tyke, but a genre exercise such as this requires, at bare minimum, a certain technical competence not to be found here. An interesting villain always helps, and the one here has to be one of the dumbest and clumsiest on record, as he consistently bungles his many attempts to nab the boy.

Even if it once worked in Hollywood, plot seems highly contrived in this context. As an attempt to crack certain levels of the international market, shooting a popularly oriented crime story in English may make some sense, but it also seems culturally and artistically inauthentic and arguably not the way to go in trying to establish a national cinema.—*Cart.*

Ticket
(SOUTH KOREAN-COLOR)

A Motion Picture Promotion Corp. release of a Jimi Films Co. production. Executive producer, Kim Ji-mi. Directed by Im Kwon-t'aek. Screenplay, Song Kil-han; camera (color), Gu Jung-mo. Reviewed at the Toronto Festival of Festivals, Sept. 18, 1987. Running time **100 MINS.**
With: Kim Ji-mi, An So-Young, Lee Heh-Young, Chun Se-Young.

Toronto — With "Ticket," prolific South Korean director Im Kwon-t'aek and constant collaborator, scripter Song Kil-han, produce an intriguing and entertaining look at a Korean coffee shop where the waitresses serve up more than just tea and sympathy.

Pic tracks three rookie prostitutes, an aging, washed-up prostie and their hard-hearted madam.

Action is set in a fishing village where the waitresses deliver take-out orders to lonely seamen in their hotel rooms. Some of the waitresses revel in this work as an easy way to make money and buy pretty clothes. Some want out to become a film star or to marry a nice boy from a good family.

There is no nudity and little softcore sex. It also offers a slice of life in Korea: the grinding poverty of the peasants, the limited opportunities for youth and the considerable difficulties women have in making their way.

The girls are adorable, vulnerable and believable. Kim Ji-mi, leading Korean actress and exec producer of the pic, hands in an exquisite performance as a seemingly-tough, stingy madam who stubbornly hangs on to notions of true love and romance. Even the customers are largely sympathetic. There are few unlikeable characters.

"Ticket" is easy to watch, easy to care about the people it portrays. Direction is polished, the scripting tight and the characters finely drawn. It will certainly do well in Asia and with the right kind of marketing could attract Western audiences.—*Zerb.*

Just Like America
(HUNGARIAN-U.S.-COLOR)

A Mafilm Hunnia Studio production. U.S. producer, Yoram Mandel. Directed by Peter Gothar. Screenplay, Peter Esterhazy; camera (color), Zoltan David. (No other credits available.) Reviewed at the Tokyo Intl. Film Festival, Oct. 1, 1987. Running time: **113 MINS.**
Frigyes . . . . Andor Lukats
Jude . . . . Trula Hoosier
Also with: Adam Szirtes, Stafford Ashani.

Tokyo — "Just Like America" is an utterly unrevealing, virtually unendurable look at the United States by young Hungarian director Peter Gothar. Partially financed by prize money Gothar won for his second feature, "Time Stands Still," in the 1985 Young Cinema competition in the first Tokyo Intl. Film Festival, pic appropriately had its world premiere here at the second fest but has no chance of commercial playoff in the country in which it is set.

Tale begins in an aggressively off-putting manner and never gets any easier to take. Opening scenes in Hungary present Frigyes as a rough, uncaring man and, shortly after arriving in New York on a small tour with his wife and son, he just skips off on his own and appears to flip out.

Without knowing a word of English, the dour, uncommunicative guy scours the city from top to bottom, with the emphasis on the latter as he sleeps in abandoned buildings and lives like a bum, while at the same time falling in with a black sidewalk cardgame hustler and lady companion.

Vague melodrama introduces on the scene in the form of two thugs who bump off the deadlocked gambler for unspecified reasons and then start threatening the befuddled Frigyes, and things do pick up just a tad when the poor fellow's enthusiastic father-in-law arrives to take him back home (although how he ever found him in the concrete jungle remains a mystery).

"Just Like America" is an ordeal because the eternally disheveled Frigyes, as embodied by Andor Lukats, is one of the most unappealing figures ever to occupy centerscreen, and Gothar spends two hours dragging the viewer with him into the darkest, dirtiest backalleys of Gotham. His roving, handheld camera style rubs one's nose in the grime, and the film is full of grating scenes in which the characters talk right past each other and never communicate with Frigyes prattling on in Hungarian and the other speaking English as if they expected him to understand. Entire effect is confoundingly thick and pointless.

Foreign writers and directors over the years have almost always had interesting, fresh ways of looking at the U.S., even if certain projects didn't coalesce, but this says nothing politically, culturally or philosophically. It's just maddeningly empty. —*Cart.*

El Diablo, el Santo y el Tonto
(The Devil, The Saint And The Fool)
(MEXICAN-COLOR)

A Peliculas Mexicanas release of a Cumbres Films production. Directed by Rafael Villaseñor Kuri. Stars Vicente Fernández. Screenplay, Adolfo Torres Portillo; camera (color), Agustín Lara; editor, Max Sánchez; music, Heriberto Aceves; associate producer, Vicente Fernández. Reviewed at Hollywood Twin theater 1, N.Y., July 31, 1987. Running time: **92 MINS.**
Refugio Romero, Carmelo Romero
& Mariano Romero . . . . Vicente Fernández
Liane . . . . Sasha Montenegro
Don Abor . . . . Pedro Weber (Chatanooga)
Rafaela Vega . . . . Carmelita González
Also with: Martha Ortiz, Felipe Arriaga, Patsy, Lalo González (Piporro), Luz María Rico, Jorge Noble, Frank Tostado.

Fans of popular Mexican ranchero singer Vicente Fernández will be delighted with his latest comedy vehicle "El Diablo, el Santo y el Tonto" (The Devil, The Saint And The Fool). Instead of taking one role, Fernández has the opportunity to exercise thesping talents by playing three separate parts.

Pic utilizes the usual Fernández crew, including helmer Rafael Villaseñor Kuri, scripter Adolfo Torres Portillo, lenser Agustín Lara, and even old-time character actors Pedro Weber (Chatanooga) and Carmelita González. While in the past the combination has proved uneven, this time it pays off.

Story has rancher Don Trinidad falling off his horse. On his deathbed, he has a confession to tell his fumbling mama's boy son Refugio (Fernández). It seems that in his younger years he was quite the ladies' man: not only did he leave an illegitimate son in Monterrey, but there is also an offspring in Guadalajara.

All three of his sons are to be cared for in the will and it is Refugio's quest to find his lost brothers. The surprise is that even though they have different mothers they all look identical. Their temperaments are not the same though: Rogelio is a 4-eyed fumbling fool; Mariano is a rancher and saint-like father of 11 daughters; and Carmelo is a demonic fun-loving rogue.

Of course the will gets things confused: the saint gets a bar, the devil gets a charity hospital and the mama's boy gets the ranch. The townsfolk also get a run for their money as the familiar nerd seems to take on new personalities. All of this leads to confusion and some genuine laughs.

Coincidentally, all three brothers sing ranchero songs. In all, there are five tunes, including the old Mexican standby "Cielito Lindo." The title track, sung at the end of the pic, is a trio with the brothers alternating verses and all joining in for the chorus.

Special effects showing all three brothers together are handled effectively. Other tech credits are adequate. Fernández is believable in the three roles and is always sympathetic.

"El Diablo, el Santo y el Tonto" is fun family entertainment, full of Mexican music and character. It should do well at home and in areas with high concentrations of Mexicans or those of Mexican descent.
—*Lent.*

Negerkys & Labre Larver
(Creampuffs & Lollipops)
(DANISH-COLOR)

A Metronome Film release of a Metronome Film production with the Danish Film Institute. DFI consultant producer, Ida Zeruneith. Produced by Tivi Magnusson. Directed by Li Vilstrup. Screenplay, Li Vilstrup, Dortea Birkedal Andersen; camera (Eastmancolor), Bodil Trier; editor, Camilla Skousen; music, Sanne Brüel; sound, Iben Haahr Andersen, Morten Degnbol; costumes, Lotte Dandanell, Manon Rasmussen; production management, Michael Christensen, Susanne Arnt Torp; assistant director, Lizzi Weischenfeldt. Reviewed at Dagmar Theater, Copenhagn, Oct. 7, 1987. Running time: **68 MINS.**
Nana . . . . .Kathrina Dauscha
Conny . . . . .Lise S. Steffensen
Anders . . . . .Thomas Hansen
Michael Jackson lookalike .Mark Jackman
Teacher . . . . .Peter Hesse Overgaard
    Also with: Teresia Madeleine Rönne, Puk Schaufus, Ulla Henningsen, Helle Ryslinge, Sabine Lindeberg.

Copenhagen — "Creampuffs & Lollipops" has neat production values and smooth cinematography, but otherwise Li Vilstrup's kiddie entertainment feature is a hodgepodge of good intentions and poor narrative judgments, stilted acting and clammy jokes.

Since "Creampuffs" has a non-plot featuring mostly young grade school girl, audiences will probably also have to be recruited from the feminine gender within the 6-8-year age group, and only because of the general clamor (from pedagogs and editorial writers rather than from exhibition professionals) for children's fare, a few offshore sales loom as a possibility.

There is no storyline at all in "Creampuffs," which seems content to toy with the setting up of sequences emulating Alan Parker's "Bugsy Malone:" girls dream of glamor on the ballet stage or as veterinarians and of marrying Michael Jackson and of having babies (if they can get a boy to mind them); boys don't seem to dream at all, although it is never clear who dreams what and when.

It may not have been the director's intent, but the girls come through as more vicious than the boys who are seen as merely boisterous and/or dumb. When vicious, the girls shy at practically no means of making one or other of their company miserable, but Vilstrup is out to do a fun picture and leaves off such hints at reality dangling in mid-air. This, unfortunately, is also where the fun is suspended. —*Kell.*

Eva Guerrillera
(CANADIAN-COLOR-16m)

A Les Films du Crepescule release of a Soleil Films production. Produced by Jacqueline Levitin, Chantal Lapaire. Written and directed by Jacqueline Levitin. Camera (color, 16m), Jean-Charles Tremblay; editor, Herve Kerlaan; music, Barry Goold; art direction, Karine Lepp; sound, Juan Gutierrez. Reviewed at the Toronto Festival of Festivals, Sept. 18, 1987. Running time: **83 MINS.**
Eva . . . . .Angelo Roa
Journalist . . . . .Carmen Ferland

Toronto— Filmmaker Jacqueline Levitin dug behind the headlines to come up with this moving portrait of a young female guerrilla fighter in war-torn El Salvador. "Eva: Guerrillera" is a modest effort that shows off the skills of Levitin, a Seattle-born film teacher at Montreal's Concordia University.

Recruited by the leftist underground guerrilla army in 1978, she abandons a comfortable middle-class home and secure future as a doctor to fight the army and its death squads. All her belongings fit into a paper bag. Her friends and lovers are killed. She is imprisoned and tortured, eventually managing to escape to Montreal where she is soon bored by speaking tours and interviews with journalists. She secretly returns to the mountains of El Salvador where she dies. There is no glamor or romance in this life, only a strong sense of purpose.

It's a simple story told in a simple way: Eva recounts her life for the benefit of a Montreal magazine writer. The effect is much like a documentary (sometimes a little too talky) but, as a drama, it is successful with emotional impact.

Pic is low-budget, despite location shooting in Central America. Some of the more dramatic events are related over simple shots of dirt roads and peasant hovels. There are no big battle scenes and prison guards and the army are rarely seen, but we can feel their menace. Freeze frames, photographs, sound and the music of Barry Goold make up for the lack of big-budget special effects and a large cast.—*Zerb.*

Sierra Leone
(WEST GERMAN-COLOR)

A Filmverlag der Autoren presentation of a Uwe Schrader Filmproduktion/Bayerische Rundfunk production. Executive producer, Renée Gundelach. Produced by Schrader, Sylvia Koller. Written and directed by Schrader. Camera (color), Klaus Müller-Laue; editor, Müller-Laue; music, Bülent Ersoy, Garnet Mimms and the Enchanters, Tony Christie, Don Gibson, Samime Sanay; sound, Günther Knon; sets, Brigit Gruse, Renate Langer; costumes, Gruse. Reviewed at the Venice Film Festival (Critics' Week), Aug. 31, 1987. Running time: **92 MINS.**
Fred .Christian Redl
Alma . . . . .Ann-Gisel Glass
Vera .Rita Russek
Rita . . . . .Constanze Engelbrecht
    Also with: Andras Fricsay, Gotfried Breitfuss, Hans Eckart-Eckhart, Nikolaus Dutsch, Peter Gavajda, Janette Rauch, Mehmet Bademsoy.

Venice — A proletarian film in the deepest sense of the word, Uwe Schrader's second feature confirms the tendencies of his earlier prestige debut, "Kanakerbraut." While he has left Berlin's mostly Turkish Kreuzberg neighborhood for the north of the country, his film still dwells on cheap bars and fleabag hotels, and deals with the working class and the vicious circle of misery which is the lot from which there is no way out.

The film's title is an allusion, in any case, since it is only in the opening sequence that any African scenery is presented, as the leading character, Fred, a driver who has left West Germany three years ago to make some money in the Dark Continent, is going back home.

He has money, but soon is to find out it offers no solution to his problems. The wife he left behind doesn't want him back, an old girl-friend is looking for a stabler relationship, and he is left with a young hotel clerk who is willing but finally unable to fill the emotional gap in his life.

A road movie by definition, following the protagonist as he drifts along the highways from one cheap motel to another, it takes the audience through a grim landscape, huge grey industrial complexes spouting smoke day and night, and human beings who even if decent, have been brutalized by their living conditions. The black humor which sometimes emerges in his encounters with old friends can't change the fact that he doesn't belong in their company any more, since he's rejected his old way of life, which is all they have.

Not always sufficiently tight in its construction, Schrader's film effectively makes his point, showing Germany's underbelly, the dark and unpleasant side of an affluent Western society, and its racist undercurrents.

Acting is lifelike all through, except for Ann-Gisel Glass, the hotel clerk who shares Fred's wanderings and displays a tendency to overact which stands against the grain of the film.

Both sound and image grittily support the film's realism, presenting a convincing, if not very tempting or flattering image of what the dark side of Western evolution looks like.—*Edna.*

Nitwits
(DUTCH-COLOR)

A Holland Film Releasing release of a Preston Prods. production. Produced by Chris Houtman. Written and directed by Nikolai van der Heyde. Camera (Kodak, Haghe Film color prints), Peter de Bont; editor, Ton de Graaff; music, Vladimir Cosma; sound, Claude Ermelin; art direction, Freek Biessiot; set decoration, Pieter Brüll; production managers, Dave Schram, Hans J. Pos; casting, Preston Casting Agency. Reviewed at Alfa 2 theater, Amsterdam, Aug. 24, 1987. Running time: **112 MINS.**
Joel Palsma . . . . .Ramses Shaffy
Danielle Kooiman . . . . .Monique Rosier
    Also with: Leen Jongewaard (receptionist), Martin Oversteegen (Eddie), Muriel Chaal-Gohier (Magda).

Amsterdam — According to writer/director Nikolai van der Heyde, "Nitwits" "tries to tell what life is in fact: a series of moments of confusion, emotion and complete idiocy." His description of life is a description of "Nitwits." The screenplay consists of loose sketches, held together by the presence of the main character, an actor, Joel Palsma is overemployed, in legit theater, in films, on tv; in vaudeville, in advertising spots — anything that pays a fee. His private life is equally full, with one wife, one daughter and a string of affairs, the current one with a girl of 22, about half his age.

The sketches vary from broad farce (false noses, flamboyant deaths on stage, in his underwear in Amsterdam's central station) to farcical broadsides, but fail to ignite the intended smiles and guffaws. Technical credits, although in the hands of experienced craftsmen, are mediocre. The actors perform adequately, and Ramses Shaffy fights valiantly (and succeeds occasionally), to make a 3-dimensional human being out of the main nitwit.

The film got a unanimous drubbing from the reviewers; the public stayed away, and pic was taken out of distribution after a week. Van der Heyde, once a great hope of Dutch cinema, and now one of the foremost directors of tv-spots, in a newspaper interview blames it all on "the hateful reviews," although he says he read only two of them.
—*Wall.*

Oridathu
(There Was A Village)
(INDIAN-COLOR)

A Suryakanti Film Makers production (Trivandrum). Written and directed by Aravindan. Camera (color), Shaji; editor, Bose; music, Aravindan; sound, Devadas; art direction and costumes, Padma Kumar; sets, Sethu. Reviewed at the Venice Film Festival (competing), Sept. 7, 1987. Running time: **112 MINS.**

Electricity super	Nedumudi Venu
Kuttan	Sreenivasan
Manager	Thilakan
Jose	Vineet
The Communist	Krishnankutty Nair
Schoolteacher	Chandran Nair

Also with: Innocent, Surya, Sithara, Valsala Menon.

Venice — Aravindan, one of Kerala's foremost experimental filmmakers, tells the tragic tale of a remote village where modernization, in the form of electricity, forever changes the inhabitants' way of life. Yet the film is much more than a simple condemnation of progress. Building slowly to a powerful, ambiguous climax, "Oridathu" paints a disquieting picture of the social fabric falling apart around human beings. Though "Oridathu" is one of the most accessible of the director's works, it may not have audiences flocking to theaters, but it could find a niche in Indian retros and quality shows.

Time is the mid-'50s, place the former state of Cochin Travancore. Film opens on a light, satiric note as the various village characters are introduced. There are the members of the town council lead by a benevolent Brahim, two teenagers in love, their fathers who are friends, etc. News that their village is soon to be "electrified" delights everyone, and when a supervisor from the Dept. of Electricity appears on the scene there is high excitement.

By second half of picture things turn sour. There are disputes over cutting down trees, but other disasters occur for reasons only casually connected to electrification. A quack doctor arrives and a girl dies after an abortion; the friendly fathers argue and separate their offspring. The boy wants to go to the city to continue his education, but just as he wins his father's blessing, he is fatally electrocuted during a village festival. The building catches fire but no one notices, caught up by fireworks and celebration.

Sensitively lensed to give a real feeling of atmosphere, film is firmly grounded in local life without demeaning traces of folklore. Though leisurely, it remains watchable from opening festival to closing one. The director also composed the music.
—*Yung.*

Delincuente
(Delinquent)
(MEXICAN-COLOR)

A Peliculas Mexicanas release of a Cinematográfica Tabasco production. Executive producer, Jose Luis Orduño. Produced by Daniel Galindo. Directed by Sergio Vejar. Stars Pedrito Fernández. Screenplay, Kiki Galindo; camera (color), Luis Medina; editor, José Liho; music, Jonathan Zarzosa, with appearance of group Chico Che and La Crisis. Reviewed at Hollywood Twin theater I, N.Y., Sept. 30, 1987. Running time: **96 MINS.**

Alejandro	Pedrito Fernández
Cecilia	Lucerito
Gonzalo	José Elías Moreno

Also with: Carlos Riquelme, Nuria Bages, Gaston Tusset, Julio Urreta, Jaime Santos, Martín Rangel.

The teen pic "Delincuente" (Delinquent) is an uneven pop vehicle for former Mexican child actor-singer Pedrito Fernández, now a teen rock idol for CBS Intl. It is directed by Sergio Vejar, helmer of other recent Fernández ventures.

Thematically, "Delincuente" is close to his childhood films and once again has Fernández playing an abandoned street kid, gushing with goodwill like a frisky puppy. He is adopted by three university students, who take him in, scrub him down, buy him new clothes and give him three squares a day. When he meets and falls for rich girl Cecilia (played by ballad singer Lucerito), the film becomes a male "Pygmalion," as the students drill Fernández in how to speak correct Spanish. He even gets a job at a neighborhood grocery store. The only flaw is that, ashamed of his shabby background, Fernández passes himself off as the cousin of one of the students and invents a loving family history. When the girl's father learns of the deceit, the boy is banned from the house. He also feels betrayed by the students and returns to the streets feeling bitter for "having been allowed to dream that he could achieve something with his life."

Film boasts plenty of music. Fernández and Lucerito get to sing two songs each, and there is also a guest appearance by popular salsa singer Chico Che and his group La Crisis singing "El Africano" — this is the third recent film where Chico Che sings this tune. Lensing for the most part is competent, but the songs are handled with little imagination and lack focus, except for the title track which could function as a video-cum-trailer.

Storyline lacks detail and characterizations too easily descend into clichés. Fernández' constant good cheer makes his later unhappiness a welcome sight, while Lucerito smiles so much it looks as if she were auditioning for a toothpaste ad. Hispanic kids probably won't mind since the movie presents them with a chance to see and hear their hero. —*Lent.*

Panchvati
(INDIAN-NEPALESE-COLOR)

A Time & Space (Bombay)-Royal Nepal Film Corp. (Katmandu) production. Produced by Shobha Doctor, Basu Bhattacharya. Directed by Bhattacharya. Screenplay, Bhattacharya, Kusum Ansal; camera (color), Rajsh Joshi; editor, Om Prahash; music, Sarang Dev; production design, Bhaswati Bhattacharya; sound, J. Rana; production managr, D. Sinha; assistant director, Prabhat Kumar. Reviewed at World Film Festival, Montreal, Aug. 25, 1987. Running time: **148 MINS.**

With: Suresh Oberoi, Dipti Naval, Jatin, Anuradha Tarafdar, Nabendu Ghosh.

Montreal — A well-intentioned melodrama about a male chauvinist Indian businessman who, at his older brother's urging, enters into a marriage with a talented Nepalese painter of a lower caste, "Panchvati" emerges as less than riveting thanks to the scrappy direction and a mountain of clichés in the screenplay.

The character of the woman, Sadhvi, is an interesting one: she's a talented, self-educated artist, who is at first excited about the idea of marrying a rich Indian, but soon finds his oafish attitudes insufferable. When he beats her, she packs her bags and walks out. Actually, she's always been attracted to his older (married) brother, Vikram; it was Vikram who first discovered her work and suggested the marriage.

Love blossoms when Vikram accompanies her home to Katmandu, and they spend a night together in a hotel (the film's title is the name of the hotel's location). As a result, Sadhvi gets pregnant and has twins, while Vikram returns to his wife.

What might have been a solid exploration of male-female relationships, and an interracial marriage, remains largely an unsatisfying film because cowriter-director Basu Bhattacharya opts for the cliché whenever invention fails him. Some of the dialog and music are exceptionally corny, the editing is choppy and the camera operator rarely has a setup that doesn't involve at least one ugly zoom, often two.

Acting is fine, and the location footage is Nepal adds to the interest, but this is an Indian pic that's unlikely to travel well.
—*Strat.*

La Raza Nunca Pierde — Huele a Gas
(The Race Never Loses — It Smells Like Gas)
(MEXICAN-COLOR)

A Peliculas Mexicanas release of a Cinematográfica Calderón production. Executive producer, Mario Gris. Produced by Guillermo Calderón Stell. Directed by Victor Manuel (Güero) Castro. Screenplay, Castro, Francisco Cavazos; camera (color), Raúl Domínguez; editor, José Lino; music, Marcos Lifshitz, with appearance of Chico Che y La Crisis. Reviewed at Hollywood Twin Theater II, N.Y., Aug. 24., 1987. Running time: **100 MINS.**

Jorge Torres	
(El Campión)	Miguel Angel Rodríguez
Magda del Río	Sasha Montenegro
El Chilo	Rafael Inclán
Flaco	Roberto (Flaco) Guzmán
Cocholata	Carmen Salinas
Lorena	Maria Cardinal
Teresa	Elsa Montes
Jorgito	Christopher Lago

Also with: Griselda Mejia, Humberto Elizondo, Güero Castro, Alma Thelma, Alfredo (Pelón) Solares, Pancho Muller, Serapio, Xorge Noble, Paty Castro, Gloria Alicia Inclan, Rafael de Quevedo, Pedrin, Carlos Bravo, Carlos Suárez, Ana Berumen, Carlhillos.

"La Raza Nunca Pierde" (The Race Never Loses), directed by Victor Manuel (Güero) Castro, is a typical Mexican sex farce with mini safety lectures scattered throughout. Already in production during the 1984 San Juanico gas refinery explosions in northern Mexico City, the film is subtitled "It Smells Like Gas." Within this context, these safety tips come off as gratuitous and artificial additions to supply social relevance to an otherwise pithy pic.

Plot centers on former welterweight boxer Jorge Torres (Miguel Angel Rodríguez), forced by health reasons to retire from the ring. When his movie star wife Magda del Río (Sasha Montenegro) fights with him about money, he leaves her and their son vowing not to return until he is financially solvent. With experience as a driver, he buys a gas truck to earn a respectable living while still pining for his son.

This is the basic framework with which Castro sets up for the subsequent collection of saucy scenes mainly employing Torres' two ribald delivermen, played by Rafael Inclán and Roberto (Flaco) Guzmán, who spend a lot of time flirting with itchy housewives and domestics.

In between the drama and the antics, the audience is told to check that the pilot light is always lit, to close the gas line off even when the tank appears empty and other such valuable information. The deliverymen even offer a short lesson on how to treat first-degree burns. And, like most Mexican sex comedies, the film ends with a party.

The acting is functional. Tech credits are rushed and barely adequate to provide plot continuity. Popular salsa singer Chico Che and his group La Crisis sing the title tune.—*Lent.*

La Vie Platinée
(Treichville Story)
(FRENCH-IVORY COAST-COLOR)

An M.F. Prods./République de Côte d'Ivoire/TF1 Films production. Directed by Claude Cadiou. Screenplay, Patrick Du Corail, Souleymane Koly; camera (color), Manuel Teran; editor, Marie-Thérèse Boiche; production design, Alma Kanate; music, François Breant; sound, Alain Curvelier. Reviewed at World Film Festival, Montreal, Aug. 26, 1987. Running time: **86 MINS.**

With: L'Ensemble Koteba d'Abidjan, Nadia Do Sacramento, Souleymane Koly, Yves Zogbo Junior.

Montreal — The sparkling local color of its Ivory Coast locations, percolating music and dancing and an attractive cast make for entertaining brio in this tale of an Abidjan folkloric troupe's determination to take its act to Paris. "La Vie Platinée" (Treichville Story) might be a bit of a longshot for U.S. theatrical distribution, but if English subtitles are provided it would be a natural for programs of either Third World or musical films.

Plot revolves around the Koteba dance company, based in the poor Treichville section of the Ivory Coast capital of Abidjan. Their reputation in their homeland has spread to France and won them a coveted invitation to stage a show at the Beaubourg Center in Paris — the dream of a lifetime for all involved. Raising the necessary travel funds seems next to impossible, however, and the troupe's plans are complicated further when the beautiful star dancer disappears, a hostage to her rich, Westernized family's objections to the sensuous native spectacle.

Director Claude Cadiou's background in photojournalism and tv is apparent in his fluid evocation of Abidjan street life, a veritable panoply of color, movement and sound. He handles the story with a breezy touch as well, balancing melodrama with generous helpings of the whimsy that foreshadows the picture's happy ending.

The characters' hopes and aspirations as well as their music and dance have undeniable universal appeal. —*Rich.*

Ni de Aquí, Ni de Allá
(From Neither Here Nor There)
(MEXICAN-COLOR)

A Películas Mexicanas release of a Producciones Vlady production. Produced by Ivan Lipkies. Directed by and starring María Elena Velasco (La India María). Screenplay, Ivette Lipkies, based on an idea by Velasco; camera (color), Alberto Arellaños; editor, Jorge Rivera; music, Chucho Zarzosa. Reviewed at Hollywood Twin theater 2, N.Y., Sept. 7, 1987. Running time: **94 MINS.**
María Nicolasa . . . . .María Elena Velasco (La India María)
Tata . . . . .Don Rafael Banquells
Cook .Cruz Infante
Mr. Taylor . . . . .Bruno Schwebel
Also with: Sergio Kleiner, Memo de Alvarado (Condorito), Poly Marichal, Pepe Romay, Blackaman, Martín Ayllet, León Escobar, Ana Arjonce, Raymond Kettles, Silvestre Méndez.

Long-time Mexican comic María Elena Velasco, better known as La India María, has delighted Hispanic audiences with depictions of an uneducated Indian woman from the countryside bumbling her way through sophisticated city life in a series of low-budget comedies she also wrote.

In her second directorial effort, Velasco brings her character to Los Angeles where, as an undocument-ed worker, she witnesses a political assassination. With the killer hot on her trail, she flubs her way through a variety of jobs while every move is recorded by the FBI, whom she suspects of being immigration officials.

Since much of the humor is based on transcultural situations, the comic possibilities surpass Velasco's usual stock of slapstick routines. Besides the genuine laughs, pic also affords a few unintentional chuckles for English speakers. Since the film was made for a Spanish-speaking audience, the Gringo extras come over as if they were simply instructed to improvise their English dialog. Thus, an employee at a Kentucky Fried Chicken outlet tells people to buy the chicken because "it is really greasy," while Velasco runs around dressed in a chicken costume.

Pic is structured as an extended flashback encompassing a series of comic sketches. Most of the film was shot on location in Los Angeles, replete with a visual pun: Velasco passes a Spanish-lingo movie theater showing an India María film.

Tech credits are low budget but competent. Actors Don Rafael Banquells and Cruz Infante put in fine performances. Native English speakers are flat, especially when they try to speak English to each other, which more often than not sounds like a junior high school Spanish conversation class.

Although most India María films bring in substantial coin at the Hispanic box office, "Ni de Aquí, Ni de Allá" should gain more at U.S. locations due to audience identification of transcultural problems and situations. Judging from the reaction here, Velasco's formula works.—*Lent.*

Lev & Bilou, Hrivou
(The Lion With The White Mane)
(CZECH-COLOR)

A Czech Film Export presentation. Directed by Jaromil Jires. Screenplay, Jiri Blazek, in collaboration with Jires, Vladimir Bor; camera (color), Jan Kurik; music, Leos Janacek. (No other credits available.) Reviewed at the Tokyo Intl. Film Festival (competing), Sept. 29, 1987. Running time: **123 MINS.**
Leos Janacek . . . . .Ludek Munzar
Zdena . . . . .Jana Hlavacova
Kamila . . . . .Zlata Adamovska

Tokyo — This is a numbingly awful biopic of Czech composer Leos Janacek, effect of which is roughly akin to what might have happened had Ken Russell been forced to direct the most conventional musician's biography at MGM in the old days. In other words, it suffers both from hysterical excess and hopeless banality. How this ended up in competition at a major film festival will remain one of the mysteries of the ages, but it is a safe bet it won't surface much in the future.

There are indications in the script that Janacek is supposed to be a charismatic artist type of some attractiveness to the ladies, but as played by Ludek Munzar he's a humorless stuffed shirt.

Janacek spends seven years writing his opera "Jenufa," which on the basis of excerpts seems like an even heavier meal than the picture, and he is spurred on by the demise of his beloved daughter, whom he practically suffocated to death while she was alive anyway. His kindly wife attempts suicide when the old lech is hanging around his favorite spa dallying with musically inclined bimbos, late 19th century vintage, and advanced age doesn't stop him from putting the make on a 26-year-old beauty who is quite happy with her husband.

The worst is director Jaromil Jires' appalling attempt to beat Ken Russell at his own game, with such embarrassments as having young Kamila hug an enormous tree trunk in a suggestion of sexual ecstasy, with Janacek's crashing melodies thundering interminably on the soundtrack.

All concerned should run and hide for a while. —*Cart.*

La Oveja Negra
(The Black Sheep)
(VENEZUELAN-COLOR)

A Gente de Cine production. Produced by Miguelangel Landa. Directed by Román Chalbaud. Screenplay, Chalbaud, David Suárez; camera (color), Javier Aguirresarobe; editor, Sergio Curiel; music, Federico Ruiz; sets, Rafael Reyeros; sound, Josue Saavedra, Orlando Andersen. Reviewed at San Sebastian Film Festival (market), Sept. 22, 1987. Running time: **90 MINS.**
La Nigua . . . . .Eva Blanco
Esotérico . . . . .Arturo Calderón
Sagrario . . . . .Zamira Segura
Evelio . . . . .Javier Zapata
Also with: Carlos Montilla, José Manuel Ascensao, Freddy Pereira, Armando Gota, Bertha Moncayo, Gonzalo J. Camacho, Orangel Delfin, Conchita Obach.

San Sebastian — Venezuela's best-known director, Román Chalbaud, has come up with a kind of hybrid parable and passion play, which takes occasional swipes at his country's society. Rhetorical and ponderous at times, pic at other moments can be absorbing.

Most of the film is set in a large, abandoned film theater where a kind of thieves' den has been set up by 20 or 30 felons and delinquents lorded over by their femme leader. Unbeknownst to the police, the assorted criminals live, love and philosophize in the building, and even parade about the streets dressed as Nazarines during the Holy Week processions. Of course, the theater looks like a sound stage and the thieves are obviously thesps.

One of those seeking honorable shelter here is a young girl who falls in love with one of the miscrants. Passions are kindled when the girl's lawful husband, a motorized cop, seeks to lure her back to his homestead. When the girl refuses, he vows to destroy the lover and all his cohorts.

From metaphor Chalbaud turns in the final sequences to explicit violence. The police get wind of a bank robbery planned by the delinquents. In a final shootout in front of the bank most of the robbers are gunned down. The cops then raid the abandoned theater and put an end to the merry, lawless challenge to society.

Offbeat, at times lyrical, pic is not likely to make much of a commercial ripple, being neither artsy nor gutsy enough to please the tastes of either of these filmic antipodes.—*Besa.*

In der Wüste
(In The Wilderness)
(WEST GERMAN-COLOR-16m)

A Deutsche Film Fernsehakademie production. Produced by Hans Willy Müller. Directed and edited by Rafael Fuster Pardo. Screenplay, Horst Stasiak, based on story by Antonio Skarmeta; camera (color, 16m), Pardo; music, Inti-Illimani, Joycelyn Bernadette Smith & Band; sound, Michael de Groot, Fuster Pardo. Reviewed at San Sebastian Film Festival, Sept. 23, 1987. Running time: **74 MINS.**
With: Claudio Cáceres Molina, Mustafa Saygili, Adriana Altaras, Meric Temucin.

San Sebastian — Shot on a shoestring budget in 16m, this film about the plight of two young, jobless exiles living in Berlin has some touching moments, but about halfway through seems to lose its direction and then wanders aimlessly to its undramatic conclusion, leaving the spectator pretty much where he was at the beginning of the film.

Occasional touches of humor help lighten yarn of a Turkish and Chilean exile living from hand to mouth in a dumpy apartment. Having spent their last pfennig, they decide to raise some cash by donating blood at a hospital. After sundry minor adventures along the way, walking miles to get to the place, they get their coin and then proceed to spend it on food, drink and a night club, accompanied by two girls. Pic ends rather abruptly after a sexual encounter between the Chilean and one of the girls.

As a film about exiles, pic breaks no new ground, nor does it try to delve into the lives of the minorities living in Germany, failing to reflect upon the social and political necessities which drove them there. Pic nevertheless has its charming vignettes, but story is too slim for a feature. A long sequence featuring Joycelyn Bernadette Smith & Band is rather obtrusive and needlessly breaks the narrative. Commercial prospects seem remote.—*Besa.*

O desejado — Les montagnes de la lune
(Mountains Of The Moon)
(PORTUGUESE-FRENCH-COLOR)

An Arion Prods./Suma Films/La Sept coproduction, with the participation of Centre National de la Cinématographic, Institut Portugais du Cinéma, Canal Plus, Sofica Investimages, RTP Lisbonne, Fondation Gulbenkian. Produced by Patrick Sandrin, Paulo Rocha. Written and directed by Rocha. Screenplay, Rocha, Jorge Silva Melo, based on Murasaki Shikibu's "Genji Monogatari;" camera (color), Kozo Okazaki; editor, Christiane Lack; music, Philippe Hersant; sound, Joaquin Pinto; art direction, Luis Montero, José Matos. Reviewed at the Venice Film Festival (competing), Aug. 29, 1987. Running time: **120 MINS.**
Joao . . . . Luis Miguel Cintra
Antonia . . . . Caroline Chaniolleau
Tiago . . . . Jacques Bonnaffe
Isabel . . . . Manuela de Freitas
Also with: Yves Afonso, Isabel Ruth, Isabel Castro, Duarte de Almeida, Graziella de Galvani, Armando Cortez, Ines de Medeiros.

Venice — "Mountains Of The Moon," art film par excellence, transcribes Murasaki Shikibu's Japanese classic "Tales Of Genji" into a modern-day Portuguese setting, with a rising young politician as its Don Juan hero. Director Paulo Rocha is a cinematic poet with little regard for trends and the marketplace, and "Mountains," though more conventional than "L'Ile des Amours," looks headed for sporadic art house play between festival outings. Yet this seductive film holds rich rewards for those curious enough to give it a try, including visual opulence, intriguing characters, and a truly sensual (but rarely erotic) atmosphere.

Joao (played with distinguished appeal by stage thesp and director Luis Miguel Cintra) is the leader of a left-wing party on his way up, equally entranced with power games and love games. Men admire him, women adore him; his dying, aristocratic godfather needs him at his bedside. His ex-wife (Manuela de Freitas) hates him but wants him back, and Joao plays with her feelings. His self-assurance only wavers when he is sent to Rome to retrieve an erring family member, the firebrand beauty Antonia (Caroline Chaniolleau), who has a terrorist lover. She alone resists his charm, falling for Joao's illegitimate son Tiago (Jacques Bonnaffe) instead. Her baby, which Joao carries in his arms as the curtain falls, could be his or Tiago's.

Rocha's skill is striking in two areas: creating complex, interesting characters who are fully believable despite their various abnormalities, and weaving their lives together in a tangled skein of passions and ambiguities. Film resonates with indefinable qualities, mixing poetic 16th century monasteries and moonlit mountains in Sintra with news reports on political crises; Portuguese landscapes and myths with Japanese imagination. Rich location work swings from Portugal to Italy and India, all lensed with palpable sensuality by cameraman Kozo Okazaki. Cast imparts believability to the most over-the-top scenes, including seductions, stabbing, natural death, miscarriage, and other solid melodramatic ingredients. Palatial interiors by art directors Luis Montero and José Matos are stunning. — *Yung.*

Sinfin, La Muerte No Es Ninguna Solucion
(Sinfin, Death Is No Solution)
(ARGENTINE-COLOR)

An Aquilea production. Directed by Cristian Pauls. Screenplay, Alan Pauls, Cristian Pauls; camera (color), Hugo Colace; editor, Pablo Mari; production design, costumes, Horacio Gallo; sound, Carlos Abbate. Reviewed at World Film Festival, Montreal, Aug. 26, 1987. Running time: **86 MINS.**
With: Alberto Ure, Lorenzo Quinteros, Susana Tanco, Jorge Marrale, Cristina Banegas, Leal Rey, Jose Maria Gutierrez, Monica Galan, Ricardo Bartis, Roberto Carnaghi, Carlos Giordano, Aldo Barbero.

Montreal — This wearisome, pretentious exercise in ersatz surrealism is excruciatingly long even at 86 minutes, offering all of the tedium but none of the originality found in the films of Chilean expatriate Raul Ruiz, upon whose work this is modeled. Theatrical prospects in the U.S. are nada, although "Sinfin, La Muerte No Es Ninguna Solucion" might reasonably be included in programs devoted to contemporary Latin American film for buffs who are interested in everything going on in the newly liberated Argentine cinema.

Scenario involves a megalomaniacal film producer who has recruited a cast of once-great but fading thespians as well as ambitious young actors to make a picture (said to be based on a Julio Cortazar story) about reclusive characters trapped in a mansion haunted by malevolent spiritual forces. The actors are compelled to sign contracts stipulating that they live in strict accordance with the conditions the film-within-a-film's script imposes upon its protagonists.

At first the actors assume there will be some flexibility in this arrangement, but they're proven dead wrong. Like the party in Buñuel's "The Exterminating Angel," there is no escape from this location. While the actors slowly begin to go crazy, bitter conflicts develop between the producer, his director and a screenwriter who spends most of his time working in bed or hallucinating in front of his typewriter. "Ideas, what ideas? I haven't had any in years," he says.

"Isolation can derange," proclaims the producer at one point. It's certainly likely that the Screen Actors Guild would never approve of set conditions that induce suicide-provoking nervous breakdowns amongst the talent.

Static still frames shot in nauseous pale greens and deep purples deepen the depressing mood. All this may be taken as a cautionary parable about Argentina's years of subjugation by military dictators, but any subtextual message is buried in the meandering narrative morass. —*Rich.*

Mas Alla Del Silencio
(Beyond Silence)
(VENEZUELAN-COLOR)

A Cinearte production. Produced and directed by Cesar Bolivar. Screenplay, Bolivar, Jose Ignacio Cabrujas; camera (color), Jose Vincente Scheuren; editor, Bolivar; music, Vinicio Ludovic; production design, Henry Ramos; sound, Josue Saavedra; assistant director, Humberto Olivieri; casting, Manuel Boffil. Reviewed at World Film Festival, Montreal (Cinema of Latin America), Aug. 30, 1987. Running time: **119 MINS.**
With: Jean Carlos Simancas, Javier Vidal, Julie Restifo, Doris Wells, Luis Rivas, Jose Manuel Pozo, Jose Fidel Martinez, Jose Gregorio Lavado, Maria Isabel Calderon.

Montreal — Several plotlines vie for attention in this muddled drama which basically centers on a deaf-mute member of a gang of armed robbers. Pic falls between too stools, being neither a serious study of the plight of the deaf, nor a satisfactory thriller. International interest will be confined to Latin American film seasons, the context in which the film unspooled in Montreal.

Fidel is the deaf-mute who's fallen in with bad guys who, in the opening sequence, rob a supermarket. A sadistic cop is on his trail, while a subplot has the cop with troubles of his own via a teenage son found with marijuana in his room; but this aspect of the story is left dangling.

Meanwhile, Fidel is learning sign language at a school for the deaf run by an erudite professor whose wife has left him. He's taped the sounds of their love-making obsessively over the years, which he plays back over the phone to her new lover. His pretty assistant wants to bed him, but he thinks he's turning gay and is attracted to a transvestite he meets. Fidel has found himself a sweet deaf girl to love, and things start to look good, except that the cop still is on his trail.

These diverse plot strands are more than the film can bear, accounting for the over-extended running time. Handling is routine, and the film is technically poor, with very flat color processing and loose editing. A couple of the actors show talent, but overall "Beyond Silence" doesn't live up to the expectations of its interesting premise. —*Strat.*

La Guerra de los Locos
(The War Of The Madmen)
(SPANISH-COLOR)

A Xaloc production. Executive producer, José María Calleja. Written and directed by Manolo Matji. Camera (color), Federico Ribes; editor, Nieves Martin; sound, Miguel Angel Polo; costumes, Gumersindo Andrés; associate producer, José G. Blanco Sola. Reviewed at San Sebastian Film Festival (market), Sept. 20, 1987. Running time: **98 MINS.**
El Rubio . . . . Alvaro de Luna
Angelito . . . . José Manuel Cervino
Don Salvador . . . . Juan Luis Galiardo
André . . . . Pep Munné
Rufino . . . . Pedro Diez del Corral
Also with: Luis Marin, Emilio Lain, Joan Potau, Patxi Catalá, Paco Algora, Alicia Sánchez, Maite Blasco, Emilio Gutiérrez Caba.

San Sebastian — The concepts that war is madness and that it is sometimes difficult to distinguish the sane from the insane are the underlying themes of this first pic by director Manolo Matji, set in the opening months of the Spanish Civil War. Well paced and with several unexpected twists, film maintains audience interest throughout, but lacks enough punch to be a crowd pleaser.

Opening scenes are set in an insane asylum somewhere in the country, run by an administrator and two nuns. When the Franco forces are pulling near, the staff flees, leaving the nuns and a relatively sane caretaker to stay on. The nuns soon are slain. After the Nationalist soldiers take over the asylum and bivouac in its grounds, a handful of the inmates steal a truck and make their getaway, with no clear idea of what they intend to do.

Film then turns into a kind of road movie, where the madmen first join up with a pocket of farmers still loyal to the government, whose leader has sworn to avenge those shot in his village by the fascists by killing the village doctor, who ordered the executions. The inmates, impartial in their madness, turn alternately upon both the Nationalists and the Republicans, though some sort of final justice is done in the last sequence of the film.

Though well lensed, we never get underneath the skin of any of the main characters, played by relatively unknown Spanish thesps. Pic had only a short run in its Spanish release and was one of the films featured in March during the Spanish film week in New York. —*Besa.*

Majdanek 1944
(W. GERMAN-DOCU-B&W)

A National Center for Jewish Film release of a Chronos Film production. Produced and directed by Bengt and Irmgard von zur Mühlen. Editor, Gisela Bienert; narrated by Peter Strauss. Reviewed at the Boston Film Festival, Sept. 22, 1987. Running time: **65 MINS.**

Boston — Bengt and Irmgard von zur Mühlen are German film archivists who have unearthed a wealth of material through a series of deals with various Eastern bloc archives. Their "Liberation Of Auschwitz" (*Variety,* Aug. 13, '86) provided previously unseen footage taken by the Russians after they liberated the Nazi death camp.

"Majdanek 1944," which was shown at the Boston Film Festival with "Auschwitz" and "Krasnodar — The Trial Of 1943," is likewise comprised of documentary material made available for the first time in the West. What makes this film especially significant is that it is the film record of one of the first Nazi war crimes trials, conducted while the war was still raging.

Soviet and Polish troops drove the Nazis out of the region in July of 1944, and uncovered the evidence of Nazi genocide. A month later a joint Soviet-Polish commission heard evidence from survivors and witnesses as to the atrocities that took place, and their testimony was preserved on film.

Several captured Germans who had run the camp testified as well, and the classic post-war "Nuremberg defense" of denying all responsibility was already being established. One soldier talks of the number of people gassed but notes that that did not include prisoners of war: "That would be immoral. That goes against international law."

As a film record of the trial and conviction of several of the operators of one of the Nazi death camps, "Majdanek 1944" may not be the most palatable film experience but it is a priceless contribution to history.
—*Kimm.*

Chi C'e C'e
(Whoever Is Here, Is Here)
(ITALIAN-COLOR)

An Azione Cinematografica production. Directed by Piero Natoli. Screenplay, Natoli, Paola Pascolini; camera (color), Carlo Cerchio; editor, Domenico Varone; music, Lamberto Macchi. Reviewed at San Sebastian Film Festival, Sept. 25, 1987. Running time: **100 MINS.**

With: Piero Natoli, Luisa Maneri, Nicola Pistoia, Anita Zagaria, Paola Nazzaro, Flavio Andreini, Claudia Poggiani, Lorenzo Alessandri.

San Sebastian — "Chi C'e C'e" is a rambling, seemingly pointless exercise in self-indulgence as Piero Natoli flips through an assortment of dull personages obsessed with the collapse of their romantic relationships and with their need to reshape their social lives.

There is a frustrated actress, a director of a publishing company who aspires to be a writer and leaves his wife and daughter, a social climber who dubs films and so on.

In lieu of a plot or story development, Natoli, is as deadpan in his acting (he plays the main part) as in his directing, wanders aimlessly to stultifying cocktail parties, pointless amorous encounters and indulges in

wayward dialog that has audiences yawning long before the film is even half through.—*Besa.*

The Sicilian
(COLOR)

Botched epic faces better overseas b.o. than domestic.

A 20th Century Fox release of a Gladden Entertainment presentation of a Sidney Beckerman production. Produced by Michael Cimino, Joann Carelli. Executive producer, Beckerman. Directed by Cimino. Screenplay, Steve Shagan, based on the novel by Mario Puzo; camera (Widescreen, Technicolor; Deluxe prints), Alex Thomson; editor, Françoise Bonnot; music, David Mansfield; production design, Wolf Kroeger; art direction, Stefano Ortolani; set decoration, Joseph Mifsud Chevalier; costume design, Wayne Finkelman; sound (Dolby), David Crozier; assistant director, Brian Cook; second unit camera, Francis Grumman; casting, Deborah Brown. Reviewed at the 20th Century Fox Studios, L.A., Oct. 16, 1987. (MPAA Rating: R.) Running time: **115 MINS.**
Salvatore Giuliano . . .Christophe Lambert
Prince Borsa . . . . .Terence Stamp
Don Masino Croce . . . . .Joss Ackland
Aspanu Pisciotta . . . . .John Turturro
Professor Hector Adonis . . .Richard Bauer
Camilla, Duchess . . . . .Barbara Sukowa
Giovanna Ferra . . . . .Giulia Boschi
Minister Trezza . . . . .Ray McAnally
Dr. Nattore . . . . .Barry Miller
Passatempo . . . . .Andreas Katsulas
Cpl. Silvestro Canio . . . . .Michael Wincott
Terranova . . . . .Derrick Branche
Cardinal of Palermo . . . . .Richard Venture
Also with: Ramon Bieri (Quintana), Stanko Molnar (Silvio Ferra), Oliver Cotton (Commander Roccofino), Joe Regalbuto (Father Doldana), Tom Signorelli (Abbot Manfredi), Aldo Ray (Don Siano of Bisacquino), Nicholas Kepros (University President), Justin Clark (Boy), Trevor Ray (Frisella the Barber).

Hollywood — "The Sicilian" represents a botched telling of the life of postwar outlaw leader Salvatore Giuliano. Just who contributed to what parts of the botching remain a mystery, since uncredited hands cut over 30 minutes from the version director Michael Cimino delivered.

Nevertheless, what unfolds onscreen feels flat, unexciting and unconvincing, and lacking in the great texture and memorable scenes that have thus far graced even Cimino's most problematic films. Cimino's 146-minute cut will be released overseas, where b.o. could be good, but domestic chances look meager.

Cimino seems to be aiming for an operatic telling of the short career of the violent 20th century folk hero, but falls into an uncomfortable middle ground between European artfulness and stock Hollywood conventions. He has also burdened himself with a leading man who, while possessing the looks, simply does not have the charisma and wild streak necessary to carry off the central role.

Saga served as the basis of Francesco Rosi's 1962 "Salvatore Giuliano," and has at its core a popular young man who, working from the mountains, employs increasingly excessive means to further his dream of achieving radical land distribution from the titled estate owners to the peasants.

Giuliano unhesitatingly kills anyone he thinks has betrayed him, and maintains a semi-adversarial, curiously equivocal relationship with both the Catholic Church and the all-powerful Mafia. Alternately interested in killing him and embracing him as one of its own, the Mafia, at the behest of local politicians, finally succeeds in enlisting Giuliano's aid in preventing a communist victory at the polls, just as the bandit and frequent kidnapper of landowners was eluding a major police manhunt.

There is clearly plenty of meaty material here for a satisfying 2-hour meal, but the ingredients have combined in a unpalatable stew. Steve Shagan's script (the one for which Gore Vidal should be happy he lost an arbitration for credit) never develops a strong dramatic line, and Cimino, so enamored of palette, omits all sorts of fascinating historical and political details.

Casting is a major problem as well, mainly because the great diversity of choices detracts from a sense of specific place. In the lead, Christophe (billed in U.S. projects as Christopher) Lambert, with his big forehead, furrowed eyebrows and fleshy lips, occasionally resembles a young Brando, which is precisely what the part needs but what Lambert can't otherwise supply. He betrays little inner conflict or sense of thought, and simply does not make Giuliano interesting. The French actor's accent is vague, and the mix of accents throughout the picture would be more representative of a NATO gathering than a bunch of Sicilians on home turf.

Why, for instance, has the fine German actress Barbara Sukowa been cast as an American? Why is John Turturro, who does an intense turn as Giuliano's second-in-command, the only one who sounds as though he just stepped off the set of a Martin Scorsese picture? Why does Terence Stamp, who speaks upper-class English, have the only witty lines in the film? And how many of the actors were dubbed, as they feel to have been, whether they were or not?

Coming off by far the best is Joss Ackland, who makes the Mafia chieftain a warm, sympathetic man one enjoys being around. Richard Bauer makes a strong impression as the brilliant, crippled professor who acts as an adviser and go-between for Giuliano and the Mafia, and Giulia Boschi is strikingly, seriously beautiful as the hero's wife.

Although the canvas is as big as ever, "The Sicilian" is actually less visually impressive than any of Cimino's films since his first — memorable scenes or even shots here seldom assert themselves. Pic never finds a rhythm, and is filled with many awkward transitions as well as last-ditch cutaways to flying birds, something the director would undoubtedly blame on those who succeeded him in the editing room, but are pretty sorry no matter who did them. David Mansfield's score, however, is excellent. —*Cart.*

Suspect
(COLOR)

Cliched legal thriller.

A Tri-Star Pictures release of a Tri-Star ML Delphi Premier production. Executive producer, John Veitch. Produced by Daniel A. Sherkow. Directed by Peter Yates. Stars Cher, Dennis Quaid. Screenplay, Eric Roth; camera (technicolor), Billy Williams; editor, Ray Lovejoy; music, Michael Kamen; production design, Stuart Wurtzel; costume design, Rita Ryack; art direction, Steve Sardanis; special effects, Jim Fredburg, Joe Ramsey; assistant director, Pat Kehoe; associate producer, Jennifer Ogden; casting, Howard Feuer. In Dolby stereo. Reviewed at Cineplex Odeon Century Plaza theater, Oct. 14, 1987. (MPAA Rating: R.) Running time: **121 MINS.**

Kathleen Riley . . . . Cher
Eddie Sanger . . . . Dennis Quaid
Carl Wayne Anderson . . . . . Liam Neeson
Judge Matthew Helms . . . . . John Mahoney
Charlie Stella . . . . Joe Mantegna
Paul Gray . . . . Philip Bosco
Grace Comisky . . . . E. Katherine Kerr
Morty Rosenthal . . . . Fred Melamed
Car jockey . . . . Michael Beach

Hollywood — Art imitates art — and not very well — in Peter Yates' latest, a gimmicky suspense drama sabotaged by a flimsy script full of clichés. Dennis Quaid valiantly struggles to breathe life into the matter, but comes up short when a surprise ending packs little punch because the audience knows in the first five minutes the prime suspect can't be guilty. Nonetheless, box-office prospects look fairly promising.

Cher stars as Kathleen Riley, a hard-working Washington, D.C. public defender unlike any ever seen before (perhaps she passed her law boards through osmosis). A day before taking a long-needed vacation, she's given a defendant charged with the brutal murder of a Justice Dept. staffer. Carl Wayne Anderson (Liam Neeson) has everything working against him: a Vietnam vet, he was rendered deaf and speechless by the psychological toll of the war, and he's homeless — he *has* to be innocent.

Audience is expected to sweat that one out while the seemingly hopeless defense begins against a backdrop of the self-righteous public defender's office. Bright light is shone by Fred Melamed, as Riley's colleague Morty Rosenthal, but even he is forced to utter some amazingly trite lines.

When asked what keeps him in his job after all the years of little pay and no thanks, he says, "the one poor bastard who didn't do it," a line that could be plagiaristic if it weren't already part of the public domain.

Just when it seems the entire film is going to be suffocated by liberal piety, Quaid shows up as Dairy State lobbyist Eddie Sanger, so persuasive that he's "dangerous," according to one congresswoman who winds up changing a key vote a day after he's seduced her.

Sanger is called in for jury duty and sparks begin to fly when he faces off against Cher in the courtroom. Scenes with the two of them are the best in the film, but there aren't enough, and Yates does not spend enough time explaining why Sanger is motivated to risk his neck to find additional evidence to buttress the defense's case.

Risk it he does, and much of the snooping around to find additional clues that seem to point to a deputy attorney general has the feeling of a police procedural.

Yates' touch in balancing courtroom action with suspense is uneven, and much of the drama from the proceedings disappears when it becomes obvious that lawyers seem to be trying the case without ever once asking or finding out about the suspect's side of the story. Biggest flaw in Eric Roth's script won't go away and it prevents any tension from building during the otherwise effective dramatic performance of Neeson.

Director and scripter also rely on poor judgment by Riley and the lack of even the most rudimentary security in D.C. government buildings for their suspenseful scenes down the stretch.

If given more time and a chance to get deeper into his character, Quaid might have saved the pic singlehandedly. As it is, he's wonderfully brash without being unctuous while playing the special interest flack of someone's dreams — or nightmares.

Supporting roles are mostly well played, with John Mahoney right on as the judge handling the case, and Michael Beach turning in a rich, hilarious bit as a parking lot attendant.

Technical credits are strong, especially the sets in and around the capital, which give film the realism that it has. Michael Kamen's score is unobtrusive and effective. —*Camb.*

No Man's Land
(COLOR)

Solid, well-acted thriller.

An Orion Pictures release. Produced by Joseph Stern, Dick Wolf. Executive producers, Ron Howard, Tony Ganz. Directed by Peter Werner. Screenplay, Wolf; camera (Deluxe color), Hiro Narita; editor, Steve Cohen; film editor, Daniel Hanley; music, Basil Poledouris; production design, Paul Peters; set decoration, Ethel Robins Richards; costume design, Jodie Tillen; sound (Dolby), Charlie Wilborne; associate producers, Jack Behr, Sandy Kroopf; assistant director, Josh McLaglen; second unit director, M. James Arnett; second unit camera, Roy H. Wagner; stunt coordinator, Corey Eubanks; casting, Judith Holstra, Marcia Ross. Reviewed at the Orion screening room, L.A., Oct. 16, 1987. (MPAA Rating: R.) Running time: **106 MINS.**

Ted Varrick . . . . Charlie Sheen
Benjy Taylor . . . . D.B. Sweeney
Lt. Vincent Bracey . . . . Randy Quaid
Ann Varrick . . . . Lara Harris
Malcolm . . . . Bill Duke
Frank Martin . . . . R.D. Call
Lt. Curtis Loos . . . . Arlen Dean Snyder
Captain Haun . . . . M. Emmet Walsh

Hollywood — "No Man's Land" is a stylish thriller about a lower class rookie cop becoming caught up in the fast lane high life of the filthy rich car thief he's assigned to nail. Psychologically convincing in its portrait of the charming villain's Mephistophelean influence over the earnest but impressionable undercover man, pic also provides a teasing peek at the world of criminals who steal $70,000-plus Porsches for a living. Audience reaction should be good, but vague, unevocative title represents a handicap going in. (Film is not related to the Harold Pinter play of same title.)

Charlie Sheen and D.B. Sweeney are both extremely effective as two young men, barely into their 20s, whose diametrically opposed backgrounds make for a dynamic and ultimately deadly relationship.

Sweeney, recently seen in "Gardens Of Stone," is assigned by boss Randy Quaid to take a job at a Porsche garage that doubles as a "chop shop," where stolen cars are broken up and reassembled as untraceable new vehicles. Quaid suspects the wealthy owner, Sheen, of having killed another policeman, and Sweeney, despite his total inexperience, is supposed to get the goods on him.

A little joyriding and partying with the handsome, crafty Sheen easily seduces Sweeney into taking a softer view of illegal activity, and the bright but gullible kid begins pulling jobs with the rationale that he's getting closer to his stated goal. Unfortunately, he comes to like Sheen a lot and, furthermore, gets sexually involved with the latter's beautiful sister, Lara Harris.

Scenarist Dick Wolf is a vet of both "Hill Street Blues" and "Miami Vice" and both influences turn up here, as he has carefully worked out the script to offer opportunities for the character nuances of the first show and the flash of the second. Sweeney's incremental swing into morally and legally ambiguous territory plays quite believably, so that it takes a heavy shock of recognition to jolt him back to reality.

Director Peter Werner, who recently guided Quaid through a superb performance in "LBJ: The Early Years," has obtained excellent work from his young thesps and, in league with lenser Hiro Narita, has turned out a visually sharp suspenser. —*Cart.*

Siesta
(COLOR)

Intense drama for specialized audience.

A Lorimar Motion Pictures release of a Lorimar and Siren Pictures presentation of a Palace/Kurfirst/King production. Produced by Gary Kurfirst. Coproducer, Chris Brown. Executive producers, Julio Caro, Zalman King, Nik Powell. Directed by Mary Lambert. Screenplay, Patricia Louisianna Knop, based on the novel by Patrice Chaplin; camera (color), Bryan Loftus; editor, Glenn A. Morgan; music, Marcus Miller; music performed by Miles Davis; production design, John Beard; art direction, Jose Marie Tapiador; costume design, Marlene Stewart; sound (Ultra-Stereo), Roy Charman; associate producer, Lisa Z. Jones; assistant director, Kuki Lopez Rodero; casting, Marci Liroff (U.S.), Mary Selway (U.K.). U.S. shoot: camera, Michael Lund; art direction, Jon Hutman; set decoration, Kara Lindstrom; sound, Jon Huck; assistant director, Joe Camp 3d. Reviewed at the Cineplex Odeon Universal City Cinema (competing in Women In Film Festival), Oct. 17, 1987. (MPAA Rating: R.) Running time: **97 MINS.**

Claire . . . . Ellen Barkin
Augustine . . . . Gabriel Byrne
Kit . . . . Julian Sands
Marie . . . . Isabella Rossellini
Del . . . . Martin Sheen
Cabbie . . . . Alexi Sayle
Conchita . . . . Grace Jones
Nancy . . . . Jodie Foster

Hollywood — First feature film by Mary Lambert is a densely packed portrait of a beautiful, disturbed woman at the end of her rope. Told in a fragmented, time-jumping style reminiscent of Nicolas Roeg, this subjective, hallucinatory recollection of a 5-day descent into hell sustains intense interest throughout, to a great extent because of Ellen Barkin's extravagantly fine performance in the leading role, but will probably prove too arty, pretentious and downbeat for mainstream audiences.

A sort-of modern-style "Under The Volcano" soaked in desperate love rather than booze, "Siesta" begins with a disheveled Barkin lying at the end of a runway in Spain, then piercingly flashes back to events of the prior five days. In its elaborate, jigsaw-puzzle way, film tells of how Barkin, a daredevil skydiver, impulsively leaves her home and husband in Death Valley for a quick trip to Spain to find the man she still loves, trapeze artist Gabriel Byrne, who also has married someone else, Isabella Rossellini.

Although due back in California imminently for a big commercial payday, Barkin lets her desire for Byrne prolong her Spanish sojourn past the deadline. She falls in with a dissolute, aimless English crowd led by Julian Sands and Jodie Foster and finally becomes utterly lost and delirious, helpless at the hands of filthy-minded taxi driver Alexi Sayle.

The story's many small mysteries and character revelations are uncovered only gradually, and it is Barkin's tremendously gutsy, all-out performance that helps overcome the occasional tendencies toward undue ambiguity and abstraction. Actress runs the emotional and physical gamut, baring soul and body in her most demanding and rewarding role to date.

Symbolically, Barkin's trip to Spain is the emotional equivalent of free flight, a fearless jump that can result in total exhilaration and liberation, or sudden death. Barkin plays Claire just that way, throwing herself entirely into everything she does and being utterly believable as a rash, driven woman for whom life without risk means nothing.

At the same time, she is a woman still madly, hopelessly in love with a man she once let go and now can't have. She awkwardly confronts Byrne and Rossellini, attempts to win him back by seduction, and ultimately has a violent fight with the wife, which has a surprising result.

Pic is mostly populated by rather arch, overly serious foreigners on Spanish soil, and viewer reaction will largely be determined by the extent of one's response to Barkin. Byrne puts on a continuous smoldering act as the sought-after lover, Martin Sheen is all congenial American hype as Barkin's abandoned husband, and Sayle is properly repulsive as the sinister driver who takes advantage of the Yankee lady when she is stranded wearing only a striking scarlet dress.

Julian Sands has some breezy moments as a self-styled English artist who briefly takes Barkin under his wing, and Jodie Foster, as a snooty but friendly socialite, has fun with a British accent. Rossellini and Grace Jones have very little to do.

Pic looks splendid, with Lambert, formerly best known for her Madonna videos, getting superior contributions from lenser Bryan Loftus, production designer John Beard and costume designer Marlene Stewart. Spanish locations are sharp, and musical score, filled with an intriguingly varied selection of songs, is highlighted by some Miles Davis solos.

Film does carry more symbolic and intellectual baggage than most viewers will care to deal with, but Lambert, working from Patricia Louisianna Knop's intricate screenplay, shows considerable talent, and Barkin's performance is rare enough to give "Siesta" a fair measure of distinction. —*Cart.*

Gandahar
(FRENCH-ANIMATED-COLOR)

A Henri Rollin and Jean-Claude Delayre presentation, coproduced by Colimason, Films A2 in association with Revcom Television. Executive producer, Léon Zuratas. Directed by René Laloux. Adapted by Leloux from novel by Jean-Pierre Andrevon, "Les Homme-machines contre Gandahar;" drawings, Philippe Caza; dialog, Raphael Cluzel; music, Gabriel Yared; associate producer, Michel Noll. Reviewed at Cine Retiro, Sitges, Spain, Oct. 9, 1987. Running time: **83 MINS.**

Sitges — René Laloux, best known for his 1973 "Fantastic Planet" and his association with Roland Topor and Moebius, comes up with a new roster of fantasy creations in this feature, but the story line is weak and adult audiences are liable to find pic rather too tame and infantile for comfort.

(N.Y.-based distributor Miramax Films is prepping domestic release at the end of the year of an Isaac Asimov-scripted new version of the film, utilizing the same animation, entitled "Light Years." *-Ed.*)

Yarn concerns an imaginary lotusland called Gandahar, one of whose young men, Syl, is sent out to discover who is killing the mirrorbirds that protect their utopia. He teams up with a group of freakish-looking monsters, victims of genetic manipulations, who help him fight the heavies, the Metal Men and an artificial brain which spawns them.

Battles are fought, our hero finds a heroine to give him a hand and at last, after half a dozen adventures, bucolic virtue triumphs over modern villainy. Some of the animation is imaginative, but much of it is static and talky. The Metal Men are poor foils (sameness is rather too abstract to be effective as a villain), and the hero too much like Prince Charming to appeal to any but under-12 moppets. The philosophical symbolism underlying the plot is yawningly simplistic. —*Besa.*

Big Bad Mama II
(COLOR)

She should have stayed in bed.

A Concorde Pictures release. Produced by Roger Corman. Executive producer, Lois Luger. Directed by Jim Wynorski. Screenplay, R. J. Robertson, Wynorski; camera (Foto-Kem color; Film House prints), Robert C. New; editor, Noah Blough, Nancy Nuttall; music, Chuck Cirino; sound, Chat Gunter; art direction, Billie Greenbaum; second unit director, Linda Shayne; second unit camera, Howard Wexler; additional camera, Troy Cook; postproduction supervisor, Steve Barnett; casting, Rosemary Weldon; associate producer, Matt Leipzig. Reviewed at Palace Quad 3, Parkchester, The Bronx, Oct. 17, 1987. (MPAA Rating: R.) Running time: **83 MINS.**

Wilma McClatchie . . . . . . Angie Dickinson
Daryl Pearson . . . . Robert Culp
Billie Jean McClatchie . . Danielle Brisebois
Polly McClatchie . . . . Julie McCullogh
Crawford . . . . Bruce Glover
Jordan Crawford . . . . Jeff Yahger
Alma . . . . Jacque Lynn Colton
Also with: Ebbe Roe Smith, Charles Cyphers, Kelli Maroney, Linda Shayne.

"Big Bad Mama II" is a very embarrassing followup to the 1974 Angie Dickinson drive-in hit. Currently in regional theatrical release, cheapie was advertised to open at three Manhattan sites but bumped to bookings in the other boroughs only.

As with producer Roger Corman's novel redoing of his "Jackson County Jail" as a "parallel world" sequel called "Outside Chance," "Mama II" is not a sequel to the original pic. Only Dickinson encores, as Wilma McClatchie, a gun-toting, tough-talking 1930s gangster in the mode of Ma Barker and Bonnie Parker. Her sexy daughters (Susan Sennett and Robbie Lee in the 1974 film; Danielle Brisebois and Julie McCullogh currently) are left fatherless in a prolog wherein villain Bruce Glover has their dad killed and the family evicted from their homestead.

Dickinson vows to get Glover, who is running for governor of Texas. She kidnaps his son (Jeff Yahger) and inducts him into her family band of bank robbers. Pic at this point becomes virtually plotless, with a hapless Robert Culp along for the ride as a Philadelphia reporter out to exploit the outlaws' story (and romance Dickinson). An action montage of footage from the first film is used to suggest scope and save money.

When not straining for idiotic "socially redeeming values" in having Dickinson show solidarity with striking miners and Hoovertown denizens, pic is one long rehash with endless machinegun fire, exploding squibs and period car chases.

Its main thrust is to provide some skin for those successors to the drive-in: homevid and paycable. Big surprise is that former tv child star of "Archie's Bunker's Place," Danielle Brisebois, goes topless in a requisite frolic in a pond with sis McCullogh and in the process handily proves to have a better bod than the former Playboy centerfold model. Dickinson has a nude bed scene with Culp, but is obviously subbed for by a body double this time.

The Peter Principle has former Corman publicist and writer for "Castle Of Frankenstein" magazine Jim Wynorski directing this mess, which falls into the "no retakes" school of cinema. Actors' readings suffer accordingly and sense of ripoff is underscored by Chuck Cirino's music which draws heavily (and without credit) upon the work of Ennio Morricone, particularly his "The Good, The Bad And The Ugly" score. Idoitic ending features Dickinson in a white wig in 1987 with great-granddaughter Willie (played by Kelli Maroney) to carry on the family tradition. —*Lor.*

Fatal Beauty
(COLOR)

Ridiculous, ultraviolent antidrug vehicle for Whoopi.

An MGM/UA Communications release in association with CST Communications, from MGM Pictures. Stars Whoopi Goldberg. Produced by Leonard Kroll. Directed by Tom Holland. Screenplay, Hilary Henkin, Dean Riesner, from story by Bill Svanoe; camera (Metrocolor, Deluxe prints), David M. Walsh; editor, Don Zimmerman; music, Harold Faltermeyer; production design, James William Newport; set decoration, Rick Simpson; costume design, Aggie Guerard Rodgers; sound (Dolby), William Nelson, Jules Strasser, Mychal Smith; assistant director, Michael Green; stunt coordinator, Walter Scott; casting, Richard Pagano, Sharon Bialy. Reviewed at National Theater, Westwood, Oct. 21, 1987. (MPAA Rating: R.) Running time: **104 MINS.**

Rita Rizzoli . . . . Whoopi Goldberg
Mike Marshak . . . . Sam Elliott
Carl Jimenez . . . . Rubén Blades
Conrad Kroll . . . . Harris Yulin
Lt. Kellerman . . . . John P. Ryan
Cecile Jaeger . . . . Jennifer Warren
Leo Nova . . . . Brad Dourif
Earl Skinner . . . . Mike Jolly
Deputy Getz . . . . Charles Hallahan
Also with: Neill Barry, Richard (Cheech) Marin, Ebbe Roe Smith, Belinda Mayne, Celeste Yarnall.

Hollywood — For the first two-thirds of "Fatal Beauty," Whoopi Goldberg continues to play the same role she has in her last two films, which is, basically, Eddie Murphy. By the time this sanctimonious antidrug film has decided to condemn violent crime rather than revel in it, the game is up and a promising coupling between Goldberg and Sam Elliott is wasted. In attempting to be morally correct *after* celebrating the comic-book violence portrayed herein, director Tom Holland and crew reveal a fundamental misunderstanding of the true villains and victims of drug abuse in America. Film should do well at the boxoffice, especially in urban houses.

(John Milius, who was originally set to write and direct the film with Cher starring, was listed as executive producer during production, but is not credited on the release print. —*Ed.*)

Violence is so gratuitous in this pic (which had an X rating changed to an R on appeal), and cultural stereotypes so pervasive, that it's scary to realize that filmmakers meant this to be some kind of message to America's youth.

Goldberg is L.A. narcotics detective Rita Rizzoli, the last line of the law in the fight to wipe out crack on the streets of the city. She does most of her work in that "Beverly Hills Cop" fantasy world where cops and robbers engage in witty verbal repartee before blowing each other away.

Clue to utter lack of plausibility in Holland's scattershot direction is given early on when Rizzoli walks into a bar disguised as a prostitute (in an outfit a prostitute wouldn't be caught dead in), rushes to the aid of a junkie contact and winds up getting beaten senseless behind the bar by a drunk who repeatedly kicks her in the head while calling her a bitch, and worse. When she's up walking and wisecracking two minutes later, tone of pic is set for good.

She's on the tail of a pair of two bit dealers who are trying to hit the big time. Leo (Brad Dourif) and Earl (Mike Jolly) are the main perpetrators of violence in the film. The almost-sexual anticipation with which they put bullet clips into their automatic weapons (and the time Holland spends building to the slaughter) would be disturbing if it was played straight. Holland seems to want to get laughs from this in the same scene.

Rizzoli also suspects that the point man for dealings is Valley businessman Conrad Kroll (Harris Yulin), who inexplicably dispatches his bodyguard Mike Marshak (Sam Elliott) to take care of the cop.

Script doesn't progress so much as meander from shooting to shooting, with Leo and Earl typically using a thousand bullets for jobs that require 10 or fewer. Almost everyone gets shot, but "good guys" only get it in the ankle or the arm, and bounce right back up.

Concluding scene is one of the most ludicrous in memory, with a multi-million dollar drug deal going down *in the middle of* a pricey clothing boutique at a Valley mall during grand opening weekend.

Ninety minutes into the film, Goldberg does a 180° turn with Rita, revealing to her increasingly more intimate friend Marshak that she once had a daughter who died in a drug-related incident. While Goldberg plays the scene well, she's essentially out of character, and seems to have little relation to the detective that walks the streets fighting crime.

While Holland and scripters Hilary Henkin and Dean Riesner have no problem showing blood spurting everywhere from that crime, they can't quite stomach the thought of the black Goldberg and white Elliott engaged in a romantic clinch. (Who cares about guns?, heaven forbid anyone should find something offensive in this film.) Pair's tender kiss near the end is the couple's only sign of involvement, as filmmakers play this one straight down the line.

In the end, its not interracial relationships or even drug abuse that sticks with the viewer, but lots and lots of useless bloodshed that seems to leave no one of any worth hurting.

In 1982's "48 HRS.," Walter Hill went about as far as one can go in letting comedy and violence coexist on the same screen. Many have tried to copy that formula since, with disappointing, occasionally revulsive results. None have failed quite so spectacularly as "Fatal Beauty," a film whose positive message is smothered by an equally le-

thal negative one that untimately seems to imply that violence is okay and that the only people really hurt from drug abuse are the dumb white kids buying the stuff from their parents. —*Camb.*

Prince Of Darkness
(COLOR)

Buggy horror flick spends too much time vamping.

A Universal Pictures release of an Alive Films presentation. Produced by Larry Franco. Executive producers, Shep Gordon, Andre Blay. Directed by John Carpenter. Screenplay, "Martin Quatermass" (Carpenter); camera (Panavision, Deluxe color), Gary B. Kibbe; editor, Steve Mirkovich; music, Carpenter, in association with Alan Howarth; production design, Daniel Lomino; set design, Rick Gentz; costume design, Deahdra Scarano; sound (Ultra-Stereo), Terry Porter, Mel Metcalfe, David J. Hudson; stunts, Jeff Imada; assistant director, Larry Franco; casting, Linda Francis. Reviewed at Universal Studios, Room 1, Oct. 19, 1987. (MPAA rating: R.) Running time: **101 MINS.**
Priest . . . . Donald Pleasence
Brian . . . . Jameson Parker
Birack . . . . Victor Wong
Catherine . . . . Lisa Blount
Walter . . . . Dennis Dun
Kelly . . . . Susan Blanchard
Susan . . . . Anne Howard
Lisa . . . . Ann Yen
Lomax . . . . Ken Wright
Mullins . . . . Dirk Blocker
Calder . . . . Jessie Lawrence Ferguson
Dr. Leahy . . . . Peter Jason
Street Schizo . . . . Alice Cooper

Hollywood — The Great Satan doesn't just reside in man's heart of darkness. Instead he lives in an opposite dimension, and manifests himself in this world in ... bugs. That's about the extent of the horror that John Carpenter conjures up in his latest, "Prince Of Darkness." Carpenter falls victim to his own worst instincts again, spending so much time turning the screws on the next scare that he completely forsakes his actors, who are already stranded with a shoddy script. Boxoffice should start out okay, then fade quickly.

Story takes place in L.A., where physics prof Birack (Victor Wong) takes his graduate class to an abandoned church in the middle of the city. He's summoned there by a priest (Donald Pleasence, who seems to have some secret sorrow), who has discovered inside the church a secret canister, guarded for hundreds of years by a forgotten sect of the Catholic church, the Brotherhood of Sleep.

Canister itself, which is supposed to be the embodiment of all evil, mostly looks like a green slime lava lamp. Pseudo-scientific discussions that take place concerning it are particularly weak. Rather than pinning the story on something, and discussing the complexities of that phenomenon, actors are given incomplete thoughts to utter, as if they have to solve the secret of the world through some metaphysical free word association game.

The students, who have been left

largely in the dark about their work, slowly begin to realize what they're up against. This happens at about the same time the green canister starts sliming various students and turning them into zombies, so they can go out and wreak even more havoc.

With the help of his new converts (and an already zombified band of killer street people, led by Alice Cooper), the devil does his work in and around the church. Rather than raining fire on everyone, he works strictly by the conventions of horror movies, throwing a bunch of slimy caterpillars into a coffee cup, some *bigger, slimier* caterpillars onto a window, a mound of spiders at a man's feet, etc.

Cumulative effect is not horrific, but rather tiresome. Carpenter knows what he wants to do, but he just doesn't have the ammunition in the script to get it done and the neglect with which he handles his actors (dialog believability is on the high school theater level) only makes matters worse.

None of the ensemble really stand out, with lovers Jameson Parker and Lisa Blount never getting a real chance to develop their relationship, and Dennis Dun's Walter completely robbed of his charm through his stilted delivery of equally wooden lines.

The last two minutes of the film are effective, with scope of danger finally realized. Had Carpenter handled cast and script with a lot more care, it could have been chilling. (Screenplay is credited to ficticious Martin Quatermass (homage to Nigel Kneale's sci-fi character) but was written by Carpenter.—*Ed.*)

Technical credits are above average, with Gary B. Kibbe's crisp photography livening up dingy settings, and Carpenter's score, with Alan Howarth, evocative, if somewhat monochromatic.—*Camb.*

The Hidden
(COLOR)

Thriller fizzles at the end.

A New Line Cinema and Heron Communications release of a Robert Shaye production, in association with Mega Entertainment and Michael Meltzer. Produced by Shaye, Gerald T. Olson, Meltzer. Executive producers, Stephen Diener, Lee Muhl, Dennis Harris, Jeffrey Klein. Directed by Jack Sholder. Screenplay, Bob Hunt; camera (Deluxe color), Jacques Haitkin; editor, Michael Knue; music, Michael Convertino; production design, C.J. Strawn, Mick Strawn; set decoration, James Barrows; costumes, Malissa Daniel; sound, Jeffrey J. Haboush, Greg P. Russell; assistant director, Hohn Woodward; casting, Annette Benson. Reviewed at the Hollywood screening room, Oct. 20, 1987. (MPAA Rating: R.) Running time: **96 MINS.**
Tom Beck . . . . Michael Nouri
Lloyd Gallagher . . . . Kyle MacLachlan
Cliff Willis . . . . Ed O'Ross
Ed Flynn . . . . Clu Gulager
Brenda Lee . . . . Claudia Christian
John Masterson . . . . Clarence Felder
Jonathan Miller . . . . William Boyett
Sanchez . . . . Richard Brooks
Barbara Beck . . . . Catherine Cannon

Brem . . . . Larry Cedar
Holt . . . . John McCann
Jack DeVries . . . . Chris Mulkey

Hollywood — "The Hidden" is a well-constructed thriller brought down by an utterly conventional sci-fi ending; a spirited 80-minute chase to a disappointing final reel in which the film's fresh perspective becomes stale and its spare, knowing script collapses under the weight of a central relationship that never matures. If film gets enough response out of the box, word-of-mouth can make it a modest financial success.

Michael Nouri finally shakes his "Flashdance" shadow by turning in the best performance of his career as the tough-but-compassionate L.A. homicide detective Tom Beck.

Just as Beck is prepared to close the books on a businessman who went on a crime spree, he's approached by taciturn FBI agent Lloyd Gallagher from Seattle (Kyle MacLachlan), who's searching for the same man, Jack DeVries (Chris Mulkey).

Gallagher is unsatisfied when Beck informs him DeVries is about to die in an L.A. hospital, and the plot begins to unfold when the dying man crawls out of his bed and forcefeeds a huge, reptilian alien life form down the throat of fellow patient Jonathan Miller (William Boyett, in a nicely drawn comic turn), a mild-mannered accountant with a perfect record and a bad heart. A few minutes later, Miller bolts out of bed, escapes the hospital, murders a record store clerk and heads on another crime spree.

While Nouri is getting suspicious, he can't pierce the creepy, cold exterior of MacLachlan's Gallagher. Taking him home for dinner with the wife doesn't help either, as Gallagher has difficulty making conversation and is not particularly adept with his utensils.

What Nouri's Beck finds out eventually is that the alien organism inside of DeVries, then Miller, can't stay there for long and can only be destroyed while it's changing bodies.

This leads to a series of calamitous, well-shot chase scenes in which Beck and Gallagher are trying to catch up with the possessed human before the alien goes mouth-to-mouth into another life form. Key to stopping it is MacLachlan's weapon (which looks like a prize from inside a box of cereal), with which he tries to kill the next transporter of evil, a stripper named Brenda (Claudia Christian, a bit *too* good-looking to be believable in her part).

By this time, Beck knows something's up and has Gallagher arrested. Gallagher is, of course, not really Gallagher and not even who the police think he is, but actually an alien life form down on earth to catch the body-hopping evil organism.

From here, matters slip into an increasingly ridiculous turn of events that has the organism jumping into a dog, a senator and a couple members of the police force, with Beck getting seriously wounded in the process. It is especially disappointing to see such a stock ending after the promise shown in the beginning of the film.

Ultimate problem seems to be lack of chemistry that needs to develop between Nouri, who barely reaches out, and MacLachlan, who barely emotes. More tangible sense of connection between the two could have made ending easier to swallow (literally).

Tech credits are good all around, with Jack Sholder's direction swift and assured, Michael Knue's tight editing adding excitement to the chase scenes and effective sound mix from Jeffrey J. Haboush and Greg P. Russell (especially when people are about to belch up the monster) leavening the believability of the incredible events.—*Camb.*

87 Days + 11
(DOCU-COLOR)

A Go For It! production. Produced and directed by Whitney Blake. Camera (color), Frances Reid; editor, Joanne D'Antonio. Reviewed at the Mill Valley Film Fesitval, Oct. 12, 1987. (No MPAA Rating.) Running time: 99 MINS.

Mill Valley, Calif. — Documentarian Whitney Blake, who once acted on the tv sitcom "Hazel" and hosted a tv talkshow in Los Angeles, has rendered a crisp, intelligent docu about a surburban Frisco high school of "special cases," tough kids who for one reason or another don't fit in to the system.

Reno Taini, once named California "teacher of the year," is an apt subject for this focus as he spreads his philosophy of candor and self-commitment to a class of offbeat, but not beaten, teens. Taini's Alternative Education class concentrates on survival, both in the outdoors and in life's daily routine.

Blake has managed forthright vérité without eliciting mugging from the kids. The quick-cutting is deft, and several clean characterizations are established. All that's lacking is an early, brief voice-over intro to mechanics of the class. A quicker setup would help set the pace.

Taini himself has acting quality, likely instinctive to any first-rate classroom instructor. He's the sort of guy viewers will find fetching, and caring.

"87 Days + 11," which means the length of the class term, has the uplifting quality that might play well on a Disney tv seg and is definitely apt for PBS airing. Its prospects as a commercial docu feature are less promising, but with proper promotion in selected situations "87 Days" might be able to attract a teen following, and thus a bit of b.o. —*Herb.*

The Killing Time
(COLOR)

Drowsy attempt at *film noir*.

A New World Pictures release. Produced by Peter Abrams, Robert L. Levy. Executive producer, J.P. Guerin. Directed by Rick King. Screenplay, Don Bohlinger, James Nathan, Bruce Franklin Singer; camera (Foto-Kem color), Paul H. Goldsmith; editor, Lorenzo de Stefano; music, Paul Chihara; production design, Bernt Amadeus Capra; set decoration, Byrnadette Di Santo; sound, Ron Judkins, Bob Jackson; costumes, Jean-Pierre Dorleac; assistant director, Matthew Carlisle; casting, Paul Ventura. Reviewed at Lions Gate Studios screening room, L.A., Oct. 16, 1987. (MPAA Rating: R.) Running time: 95 MINS.

Sam Wayburn	Beau Bridges
Brian Mars	Kiefer Sutherland
Jake Winslow	Wayne Rogers
Carl Cunningham	Joe Don Baker
Laura Winslow	Camelia Kath
Lila Dagget	Janet Carroll
Stu	Michael Madsen

Hollywood — What the filmmakers probably had in mind for "The Killing Time" (originally titled "A Perfect Stranger") was a small town *film noir*, but what they got is more like Mayberry on a bad day. Filmmaking is simply too sleepy to make this town come alive as a hot bed of corruption and desire. It just doesn't have the heart for it and result is halfhearted. Box-office outlook for the New World pickup is unexciting as well.

As Sheriff Sam Wayburn, Beau Bridges is too decent and likable to suggest a man who can be driven to murder by his passions. so when he and his married girlfriend (Camelia Kath) plan desperate measures to knock off her wealthy husband it seems like just so much posing.

The one dark tone that the film manages is supplied by Kiefer Sutherland as a revenge-crazy killer masquerading as the town's new deputy. Although he doesn't yet seem to be a great actor, he has more than his share of presence and a constant snarl and chip on his shoulder that would do his father proud.

When Sutherland blows into this California coastal town he becomes the catalyst in a none too ingenious plot in which Bridges and Kath have renewed their relationship of years earlier and want to get rid of her bullying husband (Wayne Rogers). To make sure no one misses the point that he's a bad guy, screenplay by Don Bohlinger, James Nathan and Bruce Franklin Singer has him planning a housing development which would destroy the town's rustic charm.

Director Rick King never quite captures the creepy atmosphere required for these events to take root in and story just plods along from one ridiculous plot point to another. It takes no less a sleuth than Joe Don Baker as the town sheriff and resident nice guy to sort out the evil doings.

In spite of the murder committed, Baker's declarations about the ugliness of life simply don't wash here and no one connected with the film seems to believe it for a moment either.

Rogers takes a decent turn as the villain but, with the exception of Sutherland, rest of the cast seems lost in trying to create characters where none exist.

Tech credits are fine with Paul H. Goldsmith's cinematography offering nice views of life on the Coast, but it may not be what the film needed.—*Jagr.*

Born Of Fire
(BRITISH-COLOR)

A Vidmark Entertainment release. Produced and directed by Jamil Dehlavi. Screenplay, Raficq Abdulla; camera (color), Bruce McGowan; editor, Robert Hargreaves; music, Colin Towns, Kudsi Erguner. Reviewed at the Chicago Intl. Film Festival, Oct. 13, 1987. (MPAA Rating: R.) Running time: 84 MINS.

Paul Bergson	Peter Firth
Anoukin	Suzan Crowley
Master Musician	Oh-Tee

Chicago — Halfway through "Born Of Fire," the hero, a flutist seeking a magical showdown with his nemesis, the evil Master Musician, asks where he can find the combat zone. "Your flute will guide you," a nearby holy man intones. This is the point where even the most stalwart audience members should be using their flutes to guide them to the exits.

Pretentious instead of portentious, mundane instead of mysterious, "Born Of Fire" strives mightily for mysticism, but only winds up looking ridiculous.

Picture's meandering plot is almost incomprehensible, but goes something like this. Anoukin, sexy female astronomer played by Suzan Crowley, is puzzled by violent eruptions on the surface of the sun. At the same time, Paul, a pale-faced British flutist played by Peter Firth, is disturbed by snatches of eerie music that come to him during performances. Both are also treated to a grab-bag of morbid hallucinations involving lizards, skulls and fading religious icons. Inexplicably, they are drawn together just in time to hear these words from the lips of Paul's dying mother: "You must seek the Master Musician."

That gentleman, it turns out, is no ordinary bad guy but an evil demon, a badly charred fire spirit who creeps around in the nude, noodling on a flute and shooting blue flame from his eyes. His plan is to return the Earth to a volcanic state via his hot licks. Paul's job is to go to Turkey and challenge the Master to duelling flutes while the fate of the earth hangs in the balance.

Turkey is an appropriate setting for this gobbler. In fact, the Turkish location, an ancient village with stone buildings that look like crumbling ant hills, is the most interesting thing about the picture. The exotic locale, coupled with some attractive photography by Bruce McGowan, does make "Born Of Fire" strong visually. That's not nearly enough to make up for the film's bewildering plot, tedious pace and empty sensationalism.

"Born Of Fire" is laced with the kind of peek-a-boo shock effects that mark the most hackneyed horror films. It also has gross-outs aplenty featuring snakes, blood, maggots, burnt flesh and the like. One especially revolting scene shows Anoukin giving birth — or hallucinating that she's giving birth — to some sort of giant insect.

Despite all that, "Born Of Fire" still seems about as eerie as a church picnic. The soundtrack is loaded with creepy musical cues that something ominous is going on, but they are largely unjustified. Picture is too disconnected and confused to build an emotional effect.

The actors make an earnest effort, particularly Danish actor Oh-Tee as the nasty Master Musician. They all seem lost in this labyrinth of a picture that ultimately makes no sense at all and delivers far less than it promises. — *Brin.*

Weeds
(COLOR)

Prison mishmash has limited outlook.

A De Laurentiis Entertainment Group release of a Kingsgate Films production. Produced by Bill Badalato. Executive producers, Mel Pearl, Billy Cross. Directed by John Hancock. Stars Nick Nolte. Screenplay, Dorothy Tristan, Hancock; camera (Technicolor), Jan Weincke; editor, Dennis O'Connor, David Handman, Jon Poll, Chris Lebenzon; music, Angelo Badalamenti; songs, Melissa Etheridge, Orville Stoeber; production design, Joseph T. Garrity; art direction, Pat Tagliaferro; set decoration, Jerie Kelter; costumes, Mary Kay Stolz; sound (Dolby), James Thorton; assistant director, Paul Deason; associate producer, Fred Baron, Patti Carr, Ken Kitch; casting, Cathy Henderson, Barbara Hanley. Reviewed at DEG screening room, Beverly Hills, Calif., Oct. 14, 1987. (MPAA Rating: R.) Running time: 115 MINS.

Lee Umstetter	Nick Nolte
Claude	Lane Smith
Burt	William Forsythe
Navarro	John Toles-Bey
Carmine	Joe Mantegna
Bagdad	Ernie Hudson
Dave	Mark Rolston
Lazarus	J.J. Johnson
Lillian	Rita Taggart
Lead guitar	Orville Stoeber
Thurman	Essex Smith
Mom Umstetter	Anne Ramsey
Pop Umstetter	Ray Reinhardt
Bagdad's girlfriend	Amanda Gronich
Associate warden	Felton Perry

Hollywood — There is a core of deep feeling that holds "Weeds" together and it's a good thing because this prison drama cum musical cum backstage story is one of the strangest hybrids to come along in some time. Nick Nolte gives a powerful performance as a con turned playwright but all his bluff and bluster can't cover the holes of this paper-thin story. Pic should be a short-termer at the boxoffice.

Although script by director John Hancock and Dorothy Tristan musters a good deal of passion about the plight of prisoners, it ignores many of the basic elements of good drama. When a prissy drama critic calls the work that Lee Umstetter (Nick Nolte) has finally brought to Broadway unfocused theater, he could well be referring to the film.

After Nolte, a lifer at San Quentin, becomes a literary cause celebre not unlike Jack Henry Abbott and is released, he recruits his buddies from the joint and hits the road with his play of prison life. Film is at its best in suggesting the inmates yearning for freedom and the implicit tie that binds all men who have done time.

Relationships outside prison are pasted together with homilies and declarations of love but without the action and events to back it up. Film tends to address issues too directly in a head-on style that just becomes preachy. In this manner we are informed that prisoners are "the brotherhood of the doomed" and that inmates can maintain a "free mind and spirit."

In an unconvincing love interest, Nolte gets involved with a drama critic (Rita Taggart) who arranges his release after witnessing his play in prison. An interesting sidelight that Hancock never really explores is the idea that Taggart's attraction to the play is based more on her physical attraction to the man. Throughout, the substance of their relationship is more assumed than demonstrated with Taggart mostly in the background smiling, offering support.

As for the play he's concocted, titled "Weeds," it's a pastiche of "Hair"-style musical numbers, Living Theater realism and Genet-like soulbearing.

Supporting cast is strong but sabotaged by clichéd characterizations. William Forsythe is impressive as the company loser who earns his stripes in combat. Lane Smith is believable as the brains of the operation even if what he does isn't. John Toles-Bey as Nolte's soul brother strains for a connection with his friend not supplied by the script.

Nolte, like the film itself, has moments of great conviction, mostly when he isn't trying too hard. Other times when he is acting on stage reaching for big emotions and big statements, he sounds hollow.

With scenes in prison, on the road, at colleges, on Broadway and in bed, scope of the production is impressive almost because of its loose ends. Jan Weincke's cinematography and Joseph T. Garrity's production design are generally on the money although score by Angelo Badalamenti tends towards melodramatic. Songs by Melissa Etheridge and Orville Stoeber are uneven and occasionally downright incongruous.—*Jagr.*

Nightflyers
(COLOR)

Dull space story sinks imaginative visuals.

A New Century/Vista Film Co. release of a Vista Films production. Produced by Robert Jaffe. Executive producer, Herb Jaffe. Directed by "T.C. Blake" (Robert Collector). Screenplay, Robert Jaffe, based on the novella by George R.R. Martin; camera (Foto-Kem color, Deluxe prints), Shelly Johnson; editor, Tom Siiter; music, Doug Timm; production design, John Muto; art direction, Mike Bingham; set decoration, Anne Huntley-Ahrens; costume design, Brad R. Loman; special makeup and mechanical effects, Robert Short; special visual effects, Fantasy II Film Effects — supervisor, Gene Warren Jr.; sound (Ultra-Stereo), Steve Nelson; assistant director, Kristine Peterson; casting, Nina Axelrod. Reviewed at the Hollywood Pacific theater, L.A., Oct. 23, 1987. (MPAA Rating: R.) Running time: **89 MINS.**

Miranda	Catherine Mary Stewart
Royd	Michael Praed
D'Branin	John Standing
Audrey	Lisa Blount
Keelor	Glenn Withrow
Darryl	James Avery
Lilly	Hélène Udy
Eliza	Annabel Brooks
Jon Winderman	Michael Des Barres

Hollywood — Visual imagery is all that carries "Nightflyers" in its voyage through space — and it's not enough to compensate for a rather plodding trip over what is now very familiar space fantasy ground. Though based on a novella by George R.R. Martin, story is too much a poor imitation of "Alien" and "Aliens" without any of the road blocks that made those films such heart pumpers. Trailers are excellent and this may help at the b.o.

It's notable that director Robert Collector's name is removed from the credits by his request and the fictitious name of T.C. Blake was substituted. (He exited before final editing was completed on the pic.) Whatever the reasons, Collector certainly has an eye for creating intrigue with fog machines, camera tricks and special effects even if he has very little in the way of a script to work with.

The Nightflyer (the s added in the title presumably refers to its passengers) is a whale of an old spaceship possessed by an evil thing that lurks somewhere in its mass and has a stranglehold on a handsome embryo created man (Michael Praed) who appears only as a hologram but is desperate to become mortal.

The black klunker is leased by a group of scientists on a fact finding voyage to the unexplored planet Volcryn and — as given away in the opening minutes of the film — the menacing beast will not be a cooperative host.

The screen introduction to Praed is a real eye-catcher. He appears almost translucent, materializing out of a red beam of light that represents both good and evil.

Praed's love interest in the space team coordinator, Miranda (Catherine Mary Stewart), is established in a flash of moody scenes set in the ultimate of high-tech spaceship settings.

Art director Michael Bingham production designer John Muto and set decorator Anne Huntley-Ahrens have done a magnificent job creating unique living and working spaces, eerie and desolate in most areas yet warm where it matters — the living room with its mellow indirect lighting and deceiving trompe d'oeil window ceiling.

Unfortunately, once all these images get a first showing, the adventure that is to be set to them goes flat.

Except for a sizzling decapitation with a laser of one of the crewman, everything else is either foretold or expected.

Dulling the outing is a rather uninteresting set of characters stuck on board and forced to annihilate the evil one (Michael Des Barres), who bears an uncanny resemblance — and rather amusingly so — to just about any theatrically made-up heavy metal rocker.

Adding a little humor to this dour lot's chores would have lifted the production considerably, given they had such blank personalities to work from. Even so, on a purely physical level, the crewwomen (Stewart, Lisa Blount, Hélène Udy and Annabel Brooks) are as stunning as the sets.

Rounding out the small cast is John Standing as the chief scientist, visual sighting expert/master chef James Avery and biologist Glenn Withrow — competent but not compelling in their roles.

Scoring by Doug Timm is at times melodious and at others obtrusive, though the better strains linger.

Other tech credits waver between hokey, especially exterior space shots of the ship, to the powerful interior shots of sucking winds. —*Brit.*

Survival Game
(COLOR)

Actioner sunk by too many '60s in-jokes.

A Trans World Entertainment release. Executive producer, Moshe Diamant. Produced by Gideon Amir. Directed by Herb Freed. Screenplay, Freed, Susannah de Nimes, P.W. Swann, from story by Freed; camera (color), Avraham Karpick; editor, Charles Simmons, Karen Gebura; music, Tom Simonec, Michael Linn; sound (Dolby), Jacob Goldstein; production design, Diana Morris; assistant director, Paul Samuelson; fight coordinator, Aaron Norris; second unit director, Eddie Hice; production manager-associate producer, Mel A. Bishop; production consultant, Steven E. de Souza; casting, Caro Jones. Reviewed at Palace Quad 4, Parkchester, The Bronx, Oct. 17, 1987. (MPAA Rating: R.) Running time: **91 MINS.**

Mike	Mike Norris
C.J. Forrest	Deborah Goodrich
Dave Forrest	Seymour Cassel
Sugar Bear	Ed Bernard
Charles	Jon Sharp
Ice	Rick Grassi
Mike's mon	Arlene Golonka
Harlan	Michael Halton

Its title quite misleading, "Survival Game" is a would-be action pic that ends up as a silly exercise in '60s nostalgia. Chalk it up as yet another video title receiving a token theatrical release.

Mike Norris, Chuck's similarly action-prone son, toplines as a kid who enjoys attending the War In Peace Survival Camp on weekends, where folks participate in gung-ho war games. Via a car accident, he becomes involved with Valley Girl-esque Deborah Goodrich, whose dad, Dave Forrest (played by Seymour Cassel), is just getting out of stir after serving a 17-year stretch related to his druggie activities in the 1960s, in which he foisted the hallucinogenic Forrest Fire on the public.

The FBI and Forrest's ex-partners are all hounding him as to the whereabouts of $2,000,000 in drug money, which he claims never existed. Both he and daughter Goodrich are kidnaped, but Norris and his military mentor Sugar Bear (Ed Bernard) come to the rescue.

With lame action scenes and very low-speed chases, flat pic is constantly pushed towards campiness by script's references to '60s jargon and a soundtrack filled with oldies by such groups as Bubble Puppy and the Kingsmen. Herb Freed's listless direction reaches its nadir in a prolonged foot chase through city streets and a department store that is presented silently except for "Louie Louie" blasting pointlessly on the soundtrack.

Norris and Goodrich make an attractive couple, while Seymour Cassel obviously enjoys himself, but it's a long way downhill from his hippie-esque starring role in "Minnie And Moscowitz." Film might have had a chance to work if scripted as a romantic or screwball comedy, but the need to sell it internationally as an actioner has resulted in an unpalatable mishmash.—*Lor.*

Cry Freedom
(COLOR)

Attenborough's tale of moral heroism in South Africa looms a strong b.o. entry.

A Universal Pictures release of a Marble Arch production. Executive producer, Terence Clegg. Produced and directed by Richard Attenborough. Coproducers, Norman Spencer, John Briley. Screenplay, Briley, from Donald Woods' books' ''Biko'' & ''Asking For Trouble;'' camera (Panavision, Rank color), Ronnie Taylor; editor, Lesley Walker; music, George Fenton, Jonas Gwangwa; sound (Dolby), Simon Kaye, Jonathan Bates, Gerry Humphries; production design, Stuart Craig; assistant director, David Tomblin; production managers, Allan James, Gerry Levy; costume design, John Mollo; second unit director & camera, Peter MacDonald; stunt coordinator, Peter Brace; casting, Susie Figgis, Zimbabwe — Andrew Whaley. Reviewed at Magno Preview 9 screening room, N.Y., Sept. 30, 1987. (MPAA Rating: PG.) Running time: **157 MINS.**

Donald Woods . . . . .Kevin Kline
Wendy Woods . . . . .Penelope Wilton
Stephen Biko . . . . .Denzel Washington
Ken . . . . .Kevin McNally
Kruger .John Thaw
Capt. Devett . . . . .Timothy West
Also with: Juanita Waterman, John Hargreaves, Alec McCowen, Zakes Mokae, Ian Richardson, Josette Simon, Miles Anderson, Tommy Buson, Jim Findlay, Julian Glover, Kate Hardie, Alton Kumalo, Louis Mahoney, Mawa Makondo, Joseph Marcel, John Matshikiza, Sophie Mgcina, John Paul, Wabei Siyolwe, Gwen Watford, Andrew McCulloch, Graham Fletcher Cook, Tony Vogel, Gerald Sim, James Aubrey, Judy Cornwell, Nick Tate.

With ''Gandhi'' in 1982 Richard Attenborough demonstrated a cinematic command of the broad canvas of modern history and the transfiguring power of popular social movements based on overwhelming moral imperatives. In ''Cry Freedom,'' the filmmaker returns to these sweeping concerns, but personifies the ongoing struggle of South Africa's black population against apartheid in the evolving friendship of martyred black activist Stephen Biko and liberal white newspaper editor Donald Woods. ''Cry Freedom'' consequently derives its impact less from epic scope than from the wrenching immediacy of its subject matter and the moral heroism of its appealingly played, idealistic protagonists. These qualities should make ''Cry Freedom'' a prestigious release with strong boxoffice potential.

John Briley's screenplay is based on two books by Woods, who could publish them only by escaping South Africa (where he was under virtual house arrest as a ''banned'' person) with his family in harrowing fashion. This produces the singular flaw of ''Cry Freedom'' — an overemphasis in the film's final hour on the Woods family's escape to exile in England, a narrative turn that has the unmistakable feel of commercial calculation. Attenborough may be courting controversy by abruptly shifting the film's focus from apartheid's institutionalized brutalization of an entire race of people to the narrow situational melodrama of a white family's life crisis.

This narrative imbalance could have been rectified with some judicious trimming, but as the film stands it is never boring in more than 2½ hours. More important, Attenborough redeems the thematic integrity of ''Cry Freedom'' with a climactic recreation of the South African police/military slaughter in 1976 of some 500 schoolchildren in the ghetto of Soweto. This enables Attenborough to bring the film's cumulative indictment of South African government barbarism full circle with images of indelible horror that may do more to sway world opinion against apartheid than any number of news accounts.

''Cry Freedom'' opens in 1975 with a pitiless dawn raid by bulldozers and armed police on an illegal shantytown of black squatters. Stephen Biko is at first an off-screen presence, revered by blacks as a charismatic advocate of racial self-worth and self-determination, but distrusted by whites — including liberals like Woods — as a dangerous reverse racist whose condemnation of white society carries an implicit threat of violence. Biko is a ''banned'' person, forbidden to meet with more than one other person at a time and severely restricted in his movements which are monitored constantly by the police.

Realizing he needs to form an alliance with the liberals he so dislikes, Biko (Denzel Washington) arranges to meet Woods (Kevin Kline), an invitation the dedicated newshound cannot afford to turn down. The two spar cautiously at first over their perceived differences. Biko feels liberals of Woods' ilk ultimately are concerned with preserving their comfortable status and therefore ''not qualified to teach blacks how to respond to apartheid.'' Woods argues that the intractable system can only be changed without violence if blacks and liberal-minded whites work together. As they begin to know one another the two men forge a friendship built on common goals and a personal chemistry captured in beguiling fashion by the two actors.

Kline's familiar low-key screen presence and ability to step into characters who are not flamboyant and emotionally over-charged serve him well in his portrayal of the strong-willed but even-tempered journalist. He's faced with the challenge of acting out a subtle intellectual metamorphosis as Woods' rational liberalism inches towards activism under the influence of his deepening friendship with Biko, who serves as his guide to the desperate world of South Africa's black townships. Denzel Washington, familiar to U.S. audiences as a breezily confident, thoroughly American doctor in the tv hospital series ''St. Elsewhere,'' does a remarkable job of transforming himself into the articulate and mesmerizing black nationalist leader, whose refusal to keep silent led to his death in police custody and a subsequent coverup.

Biko's death occurs roughly at the film's midpoint, although he appears in flashback as Woods launches a 1-man crusade to strip away the government coverup. It can be argued that the depiction of South African police and government officials in ''Cry Freedom'' is one of stereotypical cruelty, aimed at eliciting the maximum possible sympathy for the picture's heroes. Nevertheless, the film is grounded firmly in historical fact and gives due consideration to the fears of Afrikaaners that social change will permanently end their way of life. Woods' crusade was to remake South African society so that way of life could adjust itself to a pluralistic society. As the film shows, he sacrificed much to that end without achieving his goal.

Production values are impressive and should help ''Cry Freedom'' to attract the broadest possible audience. Particularly effective is the integration of cinematography on stunning locations in Zimbabwe and the powerful soundtrack of indigenous music. —*Rich*.

Hiding Out
(COLOR)

Back to high school comedy stumbles in its 'thriller' segments.

A De Laurentiis Entertainment Group release of an Evenmore Entertainment/Locomotion Pictures production. Produced by Jeff Rothberg. Executive producer, Martin Tudor. Directed by Bob Giraldi. Stars Jon Cryer. Screenplay, Joe Menosky, Rothberg; camera (Technicolor), Daniel Pearl; editor, Edward Warschilka; music, Anne Dudley; production design, Dan Leigh; art direction, Carol Wood; set decoration, Leslie Rollins; costume design, Susan Gammie; sound (Dolby), Kim Ornitz; assistant director, Robert Girolami; second unit director, Carol Wood; casting, Bonnie Ginnegan, Steve Jacobs. Reviewed at De Laurentiis Entertainment screening room, Beverly Hills, Calif., Oct. 21, 1987. (MPAA Rating: PG-13.) Running time: **98 MINS.**

Andrew Morenski . . . . .Jon Cryer
Patrick Morenski . . . . .Keith Coogan
Ryan Campbell . . . . .Annabeth Gish
Aunt Lacy . . . . .Gretchen Cryer
Killer .Oliver Cotton
Clinton . . . . .Claude Brooks
Ezzard .Lou Walker
Kevin O'Roarke . . . . .Tim Quill
Grandma Jennie . . . . .Anne Pitoniak
Mrs. Billings . . . . .Nancy Fish

Hollywood — When teenagers try too hard to act adult, it's silly. When they play themselves, it can be fun. Such is the uneven teen comedy, ''Hiding Out.'' Yet with a completely ludicrous plotline, it still manages a certain sense of effervescence because of the adrenalin-pumped performance of lead actor Jon Cryer. Boxoffice could be lively.

The first few minutes of this pic, that filmmakers unbelievably billed as the thriller part, are so bad it's almost questionable whether it's worth staying to see the rest.

Cryer is supposed to be a glib, high-flying Wall Street type on the high finance track with a Maserati to his name and an eye for the babes on the singles circuit.

In a matter of a few furiously paced scenes, seemingly slapped together, everything turns to panic when this slick 27-year-old is on the run from some mobsters he knows are involved in a bonds scandal. He becomes a target for their vengeance and also a key witness for the feds.

A quick shave, a bad hair-dye job and an instant pseudonym later (Maxwell Hauser, as in the coffee brand) and Cryer is enrolled as a high school senior along with his partner-in-anonymity, cousin Patrick (Keith Coogan).

All this is a bit much to take, except things settle into a plausible niche once Cryer is in with those nearer his own maturity level.

While he never passes for a Manhattan yuppie, he can carry the funny lines blowing his cover trying to play as a 19-year-old who is ''short, horny and hopelessly dorky,'' as he puts it. It's hard not to laugh when some black rapsters rope him into running for class president by breaking into a catchy number or when he graciously asks for a scotch and soda from his h.s. girlfriend's accommodating Dad.

Coogan is a good foil for Cryer, playing the true geek with more sexual dreams than experience at the same time he shows all the virtues of being a decent kid with a healthy, deprecating sense of self.

There is much fish-out-of-water stuff here and scripters Joe Menosky and Jeff Rothberg seem to have a great old time making it as hip as they can. Fashion, music, sexual identity, cars, money, even tax deductions are grist for their humor mill. Teens are perhaps too savvy today and they need to be taken down a notch, scripters seem to be saying.

Auxiliary characters are cut to form; a sugar-sweet girlfriend for Cryer (Annabeth Gish); a hard-up school teacher to cross (Nancy Fish), a former boxer who's now mellow custodian (Lou Walker) and a ditzy but loving aunt (Gretchen Cryer).

Needless to say, what's a teen pic without a soundtrack? ''Hiding Out'' is no exception. Music throbs throughout, mostly by unknown heavy metal bands and when there's no song to play there's lush scoring, notably during those mercifully brief mushy scenes between Cryer and Gish.

Editing begins abysmally enough when filmmakers tried to cram in too much at once to set up the story, but things settle into a better pace once that is done with.

Otherwise, tech credits are fine.
—*Brit.*

Le Journal d'un fou
(The Diary Of A Madman)
(FRENCH-COLOR)

A Lydie Média production and release. Coproduced by Films A2. Produced, written, directed by and starring Roger Coggio, based on the story by Nicolai Gogol. Script collaborator, Bernard G. Landry; camera (Eastmancolor), Claude Lecomte; editor, Hélène Plemmianikoff; music, Jean Musy; production design, Guy-Claude François; sound, Guy Rophé; costumes, Françoise Tournafond; Reviewed at the Georges V cinema, Paris, Oct. 13, 1987. Running time: **90 MINS.**
Auxence Popritchin . . . . Roger Coggio
Also with: Fanny Cottençon (Sophie), Jean-Pierre Darras (her father), Charles Charras.

Paris — A vain, distended adaptation of Gogol's famous black comic tale, "Diary Of A Madman" is the latest endeavor by actor-filmmaker Roger Coggio to can the literary classics in lavish motion pictures, and is the most misbegotten of his pictures to date.

Gogol's story is a disturbingly hilarious first-person chronicle of schizophrenia, but Coggio's film is nothing more than an overblown showcase for it's maker's narcissism. Wearing several overcoats (as producer, director, adaptor, star), Coggio manages to smother the literary work he loves most, since it launched his acting career as a 1-man show in the early '60s, and was the subject of his first film in 1963.

In the intervening years Coggio obviously accrued a lot more ideas about Gogol's story as a film, and they all seem to be in this overstuffed, wrongheaded production, which furnishes an excessively explicit and literal visualization to the Gogolian monolog.

Realistic but often mismatched exteriors (shot in and around Paris and in Finland), elaborate studio sets by the excellent stage designer Guy-Claude François, and an orgy of interpretative modern detail (including fornicating neighbors, masturbatory fantasy, and Freudian imagery) are the futile accoutrements to the simple story of a harrowed and humbled government clerk in St. Petersburg whose frustrated sexual and social yearnings finally lead him to the looney bin.

Most damaging however is Coggio's inability, as director and performer, to tap Gogol's unique gift of absurd, fantastic humor. There's nothing distressingly funny about Coggio's scenery-chewing reading of the flakey hero, for whom the actor-director strives (in anti-Gogolian manner) to solicit pity.

Financed (as with Coggio's preceding enterprises) by advanced ticket sales via several national teachers' unions, "Diary" gets low grades as entertainment or study aid. As latter, it will probably tag Gogol as a long-winded bore. — *Len.*

The Cure In Orange
(DOCU-COLOR)

A ASA Communications and Movie Visions release of a Fiction Film production. Executive producer, Chris Parry. Produced by Gordon Lewis. Directed by Tim Pope. Camera (color), Chris Ashbrook; editor, Peter Goddard; stage lighting, Angus MacPhail; film lighting, Zenith Lighting; sound (Dolby), David Allen, assisted by Steve Riddell, Mark Phillips; production managers, Berney Jeffrey, Mick Kluczynski, Serge Touboul. Reviewed at Charles Aidikoff screening room, Hollywood, Oct. 14, 1987. (No MPAA Rating.) Running time: **96 MINS.**
With: The Cure — Robert Smith, Simon Gallup, Porl Thompson, Boris Williams and Laurence Tolhurst.

Hollywood — Apparently, lead singer Robert Smith of The Cure, a band of no small import for today's arty under-20 set, thought the most significant way to make a statement on film was to shoot a concert straight through in front of a ponderously cool backdrop like the Roman ruins near Provence, France, with no boring interviews or foolish cinematic tricks.

Had the band showed any imagination or been willing to part with any emotion, it might have worked, but in this case it didn't. End product is so lifeless and forgettable that even the hardcore Cure fan the filmmakers are targeting as a video client will have to fib to say he really liked it.

Four-walling at AMC Century 14, promoted with record store and radio tie-ins, should raise the profile of the film enough to give it a brief career when it gets to vid stores. Business will die quickly when fans realize this film delivers about as much insight and action as a poster on the wall.

Main problem with the Cure as a concert subject is their on-stage behavior — they repress emotion as a way of building tension, or perhaps because they find it the only bearable attitude. Smith, with his former gravity-defying haircut clipped short and bristly, spends the whole time standing still behind the mike, his face half-hidden by it, glancing around furtively as he delivers his anthems of angst.

Other band members perform in desultory fashion, Porl Thompson, for example, holding his guitar as far away from him as he can and playing it like stroking a cat.

Between a reasonably interesting beginning and ending few minutes, director Tim Pope shoots the band straight on, with so many long closeups of Smith that one can watch his makeup dissolve, and a camera at the top of the amphitheater supplying repetitive long shots of the classical setting — the Theater Antique D'Orange in the French countryside — which provides growing atmosphere as night falls, but with overemphasis, begins to seem silly.

At one point, Pope jumps on-stage with a hand-held camera for some wild, careening footage that wakes things up but seems merely gratuitous, while the sight of two cameramen chasing the disdainful Smith around is a bit absurd.

Through all this, the apparently rhythm-starved French teens are slamdancing deliriously in front of the stage. Had Pope taken his camera in for a look at their faces, this flat, uninspired effort might have gained some depth.

Amid swirling fog, the band plays 23 songs from its volatile 10-year career, beginning with "Shake Dog Shake" and winding with "Killing An Arab." Smith's only gesture to the audience is to mumble song titles; during the disco hit "Let's Go To Bed," he lets go of a few smiles, but they're self-mocking ones as he sings "I don't care if you don't/I won't feel if you won't." —*Daws.*

Russkies
(COLOR)

Childish, old-hat satire.

A New Century/Vista Film Co. release of a New Century Entertainment production, in association with Vista Organization. Executive producers, Mort Engelberg, Stephen Deutsch. Produced by Mark Levinson, Scott Rosenfelt. Directed by Rick Rosenthal. Screenplay, Alan Jay Glueckman, Sheldon Lettich, Michael Nankin, from story by Lettich, Glueckman; camera (Continental and Technicolor), Reed Smoot; editor, Antony Gibbs; music, James Newton Howard; sound (Ultra-Stereo), Hans Roland; production design, Linda Pearl; art direction, John Myhre; assistant director, Louis Race; production manager, Josi Konski; stunt coordinator, Chuck Waters; costume design, Nancy Cone; special visual effects, Novocom Inc.; casting, Ilene Starger. Reviewed at Bruno Walter Auditorium, N.Y., July 22, 1987. (MPAA Rating: PG.) Running time: **99 MINS.**
Mischa . . . . Whip Hubley
Danny . . . . Leaf Phoenix
Adam . . . . Peter Billingsley
Jason . . . . Stefan DeSalle
Diane . . . . Susan Walters
Raimy . . . . Patrick Kilpatrick
Sulock . . . . Vic Polizos
Mr. Vandermeer . . . . Charles Frank
Mrs. Vandermeer . . . . Susan Blanchard
Sgt. Kovac . . . . Benjamin Hendrickson
Mrs. Kovac . . . . Carole King
Boris . . . . Vojo Goric
Capt. Foley . . . . Al White
Niedermeyer . . . . Patrick Mickler
Candi . . . . Summer Phoenix
Keefer . . . . Leo Rossi
Trawler captain . . . . Gene Scherer

"Russkies" wears its heart on its sleeve, obviously intended to be a fable for youngsters to educate them to a message of universal brotherhood and tolerance. Unfortunately, this carbon copy of Norman Jewison's 1966 United Artists hit "The Russians Are Coming, The Russians Are Coming" is ineptly handled and laughable, with a very weak cast in place of the original's heady lineup of farceurs. Aggressively themed throughout its running time to July 4th celebration atmosphere, pic faces tough sledding in its unwisely delayed until November release berth.

Handsome blond Whip Hubley portrays Mischa Pushkin (his name engenders one of the script's few laughs), a Soviet sailor washed ashore in Key West, Fla., when a submarine's landing party (to pick up military secrets being sold by traitor Leo Rossi) gets caught in a storm. Three gung-ho, junior Rambos (Leaf Phoenix, Peter Billingsley and Stefan DeSalle) reluctantly take him under their wing when they quickly realize a flesh-and-blood Russian soldier does not conform to their comic books' image of an evil enemy. In fact he makes an ideal playmate as they buy him clothes and chaperone him around town.

Of course, Hubley falls in love at first sight (and the feeling is mutual) with Billingsley's older sister Susan Walters, but the adult world is only interested in tracking down (or shooting down) this nice-guy alien, especiallly when his two nasty crewmates show up, bent on stealing U.S. military secrets and kidnaping the young heroes for protection.

To be fair, though pic's plot outline is virtually identical to that of the Jewison film (which was based on Nathaniel Benchley's novel "The Off-Islanders"), "Russkies" is probably not a ripoff, but rather a case of reinventing the wheel. Update unwisely emphasizes the underlying propaganda aspects of the piece, with director Rick Rosenthal frequently drawing the action to a halt for extended monologs by Hubley or others to drive home the too-obvious plea for understanding.

Windup even has the young trio, after everything has been sorted out, reading "War And Peace" instead of their "Sgt. Slammer" comic books; a Classics Comix version of Tolstoy would have been more believable.

Precocious Billingsley easily dominates the film while his confreres Phoenix and DeSalle are, respectively, wooden and earnest. Walters is a dish to look at, but her dreamy-eyed acting is poor. Supporting cat is quite bland, as songstress Carole King stands around blankly as Phoenix' mother, and yet another oddly named member of the Phoenix clan, cute Summer Phoenix pops up, natch, as Phoenix' little sister.

Hubley tries hard in his bloated lead role, yet another script miscalculation since his similarly styled prototype, John Phillip Law, had the advantage of playing straight to an hilarious group of comedians including Alan Arkin, Jonathan Winters and Paul Ford. This time, an audience has only Hubley, insufferable kids or paper-thin adult stereotypes to choose from and it's no fun.

Tech credits are well done, though the Key West atmosphere, layed on with a trowel, is irrelevant to theme other than location's proximity to Cuba. —*Lor.*

Adelmo
(ITALIAN-COLOR)

Produced by Nuovo Film. Directed by Rocco Mortelliti. Stars Rocco Mortelliti, Francesca Topi, Vincenzo De Angelis. Screenplay, Rocco Mortelliti, Andreina Camilleri, Roberto Pagni; camera (color), Felice De Maria; editor, Marcello Malvestito. Reviewed at Sorrento Film Festival, Oct. 9, 1987. Running time: **103 MINS.**

Adelmo	Rocco Mortelliti
Paola	Francesca Topi
Mayor	Vincenzo De Angelis
Mother	Rina Franchetti

Also with: Stefania Mortelliti, Giovanni Zaniboni, Marlo D'Orazio, Pietro Bontempo, Archimede Fala, and Bernardo Zeppari.

Sorrento — Rocco Mortelliti's "Adelmo" didn't make the grade its first time out in the Sorrento De Sica competition for young directors. The meager turnout for its festival screening thinned out noticably while the lights were down.

The 28-year old Mortelliti directs his own script and takes the lead as the village idiot of a small hill town near Rome. He lives in poverty with his aged mother, also an idiot, who recites Ave Marias when she is not beating Adelmo or eating his food. The sleazy mayor (Vincenzo De Angelis) has been cheating them out of money they are owed by the government and joins the general abuse and mistreatment Adelmo suffers as he wheels around town on his bicycle.

The unhappy equilibrium is upset by the arrival in town of Paola (Francesca Topi) as the town's new doctor. She takes an interest in Adelmo, though not from pity or concern, but because he resembles her ex-lover, recently killed in a car wreck. Adelmo follows Paola around too, though they never speak to each other and succeed only in arousing the ire of Paola's many suitors, including the mayor.

This jealousy only augments the daily violence and humiliation Adelmo suffers and, having finally had enough he retires to the woods for three days and emerges a true lunatic, assaulting his former tormentors with rocks and knives, but causing few injuries.

The townspeople assemble and chase Adelmo through the cobbled streets, when the film abruptly cuts to cameras and set equipment while Mortelliti/Director and Mortelliti/Adelmo ride off together into the sunset.

Abandoning the story was a wise choice, though it ought to have been attempted in the film's first scene rather than its last.

Lensing is tired and acting is universally insipid. Although shot for under $150,000, "Adelmo" is no bargain.—*Newm.*

Hearts Of Fire
(U.S.-COLOR)

A Lorimar Motion Pictures release of a Phoenix Entertainment Group production. Produced by Richard Marquand, Jennifer Miller, Jennifer Alward. Coproducer, Iain Smith. Executive producers, Gerald H. Abrams, Doug Morris. Directed by Richard Marquand. Screenplay, Scott Richardson, Joe Eszterhas; camera (Technicolor), Alan Hume; editor, Sean Barton; music, John Barry; musical director, Beau Hill; sound, Louis Kramer; art direction, Kit Surrey, Barbara Dunphy; costumes, Pip Newbery. Reviewed at Odeon Marble Arch, London, Oct. 12, 1987. (MPAA Rating: R.) Running time: **95 MINS.**

Billy Parker	Bob Dylan
James Colt	Rupert Everett
Molly McGuire	Fiona
Alfred	Julian Glover
Anne Ashton	Suzanne Bertish
Bones	Ian Dury
Pepper Ward	Richie Havens
Jack Rosner	Larry Lamb
Nico	Tim Cappello

London — It is unfortunate that the last film of helmer Richard Marquand, who died shortly after completing it, should be "Hearts Of Fire." As an epitaph it leaves something to be desired, failing to fire on all cylinders despite a nimble performance by the enigmatic Bob Dylan typecast as a reclusive rock star. Boxoffice prospects seem limited.

It would be more fitting for Marquand to be remembered for "Jagged Edge," since it's unlikely the cliché-ridden "Hearts Of Fire" will garner much interest, though Dylan fans eager to glom the songwriter-singer in his first acting role since "Renaldo And Clara" and "Pat Garrett And Billy The Kid," could help the b.o. At a time when movie soundtracks are boxoffice boosters, this rock 'n' roll pic commits the sin of producing no memorable songs save for the title number, and an opening ditty.

In fact that opening song, "Tainted Love" (released by British duo Soft Cell in 1982) is almost destroyed by the appalling singing of Rupert Everett, whose voice is as wet and stilted as his performance.

Pic opens with would-be rock singer Molly McGuire (exuberantly played by Yank singer Fiona) meeting rock star Billy Parker (Dylan) in her hometown Pennsylvania bar and agreeing to hop over to England with him.

In Blighty she is spotted by British popster James Colt (Everett), who takes her under his wing — and into his bed — while a drunken Dylan flies home to the security of his chicken farm.

Fiona and Everett head off on tour together and, while Fiona agonizes about the real price of success and worries about which man she prefers, the inevitable climax of the gig in her hometown and reunion with Dylan fast approaches. Everett disappears after a blind fan blows her brains out in front of him (strange chap), and Fiona is forced to take the stage alone.

As she starts her song Dylan and Everett reappear (wild applause) and everything is a wild success. Eventually Fiona decides neither man is for her, and heads off into the wild blue wonder on a black Harley-Davidson.

Dylan performs well, though he looks a mite uncomfortable during the musical numbers. He certainly appears fitter than Everett who cultivates a popster's pallor to no avail.

Photography by Alan Hume is fine, though Marquand's use of the English scenery is a bit touristy, right down to Everett's country estate replete with charming sea views, pack of dogs, and Range Rover.

It is with the music that Marquand has the most problems — apart from most of the numbers being instantly forgettable, we are asked to believe that Fiona and Dylan's heavy rock characters would find Everett's lightweight electropop superstar appealing. The two musical styles are diametrically opposed, but for "Hearts Of Fire" music is just something to be lumped together.

The supporting cast go through the paces, though Julian Glover looks embarrassed as butler/minder Alfred. In the backing band wacky drummer Nico (Tim Cappello) is on screen almost as often as Fiona during the music sections, with heavy emphasis on his pectorals and braids. Technical credits on the pic are fine.—*Adam.*

Deadly Illusion
(COLOR)

Billy Dee Williams sparkles in low-budget *film noir*.

A Cinetel Films release of a Pound Ridge Films production. Produced by Irwin Meyer. Executive producers, Michael Shapiro, Rodney Sheldon. Directed by William Tannen, Larry Cohen. Screenplay; Cohen; camera (Deluxe color), Daniel Pearl; editor, Steve Mirkovich, Ronald Spang; music, Patrick Gleeson; sound (Ultra-Stereo), David Lewis Yewdall; art direction, Marina Zurkow, Ruth Lounsbury; assistant director, Michael Tadross; associate producers, Mirkovich, Tadross, Bill Elliott; casting, Louis DiGiamo. Reviewed at Cine 1, N.Y., Oct. 30, 1987. (MPAA Rating: R.) Running time: **87 MINS.**

Hamberger	Billy Dee Williams
Rina	Vanity
Jane/Sharon	Morgan Fairchild
Alex Burton	John Beck
Det. Lefferts	Joe Cortese
Fake Burton	Dennis Hallahan
Gloria Reid	Jenny Cornuelle
Costillion	Michael Wilding Jr.
Nancy Costillion	Allison Woodward
Man with gun	Joe Spinell
Medical examiner	Michael Emil

"Deadly Illusion," formerly titled "Love You To Death," is a very entertaining tongue-in-cheek homage to *film noir*, spotlighting a charming, funny performance by lead Billy Dee Williams. Absence of exploitation values and a poverty row budget puts this effort at a disadvantage in today's action film market, however.

Writer-director Larry Cohen (he began helming this film but producers chose Willam Tannen of "Flashpoint" to complete the direction) successfully paid homage to the Edward G. Robinson style of gangster pic with his Fred Williamson-starrer "Black Caesar," and here harkens back to the lovable scoundrel personified (pre-"The Thin Man") by William Powell. Williams plays Hamberger, a detective with no license whose habit of causing accidental deaths is a career detriment (pic's body count is very high and a source of black humor).

He's hired by Dennis Hallahan to kill his wife. Williams accepts the $25,000 retainer, but goes to warn the wife, played by Morgan Fairchild in a black wig. She beds him and splits, but all hell breaks loose when Burton's *real* wife is found murdered and Hallahan turns out to be an imposter. While playing cat and mouse with his old buddy cop Joe Cortese, Williams finally tracks down a drugrunning ring set in the world of models, led by Fairchild (in her familiar blond persona).

With very clever dialog by Cohen (including a throwaway line that predicts a stock market crash, not bad for a film shot last December), Williams excels at shtick mocking his pretty boy image. One funny scene has him crashing a fashion show and enjoying the fact that he's mistaken for Reggie Jackson. As his girlfriend, Vanity provides the requisite beauty and her acting is becoming more natural than in her previous films, while Fairchild is delicious as the baddie with many a double entendre. Joe Spinell has a cute bit whipping out a gun and taking a hostage when the firearms license bureau won't honor his request for a permit.

Using hidden camera techniques and other evidence of guerrilla filmmaking, pic gives the illusion of some scale, but too many scenes are static talkathons reminiscent of quota quickies. It's the dialog and performances that carry the picture. —*Lor.*

Heart
(COLOR)

Lame boxing story.

A New World Pictures release. Produced by Randy Jurgensen. Executive producer, Michael Nicklous. Directed by James Lemmo. Screenplay, Lemmo, Jurgensen; camera, (TVC color), Jacek Laskus; editor, Lorenzo Marinelli; music, Geoff Levin, Chris Many; production design, Vicki Paul; art direction, Susan Raney; costume design, Ticia Blackburn; sound, Rolf Pardula; associate producer, Chris D'Antoni; casting, Henry Alford. Reviewed at New World Pictures screening room, L.A., Oct. 20, 1987. (MPAA Rating: R.) Running time: **90 MINS.**

Eddie	Brad Davis
Jeannie	Francis Fisher
Nicky	Steve Buscemi
Buddy	Robinson Frank Adu
Diddy	Jesse Doran
Leo	Sam Gray
Fighter	Bill Costello

Hollywood — When the boxing hero is a palooka — and a charmless one at that — it's hard to get up any enthusiasm to support him in the ring. That's the uninvolving story of

"Heart," a linear, plodding retelling of an oft-told matchup between a has-been and up-and-comer that has little more than a few moments of close-up jabs to the face to keep it from being knock-down dull throughout. Bets are off for much of a boxoffice turn for the New World pickup.

Brad Davis is the inarticulate boxer now working in a produce market who is way past his prime yet willing to continue to be humiliated in $100 fights which turn his body into mincemeat and seem to have had done some serious damage to his gray matter.

In less time than it takes to go a couple of rounds, all that is going to be told of Davis' story is revealed. His loving girlfriend (Francis Fisher) acquiesces to his fighting once more against a virile fighter 10 years his junior (Bill Costello), even as she warns him he is being set up to lose by his crooked manager (Steve Buscemi).

The seedy world of lowbrow boxing is a ripe enough arena in which to find fascinating characters with more than unidimensional personalities, yet scripters James Lemmo and Randy Jurgensen (director and producer, respectively) have stuck with depicting stock Hollywood thug types to play off against the naive Davis.

There are no subplots or twists or much of anything curious or interesting to add color or dimension to this flat story. It has the low-budget look of a documentary and about as much suspense — as if someone with a minicam trailed around a loser for a couple of days until the film ran out.

Actors, including Davis in the lead, are earnest in their portrayals, which is to say none is either wooden or charismatic — just barely credible.

Of the troupe, Buscemi shows the most depth as the high strung, wily opportunist out to make a buck at his boxer's expense. Maybe that's because much of the dialog is given over to him — talking down to Davis' trainer (Robinson Frank Adu, who has a thankless role as the spineless silent partner in conceit) and in clipped talk with his conspirators Diddy (Jesse Doran) and Leo (Sam Gray).

Tech credits are uneven; film ranges from totally grainy to appropriately smokey for the fight scenes and sound occasionally doesn't sync. Opening strains by scorer Geoff Levin are suprisingly lovely. —*Brit.*

Pinocchio And The Emperor Of The Night
(ANIMATED-COLOR)

A New World Pictures release of a Filmation presentation. Produced by Lou Scheimer. Directed by Hal Sutherland. Screenplay, Robby London, Barry O'Brien, Dennis O'Flaherty; camera (CFI color), Ervin L.

Kaplan; editor, Jeffrey Patrick Gehr; music, Anthony Marinelli and Brian Banks; original songs, Will Jennings, Barry Mann, Steve Tyrell; production supervisor, Erika Scheimer, art direction, John Grusd; sound (Dolby), B&B Sound Studios. Reviewed at USA Cinemas Copley Place, Oct. 17, 1987. (MPAA Rating: G.) Running time: **87 MINS.**
With the voices of: Edward Asner, Tom Bosley, Lana Beeson, Linda Gary, Jonathan Harris, James Earl Jones, Ricky Lee Jones, Don Knotts, William Windom.

Boston — Exhibitors looking for something else to show the moppet set over the holiday season besides Disney's rerelease of "Cinderella" could do worse than "Pinocchio And The Emperor Of The Night." Pic has already bowed in London and is set for a December opening stateside. Adults will find the animation weak and the story largely derivative, but undemanding kids should have a good time.

Story finds Pinocchio a year after his adventures in the Disney classic. He's a flesh and blood boy, but still getting into as much mischief as when he was a puppet. This time, instead of Jiminy Cricket, his Fairy Godmother gives him a living version of Whilliker, a wooden lightning bug Pinocchio had carved. As before, the talking insect serves as his conscience.

On his way to delivering a jeweled box made by Gepetto to the mayor of the village, Pinocchio is snookered by the rascally Scalawag and Igor, respectively a raccoon and monkey. This leads him to a series of adventures that mimic the first story to a surprising degree, including turns with a sinister puppeteer, a monstrous fish and a cavern where naughty little boys have all their dreams come true before being turned into puppets. A subplot involving Whilliker and a Col. Blimp-like bumblebee recalls the Fleischers' 1941 "Mr. Bug Goes To Town."

Theme of the film comes from an oddly breathy Fairy Godmother who sounds like one of the Gabor sisters when she tells Pinocchio, "If you take your freedom for granted, you might lose it. You might even turn into a puppet again." This argument for free will and responsibility is likely to go flying over the heads of most of the young audience.

The voice cast boasts a lot of well-known names with James Earl Jones the most recognizable as he lends his patented Darth Vader voice to the villainous Emperor of the Night. Songs are saccharine to the extreme but, again, the kids seem to like it. The animation is several notches above standard tv fare and will disappoint only those who remember the way animated feature films used to look.

Film already has aroused the interest of the Disney legal department, who have been known to vigorously police copyright infringement. A separate story is cited as the source for the tale, but the similari-

ties are a bit close for comfort. —*Kimm.*

Slumber Party Massacre II
(COLOR)

Inept, old-hat sequel.

A Concorde Pictures release. Produced by Deborah Brock, Don Daniel. Written and directed by Brock. Camera (Foto-Kem color), Thomas L. Callaway; editor, William Flicker; music, Richard Cox; sound, David Waelder; production design, John Eng; art direction, Franc Novak; set decoration, Rozanne Taucher; special makeup effects, James Cummins; production supervisor, Matt Leipzig; assistant director-production manager, Don Daniel; postproduction supervisor, Steve Barnett; casting, Kevin Alber, Bruce Boll. Reviewed on Embassy Home Entertainment vidcassette, N.Y. Oct. 24, 1987. (MPAA Rating: R.) Running time: **75 MINS.**
Courtney Bates . . . . Crystal Bernard
Amy . . . . Kimberly McArthur
Sheila . . . . Juliette Cummins
Matt . . . . Patrick Lowe
Sally . . . . Heidi Kozak
Driller Killer . . . . Atanas Ilitch
T.J. . . . . Joel Hoffman
Jeff . . . . Scott Westmoreland
Mrs. Bates . . . . Jennifer Rhodes
Valerie . . . . Cynthia Eilbacher
Officer Kreuger . . . . Michael DeLano

"Slumber Party Massacre II," known as "Don't Let Go" during production (title of one of its songs), is a lame, quickie followup. It had a token booking on the bottom half of a double bill in Culver City a couple of weeks ahead of its homevideo release.

Original 1982 pic was something of a *cause celèbre* because its director Amy Jones and screenwriter Rita Mae Brown concocted a scathing satire of slasher pics, particularly the "Driller Killer" subgenre then in vogue. Sequel by Deborah Brock is an utterly routine slasher pic as pointless as the hundreds of films Jones and Brown were criticizing.

Crystal Bernard portrays Courtney Bates, the young sister of Valerie (Cynthia Eilbacher), a character traumatized in the first film. She's in an all-girl band, with the highschoolers heading for a weekend at a condo on a golf course to practice songs and hang out with boy friends.

Courtney keeps having nightmares in which a rock guitarist (Atanas Ilitch) attacks her, wielding a guitar with a screw-like drill bit as its neck. Pic plods along with lots of musical filler and hallucinations until suddenly Ilitch materializes for real and starts killing the cast one by one in gory fashion. Ultimately Courtney disposes of him with a blowtorch, wakes up, surprise, it was all just a nightmare and then cornily is stuck with an open-ended nightmare conclusion.

Apart from Bernard, the cast is much too old for their roles and director Brock steadfastly refuses to deliver the genre's exploitation values which would have at least earned the picture drive-in status. For example, zaftig ex-Playboy centerfold model Kimberly McArthur costars, but has no nude scenes,

with sex scenes discreetly staged off-camera (groans only, on soundtrack). The gore is plentiful but unimaginative and instead of scares we get ridiculous footage such as a plucked chicken "jumping" out of the ice box to attack Courtney. A zit on the face of one of the girls becomes a grotesque makeup effect that spurts green pus.

Acting is subpar, with rock singer Ilitch one big ham in his greaser in black leather turn. —*Lor.*

Jilted
(AUSTRALIAN-COLOR)

A J.C. Williamson release of a Mermaid Beach production. Produced by Bill Bennett, Jenny Day. Directed by Bennett. Stars Richard Moir, Jennifer Cluff. Screenplay, Bennett; camera (color), Geoff Simpson; editor, Denise Hunter; music, Michael Atkinson; sound, Toivo Lember; production manager, David Joyce; assistant director, Phil Rich. Reviewed at Dendy theater, Sydney, Oct. 11, 1987. Running time: **89 MINS.**
Al . . . . Richard Moir
Harry . . . . Jennifer Cluff
Bob . . . . Steve Jacobs
Paula . . . . Tina Bursill
Cindy . . . . Helen Mutkins
Doug . . . . Ken Radley

Sydney — Bouncing back after his disappointing comedy, "Dear Cardholder," Bill Bennett's fourth feature is his best yet, a witty, moving rondo of relationships which bring to mind the best films of Alan Rudolph, sans the music. If pic gets the critical notices it deserves, it should perform well in arthouse situations in Australia, with fests likely to be interested abroad.

Setting for the film is Fraser Island, a holiday resort popular with Australia's urban yuppies. Al (Richard Moir) is chef at the resort hotel. He's supposed to be tops in the culinary field, but has been fired from posh city hotels because of his habit of accusing his employers of sleeping with his wife. Now he and the wife have parted.

Bob (Steve Jacobs) is the hotel manager, a slightly seedy Vietnam vet whose barmaid wife has left him. He's jealous of the fact that Al is having an affair with Cindy (Helen Mutkins), the hotel waitress who is also putting an unhappy past behind her. Then there's Paula (Tina Bursill), the hotel's rather intense accountant. She fancies the charismatic Al, rejects Bob, and still broods over the fact that she was literally jilted at the altar on her wedding day years before.

All these characters, in fact, have jilted or been jilted at least once in their lives, and tensions are already running high when Harriet (Jennifer Cluff) arrives on the scene (she was named after a cyclone, she says, but prefers to be called "Harry"). She's running from her husband, who she found in bed with another man, and is camping out in a tent near the hotel, spending her days fishing in the surf. She's quick-tempered, tough and independent, and though her hair has been shaved off until she's almost bald, she's extremely feminine.

Al falls heavily for Harry, who brushes him off at first but eventually succumbs, saying later she only did it "for the sex." Faced with the presence of this outsider, the other players in the drama regroup, with Paula and Cindy — hitherto bitterly antagonistic towards each other — forming an alliance. Paula finally allows Bob into her bed, resulting in a dramatic scene in which he cruelly blames on her his inability to perform sexually. She responds with a suicide attempt which forms one climax to the drama. Meanwhile, Harry's husband, Doug (Ken Radley) arrives on the scene wanting his wife back.

Bennett's witty screenplay contains a good deal of bitter truth about relationships, and he miraculously breathes fresh life into familiarly sad situations. The five principal actors (Radley is a very late arrival) are all first-rate, and as the rondo goes its way and the partners change, the drama intensifies, with a couple of steamy sex scenes between Al and Harry giving the film a sensual lift.

Richard Moir gives one of his best performances as the quick-tempered Al. Jennifer Cluff (the director's wife) is lovely and tough-yet-vulnerable as Harry. Steve Jacobs elicits sympathy for his inherently sleazy character. Helen Mutkins gives a real edge to the frustrations of Cindy and Tina Bursill practically steals the film as the complex Paula, inviting, yet at the same time, rejecting Bob's approaches, and riding for a very considerable fall.

Pic is atmospherically shot by Geoff Simpson. Editor Denise Hunter has done a superior job. Toivo Lember's sound is pristine. Only Michael Atkinson's music comes across as conventional at times. Above all, Bennett succeeds in depicting some genuinely touching relationships, all going through crisis, while at the same time never losing his sense of humor. Time and again, a dramatic scene is followed by one in which human foibles give the audience a chance to chuckle.

Bennett has always worked with tiny budgets: his first feature, "A Street To Die," was almost a docu-drama; "Backlash" made daring use of improvisation; and "Dear Cardholder" essayed situation comedy. "Jilted" has elements of all four, and is successful on all counts. —*Strat.*

Mankillers
(COLOR)

Tame gender switch on 'The Dirty Dozen.'

An Action Intl. Pictures presentation. Executive producers, David Winters, Bruce Lewin. Produced by Peter Yuval. Written and directed by David A. Prior. Camera (United color), Keith Holland; editor, Alan Carrier; music, Tim James, Steve McClintock, Mark Mancina; sound, David Eddy; assistant director-2nd unit director, Thomas Baldwin; stunt coordinator, Fritz Matthews; production manager, Arthur Royce; associate producers, Donald Crowell Jr., Jon Mercedes 3d. Reviewed on Sony Video Software vidcassette, N.Y., Oct. 28, 1987. (No MPAA Rating). Running time: **88 MINS.**

Jake . . . . Edd Byrnes
Joan Hanson . . . . Gail Fisher
Sgt. Roberts . . . . Edy Williams
Rachel McKenna . . . . Lynda Aldon
John Mickland . . . . William Zipp
Marla Rosetti . . . . Christine Lunde
Terry Davis . . . . Susanne Tegman
Roxanne Taylor . . . . Marilyn Stafford
Also with: Paul Bruno, Byron Clark, Lizzie Borden, Thyais Walsh, Bainbridge Scott, Cyndi Domino, Brian O'Connor, Sheila Best, Naomi Delgado, Wanda Acuma, Arlene Julian, Veronica Carothers, Julie Smith, Amber Star, Wendy Gardner, Dianne Copeland.

"Mankillers," originally titled "Twelve Wild Women," is a chintzy version of "The Dirty Dozen" using women in the he-man roles. Pic is a direct-to-video timekiller.

Beautiful blond Lynda Aldon is tapped by CIA bigwig Williams (Byron Clark) and his assistant Joan Hanson (Gail Fisher) to go after a renegade federal agent in Colombia who is wreaking havoc. Aldon used to work with the creep (William Zipp) and still dreams (or has nightmares) about him.

She insists on working with an all-girl team: "It's got to be women — women are more effective in the field," she declares. She picks up a dozen femmes out of prison and has Sgt. Roberts (Edy Williams) train them in combat. Several desultory reels later Zipp is zapped and the girls are engulfed by an unruly fog machine for an atmospheric (and inept) fadeout.

Pic essentially trades on the nostalgia value of its toplined cast, but Edd (Kookie) Byrnes, Gail "Mannix" Fisher and Edy (Cannes startlet) Williams are relegated to tiny roles. Aldon is a forceful heroine but fans will be surprised, given the vast femme cast, that there is no nudity in the entire film. Action scenes are poor, with weak sound effects and mainly static setups. Riverside, Calif. locations lack the necessary atmosphere. —*Lor.*

The Bit Part
(AUSTRALIAN-COLOR)

A Comedia Ltd. production. Produced by Stephen Vizard, John Gauci, Peter Herbert. Directed by Brendan Maher. Stars Chris Haywood, Nicole Kidman. Screenplay, Vizard, Herbert, Ian MacFadyen; camera (color), Ellery Ryan; editor, Scott McLennan; music, Paul Grabowsky, Red Symons; production design, Carole Harvey; sound, John Philips; production manager, Frank Brown; assistant director, Katherine Hayden. Reviewed at Mosman screening room, Sydney, Oct. 5, 1987. Running time: **87 MINS.**
Michael Thornton . . . . Chris Haywood
Mary McAllister . . . . Nicole Kidman
Helen Thornton . . . . Katrina Foster
John Bainbridge . . . . John Wood
Peter . . . . Maurie Fields
Bev Howard . . . . Maureen Edwards
Acting Teacher . . . . . . Deborra Lee-Furness

Molly . . . . Maggie Miller
Biker . . . . Wilbur Wilde

Sydney — An unassuming, ultra-low budget comedy about an aspiring actor, engagingly played by Chris Haywood, "The Bit Part" won't set the world afire, but it should find an appreciative minority audience. Many of the jokes and references may be a bit too "in" to appeal to mainstream audiences, but showbiz types should enjoy its barbed humor.

Michael Thornton (Haywood) is a careers counsellor who always yearned to be an actor. At mid-life, he finally decides to change careers, and luckily has an understanding wife (Katrina Foster) with a good job who's able to support him. There follow amusing scenes with drama, speech and posture coaches, including a delightful bit where Haywood is seen ineptly learning to tap dance with a flock of little girls.

He's taken on by a voracious agent, and, of course, soon finds that his dreams of playing serious drama, preferably Shakespeare, aren't going to be fulfilled. Bypassed for serious roles, he's taken on as an extra in a war film being shot by a very butch femme director, but regularly spoils takes (he sneezes when supposed to be dead, and when essaying the role of a waiter in a cafe scene his grumbling stomach reduces the topline thesps to hysterics). Despite his dreams of fame, he winds up "starring" in a tv commercial for a chocolate bar, with only his hand being on camera.

Alongside these frequently amusing (but not exactly original) showbiz jokes there's a tenuous, unfulfilled relationship between Haywood and a young actress (Nicole Kidman) who agrees to join him in an intellectual production of play readings until lured off to Hollywood to play in a horror pic called "Wormwood." Kidman has just completed a leading role in the new Philip Noyce romantic thriller "Dead Calm," and looks like emerging as a major new femme star in Australia; her vibrant personality lights up her small role here.

"The Bit Part" ends on a serious note, in much the same way that Chaplin, in "The Great Dictator," underlined his message in a serious speech at the end, so here Haywood gets to make an impassioned plea on the part of actors: it ends the light comedy on a rather serious, preachy note.

Despite flaws, the picture comes across as consistently engaging, with good performances (John Wood is in fine form as Haywood's best friend) and some bright moments of satire. Technical credits are okay, given the small budget, but the lead actor's name is inexcusably spelled "Heywood" in the opening credits. —*Strat.*

Hawaiian Rainbow
(DOCU-COLOR)

A Mug-Shot production, Secane, Pa. Produced by Robert Mugge, Ann Brandman. Written and directed by Mugge. Camera (color), Lawrence McConkey. Reviewed at Denver Intl. Film Festival, Oct. 14, 1987. (No MPAA Rating.) Running time: **85 MINS.**

Denver — Robert Mugge's new film is a requiem for Hawaiian music, a valid, exotic, but apparently passé form. This music once popular throughout the U.S. seems now to be relegated to entertainment for tourists. The film needs to be considered in the context of Mugge's efforts to focus on the diversity of American music, and as such is worth attention.

This is a music that attracts with the novelty of steel guitar, unexpected yodels, and the sometimes accompanying hulas by lei-garlanded dancers. The music celebrates Hawaii's lush lands and dazzling seas yet does not enter into lament or other intimate expression to make a personal statement.

The sweetness of these sounds continues unimpeded by the diverse influences which have come over the years, including the Spanish cowboy music which came in 1830, Christian hymns, country western, jazz and rock. Perhaps Mugge needed to point up contemporary influences by substantial examples. Without them it is hard to tell they have made their influence amount to much.

Groups shown consist of plump men and women of advanced years, always shown singing for small audiences in outdoor settings. Their spirited mastery of style compensates in part for the laid-back manner of their physical performances.

Certain musical concepts, such as single line chants, the contrasting "mele" and "ole" styles, are among those considered and explained.

Overall there is the beauty of Hawaiian landscapes and seascapes to captivate under the spell of the occasional Hawaiian rainbow. —*Alyo.*

Hostage
(COLOR)

Retrograde actioner.

A Noble Entertainment Group release of a Blue Flower/Alpine production. Executive producers, James Aubrey, Michael Leighton. Produced by Thys Heyns, Paul Raleigh. Directed by Hanro Möhr. Stars Wings Hauser, Karen Black, Kevin McCarthy. Screenplay, Norman Winski, Leighton; camera (color), Johan van der Vyver; editor, Simon Grimley; music, uncredited; sound, Shaunh Murdoch; assistant director, Richard Green; art direction, Geoff Hill; set design, Caron Hill; stunt coordinator, Reo Ruiters. Reviewed on RCA/Columbia Pictures vidcassette, N.Y. Oct. 28, 1987. (MPAA Rating: R.) Running time: **95 MINS.**
Sam Striker . . . . Wings Hauser
Laura Lawrence . . . . Karen Black
Col. Tim Shaw . . . . Kevin McCarthy
Nicole . . . . Nancy Locke

Also with: Robert Whitehead, Billy Second, Ian Steadman, Iain Winter, Robert K. Brown, John Donovan, Michael Brunner, Pamela Perry, At Botha, Marcel van Heerden, Gerhard Hametner, Limpie Basson.

"Hostage" is a scatterbrained, low-octane thriller about an airplane hijacking. Filmed last year in South Africa, it was originally titled "Colt— Flight 802."

Once more, it's nasty arabs (unconvincingly portrayed by South African thesps) who are the baddies of the piece, as members of the Holy Freedom Party of Allah hijacking a flight to Nairobi and demanding the release of their firebrand leader plus $25,000,000 in gold. Typical jeopardy pic format has a motley group aboard: softcore sex film star Laura Lawrence (Karen Black), who's tired of doing "Tarzan" skin flicks and wants her agent Harry (Robert Whitehead) to get her substantial roles; Kushu (Limpie Basson), a peaceful religious leader; and Nicole (Nancy Locke) and her young son Tommy (Gerhard Hametner), the kid needing to get to New York in a hurry for a kidney transplant.

Nicole's boyfriend Striker (her real-life husband Wings Hauser) and her dad (Kevin McCarthy) enlist the aid of their ex-army buddies from the U.S. to stage a daring rescue mission. Wings appropriately arrives via hang glider, but the climax is outrageously stupid, as little Tommy sinks in quicksand while Wings punches out the final terrorist.

Highlight is a very campy performance by Black, screaming shrilly that she's sick of being a sex symbol. "I love you," exclaims her agent Harry; Black responds: "If only you were straight." —Lor.

Il Grande Blek
(ITALIAN-COLOR)

Produced by Vertigo Films. Directed by Giuseppe Piccioni. Stars Roberto De Francesco, Sergio Rubini, Federica Mastroianni, Dario Parisini, Riccardo De Torrebruna. Screenplay, Maura Nuccetelli, Giuseppe Piccioni; camera (color), Alessio Gelsini; editor, Angelo Nicolini. Reviewed at Sorrento Film Festival, Oct. 8, 1987. Running time: 105 MINS.
Yuri .... Roberto DeFrancesco
Razzo .... Sergio Rubini
Claudia .... Federica Mastroianni
Antonio .... Dario Parisini
Marco .... Riccardo De Torrebruna

Sorrento — Small-town friendships and political radicalism set the tone for this first full-length effort by Giuseppe Piccioni, winner of the De Sica competition at Sorrento. Though clumsy and a reel too long, this nostalgia film is sure to do well with Italian teenagers and young adults, though export prospects look bleak.

Film begins with a half-hour flashback in which Yuri (Roberto De Francesco) and his sister Claudia (Federica Mastroianni — niece of Marcello) watch their much older brother Marco (Riccardo De Torrebruna) go through a difficult adolescence and then 10 years later, in 1973, find themselves in his shoes.

The 19-year old Yuri spends most of his time with Razzo, a likeable dropout beautifully played by Sergio Rubini. They cruise and booze but Yuri's growing attraction to politics and girls drives a wedge between them. Yuri begins to hang out with a new crowd: all red and full of convictions.

His political conversion is overseen by new chum Antonio (Dario Parisini), an ardent, innocent Marxist who steals politically correct books from a local bookshop. The shopgirl, who watches the thefts and says nothing, is none other than Yuri's sister Claudia. They fall in love. Further complications arise as Yuri looks for love too, but with only mixed success.

Meanwhile, Razzo has joined a gang of fascist thugs. In a showdown between the fascists and the Marxists, Razzo defends old friend Yuri. Now alienated from new friends as well as old, he slips into despair and kills himself in a car wreck.

Complex plot is moving towards some revelation or rite of passage, but never quite gets there.

Locations in and around the town of Ascoli Piceno in The Marches offer plenty of opportunities for beautiful shots, but helmer Piccioni, who used to make music videos, misses most of them. Sergio Rubini, Riccardo De Torrebruna, and Silvia Mocci (in a small role as Razzo's ex-love) are all very good.

Title refers to a '60s comic book character. —Newm.

Maramao
(ITALIAN-COLOR)

A l'Union P.N. and C.G. Silver Film production. Directed by Giovanni Veronesi. Produced by Francesco Nuti, Gianfranco Piccoli. Screenplay, Sandor and Giovanni Veronesi; camera (color), Lorenzo Battaglia; editor, Ugo De Rossi. Reviewed at Sorrento Film Festival, Oct. 10, 1987. Running time: 90 MINS.
Patrizia .... Vanessa Gravina
Sandro .... Maurizio Begotti
Giannino .... Filippo Tempesti
Pippo Querci .... Alberto Frasca
Paolo................ Romney Williams
Chiara .... Cristina Sivieri
Sailor .... Novello Novelli

Sorrento — Giovanni Veronesi won second prize in the Sorrento De Sica competition for young directors with his unfinished "Maramao," a simple, almost poetic essay on the summer which divides childhood from adolescence. It is likely to have moderate success in Italy and is easily adaptable for foreign markets, especially tv aimed at young teens.

Set at the seaside in Sardinia, the film is seen from the point of view of the six children who pass the summer together. Adults only appear from the neck down, except an old sailor (Novello Novelli) whose wisdom only children can understand.

The story is minimal and concerns Sandro (Maurizio Begotti) who, at 14, is beginning to see himself and his friends change. Patrizia (Vanessa Gravina) who is a bit further along in adolescence, is attracted to this rebelliousness and their growing closeness comes between Sandro and his best friend Pippo Querci (Alberto Frasca). Although they are all growing up, they are reluctant to abandon their innocence and leave childhood. They are forced to take their first step to adulthood when faced with Sandro's death by drowning. Ironically, only Sandro's 7-year old brother Giannino can survive the tragedy unscathed because he is still a child.

The setting is beautiful and the child actors are all superb. "Maramao" displays the sort of naturalism and lightness that eludes many more experienced helmers. Still, many scenes are too long and some cutting is clumsy. This, along with sound and color problems, ought to be solved before theatrical release. —Newm.

Charlie Dingo
(Charlie Loco)
(FRENCH-COLOR)

A UGC release of a Septembre production, in association with Cofimage and Sofica Créations. Produced by Jean Nainchrik. Directed by Gilles Béhat. Screenplay, Béhat, Jean Vautrin; camera (Fujicolor), Pierre Lhomme; editor, Geneviève Vaury; music, Christian Chevalier; art direction, Jacques Dugied; sound, Paul Lainé; assistant director, François Vantrou; production manager, Catherine Lapoujade. Reviewed at the UGC Odéon cinema, Paris, Oct. 20, 1987. Running time: 100 MINS.
Charlie Maladieu .... Guy Marchand
Georgia .... Caroline Cellier
Mathieu .... Laurent Malet
William Wolski .... Niels Arestrup
Chinaski .... Maurice Barrier
Marie .... Brigitte Rouan
Jupin .... Jean-Claude Dauphin

Paris — "Charlie Dingo" is a strained, flip side replay of the myths of the old French Poetic Realism of the 1930s, then characterized by Jean Gabin and Michèle Morgan, fogbound ports and dreams of escape to Elsewhere.

Guy Marchand is the mealy-mouthed '80s descendant of those fatalistic anti-heroes. He's a loser who's managed to make that boat, but, as this film opens, is coming home to claim the girl he left behind, not to mention 2,000,000 francs in life insurance money. His escape was sanctioned by a road accident for which he was legally declared dead.

His lady love is a Janus-faced wife (Caroline Cellier) who didn't wait long to remarry with the sleazy police inspector (Niels Arestrup), who's awaiting his cut for the insurance money.

Gilles Béhat, who trades on emphatic melodrama since the success of his loud and lurid David Goodis adaptation, "Street Of The Lost" (Rue Barbare), has toned down on the bloodletting but still remains faithful to the platitudes of failure and missed opportunities.

With his privileged collaborator, crime novelist-scripter Jean Vautrin, Béhat has fashioned a good looking but unbelievable tale of lust and greed in which Marchand runs riot, armed with Vautrin's slangy vernacular dialog, and abetted by Laurent Malet as a vulnerable seminarist who becomes his unlikely go-between.

Strikingly photographed by Pierre Lhomme on Normandy coastal locations, film has pluses in Cellier's world weary femme fatale and Arestrup's paunchy crooked cop, but otherwise remains a familiar overheated yarn of outsiders, to which the French cinema is unhealthily addicted. — Len.

Fire From The Mountain
(DOCU-COLOR-16m)

A Project of Common Sense Foundation, L.A. Produced by Adam Friedson, Deborah Shaffer. Directed by Shaffer. Camera (color), Frank Pineda; editor, Gini Reticker; music, Charlie Haden; sound, Luis Fuentes; voice of Omar Cabezas, Tony Plana; associate producer, Abbie Fields. Reviewed at N.Y. Film Festival, Oct. 15, 1987. (No MPAA Rating.) Running time: 60 MINS.

Based on the autobiographical political journey of Nicaraguan author Omar Cabezas, "Fire From The Mountain" recounts the youthful political awareness and activism of the celebrated writer. The Cabezas book was nominated for the Los Angeles Times Book Prize in 1985.

Culmination of the book, and this film, is Cabezas' joining up with fellow Sandinista rebels in the mountains, badly outnumbered and short of bullets and cigarets, soggy with cold rain. Occasionally they raid into the valleys below, purpose being overthrow of the oppressive Somoza regime, the stooge of the United States government.

Film evokes parallels to Castro, high in the Sierras of Cuba, as he suffered similar hardships to overthrow Batista, another U.S. stooge. Revolutionary fire traditionally comes from the mountains, as a metaphor for celestial purgation. In the symbolism of propaganda, divine revenge comes from on high.

Oscar-winning Deborah Shaffer (for 1985's "Witness To War: Dr. Charlie Clements") traces the personal saga of Cabezas, who after his student protest days and years of ordeal as a guerrilla commander, ultimately became Vice-Minister of the Interior of the victorious new Nicaraguan government. Cabezas is today at work on a second book about the revolutionary struggle.

"Fire From The Mountain" includes admissions by the Sandinistan government of certain faulty decisions and ineptitude, as the new administration seeks by trial and error to learn how to govern.

The film includes archival footage, interviews, and new shots of border raids by U.S.-financed Contras who attack defenseless villages.

Shaffer's film is an important contribution — with other films, and the print media — to an understanding of the conflicting points of view of the struggles in Central America. —*Hitch.*

This Is Not Our Destination
(INDIAN-COLOR)

Produced, written and directed by Sudhir Mishra. Camera (color), Devlin Bose; music, Rajat Dholakla; production design, Robin Das. Reviewed at the Tokyo Intl. Film Festival (Young Cinema competition), Sept. 29, 1987. Running time: **132 MINS.**
Shamsher Singh . . . . Manohar Singh
Akhtor Baig . . . . Habib Tanvir
Murli Manohar Joshi . . . . B.M. Shah

Tokyo — Complex material is given thoughtful but awkward treatment in "This Is Not Our Destination," a consideration of how India has and has not changed over four decades of independence. Sudhir Mishra's screenplay is a lot better than his direction, but despite the heavy flaws, this warrants further exposure on the international festival circuit.

Tackling unusually mature themes for a 29-year-old first-time director, Mishra focuses upon three cantankerous old friends, former university colleagues who, 40 years before, were activists against the British.

Attracted by the 100th anniversary celebration af their school, the opinionated threesome, all of whom can easily explain why the others have been such failures in life, make from Bombay back to Rajpur for the first time since graduation. The nephew of one of them is the local head cop, and while the chief tries to put on a good face, the city is in fact on the brink of an eruption.

Some 100 workers have died in a factory fire, resulting in a strike supported by some of the students. The arrogant factory owner's son goes unpunished as he leads a bunch of goons around beating up on protestors, and matters come to a head when, despite promises to the meek university head, the students let fly with all-out warfare just as the governor arrives for the centenary ceremonies.

Interwoven with the plot are the uneasy feelings stirred in the three old-timers as events force them to confront a traitorous act they committed together for the English years ago. At last unburdened of their horrible dark secret, they freely ask, "What's the difference between then and now?," suggesting that very little has. The specific causes may be different, but the overheat-

ed confrontations, tendency to violence in the name of some belief, tragic young deaths and stupid mistakes get repeated over and over.

Mishra tends to lose track of his protagonists once he becomes embroiled in the campus intrigue, and all of the characters, intriguing and believable enough when first presented, lack depth and dimension. The ending is absurdly melodramatic and needlessly nihilistic and, worst of all, the lighting and camerawork are dismal.

Mishra's simple and straightforward approach at least allows the value of his thoughts to be expressed, and there's enough here to chew on to warrant the more-than-two hours' running time. Very much an endorsement of the p.o.v., "The more things change, the more they remain the same," pic still offers a lively look at Indian politics and academia. If Mishra can bone up on filmmaking technique and continue to progress as a writer, he could be someone to watch. —*Cart.*

The Running Man
(COLOR)

Overdone Schwarzenegger vehicle.

A Tri-Star Pictures release from Taft Entertainment/Keith Barish Prods. of a Linder/Zinnemann production, in association with Home Box Office. Executive producers, Keith Barish, Rob Cohen. Produced by Tim Zinnemann, George Linder. Directed by Paul Michael Glaser. Stars Arnold Schwarzenegger. Screenplay, Stephen E. de Souza, from novel by Richard Bachman (Stephen King); camera (Technicolor), Tom Del Ruth; editor, Mark Roy Warner, Edward A. Warschilka, John Wright; music, Harold Faltermeyer; sound (Dolby), Richard Bryce Goodman; production design, Jack T. Collis; set decoration, Jim Duffy; set design, Nancy Patton, Nick Navarro, Richard G. Berger; costume design, Robert Blackman; production manager, Gary D. Daigler; assistant director, Richard Peter Schroer; stunt coordinator-second unit director, Bennie Dobbins; additional camera, Reynaldo Villalobos; special makeup effects, The Burman Studio; special effects coordinator, Larry Cavanaugh; special effects supervisor, Bruce Steinheimer; special visual effects supervisor, Gary Gutierrez; matte shots, Syd Dutton, Bill Taylor; casting, Jackie Burch. Reviewed at Loews Astor Plaza, N.Y., Nov. 9, 1987. (MPAA Rating: R.) Running time: **101 MINS.**
Ben Richards . . . . . Arnold Schwarzenegger
Amber Mendez . . . Maria Conchita Alonso
Damon Killian . . . . Richard Dawson
Laughlin . . . . Yaphet Kotto
Fireball . . . . Jim Brown
Capt. Freedom . . . . Jesse Ventura
Dynamo . . . . Erland Van Lidth
Weiss . . . . Marvin J. McIntyre
Buzzsaw . . . . Gus Rethwisch
Subzero . . . . Prof. Toru Tanaka
Mic . . . . Mick Fleetwood
Stevie . . . . Dweezil Zappa
Brenda . . . . Karen Leigh Hopkins
Sven . . . . Sven Thorsen

"The Running Man" is an over-produced Arnold Schwarzenegger vehicle that coarsens the star's hitherto winning formula. Costing a bloated $27,000,000 (roughly four times "The Terminator's" nut), it is a risky venture, destined to attract Arnie's army of fans but few other people.

Corny plot is almost identical to Yves Boisset's 1983 French film from a Robert ("The Tenth Victim") Sheckley story "Le Prix du Danger," which was released Stateside direct-to-video by Vestron.

Pic opens in 2017 when the world, following a financial collapse, is run by a police state, with tv a heavily censored propaganda tool of the government. Schwarzenegger is Ben Richards, a helicopter pilot who disobeys orders to fire on unarmed people during an L.A. food riot. He's slapped in prison and escapes 18 months later with pals Yaphet Kotto and Marvin J. McIntyre.

Producer-host of the popular tv gameshow "The Running Man" Damon Killian (Richard Dawson) orders Richards up as his next contestant and he is duly captured and made a runner in this lethal (and fixed) gladiatorial contest for the masses. Aided by bystander-turned good samaritan Maria Conchita Alonso and his pals in the underground, Richards quickly turns the

tables on the succession of athletes, called stalkers, summoned to kill him and ultimately the populace starts betting on him instead of these popular hitmen. The underground succeeds in capturing the satellite uplink device and scuttles Killian's show in favor of broadcasting the truth.

Format works only on a pure action level, with some exciting, but overly repetitious, roller-coaster style sequences of runners hurtling into the game through tunnels on futuristic sleds. Schwarzenegger sadistically dispatches the baddies, enunciating typical wisecrack remarks (many repeated from his previous films), but it's all too easy, despite the casting of such powerful presences as Jim Brown and former wrestlers Jesse Ventura and Prof. Toru Tanaka. Brightest element here is actor Richard Dawson, long identified as the taciturn host of tv's "Family Feud," very comfortably playing the ultimately smug and vicious gameshow emcee. Femme lead Alonso and character actor Yaphet Kotto have nothing roles.

"Running Man" originally was slated to roll in 1985 in Canada with "Rambo's" George Pan Cosmatos directing and Christopher Reeve toplining, but it got underway a full year later. Andrew Davis (of "Code Of Silence") began directing the film, but was succeeded early in the shooting by former tv star Paul Michael Glaser, helming his second feature (after Tri-Star's "Band Of The Hand"). Glaser gets poor line readings from his cast (including Schwarzenegger) and sledgehammers home the most obvious gags in Stephen E. de Souza's script, based on a Stephen King novel published under his pseudonym Richard Bachman.

The satire of tv (with such popular shows of the totalitarian future as "The Hate Boat") is paperthin and constantly contradicted by the film wallowing in the sort of mindless violence for the roller derby-addicted masses it is supposedly criticizing. Interesting premise of tv becoming a communal viewer activity (watched à la drive-in movies on giant rectangular screens outside or at "Rollerball"-style parties by hordes of rich folk) in the future instead of a private family-at-home phenomenon is not developed in the screenplay. Numerous in-jokes, such as Jesse (The Body) Ventura lampooning his tv wrestling commentator image, merely trivialize the proceedings, while a couple of "Blade Runner"-influenced matte shots do not qualify as sci-fi.

Pic's nadir comes when Dawson hastily orders up a computer simulation of a final battle between Schwarzenegger and Ventura. It plays convincingly to finish the show and is immediately refuted by Schwarzenegger's vengeful return and the truth broadcast, but destroys the story's credibility. Such an easy simulation would have been routine procedure to control the show's production and outcome (once the live-action intro with new victims was staged for the studio audience), but then you'd have no movie.

Tech credits are strong enough to cover most of the film's story lapses, but glitzy dance numbers featuring a femme chorus line instead of being futuristic, look like leftovers from tv's "Solid Gold." —*Lor.*

Hello Again
(COLOR)

Stillborn romantic comedy.

A Buena Vista release of a Touchstone Pictures presentation, in association with Silver Screen Partners III. Executive producer, Salah M. Hassanein. Produced and directed by Frank Perry. Stars Shelley Long. Screenplay, Susan Isaacs, camera (Deluxe color), Jan Weincke; editor, Peter C. Frank, Trudy Ship; music, William Goldstein; production design, Edward Pisoni; art direction, William Barclay; set decoration, Robert J. Franco; costumes, Ruth Morley; sound (Dolby), Gary Alper; assistant director, Joel B. Segal; casting, Donna Isaacson, John Lyons. Reviewed at Avco Cinema Center, Westwood, Nov. 3, 1987. (MPAA Rating: PG.) Running time: **96 MINS.**

Lucy Chadman...............Shelley Long
Zelda ....Judith Ivey
Kevin Scanlon.............Gabriel Byrne
Jason Chadman..........Corbin Bernsen
Kim Lacey....................Sela Ward
Junior Lacey...........Austin Pendleton
Regina Holt ....Carrie Nye
Phineas Devereux ....Robert Lewis
Felicity ....Madeleine Potter
Danny Chadman ....Thor Fields

Hollywood — Viewers are advised to be wary of any romantic comedy in which the ultimate resolution (and very life of the protagonist) depends on the answer to the question, "Are you really ready for me to bring the rubber bone?" That's where this runaway plotline leads to, though, as Shelley Long wanders through a script she can't carry by herself while heading a cast handled with less than a Midas touch by director Frank Perry, who seems to think he's staging a high school play. Boxoffice looks only fair to moderate.

Long plays Lucy Chadman, the dull and thoroughly domesticated housewife of Corbin Bernsen's yupscale Long Island plastic surgeon Jason Chadman. First 15 minutes fails to establish enough of a believable link between Long and Bernsen to make his grief believable when his loving wife chokes to death on a chicken ball while in the occultist boutique of her off-the-wall, down-the-hall sister Zelda (Judith Ivey).

After much hocus-pocus, Zelda brings Lucy back from her grave a year to the day after her death. Here, as the confused Lucy (who remembers nothing from the intervening year) discovers what has become of her husband and son Danny (a nicely played part by Thor Fields) film looks like it might probe

some interesting questions, such as wondering what happens if you come back to life a year after your death and find that your loved ones don't really *need* you anymore.

Instead, the most predictable thing that could happen does, and Lucy walks in on her husband with her gold-digging, glory-grabbing girlfriend Kim (played with nice salaciousness by Sela Ward, before the script forces her to go out of her character in stupidity).

Scene in which Lucy discovers the lovers is actually funny, but it should have operated as a starting point for some human comedy. Instead it's a jumping off point, into an abyss of silly plot developments as scripter Susan Isaacs brings in the media and medical researchers for a ludicrous turn of events that include a pair of hospital press conferences that leaves one embarrassed for the performers.

While all of this is going on, Long is expected to provide cohesion by drawing a zany, goofball character who is lovable in her imperfection. She's too prim for this in the first place, but matters are made worse by her attempts at physical humor; her pratfalls seem stiff and poorly timed.

The tinny, tepid Bernsen isn't much of a foil, and gets lost in the demands of his first major bigscreen role. One never gets a sense of his character thinking for himself; instead he seems buffeted by the winds of Isaacs' wayward script.

Would-be romantic interest Dr. Kevin Scanlon (Gabriel Byrne) brings a little bit of sanity to the proceedings with his noble work ethic and lack of self-centeredness. His inevitable attraction to Lucy is artificially delayed till the end of the film when it's couched in silly dialog.

This mess is a step backward for both scripter Isaacs (after the wry "Compromising Positions") and director Perry (who received an Oscar nomination for his brilliant debut with "David And Lisa"), falling victim to his most stagey, theatrical instincts in his handling of his actors.

The pair conspire to prevent much affection for the characters from carrying through to the end of the film. "Hello Again" never examines itself, or what it might be about. Instead it takes a concept — not a bad one — and lets it run wild on a ride that audience members will not find pleasant.

Nice supporting turns are given by Austin Pendleton, as billionaire Junior Lacey and the wonderful Ivey, who plays her eccentric character to the hilt.

Tech credits are competent, but for the too-dark shots of lenser Jan Weincke and the mediocre (and obtrusive) score of William Goldstein. —*Camb.*

Sure Death 4
(JAPANESE-COLOR)

A Shochiku/Asahi Broadcast production. Directed by Kinji Fukasaku. Screenplay, Tatsuo Nogami, Fukasaku, Akira Nakahara; camera (color), Koh Ishihara; music, Masaaki Hirao. No other credits available. Reviewed at the Tokyo Intl. Film Festival (Japanese Cinema section), Sept. 28, 1987. Running time: **131 MINS.**

Mondo Nakamura ....Makoto Fujita
Ofuku ....Mitsuko Baisyo
Ukyonosuke Okuda .....Hiroyuki Sanada
Sen.........................Kin Sugai

Tokyo — The samurai film reaches new levels of hokiness and facetiousness in "Sure Death 4," fourth feature offshoot of a popular Japanese television series. Maddeningly contrived and padded with tedious non-action, pic is enough to sour any fan on the genre for awhile.

Lit as brightly as any tv sitcom and scored with a combination of goofy Western and Mexican music, pic watches a supposedly cowardly samurai as he investigates some reckless killing being carried out by a band of samurai at the behest of a new local magistrate.

Like a bad television detective show, film bogs down in a lot of boring procedural stuff, and long stretches pass without any swordplay. Even when it does liven up, approach is so false and unconvincing that it doesn't rivet the attention. One senses early on that things aren't going to get any better, and they don't.

Villains are all made up to look like glitter rockers with green and pink hair and gobs of makeup, and director Kinji Fukasaku, represented here at the festival with the much better "House On Fire," gives the picture no sense of style or coherent tone. It's all a joke, an unfunny one that lasts more than two hours.
—*Cart.*

Death Wish 4:
The Crackdown
(COLOR)

Violent fun for Bronson fans.

A Cannon Group release of a Golan-Globus production. Produced by Pancho Kohner. Executive producers, Menahem Golan, Yoram Globus. Directed by J. Lee-Thompson. Stars Charles Bronson. Screenplay, Gail Morgan Hickman, based on characters created by Brian Garfield; camera (TVC color), Gideon Porath; editor, Peter Lee-Thompson; music, Paul McCallum, Valentine McCallum, John Bisharat; art direction, Whitney Brooke Wheeler; set decoration, Mark Andrew; sound, Craig Felburg; assistant director, Robert J. Dougherty; stunt coordinator, Ernie Orsatti; casting, Perry Bullington, Robert McDonald. Reviewed at the Hollywood Pacific Theater, Nov. 6, 1987. (MPAA Rating: R.) Running time: **99 MINS.**

Paul Kersey ....Charles Bronson
Karen Sheldon ....Kay Lenz
Nathan White ....John P. Ryan
Ed Zacharias ....Perry Lopez
Detective Reiner ....George Dickerson
Detective Nozaki ....Soon-Teck Oh
Erica Sheldon ....Dana Barron
Randy Viscovich ....Jesse Dabson

Hollywood — It's a risky business getting close to Charles Bronson. Since 1974 his wife, daughter and friends have been blown away in the first three installments of "Death Wish." Now the vigilante is back in "Death Wish 4: The Crackdown" to revenge the death of his girlfriend's daughter. Fortunately it's still a formula that works and Bronson fans should be pleased with the body count as well as wry touches of humor.

What raises "Death Wish 4" above the usual blowout is a semi-engaging script by Gail Morgan Hickman and sure pacing by veteran action director J. Lee-Thompson. Although it runs out of steam and becomes quite tedious about halfway through, it's Bronson's show and the old warrior can still hold his own with a machinegun and grimace with the best of 'em.

As architect turned crusader, Paul Kersey (Bronson) is a curious blend of soft-spoken family man and detached seeker of justice. When he turns up the heat he does so with a measured, methodical passion as if it were his true calling in life to measure out justice in his corner of the world.

Of course it's a narrow-minded, simplistic kind of justice founded this time on the premise that "anyone connected with drugs deserves to die." Bronson's treatment of drug trafficking is akin to chopping off the weeds and thinking that they won't grow back.

It's a good excuse for Bronson to break out some heavy ammunition in pursuit of the two rival gangs who supposedly supply 90% of the cocaine in Los Angeles. Plot takes an unexpected twist when his accomplice, crimelord John P. Ryan posing as a wealthy newspaper magnate, doublecrosses him and tries to seize control of the drug trade.

Along for the ride is Kay Lenz as Bronson's lady love and mother of the teen who succumbs to an overdose of crack. Perry Lopez is suitably slimy as the drug honcho and Ryan, rapidly becoming a stock bad guy in the Cannon acting corps, turns in another serviceable job as the most loathesome of the villains.

Film generally looks fine with Gideon Porath's camerawork capturing some unfamiliar gritty L.A. locations heightened by Peter Lee-Thompson's crisp editing. Production design, however, has a bit of a cut-rate look with the Cannon screening room serving as a theater location and the company parking lot the scene of the climactic confrontation. —*Jagr.*

Less Than Zero
(COLOR)

Shallow downer of a film with anti-drug theme.

A 20th Century Fox release, in association

with Amercent Films and American Entertainment Partners. Produced by Jon Avnet, Jordan Kerner, in association with Marvin Worth. Directed by Marek Kanievska. Screenplay, Harley Peyton, based on the novel by Bret Easton Ellis; camera (Deluxe color), Edward Lachman; editor, Peter E. Berger, Michael Tronick; music, Thomas Newman, various artists; production design, Barbara Ling; art direction, Stephen Rice; set decoration, Nancy Nye; costume design, Richard Hornung; sound (Dolby), Glenn Berkovitz; assistant director, Deborah Love; casting, David Rubin. Reviewed at 20th Century Fox studio theater, L.A., Oct. 29, 1987. (MPAA Rating: R.) Running time: **98 MINS.**
Clay . . . . Andrew McCarthy
Blair . . . . Jami Gertz
Julian . . . . Robert Downey Jr.
Rip . . . . James Spader
Hop . . . . Michael Bowen
Benjamin Wells . . . . Nicholas Pryor
Bradford Easton . . . . Tony Bill

———

Hollywood — If it's possible, the film "Less Than Zero" is even more specious and shallow than the Bret Easton Ellis book it is based on. There's a story somewhere tracking the dissipated lifestyles of the super-rich, super-hip kids and their L.A. haunts and his group looks the part, if only there was more. Surely the filmmakers didn't intend to make a high-concept, anti-drug film — but that's what resulted. For a downer picture, even a mighty pretty one, the b.o. looks weak.

"Less Than Zero" shows a particularly L.A. slice of life viewed through Edward Lachman's constantly moving camera eye, many times so close up on the images to make one's eyes cross, and at other times off-center on whatever the action is. Mostly, though, it is lusciously photographed and full of great colors.

This is how the film opens, on a lengthy closeup of three chic, tanned kids from privileged homes whose friendship began in high school and has moved on to young adult passions — escaping through drugs, partying and talking about same and each other.

As "Less Than Zero" tracks this angst-ridden trio in a cool, red Corvette contertible between their expensive homes, trendy clubs and other locales, a mood is formed that all is rotten underneath, like a big shiny red apple with a worm in it.

Things sure went sour after high school and they never improve, nor is there much of a hope that they will. Drugs take over Julian (Robert Downey Jr.), Clay (Andrew McCarthy) avoids the scene by attending an eastern college and his g.f. Blair (Jami Gertz) lost her identity, which was never much to begin with.

This is where they are at the beginning of the film — and pretty much where they are at the end.

Perhaps this wasn't the best subject matter for British director Marek Kanievska ("Another Country") to make his American debut. The feel for this distinctly Southern California story escapes him.

These kids are spoiled and very vulnerable yet only Downey elicits the kind of sympathy to distinguish this drama from a photojournalist essay of the kind that might run in "Vanity Fair." He breathes life into a cold film comprised of flashy scenes where he is mostly being rescued by his friends from oblivion as his addiction to freebasing cocaine becomes more serious.

It is probably not the fault of the actors that they have little to say and what they do say doesn't have much meaning.

Ellis' book went more into the disintegration of the families and how that affected these kids' behavior. Here, other than one brief, completely wordless and wonderful scene where McCarthy's father's ex-wife and new young squeeze politely glare at each other in the interest of harmony at Christmas dinner, this very important undercurrent is pretty much shelved.

McCarthy, Gertz and especially Downey are adrift with nothing in the way of emotional support (except for each other, which is pretty tenuous) to take off from.

It would have helped if McCarthy's character was drawn less aloof. He seems more interested in winning back the affections of Gertz' fickle heart (and having sex with her) than in seeing that his best friend cleans up his act. Even when he makes a last desperate attempt to pull Downey out of his chemical, and now criminal, rut, it appears half-hearted.

Of the secondary roles, James Spader as Downey's pusher is terrifically smarmy. He knows that threats, especially from the namby-pamby McCarthy, aren't going to slow his operation any or get him to stop feeding Downey's habit.

Unfortunately, this sick relationship Downey and Spader have doesn't become involving until the last third of the film, when Downey really begins to fall apart and is forced into male whoring to pay his drug debts. By this time, he is convincingly grotesque, his nose and mouth burned red from the pipe, and also pathetic because he is so weak an individual. Weak individuals, without much charm or personality, don't make good protagonists, however, and that's what this film needed, one person worth caring about.

Visually, the picture is a treat. Production designer Barbara Ling knows what kind of mood she wants to put over, filling each set with high-style atmosphere — much of it appropriately glitzy, as in the dance scenes at Vertigo and the Stock Exchange and other hot club spots, with the one exception in the over-produced pink party scene.

Music is well-integrated and adds to the overall "MTV" tone of the film. Curiously absent from the soundtrack is Elvis Costello's "Less Than Zero."—*Brit.*

———

Steel Dawn
(COLOR)

———

Patrick Swayze buoys up a poorly written fantasy.

A Vestron Pictures release, in association with Silver Lion Films. Produced by Lance Hool, Conrad Hool. Executive producers, William J. Quigley, Larry Sugar. Directed by Lance Hool. Screenplay, Doug Lefler; camera (CFI color), George Tirl; editor, Mark Conte; music, Brian May; production design, Alex Tavoularis; Hans Van Den Zanden; set decoration, Lindy Steinman; costume design, Poppy Cannon; sound (Dolby), David Stone; special effects, Joe Quinlivan; additional editing, Adam Wolfe; production manager, Conrad Hool; assistant director, Terry Buchinsky; stunt coordinator, John Barrett; associate producer, Edgar Bold; casting, Fern Champion, Pamela Basker. Reviewed at Mann Westwood Theater, Nov. 6, 1987. (MPAA Rating: R.) Running time: **100 MINS.**
Nomad . . . . Patrick Swayze
Kasha . . . . Lisa Niemi
Sho . . . . Christopher Neame
Tark . . . . Brion James
Cord . . . . John Fujioka
Jux . . . . Brett Hool
Damnil . . . . Anthony Zerbe
Lann . . . . Marcel Van Heerden
Makker . . . . Arnold Vosloo
Tooey . . . . James Whyle
Off . . . . Russell Savadier

———

Hollywood — "Steel Dawn" attempts to be a post-apocalyptic, nuclear wasteland sword-fu epic, but its poorly written script — characters don't have motivations as much as random impulses — and uneven pacing rob it of much tension. Patrick Swayze does his best with a broadly drawn role and his real-life wife Lisa Niemi is likeable enough, but this film never quite transcends its low-budget genre. Boxoffice prospects coming on the heels of Swayze's "Dirty Dancing" lead, could be moderately successful.

Pic's first 15 minutes show Swayze's journeyman soldier Nomad walking around in the desert like an "Ishtar" extra who took a wrong turn somewhere. Storyline hints at a long-ago nuclear holocaust but circumstances of everyday life presented here don't make sense: population is reverting back to horses and carriages, but hydroelectric generators are still being built; water is precious and most people are settling in small, barren locales, but all the lead characters seem to have had their hair done by Vidal Sassoon.

After Nomad runs into his old mentor Cord (John Fujioka) somewhere in the desert, they adjourn to somewhere else in the desert for a drink. Cord has been summoned to the town of Meridian to become its commissioned Peacemaker and protect the people from hostile raiders. (What country is Meridian in? Who commissioned the Peacemaker? Why is there an empty bar in the middle of the desert? These are some of the impenetrable details in Doug Lefler's script.)

Before he gets to Meridian, Cord is murdered by a hired sword named Sho (Christopher Neame), brought in by The Bad Guy in Meridian, the evil Damnil (Anthony Zerbe, who seems to be aspiring to a brooding, puffy countenance like Brando in "Apocalypse Now").

Seeking revenge on both the assassin and the man who ordered the job, Swayze adjourns to Meridian, where he gets a job on a water purification farm owned by Niemi as the widow Kasha (all conventional names seem to have been wiped out in the nuclear firestorm also), whose husband was a great officer in "the war."

Everything that happens from this point on is utterly predictable: Swayze saves the farm from a band of saboteurs, earning Kasha's trust, then her love; her little boy is kidnaped and she falls into Damnil's clutches trying to rescue him; Swayze journeys to Damnil's headquarters for the ultimate showdown.

Lance Hool's direction is competent, with some nice panoramas of southwest Africa's Namib Desert, but he doesn't have enough of a script to work with to build up a head of steam, and the key action sequences — the swordfights — don't add anything to what has appeared in countless other films.

That the film doesn't break down entirely is attributable to Swayze's charisma; he's not a great actor, but he remains doggedly focused on the essentials of his role, never giving a false note on what is essentially an unrealistic character.

Tech credits are adequate, but costume designer Poppy Cannon gets a little carried away with her patchwork rags theme on everyone but Niemi, who looks like she just got back from Bloomingdales' southwestern chic sale.—*Camb.*

Dear America
(DOCU-COLOR)

———

Produced by Bill Couturie, Thomas Bird. Directed by Couturie. Written by Richard Dewhurst, Couturie; camera, stock footage from NBC Video Archives; editor, Stephen Stept; music, Todd Boekelheide; sound (Dolby), Robert Shoup; re-recording mixer, Mark Berger; production manager, EZ Petroff. Reviewed at Music Hall Theater, Beverly Hills, Calif., Oct. 30, 1987. (No MPAA Rating.) Running time: **87 MINS.**
With voices of: Tom Berenger, Ellen Burstyn, J. Kenneth Campbell, Richard Chaves, Josh Cruze, Willem Dafoe, Robert De Niro, Brian Dennehy, Kevin Dillon, Matt Dillon, Robert Downey Jr., Michael J. Fox, Mark Harmon, John Heard, Fred Hirz, Harvey Keitel, Elizabeth McGovern, Judd Nelson, Sean Penn, Randy Quaid, Tim Quill, Eric Roberts, Ray Robertson, Howard Rollins Jr., John Savage, Raphael Sbarge, Martin Sheen, Tucker Smallwood, Roger Steffens, Jim Tracy, Kathleen Turner, Tico Wells, Robin Williams.

———

Hollywood — Behind the explosiveness of "Platoon" there is a harder truth about the Vietnam War that is admirably and painfully exposed in Bill Couturie's "Dear America." A seamless montage of letters home, period music and newsreel footage, documentary lets the events speak for themselves and gathers its strength from the stark power of the images. Although it is often difficult to watch, film should be mandatory viewing for anyone who ever thought war was glamorous.

"Dear America" is the first home movie of the Vietnam War. Built around letters written by soldiers, most of them teenagers, in the midst of combat, film reveals the everyday reality of the war in all its ordinary, mundane glory. As the words and pictures of soldiers, many of whom soon after lost their lives, pass on the screen, one cannot help but be struck by the waste and senselessness of it all.

If nothing else, and it is much more, film is a first-rate archival effort. Stock footage donated by NBC news is riveting in its own right, seen as if for the first time after all these years. Newsreels are supplemented by outtakes which were, in fact, never seen before and super 8 snippets shot by the servicemen themselves.

Following the chronology of the war from the Kennedy inauguration to the return of the first MIA, footage has the familiarity of a nightmare turned real. What gives the images their extraordinary power is Couturie's skillful overlay of letters home which emphasize the human dimension of the war.

Soldiers long for their families, friends, lovers and anything familiar while trying to make rhyme or reason out of what they're doing there. The result is a privileged glimpse into a score of lives that clearly will never be the same.

Equally powerful are clips of the war at home seen as if with fresh eyes. Never has the National Guard firing on students at Kent State U. seemed a more dastardly deed. The focus is squarely on the fighting men and their letters document their reactions to even these events at home.

Couturie has recruited an impressive cast to read the letters and to his credit has found just the right tone so the recitations are not sanctimonious or theatrical. As in any great performance, the readings are in service of the material and while voices such as Robert De Niro, John Heard, Michael J. Fox, Martin Sheen and Ellen Burstyn are sometimes recognizable, they sound not like actors, but the people who wrote the letters.

To round out his accomplishment, Couturie has assembled a stellar soundtrack of '60s music donated by the musicians or their estates that rivals the score for "Coming Home" as a record of what people were listening to and thinking about as the Vietnam War raged.

Especially moving here, as it is in "Coming Home," is Tim Buckley's "Once I Was," a soldier's musing about his mortality and lost love.

Blown up to 35m and re-recorded in Dolby stereo, technical credits are surprisingly strong without being slick. Indeed, the rough edges are what gives the film its enormous authority. —Jagr.

Kataku No Hito
(House On Fire)
(JAPANESE-COLOR)

Produced by Tan Takawa, Masao Sato. Directed by Kinji Fukasaku. Screenplay, Fumo Konami, Fukasaku, based on the novel by Kazuo Dan; camera (color), Daisaku Kimura; music, Takayuki Inoue. (No other credits available.) Reviewed at the Tokyo Intl. Film Festival (Japanese Cinema section), Sept. 26, 1987. Running time: **132 MINS.**
Kazuo Katsura . . . . Ken Ogata
Yoriko Katsura . . . . Ayumi Ishida
Keiko Yajima . . . . Mieko Harada
Yoko . . . . Keiko Matsuzaka

Tokyo — The rich, turbulent and troubled life of novelist Kazuo Dan has been made into a film to which the same adjectives apply. Not exactly artfully made, incident-filled drama based on the writer's last, autobiographical novel is entirely absorbing and is graced by an outstanding lead performance by Ken Ogata.

Story of an eminent writer's excessive lifestyle and countless problems with women, work, booze and his children could serve as the basis of both a major work of art and a soap opera. Director Kinji Fukasaku has more or less split the difference, loading on the melodramatic coincidences and commercially designed sex scenes, but also creating a compelling character study of a man of strong will and impulse.

Narrative has Ogata, a married man with six kids, slowly developing an affair with a spritely young actress. Although one of his children develops terminal meningitis, his wife just picks up and takes off one day, leaving him to cope with the brood as well as his volatile girlfriend and pressing deadlines.

Everything that could possibly happen does — his son dies, not one but two women leave him, and he has a very odd but touching affair with a bargirl on a trip to a distant island. Through it all, he compulsively details his misadventures in his work, to the fascination of the Japanese public, and it all ends with all his children climbing on top of him as they appropriately play a game called, "Too-Heavy-To-Bear."

Fukasaku's style sometimes skids into undue slickness, but the numerous domestic arguments and sexual interludes possess a robust earthiness, and the characters are very well developed. Ogata gives a tremendously forceful performance as a man who resembles many an obsessed European artist, a compulsive creator whose work is rooted in the juices of life.

The key women in his life are almost as 3-dimensional, with Mieko

Harada impressing as the long-term mistress who finally cracks after having an abortion and Ayumi Ishida as the wife conveying convulsive emotions under an unflappable exterior.

Any man who has experienced at least some of the trials Ogata brings upon himself will doubtlessly become extremely involved in this densely packed film, and the cast makes even the most extreme situations here entirely believable.
—Cart.

Bloody Wednesday
(COLOR)

Amateurish morality play posing as an exploitation film.

A Visto Intl. presentation of a Gilmark Pictures production. Executive producer, William F. Messerli. Produced by Philip Yordan, Mark G. Gilhuis; coproducers, Robert Ryan, Susan Gilhuis. Directed by Mark G. Gilhuis. Screenplay, Yordan; camera (United color), Ryan; editor, uncredited; music, Al Sendry; sound, Steve Fuiten; art direction, Phil Adipietro; production manager-associate producer, Michel Bonneau; assistant director, Tibor Takacs; postproduction consultant, Gene Ruggiero; associate producer, Jay Schlossberg-Cohen. Reviewed on Prism Entertainment vidcassette, N.Y. Oct. 11, 1987. (No MPAA Rating.) Running time: **96 MINS.**
Harry . . . . Raymond Elmendorf
Dr. Johnson . . . . Pamela Baker
Ben Curtis . . . . Navarre Perry
Elaine Curtis . . . . Teresa Mae Allen
Animal . . . . Jeff O'Haco
Bellman . . . . John Landtroop

"Bloody Wednesday" is a most peculiar film, styled as an exploitation pic but actually unfolding in the manner of a silent era morality play. Filmed at the end of 1984, as "The Great American Massacre," it reportedly received a token theatrical booking ahead of its current homevideo release.

Picture raises serious questions about the current bent of screenwriter Philip Yordan, once a top Hollywood scripter but now churning out demented work like this opus and the even goofier "Night Train To Hollywood." Film just vaguely resembles an episode in "Night Train" entitled "Harry," which is also the hero's name here.

Overwritten Yordan screenplay purports to investigate the social malaise which results in such phenomena as the MacDonald's massacre and other acts of senseless carnage. Harry (Raymond Elmendorf) works in an auto repair shop but is going crazy: he forgets how to put an engine back together, walks into church buck naked and fantasizes sex scenes with his attractive shrink (Pamela Baker). His brother Ben (Navarre Perry) lets Harry live in an empty hotel owned by a client, and just as in "The Shining," Harry hallucinates all manner of weird events that happened there decades before, including a suicide. Meanwhile three young punks led by Jeff

O'Haco harass him, sometimes for real, sometimes merely imagined.

Tedious, episodic presentation includes plenty of criticism of our society's corruption, with the pessimism reaching its nadir after Harry's estranged wife (Teresa Mae Allen) moves in with him at the hotel to give him a hard time and Harry asks his brother to "make me a cripple," so that he can earn his keep as a beggar. "I want to be a beggar, but you have to be a cripple to get a license," is typical of script's heavy thinking.

Ultimately, in place of the religious conversion which would climax a 1920s Cecil B. de Mille version of this sort of material, director Mark Gilhuis and scripter Yordan preposterously have Harry receive a gift of a machine gun from the nihilistic punks who have been harassing him, and he heads for a local coffee shop to blast the all-American customers in slow-motion with plenty of exploding bloodpacks. Fade to black as he sinks down, exhausted.

Yordan seems to want to wake up a corrupt world by making soap box B-movies about its ills. Unfortunately, this clunker has such monotone acting, cheap, bare sets and poor film technique it doesn't even qualify for camp. Someday it probably will be lumped in with "Reefer Madness" and other vintage exercises in naïveté.—Lor.

Nuts
(COLOR)
Histrionic courtroom drama rests on Streisand's performance.

A Warner Bros. release of a Barwood Films/Martin Ritt production. Produced by Barbra Streisand. Executive producers, Teri Schwartz, Cis Corman. Directed by Martin Ritt. Stars Streisand, Richard Dreyfuss. Screenplay, Tom Topor, Darryl Ponicsan, Alvin Sargent, based on the play by Topor; camera (Technicolor), Andrzej Bartkowiak; editor, Sidney Levin, music, Streisand; production design, Joel Schiller; art direction, Eric Orbom; set decoration, Anne McCulley; sound (Dolby), Thomas Causey; assistant director, Aldric La' Auli Porter; casting, Marion Dougherty. Reviewed at Glen Glenn Sound, Hollywood, Nov. 5, 1987. (MPAA Rating: R) Running time: **116 MINS.**
Claudia Draper . . . . Barbra Steisand
Aaron Levinsky . . . . Richard Dreyfuss
Rose Kirk . . . . Maureen Stapleton
Arthur Kirk . . . . Karl Malden
Dr. Morrison . . . . Eli Wallach
Francis MacMillan . . . . Robert Webber
Judge Murdoch . . . . James Whitmore
Allen Green . . . . Leslie Nielsen
Clarence Middleton . . . . William Prince

Hollywood — Based on the stageplay by Tom Topor, "Nuts" presents a premise weighted down by portentous performances. Issue of society's right to judge someone's sanity and the subjectivity of mental health is not only trite, but dated. While film ignites sporadically, it succumbs to the burden of its own earnestness. With little else going for it, boxoffice success depends on the appeal of its star and producer Barbra Streisand.

As Claudia Draper, an upper-crust New York kid who has gone off the deep end into prostitution, Streisand is good, but it's too much of a good thing. Martin Ritt's direction literally rubs her in the audience's face with endless closeups as if she were too lovable to deny.

For the most part it's a heroic performance, abandoning many of the characteristic Streisand mannerisms while she allows herself to look seedy. Problem is more in the conception and execution of the character and as the focus of an elaborate legal chess game where every move is a point of emotional combat, she is simply too simplistic to justify all the chest-pounding and soul-bearing.

For all its histrionics, film is remarkably unengaging. Characters don't interact and seem to exist isolated in their own worlds. Consequently, individual strong performances by a stellar cast, including Maureen Stapleton as Streisand's mother, Karl Malden as her father, Eli Wallach as the court-appointed psychiatrist and James Whitmore as the hearing judge, call attention to themselves since these star turns since these people aren't really allowed to connect with each other.

Richard Dreyfuss as Streisand's reluctant public defender is by far the film's most textured character, giving a performance that suggests a world of feeling and experience not rushing to gush out at the seams.

Arrested for killing her high-priced trick, it is Dreyfuss' job to convince a preliminary hearing that Streisand is mentally competent enough to stand trial with little help from her and against her parents' wishes.

It's a hothouse of tortured emotions and her day in court resembles a therapy session more than a legal proceeding. The suggestion that all this crying and revealing of skeletons in the family closet will leave Streisand a saner person is pure wishful thinking. Indeed, the whole notion that Streisand is as sane as the man on the street and, therefore, able to control her own destiny (romanticizes) the concept of mental illness. It may be fashionable to say that society is ill-equipped to judge who is crazy and who isn't but it's clearly a fatuous conclusion to say that no one is.

As written by Topor, Darryl Ponicsan and Alvin Sargent, Streisand is flamboyantly, eccentrically crazy in a way that implies she is just a spirited woman society is trying to crush. Her best scene is a verbal seduction of the prosecuting attorney (Robert Webber) in which she displays the guile and power she has used to get her way all along and, for a moment, the audience can understand insanity as a charmed state.

Given the clunkiness of the material, Ritt does his best to inject some life into the going-on and generally is successful in orchestrating the lengthy courtroom session. Production values are strong with Andrzej Bartkowiak's cinematography and Joel Schiller's production design successfully walking the line between a nightmare and a fairy tale.
— *Jagr.*

Zombie Nightmare
(COLOR)

Trivial horror exercise.

A Gold-Gems Ltd. production. Produced by Pierre Grisé. Executive producer, Sheldon S. Goldstein. Directed by Jack Bravman. Screenplay, David Wellington; camera (Bellevue Pathé color), Robert Racine; editor, David Franko; music, Jon-Mikl Thor, others; sound, Michael Gyzelek; art direction, David Blanchard; assistant director, John Fasano; associate producers, Charles Storms, Eleanor Hilowitz; casting, Ginette D'Amico. Reviewed on New World vidcassette, N.Y., Oct. 24, 1987. (MPAA Rating: R.) Running time: **83 MINS.**
Capt. Churchman . . . . Adam West
Tony Washington . . . . Jon-Mikl Thor
Amy . . . . Tia Carrere
Molly . . . . Manuska Rigaud
Frank . . . . Frank Dietz
Maggie . . . . Linda Singer
Also· with: Linda Smith, Francesca Bonacorsa, John Fasano.

"Zombie Nightmare" is an amateur night horror film lensed in Canada last year. At one time scheduled for theatrical release (via Filmworld Distributors), pic instead has gone directly to video via New World.

Beefy singer Jon-Mikl Thor (who susequently starred in "The Edge Of Hell") portrays a guy killed in a hit-and-run accident by some joy-riding teens. His father was also killed by youngsters when, after a baseball game, he tried to prevent their raping a young Haitian girl. The widow (Francesca Bonacorsa) is fed up and calls for the Haitian (Manuska Rigaud) to perform a ceremony to reanimate Thor and have him avenge his death. Rigaud's secret agenda is to get the rapists, including the current police chief ("Batman" Adam West).

Action scenes are very awkwardly staged and the makeup effects for Thor the zombie wouldn't pass muster at a comic book convention fashion show. Acting is poor with West very bland in his smallish role. Gimmick of the zombie killing his victims with a baseball bat is merely stupid. —*Lor.*

Sign O' The Times
(COLOR)

Prince concert performance pic could heat up winter boxoffice.

A Cineplex Odeon Films release of a Cavallo Ruffalo & Fragnoli production. Produced by Robert Cavallo, Joseph Ruffalo, Steven Fragnoli; coproduced by Simon Fields. Directed by Prince. Stars Prince. Camera (color), Peter Sinclair, Jerry Watson; production/lighting design, Leroy Bennett; editor, Steve Purcell; music supervision, Billy Youdelman, Susan Rogers; songs, Prince; production manager, Victoria Niles; postproduction supervisor, Cheri Hunter; postproduction mixing, Sheila E. Reviewed at 20th Century Fox screening room, N.Y., Nov. 13, 1987. (MPAA Rating: PG-13). Running time: **85 MINS.**
With: Prince, Sheila E., Sheena Easton, Dr. Fink, Miko Weaver, Levi Seacer Jr., Wally Safford, Gregory Allen Brooks, Boni Boyer, Eric Leeds, Atlanta Bliss and Cat.

Following his disastrous, hubris-drenched fling as a leading man in the non-musical, glossy b&w fantasy "Under The Cherry Moon," Prince Rogers Nelson of Minneapolis wisely has returned with a polychromatic concert performance film that should draw anyone who got a charge out of his classic rock 'n' roll romance pic "Purple Rain." Prince's skywalking guitar sorties into post-psychedelic funk-rock, his audacious vocals and Dionysian stage turns unfold here in a compact, rapid-fire format that could attract lots of repeat viewers.

Shot on location at a music hall in Rotterdam and at the musician's studio in Minnesota, "Sign O' The Times" is a filmed treatment of Prince's touring show of songs from his hit lp of the same name. Defiantly carnal in the face of AIDS-era safe sexiness, the Prince revue is set in a *film noir* fantasy zone where the come-hither blinking of gaudy neon honky-tonk signs flashes over an idealized back-alley netherworld. There, strong-willed, Nautilus-sinewed, lascivious women — lissom gladiatrixes of rock 'n' roll bloodsport — challenge the sexual imperatives of Princely machismo.

The bloated egotism of the spectacle might be laughable were it not for Prince's mesmerizing showmanship and riveting musical command of a broad range of rock, funk and blues idioms. He's assimilated these influences and reshaped them for delivery with a strutting, passion-powered stage persona that stands up to cinematic magnification. Prince's crystal clear debts to everything from Chicago Blues to the Beatles, James Brown to Jimi Hendrix are paid off with interest in his execution of that rare rock 'n' roll feat — finding and holding an original groove. Posing, pouting and pirouetting with androgynous abandon, pushing his guitar into ethereal, upper-register soundstorms and giving supple voice to songs of senual and emotional freefall in an anomic contemporary world, Prince provides musicvideo addicts with a pure fix of visual and aural synchronicity.

Prince has replaced the Revolution band of "Purple Rain" with a new group designed to flatter and reflect his outsized narcissism, embodied in the song "U Got The Look" and flaunted in the star's ensemble of cutaway toreador jumpsuits. He favors his newest female protege, Cat, a hardbodied singer and dancer whose greatest asset is her frenetic energy. Also prominently on display is Sheila E., an above-average rock drummer (the daughter of the late jazz percussionist Coke Escovedo) who has the requisite vulpine beauty and toughness required for the women of Prince's realm. The backing musicians are well-drilled in Prince's compositions and never stray significantly from their role as sidemen. The cumulative impact of the 14 songs performed in "Sign O' The Times" renders irrelevant some superficial dramatic byplay about romantic frictions in the band.

The intertwined motifs of sexual, emotional and musical heat are sustained by flashy, finely calibrated production design and lighting and a superior sound mix. Owners of VHS stereo-hifi players should make this a very popular item when it reaches the video stores.

It would be interesting to know why Warner Bros., which released the "Sign O' The Times" LP and batted .500 with Prince's first two films, allowed this potential hit to get away to MCA ally Cineplex Odeon. —*Rich.*

Le Cri du hibou
(The Cry Of The Owl)
(FRENCH-ITALIAN-COLOR)

A UIP release of an Italfrance Films/Ci.Vi.Te.Ca.Sa. Films coproduction. Produced by Antonio Passalia. Directed by Claude Chabrol. Screenplay, Chabrol, Odile

Barski, from a novel by Patricia Highsmith; camera (color), Jean Rabier; editor, Monique Fardoulis; music, Mathieu Chabrol; sound, Jean-Bernard Thomasson; art direction, Jacques Leguillon; assistant director, Jean-Marc Rabier; production manager, Gérard Croce. Reviewed at the Gaumont Colisée cinema, Paris, Nov. 10, 1987. Running time: **102 MINS.**

Robert	Christophe Malavoy
Juliette	Mathilda May
Véronique	Virginie Thévenet
Patrick	Jacques Penot
Commissioner	Jean-Pierre Kalfon
Marcello	Patrice Kerbrat

Paris — In "Cry Of The Owl," another partial return to form from Claude Chabrol, who showed new signs of life in his previous film, "Masques," the script remains his abiding stumbling block. An intriguing psychological suspense tale based on a Patricia Highsmith novel, the film eventually disintegrates from an intimate study in the relativity of madness into Grand Guignol melodramatics.

Christophe Malavoy is a young Parisian, in the midst of divorce proceedings form a vixenish wife (Virginie Thévenet), who moves to Vichy for a new job. Lonely and depressed, he befriends lovely Mathilda May, whose isolated country house he has begun prowling about.

May is engaged to good-looking but banal Jacques Penot, but her morbid sensitivity is aroused by Malavoy's morose reserve. She falls desperately in love with him, breaking off her engagement. Malavoy tries unsuccessfully to back off, then is confronted by Penot, who disappears in order to create the impression that his rival has killed him.

May succumbs to her morbidity and commits suicide. Malavoy, who has a record of mental disturbance, obviously is thought guilty of two deaths, and has trouble convincing the police that Penot is indeed alive and, maddened by grief and rage, is back gunning for him.

For at least half its length, pic displays some of Chabrol's erstwhile mastery in balancing characterization and suspense, as in his now-classic tale of psychopathy, "Le Boucher." When the script, by Chabrol and Odile Barski, takes a detour to develop Penot's unconvincing complicity with the vindictive Thévenet, the story and direction lose their hard-earned compulsion.

Malavoy is fine as the gentle nut who is prey to the more socially acceptable madnesses of the death-seeking May and the rabidly jealous Penot. In a supporting role, Jean-Pierre Kalfon injects an entertaining note as a police inspector. Tech credits are fine. —*Len.*

Bachelor Girl
(AUSTRALIAN-COLOR)

A Yarra Bank production, made with the assistance of Film Victoria, Australian Film Commission. Produced by Ned Lander. Directed by Rivka Hartman. Stars Lyn Pierse, Kim Gyngell. Screenplay, Hartman, Maggie Power, Keith Thompson; camera (color), John Whitteron; editor, Tony Stevens; music, Burkhart Von Dallwitz; production design, Ro Cooke; sound, John Phillips; production manager, Lynda House; assistant director, Phil Jones; associate producer, Trevor Graham. Reviewed at Mosman screening room, Sydney, Australia, Nov. 3, 1987. Running time: **83 MINS.**

Dot Bloom	Lyn Pierse
Karl Stanton	Kim Gyngell
Helen Carter	Jan Friedl
Alistair Dredge Jr.	Bruce Spence
Charles	Doug Tremlett
Aunt Esther	Ruth Yaffe
Uncle Isaac	Jack Perry
Sybil	Monica Maughan

Also with: Tim Robertson (Grant), Mark Minchinton (Gazza), Christine Mahoney (Jenny), Denis Moore (Bert), Gary Samolin (Morris Glass), Sue Jones (Audrey Amore).

Sydney — "Bachelor Girl" is an affectionate, lightweight comedy about a nice Jewish girl, 32 years old and unmarried, with, as she puts it, 82 potted plants to support. She aspires to be a serious writer, but earns her money scripting a long-running soap, "In The Real World." Question is: does she need a man? Pic decides she probably doesn't, and provides some light amusement getting to the point. Best chances are for video and the tube, as this is a bit slight for theatrical playoff.

Lyn Pierse is properly bouncy as the independent Dot Bloom, whose mother is off in Nicaragua supporting the Sandinistas. Aunt Esther (Ruth Yaffe) keeps an eye on her favorite niece, and on this particular weekend invites her over for a good feed and a look at "Fiddler On The Roof" on video.

Dot has to re-write episode 491 of the soap, and declines. Enter Karl (Kim Gyngell), a long-forgotten friend from university days, an eligible, divorced lawyer. Though she's forgotten his name, Dot allows herself to be detached from her typewriter long enough for dinner and pleasant seduction, but decides next day that Karl is really a bore. Still, she joins him on a trip out of town to meet some even more boring friends, and the soap script gets even more neglected.

Drifting around on the edges of Dot's chaotic life is Alistair (Bruce Spence), a preoccupied computer buff she rather fancies; but by the time he gets round to asking her for a date (via computer, of course) she's not even aware of the offer. She knows she doesn't want Morris (Gary Samolin), the trendy gynecologist her aunt is recommending.

Rivka Hartman, who's made some award-winning short films, has come up with a charming, if decidedly thin, first feature. Good performances and some neatly written situations (especially the restaurant scene where, somehow, Dot's underpants, which have been in her pocket, get used as a napkin, only to be spirited away by an alert and sympathetic waiter) help things along. Hartman seems to be striving for a Woody Allen-type comedy (her heroine asserts that her whole aim in life is "to tell meaningful jokes"), but "Bachelor Girl," though consistently enjoyable, is all on one level, never rising to the high spots which might have taken it onto cinema screens.

Nonetheless, Hartman shows promise, and her future work should prove interesting. —*Strat.*

Cross My Heart
(COLOR)

Comedy about relationships is too slick and sanitized.

A Universal Pictures release of a Lawrence Kasdan presentation of an Aaron Spelling/Alan Greisman production. Produced by Kasdan. Coproducers, Charles Okun, Michael Grillo. Executive producers, Spelling, Greisman. Directed by Armyan Bernstein. Stars Martin Short, Annette O'Toole. Screenplay, Bernstein, Gail Parent; camera (Deluxe color), Thomas Del Ruth; editor, Mia Goldman; music, Bruce Broughton; production design, Lawrence G. Paull; art direction, Bill Elliot; set design, Nick Navarro; set decoration, Joanne Mac Dougall; costume design, Marilyn Vance-Straker; sound (Dolby), David McMillan; assistant director, Michael Grillo; casting, Wally Nicita. Reviewed at Universal Studios, Universal City, Nov. 9, 1987. (MPAA Rating: R.) Running time: **90 MINS.**

David	Martin Short
Kathy	Annette O'Toole
Bruce	Paul Reiser
Nancy	Joanna Kerns
Jessica	Jessica Puscas
Parking attendant	Lee Arenberg

Hollywood — "Cross My Heart" wants to be both cute and incisive in its presentation of an up-to-date relationship, but proves too insipid to achieve the former and too slick to fully reach the latter goal.

Conceptually ambitious in that virtually the entire film is devoted to the detailing of one date over the course of a single night, promising material would have stood a greater chance of coming to vibrant, painful life had it been more roughly made on the cheap as an independent production, rather than as a well-appointed, highly polished studio job. There are plenty of points here that will hit both the funny bones and raw nerves of young adult viewers, but overall impact is too feeble to indicate much b.o. action.

Director Armyan Bernstein, who cowrote the script with Gail Parent, clearly has lots of things to say about relations between the sexes these days. Emphasizing how the man and woman here feel compelled to put up false fronts and are afraid to just be themselves, screenplay points up the unpleasant aspects of both social and sexual intercourse in the late 1980s. Dating, the lady here says, "is no fun," although the nightmare has been considerably softened in the interests of sitcom humor and a hokey wrap-up.

David and Kathy have known each other for 17 days as the action begins on the eve of their third date. Each thinks the other is wonderful and possessed of long-range relationship potential, but, irritatingly, neither will fess up to facts that may put the other off.

David borrows his slick friend's car and ostentatious apartment for the evening and pretends to have gotten a promotion that day when the truth is he was fired. Kathy hides the fact she has a daughter and is a smoker to boot.

Roughly the first half is devoted to embarrassingly awkward and banal dating chit-chat which is all the more exasperating since the two have dated twice before and supposedly like each other a lot. It may or may not be the point that they are inclined to talk about their ideas of, and hopes for, a relationship, rather than spontaneously getting to know each other, but in any event, this didn't seem like a very successful or enjoyable night on the town to one observer.

Nevertheless, despite coy hesitation on Kathy's part, they finally bed down and supposedly enjoy themselves, only to start with the recriminations shortly thereafter. The lies are exposed, and things get so bad that Kathy brutally says, "I want to take back the sex." Thanks to a preposterous plot contrivance, the two are able to rebound from this pit of loathing, and finale would fit snugly on any episode of "Fantasy Island."

Most intriguing aspect of the venture is the compression of the tale into one night and prolonged real-time action. This approach inevitably results in some uncomfortable, recognizable moments between the characters, but Bernstein too often takes the easy way out with comedy gags to break up the tension.

In conventional terms, Martin Short and Annette O'Toole supply good characterizations which sustain one throughout the picture. However, this sort of performance piece can be so much more powerful when the actors themselves become accomplices, when one feels they have contributed at least in an improvisational sense. All the deep emotions and problems Bernstein tries to address seem thoroughly sanitized, and the raw edge of reality is never really approached.

All one has to do is compare this to the cutting, and much funnier, indie picture about misunderstandings between the sexes, "Patti Rocks," to see by how far this one misses the intended target. —*Cart.*

Chorros
(Crooks)
(ARGENTINE-COLOR)

A Sentimientos production, distributed by Magia Films. Produced by Guillermo Saura. Directed by Jorge Coscia, Saura. Stars Victor Laplace, Javier Portales, Norberto Díaz. Screenplay, Coscia, Saura, Julio Fernández

Baraibar; camera (color), Salvador Melita; editor, Darío Tedesco, Liliana Nadal; music, Leo Sujatovich; sets, Gustavo Fidler; costumes, Mónica Mendoza. Reviewed at Monumental theater, Buenos Aires, Sept. 16, 1987 (Rating in Argentina: forbidden for under 16s.) Running time: **82 MINS.**

Pablo .... Víctor Laplace
Kaplan .... Norberto Díaz
Traverso .... Hugo Arana
Piaggio .... Javier Portales
Also with: Marita Ballesteros, Rodolfo Ranni, Alberto Busaid, Mercedes Alonso.

Buenos Aires — The Coscia-Saura team, which earlier this year released its first film, "Feelings - Mirta From Liniers To Istambul," has proven its ability to work fast, turning out its second project in a little over three months.

Current product represents a complete change of tone. Where "Feelings" was an earnest, moody examination of political repression in the university and of life in the consequent exile undertaken by the heroine, the new item is an amiable caper comedy.

The setting is a banking office which the bank owners are setting up for a fraudulent bankruptcy. This kind of situation has, in real life, been experienced several times here in recent years, when apparently unstoppable inflation led some operators to all manner of financial finagling. Situation has sparked the plots for a number of Argentine films.

In the current instance, however, the emphasis is on a group of humble bank employees who — against this backdrop of high-level swindling — are severely tempted to escape their customary financial hardships, when they see a chance to stage an apparently untraceable heist. In this sense there can be easy identification with them on the part of audiences wherever the average person has difficulty making ends meet, i.e., almost everywhere.

Humor, overall, is pleasant rather than barbed. There are titillating sex scenes, sometimes veering off into laughs, and some entertainingly offbeat characters and situations. Pacing is slightly uneven. —*Olas.*

Party Camp
(COLOR)

Going through the motions.

A Lightning Pictures release of a Mark Borde production. Produced by Borde. Executive producers, Ellen Stelloff, Larry Kasanoff. Directed by Gary Graver. Screenplay, Paul L. Brown; camera (United color), Graver; editor, Michael B. Hoggan, Joyce L. Hoggan; music, Dennis Dreith; sound, David Halbert; assistant director, Joanne Knox; production manager, Shayne Sawyer; second unit director-coproducer, Kenneth M. Raich; stunt coordinator, Denny Arnold; associate producer, Colleen Meeker; casting, Michael Harrah. Reviewed on Lightning Video vidcassette, N.Y., Oct. 29, 1987. (MPAA Rating: R.) Running time: **96 MINS.**

Jerry Riviera .... Andrew Ross
Heather .... Kerry Brennan
D.A. .... Billy Jacoby
Dyanne .... Jewel Shepard
Sarge .... Peter Jason
Tad .... Kirk Cribb
Cody .... Dean R. Miller
Winslow .... Corky Pigeon
Kelly .... Stacy Baptist
Devi .... Paul Irvine
Also with: Kevin Telles, Betsy Chasse, April Wayne, Cherie Franklin, Jon Pine, Marsha McClelland.

With "Party Camp," producer Mark Borde returns to the territory he explored in 1979 with "Summer Camp," a Chuck Vincent-directed comedy which briefly shared the same title but not the b.o. results with Ivan Reitman's smash "Meatballs." New pic, under director-lenser Gary Graver, is yet another "Meatballs" clone with t&a added.

Episodic format is set at Camp Chipmunk where Andrew Ross is a horny counselor whose dream girl is camp lifeguard Kerry Brennan. Mostly stillborn gags revolve around sexy counselor Jewel Shepard (who overacts throughout), dominatrix-nurse April Wayne and computer nerd Corky Pigeon. Excuse for a plot cornily pits Ross' squad of nerdy campers called squirrels vs. a bunch of campers of the jock variety called falcons. Surprise: the nerds get their revenge.

Tech credits are fine and cast goes through the paces with vigor. Pic opened on a regional basis this past summer via Vestron's Lightning Pictures subsidiary. —*Lor.*

Ghost Fever
(COLOR)

Antiquated ethnic comedy.

A Miramax Films release of an Infinite production. (World sales, Kodiak Films.) Executive producers, Wolf Schmidt, Kenneth Johnston. Produced by Ron Rich, Edward Coe. Directed by "Alan Smithee" (Lee Madden). Stars Sherman Hemsley, Luis Avalos. Screenplay, Oscar Brodney, Rich, Richard Egan; camera (color), Xavier Cruz Ruvalcaba; editor, Earl Watson; supervising editor, James Ruxin; music, James Hart; sound, Manuel Rincon; production design, Dora Corona; production manager, Jorge Camargo; special effects, Miguel Vasquez; animation, Jorge Perez; boxing staged by Rich. Reviewed on Charter Entertainment vidcassette, N.Y., Nov. 2, 1987. (MPAA Rating: PG.) Running time: **86 MINS.**

Buford/Jethro .... Sherman Hemsley
Benny Alvarez .... Luis Avalos
Madame St. Esprit .... Jennifer Rhodes
Linda .... Deborah Benson
Lisa .... Diana Brookes
Andrew Lee .... Myron Healey
Beauregard/
  Sheriff .... Pepper Martin
Tucker .... Joe Frazier
Tucker's manager ...... Kenneth Johnston

"Ghost Fever" is an earnest but unsuccessful attempt to resurrect the 1940s style of comedy associated with Abbott & Costello. Heavy dose of strained ethnic humor was released on a regional basis last March and is now a homevido item.

Sherman Hemsley and Luis Avalos portray Buford and Benny, a pair of cops sent to evict two old ladies from their ante bellum mansion. The place is haunted by a spirit of Beauregard, an evil former slave owner (film's previous title was

"Benny And Buford Meet The Bigoted Ghost"), who pulls practical jokes on the hapless heroes, while they dally with the beautiful blond great-granddaughters of Beauregard. Commenting on the action are two other ghosts, Andy, played by Myron Healey, who is Beauregard's son and Jethro, Buford's ancestor (dual role for Hemsley).

Shenanigans climax pointlessly with Benny agreeing to fight ex-champ Terrible Tucker (played by former Heavyweight champ Joe Frazier) in order to raise money to save the mansion. Predictably dumb finish has the heroes better off dead.

Though Hemsley and Avalos are adequate farceurs, the material is lame and only interesting on a poor taste level (endless dialog referring to "spooks" and a wacky scene of Hemsley reading an illustrated Victorian-era porn tome entitled "Groins Of The Darker Species"). Pic was directed in Mexico in 1984 by Lee Madden, but anonymous later shooting caused him to have his name removed and the fictitious Alan Smithee credited. —*Lor.*

Thessaloniki Film Reviews

Vios Ke Politia
(Living Dangerously)
(GREEK-COLOR)

A Greek Film Center-Stefi II-Home Video Hellas-Spentzos Film and Nicos Perakis coproduction. Written and directed by Nicos Perakis. Camera (color), George Panoussopoulos; editor, Yannis Tsitsopoulos; music, Nicos Mamagakis; sets and costumes, Aphroditi Kotzia; sound, Nicos Achladis. Reviewed at the Thessaloniki Film Festival, Oct. 10, 1987. Running time: **105 MINS.**

Karamanos .... Giorgos Kimoulis
Director of Communi-
  cations .... Dimitris Kalivocas
Minister .... Timos Perlemgas
Also with: Giorgos Kotanides, Pavlos Kontoyannidis, Vana Barba, Takis Mosvhos, Dimitris Poulicacos, Alkis Panayotidis, Anna Makraki, Thanassis Papageorgiou.

Thessaloniki — Nicos Perakis, one of the few Greek directors whose films have broken records at the b.o., scores again with another comedy satirizing sharply the conditions and happenings inside certain Civil Services and Organizations. Though it did not win any prize his film was the most applauded one by the festival audience. It is a witty satire full of humor and droll situations, skillfully made. It has tremendous exploitation prospects locally and good chances abroad.

The story is set inside the building of the Greek Telecommunications Organization and especially in the office of its director. One morning Karamanos, an employee enters this office with an explosive device and connects it to the director's personal computer. Karamanos demands to appear on tv before the final match of the World Soccer Cup is broadcast, threatening to blow up the building's Telecommunications, tv and satellite installations. He wants to denounce the Goverment's policy.

The director, trying to play for time, does not refuse directly, while the prosecution authorities launch a widespread hunt to track down other members of Karamanos' organization. Many former colleagues of Karamanos in the army are summoned to persuade him to abandon his plan. When the investigation fails to come up with any incriminating

evidence, police psychologists are recruited to deal with Karamanos. He surprises them in the end.

Perakis directs crisply, with good pace and rounded characters.

Acting as a whole is good, particularly the key performance of Giorgos Kimoulis. It has good lensing, editing and other technical credits are tops. —*Rena.*

O Paradisos Anigi
Me Antiklidi
(Red Ants/Pass Key To Paradise)
(GREEK-COLOR)

A Greek Film Center and Ann Film EPE production. Executive producer, Nicos Yannopoulos. Written and directed by Vassilis Buduris. Camera (color), Christos Chassapis; editor, Andreas Tsilifonis; music, Mivhalis Gregoriou; sets and costumes, Miltiades Mackris. Reviewed at the Thessaloniki Film Festival, Oct. 7, 1987. Running time: **93 MINS.**

Crippled Acrobat .... Ian Dury
Hara (Joy) .... Cassavdra Voyatzi
Her Brother .... Stephanos Elliot
Their friend .... Nicos Melas
Their mother .... Lydis Lenossi
(English soundtrack)

Thessaloniki — Vassilis Buduris, after directing films mostly for tv, presents a naive but moving feature film in an English version with Greek subtitles. His efforts, using a foreign actor and English dialog, apparently were poured into getting his picture to look like a foreign film with the idea of appealing to an international audience. Film, in spite of its serious shortcomings, comes off fairly well and could attract limited international attention with proper handling.

Story involves three youngsters: Hara, a penniless but proud girl of 12, her younger brother and their friend, a boy of 13. They are three runaway teenagers wandering all day in the streets. Their castle is an abandoned bus and their realm the inhospitable city. Hara's mother was a whore, who chased her children out of the house.

The three youngsters find a fake gun and use it like a real one whenever they are in danger. For them everything is a game, even stealing for food, but grownups think differently. The only person who really befriends them is a crippled acrobat who gambles with death everyday when his girl floats in an air balloon.

When Hara is arrested stealing a pair of shoes for her friend, the acrobat helps the boys get Hara out of the hands of the police, escaping through an underground tunnel. Before the police can get them, the acrobat puts them in his balloon, which floats in the sky.

Buduris knows how to handle his story but it is rather a modest effort. Aiming it at young audiences mostly may hold their attention but he does not make it effective dramatically.

British rocker Ian Dury delivers a stunning performance as the crippled acrobat and the rest of the cast is adequate.

Lensing, editing and music have much to commend them and all other technical credits are fairly good. —Rena.

Theofilos
(GREEK-COLOR)

A Greek Film Center and Costas Papastathis production. Written and directed by Lakis Papastathis. Camera (color), Theodoros Margas; editor, Vaguelis Toussias; music, George Papadakis; sets and costumes; Julia Stavridou; sound, Dinos Kittou, Yannis Eliopoulos. Reviewed at the Thessaloniki Film Festival, Oct. 8, 1987. Running time: 133 MINS.
Theofilos . . . . Demetris Katalifis
Therian . . . . Stamatis Fassoulis
Stratis Eleftheriadis . . Theodoros Exarchos

Thessaloniki — This is a biography of a famous primitive Greek painter which won three prizes at the festival including best picture (shared), best actor and sets & costumes.

It is a specialized folklore picture with an exceptional plastic beauty which, in spite of its weaknesses, may have an easy passage at the b.o. locally and fair prospects abroad if carefully handled and placed.

Theofilos was born in Lesvos island in 1868. After his discharge from the Army in Athens he returned to Lesvos and began to paint. An ardent lover of Greek traditions he abandoned European clothing and wore the Greek costume of *Fustanella* as did his fellow countrymen. The immortal Greek heroes were the subjects of his paintings from Alexander the Great to his contemporary heroes and characters of his home country.

His refusal to compromise was the reason he was unknown during his lifetime. He was discovered by a French art critic who made him known to the world posthumously.

Director Lakis Papastathis does a good job directing this film, neatly describing the historic environment which inspired his hero. His passion for the maintenance of Greek customs, which are running the risk of

being altered by foreign influences, is obvious throughout the film.

Working with care each segment of his picture has the actors placed according to the paintings of Theofilos, with a result that enriches the film.

Demetris Katalifis in the title role turns out an impressive and sensitive portrayal of the artist.

The picture is also greatly enhanced by the wonderful work of cameraman Theodoros Margas. Another winner is Julia Stavridou for the wonderful costumes. All other technical credits are very good.
—Rena.

Ta Pedia Tis Chelidonas
(The Children Of The Swallow)
(GREEK-COLOR)

A Greek Film Center-Costas Vretacos-ERT I production. Directed by Costas Vretacos. Screenplay, Vretacos, Soula Dracopoulou, based on the novel by Dionyssis Chronopoulos; camera (color), Aris Stavrou; editor, Christos Sarantzoglou; music, George Tsangaris; sound, Marinos Athanassopoulos; art direction, Thalia Itsicopoulou; costumes, Fanni Tsouloyanni. Reviewed at the Thessaloniki Film Festival, Oct. 10, 1987. Running time: 118 MINS.
Markianos . . . . Alecos Alexandrakis
Iason . . . . Stephanos Leneos
Spyros . . . . Vassilis Diamantopoulos
Fotini . . . . Mary Chronopoulou
Sotiris . . . . Stephanos Lionakis
Panos . . . . Elias Logothetis
Anguelos . . . . Lefteris Voyatzis
Akrivi . . . . Maria Martica

Thessaloniki — With this, his first long feature film, Costas Vretacos swept many prizes at the Thessaloniki Film Festival, including best picture (shared), screenplay (shared), best actress, best supporting actor and sound. It is a well-made dramatic rendering of the recent period in Greece presented in an original manner and style, not confined just to Greek audiences.

The plot introduces a young tv director looking for the members of a family for a tv serial, six brothers and sisters scattered to the four corners of the earth. The German occupation, the civil war and the junta had forced them to leave their village and go to Athens, Canada and Germany. The director is helped by an old journalist who had kept old interviews in his file. Events are related from a different angle by each one, except Anguelos, who refuses to speak and who lives in isolation in a place accessible only by sea.

On a second trip both director and journalist ask again for their views on the occasion of the family gathering for dividing a paternal property, but the story is not completed, again.

On the occasion of the sudden death of Anguelos the family is reunited and the director and journalist, accompanied by the tv crew try to tie up the threads. The reunion scene turns out to be a display of personal and political passions.

Vretacos, filmmaker of docu-

mentary films in the past, with this long feature film succeeds in translating into cinematic terms old incidents without the use of flashbacks. His film depicts well the dramatic events and turmoil that swept the country through the German occupation, the civil war and junta. There is an uncomfortable ring of truth apparent throughout, even to those without any intimation of the time and its historical aspects. For the dramatic incidents of the story, he gave the chance to many good thesps to turn in solid performances, like Mary Chronopoulou, winner of the best actress prize, Vassilis Diamantopoulos, best supporting actor, Maria Martica, best supporting actress, Alecos Alexandrakis, Stephanos Leneos and the rest of the cast.

The photography by Aris Stavrou is splendid and all other technical credits are good.—Rena.

O Archangelos Tou Pathous
(Potlatch)
(GREEK-COLOR)

A Greek Film Center and Nicos Verguitsis production. Written and directed by Verguitsis. Camera (color), Andreas Bellis; editor, Yannis Tsitsopoulos; music, Demitris Papademetriou; art direction, Lili Pezanou; sound, Paul le Mare. Reviewed at the Thessaloniki Film Festival, Oct. 6, 1987. Running time: 105 MINS.
Aris . . . . Antonis Kafetzopoulos
Aphrodite . . . . Isabel Otero
Grégoire . . . . Patrick Bauchau
Katerina . . . . Olia Lazaridou
(Greek and English soundtrack)

Thessaloniki — This picture from a filmmaker whose previous work had won prizes, was awaited with great expectations, not fully realized. It's a psychological drama (with a lot of erotic passion) with a hero playing a mental game which may not interest the average viewer. It was awarded four prizes by the festival jury. Meant for an international audience with half the dialog in English, it may have a good chance abroad with proper handling as well as in the local market for sophisticated audiences.

Aris, a young composer, falls in love with Aphrodite, a 14-year-old French girl sole survivor of an airplane accident. Twelve years later Aris' girl friend dies and, feeling responsible for her death he makes a deal with himself: to commit suicide if before his birthday in one month he doesn't hear the word "passion" spoken by a woman. He goes to Paris to meet Aphrodite.

She is 26 now, married to Grégoire, a 50-year-old art critic. Aris befriends them and moves into their house. He wins the sympathy and trust of Grégoire. According to an Indian tradition, (of "potlatch"), when a gift is given to a rival it must be destroyed immediately. So Grégoire sacrifices himself for Aris. Aphrodite is now a dangerous rival, and Aris' hunt for passion turns out to be a deadly game. He composes

a requiem, "The Death Of Aphrodite," and decides to go through with his deal, knowing Aphrodite will never say the word "passion," yet a few hours are left till his birthday.

Nicos Verguitsis fails to create an atmosphere to justify the agony of the man and the price of passion, which is supposed to be his life. The reasons for such a price are not defined clearly, leaving the audience guessing.

Verguitsis is helped, however, by his players. Antonis Kafetzopoulos' performance is worthy of mention as is Olia Lazaridou's (his girl). She won the prize for best supporting actress.

The visual treats offered by director of photography Andreas Bellis are an asset to the picture as is the music by Demitris Papademetriou, for which he won a prize. Editing by Yannis Tsitsoppulos and makeup by Theano Kapnia also won prizes.
—Rena.

Proini Peripolos
(Morning Patrol)
(GREEK-COLOR)

A Greek Film Center and Nicos Nicolaidis production. Written and directed by Nicolaidis. Camera (color), Dinos Katsouridis; editor, Andreas Andreadakis; sets and costumes; Marie Louise Vartholomeou, music, George Hatzinassios; sound, Elias Ionesco, Sivilla Katsouridi, Thanassis Amanitis. Reviewed at the Thessaloniki Film Festival, Oct. 9, 1987. Running time: 108 MINS.
The Woman . . . . Michelle Valley
The Man . . . . Takis Spyridakis

Thessaloniki — This picture confirms Nicos Nicolaidis as one of the top Greek helmers. He has made three previous pictures in the past for which he won prizes, but this one marks a turning point, dealing with an international subject. It is one of the most impressive films of the festival and it could find its own audiences at home and abroad.

A deserted city is the setting where a woman walks alone trying to approach and enter the forbidden zone. Traps and the Morning Patrol lurk everywhere. Electronic voices summon the (nonexistent) people to abandon the city. The tv screens present old movies with famous stars. Not a human being is seen, only the woman walking, remembering phrases of books she had read like "Rebecca" by Daphne du Maurier and "The Big Sleep" by Raymond Chandler.

A man suddenly appears to chase her, but finally tries to help her. They come close together, trying to remember what happened, while the menacing noose tightens around them. Will their love story have a future?

Nicolaidis shared the prize for best director at the festival, but refused to accept it. His film is a skillful effort which shows professional knowhow. The story unfolds forcefully at a good pace and mounting suspense, though the first part is uneventful. Some influences of the works of Tarkovsky and others are evident, but Nicolaidis maintains his personal touch.

Most of the story's impact is on the shoulders of Michelle Valley and she carries it well, as does Takis Spyridakis. Camerawork by Dinos Katsouridis is impressive as are the sets by Marie Louise Vartholomeou. Musical score by George Hatzinassios establishes the desired mood and atmosphere.

All other credits are top rate.
— *Rena*.

O Klios
(The Noose)
(GREEK-COLOR)

A Greek Film Center-ERT Land Profit Ltd. production. Produced and directed by Costas Koutsomytis. Screenplay, Vaguelis Goufas, Koutsomytis, assisted by George Bramos; camera (color), Nicos Smaragdis; editor, Panos Papakyriacopoulos; music, Argyris Kounadis; sets and costumes, Rena Georgiadou; sound, Argyris Lazaridis. Reviewed at the Thessaloniki Film Festival, Oct. 5, 1987. Running time: **120 MINS.**
With; as the six boys: Gerasimos Skiadaressis, Dinitris Karabetsis, Aeas Manthopoulos, Stelios Pavlou, Socrates Alafouzos, Vladimiros Kyriakides; as pilots, authorities, passengers: Timos Perlengas, Christos Kalavrouzos, Theodoros Exarchos, Giorgos Moschidis, Anna Fonsou, George Michlacopoulos, Kyriacos Katrivanos, Antonis Katsaris.

Thessaloniki — "The Noose" is based on a real event, reportedly the first airplane hijacking ever, at the time of World War II considered a daredevil action. Well made by Costas Koutsomytis, this film is an action thriller full of suspense which will have very good prospects locally and equal chances abroad.

The central characters of the story are six young boys who live in Thessaloniki, during the Civil War in Greece. Terrorism is prevailing everywhere, with murders in the night, thousands of arrests, court martials and exile. Many of their friends are arrested and the noose is tightening around them.

The six boys decide to go to Athens where nobody knows them. A hijacking is their only way to freedom. As passengers on board an airplane flying to Thessaloniki, force the pilot to change course and land in a nearby foreign state. Both passengers and crew are afraid to resist. The foreign land is almost hostile, but finally they are smuggled out at night to join the fighting rebels in the mountains.

Costas Koutsomytis prefers to make his picture more like political drama than action thriller, but in the end it's a combination of both. He creates the right atmosphere and conditions prevailing at the time in this country and weaves his plot with a fast pace.

Koutsomytis used new players for the roles of the six hijackers and managed to get convincing performances from them. They won an honorary citation for their acting.

The photography by Nicos Smaragdis, musical score by Argyris Kounadis, crisp editing by Panos Papakyriacopoulos, plus sets and costumes by Rena Georgiadou are great assets for the picture.
—*Rena*.

Genethlia Poli
(Birthday Town)
(GREEK-COLOR)

A Greek Film Center and Takis Papayannidis production. Directed by Papayannidis. Screenplay, Papayannidis, Thanassis Valtinos; camera (color), Lefteris Pavlopoulos; editor, Yannis Tsitsopoulos; music, Thomas Sliomis; sound, Nicos Achladis; sets and costumes, Simos Karafylis. Reviewed at the Thessaloniki Film Festival, Oct. 7, 1987. Running time: **85 MINS.**
Christos . . . . .Takis Moschos
Anna . . . . .Michelle Valley
Elena . . . . .Tatiana Papamoschou
Kosmas . . . . .Costas Tsapecos

Thessaloniki — "Birthday Town" is the third picture by Takis Papayannidis and is slightly better than his previous ones. It is a psychological suspenser made skillfully but lacking the deeper insight to give it a dramatic bite.

The central character is Christos, a businessman who visits his hometown, Thessaloniki, after many years. Inner problems torment him and he hopes his old friends and family will help him to solve them. No one understands or suspects his condition or can be of any real help.

His friend Anna lives a conventional life and Kosmas is busy preparing a historical show. Christos meets Elena, a young student and actress in the show, and soon becomes a member of the company. When Elena refuses to leave the city with him, the conflict that tormented him becomes more acute.

He again feels the inner void he had before his arrival, seeing that the values he believed in were altered or lost.

This film shows Papayannidis' directorial know-how, but is based on a weak script, full of emotional monotony. Trying to include the past with the present in an original way, using parallel shots, he creates the right atmosphere, which is to the film's credit, but it is not adequate to make it successful.

Photography by Lefteris Pavlopoulos makes the city part of the plot. Music by Thomas Sliomis and editing by Yannis Tsitsopoulos are tops.

Acting as a whole is good, particularly the key performance by Takis Moschos. All other technical credits are above standard. —*Rena*.

Oniro Aristeris Nichtas
(A Leftist Night's Dream)
(GREEK-COLOR)

A Greek Film Center and Kinotek production. Written and directed by Dinos Katsouridis, Nicos Kalogeropoulos. Camera (color), Katsouridis; editor, Katsouridis; sets and

costumes, Yannis Lekkos; sound, Giorgos Theodoropoulos. Reviewed at the Thessaloniki Film Festival, Oct. 9, 1987. Running time: **106 MINS.**
Polychronis . . . . .Nicos Kalogeropoulos
Also with: Tavyeti Basouri, Dimitris Katsimanis, Christine Avlianou, Costas Daliania, Mina Chimona, Melina Botelli, Giorgos Kendros, Dimitra Zeza, Andreas Varouchas.

Thessaloniki — This is a bitter comedy which start as a satire and ends up dramatically. Its first half is especially well made with a good pace and clear flashbacks. Last half fails on many levels; its story a surface criticism of political and social conditions. Nicos Kalogeropoulos, coauthor and codirector of the picture besides being its leading actor, charges codirector Dinos Katsouridis for spiking it. This dispute harmed the film and reduced its chances in the local market. Foreign prospects are also limited.

The story concerns Polychronis, a young man from a country village living in Athens. He struggled for freedom and democracy and now is sorry all his old collaborators and friends have settled down, forgetting the ideas they believed in. He sees them collaborating with the Establishment against which they had fought in the past.

He refuses to follow their example, but realizes the dream he had fought for has vanished. How can he live without it?

The directors avoided the use of easy comic scenes to express their political criticism. Everything is criticized in this picture but not sharply. Its satire does not substantially touch the heart of each matter. It's surface only.

Nicos Kalogeropoulos turns in an excellent, moving characterization as the main hero. The photography and editing by Dinos Katsouridis have his professional mark and all other technical credits are tops.
—*Rena*.

---

120 Decibels
(GREEK-COLOR)

A Greek Film Center-Sigma Film and ERT I production. Written and directed by Vassilis Vafeas. Camera (color), Dinos Katsouridis; editor, Katsouridis; sets, Damianos Zarifis; sound, Giorgos Theodoropoulos. Reviewed at the Thessaloniki Film Festival, Oct. 6, 1987. Running time: **90 MINS.**
Nassos .Haris Sozos
Aleca . . . . .Kariofilia Karabeti
Ersi . . . . .Aneza Papadopoulou
Rea . . . . .Roubini Vassilacopoulou
Mary . . . . .Athena Tsilyra
Yannis . . . . .Alkis Papayotidis
With special appearances by: Nellie Amguelidou, Dora Volanaki, Theodora Proussalis, Costas Voutsas.

Thessaloniki — This is the fourth picture by Vassilis Vafeas, whose previous work dealt with a man in relation with his job. It is a bitter satire on the feelings of people, a critical look at human relations of today. It is not a picture that can be easily assimilated by an average filmgoer. It needs careful handling

and launching in the local market, much more abroad.

"120 Decibels" measures the sound level of the siren of an ambulance which carries Nassos, a young man, to a hospital. He is in critical condition after an accident.

With Nassos in a coma all his friends rush to the hospital. Waiting outside his ward they try to remember the moments they had spent together, wishing to understand their friend better as well as their own actions. It is a game of remembrances full of guilt but seen from a funny side, while death lurks in the ward.

Vassilis Vafeas, making great use of flashbacks, weaves a complex plot, but fails to clearly identify the story's characters and their relations. This leads occasionally to confusion.

Dinos Katsouridis' photography and editing are excellent and the costumes by Damianos Zarifis are worthy of mention. All other technical credits are adequate. — *Rena*.

Planes, Trains & Automobiles
(COLOR)

Hughes hits mark with comic travelog; big biz looms.

A Paramount release. Produced, written and directed by John Hughes. Executive producers, Michael Chinich, Neil Machlis. Camera (Technicolor), Don Peterman; editor, Paul Hirsch; music, Ira Newborn; production design, John W. Corso; art direction, Harold Michelson; set design, Louis Mann; set decoration, Jane Bogart, Linda Spheeris; costume design, April Ferry; sound (Dolby), James Alexander; associate producer, Bill Brown; assistant director, Mark Radcliffe; casting, Janet Hirshenson, Jane Jenkins. Reviewed at the Village Theater, L.A., Nov. 17, 1987. (MPAA Rating: R) Running time: **93 MINS.**

Neal Page	Steve Martin
Del Griffith	John Candy
Susan Page	Laila Robbins
State Trooper	Michael McKean
Taxi Racer	Kevin Bacon
Owen	Dylan Baker
Joy	Carol Bruce
Marti	Olivia Burnette
Peg	Diana Douglas
Boss	William Windom
Motel Clerk	Martin Ferrero
Doobie	Larry Hankin
Walt	Richard Herd
Waitress	Susan Kellerman
Little Neal	Matthew Lawrence
Car Rental Agent	Edie McClurg
Martin	George O. Petrie
Motel Thief	Gary Riley
Gus	Charles Tyner

Hollywood — Moving away from his beloved teenagers for the first time, John Hughes has come up with an effective nightmare-as-comedy in "Planes, Trains & Automobiles." Disaster-prone duo of Steve Martin and John Candy repeatedly recall a contemporary Laurel & Hardy as they agonizingly try to make their way from New York to Chicago by various modes of transport, and their clowning sparks enough yocks to position this as a strong performer for Paramount through the holiday season.

Man versus technology has been one of the staples of screen comedy since the earliest silent days, and Hughes makes the most of the format here while combining it with a contest of wills between a pushy, obnoxious salesman and a mild-mannered regular guy who invites being put-upon. Hughes packs as many of the frustrations of modern life as he can into this calamitous travelog of roadside America. Fact that he goes all soft and mushy at the end probably will only further endear audiences to the picture.

An ultimate situation comedy, tale throws together Martin, an ad exec, and Candy, a shower curtain ring salesman, as they head home from Manhattan to their respective homes in Chicago two days before Thanksgiving.

The problems start before they even get out of midtown, but the unimaginable begins happening when O'Hare, everybody's favorite airport, gets socked in by weather and the boys' flight is diverted to Wichita, of all places.

From there, it's a series of ghastly motel rooms, crowded anonymous restaurants, a sinister cab ride, an abortive train trip, an even worse excursion by rented car, some hitchhiking by truck, and, finally, a hop on the "El" before sitting down to turkey.

Virtually from the first, Candy gloms onto Martin and, like a drooling, slurping, smelly St. Bernard, never lets the willing victim out of his sight. When he's finally had too much after sharing the last spare bed in Kansas with his hulking companion, Martin lets loose a barrage of abuse, but this only results in a better understanding between the two, and is only the first of several occasions upon which Martin insists upon going his own way, only to guiltily reconcile later on.

Premise is both loaded with opportunities and thinly artificial, but Hughes for the most part comes out on the plus side, keeping things moving at a tremendous clip as if knowing that to let down for even a moment would make it extremely difficult to get the film moving again.

Picture has a very healthy quota of laughs stemming from all-too-recognizable real-life dilemmas, and so works on a dual basis of instant, nodding identification and "there-but-for-the-grace-of-God-go-I" comic horror.

Centerstage thoughout, the two stars have plenty of opportunity to shine, although it's the ever-pushy Candy who makes things happen with his relentless character. Martin is forced into a more reactive, subdued mode than is usual, but some of his agonizing and outbursts call to mind Cary Grant's elegant squirming in Howard Hawks' comedies of anxiety and frustration.

All technical work is crisp, and Hughes, as he did in "Sixteen Candles," has a field day with goofy, exaggerated sound effects. For the record, this is the second film Hughes has shot since "Ferris Bueller's Day Off," but the one in between, "She's Having A Baby," will not be released until next year. — *Cart.*

Deadly Prey
(COLOR)

Quickie survival pic.

An Action Intl. Pictures production. Produced by Peter Yuval. Executive producers, David Winters, Bruce Lewin. Written and directed by David A. Prior. Camera (United color), Stephen A. Blake; editor, Brian Evans; music, Steve McClintock, Tim James, Tim Heintz; sound, David Eddy; assistant director, Thomas Baldwin; production manager, Peter Spring; stunt coordinator, Fritz Matthews; associate producers, Don Crowell Jr., Jon Mercedes 3d. Reviewed on Sony Video Software vidcassette, N.Y., Oct. 31, 1987. (No MPAA Rating.) Running time: **88 MINS.**

Jaimy's dad	Cameron Mitchell
Don Michaelson	Troy Donahue
Michael Danton	Ted Prior
Lt. Thornton	Fritz Matthews
Col. Hogan	David Campbell
Sybil	Dawn Abraham
Cooper	William Zipp
Jaimy	Suzzane Tara

"Deadly Prey," a direct-to-video quickie, begins as the umpteenth imitation of "The Most Dangerous Game" and ends up as an exercise in survival out of the Cornel Wilde filmmaking school.

Ted Prior plays the muscular hero, shanghaied by goons in a black van while taking out the garbage one morning. He's needed as a runner, i.e., human target, for military training exercises run by Col. Hogan (David Campbell), who demands realism to get his mercenaries up to scratch.

Too bad for Hogan that Prior coincidentally is the best man he ever trained, so instead of just giving the recruits a run for their money, Prior kills them all one by one. His father-in-law, played by Cameron Mitchell, also comes to the rescue and nearly everyone's in a body bag by the time of the corny ending, a freeze-frame as Prior reverses roles with Campbell.

Filmmaker David A. Prior believes in simple, no-nonsense action, i.e., cheap and uninteresting. Running around a wooded area in Riverside, Calif. makes for dull footage and the cast is wooden. Besides Mitchell's walkthrough, Troy Donahue pops up in a couple of scenes in the nothing role of Campbell's financial backer. There's plenty of gore but no nudity, despite several script opportunities. —*Lor.*

Three Men And A Baby
(COLOR)

Fluffy remake of French hit is hard to dislike.

A Buena Vista release from Touchstone Pictures, in association with Silver Screen Partners III, of a Jean-François Lepitit/Interscope Communications production. Produced by Ted Field, Robert W. Cort, coproduced by Edward Teets. Executive producer by Jean-Francois Lepetit. Directed by Leonard Nimoy. Screenplay, James Orr, Jim Cruickshank based on the French film "Trois Hommes et un Couffin" by Coline Serreau; camera (Deluxe color), Adam Greenberg; editor, Michael A. Stevenson; music, Marvin Hamlisch; production design, Peter Larkin; art direction, Dan Yarhi; set decoration, Hilton Rosemarin; costumes, Larry Wells; sound (Dolby), Mark Mangini; assistant director, Robert Cowan; second unit director, Joseph Reidy; second unit camera, Michael Green; casting, Dianne Crittenden. Reviewed at the Avco Theater, L.A., Nov. 16, 1987. (MPAA Rating: PG.) Running time: **102 MINS.**

Peter	Tom Selleck
Michael	Steve Guttenberg
Jack	Ted Danson
Sylvia	Nancy Travis
Rebecca	Margaret Colin
Detective Melkowitz	Philip Bosco
Baby (Mary)	Lisa Blair, Michelle Blair

Also with: Celeste Holm, Paul Guilfoyle, Cynthia Harris, Derek de Lint.

Hollywood — "Three Men And A Baby" is about as slight a feature comedy as is made — while at the same time it's hard to resist Tom Selleck, Ted Danson and Steve Guttenberg shamelessly going goo-goo over caring for an infant baby girl all swaddled in pink. It's sitcom stuff of the infectious sort with sure-fire commercial appeal to return more theatrical coin to Disney coffers.

This is an Americanized version of the French sleeper hit "Trois Hommes et un Couffin" and parallels the original's storyline almost exactly.

The lives of three confirmed bachelors — the studly sort who live, play and scheme on voluptuous women together — is thrown into confusion when a baby is left at their front door. As it happens, actor and suspected father of the infant (Danson) is coveniently out of town on a shoot, leaving architect and super pushover Peter (Selleck) and cartoonist Michael (Guttenberg) all in a quandary what to do with the precious little thing.

As a plot device, and a pretty ridiculous one at that, Selleck and Guttenberg mistakenly believe the baby is the same "package" Danson told them to expect from a director friend, which they soon find out is really a second delivery of ... heroin.

As the baby crimps these swingers' style on the home front, an undercover cop and two drug dealers are putting the squeeze on them on the outside — all quite silly and never appearing the least bit life-threatening but serving to inject some action into what would otherwise be a series of cute scenes with baby.

Big macho men tripping all over themselves trying to successfully feed, diaper and bathe a bundle of innocence and helplessness is ripe for comic development, and it certainly helps that these three are having a blast seeing it through.

For the most part, the setups are expected; it's the delivery and the actors' charms that work as the key ingredients to make this formula work. Even the hardest of hearts couldn't help but go soft watching these three harmonize "Good Night Sweetheart" to get baby to sleep. Alternate this sort of treacle with inoffensive poop jokes and the whole effect is amusing.

Filmmakers surely didn't lose sight of the potential audience. Domesticity in their ultra-designed Manhattan apartment wins out over 1-night stands with the babes — and that image is sure to strike a soothing chord with (mostly female) baby boom generation types.

Film is a good showcase for the comic abilities of this threesome, all of whom seem to have their 1-liner timing down pat.

Director Leonard Nimoy moves things along at a clip. His touch is light and airy, as it should be for this kind of fluff.

Scripters James Orr and Jim Cruickshank ("Tough Guys") have turned this effort into a very successful vehicle for the stars, appropriately writing dialog to suit each of the actors' personalities. Selleck, more often than not, is the Big Daddy, Danson the irresponsible charmer and Guttenberg the most naive. Danson, more than the others, appears self-conscious.

Adam Greenberg's lensing is fine, especially considering the too-busy sets he had to shoot in. Other tech credits are good. —*Brit.*

The Video Dead
(COLOR)

A Manson Intl. presentation of an Interstate 5 production, in association with Highlight Prods. Written, produced and directed by Robert Scott. Camera (color), Greg Becker; editor, Bob Sarles; music, Stuart Rabinowitsch, Leonard Marcel, Kevin McMahon; sound, Joshua Stein; production design, Katalin Rogers; set decoration, Elizabeth Bordock; Katalin Rogers; production manager, Jacques Thelemaque; assistant director, Billy Washington; special visual effects, Dale Hall Jr.; associate producer, William S. Weiner. Reviewed on Embassy Home Ent. vidcassette, N.Y., Nov. 11, 1987. (MPAA Rating: R.) Running time: **90 MINS.**

Zoe Blair . . . . Roxanna Augesen
Jeff Blair . . . . Rocky Duvall
April . . . . Vickie Bastel
Joshua Daniels . . . . Sam David McClelland
Henry Jordan . . . . Michael St. Michaels
The Woman . . . . Jennifer Miro
The Garbageman . . . . Cliff Watts

Living up to its title, "The Video Dead" is debuting domestically on vidcassette. This cheesy 1986 horror production is an amateurish imitation of George A. Romero and various Italian zombie epics.

A black & white tv set is mistakenly delivered to a writer (Michael St. Michaels). It plays a movie "Zombie Blood Nightmare," whose undead cast walk out of the tv screen and gorily kill people.

The new inhabitants of the writer's house, siblings Rocky Duvall and Roxanna Augesen, are in danger, but the zombies go after their neighbors instead. A goofball from Texas, Sam David McClelland, arrives to join up with Duvall to hunt the ghouls, but only Augesen is left alive. Attempted irony of the finale (her parents bring the deadly tv set to her in her hospital room) falls flat.

Pic adds little to the screen lore of zombies, as script contradictorily indicates methods of dealing with the troublesome creatures, ranging from homilies "Don't show any fear") to ineffectual concepts, e.g., use conventional killing methods because the zombies *think* they're still alive. Makeup effects are weak and acting likewise. —*Lor.*

I Miei Primi Quarant'Anni
(My First Forty Years)
(ITALIAN-COLOR)

A Columbia Pictures release of a C.G. Silver production in association with Reteitalia. Produced by Mario and Vittorio Cecchi Gori. Directed by Carlo Vanzina. Stars Carol Alt. Screenplay, Enrico Vanzina, Carlo Vanzina, based on the book by Marina Ripa di Meana; camera (Eastmancolor, color by Technicolor), Luigi Kuveiller; editor, Ruggero Mastroianni; music, Umberto Smaila; art direction, Mario Chiari. Reviewed at Quirinale Cinema, Rome, Nov. 13, 1987. Running time: **106 MINS.**

Marina . . . . Carol Alt
Editor . . . . Elliott Gould
Duke . . . . Jean Rochefort
Count . . . . Pierre Cosso

Rome — Director-scripter brothers Carlo and Enrico Vanzina have a reputation for youth-oriented pics that find favor at the boxoffice. "My First Forty Years" should enhance their domestic following as it damns them further with the critics. Tackling the scandalous, autobiographical bestseller by jet set socialite Marina Ripa di Meana, "Years" covers Italo high-life as it sweetly varies through the '60s, '70s and '80s with plenty of gusto but little art, or even basic craft. The material is racy enough, but sloppy scripting and technical work thwart a film stuffed with missed opportunities. Those unacquainted with the well-publicized adventures of the lady in question may find the whole thing unentertaining.

The idea seems to be to do a bedroom version of "Lifestyles Of The Rich And Famous." Playing the authoress, former fashion model Carol Alt brings high spirits and a beautiful face to the proceedings, which begin when Marina is a teenager circa 1962. Her well-to-do parents are no match for the headstrong girl who flashes from erotic games with the family maid to full-fledged sexual initiation at the hands of an indolent teenage count (Pierre Cosso, epitome of screen lethargy). The young couple marry and Marina goes to work as a dress designer to support them, but the more successful her designs, the more her husband beats her. She tearfully moves out with a daughter.

Though Marina claims she yearns for a man's arms, she partners with a sexless Duke (Jean Rochefort), who flaunts her to his friends. His millions aren't enough, and after a series of awkward scenes showing jet set life (doubles for Ari and Jackie included), she abruptly elopes with a Communist painter. This time the attraction is truly incomprehensible, unless the heroine enjoys humiliation, beating and abuse more than she admits.

Next affair is with Elliott Gould, appearing in one of those inexplicable cameos of classy actors in bad foreign films. Story picks up for the length of a Spanish bullfight and Riviera cruise, until summer ends and Gould's newspaper editor returns to his wife. Marina assuages her uncontainable sorrow by pouncing on a politician (embarrassingly like real-life hubby Carlo Ripa di Meana, Cultural Commissioner for the Common Market). Marriage follows seduction.

Sadly, this tale promises much more than it delivers, not least of which is the lively, amoral heroine, whose setbacks as a liberated woman never get properly examined. Content to reproduce the easiest parts of life, the Vanzinas brush through the last three decades with the most superficial of touches. Sex scenes feature an obvious, nude double for Carol Alt, fully credited in the end titles. —*Yung.*

Date With An Angel
(COLOR)

Cliché-ridden romantic comedy.

A De Laurentiis Entertainment Group presentation in association with De Laurentiis Film Partners. Produced by Martha Schumacher. Written and directed by Tom McLoughlin. Camera (J-D-C Widescreen, Technicolor), Alex Thomson; editor, Marshall Harvey; music, Randy Kerber; production design, Craig Stearns; art direction, Jeffrey S. Ginn; set design, Randy Moore; costumes, Donna O'Neal; sound (Dolby), Gary Bourgeois, Dean Okrand, Chris Carpenter; visual effects, Richard Edlund; assistant director, Bruce Moriarty; casting, Fern Champion, Pamela Basker. Reviewed at Mann Regent Theater, Westwood, Calif., Nov. 18, 1987. (MPAA Rating: PG.) Running time: **105 MINS.**

Jim Sanders . . . . Michael E. Knight
Patty Winston . . . . Phoebe Cates
Angel . . . . Emmanuelle Beart
Ed Winston . . . . David Dukes
George . . . . Phil Brock
Don . . . . Albert Macklin
Rex . . . . Pete Kowanko
Ben Sanders . . . . Vinny Argiro
Grace Sanders . . . . Bibi Besch

Hollywood — Tom McLoughlin's utterly predictable romantic fantasy plot is buoyed by winning performances from leads Michael E. Knight, Phoebe Cates and Emmanuelle Beart, and topflight technical work from lenser Alex Thomson and visual effects expert Richard Edlund. Whether soap vet Knight has enough pull to bring "All My Children" fans to the theaters will decide how pic fares at the boxoffice.

McLoughlin stumbles right out of the gate, with some painfully awkward opening scenes in which Knight seems to be paying homage to Tom Hanks. He plays Jim Sanders, a middle-class regular guy engaged to spoiled princess Patty Winston (Phoebe Cates) who has PATYKAT vanity plates on her little red corvette.

Trouble starts when Jim is kidnaped from a ritzy engagement party by his three water pistol machine-gun-toting friends, who carry him off to an impromptu bachelor party, leaving Cates sulking with daddy Ed Winston (David Dukes) and the Winston family's guests shocked and appalled.

A hungover Jim is greeted the next morning by, literally, an angel with a broken wing. Angel in question is the luminously beautiful Emmanuelle Beart, who crash-lands in his apartment complex swimming pool. After he takes her into his apartment to care for her broken wing, he is transfixed by her beauty but remains faithful to his fiancée.

In McLoughlin's heaven, angels (sent down to "bring someone back") can't talk to humans, so Beart — actress in title role of "Manon Of The Spring," the French hit — is limited to physical acting (which she does well) and communication with her radiant eyes and sultry whimpers of protest, pain and affection (which she does exceedingly well).

Middle part of pic is a lazy, cliché-ridden ride through predictable hijinks and misunderstandings, with Jim's friends (Phil Brock, Albert Macklin and Pete Kowanko, all in too broadly drawn wild-and-crazy guy roles that are more stereotypical than imaginative) trying to kidnap the Angel so they can make a marketing fortune, Ed Winston spotting the girl he wants for his next cosmetics ad campaign (damn it all if she might be his daughter's fiance's mistress) and Cates engaging in increasingly funnier tantrums to express the rage she feels at the tragic turn of events.

At the center of all this is the likable — but bland — Knight, whose limited acting range prevents him from adequately expressing his amazement at circumstances surrounding his life. McLoughlin isn't much of a help, leaving him with nothing but the faithfulness issue to guide his actions (a subplot about his musical talent is stillborn).

Conclusion, with authorities, friends, fiancée, future father-in-law and parents all trying to track down Jim and the Angel are well-paced and, again, leavened by Cates' pouty humor. Sum total is a film that is mindless and empty at the core, but still pleasantly diverting in spots.

Commendable in supporting roles are Vinny Argiro and Bibi Besch as Jim's parents, Ben and Grace. Besch plays the starry-eyed, status-conscious mother to perfection.

Best support though, comes on the technical side, with Thomson's backlit shots of angelic Beart painting a luscious picture and Edlund's marvelous visual effects, including a funny perspective shot of the fetching angel's misguided flight from the heavens, adding continuity and believability.—*Camb.*

L'Oeil au beurre noir
(A Black Eye)
(FRENCH-COLOR)

An AAA release of a Films Ariane/Lira Films coproduction. Produced by Jean Nachbaur, Raymond Danon. Directed by Serge Meynard. Screenplay, Patrick Braoudé, Jean-Paul Lilienfeld; camera (color), Jean-Jacques Tarbes; editor, Georges Klotz; music, François Bernheim; sound, Jean-Charles Ruault; art direction, Catherine Lavergne; assistant director-production manager, Michel Bernede; associate producer, Paradise Prods.

Reviewed at the Marignan-Concorde cinema, Paris, Nov. 11, 1987. Running time: **92 MINS.**

Virginie .... Julie Jezequel
Rachid .... Smain
Denis .... Pascal Legitimus
Mr. Perroni .... Martin Lamotte
Mrs. Perroni ...... Dominique Lavanant
Georges .... Patrick Braoudé
Junior .... Jean-Paul Lilienfeld
Rachid's father ..... Mahmoud Zemmouri
Mr. Picard .... Michel Berto

Paris — An amiable comedy on an unpleasant subject, racism, "L'-Oeil au beurre noir" follows the vain attempts of an Arab and a black to find an apartment in Paris, where housing discrimination is no laughing matter. Serviceably directed by newcomer Serge Meynard from a screenplay by Patrick Braoudé and Jean-Paul Lilienfeld, pic is in the same light comic vein as last year's hit feature, "Black mic-mac" and could follow commercially in its tracks, both at home and abroad.

The two hapless social rejects are Smain, a likeable Arab lowlife who cruises white girls by "saving" them from a couple of delinquent youths (in fact his cohorts in idleness, played by scripters Braoudé and Lilienfeld), and Pascal Legitimus, a penniless but respectable West Indian artist. Both end up unlikely companions when they become romantic rivals for the same girl, Julie Jezequel.

The romancing becomes secondary when they learn that Jezequel is seeking to rent out a swell apartment belonging to her parents. Mom and Dad (played with caricatural relish by Dominique Lavanant and Martin Lamotte) are typical middle-class bigots. Film's best comic sequences are those involving Smain and Legitimus' absurd courtship for respectability before the uptight white couple.

Smain and Legitimus are engaging comedians from the Paris cafe-theater scene and an apparent vanguard in a second wave of talent from that sector.

Tech credits are okay. Title, by the way, literally means a "black eye" but puns on the slang for an Arab ("beur"). —*Len.*

Flowers In The Attic
(COLOR)

Dreary rendition of V.C. Andrews suspenser.

A New World Pictures and Fries Entertainment presentation of a Charles Fries production. Produced by Sy Levin, Thomas Fries. Executive producers, Charles Fries, Mike Rosenfeld. Written and directed by Jeffrey Bloom, based on the novel by V.C. Andrews. Camera (CFI color), Frank Byers, Gil Hubbs; editor, Gregory F. Plotts; music, Christopher Young; production design, John Muto; set decoration, Michele Starbuck; costumes, Ann Somers Major; sound mixer, Arnold Braun; special effects, Dick Albain; assistant director, Peter S. Gries; associate producer, Mark Ratering; casting, Penny Perry. Reviewed at New World Pictures Theater, L.A., Nov. 16, 1987. (MPAA Rating: PG-13.) Running time: **95 MINS.**
Grandmother .... Louise Fletcher

Corinne .... Victoria Tennant
Cathy .... Kristy Swanson
Chris .... Jeb Stuart Adams
Cory .... Ben Ganger
Carrie .... Lindsay Parker
Father .... Marshall Colt
Grandfather .... Nathan Davis
John Hall .... Alex Koba

Hollywood — V.C. Andrews' tale of incestuous relationships and confined childhood always has been a superb candidate for a film treatment, but director Jeffrey Bloom has taken this narrative and squeezed the life from it. Performances are as stiff and dreary as the attic these children are imprisoned in, but story holds fascination — almost in spite of itself — all the way through to its thoroughly ridiculous conclusion (different from the book). Boxoffice success will depend on response of the book's largely teenage female constituency.

In an attempt to reach that group of adolescents, filmmakers may have test-marketed themselves into a corner. A graphic depiction of the older siblings' sexual relationship reportedly was left on the cutting room floor, as well as a key scene in which the children's mother disrobes in front of her father. The ending used was one of several shot for the film.

What ultimately winds up on screen follows the book loosely: apparently loving wife/mother Corrine (Victoria Tennant) becomes a widow at a relatively young age, with a family of four kids, no job skills and no money. Seventeen years previously, she was disinherited by her father, who didn't approve of the marriage (film never tells why, the book does) and never knew she had children.

After his death, wife takes the family — teenagers Chris (Jeb Stuart Adams) and Cathy (Kristy Swanson) and pre-adolescent twins Carrie (Lindsay Parker) and Cory (Ben Ganger) — and becomes golddigger deluxe, moving back to her parents' house, intent on winning back her father's love and, in the process, getting reinstated into his will.

Kids aren't crazy about the arrangement after meeting their sadistic, bible-toting, taskmaster grandmother (Louise Fletcher, doing a lot with this one-dimensional role) and getting locked into a guest room, where they are informed they must stay until their grandfather dies, so Tennant can win his affections.

Key to the book's effectiveness came in Andrews' atmospheric description of the small world the children create for themselves in the guest room and the adjoining attic. Film version falls short in this section, for several reasons.

Firstly, Cathy and Chris' gradual, mutual attraction has been excised and is only hinted at here. More problematic is the script, which attributes none of the qualities of

teenagers to the teens and portrays the younger children as mindless drones (their dialog is what tired parents *think they hear*, not what restless kids say).

As Corinne's visits to reassure her children become increasingly less frequent, their clashes with, and hate for, the cruel grandmother — who promises them "no kindness and no love" because they are "the devil's spawn" — reach a peak, forcing all four to turn inward and seek each other for support.

Their first planned escape is laughable, the most embarrassing part of this uneven film, save the conclusion, but later plot progressions, when Cathy and Chris finally are desperate to leave and have lost faith in their money-mad mother, carry more of a punch.

But Bloom's leaden screenplay and heavy-handed direction bog even this down. Rest of tech credits are competent, although Christopher Young's score is more bothersome than anything else.

Tennant goes crazy admirably and Kristy Swanson is believable when she remains within a controlled set of emotions, but performances of the youngest children are poorly directed and totally unbelievable, leaving the entire ensemble in trouble.

Film leaves open the possibility of sequels (this was the first in a series of Andrews' books about the same characters), but finished product here doesn't do justice to the original, regardless of what the market testing says. —*Camb.*

Teen Wolf Too
(COLOR)

Fox-less 'Wolf' toothless.

An Atlantic Releasing release. Produced by Kent Bateman. Executive producers, Thomas Coleman, Michael Rosenblatt. Directed by Christopher Leitch. Screenplay, R. Timothy Kring, from a story by Joseph Loeb 3d, Matthew Weisman; camera (Consolidated Film Labs color), Jules Brenner; editors, Steven Polivka, Kim Secrist, Harvey Rosenstock, Raja Gosnell; music, Mark Goldenberg; art direction, Peg McClellan; sound, Richard Wadell; assistant director, Tana Manners; casting, Pamela Rack. Reviewed at Atlantic screening room, L.A., Nov. 19, 1987. (MPAA Rating: PG.) Running time: **95 MINS.**
Todd Howard .... Jason Bateman
Professor Brooks .... Kim Darby
Dean Dunn .... John Astin
Coach Finstock .... Paul Sand
Uncle Howard .... James Hampton
Chubby .... Mark Holton
Nicki .... Estee Chandler
Gustavson .... Robert Neary
Stiles .... Stuart Fratkin
Lisa .... Beth Ann Miller
Emily .... Rachel Sharp

Hollywood — Usually as a film's credits unroll, one has high hopes which take at least a few minutes to get dashed. In the case of "Teen Wolf Too," things go hopelessly, irretrievably bad from the first strains of the opening song. And then it gets worse. Tame teen romp aims

for a pre-adolescent audience, but without Michael J. Fox returning in the title role, boxoffice prospects are decidedly downbeat for this dog.

Premise of a benign teenage werewolf as a college freshman is unpromising enough to start with, but screenwriter R. Timothy Kring makes matters even worse by throwing in nearly every threadbare youth comedy gag in the book. Director Christopher Leitch leans on the whole thing with a leaden touch, totally surrendering any possible charm for the most obvious setups.

As Todd Howard, cousin of the original Teen Wolf, Jason Bateman doesn't even howl, he whimpers his way through standard teen travails such as popularity, loyalty and choosing the good girl over the cool girl.

Bateman gets an edge on everyone else when his heretofore dormant family characteristic surfaces with a vengeance. Pretty soon he's big wolf on campus, kicking out "Twist And Shout" to a delighted and admiring student body. But it's a phony lip-synched moment with over-"Grease"-d choreography that's as transparent as Bateman's clumsy wolf makeup.

Plot revolves around a trumped-up boxing scholarship and a climactic battle in the ring with beefcake Robert Neary. Beth Ann Miller and Rachel Sharp are striking as the campus queens out for a good time. Fueling the wolfman furor for the glory of Hamilton U. (the real Hamilton College should sue) is the unctuous dean John Astin.

Paul Sand is incomprehensibly quirky as the beleaguered coach and Estee Chandler is sweet and lovable as Bateman's love interest. James Hampton is likable as Bateman's folksy wolfman uncle, but material is so lame, characters never get off the ground.

Production has the artificial look of a hastily done television show and has about as much soul. —*Jagr.*

Strike Commando
(ITALIAN-COLOR)

A Flora Film production. (Intl. sales, Variety Film.) Produced by Franco Gaudenzi. Directed and edited by "Vincent Dawn" (Bruno Mattei). Stars Reb Brown, Christopher Connelly. Screenplay, Clyde Anderson, from story by Anderson, "Dawn" (Mattei); camera (Telecolor), Richard Gras; music, Lou Ceccarelli; art direction, Bart Scavya; dialog director, Gene Luotto. Reviewed on Intl. Video Ent. vidcassette, N.Y., Nov. 14, 1987. (No MPAA Rating.) Running time: **102 MINS.**
Michael Ransom .... Reb Brown
Col. Radek .... Christopher Connelly
Olga .... Loes Kamma
Le Duc .... Alan Collins
Jakoda .... Alex Vitale
Lao .... Edison Navarro
Cho-Li .... Karen Lopez
Diem .... Juliet D. Lee

"Strike Commando" is a run-of-the-mill Italian war picture imitating "Rambo." Made last year, pic was recently given a token release in

Kansas City ahead of its current homevideo availability.

Reb Brown fits the bill as brawny Michael Ransom, sole survivor of a deadly mission in Vietnam by the crack Strike Commando force. Befriended by local villagers, he spots Russian officers in action and is sent back in by his commander (Christopher Connelly) to get photographic evidence of the Russkies.

With dumb dialog (beefy Russian played by Alex Vitale insists on calling the hero "Americanski"), pic slavishly imitates the second "Rambo" film leading to a touch of "Rocky IV" (bare-knuckled fight between the two musclemen) as well. At least a reel or two overlong, film has an idiotic, padded coda set about 15 years later in Manila.

Some okay minor action scenes do not disguise the fact that the film lacks the large-scale setpieces that have become de rigeur for Vietnam war pics. Worst scene has Brown unsuccessfully (in an obvious stretch) simulating tears and pathos as he holds a dyng little Vietnamese boy in his arms — cut to him with machinegun in hand bellowing a warcry, fully motivated.—*Lor.*

The Time Guardian
(AUSTRALIAN-COLOR)

A Hemdale release (Filmpac in Australia) of a Hemdale-FGH (Intl. Film Management)-Chateau Prod. Investments-Jen-Diki Film production. Executive producer, Antony I. Ginnane. Produced by Norman Wilkinson, Robert Lagettie. Coproduced by Harley Manners. Directed by Brian Hannant. Stars Tom Burlinson, Nikki Coghill. Screenplay, Hannant, John Baxter; camera (Panavision, color), Geoff Burton; editor, Andrew Prowse; music, Allan Zavod; sound, Toivo Lember; production design, George Liddle; director of additional filming, Andrew Prowse; visual effects supervisor, Andrew Mason; mechanical effects supervisor, Ted Price; production manager, Stephanie Jones; assistant director, Philip Hearnshaw; casting (Australia), Susie Maizels; (U.S.), Michael McLean, Diane Dimeo. Reviewed at Fox-Columbia screening room, Sydney, Sept. 30, 1987. (No MPAA Rating). Running time: **85 MINS.**
Ballard . . . . Tom Burlinson
Annie . . . . Nikki Coghill
Petra . . . . Carrie Fisher
Boss . . . . Dean Stockwell
Prenzler . . . . Henry Salter
Tanel . . . . Jo Flemming
Sgt. McCarthy . . . . Tim Robertson
Rafferty . . . . Jim Holt

Sydney — An ambitious attempt at making a large-scale sci-fi adventure on a relatively big budget in Australia, "The Time Guardian" is an uneven affair in which the exciting and the banal co-exist uneasily. Basic theme, of a city from the future which time-travels to present-day Australia to escape its enemies, is a good one, but pic only grabs the interest in fits and starts. When placed alongside Yank and British sci-fi outings, this one seems tame, and accordingly returns will probably be modest.

Pic begins with a rather perfunctory battle in which the citizens of the 24th century are attacked by the ferocious Jen-didi (they're supposed

to be ferocious, but these creatures come across as rather tame monsters and pic would have benefitted enormously by a more formidable enemy). Ballard (Tom Burlinson), a warrior, and Petra (Carrie Fisher), an authority on the 20th century, are sent ahead to check out the Australian desert location which has been targeted as the new site for the city. The Jen-diki follow, and Petra is wounded. Seeking help, Ballard meets Annie (Nikki Coghill), a geologist who doesn't take much convincing that her new friend has travelled back in time. Together they confront the hostile population of Midas, a small mining town, and fall in love in the process, with Annie deciding, in the end, to return with Ballard to the future — and just as well, because she's the one who despatches the chief Jen-diki in the obligatory climactic battle.

By far the best scenes in "The Time Guardian" are those in which the citizens of Midas try to come to grips with the space visitors: Tim Robertson as the local police chief and Jim Holt as his nasty assistant, steal all their scenes, and Holt's fate is one of the more effective moments in the pic. Scenes in the futuristic city are rather drab and uninspiring, with the two battle scenes indifferently handled and with Dean Stockwell hamming it up in a nothing role as the city's chief, unimaginatively referred to as "Boss."

Tom Burlinson, always a good actor, is miscast as Ballard; the part called for an older, tough type of warrior, and though Burlinson tries his best, it sometimes seems as if his heart isn't in it. Nikki Coghill, on the other hand, is charming as the resourceful Annie; she's emerging as a leading actress to watch. Carrie Fisher also is good as the other time-traveler (and the only one to expire); she makes the most of all her scenes.

Director Brian Hannant, who coscripted with sci-fi author and film critic John Baxter, has come up with a rather disappointing debut feature; he's toiled for over 15 years in the Australian film industry on docus and short fiction, and his first feature was eagerly awaited. In fairness, pic evidently has suffered some postproduction changes: editor Andrew Prowse also is credited with being "director of additional filming," indicating some reshooting occurred; and the short 85-minute running time of the release print is at odds with the 100-minute running time published during production.

Dialog seems to strive for humor, but often comes across as corny.

Pic is shot handsomely by Geoff Burton, though George Liddle's production design isn't up to his usual high standard. It probably will have a struggle at the boxoffice where it lacks the thrills and scope of more lavish sci-fi outings in what in any case seems to be a dying

genre. — *Strat.*

White Winter Heat
(DOCU-COLOR)

Ski actioner for specialized market.

An Eric/Chandler Ltd. release, presented by Audi Quattro, of a Warren Miller Enterprises production. Written, produced and directed by Miller. Executive producer, Ron Edwards. Camera (color) & production manager, Don Brolin; principal photography, Brian Sisselman, Gary Nate, Larry Gebhardt, Stephen Jackson, Fletcher Manley; editor, Michael Usher, Ray Laurent; music supervisor, Brooks Arthur; music coordinator, Daniel Segal; sound effects editor, Greg Schorer; assistant editor, Doug Kleist, associate producers, Jeff Bonafede, Sims Hind, Kurt Miller, Daniel Segal, Peter Speek. Reviewed at Magno Review 1, N.Y., Nov. 12, 1987. (No MPAA Rating.) Running time: **91 MINS.**

Moviegoers have "Star Trek IV," "James Bond 14" and now, with "White Winter Heat," "Warren Miller 38." The veteran sports filmmaker's latest specialized feature on downhill skiing, distribbed mainly on a 4-wall basis in the U.S. and Canada, should be as profitable as its predecessors now and in the longrun.

"White Winter Heat" films expert athletes doing their thing in exotic and dangerous locations. Add some judicious editing and original rock-oriented action music, and you have an event for upscale skiing singles, marrieds and families in snowtime.

"White Winter Heat" takes places in w.k. ski meccas such as Switzerland and Montana, with additional forays into locales such as New Zealand and Argentina.

Pic's sizable contingent of photographers — Miller also gets an "additional photography" credit — catches skiiers in a variety of stunts, including many beat-skipping vertical drops.

In a deadpan timbre, Miller narrates the film. Most often narration's content is educational. In the Argentine mountains known as the Remarkables, for example, the snow is as deep as 900 ft. Other times he cracks wise as he describes certain skiier moves as "a chiropractor's delight."

Although produced and promoted essentially as a skiing document, "White Winter Heat" also contains footage from horse racing, harness racing, bobsledding and mountian biking.

The 1987 Warren Miller pic (another is promised for next year and producers are also branching off into summer sports docus) is expected to unspool in 600 venues in 125-130 cities in North America and abroad.

Next stop, of course, is the lucrative homevideo market when all that's left for the audience is spring skiing, alpine sliding or wind surfing. — *Binn.*

Border Radio
(B&W)

Minimalist meditation on the L.A. rockscene.

A Coyote Films presentation. Produced by Marcus De Leon. Written and directed by Allison Anders, Dean Lent, Kurt Voss. Additional dialog by the cast. Camera (b&w, 16m), Lent; music, Dave Alvin, with Steve Berlin, Bill Bateman, John Bazz, DJ Bonebrake, John Doe; sound, Nietzehka Keene; associate producer, Robert Rosen. Reviewed at the American Film Institute, L.A. (AFI Indie Fest), Oct. 29, 1987. (No MPAA Rating.) Running time: **84 MINS.**
Jeff . . . . Chris D.
Dean . . . . John Doe
Lu . . . . Luana Anders
Chris . . . . Chris Shearer
Dave . . . . Dave Alvin
Scenester . . . . Iris Berry
Babysitter . . . . Texacala Jones
Devon . . . . Devon Anders
Expatriot . . . . Chuck Shepard
Lead Thug . . . . Craig Stark
Thug . . . . Eddie Flowers
Thug . . . . Sebastian Copeland
Themselves . . . . Green On Red

Hollywood — An inert and self-consciously arty inquest into anomie among fringe L.A. rockers, "Border Radio" still possesses sufficient grace notes to hold the attention of the intended hipster audience. No-budget black-and-white feature made over three years by a trio of Wim Wenders acolytes at UCLA has an art school look that is occasionally arresting, and soundtrack by Dave Alvin and assorted cohorts is superb. Pic will truly appeal only to music world cultists, so theatrical future resides in fests and highly specialized venues. World premiere took place Nov. 14 at the AFI Indie Fest in Los Anteles.

The influence of Wenders, and particularly "Paris, Texas," on which Allison Anders and Dean Lent, two of the three writer-directors, worked, is clearly felt, and there are also echoes of novelist Paul Bowles in this erratic, stop-and-go tale of emotional discord among smalltime musicians on the run from Hollywood to Mexico and back.

Narrative momentum is hardly the film's strong suit, but basic framework has three band members — real-life rockers Chris D., John Doe and Dave Alvin — taking off after robbing a club owner of unpaid cash owed them from a gig.

Chris D. heads for the beach in northern Mexico to face his dilemma, existentially muttering things like, "It's tough being a seminal L.A. rock artist," but, unfortunately, most of the running time is taken up by his wife, Luana Anders, trying to figure out what to do while horsing around with her dimwitted putative lover, roadie Chris Shearer.

With action consisting virtually entirely of waste motion and essential uninteresting characters doing uninteresting things, it is incumbent upon the artists responsible to create a resonant context for such emptiness. Anders Lent and Kurt Voss have crept part of the way towards this goal and clearly have "artistic" sensibilities, but the viewer is not sufficiently rewarded for indulging their many conceits.

Absolute highlight is the score by Dave Alvin, an original member of The Blasters who later joined X. The songs are expectedly good, but what really impresses is the instrumental work, which lends considerable mood and emotional shading to the threadbare drama.

Final credit — "Many curses on: Those Who Tried To Thwart Us" — is testimony to the difficulty of getting any indie feature made, and the film does have flashes of talent and interest. There's not enough substance here to develop anything greater than a marginal audience.
—*Cart.*

Forty Days Of Musa Dagh
(COLOR)

Shoddy treatment of worthy material.

A High Investments Flms production. Produced by John Kurkjian. Directed by Sarky Mouradian. Screenplay, Alex Hakobian, from the book "The Forty Days Of Musa Dagh" by Franz Werfel; camera (color), Gregory Sandor; editor, Tony De Zarraga; music, Jaime Mendoza-Nava; production manager, Thomas Selden; art direction, Randy Ser; assistant director, Richard Kanter; sound, George Mouradian; makeup, Donn Markel; costumes, Patrick Norris; casting, Wm. J. Kenney-Daniel Travis. Reviewed on Video City Prods. vidcassette, N.Y., Nov. 1, 1987. (No MPAA Rating.) Running time: **94 MINS.**
Gabriel Bagradian . . . . Kabir Bedi
Juliette Bagradian . . . . Ronnie Carol
Simon Tomassian . . . . Guy Stockwell
Maris Durand . . . . Peter Haskell
Henry Morgenthau Sr. . . . David Opatashu
Talaat Pasha . . . . Michael Constantine
Kilikian . . . . Manuel Kichian
Civil governor . . . . Maurice Sherbanée
Karoon . . . . Victoria Woodbeck
Also with: David Mauro, Sid Haig, John Hoyt, Gilbert Green, Sydney Lassick, Paul King, Robert Wood.

"Forty Days Of Musa Dagh" is a dreary little film that does no justice to its weighty subject — the Armenian holocaust, specifically the 1915 uprising in which a group of Armenian villagers, faced with relocation and eventual extermination by the Turks, holed up on Mt. Musa Dagh and fought off their terrorizers. Pic carries a 1983 copyright and an international cast, largely composed of familiar U.S. character actors. The story of Musa Dagh was long in limbo at MGM in the 1930s but ultimately went unfilmed by the major; low-grade version here has gone unreleased theatrically, appearing only on vidcassette and reviewed here for the record.

Kabir Bedi stars as Gabriel Bagradian, a wealthy Armenian businessman and loyal captain in the Turkish artillery, who attempts unsuccessfully (shades of "Casablanca") to have his French wife and son given exit visas and transported out of Armenia; he sees that trouble is near, having learned that his fellow Armenians are being driven into the Syrian desert and killed.

He gives the villagers a pep talk, and those willing to fight rather than capitulate take flight to the mountain, while those opposed to violence and trusting in God's protection are soon slaughtered by the angered Turkish authorities.

Film's exposition, via hokey dialog, is too simplistic and uni-dimensional to bear the weight of such a traumatic event in human history. Filmmakers give just enough lip service to the political and social issues at hand before settling down to the real order of the day: some unconvincing gunfights, hangings, etc. Violence, however, isn't even explicit enough to qualify pic as exploitation fare; it's simply cheesy.

One decidedly grim scene, though kept off camera, has the local civil governor, a Turk, sodomize and murder the teenage son of Bedi, thus sending Bedi's already shaky wife (Ronnie Carol) completely over the edge. While the rape goes on upstairs, another Turkish official tells a visiting German officer who appears appalled, "Our customs are different here, Hoffman." In a separate moment of 20/20-hindsight screenwriting, an enraged Armenian supporter lashes out at a lackadaisical German official: "Your refusal to stand up on a moral issue will haunt you!"

American thesp Peter Haskell shows up as a journalist purportedly covering the growing unrest in the area, but he doesn't do any reporting, rather lusting variously after Mrs. Bagradian and a way out of the country.

Save for Bedi's compassionate performance, acting overall is not notable; photography is serviceable, but editing, sound and other tech areas are weak. Filming was done in California, with a large number of crew members of Armenian heritage. —*Gerz.*

Havinck
(DUTCH-COLOR)

A Holland Film Releasing release of a Riverside Pictures production. Produced by Gys Versluys. Directed by Franz Weisz. Screenplay, Ger Thijs, from the novel by Marja Brouwers; camera (Eastmancolor, Cineco prints), Giuseppe Lanci; editor, Ton Ruys; music, Egisto Macchi; sound, Marcel de Hoogd, Gusta van Eijk; art direction, Jan Roelfs, Ben van Os; assistant director, Marianne van Wijnkoop; production manager, Anke Taverne; casting, Frank Krom. Reviewed at Bellevue theater, Amsterdam, Oct. 5, 1987. Running time: **99 MINS.**
Havinck . . . . Willem Nijholt
Eva . . . . Anne Martien Lousberg
Lydia . . . . Will van Kralingen
Maud . . . . Carolien van den Berg
Bork . . . . Coen Flink
Also with: Dora van der Groen, Max Croiset, Kenneth Herdigein.

Amsterdam — "Havinck" is Franz Weisz' best film, and he's made some good ones (e.g., "Charlotte"). At the Dutch Filmdays it got the critics' prize for best film, and won. besides numerous nominations, two Golden Calves, one for best actor (Willem Nijholt), one for best supporting actress (Will van Kralingen).

Robert Havinck is a partner in a small but prestigious law firm, well off, married to Lydia, father of 15-year-old Eva. The marriage has been on the rocks for years.

Lydia is killed in a car accident. It turns out to have been an egocentric, irresponsible way of committing suicide while killing a complete stranger. Havinck does not give the dead man a thought either, but he wants to know why Lydia acted as she did. He also wants to build some kind of relationship with his daughter. Not that he loves Eva, but there's some kind of basic, atavistic affection.

It's an intriguing movie: very un-Dutch passion in a story about a very cold fish. Pic as a whole has its own rhythm, but each major character has his own beat, his or her personal style of acting. The famous light of Holland and its sky looks mysteriously different, though quite authentic, when caught by director of photography Giuseppe Lanci (who lensed for the Tavianis, Tarkovsky, Bellocchio) and his Italian camera crew. Their compatriot Egisto Macchi's dramatic music harmonizes with the art direction — affluent distinction reminding one of late period Visconti movies. Notwithstanding the Mediterranean affinity, however, the acting of the women brings Bergman thesps to mind.

Weisz tells the story of Havinck and his daughter in the present, Lydia is in flashbacks melded seamlessly into the film. Director and producer showed courage by giving the part of the wife to Will van Kralingen, a young actress whose feature debut is profoundly moving, and that of the daughter to Anne Martien Lousberg, a girl still in high school. Weisz got brilliant performances out of both. Dora van der Groen is excellent as Lydia's mother. Carolien van den Berg and Coen Flink build distinctive personalities in parts important to the story but given little screen time.

Willem Nijholt in the title role had the near-impossible task of interesting the public in a man with whom nobody would wish to identify — a man without feeling, a psyche out of the freezer. — *Wall.*

Kiss Daddy Good Night
(COLOR-16m)

Dreary underground effort.

A Beast of Eden presentation. Produced by Maureen O'Brien, William Ripka. Directed by Peter Ily Huemer. Screenplay, Huemer, Michael Gabrieli, story by Huemer; camera (color), Bobby Bukowski; editor, Ila von Hasperg; music, Don King with Duncan Lindsay; sound, Michael Lazar; associate producer, Ica Mueller; assistant director, Matthias Leutzendorff; casting, Maureen Fremont. Reviewed at the American Film Institute, L.A. (AFI Indie Fest), Oct. 29, 1987. (No MPAA Rating.) Running time: **80 MINS.**
Laura . . . . Uma Thurman
Sid . . . . Paul Dillon
William B. Tilden . . . . Paul Richards
Johnny . . . . Steve Buscemi
Sue . . . . Annabelle Gurwitch
Nelson Blitz . . . . David Brisbin

Hollywood — The promotional line used by the filmmakers — "She was cold. He was old." — is about as appealing as the picture they have made, "Kiss Daddy Good Night." A dreary exercise in decadent New York avant-gardism, this marginal effort is made watchable only by the presence of beautiful 16-year-old model Uma Thurman in the leading role, but she certainly will be seen under more favorable circumstances in future. Commercial outlook is bleak for this low-budget indie, which played at the AFI Indiefest.

The cold one is Laura, a gorgeous blond night prowler who dons a different wig and outfit every evening, lets men take her back to their apartments but, before they can make their moves, drugs them and steals some valuable items.

The old one is William, a creepy fellow who lives in Laura's building and is obsessed with how much she reminds him of his daughter. Dignified, polite and intellectual, William wants to dominate Laura but works up to it discreetly.

The only real interest generated by director Peter Ily Huemer, a native of Vienna making his feature debut, is in the misguidedly perverse behavior of Laura. Pic makes no coherent attempt at a psychological portrait and provides no one with whom the viewer can remotely connect. It's all quite pointless and emotionally numbing, and ends with preposterous melodrama.

Technical work in 16m is good and creates a definite atmosphere of frigid loathing and malaise.—*Cart.*

Open House
(COLOR)

Okay slasher fare.

An Intercontinental Releasing presentation of a Sandy Cobe production. produced by Cobe. Executive producers, Victor Bhalla, Sultan Allaudin. Directed by Jag Mundhra. Stars Joseph Bottoms, Adrienne Barbeau. Screenplay, David Mickey Evans, from story by Mundhra; camera (Foto-Kem color), Robert Hayes; editor, Dan Selakovich; music, Jim Studer; sound, David Waelder; production design, Naomi Shohan; art direction, Zachary Spoon; production manager, Stefan N. Deoul; assistant director, Michelle Solotar; special makeup effects supervisor, John A. Naulin; second unit camera, Ron Halpern; additional camera, Gary Louzon; coproducer, Gabriella Belloni; executive in charge of production, Sharyon Reis Cobe; casting, Lori Cobe. Reviewed on Prism Entertainment vidcassette, N.Y., Oct. 10, 1987. (MPAA Rating: R.) Running time: **97 MINS.**
Dr. David Kelley . . . . Joseph Bottoms
Lisa Grant . . . . Adrienne Barbeau
Rudy Estevez . . . . Rudy Ramos
Katie Thatcher . . . . Mary Stavin
Joe Pearcy . . . . Scott Thompson Baker
Harry . . . . Darwyn Swalve
Lt. Shapiro . . . . Robert Miano
Also with: Page Moseley, Johnny Haymer,

Leonard Lightfoot, Stacey Adams, Roxanne Baird, Tiffany Bolling, Dena Drotar, Cathryn Hartt, Christina Gallegos.

"Open House," previously titled "Multiple Listings," is a well-made horror film in the slasher mode, lacking the monsters and fantasy that's back in favor among fans of genre pics. Pic has debuted domestically in video stores.

Joseph Bottoms, returning to a genre he previously starred in via Nico Mastorakis' "Blind Date" (made and released pior to the Blake Edwards film of that title), portrays a psychologist who has a radio show in L.A. called "Survival Line," in which he tries to help loonies à la Dr. Ruth. Pre-credits, pic opens gloomily as a girl, victim of incest for the past two years by her father, commits suicide on the air during a conversation with Bottoms.

Film proper concerns a serial killer who preys on beautiful women realtors, with Bottoms' girl friend, Adrienne Barbeau, looking like a key target, especially when the main suspect is a nasty chauvinist pig who is actively sabotaging her work. After several gory killings, pic climaxes with Barbeau taken hostage by the real killer (who's been calling in to Bottoms' programs regularly, monitored unsuccessfully by the police). Motive pushes film into black humor territory: he blames the realtors for the high price of housing in L.A., and displacing him when he lived as a squatter in an empty Beverly Hills mansion after its owner died. Except for the chauvinist pig (who gets his head lopped off) the film adheres to the old-fashioned format of pretty girls getting sliced, not likely to please feminists.

Biggest surprise here, and helpful for word-of-mouth in the rental area, is that star Barbeau delivers a brief topless scene after seemingly having graduated from same. She and the rest of the cast are likable, with additional pulchritude provided by such lookers as Mary Stavin (also featured in New World's "House"), Roxanne Baird and Christina Gallegos. Pic's weakest point is its corny finale and utterly pointless final scene, which looks tacked-on as an afterthought. —*Lor.*

El Ansia de Matar
(The Urge To Kill)
(MEXICAN-COLOR)

A Peliculas Mexicanas release of a Cinematográfica de Sol production. Executive producers, Gilberto Trujillo, Raúl Trujillo. Produced, written and directed by Gilberto de Anda. Stars Mario Almada, Gilberto Trujillo. Camera (color), Antonio de Anda; editor, Sergio Soto; music, Diego Herrera. Reviewed at Hollywood Twin theater 2, N.Y., Nov. 2, 1987. Running time: **82 MINS.**
Roberto Robles . . . . Mario Almada
Quillo . . . . Gilberto Trujillo
Guerrilla Captain . . . . Jorge Luke
Lorena . . . . Diana Golden
Magda . . . . Tere Velázquez
María . . . . Gabriela Ruffo
Deaf Guerrilla . . . . Raúl Trujillo

Major . . . . Valentín Trujillo
Also with: Jorge Muñoz, Alfonso Dávila, Xorge Noble, Agustín Bernal, Luis Guevara, Alberto Arvizu, Jose Chávez, Carlos East, Ricardo de Loera, Jaime Reyes, Arturo Martínez Jr., Gilberto de Anda.

In 1983, Guatemalan guerrillas invaded a refugee camp in the southern Mexican state of Chiapas and massacred Guatemalan peasants seeking sanctuary. In order to exploit this situation, Mexican director Gilberto de Anda produced, wrote and directed this routine action pic "El Ansia de Matar" (The Urge To Kill).

Toplining perennial adventure star Mario Almada as a Mexican hunter whose wife and daughter are kidnapped by the guerrillas, the movie is a drawn-out revenge story as the hunter tracks down the heartless villains and frees his brutalized family. Concurrently, Gilberto Trujillo plays a Guatemalan refugee whose own wife was killed in the raid. To round things out, two other Trujillo family members have also gotten into the act: older brother Valentín plays a tough army major while kid brother Raúl takes the part of the guerrillas' chief cook and bottle washer.

The film carefully avoids any mention of the Guatemalan Army's complicity in the ill treatment of refugees, stating again and again that it is all the fault of "independent" rebels.

Tech credits are first-rate with crisp and imaginative lensing, good locations, lots of appropriate crosscutting and boasting a bold music score that utilizes native pan flutes and guitars. Too bad the script did not receive the same care. Exposition is obvious, dialog self-conscious and the audience is asked more than once to stretch its imagination to near breaking point.

These faults probably won't hinder b.o. potential, when compensated by such pic pluses as a current Latino theme, revenge, fast action and the appearance of draws like Almada and the Trujillo clan. — *Lent.*

The Wind
(COLOR)

Tired thriller.

An Omega Pictures production. Executive producer, Isabel Mastorakis. Produced and directed by Nico Mastorakis. Stars Meg Foster, Wings Hauser. Screenplay, Fred C. Perry, Nico Mastorakis, from Nico Mastorakis' story; camera (Foto-Kem and Technicolor), Andrew (Andreas) Bellis, (L.A.), Steven Shaw; editor, Bruce Cannon, Nico Mastorakis; music, Stanley Myers, Hans Zimmer; production design (Greece), Lester Gallagher; art direction (L.A.), Lenny Schultz; assistant director (Greece), Art Nikoloudis, (L.A.), Kelly Schroeder; production manager (Greece), George Iakovidis, (L.A.), Aladdin Pojhan; associate producer, Kirk Ellis; postproduction supervisor, Elliot Conrad. Reviewed on Vestron Video vidcassette, N.Y., Oct. 31, 1987. (No MPAA Rating.) Running time: **92 MINS.**
Sian Anderson . . . . Meg Foster

Phil . . . . Wings Hauser
John . . . . David McCallum
Elias Appleby . . . . Robert Morley
Kesner . . . . Steve Railsback
Also with: John Michaels, Tracy Young, Summer Thomas, Michael Yannatos.

"The Wind" is a failed thriller which completely lacks interesting or believable plot developments. Headed straight for video domestically, pic poses no threat to the memory of the same-titled Lillian Gish silent classic.

Meg Foster stars as a mystery novelist who treks from L.A. to Monemvassia, Greece to write. After unlikely landlord Robert Morley shows her the house, Wings Hauser pops up as a threatening handyman and film collapses into a series of gothic cliches.

To begin with, Foster imagines that Hauser has killed Morley and types out a story describing same. Immediately, it turns out to be true and a dull game of cat and mouse develops between Hauser and her. A ridiculous plot ploy has Steve Railsback artificially injected into the film as a stranded sailor sitting at police headquarters who volunteers to investigate when Foster's main squeeze (David McCallum in a literally phoned-in role) calls in the Greek authorities long distance to aid Foster.

The wind machine gets a workout here, but the story is pointless. Script by director Nico Mastorakis and his collaborator Fred C. Perry does not establish any links between the characters and fails to establish even a rudimentary ambiguity to Hauser's bad guy status. The result is uninvolving. —*Lor.*

Wimps
(COLOR)

'Cyrano' reduced to college comedy.

A Platinum Pictures and Vestron Entertainment presentation. Produced and directed by Chuck Vincent. Stars Louie Bonanno. Screenplay, Vincent, Craig Horrall; camera (color), Larry Revene; editor, Marc Ubell (Vincent), James Davalos; music, Ian Shaw, Kai Joffe; sound, Peter Penguin; art direction, D. Gary Phelps; assistant director, Bill Slobodian; production manager, Buck Westminster; casting, John Amero. Reviewed on Lightning Video vidcassette, N.Y., Oct. 31, 1987. (MPAA Rating: R.) Running time: **84 MINS.**
Francis . . . . Louie Bonanno
Roxanne . . . . Deborah Blaisdell
Charles Conrad . . . . Jim Abele
Tracy . . . . Jane Hamilton
Also with: Eddie Prevot, Derrick R. Roberts, Philip Campanero, Michael Heintzman, Jeanne Marie, Gretchen Kingsley, Lori Stewart, Annie Sprinkle, Carmel Pugh, Siobhan Hunter.

"Wimps" was filmed several months before the Steve Martin pic "Roxanne," but it is still wiped off the map by it. A modern-day version of Edmond Rostand's "Cyrano de Bergerac," Chuck Vincent's film plays like a score of other routine college-hijinks comedies.

Louie Bonanno, who previously played the same nerd role in Vincent's "Sex Appeal," plays Francis, a college freshman admitted to a jocks' fraternity because his dad was a football hero. When the college cracks down on academic requirements to head off a football scholarship scandal, Francis is forced to help all his frat brothers with their studies.

In particular, Francis is helping star quarterback Charles (Jim Abele) and reluctantly agrees to help him woo lovely librarian Roxanne (Deborah Blaisdell) in return for getting fixed up with a date (it turns out to be a hooker). Ultimately, Francis finds out that Charles is merely after Roxanne to prove a point to his fellow jocks, who saw him rebuffed by her on their first meeting at the library. Of course, romance finally blooms between Francis and Roxanne at the finish.

Bonanno has got the nerd routine down pat but brings little else to the film, obviously suffering by comparison with Steve Martin's bravura turn. Blaisdell, better known to adult film fans as Tracy Adams, is pretty but overly bland, while Jane Hamilton (a.k.a. Veronica Hart) steals a few scenes as the hooker. —*Lor.*

Wonder Women
(HONG KONG-COLOR)

Produced, presented and distributed by D&B Films. Executive producer, written and directed by Kam Kwok-leung. Stars Dodo Cheng, Cecilia Yip, Michael Wong. Original theme song performed by George Lam. (No other credits provided.) Reviewed at Majestic II, Kowloon, Hong Kong, Oct. 15, 1987. Running time: **98 MINS.**
(Cantonese soundtrack with English subtitles)

Hong Kong — The intricate human relationships of bosom buddies as subject matter is something not often tackled by Cantonese cinema. However, once in a while, a film of merit comes along. Made for only about $HK2,000,000, "Wonder Women" grossed over $HK8,000,-000 which shows there's hope for unconventional portraits here of real human beings.

The title is very misleading. There are no superwomen here. The simplistic storyline concerns seven days in the life of two ambitious city girls who want to skyrocket to high society, fortune and recognition, by entering a beauty contest. Dodo Cheng is a Monroe-styled, bird-brained woman with huge ambitions but low tastes in life style, culture and speech. Yet her accidental philosophical remarks amaze and astonish friends, especially Cecilia Yip. The latter is the intelligent and unpretentious one, but lacks the physical projections or attributes of Cheng and is most unlucky in her romance with a hairdresser.

Both girls were publicized as hot contenders but neither made it even to the top five of the contest. The two ladies console each other and become friends. Cheng extends her hospitality to Yip to share her off-top bungalow for awhile.

Later, their friendship is threatened when they meet a handsome Japanese tourist (Michael Wong). The two vie for his attention, but the handsome, muscular stranger leaves them both and eventually tells them on a cassette that he was never serious about either one of them.

Written and directed by ex-actor Kam Kwok-leung, this debut film has heart, exhuberance, real sincerity, and an eye for detail. It satirizes today's westernized Oriental life that is very celebrity conscious. It is Hong Kong today as media monsters are created monthly by the press, and are consumed by the mass audience.—*Mel.*

Un Tassinaro a New York
(A Taxi Driver In New York)
(ITALIAN-COLOR)

An Italian Intl. Film production and release. Produced by Fulvio Lucisano. Directed by Alberto Sordi. Screenplay, Sordi, Rodolfo Sonego; camera (color), Giuseppe Ruzzolini; editor, Tatiana Casini Morigi. Reviewed at Eden Cinema, Rome, Nov. 15, 1987. Running time: **87 MINS.**

Pietro	Alberto Sordi
Teresa	Anna Longhi
Police chief	Dom DeLuise

Also with: George Gaynes, Giorgio Gobbi, Sasha D'Ark.

Rome — "A Taxi Driver In New York," besides being misnamed (half the film takes place in Miami), shows how flat a great comedian like director-star Alberto Sordi can fall in a quickie vehicle. Even Sordi's staunchest fans who have followed his ever less funny adventure in directing himself on the big screen have shied away from this poorly scripted, lensed and acted pic. Offshore interest should be proportionately minimal.

Pietro (Sordi) and wife Teresa (Anna Longhi) are dyed-in-the-wool Romans who have never traveled farther than Bologna. Their reason for living is a son they are putting through New York U., and who they come to visit amid all those terrifying skyscrapers. Sordi has the misfortune to witness a Mafia killing, and from that point on the Mob is on his tail. To protect him, the police give him a cab and a false name, and off he drives.

This is one of those films where everybody in America, even a black cop, is "Italian." Dialog runs to clichés about the difference between Americans (good-hearted, childlike snack-consumers) and Italians (cunning, family-loving spaghetti-eaters). Location work emphasizes East River panoramas and bridges and, of course, skyscrapers. Halfway through the action switches to Miami, where Sordi is set up by an Italo-American police captain (Dom DeLuise) to draw out the Mob's big fish.

Perhaps overdosed on "Miami Vice," filmmakers paint the city as a den of thugs, drug peddlers, killers and "scum." Most of the population seems to be Cuban when it isn't Italian. Climax takes place in a hacienda-villa belonging to the kingpin, a likable madman. Car chases and police cars with flashing red lights play an important part in creating what passes for excitement.

Camerawork is lamentably perfunctory, ditto rest of technical credits.—*Yung.*

Maladie d'amour
(Malady Of Love)
(FRENCH-COLOR)

An AMLF release of an Oliane Prods./FR3 Films coproduction, with the participation of Sofica Investimage, Images Investissement and the CNC. Produced by Marie-Laure Reyre. Directed by Jacques Deray. Stars Nastassja Kinski, Michel Piccoli, Jean-Hugues Anglade. Screenplay, Danièle Thompson, from an original story by Andrzej Zulawski; camera (Eastmancolor), Jean-François Robin; editor, Henri Lanoë; music, Romano Musumarra; art direction, Jean-Claude Gallouin; sound, Pierre Lenoir; production manager, Daniel Chevalier. Reviewed at the Georges V Cinema, Nov. 10, 1987. Running time: **116 MINS.**

Juliette	Nastassja Kinski
Clément	Jean-Hugues Anglade
Raoul Bergeron	Michel Piccoli

Also with: Jean-Claude Brialy, Souad Amidou, Jean-Paul Roussillon, Sophie D'Aulan, Jean-Luc Porraz.

Paris — Hankies may drop dry and unused at the end of "Maladie d'amour," an old-fashioned Love and Death romance that asks audiences to weep for joy because its heroine, Nastassja Kinski, overcomes fatal illness (the Big C) by strength of love. Costarring Jean-Hugues Anglade and Michel Piccoli as rivals for Kinski, pic could coast abroad on its topbilling, but is singularly lacking in heart and heat.

Major problem is miscasting — not the players, but the filmmakers. Scripter Danièle Thompson, who has coauthored the smash comedies of her father Gérard Oury and the hit teen Gaumont attraction, "La Boum," hasn't the same aptitudes for the Women's Film, and her turnabout ending is only highhanded, anticlimactic audience manipulation. Psychosomatically induced illness may have its poetic value, but Thompson's characters, though acted with authority, lack density and freshness.

Script's artificiality is compounded by Jacques Deray. His cold, precise direction is fine for the thriller genre in which he made his name, but utterly off the mark here. Deray inherited the project after two other directors, Andrzej Zulawski (credited with the original story idea) and André Techiné, came and went, reportedly in disagreement on the script.

Kinski plays a young employee in a Bordeaux hairstyling salon who becomes the kept mistress of eminent oncologist Piccoli, then falls in love with one of his interns (Anglade).

When the power-wielding Piccoli threatens to destroy his career, Anglade runs off to the sticks to hide with Kinski, landing a job as general practitioner in a small town. Kinski senses she's standing in her lover's way to professional fulfillment and returns to Piccoli, telling Anglade she no longer loves him.

Several years later, Anglade, now a crack Parisian oncologist, returns to Bordeaux for some lectures to find Kinski still living comfortably but unhappily in Piccoli's gilded cage. A physical malaise is diagnosed as Hodgkin's Disease. Kinski refuses surgery and comes up with a better treatment: shacking up again with Anglade. Medicine be damned, Love's the answer.

Where are the weepies of yesteryear?—*Len.*

Mälarpirater
(Pirates Of The Lake)
(SWEDISH-COLOR)

A Sandrew Film release of Sandrew Film production with the Swedish Film Institute, SVT-1, Film-Teknik. Written and directed by Allan Edwall, based on a novel by Sigfrid Siwertz. Camera (Eastmancolor), Rune Ericson; editor, Thomas Holéwa; music, Thomas Lindahl; sound, Lars Lundberg; production design, Göran Wassberg; costumes, Gertie Lindgren; production management, Jutta Ekman, Erik Spangenberg; assistant director, Christer Brossjö. Reviewed at Nordic Film Days, Burgtor-Lichtspiele, Lübeck, West Germany, Nov. 7, 1987. Running time: **85 MINS.**

Georg	Gustav Ljungberg
Fabian	Kristian Almgren
Erik	Jonas Eriksson
The Count	Björn Gustafson
The Beekeeper	Peter Stormare
Vilhelmina	Inga-Lil Rydberg
The Mother	Anita Ekström
The Father	Björn Granath

Also with: Anita Wall, Allan Edwall, Mathias Henrikson, Gun Arvidsson, Claes Esphagen, Carl-Magnus Dellow, Lars-Erik Berenett, Ewa Munther, Carl Olof Alm.

Lübeck, West Germany — "Pirates Of The Lake" is a crazy, mixed-up kind of a feature film by Allan Edwall whose childhood memoir film "Ake & His World" three years ago won kudos on the international fest circuit and praise for its tender-tough and funny reminiscing.

This time, Edwall works from the base of a popular Swedish novel established as a minor classic of Mark Twain's "Huck Finn" style and dash, but he comes out all wet and nearly shipwrecked with the story of three kids in a boat.

Two cleancut orphans and their devious friend "borrow" one small boat, capsize it, "borrow" a bigger one, are reported missing on the otherwise idyllic Lake Mälarn and start learning about survival isolated from their usual surroundings.

This is the stuff of strong storytelling, but Edwall loses his way in trying to hit too many targets at the same time. He resorts to tired clichés in the drawing of his juvenile leads while allowing his cast of adult oddballs to disappear in clouds of vapid whimsy.

Often abandoning straight narrative to toy with cinematic sleight-of-hand such as people jumping out of sepia photographs in silver frames, Edwall brings the action to a near standstill again and again.

When sequences of suspenseful action occur, Edwall proves curiously inept at handling them and, at the end, neither kiddie nor adult audiences are likely to have found much to hold their attention. —*Kell.*

Deathstalker II
(COLOR)

Fantasy spoof, heavy on in-jokes.

A Concorde Pictures presentation of a New Horizons Pictures production. Produced by Frank Isaac Jr. Directed by Jim Wynorski. Screenplay, Neil Ruttenberg, from story by Wynorski; additional dialog, R.J. Robertson; camera (Film House color), Leonard Solis (Leonardo Rodriguez Solis); editor, Steve Barnett; music, Chuck Cirino; additional music, Christopher Young, Oscar Camp (Oscar Cardozo Ocampo); sound, William Anderson; art direction, Marta Albert. Reviewed on Vestron Video vidcassette, N.Y., Oct. 29, 1987. (MPAA Rating: R.) Running time: **77 MINS.**

Deathstalker	John Terlesky
Evie	Monique Gabrielle
Jarek	John La Zar
Sultana	Toni Naples
Amazon queen	Maria Socas
One Eye	Marcos Wolinsky
Gargol	Deanna Booher

Aimed at the terminally hip, "Deathstalker II" lampoons the sword & sorcery genre with enough skin included to please homevideo fans. Bypassing theatrical release, Argentine-lensed pic predates and is far more entertaining than filmmaker Jim Wynorski's other current release "Big Bad Mama II."

Newie carries over one minor cast member (Marcos Wolinsky), the sets and some music from its 1983 forebear. This time John Terlesky plays the flippant hunk of a swashbuckler known as Deathstalker, teamed up with an exiled princess Evie (Monique Gabrielle) who is trying to recapture her throne. Evil sorcerer Jarek (John La Zar) has created a clone of Evie (also played by Gabrielle) to take her place.

Nonsense is loaded with anachronistic wise cracks, well-endowed women in topless scenes and colorful if chintzy sets. Terlesky displays a winning personality, remarking at the end regarding his legend: "I hope they get a good-looking guy to play me" 1,000 years hence. Gabrielle, who frequently spoofs her Penthouse centerfold model image (most recently in "Amazon Women On The Moon") finally gets to shine in a comedic role while La Zar, erstwhile transsexual villain named Z-Man in Russ Meyer's "Beyond The Valley Of The Dolls," is an effective heavy, Wrestler Deanna Booher, better known as Queen Kong, pops up to throw Terlesky around in a catch-as-catch-can match.

To pad the brief running time,

film ends with some amusing outtakes. End credits reach a nadir in the in-joke department, as instead of anglicizing the Argentine supporting cast, the actors are pointlessly credited with fictional names from composer Ennio Morricone's bio, e.g., the cleffer's pseudonyms Leo Nichols & Dan Savio, characters from his Westerns like Arch Stanton & Douglas Mortimer and even a pastiche on one of his film titles, Red Sands. —*Lor.*

F...ing Fernand
(FRENCH-W. GERMAN-COLOR)

A UGC release of a Stephen Film/UGC/Films A2/ICE Film/Richard Clause (for Delta-Film, Berlin) coproduction. Produced by Vera Belmont. Stars Thierry Lhermitte, Jean Yanne, Marie Laforêt. Directed by Gérard Mordillat. Screenplay, Jean Aurenche, Belmont, Mordillat, freely adapted from a novel by Walter Lewino; camera (color), Jean Monsigny; editor, Nicole Saunier; music, Jean-Claude Petit; art direction, Jacques Bufnoir; sound, Alain Sempé; costumes, Ulrike Schutte; production manager, Linda Gutenberg. Reviewed at the UGC Normandie cinema, Paris, Nov. 10, 1987. Running time: **84 MINS.**

Fernand Le Bâtard	Thierry Lhermitte
Binet	Jean Yanne
Lotte	Marie Laforêt
Lily	Charlotte Valandrey
La Fouine	Martin Lamotte
Von Schaltz	Hark Böhm
Vigneault	Patrice Valota

Paris — An irreverent sendup of collaboration and resistance in German-occupied France, this grossly titled Gallic feature is a gross misfire. Tale of a sexually obsessed young blind man and an escaped murderer hiding out in a bordello during World War II never strikes the perilous balance between realism and absurdity that gives this dark comedy its potency. Offshore chances are slight.

Director Gérard Mordillat, reworking an earlier script by veteran screenwriter Jean Aurenche and producer Vera Belmont, favors pace over tone, pushing his cast to broad performances that continually defuse both comedy and seriousness.

Thierry Lhermitte is the titular hero, a blind heir whose embarrassed family, a leading manufacturer of eyeglasses, has packed him away to a religious institution. At 30 he's still a virgin but ever-ready to proposition anything in skirts, even nuns.

The German invasion of 1940 is his liberation. Groping his way out of his bombed asylum, the randy Lhermitte seeks a pair of compliant female thighs, but only succeeds into falling in with killer Jean Yanne, on the run from a tenacious policeman (Martin Lamotte) who doesn't shun collaboration with the Germans.

The odd couple make their way to the south where Yanne wants to find his lady love (Marie Laforêt), a brothel mistress with a large German clientele. Lhermitte is in jubi-

lation in his new surroundings and finally loses his cherry (and discovers true love). They also become resistance heroes.

Script takes its most outrageous plunge into bad taste in a sequence in which a murdered German officer is dismembered and spirited away in a pair of valises, only to be mistaken for Black Market meat and served to a table of collaborationist Vichy militia. Image of Yanne and Lhermitte with the suitcases conjures up more memorable souvenirs of Jean Gabin and Bourvil lugging Black Market pig across Paris in Claude Autant-Lara's superb wartime black comedy, ''La Traversée de Paris,'' which Aurenche cowrote in 1957.—*Len.*

Capetan Meitanos: I Ikona Enos Mythikou Prossopou
(Captain Meitanos: The Image Of A Mythical Person)
(GREEK-COLOR)

A Greek Film Center-ERT I and Dimos Theos production. Written and directed by Theos. Camera (color), Yannis Varvarigos; editor, Theos; costumes, Dimitris Kakridas, Giorgia Fakiola; sound, Thanassis Georgiadis. Reviewed at the Thessaloniki Film Festival, Oct. 9, 1987. Running time: **120 MINS.**

With: Giorgos Michalacopoulos, Ginlio Brogi, Elena Maniati, Alexandros Veronis, Constantinos Mantilas, Pamayotis Kaldis, Panos Botinis.

Thessaloniki — This is a very ambitious effort by Dimos Theos which does not come off as expected. It is a historical drama, rich in ideas but poor in cinematic realization. It's an exceptional subject which with good handling could have become an epic biography. Due to its flat direction the film fails on many levels.

The central figure is an ex-diplomat who wanders in monasteries collecting material for the novel he is writing. The hero of his book is Captain Meitanos and his exploits in the 17th century. In a monastery he finds an icon on which the basic figure is missing. The diplomat thinks the missing person may be his hero and starts a search for the missing part of the icon.

Back in the 17th century painter Valos returning from Rome meets the beautiful slave Agatha who bears an incredible resemblance to Asanna, Meitanos' lover. Valos wishes to complete the icon of St. Serafim, the same icon the diplomat is looking for.

Each one of the monks in the monastery narrates differently the story of Meitanos. The diplomat continues his search and comes to a cave in the snowy wood, where he finds the missing part of the icon. Is he sure he sees it or it is an illusion since he is suffering high fever?

Dimos Theos wishes to point out that it is difficult to verify the historical events since everyone sees them from a different angle. He weaves his story on many levels, treating a complex plot flatly with a slow pace, burdened with a lot of dialog. It seems he cares more about creating the right medieval atmosphere than in developing his story in cinematic terms.

Acting on the whole is good, particularly the performance of Giorgos Michalacopoulos in the role of the diplomat. Camerawork is occasionally striking and all other technical credits are adequate. —*Rena.*

Holy Terror
(U.S.-DOCU-COLOR-16m)

A Cinema Guild release. Produced by Hudson River Prods. and Helsinki Films, N.Y. Produced and written by Victoria Schultz. Directed by Schultz, Nancy Kanter. Camera (color), Peter Pearce, Jeff Wayman; editor, Nola Schiff; music, Sorrel. Reviewed at Nyon Intl. Documentary Festival, Switzerland, Oct. 6, 1987. Running time: **60 MINS.**

Nyon — The 2-day Nuremburg trial began with a street parade, as people arrived by car and by the busload. A huge black-robed skull and skeleton was carried aloft. Signs proclaimed ''Abortion — the great evil that destroys our nation.'' Marchers adjourned to the motel ballroom to conduct their inquest, before black-robed justices.

The ''Nuremburg Tribunal II,'' in Nuremburg, Pa., got under way with an American flag and a swastika, drum rolls and the unfurling of a banner denouncing ''The Abortion Holocaust'' and ''Crimes

Against Humanity.'' Witnesses were sworn in and they denounced the defendants, who were tried in absentia — ''The networks, the media, the celebrities,'' and all those ''baby killers'' and others who condone the murder of ''unborn living children.''

A fetus in a glass jar was displayed. A puzzled little boy was told how to place the memorial rose on the jar. ''Is a baby in there?'' he asked. A tiny coffin was wrapped in an American flag for a symbolic funeral.

''Abortion is just like the Nazis taking Jews to the ovens'' said these so-called pro-lifers. ''The Court of Heaven must judge the abortionists and mete out a just sentence.''

The mock trial in Nuremburg, Pennsylvania, was but one of many public ceremonies and demonstrations that illustrate the new alliance of the religious right and the political right, an alliance both financial

and ideological, using the most sophisticated media technology and expensive consultants to convert the nation. The U.S. is criss-crossed with itinerant evangelical activists and pro-life lobbyists and action groups that train like commandos. Elaborate networking connects disparate groups that are united in their main purpose, opposition to abortion. City and state governments, and the school boards, are special targets for their intended reform. In Christ's name, voters are asked to use their ballots like ''an army of God.'' At these politico-religious rallies and fund-raising benefits, some people wear dynamite buttons in their lapels. These people mean business.

The other Nuremburgs in Ohio and California, and all cities and towns in America, must unite to vote out of office the targeted pro-choice candidates. Rev. Pat Robertson is seen, urging voters to put the right people into office to rescue the country from certain catastrophe.

Much of ''Holy Terror'' uses newsreel footage of the fire-bombings of abortion clinics around the country. Many burglaries, assaults, acts of vandalism and arson are documented. Also, the pro-lifers are seen with arms locked, obstructing entry to the premises of the abortion clinics. A distraught young blond woman tries to enter but is shoved aside. ''Please don't kill your baby,'' the crowd shouts. They use picket lines and bullhorns, stop traffic, block off the parking lot, pass out leaflets, sing ''We Shall Overcome,'' and scream ''murderer'' in front of the private homes of clinic personnel.

''Holy Terror'' reports these acts of intimidation and violence in ironic understatement, letting several pro-choice spokespersons tell of their determination simply to press on with their duties — their rights, according to the Supreme Court — despite the dangers.

Meanwhile, the threats increase, as pro-life leaders in open Congressional hearings are shown justifying the violence and harrassment, encouraged by the silence of the White House and the slowness of the Justice Department to investigate the bombings. ''God prevails over man'' and ''The Bible takes precedent over the laws of man'' are the pro-life slogans that justify their acts. ''We will continue to shut down abortion clinics around the country,'' they claim.

Paradoxically, the pro-lifers oppose abortion because all life is sacred, yet they are in favor of capital punishment.

''Holy Terror'' is an alarming roundup of pro and con opinion, mainly con, about abortion. One can call it an abortion war, because of the increasing, well-planned, systematic violence. The producers are to be commended for gaining access with their cameras to inner-sanctum

pro-life meetings where policy is worked out, including the how-to's of staging the sit-ins and take-overs of key buildings that house abortion clinics. These plans and logistics seem very close to military strategy.
—*Hitch.*

Hello Actors Studio
(FRENCH-DOCU-COLOR-16m)

A Copra-Prod. (Paris) and Nanouk Films (Montreal) coproduction with the participation of La Sept, TF1 (Unité de programmes Claude Otzenberger), Le Centre National de la Cinematographie, and Le Ministere de la Culture (Paris), and RAI (Rome). Executive producer, Alain Guesnier. Producer (Montreal), Anouk Brault. Directed by Annie Tresgot. Camera (color), Michel Brault, with Serge Giguere, Peter Reniers, Chris H. Leplus; editor, Variety Moszynski; musical conception, Luc Perini; sound, Dominique Chratrand, Philippe Scultety. Reviewed at Intl. Festival of Documentary Film, Nyon, Switzerland, Oct. 13, 1987. Running time: **165 MINS.**
(In English, with French subtitles).

Nyon — Despite its length, almost three hours, "Hello Actors Studio" merely drops in at Actors Studio, but does not reveal the processes by which the Studio has had, and is still having, enormous impact on American theater, cinema and tv, and beyond that, the Studio's impact on American popular culture in general.

Like some of the improvisations by young actors that it shows, the film seems unstructured, rambling, discursive, an exercise or preparation for something yet to come. The film, in three parts, is always interesting but never a spellbinder. One trouble is that perhaps too much screen time is given to little vérité sketches of ambitious young actor-students, their private part-time jobs and their full-time dreams. Among these many students, curiously, there are almost no black or Hispanic faces seen.

The film also neglects to put Actors Studio in its historical context, as an outgrowth of a disenchantment within the theater world with conventional stagecraft and acting technique.

Eli Wallach demonstrates the old hackneyed acting clichés, the gestures and grimaces, then shows us how the same lines and feelings can be expressed more honestly and with less artifice — or rather the artifice is less obviously mannered; it's a fresh artifice. Wallach's sequence in the film is invaluable but far too brief.

The connections of Actors Studio to the Moscow Art Theater, to Stanislavsky, and to the Group Theater, are not sufficiently traced and explored. We learn almost nothing about how the Studio and its Method influenced or stimulated a whole generation of playwrights, notably Williams, Miller and Inge, providing them with, in effect, a rehearsal environment within which to test and polish their plays as living performances.

Most conspicuously absent from this film is its hero, Lee Strasberg, the guiding light of Actors Studio for decades until his death. Presumably the legal wrangles in regard to the Strasberg estate, the custody and use of rehearsal tapes and other priceless materials, account for the absence of Strasberg from this film.

"Hello" abounds in celebrities, veterans of West 44th St., and their comments about their work there are partial compensation for the aforementioned weaknesses of the film. Maureen Stapleton, Lee Grant, Vivian Nathan, Harvey Keitel, Gene Wilder, Rod Steiger — a common theme is the continuing usefulness to their careers of Studio values learned as students there. Sydney Pollack, who studied with Sanford Meisner, describes the long-range benefits of Studio's effect on American entertainment, which in turn has worldwide spin-off.

Paul Newman talks of the daring required for an actor to expose himself to disaster, pushing himself to the limits of the role. At this point we see Newman in his racing car, speeding the highways, and also behind the wheel at the finish line. The racing shots, we realize, are a metaphor of Newman's point that a courageous actor must get maximum acceleration from his vehicle, despite the danger.

Group Theater co-founder Cheryl Crawford observes that the Method varies according to the personalities of the instructors. Crawford stresses the value of the Studio, and a principal motive in its founding, as a training-ground for playwrights and directors, a topic that the remainder of the film does not probe adequately.

Shelley Winters chats informally with the young-adult students, who plainly adore her. She critiques their performances and also points out nostalgically the section of the balcony where, long ago, she and Tony made love. The dedicated Artistic Director of the Studio, Ellen Burstyn, discusses its purposes and also performs a long, improvised monolog scene within the Studio's permanent set, a bedroom-kitchen suite, that serves the three or four additional improv scenes of the film.

Norman Mailer, Joseph Mankiewicz and Arthur Penn sit with other guests in the Studio's bleachers to watch student actors in several different scenes, then critique them.

Studio alumni Brando, Dean and McQueen are seen in clips — McQueen in a crime-scene kinescope with William Shatner and Ralph Bellamy. Also, Robert De Niro is glimpsed running from a stage-door to a taxi-cab.

Elia Kazan, formerly a Studio student of acting and directing, later an instructor and mentor, always a supporter and inspiration, has long employed Studio methodology and performers in his many stageplays and films as director, for almost four decades. He betrays himself, of course, as an unabashed Studio fan, and his genial smile and optimistic words close the film.

Despite the riches preceding, "Hello Actors Studio" does not hit a home run. It's good, but not good enough. Doubtlessly "Hello" will come to American public tv, and in homevideo it can prove a standard, given its unique if incomplete materials. Students of drama schools and acting academies, who presumably will receive supplementary facts from their instructors, will find the film provocative and useful.—*Hitch.*

Rights And Reactions
(U.S.-DOCU-COLOR)

A Realis Pictures and Syzygy Media production, in association with Tapestry Intl. Prods., N.Y. Executive producers, Paul Fisher, Nancy Walzog, Phil Zwickler. Produced and directed by Zwickler. Written by Jane Lippman, Zwickler; camera (color), Geoffrey O'Connor; editor, Lippman; on-line editor, Jim Burgess; art direction, Richard Kuhn, Susan Wilcox; additional photography, WNYC Foundation, Bettye Lane, Gay Cable Network, Kim Hanson, Abigail Norman/Heramedia Inc.; associate producers, Conrad Johnson, Maria Maggenti. Funded in part by North Star Fund, N.Y., and Haymarket People's Fund, Boston. Reviewed at Intl. Documentary Film Festival, Nyon, Switzerland, Oct. 14, 1987. Running time: **60 MINS.**

Nyon — "Rights And Reactions" plainly favors the civil rights of gays versus the reactionary forces of denial. However, this film is not a simplistic, strident propaganda job. Instead, it gives plenty of time and footage equally to Catholic, Jewish and other groups opposed to gay rights. All sides of this inflammatory issue receive plenty of opportunity to elucidate their positions.

Arguments pro and con this or that idea about gay rights are advanced both at the microphone, within the hallowed chambers of the N.Y. City Council, and also on the sidewalk outside. Perhaps the latter is more interesting, as dramatic expressions of deeply rooted feelings. Tempers flare as both proponents and opponents come close to cracking heads, but restraint prevails. The American democratic process is vindicated, but barely.

The film ends with the victory of gay rights after 16 years of lobbying and maneuvers within the Council. These rights, won at last, may later be cancelled. As the banners of opponents warn the legislators — "If you pass the Gay Bill, we will vote you out."—*Hitch.*

Umbruch
(Marble In Pieces)
(SWISS-DOCU-COLOR/B&W-16m)

A Swiss Film Center presentation of a Filmcooperative Zurich production. Produced and directed by Hans-Ulrich Schlumpf. Commentary, Schlumpf; camera (color), Pio Corradi; editor, Rainer Trinkler; music, Bruno Spoerri; sound, Hans Kunzi. Reviewed at Nyon Intl. Documentary Festival, Switzerland, Oct. 11, 1987. Running time: **93 MINS.**

Nyon — "Umbruch" is concerned with the human consequence of automation. The film centers on the printing industry in general and on several companies in Zurich in particular. Its message is more universal: technological development must be humanized; workers and craftspeople cannot simply be dismissed as obsolete; they must be helped to find a place within the new, ever-modernizing communications systems.

"Umbruch" emphasizes several older men, typesetters who are highly skilled, with decades of experience. Their dilemma is typical of others in the industry. Must they abandon their traditional vocation? Can they be expected to retrain at an advanced age? Can they adapt to the new equipment? They try, smiling ironically at the camera. Meanwhile, the old presses are carted away and pounded into scrap iron.

Winner at the Nyon festival of the Prize of Swiss tv, "Umbruch" was commended by the international jury for dealing with "a problem of enormous proportions, on the changes in human experience as a result of trends in modern work."
—*Hitch.*

Beirut: The Last
Home Movie
(U.S.-DOCU-COLOR-16m)

A Zohe Film production, N.Y., in association with Valley Filmworks, N.Y.; the Max M. and Majory Fisher Foundation; Public Broadcasting Stations, Corp. for Public Broadcasting; WGBH Boston. Produced and directed by Jennifer Fox. Written by John Mullen, Fox; camera (color), Alex Nepomniaschy; editor, Mullen; original music, Lanny Meyers; Lebanese music, Ziad Rahbani; sound, Jeff Brown. Reviewed at Intl. Documentary Film Festival, Nyon, Switzerland, Oct. 15, 1987. (Also in London Film Festival.) Running time: **120 MINS.**

Nyon — A Soviet commentator once remarked, misunderstanding Chekhov's play, that his "Three Sisters" is about a privileged trio of spoiled bourgeois brats who somehow can't take the train to Moscow although they have the fare.

Perhaps Jennifer Fox' "Beirut" is like that. Its three idle aristocratic Lebanese sisters languorously talk a lot (too much) about themselves and social change, but they cannot get themselves organized to do anything.

Beirut is an international trouble spot but somehow these three attractive, cultured Bustros sisters manage to survive unscratched with their mother and servants in their magnificent 200-year-old palace, untouched and unmoved by the violence around them. We keep waiting for big, dramatic action but it never comes. That's the point and that's why the film works. It's fascinating (well, mostly) because of what should happen or could happen but doesn't.

The three sisters have a kid brother, something of a sissy, whom they idolize and pamper. By the end of two hours (three months of shooting), the brother weds in a fancy, old-fashioned ceremony, a scene that culminates the film and seems to say that old aristocratic Beirut is unchanged and unchangeable. The film ends, as does its audience, convinced that the privileged brats of this world are deservedly the last holdouts of style and good manners.

Old family movie footage and stills, plus news footage of Beirut at war, are intercut with the Bustros opulence. As their chandeliers vibrate, we feel the concussion of artillery, but it's in the distance. That's the problem with this film — the problems are in the distance.

More important than "Beirut" as a film and the Bustros family is the debut of Jennifer Fox as director/producer. A recent dropout from the NYU film school, she makes an auspicious start with this film. Editing in effect is writing, nicely controlled. Although this is a documentary, here is a fiction talent, and of considerable promise, with the right material. — *Hitch.*

Henri Storck, Eyewitness
(BELGIAN-DOCU-COLOR/B&W)

A Three Lines Prods., Bergen Op Zoom, Netherlands, release of a Fugitive Cinema production, Antwerp, Belgium, with the BRT, the RTB, and the Flemish Ministry of Culture. Directed by Robbe De Hert. Written by De Hert, Rik Stallaerts, in consultation with Henri Storck; research, Maurice Noben; camera (color), Jules Van Den Steenhoven; editor & sound, Chris Verliert. Reviewed at Nyon Intl. Documentary Festival, Switzerland, Oct. 15, 1987. Running time: **100 MINS.**
(French and Dutch soundtrack)

Nyon — "Henri Storck, Eyewitness" is an affectionate tribute and career biography of the famed Belgian filmmaker, now 80, who has produced and/or directed (so far) over 70 films, mostly documentaries, shot all over the world. Among the Storck films are many important records of culture and art (his "Rubens" and other painters), social upheaval, and wry observations of the human creature at work and play.

The play began at Ostende, Belgian seaside resort (Storck's birthplace), when young Storck, a cineclub manager, was appointed Ostende's official cinematographer.

Since childhood, Storck had been familiar with many famous artists, like the Belgians Ensor and Permeke, latter the subject of a Storck feature docu only three years ago. Also, Storck assisted Jean Vigo with his classic "Zéro de Conduite" and played a priest in the film, which

was promptly banned by the French as blasphemous, but years later was released and is now esteemed as a devastating social satire.

In 1933, with the Dutch filmmaker Joris Ivens, Storck made the hard-hitting documentary "Misère au Borinage," depicting the horrendous working and living conditions of Belgian miners and their families. Several years ago, "Borinage" was revived and scored for a live orchestra for screening at the Berlin festival. Storck was present for the honor. A film of enduring relevance, "Borinage" asserts the dignity of labor and the right of workers to a decent life.

The paths of Ivens and Storck have crossed many times. The two old friends meet again in this film at the railroad station, as Ivens ricochets in from China. The two old-timers have collaborated on many projects and they are esteemed as the two preeminent filmmakers of the two lowlands nations.

"Henri Storck, Eyewitness" uses excerpts from Storck films, background stock footage of Belgium's troubled history, plus interviews with Storck and with critics and fellow filmmakers. This film, and Storck's career, were not all easy, but both have come out well. "Henri Storck, Eyewitness" is the ultimate, definitive reconstruction of the career of this elder-statesman filmmaker. —*Hitch.*

Empire Of The Sun
(COLOR)

Spielberg spectacular lacks precision. B.O. outlook okay.

A Warner Bros. release of a Robert Shapiro production from Amblin Entertainment. Produced by Steven Spielberg, Kathleen Kennedy, Frank Marshall. Executive producer, Shapiro. Directed by Spielberg. Screenplay, Tom Stoppard, based on the novel by J.G. Ballard; camera (Technicolor), Allen Daviau; editor, Michael Kahn; music, John Williams; production design, Norman Reynolds; supervising art director, Charles Bishop, Maurice Fowler (China); Norman Dorme (Spain); art direction, Frederick Hole; set decoration, Harry Cordwell, Michael D. Ford; costume design, Bob Ringwood; sound (Dolby), Colin Charles, Tony Dawe; special effects supervisor, Kit West; additional optical effects, Industrial Light & Magic, Dennis Muren, Michael Pangrazio, John Ellis; associate producer, Chris Kenny; assistant director, David Tomblin; casting, Maggie Cartier, Mike Fenton-Jane Feinberg, Judy Taylor (U.S.), Yuriko Matsubara (Japan); second unit director, Frank Marshall; second unit camera, Jimmy Devis. Reviewed at The Burbank Studios, Burbank, Calif., Nov. 24, 1987. (MPAA Rating: PG.) Running time: **152 MINS.**

Jim	Christian Bale
Basie	John Malkovich
Mrs. Victor	Miranda Richardson
Dr. Rawlins	Nigel Havers
Frank Demerest	Joe Pantoliano
Maxton	Leslie Phillips
Sgt. Nagata	Masato Ibu
Jim's Mother	Emily Richard
Jim's Father	Rupert Frazer
Mr. Victor	Peter Gale
Kamikaze Boy Pilot	Takatoro Kataoka
Dainty	Ben Stiller
Tiptree	David Neidorf
Cohen	Ralph Seymour
Mr. Lockwood	Robert Stephens

Hollywood — Steven Spielberg delves deeply into the well of seriousness in "Empire Of The Sun" and comes up with about half-a-bucket. Story of an 11-year-old boy stranded in Japanese-occupied China during World War II seems tailor-made for Spielberg's fantastical inclinations as well as his increasing artistic ambition, and sweeping picture is studded by spectacular set pieces, many staged on location in and around Shanghai. Young Christian Bale successfully carries this massive production on his small shoulders, and focus on this bright, energetic fellow, along with the Spielberg name, should guarantee good initial business. But length, sketchy characterizations, pronounced Britishness and lack of a strong narrative might well keep ultimate b.o. at a lower level than is customary for the director.

With this and "The Last Emperor" entering release, much will be made of China's current fashionability on world screens. Nevertheless, "Empire Of The Sun" actually represents an ideal companion piece to "Hope And Glory," in that both are about how young boys left to their own devices can have a bloody marvelous, adventurous time during a catastrophic war.

Although the most striking single feature of "Empire" is its central situation, Spielberg has not striven

to make a realistic or historically complex film. J.G. Ballard's autobiographical 1984 novel marked the first non-science-fiction book by the author, and both it and the film clearly are the work of sci-fi artists channelling their imaginations into a more traditional framework.

Leading the first troupe of Hollywood studio filmmakers ever into Shanghai, a city virtually unchanged since the events depicted, Spielberg turns the grey metropolis into a sensational film set as he delineates the edginess and growing chaos leading up to Japan's entry into the city just after Pearl Harbor.

Jim is in every way a proper upper-class English lad but for the fact he has never seen England. Like many a Spielberg leading boy, he dreams of the skies and the vehicles that can take him there, in this case wartime airplanes.

Separated from his parents during the spectacularly staged evacuation of Shanghai, Jim makes do for awhile on his own before hooking up with a pair of American scavengers, with whom in due course he is rounded up and sent to a prison camp for the duration of the war.

It is there that Jim flourishes, expending his boundless energy on creative projects and pastimes that finally land him a privileged place among the entrepreneurially minded Americans. He's a go-getter and a survivor, and the war, which represents his "University of Life," leads him to grow in many ways that his previous cloistered existence would never have permitted.

Except for its basic intelligence, there is no recognizing the stamp of brilliant playwright Tom Stoppard in the screenplay. Much more visible is the virtual inventory of Spielberg touches — the obsession with flight, the bicycle riding, the attempts at revival of the dead, the looks of awe, the heavily backlit E.T. fingers and the amassed loot of the world out of "Raiders Of The Lost Ark" (and "Citizen Kane").

Jim's alert inventiveness in the face of adversity is the hallmark of the story, although the point of it all by the end seems fuzzy. Picture is composed mainly of vivid vignettes stemming from the confined situation, but there is little feeling of years passing or people changing. When Jim's anticipated reunion with his parents approaches, one doesn't know whether to feel emotional relief or sadness that his life probably will once again become conventional.

John Malkovich's Basie, an opportunistic King Rat type, keeps threatening to become a fully developed character but never does, although the man remains interesting and the actor's sly, insinuating line readings frequently conjure up thoughts of Jack Nicholson.

Otherwise, the characters are complete blanks, which severely limits the emotional reverberation of the piece. No special use is made of the talents of Miranda Richardson, Nigel Havers, Joe Pantoliano and the others, so it is up to young English thesp Christian Bale to engage the viewer's interest, which he does superbly with a lively performance graced by an appealing gravity.

Noteworthy, too, is the attitude toward the Japanese. Although they are the invaders and masters of the prison camp, Jim admires them for their bravery and flying skills, saluting them on occasion and forming a special bond with a young pilot. On balance, the Japanese come off more favorably than the grubby Yanks, and surely no American film depicting Japanese behavior during World War II, especially towards prisoners, has adopted so benign an attitude toward our then-enemies.

Novel and script provide numerous opportunities for wild surrealism, notably in the area of contrast between Western fashion and Eastern convention, and Spielberg follows up on them, even if his natural instincts don't lie in this direction. One suspects a European director would have emphasized the harshness and absurdism of the situation, but Spielberg still has pulled off some riveting scenes, such as Jim secretly watching a couple beginning to make love as Shanghai is bombed in the distance, and an atom bomb blast being observed from 500 miles away.

The gritty backstreets of Shanghai and heavy facades along the Bund on the waterfront are used to maximum effect by the director, who actually got to shoot in China for only three weeks. Spectacular prison camp set was built in Spain, while other scenes were shot in the U.K.

All technical contributions are, almost by definition, monumentally good. Allen Daviau's lensing, Norman Reynold's production design, Michael Kahn's editing and John Williams' lush score are all top drawer, and a few special effects shots lend the picture added scope. Overall, this is a terrifically ambitious work, partially, but still imposingly, achieved. —Cart.

Walker
(COLOR)

Loaded historical tract on Nicaragua is going nowhere.

A Universal/Northern Distribution Partners release of an Edward R. Pressman production in association with Incine. Produced by Lorenzo O'Brien. Executive producer, Pressman. Producer, Angel Flores Marini. Line producer, Carlos Alvarez. Directed by Alex Cox. Screenplay, Rudy Wurlitzer; camera (color), David Bridges; editors, Carlos Puente Ortega, Cox; music, Joe Strummer; production design, Bruno Rubeo; art direction, Cecilia Montiel, Jorge Sainz; set decoration, Bryce Perrin, Suzie Frischette (Tucson); wardrobe design, Pam Tait; costume design (Tucson), Theda Deramus; sound design,

Richard Beggs; sound, Peter Glossop, David Batchelor, John Pritchett (Tucson), Joseph Geisinger (L.A.); associate producer, Debbie Diaz; assistant directors, Mary Ellen Woods, Michelle Pinelli (L.A.); casting, Victoria Thomas, Miguel Sandoval; second unit director, Sandoval; additional camera, Dennis Crossan, Frank Pineda, Steve Fierberg, Tom Richmond, Rafael Ruiz. Reviewed at Universal Studios, Universal City, Calif., Nov. 23, 1987. (MPAA Rating: R.) Running time: **95 MINS.**

William Walker	Ed Harris
Ephraim Squier	Richard Masur
Major Siegfried Henningson	Rene Auberjonois
Timothy Crocker	Keith Szarabajka
Captain Hornsby	Sy Richardson
Bryon Cole	Xander Berkeley
Stebbins	John Diehl
Cornelius Vanderbilt	Peter Boyle
Ellen Martin	Marlee Matlin
Raousset	Alfonso Arau
Munoz	Pedro Armendariz
Mayorga	Roberto Lopez Espinoza
Norvell Walker	Gerrit Graham
James Walker	William O'Leary
Yrena	Blanca Guerra
Don Domingo	Alan Bolt
Parker French	Miguel Sandoval

Hollywood — The potentially fascinating story of an American adventurer who installed himself as president of Nicaragua 132 years ago, "Walker" unfortunately exists for one reason and one reason only — for director Alex Cox to vent his spleen about continued American interference with the Central American country. The comic, idiosyncratic approach taken by Cox and scenarist Rudy Wurlitzer has merit in theory, but the result onscreen is a virtual fiasco, a depressing companion piece to Cox' last outing, "Straight To Hell," which is about where this is headed at the box-office, except in territories where to be anti-American is enough to ensure approval.

With the financial backing of tycoon Cornelius Vanderbilt, Walker led a mercenary band of 58 men to Nicaragua in 1855 and ruled the tiny nation with an increasingly heavy hand for two years until being kicked out. As presented here, the rigid Southerner was an extreme proponent of Manifest Destiny, and no amount of logic or rational persuasion could sway him from his belief in America's God-given right to impose its ways on everyone else.

Cox and Wurlitzer make a muddled attempt at the outset to paint Walker as an idealist who becomes fatally twisted after the premature death of his strong-willed fiancée (played in a very brief appearance by Marlee Matlin). From then on, however, Walker is ramrod stiff and impenetrable, a man given to self-seriously strutting about and delivering platitudes such as, "One must act with severity, or perish."

As written, Walker is a cardboard figure, neither human and multifaceted enough to become involved with, nor sufficiently demented to assume the dimensions of a mesmerizing villain. This unreality also kills any possible dramatic believability, since he seems to inspire no enthusiasm or real loyalty among his men. Unlike some of the

contemporary Americans who have displayed a hankering to dabble in Nicaraguan politics, this Walker is not a communicator, and Ed Harris seems trapped within the character's constricted emotional and political makeup, as well as in his formal clothes.

The film is completely unconvincing in its presentation of events and how things might have been, for reasons that have everything to do with a negligent attitude toward character, narrative and historical detail, and nothing to do with the surrealistic anachronisms that have been woven into the visual fabric in order to emphasize the modern parallels to the action. In fact, these elements are introduced rather slowly and discreetly — a copy of Newsweek here, People there, until finally a chopper comes down to evacuate the Yankees out of the country they've eviscerated.

Ironically, for someone so obviously incensed about American bullying of the Third World, Cox conveys absolutely no feeling for Nicaragua or its people. The peasants and other citizens over whom Walker tramples are scarcely seen, much less drawn in any compelling way, so no picture is offered of just what the interloper is despoiling, what suffering he is provoking. No values are spoken other than Walker's arrogant ones, so there is no political context or philosophical perspective offered. Ultimately, one learns nothing except for the barest facts of Walker's actions that can be summarized in two or three sentences, and Cox' attitude — obvious for all to see from the beginning — fails to take on any complexity or shading as things progress.

Performances pretty uniformly shoot over the top, but lensing by David Bridges gives the picture a rich look and score by former Clash leader Joe Strummer (who also pops up briefly onscreen) deftly mixes traditional and modern sounds and develops one haunting theme to help dramatize the destruction of a town.

Cox and Wurlitzer wrap matters up by giving Walker the following farewell speech: "You all might think there may come a day when America will leave Nicaragua alone, but I'm here to tell you that day will never come." This heavy-handedness is compounded by subsequent tv footage of Ronald Reagan and American military maneuvers in Honduras. Even the faithful few may be heading for exits by this time, but they'll miss the best laugh in the picture, which has the proud credit crawl announcement — "This film was made in Nicaragua in 1987" — followed by the standard promo card, "When in Hollywood visit Universal Studios Tour." —Cart.

This Is Our Home, It Is Not For Sale
(DOCU-COLOR)

A Riverside production. Produced and directed by Jon Schwartz. Camera (color), Levie Isaacks; editor, Ronald Medico; sound, Brenda Reiswerg. Reviewed at Southwest Alternate Media Project, Houston, Nov. 7, 1987. (No MPAA Rating.) Running time: **190 MINS.**

Houston — If the purpose of a documentary film is to document an event or situation, then Jon Schwartz has a winner with his very long but scrupulously crafted "This Is Our Home, It Is Not For Sale." The entertainment value of a 3-hour-plus documentary on a Houston neighborhood cannot be understated, but Schwartz has come up with a film that is compelling, challenging, thorough and watchable.

The title comes from signs posted in Houston's Riverside neighborhood during the era of blockbusting, signaling solidarity among residents to hold on to the beautiful neighborhood near Buffalo Bayou. Riverside has been a neighborhood of almost ceaseless transition and the onslaught of changes has caused virtually the same drama to be reenacted among new configurations of Riverside residents.

In the 1920s, Riverside was an alternative residential district to Houston's swanky River Oaks whose "social restrictions" effectively blocked sales to Jews. While Riverside was never an exclusively Jewish neighborhood, it became known as the Jewish River Oaks and housed some of the city's most prominent residents in huge, distinctive homes on palatial grounds. By the 1960s, blacks were buying into Riverside and a tide of white flight ensued. By the 1970s, Riverside was uneasily integrated. Today, the drama continues as white gays are purchasing houses, causing yet another wave of transition, prejudice and fear.

Schwartz traces the history of Riverside chronologically, using an interview technique which bars the viewer from ever seeing the interviewer or hearing his questions. The editing of these interviews is superlative, and the pace of the long film never flags. However, there is only one instance when Schwartz gives us the name or title of his interview subject, so the viewer is left mainly watching unknown people recall their old neighborhood.

There is no voice-over and no overt attempt to manipulate the viewer's opinions. Schwartz juxtaposes the interviews carefully, so they build on each other and consolidate the story. In a few cases respondents contradict each other, even resorting to name-calling.

One of the best portions involves interviews with the first black residents to integrate Riverside. Although much of the bitterness from those years has dissipated, the interviewees speak with firm memories about the bombing of one black's home or the sit-in at a local lunch counter.

Schwartz has interspersed his interview segments with home movies, historical footage, old photographs, and some new footage of contemporary life along Buffalo Bayou, underlaid with some wonderful jazz music from the local Arnett Cobb Quintet.

Production values in the film rank on a par with the professional quality of the interviews. —*Jole.*

Custody
(AUSTRALIAN-COLOR)

A Film Australia production. Produced by Tristram Miall. Directed by Ian Munro. Screenplay, improvised; story, Ann Charlton, Anna Grieve; camera (color), Joel Peterson; editor, Denise Haslem; sound, Rob Stalder; music, Peter Best; narrator, Peter Carroll; production manager/assistant director, Grieve; casting, Forcast. Reviewed at Mosman screening room, Sydney, Nov. 21, 1987. Running time: **92 MINS.**
Christine Byrne . . . . Judith Stratford
Andrew Byrne . . . . Peter Browne
Justin Byrne . . . . Michael Cudlin
Cathy Byrne . . . . Sheridan Murphy
Christine's solicitor . . . . Stuart Fowler
Andrew's solicitor . . . . June Musgrave
Magistrate . . . . . . Lillian Thompson-Austen
Judge . . . . Justice Eric Baker
   Also with: Rosemary Michelin, Norman Goodsell (court counsellors), Robert Lethbridge, Robert Harding (barristers), Ann Charlton (legal aid).

Sydney — A dramatized docu, made in the style of Hungarian docudramas, "Custody" is a painfully realistic recreation of a seemingly average child custody case as it goes through Australia's Family Law Courts. Thanks to fine performances and no-nonsense treatment, film effectively captures the pain and frustration of such situations, and should fare well on tv and video, with fests, especially docu fests, also likely to be interested. Theatrical possibilities are there, too, especially domestically, if pic is handled properly.

In the film, actors portray a couple, married 12 years, but now involved in an acrimonious divorce; actors also play their two children, and family friends. But all the lawyers, counsellors and court officials seen in the film, including a magistrate and a judge, are nonpros; in fact, they're playing themselves. Storyline was devised by Ann Charlton (also the film's legal consultant) and Anna Grieve; it was then workshopped with the cast, and all dialog was improvised during the 3-week shoot. Result is remarkably effective.

Christine (Judith Stratford), who hasn't worked since she had her first child, now 10, is bored and has started seeing another man. Her overworked husband, Andrew (Peter Browne), is forced to leave the family home and move into a tiny apartment. Then the legal battles begin (financed, incidentally, by the Australian taxpayer via a legal aid service): firstly Andrew's access to his children, then maintenance, then division of property — all go through the courts. Christine and the children have to sell their family home and move into an apartment; their dog has to be given away, the children have to change to different schools.

When Andrew discovers his son, Justin, was arrested for stealing a Walkman, and frequently is absent from school, he is furious Christine hadn't told him and demands full custody. The ensuing case cleverly presents the problem so even-handedly that, when the judge makes his decision, the viewer is genuinely surprised at the verdict: there has been a record of violence against Family Law Court judges in Australia after such custody decisions have been handed down, and watching this film one begins to understand why.

Film's major strength is the acting of the principals; Stratford and Browne are totally convincing in their roles, their heartbreak and anger tellingly conveyed. The various legal eagles who play themselves offer at times telling asides, such as the moment when, after the verdict is announced, the successful barrister remarks: "It never feels like a victory."

Only real flaw is the overly tight editing, presumably to bring the drama down to a requried running time. Printed synopsis supplied by Film Australia offers invaluable background material left out of the film, making for tantalizing gaps in the story.

But apart from this complaint, "Custody" admirably achieves all it sets out to do. A final title informs the viewer the cost, to the community, of settling the affairs of another broken marriage, another in a long line of gloomy statistics. —*Strat.*

Stranded
(COLOR)

Claustrophobic sci-fi effort.

A New Line Cinema release. Produced by Scott Rosenfelt, Mark Levinson. Executive producer, Robert Shaye. Directed by Tex Fuller. Screenplay, Alan Castle; camera (United color), Jeff Jur; editor, Stephen E. Rivkin; music, Stacy Widelitz; sound, Peter Bentley; aliens created and designed by Michele Burke; special visual effects, VCE Inc.-Peter Kuran; special effects coordinator, Allen Hall; assistant director, Mike Topoozian; production manager, Marie Cantin; set decoration, Lisette Thomas; stunt coordinator, John Branagan; associate producer, Sara Risher; casting, Annette Benson; additional editor, Steven Schoenberg; Alien world sequence — director, Marina Sargenti; camera, Robert Brinkmann. Reviewed at Wometco Shadowood Roxy 8 theater, Boca Raton, Fla., Nov. 23, 1987. (MPAA Rating: PG-13.). Running time: **80 MINS.**
Deirdre . . . . Ione Skye
Sheriff McMahon . . . . Joe Morton
Grace Clark . . . . Maureen O'Sullivan
Helen Anderson . . . . Susan Barnes
Lt. Scott . . . . Cameron Dye
Vernon Burdett . . . . Michael Greene
Prince . . . . Brendan Hughes
Sergeant . . . . Gary Swanson
Jester . . . . Flea
Warrior . . . . Spice Williams

Boca Raton, Fla. — "Stranded" is a modest sci-fi thriller that dares to be different, but fails to come off as a satisfying feature. Currently in regional release after test bookings, it is unlikely to prove a theatrical winner for New Line.

Story is set entirely at night (oppressively) as aliens from Outer Space land at a remote farm house in the South and take cute 17-year-old Deirdre (Ione Skye) and her grandma Grace (Maureen O'Sullivan) hostage. Problems in communication result in a lethal gun battle with country boys who arrive at the farm and a night-long siege when the local police, led by black Sheriff McMahon (Joe Morton), come to attempt to defuse the hostage situation.

Director Tex Fuller maintains adequate tension as the claustrophobic tale unfolds in nearly real-time fashion. However, Alan Castle's screenplay is severely limited in scope and fails to exploit its sci-fi elements much beyond the standard confrontational mode. Subplots revolve around the local rednecks' uneasiness with obeying a black sheriff (who naturally seems to side with the "misunderstood" aliens), the women attempting to achieve a rapport with the friendly-seeming intruders and the activities of a mysterious Dept. of Defense agent (Susan Barnes).

Michele Burke's interesting designwork for the aliens' makeup, which ranges from a modified hippie look to a "Black Lagoon"-style lizard woman, is the film's strongest suit. Visual effects emphasizing blue lighting are okay.

Cast is unusual, dominated by erstwhile "The Brother From Another Planet" Joe Morton, on the other side of the alien fence this time as the no-nonsense, very sympathetic sheriff. Ione Skye (of "River's Edge") is affecting as the ordinary teenager who almost falls in love with one of the visitorsl, while Maureen O'Sullivan contributes an okay gothic turn as her grandma. —*Lor.*

Mind Killer
(COLOR)

Imitative, minor horror opus.

A Prism Entertainment and Flash Features presentation. Executive producer, A.B. Goldberg. Produced by Sarah H. Liles. Directed by Michael Krueger. Screenplay, Krueger, Dave Sipos, Curtis Hannum, from story by Krueger, Doug Olson; additional material, Olson; camera (color), Jim Kelley; editor, Jonathan Moser; music, Jeffrey Wood; sound, Bob Abbott; assistant director, Liles; special makeup effects, Vincent J. Guastini; special effects supervisor & additional story material, Ted A. Bohus; postproduction supervisor, Jon Ackelson; coproducer, Olson; associate producer, John Fitzgerald. Reviewed on Prism Entertainment vidcassette, N.Y., Nov. 18, 1987. (No MPAA Rating.) Running time: **86 MINS.**
Warren . . . . Joe McDonald
Larry . . . . Christopher Wade
Sandy . . . . Shirley Ross
Brad . . . . Kevin Hart
Vivac Chandra . . . . Tom Henry
Mrs. Chandra . . . . Diana Calhoun
Townsend . . . . George Flynn

"Mind Killer," previously titled "Brain Creature," is a modest made-for-video horror feature from Denver filmmakers.

Joe McDonald is featured as Warren, a nerd working in the library's basement archives, who unsuccessfully hangs out with fellow nerd (and trivia expert) Larry (Christopher Wade) in singles bars where the girls won't give either of them a tumble.

When Warren finds a book by Vivac Chandra on total mind control, he is suddenly full of energy and confidence, causing women to be entranced by him. Film ventures into sci-fi territory as Warren and later Larry develop psychokinetic powers. Warren uses his new mental abilities to try and force pretty librarian Sandy (Shirley Ross) to obey his will, but several yucky makeup effects later, Larry uses a machine to subdue Warren, who has mutated into a brain monster.

Film's cheapo production values are very restricting, with the brain monster looking like a leftover from the minor horror pic "The Deadly Spawn." Vincent Guastini's makeup effects bring back the boring bladders-under-the-skin and dripping goo motifs of countless horror films. Acting is adequate, on the level of regional theater.—*Lor.*

Evil Town
(COLOR)

Shoddy horror pic.

A Trans World Entertainment presentation of a Mars production. Produced by Peter S. Traynor, William D. Sklar. Directed by Edward Collins, Traynor, Larry Spiegel; additional sequences filmed by Mardi Rustam. Screenplay, Spiegel, Richard Benson, from story by Royce Applegate; camera (United color), Bill Mann, Bob Ioniccio; editor, Jess Mancilla, David G. Blangsted, Peter Parasheles; music, Michael Linn; sound, Gerald Wolfe; art direction, Richard Gillis; assistant director, Cheryl Factor; associate producers, Joan Kasha, Michael O'Donnell; casting, Remy MacKenzie Karima. Reviewed on TWE vidcassette, N.Y., Nov. 18, 1987. (No MPAA Rating.) Running time: **82 MINS.**
Chris Fuller . . . . James Keach
Julie . . . . Michele Marsh
Linda . . . . Doria Cook
Mike . . . . Robert Walker
Dr. Schaeffer . . . . Dean Jagger
   Also with: Keith Hefner, Greg Finley, E.J. Andre, Dabbs Greer, Scott Hunter, Lynda Wiesmeier, Christie Houser, Noelle Harling, Paul McCauley, Jillian Kesner, Lurene Tuttle, Regis Toomey.

"Evil Town" is a perfunctory horror thriller, which began production in 1984 and is notable mainly for the oddity of four directors credited with shooting it. Pic is a direct-to-homevideo title.

Vet talent includes Dean Jagger as a mad scientist doing aging research involving the pituitary gland, which requires human organ donors. Various inhabitants of the remote village Smalltown (population: 666) help out by capturing unwary tourists and travelers, knocking them out and delivering them to Jagger's clinic.

James Keach is a young doctor out camping with his girl friend and another couple, whom Jagger tries to shanghai to become his research assistant. Ultimately, Keach and his gal escape, Jagger is killed and the clinic patients riot. Film seems unfinished, with unsatisfactory stock footage in place of an ending.

Standard slasher horror film action to dispatch a series of young campers is highlighted by very lengthy topless scenes by former Playboy model Lynda Wiesmeier, obviously constituting the pic's potential draw in pay-cable showings. Tech credits are weak and fans of Jagger or other vets like Regis Toomey and Dabbs Greer will be disappointed by their work here.
—*Lor.*

Caught
(COLOR)

Billy Graham-backed pic needs help.

A World Wide Pictures production Produced by Jerry Ballew. Executive producer, William F. Brown. Written and directed by James F. Collier. Camera (color), Eddie Van Der Enden; music, Ted Neeley; production design, J. Michael Hooser; production manager, Pavel Marik; sound, Michael Strong, Lester Kisling; first assistant director, Ballew; production coordinator, Marije Slijkerman. Reviewed at Knollwood Plaza, Minneapolis, Nov. 13, 1987. (MPAA Rating: PG-13.) Running time: **113 MINS.**
Tim Devon . . . . John Shepherd
Rajam Prasad . . . . Amerjit Deu
Janet Devon . . . . Jill Ireland
Abraham Ahimue . . . . Alex Tetteh-Lartey
Jacques . . . . Frederik DeGroot
Erik de Bie . . . . Marnix Kappers
Aimee Lynn . . . . Kimberly Simms
Tourist Clerk . . . . Hans Kenna
Wouter . . . . Pim Vosmaer
Sprug . . . . Erik J. Meijer
Mrs. de Bie . . . . Bruni Heincke
Tibbe . . . . Rene Klijn
Dude . . . . Peter Blok
Also with: Ethel Smyth, Kerry Cederberg, Deborah Smyth, Iris Misset, Martin Versluys, Annie de Jong, Bart Romer, Edward Kolderwijn, Elvira Wilson, Leontien de Rijiter.

Minneapolis — "Caught" is the first feature film in two years from World Wide Pictures, the film division of the Billy Graham evangelistic organization. It's also WWP's 10th production in 22 years. With such lengthy gaps between offerings, better results might have been anticipated.

Pedestrian story has Amerjit Deu as an itinerant Indian evangelistic minister encountering John Shepherd as an itinerant American junkie and ne'er-do-well in Amsterdam. The pair become friends with the American sponging off his near saintly patron. It's the standard good-versus-evil yarn, and under the auspices of Billy Graham, who is pictured addressing an evangelistic confab, the outcome is a foregone conclusion.

The proceedings are loaded with implausible situations: the principals' repeated chance meetings in a metropolis; Deu's chase on foot, wearing painfully ill-fitting shoes yet, of a jeep in which his friend is being held captive, and Shepherd's eventual conversion to religion. These and other dubious factors make the plot hard to believe, but maybe ya gotta have faith. There's also a major makeup gaffe: Shepherd suffers a severe facial laceration in a mugging, but the wound seems to disappear overnight. Faith healing, perhaps.

Shepherd, a John Ritter lookalike, is okay as the bad guy turned good guy, and Deu's turn-the-other-cheek benefactor is an effective counterpart. Some of the acting in lesser roles, however, is subpar. Technical credits generally are all right with Eddie Van Der Enden's impressive shots of Amsterdam a redeeming virtue.

"Caught" opened to disappointing business at 250 theaters in October and is playing another 250 this month. It'll take church support of miraculous proportions to make the film a boxoffice winner. —*Rees.*

The Thorny Way To The Stars
(SOVIET-COLOR)

A Gorki Studio production. Directed by Richard Viktorov. Screenplay, Viktorov, Kyr Bulychov; camera (Sovscope, Sovcolor), Aleksander Rybin; production design, Konstantin Zagorsky; sound, E. Koreshnikov. (No other credits supplied.) Reviewed at New Mandarin theater, Sydney, Oct. 19, 1987. Running time: **143 MINS.**
Niya . . . . Elena Metelkina
Nadezhda . . . . Nadezhda Sementsova
Pyotr . . . . Vatslav Dvorzhetsky
Klimov . . . . Aleksander Lazarev
Rakan . . . . Ivan Ledogora

Sydney — Made about seven years ago, this Soviet space epic from the Gorki studios is a drab, uninvolving affair which takes itself far too seriously. Enjoyment of the ecologically themed outing is further hampered by the extremely dark copy unspooled in the context of a Soviet sci-fi fest.

Pic is divided into two parts. Part One, "Niya — A Test Tube Human," which runs 76 minutes, involves a spaceship from Earth discovering an abandoned craft in outer space and, aboard, a female android they call Niya (wanly played by the aptly named Elena Metelkina). She's brought back to Earth and studied by scientists, gradually becoming more human and eventually revealing she's from the planet Dessa, which is dying because of extreme pollution. This section of the film is handled in a static, lifeless way. The pacing is slow, and revelations which could, and should, have been made in the first 10 minutes, are dragged out interminably.

Part 2, "Guardian Angels Of Space" (67 minutes), is far livelier. A spaceship, with Niya aboard, is sent to help the people of Dessa, which is by now so polluted that the wearing of gas masks has become essential. A dwarf dictator rules the planet because he controls the supply of the masks, but the Earthlings are able to subdue him and finally fly away leaving Niya behind on a planet from which the pollution has been sucked away by what looks like a giant vacuum cleaner.

Apart from the amusing character of an octopus-like scientist from the planet Ocean, who lives in a water tank but is very brilliant and very sensitive to criticism, the film lacks humor. It also lacks much suspense until quite near the end when Niya, unknowingly carrying a small bomb primed to explode, nearly destroys the Earth spacecraft.

Special effects are okay, though way below the standard of U.S. effects for this kind of film. The ecological theme is hammered home, but it just adds to the seriousness of the picture. Above all, the film isn't much fun.

An alternative title is "To The Stars By Hard Ways." —*Strat.*

Tierra de Valientes
(Land Of The Brave)
(MEXICAN-COLOR)

A Peliculas Mexicanas release of a Producciones del Rey production. Produced by Arnulfo Delgado. Directed by Luis Quintanilla Rico. Stars Juan Valentin, Pedro Infante Jr. Screenplay, José Luis Rauda Delgado, based on a treatment by Estela Inda; camera (color), Atonio Ruiz; editor, Angel Camacho; music, Rafael Carrión, with appearance of groups Alma de Apatzingan de Beto Pineda, Los Tarascos, Mariachi Zapopan. Reviewed at Hollywood Twin theater 1, N.Y., Nov. 2, 1987. Running time: **85 MINS.**
Rodrigo Pineda . . . . Juan Valentin
Gregorio Solorio . . . . Pedro Infante Jr.
Esperanza . . . . Patricia Rivera
Chamuco . . . . Fernando Casanova
Don Bruno Ortiz . . . . Roberto Cañedo
El Licenciado . . . . Noe Murayama
Antonio Alvarez . . . . Victor Alcocer
Also with: Chayito Valdez, Dacia González, Gloria Sauza, Fredy Fernández, Alfredo Gutiérrez.

The Mexican film "Tierra de Valientes" (Land Of The Brave), haphazardly thrown together by Luis Quintanilla Rico, is a confused mish-mash stuffed to the brim with a surfeit of characters, plot leads, romantic involvements and political intrigues. If this were not enough, the 85-minute pic includes the appearance of various domestic music groups, folk dancing and even a long section of mediocre stock footage of a local parade with badly superimposed images of the principals.

Convoluted story begins as two men return to their hometown to work at developing a farm cooperative, one (Juan Valentin) after years of working illegally in the U.S., and the other (Pedro Infante Jr.) touting his newly earned university degree in agrarian studies. Against them is the slimy Don Bruno (Roberto Cañedo), who has been ruthlessly profiting from local farmers by years of illegal pricing practices. Dialectics and a forced script tell us that the collective wins out over the individual.

Sloppy and uneven camerawork coupled with choppy editing render the excessive narrative barely coherent. Add to this equal degrees of cliched dialog and wooden characterizations and the result is a cinematographic mess.

Movie is a dramatized political tract set within the form of a potboiler and the end product is neither enlightening nor entertaining.
—*Lent.*

Roba da Ricchi
(Montecarlo, Montecarlo)
(ITALIAN-COLOR)

A Medusa Distribuzione release of a Scena Film Prods./Reteitalia coproduction. Produced by Augusto Caminito. Executive producer, Francesco Casati. Directed by Sergio Corbucci. Screenplay, Mario Amendola, Bruno Corbucci, Sergio Corbucci, Massimo Franciosa, Giovanni Romali, Bernardino Zapponi; camera (Eastmancolor, color by Telecolor), Sergio D'Offizi; editor, Ruggero Mastroianni; art direction, Giovanni Licheri; music, Carmelo and Michelangelo La Bionda. Reviewed at Quattro Fontane Cinema, Rome, Nov. 17, 1987. Running time: **105 MINS.**
Aldo . . . . Lino Banfi
Mapi . . . . Laura Antonelli
Priest . . . . Renato Pozzetto
Princess . . . . Francesca Dellera
Insurance agent . . . . Paolo Villaggio
Dora . . . . Serena Grandi
Also with: Milena Vukotic (doctor), Vittorio Caprioli (Monsignor), Maurizio Micheli.

Rome — Latest comedy by veteran helmer Sergio Corbucci, "Montecarlo, Montecarlo" intercuts a trio of unconnected stories set on the Côte d'Azur. All three bear a strong resemblance to Corbucci's last pic, "Rimini Rimini," and cast is a virtual photocopy. Sporting a shade less vulgarity (but enough is included for every taste), current offering could reproduce the consistent domestic rentals of its predecessor, and swing into related offshore markets.

Common denominator of the tales is a voyeuristic peek into how the other half lives on vacation (Italo title: "For The Rich"). In pic's view, the rich are a lecherous, murderous, unfaithful lot; the men are short gremlins, the women sexy but heartless. In the one relatively original episode, a hung-up Italian priest (Renato Pozzetto) is escorting his parishioners back from Lourdes when the voluptuous Princess of Montecarlo (Francesca Dellera) falls for him. It seems she has had erotic dreams about a dragoon with his face, and her fantasies are interfering with a royal marriage. Monsignor Vittorio Capriolo, the Pope and her fiancé devise a sham acting-out scene to jolt the spoiled princess back to reality. Naturally it backfires, and priest and princess couple.

Laura Antonelli is the main attraction of an episode telling how — to give her straying millionaire husband Lino Banfi a taste of his own medicine — she pretends to lose her mind over a scraggly-haired bum. Antonelli's gasping imitation of Ophelia is worth seeing.

For those who would demand their money back without generous views of cleavage, softcore sex star Serena Grandi unselfconsciously displays some extra pounds of flesh in a takeoff on "Double Indemnity," costarring comic Paolo Villaggio as an imbecilic insurance agent lured into a scheme to eliminate her husband.

Little in the way of real humor intercedes in these peculiarly Italian moral tales, dumping on the monied while it envies them their private planes and Riviera glamor. Technically approximate. — *Yung.*

Olor a Muerte
(Scent Of Death)
(MEXICAN-COLOR)

A Películas Mexicanas release of a Producciones Rodríguez-Cinemato-gráfica Sol production. Executive producer, Tonatihu Rodríguez. Written and directed by Ismael Rodríguez Jr. Stars Gilberto Trujillo. Camera (color), Francisco Colón; editor, Angel Camacho; music, Ernesto Cortázar. Reviewed at Hollywood Twin theater I, N.Y., Oct. 14, 1987. Running time: **84 MINS.**
Dr. Salvador Guízar ..... Gilberto Trujillo
Piedad .... Alma Delfina
Víctor .... Raul Trujillo
Roger .... Arturo Vázquez
Carmelita .... Carmen Salinas
Also with: Miguel Manzano, José Carlos Ruiz, Pepe Romay, Gerardo Cepeda, Toño Infante, Alejandra Meyer, Carmelita González, María José Garrido, Víctor Lozoya, Valentín Trujillo.

The Mexican film "Olor A Muerte" (Scent Of Death), written and directed by Ismael Rodríguez Jr., deals with the problem of child delinquency and gang warfare in a compassionate, albeit condescending, manner.

Although the film has good intentions, the writing is muddled and melodramatic. The main problem is the film's form: the story is told in flashback by a young sympathetic doctor (Gilberto Trujillo) over the battered corpses of three street kids. Instead of working as a film by allowing the kids to tell their own story through their actions, the narration and annoying presence of the well-wishing doctor intrudes time and again with a constant plea for understanding these homeless kids and their often desperate anti-social behavior: drugs, glue sniffing, prostitution, vandalism and gang warfare.

"We are all to blame," the doctor lectures, a clichéd and very simple answer to a complex and real problem.

The young actors put in some believable performances, assisted by a slew of guest stars. There are a few good moments in the atmosphere and the writer-director has a fine ear for street slang. Overall, the pic boils down to little more than a filmed term paper for a first-year sociology class. The movie lacks the impact or penetration of a more effective film such as "Pixote," where street kids and their world are viewed from the inside.

For all of its missed good intentions, "Scent Of Death" merely smells bad and exploits what it's trying to understand. — *Lent.*

Nionde Kompaniet
(Company Nine)
(SWEDISH-COLOR)

A Svensk Filmindustri release and production. Produced by Jan Marnell. Executive producer, Waldemar Bergendahl. Directed by Colin Nutley. Screenplay, Nutley, Sven-Gösta Holm; camera (Eastmancolor), Jens Fischer; editor, Perry Schaffer; sound, Göran Carmback; production design, Lasse Westfelt; costumes, Katja Watkins; stunt director, Johan Torén; production management, Ann Collenberg. Reviewed at the Scania, Malmö, Sweden, Nov. 16, 1987. Running time: **105 MINS.**
Bertil Rosencrantz .... Thomas Hanzon
Gunnar Jönsson .... Tomas Fryk
Mogren .... Harald Hamrell
Persson .... Jan Mybrand
Kling .... Birger Oesterberg
Andersson .... Dan Eriksson
Hodén .... Patrik Bergner
The vicar .... Krister Henriksson
His mother .... Margreth Weivers
Arvid Jönsson .... Hans Straat
Alva Jönsson .... Gunilla Nyrood
Also with: Lennart Hjulström, Sara Forsberg, Robert Sjöblom, Sten Johan Hedman, Marika Lindström, Jerry Williams.

Malmö, Sweden — "Company Nine" is not a traditional military service comedy; it's bleakly serious about its satirical intent. The swiftly told story is one of corruption at levels high and low in an army regiment and at just as many levels of a rural community next to a training camp. Without a single sympathetic character on whom to hang compassion, suspense about the outcome is minimal.

At the same time, British director Colin Nutley, graduate of Swedish tv, makes his feature film bow with an impressive display of technical wizardry in all departments other than plot structure. His work with cinematographer Jens Fischer is a thing of beauty and flash, while he coaches strongly realistic performances out of all his actors.

Story has a platoon of recruits making some quick loot by exchanging the run-down engine of a farmer's car for a new one from a military vehicle. When caught in the act by their company commander, latter is soothed by being given a piece of the action, and sooner than you can say stockade, the entire regiment is helping the recruits and themselves to shares in what becomes regular big business out of a barracks dormitory.

Nutley and cowriter Sven-Gösta Holm obviously see everybody in this world as easily corruptible and correspondingly contemptible. Even if trooper Rosencrantz, the initiator of the process to milk the military to the profit of soldiers and local farmers alike, turns out to be in it for the power rather than the money, this does not serve to make him anybody's hero.

A dependency on old-fashioned realism keeps Nutley from attaining the satirical and absurdist comedy heights of "Catch-22" or "Mash," and he indulges in an awful lot of jump-cutting to speed things up and ad-lib repartee at the expense of regular character delineations. Nutley's portrait gallery remains one of rather undefined rogues throughout, one and all ready at the drop of a beret to cheat the next guy.

The moral, if any, seems to be that the state itself is based on cheating and that any kind of military establishment is evil or, at best, ridiculous. Again, "Company Nine" remains a marvel to look at up to and including a bang-up ending that explodes the story's sense and nonsense indiscriminately along with sundry pieces of real estate and, presumably, all the miserable human sinners within miles. — *Kell.*

Leila Diniz
(BRAZILIAN-COLOR)

An Embrafilme release of a Ponto Filmes production. Executive producer, Carlos Alberto Diniz. Written and directed by Luiz Carlos Lacerda. Camera (Eastmancolor), Nonato Estrela; editor, Ana Maria Diniz; music, David Tygel; art direction, Yurika Yamasaki; costumes, Mara Santos. Reviewed at Art Palacio Copacabana theater, Rio de Janeiro, Oct. 4, 1987. Running time: **95 MINS.**
Leila Diniz .... Louise Cardoso
Luiz Carlos .... Diogo Vilela
Domingos .... Carlos Alberto Riccelli
Leila's father .... Tony Ramos
Leila's mother .... Marieta Severo
Also with: Stenio Garcia, Antonio Fagundes, Jose Wilker, Paulo Cesar Grande, Jayme Periard, Romulo Arantes, Yara Amaral, Otavio Augusto, Denis Carvalho, Hugo Carvana, Oswaldo Loureiro, Mariana de Moraes.

Rio de Janeiro — Leila Diniz was one of the leading Brazilian actresses of the late '60s and one of those mainly responsible for a revolution in local women's behavior. Diniz was known for her several husbands and lovers, for unconventional behavior in any environment and her daring attitudes and concepts. In her early 20s, she became a symbol of the youth and intelligentsia of Ipanema. At 27, she died in a plane crash in India.

Luiz Carlos Lacerda, who wrote and directed this biopic, was one of her closest friends. For several years, they shared plans, struggles, idealism and friends. Diniz became a myth in her own time, the approach attempted by Lacerda. He is determined to tell Diniz' story her own way. Everything on screen is true, starting with the characters. They are real people who inhabited Diniz' life, always called by their real names. Often, they play themselves.

The most difficult task, restoring the atmosphere of Diniz' time, is achieved perfectly. "Leila Diniz" is simple, yet daring and permanently full of joy and Louise Cardoso, in the title role, even manages to resemble Diniz physically. Diogo Vilela is fine in the role of Luiz Carlos Lacerda. Most of the cast seems to be imbued with a real love for the characters or for what such people represented for their own culture.

Rather than a nostalgic view of the '60s, "Leila Diniz" is a clear attempt to review the cultural background of a generation which coped with military dictatorship but also with the beat generation influence, drugs and predominiant tendency for excitement. Such elements are very much present in the narrative, which is linear, fluent and exciting.

A great contribution is via the precise editing by Ana Maria Diniz in her first professional work. Music by David Tygel — with several insertions of themes by Antonio Carlos Jobim and others — is fundamental to conjure up Ipanema's atmosphere at a time when Diniz became its ultimate symbol.

Other technical credits are fine and it seems doubtless "Leila Diniz" will be understood perfectly and, above all, felt, by foreign audiences. This unpretentious musical comedy will certainly touch even filmgoers for whom Diniz' name never meant anything. — *Hoin.*

La Estación Del Regreso
(The Season Of Our Return)
(CHILEAN-COLOR)

A Filmocentro release of a Kocking-Kaulen-Ramos production. Executive producer, Christián Kaulen. Directed by Leonardo Kocking. Screenplay, José Román, Kocking; camera (color), Beltrán García; editor, Pedro Chaskel; sound, Freddy González. Reviewed at El Biógrafo, Santiago, Chile, Oct. 23, 1987. Running time: **86 MINS.**
Paula .... María Erica Ramos
Gerardo .... Alejandro Cohen
Isabel .... Carmen Pelissier
Also with: Luis Alarcón, Javier Maldonado, Gloria Laso, José Soza, Mauricio Pesutic, Hugo Medina, Rubén Sotoconil, Rober to Poblete.

Santiago — "La Estación's" problem is that it tries to have it both ways: putting its finger on some of the less savory aspects of life in Pinochet's Chile and also making a commercial movie about a woman's emotional complications; the latter, to avoid complications with the censor. End result is a halfway house where neither angle is fully developed. The film is obtaining reasonable b.o. on its home ground; it also played at San Sebastian and is likely to obtain further festival exposure, plus some foreign tv sales, but without creating a splash along the way.

Director Leonardo Kocking, a crossover from commercials, used $165,000 of his own company's money for this first feature, which is technically much better than other Chilean films of recent years, although acting is not always up to par. Pic was shot in 35m and not blown up from 16m, like most local features during this last decade.

Paula's story is revealed through a series of flashbacks as she travels by bus the whole length of Chile's northern desert. Life changes for her one night when, on returning home, she sees her husband dragged out of their house and bundled into a car. Endless enquiries with the authorities as to his whereabouts lead nowhere.

The anguish of the wife's search and her suffering as she tries to readjust to life are the center of the film. She continues work as a kindergarten teacher, goes to live with a women friend, runs into Gerardo (Alejandro Cohen), an old flame who is now a pathetic standup comedian at a second-rate topless bar. Before she at last receives word of her husband's whereabouts and travels north to find him, she sleeps with Gerardo and her emotionally disturbed roommate tries to commit suicide. When she finally makes it to the remote prison camp it is empty, except for an old caretaker. The film ends rather ambiguously: the inmates have either been released or transferred elsewhere.

The initial quarter of an hour generates suspense, which revives towards the end, but in between "La Estación Del Regreso" is far too flat. It lacks emotional insight and a convincing development of Paula's situation and character. This is partly attributable to the inexperience of Maria Erica Ramos (the director's wife) as an actress and Kocking himself seems far less assured in the handling of thesps than on the technical side. The principals turn in unimpressive performances, but there is some good acting in several brief secondary roles.
— Amig.

Kelvin And His Friends
(AUSTRALIAN-DOCU-COLOR-16m)

A Brian McKenzie film production, East Malvern, Victoria. Directed and edited by McKenzie. Camera (color), McKenzie; sound, John Cruthers. Produced with assistance of the Creative Development Branch of the Australian Film Commission and Film Victoria. Reviewed at Nyon Intl. Documentary Festival, Switzerland, Oct. 13, 1987. Running time: 75 MINS.

Nyon — Kelvin is a taciturn bachelor in his 40s who lives alone in a fastidiously clean rented room, as spartan as a barracks. Kelvin is fascinated by Nazi nostalgia and the

history of the Jews. He works out at body-building and pops vitamins, mineral tablets and bee pollen.

Just as physical culture is the essence of the elixir of life for the individual man, so it must be with society. A permissive morality weakens the spiritual life of a nation. For Kelvin, Australia's droughts and floods and other natural disasters are a direct result of leniency toward homosexuality and the other unspeakable nasties of modern life.

Kelvin's friends tell us about him, and also Kelvin describes himself — a victim who fought back. A weakling boy from an unhappy home, Kelvin at age 13 was the schoolyard punching-bag for bullies until he resolved "never to be second best." Through athletics and self-discipline, Kelvin became the campus 1-punch k.o. artist.

Kelvin's need for order and explantion has taken him into a Pentecostal church group. Now "born again," Kelvin espouses a simplistic righteousness.

"Kelvin" seems like a portrait of a ticking bomb waiting to explode. The man fits the stereotype or archetype of the deranged mass killer who suddenly snaps and runs amok with a rifle in a shopping mall. Nothing so dramatic happens in "Kelvin." Filmmaker Brian McKenzie is a decent chap who sympathetically records Kelvin's silent, unacknowledged suffering but without disguising its latent menace.

Because McKenzie was on the international jury at the Nyon festival when his "Kelvin" was screened, it was not in competition. In previous years, his other long films at Nyon were "I'll Be Home For Christmas," on Australian alcoholics, and "The Last Day's Work," about that faceless army of anonymous workers that holds a country's economic system together. In these three films, McKenzie displays a sociological head and a warm heart. —Hitch.

Augstaka Tiesa
(The Last Judgment)
(SOVIET-DOCU-B&W)

Produced by Riga Studio, Latvia. Distributed by Sovexportfilm, Moscow. Produced, directed and edited by Herz Frank. Camera (b&w), Andris Seleckis. Reviewed at Intl. Documentary Film Festival, Nyon, Switzerland, Oct. 15, 1987. Running time: 69 MINS.

Nyon — Convicted of a double murder during an impulsive robbery, a young man named Dolgov now sits on deathrow awaiting the result of appeals and legal maneuvers. His execution is simply a matter of form — death by firing squad.

Director Herz Frank — whose film won the Nyon festival's grand prix, plus awards from two other juries — is a cineaste/Dostoevski who probes the heart of the seemingly indifferent and hardened killer.

Dolgov, a handsome youth with long hair, mustache and ragged stubble, has a rather too common background among Soviet delinquents: abandonment by parents at an early age, growing up unloved and unsupervised in ugly block-tenaments, and a drift into black-marketeering and currency speculation. Once Dolgov comes to their attention, the police come down hard and fast, merciless.

The detectives hand Dolgov the fatal pistol — he must re-enact the shooting. He has killed two people, a woman trade-union member and her male companion. His motive was money. Dolgov confesses everything, an open and shut case. However, the Soviet press takes an interest in Dolgov, who resembles so many other young Soviet criminals. The film asks: Why do our young men kill? Must we in turn kill them?

"The Last Judgment" of Herz Frank humanizes these young criminals. Barbared in prison, shorn of his hair and all disguises, Dolgov talks grudgingly to the camera, painfully. It is all terribly sad and futile. Over the months, as the camera grinds on without pity, as it must, Dolgov and his defenses break down. Dolgov clenches his fists, bows his shaved head, his jaw working, his body trembling. His final words — I love you all. Love, that's all that matters.

Postscript: this film has not yet been released publicly within the USSR but knowledge of its existence and private screenings have stimulated opposition to the death penalty —Hitch.

Ma Mere Est A Sri Lanka
(My Mother Is In Sri Lanka)
(SWISS-DOCU-COLOR-16m)

A Swiss Film Center presentation of a Container TV, Bern production. Written and directed by Remo Legnazzi, Jurg Neuenschwander. Camera (color), Peter Guyer, Punjam; editor, Legnazzi, Guyer; music, Baghalasinghalam; sound, Andres Litmanowitsch. Reviewed at Nyon Intl. Documentry Festival, Switzerland, Oct. 17, 1987. Running time: 90 MINS.

(In Tamil, English, German)

Nyon — The predicament of foreign workers in affluent Switzerland, coming from impoverished southern Italy, became a successful comedy in "Bread and Chocolate." The predicament of these Tamil workers from Sri Lanka (ex-Ceylon) is not funny, nor does the docu intend comedy.

Fifty lonely young Tamil men live together in a Salvation Army dorm near Bern, Switzerland's capital. They await official status of asylum, as they are refugees from the civil war in Sri Lanka. Meanwhile, they work here and there, as they can. They go by Red Cross bus to the fields, where they pick strawberries and are paid in coins. Several become gardeners at private homes; one becomes cameraman on this

film; the others find odd jobs. By cooking together, they economize. There's no money for frills, although several manage to buy audio-cassette players, for listening to the music of their native land. Several have shrines in their lockers and perform religious rites privately.

They write letters home, listen to the news, try to read about that faraway struggle, the Sri Lanka government's military campaign, assisted by India, against the Tamil secessionists. When letters come from home, they are often filled with bad news.

The 50 Tamils in their dorm are like a small tropical island in a cold northern sea. Contact with the Swiss is difficult, the government functionaries are so formal. Linguistic, cultural and religious barriers, or rather strangeness, prevent close contact with the Swiss, who are always courteous and fair to them. The Tamils long for their families, their mothers, who remain behind in Sri Lanka. — Hitch.

Nos Reimos de la Migra
(Poking Fun At The Border Patrol)
(MEXICAN-COLOR)

A Películas Mexicanas release of a Filmadora Exito production. Executive director, Mario Gris. Produced by Guillermo Calderón Stell. Directed by Víctor Manuel (Güero) Castro. Stars Isela Vega. Screenplay, Francisco Cavazos, Castro; camera (color), Raúl Domínguez; editor, José Liho; music, Marcos Lifshitz, with appearance of group Sonora Santanera. Reviewed at Hollywood Twin theater II, N.Y., Oct. 9, 1987. Running time: 98 MINS.

Mónica	Isela Vega
Meto	Rafael Inclán
Rubén	Roberto (Flaco) Guzmán
Cocholata	Carmen Salinas
Nacho	Polo Ortín
Chapatín	Joaquín García (Borolas)
Lola	Rebeca Silva

Also with: María Cardinal, Carmen del Valle, Griselda Mejía, Luis Manuel Pelayo, Claudio Tate, Angélica Ruiz, Lilly Soto, Rocio Rilke, Edith Olivia Añorve, Ana Berumén, Xorge Noble, Guero Castro.

The latest feeble effort by Mexico's most prolific director of cheapo sex comedies Víctor Manuel (Güero) Castro has gone through various name changes en route to the boxoffice. Filmed under the moniker "Destrampados y Mojados" (Degenerates And Wetbacks), advance publicity labeled it "Mañosas pero Sabrosas" (Naughty But Delicious) before it finally was released under a title guaranteed to insure interest by U.S.-based Mexicans: "Nos Reimos de la Migra" (Poking Fun At The Border Patrol).

Skimpy plot concerns a trio of picaresque Mexico City drunks (Inclán, Guzmán and Ortín) and their girlfriends, one a showgirl (Isela Vega) whose uncle is head of the Texas Mafia. Because she knows too much, she is kidnaped and locked away at her uncle's house. Thus, the trio and their gals sneak across the border to get her back — tricking both immigration officials and the Mafia.

Last part of the pic is a reverse "Born In East L.A." Being almost 1,000 miles from home and with no money, they all try to get deported to Mexico, but all their outrageous schemes fail, as do the stale jokes.

Overlong story is cluttered with lots of senseless sideplots. Supplying even more filler are four songs by the popular salsa group Sonora Santanera. Also, pic "borrows" one comic scene directly from the first "Police Academy" movie, but with less success.—*Lent.*

Ultimo Momento
(Last Moment)
(ITALIAN-COLOR)

A DMV release of a Due A Film/DMV Distribuzione coproduction, in association with RAI-TV Channel 1. International release, Sacis. Produced by Antonio Avati. Directed by Pupi Avati. Stars Ugo Tognazzi. Screenplay, Pupi Avati, Italo Cucci, Antonio Avati; camera (Technovision Eastmancolor, color by Telecolor), Pasquale Rachini; editor, Amedeo Salfa; music, Riz Ortolani, art direction, Giuseppe Pirrotta. Reviewed at Ariston Cinema, Rome, Nov. 4, 1987. Running time: **105 MINS.**
Walter Ferrari . . . . Ugo Tognazzi
Pres. Di Carlo . . . . Lino Capolicchio
Duccio . . . . Diego Abatantuono
Marta . . . . Elena Sofia Ricci
Also with: Nik Novecento (hotel boy), Cinzia De Ponti (Mrs. Di Carlo), Massimo Bonetti, Giovanna Maldotti, Marco Leonardi, Luigi Diberti.

Rome — Pupi Avati has built up a faithful following around personal, low-key films about everyday people. After last season's hit "Christmas Present," director and his crew of regulars try their hand at another tale with bitter undertones, "Last Moment." Combining Avati's popular touch and a story about the national mania, soccer, pic should at least have been engrossing. Instead the story of an underdog team's big win is a dud, and the great amounts of pathos built into it never get properly wrung out. It's for local diehards.

Ugo Tognazzi headlines as Walter Ferrari, long-time manager of a major league team he's made many personal sacrifices for over the years. When smart-alec young president of the club (Lino Capolicchio) gives him the boot right before the playoffs, Walter overcomes his initial resentment to go on and fight for the team. This includes getting daughter Elena Sofia Ricci's boyfriend back on the field. Boyfriend betrays Walter's trust by throwing the game on a penalty kick, but a 17-year-old wonder boy sent in to sub him saves the match at the last moment.

Soccer can be an engrossing and dynamic sport, but the uninitiated won't see much of its charm in this film. Little action takes place on the field.

Tognazzi's barking manager with a heart of gold dominates Avati's usual cast of stock players, many little more than endearing amateurs. "Moment" is the last role for teen thesp Nik Novecento, recently deceased.

While the game stays in the background, Tognazzi's strained relations with family and team take center stage. The drama never gels, and finale, offsetting his professional victory with a personal downfall, fails to touch the heartstrings. It's technically acceptable. —*Yung.*

Moros y Cristianos
(Moors And Christians)
(SPANISH-COLOR)

An Estela Films production. Produced by Félix Tusell. Executive producer, José Luis Olaizola. Directed by Luis Garcia Berlanga. Screenplay, Berlanga, Rafael Azcona; camera (Agfa color), Domingo Solano; editor, José Luis Matesanz; sets, Verónica Toledo, Victor Alarcón. Reviewed at Exa screening room, Madrid, Oct. 22, 1987. Running time: **120 MINS.**
Fernando . . . . Fernando Fernán Gómez
Marcial . . . . Andrés Pajares
Cuqui . . . . Rosa Maria Sardà
López . . . . José Luis López Vázquez
Agustín . . . . Agustín González
Pepe . . . . Pedro Ruiz
Marcella . . . . Maria Luisa Ponte
Monique . . . . Veronica Forqué
Also with: Antonio Resines, Chus Lampreave, Luis Escobar, Luis Ciges, Juan Tamariz, Xavier Domingo, José Luis Coll.

Madrid — The re-enactment of the historical struggles between Moors and Christians in medieval Spain is one of the highlights of the fiestas held each year in Alicante, which is also the home of *turrón,* a kind of Spanish halvah, popular at Christmastime. Director Luis Garcia Berlanga and coscripter Rafael Azcona weave their story about a patriarchal manufacturer of the traditional candy who, together with his sons, decides to drive up to Madrid for a gastronomic fair and try to promote their product, dressing up a few of them as Moors and Christians.

For two hours we witness the mostly bumbling efforts of a group of characters trying to make out in the capital. Berlanga and Azcona have a good ear and eye for the absurdities of modern life, and there are plenty of lines and situations that will have Spanish audiences laughing. Unfortunately, two hours of shenanigans, in which it is common to have three or four people in the frame all jabbering at the same time, becomes tiresome and occasionally dull.

The provincials descend en masse upon the patriarch's daughter in Madrid, who has aspirations of running for office. She hobnobs with other politicos and has a kind of manager-adviser-lover who is, with great reluctance, convinced to help the *turrón*-makers get a mention on a tv program and maybe a story in a women's weekly. Comical situations come hard and fast, most of them purely local in scope, as the bumbling family gets involved in everything from a religious order trying to promote their liqueur, to a former opera singer who goes sweet on the patriarch.

Pic ends with a typical Berlanga-Azcona touch of black humor when the patriarch dies back in Alicante, is packed into a coffin too small for him, and paraded down the street amidst the "Moors And Christians" pageant.

With good thesping all around, lots of snappy dialog and fun-poking at everyone from politicos to the media, pic is sure to make a bundle in Spain, but is not likely to find an aud outside. —*Besa.*

Apoussies
(Absences)
(GREEK-COLOR)

A Greek Film Center-George Krezias and George Katakouzenos production. Directed by Katakouzenos. Screenplay, Katakouzenos, Dimitris Nolas; camera (color), Tassos Alexakis; editor, Aristidies Karydis Fuchs; music, Stamatis Spanoudakis; sets, Marilena Aravantinou; costumes, Yannis Karydis; sound, Marinos Athanassopoulos. Reviewed at the Thessaloniki Film Festival, Oct. 7, 1987. Running time: **110 MINS.**
Eldest sister . . . . Themis Bazaca
Officer . . . . Nikitas Tsakiroglou
Younger sister . . . . Pemi Zouni

Thessaloniki — George Katakouzenos, one of the most promising directors of the Greek cinema (his first picture "Anguelos" was a prize and b.o. winner) presents a dramatic love story full of passion for life and love, with good exploitation prospects here and abroad.

His story evolves around a middle class family on the eve of the World War I. The mother had left with a lover years ago. The father keeps his three daughters as well as the bastard son of the eldest in seclusion, trying to maintain the family's dignity.

After his death, the eldest daughter tries to continue their father's policy. The youngest one, however, revolts and leaves the house with an officer. When the eldest sister dies the youngest one is wondering what to do. Their cousin representing the status quo and the officer will be the catalyst in the relationship between the sisters.

Based on a screenplay inspired by the paintings by Edvard Munch: "Three Seasons Of A Woman" and "Cry," this picture is a psychological love story trying to make the point that every woman has a right in love.

Katakouzenos makes his film an interplay of basic human nature though he leaves the identifications somewhat vague, but he evokes the period well and enriches it with visuals of plastic beauty. However, given the richness of the material and its theme of a woman who places her passion for love and happiness ahead of deeply rooted religious traditions and social conventions, the resulting film is not so compelling as it should be.

Katakouzenos received good performances from Themis Bazaca and Pemi Zouni in the roles of two sisters and from Nikitas Tsakiroglou as the lover. The music by Stamatis Spanoudakis establishes the desired mood as well as the photography by Tassos Alexakis. —*Rena.*

Strannayar Istoriyar Doktora Dzhekila I Mistera Khaida
(The Strange Case Of Dr. Jekyll And Mr. Hyde)
(SOVIET-COLOR)

A Mosfilm production. Directed by Alexander Orlov. Screenplay, Orlov, Georgy Kapralov, from Robert Louis Stevenson's novel; camera (Sovcolor), Valery Shuvalov; music, Eduard Artemyev; production design, Igor Lemeshev. (No further credits supplied.) Reviewed at New Mandarin theater, Sydney, Oct. 20, 1987. Running time: **89 MINS.**
Dr. Henry Jekyll . . Innokenti Smoktunovsky
Edward Hyde . . . . Alexander Feklistov
Utterson . . . . Anatoly Adoskin
Lanyon . . . . Alexander Lazarev
Poole . . . . Bruno Freinlich
Diana . . . . Alla Budnitskaya

Sydney — This new Russian version of Robert Louis Stevenson's perennial thriller about a drug addict with a split personality is more faithful to the original book than most earlier screen adaptations, but less dramatically satisfying. It should spark interest among aficionados of the genre, and the presence of the distinguished actor Innokenti Smoktunovsky as Jekyll is an added plus.

First half of the drama sees the lawyer, Utterson (Anatoly Adoskin) center stage as he tries to discover more about the mysterious Mr. Hyde, to whom his friend Jekyll has left all his fortune. When a politician is murdered, the blame falls on Hyde, and before the film is halfway over, the plot has run its full course, with the horrified Utterson discovering that Jekyll and Hyde are one and the same.

Then a lengthy flashback takes over as Utterson reads Jekyll's last letter to him which fills in all the details of the affair, and for the first time we're allowed to see the transformation scenes which are usually the highlight of the films based on this book. Telling the story in this way may be more faithful to Stevenson, but it's far less successful on film: there are no surprises left for the second half of the picture.

Another unusual aspect of this production is that Jekyll and Hyde are played by different actors. As Jekyll, Smoktunovsky is mature, graying, troubled, while Alexander Feklistov's Hyde is young, lithe and handsome. The two transformation scenes are handled well: in the first, Hyde covers his face and, as he removes his hand, Jekyll has taken his place. In the second, Jekyll walks behind a pillar and Hyde emerges on the other side.

Also, this version plays up the drug addiction theme: the potion that effects the changes is not liquid to be consumed orally, as in most other versions; it's injected intravenously.

What it lacks in suspense, the film makes up in atmosphere. Igor Lemeshev's sets of Victorian London are effective, and Eduard Artemyev's music contributes a great deal. Acting is variable, with some minor rules overplayed. Femme interest is minimal in this version, with Lady Diana (Alla Budnitskaya) having the most marginal of roles. —*Strat.*

En el nombre del hijo
(In The Name Of The Son)
(ARGENTINE-COLOR)

A Jorge Estrada Mora Prods. release. Directed by Jorge Polaco. Screenplay, Polaco; camera (color), Esteban Coutalon; editor, Marcela Sáenz; music, Pepe Motta; sets and costumes, Norma Romano. Reviewed at the Vigo screening room, Buenos Aires, Sept. 25, 1987. Running time: **90 MINS.**

Bobby . . . . Ariel Bonomi
Mother . . . . Margotita Moreyra
Also with: Fernando Madanes, Goly Bernal, Jorge Sabaté.

Buenos Aires — "In The Name Of The Son" could be the ideal vehicle to effect the introduction of the international art-theater public to the bizarre world of a gifted Argentine director, Jorge Polaco.

Both of Polaco's previous works, a 1984 short entitled "Margotita" and a 1986 feature called "Diapasón" (Tuning Fork) have collected prizes abroad, without, however, achieving wide distribution.

The present film, which restates his concerns with a more solid production backing than he had previously commanded, could attract attention in those art circles where unusual material constitutes a plus.

Which are Polaco's concerns? With a very assured feel for the medium, he turns out darkly gleaming, slightly surrealistic films which explore the ugly, the disturbing, the decayed and the bizarre. He likes to dwell on things like dirty toenails. Above all, he likes to dwell on the naked body of an old lady, invariably portrayed by actress Margotita Moreyra, whose name was borne by Polaco's first, short offering.

Polaco is one of those artists — necessary in a period, like this century, in which art keeps on redefining itself at a fast pace — who test art's boundaries, study its opposites, question current definitions of beauty, and indeed deny the legitimacy of restricting art to the beautiful.

In the present instance the plot concerns a rather incestuous relationship between a grown man and his mother, in which, among other things, they prance around naked together. The man also likes to pester little girls to get undressed, is occasionally cruel to animals, etc.

Amateur psychologists should have a field day assessing what would appear to be a monumental Oedipus complex on the part of the director. Latter has hitherto tended to repeat himself, though his producer (Jorge Estrada Mora) has declared that he believes in letting a director with evident filmic talent work such things out of his system. —*Olas.*

Strit og Stumme
(Subway To Paradise)
(DANISH-ANIMATED-COLOR)

A Metronome Film release of a Metronome and Dansk Tegnefilm Kompagni production, in association with the Danish Film Institute. Produced by Tivi Magnusson. DFI consultant producer, Ida Zeruneith. Directed by and chief animator, Jannik Hastrup. Screenplay, Bent Haller, Jannik Hastrup; camera (color) Jakob Koch; music, Fuzzy; sound, Leif Jensen; voices: Berthe Boelsgaard, Jesper (Gokke) Schou, Annemarie Helger, Jess Ingerslev, Per Pallesen, Kirsten Peuliche, Annemarie Helger, Louis Miche Renard, Claus Ryskjar, Berthe Qvistgaard. Reviewed at the Dagmar Bio, Copenhagen, Nov. 12, 1987. Running time: **81 MINS.**

Copenhagen — "Subway To Paradise" is a swiftly told animated feature about a tribe of humans, reduced to Stone Age simplicity and surviving in the sewers of some big city when the rest of mankind and all other specimens of animal and plant life above have been killed off by pollution.

Writer-director-animator Jannik Hastrup displays technical virtuosity, wit and much poetic tenderness in all departments of the film, which should come out a winner in offshore sales as was his preceding animated film "Samson & Sally" (it dealt with threatened whale species).

The small cast of humans, the boy Strit, the girl Stumme (stum means mute in Danish), a jovial, drunkard uncle and a granny with a vision of paradise, are pursued by the cops of a subterranean Rat Dictatorship, who want nobody to ever see daylight again. Granny tells the youngsters to keep looking for a certain bird that will lead them to a new life, but to avoid the giant Serpent (presumably a symbol of pollution) who will be around to ambush them.

Using neat trickery such as getting a guard rat drunk and music (to set all the bad guys a-dancing), the youngsters finally emerge via a subway system and a volcano into the dawn of an Earth that miraculously has regenerated into Paradise Regained. Although his narrative structuring often plays havoc with logic, Hastrup keeps the pace going through the series of anecdotes that combine to tie up his tale.

In spite of a few sequences of thoroughgoing scares, "Subway To Paradise" is tempered by a fine sense of the baroque and by shots of visual beauty and impact to rise above some portentous moments of paranoia-inspired message.

On the cliché, cartoon-strip side is the tired targeting of U.S. phenomena and persona (the Rat President wears a Stetson, wields a Smith & Wesson and wallows in curvacious blonds while gleefully ordering his human prisoners brainwashed via state-of-the-art technological means) to denote everything villainous. Still, the good clean fun and the poetic innocence prevail, and Fuzzy's music will send audiences away in a song-humming mood. —*Kell.*

Operación Marijuana
(Operation Marijuana)
(MEXICAN-COLOR)

A Películas Mexicanas release of a Cinematográfica Rodríguez production. Produced by Robert Rodríguez E. Directed by José Luis Urquieta. Stars Mario Almada. Screenplay, Jorge Patiño, based on an idea by Rodríguez E.; camera (color), Armando Arellaños Bustamante; editor, Rogelio Zúñiga; music, Susy Rodríguez. Reviewed at Hollywood Twin Theater II, N.Y., Oct. 24, 1987. Running time: **98 MINS.**

Macario . . . . Mario Almada
Benito . . . . Víctor Loza
Bruno Sánchez . . . . Narciso Busquets
Foreman . . . . José Carlos Ruiz
Muchi . . . . Ernesto Gómez Cruz
Pedro (the reporter) . . . . Raúl Vale
Also with: José Chávez Trowe, Jorge Victoria, Rojo Grau, César Sobrevals, Víctor Lozoya, Carlos Poulot, Oscar Fentánez, Juan Pelaez.

In 1984, a Mexican reporter alerted federal authorities to the existence of large marijuana plantations in the northern state of Chihuahua. A major raid on the area revealed the farms were manned by 4-5,000 slave laborers lured to the site by the promise of high-paying jobs picking apples.

Two national docu-dramas were made to exploit such a lamentable albeit headline-grabbing situation, both movies by different members of the veteran filmmaking Rodríguez family. The first, "Yerba Sangriente" (Bloody Weed), directed by Ismael Rodríguez, was "a low-budget exploitation pic out to grab a few bucks at the expense of the suffering of others" (*Variety,* April 1). The latest pic "Operación Marijuana," produced by brother Roberto Rodríguez and helmed by José Luis Urquieta, is better than its predecessor, boasting higher production values and a more responsible script that vaguely attempts to analyze the situation. Underlining the film is a sense of desperation among the poor in relation to Mexico's ailing economy.

Unimaginative storyline concerns a wetback named Macario (Mario Almada), who is deported from the U.S. only to discover that all of the money he had sent home was stolen in the mails. Since the family needed money, Macario's 13-year-old son (Víctor Loza) went to look for work and ended up at one of the plantations. Thus, Macario goes to find him and, as he discovers the horrible truth, so do we.

Although most of the guards at the farm are sadistic fiends, a few possess understanding and compassion and almost all are fearful of a general rebellion of workers. The workers themselves are a mixed lot with uneven scripting and acting. In preference to "Yerba Sangriente," this pic does not scrimp on the extras and the crowd scenes are effective.

Lensing is adequate and later scenes showing the liberation of the camps by federal police include video-transfer documentary footage from the real event. Also, interviews with actual survivors are intercut with comments by the actors.

Even though this feature sensationalizes the incident, the over-sentimental human story holds equal strength. Rather than achieving the dismal failure of the first film, this pic winds up as merely a routine melodrama. —*Lent.*

The Color Of Honor
(DOCU-COLOR/B&W-16m)

A Vox production, San Francisco, in cooperation with the National Japanese-American Historical Society. Produced, written and directed by Loni Ding. Associate producer, Beth Hyams. Camera (color), Tomas Tucker, Michael Chin, and crews in France, Japan, Hawaii and other locations; editor, Ding, Steve Kuever; music, Andy Newell, Jim McKee; sound, Tony Starbuck, Sara Chin. Sponsored by the Film Arts Foundation, S.F.; funders, National Endowment for The Humanities, and its Washington and California state affiliates; Funding Exchange/Paul Robeson Fund; Asian Cultural Council; Pacific Resources Inc.; Central Pacific Bank. Reviewed at C.W. Post/L.I.U., N.Y., Nov. 5, 1987. Running time: **101 MINS.**

"The Color Of Honor" chronicles the injustice meted out during World War II by the U.S. government to American citizens of Japanese descent. As several hundred thousand Japanese-Americans were being confined in desert internment camps, Japanese-American young men were serving with the U.S. Army in the South Pacific.

Also, the Japanese-Americans of the 442 Combat Regiment were the most decorated U.S. soldiers of the war, fighting Nazis in Italy and France, sustaining heavy casualties. The 442's exploits were the subject of director Loni Ding's 1983 "Nisei Soldier." These fighters had one rule — "Don't let down the group, we're going to prove ourselves loyal."

Accordingly, "The Color Of Honor" is an education for us all and quite rightly was screened in Washington, D.C., both at the National Press Club and at the opening of the Bi-Centennial Exhibit, "A More Perfect Union — Japanese-Americans and The U.S. Constitution," which took place in October at the National Museum of American History, within the Smithsonian Institution.

Shot on three continents, "The Color Of Honor" is an immense research and editing job, as the film spans many years, from World War II to the present, and it concerns many people and events in many locations. Among these sequences, Japanese wartime stock footage is intercut with American footage, providing a 2-sided perspective on the Pacific campaigns. Japanese and American veterans of that vicious fighting, now elderly, provide living memories.

Primarily, "The Color Of Honor" deals with the story of how U.S. Army recruiters worked the desert camps, offering the interned young Japanese-American males their freedom if they would serve in the U.S. military, appealing to their patriotism through the barbed wire. Incredibly, a great many Japanese-Americans volunteered for the action, despite our government's blatent hypocrisy. As they went off to war in Uncle Sam's uniform, their families remained behind in the camps. These young men regarded themselves as Americans, most could barely read and write Japanese, and they hoped that their distinguished service would soften our government's heart in regard to their interned families.

Some sequences concern the wartime confiscation of farms, businesses and houses owned by Japanese-Americans, and their efforts, ultimately successful, after years of protest and litigation, to receive just compensation.

"The Color Of Honor" arouses many moral and legal questions, while also documenting a little-known aspect of our American history. Hollywood has almost entirely ignored this great human drama — only "Bad Day At Black Rock" comes to mind. —Hitch.

Two Dollars And A Dream
(DOCU-B&W/COLOR-16m)

A production of Stanley Nelson and Associates, N.Y. Produced and directed by Stanley Nelson. Camera (color), LeRoy Patton; editor, Deborah Bolling, Nelson; sound, Charles Blackwell; narration by Lou Potter; narrator, Jill Nelson; associate producer, Bolling. Funding by the National Endowment for The Humanities (planning grant); Lily Endowment; Indiana Historical Society; Indiana Commission for Humanities. Reviewed at Black Filmmakers Foundation, N.Y. Cultural Center, N.Y. Oct. 2, 1987. (No MPAA Rating.) Running time: **60 MINS.**

The Guinness Book of Records lists Madame C. J. Walker as the first self-made millionairess in the world — not bad for a semi-illiterate laundress, the daughter of impoverished black ex-slaves, born three years after the Civil War; orphaned at six; married with a child at 14; widowed at 20.

It all began on her kitchen stove in a sharecropper shack of the Old South. Mrs. C. J. Walker brewed up a batch of magic ingredients that, with her "hot comb," defeated the stubborn unruliness of kinky hair. Before long, Madame C. J. was the first female in America to earn a million dollars from scratch, a thousand dollars a day.

The C. J. Walker Manufacturing Co. became the first national company run by and for blacks. Her business skills and determination inspired a generation of black entrepreneurs. Her company developed 23 cosmetic products that appealed to black women, altering their appearance and habits, emphasizing health, cleanliness and pride. Hair-straighteners and skin-lighteners were among these products, provoking nasty images of white beauty, arousing political debate. Never mind, said Marcus Garvey, at that time the father of Afro-American nationalism: the Walker Co. gave jobs to 3,000 employees.

At her death, Walker left two-thirds of her company to charity. At this midpoint in the film, her daughter A'Lelia inherited the company and became one of the richest women in the U.S., "The joy goddess of Harlem," lengendary for elaborate parties, her luxurious lifestyle, patroness of Afro-American cultural development.

As our American history slips away, its artifacts and memorabilia vanished and forgotten, some documentary films seek to snatch a moment and preserve it — so with "Two Dollars And A Dream." The film is a major contribution to Americana on celluloid. It has done its homework. It uses all surviving scholarly materials: news photographs, family albums, print advertising of the Walker Co., publicity brochures, artwork, graphics, vintage newsreels, colored slides, posters, also oral recollections by ancient witnesses, shot in color in the present, croaking out their fond memories, often hilarious. The film includes footage from the 35m b&w promotional documentary of the Walker Co., produced in 1928, now restored by the American Film Institute. Music includes the 1923 Helen Hume song "Nappy Head Blues." —Hitch.

Das Falsche Wort
(The False Word)
(WEST GERMAN-DOCU-COLOR/B&W-16m)

A Katrin Seybold Film, Hamburger Filmforderung, Munich, production. Directed by Seybold. Written by Melanie Spitta; camera (color) Alfred Tichawsky, Heiner Stadler, Klaus Bartels; editor, Anette Dorn; music, Georges Boulanger; sound, Werner Nobusch; narrators, Spitta, Thomas Munz. Reviewed at Nyon Intl. Documentary Festival, Switzerland, Oct. 12, 1987. Running time: **83 MINS.**

Nyon — A small dark-eyed gyspy boy gazes sadly at the Nazi camera. He is having his picture taken — first full-face, then a half-profile, then a side view. Then they measure his nose and ear lobes. Then they send him into the gas chamber.

Nazi efficiency at death was perhaps no better demonstrated than in the wartime extermination of the gypsies. Lacking a nation, by culture nomadic, because distrusted and forced to keep moving, the gypsies of Nazi-occupied Europe were easily identified and quickly rounded up. The Nazi genocide of gypsies was almost total.

"The False Word" uses Nazi newsreels and "racial purity" films. Nazi physicians and anthropologists, like numerologists, are shown busily at work — questioning and measuring and categorizing the gypsies, who have been herded together in special camps, housed in their own caravans. These Nazi doctors, these alleged men of science, classify the gypsies and meticulously make voluminous hieroglyphics and graphs before shipping the gypsies out to the ovens at Auschwitz. Several of these Nazi pseudo-scientists are women. We learn they are still alive and well in West Germany today.

The "false word" of the title has double application — to the assurances of the Nazis that the gypsies who cooperate will survive; and to the broken promises of the postwar West German government, in regard to insufficient or no compensation and pensions to those few elderly gypsies who escaped death. We see and hear these lonely old men and women today, former slave-laborers for the Nazis. Their entire families were obliterated.

The film recycles some footage from several earlier documentaries about Leni Riefenstahl and her wartime use of gypsies as extras in her fiction feature, "Tiefland." Also, the film makes effective use of gypsy violins over poignant photographs of lovely children and their proud parents, now all dead.

Melanie Spitta, writer of "The False Word," states that "It is not necessary to write more of the assassins of the gypsies. We all know. I am one of the victims." Her mother, brothers and all the children of her family died in Auschwitz. —Hitch.

Beaks
(Birds Of Prey)
(MEXICAN-COLOR)

An Ascot Entertainment Group presentation of a Productora Filmica Real production. Executive producer, Francis Medina. Written, produced and directed by Rene Cardona Jr. Camera (color), Leopoldo Villaseñor; editor, Jesus Paredes; music, Stelvio Cipriani; additional dialog, Roberto Schlosser, Eric Weston; English translation, David Silvain; assistant director, Schlosser; special effects director & second unit director, Rene Cardona 3d; in Dolby stereo. Reviewed on Intl. Video Entertainment vidcassette, N.Y., Oct. 14, 1987. (No MPAA Rating.) Running time: **87 MINS.**
Peter	Christopher Atkins
Vanessa Cartwright	Michelle Johnson
Carmen	Sonia Infante
Joe	Salvador Pineda
Susan	Carol Connery
Arthur Neilsen	Aldo Sambrel
Rod	Gabriele Tinti
Nurse	Carol James
Olivia	May Heatherly

"Beaks," originally titled "Birds Of Prey," is a very silly and very gory imitation of Alfred Hitchcock's "The Birds." Direct-to-video packaging lampoons the film, but it's too boring to acquire the implied camp status.

Michelle Johnson (of "Blame It On Rio") toplines as a European tv newshen (pun intended) assigned by her callous boss to cover silly stories involving birds. (She complains she's a journalism school grad who wants hard news assignments, to no avail.) Accompanied by her cameraman (Christopher Atkins), she reports on a marksman who shoots birds while he is blindfolded and then covers a "feathered mutiny" of killer chickens who pecked their owner.

Meanwhile, birds of many feathers are attacking humans all over the world, duly photographed on location in Spain, Puerto Rico, Peru,. Morocco, Rome and Mexico. There's lots of gore and pithy philosophical speculation (copying Hitchcock) on why the attacks are occuring. Consensus is that instinctually the birds are trying to survive by killing off man, who has been polluting the environment. As in Hitch's classic, the birds suddenly stop at film's end, cueing an idiotic final shot of what looks like insects or tiny flying fish getting ready at a lake for a sequel.

Mexican filmmaker Rene Cardona Jr., best known Stateside for his poor taste epic "Survive," takes time off from helming Mexican sex comedies like "Buenas y con ... Movidas" to pilot this farrago. He keeps repeating boring transition shots of flocks of birds in flight and dubs the supporting cast while the leads speak English. Acting is weak, with voluptuous Johnson given a relatively flat-chested body double for the requisite nude scenes. —Lor.

The White Monkey
(AUSTRALIAN-DOCU-COLOR-16m)

A Curtis Levy production, Birchgrove, Australia. Directed by Levy. Camera (color). David Knaus; editor, Stewart Young; sound, Leo Sullivan. Reviewed at Nyon Intl. Documentary Festival, Switzerland, Oct. 15, 1987. Running time: **60 MINS.**

Nyon — This is Liberation Theology, but unpremeditated. Father Brian Gore is a tall, jovial Catholic priest from Australia who is assigned to a remote parish in Negros, a mountainous community in the Philippines. The time is during the Marcos regime. The Negros farmers are desperately poor. The wealthy sugarcane growers enjoy great power, protected by the Marcos military.

"I came out of a reasonable, conservative Australian Catholic background," says Father Gore, remembering his arrival innocently in Negros as a fresh-faced young priest. "But it was my involvement with ordinary people that radicalized me. I was radicalized, rather than me radicalizing other people.''

For 15 years, Father Gore is the Negros priest, learning their language and customs and names, doing standard church duties.

Father Gore cannot ignore the ignorance, famine and disease among the Negros people, although these are commonplace maladies in the Philippines. Deeply disturbed by the seemingly immovable social system, Father Gore begins to encourage his parishioners to assert their rights, to seek self-determination. Soon he is targeted as a troublemaker. Rebel-farmers in the Negros are murdered by the private armies of the land-owners and tossed into the river.

Deportation proceedings against Father Gore don't work, nor does the counselling of moderation by Father Gore's superiors in Manila. Next, Gore is arrested and imprisoned by the Marcos government, accused of multiple murders. Newsreel footage documents Father Gore's months in jail, sharing a cell with a dozen others, cheerfully enduring all hardships while awaiting trial. At length, with another white priest and other alleged conspirators, Father Gore is freed, the case dismissed. He is greeted enthusiastically at the prison gates by many Filipino friends and colleagues.

The story of Father Gore, the mischievous "White Monkey" of the title, is inspiring and dramatic but is presented by the filmmaker in a casual, informal way, without heavy documentary didactics or propaganda pontificating. Father Gore laughs about the risks. He is simply doing what he must, as a Christian.
—*Hitch.*

Murieron a Mitad del Rio
(They Died In The Middle Of The River)
(MEXICAN-COLOR)

A Películas Mexicanas release of a Cineasta Realiciones Cinematográficas-Prods. Esme-Alianza Cinematográfica-Soltar Corp. production. Produced by Carlos Vasallo. Directed by José Nieto Ramírez. Stars Héctor Suárez. Screenplay, Nieto Ramírez, based on the novel by Luis Spota; camera (color), Leoncio (Cuco) Villarias; editor, Nieto Ramírez; music, Joel Goldsmith. Reviewed at XII Reseña mundial de Acapulco, Mexico, Nov. 10, 1987. Running time: **91 MINS.**
José Paván . . . . Héctor Suárez
Lupe Flores . . . . Tony Bravo
Luis Alvarez . . . . Jorge Luke
Also with: Enrique Lucero, Jorge Martínez de Hoyos, Claudio Brook, Rodrigo Puebla, Arturo Alegro, Max Kerlowe, Paola Morelli.

Acapulco — The melodramatic title of Mexican director José Nieto Ramírez latest film "Murieron a Mitad del Rio" (They Died In The Middle Of The River) tells the viewer exactly what to expect. Based on the best-selling domestic novel by Luis Spota, the movie narrates the travails of four illegal aliens who swim across the Rio Grande in expectation of the riches to be found in the great land of plenty.

As the episodic story unravels,

the quartet diminishes systematically: the first is abandoned mid-river, the second is killed, the third deported and, like the 10 little indians, we are left with one. Although pic is meant as an appeal to fellow countrymen not to abandon Mexico during this time of crisis, what emerges is an obvious piece of propaganda about the abuses that undocumented workers must suffer at the hands of greedy gringos out to line their own pockets through the unscrupulous exploitation of others.

The principals are expected to work like slaves from sunrise to sunset for $40 per week. Later they experience further degradation: one employer's wife puts Suárez to work as her private stud, they are robbed, roughed up by a redneck mob, bullied, threatened, shot at and made to grovel before power-hungry immigration officials. In short, life is hell for those without papers in such a racist country as the United States.

The illegals are no saints either. They plot to rob "the only person who is good to them," an old fisherman who gives them jobs and a place to live. A chapter in the book, which never made it to the big screen, has them knock out a fellow sufferer and rape his wife.

The exploitation of film's theme by the filmmakers far outweighs the atrocities depicted. Situations are awkward and forced, dialog stilted, acting uneven and obvious message has all the subtlety of a jack hammer.

Pic's theme may spark some international b.o. interest, but the film cannot even be compared to other movies like "El Norte," which viewed such a lamentable contemporary situation with humanity and insight. —*Lent.*

Watashi o Ski Ni Tsuretette
(Take Me Out To The Snowland)
(JAPANESE-COLOR)

Produced by Yasushi Mitsui. Directed by Yasuo Baba. Screenplay, Nobuyuki Isshiki; camera (color), Genkichi Hasegawa; editor, Ishao Tomita; art direction, Hiroshi Wada. Reviewed at the Tokyo Intl. Film Festival (Young Cinema competition), Sept. 26, 1987. Running time: **95 MINS.**
Yuh Ikegami . . . . Tomoyo Harada
Fumio Yano . . . . Hiroshi Mikami
Kazuniko Izumi . . . . Hiroshi Fuse
Hiroke Haneda . . . . Hitomi Takahashi

Tokyo — Inexplicably accepted in the Young Cinema competition here, this epic about teenagers making goo-goo eyes at each other on the ski slopes plays like an adolescent Claude Lelouch picture. A feature-length commercial for several Japanese ski resorts and innumerable fashionable items in the clothes and car lines, pic represents a product-plugger's idea of heaven. The cute kids and downhill footage make it watchable.

It's a scenario that's been played out a million times before, as the ace

skiier in the group of boys attracts the attention of a lovely, unattached girl, but is too busy shy and bumbling off the slopes to do much about it.

Finally, on New Year's Eve, Fumio takes the initiative and scenically drives five hours through the snow to claim his lady's heart, which he sort of does but then proceeds to ignore her back in Tokyo due to his terrific workload.

Then it's back to the mountains, where the flimsiest of conceits about some villains trying to sabotage the ski clothing company's fashion show provides the excuse for some admittedly striking night skiing footage, as the kids are across some forbidden slopes to arrive in time in a most notable display of loyalty to their employers.

First-time director Yasuo Baba religously make the predictable choice on every occasion, and gets those product names front-and-center just like the good publicity man (with Hitachi) he used to be. Femme lead Tomoyo Harada doesn't ski too well, but looks fabulous in her white ski suit. —*Cart.*

Ke Dyo Avga Tourkias
(And Two Eggs From Turkey)
(GREEK-COLOR)

A Sakis Maniatis production. Written and directed by Aris Foriadis. Camera (color), Sakis Maniatis; editor, Elvira Varella; music, Nicos Portocaloglou; sound, Antonis Bairactaris. Reviewed at the Thessaloniki Film Festival, Oct. 5, 1987. Running time: **98 MINS.**
Mustafa . . . . Dimitris Piatas
Yannis . . . . Antonis Kafetzopoulos
Uncle . . . . Timos Perlengas

German Girl . . . . Athena Papa
Gasolene salesman . . . . Dimitris Poulicacos
Grandmother . : . . . . Dora Colanaki

Thessaloniki — This is a featherweight entry which should not have found its way to a festival. It is a comedy which may not be enough to satisfy foreign audiences but locally would do well in popular theaters with undemanding patrons.

The story starts near the Greek-Turkish border when Mustafa, a Turk, sneaks onto Greek soil to deliver "merchandise" to Yannis, a young Greek man working for his uncle. After the delivery of the "stuff" Mustafa wishes to follow Yannis to Athens to see his grandmother who is supposed to be a Greek. Yannis does not believe a word and tries to get rid of him but Mustafa manages to get him out of trouble during their trip to Athens.

Yannis' uncle, with the appearance of a gentleman admiring the beauty of antiquities, is in reality a drug dealer. When Yannis' grandmother sees Mustafa she recognizes him as her lost grandchild from a previous relationship with a Turk. Finally it turns out that both "enemies" Yannis and Mustafa are close relatives. As friends they start an adventurous trip back to the Greek-Turkish border.

This film is the only Thessaloniki fest entry not co-produced with the Greek Film Center. It is a naive comedy suffering from a low budget, based on a sketchy screenplay.
—*Rena.*

London Film Fest Reviews

Friendship's Death
(BRITISH-COLOR)

A British Film Institute production in association with Channel 4. Produced by Rebecca O'Brien. Executive producer, Colin MacCabe. Written and directed by Peter Wollen. Camera, (color), Witold Stok; editor, Robert Hargreaves; music, Barrington Pheloung; sound, Mandy Rose; production design, Gemma Jackson; costumes, Cathy Cook. Reviewed at London Film Festival, Nov. 17, 1987. Running time: **78 MINS.**
Sullivan . . . . Bill Paterson
Friendship . . . . Tilda Swinton
Kubler . . . . Patrick Bauchau
Catherine . . . . Ruby Baker
Palestinian . . . . Joumana Gill

London — "Friendship's Death" is a fascinating piece — long on words, short on action, but with a subtle charm and wit that almost makes you forgive some of the naive sci-fi dialog. It will never be a boxoffice boomer, but may travel okay to specialist art houses.

Film is held together by fine lead performances by Tilda Swinton (Friendship) and especially Bill Paterson as a cynical journalist, and is helped greatly by excellent production design by Gemma Jackson who has created some richly at-

mospheric sets.

Pic is set in wartorn Amman, during "Black September" in 1970. It deals simply with the relationship between reporter Paterson and Friendship, a robot from the distant planet of Procyon, who accidentally is dumped in Jordan rather than her intended target, the U.S.

Paterson finally starts believing her tall tale (he initially thinks she is a PLO spy) on witnessing her capacity to drink Scotch as if it were water, and ability to pick up radio messages.

Friendship finds herself identifying with the Palestinians, and when Paterson finally gets tickets to leave the country she refuses to go, preferring to stay and fight.

The philosophical sci-fi dialog is nothing new, per such hokey lines as "you humans are a barbaric race," but Paterson's playing of the witty, cynical journalist is so good the story still comes across as intelligent and ultimately affectionate.

"Friendship's Death" gives writer-director-film theoretician Peter Wollen an outlet for his fascinations with science fiction and the

Palestinian cause. He directs ably, and his work is enhanced by excellent, lush cinematography by Witold Stok. The film's final scene of a message from Friendship in the form of computer graphics looks like it was a good idea on the page, but hasn't properly been translated to the screen. —*Adam.*

Tenku no shiro Laputa
(Laputa)
(JAPANESE-ANIMATED-COLOR)

A Tokuma Shoten Publishing Co. production. Produced by Tatsumi Yamashita, Hideo Ogata, Isao Takahata. Executive producer, Yasuyoshi Tokuma. Associate producer, Toru Hata. Written and directed by Hayao Miyazaki. Camera (color), Hirokata Takahashi; editor, Miyazaki; production design, Toshiro Nozaki, Nizo Yamamoto; music, Jo Hisaishi; sound, Shigeharu Shiba; animation director, Yoshinori Kanada. Reviewed at the London Film Festival, Nov. 15, 1987. Running time: **124 MINS.**

London — A Japanese animated film of "Star Wars" dimensions, partly set in industrial revolution-era Wales, "Laputa" is based on an extract from Swift's "Gulliver's Travels." Hayao Miyazaki's children's pic is an ambitious and stylish venture that should work in some markets.

An exuberant English-language soundtrack has been added, and pic has enough suspense and excitement for wide youngster appeal. (It's a good bet for kidvid programming.) Running time of more than two hours, though, may make it a bit dodgy from some exhibs, so a little trimming is in order.

Pic opens with little girl Sheeta being carted off by airship for interrogation. When the ship is attacked by pirates, the bungling Dola family, she falls overboard but luckily floats to earth because she is wearing a rare levitation stone.

She floats into a desolate mining town and is caught by young technician Pazu. Then follow numerous chases, escapes and captures, until it is revealed Sheeta really is a princess and her stone is a key to the legendary floating city of Laputa.

The bad guys (the military) and the good guys (the pirates) all head for Laputa, where a final battle takes place. Pazu and Sheeta are reunited, the military are all killed, and the pirates escape with bags of loot.

Animation is excellent, and the desolate scenes of the mining village contrast beautifully with peaceful Laputa, which is secretly protected by hordes of death-dealing robots. The combination of high-tech and old-fashioned machinery (airships powered with hundreds of propellers) is charming, and the story contains a good deal of wit and compassion. —*Adam.*

White Mischief
(BRITISH-COLOR)

A Columbia release of a Nelson Entertainment and Goldcrest presentation of a Michael White/Umbrella Films production in association with Power Tower Investments (Kenya) and the BBC. Produced by Simon Perry. Executive producer, Michael White. Directed by Michael Radford. Screenplay, Radford, Jonathan Gems, based on the book "White Mischief" by James Fox; camera (color), Roger Deakins; editor, Tom Priestley; production design, Roger Hall; art direction, Len Huntingford; music, George Fenton; costumes, Marit Allen; sound, Tony Jackson; casting, Mary Selway; associate producer, Simon Bosanquet. Reviewed at De Lane Lea Sound Center, London, Nov. 20, 1987. Running time: **107 MINS.**

Alice . . . . Sarah Miles
Broughton . . . . Joss Ackland
Colville . . . . John Hurt
Diana . . . . Greta Scacchi
Erroll . . . . Charles Dance
Gwladys . . . . Susan Fleetwood
Idina . . . . Jacqueline Pearce
June . . . . Catherine Neilson
Lizzie . . . . Murray Head
Morris . . . . Ray McAnally
Nina . . . . Geraldine Chaplin
Soames . . . . Trevor Howard

London — "White Mischief" goes back into Africa with a vengeance. It glossily portrays the flip side of colonial life, exposing the opulent and lush — but downright debauched — lifestyle of the British "Happy Valley" crowd in Kenya during the war years.

The latest pic from the team of producer Simon Perry and director Michael Radford (last together in "1984"), "White Mischief" displays high production values, impressive acting talent, and a strong — virtually factual — storyline. The money invested can be seen on the screen, and with an excellent lead performance (following his major role in "The Sicilian") Joss Ackland should finally receive the acting kudos he deserves. Pic should make a healthy b.o. impact worldwide.

Pic opens in 1940 with newlyweds Ackland (Sir "Jock" Broughton) and Greta Scacchi (Diana) about to leave England for the British colony in Nairobi. He needs a wife and she wants the money and a title, but when Scacchi meets handsome Charles Dance (Erroll) in Nairobi the scene is set for some philandering.

Dance plays an inveterate womanizer, popular in the debauched close-knit European community, who amazes himself by falling in love with Scacchi. With stoical British reserve Ackland seemingly accepts the affair, even suggesting a celebratory dinner for the couple when they announce their plans to go away together. Later that night Dance is shot through the head while in his car.

Suspects for the murder are plentiful, including former Dance mistresses Sarah Miles and Susan Fleetwood, but Ackland is charged with the murder. He is later acquitted, but the scandal means the end of the Happy Valley set and their dalliances.

In real life the Erroll murderer was never found, but for "White Mischief," writers Michael Radford and Jonathan Gems have decided Ackland was the killer, and even include a scene of him killing himself, though in actuality he returned to England after the trial.

There are one or two unnecessary scenes (particularly one with Sarah Miles masturbating in a mortuary while visiting Charles Dance's corpse), and some of the pukka English language is overdone in the early part of the pic, but minor gripes are far outweighed by the skill of the filmmaking.

"White Mischief" has such strength in depth of acting talent that the likes of John Hurt, Geraldine Chaplin and Trevor Howard appear all too infrequently. It is Hurt who makes the most visual impact, driving about Kenya in a battered Rolls-Royce with two Massai warriors in the back seat.

Charles Dance and Greta Scacchi are fine in the lead roles, with Scacchi certainly looking desirable and elegant bedecked in stunning costumes and sporting a seemingly endless collection of sunglasses. Helmer Michael Radford lenses skillfully and confidently, and his work is enhanced by the ever excellent cinematographer Roger Deakins. All other technical credits are fine, with music by George Fenton suitably complementing the action.—*Adam.*

Al-tauq wal-iswira
(The Collar And The Bracelet)
(EGYPTIAN-COLOR)

An El-Alamia production. Produced by Hussein Kalla. Executive producer, Hussam Aly. Directed by Khairy Beshara. Screenplay, Yehia Azmi, Beshara, Abdel-Rashman el-Abnoudi, from a short story by Yehia al-Taher Abdallah; camera (Eastmancolor), Tarek el-Telmessani; editor, Adel Mounir; production design, Mahmoud Mohsen; music, Intessar Abdel-Fattah; costumes, Mahmoud Mohsen, Beshara. Reviewed at the London Film Festival, Nov. 20, 1987. Running time: **116 MINS.**

Bekhit el-Beshari/
Mustapha . . . . Ezzat el-Alaili
Fahima/Farhama . . . . Sherihan
Hazina . . . . Fardos Abdel-Hamid
El-Haddad . . . . Ahmed Abdel-Aziz
Mohamed Effendi . . . . . Mohamed Mounir
Mansour . . . . Ahmed Bedeir

London — "The Collar And The Bracelet," set in a primitive Egyptian village between the 1930s and '50s, is about the unspoken dilemmas of impotence and adultery among three generations of women. Khairy Beshara's latest film is elegantly shot, though at 116 minutes interest in the third generation is only maintained by a climax of blood and lust.

The traditional songs that are interspersed suffer somewhat in the subtitle translations, and unfortunately give the film a melodramatic feel to what is essentially a tragic story.

"The Collar And The Bracelet" is held together by the excellent performance of Fardos Abdel-Hamid as a wife and mother who oversees her daughter and granddaughter whose lives both end in misery. Her incontinent husband dies early in the film, while absent son Mustapha is working in the Sudan.

The daughter gets married to an impotent blacksmith, and mother and daughter have to resort to magic to produce a child. The daughter dies shortly after childbirth following an illness and a particularly gruesome scene of bloodletting from her skull. When grown up, the granddaughter is murdered by a jealous suitor after she has been accused of adultery.

Beshara shoots with comfortable skill. Pic has strong acting, and excellent production design by Mahmoud Mohsen, and ably shows the ancient links between folklore and village life. —*Adam.*

Bellman And True
(BRITISH-COLOR)

A Handmade Films/Euston Films production. Produced by Michael Wearing, Christopher Neame. Executive producers, George Harrison, Denis O'Brien, John Hambley, Johnny Goodman. Directed by Richard Loncraine. Screenplay, Desmond Lowden, Loncraine, Wearing, from the novel by Lowden; camera (Technicolor), Ken Westbury; editor, Paul Green; production design, Jon Bunker; art direction, John Ralph; music, Colin Towns; sound, Tony Jackson; costumes, David Perry; associate producer, Basil Rayburn. Reviewed at London Film Festival, Nov. 12, 1987. Running time: **122 MINS.**

Hiller . . . . Bernard Hill
Stepson . . . . Kieran O'Brien
Salto . . . . Richard Hope
Anna . . . . Frances Tomelty
Guv'nor . . . . Derek Newark
Gort . . . . Ken Bones

London — "Bellman And True" is a caper movie in the traditional sense, but with overtones of a psychological thriller, and featuring an excellent lead performance by Bernard Hill, one of Britain's most watchable actors.

Helmer Richard Loncraine revels in the technical gimmicks used in the pic (he is a director of a toy company) and, teamed with experienced former BBC cameraman Ken Westbury, creates a shadowy, atmospheric pic that maintains the tension but with punctuations of excitement, terror and humor.

Pic originally was planned as a 2-part tv slot, and to a certain extent it still has the feel of having two distinct halves, but this does not distract from an exhilarating two hours viewing.

Bernard Hill as Hiller, the Bellman of the title (Bellman being crime slang for an expert at getting past alarm equipment), is a man forced to use his computer skills in a bank heist.

He and Kieran O'Brien (his stepson) are held by the ruthless gang as Hill is forced to work out how to break through the bank security. They are kept in a rambling, ramshackle building where Hill balances his boozing with his computer skills to protect the boy.

The second half of "Bellman And True" is when the pic kicks up another gear and focuses on the robbery and getaway. The robbery is both technical and tense, and features a horrifying scene when Gort (Ken Bones) is caught and crushed by a lift — he may be a bad guy, but what a way to go.

The scenes inside the bank are amusing and exciting, especially the use of computerized toys to fool the police. The mood changes again as the gang escapes, and includes some fine car scenes, as the escape vehicle gets stuck between two buildings while they try and find a shortcut.

Right to the final climax as Hill and O'Brien make their dramatic escape from the gang, "Bellman And True" is constantly gripping, always offering something new whether it be a comic aside, gripping action or psychological thrills.

Acting support is excellent, with Richard Hope especially appealing as would-be villain Salto, and the ever-good Frances Tomelty in the understated role of Anna, brought in by the gang to keep Hill and stepson company.—*Adam.*

Memoire des apparences: la vie est un songe
(Life Is A Dream)
(FRENCH-COLOR)

An INA/Maison de la Culture du Havre/-La Sept/Ministère des Affaires Etrangères/-CNC/Ministère des PTT production. Produced by Jean-Luc Larguier. Written and directed by Raul Ruiz, from the play by Pedro Calderon de la Barca. Camera (color), Jacques Bouquin; editor, Martine Bouquin; production design, Christian Olivares; music, Jorge Arriagada; sound, Jean-Claude Brisson; costumes, Pierre Albert. Reviewed at London Film Festival, Nov. 23, 1987. Running time: **105 MINS.**
With: Sylvain Thirolle, Roch Leibovici, Benedicte Sire, Laurence Cortadellas, Jean-Bernard Guillard, Jean-Pierre Agazar, Alain Halle-Halle, Jean-Françoise Lapalus, Alain Rimoux.

London — Raul Ruiz' meandering tale leaps between sci-fi baloney and political thrills and, despite an overwhelming tendency toward verbosity and pretension, there are a few fine moments of visual skill and deft humor.

"Life Is A Dream" is a labyrinthine pic about a Chilean revolutionary who takes time out to visit the local cinema while trying to remember passages from Calderon de la Barca's play "Life Is A Dream."

On one level it is an irritating and frustrating exercise connecting overwritten, poorly acted scenes, while on another it is a challenging combination of links between cinema, art and politics. At the end, you wonder if the journey was worth the bother.

The plot is secondary, mostly an excuse for a number of tenuously linked scenes originating from the cinema, punctuated by an amusing array of scenes actually in the cinema with people coming and going, and sometimes having gun battles.

The prolific Ruiz undoubtedly will fascinate some viewers with this arty number, but it fails to grip the imagination, let alone hold the attention. The cast goes through its paces well enough, and technical credits are okay. —*Adam.*

Cemil
(WEST GERMAN-COLOR)

A Johannes Schäfer Filmproduktion production. Produced, written and directed by Jo Schäfer. Camera (color), Robert Schneider; editor, Schneider, Schäfer; music, Fancy, Frank Flebig. Reviewed at London Film Festival, Nov. 19, 1987. Running time: **82 MINS.**
Cemil Ersoy . . . . Vedat Uluocak
Nina Küntzel . . . . Alexandra Küntzel
Hulya Ersoy . . . . Sissy Elbir
Hassan Ersoy . . . . Halil Yucekaya

London — Shot on Super 8m for $5,000, "Cemil" is an ambitious attempt to show how young "second generation" Turkish guest workers are coping with the problems of growing up in an often inhospitable Germany. Director Jo Schäfer and his crew worked hard to compensate for thin resources, but poor sound and visual quality means pic **won't travel far outside local youth spots.**

Brought up in Berlin, Cemil and his friends spend most of their free time outside high school hanging out in parking lots and putting together Michael Jackson-style dance routines to disco music.

The thoroughly Westernized Cemil is distraught when his parents, disillusioned with prospects in Germany, decide to return to Turkey. Cemil, who challenges his father and traditional Turkish customs by sporting a gold stud in his ear, resents the idea of being transported to a country he hardly knows. To complicate matters, he has just fallen in love with Nina, an attractive German classmate.

At the last moment, in the airport departure lounge, Cemil decides to bolt from his family and stay in Germany with Nina. But loneliness and the pressure of relying on friends for food and shelter prove too much even for the streetwise Cemil. When the relationship with his girlfriend cools (a development eagerly encouraged by Nina's parents), Cemil has to swallow his pride and catch a train back to Turkey.

Standard of acting among the mainly young, amateur thespians generally is high, with Alexandra Küntzel (Nina) outstanding as Cemil's girlfriend. Pic is overly ambitious considering financial and technical limitations, but the subject of second-generation Turkish guest workers certainly warrants more screen attention.—*Coop.*

Out Of Rosenheim
(WEST GERMAN-COLOR)

A Futura/Filmverlag der Autoren release of a Pelemele Film/Project Filmproduktion/-BR/HR production. Produced by Percy Adlon, Eleonore Adlon. Written and directed by Percy Adlon. Screenplay, Percy Adlon, Eleanore Adlon, Christopher Doherty, from story by Percy Adlon; camera (color), Bernd Heinl; editor, Norbert Herzner; sound, Heinko Hinderks; music, Bob Telson; art direction, Bernt Amadeus Capra, Byrnadette di Santo; costumes, Elizabeth Warner, Regine Baetz; makeup, Lizbeth Williamson; casting, Al Onorato. Reviewed at Rio Film Festival, Nov. 26, 1987. Running time: **108 MINS.**
Jasmin . . . . Marianne Sägebrecht
Brenda . . . . CCH Pounder
Rudy Cox . . . . Jack Palance
Also with: Christine Kaufman (Debbie), Monica Calhoun (Phyllis), Darron Flagg (Sal Jr.) George Aquilar (Caguenga), G. Smokey Campbell (Sal), Hans Stadlbauer (Muenchgstettner). Aspesanshkwat (sheriff), Alan S. Craig (Eric).

Rio de Janeiro — Percy Adlon's new film, shot entirely in English and using American locations, once again exploits the talents of Marianne Sägebrecht, the corpulent lady who was the star of his previous film, "Sugar Baby," and comes up with an even better comedy, bound to reach a wider audience than any of his earlier efforts.

Sägebrecht plays a German businesswoman whose husband drops her somewhere in the middle of the desert on the road to Las Vegas. Dragging her one suitcase and guided by sheer inspiration she reaches Bagdad, Calif., a place consisting of a rundown gas station, a dubious motel and a coffee shop known as Brenda's Palace which is anything but a palace.

Brenda is a disgruntled black woman plagued with a lazy husband she has to kick out, a son who won't be taken way from his piano, a daughter who drifts away with every biker and truck driver who happens by, and a definite case of losers blues.

The weird-looking, stout German lady, in her Bavarian costume and hunting hat, looks like a vision from another world for the Bagdadians, and when she hires a room, Brenda is worried enough to call the sheriff in to check on the strange lady, whose name, Jasmin, isn't very reassuring either.

The first timid attempts by the visitor to lend a hand and put some German order into the Palace's chaos are met by rude rejection, but with lots of shy but determined patience, Jasmin turns the trick, works her way into the hearts of each member of the small community and finally in Brenda's as well. Her inspiration not only changes the quality of the coffee served in the place, but adds a touch of life and magic and turns Brenda's Palace into a local attraction.

The film is presented as a "comedy-fable" and is indeed true to this definition. A touch of surrealism in the use of objects and sets, and plenty of lyrical ideas are effectively combined with strong, controlled performances. The sequences showing Jasmin pose for Rudy Cox, a painter smitten with her charms, wordlessly portray a warm and sincere relationship in progress.

Sägebrecht is a definite asset, making her heavy-set physical appearance which normally would limit her scope, work in her favor. If in the first sequences she looks a grim and discomfited hausfrau, by the end of the film she radiates real glamor, and it is quite easy to understand the painter's fascination with her. The same could be said of Jack Palance, who works here against his typical tough guy image and makes Rudy Cox one of the high points of his career. As for Pounder, a negligent overworked slob in the beginning, she quickly becomes a charmer in her own right.

If the proceedings in the first half of the picture are rather slow, Adlon picks up the pace in the second half, once he has soundly established the situation, and guides his cast carefully way from the various pitfalls. Pic presents a funny image of a cultural gap being closed by the sensitivity of decent human beings.

Both camera work and art direction are highly imaginative, and the film, recipient of the fest's top award, and also picked as the most popular entry in the Rio competition, could easily become a b.o. winner, given the right treatment.
—*Edna.*

Broadcast News
(COLOR)

Well-acted look at tv journalism lacks a satisfying windup.

A 20th Century Fox release. Produced by James L. Brooks. Executive producer, Polly Platt. Coproducer, Penney Finkelman Cox. Directed by Brooks. Stars William Hurt. Screenplay, Brooks; camera (Deluxe color), Michael Ballhaus; editor, Richard Marks; music, Bill Conti; production design, Charles Rosen; set decoration, Jane Bogart; sound (Dolby), Thomas Causey; costumes, Molly Maginnis; assistant director, Yudi Bennett; associate producer, Kristi Zea, Susan Zirinsky; casting, Ellen Chenoweth. Reviewed at 20th Century Fox screening room, Culver City, Calif., Dec. 1, 1987. (MPAA Rating: R.) Running time: **131 MINS.**

Tom Grunick . . . . William Hurt
Aaron Altman . . . . Albert Brooks
Jane Craig . . . . Holly Hunter
Ernie Merriman . . . . Robert Prosky
Jennifer Mack . . . . Lois Chiles
Blair Litton . . . . Joan Cusack
Paul Moore . . . . Peter Hackes
Bobby . . . . Christian Clemenson
Martin Klein . . . . Robert Katims
George Wein . . . . Ed Wheeler
Anchorman . . . . Jack Nicholson

Hollywood — Enormously entertaining for most of its 131 minutes, "Broadcast News" is an inside look at the personal and professional lives of three tv journalists. Stronger on character and nuances of behavior than the ethics of tv news, producer/director/writer James L. Brooks has provided enough brilliant dialog, beautifully realized by Holly Hunter, Albert Brooks and William Hurt, to carry the film over some thin patches and an ending that sputters to a less than satisfying conclusion. Nonetheless, picture should delight a sizable audience looking for a thoughtful night out as well as a good laugh.

"Broadcast News" is not so much about the business of the news as the personal investment each of the characters brings to his job. How these people balance their private obsessions with their professional responsibilities is the stuff of the film. The bustling Washington newsroom is a colorful and fascinating stage on which to play out the drama of high-strung ambitious careerists.

Although "Broadcast News" makes a lot of noise about the higher moral issues of tv reporting, Brooks gently punctures the self-importance of his characters with a sly satrical edge. When veteran reporter Aaron Altman (Albert Brooks) and hard-nosed producer Jane Craig (Hunter) go to the jungles of Central America to report on the revolution, the results are too humorous and self-serving to take seriously.

How these people report the news says more about them than the world events they're covering. Opening the film with a look at the three characters as kids, Brooks shows how their youthful personalities determine their professional habits. Even Craig, the most serious of the newshounds, is driven by something deeper than a search for the truth.

Where Craig and Altman are seasoned professionals with great talent, Tom Grunick (Hurt) is a slick ex-sportscaster who knows how to turn on the charm and seduce an audience. In some ways he has a more human and instinctive feel for what people respond to on television, but is it news, his colleagues wonder.

Grunick is not only a problem as an anchorman, he forms the third corner of a latent love triangle. Jane loves Tom but hates his work. Aaron loves his work and loves Jane and hates Tom. Tom loves himself and loves Jane. In short it's a case of scrambled emotions among people who heretofore have substituted work for pleasure.

It's a lively bunch and there are exchanges and confrontations that are priceless and achingly authentic. A fired oldtimer doesn't tell his boss it's okay he understands, he tells him he hopes he dies soon. These are all bright people and Brooks has given them lines worthy of their and the audience's intelligence.

Hunter is simply superb barking out orders from a mouth contorted with who-knows-what emotions. In her rare quiet moments she breaks down and cries. As the neurotic but brilliant reporter, Brooks gives an insightful performance while communicating his character's guardedness and anguish.

As the hardest of the characters to read, Hurt does a good job keeping up the mystery so one never knows when he's sincere or faking, and maybe he doesn't either.

Jack Nicholson has a small but powerful presence in an uncredited role as the network anchorman.

Brooks has also assembled a crack supporting cast down to the errand boys and veteran newsman who look born for their parts. Particularly noteworthy are Robert Prosky as the bureau chief who can read the writing on the wall before anyone else and Peter Hackes, a longtime newsman making his acting debut, as the none-too-scrupulous network news honcho. Praise goes as well to Lois Chiles and Joan Cusack as part of the extended news family.

Indeed one of the joys of the production is Brooks' attention to detail executed by Charles Rosen's production design and Michael Ballhaus' heated cinematography. If Brooks' script features some glaring continuity problems and an ending that attempts to sew up loose ends better left dangling, "Broadcast News" is still a writer's film, a good one at that. —*Jagr.*

Welcome Maria
(MEXICAN-COLOR)

A Películas Mexicanas release. Produced by Mario Arturo Moreno. Directed by Juan López Moctezuma. Stars María Victoria. Screenplay, López Moctezuma, Rubén Arvizu; camera (color), Nadine Markova; editor, Jerome F. Brady; music, Miguel Angel Alonso. Reviewed at Acapulco Film Festival, Nov. 13, 1987. Running time: **79 MINS.**

María . . . . María Victoria
Meche . . . . Allison Ernand
Ezekiah . . . . Bob Copeland
Miguelito . . . . Christian Cañada

Acapulco — Mario Arturo Moreno, son of Mexican comedian Cantinflas, makes his debut as producer on this short, unsatisfactory feature about the fate of an illegal alien working in the U.S.

Cowritten and helmed by Juan López Moctezuma, film is a dishonest look at the meandering fortunes of María (María Victoria) and her young son Miguelito (Christian Cañada), who enter the U.S. illegally to search for the boy's father. The man had disappeared two years earlier after going to Los Angeles to find a better life. He eventually finds it with a blond American wife and so María is on her own.

Every character in the pic delivers contrived speeches on the difficulties of life, yet María encounters none of these problems — except for following the stilted linear script. The first person she asks about a job gives her one, the same with lodgings and so forth. No American citizen ever had it so easy relocating in Los Angeles. There are no surprises and the corny ending, which follows an utterly absurd confrontation, is a complete cop-out.

The 79-minute pic is stuffed with useless musical filler: Victoria sings two ranchero tunes at a Mexican restaurant, and three other songs are played to accompany pretty images. —*Lent.*

Wall Street
(COLOR)

Oliver Stone stumbles with a lecture instead of entertainment.

A 20th Century Fox release of an Edward R. Pressman production, in association with American Entertainment Partners L.P. Produced by Pressman. Co-produced by A. Kitman Ho. Directed by Oliver Stone. Stars Michael Douglas, Charlie Sheen. Screenplay, Stone, Stanley Weiser; camera (DeLuxe color), Robert Richardson; editor, Claire Simpson; music, Stewart Copeland; production design, Stephen Hendrickson; art direction, John Jay Moore, Hilda Stark; set decoration, Leslie Bloom, Susan Bode; costume design, Ellen Mirojnick; sound (Dolby), Chris Newman; associate producer, Michael Flynn; assistant director, Steve Lim; casting, Risa Bramon, Billy Hopkins. Reviewed at 20th Century Fox screening room, Culver City, Calif. Dec. 3, 1987. (MPAA Rating: R.) Running time: **124 MINS.**

Bud Fox . . . . Charlie Sheen
Gordon Gekko . . . . Michael Douglas
Carl Fox . . . . Martin Sheen
Sir Larry Wildman . . . . Terence Stamp
Kate Gekko . . . . Sean Young
Darien Taylor . . . . Daryl Hannah
Realtor . . . . Sylvia Miles
Roger Barnes . . . . James Spader
Also with: Hal Holbrook, John McGinley, Saul Rubinek, Franklin Cover, James Karen, Richard Dysart, Josh Mostel, Millie Perkins, Annie McEnroe, Monique van Vooren.

Hollywood — Watching Oliver Stone's "Wall Street" is about as wordy and dreary as reading the financial papers accounts of the rise and fall of an Ivan Boesky-type arbitrageur, with one exception. Instead of editorializing about the evils of greed — and greenmailers in particular — it lectures, which is great as a case study in business school but wearisome as a film. Even with the attachment of Stone's "Platoon" reputation and a big name cast, this is a bull holiday market for new issues and "Wall Street" appears an unlikely blue chip entry.

The lure of making a bundle on Wall Street by the young broker (Charlie Sheen) totally seduced by the power and financial stature of such a megalomaniacal arbitrageur as Gordon Gekko (Michael Douglas) is as good a contemporary story as there is today in the real world of takeovers and mergers.

Core problem with this filmed version is that it is too thorough a retelling of the impact of stock manipulation, more like a docudrama than a drama.

Pic needs to be edited by a good 30 minutes (it runs just over two hours) to cut the extraneous, repetitive scenes with Douglas barking orders to buy, sell and run his competitors into the ground or otherwise delivering one of his declamatory speeches on how greed is what makes America great.

Stone and co-writer Stanley Weiser seems to have done their research on the details of how greenmailers achieve their dubious aims with a script that goes over the process step by step in wordy expositions — diluting the human consequences such actions have on the targeted airline company and its employees (led by Martin Sheen).

Film instead focuses on the cold, calculating and clichéd Douglas character and his eager protégé Sheen Jr. and their love-hate relationship on the treadmill of avarice with settings on the trading floor, in chi-chi restaurants and out in the fashionable Hamptons ringing pretty much true.

Douglas is a nasty enough manipulator and exudes the black-hearted temperament suited to his role, though his character could have used a little shading. Trouble is, Sheen comes off as a pawn in Douglas' corporate raider game and as the easily duped sort doesn't elicit much sympathy since he is only remorseful once Douglas cheats on him and changes the rules of play. Martin Sheen as his father, the airplane mechanic, is the only person worth caring about: Dramatizing the triangle among him, his son and Douglas would have been a more effective presentation of the consequences of greenmailing than cold, dispassionate scenes where it's talked about in a way that results in little emotional impact.

This is also true of Sheen Jr.'s relationship to an ambitious interior decorator, Daryl Hannah, who has no conscience to speak of and the personality of wallboard. She gets short shrift when it comes to intelligence and charm, as do the other two main female characters — Douglas' ditzy wife (Sean Young) and the loud New Yawk realtor (Sylvia Miles) — in "Wall Street's" male dominated world.

The moralizing is done by secondary characters like Hal Holbrook, sage of the trading floor, and at least one of Sheen's fellow brokers, John McGinley, who rightly calls his colleague an "a.h." to his face.

Best elements of Stone's latest work are in the production values, reuniting several parties from "Platoon."

Dizzying pace of Manhattan comes through in Robert Richardson's constantly moving camera, adding to the documentary look of the picture. Production designer Stephen Hendrickson has a keen eye for authenticity — whether it be Douglas' vast corporate offices chock-a-block with expensive modern art or in the crammed working quarters that is the trading floor of the fictitious Jackson-Steinem investment house where Sheen and rows of others go cross-eyed reading the financial tables on their VDTs and hoarse screaming orders into the phone. —*Brit.*

Marilyn Monroe: Beyond The Legend
(U.S.-DOCU-COLOR-B&W-16m)

A Wombat production. Produced and written by Gene Feldman, Suzette Winter. Directed by Feldman. Camera (color, 16m), Rick Robertson, Richard Francis; editor, Les Mulkey; associate producer, Stephen Janson; narrator, Richard Widmark. Reviewed at Festival dei Popoli, Florence, Italy, Nov. 27, 1987. Running time: **60 MINS.**
With: Robert Mitchum, Shelley Winters, Joshua Logan, Susan Strasberg, Don Murray, Celeste Holm, Sheree North, Clark Gordon, John Springer, Laszlo Willinger.

Florence — In a year of numerous books and films about Marilyn Monroe as pop icon/sex star, "Marilyn Monroe: Beyond The Legend" looks at one aspect of her career which has attracted less attention of late, Marilyn Monroe as actress. The verdict: she could act. Revisionism is popular in the MM industry, so this pic should sell well.

The numerous clips from all her films, as well as press events, show she was indeed a great comic. These are mixed with interviews with Robert Mitchum, Shelley Winters, Joshua Logan, Susan Strasberg and other "friends," more telling for what they say about themselves than about Marilyn.

Ignoring her love affairs and suicide is certainly a novel approach in the pop journalism era, and a fortu-

nate one too, as it leaves room to see the actress at work, an oft-forgotten pleasure.

Most enlightening, though, is witnessing the suppressed envy and venom she still arouses among former colleagues. Only Logan, who directed her in "Bus Stop," avoids patronizing her memory.

Pic runs a bit long and could be edited to cut a few minutes for an easy tv slot. — *Newm.*

Home Is Where The Hart Is
(COLOR)

Quirky, unsuccessful debunking of the American Dream.

An Atlantic Entertainment Group release. Produced by John M. Eckert. Executive producers, Ralph Scobie, Richard Strafehl. Written and directed by Rex Bromfield. Camera (Panavision, color), Robert Ennis; editor, Michael Todd; music, Eric N. Robertson; art direction, Jill Scott; sound, Martin Fossum; production manager, Harold Tichenor; set decoration, Lesley Beale; assistant director, T.W. Peacocke; casting, Ingrid Fischer. Reviewed at Samuel Goldwyn Pavilion, L.A., Dec. 4, 1987. (MPAA Rating: PG-13.) Running time: **94 MINS.**
Belle Haimes . . . . Valri Bromfield
Rex Haimes . . . . Stephen E. Miller
Selma Dodge . . . . Deanne Henry
Carson Boundy . . . . Martin Mull
Martin Hart . . . . Eric Christmas
Art Hart . . . . Ted Stidder
Sheriff Nashville Schwartz . . Leslie Nielsen
Pappy . . . . Joe Austin

Hollywood — This film is just the sort cinematic accident that occurs when someone (director/writer Rex Bromfield) tries to graft the quirkiest aspects of "Blue Velvet" and "Raising Arizona" onto a stock story without first considering why. The result is an uneven, slow-moving vehicle that observes the pathetic underside of American life — especially its desperate greed — without providing any real insight into the feeling of those in that position. Boxoffice prospects look doubtful, even for achieving the cult status Bromfield must have had in mind.

Film is essentially the story of longtime loser Belle Haimes (played to the utmost despicableness by Valri Bromfield), never smart enough to make money honestly or pious enough to live happily without it. Along with her whipped husband Rex (Stephen E. Miller), she takes over the care of 103-year-old billionaire Slim (Pappy) Hart, keeping one eye on his inheritance at all times.

After Belle facilitates the death of Pappy's coma-stricken wife, she sets out to acquire his fortune by marrying the senile old man, but runs into trouble when some opportunistic relatives show up to check on the ailing man's health.

The septuagenarian twins — Art (Ted Stidder) and Martin Hart (Eric Christmas) who show up at Pappy's doorstep also have an eye on the future and try to prevent Belle from marrying the unwitting Pappy and

(so as to prevent a court-ordered annulment later) consumating the relationship.

The twins engage Sheriff Nashville Schwartz (Leslie Nielsen, barely trying), who goes to work on the case and slows up matters even more. Bromfield's attempts at humorous dialog too often are couched in conversational misunderstandings that don't ring true (as when the brothers confuse him by simultaneously reporting the theft of their rental car with the disappearance of their Pappy).

Two minor characters floating around the fringes of the story meet with little success. Martin Mull plays a shifty lawyer, but he's never fully integrated into the plot. More troublesome is the suicidal Selma Dodge (Deanne Henry), Belle's hotel proprietor friend. In trying to get some bizarre, sad charm out of her desperate condition he winds up with just bad acting.

When things wind up — with a big explosion — audience doesn't know much more about any of the characters than it did in the first 10 minutes. Only exception is Bromfield, who provides a certain depressing testimony to her husband's vision of the dark side of the American Dream, but not enough to justify the last 90 minutes of the picture.

Tech credits are mostly competent. Lenser Robert Ennis' landscapes of the Vancouver wilderness are breathtaking, but some of the interiors lack crispness. Art director Jill Scott seems torn between a bizarre or down-home look. The split difference is unpalatable and unbelievable.—*Camb.*

The Trouble With Spies
(COLOR)

Inept comedy.

A De Laurentiis Entertainment Group release of an HBO Pictures presentation of a Brigade production. Produced and directed by Burt Kennedy. Executive producer, Constantine P. Karos. Screenplay, Kennedy; based on the book "Apple Pie In The Sky," by Marc Lovell; camera (Eastmancolor), Alex Phillips; editor, Warner E. Leighton; music, Ken Thorne; production design, Jose Maria Tapiador. Reviewed at DEG Studios, L.A., Dec. 3, 1987. (MPAA Rating: PG.) Running time: **91 MINS.**
Appleton Porter . . . . . . Donald Sutherland
Harry Lewis . . . . Ned Beatty
Mrs. Arkwright . . . . Ruth Gordon
Mona Smith . . . . Lucy Gutteridge
Jason Lock . . . . Michael Hordern
Angus Watkins . . . . Robert Morley
Captain Sanchez . . . . Gregory Sierra
Maria Sola . . . . Suzanne Danielle
Col. Novikov . . . . Fima Noveck

Hollywood — "The Trouble With Spies" (original title: "Trouble At The Royal Rose") is an HBO Pictures film that has been without a distributor since it was made in 1984 until a recent DEG pickup. Even if it had been left as a made-for-tv pic it would have been subpar, but on the big screen "Trou-

ble" is a stultifying 91-minute spy yarn that takes forever to unravel.

Donald Sutherland, as British Intelligence agent Appleton Porter, tries at once to be naive, sly, stupid, heroic and Clouseauesque, failing most miserably in the last endeavor. Several good character actors are lost in the cinematic rubble, with the triple-threat production, direction and screenplay of Burt Kennedy doing most of the damage. In limited regional playoff for four months, big-city boxoffice prospects are DOA.

Based on Marc Lovell's book "Apple Pie In The Sky," film casts Sutherland as a bumbling, bottom-of-the-barrel British agent sent to the island of Ibiza to unwittingly act as bait for Soviet spies, rumored to have perfected a truth serum that can be used to gain information from enemy agents.

Porter assumes the alias of Arnold Barker and heads for the assignment assuming he's looking for information on a missing agent. He sets up shop at the Royal Rose Hotel, where he is immediately attracted to proprietor Mona Smith (Lucy Gutteridge, nice but on the bland side).

After five attempts on his life, he casts a suspicious eye towards his fellow guests, among the Harry Lewis (Ned Beatty, playing a shadow of more fully realized characters he's played in the past), Mrs. Arkwright (the late Ruth Gordon, in her last film), Jason Lock (Michael Hordern) and Maria Sola (Suzanne Danielle).

What passes for clues to the identity of these minor characters are random, punchless scenes that seem used merely to fill up time and get some movement in front of the camera. Middle section of the film has all the dramatic tension of a landlocked "Love Boat" episode, and about as much sophistication.

An hour into the pic, when Sutherland starts chatting up a guard dog in order to gain entry to a building occupied by his superior (Robert Morley, in good voice still), it's obvious Kennedy has run out of script to work with, or new ideas to put on film.

Remainder involves the inevitable happy ending, with Sutherland running off with one of the supporting characters, and the complicated explanation of what has transpired, from British and Soviet intelligence heads reflecting on a failed mission. Equally dismal account could have been filed by the film's helmers.

One of the few bright spots is provided by Fima Noveck (bearing a slight resemblance to Judge Robert Bork), better known as a film dubber/subtitler, as the head of Soviet intelligence. His dry telephone conversations with his inept agent are the only semi-reliable comedy bits in the film.

Tech credits are as stale as the film itself, with atrocious dubbing on outdoor scenes and maddeningly glib score from Ken Thorne.

—*Camb.*

Off The Mark
(COLOR)

Athletic comedy never makes it to finish line.

A Fries Entertainment release. Executive producer, Marisa Arango. Produced by Temple Matthews. Directed by Bill Berry. Screenplay, Matthews, Berry; camera (color), Arledge Armenaki; music, David Frank; coproducer, Ira Trattner. Reviewed at Metcalf Theater, Overland Park, Kan., Nov. 18, 1987. (MPAA Rating: R.) Running time **90 MINS.**
With: Mark Neely, Terry Farrell, Clarence Gilyard Jr., Norman Alden, Virginia Capers, Jon Cypher, Barry Corbin, Billy Barty.

Kansas City — "Off The Mark" represents a pickup venture by Fries Entertainment into the feature film market, but it's a minimal effort. Picture was titled "Crazy Legs" during production, and that is the essence of the story.

Mark Neely is entering a college "triathlon" of marathon run, swimming and cycling, but has a pair of legs that act up crazily at times, the result of a childhood playground fall. That's revealed through flashbacks, along with those of a Russian exchange student who comes back to the U.S. to become the nemesis in the triathlon. Terry Farrell is a buxom lass competing head-on with the men, and another principal in the race is a black student. A big, tan dog is a stand-out in more than a bit.

A more disjointed triathlon would be difficult to imagine. So spasmodic is the telling that it is not too plain when the race begins and when it ends, while fitting in a variety of interrupting sequences. Writers Bill Berry and Temple Matthews come up with a few good laughs and some effective sight gags, but the total is sparse. A dream sequence of the black runner done in shining white seems tasteless, and a rivalry of the two sports announcers degenerates into slapstick. In one sequence with but a slim hook to the plotline, the camera looks in on the girls' locker room while all are in the buff preparing for showers. Picture is thin on lighting, sets and camerawork, and the direction never quite pulls it together for the starting gun.

The picture apparently never has played under the original title. Fries set it in only three small Kansas City theaters the week of Nov. 13 and grosses were very thin.—*Quin.*

La Passion Béatrice
(The Passion Of Béatrice)
(FRENCH-ITALIAN-COLOR)

An AMLF release (Samuel Goldwyn Co. in U.S.) of a Clea Prods./Little Bear/TF-1 Films Prod./Les Films de la Tour/AMLF/Scena Films (Rome) coproduction. Executive producer, Adolphe Viezzi. Directed by Bertrand Tavernier. Screenplay, Colo Tavernier O'Hagan; camera (Eastmancolor), Bruno de Keyzer; editor, Armand Psenny; music, Ron Carter, Lili Boulanger; production design, Guy-Claude François; costumes, Jacqueline Moreau; sound, Michel Desrois; production manager, Pierre Saint Blancat; assistant director, Olivier Horlait; makeup, Paul Le Marinel. Reviewed at the Marignan-Concorde cinema, Paris, Dec. 3, 1987. Running time: **131 MINS.**
François de Cortemart . . . . . Bernard-Pierre Donnadieu
Béatrice . . . . Julie Delpy
Arnaud . . . . Nils Tavernier
François' mother . . . . . Monique Chaumette
Raoul . . . . Robert Dhery
Richard . . . . Maxime Leroux
Bertrand Lemartin . . . . Jean-Claude Adelin
The priest . . . . Claude Duneton
Recluse . . . . Albane Guilhe

Paris — The eclectic Bertrand Tavernier returns to a genre in which he excels — the historical drama — for what is certainly his bleakest and most disconcerting film to date. "La Passion Béatrice" is a dark, violent tale set in the 14th century during the Hundred Years War and dramatizes the clash of wills between a feudal lord and his devout, adoring daughter. Samuel Goldwyn Co. picked up U.S. distribution rights and will need extra special handling for the arthouse trade.

Screenplay is credited solely to Colo Tavernier O'Hagan, the helmer's ex-wife, who previously had a writing hand in his "A Week's Vacation" and "A Sunday In The Country." Far from the lyrical, elegaic tone of those works, "Passion Béatrice" is an unladylike chamber play of horrors. This Theater of Cruelty includes blasphemy, rape, incest and parricide, all filtered through the essentially romantic temperament of the director, who has filmed father-daughter relations before, but never of such brutal hopelessness.

The story's ogre is François de Cortemart (Bernard-Pierre Donnadieu), an embittered nobleman taken prisoner by the English along with his son and now returning home years later thanks to a ransom paid by his daughter Béatrice (Julie Delpy), who has sold off property and land.

Béatrice's dreams of affectionate reunion are chilled quickly by her father's scorn for traditional values. Bruised as a child by his mother's infidelity with a lover he himself had murdered, and by his father's death in war, Donnadieu has suffered the ultimate humiliations of captivity and degradation. Disgusted by the cowardice and effeminate nature of his own son (Nils Tavernier, son of scripter and director), the lord seeks vengeance against God and fellow man by corrupting his own daughter.

The terrible showdown between father and daughter — beginning with his incestuous rape, his intentions to marry her in defiance of the church, her attempt to kill him by witchcraft and her final act of murder — block out a narrative of unrelieved tensions and emotional convolutions.

Impeccable in period detail and feeling of time and place, Tavernier's film charts a rocky course through an excessive sea of passions, faltering in its existential motivations though gripping in its depiction of a daughter's sullied revelations of life.

As Béatrice, 18-year-old Delpy (seen briefly in Léos Carax' "Mauvais Sang") is vibrant and credible, combining a delicate physique with unfathomed inner strength. Donnadieu, a familiar heavy who also played a homecoming medieval peasant in Daniel Vigne's "The Return Of Martin Guerre" (he was the real Martin), has demonic presence and a glimmer of pathos as the godless, death-seeking lord.

Among the fine supporting cast, Monique Chaumette cuts a sharp silhouette as Donnadieu's once-perfidious, now-pious mother, while comedy veteran Robert Dhéry does an enchanting turn as an ageing knight forever sifting through his memories of the Holy Land. Nils Tavernier is fine as the fickle son who must suffer his father's unending abuse.

Guy-Claude François, a gifted stage designer associated notably with Ariane Mnouchkine, has done a remarkable job in refurbishing a ruined Cathare castle in southwestern France as the film's principal decor, and Bruno de Keyzer, who photographed Tavernier's "A Sunday In The Country" and " 'Round Midnight" helps create a sense of lived-in texture that most period films never achieve. Other credits are fine down the line.

—*Len.*

Student Confidential
(COLOR)

Unintentional high school comedy.

A Troma release. Executive producer, James Horian. Produced, written and directed by Richard Horian. Camera (color), James Dickson; editor, Richard Horian; art direction, Robert Joyce; music, Richard Horian; lighting, Al Goldenhar; sound, Gerald B. Wolfe; production executive, H. Kaye Dyle; production design, David Wasco. Reviewed at Magno Preview 4, N.Y., Nov. 24, 1987. (MPAA Rating: R.) Running time: **94 MINS.**
Johnny Warshetsky . . . . Eric Douglas
Joseph Williams . . . . Marlon Jackson
Susan Bishop . . . . Susan Scott
Elain Duvat . . . . Elizabeth Singer
Jenny Seldon . . . . Ronee Blakley
Michael Drake . . . . Richard Horian
Also with: Paula Sorenson, John Milford, Kip King, Sarina Grant, Billie Jean Thomas, Joel Mills, Corwyn Anthony.

Calling "Student Confidential" a bad film is like saying a high school quiz with no current answers is an F. It just doesn't convey the enormity of the miscue.

It seems inconceivable that anyone, even Richard Horian who produced, wrote, directed, edited and composed the music, could watch this picture without wincing.

Plot centers around three gifted but troubled students — Johnny (Eric Douglas), Joseph (Marlon Jackson) and Susan (Susan Scott). The principal of the high school they attend calls in a fabulously wealthy friend, Michael Drake (Richard Horian), to counsel the kids.

Drake arranges hair appointments for Susan to boost her ego. He finds a big part-time job for computer whiz Joseph in order to reverse his antisocial behavior. And, in the *coup de grace,* Drake convinces Johnny's father to allow his son to stop taking accounting courses and become a machinist.

Though Drake succeeds with the kids, his own marriage falls apart and he attempts to kill himself. As a result, Johnny, Joseph and Susan assume the counseling role to save Drake.

"Confidential" abounds with unintentional humor which often evokes hearty laughter and is dotted throughout with nudity for nudity's sake.

One wonders how Ronee Blakley wound up in this film or, for that matter, Eric Douglas, son of Kirk.

Judging from the creidts, Horian obviously extended a great deal of energy in making "Student Confidential." It is unfortunate the end result is such as it is. —*Chuk.*

Bushfire Moon
(AUSTRALIAN-COLOR)

A Village-Roadshow (Australia) release of an Entertainment Media production, in association with The Disney Channel, Australian Children's Film and Television Foundation, Film Victoria. Produced by Peter Beilby, Robert Le Tet. Directed by George Miller. Stars Dee Wallace Stone, John Waters. Screenplay, Jeff Peck; camera (color), David Connell; editor, Tim Wellburn; music, Bruce Rowland; production design, Otello Stolfo; sound, Andrew Ramage; production manager, Helen Watts; assistant director, Brian Giddens; costumes, Rose Chong; casting, Adrienne Dolphin, Liz Mullinar. Reviewed at Village Roadshow screening room, Sydney, Nov. 2, 1987. Running time: **98 MINS.**
Elizabeth O'Day . . . . . . Dee Wallace Stone
Patrick O'Day . . . . John Waters
Trevor Watson . . . . Bill Kerr
Max Bell . . . . Charles Tingwell
Sarah O'Day . . . . Nadine Garner
Ned O'Day . . . . Andrew Ferguson
Angus Watson . . . . Grant Piro
Miss Daly . . . . Rosie Sturgess
Also with: Francis Bell (Sharkey), Christopher Stevenson (Jamie), Kim Gyngell (Hungry Bill), David Ravenswood (Mr. Gullett), Maggie Millar (Mrs. Gullett), Francine Ormrod (Penelope Gullett), Bruce Kilpatrick (Adam McKimmie), Callie Gray (Pip McKimmie), Christine Keogh (Heather McKimmie), Martin Redpath (Sgt. Gibbs).

Sydney — A sentimental yarn about a turn-of-the-century Christmas in drought-stricken outback Australia, "Bushfire Moon" is a misfire. Theatrical chances look dim, even with the holidays approaching, but item could have a decent career on tv and video.

Story itself is promising. An 8-

year-old, Ned O'Day (Andrew Ferguson) lives with his American-born mother (Dee Wallace Stone), father (John Waters) and teenage sister (Nadine Carner) on a rundown sheep farm. Water is short, and so is cash, and the family faces a bleak Christmas, especially when their Scrooge-like neighbor, Watson (Bill Kerr) refused O'Day's sheep access to his water supply.

Then Ned spots a white-bearded drifter and petty thief (Charles Tingwell) he assumes must be Santa Claus, and before the story is over the family's happiness is assured, Watson has turned into a nice guy, and the rains have come. All of which would be enjoyable if not for the pedestrian treatment, predictable screenplay, insipid music score and mostly poor thesping.

Director George Miller (of "The Man From Snowy River" and "Les Patterson Saves The World," not to be confused with the helmer of the "Mad Max" films and "The Witches Of Eastwick") must shoulder most of the blame, because there was potential here for a family film with heart. Sadly, he handles the tall story with sluggish detachment and a complete absence of the vital magic which might have suspended disbelief.

Of the principal actors, only Charles Tingwell as the old villain who comes to enjoy playing the Santa Claus role, makes much of an impression. As the parents, John Waters and Dee Wallace Stone are rote characters, Bill Kerr overplays his villain (a stern traditionalist who imports a genuine English yule log to burn on a sweleringly hot Australian Christmas Day and insists his perspiring guests join him in a chorus of "British To The Core"). Nadine Garner is self-conscious as the pretty daughter, Grant Piro wooden as Watson's son and young Andrew Ferguson cute but occasionally inaudible.

The only comedy comes with the disruption of Watson's stiff-necked Christmas Party. Attempts to whip up drama via an opening-reel dust storm and a climactic bush fire fall flat since neither natural disaster looks the least bit convincing or threatening. Continuity blunders are another minus. Inevitably, pic looks handsome, if a bit too well scrubbed.—Strat.

Deathrow Gameshow
(COLOR)

Vulgar, amateurish satire of tv.

A Crown Intl. Pictures release of a Pirromount production. Executive producer & sound, Sergio Bandera. Produced by Brian J. Smith. Directed by Mark Pirro. Stars John McCafferty, Robyn Blythe, Beano. Screenplay, Pirro; additional material, Alan Gries; camera (color), Craig Bassuk; supervising editor, Tim Shoemaker; music, Gregg Gross; production design, Mark Simon, assistant director, Tom Milo; production manager, Devorah Hardburger; stunt coordinator, Eric Megison; casting, John McCafferty, Kent Butler; coproducer, Glenn Campbell. Reviewed at Cine 42 #2 theater, N.Y., Dec. 5, 1987. (MPAA Rating: R.) Running time: **83 MINS.**

Chuck Toedan	John McCafferty
Gloria Sternvirgin	Robin Blythe
Luigi Pappalardo	Beano
Momma	Mark Lasky
Trudy	Darwyn Carson
Shanna Shallow	Debra Lamb
Dinko	Paul Farbman

The generic concept behind "The Running Man" is recycled to ill effect in "Deathrow Gameshow," an exercise in vulgar humor reminiscent but inferior to 1970s drive-in comedies.

John McCafferty is well cast (he supervised casting) as Chuck Toedan, toothy, ever-smiling host of the tv gameshow "Live Or Die," in which, à la "Running Man," condemned convicts are given a chance to get a reprieve or gifts for their families. Executions are conducted on the taped show if they lose.

Filmmaker Mark Pirro knows talk is cheap, so there's plenty of it and not enough gameshow segments to keep the film lively. Mostly it's Toedan's private life, dealing with unruly fans or people who hate him and the show, particularly feminist Gloria Sternvirgin (Robin Blythe) and Mafia hit man Luigi Pappalardo (the height in hissable vulgarity as played by Beano). Attempts at black humor are mainly silly, the film's only successful running gag being Debra Lamb's nonstop posing as the sexy prize presenter on the show.

Production values are on the level of a home movie and cast is instructed to overact throughout. The 1-joke premise is padded endlessly with a pointless dream sequence and very slowly rolling end credits.
—Lor.

The Stranger
(U.S.-ARGENTINE-COLOR)

A Columbia Pictures release of a Tusitala-Nolin Co. production. Executive producer, Michael Nolin. Produced by Hugo Lamónica. Directed by Adolfo Aristarain. Stars Bonnie Bedelia, Peter Riegert. Screenplay, Dan Gurskis; camera (color), Horacio Maira; editor, Eduardo López; music, Craig Safan; sets, Abel Facello; costumes, Félix Sánchez Plaza; sound, José Luis. Díaz; associate producer, Peter Marai. Reviewed at Lesser Cine 2, N.Y., Dec. 4, 1987. (MPAA Rating: R.) Running time: **88 MINS.**

Alice Kildee	Bonnie Bedelia
Dr. Harris Kite	Peter Riegert
Sgt. Drake	Barry Primus
Hobby	David Spielberg
Macaw	Marcos Woinski
Jay	Julio de Grazia
Anita	Cecilia Roth

Also with: Arturo Maly, Ricardo Darín, Adrián Ghio, Tito Mendoza, Federico Luppi, Jacques Arndt, Milton James, Marina Magall, Ernesto Larrese, Sacha Favelevic.

"The Stranger" is a psychological thriller with a built-in gimmick meant to trick the audience and carry most of the pic's momentum. Directed by Adolfo Aristarain, helmer of such gaucho features as "La Parte de León," "Tiempo de Revancha" and "Ultimos Días de la Victima," Columbia pickup opened quietly at about a half-dozen Gotham locations.

Film begins briskly with three brutal murders witnessed by Alice Kildee (Bonnie Bedelia). With killers hot on her trail, she survives a car accident only to end up in the hospital as an amnesia victim with no clue to her identity. Doctors, headed by Dr. Harris Kite (Peter Riegert), are perplexed because she suffers none of the standard signs of psychosomatic amnesia. The police meanwhile are attracted by her stories of murder, while killers make attempts on her life.

Pic was shot in English entirely in greater Buenos Aires, although the story is set in a nonexistent California town called Plainville. Lensing is quite good and flashbacks and memories are handled in black and white. Bold music score by Craig Safan keeps scenes tense.

On the other hand, the pacing is uneven and the finale limps to a close after some dizzy comic banter with the police. Bits of side business and character development also fall flat. Although Dr. Kite is described as a compulsive gambler and chain smoker, it is all in the script. He exhibits no compulsive behavior and the only time we see him smoke is at the beginning of the film. The same is true with the two hardboiled policemen, whose bumbling camaraderie never rises above cliché.

Bedelia offers a believable characterization as the amnesia victim and Argentine character actor Julio de Grazia is good as the heavy. A few secondary characters sound as if they were dubbed.

Pic's theme and surprise ending keep the audience intrigued through most of the film. Boxoffice potential should prove moderate, while eventual tv and homevid sales might be stronger. — Lent.

Amor En Campo Minado
(Love In A Minefield)
(CUBAN-COLOR)

An Icaic production. Produced by Dario Larramendi. Directed by Pastor Vega. Screenplay by Vega, based on a play by Dias Gomes; music, Chico Buarque de Hollanda. Reviewed at Rio De Janeiro Film Festival (competing), Nov. 24, 1987. Running time: **96 MINS.**

With: Daisy Granados, Adolfo Llauradó, Omar Valdés, Ana Lilian Rentería.

Rio de Janeiro — Based on a Brazilian play by Dias Gomes, "Love In A Minefield" provides few opportunities to forget its theatrical origins and, in spite of a potentially interesting subject, fails to come off as a film. President Goulart's overthrow by the military in 1964 was followed by a roundup of his supporters and leftists in general and Sergio, a writer and journalist, escapes from his paper disguised as a priest. He goes into hiding at a friend's pied-à-terre, an unpleasant surprise for a middle-aged executive who has taken his secretary there.

Sergio later is joined by his wife and the country's critical juncture is echoed in his own little world. Not only is there a crisis in his 15-year marriage, but he also has to face the fact that he neither was nor is the revolutionary he thought himself. His life as a leftist intellectual was full of contradictions of which he only now becomes aware.

The play, although by no means outstanding, made some valid points and the film fails to enrich it; for example, it fails to find an adequate visual language for the husband and wife's non-realistic roleplaying (such as priest and woman in the confessional). The two main characters have a double dimension as realistic characters in a tense situation and, at the same time, mouthpieces for ideas. These two levels are conveyed by Daisy Granados but not by Adolfo Llauradó whose performance is less subtle. Technical credits are adequate but unimpressive.—Amig.

Real Men
(COLOR)

Unfunny spy spoof.

An MGM/UA Communications release from United Artists. Produced by Martin Bregman. Executive producer, Louis A. Stroller. Directed by Dennis Feldman. Screenplay, Feldman; camera (Metrocolor), John A. Alonzo; art direction, William J. Cassidy, James Allen; set decoration, Tom Pedigo; set designer, Dan Maltese; costumes, Jodie Tillen; sound, Keith Wester; assistant director; Allan Wertheim; casting, Lynn Stalmaster, David Rubin. Reviewed at Crown Center, Kansas City, Nov. 17, 1987. (MPAA Rating: PG-13.) Running time: **96 MINS.**

Nick Pirandello	James Belushi
Bob Wilson	John Ritter
Mom	Barbara Barrie
Cunard	Bill Morey
Dolly	Iva Andersen
Sherry	Gail Berle
Bradshaw	Mark Herrier
Bob, Jr.	Matthew Brooks

Kansas City — "Real Men" is a weird spy-spoof entry, entangling the CIA with extraterrestrials to save the earth from economic ruin (pre-stock market shock of October 1987) and something about a "big gun" capable of blowing up an entire planet. Writer-director Dennis Feldman has the basis of what could have been a funny spoof, but laughs are too far between. Customers likely will be, too.

Unhinged sequence piles upon unhinged sequence and the proceedings never quite get connected into a cohesive storyline as the Russians unwittingly kill off the one CIA agent who had contact with the extraterrestrials, forcing the CIA to call in James Belushi — an "unorthodox operator, but gets the job done."

No wonder — his weapons prowess and invulnerability to an assortment of Russian firepower is impressive.

The CIA veers to a secret strategy — find a milquetoast (John Ritter) to deliver a secret map from California to Washington, D.C. Belushi's job: make sure the unassuming courier delivers.

Belushi does tongue-in-cheek with a swagger throughout, making the best of what he has to work with.

Ritter plays the straight wimp throughout, first objecting to being drafted for such a wacky project, finally agreeing and lastly emerging as a man in his own right, fully capable of bashing the neighborhood bullies who had been terrorizing his family while he was gone.

While Belushi is the lead-dog, the action leans heavily on Ritter's never-failing Mr. Average, to whom the extraterrestrials finally confide their valued plans.

Production values also are spaced out, and the whole fails to make good use of the two real men in the picture.

United Artists evidently is not making a national release of this film, spotting it into the K.C. and St. Louis markets the week of Nov. 13. Grosses in K.C. were slight in the 6-theater showcase, about $1,-500 per theater. Apparently, it will go market-by-market from here on, if at all.—*Quin.*

La Rosa dei Nomi
(The Rose Of The Names)
(ITALIAN-COLOR)

A Movie Movie/RAI-Uno production. Directed by Francesco Conversano, Nene Grignaffini. Camera (color), Maurizio Dell'Orco; editor, Valter Cappucci; music, Claudio Scannavini. Reviewed at Festival dei Popoli, Florence, Italy, Nov. 27, 1987. Running time: **61 MINS.**
With: Umberto Eco, Sean Connery, F. Murray Abraham, Jean-Jacques Annaud.

Florence — "La Rosa dei Nomi" is an irritating documentary about Umberto Eco's "The Name Of The Rose" and Jean-Jacques Annaud's film based on it. It is best forgotten.

Backstage shots of film's production and clips from finished pic are shown between mindless interviews with Eco, Annaud, Sean Connery and film's other performers. Eco's rudeness and sarcasm stand out for showing as much contempt for the filmmakers as they show for their audience. They go to great lengths to take a story that is complex and interesting on its own, and turn it into a dull, complicated essay on self-absorption.

When asked what "The Name Of The Rose" is, Eco replies, "It is eight centimeters by 17 centimeters and five centimeters thick. It is made of cellulose." He does not mention celluloid.

Maurizio Dell'Orco's lensing is pic's only mark of professionalism, while Claudio Scannavini's music is under par. — *Newm.*

The Virgin Queen Of
St. Francis High
(CANADIAN-COLOR)

A Crown Intl. Pictures release of a Pioneer Pictures production, in association with American Artists (Canada) Corp. Executive producer, Lawrence G. Ryckman. Directed, written and edited by Francesco Lucente. Camera (color), Joseph Bitonti, Kevin Alexander; editorial consultant, Rick Doe; incidental music, Danny Lowe, Brad Steckel, Brian Island; location sound, James F. Baillies; additional sound, Per Asplund; associate producer, Alex Tadich; assistant director, Anisa Lalani; casting, Olimpia Lucente, Angela Bitonti. Reviewed at the Egyptian Theater, L.A., Dec. 4, 1987. (MPAA Rating: PG.) Running time: **94 MINS.**
Mike . . . . Joseph R. Straface
Diane . . . . Stacy Christensen
Charles . . . . J.T. Wotton
Judy . . . . Anna-Lisa Iapaolo
Randy . . . . Lee Barringer
Diane's mother . . . . Bev Wotton

Hollywood — When tradesters talk of a glut on the market, stuff like "The Virgin Queen Of St. Francis High" is of what they speak. Non-exploitative exploitationer from Canada possesses such shockingly subprofessional production values that members of the opening day audience in Hollywood cussed out the awful dubbing, and one rebellious soul asked all other patrons to join him as he stormed out to the lobby to demand a refund. Two did, the rest paid the price both in lost money and numbing boredom.

It must have been the opening scene that put the fellow in such a mutinous mood, since nothing quite so technically bad has been foisted upon unsuspecting audiences since the heyday of Yugoslavian-Italian-German coproductions of the 1960s.

On film that looks like it's been run through an automated cotton-picker, a nerdy guy bets the stud of the barroom $2,000 he'll get the stuck-up blond of the title out to Paradise Bungalows for a night of hanky panky by summer's end. Dialog and acting seem bad enough, but it's distractingly hard to tell since lines sound as if they were recorded on a battery-operated tape recorder in a phone booth with actors who didn't speak the same language as those onscreen.

Not only that, but throughout the picture there is virtually no ambient sound, only the dialog and a continuous background of inane and arbitrary rock music.

Clever directors sometimes can turn such liabilities into assets, but such is not the case with first-timer Francesco Lucente, who appears to have been aiming for a clean, respectable teenpic in this tale of a dimwitted guy trying to win the heart of a girl intent upon "saving" herself for marriage. Suffice to say the lady's honor, as well as the film's utter lack of talent and interest, remain intact at pic's end.
— *Carl.*

Des Grands Événements
et des Gens Ordinaires:
Les Elections
(Of Great Events And Ordinary
People: The Elections)
(FRENCH-DOCU-COLOR)

A British Film Institute (BFI) release of an Institut National de l'Audiovisuel (INA) production. Produced by Martine Durand, Dominique Benzadon. Directed by Raul Ruiz. Screenplay, Ruiz, François Ede; camera (color, 16m), Jacques Bouquin, Dominique Forgue, Alain Salomon; editor, Valeria Sarmiento; sound, Jean-Claude Brisson, N'guyen Van Tuong. Reviewed at the French Institute, N.Y., Nov. 18, 1987. Running time: **60 MINS.**

"Of Great Events And Ordinary People," an early French venture by Raul Ruiz, was to be one of a series of docus by various filmmakers about the 1978 legislative elections, of which this was the only pic produced. Like all Ruiz films, docu eschews conventionality.

Titled ironically, the movie changes intentions several times en route. Initially, the film was to be an exploration of the filmmaker's Paris neighborhood, the 11th arrondissement, during election week, to see how an event like elections can have any effect on quotidian existence. After Ruiz realizes 80% of those approached declined to be interviewed, the focus shifts to "the elections in one Paris quarter as seen by a Chilean exile." Later, as the pic becomes self-conscious, the film begins to examine and dissect the docu form itself.

A great deal of humor and surprise emerges as Ruiz uses the elections as an outward drama that inserts itself into the fabric of everyday life. The film penetrates the surface and holds each object up to scrutiny. When questioned, a trio of people at a bistro respond with empty clichés; another woman who at first appears apathetic reveals her despair and anger at the recent death of her son.

In a move away from the talking-heads docu style, Ruiz stops listening to what people say and instead dwells on the way they express themselves. He notices how some people will go out of their way to overexplain themselves because they suspect some nebulous motive lurking behind an innocuous question. He also points out how people censor themselves.

As the election week continues, different themes emerge and we begin to lose track of the polls. The documentary itself is in question. Scenes from the beginning of the film are recapped and we discover that Ruiz has inserted a re-edited 6-minute docu within the 60-minute film. This in turn is reduced to a 60-second rapid-fire version. Playwright Tom Stoppard used a similar technique to comic effect with "Dogg's Hamlet," but Ruiz notes here that the docu remains virtually the same within the form, with nothing lost.

Ruiz' favored moving camera technique is in full service. Often a speaker is abandoned as the camera pans to survey his surroundings, sometimes in a deliberate attempt to remove the viewer from what is being said.

Since it was originally produced in 16m for French tv, "Of Great Events And Ordinary People" is more accessible than many more experimental Ruiz ventures. It is bold, humorous, intriguing, insightful, frustrating and full of a self-indulgence that works within the docu form. —*Lent.*

September
(COLOR)

An Orion Pictures release of a Jack Rollins-Charles H. Joffe production. Produced by Robert Greenhut. Executive producers, Rollins, Joffe. Written and directed by Woody Allen. Camera (Du Art color, Deluxe prints), Carlo Di Palma; editor, Susan E. Morse; production design, Santo Loquasto; art direction, Speed Hopkins; set decoration, George DeTitta Jr.; costume design, Jeffrey Kurland; sound, James Sabat; associate producer, Gail Sicilia; casting, Juliet Taylor. Reviewed at the Orion screening room, L.A., Nov. 30, 1987. (MPAA Rating: PG.) Running time: **82 MINS.**

Howard . . . . Denholm Elliott
Stephanie . . . . Dianne Wiest
Lane . . . . Mia Farrow
Diane . . . . Elaine Stritch
Peter . . . . Sam Waterston
Lloyd . . . . Jack Warden
Mr. Raines . . . . Ira Wheeler
Mrs. Raines . . . . Jane Cecil
Mrs. Mason . . . . Rosemary Murphy

Hollywood — "September" sees Woody Allen in a compellingly melancholy mood, as he sends four achingly unhappy younger people and two better adjusted older ones through a grim story drenched with Chekhovian overtones. Although exceedingly well acted and sparked by numerous outstanding scenes, drama seems a bit curtailed, as if Allen were afraid to really let loose with his characters, and result doesn't feel like a full meal. Like his previous somber drama, "Interiors," this will appeal only to certain tastes and b.o. necessarily will be limited, but the anguished emotions will register powerfully with viewers receptive to brooding fare.

Set entirely within the lovely Vermont country home of Mia Farrow at summer's end, tale is constructed around a pattern of unrequited, mismatched infatuations that drive the high-strung, intellectual characters to distraction. Neighbor Denholm Elliott loves Farrow, Farrow is a goner for guesthouse occupant Sam Waterston, and Waterston is nuts for Farrow's best friend Dianne Wiest, who is married.

Also visiting are Farrow's mother, a former screen star and great beauty played by Elaine Stritch, and the latter's husband, physicist Jack Warden. Mother-daughter relationship represents the most surprising conceit in the picture, as a quarter-century before the action is set, at age 14, Farrow reputedly killed Stritch's sleazy lover, a situation that directly parallels the Lana Turner-Cheryl Crane true-life melodrama.

Farrow bears the double burden of her hopeless yearnings for Waterston and her lifelong resentment of her successful mother, who has weathered every storm and scandal and now lives in relative, if excessively alcoholic, contentment with her utterly stable husband. Unable to pull her career as a photographer together either, Farrow is in every way pitiful, but so vulnerable and sensitive that one is enormously drawn to her.

By contrast, Mama is one tough cookie, a survivor fed up with her daughter's neuroses who lashes back by saying, "If your life hasn't worked out, stop blaming me for it." Making matters worse, Stritch takes a fancy to Waterston and invites the adman and aspiring novelist to ghostwrite her memoirs, which inevitably will dwell extensively on the sordid details of the killing and Farrow's subsequent problems.

Whenever Farrow is out of view, Waterston comes on to Wiest, who is attracted and unhappy in her marriage, but reluctant to betray her already devastated closest chum. Half of Wiest's lines seem to be, "Please don't," as she must continually ward off her persistent suitor, and Farrow is forced to utter the same to Elliott, an impeccably civilized older man who knows his cause is doomed, but still feels compelled to voice his feelings.

So it goes, a merry-go-round of frustration, resentment, heartbreak, disappointment and bitterness, described in brittle, often piercing terms in Allen's dialog. Happily, the air is cleared on occasion by the outrageous Stritch, whose rowdy, forthright comments never fail to lighten the mood and provide genuine amusement.

Allen sustains his desired tone most of the way, but everyone is so wound up that, toward the end, as all the frayed ends need to be tied up, the springs snap and a few of the exchanges emerge as unintentionally comical. One senses Allen walking a very narrow tightrope throughout, so that when he falters, it is extremely noticeable.

The writer-director also seems in too big a hurry to bring his film to a conclusion, underwriting a story so ripe with dramatic angles that it needed more time to breathe and fully come to life. The framework and characters are here, but the full potential hasn't been achieved.

Even so, there is ever-so-much to chew on for those willing to indulge the characters' angst and self-torture. The debts to Chekhov are everywhere, as Stritch resembles not only Lana Turner, but Arkadina in "The Sea Gull," the younger women recall ladies in other of the playwright's work, and Farrow is considering selling the Vermont *dacha* for a life in New York, which is discussed as a beckoning culture capital in very much the same terms as is Moscow in Chekhov.

Stritch, so seldom seen on the big screen, has the showiest role and makes the most of it, wisecracking to get through the day and speaking bluntly when it suits her. The character steamrolls over everybody, and the actress is an overpowering delight. Farrow is heart-wrenching in her portrayal of naked, undisguised pain, Wiest sharply gets across sexual desire overburdened by nervous anxiety, and Waterston evokes the requisite lust and weakness of his floundering writer. Elliott and Warden are fine in more uni-dimensional roles.

Lenser Carlo Di Palma's luminous palette creates an ironically warm context in which the abrasive relationships will play themselves out, and keeps the film visually interesting despite the limitation of the single set, wonderfully designed by Santo Loquasto. Susan E. Morse's editing is even too close to the bone. As usual with Allen, popular tunes from earlier in the century, notably Irving Berlin's "What'll I Do?" dominate the soundtrack.

This is the film Allen largely reshot with a significantly altered cast after feeling dissatisfied with his first version. Originally, Maureen O'Sullivan, Farrow's real mother, played the role finally filled by Stritch. Sam Shepard, then, briefly, Christopher Walken, had Waterston's part, and Elliott was first cast as the actress' husband, with Charles Durning in the role of the neighbor. —*Cart.*

Moonstruck
(COLOR)

An MGM/UA Communications release of a Metro-Goldwyn-Mayer presentation of a Patrick Palmer-Norman Jewison production. Produced by Palmer, Jewison. Directed by Jewison. Stars Cher, Nicolas Cage. Screenplay, John Patrick Shanley. Camera (Technicolor and Medallion), David Watkin; editor, Lou Lombardo; music, Dick Hyman; production design, Philip Rosenberg; costume design, Theoni V. Aldredge; art direction, Barbra Matis, Dan Davis; sound (Dolby), Dennis L. Maitland; associate producer, Bonnie Palef-Woolf; casting, Howard Feuer. Reviewed at the Samuel Goldwyn Theater, L.A. Dec. 7, 1987. (MPAA Rating: PG.) Running time: **102 MINS.**

Loretta Castorini . . . . Cher
Ronny Cammareri . . . . Nicolas Cage
Cosmo Castorini . . . . Vincent Gardenia
Rose Castorini . . . . Olympia Dukakis
Johnny Cammareri . . . . Danny Aiello
Rita Cappomaggi . . . . Julie Bovasso
Perry . . . . John Mahoney
Raymond Cappomaggi . . . . Louis Guss
Old Man . . . . Feodor Chaliapin
Mona . . . . Anita Gillette

Hollywood — Norman Jewison's latest film is a mostly appetizing blend of comedy and drama carried by John Patrick Shanley's snappy dialog and a wonderful ensemble full of familiar faces. Leads Cher and Nicolas Cage are both solid and appealing, but it's the pic's older lovers — especially the splendidly controlled Olympia Dukakis — who give "Moonstruck" its endearing spirit. Word of mouth should help this to a modestly strong holiday performance.

Cher is Loretta Castorini, a vaguely dour, superstitious widow who believes her previous marriage — she was wed at City Hall, her father didn't give her away, her husband was killed when he was hit by a bus — was felled by bad luck.

Film begins with her accepting a wedding proposal, on bended knee, from the altogether unprepossessing Johnny Cammareri (Tony Aiello), who shortly thereafter heads off to Sicily to be at the bedside of his dying mother. He makes one request of Loretta before she leaves: to invite his brother, whom he has not spoken to in five years, to the wedding to end the "bad blood" between the two of them.

Loretta, resigned to accepting mediocrity (she admits to her mother that she doesn't love Johnny) for the sake of security, receives a shock upon meeting his kid brother. Cage's Ronny is a brooding, vital, angry, barely contained force haunted by his past. He explains to the stunned Loretta how he lost his hand five years previous, in an accident he still blames on Johnny, and that his fiance left him a short time later.

In Shanley's gorgeously written ensuing scene, the two adjourn to Ronny's apartment above his bakery and begin to talk about one another's lives. The different reactions of two people who see a second chance at true love staring them in the face is the theme of the rest of the film, with Loretta trying to decide whether to play it safe and stick with Johnny or follow her feelings and fall in love with Ronny.

Meanwhile, Loretta's father (Vincent Gardenia) and her mother (Dukakis) are in a second-chance conflict of their own, with Gardenia's Cosmo sneaking around and the hurt, betrayed, but dignified Rose trying to figure out why men chase women.

In Rose Castorini, Dukakis fleshes out a good, tired woman who is nothing less than mystified by the actions of her husband, and what her response should be. It's a warm, lyrical performance, that provides the finest moments in the film.

All the film's conflicts are resolved in a blockbuster of a climactic dinner-table scene in which Rose confronts Cosmo, Ronny meets Johnny, and Loretta receives her second proposition from a Cammareri in less than a month. It's another scene that could be poorly played for pure farce in less skilled hands than Jewison's and Shanley's, but is once again redeemed by their sure touch.

While mostly on the mark, Jewison is hardly infallible. He often gives in to heavyhanded symbolism, as when Cher bumps into two nuns while walking out of a clothing store, which has a display of a wedding dress in its front window, on the way to a date with Cage.

These excesses are few and far between, though, as Jewison keeps his eye on the action and is aided by some assured, smooth photography from David Watkin. Dick Hyman's score is on the money, with Dean Martin's rendition of "That's Amore," providing the perfectly cheesy mood-setter to open and close the film.

Supporting performances are almost universally strong, with Louis

Guss and Julie Bovasso charming and sturdy as Rose's brother and sister-in-law, Gardenia perfectly cast as her philandering husband, and even bit parts — such as Nada Despotovich's Chrissy, pining for the strapping Ronny but unable to tell him — consistently well played.

—Camb.

Ironweed
(COLOR)

A Tri-Star Pictures release of a Taft Entertainment Pictures/Keith Barish Prods. presentation. Produced by Barish, Marcia Nasatir. Executive producers, Joseph H. Kanter, Denis Blouin. Coproduced by Gene Kirkwood, C.O. Erickson. Directed by Hector Babenco. Stars Jack Nicholson, Meryl Streep. Screenplay, William Kennedy, based on his novel; camera (Technicolor), Lauro Escorel; editor, Anne Goursaud; music, John Morris; production design, Jeannine C. Oppewall; art direction, Robert Guerra; set decoration, Leslie Pope, Elaine O'Donnell; sound, Robert J. Litt, Elliot Tyson, B. Tennyson Sebastian 2d; costumes, Joseph G. Aulisi; casting, Bonnie Timmerman. Reviewed at Tri-Star screening room, Century City, Calif., Dec. 3, 1987. (MPAA Rating: R.) Running time: **144 MINS.**
Francis Phelan . . . . Jack Nicholson
Helen Archer . . . . Meryl Streep
Annie Phelan . . . . Carroll Baker
Billy . . . . Michael O'Keefe
Peg . . . . Diane Venora
Oscar Reo . . . . Fred Gwynne
Katrina . . . . Margaret Whitton
Rudy . . . . Tom Waits
Pee Wee . . . . Jake Dengel
Harold Allen . . . . Nathan Lane
Rev. Chester . . . . James Gammon

Hollywood — Filmgoers who clamor for more serious adult fare will probably find themselves fleeing to the latest John Hughes film after seeing "Ironweed." Unrelentingly bleak, "Ironweed" is a film without an audience and no reason for being except its own self-importance. It's an event picture without the event.

Whatever joy or redemption William Kennedy offered in his Pulitzer prize-winning novel is nowhere to be found, surprising since he wrote the screenplay. What's left is the flip side of "Barfly," a lowlife fable without the laughs that just spirals endlessly downward.

The story of Francis Phelan (Jack Nicholson) who returns to his native Albany in 1938 literally carrying a lifetime of ghosts with him, film gives away its central mystery after 10 minutes and with it the possibility of any dramatic momentum. Events sound the same note throughout; no highs but lots of lows.

After spilling the beans early, the only thing for Kennedy's screenplay to do is explain the events and film is loaded with elaborate expository passages trying to account for why an obviously intelligent individual has abandoned his family for a bum's life. There is scarcely any action to move what little plot there is.

Phelan's movement around Albany is like a passage through the rings of hell, but instead of coming out at paradise, he's still the same old bum at the end. There seems no way to dispel the demons that haunt him. Under Hector Babenco's direction, a parade of spirits follow Phelan in an all-too explicit externalization of the internal workings of his mind.

Result is kind of a 2-bit medicine show of spooks complete with neon gashes and festering wounds. Life has been tough for Phelan, but where is the vision to find some meaning in the suffering? Film only occasionally approaches the wistful, elegiac tone it's desperately searching for.

In rare moments film achieves an inner glow, enhanced by Lauro Escorel's cinematography, that suggests a sweet loving core in the center of all this bitterness, but for most of the way there are not enough recognizable human benchmarks to allow an audience to share the experience.

Kennedy's Albany as filtered through Babenco's lens is so specific and specialized that it's closed off to normal folk. It's not a real place, but a manifestation of Phelan's imagination, too personal to be meaningful to anyone else. It's not the poverty that ultimately puts one off, it's the failure of the filmmakers to use the material to open up this world.

Basically these are characters who are out of reach. By sheer strength of personality, rather than his character, Nicholson is able to draw in the audience occasionally, but his feeling and experience do not strike a common human chord.

As a love story, "Ironweed" offers even less. Nicholson and Meryl Streep have approximately three scenes together and though they clearly have a great deal of affection for each other, they are beyond passion. Much is made of Helen nursing Phelan when he was "weak as a pup," and there is kindness and softness between them. Yet Helen cannot save him, nor can anyone else.

Underutilized to the point that one wonders what she's doing in the film, Streep's performance is too distant to touch, propelled by a strange voice coming out of her as if it were detached from her body. Consequently, it is impossible to become emotionally involved in her struggle.

As Phelan's sidekick, Tom Waits give probably the most textured performance in the film, which manages to suggest the distance he has come and the life he's sacrificed. Moreover, Waits seems to be right in his element wearing Salvation Army handouts and waiting on breadlines for a hot meal.

Fred Gwynne has a small, but strong presence as a saloon singer who has seen better days. Carroll Baker is sympathetic as Phelan's long abandoned wife, but Michael O'Keefe and Diane Venora as his grown children are unaccountably stiff, as indeed is the entire reunion scene. Editing throughout, in fact, contributes to the director's very staid and deliberate tone.

Production values are generally impressive but a bit overdeveloped adding to the feeling that one is watching a museum piece more than living people.

Jeannine C. Oppewall's production design and John Morris' period-flavored music cannot be faulted; they gave the filmmakers exactly what they wanted.—Jagr.

Throw Momma From The Train
(COLOR)

An Orion Pictures release of a Rollins, Morra & Brezner production. Produced by Larry Brezner. Executive producer, Arne L. Schmidt. Directed by Danny DeVito. Stars DeVito, Billy Crystal. Screenplay, Stu Silver; camera (CFI color, Deluxe prints), Barry Sonnenfeld; editor, Michael Jablow; music, David Newman; production design, Ida Random; art direction, William Elliott; set decoration, Anne D. McCulley; costume design, Marilyn Vance-Straker; sound (Dolby), Robert R. Rutledge; assistant director, Joe Napolitano; coproducer, Kristine Johnson; casting, Dennison/Selzer. Reviewed at the Academy of Motion Pictures Arts and Sciences, L.A., Dec. 4, 1987. (MPAA Rating: PG-13.) Running time: **88 MINS.**
Owen . . . . Danny DeVito
Larry . . . . Billy Crystal
Momma . . . . Anne Ramsey
Beth . . . . Kim Greist
Margaret . . . . Kate Mulgrew
Lester . . . . Branford Marsalis
Also with: Rob Reiner, Bruce Kirby, Oprah Winfrey.

Hollywood — "Throw Momma From The Train" is a fun and delightfully venal comedy that could be the sleeper hit of the Christmas season.

Very clever and engaging from beginning to end, pic builds on the notion that nearly everyone — at least once in life — has the desire to snuff out a relative or nemesis, even if 99.9% of us let the urge pass without every acting on it.

Here, it's the idle death threats of a frustrated writer and flunky junior college professor (Billy Crystal) against his ex-wife that are overheard by one of his dimwitted and very impressionable students (Danny DeVito), who distinguishes himself in class by writing 3-page murder mysteries with only two characters.

DeVito's limited creative abilities are further stifled by his crazy, overbearing Momma (Anne Ramsey), a nasty, jealous old bag whom he loathes and fears. He seeks out Crystal for help on his writing and instead is told to go see Alfred Hitchcock's "Strangers On A Train," which he does — coming away with a ridiculous scheme on the film's plot to kill Crystal's wife and then ask for a like favor in return.

DeVito makes his theatrical feature directing debut here and it's a promising beginning, supported in part by a jaunty script by Stu Silver which craftily works in a number of twists playing DeVito off Crystal and the two of them against Ramsey where it's uncertain from one scene to the next who's *it* in their zany game of tag.

Giving the production zip are the animated performances of the leads. Crystal's talent as a standup comic comes through as it appears he got away with a fair amount of ad-libbing which wisely was retained in the final cut. His tirades on his ex-wife, a routine he does several times, get funnier with each delivery and are a good counterbalance for DeVito's equally comical dumb-impish schtick.

If there were to be a first place prize for scene stealing, however, it would go to Ramsey, whose horrible looks and surly demeanor are sick and humorous at the same time.

It's not inconceivable that some viewers might be turned off by the rather blasé treatment of death and murder, as say some were for "Eating Raoul" and "Harold And Maude," but this isn't either as black a comedy or as cynical a view on life — more a fun fantasy for the participants.

Slapstick and sight gags, especially when DeVito calls Crystal from a number of phone booths in Hawaii which have been plopped down in the middle of nowhere, keep the tone light and the mood silly. You never get the feeling that anyone's really going to die, even though there is a hint of doubt that carries the suspense all the way through to nearly the end.

As a good contrast to Crystal's seemingly crazed personality is Kim Greist as his anthropologist girlfriend, very sweet and appropriately befuddled by the goings-on, as Kate Mulgrew is as his shrewish former spouse who has the kind of irritatingly self-congratulatory public profile that a lot of people would be happy to see silenced forever.

Tech credits are fine throughout.
—Brit.

Overboard
(COLOR)

A MGM/UA Communications release of a Metro-Goldwyn-Mayer presentation. Produced by Anthea Sylbert, Alexandra Rose. Executive producer, Roddy McDowall. Directed by Garry Marshall. Stars Goldie Hawn, Kurt Russell. Screenplay, Leslie Dixon; camera (Metrocolor, Technicolor prints), John A. Alonzo; editor, Dov Hoenig, Sonny Baskin; music, Alan Silvestri; art direction, James Shanahan, Jim Dultz; visual consultant, Lawrence Miller; costume design, Wayne Finkleman; assistant director, Matt Earl Beesley; sound (Dolby), Bruce Bisenz; special effects, Alan E. Lorimar; casting, Wallis Nicita Associates, Joanne Zaluski; associate producer, Nick Abdo. Reviewed at Century Plaza Cinema No. 1, Century City, Calif., Dec. 9, 1987. (MPAA Rating: PG.) Running time: **112 MINS.**
Joanna/Annie . . . . Goldie Hawn
Dean Proffitt . . . . Kurt Russell
Grant Stayton 3d . . . . . Edward Herrmann
Edith Mintz . . . . Katherine Helmond
Billy Pratt . . . . Michael Hagerty
Andrew . . . . Roddy McDowall

Charlie	Jared Rushton
Joey	Jeffrey Wiseman
Travis	Brian Price
Greg	Jamie Wild
Captain Karl	Frank Campanella
Dr. Norman Korman	Harvey Alan Miller

Hollywood — "Overboard" is an uninspiring, unsophisticated attempt at an updated screwball comedy that is brought down by plodding script and a handful of too broadly drawn characters. Only element that occasionally lifts pic above the realm of the ordinary is the work of the redoubtable Goldie Hawn, who gives a gem of a performance in guiding this cumbersome vehicle to its equally cumbersome conclusion. Team of Hawn and Kurt Russell should do fair to good in holiday traffic.

Hawn plays Joanna Stayton, a millionaire wife who has run out of things to buy long ago, and is now biding her time finding things to complain about. When she and hubby Grant (Edward Herrmann, in an oversimplified role) are forced to dock in rural Elk Cove, Ore., Joanna decides it's time to have her closet remodeled.

On deck comes Kurt Russell as carpenter Dean Proffitt, whose personality doesn't seem to go much beyond affable or angry. After Joanna goes into a wonderful tizzy over Proffitt's shelf construction (done in oak rather than cedar), she fires him and shortly thereafter, pushes him overboard.

Her comeuppance is the kind of revenge found only in film — Joanna falls off the boat trying to retrieve her wedding rock, isn't missed for some time and washes back on the Elk Cove shore with a nasty case of amnesia. After her husband decides to leave her at the mental hospital, Proffitt sees her on tv and devises a scheme to claim her as his wife Annie, and get back at her by telling her she's been in his own miserable life all this time.

It's not long after convincing her that she *is* his wife and making her do scores of chores around the house, that Marshall has Russell feeling guilty and falling in love with Hawn, who has taken his four sons under her wing and straightened them out as best she can.

As this "trust" starts building between Hawn and the family of five carrying on this deceit, audience knows it's only a matter of time before Joanna's husband returns to get her.

Return Grant does, triggering Joanna's memory recovery and nasty words for the now-devastated Dean. Again, not much tension develops in this scene since audience knows Hawn will return.

With all this in the bag, and director Garry Marshall's money-doesn't-buy-happiness message ingested fully, there is little to do but sit back and admire Hawn's performance, as she splendidly transforms herself from rich bitch to sensitive, caring wife.

Supporting roles are mostly pedestrian, except for a sweet, funny turn by Michael Hagerty, as Bad Billy Pratt, Dean's best friend and a graduate of the John Candy School of Cinematic Oafishness.

Marshall is a vet of tv production and is certainly guilty of painting some uni-dimensional characters here that, while adequate on the small screen, only serve to weaken and distract a bigscreen crowd.

Tech credits are mostly good, but for Alan Silvestri's opening credits composition, which will send some screaming for the exits before pic even gets underway. —*Camb.*

Batteries Not Included
(COLOR)

A Universal Pictures release from Amblin Entertainment. Produced by Ronald L. Schwary. Executive producers, Steven Spielberg, Kathleen Kennedy, Frank Marshall. Directed by Matthew Robbins. Screenplay, Robbins, Brad Bird, Brent Maddock, S.S. Wilson, based on a story by Mick Garris; camera (Deluxe color), John McPherson; editor, Cynthia Scheider; music, James Horner; production design, Ted Haworth; art direction, Angelo Graham; set decoration, George R. Nelson; costume design, Aggie Guerard Rodgers; sound (Dolby), Gene Cantamessa; visual effects, Industrial Light & Magic; assistant director, Jerry Grandey; second unit director (N.Y.), Joe Johnston; second unit camera, Dick Kratina; casting, Penny Perry, Deborah Brown & Associates -N.Y. Reviewed at Cineplex Odeon theater, Universal City, Calif., Dec. 12, 1987. (MPAA Rating: PG.) Running time: **106 MINS.**

Frank	Hume Cronyn
Faye	Jessica Tandy
Harry	Frank McRae
Merisa	Elizabeth Peña
Carlos	Michael Carmine
Mason	Dennis Boutsikaris

Hollywood — "Batteries Not Included" could have used more imaginative juices to distinguish it from other, more enchanting Spielbergian pics where lovable mechanical things solve earthly human dilemmas. Still, it's suitable entertainment for kids and should do well enough to attract the PG crowd this holiday season.

Instead of the suburbs, Spielberg's usual haunt, scene here is in one of the crumbling neighborhoods of Manhattan where some tenants of an old and much beloved brownstone are being harassed to move out so a sleek office/residential complex can go up in its place.

The most stubborn of the holdouts is an irascible cafe owner (Hume Cronyn) and his senile wife (Jessica Tandy), whose strange behavior is the one true thread of reality in this otherwise pretty far-out fantasy.

The preservationist theme will be lost on children and Tandy's strange behavior and forgetfulness probably will cause them more anxiety. Before too long, Tandy is visited in the middle of the night by a couple of — that is, a male and female — miniature flying saucers which take their energy from the electrical outlets in the building and repair their parts with the tenants' metal appliances. They also become little angels, repairing all that the local hoods have broken on any number of their rampages, and endear themselves to the cast of characters who have steadfastly refused to take a developer's money and relocate.

Led by the Cronyn-Tandy team, pic has a good mix of personalities, even if perhaps Elizabeth Peña as an unwed mother may raise some questions in children's minds their parents just as soon would not answer.

They are certainly not everyone's grandma-grandpa ideal. He's a bit too gruff and she acts and looks like a bag lady, but they are devoted to each other and that seems to be the image the filmmakers want to get through.

Part played by the flying saucers is a bit bizarre. They are akin to birds nesting and actually are alluded to having sex at one point in the building's rooftop shed. Later the she-saucer gives birth to two live baby saucers and one stillborn one, prompting the former boxer tenant Harry (Frank McRae) to exclaim, "Batteries not included."

Unlike E.T., which was lovable, these crafty flying objects can solder metal in an instant, are fairly bland things with almost no traits which would make kids want to adore them. What tension is created in the picture doesn't come from their imminent departure (as in birds leaving the nest), but from the arson attack that neither they, nor the tenants, can prevent.

Tech credits are terrific, as in all Spielberg pictures.

Story is too linear for fans of this type of film. We hear each of the tenants' individual woes, but it isn't enough. Neither dialog nor the situation is inventive enough, though director Matthew Robbins and the cast seem to have enjoyed working with what they had. — *Brit.*

Leonard Part 6
(COLOR)

A Columbia Pictures release of a Sah Enterprises production. Produced by Bill Cosby. Executive producer, Alan Marshall. Executive producer for Cosby, Steve Sohmer. Directed by Paul Weiland. Stars Cosby. Screenplay, Jonathan Reynolds, story by Cosby; camera (Monaco color, Deluxe prints), Jan DeBont; editor, Gerry Hambling; music, Elmer Bernstein; production design, Geoffrey Kirkland; art direction, Blake Russell; set design, Bill Beck, Paul Kraus; set decoration, Jim Poynter; costume design, Aggie Guerard Rodgers; sound (Dolby), David MacMillan; visual effects produced by Richard Edlund; choreography, Louis Falco; associate producer, Ned Kopp; additional editor, Peter Boita; assistant director, Aldric Porter; second unit director, M. James Arnett; second unit camera, Eric Andersen. Reviewed at The Burbank Studios, Burbank, Dec. 11, 1987. (MPAA Rating: PG.) Running time: **85 MINS.**

Leonard	Bill Cosby
Frayn	Tom Courtenay
Snyderburn	Joe Don Baker
Giorgio	Moses Gunn
Allison	Pat Colbert
Medusa	Gloria Foster
Joan	Victoria Powell
Nurse Carvalho	Anna Levine
Man Ray	David Maier
Jefferson	Grace Zabriskie
Andy	Hal Bokar
Madison	George Maguire
Adams	John Hostetter
Monroe	William Hall
Duchamp	George Kirby
Jane Fonda	Herself

Hollywood — Perhaps no studio deserves two "Ishtars" in a single year, but Columbia has turned the trick with "Leonard Part 6" opening as its Christmas release.

Bill Cosby is right to be embarrassed by this dud, but result really can't have come as a total surprise to him since he wrote the story and produced it. Distrib should get some extra prints of "The Last Emperor" ready to slip into theaters right after the holidays, when this will sink into oblivion.

This weird little film of meager comic conceits doesn't actually resemble any other picture in memory, but occasionally calls to mind the innumerable James Bond spy spoofs of the mid-1960s, with its facetious approach to the notion of saving the world from an unimaginably heinous villain.

Having been spared mercifully Leonard's first five adventures, the audience is presented with the multimillionaire, former secret agent being called out of retirement to solve the murders of eight CIA operatives. The sinister plot, such as it is, has the maniacal Gloria Foster training animals to turn on people in revenge for 2,000,000 years of cruel mistreatment, a scheme that ultimately will enable her to dominate the world.

The viewer is thus treated to scenes of fish, frogs, lobsters and other animals launching attacks on unsuspecting citizens, but all in a light-hearted way. Mixed in with all this is Cosby's attempt to win back his wife, who has held a 7-year grudge against him, and to prevent his young daughter's marriage to a 66-year-old Lothario.

Given picture's source of financing, it is far from a coincidence that, during his key emotional scene with his daughter, Cosby holds a large bottle of Coca-Cola prominently toward the lens. Equally implausible is an early sequence in which an enormous refrigerator in Cosby's elegant San Francisco French restaurant is revealed to be loaded with nothing but Coke. Things might be different in Atlanta, but few *haute cuisine* restaurants on the west coast are known to carry the soft drink, especially in such quantity.

Tom Courtenay, doing a riff on his turn as The Dresser in the role of Cosby's butler, attempts to make sense of things with some ongoing narration, but even when the shenanigans manage to provoke a little smile or, once or twice, a chuckle, it remains impossible to imagine the response Cosby & Co. were aiming for. The jokes are so modest in conception, the targets so innocuous, the concerns so ephemeral, that even had the picture been executed brilliantly, it wouldn't have amounted to anything.

For the record, Jane Fonda did a little special work here, talking directly to Leonard as she works out on one of her videotapes. —*Cart.*

The Lonely Passion Of Judith Hearne
(BRITISH-COLOR)

An Island Pictures release of a Handmade Films presentation of a United British Artists/Peter Nelson production. Produced by Nelson, Richard Johnson. Executive producers, George Harrison, Denis O'Brien. Directed by Jack Clayton. Stars Maggie Smith, Bob Hoskins. Screenplay, Nelson, based on the novel by Brian Moore; camera (Technicolor), Peter Hannan; editor, Terry Rawlings; music, Georges Delerue; production design, Michael Pickwoad; art direction, Henry Harris; set decoration, Josie MacAvin; costume design, Elizabeth Waller; sound, Alistair Crocker; assistant director, Gary White; casting, Irene Lamb. Reviewed at the Raleigh Studios, L.A., Dec. 3, 1987. (MPAA Rating: R.) Running time: **110 MINS.**

Judith Hearne	Maggie Smith
James Madden	Bob Hoskins
Aunt D'Arcy	Wendy Hiller
Mrs. Rice	Marie Kean
Bernard	Ian McNeice
Father Quigley	Alan Devlin
Mary	Rudi Davies
Moria O'Neill	Prunella Scales
Edie Marinan	Aine Ni Mhuiri
Miss Friel	Sheila Reid

Hollywood — An ensemble of sterling performances highlights "The Lonely Passion Of Judith Hearne," an intelligent, carefully crafted adaptation of Brian Moore's well-regarded first novel. Film's centerpiece is Maggie Smith's exceptionally detailed portrait of the title character, a middle-aged Irish spinster who tragically deludes herself into imagining herself involved in a great romance. Jack Clayton's first picture in four years is a good bet for healthy runs in class situations.

Published in 1955, when Moore was 27, the novel was long coveted by an array of top filmmakers, including Clayton himself. John Huston fancied directing Katharine Hepburn in the story and, tantalizing as that prospect might have been, it is difficult to imagine anyone embodying the part more ideally than Maggie Smith.

Judith is a fragile bird, a part-time piano teacher in 1950s Dublin who has every reason to be desperate about life but still manages to look on the bright side. Moving into a new boarding house, she takes a liking to her landlady's brother James (Bob Hoskins), a widower recently returned from 30 years in New York, and begins stepping out with him.

Life at the homestead is anything but quiet, however. Owner Marie Kean sticks her busybody nose into everybody's business, and deliberately stirs up misunderstandings between Judith and James when she fears things are going too far; her obscene layabout son Bernard (Ian McNeice), a self-styled poet indulged by his mother, lies according to his advantage in every situation and his carrying on with the teenage maid (Rudi Davies), upon whom James also is fixated.

Once James takes her to a fancy dinner at the Shelbourne Hotel, Judith is sure his intentions are serious. Unfortunately for her, however, they are strictly centered on the idea of her investing in a business proposition (a brilliant one, in fact — an American fast food joint in downtown Dublin — but 20 years ahead of its time). Judith allows the misunderstanding between them to assume traumatic proportions, and her heartbreak and disappointment lead her down a spiraling road of despair, alcoholism, ostracism and religious rejection.

At the outset, Judith meekly putters about, apologizing that, "It's only me," when she enters a room, and being referred to uniformly as "poor Judith Hearne" by her acquaintances. Smith captures the reticence and timidity implied by these remarks exquisitely, but also suggests the small reserve of resolve within her that keeps her pressing forward and prevents her from giving up.

One therefore feels for her a great deal when she sets herself for her fall, and her subsequent actions are entirely believable, if elaborated upon a bit too extensively. In all events, hers is a wonderful performance.

So, too, are those of the remainder of the actors. Hoskins, laying a brash New York accent over a hint of the Irish, brings great energy and creative bluster to this irrepressible dreamer who worked only as a hotel doorman in New York but has been instilled with Yankee get-up-and-go.

Ian McNeice is terrific as the shockingly bold son, Marie Kean is all aggressive propriety to begin with but gradually reveals the landlady's small-minded mean-spiritedness, and the boarders, seen only briefly, come instantly to life.

Director Clayton deserves considerable credit for the uniformly fine performances, which carry the picture despite slight overlength. Clayton's tasteful, traditional approach to coproducer Peter Nelson's solid adaptation of the literary material is surprisingly punctuated by a couple of rude sexual scenes, and by others of brutal emotional bluntness. Story strangely becomes somewhat more remote and less involving after Judith goes off the deep end, but some redemption is delivered by the end.

Period details are subtly conveyed, and all production contributions are solid. — *Cart.*

Raw

A Paramount Pictures release of an Eddie Murphy production. Produced by Robert D. Wachs, Keenen Ivory Wayans. Executive producers, Eddie Murphy, Richard Tienken. Directed by Robert Townsend. Screenplay, Murphy; sketch, Murphy, Wayans; camera (Technicolor), Ernest Dickerson; editor, Lisa Day; production design, Wynn P. Thomas; set decoration, James T. Fredericks; sound (Dolby), Frank Graziadei; assistant director, Dwight Williams; casting, Pat Golden. Reviewed at the Mann Chinese theater, L.A., Dec. 18, 1987. MPAA Rating: R. Running time: **91 MIN.**

With: Eddie Murphy.

Hollywood — "Raw" is raw all right — a concert film that Par trimmed by several minutes so that the MPAA would rate it an R instead of an X.

Fans of Eddie Murphy's screen roles may be somewhat put off to learn how blue his standup act really is; mostly it will be women who find his routine offensive and him a most unappealing misogynist. B.o. potential appears moderate.

What's most disappointing about Murphy's routine, given its content, is its lack of social satire, except perhaps for what passes as such when he derides personal injury and community property laws and how they manage to affect him, the multimillionaire whom everyone wants to take advantage of.

In between every other word which is some version of the F-word, is a lot of talk about sex — the act, the organs, you name it. Shock value accounts for some of the lines being so funny, none of which, of course, can be relayed here. Suffice it to say anatomical humor is a prominent feature of Murphy's nonstop 90-minute set. At one point, he swings the mike like he would throw a yo-yo on a Round the World trick to draw an analogy.

What is surprising, considering this is the era of AIDS, is how Murphy takes off on how man's true nature is to go out and sexually conquer women as if this is good health policy, not to mention the questionable morality of such behavior.

Murphy is best when he gets away from the macho tract and onto more fertile comic ground. The parody of Bill Cosby is vicious, but hilarious. In fact, Murphy's take-off of just about every famous personality is amazingly right on.

He hits a little too close to the bone when he gets to his own immediate family, however, mimicking his father the drunk and how he and his brothers were raised in such poverty they used toys and games for food and clothing and Etch-a-Sketches for birthday cakes.

There is nothing particularly distinguishing about this concert film as directed by Robert Townsend ("Hollywood Shuffle"). It is neither flat nor rich. The camera follows Murphy back and forth and occasionally shoots from stage left.

Opening sketch where Murphy is a young boy trying out his first vul-

gar comic routine before his relatives is unfunny and extraneous.
—*Brit.*

The Last Empress
(CHINESE)

A Changchun Studio production. Directed by Chen Jialin, Sun Qingguo. Screenplay, Zhang Xiaotian; camera (color), An Zhiguo. Reviewed at the Rio Film Festival, Nov. 22, 1987. Running time: **120 MIN.**
With: Pan Hong, Jian Wen, Fu Yiwei.

Rio de Janeiro — This footnote to "The Last Emperor," featured with it in the Festrio official program, will certainly benefit from the massive promotion of the Columbia release, but will also suffer by comparison, as a poor cousin to Bertolucci's visual splendors and sweep.

Probably impressed by the sheer size of the Western production they were helping to put together, the Chinese obviously decided to offer their own version of Pu Yi, their last Emperor, and of the historical background of that period. The scope here is relatively modest, covering a limited period in Pu Yi's life, and more particularly in his relations with his official wife, Wanrong, and with two concubines, Wenxiu and Tan Yuling.

The point of departure is Pu Yi's marriage to Wanrong, follows his exile and his later Manchurian attempt to reclaim his seat under Japanese protection. His personal decadence and the systematic neglect of his wife, who finally has a tragic affair with a young officer, are described here in far more detail than Bertolucci ever cared to go into.

As per the Chinese, Pu Yi was much less of an innocent and of a victim than the Western version would have him be. He is shown actively and lucidly collaborating with the Japanese enemy and his cruelty towards his wife as he beats her up and then drives her into madness, are strongly stressed.

The political activities in the background, indicating Pu Yi was prepared to sell out his people in exchange for his throne, and that the minions groveling at his feet were either seeking their own interests or were too blinded by traditions to realize their folly, obviously represent a doomed society which had to be wiped out.

All through the film, the position of all women, from queen to concubine, is constantly highlighted and deeply deplored. The first concubine, Wenxiu, demands a divorce, when she realizes that out of the court, in exile, there is no official role for a concubine at all, but her impertinence is considered criminal for a Chinese woman. The second concubine, Tan Yuling, is martyred for her insubordination and the last scene already introduces the girl in line to replace her after her death.

Very melodramatic in parts, there is also a serious attempt to show ambivalence in some of the characters, and depart from the strictly 1-dimensional characterization of a populist epic. Handsomely produced and photographed, pic could have made a stronger impression but for the proximity of the grandiose Bertolucci effort. Acting tends to be strained, particularly in the late madness scenes and in some of the smaller parts, but the film, if carefully handled, could find its own niche in Western art houses.
—*Edna.*

Way Upstream
(BRITISH)

A BBC-TV production. Produced by Andree Molyneaux. Written and directed by Terry Johnson. Camera (color), Peter Hall; editor, Howard Billingham; music, Alan Brown; production design, Geoff Powell; set decoration, Geoff Tookey; costume design, Jacqueline Parry. Reviewed at the London Film Festival, Nov. 27, 1987. Running time: **101 MIN.**
Keith .... Barry Rutter
June .... Marion Bailey
Alistair .... Nick Dunning
Emma .... Joanne Pearce
Mrs. Hatfield .... Veronica Clifford
Vince .... Stuart Wilson
Fleur .... Lizzy McInnerny

London — In this unexpectedly dark comedy of errors, familiar middle-class characters on a boating holiday are subjected to a sinister seachange. What starts out like "Tillie And Gus" ends up like "Deliverance" as a foursome of smug but inept characters are forced to battle for survival against elements which they no longer control.

Unfortunately, it's all a bit too neat, the characters too cardboard and obvious in their hangups, the theatrical effects too strained to work except intermittently.

Result is a safely trendy statement about English ineptitude and sexual repression rather than provocative drama.

Plot centers on two oddly matched couples on a boating holiday. Their bickering is turned into a battle for survival when a stranger takes over at the helm.

For a while even the audience is taken in, ready to believe that the role reversals, the bullying and the sexual tauntings the stranger instigates will be healthy. This unlikely therapist puts the two main characters, Alistair and Emma, through a session they'll never forget.

Made for BBC-TV, the play is likely to command a respectable primetime audience. Ensemble acting is good and the dialog sharp but the play's peculiar blend of British humor with simplistic psychology is not likely to appeal overmuch to foreign broadcast buyers.

(As of current date no BBC-made tv movie has ever had a theatrical release domestically or abroad, though that policy is expected to be relaxed in special cases in the future to permit cinema exposure outside the U.K.) —*Guid.*

Good Morning, Vietnam

A Buena Vista Pictures release of a Touchstone Pictures presentation in association with Silver Screen Partners III, of a Rollins, Mora & Brezner production. Produced by Mark Johnson, Larry Brezner. Directed by Barry Levinson. Screenplay, Mitch Markowitz; camera (Deluxe color), Peter Sova; editor, Stu Linder; music, Alex North; production design, Roy Walker; art direction, Steve Spence; set decoration, Tessa Davies; costumes, Keith Denny; sound (Dolby), Clive Winter; assistant director, M. Mathis Johnson, Bill Westley; coproducers, Ben Moses, Harry Benn; casting, Louis DiGiaimo. Reviewed at Cinerama Dome, L.A., Dec. 14, 1987. MPAA Rating: R. Running time: **120 MIN.**
Adrian Cronauer .... Robin Williams
Edward Garlick .... Forest Whitaker
Tuan .... Tung Thanh Tran
Trinh .... Chintara Sukapatana
Lt. Steve Hauk .... Bruno Kirby
Marty Lee Dreiwitz .... Robert Wuhl
Sgt. Major Dickerson .... J.T. Walsh
Gen. Taylor .... Noble Willingham
Pvt. Abersold .... Richard Edson
Phil McPherson .... Juney Smith
Dan (The Man) Levitan .. Richard Portnow
Eddie Kirk .... Floyd Vivino
Jimmy Wah .... Cu Ba Nguyen

Hollywood — Eddie Murphy is not the only standup comic who has a performance film out for Christmas. Although it does have the shadow of a story, "Good Morning, Vietnam" is a pure Robin Williams vehicle and gives the performer his best chance yet to display his manic talent on screen. It's an impressive act, but at the expense of other dramatic considerations. Nonetheless, turnout should be sizable to watch Williams work.

After Airman Adrian Cronauer (Robin Williams) blows into Saigon to be the morning man on Armed Forces radio, things are never the same. With a machine-gun delivery of irreverencies and a crazed gleam in his eye, Cronauer turns the staid military protocol on its ear.

On the air he's a rush of energy, perfectly mimicking everyone from Gomer Pyle to Richard Nixon as well as the working grunt in the battlefields, blasting verboten rock 'n' roll over the airwaves while doing James Brown splits in the studio. From the start, the film bowls you over with excitement and for those who can latch on, it's a nonstop ride.

However, starting on the run, there is no context for the action. Who is this little squirt with a motor mouth imported from Crete to keep the troops happy? Why, of course, it's Robin Williams. The Cronauer character is just a thin veil for Williams with few attitudes of his own.

The failure of Cronauer to establish a strong identity behond his rantings on the radio seriously limits the range of the story. Despite an outstanding supporting cast, there is too little for them to interact with at the film's center. Outside of the studio, Cronauer is a 1-dimensional creation.

Screenplay by Mitch Markowitz tries to introduce other elements and director Barry Levinson's frequent closeups of Williams are meant to suggest the soft, cuddly side of his personality, but it comes off a mere pose next to the power of Williams performing.

Although the film is set in Vietnam in 1965, at the very moment when the "police action" is about to explode into a full-fledged war, the fighting seems to take a backseat to Williams' joking. Instead of the disk jockey being the eyes and ears of the events around him, a barometer of the changes about to happen, Williams is a totally self-contained character, and despite numerous topical references, his comedy turns in on itself rather than opening on the scene outside.

At a time when the world is truly in transition, it is a bit shameful to reduce the events of Vietnam to a few good jokes. Levinson and Markowitz seem to be aware of the shortcoming and have Cronauer get involved with a Vietnamese family, including a thwarted romance with a beautiful local girl (Chintara Sukapatana), and the last half-hour of the film becomes downright soggy with emotion.

The inability of Cronauer to support a full-fledged story leaves only glimpses of the struggle through the breaks in the humor. A montage of shots against a background of Louis Armstrong crooning "What A Wonderful World" is a lovely interlude somewhat disconnected from the business of the film.

The constant stream of '60s rhythm & blues hits is appealing, but also tends to keep the film rolling over most serious issues. Still, it's one of the more eclectic soundtracks around and part of what makes the film enjoyable.

If Markowitz misses the mark on the big strokes, his eye for details of behavior is usually sharp, with supporting characters a well-drawn lot. Performances are mostly right on target with Forest Whitaker as Cronauer's sidekick creating a likable big man too timid for his own body.

Bruno Kirby as Cronauer's uptight immediate superior has a few priceless comic moments of his own as he takes to the airwaves with an array of polka music. Noble Willingham is appropriately laconic as the base commander but J.T. Walsh is a bit too tight in the writing and execution to be anything more than a paper dragon.

Shot entirely on location in Thailand, production values are first-rate with a masterful sound mix by Clive Winter using the music and ambient noise to underline the action. Alex North's score settles comfortably into the cracks and Peter Sova's camerawork offers several stirring views of the countryside, if only the film were more about the country. — *Jagr.*

Les Deux crocodiles
(Two Crocodiles)
(FRENCH)

A Sara Distribution/CDF Films release of a Sara Films/Canal Plus Prods. coproduction. Executive producer, Alain Sarde. Written and directed by Joël Seria. Camera (color), Jean-Yves Le Mener; editor, Claudine Bouché; music, Philippe Sarde; sound, Gérard Barra; art direction, Annie Sénéchal; assistant director, Eddy Jabes; production manager, Christine Gozlan. Reviewed at UGC Biarritz cinema, Paris, Nov. 3, 1987. Running time: **88 MIN.**

René Boutancard . . . . . Jean-Pierre Marielle
Emile Rivereau . . . . Jean Carmet
Julien Derouineau . . . . Julien Guiomar
Greta . . . . Catherine Lachens
Felicité . . . . Dora Doll

Paris — A distastefully unfunny comedy to which Jean Carmet and Jean-Pierre Marielle fail to bring humor and humanity, "Two Crocodiles" is a picaresque tale of a smalltime adventurer (Marielle) who sets out to fleece a drab provincial shopkeeper (Carmet) but finds himself growing fond of him.

Writer-director Joël Seria sets the audience up for an off-beat buddy-buddy chronicle with a final gay-bonding twist. The series of incidents they are involved in both together and separately are a trite patchwork of episodes involving inept gangsters (trying to settle accounts with Marielle), Carmet's senile, institutionalized mother, who is kidnaped by the hoods, and an assortment of variously unpleasant hick women.

The mean-spirited petty characterizations, and a lack of genuine comic brio shackle both Marielle and Carmet, who have played these sorts of roles better in the past. Seria, who made a reputation in truculent comedies in the '70s, has missed his comeback performance. — *Len.*

The Wild Pair

A Trans World Entertainment presentation of a Sarlui/Diamant production. Produced by Paul Mason, Randall Torno. Executive producer, Helen Sarlui-Tucker. Directed by Beau Bridges. Screenplay, Joseph Gunn, from story by Gunn, John Crowther; camera (color), Peter Stein; editor, Christopher Holmes, Scott Conrad; music, John Debney; associate producers, Alana H. Lambros, Caro Jones. Reviewed at Egyptian theater, L.A., Dec. 12, 1987. MPAA Rating: R. Running time: **88 MIN.**

Joe Jennings . . . . Beau Bridges
Benny Avalon . . . . Bubba Smith
Col. Hester . . . . Lloyd Bridges
Capt. Kramer . . . . Gary Lockwood
Ivory . . . . Raymond St. Jacques
Tucker . . . . Danny De La Paz
Debby . . . . Lela Rochon
Fern Willis . . . . Ellen Geer
Nadine Jackson . . . . . . Angelique De Windt
Dalton . . . . Creed Bratton
Farkas . . . . Randy Boone
Sgt. Peterson . . . . Greg Finley
Hank . . . . Andrew Parks

Hollywood — The long-ago oversaturated black cop/white cop action film genre gets yet another dousing with this subpar police story about a fed and a local detective (Beau Bridges and Bubba Smith) doing battle with a group of drug-dealing, street-killing white supremacists. This dull deuce of a film is drawing to an inside straight in hoping for boxoffice success.

Judging only from this, his first big screen directorial effort, Beau Bridges has been watching too much tv. His characters' actions are leaden and obvious, his script is almost impossibly simplistic and derivative, and dialog is mostly laughable.

Audience is brought into a world where a band of camouflaged, greasepainted white supremacists drive into the middle of the ghetto at night without detection and gun down a building full of black people; drug deals are made in super-secret settings in which the participants say things out loud like "500 big ones?" and "40 keys of grade A."

With that much respect for his script, it's little wonder that Bridges leaves his actors, including most of his immediate family, out in the dramatic cold.

Best acquitted in the proceedings is Smith, who adequately plays L.A. detective Benny Avalon, hot on the tail of a drug-dealer while at the same time searching for leads to a brutal ghetto mass murder. The last is being researched by undercover FBI agent Joe Jennings (Bridges), who dresses up in his best threads and flaunts money to try to get closer to his suspect, bar owner Ivory (Raymond St. Jacques). The two paths cross during a botched arrest attempt before both are informed that they are now working together on the case and — surprising dramatic complication here — don't get along at first!

Trail of crime goes past Ivory to the white supremacist organization, headed by Col. Hester, played by Lloyd Bridges in an embarrassing role.

Filmmakers are starting with easy targets to begin with, but they further simplify the process by making the colonel about as intellectually challenging as a Rambo doll and responsible for street killings, black on black murder, drug abuse and just about every other crime on humanity short of third-world country loan defaults (all that is a clue to the audience that Lloyd and his ilk are *the bad guys*).

Lots of people get beat up and lots of things get blown up during Bridges and Smith's pursuit of the criminals, with virtually none of the action scenes ringing true or even rising significantly above made-for-tv film quality (perhaps not coincidentally, this is where Bridges' three previous helming credits came from). —*Camb.*

Pelle Erobreren
(Pelle The Conqueror)
(DANISH-SWEDISH)

A Kärne Film release of a Per Holst Film production with Svensk Filmindustri, the Danish Film Institute, the Swedish Film Institute, DR/TV and SID, Denmark. Produced by Holst. Line producer, Per Kolvig. Directed by Bille August. Screenplay, August, based on volume one of Martin Andersen Nexö's novel; camera (Fujicolor), Jörgen Persson; editor, Janus Billeskov Jansen; music, Stefan Nilsson; sound (Dolby), Niels Arild Niesen; production design, Anna Asp; costumes, Kicki Ilander, Gitte Kolvig, Birthe Qualmann; assistant director, Tove Berg; production management, Jens Arnoldus. Reviewed at the Imperial, Copenhagen, Dec. 10, 1987. Running time: **160 MIN.**

Pappa Lasse . . . . Max von Sydow
Pelle, his son . . . . Pelle Hvenegaard
Farm foreman . . . . Erik Paaske
Farmhand Erik . . . . Björn Granath
Kongstrup . . . . Axel Strøbye
Mrs. Kongstrup . . . . Astrid Villaume
Rud . . . . Troels Asmussen
Schoolteacher . . . . John Wittig
Karna . . . . . . Anne Lise Hirsch Bjerrum
Miss Sine . . . . Sofie Gråbøl
The Sow . . . . Lena Pia Bernhardsson
Little Anna . . . . Kristina Törnquist
Also with: Buster Larsen, Henrik Bödker, Lars Simonsen, Thure Lindhardt, Benjamin Holck Henricksen, Nis Bank-Mikkelsen.

Copenhagen — "Pelle The Conqueror" is a feature film of epic proportions and a relentlessly unsentimental look at life among the haves and, primarily, the have-nots on a big turn-of-the-century farm.

Writer-helmer Bille August's picture clearly is destined for competition slots on the major fest circuit. With several deals looming, including one for the U.S., "Pelle" also seems assured of a healthy international future commercially.

August, already a worldwide winner with his youth meller "Twist & Shout," reaches for higher ladders with "Pelle." His ambition is richly rewarded and, in dealing with his chosen subject matter, he emerged as the peer of such explorers of similar soil as Ermanno Olmi ("The Tree Of Wooden Clogs"), the Taviani Brothers ("Padre Padrone," "Kaos") and Claude Berri ("Jean de Florette," "Manon Of The Spring").

Even Bernardo Bertolucci's "1900" comes to mind through August avoids larger social issues and stays firmly down on the farm with the story he has culled from episodes in the first, and best, volume of Danish Nobel Prize winner Martin Andersen Nexö's "Pelle The Conqueror" trilogy, an early classic in world socialist literature.

Plot is loose in structure, but August follows Nexö in being a master storyteller with no overbearing message. Artistic visions of factual conditions of the age and time suffice to keep one engrossed even when things go a bit slack around the middle due to film's 160-minute running time.

Film is a record of what happened when Lasse, an elderly and widowed farmer (Max von Sydow) and his young son Pelle (Pelle Hvenegaard) join a boatload of immigrants to escape from impoverished rural Sweden to the Land Of Plenty of their dreams, Denmark's Baltic island of Bornholm.

On Bornholm, Lasse, possessor of visions and dreams but essentially broken of spirit, comes to terms with a life of near-slavery as the lowliest tender of the farm's cows, while Pelle, during two years of misery and abuse, learns to trust mainly himself. He comes of age in more ways than one, casts off his chains and sets out, in time-honored style (a lone figure crossing the snowy fields), to conquer the world.

Arriving at Bornholm, the Swedes had been treated and traded like the black slaves elsewhere in the world a quarter-century earlier, before they were forced to accept merciless toil while being fed poorer food than the livestock and niggardly salaries on the farms that hired their services.

The Danish-Swedish cast has von Sydow offering his career's apex so far as Lasse with his long horse's face lit by the minutest registrations of hope and despair. Younger Pelle Hvenegaard plays his own namesake with never a hint of being coached beyond what comes naturally and true.

The other characters who populate August's large canvas have stock characteristics enough to float a tv soap (a wenching lord of the manor; his long-suffering alcoholic wife; the coolly cruel foreman; the sadistic trainee; the seduced and abandoned maid; the vicious school children and their somnolent teacher who talks mostly with his whip, etc.).

They all rise above cliché, however, by being written with subtle nuance and acted (by superb thesps like Axel Strøbye, Astrid Villaume, Erik Paaske, Björn Granath, John Wittig) and directed likewise.

As for the generally low-key narrative stream, it has mighty waves rising now and again: a rebellious farmhand gets his head bashed in and is reduced to a permanent zombie state; the abandoned maid drowns her newborn baby; the mistress castrates her unsuspecting, sleeping husband.

There are other scenes of violent death at sea and curiously quiet death on dry land. One sequence that will resound in anybody's mind has Pelle paying a penny to vent his spleen about everything and anybody by having a small, semi-idiot chum submit to a lashing with a rope made of burning nettles.

With all production credits in shiniest order, cinematographer Jörgen Persson ("Elvira Madigan," "The Simple-Minded Murderer") excels in particular, etching the sharpest visual marvels even within the limitations of soft-focus Fujicolor. His each and every frame is a joy as well as challenge to fastidious eyes. —*Kell.*

Little Dorrit
Part I: Nobody's Fault
Part II: Little Dorrit's Story
(BRITISH)

A Sands Films production, in association with Cannon Screen Entertainment. Produced by Richard Goodwin, John Brabourne. Written and directed by Christine Edzard, based on the novel "Little Dorrit" by Charles Dickens. Camera (Technicolor), Bruno de Keyzer; editor, Olivier Stockman, Fraser Maclean; music, Giuseppe Verdi, arranged and conducted by Michel Sanvoisin; sound, Godfrey Kirby, St. Clair Davis, Dick Lenzey; costumes, Sands Films. Reviewed at Sands Films Ltd., London, Dec. 3, 1987. Running time: Part I: **177 MIN.**, Part II: **183 MIN.**

William Dorrit	Alec Guinness
Arthur Clennam	Derek Jacobi
Frederick Dorrit	Cyril Cusack
Little Dorrit	Sarah Pickering
Mrs. Clennam	Joan Greenwood
Flintwinch	Max Wall
Fanny Dorrit	Amelda Brown
Tip Dorrit	Daniel Chatto
Flora Finching	Miriam Margolyes
Mr. Casby	Bill Fraser
Mr. Pancks	Roshan Seth
Mr. Megles	Roger Hammond
Minnie Meagles	Sophie Ward
Tite Barnacle	John Savident
Daniel Doyce	Edward Burnham
Mrs. Merdle	Eleanor Bron
Mr. Merdle	Michael Elphick
Lord Decimus Barnacle	Robert Morley
The Bishop	Alan Bennett

London — "Little Dorrit" is a remarkable achievement. For writer/director Christine Edzard the epic project was obviously a labor of love, and what she has accomplished on a small budget is astounding, and certainly well worth the critical plaudits the project has been receiving in the U.K.

"Little Dorrit" is in fact two films, each three hours long, with the latter being virtually a remake of the former. This obviously poses enormous distribution and exhibition problems, though on novelty value and overall skill of the filmmaking pic could make a nice little b.o. impact.

A version of "Little Dorrit" was made in Germany in 1933 with Anny Ondra in the lead role, but this '86 version must count among the best Dickens adaptions. A large cast of uniformly excellent British actors is topped off by quite brilliant portrayals by Alec Guinness as William Dorrit, and Derek Jacobi as Arthur Clennam. Both should reap awards when prize-giving time comes around.

The first film (and they must be seen in the right order) "Nobody's Fault" tells the story of Little Dorrit and events surrounding her through Jacobi's eyes. He returns from China to find his embittered mother (Joan Greenwood) conspiring with the gnarled Flintwinch (Max Wall). While Jacobi announces he is leaving the family company he becomes intrigued with the plight of little Amy Dorrit (Sarah Pickering) and is saddened to find out that she lives in the Marshalsea debtors prison with her father (Guinness).

Jacobi vows to help the family, and with the aid of debt collector Pancks (an excellent Roshan Seth) discovers an unclaimed inheritance owed to the Dorrit family. They leave the prison in triumph to go abroad, and at that point Jacobi's fortunes change, and eventually he finds himself in the same prison when a business venture fails.

In Part II: "Little Dorrit's Story" you see from a different angle the story of the family's plight, and why they are in prison. Sarah Pickering bestows Amy with the gentle firmness to look after her father, brother and sister, and when Jacobi appears on the scene slowly falls in love with him.

The family travels abroad and during a plush dinner in Rome to celebrate the marriage of Fanny Dorrit (Amelda Brown) and Sparkler (Simon Dormandy), Guinness finally goes mad, and delivers a speech as if he were still in the Marshalsea.

Pic then follows Pickering discovering Jacobi is in prison and her efforts to raise the money to free him. The end provides a happy conclusion, with love and right conquering all.

Six hours of viewing obviously allows full characterization and depth of story — though some characters from the novel are still missing — but the style of showing virtually the same story through two people allows charming reinterpretations of certain scenes, and presents a fully rounded piece as never usually found in the cinema.

The pic, which is set in the 1820s, was shot entirely in a studio owned by Sands Films in the middle of Dickens territory, in Rotherhide close to the Thames, and the painted sets give the film a rich theatrical texture while not deflecting from the story. Costumes and production design are excellent, and there is a feeling that the cast members are actually proud to be taking part.

A slight questionmark must stand against Jacobi's ability to play youngish romantic leads at his age, but he remains one of the few actors around to bring quizzical compassion and genuine tenderness to a role. Guinness seemingly revels in the role of multi-faceted William Dorrit, and commands the scenes he is in.

Other standouts amongst the 211 named actors are Sarah Pickering, suitably small as Amy Dorrit, but who is tall and strong through her love and faith; Miriam Margolyes is hilarious as Jacobi's former love who has gone to fat and talks rapidfire; and Joan Greenwood, frail but dominating as Jacobi's mother.

The us of music by Dickens' Italian contemporary Giuseppe Verdi is excellent, and adds to the feeling that everything is just right with this pic.

It is impossible to think of "Little Dorrit" as actually two films, and full credit should go to Christine Edzard for accomplishing such a task. The six hours offer multi-layers of political and social comment, but are also trimmed of Dickens' melodrama. Pic is an event more than just a film, or films. —*Adam.*

The Adventure Of The Action Hunters

A Troma release of a Bonner Films production. Produced by Mary Holland. Directed by Lee Bonner. Screenplay, Leif Elsmo, Bonner; camera (Technicolor), David Insley; editor, Bonner; music, John Pallumbo; sound, Richard Angelella; art direction, Vincent Peranso; production manager, Terri Trupp; casting, Jane Brinker (N.Y.), Martha Royall (Baltimore). Reviewed on Lightning vidcassette, N.Y., Dec. 18, 1987. MPAA Rating: PG. Running time: **80 MIN.**

Walter	Ronald Hunter
Betty	Sean Murphy
First gangster	Joseph Cimino
Second gangster	Art Donovan
Skipper	Steve Beauchamp
Oliver	Peter Walker

"The Adventure Of The Action Hunters" is a woefully inadequate feature, originally titled "Two For The Money." Bearing a 1982 copyright, pic went into regional release last May from Troma.

With minimal action, despite its new title, pic relies heavily on asynchronous dialog to tell a nonstory involving two bystanders in an adventure finding $500,000 at the bottom of Oyster Creek. Two bumbling gangsters are after them, but not much happens. A 1950s period setting is pointless (a few old clothes and cars) and there is no reasonable connection established between the characters (heroine has a boyfriend who mysteriously disappears from the narrative as she teams up with the hero).

Ronald Hunter makes for an unusual leading man, aiming at lighthearted dialog delivery but not convincing as an action man who would rather fix martinis.

Director Lee Bonner provides no narrative drive as the film plods along, with scenes haphazardly constructed. Lensed in Baltimore and Long Island, pic is typical of a vanity (or amateur) production in listing every extra in the end credits. — *Lor.*

Het rode huis
(Red Home)
(DUTCH-DOCU)

A Stichting Stap production. Produced by Johan Schop. Directed by Jan Dop. Camera (Kodak color, 16m, Haghefilm prints), Dop; editor, Dop; sound, H. van Rooy, Rachel Field. Reviewed at Theater Desmet, Amsterdam, Dec. 4, 1987. Running time: **70 MIN.**

Amsterdam — This docu by well-known Dutch film editor Jan Dop makes an openly partisan but cogent case in favor of some 14,000 Navajo Indians, who for the past two years have been living as "illegal squatters" on their land, behind hundreds of miles of barbed wire. Film has obvious market value among ethnic and cultural minorities and specialized fests and circuits. It won the Critics Prize at the recent Leipzig fest of docus and shorts.

The film was a more or less impromptu production, Dop being in America for another assignment. He shot it in 10 days, directing and lensing in addition to conducting the interviews. The photography is not always up to the fine editing. The soundtrack is strikingly imaginative.

Except for some moments spoken in Navajo (a language so complex the U.S. used it as a code during World War II), the film is entirely in English (there is no commentary). The Indians speak of their experiences, reminiscences, way of life and their mystical relationship with the land. They speak slowly in long sentences broken by patient silences. Without dullness, the film's rhythm reflects this deliberate sense of measure, taking its time. Time, for the Navajos, belongs to the environment, like water, earth and fire. — *Wall.*

Love Stories: Women, Men & Romance
(DOCU)

Produced by Richard Broadman, John Grady, Judith Smith, Kersti Yllo. Directed by Broadman. Camera (color, 16m), John Bishop, John Hoover; editor, Broadman; sound, Stephen Olech; line producer, Susan Steiner; production manager (N.Y.), Kate Davis; archival research, Judith Smith, Media Research. Narrated by Janice Gray. Reviewed at the Segaloff screening room, Boston, Nov. 13, 1987. No MPAA Rating. Running time: **83 MIN.**

Boston — Richard Broadman has received a good deal of local acclaim for his previous documentaries such as "Water And The Dream Of Engineers" and "Mission Hill And The Miracle Of Boston," including a citation from the Boston Society of Film Critics. In his latest film he focuses on the timeless subject of how men and women relate to one another.

Each section ("Women," "Men" and "Romance") combines interviews with archival material to show that no matter how much times and mores change, the subject of romance and gender roles continues to fascinate and confuse. At one point we are treated to excerpts from a silent-era sex-education film that instructs its viewers that one must control one's sex drive as one controls a horse.

The bulk of the material consists of interviews with women and men of different ages and backgrounds, all seemingly from the Boston area. Most interesting are a pair of older women from the Italian North End, who offer some perspective on the choices they had in their day (such as whether they would be allowed to receive an education) compared with the women of today.

The film is less successful presenting the male point of view, in that most of the men seem either too full of themselves ("Unless my old lady can knock me down, I'm going to have the last word," says one) or excessively sensitive; there's no real middle ground. The last portion of the film shows various ways men and women meet, including the bar scene and dating services.

Tech credits are good, but commercial prospects probably will be confined to festivals, specialty situations (the film opened Nov. 20 at Boston's Somerville Theater) and ultimately public television.
—*Kimm.*

La Senyora
(The Lady)
(SPANISH)

A Sharp Features release (U.S.) of a Virginia Films production. Executive producer, Paco Poch. Directed by Jordi Cadena. Screenplay, Cadena, Silvia Tortosa, based on a novel by Antoni Mus; camera (color), José G. Galisteo; editor, Amat Carreras; production design, Jonni Bassiner; costumes, Andrés Urdiciain; sets J.M. Espada; associate producers, Miguel Sánchez Infante, Joan Vivó, Silvia Tortosa. Reviewed at Cine Capitol, Madrid, Dec. 8, 1987. (In London Film Festival.) Running time: **96 MIN.**
With: Silvia Tortosa, Hermann Bonnin, Luis Merlo, Fernando Guillén Cuervo, Jeannine Mestre, Alfred Luchetti, Alfonso Guirao.

Madrid — **"La Senyora" is an offbeat, well-produced, well-thesped pic with a strong dose of suggestive eroticism running through it which could make it a strong drawing card in almost any adult market in the world. Script carefully has avoided any explicit nudity or sex. In fact, the strange tale, with some unexpected twists, relies heavily on innuendo and the considerable charms of the provocative Silvia Tortosa.**

Barring a few scenes which brush somewhat too closely to melodrama, script is tight and develops intriguingly. Story opens at the turn of century in Mallorca, when a pretty, 23-year-old is forced to marry a man in his 50s, an arranged marriage of convenience typical of the period. Her family wants security and position; he wants an heir.

Instead of consummating the nuptials on their wedding night, he merely bids her goodnight. A while later he explains to the bewildered and frustrated wife that he is too scrupulous to indulge in personal contact with her, but that he will provide his sperm to her in a golden thimble, and thus through artificial insemination she is to become pregnant. She, however, only pours the liquid into the drain in disdain. Years go by, and still no pregnancy, and the husband finds it harder and

harder to provide the thimblefuls, and thus has her undress before him and indulge in other provocative acts.

Twist comes after husband dies and the widow, now rich, can indulge her own fancies. In the past she has slaked her sexual needs with a feathery fan in the privacy of her chamber. Rather than plunge into libertine orgies, she in a sense takes up the same game as the husband using her handsome gardener.

Film, picked up for U.S. distribution by Sharp Features, aside from its erotic overtones, is also a well-limned period drama, which could attract a wide audience. Tortosa, convincingly cast in ages ranging from 23-45, is an eyecatcher from start to finish and supporting roles are excellent. — *Besa.*

Il est génial Papy!
(Gramps Is A Great Guy!)
(FRENCH)

A Gaumont release of a Clea Prod./TF-1 Films Prod./Port Royal Films/Films de la Tour coproduction. Produced by Adolphe Viezzi. Directed by Michel Drach. Screenplay, Drach, Jean-Claude Islert, Michel Lengline from Remo Forlani's play "Grandpère" (uncredited); camera (Eastmancolor/Pyral/Agfa), Daniel Vogel; editor, Jean-François Naudon, Catherine Bernard; music, François Chouchan and Brahms' Concerto for Violin and Orchestra; art direction, Jean-Pierre Bazerolle; sound, Phillip Lioret, Claude Villand; production manager, Roland Thenot. Reviewed at the Gaumont Colisées cinema, Paris, Dec. 14, 1987. Running time: **92 MIN.**
With: Guy Bedos (Sebastien), Marie Laforêt (Louise), Fabien Chombart, Valérie Rojan, Isabelle Mergault, Elisabeth Vitali.

Paris — **An uncredited adaptation of a legit comedy smash by Remo Forlani, "Grandpère," this feeble pic originally was destined to be the first Gallic vehicle for Yank comic Gene Wilder, who backed out because of personal problems. The role finally went to Guy Bedos, a sharp, witty standup comedian who is disastrously miscast as the hapless, spacey protagonist.**

Somewhat in the vein of other Gallic pediatric comedies (beginning of course with "Three Men And A Cradle"), "Papy" describes the panic and helplessness of a failed musician suddenly burdened with a runaway 10-year-old grandson whose existence he never suspected. Latter is a clever lad who can take care of himself better than his glum granddad, and goes so far as to play matchmaker between Bedos and a buxom babysitter recruited to look after the brat when Bedos sidles off to his job as violinist in a strip joint.

Michel Drach, who cowrote and coproduced, has directed without conviction. There is neither rhythm nor emotion in this stale sentimental divertissement. Among supporting parts Marie Laforêt, as Bedos' ex-wife, fails to bring relief to a film in distress. Tech credits are unremarkable. —*Len.*

Home Remedy
(U.S.)

A Xero Film Associates production. Produced by Kathie Hersch. Written and directed by Maggie Greenwald. Camera (color), Thomas H. Jewett, editor, Pamela Scott Arnold; music, Steve Katz. Reviewed at the Florence Film Festival, Italy, Dec. 13, 1987. Running time: **100 MIN.**
Richie Rosenbaum . . . . Seth Barrish
Nancy Smith . . . . Maxine Albert
PJ Smith . . . . Richard Kidney
Also with: David Feinman (Moshe), John Tsakonas (Donnie), Alexa (Mary), Cynde Kahn (Bambi).

Florence — **It's impossible to dislike Maggie Greenwald's backyard screwball comedy, "Home Remedy" (a.k.a. "Xero"), shot on a shoestring in Paramus, N.J., with a handful of actors. The duet between Nancy (Maxine Albert) and Richie (Seth Barrish) as they wage a fierce battle against suburban boredom, perceived as an existential evil, and human lack of communication is as involving as it is funny, thanks to a fine script and excellent thesps. With special handling film could find its way to a sympathetic audience.**

Richie Rosenbaum's idea is actually not to fight boredom but to learn to enjoy it. This seen-it-all 30-year-old locks himself in his empty house and embarks on a conditioning program of boring activities, like painting the walls blue and staring at them. His contact with the outside world is limited to phone sex and a video camera pointed out the window.

Soon Nancy, a crazy housewife and mother of three obnoxious teenagers, breaks into his fortress of solitude. Chatting and fighting through the window while Richie makes his tapes and Nancy constructs a "garden" out of basement junk, the pair achieves some measure of intimacy. The appearance of Nancy's husband P.J. (Richard Kidney) ends up literally blasting them out of their safe little world (Richie blows up the house).

Black comedy and understated humor keep pic hopping, while thesps Barrish and Albert synthesize the suburban malaise in larger-than-life roles. Running on little action and lots of dialog (also some good harmonica playing), "Home Remedy" sidesteps monotony while talking about it. A dark underbelly occasionally surfaces in Richie's solitary obsessions with Nazi doctors and self-amputation of a finger, disconcertingly anomalous scene that sticks out painfully. Technically okay. —*Yung.*

Zärtliche Chaoten
(Without You)
(WEST GERMAN)

A Tivoli Filmverleih release of a Karl Spiehs Film production. Produced by Spiehs. Directed by Franz Josef Gottlieb. Screenplay, Thomas Gottschalk; camera (color, 16m), Klaus Werner; editor, Ute Albrecht-Lovell;

music, uncredited, sound, Peter Hummel; assistant director, Ingetraud Kiefer; art direction, Josef Sanktjohanser. Reviewed at Kino-Center, Hamburg. Aug. 30, 1987. Running time: **90 MIN.**
Walker . . . . Michael Winslow
Ricky . . . . Thomas Gottschalk
Schmidgruber . . . . Helmut Fischer

Hamburg — **Thomas Gottschalk, blond, blue-eyed veteran of a string of lightweight film comedies and tv specials, is the biggest name in West German tv. As zany quizshow host or unflappable awards broadcast emcee, Gottschalk, 37, assures any show of to ratings. Latest pic is a slapstick vehicle drawing on his appeal among teens and young adults.**

Nothing special here, and pic's German b.o. draw will not transfer abroad, where Gottschalk is unknown.

Film historians will recognize pic plot's hoary origins in the heyday of Ufa studio comedies of half a century ago. A handsome blond guy teams up with a bumbling, stocky Austrian and with a skinny, prissy wiseguy. This unlikely trio vie for the affections of an aloof beauty and stumble through a variety of jobs in a laughable attempt to impress her.

Fifty years ago, the three roles were played by Heinz Rühmann (Ufa's blond guy from next door), Hans Moser (Austria's answer to Lou Costello) and Theo Lingen (who could steal a scene simply by mincing into a shot and rolling his eyes). Rühmann, Moser and Lingen dominated German comic cinema into the 1960s, appearing together or individually in scores of films that seldom failed to misfire at the b.o.

This time Gottschalk is in the Rühmann role. Playing the dopey Austrian is Helmut Fischer, an Austrian actor well known from a tv police action series, but who has no comic acting abilities. The only laughs he gets are due to his quaint Viennese accent, which young German audiences find hilarious. Best suited of the three is American actor and sound effects expert Michael Winslow, a regular in the "Police Academy" films. Winslow carries this film and rises above a sometimes blatantly racist script (Winslow is pic's token black) to provide film's only really funny moments.

Technical credits are adequate for 16m production. —*Gill.*

Soldati — 365 all'Alba
(Soldiers — 365 Till Dawn)
(ITALIAN)

A Cidif release of a Reteitalia/Numero Uno Cinematografica coproduction. Produced by Claudio Bonivento. Directed by Marco Risi. Screenplay, Marco Modugno, Risi, Stefano Sudrie, Furio Scarpelli; camera (Eastmancolor, color by Telecolor), Giuseppe Di Mauro; music, Manuel De Sica. Reviewed at American Cinema, Rome, Nov. 3, 1987. Running time: **100 MIN.**
Claudio Scanna . . . . Claudio Amendola
Lt. Fili . . . . Massimo Dapporto

Mrs. Fili . . . . .Agostina Belli
Also with: Ivo Garrani, Claudio Botosso (the doctor), Alessandro Benvenuti.

Rome — The boredom and frustration of Army life are the subject of "Soldiers — 365 Till Dawn," a drama shot by Dino Risi's son Marco for youth entertainment company Numero Uno Cinematografica. Though pitched for appeal and professionally lensed, pic can come up with no new twist on the old boot camp conflict between sergeant and new recruit. Audience is soon counting down to freedom-day along with the boys, except viewers who have drifted off to Nodsville along the way.

Italy still has a universal 1-year draft that catches up almost every young male. "Soldiers" struggles to show how rough, unfair and useless it all is, but compared to films on the Marines or a staunch U.S. military academy, discipline is strictly Italian-style. When furious animosity builds up between hero Claudio Amendola and bitter Lt. Fili (Massimo Dapporto), the greatest cruelty filmmakers dream up is having the lieutenant deliberately muddy the bathroom floor so Claudio has to mop it a second time.

Though the drama is highly artificial, film makes some effort to delve into character. Amendola is an up-and-coming actor of promise, imparting real concreteness to his portrayal of a slum-dweller with will of iron. Dapporto's unswerving vendetta against the boy is sparked when Claudio inadvertently humiliates him by exposing a streak of irrational jealousy for his Mrs., Agostina Belli. Claudio refuses to break down before his nemesis, and gets stuck with a year of bathroom detail.

A climactic confrontation between the two builds a fair amount of tension, and shows director Risi learning his trade.

Score is a medley of current pop from Manuel De Sica. Giuseppe Berardini's crisp camerawork, much of it in nighttime blues and blacks, is a strong plus in the quality dept. —*Yung.*

Cold Steel

A Cinetel Films release. Produced by Lisa M. Hansen. Executive producer, Paul Hertzberg. Directed by Dorothy Ann Puzo. Screenplay, Michael Sonye, Moe Quigley, from story by Sonye, Puzo, Hansen; camera (Foto-Kem color), Tom Denove; editor, David Bartlett; music, David A. Jackson; art direction, Maxine Shepard; set decoration, Scott Ambrose; sound, Rob Janiger; assistant director, Richard Kanter; associate producer, Peter Combs; casting, Barbara Claman, Margie Clark. Reviewed at Hollywood Pacific theater, Hollywood, Dec. 11, 1987. MPAA Rating: R. Running time: 90 MIN.
Johnny Modine . . . . .Brad Davis
Kathy . . . . .Sharon Stone
Iceman . . . . .Jonathan Banks
Cookie . . . . .Jay Acovone
Mick .Adam Ant
Lt. Hill . . . . .Eddie Egan
Rashid . . . . .Sy Richardson

Anna Modine . . . . .Anne Haney
Fishman . . . . .Ron Karabatsos

Hollywood — It's not every film that has a man murdered by having live fish forced down his throat, but "Cold Steel" does. Director Dorothy Puzo clearly has an eye for the gritty details of street life and if she had a sense of humor about it, this would be an auspicious directorial debut. As it is, it's a run-of-the-mill actioner targeted at a limited audience.

"Cold Steel" is considerably more impressive on a visual level than on the story side. Script by Michael Sonye and Moe Quigley is a pastiche of crime story clichés which don't add up to much in the end and don't generate a whole lot of heat along the way. Major lapse is in the poorly drawn characters and the lack of motivation necessary for a good revenge picture.

As the film opens, an old man is brutally murdered and turns out to be the father of L.A. cop Brad Davis. There's a back story to explain the slaying that doesn't come out till later, but it's hardly worth the wait.

In any case, Davis sets out to find the killer, who, it turns out, is really an old Police Academy colleague (Jonathan Banks). As in any good, cheapie cop story, the villain is deformed. This time his face has been carved up and his voice is amplified electrically through a hole in his throat.

For sidekicks he's got a deliciously idiotic and evil Adam Ant, a Brit expatriate glad to be in America for all the opportunities for violence it allows, and a black heavy (Sy Richardson).

There's also some business about Davis meeting the right woman, but when Kathy (Sharon Stone) picks him up in his local watering hole it's all too easy and conspicuous. She is, in fact, in cahoots with the bad guys, but it takes Davis much longer to figure this out than it would take an average third grader.

Numerous explosions later, everything works out for the best in this violent fairyland where justice is always delivered. Puzo, however, is a bit heavyhanded dishing out the retribution while revenge and love plots never really come together in a satisfying fashion.

Production values are inconsistent, with the film sometimes taking on the look of an accomplished production and at other times looking like a bargain basement special.

Davis is likeable but hardly believable as a tough guy. Sharon Stone is aptly named for her acting style while Ant is the one character who knows how to have some fun with this kind of stuff.—*Jagr.*

Trágico Terremoto en México
(Tragic Earthquake In Mexico)
(MEXICAN)

A Peliculas Mexicanas release of a Producciones Metropolitan production. Executive producer, Miguel Kahen. Produced by Ignacio Garcia Gardelle. Directed by Francisco Guerrero. Screenplay, Reyes Bercini, based on an argument by Garcia Gardelle; camera (color), Agustín Lara Alvarado; editor, Jorge Piña; music, Jep Epstein. Reviewed at Hollywood Twin theater II, N.Y., Nov. 29, 1987. Running time: 96 MIN.
Miguel . . . . .Miguel Angel Rodriguez
Don Nacho . . . . .Mario Almada
Paty . . . . .Diana Golden
Sarah . . . . .Charito Granados
Solorio . . . . . . .Pedro Weber (Chatanooga)
Christina . . . . .Alejandra Meyer
Chucho . . . . .Oscar Fentanes
Tepo . . . . .Sergio Ramos (Comanche)
Also with: Isauro Espinoza, Victor Lozaya, Marcos Efrén Zariñaga (La Pulga), Cecilia Tijerina, Oscar Cadedo, Blanca Lidia, Maria A. Murillo.

On Sept. 19, 1985, the first of two devastating earthquakes struck Mexico City, leaving much of its downtown area a shambles. The death toll numbered in the thousands. Even without sensurround, the Mexican feature "Trágico Terremoto en México" (Tragic Earthquake In Mexico), directed by Francisco Guerrero, won't cause much of a rumble at the boxoffice, except for morbid curiosity.

Pic is a routine melodrama based on standard "disaster movie" formulas: the initial part of the film introduces a handful of principal and secondary characters; this is followed by the disaster itself and then the final efforts of the survivors to be rescued.

The main storyline concerns an unwed mom-to-be (Diana Golden) and her responsibility-shirking singer boyfriend (Miguel Angel Rodriguez). She is rushed to the hospital moments before the tremor hits and the world caves in. Of course, the quake shakes some sense into her boyfriend's head and he realizes he really does love her and the baby. The earthquake affects other main characters in likewise fashion and those who survive are better people because of it. Ho-hum.

Due to a low budget, the disaster itself is disastrous, confined to three rooms at Mexico City's Centro Medico, destroyed in the quake. The rooms shake and collapse, some live, others die.

Director Guerrero attempts to vary the images and provide a larger scope to the quake's impact, but in the most inexpensive manner possible. Even though phones and lights are out at the collapsed hospital, survivors watch rescue efforts on a tv set which is still working. Instead of using video transfer, the pic features bleached-out video images shot directly from a monitor. From the hundreds of hours of taped footage of rescue work shot after the tremors, the scant selection of video documentary presented here

is decidedly poor. Acting styles and other tech credits never stray far from soap opera.

Overall, the scope of the film is too limited to be any real examination of the situation outside of its use of the quake as a mere element of melodrama. One wants to believe the tragic quakes meant more to Mexico City residents than the slim pickings and pithy sentiments offered in this film. — *Lent.*

Noyade interdite
(No Drowning Allowed)
(FRENCH-ITALIAN)

A Bac Film release of a Paradis Films/FR3 Films Prod./Compagine Générale d'Images/-LP Films (Rome) coproduction. Produced by Eric Heumann, Stéphane Sorlat. Directed by Pierre Granier-Deferre. Screenplay, Granier-Deferre, Dominique Roulet, from novel "Widow's Walk" by Andrew Coburn; camera (Eastmancolor), Charles Van Damme; editor, Jean Ravel; music, Philippe Sarde; art direction, Dominique André; sound, Bernard Bats; production, manager, Dominique Toussaint; assistant director, Dominique Brunner; associate producer, Leo Pescarolo. Reviewed at the Marignan-Concorde cinema, Paris, Dec. 5, 1987. Running time: 101 MIN.
Molinat . . . . .Philippe Noiret
Leroyer . . . . .Guy Marchand
Elizabeth . . . . .Elizabeth Bourgine
Marie . . . . .Anne Roussel
Jeanne . . . . .Gabrielle Lazure
Isabelle . . . . .Marie Trintignant
Hazelle . . . . .Suzanne Flon
Winny . . . . .Stefania Sandrelli
Cora . . . . .Andréa Ferreol
Keli .Laura Betti

Paris — Yet another Yank detective novel — "Widow's Walk" by Andrew Coburn — provides grist for the Gallicized screen mill in "Noyade interdite." Routinely directed by Pierre Granier-Deferre, it has some lively dialog (by Dominique Roulet) and juicy performances by Philippe Noiret and Guy Marchand, but wastes a large female supporting cast in perfunctory suspect parts.

Plot is something like "Jaws" minus the shark (and the suspense). A number of dead bodies are being washed up daily on the beach of an Atlantic resort, and the bad publicity threatens to destroy the town's upcoming summer season. All the victims are male (including a local Peeping Tom) and have been shot in the head at close range. Naturally, suspicions focus on the locale's female population.

Noiret, a police inspector who hails from the region, is assigned the case. His reluctant distaste for the job is aggravated by the arrival of colleague Marchand. Their longstanding mutual hatred only poisons the already tense ambience. While Noiret goes about his investigation sluggishly, Marchand is prying into former's shady past life, looking for compromising information to sully his reputation.

Marchand finds what he's looking for, but (in one of the film's most chilling moments) Noiret dispatches him to check out some suspects whom now he is sure are behind the murders. In sending him off, Noiret knows Marchand is going to certain (and perhaps deserved) death.

When the two cops are not dueling, the film sags badly. All the ladies, both locals and vacationers, parade before the camera in a series of unsatisfying vignettes, from lovely young nymphette Anne Roussel and jealous shrew Andréa Ferreol, to a trio of nubile sunbathers Elizabeth Bourgine, Gabrielle Lazure and Marie Trintignant. As it is an Italo coproduction, Stefania Sandrelli and Laura Betti also are pressed into (dubbed) supporting service.—*Len.*

The Pursuit Of Happiness
(AUSTRALIAN)

A Jequerity Films production. Executive producer, Richard Mason. Produced and directed by Martha Ansara. Screenplay, Ansara, Alex Glasgow, Laura Black and the cast; camera (color), Michael Edols; editor, Kit Guyatt; assistant director-casting, Madelon Wilkens; production manager, Gail McKinnon. Reviewed at Mosman screening room, Sydney, Dec. 12, 1987. Running time: **85 MIN.**
Anna .... Laura Black
John .... Peter Hardy
Mandy .... Anna Gare
Stan .... Jack Coleman
Also with: Dennis Schultz, Senator Jo Vallentine, Alec Smith, Don Allison, Mayor John Catalini.

Sydney — **Here's a passionate, political film, opposed to U.S. bases in Australia and visits by nuclear warships, which wraps its message into a fictionalized story of an average working woman who, via the influence of her teenage daughter, starts to see things in a different light. Fictional trappings may get pic's concerns across to a wider audience, not just to the converted.**

Setting is Fremantle, Western Australia, venue for the America's Cup this past year. Anna (Laura Black) is a married woman just starting a middle-aged career as a journalist. Her husband, John (Peter Hardy), is a go-getting chauvinist, who loathes the fact that Mandy, their 15-year-old daughter (Anna Gare), has taken up with a peace group ("Brown rice people," they're derisively described) and sings in a group called The Jam Tarts.

Because her daughter is so dedicated to the anti-nuclear movement, Anna herself tries to find out more about it: she watches and rewatches a video of Stanley Kramer's "On The Beach," which was set in Australia; she looks at newsreel tape in which a U.S. military spokesman won't rule out the possibility of an American first strike, and another in which a Russian notes that, while U.S. submarines are hard targets, the bases which support them, including some in Australia, could be destroyed easily.

Before long, Anna is fired from her newspaper job and starts to quarrel bitterly with her unfeeling

husband. In the end, three generations of the family, including Anna, Mandy and Stan (Jack Coleman), John's father and a member of the old Left, join to protest a U.S. nuclear ship visit to Fremantle.

Interspersed into the thread of this story are numerous suggestions of a world gone a bit mad. Ugly oil refineries dominate majestic seascapes; small children play violent video games in amusement arcades; Anna is instructed that her reporting of a council meeting must be "responsible and balanced," but that she mustn't interview Left-leaning council members.

An American friend of John's talks about believing passionately in the principles of "life, liberty and the pursuit of happiness — as long as they don't interrupt the cash flow." Meanwhile, it's suggested that one syndicate involved in the last America's Cup races was more interested in nuclear arms sales than in yachting.

At times, pic comes across as being as naive as its heroine, though there's no doubting Ansara's sincerity. This is the director's first feature-length film after many political docus, and she seems to be aiming at an uncommitted audience.

"The Pursuit Of Happiness" is briskly made on a tiny budget, and the script has some sharp touches (a newspaper-owner is described as "a legend in his own mind"). Musical sequences involving the anti-nuclear rock group are well handled, and should help get younger audiences to see the film. Ansara is calling for a change of attitude, and asking audiences to see her film to rethink their attitude to the nuclear issue, just as her protagonist does.

Several well-known West Australians play themselves in the film, including the Mayor of Fremantle and politician Senator Jo Vallentine of the Anti-Nuclear Party.—*Strat.*

El Socio de Dios
(God's Partner)
(PERUVIAN-CUBAN)

A Cinematográfica Kuntur, Peru, ICAIC, Cuba production. Directed by Federico Garcia Hurtado. Screenplay, Garcia Hurtado, Roger Rumrill; camera (color), Rodolfo López. Reviewed at the Rio Film Festival, Nov. 22, 1987. Running time: **102 MIN.**
With: Adolfo Llaurado, Ricardo Tosso, Belisa Salazar, René de la Cruz.

Rio de Janeiro — **This Cuban-Peruvian coproduction follows the career of rubber baron Julio César Arana who lived at the turn of the century and manhandled his way to fame, glory and possessions. He even managed to be considered in some circles a patriot fighting the Imperialist penetration into Peru.**

Based on fact and presented as a docu drama of sorts, the film traces his rapid ascent from adventurer in the Amazon jungles (where he was torturing and exploiting the Indians

whom he forced to work for him with the full consent of the Church) through his rise to political and economic power and eventual downfall after liberals managed to spread the information about his criminal activities all over the world, depriving him of his contract with the biggest markets in the West.

No court of justice indicted the man, however, first because there was insufficient proof to condemn him, and later because he made sure witnesses and evidence would be destroyed ruthlessly.

Moral of the story is, however, that by damning Arana, the humanitarians were playing right into the hands of the British Empire and the American industry, competing for the control of the world rubber market and interested in eliminating a cumbersome local factor. The plot also makes use of the legendary figure of Irish adventurer Fitzcarraldo, Arana's competitor for the Amazonian rubber, whose unusual story was already documented on film by Werner Herzog. Here he is devoid of any particular interest, just a romantic shadow, the lover Arana's wife wished for herself before being forced to marry her husband.

The film is quite useful as a piece of Peruvian history, even if it is clearly tendentious particularly at the end when it shows the idealists who were Arana's adversaries regretting their activities when faced with the devious play of British and American diplomacy. This is, in a way, almost an acceptance, if not a justification, of Arana's crimes, displayed in such detail all through the film.

The script doesn't go in for much character building; each type is clearly defined from the onset and destined to stay the same to the bitter end. Direction, righteous and inflexible, isn't much help either, and the acting is of the stentorian variety.

Technical credits are satisfactory, the Amazonian scenery looks authentic and the facts, as presented, are based on memoirs published by people who witnessed the events, which seem to be quite reliable. It is just that they aren't always very interestingly put forward. — *Edna.*

Testimony
(BRITISH-B&W/COLOR)

An Isolde Films production, in association with The Mandemar Group, ORF, NOS, DR, SVT, HRK for Channel Four. Executive producers, Grahame Jennings, Michael Henry, Michael Kustow. Produced and directed by Tony Palmer. Screenplay, David Rudkin, Palmer, from the "Memoirs of Dmitri Shostakovich" edited by Soloman Volkov; camera (Panavision, part color), Nic Knowland; editor, Tony Palmer; production design, Tony Palmer; art direction, Paul Templeman, Chris Bradley, Chris Browning; music, Dmitri Shostakovich; sound, John Lundsten, Ian Maclagan, David Bimson; costumes, John Hibbs; associate producer, Maureen Murray. Reviewed at the London Film Festival, Nov. 15, 1987. Running time: **157 MIN.**
Dmitri Shostakovich .... Ben Kingsley

Nina Shostakovich .... Sherry Baines
Galya .... Magdalen Asquith
Maksim .... Mark Asquith
Stalin .... Terence Rigby
Tukhachevsky .... Ronald Pickup
Zhdanov .... John Shrapnel
Brutus .... Robert Reynolds

London — **"Testimony" is quite an undertaking. Long, muddled, and abstract at times, but ultimately a beautifully conceived and executed art film with fine topline performances, it makes fascinating viewing.**

The film's length at 157 minutes (mostly in black and white), and subject matter (a somewhat obscure Russian composer) indicate it will never be a boxoffice hit, but "Testimony" is a worthy and skilful project nevertheless.

Helmer Tony Palmer also acted as producer, co-writer, editor, and production designer on the pic, which probably accounts for his reluctance to cut it to a more viable length. He and cinematographer Nic Knowland produce some stunning black and white photography, and Liverpool and Wigan, in the north of England, double well for Russia.

In essence the pic follows the life of Russian composer Dmitri Shostakovich, played by Ben Kingsley sporting a dubious wig, but especially focuses on his relationship with Stalin.

"Testimony" traces the young Shostakovich who had success after success until Stalin took a dislike to the opera "Lady Macbeth," and in a marvelous scene at the Extraordinary Conference of Soviet Musicians his work is denounced, but still he apoligizes.

Later Stalin pours on further humiliation by sending him to an International Peace Congress in New York, where he is forced to denounce his fellow musicians, such as Stravinsky, who had fled Russia.

Shostakovich's personal life is treated in a more offhand way than his relationship with Stalin, and following the death of the Soviet leader the film loses some of its strength.

Characters tend to drift in and out of the pic, and some characters are not fully explained. For instance Liza Goddard appears as Beatrice Webb, and Brook Williams as H.G. Wells, but it takes a flick through the production notes to gleam this information.

Ronald Pickup is excellent as Kingsley's friend Tukhachevsky and Robert Urquhart puts in a telling — though small — appearance as the journalist who quizzes Kingsley at the U.S. peace conference.

Tony Palmer utilizes stunning technical skill to tell his story, though at times seems to be a bit too clever for his own good. Technical credits are excellent, and Shostakovich's music suitably stiring.
—*Adam.*

Bus
(JAPANESE)

A Pia Co. production. Executive producer, Takashi Nishimura. Produced by Yutaka Suzuki. Directed by Takashi Komatsu, Screenplay, Komatsu; camera (color), Yoshihisa Fujii; editor, Komatsu; music, Kiyoshi Takeo; production design, Takeo Kasai; set decoration, Atsushi Honda; art direction, Souki Murakoshi; costumes, Morihiko Katsushima; associate producer, Tadao Hikita, Kiichi Muto. Reviewed at the London Film Festival, Nov. 14, 1987. Running time: **80 MIN.**
Micho/Bengal Tiger . . . . Hiroyasu Ito
Rinzo . . . . Kyoichi Ando
Kosaku . . . . Hidehiko Komatsu
Fool on the Hill . . . . O.W. Nicole
Kaori . . . . Tomoko Kuroiwa
Also with: Toru Usuda, Katsumi Yamanoi, Kaneo Osuga, Takehiko Suzuki.

London — "Bus" purports to be "1984" Japanese-style. It apparently is an indictment of soulless authority, best represented by a shapeless mass of wires and chips, called Mama, and a trumpet call to untrammeled youthful camaraderie, supposedly represented by an enigmatic bus and its driver.

One has to use "apparently" because the intentions of first time feature director Takashi Komatsu do not actually result in anything like intelligible allegory. Relating to the characters may have been asking too much, but at least an understanding of what they were meant to represent would have helped.

Action is set in a village where all dissent and innocent fun have been eliminated or lobotomized. Main characters, with enigmatic names like the Bengal Tiger and Fool on the Hill, have all gone into hiding or been killed off thanks to an authority figure who spends his time answering an outsized black telephone.

Although the film is visually stunning in sequences, and its pacing is exuberant, it is too wayward to have much boxoffice appeal outside a limited cult following.—*Guid.*

Shattered Dreams — Picking Up The Pieces
(BRITISH-DOCU)

A Schonfeld production with the assistance of Central tv in association with Channel 4. Produced by Victor Schonfeld, Jennifer Millstone. Written and directed by Schonfeld. Camera (color), Peter Greenhalgh, Amnon Solomon, Dani Schneuer, Zachariah Raz, Yossi Wein, Yaacov Saporta, Jimmy Dibling; music, Arik Rudich, Shlomo Bar, Shalom Hanoch; sound, Shabati Sarig, Itamar Ben-Yaacov, Vaughan Roberts, Schonfeld. Reviewed at London Film Festival, Nov. 24, 1987. Running time: **165 MIN.**

London — "Shattered Dreams" is probably the most comprehensive documentary to date on the myriad political and social tensions in Israel's pressure-cooker society. Yet after four years of filming — and at 165 minutes — director Victor Schonfeld has served up little more than an extended rehash of images, speeches and ideas frequently aired in broadcast and print media in Israel and abroad.

Film shows how a deeply divided Israel is responding to the apparent destruction of ideals that helped create the Jewish state, especially after the ill-fated Lebanese War ("Operation Peace In Galilee").

Pic is exhaustive in its coverage of virtually every contentious issue in Israel today including the clash between Western and Oriental Jews, treatment of Israeli Arabs, economic problems and unemployment, immigration and emigration, terrorism (Israeli and Palestinian) and the conflict between secular and ultra-orthodox Jews. Particular attention is paid to Rabbi Meir Kahane and his virulent anti-Arab views.

"Dreams" makes no attempt to disguise its support for the Palestinian cause, or its disapproval of Israel's continuing occupation of the West Bank and Gaza. Although Schonfeld serves up a potent indictment of current Israeli policies, there is an element of overkill that is detrimental to the docu's message.

As one person says in the film, there is much despair in Israel today, but also hope. Film fully conveys the despair, but little of the hope.

One of the best moments comes at the start, with singer Shalom Hanoch performing "The Messiah" at an evening open-air concert. Combination of song's lyrics ("The Messiah is not coming. He's not even going to phone") and shots of adoring fans holding lighted candles is a moving combination.

Pic most likely will get a run in cinemas in areas with high proportion of Jews, as well as some fest circuit exposure, but its excessive length will limit tv and theatrical opportunities. Technical credits are fine.—*Coop.*

Closing Ranks
(BRITISH)

A Zenith production, in association with Fire Pictures for Central Television. Executive producer, Roger James. Produced by Emma Hayter. Directed by Roger Graef. Screenplay, Graef, Andy Smith, based on a story by Graef; Camera (Eastmancolor), Michael Davis; editor, Thomas Schwalm; music, Tony Britten; production design, Leigh Malone; set decoration, Bruce White; costumes, Ann Hollowood. Reviewed at the London Film Festival, Nov. 21, 1987. Running time: **88 MIN.**
Rick Sneaden . . . . Rob Spendlove
Shirley Sneaden . . . . Liz Edmonds
PC Albert Thom . . . . David Hunt
Sgt. David Deakes . . . . Patrick Field
PC Walter Morse . . . . Ian Brimble
Supt. Southern . . . . Richard Ireson

London — This worthy film is an intelligent indictment of the modern British police forces — and by extension, other institutions — in their tendency to protect their own, even when in the wrong.

Perhaps because it is so well observed and well meaning, it lacks true dramatic tension. Underlying the action is a thesis, so that a conflict does not arise naturally out of the interaction among characters.

What we get is formulaic: if a bad apple is thrown into a barrel, chances are contagion will spread. The thesis may be valid and its arguments may appeal to the liberal minded, but dramatically the film is unsatisfying.

Plot focuses on the bad apple, a policeman in the special services named Rick Sneaden, observed from the beginning as having bouts of uncontrolled brutality.

Sneaden's family life suffers from the tensions, while his fellow cops alternately are suspicious and intimidated by his smartass behavior. Unfortunately, he never becomes a sympathetic character.

The two strands of the action crisscross when his unit is engaged to keep order in an anti-nuke demonstration. Not only does Sneaden spot his wife among the protesters, but he personally pummels a random hippie nearly to death.

It is over this incident that he and his mates are called to account by the chief officer. Despite their dislike, they stick by him so as not to bring dishonor on the corps and disgrace upon themselves.

The direction by U.S.-born documaker Roger Graef is well-controlled and unobtrusive. Acting overall is convincing and technical credits are fine.

Though there is already talk in Britain of video screenings of the film to provoke discussion within the police forces, a full-fledged theatrical release is unlikely.
—*Guid.*

Brand New Day
(BRITISH-FRENCH-DOCU)

An Oil Factory (U.K.)/Agav Films (France) production. Produced by John Stewart. Directed by Amos Gitai. Camera (color) Nurith Aviv; editor, Anna Ruiz; music, The Eurythmics; sound, Daniel Ollivier; assistant director, Uri Fruchtman. Reviewed at London Film Festival, Nov. 28, 1987. Running time: **83 MIN.**

London — Annie Lennox and Dave Stewart of the Eurythmics are two of Britain's most inventive and exciting rock musicians with a string of hits. As Amos Gitai's rock docu "Brand New Day" effectively demonstrates, they are also compelling live performers.

Unfortunately, Gitai's film shows offstage Lennox and Stewart say little and do even less that makes for riveting viewing. Despite assistance of exotic Japanese locations, "Brand New Day" is little more than a souped-up home movie that mainly will appeal to diehard Eurythmics fans, who should guarantee good homevideo sales.

Problem for Gitai is that most rock tours are dull. Much time between gigs is spent hanging around hotels or traveling. There is the odd foray to explore local terrain, and a fair amount of routine rock star horseplay to wile away the hours.

Stewart, who seems married to his dark glasses, spends most of his time composing music on synthesizers or strumming blues riffs on guitar. Lennox, a bold performer on stage, is ill at ease with a camera shadowing her, and is reduced to embarrassing monologs on fame and the meaning of music.

Where Gitai scores is in his filming of the concert itself. Using just one camera throughout he conveys more of the thrills of a Eurythmics concert than another director would have done using 10 cameras and the obligatory highspeed editing. It's a pleasure to concentrate on what is truly compelling — the stage presence of Annie Lennox and the Eurythmics songs.

Gitai makes other refreshing efforts to create something a little different from the traditional rock concert tour film. There are evocative glimpses of Japan viewed through the porthole-like window of the train as it speeds along at night and there's a captivating moment when Stewart demonstrates to a Japanese composer how he learned to play old style blues on the guitar using a sliding glass.

Camerawork by Nurith Aviv, especially during the concert, is excellent. Other tech credit are fine.
—*Coop.*

Himmo, Melech Yerushalayim
(Himmo, King Of Jerusalem)
(ISRAELI)

A Gelfand Films presentation of a Udi Prod./Belleville Properties production. Produced by Enrique Rottenberg. Ehud Bleiberg. Directed by Amos Guttman. Screenplay, Edna Mazia, based on novel by Yoram Kaniuk; camera (color), Jorge Gurevitch; editor, Ziva Postec; music, Ilaan Virtzberg; sound Danny Shitrit; art direction, Ron Kedmi; costumes, Suzy Barda. Reviewed at the Haifa Film Festival, Oct. 10, 1987. Running time: **84 MIN.**
With: Alona Kimchi (Hamutal), Amiram Gavriel (Frangi), Dov Navon (Assa), Amos Lavi (Marco), Yossi Graber (the doctor), Aliza Rosen (a nun).

Haifa — Amos Guttman's third feature film, while staying close to his range of subject matter (concerning marginals and their conduct) is much closer to the mainstream than in the past.

Instead of sexual deviations which separated his protagonists from the rest of society, this time he deals with soldiers wounded in battle. The script is based on a highly regarded novel by Yoram Kaniuk, and the entire action takes place in an old monastery in Jerusalem converted into a hospital, during the siege on that city in 1948.

The picture focuses on an angelic young nurse who volunteers to work in one of the improvised wards, and her shock at the encounter with the maimed young men and particularly with Himmo, once a popular leader of his peers, now blind, dumb, amputated, an almost inanimate lump of flesh except for the bloodcurdling screams he lets out once in a while.

Guttman's adaptation stresses the ambivalent relation between the rest of the ward and this human ruin, the effect it has on the young girl and her strange fascination for him and the way this is perceived by the rest of the ward. The film refers less to a specific place or time, trying to put the entire narrative in a larger perspective, as an image of the ravages of war on human beings. The basic situation might suggest a reference to Dalton Trumbo's "Johnny Got His Gun," but unlike that story, there is no attempt here to penetrate into the mind of a man who has been entirely severed from the rest of the living. It is his presence which triggers the drama in the action of the other characters.

Guttman, as usual, relies heavily on mood, which he succeeds in establishing with the help of lighting, camera movement and sets. If visually this shows Guttman to have a definite flair for filmmaking, the script suffers from pretentiousness, the acting of Alona Kimchi in the lead is wooden, and it is only partially compensated by the dedicated performances of Amiram Gavriel and Dov Navon.—*Edna.*

Der Unsichtbare
(The Invisible Man)
(WEST GERMAN)

A Neue Constantin Film release of an Ulf Miehe production. Directed by Miehe. Screenplay, Miehe; camera (color), Franz Rath; editor, Barbara von Weitershausen; music, Boris Jojic; sound, Manfred Banach, Thomas Meyer; assistant director, Helga Soboszek; art direction, Hans Gailling, Renate Ereth; special effects, Stephan Schultze-Jena. Reviewed in Hamburg, Oct. 15, 1987. Running time: **90 MIN.**
Peter Benjamin . . . . . . Klaus Wennemann
Helene, his wife . . . . Barbara Rudnik
Jo Schnell . . . . Nena
Eduard . . . . Benedict Freitag
Mother . . . . Camilla Horn

Hamburg — This update of the invisible man yarn pits a topnotch cast against some pretty impossible plot turns to produce a pic neither funny nor moving. It had a short run in West Germany and has few prospects elsewhere.

A camera-weary talk-show host (Klaus Wennemann) inherits a magical cap that makes him invisible, allowing him to move unnoticed through the world. What he sees among spouse and friends takes him aback, and leads to a series of confrontations that in another film might have been funny.

Wennemann is known best outside Germany for his supporting role in Wolfgang Petersen's "Das Boot" as the indomitable U-boat chief engineer. He has a good deal of comic talent and is a versatile actor. Yet even his magic cap can't save this pic. Barbara Rudnik and

Camilla Horn in supporting roles are given no room to put their proved acting skills to work. German songstress Nena, whose "99 Red Balloons" made worldwide charts five years ago, is not a big enough b.o. draw to help this film.

Franz Rath, whose camerawork graced "Rosa Luxemburg" in 1986, does his best in this talky pic. Special effects are not all that special.—*Gill.*

Dangerous Characters
(BRITISH-DOCU-COLOR/B&W)

A Jane Balfour Films release of an Olivella Foresta-Channel 4 production. Directed by Alfio Bernabei. Historical research, Olivella Foresta; camera, (color, 16m), Nick Hale; editor, Mike Leggett; music, Jonathan Kahn; sound, Matthew Evans. Reviewed at Festival dei Popoli, Florence, Dec. 2, 1987. Running time: **104 MIN.**

Florence — "Dangerous Characters" chronicles the little-known story of the 30,000 Italians who settled in Great Britain between 1900-1945, relating the political divisions separating them and the unjustified persecution many suffered at the hands of the British government. Using interviews with Italians who lived through the period and rare archival footage, photos and documents, director Alfio Bernabei and producer-researcher Olivella Foresta skillfully create a convincing and moving portrait of those times.

Film opens with the influx of Italian immigrants, some of whom walked from their impoverished homeland, into London's "Little Italy" in the early part of the century. The migrant community, whose members worked as barbers, shoemakers and ice cream makers, became split politically when Mussolini's Fascist party took power in 1922. Film documents the growth of the London Fascio, referred to by Mussolini as "my first-born abroad," and how the British government allowed it to become a powerful force composed of thousands of members and sympathizers who operated paramilitary schools and youth camps throughout Britain.

The anti-Fascist movement, strengthened by increasing numbers of Italian political refugees, countered through newspapers and active lobbying with warnings on the dangers of fascism. Their efforts were stymied by close British-Italian political and trade ties, and a network of spies and informers which kept close tabs on anti-Fascist activities in London and Rome.

Second part of the film covers Mussolini's declaration of war on Great Britain and the government's following detainment and internment of thousands of Italians termed "dangerous characters." The roundup included not only Fascists but many anti-Fascists, including leading anti-Fascists spokesman Decio Anzani. In the most moving scene of the film, Anzani's daughter talks of

his arrest and subsequent tragic death aboard the ill-fated Arandora Star along with 475 other Italians. The unprotected ship, carrying hundreds of internees from Britain to Canada, was torpedoes by a submarine.

Winner of the best documentary research film prize at the Festival dei Popoli, the film does drag a little in some sections. Only viewers with a good knowledge of Italian history will find segments on the migrants' home country origins interesting, while others will wish the time spent focusing on old documents and photos had been given over to lengthier interviews with the eyewitnesses.

Still, the film is a thoughtful, well-made production documenting this shadowy area of history well. Already broadcast by Channel 4, it should find release in other tv markets and on the university circuit, with a possible shot at art house release.—*Thom.*

As Time Goes By
(AUSTRALIAN)

A Valhalla release of a Monroe Stahr production. Produced by Chris Kiely. Executive producer, Phillip J. Dwyer. Directed by Barry Peak. Screenplay, Peak; camera (color), John Ogden; editor, Ralph Strasser; music, Peter Sullivan; production design, Paddy Reardon; sound, Steve Haggerty, Tim Chau; production manager, Ray Pond; casting, Peter Felmingham. Reviewed at Valhalla theater, Sydney, Dec. 3, 1987. Running time: **97 MIN.**
Ryder . . . . Bruno Lawrence
Mike . . . . Nique Needles
Joe Bogart (The Alien) . . . . . . Max Gillies
J.L. Weston . . . . Ray Barrett
Connie Stanton . . . . Marcelle Schmitz
James McCauley . . . . . . Mitchell Faircloth
Cheryl . . . . Deborah Force
Margie . . . . Christine Keogh
Also with: Don Bridges (Ern), Ian Shrives (Greaser), Jane Clifton (Mechanic), Chris Kiely (Connie's father).

Sydney — This is the most ambitious, and successful, pic produced so far by the Valhalla cinemas. Following on from "Future Shlock" and "The Big Hurt," Barry Peak's latest effort, filmed under title "The Cricketer," is a cheerfully affectionate sci-fier about a rendevous with an alien in Central Australia. Prospects look to be good for this charmer, aimed at film buffs the world over.

Behind the opening credits, a strange looking spacecraft lands in the Aussie desert. Mike (Nique Needles) is a surfer from the city traveling with two eccentric femme companions through the outback (one of the film's few miscalculations is these characters, who are uninteresting and briefly intrusive). Seems Mike has a rendezvous arranged via his mother 25 years earlier. He has to meet a certain Joe Bogart at a spot miles from anywhere, though he doesn't know why.

Abandoned by the women, Mike is sunbathing on the highway when he's picked up by a local cop Ryder (Bruno Lawrence) who's tracking down a couple of villains who've been poisoning sheep. After an inconclusive shootout, Ryder takes Mike to the ranch run by Connie Stanton (Marcelle Schmitz), alone after the death of her father. Meanwhile, a local landowner, Weston (Ray Barrett) is certain that cracks in the ozone layer will turn the desert into an oasis, and is buying up the land, while an obsessed scientist (Mitchell Faircloth) is on the track of the spacecraft.

It turns out that Mike's rendezvous is with the spacecraft — which is disguised as a 1940s diner and bar. Joe Bogart (Max Gillies) is an avuncular alien who, like the outer space creatures in Joe Dante's "Explorers," speaks mostly in lines (and voices) from old movies. Gillies, usually a more successful stage and home tube performer than film actor, has a field day here with a series of clever impersonations ranging from the obvious (Bogart, Cagney) to the more obscure (Strother Martin, George Brent); he even tries Garbo.

As can be seen from the above, "As Time Goes By" never takes itself very seriously, which is just as well because it's pretty derivative. Made on a minuscule budget, pic actually has more entertainment value than local pics which cost more than 10 times as much. Special effects are serviceable, given the film's cheerfully slapdash attitude to the sci-fi. (The "machine" that allows characters to travel back and forth in time is a cocktail shaker!) Once it's been established that Ryder, a strong performance from Bruno Lawrence, who plays his part dead straight, accidentally killed his son years earlier with a cricket ball, it doesn't take much to figure out that Mike is the supposedly dead son, caught in a time warp. Nique Needles makes Mike an endearingly spaced-out hero, and newcomer Marcelle Schmitz is sweet as his love interest. Support characters aren't so interesting, though there's a good cameo from Don Bridges as a storekeeper with a hatred for dust, something you can't escape in the outback.

Given budget limitations, pic is technically good, apart from a slight fuzziness at times in the 35m blowup from Super 16m. Pic should delight buffs and earn a cult following, but with its amusing variations on classic sci-fi/time travel themes, it could possibly go wider. Life on video looks to be busy.—*Strat.*

Kampen om den röde ko
(The Fight For The Red Cow)
(DANISH)

A Regner Grasten Film release of Regner Grasten Film production with Obber-Böv I/S and Special Assignment I/S. Written and directed by Jarl Friis Mikkelsen, Ole Stephensen. Camera (Agfacolor), Peter Klitgaard; line producer, assistant director, Sven Methling; editor, May Soya; sound, Stig Sparre Ulrich; music, Jan Gläsel, Friis Mikkelsen. Reviewed at the Palads, Copenhagen, Nov. 25, 1987. Running time: **82 MIN.**
Svend Aage . . . . Jarl Friis Mikkelsen
Niels Peder . . . . Ole Stephensen
The Lawyer . . . . Axel Ströbye
Nicolette . . . . Mari-Anne Jespersen
The Count . . . . Poul Bundgaard
Irma . . . . Anne Cathrine Herdorff
Morten . . . . Morten Eisner
Also with: Preben Kristensen, Jacob Haugaard, Hanne Borchsenius, Thomas Eje, Jens Okking, Claus Nissen, Ulf Pilgaard, Lisbeth Dhal, Claus Ryskjär, Ellen Winther-Lembourn.

Copenhagen — The combatants of "The Fight For The Red Cow" are characters out of folksy Danish film tradition of the '40s. By updating them with all kinds of cinematic trickery and tongue-in-cheek parody, writer-director-performers Jarl Friis Mikkelsen and Ole Stephensen come through with a light-hearted farce sure to enthuse local audiences. The good-humored visual silliness of it all could lead to a few offshore sales as well.

Friis Mikkelsen and Stephensen hit boxoffice bull's eyes with two previous farces, "Up At Dad's Hat" and "It's Dad's, Too," which did not pass muster as jobs of professional filmmaking. Other helmers were in charge of those, while the duo, Danish tv favorites, stuck to writing and to repeating characters they had created for the home screen.

This time, Friis Mikkelsen and Stephensen have directed themselves as a vagabond trader and a girl-crazed, romantic young farmer who come to the aid of a damsel in distress and of an indebted count and his agricultural estate. The estate is threatened with takeover by supermarket and chemical plant entrepreneurs, latter represented by a wilier-than-a-coyote lawyer.

The cow at the center of things moos to indicate who will win in next Sunday's races. Sunday is when the count's debts are due for payment. So the fight for possession of the cow is on. Drawing inspiration from Mack Sennett and the Marx Brothers, and throwing in self-invented bits as well as borrowed pieces from Monty Python-esque or "Saturday Night Live" moderns, the directors keep up pace and rhythm with fine assists from editor May Soya and line producer-a.d. Sven Methling, a veteran comedy helmer.

As performers, Friis Mikkelsen and Stephensen are wittily busy and onscreen about 85% of the time. Axel Ströbye as the lawyer and Poul Bundgaard as the count contribute finely honed farce acting, too, while their peers from Danish stage and screen deliver high spirited cameos.
—*Kell.*

Lemon Sky
(U.S.)

An American Playhouse production, in association with WGBH/Boston. Produced by Marcus Viscidi. Directed by Jan Egleson. Screenplay, Lanford Wilson; camera (color, 16m), James Glennon; editor, Jeanne Jordan, William A. Anderson; art direction, Dianne Freas; music, Pat Metheny. Reviewed at the Florence Film Festival, Italy, Dec. 12, 1987. Running time: **106 MIN.**
Alan . . . . Kevin Bacon
Douglas . . . . Tom Atkins
Ronnie . . . . Lindsay Crouse
Carol . . . . Kyra Sedgwick
Penny . . . . Laura White
Also with: Casey Affleck (Jerry), Peter Macowan (Jack).

Florence — Based on a literate and moving screenplay by Pulitzer Prize-winning writer Lanford Wilson, "Lemon Sky" is classic family drama studded with sterling performances by the entire cast. Producers American Playhouse and WGBH Boston gave director Jan Egleson a chance to keep the theatrical text with little or no attempt at "cinematizing" the material, and results may be too stagey and talky for some audiences. However, film manages to be involving just as it is, and Egleson's work with the actors

yields standout emotional results.

Wilson's story, a little too strongly reminiscent of Tennessee Williams' Southern angst for comfort, takes place in the California home of all-American father Doug (Tom Atkins) and his second wife, Ronnie (Lindsay Crouse). They live with their two young sons and two orphaned teenage girl boarders. Into their peaceful kingdom comes Alan (Kevin Bacon), Doug's son by his first marriage, accidentally unbalancing the equilibrium and sparking tensions that tear the family apart in an apocalyptic final showdown.

One source of interest is the way the story is told, jumping back and forth in time from 1957 to 1970, as the sensitive narrator Bacon (17 and 30 years old, respectively) calls on memory and various family members (even dead ones) to help recount events.

Fine performances are given by all, from Bacon in his dual role to Lindsay Crouse as the maternal second wife, comprehending husband Tom Atkins' foibles to the limit. Playing the girls, Kyra Sedgwick brings malicious sensuality to the streetsmart, tragic figure of beautiful Carol, while Laura White portrays the homely, prudish Penny with affecting realism. —*Yung.*

Teresa
(ITALIAN)

A Medusa release of an Intl. Dean Film/Dean Film/Reteitalia coproduction. Produced by Pio Angeletti, Adriano De Micheli. Directed by Dino Risi. Screenplay, Bernardino Zapponi, Graziano Diana, Risi; camera (Eastmancolor, color by Telecolor), Blasco Giurato; editor, Alberto Gallitti, music, Claudio Maioli; art direction, Fabio Vitale. Reviewed at the Rouge e Noir Cinema, Rome, Dec. 19, 1987. Running time: **100 MIN.**
Teresa . . . . Serena Grandi
Gino . . . . Luca Barbareschi
Nabucco . . . . Eros Pagni

Rome — **Veteran helmer Dino Risi has a fling at molding sexy starlet Serena Grandi into a bit more serious role than she is wont to play. As a widowed truck driver hauling her rig from Bavaria to Sicily, Grandi defeats audience expectations by never removing short shorts and revealing tops; boxoffice has been proportionally low gear. Foreign playoffs look dubious for a pic with a weak storyline, no drama, cartoon characters and a blackout on the bedroom scenes.**

From her softcore hit "Miranda" on, Grandi's screen persona has steadily evolved into a tough, aggressive, independent single girl with a head for business. In "Teresa," she takes over the debt-ridden tractor trailer of her dead husband and fearlessly hits the road. Sagely using her oversize physical charms to keep banker-admirer Nabucco (Eros Pagni) at bay, Teresa toys with the idea of marrying an eccentric German baron who

could make her a millionaire. Yet love triumphs over cash in a standard finale lifted from "The Graduate," with Teresa dashing out of a church wedding (Nabucco is at the altar) to leap into a truck with poor boy Luca Barbareschi, her good-looking second driver.

Despite some nice touches, like Barbareschi's credible performance as a trucker who wanted to be a race car driver, pic has an air of being factory-made, old concept that does it in. Grandi still has a way to go before her modest range of facial expressions and provocative poses are able to console ogling fans for the absence of nude scenes (the only spice is a dip in the ocean in a clinging blouse). Technical work is adequate, but uninspired. —*Yung.*

If Looks Could Kill

A Platinum Pictures and Distant Horizons Ltd. production. Executive producer, Anant Singh. Produced and directed by Chuck Vincent. Screenplay, Vincent, Craig Horrall; camera (color), Larry Revene; editor, James Davalos, Marc Ubell (Vincent); music, Susan Jopson, Jonathan Hannah; sound, Peter Penguin; art direction, D. Gary Phelps; assistant director, Bill Slobodian; production manager, Bill Tasgal; associate producer, Mickey Nivelli; casting, Lem Amero. Reviewed on Republic Video vidcassette, N.Y., Dec. 17, 1987. MPAA Rating: R. Running time: **89 MIN.**
Laura Williamson . . . . Kim Lambert
George Ringer . . . . Tim Gail
Bob Crown . . . . Alan Fisler
Jack Devonoff . . . . Jamie Gillis
Jeannie Burns . . . . Jeanne Marie
Carson . . . . James Davies
Mary Beth . . . . Jane Hamilton

"If Looks Could Kill" represents a departure for filmmaker Chuck Vincent, entering the thriller genre after specializing in comedies and dramas. Like his subsequent horror piece "Deranged," pic is interesting mainly for its structure. It has debuted domestically via homevideo.

Using a claustrophobic technique drawing upon Hitchcock's "Rear Window" as its model, pic details the travails of the aptly named George Ringer (Tim Gail), a young man who videotapes parties and bar mitzvahs until shady lawyer Jack Devonoff (Jamie Gillis) hires him to set up a surveillance camera on the apartment of suspected embezzler Laura Williamson (played by Kim Lambert, better known as Sheri St. Claire and previously billed as Kim Kafkaloff).

Ringer becomes obsessed with this job, peeping at the beautiful woman while recording evidence of her shady doings with her love slave Carson (James Davies), a bank employee. Ringer's girlfriend Jeannie (Jeanne Marie) gets fed up with his neglect and splits, but things really go awry when Ringer finds out Devonoff is a fake and he is being set up as the fall guy in an embezzlement/murder plot. Pic concludes with several effective plot twists but a disappointing chase and police shootout.

Pic's main surprise is an effective turn by Sheri St. Claire as the mystery woman, in a role which combines some dramatic opportunities with uninhibited (within the confines of an R rating) sexuality, drawing upon St. Claire's extensive experience in adult films. Also doing well as the villain is the ubiquitous adult film performer Jamie Gillis (billed here as J. Gillis). Leads Tim Gail and Jeanne Marie are overshadowed by the supporting cast.—*Lor.*

White Water Summer

A Columbia release of a Columbia-Delphi V production from Polar Entertainment. Produced by Mark Tarlov. Executive producer, Wolfgang Glattes. Directed by Jeff Bleckner. Screenplay, Manya Starr, Ernest Kinoy; camera (Technicolor, Deluxe prints), John Alcott; editor, David Ray; music, Michael Boddicker; art direction, Jeffrey L. Goldstein; set decoration, Bruce Gibeson; costume design, Thomas Dawson; sound (Dolby), Kirk Francis; visual consultant, David Jenkins; associate producers, Christopher Dalton, Dennis Palumbo, Bob Roe, Larry Rapaport: assistant director, Bob Roe; New Zealand unit camera, Dana Christiaansen; casting, Mary V. Buck, Susan Edelman. Reviewed on RCA/Columbia Home Video vidcassette, Dec. 25, 1987. MPAA Rating: PG. Running time: **90 MIN.**

Vic . . . . Kevin Bacon
Alan . . . . Sean Astin
Mitch . . . . Jonathan Ward
George . . . . K.C. Martel
Chris . . . . Matt Adler
Virginia Block . . . . . . Caroline McWilliams
Jerry Block . . . . Charles Siebert
Storekeeper . . . . Joseph Passarelli

Hollywood — Shot in 1985 under the title "Rites Of Summer" and given only a token regional release earlier this year, "White Water Summer" is out now on vidcassette and worthy of notice only as the second-to-last film photographed by the late, great John Alcott. Script for this Kevin Bacon starrer for Columbia is so demonstrably uneventful and feeble that the surprise lies not with the fact that pic was put on the shelf, but in that it was made at all.

Bacon plays a seemingly resourceful and confident outdoor type who is first seen lining up young Sean Astin, a reluctant, well-protected city boy, to join three other pubescent types for a summer of toughening up in the Wild West.

Of all the untoward things one could imagine happening to the group in the wilderness, nothing actually does, and opening reels are paced to achieve maximum audience torpor and impatience, as Bacon teaches the kids how to make a fire, catch fish without a pole or net, and so on.

All along, Bacon is forced to be a little tough with Astin, who, while not exactly a sissy, is spoiled and always wants to do things the easy way. When he finally goes too far, leaving Astin hanging by a rope off a cliff, the other boys conclude Bacon is nothing but a sadist, and mutiny. Bacon's leg is broken in the scuffle and it is finally left to Astin to prove his character by navigating his hated guide back to safety through some wild rapids.

Neither the scriptwriters nor director Jeff Bleckner display any knowledge of how to build dramatic tension through structuring scenes, and Bacon's character remains an unfocused enigma throughout, his motivations and true feelings about his bratty charges being unexplored. Storytelling is broken up periodically by some on-camera direct address narration by Astin, but its obnoxious tone blocks this attempt at drawing the viewer close to at least one of the characters.

John Alcott, to whom the picture is dedicated, turned in some nice nature photography, but this marks a decidedly minor effort for him. Soundtrack is larded with a number of obscenely unappealing and inappropriate rock tunes bearing no connection whatsoever to the action, such as it is.

Location shooting was done in California as well as New Zealand, and pic possesses a Nippon Film Enterprises copyright. —*Cart.*

1988

The Young Magician
(CANADIAN-POLISH)

A Les Prods. La Fête (Canada)/"Tor" Film Unit (Poland) production. Produced by Rock Demers, Krzysztof Zanussi. Written and directed by Waldemar Dziki. Camera (color), Wit Dabal; editor, Andre Corriveau; production design, Violette Daneau, Jerry Sajko, Andrzej Przedworski, Andrzej Halinski; music, Krzesmir Debski; sound, Claude Langlois. Reviewed at the London Film Festival, Nov. 29, 1987. Running time: **99 MIN.**

Peter	Rusty Jedwab
Margaret	Natasza Maraszek
Alexander	Edward Garson
Mike	Tomasz Klimasiewicz
Peter's mother	Daria Trafankowska
Peter's father	Mariusz Benoit
Inspector	Wladyslaw Kowalski

London — "The Young Magician" is the fourth in producer Rock Demers' series of 12 films collectively called "Tales For All," aimed at younger audiences. It is an amusing number that could appeal to moppets.

Pic was designed and shot in Poland, but the dialog is all English and the two leading young actors are Canadian. There is lots of slapstick action, a smattering of special effects and a teenage love affair.

Young Peter (Rusty Jedwab) discovers he has telekinetic (magical) powers and can move objects around the room with his mind. This tends to alienate him from other children and, after a major incident when he is chased by police, he is carted away for scientific examinations.

He escapes from the hospital, teams up with a young cellist, and proceeds to save his town from certain death by retrieving a capsule filled with some kind of a killer substance accidentally dropped by the military. He is declared a hero and his cellist pal goes on to play for the local philharmonic.

Helmer Waldemar Dziki films skillfully, and the young actors perform well. Especially good is Rusty Jedwab's sweetheart Natasza Maraszek as Margaret. Demers' series is a fascinating exercise and could provide much needed film fodder for young viewers. —Adam.

Code Name: Zebra

A Trans World Entertainment presentation of a Pac-West Cinema Group production. Executive producer, Deno Paoli. Produced by Joseph Lucchese. Directed by Joe Tornatore. Screenplay, Robert Leon, from concept and characters by Tornatore; camera (Foto-Kem color), Bill Dickson, Tom Denove; editor, Ed Hanson; music, Louis Febre, Peter Rotter; sound, Craig Fellberg; art direction, Gene Abel; production manager, Joan Weidman; stunt coordinator-associate producer, Eddie Donno; assistant director, Matt Hinkley. Reviewed on TWE vidcassette, N.Y., Dec. 8, 1987. No MPAA Rating. Running time: **94 MIN.**

Frank Barnes	Jim Mitchum
Carmine Longo	Mike Lane
Cougar	Timmy Brown
Voce	Joe Donte
Lt. Dietrich	Chuck Morrell
Julie	Deanna Jurgens
Police sergeant	Lindsey Crosby
Mrs. Noble	Chris Costello
Kozlo	Frank Sinatra Jr.
Crazy	Charles Dierkop
Bundy	George (Buck) Flower

"Code Name: Zebra" is a lame action pic of interest only due to its second generation B-movie cast. It's another direct-to-video release.

Mike Lane plays a mafia hitman who's just out of prison and seeking vengeance upon the Zebra Force, a group of Vietnam vets led by Timmy Brown (ex-footballer who used to be billed as Tim Brown, circa "Mash"). Lane's mafia boss Joe Donte opposes his actions but finds the hothead hard to control. Jim Mitchum becomes involved when his partner (a member of Zebra Force) is killed.

Dull feature has listless line readings (particularly by Mitchum), no sex and perfunctory action sequences. Idiotic payoff has the cops on the case, Chuck Morrell and George (Buck) Flower, literally rooting for the vigilante heroes. Frank Sinatra Jr. contributes a walk-through as a mafia lawyer and Lindsey Crosby has a bit part as a desk sergeant at police headquarters. —Lor.

For Keeps

A Tri-Star Pictures release. Produced by Jerry Belson, Walter Coblenz. Directed by John G. Avildsen. Screenplay, Tim Kazurinsky, Denise DeClue, camera (Technicolor), James Crabe; editor, Avildsen; music, Bill Conti; production design, William J. Cassidy; set decoration, Richard C. Goddard; sound (Dolby), Kirk Francis; costumes, Colleen Atwood; assistant director, Ron L. Wright; associate producers, William J. Cassidy, Douglas Seelig; casting, Caro Jones. Reviewed at Tri-Star screening room, Century City, Calif., Dec. 31, 1987. MPAA Rating: PG-13. Running time: **98 MIN.**

Darcy	Molly Ringwald
Stan	Randall Batinkoff
Mr. Bobrucz	Kenneth Mars
Mrs. Elliot	Miriam Flynn
Mrs. Bobrucz	Conchata Ferrell
Lila	Sharon Brown

Hollywood — With the trumpets blaring on Bill Conti's score, a microscopic view of a sperm impregnating an egg blown up a zillion times appears behind the credits to "For Keeps." The rest of the film is about as subtle. In characteristic fashion, director John G. Avildsen tries to wring every last bit of emotion out of this teenage pregnancy drama and with so many cannons firing, he can't help but hit the target a few times. Film should hit home for a limited number of teenage girls.

Informed by the film that some 20,000 teenage girls become pregnant weekly, this would seem to be fertile ground for a real-life drama. Yet in the hands of Avildsen and screenwriters Tim Kazurinsky and Denise DeClue, pic plays like an '80s version of "Father Knows Best."

Perhaps the one redeeming ingredient in the film is Molly Ringwald's emotion-drenched performance. Although she breaks into tears no fewer than a dozen times, it is somehow refreshing to see her expanding her repertoire and dealing with adult problems, albeit still as an adolescent.

The supposedly novel twist on the old story of the bad girl getting knocked up is that Ringwald is an "A" student and editor of her high school paper with a bright future. Her boyfriend (Randall Batinkoff) is headed for an architecture scholarship at Cal Tech, but the best laid plans...

In fact the entire film is laid out like an architectural blueprint: the clumsy coupling, the outraged parents, the troubled marriage, reconciliation with the families and vows of undying devotion.

Film never really strikes an authentic emotional note. Early going is hokey with the kids attempting to deal with emotional demands beyond their experience. Later on, they seem to become model adults, seizing control of their lives and acting with newfound maturity. Filmmakers are not beyond shamelessly manipulating the characters to get a cheap cry.

Batinkoff simply is unbelievable as the child father and seems far too young and uninteresting to be involved with Ringwald. Their deep feelings for each other, therefore, come off as a bit of a mystery.

Kenneth Mars as the working class father is encouraged to overact while Conchata Ferrell is predictably forgiving and sympathetic as the mother. Miriam Flynn is painfully obvious as Ringwald's man-hating mother. Professional values are wasted on this material. — Jagr.

The Texas Comedy Massacre
(U.S.)

A Positron Films production. Produced, written and directed by Marcus Van Bavel. Camera (Eastmancolor, 16m), editor, music, Van Bavel. Reviewed at Florence Film Festival, Dec. 13, 1987. Running time: **84 MIN.** With: Marcus Van Bavel, Nicholas Van Bavel, David Boone, Jim Presnal.

Florence — A homemade, often hilarious send-up of American tv culture in the style of Monty Python skits, "The Texas Comedy Massacre" is literally a 1-man show for debuting helmer Marcus Van Bavel. Not only has the young director written and produced the film (over a 5-year period, at a rock-bottom budget of $50,000), he also handles lighting, music, editing and plays 46 different roles, including voice-overs.

Yet despite the shoestring production circumstances, "Massacre" manages to cleverly turn its shortcomings to laughs. This entertaining entry deserves video pickup and campus screenings.

Among Van Bavel's satirical targets are "Great Moments In Star Drek" with Capt. Kork, Mr. Spook and a host of aliens naturally all limned by the plasticine-faced director, "Ze Undersea World Of Jacques Clouseau" aboard the S.S. Epilepso; and "Bachelor Kitchen." All show technical work and special effects of surprisingly high caliber, considering the limited means.

The hip college humor is spiced with a few gross jokes, some sex, and a wink at the drug subculture. The multiple incarnations of Van Bavel — a comedian worth discovering — are one of pic's funniest running gags. —Yung.

Eye Of The Eagle

A Concorde Pictures presentation. Produced and directed by Cirio H. Santiago. Screenplay, Joseph Zucchero, Nigel Hogge, from story by Catherine Santiago; camera (color), Ricardo Remias; editor, Gervacio Santos; musical director, Marita Manuel; sound, Do Bulatano; production design, Joe Mari Avellana; production manager, Aurelio Navarro; second unit directors, Avellana, Bobby Santiago; stunt coordinator, Fred Espiana; casting, Enrique Reyes. Reviewed on MGM/UA Home Video vidcassette, N.Y., Jan. 1, 1988. MPAA Rating: R. Running time: **82 MIN.**

Sgt. Rick Stratton	Brett Clark
Johnny Ransom	Robert Patrick
Sgt. Rattner	Ed Crick
Capt. Carter	William Steis
Chris Chandler	Cec Verrell
Cpt. Willy Leung	Rey Malonzo
Col. Stark	Mike Monty
Col. Trang	Vic Diaz
Col. Watkins	Henry Strzalkowski
Sgt. Maddox	David Light

Cirio H. Santiago's "Eye Of The Eagle" is a low-octane (and low interest) war picture from the prolific Filipino helmer, who has been in Roger Corman's stable off and on for the past 15 years. His 1972 effort "Savage" was a lot more fun in the same vein.

Newie, shot in 1986, relies upon a tasteless plot device, postulating that various renegade G.I.s in Vietnam, listed as POWs and MIAs, actually are making up a "lost command" unit carrying out massacres and unauthorized missions. Cec Verrell portrays a pretty newshen on the track of this exposé story, joined reluctantly by Sgt. Stratton (beefy Brett Clark) after latter conducts various minor league missions of his own.

Upshot is that the renegades are led by Sgt. Rattner (Ed Crick), who killed Stratton's brother years before. Climax is the expected 1-on-1 battle between the two soldiers.

Pic consists mainly of mindless machine gun battles, in which shooting and explosions are boring and out of context. Use of Filipino actors as the Vietnamese is utterly unconvincing, especially when the heinous North Vietnamese colonel is played by Vic Diaz, mainstay of dozen of Filipino action pics of the '60s and '70s. Lead player Clark is stiff and given to monotone line readings, while Verrell, a Santiago discovery who had a distinctive, butch persona in director's previous film "Silk," is here just another Kate Capshaw clone. —Lor.

Taxi Nach Kairo
(Taxi To Cairo)
(WEST GERMAN)

A Senator Filmverleih release of a Frank Ripploh Film production. Produced by Imagimotion. Executive producer, Joschi N. Arpa. Directed by Ripploh. Screenplay, Tamara Kafka, Ripploh; camera (color), Dodo Simoncic; editor, Peter R. Adam, Peter Clausen; music, Peter Breiner; sound, Ernst Marell; art direction, Hans Zillmann. Reviewed at Broadway Kino, Hamburg, W. Germany, Dec. 30, 1987. Running time: **90 MIN.**
Frank . . . . .Frank Ripploh
Klara . . . . .Christine Neubauer
Eugen . . . . .Udo Schenk
Bernd . . . . .Bernd Broaderup
Mother . . . . .Nina Schuehly
Psychotherapist . . . . . . .Domenica Niehoff
Vice Squad Officer . . . . . .Burkhard Driest

Hamburg — It took Berlin schoolteacher-turned-filmmaker Frank Ripploh seven years to come up with a sequel to his debut pic "Taxi Zum Klo," which promoted him to the front ranks of West German gay filmmakers and turned better coin in America than it did at home.

While the sequel does not match the original for brashness and comic freshness, it is sure to appeal once again to U.S. gay audiences more than it does to Ripploh's countrymen, who already are decrying it as a frothy, Hollywood-style farce. Pic is a natural for the fest circuit and specialty houses catering to gay audiences.

Taxi Two offers no political statements, and the storyline quickly dissolves into incoherence. The fun comes from Ripploh's digs at life in stolid West Germany. His eye for American sensibilities allows him to use German household gadgets and everyday situations to optimum comic effect. Film opens with Ripploh's recording answering machine voice blithely stating he is "tied up right now" while the camera pans across a tidy high-tech German loft apartment to reveal Ripploh half naked and tidily bound, gagged and trussed up in a leather sling. It is the contrast between Teutonic tidiness and S&M decadence that is funny — and which tidy German audiences fail to notice.

Plot picks up where Taxi One left off. Promiscuous Frank (played by Ripploh) never got back together with long-suffering lover Bernd (Bernd Broaderup), who has since despaired of gay life and decided to go straight. Frank is harried by a shrewish mother (Nina Schuehly) who, walking in on the initial S&M scene, threatens to disinherit him unless he gets married. So he gets hysterical actress (Christine Neubauer) to pose as his wife, and the unlikely pair move to a thatched-roof house in the country to set up strictly platonic housekeeping.

It is when Frank and his buxom bride both set their sights on a hand-some neighbor (Udo Schenk) that the going gets tough — and the plot gets lost. Complex themes of jealousy, envy and Frank's blossoming love for the first woman in his life are beyond the scope of this lightweight film.

Pic is enhanced by Dodo Simoncic's camera, which neatly frames raunchy Ripploh in a bucolic setting. As if to please U.S. exhibitors, there are none of the hardcore scenes that prompted gasps from audiences on both sides of the Atlantic in the first place. —Gill.

The Vision
(BRITISH)

A BBC Wales production in association with Polymuse/W.W. Entertainment. Tv and video rights from BBC Enterprises. Produced by David M. Thompson. Executive producers, Tony Elmaleh, John Befin. Directed by Norman Stone. Screenplay, William Nicholson; camera (color), Russ Walker; editor, Tom Kruydenberg; music, Bill Connor; production design, Gerald Murphy; set design, Pete Hunt, Jeffrey North; costumes, Angela Muhl. Reviewed at the London Film Festival, Nov. 26, 1987. Running time: **105 MIN.**
James Marriner . . . . .Dirk Bogarde
Grace Gardner . . . . .Lee Remick
Helen Marriner . . . . .Eileen Atkins
Jo Marriner . . . . . . .Helena Bonham Carter
Also with: Paul Maxwell, Philip O'Brien, Bruce Boa, Lynda Bellingham, Lan Curtis, David Lyon.

London — This stylish, topical tv movie conjures the British broadcaster's nightmare: that an American-backed satellite channel not only steals its audiences with glitz and glamor, but subverts the country as well. Unfortunately, the style and topicality is not enough to keep the film from bogging down in muddled moralizing.

Plot centers on the People's Channel, a not-so-futuristic satellite service bent on capturing the hearts and minds of viewers through God-fearing family entertainment and, when necessary, through blackmail and bullying.

Run with singleminded determination by the ice-cold Grace Gardner (played with chilling aplomb by Lee Remick), the channel cajoles a washed-up local tv emcee James Marriner (Dick Bogarde at his most nonchalant) to host its primetime showpiece.

As it becomes clear the People's Channel is not a vulgar but innocuous vehicle for born-again Christians, but rather a sophisticated front for right-wing political interests, Bogarde tries to disengage himself.

The bemused detachment which Bogarde brings to the role, however, does not make his moral conversion very convincing. Nor does the downbeat, derivative subplot involving Marriner's family sufficiently engage the viewer.

Film does make some interesting points about the socalled "Armageddon" psychosis which has gripped segments of the American right and takes swipes at the inability of Europeans to respond to the threat of cultural imperialism from the U.S.

Problem is these are concerns which exercise only a narrow minority. There's not enough humor or believable interaction among the characters to grip a larger audience.

Most importantly, the viewer never feels he's inside the head of any of the main characters or identifying with the plight of any. It's too much a drama of ideas rather than a drama with impact in which characters confront each other over their differing ideas.

"The Vision" is being slotted for a primetime slot early in the new year on BBC. With its big names and the wide debate currently about the future of tv in Britain a respectable audience is likely to tune in.

In the States its small-screen prospects are less clear. Some may view it as a curious, hence mildly interesting, reading of U.S. intentions abroad; others might actually find its arguments pertinent and worrying; many others will simply dismiss it as a pale imitation of Paddy Chayefsky's "Network."

— Guid.

Opera
(ITALIAN)

A CDI release of a Cecchi Gori Gruppo Tiger Cinematografica/ADC coproduction, in cooperation with RAI-TV. Produced by Mario and Vittorio Cecchi Gori. Directed by Dario Argento. Screenplay, Argento, Franco Ferrini; camera (Widescreen, color), Ronnie Taylor; editor, Franco Fraticelli; music, various; art direction, Davide Bassan; sets at the Teatro Reggio di Parma, Gian Maurizio Fercioni. Reviewed at the Adriano Cinema, Rome, Dec. 27, 1987. Running time: **90 MIN.**
Betty . . . . .Cristina Marsillach
Commissioner . . . . .Urbano Barberini
Mira . . . . .Daria Nicolodi
Also with: Ian Charleson, Antonella Vitale, William McNamara.

Rome — **Latest slasher pic from Italy's premiere blood and gore master, Dario Argento, can hardly be called one of Argento's most gripping thrillers. On another scale, "Opera" rates high for its sumptuous sets and above-average widescreen lensing. Technically pic is at the top of the B-movie heap, and its total lack of psychological finesse shouldn't discourage homevid sales and limited theatrical playoffs.**

Virtually plotless, "Opera" loosely connects a series of typically spooky Argento settings and eerie camera movements to crank out the chills. Heroine is Betty (Cristina Marsillach), a pretty young understudy who gets a crack at singing Lady Macbeth when the prima donna breaks a leg. Her performance, amid cawing ravens and sinister zooms into the balcony boxes, brings down the house and brings on the murder of an usher by a mysterious black-gloved hand.

The assassin's real pleasure, however, is tying up poor Betty and tap-ing needles under her eyes to keep them open while he forces her to watch him butcher first her lover, then her costume designer. While a rock score runs riot, scenes push on past the limits of nausea, including such delights as the masked murderer extracting a bracelet from one victim's esophagus, with the help of a pair of sheers.

Dyed-in-the-wool Argento fans won't be surprised to find colorless ciphers in the place of characters, which does nothing to advance the careers of young thesps Marsillach and Urbano Barberini as an ambiguous police commissioner. Yet protests deserve to be heard over the total absurdity of having a cageful of ravens unleashed in the midst of an opera performance to "identify" the murderer. Disregarding logic worked for Argento as long as he wrapped his films in a dream web of unconscius impulses, but "Opera" has little of that, just a feeble flashback to implicate the heroine in the bloodlust. As psychological underpinnings get thinner, the thrills get cheaper. Ditto silly camera angles, like a drain's p.o.v. or inside a pulsating brain. —Yung.

Tant qu'il aura des femmes
(As Long As There Are Women)
(FRENCH)

An AAA release of a Hugo Films/Labbefilms/AAA Prods. coproduction. Produced by Evelyne and Xavier Gélin. Written and directed by Didier Kaminka. Camera (color), Eduardo Suerra; editor, Minique Prim; music, Jean-Claude Petit; sound, Jean-Louis Ughetto; art direction, Loula Morin; assistant director, Jérôme Chalou; production manager, Claude Parnet. Reviewed at the Gaumont Ambassade cinema, Paris, Nov. 3, 1987. Running time: **85 MIN.**
With: Roland Giraud (Sam), Fanny Cottençon (Vanessa), Marianne Basler (Joanna), Fiona Gelin (Elodie), Martin Lamotte (Sacha), Philippe Lavil (Jérémie), Nicole Jamet (Madam Lebeuf), Florent Ginisty (Thomas), Camille Raymond (Alice).

Paris — **Top local comedy screenwriter Didier Kaminka (coauthor of Claude Zidi's "Les Ripoux," among other b.o. hits) tried his hand at directing back in 1975 and failed. Now he's behind the camera for a second go at it, and strikes out again.**

Ironically it's the script that trips him up. Tale's just another variation on the theme of the lovable Gallic philanderer, here played by Roland Giraud. He's a struggling screenwriter who's still quite chummy with his ex-wife (Fanny Cottençon), but now shacked up with rising actress Fiona Gélin. As is to be expected, his head is quickly turned by sexy young physician Marianne Basler, who's globetrotting activities put Giraud's tactics of infidelity to the test.

Kaminka juggles the familiar situations mechanically, shipping Basler and Giraud off to Mexico (Spain, in fact) just to let some air into the fatigued romantic farce. Direction is nothing special, though the players occasionally inject a note of freshness. — *Len.*

Prison On Fire
(HONG KONG)

A Cinema City Co. Ltd. production, released by Golden Princess; a Karl Maka production, Produced by Catherine Chang. Executive producer-directed by Ringo Lam. Screenplay, Nam Yim; music, Lowell Lo; theme song performed by Maria Cordero; art direction, Luk Tze Fung; production manager, Lim Chang. Editor, by Cinema City (Film Prod. Co., Editing United); (In color.) Reviewed at President theater, Causeway Bay, Hong Kong, Nov. 26, 1987. Running time: **98 MIN.**
With: Chow Yun Fat, Leung Ka Fai, Roy Cheung.
(Cantonese soundtrack with English subtitles)

Hong Kong — "Prison On Fire" is a Hong Kong-made prison pic that breaks the tradition of having an escape scheme, gang rape and graphic sex. Instead, there's prolonged violence, bloodbath realism, cliques as in Triad societies, warmth and sensitive, human portrayal of Chinese groupings and comradeship. Top local director Ringo Lam follows his slick, macho blockbuster ("City On Fire") with an equally potent attraction.

Ken (Leung Ka Fai) is a designer who works for an ad agency. He is young, educated, with a good family background and has a good future, until he accidentally kills a thief. Convicted for murder, Ken has grave difficulty in adjusting to the tough prison life. He feels lonely, especially when he learns that his girlfriend is going to England to pursue her studies. Later, Ken meets Tim (Chow Yun Fat), a heavy gambler who, in a quarrel with his adulterous wife, accidentally killed her.

Ken and Tim become good friends, like brothers, with the latter acting as the elder protector.

Tim gets himself deeply involved in the intricate network of gang rivalry which later arouses the malice of an unsympathetic prison officer after a serious riot.

Due to the violent fights, Ken and Tim are separated. When Ken is finally released from prison, he knows that he will not see his good friend again but they do, reunite at the prison gate when Tim is about to be re-instated to his old prison cell. Ken is suddenly reminded of Tim's advice that "life is always hopeful and that there is always a better tomorrow."

Chow Yun Fat gives another marvelous serio-comic performance that is finely honed but with more restraint this time around, while Leung Ka Fai is perfect as the weakling, innocent in hell character. The "Midnight Cowboy" relationship is touching, and special credit should also be given to the casting, slick cinematography, jet pacing, detailed character development and original soundtrack music. There is good tension built up to a predictable but effective ending à la "Midnight Express." —*Mel.*

The Magic Snowman
(U.S.-YUGOSLAV)

A Miramax Films release of a Pavlina Ltd. (N.Y.) and Film i Ton (Belgrade) production. Produced by Pavlina Proevska, Jovan Markovic. Directed by C. Stanner. Screenplay, Dennis Maitland, Lyle Morris, adapted by Markovic from story by Maitland; camera (CFS color), Karpo Godina; music, John Berenzy; postproduction supervisor, Simon Nuchtern. Reviewed at UA Eastside theater, N.Y., Dec. 19, 1987. No MPAA Rating. Running time: **84 MIN.**
Jamie ....Justin Fried
Mandy ....Dragana Marjanovic
Also with: Jack Aronson, Christian James, Kyle Morris and, as voice of Lumi Ukko, the snowman, Roger Moore.

"The Magic Snowman," previously known as "A Winter Tale," is a well-photographed but dullish children's film. Best prospects for this Christmas-themed fantasy are in ancillary markets.

Shot on strikingly picturesque, wintry locations in Yugoslavia, pic presents a simple tale of kids prepping for the annual skating race, who encounter a talking snowman (well-voiced in stentorian, echo chamber tones by former James Bond, Roger Moore). He's named Lumi Ukko in Finnish but travels all over the world courtesy of his friend The Wind.

Lumi Ukko aids the young hero Jamie (Justin Fried) in finding fish as the boy tries to help out his fisherman father, using info provided by The Wind. A sort of insider info scandal develops when Jamie foolishly passes the fishing data on to a evil ship's captain in exchange for a share of the take, leading to lessons being learned. Unfortunately, film builds up to the big race but instead fizzles with Jamie saving the kids from unsafe skating, after Mr. Wind via Lumi Ukko warns of weather conditions that have created hazardous thin ice.

Karpo Godina's photography is quite lovely and Justin Fried and the other youngsters provide capable peformances. Superstar Moore's participation is a plus, with his participation reportedly stemming from production donating a percentage of its proceeds to Unicef, his favored charity. Pic would have benefited from more action and less reliance on static shots of the snowman.—*Lor.*

I Picari
(The Picaros)
(ITALIAN-SPANISH)

A Warner Bros. release of a Clemi Cinematograficia/Dia coproduction. Produced by Giovanni Di Clemente. Directed by Mario Monicelli. Screenplay, Suso Cecchi D'Amico, Leo Benvenuti, Piero De Bernardi, Monicelli; camera (color), Tonino Nardi; editor, Ruggero Mastroianni; music, Lucio Dalla, Claudio Malavasi; art direction, Enrico Fiorentini. Reviewed at Reale Cinema, Rome, Dec. 30, 1987. Running time: **125 MIN.**
Lazarillo ....Enrico Montesano
Guzman ....Giancarlo Giannini
Baron ....Vittorio Gassman
Beggar ....Nino Manfredi

Whore ....Giuliana De Sio
Also with: Bernard Blier, Enzo Robutti, Paolo Hendel, Vittorio Caprioli.

Rome — "The Picaros" are roguish heroes from the picaresque novels of 17th-century Spain, and in Mario Monicelli's elaborately staged period piece there is a whole gallery of the rascals. Film is a literary-historical comedy harking back in spirit to the director's famed "Brancaleone's Army," but early returns have not shown equivalent local interest in this offbeat pic, despite its all-star cast. "Picaros" is an unmistakably classy production with lots of invention and pro craftsmanship to spare. More's the pity it loses steam by the end.

Part of the problem lies in scripters' use of the picaresque form of story-telling itself, individual episodes that don't build to anything. Thus, the first half is a surprising treat, but as the novelty fades one off-target episode is enough to make attention stray.

Main characters are Lazarillo (Enrico Montesano), offspring of a prostitute, whose procurer-father sells him as a boy to a terrible blind beggar (Nino Manfredi), and Guzman (Giancarlo Giannini), son of a gambler hanged for cheating. Our heroes recount their cruel childhoods to each other while chained together in the galley of a prison ship. The humor is black, quick as a knife in the back and told with a masterful economy of images, against a colorful Spanish background.

Fortune smiles on the hapless prisoners and frees them during a mutiny aboard ship (they choose the wrong side and are tossed overboard by the mutineers). Here their ways part. Guzman becomes the servant of penniless nobleman Vittorio Gassman; Lazarillo joins an itinerant theater company and seduces nuns with his San Sebastian act. They pair up again for an amusing roguery called "the cannoli trick," but waste their ill-gotten gains by buying headstrong whore Giuliana De Sio, who refuses all but attractive clients. This is the episode that cuts film's speed and brings it down for a slow — too slow — landing.

Period re-creation is exceptional and Tonino Nardi's lensing a visual treat recalling various period painters. Cast is uneven, with Giannini turning in the on-target performance, neither caricature nor flat. Montesano falls back on his usual monkeyshines without adding much to the film. Vets Gassman and Bernard Blier contribute fine cameos. — *Yung.*

Buisson ardent
(Burning Bush)
(FRENCH)

A Films de l'Atalante release of a Scopitone

Films/Maison de la Culture of Le Havre/-Films de l'Atalante/Sept coproduction. Produced by Jean-Luc Ormières. Directed by Laurent Perrin. Screenplay, Benoît Jacquot, Guy Patrick Saindrichin, Perrin, Marguerite Arnaud; camera (Eastmancolor), Dominique Le Rigoleur; music, Jorge Arriagada; sound, Philippe Sénéchal, Gérard Lamps; art direction, François-Renaud Labarthe; assistant director, Jérôme Jeannet; production manager, Joey Faré. Reviewed at Studio 43, Paris, Oct. 6, 1987. Running time: **84 MIN.**
With: Jessica Forde (Julie), Jean-Claude Adelin (Jean), Alice de Poncheville (Caroline), Simon de la Brosse (Henri), Anne Brochet (Elizabeth), Anouk Ferjac (Christine), Catherine Rich, Philippe Morier Genoud, Jacques Boudet, Corrine Cosson, Serge Riaboukine.

Paris — Winner of the 1987 Jean Vigo Prize, "Buisson ardent" is a drama of adolescent passion that produces no heat or emotion. Laurent Perrin, a Cahiers du Cinéma scribe-turned-filmmaker, does somewhat better here than in his dull debut feature, "Passage Secret" (1985), but the gain in technical skill is not matched by improved direction of actors.

Jessica Forde and Jean-Claude Adelin were childhood sweethearts of different social classes: she a bourgeois, he the son of the family maid.

Adelin was shipped off one day to live with his father abroad and Forde has grown up to become the fiancee of a childhood friend of her own social standing (Simon de la Brosse).

Adelin's unheralded return years later reignites Forde's pasion for him and drives Brosse to jealous extremes. The mysterious and taciturn Adelin keeps his distance and one day again disappears. Forde follows his trail to Paris but fails to win him back.

Perrin, who inherited the story from director Benoît Jacquot, tells the story with clarity but not much feeling. Though Adelin is adequate as the inscrutable prole, Forde (featured in Eric Rohmer's "Four Adventures Of Reinette And Mirabelle") is lacking in relief as his still-burning flame.

Dominique Le Rigoleur's lensing is excellent. —*Len.*

Le Vie del Signore Sono Finite
(The Ways Of The Lord Are Finite)
(ITALIAN)

A Columbia Pictures Italia release of an Esterno Mediterraneo Film production. Produced by Mauro Berardi. Directed by Massimo Troisi. Screenplay, Troisi, Anna Pavagnano; camera (color), Camillo Bazzoni; editor, Nino Baragli; music, Pino Daniele; art direction, Francesco Frigeri. Reviewed at Barbarini Cinema, Rome, Dec. 25, 1987. Running time: **103 MIN.**
Camillo ....Massimo Troisi
Vittoria ....Jo Champa
Brother ....Marco Messeri
Orlando ....Massimo Bonetti

Rome — One of Italy's most original young comics, Massimo Troisi, embarks on his fourth self-directed film, "The Ways Of The Lord Are Finite," with a commendable search for new ground to exhibit his talents. Results, unfortunately, are not up to snuff. This costume pic set in the early years of Fascism is thrown together with too little structure and filming savvy, to the detriment of both humor and whatever point it was striving to make. Local fans have demonstrated a willingness to wait patiently for the comedian's signature jokes, told in a Neapolitan accent. Chances for offshore playoff look remote.

Story, put together by Troisi and Anna Pavagnano, has Camillo (Troisi) hysterically — i.e., psychosomatically — paralyzed from the waist down when his French fiancee Vittoria (Jo Champa) breaks off their engagement. Exactly why a small-town barber like Camillo would have a doctor "psychoanalyze" him in the first place is never explained. Nor do we ever see patient and doctor together, just the medico writing vain letters to Vienna for advice on the case.

Many overlong scenes later, we find Camillo at home being taken care of by barber-brother Marco Messeri. Out of friendship for a sensitive, shy poet who's also paraplegic, Orlando (Massimo Bonetti), Camillo engineers an introduction to a girlfriend of Vittoria's, but the plan backfires; the g.f. is a card-carrying Fascist, and his pal falls for Camillo's own girl instead. Camillo regains the use of his legs for a while when Vittoria comes back to him, but loses them when he thinks she's taken up with Orlando. In the meantime he gets thrown in jail by the Fascists for two years. Guess who gets him out? The loyal Orlando, now inexplicably a member of the Fascist hierarchy ... so much for character consistency.

All is resolved in a sentimental ending set in postcard Paris.

Troisi is unquestionably a likable comic who gets a lot of mileage out of very little really funny businss. In "Ways Of The Lord," he hits the mark with a few good lines, but hardly enough to carry a feature-length film. Like many youngsters who have fallen victim to their own poor scripting, lensing and direction, Troisi radiates hidden talent begging for some professional discipline. Technically, this film is undistinguished, jumpy and hard to follow. Supporting actors Jo Champa and Marco Messeri are fetching and hold the line a hair's-breadth this side of schmaltz. — *Yung.*

Bouba
(ISRAELI)

A Hetz 2 production. Produced by Jacob Kotzky. Directed by Ze-ev Revach. Screenplay, Hillel Mittelpunkt, Revach, Kotzky, based on play by Mittelpunkt; camera (color), Ilan Rosenberg; editor, Zion Avrahmian; music, Dov Seltzer; sound, Itamar Ben-Yaakov; art direction, Eitan Levy. Reviewed at the Rio Film Festival, Nov. 22, 1987. Running time: **87 MIN.**
Bouba . . . . Ze-ev Revach
Rachel . . . . Etty Steinmetz-Nahmias
Eli . . . . Eli Dankner
   Also with: Yossi Graber, Yona Elian, Asher Tzarfati, Shlomo Wishinsky, Shlomo Tarshish, Ezra Kafri, Ruth Segal.

Rio de Janeiro — This is the second attempt by actor-director Ze-ev Revach to depart from his role as a highly successful popular comic and make a more ambitious statement. Again he chooses to deal with marginal losers who have been either forgotten or ignored by society, and again he has confused his local fans completely by the total change of style.

Bouba (Hebrew for "doll") is the nickname of the hero, a man who once distinguished himself in action, saving a comrade by pulling him out of a burning tank. Stunned from shellshock, he has lived since as a recluse, in a bus wreck, near a gas station, working the pumps and sweeping the floor to make a living and hardly speaking with anybody.

Ten years later his self-imposed solitude is disrupted by two separate events. His brother, Eli, a former prizefighter turned goon, seeks refuge in Bouba's bus from the wrath of his boss, whom he has swindled. At the same time, a young girl from a slum, on her way to a disco competition, is stranded in the gas station, and asks for a 1-night shelter. This encounter between three persons, evidently all losers and each facing his lot in a different way, leads to disappointment, misery and death. At the end, Bouba realizes he has to take a stand after all, and by doing so gets a second lease on life.

Shot in the southern part of Israel, chosen for its barren and desolate landscape of yellowish hills on which Bouba roams alone most of the time, a physical reflection of his state of mind, the film captures the special atmosphere of the place and integrates it effectively into the context.

Revach's acting is totally committed to the character, depicted as a social victim who has given up, Etty Steinmetz-Nahmias is keen but still rough at the edges as the aspiring disco queen and Eli Dankner manages to infuse a touch of emotion and humanity under a rough and tough exterior. Some stage veterans, in smaller parts, forget they are playing for the camera and provide some grossly overdone performances.

Ilan Rosenberg's camera uses the locations to the best advantage and Dov Seltzer's music adds its own bit to the pathos. Not a perfect film, it is still worth more than the brief career it had on Israeli screens last winter, but may do better with audiences which do not identify Revach with a certain genre and thus aren't disappointed when he doesn't deliver as expected. Reception in Rio was highly appreciative and film won Intl. Film Critics' (Fipresci) award. — *Edna.*

Nocturno Amor Que Te Vas
(Nocturnal Love That Goes Away)
(MEXICAN)

A Peliculas Mexicanas release of a Universidad Nacional Autonoma de México (UNAM)-Dirección de Actividades Cinematográficas production. Produced by Patricia Weingartshofer. Directed by Marcela Fernández Violante. Screenplay, Jorge Pérez Grovas, adapted by Pérez Grovas, Fernández Violante; camera (color), Arturo de la Rosa; editor, Ramón Aupart; sound, Raúl Sinobas. Reviewed at Acapulco Film Festival, Nov. 13, 1987. Running time: **101 MIN.**
Carmen Pérez . . . . Patricia Reyes Spíndola
Trompetas . . . . . Sergio Ramos (Camanche)
Alcoholic mother . . . . Leonor Llansas
Chuy . . . . Uriel Chávez
   Also with: Dunia Saldivar, Ivone Chávez, Yair de Rubi.

Acapulco — Mexican director Marcela Fernández Violante's latest feature "Nocturnal Love That Goes Away" is an artistic and technical failure owing to an intriguing but underdeveloped script and obvious low budget. Pic was produced by the National U., where Fernández Violante heads the film department CUEC.

It concerns a divorced domestic (Patricia Reyes Spíndola) with two children and an alcoholic mother. She remarries a Mexico City taxi driver (Uriel Chávez) who, the night after the wedding, picks up a mysterious mariachi (Sergio Ramos a.k.a. Camanche) on his way to a local pilgrimage. To the taxi driver's chagrin, the pilgrimage takes place many hours away from the capital and he doesn't return home until late the next night. Although his wife has been worried, the extra fare can help the family.

A month later, the cabbie meets up with the mariachi once again, this time he's looking for a ride for his friend. The taxi driver takes off with his new fare, disappearing into the night never to return, although his blood-stained taxi is seen abandoned in the parking lot of a shopping mall. Back home, Reyes Spíndola does not give up hope. She continues looking for her husband even after weeks pass and her search puts her in danger.

Meandering script follows the misadventures of the alcoholic mother (Leonor Llansas), the children, the callous employer, et al. It makes illogical leaps in the narrative bringing Reyes Spíndola back to the mariachi and following him on the street, juxtaposed with cutaways showing the solitary taxi bearing still-wet blood a full month after the disappearance. Pic's ending is neither convincing nor satisfying.

Fernández Violante inserts various fantasy sequences, using Christian and indigenous Mexican symbols, but they are obvious and awkward in design and tend to distance the viewer. In one scene a technician clearly is seen trying to hide from the camera.

In the past, Fernández Violante has demonstrated she can work with limited resources and within a rushed production sked, as in her meritorious 1979 "Mistero." But "Nocturnal Love" lacks this inventiveness. Most shots appear to have been executed in only one take, with no way to eradicate tech errors. The finished film here is only a frustrating bare-bones outline. — *Lent.*

Macu, La Mujer Del Policia
(Macu, The Policeman's Wife)
(VENEZUELAN)

A Macu Films and Cinearte production. Directed by Solveig Hoogesteijn. Screenplay, Hoogesteijn, Milagros Rodriguez; camera (color), Andrés Agusti; editor, José Alcade; music, Víctor Cuica. Reviewed at Rio de Janeiro Film Festival (competing), Nov. 20, 1987. Running time: **91 MIN.**
   With: Daniel Alvarado, María Luisa Mosquera, Frank Hernández, Tito Aponte, Ana Casteli, Carmen Palma, Iván Feo, Ana María Paredes, Daniela Alvarado, Carlos Daniel Alvarado, Argelia Bravo, Angeli Gutierrez, Mónica Juarez, Douglas Reyes, María Fernanda Urguelles, Hugo Vargas.

Rio de Janeiro — Three youngsters have disappeared and, although no proof is available, the main suspect is Ismael, a burly policeman in his mid 30s. Only a few years earlier he had married Macu, an 11-year-old child who, within three years, bore him two children. She now has fallen in love with Simon, also a teenager, and it is he and two of his friends who have disappeared. Their families and neighbors point an accusing finger at Ismael.

The physical environment and atmosphere of a Venezuelan barrio is well caught by director Solveig Hoogesteijn, but although María Luisa Mosquera (Macu), Daniel Alvarado (Ismael) and Frank Hernández (Simon) do quite well in the main roles, the film fails to generate the story's potential suspense and emotional impact although it does, at times, convey the social background that lead up to the triple murder.

Due to its factual background, well known in Venezuela, the film could be successful on its home ground, but it is unlikely to travel well. — *Amig.*

Las Movidas del Mofles
(Mofles' Escapades)
(MEXICAN)

A Peliculas Mexicanas release of a Tijuana Films production. Produced by Juan Abusaid Ríos, Pedro Martin Gurrido. Directed by Javier Durán. Screenplay, Francisco (Pancho) Sánchez, Marco Eduardo Contreras; camera (color), Antonio Ruiz; editor, Sergio Soto; music, Gustavo Pimentel, with the appearance of the groups Generaciíon 2000, Los Infieles. Reviewed at Hollywood Twin theater II, N.Y., Nov. 28, 1987. Running time: **89 MIN.**
Mofles . . . . Rafael Inclán
Abrelatas . . . . Manuel (Flaco) Ibáñez
Chopo . . . . Joaquín García (Borolas)
Don Gastón . . . . Charly Valentino
Rebeca del Mar . . . . Merle Uribe

Also with: Myrra Saaveda, Maria Cardenal, Alejandro Ciangherotti, Victor Junco, Raul (Chato) Padilla, Yirah Aparicio, Leo Villanueva, Oscar Fentanes, Sonia Piña, Polo Ortín, Estrella Fuentes, Alfredo (Pelón) Solares, Arturo Cobo, Gina Leal.

Mexican feature "Las Movidas del Mofles" (Mofles' Escapades), starring comedian Rafael Inclán, is a half-hearted sequel to the 1986 picaresque comedy "Mofles y Los Mecánicos." If the first venture, directed by Victor Manuel (Güero) Castro, lacked much in the way of a storyline, the second, helmed by Javier Durán, is completely devoid of narrative. Pic is little more than a series of spicy scenes featuring a group of garage mechanics and their drunken exploits.

Lots of inane filler has been inserted between these vacuous scenes, two party sequences, a poolside wingding and several nightclub episodes featuring various musical numbers by groups Generación 2000 and Los Infieles.

Tech credits are passable and acting is strictly caricature. "Mofles' Escapades" needs more than a few naughty mechanics to get its motor started. — Lent.

The Couch Trip

An Orion Pictures release. Produced by Lawrence Gordon. Directed by Michael Ritchie. Screenplay, Steven Kampmann, Will Porter, Sean Stein, from Ken Kolb's novel; camera (Deluxe color), Donald E. Thorin; editor, Richard A. Harris; music, Michel Colombier; production design, Jimmie Bly; set decoration, Gary Fettis; sound, Richard S. Church; James R. Alexander; assistant director-associate producer, Tom Mack; coproducer, Gordon A. Webb; casting, Patricia Mock. Reviewed at Mann Plaza theater, Westwood, Calif., Jan. 5, 1988. MPAA Rating: R. Running time: **98 MIN.**

John Burns	Dan Aykroyd
Donald Becker	Walter Matthau
George Maitlin	Charles Grodin
Laura Rollins	Donna Dixon
Harvey Michaels	Richard Romanus
Vera Maitlin	Mary Gross
Lawrence Baird	David Clennon
Perry Kovin	Arye Gross
Robin	Victoria Jackson
Condom Father	Chevy Chase

Hollywood — "The Couch Trip" is a relatively low-key Dan Aykroyd vehicle that restores some of the comic actor's earlier charm simply by not trying too hard. Relying as much on character as shtick, Aykroyd is a likable everyman here out to right the minor indignities and injustices in the world. Although film never really fires on all cylinders and Walter Matthau is underutilized in a buddy subplot, "The Couch Trip" is moderately diverting and could be a welcome relief after the frenzy of Christmas pictures.

At his best, Aykroyd's appeal is his cool command of every situation and here, as an escaped mental case impersonating a psychiatrist, he can get out of any jam, even a straight jacket, with no sweat.

As an obstreperous prisoner biding his time in a Cicero, Ill. looney bin, Aykroyd trades places with his attending shrink, Dr. Baird (David Clennon), and moves to L.A. to fill in for radio therapist Dr. Maitlin (Charles Grodin) who is having a mental breakdown of his own.

Screenplay by Steven Kampmann, Will Porter and Sean Stein doesn't break any new ground in suggesting there is a thin line between the certifiably crazy and certifiably sane, but it still manages some gentle jabs at the pretensions of the psychiatric profession. When, in the guise of Dr. Baird, Aykroyd takes several busloads of patients to a baseball game as group therapy, the suggestion that people should just go out and have some fun instead of spending years on the couch makes a lot of sense.

While radio gurus are an apt target for satire, the film is over its head when it proposes that all mental illness can be treated by the equivalent of two aspirins and a pat on the back. Director Michael Ritchie displays once again a keen eye for the flimsiness of social conventions, but gets in trouble when he tries to stuff too much plot into the picture.

As a mock priest and another fringe member of society, Matthau is Aykroyd's soulmate, but the connection between the men is too thinly drawn to have much meaning. Donna Dixon, stunningly beautiful though she is, is impossible to swallow as a brilliant psychiatrist, particularly since her duties include signaling commercial breaks on radio and standing around posing.

As Grodin's greedy lawyer, Richard Romanus is delightfully slimy and with a few glances reveals all the loathesomeness of his character. Grodin and Mary Gross as his wife both deliver fine comic performances and seem as if they could actually be a couple, a rarity in films. Matthau apparently wants to make up for the briefness of his role by overdoing it in his limited time on screen.

Tech credits are fine with Jimmie Bly's production design creating the feel of Southern California opulence without going overboard while Donald E. Thorin's camerawork suggests the shadows in the sunshine. It's Aykroyd's film and he seems right at home playing someone who may or may not be mad. — Jagr.

Kandyland

A New World Pictures release. Produced by Rick Blumenthal. Executive producer, Robert Schnitzer. Coproduced by Leo Leichter, Richard Hahn. Directed by Schnitzer. Screenplay, Schnitzer, Toni Serritello; camera (Technicolor), Robert Brinkman; editor, Jeffrey Reiner; music, George Michalski; production design, Paul Sussman; art direction, Archie D'Amico, Billie Greenbaum; set decoration, John Edgerton; sound, Edwin J. Somers; costumes, Vicki Graef; assistant director, Herb Shulman; associate producers, Serritello, Ron Shapiro; casting, Joyce Maio, Louis Goldstein. Reviewed at New World Pictures screening room, L.A., Jan. 6, 1988. MPAA Rating: R. Running time: **93 MIN.**

Joni	Kim Evenson
Frank	Charles Laulette
Harlow	Sandahl Bergman
Roy	Cole Stevens
Mad Dog	Bruce Baum
Eppy	Alan Toy
Biff	Irwin Keyes
Bruce Belnap	Steve Kravitz
Diva	Catlyn Day
Vampira	Ja-Net Hintzen
Scarlet	Chrissy Ratay
Betty	Brenda Winston

Hollywood — Women's lib goes full circle in "Kandyland" where being your own person means having a career as a stripper. This insipid premise is carried off with a straight face and a heavy hand and results are predictably lifeless. Box-office interest will be minimal as New World continues a mandatory regional release before putting it on the homevid shelf the end of this month.

Kandyland is just your friendly neighborhood strip joint, but it's a respectable club. Customers wear 3-piece suits and are nice guys just blowing off some steam. Into this clubby atmosphere comes young Joni Sekorsky (Kim Evenson) looking to change her life.

For some reason Joni seems to find self-expression in taking her clothes off in front of cat-calling, horny men. As her mentor Harlow (Sandahl Bergman) tells her, "it's an art form, it takes commitment." Screenplay by Robert Schnitzer and Toni Serritello is full of such howlers delivered with great seriousness.

"Kandyland" is, in fact, the brainchild of Schnitzer who also directed and exec produced. Staging and editing are clumsy and the real justification for the film seems to be to show as much flesh as possible, but even that becomes numbing after a while.

Performances are mostly awful with the exception of Evenson who is appealingly playful but trapped by the limitations of her role. Forced to ask her boyfriend (Charles Laulette) for permission to become a dancer, she is reduced to the stereotypical dumb blond who happens to have a great body. Despite flashes of charm and vulnerability, it is impossible to make this part more than it is.

As her greasemonkey boyfriend, Laulette is too stiff to suggest any real feelings or affection and Bergman seems lost in her own world half the time. Bruce Baum as the club comic is likeable and adds a few moments of needed humor.

It's all pretty foolish stuff shot with a minimum of style and a maximum of crudeness and despite lines like "there are no mistakes, only lessons," this one is a mistake.
—Jagr.

Cobra Verde
(Slave Coast)
(WEST GERMAN)

A UGC (France) release (DEG in U.S.) of a Werner Herzog Filmproduktion production, in association with ZDF and the Ghana Film Industry Corp. Executive producers, Walter Saxer, Salvatore Basile. Produced by Lucki Stipetic. Written and directed by Werner Herzog, based on Bruce Chatwin's book "The Viceroy of Ouidah;" camera (color), Viktor Ruzicka, Thomas Mauch; editor, Maixmiliane Mainka; music, Popol Vuh; production design, Fabrizio Carola; costumes, Gisela Stoch; sound (Dolby), Haymo H. Heyder; makeup, Berthold Sack; assistant director, Salvatore Basile. Reviewed at the Havas screening room, Neuilly, France, Jan. 6, 1988. Running time: **110 MIN.**

Francisco Manoel da Silva	Klaus Kinski
Taparica	King Ampaw
Don Octavio Coutinho	Jose Lewgoy
Captain Fraternidade	Salvatore Basile
Bossa Ahadee	His Royal Highness Nana Agyefi Kwame II de Nsein

(English-language dialog)

Paris — Werner Herzog has another bout with tropical madness in "Cobra Verde," a picaresque tale of a 19th century Brazilian slave trader in Africa. The German helmer's favorite themes of lunatic exploits and the conflict of civilizations run riot and alter ego Klaus Kinski is along for the trip, but the hallucinatory jungle fever of earlier Herzog work such as "Aguirre" and "Fitzcarraldo" unfortunately has broken. "Cobra Verde" seems a perfunctory scrapbook of Herzog eccentricities that will have followers connecting the dots to previous pics, but will leave the uninitiated bored or indifferent.

It won't help that Herzog again has opted for an English-language soundtrack. Apart from being a real rip in the film's texture, the post-synchronization is egregiously poor. Why all this maniacal pursuit of geographic and ethnographic accuracy (with location lensing in Colombia, Brazil and Ghana), when it's all to be sabotaged by a Babel of assorted English-speaking voices that seem thrown by slightly drunken ventriloquists?

The corker is the script. Herzog has loosely adapted Bruce Chatwin's novel, "The Viceroy Of Ouidah," based on the life of a legendary Brazilian slave dealer, who despite his metier was known to have certain humanitarian graces.

Herzog trashes the biographical and historical for a dash through his familiar gallery of the batty and the battered.

Kinski, donning his Claws Kinky mask (wild haired, mad-eyed, lips twisted into a permanent snarl), is Francisco Manoel da Silva, a ruined Brazilian rancher driven to banditry under the awesome moniker Cobra Verde (Green Serpent). Ironically, this early outlaw career is dispensed with in an expository sequence so hurriedly elliptical it seems to have been edited with a machete.

Tiring of his current life, Kinski soon slithers into the employ of a wealthy and libidinous plantation owner, where he emulates the boss by promptly impregnating his three daughters.

Rather than being put to death, Kinski is "rewarded" by local officials by being dispatched on a special mission to Western Africa to revive a slave network broken by the unhospitable bloodletting of a tribal king. Kinski's patrons of course expect him to meet an immediate death upon arrival.

Kinski fools them all by succeeding. Overthrowing the mad king with the help of a rival (and apparently no less nutty) brother, Kinski builds a new slave empire with himself as its lord.

It's of short duration, Kinski all along has been swindled by his correspondents back home, slavery is suddenly abolished and, to top it off, the mad sovereign whom Kinski has put on the throne turns out to be not as looney as all that and deposes the white invader. Kinski flees, pursued by a spidery black cripple, and is swept away by the tide as he vainly tries to gain the sea in a skiff. Back in the village, a coquettish black girl leads a local chorus in exultant song. Ah, the noble savages.

Herzog has nothing to say about his protagonist, who is not over-reaching utopian dreamer in the Herzog mode, but a jaded, cynical being who follows his destiny, rather pulling it along behind him. As played by Kinski, he is an inscrutable cynic, at best stupidly audacious but never noble or earthstriding.

Without the usual Kinski fire, the film plods through familiar ground of exploiter-and-exploited melodrama with no new variations. A few sequences stand out in the general tedium, such as Kinski's training of an Amazon army to fight the crazy king (which leads to an anticlimactic, bloodless victory).

None of the supporting professional cast deserves mention. A real African chieftain by the name of His Royal Highness Nana Agyefi Kwae II de Nsein plays the mad king with some juvenile panache.

Tech credits are okay though lensing suffers due to replacement of Thomas Mauch (who is said to have quit because of Kinski) by Viktor Ruzicka. The score is unmistakably Popol Vuh, but not the group's best.—*Len.*

Scavengers

A Triax Entertainment Group release. Produced by Chris Davies, David Barrett. Written and directed by Duncan McLachlan. Camera (J.T. Avanti color), Johan Van Der Veer, Nic Heroldt; editor, Patti Regan; music, Nick Picard; production design, Roy Rudolphe; art direction, Jay Avery; set decoration, Chelsea; sound, Dale Ray; costume design, Ele Parker; associate producer, Harriet Ephraim; casting, Mariah Cunningham. Reviewed at the UA Egyptian, L.A., Jan. 8, 1988. MPAA Rating: PG-13. Running time: 94 MIN.

Tom Reed	Kenneth Gilman
Kimberly Blake	Brenda Bakke
Col. Chenko	Crispin De Nys
February	Cocky (Two Bull) Tlhothalemaj

Hollywood — "Scavengers" wavers from being a bad parody of a high adventure movie to just being a bad high adventure movie. In any case, it's on the fast, low road to video.

Creaky organ grinder soundtrack sets the tone for this silly KGB-CIA caper where a swarthy ornithologist (Kenneth Gilman) and his g.f. (Brenda Bakke) become entwined in a drug operation involving the two agencies that has something to do with a Bible the Russkies fear could destroy the USSR's reputation.

It's a ludicrous idea which, combined with the mistaken identity theme, might have made a funny spoof. It is neither a spoof nor funny, except for a couple of unintentional laughs when the Russkies are uttering one or another of their stilted lines of dialog that half the time doesn't synch with their lips.

In fact, pic is made so crudely as to be at all time distracting to whatever else is going on in the way of action. The scoring seems as if someone went to a music store and bought an old album of instrumentals that have themes to suit certain moods and inserted them in the film without much thought to suitability.

Essentially, "Scavengers" is one lengthy chase scene that has the hero and heroine dangling dangerously out of vintage bomber planes, driving Land Rovers and tanks and shooting bazookas at their pursuers — all the while managing to escape unscathed and smiling, looking most times as if they just stepped out of Banana Republic.

Cheerful rapport between Gilman and Blake gives some life to the production. Even if they aren't given many lines of repartee to work from, they manage to create a certain bonding out of a lot of hysteria.

As opposed to the awful assembly of this pic and generally low production values, oddly enough there seems to be a certain authenticity to the location, unidentified in the credits (reportedly Zimbabwe). The village people and the village itself look African.—*Brit.*

Cop

An Atlantic Entertainment Group release of a Harris-Woods production. Produced by James B. Harris, James Woods. Executive producers, Thomas Coleman, Michael Rosenblatt. Directed by Harris. Screenplay, Harris, based on novel "Blood On The Moon" by James Ellroy; camera (color), Steve Dubin; editor, Anthony Spano; music, Michel Colombier; production design, Gene Rudolf; costumes, Gale Parker Smith; assistant director, Richard Wells; casting, Pamela Rack; associate producer-production manager, Ann Gindberg. Reviewed at Magno Review 2, N.Y., Nov. 12, 1987. MPAA Rating: R. Running time: 110 MIN.

Lloyd Hopkins	James Woods
Kathleen McCarthy	Lesley Ann Warren
Dutch Peltz	Charles Durning
Whitey Haines	Charles Haid
Fred Gaffney	Raymond J. Barry
Joanie Pratt	Randi Brooks
Bobby Franco	Steve Lambert
Amy Cransfield	Annie McEnroe
Penny Hopkins	Vicki Wauchope

Shot under the title "Blood On The Moon," one of three James Ellroy novels with same central character, "Cop" is a modestly executed, off-target police drama giving actor James Woods another outlet for his compellingly schizophrenic persona. As star vehicles go, this one's good, but the overall package fails to fill the big screen.

Given his reputation for depicting amoral, maniacal outcasts, perhaps the only producer that would give Woods a chance to play a sympathetic guy is, well, himself. Joining Woods' for his first production, coproducer James B. Harris' screenplay and direction gives his star partner complete freedom to deliver everything in his bag of tricks plus a new one: warmth.

Lloyd Hopkins (Woods) is a good cop who clearly loves his work and his 8-year-old daughter; in that order, harps his ever-critical wife (Jan McGill). Although Hopkins' bedtime stories about L.A.P.D. detective work tickle the little girl (Vicki Wauchope), the parents disagree vehemently on how much their daughter should know about daddy's work in the cruel world.

"Cop" fortunately avoids the cliché device of the workaholic cop/estranged wife since it begins with the marriage already on the rocks. She's soon out of the picture as Mrs. Hopkins moves out with the child, leaving a note labeling Woods "deeply disturbed."

She may be right. Domestic pressures and a hard-to-crack serial murder case lead to the detective's lapses in judgment. His affairs with women he meets in the course of his investigation get him into trouble with his superiors (including Charles Durning).

One of the implicated is Lesley Ann Warren, a chain-smoking, feminist poet and bookshopkeeper who turns out to play a pivotal role in the murder mystery hounding Woods.

Warren's character and tantalizing performance appear fully 50 minutes into the running time, a fact that adds to pic's off-balance feeling. Likewise, fourth-billed Charles Haid never shows up until 40 minutes into the film. (Also, why did the "Hill Street Blues" alumnus take another role as a policeman?)

For the abrupt ending, Woods' cop finally snaps and luckily it's the killer who's in the way, a character that's introduced only to die in the minimally suspenseful 1-on-1 showdown in a ill-lit gymnasium.

Technical contributions are routine. Fun-to-watch performances of Woods, Warren and Durning notwithstanding, "Cop" is a bit of a muddle singularly suited to a sturdy post-theatrical shelf life. — *Binn.*

Return Of The Living Dead Part II

A Lorimar Film Entertainment release of a Greenfox production. Produced by Tom Fox. Coproducer, William S. Gilmore. Executive producer, Eugene C. Cashman. Written and directed by Ken Wiederhorn. Camera (color), Robert Elswit; editor, Charles Bornstein; music, J. Peter Robinson; music supervision, David Chackler; special makeup, Kenny Myers; production manager, Robin S. Clark; sound, Glenn Anderson; casting, Shari Rhodes. Reviewed at Warner theater, N.Y., Jan. 11, 1988. MPAA Rating: R. Running time: 89 MIN.

Ed	James Karen
Joey	Thom Mathews
Jesse Wilson	Michael Kenworthy
Lucy Wilson	Marsha Dietlein
Tom Essex	Dana Ashbrook
Doc Mandel	Philip Bruns
Brenda	Suzanne Snyder

Also with: Thor Van Lingen, Jason Hogan, Suzan Stadner, Jonathon Terry, Sally Smythe, Allan Trautman, Don Maxwell, Reynold Cindrich, Mitch Pileggi, Arturo Bonilla, Terrence Riggins, James McIntire.

While raising an army of zombies from their graves, "Return Of The Living Dead Part II" succeeds in burying itself so deep, even home-video may not be able to resurrect it after it dies at the boxoffice. Billed as a comedy/horror flick, it is neither scary nor funny and adds salt in the wound with an obnoxious soundtrack of grating rock music.

Story is familiar to "Living Dead" followers. This time a canister falls off an army truck and three kids — including Jesse Wilson (Michael Kenworthy) — discover it. Curiosity leads Jesse's two friends to fool around with a few buttons and suddenly a weird fog spews from the container, awakening a ghoul who is packed inside as neatly as tuna fish.

As the fog spreads, it is a call to arms for the occupants of a cemetery, unleashing a throng of decaying cadavers. The balance of the film is a prolonged chase scene as these creatures pursue Jesse, Lucy (Marsha Dietlein), Tom (Dana Ashbrook) and Doc (Philip Bruns) through the streets of a small town.

The overall effect of "Living Dead" is supposed to be tongue-in-cheek but turns out to be foot in mouth as dialog seems aimed at 4-year-olds.

The only saving grace in a totally misguided effort is the performance of character actor Philip Bruns who is quite funny as a slightly off-the-wall doctor. He mugs for the camera and delivers his lines with fine-tuned comedic timing. — *Chuk.*

Rent-A-Cop

A Kings Road Entertainment release. Produced by Raymond Wagner. Directed by Jerry London. Screenplay, Dennis Shryack, Michael Blodgett; camera (Technicolor prints), Giuseppe Rotunno; editor, Robert Lawrence; music, Jerry Goldsmith; sound (Dolby), Amelio Verona; production design, Tony Masters; art direction, Aurelio Crugnola; set decoration, Franco Fumagalli; costume design, Moss Mabry; assistant director, Tony Brandt; associate producer, John D. Schofield; casting, Judith Holstra, Marcia Ross. Reviewed at Manhattan theater, N.Y., Jan. 5, 1988. MPAA Rating: R. Running time: 95 MIN.
Church . . . . .Burt Reynolds
Della . . . . .Liza Minnelli
Dancer . . . . .James Remar
Roger . . . . .Richard Masur
Beth . . . . .Dionne Warwick
Lemar . . . . .Bernie Casey
Pitts . . . . .Robby Benson
Alexander . . . . .John Stanton
Wieser . . . . .John P. Ryan

Burt Reynolds racks up three flops in a row on his current comeback trail (with two more pictures in the can) via "Rent-A-Cop," a cheesy little crime thriller. Maiden release from Kings Road Entertainment pointlessly reunites Reynolds with "Lucky Lady" costar Liza Minnelli, but even her flamboyant thesping in a stock role fails to make this one watchable.

Pic starts off promisingly as a sort of followup to Reynolds' "Sharky's Machine," with him working again with fellow cop Bernie Casey on a big drug bust. Nutcase James Remar wipes everybody out except Reynolds, who is suspected of being crooked and bounced from the force. He gets work as a "rent-a-cop," working undercover (dressed as a Santa Claus) in a department store. In an awkwardly staged but key subplot, Minnelli, as a Chicago hooker, has been saved from Remar by Reynolds and now attaches herself to him for protection.

He laboriously traces the killer to a potential scandal involving hookers and ex-cops, with shady Richard Masur the key link in the underworld chain. Loose ends of the plot are sorted out via gunplay.

Lowgrade programmer is an inauspicious feature from tv helmer Jerry London, and plays on the big screen like a subpar episode of "Starsky & Hutch." Interiors were filmed in Rome evidently to save a buck, but not noticeable except in a disco sequence where all the extras look Italian. Top creative team including cinematographer Giuseppe Rotunno and scorer Jerry Goldsmith turn in uncharacteristically ho-hum jobs.

Reynolds looks bored and is boring here, with an ill-fitting toupé that is downright embarrassing from one closeup angle. Minnelli is a lot of fun as the flamboyant prostie, but one inevitably wonders why no better role (or screen vehicle) can be concocted for the star, to exploit her musical talents. Ditto Dionne Warwick, absent from the screen since "Slaves" in 1969, and thoroughly wasted here as head of a callgirl ring. Remar is laughably hammy as the narcissistic killer.
—*Lor.*

Montecarlo Gran Casinò
(ITALIAN)

A Filmauro release and production. Produced by Luigi and Aurelio De Laurentiis. Executive producer, Maurizio Amati. Directed by Carlo Vanzina. Screenplay, Carlo & Enrico Vanzina; camera (Technicolor), Luigi Kuveiller; editor, Ruggero Mastroianni; music, Manuel De Sica. Reviewed at Fiamma Cinema, Rome, Dec. 25, 1987. Running time: 97 MIN.
Furio . . . . .Christian De Sica
Gino . . . . .Massimo Boldi
Silvia . . . . .Florence Guérin
Oscar . . . . .Ezio Greggio
Patrizia . . . . .Lisa Stothard
Also with: Paolo Rossi, Enrico Beruschi, Philippe Leroy.

Rome — Director-scripter frères Carlo and Enrico Vanzina pop their second film of the season out of the oven, an Xmas quickie of considerably less interest than their Carol Altstarrer "My First 40 Years." In "Montecarlo Gran Casinò" the Vanzinas drag out their stock company of comic thesps (Christian De Sica, Massimo Boldi, Ezio Greggio), pair them with leggy femmes and plug in a series of dully familiar gaming tales. Pic has done so-so, with better biz in small towns.

The three stories are edited together but unconnected. In one, De Sica is a big winner at the casino; soon fleeced of his cash, he is forced to spend "a night of love" with a flabby old millionairess. Conclusion is as distastefully misogynist as it is unfunny.

In another episode, Massimo Boldi and his brother come to Montecarlo to buy an apartment, but lose their liras when Boldi lets beautiful gambler Florence Guérin twist

him around her finger. Guérin, who sleeps where the money is, is the mistress of a rich Italian and together the three stage an inept robbery of a diamond necklace. It's a fake.

Ezio Greggio plays a professional card shark who meets his match, a French gambler more sly than he is. Teaming up with a young cheat, he wins against the Frenchman and gets back his girl Lisa Stothard, another fortune-hunter of easy virtue.

Location work in Monaco and its highlife hotels is atmospheric. De Sica and Boldi are likable thesps unable to salvage unsavory, standardized parts. The girls are pretty.
—*Yung.*

The Lone Runner

A Trans World Entertainment release of an Ovidio Assonitis production. Produced by Maurizio Maggi. Directed by Roger (Ruggero) Deodato. Screenplay, Chris Trainor, Steven Luotto; camera (Technicolor), Robert Bennet (Robert Forges Davanzati); editor, Eugene Miller (Eugenio Alabiso); music, Charles Cooper (Carlo Maria Cordio); art direction, Bob Glaser; sound, Carl Schaefer; special effects supervisor, Burt Spiegel; associate producer, Peter Graf (Romeo Assonitis); assistant director, Jerry Vaughan. Reviewed at the UA Egyptian Theater, L.A., Jan. 10, 1988. MPAA Rating: PG. Running time: 85 MIN.
Garrett, the Lone Runner . .Miles O'Keeffe
Analisa Summerking . . . . . .Savina Gersak
Emerick . . . . .Michael J. Aronin
Skorm . . . . .John Steiner
Nimbus . . . . .Hal Yamanouchi
Mr. Summerking . . . . .Donald Hodson
Misha . . . . .Ronald Lacey

Hollywood — "The Lone Runner" is a waste-of-time adventure opus that won't even please the 12-year-olds it was designed to attract. Yawning audience of two at an opening weekend show bore witness to the fact that this has no business (and will do none) in theatrical release, and pic is a painfully poor example of the sort of product polluting theaters due only to homevideo contractual obligations.

A basically Italian production lensed in Morocco in early 1986, Ovido Assonitis production betrays its debt to spaghetti Westerns not only through its shooting title — "Fistful Of Diamonds" — but via the imitation Ennio Morricone score and the loner figure cut by star Miles O'Keeffe.

American thesp plays the eponymous bounty hunting hero who dressed very much like the Man with No Name, says even less, and rides a horse through modern Arab lands toting only a crossbow which he loads with explosive-tipped arrows. Fortunately for him, no one in these parts has ever heard of guns.

Inane, never-never-land plot has O'Keeffe performing several daring rescues of European rich girl Savina Gersak, whose main talent resides in getting kidnaped by a succession of baddies. Gersak's dad is in possession of a stash of invaluable diamonds, which suffer no end

of indignities at the hands of the villains, unlike Gersak herself, who is tied up a lot but never molested even by O'Keeffe, for whom she clearly has eyes.

Technical quality is subpar, with postsynch work sounding as though it were done in a phone booth, and violence quotient in the physical action proves very mild, befitting the PG rating. With his 3-day stubble and long hair, O'Keeffe looks to be posing for fashion photos, while Gersak manages to convey some attractive spunk under adverse circumstances.—*Cart.*

Hard Rock Zombies

A Cannon Films release (in 1985) of a Patel/Shah Film Co. production. Executive producer, Shashi Patel. Produced and directed by Krishna Shah. Screenplay, David Ball, Shah; camera (color), Tom Richmond; supervising editor, Ami Bosé; music, songs, Paul Sabu; sound, Steve Nelson; art direction, Cynthia A. Sowder; production manager-assistant director, Reuben Watt; special effects makeup, John Buechler; second unit camera, Toyomichi Kurita; additional camera, Peter Austin; associate producers, Sigurjon Sighvatsson, Steve Golin; casting, Allison Jones. Reviewed on Vestron Video vidcassette, N.Y., Dec. 22, 1987. MPAA Rating: R. Running time: 94 MIN.
Jesse . . . . .E.J. Curcio
Chuck .Sam Mann
Tommy . . . . .Geno Andrews
Robby . . . . .Mick McMains
Cassie . . . . .Jennifer Coe
Elsa . . . . , .Lisa Toothman
Also with: Ted Wells, Crystal Shaw, Jack Bliesener, Susan Prevatte, H.G. Golas, Nadia.

"Hard Rock Zombies," a pickup briefly released by Cannon in 1985, is a not-bad cult item combining rock music and horror spoofing. Picture was lensed in California in 1983 in tandem with "American Drive-In," with latter film economically using the "Zombies" feature as the film-within-the-film playing at the drive-in.

E.J. Curcio plays the lead singer of a heavy metal band on tour, which gets mixed up with a Hitler cult after picking up a pretty blond hitchhiker (Lisa Toothman, a.k.a. Donna Boise). The band is murdered, but fortunately Curcio was toying with some satanic lyrics taken from a book on raising the dead and, sure enough, this music is used to reanimate them as zombies.

Plot involves some silly run-ins with local types intent on banning rock music from their municipality, but catchy music and some effective satire, especially the zombies' rhythmic strutting, are the film's highlights. Horror buffs will note an inconsistency in pic's solutions to dealing with the problem of annihilating the undead and a silly sequence of good guys obtaining large blowups of celebrity posters (Jimi Hendrix, Marily Monroe, James Dean, etc.) to scare the zombies with is thoroughly unconvincing.

Pic would make an interesting college campus booking with "American Drive-In." —*Lor.*

Vernehmung der Zeugen
(Interrogation Of The Witness)
(EAST GERMAN)

A Defa Spielfilme production. Directed by Gunther Scholz. Screenplay, Manfred Richter, Scholz; camera (color), Claus Neumann; editor, Thea Richter; music, Friedbert Wissmann; art direction, Harri Lenpold. Reviewed at the Cairo Film Festival, Dec. 8, 1987. Running time: 76 MIN.
Maximilian . . . . Rene Steinke
Rainer . . . . Mario Gericke
Viola . . . . Anne Kasprzik
  Also with: Johanna Schall, Christine Schorn.

Cairo — Latest feature by East German helmer Gunther Scholz, "Interrogation Of The Witness," adopts a legal-scientific method of grilling actors to explore the making of a juvenile murderer. This novel approach is pulled off by a topnotch cast of thesps, who bring to life a convincing middle-class world. A watchable entry of serious intent, film should make fest rounds.

As the curtain opens, a woman doctor bends over the corpse of a teenage boy and announces to police, "My son killed him." Maximilian, the son (Rene Steinke), is at that moment trying to swallow a lethal dose of pills, but he's saved and his tragic story is recounted by the "witnesses" to his life.

First is obviously the mother, a tough career woman who makes Max leave Berlin and his granny to live in a country village with her and her new husband. Possessing a good amount of egotism himself, Max wars with family and classmates alike. Eventually, his natural dominance imposes itself at school, and he co-rules the class with Rainer (Mario Gericke), son of a poor drunk. The two boys even share a crush on pretty Viola (Anne Kasprzik), until Rainer and Viola become lovers under Max' eyes in one of pic's most plaintive scenes. Tragedy isn't far off, and when Max finds his dog slain (a gift to Viola), he knifes his rival Rainer in rage.

Leaning heavily on the psychological, "Interrogation" suffers a little from lack of action. Its teen characters are believable, however, and Steinke in the role of Maximilian is particularly appealing in his unhappy ambiguity. The interview gimmick lends pic consistency without being too restrictive. Overall, it's an interesting effort from a director worth watching. — Yung.

Van geluk gesproken
(Count Your Blessings)
(DUTCH)

A Cannon Tuschinski Film Distribution release of a Verenigde Nederlandsche Filmcompagnie production. Produced by Rob Houwer. Directed by Pieter Verhoeff. Screenplay, Jean van de Velde, Verhoef, from the novel by Marijke Höweler; camera (Eastmancolor, prints by Cineco), Paul van den Bos; editor, Ot Louw; music, Cees Bijlstra; art direction, Dorus van der Linden; assistant director, Wilfried Depeweg; production manager, Remmelt Remmelts. Reviewed at City Theater,

Amsterdam, Nov. 23, 1987. Running time: 99 MIN.
Martje . . . . Mirjam Sternheim
Karin . . . . Marijke Veugelers
Sjef . . . . Gerard Thoolen
Leo . . . . Peter Tuinman
Mother Kalk . . . . Loudi Nijhoff
Kalk . . . . Aart Lamberts
Harrie . . . . '. . . . . Michiel Romeyn
  Also with: Olga Zuiderhoek, Geert de Jong, Arend Jan Heerma van Voss.

Amsterdam — Chosen as the official Dutch candidate for the foreign-language Oscar nomination race prior to its domestic release, "Count Your Blessings" is an innovative gamble that has paid off here with press and public and could find favorable response abroad with imaginative marketing.

Scripted by director Pieter Verhoeff and Jean van de Velde from an ironic, sometimes satiric bestseller, pic is a group study of life in an apartment house in one of Amsterdam's poorer districts, with its protagonists drawn from various social strata.

Film observes the tenants with a sort of cool sympathy, as if they were specimens of a terrarium. The narrative is fragmented, ostensibly haphazard, though in fact artfully constructed, with camerawork and editing creating a hard, neutral, investigative texture. The soundtrack is richly composed of voices, sounds and pop, songs, inducing both a sense of familiarity yet keeping its distance with the characters.

The acting is uniformly excellent, with special kudos for newcomer Mirjam Sternheim, whom the helmer literally discovered in a café. A provincial drama school student, Sternheim brings exacting nuance and professionalism to the role of Martje, a student who shares an apartment with her brother.

Marijke Veugelers, as a blond with a couple of darkskinned daughters and Gerard Thoolen, as a grubby wheeler-dealer, also hand in fine performances.

Tech qualities stand out, notably soundwork and scoring. Unusual in conception and telling, "Count Your Blessings" remains always accessible and should appeal to audiences appreciative of new ways of filming, while being uninhibited enough to provoke lively criticism. — Wall.

Abba Ganuv
(The Skipper)
(ISRAELI)

A Ro'i Films production. Produced by Yehuda Barkan. Directed by Yankul Goldwasser. Screenplay, Haim Marin, based on idea by Pini Idan; camera (color), Ilan Rosenberg; editor, Anath Lubransky; music, Shlomo Gronich; songs composed and performed by Moshe Hillel, Boaz Shar'abi; sound, Shabtai Sarig; art direction, Ariel Glazer; costumes, Inbal Ba'al Taksa; casting, Nirith Yaron-Gronich. Reviewed at the Ben Yehuda Cinema, Tel Aviv, Dec. 17, 1987. Running time: 90 MIN.
Chico . . . . Yehuda Barkan
Ben . . . . Ben Zion

Galia . . . . Alona Kimchi
Maggie . . . . Karen Mor
Kugler . . . . Uri Shamir
  Also with: Geta Luca, Ilana Berkovitz, Zarah Vartanian, Dan Ardan, Lenny Ravitz, Yael Amit.

Tel Aviv — Yehuda Barkan has produced this melodrama to exploit his own thespian talents, after a series of lucrative candid camera epics which established him as a highly popular entertainer.

However, as an actor in a "Kramer vs. Kramer" type of story he fares less well, for beyond his affable personality, which comes through all right, he has trouble coping with the more emotional aspects of the plot he has chosen for himself. This is painfully evident since the story itself is indeed transparent and without strong performances, it doesn't stand up on its own merits.

What's more, Barkan enlisted the help of helmer Yankul Goldwasser and scripter Haim Marin, who are both obviously out of their depth with this kind of material and fail to deliver either the tears or the laughs which could have saved it.

Chico, a dedicated but not very responsible father refuses to hand his son, Ben, back to his estranged wife, when she returns after a five year absence with a new husband, an American millionaire, to ask for the boy. The case is taken to court, with a crooked lawyer, Kugler, trying to cheat the nice father, who finds a pretty legal adviser to save him at the last moment.

If Barkan has no trouble playing himself on camera, the rest of the cast is terribly self-conscious and amateurish, except for some veterans like Geta Luca who have too little to do. With a script that offers no substance to rely on, landscapes and aerial shots of Tel Aviv are thrown in at the slightest excuse, to add some footage necessary to fill up the required feature film length. Music is far too evident in its efforts to elicit the kind of emotions lacking in the story itself and commercial tie-ins, spread all through the picture, are a bit too obvious for comfort.

Technical credits are acceptable but not much more, and initial public reception has been lukewarm. — Edna.

Ennemis intimes
(Intimate Enemies)
(FRENCH)

An AAA release of a Films Ariane/FR3 Films Prod./Slav 1 coproduction. Executive producer, Jean Nachbaur. Directed by Denis Amar. Screenplay, Bruno Tardon, Amar; camera (Eastmancolor), Gérard de Battista; editor, Jacques Witta; music, Philippe Sarde; production design, Jean-Pierre Kohut-Svelko; sound, Guillaume Sciama, Paul Bertault; stunt coordinator, Daniel Verité; production manager, Philippe Schwartz. Reviewed at the UGC Odéon cinema, Paris, Dec. 22, 1987. Running time: 95 MIN.
Baudin . . . . Michel Serrault
Tayar . . . . Wadeck Stanczak

Mona . . . . Ingrid Held
Billie . . . . Anne Gautier
Schiltz . . . . Thierry Rey
El Loco . . . . Roch Leibovici
Tendinite . . . . Yannick Soulier
Feeling . . . . Sylvie Coffin

Paris — Costar Michel Serrault gave "Ennemis intimes" some negative publicity by rapping it in a newspaper interview. Not a very elegant thing to do, especially on the day of the national release, but Serrault's remarks about inconsistent characterizations and impoverished plot are unfortunately all too true.

With "Ennemis intimes" filmmaker Denis Amar confirms a certain technical know-how for action and production polish (he got his training in commercials), but continues to flaunt his contempt for solid story and dramatic logic.

Tale, thrown together by Amar and Bruno Tardon (scripter of the equally disastrous local actioner, "Cayenne-Palace"), has Serrault and young Wadeck Stanczak holding off the siege of a gang of juvenile delinquents in a clifftop cinema in a far-flung corner of Madera.

Story is elementary, not elemental as its makers no doubt hoped. Amar simply alternates the noisy and incoherent confrontation of his costars (the fur is flying over some mysterious young girl, who appears in opening and closing scenes) with more spectacular setpieces of the reluctant allies trying to keep the hordes outside from getting into the bunkerlike building (designed by Jean-Pierre Kohut-Svelko) and tearing them apart.

Amar, a sucker for mimickry, evokes Mad Max, westerns, samurai movies and chopsocky pics (Stanczak meets the hordes with nothing less than a samurai sword and surprising karate prowess). As for dramatic substance, characters and meaning, there's nothing on the horizon.

Tech credits, excepting Philippe Sarde's dull score, are first-rate, notably Gérard de Battista's pristine lensing. — Len.

Io e Mia Sorella
(Me And My Sister)
(ITALIAN)

A Columbia Pictures Italia release of a C. G. Silver Film/RAI-TV coproduction. Produced by Mario and Vittorio Cecchi Gori. Directed by Carlo Verdone. Screenplay, Leo Benvenuti, Piero De Bernardi, Verdone; camera (color), Danilo Desideri; editor, Antonio Siciliano; music, Fabio Liberatore. Reviewed at Quirinale Cinema, Rome, Jan. 2, 1988. Running time: 89 MIN.
Carlo . . . . Carlo Verdone
Silvia . . . . Ornella Muti
Serena . . . . Elena Sofia Ricci
  Also with: Sebastiano Balaw.

Rome — Comedian Carlo Verdone has turned his talents to directing himself in a series of ever less inventive films that nevertheless click with Italo audiences. Current effort, "Me And My Sister," tantalizes with the untried pairing of director-headliner Verdone and popular actress Ornella Muti, but turns out a coupling lacking spark. Onshore response has been good.

Attempting to dissect a brother-sister relationship in a comic key, ''Sister'' upgrades Verdone's screen persona from bungling weirdo to boring hubby from the provinces, an orchestra musician like his humorless wife Serena (Elena Sofia Ricci). Carlo retains just enough of the underdog to be sympathetic in his dealings with sis Silvia (Muti), a free-spirited black sheep who comes home after many years for their mother's funeral.

Swathed in voluminous overcoats and looking pregnant throughout the film, Muti is definitely low-key in the role of self-centered sibling who jumps irresponsibly from one love affair to another. Carlo is always one step behind her, clucking in affectionate reproach and trying to clean up the mess, which includes a baby boy in a Budapest children's home. Predictably, firebrand Silvia convinces reluctant Carlo to kidnap the child (location work in Hunary), but once back in Italy abandons son and brother for a fling with a British rock star.

Muti imparts more brattiness than spunk to Silvia, and audience never warms up to the character enough to care about her misfortunes. Despite his towering dullness, Carlo is a more human figure and has the funny lines. Technically there is little to write home about in a film that seems aimed at consolidating Verdone's place in the army of middle-range Italo comedians, despite his superior talents.
— Yung.

Man Outside
(U.S.)

A Virgin Vision release (London) of a Stouffer Enterprise Film Partners production. Produced by Mark Stouffer, Robert E. Yoss. Executive producers, Tom Earnhart, Ross Barrows. Written and directed by Stouffer. Camera (color), William Wages; editor, Tony Lombardo; music, John McEuen. Reviewed at the Florence Film Festival, Dec. 11, 1987. MPAA Rating: PG-13. Running time: **109 MIN.**

Jack Avery	Robert Logan
Grace Freemont	Kathleen Quinlan
Frank Simmons	Bradford Dillman
Sheriff Leland Laughlin	Levon Helm

Florence — Feature debut of nature documentarist Mark Stouffer, ''Man Outside,'' is a professionally lensed, conventionally plotted drama for family audiences. As the traumatized hero takes to the woods to lead a natural life, pic leaves lots of room for describing the great outdoors in the bayous of Arkansas. It should find tv markets a natural habitat. Original moniker for the film was ''The Tuscaloosan: A Solitary Man.''

Scripters stick to the tried and true. Jack Avery (Robert Logan) was a lawyer before running his Porsche into the ground and reverting to a hermit's existence in the woods. As pretty anthropologist Grace Freemont (Kathleen Quinlan) smugly tells her students, solitary isolation is a form of self-punishment. Sure enough, Jack has a skeleton in the closet — he feels responsible for his wife's death in a fire. It takes Grace half the film to coax the rugged neo-caveman into some semblance of human communication, and eventually a romance.

The long arm of civilization is out to get Jack anyway, when a little boy is kidnapped by psycho Bradford Dillman. The evidence (a shoe) points to Jack as the pervert, and sheriff Levon Helm (musician from The Band) arrests him over Grace's protests. The spunky anthropologist springs Jack from jail and together they track down Dillman.

In a story this obvious, spiced with car and jeep chases and a little rugged romance, tone is set by sympathetic performances from principals Logan and Quinlan. Dillman also stands out as the crazed kidnaper with a nasty mother upstairs. With its mid-America setting and values, pic shies away from directly confronting sexual molestation, though it's certainly implied.

There's good technical work in a picture lensed on a modest $3,-500,000 budget. — Yung.

Valdei Stalin
(Stalin's Children)
(ISRAELI)

A Nachshon Films presentation. Produced by Doron Eran. Written and directed by Nadav Levithan; camera (color, 16m), Gad Danzig; editor, Shimon Tamir; sound, Danny Matalon; art direction, Ella Skagiu. Reviewed in Tel Aviv, Jan. 1, 1988. Running time: **90 MIN.**
With: Shmuel Shilo, Yossi Kantz, Hugo Yarden, Rachel Dobson, David Rona, Doron Golan, Rachel Wallach, Ezra Dagan, Aharon Almog, Dudik Semadar, Athalia Kaplan, Ran Apfelberg.

Tel Aviv — One of the major turning points the kibbutz ideology in Israel has experienced is treated quite earnestly by Nadav Levithan, a former kibbutz member. No real drama, however, emerges out of this clash of moral and political opinions, which at best remain on a theoretical level.

Levithan starts with the news of Stalin's death and all the purges following it, shaking three cobblers, all fanatical believers in the Moscow gospel, living in a kibbutz. At the same time, a second crisis erupts with the advent of the Compensations Agreement with West Germany, which presented several kibbutz members with a moral dilemma: should they accept it at all, and if so, should they have the money for private use or give it to the kibbutz, as the ideological principles of this society require.

Both subjects have been debated for years and have caused many dramatic incidents, but the film itself fails to build any interest either in the characters — too easily stereotyped as ''the artist,'' ''the fanatic'' or ''the leader'' — or in the personal problems born out of the dilemma.

Done on a shoestring budget, the number of camera set-ups has been reduced to the barest minimum, to save time, and framing goes haywire after blowup from 16m. Acting is slack and the use of Dvorak's New World Symphony is an unhappy choice to stand in for original music, as it has little to do with the subject at hand.

Levithan can at most claim having done an extremely personal picture, which may become useful, in later days, to fill in details in the historical development of the kibbutz society. His attempt to explain this as a condemnation of any fanaticism at all isn't quite substantiated by his treatment.—Edna.

Rome, 2072 A.D. — The New Gladiators
(ITALIAN)

A Regency production. Executive producer, James Vaughan. Directed by Lucio Fulci. Screenplay, Elisa Briganti, Dardano Sacchetti, Cesare Frugoni, Fulci, from story by Briganti, Sacchetti; camera (Telecolor), Giuseppe Pinori; editor, Vincenzo Tomassi; music, Riz Ortolani; art direction, Frank Vanorio, Jerry Mitchell; assistant director, Rinaldo Ricci; special effects, Corridori; stunt coordinator, Sergio Mioni; post-synch director, Nick Alexander. Reviewed on Media Home Entertainment vidcassette, N.Y., Dec. 23, 1987. No MPAA Rating. Running time: **90 MIN.**
With Jared Martin, Fred Williamson, Howard Ross, Eleanor Gold, Cosimo Cinieri, Claudio Cassinelli, Al Cliver, Haruiko Yamanouchi, Valerie Jones, Donal O'Brian, Penny Brown, Tony Sanders.

''Rome 2072 A.D. — The New Gladiators'' is a 1983 Italian film that is yet another forerunner of ''The Running Man.'' A meek sci-fi effort from horror maestro Lucio Fulci, pic adds nothing to the tv paranoia genre.

Following inadequate model shots of a futuristic cityscape cribbed from the ''Blade Runner'' style, pic posits two rival international tv networks of the future competing for popular, violent programming. One has the hit ''Kill Bike'' show, of which Jared Martin is a top competitor in deadly motorcycle battles. Rival network decides to create the ''Battle Of The Damned,'' a throwback to gladiators and set in Rome.

Boring film focuses on the preparations and arguments concerning the game, which actually does not begin until one hour into the picture. Key plot element of a renegade computer program (named Junior) responsible for the evil game doesn't work. The actual game is modeled after chariot races, with 2-man motorbikes used as the modern version.

Cast, including the since deceased Claudio Cassinelli, is operating on half power. Fulci's fans are bound to be disappointed. —Lor.

Thrillkill
(CANADIAN)

A Brightstar Films presentation of a Thrillkill production, in association with Manesco Films. Produced by Anthony Kramreither. Directed by Kramreither, Anthony D'Andrea. Screenplay, D'Andrea; camera (Filmhouse color), John Clement; editor-associate producer, Nick Rotundo; music, Tim McCauley; sound, Urmas Rosin; art direction, Andrew Deskin; production manager, Robert Wertheimer; assistant director, Otta Hanus. Reviewed on Fox Hills vidcassette, N.Y., Dec. 8, 1987. No MPAA Rating. Running time: **87 MIN.**

Frank	Robin Ward
Bobbie	Gina Massey
Adrian	Laura Robinson
Carly	Diana Reis
Parrish	Colleen Embree
Schofield	Kurt Reis
Grissom	Eugene Clark
Caspar	Frank Moore
Maggie	Joy Boushel

''Thrillkill'' is a dated (copyright is 1984) Canadian quickie about using computers to embezzle funds. It's currently a direct-to-video release Stateside.

Gina Massey finds herself a target of various greedy folks when her sister (Diana Reis) disappears. Sis has been a key cog in an embezzling scheme, with millions of dollars stolen from a bank via computer. The key to unlocking the scam has been hidden by Reis in a computer game named Thrillkill.

Naturally, not only the gangsters and their goons are out to get the info from innocent Massey, but the cop on the case (Robin Ward) is actually a baddie in disguise. Massey and Ward predictably fall in love, and a ridiculous happy ending has the two of them getting away with some of the ill-gotten money.
—Lor.

The Telephone

A New World Pictures release of a New World and Odyssey Entertainment presentation. Produced by Robert Katz, Moctesuma Esparza. Directed by Rip Torn. Screenplay, Harry Nilsson, Terry Southern; camera (Monaco color), Sandra Adair; music, Christopher Young; visual consultant, David Myers; art direction, Jom Pohl; set decoration, Antonio Vincent; sound, Agamemnon Adrianos; assistant director, Lope Yap Jr., associate producer, Joel Glickman. Reviewed at New World screening room, L.A., Jan. 11, 1988. MPAA Rating: R. Running time: **82 MIN.**

Vashti Blue . . . . Whoopi Goldberg
Max . . . . Severn Darden
Honey Boxe/Irate neighbor . . Amy Wright
Rodney . . . . Elliott Gould
Telephone man . . . . —John Heard
Saxophone player . . . . . Ronald J. Stallings

Hollywood — Anyone who likes the sound of chalk scraping on a blackboard should enjoy the experience of being locked in a room with a deranged Whoopi Goldberg in "The Telephone." Performance is nothing if not excruciating in a film so slight one wonders why it was even considered for production. Only masochists will want to see this one.

In a lawsuit by Goldberg against New World and the film's director Rip Torn, Goldberg charged she was denied a final cut specified in her contract. Although L.A. Superior Court ruled in favor of the director, it is highly unlikely that Goldberg's version would have improved matters since editing is not the problem here.

The problem is the material and the execution. As an out-of-work actress, Goldberg goes through a series of monologs in her apartment which just become tedious and tiresome. Things are so bad that her pet owl is relied on for reaction shots.

With a screenplay credited to Harry Nilsson and Terry Southern, it is a bit surprising how flat the writing is. Goldberg fails to salvage a character of any depth or interest and her bits lack any wit or sense of timing.

The one surprise the film conceals is held until the very end, by which time it is too flimsy and too late to rescue this disaster. One suspects long before the final revelation that the character is cracked.

Obviously a low-budget venture, production credits are often crude and are made to look worse by the film's 1-set location.—*Jagr.*

Terre Para Rose
(Land For Rose)
(BRAZILIAN-DOCU)

An Embrafilme release of a Vemver Comunicação production. Produced by Hilton Kaufman, Maria Kaufman, Maria Augusta. Directed by Tetê Moraes. Screenplay, José Joffily, Moraes; narration, Lucélia Santos; camera (color, 16m), Walter Carvalho, Fernando Duarte; additional photography, Peter Overbeck, Antônio Oliveira; editor, Manfredo Caldas, Alzira Cohen, Amauri Alves, Alda Marques, Dominique Paris; music, Ricardo Pavão, Paulo André, Marcelo Pascoal. Reviewed at Havana Intl. Film Fest (competing), Dec. 18, 1987. Running Time: **83 MIN.**

Havana — "Terre Para Rose" (Land For Rose), by Tetê Moraes, documents the continued struggle from the founding of Brazil's New Republic for agrarian land reform, something politicians have been promising for decades. Docu garnered top film awards at the Havana and Brasilia film fests.

Pic begins with archive footage to give historical perspective and reference to the problem, before launching into the story of Rose, one of 1,500 families that in 1985 invaded and occupied the large 74,000-acre Anoni Farm in Rio Grande do Sul. The families set up a community and Rose gives birth to the first citizen of the new township.

When local authorities demand they leave, the community begins negotiations and puts pressure on federal officials through marches and sit-ins. To draw media attention to their situation, the citizens march the 300-plus miles to Porto Alegre to state their case.

The film's principal failure is that even though the audience meets many members of the community through talking-head appearances, the audience never really gets to know them as people, only as voices in a struggle. Later, when it reveals that Rose dies in a 1987 accident when the brakes give out on a truck, there is no impact. The audience feels nothing for Rose or the others whose paths we cross in the pic: they are merely elements of the process without personal substance or depth.

Even though the film ends in stand-off and tragedy (with pressing allegations), the docu functions first as a model for political action through collective effort. As political propaganda, it documents a continuing dialectical struggle for social change. —*Lent.*

De Grande
(Growing Up)
(ITALIAN)

A Titanus release of a Gruppo Bema/Reteitalia coproduction. Produced by Achille Manzotti. Executive producer, Raffaello Sarago. Directed by Franco Amurri. Screenplay, Amurri, Stefano Sudriè; camera (Eastmancolor), Luciano Tovoli; editor, Raimondo Crociani; music, Pino Massara; art direction, Giorgio Luppi. Reviewed at Empire Cinema, Rome, Dec. 23, 1987. Running time: **96 MIN.**

Marco . . . . Renato Pozzetto
Francesca . . . . Giulia Boschi
Marco's father . . . . Alessandro Haber
Marco's mother . . . . Ottavia Piccolo
Also with: Ioska Versari (little Marco), Gaia Piras (sister), Alex Partexano (detective).

Rome — A pleasant Italo comedy for a change, "Growing Up" makes the most of a good idea — what happens when a little boy suddenly finds himself living in a grown-up's body. Newcomer Franco Amurri directs his second feature with assurance and shows a talent for working charming variations into the tired Italian comedy mold, one of whose mainstays, Renato Pozzetto, leads the cast. Not a pic for kids, "Growing Up" has had to contend with the Xmas rush at local wickets, but could have a chance or two offshore with special handling.

The 8-year-old Marco (Ioska Versari), rebuked by mom Ottavia Piccolo for bed-wetting, teased by the kids at school, and disappointed in papa Alessandro Haber's failure to produce a Lego set for his birthday, can stand no more. His fervent wish to be big is granted, and in the place of the cute boy a lumpy, overweight Renato Pozzetto appears bursting out of Marco's clothes. This new Marco — who still thinks like an 8-year-old — flees the house and takes a room with his schoolteacher Francesca (pretty Giulia Boschi), who he has a crush on.

Most gags revolve around the incongruous ways kids and adults think, but Pozzetto does a good job ad-libbing body movements and posturing. It's soon discovered he has a way with children, and he becomes the world's greatest babysitter, albeit a selfish one. Climax comes when Marco the Big is mistaken by police detective Alex Partexano for Marco the Small's kidnaper, and a raucous car chase follows. Ending is on the predictable side.

All hands turn in credible performances, especially stage thesp Piccolo as Marco's harassed but loving mother. Lensing and technical work is professional, without straying from the tried and true.
—*Yung.*

Braddock: Missing In Action III

A Cannon Group release of a Golan-Globus production. Produced by Menaham Golan, Yoram Globus. Directed by Aaron Norris. Screenplay, James Bruner, Chuck Norris, based on characters created by Arthur Silver, Larry Levinson, Steve Bing; camera (Rank color, Philippine Information Agency Film Lab prints), Joao Fernandes; editor, Michael J. Duthie; music, Jay Chattaway; production design, Ladislav Wilheim costume design, Tamy Mor; sound (Ultra-Stereo), Paul LeMare, Eli Yarkoni; second unit director-stunt coordinator, Dean Ferrandini; second unit art direction, Rodell Cruz; second unit set decoration, Piz Fernandez; second unit sound, Nitoy Clemente; associate producers, Michael Hartman, Michael R. Sloan; casting (U.S.), Perry Bullington, Michael Olton; casting (Philippines), Ken Metcalfe, Maria Metcalfe. Reviewed at Cannon screening room, L.A., Jan. 14, 1988. MPAA Rating: R. Running time: **103 MIN.**

Braddock . . . . Chuck Norris
General Quoc . . . . Aki Aleong
Van Tan Cang . . . . Roland Harrah 3d
Lin Tan Cang . . . . Miki Kim
Reverend Rolanski . . . . Yehuda Efroni
Mik . . . . Ron Barker

Hollywood — Chuck Norris manages to pull off a strangely timely and involving story about getting a bunch of Amerasian kids out of Vietnam within the confines of his usual 1-man army action meller parameters. Not to say this is emotional stuff, just up a notch from past chapters that have managed to attrack mostly a redneck following at the b.o.

In order to come up with another reason to get Norris' character Col. James Braddock back inside Vietnam, Norris and co-scripter James Bruner came up with a Vietnamese wife for him who has had his son after he left her for dead during the Saigon airlift.

Norris learns 13 years later of his wife and child from a priest who runs a mission for Amerasian children outside old Saigon on a visit to D.C. to track down the fathers. Initially, Norris doesn't believe it until the CIA — however implausibly — tries to dissuade him from trying to go back and get them out.

With the Philippines again serving for jungle scenes, Norris zooms in James Bondian style to the exact location where now outcast wife (Miki Kim) and bitter son (Roland Harrah 3d) are living. Before you can say Ho Chi Minh, comic book bad guy Gen. Quoc (Aki Aleong) is after them — setting up for the fury of firepower pitting the incredibly deft Norris against a legion of commies, who he manages to pick off or blow away while escaping with 20 others as a zillion bullets and rockets land all around.

At least in this "Missing In Action" sequel, the Asians depicted are given a break when it comes to characterization. There's still a jingoistic slant branding most of them as red enemies, but Norris' apparent love for his family (we presume that's somewhere deep inside his steely demeanor) and concern for the other innocents moves beyond the simplistic black versus white conflict.

Harrah, himself a child of a vet and a Vietnamese woman, plays well as Norris' son given the limited depth of their relationship and Norris' unwillingness to smile, cry, frown or otherwise exhibit any outward signs of vulnerability more than an occasional embrace.

Along with the other well-cast Amerasian offspring in this pic, Harrah gives viewers a very real and current cause to care about, considering all the news stories about this disenfranchised segment of Viet society that are running today.

Film is still mostly a vehicle for Norris and his particular style of search and destroy — a combination of Rambo and Bruce Lee. Particularly impressive is his single-handed annihilation of an army compound from which he escapes with a truckload of kids before hijacking an enemy plane and finally managing to level the Viet-Thai border before crossing it.

Physical scope of the pic is fairly standard for the genre. Manila passes for both Saigon and Bangkok well enough and a rice paddy is a rice paddy in most westerners' eyes.

Now, if only next time around Norris could relish killing less and emoting more, he might have something. —*Brit.*

Imagen Latente
(Latent Image)
(CHILEAN)

A Colectivo de Actores y Tecnicos y Productores Chilenos-Ictus production. Produced by Freddy Ramsy, Patricia Varela. Written and directed by Pablo Perelman. Camera (color, 16m), Beltrán Garcia; editor, Fernando Valenzuela Q.; music, Jaime de Aguirre; sound, Marcos de Aguirre. Reviewed at Havana Intl. Film Festival, Cuba, Dec. 14, 1987. Running time: **92 MIN.**
Pedro . . . . Bastián Bodenhófer
Hochi . . . . María Isquierdo
Carlos . . . . Gonzalo Robles
Brother's friend . . . . . . Gloria Munchmeyer
Emilia . . . . Elena Muñoz
Also with: Schlomit Baytelman, Héctor Noguera, Patricio Bunster, María Teresa Fricke, Elsa Poblete, Jorge Gayardo, Claudia Arredonde, Gabriela Madina.

Havana — Within the context of New Latin American cinema, the Chilean feature "Imagen Latente" (Latent Image), by Pablo Perelman, deals with a familiar theme. It concerns a problem shared by many countries living under repressive regimes: What has happened for those who have disappeared for political reasons? This haunting subject has been explored in films as diverse as "Missing," by Constantin Costa-Gavras, Argentine Oscar Barney Finn's "Contar Hasta Diez" (Count To 10) and even the recent "La Estación del Regreso" (The Season Of Our Return), by fellow countryman Leonardo Kocking.

Action begins in 1983 and concerns professional advertising photographer Pedro (Bastián Bodenhófer), whose politically active older brother disappeared in 1975. At the time, Pedro didn't want to know anything about it, but after almost a decade he is suddenly obsessed with discovering his sibling's fate. He is set to brooding, talking to his father, checking through official and non-official channels and meeting his brother's old friends. He eventually becomes paranoid fearing that his search will result in his own arrest.

Perelman handles these elements well in a complex personal story of how disappearances affect those who remain. Pedro is restless. He views his brother through a veiled vision of guilt: his brother was the better one in every way, the most ideal, most generous, pure, but also the most political. The brother was the sacrificial lamb to his own existence and coming to odds with this is fundamental in coming to grips with Pedro's own self-acceptance.

The photography is tight and keeps focus clearly on Pedro and his story. Insertion of 8m home movies, Pedro's b&w photos which he develops in the bathtub and other images add yet another level to the visual texture of the film.

Although "Imagen Latente" breaks no new ground, it is obviously a cathartic theme which will pop up again and again as each country which has suffered repression learns to grapple with its own lamentable experiences and political realities.

The film was edited and blown up to 35m in Canada. It is currently awaiting official okay for domestic exhibition. —*Lent.*

Y'a Bon les blancs
(Um, Good, De White Folks)
(FRENCH-SPANISH-ITALIAN)

A Gaumont release of a Camera One/JMS Films/Cia Iberoamericana de TV (Madrid)/23 Giugno (Rome) coproduction. Executive producer, Andres Vicente Gomez. Produced by Armand Barbault. Directed by Marco Ferreri. Screenplay, Ferreri, Rafael Azcona, with Evelyne Pieiller, Cheick Doukouré; camera (Eastmancolor), Angel Luis Fernandez; editor, Ruggero Mastroianni; music, Guy Eyoum, Armand Antonio-Tamba Kyata, Jacob Diboum, Alejandro Castillo, Cisse Fode, the Tissinitg group; sound, Jean-Pierre Ruh; art direction, Ferreri, Fernando Rosales Sanchez; production managers, Jesus Maria Lopez Patino, Abderrahmane Khayat. Reviewed at the Gaumont Colisée cinema, Paris, Jan. 24, 1988. Running time: **100 MIN.**
Nadia . . . . Maruschka Detmers
Michel . . . . Michele Placido
Diego Ramirez . . . . Juan Diego
Father Jean-Marie . . . . Michel Piccoli
Peter . . . . Jean-François Stevenin

Paris — Marco Ferreri, the European cinema's erstwhile scandalmonger, turns his satiric sights on European relief organizations for Third World trouble spots, but "Y'a Bon les blancs" has as much shock impact as spitballs on an elephant. This Franco-Spanish-Italian coprod marks another step down in Ferreri's reputation as provocateur and filmmaker and will be a hard sell in overseas markets.

Humanitarian aid operations have been the subject of much hot discussion and debate and are juicy targets for satire. But Ferreri shoots wide of the mark with a script that makes facile fun of well-meaning nincompoops rather than take apart the socio-political ambiguities of the theme.

Script follows the misadventures of a motley band of Europeans who are bringing a convoy of foodstuffs (spaghetti, tomato sauce and powdered milk) to a famine zone in North Africa's Sahel region. Sidetracked by corrupt local officials and fleeced by a resort hotel manager, the 5-truck expedition soon is lost in the desert, where it runs the gauntlet of sundry guerrillas and mad tribal chieftains, not to mention an occasional African who has lived in France but has returned home.

Ferreri feebly tries to revive memories of his "La Grande bouffe" in a macabre climax in which costars Maruschka Detmers and Michele Placido decide to quit the convoy and are eaten by a tribe of nomads, infuriated that the whites have polluted their oasis water hole.

Rather than enforce Ferreri's message that Europeans have no business being in Africa and that in any case the latter couldn't care less for their aid, the cannibal twist merely deflects attention from the central theme. Ferreri doesn't show us what happens to the food when the convoy reaches its (offscreen) destination.

Detmers and Placido are listless as two Europeans along for the ride for the wrong reasons, while Michel Piccoli makes a disappointing guest star turn as a disgusted missionary who only wants to go home. Juan Diego fares a little better as the fumbling expedition leader.

Script and cast are disserved by Ferreri's limp direction, which lacks the aggressive vitality of effective satire. Tech credits are mediocre. Pic was shot on location in Tunisia. —*Len.*

U.S. Film Festival Reviews

Hairspray

A New Line Cinema release in association with Stanley F. Buchthal. Produced by Rachel Talalay. Coproducers, Buchthal, John Waters, Line producer, Robert Maier. Executive producers, Robert Shaye, Sara Risher. Written and directed by Waters. Camera (color), David Insley; editor, Janice Hampton; music supervisor, Bonnie Greenberg; art direction, Vincent Peranio; costume and makeup design, Van Smith; hair design, Christine Mason; sound (Ultra-Stereo), Rick Angelella; choreographer, Edward Love; assistant director, Stephen Apicella; casting, Mary Colquhoun, Pat Moran (Baltimore). Reviewed at the Lorimar screening room, Culver City, Jan. 11, 1988. In competition — U.S. Film Festival.) MPAA Rating: PG. Running time: **90 MIN.**
Franklin Von Tussle . . . . Sonny Bono
Motormouth Maybell . . . . Ruth Brown
Edna Turnblad/Arvin Hodgepile . . . Divine
Amber Von Tussle . . . . Colleen Fitzpatrick
Link Larkin . . . . Michael St. Gerard
Velma Von Tussle . . . . Debbie Harry
Tracy Turnblad . . . . Ricki Lake
Penny Pingleton . . . . Leslie Ann Powers
Seaweed . . . . Clayton Prince
Wilbur Turnblad . . . . Jerry Stiller
Tammy . . . . Mink Stole
Corny Collins . . . . Shawn Thompson
Beatnik Cat . . . . Ric Ocasek
Beatnik Girl . . . . Pia Zadora

Hollywood — A longtime John Waters fan may find it hard to believe the modern cinema's foremost connoisseur of bad taste actually has made a picture rated PG. What's a Waters film, after all, without some poodle doo, mass murder or mind-bending sexual confusion? His admirers needn't worry, however, since his appreciation for the tacky side of life is in full flower in "Hairspray," a slight but often highly amusing diversion about integration, big girls' fashions and music-mad teens in 1962 Baltimore. With its high spirits and goofball cast, pic should deliver okay b.o. results.

Operating in a low-budget Frank Tashlin world of ghastly lower-middle class apartments, a rinky-dink local tv station and gaudy neighborhood shops, Waters has made his slickest pic to date with this perky comedy which is unfortunately bogged down somewhat by the serious intentions of its latter section.

First two or three reels are sometimes hilarious, as Ricki Lake, chubbette daughter of Divine and Jerry Stiller, overcomes all to become queen of an afternoon teenage dance show, much to the consternation of stuck-up blond Colleen Fitzpatrick, whose parents are Debbie Harry and Sonny Bono.

Divine spits out some choice bon mots while denigrating her daughter's pastime, but finally rejoicing in her success, takes Lake off for a pricelessly funny visit to Hefty Hideaway, where full-figure girls can shop to their hearts' content.

More silliness of varying degrees of inspiration follows, and little by little Waters brings to the fore his integration theme, pointing out how black music was played and danced to endlessly by whites happy to enjoy it and make money off it, but how blacks were rigorously kept off such shows and out of other bastions of white culture and commerce.

Being John Waters, he sends up the clichés of his little exposé just as he delivers it, having the young black lead, a fellow named Seaweed, exclaim to his blond girlfriend, "Our love is taboo!" and setting a race riot in a kiddies fun fair called "Tilted Acres." Nevertheless, the steam and fun seep out of the picture during this latter segment, leaving "Hairspray" about half a funny film.

Divine, so big he wears a tent-like garment big enough for three ordinary mortals to sleep in, is in otherwise fine form in a dual role. Debbie Harry has little to do but act bitchy and sport increasingly towering wigs, while Pia Zadora is virtually unrecognizable as a beatnik chick. All the kids in the predominantly teenage cast are tirelessly enthusiastic.

No doubt, special credit should go to hair designer Christine Mason, who has made every woman in the cast look as though she's wearing frozen cotton candy on her head, and costume designer Van Smith, whose period recreations provoke constant amusement. Also splendid is the chock-full soundtrack, which features some new tunes but is distinguished by its great tunes from the past, such as

"Town Without Pity" and "Duke Of Earl." —Cart.

Promised Land

A Vestron Pictures release of a Wildwood production with the Oxford Film Co., presented in association with Great American Films Ltd. Partnership. Produced by Rick Stevenson. Executive producers, Robert Redford, Andrew Meyer. Written and directed by Michael Hoffman. Camera (color), Ueli Steiger, Alexander Gruszynski; editor, David Spiers; music, James Newton Howard; production design, Eugenio Zanetti; art direction, Jim Dultz; set design, Clif A. Davis; set decoration, Michael Marcus; costume design, Victoria Holloway; sound (Dolby), Darrell Henke; associate producers, Dennis Bishop, Mark Bentley, Andy Paterson; assistant director, Matthew Carlisle; second unit director, Paterson; second unit camera, Matthew Williams; casting, Risa Bramon, Billy Hopkins, Lora Kennedy. Reviewed at the Lorimar screening room, Culver City, Calif., Jan. 5, 1988. (In competition — U.S. Film Festival.) MPAA Rating: R. Running time: **100 MIN.**
Davey Hancock . . . . Jason Gedrick
Danny Rivers . . . . Kiefer Sutherland
Bev . . . . Meg Ryan
Mary . . . . Tracy Pollan
Baines . . . . Googy Gress
Pammie . . . . Deborah Richter
Mr. Rivers . . . . Oscar Rowland
Mrs. Rivers . . . . Sondra Seacat
Circle K clerk . . . . Jay Underwood
Mrs. Higgins . . . . Herta Ware

Hollywood — "Promised Land" is a pregnant drama about aimless Middle American lives that never delivers. Produced in Utah near where it was developed at the Sundance Institute, pic covers familiar, unexciting ground as it looks at four thoroughly unremarkable young people who never come close to getting things together. Muted tale, which premiered at the U.S. Film Festival in Park City, Utah, looms as an unpromising b.o. performer for Vestron.

Writer-director Michael Hoffman starts his story off on the basketball court, where Jason Gedrick wins the game for the high school home team, much to the delight of friend and admirer Kiefer Sutherland and g.f. Tracy Pollan.

The glories of youth soon fall into the shadow of adult realities and the friends go their separate ways. Within two years, Gedrick's life consists of making the rounds of sleepy Ashville as a cop in a squad car, and Pollan has matured at college but is still tempted by the idea of a quiet family existence full of babies.

By contrast, the bashful Sutherland has left town to find himself, only to return with a bride, hellcat Meg Ryan, whom he married three days after meeting her. Unfortunately, once she arrives in Ashville to meet the folks, this outsider brings senseless tragedy to the group of old friends, making for a contrived, downbeat ending that resolves nothing.

Many scenes are extended to the point that all potential dramatic tension is drained out of them.

A cattle prod would have been a useful tool on the set, as the actors show boundless earnestness and lit-

tle energy except for Ryan, whose role calls for her to be dangerously wild and reckless in a sexy, silly way, something she manages just fine.

Film is technically handsome, but evinces no spirit or burning creative drive behind it. It's careful, safe and uneventful. —Cart.

The Silence At Bethany

An American Playhouse Theatrical Films presentation. Produced by Tom Cherones. Executive producers, Lindsay Law, Joyce Keener. Coproducer, Fred Gerber. Directed by Joel Oliansky. Screenplay, Keener. Camera (Foto-Kem color), Charles Minsky; editor, Pasquale Buba; music, Lalo Schifrin; second editor, Norman Hollyn; production design, Cletus Anderson; costume design, Barbara Anderson; sound, Klaus Landesberg; associate producer, Tom Spezialy; assistant director, Mike Katleman; casting, Al Onorato, Jerold Franks (L.A.), Elina de Santos Associates (east coast). Reviewed at the U.S. Film Festival (in competition), Park City, Utah. Jan. 16, 1988. Running time: **90 MIN.**
Ira Martin . . . . Mark Moses
Pauline Mitgang Martin . . . . Susan Wilder
Phares Mitgang . . . . Tom Dahlgren
Sam Mitgang . . . . Dakin Matthews
Elam Swope . . . . Richard Fancy

Park City, Utah — Though it says worthwhile things about the limitations of absolutism and presents a vivid picture of a struggle of faith, "The Silence At Bethany" never achieves the vibrancy and energy needed to bring it to urgent dramatic life. A typically serious-minded and ethnographically exploratory film from American Playhouse, this has very limited theatrical prospects.

Written with evident personal commitment by Joyce Keener, tale tells of a departed son, Mark Moses, who returns to his rural Pennsylvania homeland in 1939 to build a life in a tiny Mennonite community.

Welcomed by the stern, solid elders, Moses soon marries an intelligent, pious young woman, Susan Wilder, and is ordained as a minister. He is a caring liberal compared to the severe, doctrinaire bishop, who also happens to be his wife's uncle, and the rift between him and the local establishment widens when he makes an impassioned speech in defense of a farmer who want to defy orthodoxy by doing business on Sunday rather than go bankrupt.

Resulting moral dilemma forces Moses and his wife into a convulsive choice between their faith and their personal convictions, and climax is apt if not surprising. Nothing in this picture quickens the pulse at all, as it is directed by Joel Oliansky at a very measured pace that confers dignity on the proceedings but develops little involvement.

Setting among the Mennonites is certainly unusual and their practices at church services are, if anything, dwelled upon to undue length, but one learns disappointingly little about them, and nothing of what distinguishes them from the Amish

or other groups.

Performances are believable, particularly those of Susan Wilder and Dakin Matthews as her father, and pic looks sharp on a low budget. The drama presented here will remain remote for most audiences.
— Cart.

Zelly And Me

A Columbia Pictures release of a Cypress Film and Mark/Jett production. Produced by Sue Jett, Tony Mark. Executive producers, Elliott Dewitt, Tina Rathborne. Written and directed by Rathborne. Camera (Technicolor; Deluxe prints), Mikael Salomon; editor, Cindy Kaplan Rooney; music, Pino Donaggio; production design, David Morong; art direction, Diana Fress; costume design, Kathleen De Toro; sound, Scott Brindi; associate producer, Helena M. Consuegra; assistant director, Dick Feury; casting, Barbara Shapiro. Reviewed at the U.S. Film Festival (noncompeting), Park City, Utah, Jan. 23, 1988. Running time: **87 MIN.**
Zelly . . . . Isabella Rossellini
Coco . . . . Glynis Johns
Phoebe . . . . Alexandra Jones
Nora . . . . Kaiulani Lee
Willie . . . . David Lynch
Earl . . . . Joe Morton

Park City, Utah — Directing her first feature, Tina Rathborne has no doubt accomplished exactly what she set out to do, as she displays evident care and skill with both actors and camera. But this precious story of the tensions within a rich orphan girl's tiny private world will be as off-putting to some people as it will be moving to others. There is no doubt an audience, particularly among women, for this well-wrought picture, but Columbia's marketing department will have to work hard to identify and tap it.

Set in the beautiful Virginia countryside in 1958, concentrated tale presents little Phoebe, played with appealing pensiveness by Alexandra Jones, as a smart girl being raised by her grandmother Coco (Glynis Johns) and a European nanny Zelly (Isabella Rossellini).

Phoebe is pampered and doted over endlessly by Zelly and the other help — Kaiulani Lee's maid and Joe Morton's gardener — and the opening reels are nearly suffocating and fetishistic in their creation of a world dominated by cooing women, stuffed animals, immaculate gardens, cupcakes and lace; anyone liking a certain edge on films will find all this rough going.

Since Phoebe is obsessed with Joan of Arc and the pain of fiery death (her parents were killed in a plane crash), one keeps waiting for dark, disturbing undercurrents to assert themselves dramatically. At long last, they do, as stern Coco dismisses, first the black gardener, then Zelly, because it's clear to her than Phoebe loves them more than she does her.

As Coco's punishments for the child become increasingly severe and unjust, so does Phoebe begin torturing herself by burning herself with matches. Finally, Zelly and her

mysterious suitor, played by "Blue Velvet" director David Lynch, concoct a kidnaping scheme, which produces a couple of twists of its own.

Rathborne has constructed her screenplay precisely and deliberately, making all the points she considers important but also laying on the sweetness to an excessive degree.

Accumulation of private details gives the picture an autobiographical feel, but concentration on Phoebe's point-of-view overlooks some potentially rich angles. What, for example, is Coco's problem, why must she act in such an obviously hurtful way to her grandchild? And what is Zelly's story, why is she so afraid to start a family of her own instead of making do with this surrogate one? These stories could have made films of their own, but lack of probing into their makeup and motivations leaves these characters 1-dimensional despite the considerable time spent with them.

Nevertheless, it is far from impossible to become engaged with these women, and many will no doubt be deeply absorbed emotionally. Performances help to that end, as Jones nicely carries the picture, Rossellini conveys both love and desperation with admirable directness, and Johns is convincing as an emotional tightwad. In a small role, Lynch is all earnest sincerity.

Mikael Salomon's lensing richly captures the beauty of the women as well as the surroundings. —Cart.

Avalon

A Rapid Eye Movement production. Produced, directed, written, photographed (color) by John J. Anderson; editor, Rick Barnes, Julie Duvio, Jim Sander; costume design, Gail Cuen, Jerry Chin; sound, Matt Clark; additonal sound, Rick Barnes. Reviewed at the U.S. Film Festival (in competition). Park City, Utah, Jan. 19, 1988. Running time: **75 MIN.**
Fenian . . . . James Liu
Olwyn . . . . Elizabeth Yoffe
Priest . . . . Leroy Logan
Anscombe . . . . Reinhard Mayer

Park City, Utah — "Avalon" is a rare bird, an uncompromising attempt at a serious, metaphysical American art film. Graced by often striking photography on spectacular international locations, extreme maverick picture is done in by its static pace, risible performances and intellectual fuzziness. This has no commercial future in conventional venues, but fests and specialized outlets receptive to weird, eccentric works might give it a look.

First reel makes one think the film will be virtually unendurable, as protracted scenes, seemingly shot from as far away as the next county, give the viewer no access into the proceedings.

Story, such as it is, involves a young man named Fenian who is exiled from his village in the 15th century for reporting his dream that the plague of two centuries before will return. Thus begins Fenian's quest for the fabled island of Avalon, which takes him through some extraordinary land- and seascapes but results in only marginally dramatic events until he finally returns to his village for a mystifying conclusion.

Obviously influenced by the mystical elements and languid storytelling techniques of Werner Herzog, first-time American director John J. Anderson has traversed some of the most stunning areas in Scotland, Ireland, Wales, Washington, Oregon and British Columbia with a bare-bones crew to capture some scenes of rapturous beauty. Director, who shot the picture on Super-16, which was blown up to 35m, studied with Ansel Adams, and his skill photographing scenes with available natural lighting is evident everywhere.

Dramatically, it's another story, however. Scenes possess no tension or conflict, motivation is vague or nonexistent, acting is of high-school caliber, and the grossly American accents emerging from the mouths of these Middle Ages characters sound ludicrous.

Given the extreme artiness of the project, Anderson should have gone all the way and had the characters speak in some obscure tongue, then supplied subtitles. This at least would have removed the unwanted laughs from the picture. —*Cart.*

The Unbearable Lightness Of Being

An Orion Pictures release of a Saul Zaentz Co. presentation. Produced by Zaentz. Executive producer, Bertil Ohlsson. Directed by Philip Kaufman. Screenplay, Jean-Claude Carrière, Kaufman, based on the novel by Milan Kundera; camera (Technicolor; Deluxe prints), Sven Nykvist; supervising film editor, Walter Murch; editor, B.J. Sears, Vivien Hillgrove Gilliam, Stephen A. Rotter; production design, Pierre Guffroy; costume design, Ann Roth; sound (Dolby), Chris Newman; associate producer, Paul Zaentz; assistant directors, Charles Paviot, Eric Bartonio; special consultant, Jan Nemec; casting, Dianne Crittenden (U.S., U.K.), Margot Capelier (France). Reviewed at the Orion screening room, L.A., Jan. 8, 1988. MPAA Rating: R. Running time: **171 MIN.**

Tomas	Daniel Day-Lewis
Tereza	Juliette Binoche
Sabina	Lena Olin
Franz	Derek de Lint
The Ambassador	Erland Josephson
Pavel	Pavel Landovsky
Chief Surgeon	Donald Moffat
Interior Ministry	
Official	Daniel Olbrychski
The Engineer	Stellan Skarsgard

Hollywood — Great films are seldom made from great novels, but "The Unbearable Lightness Of Being" stands as a stunning and surprising exception. Milan Kundera's 1984 international bestseller of love and erotica set against the Russian invasion of Czechoslovakia has been regarded as essentially unfilmable by many observers, so Philip Kaufman has pulled off a near-miracle in creating this richly satisfying adaptation. With a 3-hour running time, a non-boxoffice cast and a title that may be unfamiliar and awkward to the general public, this Saul Zaentz production represents the definition of a tough sell, at least in the U.S. Kaufman has put it all together here in what might well be a masterpiece, so critical reaction should give the film a running start.

Kaufman and co-scenarist Jean-Claude Carrière have reorganized the time-jumping novel's tale in conventional chronological order, changed some minor details and omitted others, but have managed to produce an adaptation that very closely approximates the feel of the book — emotionally charged, even passionate, but somewhat distanced by an intellectual cool. The film can therefore please lovers of the book, but also it takes on an integrity and separate life of its own.

In its basic outline, story is quite simple. Tomas, a top surgeon and compulsive ladies' man in Prague, takes in and eventually marries a lovely country girl, Tereza. He continues his womanizing, however, particularly with his voluptuous mistress Sabina, an artist who takes off for Geneva as soon as Russian tanks put a halt to the Prague Spring of 1968.

Galvanized into a certain consciousness by the invasion, Tomas and Tereza follow to Switzerland soon thereafter. After experiencing the weight of freedom, Tereza, and

later Tomas, return to Czechoslovakia, where their love deepens even as they suffer in squalor under increasing political oppression and humiliation.

Daring to take his time with this intimate epic, Kaufman bracingly breathes life into the principal characters and the world they inhabit, defying and triumphing over may potential clichés and traps in the process.

The sexuality which drenches the entire film possesses a great buoyancy and spirit in the first act, set during the exciting liberalization of communism under Alexander Dubcek. The intoxicated atmosphere of the period is manifest, but shockingly aborted by the Soviets, and Kaufman has recreated the invasion in a tour-de-force combination of newsreel footage and newly filmed material with the actors.

Second act, in Geneva, is comparatively somber and spare, but is punctuated by Sabina's new affair with a married man and by the growing friendship between Sabina and Tereza, which is illustrated by a daringly but successfully protracted sequence in which the two women photograph each other in the nude.

Tale takes on a tragic inevitability in the third act, in which the characters meaningfully explore the profound differences between love and sex just as they are ground under the heel of totalitarianism.

Kaufman's visual strategies, echoing motifs, dramatic oppositions and balancing of contrasts could provide the stuff of extended analysis. Suffice it to say the director's mastery of his material is total, his modulation of it over the course of three hours standing as an exceedingly rare example of sustained artistry.

Kaufman and Zaentz, who produced the film independently, with distrib Orion only coming aboard late last year, showed guts in casting, putting the ideal choice above commercial name value. The two main women in Tomas' life, Tereza and Sabina are, respectively, a child-woman, a peasant girl who gives herself up entirely to her man, and an older, sophisticated woman of the world who runs the other way if a man tries to possess and trap her.

As played by Juliette Binoche and Lena Olin, the two women are absolutely enchanting; one of the keys to the film's success is that one simply cannot choose between them. Binoche is adorably doll-like and frisky at first, compellingly introspective later on, while Olin is simply striking as a woman who lives her sexual and artistic lives just as she pleases, but knows she always will be fundamentally alone.

Attractive in some ways, Tomas is irritatingly uncommunicative and

opaque at others, and Daniel Day-Lewis at times overdoes the self-consciously smug projection of his own appeal. He also admirably and quietly conveys Kundera's creation, a man always in the process of becoming, whose ambivalence only slowly sprouts resolve and convictions.

Film is convincing in all details, emotional and physical. Using locations in Lyon, Paris and Switzerland, production designer Pierre Guffroy conjures up an utterly believable impression of Eastern Europe, which is enhanced immeasurably by some of the loveliest work cinematographer Sven Nykvist has ever done.

Walter Murch has overseen a seamless job of film editing, and much of the effective score consists of pieces by Czech composer Leos Janacek, who died in 1928. Also noteworthy are the accents which, despite the diverse national backgrounds of the players, are appealingly light and remarkably consistent.

End result is mature, serious and intellectual, but not arty. It is certainly among the most fully realized ambitious films in a very long time. —*Cart.*

She's Having A Baby

A Paramount Pictures release. Produced, written and directed by John Hughes. Executive producer, Ronald Colby. Camera (Technicolor), Don Peterman; editor, Alan Heim; music, Stewart Copeland; additional music, Nicky Holland; production design, John W. Corso; set design, Louis M. Mann; set decoration, Jennifer Polito; costume design, April Ferry; additional editing, George Bowers, Eric Strand; stunt coordinator, Conrad E. Palmisano; choreography, Tony Stevens; sound (Dolby), James Alexander; production manager, Colby; associate producer -second unit director, Bill Brown; assistant director, Mark Radcliffe; casting, Janet Hirshenson, Jane Jenkins; N.Y. casting, Steven Jacobs. Reviewed at the Mann National theater, L.A., Jan. 26, 1988. MPAA Rating: PG-13. Running time: **106 MIN.**

Jake Briggs	Kevin Bacon
Kristy Briggs	Elizabeth McGovern
Davis McDonald	Alec Baldwin
Fantasy Girl	Isabel Lorca
Russ Bainbridge	William Windom
Gayle Bainbridge	Cathryn Damon
Sarah Briggs	Holland Taylor
Jim Briggs	James Ray

Also with: Dennis Dugan, Nancy Lenehan, John Ashton, Edie McClurg, Paul Gleason, Larry Hankin, Valeri Breiman.

Hollywood — The films of John Hughes are growing up in strange ways. His last one, "Planes, Trains & Automobiles," moved him beyond his beloved teens and into more satisfying adult territory. Now he's taken a giant step backward with "She's Having A Baby" (filmed prior to "Planes"), an oddly uneven and quasi-serious look into the angst of the early years of a contemporary marriage that parallels tv's "thirtysomething" and would seem to appeal to mostly an audience of the exact age and situation that in this case is twentysomething. This may narrow, not expand, Hughes' b.o. following.

There are many comedic setups in "She's Having A Baby" which, if they were with less archetypally drawn characters, might have delivered the laughs with the refreshingly innocent joy that has been the hallmark of other Hughes pics.

In the lead role, Kevin Bacon is written to take on all the complexity and shading that all but one of those he plays against is deprived. He is enthusiastic and believable, but even his energy can't carry what boils down to a fairly limp story told from his p.o.v. about buying into the comfortable suburban dream possibly before his time.

Bacon ties the knot with teenage sweetheart Kristy (Elizabeth McGovern) and begins to fantasize about what he's going to be missing out on as a married man from the moment they take their vows.

His desires and fears about becoming a responsible adult while still in his early 20s manifests itself in unexpected and quixotic ways. In the opening scene, the minister asks if he will promise to uphold the yuppie standard of assuring his wife a big, comfy house, credit cards and a Mercedes in the driveway.

Well, he does (except it's a new BMW instead of a Benz) with occasional timeouts to wonder whether perhaps he should be accepting it all so easily, seeing as everything seems to be falling into place so nicely anyway.

Though an ad copy writer by day, Bacon fancies himself a writer of fiction in the wee hours. This is supposed to give him the appearance of creativity and in some scenarios, it does. One minute he's looking down the street and listening to his neighbors argue about power lawn mowers and the next, the homeowners are dancing with their machines to a synchronized number that's been choreographed like a Broadway musical.

What normal guy could go through this anxiety without there being another woman. Hughes has most fun having her be a tantalizing, blond, French-speaking babe (Isabel Lorca, who bears an uncanny resemblance to Donna Rice) whom Bacon eyes in a dance club and then later finds back home sitting on the family sofa.

It soon becomes evident why Bacon is endlessly dreaming: take away his imaginings and his home life is dull indeed.

For one thing, he's got a Stepford wife for a mate. McGovern is so uncomplicated and unabashedly adoring towards her husband, it gets one wondering what such a bright guy is doing with her. They never seem to connect as a couple. He's too self-absorbed and it's anyone's guess if she's thinking much of anything at all.

What about friends? They have exactly one, it seems. Bacon's wayward buddy Davis (Alec Baldwin) shows up too infrequently to spar with his good chum and ruffle McGovern's feathers by bringing along just the kind of girl she would loathe.

With Baldwin, Bacon actually has someone interesting around to talk to. Isn't conversation and interaction with peers what Hughes pics excel in?

When McGovern gets to scheming about having a baby halfway through the film, the story loses momentum and after some light moments here and there joking about ovulation and specimen gathering, takes an irreversible, somber turn downwards. Presumably, Hughes meant for this to be a living portrait of a couple growing closer, when it seems they really were never in sync to begin with.

For whatever reason, about the only other people they entertain besides Baldwin is their parents, a particularly overbearing, typecast bunch led by her obnoxious father, played to the max by William Windom.

Technically, this probably is the most textured of Hughes' films. Good use is made of numerous black & white flashbacks and shots taken looking up from below eye level that give a curious perspective to the already curious proceedings.

— *Brit.*

Thy Kingdom Come ... Thy Will Be Done
(BRITISH-U.S.-DOCU)

A Roxie Films release (U.S.) of a Central Independent Television production for Viewpoint '87 with WGBH for "Frontline." Executive producers, Roger James, David Fanning. Produced, written and directed by Antony Thomas. Camera (color), Curtis Clark; editor, MacDonald Brown. Reviewed at the U.S. Film Festival (in competition), Park City, Utah, Jan. 20, 1988. Running time: **107 MIN.**

Park City, Utah — The Christian Fundamentalist Right is expertly laid out and dissected in "Thy Kingdom Come ... Thy Will Be Done." This fascinating 2-part documentary by Britain's Antony Thomas was bumped mysteriously from its scheduled PBS showings last summer, but has now won a prize at the U.S. Film Festival, opened to big numbers in a San Francisco theatrical run and been reslated for a PBS airing April 6. A superior documentary by any standard, it looks to stir up considerable interest no matter where, and in what media, it plays.

Thomas, who made the controversial "Death Of A Princess," as well as the awardwinning "South African Experience" and "The Most Dangerous Man Alive: Frank Terpil," begins his investigation by having born-again Christians describe what drew them to Jesus; almost invariably, the reasons have to do with troubled earlier lives bedeviled by abusive parents or mates, alcohol and drugs.

It doesn't take long, however, for Thomas to zero in on his main point of inquiry, namely, the intense, unprecedented and financially stupendous links between fundamentalist Christians and right-wing politicians, a marriage the filmmaker tends to see as essentially illogical.

With the great good fortune of the lucky reporter, Thomas devoted a considerable portion of Part I to a visit to Jim and Tammy Bakker's Heritage USA park, where the faithful are seen flocking to dwell in a mind-boggling display of whitebread, Middle American kitsch so ostentatious that the pair surely qualify as the true inheritors of Liberace's mantle.

All of this was filmed before the Bakker scandal exploded and, far from making the documentary dated, as "Frontline" exec producer David Fanning suggested when canceling the PBS showings last year, the Bakker material represents, in retrospect, a major coup that adds immeasurably to the program's commercial value.

As one hears born-again Christianity described as the only true religion, learns that even Mother Teresa will burn in hell if she doesn't doesn't undergo the born-again experience, and watches these self-righteous, squeaky-clean, smoke-free, teetotaling, pure white and mostly grotesquely fat try to will into existence an America that never was and never will be, the message comes through loud and clear that the main motivating factor behind the entire movement is fear — fear of the other, the different, the foreign.

Part I goes on to survey the television evangelists and to illustrate the ways these men have used the airwaves, cable, telephones and computers to raise huge sums of money, and the manner in which such reactionary political operators as Morton Blackwell and Gary Jarman have seized upon this movement to create a new voting constituency.

Part II concentrates on Dallas, "the buckle on the Bible Belt," the U.S. city which boasts the highest percentage of paid-up church members as well as the nation's highest crime rate, perhaps the most Christian metropolis in the world, in Thomas' view.

The filmmaker sharpens his lens with particular precision on the money-drenched First Baptist Church of Dallas and its pastor, Dr. W.A. Criswell. Contrasting the haves and have-nots and delineating how this enormously influential institution segregates its congregations on a racial, as well as financial, basis, Thomas underlines the fundamental inconsistency of the church's practices and makeup with Jesus' own life and teachings.

Criswell has rationalized it all and deflects all of Thomas' barbed questions with patronizing comments about how blacks prefer to worship with their own kind, and how the high local crime rate can be attributed to all those who are not Christian. It's amazing stuff.

In this and other instances during the film, Thomas can't help but editorialize. At the same time, he handles his investigation in a thorough responsible manner, as one genuinely interested in and concerned with the events at hand, not as an outraged muckraker. Film deserves as wide a public as can be found. — *Cart.*

Tapeheads

A DEG release of an NBC Prods. and Pacific Arts presentation of a Peter McCarthy/Front Films production. Produced by Peter McCarthy. Executive producer, Michael Nesmith. Coproducer, Robert Lecky. Directed by Bill Fishman. Screenplay, Fishman, McCarthy, from story by Fishman, McCarthy, Ryan Rowe, Jim Herzfeld; camera (Deluxe color), Bojan Bazelli; editor, Mondo Jenkins; music, Fishbone; music supervisor, Nigel Harrison; production design, Catherine Hardwicke; art direction, Don Diers; costume design, Elizabeth McBride; sound (Ultra-Stereo), John Pritchett; associate producers, Andrew Davis, Eric Barrett; assistant director, Josh King; second unit camera, Bryan Duggan; casting, Victoria Thomas. Reviewed at the U.S. Film Festival (noncompeting), Park City, Utah, Jan. 22, 1988. MPAA Rating: R. Running time: **97 MIN.**

Ivan Alexcov	John Cusack
Josh Tager	Tim Robbins
Sidney Tager	Doug McClure
June Tager	Connie Stevens
Norman Mart	Clu Gulager
Samantha	Mary Crosby
Belinda Mart	Katy Boyer
Thor Alexcov	Lyle Alzado
Roscoe	King Cotton
Mo Fuzz	Don Cornelius
Kay Mart	Jessica Walter
Billy Diamond	Sam Moore
Lester Diamond	Junior Walker
Also with: Susan Tyrrell.	

Park City, Utah — A smirky and jerky comedy about rising to the top in the world of music-videos, "Tapeheads" is so loaded with inside jokes about the music business that it will no doubt generate a small cult following. Pic's unflappable hipsterism and desperate sense of energy and inventiveness first prove irritating, then simply exhausting, as every gag comes across as arbitrary and gratuitous. Commercial outlook appears limited, although proper marketing could locate enclaves of partisans.

First film by vid director Bill Fishman is constructed as an excuse to send up any number of music-video formats. As even fans of the genre agree, a little bit of it goes a long way, and protracted exposure to the frantic, superficial, aggressive style can produce a deadly overdose.

Plot per se is of little consequence, as security guards John Cusack and Tim Robbins junk their jobs to seek fame and fortune in the L.A. music scene. Along the way, they also become involved in political intrigue, with a tape of theirs showing a wealthy Presidential contender indulging in compromising sexual activity developing into an excuse for blackmail, hit man shoot-outs and humiliation on an unimaginable international scale.

Taken individually, some of Fishman's video parodies are amusing enough, notably a fried-chicken commercial done as a rap number and a heavy-metal tape about death that assumes new meaning when it must be aired posthumously in the wake of the band's sudden demise.

Along the way, Cusack, with his little mustache, who looks disconcertingly like Adolf Hitler, and Robbins resurrect an old blues twosome, impersonated by Junior Walker and Sam Moore, who have some self-kidding fun with their roles.

In general, casting is clever in a hokey way, with Connie Stevens and Doug McClure in as middle-class parents, Susan Tyrrell dropping by for a kinky moment, Jessica Walter popping in for a society party, Don Cornelius offering the boys as much spec work as they want and Lyle Alzado, in what must be an inside dig by producer Peter McCarthy and exec producer Michael Nesmith, portraying a proud veteran Universal Tour guide.

While indulging in some gentle chewing on the hand that's fed him, Fishman seems to adopt the general cynical attitude of his leading characters. —Cart.

You Can't Hurry Love

A Lightning Pictures release. Produced by Jonathan D. Krane. Executive producers, Lawrence Kasanoff, Ellen Steloff. Written and directed by Richard Martini. Camera (Duart color), Peter Lyons Collister, John Schwartzman; editor, Richard Candib; music, Bob Esty; art direction, Douglas A. Mowat; set decoration, Garreth Stover; sound (Dolby), Nicholas Allen; costumes, Colby Bart; coproducer, Simon R. Lewis; assistant director, Jan Ervin; associate producer, Anthony Santa Croce. Reviewed at Hollywood Egyptian theater, Hollywood, Jan. 28, 1988. MPAA Rating: R. Running time: 92 MIN.
Eddie ....David Packer
Skip ....Scott McGinnis
Peggy ....Bridget Fonda
Newcomb ....David Leisure
Tony ....Anthony Geary
Chuck Hayes ....Frank Bonner
Miss Friggett ....Lu Leonard
Monique ......Merete Van Kamp
Kelly Bones ....Sally Kellerman
Mr. Glerman ....Charles Grodin
Rhonda ....Kristy McNichol
Glenda ....Judy Balduzzi
Tracey................Danitza Kingsley

Hollywood — "You Can't Hurry Love" is a film with the consistency of Velveeta. It's a skin-deep teen comedy pretending to be a penetrating look at contemporary romance, but it has nothing to say beyond the most banal and hackneyed observations about life in L.A.'s fast lane. As a film that tries to please everyone, it should please hardly anyone.

Film is constructed around the novel premise that you must be yourself to find love. Not a bad idea in itself, but writer-director Richard Martini can't think of anything that hasn't already been said and done on the subject. What's worse, he has smoothed out all the rough edges, making L.A. (continually referred to as "this town") seem like a parody of itself.

Young Eddie (David Packer) is a nice kid fresh off the plane from Ohio who tries to keep in step with the dress, jargon and attitudes of life in this town. Film parodies L.A. cool while patting itself on the back for its own hipness.

Taking Eddie underwing is his swinging-single cousin Skip (Scott McGinnis) who through a scam lives in a Beverly Hills mansion and has girls waiting in line to pull off his torn jeans. When things don't go so well for Eddie, he winds up passing out circulars on Venice beach for his professional life and joining a video dating service for his social life.

Trying to strike the right pose to win friends and score with women, Eddie goes through a series of mindless misadventures which have him making love in the window of a Melrose Avenue boutique. After experiencing life as a freak show, he reclaims his solid American values which somehow transform this town back into his town.

Packer is likable in a star turn that owes more than a little to Tom Hanks (Packer even looks a bit like him). McGinnis is stiff and pretty while most everyone else is just pretty.

On the plus side, Bridget Fonda (Peter's daughter) gets passing grades in her first film role and manages a kind of vulnerable sweetness. David Leisure as an ad exec does an amusing version of corporate s.o.b. and Charles Grodin turns up in a cameo that is a virtual non sequitur. Kristy McNichol is ludicrous in another cameo as a performance artist.

Douglas A. Mowat's art direction looks right but Peter Lyons Collister and John Schwartzman's cinematography, like the rest of the film, offers a murky view of this town. —Jagr.

The Serpent And The Rainbow

A Universal Pictures release. Produced by David Ladd, Doug Claybourne. Executive producers, Rob Cohen, Keith Barish. Directed by Wes Craven. Screenplay, Richard Maxwell, A.R. Simoun, inspired by Wade Davis' book; camera (Duart color), John Lindley; editor, Glenn Farr; music, Brad Fiedel; percussion, Babatunde Olatunji; production design, David Nichols; art direction, David Brisbin; set design, Dawn Snyder; sound (Dolby), Donald Summer; special makeup effects, Lance Anderson, David Anderson; special visual effects supervisor, Gary Gutierrez; special mechanical effects, Image Engineering; costumes, Peter Mitchell; assistant director, Bob Engelman; associate producer, David B. Pauker; casting, Dianne Crittenden. Reviewed at Universal Pictures screening room, Universal City, Calif., Jan. 28, 1988. MPAA Rating: R. Running time: 98 MIN.
Dennis Alan ....Bill Pullman
Marielle..................Cathy Tyson
Dargent Peytraud ....Zakes Mokae
Lucien Celine ....Paul Winfield
Mozart ....Brent Jennings
Christophe............Conrad Roberts
Gaston ....Badja Djola
Simone ....Theresa Merritt
Schoonbacher..........Michael Gough
Andrew Cassedy ....Paul Guilfoyle
Mrs. Cassedy ....Dey Young
Celestine ....Aleta Mitchell

Hollywood — Wes Craven's "The Serpent And The Rainbow" is a better-than-average supernatural tale that offers a few good scares but gets bogged down in special effects. Distinguished by superior production values, film is intriguingly eerie as long as it explores the secrets of voodoo in a lush Haitian setting alive with mysteries of the spirit. Pic should enjoy a few good weeks at the boxoffice.

Although Richard Maxwell and A.R. Simoun's screenplay doesn't offer much of a story, thanks to Craven's skill the film gets along mostly on atmosphere. From the start one is caught up in the moody music by Brad Fiedel and John Lindley's humid photography. Unfortunately the explanations for it all are less than meets the eye.

When Craven relies on the traditional elements of good filmmaking — light and shadow, editing and camera movement, "The Serpent And The Rainbow" is good, gripping entertainment. Yet he can't resist the temptation to have snakes jumping out of people's mouths and blood gushing from every orifice.

Dennis Alan (Bill Pullman), a Harvard anthropologist looking for a magic zombie powder at the behest of an American drug company, is sort of a second-rate Indiana Jones. Character never strikes the right balance between cynicism and commitment and consequently he is unconvincing despite an earnest voice-over narration.

In Haiti, Alan gets involved with psychiatrist Marielle Celine (Cathy Tyson) who is battling the cumulative effects of deep-rooted black magic, religion and everyday mental illness. Film is at its best when it captures the complexities of the native culture and the conflicting cross-currents.

Opposing the more progressive Marielle are the reactionary political and supernatural forces of police chief Dargent Peytraud, played with evil zeal by Zakes Mokae. Speaking out of the side of his gold-toothed mouth, Mokae walks a narrow line between being truly frightening and truly hilarious.

Along for the ride are various zombies and practitioners of the ancient art. Paul Winfield does a convincing turn as the patriarch of the people while Conrad Roberts is a walking, talking zombie. Although the love story subplot between Pullman and Tyson never realy generates much feeling, Tyson projects a calm, magical command of the screen. Pullman is less magnetic but generally likable.

Special effects are well done, but fail to capture the creepy undercurrents of voodoo conveyed with greater impact through more human scale filmmaking. —Jagr.

Mariana, Mariana
(MEXICAN)

A Películas Mexicanas release of an Instituto Mexicano de Cinematográfica (Imcine) production. Executive producer, Héctor López Lechuga. Directed by Alberto Isaac. Screenplay, Vicente Leñero, José Estrada, based on the novel "Las Batallas en el Desierto" by José Emilio Pacheco; camera (color), Daniel López, Angel Goded; editor, Carlos Savage; art direction, Xavier Rodríguez, Jorge Morales; music, Carlos Warman. Reviewed at Acapulco Film Festival, Nov. 12, 1987. Running time: 110 MIN.
Carlos (adult) ....Pedro Armendáriz
Carlos (boy) ....Luis Mario Quiroz
Mariana................Elizabeth Aguilar
Jim ....Juan Carlos Andrews
Carlos' mother ....Saby Kamalaich
Carlos' father ....Aarón Hernán
Also with: Fernando Palavicini, Héctor Ortega, Ignacio Retes, José Carlos Cruz, Adolfo Olmos, Isabel Andrade, Gerardo Quiroz.

Acapulco — Mexican filmmaker Alberto Isaac has made a sensitive and disturbing picture dealing with the precocity of childhood in the small but carefully helmed "Mariana, Mariana." Isaac, former head of the Mexican Film Institute Imcine, took over the venture upon the sudden death of original director José Estrada in late 1986, just a week before the production was to

Based on the short autobiographical novel "Las Batallas en el Desierto" (Battles In The Desert), by José Emilio Pacheco, the film recounts the confused childhood crush that young Carlos (Luis Mario Quiroz) has on his best friend Jim's mother Mariana (Elizabeth Aguilar). Carlos' own family frowns on his association with Jim because his friend is illegitimate and the mother of doubtful morality, and they are upset when they discover the boy has gone off on an overnight picnic with Jim and his mother and even more distraught when Carlos skips school to declare his love for Mariana.

Story is told in retrospect as two men, the now grown Carlos (Pedro Armendáriz) and another former school chum are stuck in Mexico City's modern traffic nightmare and choked by smog. These scenes are contrived and unconvincing, especially when compared to the loving attention with which Isaac recreates a halcyon vision of Mexico's capital city as it existed during the early 1940s.

Isaac deftly gets inside the mind of the child Carlos and presents the cryptic world from this disturbing vantage point, one where adults follow different rules and the larger picture is that of incomprehensible mystery.

The young actors give complex and sensitive portrayals. Set and art directors Xavier Rodríguez and Jorge Morales provide detailed period work. Aguilar, as Mariana, offers a full portrait of a beautiful and touching woman. —Lent.

Lou, Pat & Joe D
(B&W)

A Marshall Entertainment Group release of a Vittoria/Furris production. Produced by Nicholas Furris. Coproducer, Michelle Materre. Written and directed by Stephen Vittoria. Camera (b&w), Tom Denove; editor, Leland Thomas; music, Daryll Dobson; sound, Edward Novick; production design, J.C. Svec; production manager, Hanif Shabazz; costume design, Anna Torres; assistant directors, Roderick Giles, Tyrone Henderson; associate producers, Michael Peluso, Todd Shane. Reviewed at Magno Preview 9 screening room, N.Y., Jan. 14, 1988. No MPAA Rating. Running time: **104 MIN.**

Pat Corelli	Nick Furris
Jacob Branch	Kim Delgado
Pat (older)	Ben Vittoria
Pat (younger)	Vince Mazzilli
Jacob (younger)	Richard Habersham
Pop	Frank Vincent
General Craig	Eddie R. White
Ben	Jerry Marino

One of the most quoted pearls of wisdom from the old Hollywood guard is the acerbic "If you want to send a message, use Western Union." "Lou, Pat & Joe D" ignores that vintage advice and tries very hard to make a definitive social statement. Visually, it succeeds, but much of the dialog might have been better served via a telegram.

"Lou" is a feast of frigid frames starkly chronicling events in the life of two friends growing up in 1930s New Jersey. Lensed in black & white, pic elicits the same melancholy feeling which results from flipping through an old scrapbook.

Scrapbook notion is reinforced as film opens with an older Pat Corelli (Ben Vittoria) reminiscing about his youth.

Flashbacks capture vignettes of painful realism as a younger Pat (Vince Mazzilli) — who is white — is seen meeting Jacob Branch (Richard Habersham), who is black. Though a friendship develops between them, racial tension of the period subtly serves to chip away at their camaraderie.

So does puberty. When teenage Pat (Nick Furris) becomes enamored with a girl, the chasm separating him from now adolescent Jake (Kim Delgado) widens and they wind up not speaking to each other.

Death — Pat's sister — morosely provides the catalyst for a reunion as Pat's anguish sends him seeking consolation from his old pal Jake.

The duo is separated again, this time by Uncle Sam, and Pat returns from Korea having lost a leg. His attitude is pragmatic regarding his injury, but he seems devastated to learn Joe DiMaggio (the Joe D in the title) has retired. Later, when Lou Costello dies (the Lou is the title), that event is depicted as hammering another nail of resignation into Pat.

Pat's hero worship of DiMaggio and admiration for Costello might sound trivial or contrived but actually provides a basis by which the insidious evolution of Pat's youthful enthusiasm into a chronic sense of helplessness can be gauged.

There is an analogy here too, since everything that happens in Pat's life happens to him, not because of any action on his part.

When Jake — on his way to a professional baseball tryout in the South — is lynched by Klan types, Pat's spirit is broken, his notion of self-determination invalidated.

This is the story the film conveys cinematically. Unfortunately, the dialog strains to tell a different story, one of racial unrest. The fact Pat is white and Jake is black really has no bearing on the ultimate condition of Pat's pitiful existence. In fact, the dichotomy between image and word is so acute, there actually are two distinct endings.

The cinematic finale occurs as an older Pat walks through the neighborhood — now in urban decay — and wistfully wails, "Jake was the closest thing to a hero the neighborhood ever produced." It is a moving scene and fitting conclusion.

Then the film lurches into a meaningless wrapup (made necessary by an early scene showing Pat talking to an unseen "doctor") which adds nothing pertinent.

There are a lot of other things wrong with this film but none worth dredging up in light of its low budget and first-time feature filmmakers. It tackles a very complex subject in a genuine enough way. Besides, with its b&w frames and bleak subject matter, it's not the typical commercial zinger with designs on mega-boxoffice performance.

Considering its humble origins, it delivers what one might expect and perhaps a bit more. — *Chuk.*

Time Out
(DANISH)

An Obel Film Release of a Gunnar Obel production. Executive producers, Bo Christensen, Gunnar Obel. Written and directed by Jon Bang Carlsen; camera (Eastmancolor), Alexander Gruszynski; editor, Bruce Cannon; music, Tomas Gislason; music, Anne Linnet; art direction, Viggo Bentzon; sound (Dolby), Henrik Langkilde, Leif Jensen; production management, Gerd Roos; casting, Barbara Remsen, Ann Remsen Manners. Reviewed at the Dagmar, Copenhagen, Jan. 27, 1988. Running time: **92 MIN.**

John	Alan Olsen
Lucy	Patricia Arquette
Smith	Geoffrey Lewis
Mrs. Smith	Nina Van Pallandt
Nixon	Dan Priest
The Sheriff	Richard Bright
Motel owner	Vincent Schiavelli
The derelict	Mike Gomez

Also with: Kirsten Olesen, Nonny Sand, Lars Bom Olesen, Julian Kyhl, Jack Jozefson, James R. Jarrett, Jonas Hoffenberg.

(English dialog)

Copenhagen — "Time Out" is a comedy thriller with English dialog and an American cast shot on location in New Mexico and Santa Monica, Calif., but it's as Danish as writer-director Jon Bang Carlsen, who is enamored with the American Gothic film. His picture falls somewhere between Joel Coen's "Blood Simple" and "Raising Arizona" and lands neatly on its artistic and technical feet.

Looking rather like the classical road movie, "Time Out" has John, a young Dane (gangly, sincere Alan Olsen) en route to Los Angeles to look for his long-lost father. He is trapped in a fly-speck New Mexico town where his money is stolen, presumably by Lucy, the young waitress (Patricia Arquette), who promptly offers him her bodily charms in return.

In rapid succession, John encounters smalltown xenophobia and rough treatment from the shifty-eyed motel-owner (Vincent Schiavelli) and the local sheriff (Richard Bright), who also has designs on Lucy. So does Lucy's father for that matter. He is a fire-and-brimstone lay preacher and the leader of a shoot-first Survival School in the desert. Bound to her father in an incestuous relationship, which she is not quite sure she dislikes, Lucy, in a neat "Baby Doll" takeoff, keeps everybody dangling.

John joins the Survival School to avoid being run out of town by the sheriff. His romance with Lucy blossoms. Lucy's father rolls his mean eyes and soon crosses the borderline to murderous insanity, but guess who gets shot first and by whom?

Hoping to find themselves a better father figure to cling to, the youngsters finally make it to the Coast, where a ghoulish surprise is in store for them. Aided by Alexander Gruszynski's fleet cinematography, Bruce Cannon's intelligent editing and actors who bring their Madame Tussaud characters wittily to life, Bang Carlsen gets away with almost everything except maybe his wish to be also taken seriously as a social satirist. —*Kell.*

Les Innocents
(The Innocents)
(FRENCH)

A UGC release of a T. Films/Cinéa/Films A2 coproduction, in association with Sofinergie and the CNC. Produced by Alain Terzian, Philippe Carcassonne. Directed by André Téchiné. Screenplay, Téchiné, Pascal Bonitzer; camera (Eastmancolor), Renato Berta; editor, Martine Giordano; music, Philippe Sarde, based on an 18th century melody; art direction, Ze Branco; sound, Jean-Louis Ughetto, Dominique Hennequin; song lyrics, Téchiné; song performed by Marie-France; assistant director, Michel Bena; casting, Philippe Landoulsi; production manager, Frédéric Sauvagnac. Reviewed at the UGC Champs-Elysées cinema, Paris, Jan. 10, 1988. Running time: **96 MIN.**

Jeanne	Sandrine Bonnaire
Stéphane	Simon de la Brosse
Said	Abdel Kechiche
Klotz	Jean-Claude Brialy
Alain	Stéphane Onfroy
Myriam	Tanya Lopert
Maïté	Christine Paolini
Hotel owner	Marthe Villalonga

Paris — Emotion yields to mannerism in André Téchiné's new film about a northern French girl who becomes tragically involved with two Mediterranean youths at daggers drawn in an ambience of racist tensions. Fuzzy characterizations in script by Téchiné and Pascal Bonitzer and some curiously elliptical direction make this inferior to the helmer's two previous films, "Rendez-vous" and "Scene Of The Crime," also produced by Alain Terzian.

Film's main disappointment is blandly unconvincing Sandrine Bonnaire as an orphan who comes to Toulon to attend her sister's marriage to an Algerian and retrieve her deaf and speechless kid brother, who's drifted into the shady company of a young Arab (Abdel Kechiche). Latter dreams of returning to a homeland he never knew and has promised to take Bonnaire's sibling with him.

Searching for her brother, Bonnaire meets and falls in love with Simon de la Brosse, the convalescing son of an embittered orchestra conductor (Jean-Claude Brialy) with a homosexual lien to Kechiche. Later on she also gets entangled with Kechiche unaware he stabbed La Brosse in a racial confrontation. She is unable to prevent the final explosion of hate in which both boys die side by side.

Though shooting in natural locations, Téchiné inflects realism towards a certain mythical quality (film opens with a "once upon a time..." intertitle, and closes with a quote from Sophocles), but the central performances lack conviction. Some emotion surfaces however in Brialy's desperation and that of the deaf-mute brother, whose puppy-dog devotion to Kechiche seems poignantly boundless.

Some of the supporting roles, notably Christine Paolini as Bonnaire's sister, and Marthe Villalonga as a hotel proprietress, have relief. Film technically is up to Téchiné's stylish standards.—*Len.*

Galactic Gigolo

An Urban Classics release from Titan Prods. and Generic Films. Produced by Gorman Bechard, Kris Covello. Directed by Bechard. Screenplay, Bechard, Carmine Capobianco; camera (Foto-Kem color), Bechard; editor, Joe Keiser; music, Lettuce Prey (Bob Esty, Michael Bernard); sound, Shaun Cashman; set design, Cashman, George Bernota; assistant director, Covello; production manager, Cashman; postproduction coordinator, Juliet Avola; associate producers, Capobianco, Cashman. Reviewed at Cine 42 #2, N.Y., Jan. 30, 1988. MPAA Rating: R. Running time: **82 MIN.**

Eoj	Carmine Capobianco
Hildy Johnson	Debi Thibeault
Dr. Pepper	Ruth Collins
Peggy Sue Peggy	Angela Nicholas
Waldo	Frank Stewart
Sonny Corleone	Michael Citriniti
Carmine	Tony Kruk
Tony	David Coughlin

Also with: Donna Davidge, Will Rokos, Todd Grant Kimsey, Barry Finkel, Bill Gillogly, J.E.L. Gitter, Lee Anne Baker, Toni Whyte, Lisa Schmidt, Jenny Bassett.

"Galactic Gigolo" is a home movie masquerading as a feature

film. Lensed a year ago as "Club Earth," pic is an interminable attempt at tasteless comedy which proves to be unwatchable.

Carmine Capobianco, whose smug charm is eminently resistible, toplines (and like the rest of cast and crew, fills many different production capacities) as Eoj, a broccoli from Outer Space who wins on a quiz show a 2-week vacation to Earth, i.e., Prospect, Conn. Pic consists of him using his hypnotic powers to go to bed with every woman in town, while two newshounds (Debi Thibeault and Frank Stewart) record his sexual escapades for the tabloids.

Idiotic subplots feature a mafia gang out to get Eoj and a family of backwoods rednecks, who happen to be, yuk, yuk, Jewish. Would-be auteur Gorman Bechard's mixture of bad puns, in-jokes, dumb namedropping and failed slapstick is a chore to endure, especially given the backyard filming absence of production values. Pic's running gag that Elvis Presley (and his subsequent imitators) was a spaceman is about as funny as its riproaring potshots at Prospect, Conn.—*Lor.*

The Nest

A Concorde Pictures release. Produced by Julie Corman. Directed by Terence H. Winkless. Screenplay, Robert King, from Eli Cantor's novel; camera (color), Ricardo Jacques Gale; editor, James A. Stewart, Stephen Mark; music, Rick Conrad; art direction, Carol Bosselman; set direction, Craig Sulli; associate producer, Lynn Whitney. Reviewed at AMC Towne 4, Oak Park, Mich., Jan. 23, 1988. MPAA Rating: R. Running time: **88 MIN.**

Mayor Elias Johnson	Robert Lansing
Elizabeth Johnson	Lisa Langlois
Richard Tarbell	Franc Luz
Dr. Morgan Hubbard	Terri Treas
Homer	Stephen Davies
Mrs. Pennington	Diana Bellamy
Shakey Jake	Jack Colins
Lillian	Nancy Morgan
Church	Jeff Winkless
Mr. Perkins	Steve Tannen
Jenny	Heidi Helmer
Diner	Karen Smyth
Stuntman	Noel Steven Geray

Oak Park, Mich. — Just when you thought it was safe to go back to the movies, here comes another low-budget "Aliens"/"Jaws"/-"Willard"/"The Swarm" derivative with enough humor and believable special effects to make its 88 minutes pass quickly. Little new ground is broken here in a tale of biogenetic experimentation gone amok. Its erstwhile acting and care for the genre should appeal to horror cultists.

There's something amiss in North Port, a small (pop. 700) west coast island resort town where Sheriff Richard Tarbell usually spends his days helping lost tourists find their way and courting the pretty owner of the local diner.

Tarbell soon learns that a couple of tourists are missing. The problem is Mayor Elias Johnson (Robert Lansing) who in an effort to entice a major corporation to develop his sleepy town, has made a deal with the devil in the form of INTEC, a mysterious corporation on the mainland.

The mayor has allowed the company to do some sort of secret experimenting and research in the town. Soon he realizes, however, that the experimenting has backfired.

When Tarbell confronts the mayor with the carcass of a devoured watchdog, Johnson calls in Dr. Morgan Hubbard (played with a delightful sense of maniacal devotion to science by Terri Treas) from INTEC.

Dr. Hubbard uses a playful cat to lure the frenzied cannibalistic cockroaches into a trap. The cat is quickly eaten alive, and Dr. Hubbard just as quickly realizes that an earlier experiment of hers seems to have gone awry.

At first, Dr. Hubbard believes she can destroy the roaches, but they have become immune to her poisons. Worse yet, they genetically mutate to the point where they literally become what they eat. In some of the film's best scenes, the cat turns into a wild half/cat roach monster. The outcome is even more morose when the super roaches start eating humans.

The only way to stop the roaches is to find their nest and kill the queen mutant roach. Tarbell and Elizabeth Johnson (Lisa Langlois), the mayor's daughter and an old flame of the Sheriff who has returned home to be with her father, join Hubbard in racing to the caves where the roaches colonize.

They have to hurry. INTEC, thinking the island has been evacuated, plans to spray North Port at sunrise with a chemical that may kill the roaches, but is certain to kill humans.

The science-gone-amok motif has worn pretty thin, but director Terence H. Winkless provides enough jokes and thrills to keep the film moving.

Staring at huge cockroaches crawling up people's legs — and there are plenty of scenes of those — can send shivers down your back. Homer (Stephen Davies), the local frizzed-out pest control man who sees this menace as the ultimate test of his anti-entomology skills, provides nice comic relief.

The film's stars, however, are the special effects, which start out slowly but build to a nice, gory finale where bug meets man. —*Advo.*

Emanon

A Paul Releasing release of a Paul Entertainment production. Executive producer, Steven Paul. Produced by Hank Paul, Dorothy Koster-Paul. Written and directed by Stuart Paul. Camera (Deluxe color), John Lambert; supervising editor, Richard Meyer; editor, Janet Riley; music, Lennie Niehaus; sound, Glenn Berkovitz; art direction, Donna Stamps; set decoration, Christina Volz; second unit director, Patrick Wright; casting, Koster-Paul. Reviewed on Charter Entertainment vidcassette, N.Y., Dec. 12, 1987. MPAA Rating: PG-13. Running time: **98 MIN.**

Emanon	Stuart Paul
Molly	Cheryl M. Lynn
Jason	Jeremy Miller
Max	Patrick Wright

Also with: B.J. Garrett, Robert Hackman, Tallie Cochrane, William F. Collard, Bonnie Paul, Steven Paul.

"Emanon" is a well-meaning but unsuccessful throwback to inspirational cinema, combining elements that would have fit in a Shirley Temple film in the 1930s with a plotline suited for a "Highway To Heaven" tv episode. Pic, a family effort by two generations of the Paul brood, was self-distributed briefly in 1986 ahead of current homevideo availability.

Writer-director Stuart Paul also appears as Emanon (that's No Name spelled backwards), a young Bowery bum in New York who performs very minor "miracles" such as delivering a baby and convincing a young model (real-life sister Bonnie Paul) not to jump off a church roof in despair.

Emanon is befriended by rich, crippled kid Jason (Jeremy Miller) whose beautiful mom Molly (Cheryl M. Lynn) is struggling to run her late husband's fashion business. With Emanon's help, Molly "creates" a new line of peasant garb to save her nest egg, while Jason miraculously throws his crutches away at the climax. Absurd overstatement has Emanon literally crucified by an angry New York mob, mad that he is not the messiah they thought he was.

Picture is overly saccharine in driving home its message of faith, while the casting of the two leads, Paul himself and Lynn, leaves it sorely lacking in acting skills. Jeremy Miller as the cute kid handles the thesping quota while Patrick Wright, a familiar face from B pictures, provides comic relief as the kid's chauffeur. — *Lor.*

Derrumbe
(Collapse)
(MEXICAN)

A Distribuidora y Exportadora de Cine de Latino América (Decla) release of a Canario Rojo production. Executive producer, Héctor Cervera Gómez. Produced and directed by Eduardo Carrasco Zanini. Screenplay, Luis Felipe Ybarra, Carrasco Zanini; camera (color), Jaime Carrasco Zanini; editor, Sigfrido García; music, Alberto Nuñez Palacio. Reviewed at Mecla, Havana Intl. Film Festival, Cuba, Dec. 16, 1987. Running time: **91 MIN.**

Fabián	Eduardo Palomo
Amadeo	Simón Guevara
Mirna	Yira Aparacio
Lucía	Marta Papadimitriou
Captain	Carlos Duering
Victoria	Tere Minghet
Elvira	Patricia Paramo

Havana — "Derrumbe" (Collapse) is a pretentious, offbeat Mexican art film that uses the destroyed rubble of the 1985 earthquakes as an almost sci-fi backdrop to this tale of moral collapse.

Improbable plot is full of outrageous scenes and hilarious overacting. After losing his job as a security official, Fabián (Eduardo Palomo) goes on a maniacal rampage, raving to himself and robbing a bank at gunpoint. He takes a woman hostage and rapes her. When the woman's son Amadeo (Simón Guevara) enters, Fabián shoots him and escapes. Amadeo's reaction is to call his mother a whore and vow revenge. Later Fabián, who has established a publishing empire with his robbery loot, invites the wounded Amadeo to rape his own wife in exchange and give him a job. Amadeo takes both, but plots something more grievous, which eventually takes place at a candlelight dinner among the ruins with a string quartet perched in the rubble of a collapsed building.

The film reads like a misplaced fable, yet the melodramatic plot twists and ham acting make for high camp throughout. The stark panorama of destroyed modern buildings in the background comes off as eerie urban monoliths of a familiar long-past culture.

"Collapse" should make for shambles at the boxoffice. Its unrestrained hysteria will alienate the art crowd and provoke a host of chortles from the general public.
—*Lent.*

Tequimán
(ECUADORAN)

An Asocine production. Written and directed by Jorge Vivanco. Camera (color), Criconbe Pérez; editor, Poncho Alvarez; music, Julio Bueno; animation, Eoumundo García. Reviewed at Havana Intl. Film Festival, Cuba, Dec. 12, 1987. Running time: **73 MIN.**

With: Rodrigo Vega, Edison Saime, Ivone Acumán, Guillermo Vega.

Havana — The Ecuadoran feature "Tequimán" is a super low budget kid pic with a tacked-on social message. The basic idea of the film would make for an interesting half-hour short perhaps, but its current 73-minute length is full of tedious repetition that drags out to unbearable proportions.

Pic's theme concerns three rich toddlers who dress up in comic book superhero costumes, while the adults are occupied with an outdoor wedding reception. These caped crusaders begin playing with the neighbor kids, who are poor children of nearby construction workers. The games are intercut with fantasy scenes, comic book-style animation and even a few musical numbers.

Sound qualities range from adequate to bad, while the photography lacks color correction. Color and light values shift continually from shot to shot making it difficult to follow the drawn-out storyline. Animation sequences are well handled.
—*Lent.*

De guerre lasse
(For The Sake Of Peace)
(FRENCH)

A Sara/CDF release of a Sara Films/Canal Plus Prods./Générale d'Images/TF 1 Films Prod. coproduction. Executive producer, Alain Sarde. Directed by Robert Enrico. Screenplay, Jean Aurenche, Didier Decoin, Enrico, based on the novel by Françoise Sagan; camera (Eastmancolor/Fuji), François Catonné; editor, Patricia Neny; music, Philippe Sarde; sound, Pierre Gamet, Guillaume Sciama, Jacques Thomas Gérard; art direction, Alain Veissier; costumes, Olga Berluti; production manager, Christine Gozlan; assistant director, Clément Delage. Reviewed at the Gaumont Ambassade cinema, Paris, Jan. 5, 1988. Running time: **123 MIN.**
Alice . . . . Nathalie Baye
Jérome . . . . Pierre Arditi
Charles . . . . Christophe Malavoy
Louise . . . . Geneviève Mnich
Paul . . . . Philippe Clevenot
Roth . . . . Jean Bouise

Paris — Director Robert Enrico, who scored one of his biggest commercial successes and a French César award for his 1976 wartime melodrama, "The Old Gun," returns to that mode in "De guerre lasse," based on a recent novel by Françoise Sagan about a romantic triangle during the German Occupation.

Performances by Pierre Arditi and Christophe Malavoy as rivals for Nathalie Baye, herself back in fine form after a 2-year absence, are main plusses in this otherwise familiar love-and-resistance drama.

Adaptation by veteran scripter Jean Aurenche and Didier Decoin (son of classic director Henri Decoin) adroitly but prosaically stitches together a plot of by-now-obligatory scenes of collaboration, resistance and Nazi sadism. Admirers of Sagan's novel have rapped the film for betraying the lyrical ambiguities of her characters.

Baye plays the widow of a Viennese Jewish surgeon and Arditi a former diplomat to Austria who, when France falls to the Germans, join the Resistance to help smuggle Jews out of the country.

They visit an old friend of Arditi's in the Free Zone (Malavoy) with the hopes of convincing him to participate in their activities. Malavoy, a shoe manufacturer with an uncle in the Vichy Government and an easy life, seems an unlikely recruit

Malavoy is not indifferent to Baye and accompanies her back to Paris when Arditi dispatches her on an assignment. Picked up and humiliated by a German patrol for violating curfew, Baye and Malavoy become lovers.

Baye finally chooses to remain with Malavoy, but when she later learns that Arditi has been arrested by the Gestapo she returns to the Maquis. Malavoy follows by enrolling as a freedom fighter.

Enrico's direction is workmanlike, without surprises and without mystery. His heroes are sympathetic but lack depth.

Supporting cast is good, notably the excellent stage actor Philippe Clevenot, who plays Baye's Viennese husband in an early flashback sequence. Clevenot's pained and thoughtful limning give these scenes their validity.

Period reconstruction is par for the course, and pic is technically slick.—*Len.*

Border
(BRITISH)

A BBC-TV production, in association with the Arts & Entertainment Network. Produced by Terry Coles, Directed by Misha Williams. Screenplay, Tim Rose Price, from a story by Jiri Stanislav; camera (color), Andrew Dunn, Graham Veevers; editor, Kate Evans; music, 'Jiri Stanislav; production design, Stuart Walker; set decoration, Graham Ross, Michael Horwood, Jane Rowson; costumes, Charlotte Holdich. Reviewed at the London Film Festival, Nov. 28, 1987. Running time: **96 MIN.**
Jan . . . . Shaun Scott
Eva . . . . Edita Brychta
Jiri . . . . Daniel Hill
The actress . . . . Catherine Schell
Also with: Christopher Hammond, Norman Jones, Lynn Farleigh, Hugh Dickson, Nicola Wright, Bob Sherman, Kate Fowler, Andre Thornton-Grimes.

London — Based on carefully researched historical incidents, "Border" is a gripping account of an attempted escape across the Iron Curtain by Czech refugees in 1952. To heighten the horror, it turns out that the supposed "border" was a false one — a ploy used by the regime to trap unsuspecting escapees, who would unknowingly denounce fellow conspirators back home.

Plot focuses on a core group of escapees: a young couple in love (played effectively by Edita Brychta and Daniel Hill) and their rebellious Jewish friend (Shaun Scott).

Much attention is lavished on the recreation of the atmosphere of Prague; thanks to set designer Stuart Walker, unremarkable Bradford, England, doubles credibly as the Czech capital.

A farewell dinner featuring a stolen carp perfectly conveys the differing reactions of people forced to cope with the repressive regime in Czechoslovakia.

The actual escape through an inhospitable landscape is a harrowing sequence, perfectly enhanced by the gritty, jittery camerawork. To compound the chillingness, the interrogators in the "Free West" debrief their unsuspecting victims in reassuring American accents. Only slowly does it dawn on Jiri (and on the viewer) that all is not quite right in the "free" western zone.

Although it is reported the BBC latched on to this project as a way of countering criticism of its left-wing bias in programming, "Border" manages to rise above its ideological underpinnings. Though not large-scale or star-studded, it tells its tale with style. Technical credits are fine and even the minor roles are well-performed. — *Guid.*

Cayenne-Palace
(FRENCH)

A UGC release of a Films Plain Chant Prods./Mikado Films/Canal Plus/UGC/Georges Reinhart Prods./Films 13 coproduction. Produced by Philippe Diaz. Directed by Alain Maline. Screenplay, Bruno Tardon, from story by Maline, Jérôme Tonnerre. Philippe Leguay; camera (Fujicolor), Jacques Steyn; editor, Hugues Darmois; music, Jean-François Léon; sound, Harald Maury, Paul Bertault; art direction, Bruno Held; production manager, Jean-Loup Monthieux. Reviewed at UGC Odéon cinema, Paris, Dec. 27, 1987. Running time: **96 MIN.**
Noël Caradec . . . . Richard Berry
Equateur . . . . Jean Yanne
Mathieu . . . . Xavier Deluc
Alice . . . . Olivia Brunaux
Lola . . . . Anna Karina
Lionel . . . . Jean-Roger Milo

Paris — A preposterous adventure yarn set and shot in French Guiana, "Cayenne-Palace" follows a young Frenchman's quest for his father, a convicted murderer who years before had escaped from a Guianese prison.

It's Richard Berry, absurdly clad in black hat and trenchcoat (this is a green *film noir*), who combs the jungles and rivers for his long-lost daddy, but only runs into a sleazy army of adventurers, mercenaries and other forms of local lowlifes. Many answer to local villain Jean Yanne, owner (with faded sexpot Anna Karina) of a seedy hotel-bar, Cayenne-Palace.

Berry's only allies are his half-brother, Xavier Deluc, an employee at a local French missile base, and Berry's girlfriend Olivia Brunaux who dizzily comes running from Paris six months later, having had no word from him.

There's also a tribe of local natives who for no reason take a liking to Berry and company. It's the Indians who rush to Berry's rescue when he falls into the clutches of the bad guys. Latter string Berry up by his feet and stick his head into a sack with a lethal snake. It's Berry who bites the reptile to death! A chip off the old block no doubt, since dad was something of a snake himself.

From Dreyfus to Papillon, the former penal institutions of Guiana have earned a dark mythical renown rarely exploited by French filmmakers. It's a shame Bruno Tardon's script (from an original story by Alain Maline, Jérôme Tonnerre and Philippe Leguay) is nothing more than a clichéd, hyperrealistic Gallic potboiler relocated abroad in the expectation that the exoticism will veil the stereotypes and trite situations. Director Maline has an eye for travelog shots and doesn't spare us the torrential rains, tropical fauna and carnival capers. — *Len.*

Terirem
(GREEK)

A Greek Film Center and Apostolos Doxiades production. Written and directed by Doxiades. Camera (color), Andreas Bellis, George Panoussopoulos; editor, G. Mavropsaridis, Panoussopoulos; sound, Nicos Achladis; sets, Alexis Kyritsopoulos. Reviewed at the Thessaloniki Film Festival, Oct. 4, 1987. Running time: **85 MIN.**
Costas Kavadias . . . Antonis Kafetzopoulos
Maria Kavadias . . . . Olia Lazaridou
Smuggler . . . . Demetris Poulicacos
Maria . . . . Vassia Panagopoulou
Leonidas . . . . Sophocles Pepas

Thessaloniki — This is the second picture by Apostolos Doxiades, but it turns out to be a halfway effort due to its unbelievable story, unevenness in construction and treatment and incredible characters.

The plot introduces Costas Kavadias, a player of shadow theater and his wife Maria, who cannot speak due to a brain tumor. They both arrive at a village for a series of performances when strange things are happening. An old woman sees visions which lead her nephew Leonidas to dig up a precious Byzantine icon, and sell it to a smuggler of antiquities. The local priest, unable to explain the happenings asks his uncle, a monk, for advice. Latter arrives in the village accompanied by a novice monk.

Meanwhile, Maria confesses to her husband that she had deceived him with her doctor. Costas, in a fury, deserts her and turns to his assistant. Maria attempts suicide but is saved by the young monk, who teaches her how to pray.

The smugglers kill the old woman, fearing she knew too much. When the Costases' new girl walks out with another lover, he sets fire to his wooden theater and goes to his wife crying. Maria takes him in her arms and begins to talk. She has been healed.

Doxiades, trying to avoid melodramatic pitfalls, narrates his story by simply combining several incidents. He fails to make this naive story or its message believable, namely, whoever believes in something may get it. Terirem is a Byzantine psalm meaning the hymn of the angels. Due to the unevenness of his treatment there is a lack of balance in various scenes and the sex scene of Maria and her doctor obviously was added for exploitation value.

Olia Lazaridou's good performance does not save the film. Antonis Kafetzopoulos turns in a competent performance.

All technical credits are above standard.—*Rena.*

Les Keufs
(The Flatfoots)
(FRENCH)

An AMLF release of a GPFI/Films Flam/Film A2 coproduction. Produced by Jean-Claude Fleury. Directed by Josiane Balasko. Screenplay, Christian Biegalski, Jean-Bernard Pouy, Balasko; camera (color), Dominique Chapuis; editor, Catherine Kelber; music, Manu Dibango, Stéphan Sirkis, Raoul and Francis Agbo, Charles Trenet; art direction, Carlos Conti; sound, Gérard Lamps; production manager, Charlotte Fraisse. Reviewed at the Gaumont Colisée cinema, Paris, Dec. 25, 1987. Running time: **97 MIN.**

Mireille Molyneux . . . . Josiane Balasko
Blaise Lacroix . . . . Isaach de Bankolé
Inspector Blondel . . . . Ticky Holdago
Inspector Averell . . . . Patrick Olivier
Comm. Bouvreuil . . . . . . Jean-Pierre Léaud

Paris — Comedienne Josiane Balasko struck out with her Warner Bros.-backed writing-helming debut "Un Sac de noeuds" (1985), a black comedy in which the blackness smothered the comedy. She fares much better in her second directorial outing, "Les Keufs," a police comedy-drama in which humor and seriousness are better balanced. Cut from a more conventional pattern by scripters Christian Biegalski and Jean-Bernard Pouy, tale of an aggressive woman cop and a black detective provides an entertaining vehicle for Balasko, the actress, and Isaach de Bankolé.

Balasko, a saucy, plump redhead, is leading a personal crusade against a dangerous pimp when she runs into Bankolé, who's been put on her trail to check an accusation of corruption. At first antagonists, the red and the black merge, become colleagues, and simultaneously lovers.

Balasko (who adapted the script and wrote the dialog) is sharp behind and in front of the camera and Bankolé (laureled for his performance in last year's comedy hit, "Black mic-mac") confirms a winning personality. The tandem is impertinent and charming. Taken as a straight Gallic thriller, it often convinces better than more heavy-breathing recent efforts.

Among a good supporting cast is Jean-Pierre Léaud, who offers his usual contortions as Balasko's hysterical superior. Tech credits are okay. —*Len.*

Der Flieger
(The Flyer)
(WEST GERMAN)

A Xenon Films production, Hamburg, West Germany. Executive producer, Michael Bergmann. Produced by Anke Apelt. Directed by Erwin Keusch. Screenplay, Uwe Timm; camera (color), Jürgen Jürges; editor, Barbara Hennings; music, Andreas Kobner; sound, Wolf D. Peters-Vallerius; set design, Gabriele Hochheim; costumes, Regina Troester; props, Volkmar Vittinghoff; makeup, Karin Patschke; assistant director, John P. Meade. Reviewed at the Chicago Intl. Film Festival, Oct. 6, 1987. Running time: 102 MIN.
Bernd Klinger . . . . Martin May
Rita . . . . Ulrike Kriener
Moni . . . . Birgit Franz
Ewald . . . . Norbert Mahler
Vater Klinger . . . . Dieter Augustin
Mutter Klinger . . . . Ilse Schorner
Bollwieser . . . . Eberhard Wagner
Also with: J. Drew Lucas, Heiner Stadelmann, Karl Huls, Lisa Helwig, Joost Siedhoff, Douglas Welbat, Peter Weintritt, Herbert Lehnert, Herrmann Motschach, Gabriele Kastner, Silvia Guhr-Hildebrand.

Chicago — "The Flyer" might have been an uninteresting film if it had merely presented, one more time, the story of a youth who gets the chance to achieve a dream of glory. Fortunately, this film takes that old cliché and turns it inside out, revealing the dismay of a kid who has a private dream forced on him in reality.

Title character is Bernd Klinger, an amateur hang glider from a small town in Germany who dreams of breaking a world record by flying from Mt. Palomani in the Andes, over an uncharted jungle full of headhunters to a distant village. At first, Klinger's plan is strictly kid's stuff, little more than a fantasy shared with two close friends. An ambitious journalist enters the scene and before he's fully prepared, Klinger finds himself en route to a very dangerous rendezvous with destiny.

Most enjoyable aspect of "The Flyer" is Uwe Timm's tightly constructed script, layered with ironies that give the film a dark undercurrent of humor. For example, Klinger's small town already has one heroic world-record holder, a young man who walks 60 feet on raw eggs.

The cast turns in uniformly solid performances, particularly Martin May as Klinger, the dreamer who finds reality to be a rude awakening. Director Erwin Keusch moves things along at a brisk pace that builds nicely, right up to the end.

Unfortunately, the picture has an ambiguous ending that comes as surprise and a bit of a disappointment. Despite that drawback, there's a lot to recommend about "The Flyer," a charming and absorbing film that deserves to find an appreciative audience. —*Brin.*

Shoot To Kill

A Buena Vista release of a Touchstone Pictures presentation, in association with Silver Screen Partners III, of a Philip Rogers production. Executive producer, Rogers. Produced by Ron Silverman, Daniel Petrie Jr. Directed by Roger Spottiswoode. Screenplay, Harv Zimmel, Michael Burton, Daniel Petrie Jr., from story by Zimmel; camera (Widescreen, Alpha Cine color), Michael Chapman; editor, Garth Craven, George Bowers; music, John Scott; production design, Richard Sylbert; art direction, John Willett; set decoration, Jim Erickson; costume design, Richard Bruno; sound (Dolby), Simon Kaye; assistant director, Michael Steele; special effects supervisor, John Thomas; second unit director-stunt coordinator, Fred Waugh; additional photography, Robert Stevens; second unit camera, Curtis Peterson; associate producer, Fredda Weiss; casting, Penny Perry; Canadian casting, Lynne Carrow. Reviewed at the AMC 10 Theaters, Burbank, Calif., Feb. 3, 1988. MPAA Rating: R. Running time: 110 MIN.
Warren Stantin . . . . Sidney Poitier
Jonathan Knox . . . . Tom Berenger
Sarah . . . . Kirstie Alley
Steve . . . . Clancy Brown
Norman . . . . Richard Masur
Harvey . . . . Andrew Robinson
Ben . . . . Kevin Scannell
Ralph . . . . Frederick Coffin
Fournier . . . . Michael MacRae
Minelli . . . . Robert Lesser

Hollywood — Everybody, including the audience, gets a good workout in "Shoot To Kill," a rugged, involving manhunt adventure in which a criminal leads his pursuers over what is perhaps the most challenging land route out of the United States. Sidney Poitier makes an effective and welcome return to the screen after more than a decade's absence, and Buena Vista should be able to overcome the meaningless, vaguely exploitation-sounding title to rack up some decent late-winter grosses.

Originally titled "Mountain King," pic actually was Poitier's second recent outing as an actor, as it was lensed in the spring of 1987 after he completed the as-yet-unreleased "Little Nikita." Here, he establishes his authority immediately as a veteran FBI man in San Francisco who, despite handling the crisis with calm assuredness, cannot prevent the getaway of a jewel thief who kills hostages on a foggy night on Frisco Bay.

Another shooting of a similar type takes Poitier up to the Pacific Northwest, where he is forced to engage the services of tough backwoodsman Tom Berenger to lead him up into the mountains to apprehend the villain before he makes it over the border into Canada.

In a certain sense, Harv Zimmel's story represents a mere recasting of the basic situation in "In The Heat Of The Night," with big city cop Poitier teamed up with a white man who wants no part of him. The times and tone have changed completely, however, and Berenger's objections to the assignment have nothing to do with race (in fact, any reference to racial matters is withheld for so long one imagines it might be avoided altogether, but Poitier himself finally lets the lid off with a good joke).

A self-styled macho hermit, Berenger considers Poitier a cityfied softy incapable of making it in the mountains. This sets up a cliched enmity between the two men that one knows will have to be broken down in the course of the picture, as indeed it is, but not without some predictable jibes at Poitier's awkwardness outdoors and some revelations of Berenger's own vulnerabilities.

Fortunately, screenwriters Zimmel, Michael Burton and Daniel Petrie Jr. have come up with some inventive twists that, for the most part, lift the story out of conventional territory. The murderer joins up with a band of backpackers led by Berenger's girlfriend, Kirstie Alley, and the long second act consists of alternation between the two men's increasingly difficult chase through imposing terrain, and the tense journey of the criminal and his resourceful hostage.

After "Under Fire" and "The Best Of Times," director Roger Spottiswoode has set himself a formidable technical exercise here and passed with plenty of room to spare. Muscular handling of visceral action scenes on remote locations occasionally brings memories of "Deliverance" to mind, and the director seems to have delighted in subverting viewer expectations in some sequences and surpassing them in others.

Although it has a couple of surprises up its sleeve, climactic action rests upon some coincidences that strain credulity, and goes on at undue length. Situation also is a bit perplexing in that Poitier pursues his prey, first into Canadian territory, then into the City of Vancouver, all the while behaving as though this still were his turf despite the change of jurisdiction and without a murmur of protest from the Mounties.

Poitier, 63 when the film was shot, looks little more than 40 and perhaps now qualifies as the youngest-looking leading man of a certain age since Cary Grant (who was 62 when he made his last film, "Walk, Don't Run"). The actor's directness and easiness on the screen are refreshing, his humor self-deprecating and understated.

Berenger solidly fills the bill as the confident mountain man, and Kirstie Alley, despite the extreme limitations of her role, proves entirely believable as his female counterpart.

British Columbia locations give the film tremendous scenic impact, and Michael Chapman's camera has captured the surroundings beautifully and from many angles. John Scott's varied and subtle score also greatly adds to the story's power.
—*Cart.*

Die Katze
(The Cat)
(WEST GERMAN)

A Bavaria Film production of a Neue Constantin Film release. Produced by Georg Feil. Directed by Dominik Graf. Screenplay, Uwe Erichsen, Christoph Fromm from a novel by Erichsen; camera (color), Martin Schäfer; editor, Christel Suckow; music, Andreas Koebner; theme song "Good Times" by Eric Burdon; art direction, Matthias Kammermeier; costumes, Susanne Wemcken. Reviewed at Ufa Palast, Hamburg, Feb. 3, 1988. Running time: **108 MIN.**
Probek . . . . Götz George
Jutta . . . . Gudrun Landgrebe
Also with: Heinz Hoenig, Joachim Kemmer, Ralf Richter, Ulrich Gebauer, Sabine Kaack, Iris Disse, Heinrich Schafmeister, Uli Krohm, Erich Will.

Hamburg — Fast paced, well-written, well-acted and tightly directed actioners are rare in West Germany. "The Cat" is all of the above and should have its producers purring all the way to the bank.

Every word of this taut screenplay counts — a plus for Götz George, the hairy-chest heartthrob of many a housefrau due to a prime-time crime skein. He's at his best grimacing and leaping over banisters, and is used to good advantage here as the cool-headed mastermind of a high-tech bank heist in a highrise complex. No one knows he has the bank director's wife (Landgrebe) wrapped around his little finger — or is it the other way around?

Plot takes about as many twists and turns as Gudrun Landgrebe's car does as she snakes out of a traffic jam with 4,000,000 marks in unmarked bills in the trunk and the law on her bumper.

There's good acting by all hands as well as sexual situations and rough language. The inevitable bloodbath is reserved for the final reel. —*Gill.*

Les Possédés
(The Possessed)
(FRENCH)

A Gaumont production and release. Coproducer, Films A2. Produced by Margaret Menegoz, Les Films du Losange. Directed by Andrzej Wajda. Screenplay, Jean-Claude Carrière, Wajda, Agnieszka Holland, Edward Zebrowski, from novel by Fyodor Dostoevsky; camera (Agfa color), Witold Adamek; editor, Halina Prugar Kettling; music, Zugmunt Konieczny; art direction, Allan Starski; sound, Piotr Zawadzki; makeup, Krystyna Leszcynska; costumes, Krystyna Zachwatowicz; assistant director, Krystyna Grochowicz; production manager, Barbara Pec-Slesicka. Reviewed at the Publicis screening room, Paris, Feb. 2, 1988. (In Berlin Film Festival — competing.) Running time: **116 MIN.**
Peter Verkhovensky . Jean-Philippe Ecoffey
Nikolas Stavrogin . . . . Lambert Wilson
Ivan Shatov . . . . Jerzy Radziwilowicz
Maria Shatov . . . . Isabelle Huppert
Liza . . . . Philippine Leroy Beaulieu
Maria Lebyatkin . . . . Jutta Lampe
Alexei Kirilov . . . . Laurent Malet
Stephan Verkhovensky . . . . . . Omar Sharif
Schigalov . . . . Philippe Chambon
Fedka . . . . Serge Spira
Lebyatkin . . . . Wladimir Yordanoff
Virginsky . . . . Jean-Quentin Chatelain
Erkel . . . . Rémi Martin

Paris — Andrzej Wajda has made a wild and woolly film of Fyodor Dostoevsky's 1870 political novel "The Possessed" (a.k.a. "The Devils"), in which the Russian writer settled his accounts with the revolutionary movement to which he had once belonged. Manipulating a motley European cast in a French-language period recreation (shot on location in Poland), Wajda captures the feverish, often pathological climate of Dostoevsky's hothouse universe. Yet pic's success as literary adaptation is comprised by an often ragged screenplay and a group of young Gallic leads who aren't quite up to the demands of stylization Wajda makes on them. Film is competing at the Berlin festival and should have tongues wagging one way or another, which will help it to a healthy arthouse career internationally.

Spectators unfamiliar with the book (for which one needs a scorecard to keep tabs on characters and incidents) will.no doubt be confused by the adaptation Wajda has entrusted to jack-of-all-trades scripter Jean-Claude Carrière, with whom he made "Danton," his first French-language production, in 1983.

Understandably, much of Dostoevsky's overheated and raggedly disgressive plot has been shorn away and numerous secondary characters eliminated, but rather than gain in clarity and dramatic force, the film often loses in density and thematic design.

The writer's personages essentially are marionettes in a shadow show of ideological conflicts, articulated by a brilliant if undisciplined dramatist-puppeteer. Wajda's breathless direction beguilingly catches the nervous energy of the erratic Dostevsky style, but the cut-and-paste thinness of the script reduces the social background to a matter of art direction, and the plot's made protagonists are revealed in all their propagandistic nudity.

Impression of theatricality that both propels and hinders the action is due to the nature of Dostoevsky's melodramatic narrative, but certainly also owes something to the fact that Wajda has staged several legit adaptations of the novel, including an American production at Yale in 1974.

Wajda and Carrière take a running leap into the story with nothing more than an opening intertitle to provide the barest of exposition: a group of young nihilists from a provincial Russian city return from a stay abroad with plans for fomenting social disorder as part of a would be large-scale revolution.

The rabid ringleader is cynical Peter Verkhovensky (Jean-Philippe Ecoffey), who employs pre-Stalinist methods to sway the local revolutionary cell composed of cowardly and gullible local functionaries, whom he finally leads to an act of murder.

Ecoffey's professed model and mentor is decadent dandy Nikolas Stavrogin (Lambert Wilson), whom former wants to apotheosize as the movement's messiah. Wilson remains aloof from his demonic colleagues, bent on a personal destiny of depravity and self-degradation.

Ecoffey's destructive social agitations hide personal motives: he seeks revenge against Shatov (Jerzy Radziwilowicz), a repentant activist who wants out of the movement. Humiliated in the past by Radziwilowicz, Ecoffey convinces his fellow fanatics that former is planning to denounce the group to the authorities.

In a terrifying climax that doesn't betray the book, Radziwilowicz, thrown off guard by the unexpected return of an estranged wife (Isabelle Huppert) who is about to deliver Wilson's baby, is lured out to a remote spot and brutally executed by Ecoffey and company.

Wajda, working with his French actors via an interpreter, guides them through the gesticulating motions of their roles, but most of the players seem ill at ease with this exaggerated style of performance. Laurent Malet particularly is inadequate in the marvelous part of Kirilov, a mystical looney who advocates suicide as the supreme expression of free will and finally blows his brains out as part of Ecoffey's overall design of murder and arson.

Not surprisingly the film's most convincing performance comes from Radziwilowicz, who was Wajda's Man of Marble and Iron and clearly is on the director's wavelength. His is the only humanly sympathetic characterization, based as it is on Dostoevsky's own activist youth. As the naive and hesitant Shatov, rapturously and fatally confused by the return of his wife, Radziwilowicz activates the potboiling action with pathetic humanity.

Omar Sharif is oddly miscast as Ecoffey's intellectual father, a basically comical figure who is the butt of Dostoevsky's scorn for spineless liberals who toady to the younger generation of revolutionary ideals. Unfortunately Wajda has no feeling for the book's often savage humor.

Moodily lensed by Witold Adamek, and smartly executed by a mostly Polish tech crew, Wajda's film is unsatisfying on many accounts, but in its best moments comes closer than many other films in translating Dostoevsky's fury with the godlessness of society on the edge of the abyss.

It will be fascinating to see what political readings this film will give rise to. —*Len.*

Skyggen af Emma
(Emma's Shadow)
(DANISH)

A Metronome Film release of Metronome Film production with the Danish Film Institute. Produced by Tivi Magnusson, DFI consultant producer, Ira Zerunejth. Directed by Sören Kragh Jacobsen. Screenplay, Jacobsen, Jörn O. Jensen; camera (Eastmancolor), Dan Lausten; editor, Leif Axel Kjeldsen; music, Thomas Lindahl; art direction, Lars Nielsen; sound, Morten Degnbol; costumes, Jette Terman; production management, Ib Tardini, Jens Arnoldus; assistant director, Birger Larsen. Reviewed at the Palads, Copenhagen, Jan. 25, 1988. Running time: **98 MIN.**
Emma . . . . Line Kruse
Malthe Eliasson . . . . Börje Ahlstedt
Emma's father . . . . Henrik Larsen
Emma's mother . . . . Inge Sofie Skovbo
Malthe's lady friend . . . . . Ulla Henningsen
Gustav . . . . Bent Nalepa Steinert
Albert . . . . Ken Vedsegaard
Eatery owner . . . . Otto Brandenburg
Chauffeur . . . . Jesper Christensen
Chief of detectives . . . . Erik Wedersöe
Also with: Sanne Grangaard, Pernille Hansen, Lene Vasegaard, Jeanne Boel, Sören Oestergaard.

Copenhagen — Due for an immediate international sales launch, "Emma's Shadow" is a soft-spoken comedy thriller about a poor little rich girl runaway who seeks refuge and solace with a poor Swedish immigrant sewer-worker in the slums of 1931 Copenhagen. Although limiting picture's appeal to the 8-14 age group, writer-director Sören Kragh Jacobsen may see quite a few older relatives joining their kids in an enthusiastic sob or two.

Plot is contrived to the point where unlimited Damon Runyon-esque fun would seem the right narrative solution, but Kragh Jacobsen is burdened heavily with an old-fashioned social conscience, so he insists on his characters being believable. They are not. The 11-year-old girl Line and the abjectly naive and downtrodden Swede Malthe are seen in a relentlessly sentimental light, while the girl's parents are never allowed a single breather from the rigid Stupid Rich cliché.

When things work to a certain degree of cinema magic, it's mostly thanks to Line Kruse as Emma. She has some stage experience, and on film Kragh Jacobsen elicits her coquettish charm and vicious temper to match any adult diva.

The shadow of the film's title has no discernible meaning. Emma tells her slum friend she is a Russian aristocrat on the run from the Bolsheviks. He believes her absolutely while playing moodily on his broken-down pipe organ. The girl has mailed a fake ransom note to her parents, inspired by the current newspaper coverage of the Lindbergh kidnap case.

When the ransom actually is delivered, Line invites the Swede and a couple of small slum boys to a hotel suite, where a champagne-and-caviar dinner is laid out. Meanwhile, the police search turns into an outright chase, and the comedy pales as Kragh Jacobsen generates genuine cinematic energy in his film's thriller element.

The theme of friendship growing between the refined girl and the clumsy Swede (played with discreet bumbling by Börje Ahlstedt) is developed with rather too languid care, while Kragh Jacobsen vacillates between twinkle-eyed fun and straight suspense. —*Kell.*

Sagolandet
(The Fairytale Country)
(SWEDISH-DOCU)

A Swedish Film Institute release of a Bold production with SVT-Malmö and the Swedish Film Institute. Produced by Göran Setterberg. Executive producer, Bengt Linné. Conceived (no screenplay credit), camera (Eastmancolor), edited and directed by Jan Troell. Music, Tom Wolgers; sound, Studio Lagnö. Reviewed at Gothenburg Intl. Film Festival (official entry), Jan. 30, 1988. Running time: **185 MIN.**
Interviewees: Rollo May, Ingvar Carlsson, Tage Erlander, Anita Grede. With Johanna Troell as herself.

Gothenburg — This docu certainly is overlong even if cut down from a reported 80 hours to 185 minutes, and its traveling prospects outside of specialized situations — even to other Nordic lands — must be deemed dim. Still, Jan Troell, who took five years off from feature filmmaking to docu the state of his native Sweden, has brought "The Fairytale Country" off as a tour de force of a strength that runs deep and a stubborn honesty that will reward any patient audience with new and often frightening insights.

Never resorting to scare tactics or to the traditional, hurried hectoring of opininated tv documentarists, Troell has all his interviewees given plenty of time to think before speaking their little pieces about their chosen professions or pursuits. They represent such diverse ways of life as those of the parliamentary and local politician; the rural road planner; the plant exterminator; the municipal dog-killer-cum-mortician; the woodsman with the saw that fells six trees at a time; and an artist-weaver.

Generally, they contribute to a picture of Sweden as a tightly regulated nation where social progress is identified with technical progress at the expense of free will and independent thinking, let alone imagination. The artist-weaver is, of course, an exception. So is Johanna, Troell's daughter, who is followed from her moment of birth and on to her early fumbling and stumbling into a world that will not, one hopes along with her father, regulate her to the numbness of playing computerized bingo games, as many adult Swedes do.

One would also hate to see her one day join in the hunting down of Sweden's last surviving wild beast, the wolf. One such wolf is seen being freed for the sake of scientific research; another is shot and dissected before being skinned and strung up.

Troell frames his own mute pleas for sanity with little speeches made by U.S. psychotherapist and moral philosopher Rollo May and by Sweden's new Social Democrat premier Ingvar Carlsson and the same party's Grand Old Man, since deceased Tage Erlander. The lastnamed pair defend conformity by claiming only well-fed and well-housed people will feel any impetus to use their imagination, while Rollo, who knows Sweden well, spouts trite wisdoms about the state being too good a parent by offering the kids too many playthings and leaving them too little room to think up games themselves.

Rollo May is seen going down a kindergarten slide and having great fun while moaning about the near-impossibility of "resuscitation of the dead soul of Western civilization." Here is exactly the hectoring that Troell himself backs away from. Still, the director obviously felt he needed May's platitudes in order not to leave the audience entirely dangling, as he clearly does himself, between optimism and pessimism.

It is exactly when posing questions rather than when offering answers that "The Fairytale Country" retains wonder, magic and hope, as in the end vignette where little Johanna plucks a red poppy and sticks in into the pocket of a black scarecrow. — *Kell.*

Born To Race

An MGM/UA Distribution Co. release from United Artists of a Romax production. Produced by Andrew Bullians, Jean Bullians. Directed by James Fargo. Screenplay, Dennis McGee, Mary Janeway Bullians, from story by Mary Janeway Bullians; camera (color), Bernard Salzmann; editor, Tony Lombardo, Thomas Stanford; music, Ross Vannelli; production manager, John J. Smith; associate producer, Nicholas Longhurst; production design, Katherine G. Vallin; assistant director, Dennis White; rerecorded in Ultra-Stereo; opticals by Lorimar Telepictures. Reviewed at AMC Towne 4, Detroit, Feb. 2, 1988. MPAA Rating: R. Running time: **98 MIN.**

Al Pagura	Joseph Bottoms
Kenny Landruff	Marc Singer
Vincent Duplain	George Kennedy
Andrea Lombardo	Marla Heasley
Enrico Lombardo	Antonio Sabato
Theo Jennings	Robert F. Logan
Bud	Dirk Blocker
Walt	Michael McGrady
Jenny	LaGena Hart

Detroit — Even if the race scenes were going at 100 miles per hour, stilted acting, atrocious dialog and a predictable, hackneyed plot conspire to throw "Born To Race" into a tailspin of mediocrity. The plan to confine theatrical release of this film to Detroit, Texas and North and South Carolina before rushing it into video seems about the best decision made around this movie, which is unlikely to appeal to race car or action/adventure fans, about the only groups it ever had a chance of reaching.

Even George Kennedy, who limps around both literally and figurative-ly as the heavy in what appears to be "The Hardy Boys Meet Heart Like A Wheel," fails to bring a spark to this story of deceit and corruption set against a North Carolina stock car race.

Marla Heasley, an attractive Italian auto designer, has come up with a "revolutionary" design for an auto engine. So where does her wealthy father send her to show off this new technology? To the weekend Hickory Speedway race in Charlotte, N.C.

The bad guys kidnap her to steal her engine designs (we know they're the bad guys because they have black T-shirts, black greasy hair and need shaves). The good guys (light hair, bright shirts and shaven) rescue her, but spend the rest of the movie trying to get back the engine blueprints.

Heasley and Joseph Bottoms, who plays good-guy race car driver Al Pagura, fall in love, fight a lot, fall out of love, fight a lot and finally fall in love again.

Robert F. Logan as Theo Jennings, Bottoms' race car mentor, lends an easy acting style to the film, despite such lines as "You know, pride is like oysters. They're both hard to swallow."

Also hard to swallow is the notion that 1) no one in Italy has a copy of the engine plans, 2) one lone engineering graduate has revolutionized auto design, 3) an engine can be completely overhauled in an evening, and more.

While the film is technically competent, its limping pace makes even the "big race" finale seem unimportant. —*Advo.*

Sorority Babes In The Slimeball Bowl-O-Rama

An Urban Classics release of a Titan production. Produced by David DeCoteau, John Schouweiler. Directed by DeCoteau. Screenplay, Sergei Hasenecz; camera (Foto-Kem color), Stephen Ashley Blake; editor, Barry Zetlin, Tom Meshelski; music supervision, Jonathan Scott Bogner; music, Guy Moon, including excerpts from "Creepozoids;" sound, Mary Kasparian; production design, Royce Mathew; special makeup & creature effects, Craig Caton; assistant director, Will Clark; additional photography, Scott Ressler; postproduction coordinator, Juliet Avola. Reviewed at Cine 42 No. 2 theater, N.Y., Jan. 30, 1988. MPAA Rating: R. Running time: **78 MIN.**

Spider	Linnea Quigley
Lisa	Michelle Bauer
Calvin	Andras Jones
Babs	Robin Rochelle
Taffy	Brinke Stevens
Rhonda	Kathi Obrecht
Frankie	Carla Baron
Jimmie	Hal Havins
Keith	John Stuart Wildman
Janitor	George (Buck) Flower

This film, with its mouthful of a release title, began its life as simply "The Imp," constituting an enjoyable (for exploitation film fans) mishmash of fantasy, horror and t&a. Pic's theatrical prospects are meager but it should attract attention among homevideo loyalists.

Opening is in the wornout genre of three young nerds/Peeping Toms glomming the pretty girls who get paddled as part of the Tri Delta sorority initiation rites. Pic then slides into even cornier territory (e.g., "The Initiation") of the pledges (Michelle Bauer, Brinke Stevens) sent to a shopping mall after dark to break in and capture a bowling trophy. The three nerds are sent along for the ride by dominatrix-styled sorority girl Babs (Robin Rochelle), who plans to pull practical jokes on them at the mall.

Story takes a more interesting turn when the kids drop their bowling trophy which releases a cute, demonic puppet, The Imp. It grants each of them a wish, but in perverse fashion changes the girls into marauding monsters. Filmmaker David DeCoteau (who makes fun here of his nom de plume David McCabe) has fun with the concept.

The Imp is an okay creation by Craig Caton, voiced by one "Dukey Flyswatter," a pseudonymn used by Michael D. Sonye. Among the gals, Michelle Bauer (billed as Michelle McClellan) is more than an eyeful and feisty Linnea Quigley makes an engagingly sarcastic and resourceful heroine. —*Lor.*

Doxobus
(GREEK)

A Greek Film Center-ERT I and Lampa Ltd. production. Directed by Fotos Lambrinos. Screenplay, Lambrinos, Panos Theodoridis; camera (color), George Arvanitis; editor, Aristidis Karydis Fuchs; music, Costas Vomvolos; sets, Mikes Karapiperis; costumes, Ioanna Papantoniou; sound, Yannis Haralambidis. Reviewed at the Thessaloniki Film Festival, Oct. 5, 1987. Running time: **105 MIN.**
Xenos ... Tassos Palaitzidis
Also with: Stelios Capatos, Barbara Mavromati, Panos Theodoridis, Alexis Megas, Stephanos Kyriakidis, Vassilis Gopis, Nicos Vretos.

Thessaloniki — Though this film won four prizes at the festival, including best new director, photography, sets and makeup, it received whistles and catcalls during its screening. Title became a slogan to the audience to express disappointment whenever they did not like a subsequent picture.

It is not a bad film in itself. On the contrary, it is a historical picture of extreme beauty, but it has a weak script. It takes place in the 14th century, following the life and exploits of a young man in a remote Balkan village during a period of unrest in the Byzantine Empire.

Doxobus is a village near the Strymon river belonging to the Byzantine Empire. Zoranna, a widow, lives there with her son Xenos, adopted by the village elder Mazaris. When Zoranna gives birth to another son with Mazaris, Xenos is sent into a monastery.

Seven years later, Xenos leaves the monastery but Doxobus is seized by the emperor's forces. Xenos joins the Army and quickly becomes an officer. He is rewarded by being given control over Doxobus. The film ends with the king's visit to Doxobus and a further reward to Xenos.

Fotos Lambrinos worked hard to collect the historical facts for his film, but could not overcome the weakness of his script, caring more for the making of graphic sequences rather than enriching his film with a firm plot. He means to present in an allegorical way the conditions of life in that area as well as the important role of the clergy in political and social life, the misery of the people and the unrest prevailing at the time. Without a firm plot to tie these scenes together, a central hero, rounded characters, or dramatic and emotional elements, the result is an unmoving parade of beautiful pictures, meaning very little. The photography by George Arvanitis is striking and rightly won the festival prize.—*Rena.*

Blue Movies

A Blue Partners production. Executive producers, Kent Snyder, Roger DeYoung. Produced by Maria Snyder. Written and directed by Paul Koval, Ed Fitzgerald. Camera (color), Vance Piper; editor, John Currin; music, Patrick Gleeson, Michael Shrieve; sound, Mary Jo Devenney; art direction, John Wade; set decoration, Terese Mitchell; assistant director, Terry Edwards; production manager, Michael Holt; second unit camera, Robert Brinkmann; casting, Stanzi Stokes; associate producer, Shi Sun. Reviewed on Academy Ent. vidcassette, N.Y., Jan. 16, 1988. MPAA Rating: R. Running time: 92 MIN.
Buzz . . . . Steve Levitt
Cliff . . . . Larry Poindexter
Randy Moon . . . . Lucinda Crosby
Kathy . . . . Darian Mathias
Brad . . . . Christopher Stone
Max . . . . Don Calfa
Also with: Larry Linville, Russell Johnson, Hardy Rawls, Seth Mitchell, Vickie Benson, Leland Crooke, Bert Rosario.

"Blue Movies" covers familiar ground, pinpointing the comic travails of would-be porno filmmakers, but with a disarming, pleasant approach to the potentially smutty subject. It's an okay homevideo title.

Steve Levitt and Larry Poindexter are the nerd and his would-be standup comedian pal, who raise a little money to get rich quick in the adult film biz. They hire a down-and-out veteran screenwriter (Don Calfa in an effective supporting role) and a whiz kid director just out of film school (Leland Crooke). Project moves closer to reality when a bona fide sex star Randy Moon (well-limned with panache by Lucinda Crosby) agrees to work for them, but that also gets them into hot water since the mob doesn't want her working for an independent.

Though pic becomes silly in the final reel of chasing around one step ahead of the mafia, filmmakers Paul Koval and Ed Fitzgerald show an apt talent for satire that puts their pic head and shoulders above such crude forerunners as "Let's Make A Dirty Movie" and "Screen Test."

An added bonus, probably unintentional, is that lead actress Crosby looks a lot like real-life porn star Janey Robbins, lending verisimilitude to the picture. Other roles and various inside jokes are competently executed. —*Lor.*

Voyage Of The Rock Aliens

An Inter Planetary Curb production. Produced by Micheline H. Keller, Brian Russell. Executive producers, Max A. Keller. Tino Barzie, Mike Curb. Directed by James Fargo. Initial "When The Rain Begins To Fall" sequence directed by Bob Giraldi. Screenplay, S. James Guidotti, Edward Gold, Charles Hairston; camera (Deluxe color), Gil Taylor; camera ("Rain" sequence), Dante Spinotti; editor, Malcolm Campbell; editor ("Rain" sequence), Billy Williams; music, Jack White; sound, Ron Judkins; production design, Ninkey Dalton; special visual effects, Image Engineering; spaceship design and miniatures, Tony Tremblay; additional optical effects, Apogee Inc.; assistant director, Stu Fleming, Conrad Irving; production manager, Bert Gold; choreography, Dennon Rawles, Sayhber Rawles; coproducers, Gold, Hairston; postproduction supervisor, Amanda Digiulio; casting, Barbara King. Reviewed on Prism Ent. vidcassette, Jan. 23, 1988. MPAA Rating: PG. Running time: 95 MIN.
Dee Dee . . . . Pia Zadora
Abcd . . . . Tom Nolan
Frankie . . . . Craig Sheffer
Diane . . . . Alison LaPiaca
Chainsaw . . . . Michael Berryman
Sheriff . . . . Ruth Gordon
Rain . . . . Jermaine Jackson
Also with: Rhema band, Jimmy & The Mustangs.

"Voyage Of The Rock Aliens" is an odd bird indeed, a combo beach party/sci-fi/musical spotlighting Pia Zadora. After being on the shelf for four years (a 1985 plan for a national saturation release pegged to pic's hit song "When The Rain Begins To Fall" fell through), pic is an intriguing direct-to-homevideo title.

The filmmakers clearly were aiming at a mass audience crowdpleaser in the vein of "Grease" but the material is not there. An awkward opening sequence establishes a spaceship of aliens (played by Tom Nolan and a Devo-esque band called Rhema) hunting for intelligent life in the universe, i.e., a planet boasting rock music. They reject a planet wherein Zadora and guest star Jermaine Jackson perform their 6-minute music video "When The Rain Begins To Fall." As helmed by Bob Giraldi, it is a pleasant diversion but has nothing to do with the rest of the film.

James Fargo directs the remainder, a contrived beach party movie in which frustrated singer Dee Dee (Zadora) befriends the odd spaceman Nolan who gives her a chance to sing. There is very little time devoted to narrative between a series of forgettable musical numbers. Zadora displays a lot of potential as a screen musical star, but the material is unyielding.

The late Ruth Gordon has a nothing role as the sheriff of the little town of Spielburg (typical of script's lame jokes). Horror mainstay Michael Berryman has a surprisingly sympathetic role and even gets the girl.

Pic has a big, expensive look in all technical departments, meaning somebody took a bath when it failed to get a theatrical release.—*Lor.*

Laura
(From Heaven To Hell)
(SPANISH)

An IPC-Laurenfilm production, in association with Televisió de Catalunya. Produced by Enrique Viciano. Directed by Gonzalo Herraldo. Screenplay, Herraldo, Gustavo Hernández, Viciano, based on the novel by Miguel Llor; camera (Agfa color, Eastmancolor prints), Xavier Aguirresarobe; editor, Ernest Blasi; sound, Licio Marcos; sets, Marcelo Grande; music, Jordi Cervelló. Reviewed at Cine Luchana, Madrid, Nov. 15, 1987. Running time: 97 MIN.
Laura . . . . Angela Molina
Tomás . . . . Juan Diego
Adrián . . . . Sergi Mateu
Teresa . . . . Terele Pávez
Also with: Alfred Luchetti, Carlos Lucena, Maruchi Fresno, Albert Vidal.

Madrid — This rural melodrama set in 1927 Cataluña only intermittently works up passions; by modern standards pic is markedly tame, dealing as it does with a love triangle among hot-blooded Spaniards.

Laura, a middle-class city girl, marries a rich and dour nobleman more interested in hunting and gambling than in domestic bliss. The somewhat rebellious wife, refusing to sink into housewifely resignation, casts her eye and then her body on a handsome village textile manufacturer. After various incidents, in which Laura's small child dies and her affair with the textile man flames up, the inevitable violent denouement arrives, all in a tragic key.

Complicating the relationships is the fact that the lover and the macho husband are half brothers. A good deal of footage is spent on the husband's slow burn turning into indignation, fury and finally mayhém, but all handled with exemplary moderation by helmer Gonzalo Herraldo.

Pic is well produced and directed, though sets trying to recapture Barcelona in the '20s are necessarily skimpy; earlier scenes are rather too poorly lit for comfort, but on the whole production is handsome, with topnotch thesping by Angela Molina as Laura, fine performance by Juan Diego as the simmering spouse and good support by the photogenic Sergi Mateu.

Item could generate some sales in secondary territories where passions and melodrama are come-ons and explicit sex and violence are not required. —*Besa.*

Apprentice To Murder

A New World Pictures release of a Hot Intl. presentation. Produced by Howard K. Grossman. Executive producer, Michael Jay Rauch. Directed by R.L. Thomas. Screenplay, Alan Scott, Wesley Moore; camera (color), Kelvin Pike; editor, Patrick McMahon; music, Charles Gross; production manager, Svein H. Toreg; assistant director, Torill Ek; production design, Gregory Bolton; costume design, Elizabeth Ann Seley; sound, Jan Brodin; associate producer, Michael R. Haley; casting, Lynn Kressel. Reviewed at Magno Preview 4 screening room, N.Y., Jan. 21, 1988. MPAA Rating: PG-13. Running time: 94 MIN.
John Reese . . . . Donald Sutherland
Billy Lowe . . . . Chad Lowe
Alice Spangler . . . . Mia Sara
Lars Hoeglin . . . . Knut Husebo
Elma Kelly . . . . Rutanya Alda
Tom Kelly . . . . Eddie Jones
Also with: Mark Burton, Adrian Sparks, Tiger Haynes, Minnie Gentry, Blain Fairman, Mert Hatfield, Keith Edwards, Chris Langham, Lars Hiller, Ed Wiley, Agnette Haaland, Irina Eidsvold, Bembo Davis, Tor Hansen, Edel Eckblad.

A dark and brooding effort, "Apprentice To Murder" is enhanced — and perhaps saved — by a scintillating performance by Donald Sutherland. His portrayal of John Reese, a devoutly religious country "doctor" who practices a medieval magic called "Pow Wow Medicine," bristles with eerie energy.

Lensed in Norway as "The Long Lost Friend," pic centers around Reese's notion he is on the wrong end of a hex cast by Lars Hoeglin (Knut Husebo). Hoeglin as meanlooking as they come, is presented as a personification of Satan. He appears unexpectedly throughout the film, offering no dialog but glowering demonically into the camera instead.

Reese, who has the power to silence mad dogs and cure myriad diseases, becomes the object of fascination for young Billy Kelly (Chad Lowe). Billy finally approaches Reese about his drunken father (Eddie Jones) and implores Reese to use his spells to stop ol' Dad from imbibing.

Reese agrees to help, striking a wild-eyed countenance.

The magic works, Dad becomes an upright citizen and Billy now is obsessively enthralled by Reese and his supernatural power.

Thus begins the association between Reese and Billy which grows into a smothering interdependence for both of them. Billy starts out by drawing hexagrams for Reese's Pow Wow spells — "The Lord loves artists, Billy," Reese points out — and quickly comes to believe he is Reese's protector and rightful heir to the "Pow Wow" secrets.

Enter "the girl." Alice (Mia Sara) vies for Billy's attention and succeeds in seducing him. This brings about "the conflict" — amulets or affection. Which will Billy choose?

This leads to "the resolution" in which reality blurs into fantasy until one is imperceptibly different from the other. The result of this amorphous intertwining of realms provides the impetus for the "surprise" ending.

Though the final act shall remain a mystery in this review, here's a clue: "Apprentice" was based on the actual events in the life of three York, Pa. residents on Nov. 28, 1928.

In many ways, pic is a parable. Every character represents some icon of good or evil, and theological analogies — if one wishes to examine them — are rampant throughout. Essentially, "Apprentice" chronicles the basic struggle between diametrically opposed universal forces with mortals acting as combatants.

Overall film is reasonably good entertainment with the sometimes slow-moving story being redeemed by Sutherland's ardent Reese. One potential problem might be the fact "Apprentice" doesn't have enough special effects and gore to please the horror flick fan and too much cinematic trickery for the purist.

Yet, despite its defiance of genre classification, Sutherland's "Pow Wow" act is worth catching. — *Chuk.*

Stand And Deliver

A Warner Bros. release of an American Playhouse Theatrical Film and a Menendez/-Musca & Olmos production. Produced by Tom Musca. Executive producer, Lindsay Law. Directed by Ramon Menendez. Screenplay, Menendez, Musca; camera (Foto-Kem color; Technicolor prints), Tom Richmond; editor, Nancy Richardson; music, Craig Safan; art direction, Milo; costume design, Kathryn Morrison; sound, Steve Halbert; associate producer, Iya Labunka; assistant director, Elliot Rosenblatt; casting, Jaki Brown, Toni Livingston. Reviewed at the Warner Hollywood studios, L.A., Jan. 29, 1988. MPAA Rating: PG. Running time: **102 MIN.**
Jaime Escalante . . . . Edward James Olmos
Angel . . . . Lou Diamond Phillips
Fabiola Escalante . . . . Rosana De Soto
Ramirez . . . . Andy Garcia

Hollywood — Inspiration rather than inspired, "Stand And Deliver" tells a story that seems too good to be true, although it is based closely on fact. It's a heartwarming message picture about how a gifted teacher raises a bunch of East L.A. high school students to unimagined heights of academic excellence. Pic was independently produced, made under the title "Walking On Water," picked up by Warner Bros. for a reported $5,000,000 and should do well with kids, family and, especially, Hispanic audiences, who have rarely, if ever, had a film of this nature made for and about them.

Edward James Olmos portrays Jaime Escalante, who arrived at Garfield High School in 1982 and faced a mathematics class populated both by nice, willing kids and surly, gang-member types defiant of any attempts to improve them.

Not only did Escalante succeed in interesting them in math, he proved so exciting as a teacher of a particularly dry subject that he managed to get some of the kids to come in for extra study sessions during the summer, on weekends and before and after school to cram for the advance placement test in calculus and triumph on them. Number of Garfield students passing the test has increased every year since.

Story is simple and straightforward, as is the manner of its telling. Director Ramon Menendez and his producer and cowriter Tom Musca clearly have set as their goal the delivery of the message that one can succeed if one tries, that seeming limitations of environment and resources are only artificial barriers that can be overcome with hard work and the right attitude.

Some of the obstacles — the criminal element among the students, lack of money and unimaginative teachers — are presented, but pretty much glossed over. Pleasantness and an upbeat mood prevail, but this dramatization never gets under the skin of any of the characters, even Escalante, who brushes off a heart attack as if it were a cold and proceeds with his teaching.

Adopting a pronounced stoop, nerdy clothes and balding pate, Olmos still is commanding, and does convince that he could whip all but the most unruly kids into shape. In this regard, he represents the saving grace of the film. As a young tough, Lou Diamond Phillips persists in his insolent posing, but comes around to Olmos' p.o.v. remarkably easily.

Settings are authentic, lenser Tom Richmond makes the picture look richer than it probably was, and soundtrack is dense with mostly Latin-oriented rock. — *Cart.*

School Daze

A Columbia Pictures release of a Forty Acres And A Mule Filmworks production. Produced by Spike Lee. Executive producer, Grace Blake. Coproduced by Monty Ross, Loretha C. Jones. Written and directed by Lee. Camera (Duart color; Deluxe prints), Ernest Dickerson; editor, Barry Alexander Brown; music, Bill Lee; production design, Wynn Thomas; art direction, Allan Trumpler; set decoration, Lynn Wolverton; sound (Dolby), Rolf Pardula; choreography, Otis Sallid; costumes, Ruthie Carter; assistant director, Randy Fletcher; casting, Robi Reed. Reviewed at the Directors Guild theater, L.A., Calif., Feb. 5, 1988. MPAA Rating: R. Running time: **120 MIN.**
Dap Dunlap . . . . Larry Fishburne
Julian . . . . Giancarlo Esposito
Jane Toussaint . . . . Tisha Campbell
Rachel Meadows . . . . Kyme
President McPherson . . . . Joe Seneca
Odrie McPherson . . . . Ellen Holly
Cedar Cloud . . . . Art Evans
Coach Odom . . . . Ossie Davis
Half-Pint . . . . Spike Lee

Hollywood — Filmgoers who admired the freshness and energy of Spike Lee's "She's Gotta Have It" are bound to be thrown by his followup film, "School Daze." A loosely connected series of musical set-pieces exploring the experience of blackness at an all-black university, film is a hybrid of forms and styles that never comes together in a coherent whole. Surprising, too, is the almost dour tone of the film, sure to keep the audience to a minimum.

Although it starts out something like a black "Animal House," "School Daze" has other more serious things on its mind. Issues raised all center around the nature of black identity which Lee tackles head-on rather than integrating into a larger dramatic framework.

Almost as if he were trying to create a new genre single-handedly, Lee throws traditional rules of narrative filmmaking out the window in exchange for a collection of awkwardly staged production numbers, one remarkably like the other. Lacking are characters to care about with compelling everyday problems. Film bumps and grinds along from the funky to the preachy but without enough emotion. Production seems to have been conceived more in Lee's head than his heart.

Story, such as it is, focuses on the conflict between the militant activists on campus and the goodtime boys of Gamma Phi Gamma fraternity which comes to a head during homecoming week. Leading the freshman pledges class and begging for acceptance is the diminutive Half-Pint (Spike Lee). In the course of becoming a frat brother he is caught between the demands of fraternity life and the responsibilities of being black advanced by his cousin Dap Dunlap (Larry Fishburne).

Making life miserable for Half-Pint is his pledge-master and Dap's archrival Julian (Big Brother Almighty) Eaves (Giancarlo Esposito). On the female side, it's the Gamma Rays vs. the Jigaboos illustrating the tensions between the light-skinned, straight-haired blacks and the dark-skinned sisters. On top of the already-complicated picture, Lee throws in the problems of male-female relations.

Feeling compelled to accurately represent the realities of black life, Lee may have been too ambitious and tried to cover too much ground. The result is rather superficial without offering any great insights and ends with a conclusion that really begs the issue.

Along the way Lee has assembled a massive cast which more often than not breaks into intricately choreographed musical numbers borrowed from '50s musicals. Tisha Campbell as the leader of the Gamma Rays has one hot routine battling the Jigaboos in a mock beauty salon set. Choreography is downhill from there and frequent musical interruptions only serve to short-circuit the action.

As a director, Lee fails to strike the right note between realism and fantasy, and the heavy subject matter just falls with a thud. As an actor, however, Lee does a good job creating a sort of black babe in the woods. Fishburne brings great authority to his role as the campus conscience while his adversary Esposito struts around like a black Groucho Marx but without a sense of humor.

While "School Daze" touches on some important themes and it is refreshing to see so much new black talent on screen, one wonders whether such a miscalculated film would have been made if Lee hadn't been burdened with the responsibility (and freedom) of making The Great Black Film. — *Jagr.*

Halodhia Choraye Baodhan Khai
(The Catastrophe)
(INDIAN)

A Patkai Films production. Produced by Sailadhar Barua, Jahnu Barua. Written and directed by Jahnu Barua, based on the novel by Homen Bogohain. Camera (color), Anoop Jotwani; art direction, Phatk Barua; editor, Heu-en Barua; music, Satya Barua. Reviewed at the Indian Film Festival, Trivandrum, Jan. 16, 1988. Running time: **120 MIN.**
With: Indra Bania (Bora), Pumima Pathak, Pranjol Saikai, Hemen Choudhury, Badal Das.

(In Assamese)

Trivandrum — "The Catastrophe," set in present-day rural Assam, is a harsh social outcry against the nauseating exploitation of the poor by richer and more educated men. Well lensed by helmer Jahnu Barua, pic was the most sophisticated political film from this year's Indian Panorama. The painful subject matter doesn't make for easy entertainment, as an implacable chain of consequences beats down the farmer-hero. Yet out of the catastrophe comes a positive ending of increased social awareness. Also interesting as an ethnographic portrait of the Asiatic Indian state of Assam, pic merits attention.

Rakkheshwar Bora (Indra Bania) is waiting for rain to plow up his small paddy field, from which he ekes out a meager living for his family. Catastrophe arrives when a local land owner, Sharma usurps the paddy, claiming it was mortgaged to him by Bora's father and never redeemed. Bora has seen his father pay back the mortgage with interest, but because the farmers naively failed to make Sharma give them a receipt for the money, they have no legal leg to stand on.

Bora goes to the registrar (one of Sharma's men), and is advised to start court proceedings. Brutally demanded bribes cost the pecunious farmer his milk cow, then his oxen, and finally his bright little son, sent to work as an errand boy. Finally, to earn money, he is reduced to pasting up election posters of the man who ruined him.

A sympathetic official gets Bora's land back, but by now the ignorant farmer has lost his innocence and become angry and politicized.

Not a pretty picture of human beings, "Catastrophe" tends toward the heavy-handed in limning crass villains and indifferent villagers. Barua opts for simplicity in telling the tale, aided by a moving performance from main thesp Bania.

— *Yung.*

Bernadette
(FRENCH)

A Cannon France release of a Films de l'Etoile d'or/Bernadette Assn. Intl. production. Executive producer, Jacques Quintard. Directed by Jean Delannoy. Screenplay, Delannoy, Robert Arnaut; camera (Eastmancolor), Jean-Bernard Penzer; editor, Annick Charvein; music, Francis Lai; art direction, Alain Paroutaud; costumes, Laurence Brignon; makeup, Odette Berroyer; sound, Guy Villette, Pierre Vuillemin; production manager, Jean-Claude Vieu; assistant director, Michel Leroy. Reviewed at the Cannon France screening room, Paris, Feb. 10, 1988. Running time: **118 MIN.**

Bernadette Soubirous . . . . . Sydney Penny
Peyramale . . . . Jean-Marc Bory
Louise Soubirous . . . . Michele Simonnet
François Soubirous . . . . . . Roland Lesaffre
Dr. Dozous . . . . Bernard Dheran
Jacomet . . . . François Dalout
Nicolau . . . . Stephan Garcin
Mme. Milhet . . . . Arlette Didier
Mme. Pailhasson . . . . . . Beata Tyszhiewicz
Napoleon III . . . . Michel Duchaussoy
Destrade . . . . Frank David

Paris — Two years after Alain Cavalier's sublime "Thérèse," here is Jean Delannoy's "Bernadette," a plodding, artless but sincere biopic about Bernadette Soubirous, the simple and sickly miller's daughter whose visions of the Virgin Mary in a grotto transformed Lourdes into a Catholic shrine and pilgrimage site. Made by people who believe for audiences who believe, it may have little commercial potential outside nontheatrical religious presentations and television.

Delannoy, 79, back in the 1940s was one of France's most distinguished filmmakers before the New Wave generation laid him low for the arid earnestness and cold, technical perfection of his prestige productions. Unlike some of his other colleagues, he survived the auteurist onslaught and continued his career, albeit without distinction, working exclusively in tv since 1972.

Delannoy scripted "Bernadette" (with Robert Arnaut), fastidiously recreating the known highlights of the future saint's life and the conflicting reactions of population, church and state.

Apart from the feebleness of the dialog, the stock characterizations and mechanical performances, film stumbles on an insurmountable dramatic obstacle: its heroine is not interesting.

Unlike the impassioned Thérèse, who knew where she was going, Bernadette was apparently humble, ignorant and bland, a passive medium for a divine message. Delannoy's attempts to counterbalance this weakness with sketchlike dramatizations of those directly and indirectly affected by her revelations reek of telefilm turgidness. His art isn't where his heart is.

Young American actress Sydney Penny plays Bernadette (dubbed into French) with unaffected simplicity that is far from the coy, Holywooden ingenuousness of Jennifer Jones in Henry King's monstrously glossy "The Song Of Bernadette." Though she has the right age, her clean, healthy features mask the grinding poverty and rustic sickliness she is meant to suggest. Nor does she communicate any sense of wonderment or mystery during her visions (which require a puff of wind and an extra light on her face to tell us something supernatural is going on).

Delannoy had permission from religious authorities to shoot some of his scenes at the Lourdes shrine. Cannon France, which is distributing the film here, last year released "Le Miraculé," Jean-Pierre Mocky's irreverent Lourdes pilgrimage satire. How ecumenical!

— *Len.*

Action Jackson

A Lorimar Film Entertainment release. Produced by Joel Silver. Directed by Craig R. Baxley. Screenplay, Robert Reneau; camera (Metrocolor), Matthew F. Leonetti; editor, Mark Helfrich; music, Herbie Hancock with Michael Kamen; art direction, Virginia Randolph; set decoration, Phil M. Leonard; costume design, Marilyn Vance-Straker; sound (Dolby), Jim Webb; associate producer, Steve Perry; assistant director, Benjamin Rosenberg; casting, Karen Rea. Reviewed at the Lorimar Cary Grant theater, Culver City, Calif., Feb. 8, 1988. MPAA Rating: R. Running time: **95 MIN.**

Action Jackson . . . . Carl Weathers
Peter Dellaplane . . . . Craig T. Nelson
Sydney Ash . . . . Vanity
Patrice Dellaplane . . . . Sharon Stone
Officer Kornblau . . . . . Thomas F. Wilson
Also with: Bill Duke, Robert Davi, Jack Thibeau, Nicholas Worth, Sonny Landham.

Hollywood — "Action Jackson" certainly lives up to its title. It's noisy and violent, all right, and would have succeeded as a cartoon, but the filmmakers mucked it up by trying to get serious with some outdated, melodramatic, potboiler material. Carl Weathers moralizing with Vanity probably isn't the dynamic pairing that makes for cinematic memories. B.o. looks weak.

This clearly is meant as a star vehicle for Weathers, who up to now has played second banana to other macho men like Stallone and Schwarzenegger. Nice that he got a sexy singer like Vanity as his costar, but his character still is second-rate stuff — more brawn than brain and

hardly the kind of casting to get him out of this rut.

"Action Jackson" very simply is an overly busy good guy/bad guy actioner pitting Weathers, a no-nonsense Detroit cop, against Craig T. Nelson, a megalomaniacal auto magnate.

Nelson has a band of thugs blowing up various auto union officials so he can put in their place one of his own puppets, thereby assuming power over the too-powerful organization.

Hot on his trail is the righteous Weathers, recently demoted to sergeant because of some past no-no over the handling of Nelson's criminal son and now bent on ridding Motown of Nelson's corruptible influence as it becomes evident he is behind the fiery deeds.

Vanity rides the tide first with Nelson; she indulges his sexual appetite and he supplies her with heroin; then with Weathers, who refuses to acknowledge the sinful side of her and tries to bring out some of that wholesomeness she's been suppressing.

With such heartwarming intentions as this, pic could have been made 40 years ago, except perhaps that the lyrics to Vanity's songs surely would have been a lot less salacious.

Weathers is up to the task of filling the screen as a larger-than-life force to be reckoned with. In fact, he's indestructible. Not only does he excel at all the ordinary physical skills that his muscled body suggests, but goes one better by being superhuman. He can dodge a rain of bullets while clutching the roof of a speeding car and survive the ordeal by doing a backflip onto the street while the bad guy driver gets munched as the vehicle careens out of control and into a storefront.

There's lots of this "action," but not a heck of a lot of story propelling it. Nelson is venal enough, if perhaps too archetypically drawn to be credible for a second, though he has the stature to play off against Weathers' overpowering persona.

Throw in Vanity to bring out the cop's soft side, that part of him where he gets to emote, and things become unintentionally silly. They do have remarkably well-matched cleavages, however.

Trying to bring some sentimentality to what basically is a film comprised of speeding cars, explosions and the bloody wasting of lives is not a successful formula in this case.

The fault lies not with the actors, but with the scripter, Robert Reneau, who has tried to complicate matters when the opposite would have worked better.

A little humor would have helped. Unfortunately, what laughs there are, are unintentional.—*Brit.*

Secondo Ponzio Pilato
(According To Pontius Pilate)
(ITALIAN)

A UIP release of a Massfilm/Reteitalia coproduction. Produced by Franco Committeri. Written and directed by Luigi Magni. Camera (Eastmancolor), Giorgio Di Battista; editor, Ruggero Mastroianni; music, Angelo Branduardi; art direction, Lucia Merisola. Reviewed at Fiamma Cinema, Rome, Jan. 30, 1988. Running time: **105 MIN.**

Pontius Pilate . . . . Nino Manfredi
Claudia Procula . . . . Stefania Sandrelli
Tiberio . . . . Mario Scaccia
Herod . . . . Flavio Bucci
Valeriano . . . . Lando Buzzanca
Also with: Antonio Pierfederici, Nelija Bosic.

Rome — Helmer Luigi Magni's predilection for lensing chunks of religious history in a semi-comic, semi-reverent vein has found better expression before his current offering, "According To Pontius Pilate." The humor is supposed to be supplied by Nino Manfredi's hamming, gesticulating Pilate, a nice guy with the cynical horse sense of a Roman taxi driver, and an accent to match. Local audiences haven't been much taken with this improbable figure — also because the tale is overly familiar and the twists few.

Pic is the second Italo Pontius Pilate story in a year, its predecessor being a Damiano Damiani picture, "The Inquiry," with Keith Carradine, Harvey Keitel and Phyllis Logan.

Taking the New Testament as a basis and imaginatively embellishing, filmmakers depict Pilate as a weak, vacillating perfect of Judea, whose prosaic Roman rationality prevents him from perceiving the obvious: that Jesus is God. Not so his wife Claudia Procula (Stefania Sandrelli), whom we first meet sleeping with her nightgown around her waist. Beset by dreams and encouraged by Pilate's adjutant Valeriano (Lando Buzzanca), Claudia is firm in her belief in Jesus.

Pilate pooh-poohs incontrovertible signs like giant statues crashing to the ground during the Crucifixion, Roman centurions who involuntarily pay homage to Jesus as he passes, and a good-looking angel who keeps popping up and preaching the good news.

Though a liberal at heart (more than once he underlines it isn't the Jewish people who want Jesus dead, but the fats cats at the temple), Pilate just can't overcome his native skepticism and see the light. In an unhistorical finale, Pilate dies a here in the old Roman tradition, letting the emperor Tiberius cut his head off, taking the responsibility for Jesus' death entirely on his shoulders, so that Tiberius will stop persecuting the Jews.

Pic is graced with Lucia Merisola's colorful, theatrical sets and deluxe costumes, contributing to the Classics Illustrated atmosphere and fundamentally pleasant to look at.

Low-key guitar score is by Angelo Branduardi. To liven things up there are cameos by great character actors Mario Scaccia and Flavio Bucci, plus some generous views of naked female slaves cavorting at Herod's court. — *Yung.*

Les Saisons du plaisir
(The Seasons Of Pleasure)
(FRENCH)

A Bac Films release of an AFC/Canal Plus Prods./FR3 Films coproduction. Produced by Maurice Bernart. Written and directed by Jean-Pierre Mocky. Camera (color), William Lubtchansky; editor, Mocky; music, Gabriel Yared; art direction, Clorinde Méry; sound, Bernard Rochut; costumes, Marie Rodriguez; production manager, Louis Wipf. Reviewed at the Gaumont Ambassade theater, Paris, Feb. 10, 1988. Running time: **88 MIN.**
Charles . . . . Charles Vanel
Emmanuelle . . . . Denise Grey
Jacqueline . . . . Jacqueline Maillan
Jeanne . . . . Bernadette Lafont
Paul . . . . Jean-Luc Bideau
Bernard . . . . Jean Poiret
Marthe . . . . Eva Darlan
Hélène . . . . Fanny Cottençon
Jacques . . . . Jean-Pierre Bacri
Adam . . . . Richard Bohringer
Simon . . . . Bernard Menez
Dominique . . . . .Sylvie Joly
Bernadette . . . . Stéphane Audran
Daniel D. . . . . Darry Cowl
Gus . . . . Roland Blanche
Also with: Jean Abeille, Jean-Claude Romer, Michel Varille, Sophie Moyse, Hervé Pauchon.

Paris — A rollicking good, all-star cast partially saves a mostly trite, vulgar script in "The Seasons Of Pleasure" by prolific, local bad boy Jean-Pierre Mocky, whose anarchistic entertainments would be tonic if they weren't so often second-hand. Pic, backed by a tastelessly clever poster campaign, has unzippered to plenty of public inspection at home and could arouse some interest in other markets.

Mocky has cooked up a sort of "Libidinous Charms of The Bourgeoisie" with a wide, multi-generation sampling of horny Gauls on the make in the sensuous surroundings of a southern French chateau.

Occasion is the annual convention for shareholders and execs organized by centenarian perfume mogul Charles Vanel, who despite his great age has decided to remarry to equally ancient Denise Grey, and appoint a successor to his industrial throne.

Vanel's announcement naturally excites the dormant ambitions of some conventioneers, though the plotting and backbiting remain secondary to the satisfaction of carnal appetites.

Mocky's portrait gallery of deep-throat France is composed with brio, if not much imagination, but there are some fitfully hilarious scenes in this crazy-quilt sex farce. Though better made than many previous Mocky mockeries (photography by the ace William Lubt-

chansky, adroit editing by the director himself), pic's energies peter out in the final third. Unable to find an apt conclusion, Mocky merely erases the entire drooling mass of humanity with an apocalyptic *deus ex machina* (an accident from a nearby nuclear power plant).

Performances from a large name cast are film's principal saving grace, carrying the script with relish and style, even when the dialog wallows in the scabrous (actual dirty deeds are kept off-screen or out of the frame).

Among the fast-paced farceurs are Jean Poiret, as the group's principal dirty old man and perfume conspirator, Bernadette Lafont, as a hypocritically prudish mother hen, Darry Cowl, as a pathetic aging queen, Roland Blanche, as a frustrated loser with a huge reserve of randiness, Sylvie Joly and Stéphane Audran, as a couple of porn-video pickup artists, and Richard Bohringer and Bernard Menez as two nuclear plant guards who service one another.

Golden palm for inspired foolishness however must go to legit comedienne Jacqueline Maillan, who, dressed in a tutu, compensates for an impotent husband by running a phone-teletext service for lonely, perverted callers.

Mocky fails to make the most of the December romance between Vanel and Grey, who are whisked out of the film once their catalyst functions are done with. Vanel, by the way, is 95, and Grey, a still active stage thesp, is 91. They make a charming couple of lovers. —*Len.*

A Better Tomorrow II
(HONG KONG)

A Cinema City Co. Ltd. presentation and production, distributed by Golden Princess. Produced by Tsui Hark. Directed by John Woo. Screenplay, Woo, Hark; camera (color), Wong Hing Hung; music, Joseph Koo, production manager, Won Kar Man; post-production manager, Tony Chow; action direction, Ching Siu Tung; art direction, Andy Li; costume design, Pauline Lau. Reviewed at President theater, Hong Kong, Dec. 29, 1987. Running time: **98 MIN.**
Cantonese soundtrack with English subtitles.

Hong Kong — This is a highly commercial, overblown but entertaining followup to last year's attraction that broke boxoffice records and reaffirmed the gangster genre's popularity in Cantonese cinema.

Superb actor Chow Yun Fat (his character Mark died in the last reel of Part I), returns as the twin brother called Ken, who lives in New York. Kid brother of Ti Lung, young cop Leslie Cheung is still stubborn as ever and dies a hero's death.

This time Ti Lung is forced by circumstances to join an international counterfeit syndicate, his way out from prison. His brother Leslie

Cheung is secretly assigned to collect evidence by the police department against the illegal activities of the Lung Ship Building Co. headed by Dean Shek.

Villain Ko plans to have Shek murdered to take over his shipyard and full control of the profitable trading. Somehow, Shek is saved from assassination attempts and smuggled to New York where Chow Yun Fat (now Ken) is running a Chinese restaurant. The on-location Manhattan scenes are interesting. A deep friendship is developed between catatonic Shek and Ken, who both return to Hong Kong to set things right. —*Mel.*

Phera
(The Return)
(INDIAN)

Produced, written and directed by Buddhadeb Dasgupta. Camera (color), Dhrubajyoti Bose; editor, Ujjal Nandi; music, Jyotishka Dasgupta; production manager, Somnath Das. Reviewed at the Indian Film Festival, Trivandrum, Jan. 16, 1988. (Also in Berlin Film Festival — competing.) Running time: **94 MIN.**
Sasanka . . . . Subrata Nandy
Saraju . . . . Aloknanda Dutt
Kanu . . . . Aniket Sengupta
Also with: Sunil Mukherjee, Chanda Dutt, Debika Mukherjee, Biplab Chatterjee, Kamu Mukherjee, Samit Bhanja.
(In Bengali)

Trivandrum — India's competition entry at the Berlin Film Festival, "The Return," explores the dilemmas of a creative artist at odds with both his public and himself, locked in a frozen state of non-communication with the world around him. Fascinating in its setting, a decaying mansion in rural Bengal, and touching in its portrait of artistic solitude, "The Return" is a good candidate for art house playoff and more fest screenings for director Buddhadeb Dasgupta.

Within the crumbling walls of his ancestral home, Sasanka (refreshingly underplayed by Subrata Nandy) lives in mournful, often drunken solitude with his servant and pens plays for *jatra,* the traditional Bengali folk theater, in which he also acts. Times are changing, however; as the powerful opening scene shows, folk art is in the process of being supplanted by more commercial, modern plays. Sasanka lives with his ghosts and memories (especially of being abandoned by his young bride).

The arrival of his widowed sister-in-law Saraju and her little son Kanu (another adorable child thesp, Aniket Sengupta) is both welcome relief and further torment. Saraju (played coldly by Aloknanda Dutt) becomes his mistress in a relationship based on economic dependency and sexual exploitation. Not a well-defined character, she is treated as expendable both as companion and mother.

It is with the bright, lively Kanu that Sasanka develops a fully human relationship. The little boy finds Sasanka's theater costumes and rehearsing magically fascinating. Gradually the bond between middle-aged, disillusioned actor-writer and little boy deepens, as they stroll around the melancholy, abandoned property of a fading world. Kanu turns his back on his soulless mother to walk with Sasanka in a gentle, upbeating ending.

Short for an Indian film (94 minutes) and quite Western in its understatement and way of leaving things half-said, "The Return" benefits from poetic lensing by Dhrubajyoti Bose that tastes of the past and memory plus an atmospheric score by Jyotishka Dasgupta. Soundtrack in general is highly elaborated and contributes substantially to pic. —*Yung.*

Satisfaction

A 20th Century Fox release of an Aaron Spelling/Alan Greisman production. Produced by Aaron Spelling, Alan Greisman. Executive producers, Rob Alden, Armyan Bernstein. Directed by Joan Freeman. Screenplay, Charles Purpura; camera (Deluxe color), Thomas Del Ruth; editor, Joel Goodman; music, Michel Colombier; sound (Ultra-Stereo), Willy Burton; production design, Lynda Paradise; set decoration, Ernie Bishop; costume design, Eugenie Bafaloukos; assistant director, Jerry Ketcham; associate producer, Ilene Chaiken; casting, Johanna Ray. Reviewed at 20th Century Fox Studio, L.A., Feb. 12, 1988. MPAA Rating: PG-13. Running time: **92 MIN.**
Jennie Lee . . . . .Justine Bateman
Martin Falcon . . . . .Liam Neeson
May (Mooch) Stark . . . . Trini Alvarado
Nickie Longo . . . . Scott Coffey
Billy Swan . . . . Britta Phillips
Daryle Shane . . . . Julia Roberts
Tina . . . . Debbie Harry

Hollywood — "Satisfaction" doesn't live up to its title and Justine Bateman singing the immortal Rolling Stones song, or any song for that matter, can't save this adolescent tale from being a bore. B.o. looks unsatisfactory as well.

First, it was "Family Ties" costar Michael J. Fox to get a starring role as a rocker in "Light Of Day," and now Bateman. She can't sing either, but even if she could, the part she plays here only hurts her act.

Bateman is the lead singer in a garage band that plays classic tunes like "Satisfaction," "Knock On Wood" and "Lies," which takes its inner-city routine on the road to a dull, no-name, beach community where they win an audition to play at a local pub for the summer.

What happens for these short, hot months is about the same as what happens in every other low-budget, teen beach pic that's ever been made — not much. About the only distinction this one has is that its production values are well above the standard for this genre.

To satisfy the target audience that presumably is the same that follows the actress' tv career, Bateman is cast to type as kind of a sassy good girl backed up by a band comprised of three equally impudent femmes and a freckle-faced keyboardist who is the cleanest of the bunch.

In between night-time gigs, they hit the sand, a volleyball game, a party with law students and other such exciting activities.

If not for a song ever 10 minutes or so, even a poorly performed one, even the most easily entertained viewer might start nodding off.

Liam Neeson comes in as Bateman's love interest playing an aging Irish-rogue type who owns the pub and turns out to be a Grammy-winning songwriter gone bitter and alcoholic. He's most unappealing and hardly convincing, but wisely Bateman comes to her senses in the end and realizes it wasn't love, but just a schoolgirl crush she's had on him all along.

To spice up this PG-13 fare, the kids occasionally cuss and smoke; blond Billy, the band's dog-loving soprano (Britta Phillips) o.d.'s on whatever pills she's popping, while dumb, sexy bass player Daryle (Julia Roberts) spends at least 24 hours in the back of a van with her boyfriend.

While situations are almost all forgettable, including Debbie Harry's 90-second, 2-line cameo, effort isn't embarrassingly bad. It just reinforces what most adults have known for a long time — being a teenager can sure be dull. —*Brit.*

I morgen er det slut
(Tomorrow It Is Over)
(DANISH)

A Scala Film release of a Jysk Filmproject production, with the Danish Film Institute. Produced by Sigfred Aagaard. DFI consultant producer, Kirsten Bonnén Rask. Written and directed by Aagaard. Camera (Eastmancolor) and editor, Jörgen Vestergaard; music, Gounod, Jörgen Vestergaard; sound, Kristian Bro; assistant director, Jonna Green. Reviewed at the Dagmar, Copenhagen, Feb. 10, 1988. Running time: **82 MIN.**
Schoolteacher . . . . Sigfred Aagaard
Mikkel Borgen . . . . Ejnar Johansen
Johannes . . . . Bent Berg
Also with: Karen Margrethe Burmölle, Poul Poulsen, Anna Schmidt, Hans Post, Mogens Tarp, Inge Provstgaard, Jonna Green, Georg Hougaard, Jens Galsgaard, Karen Ernst.

Copenhagen — Carl Theodor Dreyer based one of his major films, "Ordet" (1955), on a stage play by Kaj Munk, a noted European playwright, who also happened to be the vicar in a windswept, remote village on Jutland's North Sea coast. "Ordet"'s action took place among the local peasants, and now Sigfred Aagaard, an amateur jack-of-all-arts, has fashioned his own feature film about the descendants of those very same peasants, not noticeably different from their grandparents, doing "Ordet" as their annual amateur stage offering in the village assembly house.

Writer-director Aagaard is seen as story's only outsider, a deputy schoolteacher who is asked to direct the amateurs in some silly British comedy. He talks them into doing "Ordet" instead, playing more or less themselves, which they proceed to do. They actually do a better acting job with their roles in the stark play about the power of Faith to wake up the dead than they do of trying to act natural as themselves.

Media representatives arrive with a mind to ridicule the amateur performance, but come away lauding it. Life in general is slightly changed for some of the acting amateurs. A minuscule subplot has the teacher spotted in an embrace with the mailman's wife, just risen from the dead on stage, and is forced to leave the tiny community that he had inspired in so many ways.

Midway through the shooting, distributor Finn Dyhre of Scala Film convinced the Danish Film Institute that Aagaard's film deserved some public subsidy coin and other support. Now in commercial release, "Tomorrow It Is Over" will charm local audiences with its determined nonsophistication, but offshore the fun and pleasure of hearing Munk's High Drama lines spoken in local west coast dialect naturally will be limited. Film, however, leaves no doubt the road to film professionalism lies open for Aagaard, who also happens to shine as by far the best actor of the troupe.—*Kell.*

Noistottus
(ITALIAN-DOCU)

A Centro Sperimentale di Cinematografia production. Executive producer, Istituto Luce/Italnoleggio Cinematografica. Written and directed by Piero D'Onofrio, Fabio Vannini. Camera (Eastmancolor), Franco Lecca; editor, Maddalena Colombo, D'Onofrio, Vannini; music, Mauro Di Renzi; art direction, Michele Della Cioppa; sound, Stefano Savino; costumes, Alessandro Ciammarughi. Reviewed at the Capranica Cinema, Rome, Dec. 16, 1987. Running time: **145 MIN.**

Rome — "Noistottus," a dialect word meaning "All Of Us," is a 2½-hour docu on the history of coal mining in Sardinia. Though subject may not seem compelling, film has the merit of allowing a glimpse at a fascinating world of considerable social implications. It has the demerit of not succeeding in organizing this rich material into watchable form. Lensed by two graduates of Rome's filmschool, the Centro Sperimentale di Cinematografia, Piero D'Onofrio and Fabio Vannini, "Noistottus" is a cautionary tale that shows what can happen when academics move too glibly into film. The young directors hopefully will learn their lesson and produce more successful projects.

A lot of research obviously has gone into the lengthy script, reaching back to a Socialist newspaperman's visit to Sardinia in 1906 and his exposé of the poverty and exploitaton of the miners. Film stages a confused reconstruction of a parliamentary investigation of mining conditions, enacted tableaux-style by inexpert thesps. One good piece involves a Frenchman named Bedaux who explains, in pompous French, the advantages of his system for speeding up the work by timing each movement involved in mining. Another point of interest is Fascist newsreels from the 1930s designed to propagandize coal mining in the interest of arms production.

A great deal of dead weight is constituted by long interviews with oldtimers, a little of which would have sufficed. Though film takes a strong political stance against the miners' exploitation, excess length and unsystematic structure undercut its message badly. Camerawork by Franco Lecca, however, is atmospheric and engaging.

Pic was to be the first in a series of films produced by the Centro Sperimentale's Research Dept., but it could also be the last if the school's current state of semi-paralysis continues. — *Yung.*

Doom Asylum

A Filmworld Distributors presentation from Manhattan Pictures and Filmworld Prods. Executive producers, Alexander W. Kogan Jr., Barry Tucker. Produced by Steve Menkin. Directed by Richard Friedman. Screenplay, Rick Marx, from story by Friedman, Menkin, Marx; camera (Precision color), Larry Revene; editor, Ray Shapiro; music, Jonathan Stuart, Dave Erlanger; sound, Steve Rogers; production design, Kosmo Vinyl; art direction, Hank Liebeskind; assistant director, Bill Tasgal; production manager, Ted Hope; second unit director, Jeff Folmsbee; second unit camera, Steve Ross; special makeup effects, Vincent J. Guastini. Reviewed on Academy Entertainment vidcassette, N.Y., Feb. 3, 1988. MPAA Rating: R. Running time: **78 MIN.**
Judy/Kiki . . . . Patty Mullen
Tina . . . . Ruth Collins
Jane . . . . Kristin Davis
Mike. William Hay
Dennis . . . . Kenny L. Price
Darnell . . . . Harrison White
Also with: Dawn Alvan, Farin, Michael Rogen.

"Doom Asylum" is a modest yet effective satire of horror films, going direct to video. As he did in "Deathmask," director Richard Friedman demonstrates his ability to transcend genre limitations, aided here by witty, off-the-wall dialog by Rick Marx.

New Jersey-lensed pic is set at a deserted asylum where a monstrous guy (Michael Rogen), who rose from the autopsy table 10 years ago, preys on unwary youngsters. In attendance is a 3-girl punk band led by Ruth Collins, plus Patty Mullen, whose mom was killed in a car crash with Rogen a decade back.

With gory makeup effects, film closely follows the killing-every-7-minutes pattern of slasher pics, but finds considerable black humor in the situation. The young cast is energetic. Pic's highlight is well-preserved b&w clips from five vintage Tod Slaughter horror epics, which punctuate the action and hopefully will spur renewed interest in the lip-smacking British thesp.
—*Lor.*

La Coyota Dos (La Venganza de la Coyota)
(Coyota II — Coyota's Revenge)
(MEXICAN)

A Peliculas Mexicanas release of a Cinematográfica Rodríguez production. Produced by Roberto Rodríguez E. Directed by Luis Quintanilla Rico. Screenplay, Ramón Méndez, Ernesto Juárez, based on an idea by Carlos E. Taboada; camera (color), Fernando Alvarez Colín; editor, Angel Camacho; music, Susy Rodríguez; special effects, Miguel Vázquez. Reviewed at Hollywood Twin Theater II, N.Y., Oct. 26, 1987. Running time: **86 MIN.**
Rosalba (La Coyota) . . . . Rebeca Silva
Mateo . . . . Mario Almada
Captain Lucio . . . . Noe Murayama
Rogelio . . . . Juan Valentín
Margarita . . . . Claudia Guzman
Also with: Lorenzo de Monteclaro, Marcko D'Carlo, Elsa Montes, Alfredo Gutiérrez, Ernesto Juárez.

As its title implies, "La Coyota Dos" is a sequel to Mexican filmmaker Luis Quintanilla Rico's 1986 historical drama of the same name. The second installment continues the adventures of former landowner Rosalba, who was sparked by the treacherous murder of her lover to join the 1910 Mexican Revolution under the moniker "La Coyota" (The Female Coyote).

"The Coyota's Revenge" takes up where the first pic ended and uses many of the same actors with one major exception: actress Rebeca Silva dons the hat of the rebel Coyota in the sequel, replacing original lead Beatriz Adriana. Besides adding a small change in character interpretation, this also accounts for a lack of bothersome flashbacks.

Pic narrates a half-hearted tale of passion, betrayal and mismatched love set against a tumultuous backdrop of battle and social upheaval. Although Fernando Alvarez Colín's able photography tries to capture the richness of the period, the film falls into the too-oft romanticized vision of the Revolution: all campesinos are pictured as colorful noble folk who fight to the death for what they believe. In their free time, they sit around the campfire and sing *corridos* (narrative ballads). There is very little realism either in their idealized depiction or in the savage portrayal of the ruthless Federal Army, led by the egregious villain Captain Lucio (Noe Murayama).

Most of the time the sets and

reconstructed battle scenes are quite effective in carefully creating a feeling for the epoch.

"La Coyota Dos" should find its most receptive audience either at home or in places with high concentrations of Mexicans and Mexican descendants. —*Lent*.

With Time To Kill
(AUSTRALIAN)

A Kim Lewis Marketing release of a Chair Films production. Produced and directed by James Clayden. Screenplay, Clayden; camera (color), Laurie McInnes; editor, Gary Hillberg; music, Chris Knowles, Stephen Cummings, Ollie Olsen; sound, Steve Burgess; assistant director, Laurie McInnes; associate producer, Fred Harden. Reviewed at Mosman screening room, Sydney, Dec. 5, 1987. Running time: **71 MIN.**
Lt. Nick Yates................Ian Scott
Louise Yates..........Elizabeth Huntley
Sgt. Max Clements.......James Clayden
Janet Golding..............Lin Van Hek
The Laundryman...........Peter Green
Adam Sayer ....John Howard
Terry Bendix.............Barry Dickins
Jack Keane...............Tim Robertson
Also with: Stephen Cummings (Tony Shaw), Val Kirwan (Clairvoyant), Phil Motherwall (Frank Williams), Marie Hoy (Sarah Davis), Nigel Buesst (Wilson Manning).

Sydney — "With Time To Kill" is a first feature by 8m filmmaker James Clayden, who wrote, produced, directed and plays a leading role. Entire enterprise harks back to those '60s pics in which young intellectuals paid "tribute" to Hollywood genre films, usually thrillers, while at the same time adding an existential dimension. Sadly, Clayden's film is a thoroughly botched effort which fails to work on any level. Prospects are dismal.

At first, it seems promising. Pic opens with a striking scene of a man gazing on the corpse of a woman in a bathtub. Then a wry narrator informs us we're in Melbourne, "Not far away from Antarctica," before introing two cops, Yates (Ian Scott) and Clements (director Clayden), members of the Drugs and Homicide squad, who've decided the courts aren't doing their job. They decide they have to "get rid of some of the garbage," especially The Laundryman (Peter Green), a crime kingpin.

Unhappily, any expectations that opening arouses are dashed quickly. Plotting and scripting are dullsville when not thoroughly confusing. Characters, some played by proficient thesps, are briefly introed and then, before they have time to make an impact, dispatched, usually by a bullet in the back of the head. Acting is listless, with the non-synch dialog a further distraction (some actors don't even use their own voices; the credits inform us that Elizabeth Huntley was voiced by Jan Freidel).

Technically, film is ugly and scrappy — presumably deliberately so, since cinematographer Laurie McInnes has proved he can do bet-ter on other occasions. Handouts describe the film as "experimental" (which it might have been 20 years ago) and "a mixture of Chandler and Dostoyevsky." Suffice to say neither would be terribly happy to find his name linked with something as poor as "With Time To Kill."
—*Strat*.

La Fuga del Caro
(Maten a Fugitivo)
(Caro's Escape—Kill The Fugitive)
(MEXICAN)

A Peliculas Mexicanas release of a Puma Producciones production. Directed by Raúl Fernández Jr. Screenplay, Raúl and Rolando Fernández, adapted by Carlos Valdemar; camera (color), Armando Castillón; editor, Jorge Rivera; music, Ernesto Cortázar Jr., with appearance of Grupo Audáz and Rigo Dominguez. Reviewed at Hollywood Twin Theater II, N.Y., Oct. 12, 1987. Running time: **100 MIN.**
Ramiro Caro........Rolando Fernández
Dr. Navarro.......Rosa Gloria Chagoyán
Diana....................Diana Ferreti
Diana's mother.......Ana Luisa Peluffo
Lawyer ....Frank Moro
Col. Castro ....Alfredo Leal
Dr. Navarro ....René Cardona Sr.
Also with: Edna Bolkan, Guillermo Rivas (El Borras), Charly Valentino, Augustln Bernal, Carlos East, Carlos Rotzinger, Toño Camacho.

Over the past several years, Mexican filmmaker Raúl Fernández Jr. has directed a series of domestic b.o. hits based on the misadventures of "Lola la Trailera" (Lola The Trucker). His latest venture, titled alternately "La Fuga del Caro" (Caro's Escape) and "Maten a Fugitivo" (Kill The Fugitive), is almost incomprehensible. It is a chase film in the extreme: all chase and no plot.

Storyline, if that's what it can be called, begins with the capture of major cocaine smuggler Ramiro Caro (Rolando Fernández). He escapes and the rest of the film pits Ramiro against squads of cops and later armies of commandos who, although they fire enough bullets and bombs to win a small war, never manage to slow Ramiro down either on city streets or stomping around in jungles. Of course Ramiro mows down his pursuers by the score.

The main problem with the film is that the audience is never quite sure who are the good guys and who are the bad, much less what is going on. We learn nothing about any of the characters and the sparse dialog doesn't help. —*Lent*.

Hollywood Cop

A Peacock Films production. Produced by Moshe Bibiyan, Simon Bibiyan. Written and directed by Amir Shervan. Camera (color), Peter Palian; editor, Ruben Zadurian, Bob Ernst; music, Elton Farokh Ahi; sound, Scott Smith; assistant director, Bob Medora; special effects, Bill Kulzer; casting, Debbie Sipos. Reviewed on Celebrity Home Entertainment vidcassette, N.Y., Jan. 28, 1988. MPAA Rating: R. Running time: **100 MIN.**
Feliciano.................Jim Mitchum
Capt. Bonano ....Cameron Mitchell
Turkey....................David Goss
Rebecca..............Julie Schoenhofer
Jaguar ....Lincoln Kilpatrick
Lt. Maxwell ....Troy Donahue
Fong ....Aldo Ray
Joe Fresno ....Larry Lawrence

"Hollywood Cop" is an enjoyable B-picture, crudely made but suitable for the homevideo action market. Its roster of familiar character actors will generate some interest.

David Goss plays the title role, a handsome young cop assigned to undercover work. Susan Schoenhofer appeals to him for help when her son is kidnaped by the mob to put pressure on since her husband (Larry Lawrence) stiffed them for $6,000,000. With the aid of his partner Lincoln Kilpatrick, Goss goes.up against the baddies and blows them away.

Loaded with extraneous t&a footage, picture substitutes energy for sense in many scenes but is fun to watch. As fellow cops, Cameron Mitchell and Troy Donahue take a tongue-in-cheek approach to the proceedings, while lead Jim Mitchum is cast against type in a smallish role as a Mafia boss. —*Lor*.

End Of The Line

An Imagine Entertainment presentation of an Orion Classics release, produced in association with Guadalupe-Hudson Prods. and the Sundance Institute. Executive producer, Mary Steenburgen. Produced by Lewis Allen, Peter Newman. Coproduced by Walker Stuart. Directed by Jay Russell. Screenplay, Russell, John Wohlbruck; camera (Duart color), George Tirl; editor, Mercedes Danevic; music, Andy Summers; sound, Gary Alper; production design, Neil Spisak; costumes, Vanbroughton Ramsey; casting, Pat McCorkle. Reviewed at Orion screening room, N.Y., Feb. 17, 1988. MPAA Rating: PG. Running time: **105 MIN.**
Will Haney ....Wilford Brimley
Leo Pickett ....Levon Helm
Rose Pickett ....Mary Steenburgen
Jean Haney ....Barbara Barrie
Thomas Clinton .....Henderson Forsythe
Warren Gerber ....Bob Balaban
Everett ....Kevin Bacon
Alvin....................Michael Beach
Charlotte ....Holly Hunter
Also with: Missy Platt, Carroll Dee Bland, Trey Wilson, Don Hood, Clint Howard, Rita Jenrette, Lillian Grimes, Dan DeMott, Bruce McGill, Howard Morris, Armando Garza, Velva Walthall, Clay Crosby.

A capably made morality tale about two Arkansas railroad men who journey by locomotive from the backwoods to Chicago to rescue their jobs from a callous corporation, "End Of The Line" makes all the obvious thematic whistle-stops: the alarming decline of America's industrial health, the virtues of old-fashioned initiative and close-knit friendships, the sin of pinstriped greed and the trauma of unemployment in heartland company towns.

Initially released in regions where its plodding accents and jes' folks mise en scène would be at home, the picture's credible cast and predictable direction are on track for small-screen programming, but "End Of The Line" figures to stall in major theatrical markets.

Will Haney (Wilford Brimley) and Leo Pickett (Levon Helm) are salt-of-the-earth types with twangs in their voices, beer in their bellies and deeply embedded soil on their hands from long days of honest labor on the Southland Railroad. Their friendship's father-and-son overtones are deepened by the portrayal of Brimley's son as an easygoing rodeo bum who never followed the old man's footsteps into brakeman's overalls. They live in Clifford, Ark., a company town where no one wants to believe rumors that Southland is closing the railroad to enter the air freight business. When the unthinkable comes to pass, the rural hamlet is helpless to respond to the abrupt draining of its life blood.

Brimley challenges his coworkers to take a Southland train up to Chicago and confront the company's chairman, but Helm is the only one who joins him. The concept of two hicks setting off for the big city in a stolen railroad car is an appealing one that for a while manages to sustain the picture's narrative flow with romantic camaraderie. Brimley and Helm examine their existence and — after contemplating suicide at the low point of the trip — decide instead to press on and take direct action for the first time in their lives against the distant powers that dominate them.

When they arrive in the Windy City, Southland's yuppie martinet president, Warren Gerber (Bob Balaban) attempts to co-opt the two hayseeds for p.r. purposes in a scenario that probably looked funnier in the script than it plays on the screen. Not surprisingly, Brimley and Helm stick to their guns and take their case to Balaban's father-in-law, Southland chairman Thomas Clinton (Henderson Forsythe) who's been relegated by his callow son-in-law to a ceremonial role and passes his days playing with model railroad trains. Hitting it off immediately with the yokels, the aging exec agrees to be "kidnaped" and joins them on the locomotive for a triumphant ride back to Dogpatch country.

Brimley and Helm (who by this time have perfected the behaviorist approach to hayseed roles) acquit themselves well as does Kevin Bacon as a rambunctious railroad worker with a fondness of heavy metal, beer, gambling and Brimley's daughter Charlotte (Holly Hunter). Hunter plays her abrasive character with virtually the same regional accent she used in "Broadcast News," but like Mary Steenburgen (as Helm's lazy wife) and other citizens Brimley and Helm leave behind for the bright lights of Chi, she's stuck with a role shaped by the strained realism with which the film treats life in its forgotten corner of America.—*Rich.*

Moon In Scorpio

A Trans World Entertainment presentation. Executive producer, Yoram Pelman. Produced by Alan Amiel. Coproduced by Fred Olen Ray. Directed by Gary Graver. Screenplay, Robert S. Aiken; camera (Foto-Kem color), Graver; editor, uncredited; music & songs, Robert Ragland; sound, David Waelder; production manager-associate producer, Herb Linsey; assistant director, Scott Yagemann; second unit camera, Scott Ressler. Reviewed on TWE vidcassette, N.Y., Jan. 27, 1988. MPAA Rating: R. Running time: **87 MIN.**
Linda . . . . Britt Ekland
Allen . . . . John Phillip Law
Burt . . . . William Smith
Mark . . . . Louis Van Bergen
Isabel . . . . April Wayne
Dr. Khorda . . . . Robert Quarry
Claire . . . . Jillian Kessner
Also with: James Booth, Donna Kei Benz, Don Scribner, Bruno Marcotulli, Ken Smolka, Thomas Bloom.

"**Moon In Scorpio**" is a ridiculous attempt at a thriller, combining three sets of separate footage (plus stock footage) into an indigestible whole. TWE quietly released the pic to video stores last year.

Original intent undoubtedly was to fashion yet another unwanted

film about a Vietnam vet suffering oodles of angst over his war guilt. Accompanied by horrendously phony reenactment footage of war atrocities in a California forest area plus poor stock footage, John Phillip Law is the sufferer.

Gary Graver, who has several different careers as cinematographer, director and adult filmmaker, is credited with the principal footage and it is very dreary. Perhaps he was aiming at his late mentor Orson Welles' "Lady From Shanghai" or unfinished "The Deep" in the central motif of a group of scabrous individuals trapped on a yacht together, as part of a wedding gift to Law and his bride Britt Ekland.

In any event, Fred Olen Ray and finally Alan Amiel were brought in to try and save the picture. Result is a lot of extraneous footage, some of it lamely building a cover story involving an escaped lunatic who slashes various people to death including most of the cast of Graver's film; roundtable discussions by shrink Robert Quarry (playing Dr. Khorda, his character name from Ray Danton's 1972 film "The Deathmaster") and his associates James Booth and Donna Kei Benz; or idiotic voiceover by Ekland matched with additional footage of her interviewed by Quarry. End result is risible, with exposition spoonfed and reinforced repetitiously to the viewer, who is assumed to be braindead.

Technical credits are poor, and the cast is awful, particularly hammy Ekland, and, in undoubtedly his worst performance, William Smith. Graver's starlet (from his "Party Camp" pic) April Wayne is embarrassing. —*Lor.*

Aloha Summer

A Spectrafilm release of a Hanauma Bay production. Produced by Mike Greco. Executive producer, Warren Chaney. Directed by Tommy Lee Wallace. Screenplay, Greco, Bob Benedetto, story by Greco; camera (CFI color), Steven Poster; editor, James Coblentz, Jack Hofstra, Jay Cassidy; music, Jesse Frederick, Bennett Salvay; art direction, Donald Harris; set decoration, Airick Kredell; sound, Richard Goodman, Ray Barons; special water photography, Ron Condon, Bob Condon, Tom Boyle; surfing technical advisor, Rabbit Kekai; Jet-Cam, Team Hot Shots; special kendo choreography, Sho Kosugi; production manager, Jack Grossburg, assistant directors, Brian Frankish, Harry Hogan; casting, Caro Jones. Reviewed at Carolco screening room, L.A., Feb. 17, 1988. MPAA Rating: PG. Running time: **97 MIN.**
Mike . . . . Chris Makepeace
Kenzo . . . . Yuji Okumoto
Chuck . . . . Don Michael Paul
Lani . . . . Tia Carrere
Yukinaga Konishi . . . . Sho Kosugi
Amanda . . . . Lorie Griffin
Jerry . . . . Blaine Kia
Kilarney . . . . Warren Fabro
Kimo . . . . Andy Bumatai
Angelo Tognetti . . . . Ric Mancini
Scott . . . . Scott Nakagawa

Hollywood — A well-made and harmless entertainment, "Aloha

Summer," targets male teens in a wistful look back at an idyllic summer spent on the Hawaiian islands in 1959. Typical elements include surfing, drinking and the pursuit of females among six new friends, but added themes of interracial tension and violence will give viewers something more than popcorn to chew on.

With an abundant period soundtrack and some spectacular surfing footage, pic is likely to be an agreeable date-night attraction, but won't generate much momentum as it's simply too unimaginative to catch on.

Set in the year Hawaii attained statehood, 1984-lensed pic comes uncannily close to the robust look and feel of '50s films. Shy, middle-class Mike (Chris Makepeace) is stuck for the summer in his parents motel room, but soon escapes into the company of newfound friends, a girl-getting rich kid (Don Michael Paul), two Japanese-Americans (Yuji Okumoto, Scott Nakagawa) and two Hawaiian beach boys (Blaine Kia, Warren Fabro).

Majority of the tension comes from their mismatched backgrounds; the boys, embodying the "spirit of aloha," don't mind at all, but their parents do, and so do some aggressive sailors and an islander (Andy Bumatai) who doesn't like haoles (pronounce that "howlies," for mainlanders). It all leads to trouble, including a surprisingly vicious brawl with the sailors, but in the end, the bonds of friendship prevail, and the boys set an example for the less enlightened oldsters.

Sadly, filmmakers' magnanimous approach to human relations doesn't extend to females, who must all walk through 1-dimensional roles as sex objects. It's definitely a period piece.

Star Chris Makepeace makes a rather mushy core for the film, especially in the scenes with the girls, in which he wears an expression indicating he has just been struck over the head with a telephone pole.

Charm of Don Michael Paul pretty much carries the film. Both he and Lori Griffin bring the appropriate veneer of privilege and ease to the roles of the rich brother and sister.

Various standard plotlines weave the raft of momentum on which characters float through that Special Summer, until the final, spectacular bonding scene when the gang tackles the 18-ft. surf during a hurricane. Kudos to the camera team, who filmed from jet skis.

Film offers added interest in scenes depicting the martial art of kendo, a form of sword battle, choreographed by Sho Kosugi ("Enter The Ninja") who plays the stern father of Yuji Okumoto.

Overall happy ending is a bit much, but probably will go over fine with intended audience.
—*Daws.*

Baja Oklahoma

An HBO Pictures presentation in association with Rastar Prods. Produced by Marykay Powell. Executive producer, Hunt Lowry. Directed by Bobby Roth. Screenplay, Roth, Dan Jenkins, based on Jenkins' novel; camera (CFI color), Michael Ballhaus; editor, John Carnochan, Gail Yasunaga; music supervisor, Dick Rudolph; original music, Stanley Myers; production design, Al Brenner; art direction, David M. Haber; costume design, Ruth Myers; associate producer, Fred Baron; assistant director, Josh McLaglen. Reviewed at the Beverly Center Cineplex, L.A., Feb. 3, 1988. Running time: **99 MIN.**
Juanita Hutchins . . . . . Lesley Ann Warren
Slick Henderson . . . . Peter Coyote
Doris Steadman . . . . Swoosie Kurtz
Lonnie Slocum . . . . Billy Vera
Ol' Jeemy Williams . . . . Anthony Zerbe
Tommy Earl Browner . . . William Forsythe
Lee Steadman . . . . John M. Jackson
Dove Christian . . . . Bruce Abbott
Candy Hutchins . . . . Julia Roberts
Roy Simmons . . . . Carmen Argenziano
Minister . . . . Paul Bartel
Beecher Perry . . . . Jordan Charney
Tina Busher . . . . Carole Davis
Patsy Cline . . . . Alice Krige
Bob Wills . . . . Bob Wills Jr.
Emmylou Harris . . . . Herself
Willie Nelson . . . . Himself

Hollywood — "Baja Oklahoma" is an amiable little country-western fairytale none too high on plausibility but pleasant enough while it's happening. Produced by HBO in association with Rastar with strong feature film talent both in front of and behind the camera, pic debuted on HBO last week but also will play a limited theatrical engagement, at least in Los Angeles.

Adaptation by director Bobby Roth and Dan Jenkins of Jenkins' popular novel ranges in tone from the broadly comic to the melodramatic in telling of how a hard-luck Fort Worth barmaid rises to at least the beginning of success in the c&w music world.

A beautiful gal, Juanita just hasn't been dealt a very good hand in life thus far. One of her two marriages has produced a teenage daughter who runs off with a drug dealer, she tends to drink too much, and the last thing she needs — her own teenage flame, Peter Coyote — walks back into her life in the early going, confusing her to the point of distraction.

All along, Juanita tries to escape her bartending life by writing a good country song, but she can't get her buddy, singer Billy Vera, to listen to it. Heartbreak, disappointment, lonely nights and frustration, all in lively Texas style, make up her life, but it's so full of incident it's never dull.

Slaphappy tone suggests nothing too awful will happen to Juanita no matter how desperate her situation becomes, and when the film does get serious with the reappearance of the daughter's drug-pushing b.f. it also becomes unconvincing.

But good times prevail in the end, with no less a personage than Willie Nelson coming on to give Juanita's song its public debut, and all's well down home. Along with its easygoing predictability, film has no strong urgency about it, and Coyote, always hovering around the edges of Juanita's life as well as the picture, lacks dramatic tension in a sketchily defined role.

But in the leading role, Lesley Ann Warren is a delight to watch. Character — and actress — wears all her emotions on her sleeve and is so eager to please that one wants things to finally go right for her. Other performers are similarly vibrant in colorful roles, including Swoosie Kurtz as a vulgar barroom habitue who has her husband well under her thumb, Billy Vera in a tailormade part, Anthony Zerbe as a promoter who gives Juanita a break and William Forsythe as another regular on the barstools.

Everyone involved seems to have enjoyed themselves on this one and the feeling comes across, even if the material is of no great consequence and proves rather ephemeral. Seen on the big screen, all technical contributions, notably Michael Ballhaus' lensing, look sharp. — *Cart.*

The Courier
(BRITISH)

A Vestron Pictures release of a Euston Films and Palace Productions present at City Vision Film. Executive producers, Neil Jordan, Nik Powell, John Hambley. Produced by Hilary Mcloughlin. Coproducer, Steve Woolley. Directed by Frank Deasy, Joe Lee. Screenplay, Deasy; camera (Technicolor), Gabriel Beristain; editor, Derek Trigg; annette D'Alton; music, Declan MacManus (Elvis Costello); sound, Pat Hayes; production design, David Wilson; costumes, Consolata Boyle. Reviewed at the Century Preview theater, London, Feb. 2, 1988. Running time: **86 MIN.**

Mark . . . . Padraig O'Loingsigh
Colette . . . . Cait O'Riordan
Val . . . . Gabriel Byrne
McGuigan . . . . Ian Bannen
Christy . . . . Patrick Bergin
Danny . . . . Andrew Connolly
Sharon . . . . Michelle Houlden

London — No rolling green hills of Eire or cute "begorrah" Irish accents for "The Courier," a grim, occasionally violent, contempo thriller that works well for the low-budget affair it is.

A strong supporting cast, excellent photography by Gabriel Beristain ("Caravaggio"), and a fine soundtrack from young Irish bands, go some way to covering up many of pic's shortcomings, which stem from the inexperience of the two lead actors and the tyro writer/director team.

"The Courier" offers an arresting alternative look at life in Dublin, depicting youngsters turning to the burgeoning drug trade that grips modern industrial Ireland. Offshore prospects (the accents may be a problem) will be limited, but worthwhile.

Pic opens with a jewelry robbery by Andrew Connolly to get money

for drugs from vicious dealer Gabriel Byrne, who in turn kills Connolly when he betrays Byrne to the police.

While all this is going on, motorcycle courier Padraig O'Loingsigh re-embarks on a relationship with Cait O'Riordan, Connolly's sis, and begins investigating Connolly's death, discovering links between drug-dealing Byrne and police detective Ian Bannen.

What follows is a cat-and-mouse game between O'Loingsigh and Byrne, with a violent end for the villain, and love and a new life for O'Riordan and O'Loingsigh. It's your basic happy ending all things told.

O'Loingsigh looks the part with his dark good looks, but is too mild-mannered to play the hero, while O'Riordan acts with a lot of character, but not a great deal of finesse. Honors on the thesping front should go to Byrne and Bannen, whose professional playing gives the film a finer edge.

Music from some of Ireland's top rock bands adds to the contempo feel, and just to keep it in the family the score is by one Declan MacManus, a.k.a. musician Elvis Costello, and hubby of Cait O'Riordan.

The joint directing method of Frank Deasy and Joe Lee (one directing the camera, the other the actors) works fine, though Gabriel Beristain makes them look better. A badly handled bank robbery scene towards the end of the pic blots their copybook somewhat, and the idea that love scenes must be equated to bodies covered by shadows from venetian blinds is plagiarism of the most unadventurous kind.

— *Adam.*

La Vie est un long fleuve tranquille
(Life Is A Long Quiet River)
(FRENCH)

An MK2 release of a Téléma/MK2/FR3 Films coproduction. Executive producer, Charles Cassot. Produced by Florence Quentin. Directed by Etienne Chatiliez. Screenplay, Chatiliez, Quentin; camera (color), Pascal Lebèque; editor, Chantal Delattre; music, Gérard Kawczynski; art direction, Geoffrey Larcher; costumes, Elisabeth Tavernier; sound, Harrik Maury, Dominique Dalmasso; assistant director, Patricia Eberhard; casting, Romain Brémond; production manager, Louis Becker. Reviewed at the Gaumont Colisée theater, Paris, Feb. 10, 1988. Running time: **90 MIN.**

With: Benoit Magimel (Momo), Valérie Lalande (Bernadette), Hélène Vincent (Mme. Le Quesnoy), André Wilms (Mr. Le Quesnoy), Christine Pignet (Mme. Groseille), Maurice Mons (Mr. Groseille), Daniel Gélin (Dr. Mavial), Catherine Hiegel (Josette), Patrick Bouchitey (Father Aubergé), Claire Prevost (Roselyne), Tara Romer, Jérome Floch, Sylvie Cubertafon, Emmanuel Cendrier, Guillaume Hacquebart, Jean-Brice Van Keer, Praline Le Moult, Axel Vicart, Abbes Zahmani, Khadou Fghoul, Ismael Bourabaa.

Paris — Prize-winning commercials helmer Etienne Chatiliez

makes a zestful feature film debut with "Life Is A Long Quiet River," a comic tale of two families and some cradles (yes, those again).

Boasting no name actors, but plenty of talent, it's the first runaway local smash of the new year and has chances to travel. It also has remake possibilities.

Original script by Chatiliez and Florence Quentin borrows a premise used by Mark Twain in his 1894 novel, "Pudd'nhead Wilson," in which the identities of a slave's baby and its master's child are switched. Chatiliez, playing basically on the level of social farce, traces the consequences of switched babies from a provincial Catholic middle class family and a vulgar clan of lowlifes from the other side of town.

Film's tool of fate is the adoring nurse of a philandering local physician, who out of frustration and rage (he's only interested in her for occasional sex, she wants more) swaps the cradles of two babies he's just delivered.

She holds her tongue for some 15 years but finally breaks down when she realizes he'll never be hers. Her revenge is to post letters about her erstwhile deception to the doctor and the two families concerned. Then all hell breaks loose.

The God-fearing, pious Le Quesnoy family sees its hard-won insular harmony destroyed when it learns their sweet darling daughter (one of five children) is of lowly origins. The revolting Groseille clan, also blessed with five mouths to feed, take advantage of the revelation by "selling" its delinquent dear Momo back to his real parents to keep a scandal from erupting.

Comedy revolves around the facile but funny contrast of two families who should never have met and the corrupting presence of Momo among his hereditary own, who try to accept the domestic disaster as a trial from Above.

Clever as the script is, it is not always thorough. Chatiliez and Quentin fail to folow through on certain elements (Momo's unnatural interest in his real mom's body) and don't really come up with a conclusion. They just pack up once they've shaken up their droll ingredients for sufficient length (though that lovelorn nurse, whom one has forgotten, does get her man in the end).

Performances from a large cast of adults and kids are perfectly tuned, notably legit thesps Hélène Vincent and André Wilms as the befuddled bourgeois parents. Daniel Gélin (the pic's only name actor) is delightful as the self-absorbed doctor and Catherine Hiegel is fine as his avenging nurse. Tech credits are smart. —*Len.*

Amsterdamned
(DUTCH)

A Concorde Film release of a First Floor Pictures production. Produced by Laurens Geels, Dick Maas. Executive producer, Geels. Written and directed by Maas. Camera (Kodak color; Cineco prints), Marc Felperlaan; editor, Hans van Dongen; music, Maas; sound, Georges Bossaers; art direction, Dick Schillemans; assistant director, Myrna van Gilst; production manager, Yvonne C. Belonje; stunt coordinator, Dickey Beer; casting, Dorna van Rouveroy. Reviewed at Cinema Intl., Amsterdam, Feb. 8, 1988. Running time: **105 MIN.**

Eric . . . . Huub Stapel
Laura . . . . Monique van de Ven
Ruydael . . . . Hidde Maas
Vermeer . . . . Serge-Henri Valcke
Also with: Lou Landré, Tatum Dagelet, Lettie Oosthoek, Pieter Lutz, Helmert Woudenberg, Bert Haanstra.

Amsterdam — Following his successful debut feature, "The Lift" (world distribution rights acquired by Warner Bros.) and the merry, moneymaker "Flodder" (seen by nearly a quarter of the total Dutch population), Dick Maas delivers something of a disappointment with "Amsterdamned."

Impressive lensing by Marc Felperlaans, excellent stunt work by Dickey Beer, and lengthy speedboat pursuits through the canals of Amsterdam can't make up for the thin characterizations and lack of genuine suspense. It remains to be seen if the fame of "Flodder" and an avalanche of publicity can again bring the Dutch out by the millions. Chances abroad look iffy.

Horribly mutilated corpses are turning up with disturbing regularity in Amsterdam's canals on the eve of tourist season. A police investigation led by Huub Stapel turns up no leads, but at least gets the hero somewhere with Monique van de Ven, an attractive museum guide, member of the diver's club and patient of psychiatrist Hidde Maas, also an amateur diver. As it happens, the murder victims are being done in by a mysterious diver.

Maas tows a fat red herring through the murky canals for much of the screen time, only to dock on a solution due to a gratuitously injected case of atomic energy-induced insanity.

Except for Stapel, none of the large cast is developed dramatically and there are too many stereotypes, though performances are adequate.

It's a shame that the filmmakers concentrate their energies on technical effects. Spectacular sequences are flawlessly executed but they can't compensate for the dullness of the more mundane scenes. Tech credits are top flight all around.
—*Wall.*

La Maison de Jeanne
(Jeanne's House)
(FRENCH)

An AMLF release of a M.D.G./FR 3 Films coproduction. Produced by Marie-Dominique Girodet. Written and directed by Magali Clément. Camera (Eastmancolor), Pierre Novion; editor, Amina Mazani; music, Raymond Allessandrini; sound, François de Morant; art direction, Bruno Bruneau; technical advisor, Claude Barrois; script consultnat, Elvire Murail. Reviewed at the Gaumont Colisée theater, Paris, Feb. 12, 1988. Running time: **85 MIN.**

Jeanne	Christine Boisson
Georges	Jean-Pierre Bisson
Pierre	Benoit Regent
Mother	Pascale Audret
Marie	Michelle Goddet
Martine	Marie Trintignant
Father	Jacques Richard
Marc	Maxime Leroux

Paris — Typical French pastry about Amour and bourgeois values, "La Maison de Jeanne" is the debut feature by former actress Magali Clément, who wrote and directed, not very well on either count. Film's exportable charm, however, won it a European Film Special Jury Prize at the recent Brussels Film Festival.

Clément paints a portrait of a hive-like provincial hotel-restaurant run by a matriarchal family, over which presides Jeanne (Christine Boisson). Apart from her cook-husband (Jean-Pierre Bisson), their children, and her two eccentric sisters (Michelle Goddet and Marie Trintignant), Boisson must cope with a hysterical pharmacist mother (Pascale Audret) and philandering father (Jacques Richard).

The delicate balance of this disparate tribe is broken by the arrival of the property's new landlord, Benoit Regent, who no sooner settled in the household begins to court Boisson, who is soon torn between meek husband and bold but straightforward potential lover.

Clément's script abounds in scenes of homey anarchy and tenderness, romantic effusions, tantrums and tears, none of it informed by any insight or genuine pathos. Film's conclusion is especially false; Boisson decides to keep both hubby and lover, without apparent protest from either.

Cast is attractive at first but soon gets on the nerves as players indulge in a style of affected naturalism (and ostensible improvisation) that weakens character credibility. Tech credits are fair. — *Len.*

Rouge
(The Legend Of Flower)
(HONG KONG)

A Golden Way production, released by Golden Harvest. Executive producers, Jackie Chan, Willie Chan. Directed by Stanley Kwan. Screenplay and story, Li Pik-wah; camera (color); theme song performed by Anita Mui. (No other credits provided by producer/distributor.) Reviewed at State theater, Hong Kong, Jan. 19, 1988. Running time: **98 MIN.**

With: Anita Mui, Leslie Cheung, Alex Man, Emily Chu.
(Cantonese soundtrack with English subtitles)

Hong Kong — Definitely one of the best Hong Kong films of 1988, classy, elegant, artistic, believable and enjoyable love story with a ghost framework. The movie is set in colorful 1900 and retells the sad story of a high-class prostitute from an exclusive brothel patronized by rich men.

There is a woman called Flower (Anita Mui, a singer who proves that she's also a dramatic actress), who falls in love with a customer (Leslie Cheung, perfect typecasting) as a spoiled, passive young man controlled by family ties. Love blossoms, but things go awry when they plan to marry and must face the opposition of the young man's family.

With no help from anybody, the young man tries several jobs but fails and Flower must continue her trade. The outcome is that they decide to end their existence by swallowing raw opium. Flower dies but the young man loses his nerve and survives. They are expected to meet in "hell" and Flower waits for years in the spiritual dimension. When he does not come, she returns to earth to look for her lost lover.

"Rouge" has the technical gloss of an art movie, detailed cinematography to suit the mood, superb art direction and well-balanced acting, especially Alex Man who underacts for a change.

It was first released in Taiwan, was a boxoffice sensation and won three major Golden Horse awards for best actress, cinematography and art direction. In Hong Kong, it was greeted with $HK18,000,000 at the Golden Harvest theater chains during its long run. —*Mel.*

Cubagua
(VENEZUELAN-CUBAN-PANAMANIAN)

A Universidad de los Andes Depto. de Cine-Instituto Cubano del Arte y Indústria Cinematográfica (Icaic)-Grupo Experimental Cine Universitario (GECU) production. Produced by Donald Myerstón (Venezuela), Camilo Vives (Cuba), Pedro Rivera (Panama). Directed by Michael New. Screenplay, New, Ednodio Quintero, Luis Rogelio Nogueras, based on the novel by Enrique Bernardo Nuñez; camera (color), Adriano Moreno; editor, Justo Vega, Roberto Siso; music, Gilberto Márquez; sound, Stefano Gramitto. Reviewed at Havana Intl. Film Festival (competing), Cuba, Dec. 13, 1987. Running time: **81 MIN.**

Ing. Leiziaga/Count of Lampugnano	Herbert Gabaldón
Nila/Indian Woman	Sonia López
Stakelum/Carballo/ Diego de Ordáz	Reinaldo Miravalles
Dr. Figuerias/Mayor	Héctor Myerston
Fr. Dionisio	Julio Mota

Also with: Oscar Berrizbeitia, Jacinto Cruz, Yovan Rodríguez, Otilia Docaos, Rolf Clemens, Roland T. Ely, Rafael Salvatore, Antonio Dagnino, Valmore Gómez, Ramón Morales, Jesús Ortol.

Havana — The didactic Venezuelan-Cuban-Panamanian coprod "Cubagua" flits capriciously back and forth through time covering almost half a millennium to drive home its point that history repeats itself endlessly until some one with a dialectical view of history breaks the chain.

Three separate storylines using the same actors set in different time periods overlap on the accursed isle of Cubagua, showing the early rape of the Americas in the name of the Spanish crown is the same as today's exploitation of underdeveloped countries by transnational industries. For those who may not understand this point immediately, there is plenty of repetitious cross-cutting to make this perfectly clear.

At the center of the story is actor Herbert Gabaldón, who plays alternately the 16th century Count of Lampugnano and two separate incarnations of a civil engineer named Leiziaga. All three characters in this trinity are appalled at the treatment of the local indians, but powerless to halt their exploitation. It is up to our final engineer, who finally learns two and two make four, to break the process by blowing a covert corporate plan. He teams up with investigative reporter Nila (Sonia López), who also has gone through various historial incarnations.

All this makes for pretty tedious viewing. There are some nice touches to the scenery and clear visual depiction of the different time periods, but following the pamphlet-like script is like beating the proverbial dead horse into hamburger. Rather than characterization and involvement, the audience is treated to an extended lecture on the dynamics of dialectics geared to lull the viewer to sleep through repetition and overstatement. —*Lent.*

El Juego Mas Divertido
(The Most Amusing Game)
(SPANISH)

A Kaplan-TVE production. Produced by Emilio Martinez-Lazaro, Fernando Trueba. Directed by Martinez-Lazaro. Screenplay, Martin-Lazaro, Luis Arino; camera (color), Juan Amoros; editor, Nieves Martin; music, Angel Munoz-Alonso; sound, Gilles Ortion; production manager, Cristina Huerte. Reviewed at Miami Film Festival, Feb. 6, 1988. Running time: **92 MIN.**

Ada Lasa/Sara	Victoria Abril
Bruno Laforque	Antonio Valero
Tomas	Antonio Resines
Betty	Maribel Verdu
Dionisio	Santiago Ramos
Longinos Vazquez	Miguel Rellan
Jose Retama	Richard Borras
Ricardo Almonte	El Gran Wyoming
Robert Moreno	Nancho Novo

Miami — One of the bright lights of post-Franco Spanish cinema, Emilio Martinez-Lazaro ("Everything's Wrong," "Lulu By Night") has turned to screwball comedy, and the results are rambunctious fun. Mix of sex and sight gags is paced fast enough to vault the language gap, though some gags, naturally, are lost in translation, and outlook in specialty situations should be bright.

Film has to do with a national soap-opera obsession, with sexual frustration worthy of the best of the Doris Day/Rock Hudson era, and with a tangle of identities so confused and confusing that it's possible to spend a good part of the film just figuring out who is supposed to be doing what to whom.

The basic plot concerns a Spanish nighttime soap (with no small measure of bedroom romps, steamy enough to make "Dallas" seem quite tame) in which the characters of Sara and Bruno are having a sometimes torrid, sometimes stormy love affair.

In real life Sara is played by Ada (Victoria Abril), who is supposed to be with Dionisio (Santiago Ramos), the program's writer. Ada is actually pursuing and being pursued by her costar Bruno (Antonio Valero, who also plays Bruno on the soap), in their frenzied but always-foiled attempts to find a spot where they can be alone long enough to consummate their love. It's an old situation that Martinez-Lazaro milks to surprisingly fresh comic effect. At one point the lovers find themselves in glorious anonymity in a remote mountain village, only to discover that the only amenity the inhabitants enjoy is television. (Since everyone in Spain watches the soap, which is mysteriously called "Hotel Fez," the two are forever being recognized.)

It's not their only problem: The show's producer, Tomas (played by the always perplexed Antonio Resines), has the habit of turning up unexpectedly; Dionisio is no cuckold at all, but has been having a fling with Betty (the dazzling Maribel Verdu), a young actress about to get her big break on the show; and a 2-man gang of perverts, one of whom used to court Ada with ice cream in her schoolyard, is plotting to kidnap Ada and sell the story to a dimwitted "investigative reporter" for a gossip sheet.

Martinez-Lazaro has a deft way with the logistics required by a story so dependent on physical comedy. He also gets off some wicked shots at celebrity worship, journalism and contemporary mores, and he gets the expected collection of comic turns from his ensemble, topped by Abril's hysterically overwrought sexuality. It's one, long, shaggy-dog story — frisky, likable and just naughty enough.

Tech credits are adequate or better; Juan Amoros' lensing is crisp, and production has a first-rate, exportable look to it. —*Cos.*

Szerelem Masodik Verig
(Love Till Second Blood)
(HUNGARIAN)

A Dialog Studio, Mafilm, production. Directed by György Dobray. Screenplay, Dobray, Istvan Csörsz, Peter Horvath; camera (Eastmancolor), Tamas Andor; editor, Zsuzsa Posan; music, Laszlo Des; sound, Janos Reti. Reviewed at Hungarian Film Week, Budapest, Feb. 11, 1988. Running time: **88 MIN.**
With: Ary Beri, Mariann Szilagyi, Attila Epres, Denes Ujlaki, Agnes Olasz, Ilona Kallai.

Budapest — A sequel to last year's local hit "Love Till First Blood," this new one's the mixture as before. The skinny hero and his pregnant girl sing in a rock band, but at a concert riot she's hurt and loses the baby. That's the start of a teen movie, Magyar-style, that's pure fantasy and pure soap.

Füge, our hero, inherits his father's taxi when Dad takes a job in Africa; and when he quarrels with his girl and she heads off to America, he dallies with someone else. There are jealousies and petty rivalries, all set against a well-scrubbed, prosperous-looking background in which young people drive cars and live in smart apartments.

There's some mild sex, and lots of teasing, but what's most surprising is the lack of a music track, which might have enlivened these dull proceedings. The young thesps are adequate, and the production is good to look at thanks to Tamas Andor's pro camerawork; but it's very slight stuff. — *Strat.*

La Boheme
(FRENCH-ITALIAN)

A UGC release of an Erato Films/La Sept/SFPC générale d'Images/Traveling Prods./Videoschermo (Rome) coproduction. Executive producers, Claude Abeille, Massimo Patrizi, Daniel Toscan du Plantier. Produced and directed by Luigi Comencini. Screenplay from the opera libretto by Giuseppe Giacosa, Luigi Illica, inspired by Henri Murger's "Scènes de la vie de bohème;" camera (Eastmancolor), Armando Nannuzzi; editor, Sergio Buzi; music, Giacomo Puccini; musical direction, James Conlon; production design, Paola Comencini; costumes, Carolina Ferrara; sound, Guy Level, Alain Duchemin; assistant director, Mathilde Bocchi. Reviewed at UGC, Neuilly, Feb. 16, 1988. Running time: **106 MIN.**
Mimi . . . . Barbara Hendricks
Rodolphe . . . . Luca Canonici, sung by José Carreras
Musette . . . . Angela Maria Blasi
Marcel . . . . Gino Quilico
Schaunard . . . . Richard Cowan
Colline . . . . . . Francesco Ellero d'Artegna
The old suitor . . . . Massimo Girotti

Paris — "La Bohème" is an inert, unimaginative film of the famous Puccini opera by Italo director Luigi Comencini for producer Daniel Toscan du Plantier, one of the chief purveyors of the genre.

It is latter's first opera film under his indie banner Erato Films, cinema spinoff of the Erato classical records house, a former affiliate of Gaumont, where Toscan du Plantier produced Joseph Losey's "Don Giovanni" and Francesco Rosi's "Bizet's Carmen."

Contestable as those two previous productions may have been as cinema, they at least had superb natural locations and decors. With the exception of one scene, Comencini opts for a studio-bound transposition that is graceless and unhappily matches the stiff, stagy acting style. For a tale that celebrates the youthful insouciance and romantic melancholy of Bohemian Paris (here pointlessly updated to 1910), the film is remarkably devoid of spontaneity and passion.

Music buffs will probably find their money's worth in the singing, and might be tempted to shut their eyes and imagine their own staging.

Comencini is not the man for the job (the producer spent years courting Woody Allen for the project). He has a few ideas of his own, but they don't enrich the film. A particularly pointless interpolation is that of a mute role, an elderly gentleman suitor, in the double separation scene between the story's two pairs of lovers. Incarnated by Massimo Girotti, the character confuses and upsets the simple theatrical symmetry that gives the act its effect.

In her first film appearance, soprano Barbara Hendricks performs Mimi with musical emotion, but dramatically she lacks fire, and her highly photogenic face belies to the very end any signs of fatal illness.

Originally cast as her lover, the struggling playwright Rodolphe, José Carreras fell seriously ill three days into shooting and was quickly replaced by young Italian singer Luca Canonici, whose dramatic inexperience shows. Since it's Carreras' prerecorded voice we hear, what was the point of recruiting an opera singer for a lip-sync performance?

As Canonici's comrades-in-penury, Gino Quilico (as the painter Marcel, a cubist!), Richard Cowan (the musician Schaunard) and Francesco Ellero d'Artegna (the philospher Colline) are stolid and interchangeable. Only Angela Maria Blasi's Musette has some welcome animation. —*Len.*

Der Madonna Mann
(The Madonna Man)
(WEST GERMAN)

An Impuls Film Verleih release of a Radiant Film production, in conjunction with Studio Hamburg, Friedlander Filmproduktion and Norddeutscher Rundfunk (NDR). Produced by Michael Bittins. Directed by Hans-Christoph Blumenberg. Screenplay, Jonathan Thornhill, Blumenberg; camera (color), Theo van de Sande; editor, Annette Dorn; sound, Gunther Kortwich; music, Manfred Schoof; art direction, Christian Bussmann. Reviewed at Holi Kino, Hamburg, W. Germany, Jan. 18, 1988. Running time: **83 MIN.**
Martin . . . . . . Marius Muller-Westernhagen

Juliane Mundt . . . . Renée Soutendijk
Tanzmann . . . . Michael Lonsdale
Wiegand twins . . . . Heinrich Schweiger
Schirmer . . . . Peter Kraus
Wiegand's ex-wife . . . . . . Ingmar Zeisberg
Charly . . . . Ingrid van Bergen
Gronski . . . . Matthias Fuchs

Hamburg — Hans-Christoph Blumenberg was one of West Germany's leading film critics before trying his hand at directing. Now he has come out with his third film, an attempt at Hitchcock-style dry wit, action and suspense that is witless, leaden and inspires mostly yawns. That is, except when it inspires unintended hoots and guffaws.

No chance of turning coin from this clunker, whose main reason for existence seems to be to promote its shooting location, the city of Hamburg, which put up film subsidy coin.

At times Blumenberg's sense of setting and atmosphere and Theo van de Sande's camera seem on the verge of rescuing this film, but the lack of any kind of coherent plot sabotages the whole shebang.

Unbelievable storyline involves an Australian (Marius Müller-Westernhagen) whose flight to Helsinki is interrupted by a weather-induced layover in (where else?) Hamburg. In no time he's mistaken for a hired killer and finds himself on the run with a Dutch accomplice (Renée Soutendijk).

Two leads haven't got a chance with an implausible screenplay that reduces them both to walking clothespins stumbling through a series of illogical mishaps while the viewer wonders, "Who are these people and why should I care what happens to them?"

Technical credits, on the other hand, are tops. —*Gill.*

The Dark Side Of Midnight

A Troma release. Written, produced and directed by Wes Olsen. Camera (color), Wes Page; editor, Olsen; music, Doug Holroyd; sound, Misty Walls, Tony Medeiros, Bill Prudhomme; art direction, Bob Olsen; special makeup effects, Susan Frawley; associate producer, MaryAnn Olsen; casting, James Hull. Reviewed on Prism Entertainment videcassette, N.Y., Feb. 3, 1988. No MPAA Rating. Running time: **89 MIN.**
Chief Cooper . . . . James Moore
Brock Johnson . . . . Wes Olsen
Jan Cooper . . . . Sandy Schemmel
Mayor Reilly . . . . Dave Bowling
The Creeper . . . . Dan Myers
Ben Fischer . . . . Dennis Brennan
Cheryl . . . . Susan Frawley
Timmy . . . . Eliot Fisher
Lt. Nelson . . . . Rocky Jackson
David Griffin . . . . Ron Posey
Kathy . . . . June Asher

"The Dark Side Of Midnight" is another amateur production released by Troma, the N.Y.-based distrib yet to upgrade its product. Pic bears a 1984 copyright and was released briefly to theaters in 1986 ahead of current homevideo availability.

Wes Olsen performs virtually all credits here in a relentlessly dull attempt at a "thriller" about a slasher preying on folks in Fort Smith, Ark. (where the pic was lensed). He's called in as a specialist private eye when local police are baffled by the murderer called "The Creeper."

Nominal plot has the local mayor (Dave Bowling) obstructing the course of James Moore's investigation in order to further his own scheme to sell some local land to developers planning to build a university in Fort Smith.

The acting is extremely stiff and amateurish, and action scenes are kept to a minimum. With violence off camera, no sex and no nudity, pic has nothing to offer to the exploitation market. On any other level, it is inept. Casting of the tall killer to look a lot like cop James Moore doesn't pay off, it's just a mistake. Lack of an ending is another problem. —*Lor.*

Nadie Escuchaba
(Nobody Listened)
(DOCU)

A Cuban Human Rights Film Project production. Produced, written and directed by Nestor Almendros, Jorge Ulla. Camera (color), Orson Ochoa; editor, Esther Duran; sound, Phil Pearle; associate producers, Marcelino Miyares, Jorge A. Rodriguez, Albert E. Jolis; narrators, Geoffrey Carey, Sondra Lee. Reviewed at Miami Film Festival, Feb. 12, 1988. Running time: **117 MIN.**

Miami — "Nobody Listened" (Nadie Escuchaba), a strong U.S. docu on three decades of oppression, torture and systematic human rights violations by the Castro regime in Cuba, joins "Improper Conduct," "The Other Cuba" and "In Their Own Words" in the documentary record of the tragedy of Cuba.

The noted cinematographer, Nestor Almendros, and Cuban exile director Jorge Ulla each was involved with one or another of these films; "Nobody Listened" marks thier first collaboration, as coproducers and codirectors.

It's a productive one. Some 30 survivors of Castro's jails are interviewed, most of whom drew sentences as long as 20 years for merely criticizing the regime, often from among its own ranks. The procession of "talking heads" recounting miseries is testament to the existence of a reign of terror where, for years, outside observers saw and heard no problems at all. Hence the title, which describes the situation in which many Cubans, exiled or not, found themselves throughout the 1960s and '70s. The rest of the world did not want to know, or found it easier not to know, or knew but denied the knowledge.

Film has been assembled with care, and easily is the most technically accomplished of the documentaries on the subject; though short on revelations, it's long on emotional impact. The testimony of victims from Huber Matos (once a Castro commandant) to Armando Valladares (whose memoirs were published as "Against All Hope") have been well documented elsewhere, but are reprised here in context of witnesses whose stories are less well known. Film essentially is a procession of "talking heads," but the tales they tell are harrowing.

Orson Ochoa's camerawork is exemplary, though it is in routine documentary style — zoom in, zoom out, add the illusion of action where there is only speech. Ulla proves a determined interrogator, somewhat in the fashion of Claude Lanzmann in "Shoah."

The essential human drama of "Nobody Listened" is riveting and, because of its basic truth, terribly sad. To the extent that the word is out on Castro, docu merely adds to the evidence, but in those areas where he's still a hero, particularly in Europe and among the American left, "Nobody Listened" should come as news, and controversial news at that. Film's polish is high for a project budgeted at less than $200,000. That, plus built-in appeal to Latin audiences as well as allure of Almendros' name, should spur much more than the usual docu biz. —*Cos.*

Felix
(WEST GERMAN)

A Filmverlag der Autoren release of a Futura Film production, with support from the Hamburg Wirtschaftsförderung. Produced by Theo Hinz. Directed by Christel Buschmann, Helke Sander, Helma Sanders-Brahms, Margarethe von Trotta. Screenplay, Buschmann, Sander, Silvo Lahtela, Sanders-Brahms, Von Trotta; camera (color), Frank Brühne, Mike Gast, Martin Gressmann, Franz Rath; editor, Jane Seitz; costumes, Heidrun Brandt, Mascha Braun; production manager, Pit Schröder. Reviewed at Broadway Kino, Hamburg, Feb. 1, 1988. Running time: **100 MIN.**

Felix . . . . Ulrich Tukur
Eva . . . . Eva Mattes
Also with: Barbara Auer (Luci), Annette Uhlen (Susanne), Danuta Lato (Danuta), Gabriela Herz (Gabi), Eva-Maria Hagen (hotel clerk), Gerhard Olschewski (drunk), Stefan Aust (Stefan), August Zimer (Luci's husband), Nadine Rensing (little girl).

Hamburg — Ulrich Tukur, 27, is one of West Germany's leading young stage actors — able to tackle anything from Shakespeare's Marc Antony to a crooning song & dance man, reflecting on his offstage musical interests. Even he needs a good screenplay, and this tag-team directorial outing by four filmmakers fails to provide that.

Distribution prospects are sadly limited for this pic, whose disjointed screenplay often puts tedious monologs in the mouth of a thesp worthy of much better. Plot follows Felix (Tukur) through the aftermath of a material breakup, with segments divvied up between pic's four directors.

Best segment is by Margarethe von Trotta and teams Tukur with Eva Mattes, a gifted thesp who has worked before with Tukur on the legit stage. Capable of handling the most difficult role, she even donned male drag to play a convincing Rainer Werner Fassbinder in "A Man Like EVA" after the director's death in 1982. Von Trotta brings this pair together in an ice cream parlor to play strangers grieving their respective lost loves, and gives Tukur and Mattes lines they can work with.

Technical credits are good, especially editing by Jane Seitz, who does her best to give the rocky pic some continuity. —*Gill.*

Souvenir
(BRITISH)

A Palisades Entertainment release of an Andre A. Blay and Tom Reeve presentation in association with Intl. Contracts of a Fancy Free production. Produced by Tom Reeve, James Reeve. Executive producer, Blay. Coproducer, Bernard Krichefski. Directed by Geoffrey Reeve. Screenplay, Paul Wheeler, based on the novel "The Pork Butcher" by David Hughes; camera (Technicolor), Fred Tammes; editor, Bob Morgan; costume design, Raymond Hughes; sound (Dolby), Bob Allan; assistant director, Fraser Copp; second unit camera, Henk Risch; casting, Maude Spector (U.K.), Margot Capellier (France). Reviewed at the Executive screening room, L.A., Feb. 17, 1988. MPAA Rating: R. Running time: **93 MIN.**

Ernst Kestner . . . . . . Christopher Plummer
Tina Boyer . . . . Catherine Hicks
Xavier Lorion . . . . Michaël Lonsdale
William Root . . . . . . Christopher Cazenove
Young Kestner . . . . Patrick Bailey
Janni . . . . Amelie Pick
Madame Lorion . . . . Lisa Daniely
Henri Boyer . . . . Jean Badin

Hollywood — A potentially dramatic story has been flattened out into a string of unconvincing confrontations and coincidences in "Souvenir," an earnest but bland film about a former Nazi soldier's need to unburden himself of guilt 40 years after the war.

An English production lensed entirely in France, pic had its world premiere last week at the Monterey Film Festival and faces a dim American theatrical future.

Based on David Hughes' acclaimed novel "The Pork Butcher," tale sees German native Christopher Plummer leaving his adopted country of the U.S. for the first time since the war to see his daughter in Paris. His real mission, however, is to return to the French village of Lascaud where, as a young recruit, he had an unforgettable love affair with a local girl and, it turns out, he played an unwitting part in the massacre of more than 100 townsfolk.

Unfortunately, most of the first half of the picture has his immature, unhappy, incredibly irritating daughter, played by Catherine Hicks, acting very intolerant and impatient with her old man. Furthermore, most of her dialog consists of questions, designed to elicit expository ramblings from Plummer, but this just results in all the story points being hit dead on, in increasingly laborious ways.

Shady Brit journalist Christopher Cazenove turns up to interrogate the principals further, and to provide Hicks with some distraction while Plummer revisits the scenes of his youth and broods about his crimes and lost love.

Not once but twice, Plummer publicly pours out his guilt and demands to be tried and punished. But local mayor Michaël Lonsdale, who has grand political ambitions centered upon his dream of a united Europe, will have none of it, as he sees no point in opening up old wounds. The double irony inherent in the climax proves just too coincidental to swallow, making one reject the whole thing as an overly pat treatment of difficult material.

Plummer looks appropriately tortured throughout, but Geoffrey Reeve, making the transition from producer's desk to director's chair, never gets under his skin or draws the audience close to him. Hicks is mannered and psychologically unfathomable, while the others are just along for the ride. Amelie Pick is quite lovely as Plummer's young love, seen in flashbacks.—*Cart.*

Linie 1
(Line 1)
(WEST GERMAN)

A Bioskop-Film. Produced by Eberhard Junkersdorf. Directed by Reinhard Hauff. Screenplay, Volker Ludwig, Hauff, based on an original musical by Ludwig; camera (color), Frank Brühne; editor, Peter Przygodda; sound, Christian Moldt, Ralf Krause; music, Birger Heymann; art direction, Benedikt Herford, Matthias Fischer-Dieskau; make-up, Rüdiger Knoll, Margit Neufink; choreography, Neva Howard. Reviewed at Berlin Film Festival, Feb. 12, 1988. Running time: **99 MIN.**

With: Ilona Schulz, Dieter Landuris, Thomas Ahrens, Christian Veit, Petra Zieser, Claus-Peter Damitz, Dietrich Lehmann, Else Nabu, Christiane Reiff, Rainer Strecker, Inka Groetschel, Andreas Schmidt, Johannes Kresch, Karen Rasenack.

Berlin — This much anticipated, homegrown musical world premiered on its own turf. The first German musical with non-operatic pretensions to come along in some time, "Linie 1" is based on a very successful local stage production with book and lyrics written by Volker Ludwig for his base, the Grips Theater Co.

Berliners were out in force to cheer the home team on, even attracting demonstrators, many the very subjects the film's about, protesting the fact that while their lifestyle is being glorified in film, the local government is doing its best to make it harder for them to live in the divided city.

While the film is chock full of excellent performances, some dazzling ensemble playing, a still impressive number of witty, biting lyrics and situations, filming has tended to dilute the theatrical impact. Rather than opening the piece for the screen, the production remains somewhat stagebound, and the sets unfortunately look like sets, no matter how cleverly distressed they were to resemble the real settings. One wonders why the production didn't bother to use authentic Berlin locations.

About the travellers on one of Berlin's popular subway lines, the story deals with some gritty character and subject matter, including a moving condemnation of Nazi accommodation. There are portraits of desperate people, young and old, many living on the emotional and physical edge. Indeed, one self-destructive lass succeeds in getting the attention she craves by throwing herself in front of an oncoming subway train.

The worst kinds of low-lifes are depicted very much in the Brecht-Weill tradition of "Three-penny Opera," but tailored to contemporary Berlin.

Bigotry, violence and petty officialdom are all savagely satirized, but the storyline of a young girl's search for a rock star who after a 1-night stand promised to help her if she ever needs him, proves rather thin on the big screen. However, the street types she meets and interacts with have substantial weight.

Director Reinhard Hauff has turned in a well-paced, colorful production, though the soundstage and the familiar faces of the same extras throughout make things a bit claustrophobic.

Not the kind of musical you leave humming the tunes, one is left with some very strong impressions of Berlin street life. No doubt the pic will play well in the rest of West Germany and Europe. Whether it paints the kind of tourist-oriented atmosphere the city fathers would prefer in a town whose main industry is politics, is an open question.

About the film crossing the Atlantic there appears less certainty. While dubbing for the U.S. market is the only way to go — the subtitling in the reviewed version is more than adequate but reading detracts from enjoying the more subtle moments — can a dubbed translation truly do justice to the special Berliner schnauze or cant?

The cast is composed primarily of the musical's original performers, an extremely talented and versatile ensemble, many of whom convincingly essay a number of roles in well-articulated performances.

Dieter Landuris is a standout for his street-smart drug dealer, zonked-out rapper and Wilmersdorfer widow, among other roles. So are Ilona Schulz and Petra Zieser, as the archetypical sadistic school girls.

Perhaps the high point of the film, as in the original stage version, is the biting Wilmersdorfer widows number — played by four men in drag — brutally satirizing the complacency of Nazi widows living comfortably on their husbands' pensions.

One wants the filming of the musical to succeed more than it has. There are highly entertaining, witty moments that will translate wherever the film goes, but it seems an opportunity to really do a film about contemporary Berlin has been left unfulfilled. —*Owl*.

Die Alleinseglerin
(The Solo Sailor)
(EAST GERMAN)

An East German DEFA Studios production and release. Produced by Garrit List. Directed by Hermann Zschoche. Screenplay, Regine Sylverster, from novel by Christine Wolter; camera (color), Günther Jaeuthe; editor, Monika Schindler; music, Günther Fischer; sound, Werner Dibowski; art direction, Paul Lehmann; production manager, Dieter Anders. Reviewed at Berlin Intl. Film Festival (Panorama section), Feb. 14, 1988. Running time: **90 MIN.**
Christine . . . . Christina Powileit
Also with: Johanna Schall (Veronika), Manfred Gorr (Werner), Gotz Schubert (Georg), Monika Lennartz (father's widow), Gunter Schob (professor).

Berlin — No smooth sailing for this morose East German pic about a woman's lonely struggle to hold a steady course through the troubled waters of a sea of egoistic men. A vortex of audience depression drains export prospects from this otherwise well-scripted low-budgeter.

Pic's central figure, Christine (Christina Powileit), is thwarted at every turn by men. First there's the father who abandons her. Then there's her womanizing husband, whom she divorces. A sexist professor blocks her academic career. Then her father dies, leaving her his pride and joy — a 20-foot sloop. Her decision to restore and refloat the boat meets derision from men at the boat docks. A boyfriend splits after she starts devoting her weekends to her boat. Her toddler son also feels neglected.

When boat is at last seaworthy after an arduous winter, it turns out to be masculine too — the jib knocks her senseless, the mainsail rips into tatters reminiscent of the relationships and academic career she has lost. Determined more than ever to

make at least the boat go, she repairs it and sets out anew, only to capsize on a sandbank. Fade to black with her laughing hysterically atop the sunken hull.

Ho-hum camera and tech credits can't bail this one out. — *Gill*.

Brise-glace
(Icebreaker)
(FRENCH-SWEDISH)

A Ministry of Foreign Affairs (France)/Swedish Film Institute coproduction, with the participation of the SFP, SEPT, Radio-France, la Muse en circuit, the Maison de la Culture de Le Havre. Conceived and produced by Pascal-Emmanuel Gallet. Executive producers, Gallet and Lisbet Gabrielsson (second episode). Directed by Jean Rouch, Titte Törnroth, Raul Ruiz. Camera (color), Rouch, Andra Lasmania, Patrice Cologne; editor, Jean Ravel, Valeria Sarmiento; music (third episode), Jorge Arriagada, David Jisse; sound, Patrick Genet, Peter Eklund, Jean-Paul Buisson; still photography, Katalin Volcsanszky. Film in three sections: "Bateau givre" (Rouch), "Hans Majestät Isbrytaren Frej" (Törnroth), "Histoires de Glace" (Ruiz). Reviewed at Forum-Horizon theater, Paris, Feb. 11, 1988. (In Berlin Film Fest — Panorama section.) Running time: **90 MIN.**
With: captain and crew of the Swedish icebreaker Frej, and Jacques Wenger, Ewin Hansen, Yves Leroy, Claude Becker, and the voices of Alain-Halle Halle, Jean-François Lapalus, Alain Rimoux.

Paris — Filmmakers Jean Rouch, Titte Törnroth and Raul Ruiz shipped out on a Swedish icebreaker in March 1986, at the invitation of the French Ministry of Foreign Affairs. What they brought back and edited has been combined to make a visually haunting feature film that is a must for the festival circuit (it is being shown at the Berlin Fest's Panorama program), and should find specialized playoffs and tv exposure.

Film, coproduced by the Swedish Film Institute, had a 3-week, 1-screen commercial run here and was broadcast on French tv to considerable media comment.

Project was conceived, coordinated and produced by Pascal-Emmanuel Gallet, head of a new multimedia division at the foreign affairs ministry, who invited a number of artists (there were also a composer, a photographer and a writer) to sail for two weeks during one of the ship's regular service runs in the ice-bound Bothnian Sea.

Each filmmaker shot with reduced crews according to their own aesthetic inclinations, letting the ship, its crew and the majestically eerie polar scapes fire their imaginations.

French documentarian Jean Rouch, far from the tropical climes of his beloved Africa, checks in first with "Bateau-givre" (a pun on the title of a famous Rimbaud poem, "Le Bateau-ivre" — "The Drunken Boat" — here meaning "The Frosted-boat"). Shot in a straightforward cinema vérité style, sans commentary, the episode captures the hypnotic, allegorical beauty of the icebreaker, a massive metallic Saint-

Bernard of the northern seas.

Sweden's Titte Törnroth, a woman film and tv helmer, retraces much of Rouch's on-board itinerary, but introduces the human element of voiceover snatches of interviews with the ship's captain and navigator.

Finally, the prolific Raul Ruiz sifts the material through his eccentric sensibility to imagine an enigmatic sci-fi fiction that uses the literary first-person narrative, filmed footage and stills (many of Katalin Volcsanszky, the project's guest photographer, whose work has been published in a superb album).

Though each film (running about 30 minutes) is automatically interesting, they all overlap, complement, extend one another, as panels in a triptych. There is a fascinating progression from the objective, wordless impressions of Rouch to the wordy, kaleidoscopic fantasies of Ruiz, which will provide plenty of grist for analytical mills.

Film was shot in 16m and (well) blown up to 35m for theatrical screenings. The multi-media experiment has also produced a prize-winning musical work by Luc Ferrari, a radio documentary by David Jisse (whose own music is used in the film by Ruiz), a photo album and even a 1,000-piece jigsaw puzzle! — *Len*.

Talking To Strangers
(U.S.)

A Baltimore Film Factory production. Produced by J.K. Eareckson. Directed by Rob Tregenza. Screenplay and camera (Duart color), Tregenza; editor, none; sound, Jay Harrison. Reviewed at Berlin Film Fest (Panorama), Feb. 15, 1988. Running time: **92 MIN.**
Jesse . . . . Ken Gruz
The Woman . . . . Sarah Rush
Ms. Taylor . . . . Caron Tate
The Priest . . . . Henry Strozier
Red Coat . . . . Dennis Jordan
The General . . . . Marvin Hunter
The Angry Man . . . . . . Brian Constantini
Also with: Bill Sanders, Joanne Bauer, Lois Nettles, Sharri Valero, Lois Evans, Richard Foster, Linda Chambers.

Berlin — Firsttime director Rob Tregenza is to be congratulated on the elaborately inventive camerawork for which he's responsible and which makes "Talking To Strangers" an interesting experience; but as the film's writer he has come up with a weak concept and screenplay to go with his visual ideas.

Result is a fascinating but frustrating pic, which might do modest biz in small houses if the curious can be attracted.

Pic consists solely of nine 10-minute takes (no editor was employed), the only link between them being the dull character of Jesse (Ken Gruz), a would-be writer. There's no overall narrative, and some episodes are a lot more interesting than others, while a couple are just fillers.

First segment is a clever overhead shot of a city intersection, looking

down on an indecisive type, uncertain which bus to catch. This curtain-raiser smacks of a smart film school graduate pic rather than an establishing shot for a feature. Next, The Soup Kitchen, has the cleverest camerawork of the film, with some intricate camera moves (forcing some of the extras visibly to duck to avoid the camera as it passes over them) climaxing in a smooth exit from the building out onto the street. It earns full marks for ingenuity.

The Photographer, shot under an underpass, is one of the weakest segs, but is followed by one of the best, The Bank, in which a femme employee is assailed by a frustrated customer while hassled by her husband who keeps phoning her with his domestic troubles. It's the best-written segment.

The Priest is a routine dialog in a confessional. The Water Taxi, also well shot, has the unpleasant Jesse annoying some shy nuns on a sight-seeing boat. The Bus is a nasty item about a hijacked bus and the rape of a middle-aged woman. The Woman involves Sarah Rush as a prostie-turned-ceramic artist who's spent a night with Jesse and finds getting to know him as boring as we could have told her it would be. Final, and completely extraneous, seg has Jesse spray-painting an apartment; when he turns his paint-spray on the camera, the film ends.

Now that he's proven he's an inventive cameraman, with skill in staging long, elaborate takes, Tregenza should find himself a writer. He could make a really interesting film in the future, but "Talking To Strangers" works only for about a third of its length. —*Strat*.

La Deuda Interna
(The Debt)
(ARGENTINE-BRITISH)

A British Film Institute presentation of a Yacoraite Films-Mainframe Films coproduction. Produced by Julio Lencina, Sasha Menocki. Directed by Miguel Pereira. Screenplay, Pereira, from a book by Fortunato Ramos, dialog, Pereira, Eduardo Leiva Muller; camera (color) and editor, Gerry Feeny; music, Jaime Torres; production design, Kiki Aguiar; sound, Juana Sapire; executive producers in charge of postproduction, Colin MacCabe, Jill Pack; assistant director, Ariel Piluso. Reviewed at Berlin Film Fest (competing), Feb. 14, 1988. Running time: **100 MIN.**
The Teacher . . . . Juan Jose Camero
Veronico . . . . Gonzalo Morales
Grandmother . . . . . . Anna Maria Gonzales
Juanita . . . . Juanita Caceres
Also with: Guillermo Delgado, Rene Olaguivel, Titina Gaspar, Raul Calles.

Berlin — Despite a very slow first half, this unique Argentine-British coproduction winds up as a moving drama about the effects of the country's notorious military junta, and the 1982 Falklands War, on people even in remote country backwaters.

If properly handled, pic could spark interest in Spanish-lingo territories, and also in Britain, where there's likely to be a controversy over the government-financed British Film Institute's involvement in the project.

Director Miguel Pereira, 30, graduated from the London Film School the day the Falklands (or Malvinas) conflict started. He's from the northwestern Argentine province of Jujuy, and the setting for "The Debt" is the village of Chorcan in that bleak, arid area. First 40 minutes or so of the pic are, unfortunately, over-extended and even cliched as Pereira establishes the death of a peasant woman in childbirth and the departure of her bereaved husband to seek work, leaving his infant son, Veronico, with his old mother. These scenes cover very familiar territory, and are handled without much originality, and with camerawork that's too pretty for its own good.

But just before the film's halfway point, the military junta takes over in Buenos Aires, and the film becomes more interesting. Soldiers arrive in the village and put the local cop in charge of things, over the village mayor. The teacher, who has come from the city, has to surrender books deemed "political." Meanwhile, young Veronico's grandmother has died, and he's cared for by the teacher, who even takes him to the provincial capital in search of his father. This visit results in one of the film's strongest scenes, as the teacher is interrogated by the police since the missing father, apparently, was involved in the outlawed labor movement.

Sometime later, the teacher is moved back to the city, and when he visits the village again during 1982 he discovers that Veronico was a sailor aboard the ill-fated General Belgrano, sunk by a British submarine during the conflict. It's ironic, because the teacher had fostered the boy's curiosity about the sea when they'd lived together.

If the first part of the film could be trimmed, result would be a much more successful pic, because the elements are there for a moving tale. Performances are fine, and technically the film is first-rate; postproduction was handled entirely in Britain, and financing was equally British and Argentine. International sales are handled by the British Film Institute. The British participation is unusual, although the film's villains are undoubtedly the military junta that misgoverned the country from the mid-'70s. Yet, it's stressed that the General Belgrano was sunk when it was situated outside Britain's own exclusion zone, a tender point for the Thatcher government (which funds the BFI). Pic may be expected to be in demand at fests, and should have modest commercial success in art houses, especially if tightened. —*Strat.*

Hong Gaoliang
(Red Sorghum)
(CHINESE)

A China Film Export presentation of an Xi-an Filmstudio production. Directed by Zhang Yimou. Screenplay, Chen Jianyu, Zhu Wei, Mu Yan; camera (Widescreen, color), Gu Changwei; editor, Du Yuan; music, Zhao Jiping; production design, Yang Gang. Reviewed at Berlin Film Fest (competing), Feb. 15, 1988. Running time: **91 MIN.**
The Bride .... Gong Li
Grandfather .... Jian Weng
Child .... Jiu Ji
Bandit Chief .... Ji Cun Hua
Also with: Teng Rujun, Cui Cun-Hua.

Berlin — With "Red Sorghum," China has come up with a film with genuine arthouse possibilities around the world. A fable set in the '30s and '40s, pic starts off as a light-hearted love story, then abruptly shifts into harrowing indictment of Japanese wartime artocities. Throughout it is visually splendid, the work of a filmmaker of considerable talent.

In fact, it's the first film directed by Zhang Yimou, hitherto known as the gifted cameraman of such key Chinese films as "Yellow Earth," "The One And The Eight" and "The Big Parade." Tale is structured as a recollection of the lives of the grandparents of an unseen narrator. His grandmother, at age 18, was sold by her father into marriage with a 50-year-old brandy-maker suffering from leprosy. On her wedding day, gowned in red and with a red veil, she's carried by bearers in a red sedan chair to meet her husband. The bearers sing cheerfully as they bounce the unhappy bride along.

The wedding party is waylaid by a masked bandit, supposedly the notorious bald bandit who haunts the vast sorghum fields of the district. He's a fake, though, and when he tries to rape the bride, one of the bearers kills him. The bearer now becomes besotted with the girl, and she with him, and a short while later he lays in wait for her and makes love to her amid the sorghum, as the tall plants blow furiously in the wind about them. Soon after, the leprous husband (whom we never see), is murdered, and the wife takes control of his distillery business.

The bearer turns up to claim his woman, but she rejects him at first, and in revenge he urinates in several caskets of brandy; however, the distillery foreman tastes the drink and pronounces it outstanding. Then the real bandit turns up and kidnaps the girl, though she escapes rape because he's frightened of getting leprosy. The vengeful lover attempts to rescue her from the bandit's lair — which, incongruously, is a butcher's shop — and, despite the odds, succeeds.

Years pass and the couple have a 9-year-old son. The Japanese invade, and the distillery foreman becomes a leader of the resistance. In the film's most shocking scene, the foreman and the bandit chief are captured by the enemy and sentenced to be skinned alive. One villager refuses and is shot, his assistant complies, fortunately offscreen (there's a rather jarring cut at this point, suggesting that the harrowing sequence might have originally gone further than it does). Pic climaxes with a bloody confrontation with Japanese troops, resulting in many deaths, and a symbolic eclipse of the sun.

Zhang Yimou tells this legendary tale with brio. Early scenes are good-humored and fun, with the bandit appearing dramatically from behind the wide-screen camera like a Mifune character in a Kurosawa film. Last part, though, is grim. Color is boldly used, with red dominating: the red bridal costume, the bright red brandy, red blood, and the red that fills the screen during the final scenes of the eclipse. Music is also used very dramatically and to great effect.

It's invigorating to see the wide screen used with such confidence and distinction, and exciting to find a film which, despite a few loose ends (partly brought about, perhaps, by the inadequate subtitling of the copy unspooled in Berlin) is handled in such a masterly way. "Red Sorghum" is definitely in the running for a major prize in Berlin, and should play the world's art house circuit where the best Asian films are becoming increasingly acceptable. —*Strat.*

Karhozat
(Damnation)
(HUNGARIAN-B&W)

A Hungarian Film Institute-Mokep-Magyar TV production. Produced by Jozsef Marx. Directed by Bela Tarr. Screenplay, Tarr, Laszlo Krasznahorkai; camera (b&w), Gabor Medvigy; editor, Agnes Hranitzky; music, Mihaly Vig; sound, Peter Laczkovich. Reviewed at Hungarian Film Week, Budapest, Feb. 7, 1988. (In Berlin Film Fest — Panorama Section.) Running time: **114 MIN.**
Karrer .... Miklos B. Szekely
Wife .... Vali Kerekes
Willarsky .... Gyula Pauer
Old Woman .... Hedi Temessy
Husband .... György Cserhalmi

Budapest — A bleak, cheerless film about defeated, desolate characters, "Damnation" remains watchable thanks to the rigorous style with which it's made. It's been picked for the Panorama section of the Berlin fest, and could find specialist art house audiences.

The film is set in dingy apartments, rundown backstreets, and a cheerless bar called the Titanic. It seems to be permanently raining, and stray dogs wander mournfully around seeking food. Central character is Karrer (Miklos B. Szekely), an intense, gloomy figure fixated on a singer (Vali Kerekes) with whom he's had an affair, though she's married. She wants to call a halt, but Karrer involves her husband (György Cserhalmi) in some smuggling proposed by the Titanic's manager, which gets him out of the way so that the cheerless romance can continue. When the wife again calls a halt, Karrer betrays the husband to the police.

The characters are a gloomy lot, and the world they inhabit is even gloomier, with the never-ending rain emphasizing the wretchedness of it all. Pic would be unendurable if not for the striking camerawork (by Gabor Medvigy) which involves lateral tracking shots in virtually every set-up. Longish takes, in which the camera placidly observes characters going about their routine lives, are reminiscent of the style of certain Greek films.

Nobody is happy in this film. The wife wants to be beautiful again, Karrer still broods over the suicide of his wife years earlier, the barman is up to his ears in shady deals (and is sexually involved with the wife, also), while the gullible husband is doomed because he goes after the easy money. There's also an old woman who appears periodically to quote from the Bible and offer unheeded advice. Apart from the principal characters, inhabitants of the neighborhood stand passively in the drenching rain waiting for who knows what, or join in a plodding communal dance in the scrungy bar. One solitary man dances alone in the rain, in a forlorn imitation of Gene Kelly.

Pic won't be to everyone's taste (and prompted lotsa walkouts at the screening caught), but it exerts a certain spell over the viewer thanks to its rigorous approach to a very depressing theme. Final image, of a pile of sodden mud, seems to sum it all up.—*Strat.*

Is-Slottet
(The Ice Palace)
(NORWEGIAN)

A Norsk Film production. Produced by Gunnar Svendsrud. Directed by Per Blom. Screenplay, Blom, from the novel by Terjei Vesaas; camera (color), Halvor Naess; editor, Margit Nordqvist; music, Geir Bohren, Bent Aserud; production design, Ingeborg Kvamme; sound, Havard Rype; assistant director, Sirin Eide. Reviewed at Berlin Film Fest (Panorama), Feb. 16, 1988. Running time: **76 MIN.**
Siss .... Line Storesund
Unn .... Hilde Nyeggen Martinsen
Bente .... Urda Bratternd Larsen
Aunt .... Merete Moen
Father .... Vidar Sandem
Mother .... Sigrid Huun
Kari .... Charlotte Lundestad

Berlin — A very powerful and disturbing film about friendship and a strong and strange attraction between two pre-teen schoolgirls, one of whom disappears, "The Ice Palace" is a mood piece of style and

distinction.

Its very slow pacing may make it a tough international sell, but it could find audiences for its mysterious and extremely beautiful story.

Apparently set in the '50s, in a remote, snowbound village, pic intros 11-year-old Unn, whose mother has recently died and who never knew her father; she lives with a kindly aunt. She has no friends, except for Siss, who's the same age and who comes from a stable family background. One evening, Siss visits Unn's home for the first time, and in a very long, and quite strange, sequence, an unspoken sexuality between the two children results in their undressing and just gazing at each other. Then, frightened and shy, they dress again, and Unn swears Siss to keep what they've done a secret.

Next day, on her way to school, Unn slips and falls into a frozen waterfall. Unable to find her way out of this "ice palace," she slowly freezes to death in another long, beautifully handled, and very moving, sequence. As she dies, she speaks the name of her friend.

Siss is dismayed at Unn's disappearance, and takes part in the fruitless search. But eventually spring comes, Unn's aunt comforts the forlorn child, a new girl takes Unn's place in class, and life goes on.

"The Ice Palace" has interesting parallels with Peter Weir's "Picnic At Hanging Rock." Here, too, there's the undefined sexual attraction between very young girls, a disappearance, and a feeling for the powerful forces of nature that shape the lives of mere humans. Director Per Blom doesn't shrink from the sexual aspects of the story, and images of the shy, naked girls are handled with tact and a calm beauty. A magnificent music score by Geir Bohren and Bent Aserud is a major factor in the film's success, as is the extremely handsome photography of Halvor Naess.

As the two girls, Line Storesund and Hilde Nyeggen Martinsen give lovely, unaffected performances. They enact difficult, even at times embarrassing, roles with confidence and serenity.

Blom takes his time to capture the spirit of this strange story, and despite the film's short running time, many will find the picture very slow. This may harm commercial chances, but this is one Norwegian film which could find foreign audiences, given careful and tactful handling of the tricky theme. — Strat.

Uma Pedra No Bolso
(Tall Stories)
(PORTUGUESE)

A GER production, produced by Joao Pedro Benard. Directed by Joaquim Pinto. Screenplay, Pinto; camera (color), Rui Henriques, Pinto; editor, Pinto; sound, Francisco Veloso. Reviewed at Berlin Film Fest (Panorama), Feb. 16, 1988. Running time: 92 MIN.
Miguel . . . . Bruno Leite
Joao . . . . Manuel Lobao
Luisa . . . . Ines Medeiros
Dona Marta . . . . Isabel de Castro
Dr. Fernando . . . . Luis Miguel Cintra

Berlin — A sensitive first feature, shot in 2½ weeks with a crew of only four, and using nonprofessional actors in the key roles, "Tall Stories" is a modest achievement. The story it tells is a familiar one, and commercial chances look to be tough, but fests could be interested.

Miguel, the film's 12-year-old hero, has been shirking his studies and is sent to spend the summer at the seaside hotel run by his aunt. There the boy meets Luisa, a pretty maid, and Joao, who's a bit older than he is, and full of tall stories about his amorous conquests with women holidaymakers.

Miguel and Joao become friends, despite the opposition of the aunt. When valuables are stolen from the hotel, Miguel suspects his friend who protests his innocence. Confused, Miguel finds that truth is, after all, relative; and he eventually leaves his aunt's place wiser than he was when he arrived.

Given the film's tiny budget and constricted production, it's not surprising it's a bit rough at the edges. Pacing is overly slow, but by the end the director has made the points he was striving for with economy and charm.

Not a world-beater, but a film that marks the arrival of a sensitive and obviously dedicated young director. —Strat.

In Georgian
(In Georgia)
(EAST GERMAN-DOCU)

A DEFA-Studio for Documentary Film production. Production managers, Frank Löprich, Kerstin Lindenberg, Dia Kurdgelia. Written and directed by Jürgen Böttcher. Camera (color), Thomas Plenert; editor, Gudrun Plenert. Reviewed at the Berlin Film Festival (Forum), Feb. 13, 1988. Running time: 100 MIN.

Berlin — With "In Georgia" East Germany's docu star Jürgen Böttcher leaves his native land for the first time in his 30-year career to lens a laid-back trip through the most fascinating of USSR republics.

Given the reputation of the director (whose last short, "The Kitchen," was a small miracle of hyperrealist, minimalist filmmaking, set in a big factory kitchen), and the potential of the subject, it is mystifying how pedestrian and flat this film is. It could have been made for Intourist as Soviet travel promotion.

Avoiding intelligible (and possibly controversial?) discussion with the natives, other than questions about what time they milk their goats, film eliminates the social fabric as a field of exploration a priori.

Böttcher's keen interest in art, on the other hand, is given full rein. Film opens with a series of fine old cathedrals and fortresses perched atop extraordinary mountain ranges, and pumps in frequent side-trips on which the crew goes icon-hunting.

There is a sequence in the museum that houses the work of Pirosmani, Georgia's famed naif painter, and it's not difficult to see "In Georgia" as a modest attempt to recapture the master's spirit in frozen, whimsical images. The question is whether this painterly approach is adequate, or even appropriate, to reflect reality.

Pic is top-heavy with posed bulls, goats and horses, which — pretty as they are — tell very little about life in mountain villages, said to be isolated from civilization up until 1937. Not surprisingly, this style privileges the picturesque and folkloric, the bane of serious travelog. What of sophisticated, modern-day Tbilisi, home of Stalin as well as precocious *perestroika*?

To its credit, film is economic with voiceover, letting the often striking images speak for themselves. Nature plays a big role, suggesting the diversity of the land from icy mountains to almost tropical tea plantations. Camera lovingly dwells on the people's strong faces bursting with character, though it prefers to leave the mysteries veiled. — Yung.

Reefer And The Model
(IRISH)

A Berber Films production, in association with the Irish Film Board and Radio Telefis Eireann. (World sales: Film Four Intl., London.) Produced by Lelia Doolan. Directed by Joe Comerford. Screenplay, Comerford; camera (Agfacolor), Breffni Byrne; editor, Se Merry; music, Andy Roberts; sound, Kieran Morgan; production design, John Lucas; assistant director, Dave Murphy; production manager; Darryl Collins. Reviewed at Berlin Film Fest (Panorama), Feb. 15, 1988. Running time: 93 MIN.
Reefer . . . . Ian McElhinney
Teresa (The Model) . . . . Carol Scanlan
Spider . . . . Sean Lawlor
Badger . . . . Ray McBride
The Mother . . . . Eve Watkinson
Also with: Birdy Sweeney, Maire Chinsealach.

Berlin — Lots of Irish charm, and glorious locations, bolster this slight, uneven yarn about a reformed IRA man and his involvement with a pregnant woman. Commercial chances are only fair, since Joe Comerford's film suffers from poor scripting which makes the early scenes too diffuse and prevents audience identification with the characters for too much of the film.

Reefer, played with great authority by Ian McElhinney, is retired from the IRA ("He Ran Away," says his mother, derisively) and works as a fisherman. Teresa, quickly dubbed The Model by mom, is hitchhiking in the middle of nowhere with only a canary. Reefer gives her a ride and soon discovers she's a former prostitute and drug addict, and is suspected of having IRA sympathies (her brother had been killed in the ongoing conflict).

Ensuing scenes drag a bit, because the writing isn't nearly sharp enough. So we meet Reefer's mates, the macho Spider and the gay Birdy, and plod along with these characters until the film picks up two-thirds of way through. Birdy flirts with a soldier in a dance-hall, Spider gets into a fight with a tough army sergeant, their boat breaks down, and they decide to revert to a life of crime. That means robbing a mobile bank, but it all goes wrong and a cop is killed. Spider and Badger are trapped, and the pregnant Model sails to the rescue of Reefer, inconveniently going into labor as she does.

Closing scenes pack a punch, and there's an amusing cameo from Eva Watkinson as Reefer's sprightly mother, but Carol Scanlan invests The Model with less personality than she deserves.

Video and cable possibilities loom for this uneven effort, with lovers of all things Irish a natural audience for this wayward romance-turned-thriller. —Strat.

Marie S'en Va-T-En Ville
(Marie In The City)
(CANADIAN)

A Films Transit (world sales) release of a Prods. du Lundi Martin production. Produced by François Bouvier. Written and directed by Marquise Lepage. Camera (color), Daniel Jobin; editor, Yves Chapat; music, Michel Rivard; production design, François Seguin; sound, Marcel Fraser; artistic collaborator, Jean Beaudin; assistant director, René Pothier; production manager, Claude Cartier. Reviewed at Berlin Film Fest (Market), Feb. 14, 1988. Running time: 72 MIN.
Sarah . . . . Frederique Collin
Marie . . . . Genevieve Lenoir

Berlin — "Marie In The City," which has already unspooled at the Mannheim fest and the New York Independent fest, is an all-too-brief 2-hander about the relationship between two women. At only 72 minutes, it's almost too short for theatrical playoff, but there are definite homevid and tv possibilities.

The 13-year-old Marie leaves home when she's abused by her brother while she's taking a shower. The vulnerable child, very sweetly played by Genevieve Lenoir, winds up on the streets of Montreal and soon befriends a hooker, Sarah, played with world-weary charm by Frederique Collin. Marie doesn't cotton on to her new friend's profession, nor her involvement with cocaine dealing, and the two develop a relationship that's partly mother-daughter and partly, a bit disturbingly, something more. All that changes when Sarah's pimp arrives to beat her up and for the first time Marie realizes her friend isn't a waitress as she'd supposed. However, she wants to stay with Sarah and here the film abruptly, and frustratingly, ends.

It's a pity, because until that point writer-director Marquise Lepage has been adept at building up characters and the central relationship; it's almost as if money, or inspiration, ran out before anything was done with the engaging characters established. Audiences are liable to go home frustrated as a result.

Though evidently made on a very tight budget, pic is technically tops, apart from slightly schmaltzy music. It's certainly to be hoped that young Lenoir pursues her career as an actress, because she leaves a lasting impression as the waif-like Marie. —*Strat.*

Kung Fu Master!
(FRENCH)

A Capital Cinéma release of a Ciné-Tamaris/Sept coproduction. Produced, written and directed by Agnès Varda, from a story idea by Jane Birkin. Camera (color), Pierre-Laurent Chenieux; sound, Oliver Schwob; editor, Marie-Josée Audiard; music, Joanna Bruzdowicz. Reviewed at the Club de l'Etoile, Paris, Feb. 17, 1988. (In Berlin Film Festival - competing.) Running time: **80 MIN.**
With: Jane Birkin (Mary-Jane), Mathieu Demy (Julien), Charlotte Gainsbourg (Lucy), Lou Doillon, Eva Simonet, Judy Campbell.

Paris — **Second feature in Agnès Varda's Berlin fest-competing double-header devoted to actress Jane Birkin, "Kung Fu Master!" is still brittle fare, but in every respect superior to the self-conscious shenanigans of "Jane B. By Agnès V."**

"Kung Fu Master!" was a relatively impromptu idea amid the more elaborate production of Film One. Birkin showed Varda an original script treatment she'd written but was shy about promoting.

Director was intrigued by the story as a fictional vehicle for Birkin's talent and personality and decided to adapt and produce it as a separate film, though as a complement to "Jane B." In fact, "Kung Fu Master!" was shot before the first film was even completed.

The apparent spontaneity with which it was made was probably beneficial, for it prevented Varda from theorizing her directorial approach as she'd done in the first film. Though it merely skims its subject and stops short of any thorny situations, film is simple and affecting, in the image of Birkin herself. In a way it accomplishes what Varda's first film failed to do.

Birkin's tale, as developed by Varda, relates a mutual infatuation between a middle-aged divorcee with two children and the 14-year

old classmate of her daughter, who is hurt and revolted when she surprises them one day in an embrace.

Birkin of course is the protagonist, who is endowed with thesp's vulnerability and melancholy charm. Happily Varda spares us the head-banging psychodramatics that Birkin has indulged in for the films of her director-mate Jacques Doillon.

Picture is a family affair since the cast is entirely composed of Birkin and Varda's own families. Former's teen heartthrob is winningly portrayed by Mathieu Demy, Varda's son. Birkin's children are her own daughters, Charlette Gainsbourg (already a laureled teen thesp) and little Lou Doillon. Birkin's parents (mom is British actress Judy Campbell) also get into the act in a sequence set during an Easter holiday trip to London, where the romance takes another turn.

Though a minor effort, "Kung Fu Master!" (title refers to one of Demy's obsessive video games) has a confidential, low-keyed appeal due to its performers and Varda's discreet, unfussy direction. Tech credits are fine. —*Len.*

Jane B. par Agnès V.
(Jane B. By Agnès V.)
(FRENCH)

A Capital Cinéma release of a Ciné-Tamaris/Sept coproduction. Written and directed by Agnès Varda. Camera (Fujicolor), Nurith Aviv, Pierre-Laurent Chenieux; editor, Varda, Marie-Josée Audiard; music, Manfredini, Chopin, Serge Gainsbourg; sound, Olivier Schwob, Jean-Paul Mugel. Reviewed at the Club de l'Etoile, Paris, Feb. 15, 1988. (In Berlin Film Festival — competing.) Running time: **96 MIN.**
With: Jane Birkin, Philippe Léotard, Jean-Pierre Léaud, Farid Chopel, Alain Souchon, Laura Betti, Charlotte Gainsbourg, Mathieu Demy, Agnès Varda.

Paris — **A frustrating exercise in complicating what should be simple, "Jane B. By Agnès V." is the first of director Agnès Varda's 2-feature valentine to Jane Birkin, the British actress who has become a French screen star.**

Both films were shot back-to-back last year and are autonomous feature films, to be being released theatrically next month in two consecutive weeks. Second part of the "dyptych" portrait is "Kung Fu Master," a fiction imagined by Birkin and adapted by Varda.

Despite more than 90 minutes in her company, the viewer learns little about Birkin. She is sweet, frank and sometimes funny (a deft comedienne, she's more often cast as hysterics, notably in the films of her current mate Jacques Doillon), but there is little more than anecdotal interest. Doillon is absent, her children barely glimpsed, and her previous boyfriend and Pygmalion, songwriter-provocateur Serge

Gainsbourg, appears briefly in one of her recording sessions (she has an inadequate singing voice, but has gotten by on a number of fine songs by Gainsbourg).

Film's essential problem is indicated in its title: this is Varda's Birkin. Where her subject is simple and straightforward, the filmmaker is all affectation and artiness, as if she were more concerned about generating copy in theoretical film journals.

So we get a "collage" picture, with Birkin mediated by Varda's cinematic pirouettes. Director casts her in a series of fantasy sketches: as muse, Dickensian victim, Calamity Jane, Joan of Arc, etc. She plays a variety of lovers opposite guest stars Jean-Pierre Léaud, Alain Souchon, Farid Chopel and Philippe Léotard. In the most embarrassing skit, Birkin plays Laurel to Laura Betti's Hardy. None of this flatters Birkin's modest acting abilities or Varda's sense of film imagination.

Though conceived as a theatrical feature, this is at best homescreen filler and art festival fodder. Amazingly, it is repping France in the Berlin fest competition.—*Len.*

Dani, Michi, Renato And Max
(SWISS-DOCU)

A Cactus Films presentation of a Richard Dindo, Alfred Richterich, Fredi Leu production. Written and directed by Dindo. Camera (color, 16m), Jürg Hassler, Rainer Trinkler; editor, George Jannett; sound, Dieter Gränicher, Alain Klarer; music, KPM-Music, Patti Smith; narration, Dindo, Bettina Schmid, Regula Schiess. Reviewed at the Berlin Film Festival (Forum of Young Cinema), Feb. 15, 1988. Running time: **138 MIN.**

Berlin — **A meticulous and careful reconstruction of four separate deaths of very young men caused by police brutality in the early '80s, Richard Dindo's documentary sheds a grim light on the desperate underbelly of the Swiss paradise.**

The four victims all were associated one way or another with the struggle of Zurich youth to get its own youth center in town, against the opposition of the entire establishment. In a brief prolog, using mainly video footage from Swiss tv and private sources, Dindo starts by showing the demonstrations asking for the youth center, the police reaction and the final failure of the center, before moving to each particular case.

Dani and Michi, both 17, stole a neighbor's motorcycle for a ride, were chased by police for speeding and were killed during the chase. Renato, 22, a drug addict with a record for peddling narcotics to finance his own addiction, stole a car, was chased by the police and shot while trying to escape, never regained consciousness and later was stabbed to death by his girlfriend

who couldn't stand to see him in this state. Max, 27, was bludgeoned by a helmeted policeman while standing on a sidewalk, not far from the scene of a particularly violent demonstration. He died a couple of years later in a Barcelona hospital from the aftereffects of the blows.

Dindo, an experienced documentarist, unfolds each of the three stories with the utmost thoroughness. He uses narrators to express the details, interviews the people who knew the four youngsters and eyewitnesses; police spokesmen refused to comment.

He leaves no stone unturned, carefully avoids the temptation to jump to conclusions, repeats again and again the facts as they are known and reconstructs the scene, whenever possible. In this fashion he shows that Dani and Michi most probably were pushed off the road to their death by police car, Renato was shot ostensibly while the guns were pointed at the car's tires while Max was attacked for no obvious reason.

Dindo also follos the judicial proceedings in all these cases, as relatives and parents lodged complaints, and leaves no doubt the Swiss courts were fully supportive of the police, even granted a compensation to the cops for their performance and turned a blind eye on all evidence produced to shake the official version.

Dindo also follows the judicial proceedings in all these cases, as relajustify their conduct which, at least, in the first two cases, required the involvement of the law. But the inevitable conclusion is that all four were felled by the intense animosity of the police for anyone who dares to step out of line, and its preference to eliminate rather than correct, their tendencies.

The combination of cool, detailed presentation of facts with moving interviews and of spruced up streets with angry graffiti spoiling the sterilized effect are very effective. So is the feeling that the protest of the new generation already has defeat built in, since none of the demonstrators really believed they stood a chance, and in each one of them there are clear traces of a death wish.

The film eloquently shows the squelching of the spirit which activated the Zurich demonstrations, but which led to victory for the police and defeat for a society which refuses change. It's overlong and too elaborate at times, only because Dindo insists on being thorough beyond doubt.—*Edna.*

Die Russen Kommen
(The Russians Are Coming)
(EAST GERMAN-B&W)

An East German DEFA Studios production and release. Produced by Dieter Dormeier. Directed by Heiner Carow. Screenplay, Claus Küchenmester, Carow, from a story by Egon Richter; camera (Cinemascope, b&w), Jürgen Brauer; editor, Evelyn Carow; music, Peter Gotthardt; sound, Hans-Joachim Kreinbrink, Werner Klein; production manager, Wolfgang Glomm; associate director, Haral Fischer. Reviewed at Berlin Film Festival (Panorama section), Feb. 13, 1988. Running time: **106 MIN.**

Günter . . . . .Gert Krause-Melzer
Igor . . . . .Viktor Perevalov
Christine . . . . .Dorothea Meissner
  Also with Karla Runkehl (Herr Bergschicker), Vsevolod Saonov (Golubkov), Rolf Ludwig (Herr Walcher), Lissy Tempelhof (Frau Walcher), Hans Hardt-Hardtloff (policeman), Claus Kuchenmeister (Willi).

Berlin — Whatever chance this East German reissue of a 1968 release may have had for showing how the Nazis warped young minds is totally thwarted by a hamfisted attempt to portray the Soviets as unerring liberators.

No sign of any Gorbachev-style openness is in this dated, Cold War treatment of a longstanding DEFA theme — The Nazis told us to fear the Russians, but in fact they are our friends.

Story is set in April and May 1945 as the Nazi reich is crumbling under advancing Allied forces. Impressionable 16-year-old Günter (Gert Krause-Melzer) is a stalwart Hitler Youth member who won the Iron Cross when he unwittingly aided the shooting death of a Soviet prisoner (Viktor Perevalov). He dutifully abandons girlfriend (Dorothea Meissner) to join other youths in a last stand against encroaching Soviet tanks. Taken prisoner, he must answer for his part in the shooting death.

All of this has been done before by better hands, most notably by Bernhard Wicki, who directed the West German classic "Die Brücke" (The Bridge) in 1959, using teens with no acting experience.

Best part of this East German pic is a film-within-film scene set in a Nazi-era cinema. Teens neck in the balcony during the unspooling of Viet Harlan's infamous "Kolberg," the Nazi propaganda machine's last major cinematic attempt to whip up support for the war effort. Ironically, the juxtaposition reveals how a convincing screenplay and good acting (in "Kolberg" by Heinrich George and Horst Caspar) can produce effective propaganda. The DEFA effort is lame by comparison.

Print screened at the Berlin Film Fest was poor. What at first appeared to be an artsy effect turned out to be just bad production values. —*Gill.*

The Big Blue
(U.S.)

An Angelika Films release of a Big Blue Second German Channel (ZDF) production. Executive producers, Joe & Angelika Saleh. Produced by Yoram Mandel. Directed by Andrew Horn. Screenplay, Jim Neu, based on short story by Horn; camera (color), Carl Teitelbaum; editor, Ila von Hasperg; sound, Dan Walworth; music, Jill Jaffe; art direction, Ann Stuhler. Reviewed at Berlin Film Fest (Forum of Young Cinema), Feb. 13, 1988. Running time: **100 MIN.**
  With: David Brisbin, Taunie VreNon, John Erdman, Jim Neu, Sheila McLaughlin, Bill Rice.

Berlin — This is a movie designed first and foremost for film buffs. Director Andrew Horn is concerned exclusively with film clichés and tributes to Hollywood's private eye tradition, from the days of Bogart to Coppola's "The Conversation," and doesn't really take the time to breathe some life of its own in the picture, outside the old-fashioned conventions.

Calling his characters Arthur Murray, Myrna Monroe or Carmen, and building them up to be something like the models indicated in the names, only shows Horn's intentions.

A detective story which starts in fiction, since we are introduced to a black and white movie on tv before we know there is life outside it, the film features hard-boiled Raymond Chandler-like narration, tough dialog of the kind associated with James Cagney and George Raft, on camera monologs and narrative strictly limited to very visible studio sets, except for one street sequence.

Everything, however, is used to excess, particularly the elaborated smart-ass dialog, leaving no doubt this is a send-up, on the one hand, and a study of the genre, on the other. Judicious use of the frame is displayed all through, with painted backdrops enhancing the unreal atmosphere.

Straight-facedly played by the entire cast, the picture is amusing for those who realize what Horn tries to achieve, but it slows down dangerously in the second half, when every trick of the trade has already been revealed and reliance on plot becomes more necessary. Plot, concerning a private investigator asked to spy on a cop whose wife suspects infidelity, and who discovers instead of another woman a drug operation, is far too thin to offer any support. At least the final surrealistic climax fits in with the film's nature.

As style is more important than story in this instance, the spare construction of the sets, the careful set-up of each camera angle and the smart use of sound are of major importance. Horn handles himself well in all departments, taking into consideration this is a low-budget film which has to go a long way on small resources. Sometimes too gimmicky for its own good in its belabored use of established mannerisms, it is still the stuff art houses dream of. —*Edna.*

Geierwally
(WEST GERMAN)

A Filmverlag der Autoren release of an Entenproduktion, in association with Pro-ject Filmproducktion. Produced by Rolf Bührmann. Directed by Walter Bockmayer. Screenplay, Bockmayer; camera (color), Wolfgang Simon; editor, Alexander Rupp; music, Horst Hornung; production design, Thomas Schappert; sound, Christian Moldt, Helmut Röttgen; costumes, Barbara Langenberg. Waltraud Lindner, Bockmayer; assistant director, Bernd Holzmüller. Reviewed at Berlin Film Fest (New German Cinema section), Feb. 16, 1988. Running time: **91 MIN.**
Geierwally . . . . .Samy Orfgen
Vinzenz . . . . .Christoph Eichhorn
Baron Joseph . . . . . . .Gottfried Lackmann
Aunt Luckard . . . . . . .Ralph Morgenstern
  Also with: Ortrud Beginnen (Genoveva), Brigitte Janner (Afra), Karl-Heinz von Hassel (Stromminger), Elisabeth Volkmann, Sonja Neudorfer, Walter Bockmayer, Barbara Valentin, Stephen Wald.

Berlin — After a 5-year gap, Walter Bockmayer bounces back as Germany's No. 1 director of broad camp comedies with this musical parody based on a famous Tyrolean story.

Backgrounds are the lovingly filmed mountains of southern Germany, but everything else is deliberately artificial, with garish colors, drag queens and the least subtle kind of humor. It's strictly for audiences amused by this kind of over-the-top treatment; others will cringe with embarrassment.

Geierwally is the name of the buxom heroine, who has a pet vulture and who loves Joseph, who affects a kiss-curl on his toupee. Her father insists she marry Vinzenz, whom she hates, so she and the vulture go to live in a mountain hut, returning only to take her revenge.

Film is staged as high (or, if you prefer, low) camp. The jokes are not very funny, and mostly center on male sex organs, excrement or flatulence. Characters lose their wigs or fake moustaches midscene, but carry on. Song lyrics and dialog are strenuously suggestive. It plays a bit like an English pantomime, with the heroine's maiden aunt played by a man in drag; or like a school romp. Occasionally, a joke works: in one ballad, a cow's tail is seen to twitch in time with the music until the camera pulls back to reveal a technician with fake tail. Most of the humor is so gross and unsubtle that audiences who crave a bit of sophistication will be appalled.

Of course, the film wasn't made for such audiences, but for the crowd that's willing to go along with Bockmayer's concept. Outside Germany, pic could make its mark as a cult item.

It's useless to talk about acting in this context. Bockmayer himself does a wild turn as the local postman, Christel von der Post, who wears a tutu and a telephone on his/her hand. The vulture is played by a turkey, and some would say that sums up the picture. —*Strat.*

Pirates Ni Yoroshiku
(Pirates In The City)
(JAPANESE)

A Kinoshita production. Produced by Kei Sasaki. Directed by Koichi Goto. Screenplay, Toshimichi Saeki, from a story by Ran Kawanishi; camera (Eastmancolor), N. Shinoda; sound, M. Seto. (No other credits supplied.) Reviewed at Berlin Film Fest (Panorama section), Feb. 13, 1988. Running time: **105 MIN.**
Toru . . . . .Ken Ishiguro
Akira . . . . .Hiroshi Mikami
Asuka . . . . .Mari Torigoe
Mariko . . . . .Yoko Takahashi
Man . . . . .Leo Morimoto
Matilda . . . . .Aiko Asano
Akko . . . . .Hazuki Kozu'
Hitoshi . . . . .Tamotsu Ishibashi

Berlin — A trendy youth pic which seems to be saying something significant about today's listless generation, as contrasted to the radicals of the '60s; "Pirates In The City" is too langorous and diffuse to make much of an impact. Offshore chances are poor.

Pic, also known as "Regards To Pirates," centers on a trio of none-too-interesting characters. Toru is a student hooked on a pirate radio serial ("A Man And A Woman In The Driveway") hosted by a mysterious deejay; Akira, with blond-dyed hair, is a computer whiz with a life-size, plastic female doll in a hot-house garden alongside his living room; and Asuka is a bright girl, who seeks love from both men (both reject her) and who works as cartoonist on an action-packed comic strip. The three have teamed up to design a computer game.

Since there seems to be little communication between these three, though they're all involved in the communication business, other characters are introed to fill in the details, including Mariko, Asuka's assistant, and Matilda, a sweet prostie. There are also the inhabitants of a German bar, where a picture of Hitler is prominently displayed. Talk about the destructive legacy of the '60s generation comes across as woolly and contrived.
— *Strat.*

Neprofessionaly
(The Nonprofessionals)
(SOVIET-B&W)

A Kazakhfilm production. Directed by Sergei Bodrov. Screenplay, Bodrov, Alexander Buravski, Ashar Aiapova; camera (b&w), Fedor Aranishev; editor, V. Kulagina; music, Tuligen Muchamedshanov, the Beatles, Bulat Okudshava. Reviewed at Berlin Film Festival (Forum), Feb. 15, 1988. Running time: **70 MIN.**
  With: Valentina Talisina, Amangelis Eselbaiev, Anis Sadikov, Igor Solotovitski, Luisa Mosends, Galina Kalashnikova.

Berlin — A rock band traveling through the barren steppes of Kazakhstan is the focus of what can only be called a Soviet road movie. "The Nonprofessionals," made by far flung Kazakhfilm Studio in 1985 and released last year, offers an innocent but intriguing glimpse into two lifestyles: the free and hungry rockers with no fixed abode, always in search of their next gig for grocery money, and the elderly residents in an old folks' home with nowhere to go. Film is a curiosity item for glasnost fans, who are still a limited audience.

Lensed in limpid, 35m black & white, pic has a strong documentary feel woven into its slight story. At the beginning a girl's voice announces the group (going by the sugary moniker "Rainbow") was traveling through the provinces playing "music allowed by the chiefs" — i.e., pap about flowers and springtime. The band is indeed unexceptional musicwise, but it's enough of a novelty to draw audiences of all ages in the middle of the steppe.

While the kids drive around in an old bus looking for gigs, other characters are introduced from the old folks' home. There is a woman whose cow has followed her to the home; milking it each morning is her main occupation. The home director wants to throw a party but has no money to feed all the residents; the cooks suggest eating the cow.

Instead the young musicians load the cow on their bus as a joke. When they're stopped by police, they kill it to keep from getting into trouble. They threaten the shocked old lady to make her keep quiet; but later, at their concert at the home, she is their most rapt listener.

Final voiceover informs us one member of the band was later killed in Afghanistan. "Why?" the voice wonders.

As mellow and inconsequential as it may seem, "The Nonprofessionals" strikes a rule-breaking note just because it is so laid back, ironic, even pointless. Echoing frank Soviet docus like "Is It Easy To Be Young?" film demonstrates an impressive lack of rhetoric and ability to get up close to the frustrations of a nation caught between restlessness and resignation. — *Yung.*

Neco z Alenky

(Alice)
(SWISS)

A Film Four Intl. presentation of a Condor Films, Hessisches Rudfunk, Frankfurt, German Swiss TV, Zurich (SRG), Film Four Intl., London, production. Directed by Jan Svankmajer. Screenplay, Svankmajer, based on Lewis Carroll's book "Alice's Adventures In Wonderland;" camera (Eastmancolor), Svatopluk Maly; editor, Maria Drvotova; animation, Bedrich Glaser; sound, Ivo Spalj, Robert Jansa; sets, Eva Svankmajerova, Jan Svankmajer. Reviewed at the Berlin Film Festival (official selection, noncompeting), Feb. 13, 1988. Running time: **84 MIN.**
With: Kristyna Kohoutova (Alice).

Berlin — In spite of the Swiss flag it flies, and the British and German partners in the production, this is still first and foremost a Czech picture, a combination of live action and animation of the kind this country in general, and director Jan Svankmajer in particular, has specialized in for many years.

Svankmajer, a veteran animator and specialist in puppet theater, has made numerous short subjects but this is the first time he has tried a feature film. The results indicate he might be more comfortable sticking to shorts.

His close relations with the surrealist movement in his country explain the references he makes to Sigmund Freud and Andre Breton when trying to explain his film as a blending of reality and dream. Yet the dreams Svankmajer introduces here are the nightmare variety; stuffed animals, shrunken skeletons and bird skulls playing an important part in Alice's visions, inspired if not quite adapted from Lewis Carroll's classic.

To its credit, the film states from the very beginning it is not necessarily intended for very young audiences, and indeed children might have nightmares after this. On the other hand, it is not quite for adults, as Svankmajer's inspiration fails at times.

Semiologists may have a field day with it, discussing for instance the frequent use of drawers as mystery reservoirs, but even for them, the film doesn't quite fill the bill.

Puppet animation used here around Alice, as the objects in her dreamworld, are effectively moved, sometimes even with a degree of self-humor, like the Mad Hatter activating the spring in the March Hare's back to make it move, but even in this respect Svankmajer is only partially successful.

As it is, the picture will appeal mainly to animation buffs, while those in search of a fully satisfactory adaptation of Carroll's tale to the screen, will go on looking. —*Edna.*

Tilinteko

(The Final Arrangement)
(FINNISH)

A Villealfa Filmproductions production. (World Sales: Jörn Donner Productions, Helsinki.) Produced by Aki Kaurismäki. Directed by Veikko Aaltonen. Screenplay, Aaltonen, Kaurismäki; camera (Eastmancolor), Timo Salminen, Timo Markko; editor, Juha Jeromaa; music, Leo Friman; sound, Jouko Lumme. Reviewed at Berlin Film Fest (market), Feb. 16, 1988. Running time: **70 MIN.**
Nieminen . . . . Juhani Niemelä
Timo Varjola . . . . Esko Nikkari
Leena . . . . Kaija Pakarinen
Reidar . . . . Seppo Mäki
Town clerk . . . . Leo Friman
Mrs. Varjola . . . . Riitta Huhtasalo

Berlin — This first feature by Veikko Aaltonen is a thriller along the classic lines of Hollywood or French *film noir*. It's briskly made, grippingly handled, and confidently acted, but its brief running time and abrupt ending may count against it internationally. It's fine for tv or video, though.

Nieminen and Varjola pose as policemen to rob a mail van in the film's no-nonsense opening sequence. The mail van driver is killed, and Varjola double-crosses his partner, shooting him in the back. Nieminen survives, but doesn't squeal on his treacherous mate. Some years later, he's given a 3-day pass from prison, and sets off to track down Varjola who's now a pillar of the establishment. He's married with a child; he's mayor of a small town, a churchman, and chairman of the Lion's club — he's also running for parliament in upcoming elections, and hoping one day to be Minister of Justice!

In the grand tradition of this kind of film, Nieminen (the strong, silent type) arrives in town and checks into the local hotel. He attends one of Varjola's political rallies, giving the candidate a terrible fright. Varjola tries to buy off his former partner with what's left of the stolen money, but Nieminen stays on in town, and has an affair with a lonely, pretty hairdresser. He takes his final revenge on the night the election results are declared.

The inspiration for the film is as much Western as thriller, but the formula works until the somewhat unconvincing fadeout. Juhani Niemälä is suitably imposing as the taciturn hero, while Esko Nikkari is properly sinister as the threatened mayor. Very well photographed, and tightly edited, the film is marred by the overemphatic music by Leo Friman, who's more successful playing the mayor's toadying assistant.

One surprising flaw, though, is the very clear shadow of a boom mike in the key election sequence, a technical gaffe that shouldn't have happened. — *Strat.*

Tot Oder Lebendig

(Dead Or Alive)
(WEST GERMAN)

A Suprise Co. production under consignment from West German ZDF tv. Produced by Goggo Gensch. ZDF supervising editor, Sibylle Hubatschek-Rahn. Directed by Gisela Zimmermann. Screenplay, Zimmermann; camera (color), Klaus Moderegger; editor, Hildegard Schröder; music, Wolfgang Dauner; sound, Jens Hasler; art direction, Chris Gill, Wolfgang Diehl; costumes, Jochen Kleber; production manager, Marianna Deissler. Reviewed at Berlin Film Festival (market), Feb. 16, 1988. Runing time: **125 MIN.**
Bruno Morlock . . . . Ludwig Hirsch
Karl . . . . Sara Kellenberger
Dr. Tanzgeschirr . . . . Elsbeth Janda
Mendelsohn . . . . Gerhart Hinze
Hasso . . . . Wolfgang Büttner
Kalbstall . . . . Wolfgang Höper
Dr. Holzwarth . . . . Klaus Steiger

Berlin — This marvelously haunting pic is nothing for people who like to see tv sets possessed by demons or a man transformed into a fly. Nor is it anything for those who hum "omm" at sunrise during astrological conjunctions.

This is genuine occult, as studied by those who pore over dusty tomes on the esoteric Cabala, and as practical by those who bow down before graven images not worshipped since before the fall of Troy — which all rather limits export possibilities for this difficult film.

Pic starts out as a standard horror flick with plenty of graveyard atmosphere. At length (too late for most viewers at this Berlin market screening), it deftly shifts away from chills and toward — well, the stuff that's in those tomes.

Big city cop, tired of life, finds that when his occultist mother dies, she leaves him a weird teenage boy who cannot speak but who has long fingernails that rip flesh easily. Cop (Ludwig Hirsch) takes home the kid (Sara Kellenberger, a girl). In following days — it's the Winter Solstice — the cop investigates a spate of uncanny murders. At least the victims *appear* to be dead.

Hirsch is well-cast as the despairing, cynical detective whose growing love for his ward finally gives him an insight into what life is about. Kellenberger, in a virtually mute role, is at times angelic, at times monstrous. Elsbeth Janda is convincing as the baffled coroner whose straight-laced training does not prepare her for the kind of out-of-body experiences her very stiff charges seem to be having.

Film's slow pace, especially in early reels, could be made snappier by judicious cutting of overlong, 125-minute running time.

Jazz pianist Wolfgang Dauner's music fittingly alternates between the mundane and the other worldly. Klaus Moderegger's agile camera makes scenes in stuffy apartments and police offices claustrophobic, while the camera at other times soars dizzyingly, like the canary's soul which is "liberated" at one point near pic's end. Through it all, director Giesela Zimmermann's macabre humor is so dry that it crackles past most German ears. —*Gill.*

Yasemin

(WEST GERMAN)

A Hark Bohm Filmpoduktion by the Hamburger Kino Kompanie in conjunction with West German ZDF tv with subsidy support from BMI, the Filmförderungsanstalt and the City of Hamburg. Written and directed by Hark Bohm. Camera (color), Slawomir Idziak; editor, Moune Barius; art direction, Christian Bussmann; music, Jens Peter Ostendorf; sound, Gunther Kortwich. Reviewed at Berlin Film Festival (competing), Feb. 18, 1988. Running time: **86 MIN.**
Yasemin . . . . Ayşe Romey
Jan . . . . Uwe Bohm
Also with: Şener Şen, Ithan Emirli, Katharina Lehmann, Nedim Hazar, Sevigi Oezdamar.

Berlin — West German actor-director Hark Bohm has updated the Romeo and Juliet story to spotlight the plight of ethnic Turks in

West Germany and the result is one of the best German films 1988 is likely to produce.

Wit, poignancy and suspense are blended deftly to tell this tale of a 17-year-old Turkish schoolgirl (Ayşe Romey) who is wooed by a rakish, middle-class German youth (Uwe Bohm).

Key to film's success are performances by Romey and Uwe Bohm, director's son. Raven-haired, lithe Romey offers just the right balance of girlish, giggling naiveté and self-confident womanhood. She's got a difficult role here first having to show her gradual warming to an impetuous youth's uncouth advances, and then having to show a dawning realization that her loving family poses a roadblock to her happiness. Romey handles it well.

Uwe Bohm is wellknown in Germany as the actor who bared his bottom on the legit stage in Hamburg's Schauspielhaus playing the lead as a doomed street kid in a highly popular rock musical last year. His streetwise bravado is tempered by a tenderness that seduces not only Yasemin but the audience as well. Hard to say, though, whether Bohm is acting or just playing himself.

Kudos to strong supporting cast, especially Şener Şen as Yasemin's father, torn by love for his daughter and by outraged shame over his perceived loss of face.

Pic starts off a tad too slowly but picks up as Bohm's direction and Slawomir Idziak's poetic photography combine to show what it means to be an immigrant family in a new world. Scene aboard a river cruise boat, the site of the couple's first secret date, touchingly captures the full rush of first love. Fleeting final scene with Yasemin clinging to Jan on a motorbike sticks with the audience long after credits have rolled. —*Gill.*

Horsenschimmen
(Mind Shadows)
(DUTCH-CANADIAN)

A Filmproduction Co. De Nieuve Unie BV (Amsterdam)-Imagex Ltd. (Halifax) coproduction. (World sales: Film Transit, Montreal.) Produced by Rolf Orthel, Christopher Zimmer. Directed by Heddy Honigmann. Screenplay, Honigmann, Goert Giltay, from the novel by J. Bernlef; camera (Eastmancolor), Giltay; editor, Jan Wouter van Reyen; production design, Dick Schillemans; sound, Piotr van Dijk; assistant director, Dick van den Heuvel. Reviewed at Berlin Film Festival (Panorama), Feb. 17, 1988. Running time: **112 MIN.**
Maarten Klein . . . . Joop Admiraal
Vera Klein . . . . Marja Kok
Phil Taylor . . . . Melanie Doane
William . . . . Robert Dodds
Lotje . . . . Inge Marit van der Wal
Sylvie . . . . Catherine ten Bruggencate
Karl Simic . . . . Peer Mascini
   Also with: Lionel Doucette (Dr. Eardly), Rick Collins (Phillip), Catherine Kuhn (Girl in cafe), Max MacDonald (Montpellier), Chris de Vries (Maarten's father), Sasa Spanjerberg (Maarten's mother).

Berlin — A finely made and very absorbing tragic drama about a man suffering from Alzheimer's disease, "Mind Shadows" won't be everyone's idea of a night at the movies but could find appreciative audiences in special situations.

Maarten Klein is a Dutch-born businessman who lived for many years with his Dutch wife Vera in the countryside outside Halifax, Nova Scotia. His wife is troubled because Maarten's mind is slowly going. He's chronically forgetful, even turning up one day at the office where he hasn't worked in four years, or taking his dog into town and leaving the animal behind.

Though seemingly in good physical shape, Maarten talks to himself a lot and is haunted by disconnected memories of the past: of his parents and his grandfather's house; of his first sweetheart and the beauty of first love one long-ago summer; of a girl he once met, and romanced, in Paris; and, constantly, of a friend who'd committed suicide.

Vera increasingly is troubled by her husband's irrational behavior but finds herself powerless to help. Hospital treatment in the end is the only solution.

The bleak, snowbound Canadian settings are a perfect background for this sad little drama, for Maarten believes the winters are the cause of his illness. Femme director Heddy Honigmann handles the story with great delicacy and sensitivity and is aided immeasurably by the intelligent and moving performance of Joop Admiraal as Maarten.

Pic is a bit long and could be tightened somewhat but overall the problems inherent here have been triumphantly overcome. By nature of the subject, though, audiences will be limited. —*Strat.*

Die Nacht Des Marders
(The Night Of The Marten)
(WEST GERMAN)

An Alpha Film production, in association with Seybusch, WDR. Produced by Reinhild Gräber, Rainer Thilo Pongratz. Written and directed by Maria Theresia Wagner. Camera (color), Weidigo von Schultzendorff; editor, Juliane Lorenz; production design, Hans Gailling; music, Ranier Fabich; sound, Georg Krautheim; assistant director, Sabine Bachthaller. Reviewed at Berlin Film Festival (New German Cinema section), Feb. 17, 1988. Running time: **95 MIN.**
Elizabeth . . . . Annamirl Bierbichler
Max . . . . Claus Eberth
Ignaz . . . . Franz Buchrieser
Grandmother . . . . Herta Böhm-Wildner
Franz . . . . Claus Peter Seifert
Ida . . . . Renate Muhri

Berlin — An overwrought rustic melodrama very similar in theme to the recent Aussie pic "The Good Wife" (a.k.a., "The Umbrella Woman"), "The Night Of The Marten" won't do much biz outside Germany as it's too predictable and insular.

Set in a Bavarian village, opening scenes establish farmer Ignaz and his rather bored wife, Elizabeth. Their daughter is getting married and moving away; the work is hard; and their lovemaking is perfunctory and, for the wife, uninspiring.

Then along comes Max who's the strong, silent type: literally silent, because he can't speak. The couple take him on to help with the farm work and Elizabeth, at first disdainful of the newcomer, gradually becomes infatuated with him especially after he charms all the local women at the daughter's wedding.

Ignaz takes a trip to the city and Elizabeth gets drunk and goes to the local pub to find Max; they sleep together causing a public scandal. Ignas forgives his wife, however, and Max goes away, but not far. Elizabeth becomes obsessed with the mute and eventually goes after him, dressing up like the prostitute he's been seeing. There's more scandal and eventually tragedy.

First-time director Maria Theresia Wagner gives this tale rather stolid treatment, with the characters coming across as types rather than as real people. Technically the film is fine with a nice feel for the gossipy little community.

Title is derived from Max' success in killing a marten, a symbolic predator which has been eating the farm eggs and which had hitherto proved too wily to be trapped. — *Strat.*

Switching Channels

A Tri-Star Pictures release of a Martin Ransohoff production. Produced by Ransohoff. Executive producer, Don Carmody. Directed by Ted Kotcheff. Screenplay, Jonathan Reynolds, based on the play "The Front Page" by Ben Hecht, Charles MacArthur; camera (Medallion color), François Protat; editor, Thom Noble; music, Michel Legrand; production design, Anne Pritchard; art direction, Charles Dunlop; set decoration, Mark Freeborn, Rose Marie McSherry; Lynn Trout (Montreal); costume design, Mary McLeod; sound (Dolby), David Loe; Bernie Blynder (Miami); assistant directors, Jim Kaufman, James Giovannetti (Chicago), Michelle Marx (Miami); casting, Lynn Stalmaster & Associates, Stuart Aikins (Toronto). Reviewed at Screening Room, L.A., Feb. 26, 1988. MPAA Rating: PG. Running time: **105 MIN.**
Christy Colleran . . . . Kathleen Turner
John L. Sullivan 4th . . . . Burt Reynolds
Blaine Bingham . . . . Christopher Reeve
Roy Ridnitz . . . . Ned Beatty
Ike Roscoe . . . . Henry Gibson
Siegenthaler . . . . George Newbern
Berger . . . . Al Waxman
Warden Terwilliger . . . . Ken James
Zaks . . . . Barry Flatman
Tillinger . . . . Ted Simonett
Carvalho . . . . Anthony Sherwood
Morosini . . . . Joe Silver
The Governor . . . . Charles Kimbrough

Hollywood — "Switching Channels" is a broad, sometimes silly transfer of "The Front Page" or, more specifically, "His Girl Friday," from the old world of smoke-filled newspaper offices to the gleaming modern setting of a satellite tv news station. Appeal of the three stars and enduring strength of the Ben Hecht-Charles MacArthur plot lend the film some undeniable mainstream entertainment value, giving it some decent b.o. potential, but this is the least distinguished rendition of the classic piece on record.

Instead of holding it up to earlier filmed versions of the play, modern audiences are more likely to contrast the picture to the recent "Broadcast News," which also

---

Original 1931 Version

A Howard Hughes production; Caddo release through United Artists. Directed by Lewis Milestone. Featured players: Adolphe Menjou, Pat O'Brien, Mary Brian, Edward Everett Horton. Adapted for the screen, story and some added dialog, by Bartlett Cormack from stage hit, same title, by Ben Hecht and Charles MacArthur. Glen MacWilliams, camera (b&w). Asst. director, Nate Watt. At Rivoli, New York, on grind run, March 19, 1931, indef. Running time: **100 MIN.**
Walter Burns . . . . Adolphe Menjou
Hildy Johnson . . . . Pat O'Brien
Peggy . . . . Mary Brian
Bensinger . . . . Edward Everett Horton
Murphy . . . . Walter Catlett
Earl Williams . . . . George E. Stone
Molly . . . . Mae Clarke
Pincus . . . . Slim Summerville
Kruger . . . . Matt Moore
McCue . . . . Frank McHugh
Sheriff Hartman . . . . . . Clarence H. Wilson

comically details a competitive love triangle against a network backdrop. Comparison strongly favors the earlier release, although this one does manage to score a few points against the inanity of much news broadcasting.

Although the obvious, almost slapstick style is apparent from the outset, opening stretch proves somewhat amusing, as ace anchorwoman Kathleen Turner leaves Chicago for a much-needed Canadian vacation and is swept off her feet by the dashing and obscenely rich Christopher Reeve.

Upon her return, Turner announces to her crafty, manipulative boss, Burt Reynolds, that she is through with the news game and intends to settle down in New York with her new love. Reynolds also is her ex-husband and, though he'd never admit it, still is in love with her, so he launches into a frantic campaign to keep her on the station.

As in "The Front Page," this involves her in covering the scheduled execution of a hapless man, played in a nice touch by Henry Gibson, who escapes just as his electrocution is about to be covered live by the tv cameras. Turner and Reynolds proceed to hide this victim of a miscarriage of justice from evil politicos as well as the competing newshounds, and there can be little doubt as to which man the lady will choose in the end.

Partly, this is due to the softening of the original "Walter Burns" boss

His Girl Friday

A Columbia release of Howard Hawks production. Stars Cary Grant, Rosalind Russell; features Ralph Bellamy, Gene Lockhart, Helen Mack. Directed by Howard Hawks. Screenplay by Charles Lederer, based on 'The Front Page' by Ben Hecht and Charles MacArthur; camera (b&w), Joseph Walker; editor, Gene Havlick. Previewed in the Projection Room, N.Y., Jan. 3, 1940. Running time: **92 MIN.**

Walter Burns	Cary Grant
Hildy Johnson	Rosalind Russell
Bruce Baldwin	Ralph Bellamy
Sheriff Hartwell	Gene Lockhart
Mollie Malloy	Helen Mack
Murphy	Porter Hall
Bensinger	Ernest Truex
Endicott	Cliff Edwards
Mayor	Clarence Kolb
McCue	Roscoe Karns
Wilson	Frank Jenks
Sanders	Regis Toomey
Louis	Abner Biberman
Duffy	Frank Orth

role from a terroristic s.o.b. to a scheming nice guy. Reynolds is good at the part's sardonic insincerity, but isn't really intimidating.

At first, it appears that the classic "Ralph Bellamy role" of the new suitor will be given much more forceful dimensions by Reeve, who comes off as the last word in confident swank in the seduction scenes. Unfortunately, he turns into a wimp almost from the moment he meets Reynolds, making it no contest, and sending the picture in silly directions in the bargain. The idea of giving Superman a fear of heights should have been thrown out in the first rewrite.

Turner suits her superstar newshen role to a T but she, along with everyone else, has been directed to a very broad performance by Ted Kotcheff, who has at least temporarily forgotten about the virtues of subtlety. Pic is most arch in the

city newsroom sequences that weakly ape terrific scenes from the play, and screenwriter Jonathan Reynolds has found no good substitutes for the great wisecracking supporting characters in the original.

Emptyheaded, inexperienced tv reporters get their share of barbs here, and some good exchanges have to do with the antipathy be-

1974 Version

A Universal Pictures release. Produced by Paul Monash; executive producer, Jennings Lang. Stars Jack Lemmon, Walter Matthau. Directed by Billy Wilder. Screenplay, Wilder, I.A.L. Diamond, from play by Ben Hecht, Charles MacArthur; camera (Technicolor), Jordan S. Cronenweth; editor, Ralph E. Winters; music supervision, Billy May; art direction, Henry Bumstead; set decoration, James W. Payne; sound, Robert Martin; asst. director, Howard G. Kazanjian; second unit director, Carey Loftin. Reviewed at Academy Awards theater, L.A., Dec. 3, 1974. (MPAA Rating: PG.) Running time: **105 MIN.**

Hildy Johnson	Jack Lemmon
Walter Burns	Walter Matthau
Mollie Malloy	Carol Burnett
Peggy Grant	Susan Sarandon
Sheriff	Vincent Gardenia
Bensinger	David Wayne
Kruger	Allen Garfield
Earl Williams	Austin Pendleton
Murphy	Charles Durning
Schwartz	Herbert Edelman
Dr. Eggelhofer	Martin Gabel
Mayor	Harold Gould
City Editor Duffy	John Furlong
Jacobi	Cliff Osmond
McHugh	Dick O'Neill

tween the ink-stained wretches still working for traditional newspapers and the modern electronic generation.

Lensed mostly in Toronto, production looks a little thin around the edges and makes the setting, Chicago, look more like a suburb than a metropolis.—*Cart.*

Vice Versa

A Columbia Pictures release. Written, produced by Dick Clement, Ian LaFrenais. Executive producer, Alan Ladd Jr. Directed by Brian Gilbert. Camera (Deluxe color), King Baggot; editor, David Garfield; music, David Shire; production design, Jim Schoppe; art direction, Eva Anna Bohn; set decoration, Karen O'Hara; costume design, Jay Hurley; sound, Scott D. Smith; assistant director, Jerry L. Ballew; casting, Penny Perry. Reviewed at the AMC theater, L.A., Feb. 26, 1988. MPAA Rating: PG. Running time: **98 MIN.**

Marshall	Judge Reinhold
Charlie	Fred Savage
Sam	Corinne Bohrer
Tina	Swoosie Kurtz
Turk	David Proval
Robyn	Jane Kaczmerek
Secretary	Gloria Gifford

Hollywood — When two films are released only six months apart with a nearly identical plot — even if the second one is better — marketing and distribution folks are in for a real challenge. Such is the situation with Columbia's "Vice Versa," which is more clever and funny than Tri-Star's "Like Father Like Son" while it is questionable whether audiences will pay twice for a few more laughs over the same kind of jokes.

With "Like Father Like Son," it

was Dudley Moore, a doctor, and his teenage son, Kirk Cameron, who drank a magical potion and ended up with each others' personalities. Cameron went to school as a smarty pants and Moore to the hospital acting like a dope. "Vice Versa" finds Judge Reinhold, a tony Chicago department store exec named Marshall, and his junior high school age son, Charlie (Fred Savage), in a similar predicament after they both touch a mystical oriental skull.

What this latest comedic reworking of the much used fish-out-of-water story has over its predecessor is much more engaging stars involved in slightly less predictable situations delivering considerably wittier dialog.

Judge Reinhold, who is good at playing a goofy character such as his "Beverly Hills Cop" role, is in his element acting like an 11-year-old more interested in heavy metal rock and his pet frog than girls and other yucky things.

No one knows what to make of this grown-up looking kid wearing sneakers and pounding away on the drums in the store's music department or toppling a display when he misfires a crossbow in the adult toy section. Just yesterday he was a colorless, humorless yuppie type eating at chic restaurants and drinking Evian water. The store's chief honcho is ready to fire him, but his fellow execs, all coveting his job, are relishing his antics.

Gloria Gifford as his secretary is particularly good, looking him straight in the eye for any telltale signs of insanity. Things get a bit too sappy, though, with his love-struck girlfriend, Sam (Corinne Bohrer); the more immature he acts, the more enamored she becomes. However, the scene with the two of them rockin' out at a Malice concert (clearly a parody of Kiss or Motley Crue), when Reinhold manages to get the lead singer's autograph — ostensibly for his "son" — and later falls asleep in the car, exhausted like any other growing boy, is pretty funny stuff.

It is really Savage, best known for his role as the little boy in "The Princess Bride," who is particularly winsome as the smart-alecky Dad stuck in his kid's pint-size body.

Adults soon realize that he's more than a little precocious, they're bowled over by his slick talk and abrasive manner.

Savage manages to carry off some fairly deadpan expressions when he gets beyond himself, especially when his homeroom teacher thinks he's passed her a love note, but is a good little tyrant too, barking orders to limo drivers, fellow school squirts and an assortment of others too foolish to misread his tenacity.

Swoosie Kurtz and David Proval get a couple of stock roles as sleazy and incompetent smalltime art dealers, but manage to have a good time

at it.

Except for the overuse of profanity for Savage's character, this is fun family fare. —*Brit.*

Frantic

A Warner Bros. release of a Mount Co. production. Produced by Thom Mount, Tim Hampton. Directed by Roman Polanski. Screenplay, Polanski, Gérard Brach; camera (color), Witold Sobocinski; editor, Sam O'Steen; music, Ennio Morricone; production design, Pierre Guffroy; costume design, Anthony Powell; sound (Dolby), Jean-Pierre Ruh; assistant director, Michel Cheyko; casting, Margot Capelier (France), Bonnie Timmermann (U.S.). Reviewed at the Village theater, L.A., Feb. 22, 1988. MPAA Rating: R. Running time: **120 MIN.**

Richard Walker	Harrison Ford
Michelle	Emmanuelle Seigner
Sondra Walker	Betty Buckley
Williams	John Mahoney
Shaap	Jimmie Ray Weeks
The Kidnapper	Yorgo Voyagis
Peter	David Huddleston
Gaillard	Gérard Klein
Hotel Manager	Jacques Ciron
Wino	Dominique Pinon
Rastafarian	Thomas M. Pollard
Edie	Alexandra Stewart

Hollywood — Roman Polanski brings little of his customary film-making flair or brilliantly perverse imagination to bear upon "Frantic," a thriller without much surprise, suspense or excitement.

Drama about an American doctor's desperate search for his kidnapped wife through the demimonde of Paris reveals its director's personality and enthusiasm only in brief humorous moments, and doesn't really make the grade either as the commercial entertainment it was clearly intended to be. Warner Bros. opened the pic in more than 1,100 sites, which is the only way to go given the damp word-of-mouth sure to ensue.

Polanski's most commercially successful films — "Rosemary's Baby," "Chinatown" and "Tess" — all have been based on material not his own, while some of his smaller pictures — "Cul-de-Sac," "The Tenant" — probably best represent the director's character in undiluted form.

Although designed for a wide public, "Frantic" falls in neither camp and exhibits little of the intensity or feeling of obsession Polanski normally brings to his work. Result is a disappointingly conventional mystery in which the filmmaker's apparent lack in engagement translate into insufficient stimulation for the viewer.

Adopting the Hitchcockian principle of thrusting an ordinary man into extraordinary circumstances, pic devotes much of its leisurely first reel on little travel jokes, as San Francisco medic Harrison Ford arrives in Paris with wife Betty Buckley to deliver a paper at a conference and, incidentally, to revisit the scene of their honeymoon 20 years before.

While Ford is showering, Buckley disappears from the hotel room, thus setting off an urgent womanhunt that takes the distraught husband, initially, to French police and officious American embassy authorities, but more critically connects him, through mixed-up luggage, to young Emmanuelle Seigner, a sleek, punky drugette and nightclubber who appears to be the only lead to the kidnappers.

Despite his sustained proximity to this sexy kid, Ford's love and loyalty to his wife never waivers. While this may be an impressive character trait, it also leaves the film rather undernourished, since Ford's Richard Walker never develops or fleshes out in interesting ways. Straight, sincere in every way normal, he seems untouched by his contact with both Seigner and the cops, pushers, terrorists and general run of weirdos he meets, and seems unafflicted with truly dark recesses of personality.

The McGuffin, or object of everyone's pursuit, here is a miniature Statue of Liberty which contains an object that, predictably, could endanger the Free World. Action climax takes place alongside the small-scale replica of France's gift to New York Harbor, but the symbolism of the hollow statue with sinister contacts lacks resonance, as does the near-concluding garbage truck imagery reminiscent of "Once Upon A Time In America."

The few clever gags and lines Polanski pulls off only serve to point up how lacking in edge is the picture as a whole. For those on the lookout for such things, there are a few ruefully funny observations on what an older man must put up with to keep company with a coltish young lady. On the downside are the uniformly caricatured portraits of evil Middle Easterners.

Ford sweats a lot while conveying Polanski's view that anxiety is the natural state of the human condition. His latest discovery, Seigner, certainly is eye-catching and proves servicable in her part, but no one else, including Buckley, gets much screen time.

As opposed to Polanski's often technically brilliant earlier films, this one appears routine in most respects. Ennio Morricone's jazzy score is unusally loud and abrasive.
—Cart.

A Jumpin' Night In The Garden Of Eden
(DOCU-COLOR/B&W)

A First Run Features release. Produced, directed and edited by Michal Goldman. Camera (color, 16m), Boyd Estus, Dyanna Taylor; sound, Colin Macnab, John Dildine; associate producer, Anne O. Craig. Reviewed at Film Forum 1, N.Y., Feb. 23, 1988. No MPAA Rating. Running time: **80 MIN.**
With: Henry Sapoznik, Hankus Netsky, Kapelye and the Klezmer Conservatory Band.

Essentially a documentary on the revival of klezmer — Yiddish dance-band music which has survived centuries of migratory permutations — "A Jumpin' Night In The Garden Of Eden" also looks at assimilated young American Jews unearthing their links to a buried cultural heritage. The film's uncomplicated presentation and musical vitality should provide satisfying programming for eclectic festivals and public tv.

Literally "instruments of song," klezmer is an emotionally irrepressible, free-wheeling music, propelled by horns, violins and bouncy syncopation. During its evolution, this party music of Eastern European Jewry became overlain with gypsy, Turkish and Balkan influences. The skilled young musicians featured in the film have used the inherent improvisational freedom of klezmer to reinvent the old-time music with modern arrangements while retaining the boisterous character that accompanied it on its emigration from the *shtetls* of the old world to the Yiddish theater of early 20th century America.

Focus is on two klezmer revival bands that sprung up around 1980: the New York-based Kapelye, led by Henry Sapoznik, and the Boston-based Klezmer Conservatory Band, led by Hankus Netsky. Both were accomplished, academically trained musicians when they separately rediscovered klezmer through old recordings.

Sapoznik, a cantor's son whose parents spoke "with accents," was fulfilling a desire "to be an American" by playing country and bluegrass with his Delaware Water Gap band, when curiosity about klezmer led him to recordings in the achives of the YIVO Jewish research institure in New York. Netsky, whose primary interest was jazz, had links to the Yiddish swing music through family members who played in klezmer bands and recorded for RCA and Columbia ethnic specialty labels in the 1920s.

Klezmer Conservatory vocalist Judy Bressler, grand-niece of Yiddish theater star Menasha Skulnik, says she did not grow up speaking the language but learned Yiddish in order to perform the exuberant, lyric-scatting klezmer songs. (The best known klezmer-derived crossover hit was the Andrews Sisters' prewar rendition of "Bei Meir Bis Du Schoen," with English lyrics penned by Sammy Cahn.)

Kapelye vocalist Michael Alpert says klezmer provides a tangible connection to the world of European Yiddish culture that vanished in the firestorm of the Holocaust. Filmmaker Michal Goldman reinforces the documentary's theme of cultural regeneration through snippets of b&w archival footage (which might have been used a little more generously) and interviews with old-time klezmer players like clarinetist Dave Tarras that fill out her portrait of what one musician calls "a kind of screaming music that blares out its roots." —Rich.

A Night In The Life Of Jimmy Reardon

A 20th Century Fox release of an Island Pictures presentation. Produced by Russell Schwartz. Coproducer, Richard H. Prince. Executive producers, Mel Klein, Noel Marshall. Written and directed by William Richert, based on his novel "Aren't You Even Gonna Kiss Me Goodbye?" Camera (Metrocolor; Deluxe prints), John J. Connor; editor, Suzanne Fenn; music, Bill Conti; production design, Norman Newberry; art direction, John R. Jensen; set decoration, Hilton Rosemarin; costume design, Bob De Mora; sound (Dolby), Scott Smith; associate producer, Lauren Graybow; assistant director, Craig Huston; casting, Elisabeth Leustig, Alderman & Andreas (Chicago). Reviewed at the 20th Century Fox Studios, L.A., Feb. 25, 1988. MPAA Rating: R. Running time: 92 MIN.
Jimmy Reardon . . . . River Phoenix
Joyce Fickett . . . . Ann Magnuson
Lisa Bentwright . . . . Meredith Salenger
Denise Hunter . . . . Ione Skye
Suzie Middleberg . . . . Louanne
Fred Roberts . . . . Matthew L. Perry
Al Reardon . . . . Paul Koslo
Faye Reardon . . . . Jane Hallaren
Matthew Hollander . . . . Jason Court

Hollywood — As a reflective, serious-minded teen comedy, "A Night In The Life Of Jimmy Reardon" thankfully avoids many of the traps and clichés of the overworked genre. Also it is a bit indulgent and at times flat in its presentation of the misguided escapades of a slick young fellow who crams a lot of desperate activity into the 36 hours before his friends start leaving for college.

Produced and intended for release by Island Pictures last year as "Jimmy Reardon," film was sold to Fox, who expanded its title and should draw okay b.o. in broad release.

In his third picture after the striking black comedies "Winter Kills" and "Success," William Richert draws upon an autobiographical novel he wrote in 1963, when he was 19 years old. Set the year before that in Evanston, Ill., tale tells of the sexually precocious title character who, in the course of two nights and one day, beds down his best friend's girlfriend, alienates that same friend by making out with another girl intended for him, and gets it on with his father's mistress, all while he is trying to raise enough money to accompany his true love, who will not sleep with him, to Hawaii.

Overlaid on these frantic adventures are detailings of Jimmy's troubled relationship with his officious father, little demonstrations of his abilities as a con artist, intimations of his writerly future, and a half-baked poetic acceptance of the notion that, whatever messes one gets into are just fate's way of helping one define oneself.

The suburban fringes of the late beatnik scene are to be glimpsed around the film's edges, and the specter of J.D. Salinger's "The Catcher In The Rye" looms large in the storyteller's callow, poetic outsider's frame of reference.

With the demands of mainstream entertainment calling, Richter also tries to force some antic humor out of the situations, with only marginal results. A teenage bedroom farce might have been fine, but Jimmy's activities are so unfocused and confused that he emerges, finally, as unsympathetic, a kid who ends up aggravating everyone around him, including the audience.

Although, presumably, Richert should know because he was there, the kids here appear remarkably sophisticated, hip and experienced for early 1960s suburban WASPs; one girl's claim that there are only four female virgins left in the high school graduating class seems especially dubious. Everyone is just a bit too cool and sure of themselves for their ages and the age, and the uniform inability of the characters to enact real emotions rather than posing or scheming lends a vaguely sour taste to the proceedings.

Nevertheless, pic operates on a level of intelligence many rungs higher than the norm for the genre, and cast is filled with any number of lively performers doing interesting things. Despite his character's severe limitations, River Phoenix suggests the craftiness and nascent artistic bent essential in Jimmy, and successfully holds centerscreen.

Ann Magnuson has delicious fun as a provocative divorcée with a taste for father and son, Meredith Salenger, Ione Skye and, particularly, Louanne — who has a nice way with tart, frank dialog — are on the money as the three main girls in Jimmy's circle, and Paul Koslo and Jane Hallaren sketch vivid portraits as his parents.

Pic was lensed in Evanston, and looks sharp, in large measure due to the fine camerawork of John J. Connor, formerly Vilmos Zsigmond's operator, who makes his debut as a d.p. here.—Cart.

Bloodsport

A Cannon Group release. Produced by Mark DiSalle. Directed by Newt Arnold. Screenplay, Sheldon Lettich, Christopher Crosby, Mel Friedman, story by Lettich; camera (TVC color), David Worth; editor, Carl Kress; music, Paul Hertzog; production design, David Searl; costume design, Wei Sau Ling; sound (Ultra-Stereo), George Weis; fight coordinator, Frank Dux; stunt coordinator, Steve Le Ka Ding; production manager, Burt Bluestein; assistant director, O.J. Tan; casting, Michael Olton. Reviewed at Hollywood Pacific theater, L.A., Feb. 26, 1988. MPAA Rating: R. Running time: 92 MIN.
Frank . . . . Jean Claude Van Damme
Jackson . . . . Donald Gibb
Janice . . . . Leah Ayres
Helmer . . . . Norman Burton
Rawlins . . . . Forrest Whitaker
Tanaka . . . . Roy Chiao
Capt. Chen . . . . Philip Chan
Chong Li . . . . Bolo Yeung

Hollywood — Cannon has bred a champion fight film in "Bloodsport," based on the true story of Frank Dux, American who became the world master of a deadly clandestine martial arts contest called

Kumite.

Director Newt Arnold, working from a tight script, is in full control from start to finish, and film, though packed with spectcular physical conflict, says more about friendship, integrity and achievement than gratuitous violence.

With word of mouth likely to pull an audience greater than the norm for this genre, project looks like a muscular b.o. contender.

Jean Claude Van Damme stars as Dux, who seeks out the Kumite arena hidden in the grim slums of Hong Kong to fulfill a bond of honor with his ailing martial arts teacher. Valuable to special forces of the U.S. government, he's pursued by agents charged with keeping him away from the deadly contest, as well as by a spunky female reporter (Leah Ayres) who falls for him and decides she'd rather doublecross him than see him risk his life.

At the Kumite, Dux becomes friends with another American fighter, a bearded, beer-guzzling backwoods giant (Donald Gibb), and confronts his ultimate foe, the smiling, undefeated Chong Li (Bolo Yeung), who's not above fighting dirty or killing his opponents.

As the kind of clean-cut, softspoken hero who says "excuse me" to bystanders jostled in a chase scene, Van Damme has wide appeal that could see him giving Arnold Schwarzenegger a run for the action pic roles. A scene in which he uses a swift coin trick to rescue the gal from menacing males is particularly charming.

The film is about combat, and at its core is Van Damme's amazing physical prowess, shown in eye-popping scenes of strength and grace that, mixed with deft strokes of character comedy, had house howling with delight.

Pic earns its R rating when the first punch of the Kumite tournament is thrown, as blood sprays from a fighter's mouth. One warrior ends up with a broken bone hanging from his leg, Dux' big pal is hospitalized, and another ends up dead.

As pic builds toward the inevitable final contest, suspense is skillfully orchestrated by script and director.

Skillful, sparing use of slo-mo makes the most of fight scenes, for which the real Frank Dux was a consultant and editor Carl Kress, from the beginning, builds scenes of conflict to a percussive momentum. A better-than-average score for this genre also elevates tension.

Refreshing aspect of this film is that skill and dedication, not guns and money, are the source of power. Final showdown has Dux escape death by reaching for resources he developed in his past.

Decidedly international milieu, in which warriors are ranked based on personal achievement and nothing else, might even erase some prejudice.

Director of photography David Worth contributes spectacular aerial views of Hong Kong harbor.

— *Daws.*

The House On Carroll Street

An Orion Pictures release. Produced by Peter Yates, Robert F. Colesberry, Executive producers, Arlene Donovan, Robert Benton. Directed by Peter Yates. Screenplay, Walter Bernstein; camera (Duart Color, Deluxe prints), Michael Ballhaus; editor, Ray Lovejoy; music, Georges Delerue; production design, Stuart Wurtzel; art direction, W. Steven Graham; set decoration, George DeTitta Jr.; costume design, Rita Ryack; sound, Tod Maitland; assistant director, Joseph Reidy; associate producer, Nellie Nugiel; casting, Howard Feuer. Reviewed at Orion Pictures screening room, L.A., Feb. 26, 1988. MPAA Rating: PG. Running time: 100 MIN.
Emily Crane . . . . Kelly McGillis
Cochran . . . . Jeff Daniels
Salwen . . . . Mandy Patinkin
Stefan . . . . Christopher Rhode
Miss Venable . . . . Jessica Tandy
Alan . . . . Jonathan Hogan

Hollywood — If Nancy Drew were to grow up and move to New York to be a sleuth trailing improbable characters involved in a ridiculous conspiracy, she might find herself solving such dumb cases as "The House On Carroll Street." The pic isn't based on any of Carolyn Keene's popular book series, but it also has in common with them amateur plotting and a guaranteed shelf life — at the video store.

Pic has been sitting around for a while (it wrapped in late 1986) and it's easy to see why. It succeeds at neither characterization of being a "romantic thriller" as filmmakers intended.

Kelly McGillis is the idealistic and hardly convincing political activist who is fired from her job at Life magazine circa 1951 when she refuses to answer questions before a Senate hearing on her involvement in a controversial organization. That puts a couple of FBI agents on her trail.

She then takes a job reading to a crotchety old blind lady (Jessica Tandy) whose row house garden is adjacent to another brownstone where there are mysterious goings-on. It just so happens the same Senator (Mandy Patinkin) who grilled her about her political leanings is in the house shouting as an interpreter translates into German. McGillis is intrigued.

With the inquisitive enthusiasm of a glamor girl off an adventure in the big city, McGillis collects about three clues and figures out Patinkin is smuggling Nazis in by having them take the names of dead Jews.

Georges Delerue's gangster 1950s tv music that comes in every time German is being spoken sets up for the hokeyness of the story which follows.

The motive for why Patinkin, who is more a bad parody of a Godfather-type character, would harbor Nazis, let alone how he manages to get the Immigration and Naturalization Service agents to cooperate, was left out of the script — and effectively neutralizes whatever excitement was planned before it even gets going.

Jeff Daniels is Ned to McGillis' Nancy Drew. He is the FBI agent who manages to come in at exactly the right moments to save her from whatever perilous predicament she is in at the time — no matter how preposterous. Their dialog is even sillier, like when she says to him how their relationship is like "oil and water" except he counters, when they're between the sheets.

Besides how cliched an analogy this would be to describe any couple's relationship, it is just bad dialog writing and pretty much is indicative of the whole film.

Production design by Stuart Wurtzel, set decoration by George DeTitta Jr. and art direction by W. Steven Graham are the saving grace of this effort. Scenes of treesy New York streets cluttered with roadsters and clean, sleek, moderne-style subway cars beautifully harken back to the times of the city in its heyday.

—*Brit.*

Prison

An Empire Pictures release. Executive producer, Charles Band. Produced by Irwin Yablans. Directed by Renny Harlin. Screenplay, C. Courtney Joyner, from Yablans' story; camera (color), Mac Ahlberg; editor, Ted Nicolaou; music, Richard Band; sound (Ultra-Stereo), Jan Brodin; costumes, Stephen Chudej; art direction, Phillip Duffin; set decoration, Patti Garrity; production manager, Barin Kumar; stunt coordinator, Kane Hodder; casting, Anthony Barnao. Reviewed at Mark Goodson theater, N.Y., Feb. 29, 1988. MPAA Rating: R. Running time: 102 MIN.
Sharpe . . . . Lane Smith
Burke . . . . Viggo Mortensen
Katherine . . . . Chelsea Field
Sandor . . . . Andre De Shields
Cresus . . . . Lincoln Kilpatrick
Lasagna . . . . Ivan Kane
Rhino . . . . Steven Little
Brian Young . . . . Mickey Yablans
Big Sam . . . . Tom (Tiny) Lister Jr.
Rabbitt . . . . Tom Everett

A veritable "Poltergeist Penitentiary," "Prison" should be a breeze to market because of the clearcut audiences out there for both rough penal pics and special effects-laden horror stories. This rare amalgam should guarantee strong initial business, but the routine lensing, acting and ending foreshadows a short theatrical run.

Starring as the prison in the pic is the 87-year-old Wyoming State Penitentiary, which has attracted tourists rather than cons since 1981. Thanks to movie magic conjured up by an L.A. crew, the structure takes on all the menace of the house in "Amityville Horror" or hotel in "The Shining."

The crumbling stone fortress is grounds for revenge because, as aged inmate Cresus (Lincoln Kilpatrick) points out toward the end, "things won't stay buried." It turns out that in 1964 guard Ethan Sharpe (Lane Smith, in last year's "Weeds" as an inmate) watched an innocent man fry in the electric chair.

The execution took place in the prison which is reopened despite protests from the fair, fervent prison board member Katherine (Chelsea Field). Sharpe, now a warden, is appointed to the prison's helm despite recurrent nightmares brought on by a guilty conscience.

Before dispatching the warden in a conflagatory, monster-revealing ending that packs only a modest punch, the wronged convict's evil spirit is mad enough to eliminate a few of the new guards and inmates, including Tom Everett, Andre De Shields, Ivan Kane and Steven Little. Last named was recruited from real-life inmate extras.

The suspensefully and creatively staged deaths found two of the victims tangled up in barbed wire and metal tubing like bloody marionettes, suggesting the supernatural force might have been a puppeteer in another life.

Viggo Mortensen plays Burke, a James Dean type antihero spared death but not a lot of bumps and bruises. His resemblance to the electrocuted con (Katherine did her homework in a local newspaper morgue) apparently is just a coincidence in C. Courtney Joyner's screenplay of producer Irwin Yablan's story.

Although touted as one of Empire's bigger-budget offerings, "Prison" clearly was a frugal production. For example, Richard Band's original score is performed entirely on a synthesizer instead of using an orchestra, his past modus operandi which the press data so proudly points out.

Finnish director Renny Harlin ("Born American") and cinematographer Mac Ahlberg did okay jobs, while the special effects crews (mechanical SPFX coordinated by Eddie Surkin and makeup SPFX, John Buechler) all earned their salaries, and then some.—*Binn.*

Saxo
(FRENCH)

A UGC release of a Partner's Prod./Canal Plus Prods./Films A2 coproduction. Produced and directed by Ariel Zeitoun. Screenplay, Zeitoun, Gilbert Tanugi, Jacques Audiard, from novel "Saxo jaune" by Tanugi; camera (color), Bruno de Keyzer; editor, Hugues Darmois; music, Gene Barge; Denise Osso, Roy Buchanan, Donald Kinsey, performed by Archie Shepp, Roy Buchanan; additional music, François Bréant, art direction, Jacques Bufnoir; sound, Harald Maury, Claude Villand, Bernard Leroux, William Flageollet; assistant director, Philippe Besnier. Reviewed at the Gaumont Ambassade cinema, Paris, Feb. 16, 1988. Running time: 116 MIN.
Sam Friedman . . . . Gérard Lanvin
Puppet . . . . Akosua Busia
Joe . . . . Richard Brooks
Esther . . . . Laure Killing
Tonia . . . . Clément Harari
Scorpio . . . . Roland Blanche

Manager ....Thomas Pollard
Meicha ....Jany Holt
Lawyer ....Francis Girod

Paris — Producer Ariel Zeitoun displayed vigorous promise as a director in his first feature, "Souvenirs, souvenirs," (1984) a '60s youth chronicle about an aspiring pop singer (acquired by MGM/UA but never released Stateside). The promise still is good in his new film, "Saxo," a flamboyant jazz thriller, but the script betrays the energetic direction.

The premise has good *film noir* qualities. A debt-ridden young Parisian music producer (Gérard Lanvin) comes upon what he thinks is his professional salvation — an unknown American brother-and-sister jazz duo. Digging himself even deeper into a debtor's grave, Lanvin succeeds in signing an exclusive recording contract with them.

Dream turns to nightmare however when Lanvin learns that the superb saxophonist is a sexual psychopath. When latter murders a prostitute, Lanvin decides to take the rap so that his million-dollar record will still be made. Then suddenly the two blacks disappear.

Up to this point the script holds, despite the genre clichés and perfunctory supporting roles. Unfortunately, Zeitoun and his coscripters (including the author of the source novel) have to strain mightily and melodramatically to pull the situation to its bloody climax and ironic coda, which don't convince.

Despite the plot fumblings, Zeitoun's kinetic direction is often riveting, breathless. What he needs is to fully assimilate his American influences and find a solidly original script.

Lanvin is good as the taciturn, tense hero-loser, but most striking performances come from Yanks Richard Brooks and especially Akosua Busia as the black brother-sister act (musically transfigured by the off-screen playing of Archie Shepp and Roy Buchanan). The music track is exciting. —*Len.*

Aaj Ka Robin Hood
(The Return Of Robin Hood)
(INDIAN)

An R.A. Jalan-Gaurang Films/The Children's Film Society coproduction. Produced, written and directed by Tapan Sinha. Camera (color), Kamal Nayak; editor, Subodh Roy; music, Tapan Sinha; art direction, Ashok Bose. Reviewed at the Indian Film Festival, Trivandrum, Jan. 14, 1988. Running time: **111 MIN.**
With: Utpal Dutt, Anil Chatterjee, Satish Shah, Nan Patekar, Rabi Ghosh, Master Ravi, Suraj Ritesh Talwat.
(In Hindi)

Trivandrum — Kidpic with a strong social message, "The Return Of Robin Hood" is an adventure-fable championing the underprivileged classes by veteran Hindi director (32 features) Tapan Sinha.

Though the cruel oppression of pint-size hero Tetra often heads into the maudlin, pic's fable-like quality and a credible supporting cast pull it out of the swamp in time for a stirring finale. It's indicated for children's audiences anywhere.

Tetra (Master Ravi), son of a poor villager, works in the Singh family's private school, fanning the pupils to keep them cool. The boys are the sons and relations of three brothers: Ram Yadav Singh, domineering family head, a wastrel younger brother interested only in cards and horses, and a comical fat brother living in Ram Yadav's shadow.

Endowed with a great gift, a photographic memory, Tetra outlearns the regular pupils, to the secret joy of good-hearted schoolmaster Jatin Babu. Tetra's gift doesn't go unnoticed, and Ram Yadav callously plans to make an accountant out of him to get more money out of the villagers, whom he cheats after making high-interest loans. Discovering his treachery and inspired by the tale of Robin Hood, little Tetra manages to return the loan receipts to the villagers, with the help of another boy. Ram Yadav orders him killed, but the family rebels and allows Tetra to escape on a wonderful horse.

This pleasant kidpic clocks in at an overly long 111 minutes; technical work is pro, however. Thesps, young and old alike, are sharply delineated types. Pic ends with a call for education for the poor. — *Yung.*

Muelle Rojo
(Red Dock)
(MEXICAN)

A Peliculas Mexicanas release of an A.T.A.-Gremio Unido de Alejadores production. Directed by José Luis Urquieta. Screenplay, Xavier Robles; camera (color), Alberto Arellanos; editor, Enrique Murrillo; music, Rafael Carrión. Reviewed at XII Reseña Mundial de Acapulco, Mexico, Nov. 9, 1987. Running time: **101 MIN.**
El Ostión ....Roberto (Flaco) Guzmán
Gerardo Gómez
Castillo..........Ignacio López Tarso
Isauro Alfaro ....Manuel Ojeda
Emilio ....Eric del Castillo
Samuel Kelly.........Fernando Balzaretti
Fernández ....Raul (Choforo) Padilla
Esteban Hernández ....Mario Cid

Acapulco — The Mexican feature "Muelle Rojo" (Red Dock), helmed by José Luis Urquieta, is a mixed bag of film styles and forms that leave the viewer wondering exactly what the director had in mind.

Produced by the film cooperative A.T.A. (Artistas y Técnicos Asociados) and the dock workers union Gremio Unido de Alijadores, the pic functions only as a confused in-house docu-entertainment meant to celebrate the syndicate's 75th anni, which took place in 1986. It makes little sense to a general domestic audience and offers zero international interest.

Besides an almost religious reverence bestowed on the union's martyred founder Isauro Alfaro, pic is a sappy and forced homage to its current leader Gerardo Gómez Castillo. At times the pic seems like a weak justification for Gómez Castillo's 20-year-plus tenure as union boss.

Technical aspects of the film are well handled with care given to recreating the period depicted at pic's beginning. The film falls completely apart with its plodding script that meanders between hagiography, documentary and a cheap comedy about a couple of drunks, watched over by the ghost of the founder. Union objectives are awkwardly inserted throughout with the inclusion of boring public speeches and 1-sided arguments about collective benefits.

Given the tremendous strength of Mexican labor unions, the film will find a forced audience nationally within the confines of darkened union halls, but b.o. potential is zilch. — *Lent.*

Shallow Grave

An Intl. Film Marketing release of an E.L.F. production. Executive producers, George E. Fernandez, Ed Fernandez. Produced by Barry H. Waldman. Directed by Richard Styles. Screenplay, George E. Fernandez, from story by Fernandez, Carolyn J. Horton; camera (Continental color), Orson Ochoa; editor, Horton; music, Mason Daring; sound, Henry Lopez; art direction, Alan Avchen; set decoration, Suzi Margolin; assistant director, Corky Irick; production manager, Mel Kiser; second unit director, Ralph R. Clemente; second unit camera, Henry Lynk; associate producers, John Dinicola, Clemente, Shelley E. Reid. Reviewed on Prism Ent. vidcassette, N.Y., Jan. 16, 1988. MPAA Rating: R. Running time: **89 MIN.**
Sheriff Dean ....Tony March
Sue Ellen ....Lisa Stahl
Deputy Scott ....Tom Law
Patty ....Carol Cadby
Rose ....Donna Baltron
Cindy ....Just Kelly
Chad ....Vince Tumeo
Owen ....Gregory Todd Davis
Also with: Merry Rozelle, Roy Smart, Kimberly Johnson, Heidi Brown.

"Shallow Grave" is a well-made but overly contrived thriller. It didn't create much interest in its theatrical run last year, but is a useful homevideo rental title.

Florida-made effort essays a familiar tale (best version being the Yvette Mimieux-starrer "Jackson County Jail") of young girls getting in trouble with the law on a trip down south. After a misjudged, student film-style opening (which restages the "Psycho" shower scene shot-for-shot as a dumb gag), pic has four pretty college girls headed to Fort Lauderdale on vacation. They have a flat tire in Medley, Ga., and looking for help one of them witnesses a couple making love in the woods.

Post coitus, the guy has an argument and kills his girlfriend. Two of the other girls stumble on him digging a grave and he blows them away, burying them with his lover. Surviving coeds are thrown in jail when their story is disbelieved and it turns out that the young sheriff (Tony March) is the killer. A friendly deputy (Tom Law) tries to help out, but a cynical, unsatisfying, freeze-frame ending has the last girl left in the clutches of the evil sheriff.

Acting and technical values are fine here, but the numerous plot twists range from unbelievable to downright stupid (a running bit involving two guys from Michigan who fail to arrive in time to help the girls). Better scripting and some name casting could have made this one a winner. —*Lor.*

L'Ane qui a bu la lune
(The Donkey That Drank The Moon)
(FRENCH-B&W/COLOR)

A Bac Films release of an ACS/Sept coproduction. Produced by Guy Cavagnac. Written and directed by Marie-Claude Treilhou, based on regional folk tales. Camera (Eastmancolor and Fuji, b&w and color), Lionel Legros; editor, Khadicha Bariha; sound, Michel Mellier; costumes, Nathalie Cercuel; art direction, Patrick Durand; assistant director, Michel Gauthier. Reviewed at the Publicis screening room, Paris, Feb. 4, 1988. Running time: **95 MIN.**
With: José Pech (storyteller), Térence Le Deschault de Montredon, Christian Conejero, Jean-Pierre Olive, Didier Serre, Denis Bonnes, Jean-Henri Meunier, Charles Serres, Jean Labeyrie.

Paris — Marie-Claude Treilhou made a sympathetic albeit amateurish debut feature in 1979, "Simone Barbès," about a porno house usherette. She's since gone home to her native southwestern France where she's been making docus and shorts about progress, tradition and provincialism, notably "Lourdes In Winter," a hilarious short set in the famous pilgramage site during off-season.

In "L'Ane qui a bu la lune," Treilhou has adapted five folk tales, to mixed results. Using as linking device a local storyteller who spins his yarns to a child, she cleverly visualizes oral tradition by using such devices as jerky silent film pastiche and the sequence shot.

This provides a charming cinematic equivalency for the first two tales: about three yokels who want to learn French but only succeed in confessing to a murder with the few words they ignorantly spout; and a fable about a pig who's elected mayor of a village in a perfectly legal manner.

The style of the remaining sketches is more conventional and less satisfying, and the mostly amateur local cast doesn't help. Last story in particular, about a young man haunted by a dead girlfriend during a local carnival, is prosaic and overlong, underlying Treilhou's abiding problem with rhythm. Technically, film suffers from its obviously low budget. —*Len.*

Ekti Jiban
(Portrait Of A Life)
(INDIAN)

A Chalchitra production in association with the National Film Development Corp.

Executive producer, Dilip Ghosh. Written and directed by Raja Mitra. Camera (color), Kamal Nayak; editor, Bulu Ghosh; music, Raja Mitra; art direction, Satadal Mitra. Reviewed at the Indian Film Festival, Trivandrum, Jan. 14, 1988. Running time: **130 MIN.**

Gurudas .... Soumitra Chatterjee
Also with: Madhavi Chakrabarty, Avory Dutta, Munna Chakrabarty, Gyanesh Mukherjee.

(In Bengali)

Trivandrum — "Portrait Of A Life" is that rare avis, a film that manages to turn abstract pleasures like the thirst for knowledge and the joy of words into cinematic material. Told like the life of a saint, film traces a humble, country schoolteacher's struggle to write the first Bengali dictionary, an undertaking of no small scope.

Though it suffers from the national vice of excessive length (first-time director Raja Mitra, a documentarist, asserts his willingness to trim), "Portrait" marks a significant feature debut and should circulate through the fest and specialized art house circuits.

The time is the 1930s, the place rural Bengal, and Partition still seems a long way off. Gurudas (played with quiet finesse by Soumitra Chatterjee) teaches Sanskrit in a poor country school. One day, when casually asked to take over a Bengali lit class, he is thunderstruck by the origin of some words of common parlance. Positively suffering an anxiety attack over the expressions' ambiguity, he feverishly scans extant dictionaries as tension builds à la a good detective story.

Convinced of the need for a comprehensive Bengali dictionary, Gurudas modestly hesitates before accepting the mighty task. His is an interior acceptance of a vocation, carried out through years of patient, unpaid labor, sacrifice, and family tragedy. Despite his wife's mistrust of the project and the cash outlay it involves (Gurudas even has to pay press costs himself), he perseveres. Years pass; he frequents shady places to find colloquial expressions, makes regular research trips to Calcutta, buries his daughter, son, and wife. He completes his life's work with the aid of his faithful daughter-in-law, who attends him as though waiting on a saint. Belatedly, official recognition arrives when Gurudas is on his deathbed in a miserable hovel. He has the officials thrown out.

Unbelievably, Mitra transforms an academic hagiography into compulsive viewing, despite pic's drawn-out length and uncertain, faded photography. Story is the fictionalized account of a real person.
— *Yung.*

La Passerelle
(The Catwalk)
(FRENCH)

A UGC release of a T. Films/TF-1 Films coproduction. Produced by Alain Terzian. Directed by Jean-Claude Sussfeld. Screenplay, Sussfeld, Paul Berthier, inspired by "Savage Holiday" by Richard Wright; camera (color), Robert Fraisse; editor, Monique Prim; music, Hervé Lavandier; art direction, Serge Douy; sound, André Hervée, Dominique Dalamaso; assistant director, Michel Thibaud. Reviewed at the UGC Normandie cinema, Paris, Feb. 24, 1988. Running time: **90 MIN.**

Jean Nevers .... Pierre Arditi
Cora Eden .... Mathilda May
Maminouche .... Jany Holt
Virginie .... Aurelle Doazan
Richard .... Jean-Marie Marion

Paris — A moderately interesting, intimate drama from Jean-Claude Sussfeld, who previously directed a couple of light comedies, "Passerelle" casts Pierre Arditi and Mathilda May as two nextdoor neighbors with no contact until latter's 5-year-old son falls from an inner court catwalk outside Arditi's bathroom window.

Arditi is the catalyst of the accident. Shut out of his apartment by a sudden gust of wind, the stark naked bachelor rushes panic-stricken onto the catwalk and frightens the boy, who clambers onto the railing and falls three floors. He is hospitalized in a coma.

Script by director and Paul Berthier, loosely drawn from an American novel, centers on the attraction-repulsion between the middle-class intellectual, afraid to admit his part in the accident, and the liberated single mother estranged from and contemptuous of her uptight neighbors. Sudden switch of attention from the adults to the recovered but somewhat troubled child belatedly buries pic in psychoanalytical murk.

Apart from inevitable buff quotations ("Rear Window," quite naturally, as well as Stanley Kubrick) Sussfeld directs adequately, with Arditi and May giving their roles personable substance. Tech credits are acceptable.— *Len.*

A másik ember
(The Other Person)
(HUNGARIAN)

A Hungarofilm presentation of an Objektiv Studio production. Written and directed by Ferenc Kosa. Camera (Eastmancolor), László Baranyiai; editor, Margit Galamb; sound, György Pintér; art direction, Zsolt Khell; costumes, Márta Jánoskúti. Reviewed at Hungarian Film Week, Budapest, Feb. 9, 1988. Running time: **220 MIN.**
With: Csaba Jakab, Anna Ráckevei, Zóltan Varga, Zsolt Szerényi, Ferenc Bessenyei, János Konyorcsik, Károly Eperjes, László Méhes, István Holl, Lajos Kovács, Johanna Bodor, Józef Balogh.

Budapest — The most ambitious production of Hungary this year, Ferenc Kosa's 2-part historical drama shows impressive visual imagination and some courageous political statements, not always supported by an equally dramatic sweep.

The first part is the tale of two survivors of an Hungarian battalion completely annihilated on the battlefront in 1944, who are facing a court-martial, both suspected of having deserted their unit. Saved in the nick of time by a fascist who believes they are just the human material the national socialist revolution requires, they soon discover what they are expected to do. One of them, Antal Bojtar, manages to escape and reaches his home in the village, but the fascists are on his tracks and refuse to give up.

The second part takes place 12 years later, dealing with Bojtar's son. It begins with a huge student assembly around the bodies of their colleagues killed in the first stages of the 1956 insurgence. Young Bojtar rejects the offer to be a student leader, trying to preach non-violence, as he was taught by his father. Once again, the brutality of weapons is going to carry the day, just as in his father's case.

Kosa makes a clear stylistic division between the two parts. While both are pictorially striking in their compositions and color patterns, the first takes place entirely in the countryside and shows more concern for action and drama. At least one emotional climax, when the news of a man's death is conveyed by his wife to his father only through the expression on their faces, is truly exceptional in every sense.

In the second part, Kosa moves to the stentorial tones of the socialist drama, starts with the majestic shots of the student meeting around the neatly arranged bodies of the victims, and proceeds with equally impressive images of the uprising, mass movements on the streets, imposing distribution of figures all over the urban landscape in large and richly detailed frescoes.

By placing the audience's sympathy exclusively on the insurgents' side, and by juxtaposing this historical episode with the fascist rule of Hungary in World War II, Kosa draws a courageous parallel between the identity of the villains in both instances.

He stresses the fact that all villains in this piece, without exception, are Hungarians shooting at other Hungarians. One sequence, when demonstrators break into an army camp, each side flying identical Hungarian flags in the name of which they butcher each other, is particularly significant in this instance.

The problem in this part is that Kosa seems carried away by the importance of the message he has to convey. The construction consists of alternate soliloquies written and delivered in a declamatory fashion, and spectacular mass scenes. Every time an actor launches into a monolog the action grinds to a standstill, to be picked up only after he has thoroughly explained himself.

Technically, this is a remarkable achievement. Kosa's actors have strong personalities, particularly in the country scenes, but at over 3½ hours, with its clear tendency towards the historical pageant, the picture's appeal inevitably will be restricted to specialized positions.
— *Edna.*

Egy teljes nap
(A Full Day)
(HUNGARIAN)

A Hungarofilm presentation of a Mozgókép Innovációs Társulás production, Budapest. Written and directed by Ferenc Grunwalsky. Camera (video, Eastmancolor), Grunwalsky; editor, Klára Majoros; sound, András Vámosi. Reviewed at the Hungarian Film Week, Budapest, Feb. 9, 1988. Running time: **80 MIN.**

Jószi .... Károly Nemesák
Eva .... Erika Pék
Gáspár .... Sándor Gáspár
Kálmán .... Béla Ivánfi
Blind man .... Péter Andorai

Budapest — Entirely shot on video and transferred to 35m, this independent production, an exception for the Hungarian industry, seems dedicated to three working-class obsessions. The easiest to identify is sexual, but there is also big city social and economic anxiety and macho self-esteem.

The film's opening sequence shows a young cab driver and his pretty wife getting up in the morning, no inch of actress Erika Pék's naked body left unexplored, as her excited husband barely manages to tear himself away from her and go out to hustle some money he badly needs in order to pay a big debt to one of his fellow drivers.

Leaving his wife lasciviously loitering at home mostly with no clothes on, he sets out to fight the traffic, the other drivers and the customers, while his CB set is blaring constantly, both at home and in his taxi, allowing him to keep in touch with his spouse, but with no privacy at all. By the end of a frustrating day, she tells him his creditor has paid her a visit and raped her, leaving him no alternative but to find the man he had tried to avoid and demand an explanation.

The inevitable tragic ending leads again to the desperate conclusion many Hungarian films point out. The social conditions push these characters into a sort of primitive bestiality, explaining the macho attitude of the men and the submissive consent of the woman.

This is dutifully reflected in the passive performances of all the actors, who seem to submit to their parts rather than master them and also explains the use of video technique for the entire picture. Not only does it make it much easier on the budget, it also allows a greater measure of flexibility for director Ferenc Grunwalsky (who is also his own cameraman), while lending the image a kind of gritty, pseudodocumentary quality, particularly in medium and long shots. Closeups often are remarkably textured, a credit to the laboratory work done here.

The script, however, once it states its basic premise, doesn't really elaborate on it, develop it or the characters to any degree of interest. The dialog is purposely kept on a monosyllabic level and use of numerous classical music excerpts is both pretentious and generally unnecessary in this context.—*Edna.*

Hótreál
(Damn Real)
(HUNGARIAN)

A Hungarofilm presentation of a Hunnia Films production. Written and directed by Ildikó Szabó. Camera (Eastmancolor), Zoltán Dávid; editor, Zsuzsa Pósán; music, János Másik; sound, Tamás Márkus; art direction, Pál Lovas; costumes, Emőke Csengey. Reviewed at Hungarian Film Week, Budapest, Feb. 9, 1988. (In Berlin Film Fest — Panorama section.) Running time: **80 MIN.**
With: Ildikó Czakó, Géza Vincze, Sándor Szótér, Attila Berencsi.

Budapest — The Hungarian reality takes on its grimmer aspects for this first film by Ildikó Szabó, a former actress, about marginal youth and its doomed future.

Selected by the Berlin Panorama program, Szabó's script focuses on four youngsters, all in their early 20s. Lili, a dressmaker, is determined to do everything in order to save her brother Gyuri, she adores, as he is released from a 3-year stint in jail. For that she enlists the help of another boy, Adam, who spent time with Gyuri in jail and nurtures a strong homosexual affection for him, and of David, an officer's son who is her boyfriend.

The story moves in circles describing Lili's efforts necessary

to release Gyuri from his debts and buy him a passage abroad, where he might get a fresh start, and the self-destructive conduct of all four members of this quartet, each one of them struggling in his own private hell, either against apathy, drugs, sexuality or parental and social rejection.

Szabó's disjointed style, her sudden jarring moves from mood to mood, and her constant use of handheld camera techniques will irk many viewers, while her overuse of clichés to define a hopeless vision of youth wasted tends to limit itself to a description of a given situation rather than its analysis. If anything, it shows socialist youth going through crises that are only too familiar to the West and one is bound to wonder what exactly Gyuri, who evidently lacks any incentive whatsoever to care for himself, will do once he crosses the border.

The real problem is that script does not work sufficient sympathy for the four characters. —*Edna.*

Valahol Magyarorszagon
(Rear-Guard)
(HUNGARIAN)

A Dialog Studio, Mafilm, production. Written and directed by Andras Kovacs. Camera (Eastmancolor), Ferenc Szecsenyi; editor, Maria Szecsenyi; sound, Gabor Erdelyi. Reviewed at Hungarian Film Week, Budapest, Feb. 10, 1988. Running time: **91 MIN.**
Balint Bodnar . . . . Peter Blasko
Veres . . . . Imre Csiszar
Agnes . . . . Anna Kubik
Harmati . . . . Istvan Fonyo
Jakas . . . . Andras Fekete
Also with: Mari Szemes, Gabor Madi Szabo.

Budapest — "Rear-Guard" is a political drama with a fascinating subject — grassroots politics in a socialist nation — but weighed down by static, stolid handling. This one's unlikely to travel far from home.

Electoral reforms took place in Hungary a few years ago, and it's now compulsory for more than one candidate to stand for an election. Story, based on documented facts, is set in a small town where the Communist Party machine is putting up two aging comrades for election. However, a write-in candidate unexpectedly is added to the ticket: Bodnar, director of the local rural research institute, who has opposed construction of a quarry on environmental grounds, thus annoying the local Party clique.

The Establishment will do anything to stop Bodnar's unwanted election: They try vilifying his father, but this backfires on them and Bodnar becomes even more popular. Eventually they withdraw both their candidates so that the election has to be postponed, but finally their machinations fail. Bodnar is elected, though his deputy is a bland young Party man who previously spearheaded attempts to engineer his downfall.

Americans embarking on the long electoral process might have found the goings-on in this Hungarian backwater fascinating and timely, but unfortunately director Andras Kovacs handles the drama so listlessly that, in filmic terms, "Rear-Guard" almost is of no interest. The story is told in endless scenes in which two or three people argue, and even in the larger scenes of electoral meetings and rallies, no cinematic flair is provided to try to tell the story in more visual terms.

It's a shame, because the basic material, which is strikingly similar to that found in Gyula Gazdag's remarkable docu "The Resolution," is potentially explosive: what was needed was the skill of a Frank Capra to take this tale of the underdog coming out on top and make a movie out of it. Fact that it's a true story makes the wasted opportunity even more regrettable.—*Strat.*

A Szárnyas Ugynök
(Peter In Wonderland)
(HUNGARIAN-WEST GERMAN-B&W)

A Bela Balazs Studio (Budapest)-DFFB (Berlin) coproduction. Directed by Sándor Soth. Screenplay, Soth, Géza Bereményi; camera (b&w), Andras Mesz, Sandor Csukas; editor, Gabriella Koncz; music, Ferenc Darvas, Neurotic Group; production design, Daniel Bartos; sound, Otto Olah; assistant director, Elemer Kaldor. Reviewed at Hungarian Film Week, Budapest, Feb. 9, 1988. Running time: **73 MIN.**
Peter . . . . Laszlo Kistamas
The Agent . . . . Tamas Pajor
Ilona . . . . Valeria Zsoldos
Mari . . . . Beatrice Manowski

Budapest — A first feature from 23-year-old director Sándor Söth shows some promise, but also clearly indicates a malaise among Hungarian youth evident also in other new Magyar pics. This one completely lacks the sense of adventure and *joie de vivre* that characterized young cinema in Eastern Europe 20 years ago; its characters are morose, self-centered, and frankly dull.

Peter, Ilona and Mari are three young Hungarians who seem to hate life. Their goal is Wonderland (spelled Wunderland), a country where, they seem to feel, everything will be better. A secret agent from Wonderland arrives in town, and before long is involved with the trio, sleeping with both girls and befriending Peter. The girls don't find happiness with him; he worms secrets from Maria, and brings about Ilona's death. Eventually, Peter sets out for Wonderland, by train — Wonderland, it seems, is West Berlin, held up as some kind of ironic image of Paradise.

This Paradise consists of seedy strip-clubs and brothels and more unhappiness. Peter returns home, to an even gloomier future. Gloom is all-pervading here, swamping the film and preventing the viewer from having much sympathy for, or interest in, these self-pitying types. Film is well made, and indicates

that young Söth may go on to do more interesting things. It's sad to see someone so young make a film so depressingly pessimistic and lifeless.

Pic's original title translates as "Winged Agent," and an end credit thanking the U.S. Army must be some kind of a first for Hungarian cinema. —*Strat.*

Mr. Universe
(HUNGARIAN)

A Hunnia Studio, Malev, production, in association with Cine Universe. Directed by György Szomjas. Screenplay, Szomjas, Ibolya Fekete, Ferenc Grunwalsky; camera (color), Grunwalsky; editor, Anna Kornis; sound, György Kovacs; assistant director, Judith Toth. Reviewed at Hungarian Film Week, Budapest, Feb. 10, 1988. Running time: **98 MIN.**
Laszlo . . . . Laszlo Szabo
Lord . . . . George Pinter
Mickey Hargitay . . . . Himself

Budapest — Made on an extremely small budget, "Mr. Universe" is the second U.S.-located Hungarian film produced in the last 12 months; however, unlike Peter Gothar's disappointing "Just Like Amerika," György Szomjas' film is a modest delight.

Basically, it's an extended shaggy dog story with a road movie construction. Laszlo (Laszlo Szabo) sees a tv interview with Hungarian-born Mickey Hargitay, who was the first world-famous body-builder, a Mr. Universe, husband of Jayne Mansfield and, for a while, an actor. Laszlo thinks it would be great to make a movie with Hargitay, and sets off for New York to locate Lord (George Pinter), a friend of the former athlete and a would-be film director. He discovers a disconsolate Lord driving a cab and bemoaning his latest unsuccessful romance; after some delays, the pair set out in the cab to drive across the country to L.A.

Bulk of the film, which was shot last September, takes place on the road, with truck stops and gas stations being principal locations. As they drive, Laszlo and Lord argue about their project, about Hargitay and his life, about Hungary and about America, while radio programs, and the inevitably bizarre ads, fill the soundtrack. They're welcomed warmly by Hargitay, who introduces them to his family and shows them around his palatial home (which flies U.S. and Hungarian flags), but then he flatly refuses to make a film with them. Their trip was all for nothing.

Though "Mr. Universe" is rough at the edges, its sense of humor and love of the film medium set it apart from the current crop of Magyar pics. It's not a depressing slog through upheavals and injustices of the past or present; it's simply fun. It's fun when Szomjas follows Laszlo around a variety of New York Hungarian restaurants and cafes, and a caption playfully points out a painting of King Mathias The Just on a restaurant wall. It's fun when a series of famous (and some not-so-famous) movie quotes appear to comment on the action, as for example a quote from Judy Garland ("What comeback? I've never been away") when, 85 minutes into the film, Hargitay himself finally appears. Other quotes are by the likes of Griffith and Godard, Hitchcock and Warhol, Welles and Lugosi, plus the famous sign that once graced a wall at MGM: "It's not enough to be Hungarian, you have to have talent too."

Talent György Szomjas certainly has: his previous films, including "Bald Dog Rock," "Light Physical Injuries" and "The Wall Driller" were abrasive, hard-hitting comedies. This time he's come up with an affectionate film about the U.S. which has a lot more to say — about Americans and Hungarians — than meets the eye. Film was shot in 16m, and top marks go, also, to cameraman Ferenc Grunwalsky for outstanding work. —*Strat.*

film is Tina Engel. Best known as Oskar's 4-skirted grandmother (as a young woman) in "The Tin Drum," Engel fills the bill here as a basically good hausfrau with a slightly wanton side.

She is not the only temptation Rudi faces. He is pulled in all directions and, keeping his thoughts to himself, he gets along with everyone. It is when he asserts himself that decisions have to be made and at least one fantasy comes true.

Fantasy Bardots and dream landscapes mix with a larger-than-life Vienna thanks to art direction by Rudi Czettel and Frank Brühne's camera. Other technical credits also help give a big-budget look to this production. —*Gill.*

Out Of Order
(BRITISH)

A British Film Institute-Channel 4 presentation of a Birmingham Film & Video Workshop production. (World sales: BFI, London.) Produced by Lucy Hooberman, Roger Shannon. Directed by Jonnie Turpie. Screenplay, Turpie, Graham Peet, The Dead honest Soul Searchers; camera (video, color), Terry Flaxton; music, Working Week, Wee Papa Girl Rappers; sound, Diana Rushton; production design, Jock Scott; assistant director, Rupert Ryle-Hodges; production manager, Sally Randle; casting, John Hubbard. Reviewed at Berlin Film Festival (market), Feb. 19, 1988. Running time: **95 MIN.**
Anthony Campbell . . . . Gary Webster
Sharon . . . . Sharon Fryer
Billy . . . . Pete Lee-Wilson
  Also with: Cheryl Maiker, Natasha Williams, Timmy Lawrence, Sandra Lawrence, George Baker, David Yip, Stephen Lewis, Frank Windsor, Glynn Edwards, Ricky Tomlinson, Sue Hanson, Roland Gift.

Berlin — "Out Of Order" is a low-budget, lively offering, shot on video, with an infectious music track. Pic makes fun of authority figures in Britain today via a comedy about an unemployed lad who joins the police force. It's good for tv spots.

Anthony needs a job, but his girl Sharon is appalled when he announces plans to join the police force. At a smart police dinner-dance, she insults the police chief and pursues him into the men's room to continue giving him a piece of his mind.

Meanwhile Billy, a telephone freak, has been fired because he used a phone at work to call a Washington, D.C., radio station to request a disk be played. He lands in prison, and Sharon decides to help him.

The slight storyline is amiably acted, bolstered by a gallery of well-known tv stars in cameo roles, playing traffic warden, bus drivers, senior police and the like. The music is a particular plus, and editing makes full use of video possibilities. The whole thing has a lively sense of fun. —*Strat.*

Friends
(SWEDISH-JAPANESE)

A Tiger Film (Stockholm)-Seibu Saison Group (Tokyo) production, in association with the Swedish Film Institute, Sverige TV, 41 Kobe. (World sales: Swedish Film Institute.) Produced by Börge Hansson, Yoichi Matsue. Directed by Kjell-Åke Andersson. Screenplay, Andersson, based on a play by Kobo Abe; camera (Eastmancolor), Peter Mokrosinski; editor, Michael Leszsczylowski; music, Anders Hillborg; production design, Kaj Larsen; sound, Po Persson; assistant director, Bamse Ulfing; production manager, Hans Lonnerheden; casting, Bonnie Pietila. Reviewed at Berlin Film Fest (market), Feb. 20, 1988. Running time: **84 MIN.**
John . . . . Dennis Christopher
Zeb . . . . Sven Wollter
Matt . . . . Stellan Skarsgård
Sue . . . . Lena Olin
Jennifer . . . . Anita Wall
Sally . . . . Edita Brychta
  Also with: Aino Taube (Matilda), Helena Bergstrom (Bonnie), Richard Craig Nelson (Client), Anki Liden (Blond).
  (English soundtrack)

Berlin — This Swedish-Japanese coproduction, based on a Japanese play, is set in an unnamed North American city (film was shot in Calgary, Alberta) and spoken in multi-accented English. It demonstrates all the pitfalls of an international production.

Though brilliantly photographed, and with an intriguing central theme, the film misses out because it has no roots. It doesn't ring true, so that the strange story has no realistic base on which to build.

John is a yuppie bachelor living in a swank apartment and working as an investigator on divorce cases. He's engaged to the beautiful Sally, and life seems to be good until a model plane crashes through his window one day, followed by an obnoxious child. This event is the precursor of an invasion by a strange family, who simply walk into the apartment and take over. They consist of husband and wife, grandmother, son and two daughters, and they blithely ignore John's protests; he calls the police, but they do nothing.

The strangers keep telling John they're his friends. The older daughter seduces him, the younger flirts with him, and the son makes a play for his fiancée. He finds himself powerless to do anything, his work is affected, and he becomes, literally, a prisoner when they strait-jacket him, though he's a strangely willing one.

On the stage in Japan, this might have worked very well, because in the Japanese context what seems rather silly in the film might have been convincing. Relocating the film to Anywhere, U.S.A., has been no help, although the city is brilliantly photographed by Peter Mokrosinski. On the other hand, had director Kjell-Åke Andersson (who replaced Czech helmer Jan Nemec during production) played up the erotic aspects of the story he might have come up with a sexually interesting arthouse item; but the various sexual encounters are

---

Berlin Film Reviews

Vergessen Sie's
(Just Forget It)
(WEST GERMAN)

A C. Cay Wesnigk Film production in conjunction with West German ZDF television and Hamburg Filmburo. Written and directed by C. Cay Wesnigk. Camera (color, 16m), Bernd Meiners; editor, Christoph Janetzko; music, Thomas Bauer; sound, Alf Olbrisch. Reviewed at Berlin Film Festival (New German Cinema section), Feb. 20, 1988. Running time: **80 MIN.**
Thomas Novak . . . . Edgar Marcus
Karl Fischer . . . . Bernd Blasen
Ali Chrysosto . . . . Necati Sahin

Berlin — C. Cay Wesnigk, 25, makes an impressive bow with his first feature-lengther, which follows in the "Silkwood" vein of films about hapless individuals up against corporate monsters.

Wesnigk's film is flawed by a plodding storyline and stolid acting, but his action sequences indicate he has potential. German lingo and 16m format limit export possibilities from the start.

A taxi driver (Edgar Marcus) thinks he sees a human arm flop out of a garbage bin as trashmen heave it into a truck. Despite a policeman's advice to "just forget it," he checks out the municipal waste treatment plant, where he is pursued by guards with dobermans and, later, is almost run off the road by snowplows.

Meanwhile, a plant official (Bernd Blasen) learns the reason for such tight security — a special team of workers daily pokes through trash from selected addresses in search of evidence that could incriminate enemies of the state.

Plot may sound farfetched to non-Germans, but Wesnigk's message is not lost on audiences in a country where some older persons would still prefer to "just forget" what happened in the 1930s and 1940s.

The taxi driver's headlong flight through an eerie garbage treatment plant is effectively harrowing, and there is some good camerawork here, underscored by chilling music.

The screenplay is too weak to get Marcus and Blasen through the slow parts when they are required to speak laughable lines.

Tech credits are above average for a 16m production. —*Gill.*

Die Verlockung
(The Temptation)
(AUSTRIAN)

A Heinz Scheiderbauer production. Directed by Dieter Berner. Screenplay, Peter Turrini, Rudi Palla; camera (color), Frank Brühne; editor, Ingrid Koller; music, Matthias Rüegg; art direction, Rudi Czettel; sound, Ekkehart Bauming, Karl Schlifelner. Reviewed at Berlin Film Festival (Panorama), Feb. 20, 1988. Running time: **90 MIN.**
Rudi Baha . . . . Levin Kress
Manfred . . . . Fritz Karl
Brigitte Bardot . . . . . . Therese Jagersberger
Fritz Anders . . . . Dominic Raacke
Gitti . . . . Sabine Gautier
Frau Priessnitz . . . . Tina Engel
  Also with: Hans Brenner (Herr Priessnitz), Hilde Berger (Olga Blaha), Helmut Berger (Karl Blaha), Bela Erny (Johannes Heesters), Johann Ivancits (union leader).

Berlin — This handsome production is a visual delight, vividly creating Vienna of the early 1960s as seen through the eyes of an impressionable 17-year-old daydreamer. Film should travel, despite Austrian dialect and a storyline that stalls when attempting too much.

In the eyes of adolescent Rudi (Levin Kress), Vienna is big, colorful and exciting — there's a fantasy in every billboard and at every snackbar. Somehow a lot of the women in ads and on posters look just like Brigitte Bardot, his not-so-secret love. He and his pal Manfred are so concerned for her welfare that they have decided to go to St. Tropez to protect her. The head of the local Young Socialists group wants Rudi to work on a film project. Then there's Gritti, whom both boys are interested in, not to mention an "older woman" who just moved into the neighborhood.

Kress handles his challenging role well, showing the embarrassment, jealousy and swagger of a 17-year-old. The other bright spot in this

rigorously downplayed, and seen, at most, in silhouette.

In the pivotal central role, Dennis Christopher is ill-at-ease and strident. The Swedish actors who play the members of the strange family are professional, and speak with light Swedish accents. Stellan Skarsgard as the slightly sinister son is impressive. As the hero's beleaguered fiancée, Edita Brychta makes an impression.

Film technically is sumptuous, with an interesting Japanese-style music score by Anders Hillborg and very sharp sound recording. It will be tough to find an audience for this one, because the compromises made in the concept will alienate arthouse audiences, while the pic doesn't deliver enough to make it acceptable in broader venues. Even on video, it may find the going tough, unless very provocatively packaged.

—*Strat.*

Enigma
(FRENCH-ITALIAN)

A KWK Kinowerke/CNRS/INA coproduction. Written and directed by Jean Rouch, Alberto Chiantaretto, Marco di Castri, Daniele Pianciola. Camera (color), Rouch, Di Castri; editor, Françoise Beloux; art direction, Unistudio, Galliano Habitat. Reviewed at the Berlin Film Festival (Forum), Feb. 17, 1988. Running time: **80 MIN.**

Gilbert ....Gilbert Mazliah
Patron ....Gianfranco Barberi
Sabina ....Sabina Sacchi
Also with: Philo Bregstein, Giorgio Bono, Sandro Franchina, Sauro Roma.

Berlin — "Enigma," a co-effort between Jean Rouch and three young Italo helmers making their feature film bow, fails to bridge satisfactorily the gap between all its heterogeneous elements.

Though filmmakers would no doubt describe its mysterious plot concerning an artist assigned to forge a De Chirico painting as enigmatic, it comes across as simply unreadable, and quite often uninteresting. A hard sell, pic may find some tv viewership with a little luck.

Premise is not without merits: curly-locked French painter Gilbert (Gilbert Mazliah) is invited to live in a fairy tale castle that has been transformed into a private art museum by millionaire collector Sir Richard (Gianfranco Barberi). His assignment is to produce a metaphysical painting of the city of Turin, a work projected by Giorgio De Chirico but never begun.

While Gilbert scours the modern city in search of inspiration (tailed by Sir Richard's beautiful, sphinx-like cohort Sabina Sacchi), he meets a group of kids and joins them on their outings. Though whole cast has a distinctly non-pro look, Mazliah is good at projecting a quality of childlike curiosity, making his honorary membership in the kids' gang plausible. Best of all, he's a real artist able to make drawings on-camera.

In the empty, echoing halls of the castle, Gilbert plows ahead on a modern painting full of bright colors — more children's art than De Chirico, but the creative process is fun to watch. Outside, he seriously discusses with the band how they can get an old WWI submarine to work and take them to Egypt. They meet other characters including an eccentric philosopher (Philo Bregstein) and a magician (Sandro Franchina) who works in a car factory. The final voyage to Egypt, we are given to understand, is no less real for taking place in the kids' imagination.

Gilbert's final output, meanwhile, is three paintings of metaphysical intent. Their meaning remains as puzzling to the viewer as it is to his philistine patron; the one nice, comprehensible touch is a submarine in the background of one.

It may be a case of too many cooks (and Rouch can't resist throwing in some footage from one of his African ethnographic docus, for good measure), but "Enigma" is enough to send any adult scurrying for the nearest sub to Luxor. Or is it the first metaphysical kidpic?

—*Yung.*

Einer Trage des Anderen Last
(Bear Ye One Another's Burdens)
(EAST GERMAN)

A DEFA Feature Film Studio (Babelsburg Group) production. Directed by Lothar Warneke. Screenplay, Wolfgang Held; camera (Orwocolor), Peter Ziesche; editor, Erika Lehmphul; art direction, Alfred Hirschmeier. Reviewed at Berlin Film Festival (competing), Feb. 15, 1988. Running time: **118 MIN.**

Josef Heiliger ....Jorg Pose
Hubertus Koschenz ......Manfred Mock
Sonja Kubanek ....Susanne Lüning
Sister ....Karin Gregorek
Dr. Stülpmann ......Hein Dieter Knaup
Sister Inka ....Doris Thalmer

Berlin — Don Camillo meets Thomas Mann in "Bear Ye One Another's Burdens," an improbable, often funny drama of Communism and Christianity battling it out in a "Magic Mountain"-style sanatorium.

Lothar Warneke, one of East Germany's top helmers, is peculiarly qualified for the assignment, having been a Protestant vicar before he left the church. Film is one of the most accessible entertainments to come out of East Germany in some time, with a winning cast and fine Old World setting.

Gentle fun gets poked at both ideologies, offending no one, and concluding with a plea no one can take issue with — better understanding and tolerance between men. This diplomatic film for the era of detente could well find audiences East and West with special handling.

Josef Heiliger is a youthful People's Commissar in 1950, sent to a private sanatorium (as pic opens) to recover from acute tuberculosis. As

played by Jörg Pose, Heiliger is an idealistic bigot in a uniform, whose first act is to put a portrait of Stalin over his bed. He is rudely surprised to find a young Protestant vicar, Hubertus Koschenz (Manfred Möck), assigned as his roommate. Koschenz tacks a picture of Jesus over his bed.

The symmetrical antagonism begins — Heiliger calls a party meeting, Koschenz a prayer meeting; one hums the "Internationale" while shaving, the other "A Mighty Fortress Is Our God." As the minister, Möck is a good comic foil for Heiliger, even if script makes him into too much of a mirror image to be equally believable as a character. When they demand separate rooms, the good doctor who runs the clinic (Hein Dieter Knaup) counsels tolerance — Christians and Socialists have to live in the same world, after all. The limits of this rather too simplistic message are the limits of the film.

Echoes of Thomas Mann notwithstanding, "Bear Ye" unfolds predictably. There is an innocent young girl (Susanne Lüning) for romance, and later tragedy. There is a new wonder drug that could save Heiliger, but difficult to procure. Koschenz silently obtains it for his archrival. The inevitable clashes between the two naturally end in undying friendship and symbolic last handshake in a churchyard.

Whatever its shortcomings, however, film is significant for its liberal message put over in an appealing, popular style. Peter Ziesche's lensing is adept and smooth; music score is on the hackneyed side.

—*Yung.*

Off Limits

A 20th Century Fox release. Produced by Alan Barnette. Directed by Christopher Crowe. Screenplay, Crowe, Jack Thibeau; camera (Deluxe color), David Gribble; editor, Douglas Ibold; music, James Newton Howard; production design, Dennis Washington; set decoration, Chrispian Sallis; art direction, Scott Ritenour; sound (Dolby), David Lee; assistant director, Doug Metzger; associate producer, Michael S. Glick; casting, Mike Fenton, Jane Feinberg, June Taylor. Reviewed at 20th Fox Zanuck theater, L.A. March 3, 1988. MPAA Rating: R. Running time: **102 MIN.**

Buck McGriff ....Willem Dafoe
Albaby Perkins ....Gregory Hines
Dix.....................Fred Ward
Nicole ....Amanda Pays
Line Green ....Kay Tong Lim
Col. Armstrong ....Scott Glenn

Hollywood — Exploitation films aren't usually associated with major studios like Fox and maybe "Off Limits" wasn't intended to turn out so. For what it is — a black-white buddy cop story set in 1968 Saigon — pic is mildly entertaining, if clearly derivative of more thoroughly executed actioners.

Pic should earn some decent coin for its appeal to the crowd that enjoys macho posturing, done well by the duo of Willem Dafoe and Gregory Hines.

"Off Limits" is a well-crafted story by Christopher Crowe and Jack Thibeau that explores the underbelly of Saigon well enough as two undercover detectives (Dafoe, Hines) go about to solve a string of prostitute murders by a high-ranking Army officer. While the plot and characterizations are well worked out, what this production lacks is enough pizzazz to distinguish it from others of this genre.

Dafoe and Hines stick together like glue, working diligently in the sticky Saigon heat with equally racist attitudes about "gooks" and "slopes." Dafoe is a little more hot-tempered and Hines only slightly less intense.

So serious are they, even when tracking AWOL soldiers, that the production is at nearly all times gloomy, especially after they realize the importance of their assignment — finding which Army officer is cavorting with whores and then wasting them.

With Bangkok backstreets acting as Saigon, plainclothes Criminal Investigations Detachment Officers Buck McGriff (Dafoe) and Albaby Perkins (Hines) find the last months of their tour of duty not exactly to be the winding-down period they anticipated, being that they're not in a combat zone.

Vietnam certainly is fast becoming an exploited territory for all kinds of films these days, but an exotic war zone setting doesn't really add much intrigue to this urban cop caper. This is much more a civilian story that only twice puts the action out in the country where the bombs are exploding. As such, with the exception of one scene where a sadist colonel, whom Dafoe and Hines suspect of being the sicko murderer, is pushing Vietcong out of a helicopter, lensing could have been accomplished on the backlot.

Director Crowe has tried to make a tough picture with sensitivity, though it's the former that mostly prevails. Dafoe has a platonic affection for a nun (Amanda Pays) who counsels prostitutes and takes care of their children. Hines fancies himself a red-blooded American who loves well-endowed women and UCLA basketball. There is little tension between them and so all the aggression is against the Vietcong and the unknown suspect.

Fred Ward is particularly good as the partners' superior, Master Sgt. Dix. He acts like the good soldier who plays it right by his men, which turns out to be crucial to how things are solved in the end.

There are about as many unbelievable coincidences as one would find in the average "Missing In Action" or "Rambo" pic, but the scripters finessed them by busying things up with frequent changes of scenery and some clever twists they are less noticeable. Why is it always with this type of genre picture that the U.S. Army always manages to show up when the protagonists are in dire straits? Again here, it's as if Saigon were a 2-street town where nothing goes unobserved — except for the purposes of serving the story.

Editing by Douglas Ibold continues to the film's fast pace and David Gribble's camerawork is fine for exploring the ins and outs of undesirable places. —*Brit.*

The Everlasting Secret Family
(AUSTRALIAN)

A Hemdale Film Corp. release of an FGH presentation for Intl. Film Management Ltd. Executive producer, Antony Ginnane. Co-produced by Sue Carelton. Produced and directed by Michael Thornhill. Screenplay, Frank Moorhouse, based on his book of short stories "The Everlasting Secret Family And Other Secrets;" camera (Eastmancolor), Julian Penney; editor, Pam Barnetta; music, Tony Bremner; art direction, Peta Lawson; production manager, Elizabeth Symes. Reviewed at the Crown Preview theater, London, Jan. 21, 1988. Running time **94 MIN.**

Senator	Arthur Dignam
Youth	Mark Lee
Eric	Dennis Miller
Senator's wife	Heather Mitchell
Son	Paul Goddard
Judge	John Mellion
Potter's woman	Beth Child

London — "The Everlasting Secret Family" is something of an oddity. A contempo Australian pic dealing with a secret homosexual society, it succeeds in being ponderous and dull when it could and should have been provocative and controversial.

A distinguished cast of Oz thesps perform well but cannot make the material convincing let alone interesting, leaving the blame squarely with scripter Frank Moorhouse (who wrote "The Coca-Cola Kid")

and helmer Michael Thornhill. Box-office prospects look equally dull.

Pic opens with a senator (Arthur Dignam), visiting a boys' school where he selects a youngster (Mark Lee) to have his wicked way with. Lee proves to be a petulant boy-toy, and after a brief attempt to leave the decadent world of Dignam he settles into his sexually corrupt "secret family."

To further his career Dignam marries Heather Mitchell and they have a son. Lee sets about corrupting the boy, Paul Goddard, and despite Mitchell's disapproval he and Dignam introduce Goddard to the shrouded society of homosexuals.

Arthur Dignam and Mark Lee are excellent as the senator and his young lover, and try hard to give the pic deeper nuances despite a pretentious script. John Mellion also is fine as the elderly judge whose tastes run towards bondage and masochism.

Producer/director Michael Thornhill gives the film an elegant, rich quality, and though he quite obviously wants to be provoking many scenes come across as just bland. Inadvertently amusing are scenes of initiation into the "secret family" where chaps hop about doing a sword dance while wearing costume masks.

Technical credits for "The Everlasting Secret Family" are all fine, but while the pic undoubtably is original and oddly surreal it also is humorless, empty and more importantly disappointing considering the talents involved.—*Adam.*

And God Created Woman

A Vestron Pirctures release in association with Crow Prods. of a Braunstein & Hamady production. Produced by George G. Braunstein, Ron Hamady. Executive producers, Steven Reuther, Mitchell Cannold, Ruth Vitale. Co-executive producers, Emilia Crow, Robert Crow. Supervising producer, Patrick McCormick. Directed by Roger Vadim. Screenplay, R.J. Stewart; camera (Deluxe color), Stephen M. Katz; editor, Suzanne Pettit; music, Thomas Chase, Steve Rucker; production design, Victor Kempster; set decoration, Robin Laughlin, Guido DeCurtis; costume design, Sharman Forman-Hyde; sound (Dolby), Frank Stettner; assistant director, Peter Giuliano; casting, Amanda Mackey. Reviewed at the Directors Guild of America Theater, L.A., Feb. 29, 1988. MPAA Rating: R. Running time: **94 MIN.**

Robin Shay	Rebecca DeMornay
Billy Moran	Vincent Spano
James Tiernan	Frank Langella
Peter Moran	Donovan Leitch
Alexandra Tiernan	Judith Chapman
Timmy Moran	Jaime McEnnan
Blue	Benjamin Mouton
David	David Shelley
Einstein	Einstein Brown
Hawk	David Lopez

Hollywood — A remake in name only of his first feature, made 32 years ago, Roger Vadim's new film called "And God Created Woman" is considerably more legitimate dramatically than one might have expected from such an undertaking. At the same time, it betrays no compelling reason for being, meaning

that audiences probably will feel little reason to put this high among their viewing priorities.

Original 1956 pic was one of the breakthrough French sex imports and made Brigitte Bardot an international sensation. The St. Tropez locations, frank eroticism and Bardot's casual amorality proved titillating, even perhaps mildly shocking, in the context of the times.

Well, the times have changed a bit, and Vadim, accepting the dubious task of reapplying himself to his most famous work, wisely jettisoned the original plot and avoided any temptation to try to outdo himself here.

Rather, he has taken a relatively unpromising story and, with a surprisingly sound script by R.J. Stewart, told a modestly involving tale about how a woman with two strikes against her gives herself a shot at life through a combination of sex, imagination, energy and plenty of scheming.

Attention-grabbing opening has inmate Rebecca DeMornay escaping from prison and hitching a ride in a limo belonging to New Mexico gubernatorial candidate Frank Langella, only to be deposited right back where she came from.

In the picture's hottest scene, she then gets it on with carpenter Vincent Spano and wins early parole by convincing this earnest young single father to marry her. She takes up residence in the Santa Fe home Spano shares with his musician brother, but DeMornay lays a major surprise on her husband when she announces that their marriage contract does not include sex, which instantly puts a major strain on the relationship.

Nor is the tough, willful, hardbitten young lady very interested in doing housework. Instead, she spends her time trying to put together a rock band, as well as seducing the would-be governor while his wife is away.

DeMornay's best-laid plans eventually come crashing down on her but she pulls things out in the end with a raunchy display of rock 'n' roll form that wins over even the starchiest members of the community.

Some of the dramatic developments, particularly the later ones, are farfetched and implausible, but they tend to play better than they

read on paper because screenwriter Stewart had endowed the proceedings with an emotional validity that is as unexpected as it is welcome. Principal characters all come alive and behave in utterly believable ways given developments, which is rare enough in any film.

Credit for this also belongs to the actors, who without exception delivery serious performances that yield continuous insights into their characters. DeMornay has thrown herself deeply into the part and makes a strong impression as a life-long loser now determined to win at all costs. Spano's macho exterior is nicely modified as the story progresses with considerable emotional shading, and Langella is just right as the politico who is most intrigued by DeMornay but knows he could get burned by her.

Nice Santa Fe settings help the film look good. Pic is ultimately of small consequence, but is handled more capably than anything else Vadim has done in many years and possesses a certain appeal. — *Cart.*

Et Dieu ... Créa La Femme
(FRENCH)

A Cocinor release of a Raoul Lévy-Iéna-UCIL-Cocinor production. Stars Brigitte Bardot, Curt Jurgens, Jean-Louis Trintignant; features Christian Marquand, Georges Poujouly. Written and directed by Roger Vadim. Camera (Cinemascope, Eastmancolor), Armand Thirard; editor, Victoria Mercanton; music, Paul Misraki. At Normandie, Paris, Jan. 15, 1957. Running time: **90 MIN.**

Promis .. Juré!
(Cross My Heart)
(FRENCH)

A Gaumont production and release. Produced by Alain Poiré. Directed by Jacques Monnet. Screenplay, Monnet, Gérard Carre; camera (Eastmancolor), Claude Lecomte; editor, Françoise Garnault; music, Vladimir Cosma; art direction, Pierre-Louis Thevenet; costumes, Agnès Negre; sound, Alain Lachassagne; assistant director, Vincent Monnet; casting, Mamade; production manager, Marc Goldstaub. Reviewed at the Gaumont Ambassade cinema, Paris, Jan. 22, 1988. Running time: **98 MIN.**

Pierre Marie	Michel Morin
Jean Charles	Roland Giraud
Madeleine	Christine Pascal
Dora	Andréa Ferréol
Hans	Mandred Andrae
Frédo	Stéphane Legros

Also with: Marie Constant, Henele Duc, Annik Alane, Kathy Kriegel, Penelope Schellenberg, Céline Samie.

Paris — "Promis .. Juré!" is another entry in the current childhood wartime memoirs trend exemplified by John Boorman's "Hope And Glory" and Louis Malle's "Au revoir, les enfants." Lacking the style and historical texture of these prior pics this Gaumont production does have some anecdotal charm.

Jacques Monnet, a commercials helmer who has two Gaumont feature comedies to his credit, wrote and directed from his own souvenirs as a child in occupied Normandy just before D-Day. His young alter ego, Pierre Marie (portrayed by newcomer Michel Morin), is a 12-year-old student somewhat neglected by his parents and feeling inferior because of a slightly protuberant nose (though he's no Cyrano).

Monnet's script revolves around some of the boy's misadventures with schoolmates, the Black Market, and climactically a German deserter who decides to hole up in the family basement until the war ends.

When the Americans liberate the town, the child finds himself leading the German out at machine-gun point and becomes a local hero.

Monnet puts the accent on humor but doesn't really succeed in communicating the underlying anxiety of the time. The period recreation is adequate as are supporting performances. —Len.

Moving

A Warner Bros. release. Produced by Stuart Cornfeld. Directed by Alan Metter. Screenplay, Andy Breckman. Camera (Technicolor), Donald McAlpine; editor, Alan Balsam; music, Howard Shore; production design, David L. Snyder; art direction, Joe Wood; set decoration, Linda DeScenna; costume design, Deborah L. Scott; sound (Dolby), Jim Tanenbaum; associate producer, Kim Kurumada; assistant director, Marty Ewing; second unit director, Terry Leonard; second unit camera, Don Burgess, Tom Ackerman; casting, Marion Dougherty. Reviewed at the Chinese theater, L.A., March 4, 1988. MPAA Rating: R. Running time: **89 MIN.**

Arlo Pear	Richard Pryor
Monica Pear	Beverly Todd
Gary Marcus	Dave Thomas
Brad Williams	Dana Carvey
Frank/Cornell Crawford	Randy Quaid
Casey Pear	Stacey Dash
Marshall Pear	Raphael Harris
Randy Pear	Ishmael Harris
Perry	Robert La Sardo
Edwards	Ji-Tu
Gorgo	King Kong Bundy
Rudy	Morris Day
Banker	Rodney Dangerfield

Hollywood — At one point in "Moving," Richard Pryor comments that, rather than being one big joke, "Life is a series of 89,000 little jokes." Unfortunately, very few of them made it into the picture, a meek little comedy that Warner Bros. declined to screen in advance and which looks to open well but pull out of the neighborhood within a few short weeks.

In a far cry from his earlier wild characters, Pryor here plays a full-fledged Oreo, an upper-middle-class buppie so unstreetwise that he flashes the wrong finger at his boss when fired from his well-paid job in New Jersey.

The mild-mannered fellow, whom everyone picks upon and takes advantage of, finally secures a first-class job in his line of mass-transit engineering, but it's in Boise, Idaho. His wife, Beverly Todd, quickly comes around to the idea of transplanting the family, but their trendy princess of a daughter, Stacey Dash, can't abide leaving her boyfriend and Friday nights at the mall, so she goes to extreme lengths to sabotage all efforts to sell the house.

Also making life no easier are next-door neighbor Randy Quaid, a raving madman who might have been Rambo's partner in Vietnam, and a sinister 3-man moving team whose members look like they strayed off the set of "The Road Warrior."

What with all the hitches and complications, it takes Pryor and family a full hour of screen time to get out of the house and on the road. When he finally arrives in Idaho, Pryor is crossed once too often, the lamb turns himself into a lion, jumps into his Mad Max mobile and kicks some butt from Boise to Butte.

Watching the usually tenacious, clever and hip Pryor playing this milquetoast Arlo Pear is a bit disconcerting. The character resembles one of his classic "white" impersonations in his standup comedy routines, and it's almost as if he had been neutered and drained of all his cool.

Supporting performers all put in energetic turns, and Rodney Dangerfield, star of director Alan Metter's previous comedy, "Back To School," puts in an uncredited couple of minutes as an amoral bank loan officer.

The concept and plotting of Andy Breckman's story remain irredeemably thin, and matters aren't helped by the somewhat cheesy-looking production values. —Cart.

Pass The Ammo

A New Century/Vista release of a Vista Organization production. Produced by Herb Jaffe, Mort Engelberg. Line producer, David Strait. Directed by David Beaird. Screenplay, Neil Cohen, Joel Cohen; camera (Deluxe color) Mark Irwin; editor, Bill Yahraus; music, Carter Burwell; production design, Dean Tschetter; art direction, Mayling Cheng; set decoration, Michele Starbuck; costume design, Reve Richards; sound (Ultra-Stereo), Walt Martin; special effects coordinator, Rick Josephson; assistant director, Steven Buck; associate producer, Bill Yahraus; casting, Nina Axelrod. Reviewed at AMC Century 14 theater, L.A., Feb. 23, 1988. MPAA Rating: R. Running time: **97 MIN.**

Jesse	Bill Paxton
Claire	Linda Kozlowski
Ray	Tim Curry
Darla	Annie Potts
Big Joe	Dennis Burkley
Arnold	Glenn Withrow
Stonewall	Anthony Geary

Hollywood — Timing of the Jimmy Swaggart scandal was a major stroke of luck for this lampoon of tv evangelists, but it would take an act by a higher source than Swaggart to save this effort. Where messed-up ministries are concerned, there's better entertainment on the nightly news.

Hereafter of video rentals is pic's only hope for glory, as b.o. collection plate will come up wanting.

Tim Curry and Annie Potts play the Reverend Ray and his wife Darla, who broadcast from the garish "Tower Of Bethlehem" studios somewhere in deepest Arkansas. A band of 2-bit backwoods thieves, led by Bill Paxton and Linda Kozlowski (last seen in "Crocodile Dundee"), break into the studio vaults to recover money bilked from the gal's grandma. Cops show up, so the burglars burst into the studio to hold the evangelists hostage during their live tv broadcast.

Plot, barely clunking along, stalls out at this point. Endless live tv standoff between cops and robbers (who never get around to stating their demands) puts pressure on the ordained hosts, who break down and reveal what charlatans they are. It's all grand entertainment for the simple folk shown fastened to their tv screens at home — so much so that a Jerry Falwell-like church heavyweight (Richard Paul) orders the guv to have the National Guard blow the whole studio to its just reward — with everyone inside.

Not before Paxton, an anti-hero with a Robin Hood complex, can shake down his captive guests with lines like "Ministry, huh? What about your two Rolls Royces, your house in Palm Desert, and the one in Bermuda?"

At one point Rev. Ray turns to the camera and confesses, "I have sinned." Line drew howls from the house in light of recent events.

Basic idea could have been a hoot, if only pic didn't keep veering out of control.

Screenwriters Neil Cohen and Joel Cohen seem to have only the vaguest idea of who their characters are or what their story is about, and rely on the weariest clichés — like the shoot 'em up finale — to fill out the plot. Minus all the guns being waved around, pic would have no tension at all.

Director David Beaird seems to equate comedy with dumbness. Effort to make support characters memorable backfires, as woolly backwoods locals become as laughable as the evangelists, and a sympathetic Cajun sheriff (Leland Crooke) seems totally out of place.

Only Annie Potts, as the Rev.'s slightly unhinged wife, and Anthony Geary, as a subversive studio technician, create credible characters. Kozlowski should have waited this one out. Curry plays himself, and Paxton is justifiably lost.

Affable score mixes country hoke and hosannahs in the right spirit with songs like "Lay Your Money Down For Jesus" and production numbers like "Samson & Delilah."

Game-show like production design for Tower of Bethlehem interiors is garish enough to embarrass Las Vegas.

Casting of identical twins John and Paul Cody, who resemble Robert Goulet in rhinestone cowboy suits, as co-hosts on the show is a classic touch.—Daws.

Rorret
(ITALIAN)

A Nuova Dimensione production in association with RAI-TV Channel 1. Directed by Fulvio Wetzl. Screenplay, Wetzl, Enzo Capua; camera (Eastmancolor), Carlo Cerchio; editor, Massimo Palumbo Cardella; music, Florian Schneider, Ferruccio Busoni; art direction, Bruno Rapisarda; costumes, Alessandra Montagna; production manager, Giannandrea Pecorelli. Reviewed at the Berlin Film Festival (Forum), Feb. 18, 1988. Running time: **103 MIN.**

Rorret	Lou Castel
Barbara	Anna Galiena
Carlo	Massimo Venturiello
Sara	Enrica Rosso
Sheila	Rossana Coggiola

Also with: Claudia Giannottio, Fabrizio Temperini, Patrizia Punzo (Cecilia).

Berlin — Three years in the making, debut feature by Fulvio Wetzl (former manager of a Rome film club) is a thriller made by and for cinephiles. Its audience may not be much larger than that.

Those up on their movies will get a charge out of identifying pastiche excerpts from famous classics, which dot the tale of a psychopathic theater owner who lives behind the screen of his cinema. Regular filmgoers will identify most excerpts, anyway (who can miss the shower sequence from "Psycho?"). What they'll have trouble with is following the convoluted, often incoherent plot, which leads to nothing but trouble as it progresses.

Cast of barely-pros is one problem; only thesp able to carry out the demands of the difficult role is Lou Castel as the murderous exhib, Rorret. Dressed like Peter Lorre in "M," Castel makes Rorret a sympathetic, intense, but not really penetrable nut, unable to restrain his rampaging unconscious desire to do away with the female part of his cast. For some reason (the first, fatal credibility gap), pretty girls find this short, tongue-tied introvert irresistible. He chooses his victims from the audience; whoever shows the most fright at the scary scenes attracts him. He strangles Rossana Coggiola in an amusement park funhouse; then takes the corpse home. Conveniently, the theater is attached to an abandoned church, where he lays out the body in a crypt.

Lively artist Anna Galiena accidently stays alive through several scenes, but eventually ends up under glass in the church, too. The ticket-taker Enrica Rosso, married to dumb theater manager Massimo Venturiello in a senseless subplot, plays detective Nancy Drew-style, and stumbles onto the truth just in time to save hysterical actress Patricia Punzo from meeting the other girls' fate.

In his directorial bow, Wetzl demonstrates a great number of ideas, but few of them are very original. The recreated scenes from "Psycho," "Strangers On A Train," "Dial M For Murder," Michael Powell's "Peeping Tom" and Otto Preminger's "Bunny Lake is Missing" are cute pieces and quite fun. Whole film is such a medley of influences, however, it has the taste of warmed-over lunch. Wetzl nevertheless shows he knows his masters, and is striving after quality work. His next effort could be a surprise if it breaks out of the cineaste mode. —Yung.

Who Killed Vincent Chin?
(DOCU)

A film by Christine Choy and Renee Tajima. Produced by Film News Now Foundation and WTVS Detroit. Executive producer, Juanita Anderson. Directed by Choy. Camera (color, 16m), Choy, Nick Doob, Kyle Kibbe, Al Santana; editor, Holly Fisher; interviews, Tajima; associate producer, Nancy Mei-Yu Tong; sound, Ira Spiegel, Mark Rance, Sylvie Thouard. Reviewed at Roy & Nuita Titus Theater 2, N.Y. (In New Directors/New Films), Feb. 29, 1988. No MPAA Rating. Running time: 87 MIN.

It's sadly appropriate that this documentary about racism and the paradoxical nature of American justice should be ironically titled. Not only is the killer of Chinese-American auto engineer Vincent Chin known, but Detroit autoworker Ron Ebens, who battered Chin lifeless with a baseball bat in the aftermath of a 1982 barroom brawl, is a willing participant in this disturbing study of how he got away with murder.

Destined for public tv via its WTVS Detroit production genesis, "Who Killed Vincent Chin?" should be a candidate for the docu sections of various international film festivals.

Filmmaker Christine Choy examines the Chin case from the perspective of the American dream gone bad in Detroit. Gritty Motown -- the once monolithic automaker to the world and magnet of opportunity for American workers — is depicted as a city angry and defensive about the encroachment of Japanese automobile imports and the subsequent ravages of unemployment amongst formerly prosperous skilled craftsmen.

Conflicting accounts of the events leading up to Chin's death deepen the sense of capriciousness surrounding the tragedy, but it's apparent that anti-Asian racism, fueled by bitterness over Japanese competition, was a crucial factor. Most witnesses suggest that the barroom confrontation between Ebens and Chin began with differing opinions on the virtues of a topless dancer, escalated into ethnically barbed insults about Japanese and local unemployment and led to a fistfight in which Ebens got the worst of it.

A drunk and furious Ebens, together with his stepson Michael Nitz (an unemployed auto worker), pursued Chin to a nearby hamburger stand and murdered him in a brutal beating that was witnessed and broken up too late by an off-duty police officer.

Ebens, a white, middle-aged Chrysler worker who had come to Detroit from a Wisconsin farm, contritely admits his deed, attributes the incident to unfortunate timing and too much drinking and flatly denies harboring racist sentiments. Following a guilty plea to manslaughter, Ebens was let off with a suspended sentence and a $3,000 fine. To Chin's inconsolable mother — whose grief is used by the filmmaker to hammer home the outrage of the victim's family and friends — it was an unconscionable injustice that the killer of her son would not spend a single day in jail.

The case was kept alive by Chin's family, friends and sympathetic activists who succeeded in bringing federal civil rights violations charges against the killer. Ebens was found guilty by a Detroit Federal Court and sentenced to 25 years in jail, but his appeal was upheld by the Cincinnati Circuit Court which set him free. In his low-key but aggrieved interviews with the filmmakers Ebens portrays himself as a victim of media witch-hunting.

Local tv news coverage of the case indicates that many in Detroit were outraged by the perceived miscarriage of justice but, like Chin's family, eventually were thwarted in seeking redress. The ultimate irony of the Chin case and the film's unifying theme is the location of possible answers to its titular question far from the fateful night when two strangers locked destinies in a chance confrontation. —Rich.

Slaughterhouse Rock

A Taurus Entertainment Co. release of a First Intl. Film Capital/Arista Films presentation. Produced by Louis George. Executive producers, Nick Celozzi Sr., Joseph Medawar. Directed by Dimitri Logothetis. Screenplay, Ted Landon; camera (color), Nicholas Von Sternberg; editor, Daniel Gross; music, Mark Mothersbaugh, Gerald V. Casale; music performed by Devo; production coordinator, Jennifer West; assistant director, Richard Hench; production design, Peter Paul Raubertas; associate producers, Orlando Vestuto, Maurice Ettleson, Daniel Somrack. Reviewed at the Davis Theater, Chicago, Feb. 28, 1988. MPAA Rating: R. Running time: 90 MIN.

Alex Gardner . . . . Nicholas Celozzi
Richard Gardner . . . . Tom Reilly
Carolyn Harding . . . . Donna Denton
Sammy Mitchell . . . . Toni Basil
Krista Halpern . . . . Hope Marie Carlton
Jack . . . . Steven Brian Smith
Marty . . . . Ty Miller
The Commandant . . . . Al Fleming

Chicago — "Slaughterhouse Rock" is an ambitious, low-budget horror pic with a concept that is rich with potential — imagine "Nightmare On Elm Street Goes To The Slammer." Unfortunately, like the cannibal demon that provides the title carnage by turning most of the cast into snack food, "Slaughterhouse" bites off more than it can chew. The result is a mess.

B.o. potential is limited to word of mouth among hardcore horror-philes, who certainly will be attracted to the film's jucier moments.

Complicated plot centers around Alcatraz Island, supposedly that not-so-final resting place of U.S. cavalry commandant Mordecai G. Langston, a model officer in all respects except for his pact with the devil and his habit of killing, torturing and eating people. Occult-buff femme rock 'n' roller Sammy Mitchell (Toni Basil) takes a tour boat to the island and unleashes Langston's evil spirit to learn his dark secrets. Instead, his spirit kills and possesses Mitchell, who in turn kills everybody who happens to be standing around, including the members of her wholesome band, Bodybag. Repentant, Mitchell's spirit makes a psychic search for a champion to do battle with the demon she revived.

That huge chunk of exposition is revealed only in flashback, late in the film, a ploy that results in confusion instead of mystery. Picture opens with Alex Gardner (Nicholas Celozzi), suffering some unexplained nasty visions involving Alcatraz and the Commandant. On the questionable advice of one of his teachers, he goes to Alcatraz with several friends to confront the dreams at their source. One of the party is possessed by the demon and begins killing off the others while Gardner, aided by Mitchell, tries to destroy the source of the evil spirit's power.

A whopping story, but it's simply too much for a production of such limited means to handle. The picture becomes completely incoherent at times, with many straying plot threads, and many of the largescale special effects come across as ludicrous. One scene in particular, when the demon is supposed to be pounding a prison wall hard enough to shake it to its foundations, simply looks like he's beating his fists in a temper tantrum. The illusion of supernatural power just isn't there.

"Slaughterhouse" also has other technical problems. Cinematography alternates between washed-out & dull and shadowy & dull. Editing often is choppy and jarring. Synthesized ghost-voices of the demon's victims are difficult, sometimes impossible, to understand. During the climactic battle sequence, it's raining in one scene and dry in the next.

Worst of all, the picture never builds suspense. Despite the presence of plentiful shock scenes, some of which hold interest if only because they are so excessive, "Slaughterhouse Rock" isn't scary.

It's a pity, because the picture does have some interesting elements. The script provides some snappy dialog and a few of the actors turn in fun performances. Ty Miller and Steven Brian Smith help move things along as wise-cracking roommates and Toni Basil is a standout as the goofy rock star who starts all the trouble. — Brin.

Nilouhe Nuer
(Daughter Of The Nile)
(TAIWANESE)

A Fu Film production. Produced by Lu Wen-jen, Ts'ai Sung-lin, Wang lin-jui. Directed by Hou Hsiao-hsien. Screenplay, Chu T'ien-wen; camera (color), Ch'en Huai-en; editor, Liao Ch'ing-sung; music, Ch'en Cih-yuan, Chang Hung-yi; production design, Liu Chih-hua, Lin Chu; sound, Hsin Chiang-sheng, Tu Tu-chih, Yang Ta-ch'ing; assistant director, Chiang Pao-te. Reviewed at Berlin Film Fest (market), Feb. 19, 1988. Running time: 91 MIN.

Lin Hsiao-yang . . . . Yang Lin
Lin Hsiao-fang (brother) . . . . Kao Jai
Ah-sang . . . . Yang Fan
Grandfather . . . . Li T'ien-lu
Father . . . . Ts'ui Fu-sheng

Also with: Hsing Shu-fen, Yu An-shun, Wu Nien-chen, Huang Ch'iung-yao, Ch'en Chien-wen, Yang Tzu-t'ei, Lin Chu, Ch'en Shu-fang.

Berlin — The latest film from Hou Hsiao-hsien ("A Summer At Grandpa's," "Dust In The Wind") is one of the best from this gifted filmmaker, and marks a change in pace. Unlike his earlier, mainly non-urban family dramas, this one's set in the city, has more plot, and is more tightly constructed. A major fest outing this summer is indicated, followed by international arthouse release.

The central character is Hsiao-yang, a teenage schoolgirl who's an avid reader of the popular comic strip "Daughter Of The Nile." Since her mother died of cancer, she's cared for her father, grandfather, older brother and younger sister, doing cooking and housework as well as working in a Kentucky Fried Chicken outlet after school. Still, she has time for her daydreams.

The brother is a petty criminal who, together with his charming friend Ah-sang, runs a trendy restaurant. He still commits the occasional burglary, and his sister has to bind his wounds after one such incident. Gang warfare erupts for unspecified reasons, and after one shooting Ah-sang comes to borrow money from Hsiao-yang before taking off. The police catch him, and he's gunned down. Later, the brother meets a similar fate.

There's trouble at school too, with the class teacher forced to resign because he's been branded "a red" by a student. Hsiao-yang has little time for normal teenage pursuits, and regrets the fact that time passes so quickly.

Hou's film often looks more like the work of his equally talented compatriot Edward Yang, indicating quite a change in style for him. The seemingly effortless directing style is distinctively Hou's, together with the perfect compositions of this beautifully photographed film. Repeated establishing shots of the interior of the family home, the exterior of the restaurant and the fast food outlet are reminiscent of Japanese master Yasujiro Ozu.

Lead actress Yang Lin, a popular singer in Taiwan, is tops as the put-upon teenager who never complains about the way she's casually exploited by everyone around her. Kao Jai, in real life a Taipei fashion boutique owner, makes an impression as the doomed brother, while another pop star, Yang Fan, also is good as his partner. Li Ti'en-lu as the cheerful old grandfather is charming as another of Hou's lovable old people (e.g., the grandmother in "Dust In The Wind").

The comic strip allusions, which will be taken for granted in Asia, where the comic is well known, comes across as tenuous, but it doesn't matter. The fact that the film moves much more briskly than Hou's earlier efforts should bring him a whole new audience. —*Strat.*

The Milagro Beanfield War

A Universal Pictures release of a Robert Redford/Moctesuma Esparza production. Executive producer, Gary J. Hendler. Produced by Redford, Esparza. Coproducer, Charles Mulvehill. Directed by Redford. Screenplay, David Ward, John Nichols, based on Nichols' novel; camera (MGM color), Robbie Greenberg; editor, Dede Allen, Jim Miller; music, Dave Grusin; sound (Dolby), Jim Webb; art direction, Joe Aubel; set decoration, Tom Roysden; visual consultant, Peter Jamison; second unit camera, Jack Couffer; production manager, David Wisnievitz; additional editor, Stan Frazen; casting, Nancy Foy. Reviewed at Universal Studios, Universal City, Calif., March 14, 1988. MPAA Rating: R. Running time: **117 MIN.**
Sheriff Montoya . . . . Rubén Blades
Ladd Devine . . . . Richard Bradford
Ruby Archuleta . . . . Sonia Braga
Nancy Mondragon . . . . Julie Carmen
Horsethief Shorty . . . . James Gammon
Flossie Devine . . . . Melanie Griffith
Charlie Bloom . . . . John Heard
Amarante Cordova . . . . . . Carlos Riquelme
Herbie Platt . . . . Daniel Stern
Joe Mondragon . . . . Chick Vennera
Kyril Montana . . . . Christopher Walken
Mayor Sammy Cantu . . . . . . Freddy Fender
Coyote Angel . . . . Robert Carricart
Governor . . . . M. Emmet Walsh
Nick Rael . . . . Tony Genaro
Emerson Capps . . . . Jerry Hardin

Hollywood — "The Milagro Beanfield War" is a charming, fanciful little fable built around weighty issues concerning the environment, the preservation of a cultural heritage and the rights of citizens versus the might of the dollar.

Robert Redford's second film as a director has been eight years coming and surprisingly, given the earnestness of his commitment to these matters, the tone here is considerably lighter and jokier than that of his compelling, sober Oscar-winner, "Ordinary People." Breezy humor and an enjoyable cast create enough intrinsic appeal to please a sizable public, but conveying these qualities represents a considerable marketing challenge even with Redford's name above the title.

The director and his screenwriters, David Ward and John Nichols, who adapted Nichols, 1974 novel, adeptly juggle at least a dozen major characters in telling the story of how one man's decision to cultivate his land, which is coveted by outside developers intent upon building a resort, leads to a standoff between natives of the area and the big boys.

Such yarns of so-called little people fighting a seemingly stacked deck have been spun countless times before, so it's a relief that Redford and company have put a quirky twist on the material, investing it with a quasi-mystical aspect as well as some raw comedy. Happily, filmmakers also have resisted any impulse to falsely ennoble or idealize the characters, an easy trap in such stories.

Set in modern-day New Mexico, tale is set in motion when impoverished farmer Joe Mondrago (Chick Vennera) improperly diverts some water from a main irrigation channel onto his own modest plot of land in order to start up a beanfield. This little act of defiance stirs up the handful of activists in the affected village, notably garage owner Ruby Archuleta (Sonia Braga), who recruits dropped out radical attorney and newspaperman Charley Bloom (John Heard) to rally 'round the cause.

Gradually, Mondragon's obstinance grows from a thorn in the side of developer Ladd Devine (Richard Bradford) to a major annoyance, so he calls in goon Kyril Montana (Christopher Walken) to take matters into his own hands. Unfortunately for him, the local authorities, led by Sheriff Bernabe (Rubén Blades), are seriously divided in their loyalties, and the situation eventually becomes too messy for even the state governor (M. Emmet Walsh) to want to deal with.

Mixed into the brew are the antics of the ancient Amarante (Carlos Riquelme), an unreliable gun-toter often seen in the company of the mysterious, light-on-his feet Angel (Robert Carricart), and the naive probings into local ways of New York sociology student Herbie Platt (Daniel Stern).

Although paced somewhat leisurely, pic tucks needless exposition away, and Redford generally has well judged how much time can be spent with amusing digressions and when the moment has arrived to speed along the narrative. The mark of the ultra-careful craftsman of "Ordinary People" is present here, but he has opened up somewhat to embrace the humorous vulgarities that help spark the picture to life (and give it its R rating), as well as the odd and unexpected.

In fact, Redford has gone so far to reduce the conventional melodrama inherent in this confrontational story that he has reduced its potency from what it could have been. Walken's bad guy character pursues his nasty business, but the actor plays him softly, certainly less threateningly than he might have.

Initially poised as a heavy, slit-eyed James Gammon end up making one of Bradford's henchmen extremely appealing. As played, there is an easy, often funny way out of every tough situation, and when the ultimate decision regarding the farm versus the development must be made, one doesn't really understand why the governor reasons as he does. Lyrical, unrealistic tone, which is well-sustained throughout, essentially lets filmmakers off the hook as far as the hard issues are concerned.

Bulk of the picture was shot in the latter half of 1986, and inclement weather which helped protract lensing and necessitated further shooting last year is visible only in occasional matching problems. Northern New Mexico settings make the film easy on the eye, and Dave Grusin's score makes it a pleasure to listen to as well.

All the performers are exceedingly pleasant, and result is an appealing if modest achievement that sees Redford treading new ground cautiously but with spirit. —*Cart.*

18 Again

A New World Pictures release. Produced by Walter Coblenz. Executive producers, Irving Fein, Michael Jaffe. Directed by Paul Flaherty. Screenplay, Josh Goldstein, Jonathan Prince; camera (Deluxe color), Stephen M. Katz; editor, Danford B. Greene; music, Billy Goldenberg; production design, Dena Roth; costume design, John Buehler; sound, Russell Williams; associate producers, Arthur Schaefer, Yvonne Ramond; assistant director, Stephen McEveety; casting, Melissa Skoff. Reviewed at Mann's Westwood Theater, L.A., March 12, 1988. MPAA rating: PG. Running time: **100 MIN.**
Jack Watson . . . . George Burns
David Watson . . . . Charlie Schlatter
Arnold . . . . Tony Roberts
Madelyn . . . . Anita Morris
Betty. . . . . Miriam Flynn
Robin . . . . Jennifer Runyon
Charlie . . . . Red Buttons
Coach . . . . George DiCenzo
Horton . . . . Bernard Fox
Prof. Swivet . . . . Kenneth Tigar
Russ . . . . Anthony Starke
Barrett . . . . Pauly Shore

Hollywood — In a season when the body-switching ploy as a film premise is beginning to seem as old as, well, George Burns, New World is banking on a film about an old man who gets to spend some time in a young man's body. This one stars George Burns, and there's a difference.

At 92, Burns' sly 1-liners and canny delivery are as on-target as ever, and boxoffice could be almost as snappy for this generation-spanning fantasy. Pairing with Charlie Schlatter as his shy grandson is charmed.

Burns plays Jack Watson, a wealthy bon vivant celebrating his 81st birthday and a lifetime of success. Schlatter, at 18, is an uncertain college student who gets pushed around by everyone but grandpa, with whom he shares a close-knit friendship. Pair take a drive after the birthday party, and there's a car accident. Burns, who has just made a birthday wish to be 18 again, wakes up in his grandson's body, while his own body remains unconscious and hospitalized.

Young again and plunged into his grandson's world, Burns quickly discovers things have not been going well. The film's hook is the personality difference — the old man, with confidence and charm to burn, turns things around in delightful style. Pic becomes a fantasy for both generations, as kids will imagine what they could do if equipped with comparable panache.

Burns gets the girls, gets ahead of the bullies, and becomes wildly popular as the gleeful, wise-cracking fraternity ringleader. His sensitive grandson, an aspiring artist, has talents he can't duplicate, so grandpa begins to appreciate what the kid is all about.

Schlatter is a natural in the Burns

role — clicking into the timing, the walk and the mannerisms with flair, and offsetting the old man's provocative cockiness with his own sweet-spirited appeal.

Burns, though off screen a significant chunk of the time, is a constant presence through voice-over, and writers Josh Goldstein and Jonathan Prince have given him a fine vehicle.

Film falters in some places — its clichéd college-life situations, such as the rivalry over a girl between young Burns and the bullying frat president (Anthony Starke) are a tad wearisome. Even less imagination has been applied to the female roles, such as the "dream girl" (Jennifer Runyon), who's only there to react to the men.

Anita Morris makes the most of a turn as old man Burns' curvaceous "companion" with a heart of brass and Red Buttons does a good, sentimental turn as Burns' best friend, who's a little nonplussed by what's happened to him.

Ostensibly set in Ohio, pic was lensed around Los Angeles and at USC, and has a Southern California feel. Production values are good, especially in an elaborate party scene at the USC fraternity. A scene at Club Lingerie, a Sunset Blvd. nitery, is amusing, if exaggerated.

Meanwhile, film's ending is pumped up to melodramatic excess, but that's apparently a requirement of the form.

Filmmakers are at their best with simple scenes that mine the film's premise, such as when Burns, nearly discovering his young body, romps ecstatically through a track and field course at night. — *Daws.*

D.O.A.
(COLOR/B&W)

A Buena Vista Distribution release of a Touchstone Pictures presentation, in association with Silver Screen Partners III, of a Ziskin/Sander production. Produced by Ian Sander, Laura Ziskin. Coproducers, Cathleen Summers, Andrew J. Kuehn. Directed by Rocky Morton, Annabel Jankel. Screenplay, Charles Edward Pogue, from story by Pogue, Russell Rouse, Clarence Greene (based on Rouse & Greene's 1949 screenplay); camera (CFI color, Duart b&w), Yuri Neyman; editor, Michael R. Miller; music, Chaz Jankel; sound (Dolby), Thomas Brandau; production design, Richard Amend; set decoration, Michael O'Sullivan; assistant director, Louis D'Esposito; production manager, Jeanne M. Van Cott; additional photography, Stephan Czapsky; casting, Nancy Foy. Reviewed at Plaza theater, N.Y. March 14, 1988. MPAA Rating: R. Running time: 96 MIN.
Dexter Cornell . . . . Dennis Quaid
Sydney Fuller . . . . Meg Ryan
Mrs. Fitzwaring . . . . . . Charlotte Rampling
Hal Petersham . . . . Daniel Stern
Gail Cornell . . . . Jane Kaczmarek
Bernard . . . . Christopher Neame
Cookie Fitzwaring . . . . Robin Johnson
Nicholas Lang . . . . Rob Knepper
Graham Corey . . . . Jay Patterson
Det. Ulmer . . . . Brion James
Det. Brockton . . . . Jack Kehoe
Elaine Wells . . . . Elizabeth Arlen
Also with: Karen Radcliffe, William Forward, Lee Gideon, Bill Bolender, Hillary Hoffman, John Hawkes, Timbuk 3 group (Barbara MacDonald, Pat MacDonald).

An excessively morbid and unsubtle second remake of the 1949 film noir classic, "D.O.A.," is an unlikely entry for general audiences to come from Disney's hitprone Touchstone banner. Despite a barnstorming central performance by Dennis Quaid, pic remains unbelievable and unappealing.

Heir apparent to the Victor Drai mantle of recycling old film plots, scripter Charles Edward Pogue ("The Fly," "Psycho III") uses two central MacGuffins to get the pot boiling. First, a premise identical to "Throw Momma From The Train" introduces Quaid as an Eng-

Original Film
(B&W)

A United Artists release of a Harry M. Popkin production. Stars Edmond O'Brien, Pamela Britton; features Luther Adler, Beverly Campbell, Lynn Baggett, William Ching, Henry Hart, Neville Brand, Laurette Luez. Directed by Rudolph Maté. Story and screenplay, Russell Rouse, Clarence Greene; camera (b&w), Ernest Laszlo; music, Dimitri Tiomkin; editor, Arthur H. Nadel. Previewed Dec. 22, 1949. Running time: 83 MIN.
Frank Bigelow . . . . Edmond O'Brien
Paula Gibson . . . . Pamela Britton
Majak . . . . Luther Adler
Miss Foster . . . . Beverly Campbell
Mrs. Philips . . . . Lynn Baggett
Halliday . . . . William Ching
Stanley Philips . . . . Henry Hart
Chester . . . . Neville Brand
Marla Rakubian . . . . Laurette Luez
Sam . . . . Jesse Kirkpatrick
Sue . . . . Cay Forrester
Jeanie . . . . Virginia Lee
Dave . . . . Michael Ross

lish prof who's unwilling to read his precocious student Nick Lang's (played by Rob Knepper) novel "Out Of Whack" despite the kid's pleas. Just as hard-drinking Quaid marks an A on the still unread manuscript, Nick falls to his death past Quaid's window, an apparent suicide. Visual and verbal emphasis on the novel sets up film's delayed final twist, which also is the same as "Throw Momma."

Second, pic's structure (bookended with black & white sequences at the police station) and catalyst are from Russell Rouse and Clarence Green's 1949 screenplay for "D.O.A.," filmed for UA by Rudolph Maté. In the third reel Quaid (like Edmond O'Brien before him) is diagnosed as having ingested a luminous poison, with only 1-2 days left to live. As Pogue's overly spoonfed dialog proclaims (several times), the protagonist who has given up on life since publishing his last novel four years back now has an obsession to live for: find his own killer.

Convoluted trail of murder and suicide (all but one of the pic's lead cast are dead at the finale) teams Quaid with his "Innerspace" costar Meg Ryan, as a pretty coed with a

crush on him. Spoofing "The 39 Steps," Quaid literally bonds himself to Ryan at one point by superglue at the wrist (this continues a morbid obsession with toilet scenes that litters the picture).

Unbelievable central mystery (a red herring to boot) revolves around Nick — he was sleeping with Quaid's wife (Jane Kaczmarek) and was the son of rich matron Charlotte Rampling's husband's murderer. Rampling implausibly sponsored the boy's education and is jealous of his affair with her daughter Cookie (Robin Johnson). Plot unravels with revelation of bigamy, murdering two husbands back-to-back and "Tom

1969 Version:
Color Me Dead
(AUSTRALIAN)

A Commonwealth United release of a Goldsworthy production. Stars Tom Tryon, Carolyn Jones. Directed and produced by Eddie Davis. Screenplay, uncredited; based upon a screenplay by Russell Rouse and Clarence Greene; camera (Eastman color), Mick Borneman; music, Bob Young; editor, Warren Adams; art director, Sid Fort. Reviewed at New Amsterdam Theater, N.Y., Dec. 29, 1969. MPAA Rating: R. Running time: 97 MIN.
Frank Bigelow . . . . Tom Tryon
Paula Gibson . . . . Carolyn Jones
Bradley Taylor . . . . Rick Jason
Marla Rukubian . . . . . . Patricia Connolly
Halliday . . . . Tony Ward
Miss Foster . . . . Penny Sugg
Eugene Phillips . . . . Reg Gillam
Mrs. Philips . . . . Margot Reid
Stanley Philips . . . . Peter Sumner
George Reynolds . . . . . . Michael Lawrence
Chester . . . . Sandy Harbott

Jones"-like hidden parentage. Climax is an unconvincing and pretentious confrontation of Quaid with the least likely (and hence guilty) suspect.

Hailing from music videos and tv's "Max Headroom," married helmers Rocky Morton and Annabel Jankel overload their maiden feature with visual gimmickry: lots of tilted, or swivelling first-person camerawork plus moiré-patterned lighting to create distortion. Some of it is arresting (cinematographer Yuri Neyman did striking work on "Liquid Sky"), but the action scenes are shot too close up, becoming claustrophobic and messy. Acting, particularly by Quaid, Ryan and Knepper, is fine, but villainess Rampling is very unflatteringly styled and photographed.

Except for some moments of romantic lyricism, Chaz Jankel's noisy rock score sabotages most key scenes.

Unlike other recent films noirs, such as "Body Heat," "No Way Out," "Masquerade" and Quaid's "The Big Easy," pic misses the boat by eliminating eroticism entirely.
— *Lor.*

Masquerade

An MGM/UA Communications Co. release from MGM Pictures of a Michael I. Levy Enterprises production. Produced by Levy. Directed by Bob Swaim. Screenplay,

executive producer, Dick Wolf; camera (Duart color, Deluxe prints), David Watkin; editor, Scott Conrad; music, John Barry; production design, John Kasarda; art direction, Dan Davis; set decoration, Steve Jordan; costume design, John Boxer; sound (Dolby), James Sabat; assistant director, Michael Tadross; assistant camera, Cary Fisher; associate producer, Kelliann Ladd; casting, Wallis Nicita. Reviewed at MGM screening room, Culver City, Calif., March 10, 1988. MPAA Rating: R. Running time: 91 MIN.
Tim Whalen . . . . Rob Lowe
Olivia Lawrence . . . . Meg Tilly
Mike McGill . . . . Doug Savant
Brooke Morrison . . . . Kim Cattrall
Tony Gateworth . . . . John Glover
Anne Briscoe . . . . Dana Delany

Hollywood — "Masquerade," set in the Hamptons among the genteel with their weathered mansions and racing yachts, is like many poor little rich girl stories; a beautiful backdrop and dreamy settings aren't enough to compensate for uninvolving characters caught in an unsuspenseful scheme. Pic is a cold, if lovely, production and too much of a downer to win much of a b.o. following.

Latest picture from director Bob Swaim is better executed than his "Half Moon Street," but suffers the same flaw of incredulity and lack of chemistry between the stars — here Meg Tilly and Rob Lowe.

Dick Wolf's script is partially to blame by trying to cram too many superficially workable twists into this predictable tale of deception, greed and murder.

Tilly's womanizing, drunkard stepfather (John Glover) is in on a plot with Lowe who, unbeknownst to her, is intent upon securing her hand in marriage so that he and his buddy will be set for life.

From a structural standpoint, just when it seems the scheme is going to be carried off, something happens to thwart its execution. For the most part, it's Lowe's guilt feelings — and change of heart toward his intended victim — that get in the way, even as he isn't for a minute convincing either as a villain or a lover.

In the beginning, Lowe is a rake, the cocky captain of the racing boat Obsession while at the same time making it with the boat owner's much younger wife (Kim Cattrall).

Tilly's just out of a Catholic women's college, innocent and apparently chaste (it's never explained later why, then, she needed to be on the pill) — just the sort who would fall for such a dashing and handsome gent like Lowe, who seems to have become Mr. Nice Guy overnight, dumping Cattrall for bigger bait.

It seems the Hamptons is not the bucolic haven it's cracked up to be. The police take their oath as peace officers to heart — that is, not upsetting the influential and wealthy community that pads the wallets for off-duty cops moonlighting at ritzy parties.

That leaves the snooping to an eager rookie (Doug Savant), seemingly wanting to protect the interests of Tilly, the girl he's always loved, as she takes the fall for a murder she didn't commit.

The crucial plot point that comes halfway through the action blows the whole picture. When the only good, strong person with a clear sense of identity comes out a bad guy, the drama falls apart.

Dana Delany as Glover's sassy g.f. has a small, but memorable part, equally convincing as the loose femme representing the other side of the tracks and the one most interested in seeing justice done.
—*Brit.*

Stars And Bars

A Columbia Pictures release. Produced by Sandy Lieberson. Executive producer, Sheldon Schrager. Coproducer, Susan Richards. Directed by Pat O'Connor. Screenplay, William Boyd, from his novel; camera (Duart color; Deluxe prints), Jerzy Zielinski; editor, Michael Bradsell; music, Stanley Myers; song, Sting; sound (Dolby stereo), John Pritchett; production design, Leslie Dilley, Stuart Craig; art direction, Becky Block; production manager-associate producer, Jack Cummins; assistant director, Ned Dowd; casting, Risa Bramon, Billy Hopkins. Reviewed at Columbia screening room, N.Y., March 2, 1988. MPAA Rating: R. Running time: 94 MIN.

Henderson Dores . . . . . . Daniel Day-Lewis
Loomis Gage . . . . Harry Dean Stanton
Bryant . . . . Martha Plimpton
Beckman . . . . Matthew Cowles
Irene Stien . . . . Joan Cusack
Freeborn . . . . Maury Chaykin
Shanda . . . . Deirdre O'Connell
Duane . . . . Will Patton
Pruitt . . . . Steven Wright
Teagarden . . . . Keith David
Melissa . . . . Laurie Metcalf
Cora . . . . Glenne Headly

Also with: Kent Broadhurst, Rockets Redglare, Spalding Gray, Celia Weston, Beatrice Winde, Bill Moor.

In David Puttnam's film legacy at Columbia Pictures, "Stars And Bars" represents a major *faux pas*. Unfunny mixture of farce and misdirected satire has no conceivable audience apart from undiscriminating pay-cable viewers.

Project was developed by Puttnam, but given to his ex-partner Sandy Lieberson to produce after Puttnam acceded to head of Columbia. Though an American picture, it features a high complement of U.K. personnel behind the camera.

Scripted by William Boyd from his novel, thin storyline follows the misadventures of a Brit in America, or rather someone's view of what America is like (targets of Boyd's satire are all straw men). Daniel Day-Lewis plays the hapless hero, an art expert sent by his boss to acquire a rare Renoir painting (worth about $10,000,000) from hayseed Harry Dean Stanton, who claims to have bought it for $500 in France in 1946.

Bulk of pic deals with Day-Lewis' interactions with Stanton's weird brood, including Maury Chaykin as his Elvis-imitating son who already has sold the painting to unscrupulous, rival New York art dealers. Nonsensical gags and caricatures represent a real comedown from Hollywood's cutesy but effective portrayal of Southern goofballs, especially in such funny films as the 1945 Fred MacMurray vehicle "Murder, He Says."

Add to this concoction some awkward bedroom farce (Day-Lewis unconvincingly juggling his new pickup, Joan Cusack, at an Atlanta hotel with his fiancée Laurie Metcalf) that wouldn't pass muster as a West End farce for the tourist trade and pic self-destructs rapidly. Helmer Pat O'Connor evidences no feel for comedy, having the cast overact unmercifully, except for standup comic Steven Wright (as Day-Lewis' business rival) who maintains his familiar deadpan persona.

Day-Lewis is downright embarrassing, suffering through two extended nude chase scenes and nearly bursting a blood vessel in his uncharacteristic turn. Stanton is wasted in the sort of role he graduated from a decade ago and juve actress Martha Plimpton is miscast in a precocious temptress role.

Supporting cast is one long in-joke, featuring tons of New York talent whose presence will mean nothing to national audiences and add nothing to the picture, e.g., Spalding Gray, Rockets Redglare. Structurally the fact that Will Patton (recently impressive as the villain in "No Way Out") has a key role but doesn't show up on screen until two brief scenes in the final reel is mystifying.

Sting contributes an excellent theme song "An Englishman In New York," from his latest LP, which is pointlessly reprised near the end of the film. —*Lor.*

Powaqqatsi
(U.S.-DOCU)

A Cannon Group release of a Francis Ford Coppola and George Lucas presentation of an IRE production. Executive producers, Menahem Golan, Yoram Globus. Line producers, Marcel Kahn, Tom Luddy. Produced by Mel Lawrence, Godfrey Reggio, Lawrence Taub. Directed by Reggio. Screenplay, Reggio, Ken Richards; camera (color), Leonida Zourdoumis, Graham Berry; editor, Iris Cahn, Alton Walpole; music, Philip Glass. Reviewed at the Berlin Film Festival (official program, non-competing), Feb. 22, 1988. MPAA Rating: G. Running time: 100 MIN.

Berlin — Godfrey Reggio earned a small cult following with his first docu, "Koyaanisqatsi." During its screening at the Berlin Film Festival in 1983, he was inspired to make it the first part of a trilogy. "Powaqqatsi," the second part, was lensed on a larger, $4,300,000 budget.

It has greater scope (pic was lensed in Asia, India, Africa and South America) than its predecessor and Reggio is more surefooted technically, but "Powaqqatsi" is visually and musically (another superb Philip Glass score) a continuation of the first effort, likely to satisfy old customers and earn some new ones in limited playoff situations.

Less a documentary in the usual sense of the term than a medley of images set to music, film will stir up the same controversy as its predecessor over the way it uses images of the Third World in a highly estheticized film language. Title of the film comes from two Hopi Indian words meaning a magician who lives at the expense of others.

The evil magician is the North of industrial exploitation; but film shows only its victim, the native cultures of the South (i.e., Third World), disappearing into misery. The professed intention of the filmmaker, who has a background in social work and who spent 14 years with the Christian Brothers Teaching Order, is to send the viewer into a "conscious trance," from which to feel the exploitation of Third World culture more profoundly than via rational thought.

Film's opening sequence is one of the strongest examples of what this means in practice. With Glass' hypnotic score controlling the image, we see dozens of mud-covered men bent double under unidentifiable loads they are struggling to carry up a hill Sisyphus-style. One of them falls and thus becomes another burden to get up the hill. It is a stunning tour-de-force of refined camerawork wedded to music in a visual ballet, but one which largely cancels out horror or discomfort at what is actually represented.

Completely wordless, "Powaqqatsi" derives its impact exclusively from the rhythm of the cutting. Glass' original score was composed along with the editing, and is a powerful emotional experience that helps put the film in a category of its own.

Chief cameramen Leonida Zourdoumis and Graham Berry deliberately emphasize the high-tech end of their profession. The preference is for telephoto lensing, soft focus and striking camera angles that make a boat seem to sink below the waves, or a boy and his horse appear to be frolicking in the middle of the ocean. High-speed photography futher abstracts the images into a slow-motion dance, turning exotic subjects and locales into a world of shimmering chimeras that are as beautiful to look at as they are hard to grasp concretely. — *Yung.*

Dominick And Eugene

An Orion Pictures release of a Farrell-Minoff production. Produced by Marvin Minoff, Mike Farrell. Directed by Robert M. Young. Screenplay, Alvin Sargent, Corey Blechman, story by Danny Porfirio; camera (Duart color; Deluxe prints), Curtis Clark; editor, Arthur Coburn; music, Trevor Jones; production design, Doug Kraner; set decoration, Derek R. Hill; costumes, Hilary Rosenfeld; sound (Dolby), David E. Kirschner; associate producer, Lee R. Mayes; assistant director, Christopher Griffin; casting, Julie Hughes, Barry Moss. Reviewed at Orion screening room, L.A., March 8, 1988. MPAA Rating:

PG-13. Running time: 111 MIN.
Dominick Luciano . . . . Tom Hulce
Eugene Luciano . . . . Ray Liotta
Jennifer Reston . . . . Jamie Lee Curtis
Larry Higgins . . . . Todd Graff
Mrs. Gianelli . . . . Mimi Cecchini
Dr. Levinson . . . . Robert Levine
Jesse Johnson . . . . Bill Cobbs
Martin Chernak . . . . David Strathairn
Mikey Chernak . . . . Tommy Snelsire
Teresa Chernak . . . . . . Mary Joan Negro
Father T . . . . Tom Signorelli
Guido . . . . Joe Maruzzo

Hollywood — A heart-tugging tale of twin brothers, one a med student, the other retarded, "Dominick And Eugene" lays all its emotional cards right out on the table. As such, its blatant sentimentality will put off more sophisticated viewers, while its direct approach might hit the mark with a more general public if its attention can be directed toward the picture, which is questionable.

In any event, Orion will have to work hard to cultivate an audience for this tale of sibling responsibility.

Parentless title characters live in a working class section of Pittsburgh. Supposedly the victim of a childhood accident, Dominick (Tom Hulce) represents a tragic case of a young man who is "slower" than other people, but smart enough to function nominally in society.

Dominick's work as a garbageman is helping to put his hard working brother Eugene (Ray Liotta) through school, which seems like a fair trade since Eugene, despite his short temper, virtually is the ideal supportive brother, who has selflessly taken care of his disadvantaged twin all his life.

Problem surfaces when Eugene is accepted at Stanford to finish his medical studies. Unfortunately, pic never explains why Eugene can't take his brother with him, but in any event, the point is to create a situation in which Dominick must fly on his own.

Dominick is mildly taken advantage of at times, by local thugs and a drug dealer who sees in the trusting innocent an ideal courier, but also makes life difficult for his brother, barging in at all the wrong times when Eugene is trying to get something going with friendly aspiring medic Jamie Lee Curtis.

Things finally come to a melodramatic head after Dominick's dog is run over by a car, when the fellow witnesses an abused boy being pushed down some stairs and killed by his father. As in coscreenwriter Alvin Sargent's script for "Ordinary People," this leads to a crucial revelation about an earlier event between brothers that represents the key to the entire drama, and a liberation for the afflicted one.

Acting by the principals is acutely sensitive, but its demonstrative emotionalism plays directly into the hands of the obvious approach of both the script, written by Sargent and Corey Blechman, and director

Robert M. Young, in which every intended effect is pushed front-and-center, to the point where everything is on the surface, and nothing under it.

Explicit attack on the viewer's feelings obliterate the shadings and subtlety that would have been welcome, and ever-so-neat wrapup strains credulity.

Still, coming after his memorable villainous turn in "Something Wild," Ray Liotta impresses in a very different characterization here, conveying real substance, integrity and love in his relationship with his brother, which transfers in turn to his overall approach to life.

Hulce also is believable and will move many with his valiant attempt to lead a normal life, while Curtis, stuck with a mostly standby role, is appealingly lowkeyed.

Soundtrack is filled mostly with nicely varied pop songs, while stretches of Trevor Jones' original score are extremely effective. Other behind-the-scenes contributions are fine. —*Cart.*

The Drifter

A Concorde Pictures release of a New Horizons production. Produced by Ken Stein. Executive producer, Roger Corman. Coproducer, Matt Leipzig. Written and directed by Larry Brand. Camera (color), David Sperling; editor, Stephen Mark; music, Rick Conrad; casting, Al Guarino; set decoration, Cara Haycak; makeup/hair, Deborah Zoller; costume design, Daryl Binder. Reviewed at AMC Americana 8, Southfield, Mich., March 3, 1988. MPAA Rating: R. Running time: **90 MIN.**

Julia . . . . Kim Delaney
Arthur . . . . Timothy Bottoms
Kriger . . . . Al Shannon
Trey . . . . Miles O'Keeffe
Matty . . . . Anna Gray Garduno
Willie Munroe . . . . Loren Haines
Morrison . . . . Larry Brand
Captain Edwards . . . . Thomas Wagner
Also with: Ernest Alexander, Joanne Willette, Gil Christner, Charles Zucker, Patrick McCord, Ken Stein, Myvanwy Jenn, Bruce Vilanch, Kerry Barden.

Southfield, Mich. — "The Drifter" has a little style and very little suspense. There is a curiosity factor running throughout this exploitation film. Having attractive Kim Delaney bare her all early in the movie doesn't hurt either.

While returning from a business trip, Julia (Delaney), a successful interior designer, gets a flat. Against her better judgment, she lets a rugged looking hitchhiker named Trey (Miles O'Keeffe) change her tire. In return she gives him a lift and — in these safe-sex times of "Fatal Attraction" phobia — invites him to spend the night in her motel room.

Once back at work, however, she finds that out of sight is not necessarily out of mind. Trey won't leave her alone. He calls her at home, calls her at work, even shows up at work, demanding that they get together.

That's only half of Julia's troubles. Her loose-moraled attorney boyfriend (Timothy Bottoms) has hired a private detective to trail her

and knows all about the business trip tryst. Worse still, someone has just killed Julia's best friend. The obvious suspect is the drifter, and the next victim apparently is Julia herself.

The plot of this latest Roger Corman production starts weak and never builds strength. We don't know who Julia's tormentor is, but we feel comfortable in ruling out the Drifter. Too easy.

Because the plot is so threadbare, "The Drifter" never builds any suspense. Try as he might to emulate Clint Eastwood's laconic style, Trey's laid-back approach to mania never convinces us he's much of a threat.

With so few characters, if Trey is not the menace, who is?

It's this curiosity coupled with a film style sparingly reminiscent of "Manhunter" that carries the audience to a predictable conclusion that binds every loose end.

Concorde hasn't decided on a national release schedule. With the proper promotion, however, "The Drifter" could stoll around video-store shelves for many months.

— *Advo.*

Little Nikita

A Columbia Pictures release. Produced by Harry Gittes. Directed by Richard Benjamin. Screenplay, John Hill, Bo Goldman, from story by Tom Musca, Terry Schwartz; camera (Deluxe color), Laszlo Kovacs; editor, Jacqueline Cambas; music, Marvin Hamlisch; production design, Gene Callahan; art direction, Hub Braden; set design, Ann Harris; set decoration, Lee Poll; costume design, Patricia Norris; sound (Dolby), Jerry Jost; special effects, Michael Edmonson; production manager-coproducer, Art Levinson; assistant director, Dennis Maguire; stunt coordinator-second unit director, Conrad Palmisano; 2d unit camera, Rexford Metz; associate producer, Gail Mutrux; casting, David Rubin. Reviewed at Columbia screening room, Burbank, Calif., March 7, 1988. MPAA Rating: PG. Running time: **98 MIN.**

Roy Parmenter . . . . Sidney Poitier
Jeff Grant . . . . River Phoenix
Richard Grant . . . . Richard Jenkins
Elizabeth Grant . . . . Caroline Kava
Konstantin Karpov . . . . . Richard Bradford
Scuba . . . . Richard Lynch
Verna McLaughlin . . . . Loretta Devine
Barbara Kerry . . . . Lucy Deakins

Hollywood — "Little Nikita" never really materializes as a taut espionage thriller and winds up as an unsatisfying execution of a clever premise.

A teen's traumatic discovery that his parents are Soviet spies provides ample cinematic tension but narrative unravels in the latter third of the film as chaotic and jumbled action takes over completely. There's little reason to expect more than a meager b.o. performance.

Film opens strongly as parallel storylines unfold and audience is drawn in by the need to decipher the link between the mission of a Soviet agent and an all-American family in the mythical San Diego suburb of Fountain Grove.

Poised at the juncture of these developments is FBI agent Sidney

Poitier, whose natural intensity seems just right for the role (he played a similar FBI part in "Shoot To Kill," filmed after "Nikita"). His presence is the film's real strength, particularly early on.

Poitier encounters River Phoenix, a youngster who decides to apply for the Air Force Academy, on a routine FBI check. When some peculiar data turns up on Phoenix' parents — convincingly portrayed by Richard Jenkins and Caroline Kava — Poitier begins an investigation that leads to an almost avuncular bonding with Phoenix.

Simultaneous action finds KGB agent Richard Bradford immersed in a desperate attempt to capture a renegade Soviet spy who wants a large cash payoff or he'll continue eliminating some of his most valued colleagues. In an especially believable performance, Bradford as the experienced villain becomes the film's most compelling character.

Poitier and Bradford are adversaries from two decades ealier and that history is designed to intensify the personal conflict. Just as that connection is solidified, the one between Poitier and Phoenix takes hold.

Plot begins careening out of control, however, as Bradford zeroes in on the parents — identified now as "sleeper" agents who were smuggled into the country years ago — and drags them unwillingly into his pursuit.

While Richard Benjamin's direction up to this point is strong (in his fifth venture at the helm), intrigue is overwhelmed by a series of implausible and disjointed events that tumble out with blazing speed. One gets the sense that perhaps a committee of writers decided that only a few minutes were left for the big climactic chase, so on with the action.

Unfortunately, resorting to such a tiresome approach destroys the dramatic possibilities. Resolution really becomes inevitable, relegating film to the wornout tradition of far less inventive plots. — *Tege.*

Shame
(AUSTRALIAN)

A Hoyts Distribution release of a Barron Films production. Produced by Damien Parer, Paul Barron. Directed by Steve Jodrell. Screenplay, Beverly Blankenship, Michael Brindley; camera (color), Joseph Pickering; editor, Kerry Regan; music, Mario Millo; production design, Phil Peters; associate producer, Pru Donovan; assistant director, Stuart Wood. Reviewed at Hoyts cinema complex, Perth, Feb. 25, 1988. (In New Directors/New Films series, N.Y.) Running time: **92 MIN.**

Asta Cadell . . . . Deborra-Lee Furness
Tim Curtis . . . . Tony Barry
Lizzie Curtis . . . . Simone Buchanan
Tina Farrel . . . . Gillian Jones
Sgt. Wal Cuddy . . . . Peter Aanensen
Norma Curtis . . . . Margaret Ford
Danny Fiske . . . . David Franklin
Also with: Bill McClusky (Ross), Allison Taylor (Penny), Phil Dean (Gary), Graeme Wemyss (Bobby).

Perth — Taut, uncompromising, and often disturbing, "Shame" is one of the toughest dramas to come out of the Aussie film industry in some years. However, confronting subject matter — rape in a small, uncaring country town — could make it a hard sell to attract a broad audience.

Film also marks a powerful feature directing debut for Steve Jodrell, and is the best offering yet from Perth-based producer Paul Barron.

"Shame" centers around Deborra-Lee Furness, a strong-minded barrister touring solo on a motorbike, who's forced to stay in a small town for repairs. Town boasts a brace of layabout adolescents, and a not much better bunch of older men, many fathers of the recalcitrant youths. With the arrival of the single, leather-clad motorcyclist, townspeople's caliber is quickly gauged.

Furness lodges with the local mechanic (Tony Barry), while she fixes her bike. There she meets Barry's teenage daughter, Simone Buchanan, who it turns out, has been recently raped — intimation is by more than one assailant. Her trauma — her shame — is compounded by Barry's inability to come to grips with such violation, and a pervading attitude amongst the townspeople that she brought it on herself by being a "loose" girl.

Catalytic presence of Furness — who herself has various brushes, directly and indirectly, with some of the youths plus the town's (including the local police) general apathy towards what's going on — spurs Buchanan to face her ordeal and bring charges against her attackers despite a previous failed attempt by another woman in the town.

That leads ultimately to a confrontation firstly between Furness, Barry and family in a "Straw Dogs"-type attack on their house, then between the main youth element and an increasing amount of townspeople (principally the women), finally spurred to action after years of turning a blind eye. That recognition, however, is only properly brought home after the violent death of Buchanan at the hands of two of the youths.

Under Jodrell's handling, potential clichés of this scenario are avoided; he presents a tense buildup and a growing sense of menace that erupts angrily at film's end.

Pace could be tightened in pic's first half, and some more depth added to such characters as Barry's girlfriend, Gillian Jones, who also changes thanks to Furness' presence, and some of the other rape victims who emerge during the film. Nevertheless, they're minor quibbles, easily countered by the film's compellingness and some excellent performances, notably Furness, displaying a credible image of independence rather than just a tough-girl look, as well as Barry and Jones; the young Buchanan deserves special mention in what emerges as the film's lynchpin role.

Tech credits are up to usual Aussie high standards. "Shame" already has representation in the U.S. (PRO), internationally via Safir (excluding Australia/N.Z.) and has garnered various fest invites; a disturbing film, it'll require some sensitive targeting and, more than usual, could work better here and abroad off word of mouth rather than any specific marketing push.
— *Doch.*

Biloxi Blues

A Universal Pictures release of a Rastar production. Produced by Ray Stark. Executive producers, Joseph M. Carraciolo, Marykay Powell. Directed by Mike Nichols. Screenplay, Neil Simon, based on his play; camera (Super 35, color), Bill Butler; editor, Sam O'Steen; music, Georges Delerue; production design, Paul Sylbert; set decoration, John Alan Hicks; costume design, Ann Roth; sound (Dolby), Allan Byer; assistant director, Michael Haley; casting, Juliet Taylor. Reviewed at Universal Studios, Universal City, March 10, 1988. MPAA Rating: PG-13. Running time: **106 MIN.**

Eugene Morris Jerome	Matthew Broderick
Sgt. Toomey	Christopher Walken
Wykowski	Matt Mulhern
Epstein	Corey Parker
Selridge	Markus Flanagan
Carney	Casey Siemaszko
Hennessey	Michael Dolan
Daisy	Penelope Ann Miller
Rowena	Park Overall

Hollywood — "Biloxi Blues" is an agreeable but hardly inspired film version of Neil Simon's second installment of his autobiographical trilogy, which bowed during the 1984-85 season. Even with high-powered talents Mike Nichols and Matthew Broderick aboard, World War II barracks comedy provokes just mild laughs and smiles rather than the guffaws Simon's work often elicits in the theater, so the playwright's record of seeing his work reach the screen in diluted form remains consistent. Boxoffice prospects look good.

In fact, there is nothing at all wrong with the picture — it is perfectly well acted, directed and produced, looks and sounds fine, and has engaging enough charac-

Original Play

An Emanuel Azenberg, in association with Center Theater Group/Ahmanson Theater, presentation of a comedy in two acts by Neil Simon. Staged by Gene Saks. Settings, David Mitchell; costumes, Ann Roth; lighting, Tharon Musser; general manager, Robert Kamlot; stage managers, Charles Blackwell, Henry Velez; company manager, Leslie Butler; publicity, Bill Evans Assocs. Stars Matthew Broderick. Opened March 28, 1985 at the Neil Simon Theater, N.Y., $35 top.

Roy Selridge	Brian Tarantina
Joseph Wykowski	Matt Mulhern
Don Carney	Alan Ruck
Eugene Morris Jerome	Matthew Broderick
Arnold Epstein	Barry Miller
Sgt. Merwin J. Toomey	Bill Sadler
James Hennessey	Geoffrey Sharp
Rowena	Randall Edwards
Daisy Hannigan	Penelope Ann Miller

ters. Yet the wisecracks that reportedly brought down the house onstage frequently stick out like corny Broadwayisms, to the extent that, for all the film gains through its 1-liners, it equally suffers due to the accumulation of artificiality.

Graced with a beautiful opening song and shot, of a steam-driven train carrying new recruits down South, film is narrated from an adult perspective by Simon's alter ego, Eugene Morris Jerome, an aspiring writer called up for service in the waning months of the war.

With 10 weeks of boot camp ahead of them, it's not at all sure that Eugene and his cohorts will ever see action, but that doesn't prevent basic training from being a living hell relieved only by an excursion into town to party and look for ladies.

In Eugene's case, the matter of women looms particularly large, as he'd keenly like to be promoted from the rank of virgin before eating sand on some Pacific island.

In the meantime, he must contend with Sgt. Toomey, whose soft-spoken, articulate manner ill-conceals a sadistic heart, a twisted mind and a metal-plated head. Toomey specializes in turning the men against one another by forcing one of them — often Eugene — to select one of the others for unpleasant assignments or punishment.

The Army wasn't yet integrated at this point in history, but the company here still has its share of strife, stemming from tension between the gung-ho macho men and the intellectual Jews, as well as from a gay incident that surfaces late in the game. Eugene is taunted for writing down all his observations about the others in his journal, but he gets off easy compared to Epstein, a difficult, stubborn, brainy kid who doesn't hide his contempt for everyone around him, and is repaid in kind.

Simon's excellent craftsmanship keeps the story moving smartly, and the actors' winning personalities provide easy and comfortable access into the picture. After the punch to the solar plexus provided by "Full Metal Jacket," the equivalent boot camp sequences here have the impact of a mosquito bite.

Nor can other comparisons be avoided. Although he has collaborated with Simon four times in the theater, Nichols had heretofore declined to direct the films of any of the writer's plays. "Biloxi Blues" is certainly superior to most Simon stage-to-screen transfers, but judged on the basis of Nichols' previous work, one sorely misses the acid humor and incisive social critiques prevalent in "The Graduate," "Carnal Knowledge" and the best scenes of "Catch-22." His mark is much less apparent here than in any of his other pics.

Playing a character perched precisely on the point between adolescence and manhood, Broderick is enjoyable all the way. Of his five fellow recruits, Matt Mulhern repeats his Broadway characterization as Wykowski, the threatening hulk, in strong fashion, while newcomers Corey Parker, Markus Flanagan, Casey Siemaszko and Michael Dolan are equally on the money.

Also carrying over from the stage is Penelope Ann Miller, adorable as the girl who inspires love at first sight in Eugene at a dance. Park Overall proves deliciously sly and knowing as the prostie who introduces the protagonist to the mysteries of life.

The most intriguing performance comes from Christopher Walken as the weird sergeant. Refusing to indulge the cliché of the screaming, vein-popping D.I., Walken underplays dramatically and to pointed effect; by starting so coolly, his subsequent aberrations seem all the more shocking. Walken would hardly have been the first actor to come to mind for this role, but he makes it his own.

All technical contributions are ultra-smooth. —*Cart.*

A New Life

A Paramount Pictures release of a Martin Bregman production. Produced by Bregman. Executive producer, Louis A. Stroller. Written and directed by Alan Alda. Camera (Medallion color, Technicolor prints), Kelvin Pike; editor, William Reynolds; music, Joseph Turrin; production design, Barbara Dunphy; art direction, Lucinda Zak; set decoration, Anthony Greco, Alan Hicks (N.Y.); costume design, Mary McLeod; sound, Bruce Carardine, Al Mian (N.Y.); associate producers, Barbara Kelly, Michael Scott Bregman; assistant director, Yudi Bennett; casting, Mary Colquhoun. Reviewed at the Bruin theater, L.A., March 15, 1988. MPAA Rating: PG-13. Running time: **104 MIN.**

Steve Giardino	Alan Alda
Jackie Giardino	Ann-Margret
Mel Arons	Hal Linden
Kay Hutton	Veronica Hamel
Doc	John Shea
Donna	Mary Kay Place
Judy	Beatrice Alda
Billy	David Eisner

Hollywood — Perhaps trying to break his image as the most conscientiously nice guy of the latter half of the 20th century, Alan Alda has tried to give himself an edge in "A New Life." As the newly divorced Steve Giardino, he is loud, obnoxious, neurotic, argumentative and manic; he also has permed hair and a beard, smokes, drinks hard liquor rather than wine, and eats red meat instead of chicken and fish.

These traits make this Alda more palatable for non-fans of his endlessly caring and understanding persona, but still can't disguise the fact he is *still* a nice guy, and that this is a middle-aged yuppie comedy to its core. If baby humor is still in this spring, Paramount should be seeing some good returns from this mildly pleasant entry.

Almost everything that happens here has a familiar ring to it. After some 20 years of marriage, New Yorkers Alda and Ann-Margret decide to call it quits, more at her instigation than his. Alda's screenplay follows the two equally as each endures the predictably excruciating blind dates, singles parties and matchups, solicits advice from close friends and, in Alda's case, frets over ever meeting anyone decent again.

They are tenacious and game, and some months later each meets an attractive new prospect, she a dreamy, younger TriBeCa sculptor (John Shea), he a sharp and similarly younger doctor (Veronica Hamel).

Swept off her feet at first by her handsome beau, Ann-Margret finally has to confront the wimpier side of Shea's personality, while Alda is drawn quickly toward marriage and encores in fatherhood at a time when his daughter is making him a grandfather.

Alda seems to be protesting, complaining and just plain jawing about everything at all times, and many of his put-upon single man remarks sound like sharp echoes of lines written a long time ago by Neil Simon and Woody Allen. There also is no denying some of the jokes and situations possess tart comic effect, much of it based on the utter recognizability and universality of the emotional drama being played out.

Alda's character is just uningratiating enough to make all the mishaps and unpleasantries he experiences rather enjoyable. Sufficiently vain to dye his graying hair and beard black when hitting the singles trail, he frequently is an insufferable jerk, but a fairly engaging one.

His best friend, played with high humor by Hal Linden, is proudly shallow in his interests, and unsuccessfully tries to introduce his buddy to the pleasures of stupid young disco girls. Ann-Margret's ally, Mary Kay Place, seems even more singlemindedly sexual in her preoccupations, but Ann-Margret's social shyness holds her back even though she looks like a million bucks.

All the actors have the upper-middle-class mannerisms down pat, and make for perfectly agreeable company despite the familiarity of the terrain. Shot mainly in Toronto, pic looks and sounds good. —*Cart.*

Police Academy 5: Assignment Miami Beach

A Warner Bros. release of a Paul Maslansky production. Produced by Maslansky. Directed by Alan Myerson. Screenplay, Stephen J. Kurwick, based on characters created by Neal Israel and Pat Proft; camera (Technicolor), Jim Pergola; editor, Hubert De La Bouillerie; music, Robert Folk; production design, Trevor Williams; costume design, Robert Musco; sound, Howard Warren; stunt coordinator, Gary Hymes; coproducer, Donald West; assistant directors, Bill Baker, Marty Ewing. Reviewed at Mann's Chinese theater, Hollywood, March 18, 1988. MPAA rating: PG. Running time: **90 MIN.**

Nick	Matt McCoy
Kate	Janet Jones
Cmdt. Lassard	George Gaynes
Capt. Harris	G.W. Bailey
Tony	René Auberjonois
Hightower	Bubba Smith
Tackleberry	David Graf
Jones	Michael Winslow
Callahan	Leslie Easterbrook
Hooks	Marion Ramsey
Proctor	Lance Kinsey
House	Tab Thacker

Hollywood — Negative five plus five equals zero, and the fifth installment of this genre-in-itself arrives at just that stunning plateau. Miami field trip only brings a pastel backdrop to the insipid infighting of the boobs in blue. With a

$455,000,000 worldwide gross for the series to date, pic will probably shake a few more coins from an audience eager for another spoonfeeding.

The jokes are all on Capt. Harris (G.W. Bailey) this time out, as he makes a disastrous attempt to unseat Cmdt. Lassard (George Gaynes), aging leader of this duncecap police academy, by pulling out a mandatory retirement clause.

Lassard's last act is supposed to be to address a Miami police convention, which gives his downhearted but loyal graduates, rallying behind him, an excuse to follow him there for some surfside antics.

At Miami airport, Lassard crosses paths with some more excitable crooks, and in the old luggage switcheroo, ends up in possession of some diamonds they've heisted.

The trio of baddies, led by René Auberjonois, who plays the Moe part in what amounts to a watered-down Three Stooges routine, spends the rest of the film trying to get them back from the blissfully unaware, graciously idiotic Lassard.

Meanwhile, Harris and his yes-man assistant, Proctor (Lance Kinsey), are trying to trip up Lassard at every turn, only to have their schemes backfire. Sometimes the gags are funny, as when Proctor sets Harris' hat on fire while he's trying to pick up a girl in a bar. Other times, they're just dumb. Raunchy humor — mostly consisting of the kind of language fourth-graders use to insult each other — gives the film a PG rating, but other than that it's safe stuff.

The usual crew — minus Steve Guttenberg or Bobcat Goldthwait, but with Tab Thacker, a Fat Albert lookalike, taking both seats — is ostensibly on vacation while in Miami, and takes a backseat to the action, lethargic pace suited to the resort environs.

Water-skiing stunt scenes are roughly edited, and Alan Myerson contributes by-the-numbers direction. —*Daws.*

La Ligne De Chaleur
(The Heat Line)
(CANADIAN)

An ACPAV production (world sales: Film Transit, Montreal). Produced by Marc Daigle. Directed by Hubert-Yves Rose. Screenplay, Micheline Lanctôt, Rose; camera (Eastmancolor), Michel Caron; music, Richard Gregoire; production manager, Danny Chaifour; sound, Yvon Benoit; assistant director, Lise Abastado; casting, Deirdre Brown. Reviewed at Berlin Film Festival (market), Feb. 17, 1988. Running time: **88 MIN.**

Robert Filion	Gabriel Arcand
Maxime Filion	Simon Gonzalez
Norman G. Simpson	Gerard Parkes

Berlin — A finely wrought road movie about loneliness, loss and alienation, "The Heat Line" is not a cheerful night's entertainment but succeeds very well indeed as a thought-provoking and beautifully

handled drama.

Pic was sneaked in the Berlin market and may be bound for other major fests this year before enjoying a prestige arthouse career; it will need very careful handling.

The drama begins in Montreal in midwinter. Robert (Gabriel Arcand) recently divorced from his wife and still adjusting to life alone, hears that his father, whom he hasn't, seen in several years, has died in Florida. Robert takes his young son Maxime (Simon Gonzalez) down south with him and they decide to drive the father's car back to Canada. After initially contrasting Montreal's snowbound chills with Florida's steamy heat, first-time director Hubert-Yves Rose sets the rest of the movie on the road, in Georgia, the Carolinas and Virginia.

The trip doesn't go smoothly. Motels are all full and father and son are sleeping in the car when Georgia cops abruptly awake them and move them on. Later they meet an avuncular, talkative, over-friendly man (Gerard Parkes) who writes travel books. Robert finds him a bit sinister but his rather corny charm appeals to the child, which makes the father even more tense. When the stranger confesses he's dying of a terminal disease Robert is made even more uneasy.

Things come to a head at the aptly named Drama Motel in Chesapeake Bay, Va., which is said to be on the socalled "heat line" that divides southern climes from the northern cold. Robert gets drunk and decides he won't return Maxim to his mother; the boy is frightened by his father's increasingly irrational behavior and the unexpected return of the stranger doesn't help.

"The Heat Line," which director Rose has dedicated to his father, primarily is about father-son relationships and loss. At first Robert isn't unduly disturbed by his father's death but the reality of it finally sinks in and by the end he's literally haunted by it. He also has difficulties coming to terms with his own son, especially since the divorce.

This is a difficult theme to put across in a film and even more difficult to make work commercially. The film lacks meaningful femme roles and is played out between three male principals: father, son and stranger. Rose skillfully builds up a sense of dislocation and undefined angst thanks to three fine performances and top camerawork. Film could win critical kudos and find an appreciative if limited international audience, but it will be a tough sell. Pic is good enough to make the effort worthwhile, however. — *Strat.*

The Thin Blue Line
(DOCU)

An American Playhouse presentation of a Third Floor production. Produced by Mark Lipson. Executive producer, Lindsay Law. Directed by Errol Morris. Camera (Duart color), Stefan Czapsky, Robert Chappell; editor, Paul Barnes; music, Philip Glass; production design, Teddy Bafaloukos; art direction, Lester Cohen; sound (Dolby), Brad Fuller; associate producer, Fuller; additional camera, Philip Carr-Foster, Ned Burgess, Peter Sova, Tom Sigal; additional sound, Steven Aaron. Reviewed at the Aidikoff screening room, L.A., March 18, 1988. (In San Francisco Film Festival.) No MPAA Rating. Running time: **106 MIN.**

Hollywood — Rather like the cinematic equivalent of Truman Capote's literary achievement in "In Cold Blood," Errol Morris' "The Thin Blue Line" constitutes a mesmerizing reconstruction and investigation of a senseless murder. Employing strikingly original formal devices to pull together diverse interviews, filmclips, photo collages and recreations of the crime from many points of view, pic cannot be easily classified, which is all to its credit.

World premiered March 18 at the San Francisco Film Festival, this compelling, real-life drama will certainly win the top reviews it needs to push it to successful runs in specialized release prior to eventual PBS airing.

Morris is known by buffs for "Gates Of Heaven" (1978) and "Vernon, Florida" (1981), oddball documentaries that were sometimes outrageously humorous due to their deadpan, highly controlled approach to the bizarre fringes of Americana.

After a long layoff, filmmaker has continued in the same individualistic language but has expanded significantly his vocabulary to tackle more substantive material. Case in question centers upon the 1976 murder of a Dallas policeman. Late one night, Officer Robert Wood and his partner pulled over a car that was traveling without its headlights on. When Wood approached the driver's window, he was shot five times and killed, and his partner failed to catch the license number or even remember the make of car correctly.

Some time later, David Harris, 16, was arrested in Vidor, Texas, after having bragged to friends that he'd killed a Dallas cop. The murder weapon was found in a nearby swamp, but Harris later insisted his boasting was only meant to impress his buddies, and that the real murderer was a hitchhiker he'd picked up earlier in the day, one Randall Adams.

Despite Harris' extensive criminal history and Adams' unblemished past, the teenager got off scot-free, while the older man was convicted and sentenced to death (later committed to life imprisonment).

Morris first introduces the two

men via freshly filmed, straightforward interviews, then stages the crime for the camera from a variety of angles and at an assortment of speeds. Eventually entering the picture are other key players, including Adams' two attorneys, the judge, various law enforcement officials and three eyewitnesses of seemingly dubious credibility.

It doesn't seem to have been Morris' original intent to prove either of the men's guilt or innocence, but the weight of all the evidence provided heavily suggests justice was not done.

In a shocking final scene, Harris, now on death row for a later murder, as much as confesses to Morris on audiotape that Adams is innocent after all. While such a conversation is inadmissible in court, the film makes such a strong case for Adams that the viewer cannot help feeling a new trial would be in order. Almost incidentally, the film also emerges as a potent critique of the death penalty.

Clearly a self-conscious artist rather than a socially conscious documentarian, Morris has in spite of himself, made a film that succeeds both as an *objet d'art* and a nonfiction narrative. The things he chooses to show, and the way he reveals them, betray the eye of a highly creative filmmaker, one in which a passion for legal justice is only slowly awakened during the course of the investigation.

Visual design, lighting and editing are impeccable, with all these elements carefully planned in a way entirely at odds with the technique of the ordinary documentary. Also of critical importance is Philip Glass' rushing score, which bestows the drama with a relentless propulsiveness. Title refers to the police, said by the judge here to be the only thing that separates the public from the rule of anarchy. —Cart.

Av Zamani
(Hunting Time)
(TURKISH)

A Metropolis Films presentation of a Mine Film, Istanbul, production. Produced by Kadri Yurdatap. Directed by Erden Kiral. Screenplay, Ferit Edgü; camera (color), Kenan Ormanlar; editor, Nevzat Dislacik; music, Sarper Öszan; sound, Serdan Isin; art direction, Nur Özalp. Reviewed at Berlin Film Festival (competing), Feb. 14, 1988. Running time: **96 MIN.**
Writer . . . . Aytac Arman
Housekeeper . . . . Serif Sezer
Ali . . . . Zihni Kucumen
Murder victim . . . . Nüvit Özdogru
Fisherman . . . . Dilaver Uyanik

Berlin — Director Erden Kiral, who won an award in Berlin five years ago for his "Season In Hakkari," now moves the issue of terrorism onto Turkish ground in order to show once again the intellectual's impotence to deal with it.

A writer retreats to is native island after the vicious murder of a close friend and spiritual guide. He hopes to find in the old parental home, abandoned years ago, the calm and security he badly needs. He has lost all confidence in himself and in his writing which he finds obsolete in a world addicted to violence.

A childhood friend, Ali, helps him settle down, arranges for a housekeeper that evidently has designs on the handsome author and tries to convince him that nothing can happen in this idyllic spot removed from the turbulence of the big city.

Terrorism is a spreading disease: the tormented writer witnesses a second murder during one of his morning walks, which nobody believes until the victim's body is fished out of the sea, because nothing like this has ever happened before on the peaceful little island.

Like his previous films, Kiral's new one relies on mood rather on than on story. There are numerous travelings over barren landscapes, the pace is excruciatingly slow and there are frequent flashbacks of encounters with the dead friend, the two of them trying to make sense of life. All of it takes place as the main character walks around speechlessly with a grim, desperate expression which leaves little room for hope.

Serif Sezer, as the gaunt, devoted and yet very reserved housekeeper, is the only one of the cast who manages to create an interesting character, the others going through the motions none too convincingly. Kiral's insistence to deal with his issue only on the most abstract level, never specifying its reasons, deprives his statement of the dramatic impact it should have had. —Edna.

Miss Arizona
(HUNGARIAN-ITALIAN)

A Hunnia Studio (Mafilm)-Video Distributori Associati/Reteitalia coproduction. Directed by Pal Sandor. Screenplay, Alfredo Giannetti, Sandor; camera (Eastmancolor), Elemer Ragalyi, editor, Nino Baragli; music, Armando Trovajoli; sound, György Kovacs. Reviewed at Hungarian Film Week, Budapest, Feb. 11, 1988. Running time: **108 MIN.**
Sandor Rozsnyai . . . . Marcello Mastroianni
Mitzi . . . . Hanna Schygulla
Eva . . . . Dorottya Udvaros
Also with: Alessandro Martinez, Urbano Barberini, Augusto Poderosi, Sandor Zsoter, Juli Basti, Gabor Reviszky, Deszö Caras, Karoly Eperjes, Pal Hetenyi.
(Hungarian language version)

Budapest — One of those elaborate, large-scale romantic melodramas spanning 25 turbulent years, "Miss Arizona" will have to succeed on the strength of its two lead actors, Marcello Mastroianni and Hanna Schygulla, because it's an otherwise bland and familiar offering.

Pal Sandor's career has been one of ups and downs, with excellent pics such as "Daniel Takes A Train" offset by clinkers such as "Just A Movie." This new one falls somewhere in between.

Hungarian cinema hit paydirt with two lavish West German coproductions helmed by Istvan Szabo, and there's a third on the way. This coprod with Italy seems like a conscious attempt to milk the same formula, but Sandor doesn't have the abilities of Szabo to turn familiar themes into something more, and "Miss Arizona" pales beside both "Mephisto" and "Colonel Redl." However, it does have Mastroianni, giving yet another thoroughly charming and professional performance, and Schygulla, who looks elegant throughout. Both miraculously survive being dubbed into Hungarian (the international version of the film will be the Italian one).

Story is based on the careers of real-life characters. Pic opens in Budapest in 1920 with the slaying of Stein, an elderly Jew, by right-wingers looking for some diamonds he's known to possess. Stein leaves behind Mitzi (Schygulla), his flighty wife, and a small son (the diamonds are hidden in the child's toy monkey). Mitzi is aided by Sandor (Mastroianni), an ebullient entertainer temporarily down on his luck. He's half-Italian, half-Jewish but, as he notes, all Hungarian. The three escape to Italy, where Mitzi uses her charms to keep them in funds.

By the mid-'30s, they're back in Budapest running the famous Arizona club, a night-spot that quickly becomes the in place for the city's elite. They're riding high, except that Mitzi becomes involved with a Yank journalist who's spying on the Magyar fascists, and their son has fallen for a girl who has links with powerful Germans.

Comes the war, and the Jewish purge begins in Hungary. The son is shocked to discover he's half-Jewish, and also to see his young wife flirting with his stepfather. His suicide comes across, though, as abrupt and unmotivated, one of many loose ends in the Hungarian version of the film. Eventually, the Arizona club is bombed. Jews, including Sandor, are rounded up for transportation, but there's an ironic twist at fadeout.

Given the pitfalls of international coprods of this nature, the film is a lot better than might have been expected. Pal Sandor brings off many scenes with flair and charm, such as an impromptu sing-song on a ship in Italian waters, or the visit of two Jewish friends to the nightclub (they will, of course, be rounded up later in the film). Given the mixed Hungarian-Italian cast, acting styles meld smoothly together, and the Hungarian dubbing is impeccably handled. Production dress is excellent, and there's the usual fine camerawork of Elemer Ragalyi, plus a jaunty Armando Trovajoli score.

On the minus side there are gaps in the narrative that suggest the ruthless cutting down of a much longer film, and some of the moments of melodrama are awkwardly handled — the viewer only has to consider how, say, Fassbinder might have handled this story to sense that a bland middle road has been taken.

Pic will play better in Europe than elsewhere, since it's too familiar and soft-centered to attract much attention in other markets. However, Mastroianni's following is considerable, and his fans won't be disappointed with his playing in this role, so adroit handling could result in useful runs in key cities. —Strat.

Italian Language Version:

Rome — "Miss Arizona" opened to scant interest among local filmgoers in spite of a roaring publicity campaign by Italy distribs Artisti Associati and the presence of Marcello Mastroianni in the cast. In Italian, Mastroianni is an entertaining showman of Fellini stamp; Schygulla, dubbed, a blander slapstick as the eternal femmina. The jumpy, at times disconnected editing and familiar story smack of a tv cut-down, and indeed tale seems destined to the small screen for most of its Euro exploitation. —Yung.

Pabo Sunon
(Fool's Manifesto)
(SOUTH KOREAN)

A Hwa Chun Trading Co. production. Produced by Park Chong-Chan. Directed by Lee Chang-Ho. Screenplay, Yoon Si-Mon, based on novel by Lee Dong-Chul; camera (color), Suh Jung-Min; editor, Kim Hee-Su; music, Lee Jong-Ku; sound, Kim Kyung-Il, Kim Byung-Su; art direction, Kim Yoo-Jung. Reviewed at Berlin Film Festival (Forum of Young Cinema), Feb. 13, 1988. Running time: **87 MIN.**
Hae-Yong . . . . Lee Bo-Hee
Dong-Chil . . . . Kim Myung-Kon
Fatso . . . . Lee Hui-Sung

Berlin — The most accurate definition for this 1983 picture would be slapstick tragedy. It's based on an enormously successful novel written by a former convict, which has shocked Korean readers by describing the low life of prostitutes and bums.

This film adaptation uses silent movie gags, speeded up motion, children's drawings for credits, and a child's voice for the narrator. It will take Wesern audiences by surprise, which might find it difficult to categorize.

The trio of characters it deals with are a dimwit vagabond, a fat taxi driver and a young hooker. The dimwit falls for the girl, believing she is a student, he secures the taxi driver's help in order to abduct her and discovers her real identity.

Moving often haphazardly from one situation to another, trying to avoid clichés but often falling into this trap, the picture is a hodgepodge of refreshing ideas and stale jokes, with some astonishingly moving moments stuck in between.

Well shot, dynamically cut and featuring nice performances by the girl (Lee Bo-Hee) and Fatso (Lee Hui-Sung), this could be an easily accepted introduction to a cinema barely known in the West. —*Edna.*

Johnny Be Good

An Orion Pictures release. Executive producers, Steve Zacharias, Jeff Buhai, David Obst. Produced by Adam Fields. Directed by Bud Smith. Screenplay, Zacharias, Buhai, Obst; camera (Foto-Kem color, Deluxe prints), Robert D. Yeoman; editor, Scott Smith; music supervisor, Dick Rudolph; original music, Jay Ferguson; sound, Mike Dobie; costumes, Susie DeSanto; production design, Gregg Fonseca; art direction, Sharon Seymour; set decoration, Doree Cooper, production manager, Jeffrey Chernov; stunt coordinator, Russell Towery; associate producer, Karen Penhale; assistant director, Paul Moen; casting, Gary M. Zuckerbrod. Reviewed at Festival theater, N.Y. March 17, 1988. MPAA Rating: PG-13. Running time: **84 MIN.**

Johnny Walker	Anthony Michael Hall
Leo Wiggins	Robert Downey Jr.
Wayne Hisler	Paul Gleason
Georgia Elkans	Uma Thurman
Coach Sanders	Steve James
Wallace Gibson	Seymour Cassel
Tex Wade	Michael Greene
Chief Elkans	Marshall Bell
Mrs. Walker	Deborah May
Vinny Kroll	Michael Alldredge

Also with: Howard Cosell, Jim McMahon, Robert Downey Sr., John Pankow, Jennifer Tilly, Jon Stafford, Pete Koch, George Hall, Lucianne Buchanan, Tony Frank, Tim Rossovich.

Easily amused high schoolers will be glad to know that the makers of "Johnny Be Good" have ignored the demise in profitability of the teen comedy. Fact that almost any of the many films in the marketplace is better than this dull bulb, however, suggests youths won't be grateful enough to show up in large numbers.

An embarrassing directorial debut for "Exorcist" and "Flashdance" editor Bud Smith, "Johnny Be Good" takes the "Porky's"-inspired bawdy cartoon approach to a serious issue. As true events have shown, college officials will go to unethical lengths to sign up gifted high school athletes.

Anthony Michael Hall plays Johnny Walker — no scotch whiskey jokes, surprisingly, given pic's unbroken string of cheap jokes — a quarterback who's so good, he is besieged by dozens of leisure-suited university recruiters from the moment he won his last high school game, 52-0.

All there is to the plot really is Johnny's all-expenses paid, no-holds-barred visits to various colleges (fictionally named, luckily for the colleges actually punished for illegal recruiting). Slick and sleazy, the college scouts (Seymour Cassell, Michael Green, John Pankow, mainly) ply him with booze, bimbos and kickbacks, everything except a guarantee of an education.

First Johnny is indifferent, then he's sucked into the glitz until his girl friend (Uma Thurman in her debut), family (Deborah May, George Hall, Adam Faraizl, Megan Morris) and a night in jail help him see What's Important.

The screenwriters' biggest mistake, although they certainly aren't the first to make it, is confusing funny with obnoxious. There are several excrement jokes and their idea of sight gags include pizza in the face and an obese couple necking when idiot coach Hisler (Paul Gleason) is trying to eat his lunch.

Gleason isn't the only supporting actor to suffer in this misfired comedy. As Johnny's best friend, Robert Downey Jr. has no material to work with so tries to inject his otherwise appealing manic humor. He seems to be improvising most of his time here. His father, the director Robert Downey Sr., crops up as an NCAA investigator who gathers evidence against the scurrilous scouts.

Chicago Bear quarterback Jim McMahon is an onscreen briefly as Hall visits him on the set of a commercial. In the least subtle and arguably most offensive example of product placement, the whole commercial for Adidas is shown. Neither McMahon's nor Howard Cosell's cameos are likely to boost patronage in a big way.

Hall, now 19 going on strike 3 as a topliner following "Out Of Bounds" and this pic, is not getting better as he's getting older. Screenwriters Steve Zacharias, Jeff Buhai and David Obst (of "Revenge Of The Nerds") didn't give Hall much room to stretch anyway.

After a forgettable soundtrack of contempo rock music, audience finally gets to hear Chuck Berry's "Johnny B. Goode" just as the end credits are rolled over tv-tempoed sequences depicting the comeuppance of those who would lead an innocent lad down a greedy and immoral path. —*Binn.*

Hamlet Liikemaailmassa
(Hamlet Goes Into Business)
(FINNISH-B&W)

A Christa Saredi presentation of a Villealfa Films production. Produced, written and directed by Aki Kaurismäki. Camera (b&w), Timo Salminen; editor, Raija Talvio; sound, Veikko Aaltonen, Jouko Lumme; art direction, Pertti Hikamo; costumes, Tuula Hilkamo. Reviewed at Berlin Film Festival (Forum of Young Cinema), Berlin, Feb. 17, 1988. Running time: **86 MIN.**

Hamlet	Pirkka-Pekka Petelius
Klaus	Esko Salminen
Ophelia	Kati Outinen
Gertrud	Elina Salo
Polonius	Esko Nikkari
Lauri	Kari Väänänen

Also with: Hau Valtonen, Mari Rantasila, Turo Pajala, Aake Kalliala, Pontti Auer, Matti Pellonpää.

Berlin — This isn't exactly a parody or a send-up of the Shakespeare classic, nor quite an adaptation of it but rather an attempt to update it sarcastically in terms of Finland today.

Hamlet Sr. is a big paper baron, one of the more lucrative industries in the country. His son is a spoiled brat, a playboy devoid of any sense of responsibility. After his father's demise, he inherits the bulk of the family's fortune, but doesn't seem to be particularly interested, his main concern being to bed down Ophelia, the daughter of his father's chief counselor. When he has his meeting with his father's ghost, introduced at a relatively late stage, he starts acting strange, after warning his friends to expect his weirdness.

Less concerned with the psychological aspects, director Aki Kaurismäki focuses on economic and social issues. Klaus, Hamlet's uncle who marries his mother, is blamed less for attempted murder, his real crime being economic manipulations which will leave thousands of workers unemployed, dockyards and factories will close down, while the traditional family business will be reprofiled to produce rubber ducks. Class distinctions are further stressed by presenting Hamlet's cronies as his servant staff, subalterns to be ordered around rudely.

Alternately amusing and angry, using at times obvious humor, but also cynical social and even national criticism, Kaurismäki's main problem is choosing a clear point of view. At times he seems bent on broad farce, Hamlet's unpleasantness and stupidity being overplayed when he writes ridiculous poetry or when he is sneered at by the ghost. Other times, he is almost a smart schemer, with his remarks on class struggle or Finland's economic status. Greed seems to be the only human feature taken seriously in this picture, the undoing of all characters, more than any other moral issue.

The tongue-in-cheek approach chills any eventual emotion, but the actors are careful to keep a straight face, even in childishly awkward situations.

Never intended as more than a joke, with black and white photography effective in its own way, this could be an offbeat type of entertainment, as long as it isn't taken too seriously. —*Edna.*

Tüske A Köröm Alatt
(A Thorn Under The Fingernail)
(HUNGARIAN)

A Budapest Studio, Mafilm, production. Directed by Sandor Sara. Screenplay, Sara, Sandor Csoori; camera (Eastmancolor), Sandor Kurucz; editor, Mariann Tuba; music, Peter Eötvöss; production design, Erzebet Mialkovszky; sound, György Fek; assistant director, Ferenc Jeli. Reviewed at Hungarian Film Week, Budapest, Feb. 7, 1988. Running time: **90 MIN.**

Andras Hodosi	György Cserhalmi
Zsuzsa	Anna Rackevei

Also with: Erika Szegedi, Attila Tyll, Tibor Kenderesi, Gabor Koncz, Gabor Reviczky.

Budapest — This handsomely produced political thriller is the first fiction film in 10 years by cameraman-turned-director Sandor Sara, who's been making probing docus in the meanwhile. Tale, which has many of the elements of a western thriller, including a climax borrowed from "North By Northwest," is a bit remote for non-Hungarians, dealing as it does with corrupt Party officials and their scams, so theatrical chances outside Hungary are poor.

Drama centers on Andras, played by popular lead actor Györy Cserhalmi, an artist who has opted out and lives as a shepherd on the visually spectacular Plain. As a 13-year-old, he'd been caught with a gun during the 1956 uprising and sent to a reformatory where a cruel administrator had driven another youngster to suicide. On the Plain, Andras meets the man from his past again; he's now working as chauffeur for an important Party member.

Although engaged in a desultory affair with a married woman, Andras is attracted to Zsuzsa (Anna Rackevei), the Paris-educated daughter of the Party man, who has a French boyfriend in tow. Infuriated by the liaison, and also because Andras had interfered when he and his highly placed friends had been enjoying some illicit hunting of wild boar in a protected area, the Party man starts to put the squeeze on Andras, leading to a climax involving a cropduster that brings the film to an abrupt, downbeat, freeze-frame fade-out.

Non-Magyars may be a bit confused about the details of the Party man's corruption, which centers on a scam involving wrongly registered geese. Leaving aside the plot mechanics, the film is entertaining enough, though a bit more action and a bit less introspection might have made it more accessible. It seems to strive to be a romantic thriller, an exposé, and a serious study of an alienated artist all at once, and Sara doesn't integrate all these elements with complete success.

Nonetheless, the film is always watchable thanks to very handsome camerawork which uses the stark beauty of the Plain to very good effect. Rackevei has a brooding presence which suggests she'll be much in demand in future pics. —*Strat.*

Return To Snowy River
Part II
(AUSTRALIAN)

A Hoyts (Australia) release (Buena Vista Distribution in U.S.) of a Burrowes Film Group-Hoyts Entertainment production. Executive producers, Dennis Wright, John Kearney. Produced and directed by Geoff Burrowes. Screenplay, Burrowes, John Dixon; camera (Panavision, Eastmancolor), Keith Wagstaff; editor, Gary Woodyard; music, Bruce Rowland; production design, Leslie Binns; sound, Gary Wilkins; 2d unit director/camera, David Eggby; production supervisor, Bill Regan; costumes, Jenny Arnott; production manager, Stuart Menzies; assistant director, John Powditch; horse master, John Lovich; casting, Susie Maizels. Reviewed at Hoyts screening room, Sydney, Jan. 15, 1988. Running time: **97 MIN.**

Jim Craig	Tom Burlinson
Jessica Harrison	Sigrid Thornton
Harrison	Brian Dennehy
Alistair Patton	Nicholas Eadie
Harry Hawker	Bryan Marshall
Patton Sr.	Rhys McConnochie
Seb	Mark Hembrow
Jake	Peter Cummins
Mrs. Darcy	Cornelia Francis
Jacko	Tony Barry

Sydney — In 1982, "The Man From Snowy River," produced by **Geoff Burrowes** and directed by **George Miller**, grossed some $A25,-000,000 in Australia, at the time a record amount for a local pic (it has since been swamped by "Crocodile Dundee"); pic's world gross was reported to be $A50,000,000. The sequel is very much the mixture as before, with the same pluses and minuses, and should perform almost as well at the local wickets, with a useful international career also indicated.

Biggest plus, once again, is the film's great look. Shot on rugged locations in Victoria's High Country, with Keith Wagstaff once again responsible for the beautiful camerawork, images of galloping horses and riders are genuinely exciting. There's also a bit more action this time around, with a hissable villain (Nicholas Eadie) who wields a saber in a climactic struggle with the unarmed hero.

Latter is Jim Craig, played again by Tom Burlinson, with love interest once more in the capable hands of Sigrid Thornton. However, Kirk Douglas, who essayed two roles in Part I, is not back for a second ride, nor is Jack Thompson, who played a marginal character originally. George Miller has been succeeded as director by producer Burrowes (coincidentally, the producer of "Crocodile Dundee," John Cornell, also has taken over from that pic's director, Peter Faiman, as helmer of "Croc II"). Change of director has made no noticeable difference to pic's style.

Newcomer to the cast is Brian Dennehy, lending his considerable presence to one of the Kirk Douglas roles, that of Harrison, Thornton's father and a local landowner.

Plot takes up sometime after Part I left off. Jim has been away for some months in the desert mustering horses, and returns to find Jessica (Thornton) has been forced by her father to become engaged to the unctuous Alistair Patton (Eadie), son of the local banker. Reviled as a hick and a drifter and a member of "the hairy unwashed" by the conservative landed gentry, Jim has to prove his worth all over again.

Matters are complicated by the fact that his stallion has been luring away valuable mares. As a parallel to this theme, Jim persuades Jessica to join him in his mountaintop home, a breaking of taboos which doesn't seem to outrage the community as much as one might expect.

Story climaxes when the evil Alistair and his mates steal a clutch of horses and head for the border, with everyone else in pursuit. Final conflict between Jim and Alistair ends in the latter's defeat, and pic ends with a wedding (in white).

Story owes much to "Green Grass Of Wyoming" and its ilk, and comes across as old-style Disney family fare. It completely lacks the mythic allusions to the Banjo Patterson poem (beloved of all older generation Aussies) that inspired Part I, and this could diminish its local b.o. chances. Dialog is often clinched, while plotting is mechanical.

Direction of early scenes is slow at times, but thesping is better than its was first time round, with Burlinson, especially, giving a rugged performance as the youthful hero, and Dennehy less inclined to camp things up than was Douglas. Film comes into its own with the horse scenes, and there's a heartstopping moment when Jim rides his mount down an almost vertical slope (idea is a repeat from Part I, but still works well). There's also more pathos. Youngsters should love the horses, though might get restless as the plot unfolds. Overall this should earn plenty of dollars on its home territory without, perhaps, quite coming up to the original's figures.

Production is sumptuous in every department, with snappy editing by Gary Woodyard, handsome production design by Leslie Binns and rousing music from Bruce Rowland, latter two on hand again as they were first time round. — *Strat.*

Espérame En El Cielo
(Wait For Me In Heaven)
(SPANISH)

A BMG production with collaboration of Televisión Española. Executive producer, José Maria Calleja. Directed by Antonio Mercero. Screenplay, Mercero, Horacio Valcárcel, Román Gubern; camera (color), Manuel Rojas; music, Carmelo Bernaola. Reviewed at Cine Carlos III, Madrid, Feb. 13, 1988. Running time: **106 MIN.**

With: Pepe Soriano, José Sazatornil, Chus Lampreave, Manolo Codeso, Amparo Valle, J. Luis Barceló, Federico Cambres, Francisco Javier, Miguel de Grandi, Chari Moreno, Pedro Civera.

Madrid — Did General Franco have a double? The supposition that he could have is the basis for this occasionally droll flight of fancy toplining the Argentine thesp Pepe Soriano. Though there are occasionally some amusing situations and clever parodies, pic drags on far too long and the script never picks up momentum. Also, Soriano doesn't look enough like Franco to be really convincing.

The weak story has a Madrid shopkeeper who sells prosthetic equipment kidnaped by Franco's henchmen. After clipping his hair, pasting a moustache on him and training him in the personal quirks and mannerisms, the henchmen oblige the bewildered double to take Franco's place in official ceremonies. His wife, who believes she is now a widow, tries to communicate with him via spiritualistic seances, when to her surprise the double slips away one night to visit her.

Thereafter, he returns to live out his years in Franco's palace, but he lets her know when it is he appears in the newsreels and not Franco, by touching his ear.

Most of the humor will be lost on all but local audiences, or those well-versed in the Franco period, though there are occasionally comic situations such as when Franco and his double are confused by the palace guards. Soriano is rather too deadpan, but Chas Lampreave and José Sazatornil manage to liven up some of the scenes. A point of some interest is that numerous sequences are shot on the true locations, such as the Pardo Palace, the Valley of the Fallen, the Entrepeñas reservoir and on Franco's yacht. — *Besa.*

La Visione del Sabba
(The Witches' Sabbath)
(ITALIAN-FRENCH)

A Titanus release of a Gruppo Bema/Reteitalia/Cinemax (Paris) coproduction. Produced by Achille Manzotti. Executive producer, Claudio Mancini. Directed by Marco Bellocchio. Screenplay, Bellocchio, Francesca Pirani; camera (Luciano Vittori color) Beppe Lanci; editor, Mirko Garrone; music, Carlo Crivelli; art direction, Gianni Burchiello; choreography, Raffaella Rossellini. Reviewed at Ariston 2 Cinema, Rome, Feb. 28, 1988. Running time: **100 MIN.**

Maddalena	Béatrice Dalle
Davide	Daniel Ezralow
Cristina	Corinne Tauzet
Prof. Cadò	Omero Antonutti
Hysteric	Roberta Palladini

Also with: Jacques Weber.

Rome — Psychoanalysis has had a hold on helmer Marco Bellocchio for most of his filmmaking career, often enriching his characters and putting a dark and disturbing stamp on their behavior. "The Witches' Sabbath," like last year's perversely fascinating "Devil In The Flesh," centers on a woman labeled mad by a society unwilling to tolerate her divergence from the norm.

Here, however, Bellocchio's sympathy for the ostracized female flounders in a poorly constructed narrative banally designed to manipulate limits between the real and the imaginary. Art house sex star Béatrice Dalle ("Betty Blue"), the virgin-seductress who believes she's a witch, remains pic's best hope of drawing an audience beyond the director's personal following, who probably will account for most of the ticket sales at home and abroad for this disappointing offering.

Film's other point of interest is the witch/sabbath theme, associated with several bold scenes of torture, orgies and female nudity. Amply publicized, in the wake of choreographer Raffaella Rossellini's lawsuit against the production company for allegedly subjecting her to extra-contractual nudity and physical mistreatment, film's set piece, the long sabbath dance sequence, is a major letdown. Running almost 20 minutes of screen time, the sequence (including a stylized orgy, performed by the dancers with their clothes on) falls far short of the emotional excitement it obviously wants to generate. The dancing is good, the choreography modern, but somewhere in the editing process the sabbath has lost its bite.

With a story of gossamer weight, "Sabbath" hangs on mood and striking images, at times brilliantly captured by Beppe Lanci's refined camerawork coupled to filmer's very visual imagination. Davide (Daniel Ezralow) is a young psychiatrist who has lost none of his idealism. A forceful opener has him dreaming of a grisly Medieval trial and autopsy of a comely nude witch (Dalle), whom he publicly embraces. In reality, he has yet to encounter the present-day Dalle, locked up as criminally insane after she shoots to death a voyeur she claims was spying on her.

Davide's field method is to put his own humanity on the line when he is dealing with a patient, as his violent confrontation with a hysteric (Roberta Palladini) in a hospital demonstrates. When he meets Maddalena (Dalle), his empathy is so strong he enters her world, having visions on a regular basis: he sees her hanging from a wall in an iron cage; he watches her disappear underwater and not come back up; he projects himself into the Sabbath as the main protagonist of a wild celebration involving dozens of frenzied dancers. He sees her burn at the stake and survive the flames. Worst of all, from the p.o.v. of his understandably distraught wife Corinne Tauzet and his medical colleagues, he falls in love with the patient and lets no rational consideration stand in the way of his passion.

Ezralow, a dancer-turned-actor ("Camorra") with some screen presence but limited expressive range, makes an overly soft, ingenuous psychiatrist. Dalle, in contrast (and most of the other female members of the cast) is painted in starkly primitive colors — she produces a ferociously immediate impression, but her motivation and psychology, in the most general sense, remain distressingly unclear. Film indulges in a lot of hocuspocus with what's real and what's imaginary without producing any additional depth. Most seriously, it forgets to develop sympathy for Maddalena, making her ultimate fate of very little interest. — *Yung.*

Il Volpone
(The Big Fox)
(ITALIAN)

A CDI release of a Tiger Cinematrografica production in association with RAI-TV Channel 1. Produced by Mario & Vittorio Cecchi Gori. Associate producers, Bruno Altissimi and Claudio Saraceni for Maura International Film. Directed by Maurizio Ponzi. Screenplay, Leo Benvenuti, Piero De Bernardi, Ottavio Jemma, Ponzi, from play "Volpone," by Ben Jonson; camera (color), Alessandro D'Eva; editor, Sergio Montanari; music, Fabio Liberatore; art direction, Maurizio Tognalini. Reviewed at Barbarini Cinema, Rome, March 11, 1988. Running time: **111 MIN.**

Ugo Maria Volpone . . . . . . Paolo Villaggio
Mosca . . . . Enrico Montesano
Raffaele . . . . Renzo Montagnani
Corvino . . . . Enrico Maria Salerno
Corbaccio . . . . Alessandro Haber
　　Also with: Eleanora Giorgi (the mayor), Maria Angela Giordano, Athina Cenci.

Rome — **"The Big Fox" is a decently funny farce lampooning the greed of heirs and the fawning of ambitious servants. Helmer Maurizio Ponzi, who began his career with more serious subjects, has shown great aptitude in handling light comedy without pretense or vulgarity.**

Aided by a strong cast, "Fox," based on a celebrity play by Ben Jonson, ought to reward the care with which it was made with a good domestic showing. Foreign playoff will be limited to Italo comedy markets.

One of pic's pluses is the room it gives thesps to work to the best of their ability. Paolo Villaggio is strikingly different from his usual incarnations as millionaire Ugo Maria Volpone, a role he plays with believable finesse. Enrico Montesano is his new butler Mosca, an operator even smoother than the master. The two hit it off at once and join forced to play dirty tricks on a trio of would-be heirs to the Volpone fortune. Twist at the end sees the riches ably maneuvered into Mosca's lap, while Volpone remains a prisoner in his luxuriously appointed fallout shelter.

The secondary roles are covered by a fine trio of veterans. When servant and master make them believe Volpone is on his deathbed, they scurry for favor, offering the thing they prize most in life. Renzo Montagnani is convinced he should transfer the title of his biggest yacht to the dying man, in the belief he'll soon have it back when the will is read. Enrico Maria Salerno offers his sexy wife Eleanora Giorgi, mayor of the town, for a night of love with the old man. The hysterical Alessandro Haber reluctantly hands over the keys to his beloved million-dollar Maserati at the behest of wife Athina Cenci; he watches it totaled in the next scene.

Ponzi choreographs this not overly original material in a lively dance of one-up-manship. Important is the princely backdrop of Volpone's breathtaking mansion and the picturesque angles of Santa Margheri-

ta Ligure on Italy's northeast coast. Technical work is fine. — *Yung.*

Bright Lights, Big City

An MGM/UA Communications release from United Artists. Produced by Mark Rosenberg, Sydney Pollack. Directed by James Bridges. Screenplay, Jay McInerney, from his novel; camera (Technicolor), Gordon Willis; editor, John Bloom; music, Donald Fagen; production design, Santo Loquasto; art direction, Thomas C. Warren; set decoration, George Detitta; costume design, Bernie Pollack; sound (Dolby), Les Lazarowitz; assistant director, David McGiffert; Coma baby created by Chris Walas Inc.; associate producer, Jack Larson; casting, Mary Colquhoun. Reviewed at Mann's Village theater, Westwood, Calif., March 24, 1988. MPAA Rating: R. Running time: **110 MIN.**

Jamie . . . . Michael J. Fox
Tad . . . . Kiefer Sutherland
Amanda . . . . Phoebe Cates
Megan . . . . Swoosie Kurtz
Clara . . . . Frances Sternhagen
Vicky . . . . Tracy Pollan
Mr. Vogel . . . . John Houseman
Michael . . . . Charlie Schlatter
Alex Hardy . . . . Jason Robards
Rittenhouse . . . . David Warrilow
Mother . . . . Dianne Wiest
Yasu Wade . . . . Alec Mapa
Ferret man . . . . William Hickey

Hollywood — **This novel-cum-feature film is neither very entertaining nor very enlightening. It is, instead, a distinctly morose and maudlin journey through one man's destructive period of personal loss. Fans of the book by Jay McInerney — who also gets screenplay credit — and those curious about how Michael J. Fox handles this serious part should spin a decent number of turnstiles in the early going, but overall b.o. receipts are likely to plateau at modest levels.**

Opening scene establishes Fox as a lonesome barfly with a cocaine habit in the Big Apple. First reason given is that his wife (Phoebe Cates) has dumped him to pursue modeling in Paris. It's later learned that he's also grieving over the death of his mother (Dianne Wiest) a year earlier.

To make such material palatable, a story must clearly establish some reason for the audience (or readers) to empathize with the character. That never happens on screen.

Fox is cast here as Jamie, a would-be writer marking time as a fact checker for literary giant Gotham magazine (subbing for a venerable real-life publication in the same city). There's hope for fine interaction early on as his editorial chiefs, Frances Sternhagen and John Houseman, provide the harsh counterpoint to all-night carousing and drug consumption.

Jamie quickly slides so badly that he's fired during a scene with Sternhagen — an exchange that points up the benefit of placing the youthful Fox in situations with seasoned veterans. That opportunity is completely missed with Houseman, who is barely involved and thus sorely missed.

Jason Robards' appearance as a drunken fiction writer is all to familiar and becomes virtually a caricature. There's one okay luncheon scene but that's almost it for

Robards.

A brief encounter with the fascinating William Hickey and a pittance of time with Wiest round out these cameos. They leave one feeling cheated by clever casting that doesn't match expectations.

As Jamie sinks deeper and deeper into his abyss, he confronts his wife as she works a chic fashion show. He makes a fool of himself, but the confrontation only accentuates the miscasting of Cates as a supposedly alluring femme fatale.

Diamond in the rough is Swoosie Kurtz, whose office-based friendship is genuine. Even as a drunken soliloquy by Fox deteriorates into a lame sexual advance, Kurtz is endearing. But again she, too, is denied adequate time.

Fox' failure to generate much concern over his well-being is perhaps his own doing, or more likely it's the fault of the McInerney script/novel and certainly the direction. In any case, by the time nearly two hours have passed, one easily concludes: who cares, and, more importantly, who cares to spend so much time with this particular guy?

It's understandable that Fox would want to stretch his acting experience by tackling such a part, and at a few points he's quite convincing. But his overwhelming amount of screen time does him a disservice. No thanks to director James Bridges, who was either constrained by the material or lacked adequate rapport with Fox.

Kudos to Chris Walas Inc. for creation of an intriguing coma baby, which was the centerpiece of a metaphorical subtext. — *Tege.*

En toute innocence
(No Harm Intended)
(FRENCH)

An AMLF release of an AJ Films/TF-1 Films coproduction, with the participation of Slav 1 and Images Investissement. Produced and directed by Alain Jessua. Screenplay, Jessua, Luc Béraud, Dominique Roulet, from novel "Suicide à l'amiable" by André Lay; camera (color), Jean Rabier; editor, Hélène Plemiannikov; music, Michel Portal; sound, Paul Lainé, Claude Villand; art direction, Gérard Daoudal. Reviewed at the Marignan-Concorde cinema, Paris, Feb. 14, 1988. (In French Perspectives series at N.Y.'s Museum of Modern Art.) Running time: **95 MIN.**

Paul Duchêne . . . . Michel Serrault
Catherine . . . . Nathalie Baye
Thomas . . . . François Dunoyer
Clémence . . . . Suzanne Flon
Didier . . . . Philippe Caroit
Geneviève . . . . Sylvie Fennec
Serge Cohen . . . . Bernard Fresson
Meunier . . . . André Valardi
Anna . . . . Anna Gaylor

Paris — **"En toute innocence" is a psychological thriller in which a conniving young wife and her invalid father-in-law square off for an unto-the-death showdown. Passably directed by Alain Jessua, main interest is in its players, not the contrived suspense plot adapted from a novel.**

Nathalie Baye, often typecast as the girl-next-door, gets nasty with

Michel Serrault when latter discovers her with a lover. Upset he rushes off the premises and promptly smashes his car. He survives but is brought home in a wheelchair and apparently speechless.

Baye at first seeks reconciliation, anxious to avoid her adoring husband finding out. Serrault's mute refusal leads her to arrange a fatal accident for her formerly devoted father-in-law. Serrault plans a counter-offensive by boobytrapping her shower with electrical wiring. He comes out the victor.

Though her character is somewhat murkily composed, Baye is promising in a malevolent role, while Serrault is unsurprisingly pithy as her antagonist. Among the small supporting cast, Suzanne Flon is excellent as Serrault's long-suffering governess.

This is Jessua's best made film in a long while, but remains middling commercial fare with fair chances in other markets. —*Len.*

Beetlejuice

A Geffen Co. release through Warner Bros. Produced by Michael Bender, Larry Wilson, Richard Hashimoto. Directed by Tim Burton. Screenplay, Michael McDowell, Warren Skaaren from story by McDowell, Larry Wilson; Camera (Technicolor), Thomas Ackerman; editor, Jane Kurson; music, Danny Elfman; sound (Dolby), David Ronne; production design, Bo Welch; set decoration, Catherine Mann; art direction, Tom Duffield; set design, John Warnke, Dick McKenzie; creatures & makeup effects, Robert Short; special effects supervisor, Chuck Gaspar; special visual effects, VCE Inc., Peter Kuran; assistant director, Bill Scott; casting, Jane Jenkins, Janet Hirschenson. Reviewed at the Mann Village theater, L.A., March 24, 1988. MPAA Rating: PG. Running time: **92 MIN.**
Adam . . . . Alec Baldwin
Barbara . . . . Geena Davis
Betelgeuse . . . . Michael Keaton
Delia . . . . Catherine O'Hara
Otho . . . . Glenn Shadix
Lydia . . . . Winona Ryder
Charles . . . . Jeffrey Jones
Juno . . . . Sylvia Sidney
Also with: Patrice Martinez, Robert Goulet, Dick Cavett, Annie McEnroe, Simmy Bow.

Hollywood — "**Beetlejuice**" springs to life when the raucous and repulsive Betelgeuse (Michael Keaton) rises from his moribund state to wreak havoc on fellow spooks and mortal enemies — if only he popped on the scene more often. When he's not, this supernatural comedy mostly is silly and mildly amusing, which probably translates to an equally lukewarm b.o. reception.

Geena Davis and Alec Baldwin are a couple of affectionate New Englanders who live in a big barn of a house that they lovingly are restoring. Just when they are to start a vacation, they crash over a covered bridge and drown — consigned to an afterlife that keeps them stuck at home forever invisible to anyone not similarly situated.

No sooner is their funeral over when their beloved house is sold to a rich New York financier (Jeffrey

Jones), his wife, the affected *artiste* (Catherine O'Hara), her overweight, gay friend Otho (Glenn Shadix) and stepdaughter Lydia (Winona Ryder), dressed in black with a mood to match.

The artiste and her terribly hip sidekick waste no time turning gingham haven into a new wave showcase while Davis and Baldwin fret about how to oust these city rascals. Help comes via a cryptically written book for the newly deceased that takes them into the afterlife — kind of a comical holding cell for people who died of unnatural causes like themselves — but better yet, from this freak of a character named Betelgeuse that lives in the graveyard that's part of the miniature tabletop town that Baldwin built.

In Michael McDowell and Warren Skaaren's script, things above ground aren't nearly as inventive as they are below. Luckily, Keaton pops up from his grave to liven things up when the antics pitting the good ghosts against the intruders become a trite cat & mouse game.

Director Tim Burton seems to like comical actors who are uninhibited in their roles. It was Pee-wee Herman who really brought all his originality and delightfulness to "Pee-wee's Big Adventure," but Keaton's part too often is playing second banana to less-funny eccentrics.

He's a cross between a P.T. Barnum-type pitchman for the hellish and fiendish and an ordinary rascal looking for a little trouble. Keaton looks the part, made up to appear as if he has open sores on his face and worms for coffinfellows. There's more energy in what he does than practically the whole rest of the cast, except for the grand entrance made by the shrill O'Hara as she first attacks the house with a can of spray paint.

It's a pretty hokey story that to some extent succeeds at poking fun at serious horror pictures, the most comical situations and characters found when the cute couple ventures into the underworld to visit their afterlife case worker (Sylvia Sidney), a sassy, chain-smoking parody of a government worker who pours smoke from her neck as well as her mouth and nose.

The living dead include a funny troupe of football players, a 1-dimensional man who was squished to death, and the best specimen, a woman severed at the waist — the bottom half sitting legs crossed on one side of the couch and her top half posing quite sexily on the other. Closing scene with her and Keaton is a hoot. —*Brit.*

Ti Presento Un'Amica
(Quite By Chance)
(ITALIAN)

A Medusa release of a Racing Pictures/Reteitalia coproduction. Produced by Alessandro Fracassi. Directed by Francesco

Massaro. Screenplay, Suso Cecchi D'Amico, Franco Ferrini, Enrico Vanzina, Massaro; camera (Luciano Vittori color), Luigi Kuveiller; editor, Sergio Montanari; music, Celso Valli; art direction, Raffaele Balletti. Reviewed at Rivoli Cinema, Rome, March 14, 1988. Running time: **104 MIN.**
Nagra . . . . Giuliano De Sio
Lionello . . . . Michele Placido
Brunetta . . . . Kate Capshaw
Mauro . . . . David Naughton
Claudio . . . . Luca Barbareschi
Marina . . . . Carolina Rosi
Also with: Sergio Fantoni, Lina Polito, Micaela Goodwin, Silvio Ciammarughi.

Rome — The sentimental and sexual adventures of a group of characters, told not as the usual Italo bedroom farce but as a *la ronde* of overlapping love affairs, is what mainly distinguishes "Quite By Chance." Though the players are updated to reflect the times, offshore viewers may find their behavior a little hard to swallow anyway. Local product got off to a good start at domestic wickets, and could pass over to related markets.

Nagra (Giuliana De Sio) is an aggressive, unscrupulous radio journalist determined to claw her way to the top at all costs. The path to success passes over the bodies of several disappointed men. Her admirer and housemate Mauro (David Naughton), a struggling actor, is her first victim. Claudio (Luca Barbareschi), a young tv exec, beds her but loses his job to her after she sleeps with the boss. Nagra's punishment is to be left with a sense of emptiness when she achieves success.

Brunetta (Kate Capshaw) is a p.r. woman for a big fashion house, in love with a surgeon named Lionello (Michele Placido). Lionello barely bothers to hide her — or his long chain of mistresses — from his wife. Tired of Brunetta, he picks up ingenuous swimming teacher Marina (Carolina Rosi). When he gets tired of her, he goes back to Brunetta and convinces her to get rid of Marina for him. Not only does his ex-flame stoop to this task, she watches in chagrin while he picks up Nagra in the final scene.

It's not a pretty picture, but some of the egotistical misdeeds are outrageously true enough to win smiles. Pic is too timid to turn the screw all the way to tragedy, and in the end most of the characters seem consoled, older but wiser, or at least reconciled to living with their weaknesses. "Quite By Chance" steers a safe middle track between a critical look at modern love and a typical bedroom comedy.

Cast is adequate, if tending too much to stereotype their roles. Technical work is up to par.
—*Yung.*

Pound Puppies And The Legend Of Big Paw
(ANIMATED)

A Tri-Star Pictures release of a Family Home Entertainment and Tonka Corp. pre-

sentation of an Atlantic/Kushner-Locke production with the Maltese Cos. Produced by Donald Kushner, Peter Locke. Executive producers, Edd Griles, Ray Volpe. Directed by Pierre DeCelles. Screenplay, Jim Carlson, Terrence McDonnell; in color; editor, John Blizek; music, Steve Tyrell; original songs, Tyrell, Stephanie Tyrell, Ashley Hall; original score, Richard Kosinski, Sam Winans, Bill Reichenbach; art direction, DeCelles; sound, A/K-L Sound Design; coproducers, Diana Dru Botsford, Beth Broday; assistant director, Chiou Wen Shian; voice directors, Ward Botsford, Diana Dru Botsford; voice casting, Brenda K. Kyle. Reviewed at Tri-Star, L.A., March 22, 1988. MPAA Rating: G. Running time: **76 MIN.**
Voices: George Rose (McNasty), B.J. Ward (Whopper), Ruth Buzzi (Nose Marie), Brennan Howard (Cooler), Cathy Cadavini (Collette), Nancy Cartwright (Bright Eyes).

Hollywood — "Pound Puppies And The Legend Of Big Paw" is an uninvolving and endlessly derivative crime caper that takes the perky pups from the Saturday morning tv show on a walk to nowhere. With nothing to offer the kiddies, filmmakers are obviously hoping for a payoff from the stuffed toy tie-ins the tykes will end up squalling for, sold by production partner The Tonka Corp. Call the dogcatcher.

Story involves something called "Puppy Power," which enables kids and dogs to speak to each other. It only works when a mystical relic called the Bone of Scone is intact, and at the outset of this misadventure, it's broken in half by thugs trying to steal it from a museum. Until our yelping heroes can restore the status quo, all kinds of heck break loose.

This involves foiling the villain, a very unoriginal nasty old man with an evil laugh (George Rose) whose goal is to take over the world, something the bone apparently will empower him to do.

As for the legend of Big Paw, it's almost an afterthought, involving an enormous dog with a bad case of low self-esteem who's hiding from life in a swamp until the mutt pack befriends him and he helps them out of their jam. Surprise.

It all might fit nicely into a 30-minute Saturday morning format, but stretching it to 76 minutes involves adding a lot of inane, repetitive dialog and visual gimmicks to add interest where a story should have been.

On the plus side, there's the music by Steve Tyrell — bright, upbeat, well-produced remakes of '50s pop hits that have been reworded in halfway-clever doggie lingo.

B.J. Ward does a nice job with the voice of Whopper, the yarn-spinning protagonist. George Rose is just tiresome as the cliched villain.

Animation is what we've come to accept — flat characters moving jerkily through still-life backgrounds. The backgrounds, at least, display a certain amount of style, with a touch of '50s surrealism. Colors have been sweetened for the big screen, and some of the settings, such as the evil forest and the swamp, show some imagination.

Overall art direction, though, is not good, moving non-cohesively from the Dark Ages to the '50s to the present, and visuals disjointed and hard to follow. —*Daws.*

Dandin
(FRENCH)

An AAA release of a Films du Losange/-Séléna Audiovisuel/Sept/Films A2 coproduction. Produced by Margaret Menegoz. Written and directed by Roger Planchon, based on Molière's play "Georges Dandin;" camera (color), Bernard Lutic; editor, Hélène Viard; music, Jean-Pierre Fouquey; art direction, Thierry Leproust; costumes, Jacques Schmidt; sound, Georges Prat; assistant director, Frédéric Planchon. Reviewed at the Gaumont Ambassade cinema, Paris, Feb. 25, 1988. Running time: **110 MIN.**

Georges Dandin	Claude Brasseur
Angélique	Zabou
M. de Sotenville	Daniel Gélin
Mme. de Sotenville	Nelly Bourgeaud
Clitandre	Jean-Claude Adelin
Claudine	Evelyne Buyle
Lubin	Marco Bisson
Colin	Vincent Garanger

Also with: Martine Merri, Marie Pillet, Philippe Leroy-Beaulieu, Roger Planchon.

Paris — There's brio, flavor and visual delight, as well as attendant irritation, in "Dandin," the sumptuous debut feature by Roger Planchon, 57, one of the celebrity directors of the contemporary French theater.

Inspired by a Molière farce, this is Planchon's cornerstone production for a planned series of costume films devoted to society and culture in the 17th century, "Grand siècle." Despite its shortcomings, "Dandin" puts Planchon in the front ranks of France's most promising new directors. Though it's been sadly shrugged off by local audiences, it has the stuff to travel.

Molière's "Georges Dandin" is considered minor farcical fare by many specialists, though Planchon is among those who see serious underpinnings to its knockabout antics. Planchon in fact staged it last year with Claude Brasseur and Zabou and recruited the same actors for his film.

This isn't filmed theater, however, nor an aired-out adaptation of Molière. Planchon has used the play as armature for a personal recreation of provincial life in Molière's time, developing the piece's plot and characters far beyond what the playwright imagined. Significantly, screen credits read: "Story and dialog by Molière." The rest is Planchon.

Brasseur has one of his best screen roles as Dandin, the rich peasant who acquires a ridiculous title, social standing and a wife, Angélique, daughter of impoverished nobles who accept the marriage as means to save their estate and prestige.

Dandin also sets himself up as one of Molière's potential cuckolds, at first blind to the fact that Angélique, played zestfully by Zabou, is being pursued by a libertine (Jean-Claude Adelin).

Molière's plot was a simple repetition of scenes and variations on the situation of Dandin's attempts to convince his in-laws of their daughter's infidelities and latter's cunning in turning the tables on the rich rube.

Planchon embroiders richly on this basic story, adding new, more complex tensions: notably that Angélique is torn between her outrage at having been part of a business deal and her genuine but suppressed love of Dandin. To Planchon, Angélique uses her decadent suitor as a tool of revenge and a lever towards reconciliation. In the film's final scene, which is not in Molière, Brasseur and Zabou finally sit down as equals at the breakfast table.

Among other important interpolations Planchon makes is the addition of numerous characters, notably a trio of mischievous witches who open the film by popping out of the earth, and return regularly as traditional chorus and Dandin's conscience. Planchon himself, is seen briefly as a player in an extravagant outdoor royal legit performance.

Planchon directs with virtuosity — too much so. There's not a scene that's staged dully, but like many a gifted newcomer Planchon feels the need to keep actors and cameras constantly on the move, running, jumping, pirouetting in an unceasing ballet of sight and sound (the soundtrack offers little respite, with its orgy of stomping, overturned furniture, slamming doors, etc.).

One also can criticize Planchon for sacrificing the elementary laughter of Molière. Like many of his theatrical colleagues Planchon is prey to that professional malady, Revisionist Seriousness, in which many a comedy classic has been restaged portentously with all the gaiety of a wake. "Dandin" certainly has vigor and an underlying sense of joie de vivre, but it's not essentially jocular, and the farce reversals of the play seem quite artificial.

Working with theater designer Thierry Leproust and costumer Jacques Schmidt, Planchon has invested several particularly splendid chateaux for the production, notably Chenonceaux in the Loire river valley. The lush camerawork is by Bernard Lutic and the fluid editing is by Hélène Viard.

Among a well-chosen supporting cast, Daniel Gélin and Nelly Bourgeaud stand out as Brasseur's in-laws, the foolish but basically decent Sotenvilles. —*Len.*

Demonwarp

A Vidmark Entertainment presentation, in association with Design Projects. Executive producer, Mark Amin. Produced by Richard L. Albert. Directed by Emmet Alston. Screenplay, Jim Bertges, Bruce Akiyama, from story by John Buechler; camera (color), R. Michael Stringer; supervising editor, W. Peter Miller; editor, John Travers; music, Dan Slider; sound, Marty Kasparian; special makeup effects, Bruce Barlow, Ed Yang; Bigfoot design, Buechler; additional photography, Alex Leyton; casting, Ted Warren, Jeanette O'Connor. Reviewed on Vidmark videassette, N.Y., March 5, 1988. No MPAA Rating. Running time: **91 MIN.**

Bill Crafton	George Kennedy
Jack	David Michael O'Neill
Carrie	Pamela Gilbert
Tom	Billy Jacoby
Cindy	Colleen McDermott
Fred	Hank Stratton
Betsy	Michelle Bauer
Tara	Shannon Kennedy

Also with: John Durbin, Joe Praml, Jill Mern.

"Demonwarp" is a moderately successful sci-fi/horror pic that could have used more sci-fi and less routine horror. Film is going out as a direct-to-video entry, presumably to avoid cutting its gory and sexy material to achieve a theatrical R rating.

A group of teens for the umpteenth time in the past decade is camping at a remote cabin in the woods, attacked by a Bigfoot monster (well-executed by makeup specialist John Buechler, but shown too often to be credible). George Kennedy's daughter was carried off by Bigfoot from the same cabin a while back and he shows up to help the teens fight the unknown.

Farfetched plot peg has Bigfoot turning out to be the creation of space aliens who landed nearby many years back. Pic climaxes with the aliens' stooges sacrificing nubile, topless Earth girls (Michelle Bauer and Pamela Gilbert) to their gooey monster boss. A corny multiple-nightmare ending sabotages much of the builtup effect.

Technically well made, "Demonwarp" is ultimately an excuse to show off naked women (definitely prime voyeur material), gory makeup and some interesting monster garb. More creativity and less exploitation could have qualified for theatrical usage. —*Lor.*

Chouans!
(FRENCH)

A UGC release of a Partner's Prod./Films-A2/Canal Plus coproduction. Executive producer, Ariel Zeitoun. Produced by Daniel Deschamps, Maurice Illouz. Directed by Philippe de Broca. Screenplay, De Broca, Daniel Boulanger, Jérôme Tonnerre; camera (Panavision, Eastmancolor), Bernard Zitzermann; editor, Henri Lanoë; music, Georges Delerue; art direction, Jacques Bufnoir; costumes, Yvonne Sassinot de Nesle; sound, Jean Charles Ruault, Renée Deschamps; stunt coordinator, Daniel Perche; assistant director, Laurent Laubier; casting, Shula Siegfried. Reviewed at UGC Normandie cinema, Paris, March 14, 1988. Running time: **146 MIN.**

Savinien de Kerfadec	Philippe Noiret
Céline	Sophie Marceau
Tarquin	Lambert Wilson
Aurele	Stéphane Freiss
Baron de Tiffauges	Jean-Pierre Cassel
Olympe	Charlotte de Turkheim
Grospierre	Raoul Billery
Refractory priest	Maxime Leroux
Bouchard	Roland Dumas
The Chaplain	Jean Parédès

Paris — Philippe de Broca, veteran confectioner of light Parisian comedies and tongue-in-cheek adventures, tried to expand his scope in the ill-fated cinema/tv item "Louisiana." Now he returns to the historical fresco with "Chouans!" another theatrical feature/tv miniseries hybrid.

De Broca has fashioned a colorful romance with good acting, striking Britanny locations and adequate widescreen movement, though it lacks the panache of the best film epics. It should do well on home territory and possibly find a niche in other theatrical markets.

There have been plenty of films about the French Revolution but few about the bloody, unromantic civil war of 1793, when Republican armies decimated entire regions of western France to put down a royalist counterrevolution revolt by aristocrats, clergy and peasants. Jean-Paul Rappeneau did use it as backdrop in his 1971 costume romp, "Les Mariés de l'An Deux," with Jean-Paul Belmondo.

De Broca and his scripters Daniel Boulanger and Jérôme Tonnere recognize the fundamental tragedy of the Chouan uprising (named after one of its peasant ringleaders, Jean Chouan) and take some pains to dramatize its violence and atrocities, though mainly those of the Chouans. The wholesale slaughter of rebel villages by the revolutionary armies is glossed over, and the climactic rout of the peasant forces is tamely represented.

This is basically romantic melodrama, masking the profound horror of civil war with conventional movieland trappings. At centerstage are two childhood friends, Stéphane Freiss and Lambert Wilson, who find themselves in opposing camps, though their differences are less ideological than amorous — both are in love with Sophie Marceau, who was adopted and raised by Freiss' father, an enlightened pacifist Breton nobleman, played with class by Philippe Noiret.

Wilson's now-familiar dark angel romanticism fires the role of a Republican commissioner who favors duty and principle over heart and compassion, while Freiss, a promising newcomer, is the nobleman's son who has made his fortune in the New World and returns home to find himself forced into the rebel camp, though his allegiances waver. He, of course, gets the girl while Wilson gets the bullet from Marceau, who is photogenically adequate.

Noiret is the film's most appealing and original character, an aristocratic inventor who concocts a flying machine, which in a fancifully incredible climax whisks Freiss and Marceau from a clifftop guillotine off to the Happy Ever After (though where they land nobody knows).

Miniseries *oblige*, the theatrical version (which runs nearly 2½ hours) is often superficial in its exposition and dramatic progression, which probably explains some of the jarring discontinuities (such as Marceau passing from the Republican stronghold to a Chouan village without explanation).

Secondary characters also suffer from the feature film compression, such as Jean-Pierre Cassel's treacherous aristocrat, embodying the uprising's inhumanity, and Charlotte de Turkheim's unladylike marchioness.

Production enjoyed a more than handsome budget though there never seem to be enough extras around for the big-scale scenes.

Technically pic is glossy, and one shudders to think of what will become of Bernard Zitzermann's lush Panavision compositions on the home screen. Yvonne Sassinot de Nesle's costumes look lived-in and Georges Delerue's themes are aptly romantic. —*Len.*

Avoda Ba 'Eynayim
(Tongue In Cheek)
(ISRAELI)

A Cannon Films presentation of a Pygmalion production. Produced by Hadassa Dgani, Itzhak Kol. Directed by Igal Shilon. Based on ideas by Shilon, Kol, Dgani, Nathan Datner, Avi Kushnir, Udi Sofer, Meir Remez, Yair Nitzani; camera (color, 16m), Benny Carmeli, Oren Shmukler; editor, Zion Avramain; theme song, Uzi Hitman, Kobi Oshrath; art direction, Yossi Peled; production manager, Nancy Hakim. Reviewed at the Hod cinema, Tel Aviv, March 15, 1988. Running time: **83 MIN.**
With: Nathan Datner, Avi Kushnir, Yair Nitzani, Yossi Barak, Eyal Geffen, Dudu Dotan, Tom Soffer, Daniela.

Tel Aviv — Candid camera is still highly popular in this country and Igal Shilon, who has been associated with most of the previous efforts in this genre but left most of the credit to his partners, is now flying under his own flag.

The result is a good-natured, often amusing series of gags, built around the personalities of Nathan Datner and Avi Kushnir, two legit actors whose parody of the Blues Brothers for a tv show has rocketed them into fame as the Batlanim (the Lazy Bums), the name they adopted for the show.

As usual when dealing with this brand of humor, some of the gags are funnier than others, the more entertaining in this case showing Datner as he chastizes guests at a Bar Mitzvah for the modesty of the checks they bring, or Kushnir's head replacing that of a mannequin. Another sequence shows an unsuspecting temporary receptionist being assaulted by fake calls from political figures, which she is forbidden to pass on to her boss, whom she hasn't even seen.

The scene showing a little boy left in charge of chocolate eggs whose temptation he can't resist for long works because of the natural charm of roly-poly Tom Soffer.

Less offensive and insulting than many of the earlier forays in this genre, the film obviously was made on a small budget. The picture is populated with local celebrities, entertainers and tv personalities, who are gently kidded to the delight of the public who recognizes them.

Initial response by local audiences is enthusiastic and picture, released for the Passover holidays, is bound to show a profit quickly. Tv marketing seems more likely for foreign territories. —*Edna.*

Livsfarlig Film
(Deadly Film)
(SWEDISH)

A Sandrew Film release of a Göran Lindström production with Sandrew Film, the Swedish Film Institute, SVT-1, Sandrew 87 KB and Film Teknik. Produced by Göran Lindström. Directed by Suzanne Osten. Screenplay, Etienne Glaser, Osten, Niklas Radström; camera (Eastmancolor), Göran Nilsson; editor, Darek Hoder; music, Fläskkvartetten; sound, Ulf Darin; art direction, Roland Söderberg; costumes, Maria Geber, Eva Fänge; choreography, Iris Scaccheri; production management, Jutta Ekman, Brita Werkmäster; assistant director, Finn Zadén. Reviewed at Metropol, Malmö (Sweden), March 7, 1988. Running time: **108 MIN.**
Emil Frankenstein . . . . Etienne Glaser
Maenad . . . . Stina Ekblad
Foreman . . . . Henrik Holmborg
Ingrid Stromboli . . . . Lena T. Hansson
Görel Key . . . . Agneta Ekmanner
Ixion . . . . Helge Skoog
Cherberos . . . . Claes Mandsson
Lucho . . . . Philip Zanden
Ella . . . . Gunilla Röör
Also with: Demba Conta, Curre Hillfon, Henry Bronett, Zoey Finer, Björn Gedda, Ewa Maria Björkström, Niklas Ek, Lars Göran Persson, Iris Scaccheri, Ana-Yrsa Falenius, Pia Johansson, Rakel Seron, Maria Lustron.

Malmö (Sweden) — "Deadly Film" is a morbidly funny takeoff on assembly-line work in what might be termed a Fright Factory, a film studio serving the horror trade.

With a sumptuous production dress and a cast of 800, most of them grotesque, plus a sweet and nervous clown-type actor-director at its center, the picture will not avoid being labeled Felliniesque. Still, helmer Suzanne Osten, working from a screenplay she co-wrote with Etienne Glaser and Niklas Radström, stands solidly on her own stylistic feet. She does so in a sea of gore & guffaws that is sure to spill over into art-oriented offshore situations.

Etienne Glaser plays Emil Frankenstein, the studio's balding, hangdog yet stubbornly hopeful ace actor-director, who tries to talk his two bosses, a female twosome of no-nonsense attitudes (Agneta Ekmanner, Stina Ekblad), into allowing him a shot at doing a film about real people. His immediate urge to do this is prompted by disgust with his life and work, a disgust shared by his daughter. His sole companion, she ups and leaves him in protest. The rest of the film describes his Orpheus-like search for his lost Eurydice and for the real people he

---

wants to put in his new film.

Suzanne Osten's guided tour of the Dante's Inferno film enterprises has Ingrid Stromboli (Lena T. Hansson), a more-vamp-than-vampire star of the director's worst films, forced upon him as a Beatrice hell-bent on seeing her own light at the end of tunnels, corridors and in and out of men's rooms an commissaries with dangers lurking everywhere.

Homosexual attacks interchange with cruel pranks played by one and all on each other (flying, blood-oozing limbs everywhere and even out of the lunch-time soup). There are also the odd high emotional moments of Emil's attempts at escape from himself and from it all.

In the subterranean store rooms visited by Emil and his crew, they come upon the real people they look for, a tiny flock of either unwanted aliens or political refugees, but the foreigners all seem keen on acting roles of happy, lusty human beings rather than playing the victims Emil has in mind.

At some time or other the narrative flow is interrupted by displays of stagey fireworks and, of course, special effects orgies. Finally, the narrative disappears completely. It turns out that there has been no film in the crew's camera, and Emil winds up *sans* his head, which is seen in the fade-out floating — while singing softly — under some Aegean waves.

Everybody seems to have a high old time as participants, in front of or behind the camera, and undoubtedly the whole show is cinema as theater-within-theater. The director's professed intent of unmasking the scare trade as a diminisher of our sense of the world's real dangers, should be taken as a tongue-in-cheek. —*Kell.*

Z.B. ... Otto Spalt
(Mr. Spalt — For Instance)
(WEST GERMAN)

A Filmproduktion Perraudin (Berlin) production. Written, directed and edited by René Perraudin. Camera (Kodak, Fujicolor), Werner Nitschke; lighting, Michael Schuff; sound, Erich Lutz; music, Klaus Doldinger; set decoration and costumes, Olga vn Wahl; makeup, Dörte Eben; production supervisor, Renée Gundelach; production manager, Christine Däumling. Reviewed at Berlin Film Festival (Arsenal section), Feb. 13, 1988. Running time: **100 MIN.**
With: Otto Sander, Katharina Thalbach, Udo Samuel, Rolf Zacher, Helmut Krauss, Alfred Edel, Günter Meisner, Heinz Meier, Inge Steiert, Irm Hermann, Romy Haag.

Berlin — This is a satirical look at the rigors of petty officialdom German filmmakers are subjected to on attempts to get government subsidy money for their films.

Otto Sander plays a fairly established filmmaker — obviulsy meant to be director René Perraudin's alter ego — presenting his short films to a review panel of picky officials and clergy.

This is a great opportunity for Perraudin to recycle his old films — about five going back to 1978 — in the plot mechanism of showing the panel a sampling of his filmmaker character's earlier *ouevre*. He also gets into the credits a number of German actors who may not have been so well known when the earlier films actually were made.

Many of the jokes depend on situations and faces familiar to those in the German film business. In one scene he has gathered quite a number of contemporary Berlin directors and production people for a sight gag of having them all holding film cans waiting their turn in line to go before the panel.

There are some amusing effects like reversing the film and other trick work that all contribute to the general lunacy. Whether this can move beyond a local audience remains to be seen. It may be one of those situations where you had to be there to get it. —*Owl.*

Maroc, Corps et ames
(Morocco, Bodies And Souls)
(FRENCH-MOROCCAN-DOCU)

An OHRA (SOGEAV) production and release. Written and directed by Izza Genini. Camera (color, 16m), Jean-Jacques Flori; editor, Marie-Catherine Miqueau; sound, Antoine Rodet, Alain Garnier. Reviewed at Rotterdam Film Festival, Feb. 3, 1988. Running time: **78 MIN.**

Rotterdam — First of a planned 3-part film docu series about Moroccan music is the surprising, audiovisually exciting debut of Izza Genini, 45, born in Casablanca, who is based in Paris. In the '70s she managed the famous (film) Club 70 with Louis Malle and has produced and distributed Moroccan films.

Her film seeks to trace the foreign influences of Moroccan music and its role in local society. Not only its Arab neighbors, but also other Mediterranean cultures — Spain notably — helped shape Moroccan civilzation.

Genini isn't content with conventional docu footage of instruments, singers and dancers. She shows us the land and towns into which the music is integrated; catches the light that moulds land, fauna, peoples and architecture into one grand setting. Camerawork is unobtrusive but effective.

Film is informative but never didactic. Genini is an adroit teacher who understands that facts go down best when coated with anecdote — cultural history without pain. —*Wall.*

Abierto de 18 a 24
(Open From 6 To Midnight)
(ARGENTINE)

A Cinematográfica de Santa Fe release of a Kankún production. Produced by Alberto Trigo. Written and directed by Víctor Dinenzón. Camera (color), Hugo Colace; editor,

Juan Carlos Macías; music, Emilio Kanderer; sound, Anibel Lebenson; sets and costumes, Alfredo Iglesias; associate producer, Claudia Kohen. Reviewed on video at Havana Intl. Film Festival Market, Mecla, Cuba, Dec. 17, 1987. Running time: **80 MIN.**

Julio .... Gerardo Romano
Dory .... Silvia Peyrou
Carla .... Horacio Peña
José .... Jorge Luz
Also with: Cora Sánchez, Carmen Reynard, Omar Pini, Nora Sajaroff, Zulmagrey, Aldo Piccioni, Nestor Zacco, Silvana Sigal, Bernardo Baras, Eduardo Santoro, Amalio Garbulsky, Cris Lavalle, Antonio Devitta, Susana Devitta, Eugenio Troisi.

Havana — The Argentine dance pic "Abierto de 18 a 24" (Open From 6 To Midnight) is a bittersweet reflection on the complexities of human nature and interrelationships as seen through the microcosm of an evening tango class. Director Victor Dinenzón borrows heavily in tone and atmosphere from Ettore Scola's 1983 dance film "Le Bal."

Pic's starting point begins with the death of Vicente, who carried a longtime relationship with Carla, director of the class. The students are a tawdry mix of housewives and low-level businessmen who find escape through torrid tango rhythms.

One day the class is interrupted by the appearance of handsome countryboy Julio, Vicente's nephew. He is the catalyst who brings out the intrigues, jealousies and more tender feelings of those who frequent this nighttime world. He begins an affair with Dory, the class vamp, to the chagrin of her former paramours and his potential admirers.

Dinenzón keeps a keen eye on parody and incidental humor through character detail and gesture, amplifying the quirks and tensions of the class regulars. It is not until the pic's end that Carla lets her mask fall and we understand the tender "Cage aux Folles" relationship she has shared with Uncle Vicente. This scene is touching and underlines the basic world of fragile emotions revealed by the class and underlying passions expressed in the tango.

Acting is strong, especially Horacio Peña, who plays a transvestite role believably and sensitively. Carla and Uncle Vicente's story is only part of the larger life picture portrayed in the film.

Cinematographer Hugo Colace has created a dream-like tone through use of artificial lights and deft close-ups. Dance detail focuses on the complicated footwork.
—*Lent.*

Natshalo Nevedomogo veka
(The Beginning Of An Unknown Century)
(SOVIET-B&W)

Produced by the Moscow Studio for Creative Experiments. In two episodes. "Angel;" written and directed by Andrei Smirnov, based on a short story by Yuri Olesha. Camera (b&w), P. Lebeshov; editor, L. Badorina; music, Alfred Schnittke, L. Ledenev, Bulat Okudhsava; art direction, V. Korovin. With: L. Kulagin, N. Gubenko, L. Poliakova, G. Bzurkov, S. Wolf. "The Homeland Of Electricity:" written and directed by Larissa Shepitko, based on a short story by Andrei Platonov. Camera (b&w), Dmitri Korshichin; music, R. Lebediev; art direction, W. Konovalov, W. Kostrin. With: S. Gorbachuk, A. Popova, F. Gladkov, I. Gurtchenkov. Reviewed at Berlin Film Festival (Forum), Feb. 22, 1988. Running time: **74 MIN.**

Berlin — Shot in 1967 and held back for release until 1987, "The Beginning Of An Unknown Century" is a historically key work in the careers of two noted Russian helmers, Larissa Shepitko and Andrei Smirnov. Their two shorts have been yoked together as a feature, which should attract attention because of its directors, its sophistication in bringing stories from the '20s to the screen, and its superb recreation of the expressive b&w style of filmmaking used by the great Russian directors of the 1920s.

Both films are impressive efforts, though not always easy to watch or penetrate. College circuits and very specialized venues might handle this one.

"Angel," Smirnov's first film, was shot at Leningrad Studio. Based on a short story by Yuri Olesha and set in 1920 during the scattered battles between Reds and Whites in the countryside, it could use some kind of explanatory opening title with a few words of background to help orient offshore viewers.

A ragged trainload of refugees chugs along; it's fueled by chopped-up heirloom chairs and other detritus of the revolution. When it runs off the tracks, only a handful of hard-core survivors stick around to put it back on the rails and get it running again. They milk a cow on board and sing songs (side of the car reads "Workers Solidarity") until they are captured by the dreaded, half-mad, counterrevolutionary Angel and his band. Angel savagely sinks a sledge hammer into the skull of a blond Commissar. The others walk away with a young girl, who has been raped but still holds her head high.

This brief film is full of resonant dialog with philosophical political overtones, and disturbing paradoxes — like the executioner calling himself the Angel of God, and believing it. Lebeshov's camerawork is a dazzling frame for Smirnov's careful staging, though image has whited out a little with time. Actors are top-notch as is Alfred Schnittke's score.

Shepitko's "The Homeland Of Electricity," from an Andrei Platonov story, turns the classic boy-meets-tractor plot into stirring cinema. A young student arrives in a remote Turkmenistan village, apparently on assignment to assist the local drought-stricken population. The first thing he sees in the desolate steppe is an eerie religious procession of old folks praying for help. The boy is bright enough to realize they can adapt an old motorcycle engine into a water pump and irrigate a field.

The villagers feverishly join in the project, contributing their samovars to be melted down into the pump. When the first water gushes forth, they celebrate. That night, however, the overloaded pump explodes. As the townsfolk silently weep in front of the conflagration it begins to rain. They're so absorbed in their grief they don't notice it's pouring.

Lensing in Kiev, Shepitko and her cameraman Dmitri Korshichin come close to the ineffable silent school of Dovzhenko (her prof at VGIK); dialog is minimal. Landscape and faces are central. —*Yung.*

Preuve d'amour
(Love Token)
(FRENCH)

A Sara CDF Films release of a Sara Films/Canal Plus coproduction. Produced by Alain Sarde. Directed by Miguel Courtois. Screenplay, Courtois, Philippe Combenegre; camera (color), Yves Dahan; editor, Marie Castro-Vazquez; music, Preface; sound, Pierre Lorrain; art direction, Denis Barbier; production supervisor, Philippe Guez; production manager, Catherine Mazières; assistant director, Eric Belassen; casting, Marie-Christine Lafosse. Reviewed at the Gaumont Colisée cinema, Paris, March 12, 1988. Running time: **92 MIN.**

With: Gérard Darmon, Anais Jeanneret, Philippe Combenegre, Sylvie Orcier, Jean Rougerie, Michel Auclair, Jacques Spiesser, Jean-Michel Dupuis, Isabelle Nanty.

Paris — A typically self-indulgent first feature, "Preuve d'amour" builds a B-movie intrigue out of genre clichés involving a journalist wrongly accused of murder and a femme fatale with a dark secret.

Newcomer Miguel Courtois weaves an incoherent plot around his leads Gérard Darmon and the nubile Anais Jeanneret, throws in a mysterious bald-headed killer straight out of Jean-Jacques Beineix' "Diva," and extends the screen time pointlessly with a number of subsidiary characters (a police team investigating the murders).

Though Courtois' effects are often pretentious (the murder of a woman by suffocation intercut with the agony of a pinned butterfly), there are some scattered moments that suggest genuine skill.

Film is dedicated to the late Michel Auclair, who had his last screen role here as a corrupt movie producer. —*Len.*

Uppu
(Salt)
(INDIAN)

An Erandan Films production. Produced by KMA Rahim. Directed by (Vattaparambi Krishnan) Pavithran. Screenplay, K.M.A. Rahim; camera (color), Madhu Ambat; editor, Venugopal; music, Sarath Chandra Maratte; art direction, Sithara. Reviewed at Berlin Film Festival (Forum), Feb. 18, 1988. Running time: **117 MIN.**

Amina .... Jayalitha
Abu .... Mohammed
Moosa Meleri .... Vijayan Kottarathil
Musaliar .... Sree Raman
Also with: Madhavan (Moidutty), Sidiq (Salim), Mullanezhi, Renu Nair (Jasmine), Bharati, Valsala Menon (Mariambi).
(In Malayam)

Berlin — The plight of women is a theme that has often attracted crusading Indian helmers. In "Uppu" the cruel, atavistic Moslem practice of male polygamy is condemned in a languid, poetic work from Malayam helmer V.K. Pavithran. Film is entirely on the side of the wronged wives, mounting a strong criticism of this aspect of the Moslem religion.

Though the heroine may seem too obedient and resigned to her fate for Western feminist tastes, tale concludes with her daughter's courageous rebellion when it's her turn to be treated as chattel. Main problem with foreign playoffs will be that slow Indian rhythm that spins out running time to almost two hours.

Story begins when old patriarch Moosa Meleri arrives in a quiet Kerala village with his adopted son Abu (Mohammed) and daughter-in-law Amina (Jayalitha). He has lost all his money in litigation, and now the once-proud family is forced to live in a warehouse.

Despite their hard life, the young couple is happy to have each other; they industriously set about repairing their hut, and Abu becomes a fisherman. Storm clouds gather when their rich landlord (Sree Raman) conceives a passion for the girl. He proposes that Amina divorce Abu and marry him as his second wife.

Naturally, there is money in it for Moosa. Abu, pained but feeling dutybound to his foster-father, agrees. Amina weeps and changes husbands.

To underline the point, the marriage ceremony shows the menfolk chanting about how Allah says celibacy is a sin, and a man can have four wives as long as he treats them equally.

Twenty years later, Amina has two grown children by the landlord, a dissolute son devoted to women and booze, and a daughter nobody wants to marry. The daughter runs off with the family chauffeur and bravely stands up for her rights in a court battle. Grey-haired Amina returns to grey-haired Abu, and the tradition-crossed lovers burn themselves in a conflagration on the beach.

Pavithran pads story out with so much naturalistic detail that the pace is lethargic, and the 2-generation story seems like two films put back to back. Yet Amina's tragedy is touching all the same. Tropical Kerala makes a splendid backdrop. — *Yung.*

Rami og Julie
(Rami And Juliet)
(DANISH)

A Metronome release of a Filmkooperativet Danmark production with C. Cosmos C., the Danish Film Institute and K-Films (Paris). DFI consultant producers, Claes Kastholm Hansen, Peter Poulsen. Directed by Erik Clausen. Screenplay, Clausen, Fayez Kanafani; camera (Panavision, Eastmancolor), Morten Bruus; editor, Ghita Beckendorff; music, Tchaikovski; sound, Henrik Langkilde; art direction, Thorkil Slebsager; casting, Bent Erik Kröyer, Vibeke Wrede Höffner, Lene Kramshöj; production management (Denmark), Marianne Christensen, (Duisburg, W. Germany), Edmund Labonté. Reviewed at Dagmar Theater, Copenhagen, Feb. 26, 1988. Running time: **90 MIN.**

Julie . . . . Sofie Graböl
Rami . . . . Saleh Malek
Frank . . . . Steen Jörgensen
Mohammed . . . . Jamal El Khatib
Bob . . . . Kjeld Löfting
Mawan . . . . Mohammed Bakri
Julie's mother . . . . Anne Nöjgaard
Rami's brother . . . . Khalid Ibrahim Alsbeihi
Also with: Paprika Steen, Mohammed Laraj, Fredy Madcapps, MohammedLaraj, Samir Al-Subehi, Peter Thiel, Brian Hansen, Ibrahim Ali Aslbeihi, Bente Hansen, Ghada Hasan, Haliman Yusef, Mahmoud El Awad, Ismat Arslan.

Copenhagen — Danish writer-director Erik Clausen has reached international audience for his exquisitely crafted pictures about, mostly, the Danish underdog. With "Rami And Juliet," a combined paraphrase of Shakespeare's "Romeo And Juliet" and Bernstein-Sondheim's "West Side Story," transferred and updated to deal with doomed young love and racial hatred in the concrete desert of a lower middle class Copenhagen suburb, Clausen may have forsaken melodrama and thrills for art, but he should still be assured of international acclaim.

Saleh Malek has innocence to near-excess in his role as Rami, the Palestinean guest worker, who has hardly met and fallen in (reciprocated) love with lonely Julie, the blond on nighttime duty at a service station, before he is sent on a secret mission to West Germany. The youngsters cannot run away together as they had otherwse decided to do — from all the hatred surrounding them. Rami gets killed while trying to smuggle his cousin Mawan (on the run from persecution in Beirut), into Denmark. Julie survives after having been molested by the leader of the gang of young Danes. This youngster, himself a victim of circumstance, soon has a knife plunged into his guts by Rami's brother.

The traps of cliché inherent in his material have been avoided by Clausen. Not only does he pull his punches (blood and tears are shed, but never wallowed in), he also opts for the highly stylized in all his narrative devices. A laundromat manager, who is a failed actor-dancer, breaks the action intermittently by coming forward to speak appropriate lines from Shakespeare, and nearly all movement by actors and camera has a choreographed feel.

Sofie Graböl (who played Gauguin's nude teenage model opposite Donald Sutherland in Henning Carlsen's "Wolf At The Door") has plenty of innocence, too, as Julie, but she displays a winning toughness also, and her pert little face radiates an inner beauty. Mohammed Bakri, a veteran of several Israeli films such as Uri Barbash's "Beyond The Walls," has quiet strength as the Palestinean on the run. Entire cast puts in convincing performances, including Steen Jörgensen as the Danish gang leader.

Clausen and his regular cinematographer Morten Bruus hew closely to the narrative line with frames composed with striking imagination and lit to perfection. Editing and all other technical credits also are topnotch. —*Kell.*

Bantsuma — Bando Tsumasaburo no shogai
(Bantsuma — The Life Of Tsumasaburo Bando)
(JAPANESE-DOCU-COLOR/B&W)

Produced and directed by Shunsui Matsuda. Written by Tadao Sato; camera (color), Hiroshi Takasaka, Masayuki Ike, Ichiro Sakamoto; editor, Yoshio Ebara; music, Omoide Ensemble; sound, Takeshi Shirafuji; narrators, Matsuda, Midori Sawato. Reviewed at Berlin Film Festival (Forum of Young Cinema), Feb. 19, 1988. Running time: **91 MIN.**

Interviewees: Takahiro Tamura, Daisuke Ito, Shizuko Mori, Hiroshi Inagaki, Utako Tamaki, Ryu Kuze, Kenichi Adachi, Toshi Ota. Excerpts from "Kosuzumetoge" (1924), "Kageboshi" (1925), "Ooka Seidan" (1928), "Kurama tengu" (1928), "Sakamoto Ryoma" (1928), "Hatamoto taikutsuotoko" (1930), "Kyokaku harusamegasa" (1930), "Kokushi muso" (1932), "Shinno tsuruchiyo" (1935), "Chushingura" (1938), "Jigoku no mushi" (1938), "Shogun to sanbo to hei" (1942), "Muho matsu no issho" (1943), "Kitsune no kureta akanbo" (1945), "Osho" (1945), "Yabure taiko" (1949), "Abare shishi" (1953).

Berlin — Avid followers of Japanese cinema will welcome this biographical docu, a combination of interviews and numerous film excerpts, dedicated to one of its great stars, Tsumasaburo Bando, whose early death at the age of 51 (in 1953) was considered a great loss for the industry.

Shunsui Matsuda, who made the film in 1979 and died last summer, used a wealth of material from his enormous private archive of silent film excerpts, most of them never seen before outside Japan, with additional footage contributed by Shochiku, Daiei and Nikkatsu. Noted film critic and historian Tadao Sato was responsible for the script and the interviews with directors and actors as well as the family, contributing to this profile of the star. At least for one of the silent film excerpts, "Orochi" (1925), director Matsuda's voice is heard explaining the action in the famous *Benshi* style, a staple feature during the silent period in Japan, when a narrator accompanied each screening, saying the dialog mimed on screen and adding his own commentaries. Matsuda, who learned this trade from his father, was the last of his kind in Japan to make a living out of it.

The film documents Tsumasaburo Bando's career painstakingly, elaborates on his own contribution to the historical pageants *(jidaigeki)*, his own innovations in the technique of spectacular samurai battle scenes, his position as his own producer since 1925, and his personality both as an actor and as a pater familias, reflected in home movies.

Most of the interviews are done in the most traditional fashion but at least in one case, choreographer Ryu Kuze demonstrates for the benefit of the camera, some of the finest points used in staging Bando's battle scenes.

Film buffs will certainly want to have a look at this, and film archives will probably apply for a copy to add to their catalogs. In spite of production date, film was never shown before, Berlin fest hosting its world premiere. —*Edna.*

Yi Ge Si Zhe Dul Sheng Zhe De Fang Wen
(A Dead Man Visits The Living)
(CHINESE)

A Beijing Studios production. Directed by Huangjian Zhong. Screenplay, Liu Shu Gang, based on his stage production; camera (color), Zhao Fei; music, Qu Xiao Song; sound, Zheng Kun Yu; sets, Kant Wei Chang; costumes, Fan Gang; make-up, Song Hong Hui, Sun Bing, Li Na; special effects, Yuan Qing Ye. Reviewed at Berlin Film Festival (Forum of Young Cinema), Feb. 15, 1988. Running time: **105 MIN.**

With: Chang Lan Tian (Xiaoxiao), Ling Fang Bing (Tiantian), Yü Jun Wun, Da Li, Ji Yuan, Shi Ke, Zhao Tong, Wang Xiao Yen, Na Xi Mo Zuo.

Berlin — This is an amazing item to emerge from Red China, both in form and in content. As the title indicates, this is a surrealistic picture, set between fantasy and real life. It displays a remarkable visual imagination and offers critical, unflattering comments on present-day Chinese society.

Xiaoxiao, a bit player in a theater company, is knifed on a bus, when he accidentally catches a gang of pickpockets at work. After his death, however, his spirit is brought back to earth by Tiantian, an avant garde artist, burdened by the guilt of never having fully returned his love for her.

In her company and on his own, he tours the land and tries to understand why nobody on the bus lifted a finger to help him. From one encounter to another it becomes evident his death is the responsibility of an insensitive society, egotistical, scared and corrupt. Mention is made of artistic censorship, of narrow-minded bureaucrats hiding behind regulations and formulas, and a party machine indifferent to private persons.

Visually too, there is much to praise in this film. Not only the presence of nudity, the trendy short skirts donned by the artist practically all through the film, and a witches sabbath in the best demonic tradition, are visions of the kind one does not expect from an industry weaned on socialist realism. These sights are not used for their shock effect, but as an integral part of a conception. —*Edna.*

Mercenary Fighters

A Cannon Group release of a Golan-Globus production. Executive producer, Avi Lerner. Produced by Menahem Golan, Yoram Globus. Directed by Riki Shelach. Screenplay, Bud Schaetzle, Dean Tschetter, Andrew Deutsch, from story by Schaetzle, Tschetter; additional dialog, Terry Asbury; camera (Irene color), Daniel Schneor; editor, Michael Campbell, Dean Goodhill; coeditor, Omer Tal; music, Howard Morgan; sound, John Bergman; production manager, Michael Games; stunt coordinator, B.J. Davis; second unit director, D. Bruce McFarlane. Reviewed at 42d St. Times Square theater, N.Y., March 26, 1988. MPAA Rating: R. Running time: **91 MIN.**

Virelli . . . . Peter Fonda
D.J. Christian . . . . Reb Brown
Cliff Taylor . . . . Ron O'Neal
Wilson . . . . Jim Mitchum
Col. Kjemba . . . . Robert DoQui
Nurse Warwick . . . . Joanna Weinberg
Also with: Jerry Biggs, Henry Cele, Ian Steadman.

"Mercenary Fighters" is a lamebrained action pic made in South Africa in 1986 under the title "Freedom Fighters." Cannon released it regionally last month, and dumped it in N.Y. at a 42d Street fleapit with zero advertising.

Peter Fonda toplines as a U.S. soldier of fortune hired by the government of the fictional central African nation of Shinkasa (an anagram for Kinshasa, ex-Leopoldville, capital of Zaire) to wipe out some rebels blocking a vast dam project which would force the Kurubu tribe off its homeland.

Of Fonda's motley crew of mercenaries, kindhearted beefcaker Reb Brown (after falling for a pretty white nurse, Joanna Weinberg) realizes he's fighting for the bad guys and takes up with the rebels. Dissension among the mercenaries pushes Ron O'Neal to do the right thing in the final reel but Fonda is a gamy-legged bad guy only out for a buck till the end.

Slapdash script and ineffectual direction (an explosion every once in a while) drain this programmer of any believability. Such is its miscalculation that miscast Robert DoQui as the heinous villain was mightily cheered on by the predominantly black 42d Street audience when he viciously slaps down the nurse, who's only been trying to protect women and children in villages from being murdered by DoQui's troops. Equally ridiculous is the scene of Brown named new leader of the

Kurubu rebels by their dying chief, just after Brown in Rambo pose has mowed down Kurubus with a machine gun as he was hired to do.

Tech credits are acceptable except for the tinny music track. A sloppy touch has erstwhile "Superfly" star Ron O'Neal misspelled as "O'Neil" in the opening credits. —*Lor.*

Xaver
(WEST GERMAN)

A Kora Film release of a Calypso Film production, with support from the West German state of North Rhine-Westphalia. Produced by Uwe Franke. Directed by Werner Possardt. Screenplay, Possardt; camera (color), Jakob Eger; music, Hans Jürgen Buchner Baindling. Reviewed at Berlin Film Festival (market), Feb. 16, 1988. Running time: **90 MIN.**
Xaver .Rupert Seidl
Alois . . . . .Carlos Pavlidis
Farm girl . . . . .Gabi Fischer
Also with: Marinus Brand, Heinz Josef Braun.

Berlin — This lightweight comedy about a little man from space who lands in the Alpine foothills and is mistaken for a Munich tourist actually succeeds in provoking laughs in parts. Export possibilities are limited by the Bavarian dialect gimmick, which is responsible for most of the yuks.

A gangly hayseed named Xaver (played to full buck-toothed capacity by Rupert Seidl) stumbles onto a ditched spacecraft bearing a small humanoid he dubs "Alois" (Carlos Pavlidis). Decked out in a pointy Alpine hat and lederhosen, Alois easily passes as just another flatland city dweller as Xaver and his buxom girlfriend (Gabi Fischer) help the wee alien through a series of misadventures in search of a fuel pump to make his ship spaceworthy.

Standard chase antics are performed against a backdrop of glorious Alpine scenery. —*Gill.*

Joshua, Joshua
(ISRAELI)

A Paris Cinema presentation of a Halom production. Produced by Itzhak Ginsberg, Doron Eran. Directed by Avi Cohen. Screenplay, Ginsberg; camera (color, 16m), Yoav Kosh; editor, Lina Kadish; music, Adi Rennert; art direction and animation, Tali Van der Vouden. Reviewed at the Paris Cinema, Tel Aviv, March 10, 1988. Running time: **87 MIN.**
With: Avri Gil'ad, Ossi Hillel, Matti Seri, Mira Almog, David Moonshine, Davey Cohen, Elisheva Michaeli.

Tel Aviv — One of the most prolific directors of commercials in the country, Avi Cohen is trying his hand for the second time with a full-length feature, and once again fails to make the grade.

Supposedly a madcap comedy about a juvenile pulp writer (Avri Gil'ad) whose only satisfactory relationship is with his typewriter, the script is chaotic, the humor is sub-adolescent and the production is surprisingly sloppy for someone

who normally has to meet the sleek standards of advertising agencies.

The plot has the hero ghostwriting the autobiography of a stud (Matti Seri), falling in love with the stud's latest conquest (Ossi Hillel) but being too scared to do anything about it. Gags are mostly verbal, heavy-handed and obvious, acting is amateurish at best and technical credits way below par. Using a brand of humor introduced here by a popular radio show featuring the same Gil'ad who plays the lead, the film has gathered a limited following at home, but it is doubtful whether this is sufficient to recoup production costs or carry it across the borders. —*Edna.*

Hollywood Chainsaw Hookers

A Camp Motion Pictures release, in association with American-Independent Prods., of a Savage Cinema production. Executive producers, Salvatore Richichi, James Golff, Nick Marino. Produced and directed by Fred Olen Ray. Screenplay, Ray, T.L. Lankford; camera (United color), Scott Ressler; editor, William Shaffer; music, Michael Perilstein; sound, Dennis Fuller; production design, Corey Kaplan; costume design, Jill Conner; production manager, Tony Brewster; associate producers, Nancy Paloian, Gary J. Levinson; second unit camera, Gary Graver. Reviewed on Camp vidcassette, N.Y., March 25, 1988. No MPAA Rating. Running time: **74 MIN.**
Cult leader . . . . .Gunnar Hansen
Samantha Kelso . . . . .Linnea Quigley
Jack Chandler . . . . .Jay Richardson
Mercedes . . . . .Michelle Bauer
Laurie . . . . .Dawn Wildsmith
Also with: Dennis Mooney, Jerry Fox, Esther Alyse, Tricia Burns, Michael D. Sonye, Jimmy Williams.

"Hollywood Chainsaw Hookers" is a self-styled cult film that is entertaining for its intended fringe audience. Minor effort deserves college campus bookings, but this will be hampered by its extremely brief window between west coast midnight bookings in March and an April 14 homevideo release.

Filmmaker Fred Olen Ray uses a film noir format involving private dick Jay Richardson hired to find runaway teenage beauty Linnea Quigley, whose dad had been suspected of child abuse. He finds her stripping in a topless club; she slips him a mickey and he awakes to find himself in the midst of a blood cult ritual presided over by Gunnar Hansen (Leatherface in "The Texas Chainsaw Massacre").

Spoof goes over the edge when cult is revealed to be worshiping the chainsaw: "the cosmic link by which all things are united." Supposedly Hansen is staying alive perennially by his human sacrifices, and film tips its hat to Herschell Gordon Lewis' 1963 "Blood Feast," which started the gore/grossout genre.

Pic's highpoint is an outrageous sequence when voluptuous Michelle Bauer, posing as a hooker, covers her Elvis wall poster with plastic as

she strips to an Elvis soundalike record and then bloodily cuts up her customer with a chainsaw. Scene is tongue-in-cheek but wild. Pic climaxes with a dueling chainsaws battle between Quigley and Bauer.

Richardson is okay as the private eye given to clutzy voiceover, but Hansen's line readings are flat. Mainstream audiences probably are not ready for the trashy mixture of naked girls and buckets of blood, or the numerous in-jokes (including spurious credits). —*Lor.*

Kiattas és Kialtas
(Cry And Cry Again)
(HUNGARIAN)

A Budapest Studio, Mafilm, production. Directed by Zsolt Kezdi-Kovacs. Screenplay, Kezdi-Kovacs from novel by Gyula Hernadi; camera (Eastmancolor), Janos Kende; editor, Eva Karmento; music, György Selmeczi; sound, Peter Kardos. Reviewed at Hungarian Film Week, Budapest, Feb. 8, 1988. Running time: **86 MIN.**
Karoly Gerencser . . . . .Jerzy Trela
Maria .Maria Varga
Tibor . . . . .Peter Andorai
Anna . . . . .Lili Monori

Budapest — "Cry And Cry Again" is a sad little love story set in 1958 and adapted from a novel by Gyula Hernadi, a long-time screenwriter for Miklos Jancso. Story deals with a relationship literally crushed by the system, and has universal application.

Focus is on Karoly (Jerzy Trela), a middle-aged ex-POW who works in a slaughterhouse. He's lonely since his wife left the country after the so-called "counter revolution" of 1956. Karoly has been having an affair with fellow worker Lili Monori, but when he discovers she's cheated on him, he leaves her.

He becomes attracted to Maria, a new worker at the place. Her husband, too, had ankled in '56, but she'd been arrested when she tried to follow him to the West. The two of them fall in love and start an affair: only then does Maria reveal that she's the reluctant mistress of a powerful Party man and ex-secret policeman who'd interrogated her after she was arrested and forced her to sleep with him. Terrified she's being followed, Maria goes along with Karoly to the countryside where they have a few days of happiness before goons arrive and kidnap her; Karoly is beaten senseless.

Determined to get the girl back, Karoly starts a hopeless quest for her. Police are no help, she's left her job and apartment, and every time he gets too close, he gets beaten again, winding up a basketcase in an asylum, supposedly the victim of a drunken brawl. Two years later, Maria, now married to the Party man and mother of his child, accidentally sees the man she once loved, though he's unable even to speak to her.

Director Zsolt Kezdi-Kovacs depicts a period when secret police

and Party officials wielded awesome power. His Mr. Average is a dissenter crushed for stepping out of line. Jerzy Trela is rightly wan as the unfortunate protagonist, while lovely Maria Varga shines as the girl for whom he gives up everything. As her unwanted lover, Peter Andorai has two brief but impressive scenes.

Director overdoes the lyrical central section (slow-motion images of lovers in the rain have been passé for years), but recovers to depict the destruction of the hero with unflinching horror. Pic's downbeat ending is inevitable.

Production dress is impeccable, and director and his editor Eva Karmento are to be commended for keeping the running time down to a tight 86 minutes. English title makes pic sound like a weepie, and a better translation of the original might be "Shout And Shout Again," since it's a cry of anger that's involved, anger against events that happened at a time when many Hungarians already felt, wrongly as it turned out, that such things belonged to the past. —*Strat.*

Bol'se Sveta!
(More Light!)
(SOVIET-DOCU-B&W)

A Sovkinochronika SU-Moscow production. Directed by Marina Babak. Screenplay, Igor Itzkov; camera (color, b&w), Ivan Filatov; music, L. Ovtshinskaia; sound, Viktor Brus, J. Ignatov. Reviewed at Berlin Film Festival (official program, noncompeting), Feb. 23, 1988. Running time: **93 MIN.**

Berlin — Filling in the blank pages of Soviet history — i.e., those periods, personages, and events that have long been kept out of the public eye — is for many contemporary documakers something of a holy task. In "More Light!" filmer Marina Babak plunges enthusiastically into the 20th century, beginning with long unsung heroes of the October revolution like Trotsky and Bukharin, and following the train of history right up to 1987 *glasnost.*

Advertised as a compilation of unknown and banned docu footage, "More Light!" ought to find a ready audience at home. Offshore viewers will see it more as a curiosity item with a pompous, self-righteous commentary firmly steering the audience to the latest correct interpretation of history. It is as conventional in form as any of its predecessors of greyer years.

True, Babak and scriptwriter Igor Itzkov have a lot of history to rehabilitate, and they do it with vigorous assurance. There's rarely a dull minute in this fast-moving docu, full of the colorful posters of the times and unusual newsreels of people great and small.

Lenin is the film's godfather, oft reappearing to lend his supreme authority to any dark patch of the past. If he felt Trotsky was the most intelligent member of the Central Committee, and Stalin too dangerous to be made head of the Party, that's how these figures should be seen today. Film is outspoken in decrying Stalin as the instigator of the mass repression of the late '30s; camera pans down a list of official obits to illustrate how many died in '37 and '38.

The narrator appears on screen several times to rouse a spirit of indignation in the viewer: "Why gloss over our historical difficulties? We're not stupid." Unfortunately, his emotional reading is an uncomfortable drag on the commentary.

Film leaps through 10-year annis of the revolution. In 1937 the New Economic Policy creates an army of NEP-men whose private initiatives (according to the filmmakers) the Soviets might learn from today. A startling newsreel shows churches getting their crosses and bells knocked off and being blown up. By 1947 the hard days of the war are past. Stalin is buried; Khrushchev appears on the scene to courageously denounce Stalin and stir hope at the 20th Party Congress.

In 1967, a backward step with Brezhnev: film mocks the new leader for collecting medals while acute social ills go untreated. Yet by 1987 the country is back on the right track; Gorbachev, like Lenin, calls for "more socialism, more democracy, more light!"

Technically high quality, film benefits from good pacing and some splendidly lensed historical footage. —*Yung.*

Das Mikroscop
(The Microscope)
(WEST GERMAN)

A Moana Films production. Written and directed by Rudolph Thome. Camera (color), Martin Schäfer; editor, Dörte Völz-Mamarella; music, Hanno Rinné, Gabriela di Rosa; sound, Hermann Ebling; costumes, Anina Diener; production manager, Jochen Brunow. Reviewed at Berlin Film Festival (Forum of Young Cinema), Feb. 17, 1988. Running time: **97 MIN.**
Franz . . . . Vladimir Weigl
Maria . . . . Adriana Altaras
Tina . . . . Malgoscha Gebel
Klaus . . . . Alexander Malkowsky
Johanna . . . . Barbara Beutler
Also with: Ganeschi Becks, Max Below, Antje Goldau, Beate Stope, Alf Bold, Thomas Kempas, Brigitte Kolb, Martin Haupl, Oberpfleger Barth, Johannes Herschmann, Bernhard Schütz.

Berlin — An intelligent, low-key satire on troubled relations between men and women, Rudolph Thome's new film is intended as a first part of a trilogy on "the forms of love."

Here he starts by dealing with the unwillingness of Franz to assume his responsibility and bring a baby into the world. He prefers to leave his girlfriend Maria, but at the same time falls prey to an obsessive fascination with aquariums, fish being a symbol for the fertility he rejects. He embarks on a new relationship, with Tina, who turns out to be as-

sociated with Maria as well, and the relationship reaches its satirical climax when Franz, who has his arm broken accidentally, demands full female attention and care round the clock, which finally brings him back into Maria's arms.

All through the film, Franz' troubled relations with the women in his life are juxtaposed with the perfect bliss of another couple, Klaus and Johanna, who have two children and who represent the kind of successful solution Franz should adopt for himself.

Thome's approach, both humorous and earnest, is well balanced and the actors identify convincingly with their parts. The ending is somewhat disappointing, but on the whole, this is an interesting and often amusing psychological study. The film's title refers not only to another one of the protagonist's obsessions (observing cell fusion through a microscope), but also to scientific survey of human behavior glanced at through the impartial eye of a lens, this time attached to a movie camera.—*Edna.*

Wo-te ai
(This Love Of Mine)
(TAIWANESE)

A Central Motion Picture Corp. production. Executive producer, Hsu Hsin-chih. Produced by Lin Teng-fei. Directed by Chang Yi. Screenplay, Hsiao Sa, Chang Yi; camera (color), Yang Wei-ban; editor, Wang Chin-ch'en; production design, Wang Hsia-chun; music, Chang Hung-yi; sound, Tu Tu-chih; costumes, P'an Mei-li; associate producers, Hsu Kuo-liang, Chao Ch'i-pin. Reviewed at the London Film Festival, Nov. 25, 1987. Running time: **107 MIN.**
Wei-liang . . . . Yang Hui-shan
Wei-yeh . . . . Wang Hsia-chun
Wei-liang's mother . . . . Ch'en Yen-yen
An-ling . . . . Yang Li-ching
An-p'ing . . . . Ting Yeh-t'ien
Yuan-yuan . . . . Wu Jo-mei
Chiao-chiao . . . . Ho Ch'eng-hai

London — This is doom, gloom and despondency Taiwanese style. "This Love Of Mine" is a simple tale of a housewife whose moods shift from paranoia to suicidal as her family is shattered around her, with not a smile to be found anywhere.

Helmer Chang Yi shot with an abundance of elegance and class, attempting to film in the style of Ingmar Bergman, but the story is too shallow to support the effort.

Plot is pretty simple. Wife Yang Hui-shan finds out from her best friend that hubby is having an affair with a dancer. She dumps their two youngsters on momma and heads off to carve a new life for herself.

Part of this search for life without husband involves cutting most of her hair off so she looks like a punkette. Before long she finds she can't cope, so she goes back to her husband, emotionally blackmailing him into staying with her and the children.

This upsets the girlfriend, who tries to kill herself, and Yang Hui-shan, seeing she will never regain her husband's love, sets about gassing herself and the family.

Pic is high drama indeed, and features suitably stoney-faced performances from the lead players, especially Yang Hui-shan as wronged wife Wei-liang, who smiles just once in the whole film.

Script by Chang Yi and Hsiao Sa is literate and intelligent, but a respite — even a brief one — from the unrelenting gloom would have been welcome. Cinematography by Yang Wei-ban is excellent, and other technical credits are fine.—*Adam.*

Missile
(U.S.-DOCU)

Produced by Zipporah Films. Directed, written, edited and sound by Frederick Wiseman. Camera (color), John Davey. Reviewed at the Berlin Film Festival (Panorama), Feb. 19, 1988 (Also in AFI Fest, L.A.) Running time: **120 MIN.**

Berlin — Frederick Wiseman's docus are always interesting. Through the years he has fine-tuned his technique for letting his subjects speak for themselves to perfection. This time he takes on the military establishment.

Over two months he shot 60 hours of film at a California SAC base. The camera follows a training group who at the completion of their instruction will man the controls that launch the deeply buried defense missiles in the California desert.

We attend various preparatory lectures, range practice, freetime baseball game, church service and eavesdrop on conversations.

Though not as fascinating as some of his other work, that fact, ironically, is what makes this one doubly scary. He portrays the dull day-to-day lives of squadron recruits and officers who are trained to follow orders unquestioningly and with potentially deadly dedication.

These are the people who can determine our future since they have a finger on the button that controls the missiles. It's not so much that they seem incompetent, though no one imparts great wisdom or depth, but it's awesome that such potential for destruction, after the President gives the word, depends on their judgment and loyalty.

"Missile" offers a chilling look at the U.S. military climate and the bomb's potential. The beauty of Wiseman's approach is that another viewer might be inspired to recruitment. —*Owl.*

Dias Dificiles
(Difficult Days)
(MEXICAN)

A Distribuidora y Exportadora de Cine de Latino América (Decla) release of a Cooperativa José Revueltas-Producciones Penichet

production. Produced by Penichet, Alejandro Pelayo Rangel. Directed by Pelayo Rangel. Screenplay, Pelayo Rangel, Víctor Hugo Rascon; camera (color), Arturo de la Rosa; editor, Sigfrido Barján; music, Arturo Martínez. Reviewed at Havana Intl. Film Festival, Cuba, Dec. 11, 1987. Running time: **83 MIN.**
Edmundo Castelar . . . . . . Alejandro Parodi
Domingo Goycochea . . Enrique Hernández
Salvador Acevedo . . . . . . Ramón Menéndez
Himself . . . . Ricardo López Nava
Ricardo Castelar . . . . . Fernando Balzaretti
Luisa Castelar . . . . Blanca Guerra
Doña Amalia Castelar . . . . Beatriz Aguirre
Also with: Luisa Fernanda González, Sofia Olhovich, Luis Manuel Pelayo, Chuy Ramírez, Héctor E. Rascon, Mario Arras, Salvador Sánchez, Ricardo Aziz, Jorge Luis Castañeda.

Havana — In his new film "Dias Dificiles" (Difficult Days), Mexican director Alejandro Pelayo Rangel continues his investigation of power structures which began with his 1982 pic "La Vispera" (The Eve). This time, Pelayo structures his melodrama around the power struggles within the private sector by presenting the audience a complicated story of an industrialist family living in a nonexistent factory town in the north of Mexico.

Film begins with the death of the family patriarch, a workaholic who founded a major chemical processing plant. Control passes to eldest son Edmundo (Alejandro Parodi), a hard-working, honest man. Things complicate when he discovers young brother Ricardo (Fernando Balzaretti) plotting against him for rule. Two other actions complicate the tale even further: Edmundo is kidnaped by unknown assailants and held for $3,000,000; and ecological contamination from the factory suddenly has the community up in arms. While Ricardo meets with federal officials to secure his brother's release, media pressure is on to close the plant.

Pelayo keeps firm control on the diverse plot elements by balancing tensions between scenes. Acting is strong with a solid core of local talent led by Parodi and Blanca Guerra as Edmundo's wife Luisa.

Film also involves some of Mexico's current problems. The plant clearly should be closed down for ecological reasons, but in a country hard hit with economic problems, the closure would financially depress the region. Politicians are seen debating between the public good and private interests. It is a no-win situation for everyone involved.

Lensing is sharp and other tech credits help focus the drama toward its obvious solution. Pelayo shows once again that he is up to the task of tackling a difficult theme in an absorbing fashion. —*Lent.*

Tabarana Kathe
(Tabara's Tale)
(INDIAN)

A National Film Development Corp. production. Produced by Apoorva Chitra. Written and directed by Girish Kasaravalli. Story and dialog, Pooma Chandra Tejaswi; camera

(Eastmancolor), Madhu Amba; editor, M.N. Swamy; music, L. Vaidyanathan; art direction, Srinivas, Mohan. Reviewed at the Indian Film Festival, Trivandrum, Jan. 17, 1988 Running time: **140 MIN.**

Tabara Setty . . . . Charuhasan
Appi . . . . Nalina Murthy
Babu . . . . Santosh Nandavanam
Krishnappa . . . . Ha-Saa-Kru
Tehasildar . . . . R. Nagesh
   Also with: Madhav Rao (clerk), A.B. Jayaram (Eerey Gowda), Vaishali Kasaravalli, Sreenivas.

(In Kannada)

Trivandrum — The Kannada film that won all the national awards for 1986 (Golden Lotus for best feature film; best actor) "Tabara's Tale" is a nonstop indictment of how the poor get poorer and more miserable under the all-prevailing cancer of petty bureaucracy and the inhumanity of their fellow men.

Hero is a small tax collector whose tragedies, by pic's end, make melodrama look bland. To Western eyes, film errs in hammering out a message with relentless repetition for 140 numbing minutes. It may go down in history as a watershed of anti-bureaucratic rage, but audiences will be hard to rustle up for this painfully told tale of a painful life.

When we meet Tabara he's weeks away from well-earned retirement, fondly remembering the happy days when he worked for the British and watched them beat up Gandhi supporters. There was order then. Today it's a headache for the simple-minded taxman to get a tithe out of anybody.

All his efforts get him is a cut in pay due to a silly technicality about writing out receipts. It comes at the wrong time: his gentle wife Appi (Nalina Murthy) hurts her foot; complications lead to gangrene and diabetes is discovered. Too poor to arrange proper medical treatment, Tabara increases his efforts to get the pension that is coming to him. His file is at the bottom of a thick, dusty pile. He tries bribes; he tries the help of a local left-wing politician, whose good intentions backfire by getting Tabara into more trouble.

As the situation worsens, Tabara tries begging for a loan. Another self-interested politician helps him out, but by then it's too late to save Appi. Their simple-minded adopted son, Babu (Santosh Nandavanam), is lost in the city crowds while Tabara stumbles down the street, overwhelmed by grief.

The sight of the distraught man disturbs his fellow villagers, who openly wish he'd go mad. It creates other bureaucratic hassles for an official who "went out on a limb" by once declaring him sane and writing it on a document. Then the pension comes — ironically, a fabulous sum — and Tabara, completely destroyed, disdainfully donates it to the celebrations for India's silver jubilee of independence.

Filmmaker Girish Kasaravalli has

obviously worked painstakingly on his script and its symbology. There are many striking moments and heart-rending scenes, underlined by touching performances. If all that injustice to innocents seems excessive to outsiders, native viewers may find it far more proportional to reality. — *Yung.*

Consuming Passions
(BRITISH-U.S.)

A Samuel Goldwyn Co. release of a Samuel Goldwyn Co. and Euston Films Ltd. presentation. Produced by William Cartlidge. Directed by Giles Foster. Screenplay, Paul D. Zimmerman, Andrew Davies, from play "Secrets" by Michael Palin, Terry Jones; camera (Technicolor), Roger Pratt; editor, John Grover; music, Richard Hartley; sound (Dolby), Tony Dawe; production design, Peter Lamont; art direction, Terry Ackland-Snow; set decoration, Michael Ford; assistant director, Roger Simons; production manager, Patricia Carr; special effects supervisor, Ian Wingrove. Reviewed at Magno Preview 9 screening room, N.Y., March 9, 1988. MPAA Rating: R. Running time: **98 MIN.**

Mrs. Garza . . . . Vanessa Redgrave
Farris . . . . Jonathan Pryce
Ian Littleton . . . . Tyler Butterworth
Chumley . . . . Freddie Jones
Felicity Stubbs . . . . Sammi Davis
Ethel . . . . Prunella Scales
Mrs. Gordon . . . . Thora Hird
   Also with: William Rushton, John Wells, Timothy West, Mary Healey, Andrew Sachs, Bryan Pringle, Patrick Newell, Preston Lockwood.

"Consuming Passions" is a thoroughly unfunny misfire, equating poor taste with black humor. British-made effort from Samuel Goldwyn Co. (of which the late Goldwyn Senior would clearly disapprove) integrates cornball elements from such warhorses as "Sweeney Todd" into a very flat satire that is barely suitable for midnight screenings.

Pic originally was developed with the active participation of several Monty Python members, with Goldcrest (since departed from the project) involved as well under working title "The Chocolate Factory." Final result is credited as based on a (little-known) play "Secrets" by Pythonites Michael Palin and Terry Jones, but Paul D. Zimmerman ("The King Of Comedy") and Andrew Davies' script is witless and vulgar.

Nominal plot, a sketch stretched to feature length, has naive management trainee Tyler Butterworth arriving at Freddie Jones' chocolate factory and accidentally pushing three workmen into a vat. Unable to stop the assemblyline, Butterworth to his horror discovers the men have been processed into the first batch of Passionelles chocolates, a brainchild of new company manager Jonathan Pryce.

Under Giles Foster's mechanical direction, every plot twist is telegraphed at least a reel ahead: Jones and Butterworth's unsuccessful, frenzied attempt to retrieve the tainted chocolates; test results which prove that only the cannibal-contents Passionelles meet with consumer approval; lengthy segue to Butterworth's "Burke And Hare" assignments to fetch corpses to keep the popular 6% human content Passionelles in production, etc..

Only surprise here is topbilled Vanessa Redgrave, taking an ill-advised stab at comedy by playing, with Melina Mercouri-esque voice,

a Maltese woman whose insatiable sexual appetite gets Butterworth in trouble. Redgrave's extraneous cameo, at first amusing, is padded via endless repetition and becomes embarrassing. Toilet humor here makes the "Carry On" films seem a paragon of good taste by comparison, and at least they were amusing.

Pryce gets a few cheap laughs from his garish clothing, but his facial tics and affected vocal pattern (punctuating each sentence with "Yeah?") are tiresome. Jones hams to no effect and Prunella Scales, erstwhile perfect comedy foil for John Cleese in his "Fawlty Towers" tv series, has little to do as a secretary wearing funny-looking miniskirts. Sammi Davis, as Butterworth's romantic interest and the closest to normal character, is very appealing with a Liverpudlian accent.

Helping to sink the dubious enterprise is casting of Butterworth in the lead role — he simply isn't funny in a part that would require an established talent on the level of Michael Palin to carry the picture. Tech credits are solid down the line, offering needed visual distraction.

A tasteless sight gag involving an AIDS-prevention warning got the only belly laugh at the screening. — *Lor.*

The Invisible Kid

A Taurus Entertainment release of an Elysian Pictures production. Executive producers, Philip J. Spinelli, Avery Crounse. Produced by Spinelli. Directed by Crounse. Screenplay, Crounse; camera (United color), Michael Barnard; editor, Gabrielle Gilbert; music, Steve Hunter, Jan King; sound (Ultrastereo), Jan Brodin, Jerry Wolfe; art direction, Charles Tomlinson; special mechanical effects, Tassilo Baur; makeup design, Annie Maniscalco; production manager, Nancy Nickerson; assistant director, Tom Rolapp; second unit director, Spinelli; second unit camera, Sam Dodge; special visual effects, Ernie Farino; coproducers, Nickerson, Rolapp; casting, Carole Dudley, Reuben Cannon & Associates; stunt coordinator, John Stewart. Reviewed at Criterion 3 theater, N.Y., April 1, 1988. MPAA Rating: PG. Running time: **95 MIN.**

Grover . . . . Jay Underwood
Mom . . . . Karen Black
Milton . . . . Wally Ward
Cindy Moore . . . . Chynna Phillips
Dr. Theodore . . . . Brother Theodore
Officer Chuck . . . . Mike Genovese
Singer . . . . Jan King
   Also with: Nicolas de Toth, John Madden Towen, Thomas Cross, John Miranda.

"The Invisible Kid" is an inept teen fantasy; one hesitates to call it a comedy though that was the intention. It's another video given a theatrical release.

Pic belongs not to the flop teen science genre of three years back (e.g., "My Science Project," "Real Genius") but rather the tease sleaze of "Zapped!" Jay Underwood portrays a high school nerd using his late science teacher dad's notes to complete dad's work. Pigeon droppings fall in the compound (unbeknownst to Underwood), creating a powder that makes one invisible for

30 minutes when ingested. Stupid script has the invisibility period reduced by five minutes each time; dumb twist gives you a full 30 the eighth time around.

This is strictly an excuse for peeping in the girls' locker room, hoping leading lady Chynna Phillips will flash a bare chest (she doesn't) and failed slapstick. Low point probably is when the hero hides in the principal's office and we are treated to a flatulence gag. An inane subplot involving a basketball tournament is injected to give Underwood some licks imitating Michael J. Fox on the court in "Teen Wolf."

Threadbare production has most of the invisibility "achieved" via first-person Steadicam, plus some token effects work. Avery Crounse's direction is strictly amateurish.

Young cast tries, but Karen Black is a joke as the boy's dizzy mom, right down to a pointless outtake of her following the end credits. Brother Theodore has nothing to do as a Dr. Ruth-type tv advice show host, presumably cast because (like Dr. Ruth) he has a thick accent.—*Lor.*

The Seventh Sign

A Tri-Star Pictures release from Tri-Star ML Delphi Premier Prods. of an Interscope Communications production. Produced by Ted Field, Robert Cort. Executive producer, Paul R. Gurian. Direced by Carl Schultz. Screenplay, "W.W. Wicket," "George Kaplan" (Clifford Green, Ellen Green); camera (Panavision, Technicolor), Juan Ruiz-Anchia; editor, Caroline Biggerstaff; music, Jack Nitzsche; production design, Stephen Marsh; art direction, Francesca Bartoccini; set decoration, Cricket Rowland; costume design, Durinda Rice Wood; sound (Dolby), Emile Razpopov, Dessie Markovsky; special makeup effects, Craig Reardon; additional makeup effects, Kevin Yeager; assistant director, Chris Soldo; coproducer, Kathleen Hallberg; stunt coordinator, Gary Hymes; second unit director-visual effects supervisor, Michael L. Fink; special visual effects, Dream Quest Images; casting, Pennie du Pont. Reviewed at Tri-Star Pictures screening room, L.A., March 29, 1988. MPAA Rating: R. Running time: **97 MIN.**

Abby Quinn . . . . Demi Moore
Russell Quinn . . . . Michael Biehn
The Boarder . . . . Jürgen Prochnow
Avi . . . . Manny Jacobs
Lucci . . . . Peter Friedman
Also with: John Heard, Akosua Busia, John Taylor, Arnold Johnson, Leonardo Cimino, Lee Garlington, Richard Devon.

Hollywood — If the seventh sign of the apocalypse is anything like the film "The Seventh Sign," the world needn't worry. There's about two minutes of suspense with the rest a fairly tame dramatization of revelations from the Bible. It's doubtful this will excite film audiences much.

Demi Moore as an expectant mother leads the cast for what evolves into a religiously based melodrama drawn from the Judeo-Christian belief that God will end life on earth when the last martyr dies and the next child born is soulless, which turns out to be Moore's baby.

This is a terrifying prospect for those who believe in such things and

could have made an equally horrifying picture as well even for those who don't.

Instead, scripters Clifford and Ellen Green (using the pseudonyms W.W. Wicket ànd George Kaplan) have things move too perfectly back and forth from allegory to reality. The last martyr is a convicted criminal (John Taylor) represented by Moore's lawyer husband (Michael Biehn); and the priest from Rome (Peter Friedman) investigating the various incidences just happens to be the one who later gives the martyr last rites before he's to be sent to the gas chamber.

Jürgen Prochnow walks through a coastal town in Haiti (filmed in Dominica) while the locals stand and stare. When he reaches shore, he breaks open a sealed envelope and this triggers the first revelation where the fish of the sea die.

Prochnow is God's messenger and a fairly stoic one at that. He later turns up at Moore's door to rent a garage apartment and becomes more of an apologetic friend of hers even after she discovers he's going to cause the death of her child.

When the harbinger of evil seems to be having second thoughts, the suspense goes right down the tubes.

Cut several times with the linear story is a cryptic scene showing an ancient Roman soldier hitting another followed by the smashing of a jug. Their faces are never shown until the end of the film, but all the lead-ins serve to merely distract the viewer than further the story.

Director Carl Schultz jumps around too much — stopping the action as Moore takes a bath and contemplates suicide when she thinks things are getting beyond her, then back to her husband's office where he frenetically works on an appeal to the California Supreme Court to stay the execution.

With so many changes of mood and tone, Schultz never is able to build any excitement or tension.

This is not the fault of the actors either, but more their characterizations. Biehn isn't much of a husband. He dismisses Moore's theories about the end of the world as the imaginings of a suicidal woman and is more concerned about exploring all the legal maneuvers to get his client off than whether he is a religious symbol.

Manny Jacobs gets the best role as the student of Hebrew who does some translating for Moore. His visit with a white-bread minister (John Heard) for an explanation of the Christian view of the apocalypse versus the Jewish view is one of the film's better scenes. —*Brit.*

Mujeres al Borde de Un Ataque de Nervios
(Women On The Verge Of A Nervous Breakdown)
(SPANISH)

An El Deseo and Lauren Films production. Executive producer, Agustin Almodóvar. Written and directed by Pedro Almodóvar. Camera (Eastmancolor), José Luis Alcaine; editor, José Salcedo; music, Bernardo Bonezzi, production manager, Ester Garcia; costumes, José Maria de Cossïo; sound, Guilles Ortión; associate producer, Antonio Llorens. Reviewed at Cine Proyecciones, Madrid, March 28, 1988. Running time: **98 MIN.**

Pepa . . . . Carmen Maura
Carlos . . . . Antonio Banderas
Iván . . . . Fernando Guillén
Lucia . . . . Julieta Serrano
Candela . . . . Maria Barranco
Marisa . . . . Rossy de Palma
Paulina . . . . Kitty Manver
Also with: Chus Lampreave, Yayo Calvo, Lotes León, Angel de Andrés López.

Madrid — The ever-growing cult following, both in and out of Spain, of Pedro Almodóvar should increase appreciably with the release of this often hilarious, irreverent and offbeat comedy, the most coherent the young Spanish filmmaker has limned thus far.

Almodóvar has honed his humor and knows just the right moment for springing nuances, or comic silences, or letting loose the unexpected wisecrack or slap in the face. No need here for sex and drugs and the gay scene (only marginally touched upon in a humorous vein), since the dilemma of a woman on the verge of a nervous breakdown after breaking up with a married man is fascinatingly treated in a comic vein. Almodóvar understands his women, and there always is underlying sympathy for them, even when he turns their personal tragedies into whimsy.

Central character is Pepa, superbly played by the helmer's Muse, Carmen Maura. Using mostly the interior of her apartment as the scenario of the action, Almodóvar introduces her zany girlfriend, then the son of the man who has jilted Pepa, his outraged wife, a second girlfriend, two policemen, a distaff lawyer and a gay taxi driver. All come wonderfully together in a script solid and witty enough to please not only cult followers but wider audiences as well.

Pic winds after an amusing taxi vs. motorcycle race to the airport, where one of the "nervous" women is collared by the police after trying to shoot her husband (who had been Pepa's lover).

Good production values, crisp lensing, fine editing and mock-heroic music all add up to a thoroughly enjoyable film which should do brisk business in all territories, helped by the already considerable reputation Almodóvar has established for himself. Pic was given an "all audiences" classification in Spain.—*Besa.*

Above The Law

A Warner Bros. release. Produced by Steven Seagal, Andrew Davis. Executive producer, Robert Solo. Coproduced by John Wilson. Directed by Davis. Screenplay, Steven Pressfield, Ronald Shusett, Davis; from story by Davis, Seagal; camera (Technicolor), Robert Steadman; editor, Michael Brown; music, David M. Frank, production design, Maher Ahmad; assistant director, Peter Guilliano; second unit camera, Davis; casting, Richard S. Kordos, Nan Charbonneau, Billy Damota. Reviewed at Warner Bros. screening room, L.A., March 29, 1988. MPAA Rating: R. Running time: **99 MIN.**

Nico Toscani . . . . Steven Seagal
Delores Jackson . . . . Pam Grier
Zagon . . . . Henry Silva
Lukich . . . . Ron Dean
Salvano . . . . Daniel Faraldo
Sara Toscani . . . . Sharon Stone
Agent Neeley . . . . Nicholas Kusenko
Father Gennaro . . . . Joe V. Greco
Nelson Fox . . . . Chelcie Ross
Crowder . . . . Thalamus Rasulala

Hollywood — "Above The Law" is an ultraviolent actioner from Andrew Davis that's not unlike his "Code Of Silence" — or many other Chuck Norris pics — except here it's Steven Seagal playing the aikido-chopping cop on a oneman crusade to clean up Chi streets. Fans of the genre will not go away unsatisfied, but for others the gore may be a bit much.

Seagal takes on the same steely demeanor as many of Norris' characters. He's a man of action, not one of words.

His mission at first appears straightforward — to get rid of the cocaine-pushing scum that are destroying the peace and cohesiveness of his Italian working class neighborhood.

As Nico Toscani, Seagal is a no-nonsense cop with a cynical eye towards authority, an attitude shaped from his experiences working with the CIA in Vietnam and now, many years later, finding them moving in on his beat where they should have no business.

When he's taken off the trail of a suspected drug dealer, he smells a rat or two at the top of his chain of command. Late one night, he gets a call from an old war buddy now with the CIA warning him to cool his jets, but audiences can be assured this will only fuel Seagal's fire.

With the support of a couple dozen stunt persons and an earthy, warm and supportive partner (Pam Grier), Seagal kicks, kills and crushes with his skillful hands one handful after another of street hoods who try to thwart his mission.

In the context of this rather limiting and convoluted scheme, somehow is worked in an assassination plot against the U.S. senator who's about ready to expose a drug trafficking trade in Central America and a group of Salvadoran refugees hiding out in the basement of Seagal's neighborhood Catholic church.

Given the true accounts of CIA involvement in Central America these days, this may not be so out of the realm of possibility.

Henry Silva is a sicko sadist who gets off shooting his victims in the arm with truth serum and then threatening to chop their limbs off one by one until they talk.

Noise factor of the production almost always is at fever pitch with successive fighting scenes broken up by a couple of screeching car chases and a church bombing. Quiet moments like the ones with Seagal and his emotional wife (Sharon Stone) comprise about 1% of the film.

Davis makes good use of Chi's cityscape as he did in "Code Of Silence." Robert Steadman's eye for capturing all of the action without crowding the picture is well executed. —*Brit.*

Slugs
(SPANISH)

A New World Pictures release of a Dister Films production. Produced by José A. Escrivá, Francesca de Laurentiis, Juan Piquer Simón. Directed by Juan Piquer Simón. Screenplay, Ron Gantman, based on novel by Shaun Hutson; camera (color), Julio Bragado; editor, Richard Rabjohn; special effects, Emilio Ruiz; makeup effects, Carlo de Marchis. Reviewed at Fotofilm screening room, Madrid, April 1, 1988. MPAA Rating: R. Running time: **92 MIN.**

Mike Brady	Michael Garfield
John Foley	Santiago Alvarez
Don Palmer	Philip Machale
Maureen Watson	Alicia Moro
Kim Brady	Kim Terry
Maria Palmer	Concha Cuetos
David Watson	Emilio Linder

Madrid — Lively pacing, convincing special effects & makeup and snappy direction help to maintain interest in this horror pic being released by New World which has enough thrills and spills in it to keep youth audiences alert.

Yarn concerns a plague of slugs invading a smalltown American community. The creepers, about four or five times the size of a regular slug, have turned carnivorous after being exposed to toxic waste and slowly start to take over the town, sliming out of faucets in kitchens and crawling through innocent-looking gardens.

After the local authorities prove unresponsive to the threat, the local health inspector (Michael Garfield) and a friend start to take action on their own and discover that some old sewers running under the town are the breeding place of the killer slugs.

As the corpses pile up around the village, the two men and a university doctor, armed with a special toxin, set out to destroy the slugs in their lair. Pic provides scenes which should appeal to horror buffs, as the slugs attack some of the townspeople. Final 15 minutes build to a satisfying climax as the slugs are hunted down in the sewers, providing several appropriately thrill-packed scenes.

Thesping, direction, special ef-

fects and production credits are good. Pic could appeal to a wide audience in most territories around the world. —*Besa.*

Der Werwolf von W.
(The Werewolf Of W.)
(WEST GERMAN)

A Reinery Publication and Film commissioned by ZDF, Mainz. Produced by Peter Wohlgemuth-Reinery, Wolfgang Schulte. Directed by Manfred Müller. Screenplay, Müller, Werner Pilz; camera (color), Wolfgang Pilgrim, Niki Stein; editor, Brigitte Lippmann, Marion Schwarz; sound, Günter Knon; music, Voker Rogall; sets, Achim Feles, Eckard Kuchenbecker; costumes and makeup, Brigitte Gruse, Dagmar Bergfeld. Reviewed at Berlin Film Festival, Feb. 18, 1988. Running time: **82 MIN.**
With: Henry Hübchen, Michael Gwisdek, Martina Schieber, Werner Brehm, Horst Fechner, Erwin Brunn, Rudolf Mölders, Herbert Meurer, Peter Schwab, Ralph Willmann, Til Uhlenbrock, Klaus Frohwein.

Berlin — **First-time director Manfred Müller here has mistaken slow pacing for suspense. A night watchman is found dead under mysterious circumstances. There seems to be have been other mysterious deaths associated with the land the industrial site was built on that go as far back as the 16th century.**

The dead man's nubile daughter seems to be looking for clues, so is a detective and the night watchman's successor.

Other than these basic facts it's hard to make sense of this film. Rather than offering any substantial clues, or even delivering a glimpse of the title character, we get a series of vague scenes, more unexplained deaths and a factory owner with some kind of secret. The film goes after atmosphere but achieves tedium.

Technically, there's good work. The pic was well photographed and framed but the story goes nowhere. —*Owl.*

Bad Dreams

A 20th Century Fox release, in association with American Entertainment Partners II, of a No Frills Film production. Produced by Gale Anne Hurd. Directed by Andrew Fleming. Screenplay, Fleming, Steven E. de Souza, from story by Fleming, Michael Dick, Yuri Zeltser, P.J. Pettiette; camera (Deluxe color), Alexander Gruszynski; editor, Jeff Freeman; music, Jay Ferguson; sound (Dolby), John Geisinger; production design, Ivo Cristante; art direction, A. Rosalind Crew; special makeup effects, Michele Burke; visual effects, Fantasy II Film Effects; assistant director, John Woodward; production manager, Charles Skouras 3d; stunt coordinator, Tony Cecere; costume design, Deborah Everton; associate producer, Ginny Nugent; casting, Mindy Marin. Reviewed at Criterion 4 theater, N.Y., April 2, 1988. MPAA Rating: R. Running time: **84 MIN.**

Cynthia	Jennifer Rubin
Dr. Alex Carmen	Bruce Abbott
Harris	Richard Lynch
Ralph	Dean Cameron
Dr. Beresford	Harris Yulin
Connie	Susan Barnes
Lana	E.G. (Elizabeth) Daily
Detective	Sy Richardson
Young Cynthia	Missy Francis

Also with: John Scott Clough, Damita Jo Freeman, Louis Giambalvo, Alba Francesca.

"Bad Dreams" is a dull, unscary horror shlocker. New Line's Bob Shaye won't lose any sleep over this failed Fox imitation of his hit "Nightmare On Elm Street" pics.

Five writers are credited for a laughably inept story and screenplay, ostensibly concerning a young girl (Missy Francis) who survives a Jonestown-style suicide ritual presided over by a cult leader (Richard Lynch). After 13 years in a coma she awakes (as Jennifer Rubin), put by mad shrink Harris Yulin into a group therapy session (suspiciously similar to that of "Nightmare 3") run by Bruce Abbott.

Reductio ad absurdum plot has group members killed off one by one, each time looking like a suicide, with frequent fantasy appearances by Lynch, alternately as himself, or illogically covered in gooey red makeup (to vaguely resemble a hatless Freddy Krueger from "Nightmare"). These appearances and the deaths aren't scary at all, but lots of extraneous gore is featured for the low-end fans. Loads of supernatural material is all explained away in the final reel (an instant turnoff) as drug-induced hallucinations caused by the mad doc to incite his patients to suicide.

Debuting helmer Andrew Fleming muffs this audition by emphasizing comic relief (primarily wisecracks by a hip patient, well played by Dean Cameron), but the preview audience at a postage stamp-sized Times Square theater laughed in all the wrong places. Rooftop climax culminating numerous red herrings and fake plot twists is an embarrassing example of poor construction.

Leading lady Jennifer Rubin is a very bland lookalike for Amanda Pays, while costar Abbott had a much better time in "Re-Animator." Lynch, overused as a villain (one look at him sunk "Little Nikita's" suspense recently), is cast in extremely poor taste whereby his heavily scarred (from a real-life incident) face and neck give way to Michele Burke's post-fire makeup effects. Diminutive actress Elizabeth Daily is given a Veronica Lake peekaboo hairstyle and credited under her latterday rock singer name E.G. Daily.

Tech credits are below average, particularly the very fake-looking superimposed fire effects during a reprise of the suicide cult's demise. —*Lor.*

Landlord Blues

Produced and directed by Jacob Burckhardt. Coproducer, Howard David Deutsch. Codirector, William Gordy. Written and edited by Burckhardt, Gordy, from story by George Schneeman; camera (Kodak color), Carl Teitelbaum; music, Roy Nathanson, Marc Ribot, Nona Hendryx, Oliver Lake;

sound, L.B. Dallas; production design, Wendy Walker; production manager, Nick Smithberg. Reviewed at Berlin Film Festival (Panorama), Feb. 19, 1988. Running time: **96 MIN.**

Berlin — **Ever wanted to believe your New York landlord was a no-good cocaine dealer? Then this second feature from director Jacob Burckhardt might be of interest.**

At moments the dialog and situations of this low-budgeter stretch credibility, but pic is well intentioned and is a kind of urban morality tale with the villain truly villainous and the tenants thoroughly victimized.

A bike chase scene is good if you can believe a middle-aged man in not particularly good shape can keep up with a teenager darting in and out of New York traffic.

The basic story involves a greedy landlord who wants to evict a bicycle shop — non-polluting, non-environment-threatening — and replace it with a high-rent-paying art gallery. Bike shop owner (Mark Boone Jr.) becomes a neighborhood hero when he is able to thwart the landlord's intentions.

Pic shows promise and could find limited distribution in special situations. —*Owl.*

Pandemonium
(AUSTRALIAN)

A KFM Pandemonium production, in association with Smart Street Films-Tra La La Films. (Intl. sales, Shining Armour Communications.) Executive producer, Patric Juillet. Produced by Alex Cutler, Haydn Keenan. Directed by Keenan. Screenplay, Keenan, Peter Gailey; camera (Eastman color), David Sanderson; editor, Paul Healy; music, Cameron Allan; sound, Phillip Keros; production design, Melody Cooper; special effects, Monte Fieguth. Reviewed at Chauvel, Sydney, March 11, 1988. Running time: **88 MIN.**

Kales Leadingham/Ding the Dingo	David Argue
The Dingo Girl	Amanda Dole
E.B. De Woolf	Esben Storm
P.B. De Woolf	Arna-Maria Winchester
1st twin	Rainee Skinner
2nd twin	Kerry Mack
Little Adolph/paperboy	Ashley Grenville
Morticia	Mercia Deane-Jones
Dr. Doctor	Haydn Keenan
Det. Sgt. Dick Dickerson	Lex Marinos
The Holy Ghost	Gary Foley

Also with: Henk Johannes (The Count), Greg Ham (Marvo the Magician), Pete Smith (Peter Kong), Ignatius Jones (Marriage Celebrant), Ian Nimmo (Mr. David).

Sydney — **Evidently inspired by "The Rocky Horror Picture Show," "Pandemonium" is a frantic, over-the-top affair filled with eccentric characters and incidents that strive to be as tasteless as possible. It has something to offend just about everybody, and yet there's a naïveté and innocence about it that's quite touching. Best commerical bet is to appeal to would-be cult audiences.**

Setting is a disused, apparently haunted, film studio located at Sydney's famous Bondi Beach. The place is occupied by the lecherous film director E.B. De Woolf (Esben Storm with a phony Yank accent) and his crippled, ex-beauty queen wife (Arna-Maria Winchester) who's as mad as the proverbial hatter.

Pic begins with the arrival of a buxom, near-naked beauty (Amanda Dole) who, as a baby, was abandoned by her parents and raised by dingos in the desert. Clad only in a loincloth, the beauteous innocent is searching for her long-lost mom and pop.

Hero of the piece is Kales Leadingham (David Argue), described in hand-outs as "a cross between Indiana Jones and Daffy Duck." He takes a shine to the girl, and tries in his clumsy way to help her.

Characters also include a diminutive descendent of Hitler, neo-Nazi twin femmes who buzz around on roller skates, vampires and other monsters, a corrupt cop and an aboriginal Holy Ghost who, it seems, is the Dingo Girl's true father, though that doesn't stop him having sex with her in the film's calculatingly blasphemous climax.

Haydn Keenan has always worked on the fringes of the film industry (his last was the gritty drama "Going Down") and here he cheerfully lets it all hang out. He's packed his film with bizarre characters and situations, insuring that it will appeal mainly to a young, hip crowd. Direction is chaotic, and the pic is never as funny as it thinks it is, but it has an undisciplined energy that's infectious, at least for a while.

Thesping is all over the place, with a variety of actors and local personalities mugging away in widely differing styles.

It all adds to the off-the-wall mood the director obviously sought. Given the low budget involved, pic is technically okay.

Late last year, "Pandemonium" played at the Hof fest in Germany, and this month it participates in the Hong Kong fest. Commercial chances look iffy. —Strat.

Risk
(SOVIET-DOCU-B&W/COLOR)

A Gorky Studio production (Moscow). Directed by Dmitri Barshtchevski. Written by Natalia Violina, F. Bortvik, Vitali Ignatenko, Vladimir Kusnotzov, Lev Kulidjanov, Konstantin Slavin; camera (b&w, color), Aleksandr Kulidjanov, V. Berger, N. Shutnik; sound, Vladislav Nabatnikov. Reviewed at Berlin Film Festival (Panorama), Feb. 19, 1988. Running time: 94 MIN.

Berlin — There is an unquestionable fascination in seeing history recounted from the other side; in the case of "Risk," Dmitri Barshtchevski's docu on the international politics of nuclear missiles, the other side is the Russian view of some of the most significant events of the 20th century.

Hard facts may overlap; but not always the p.o.v., as for example in filmmaker's critical view of J.F.K. In a film of proclaimed pacifist intent, however, discrepancies with the Western schoolbook version are rather intriguing. Stumbling block to pic's circulation lies in the blurriness of the whole.

Produced by Gorky Studio, which has been under attack for allegedly holding out against the new regime of glasnost, "Risk" nevertheless purports to be a new wave work — suffice it to say that in the plethora of political figures parading across the screen there is not a single image or mention of Brezhnev. Stalin, who abounds in key moments of Soviet nuclear history, gets chided for loving crowds and parades in his honor. Lacking is a clear, coherent or new p.o.v. on the nuclear issue, much less a controversial one.

After opening with a speech by Gorbachev, film starts back at Stalin's meeting with Truman and Churchill at Potsdam in 1945 — featuring some rare color footage. Next comes Hiroshima (again, excellent quality footage, which characterizes the film), the announcement the Russians have the bomb in 1949, and on to the McCarthy hearings and the Rosenbergs' trial, admittedly eerie as viewed from faraway Gorky Studio.

Bomb builders are reviewed, from Werner Von Braun (whose Nazi past is underlined, along with the irony of his going to work for the "unscrupulous" Americans) to Soviet missile builders like Koroliov. Khrushchev's applauded UN address in 1959 segues into the Gary Powers U2 trial; Kennedy's assassination, cosmonauts, then Challenger and Chernobyl make their bow, under the general heading "risk." Thus concludes an inconclusive docu, albeit one with superb technical reproduction of historical footage and an effective soundtrack drawn from the classics. —Yung.

Flag
(Flagrante Delicto)
(CANADIAN-FRENCH)

An AAA release of a Films Ariane/Cinévidéo/FR3 Films/Soprofilm (AAA) coproduction. Executive producer, Jean Nachbaur. Produced by Justine Heroux, Santi, Simon Mickael, Tansou; camera (Eastmancolor), François Protat; editor, Françoise Javet; music, Jean-Pierre Mas; sound, Bernard Aubouy; art direction, Dominique André; assistant director, Michel Thibaud; production manager, Raymond Leplont; casting, Mamade. Reviewed at Trois Balzac theater, Paris, Feb. 11, 1988. Running time: 101 MIN.
Simon . . . . Richard Bohringer
Tramoni . . . . Pierre Arditi
Sax . . . . Philippe Pouchain
Fanny . . . . Philippine Leroy-Beaulieu
Josy . . . . Anne Letourneau
Léon Terzakian . . . . Julien Guiomar
Also with: Smain, Philippe Besson, Philippe Sfez.

Paris — Nominated for a César award for best first feature, "Flag" is a lean, well-paced minor thriller and a good vehicle for Richard Bohringer as a police detective slumming in an underworld of gambling dens.

Former actor and assistant director Jacques Santi debuts with straightforward skill, attentive both to actors and technical efficiency. For the screenplay he had the collaboration of Simon Mickael, a former flic turned scripter, whose experience has authenticated a number of genre efforts (including Claude Zidi's police comedy, "Les Ripoux").

Bohringer is in fine, low-keyed form as a veteran cop who's remained in the ranks while colleague Pierre Arditi has succeeded in becoming department boss.

Their cooling friendship takes a hard blow when Bohringer, after a failed effort to back some dangerous thieves, begins to suspect Arditi of taking bribes to cover the activities of a professional fence (Julien Guiomar).

Arditi orders him off the job. Bohringer, known once to have hit the skids as an inveterate gambler, suffers an apparent relapse and begins to haunt the gambling dives, especially those run by Guoimar, where he runs up a high debt.

In fact, Bohringer is preparing a roundabout vengeance against his corrupt colleague, who in the end is forced to shoot down the hood he was protecting.

Script is well-constructed though it doesn't instill enough ambiguity about Bohringer's supposed regression.

Perfunctory female presence is provided by Philippine Leroy-Beaulieu, as Bohringer's girlfriend, and Canada's Anne Letourneau (courtesy of a Franco-Canadian coprod arrangement).

Tech credits are fine. —Len.

Clandestinos Destinos
(Clandestine Destinies)
(MEXICAN)

A Clasa Films Mundial release of a Universidad de Guadalajara production. Presented by Manuel Barbachano Ponce, Pablo Barbachano. Produced by Lourdes Rivera, Norma Castañares. Written and directed by Jaime Humberto Hermosillo. Camera (color), José Antonio Asencio, Francisco Bajorquez; editor, Laura Imperiale; music, Carlos Esege, with songs by Jaime López; sound, Fernando Cámara; art direction, Laura Santacruz, Marta Vidrio. Reviewed at Havana Intl. Film Festival, Cuba, Dec. 10, 1987. Running time: 81 MIN.
Lila/Odinette Orozco . . . . . Magnolia Rivas
Eduardo Zuringa . . . . Rafael Monroy
Angel . . . . Alonso Téllez
Isabel . . . . Denise Montiel
Salvador . . . . Arturo Villaseñor

Havana — Never one to work with conventional themes, Mexican helmer Jaime Humberto Hermosillo mixes his continued exploration of socio-sexual role-switching, which was best expressed in the 1986 "Doña Herlinda And Her Son," with politics in his latest offering "Clandestine Destinies."

Add to this a low-budget sci-fi setting, camp posturing, lots of black humor and horrendous acting and we are served an unappetizing salad of diverse themes and ideas that make for unpalatable viewing.

Story is set in some vague police-state future when the northern half of Mexico has been annexed to the United States. Sex has been outlawed and the Second American Civil War looms imminent. Characters include: Eduardo, whose suicide attempts clutter the plot like a running joke; spoiled movie princess Lila, a.k.a. Odinette Orozco or more simply O.O.; gay artist Angel, who plots with O.O. to get into Eduardo's pants; sweet Isabel, Eduardo's ex on the eve of her wedding; Isabel's conservative boyfriend Salvador who wants to throw a damper on the entire proceedings; and Ninón, Eduardo's neurotic dog.

In order to distract Eduardo from mortal thoughts, the characters go on a camping trip where they can frolic in sexual freedom. Rather than talk Eduardo out of suicide, he convinces them to make a death pact, and things go on from there.

There are some amusing moments to the film but technically it's a mess. Thesping is awkward and substandard, and the high-tech props are hilarious. Pic has the feel of an early '60s underground film, and the ending is totally predictable.

For all the film's faults, it is interesting to see that Hermosillo is continuing to explore new themes. He still lacks control over them.
—Lent.

Entre Compadres Te Veas
(Dirty Dealings Between Buddies)
(MEXICAN)

A Peliculas Mexicanas release of a Cumbre Films production. Executive producer, Luis Berkis. Directed by Rafael Villaseñor Kuri. Screenplay, Adolfo Torres Portillo, based on an idea by Oscar J. Brooks, Ernesto Cortázar, with additional dialog by Eulalio González; camera (color), Agustin Lara; editor, Max Sánchez; music, Cortázar; associate producer, Vicente Fernández. Reviewed at Hollywood Twin, N.Y., Nov. 20, 1987. Running time: 94 MIN.
Juan Benegas . . . . Vicente Fernández
Pablo Benegas . . . . Andrés García
Pedro Benegas . . . Lalo González (Piporro)
Rossy Orino . . . . Olivia Collins
Also with: Merle Uribe, Polo Ortín, Pancho Muller, Luis Manuel Pelayo.

"Dirty Dealings Between Buddies" is the latest comedy vehicle for popular Mexican ranchero singer-actor Vicente Fernández and is directed by perennial Fernández helmer Rafael Villaseñor Kuri.

This time Fernández teams up with Mexican leading man Andrés García and the two look as if they share 400 gleaming white teeth between them. They play brothers brought up under a strict, domineering mother, who has ruled the house with an iron hand. At her death, the two join with their father (Lalo González a.k.a. Piporro) and declare themselves to be good buddies out to have fun for the first time in their lives. Out come the bottles, the cigarets and the lustful thoughts.

In need of funds, the trio rush to town where they pretend to be strangers so they can bilk townsfolk at the card table. Their large cash winnings attract the attentions of a beautiful bank robber (Olivia Collins), who knows how to twist these macho men around her finger with a bit of flattery. Of course all three men fall for her, and best-buddy relations go out the window.

Pic follows standard Fernández formula. As usual, comedy is genial. Things get exaggerated, Fernández has the last word and all's well that ends well. Lensing is functional and other tech credits are up to par. Fernández fans also are treated to several ranchero tunes accompanied by mariachi.—*Lent.*

Como Ves?
(Whaddya Think?)
(MEXICAN)

A Distribuidora y Exportadora de Cine de Latino América release of a Zafra Films-Consejo Nacional de Recursos Para la Atención de la Juventud (CREA) production. Produced by Dulce Kuri. Directed by Paul Leduc. Screenplay, Leduc, José Joaquín Blanco; camera (color), Toni Kuhn; music, El Trí, Rockrigo González, Jaime López, Tito Vasconcelos, Cecilia Toussaint, Son de Merengue; sound, Carlos Aguilar. Reviewed on video at Havana Intl. Film Festival Market, Mecla, Cuba, Dec. 12, 1987. Running time: 75 MIN.
With: Blanca Guerra, Roberto Sosa (hijo), Rafael Pérez Fons, Javier Pérez Fons, Ana Ofelia Mungula, Eduardo López Rojas, Homero Matturano.

FRISCO FEST REVIEWS

La Gentilezza Del Tocco
(The Gentle Touch)
(ITALIAN)

An Arte & Spettacoli production. Directed by Francesco Calogero. Screenplay, Antonino Bruschetta, Calogero; camera (color), Franco Lecca. Reviewed at San Francisco Film Festival, March 20, 1988. Running time: 80 MIN.
Giorgio . . . . Maurizio Puglisi
Carlo . . . . Antonio Alveario
Giuliana . . . . Rosalba Scimone
Irene . . . . Daniella Pacetto
Professor . . . . Antonio Bruschetta

San Francisco — This all-Sicilian production, which has nothing to do with sheep or capos, has the feel of a '30s screwball comedy. The opening credits not only set a light-hearted tone but rank as the most unique set of credits one's bound to see, particularly to read fully.

Because the hero of the piece is a proofreader, the credits are proofed as they're rolling. Natch, there are

Havana — This 1986 film "Como Ves?" (Whaddya Think?), by Mexican director Paul Leduc, has the texture and look of a student work rather than the handling of the mature filmmaker who made "Reed: Mexico Insurgente" and "Frida."

Film is a mish-mash of story fragments, visual meanderings, fantasies and pretty images of street kids and residents of a poor Mexican neighborhood, intercut with concert footage of various domestic rock groups.

Sound quality is good throughout, especially the music. Appearing are such local bands and soloists as El Trí, with over 15 years of performing, Cecilia Toussaint, and a rare look at urban folksinger Rockrigo González before his tragic death in Mexico's late-1985 earthquakes.

Besides night wandering through the city, mariachi bars and "queer bashing" at a transvestite club, there is an exploration of Mexico City's notorious "hoyos funquis," run-down halls and warehouses where poor kids come to listen to groups and forget their quotidian miseries through drugs, booze and glue-sniffing.

Overall, the diverse elements of this pic never gel. At times the film seems like an illustrated coffee-table book full of socially conscious photos set to music. The film will probably draw in local rock fans and those interested in Leduc's work, but mass appeal will prove limited.

As for the question: "Whaddya Think?" Not very much. — *Lent.*

built-in misspellings and wrong spacing, all corrected under viewer's studious ogling. It's much fun, bright in execution and a swell lead-in.

Giorgio (Maurizio Puglisi in the sort of role Tom Hanks owns) is a career proofreader at a newspaper and considers his work "a mission." He had a mentor once inform him, "One has to live life without correcting. Erasing is forbidden." This 2-penny philosophy eventually is translated into "avoid looking at your own flaws; accept yourself" at pic's end. In between, the tone is less analytical and more pranksterish.

Our hero and newsvendor buddy Carlo are enamored of a young pianist whose review is about to run in Giorgio's paper.

It's all frothy but moves quickly, backed by a silky sax-piano jazz score. Sometimes director Frances-

co Calogero bogs himself down with studied slow pans.

Picture has a healthy innocence to it, a truly gentle touch. Generations of anonymous proofreaders deservedly will find their profession lionized at last. — *Herb.*

King James Version

A Joseph E. Taylor/Vitascope Inc. production. Produced by Taylor, Robert Gardner. Directed by Gardner. Screenplay, Judy Simmons, Renee Roper, Gardner; camera (color), Judy Irola; editor, Jonathan Weld; music, Wendy Blackstone; associate producer, Louise Fleming. Reviewed at the San Francisco Film Festival, March 20, 1988. No MPAA Rating. Running time: 91 MIN.
Rachel Daniels . . . . Christina Braggs
Esther Pearl Daniels . . . . Joan Pryor
Jesse Daniels . . . . Ellwoodson Williams
Grandmother . . . . Louise Mike
Rev. Swan . . . . Lee Roy Giles
Rev. Turner . . . . Neal Harris
Annette . . . . Hope Branford
Child evangelist . . . . Eddie Owens
Spud . . . . Wayne Outlaw
Digger . . . . William Outlaw
Sister Johnson . . . . Roberta Watson
Harmonica player . . . . Charles Sayles
Church trombonist . . . . Leon Comegys
Church drummer . . . . Joe Ham

San Francisco — This 1987 pic took five years to make because, per director Robert Gardner in post-screening comments, a key investor and two actors died. "Things we wanted to do, we couldn't," he said.

Still, Gardner ("Clarence And Angel," "Forest Of Bliss"), has managed an often-moving study of a 12-year-old girl roiled by the different religious values of her parents. Dad is a traditionalist, mother a streetcorner preacher. Each tugs at the girl's sense of values.

One of the film's flaws is that Christina Braggs, as the child Rachel, is simply too mature to look like a 12-year-old. There's a feeling she's really old enough to walk away from the bickering, "take my side" parents.

The mother-dad contrasts are not the only shadings in the pic. Rachel spends a vacation away from Harlem with her relatives in the rural South (actually lensed on the eastern shore of Maryland) and finds yet another lifestyle. Footage in this seg is exemplary.

Gardner's strength is pulling fine performances from supporting players, particularly preachers portrayed by Lee Roy Giles and Neal Harris, who are as realistic in their sermonizing as folks you'll find in a pulpit.

There is a tone of dignity to "King James Version," but the uneven storyline evidences Gardner's off-screen problems.—*Herb.*

Magyar Stories
(HUNGARIAN-DOCU)

A Hungarofilm release of a Hunnia Studio production. Directed by Pal Schiffer, Balint Magyar. Camera (color), Gabor Balog, Ferenc Kaplar. Reviewed at San Francisco

Film Festival, March 19, 1988. Running time: 126 MIN.

San Francisco — This is a clean piece of documentation of the post-war impact of Communism on Hungary and particularly of events tied to the attempted late 1956 anti-Communist uprising.

Directors Pal Schiffer and Balint Magyar tell their history-rich tale through seven men who lived in the same town, Dunapataj, in those strife-torn years.

Because so many principals, not to mention principles, are involved, the docu takes time to build. It's necessary not only to meet all the characters and absorb the specifics of their background but to deal with the interweaving references. Eventually, the viewer gets to know and understand them all and must conclude that these men must be accepted on their own terms.

Each has a rationale for his actions, and the distancing of time appears to have diluted any lingering animosities. Their revelations unflaggingly point out the fact plainfolk somehow always muddle through large events beyond their control.

All the men appear at ease with the camera, much as talking to a friend, reminiscing with clarity. It's possible they'd been waiting decades to put their actions on the record, to explain themselves, perhaps to cop a plea.

That a story so intricate, so fact-laden could be etched with such clarity is a tribute to the docu-makers. "Magyar Stories," also labeled by production press copy as "At The Danube," is a splendid visual example of oral history.

—*Herb.*

Colors

An Orion Pictures release. Produced by Robert H. Solo. Directed by Dennis Hopper. Screenplay, Michael Schiffer, from story by Schiffer, Richard Dilello; camera (Metro-color, Deluxe prints), Haskell Wexler; editor, Robert Estrin; music, Herbie Hancock; production design, Ron Foreman; art direction, Chas. Butcher; set decoration, Ernie Bishop; sound (Dolby), Jim Webb; stunt coordinator, Chuck Waters; assistant director, Elie Cohn; casting, Lauren Lloyd. Reviewed at UA Coronet, Westwood Calif., April 5, 1988. MPAA Rating: R. Running time: 120 MIN.

Danny McGavin ....Sean Penn
Bob Hodges ....Robert Duvall
Louisa Gomez ....Maria Conchita Alonso
Ron Delaney ....Randy Brooks
Larry Sylvester..............Grand Bush
Rocket ....Don Cheadle
Bird ....Gerardo Mejia
High Top ....Glenn Plummer
Melindez ....Rudy Ramos
Bailey ....Sy Richardson
Frog ....Trinidad Silva
Reed ....Charles Walker
T-Bone ....Damon Wayans
Also with: Seymour Cassel, Virgil Frye, Courtney Gaines, Jack Nance.

"Colors" is a solidly crafted depiction of some current big-city horrors and succeeds largely because of the Robert Duvall-Sean Penn teaming as frontline cops. They're terrific together as members of the gang crime division of the LAPD. Backed by excellent-work from director Dennis Hopper and cinematographer Haskell Wexler, duo just might carry this gritty release into the respectable ranks of b.o. business.

Filmmakers alert the uninitiated right off that theirs is a tale of unequal odds, pointing out that 600 street gangs with more than 70,000 members roam America's second-largest city while local and county police directly assigned to the problem number only 250. Just last year there were nearly 400 gang-related killings in L.A. County.

Drawn into this fracas is officer Bob Hodges (Duvall), married, the father of three, who's inexplicably been forced back into the action. He's been returned to the socalled Crash unit — a pungent acronym for Community Resources Against Street Hoodlums.

He's savvy about his dealings with punks in "bozoland," as Hodges calls the streets, and is unhappy about getting greenhorn Danny McGavin (Penn) as his sidekick. Latter is a high strung and cocksure volunteer to Crash. He not only busts them with bravado but roughs 'em up out there and soon gets pegged for particular street hatred — notwithstanding Duvall's avuncular guidance.

Penn's active on-the-job libido leads to a quickie fling with gang relative Louisa Gomez (Maria Conchita Alonso). There's a steamy bedroom scene but little else to merit this subplot and it winds up as one of the film's weakest points.

Development of the tensions over conflicting work styles by Duvall and Penn give the film its compelling quality. Credit there must extend to first-time screenwriter Michael Schiffer, who created the story with Richard DiLello. Every word, phrase and gesture seems just right. Humor relieves the heavy material at the proper moments.

Plot takes Duvall and Penn through investigation of the latest offing of a "Blood" gangmember by the rival "Crips" and shows the police frustrations in working the case against nearly insurmountable obstacles. There's one of the best-ever car chases and plenty of explicit — and appropriate — violence.

While nicely avoiding the feel of a docu, film seems to effectively capture the gang "culture" — the deep bonding among members who will die for the other "homeboys." One says: "Want me to walk away from this? No way, man."

Giving the audience necessary access to such a mindset via the reasonable, but not too likable a character called Frog is Trinidad Silva, who handled similar chores on "Hill Street Blues" appearances.

When Silva leads his boys on a retaliatory strike, Duvall and Penn pursue and a startling development occurs — one that jolts the spirit and cinematically unleashes the furor of the gods.

Through it all, the soundtrack perfectly complements the screen action. Herbie Hancock's pulsating score is eerie. And the title song by Ice-T speaks volumes with such lyrics as "My color's my honor ... my game ain't knowledge; my game is fear."

These are indeed fearful times in some quarters of overpopulated L.A., which is plagued by gangs practicing the high-stakes business of drugdealing. "Colors" vividly portrays that world and leaves one thinking this picture will wind up having considerable impact in community, law enforcement and perhaps political circles in this election year. —Tege.

Deux minutes de soleil en plus
(Two Minutes More Of Sunlight)
(FRENCH)

An AMLF release of a TCA Prods./TF-1 Films coproduction. Produced by Denis Mermet. Direced by Gérard Vergez. Screenplay, Vergez, from the novel "Le Piège" by Francis Ryck; camera (color), André Diot; editor, Jacques Witta; music, Michel Portal; art direction, Jean-Jacques Caziot; sound, Jean-Bernard Thomasson; assistant director, Michel Such; production manager, Catherine Lapoujade. Reviewed at the Marignan-Concorde theater, Paris, March 27, 1988. Running time: 98 MIN.

Vic.................Christophe Malavoy
Cat.................Pauline Lafont
Aina.................Catherine Wilkening
Marc.................Jacques Pozzallo

Paris — Two certified loonies (Pauline Lafont and Catherine Wilkening) and one supposedly normal neurotic (Christophe Malavoy) enjoy an itinerant escapade in southern France in "Deux minutes de soleil en plus," based on a novel by renowned Gallic suspense author Francis Ryck.

Gérard Vergez scripted and directed this tale of a writer who's made a fortune with a book about his unstable young wife (Lafont), institutionalized after an indictment for infanticide. Hubby Malavoy comes to pick her up upon her release with an ulterior motive: make her sign a new commercial contract, which will sponge up his heavy gambling debts.

The reunion is marred by a third party, Wilkening, a fellow inmate who joins the party. Not only has she a few more screws loose, but she is inordinately fond of Lafont and understandably not keen on Malavoy. Worse she has a disturbing way with a pair of scissors...

This psycho-neurotic threesome is not enchanting company, despite the forwardmoving energy Vergez puts into their picaresque adventures. Performances by all are too mannered to be touching.

Tech credits, however, are first-rate, from André Diot's vivid lensing to Michel Portal's jaunty music. —Len.

The Moderns

An Alive Films release of a Pfeiffer/Blocker production, in association with Nelson Entertainment. Executive producer, Shep Gordon. Produced by Carolyn Pfeiffer, David Blocker. Directed by Alan Rudolph. Screenplay, Rudolph, John Bradshaw; camera (CFI color), Toyomichi Kurita; editor, Debra T. Smith, Scott Brock; music, Mark Isham; songs performed by, CharlElie Couture; production design, Steven Legler; set decoration, Jean-Baptiste Tard; costume design, Renee April; sound (Dolby), Ron Judkins, Robert Jackson; paintings by David Stein; associate producer, Stuart Besser; assistant director, Michael Williams; casting, Pam Dixon, Ginette D'Amico (Montreal); additional camera, Jan Kiesser. Reviewed at the Carolco screening room, L.A., March 2, 1988. No MPAA Rating. Running time: 126 MIN.

Nick Hart ....Keith Carradine
Rachel Stone ....Linda Fiorentino
Bertram Stone ....John Lone
Oiseau ....Wallace Shawn
Libby Valentin ....Genevieve Bujold
Nathalie de Ville ......Geraldine Chaplin
Hemingway ....Kevin J. O'Connor
L'Evidence............CharlElie Couture
Gertrude Stein ....Elsa Raven
Alice B. Toklas ....Ali Giron
New York Critic ....Gailard Sartain
Surrealist Poet ....Michael Wilson

Hollywood — The artistic world of Paris in the 1920s comes to life as if in a lustrous dream in "The Moderns," Alan Rudolph's long-cherished project which he has succeeded in turning into his best film. A romantic's lush vision of a group of expatriate Americans at a time and place of some of the century's most tumultuous creative activity, pic is nevertheless entirely unsentimental in its blunt assessment of affairs of the heart, imagination and pocketbook. A strong critical reception will provide a solid launch on the domestic art circuit, but Alive will have to work overtime to translate this into crossover business.

Given a time machine, anyone with an artistic bent would probably put the Left Bank, circa 1926, at or near the top of the list of places to visit; certainly, thousands of Americans migrated there, either to pursue the muse or just rub shoulders with Hemingway, Fitzgerald, Picasso, Stein, the surrealists and all the rest.

Rudolph, who has frequently constructed his films around isolated, self-contained worlds populated by a limited number of characters, has here focused upon life in cafes, art galleries and painters' lofts. In his supple, bank-shot style, he introduces several of his major characters in a striking opening bar scene.

There is Nick Hart (Keith Carradine) who, at 33, is viewed suspiciously for not having made it yet as an artist — as Gertrude Stein says, "American painters are 26 this year;" Oiseau (Wallace Shawn), a gossip columnist for the Tribune, who dreams only of going to Hollywood; Bertram Stone (John Lone), an elegant, rich, philistine art dealer with a disturbing violent streak; his wife, Rachel (Linda Fiorentino), with whom Nick has a past and, he hopes, a future, and Hemingway himself (Kevin J. O'Connor), who amusingly careens through the action in varying states of inebriation, trying out titles for a new book — "Life is a portable picnic ... no, life is a bon repas ... a traveling banquet..."

Also critical to the assorted personal equations pertaining here are Libby (Genevieve Bujold), an impoverished gallery owner with values diametrically opposed to those of Stone, and Nathalie (Geraldine Chaplin), a patroness of the arts who convinces Nick to execute some spectacular forgeries.

From the outset, the viewer is steeped in the heady atmosphere of colorful, art deco bistros and rooms festooned with glorious paintings, the experience of which is made more intense by the wonderful music of Mark Isham which runs almost continuosly under the action.

The emotional connections in Rudolph and the late Jon Bradshaw's imaginative script are made almost as quickly. Nick and Rachel, it turns out, were married in Chicago some years before, and Nick wants to start things up again with this alluring femme fatale. Recognizing the rivalry, Stone takes Nick on in a duel, not with the traditional pistols, but in the boxing ring (in one of the film's occasional missteps, a drunken Hemingway is put in charge of clanging the bell between rounds; more accurately, the writer would have coached his pal and worked as corner man).

Stone's overbearing tendencies toward everyone around him, Oiseau's desire to escape, Nick's passion for Rachel, Libby and Nathalie's respective hopes for Nick as an artist — all the threads have their surprising dramatic resolutions. The most startling one comes at Stone's exhibition at which three paintings by Cezanne, Modigliani and Matisse, which may or may not be copies by Nick, are declared to be forgeries by the "experts" and are summarily burned, giving rise to conflicting feelings and debate over where the true meaning and achievement of art may lie.

Film's final section veers off in some eccentric, fantastical directions, some of which are momentarily off-putting, notably a shock cut to some 1980s-style punks in a cafe, obviously meant to draw a connection between the two eras. The readiness of some of the characters to leave Paris for the even greedier environs of Hollywood seems rather odd as well.

The mood is brilliantly captured and sustained by Rudolph; his superb production designer Steven Legler, who has come up with a myriad of evocative sets and gotten across the feeling of Paris even though the picture was entirely shot in Montreal; cinematographer Toyomichi Kurita, who has drenched everything in exquisitely soft, burnished hues; editors Debra T. Smith and Scott Brock, who have nicely integrated vintage documentary footage of the French capital with the fictional material, and composer Isham, whose score makes one want to run right out and buy the record.

Similarly, the actors are uniformly outstanding. Carradine has never been better, as he conveys the strong feelings he has for art and his estranged wife as well as the diffidence that has set in due to years of frustration and lack of recognition. Lone is the picture of disciplined decadence, a magnetic figure who commands fascination, and Fiorentino is ideal as the gorgeous American of a prosaic background over whom men may lose their hearts, mind and lives.

O'Connor's Hemingway is a curiously introspective and quiet characterization but appealing as such and far preferable to the loudmouthed boor on view in last year's "Waiting For The Moon." Shawn, Bujold and Chaplin are all amusingly on target. —*Cart.*

A Time Of Destiny

A Columbia Pictures release of an Alive Films presentation of an Anna Thomas production, in association with Lantana Prods. Executive producers, Carolyn Pfeiffer, Shep Gordon. Produced by Anna Thomas. Directed by Gregory Nava. Screenplay, Thomas; camera (Deluxe color), James Glennon; editor, Betsy Blankett; music, Ennio Morricone; sound (Dolby), Stephan von Hase-Mihalik; production design, Henry Bumstead; art direction, Les Gobruegge; set decoration; Anne Kuljian; casting, Wally Nicita. Reviewed at Columbia screening room, N.Y., March 23, 1988. (In Cleveland Film Festival.) MPAA Rating: PG-13. Running time: **118 MIN.**

Martin .... William Hurt
Jack .... Timothy Hutton
Josie .... Melissa Leo
Margaret .... Stockard Channing
Irene .... Megan Follows
Jorge .... Francisco Rabal
Also with: Concha Hidalgo, Frederick Coffin.

A heavy-handed melodrama of familial conflict, obsessive vengeance and starcrossed romance set in a World War II milieu, "A Time Of Destiny" stumbles awkwardly over a stiff, conventional screenplay laden with tedious and lachrymose plot-rigging.

The teaming of William Hurt and Timothy Hutton as blood-brother antagonists may produce a decent initial boxoffice, but word of mouth is almost certain to scuttle the prospects of a lackluster film that's particularly disappointing coming from the creators of the superb 1983 benchmark independent project, "El Norte."

The film's gripping, visceral battlefield scenes suggest that if "Destiny" (pic's working title) had been a straight combat opus it might have been more compelling. During a riveting opening sequence set on the Italian front, director Gregory Nava presents Hurt and Hutton as shell-shocked comrades-in-arms who exchange a solemn promise to make it together "through this goddamned war."

Hutton has someone very special to live for, his new wife Josie (Melissa Leo), who lives on her family's ranch in the idyllic countryside near San Diego. An overlong setup flashback relates how Hutton's bride was virtually abducted from her marraige bed by her stern autocratic father (Francisco Rabal) — a rough-hewn Basque immigrant with Old World values who reacts violently to his daughter's elopement with the penniless G.I.

The successful patriarch feels especially betrayed because Leo is the favorite of his three daughters. One of his two sons has died of tb, the other, Martin, is a G.I. and the family outcast. Rabal hates this black sheep son for unspeakable transgressions that are never spelled out clearly but have something to do with incorrigible dishonesty and sneakiness. Determined to reclaim his most precious daughter, Rabal tracks her down to the couple's honeymoon hotel, then makes off with her through a monsoon rainstorm with Hutton in hot pursuit.

Predictably, father and daughter crash into a lake, and notwithstanding Hutton's heroic rescue effort (strangely similar to previous dives taken by the actor in "Ordinary People" and "Made In Heaven") the old man drowns.

That same night, the pariah son Martin materializes in the person of none other than Hurt, who is immediately obliged by the scenario's embarrassing contortions to squint his way through a weeping scene over Rabal's warm corpse.

The previously purposeless young

man seizes the occasion for a motivational epiphany — he will track down and wreak vengeance on Hutton.

In one of the film's cluster of clumsy ironies, Hurt dedicates himself to his father's memory unaware that the unforgiving crumudgeon has cut him out of his will. The ranch is left in Leo's hands, and this next-to-saintly sweetie is determined to shield Hurt from Rabal's posthumous cruelty.

Ever the consummate conman, Hurt improbably has himself assigned to Hutton's platoon deep in the thick of some of the bloodiest fighting in the European theater. One fateful night the two infantrymen save each others lives and are awarded bronze stars for heroism. Strong chemistry of friendship seems to bind Hurt and Hutton (who still has no clue to his pal's true indentity) and for awhile it seems that Hurt may emerge from the purgatory of battle cleansed of his compulsion for vengeance.

No sooner does the war end, however, than Hurt's darker impulses reemerge. By the time Hurt turns on his best pal and spills the beans about who he is, the revelation is dully anticlimactic.

This does not prevent Nava from dragging the film onward to an absurdly choreographed denouement whose blood vengeance motif ineptly echoes Hitchcock and the Spanish playwright Federico Garcia Lorca. Neither the picture-postcard cinematography of James Glennon, the meticulous period production design of Henry Bumstead nor the self-Xeroxed score by Ennio Morricone can rescue the cast from the unremitting lameness of the story. —*Rich.*

Plain Clothes

A Paramount Pictures release of a Sierra Alta production. Executive producer, Steven-Charles Jaffe. Produced by Richard Wechsler, Michael Manheim. Directed by Martha Collidge. Screenplay, A. Scott Frank, from story by Frank, Dan Vining; camera (CFI color, Technicolor prints), Daniel Hainey; editor, Pat Kennedy, Ed Abroms; music, Scott Wilk; sound (Ultra-Stereo), Dan Gleich; art direction, William Apperson; set decoration, Marya Delia Javier; costume design, Tracy Tynan; production manager-associate producer, Don Goldman; assistant director, Peter Gries; special effects, Robert Riggs; casting, Jackie Burch. Reviewed at Paramount 30th floor screening room, N.Y., March 30, 1988. MPAA Rating: PG. Running time: **98 MIN.**

Nick .... Arliss Howard
Robin Torrance .... Suzy Amis
Chet .... George Wendt
Jane .... Diane Ladd
Ed .... Seymour Cassel
Coach Zeffer............... Jackie Gayle
Principal .... Robert Stack
History teacher .... Abe Vigoda
Simon Feck............... Harry Shearer
Kyle Kerns .... Peter Dobson
Daun-Marie .... Alexandra Powers
Matt .... Loren Dean.

"Plain Clothes" is an entertaining variant on the formula teen comedy, with better casting and gags than its forbears. Problem for

Paramount will be to get an audience's attention with such familiar-sounding material.

Story hook is identical with DEG's 1987 release starring Jon Cryer, "Hiding Out," in which an adult becomes the fish out of water posing as a student back in high school. This time around it's personable Arliss Howard as a cop who goes undercover (unauthorized since he's been suspended for punching a superior) to find the real killer of a teacher at Adlai Stevenson High School where his brother (Loren Dean) has been arrested as chief suspect.

Howard, adopting the name Nick Springsteen as an old-looking teen (gag line by fellow students: "Are you related?"), has the usual quota of misadventures including a budding romance with the pretty daughter (Alexandra Powers) of the gym teacher (Jackie Gayle) and a crush on the very appealing home room teacher (Suzy Amis, who bears a striking resemblance to the late Elizabeth Hartman).

It's all handled in very tongue-in-cheek fashion by helmer Martha Coolidge, with ample emphasis on black humor. Solution of the mystery, involving a romantically thwarted teacher, is mainly on the back burner.

Howard is a find, carrying the picture with an easy charm that bridges the gap between straight scenes and silly ones. Amis also impresses, but the picture is stolen by a roster of character actors who make the most of briefer assignments: Robert Stack, cast against type as the dimwitted principal; Diane Ladd as his goofball secretary; Seymour Cassel a treat as Howard's cop partner who pretends to be his dad and Harry Shearer, with no dialog but perfect as the suspicious "wheezer" who ends up an excellent corpse.

Tech credits for this Seattle-lensed (under the working title "Glory Days") picture are fine, but a blatant continuity/construction error in the final reel is harmful to the total effect, as time unbelievably seems to stand still for everyone waiting for Howard to arrive as King of the Mayfest while he's involved as a cop in nearly a full reel of action. —*Lor.*

Al Bari
(The Innocent)
(EGYPTIAN)

A National Center of Cinema release of a Video 2000 production. Produced by Safwat Ghattas. Directed by Atef El Tayeb. Screenplay, Wahid Hamed; camera (color), Said Shimy. Reviewed at San Francisco Film Festival, March 23, 1988. Running time: **117 MIN.**

Soldier .... Ahmed Zaki

San Francisco — "The Innocent" was made in 1985 and, per Friscofest assistant programmer Laura Thielen, trimmed by the

Egyptian government because "they felt panicky how soldiers might react to it." Print shown at S.F. fest is, Thielen said, "the only existing uncut version."

Screenplay is an often overly melodramatic exposition of the violent reaction by one young peasant turned soldier against the government and military. Ahmed Zaki is impressive as the ingenuous army recruit who lacks brains but brims with valor, loyalty and a sense of right. The full force of Zaki's performance is evidenced when he realizes how his commander has manipulated him and perceives the sadism in his midst.

Director Atef El Tayeb nicely establishes the roots of Zaki's character, giving the viewer a strong sense of the place and people from which this eventually heroic figure sprung.

We're taken through basic training, the military's brutal handling of a dissident prison population and a compelling escape attempt. There's a later scene of snakes being let loose in a cell that's a tingler.

Too often, a heavy-handed score mars the impact of the action, and some of the cuts in this supposedly uncut version feel incursive.

On the whole El Tayeb keeps his picture and story moving; even anticipated twists are woven smartly.—Herb.

Tokyo Pop

A Spectrafilm release in association with Lorimar of a Kuzui Enterprises production. Produced by Kaz Kuzui, Joel Tuber. Executive producers, Jonathan Olsberg, Kaz Kuzui. Directed by Fran Rubel Kuzui. Screenplay, Fran Rubel Kuzui, Lynn Grossman, original story by Kuzui; camera (TVC color), James Hayman; editor, Camilla Toniolo; music, Alan Brewer; production design, Terumi Hosoishi; costume design, Asako Kobayashi; sound (Dolby), Yutaka Tsurumaki, William Sarokin (N.Y.); assistant director, Yoshikuni Matsunaga; second unit camera, Shiguchi Hirabayahi, Kenji Takama, Norimichi Kazamatsu (Japan), Hart Perry (N.Y.); associate producers, Akira Morishiga, Nancy Tuber; casting, Ellen Lewis, Julie Alter, Yoshikuni Matsunaga. Reviewed at Glen Glenn Sound, L.A., Feb. 18, 1988. MPAA Rating: R. Running time: 99 MIN.
Wendy Reed . . . . Carrie Hamilton
Hiro Yamaguchi . . . . Yutaka Tadokoro
Grandfather . . . . Taiji Tonoyama
Dota . . . . Tetsuro Tamba
Mother . . . . Masumi Harukawa
Mama-san . . . . Toki Shiozawa
Seki, the Club Manager . . . Hiroshi Mikami
Mike . . . . Mike Cerveris
Holly . . . . Gina Belafonte
Yoji . . . . Daisuke Oyama
Kaz . . . . Hiroshi Kobayashi
Taro . . . . Hiroshi Sugita
Shun . . . . Satoshi Kanai

Hollywood — The odyssey of an American girl who moves to Japan to seek rock 'n' roll fame is documented in "Tokyo Pop," a light entertainment that diverts with its hefty supply of local color even when the central story falls flat. Unusual cultural aspects and musical angle provide what b.o. allure may exist, but prospects for the Spectrafilm release appear modest.

Carrie Hamilton plays a bummed

out Gotham punker who, deciding that things can't get any worse, impulsively takes off to check out the music scene across the Pacific. Early scenes of the destitute traveler's hopeless disorientation upon arriving in Tokyo's teeming neon jungle will strike a responsive chord with anyone who has ventured to the Orient, and quite a few familiar incidents are sketched in with knowing humor.

Regardless of whether she has any talent, Hamilton's Wendy is employable locally on the basis of her being a tall American with dyed blond hair, but her first gig, as a hostess in a tacky club, where she is obliged to sing "Home On The Range" for the benefit of a bunch of drunken businessmen, isn't exactly what she had in mind.

She manages to hook up with a band that thinks it might benefit from a *gaijin* lead singer, and while their performances are pretty routine, they finally make it big on the basis of novelty.

Predictably running through their ascent to dubious stardom is a slow-to-grow romance between Wendy and the Japanese band leader (Yutaka Tadokoro). He initially turns her off by taking her directly to a love hotel, but they gradually fall into each other's arms, only to split apart due to different habits and cultural priorities.

Wendy, for instance, becomes frustrated with her boyfriend's uncommunicativeness, which he regards as normal. She, on the other hand, is too upfront and assertive for him. Ultimately, Wendy plausibly falls prey to depression and a sense of isolation, and comes to feel that, if she has been a success in the Orient, it's only because she was a freak.

The cross-cultural observations represent the most satisfying element of the picture. The filmmakers obviously know whereof they speak on this score, and the locations throughout Tokyo have been selected imaginatively.

By contrast, the lead couple make for a less than thrilling pair, making for something of a hole in the center of the film. They don't seem to go together, so the protracted scenes of their breakup, and her decision-making about leaving Japan, create severe impatience through the final section.

Music also is largely unexciting and repetitive. Band mainly sings warmed-over 1960s American tunes, making it seem like a pretty useless addition to the pop scene. That may be part of the point, but doesn't make listening to the songs very enjoyable.—Cart.

32 Dicembre
(The 32d Of December)
(ITALIAN)

A Medusa Distribuzione release of a Retei-

talia/Eidoscope coproduction. Produced by Mario Orfini, Emilio Bolles. Directed by Luciano De Crescenzo. Screenplay, Lidia Ravera, De Crescenzo; camera (color), Danilo Desideri; editor, Anna Napoli; music, Tullio De Piscopo; art direction, Carlo Leva; costumes, Tiziana Mancini; production organizer, Pino Mangogna. Reviewed at America Cinema, Rome, March 4, 1988. Running time: 109 MIN.
Antistene . . . . Benedetto Casillo
Socrates . . . . Silvio Ceccato
Carlotta . . . . Caterina Boratto
Oscar . . . . Renato Scarpa
Gen. Anselmi . . . . Riccardo Cucciolla
Alfonso Caputo . . . . Enzo Cannavale
Psychiatrist/priest/-
astronomer . . . . . . Luciano De Crescenzo
Also with: Sergi Solli, Parrizia Loreti, Massimo Serato, Riccardo Pazzaglia.

Rome — "The 32d Of December," latest from pop philosopher/humorist Luciano De Crescenzo ("Thus Spake Bellavista"), is an offbeat comedy in three episodes dedicated to the proposition that time, in the last analysis, doesn't exist. More wordy than visual, film hangs precariously on the thread of appealing, slightly surrealistic characters and gentle humor with a point behind it.

Though two skits are set generically outside Naples, it's the third, very Neapolitan tale that clinches pic's good intentions and produces something substantial. Playoff returns have been middling onshore; it'll take delicate handling to move to foreign markets.

Linking the trio of tales is the concept that time is relative. In the first, a concerned wife hires two bumbling actors to impersonate "disciples" of her cultured husband Silvio Ceccato, who thinks he's Socrates and lives in Greek times. In the end, the wife's sanity is cast in doubt, and then that of the psychiatrist (De Crescenzo) following the case.

Second part plays on the paradox of an attractive 65-year-old widow (the great Caterina Boratto, still every inch a diva) so young in heart she acts like a teenager. Her romantic adventures are opposed by an old-fogey son (Renato Scarpa) and daughter-in-law, fearful she'll spend their inheritance.

The episode that stands out, however, is the last. A poor man (Enzo Cannavale in a surprisingly moving low-key performance) without a job or a lira in his pocket roams the backstreets of Naples on the last day of the year, humbly looking for enough credit to buy the fireworks he's promised his two boys. At the end of a grueling, unsuccessful search, an astronomy prof (De Crescenzo again) explains how time is relative: due to a calendar mixup we should really celebrate New Year's a week later. This is what Alfonso finally does, setting off a cherry bomb in mid-January and being arrested for it. Episode combines originality, emotion, and good storytelling to make an effective point, and not just about how conventionally we measure time.

A large cast of well-selected thesps helps pic over the hump of excessive dialog; technical work is adequate. —Yung.

Lady In White

A New Century/Vista Film Co. release. Produced by Andrew G. La Marca, Frank LaLoggia. Executive producers, Charles M. LaLoggia, Cliff Payne. Written and directed by Frank LaLoggia. Camera (Deluxe color), Russell Carpenter; editor, Steve Mann; music, Frank LaLoggia; production design, Richard K. Hummel; set decoration, Sarah Burdick; art direction, Howard Kling; Kenneth Wolf; costume design, Jacqueline Saint Anne; sound (Dolby), Robert Anderson Jr.; special effects, Image Engineering, Fantasy II Film Effects; visual effects supervisors, Ernest D. Farino, Gene Warren Jr.; casting, Lynn Stalmaster & Associates, Mali Finn. Reviewed at the AMC theater, L.A., March 17, 1988. MPAA Rating: PG-13. Running time: 112 MIN.
Frankie . . . . Lukas Haas
Phil . . . . Len Cariou
Angelo . . . . Alex Rocco
Amanda . . . . Katherine Helmond
Geno . . . . Jason Presson
Mama Assunta . . . . Renata Vanni
Papa Charlie . . . . Angelo Bertolini
Donald . . . . Jared Rushton
Louie . . . . Gregory Levinson
Melissa . . . . Joelle Jacob

Hollywood — "Lady In White" is a superb supernatural horror film from independent filmmaker Frank LaLoggia which, with good word of mouth and a strong ad campaign, could make a spellbinding b.o. run.

LaLoggia all but developed his own film. He directed and co-produced this semi-autobiographical tale of the dark side from his own script as well as composed the music. With the help of cousin Charles LaLoggia, he raised production money from 4,000 investors — many of whom live in and around the small town of Lyons in upstate New York that doubles for the fictional spooky Willowpoint Falls of the early 1960s.

However modest its origins, "Lady In White" succeeds where many bigger-budgeted pictures fail — by not letting special effects get in the way of a good story.

At the center of it is big-eyed Lukas Haas, the youngest boy of a loving and earthy Italian family that is headed by his widowed dad, Angelo (Alex Rocco), fed and cared for by his grandmother, Mama Assunta (Renata Vanni), with comic relief provided by her henpecked old-country husband, Papa Charlie (Angelo Bertolini), whose sole purpose in life is evading his squawking wife to sneak cigarets.

As an elementary school kid, Haas has an inventive mind and, we soon find out, an even more vivid imagination.

On Halloween night, his school chums lock him in his classroom cloakroom where he is visited by those who wouldn't ordinarily be there — the ghost of a young girl about his age and a masked man searching for something in the heating grate. He seems real, but is she?

As the mystery unravels, it is revealed how they are connected. What is crucial to the way this strange tale so effectively works on the audience, the Haas character is so without guile that his encounters with human forms — both transparent and mortal — are nearly believable.

Even with a PG-13 rating, this is too intense for older children, especially given that underlying theme involves an old family friend who turns out to be the mass murderer.

LaLoggia manages to direct Haas equally well as a junior sleuth as he does the innocent youngster who fights with his older brother Geno (Jason Presson) and is easily influenced to go places he shouldn't by his bike-riding pals, Donald (Jared Rushton) and Louie (Gregory Levinson).

On one of these "adventures," the boys meet up with the town crazy, a Miss Havisham type played by a wonderfully scary Katherine Helmond.

Her role, like several others in this suspenseful tale, is drawn from the short roster of must-be-used horror characters.

What singles out this production is the normalcy, even humor, that those not privy to Haas' sightings maintain.

Alex Rocco is particularly successful as a concerned father fearful his boy will be the next murder victim, but not overplaying his part by becoming hysterical.

Equally solid is Haas' brother, a good casting in Jason Presson, who turns out to be much less precocious than his younger sibling and yet not so grown up that he doesn't believe in ghosts and the places they haunt.

This probably is as good a nightmare as any impressionable boy could have and still be suspenseful enough to get most adults' hearts going.

Special visual effects created by Image Engineering and Fantasy II Film Effects and supervised by Ernest D. Farino and Gene Warren Jr. range from the terrific — especially the holographic-looking ghost walks taken by dead Melissa (Joelle Jacobi) — to the hokey.

End scene, clearly derivative of every cliffhanger picture ever made, is very obviously a matte job where the murderer flails precipitously over the edge, hanging on for dear life, superimposed over a darkened daytime shot of the ocean crashing on the rocks beneath. —*Brit.*

Strul
(Trouble)
(SWEDISH)

A Svensk Filmindustri production and release. Produced by Waldemar Bergendahl, Jan Marnell. Directed by Jonas Frick. Screenplay, Bengt Palmers, Björn Skifs; camera (Eastmancolor), Stefan Kullänger; editor, Christjan Persson, Leon Flamholc, Jan Persson; sound, Anders Larsson; stunts, special effects, Johan Thoren, Svenska Stuntgrup-pen; costumes, Inger Persson; 2d unit director, Magnus Nanne; 2d unit camera, Roland Skogfeldt; art direction, Bengt Fröderberg; production management, Anita Tesler. Reviewed at the Palladium, Malmö, Sweden, March 8, 1988. Running time: **100 MIN.**
Conny . . . . Björn Skifs
Susanne . . . . Gunnel Fred
Hjelm . . . . Gino Samil
Pege . . . . Johan Ulveson
Gränges . . . . Magnus Nilsson
Norinder . . . . Mikael Druker
Sörman . . . . Kare Sigurdson
Brinke . . . . Stefan Sauk
Also with: Hans Rosenfeldt, Peter Palmer, Roland Stenström.

Malmö, Sweden — Turning out fastpaced musicvideos and other shorts made Jonas Frick a Swedish household name via tv. Making his feature film bow with "Trouble," Fricks falls into all the traps of his acquired mastery.

He has an action comedy-thriller screenplay to turn into a picture, and what he does is let loose an uninterrupted deluge of special effects, camera gimmickry, crashes and chases. True humor, let alone human comedy, goes down the drain in spite of the charming and valiant efforts of actor-cowriter Björn Skifs.

Strul, Swedish slang for trouble, overcomes Conny, a young chemistry teacher, when he is wrongly jailed for manufacturing amphetamines in his home. His fellow prisoners are brutal in the realistic prison film way, but somehow Conny avoids their worst abuse by showing them a secret passageway to the outside. He goes back and forth with them on thieving outings, and he also goes along on their scheme to rob the Royal Mint.

The plotters are fools; Conny is foolhardy. To keep himself afloat he slides down steep roofs; saves Susanna, a woman cop, from getting killed by a runaway car; barges in and out of hospital operating rooms just ahead of a hypodermic needle, etc. Everything that can happen in a chase thriller does — so furiously that nothing gets a chance to settle on your retina, let alone in your mind.

None of the characters get a chance to develop their roles, and the romance between Conny and Susanne soon gets a wallop by the camera swinging from its Louma crane hoisting. Skits, an established talent both as an actor and a pop music performer, displays a limited range of befuddled charm. Susanne is played against the wanton assaults of the action by Gunnel Fred, and so her character is lost.

The actors cast as prisoners somehow come off better than the rest, if only for the fanciful way Inger Persson has dressed them up. It is quite clear why Persson was the obvious choice to win this year's Ingmar Bergman Special Talent award. Too bad that costume alone does not make a character work.—*Kell.*

Der Indianer
(The Red Indian)
(WEST GERMAN-DOCU)

A Oase Film, ZDF production. Produced by Michael Lentz. Directed by Rolf Schübel. Screenplay, Leonhard Lentz, Schübel; camera (color, 16m), Rudolf Körösi, Ursula Körösi; editor, Harald Reetz; music, Jan Garbarek; sound, Reetz; narrator, Peter Striebeck. Reviewed at Berlin Film Festival (Forum of Young Cinema). Feb. 16, 1988. Running time: **93 MIN.**

Berlin — Film journalist Michael Lentz produced this documentary based on the diary of his brother, Leonhard, a courageous tale of a man who stood up to cancer and learned to live with it.

A furniture salesman who suffered from a sore throat, he went to the hospital and was told he had cancer of the larynx. Leonhard Lentz describes in minute detail all the treatments he went through and the psychological effects they had on him, such as a profound feeling of solitude that rejected any moral support, extreme egotism in every reaction and frequent nostalgia bouts.

This also is the tale of a man who keeps fighting both for his sanity and his life, even when he comes out of surgery with half a neck and an angry red scar which made him look like a "red indian."

Gradually he reeducates himself, starts writing (among other things this autobiography) and even manages to regain a sort of speech. Being a naturally happy person and a storyteller by nature, learning to speak again without the help of a machine was crucial in regaining his self-confidence.

Documentarist Rolf Schübel chose to reconstruct the entire story with the help of a subjective camera, standing in for Lentz and a narrator reading his first-person account of the sickness' progress. The film tries to stay as cool as possible during the entire proceedings, but interviews with Lentz' wife, brother and friend lend it a touch of pathos nevertheless.

A picture which could be an inspiration to anyone facing this kind of tragedy, the film ends with a moving epilog. Lentz died nine months after the film (in which he appears on camera at beginning and end) was finished. He left behind an afterword, which is used as the closing statement, saying how often he was afraid during the nine years between the time he contracted the disease until his death, but also how often he was happy, maybe more than ever before. "Everything I do is life," he wrote, "including death, which is its final chapter. It's only a pity I couldn't sing anymore."
—*Edna.*

Pestonjee
(INDIAN)

A National Film Development Corp. production. Directed by Vijaya Mehta. Screenplay, B.K. Karanjia, Mehta; camera (color), Rajan Kothari; editor, Renu Saluja; music, Vanraj Batia; art direction, Roshan Kalapesi. Reviewed at the Indian Film Festival, Trivandrum, Jan. 21, 1988. Running time: **124 MIN.**
Pesi . . . . Anupam Kher
Piroj . . . . Naseeruddin Shah
Jeroo . . . . Shabana Azmi

Trivandrum — Offbeat, sophisticated and atmospheric, "Pestonjee" is set in the Parsi community of 1930s Bombay, from which viewpoint it explores the idea of human happiness. Vijaya Mehta, a well-known stage director and actress, and one of India's scarce femme helmers, steers her third feature into novel territory of potential fest interest.

If the 2-hour running time leaves ample room for repetition, cast is buoyant and enjoyable. It's very much an actors' picture.

Hero is Piroj (Naseeruddin Shah), a slope-shouldered, weak-chinned fussbudget of ironclad morals. Too sleepy to grab a marriage offer, he lets the bride fall to the lot of his best friend, Pestonjee (or Pesi, played by Anupam Kher). When Piroj meets the beautiful Jeroo (Shabana Azmi) at the wedding, he falls in love on the spot, and comically turns into her platonic knight and defender.

His infatuation blinds him to Jeroo's masochistic nature, which turns the initially happy marriage into hell for Pesi. Unable to accept Pesi's relations with another woman, Piroj breaks with him in disgust, and spends many years in another town. He returns to Bombay just in time to see Pesi die of a heart attack, and loses his illusions about many matters he thought he was sure about.

Besides top-flight performances from the three principals, who all know how to give a touch of sly comedy to the drama, pic is of interest for the glimpses it furnishes of the Parsis (ancient religion of Indians who migrated from Iran) and its recreation of middle-class life in the '30s as a round of clubs and parties. Story is based on a tale by B.K. Karanjia, editor of Indian Screen.
—*Yung.*

Parinati
(INDIAN)

A National Film Development Corp. production. Produced and directed by Prakash Jha. Based on Vijay Dan Detha's short story "Anaadi Anat." Music, Regunath Seth. In color. Reviewed at the Indian Film Festival, Trivandrum, Jan. 21, 1988. Running time: **120 MIN.**
Ganeesh . . . . Basant Josalkar
Wife . . . . Surekha Sikri

Trivandrum — Prakash Jha's solemn fable "Parinati," set in the bleak red deserts of Rajasthan in ancient times, warns against the evils of greed in a harrowing but beautifully crafted parable. Packed with folklore and colorful costumes, and graced with regal performances from local principals, film offers particular appeal to offshore audiences.

Ganeesh (Basant Josalkar) is a gifted potter, respected by his neighbors. His hard existence is lightened unexpectedly when, to reward his honesty and goodness, a benevolent businessman chooses him and his wife (Surekha Sikri) to run a charity inn. Their life is happy, until one day a caravan of merchants persuades them to give their young son Laxman to them to be trained in business and become rich.

Surrendering the boy with a heavy heart, the parents pine away for years. The seed of avarice has been planted, however, and they begin killing rich travelers for their gold. At last the old couple's bloodlust leads them to a final crime, when Laxman returns a grown man and they fail to recognize him.

Story is told with the directness and simplicity of all classic fables. Actors (essentially it's a 2-thesp show) toe the line between obsessive behavior and credible motivations — both paradigms and human beings.

Music by Regunath Seth joins the mystical natural landscape and spectacular traditional costumes to create an air of princely old Rajasthan. Pace is as slow and steady as that of the camels who lope across the screen, but in this case in tune with the mood. — *Yung.*

Es Cosa Con Plumas
(With Feathers)
(SPANISH)

A Leon Films production. Produced by Felix Rodriguez. Directed by Oscar Ladoire. Screenplay, Azucena Rodriguez; camera (color), Jose Garcia Castillo; editor, Miguel A. Santamaria; music, J.M. Pagan. Reviewed at Miami Film Festival, Feb. 8, 1988. Running time: **90 MIN.**
With: Oscar Ladoire, Maureen Herero, El Gran Wyoming, Eulalia Ramon, Mary Paz Pondal.

Miami — Actor-screenwriter Oscar Ladoire of Spain has collaborated in the past to comic effect with director Fernando Trueba — they made "Opera Prima" and "Bad Taste," for example. Both those films were funny; the former was insightful, even touching. Now Ladoire is on his own, and his first film as a director, "With Feathers" (Es Cosa Con Plumas), suggests that he still needs Trueba — a lot.

"With Feathers" is about a hapless Woody Allen figure (even a cartoon rendering of the director over the opening credits is stylized to suggest Allen) whose sexual longings have been frustrated since before puberty by constant rejection and a bad case of hives. Film does not seem to know if it is a farce, a

character drama or a meditation on the genders. Worse, it's never comfortable, nor at all wise, in any of those modes, much less in combination. More than anything else, Ladoire's sensibility seems simply puerile. (Film's title is a variation on "Without Feathers," a published collection of Woody Allen pieces.)

Ladoire is also the star, and performer Ladoire gives director Ladoire better than he deserves, though not much. He lacks that sense of the underdog's refusal to be beaten that Allen inherited from Charlie Chaplin and Buster Keaton, a quality that might have made his nerd character interesting.

The story serves largely as a framework for a series of blackout sketches and sight gags, and involves the unexpected liaison of a neurotic guy (Ladoire) with a beautiful rock star on the lam from her own celebrity. This relationship, which is pointed towards the inevitable domestic bliss from the very first, is never believable

Film ends in a blaze of nonsense bordering on the surreal, with the scrawny anti-hero decked out as Rambo and amazing everyone with his emergence into the wild world of macho. In between, there is much noodling about the relationship of birds and man, part schoolyard philosophizing and part merely incomprehensible.

Production values are ragged, and the low budget shows. Outlook, considering that the film is too broad for the arthouse circuit and way too unpolished for wider audiences outside Spain, appears bleak.—*Cos.*

Appointment With Death

A Cannon Group release of a Golan-Globus production. Executive producers, Menahem Golan, Yoram Globus. Produced and directed by Michael Winner. Screenplay, Anthony Shaffer, Peter Buckman, Winner, based on novel by Agatha Christie; camera (Rank color), David Gurfinkel; editor, Arnold Crust (Michael Winner); music, Pino Donaggio; production design, John Blezard; costumes, John Bloomfield; associate producer, Mati Raz; casting, Dyson Lovell. Reviewed at the Cannon Prince Charles, London, Jan. 28, 1988. MPAA Rating: PG. Running time: **108 MIN.**

Hercule Poirot	Peter Ustinov
Lady Westholme	Lauren Bacall
Nadine Boynton	Carrie Fisher
Colonel Carbury	John Gielgud
Mrs. Emily Boynton	Piper Laurie
Miss Quinton	Hayley Mills
Sarah King	Jenny Seagrove
Jefferson Cope	David Soul
Raymond Boynton	John Terlesky
Carol Boynton	Valerie Richards
Lennox Boynton	Nicholas Guest

Also with: Amber Bezer, Douglas Sheldon, Mike Sarne, Michael Craig.

London — Peter Ustinov hams his way through "Appointment With Death" one more time as ace Belgian detective "Hercuool Pwarow," but neither he nor glitz can lift the pic from an impression of little more than a routine who-

dunit.

Cannon once again (as with the "Superman" sequels) seems to have latched onto a series that appears to have run its b.o. course, and even the normally amusing Ustinov looks a bit jaded in his third big-screen outing as the sleuth as well as several tv productions. Business outlook is only so-so.

Director Michael Winner has some fine Israeli locations to play with, but his helming is only lackluster, the script and characterizations bland, and there simply are not enough murders to sustain the interest of even the most avid Agatha Christie fan.

Lauren Bacall and John Gielgud both make second appearances in the series, having appeared in "Murder On The Orient Express" which had Albert Finney as Poirot.

The film opens in 1937 in a New Jersey mansion with the obligatory reading of the will, a scene that also establishes Piper Laurie as the villainess of the piece as she fixes the will to get all hubby's money and for his four children to get nothing.

She takes them off on a trip to Europe and the Holy Land, and it is while they are en route to Palestine by liner that they meet Ustinov, Bacall (playing a British Member of Parliament), Jenny Seagrove and Hayley Mills. The opening credits sequence takes place over cheap-looking touristy shots of their tour through Europe to awful, inappropriate music.

Ustinov overhears all sorts of murderous intent as characters conspire with each other and try to hide aspects from their murky past, until Piper Laurie finally is poisoned while the troupe is at an archaeological dig, leaving Ustinov to twiddle his moustache and pinpoint the killer (who actually is quite easy to spot).

The actors seem to be merely going through the motions, with Gielgud looking particularly uncomfortable in an ill-fitting military uniform, and Bacall having a wonderful time overacting madly. Seagrove and Mills perform well, and at least seem to be trying to take the whole affair seriously.

Technically "Appointment With Death" is fine, with cinematographer David Gurfinkel making the Israeli locations look lush and elegant, and Winner again using his nom de plume Arnold Crust for the editing chores. In all it is quite well-made hokum that at least delivers the sleuthing goods. —*Adam.*

Mondo New York
(DOCU)

A Fourth and Broadway Films (Island Pictures) release of an Intl. Harmony production. Executive producer, Dorian Hendrix. Produced by Stuart S. Shapiro. Directed by Harvey Keith. Screenplay, David Silver, Keith; camera (color), Leonard Wong; editor, Richard Friedman; music, Johnny Pacheco, Luis Perico Ortiz; production design, Jacquiline Jacobsen; associate producers, John Paige, Steven Menkin; production consultant, Alan Douglas. Reviewed at Magno Preview 9 screening room, N.Y. March 2, 1988. No MPAA Rating. Running time: **83 MIN.**
With: Joey Arias, Rick Aviles, Charlie Barnett, Joe Coleman, Emilio Cubiero, Karen Finley, Dean Johnson, Phoebe Legere, Lydia Lunch, Ann Magnuson, Frank Moore, John Sex, Shannah Laumeister.

A documentary with the most unconventional subject matter, "Mondo New York" captures a part of the city not even many New Yorkers have seen — or would want to see. This feature disgusts and enrages as much as it enlightens and entertains, which foretells a narrow but fervent following in the specialized market.

Instead of globetrotting for visual evidence that ours is "a dog's world" like its 1962 Italo namesake "Mondo Cane," "Mondo New York" focuses on the actions of several performance artists and other denizens of Gotham's East (Greenwich) Village.

An opening monolog by "avant-retard" (presskit's words) singer-actress Lydia Lunch sets the tone of the pic. She refers to New Yorkers "clawing their way to the top of the garbage heap." What some people will do to get to the top, and indeed, what some people call art, is stunningly unveiled in "Mondo New York."

"Escorted" from scene to scene by pretty blond teenager Shannah Laumeister (who's silent throughout), viewer catches a cockfight, a slave auction in Chinatown and a voodoo rite in which a chicken's head is bitten off. These grisly acts, of course, are illegal, and perhaps the film should be required viewing for urban vice squads.

As scripted by cult film producer Stuart S. Shapiro and directed by Harvey Keith (in his unforgettable debut), viewer's sympathies alternate from repugnance over the acts of cruelty to animals to enjoyment of its truly entertaining aspects.

Some of the acts are refreshingly amusing, namely, black comedians Charlie Barnett and Joey Aviles. Ann Magnuson, Karen Finley, Phoebe Legere and Dean Johnson offer outlandish yet compelling performances. The Latin- and punk-flavored soundtrack is *au courant.*

"Mondo New York" has the twisted sense of humor and commitment to artistic upheaval for which filmmaker John Waters has been known ("Mondo Trasho" is his 1970 film). Following a painfully long closeup of an addict administering a dose, the addict cheerfully talks about making it in New York. Hookers sing "I Love New York."

Paramount was prepared to release "Mondo New York" in some media until it discovered sometime during postproduction that Shapiro was unprepared to cut the docu to fit an R rating. Island Pictures, perhaps to distance itself from controversy that's sure to arise if pic plays in some territories, makes "Mondo New York" the maiden release for its Fourth and Broadway Films arm.

The filmmakers succeeded in producing a celebration of the darker side of the Big Apple. "Mondo New York," however, also stands as a celebration of the First Amendment. Perhaps only in America (only in New York?) could such aberrant and illegal behavior be presented for public consumption.

In contrast to its shadowy content, commercial cinematographer Lenny Wong's sharp work is uncompromisingly well-lit. —Binn.

Illustrious Energy
(NEW ZEALAND)

A Mirage Entertainment Corp. presentation in association with the N.Z. Film Commission. Produced by Don Reynolds, Chris Hampson. Directed by Leon Narbey. Screenplay, Narbey, Murray Edmond; camera (color), Alan Locke; editor, David Coulson; music, Jan Preston; production design, Janelle Aston; sound, Bob Allen. Reviewed at Odeon cinema, Palmerston North, N.Z., March 15, 1988. Running time: **100 MIN.**

Chan	Shaun Bao
Kim	Harry Ip
Wong	Peter Chin
Li	Geeling
Rev. Don	Peter Hayden
Surveyor	Desmond Kelly
Mrs. Wong	Heather Bolton

Palmerston North, N.Z. — Leon Narbey's first feature, "Illustrious Energy," heralded during its shooting as "unashamedly an art movie," cannot conceal missed opportunities — on or off a regular commercial circuit.

Cinematographer on four Kiwi features since the industry's surge a decade ago, Narbey shapes but fails to realize a classic tale of fortune won and lost by two Chinese miners enduring alienation and suspicion on the predominantly European New Zealand goldfields of the late 19th century. The human story emerges undeveloped and disjointed with the landscape disproportionately *uber alles*, weakening any dramatic drive and the chances of sustained viewer involvement.

As can be a temptation with first-time lensers turned helmers, little facility is offered the actors to run with the story, even given the added difficulties, in this instance, of imported Chinese thesps with little apparent English fluency. The eye seems too doggedly fixed on the stasis of a single shot rather than the flow of the whole.

Visually, "Illustrious Energy" opens strongly as young Chan (Shaun Bao) and his aging father-

in-law Kim (Harry Ip), in silence, disinter the bones of a former mining partner and prepare them for the journey to ancestral China. The old man is anxious to strike it rich and return home before he dies. Chan, even with a wife and young child in the homeland, appears not so sure.

Land surveyors are moving in on the old gold claim the pair are reworking, adding urgency to their task.

The miners make a strike. Chan goes to town with some of the gold to buy food and pay off debts. He is harassed by Europeans and tempted into illicit pleasures by town Chinese before enjoying a brief idyll with a traveling circus.

When Chan returns to the lonely rock shelter he shares with Kim, tragedy and misfortune strike together, challenging his fortitude yet again.

The disappointment with "Illustrious Energy" is its inability, as a statement, to sustain its title. The lead performances fail to provide coherence and the sweep of human emotion that could have made cultural difference and strangeness irrelevant in the final analysis.

Why a Chinese language track with English subtitles was not used, where it is logical to be used, also is a question that begs asking. —Nic.

Backstage
(AUSTRALIAN)

A Hoyts (Australia) (Skouras Pictures in U.S.) release of a Burrowes Film Group production. Produced by Geoff Burrowes. Executive producers, Dennis Wright, Kent C. Lovell. Directed by Jonathan Hardy. Screenplay, Hardy, Howson; based on an idea by John Lamond; camera (color), Keith Wagstaff; editor, Ray Daley; music, Bruce Rowland; production design, Leslie Binns; sound, Terry Rodman, John Schiefelbein; production manager, Bill Regan; assistant director, Bob Donaldson; costumes, Jane Hyland; coproduced by Frank Howson; casting, Liz Mulliner. Reviewed at Hoyts screening room, Sydney, April 5, 1988. Running time: **91 MIN.**

Kate Lawrence	Laura Branigan
Robert Landau	Michael Aitkens
Mortimer Wynde	Noel Ferrier
Evelyn Hough	Rowena Wallace
Bill French	Phillip Holder
Milton	Len Kaserman
Paarvo	Kym Gyngell
Steven Williams	David Letch
Geraldine Woollencraft	Mary Ward
Myles Frewe	Henry Cutherbertson

Also with: John Tarrant (Bruce Tendon), James Condon (Frank Turner), Penelope Stewart (Mary Foote), Ian Mune (Mangin), Nancy Kiel (Evie), John Frawley (Metheny), Robin Dene (Bollinger), Randall Berger (Roger Weiss).

Sydney — Yank warbler Laura Branigan came to Melbourne to make a film about a Yank warbler who comes to Melbourne to act in a play.

The resulting production is a witless comedy coupled with a lifeless romance which will not enhance the reputations of anyone involved. Even with the Branigan name, box-office chances look glum.

She plays Kate Lawrence, a popu-

lar singer who just wants to be taken seriously as an actress. Despite being told by her agent that "as an actress, you're Siberia," she accepts an offer to tread the boards in far-off Melbourne without, apparently, reading the script of the play in question.

The play, it turns out, is a sub-sub-Noël Cowardish piece, set in '30s Britain, called "The Green Year Passes." The producer is a dimwitted buffoon (ludicrously portrayed by Noel Ferrier), the director is a Finn (Kym Gyngell) into communicating on a Higher Plane, and the supporting actors are a clutch of incompetent bores.

At a Meet The Press function, Kate is upset by the hostile questioning of Robert Landau (Michael Aitkens), supposedly one of Melbourne's leading theater reviewers, and the son of a famous playwright: Landau, we're informed scathingly, is "only a critic" who "didn't live up to his potential." Kate hurls a glass of red wine at the scribe, but at the same time falls for him, and after a stroll in the park and a frolic in a fountain, winds up in his bed.

The play turns out to be a complete disaster (presented in the film on about the level of a pre-school production) and Landau writes a savage review. He and Kate quarrel, but he agrees to teach her the art of acting (he's some critic!) before she returns home. He also writes a rave review of her performance in *Variety*, which helps her get a starring role on Broadway — as Nina in "The Seagull."

Pic climaxes with generous chunks of Branigan as Nina, after which, despite the fact that she clearly fails to give an acceptable performance, she gets a standing ovation. Her triumph is made complete by the fact that Landau has winged in from Australia to be waiting in the wings at curtain.

"Backstage" presents a ridiculous world with no semblance of fact. It's impossible to believe in the syrupy romance, because nothing in the film rings true. Every role in the film is caricatured, starting with the singer who only wants to be taken seriously as an actress, and continuing with the critic who secretly wants to write plays like his father did, the theater producer who, when told his investors want a meeting, says: "Put it down for the next Jewish holiday," the singer's manager, who weeps during her truly awful Broadway debut, the Broadway producer who keeps a straight face during her embarrassing audition, and so on.

Given the dire screenplay by director Jonathan Hardy and coproducer Frank Howson, it's no wonder the cast give performances ranging from poor to awful. Keith Wagstaff's camerawork is pro, and the film is well crafted in every department, including Bruce Row-

land's music score. Overall, the film fails not only because of its hoary clichés but because writers and director fail to give this American in Melbourne a real world against which to react. — Strat.

Brain Damage

A Palisades Entertainment release of a Henenlotter/Ievins production. Executive producers, Andre Blay, Al Eicher. Produced by Edgar Ievins. Written and directed by Frank Henenlotter. Camera (TVC color), Bruce Torbet; editor, James Y. Kwei, Henenlotter; music, Gus Russo, Clutch Reiser; sound, Russell Jessum; set design, Charles Bennett; art direction, Ivy Rosovsky; special makeup effects, Gabe Bartalos; Elmer created by Bertalos, David Kindlon; special visual effects, Al Magliochetti; production manager, Ed Walloga; assistant director, Gregory Lamberson; associate producers, Bennett, Ray Sundlin; casting, Frank Calo. Reviewed at Cine 42 #1 theater, N.Y., April 16, 1988. MPAA Rating: R. Running time: **94 MIN.**

Brian	Rick Herbst
Mike	Gordon MacDonald
Barbara	Jennifer Lowry
Morris	Theo Barnes
Martha	Lucille Saint-Peter
Blond in Hell club	Vicki Darnell
Man with basket	Kevin Van Hentenryck

"Brain Damage" is an overly ambitious but nonetheless rewarding low-budget horror film using the monster genre as a timely metaphor for drug addiction and its ills.

Unfortunately, pic has been poorly promoted and instead of a careful launch it preemed at the sleaziest theater on 42d Street in Manhattan.

Filmmaker Frank Henenlotter showed promise with his 1982 pic (shot in 16m) "Basket Case," with many of his collaborators encoring on this 35m followup, which includes a funny cameo (with basket) by the first pic's lead Kevin Van Hentenryck.

Rick Herbst stars are Brian, a youngster who's bitten by Elmer The Parasite (film's working title), a centuries-old eel-like monster being kept alive on animal brains by goofball neighbors Theo Barnes and Lucille Saint-Peter. As Brian quickly learns, Elmer gives his host a periodic jolt of "juice," blue fluid injected into the brain which provides a psychedelic high.

Brian becomes addicted to this pleasure and carrying Elmer around under his shirt gives the monster access to human victims, whose brains Elmer dines upon. Pic climaxes when Elmer goes after the heroine, Brian's pal Barbara (Jennifer Lowry).

At every step, Henenlotter makes clear the analogy between Brian's plight and drug addiction, including going cold turkey and radical behavior changes as a tipoff to family (Brian's brother Mike, played by Gordon MacDonald) and friends, etc. Horror format is useful in this regard, heavily leavened by outbreaks of black humor.

Elmer, created by Gabe Bartalos and David Kindlon, is an admirable achievement, a mobile puppet-like monster that pays homage to films ranging from "Fiend Without A Face" to "The Tingler." With a wisecracking voice (uncredited, but sounding like tv horror movie host Zacherly) and cute eyes, Elmer is funny as well as scary in context.

Acting is over-the-top and film could have benefited from the casting of name talent in order to cross over to mainstream audiences with its timely thematics. As it is, Henenlotter, cinematographer Bruce Torbet and their team have maintained a harsh, cheap, underground look that fits the picture's cult ambitions. Overuse of blue filters is one drawback, however. Keyboards musical score by Gus Russo and Clutch Reiser is extremely effective. — *Lor.*

Seppan
(SWEDISH)

A Movie Makers Sweden production. (World sales: Swedish Film Institute, Stockholm.) Produced by Bert Sundberg. Directed by Agneta Fagerström-Olsson. Screenplay, Fagerström-Olsson; camera (color), John O. Olsson; editor, Christin Loman; music, Mikael Renliden; sound, Lennart Duner; production design, Lena Billingskog; production manager, Anders Durvall. Reviewed at Berlin Film Festival (market), Feb. 20, 1988. (Also in AFI Fest, L.A.) Running time: **120 MIN.**

Pirjo	Nina Lager
Sara	Sofie Mällström
Seppo	Jesper Lager
Jari	Jani Nimemimaa
Fransiska	Marian Vodovosoff

Berlin — This is a Swedish film about a group of youngsters whose parents were refugees from all over Europe and who lived in overcrowded conditions in a hostel known as Seppan.

Though far too long, the film mixes pathos and humor to good effect, and the children are wonderfully well directed. With trimming, pic might have a cinema career.

The year is 1961 and Russian sputniks are flying in the night sky. The children come from all over Europe: there are Finns and Poles, Russians and Estonians, Hungarians and Latvians. Naturally enough, there are rivalries and problems galore among the adults, which are seen through the wide eyes of the kids. There are fights and drunkenness and infidelities: a child comes home unexpectedly to find her mother in bed with another child's father.

There are tragedies, too. One child drowns in the river, another is killed while walking along the nearby railway tracks. Life goes on and the children take all the frustrations better than their parents. For them, life in Seppan is all they know, and their parents remember a better life, before the war.

Classes are run by a severe-looking teacher and discipline is strict. Seppo is thrown out of the class because he won't do as he's told. Pirjo and Sara are best friends and share secrets together.

Adults break the monotony of life with a summer barbecue and outdoor dance, but it's hard to disguise the ugliness of the place where they all have to live.

Though composed of many beautifully handled incidents and episodes, "Seppan" is marred by exceedingly slow pacing and a consequently long running time. Yet it obviously was a labor of love, and the director's warmth and humanity shines through. — *Strat.*

Lola la Loca

Produced by Martha Fowlkes, Enrique Oliver. Directed by Oliver. Screenplay, Oliver; camera (Duart color), Bobby Bukowski; editor, Scott Davis; music, Daniel Indart; sound, Mario Cardnas, Jose Quintero, Susan Welsh, Josh Margoles; production design, Liz Barrows; creative consultant, Robert Sampson; coproducer, Heidi Price; associate producers, Quintero, Jose Berrios. Reviewed at Remis Auditorium, Museum of Fine Arts, Boston, March 24, 1988. (In the AFI Festival, L.A.) No MPAA Rating. Running time: **85 MIN.**

Lola	Myrna Cruz
Social Worker	Heidi Egloff
Robertico	Enrique Oliver
Glendaly	Jeanne Bukowski
Grampa	Silvestre Oliver
Lalo	Armandine San Martin
Jane	Carmen Z
Cundi	Sonia Brava
Pimp	Jose Berrios
Nena	Zoyla Oliver
Carmela	Josefina Miranda
Perla	Ana Margarita Campos
Lupe	Beatrice Dobelle

Boston — With Hispanic-Americans currently represented on screen by the happy peasants of "The Milagro Beanfield War" and the cutthroat gangs of "Colors," Enrique Oliver's feature bow is a breath of fresh air.

Oliver first gained attention with his awardwinning student short, "Photo Album." A native of Cuba who lives in Boston, he pokes good-natured fun at the lives of Hispanic immigrants as well as at the outsiders who try to understand them.

"Lola la Loca" (literally, "Lola The Crazy One") is set up as a shaggy dog story. A social worker (Heidi Egloff) assigned to Lola's (Myrna Cruz) case arrives at the housing project to find that Lola isn't home. All her neighbors, however, have very definite opinions about her which they are happy to share not only with the social worker but with the rest of the neighborhood.

As the afternoon progresses, more and more people gather to give their stories which are not only contradictory but often mutually exclusive. Writer-director Oliver appears as one of the neighbors and as the narrator in a framing device where he is introducing the film to a group of people who turn out to be the cast and crew. Device doesn't always work, but Oliver has many droll asides about neighborhood life: "I always thought the meaning of life was for something to happen so we could talk about it."

And talk they do. Everyone from a practicing witch doctor to a cosmetics saleswoman to a woman who predicts the weather from a bullet lodged in her neck give their own version of why Lola is known as the Crazy One, usually projecting their own problems onto Lola in the process. In a brief animated sequence even the neighborhood cat gets to put in his two cents.

"Lola" would seem to have definite possibilities on screens catering to Hispanic audiences, as well as houses known for taking risks on such specialty fare as "Chan Is Missing" or "She's Gotta Have It." Chief problem limiting wider appeal concerns some of the accents, which make it the toughest sledding for domestic audiences this side of the Liverpudlians in "Letter To Brezhnev." Additionally, shaggy dog nature of the plot means that film stands or falls on the success of the individual segments since there's no real payoff to the story.

Cast and tech credits are professional if a bit on the low-budget side. Pic was underwritten in part by the National Endowment for the Arts and the Masssachusetts Council for the Arts. —*Kimm.*

Kiss The Night
(AUSTRALIAN)

A Rainy Day production. (Intl. sales, Fox/Lorber Associates.) Produced by Graeme Isaac. Directed by James Ricketson. Executive producer-screenplay, Don Catchlove; camera (Fuji color), Michael Edols; editor, Tony Stephens; music, Graeme Isaac; production design, Rob Ricketson; sound, Ross Linton; production manager, Brenda Pam; assistant director, John Warran; casting, Michael Lynch. Reviewed at Australian Film Commission screening room, North Sydney, Dec. 12, 1987. Running time: **99 MIN.**

Candy Regentag (Jenny)	Patsy Stephen
Reg	Warwick Moss
Ian	Garry Aron Cook
Fleur	Rainee Skinner
Bibi	Maxine Klibingaitis
Gail	Toni Scanlon
Wendy	Jacqui Phillips
Lola	Beth Child
Sacha	Imogen Annesley

Sydney — This rather bleak, but quite gripping, drama centers around a disturbed young woman who works as a prostitute in a Sydney brothel. Pic combines a surprisingly detailed examination of brothel life (a bit akin to Lizzie Borden's "Working Girls") with a painful personal story which leads to murder. It makes for a modestly effective film which, if it gets upbeat reviews, could work in selected venues in most large cities.

Low-budgeter was filmed as "Candy Regentag," the name taken by Jenny, the hooker at the center of the drama ("Regentag" is German for "rainy day," which is the name of the film's production company). Candy shares an apartment with Ian (Garry Aron Cook), her surly boyfriend, but spends most of her time at Bambi's, a gaudy broth-

el in the racy King's Cross section of Sydney.

Early on, a scene in which three very young men arrive seeking femme company is presented in an unusually frank manner. One of them's assigned to Candy, who goes through what's obviously a long-standing routine, including supervising the lad's shower and inspecting his privates.

Most of the film, however, concerns Candy's relationship with the mysterious Reg (Warwick Moss), who comes to her aid one night out on the street. He visits her in the brothel, and, almost against her will, Candy finds herself falling in love with him. She breaks with Ian, but, too late, discovers that Reg's attitudes to life are hardly normal, a revelation that results in a fatal stabbing at fadeout.

"Kiss The Night' is a comeback for director James Ricketson, who made some very personal and interesting low-budgeters many years ago. Working from a screenplay by executive producer Don Catchlove, Ricketson has done a good job in capturing the strange, perverse world of the brothel, its women and its clients. The result is a drama that's never predictable and which combines unsensational, but full-frontal nudity in sex scenes with a strong personal drama.

The cast is composed mostly of unknowns. Patsy Stephen gives a powerful performance as Candy, her looks and style reminiscent at times of Judy Davis. Warwick Moss makes the enigmatic Reg an interesting character, but Garry Aron Cook can't do much with the under-developed role of Ian. Supporting players are all okay.

Pic is technically solid down the line. —*Strat.*

Permanent Record

A Paramount Pictures release of a Frank Mancuso Jr. production. Produced by Mancuso. Coproducer, Herb Rabinowitz. Executive producer, Martin Hornstein. Directed by Marisa Silver. Screenplay, Jarre Fees, Alice Liddle, Larry Ketron; camera (Technicolor), Frederick Elmes; editor, Robert Brown; music, Joe Strummer; production design, Michel Levesque; art direction, Steven Karatzas; set design, Lachlin Loud; set decoration, Woody Crocker; costume design, Tracy Tynan; sound (Ultra-Stereo), Robert Gravenor; assistant director, Eric Heffron; casting, Amanda Mackey. Reviewed at Paramount Studios, L.A., April 15, 1988. MPAA Rating: PG-13. Running time: **91 MIN.**

David Sinclair	Alan Boyce
Chris Townsend	Keanu Reeves
M.G.	Michelle Meyrink
Lauren	Jennifer Rubin
Kim	Pamela Gidley
Jake	Michael Elgart
Leo Verdell	Richard Bradford
Mr. McBain	Dakin Matthews
Jim Sinclair	Barry Corbin
Martha Sinclair	Kathy Baker
Lee Sinclair	Joshua Taylor
Mr. Townsend	Sam Vlahos
Dr. Moss	David Selberg
Lou Reed	Himself

Hollywood — If "River's Edge" was a chillingly matter-of-fact, genuinely tough portrait of lost youth, "Permanent Record" is pretend tough.

A look at how a bunch of high schoolers try to deal with the suicide of their class' most promising member, pic is populated by profoundly unrewarding characters doing and saying utterly uninteresting things, which should mean a washout at the b.o.

Bland is the operative word here, as suburban white bread kids variously hang out, play a little rock 'n' roll and audition for the school production of "H.M.S. Pinafore." The only potentially distinguished one of the lot is David (Alan Boyce), who is the best-looking, smartest and possibly a talented composer.

At the same time, David is prone to inexplicable bouts of doubt, anguish and indecision, until he finally just plunges off a cliff into the sea. Shocking event forces everyone to face their own insecurity and vulnerability, but it is especially painful to Chris, David's best friend, who looked up to him as a shining example for his own comparatively aimless, irresponsible life.

Chris' gradual coming to grips with his sense of self gives the film its only point of interest, largely due to Keanu Reeves' performance, which opens up nicely as the drama progresses. Pic builds to a goofy climax which actually intercuts the posthumous recording of David's last composition with a performance of the Gilbert & Sullivan musical, resulting in a predictable cleansing of everyone concerned.

Boyce is appealing enough as the doomed bright boy, and Richard Bradford contributes a highly sympathetic turn as the school principal. All the girls are vapid dips, and in a film directed by a woman, yet.

Marisa Silver and lenser Frederick Elmes have opted for a lot of show-offy crane and moving camera shots, often in long takes, but this display of technical virtuosity has been applied senselessly to this thin concoction cooked up by three screenwriters who, maddeningly, go completely unidentified in Paramount's press materials even though the art director and musical supervisor, among others, are accorded extensive bios.

Joe Strummer (of Clash fame) was brought in to lend a little distinction to the soundtrack, and Lou Reed makes a cameo appearance as himself. — *Cart.*

young and bland to carry a picture designed for a young Robert Mitchum, and Pamela Gidley way too young and low-key to be the tough-as-nails cafe owner.

Tech credits are impressive.

—*Lor.*

Stormy Monday
(BRITISH)

An Atlantic Entertainment Group release, in association with British Screen and Film Four Intl., of a Moving Picture Co. production. Produced by Nigel Stafford-Clark. Written and directed by Mike Figgis. Camera (Rank Agfa color), Roger Deakins; editor, David Martin; music, Figgis; sound (Dolby), Tony Jackson; production design, Andrew McAlpine; art direction, Charmian Adams; assistant director, John Watson; costume design, Sandy Powell; stunt coordinator, Denise Ryan; associate producer, Alan J. Wands; casting, Mary Selway, Teresa Topolski; U.S. casting, Deborah Brown, Pamela Rack. Reviewed at 20th Century Fox screening room, N.Y., March 28, 1988. (In Cannes Film Festival, Directors Fortnight.) MPAA Rating: R. Running time: **93 MIN.**

Kate	Melanie Griffith
Cosmo	Tommy Lee Jones
Finney	Sting
Brendan	Sean Bean

Also with: James Cosmo, Mark Long, Brian Lewis, Derek Hoxby, Heathcote Williams, Prunella Gee, Guy Manning, Alison Steadman, Al Matthews, Caroline Hutchison, Fiona Sloman.

The attempt to come up with another stylish British *film noir* in the vein of "Mona Lisa" comes a cropper in "Stormy Monday." Debut theatrical pic for Mike Figgis is all visual flash and no script, with comatose performances to boot.

Melanie Griffith, styled unattractively (and overweight) with unkempt red hair, toplines as a sort of B-girl working for U.S. gangster/real estate magnate Tommy Lee Jones. Jones is in Newcastle to run an American Week promotion to boost U.S./U.K. business development, and also is trying to run Sting out of business, operating a local jazz club.

Griffith unbelievably is moonlighting as a waitress in a local cafe, but soon becomes involved romantically with a handsome Irish lad, Sean Bean, who is doing odd jobs at Sting's club. Plot unfolds as a string of ridiculous coincidences, set in motion when Bean at lunch overhears two of Jones' hitmen plotting to do in Sting. Truly absurd finale has Bean and Griffith narrowly being exploded in a Jaguar by Jones, who calmly asks Griffith if she wants to go home with him after being found out as a ruthless killer.

Figgis, who also composed the film's musical score, gets one good laugh when he has the Cracow Jazz Ensemble (actually a sextet of Brits given to '60s-style free jazz) play a funky, tongue-in-cheek version of "The Star Spangled Banner" at a U.S./U.K. cooperation banquet presided over by the local mayor (Alison Steadman in a cameo). One other good scene has Sting playing an acoustic bass solo all alone in his club.

Otherwise, film merely is a showcase for Roger Deakins' glossy visuals, in support of a sketchy storyline. Chance for another atmospheric classic like Mike Hodges' 1971 set-in-Newcastle thriller "Get Carter" is muffed. Jones walks through his idiotic role with barely hidden embarrassment. Griffith hasn't missed many meals, sporting an unbecoming figure resembling latter-day Anita Ekberg. Her romantic scenes with hero Sean Bean are so low-key one thinks they must be a put-on. Sting's acting, using his own hometown Newcastle accent, is fine, but like Mick Jagger he can't seem to find a successful film vehicle for his talents.

Tech credits, including Deakins' camerawork and Figgis' own score, are arresting but shouldn't have been ends in themselves, supporting a creative vacuum in Figgis' writing and direction of actors. —*Lor.*

EARLY CANNES REVIEWS

The Blue Iguana

A Paramount Pictures release of a Polygram Movies presentation in association with Propaganda Films. Executive producers, Michael Kuhn, Nigel Sinclair. Produced by Steven Golin, Sigurjon Sighvatsson. Written and directed by John Lafia. Camera (CFI color), Rodolfo Sanchez; editor, Scott Chestnut; music, Ethan James; sound (Dolby), Bob Dreebin; production design, Cynthia Sowder; second unit director, Chestnut; stunt coordinator, John Escobar; coproducers, Othon Roffiel, Angel Flores-Marini; associate producer, Winnie Fredrisz; casting, Jeff Gerrard; Mexico casting, Claudia Becker. Reviewed at Paramount 29th floor screening room, N.Y., Feb. 4, 1988. (In Cannes Film Festival, official selection, noncompeting.) MPAA Rating: R. Running time: **90 MIN.**

Vince Holloway	Dylan McDermott
Cora	Jessica Harper
Reno	James Russo
Dakota	Pamela Gidley
Vera	Tovah Feldshuh
Det. Carl Strick	Dean Stockwell
Mona	Katia Schkolnik
Floyd	Flea
Yano	Yano Anaya
Bartender	Michele Seipp
Boat captain	Don Pedro Colley

"The Blue Iguana" is a likable problem child: a hip, modern *film noir* that is too wacky and too specialized in its allusions to attract general audiences. Add problematic casting of the central roles and you have an iffy theatrical entry destined for cult status in future.

Title, conjuring up *noir* goodies "The Blue Dahlia" and "The Blue Gardenia" (and also, alas, Par's laughable *brat noir* "Blue City") refers to a cafe in the tough south-of-the-border town of El Diablo, operated by tough young Pamela Gidley. With Ethan James right-on brassy musical score and cars and costumes out of the 1950s, pic at the outset suggests a hip spoofing of Orson Welles' stylish 1958 "Touch Of Evil."

Ultimately pic takes on elements of a Spaghetti Western, especially the revisionist model (replete with 1950s Buicks everywhere) of Alex Cox' "Straight To Hell." Dylan McDermott portrays a private dick coerced into a suicide mission to El Diablo by goofball IRS agents (Tovah Feldshuh and Dean Stockwell) to recover money laundered at the local bank. Jessica Harper, with slicked-back hair, runs the bank, assisted by her chief goon James Russo.

Well-staged action scenes punctuate the tongue-in-cheek proceedings, in which McDermott ultimately resorts to plot manipulations familiar from "A Fistful Of Dollars" out of "Yojimbo."

Pic's rogues gallery of eccentric players is a delight: Feldshuh as butch as they come; Harper camping it up Eva Peron-style; Russo out of control hobbling around like Richard III; Stockwell in thick glasses and neckbrace; Flea as a hambone geek in the Elisha Cook slot; and Michele Seipp as punk-styled bartender Zoe.

Unfortunately, the lead players are colorless; McDermott too

Hanna's War

A Cannon Group release of a Golan-Globus production. Executive producer, Otto Plashkes. Produced by Menahem Golan, Yoram Globus. Written and directed by Golan based on "The Diaries Of Hanna Senesh" and "A Great Wind Cometh" by Yoel Palgi; camera (color), Elemer Ragalyi; editor, Alain Jakubowicz; music, Dov Seltzer; sound (Ultra-Stereo), Cyril Collick; art direction, Tividar Bertaian; set decoration, Fred Carter; costume design, John Mollo; second unit director-associate producer, Carlos Gil; assistant director, Miguel Gil; production managers, Andras Elek (Hungary), Itzik Kol (Israel); casting, Noel Davis, Jeremy Zimmerman. Reviewed in Tel Aviv, April 14, 1988. Running time: **158 MIN.**

Katalin . . . . Ellen Burstyn
Hanna . . . . Maruschka Detmers
McCormack . . . . Anthony Andrews
Rosza . . . . Donald Pleasence
Cpt. Simon . . . . David Warner
Yoel . . . . Vincenzo Ricotta
Ruven . . . . Christopher Fairbank
Peretz . . . . Rob Jacks
Tony . . . . Serge El-Baz
Aba . . . . Eli Gorenstein
Yona . . . . Josef El-Dror
Also with: Rade Serbedzjia (Capt. Ivan), Miodrag Krivokapic (Col. Illya), Dorota Stalinska (Maritza), George Dillon (Milenko), Teri Tordai (Baroness Hatvany), Yehuda Efroni (Sandor), Agi Margitai, John Stride, Patrick Monckton, Jeff Gerner, Shimon Finkel, Ingrid Pitt, Jon Rumney, Magda Faluhelyi, Emma Lewis, Russell Porter.

Tel Aviv — Cannon topper Menachem Golan took time off from corporate wars to direct this biopic of Hanna Senesh, a project he had nursed in various forms for many years. Golan's picture is bound to become the official film version by definition.

Senesh, a talented poet and a martyr who died in a Hungarian jail in 1944, before her 24th birthday, is a mythical figure in Israel, a symbol of gentle but determined heroism.

In Golan's version, heroes and villains are easily distinguished, characters are respectfully observed and admired, or duly abhorred and discredited, and no time is spent dwelling on psychological niceties. As for Hanna herself, she is a bigger-than-life, idealized figure, not surprisingly put by the film on equal footing with Joan of Arc.

The straightforward script systematically follows her steps from the point she decides, on graduating high school, to part with her family and leave antisemitic Hungary to go to Palestine for a new start. She spends time at agricultural school, and happy years in Sdoth Yam, the kibbutz she joins as a fisherwoman. While there, she is drafted by the British for a special operation behind German lines in Eastern Europe and after a brief Yugoslav interlude, she crosses the border back into Hungary.

This fills up about half of the picture, the rest being dedicated to the time she spent in Hungarian jail, the tortures she suffered as while refusing to divulge her identity and the nature of her assignment, until the moment she thinks the Allies have ensured her mother's safety. Only then does she reveal her real name, which causes the immediate arrest of her mother and an attempt to blackmail more information out of her.

As the Russians are about to enter Budapest, she is taken off the trucks dispatching prisoners into the hands of the Gestapo, and is executed by the Hungarians without a trial.

Using the stentorian tones of a heroic saga, the script skips over the many controversies involved. The exact intentions of British intelligence in organizing the operation aren't clear, and the reasons which determined the Hagana, the official military arm of the Jewish struggle for independence in Palestine, to cooperate with their enemies aren't sufficiently explained.

Hanna's capture, the conduct of her jailers — who, once they discover her true identity, seem to lose all interest in her assignment and execute her at a moment when saving her life might have counted in their favor once the Allies stepped in — all these details are left for the audience to sort out.

Maruschka Detmers in the lead may not radiate the spiritual strength required by her role, but she is dedicated and often moving during the prison sequences. Donald Pleasence and David Warner each notch another villain to their credit. Topbilled Ellen Burstyn has at most a supporting part as Hanna's mother, and Anthony Andrews is a bit top-heavy as the British instructor who leads the expedition.

Lensed in Hungary and Israel by top Magyar cinematographer Elemer Ragalyi, this is a handsome production, sometimes even too handsome and picturesque for its good. Dov Seltzer's gushing music track stays constantly on a high emotional level and Alain Jakubowicz' editing is brisk in spite of pics considerable length.

Obviously Golan spared no effort to make this a moving, highly emotional statement, and scheduling the world premiere in Israel on the eve of the 40th anniversary of its independence indicates he would like it to be considered first of all a national epic. —*Edna.*

Terror Squad

A Manson Intl. presentation of a Matterhorn Group production. Executive producer, Ken Kimura. Produced and directed by Peter Maris. Screenplay, Chuck Rose, from story by Mark Verheiden; camera (United color), Peter Jensen; editor, Jack Tucker; music, Chuck Cirino; sound, Gerry Wolfe; art direction, Joe Dea; assistant director, Lisa Yesko; production manager, Richard Kanter; second unit director & camera, Mark Morris; postproduction supervisor-associate producer, Sunny Vest; coproducer, Richard Allen; casting, Barbara Remsen. Reviewed on Forum Home Video vidcassette, N.Y., April 6, 1988. No MPAA Rating. Running time: **92 MIN.**

Chief Rawlings . . . . Chuck Connors
Capt. Steiner . . . . Brodie Greer
Johnny . . . . Bill Calvert
Jennifer . . . . Kerry Brennan
Yassir . . . . Kavi Raz
Gamel . . . . Joseph Nasser
Mr. Nero . . . . Budge Threlkeld
Norman . . . . Dennis Moynahan
Also with: Ken Foree, Nathan Dyer, Lisa Ross, Baggie Hardiman, Jill Sanders.

"Terror Squad" is an exciting B-actioner, despite its absurd premise of Libyan terrorists invading Kokomo, Ind. Unluckily, pic failed to get a theatrical tryout, going directly to homevid shelves.

Chuck Connors, back in his trademark Brooklyn Dodgers jacket, is the local police chief when a commando squad from Khaddafyland attacks a nuclear power plant. There ensues a spectacular car chase, the lengthiest and one of the best since the classic Barry Newman pic "Vanishing Point" of 1971. Terrorists, led by Kavi Raz and hothead Joseph Nasser, kidnap a high school class and hold them hostage while Connors comically uses "Dog Day Afternoon" explicitly as his guidebook to negotiations.

Topnotch action directed by Peter Maris lifts this one out of the lookalike boredom of made-for-vid titles, and indicates he is ready for a theatrical assignment. Young cast, essaying stet roles in a "Breakfast Club" detention setting, is okay and tech credits are impressive.
—*Lor.*

Salome's Last Dance

A Vestron Pictures release. Executive producers, William J. Quigley, Dan Ireland. Produced by Penny Corke. Coproducer, Robert Littman. Directed by Ken Russell. Screenplay, Russell, incorporating Oscar Wilde's play "Salome," translated from French by Vivian Russell; camera (Technicolor), Harvey Harrison; editor, Timothy Gee; music, classical selections, conducted by Richard Cooke; sound (Dolby), Ray Beckett, art direction, Michael Buchanan; set design, Christopher Hobbs; additional designs, Michael Jeffery; costume design, Michael Arrals; choreography, Arlene Phillips; assistant director, Mike Gowans; casting, Rebecca Howard. Reviewed at Broadway screening room, N.Y., April 22, 1988. (In Seattle Film Festival.) MPAA Rating: R. Running time: **89 MIN.**

Herodias/Lady Alice . . . . . Glenda Jackson
Herod/Alfred Taylor . . . . . Stratford Johns
Oscar Wilde . . . . Nickolas Grace
John the Baptist/Bosie . . . . Douglas Hodge
Salome/Rose . . . . Imogen Millais-Scott
Tigellenus/Chilvers . . . . Denis Ull
Pageboy . . . . Russell Le Nash
Cappadocem . . . . Alfred Russell
Kenneth . . . . Ken Russell
Also with: David Doyle, Warren Saire, Kenny Ireland, Michael Van Wuk, Paul Clayton, Imogen Claire, Tim Potter, Matthew Taylor, Linzi Drew, Tina Shaw, Caron Anne Kelly, Doug Howes (phony Salome).

"Salome's Last Dance" is an outstanding film, marking a new career bent for filmmaker Ken Russell in his adaptations of works by and about creative artists. Specialized nature of the subject matter and particularly rigorous treatment of same mark this one for limited, highly sophisticated audiences. Pic preems at Seattle Film Festival.

The biblical tale of Salome and her demand of King Herod: "Bring me the head of John the Baptist" is quite familiar from numerous films, notably the Rita Hayworth/Charles Laughton version of 1953. Carmelo Bene directed an experimental version of Oscar Wilde's play in 1972 starring Donyale Luna, while Claude d'Anna's 1986 Cannon adaptation of the Wilde play, starring Jo Champa, was singularly unsuccessful, updated to the Nazi era with futuristic overtones.

Russell pulls a fast one here by paying strict attention to the text of Wilde's play (translated by Russell's wife Vivian and enunciated precisely in a wide range of accents including Cockney and Scots) while simultaneously capturing its spirit and trashing it with outlandish visuals. Play is enacted virtually in its entirety, set in the context of a surprise premiere performance (it was banned) on Nov. 5, 1892 in a brothel for Wilde (Nickolas Grace) to watch, staged by brothelkeeper Alfred Taylor (Stratford Johns). Following the play's conclusion, picture climaxes with the arrest of Wilde and an odd twist involving Salome (the actress, actually) fate.

The key surprise here is not Russell's numerous shock effects (including a voluptuous woman or two, topless in almost every shot, full male nudity, flatulence out of Mel Brooks' "Blazing Saddles" and caricatures of the Jews as three lustful dwarves wearing Hasidic garb) but rather the often static, intense concentration on the play, almost reaching the minimalism of Andy Warhol at times. (In fact, the approach oddly resembles Warhol's homoerotic 1965 adaptation of Anthony Burgess' "A Clockwork Orange," titled "Vinyl.")

Severe structure brings out Wilde's themes and apocalyptic symbols, while Russell frequently intercuts Wilde in the audience reacting or carrying on with a young male lover. Much in the manner of his controversial 1971 adaptation of Sandy Wilson's "The Boy Friend," Russell also introduces another point-of-view by appearing himself as Kenneth, a still photographer in a Santa Claus beard who handles various stage effects while occasionally interrupting the action with a flash photo montage to preserve it for posterity. Play itself is kept within the proscenium confines, though captured via numerous camera angles.

The overwhelming homophilic nature of the production is balanced by Russell's emphasis on half-naked, busty women, including several popular from British men's magazines, such as Linzi Drew (who previously starred in his segment of "Aria"). One undeniable shock is provided by substituting a male dancer (Doug Howes) for Salome during the Dance of the Seven Veils, which makes sense in context.

Also helping to make this work is the casting of boyish young actress Imogen Millais-Scott as Salome, as well as the brothel's Cockney maid, as she cutely overacts the role in the eye-rolling manner of the ingenues of "The Boy Friend." Stratford Johns adds a good deal of panache to his dual role of Herod and the brothelkeeper, while Douglas Hodge is appealing and holds his breath well as Wilde's lover Bosie and on stage as John the Baptist.

Nickolas Grace is well-cast in the small, mainly reactive Wilde role, while Glenda Jackson, back with Russell for the first time since "The Boy Friend," gives delicious readings, handles fun in-jokes (including references to her current Lady Macbeth role) and is basically a good sport in many a tasteless scene. One of Russell's favorite players, Imogen Claire (who played Salome in his 1969 banned BBC program "Dance Of The Seven Veils" on Richard Strauss), is striking as a Nazarean woman.

Reportedly denied by the Strauss estate from using any of the appropriate music here, Russell resorts to a tongue-in-cheek pastiche of light classical themes, ranging from Delius to Debussy. Visually, the film is shot in highly saturated colors, harshly lit by Harvey Harrison (currently Nicolas Roeg's cameraman) and illuminated by outlandish costumes by Michael Arrals and Christopher Hobbs' gaudy set. They're all operating on the director's wavelength. —*Lor.*

Contagion
(AUSTRALIAN)

A Premiere Film Marketing Ltd. presentation of a Reef Films production. Executive producer, Tom Broadbridge. Produced by Leo Barretto, Ken Methold. Directed by Karl Zwicky. Screenplay, Methold; camera (Atlab color), John Stokes; editor, Roy Mason; music, Frank Strangio; sound, Tony Vaccher, John Dennison; assistant director, David Munro; associate producer, Richard Rooker. Reviewed on Sony vidcassette, N.Y., March 12, 1988. Running time: **90 MIN.**

Mark	John Doyle
Cheryl	Nicola Bartlett
Bael	Roy Barrett
Cleo	Nathy Gaffney
Helen	Pamela Hawksford
Trish	Jacqueline Brennan

The direct-to-video Aussie feature "Contagion" takes a long time to get to the point and, when it does, it turns out to be a rather pointless ghost story.

John Doyle toplines as a real estate salesman lured by two blond beauties to a fantasy-like mansion where Ray Barrett holds court. Barrett prattles on cult-wise about the "Threefold Powers" and induces Doyle to try and kill a colleague to "prove himself." Later, "voices" urge him to fetch a sexy girl for Barrett the voyeur to ogle.

Fantasy payoff, that the mansion is actually old and rundown, its inhabitants long since dead, is an anticlimax, leading to a downbeat ending.

Technically it's okay, except for a misjudged fast-forward sequence which only makes sense in terms of a video, not a feature film format. —*Lor.*

Da

A Film Dallas Pictures release of a J. Corman-Sheen/Greenblatt/Auerbach production Executive producers, William R. Greenblatt, Martin Sheen, Sam Grogg. Produced by Julie Corman. Directed by Matt Clark. Screenplay, Hugh Leonard, from his play "Da" and book "Home Before Night;" camera (color), Alar Kivilo; editor, Nancy Nuttal Beyda; music, Elmer Bernstein; associate executive producer, Jeffrey Auerbach; costumes, Carol Betera, Jill Spalding; casting, Nuala Moiselle. Reviewed at Broadway screening room, N.Y., April 12, 1988. MPAA Rating: PG. Running time: **102 MINS.**

Da	Barnard Hughes
Charlie	Martin Sheen
Drumm	William Hickey
Young Charlie	Karl Hayden
Mother	Doreen Hepburn
Boy Charlie	Hugh O'Conor
Polly	Ingrid Craigie

Also with: Joan O'Hara, Jill Doyle, Peter Hanly, Maurice O'Donoghue, Aimee Clark, Frank McDonald, Marie Conmee, Ronan Wilmot, Kathy Greenblatt, Martin Dempsey, Marcus Colley and Fly.

The filmed adaptation of Hugh Leonard's autobiographical play about an Irish-American playwright's journey of self-discovery from New York to his father's funeral in the Old Sod casts a beguiling spell, thanks to the playful richness of its language and the finely knit acting of Martin Sheen, Barnard Hughes and their supporting cast.

"Da" represents the best opportunity since "The Trip To Bountiful" for a Film Dallas production to become an arthouse success, but critical blessings will be crucial to the marketing of this low-key film that's wistful and droll in turn.

The linchpin of the affecting story is provided by Leonard's dramaturgic sleight of hand in presenting Charlie's (Sheen) dead father, Da (Hughes), and mother (Doreen Hepburn) as living, breathing temporal characters animated by the successful playwright's grief-catalyzed imagination. The scenario's supernatural presupposition is made easy to swallow by its setting in pastoral Ireland, land of leprechauns and tall tales, but Leonard never lays on the blarney. Instead, Hughes informs the character of the garrulous, obstreperous Da with a larger-than-death humanity that succeeds in making the old ma's omnipresence enjoyably believable.

With Hughes' beyond-the-grave tangibility established, Leonard guides Sheen through a series of timeshifting visitations to episodes in his past, as the adult playwright — whom we learn was adopted from a foundling hospital — plunges into an emotionally wearing crisis of self-confrontation.

There's a universal poignance in the grown man's perspective on his long-dead mother, played by Hepburn with a beautifully balanced sensitivity to the character's mood swings from martyred, lonely self-pity to compassionate caring for the men in her home. The ineffable nature of familial love, overlain with the complex complications imposed by religion, culture, history and economic class, serves as the subtle thematic hypotenuse in the household's fractious triangular relationships.

Sheen's performance is also distinguished by its subtlety, as he's swept up in the conflicting emotions that animate his wry encounters with his stubborn adolescent self (very capably rendered by Karl Hayden), his domineeirng mother and, most indelibly, the hard-headed, lyrically aphoristic gardener whose failings as an adoptive father the mature playwright must reconcile with his own hard-earned knowledge of human fallibility. When Sheen's grief-battered emotional dam finally bursts the restraint with which he's approached the climactic moment enables him to unleash Charlie's pent-up rage with expiatory abandon.

William Hickey gives a notable supporting performance as Drumm, young Charlie's churlishly Dickensian employer. Leonard, however, flushes out Hickey as more than a one-dimensional character and the strait-laced office over which Drumm reigns and his own inarticulated but deeply suffered emotional repression stand as a metaphor for the stultifying moralistic restraints of Ireland itself. The playwright's return from his self-liberating escape to America is rendered by Leonard in explicitly affirmative terms, mercifully free of lachrymose sentimentality.

First-time director Matt Clark (better known as an actor) handles the recollective flashbacks with a sensitivity to dramatic rhythm, and keeps the structural device from calling undue attention to itself. Cinematography and production design on location in Leonard's home village of Dalkey measurably enhance the dreamy mood of the piece. —*Rich.*

World Gone Wild

A Lorimar Film Entertainment release of an Apollo Pictures presentation of a Robert L. Rosen production. Produced by Rosen. Directed by Lee H. Katzin. Screenplay, Jorge Zamacona; camera (Foto-Kem color), Don Burgess; editor, Gary A. Griffen; music, Laurence Juber; production design, Donald L. Harris; set decoration, Andrew Bernard, Christian W. Russhon; costume design, Dona Granata; sound, Stephan von Hase; special effects supervisor, Cliff Wenger; associate producer, Donald C. Klune; assistant director, Jerram Swartz; second unit/aerial photography, Stephen C. Confer. Reviewed at the Plaza theater, L.A., Apr. 23, 1988. MPAA Rating: R. Running time: **94 MIN.**

Ethan	Bruce Dern
George Landon	Michael Paré
Angie	Catherine Mary Stewart
Derek Abernathy	Adam Ant
Ten Watt	Anthony James
Exline	Rick Podell
Nitro	Julius J. Carry 3d
Hank	Alan Autry

Hollywood — "World Gone Wild" feels like a facetious "The Magnificent Seven" with a hippie mentality played out on "Mad Max" territory. In other words, it's a hybrid with no identity of its own, and a boring, silly and underproduced one to boot. The road to video stores will be a short one for this time killer.

Jorge Zamacona's lame screenplay is yet another piece of post-apocalyptic hokum, about a society a hundred years hence which suffers from the lack of rainfall in the 75 years since a massive nuclear war.

Blessed by some natural deposits of water, a desert community of flower children types called Lost Wells is raided by cult creep Adam Ant, prompting laid-back magician Bruce Dern and teacher Catherine Mary Stewart to head to a metropolis to round up a gang capable of teaching Mr. Ant a lesson or two.

Excursion to the nightmarish city is so darkly photographed that it's virtually impossible to tell what's going on, and the subsequent waiting around at the remote compound for Ant and his biker minions to make their assault is padded with woefully unimaginative occurrences. When they finally do come, major action sequences are staged with less imagination than a routine Indians vs. settlers standoff in an old B Western.

Only source of amusement herein is Dern's characterization. Festooned with 1960s-era buttons and patches and adopting an ultramellow pose throughout, actor

---

Original Play

A Lester Osterman, Marilyn Strauss & Marc Howard presentation of a Hudson Guild Theater-Craig Anderson production of a play in two acts, by Hugh Leonard. Staged by Melvin Bernhardt; setting, Marjorie Kellogg; costumes, Jennifer von Mayrhauser; lighting, Arden Figerhut. Stars Barnard Hughes, Brian Murray; features Sylvia O'Brien, Richard Seer, Ralph Williams, Mia Dillon, Lois de Banzie, Lester Rawlins. General manager, Richard Horner; publicity, Howard Atlee, Becky Flora; company manager, Bruce Laffey; stage managers, Edward R. Fitzgerald, David Naughton. Opened May 1, 1978, at the Morosco Theater, N.Y.; $15 top weeknights, $16.50. weekend nights.

Charlie Now	Brian Murray
Oliver	Ralph Williams
Da	Barnard Hughes
Mother	Sylvia O'Brien
Young Charlie	Richard Seer
Drumm	Lester Rawlins
Mary Tate	Mia Dillon
Mrs. Prynne	Lois de Banzie

looks like he just stepped out of his 20-year-old features "The Wild Angels" and "Psych-Out," so it seems a shame he wasn't given a few more clever lines to toss off.

As it is, script is littered with dumb 1960s-80s references and colloquialisms. Ant, for instance, uses a tome called "The Wit And Wisdom Of Charles Manson" as his Bible at prayer meetings, and warrior hero Michael Paré, noticing the "Iacocca" autobiography in Stewart's meager book collection, remarks, "Iacocca — I understand he was a great president."

Shot in Arizona, pic bears a threadbare look from top to bottom. -- *Cart.*

The Night Before

A Kings Road Entertainment release. Produced by Martin Hornstein. Directed by Thom Eberhardt. Screenplay, Gregory Scherick, Eberhardt, from story by Scherick; camera (color), Ron Garcia; production design, Michel Levesque; production coordinator, William Chapman; assistant director, Steven Pomeroy; casting, Reuben Cannon & Associates, Monica Swann. Reviewed at Shelard Park theater, Minneapolis, April 19, 1988. MPAA Rating: PG. Running time: **85 MIN.**

Winston Connelly	Keanu Reeves
Tara Mitchell	Lori Loughlin
Rhonda	Theresa Saldana
Tito	Trinidad Silva
Lisa	Suzanne Snyder
Mom	Morgan Lofting
Dad	Gwil Richards
Brother	Chris Hebert
Capt. Mitchell	Michael Greene
Burly Waitress	Pamela Gordon
Danny Boy	David Sherrill
Rat's Nest Band	P-Funk All Stars

Minneapolis — Though it's no great shakes as film fare, "The Night Before" deserved a better fate than empty filmhouses considering what's going down these days.

Carrying two strikes against it — puny promotion and a lackluster title — teenagers' pic is down the tube for the outset. A more appropriate handle might have been "Ferris Bueller's Night Before" or "Back To The Present."

Storyline involves Keanu Reeves (currently toplining in Par's "Permanent Record") as a teen nerd, recovering from a mickey which wiped out memories of the previous night. Via flashbacks, Reeves reconstructs the series of midadventures he encountered on a date with the school beauty, a police captain's daughter who Reeves sold to a universally feared pimp.

It develops that the young suburban pair, while on the way to a school prom, inadvertently wound up on the wrong side of the tracks where they were threatened repeatedly by an assortment of creeps, misfits and weirdos. The couple survives all perils and the girl (Lori Loughlin), falls in love with Reeves whom she had dated on a lost bet.

The premise is so ridiculous and the situations so cockeyed that credibility flies out the window in the opening scenes. Though most of its laughs are of the snicker variety, pic seems as screenworthy as other unbelievable adventure comedies that have fared better at the box-office. It also treads more lightly on raw sex, gutter language and gratuitous violence than most of the current film crop.

Reeves and Loughlin are attractive youngsters who perform reasonably well as the beleaguered couple. Trinidad Silva, in a cameo role mirroring his "Hill Street Blues" gang leader, is okay. Theresa Saldana and Michael Greene also are adequate in minor parts. Thom Eberhardt's direction is uneven and is scrambled by the endless flashbacks which tend to confuse.

The word obviously is out that the film is a dud. At the weeknight unspooling caught, the reviewer and his companion were the only souls in the theater. That was two more than attended the following showing. — *Rees.*

The Unholy

A Vestron Pictures release, presented by Limelite Studios, of a Team Effort production. Executive producers/Vestron, William J. Quigley, Dan Ireland. Executive producers, Frank D. Tolin, Wanda S. Rayle, Duke Siotkas. Produced by Mathew Hayden. Directed by Camilio Vila. Screenplay, Philip Yordan, Fernando Fonseca; camera (CFI color), Henry Vargas; editor, Mark Melnick; music, Roger Bellon; production design, Fonseca; set decoration, Carterlee Cullen; art direction, Jose Durate; costume design, Beverly Safier; sound (Dolby), Henri Lopez; director of special effects, Bob Keen; associate producers, Oscar L. Costo, Michael Economou; assistant director, Douglas Bruce; second unit director, Andy Armstrong; second unit camera, Orson Ochoa; casting, Reuben Cannon & Assoc., Carol Dudley. Reviewed at Mann Chinese theater, L.A., April 22, 1988. MPAA Rating: R. Running time: **100 MIN.**

Father Michael	Ben Cross
Archbishop Mosley	Hal Holbrook
Millie	Jill Carroll
Luke	William Russ
Father Silva	Trevor Howard
Teresa	Claudia Robinson
Lt. Stern	Ned Beatty
Demon	Nicole Fortier

Hollywood — Ben Cross leads a terrific cast through this better than average horrific religious tale that doesn't fall into the hokey monster-devil rut until the very end. B.o. looks average for the genre, but title should do well in vid release.

Films like "The Unholy" are evidence that getting good actors to play in not exactly high-brow pictures can make all the difference in whether their characters are believable. With Cross are Ned Beatty as a nervous police investigator, Hal Holbrook as a righteous archbishop and Trevor Howard as an aging blind priest.

Cross is a compelling, stern and invincible Catholic priest chosen by God (by way of Holbrook's order) to rid the devil from continuing his deathly visitations on a New Orleans parish church.

The two priests assigned to the church before Cross had their throats slashed by a she-devil seductress who tempted each of them to sin while they kneeled in prayer on the high altar. It's easy to understand why once she (Nicole Fortier) walks into view basically naked with only a transparent chiffon sheath covering her lithe body.

In settings mostly backlit and too often obviously made to look eerie with the overuse of fog machines, Cross manages his difficult role of tending his mostly poor black flock, denying the existence or evidence of the devil while playing detective by trying to solve the murders along mortal lines.

Scripters Philip Yordan and Fernando Fonseca manage to integrate well a subplot involving Luke (William Russ), the operator of a satanic club and his attachment for a club waitress Millie (Jill Carroll), who as a vestal virgin also tempts the chaste Cross.

Roger Bellon's scoring more often than not adds the needed element of scariness when things drag while Cross makes his investigative rounds between the club or has those somber priestly talks with his superiors.

There is a certain amount of intensity in all the actors with the only brevity and warmth given over to the role of the church caretaker, Teresa, nicely played by Claudia Robinson.

The filmmakers resort to having the devil finally emerge a goopy, slobbering monster at the end when the suspense was built up well enough without showing him/her, an example of lazy creative thinking.

Otherwise, special effects showing bloody carnage, blown-in stained glass windows and creepy dark shots that jump from the shadows into the face of the devil are deftly handled by editor Mark Melnick and special effects director Bob Keen.

Carroll is particularly good in her secondary role as a psychotic sexpot turned goody-two-shoes. Also fine is Russ, who must be a good actor considering he has to fake being a punk satanic leader out to make a few bucks on the unsuspecting devil-worshipping scene and be convincing as Cross' chief suspect for committing the murders of two priests and worse — the church's faithful dog, Francis. — *Brit.*

A Killing Affair

A Hemdale release from Tomorrow Entertainment. Produced by Michael Rauch, Peter R. McIntosh. Executive producers, John D. Backe, Myron Hyman. Written and directed by David Saperstein, based on the novel "Monday, Tuesday, Wednesday" by Robert Houston; camera (Technicolor), Dominique Chapuis; editor, Patrick McMahon; music, John Barry; production design, John J. Moore; set decoration, Lynn Wolverton; costume design, Elisabeth Ann Seley; sound, Tom Braden; assistant director, Alex Hapsas; casting, Pat McCorkle. Reviewed at the American Film Institute, L.A. (AFI Fest), March 22, 1988. MPAA Rating: R. Running time: **100 MIN.**

With: Peter Weller (Baston Morris), Kathy Baker (Maggie Gresham), John Glover, Bill Smitrovich.

Hollywood — Lensed three years ago as "Monday, Tuesday, Wednesday," the title of the novel on which it is based, "A Killing Affair" is a subdued, listless account of the odd complicity between a backwoods woman and the man who just murdered her husband.

Feature directorial debut by David Saperstein, former documentary marker and author of the novel "Cocoon," approaches its bizarre Southern Gothic story with a straight face and a plain style and is resolutely uncommercial.

Set in the West Virginia hill country in 1943, film spends its initial reel illustrating how cruel the local labor boss, Pink Gresham, is to his workers and prospective employees. When he is killed and left in an outhouse by mysterious stranger Baston Morris (Peter Weller), one can only feel that justice has been done and that the world might now be a slightly better place.

Instead of taking off, Morris sticks around the isolated Gresham cabin and enters into a variously threatening, provocative and amorous relationship with the widow Maggie (Kathy Baker). Predictably for a piece of Southern literature, all sorts of nasty facts are buried in the pasts of both characters, and they take their own sweet time coming to the surface. Just as predictably, it all ends in an explosive burst of violence that must arrive to purge all the murky feelings and wipe the slate clean.

Because the overall atmosphere is so muted, every little misstep in Saperstein's telling assumes exaggerated importance. Several story points are so baffling they induce considerable head scratching, then dismissal of the whole thing as unconvincing. Among these are Maggie's leaving her husband's corpse in the outhouse for the longest time without doing anything about it, her willingness to sympathize with all of the killer's problems in the face of her own great loss, and her ultimate shrugging off of the murder; one never knows what she really thought of her mate, who seemed so repellent to everyone else.

These problems represent holes in Maggie's character that Kathy Baker can't fill, and Peter Weller comes off only slightly better in a part that called for a more dangerous, physically threatening presence.

Shot in the Atlanta area, pic looks okay but proves very slow going. John Barry composed the appealing, low-key score. —*Cart.*

In A Shallow Grave

A Skouras Pictures release of an American Playhouse Theatrical Film, presented in association with Lorimar Home Video, Film Trustees Ltd. and John Wolstenholme. Executive producers, Lindsay Law, Marilyn G. Haft. Produced by Kenneth Bowser, Barry Jossen. Line producer, Ron Wolotzky. Coproducer, Sandra Mosbacher. Written and directed by Bowser, based on the novel by James Purdy; camera (Foto-Kem color), Jerzy Zielinski; editor, Nicholas C. Smith; music, Jonathan Sheffer; production design, David Wasco; art direction, Sharon Seymour; set decoration, Sandy Reynolds Wasco; costume design, Molly Maginnis; sound, Russell C. Fager; makeup design, Michele Burke; associate producer, Ron Tippe; assistant director, Elliot Lewis Rosenblatt; casting, Pam Dixon. Reviewed at the American Film Institute, L.A. (AFI Fest), March 30, 1988. No MPAA Rating. Running time: **92 MIN.**

Garnet Montrose . . . . Michael Biehn
Georgina Rance . . . . Maureen Mueller
Quintas Pearch . . . . Michael Beach
Potter Daventry . . . . Patrick Dempsey
Edgar Doust . . . . Thomas Boyd Mason
Milkman . . . . Mike Pettinger
Postman . . . . Prentias Rowe

Hollywood — "In A Shallow Grave" represents an intriguing and wellmade, if not entirely successful, rendition of James Purdy's novel, the first adaptation of one of the author's works for the screen. Symbolic tale of a horribly scarred soldier's slow reentry into life, and his ultimate redemption, is anchored on a strong central performance by Michael Biehn, but is held back by miscasting and pacing problems.

World premiered at the AFI Fest, somber, intense drama will require special attention by domestic distrib Skouras to break through on the specialized theatrical circuit.

Striking prolog has the good-looking Biehn hit by an explosion at Guadalcanal in 1943. A year later, he is back on his farm in Virginia, gruesomely disfigured and alone but for a black worker who helps him out a bit. His face and one hand look as though they have been put through a meat grinder, and the young man understandably keeps his distance from most folks.

Still living down the road is his old sweetheart, played by Maureen Mueller. The two do not meet face to face, but Biehn spies on her as she goes about her dull daily business and sends her messages when he can find someone to deliver them.

Into this unfortunate situation comes a young stranger portrayed by Patrick Dempsey. Biehn hires him to do odd jobs, including dropping off notes to his beloved, and takes a strong liking to the kid until he becomes convinced Dempsey is doing more with her than giving her letters.

A melodramatic development makes possible a reconciliation of Biehn and his lady on the common ground of bereft sorrow, and writer-director Kenneth Bowser, in his feature debut, has handled the delicate material with great care and reverence. Although it remains difficult to really get inside the head of such a withdrawn, moody individual, Bowser and Biehn effectively convey his states of mind and his new existence within a virtual void imposed on his inner life by his outward appearance.

Unfortunately, Dempsey is not too convincing as the go-between who becomes something of an obsession for both correspondents, and this both reduces the story's credibility and makes one anxious for matters to be resolved. Mueller is also less than bewitching as Biehn's inamorata, so the intensity of Biehn's feeling must be partly imagined rather than directly experienced.

Even if the full potential of the tale has not been reached, the haunted, eerily quiet mood is well maintained, and pic looks good on a low budget.—*Cart.*

The Further Adventures Of Tennessee Buck

A Trans World Entertainment release and production. Executive producer, Moshe Diamant. Produced by Gideon Amir, coproducer, Peter Shepard. Directed by David Keith. Screenplay, Barry Jacobs, Stuart Jacobs, from story by Paul Mason; camera (color), Avraham Karpick; editor, Anthony Redman; production design, Erroll Kelly; stunt coordinator, Gregg Brazzel; sound, Jacob Goldstein; makeup, Camille Calvet; special effects supervisor, Adams Calvert. Reviewed at Northland theater, Southfield, Mich., April 13, 1988. MPAA Rating: R. Running time: **90 MIN.**
Buck Malone . . . . David Keith
Barbara Manchester . . . . Kathy Shower
Ken Manchester . . . . . Brant Van Hoffman
Sinaga . . . . Sillaiyoor Selvarajan
Che . . . . Tiziana Stella
Monique . . . . Patrizia Zanetti
Chief . . . . Sumith Mudanayaka
Chief's mother . . . . Pearl Vesudeva
Witch doctor . . . . Somi Ratanayaka
Tui . . . . Solomon Hapte-Selassie
Argo . . . . Steve Davis

Southfield, Mich. — You know you're in trouble when even the lettering of the title of "The Further Adventures Of Tennessee Buck" is written in a style reminiscent of the "Indiana Jones" movies.

Indeed, everything about this movie suggests the idea has been taken from somewhere else, where it was done better.

Usually, one has to go to a World Wrestling Federation exhibition to see acting of the caliber that David Keith ("An Officer And A Gentleman") and his entourage bring to this tale of a world-class hunter gone to waste in mourning over the death of his family.

Stuck in Borneo, content to drown his sorrow in alcohol when he is not dickering with the natives over alligator hides, Keith meets Ken and Barbara Manchester, wealthy urbanites out for a lark in the jungle, where Ken hopes to back up his boast back east with a real tiger skin.

Keith doesn't like the idea because of the cannibals in the jungle, and Barbara doesn't like Keith, because he's an uncouth, alcoholic womanizer.

By movie's end, of course, Ken is out of the picture and Barbara has fallen for Keith. Along the way, we're treated to a host of racial and sexist jokes from the wink, wink/-nudge, nudge school of humor.

Here comes Keith bowling over village bullies in his pursuit of the sex starved love native. There goes Keith satisfying himself with the buxom, bare-breasted jungle dancer a tribal chief has just given him as a dinner gift. Here comes Keith again, drinking himself into a stupor as two natives fight over who can undress him first.

There is even a scene in which former Playmate of the Year Kathy Shower — who must have studied under the roll-your-eyes and shout-your-lines method school of acting — is shot in the crotch with a venemous arrow, and Keith valiantly offers to suck out the poison.

With such tedious fare, it's easy to get bored with the hunt for the tiger, and even more bored with whether Keith, et al., will escape the clutches of a cannibal tribe that intercepts them.

Indeed, by the time Keith utters his final line, "Let's get the hell out of here," moviegoers will likely have already done so. —*Advo.*

The Order Of The Black Eagle

An Intl. Film Marketing release of a Polo Players Ltd. production. (International sales, Manson Intl.) Executive producers, Betty J. Stephens, John A. Stephens. Produced by Betty J. Stephens, Robert P. Eaton. Directed by Worth Keeter. Screenplay, Phil Behrens; camera (Technicolor), Irl Dixon, editor, Matthew Mallinson; music, Dee Barton; sound, David Henson; art direction, Mack Pittman; production manager, Thom McIntyre; associate producer, Mallinson. Reviewed on Celebrity Home Entertainment vidcassette, N.Y., April 13, 1988. MPAA Rating: R. Running time: **93 MIN.**
Duncan Jax . . . . Ian Hunter
Star . . . . C.K. Bibby
The Baron . . . . William Hicks
Maxie Ryder . . . . Anna Rapagna
Tiffany . . . . Jill Donnellan
Spike . . . . Flo Hyman
Sato . . . . Shan Tai Tuan
Also with: Stephan Krayk, Gene Scherer, Wolfgang Linkman, Typhoon the Baboon.

"The Order Of The Black Eagle" proves one can make a low-budget James Bond imitation in North & South Carolina, but the results aren't appealing. Shot in 1985, pic received limited theatrical runs commencing last December and now is in video release.

Designed as a sequel to helmer Worth Keeter's "Unmasking The Idol," pic toplines Ian Hunter (not very impressive compared to the late British thesp by that name — he's also not the rock performer) as Duncan Jax, a government agent imitating 007. Unfortunately, he is cryptically saddled with a baboon (literally, played by a trained animal named Typhoon) sidekick who wears a tux and makes rude gestures and noises for socalled comic relief. Everyone in the film takes the simian's presence for granted, but the audience is bound to wonder.

Jax' mission provides a very skimpy storyline: it seems a group of cartoonish baddies led by portly William Hicks is attempting to take over the world by using stolen laser technology to destroy the major communications satellites. Adolf Hitler is in deep freeze and will be revived to take over.

Pic consists of mainly okay action scenes involving lots of explosions, as well as irritating Bond imitation, especially from "Dr. No" and a Q-figure played by Shang Tai Tuan. The girls are pretty but Hunter's performance is flat. An Amazonian black actress, Flo Hyman plays Spike; film is dedicated to her, listing her as having died in 1986.

Lensing at Earl Owensby Studios and on locations in the Carolinas is quite unconvincing for the globe-hopping plot, especially when feathers are used for snow in a Geneva-set sequence. —*Lor.*

Casual Sex?

A Universal Pictures release of a Jascat production. Executive producer, Ivan Reitman. Produced by Ilona Herzberg, Sheldon Kahn. Directed by Genevieve Robert. Screenplay, Wendy Goldman, Judy Toll, based on their play, "Casual Sex;" camera (CFI color), Rolf Kestermann; music, Van Dyke Parks; sound (Dolby), David Brownlow; production design, Randy Ser; art direction, Phil Dagort; set decoration, Julie Kaye Towery; costume design, Grania Preston; assistant director, Betsy Magruder; casting, Stanzi Stokes. Reviewed at Universal Pictures screening room, L.A., April 20, 1988. MPAA Rating: R. Running time: **97 MIN.**
Stacy . . . . Lea Thompson
Melissa . . . . Victoria Jackson
Nick . . . . Stephen Shellen
Jamie . . . . Jerry Levine
Vinny . . . . Andrew Dice Clay
Ilene . . . . Mary Gross

Hollywood — In this age of AIDS, the idea of casual sex has lost its image of playfulness. Playwrights Wendy Goldman and Judy Troll try to address this in adapting their Groundlings stage production "Casual Sex" to the screen by adding doubt — ergo a slightly different title, "Casual Sex?"

Increased awareness makes this slightly more contemporary and a lot less amusing. B.o. looks limp.

Scripters Goldman and Toll have moved the setting of the stage version from the loose environs of a Club Med-type playground to a health and fitness resort, the Oasis.

Now it's Lea Thompson and Victoria Jackson huffing and puffing through exercises as the excuse to meet an athletic guy who they suppose will have equally healthy attitudes about sex in these precarious times.

This isn't the place for serious entanglements, but one-night stands aren't what they have in mind either. So, they spend a lot of time talking about the joys and disappointments of sex and how much each of them — especially Thompson as the formerly promiscuous Stacy — misses the occasional romp in the sack.

To this end, film is comprised mostly of a lot of talk about sexual frustration with not a lot of buildup to anything.

With a late '80s sensibility, their sex conversations, which often touch on intimate details of the male anatomy and how to achieve satisfaction from coupling (pic's R-rating reflects frank conversation on these subjects more than nudity or sex scenes) are peppered with the girls' finding their own identities in relationships with men outside the sex act.

Is it mature? Yes. Is it funny? No.

Humor ostensibly comes from the male guests at the Oasis who still are bent on easy conquests — with these girls as targets.

Andrew Dice Clay stands out as the Italian palooka from Jersey with the thick New Yawk accent and equally unsophisticated approach to the opposite sex. Desperate to land Thompson, he attempts reading the "Pretend You're Sensitive Handbook" obtained at the Oasis gift shop but finds ultimately that affecting an attitude too foreign from his roots makes him feel even more silly and dejected.

Stephen Shellen and Jerry Levine, objects of desire for Thompson and Jackson respectively, are typecast as nice dumb jocks and Oasis exercise instructors.

When they are incorporated into the actresses' dream sequences, they at least have something to do other than flex muscles and look studly.

Actually, all of the inventiveness on this subject comes through when the girls' imaginations take over and director Genevieve Robert makes more of these diversions than any other.

Thompson's ethereal and romantic walk with Shellen turns into a very funny sequence where she runs into a few of the men she's bedded, with embarrassing results. Jackson's hallucinations are nearly every woman's fantasy — having a number of handsome gents seek your hand in marriage as she stands at the altar about ready to marry a guy she's not wild about.

Film begins and ends with the two of them talking against a black background directly to the audience with a few asides during the picture similarly delivered as a running commentary to how they're reacting to a given situation. This works in theater, not so well here.

Theme eventually boils down to a sappy, old-fashioned concoction, never really addressing the issue at

hand other than a couple of mentions that it's high time men take precautions for birth control and against spreading disease.

For a production where women have many of the key positions, surely more realistic endings than living happily ever after in married bliss should come from exploring the options of being single and sexually active. Or at least, they could give us more things to laugh at while we figure it out. — *Brit.*

Strana la Vita
(Life Is Strange)
(ITALIAN)

A Medusa release of a Dania Film/Medusa Distribuzione/AMA Film coproduction, in association with Reteitalia. Produced by Gianni Minervini. Directed by Giuseppe Bertolucci. Screenplay, Bertolucci, Paolo Biagetti; camera (Telecolor), Renato Tafuri; editor, Nino Baragli; music, Nicola Piovani; art direction, Angelo Frigato. Reviewed at King Cinema, Rome, April 3, 1988. Running time: **94 MIN.**
Dario . . . . Diego Abantantuono
Anna . . . . Monica Guerritore
Maria . . . . Lina Sastri
Esther . . . . Amanda Sandrelli
Silvia . . . . Domiziana Giordana
   Also with: Maria Monti, Massimo Laurenzi.

Rome — "Life Is Strange" is a film that fails. Like all helmer Giuseppe Bertolucci's work, it starts out ambitiously with the aim of doing something new with style and intelligence. In this case, tale of a man who takes over a dead pal's wife and mistress never gets off the ground. After a brief round of local screens, pic will be in demand mostly by those interested in this curious director's career.

On paper, "Life" certainly has potential, beginning with a kinkily mixed cast of femmes evenly divided between cerebral (Monica Guerritore, Lina Sastri) and earthy types (Amanda Sandrelli, Domiziana Giordana). Leading the harem, or rather being led by it, is distracted psychologist Dario (Diego Abantantuono, firming his stature as a surprisingly versatile talent).

Dario has a tepid relationship with schoolmarm Sastri, a comfortable companion he's reluctant to marry. Fate steps in when he meets an old buddy who has married the girl he loved (Guerritore). Over a drink the friend drops dead, leaving Dario with a snapshot of a young girl (Sandrelli) with whom he's having an affair. Dario finds himself paying calls on both widow and girlfriend, and establishing ambiguous (i.e., not immediately sexual) relations with both. Meanwhile, he winds up in bed with a crazy patient (Giordana) and breaks up with Sastri.

Bertolucci sets all the elements in motion via intriguing settings and staging, then seems to have nowhere to go with his offbeat characters. The ending, in which Dario brings

his women together and spies on them behind a tree, is frustratingly inconclusive. Camerawork (by the excellent Renato Tafuri) and technical credits are topnotch. — *Yung.*

Afraid To Dance
(AUSTRALIAN)

An Andrena Finlay production (Intl. sales, Overview Films, London). Executive producers, Grahame Jennings, Juliet Grimm. Produced by Andrena Finlay. Directed by Denny Lawrence. Screenplay, Paul Cockburn; camera (Eastmancolor), Steve Arnold; editor, Richard Hindley; music, Chris Neal; production design, Jane Norris; sound, Bob Clayton; production manager, Sue Seeary; assistant director, Jake Atkinson; casting, Christine King. Reviewed at Hoyts Center 2, Sydney, April 10, 1988. Running time: **89 MIN.**
The Male . . . . Nique Needles
The Female . . . . Rosey Jones
Jim Pratt . . . . Grigor Taylor
Driving Woman . . . . Tina Bursill
Betty . . . . Annie Byron
Terry . . . . Mervyn Drake
Don Chapman . . . . Tom Richards
   Also with: Steve Spears (Garage Man), Bill Young (Publican), Allan Penney (Newsagent), Stuart Halcroft (Supermarket attendant), Marina Finlay (Checkout girl), Fred Welsh (Tom the mailman).

Sydney — The marketing challenge facing "Afraid To Dance," an extremely likable romantic comedy-drama, is that it's hard to describe in a nutshell what the film's about without making it sound like familiar territory.

In fact, screenwriter Paul Cockburn and director Denny Lawrence succeed in breathing new life into a story of an odd couple who meet and fall in love, and audiences are likely to be touched and amused by the film and its characters.

The first third of the pic establishes Nique Needles as a flip, devil-may-care character. He lives in a roach-infested city apartment, has no job, and is ripped off by socalled friends; so he decides to hitchhike out of the city.

He's soon picked up by an attractive and apparently available woman (an excellent cameo from Tina Bursill), and is considering robbing her when she turns the tables and robs him instead. Stranded, he comes across lonely Rosey Jones when he's trying to steal her car just as she's attempting a quick getaway after pilfering groceries from a small store.

She lets him sleep on her couch, but keeps him at arm's length, and we eventually discover her mistrust of men stems from a father who abandoned her, office coworkers who raped her, leaving her with VD, and a boyfriend who'd left her bleeding by the roadside after a motorbike accident; she's a wounded lady.

Back in the city, the couple clumsily attempt to rob a mail van, hoping for social security checks. Instead, they wind up with a sackful of letters, which they read while

holed up in a house they've broken into (during production, pic was at various times called "Letters" and "Kick Start").

Moved by some of the letters, and by a video in which a man (Grigor Taylor) addresses his as yet unborn daughter, the couple are drawn together, but a night of lovemaking is followed the next day by tragedy.

Lawrence, directing his second cinema feature after "Emoh Ruo," handles the changes in mood with skill. Early scenes consist of laid-back encounters between the antisocial Needles and a variety of characters he meets along the way, and most of the material is played for laughs, leading up to an awful dinner hosted by a religious type and his wife.

Once the couple start to read the letters, the mood changes and becomes melancholy, culminating in passionate lovemaking and its sad aftermath.

Nique Needles gives his usual cool performance, but the film is stolen by newcomer Rosey Jones as the troubled woman who nervously decides to try for love once again. Production credits are tops, and there are two excellent songs on the soundtrack, one of them the title number.

Pic won't be an easy sell, but it may perform once the word gets around. — *Strat.*

A notre regrettable epoux
(To Our Late Unlamented Husband)
(FRENCH)

A Prods. du Daunou production and release. Coproducer, TF-1 Films. Produced by Denise Petitdidier. Directed by Serge Korber. Screenplay, Korber, Christian Watton; camera (color), Jean Rabier; editor, Marie-Claire Korber; songs and music, Alain Goraguer; sound, Guy Villette; costumes, André Lavasseur. Reviewed at the Georges V cinema, Paris, March 2, 1988. Running time: **86 MIN.**
Hermione . . . . Jacqueline Maillan
Catarina . . . . Alida Valli
Romeo . . . . Jacques Dufilho
Radetsky . . . . Pierre Tornade
Alexandre . . . . Jean-Pierre Aumont
Henri . . . . Henri Marteau
Bel brothers . . . . Francis Lemaire

Paris — A lifeless black comedy involving buried gold, a restless corpse and sundry other bodies in the basement, "A notre regrettable epoux" is a flagrant waste of talent, strictly for local consumption.

Jacqueline Maillan, a popular comedienne of the Paris stage, and the classy Alida Valli play the widows of a deceased bigamist and international swindler (Jean-Pierre Aumont, quickly replaced by a dummy), who's left his booty hidden somewhere in his French manor house, where Maillan lives alone in the company of her secretly adoring majordomo (Jacques Dufilho).

At first rivals, the two women become allies as a small horde of crooked lawyers, notaries and gangsters descend on the property to get their mitts on the treasure.

There are plenty of corpses along the way, with the starring players at the center of an artistic hecatomb. Serge Korber cowrote and directed with a dead hand. —Len.

Ödipussi
(WEST GERMAN)

A Tobis Filmkunst release of a Bavaria Film and Rialto Film coproduction. Produced by Horst Wendlandt. Written and directed by Loriot. Camera (color), Xaver Schwarzenberger; editor, Dagmar Hirtz; music, Rolf Wilhelm; sound, Rainer Wiehr; art direction, Rolf Zehetbauer, Werner Achmann. Reviewed at the Savoy Kino, Hamburg, March 28, 1988. Running time: **90 MIN.**
Paul (Pussi) Winkelmann . . . . Loriot
Margarethe Tietze . . . . Evelyn Hamann
Mother Winkelmann . . . Katharina Brauren
Gerda Tietze . . . . Edda Seippel
Kurt Tietze . . . . Richard Lauffen
Also with: April de Luca (Fräulein Hagebusch), Dagmar Biener (Frau Mengelberg), Rosemarie Fendel (Frau Wetphal), Rose Renee Roth (Aunt Mechthild).

Hamburg — This much-awaited debut film by Loriot, West Germany's foremost cartoonist, is a sure-fire hit for the German-lingo market, particularly in Austria, Switzerland and southern West Germany, where Loriot's takeoff on stiff-necked Prussians will go down well. Prospects are limited elsewhere, though, where this cold, low-key satire will come across as humorless.

It's exactly this northern German compulsiveness and lack of humor that is being spoofed in this handsome film, which has a high-budget look thanks to top-drawer lensing by Xaver Schwarzenberger.

This film is a good intro to the works of Loriot, whose real name is Vicco von Bülow, himself a product of the prewar Prussian landed gentry he has been spoofing in Thurberesque cartoons and tv specials for some 35 years.

Loriot plays a nervous, aging upholstery merchant still dominated by his matronly mother, played to Margaret Dumont perfection by one-time Ufa starlet Katharina Brauren. In steps a dowdy, middle-aged clinical psychologist, played by Loriot's veteran tv partner Evelyn Hamann. Plagued by screwy parents herself, she soon falls for the nerd. Then begins a painfully awkward courtship. By the end of the film they are on a first-name basis and nearly ready for their first kiss.

Loriot and Hamann put in the "*Verklemmt*" (uptight) performances their tv audiences have come to expect, shored up by a solid supporting cast, with kudos to Rose Renee Roth as the dotty old Aunt Mechthild.

Audiences delight at the fact that Loriot's stuffed-shirt character is called "Pussi," which combined with "Oedipus" provides the film's

title. Most of the laughter comes from recognition of tv sketches and cartoon elements Loriot fans have enjoyed for years since he's offering them very little new here. For true Loriot fans — and his subtle humor is an acquired taste — that doesn't matter. They leave the theater longing for more of the same. —Gill.

I Married A Vampire

A Troma release of a Full Moon production. Produced by Vicky Prodromidov, Jay Raskin. Written and directed by Raskin. Camera (Duart color), Oren Rudavsky; editor, Raskin; music, Steve Monahan; sound, Phil Kramf, Chris O'Donnell; art direction, Prodromidov; assistant director, Maria Mann-Scherzer. Reviewed on Prism Entertainment videassette, N.Y., March 5, 1988. No MPAA Rating. Running time: **93 MIN.**
Viola . . . . Rachel Golden
Robespierre . . . . Brendan Hickey
Gluttonshire . . . . Ted Zalewski
Olivia . . . . Deborah Carroll
Portia . . . . Temple Aaron
Also with: David Dunton, Kathryn Karnes, Marcus Chase, Steve Monahan, Ken Skeer, Rit Friedman.

"I Married A Vampire" is another student-type film released by the Troma Team, or at least sent to the marketplace. Originally a 16m effort shot in Boston by Jay Raskin five years ago, pic got a blowup and token theatrical release in 1986 ahead of homevideo status.

Title is somewhat misleading, as pic is a throwback to the '60s indie feature movement, a rites-of-passage tale about young Viola (Rachel Golden) who goes to the big city (Boston) to make it on her own. Her boring and trite tribulations are delineated in detail: cheated by a real estate agent, swindled by a lawyer and ripped off by a religious cult. She's even raped (off-screen) by a businessman who then gets her a job working as a washerwoman.

Upshot is that her best friend introduces her to her brother Robespierre (deadpan Brendan Hickey) who is a 100-year-old-plus vampire. He helps her get revenge on all her tormentors and they marry, celebrating by attending a screening of Carl Th. Dreyer's "Vampyr."

Bookending cover story has Viola telling her just-arrived parents the dreary trale and then tkaing them home to meet hubbie — cue the off-camera screams.

Pic has a vanity production look with acting to match, though Viola's kleptomaniac friend Portia is a promising turn by actress Temple Aaron. —Lor.

Rikky And Pete
(AUSTRALIAN)

An MGM/UA Communications release from United Artists of a Cascade Films production. Executive producer, Bryce Menzies. Produced by Nadia Tass, David Parker. Directed by Tass. Screenplay & camera (Eastman color), Parker; editor, Ken Sallows; music, Phil Judd, Eddie Raynor; sound, Lloyd Carrick; production design, Josephine Ford;

production manager, Lynda House; assistant director, Tony Mahood; associate producer, Timothy White; casting, Tass. Reviewed at UIP screening room, Sydney, April 14, 1988. Running time: **101 MIN.**
Pete . . . . Stephen Kearney
Rikky . . . . Nina Landis
Flossie . . . . Tetchie Agbayani
Whitstead . . . . Bill Hunter
Sonny . . . . Bruno Lawrence
Ben . . . . Bruce Spence
Mrs. Menzies . . . . Dorothy Alison
Mr. Menzies . . . . Don Reid
Adam . . . . Lewis Fitz-gerald
Delahunty . . . . Peter Cummins
Police Officer . . . . Peter Hehir
George . . . . Ralph Cotterill

Sydney — In their charming first feature, "Malcolm," husband/wife team David Parker and Nadia Tass came up with an unexpected success, a charmer which won prizes, critical kudos and boxoffice success at home, and overseas played with success at fests and, more modestly, in theaters. Much was therefore expected of the team's second effort, "Rikky And Pete," which was backed by United Artists, but the result is a considerable disappointment.

The new film, obviously produced on a more lavish budget than its predecessor, has a clutch of potentially interesting characters and a promising storyline; but the characters are inadequately developed, and the plotting doesn't live up to expectations.

Pete, like Malcolm in the earlier film, is an inventor, and the cheerful opening scene, set in Melbourne, displays one such invention: a motorized device for delivering newspapers door to door. It's a good opening sight-gag. For reasons barely specified, Pete is in the middle of a vendetta with a burly police officer (Bill Hunter) who's out to get him; his sister, Rikky, meanwhile, is tired of her latest beau (Lewis Fitz-gerald) and of singing to unappreciative audiences in a bar. When the siblings quarrel with their rich, stuffy father, they decide to leave the city, and take off in their mother's magnificent Bentley for the outback.

Eventually, pursued by Hunter, they arrive in a mining town, buy a small mining lease and, thanks to another of Pete's inventions, strike it rich. They make friends among the miners, and Pete has an affair with a pretty Filipino girl (Tetchie Agbayani), but winds up in prison where the pursuing cop finally locates him.

Tass and Parker have cast two film newcomers in the leads; Stephen Kearney gives Pete plenty of raffish charm, and Nina Landis has a warm personality as Rikky. Unfortunately, their roles remain sketchy; their scenes together never explain why brother and sister maintain such strong ties, and their scenes with other characters are similarly perfunctory. Landis suffers particularly, since a romance with miner Bruno Lawrence is sug-

gested but never followed through, leaving a void in the film.

Ken Sallows' ragged editing leaves plenty of gaps, Characters disappear for stretches of the film, then reappear in unlikely situations (usually prison) without explanation. It's as if the pic was originally much longer and has been severely cut down, with resulting lack of clarity. Despite, or because of, the poor cutting, pacing is very slow; the plot and characters need a brisk, light-hearted approach, but Tass directs with a very deliberate pace, which drags the film down. Also, there are probably too many characters in the film, none of them given enough screentime to come across.

David Parker's camerawork is excellent, a lot better than his under-developed screenplay. Entire cast members acquit themselves well, but lacking, as it does, the tight structure of "Malcolm," "Rikky And Pete" looks to have a tough time ahead, even in the Australian marketplace. —Strat.

Die Seele Des Geldes
(The Soul of Money)
(WEST GERMAN-DOCU)

A Barfuss Film production and release in conjunction with West German NDR television. Direction, screenplay, camera (color, 16m) and editing by Peter Krieg. Sound, C. König, Uthea; narrators, Ullo von Peinen, Ilse Böttcher. Reviewed at Berlin Film Festival (New German Cinema section), Feb. 17, 1988. Running time: **135 MIN.**

Berlin — The psycho-historian view that the ups and downs of the stock market and the dollar are attributable directly to the American psyche's genital fixation gets a good, long airing in this plodding docu — 135 minutes of talking heads interspersed with surprisingly tedious Third World market scenes.

Pic is steeped in German leftwing ideology with an overwhelming cynicism that implies the world would be better off returning to the barter system practiced by African tribes before European colonists arrived. Docu does not measure up to the standards of some of director Peter Krieg's earlier films, most notably "Septemberweizen" (September Wheat), which linked commodity market speculation to Third World famine.

This time around unimaginative camerawork, rambling interviews and a so-what-else-is-new premise ("Money has no soul") all combine to undermine Krieg's valid contention that the world economic system is in drastic need of reform —Gill.

Man Spricht Deutsh
(WEST GERMAN)

A Neue Constantin Film release of a Vision Filmproduktion. Produced by Hans Weth.

Written and directed by Hanns Christian Muller. Screenplay, Muller, Gerhard Polt; camera (color), James Jacobs; editor, Hannes Nikel; music, Muller; sound, Haymo Heyder; art direction, Winfried Hennig; costumes, Claudia Bobsin; production managers, Harry Nap, Maurizio Pastrovich. Reviewed at Ufa Palast, Hamburg, March 20, 1988. Running time: **90 MIN.**
Erwin Loffler . . . . .Gerhard Polt
Irmgard Loffler . . . . . .Gisela Schneeberger
Dr. Eigenbrodt . . . . . . .Dieter Hildebrandt
Von Bronstedt . . . . .Werner Schneyder
Violetta . . . . .Pamela Prati
Paolo, beach attendant . . .Enzo Cannavale
Dr. Wilms . . . . .Michael Gahr
Herr Endress . . . . .Siegfried Mahler
Frau Endress . . . . .Elisabeth Welz
Heinz-Rüdiger . . . . Thomas Geier

Hamburg — The average West German gets at least five weeks vacation a year, has lots of disposable income and can't wait to get away from a cold and clammy climate at home to soak up as much sunshine as possible. That is the premise for Hanns Christian Müller's at times scathingly funny look at his fellow countrymen on vacation away from home.

The biting satire of this portrayal of uncouth Teutonic sunbathers at the polluted Italian Adriatic seaside earns embarrassed laughter from German audiences. This film's prospects in other markets are limited by the German lingo barrier and injokes few non-Germans will understand. The title itself (roughly translated: "German Spoken Here") contains an intentional misspelling of "deutsch" (German) — a subtlety, to say the least.

Beer-bellied, toothy Gerhard Polt is ideal as an obnoxious Bavarian spending his hard-earned vacation at a miserable — but sunny — Italian beach with his ditzy wife (Gisela Schneeberger) and bratty son (Thomas Geier). The beach is populated by an assortment of stereotypical German tourists, with comic character actor Dieter Hildebrandt heading a suitably loony supporting cast. Clichés and stereotypes are played to the hilt as the coast-loving Krauts go to great lengths to ensure nothing even remotely Italian intrudes on their holiday fun — certainly not Italian food or any Italians themselves.

Polt carries the film through weak spots when the vignettes of stereotypical tourist behavior become somewhat boring for lack of any real storyline. After a while, even expert camerawork by James Jacobs and the outlandish beach wardrobes by Claudia Bobsin are not enough to keep up audience interest between vignettes.

Tech credits are well above average. —*Gill.*

The Road Home
(BRITISH-POLISH)

A Film Four Intl. presentation of a Zed Ltd. production, in association with Tor Unit of Film Polski. Produced by Sophie Balhetchet, Glenn Wilhide. Directed by Jerzy Kaszubowski. Screenplay, Kaszubowski; camera (Metrocolor), Wit Dabal; editor, Marek Denys; music, Zygmunt Konieczny; production design, Andrzej Kowalczyk; assistant director, Maria Kuzemko; production manager, Wojciech Bednarek; artistic director of Tor Unit, Krzysztof Zanussi. Reviewed at Berlin Film Festival (market), Feb. 21, 1988. Running time: **103 MIN.**
Jerzy . . . . .Rafal Synowka
Edward . . . . .Boguslaw Linda
Maria . . . . .Marzena Trybala
Jozef . . . . .Jerzy Binczycki
Martha . . . . .Slawa Kwasniewska
(In Polish and German)

Berlin — Coming from a British production company, this is a most unusual film in that it's an entirely Polish-made production.

It's a symbolic, atmospheric story about the immediate postwar period, as seen through the troubled eyes of a child, and is made with enough sensitivity and style to be of specialized arthouse interest. Fest outings also are indicated.

During the war, the Germans took many thousands of blond, blue-eyed Polish children away from their families and brought them to Germany; this was the socalled "Lebensborn" program, designed to enrich Aryan bloodlines within the Reich. As the war comes to an end in 1945, young Georg realizes for the first time his "parents," a Bible-thumping preacher and his wife, aren't his real parents. Wandering off, he's found by Polish soldiers who realize he's a Pole, though he can't speak the language well.

Eventually Jerzy (that's his real name) is reunited with Maria, his mother, who hasn't seen him in five years; her husband disappeared right at the beginning of the war. Life in a small Polish town is difficult for the boy, since the other kids derisively bait him for being "German" but gradually he learns to speak Polish, and is happy with his mother and grandparents.

Grandfather is an old-fashioned romantic, dreaming about a prewar Poland that will never come back. He's contrasted with Maria's new lover, Edward, the local communist boss, who lets the family live on in a big, old farmhouse which might otherwise have been requisitioned. Jerzy mistrusts Edward, and longs for his father's return. Every night, grandfather puts out a lantern to guide his son home. The old man tries to capture and break a wild white horse (a symbol of prewar Poland), but his accidental death is the result of this attempt to recapture the past. The boy is even more isolated, and dreams of killing his new stepfather, but the film's ambiguous ending suggests Edward — and, by extension, rigid communism in Poland — is morally corrupt and will lose power eventually.

Though the film's underlying themes are handled obliquely, it works as a drama of a disoriented child coming to terms with the abrupt changes in his life. The atmos-phere of the period is handsomely evoked in scenes in the town square, in the bar or at the local cinema (where Maria remembers the old days of Garbo and Gable while watching a polemical documentary attacking Poland's prewar leaders).

Technically firstdate, with solid performances down the line, "The Road Home" obviously is specialized fare but should find audiences, especially in cities with large Polish populations. A fine music score is a plus.—*Strat.*

Vargens tid
(Age Of The Wolf)
(SWEDISH)

An SF (Svensk Filmindustri) release of an SF production with Skrivstugan, the Swedish Film Institute and Nordisk Film (Denmark). Produced by Hans Alfredson, Waldemar Bergendahl. Directed by Hans Alfredson. Screenplay, Alfredson, based on Vagn Lundbye's treatment; camera (Eastmancolor), Jörgen Persson; editor, Jan Persson; music, Stefan Nilsson; sound, Björn Gunnarsson, Stefan Ljungberg; costumes, Kicki Ilander; art direction, Stig Boquist; production management, Marianne Persson, Per Arman. Reviewed at the Palladium, Copenhagen, April 6, 1988. Running time: **87 MIN.**
Inge/Arild . . . . .Benny Haag
Isis . . . . .Melinda Kinnaman
Cassandra . . . . .Lill Lindfors
Horace . . . . .Gunnar Eyjolfsson
Quattara . . . . .Per Mattsson
Louis . . . . .Lars Carlsson
Peder Ulfstand . . . . .Stellan Skarsgard
Innkeeper . . . . .Gösta Ekman
Alchimedes . . . . .Baard Owe
The poet . . . . .Vagn Lundbye
The singer . . . . .Hanne Methling
Also with: Kenneth Milldoff, Per Burell, Klaus Pecsen, Pierre Lindstedt, Carl-Gustav Lindstedt, Georg Arlin, Stig Olin.

Copenhagen — Writer-director Hans Alfredson took artistically strong issue with the common folks' crypto-fascism in 1930s Sweden in his internationally acclaimed meller "The Simple-Minded Murderer." A high moral tone permeates his new one, "Age Of The Wolf," to such a degree that the picture comes out drained of drama.

Based on a story treatment by Danish author Vagn Lundbye, "Wolf" employs Jörgen Persson's exquisite cinematography, fine production values and beautiful Swedish forest landscapes to tell the story (a clear parallel to current racist attitudes towards Sweden's foreign labor force) of a young boy's wanderings with a band of gypsies in the 16th century, when a royal decree had just made it lawful, indeed obligatory, to shoot any gypsy on sight.

The boy is not who the gypsies take him to be. He is the twin of a lad who somehow disappeared just after his engagement to the gypsy chieftain's daughter. Hans Alfredson half-heartedly juggles the mistaken identity cum identity crises possibilities, but mostly he plods along with the main storyline that confronts the boy and the girl in poetic exchanges, while the band is fleeing the mercenary soldiers of the twins' ignoble nobleman father.

With one exception, all the gypsies are brave and good souls who speak mostly in lofty proverbs. All Swedes except the fairhaired boy are baddies. The two juvenile actors have faces of chubby vacuity. The gypsies' flight comes to an end in a gory massacre that will make "Wolf" a hard sell even to tv youth-programming slots.—*Kell.*

Betzilo shel Helem Krav
(China Ranch)
(ISRAELI)

A Gelfand Films presentation of a Maya-Sharon production. Produced by Yekhiel Yogev, Meir Amsalem, Yoel Sharon. Directed by Yoel Sharon. Screenplay, Sharon, with Michael Cahana, Meir Doron, Rachel Michaeli; camera (Technicolor, 16m), Yoav Kosh; editor, Zohar Sela; music, Erich Rudich; sound, Riccardo Levy; art direction, Ariel Glazer; costumes, Tal Amir. Reviewed at Gordon cinema, Tel Aviv, April 2, 1988. (In Israel Film Festival, N.Y.) Running time: **90 MIN.**
Gideon . . . . .Asher Tzarfati
Micha . . . . .Dan Turgeman
Dana . . . . .Anath Atzmon
Tali . . . . .Gilli Bon-Ozillio
Dr. Klein . . . . .Stanislaw Chaplin
Also with: Amnon Berenson, Babai Jihd, Oded Naier, Shlomo Ostrovsky, Yoram Boker.

Tel Aviv — War traumas have become a favorite subject with Israeli filmmakers, and Yoel Sharon's tyro effort deals with one of it smore painful aspects.

Sharon himself was wounded in 1973 and lost the use of his legs, and spent almost two years in a hospital before he could function again, walking on crutches. "China Ranch" (a.k.a. "Shellshock") deals with some of the cases he observed during that period.

Two officers share a room in a hospital. Both are unable to rid themselves of dreadful nightmares resulting from their war experiences which prevent their return to normal socity. The pic follows their treatment and, once they are released, their desperate attempts to function outside the sheltered surroundings of the treatment center.

Using fictive cases and characters that are almost identical to real persons and events associated with the Yom Kippur War, the script touches a nerve in the local audience, only too familiar with this background. The approach is almost documentary, unadorned and quite rough. Plot construction, however, suffers from certain shortcomings as the exact nature of the traumas isn't clear and therefore the mysterious circumstances behind it all that have to be unraveled are not evident.

With a restricted budget, Sharon lacked the means to supply a more detailed image of the clash between the two heroes and society around them, and stayed pretty close to the two outcasts and their personal problems.

Dan Turgeman is commendable as the younger of the two officers, but Asher Tzarfati tends to be rather theatrical as the disturbed commander who may be carrying somebody else's guilt on his shoulders. Both female roles offer Anath Atzmon and Gilli Ben-Ozillio little more than a chance to be alternately shocked and sympathetic.

Blowup of original 16m negative is acceptable, like the rest of technical credits, considering the budgetary restrictions. Film opened to a generally positive reaction and is showing at Israel Film Festival in New York. —Edna.

El Vent De L'illa
(The Island Wind)
(SPANISH)

A Septimania Films-Gormezano Films production. Produced by Manuel Valls. Directed by Gerardo Gormezano. Screenplay, Gormezano; camera (Fuji color), Xavier Gil; editor, Jose Cano; music, Alexandro Marcello, Robert Schumann; sound, Manuel Almiñana; production design, Albert Sagales. Reveiwed at Berlin Film Festival (Panorama), Feb. 20, 1988. Running time: **91 MIN.**
John Armstrong . . . . Simon Casel
Ariel Kane. . . . . Mara Truscana
Anna . . . . Ona Planas
Also with: Anthony Piley, Pitus Costa, Maxim Perez, The Incredible Orlando, Naco Nadal.

(In English and Catalan)

Berlin — This first feature, by an established Spanish cameraman, is a genuine curiosity. It boasts glorious photography, but looks as if it were made by someone who's seen "The Draughtsman's Contract" once too often.

Set and filmed on the island of Minorca, the film is about a British engineer, John Armstrong, sent there in 1738 to map the island and record its history, flora and fauna. In doing so, according to the film, Armstrong falls afoul of the island's British governor, is attracted to a local girl, is befriended by a reclusive Englishwoman (a well-known artist) and is non-fatally stabbed by one of the locals.

It's not much of a plot on which to hang a film, but matters are made worse by the stilted acting (apparently by non-pros) and English dialog that's written, and played, sans any feeling for the language.

A major plus, though, is Xavier Gil's glowing camerawork, with its pristine compositions which appear to have been inspired by the films of Peter Greenaway. What the film crucially lacks is Greenaway's sly sense of humor; Gerardo Gormezano takes it all very seriously indeed.

Dialog is spoken about half in English, half in Catalan. The music score includes a number of classical songs by Richard Schumann, which are sung in German, adding to the curious tone of the film. It will be hard to find an audience for this

one, despite the care lavished on it. —Strat.

Partition
(BRITISH-COLOR/B&W)

A Bandung production, for Channel 4. (World sales: Jane Balfour Films, London.) Executive producers, Tariq Ali, Darcus Howe. Produced by Lynn Horsford. Directed by Ken McMullen. Screenplay, McMullen, Tariq Ali, based on a short story by Saadat Hasan Manto; camera (color, b&w), Nancy Schiesari; editor, Robert Hargreaves; production design, Paul Cheetham; sound, John Anderton; assistant director, David Gilbert; production manager, Eileen Morgan. Reviewed at Berlin Film Festival (market), Feb. 21, 1988. Running time: **78 MIN.**
Roshan . . . . Roshan Seth
Everywoman . . . . Zohra Segal
Toba Tek Singh . . . . Zia Mohyeddin
Saeed . . . . Saeed Jaffrey
General John Flood . . . . John Shrapnel
Medal Lal . . . . Tariq Yunus
Also with: Tusse Silberg, Bhasker, Shaheen Khan, Dhivendra, Leonie Mellinger, Sunil Tanna.

Berlin — An adaptation of "Toba Tek Singh," a short story by Urdu writer Saadat Hasan Manto, "Partition" is a highly stylized, even theatrical, polemic about the partition of India in 1947 when the British Raj moved out.

Establishment of the separate Muslim country of Pakistan brought about much bloodshed (a million died), which is handled in an overly precious way here. Chances are limited to enterprising tv programmers.

Scenes are more or less evenly divided between those set in an insane asylum and those in civil servant offices; actors mostly play dual roles, appearing both as lunatic and bureaucrats. The asylum scenes are repetitive and emotionless, leaving the civil servant sequences to carry the drama. Here, too, the deliberately artificial style chosen by director Ken McMullen ("Zina") and writer Tariq Ali prevent much audience involvement.

A fine cast, including many actors familiar from key British films of recent years, can't bring the drama to life. There's a fascinating story to be told about the way India was divided, and the results of those decisions, but "Partition" handles the theme far too heavily. Audiences seeking to be informed about the events of 1947 are likely to come away frustrated.—Strat.

Opbrud
(Closing Time)
(DANISH)

An Obel Film release of Obel Film (Gunnar Obel) production with the Danish Film Institute (consultant producer, Claes Kastholm Hansen). Produced by Gunnar Obel. Directed by Claus Ploug. Screenplay, Morten Sabroe; camera (Eastmancolor), Henrik Heger; editor, Jörgen Kastrup; music, Elit (Nulle) Nykjär; sound, Jan Juhler; art direction, Tove Robert Rasmussen; production management, Henriette Cornet Sörensen.

Reviewed at the Danish Film Studio, Lyngby, March 7, 1988. Running time: **90 MIN.**
The Guy . . . . Kim Jansson
The Man . . . . Claus Strandberg
The Girl . . . . Pernille Sue Winton
Also with: Tina Myra Matharu, Jytte Pilloni, Henrik Jandorf, Morten Surballe, Sören Thomsen, Gunhild Larsen.

Stockholm — "Closing Time" is a low-budget but meticulously crafted black comedy suspenser, too short on humor and menace to work as much more than a neat tribute to the Harold Pinter drama tradition, with a nod to Jim Jarmusch's tableaux style. Picture may attract some attention at festivals, but its commercial future looks dim.

Director Claus Ploug has fine actors working for him, and with cinematographer Henrik Heger, he has set up striking visuals, but writer Morten Sabroe has failed to deliver a screenplay with enough dynamics to go with all its loose-ended plot suggestions. Without more finely developed interplay between characters, moods and situations, audience interest in the proceedings is bound to flag.

The promise of great adsurdist entertainment is there, however. A young bum steals a taxi cab to escape a debt to some underworld character. He soon finds himself with a passenger, a stylish businessman, who wants to be taken to some city at the other end of the country. First, a stop has to be made at the gentleman's home, where he rereads the letter that seems to have prompted his sudden urge to travel. He also packs a gun.

Picture's Danish title translates literally both as Departure and Break-Up. Off the two men are, taciturn most of the time and probably aware the other guy is not quite on the up and up. They stop at a ghost-townish motel as they proceed through a barren landscape, and the wasteland mood is stressed throughout.

A sexy young girl they pick up enlivens things a bit by introducing choice morsels of humor the picture otherwise lacks. Unfortunately, she soon decamps, and when the men both feel she has ditched them, they in turn ditch first the gentleman's gun, then the stolen cab. On the platform of a whistle-stop station they exchange wry smiles.

That's it, and it might have been enough if menace, suspense and humor had been given their due as essential elements in absurdist drama. —Kell.

La Comédie du travail
(The Work Comedy)
(FRENCH)

A La Lasa Films release of a Vidéo 13/La Sept/Films d'Ici/Ministry of Culture co-production. Produced by Michèle Cretel, Paul Saadoun. Written and directed by Luc

Moullet. Camera (Eastmancolor), Richard Copans; editor, Françoise Thevenot; sound, Patrick Fredrich; art direction, Marie-Josèphe Medan. Reviewed at 3 Luxembourg cinema, Paris, March 12, 1988. Running time: **85 MIN.**
With: Roland Blanche, Sabine Haudepin, Henri Déus, Antonietta Pizzorno, Jean Abeille, Michel Delahaye, Paulette Dubost, Dominique Zardi, Noel Simsolo.

Paris — Luc Moullet, a onetime Cahiers du Cinéma scribe turned filmmaker, is an advocate of minimalist cinema and the idea that less is more. Less can be less too, especially when the shoestrings of budget apply to the script as well.

"La Comédie du travail" is a comedy about unemployment. Moullet zeroes in on three individuals whose paths cross momentously: a bank clerk who loses his job and is ashamed to admit it; a professional layabout who prefers climbing mountains, and a zealous employment agency job counselor in love with the layabout and determined to find him decent labor. *

For lack of funds, Moullet has a good reserve of irony and humor. Unfortunately, the tale is scrappy and the direction lacks imagination. The three leads, Roland Blanche, Henri Déus and Sabine Haudepin, are good, but they would have been better with a more substantial screenplay and production. Nothing comes of nothing. —Len.

Anantram
(Monolog)
(INDIAN)

A General Pictures production. Produced by K. Ravindranathan Nair. Written and directed by Adoor Gopalakrishnan. Camera (Eastmancolor), Ravi Varma; editor, M. Mani; music, M.B. Srinivasan; art direction, N. Sivan. Reviewed at the Indian Film Festival, Trivandrum, Jan. 15, 1988. Running time: **125 MIN.**
Ajayan . . . . Ashokan
Ajayan as a boy . . . . Sudheesh
Ajayan as a child . . . . Sooraj
Balu . . . . Mammootty
Suma/Nalini . . . . Shobana
Doctor-uncle . . . . N.B. Thampi
Also with: B.K. Nair (compounder), Vempayam (cook), Bahadur (driver).
(In Malayam)

Trivandrum — "Monolog" (also translated "And Then..." to underline this is a film about storytelling) is a complexly structured, sensitively lensed work by Kerala helmer Adoor Gopalakrishan ("Rat-Trap," "Face To Face").

A first-person narrator tells the story of his life from birth to college; then he retells the same life, using a different set of facts and incidents. Luckily, interest of film is not only in its form, but in the character of the young hero, a genius unable to realize his potential. Of sure fest interest, "Monolog" is lensed with grace and aplomb, enjoyable enough for playoff in specialized venues.

It is Ajayan Kumar as a young man (played with more wide-eyed innocence than force by Ashokan) who offers the twin accounts of his life. In the first, he starts life as an abandoned child in a hospital. A kindly doctor (N.B. Thampi) brings him up like his own son. Sharp-witted, a brilliant student and natural sportsman, Ajayan is cold-shouldered by schoolmates because of his exceptional talents. As a youth, his outsider status leads him to neurotic dejection, while forbidden feelings for his foster-brother's young bride Suma (Shobana) torment him with guilt.

In the second story, Ajayan chooses other highpoints from his experiences to weave a coherent life's tale, deepening our first glimpse of him. The dominating figure this round is Nalini (again played by the shy, magnetic Shobana), a lookalike for the lusted-after sister-in-law, but maybe just a figment of his over-excited imagination. As Ajayan increasingly confuses the real with memories and fantasies, he reaches the brink of madness.

Of note are the two child actors (Sudheesh and Sooraj) and the sinister scenes of growing up in an empty house with a trio of scary old servants. —*Yung.*

235,000,000
(SOVIET-DOCU-B&W)

A Riga Studios production (Latvia). Directed by Uldis Brauns. Camera (Widescreen, b&w), Rihards Piks, Ralfs Krumins. (Other credits unavailable.) Reviewed at Berlin Film Festival (Panorama), Feb. 21, 1988. Running time: **100 MIN.**

Berlin — Reviewed for the record, this 1967 Latvian docu by director Uldis Brauns is a bewitching panorama of everyday life in the USSR, lensed for the 50th anni of the revolution.

Nothing political, nothing heavy, "235,000,000" (population of the country at that time) simply presents people and places in a tender, Candid Camera-like style, using a sweeping widescreen image. It is a prime example of the poetic documentary style popular in the '60s. Today its charm hasn't faded, and it looks surprisingly undated.

Part of pic's secret is the way it cleverly contrasts the multiple faces and facets of the Soviet Union, bringing out an astonishing diversity of national cultures. Asians, Central Asians, Eskimos, Georgians and northerners from the Baltic appear alongside the more familiar Russian images of Kremlin guards and bigwigs.

There's a wedding, a new baby, two toddlers taking their first steps on the beach and kids swimming with papa in a hole cut in the ice. From a homey scene film jumps to Uzbek riders galloping across the steppes. Skillfully juxtaposing their sequences, the filmmakers play up the vastness and variety of a truly giant land.

There is no narrator and not a single voice heard in the film — images tell their own story with wit and humor. All is underscored by an easy-listening '60s jazz track.
— *Yung.*

Aetherrausch
(WEST GERMAN)

A coproduction of Senso Film and Bavarian Broadcasting and Hessian Broadcasting. Produced by Georg Killan. Written, directed and edited by Klaus Gengnagel. Camera (video, color), Mike Bartlett; music, Kristian Schultze; sound, Stefan Meisel. Reviewed at Berlin Film Festival (market), Feb. 19, 1988. Running time: **93 MIN.**
Wolfgang Senne . . . . Klaus Grünberg
Sussane/Vera . . . . Sabine Dornblut
Franz Wismuth . . . . Rudolf Schündler

Berlin — West German director Klaus Gengnagel says he wanted to make a non-rational "video thriller" that cannot be comprehended in traditional terms. He got what he wanted.

His gimmick of taping entire pic on ¾-inch videotape and bumping up to 35m succeeds in creating the all-pervading television effect he wants. The monotone delivery of disjointed lines by his cast of three does more than show that tv has a numbing effect. It also numbs the audience.

The plot, to the extent there is one, involves a consumer electronics r&d man (Klaus Grünberg) who is developing a thought-controlled video system that apparently can also project thoughts. He is haunted by his wife's murder. A second love affair (or possibly a revival of the first) appears destined for the replay mode.

Unclear through it all is whether Gengnagel is putting down the tv medium or has, himself, become obsessed with it. Video-to-film technique is effective, especially using the British German PAL system with 625 scan lines and ever-perfect color. The viewer is often only vaguely aware of the difference, but the medium still requires a message.
—*Gill.*

Bony A Klid
(Big Money)
(CZECH)

A Barrandov Film Studios production. Directed by Vit Olmer. Screenplay, Radek John, Olmer; camera (color), Antonin Kopriva; music, Ondrei Soukup; art direction, Ludvik Široký. Reviewed at Berlin Film Festival (Panorama), Feb. 16, 1988. Running time: **86 MIN.**
Martin . . . . Jan Potměšil
Eva . . . . Veronika Jeníková
Biny . . . . Roman Skamene
The banker . . . . Miloslav Kopečný
Harry . . . . Tomáš Hanák

Berlin — "Big Money" is a hip Czech film with a lot of surprises: a completely open treatment of the local underworld; a clear depiction of police corruption and the ordinariness of the black market; even some explicit sex scenes. Definitely (and somewhat self-consciously) a film for the era of *glasnost,* which appears to be overtaking one Eastern European country after another, film should attract fest interest on that basis alone.

Judged by filmic criteria, director Vit Olmer, with eight features under his belt, has mastered the art of storytelling, but can't manage to keep out some jarringly naive moments that might hinder wider playoff abroad. Finally, film's reliance on its 2-tune rock score to snazz up scenes becomes overdone before it's half over. By the end, the continually repeated ditties occasion hoots of laughter from the audience.

Film chooses an intriguing candid camera-type opening on a busy Prague street, where a line of hustlers are offering to change money for passersby. When 20-year-old country boy Martin (Jan Potměšil) turns up as an eager customer we're in the heart of "Big Money." His pals have sent him to buy $1,000 worth of dollars to purchase some Western goods. Unluckily, he gets counterfeit greenbacks, and by the time he makes the discovery the hustler has vanished.

Incredibly, he goes to the police with his complaint, but is discouraged by their lack of interest. Setting about cornering the dealers by himself, he is threatened, beaten up, and meets Eva (Veronika Jeníková). Finally the beleaguered dealers offer to take him into the business. He moves into a spacious apartment with Eva and lives it up as a mini-gangster: discos, fast cars, fun with ringleader Harry (Tomáš Hanák). Though Prague highlife looks a little limited, there are some surprisingly explicit sex and orgy scenes (background shows porn videos on tv).

Action is fast-paced with many a bow to Western thrillers, particularly in the gang's final tangle with a rival band and a police chase. Retribution — prison for all — brings out a trite moral of crime doesn't pay.

In its best moments, film captures a breathless atmosphere through a nervous, handheld camera on the move; one just wishes the ad nauseum score could have been left off. Young thesps are more passable than exciting as performers. —*Yung.*

Jarrapellejos
(SPANISH)

A Producciones Cinematograficas Penelope production. Executive producers, José Maria Calleja, Juan Lopez Galiardo. Produced by José G. Blanco Sola, José Joaquin Aguirre. Directed by Antonio Gimenez-Rico. Screenplay, Gimenez-Rico, Manuel Gutierrez Aragon, from the novel by Felipe Trigo; camera (Eastmáncolor), José Luis Alcaine; editor, Miguel Gonzalez Sinde; music, Carmelo A. Bernaola; sound, Miguel Angel Polo; production design, Rafael Palmero; costumes, Javier Artiñano; assistant director, Kuki Lopez Rodero; production manager, Martin Cabañas. Reviewed at Berlin Film Festival (competing), Feb. 21, 1988. Running time: **108 MIN.**
Pedro Jarrapellejos . . . . Antonio Ferrandis
Saturnino . . . . Juan Diego
Ernesta . . . . Lydia Bosch
Isabel . . . . Aitana Sanchez-Gijon
Purita . . . . Amparo Larrañaga
Juan Cidoncha . . . . Joaquin Hinojosa
Gato . . . . Miguel A. Rellan
Also with: Carlos Tristancho (Mariano), Florinda Chico (Maria del Carmen), José Coronado (Octavio), Carlos Lucena (Don Roque), José Maria Cafarell (Richter), Gabriel Llopart (Dr. Barriga), Concha Leza (Asuncion), Juan Jesus Valverde (Gregorio).

Berlin — Spain's film which competed at the Berlin fest is a handsomely produced period piece set in 1912 in a small town where a local businessman, Jarrapellejos, is all-powerful.

Title is a mouthful in any language, and the film takes too long to get to its dramatic, if familiar climax.

The protagonist is an inveterate womanizer who has influence over the local police and judiciary. He's had his way with most of the women in the area, except for the lonely Isabel, daughter of peasants. When Isabel and her mother are raped and murdered, the local schoolteacher, who has leftist leanings, is accused of the crime by the town's inept judge.

Jarrapellejos knows the killing was done by his own nephew, and the nephew of another aristocrat, and he manages to manipulate the court — and even order the murders of two witnesses — to keep the identities of the killers a secret.

In fact, most of the plot takes place in the last third of the film, with the first two-thirds taken up with establishing the various characters in the town, including Ernesta's wedding to an old man she doesn't love (she keeps seeing her young lover, though) and Purita's revelation that she was made pregnant by a shepherd.

Attractive production dress is an asset, with fine camerawork, settings and costumes. The narrative tends to drag too slowly in the first section of the film, and more could have been made of the aftermath of the murder.

The rape and murder scene itself is quite strongly presented, and packs a punch. Thesping is fine, with Antonio Ferrandis stealing the limelight as the wily old town boss. On the whole, pic is too familiar and bland to make much international impact. — *Strat.*

Thinkin' Big

An AFC Pictures production. (Intl. sales, Arista Films.) Produced by Jim C. Harris. Directed by S.F. Brownrigg. Screenplay, Robert Jospeh Sterling, Loretta Yeargin; camera (color) & editor, Brian H. Hooper; music, John Boy Cooke; sound, Stacy Brownrigg; assistant director, Joe Sterling; production manager, Carl Simmons. Reviewed on Prism Entertainment vidcassette, N.Y., April 7, 1988. MPAA Rating: R. Running time: **94 MIN.**

Pud	Bruce Anderson
Morgan	Nancy Buechler
Liz	Darla Ralston
The Chief	Kenny Sargent
Wong	Randy Jandt
Barry	Derek Hunter
Dee-Dee	Regina Mikel
Wendy	Claudia Church
Georgia	April Burrage

"Thinkin' Big" is a B movie that poses the pointless question: can a full-length feature be constructed from jokes about penis size? Answer is: yes, but a very bad time-killer will result.

Shot in Texas at the end of 1985, pic received a brief release in 1986 in California ahead of its current homevideo slotting. Helmer S.F. Brownrigg is known for his horror and exploitation pics: "Don't Look In The Basement," "Keep My Grave Open" and "Poor White Trash, Part II."

Skimpy plotline has four guys and five gals heading south for the Texas coast in a parody of spring break frenzy. They arrive (the South Padre Island and Port Isabelle locations look cold and foreboding), get together and party — cue the wet t-shirt contest.

Pic is mainly an excuse for innumerable shots of topless girls, of which Regina Mikel and April Burrage take honors as the best chests. However, an endless stream of stupid double entendres revolves around fat hero Pud (Bruce Anderson) believing his Asian-American pal Wong (Randy Jandt) has a 3-ft.-long sex organ. Though pic is R-rated, on-screen displays of a vibrator and penis expander are typical of its poor-taste approach.

Heroine Darla Ralston is Texas' answer to Annette Funicello, while hero Kenny Sargent shows the most acting promise here. Tech credits are acceptable on the level of regional filmmaking. — *Lor.*

Donna Donna!
(DUTCH)

A Meteor Film release of a Movies Film production. Produced by Chris Brouwer, Haig Balian. Executive producer, Anna Brouwer. Directed by Hans and Luc van Beek. Screenplay, Luc van Beek; camera (Fuji color, Cineco prints), Peter de Bont; editor, Wim Louwrier; music, Bert Hermelink; sound, Arno Hagers; art direction, Harry Ammerlaan; production manager, Kees Groenewegen. Reviewed at Bellevue theater, Amsterdam, Dec. 21, 1987. Running time: **85 MIN.**

Felix	René van 't Hof
Esther	Simone Walraven
Coby	Joke Tjalsma

Also with: Glenn Durfort, Guusje van Tilborgh, Bridget George, Heleen van Meurs, Marlies van Alemaer.

Amsterdam — A screwball comedy with a good premise, a few surprises and some good belly-laughs, "Donna Donna!" doesn't quite come off, essentially due to the inexperience of some key people.

Felix, a brilliant student, pride of his school, quite popular with his mates, has problems with girls — they're unobtainable. He's forever falling in love and out of it when a pretty new face shows up. To stop tongues wagging, he arranges a fake engagement with a model he's never met, then falls for the new girl next door, who's sexy (and engaged), but suddenly jilted and available. Felix then finally meets his fake fiancée and gets to know her, in the biblical sense. There are consequences.

Film was written and directed by twin brothers, who have only some uncredited minor work in tv. Male lead was given to a mime artist with only one small film role to his credit. Main actress previously did some radio work, but never acted. The composer too is a tyro. Generally, the film suffers from slack handling of story structure, pacing and rhythm.

Still, it opts for a style and sticks to it: a deadpan account of preposterous events, which gives the oddball characters a semblance of plausibility and their fanciful actions a topsy-turvy logic. Though not always well served by the directors, the actors get by well enough, especially the leads.

Production values from a trained crew ostensibly allowed much license by the debutant helmers help bolter this pleasant, featherweight entertainment, best marked for tv exposure. — *Wall.*

Isten Veletek, Barataim
(Farewell To You)
(HUNGARIAN)

A Hunnia Studio, Mafilm-Magyar TV coproduction. Directed by Sandor Simo. Screenplay, Simo, Zsuzsa Biro, from the novel "The Story Of A Barrow" by Jenö Jozsi Tersanszky; camera (Eastmancolor), Tamas Andor; editor, Maria Rigo; music, Zdenko Tamassy; sound, Karoly Peller. Reviewed at Hungarian Film Week, Budapest, Feb. 8, 1988. Running time: **100 MIN.**

With: Cecilia Esztergalyos, Laszlo Sinko, Kornel Gelley, Sandor Zsoter, Vera Papp, Sandor Gaspar, Peter Müller, György Kari.

Budapest — "Farewell To You" will remind aficionados of Hungarian cinema of Istvan Szabo's 1973 pic "25 Fireman's Street," since it's also about the inhabitants of a rambling old apartment house in Budapest. However, Sandor Simo's new film lacks the poetry and magic of Szabo's.

Story takes place on three September days, in 1938, 1942 and 1944. Before the war, the characters in the building go about their business without really thinking that it could all change so quickly. They include a famous actress (Cecilia Esztergalyos) who has a married lover; a student with a widowed mother, pregnant by her lover; the student's secret mistress (Vera Papp of "Angi Vera" fame); a Jewish doctor; a music teacher impressed by the Nazis after he attended a Nuremberg rally; and a nouveau-riche upholsterer who's so besotted with the actress that he marries her sappy maid.

Pre-war there are petty affairs, jealous husbands, young lovers, cafe talk about politics and nervousness about the future (it's the time of the Munich crisis). Come 1942 and bombing raids have begun, even horses wear gas masks and political lines are much more sharply drawn. The third act (1944), involves betrayal and blackmail, suicide and terror as rival fascist groups emerge and the Jewish doctor is cruelly threatened by his former patients and friends. Pic ends with an air raid that destroys the building and its inhabitants (and, by implication, the entire pre-war way of life).

Simo handles all this without much flair. Pic looks fine, with top camerawork and production design. Acting is good down the line; breaking-up of the three episodes with old cinema advertising slides is a neat device. It's all familiar stuff, however, and the treatment is decidedly flat, lacking the tension brought to Simo's well-regarded 1977 film, "My Father's Happy Years." Occasionally there are good moments — the actress "performing" in a scarlet dress in the air raid shelter; the grim scene of Jew-baiting — but overall "Farewell To You" is decidedly bland.—*Strat.*

L'Age de monsieur est avancé
(Monsieur Is Getting On In Years
(FRENCH-COLOR/B&W)

A Neuf de Coeur release of a Vamp Prods./FR3/Sept coproduction. Produced by Jean-Daniel Verhaege. Written and directed by Pierre Etaix, based on his play. Camera (color, b&w), Edmond Sechan; editor, Jean-Baptiste de Battista, René Garat; music, Verdi, Jean Wiener, Doucet; sound, Alain Duprat, Hubert Juzanx, Jean-Louis Garnier; art direction, André-Roland Palis. Reviewed at the Reflet Medicis Logos theater, Paris, Jan. 5, 1988. Running time: **91 MIN.**

The author	Pierre Etaix
Suzanne/Jacqueline	Nicole Calfan
Stage manager/Désiré	Jean Carmet

Paris — Pierre Etaix, the gifted funnyman-filmmaker whose last feature dates back to 1970 ("Pays de Cocagne"), makes a disappointingly minor comeback with this film of his own recent Paris legit success, "L'Age de monsieur est avancé."

Coproduced by pubcaster FR-3 and culture net La Sept, it had a brief theatrical run here but essentially is tv entertainment.

Etaix' piece is a frothy, Pirandellian conceit and an extended homage to the witty Boulevard theater of Sacha Guitry. Smart, brittle repartee and theatricalist sleight-of-hand, amplified by the movie camera, are the essential elements in this plotless give-and-take between Guitryesque author (Etaix) and his problematic mistress (Nicole Calfan).

As actor and director, Etaix is versatile and charming, but at 90 minutes this is a long haul for such fragile material, which falls back on flash reaction shots of a theater audience to enliven the repetitive situations. Jean Carmet acts the bemused stage manager of Etaix' play-within-a-play-and-film fantasies and quietly steals the show. — *Len.*

Einstweilen Wird es Mittag
(Meantime, It's Already Noon)
(AUSTRIAN-WEST GERMAN)

A MR-TV, ORF, ZDF production. Directed by Karin Brandauer. Screenplay, Brandauer, Heide Kouba, based on the research "The Unemployed Of Marienthal" by Marie Jahoda, Paul F. Lazarsfeld, Hans Zeisel; camera (color), Helmut Pirnat, Heinz Menzik; editor, Maria Homolka, Monica Parisini; music, Christian Brandauer; sound, Walter Amann, Peter Paschinger; art direction, Peter Manhard; costumes, Uli Fessler. Reviewed at Berlin Film Festival, Intl. Forum of Young Cinema, Feb. 21, 1988. Running time: **95 MIN.**

Researchers: Franziska Walser, Nicolas Brieger, Stefan Suske, Johannes Nikolussi.

Unemployed: Herman Schmid, August Schmolzer, Georg Staudacher, Bernd Spitzer, Peter Moucka, Kristina Walter, Karina Thayenthal, Andrea Kiesling, Inge Maux.

Berlin — Based on an Austrian sociological research published in the late '30s, Karin Brandauer's new effort is closer to documentary, even if it does play as fiction with actors reading a written script.

Taking place in 1933, the film deals with a whole town, Weiszenberg, thrown into an acute state of crisis when the thriving textile plant which supplied the livelihood for most of the inhabitants is closed down during the economic recess of that period. The subject is timely since unemployment once again is a top issue in Austria, as the steel industry has drastically reduced its activities in recent years.

Brandauer adopts the point-of-view of the researchers, three Viennese students coming from well-to-do families, and their professor, but adds her own comments about the researchers themselves, who often act like peeping toms prying into private lives, and sympathizing with the subject of their study but insisting that ethically, they should do nothing more than observe.

Keeping the action low-key and lifelike, with performances sometimes as stilted as authentic testimonies, Brandauer makes some obvious points, e.g., unemployment does not affect just those who are out of work but the entire economy of the place, and some relevant ones, e.g., indicating turmoil of this kind is the best breeding ground for racism and extremist politics.

Since the script criticizes invasion of privacy, it also seems loath to define too clearly its characters, who lack the strength required for audience identification. The tempo is slow, with warning of the historical lesson made perfectly clear in an epilog. The picture, at times a bit too didactic, probably will have an easier time on tv than in theaters.
— *Edna.*

Folie Ordinaire d'une Fille de Cham
(The Ordinary Madness Of A Daughter Of Ham) (FRENCH)

An INA, RFO, CNRS Audiovisuel production. Directed by Jean Rouch. Based on a play by Julius Amédé Laou, produced on stage by Daniel Mesguish; camera (color, 16m), Rouch, Philippe Costantini; editor, Françoise Beloux; sound, Jean-Claude Brisson. Reviewed at the, Berlin Film Festival Intl. Forum of Young Cinema, Feb. 22, 1988. Running time: **75 MIN.**
With: Jenny Alpha-Villard, Sylvie Laporte, Catherine Rougelin.

Berlin — This is an almost straightforward version of a play by Julius Amédé Laou, a student of filmmaker Jean Rouch, as produced on the Paris stage by actor-director Daniel Mesguish.

The play, a delirious dialog between a black woman from Martinique who has spent the last 50 years of her life in a mental institution, and a young nurse who comes from the same island, displays the unconscious conflicts, frustrations, fears and guilts carried by the two women because of their sex, the color of their skin, their religious upbringing and their nationality.

The title is a Biblical reference, Ham being Noah's son, who uncovered his father's nakedness, was cursed and all his descendants — black people — are supposed to atone for this sin.

Rouch left the Mesguish staging intact, using two cameras, one operated by himself the other by his assistant, both following the actresses rather than imposing their presence on them, and using very long takes in order to disturb them as seldom as possible. The only addition is an introduction, showing a psychiatrist called Charcot (the name of a famous pre-Freudian doctor) who invites some of his colleagues to watch the strange case of the two women, thereby making them part of audience. The same persons appear at the end. (The entire picture was shot in two days.)

Jenny Alpha-Villard and Sylvie Laporte, who carry the entire show on their shoulders, obviously are intimate with the enormous amount of text they have to deliver in a relatively brief span of time. They manage their parts remarkably well, and a certain feeling of theatricality which might bother the viewer in the early stages disappears gradually as the viewer is drawn into the unlikely situation.

The strong performances which keep tension high and the remarkable flexibility of both cameras and sound help to connect with a screen audience.

Still, this essentially is a film played, very static and relying mostly on the spoken word, but it might appeal to fans of the genre Rouch defines as "cinetheater," on one condtion: that they speak French perfectly. It is not the kind of film one would like to see either dubbed (if that is at all possible) or subtitled. —*Edna.*

Dogura Magura
(Abracadabra) (JAPANESE)

A Katsujindo Cinema, Toshikankyo Kaihatsu production. Produced by Shuji Shibata, Kazuo Shimizu. Directed by Toshio Matsumoto. Screenplay, Matsumoto, Atsuhi Yamatoya, based on novel by Yomeno Kyusaku; camera (color), Tatsuo Suzuki; editor, Hiroshi Yoshida; music, Haruna Miyake; sound, Shimpei Kikuchi; art direction, Takeo Kimura, Iwao Saito. Reviewed at Berlin Film Festival (Intl. Forum of Young Cinema), Feb. 20, 1988. Running time: **109 MIN.**
Ichiro Kure . . . . Yoji Matsuda
Prof. Masaki. . . . . Shijaku Katsura
Prof. Wakabayashi . . . . Hideo Murota
Also with: Eri Misawa, Kyoko Enami, Kaori Kobayashi, Jun Haichi, Reo Morimoto, Daisuke Ijima, Fumio Watanabe.

Berlin — This is a psychiatric puzzle, in which every solution is possible, every interpretation is valid, reality and fantasy are inseparable and even the identity of the fantasy is unclear most of the time.

Ichiro Kure is a young man who arises from a fetal nightmare into apparent amnesia. Two psychiatrists in the university hospital, one of them possibly dead for a month already, have been treating the young man, telling him he has murdered his mother and later his bride, and that his madness is hereditary, as he is the descendant of a mad painter who lived 1,100 years ago. In the room next to the patient, a girl constantly sighs and moans but when she sees Kure she immediately identifies him as her brother-in-law, but he was supposed to have killed her too.

It seems for a while this might be the sort of psychodrama whose unraveling at the end will offer the key to the riddle, but it soon turns out the object is much more ambitious: tangible proof is produced for one theory only to be denied. Nothing said or shown can be taken at face value, and the viewer will come out of this advant-garde walk through the unconscious even more mystified than he walked in.

The film offers plenty of intriguing visuals lending themselves to Freudian interpretations. It constantly jumps backward and forward in time, indulging here in gruesome images. Matsumoto keeps a stream of unsolved mysterious coming at top speed, and uses the two psychiatrists, one of them a jeering hyena, the other a mournful scavenger, as the two masters of ceremonies.

Acting is solid and Yoji Matsuda in the lead role looks desperate enough as a man who refuses to believe the monstrous takes he is told about himself and the supposedly logical explanations for his conduct.

This curiosity could find its niche on the art circuit. — *Edna.*

Judgment In Berlin

A New Line Cinema release of a Bibo TV/January Enterprises/Sheen-Greenblatt production. Produced by Joshua Sinclair, Ingrid Windisch. Executive producers, Martin Sheen, William R. Greenblatt, Jeffery Auerbach. Directed by Leo Penn. Screenplay, Sinclair, Penn, based on a book by Herbert J. Stern; camera (Eastmancolor), Gabor Pogany; editor, Teddy Darvas; music, Peter Goldfoot; art direction, Jan Schlubach, Peter Alteneder; costumes, Ingrid Zore; sound, Karl Laabs; production coordinator, Gabriele Scheiger; casting, Horst D. Scheel, Joyce Gallie. Reviewed at the Mark Goodson theater, N.Y., April 20, 1988. MPAA Rating: PG. Running time: **92 MIN.**
Herbert J. Stern . . . . Martin Sheen
Bernard Hellring . . . . Sam Wanamaker
Judah Best . . . . Max Gail
Uri Andreyev . . . . Jürgen Heinrich
Helmut Thiele . . . . Heinz Hönig
Bruno Ristau . . . . Harris Yulin
Günther X . . . . Sean Penn
Edwin Palmer . . . . Carl Lumbly
Hans Schuster . . . . . . Max Volkert Martens
Marsha Stern . . . . Cristine Rose
Kim Becker . . . . Marie-Louise Sinclair
Alan Sherman . . . . Joshua Sinclair
Sigrid Radke . . . . Jutta Speidel

The desperation that drives people in the pursuit of freedom from oppression is a recurring theme in the current political impasse separating the two Germanys. The everyday political realities of the division are being confronted constantly. The new Martin Sheen film, "Judgment In Berlin," succeeds in defining that experience with one atypical defection that occurred in West Berlin in the late 1970s.

An East German couple traveling with a child hijacked a Polish airliner headed for East Berlin, forcing the pilot to land at a West Berlin airport that serves as a U.S. military installation.

The big question is who has legal jurisdiction to prosecute the hijackers. The West German government won't touch it, and U.S. officials are reluctant to hand the hijackers over to the Soviet-influenced East Germans and certain harsh penalties. It is decided that since they landed in U.S.-occupied territory, a trial conducted by a U.S. judge is the humane solution.

Though the film's action essentially evolves around a courtroom drama and raises questions of American constitutional law, we also get glimpses of the personal lives of the principal characters, including the trial judge (Sheen), and the couple accused in the hijacking, effectively played by Heinz Hönig and Jutta Speidel.

Dramatically and cinematically no new ground is covered here, but the ironies of the political situation pack a heavy emotional wallop. There is good work by all concerned, including Leo Penn's deft, understated direction and the serviceable screenplay credited to Penn and producer Joshua Sinclair, and adapted from an actual account written by the story's real trial judge Herbert J. Stern.

Sean Penn (Leo's son) has a plum

role as an airline passenger who decided to defect when the opportunity presented itself. His trial testimony provides the film's dramatic center.

This is a quality production made on a tight budget but with obvious care and commitment. Avoiding the didacticism that such an explosive political situation can sometimes evoke, the filmmakers wisely opted to dramatize the human scale at the heart of the matter.—*Owl.*

Critters 2: The Main Course

A New Line Cinema release of a New Line/Sho Films production. Produced by Barry Opper. Executive producer, Robert Shaye. Directed by Mick Garris. Screenplay, D.T. Twohy, Mick Garris; camera (Deluxe color), Russell Carpenter; editor, Charles Bornstein; music, Nicholas Pike; production designer, Philip Dean Foreman; set decorator, Donna Stamps Scherer; costumes, Lesley Lynn Nicholson; sound (Ultra-Stereo), Don Summer; Critters created by Chiodo Bros. Prods.; special effects & pyrotechnics, Marty Bresin; stunt coordinator, Dan Bradley; assistant director, Jerry Ketcham; associate producer, Daryl Kass; casting, Robin Lippin. Reviewed at 20th Century Fox Zanuck Theater, L.A., April 27, 1988. MPAA Rating: PG-13. Running time: **87 MIN.**

Brad Brown	Scott Grimes
Megan Morgan	Liane Curtis
Charlie McFadden	Don Opper
Harv	Barry Corbin
Wesley	Tom Hodges
Mr. Morgan	Sam Anderson
Cindy Morgan	Lindsay Parker
Nana	Herta Ware
Sal Roos	Lin Shaye
Ug, Bounty Hunter	Terrence Mann
Lee, Bounty Hunter	Roxanne Kernohan
Quigley	Doug Rowe

Hollywood — Cruncha, Cruncha, Cruncha. Those cute, but deadly critters are back in an amusing sequel that should nicely do the job for fans of this genre. New Line Cinema may well chomp itself a decent slice of the spring boxoffice.

All concerned are back in small Grovers Bend, where Krites terrorized residents just two years earlier. Tipoff that they've returned is appearance of dozens and dozens of large eggs with colorful patterns on them.

Outer space bounty hunters Ug and Lee (Terrence Mann and Roxanne Kernohan), as well as Charlie (Don Opper), are dispatched to planet Earth to complete their earlier attempt to obliterate the nasty little killers.

Coincidentally, young Brad Brown (Scott Grimes) comes to visit his Nana (Herta Ware) and gets blamed again by some townfolk for arrival of the critters, which are now hatching and eating at a furious pace.

Director Mick Garris, who co-wrote the pic with D.T. Twohy, perfectly weaves together the gruesome behavior of these blood-thirsty creatures and the comic asides that keep things gliding along.

Story is fairly predictable but that hardly matters since nifty visuals,

such as critters hauling themselves down the streets like bowling balls, keep one's interest. Occasionally, filmmakers resort to gratuitous violence, such as one scene in which the bounty hunters try to blow away the critters inside a fast food joint.

There are two particularly notable aspects that give the film real strength overall. One is the superb job by Barry Corbin, succeeding M. Emmet Walsh from the first film as sheriff Harv (here brought out of retirement). He's topnotch and provides repeated levity with 1-liners, such as labeling the critters "man-eating dust mops." Corbin must be one of the best character actors around.

Second, music by Nicholas Pike is of the caliber of John Williams' work on several of those monstrously successful space films of the past decade. The orchestration here works so well as complement and accentuator, while seeming to flirt playfully with the grandeur of Williams' overpowering scores.

Also due for kudos is Chiodo Brothers Prods., which created the critters, making them vicious and almost lovable at the same time. It's the ideal metaphor for the whole pic — which just might wind up being seen mostly as a clever sendup of monster pics. — *Tege.*

Two Moon Junction

A Lorimar Film Entertainment release of a DDM production. Produced by Donald P. Borchers. Executive producers, by Mel Pearl, Don Levin. Directed by Zalman King. Screenplay, King from story by King, MacGregor Douglas; camera (CFI color), Mark Plummer; editor, Marc Grossman; music, Jonathan Elias; sound, Stephen Halbert; production design, Michelle Minch; costume design, Maria Mancuso; casting, Linda Francis. Reviewed at the Beverly Cineplex Odeon, L.A., April 29, 1988. MPAA Rating: R. Running time: **104 MIN.**

April	Sherilyn Fenn
Perry	Richard Tyson
Belle	Louise Fletcher
Patti-Jean	Kristy McNichol
Chad	Martin Hewitt
Sheriff Hawkins	Burl Ives

Also with: Millie Perkins, Don Galloway, Hervé Villechaize, Dabbs Greer, Juanita Moore, Screamin' Jay Hawkins.

Hollywood — "Two Moon Junction" is a bad hick version of "Last Tango In Paris" down to the poor imitative scoring by Jonathan Elias. Sexual obsession might be the aim, but the result is anything but hot.

Director Zalman King, working from his and MacGregor Douglas' painfully convoluted story, tries hard to be arty with very conventional characters playing the passionate lovers drawn together like magnets.

In the Maria Schneider role is Madonna-clone Sherilyn Fenn (same bleached hair, pretty eyes, milky skin, but the beauty mark is on her forehead, not near her mouth), who decides to give her virginity to a guy who works at the

traveling midway (Richard Tyson) instead of her fiancé (Martin Hewitt).

She wears white all the time, along with everyone else in her privileged Southern family, and acts pure when on her home turf. When her hunk of a man from the road show is anywhere within view, she not only gets weak in the knees, she can't wait to strip her clothes off *and his* and get down to it.

Okay, so repression breeds obsession — that's nothing new though King instead manages to have created a film one notch higher than softcore porn in his efforts of making a compelling drama from this potentially interesting quandary.

Plot has all the ingredients of a '40s meller with the obvious exception that poor little rich girl Fenn unabashedly defrocks at the drop of a hat while the object of her desire (Tyson, who would be better cast in a "Conan The Barbarian"-type actioner) manages to never bare much more than his chest.

There is a lot of giant screen closeups of them kissing and going at it, including a not so kinky or titillating video replay of one such encounter, that are juxtaposed with ordinary scenes at her genteel family's ante bellum white colonnaded mansion or what passes for his home among the lowlifes working the midway.

Fenn does all right playing the mixed-up femme awakening to her sexuality and trying hard to remain as anonymous a lover as possible with Tyson while he never says much of anything, which probably is not such a bad thing.

Kristy McNichol appears as a midway groupie whose subtle bisexual scenes dancing with Fenn have more electricity than Fenn's clandestine heterosexual encounters with Tyson.

Source of considerable unintentional hilarity is the drippy dialog, infused with nonsense about the Southern way of life and the importance of lineage that Louise Fletcher, in her minor role as the matriarch, bears with little dignity.

Shot in and around Los Angeles, pic seldom looks like Alabama. For one thing, except for Fenn's car, license plates are all blue.

Look of the production is cheesy as well. Opening scene at the fraternity-sorority ball doesn't have the words synching with the picture.

—*Brit.*

Sunset

A Tri-Star Pictures release of a Hudson Hawk production from Tri-Star-ML Delphi Premier Prods. Produced by Tony Adams. Written and directed by Blake Edwards, story by Rod Amateau; camera (Panavision, Technicolor), Anthony B. Richmond; editor, Robert Pergament; music, Henry Mancini; production design, Rodger Maus; art direction, Richard Y. Haman; set decoration, Marvin March; costume design, Patricia Nor-

ris; sound (Dolby), Jerry Jost; assistant director, Mickey McCardle; second unit director, Joe Dunne; associate producer, Trish Carolselli; casting, Nancy Klopper. Reviewed at the Tri-Star screening room, L.A., April 27, 1988. MPAA Rating: R. Running time: **107 MIN.**

Tom Mix	Bruce Willis
Wyatt Earp	James Garner
Alfie Alperin	Malcolm McDowell
Cheryl King	Mariel Hemingway
Nancy Shoemaker	Kathleen Quinlan
Victoria Alperin	Jennifer Edwards
Christina Alperin	Patricia Hodge
Captain Blackworth	Richard Bradford
Chief Dibner	M. Emmet Walsh
Dutch Kieffer	Joe Dallesandro
Arthur	Andreas Katsulas
Michael Alperin	Dermot Mulroney

Hollywood — "Sunset" is a silly Hollywood fiction, unconvincing in all but a couple of its details. Premise of teaming up righteous cowboy star Tom Mix and real-life lawman Wyatt Earp to solve an actual murder case may have looked good on paper, but it plays neither amusingly nor excitingly.

Even the tallest tale needs some link to reality, and one just gets the feeling that nothing at all happened the way it is shown here, nor should it have. B.O. looks bleak.

Despite the tough guy charm he has exhibited elsewhere, Bruce Willis is one of the least likely choices imaginable to play Mix, perhaps the top Western star of the 1920s. Willis adds "pardner" to the end of some sentences and throws in a token twang every now and then, but otherwise sounds as much like a cowpoke as Sylvester Stallone.

That's just the beginning of the film's lack of plausibility, even on its own terms. The notion of English, Chaplin-like former star (Malcolm McDowell) becoming the venal head of a studio bears no resemblance to anything that ever occurred in Hollywood, the idea of multiple murders taking place at the first Academy Awards ceremony is nasty and far-fetched, and what's a Mae West lookalike doing sashaying around in 1929, three years before the great lady made her first picture?

Murder plot, involving the death of the owner of a ritzy cathouse, never generates much interest because one never meets the victim and couldn't care less about her. Tracking the killer puts Mix and Earp into one tight squeeze after another, which they take turns getting themselves out of, but too much time is taken up with thoroughly unattractive, disagreeable characters.

In particular, just about all the women here have been made up and coiffed in extremely unflattering ways, and beyond that have been directed to very shrill performances. Mariel Hemingway (deliberately) looks very butch, while neither Kathleen Quinlan nor Jennifer Edwards has ever been seen to worse advantage.

Fortunately, there is James Garner as Earp (a role he essayed in John

Sturges' 1967 "Hour Of The Gun") as relief from all the nonsense around him. In fact, the man from Tombstone seems a little too sophisticated and at ease in Tinseltown, but the actor's natural charm and fine sense of one-upmanship wins the day in virtually all his scenes. The other thesp to make a strong impression is former Andy Warhol leading man Joe Dallesandro, who is excellent as a supremely self-confident gangster.

In all, this represents one of Blake Edwards' least sparkling efforts, one in which a great deal of money has been lavished on something that wasn't worth doing in the first place. Even the much-publicized re-creation of the first Oscar ceremony is a major disappointment, as the recruited lookalikes of the era's celebrities fail to materialize in any noticeable way.—*Cart.*

Sticky Fingers

A Spectrafilm release of a Hightop Films production. Produced by Catlin Adams, Melanie Mayron. Executive producer, Jonathan Olsberg. Coproducer, Carl Clifford. Directed by Adams. Screenplay, Adams, Mayron; camera (Duart color), Gary Thieltges; editor, Bob Reitano; music, Gary Chang; production design, Jessica Scott-Justice; art direction, (N.Y.) Susan Beeson, (Toronto) Reuben Freed; set decoration, (Toronto) Brendon Smith; costume design, David Norbury, Cynthia Schumacher; sound, (N.Y.) John (Sol) Sutton 3d, (Toronto) David Joliat; line producer/production manager (Toronto), John Ryan; associate producer, Sam Irvin; assistant director, (N.Y.) Lewis H. Gould, (Toronto) Stephen Reynolds, Neil Huhta. Reviewed at Spectrafilm screening theater, L.A., Feb. 16, 1988. MPAA Rating: PG-13. Running time: 97 MIN.
Hattie .... Helen Slater
Lolly .... Melanie Mayron
Evanston ., ... Danitra Vance
Stella .... Eileen Brennan
Kitty .... Carol Kane
Diane .... Loretta Devine
Eddie .... Stephen McHattie
Sam .... Christopher Guest
Marcie .... Gwen Welles
Tenant .... Shirley Stoler

Hollywood — Spectrafilm has a gem of a picture on its hands with "Sticky Fingers," a snappy, offbeat urban comedy about two N.Y. gal pals — starving artist types — who get caught up in the shopping spree of a lifetime. Too bad the money isn't theirs.

Extraordinary feature directing debut turn by Catlin Adams spins gold from the premise, and savvy marketing could bring the same result at the boxoffice. Knockout production design puts this one on a visual par with Jonathan Demme's "Something Wild."

Story, cowritten by Adams and Melanie Mayron, casts Mayron and Helen Slater as struggling musicians on the verge of eviction from their N.Y. walkup until a bagful of drug money — nearly a million bucks — lands in their laps. They've been asked to "mind it" for a spacey friend-of-a-friend (Loretta Devine)

who's clearing out of town in a hurry.

Initially panicked, they wind up using it to pay their rent; then to replace their instruments, a cello and a violin, after a burglary. As days pass, the urge to spend becomes insatiable, and they give in with gusto.

Abundant talent of design team, including Jessica Scott-Justice, and costume designers David Norbury and Cynthia Schumacher, makes it all very amusing, as the gals mix decadent consumption with pop art sensibilities. Apartment, once decorated in funky castoffs, becomes a palace of purchases. Petty squabbles increase too, as filmmakers convey that money doesn't buy satisfaction.

Meanwhile they're being tailed by a couple of shadowy figures who're keeping a close eye on everything they do.

Then Devine calls, back in town wanting to collect her bag, and the real action begins. Much aggrieved at their own behavior, gals venture into a Chinatown gambling parlor in a ludicrous attempt to win a quarter-mil by the next day. It works, but their troubles are far from over, since they're not very good at holding onto money, even when it's theirs.

By the time it's all over, script qualifies as a model for writing classes, since everything comes full circle, working out on a variety of satisfying levels.

Adams directs with startling flair, finding visual punchlines for much of the character comedy. Lensing is evocative and inventive throughout, conveying equally, for example, the mixed feelings of Slater's encounter with her ex-husband at a crowded art loft party and the high anxiety of Mayron's encounter outside a museum with her boyfriend, who has his arm around another woman.

A latter scene in which the gals try to escape the drug thugs while dressed as dancing marshmallows in the cast of a performance art piece is hilarious.

Core of the film's appeal is the credible relationship between Mayron and Slater as the roomies, but memorable supporting roles abound, including Danitra Vance as a fellow musician and Stephen McHattie as a tough but romantic undercover cop posing as a parking lot attendant across from their building.

Eileen Brennan is right on as the ailing landlady and Carol Kane delightful as her sister, who has a romance with the cop.

Christopher Guest is near perfect as Mayron's uncertain boyfriend, a newly published novelist pursued by a spooky ex-girlfriend (Gwen Welles).

Shirley Stoler does a cameo as a tenant whose ample girth comes in handy during the final crisis.

Rarely heard femme humor adds to film's freshness — Mayron, panicking after a burglary, runs through the house muttering "Oh my goddess, oh my goddess."

A more memorable score could have put this film over the top. Bookend classical music segments at beginning and end are a nice touch, and add authenticity to the main characters.—*Daws.*

Outlaw Force

A Trans World Entertainment and TBJ Films presentation of an Outlaw Film production. Executive producers, Sid Caplan, Tom Jenssen. Produced by David Heavener, Ronnie Hadar. Written and directed by Heavener. Camera (Foto-Kem color), David Huey, James Mathers; editor, Peter Miller; music, Donald Hulette; songs, Heavener; sound (Ultra-Stereo), Hamond Kouh, John Lifavi; art direction, Phil Schmidt, Naomi Shohan; special effects, Fritz Matthews; assistant director, Jonathan Tzachor; casting, Jacov Bresler. Reviewed on TWE vidcassette, N.Y., March 30, 1988. MPAA Rating: R. Running time: 95 MIN.
Billy Ray Dalton .... David Heavener
Insp. Wainwright .... Paul Smith
Grady .... Frank Stallone
Washington .... Robert Bjorklund
Jesse .... Devin Dunsworth
Holly Dalton .... Stephanie Cicero
Capt. Morgan .... Warren Berlinger
Billy's wife ., ... Cecilea Xavier
Also with: Mickey Morton, John Reister-ter, Steve Keeley, Mark Richardson, Arvid Homberg, Jeff D. Patterson, Francesca Wilde.

"Outlaw Force" is a vanity production for singer David Heavener, who obviously fancies himself a new Clint Eastwood. TWE released this one directly to homevideo stores.

Cornball motivation is generated when Heavener saves a local black gas station attendant from young rednecks, who later return to gang rape Heavener's wife, kill her and kidnap her daughter. They plan to sell her to a kiddie porn magnate.

With no help from the L.A. police (Paul Smith and a miscast Frank Stallone), Heavener goes on the predictable oneman crusade to save his kin and mete out revenge. As writer-director, he stages the action scenes awkwardly (and cheaply), while proving totally unconvincing as an action man. Many visual nods to Sergio Leone Westerns come off as silly.

Only point of interest here is Heavener pleasantly warbling several of his own songs. Attractive actress Cecilea Xavier, a Cristina Raines type, is wasted. — *Lor.*

Les Années sandwiches
(The Sandwich Years)
(FRENCH)

A UGC release (Galaxy Intl. Releasing in U.S.) of a Philippe Dussart production; co-produced by Société Française de Production Cinématographique/Films A2/Sept/Hachette Première, in association with Sofinergie and with participation of the CNC. Directed by Pierre Boutron. Screenplay, Boutron, Jean-Claude Grumberg, from Serge Lentz' novel; camera (Eastmancolor), Dominique Brabant; editor, Robert Coursez; music, Roland

Romanelli; sound, Paul Granger; costumes, Pierre Cadot; production manager, Michel Choquet. Reviewed at the UGC Champs-Elysées cinema, Paris, April 23, 1988. Running time: **100 MIN.**
Max .... Wojtek (Wojciech) Pszoniak
Victor .... Thomas Langmann
Felix .... Nicolas Giraudi
Uncle Jean .... Michel Aumont
Bouboule .... Clovis Cornillac

Paris — A tenderized post-war "kosher" chronicle with little depth but enough ethnic sentiment to see it abroad, "Les Années sandwiches" is the second theatrical feature by seasoned tv helmer Pierre Boutron, whose talents seem more suited to the home screen on the basis of his work here. Galaxy Intl. Releasing bagged it for stateside distribution.

Boutron and Jean-Claude Grumberg (author of several successful plays such as "Dreyfus" and "The Atelier") adapted a novel by Serge Lentz about a young French Jewish orphan, whose parents were deported during the German Occupation, and a Polish Jew who gives him a roof and a job in his second-hand goods shop in a Paris suburb.

Boutron and Grumberg don't mess around with subtleties and insight. As played by the fine Polish actor Wojciech (now Wojtek) Pszoniak, the Jewish dealer is that sure-fire stock character: the gruff closet philosopher with a Heart of Gold. Pszoniak enacts the part with hammy relish that is the firm's principal appeal.

Script is more neglectful of the young orphan (Thomas Langmann) and his aborted friendship with a boy from the upper (anti-Semitic) bourgeoisie. A long section of the film involves both youths in a black market misadventure, which is gauche in writing and direction. Boutron's inconspicuous helming is effective when it stays away from the plotting and concentrates on the heartwarming. Tech credits are okay. —*Len.*

The Man Who Mistook His Wife For A Hat
(BRITISH)

An ICA production, for Channel 4. (World sales: Jane Balfour Films, London.) Produced by Debra Hauer. Directed by Christopher Rawlence. Screenplay, uncredited (based on a story by Oliver Sacks); camera (color), Christopher Morphet; editor, Howard Sharp; music, Michael Nyman; libretto, Rawlence; sound, Greg Bailey; production design, Jock Scott. Reviewed at Berlin Film Festival (market), Feb. 22, 1988. Running time: **67 MIN.**
The Neurologist .... Emile Belcourt
Dr. P. .... Frederick Westcott
Mrs. P. .... Patricia Hooper
Himself .... Oliver Sacks
Himself .... John Tighe

Berlin — A quirky, curiously charming pic based on the London stage production of Michael Nyman's "neurological opera," this is a pic which might well find specialized, even cult, audiences around

the world.

Pic starts off as a straightforward case history, with neurologist Oliver Sacks describing the sad case of a gifted musician suffering from Alzheimer's Disease. As a result, he starts to lose the faculty of sight, and is unable to recognize photos of himself and his family. At the doctor's consulting room, he mistakes his wife for a hatstand.

John Tighe, a pathologist, takes the story further, demonstrating with a human brain how the dreadful disease effects part of the human response system.

This isn't a gloomy case history. It is, of all things, an opera, with music by Michael Nyman (the composer usually associated with the films of Peter Greenaway). Most of the film is taken up with song, as Emile Belcourt (a tenor) plays Sacks, Frederick Wescott (a baritone) plays the unfortunate Dr. P. and soprano Patricia Hooper is the sick man's long-suffering wife.

The opera was originally staged, by Michael Morris, at the ICA in London, but transfers well to film. The singers invest their characters with a great deal of charm, with Wescott making Dr. P. a genuinely endearing character, whether asking street directions from a parking meter or beating the doctor at chess, even though he's unable to see the figures on the chess board.

It's a good bet for tv and video, and theatrical chances are there, too, though pic's short running time must be taken into account. It's a film that will have people talking, and is a positive way of discussing a dreadful illness. —Strat.

Hudodelci
(The Felons)
(YUGOSLAVIAN)

A Jugoslavija Film presentation of a Viba Film production. Directed by Franci Slak. Screenplay, Slak, based on novel by Marjan Rožanc; camera (color), Boris Turkovic; editor, Vuksan Lukovic; music, Bugenhegen, Laibach; sound, Hanna Preuss; art direction, Janez Kovic; costumes, Bjanka Adžić-Ursulov. Reviewed at Berlin Film Festival (competing), Feb. 22, 1988. Running time: 90 MIN.
Peter Berdon . . . . Mario Selic
Stefka . . . . Anja Rupel
Preiskovalni . . . . Bata Zivojinovic
Raka . . . . Rade Serbedzija
Florence . . . . Elisabeth Spender
Also with: Mustafa Nadarevic, Vlado Repnik, Zijah Sokolovic, Paolo Magelli.

Berlin — The separation of the Yugoslav regime from the Socialist bloc in the late '40s, and its painful efforts to assert its independence and personal brand of communism seem to be very fashionable in the recent cinema of this country.

Franci Slak's film returns to the same theme, but with a much grimmer version of the events, unrelieved by that special dimension of humor and profound sympathy

for human nature, which made "When Father Was Away On Business," and "Happy New Year" attractive.

Politically, the picture tries to break new ground as it shows traditional Moscow-oriented communism in a bad light, but puts the nationalistic variety in an even worse one. Arbitrary arrests, tortures, fears and terror reign supreme here, political tyranny being the only concern of the law enforcement agencies, the rest, including murder and robberies, being of secondary importance in their eyes.

Peter Berdon, whose father was killed by the Nazis, joins a Stalinist group and is sent to Trieste for them. Coming back, he finds out the cell has been disbanded, its members arrested and he embarks, with another outcast and his girlfriend, in a kind of Bonnie & Clyde career.

The film starts with Berdon's arrest and then works its way into his past, on the one hand, and follows him through the process of human degradation and infamy, inflicted on him in prison not only by the jailers but by the other prisoners as well.

However, for someone who is not intimately familiar with the history of Yugoslavia, the plot itself is baffling and character motivation muddled. Slak doesn't control his story material, and if ideological points are perfectly clear, narrative appears constantly arbitrary.

Given these circumstances, the actors do their best but can't go very far with characters that are mostly flat, while technically the film is acceptable but not much more. The upbeat ending may lend the picture a silver lining, but doesn't make much sense. —Edna.

Daddy's Boys

A Concorde Pictures release. Produced by Roger Corman. Directed by Joe Minion. Screenplay, Daryl Haney; camera (Foto-Kem color), David G. Stump; editor, Norman Hollyn; music, Sasha Matson; production design, Gabrielle Petrissans; art direction, Hernan G. Camacho; sound, Steve Hawk; stunt coordinator, Mike Ryan; associate producer, Anna Roth; assistant director, Melitta Fitzer. Reviewed at the American Film Institute (AFI Fest), L.A., April 26, 1988. MPAA Rating: R. Running time: 85 MIN.
Jimmy . . . . Daryl Haney
Christie . . . . Laura Burkett
Daddy . . . . Raymond J. Barry
Hawk . . . . Dan Shor
Otis . . . . Christian Clemenson
Madame Wang . . . . Ellen Gerstein
Axelrod . . . . Robert V. Barron
Traveling Salesman . . . . Paul Linke

Hollywood — In legendary Roger Corman tradition, "Daddy's Boys" was supposedly written and cast in a week and shot practically overnight simply to take advantage of standing sets built for Corman's more expensive "Big Bad Mama II." Under the circumstances, this

bastard son of "Bonnie And Clyde" and "Bloody Mama" isn't all that bad, thanks to some perverse plotting and decent performances.

An unlikely closing night attraction at the AFI Fest, pic has limited prospects in undemanding action situations, but might do better with a more pointed, evocative title, such as "Bloody Daddy."

As could be guessed, clan of three sons is lorded over here, not by a hot pistol-packin' mama, but by a lean, mean daddy. Ever since Mama died, Daddy has been a little hard to take, as he endeavors to keep the family together while robbing banks and scouring the West in search of a new woman.

Son Jimmy has had enough of Daddy's manipulative ways, flies the coop and takes up with a prostitute named Christie from Madame Wang's whorehouse in Barstow. Falling in love, as young folks will, the pair hit the road and start a crime spree of their own under the names of Adam and Eve.

Daddy, wanting to keep it all in the family, puts a stop to this by kidnapping the rebellious Jimmy and even threatening to crucify him. Blazing shootout between the Haggard clan and some evil real estate owners brings a surprising result, and ending is heavily ironic.

Action possesses the usual Corman light-hearted attitude toward crime, which still doesn't go well, and perhaps the worst element of the production are those pre-existing sets, which look phony and freshly painted.

By contrast, script by Daryl Haney, who also plays Jimmy, is several notches above the norm for such fare and provides quite a few sharp lines for Daddy, which Raymond J. Barry delivers very entertainingly.

Haney, Dan Shor and Christian Clemenson fill the bill as the diverse sons, Laura Burkett is satisfactory as the prostie turned gun moll, and Robert V. Barron lends his highly distinctive voice to the character of the villainous landowner.

Joe Minion, screenwriter of "After Hours," was given his shot at directing here by Corman, allegedly on a week's notice, and has gotten things up on the screen in presentable fashion. No major new talent is revealed under these constrained conditions, but he doesn't embarrass himself either.

Ultimately, format and genre are too tired and familiar to allow "Daddy's Boys" to flower into something worth going out of one's way to see, but it's better than a lot of other pics cranked out at this level of filmmaking. —Cart.

Jakob Hinter Der Blauen Tür
(Jacob Behind The Blue Door)
(WEST GERMAN)

An Igelfilm release of an Alpha Film production. Produced by Lutz Mayer-Lueen. Directed by Haro Senft. Screenplay, Josef Rölz, Sylvia Ulrich, Senft, from novel by Peter Härtling; camera (color), Wedigo von Schultzendorff; editor, Christine Fritz, Hans-Jürgen Teske; music, David Knopfler; sound, Robi Güver. Reviewed at Berlin Film Festival (market), Feb. 19, 1988. Running time: 96 MIN.
Jacob . . . . Thomas Speilberg
Mother . . . . Dagmar Deisen
Shot . . . . Marquard Bohm
Also with: David Knopfler, Hannelore Hoger.

Berlin — This sensitive but heavygoing film about a boy's coming to terms with the death of his father will prove difficult to peddle, despite a cameo by former Dire Straits pop star David Knopfler.

Twelve-year-old Jacob (Thomas Spielberg) becomes obsessed with death. His school grades suffer. His mother, herself still in mourning, loses all control over him. It is only when he runs into a down-and-out jazz cornet player (Marquard Bohm) that the turning point comes and the unlikely duo help each other carry on.

Child actor Spielberg must bear much of this film alone. He is fine in the scenes calling for obstinacy, but less so when emotions are called for. That's a minor point in an otherwise moving film.

Cameraman Wedigo von Schultzendorff makes good use of color during a jazz-rock concert which heralds Jacob's return to the living. Technical credits are above average for this modestly budgeted production. —Gill.

Moziklip
(Movie Clip)
(HUNGARIAN)

A Hungarofilm presentation of a Dialog Studio production. Written, directed and edited by Péter Timar. Camera (Eastmancolor), Timar; sound, Tamás Márkus; art direction, László Gárdonyi; costumes, Zsuzsa Stenger. Reviewed at Hungarian Film Week, Budapest, Feb. 10, 1988. Running time: 82 MIN.

Budapest — The 18 clips strung together here into a feature film allow director Péter Timar the opportunity to experiment with a different kind of approach to the overexposed music promo genre.

Timar, who has quite a reputation in special effects, shows impressive mastery of the technique. This collection of separate illustrations is a kind of impressionistic picture of the society in which he lives.

Some of the visions he offers are starkly realistic and avoid the habitual glamor of the traditional clip, whether it is the solitary daydreams of a young girl working in a laundry or the ironic image of the marriage cycle.

In the first three or four episodes, he does manage to find different and original ideas, but the longer the film goes on, the more difficult it is to keep it up. The subjective shot of a baby looking out at the obstretician in birth, or the couples plummeted by ski lift into their prefabricated flats, are felicities that Timar does not match in later episodes, displaying at best solid workmanship but a lesser degree of inspiration.

To his credit, Timar avoids excessive use of tricks, sticks to a narrative format in all 18 pieces, inspired by remarkably well-written and produced numbers by Hungarian pop groups. All of them sing in English, which could add to this picture's appeal.

Timar masters thoroughly all technical tasks, but it will be interesting to find out whether potential buyers will be interested to show this feature film integrally, as displayed in Budapest, or cut it into individual items for separate use, since there is no clear continuity holding the clips together. —*Edna.*

Wohin?
(Where To Go?)
(WEST GERMAN)

A Herbert Achternbusch Filmproduktion. Distributed by Exportfilm Bischoff, Munich. Written and directed by Achternbusch. Camera (Fujicolor), Adam Olech; editor, Micki Joanni; music, Tom Waits; sound, Heike Pilleman; set decoration, Ann Poppel. Reviewed at Berlin Film Festival (competing), Feb. 23, 1988. Running time: **96 MIN.**

With: Herbert Achternbusch, Gabi Geist, Annamirl Bierbichler, Franz Baumgartner, Josef Bierbichler, Kurt Raab.

Berlin — This pic gets off to an interesting start, but soon bogs down trying to mix different styles of comedy.

There are running jokes about a mysterious trunk, suspected terrorist activity by an otherwise unremarkable businesswoman, and a surly waitress with a look that literally kills. An oft alluded-to gag about an official having been infected with AIDS virus by the businesswoman's bite is meant to be satirical.

Little of what happens is believable, nor is it meant to be. The occasional gag that works comes too seldom. —*Owl.*

Inseln Der Illusion
(Isles Of Illusion)
(WEST GERMAN)

Produced by Baumhaus Film, Hamburg. Directed by Herbert Brödl. Screenplay, Jobst Grapow; camera (color), Jörg Jeshel; editor, Margot Neubert-Maric, Carlo Carlotto; sound, Steve MacMillan; production manager, Thomas Dierks; location manager, Chris E. Strewe. Reviewed at Berlin Film Festival (New German Cinema section), Feb. 20, 1988. Running time: **99 MIN.**

With: Ulrich Wildgruber, Helen Mafua, Mikael, Kirk Huffman, Norman Shackley, Joan Omawa, John Drake, Salome Zeitler.

Berlin — This is a fictional film inspired by actual incidents — a hybrid between fiction and nonfiction.

A German actor becomes fascinated with a book of published correspondence written by an Englishman who lived in the South Seas in the early part of this century. Dog-eared book in hand, he embarks on a journey to retrace the adventurer's route in the New Hebrides and Society Islands.

The protagonist identifies very strongly with the man he knows only from his letters, and soon comes to love the islands and the people as his predecessor seemingly had. He discovers that the adventurer, named Fletcher, sired a son with one of the native women, and he sets out to other islands to find him, only to discover the son died some time ago.

Other events enhance his experience. He helps nurse a sick native boy through a bout of malaria. He shares the food and living quarters of the local people. Soon he discovers that what he believed about Fletcher's death was incorrect, and that instead of dying in the 1920s, he had returned to England and lived well into the 1960s.

This is a personal film and one has to care about the story and characters. Though director Herbert Brödl sought to expand the story, the result is too long, not very well paced and ultimately not that interesting to the uninitiated. —*Owl.*

Schmetterlinge
(Butterflies)
(WEST GERMAN-B&W)

A production of DFFB, Berlin. Directed by Wolfgang Becker. Screenplay, Becker from story told by Ian McEwan; camera (b&w), Martin Kukula; editor, Becker, Verena Neumann; sound, Jochen Isfort, Uwe Thalmann. Reviewed at Berlin Film Festival (New German Cinema section), Feb. 21, 1988. Running time: **62 MIN.**

Andi . . . . .Bertram von Boxberg
Kaja . . . . .Lena Boehncke
Charlie . . . . .Dieter Oberholz
Police Inspector . . . . .Uwe Helfrich
Father . . . . .Peter Franke

Berlin — "Butterflies" is a quiet pic packing a cumulative wallop. Told in a series of flashbacks, the story shifts back and forth, sometimes imperceptibly, between past and present. A little girl (Lena Boehncke) is found dead and the film's protagonist, Andi (Bertram von Boxberg), was the last to see her.

The girl died under mysterious circumstances. Andi and the demanding youngster had passed the afternoon exploring the abandoned railroad tracks that run along a little used canal. He had promised to show her a place where butterflies were plentiful, thus the title. Instead, during their outing, she falls and dies.

Rather than give the film's one revelation away, suffice it to say this is a striking debut film for director Wolfgang Becker. It's not a big story, but one told effectively, creating a nice mood. Apparently based on an actual incident, pic is done with economy and style. —*Owl.*

Imagens do inconsciente
(Pictures From The Unconscious)
(BRAZILIAN-DOCU)

Produced by Jessel Buss, Luis Fernando Guimarães. Directed by Leon Hirszman. Camera (color, 16m), and editor, Luis Carlo Saldanho; music, Edu Lobo. (No further credits available). Reviewed at Rotterdam Film Festival, Feb. 3, 1988. Running time: **205 MIN.**

Rotterdam — "Pictures From The Unconscious" is a documentary in the form of three case histories — three lectures with moving images about two men and a woman. They're mental patients trying to find through painting a means of communication between their turbulent inner lives and their humdrum, institutionalized environment.

Brazilian psychiatrist Nise da Silveira founded the Museum of Pictures from the Unconscious in 1952. Drawings and paintings from mental institutions all over the country were assembled and studied in the hope of finding a cure for insanity. Some of the artist-inmates were brought to the museum to live. Their work is often impressive and beautiful, not "insane" at all.

The case histories are fascinating: changes of subject matter, the breaks in style in each painter's work; the mostly self-taught mastery of color and technique; the way the artist comes to life while painting. These ciné-lectures are most stimulating material for all intrigued by insanity and art, and the mysterious no-man's-land between them.

Director Leon Hirszman died tragically last year at age 49, the victim of an AIDS-polluted blood transfusion. —*Wall.*

Dorst
(Thirst)
(DUTCH)

A Cor Koppies release. Produced by Olga Madsen. Directed by Willy Breebaart. Screenplay, Breebaart, Rogier Proper, camea (Kodak color; RCM prints, 16m), Jules van den Steenhoven; editor, Rob van Steensel; music, Boudewijn Tarenskeen; sound, Lukas Boeke; art direction, Harry Ammerlaan. Reviewed at Cinecenter, Amsterdam, Feb. 26, 1988. Running time: **88 MIN.**

With: Alexander van Heteren (Peter), Gijs Scholten van Aschat (Harry), Carla Hardy (Nanny), Sylvia Millecam (Linda), Pollo Hamburger (Ben).

Amsterdam — A quest for perfection and meticulous care for detail are laudable traits in a first feature, but one can have too much of a good thing. The story in "Thirst" is slight and needed deft treatment. Instead, it gets a hefty dose of over-direction.

From the flutter of a curtain in the opening sequence to the angle of a beer glass in the final shot, nothing is left to chance. The rhythm is slowed down and life goes out of the acting, photography, everything.

Alexander van Heteren is an alcoholic, a charmer and a journalist, in that order. He could not keep a job at any paper, except at the most improbable publication shown in this film. He charms all women and most men to do his bidding. He is one of those alcoholics who think they can stop whenever they like, which ain't necessarily so.

Van Heteren has a loving, always forgiving girlfriend and an ever-faithful buddy. They are reliable. He is utterly unreliable, and assumes, moreover, that all this is as it should be. The story meanders along and has some openings for either more substantial or frothier sequences, but they don't materialize. —*Wall.*

Urgences
(Emergencies)
(FRENCH-DOCU)

A Pari Films release of a Double D Copyright Films/TF-1 coproduction. Produced by Pascal Dauman, Raymond Depardon. Directed by Depardon. Camera (color), Depardon; editor, Roger Okhlef; sound, Claudine Nougaret. Reviewed at Rotterdam Film Festival, Feb. 2, 1988. Running time: **105 MIN.**

Rotterdam — A disturbing film about disturbed people, "Urgences" is the result of two months filming in the psychiatric service at the Môtel Dieu, one of Paris' largest hospitals. It is documentarist Raymond Depardon's second feature docu on the subject, after his "San Clemente," shot at the Venetian psychiatric hospital.

Unrelieved by humor, unmediated by commentary, pic starkly records the distress of emergency patients at the hospital, some flanked by police, others coming on their own volition. Manic-depressives, suicides, paranoiacs and other victims of the unrelenting pressures of modern urban life compose this harrowing gallery of society's losers.

Depardon, who did his own camerawork (accompanied only by a sound person), has filmed with his usual discretion, but the close-quarters intensity of certain sequences is sure to leave many viewers feeling uneasy and voyeuristic.

Opening credits make it clear that all the patients gave their accord to being filmed. Can many of them be said to have been in their right mind?

Filmed with available light, film's picture and sound qualities are variable, from poor to mediocre. It's obviously an item for very specialized exposure. —*Len.*

Om Dar B Dar
(INDIAN)

Produced, written and directed by Kamal Swaroop. Camera (color), Ashwini Kaul. (Other credits unavailable.) Reviewed at Berlin Film Festival (Forum), Feb. 22, 1988. Running time: **90 MIN.**
With: Aditya Lakhia, Laxmi Narayan, Sastri, Gopi Desai, Anita Kanwar, Manish Gupta, Lai, Laiit Tiwari.

(In Hindi)

Berlin — "Om Dar B Dar" **marks the feature film debut of Kamal Swaroop. A first-person narrator recounts his life as a kind of surrealistic dream in this offbeat film brimming with rule-breaking. Unfortunately, the delightful, brisk pace with which pic so auspiciously begins falls apart somewhere along the line, degenerating into an incoherent mishmash that leaves audience with few smiles on the way out.**

Swaroop certainly demonstrates a unique talent, but it needs some reining in to become intelligible.

Part of the difficulty lies in pic's ambition to blur the boundaries between fantasy and reality. The tongue-in-cheek humor of the rapid-fire opening scenes sets a tone of high fun, as the little hero, Om, is introduced along with his eccentric family. His father, who was suspended from the civil service for issuing false caste certificates, now practices astrology.

Om has trouble with school discipline, but is fascinated by magic and religion. From what one can gather, Om leaves school and goes to the fantasy city of Pushkar. Eventually, exploiting his extraordinary ability to hold his breath for long periods, he goes to live at the bottom of a frog pond.

More coherent is the story of Om's sister Gayatri, a burgeoning feminist unmarried at 30, who even goes to the cinema alone. One day she's followed home by an earnest young man on a bike. Om borrows the bike and throws it off a cliff. Years later, Gayatri finally seduces her timid suitor in a comic bedroom scene, but in the end he shows he's shallow and unworthy of her.

Strewn with nonsense songs and verses, puns and silly bits of business, "Om Dar B Dar" vacillates between amazing inventiveness and soporific self-indulgence. The latter tends to predominate as pic goes along. Nevertheless, it's a rare example of experimental filmmaking in Indian cinema, and could well be followed up by more successful efforts. —*Yung.*

Tres menos eu
(Three Minus Me)
(PORTUGUESE-FRENCH)

A Filmargem/Films du Passage production. Produced by Paolo Branco, Paolo Sousa. Directed by João Canijo. Screenplay, Canijo, Paolo Tunhas; camera (color, 16m), José Luis Carvalhosa; editor, Jaime Silva; music, José Mária Branco; sound, Joaquim Pinto; production manager, António Goncalo. Reviewed at the Rotterdam Film Festival, Feb. 2, 1988. Running time: **90 MIN.**
With: Rita Blanco, Anne Gautier, Isabel de Castro, Pedro Ferreira, Joano Cabral.

Rotterdam — **Debut feature by João Canijo, who served as assistant to Manoel de Oliveira, Wim Wenders and Werner Schroeter, "Three Minus Me" is sympathetic enough, but remains slight and timid considering tyro helmer's robust tutors. Chances abroad seem weak.**

Tale focuses on the unruly emotions of two 18-year-old girls. Portuguese Rita is annoyed when her (distant) Parisian cousin, Anne, announces a visit. The girls don't get on well. Nervous Rita quarrels with boyfriend Antonio, which leads to a rapprochement between cousins. Then Anne and Antonio fall in love. Rita, hurt and betrayed, tries successfully to break things up. Anne returns to France, and Antonio to Rita. A Pyrrhic victory; for a boyfriend regained, a girlfriend lost.

Canijo has directed this bittersweet little item adequately, though he's yet to acquire the skill and flair to camouflage a low budget.

Rita Blanco is properly gauche and determinedly mean as the Portuguese girl, but Anne Gautier's Parisian lacks animation. — *Wall.*

Zina-Zinoulia
(Zina, Dear Zina)
(SOVIET)

A Mosfilm production. Directed by Pavel Chukhrai. Screenplay, Alexander Gelman; camera (Widescreen, Sovcolor), N. Nemolyaven; music, M. Minkov; production design, S. Agoian. Reviewed at Mandolin theater, Sydney, April 6, 1988. Running time: **85 MIN.**
Zina ....Yevgenia Glushenko
Petrenko ....Viktor Pavlov
Also with: Vladimir Gostyukhin, A. Zbruyev, T. Agafonova, E. Shotov.

Sydney — **Back in the early '70s, screenwriter Alexander Gelman wrote "Premia" (The Bonus), a controversial Soviet pic about a group of factory workers who refuse a production bonus because they know their plant is being mismanaged. Gelman's new screenplay also is about mismanagement, and is a strong piece of propaganda for Mikhail Gorbachev's policy of** *perestroika.*

Drama is set at a provincial construction site where Zina (Yevgenia Glushenko) works as a dispatcher. Earlier, she'd fallen foul of an ill-tempered truck driver, Petrenko (Viktor Pavlov), and he tries to get even by falsely stating she'd ordered him to deliver cement to the wrong location. Though she protests her innocence, Zina is demoted by her boss.

Determined to prove her innocence, Zina goes on strike. She sits on a tree stump near the site and vows not to move until Petrenko admits he lied and she gets her job back. Her friends and workmates plead with her to give up, but she stays put. Her boss can't shift her, and when his superior comes on the scene with strongarm men and even an ambulance to remove the woman, he softens his attitude toward Zina. At film's end nothing's resolved and she's still sitting on the stump, seeking justice.

Pic is more a political statement than a well-rounded drama, but it's fascinating nonetheless. The setting of the muddy construction site with its dormitories for women and single cubicles for men is sharply etched. Zina is no goodie-goodie, as she's having an affair with a married man; pic begins as she awakens in his bed, then slips into her dorm before the other women wake up.

Yevgenia Glushenko is fine in the lead role, and though Pavel Chukhrai's direction is routine, the film fascinates.—*Strat.*

Moloka'i Solo
(DOCU)

A Bob Liljestrand production. Produced, written, directed, edited, camera (color, 16m), by Liljestrand; music, Kapono Beamer. Reviewed at the American Film Institute (AFI Fest), L.A., March 25, 1988. No MPAA Rating. Running time: **69 MIN.**
With: Audrey Sutherland.

Hollywood — **Considerable patience and a desire to contemplate beauty vicariously are requirements to enjoy "Moloka'i Solo," an exceedingly relaxed and indulgent documentary about a woman who has spent much of the last 25 years paddling around the northern coast of this Hawaiian Island in a kayak. Distribution possibilities are limited, to say the least.**

Audrey Sutherland's course takes her along an extremely rugged and impressive coastline, and filmmaker Bob Liljestrand has indeed an abundance of exquisite vistas and majestic views.

As the viewer is subject to endless shots of Sutherland slowly moving through the water, taking a natural bubble bath and bedding down in the wilds for the night, one also learns more than one ever wanted to know about local history and the primitive mythology of the region, by way of Sutherland's painfully slow, deliberate narration.

For all but the most mellowed-out souls, this would have been infinitely more rewarding and enjoyable as a 20-minute short. —*Cart.*

The Antarctica Project
(WEST GERMAN-DOCU)

An Eugstfeld Film Prods., Greenpeace Intl., West Deutsches Rundfunk (WDR) production. Directed by Axel Eugstfeld. Screenplay, Eugstfeld, Gisela Keuerleber; camera (color, 16m), Bernd Mosblech; editor, Jean-Marc Lesguillons; music, Marcel Wengler; sound, Karsten Ullrich, Michael Locken, Bruce Adams; research, Hans G. Helms, Carlos Echeverria, Ingrid Echeverria, Gisela Keuerleber, Florence Ogawa, Gunther Schwedheim. Reviewed at the Berlin Film Festival, Intl. Forum of Young Cinema, Feb. 19, 1988. Running time: **97 MIN.**

Berlin — **The documentation of the South Pole conservationist expedition undertaken in order to denounce the intention to destroy the ecological balance in Antarctica for profit, comes naturally out of West Germany. Naturally, because in this country, the efforts to preserve the world's natural resources probably has been the most insistent.**

Filmmaker Axel Engstfeld joined the activists on the Greenpeace ship which undertook its well-publicized trip to the Antarctic in the winter of 1986. Totally engaged in its approach (after all, Greenpeace coproduced), this is a traditionally made documentary, with a narrator tying together the various archive excerpts with footage shot before, during and after the expedition, proving the concerns for the future of this continent certainly are justified.

The official purpose of the Greenpeace adventure was to establish a kind of civil park in a continent controlled almost exclusively by the military, but practically, they wanted to draw attention to the dangers of irresponsible exploitation of this continent, once the present international agreements which ensure some kind of order expire in 1991.

Solid research work, a wealth of information, video diagrams and historical material from the first expeditions to the Pole are used judiciously in what easily could become a useful tv program, if pruned to a more manageable length. Narration can be easily dubbed without problems and the few authentic voices recorded do not speak German.

It's shot in gritty 16m which doesn't always do justice to the astounding landscapes. — *Edna.*

Wann, Wenn Nicht Jetzt
(When, If Not Now?)
(WEST GERMAN)

A Filmverlag der Autoren release of an Olga Film production, with ZDF. Produced by Harald Kügler. Directed by Michael Juncker. Screenplay, Juncker, Doris Dörrie; camera (color), Helge Weindler; editor, Raimund Barthelmes; music, Claus Bantzer; production design, Erhard Engel; sound, Michael Etz; assistant director, Elke Vogt; production manager, Danny Krausz. Reviewed at Berlin Film Fest (New German Cinema section), Feb. 18, 1988. Running time: **100 MIN.**
Elisabeth Merz........Hannelore Schroth
Franz.............Hans Peter Hallwachs

Heinrich Merz........Friedrich von Thun
Charlotte ....Gudrun Gabriel
   Also with: Elma Karlowa (Else), Thomas
Kylau, Helga Lehner-DuMont, Victoria Stet-
ter, Daniel Muck, Daniel Krausz, Werner Al-
bert Püthe.

———

Berlin — This is the first feature
of Michael Juncker, who worked as
assistant to Doris Dörrie on all her
films to date. Dörrie collaborated
on the screenplay of "When, If Not
Now?" and it's tempting to see its
links with her films, especially
"Men." Since this is a tale of two
elderly characters who'd been rivals
in the past and become rivals again.
In this case, an intriguing situation
is set up only to be frittered away in
routine non-events. It's a tough sell.

Heinrich and Elisabeth Merz return to Germany after 40 years in
America where Heinrich was a top
scientist and presidential adviser.
Their return is welcomed with very
mixed feelings by Heinrich's old
friend and professional and personal rival, Franz, who makes petty attempts to embarrass Heinrich.
Franz is one of life's perennial
losers.

Elisabeth is sick, and so Heinrich
hires a nurse, Charlotte, to care for
her. Charlotte is a bespectacled
frump, so we know from the start
she'll get rid of those glasses and
turn beautiful, which she does.

For reasons that make sense only
to the screenwriters, Charlotte
moves in not with her patient and
her husband, but with Franz. Soon,
the two men are vying for her
favors, their old rivalries gaining
new strength as the girl flirts with
them both in turn. When all four
take off for a holiday in Spain, the
plot goes all to pieces.

It's a pity, because the film is
technically assured and has a quartet of solid performances, with Gudrun Gabriel especially good as the
winsome Charlotte. Allusions to
bullfighting and images of the death
of a bull are as superfluous as the
portentous credit sequence composed of familiar newsreel footage
of the infamous Nazi era.—*Strat.*

———

Das Mädchen Mit
Den Feuerzeugen
(The Cripples Go Christmas)
(WEST GERMAN)

———

An Elan Film Gierke & Co. production in
conjunction with West German ZDF tv.
Directed by Ralf Huettner. Camera (color,
super 8m), Diethard Prengel; editor, Lydia
Piegler; music, Andreas Köbner; sound,
Manfred Banach, Marc Parisotto. Reviewed
at Berlin Film Festival (New German Cinema
section), Feb. 19, 1988. Running time: **100
MIN.**
Ringo ....Enrico Böttcher
Aga ....Arnold Frühwald
Blond Giant................Rupert Seidl
Spasski ....Stefan Wood
Angel ....Eva Ordonez

———

Berlin — West German director
**Ralf Huettner, 33, chose an unfor-
tunate metaphor for his first**

feature-length film — the wheelchair. Any discussion of this film
necessarily centers on this metaphorical device and his use of it
(why no disabled actors?). Director's goal of showing how people
can "rise above" themselves gets
lost.

Four disabled young men steal
Christmas donations from their
home for the handicapped and go
out for a joy ride in their wheel-
chairs on Christmas Eve. They encounter a yuletide angel who grants
them each three wishes. One of
them reserves his last wish, and
when tragedy befalls the others, he
grudgingly uses it to set things
aright. Battered but none the wiser
from their "Monkey's Paw" escapades — the four steal the money
again the next day and start out
anew.

Huettner is trying for comedy
and pathos, but succeeds only in
making his audience cringe with
embarrassment. Thesps seem unsure how they are supposed to play
their roles — for laughs or for tears.
Technical credits are adequate
for pic bumped up from Super 8 to
16m. —*Gill.*

———

Gezocht: Lieve Vader
en Moeder
(Wanted: Loving Father
And Mother)
(DUTCH-DOCU)

———

A Stichtung D.D. production. Written and
directed by Sarah Marijnissen, Agna Rudolph. Camera (color, 16m), Dorith Vinken;
editor, Ot Louw; music, Ig Henneman;
sound, Gusta van Eijk, Eric Langhout; art
direction, Inger Kolff, Rebecca Geskus. Reviewed at Berlin Film Festival (Forum of
Young Cinema), Berlin, Feb. 19, 1988. Running time: **74 MIN.**
Father ....Wick Ederveen
Daughter.................Tineke Rosing
Young daughter ....Amber Leijdens
Mother ....Saskia Grotenhuis

———

Berlin — This dramatized documentary on child abuse combines stunning interviews with two
adult women who were forced by
their parents to have sexual relations with them for many years,
with the portrait of a fictional family in which the daughter dreams
constantly of her father's death.
Margo and Jeanne, both 30, spin
tales of woe that are even more
damning considering the respectable background of the family, in
one case the father being a social
worker whose specific job was to
counsel on child relations. It also
turns out that in both cases, the
mother knew and condoned these
acts in order to preserve family stability. The relations went on for
many years, in one case from age
seven to age 21, in the other from
four to 18, the first stopped when
the daughter left home, the second
when she finally mustered up the
courage to tell a cousin about it.
Pic makes a strong case for the

defense of children who dare not
complain and are at the total mercy
of their parents, pointing out the
emotional damage caused by such a
childhood (both women look amazingly normal but confess they are
not rid of the horrific memories).
Filmers go out to visit institutions
taking care of such cases, and look
at drawings made by the children,
who are probably the most shocking and moving testimony of the entire film.

The dramatized section builds a
composite picture of a typical case,
to leave no doubt about the nature
of this crime.

In its quietly impassioned plea,
the film makes its points succinctly
and should be largely in demand for
social work purposes. —*Edna.*

———

Irgendwie Power Machen
(Get Your Finger Out)
(WEST GERMAN-DOCU)

———

Produced by Mediengruppe Schwabing
Filmproduktion, Munchen, with assistance
from ZDF-TV, Mainz/WDR-TV, Cologne.
Written and directed by Wolfgang Ettlich.
Codirector, Klaus Lautenbacher. Camera
color), Lautenbacher, Henry Hauck; editor,
Monika Abspacher, Mary Lou; sound, Paul
Spitzkopf; production manager, Johanna
Aschenbrenner. Reviewed at Berlin Film Fest-
ival, (New German Cinema section), Feb. 20,
1988. Running time: **73 MIN.**
With: Oliver Neumann, Nicola Bell, Jo-
hanna Collier.

———

Berlin — At times an absorbing
look at the problems confronting
alienated young people in the new
Germany, this docu focuses on the
teen years of Oliver Neumann beginning in 1980 when he was a 14-
year-old grammar school student
prepared to throw his life away because he believed there was no future for him, to the day he graduates
seven years later from the Gymnasium completing his Abitur, a very
rough equivalent of American high
school but a great deal more comprehensive and stressful.

As the film opens, Oliver's deciding between joining a Baghwan
sect or getting into the punk scene.
He chooses the latter. He's always at
odds with his seemingly liberal parents, a pretty permissive couple obviously out of the 1960s generation,
who soon divorce.

First he lives with his mother, but
when she puts too much pressure on
him, he moves in with his father. All
the while his live-in girlfriend remains at his side, and they live as it
suits them, mostly in messy, littered
rooms practicing punk guitar.

The docu follows Oliver without
comment, including long and sometimes acrimonious discussions with
his parents, and footage of him attending a punk music concert where
he initiates a round of sometimes
brutal slam dancing.

Director Wolfgang Ettlich in this
longterm project has captured many
elusive aspects of growing up. Even

the tedious moments are justifiable
in the context of film as document.
There's something here for all
young people and their families. Pic
provides interesting insights into the
children of post-war German af-
luence. —*Owl.*

———

Komplizinnen
(Accomplices)
(WEST GERMAN)

———

An Elephant Film-ZDF production.
(World sales: Filmverlag der Autoren.) Produced by Sibylle Hubatschek-Rahn. Directed
by Margit Czenki. Screenplay, Czenki; camera (color), Hille Sagel, Pascal Mundt, editor,
Ursual Höf, Angela Tiedt; music, Franz
Hummel; sound, Wolfgang Schukrafft; production design, Wolfgang Rux; assistant
director, Lars Becker; production manager,
Martin Schulz. Reviewed at Berlin Film Festival (New German Cinema section), Feb. 20,
1988. Running time: **109 MIN.**
With: Pola Kinski, Therese Affolter, Gerlinde Eger, Marianne Rosenberg, Ilse Pagé,
Petra Rennert, Astrid Meyer-Gossler, Agathe
Taffertshofer, Gabi du Vinage.

———

Berlin — A grim, heavy-handed
drama set in a women's prison,
"Accomplices" is too familiar, and
too leaden, to make much impact
outside its home turf.

First-time director Margit Czenki
has first-hand experience of the subject, because she served a 5-year
prison term after being convicted of
armed robbery (the former teacher
of handicapped children robbed a
bank when she was a member of a
radical political group; her story
was told to Margarethe von Trotta
in her first solo feature "The Second Awakening of Christa Klages").

Having first-hand experience
doesn't necessarily a good film
make. Czenki seem unable or unwilling to tell her story (which,
presumably, is autobiographical)
straight. So her angry heroine, in
solitary confinement for weeks on
end, is photographed from a variety of relentlessly odd angles, with
the camera sometimes turning sideways or upside down to observe her
in her cell. The tricks add nothing to
the drama.

Film's main interest in some solid acting from an almost all-femme
cast (prisoners and guards), and an
intriguingly composed soundtrack.
First reel of print caught had very
soft focus, which was not a projector fault, apparently.

Even sympathetic audiences will
find the going tough when confronted with nearly 110 minutes in company with the slobby protagonist
and her friends, despite a brave performance from Pola Kinski in the
lead. —*Strat.*

———

Verbieten Verboten
(Forbidden To Forbid)
(WEST GERMAN-B&W)

———

Produced, written, directed and edited
Lothar Lambert. Camera (b&w) and sound,

Albert Kittler, Lambert. Reviewed at Berlin Film Festival (Panorama), Feb. 23, 1988. Running time: 60 MIN.

With: Dagmar Beiersdorf, Dorothea Moritz, Dennis Buczma, Stefan Menche, Slavko Hitrov, Lothar Lambert, Renate Soleymany, Doreen Heins, Inga Schrader, Milgun Taifun, Ismet Elci, Susanne Gautier, Sigurd Wendland, Robert Cutts, Ingrid Caven, Dieter Schidor, Klaus Marner.

Berlin — A winner from veteran director Lothar Lambert, this low-budget, black and white gem is full of bawdy humor and good fun. Lambert always has had a slightly warped sense of humor and this series of short vignettes strung on a common thread of lust and lechery could travel quite well.

It's a possibility not gone unnoticed by the filmmaker, who besides doing practically everything including holding the camera, had the forethought to prepare a print with English subtitles.

Each of the eight short pieces takes an amusing look at people and their foibles. Though the people from story to story never seem directly related, except for the opening and closing that provide the frame, it's almost as if Lambert's camera found these stories lurking about on a random shoot around Berlin.

He also manages to take a swipe at last year's big hoopla over the city's 750th anniversary, and a few more pokes at other Berlin stereotypes.

The opening bit is one of the better sustained with two housewives standing in front of a famous Berlin legit house which happens to be situated directly across from a porno district of peeps and flicks. While the ladies chat, the inevitable happens: one of their husbands is seen going in.

In another, one guy tries to pick up another, and they discover after going to great lengths that they're after the same kick. One or two of the vignettes may get a little lost in translation, but there's enough funny business to keep things moving. This film could get mileage with the right distribution in special venues. —Owl.

Die Letzte Geschichte von Schloss Königswald
(The Last Story Of Königswald Castle)
(WEST GERMAN)

An Allianz-Film, Berlin/Peter Schamoni Film, Munich/Zweites Deutsches Fernsehen, Mainz, production. Directed by Peter Schamoni. Screenplay, Horst Bienek, Schamoni; camera (color), Gerard Vandenberg; editor, Angelika Siegmeier; music, Ralph Siegel; sound, Martin Mueller; costumes, Charlotte Flemming; production manager, Peter Rothkopf; assistant director, Harald Eberhard. Reviewed at Berlin Film Festival (New German Cinema), Feb. 22, 1988. Running time: 87 MIN.

With: Camilla Horn, Dietlinde Turban, Marianne Hoppe, Carola Hoehn, Rose Renee Roth, Ortrud von der Recke, Fee von Reichlin, Anja Kruse, Claudia Vandenberg, Hanna Bergmann, Marika Roekk, Wolfgang Fierek, Wolfgang Greese, Jockel Tschiersch, Helmut Ketels, Michael Goldberg, Sherman Steward.

Berlin — The premise of this film is a lot funnier than the actual execution. Yet the script provides a golden opportunity to assemble a stellar cast of veteran German stars and character actors, who give this would-be romp more class than it could muster without them.

A Bohemian castle full of aristocratic old ladies has managed to sit out World War II untouched and in grand style. Hearing that the war's over, they expect the Russian army to appear at any moment, only instead a group of fleeing Nazi soldiers arrive. The Nazis briefly occupy the castle, threatening to make their last stand from the turrets, but the ladies, fearful of the castle being destroyed, hatch a scheme to get rid of them.

When the next group of soldiers arrive, thinking for a moment it's the Russians, the baroness dons her sable fur hat to welcome them. When the butler informs her it's the Americans — one of the soldiers is black — she immediately switches to a feather boa.

This well-intentioned comedy might've proved a gem. All the elements are there, including gorgeous settings, a roster of scene-stealing veterans, and a germ of an idea that would easily have played internationally. Only in the hands of director Peter Schamoni, things fall a little flat. — Owl.

Three To Get Ready
(DOCU-B&W)

A Brooks/Gasperik production. Produced by Carolyn Brooks. Directed by David Gasperik. Camera (b&w, 16m), Gasperik; editor, Alan Baumgarten; music, Duran Duran. Reviewed at the American Film Institute (AFI Fest), L.A., March 23, 1988. No MPAA Rating. Running time: 71 MIN.

With: Simon Le Bon, Nick Rhodes, John Taylor.

Hollywood — Pretty boy technorockers Duran Duran can't stand up even to the mild scrutiny they are subjected to in "Three To Get Ready," a short documentary feature about the four weeks leading to their "Notorious" world tour a couple of years ago.

Simultaneously boring and fascinating for the utter banality it reveals, pic now emerges past its time with the group apparently off the map, so there will be few viewers for this outside diehard fans in the homevid arena.

It is entirely possible that band members Simon Le Bon, Nick Rhodes and John Taylor approved this film as flattering to their talent, good manners and heads for business. After all, they don't sit around in hotel rooms doing drugs and throwing tv sets out of windows, nor do they come off like abrasive egomaniacs like the Bob Dylan of "Don't Look Back."

To the contrary, David Gasperik's camera reveals the three English lads to be entirely colorless and bland, lacking in the eccentricity and charisma one has come to expect from major music world stars. They seem like nothing so much as young entrepreneurs molded in the Thatcher era, and the viewer has no doubt that every penny they ever made has been accounted for and wisely invested.

Shot in Los Angeles before the group's scheduled departure for Japan, picture shows the boys having lunch in the Capitol Records executive dining room, signing autographs for the staff, rehearsing, doing radio spots, auditioning backup singers, posing for photographs, doing phone interviews and agonizing about whether appearing on "The Late Show Starring Joan Rivers" would be right for their image.

Ultimately, they appeared on both that program and "Soul Train," but the topper comes when they issue stern demands that under no circumstances must fish, exotic cheeses or chicken with bones in it be present on their dressing rooms on tour. For some reason, scenes like this didn't pop up in late 1960s rock docus.

From a technical point-of-view, film is refreshing in black-and-white. — Cart.

Blue City Slammers
(CANADIAN)

A Cineplex Odeon Films (in Canada) release of a Bruce Raymond Intl./Shatalow presentation. Produced by Bruce Raymond. Directed and coproduced by Peter Shatalow. Screenplay, Layne Coleman, Peter Shatalow, based on a play by Layne Coleman; camera (color), Bob New; editor, John Victor Smith; music, Tim McCauley; sound, Marc S. Green; production manager, Anthony B. Armstrong. Reviewed at Cineplex Odeon Eaton Center, Toronto, April 29, 1988. Running time: 93 MIN.
Butter .... Eric Keenlyside
Kim .... Tracy Cunningham
Lori .... Paula Barrett
Gary .... Barry Green
Bill Walker .... Murray Westgate
Chicken .... Mary Ellen Mahoney
Doug .... Gary Farmer
Barb .... Fran Gebhard
Jean .... Samantha Langevin
Jimbo .... Stuart Clow

Toronto — Small town folk, with emotions in high gear and pulled together for a women's amateur softball championship on a Labor Day weekend, in this case make for a limp match-up.

Sluggishly directed effort, bogged down by weak, legit-sounding script, hinges on apparently strong women on and off the field pitted against their boozy and otherwise straying males. Characterizations are 1-sided and pale. Acting is lacklustre, except for cheated-on housefrau Fran Gebhard and lonely grandfather Murray Westgate.

Other production values are flat. Possibilities in all media: dim.
—Adil.

Eternal Evil
(CANADIAN-U.S.)

A Seymour Borde & Associates release of a Filmline Intl./New Century Prods. Ltd. production. Executive producers, Nicolas Clermont, David J. Patterson. Produced by Pieter Kroonenburg. Directed by George Mihalka. Screenplay, Robert Geoffrion; camera (Sonolab color), Paul van der Linden; editor, Yves Langlois, Nick Rotundo; music, Marvin Dolgay; sound, Gabor Vadnay; art direction, John Meighen; production manager, Luc Campeau; assistant director, Mike Williams; casting, Nadia Rona, Elite Prods. Reviewed on Lightning Video vidcassette, N.Y., April 13, 1988. MPAA Rating: R. Running time: 85 MIN.
Paul Sharpe .... Winston Rekert
Janus .... Karen Black
Det. Kaufman .... John Novak
Matthew .... Andrew Bednarsky
Jennifer Sharpe .... Patty Talbot
Monica .... Lois Maxwell
Scott .... Vlasta Varna
John Westmore .... Walter Massey
Iris .... Bronwen Booth
Helen .... Joanne Côté

"Eternal Evil," originally entitled "The Blue Man," is a 1985 Canadian-made horror pic that makes little use of an interesting supernatural premise. Pic was briefly released last year ahead of current homevideo availability.

Winston Rekert portrays a tv commercials helmer whose studies of astral projection (i.e., leaving one's body on psychic trips) get him into trouble as the main suspect in a series of brutal killings he's seemingly witnessed in his sleep. As the police, led by ineffectual Det. Kaufman (John Novak), plod along miles behind the audience in solving the case, it turns out that an ancient couple is mystically inhabiting a succession of other people's bodies and responsible for the killings.

Director George Mihalka emphasizes swooping, wide-angle, first-person camera for the astral traveling sequences but otherwise fails to make the necessary plot connections. Rekert is an earnest antihero and costar Karen Black is convincingly strange in a lesbian role that turns out to be more complicated than that. Erstwhile Miss Moneypenny of the James Bond films Lois Maxwell shows up in a brief cameo.
— Lor.

Jack's Back

A Palisades Entertainment release. Executive producer, Elliott Kastner. Produced by Tim Moore, Cassian Elwes. Written and directed by Rowdy Herrington. Camera (color), Shelly Johnson; editor, Harry B. Miller 3d; music, Danny Di Paolo; sound, Robert J. Anderson Jr.; production design, Piers Plowden; set decoration, Deborah Evans; production manager, Mary McLaglen; assistant director,

Ellen Rauch; special effects makeup, John Naulin; casting, Kimba Hills. Reviewed at Magno Review 2 screening room, N.Y., April 28, 1988. MPAA Rating: R. Running time: **97 MIN.**

John/Rick Wesford	James Spader
Christine Moscari	Cynthia Gibb
Dr. Sidney Tannerson	Rod Loomis
Jack Pendler	Rex Ryon
Dr. Battera	Robert Picardo
Sgt. Gabriel	Jim Haynie
Capt. Prentis	Wendell Wright
Scott Morofsky	Chris Mulkey
Denise Johnson	Danitza Kingsley

"Jack's Back" is a tedious, unappealing attempt at a thriller updating the Jack the Ripper saga to contemporary Los Angeles. Theatrical prospects are nil, the main question raised where to file it on one's homevideo store shelves, under horror or mystery?

Debuting helmer Rowdy Herrington (currently directing Patrick Swayze in UA's "Road House") provides a woebegone script, featuring clichéd dialog, including enough extraneous swearing to cop an R rating but otherwise playing like a tv episode. Two plot gimmicks, the psychic linkup of identical twins and hypnosis as the key to the police investigation, are presented unconvincingly.

James Spader stars as John Wesford, a dedicated young doctor in hot water with his no-nonsense clinic boss Dr. Tannerson (Rod Loomis), who becomes the chief suspect in a Ripper-styled set of serial killings of L.A. prosties, each timed 100 years to the day from Bloody Jack's grisly deeds. He's not a suspect for long, as suspect No. 2, a jock-styled young doctor named Jack (Rex Ryon) kills Wesford after the second reel by hanging him after he sees him with the next victim Danitza Kingsley, and makes it look like suicide. Police pronounce case closed, with dead Wesford the fall guy for the killings.

Pic climaxes at this early point, as Wesford's twin brother Rick (also played by Spader) wakes up from a nightmare, having psychically witnessed his bro's murder while sleeping. He teams up with bro's pretty colleague Cynthia Gibb to find the real killer, whose identity is immediately telegraphed since there's only one other suspect on view. With no suspense, Herrington lamely uses a red herring in the form of police shrink Robert Picardo, to ill effect.

Film has threadbare production values, boringly static exposition scenes (nothing seems to be happening in the frame, no life or background atmosphere) and no exploitation values. Spader's performance is heavy and mannered, speaking in a near whisper in both roles, and a decided step down from his recent typecasting as the hissable yuppie in "Less Than Zero," "Mannequin" and "Baby Boom." Gibb is merely decorative, though Herrington perversely leaves out her built-up-to nude scene; the various heavies are

1-note. Only funny line is enunciated by Chris Mulkey as a police detective, otherwise a waste of the talents of the "Patti Rocks" star. Synthesized musical score is poor.—*Lor.*

L'Amoureuse
(Women In Love)
(FRENCH)

A Lola Films presentation of a Sept Films-FR3 production. (World sales: World Marketing Film, Paris.) Directed by Jacques Doillon. Screenplay, Doillon, Jean-François Goyet; camera (color), Caroline Champetier; editor, Marie Robert; music, Les Rita Misouko; production design, Simon Duhamel. Reviewed at Berlin Film Festival (Panorama), Feb. 21, 1988. (Also in Cannes Film Festival Market.) Running time: **94 MIN.**

Marie	Marianne Cuaul
Camille	Catherine Bidaut
Dick Diver	Dominic Gould
Elsa	Eva Ionesco
Aude	Aurelle Doazan
Vanessa	Valéria Bruni Tedeschi
Laurence	Laura Benson
Hermine	Hélène De Saint Pere
Irène	Isabelle Renauld

Also with: Marc Citti (Mathieu), Thibault de Montalembert (Thomas), Pierre Romans (Roman), Bruno Todeschini (Guy).

Berlin — Jacques Doillon comes up with a modest, sub-Eric Rohmer comedy about a gaggle of girls, with men on their mind, vacationing in a large empty house by the sea in the off-season. The chatter quickly becomes tiresome, but there are some appealing fresh faces among the cast.

The eight girls come to stay with a ninth whose family is away. Almost all their talk, and they never stop talking, is of men and love affairs. Hermine, for instance, is worried that, since she started working recently, she's lost her looks; she spends her time waiting for a boy, but as soon as he arrives, they quarrel. Vanessa, the hostess, also is upset over a man; she sits in a bathtub playing with plastic ducks, and as soon as her guy calls, she takes off leaving her friends behind.

Audie is used to sleeping with someone, boy or girl; she's the least mature of the bunch. Elsa, who lives locally, is a more worldly type with troubles of her own. Camille arrives on a motorbike with her friend Marie, whom she seems to need to protect. Soon, she spots an American tourist in a bar, and invites him to the house. Elsa steals his passport so he can't leave, but when Marie offers herself to him, he politely declines; seems he's troubled over the woman and child he left behind in the states.

The character of the American, played by Dominic Gould, is absurdly written and played, with the character (who speaks fluent French) acting like no American tourist in history.

Still, many of the young actors — apparently fresh from acting class-

es — are pleasant company, especially Marianne Cuaul as the strong-willed Marie. Essentially, the film's about nothing at all, but Cuaul and her costars keep your eyes on the screen, rising above their material. It's not a film that's likely to find an international audience, outside possible fest exposure. —*Strat.*

My Best Friend Is A Vampire

A King Road Entertainment release. Produced by Dennis Murphy. Directed by Jimmy Huston. Screenplay, Tab Murphy, camera (Technicolor), James Bartle; editor, Janice Hampton, Gail Yasunaga; music, Steve Dorff; sound, Art Names, Tim Himes; production design, Michael Molly; set design, Richard Huston; set decoration, Jeanette Scott; costume design, Rona Lamont; makeup, Christy Belt; associate producer, Tab Murphy; assistant director, Sanford Hampton; casting, Pennie du Pont. Reviewed at AMC Burbank 10 theater, Burbank, Calif., April 29, 1988. MPAA Rating: PG. Running time: **90 MIN.**

Jeremy Capello	Robert Sean Leonard
Ralph	Evan Mirand
Darla Blake	Cheryl Pollak
Modoo	René Auberjonois
Nora	Cecilia Peck
Mrs. Capello	Fannie Flagg
Mr. Capello	Kenneth Kimmins
Professor McCarthy	David Warner
Grimsdyke	Paul Willson

Hollywood — Yet another in the endless parade of films that mix and match genres for lack of a new idea, "My Best Friend Is A Vampire" wins a few laughs for casting blooddrinkers as just another oppressed minority with a bad rap. Script quickly loses momentum, relying on contrivances to move ahead, and pic is neither stylish nor funny enough to really hook teens. Boxoffice prospects look anemic.

Director Jimmy Huston and cinematographer James Bartle have done a lot with a little, creating a pic with a richer look than its premise deserves. Everyday suburban world of its teen protagonists is blended to intriguing effect with Gothic graveyards and churches discovered in Houston lensing locales.

Robert Sean Leonard plays Jeremy Capello, a nice-as-can-be high schooler who goes to a decrepit mansion to deliver groceries and gets seduced by a sexy Elvira type who seems to be living there.

The love bite she gives him has strange consequences. Howling dogs begin to gather under his bedroom window and his bathroom mirror doesn't work anymore.

Just as he's about to panic, René Auberjonois shows up as a friendly, avuncular bloodsipper who tells him it's not all bad — vampires can be nice people with normal lives, so long as they stock up on pig's blood down at the butcher shop. To him, it's just an alternative lifestyle.

To the pic's credit, Jeremy clicks into it, taking a kind of hip pleasure in his newfound status. Meanwhile, he and his best friend Ralph (Evan Mirand) are being followed by car-

toonish, vampire-hating thugs who want to kill them.

Then there's the girl at school Jeremy's smitten with (Cheryl Pollak), who likes him but thinks he's a little too weird — especially now.

His model middle-class parents deduce from his odd behavior that he's a homosexual and start figuring out how they can be supportive.

Film's main problem is the story by Tab Murphy — after establishing the basic situation, it has no reason to be, and relies on the unconvincing threat of danger from the anti-vampire brigade for suspense. Car chases, at least four of them, are used for action — not very funny.

Small moments between characters often fall flat, and some of the goofy-sweet teen love scenes are genuinely clunky.

Keeping the pic afloat is a team of seasoned character actors, including Fanny Flagg, refreshingly real as the solid Southern mom, and Auberjonois, a gem as the kindly, cultivated vampire. Leonard does fine in the lead role, though it's no star turn, and Mirand adds some energy as his nuts-and-bolts pal, while Pollak makes an agreeable impression as Jeremy's slightly offbeat love interest.

David Warner and Paul Willson can't overcome tedious roles as the vampire haters.

After the basic setup is established, pic hits its stride only once — in a brief montage when Jeremy transforms himself into a hip, happy bloodseeking nightstalker.

Result is a pic teens will find mildly diverting, but nothing to line up for.

Steve Dorff's snappy soundtrack, with songs by Blondie, Oingo Boingo and Timbuk 3, does a lot to aid momentum.—*Daws.*

Shakedown

A Universal Pictures release of a Shapiro/-Glickenhaus Entertainment production. Produced by J. Boyce Harman Jr. Executive producers, Leonard Shapiro, Alan Solomon. Written and directed by James Glickenhaus. Camera (TVC color), John Lindley; editor, Paul Fried; music, Jonathan Elias; production design, Charles Bennett; costume design, Peggy Farrell Salten; sound (Dolby), William Daly; stunt coordinators, Alan Gibbs, Jack Gill; special effects coordinator, Michael Wood; visual and optical effects sequences, Apogee Prods.; assistant director, Joel B. Segal. Reviewed at Directors Guild theater, L.A., April 27, 1988. MPAA Rating: R. Running time: **90 MIN.**

Roland Dalton	Peter Weller
Rickie Marks	Sam Elliott
Susan Cantrell	Patricia Charbonneau
Gail Feinberger	Blanche Baker
Nicky Carr	Antonio Fargas
Michael Jones	Richard Brooks

Hollywood — An entertaining, well-made urban actioner with a couple of great stunts, "Shakedown" lacks the originality or star-power to make much b.o. impact. After a modest theatrical run, expect to see this on the small screen.

Writer-director James Glickenhaus ("The Exterminator") describes a New York Police Dept. precinct where cops find it more profitable to pocket the cash they seize from drug dealers than salt it away in the evidence room. To keep the cash rolling in, they're willing to let the big boys stay out on the street.

Into this web of corruption stumbles Peter Weller as a legal aid lawyer about to take a right turn onto Wall Street when he takes up an unlikely crusade — the case of a drug dealer claiming self defense in the slaying of a cop. The hook: the ex-love of his life (Patricia Charbonneau) will be the prosecuting attorney.

Burned out on the criminal world but uneasy about a pinstriped future, Weller rediscovers in Charbonneau the social conscience he longs to listen to. The two of them, in their hastily enacted love affair, however, don't generate much heat.

Glickenhaus never commits to who Charbonneau's character is, and she's not very credible paying lip service to "the good fight" from her Central Park view penthouse. In court, she hasn't the depth or fire to be the figure she supposedly is.

Meanwhile, Weller's got another new compadre, a seedy but self-assured undercover cop (Sam Elliott) who suddenly realizes just how much he wants to bring down the bad guys.

These two piece the puzzle together in the harsh, amoral urban world Glickenhaus creates, full of vicious baddies high on cash.

Action scenes take up much of the screen time, with some imaginative stunts, such as a Coney Island rollercoaster that jumps track, takes flight and crashes atop a concession stand. A spectacular smash 'em up car chase down 42d Street is a gritty centerpiece.

Best stunt is saved for the climax, when Elliott leaps from a speeding Porsche onto the landing gear of the plane in which the drug kingpins are escaping, shoots it down over New York harbor, and then splashes down to safety. It's implausible, but fun filmmaking.

As a director, Glickenhaus fares best in the underworld, creating a lurid, frightening crack den on the Lower East Side and some truly menacing, amoral characters. Above ground, relationship scenes seem overwritten and forced, but snappy dialog, at least, keeps things moving.

Weller and Elliott do fine in the lead roles, endowing both with a bit of quirky texture, and Richard Brooks makes a particularly strong impression as the drug-dealing defendant. Of all the femmes, only Kathryn Rossetter seems to fit in comfortably as the wife of the slain cop.

John Lindley contributes no-frills cinematography.

Glickenhaus, in a touch of whimsy, includes scenes from his own 1982 spy thriller "The Soldier," playing in a sleazy downtown theater. — *Daws.*

A Hungry Feeling: The Life And Death Of Brendan Behan

(DOCU)

A First Run Features release. Executive producer, Walter Scheuer. Produced and directed by Allan Miller. Camera (color), Don Lenzer; editor, Tom Heneke; postproduction manager and assistant editor, Donald Klocek; production coordinator, Kathryn Quinn. Reviewed at Film Forum, N.Y., May 2, 1988. No MPAA Rating. Running time: **85 MIN.**
With: Liam Clancy as the narrator.

The late Irish playwright Brendan Behan drew scandalous headlines from the very beginning of his brief incandescent literary career. Academy Award winning producer-director Allan Miller's latest docu is an affectionate, straightforward portrayal of a man gone wild with drink and fame. Pic's a natural for public tv, festivals and special bookings.

Intercutting recollections of friends and family gathered in a favorite Dublin pub is archival footage of Behan's interviews and many arrests for public drunkenness. He seemed to revel in the attention, and was such a determined drunk that his wife Beatrice reports he threatened to drink himself to death if she made any attempt to have him hospitalized or treated against his will.

The docu traces Behan's origins as one of six children born to a working class family in the North Dublin slums of the 1920s. He became active with the IRA very early and by the time he was 15 was serving time in an English juvenile detention facility for smuggling explosives into Liverpool with the intent of blowing up a ship.

A subsequent police confrontation earned him further incarceration bringing his total time served to nine years by age 24.

One interviewee comments Behan was no wittier or smarter than the next Irishman, but his edge was that he wrote it down. Behan's tragedy was that in the years following the worldwide success of his play "The Hostage" he wrote less and drank more. Near the end his concentration was so badly shattered he tried dictating his stories to a typist but with diminishing success.

Miller has skillfully captured the sad spiral of a man out of control. Nothing prepared Behan for instant fame and in the end he was never quite able to come to grips with it. In his native Dublin he became something of an outcast: other artists became jealous of his success, and friends and neighbors turned against him. because of his drinking binges.

One anecdote perhaps sums up the man's devilish character best. He once approached a line of people waiting outside a meat market and begged for money claiming he had 10 hungry, bawling children at home to feed. However, he didn't want the money to feed them, but rather to put on a good drunk so he could forget about the problem.
—*Owl.*

Salsa

A Cannon Group release of a Golan-Globus Production. Produced by Menahem Golan and Yoram Globus. Directed by Boaz Davidson. Screenplay, Davidson, Tomas Benitez, Shepard Goldman, from story by Davidson, Eli Tabor. Camera (TVC color), David Gurfinkel; editor, Alain Jakubowicz; music, supervision, Jack Fishman, Michael Linn; music editor, John Strauss, S.M.E.; production design, Mark Haskins; costumes, Carin Hooper; sound (Ultra-Stereo), Peter Bentley, Kim Ornitz; choreography, Kenny Ortega; associate choreographer, Miranda Garrison; stunt coordinator, Al Jones; production managers, John Zane, Daniel Schneider; associate producer, Ortega; assistant directors, Elie Cohn, Michael Kennedy; second unit director, Ortega; casting, Nancy Lara; dance casting coordinator, Gregg Smith. Reviewed at Paramount theater, L.A., May 6, 1988. MPAA rating: PG. Running time: **97 MIN.**

Rico	Robby Rosa
Ken	Rodney Harvey
Rita	Magali Alvarado
Luna	Miranda Garrison
Lola	Moon Orona
Vicki	Angela Alvarado
Mother	Loyda Ramos
Chuey	Valente Rodriguez

Hollywood — "Salsa" is all elements, no story. What might have been a craze-making pic, with its hot styles and sounds, flashy choreography and good-time atmosphere, is deflated by rushed, low-budget execution.

Initial business should be high in a 1,125-print release backed by a sizzling ad campaign and music-videos, but momentum isn't likely to build.

Imprint of "Dirty Dancing" choreographer Kenny Ortega is all over this film. Ortega not only molds the remarkable dances, but also fronts a live band to perform an energetic "Good Lovin'," leaps into the crowd to join the dancers, and gets associate producer and second-unit director credits.

Pistol-hot dancer Robby Rosa, 19, a veteran of four years with Puerto Rican pop sensation Menudo, plays Rico, an auto shop worker obsessed with dancing salsa. In pic's first dialog — after a fantasy-like sequence in which shop workers dance all over the garage — we learn there's a big contest coming that he just has to practice for.

Since his girlfriend (Angela Alvarado) isn't quite the dance partner he needs to put him over the top, he falls into the clutches of Luna (Miranda Garrison), an aging former "Queen Of Salsa" who sees him as her ticket back into the limelight. (Garrison is pic's associate choreographer, as she was on "Dirty Dancing," in which she also acted.)

Meanwhile his Anglo buddy Ken (Rodney Harvey) is secretly romancing Rico's 14-year-old sister (Magali Alvarado), a development the macho, overprotective Rico just can't handle. And sis' slightly older friend (Moon Orona) is trying to get her hooks into dreamy Rico.

It's a situation, but somewhere along the way someone forgot to write a script. Leaden dialog abounds, and there's no end of bad acting. Plot waltzes through one cliched half-turn after another. Characters are underdeveloped, though not for lack of screen time.

A film that might have been at least as involving as "Saturday Night Fever" or "Urban Cowboy" is instead shallow and boring, about as memorable as a music-video. Unsubtle camera work and a couple of flashy editing sequences also are reminiscent of musicvideo.

However the dancing doesn't disappoint. Rosa is dynamite in unabashedly sensual pairings with all three of the women who pursue him, while solo, he's got precision and electricity to rival Michael Jackson.

Soundtrack, with numerous live performances at film's nightclub setting by salsa stars like Celia Cruz and Tito Puente, brings a party atmosphere to theaters. A few rock chestnuts are included to broaden appeal.

Carin Hooper's costumes are an asset, and the imaginative nightclub set captures a sense of the streets with freeway ramps, classic cars and neon.

L.A. setting for a tale with Puerto Rican focus is a puzzler (New York would be more accurate), but pic scarcely concerns itself with any kind of ethnic allegiance. In fact, first dance scene has Rosa kissing the hood ornament of a Rolls-Royce and fondling handfuls of cash to a tune called "Mucho Money." Some values.

Cannon released 21 Spanish-language prints, four in New York and 17 in the Los Angeles area.

— *Daws.*

Dead Heat

A New World Pictures release of a Helpern/Meltzer production. Produced by Michael Meltzer, David Helpern. Directed by Mark Goldblatt. Screenplay by Terry Black; camera (Technicolor), Robert D. Yeoman; editor, Harvey Rosenstock; music, Ernest Troost; sound (Dolby), Walt Martin; production design, Craig Stearns; art direction, Jon Gary Steele; set decoration, Greta Grigorian; costume design, Lisa Jensen; stunt coordinator, Dan Bradley; special visual effects supervisor, Patrick Read Johnson; prosthetics and special mechanical effects, Steve Johnson's XFX Inc.; assistant director, Mike Topoozian; associate producer, Allen Alsobrook; casting, Steve Jacobs. Reviewed at Cineplex Odeon theaters, Universal City, Calif., May 6, 1988. MPAA Rating: R. Running time: **86 MIN.**

Roger Mortis	Treat Williams
Doug Bigelow	Joe Piscopo
Randi James	Lindsay Frost
Dr. Ernest McNab	Darren McGavin
Arthur P. Loudermilk	Vincent Price
Rebecca Smythers	Clare Kirkconnell
Mr. Thule	Keye Luke
Bob	Ben Mittleman
Smitty	Peter Kent

Hollywood — There was plenty of poor judgment all around at New World in thinking "Dead Heat" could be either funny or thrilling — as it's billed — and involvement by Treat Williams, Joe Piscopo, Darren McGavin and certainly Vincent Price must stand as a huge embarrassment.

Word of mouth will likely sink this Titanic early, notwithstanding its early ad blitz.

The shabbiness starts early as L.A. cops Williams and Piscopo participate in a shootout at a jewelry store. Baddies take many direct hits but don't go down quickly, and gunplay goes on ad nauseam.

Williams finally bashes one to death with a p.d. car and assistant coroner (Clare Kirkconnell) later reveals that the robbers had come back from the dead. It seems she'd previously cut them open for an autopsy.

Investigation leads to a drug lab where Piscopo stumbles onto Dr. Frankenstein-like equipment and a disfigured bruiser who's been electrified back from the dead. More shootings and major brawl lead to Williams' demise — but not for long as Kirkconnell miraculously figures out how to resurrect him with a bolt from the same machinery.

The leads now begin a furious chase — Williams having only a few hours before disintegrating — and they're joined by lab p.r. femme Lindsay Frost, whose empty performance is on a par with the pic. She later exits in an obnoxious special effects meltdown of human flesh certain to tantalize the most depraved among the audience.

By now, Price has made a small entry into the plot and McGavin's

role as the evil coroner is gathering steam. Trio of Williams, Piscopo and Frost are in hot pursuit — that is, until Piscopo is unceremoniously bound and drowned in a living room water tank.

Doubly determined for revenge, Williams heads toward the climactic shenanigans depicting the Price-McGavin attempt to defy death and achieve immortality. Price and McGavin should each have recognized the folly of earning any on-screen immortality with such dumb material.

Windup is as offensive as rest of the pic and serves only to point up the lame writing by Terry Black and weak direction of Mark Goldblatt. Their work is of a piece with the comment by Williams' character at one juncture; "just weird ... approaching degenerate." Or as Piscopo's cop declares at another point, "that's really disgusting."

— *Tege.*

Assault Of The Killer Bimbos

An Empire Pictures release of a Titan production. Produced by David DeCoteau, John Schouweiler. Executive producer, Debra Dion. Directed by Anita Rosenberg. Screenplay, Ted Nicolaou; story by Rosenberg, Patti Astor, Nicolaou; camera (color), Thomas Calloway; editor, Barry Zetlin; music supervisor, Jonathan Scott Bogner; music, Fred Lapides, Marc Ellis; sound, D.J. Ritchie; production design, Royce Mathew; costume design, Susan Rosenberg; stunt coordinator, John Stewart; coproducer, Thomas A. Keith; production manager, Ellen Cabot; assistant director, Will Clark; second unit director, DeCoteau; second unit camera, Voya Mikulic. Reviewed at Pickwick Drive-In theater, Burbank, Calif., May 4, 1988. MPAA Rating: R. Running time: **81 MIN.**

Peaches	Christina Whitaker
LuLu	Elizabeth Kaitan
Darlene	Tammara Souza
Wayne-O	Nick Cassavetes
Troy	Griffin O'Neal
Billy	Jamie Bozian
Vinnie	Mike Muscat
Poodles	Patti Astor
Shifty Joe	David Marsh

Hollywood — Empire Pictures may be hitting its stride with "Assault Of The Killer Bimbos," creating the kind of engagingly dumb, slyly hip pic that is tailor-made for cult enjoyment.

Bound to be a hoot for followers of light, campy diversion, under-$1,000,000 outing could uncover an enthusiastic, if limited, following in a 70-print release.

First-timer Anita Rosenberg is decidedly the right choise as director, fashioning a pic that dips and sways with its own kind of bimbotic integrity.

(The catchy title originally was assigned by Empire to Gorman Bechard for a film ultimately receiving the moniker "Hack 'Em High," following which Rosenberg's version was shot. — *Ed.*)

With plenty to ogle in the form of its leggy, curvaceous and brazen protagonists, it nonetheless scores, of all things, a few feminist points in its portrayal of the resilient air-

heads.

Chief bimbos are played by Christina Whitaker and Elizabeth Kaitan as go-go dancers in a dead-end nightclub who are mistakenly taken for murderers after their boss, who's just fired them, gets bumped off by hoods.

On the lam to Mexico, they pick up a willing hostage — Tammara Souza as a truckstop waitress who's bored with her job — and three unwelcome admirers in the form of cartoonish surf bums played by Jamie Bozian and moviebiz brats Nick Cassavetes and Griffin O'Neal.

Road adventures, which includes a wacky high-speed chase on the desert highway, complete with a flying police car stunt, end in a low-rent Tijuana motel where they encounter the true killers, vacationing in kitschy style, lure them into their room, and justice, in effect, is served.

Fueling this unabashedly low-octane outing is filmmaker's innate feel for the material. Camera angles now and then achieve a skewed style similar to current cult fave "Blood Simple," and Ted Nicolaou's script is frequently a hoot.

Head bimbo Whitaker has the kind of unshakable cool that makes her look like she's cruising Ocean Avenue even while driving a getaway car out of a truckstop, and Kaitan makes the perfect dopey sidekick.

The bimboys, unfortunately, don't fare as well.

David Marsh is memorably smarmy as the nightclub owner, and Eddie Deezen is inspired casting as the froggy little deputy who tries to get in the bimbos' way.

Pic is rated R for language that saunters crudely into the vernacular, brief nudity and numerous titillation shots. — *Daws.*

Midnight Crossing

A Vestron Pictures release of a Team Effort/Limelight Studios production. Produced by Mathew Hayden; coproduced by Doug Weiser. Executive producers, Dan Ireland, Gary Barber. Gregory Cascante, Wanda Rayle. Directed by Roger Holzberg. Screenplay, Holzberg, Doug Weiser from story by Holzberg; camera (color), Henry Vargas; editor, Earl Watson; music, Steve Tyrell; original score, Paul Buckmaster, Al Gorgoni; line producer, Jack Lorenz; associate producers, Frank Tolin, Oscar Costo, Duke Siotkas; casting, Reuben Cannon & Associates/Carol Dudley CSA. Reviewed at Egyptian theater, Seattle Film Festival, May 7, 1988. MPAA Rating: R. Running time: **104 MIN.**

Helen Barton	Faye Dunaway
Morely Barton	Daniel J. Travanti
Lexa Shubb	Kim Cattrall
Jeff Shubb	John Laughlin
Ellis	Ned Beatty

Seattle — "Midnight Crossing" is tedious, grossly over-acted attempt at a modern-day pirate adventure filled with gratuitous sex and violence.

The plot is passable, but it be-

comes buried beneath awful dialog, unbelievable characters and disjointed scenes which make no sense. It's hard to image anyone lining up to see this one, either at the box-office or at homevid stores. Film had its world preem at the Seattle Film Festival.

Faye Dunaway stars as Helen, who apparently is an ophthalmologist who goes blind because of glaucoma. ("Why me?" she wonders aloud.) Her apparent blindness is just one example of an unrealistic device employed to move along the limp plot.

She's married to a sleazy insurance salesman (Daniel J. Travanti) bent on retrieving the fortune he and a former naval buddy buried on an island off the coast of Cuba during Castro's takeover in 1959. Dunaway and Travanti set sail for the Caribbean — purportedly to celebrate their 20th anniversary — on a boat owned by John Laughlin, the son of Travanti's now-deceased naval buddy, and Laughlin's tawdry wife, Kim Cattrall.

Cattrall, it turns out, is having an affair with her boss — Travanti. That is but one of many double and triple crossings, many of which don't make too much sense, which emerge during the film.

There are also assorted run-ins with Ned Beatty, a debauched sailor with some sort of British accent, who seems to serve no more purpose than another opportunity to introduce more violence into the film.

— *Magg.*

Slime City

A Slime City Co. production and release. Produced by Gregory Lamberson, Peter Clark, Marc Makowski. Written and directed by Lamberson. Camera (Lab-link color, 16m), Clark; editor, Lamberson, Britton Petrucelly; music, Robert Tomaro; production design, Bonnie Brinkley; special makeup effects, J. Scott Coulter; additional effects, Tom Lauten; production manager, Makowski; assistant director, Ed Walloga. Reviewed at Bleecker St. 2 cinema, N.Y., May 6, 1988. No MPAA Rating. Running time: **85 MIN.**

Alex	Robert C. Sabin
Lori/Nicole	Mary Huner
Jerry	T.J. Merrick
Irish	Dick Biel
Lizzy	Jane Reibel
Ruby	Bunny Levine
Roman	Dennis Embry
Selina	Marilyn Oran

"Slime City" is a minor horror film with spoof elements, shot in Brooklyn on a $50,000 budget. Currently unspooling midnights in Greenwich Village, it is destined for fringe audiences.

Title promises more than is delivered, in a tale of an apartment building whose denizens aren't what they seem. Student Robert C. Sabin moves in and after dining with a poet neighbor starts dripping slime from his forehead, his face starting to look like a pizza via makeup effects. Goopy look is only temporary but recurs and Sabin turns into a murderous monster.

An occultist named Zachary was the cause of the problem, having turned the inhabitants of the building into monsters who possess their victims' bodies. Pastel-colored concoctions stored in the basement do the trick.

Pic climaxes in a repulsive, extended scene of grotesque makeup effects where heroine Mary Huner awkwardly hacks Sabin into little pieces but he just won't die. The fact that when his entrails spill out they look just like a breakfast of sausage and eggs appears to be tongue-in-cheek.

Lighting and sound recording are amateurish but the film plays acceptably, with tolerable acting. A harsh jumpcut (scene deleted) during a dinner scene with the heroine's parents is jarring and ineffectual.

Sabin is a bland antihero, but Huner shows promise in her dual role as heroine and contrasting vamp in black Nicole, who seduces the hero.—*Lor.*

Phobia
(AUSTRALIAN)

A Jadee production. Executive producer, Will Davies. Produced by John Mandelberg. Written and directed by John Dingwall. Camera (color), Steve Newman; editor, Mandelberg; music, Ross Edwards; art direction, Robert Michael. Reviewed at Australian Film & TV School screening room, Sydney, May 4, 1988. Running time: **85 MIN.**

Renate Simmons . . . . . Gosia Dobrowolska
David Simmons . . . . Sean Scully

Sydney — Although the title might lead one to expect a slasher-thriller, this actually is a gripping psychological drama about the final hours of a 9-year marriage.

Obviously made on a modest budget, with only a 3-week shooting schedule, pic, first one directed by screenwriter John Dingwall ("Sunday Too Far Away," "Buddies") triumphantly overcomes its monetary limitations, and boasts two outstanding performances. Arthouse release is indicated ahead of a strong video and tube life.

Film takes place over two nights and days in the leafy, waterside suburban home of Polish-born Renate Simmons and her husband, David. Right from the first scene, Dingwall creates a tense mood as Renate waits anxiously for the drunken David's latenight return. This marriage, we quickly discover, is over. "The heat of battle's died," says David, and Renate has made up her mind to leave.

Problem' she suffers from agoraphobia, a fear of open spaces, and the tensions brought about by her collapsing marriage have aggravated the illness. David knows how sick she is (very late in film it's revealed just to what extent he knows) and plays on her phobia.

Early scenes establish David as charming, cheerful and matter-of-

fact, while Renate is anguished, tearful and edgy. She plans to stay with a girlfriend when she leaves, but David sabotages those plans along with every other attempt she makes to get out of the house. He accuses her of being selfish and demanding, while she struggles to overcome her phobia.

Midway through the film, the roles begin to change. Renate summons almost superhuman strength to overcome her fears, and David, realizing she may, after all, be able to leave him, becomes morose, then angry and finally violent. Pic builds to a gripping climax, though audiences shouldn't expect a bloody end to the drama; "Phobia" isn't a thriller in that sense.

The pic is a 2-hander, and Dingwall relies heavily on his actors to carry it off. They don't let him down. Gosia Dobrowolska is superb as the wife who, with great effort, finds the strength to fight back against her Machiavellian spouse. It's a touching, beautifully crafted performance.

Former Disney child star Sean Scully ("Prince And The Pauper") is a revelation as David, whose charm masks his own severe psychological problems. The edgy relationship between the two is sharply maintained throughout the film.

Credits are modest but proficient, with Steve Newman's fluid camerawork and Ross Edwards' spare, haunting music worthy of mention. Dingwall's screenplay, intelligent and sometimes grimly amusing, keeps the viewer wondering whether husband or wife is the one worthy of sympathy.

Obviously a pic with only two characters about a marriage breakup won't be to everyone's taste, and marketing must be handled carefully; but "Phobia" deserves to find an audience, and probably will. Fest outings are also indicated.   —*Strat.*

Tango Bar
(ARGENTINE-PUERTO RICAN)

A Beco Films/Zaga Films production. Produced by Roberto Gandara, Juan Carlos Codazzi. Executive producer, Codazzi. Directed by Marcos Zurinaga. Screenplay, Jose Pablo Feinnman, Codazzi, Zurinaga; camera (color), Zurinaga; editor, Pablo Mari; music, Atilio Stampone; production design, Maria Julia Bertozio; associate producers, Porfirio Guzman, Daniel Lugo. Reviewed at the American Film Institute (AFI Fest), L.A., April 13, 1988. Running time: **90 MIN.**

Ricardo . . . . Raul Julia
Elena . . . . Valeria Lynch
Antonio . . . . Ruben Juarez

Hollywood — "Tango Bar" represents a 1-dimensional but spirited spin through the history of the Argentine dance form, with dashes of melodrama and politics thrown in for good measure.

Episodic, anthology format dominates the simple, schematic storyline, but strong production numbers and almost continual music should

create a domestic audience for this Spanish-language import.

Dancers from the "Tango Argentino" stage show execute many of the exciting numbers mounted here, and this film could have the sort of popularizing effect on willing crossover viewers that the theatrical piece had. On the other hand, those for whom a little tango music goes a long way will be in for a long evening.

Pic is framed around the anticipated reunion, after 11 years, of popular cabaret performers Ricardo (Raul Julia) and Antonio (Ruben Juarez). As extensive flashbacks reveal, Antonio felt compelled to leave Argentina when the censorship directives of the military dictatorship began affecting even something as seemingly innocuous as the tango, while Ricardo opted for staying in Buenos Aires and seeing the thing through.

Complicating matters further was the decision of the club's third singer and Antonio's ladyfriend, Elena (Valeria Lynch), to remain behind and take up with Ricardo.

Neat little triangle provides the most meager of propellents to the picture, and in microcosm illustrates the impulse toward reconciliation between those who fled and those who stayed.

All this just lends a mildly melancholy context to the overview of tango that director Marcos Zurinaga ably provides. Julia and Juarez (considered the leading tango singer in Argentina today) perform a number of tunes themselves and the Tango Argentino dancers enact others, but the highlights undoubtedly are the clips of the ways tango has turned up in international films through the decades.

Beginning with excerpts featuring Carlos Gardel, who is credited with exporting the form in the 1920s and '30s, pic offers up sometimes hilarious, sometimes electrifying snippets from numerous American and French pictures featuring the tango, from Chaplin, Valentino and Gene Kelly to Laurel & Hardy and the Flintstones.

Song lyrics, and the film itself, lean a bit heavily on the "life is but a tango" notion, and nightclub setting becomes rather claustrophobic after an hour or so. Zurinaga, a Puerto Rican cinematographer whose sole previous directorial outing was "La Gran Fiesta," has shot the dance numbers exceptionally well, showing the performers to maximum advantage, and pic has a very polished technical sheen.

As for the actors, Raul Julia doesn't seem as entirely at home on the small cabaret stage as Juarez and Lynch, but all three contribute to the energy and spirit of the occasion. —*Cart.*

Deep Space

A Trans World Entertainment presentation. Executive producer, Yoram Pelman. Produced by Alan Amiel. Coproduced and directed by Fred Olen Ray. Screenplay, Ray, T.L. Lankford; camera (Foto-Kem color), Gary Graver; editor, Natan Zahavi, Bruce Stubblefield; music, Robert O. Ragland, Alan Oldfield; sound, David Waelder; art direction, Corey Kaplan; assistant director, Gary Bettman; production manager-associate producer, Herb Linsey; creature effects, Steve Patino, Sho-Glass Effects; special effects makeup, Steve Neill; stunt coordinator, John Stewart; postproduction supervisor, Zahavi. Reviewed on TWE vidcassette, N.Y., April 30, 1988. MPAA Rating: R. Running time: **90 MIN.**

Det. Macliamor . . . . Charles Napier
Carla Sanborn . . . . Ann Turkel
Capt. Robertson . . . . Bo Svenson
Jerry . . . . Ron Glass
Elaine Wentworth . . . . Julie Newmar
Dr. Forsyth . . . . James Booth
Gen. Randolph . . . . Norman Burton
Dr. Rogers . . . . Anthony Eisley
Hawkins . . . . Michael Forest
Also with: Peter Palmer, Elisabeth Brooks, Jesse Dabson, Fox Harris, Dawn Wildsmith, Sandy Brooke, Susan Stokey.

Something went wrong with "Deep Space," a horror sendup that reportedly went through extensive postproduction reshooting and tinkering before its recent direct-to-video release. Finished product doesn't fit its title in the slightest.

Both Charles Napier and Ron Glass are typecast as a couple of L.A. police detectives, partnered on a case when a monster from Outer Space crash lands and starts killing people. The monster was created by U.S. scientists for military research that went awry, with project director James Booth feeling the heat from his supervisor, a general played by Norman Burton.

Pic is essentially a too literal, tired homage to Ridley Scott's modern classic "Alien," which already has been the model for several alien-on-Earth cheapies such as "Scared To Death" and "Alien Contamination."

Helmer Fred Olen Ray goes to absurd lengths to mimic "Alien," including a scene of a guard calling for his kitty cat which is staged identically, the monster dripping KY jelly, it striking with same rapid movement (but ropelike tentacles), having a young version that is shaped like an oversize scorpion (instead of the octopus look) and even a variation on the chest-burster scene. It's all silly, not funny or scary.

Cast includes numerous unimpressive cameos, including erstwhile "Li'l Abner" star Peter Palmer popping up as a fellow cop; he has no scenes with his onetime costar Julie Newmar, however. Lead players are okay, maintaining a flippant attitude. The monster vaguely resembles the beastie inserted at the climax of Jacques Tourneur's classic "Night Of The Demon," and Napier ultimately wields a chainsaw against it. — *Lor.*

A World Apart
(BRITISH)

An Atlantic release and presentation with British Screen of a Working Title production, in association with Film Four International. Executive producers, Tim Bevan, Graham Bradstreet. Produced by Sarah Radclyffe. Directed by Chris Menges. Screenplay, Shawn Slovo; camera (Metrocolor), Peter Biziou; editor, Nicolas Gaster; music, Hans Zimmer; sound (Dolby), Judy Freeman; production design, Brian Morris; art direction, Mike Philips; costume design, Nic Ede; assistant director, Guy Travers; associate producer, Slovo; casting, Susie Figgis. Reviewed at Atlantic screening room, L.A., May 6, 1988. (In Cannes Film Festival, competing). MPAA Rating: PG-13. Running time: **113 MIN.**

Diana Roth .... Barbara Hershey
Molly Roth .... Jodhi May
Muller .... David Suchet
Gus Roth .... Jeroen Krabbé
Kruger .... Paul Freeman
Harold .... Tim Roth
Elsie .... Linda Mvusi
Bertha .... Yvonne Bryceland
Solomon .... Albee Lesotho
Yvonne Abelson .... Nadine Chalmers
Miriam Roth ..... Carolyn Clayton-Cragg
Jude Roth .... Merav Gruer

Hollywood — **"A World Apart" provides a sharp glimpse of conditions at a particular time and place — what it was like to be politically contrary in the early 1960s in South Africa. Although its politics are very clear, this first feature from ace cinematographer Chris Menges and writer Shawn Slovo is neither a polemic nor an analysis of apartheid, since it is mostly told from the p.o.v. of a 13-year-old girl whose life becomes dramatically disrupted as a result of her parents' subversive activities.**

Critical reception for this absorbing Cannes Film Festival competition entry should be strong, paving the way for a good run on the specialized circuit internationally.

Set in 1963, story is described as a fictionalized account of what happened to young Shawn and her family when the authorities began cracking down on them. Pic's dramatic arc traces the growing emotional and political awareness of the youngster, but also represents a daughter's critique of what she perceives as her mother's selfish absorption in concerns she condescendingly considers above her offspring's head.

Film opens with Papa Jeroen Krabbé's quick flight from the house and the country for what he describes as a "business" trip. This leaves the lovely suburban Johannesburg home full of women — Diana (Barbara Hershey), an activist journalist, three daughters, of whom Molly (Jodhi May) is the oldest, and the black live-in maid Elsie (Linda Mvusi).

The casual cruelties and injustices of the South African system and the attitudes it encourges and condones are displayed as part of life's fabric, but what's really going on with Molly's parents, as well as the friendly blacks who often visit the house, remains unclear and out of reach to the girl.

Reality begins rudely intruding, however, first with hateful taunts about her father at school, then with much more serious incidents stemming from her mother's arrest under the 90-day Detention Act. At this, Molly's grandmother comes to try to hold the family together, but can't handle it, leading Molly to board at school, where even her best friend won't talk to her anymore.

Diana commences her incarceration stoically and refuses to cooperate with her interrogators. During a second 3-month stretch, she begins cracking. A suicide attempt lands her back home under house arrest, setting the stage for Molly's outpouring of resentment over having been denied her mother's love and kept in the dark for so long about why events unfolded as they did.

Little that takes place here is very surprising, and the ending, which unites the family literally and figuratively with the masses of blacks whose cause it has taken up, feels somewhat soft and generalized in the wake of the very specific story that has led up to it.

After a distinguished and varied career as a lenser of mostly socially committed documentaries and features, Chris Menges shows a sensitive and sure hand as a director. Muted, unemphatic approach reveals the influence of his longtime collaborator Ken Loach, but Menges moves things along much more crisply than Loach ever has, and for the most part steers clear of 1-note didacticism. Unlike the case in "Cry Freedom," for instance, the chief prison investigator, vividly portrayed by David Suchet, is allowed a fair share of humanity.

Barbara Hershey represents a solid central figure for the film. Her commitment to her own ideals is convincingly unshakable, and the actress conveys strength that could only be worn down with considerable time and difficulty. Nevertheless, the limited, daughter's eye viewpoint restricts one's access to the woman's inner self, the source of her political beliefs and her self-image. Ultimately, the viewer knows little about her except for her particular politics vis-à-vis apartheid.

Happily, Jodhi May is at all times engaging as Molly, sustaining the film with no problem. Performances throughout are uniformly naturalistic and believable, and pic, which was shot in Zimbabwe, possesses a rich, luminous look despite what was assuredly a limited budget.

As final title partially informs, the real-life family moved to London in 1964. Shawn Slovo's father Joe is a Communist Party leader, the only white member of the executive committee of the African National Congress, and continues to work for his cause out of Zambia. Her mother, however, was killed by a parcel bomb in 1982. —*Cart.*

El Lute II
(Mañana Seré Libre)
(Tomorrow I'll Be Free)
(SPANISH)

A Multivideo production. Produced by Isabel Mula, José María Cunillés. Directed by Vicente Aranda. Screenplay, Aranda, Eleuterio Sánchez, Joaquin Jordá; camera (Fujicolor), José Luis Alcaine; editor, Teresa Font; music, José Nieto; sets, Josep Rosell; sound, Jim Willis. Reviewed at Cine Lope de Vega, Madrid, April 21, 1988. (In Cannes Film Festival, competing.) Running time: **127 MIN.**

Eleuterio (El Lute) .... Imanol Arias
Lolo .... Angel Pardo
Toto .... Jorge Sanz
Esperanza .... Pastora Vega
Maria .... Blanca Apilanez
Also with: Silvia Rodriguez, Montserrat Tey, Antonio Iranzo, Nuria Hosta, Pedro Diaz del Corral.

Madrid — **The second part of the adventures of Spain's best-known delinquent and escape artist during the last years of the Franco era is an entertaining, fast-moving sequel to the grimmer first part. It has all the ingredients for becoming a crowd-pleaser both in Spain and abroad.**

For those who haven't seen the earlier adventures of "El Lute," pic holds up on its own. Script alternates between action scenes with the Civil Guards, who are hunting El Lute and his family throughout Andalucia, and touches of wry humor and folklorish insights into the lives of Spanish gypsies, a mix that should prove appealing to foreign audiences as well.

Pic kicks off with El Lute again breaking out of a prison on New Year's Eve, eventually joining up with his two brothers. Partly alone, and partly together with his brothers, their wives and their children, the delinquents elude the police, sometimes setting up house in sewers, sometimes appearing as respectable businessmen, and even buying a swank apartment overlooking the Alhambra.

The action scenes, including shootouts with the Civil Guards, bank robberies and persecutions are excellently handled by director Vicente Aranda and Spain's top lenser, José Luis Alcaine; the dialog is fast, witty, but sometimes hard to follow since it's spoken in the gypsy dialect. Carrying the film along brilliantly is Imanol Arias, who is as captivating in this part as in the first.

Supporting cast is topnotch, and all technical credits excellent. Story ends with El Lute's recapture by the Civil Guards in 1973, and an explanation by narrator that the criminal was pardoned after Franco died, two years later.

Pic should prove of interest to all audiences. There are no unpleasant torture scenes, as there were in Part I. Presence of the real Eleuterio Sánchez at Cannes should further help in promoting the film internationally. —*Besa.*

Drowning By Numbers
(BRITISH)

Film Four Intl. and Elsevier Vendex Film presentation of an Allarts production in association with VPRO Television Holland the coproduction fund for the Dutch Broadcasting Corp. Produced by Kees Kasander and Denis Wigman. Written and directed by Peter Greenaway. Camera (Kodakcolor), Sacha Vierny; editor, John Wilson; music, Michael Nyman; production design, Ben Van Os, Jan Roelfs; costumes, Heather Williams. Reviewed at Bijou Preview Theater, London, May 6, 1988. (In Cannes Film Festival, competing.) Running time: **118 MIN.**

Madgett .... Bernard Hill
Cissie Colpitts 1 .... Joan Plowright
Cissie Colpitts 2 .... Juliet Stevenson
Cissie Colpitts 3 .... Joely Richardson
Smut .... Jason Edwards
Jake .... Bryan Pringle
Hardy .... Trevor Cooper
Bellamy .... David Morrissey
Also with: Joan Rogan, Paul Mooney, Jane Gurnett, Kenny Ireland, Michael Percival, Joanna Dickens, Janine Duvitski.

London — **With "Drowning By Numbers" British writer-producer Peter Greenaway has fashioned an altogether more easily enjoyable pic than his last two efforts, and is greatly aided by an excellent cast of English actors who finely complement the helmer's skilled use of camera and location.**

Greenaway's last pic, "The Belly Of An Architect," was an attempt to break more into the mainstream, while this pic seems to reflect what Greenaway does best ... a compact, more clearly defined film (though still packed with provoking asides and esoteric nuances), that is both intellectually stimulating and darkly funny. Its eccentricities are peculiarly British, but the pic could work for offshore audiences, and undoubtedly will be a winner on the film festival and art circuits.

Peter Greenaway seems to fall into the love-him or hate-him category, and reaction to "Drowning By Numbers" again will be game-playing the all-important ingredients.

In previous features Greenaway has ably shown his brilliance as a director of staged and structured scenes (with regular cinematographer Frenchman Sacha Vierny giving the films a beautiful look), but his failing always has been his direction of actors. In "Drowning By Numbers" the confident talents of Joan Plowright (especially), Juliet Stevenson, Joely Richardson and Bernard Hill give the film a more rounded feel than any of his previous efforts.

Pic follows the darkly murderous acts of three women all named Cissie Colpitts (Plowright, Stevenson and Richardson) and their friend the local coroner Madgett Mill) and his son Smut (Jason Edwards).

Pic opens with Plowright drowning her husband in a tin bath.

The families and friends of the three murdered men suspect the three women of the killings and meet under a water tower. When none of the three Colpitts women submit to Madgett's sexual advances he decides to admit his part in the murders. But his game-playing instincts take the better of him, and he organizes a game of tug-of-war between the conspirators and the women.

Pic ends with young Jason Edwards (Smut) killing himself and the three Cissie Colpitts taking their affectionate leave of Hill and leaving him to drown in a sinking row boat.

"Drowning By Numbers" deals with metaphorical game-playing of sex and death in the best traditions of black humor, all set in an idyllic English summer (actually pic was filmed in the fall and some actors look decidedly cold) and pays tribute to the games, landscape and especially a conspiracy of women.

As an aside Greenaway has placed the numbers 1-100 throughout the film (for example 1 appears on a tree, 36 is on Joely Richardson's swimsuit, 76 and 77 are on the rumps of cows and 100 is on Madgett's rowing boat) — yet another exercise in game-playing and a challenge for the viewer to spot all the numbers.

The acting is uniformly excellent, with Joan Plowright and Juliet Stevenson especially good, and Jason Edwards making an appealing film debut. Technical credits are all fine, with Vierny's cinematography making the landscape look lush and beautiful.

Greenaway has written and directed a pic that should appeal to his admirers and possibly convert a few previously disinterested filmgoers.
—*Adam.*

The Navigator
(NEW ZEALAND-COLOR/B&W)

An Arenafilm and Film Investment Corp. of New Zealand presentation. Produced by John Maynard. Directed by Vincent Ward. Screenplay, Ward, Kelly Lyons, Geoff Chapple; camera (color, b&w), Geoffrey Simpson; editor, John Scott; music, Davood A. Tabrizi; production design, Sally Campbell; sound (Dolby), Dick Reade; coproducer, Gary Hannam. Reviewed at National Film Unit theater, Wellington, N.Z., March 19, 1988. (In Cannes Film Festival, competing). Running time: 93 MIN.
Connor . . . . Bruce Lyons
Arno . . . . Chris Haywood
Griffin . . . . Hamish McFarlane
Searle . . . . Marshall Napier
Ulf . . . . Noel Appleby
Martin . . . . Paul Livingston
Linnet . . . . Sarah Peirse

Wellington — "The Navigator" is a remarkable second feature from director Vincent Ward, whose first full-length film, "Vigil," was selected for main competition at Cannes in 1984. It is remarkable because of its absorbing story that links medieval fears and fortunes to our times, while confirming Ward as an original talent.

The story begins in Cumbria in 1348, the year of the Black Death. A mining village lives in fear of the advancing plague. Young Griffin (Hamish McFarlane) is anxious for the return of his beloved, much-older brother Connor (Bruce Lyons) from the outside world. He is haunted by a dream about a journey, a quest to a great cathedral in a celestial city, and a figure about to fall from a steeple.

When his brother returns to the village with tales of impending doom, 9-year-old Griffin recounts his dream which reveals a way whereby the community might escape.

The two brothers, with four comrades, set out on the journey fired by Griffin's prophetic vision. It takes them to a city of the late 1980s and on a mission against time if their village is to be saved. There is no triumph without sacrifice — in the dream and in reality.

The formidable skills of Ward are shown in the way his story works, not only as adventure, but as the love story of two brothers and a parable of faith and religion.

As the medievals joust with the paraphernalia of a night-bound, modern city, in their striving to reach the cathedral at its heart, Ward conjures a series of striking sequences and images.

The best affirm, invariably with humor, the timeless ascendancy of individual human spirit against the forces that would dehumanize, whether it is Griffin momentarily mesmerized by a wall of tv screens beaming their message or Connor hurtling through the night clinging to the front of a "monster" train.

From the convincing detail of the 14th century locations to the uneasy, slumbering, contemporary metropolis, Ward's inspiration is apparent, and actors and technicians give their best.

Geoffrey Simpson's photography — stark black and white for the Cumbrian sequences, color for the enactment of Griffin's dream and visions — is of the highest order, with score by Iranian composer Davood Tabrizi (domiciled in Sydney) empathetic with the whole.

Fine performances are delivered by McFarlane and Lyons, and also Marshall Napier and Paul Livingston as the Cumbrians Searle and Martin.

"The Navigator" should find broader acceptance and do greater business on and off the festival and art-house tracks, than the director's earlier "Vigil." As the first coproduction between the New Zealand and Australian film commissions, following producer John Maynard's difficulty in raising all the necessary finance in Ward's homeland, it sets a sterling precedent for future joint enterprises in feature filmmaking between the two countries. —*Nic.*

El Dorado
(SPANISH-FRENCH)

An Iberoamericana de TV, coproduction with Chrysalide Films, Canal Plus and FR 3 Films, with collaboration of the Quinto Centenario, and participation of TVE and RAI-Sacis. Produced by Andrés Vicente Gómez. Written and directed by Carlos Saura. Camera (Agfa Gevaert color), Teo Escamilla; editor, Pedro del Rey; musical direction, Alejandro Masso; art direction, Terry Pritchard; production manager, Victor Albarran; special effects, Reyes Abades; production manager, Pablo Buelna; sound (Dolby), Gilles Orthion; casting, Carlos Cordero. Reviewed at Cinema Real, Madrid, April 20, 1988. (In Cannes Film Festival, competing). Running time: 151 MIN.
Aguirre . . . . Omero Antonutti
Pedro de Ursúa . . . . Lambert Wilson
Guzmán . . . . Eusebio Poncela
Inés . . . . Gabriela Roel
Elvira . . . . Inés Sastre
La Bandera . . . . José Sancho
Pedrarias . . . . Patxi Bisquert
Llamoso . . . . Francisco Algora
Montoya . . . . Feodor Atkine
Also with: Abel Vitón, Paco Merino, Mariano González, Gladys Catania, David González, Alfredo Catania, Luis Fernando Gómez, Rodolfo Cisneros, Gerardo Arce, Manuel Ruiz, Adrián Diaz, José Solano, Gustavo Rojas, Aidee de Lev, Franklin Huezo, Rubén Pagura, Wilson Morera.

Madrid — Touted as the most expensive Spanish film ever ($8,000,000), Carlos Saura's epic on the Conquistador Lope de Aguirre is a project that has been kicking around for close to a decade.

Saura's film is a linear, chronological version of the ill-fated Conquistador's trip up the Amazon River. There are some beautiful sequences and moments of superb footage, but somehow the story unravels at a distance.

Thanks to hefty coin from the Spanish Culture Ministry, the Foundation for the 500th anniversary of the discovery of America and various coproduction deals with Spanish, Italo and French tv, producer Andrés Vicente Gómez managed to film the epic using locations in Costa Rica.

Despite some dramatic moments, much of the overlong film is anticlimactic and far too talky. The slow pacing is punctuated occasionally by a violent sequence, but there is never any build-up of tension or real suspense.

Yarn, familiar to those who have seen Werner Herzog's "Aguirre, The Wrath Of God," concerns an expedition undertaken in 1560 from Peru by Pedro de Ursúa to discover the fabled land of El Dorado. Setting out with 300 Spanish soldiers and 300 natives, Ursúa slowly made his way up the river, accompanied by his pretty mulatto mistress, Inés.

As the expedition penetrated deeper into the jungle, supplies ran short, the expedition was harassed by hostile tribes and finally mutiny broke out among the Spaniards. The leadership eventually was seized by Aguirre, who, after going slowly mad, also was killed by the surviving soldiers.

Saura does provide some spectacular scenes. One certain to be much commented upon is a sequence in which the Spaniards run short of food and decide to sacrifice the horses. The knifing is graphically portrayed. Then the story reverts to lethargy. A pitched battle between the Spaniards and the natives never occurs; indeed, there is virtually no fighting in the film, only the successive assassinations of the various leaders.

Italo thesp Omero Antonutti, who has put in superb performances in other Spanish and Italian films, is rather too bland for the part of Aguirre, and can't hold a candle to Klaus Kinski's interpretation in the Herzog film. Lambert Wilson as Ursúa is the most convincing, although he, too, hardly comes across as a ruthless Conquistador.

Saura has not tried to whitewash history, but the episodes showing Spanish cruelty are limited mainly to one scene in long shot in which the natives, refusing to work, are shot down by Spanish arquebusiers. None of the captains arouses sympathy, but neither do they inspire hatred.

Commercially, pic may have a hard time even in art circuits, even if cut by a half hour. Carlos Saura's name may draw some audiences, but it is hard to imagine how the production cost can ever be recouped by this technically well made, but ultimately nondramatic retelling of the Aguirre story.
—*Besa.*

CANNES MARKET

A Handful Of Dust
(BRITISH)

A New Line Cinema release of an LWT/Stagescreen production. Executive producers, Jeffrey Taylor, Kent Walwin. Produced by Derek Granger. Directed by Charles Sturridge. Screenplay, Tim Sullivan, Granger, Sturridge, based on the novel by Evelyn Waugh; camera (Technicolor), Peter Hannan; editor, Peter Coulson; music, George Fenton; production design, Eileen Diss; costumes, Jane Robinson; associate producer, David Wimbury. Reviewed at Century Preview theater, London, April 14, 1988. (In Cannes Film Festival Market.) Running time: 118 MIN.
Tony Last . . . . James Wilby
Brenda Last . . . . Kristin Scott-Thomas
John Beaver . . . . Rupert Graves
Mrs. Rattery . . . . Anjelica Huston
Mr. Todd . . . . Alec Guinness
Mrs. Beaver . . . . Judi Dench
Jock . . . . Pip Torrens
Milly . . . . Cathryn Harrison

London — "A Handful Of Dust" is classy stuff from the producer-director team behind the British tv series "Brideshead Revisited." Pic, also based on an Evelyn Waugh novel, is up to the same high production standard, but with an essentially empty story.

Kristin Scott-Thomas as a lovely but fickle aristocrat is excellent, with an appealing fey manner in a role that's central to holding the film together. (Recently in the Catherine Deneuve film "Agent Trouble," her only other English-language pic is Prince's "Under The Cherry Moon.") The virtual cameo appearances of Alec Guinness, Anjelica Huston and Judi Dench go some way to giving "Dust" a pedigree it might otherwise not be able to claim.

Given proper handling, pic could fare well offshore, though the two male leads, James Wilby and Rupert Graves (recently together in "Maurice"), still are somewhat lightweight to carry a film.

Set in Britain of the 1930s, the upper classes lead a happy, cloistered life and, at the beautiful country house Hetton Abbey, Wilby and Scott-Thomas and their young son seem content until the weekend visit of idle socialite Graves.

Scott-Thomas slips into an affair with the penniless Graves while Wilby happily wanders his estate unaware he is being cuckolded. Their son is killed in a freak riding accident, prompting Scott-Thomas to tell her husband she is leaving him and wants a divorce.

When Wilby finds the divorce settlement would mean selling Hetton he cancels proceedings and promptly sets sail for South America in search of a lost Amazonian city with an eccentric explorer. Pic ends with Scott-Thomas' affair petering out and Wilby being held by the mysterious Mr. Todd (Guinness), destined to spend the rest of his years reading the novels of Dickens to the oddly threatening man.

Technically, "A Handful Of Dust" cannot be faulted, with the design of Eileen Diss, costumes by Jane Robertson and cinematography of Peter Hannan combining for a visual feast. Where the film disappoints is the story, which though it ably highlights the vacuous attitudes of the English upper clases, is essentially slight.

Guinness is fine as a half-caste, though he doesn't really have to stretch himself; ditto Anjelica Huston, who at least has some humorous scenes with Wilby as he consoles him over the death of his son by playing animal snap. Also good is Pip Torrens as the couple's best friend, a lawmaker, who spends most of the pic trying to find someone who can tell him about pigs so he can help his farming constituents. —*Adam.*

Der Gläserne Himmel
(The Glass Heaven)
(WEST GERMAN)

An Avista Film production, in association with Voissfilm, Nina Grosse Film. World Sales; Transocean Intl., Munich. Produced by Alena & Herbert Rimbach. Written and directed by Nina Grosse. Camera (color), Hans Bücking; editor, Patricia Rommel; music, Flora St. Loup; production design, Reiner Schaper, Christine Pendellé; sound, Holger Gimpel, Günther Hahn; assistant director, Harry Göckeritz. Reviewed at Berlin Film Festival (New German Cinema section), Feb. 18, 1988. (Also in Cannes Film Festival Market.) Running time: **87 MIN.**

Julien Lerner	Helmut Berger
Bichette	Silvie Orcier
Julien's mother	Agnes Fink
Irene Lerner	Maria Harmann
Cortez	Tobias Engel
Kiki	Flora St. Loup

Also with: Klaus Mikoleit (Antoine), Jean François Derec (Leduc), Circe (Hotel manager), Jodie Pavlis (Woman in Black), Kathryn Walton Ward, Noel Vergo.

Berlin — "The Glass Heaven" is a moody, smartly handled first feature about a respectable businessman tormented by a nightmare in which he sees a woman strangled in an aquarium. Nina Grosse shows she has plenty of style and ideas and this debut augers well for her future. Distribs looking for offbeat fare should take a look.

Pic is set entirely in Paris, though everything is spoken in German, which is distracting at times. Julien lives with his bedridden, demanding mother and his bed-minded wife, but seems bored with it all. The woman he saw killed was dressed in black and wore a distinctive bracelet. Coincidentally, there has been a series of unsolved stranglings in the city, seven to date.

On his way to work one day, Julien sees the woman of his nightmare. He follows her to a bar where she disappears, but he reconizes a customer in the bar as the strangler in the dream. Before long he's attracted to Bichette, a prostitute who's friendly with the supposed killer. Julien stops going to work and moves into a seedy hotel near the glass-ceilinged arcade where Bichette works the "glass heaven" of the title).

It all gets more and more mysterious, and Grosse keeps the viewer on edge until the slightly predictable ending. She shows a sure touch for the imposing image, such as the strange-looking fish in the aquarium.

Thesping is fine and camerawork tops, with sharp editing adding to the enjoyment. Flora St. Loup not only provides the music, but plays another prostie. —*Strat.*

The Nature Of The Beast
(BRITISH)

A Film Four Intl.-British Screen presentation of a Rosso production. Produced by Joanna Smith. Directed by Franco Rosso. Screenplay, Janni Howker, from her novel; camera (color), Nat Crosby; editor, George Akers; music, Stanley Myers, Hans Zimmer; production design, Jamie Leonard; sound, Mike Shoring; assistant director, Ray Corbett; production manager, Linda Bruce; casting, Doreen Jones. Reviewed at Berlin Film Festival (market), Feb. 20, 1988. (Also in Cannes Film Festival Market.) Running time: **95 MIN.**

Bill Coward	Lynton Dearden
Mick Dalton	Paul Simpson
Chunder	Tony Melody
Ned Coward	Freddie Fletcher
Oggy	Dave Hill
Mrs. Dalton	Roberta Kerr
Jim Dalton	David Fleeshman

Also with: Willie Ross (Danny), Georges Malpas (Bill Howgill), Howard Crossley (Big Man), Jonathan Parkinson (Hargreaves), Julian Walsh (Tinker), Simon Molloy (Mr. Arkwright).

Berlin — A low-key drama set in a small Lancashire mill town which, like many other north country centers in Britain today, has been hard hit by unemployment, "The Nature Of The Beast" is a modest, but very sympathetic, evocation of a bleak and cheerless world as seen through the eyes of two lively schooldays.

Despite lack of names, sometimes puzzling accents and slang and a downbeat plot pic is interesting enough to enjoy okay returns in class venues.

The drama is reminiscent of Kenneth Loach's 1969 "Kes" in that it's seen exclusively from the point of view of its 14-year-old protagonists. Young Bill is fascinated by stories about a "beast" that's been killing sheep on the moors outside town, and also killed his grandfather's chickens. Bill, who is bored with school and regularly cuts classes along with his pal, Mick, is determined to hunt down the mysterious predator.

For his father, the "beast" is unemployment. Like other men in Haverston, he's worked in the mill all his life, and now it's closing down. The union organizes a strike, but it's a hopeless gesture, and Ned despises Jim Dalton (Mick's father), the shop steward, for his weakness. Ned's wife has left long ago, and he lives with his alcoholic father and his son, whom he can barely control. Eventually, he leaves to try to find work in Scotland.

For Bill, his father's departure is yet one more blow. He and Mick resort to petty stealing, even taking the expensive camera of Oggy, their sympathetic but ineffectual schoolteacher, to try to take photos of the beast. Bill's future, along with the other children of unemployed parents, looks like a grim one.

However, the film isn't grim, but filled with a sardonic humor and optimism that's refreshing. Director Franco Rosso (whose last film, "Babylon," was an all-black drama made in 1980, and who's been toiling in tv since then) gives his sad little story plenty of life.

Nat Crosby's camerawork is exemplary, and first-time producer Joanna Smith, still in her 20s, has done a super job in bringing Janni Howker's novel to the screen.

Without a doubt this will be a hard pic to market, but if handled carefully it could find an audience who'll enjoy meeting these plucky characters and experiencing a Britain away from the affluent South.
—*Strat.*

Girl Talk
(DOCU)

A Davis/Denny production. (Sales, Double Helix Films.) Produced and directed by Kate Davis. Camera (Duart color, 16m) Alyson Denny, Richard Leacock; editor, Davis, Denny; sound, Davis; technical adviser, Michael Callaghan; associate producer, Pat Gross. Reviewed at the Brattle theater, May 7, 1988. (In Cannes Film Festival Market.) No MPAA Rating. Running time: **85 MIN.**

Boston — If, as Alfred Hitchcock observed, drama is life with the dull bits cut out, then cinéma vérité might be defined as life with the dull bits left in. A case in point is Kate Davis' "Girl Talk," a fascinating 1-hour look into the lives of three troubled adolescent girls that, unfortunately, runs for 85 minutes.

Film is often effective, but it lacks the punch of the similarly themed docu "Streetwise."

Produced locally, film presents three lives for examination: Pinky, 14, who skips school and tries to stay one step ahead of the social workers who want to place her in a foster home; Mars, a runaway since she was 13, now working as a stripper in Boston's Combat Zone; and Martha, 19, who is unmarried and having her first child. Their stories are presented separately, although some attempt is made to tie them together by briefly intercutting between them toward the end of each segment.

Pinky's segment is the most annoying. Basically a child desperately in need of caring, adult supervision (her mother largely has absented herself from that role), she spends her days putting on makeup and gorging herself on candies. She is so self-absorbed that watching this for almost half an hour deadens whatever impact it might initially have.

The segment with Mars is perhaps the most heartbreaking as we watch her perform her strip routine at the now shuttered Pussycat Lounge, where she rides out on a tricycle in a schoolgirl's outfit. Subject to a great deal of abuse in her life, she claims to have found a substitute family among the bartenders and strippers at the bar.

Martha is the most articulate of the three, and is able to discuss the problems of her life including — alone among the three — her willingness to accept at least some of the responsibility for her problems. Her segment also goes on too long, as she reads several poems she has written and talks to her infant son.

While the filmmakers succeed in getting their subjects to open up about the pain in their lives, they spend too much time recording atmospheric details (Pinky running down the stairs of her apartment building, Mars washing her tricycle) instead of trying to get beyond the surface.

We never learn, for example, what has become of the father of Martha's son, a subject that does not appear to have come up during the filming. The result may be true to the spirit of cinéma vérité, but it seems more like an opportunity missed.

Tech credits are good, with noted filmmaker Richard Leacock credited with "additional photography."
— *Kimm.*

Cowboy's Don't Cry
(CANADIAN)

A Cineplex Odeon films release (Canada) of an Atlantis Films Ltd. production, in association with the Canadian Broadcasting Corp. and the Beacon Group. Executive producer, Peter Sussman. Produced by Janice L. Platt. Written and directed by Anne Wheeler, based on novel by Marilyn Halvorson. Camera (color), Brian R.R. Hebb; editor, Peter Svab; music, Louis Natale; production design, John Blackie; production manager, Tom Dent-Cox; art direction, Ted Kuchera; costume design, Jill Concannon; makeup, Dianne Pelletier; associate producer, Wheeler. Reviewed at Filmhouse screening room, Toronto, April 29, 1988. (In Cannes Festival Market.) Running time: **106 MIN.**
Josh Morgan . . . . Ron White
Shane Morgan . . . . Zachary Ansley
Lindsay Sutherland . . . . Janet-Laine Green
Janet . . . . Val Pearson
Casey Sutherland . . . . . . Candace Ratcliffe
Roger Sutherland . . . . Thomas Hauff
Lucy Morgan . . . . Rebecca Jenkins
Ron Grady . . . . Michael Hogan
Mr. Thorpe . . . . Thomas Peacock

Toronto — The lush vistas of big sky country in Alberta take front seat to the emotionally charged father-son relationship in Anne Wheeler's "Cowboys Don't Cry," based on Marilyn Halvorson's children's novel.

It's likable family fare with fine lead performances that don't allow the pic to slip into cloying sentimentality. Because it's an exploration of the intimacies of a parent and child, it probably will fare better on tv.

As country guitar strings pluck away, Josh Morgan (Ron White) rides the bulls as a rodeo cowboy, a former champ on the circuit. He's a beer guzzling, hard-driving rider who's always being implored by his wife Lucy (Rebecca Jenkins) and son Shane to settle down. When drunk Josh crashes the family pickup truck during a blowout, killing Lucy, it's time for father and son (Zachary Ansley) to align forces and carry on.

Shane's grandfather leaves him the family ranch upon his death, and he and his father move there, but with hardships to follow. Dad can't hold a job. Shane, now an adolescent, has to act as disciplinarian, supporter and promoter in a stressful, put-upon relationship. The friendship of a soon-to-be-divorced neighbor veterinarian

(Janet-Laine Green), who tends Shane's injured palomino, is one that tries to heal the indelicate father-son bond.

Wheeler and cinematographer Brian R.R. Hebb establish a vivid sense of place and rhythm, which is integral to the story, as the details of the rodeo circuit and its flashy characters are explored.

White brings a rich texture to the Peter Pan syndrome father and young Ashley crystalizes the trauma of adolescent tribulations, especially those dealing with an immature parent.

Economical script results in many volatile outbursts between father and son without enough introspective interchange. Rodeo stunts around the conflict are fine, if not menacing.

Other cast highlights include Michael Hogan as White's beer buddy and Thomas Peacock as a principal from the John Houseman school of discipline.

Wheeler has a clear attachment to the rodeo world and the geography of the Canadian west, which are the strongest suits of this tale that occasionally plucks too many heartstrings. —*Devo.*

Vroom
(BRITISH)

A Motion Pictures production for Film Four Intl. and British Screen. Produced by Paul Lister. Coproducer, Raymond Day. Directed by Beeban Kidron. Screenplay, Jim Cartwright; camera (color), Gale Tattersall; editor, Stephen Singleton; music, Adam Kidron, Michael McEvoy; art direction, Caroline Hanania; costumes, Anne Hollowood. Reviewed at Bijou Preview theater, London, May 5, 1988: (In Cannes Film Festival Market.) Running time: **89 MIN.**
Susan . . . . Diana Quick
Jake . . . . Clive Owen
Ringe . . . . David Thewlis
Fat Sam . . . . Jackie O'Broad
Donald . . . . Jim Broadbent
Shane . . . . Philip Tan
Also with: Melani Kilburn, Rosalind Bennett, Moya Brady, Sheila Reid, Michael Irving, Bill Rodger, Tim Potter.

London — "Vroom" has an easy, infectious charm with three appealing lead characters, but somewhere along the way the pic runs out of steam, and features an ending that will work for some, but make most viewers grimace.

Helmer Beeban Kidron directs with confidence and awareness, though with perhaps too much inclination to use a pop-promo style in the first half-hour, and her work is complemented by a witty script from Jim Cartwright. Pic could appeal to a young audience if handled properly.

Olive Owen (Jake) and David Thewlis (Ringe) live an okay life in a bleak north of England town, but they have a secret ... a gleaming '50s American car ready and waiting for the moment they can't stand things any longer.

That moment comes when Jake

falls for divorcée Diana Quick (Susan) and Ringe is thrown out of his house. The three drive off exhilarated and happy, reveling at life in their freedom machine. Soon they are duped out of their money, but start an apparently idyllic life in a cottage high in the beautiful Lake District.

Owen starts to get restless again and finds the others don't truly share his vision of freewheeling independence. He takes them home, the car gradually becoming more and more battered, and the pic ends with Owen flying above his hometown at the wheel of his dream car.

"Vroom" is of two distinct halves — the first features the two happy-go-lucky lads around town, Owen whom all the girls adore and Thewlis of the wacky personality and orange hair; the second deals with the trio's escape and eventual demoralization before Owen's final expression of his free spirit.

The first half is quite amusing and works well as light comedy, but when the pic takes itself more seriously the problems set in. The friend's downhill path is too obvious and has been covered in road movies before.

Owen has copious amounts of charm (though his sex appeal is rather overplayed), but has the physical problem of being rather flatfooted, which shows up regularly as Kidron has many shots of him running around. Thewlis is excellent as the wacky sidekick, but has to rely on his physical acting rather than the lines he gets.

It is easy to see why Owen should fall for Diana Quick who seems quite comfortable in the older divorced woman role, though her northern accent varies from time to time. The pic suffers from a couple of basic continuity errors and an ending that just doesn't work, but on the plus side has a certain charm and youthful fervor. —*Adam*

The Dressmaker
(BRITISH)

A Shedlo/Freeway production for Film Four Intl. and British Screen. Produced by Ronnie Shedlo. Directed by Jim O'Brien. Screenplay, John McGrath; camera (color), Michael Coulter; music, George Fenton; production design, Caroline Amies; associate producer, Steve Clark Hall. Reviewed at Market theater, Seattle Film Festival, April 30, 1988. (Also in Cannes Film Festival Market.) Running time: **90 MIN.**
Aunt Nellie . . . . Joan Plowright
Aunt Margo . . . . Billie Whitelaw
Rita . . . . Jane Horrocks
Wesley . . . . Tim Ransom

Seattle — Led by Joan Plowright and Billie Whitelaw, "The Dressmaker" is a well-made, intriguing family drama that nicely balances tension and humor within a fast-paced plot, but, unfortunately, fails to arrive at a wholly satisfying conclusion.

Still, the film has boxoffice

potential in the arthouse circuit should it find a distributor. Pic had its world premiere at the Seattle Film Fest.

Set in Liverpool in 1944, World War II is drawing to a close. The story focuses on 17-year-old Rita, who is being brought up by her two aunts — Aunt Nellie, an oldish-spinster who tries to shield Rita from the changing world around them, and flighty Aunt Margo, who takes a more liberal view of boy-girl relations and believes in enjoying life to its fullest.

As opposite personalities, Nellie and Margo suffer through a love-hate relationship as sisters. Nellie clearly dominates the household and at times barely tolerates her sister's actions. Yet it is the more youthful Margo to whom Rita naturally turns for counsel and friendship.

Enter American G.I. Wesley, a poorly educated Southern boy who captures Rita's fancy at a party. To Rita, he represents romance, excitement and escape. She longs to share her thoughts and heart with him, but her strict upbringing inhibits her from responding to his sexual advances.

Margo encourages Rita in her clandestine affair with Wesley, warning Rita to be more willing to give of herself or she will lose him. To Nellie, Wesley symbolizes the erosion of the old high standards, and she orders Margo to stop encouraging Rita and to stay away from her.

The resulting tension in the household unleashes long-suppressed bitterness between Margo and Nellie, and propels Rita toward womanhood and self-sufficiency. The rather abrupt resolution of this conflict, however, is a somewhat jarring departure from the smooth pacing delivered throughout the rest of the film. The pieces fall almost too conveniently into place, even if only temporarily.

This plot type — family conflicts — has the tendency to become tedious and repetitious. "The Dressmaker," however, moves quickly under the direction of Jim O'Brien, and with script by John McGrath (based on the novel by Beryl Bainbridge) it fully engages the audience throughout.

Highly polished performances are offered by all, including Jane Horrocks, in her screen debut as Rita.—*Magg.*

Murder One
(CANADIAN)

A Miramax Films release of an SC Entertainment production. Executive producer, Syd Cappe. Produced by Nicolas Stiliadis. Directed by Graeme Campbell. Screenplay, Tex Fuller; camera (color), Ludek Bogner; editor, Michael McMahon; music, Mychael Danna; casting, Paul Ventura; associate producer, George Flak. Reviewed at Famous Players screening room, Toronto, May 2, 1988. (In Cannes Film Festival Market.) Running time: **95 MIN.**

Billy Isaacs	Henry Thomas
Carl Isaacs	James Wilder
Wayne Coleman	Stephen Shellen
George Dungee	Erroll Slue

Toronto — Despite a potentially chilling true storyline about the 1973 mass slayings by the Isaacs brothers gang, "Murder One" turns out to be a dud.

Director Graeme Campbell doesn't give the audience a chance to be shaken by the coarse drama and he's not inside the material. Curiosity factor associated with the "In Cold Blood"-style story could peak initial interest, but after that it's an iffy theatrical prospect.

Tex Fuller's screenplay is told from the point-of-view of young innocent Billy (Henry Thomas), who gets whisked into a joyride with his two half-brothers Carl (James Wilder) and Wayne (Stephen Shellen) and their black prisonmate George (Erroll Slue) after their escape from a Maryland jail. Thomas' voiceover is flat and matter-of-fact as he narrates the spiraling horror of their escapade.

Wilder and Shellen can't absorb their characters' psyches because they're inadequately developed, and so inner machinations of the criminal mind are not revealed. They

need money and gasoline and when trying to hijack a car on a rural road, they kill a smarmy college student.

After some ambling highway driving and drinking, they arrive at a Georgia farmhouse, planning to rob it and get some gas. One by one, six family members arrive, and Wayne and Carl mechanically shoot each one. Billy is horrified, but only starts breaking down at this point. His somnambulent narration tries to rationalize why he stays — they're his only family — but it doesn't support his lack of action.

Campbell doesn't build any dramatic tension, but ambles into the murders without any emotional involvement or motivation. The actual murders may have been numbing, but so is the filming.

Although the gang knew they'd be caught there's no tension in the inevitability of it all. Carl, Wayne and George were sentenced to death over 10 years ago, but all their cases are coming up for appeal. Billy, who testified at his brothers' trial (and apparently never actually murdered anyone) is sentenced to 100 years in prison. —*Devo.*

CANNES INVITED BUT NON COMPETING

Ville étrangère
(Foreign City)
(FRENCH)

A Films Plain Chant production and release. Coproducer, La Sept. Produced by Philippe Diaz. Directed by Didier Goldschmidt. Screenplay, Goldschmidt, Jérôme Tonnere, based on Peter Handke's story "A Moment Of True Feeling;" camera (Fujicolor), Denis Lenoir; editor, Isabelle Dedieu; music, Dimitri Shostakovich; art direction, François-Renaud Labarthe; sound, Philippe Lioret, Eric Devulder, Jean-Paul Loublier; assistant director, Serge Pescetelli; production manager, Michèle Arnould. Reviewed at the CNC, Paris, April 28, 1988. (In Cannes Film Festival, Perspectives on French Cinema.) Running time: **102 MIN.**

Gregor Keuschnig	Niels Arestrup
Stéphanie	Anne Wiazemsky
Béatrice	Isabelle Otero
The writer	Roland Bertin
Françoise	Christiane Cohendy
Agnès	Marguerite Bonnin

Paris — Former critic Didier Goldschmidt, 29, bites off more than he can chew for his feature film debut in tackling a Peter Handke novella, "A Moment Of True Feeling," which is set in Paris.

Handke's study in alienation is hypnotic in its description of the mundane perceived by a man who is suddenly estranged from it. Goldschmidt's transcription is banal and boring because it cannot get into the protagonist's head as the writer does.

Handke's tale deals with an official at the Austrian Embassy in Paris who dreams he has committed murder and wakes up in the morn-

ing feeling entirely alienated from himself and his environment. He goes through his daily activities — a visit to his mistress, a presidential press conference, etc. — but is constantly aware of the absurd banality of his life.

Goldschmidt (whose father is Handke's French translator) follows the literary text faithfully, but finds no equivalent for Handke's style. One measures the failure of the film in scenes during which the protagonist (embodied by Niels Arestrup) revolts against his routine, e.g., during a dinner party at home he suddenly strips naked and tries to rape one of the guests. Grotesque and horrifying on the page, these moments manage only to be ludicrous in Goldschimdt's overly literal illustration. —*Len.*

Domani Accadrà
(It'll Happen Tomorrow)
(ITALIAN)

A Titanus release of a Sacher Film/Sofina coproduction, in association with RAI-TV Channel 1. Produced by Nanni Moretti, Angelo Barbagallo. Directed by Daniele Luchetti. Screenplay, Luchetti, Franco Bernini, Angelo Pasquini, with Sandro Petraglia; camera (Technicolor), Franco Di Giacomo; editor, Angelo Nicolini; music, Nicola Piovani; art direction, Giancarlo Basili, Leonardo Scarpa; costumes, Albert Barsacq, Marina Sciarelli. Reviewed at Holiday Cinema, Rome, March 23, 1988. (In Cannes Film Festival, Un Certain Regard section.) Running time: **90 MIN.**

Lupo	Paolo Hendel
Edo	Giovanni Guidelli
Duchess	Angela Finocchiaro
Allegra	Agnese Nano
Vera	Margherita Buy
Brigand	Ciccio Ingrassia
Count Lucifero	Ugo Gregoretti
Abbott	Dario Cantarelli

Rome — Debutant helmer Daniele Luchetti and his patrons Nanni Moretti and Angelo Barbagallo of Sacher Film hit paydirt in "It'll Happen Tomorrow," a captivating neo-Western comedy. Film shows every sign of being the discovery of the year, and judging by opening returns, a local boxoffice hit.

It should travel through fests and Italian shows abroad, with playoff possibilities in special situations.

Simplicity and originality are the key ingredients in this offbeat comedy, tracing the Jules Verne-type of fantastic adventures of two Italo cowboys in the last century. Setting is the Maremma, a malaria-infested swamp bordering the coast of Tuscany, where outlaws fled to escape the long arm of the law. Lupo (Paolo Hendel) and his young sidekick Edo (Giovanni Guidelli) instead try to leave the Maremma after stealing a few pieces of gold. The robbed man's idealist son and three ruthless Austrian mercenaries pursue the pair through a series of outlandish adventures.

Film is divided by titles into six sections. In one episode Edo and Lupo attempt to join forces with the famous bandit Ciccio Ingrassia, who has just kidnaped an uppity English noblewoman (Angela Finocchiaro). In another, handsome Edo falls under the spell of Agnese Nano, daughter of decadent (and hilarious) Count Lucifero (Ugo Gregoretti). While she gives the boy lessons in Tasso that are far from innocent, Lupo departs and falls in with a group of utopians called the Harmonics. Their enlightened commune proves short lived, but it gives the unprepossessing Lupo a chance to fall in love with sweet Harmonic chemist Margherita Buy.

Italo audiences have shown their appreciation of this intelligent, offbeat work, lensed without stars or a big budget. Art directors Giancarlo Basili and Leonardo Scarpa, and costume designer Albert Barsacq perform miracles. In the leading roles, neo-thesps Hendel and Guidelli strike the right note of ingenuous buffoonery, in sync with the rest of the cast. — *Yung.*

The Penitent

A Cineworld release of a Vista Organization/Michael & Kathy Fitzgerald presentation of an Ithaca-Cinevest production. Produced by Michael Fitzgerald. Written and directed by Cliff Osmond. Camera (Technicolor), Robin Vidgeon; editor, Peter Taylor; music, Alex North; sound, Grieve Smith; assistant director, Ruben Gonzalez R. Reviewed at Aidikoff screening room, L.A., May 11, 1988. MPAA Rating: PG-13. Running time: **94 MIN.**

Ramon Guerola	Raul Julia
Juan Mateo	Armand Assante
Celia Guerola	Rona Freed
Corina	Julie Carmen
Margarita	Lucy Reina

Hollywood — "The Penitent" is an exceedingly odd tale that is competently and simply told but would have to have been absolutely brilliant for anyone to feel compelled to see it.

Nearly 2-year-old low-budgeter has a sort of 1950s earnestness and discretion about it, and won't exactly pack 'em in at theatrical venues.

Directorial debut of character actor Cliff Osmond concerns some remote villagers of Mexican extraction (whether action is set in Mexico or the U.S. is never specified) who carry on a 200-year-old ritual of re-enacting the crucifixion every spring.

A local annually is selected to be hung on a cross all day, but even though they mercifully use only rope and not nails, the survival rate for this ritual appears to be zero, based on the swarm of widows avidly attending the spectacle.

Unlikely suspects who end up being drawn into this obscure rite are longtime chums Raul Julia and Armand Assante. Julia has married a hysterical young woman, Rona Freed, who's so uptight she won't even have sex with him. So when the mysterious, rugged Assante appears at the farm after five years in the slammer, it's the proverbial fox in the chicken coop, with Assante moving in on Freed literally in front of the frustrated Julia's nose.

All this unfolds convincingly but slowly and predictably, as the strong, bold man has his way in the world while the weaker, more reticent one stands by helplessly. Suddenly, just when Assante has made his conquest, Julia is called upon unexpectedly to substitute as this this year's Christo when the original candidate falls ill.

Obediently, the man strips down, lies down on catctus thorns, pulls a wagon bearing a figure of death through the streets of the village while various men flagellate themselves, then must carry a heavy cross up an enormously steep hill.

Apparently crazy about Freed and expecting Julia to die on the cross (tradition prohibits widows from every having sex again), Assante deviously talks his friend into letting him take his place. Without revealing the final ironies, suffice it to say the joke is on Assante.

Such a story possessed a huge potential for heavy pretentiousness, so there is something resembling pleasure in the film's general avoidance of symbolism and grandiosity. What takes place is believable from every character's point of view, except for the bigger question of why these people believe they must go through with this incredibly masochistic bit of theater.

Osmond never questions or explores the isolated phenomenon of the ceremony and shows no one, other than the atheistic outsider Assante, doubting the value of the tradition. The ideal director for this material, of course, would have been the late Luis Bunuel, who could have inspected the underside of this rock with perverse interest while getting at the psychology behind this extreme manifestation of Catholicism.

By contrast, Osmond plays it perfectly straight, with respectable but limited results. Julia and Assante are both very good, and the latter proves particularly effective as he suffers more than he imagined he would up on the cross. He tries to look away from a carved Christ figure set up directly opposite him, but he can't sustain the aversion of his eyes.

Freed is okay as the virginal wife, and Julie Carmen is quite foxy as Assante's initial fling in town. Alex North's score confers a respectable seriousness on the proceedings, but the sound leaves something to be desired, as ambient sound has often been forgotten and considerable dialog seems post-synched. Michael Fitzgerald, who backed John Huston's "Wise Blood" and "Under The Volcano," produced in Mexico. —Cart.

Broken Victory

A Carstens/Smith production. (Sales, Double Helix Films.) Executive producers, David Carstens, Jonathan Smith. Directed by Gregory Ström. Screenplay, Smith, Ström, from story by Smith; camera (color), Brett Webster, Carstens; editor, Pat Edmondson; music, Tom Howard; sound, Margaret Duke; production design, Heather Roseborough; art direction, Paul Kinike; set decoration, Susan Ström; production manager-assistant director, Tad Fettig; costume design, Diana Creekmore. Reviewed on videocassette, N.Y., April 30, 1988. No MPAA Rating. Running time: **79 MIN.**

Sarrah	Jeannette Clift
Matthew	Ken Letner
Colonel	Jon Sharp
Joshua	Jonathan Turner Smith
Kevin	John Shepherd
Elizabeth	Bonnie Hawley
Nathanael	Elias McCabe
Miriam	Cheryl Slean
Johnson	Gerald Sharp
Ben	Michael Conn
Gregory	Jeff Kemnitz
Jeff	Gary Ballard

"Broken Victory" is a rather flat sci-fi parable about a dystopia of the future where religious Christians are being persecuted and forced to give up their faith. Well-meaning effort fails to scintillate or shed new light on a familiar theme of speculative fiction.

Central characters comprise a Christian family hounded by the evil Colonel (Jon Sharp) to relinquish their faith or face death, with the kids used and abused by the state to put pressure on their stubborn elders. Subplots are mainly of the soap opera variety and fail to hide a serious absence of plot development in Gregory Ström and Jonathan Smith's 1-note screenplay.

It is easy to identify with this clan led by matriarch Jeannette Clift, but films does not sketch in details of how the future/parallel society works. The religious presecution theme is a universal one, but absence of an interesting storyline or imaginative futuristic trappings reduces the film to the level of unfounded paranoia.

In particular, a scene of the Colonel spitting on and burning a bible is meant to conjure up the loss of freedom embodied in "Fahrenheit 451," yet without a specific context the viewer cannot tell if this is a liberation work or merely propaganda from the fundamentalist right.

Production has a threadbare look and lacks action. Cast is adequate. — Lor.

Grievous Bodily Harm
(AUSTRALIAN)

An Intl. Film Management Ltd. presentation of a Smiley Films/FGH production. Executive producers, Antony I. Ginnane, Errol Sullivan. Produced by Richard Brennan. Directed by Mark Joffe. Screenplay, Warwick Hind; camera (Eastmancolor), Ellery Ryan; editor, Marc Van Buren; music, Chris Neal; sound, Andrew Ramage; production design, Roger Ford; production manager, Julie Forster; assistant director, Evan Keddie; casting, Forcast. Reviewed at Colorfilm screening room, Sydney, April 22, 1988. Running time: **96 MIN.**

Tom Stewart	Colin Friels
Morris Martin	John Waters
Det.-Sgt. Ray Birch	Bruno Lawrence
Claudine	Joy Bell
Allen	Chris Stalker
Mick	Kim Gyngell
Stephen Enderby	Shane Briant
Vivian Enderby	Caz Lederman
Barbara Helmsley	Sandy Gore
Annie Stewart	Kerry Armstrong
Bradshaw	John Flaus

Sydney — "Grievous Bodily Harm" is a genuinely exciting thriller, combining an ingenious screenplay by Warwick Hind, racy direction from first-time feature director Mark Joffe, topflight technical credits marshaled by producer Richard Brennan and a top Aussie cast. This should be a solid commercial success in Australia, with worldwide possibilities indicated.

Pic intros three men whose paths cross as the drama proceeds. Tom Stewart (Colin Friels) is an unscrupulous crime reporter for a Sydney newspaper. In an early sequence, he's at the scene when a petty criminal (Gary Waddell) is fatally injured trying to escape with an airline bag filled with money; the dying hood begs Stewart to take the loot to his girl, but Stewart only gives her a small amount of cash, stashing the remainder for himself.

Ray Birch (Bruno Lawrence) is a rugged cop, the type who shoots first and asks questions later. He's always fighting with his superiors, who, with good reason, don't really trust him.

Thirdly, there's Morris Martin (John Waters), a schoolteacher still brooding because his beautiful wife (Joy Bell) left him and later was apparently killed in a car crash in Paris. A man barely able to control his own violence, Martin spends much of his spare time alone obsessively watching porno videos in which the wife participated with another couple.

One night, in a crowded bar, Martin briefly glimpses a woman he believes to be his wife. He becomes convinced she's still alive, and tracks down her old friends, starting with the woman (Caz Lederman) who costarred with her in the porn film; when she refuses to confirm the wife is alive, Martin loses his grip and stabs her to death. It's the first of several such murders he'll commit.

Birch is in charge of the investigations, and Stewart is assigned to cover the crimes for his paper. Via a series of clues and illegal searches, Stewart actually discovers the missing girl's whereabouts — she's working in a high-class brothel in the mountains. Thus, the stage is set for a confrontation between the three men, which is cleverly resolved with a couple of twists to keep audiences on edge until the film's final, wry, image.

Joffe and cameraman Ellery Ryan pay tribute to some *film noir* classics via various moody settings and images, and the rain-lashed city is contrasted sharply with the great outdoors where some of the film's best scenes take place. Marc Van Buren has done a great job of editing, keeping the film zipping along, and Chris Neal's music score is another major plus. Production design is excellent, with opening credits strikingly handled.

John Waters steals the film as the deranged Martin; Aussie actor is starting to look a lot like the mature Peter Finch, and he plays the killer with charm while subtly conveying his frightening propensity for violence.

Bruno Lawrence is great as the cop, Colin Friels fine as the dogged newshound and newcomer Joy Bell, though she has a tiny part, is a looker who shows talent as the missing wife. Small parts are expertly filled, with Kim Gyngell's news photographer, John Flaus' news editor and Kerry Armstrong, as Stewart's ex-wife with whom he finds time to renew his relationship, all worthy of mention. —Strat.

Friday The 13th Part VII — The New Blood

A Paramount release. Produced by Iain Paterson. Directed by John Carl Buechler. Screenplay, Daryl Haney, Manuel Fidello; camera (Technicolor), Paul Elliott; editors, Barry Zetlin, Maureen O'Connell, Martin Jay Sadoff; music, Harry Manfredini, Fred Mollin; production design, Richard Lawrence; costume design, Jacqueline Johnson; sound (Ultra-Stereo), Jan Brodin; stunt coordinator, Kane Hodder; mechanical effects coordinator, Lou Carlucci; special makeup effects, Magical Media Industries; associate producer, Barbara Sachs; assistant director, Francis R. (Sam) Mahony; casting, Anthony Barnao. Reviewed at Loews 34th Street Showplace, N.Y., May 13, 1988. MPAA Rating: R. Running time: **90 MIN.**

Young Tina	Jennifer Banko
Mr. Shepard	John Otrin
Mrs. Shepard	Susan Blu
Tina	Lar Park Lincoln
Dr. Crews	Terry Kiser
Nick	Kevin Blair
Melissa	Susan Jennifer Sullivan
Sandra	Heidi Kozak
Jason	Kane Hodder

Also with: William Butler, Staci Greason, Larry Cox, Jeff Bennett, Diana Barrows, Elizabeth Kaitan, Jon Renfield, Michael Schroeder, Debora Kessler.

A dozen teenagers and two adults comprise the body count in the newest installment of Paramount's handheld horror annuity. Familiar monster wreaking familiar havoc equals strong initial b.o. for "Friday The 13th Part VII — The New Blood," but there's nothing to suggest a leggy run or to entice new patronage.

After a prolog with scenes from earlier "Fridays," routine screenplay introduces Tina (Lar Park Lincoln), a pretty young blonde who is under psychiatric care because flashbacks of her father's death won't go away. Her troubled mind's eye also sees tragedies before or just after they happen, and she can move objects without touching them.

On the advice of her less-than-dedicated shrink (Terry Kiser), Tina and her mother (Susan Blu), head up to Crystal Lake for a little on-site therapy. (Never mind neither they nor the partying youths next door heard about the murder sprees over the years.)

Seems that amid these picturesque surroundings about 15 years earlier, little Tina (Jennifer Banko) got angry at her wife-abusing father (John Otrin) and sent him crashing off a dock (telepathically) and into the same lake where Jason has been dead in the water, anchored by a rock and chain, since the last sequel.

When a guilt-ridden young adult Tina wishes her father back, she accidentally releases Jason from his watery grave. The rest is formula in both content and execution. The screenplay is replete with paper-thin characters who're only good for a roll in the sack and then a knife in the back (or worse).

The still indestructible Jason (played by stunt coordinator Kane Hodder) has deteriorated so much so that parts of his skeleton protrude from flesh and rags. When his trademark hockey mask comes off, he's gruesome enough for a makeup Oscar nomination.

After Jason is through spiking, macheting, chainsawing, knifing, drowning, scything or battering just about everybody else, he meets his match with the girl who cooks up her own storm with a willful stare. Although their duel offers original effects-laden thrills and stunts, it's too little and too late.

Tech credits in addition to makeup and stunts are pretty good; acting is passable, and no imagery is lost in the Alabama forest night scenes or underwater. — *Binn.*

Lurkers

A Crown Intl. Pictures release of a Reeltime Distributing Corp. production. Produced by Walter E. Sear. Directed by Roberta Findlay. Screenplay, Ed Kelleher, Harriette Vidal; camera (Studio Film Labs Color), Findlay; editors, Sear, Findlay; music, Sear; art direction, costumes, Ivy Rosovsky, Jeffrey Wallach; sound, William Titus; assistant camera, Richard Eliano; casting, Findlay, James M. Cirile. Reviewed at the Vine Theater, L.A., May 14, 1988. MPAA Rating: R. Running time: **90 MIN.**
Cathy ....Christine Moore
Bob ....Gary Warner
Monica ....Marina Taylor
Sally ....Carissa Channing
Leo "The Hammer" ....Tom Billett
Cathy (as a girl) ....Dana Nardelli

Hollywood — "Lurkers" is the terrifying story of a little girl forced to grow up with a mother who can't act. Unfortunately, this means the little girl will grow into a beautiful young woman who can't act, either. Doubly unfortunately, Crown chose to distribute the picture.

Little Cathy (Dana Nardelli) is first introduced at home in an old New York City brownstone by a screen notation that says "15 years earlier." Since this is a metaphysical film, it's quite acceptable that it can be 15 years earlier inside the brownstone and 15 years later on the outside, judging from the late-model cars parked out front.

No matter. It's clear in the first five minutes that "Lurkers" is never going to make any sense, no matter when it's taking place. After an unhappy childhood of being burned with an iron and watching dead people float through the walls of her bedroom, Cathy grows up to play the cello.

Adult Cathy (Christine Moore) is engaged to Bob (Garry Warner), which is kind of interesting. Many young ladies choose a fiancé who remind them of their fathers. But Cathy obviously sees in Bob exactly the same acting talent as her mom. It's just a shame mother died before she ever had a chance to meet her future son-in-law. It could have been a scene for acting schools

to study forever.

We learn of mother's death through flashbacks. Such is the continuity constructed by director Roberta Findlay, however, that in one recollection we see mother murder dad and chase little Cathy into the street, looming over her with a knife. In the very next recollection, mom herself is being carried out of the apartment building with the knife sticking out of her chest.

Does what happened in between have something to do with the rest of the film? Did what happen before have anything to do with the rest of the film? Is the rest of the film going to have anything to do with the rest of the film?

Sadly, no. But dead mom does continue to torment Cathy, even in the bubble bath. Presumably, mother does this because she once told Cathy never to bathe with her bikini bottoms on, though it's okay to show her bare top. Either that, or the camera work, also by Findlay, is as askew as the directing.

Ultimately, Bob lures Cathy back to the old brownstone, where he introduces her to his weird friends, including all the dead people who used to float through her bedroom as a child. Even this late, there's still hope for one last scene that will explain everything that's gone before. The last scene, however, proves to be as confusing as the rest.

But at least it's the last scene.

— *Har.*

The Wrong Guys

A New World Pictures presentation of a Gordon Co. production. Produced by Chuck Gordon, Ronald E. Frazier. Executive producer, Lawrence Gordon. Coproducer, Paul De Meo. Directed by Danny Bilson. Screenplay, De Meo, Bilson. Camera (CFI color), Frank Byers; editor, Frank J. Jiminez; music, Joseph Conlan; production design, George Costello; sets, Damon Medlen; costume design, Jill Ohanneson; sound (Dolby), Bernie Kriegel; associate producer, Lloyd Levin; assistant director, Mary Ellen Woods; production manager, Vic Schiro; casting, Nan Dutton. Reviewed at Hollywood Pacific Theater, L.A., May 13, 1988. MPAA Rating: PG. Running time: **86 MIN.**
Louie ....Louie Anderson
Richard ....Richard Lewis
Belz......................Richard Belzer
Franklyn ....Franklyn Ajaye
Tim....................Tim Thomerson
Glen Grunski ....Brion James
Mark Grunski ....Biff Manard
Duke Earl ....John Goodman
Dawson ....Ernie Hudson
J.T................Timothy Van Patten

Hollywood — They got the right guys. Comics Louie Anderson, Richard Lewis, Richard Belzer and character actor John Goodman are the only reasons anyone would sit through this bonehead backpacking trip, and probably the only ones who could have been persuaded to star in it.

Dumber-than-dumb "Police Academy" ripoff should draw middling initial business and then quickly fade.

So thinly concocted that the

characters go by their real-life names, pic has five adults successful in different jobs fly cross-country for a reunion campout with members of their cub scout den. If that weren't ludicrous enough, add Goodman as crazed machine-gun-toting ex-con who mistakes them for FBI agents and chases them around the mountain.

Sadly, his repeated attempts to shoot them fail, and we're left with "Meatballs" meets "Deliverance" as the overaged scouts go through the goony inept campers routine, all the way up to infiltrating a nearby femme health spa in search of a score. Meanwhile, Goodman visits their tent and riddles it with bullets. Shucks, missed again.

Pic's only redeeming aspect is Lewis as an urban neurotic trapped in a wilderness nightmare and Belzer as his slick, fastidious foil. Pair's personas and delivery are good for many a hoot. Goodman ("True Stories," "Raising Arizona") also conjures up marvelous menace as the psycho gunslinger.

Franklyn Ajaye plays a radio call-in counselor who's heavy into human relations, and Tim Thomerson is an aging emptyheaded surfer.

Director Bilson, who cowrote the script, keeps things reasonably well paced and more entertaining than they deserve to be. Lensing on Wyoming locations by Frank Byers is unremarkable except for some weirdly imaginative scenes inside the den of an aggressive squirrel. Editor Frank Jiminez adds an amusing sequence during a downhill spill.

In case the debt owed "Police Academy" is missed, there's even a ceremony at the end where the middle-aged scouts, dressed in cub uniforms, get their medals. On-screen audiences for this consist of 8-year-olds. Theater audiences should match it, mentally. — *Daws.*

Bulletproof

A Cinetel Films release. Produced by Paul Hertzberg. Executive producer, Lisa M. Hansen. Coproduced by Neil C. Lundell. Directed by Steve Carver. Screenplay, T. L. Lankford, Carver from a story by Lankford, Fred Olen Ray; camera (United color), Francis Grumann; editor, Jeff Freeman; music, Tom Chase, Steve Rucker; production design, Adrian H. Gorton; associate producer, Fred Olen Ray; casting, Barbara Claman, Margaret McSharry. Reviewed at the Fox theater, L.A., May 13, 1988. MPAA Rating: R. Running time: **94 MIN.**
Bulletproof McBain ....Gary Busey
Lt. Devon Shepard ......Darlanne Fluegel
Col. Kartiff................Henry Silva
Pantaro ....Juan Fernandez
Gen. Brogado ....Rene Enriquez

Hollywood — Lest anyone forget, truly awful pictures are still being made, latest example being "Bulletproof."

Pic has stale topic, comic book characters and a ludicrous plot with more holes than bullets shot in the

film. It's not one to remember Gary Busey by or to pay any coin for, either in theaters or in video stores.

Busey is Bulletproof, a vigilante-type cop in a no-name city forced by the government on a mission to recover a super-duper tank from a group of Communist insurgents just over the border in Mexico. For a reason never explained, the tank was brought there by U.S. Army soldiers led by a beautiful blond (Darlanne Fluegel), entrusted to operate the hardware but amazingly never told what she was supposed to be doing with it once she gets there.

Henry Silva plays the bad guy, Col. Kartiff, leader of ragtag troupe of B actors wearing kafias (they're supposed to be Arabs) or marine surplus fatigues (those are the Mexicans) or fur hats (the Russkies).

Busey adapts his 1-man army technique from an urban setting to dusty, isolated Mexican countryside. More skillful than Houdini, he escapes a continuous barrage of bullets, grenade attacks, knifings — even stinger missiles. He is immortal (it's revealed he's pulled 37 bullets out of himself over the years), though a lot of others are fairly easily wasted. No expense was spared on red dye here.

Filmmakers attempt inserting slomo flashbacks on Busey's various encounters with city scum, as if this is supposed to make his character more interesting.

For his part, Busey doesn't ever look embarrassed for playing this type of role, though he should. If it's possible, Silva is more wooden than ever as he goes through the motions barking orders and looking menacing but at no time really seeming as if he means it.

About the only exceptional feature of this production is the amount of money wasted on blowing up trucks and men and structures for such a dreadful script.

— *Brit.*

CANNES INVITED BUT NON COMPETING

Willow

An MGM/UA Communications release from MGM Pictures of a Lucasfilm Ltd. production, in association with Imagine Entertainment. Produced by Nigel Wooll. Executive producer, George Lucas. Directed by Ron Howard. Screenplay, Bob Dolman, from story by Lucas; camera (Panavision, Rank color, Deluxe prints), Adrian Biddle; editor, Daniel Hanley, Michael Hill, Richard Hiscott; music, James Horner; sound design (Dolby), Ben Burtt; production design, Allan Cameron; special visual effects, Industrial Light & Magic, Dennis Muren, Michael McAlister, Phil Tippett; special effects supervisor, John Richardson; makeup & creature design, Nick Dudman; fight arranger, Bill Hobbs; stunt coordinator, Gerry Crampton; second unit director, Micky Moore; second unit camera, Paul Beeson; associate director, Joe Johnston; casting, Davis & Zimmerman, Jane Jenkins, Janet Hirshenson. Reviewed at Village Westwood theater, L.A., May 12, 1988. (In Cannes Film Festival, official selection, noncompeting.) MPAA Rating: PG. Running time: **125 MIN.**

Madmartigan	Val Kilmer
Sorsha	Joanne Whalley
Willow	Warwick Davis
Queen Bavmorda	Jean Marsh
Raziel	Patricia Hayes
High Aldwin	Billy Barty
Kael	Pat Roach
Airk	Gavan O'Herlihy
Meegosh	David Steinberg
Vohnkar	Phil Fondacaro
Burglekutt	Mark Northover
Rool	Kevin Pollak
Franjean	Rick Overton
Cherlindrea	Maria Holvöe
Kiaya	Julie Peters

Hollywood — "Willow" is medieval mishmash from George Lucas, a sort of 10th century "Star Wars" tossed together with a plethora of elements taken from numerous classic fables.

Even if Lucas has bastardized his own story with derivative and unoriginal elements, kids probably will love it. For MGM Pictures, b.o. should mean recoupment of its large investment.

There's a baby princess, an evil queen, trolls, fairies, little people, warriors, sorcerers and a community of midgets called Nelwyns. Willow is a Nelwyn.

Most of the characters have unpronounceable names, an attempt perhaps to disguise from whence they come: Han Solo, R2 D2 and C-3PO, Princess Leia and Darth Vader from "Star Wars," Bilbo Baggins from "The Hobbit," the lilliputians from "Gulliver's Travels," Glinda, the Good Witch of the North from "The Wizard Of Oz" and even Moses from the Old Testament, to name a few.

They serve to clutter a simple story, saving their kingdom from an evil queen (Jean Marsh) who makes it her crusade to kill every newborn in the land to ensure that baby Elora Danan, a princess, never ascends to her throne.

The most engaging thing about "Willow" is the baby, played by twins Ruth and Kate Greenfield, whom filmmakers must have spent many hours photographing to get the amazingly varied expressions that sync so beautifully with the storyline.

The baby is floated downriver by a sympathetic midwife fearing she will be killed (read: Moses) and ends up on the banks of the Nelwyn's peachful settlement where Willow (Warwick Davis) is commanded by the Nelwyn's leader, High Aldwin (Billy Barty) to return her to her people, the Daikinis. Davis is terrified of his mission for Daikinis are in the midst of a war with the forces controlled by the sinister and all-powerful sorceress Queen Bavmorda — Marsh, made up as the spitting image of the evil queen in Disney's "Snow White And The Seven Dwarfs."

Not since the munchkins came out to sing for Dorothy have there been so many midgets on screen (except perhaps in "Under The Rainbow"), here depicted whooping it up like they were at a Renaissance Faire.

Willow gets a loving send-off, baby on his back papoose-style, and sets off for what surely should be an adventure but turns out more a series of haphazard encounters with mostly nonthreatening creatures on a journey through some fantastic matte paintings done up to look like The Middle Kingdom.

Along the way, he teams up with a wisecracking Han Solo renegade warrior named Madmartigan (read: Mad Max), played well enough by Val Kilmer, and the two of them — cute baby giving the appropriate silent commentary the whole time — manage to avert real danger that the Queen is plotting back at her castle.

Good versus evil is much more watered down in "Willow" than any of the "Star Wars" chapters, due in large part to so many different distractions constantly coming at the protagonists. Darth Vader shows up as a shadow of his former self, an evil warrior named General Kael (Pat Roach) made up with a skeleton mask.

If there isn't a couple of jokester little people nipping at their heels, Willow and Madmartigan are talking to ghostly friendly spirits and animatronic rodents, and fighting an "Alien"-looking 2-headed monster, warthogs and trolls that look like apes.

Dialog waivers from the truly banal — Willow himself is very earnest and boring — to some very clever interplay between the secondary characters, including a delightful scene between Madmartigan, dusted with love sparkles, and the object of his desire, Sorsha (real life wife, Joanne Whalley), the evil Queen's daughter.

Ron Howard directed, but only Lucasness shows up on the screen, particularly towards the end when the special effects start to come on at full bore.

Much of it has been seen before in Lucas productions, notably the ending where Marsh and a good sorceress claw at each other while the baby is squirming on a sacrificial altar about to be obliterated by a supernatural force à la "Raiders Of The Lost Ark." Inventiveness shows up in the transformations of humans into pigs, a particularly funny scene, and in the metamorphosis of a possum sorceress into a crow, a goat, an ostrich and finally an old lady.

Sword-brandishing scenes are, for the most part, a muddled mess as the camera rarely pulls back far enough to give the feel of battle. Exceptions are the aerial shots down on Madmartigan and Willow slashing away at an incredibly fake-looking, 2-headed sci-fi monster — technically something of an achievement, but way out of place with the magical sorcery theme of the overall film.

The scenery, that which isn't matte paintings, is stunning. "Willow" was lensed in England, Wales and New Zealand. It's not surprising the overall flavor of the production looks familiar. Production designer Allan Cameron ("Aliens") and cinematographer Adrian Biddle ("Aliens," "The Princess Bride") have put their stamp on the film. Industrial Light & Magic wizards, too numerous to mention, are up to usual Lucasfilm standards of excellence.—*Brit.*

The Raggedy Rawney
(BRITISH)

An Island Pictures release (U.S.) of a Handmade Films production. Produced by Bob Weis. Executive producers, George Harrison, Denis O'Brien. Directed by Bob Hoskins. Screenplay, Hoskins, Nicole De Wilde; camera (color), Frank Tidy; editor, Alan Jones; music, Michael Kamen; production design, Jiri Matolin; art direction, Jindrich Koci; costumes, Theodor Pistek; sound, David John; assistant director, Luciano Sacripanti; associate producer, Garth Thomas; casting, Irene Lamb. Reviewed at Cannes Film Festival (Un Certain Regard), May 13, 1988. Running time: **102 MIN.**

Darky	Bob Hoskins
Tom	Dexter Fletcher
Jessie	Zoe Nathenson
Lamb	Dave Hill
Weasel	Ian Dury
Elle	Zoe Wanamaker
Jake	J.G. Devlin
Victor	Perry Fenwick
Simon	Timothy Lang

Cannes — Bob Hoskins brings to the screen an intriguing and particularly insightful perspective on the horrors suffered by the innocent amidst warfare.

"The Raggedy Rawney" story certain meets, and may well exceed, expectations for the British actor's initial foray into directing and scripting. With its fascinating characterizations and superb cinematography, film is marked for success and should appeal to discerning audiences worldwide.

Heading an ensemble cast as Darky, Hoskins plays the gritty leader of a gypsy-like band of refugees on the run from a war purposely set in an unspecified period somewhere in Europe. As Hoskins explained here, the idea was to portray that "the enemy is war" — on whatever soil, whoever the adversaries.

In this circumstance, a young soldier named Tom (Dexter Fletcher) deserts after an attack on his unit sends him into a panic. He stumbles upon Hoskins' group and is consoled by Hoskins' daughter Jessie (Zoe Nathenson).

The "gypsies" are swiftly on their way, desperately attempting to outmaneuver the war machines. Tom comes upon a farmhouse where a little girl innocently paints his face with her mother's makeup and dress, a bizarre turn that holds plausibility due to the shock he's experienced and the seeming innocence of this interaction.

Event suddenly turns nightmarish as it's revealed her family has been tortured by marauding troops who have discovered a deserter on their property. Tom concludes his survival may depend on perpetuating a ruse that he is a woman, one who cannot speak.

By the time he catches up with Darky, et al., Tom is deemed to be a "rawney" — a person who is half-mad and half-magic. The film then opens its direct passageway into this closed community of near medieval attitudes, with fears of evil spirits and the unknown.

Hoskins the director, director of photography Frank Tidy and production designer Jiri Matolin convey the sentiments and living patterns in exquisite detail, particularly through a pastiche of vehicles, clothing and especially via a wedding celebration. Landscapes of film's Czechoslovakian location are perfect.

Set against this backdrop a love affair unfolds between Tom and Jessie, even as he maintains the female pose. They are discovered one night by the retarded Simon, played by Timothy Lang of Robert Titlady's theater group for Down's Syndrome and handicapped people. Simon falls into the river, drowns and later is accused by Jessie of having raped her — a charge she makes to protect Tom from being discovered.

Demanding an abortion, and eventually tricking his daughter into one, Darky becomes less and less likable, as Hoskins' work on screen and at the helm become all the more commendable. Also deserving of particular credit are Fletcher and Nathenson, who make the couple's relationship genuine and tender.

As Jessie loses her baby, resolution of the film begins as the almost-forgotten reality of war's brutality crushes in on the "gypsies," whose caring one for another has become most endearing. Theirs is the human spirit at its best, which is really the most compelling attribute of the film itself. —*Tege.*

Le Grand bleu
(Big Blue)
(FRENCH)

A Gaumont production and release (France); Weintraub Entertainment Group release through Columbia (U.S.), 20th Century Fox (foreign). Produced by Films du Loup. Executive producer, Patrice Ledoux. Directed by Luc Besson. Screenplay, Besson, Roger Garland, with collaboration of Marylin Goldin, Jacques Mayol; camera (color, Cinemascope, 70m), Carlo Varini; editor, Olivier Mauffroy; music, Eric Serra; art direction, Dan Weil; costumes, Creation-Express; sound, Pierre Befve, Gérard Lamps; production manager, Bernard Grenet. Reviewed at Gaumont Ambassade cinema, Paris, May 11, 1988. (In Cannes Film Festival, out of competition.) Running time: **135 MIN.**
Jacques Mayol .... Jean-Marc Barr
Enzo Molinari .... Jean Reno
Johana .... Rosanna Arquette
Laurence .... Paul Shenar
Also with: Sergio Castellito, Jean Bouise, Marc Duret, Griffin Dunne, Andreas Voutsinas, Valentina Vargas, Kimberly Beck, Alessandra Vazzoler, Bruce Guerre-Berthelot, Gregory Forstner, Claude Besson.
(Original English soundtrack)

Paris — Luc Besson, the French wonder boy who moved into the commercial major leagues with his $3,000,000 Gaumont picture "Subway," has joined the international spendthrifts club with "Big Blue," a waterlogged yarn about a couple of rival championship divers.

Produced on a disproportionately large scale ($12,000,000 budget, a 9-month shoot on international locations from Greece to Peru), this English-language adventure is indigently plotted and lacking in genuine dramatic and human interest. Besson has tried to make a film about the passion of diving, the mystical lure of the deep, but much of his ploddingly overlong film reeks of soggy banality.

Besson was in part inspired by the life and exploits of French champion free diver Jacques Mayol, who served as technical adviser on the film and allowed his name to be retained for the protagonist, played by Jean-Marc Barr.

Hero has a life-long competitive friendship with a Sicilian diver, played with self-mocking Latin bravado by Jean Reno, Besson's favorite actor. We first meet them as youths in Greece, where Barr's father, a coral fisherman, dies in a diving accident.

Years later Barr is a renowned experimental diver based on the French Riviera. During an assignment at a frozen lake high in the Peruvian mountains, he runs into Rosanna Arquette, a flighty New York insurance agent who immediately falls in love with him and trails him to Taormina where he is facing off Reno in a diving meet.

Apart from Arquette's increasingly giddy pursuit of the somewhat absent Barr (more concerned with dolphins he befriends than humans who love him) and the struttings of the equally preoccupied Reno, nothing much happens until a climactic runoff in which latter tries to beat his friend's world free-diving depth.

Besson has fatally misjudged the cinematic interest of his theme. The underwater sequences, as splendidly lensed as they are (by Carlo Varini), have little intrinsic suspense and quickly become repetitious. The land scenes are boring because Besson has been unable to give his characters any psychological density. Accordingly none of the performances merit any mention.

Despite some welcome comedy, "Big Blue" reflects a solemnity of purpose that longs for lyrical climaxes. Waltzing dolphins aside, Besson misses the boat.

Supporting cast is largely neglected, among them Jean Bouise as Barre's uncle, Valentina Vargas as Reno's frustrated girlfriend, Andreas Voutsinas in a cameo as a Greek priest and Griffin Dunne, still working neurotic after-hours as Arquette's boss.

All tech credits are lushly first-rate.—*Len.*

La Maschera
(The Mask)
(ITALIAN)

An Istituto Luce/Italnoleggio Cinematografica release of an RAI-Channel 2/Istituto Luce/Italnoleggio Cinematografico/Best Intl. Films coproduction. Produced by Lilia Smecchia, Ettore Rosboch. Directed by Fiorella Infascelli. Screenplay, Andriano Aprà, Infascelli, with Ennio De Concini, Enzo Ungari; camera (Eastmancolor, Cinecittà lab), Acacio De Almeida; editor, Francesco Malvestito; music, Luis Bacalov; art direction, Antonello Geleng, Stefania Benelli. Reviewed at Cinecittà, Rome, May 5, 1988. (In Cannes Film Festival, Un Certain Regard.) Running time: **90 MIN.**
With: Helena Bonham Carter (Iris); Roberto Herlitzka (Elia), Michele De Marchi (Capocomico), Alberto Cracco (Viola), Valentina Lainati (Maria), Saskia Colombaioni, Feodor Chaliapin, Michael Maloney.

Rome — In "The Mask," Helena Bonham Carter's fresh, old-fashioned innocence, which worked so delicately in "A Room With A View," conjures the same enchantment in a make-believe 18th century Italian setting.

The feature debut of Fiorella Infascelli is a highbrow fable about play-acting roles in and out of the theater, artfully colored with mystery and romance. While the hide-and-seek love affair between a decadent nobleman and a high-spirited young actress seems tailored for the readers of Gothic romances, "Mask" is complicated enough to have trouble circulating beyond local art houses and foreign fest play.

Iris (Carter) is the 17-year-old prima donna in a company of traveling actors. One day the picturesque caravan performs for aged count Feodor Chaliapin (son of the famed Russian-singer actor, fine in this small character role) and his dissipated son Leonardo (Michael Maloney who, despite bad habits like wine and cards, has the heart-breaking suavity of the quintessential romantic hero). Iris rebuffs his first, blunt passes.

To win her heart, Leonardo applies to a sinister mask maker whose creations give him the courage to express his innermost feelings. Iris falls hard for the mysterious **masked stranger, putting aside her professional mask for love. Leonardo hasn't the courage to reveal his real identity, now that his love is returned. After a good deal of sighing and dallying beside idyllic rivers and ancient fountains, the lovers unite in a happy ending.**

Typically Italian in its eye-catching settings that recall Venice without specifically being set there, "Mask" gets a lot of mileage out of atmospheric backgrounds, costumes and Luis Bacalov's score. All hands turn in idiosyncratic performances between the Gothic and the literary. Results are delicate and curious but not very emotionally involving, though Infascelli is a new director to be watched for developments. — *Yung.*

Na Srebrnym Globie
(The Silver Globe)
(POLISH)

A Zespoly Filmowe, KADR Unit production. Written and directed by Andrzej Zulawski, based on Jerzy Zulawski's novel "Moon Trilogy." Camera (color), Andrzej Jaroszewicz; editor, Krzysztof Osiecki; sound, Michal Zarnecki; music, Andrzej Korzynski; production manager, Tadeusz Lampka; art direction, Tadeusz Kosarewicz, Jerzy Sniezawski. Reviewed at the Cannes Film Festival (Un Certain Regard), May 12, 1988. Running time: **166 MIN.**
With: Andrzej Seweryn (Marek), Grazyna Dylag, Jerzy Trela, Waldemar Kownacki, Iwona Bielska, Jerzy Gralek, Elzbieta Karkoszka, Krystyna Janda (the actress), Maciej Goral, Henryk Talar, Andrzej Frycz, Henryk Bista.

Cannes — In 1977, two years into the production of Andrzej Zulawski's "The Silver Globe" and with 20% of the film left to shoot, Polish authorities closed down the film and set the stage for director Zulawski's successful emigration to Paris ("Possession," "Le femme publique").

In the friendlier times of 1987, filmer got the official greenlight — albeit a decade late — to complete the picture. Having lost his costumes, sets, actors and momentum, Zulawski understandably opted to release the film in its "amputated" form, using voiceover to narrate the missing pieces.

In its present 2-hour 46-minute version, "The Silver Globe" is a shrill scream for freedom and love under the guise of a highly original work of science fiction. It's all-out, no-holds-barred cinema, lensed in aggressive handheld p.o.v. shots with a range of distorting lenses to go with the near-hysterical shouting and screaming performances of cast. Pic's excesses could prove a boon or bar to it at the wickets.

It remains an impressive tour de force on the technical end and an intriguing attempt to turn sci-fi into a vehicle for intense philosophizing. Film's uncompromising auteurism and esoteric thrust, as much as its "subversive" content, probably are responsible for the minister of culture's cold feet back in '77.

The immediate problem facing viewers is making sense of the plot. Zulawski's elliptical storytelling style is the culprit, not the narrative holes, which come well into the picture. Film can be divided into three parts. The silver globe in question is the moon, and action takes place on its dark side.

In the first part, a small group of cosmic explorers, including a woman, leave Earth to find freedom and start a new civilization. They don't realize that within them they carry the end of their own dream. In anguishing p.o.v. shots (this whole segment is supposedly being filmed by one of their number), the idealists die one by one, while their children revert to the primitive native culture and lose no time creating new myths and a new god.

Some time later, Marek (Andrzej Seweryn), a smalltime space bureaucrat on the run from a broken heart, arrives to find the colonizers' descendants have been enslaved by bird-monsters called Cherns. Society is divided into all kinds of classes and subclasses, and what everyone is waiting for is the arrival of a messiah.

Marek is judged a suitable candidate, and for a while he literally lives as a god. His constant search for the meaning of his life, as tortured as it is improbable, gets a bit tedious, especially as Seweryn is kept in high gear acting-wise. While he shrieks his bewilderment over questions (and dialog) that would throw Kierkegaard, he finds himself in love with a local girl, but loses her to a more virile Chern. He winds up crucified by his people in a gory, if godlike, finale.

In the third story which gets short shrift, Zulawski takes an ironic view of life back on Earth, where male-female relations are proceeding as badly as usual, amid planetary decay. Krystyna Janda is featured as a cold, rather tacky beauty who spurned Marek and sent him off on his tormented adventures.

Art direction and costume design are knockouts and makeup a blast in a film that refuses to blush before outrageous excess. As to comprehension, the narrated summaries where footage is missing are the easiest to follow. Aboard the "Silver Globe" roller coaster, however, understanding what it's all about is only part of the experience. — *Yung.*

Amagleba
(Living Legends)
(SOVIET)

A Gruziafilm Studio production. Directed by Nodar Managadze. Screenplay, Erlom Akhvlediani, Managadze, David Djavakhichvilli; camera (color), Nugzar Erkomaichvili; music, Nodar Gabunia. Reviewed at Cannes Film Festival (Directors Fortnight) May 12, 1988. Running time: **65 MIN.**

Ivane	Zurab Kapianidze
Naskida	Temo Djaparidze
Kirile	Djemal Moniava
The monk	Temur Chkheidze

Cannes — "Living Legends" (the original Georgian title might be translated as "uprising"), a 1977 production just off the shelf, combines helmer Nodar Managadze's notable lensing talent with his homeland's natural beauty.

Result is a small film of stirring pictorial beauty with a great-hearted theme: Georgian nationalism. This brief work takes some patience to get into, but pays off in a rousing climax that brings all the ends together.

Film is dedicated "to the unknown heroes who died for their country," and a sense of fatality pervades the quiet first half, tracing the simple lives of four men. Stonecutter Nazkida works humbly on carvings for a tiny church under construction in the mountains, aided by his angelic ox.

The monk Béka paints pictures on his monastery's walls; field hand Ivane struggles to keep his brood of kids fed; a young nobleman thinks of his future bride. All are called to war to defend their homeland and give their lives unselfishly.

Particularly striking are the fairytale Georgian landscapes, lovingly painted by cameraman Nugzar Erkomaichvili. Film has slow stretches, but they're punctuated with poetic sequences of great beauty and power. At once pious and nationalistic, "Living Legends" is a parable that, like the films of Sergei Paradjanov, has thought-provoking ramifications. — *Yung.*

Soursweet
(BRITISH)

A British Screen-Zenith presentation of a First Film Co. production in association with Film Four. (Intl. sales: The Sales Co.) Produced by Roger Randall-Cutler. Directed by Mike Newell. Screenplay, Ian McEwan, from the novel by Timothy Mo; camera (Metrocolor), Michael Gerfath; editor, Mick Audsley; music, Richard Hartley; sound, David Stephenson; assistant director, Michael Zimbrick; production manager, Wendy Young; casting, Patricia Pao, John Hubbard. Reviewed at Cannes Film Festival (Directors Fortnight), May 15, 1988. Running time: **110 MIN.**

With: Sylvia Chang, Danny Dun, Jodi Long, Soon-Tech Oh, William Chow, Shih Chieh King, Speedy Choo.

Cannes — Cinema audiences who responded to Wayne Wang's "Dim Sum" should be equally enthralled by "Soursweet," an aptly titled charmer about a Chinese family living in a dismal suburb of London.

Pic's great quality is that it sympathetically explores the insidious ways in which Chinese emigrants have to adapt to life in Britain after moving to London from Hong Kong. Good arthouse prospects worldwide are indicated.

The film opens with an elaborate wedding ceremony for a young couple (Sylvia Chang, Danny Dun) held on the outskirts of Hong Kong. Shortly after, the couple moves to London, where Dun finds work as a waiter in a crowded Chinatown restaurant. They have a son and are joined first by the wife's sister and later by the husband's old father.

Dun goes through a period in which he loses money gambling and becomes indebted to a seedy moneylender who works for one of the two gangs who seem to control the Chinatown underworld. The couple soon moves to the suburbs, where they start a modest Chinese restaurant in a rented house. After a slow start, the place prospers, and gradually friendly links are formed with the locals (the sister becomes pregnant by a Belgian; the grandfather makes friends among the community's old people).

Fate catches up with Dun, who simply disappears one day, a victim of gang rivalry. It makes for a touching last section of the film as Chang carries on bravely alone, not really knowing if her man is dead or alive.

"Soursweet," adapted from Timothy Mo's novel, covers a lot of ground and is, perhaps, a shade long at 110 minutes; some incidents, charming as they are, could be trimmed. Also, the behind-the-scenes rivalries between the gangs come across as confusing at times. These are minor criticisms given that director Mike Newell's great achievement is to capture the world of ordinary Chinese-Londoners with such affection and insight.

It's the small details that are most significant. The way a little boy discovers at school that the Chinese way of fighting, taught to him by his mother, is considered unfair. The conversations about Westerns who've "got feelings like everybody else." Or the way traditional Chinese customs give way in the face of British culture and lifestyle; french fries replaces noodles.

Newell gets fine performances from an almost all-Chinese cast, and technical credits are perfect right down the line. "Soursweet" should find appreciative audiences, especially since "The Last Emperor" proved films about Chinese life and culture can succeed in the marketplace if they're good enough.—*Strat.*

Distant Voices, Still Lives
(BRITISH)

A British Film Institute production, in association with Film Four Intl. Produced by Jennifer Howarth. Executive producer, Colin MacCabe. Written and directed by Terence Davies. Camera (color), William Diver, Patrick Duval; editor, Diver; production design; Miki van Zwanenberg, Jocelyn James; costumes, Monica Howe; sound, Moya Burns, Colin Nicolson; production managers, Sarah Swords, Olivia Stewart; assistant directors, Andy Powell, Glynn Purcell. Reviewed at Cannes Film Festival (Directors Fortnight), May 14, 1988. Running time: **84 MIN.**

Mother	Freda Dowie
Father	Pete Postlethwaite
Eileen	Angela Walsh
Tony	Dean Williams
Maisie	Lorraine Ashbourne
Micki	Debi Jones
Jingles	Marie Jelliman

Also with: Sally Davies (Eileen as a child), Nathan Walsh (Tony as a child), Susan Flanagan (Maisie as a child), Michael Starke (Dave), Vincent Maguire (George), Antonia Mallen (Rose), Chris Darwin (Red), Andrew Schofield (Les), Anny Dyson (Granny).

Cannes — This is a unique, special film, a labor of love that should communicate its deeply felt emotions about British family life to all who see it.

Stylized drama, bursting with life and music while dealing with basically drab and unfulfilled lives, will be extremely hard to market, especially outside Britain, but critical support and word-of-mouth should ensure an international arthouse career.

This is the first feature film of Liverpudlian Terence Davies, though he's known for a trio of stark short dramas about the Catholic working class of his home city. His new film is obviously autobiographical, dealing with a family called Davies and their lives during the '40s and '50s.

The film is divided into two parts: "Distant Voices," which runs 45 minutes, centers on the wedding of Eileen, eldest of the three Davies children, and the funeral of her father, events which spark memories of the past, including the frightening war years when the city was bombed frequently; part two, "Still Lives," at 39 minutes (including end credits), actually was filmed two years after the first part, with the same actors but with a substantially different crew. It's a seamless continuation which climaxes with the wedding of another of the clan, son Tony.

For the Davies family, life always has been hard and pleasures simple. The film is full of singing, as the characters break into familiar songs at family gatherings or in the local pub. In addition, familiar standards (including "Taking A Chance On Love," "There's A Man Goin' 'Round Taking Names," "Love Is A Many Splendored Thing" and many others) are heard over the radio as are excerpts from popular British radio shows of the era ("The Billy Cotton Band Show," "Family Favorites," "Take It From Here") which will appeal enormously to British auds who recall those radio days.

This isn't a film based on nostalgia, though; its very special qualities stem from the beautiful simplicity of direction, writing and playing, and the accuracy of the incidents depicted. A woman can confess she married her husband because "he was a good dancer," and that's reason enough. Close girlfriends can drift irrevocably apart when they marry and their husbands reject their former friends. An evening in the pub, or at a smoke-filled cinema, brings romance. Despite the cruelties and disappointments of life, the memories of pleasant times outweigh those of pain.

The wonderful cast perfectly complements Davies' personal style, and the result is a film which, while its pacing and very structure may exasperate some, should envelop receptive audiences with its special magic. — *Strat.*

Ei
(Egg)
(DUTCH)

A Seventh Heaven (Amsterdam) presentation of a René Scholten production for Studio Nieuwe Grondon. Produced by Scholten. Written and directed by Danniel Danniel; Camera (Eastmancolor), Erik van Empel; editor Menno Boerema; music, Michel Mulders; sound, Mark Glynne; art direction, Michal Shabtay; production manager, Stienette Bosklopper. Reviewed at Cannes Film Festival (Directors Fortnight), May 13, 1988. Running time: **58 MIN.**

Johan	Johan Leysen
Eva	Marijke Veugelers
Johan's mother	Coby Timb
Paul	Jake Kruyer
Peter	Peter Smits
Gerard	Piet Kamerman

Also with: Anneleun Schram, Maddaleen Jansen, Andri de Bruyn, Henk Admiraal, Joan Berkheimer, Hetty van Breukelen, Lou de Boer, Alie Ende, Bram Stam.

Cannes — In spite of its brevity, Danniel Danniel's "Egg," a first feature, has done well in Holland and its producer was approached by serious buyers immediately after the first showing in Cannes.

It is not hard to understand why, since "Egg" has some of the charm of early Jacques Tati, while keeping a straight face about its characters.

Johan, 35, works in his own bakery shop and puts meticulous care into every detail of his work. He can also stand an egg on its end without breaking it. Assistants Paul and Peter are his lean, taciturn lookalikes. After hours, they throw pebbles at a store in the village square while watching the bus make its one daily stop to unload passengers and mail.

Johan lives alone with his mother and we know his life is never going to change much. Or wouldn't have, if Paul had not one day suggested Johan might get himself a wife by answering an ad in the local newspaper's personal column. Paul does the writing for Johan, who knows what he wants to say.

A correspondence begins between

Johan and a lady from some foreign shore. Johan is enriched by the experience, but doesn't even reveal his identity when one day he watches a handsome woman of about his own age descend from the bus and is asked to carry her bags. She says she has come to marry the the local baker!

The lady tells Johan's mother the same thing and is admitted grudgingly to her house. After an afternoon of embarrassing waiting, Johan shows up for supper and tells her it is not customary to speak during meals here.

Romance will have its way, but through to the happy ending, everybody remains either silent or saying very little. The story is told in tableaux with interspersed titles as in silent movies.

Johan Leysen and Marijke Veugelers are likable leads. The village of Kockengen and its population are seen with warmth and sympathy. The thoroughly sunny mood is enhanced by the lilt and bounce of Michel Mulders' recurring theme music, played mostly on harp and guitar. —*Kell.*

Amerika, Terra Incognita
(America, Unknown Land)
(VENEZUELAN)

A Cuakamaya Prods. film. Produced by Morelba Pacheco, G. Radonski. Written and directed by Diego Risquez. Camera, Andrès Agusti; editor, Leonardo Henriquez; sets, Oscar Armitano; music, Alejandro Blanco Uribe. Reviewed at Cannes Film Festival (Directors Fortnight), May 16, 1988. Running time: **98 MIN.**
With: Alberto Martin, Maria Luisa Mosquera, John Phelps, Luis Mariano Trujillo, Amapola Risquez, Nelson Varela, Boris Izaguirre, Blanca Baldo.

Cannes — **This is a highly stylized art pic with no dialog, giving an impressionistic recreation of the Spanish court after the discovery of America.**

Risquez uses lotsa tilted camera angles and ponderously slow scans of the court, sometimes slipping into static poses simulating famous Velàzquez paintings.

In lieu of a plot, we see the court botanist puttering about with exotic plants brought from the New World, a real live native who wanders about the palace and eventually is baptized in an elaborate church ceremony, shots of court jesters and nuns (toting heavy lipstick) and other miscellanea.

What the point of it all is may be lost on most viewers of this low-budget item. Commercial prospects seem pretty remote. — *Besa.*

De sable et de sang
(In Blood And Sand)
(FRENCH)

A UGC release of a Septembre Prods./Films A2/Le Sept coproduction. Produced by Jean Nainchrik. Written and directed by Jeanne Labrune. Camera (color),

André Néau; editor, Nadine Fischer; music, Anne-Marie Fijal, Nina Corti; art direction, Patrice Mercier; sound, Eric Devulder, Jacques-Thomas Gérard; assistant director, Alain Baudy; production manager, Philippe Desmoulins. Reviewed at UGC Biarritz cinema, Paris, May 12, 1988. (In Cannes Film Festival, Un Certain Regard.) Running time: **100 MIN.**
Manuel Vasquez . . . . .Sami Frey
Francisco Almeira . . . . . . .Patrick Catalifo
Marion Vasquez . . . . . .Clémentine Célarié
Dolores Vasquez . . . . .Maria Casarès
Carmina . . . . .Catherine Rouvel
Also with: Pierre Forget, Andre Dussollier, Camille Grandville, Stéphane Albouy.

Paris — Jeanne Labrune, one of the most talented of the new generation of telefilm helmers, takes the leap to the big screen but misses her footing in this unconvincing drama about the unladylike world of bullfighting.

Labrune's fascination with the bullring already was manifest in her last tv film, "La Part de l'autre." Here she confronts two dissimilar men, a doctor and a bullfighter, and tries to imagine their uneasy friendship.

Sami Frey is a genteel radiologist of Spanish origin whose phobia of the bullring is associated with the murder of his father by Franco in an Andalusian arena. Since leaving Spain at an early age to settle in southern France, he cannot envisage going back to his birthplace.

Patrick Catalifo is a poor gypsy who's managed to become a local glory in the arenas of Nîme and who has an opportunity to enter the major leagues in Spanish rings.

Their fortuitous meeting is the beginning of soul-searching for both, with Catalifo suddenly losing interest in his sport. Frey agrees to accompany him to Spain for his first important corrida, but the torero throws his sword down at the moment of the coup de grâce.

In her tv work, Labrune proved her ability to create unusual physical and psychological climates (with the aid of her habitual lenser André Neau), but here she remains exterior to her subject matter and personages, failing to give any density or tension to the diffuse action.

Especially disappointing is the neglect of her supporting cast which includes Maria Casarès as Frey's mother, Clémentine Célarié as his uncomprehending wife and Andre Dussollier as Catalfo's agent. It's ironic the two fine actresses should remain so peripheral in a film directed by a woman.

Labrune does succeed in conveying the barbarousness of the bullring as well as some of its perverse lyricism. Viewers made queasy by sight of bulls being put to death should abstain. —*Len.*

Gece Yoloulugu
(Night Journey)
(TURKISH)

An Alfa Film production and release. Written and directed by Ömer Kavur. Camera (color), Salih Dikisçi; editor, Mevlut Kocak;

music, Atilla Ozdemiroğlu. Reviewed at the Istanbul Film Festival, April 22, 1988. (In Cannes Film Festival, Un Certain Regard.) Running time: **107 MIN.**
Ali . . . . .Aytaç Arman
Yavuz .Macit Koper
Also with: Zuhal Olcay, Sahika Tekand, Arslan Kacar, Orhan Cagman, Osman Alyanak, Nurseli Camlibel.

Istanbul — Ömer Kavur, Turkey's leading exponent of sophisticated, European-style cinema, has crafted a sensitive, psychological road movie in "Night Journey."

Tale about a tormented film director's trip inside himself is an attractive piece of autobiographical soul-searching that will find supporter among arthouse habitués. It doesn't have enough plot or forward movement to widen its appeal much farther.

Fans of Kavur's "Motherland Hotel," which found favor at many fests, will recognize the angst-ridden hero's quiet desperation and the eerie emptiness at pic's center as signposts of this director's poetic universe.

Ali (Aytaç Arman, looking very much like a Turkish William Hurt in his wire-rimmed glasses) starts location hunting with scriptwriter Yavuz (the versatile and always convincing Macit Koper). An abandoned Greek village on the seacoast — the real star of the film — attracts Ali immensely and he sends the writer back to Istanbul while he moves into a crumbling old church. Never much of a communicator, Ali breathes freely in this picturesque solitude, where he finds the inspiration to write his script. Yavuz returns with a new, more down-to-earth director and finds the script scattered to the four winds. Ali has vanished.

Reminiscent of Wim Wenders' "The State Of Things," "Night Journey" revolves around a stalled film and a creative block. The lucre-eyed producer and cooing star who hover on the other end of the telephone make banal villains, but hero Ali can be exasperatingly pretentious, too. It's the familiar conflict between art and money, with little substance to keep it afloat.

To its credit are savvy, modern editing, atmospheric lensing by Salih Dikisçi, a sophisticated score by Atilla Ozdemiroğlu and, of course, the splendors of the Aegean coast.
— *Yung.*

Slucaj Harms
(The Harms Case)
(YUGOSLAVIAN-COLOR/B&W)

An FIT (Belgrade) production; U.S. and Canada distribution sales, Eurofilm (L.A.). Producer Jovan Marković. Executive producer, Slobodan Stojičić-Lesli. Directed by Slobodan D. Pesić. Screenplay, Alexander Ciric, Pesić, camera (Eastmancolor, ORWO NP 55 black & white), Milos Spasojević; editor, Neva Habić; music, Alexandar Habić; art direction, Snezana Petrović; costume design, Olgica Pavković; sound, Srdjan Popović; assistant director, Snezana Zitnik; dialog consultants, Brana Crncević, Jovan Mar-

ković. Reviewed at Cannes Film Festival (Un Certain Regard), May 13, 1988. Running time: **90 MIN.**

Harms . . . . .Frano Lasić
The angel . . . . .Damjana Luthar
Irinia Mazer . . . . .Milica Tomić
Maria Vasilevna . . . . .Branko Cvejić
Zabolotsky . . . . .Mladen Andrejević
Prof. Sobakov . . . . .Stevo Zigon
Also with: Francisco—Kiko-Zegarac (Harms as a boy), Milutin Karadzić, Predrag Lakovic, Oliver Viktorivić, Alexandar Lukać, Danko Djurić, Dragan Velićković, Zoran Miljković, Dijana Sporcić.

Cannes — Last year at Cannes, it was "Repentance" by Tengiz Abuladze of Soviet Georgia; this year it is Yugoslavia's Slobodan D. Pesić, who with "The Harms Case" takes a lopsided surrealistic look at Stalin-era persecution of all who deviated from the party line.

Using the story of experimental poet Danil Harms, who died at 36 in a Leningrad prison hospital, as his takeoff point, Pesić comes up with a dashing, vigorous tragicomedy of the absurd with lots of intriguing action within strikingly composed frames, abetted by a narrative flow that swells and moves in rhythm with deft camera movements. A neat international future in specialized situations can hardly fail to follow.

In a prolog, a scientist holds up what we may surmise to be the late poet's brain in a glass jar, and we are given a lecture on that same brain's aberrations into useless, decadent, nonsensical poetry.

The prolog is in color, the rest of the film is in black & white, with red used only occasionally as in a sky suggesting a revolutionary dawn (as people in the streets are gunned down) or a trickle of blood.

Biographical facts of Harms' life are juggled in a freeform manner the writer-director thinks would please the poet of the absurd himself. Harms is being paid a visit by an angel, whose detachable wings are put under the bed while the two of them wander along streets where old women are getting instructions in putting on gasmasks, and into a factory dining room where they are whirled into an exchange of fisticuffs between Believers and Unbelievers.

One surrealist episode follows another, tied together by the trouble caused the poet by a sturdy wooden beam sent him by registered mail. Is it the symbol of his Staff of Life as a free poet or part of the cross to which he eventually is to be nailed and shot?

There is plenty to guess about. The physical attractions of a girlfriend's stockinged leg, especially the unstockinged upper part, rates careful attention, but there always is something to upset the mood, generally personified by a variety of commissars and cops.

An epilog, again in color, has the poet flying past his girlfriend's window on his own wings. Before that, the down-below entertainment has been marvelous, chilling at times perhaps, but never enough for anybody to leave Pesić's film with a heavy heart. On the contrary, a martyred poet's redemption has been accomplished in a satirical form that is downright jubilant if not devilishly angelic. —*Kell*.

Katinka
(SWEDISH-DANISH)

A Nordisk Film release of Nordisk Film (Denmark) production in association with Svensk Filmindustri (Sweden), the Danish Film Institute, the Swedish Film Institute and Film Four Intl. (U.K.) Produced by Bo Christensen. Executive producer, Katinka Farago. Producer consultant, Peter Poulsen. Directed by Max von Sydow. Screenplay, Klaus Rifbjerg, based on the novel by Herman Bang; camera (Eastmancolor), Sven Nykvist; editor, Janus Billeskov Jansen; music, Georg Riedel; art direction, Peter Höimark; sound, Michael Dela; costumes, Annelise Hauberg, Pia Myrdal, Ole Gläsner; choreography, Niels Björn Larsen; production manager, Lene Nielsen; assistant director, Tom Hedegaard. Reviewed at Cannes Film Festival (Un Certain Regard), May 15, 1988. Running time: **96 MIN.**

Katinka	Tammi Öst
Bai, her husband	Ole Ernst
Huus, estate manager	Kurt Ravn
Agnes	Tine Miehe-Renard
Reverend Linde	Erik Paaske
Helene Jensen	Ghita Nörby
Mrs. Abel	Birthe Backhausen
Ida Abel	Vibeke Hastrup
Louise Abel	Bodil Lassen

Also with: Henrik Kofoed, Kim Harris, Kjeld Nörgaard, Birgitte Bruun, Dick Kaysöe, Paul Hüttel, Sören Sätter-Lassen, Bjarne G. Nielsen (as Herman Bang), Anna Lise Hirsch Bjerrum.

Cannes — In picking Herman Bang's slim 1986 novel about a sturdy provincial stationmaster's consumptive wife's never-to-be love affair with a handsome estate manager as the base for "Katinka," his bow as a director, Max von Sydow was asking for trouble.

He overcomes enough of it to show considerable skill in his new trade, but not enough to assure his film an international theatrical future beyond art situations.

We attend Katinka's funeral and are faced with her deeply moved husband, eliminating all hope of a happy ending, concentrating on the exceedingly slow development of tender feelings between the frail, coughing 30ish woman and Huus, the newcomer to the small community, whose inhabitants are described along the way in sharp, witty vignettes.

Huus is not the man to sweep a woman off her feet, hurting from an earlier rejection. Bai, the stationmaster, loves his wife in an old-fashioned, chauvinistic way, but it is obvious he longs for a lustier female response.

Maybe it's because she knows she's dying, but it could also be Katinka just does not have the guts to face Life as it supposedly is lived outside the small community, and as it is symbolized by the trains that chug into this whistlestop only to rush off again.

A Chekhovian mood permeates von Sydow's film, and his lead actors beautifully live up to their non-participant roles. Tammy Öst has poetry and longing in her every move as Katinka, and as Huus, Kurt Ravn is the epitome of the suppressed male, essentially content to express tenderness.

As Bai, Ole Ernst is a marvel of madness that seeks but is not granted expression, a performance as gutsy as it is sensitive.

Unfortunately the dialog, when not serving the leading trio, thwarts the director. It may have read well, but is sounds bookish and stilted. Similarly, a series of "occasions," serving to flesh out proceedings (a New Year's Ball, an outing to a country fair, etc.) have a contrived look.

Otherwise, "Katinka" is a most handsome production. Sven Nykvist's cinematography is at the height of its poetic power and in rhythm with the core tragedy. Had von Sydow chosen a story of more obvious dramatic impact, and had he dared to have stronger and more prolonged interplay between the dream lovers in his film, he might have delivered a more personal work of art instead of merely a sensitive, intelligent adaptation. —*Kell*.

Kholodni Mart
(Cold March)
(SOVIET)

An Odessa Studio production. Directed by Igor Minaev. Screenplay, Alexander Gorokhov; camera (color), Vladimir Panlov; art direction, Anatoli Naumov; music, Anatoli Dergachev. Reviewed at Cannes Film Festival (Directors Fortnight), May 13, 1988. Running time: **107 MIN.**

Mitia Koronienko	Maxim Kisilev
Andrei Ivanovich	Andrei Tolubeev

Also with: Ludmilla Davidova, Igor Antov.

Cannes — First film by young Kiev helmer Igor Minaev is a pedes- trian work of hyper-classic, old-fashioned Russian filmmaking, with little to interest the offshore viewer.

This overwritten drama set in a boys' technical school in the provinces remains uninvolving, in spite of appealing thesps and pro lensing. Now that Minaev has demonstrated a good grasp of technique, it can be hoped he'll try more exciting subject matter next time around.

Story opens with Mitia (Maxim Kisilev), a new arrival, turning up at the technical school. His classmates put him through the mildest of "initiations" before accepting him into their band. He never quite blends in, however, because of his preoccupation with a secret girlfriend. The trio of good-hearted teachers is headed by Andrei Ivanovich (Andrei Tolubeev), who is just a little harder than the rest.

Shying away from strong drama, "Cold March" contents itself with little. The boys' hijinx lead to no worse than a broken store window, but the incident mushrooms into the threat of a court trial and a year in jail for the towheaded rascal involved. Maxim loses his girl when her mother comes to take her away, and Andrei Ivanovich's wife falls seriously ill. To its credit, film doesn't try to soften the edges or tack on a fake happy ending.

Besides the overall familiar boarding school setting, used much more convincingly elsewhere, "March" drags over its conformist characters who — at least to Western eyes — are too good to be true. The only rotten apple around is an older boy, a malevolent outside influence who teaches the band to fight and act big. The boys remain distant and undifferentiated.

Of no help is the muddy yellow-green cast to the film stock, blurring faces and background. —*Yung*.

CANNES COMPETING

Patty Hearst

An Atlantic Entertainment and Zenith Group release. Produced by Marvin Worth. Executive producers, Thomas Coleman, Michael Rosenblatt. Directed by Paul Schrader. Screenplay, Nicholas Kazan from the book "Every Secret Thing" by Patricia Campbell Hearst with Alvin Moscow; camera (Deluxe), Bojan Bazelli; editor, Michael R. Miller; music, Scott Johnson; production design, Jane Musky; art direction, Harold Thrasher; set decoration, Jerie Kaelter; costumes, Richard Hornung; sound, Ed White; assistant director, Stephen Dunn; associate producer, Linda Reisman; casting, Pamela Rack. Reviewed at Cannes Film Festival (competing), May 13, 1988. Running time: **108 MIN.**

Patricia Hearst	Natasha Richardson
Teko	William Forsythe
Cinque	Ving Rhames
Yolanda	Frances Fisher
Wendy Yoshimura	Jodi Long
Fahizah	Olivia Barash
Celina	Dana Delany
Zoya	Marek Johnson
Gabi	Kitty Swink
Cujo	Pete Kowanko
Jim Browning	Tom O'Rourke
Steven Weed	Scott Kraft
Randolph A. Hearst	Ermal Williamson

Cannes — "Patty Hearst" puts forth much less than its pretensions. Frequently wrapped in surrealistic stylization, film manages only to tell Hearst's side of her kidnapping ordeal.

While she may be entitled to do so, even on the big screen, version here is largely flat and often dull. There'll be some business from the curious in the U.S. and even abroad since the extraordinary saga riveted so many millions for so long.

Paralleling Hearst's book "Every Secret Thing," on which Nicholas Kazan based the script, story quickly recounts Hearst's early life and picks up cinematically with the kidnaping at the Berkeley apartment she shared with fiancé Steven Weed.

Stuffed into a closet and blindfolded for nearly 50 days, Hearst is subjected to verbal abuse by the deranged band of self-styled revolutionaries that called themselves the Symbionese Liberation Army. The real events begin tumbling out of one's memory bank.

What had not been witnessed by the media was the bleak traumatizing Hearst underwent — critical to the question of whether she was so psychologically abused that a form of brainwashing impaired all judgment. A highly sympathetic portrait, not surprisingly, is painted of this initial phase via black & white imagery and is augmented with the eerie sounds of a creaking closet door opened only for verbal and later sexual assaults.

By the time Hearst is offered her freedom or membership in the SLA, one is bound to accept that the latter was chosen at least as much for survival as for any other motive.

Film often utilizes voiceover stream of consciousness by Hearst to convey her confusion, perceptions, frustrations and increasingly detached mental state. While effective as technique, it simply attempts to overwhelm the audience with a singular p.o.v. that is nearly as overbearing as the very circumstances she encountered.

Director Paul Schrader cleverly manages that indoctrination while maintaining a posture of inventive demystification of an overexposed — at least during the 1974-79 period of this story — media celebrity. His approach might have worked in a truly fictionalized case such as his script for "Taxi Driver," but here it virtually panders to the material.

In portraying Hearst, Richardson — daughter of Vanessa Redgrave and director Tony Richardson — is quite effective. She manages to convey all the sympathy clearly intended. Not so fortunate are the actors playing the real-life characters of father Randolph, mother Catherine and fiancé Weed. They're merely stick figures lacking any human dimension.

The SLA Members, from the notorious Cinque to the ruthless Harrises, certainly are mean-spirited and seemingly authentic in their depictions by Ving Rhames, William Forsythe and Frances Fisher. Their work may serve them well in future casting.

The sum of it all, however, remains an unsatisfying exercise.
— *Tege*.

Bird

A Warner Bros. release of a Malpaso production. Produced and directed by Clint Eastwood. Executive producer, David Valdes. Screenplay, Joel Oliansky; camera (Technicolor), Jack N. Green; editor, Joel Cox; music, Lennie Niehaus; production design,

Edward C. Carfagno; set design, Judy Cammer; set decoration, Thomas L. Roysden; sound (Dolby), Willie D. Burton; assistant director, L. Dean Jones Jr.; casting, Phyllis Huffman. Reviewed at The Burbank Studios, L.A., May 5, 1988 (In Cannes Film Festival, competing). No MPAA Rating. Running time: **161 MIN.**

Charlie (Bird) Parker	Forest Whitaker
Chan Parker	Diane Venora
Red Rodney	Michael Zelniker
Dizzy	Samuel E. Wright
Buster Franklin	Keith David
Brewster	Michael McGuire
Esteves	James Handy
Young Bird	Damon Whitaker
Kim	Morgan Nagler

Hollywood — **In taking on a bi-opic of late jazz great Charlie Parker, Clint Eastwood has had to chart bold new territory for himself as a director, and he has pulled it off in most impressive fashion.**

Sensitively acted, beautifully planned visually and dynamite musically, this dramatic telling of the troubled life of a revolutionary artist certainly will surprise those stragglers who believe Eastwood's talents lie strictly with mayhem and monkeys.

But as creatively successful as the picture is, major problems lurk on the commercial front, primarily due to its length and secondarily because of the jazz milieu and downward spiral of Bird's life. Going out in exclusive runs in the fall, when it will open, after Eastwood's next Dirty Harry actioner, and relying upon reviews and word-of-mouth seems the only way to go.

Parker and Dizzy Gillespie were the primary innovators in the bebop style that overhauled the sound of jazz in the 1940s and has had a profound influence on musicians to this day. That Parker, who died in 1955 at 34, was the greatest sax man of them all is virtually undisputed, but he also lived a messy, complicated life, mixing drug addiction and a multitude of women with an ongoing attempt at a home life with his wife Chan and their two children.

Joel Oliansky's big-framed script, originally written for Richard Pryor at Columbia some years back, jumps around considerably at the beginning, skipping strikingly from Parker's childhood to a suicide attempt in 1954, then to some other key incidents. Eastwood bridges these gaps with some deftly designed transitional devices, but the constant shifting in the early going undoubtedly will prevent easy access into the characters for viewers totally unfamiliar with their world.

But outstanding scene begins mounting upon outstanding scene, from a collection of saxophone auditioners warming up in a hallway to Bird and Chan's first major encounter, from a nocturnal, anonymous visit Bird makes to Stravinsky's home in Los Angeles to his forcing white musician Red Rodney to sing the blues in the deep South.

Pic underlines the irony of one of jazz' most famous figures having been virtually unemployable, and therefore broke, at various periods; of having a club, Birdland, named after him that he often couldn't play in because of lack of a cabaret card, and of a man of such sophistication and elevated tastes having been trapped by "the life," of which drugs and irresponsible behavior were primary components.

Oliansky and Eastwood's approach remains admiring and sympathetic through the thick and thin of Bird's career. Although the effects of his self-abuse are amply displayed, actual drug use is kept almost entirely offscreen. The one scene which seems present just for its anti-drug message actually is one that Red Rodney has recounted himself, in which Bird lectured him to the effect that, just because he was a junkie didn't mean everyone else had to shoot up in an attempt to play better.

Film also makes no particular mention of the difficulties of the Parkers' mixed marriage, quite uncommon in the era, and any problems Bird may have had because of his race remain implicit.

Naturally, the prolific artist's music provides the continuing thread for the film, and jazzman Lennie Niehaus has done a sensational job in blending Bird's actual sax solos with fresh backups by contemporary musicians. Unlike the unique case of "'Round Midnight," in which Dexter Gordon blew his own horn, this has Forest Whitaker miming his playing, but doing so very convincingly indeed.

Large and rambling, Whitaker, last seen as Robin Williams' buddy in "Good Morning, Vietnam," makes an imposing, likable, very hip genius, a well-spoken man whose decisions to do as he pleases don't always have the best repercussions. It's an excellent performance, with an especially memorable death scene.

As Chan, Diane Venora is so riveting that her occasional long absences from the story are sorely missed. The one person who could really understand Bird is presented as a feisty woman of great character, awareness and strength, and Venora makes her come totally alive.

Michael Zelniker etches a vivid portrait of Rodney, and the multitude of smaller parts are more than capably filled.

Working largely in studios and on the Burbank New York Street, production designer Edward C. Carfagno and lenser Jack N. Green have fashioned a carefully controlled dark look for the picture. Only problem is the length, which is more a commercial consideration than an artistic one.

Film does not seem slow or overly drawn out while watching it, and the abundance of musical sequences and grace note scenes, while perhaps not advancing the story, is one of its distinctions. But pic has an undeniable weight, and marketing it successfully will pose a considerable challenge.

In the end, however, Eastwood has tested himself with an ambitious labor of love and emerged standing taller as a filmmaker than he ever has before.—*Cart.*

Paura e Amore
(Three Sisters)
(ITALIAN-FRENCH-GERMAN)

An Erre Produzioni-Reteitalia (Rome)/-Bioskop Film (Munich)/Cinemax (Paris) co-production. Produced by Angelo Rizzoli. Executive producer, Romano Cardarelli. Directed by Margarethe von Trotta. Screenplay, Dacia Maraini, von Trotta; camera (Eastmancolor, Technicolor prints), Giuseppe Lanci; editor, Enzo Meniconi; art direction, Giantito Burchiellaro; music, Franco Piersanti. Reviewed at Fiamma Cinema, Rome, May 7, 1988. (In Cannes Film Festival, competing). Running time: **112 MIN.**

Velia	Fanny Ardant
Maria	Greta Scacchi
Sandra	Valeria Golino
Roberto	Sergio Castellito
Federico	Paolo Hendel

Also with: Peter Simonischek (Massimo), Agnès Soral (Sabrina).

(Italian language version)

Rome — **"Paura e Amore" (literally, "Fear And Love," but going under the moniker "Three Sisters" to underline its vague Chekhov connection) is one of German director Margarethe von Trotta's least compelling works.**

Sewing together patches of small-town passion, film never clarifies its aim or p.o.v., leaving viewer adrift in a kind of murky arthouse world of telenovellas.

The trio of Euro leads, Fanny Ardant, Greta Scacchi and Valeria Golino (singularly hard to imagine as genetically related), embodies the problems of the modern woman in achieving personal fulfillment on the emotional and professional planes, yet remain distant fictional types. Film was shot in the sleepy northern Italian town of Pavia and has a quality Italo look, thanks to efforts of a fine technical crew. It should do respectably on the Continent and find limited release abroad, where stars and setting are less familiar.

Velia (Ardant) is the steady elder sister, an academic often passed over for promotion. She falls for a married physics prof Massimo (Peter Simonischek), a self-styled Latin lover whose appeal for Velia and, later her gentle sibling Maria (Scacchi), remains film's great mystery. Maria is married to a tv comedian (Paolo Hendel, one of the discoveries of the year and a delight whenever he appears on screen). He bores her and she lets the suave prof pick her up, causing a rupture with Velia.

Little sis Sandra (Valeria Golino, giving one of her lively teenage performances), just 18, is at odds with premed studies and political commitment (ecology). Her nice biology prof becomes her lover until he dies in a car accident one foggy night.

There also is a brother, versatile thesp Sergio Castellito, whose unhappy marriage to floozy Agnès Sorel turns him away from the violin, into the insurance biz. With all the other stories film is attempting to juggle, his is just too much. It does fit the spirit of stereotype weighing down the von Trotta-Dacia Maraini script.

Maybe led astray by a desire to parallel Chekhov's characters and play, "Three Sisters" never zeroes in on one theme or problem that could focus all those passions and emotions. There is a lot of feeling depicted by principals, all of whom project strong screen personalities. Ensemble acting is weak, reflecting pic's bits-and-pieces structure; drama seems always just around the corner, but never quite makes it into the open. In the end it's the audience which takes the Chekhovian part, waiting and waiting for the loose ends to come together in a meaningful finale. Alas, they don't.

Nothing remains but to enjoy "Sisters" for its soap opera components unrequited love, adultery, the suffering of the sensitive. The U. of Pavia provides an Ivy League touch of class, while camerawork by Giuseppe Lanci is suitably moody, but not despairing, as the filmmaker would have it. — *Yung.*

Haizi Wang
(King Of The Children)
(CHINESE)

A China Film Corp.-Xi'an Film Studio production. Executive producer, Wu Tianming. Directed by Chen Kaige. Screenplay, Kaige, Wan Zhi, from a short story by Ah Cheng; camera (color), Gu Changwei; editor, Liu Miaomiao; production design, Chen Shaohua; music, Qu Xiaosong; sound, Tao Jing, Gu Changning; production manager, Mao Yuwen; assistant director, Qiang Xiaolu. Reviewed at Cannes Film Festival (competing), May 16, 1988. Running time: **107 MIN.**

Lao Gar	Xie Yuan
Wang Fu	Yang Xuewen
Headmaster Chen	Chen Shaohua
Laidi	Zhang Caimei
Lao Hei	Xu Guoqing
Cowherd	Le Gang
Village team-leader	Tan Tuo
Secretary Wu	Gu Changwei

Cannes — **Chen Kaige's eagerly awaited third film (after "Yellow Earth" and "The Big Parade") is a mood piece deeply saturated with comment on the mistakes of the Cultural Revolution.**

It can be enjoyed simply as an intimate drama of a schoolteacher working in a remote country school and learning as much from his pupils as they learn from him, but the inquisitive viewer can find much more beneath the surface.

Story is set in China's southwest (Yunnan province) where the locals belong to an ethnic minority; their first language is not Chinese. It's 1976; Mao's Cultural Revolution is 10 years old, and the authorities have been trying to stifle 7,000 years of Chinese history. Young people from cities have been uprooted forcibly and made to work in remote areas, on the surface a destructive policy, but one which allowed city folk a greater understanding of the hinterlands.

Lao Gar is such a youth, who was taken from the city and may never return. He's spent seven years working as a farm laborer, but now is told he's to teach at the local school, an exciting but intimidating prospect for him. He discovers a rather unruly class with no textbooks provided, but sets out dutifully to teach in the approved Mao manner.

Gradually, though, he adapts his teaching methods and personalizes his work. This brings success, but also the disapproval of the local Party Secretary, who eventually dismisses him.

This simple story is told with haunting images, beautifully composed and gracefully assembled. It's a slow-moving film, but one charged with emotion. Western audiences may puzzle over the significance of some obviously key points, such as the scene in which Lao "invents" a Chinese character which doesn't exist; but there's no denying the talents of director Chen Kaige.

Mop-haired Xie Yuan is fine as Lao Gar, and the supporting cast also is praiseworthy. There's plenty of humor in the film, much of it derived from the primitive conditions found at the school, with its lopsided classrooms and furniture. Ultimately, the points Chen is making about the impact of the Cultural Revolution, on both city and country folk, come over strongly in this challenging, beautiful pic.
—*Strat.*

Arashi Ga Oka
(Onimaru)
(JAPANESE-SWISS)

A Seiyu Ltd.-Mediactuel coproduction. (Foreign sales outside Far East, Cofimedia.) Coproduced by Kazunobu Yamaguchi, Francis Von Buren. Written and directed by Kiju Yoshida, based on "Wuthering Heights" by Emily Brontë. Camera (Fujicolor), Junichiro Mayashi; editor, Takao Shirai; music, Toru Takemitsu; art direction, Yoshiro Muraki; costumes, Reiko Yamada; sound (Dolby), Tadaski Shimada. Reviewed at Cannes Film Festival (competing), May 13, 1988. Running time: **130 MIN.**
Onimaru . . . . Yusaku Matsuda
Kinu . . . . Yuko Tanaka
Mitauhiko . . . . Tatsuo Nakaka
Tae . . . . Eri Ishida
Hidemaru . . . . Nagare Hagiwara
Shino . . . . Keiko Itoh
Ichi . . . . Masso Imafuku
Sato . . . . Tokuko Sugiyama
Suka . . . . Shun Ueda
Kinu (daughter) . . . . Tomoko Takaba
Yoshimaru . . . . Masato Furuoya
Takamaru . . . . Rentaro Mikuni

Cannes — Setting Emily Brontë's "Wuthering Heights" in medieval

Japan is an interesting conceit that gets outsized treatment in this period costumer from Kiju Yoshida, who scored nicely in Cannes two years ago with "Promessu," a tight, tough look at sickly geriatrics and their children.

With "Arashi Ga Oka," however, Yoshida seems to have gone too far in the style department. Costumes are gorgeous as is camerawork by Junichiro Hayashi, but overall performances make the late John Belushi's "Saturday Night Live" samurai routines seem restrained by comparison.

This combined with a hefty 2-hour 10-minute running time make "Arashi" a tough sell in the West and an iffy prospect in Japan where Toho is rolling out the distribution May 28.

Pic isn't, obviously, an exact duplication of much-filmed "Wuthering Heights." Director Yoshida says he has for decades been struck by the fearsomeness and essential mysteriousness of the Brontë love story set in the Yorkshire moors of the mid-19th century. Amid the anguish, he sees steamy eroticism and abrupt violence.

The best parts of "Arashi" are alternately — and occasionally at the same time — violent or erotic. To research the feverish pitches required to set the stage for such primal emotion, Yoshida seems to have worked up his cast so routine dialog is emoted at a high energy level. Must characters shout imprecations as they dig ditches?

The mythic approach taken by the film to its subject — this is hardly a model of logical unfolding of a storyline — also makes continuity difficult to grasp. Audience is left to piece together seemingly random scenes into a thematic jigsaw.

Central focus of the plot is passionate love gone berserk. Onimaru (Yusaku Matsuda), a strapping, homeless youth, is taken in by a family of priests engaged in various rites aimed at defusing the anger of the Mountain of Fire. In this pic, physical surroundings, things, take on human characteristics.

Youth's downfall is Kinu, the family's daughter, whom Onimaru deflowers (in a smoothly staged erotic scene) before she marries the heir to a rival family. She bears a daughter, dies and Onimaru goes off the deep end mourning the loss.

There are undercurrents of incest and psychological violence in the film. Yoshida is intrigued by social reversals, when the inmates take over the asylum and the beggar becomes king. "Arashi" is a film with psychological depth and insight.

The crusher is the acting. Matsuda, a versatile performer seen in "The Family Game" and three years ago at Cannes in "Sorekara," is urged to mug it up. The actor moves gracefully and gives a balletic touch to the heavily physical scenes.

Yuko Tanaka as the daughter is sufficiently rarefied to appear zonked out during much of the film. Tanaka explains that long lapses in the film's production — at Gotamba near Mount Fuji and near the Aso volcano on Kyushu, Japan's southern island — allowed her to empty out her emotions. The draining shows onscreen.

Pic is a Japanese-Swiss coprod, costing some $10,000,000 to lens. Japanese side is the innovative Seibu Dept. Store group, which produced director Yoshida's last, and far superior, pic. —*Sege.*

L'Oeuvre au noir
(The Abyss)
(BELGIAN-FRENCH)

A UGC release of a Philippe Dussart/La Sept/Films A2/La Nouvelle Imagerie (Brussels) coproduction. Executive producer, Jean-Claude Batz, Philippe Dussart. Written and directed by André Delvaux, from novel by Marguerite Yourcenar. Camera (color), Charlie Van Damme; editor, Albert Jurgenson; music, Frédéric Devreese; sound, Henri Morelle; art direction, Claude Pignot, Françoise Hardy; costume design, Jacqueline Moreau; makeup, Laurence Azouvy; assistant director, Susana Rosberg; production manager, Jacqueline Louis. Reviewed at UGC, Neuilly, May 2, 1988. (In Cannes Film Festival, competing.) Running time: **110 MIN.**
Zenon . . . . Gian Maria Volonté
Prior . . . . Sami Frey
Myers . . . . Jacques Lippe
Catherine . . . . Anna Karina
G. Rombaut . . . . Johan Leysen
Cyprien . . . . Pierre Dherte
Campanus . . . . Jean Bouise
Henri-Maximilien . . . . Philippe Léotard
Hilzone . . . . Marie-Christine Barrault
Martha . . . . Marie-France Pisier

Paris — André Delvaux' film of Marguerite Yourcenar's 1976 novel about a physician-alchemist pursued by the Inquisition in 16th century Flanders is respectful, conscientious and somewhat tedious.

Competing at Cannes, this Belgian-French coprod has European arthouse product written all over it and should find an audience there.

Yourcenar, the only woman writer to be admitted to the Académie Française, gave a nod to Delvaux' adaptation but died earlier this year before the director could show her the film. Yourcenar had been disappointed by Volker Schlöndorff's 1976 adaptation of her story "Coup de grâce" and was not eager to renew her contact with the cinema, so her support of Delvaux' project was unusual.

But Delvaux' film is a conventional literary adaptation of the cut-and-paste school. Handsomely mounted and adequately acted, it cannot bridge the gap between Yourcenar's tapestry-rich literary style and the demands of the screen. It also suffers from the remoteness of period and situation that makes most costume pictures emotionally uninvolving.

Delvaux in fact has dramatized only the last part of the novel concerning the tragic homecoming of Zenon, a Flemish-born doctor who

has wandered throughout Europe and who now returns incognito to his native Bruges where Inquisition authorities finally arrest him and try him for heresy.

The director has rendered well the brooding, oppressive background of medieval intolerance pitted against progressive humanity, the latter embodied with dignity by the white-maned Gian Maria Volonté. But the dank, dark Middle Ages have become too much of a cinematic cliché, which Delvaux only rarely transcends.

A good supporting cast is weakened by sketchy scripting and episodic nature of the roles, deprived of their philosophical and human density. Sami Frey comes across best as a Bruges prior who befriends Volonté even though he is aware of his true identity.

Tech credits, led by Charlie Van Damme's striking lighting, are first-rate. —*Len.*

Sur
(South)
(ARGENTINE-FRENCH)

A Cinesur (Buenos Aires)/Pacific Prods./Canal Plus (Paris) coproduction. Produced by Fernando E. Solanas, Sabina Sigler, Djamila Olivesi. Executive producers, Solanas, Envar El Kadri, Patricia and Pierre Novat. Written and directed by Solanas. Camera (color), Felix Monti; editor, Juan Carlos Macias; music, Astor Piazzolla; production design, Solanas; sound, Anibal Libenson; makeup, Mirta Blanco; costumes, Nene Murua; assistant director, Horacio Guisado. Reviewed at Publicis screening room, Paris, May 2, 1988. (In Cannes Film Festival, competing.) Running time: **127 MIN.**
Rosi . . . . Susu Pecoraro
Floreal . . . . Miguel Angel Sola
Roberto . . . . Philippe Léotard
El Negro . . . . Lito Cruz
Emilio . . . . Ulises Dumont
Amado . . . . Roberto Goyeneche
Blondi . . . . Gabriela Toscano

Paris — Fernando E. Solanas' "Sur," competing at Cannes, is a kaleidoscopic companion piece to the Argentine helmer's Venice-laureled "Tangos — Gardel's Exile" (1985).

Made possible by the success of latter film, this new Argentine-French coprod is often stylistically similar — and just as overlong — as Solanas' earlier evocation of exile and nostalgia.

Exile again is at the heart of "Sur," but this time it is the interior exile of imprisonment under Argentina's military dictatorship, and the difficulty of homecoming and adjustment.

Central narrative line of Solanas' original screenplay is a painful reunion of a couple torn apart when the husband (Miguel Angel Sola) was imprisoned for subversive activities. Now, five years later in 1983, he is liberated but has a night-long reckoning with himself and his past before he can summon up the courage and love to return home.

His long-suffering wife (Susu Pecoraro) has been through her own hell during these years, and in her desperation and loneliness had become the lover of Sola's best friend, a Corsican (Philippe Léotard) who had found friendship and purpose in Argentina.

Solanas describes a long night's journey into day as his protagonist wanders through the dreamlike streets of his neighborhood, strewn with banners and leaflets celebrating the return of democracy. As he roams he meets ghosts of his past who help him recollect the moments and people of the past years that marked his broken life.

As with "Tangos," music is the soul and motor of the film, with Astor Piazzolla and his quintet performing superb choral duties and Roberto Goyeneche crooning with soulful abandon.

More emotionally involving than "Tangos," film does tend to meander in a mosaic of anecdotes and might benefit from some trimming, especially since foreign audiences may be confused by some of the peripheral incidents and characters.

Technically the film is dazzling, though Solanas goes overboard on the smoke machines and Felix Monti's virtuoso lighting effects.

Sola and Pecoraro are both poignant, while Léotard (who was in "Tangos") makes the most of an episodic but eloquent role.

Shot and edited entirely in Argentina, film owes much to its French partners, who hung on through a series of contretemps that nearly sank the production.—*Len.*

Pascali's Island
(BRITISH).

An Avenue Pictures release of an Avenue-Initial production, in association with Film Four Intl. and Dearfilm Ltd. Produced by Eric Fellner. Executive producer, Cary Brokaw. Directed by James Dearden. Screenplay, Dearden, from novel by Barry Unsworth; camera (color), Roger Deakins; editor, Edward Marnier; music, Loek Dikker; production design, Andrew Mollo; sound, Ian Voigt; costumes, Pam Tait; production manager, Angela Petropoulakis; assistant director, Guy Travers; casting, Noel Davis, Jeremy Zimmerman. Reviewed at Cannes Film Festival (competing), May 11, 1988. Running time: **104 MIN.**
Basil Pascali . . . . Ben Kingsley
Anthony Bowles . . . . .Charles Dance
Lydia Neuman. . . . . .Helen Mirren
Herr Gesing . . . . .George Murcell
Mrs. Marchant. . . . . .Sheila Allen
Pasha . . . . .Nadim Sawalha
Izzet Effendi . . . . .Stefan Gryff
Pariente . . . . .Vernon Dobtcheff
Also with: T.P. McKenna (Dr. Hogan), Danielle Allan (Mrs. Hogan), Nick Burnell (Chaudan), Josh Losey (Turkish soldier).

Cannes — Intrigue on a Turkish-occupied Greek island in 1908 is the theme of this mildly exotic British pic which, despite an eye-catching but mannered central performance from Ben Kingsley, looms as too languid and remote to make much of a dent in the market. Initial production of Avenue Pictures looks like it's heading down a one-way street.

Kingsley plays Pascali, a seedy little Turkish spy who's lived on the small island of Nisi for 20 years, regularly transmitting reports to Constantinople. The ever-watchful agent is a very minor cog in the crumbling Ottoman Empire, yet is filled with self-importance. Sexually ambivalent, he carries a half-hearted torch for a comely, middle-aged Austrian painter, Lydia (Helen Mirren), though is incapable of making a move in her direction.

Enter Charles Dance as Bowles, a bronzed British adventurer professing to be an archeologist, actually planning to loot the island of its ancient treasures. Before long he's involved in an affair with Lydia, observed by the frustrated and jealous Pascali who is, perhaps, even more attracted to Bowles than to the woman. The stage is set for a final-reel tragedy.

"Pascali's Island" marks James Dearden's return to direction after his Academy-Award nominated screenplay "Fatal Attraction;" he previously helmed "The Cold Room" (1984) for HBO. Despite its evocative settings (filmed on the islands of Rhodes and Simi), lush camerawork by Roger Deakins and top production design by Andrew Mollo, pic remains listless and uninvolving.

Kingsley gives a technically impressive performance as the frustrated, bitter spy, but his mannerisms are becoming as bothersome as those of Rod Steiger in his lesser roles. Charles Dance reprises his "White Mischief" role as a handsome he-man with an unscrupulous eye for the ladies who meets a sticky end. The best is Helen Mirren who, 20 years after her film debut in Michael Powell's "Age Of Consent," still can disrobe to play a love scene with elegance and style; she brings much-needed warmth to an otherwise cold pic.

Dearden's pacing is slow, spending more time on local color than advancing the plot. In adapting Barry Unsworth's novel, which consisted of Pascali's reports to his superiors, he's done a workmanlike job. Pic looks like a tough sell since it lacks mass appeal and the dramatic highlights required for arthouse success. Downbeat ending won't help either. Loek Dikker's score is worth a nod. — *Strat.*

Chocolat
(Chocolate)
(FRENCH)

An MK2 release of a Cinémanuel/MK2-/Wim Wenders Produktion/Cerito Films/La Sept/Caroline Prods./Fodic/TF1 Films coproduction. Produced by Alain Belmondo, Gérard Crosnier. Directed by Claire Denis. Screenplay, Denis, Jean-Pol Fargeau; camera (color), Robert Alazraki; editor, Claudine Merlin; music, Abdullah Ibrahim; art direction, Thierry Flamand; sound, Jean-Louis Ughetto, Dominique Hennequin; assistant directors, Bassek Ba Kobhio, Luc Goldenberg; associate producers, Samuel Mabom, Pierre Ilouga Mabout. Reviewed Publicis screen room, Paris, April 20, 1988. (In Cannes Film Festival, competing.) Running time: **105 MIN.**
Protée . . . . .Isaach de Bankolé
Amiée . . . . .Giulia Boschi
Marc . . . . .François Cluzet
Luc. . . . . .Jean-Claude Adelin
France (child) . . . . .Cécile Ducasse
France (adult). . . . . .Mireille Perrier
Also with: Emmet Judson Williamson, Laurent Arnal, Jean Bedière, Jean Quentin Chatelain, Emmanuelle Chaulet, Jacques Denis.

Paris — Newcomer Claire Denis dissects domestic life in French colonial Cameroon in the 1950s in "Chocolat," which is a French competing entry at Cannes.

A former assistant to Wim Wenders ("Paris, Texas" and "Wings Of Desire"), who helped finance films by securing distrib rights for West Germany, Denis displays subtle skill in this impressionistic chronicle, based in part on her own childhood memories.

Denis' script (adapted with Jean-Pol Fargeau) centers on the isolated provincial homestead of a French colonial administrator (François Cluzet), his wife (Giulia Boschi) and their daughter (Cécile Ducasse). With husband often absent on inspection tours, Boschi is left on her own in a cultural and social desert, while the child connives with the native houseboy (Isaach de Bankolé).

The semblance of order is broken one day when an airplane sets down nearby with engine trouble. With spare parts not to be had for weeks, the motley group of passengers become Cluzet and Boschi's problematic houseguests.

The alien presence especially affects the delicate rapport between the lonely and frustrated Boschi and the virile Bankolé, who is aware of his mistress' sexual attraction. When he rebuffs her desperate advance, she has him transferred to another post outside the house. The young black exacts a minor but indelible revenge via the child.

Though most of the acting ranges from wooden to passable — the exception being the César-winning Bankolé, fine as the servant anxious to maintain social roles — Denis gives evocative relief to her scenes from colonial life, demonstrating an acute sense of detail, rhythm and ambience. Lenser Robert Alazraki deserves special mention for helping her achieve her vision.

The central story set in the past is framed in the present-day return of the daughter, now an adult (Mireille Perrier), who gets a lift from a black American and his son. Both find a country in which they are strangers.

This bookending device sets the stage for a poetic coda: at the airport where Perrier is to catch a plane back to France, some black workers load tourist goods on an aircraft before taking shelter from a sudden storm, to the accompaniment of gay, jaunty music. It is a joyous, lyrical image of independence and self-confidence.

"Chocolat" also is a debut effort in indie production from veteran production managers Gérard Crosnier and Alain Belmondo. Latter is brother of screen star Jean-Paul Belmondo, who chipped in coproduction coin. — *Len.*

Viper

A Fries Distribution release of a Maris Entertainment Group production. Produced and directed by Peter Maris. Screenplay, Frank Kerr; camera (United color), Gerald Wolfe; editor, Jack Tucker; music, Scott Roewe; sound, Bill Robbins; assistant director, Jeff Mallians; stunt coordinator, Peter Horak; associate producer, Sunny Vest; assistant producer, Bradley Chambers; casting, Valerie McCaffrey. Reviewed at Cannes Film Festival (market), May 14, 1988. MPAA Rating: R. Running time: **94 MIN.**
Laura McCalla . . . . .Linda Purl
Col. Tanzer . . . . .James Tolkan
Richard Gelb . . . . .Jeff Kober
Harley Trueblood . . . . .Ken Foree
Jim McCalla . . . . .Chris Robinson
Powell . . . . .David M. Sterling
Broadnax . . . . .Charles Hoyes

Cannes — "Viper" is a genuine sleeper, a well-crafted, riveting action drama which gets the job done efficiently and entertainingly. Newcomer indie Fries Distribution has the challenge of getting the word out on this one.

Pic is a companion piece to filmmaker Peter Maris' previous action-er "Terror Squad," which dealt with a group of Libyan terrorists who invade America via Indiana (!) and hold a classroom of kids hostage. In "Viper," it is a special U.S. military unit that pretends to be Middle Eastern terrorists and takes over a building at a university in Indiana, in order to fake an incident that will allow our government to launch a reprisal mission.

The plan goes awry quickly when a soldier (David M. Sterling) kills a hostage during a scuffle, resulting in the evil mission commander Col Tanzer (James Tolkan) ordering our hero Jim McCalla (Chris Robinson) to execute all the hostages as part of a coverup. He refuses, but they're murdered anyway.

McCalla steals Tanzer's top-secret file on the project in order to go public, but is killed ruthlessly by a car bomb. This leaves his mousy wife Laura (Linda Purl, very well cast) as a target for the heavies who want the file back and no traces, as the government is going ahead with the invasion reprisal.

Film becomes a tightly paced, familiar saga at this point, with Purl as the innocent who must take matters in her own hands and develop survival smarts in a hurry, not unlike Amy Madigan did in the similar "Nowhere To Hide" saga. The difference is that Maris has learned many of the tricks of The Master, Alfred Hitchcock, and rather than aping him with tiresome homages, he puts the knowledge to use. There is classical daylit horror during Purl's extended chase, a real feeling of danger, and exploitation of sinister aspects of commonplace objects, locales and situations. A simple scene in a diner when Purl finally gets to read the classified file (code name: Viper) illustrates the film's ability to generate sleek suspense.

Ultimately, she's given a backbone and taught how to fight back (with hand grenades and automatic weaponry) by her husband's army buddy Trueblood (Ken Foree). Maris develops a fascinating relationship between these two opposite types and scores a thrilling surprise in the cleverly structured scene where Foree is ambushed. Key plot twist involving Purl and a newspaper reporter (Jeff Kober) who's not what he appears to be works effectively.

Helping put "Viper" over is a topgrade cast, with Purl utterly believable and mucho sympathetic as the every-woman heroine, Tolkan the epitome of a no-nonsense, brute force military nut (acting in the name of "national security") and Foree offering one of the most shaded, interesting macho figures in some time. In smaller roles, Kober, Robinson and Sterling are on target.

Vivid chase scenes and tech credits are fine, except for a couple of insert shots that aren't color-corrected.—*Lor.*

The Chair

An Angelika Films release of an Urban Entertainment production. Produced by Anthony Jones. Executive producers, Angelika Saleh, Joseph Saleh. Directed by Waldemar Korzeniowsky. Screenplay, Carolyn Swartz; camera (color), Steven Ross; editor, Swartz; music, Eddie Reyes; sound, Scott Breindel; production design, Robert Pusilo; special makeup effects, Tom Lauten; line producer, Norman Berns; coproducer, Jerry Lott; casting, Barbara Shapiro. Reviewed at Cannes Film Festival (market), May 13, 1988. Runnin time: **90 MIN.**

Dr. Harold Langer . . . . James Coco
Lisa Titus . . . . Trini Alvarado
Eddie Dwyer . . . . Paul Benedict
Rick . . . . Gary McCleery
Roach . . . . Stephen Geoffreys
Also with: Ron Taylor, Calvin Levels, Brad Greenquist, Jihmi Kennedy, John Bentley, Richard Edson.

Cannes — "The Chair" is a curious combination of black comedy and horror that features both impressive scenes and harmful lapses in taste. Angelika Films faces a tough challenge to find an audience for this oddity.

Film's basic premise is similar to that of Irwin Yablans' recent horror thriller "Prison" — the spirit of a man (the warden) executed 20 years ago at High Street correctional facility haunts the place, seeking revenge on the guard Eddie (Paul Benedict) who failed to come to his aid when the rioting inmates put him in the electric chair.

To this story, which also features the "Prison" genre animated effects when the spirit attacks prisoners and other people, is added a most unusual tale of unbalanced prison psychologist Dr. Langer (played by the late James Coco), who uses the nine prisoners transferred to his decrepit institution as guinea pigs for his experiments in conditioning. With his pretty new assistant Lisa (Trini Alvarado), the nutty doctor (who fancies himself as Doc in John Steinbeck's "Cannery Row") subjects his charges to idiotic word games and feeds them Chinese food before bedtime to increase their dream output.

He also covers up several murders caused by the phantom, before the prisoners finally mutiny and murder him right ahead of the phantom's revenge against Eddie.

With Coco giving a fascinating performance that adds sympathy for a generally negative character, film occasionally soars, abetted by solid ensemble playing by the cast of prisoners plus sympathetic readings by Alvarado and her prisoner beau Gary McCleery.

However, the horror elements frequently intrude, particularly the grisly murders of Coco's character and, in flashback, the previous warden whose spirit lives on. Repeated use of a stop-motion animated effect for an eyeball creature superimposed on a light bulb which torments the paranoid Eddie is silly, as is attempted comical music.

Director Waldemar Korzeniowsky sustains a gritty, realistic backdrop for the proceedings, but fails to maintain the proper tone.
—*Lor.*

Pin
(CANADIAN)

A New World Pictures release (U.S.), Malofilm Distribution in Canada of a Pierre David and Rene Malo production. Sales, Image Organization. Produced by Rene Malo. Executive Producer, Pierre David. Written and directed by Sandor Stern. Camera (color), Guy Dufaux; editor, Patrick Dodd; art direction, François Seguin; music, Peter Manning Robinson; sound, Richard Nichol; sound editing, Patrick Dodd. Reviewed at Cannes Film Festival (market), May 16, 1988. Running time: **102 MIN.**

Leon . . . . David Hewlett
Ursula . . . . Cyndy Preston
Sam Fraker . . . . John Ferguson
Dr. Linden . . . . Terrance O'Quinn
Mrs. Linden . . . . Bronwen Nantel

Also with: Jacob Tirney, Michelle Anderson, Steve Bernarski, Katie Shengler.

Cannes — One would assume by reading the ad that "Pin" is a horror film on the order of the "Friday The 13th" series, but this is a well-made thriller nicely photographed by Genie Award-winning cameraman Guy Dufaux ("Un Zoo La Nuit"). This is subtle suspense, not quite up to the levels of a Hitchcock, but deserving a better fate than the marketing programs planned by its distributors.

The plot follows Leon and Ursula Linden over the course of 15 years, from childhood through adolescence to adulthood. It also traces their relationship with their doctor-father's anatomically correct dummy Pin.

To Leon, Pin is a brother figure and he soon learns how to "talk" to the dummy through the same ventriloquist's tricks used by his father. Unlike his father, who used ventriloquism to calm nervous young patients, Leon creates a best friend out of the dummy, soon forgetting Pin is not real. The game continues long after his parents' death in a car accident. Eventually, Leon creates a 3-member family and vows to do whatever it takes to protect it from outsiders.

Although the film is far better than the ads suggest, theatrical potential is limited. It is difficult to imagine horror fans giving good word-of-mouth to a pic that contains not a single murder. A well-packaged video campaign could work, particularly if the campaign targets younger teens who want to be scared, but not terrified.
— *Cadd.*

Send A Gorilla
(NEW ZEALAND)

An Energy Source Intl. presentation of a Pinflicks Prod. Produced by Dorothee Pinfold. Executive producers, Peter Sainsbury, Pinfold. Written and directed by Melanie Read. Camera (color), Wayne Vinten; editor, Paul Sutorius; music, Peter Blake; production design, Kirsten Shouler; sound, Brian Shennan; production manager, Jane Gilbert; assistant director, Joe Nolan. Reviewed at Cannes Film Festival (market), May 14, 1988. Running time: **93 MIN.**

Clare . . . . Carmel McGlone
Joy . . . . Katherine McRae
Vicki . . . . Perry Piercy
Chris Dean . . . . John Callen
Ian Hunter . . . . Larney Tupu
Ned . . . . William Kircher
Joe . . . . Jim Moriarty

Cannes — A Kiwi offering with a bright central idea shot down by vulgar, incoherent handling, "Send A Gorilla" is a farcical flop.

First production of Energy Source Intl. is likely to perform only on its home turf, and that's if local auds are tolerant.

Film is a major disappointment coming from writer-director Melanie Read, whose first feature "Trial Run" was a modest winner. Read is aiming for farce this time, but right from the first scene it's clear comedy's not her forte: principal characters are introed chaotically and prove supremely uninteresting.

Action is set on St. Valentine's Day and centers around an all-femme singing telegram operation. Outfit is having a bad day, since the manager has ankled and a key member of the group has lost her voice. Of the three women who have to deliver 50 love messages during the day, one has just broken off with her lover, another is fighting her ex over child custody and the third ought to be at an operatic audition.

Under Read's frantically energetic, but empty direction, the principal actresses can only flounder helplessly. They come across as a strident and unappealing trio, matched only for charmlessness by the men in the film, who include a misogynistic deejay, a property developer and the philandering ex-hubby.

Overflowing with subplots, including one involving the deejay's beloved dog which is attracted to the gorilla outfit worn by one of the femmes, pic bustles along at a busy pace but never comes close to hitting the target. Technical credits are okay, but on the garish side. — *Strat.*

Sebastian And The Sparrow
(AUSTRALIAN)

A J.C. Williamson Distributors P/L release of a Kino Film production. A Colour & Movement film. Executive producer, Terry Ohlsson. Produced, written and directed by Scott Hicks. Camera (color), David Foreman; editor, Pip Karmel; music, Allan Zavod; production design, Anni Browning; sound, Toivo Lember; creative consultant, Kerry Heysen; associate producer, Darryl Sheen; assistant director, Gus Howard; casting, Jan Killen. Reviewed at Cannes Film Festival (market), May 14, 1988. Running time: **90 MIN.**

Sebastian Thornbury . . . Alexander Bainbridge
Sparrow . . . . Jeremy Angerson
Peter Thornbury . . . . Robert Coleby
Jenny Thornbury . . . . . Elizabeth Alexander
Mick . . . . Vincent Gil
Country Cop . . . . John Clayton
Also with: Alice Ramsay (Maude Thornbury), Jethro Heyson-Hicks (Jethro Thornbury), Chris Roberts (Turbo), Peter Crossley (Red), Patrick Frost (schoolteacher).

Cannes — A lightweight family film about friendship between two 15-year-old boys, one from a rich home, the other a street kid, "Sebastian And The Sparrow" is more suited to tube transmission and family video packaging than theatrical release.

Basically familiar tale is just too slight to get by in the competitive world of commercial cinema.

That's not to say Scott Hicks' film, made in Adelaide, doesn't have qualities. Jeremy Angerson is a find as young Sparrow, a half-Vietnamese boy whose father, a war vet, died in an accident and whose mother is missing. Sparrow lives on the streets by his wits, scavenging food and money and avoiding a welfare officer (Vincent Gil).

Sebastian (Alexander Bainbridge) on the other hand comes from a privileged home and attends an expensive private school where he's rehearsing piano for an upcoming concert, until diverted by Sparrow into a trek into the hinterlands to find the missing mother.

Trouble is, the adventures of the two boys aren't particularly exciting, amusing or original. Result is a perfectly decent but bland film. Another problem is that young Bainbridge doesn't register as interestingly as Angerson, making the central relationship lopsided.

A few clichés creep into the tale, too, especially at the all-too-rosy finale. Adult players are fine, with professional performances from Robert Coleby and Elizabeth Alexander as Sebastian's worried parents, and from John Clayton as a country policeman.

Best slot for the film is early evening tv since youngsters might identify with the characters. Childrens' film fests also could be interested. Technical credits are all fine. — *Strat.*

The Prince of Pennsylvania

A New Line Intl. release. Produced by Joan Fishman. Coproduced by Kerry Orent. Written and directed by Ron Nyswaner. Camera (color), Frank Prinzi; editor, Bill Sharf; production design, Toby Corbett; set decoration, Marlene Marta; costumes, Carol Wood; sound, Alan Byer; assistant director, Michael Topoozian; casting, Alan Amtzis (N.Y.), Donna Belajac (Pittsburgh). Reviewed at Cannes Film Festival (market), May 15, 1988. Running time: **87 MIN.**

Rupert Marshetta	Keanu Reeves
Carla Headlee	Amy Madigan
Pam Marshetta	Bonnie Bedelia
Gary Marshetta	Fred Ward
Roger Marshetta	Joseph De Lisi
Jack Sike	Jeff Hayenga
Lois Sike	Tracy Ellis
Trooper Joe	Jay O. Sanders

Cannes — "The Prince Of Pennsylvania" is a gem of independent filmmaking. Writer-director Ron Nyswaner addresses the themes of alienated youth and confused adults with exquisite care.

His superb script, with its inventive plot and empathetic characters, captures the textbook elements of fine drama: conflict, tension, uncertainty and humor. Film will likely need narrow release for building of its deserved word-of-mouth and critical backing. That should mean success domestically while overseas appeal hinges on whether pic can be marketed as a universal story of human relationships.

Setting is a rural Pennsylvania coalmining town where young Rupert Marshetta (Keanu Reeves) is coming of age in a rebellious mood. He's at cross purposes with father Gary (Fred Ward), a stern Vietnam vet who thinks Oliver North is a hero.

Gary has decided his son should follow him into the mines. His wife Pam (Bonnie Bedelia) considers

that a betrayal of an earlier pledge that their sons would find a better life. Pam herself, however, is betraying her husband via an affair with his best friend, Jack (Jeff Hayenga).

Rupert's discovery of his mom's liaison compounds his own frustrations, pushes him further into outrageous behavior and finally into the arms of ex-hippie and roadside diner operator Carla Headlee (Amy Madigan). They team for an outlandish escapade to settle the score with dad.

By the time this scheme is launched, one clearly appreciates the perspective of each character — whether it's with sympathy or enmity.

Lending considerable quality to the venture are performances of each of the key castmembers. Reeves' depiction of a teen in turmoil conveys a dimension too often lacking in similar circumstances.

Ward and Bedelia certainly are figures representative of parents whose energies are centered on the trials of their responsibilities. Struggling to make some sense of their lives, couple slides into pitfalls indeed but with a believability frequently absent in many cardboard figures whose singular dimension is devoid of purpose. Each is a fully depicted individual against whom the son's actions can be gauged.

Madigan's idiosyncratic carryover from an earlier era is a stunning example of one who never does quite adapt to the 1980s — notwithstanding a media-generated notion that all such singular souls have gone Gucci. She lifts her character above that of caricature.

Nyswaner has brought the material to life.—*Tege.*

Corentin, ou les infortunes conjugales
(Corentin, Or The Conjugal Misfortunes)
(FRENCH)

An AAA release of a Films du Chantier/-ARP/Ciné 5 coproduction. Produced by Jean Marboeuf, Laurent Petin. Directed by Marboeuf. Screenplay, Marboeuf, Josiane Leveque; camera (Fujicolor), Jean Rozenbaum; editor, Anne-France Lebrun; music, period songs performed by Les Arts Florissants; art direction, Jérôme Clément; sound, Alix Comte, Gérard Lamps; costumes, Odile Sauton; production manager, Marie-Annick Jarlegan. Reviewed at the Marignan-Concorde cinema, Paris, May 3, 1988. (In Cannes Film Festival Market.) Running time: **98 MIN.**

Corentin	Roland Giraud
Athenais	Andréa Ferréol
Marquis	Patrick Chesnais
Clémence	Muriel Brener
Lisette	Olivia Brunaux
Blaise	Jacques Chailleux
Quack doctor	Jean Poiret

Paris — Writer-director Jean Marboeuf applies an overly broad hand to a potentially good comic script in "Corentin," his first attempt at a costume film. It should

have had more finesse in the direction and especially more vigorously stylish performances.

Marboeuf based his screenplay on a true 17th century case of a wealthy French rube who married a 16-year-old girl but was unable to perform his marital duties. Under church law the husband was threatened with loss of property and annulment of the marriage, unless he could consummate his marriage during a public tribunal.

There are some juicy farce situations here worthy of Molière, but Marboeuf's inexperience with period dialog and his usual problems of pacing trip him up. Roland Giraud plays the title role with his usual bemused wryness but fails to give it sympathy or comic relief. Andréa Ferréol is the outraged mother-in-law hankering to get her hands on Giraud's wealth and remarry her daughter to a libertine nobleman.
— *Len.*

Chief Zabu

An IFM release of a Zabu Co. production. Produced by Norman Leigh. Directed by Howard Zuker (Zack Norman), Neil Cohen. Coproducers, Cohen, Howard and Nancy Zuker. Screenplay, Cohen, Zuker, Nancy Zuker; camera (color), Frank Prinzi; editor, Fima Noveck; music, Andrew Asch; production design, John Loggia, Tom Surgal; special effects and sound supervision, Scott Briendal; costumes, Hali Briendal. Reviewed at Cannes Film Festival (market), May 15, 1988. Running time: **80 MIN.**

Ben Sydney	Allen Garfield
Sammy Brooks	Zack Norman
Dankworth	Allan Arbus
Zabu	Manu Tupou
Monica	Lucianne Buchanan
Skip	Ed Lauter
Jennifer	Marianna Hill

Cannes — Take a preposterous premise and dialog that fizzles rather than sizzles, play it way over the top and shoot it sloppily, and you have "Chief Zabu."

Not so much a comedy as an unintentional farce, this dismal effort has no discernible commercial value. Pin most of the blame on Zack Norman, the actor who figures here as co-lead, codirector (under real name Howard Zuker), coproducer and cowriter.

Norman and Allen Garfield play New York real estate salesmen, somewhat below the Donald Trump level, who dream of making it rich. Answer to their prayers, it appears, is the chief of a Polynesian island (Manu Tupou) who's willing to award lucrative business concessions in return for the greasing of his application for United Nations membership.

Hare-brained scheme comes unstuck when it's learned the French have been testing nuclear weapons in close proximity to the island.

No matter, for Sammy (Norman) realizes his other ambition of doing standup routines in Las Vegas, at a stroke ruining that resort's reputation for high-class acts, and Ben (Garfield), after a puzzling leap in

the narrative, gets married and launches a promising (?) political career in Beverly Hills.

No Hope and Crosby, Garfield and Norman are an illmatched couple and often seem to be competing rather than complementing each other. Their air of manic desperation (perhaps in fruitless pursuit of gags in the script) infects the other players.

Making his helming debut, Zuker/Norman favors a lot of closeups which don't convey a lot, and an odd preference for aiming upwards toward the actors' nostrils.

Typical of the all around technical sloppiness, boom mikes move into view numerous times. Not just one, but two mikes appear at one point, and like the rest of the picture, that's not funny. — *Dogo.*

Blueberry Hill

A Fox/Lorber release of a Mediacom Industries production in association with MVA-I and Tricoast Prod. Partners. Produced by Mark Michaels. Executive producers, Ronald S. Altbach, A.J. Cervantes. Directed by Strathford Hamilton. Screenplay, Lonon Smith; camera, (color), David Lewis; editor, March Hamilton; music, Ira Ingber. Reviewed at Cannes Film Festival (market), May 12, 1988. Running time: **87 MIN.**

Becca Dane	Carrie Snodgress
Ellie Dane	Jennifer Rubin
Hattie Cole	Margaret Avery
Danny Logan	Matt Lattanzi

Cannes — "Blueberry Hill" is yet another small American film trying to cash in on a nostalgia craze that looks to be past its peak.

Pic toplines two former Academy Award nominees — Carrie Snodgress ("Diary Of A Mad Housewife") and Margaret Avery ("The Color Purple"), which could be a marketing error. Neither has a high profile in the theatrical or video market. Distrib Fox/Lorber might be better off promoting young costars Jennifer Rubin and Matt Lattanzi.

Pic is set in a California town in 1956. Snodgress is a woman whose husband drowned in a local creek the night their daughter Ellie was born. She has never quite recovered from his death and has turned her house into a shrine with his pictures lining the living room walls. The only person who knows the truth about the husband is local piano teacher Avery who remembers him as a womanizing piano player. When Ellie — now 6 — wants to know what he was like, her piano teacher takes her to the club where he played.

Best feature is the music. Avery sings '50s jazz numbers and the soundtrack features some hit songs of the era including the title tune. The acting doesn't quite measure up to the story's potential. Particularly poor is Snodgress, who chews up the scenery in a pic that might have worked better with a softer approach to the mother/daughter relationship.

The interaction between Snodgress and Rubin is too overbaked to appeal to teens. Avery's performance is the best of the four toppers. She brings the same sense of energy to the role of the piano teacher that she brought to Shug in "The Color Purple." —*Cadd.*

Hotel St. Pauli
(NORWEGIAN)

A VCM (Oslo) release of Mefisto Film production. Produced, written and directed by Svend Wam and Petter Vennerød from Erland Kiösterud's novel. Camera (Eastmancolor), Philip Ogaard; editor, Inge-Lise Langfeldt; music, Svein Gundersen; art direction, Tone Skjelfjord, Viggo Jönsberg; sound, Ragnar Samuelsson; costumes, Eirin Osen; production manager, Finn Thome. Reviewed at Cannes Film Festival (market) May 15, 1988. Running time: **118 MIN.**
Jor ....John Ege
Gerda ....Amanda Ooms
Morgan ....Oyvin Berven
Also with: Sossen Krogh, Jorunn Kjellsby, Ingrid van Bergen, Jöns Andersson, Lasse Lindtner, Linn Stokke.

Cannes — Given a strong pitch at Cannes and already a *success de scandale* **in Norway, the ever outrageous writer-director-producer team Svend Wam and Petter Vennerød's "Hotel St. Pauli" is a rough-and-tumble recounting of the drug-induced attempts at coming of age of three young people in the early '60s.**

Picture is dramatically efficient in a crude way. It has nothing to add to the drug culture portrait seen by so many earlier filmmakers, but it has explicit sex in abundance.

A young Norwegian boy dresses up as a cowboy and goes to Denmark in search of a whore to take care of his sexual initiation. Instead he finds sweet and willing Gerda (Sweden's Amanda Ooms) who hopes to have the boy help her get away from Jor, the obsessive writer of autobiographical fiction with whom she lives in a kind of bondage.

Starting with marijuana, the trio begin their descent into a hell of their own making. The youngster is hospitalized, but escapes, heading back to Gerda and Jor. Jor kills the boy and Gerda runs away to Hamburg to work in a brothel. When Jor finds her, she is a ruin.

In Norway, the picture has been compared to "Betty Blue." The comparison is hardly merited but the raw punch is there. —*Kell.*

Something About Love
(CANADIAN)

An Image Organization Release of an Allegro Films production. Produced by Franco Battista, Thomas Berry and Stefan Wodoslawsky. Directed by Berry. Screenplay, Berry, Wodoslawsky; camera (color), Rodney Gibbons; editor, Battista; music, Lou Forestieri; art direction, Guy Lalande; costumes, Nicole Pelletier; sound, Jacques Drouin; sound editing, Andre Galbrand. Reviewed at Cannes Film Festival (market), May 14, 1988. Running time: **94 MIN.**

Wally Olynyk ....Stefan Wodoslawsky
Stan Olynk ....Jan Rubes
Bobbie ....Jennifer Dale
Elaine ....Diana Reis
Also with: Ron James, Lendie Zann.

Cannes — Canadian filmmakers with roots in the Nova Scotia region of Cape Breton seem to delight in returning home to make movies. This is the third such film of recent vintage, following on the heels of 1985's "The Bay Boy" and last year's "Life Classes."

While its predecessors won several Genie nominations — Canada's Oscar — neither found much of a market outside Canada's Cape Breton emigrant communities.

This pic probably will follow that dubious tradition. It has some nostalgia value, but spends too much time examining the relationship between a Cape Breton man now living in Los Angeles and his 63-year-old Ukranian-Canadian father. The father, a mortician in a steel mill town, has Alzheimer's disease but refuses to admit he's in trouble.

Most entertaining moments come at a high school reunion, but the pace slows when Rubes and Wodoslawsky get together for the traditional father-son clash. Hardest to watch are the mortuary scenes.

"Something About Love" has nothing to add about the strain of going home again. Fortunately, the producers presold the pic to Canadian cable tv, it has very limited foreign market potential. Despite its universal themes and some good acting by Rubes, it probably won't sell beyond Canada's borders.
—*Cadd.*

Buying Time
(CANADIAN)

An Arista Films release of a Louis George presentation. Produced by Richard Gabourie. Directed by Mitchell Gabourie. Screenplay, Richard and Mitchell Gabourie; camera (color), Manfred Guthe; editor, Michael Todd; music, David Krystal. Reviewed at Cannes Film Festival (market), May 14, 1988. Running time: **103 MIN.**
With: Jeff Schulz, Laura Cruickshank, Page Fletcher, Leslie Toth, Dean Stockwell.

Cannes — Two young carwash attendants are drafted by the police against their will to moonlight in a murder investigation. Working as waiters in an old people's home, they unearth a plot to doctor races by drugging the horses, but in the process become themselves living targets for the criminals.

After a slow start, "Buying Time" goes into high gear, but violence and sex are kept under control to keep product on a youth-oriented level. The "Fatal Attraction"-type double climax leads to a pious moral, with the two protagonists changing the carwash for horse stables.

A typical, unmemorable exploitation movie with an uninspired cast of beginners and a tired performance by Dean Stockwell as the

scheming police detective, its technical credits are satisfactory enough to help it make a quick transition to the video market where it may stand a better chance. —*Edna.*

Iguana
(SWISS)

An Enterprise Iguana Filmproduction. Produced by Franco di Nunzio. Directed by Monte Hellman. Screenplay, Hellman, David M. Zehr; camera (Telecolor), Jose Maria Civit; editor, Hellman; music, Franco Campanino; production design, Paolo Petti; costumes, Leslie Ballard; production manager, Mario Pedraza; assistant director, Yousef Bokhari. Reviewed at Cannes Film Festival (market), May 12, 1988. (Also in Seattle Festival.) Running time: **97 MIN.**
Oberius................Everett McGill
Carmen ....Maru Valdivielso
Gamboa ....Fabio Testi
George ....Tim Ryan
Also with: Michael Madsen, Joseph Culp, Augustin Guevara.
(In English and Spanish)

Cannes — Cult director of the '60s Monte Hellman returns after a long absence with one of those infuriating "international" productions that boasts a cast of mixed nationalities and clashing accents.

Downbeat swashbuckler is only of minor interest for buffs, with theatrical possibilities poor save for undemanding grindhouses.

Everett McGill plays an evil-tempered sailor with a badly disfigured face; after undergoing a lashing as punishment for disobeying an order, he jumps ship, winding up on a desert island where he can rule as self-styled king. He takes as his prisoners sailors lucky enough to be washed ashore, plus a beautiful Spanish noblewoman, Carmen, whom he takes as his mistress and rapes repeatedly.

Hellman's theme seems to be that the disfigured antihero has declared war on all mankind because he can't cope with his ugly face. The director is unable to make McGill a genuinely tragic figure, however, and all we get is a second-rate actioner, with some perfunctory swordfights, a touch of cruelty and some amazingly rugged depictions of sexual activity (which place the film into the hard R category).

Frantic crosscutting during the first third of the film makes the action needlessly confusing at times for which Hellman, as editor, must take the blame. Basically, "Iguana" is another example of no-nonsense Yank director trying to cope with the problems of a European production, and making heavy weather of it. Dialog often is unintentionally funny.

Technically, pic is adequate, but overall "Iguana" is a major disappointment and a quick trip to the homevid shelf is the best option.
—*Strat.*

Helsinki Napoli All Night Long
(FINNISH-SWISS)

A Finnkino (Finland), Senator Film (West Germany) release of a Villealfa (Finland), Francis van Buren/Mediactuel (Switzerland) production in association with Salinas (Berlin), Condor Features/Christa Saredi (Zurich), Felix Film/Nova Film/Claudio Pappalardo/Wiz Music (Milano) and Finnkino (Helsinki). Produced and directed by Mika Kaurismäki. Screenplay, Kaurismäki, Richard Reitinger; camera (Eastmancolor), Helge Weindler; editor, Helga Borsche; music, Jacques Zwart; sound, Paul Jyrala; art direction, Olaf Schiefner; associate producers, Peter Christian Fueter, Christa Saredi; production supervisor, Uli Moeller. Reviewed at Cannes Film Festival (market), May 12, 1988. Running time: **105 MIN.**
Alex ....Kari Vaananen
Stella, his wife ....Roberta Manfredi
Stella's father ....Nino Manfredi
Igor ....Jean-Pierre Castaldi
Mara the prostitute ....Margi Clarke
Lilli ....Melanie Robeson
Gangster boss ....Samuel Fuller
Older henchman ......Eddie Constantine
Younger henchman .....Saku Kuosmanen
Also with: Wim Wenders, Jim Jarmusch, Katharina Thalbach, Harry Baer, Gerd Jochum, Werner Masten, Remo Remotti, Ugo Fangarezzi, Carlo Hafzalla.

Cannes — The art of cinematic spoof is tricky. In "Helsinki Napoli All Night Long," Finnish producer-writer-director Mika Kaurismäki serves up with (mostly) English dialog, a jagged mix of film noir clichés and visual slapstick nonsequiturs as a farce that sometimes works with bounce and buoyancy and at other times falls confusedly on its face.

Already a moderate boxoffice hit in Finland and released in West Germany, pic is likely to find limited international exposure primarily because of its name actors from many lands plus supporting bits or cameos by helmers Sam Fuller, Jim Jarmusch and Wim Wenders.

Plot has West Berlin's only Finnish cabbie riding around one long night with a couple of stiffs and a briefcase full of $100 bills in the back seat. He is forever thwarted in getting rid of the dead men and his Italian wife is allergic to stolen loot. The cabbie is being chased by a top mobster (Fuller, waving his cigar like a flag) and his sidekick (Eddie Constantine).

Car chases, beatings, etc., alternate with dumb conniving and kidnapping. Italian comedy actor Nino Manfredi stumbles around in an alcoholic daze as a babysitting grandfather, and England's Margi Clarke ("A Letter To Brezhnev") and France's Jean-Pierre Cristaldi are left to their own devices as a prostitute and Russian truckdriver, in roles left undeveloped by the writers.

Finland's Kari Vaananen mostly looks foolish in a part designed by writers who claim to have a moralistic ax to grind. The pretense is best forgotten and soon lost anyway in flashy production (Berlin after-hours locations are used to great advantage) and in the general hubbub of smart repartee. This film is fun on

the run, but too often out of breath.
—*Kell.*

Assa
(SOVIET)

A Mosfilm production. Directed by Sergei Soloviov. Screenplay, Sergei Livnev, Soloviov; camera (color), Pavel Lebeshev; art direction, Marken Gauchman-Sverdiov; music, Boris Grebenschikov, Aquarium, Kino, Bravo, Soyuz Compozitorov. Reviewed at Cannes Film Festival (market). May 13, 1988. Running time: **150 MIN.**

Alika	Tatiana Drubich
Krymov	Stanislav Govorukhin
Bananan	Sergei Bugayev

Cannes — "Assa," one of the first films of the perestroika age, opens a luminous window on what Gorbachev's new cinema may look like. This stylish, 2½-hour rock-thriller is crammed with a wealth of invention.

Technically innovative (as was helmer Sergei Soloviov's previous film, "The Wild Dove"), with a fresh approach to thesping and explanation-less storytelling, "Assa" is watchable and surprising. With the right handling it should pique the curiosity of adventurous Western audiences, if nothing else for its music track featuring four of the USSR's top rock bands.

Yalta in winter, covered in snow, Brezhnev's 1980 is the setting for the arrival of Andrei Krymov (Stanislav Govorukhin). This gentleman-mobster, who's swindled millions and murders with regret, has come to meet his young mistress Alika (Tatiana Drubich).

The snowstorm gives Alika time to get acquainted with Bananan, irrepressible singer in a rock band and burgeoning composer. She likes his style, but has other things on her mind. Without false moralizing, film depicts her relationship to the gangster as deeper than just an attraction to the luxuries he showers upon her. (Curiously missing are the implicit bedroom scenes.)

Their life in the oak-paneled hotel suite is punctuated by Alika's outings with Bananan and Krymov's contacts with old cronies in the Yalta underworld. All three are highly individualized, likable characters, thanks to the original script (coauthor, Sergei Livnev) and excellent performances by principals.

Film unspools as an enjoyable cat-and-mouse game between the rivals for Alika's love, but gradually turns more somber. First victim of Krymov's deviltry is a midget who has left the gang and gone straight as an entertainer. Rather than hide in a double-bass case and steal a priceless violin, the midget jumps off Krymov's yacht. Ignoring all warnings, Bananan stubbornly sticks around and, in a chilling and quite effective chase sequence, winds up the same way. When Alika learns the truth, she hysterically puts an end to Krymov's crimes with his own revolver.

An intricate film with a sense of humor and, more important, a sense of cinema, "Assa" takes a popular gangster story to the edge of surrealism. Its experimental inclination is evident in the background soundtrack, which sounds like a special effects track from Mars, and such strange devices as visualizing, every so often, the book Krymov is reading about the assassination of a Russian emperor. Pavel Lebeshev's superbly versatile camerawork helps carry the whole thing off with style.

Aficionados will recognize the influence of Soloviov's master Alexei Gherman, who put the experimental gangster film on the map of new Soviet cinema with "My Friend Ivan Lapshin." Soloviov has not yet achieved the originality or weightiness of his model, but has absorbed well the exploratory spirit. —*Yung.*

The American Scream

A Genesis Home Video presentation and production. Produced by Lori Levine and Mitchell Linden. Executive producers, Icek Tenenbaum, Elliott Siegel. Written and directed by Mitchell Linden. Camera (Eastmancolor), Bryan England; editor, Noreen Zepp; music, Richard Cox; art direction, Peggy Gilder. Reviewed at Cannes Film Festival (market), May 15, 1988. Running time: **85 MIN.**

Mr. Benzinger	Kevin Kaye
Mrs. Benzinger	Jennifer Darling
Barbara	Kimberlee Kramer
Charlotte	Jeanne Sapienza
Ben	Matt Borlenghi
Ben's friend	James Cooper
Stripper	Edy Williams

Also with: Blackie Dammett, Pons Marr.

Cannes — **In spite of its widescreen format; reasonably neat production values and good comedy in several parts, Mitchell Linden's horror comedy feature "The American Scream" is not likely to resound in too many cinemas. Homevideo future as unassuming family entertainment except for the very young looks okay.**

Benzinger family — Mom, Dad and teenagers Ben, Barbara and Charlotte, plus a funny guy boyfriend — are lured by a Wilson Creek tourist folder ("Bring the kids...") to spend a holiday in California's Sierra Mountains. It turns out Wilson Creek is inhabited by weirdos who hate young people and young ideas. While the naïve parents are left alone, all kinds of horror tricks (or are all these deaths real?) are played on the kids. Only Edy Williams as a stripper seems real.

Everything is definitely tongue-in-cheek, but some of the chills are really freezing. Near the end, the youngsters turn the tables on the natives by going them one better and taking on some ghoulish roles themselves.—*Kell.*

Angel III:
The Final Chapter

A New World Pictures release. Produced by Arnold Orgolini. Executive producers, Mel Pearl, Don Levin. Directed by Tom DeSimone. Screenplay, DeSimone, based on characters created by Joseph M. Cala, Robert Vincent O'Neill; camera (Getty color), Howard Wexler; editor, Warren Chadwick; music, Berlin Game; additional music, Don Great, Alan Ett; sound, Mary Jo Devenney; art direction, Alexandra Kicenik; set decoration, Monette Goldman; production manager, Johnine Novosek; stunt coordinator, John Branagan; casting, Tedra Gabriel. Reviewed at Cannes Film Festival (market), May 15, 1988. MPAA Rating: R. Running time: **99 MIN.**

Nadine	Maud Adams
Molly	Mitzi Kapture
Spanky	Mark Blankfield
Neal	Kin Shriner
Shahid	Emile Beaucard
Lt. Doniger	Richard Roundtree
Michelle	Tawny Fere
Gloria	Anna Navarro
Pam	Susan Moore

Also with: Barbara Treutelaar, Floyd Levine, Kyle Heffner, Dick Miller, Tony Basil, Steve Basil.

Cannes — **Third entry in New World's "Angel" series is a tired-blood melodrama about sisterly devotion. Prospects are extremely weak, even among devotees of the first two sexploitationers.**

All-new cast (though several of the characters are the same) is headed by Mitzi Kapture as Angel, now a 26-year-old shutterbug in New York City, who recognizes her long-gone mom Gloria (Anna Navarro) in a photo and tracks her to L.A. Mom reveals Angel has a 14-year-old sister, Michelle (Tawny Fere), who is involved with bad company. Mom is killed by a car bomb and Angel decides to go back out on the street as a fake prostie to find sis and avenge her mom.

Baddies are led by Maud Adams, running a combo white slavery and drug smuggling ring. Padded film wallows (with too many in-jokes) in the world of porn filmmaking as Angel takes many risks en route to saving sis and a poorly staged shootout finale.

Kapture is miscast as Angel, playing it too hard-edged to generate any sympathy and Fere too mature and far from innocent-looking in the youngster role. Comedian Mark Blankfield gets no laughs (his dialog is awful) as Angel's stereotyped street-person friend, played as if written for Craig Russell in "Outrageous." Rest of the cast phones it in.

Technical credits are chintzy.
—*Lor.*

Crack In The Mirror

A Jubran Group production, in association with Rebo High Definition Studio. (Intl. sales, Paul Intl.). Produced by Fred Berner, Jubran Jubran. Executive producers, Denis Bieber, Jubran, Michael Marrone, Barry Rebo, Tomio Taki. Directed by Robby Benson. Screenplay and story, Robert Madero; camera (color), Neil Smith; editor, Alan Miller, Craig McKay; music, Nile Rodgers; additional music, Philippe Saisse; sound (Dolby), Juan Rodriguez; production design, Rueben Freed; assistant director, David Dreyfuss; associate producer, Phyllis Jubran. Reviewed at Cannes Film Festival (market), May 13, 1988. Running time: **95 MIN.**

Scott	Robby Benson
Charlie	Danny Aiello
Vanessa	Tawny Kitaen
Butchie	Kevin Gray

Also with: Tony Gillan, Alan Hunter, Jihmi Kennedy, Mark Margolis, Judy Tenuta, Sally Kirkland.

Cannes — **"Crack In The Mirror" (alternately known as "Do It Up," name of its title song) is a grueling, cautionary tale about drug addiction. Misguidedly overdirected, it often plays more as a tract than entertainment.**

Feature's claim to fame is that it is the first full-length U.S. film shot via high definition video, following the trailblazing Italian production "Julia & Julia." Good news is that "Crack" demonstrates that a visually pleasing 35m film transfer can be achieved with this technology, though a few bugs (particularly the slight jerkiness of rapid movement in the frame) need to be ironed out.

Unfortunately, Robert Madero's script, directed by debuting helmer Robby Benson (who doubles as leading actor), is a compendium of clichés about the lives of crack-addicted yuppies. Worse, the grafting on of many sleazy, exploitation film elements tends to reduce the high-minded project to drive-in style fodder.

Benson rather uncomfortably plays Scott, a young New Yorker deeply in debt whose beautiful better half (luscious Tawny Kitaen) is becoming addicted to cocaine and crack. Rather silly story premise has Scott returning a lost pound bag of coke to local dealer Butchie (Kevin Gray) just as Gray is about to go on the lam to avoid a hit put out on him by mafioso boss Charlie (Danny Aiello).

Butchie agrees to wipe out Scott's debts and instantly set him up in the lucrative business of drug dealing in return for looking after Butchie's fabulous apartment and drug empire during his forced 2-week absence.

Benson reluctantly agrees, lying to Kitaen that he is taking a trip to Paris, and film builds dizzyingly and foolishly from there. Benson goes through instant personality changes, switching from nebbish to hardened gangster and soon a sniveling crackhead. Kitaen quickly discovers his deception, joins the highflying world and is seduced by their best friend in exchange for more crack.

Story climaxes with Butchie's return, leading to several shootouts and a repellent, disgusting vigilante finale as Benson and his young nebbish counterpart in the mafia mete out graphic and symbolic revenge upon Butchie. Extended scene is meant to scare the viewer straight, but is likely to enrage rather than enlighten the audience.

Apart from Benson's overwrought performance, which includes a rather graphic sex scene involving him and Butchie's pretty blond girlfriend, acting is commendable. Aiello has a lot of fun as the ruthless mafioso who auditions girls (including offbeat comedienne Judy Tenuta) for a Broadway play he's planning.

Kevin Gray is chilling in a rather subtle reading of the devil-figure dealer and Jihmi Kennedy is scary as a black henchman who loses control during a big-bucks drug sale. Future Oscar nominee Sally Kirkland pops up briefly and very effectively as a junkie with a tale of woe.

Nile Rodgers' funky musical score, including songs by Benson and his wife Karla DeVito, is a big asset. Neil Smith's camerawork creates nicely moody compositions, and via the processing and transfer to 35m by Rebo High Definition Studio is virtually indistinguishable from 35m lensing in closeups. Besides the noticeable jerky movements, some longer shots, especially a crane-effect in the apartment during the final reel, carry telltale grain and crosshatching.—*Lor.*

Beyond The Rising Moon

A Common Man Motion Picture production. (Intl. sales, Films Around The World.) Produced by John Ellis. Written, directed and edited by Philip Cook. Camera (color), Cook; associate producer, Pamela Hoeft; visual effects director, Cook; music, David Bartley; art direction, John Ellis; model supervisor, Norman Gagnon; conceptual artist, John Poreda; costume design, Helen Cook, Nancy Handwork. Reviewed at Cannes Film festival (market), May 14, 1988. Running time: **97 MIN.**
With: Tracy Davis, Hans Bachmann, Michael Mack, Ron Ikejiri, Rick Foucheaux, James Hild, Reggi Vaughn and Judith Miller.

Cannes — "Beyond The Rising Moon" is a victim of the emphasis on special effects placed on the sci-fi genre these days; pic is enslaved by a topheavy emphasis on effects at the expense of plot and, while not unlikable, it could've benefited by more work on plot to uplift it from the clearly homevideo-oriented niche it's heading for.

In 21st century Earth, life and business have changed radically with the discovery of a deserted alien spacecraft and the technology it offers; when information about the discovery of a second craft is intercepted by the scheming heads of conglomerate Kuriyama Enterprises, plans are made to claim salvage rights to the priceless find.

Enter Tracy Davis as Pentan, a genetically engineered "superbeing" the company has made as a troubleshooter; she's assigned to intercept the information but rebels at the prospect of unnecessary killing. She teams up with handsome space trader Hans Bachmann and the race is on, first to remove an implant in Pentan's head set off by the compa-

ny in just such a case, second to salvage the alien ship for themselves. Along the way she has to come to grips with the notion of independence and human emotion spurred naturally by romantic intentions on Bachmann's part.

Climax sees a new typical space dogfight against the pursuing company henchmen, and the none-too-clear survival of Pentan in a thermonuclear blast.

It's basic stuff, but handled well enough; problem is the surfeit of special effects, all model-based. Helmer and visual effects designer Philip Cook comes up with some excellent scenes, then clouds them with some quite poor shots; some judicious cutting wouldn't have been amiss. Thesping is okay, but, like "Beyond The Rising Moon's" plot, the effects have taken precedence, to the detriment of the film. — *Doch.*

36 Fillette
(Size 36 Girls)
(FRENCH)

A Gaumont release of a French Prod./CB Films/CFC coproduction. Executive producers, Emmanuel Schlumberger, Valérie Seydoux. Produced by Pierre Sayag. Directed by Catherine Breillat. Screenplay, Breillat, from her novel; script collaborator, Roger Salloch; camera (color), Laurent Dailland; editor, Yann Dedet; sound, Jean Minondo; art direction, Olivier Paultre. Reviewed at the Gaumont Ambassade theater, Paris, March 25, 1988. (In Cannes Film Festival Market.) Running time: **85 MIN.**
With: Delphine Zentout (Lili), Etienne Chicot (Maurice), Olivier Parnère (Bertrand), Jean-Pierre Léaud (Boris Golovine), Berta Dominguez D. (Anne-Marie), Jean-François Stévenin (the father), Diane Bellego (Georgia), Adrienne Bonnet (the mother).

Paris — "36 Fillette" is an unsentimental rites-of-passage chronicle about a 14-year-old girl's attempts to become an adult in the bed of a 40-year-old man she meets while vacationing with her family at a Biarritz camping site.
Written and directed by Catherine Breillat, pic avoids the bittersweet gilding of many other such films. Her heroine, played with sullen intensity by 16-year-old newcomer Delphine Zentout, is no charmer, wavering unexpectedly between coarse aggression and shyness, but she deserves some attention. Her clumsy pursuit of a burned-out lounge lizard (subtly embodied by Etienne Chicot) has occasional poignancy.

Yet the film as a whole lacks the piquant quality of its various scenes. Breillat, who worked with Maurice Pialat on his disappointing "Police," has affinities with that director's style of brute realism, but her sense of pacing and tone is faulty and sometimes monotonous. Though this is the third film she's directed, her strengths seem to be in writing. —*Len.*

Midnight Movie Massacre

A Wade Williams production, produced at the Film Works. (Sales, Reel Movies Intl.) Produced by Williams. Executive producer, Aaron Wilson. Directed by Mark Stock. "Space Patrol" live-action sequences directed by Larry Jacobs, inspired by ABC-TV series created by Mike Moser. Screenplay, Roger Branit, John Chadwell, David Houston, Stock; camera (color), Branit; music, Bill Crain; sound (Ultra-Stereo), Ken Ross; set design, Dickie Stafford; miniatures, David & Ellie Merriman; glass paintings, Joel Andrews, Ric Lee; special makeup effects, Ken Wheatly; "Space Patrol" camera (live-action), Nicholas von Sternberg. Reviewed at Cannes Film Festival (market), May 14, 1988. Running time: **85 MIN.**
Col Carlyle . . . . Robert Clarke
Dr. Van Buren . . . . Ann Robinson
Also with: David Staffer, Tom Hutsler, Margie Robbins, Brad Bittiker, Duke Howze, Susan Murphy, John Kelly, Mary Stevens, Carl Robertson, Charity Case, Lori Davis, Tamara Sue Hill, Andrew Goodman, Stuart Allen, Sara Strnad, Heidi Thomas.

Cannes — The potential of a knowing homage to '50s sci-fi is wasted in "Midnight Movie Massacre," a poorly scripted pastiche film. Even midnight bookings will be hard to come by for this one, which bears a 1986 copyright.
Pic actually is two films (often at odds) in one: the gory horror story of folks at the Granada Theater in 1956 being killed by a yucky, tentacled monster, and the movie serial "Space Patrol" (inspired by the actual tv series) that's playing there. An immediate probelm in tone and style is that the horror footage combines idiotic slapstick with latterday grossouf effects, while "patrol" is a benign recreation of old sci-fi films. The two don't mix well.

Genre faves Robert Clarke and Ann ("War Of The Worlds") Robinson topline with smallish roles in "Patrol," the episode "Back From The Future" dealing with a mad scientist and time travel. The clichéd dialog is merely boring, meant to be corny, but not sharp or clever enough to be funny. Best touches are the careful simulations of '50s matte shots, cheapo models and junky robots (which dance) plus too-fleeting cameos by Robby the Robot and his predecessor Gort.

Surrounding film is mainly running gags (each one extended past the breaking point) involving stereotyped audience members. Promising jokes like the fat wife (played by a thesp named Charity Case) who eats a ton start well but peter out, and others (particularly a girl who can't stop sneezing) prove to be mere timekillers.

Acting ensemble fits the lampooning roles, while tech credits capture the spirit of the cheesy originals. Unfortunately, the naiveté of the 1950s that made the sci-fi B's campy eludes this studied concoction. —*Lor.*

Doin' Time On Planet Earth

A Cannon release of a Golan-Globus production. Produced by Menahem Golan, Yoram Globus. Directed by Charles Matthau. Screenplay, Darren Star, from story by Star, Andrew Licht, Jeffrey A. Mueller; camera (TVC color), Timothy Suhrstedt; editor, Alan Balsam, Sharyn L. Ross; music, Dana Kaproff; sound (Ultra-Stereo); production design, Curtis A. Schnell; art direction, Colin D. Irwin; set decoration, Douglas A. Mowat; costumes, Reve Richards; visual effects designer, Bill Millar; assistant director, Frank Bueno; associate producer, Karen Koch; casting, Don Pemrick (L.A.), Paula Herold, N.Y. Reviewed at Cannes Film Festival (market), May 12, 1988. Running time: **85 MIN.**
Ryan Richmond . . . . Nicholas Strouse
Fred Richmond . . . . Hugh Gillin
Mary Richmond . . . . Gloria Henry
Richard Camalier . . . . Hugh O'Brian
Virginia Camalier . . . . Martha Scott
Jeff Richmond . . Timothy Patrick Murphy
Jenny Camalier . . . . Isabelle Walker
Marilyn Richmond . . . . Paula Irvine
Lisa Winston . . . . Andrea Thompson
Charles Pinsky . . . . Adam West
Edna Pinaky . . . . Candice Azzara

Cannes — "Doin' Time on Planet Earth" intends to be a comedic tale about an awkward teen who decides the only explanation for his peculiarities must be that he's an extra-terrestrial. Pic falls flat on all counts and is unlikely to generate much business in the U.S. or offshore.
Set in the mythical town of Sunnydale, Ariz., film centers on young Ryan Richmond (Nicholas Strouse), who is an embarrassment to his family amidst wedding preparations of brother Jeff (Timothy Patrick Murphy), a pretentious preppy, and the daughter of an ex-v.p. of the U.S. (Hugh O'Brian).

Convinced by his computer he's an alien, Ryan initially warms to the idea as a way of validating his off-center and generally nerdish behavior. He then is visited by self-proclaimed kindred spirits Edna (Candice Azzara) and Charles (Adam West). Latter's wacky persona is characteristic of his earlier Batman eccentricities, but it's hardly enough to carry the film.

Ryan is told by Edna and Charles that he is their leader and must take them back to their home planet. The secret of its location supposedly is buried within Ryan's DNA packet, which can be accessed only by a jolting experience.

To Ryan that means trying to lose his virginity to lounge singer Lisa Winston (Andrea Thompson). While previously repulsed by Ryan, Lisa curiously finds his outlandish circumstances beguiling enough to do an about-face.

Next stop is his sibling's wedding inside the spaceship-like bar of his father's Holiday Inn, which Charles believes actually is the aliens' vehicle for interplanetary escape.

Story is the work of first-time screenwriter Darren Star, whose black humor has a certain appeal but is not quite developed into engrossing farce.

Directorial debut of Charles Matthau, fils of actor Walter, is serviceable enough, considering the material. There is, however, a lack of vitality in the proceedings.

O'Brian's presence adds little and not much is gained either with cameos by Roddy McDowall and Maureen Stapleton.

Hugh Gillin as Ryan's father is comically on target. As for Strouse, his big-screen bow is strained at best. —Tege.

Blood Money

An ITC Entertainment Group production. Produced by Donald March. Directed by Jerry Schatzberg. Screenplay, Robert Foster; camera, Isidore Mankofsky; editor, David Ray; music, Jan Hammer; production design, Howard Barker; costumes, Brad Loman; sound, Michael Tromer; assistant director, Jerram Swartz; associate producer, Brad Loman; casting, Paula Herold. Reviewed at Cannes Film Festival (market), May 14, 1988. Running time: **90 MIN.**
Clinton Dillard ....Andy Garcia
Nadine Powers ....Eilen Barkin
Dorsey Pratt ....Morgan Freeman
Conrad ....Michael Lombard
Anson ....Brad Sullivan
Jewell ....Bill Raymond
Rayburn....................Alan North
Turner ....John McGinley

Cannes — Execution of this film bears a remarkable likeness to "Miami Vice," which is suitable since pic will go out in the U.S. via HBO under the title "Clinton And Nadine."

They're the lead couple who muddle through a murder mystery tale linked to illicit Contra•fundraising. Exploitation of that timely theme, despite substantial flaws, may generate some business in certain overseas quarters, but little else.

Andy Garcia, who performed so solidly in 'The Untouchables," is cast as Clinton, a parrot smuggler who stumbles onto his brother's slaying and foils murderers' attempts to escape with a backpack containing some audiocassettes. One of them, he learns, inexplicably includes the recording of another murder and references to certain individuals.

Clinton also came away from the crime scene with a purse belonging to Nadine Powers (Ellen Barkin), a hooker on the run from the refuge of his brother's home. She has a "business" involvement with a Miami kingpin with vague connections. Lonely and confused, she is drawn reluctantly into Clinton's attempt to track down those responsible for the murders.

Trail leads to attorney Dorsey Pratt (Morgan Freeman), who was mentioned on the tape. Uncertain of Pratt's role, Clinton plays it cagey and himself becomes a target so the evidentiary tape can be retrieved.

Clinton's generally single-minded demeanor provides the audience little accessibility — nothing at all is really known about him beyond the bird smuggling — and Nadine's

screechy and combative manner is equally offputting. Script and direction thereby combine to create further enigma in an already elusive portrait.

By the time the pair become lovers, one hardly cares and problem is compounded when the story becomes bewildering as everyone is transposed suddenly to Costa Rica for the denouement. Disjoined sequencing is more of a distraction than a reward, with storyline being sacrificed for action and moodish cinematography.

Once Clinton prevails and resumes interrupted liaison with Nadine, windup cannot come soon enough. —Tege.

The Passage

A Manson Intl. release of Spectrum/Carrera production. Produced by Raul Carrera. Executive producer, Brandon Baade. Directed by Harry Thompson. Camera (Eastmancolor), Peter Stein; editor, Peter Appleton; music, Paul Loomis, others. No further credits available. Reviewed at Cannes Film Festival (market), May 15, 1988. Running time: **105 MIN.**
Annie May Bonner ....Alexandra Paul
Matthew Bonner ....Ned Beatty
Rachel Bonner ....Barbara Barrie
Byron Monroe ....Brian Keith
Jesse ....Dee Law

Cannes — In spite of vigorous playing by Ned Beatty and Brian Keith as, respectively, mean old guy and good old guy, Harry Thompson's "The Passage" is stolid and turgid throughout. Theatrical chances seem nil and even in homevideo it will have very limited appeal.

Picture is a weepie about stubborn Southern estate owner Matthew Bonner (Beatty) who turns his pretty Radcliffe-graduate daughter out of the family mansion when she gets pregnant. Her lover Jesse is the son of Bonner's trusty old lumber logger Byron Monroe (Keith), but Jesse is considered an unsuitable match.

The older Bonner remains stubborn even when his wife dies of heartbreak and the youngsters marry and settle down to raise a family that soon boasts four children. Bonner causes the new family a lot of harm before he forgives, forgets and settles down in a role as grandfather (Byron Monroe having vacated his job as senior head of the family by dying of heart failure).

"The Passage" is a Depression period meller and its production dress is neat enough. Life within the frames is just a set of clichés, however, and dully told. Alexandra Paul and Dee Law as the young couple look prettier in a squaredance than as movers of melodrama.—Kell.

Deadly Stranger

A Manson Intl. release of an MJK Prods.

production. Produced, directed and written by Max Kleven. Camera (color) Tony Gaudioz; editor, Stanford C. Allen; music Chuck Cirino; additional music, Mayf Nutter. Reviewed at Cannes Film Festival (market), May 14, 1988. Running time: **93 MIN.**
Peggy Martin...........Darlanne Fluegel
J.C. Ryan ....Michael J. Moore
Mitchell....................John Vernon
Red ....Taylor Lacher
Larkin ....Ted White
Juan ....Tommy Rosales

Cannes — If the B-grade picture is a fast fading phenomenon, this turkey will hasten its demise. For "Deadly Stranger," read deadly dull.

Limp actioner fails to develop even a smidgin of dramatic tension and sans promotable names seems destined to be a theatrical nonevent most everywhere.

Frequent use of 4-letter words and other vulgarities will have to be cleaned up to give item any chance of tv exposure.

Homevideo consumers who latterly have shown more discriminating taste are not likely to devour this lowercase offering.

Drifter J.C. Ryan (Michael J. Moore) gets inveigled into picking peppers for plantation owner Mitchell (John Vernon) who's in cahoots with corrupt union boss Larkin (Ted White). Workers — mostly Mexican wetbacks — are being grossly exploited and if they kick up too much of a stink are likely to disappear.

Mitchell's mistress Peggy (Darlanne Fluegel) in a blink of an eyelid has Ryan jump into the jacuzzi with her. Desiring more than his body, she wants his help in getting her greedy hands on the proceeds from the union racketeering.

It's clear to just about everyone except dimwitted Peggy that Ryan's sympathy for the downtrodden pepperpickers sets him apart from the usual solitary drifter, and the stage is set for a confrontation with Mitchell and henchmen.

The fist fights are staged poorly, Fluegel does not exhibit much flesh out of the hot tub, and the dialog never rises above the comic strip caliber of "You're never going to get away with this, punk."

Writer-producer-director Max Kleven demonstrates no particular flair in any department, and tech credits are passable. —Dogo.

Dixie Lanes

An SC Entertainment release (Miramax Films in U.S.) of a David H. Brady-Gateway Entertainment production. Executive producers, Saul Wilen, Jack Granat, Alan R. Vogeler Jr., George Flak. Produced by Brady. Directed by Don Cato. Screenplay, John Howbrook; camera (color), Bill Wages; editor, Michael McMahon, Stephen Withrow, Harvey Zlatarits; music, Pat Coleman, Paul Novotny; production design, Ed Richardson; associate producers, Stolp Fraser, Robert G. Rosenblatt. Reviewed at Cannes Film Festival (market), May 3, 1988. Running time: **87 MIN.**
Clarence Laidlaw...........Hoyt Axton
Zelma Putnam...............Karen Black
Louis Clark ....Art Hindle

Elmer Sinclair ....John Vernon
Betty Conklin ....Ruth Buzzi
Hazel Laidlaw ....Nina Foch
Violet....................Tina Louise
Chester Conklin ...........A.J. Freeman
Popinjay ....Moses Gunn
Judy ....Pamela Springsteen
Everett ....Chris Rydell

Cannes — Toronto-based distrib SC recently purchased Creswin Film Distribution and has plans to add a video label to the mix. One of the first pics to go to video could be "Dixie Lanes" an awkward marriage of comedy and drama set in Washington State immediately following World War II.

Producer Gateway Entertainment brought together an ensemble of performers with little theatrical release sales potential — including Karen Black, Hoyt Axton, Art Hindle and Ruth Buzzi. Black is Zelma Putnam, a woman who wants to keep her favorite nephew, Everett Laidlaw, from the bad influence of "Laidlaw luck."

The "disease" already has claimed his mother, who ended life as an entree on a New Guinea tribe's dinner menu. She was Zelma's sister and the latter still blames her brother-in-law's inherited bad luck for her death. She hopes to save her son Everett from the same kind of tragedy by employing him as a runner in his illegal war-ration selling scheme, hoping he will be out of town enough on business so the lack of proximity to his clan will free him of the curse.

John Howbrook's script is a cross between Robert Altman's "Popeye" and "The Best Years Of Our Lives." If that sounds like an awful combination, on screen it is worse. Black acts with all the dignity of Shelley Duvall's Olive Oyl, while Axton, who plays her brother-in-law, appears to be auditioning for the Fredric March role in "Best Years."

The actors can't be blamed for their inability to choose between Marx Bros. and melodrama. Director Don Cato never gets a handle on the material, maneuvering along the thin line that separates black comedy from drama with the grace of a tank driver. —Cadd.

Dear John
(CANADIAN)

A Simcom (in Canada) release of an Ordinary Film production. Produced by Catherine Ord, Don Haig, Bill Robertson. Written and directed by Ord. Camera (color), Douglas Koch; editor, Ord; art direction, Allan Fellows; costumes, Melinda Forster; sound, Robert Vollum; sound editing, Michael Werth. Reviewed at Cannes Film Festival (market), May 16, 1988. Running time: **115 MIN.**
Janet ....Valerie Buhagiar
Pocket ....Stan Lake
Hunter ....Thomas Rickert
Joe-Ann................David Maclean
Eonnie ....Evelyn Kaye

Cannes — There might have been a market for this Canadian film had last year's "Too Outrageous" had

boxoffice legs, but a second film about the relationship between straight women and drag queens so soon after a flop on the same subject should prove hazardous to "Dear John's" health.

"Too Outrageous" and 1977 predecessor "Outrageous" had female impersonator Craig Russell to help sell tickets, but this low-budget film has no name help. It stars Valerie Buhagiar as a young would-be prostitute who gets friendly with a drag queen named Rocket and decides to change him into a "real man."

The process is initiated by the death of their friend George, a male prostitute. The grieving friends find themselves in each other's arms. Janet wants it to lead to white picket fences, but Rocket sees it all as a lost cause. When she takes off with the same customer they suspect of killing George, Rocket decides to play white knight to her damsel in distress.

The only element worth noting is the performance of Stan Lake as the cynical Rocket. He brings a little depth to a pic that doesn't have much to say about street life. The other performers hardly scratch the surface of their characters or manage to give reason to their choice of the streets as a career. —*Cadd.*

Deadly Intent

A Fries Distribution presentation. Executive producers, Thomas Fries, Jackelyn Giroux. Directed by Nigel Dick. Screenplay, John Goff; camera (color), Daniel Yarussi; editor, Craig Bassett; music, Ethan James; sound (Ultra-Stereo), Dennis Fuller; production design, Anthony Brockliss; assistant director, Brian Demellier; stunt coordinator, Solly Marx; second unit camera, Gary Graver; associate producer, Richard Bennett Warsh; casting, Donna Schlueter. Reviewed at Cannes Film Festival (market), May 13, 1988. Running time: **87 MIN.**

Laura Keaton	Lisa Eilbacher
Jeff Kirkwood	Steve Railsback
Elise Marlowe	Maud Adams
Curt Slate	Fred Williamson
Francesca Slate	Persis Khambatta
Raymond Keaton	Lance Henriksen
Myron Weston	David Dukes
Nadine Weston	Pamela Seamone
Harley	Solly Marx
Vicky	Pamela Roylance
Hernando Ramirez	Curt Lowens
Scott	Clayton Rohner

Cannes — "Deadly Intent" unfortunately lives up to its title: it's a dull, low-energy attempt at a suspense yarn. Absence of sex and much violence mark this one for tv syndication use primarily.

John Goff's 1-note story concerns an unsympathetic group of people all out to find the fabulous jewel known as the Window Stone of Naboth, brought back from an expedition to South America by the ruthless Raymond Keaton (Lance Henriksen). After a party celebrating his return, Keaton is killed at the end of the first reel by Harley (Solly Marx), a guy he doublecrossed.

This sets in motion a series of intrigues as Keaton's boss (Maud Adams) and numerous nogoodniks give his widow (Lisa Eilbacher) a hard time, hoping to discover the stone's whereabouts (solution of which is pic's one good element). Though the body count is quite high by film's end, it feels like they all talked each other to death under Nigel Dick's uneventful, by-the-numbers direction.

Henriksen is impressively mean and hissable during his brief screen time, but the film seems to die with him. The other cast members mainly walk through it except for David Dukes and Pamela Seamone, who generate a few laughs as a fake priest/nun conman team.

Technical credits, especially the flat lighting, are mundane.—*Lor.*

On The Black Hill
(BRITISH)

A British Film Institute production for Channel Four, in association with British Screen Finance Ltd. Executive producer, Colin MacCabe. Produced by Jennifer Howarth. Written and directed by Andrew Grieve, from the novel by Bruce Chatwin; camera (Kodak color), Thaddeus O'Sullivan; editor, Scott Thomas; music, Robert Lockhart; sound, Moya Burns; art direction, Jocelyn James; costumes, Phoebe de Gaye. Reviewed at the Century Preview theater, London, March 7, 1988. (In Cannes Film Festival Market.) Running time: **116 MIN.**

Benjamin Jones	Mike Gwilym
Lewis Jones	Robert Gwilym
Amos Jones	Bob Peck
Mary Jones	Gemma Jones
Hannah Jones	Nesta Harris
Arkwright	Benjamin Whitrow
Lotte Zons	Catherine Schell
Tom Watkins	Eric Wynn
Rosie	Nicola Beddoe

London — A low-budget drama about Welsh hill farmers may not sound broadly appealing, but Andrew Grieve's "On The Black Hill" is a remarkably moving and entertaining film offering a fascinating view of life in the border country between Wales and England.

Pic follows the Jones family from 1895-1980, but mainly centers around twin brothers Benjamin and Lewis Jones (played by brothers Mike and Robert Gwilym). It is through their inseparability, and the traumas and humor that inspires, that the story is told.

"On The Black Hill" may be a finely acted, written and directed piece, but marketplace reality dictates it won't set the boxoffice alight. Pic is destined for limited release, but likely to appreciative audiences.

Pic opens with Mike and Robert Gwilym on their 80th birthday waiting for their great-nephew to take them out, before cutting back to 1895 and Bob Peck's wooing of Gemma Jones, daughter of an English vicar.

From then on the pic follows the birth of the twins and the ways in which their lives are forever linked — through World War I, their failed attempts at love and the eventual death of their parents. What remains the same is their farm The Vision, the Welsh countryside and their need for each other.

Eventually they meet their long-lost great-nephew and heir, who in 1980 takes them for a flight over their farmland as a birthday gift. Pic ends in tragedy as one of the twins dies in a tractor accident.

"On The Black Hill" spends a good deal of time dealing with the psychological problems of twins, most of which are well presented. One section, though, has the brothers meeting a Viennese woman (Catherine Schell) who has made a study of twins. She pontificates about things the viewer has already gathered, making the scene somewhat contrived and unnecessary.

Bob Peck and Gemma Jones are excellent as the Welsh farming couple, and the pic ably displays the hardship of their life. Mike and Robert Gwilym perform well and are especially good in the twins' latter years, aided by excellent make-up by Jenny Shircore.

Andrew Grieve directs confidently and seems aided by a crew that obviously relished the outdoor life. His screenplay suitably captures the complex themes of Bruce Chatwin's novel, but as importantly his camerawork, by Thaddeus O'Sullivan, brings the bleak Welsh hills beautifully to life. It should certainly be a popular film in Wales.
—*Adam.*

Pohjanmaa
(Plainlands)
(FINNISH)

A Finnkino release of National Filmi production. Produced by Marko Röhr. Directed by Pekka Parikka. Screenplay, Parikka, Antti Tuuri, based on Tuuri's novel; camera (Eastmancolor), Kari Sohlberg; editor, Keijo Virtanen; music, Antti Hytti; art direction, Pertti Hilkamo; sound, Paul Jyrää; costumes, Tuula Hilkamo. Reviewed at Cannes Film Festival (market), May 14, 1988. Running time: **127 MIN.**

Errko	Taneli Mäkelä
Veikko	Esko Salminen
Seppo	Vesa Mäkelä
Paavo	Esko Nikkari
The Teacher	Kalevi Kahra
Sarah	Eeva Eloranta

Also with: Paavo Pentikäinen, Heikki Paavilainen, Rea Mauranen, Kirsti Ortola, Tarja Keinänen, Sari Mällinen.

Cannes — Based on her sprawling novel about common folk in the rural Baltic province of Pohjanmaa, "Plainlands" author Annti Tuuri worked with director Pekka Parikka on the screenplay, but the transition to film, while looking good, moving well and full of fine acting, is messy.

It worked in Finnish cinemas, where audiences are familiar with the characters and the actors, but offshore appreciation is less likely.

In a small agricultural-industrial village four brothers gather on a Sunday with wives and children in their dying grandmother's house to split an inheritance left by a distant relative. What follows has nothing to do with the inheritance. Instead we got an uneasy mix of comedy and tragedy in a description of how common Sunday ennui is overcome in Pohjanmaa.

Three of the brothers soon drink on the sly. Erkki, the sober, youngest, has found a machine gun buried in his field. He puts it in the trunk of his car and takes his brothers into the woods for swimming, target practice and more drinking. The women are left to sulk at home, while three youngsters go to a neighbor's home and kidnap him violently. They mean to settle an old family business score, but one of the boys winds up in the hospital, blinded by a knife wound inflicted upon him by the desparate victims.

Scenes of violence alternate endlessly with drunken cavorting. In between, Errko beds down neighbor's pretty, willing wife. Everybody ends up either in jail or the hospital, while grandmother moans about women alone possessing goodness and wisdom. All men, she adds, are mad.

Helmer Parikka drags out every episode far too long for dramatic suspense to work. The drinking is gargantuan throughout, but is seen mostly as dull and dumb rather than initially funny and then tragic.

The ending has the wildest brother steal the machine gun, but when he is found dead, it is from a heart attack. By this time, you don't much care, especially since there's nothing to indicate family life in Pohjanmaa will not go on like this forever. —*Kell.*

Rambo III

A Tri-Star Pictures release of a Carolco production. Produced by Buzz Feitshans. Executive producers, Mario Kassar, Andrew Vajna. Directed by Peter Macdonald. Screenplay, Sylvester Stallone, Sheldon Lettich, based on characters created by David Morrell; camera (J-D-C Widescreen, Technicolor), John Stanier; editor, James Symons, Andrew London, O. Nicholas Brown, Edward A. Warschilka; production design, Billy Kenney; music, Jerry Goldsmith; sound (Dolby), William B. Kaplan, Eli Yarkoni; unit production manager, Charles Murray; first assistant directors, Terry Needham, Andrew Stone; stunt coordinator, Vic Armstrong; special effects supervision, Thomas L. Fisher (Israel), William Mesa (Arizona); associate producer, Tony Munafo; casting, Joy Todd. Reviewed at the Gemini theater, N.Y., May 18, 1988. MPAA Rating: R. Running time: **101 MIN.**

Rambo	Sylvester Stallone
Trautman	Richard Crenna
Zaysen	Marc de Jonge
Griggs	Kurtwood Smith
Masoud	Spiros Focas
Moussa	Sasson Gabai
Hamid	Doudi Shoua
Kurov	Randy Raney

Also with: Marcus Gilbert, Alon Abutal, Mahmoud Assadollahi, Yosef Shiloah, Harold Diamond, Seri Mati, Hany Said El Deen, Shaby Ben-Aroya, Marciano Shoshi.

Producers of mega-budget motion pictures like to say the money is "up on the screen," and the lavishly made "Rambo III" spectacularly tops its predecessors in the sheer magnitude of its panoramic action pyrotechnics. Only the accountants can tell how much of the pic's whopping budget was essential to making Sylvester Stallone's showdown Armageddon with the Red Army, but this high-stakes gamble should pay off at the global boxoffice.

The legions of fans who have nurtured the Rambo phenomenon through "First Blood" (Orion, 1982) and the far more successful "Rambo: First Blood Part II" (Tri-Star, 1985) have every reason to return in droves for the muscular, monosyllabic warrior's mission to Afghanistan. Stallone (whose $20,-000,000 fee was not in the budget, but advanced against a percentage of boxoffice), and the producers can only benefit by the Russian withdrawal from that beleaguered country commencing just as their picture is released. It's not too farfetched to conjecture that some Rambo devotees will believe their man actually had a hand in real-world events.

"Rambo III" stakes out a moral high ground for its hero missing or obscured in the previous two pictures. In the Soviets' heinous 9-year occupation of Afghanistan, this mythic commando and quintessential outsider is enlisted in a cause that — *glasnost* notwithstanding — is indisputably righteous. This may prompt some moviegoers who shunned the retro-Vietnam "Rambo II" on ideological grounds to queue up out of curiosity.

Indeed, as this picture opens, the character of John Rambo has been demilitarized and transported to exotic self-exile in Thailand, where he

lives in a Buddhist monastery and supports himself by engaging in slam-bang mercenary martial arts contests. At one such affair, a brutal stick-fighting match in a warehouse full of screaming, money-waving Orientals (that's a direct lift from the Russian roulette arena in "The Deer Hunter"), Rambo is observed by none other than his old mentor Colonel Trautman (Richard Crenna), the Green Beret who's stood by him through thick and thin.

Crenna has come halfway around the world to Bangkok to ask Stallone for payback — Rambo's participation in a clandestine operation to destroy a "brutal' Russian general who rules a remote province in occupied Afghanistan. But the newly spiritual Rambo refuses. "My war's over," he tells the Colonel. "Not the war inside you," is Crenna's platitudinous response, but Rambo is unmoved. He remains in the paradisiacal Thai countryside until word arrives that the Colonel has been captured and imprisoned in the Russkies' Afghan fortress of evil.

With the grudging help of the CIA, Rambo arrives in Peshawar, Pakistan, where he contacts mujahadeen freedom fighters who will guide him to Afghanistan. Locations in Israel and Arizona serve remarkably well in recreating the look and atmosphere of Afghanistan's dusty towns, and rugged mountainous landscape. Rambo and Moussa (Sasson Gabai) travel to a guerrilla camp, where the strong sullen American is soon tested in a bloody helicopter raid by the Russians.

The battle scenes in "Rambo III" are explosive, conflagratory tableaux that make for wrenching, frequently terrifying viewing. Always at ground zero in the chaos is Rambo — gloriously, inhumanly impervious to fear and danger (who else could outrun a bullet-spitting helicopter?) — whose character is inhabited by Stallone with messianic intensity. When Rambo ignores the advice of battle-hardened mujahadeen to turn back from his suicidal rescue mission, he replies, "So, I die." Stallone, to his credit, makes this insane singlemindedness believable in its fantastical context.

Cruel Russian general Kurov (Randy Raney), abetted by some of the most villainous comrades this side of the World Wrestling Federation, has tortured Crenna beyond human endurance, but the Colonel won't betray the location of guerrilla missiles. His successful rescue by Rambo and two Afghans puts credibility on another planet, but no matter. Action audiences worldwide are certain to bellow approval for the picture's frenetic and protracted denouement in which Rambo overcomes a nasty wound with some gruesome self-surgery and wins out once more against all odds.

Stallone and the fireworks are essentially the whole show, but Crenna seems to be enjoying the ride and Stallone permits the two characters to poke a little fun at themselves and the Rambo saga, as may be inevitable in this kind of triptych. The complexities of the Afghan war, the bitter divisions among the guerrilla factions, and the crucial importance of the Islamic religion to the freedom fighters are glossed over or ignored in a screenplay whose simplistic formlations and exploitation of the war's violence will not matter to ticket buyers.

John Stanier's cinematography nicely serves the production's impressive logistical accomplishments. Jerry Goldsmith's music is bombastic, but enhances the pulse-pounding wall-to-wall bloodshed as intended. —*Rich.*

Crocodile Dundee II

A Paramount Pictures release. Produced by John Cornell, Jane Scott. Executive producer, Paul Hogan. Directed by John Cornell. Screenplay, Paul Hogan, Brett Hogan; Camera (Duart color), Russell Boyd; editor, David Stiven; music, Peter Best; production design, Lawrence Eastwood; art direction, Jeremy Conway; set decoration, Leslie Pope; costume design, Norma Moriceau; sound (Dolby), Ron Brandau; associate producer, Mark Turnbull; assistant director (Australia), Turnbull; second unit camera (Australia), Steve Windon. Reviewed at Mann National theater, L.A., May 18, 1988. MPAA rating: PG. Running time: **111 MIN.**

Mick (Crocodile) Dundee	Paul Hogan
Sue Charlton	Linda Kozlowski
LeRoy Brown	Charles Dutton
Rico	Hechter Ubarry
Miguel	Juan Fernandez
Walter	John Meillon

Hollywood — "Crocodile Dundee II" is a disappointing followup to the disarmingly charming first feature with Aussie star Paul Hogan. Sequel is too slow to constitute an adventure and has too few laughs to be a comedy — resulting in a mildly entertaining 111 minutes that has much less of the freshness and spark that legions of filmgoers loved in the original.

Par is putting "Dundee II" into a record 2,500 houses where initial b.o. probably will be good until word of mouth gets out.

As coscripter with son Brett, Hogan picks up where "Dundee" left off, in New York City. Fish-out-of-water theme literally is the opening scene where Hogan is sitting in a rowboat offshore of Manhattan throwing dynamite into the water to catch fish. The Harbor Patrol comes along, calls him by his name, Mick Dundee, gives him a little tongue-lashing and goes on their merry way. Dundee has charmed the cops. Who is this guy, anyway?

One of the failings of the script is that it's never explained what brought this outback cowboy to be living the lush loft life with g.f. Linda Kozloswki, or any other background on either of them from which to launch this second chapter.

The audience is presumed to care about them being happy and together, though it's never addressed why we should when we never learn much about them.

Nevertheless, story unfolds with Hogan making a passable attempt to find gainful employment at just about the time Kozlowski's ex-lover is killed in Colombia for taking photos of a cocaine king as he shoots one of his runners. The nefarious Rico (Hechter Ubarry is much too cute for this role) learns the photos were sent to Kozlowski and in a flash he sets up an operation in a Long Island fortress with a handful of stereotypical Latino henchmen to get the incriminating evidence back. Hogan has the photos, which means Rico has Kozlowski kidnaped.

In his inimitable fashion, Hogan works his wiles first on LeRoy Brown (Charles Dutton), who parades as a streetwise cool cat, but really pushes stationery (this actually is one of the more humorous discoveries in the plot), and then on a band of punked-out gang members to help him get Kozlowski back.

Using outback strategy, that is, getting the punks to yelp like a pack of wild dogs, Hogan gains entrance and frees his woman. Kozlowski basically does little but wait at the sidelines as Hogan flies into action, though she's dressed less ridiculously than in the first "Dundee."

It's a poor excuse to move the production to Australia, but Hogan finds one — having the Drug Enforcement Agency give them the okay, but no support, to venture Down Under and hide out in the bush. There Hogan knows the territory and puts his outback strategy into full use with the drug runners in hot pursuit.

Aborigines, bats, reptiles — big and small — and a water buffalo help Dundee out of his dilemma, but get too little screen time to keep the energy level up during this overlong chase scene between Hogan and the Latino baddies.

Without much dialog, nearly everything is a sight gag. Hogan could have used more situations to verbally joke around with whomever is the current target for kidding, since that's what he does best.

Giving a dour tone to the beautiful, unspoiled scenery is the monotonous beat of Peter Best's scoring. —*Brit.*

Besökarna
(The Visitor)
(SWEDISH)

A Sonet Film release of an MVM Entertainment production. Produced by Hakan Ersgard. Directed by Joakim Ersgard. Screenplay, Joakim, Ersgard, Patrik Ersgard; camera (Eastmancolor), Hans-Ake Lerin; editor, Martin Jordan; music, Peter Wallin; sound, Kjell Jansson; art direction; Jean-Louis von Dardel; special effects, Olov Nylander; costumes, LenaMari Wallström, Lena

Söderström; production management, Ann Collenberg; assistant director, Patrik Ersgard; stunt coordinator, Mats Lundberg. Reviewed at the Camera, Malmö, Sweden, April 3, 1988. Running time: **104 MIN.**

Frank . . . . Kjell Bergqvist
Sara, his wife . . . . Lena Endre
Lotta, their daughter . . . . Joanna Berglund
Peter, their son . . . . Jonas Olsson
Allan, occult researcher . . . Johannes Brost
Mailman . . . . Patrik Ersgard
The sheriff . . . . Bernt Lundquist

———

Malmö, Sweden — Joakim and Patrik Ersgard, sons of tv producer Hakon Ersgard, have made an occult thriller fit to chill audiences anywhere to the bone. Film's dialog is sparse enough to secure shots uncluttered by more than a minimum of subtitling necessary for offshore sales.

There is nothing new in story, setting or delivery, but everything works with eerie precision from the start. Young ad agency whiz Frank, his pretty wife Sara and their two small children arrive at their newly acquired dream house hidden away in a forest. Everything promises to be undiluted idyl even if Frank is overwrought with the need to develop ''a new line to save an important account.''

Sighs, knocks, water gurgling in the toilet, and even footprints of blood-mixed mud are signs of the supernatural noted by Frank but ignored by his pragmatic wife and the kids. This makes Frank no less testy, so he bawls everybody out, including the local mailman (who is played as a rather mischievous rural rube in a comic cameo by picture's cowriter Patrik Ersgard).

The tension builds so subtly, notably via special effects and music, that the audience will remain as incredulous as Frank's wife. Sara is furious when Frank calls a self-styled occult researcher to look into things. The researcher makes dramatic contact with what or whoever is hidden in the sealed-off attic and winds up drowned in a pool outside.

Sara takes flight, not in fright but in anger. When she decides, late at night, to return after all, she finds the house ablaze, the children screaming and her husband hanging by his heels in the attic, fighting off an invisible but obviously hardhitting enemy. We get a glimpse of this brutal antagonist as an octogenarian E.T., but we may just have been sharing what Frank thinks he sees from his pendular upside-down position.

Character delineations are sketchy throughout. The actors are hard put to maintain their balance between realism and wide-eyed fantasy but, miraculously, they succeed.

''The Visitors'' has a teaser denouement, a tongue-in-cheek indication that the horror isn't really over even if the house lights are up again. — *Kell.*

Not Of This Earth

———

A Concorde Pictures release of a Roger Corman production. Produced by Jim Wynorski, Murray Miller. Directed by Wynorski. Screenplay, R.J. Robertson, Wynorski, based on the original script by Charles B. Griffith, Mark Hanna; camera (Foto-Kem color), Zoran Hockstatter; editor, Kevin Tent, art direction, Hayden Yates; costume design, Libby Jacobs; sound, Al Ramirez; assistant director, Sam Braslau; assistant camera, Ron Bahara; casting, Al Guarino. Reviewed at Hollywood Pacific, L.A., May 20, 1988. MPAA Rating: R. Running time: **80 MIN.**

Nadine Story . . . . Traci Lords
The Alien . . . . Arthur Roberts
Jeremy . . . . Lenny Juliano
Dr. Rochelle . . . . Ace Mask
Harry . . . . Roger Lodge
Vacuum cleaner salesman . Michael Delano

———

Hollywood — What could bring the remake of the 30-year-old Roger Corman special ''Not Of This Earth'' into the 1980s? Why, by having former porn star Traci Lords in the starring role. Lords still manages to expose most of herself while also showing a surprising amount of high-camp acting ability as well.

''Not Of This Earth'' is an enjoyable visit with some pretty strange characters. Lords takes the straight

Original Film
(B&W)

———

Allied Artists release of Roger Corman production, directed by Corman. Stars Paul Birch, Beverly Garland, Morgan Jones; features William Roerick, Jonathan Haze, Richard Miller, Anne Carroll, Pat Flynn, Roy Engel. Screenplay, Charles Griffith, Mark Hanna; camera (b&w), John Mescall; editor, Charles Gross; music, Ronald Stein. Previewed March 14, 1957. Running time, **67 MIN.**

Paul Johnson . . . . Paul Birch
Nadine Storey . . . . Beverly Garland
Harry Sherbourne . . . . Morgan Jones
Dr. F.W. Rochelle . . . . . . William Roerick
Jeremy Perrin . . . . Jonathan Haze
Joe Piper . . . . Richard Miller
Davanna Woman . . . . Anne Carroll
Simmons . . . . Pat Flynn
Sgt. Walton . . . . Roy Engel
Joanne . . . . Tamar Cooper
Specimen . . . . Harold Fong

———

role, which could attract an interesting cross-section of the filmgoing public.

Producer-director-coscripter Jim Wynorski shows a certain flair for turning a ridiculous sci-fi story about an alien in dark glasses into a sometimes hilarious parody of low-budget genre pictures.

At no time does any of the alien's special abilities ring true, though there is a quirky, involving manner about his particular dilemma that keeps interest at a peak throughout.

Arthur Roberts is the alien who comes to earth in dire need of constant infusions of blood in addition to having to find a new supply for his dying planet's population. He goes to a blood bank where Lords is the nurse, hiring her away for $2,000 a week to become his personal attendant.

The alien's no dummy. He chooses for victims mostly scantily or sexily attired, well-endowed wo-

men.

Plot is hokey and special effects even more so, which leaves all the fun to be had in the hands of the actors. Most everyone, especially Ace Mask as the nosy doctor, plays it right — not too silly, not too seriously.

Lords is sassy throughout and a good foil for Lenny Juliano, who plays the alien's dumb chauffeur, and her cop b.f. Roger Lodge (there's a joke here on Lords' past).

No one would expect great dialog though there are a few choice tidbits worth noting — Lords' preference for Chardonnay and lobster (not burgers and fries) and a discussion with Mask on the molecular structure of blood.

Ending is kind of a ''Carrie'' ripoff, but even so, is amusing for its lack of pretensions. —*Brit.*

Lo que vendrá
(What Is To Come)
(ARGENTINE)

———

A Faro Films presentation of a Tripiquicios production. Executive producer, Maria Angeles Mira. Directed by Gustavo Mosquera. Screenplay, Mosquera, Alberto Delorenzini; camera (color), Javier Miquelez; editor, Oscar Gómez; music, Charly Garcia. Reviewed at Astro theater, Buenos Aires, April 5, 1988. Running time: **98 MIN.**

Galván . . . . Hugo Soto
Morea . . . . Juan Leyrado
Male nurse . . . . Charly García
Also with: Rosario Blefari, Osvaldo Flores, Luis Minces, Roxana Randón, Inés Estévez, Aldo Braga.

———

Buenos Aires — A political tale with something of the feel of science fiction and a lot of the look of videoclips, ''Lo que vendrá,'' a smooth, glossy first feature by director Gustavo Mosquera R., primarily is a visual and aural experience for a video generation.

Locally, the picture banks on the attraction of having one of the country's top rock musicians, Charly García, in the cast and on the soundtrack, and the film's ads call it ''Charly's picture'' above the title.

García comes across as a relaxed genial figure with a ready wink behind his glasses and an ever-present hint of a smile beneath his greying mustache, and his friendly aura communicates itself to the film as a whole, which emerges as a pleasant piece despite intellectual shortcomings.

Although the title sets the action in the future, the story feels more like an occurrence of the fairly recent past under military dictatorship. The hero, Miguel Galván, an innocent bystander played by Hugo Soto, is injured by a policeman's accidental shot during a political demonstration. The injury is to his head, leading Soto to spend much of the picture with a lost expression akin that with which he distinguished himself in ''Man Facing Southeast.''

The authorities take him to hospi-

tal and try to hush the incident up, but the lid comes off the case, and the cop who fired the shot (Juan Leyrado) uses increasingly brutal methods in the attempt to put it back on. Meanwhile, Galván is watched over by a kind of guardian angel, a male nurse and ambulance driver (García). At the end, with another wink, there is a gag concerning the identity of that angel.

It isn't clear why the authorities would go to such trouble, not to mention extremes, to hide an accidental injury, particularly when far worse crimes are committed on purpose. But the point obviously wasn't to make consistent sense — it was to employ recognizable character types, such as those of a sexy female nurse, the brutal cop, or the latter's manipulative superior, in snazzy sequences.

The production, relying considerably on close shots to isolate a figure or situation from a suggestively fuzzy background, makes use of well chosen and adapted locations, including a ship in dry dock, to create a slightly unreal atmosphere for the cartoon-strip proceedings. —*Olas.*

Alouette, je te plumerai
(The Lark)
(FRENCH)

———

A UGC release of a Cinéa/Films A2 coproduction. Produced by Philippe Carcassonne. Written and directed by Pierre Zucca. Camera (Eastmancolor, Pyral, Agfa), Paul Bonis; editor, Nicole Lubtchansky; art direction, Max Berto; sound, Michel Vionnet; music, Jean-Philippe Rameau; assistant director, Chantal Desanges. Reviewed at the UGC Biarritz cinema, Paris, May 10, 1988. Running time: **95 MIN.**

Pierre Vergne . . . . Claude Chabrol
Françoise . . . . Valérie Allain
Jacques . . . . Fabrice Luchini
Lady with jewels . . . . Micheline Presle
Coal-burner . . . . Jean-Paul Roussillon

———

Paris — Veteran New Wave helmer Claude Chabrol, who's done cameo bits in numerous films over the years, gets his first lead thesping opportunity in this would be sardonic comedy by Pierre Zucca. The nicest thing one can say is that Chabrol is better behind the camera than in front of it.

True, he hasn't been helped by the unbelievable screenplay and leaden direction. Chabrol plays a chronic fabulist and professional parasite who worms his way into the home of a young nurse (Valérie Allain) and her ambulance-driver hubby (Fabrice Luchini) by making them believe he is fabulously wealthy, has one step in the grave, and is willing to make the couple his sole heirs.

Chabrol's self-conscious grimacing and muttering diction do not give substance to a part Zucca originally wrote with Michel Bouquet in mind. Two seasoned thesps, Micheline Presle and Jean-Paul Roussillon, are around in minor roles but only succeed in showing up Chabrol's inadequacy as an actor.

—*Len.*

Love Story Wo Kimi Ni
(Memories Of You)
(JAPANESE)

A Toei release of a Toei-Oscar Promotion production. Produced by Ryoji Ito, Yoshihiro Kojima. Directed by Shinichiro Sawai. Screenplay, Koichi Maruyama, from novel by Didier Decoin; camera (color), Seizo Sengen; editor, Kioaki Saito; art direction, Tadayuki Kuwana; sound, Fumio Hashimoto; music, Akiyuki Asakawa. Reviewed at Toei screening room, Tokyo, April 15, 1988. Running time: **104 MIN.**

Yumi Hirose .... Kumiko Goto
Akira Kamijo .... Toru Nakamura
Tomoko Hirose .... Yumi Sato
Kinichi Araki .... Shingo Yanagisawa
Kojiro Tanaka .... Osami Nabe
Hatsumi Imamura .... Michiko Kawai
Setsuo Nakada .... Ken Ogata

Tokyo — Kumiko Goto is being touted and touted and touted as the domestic version of the early Brooke Shields. Not yet 14, she paradoxically seems to have been around forever, her comely countenance beaming eternally from kiosks, newsstands, bookstores and tv screens around Japan.

This marks her widescreen debut and she does a commendable job with an almost unbelievably goody-goody role.

Because it comes bearing the seals of approval of numerous organizations devoted to moral uplift, including the Ministry of Education and the national PTA, the film lays on the sweetness and light pretty thickly. No one is selfish or unkind or thoughtless.

Goto plays a junior high school student who is relentlessly cheerful, an accomplished flutist, a student of the tea ceremony, who obeys her mother and loves her father, even though he lives in a foreign country with his new family. Also a paragon of virtue is Toru Nakamura, a serious college student who one day wishes to become a teacher, a development about as unexpected in a film approved by the Ministry of Education as pectoral flexing in "Rambo III."

When the good Nakamura learns the good Goto is dying of leukemia, he accedes to her mother's request that he instigate a puppy love romance with the doomed girl so that she will at least have an inkling of what amour is all about before dying.

Further, he accedes to the girl's request that they climb a mountain she has long had a hankering to conquer, and it is during their ascent of this peak that she expires in his arms.

For what the Japanese call a "nakaseru eiga" (a film to make you cry), "Love Story Wo Kimi Ni" is surprisingly free of the almost brutal tearjerking that characterizes most examples of this genre. Goto is a gentle, understated presence, and Ken Ogata, known to

most Westerners for his roles in "Mishima" and "Narayama Bushiko," is fine in the almost cameo-sized role of her father.—*Bail.*

Cuibil De Viespi
(The Wasps' Nest)
(RUMANIAN)

A Romaniafilm production. Directed by Horea Popescu. Screenplay, Popescu, based on the play "The Rattlers," by Alexander Kiritescu; camera (color), Vivi Vasile Dragan; editor, Maria Neagu; art direction, Traian Buciueanu; sound, Horea Murgu, music, Paul Urmuzescu. Reviewed at Rivertown Film Festival, Minneapolis, May 14, 1988. Running time: **115 MIN.**

With: Tamara Buciueanu, Coca Andronescu, Raluca Zamfirescu, Marin Moraru, Gheorghe Dinica.

Minneapolis — "The Wasps' Nest" is infested with the worst swarm of human parasites since Lillian Hellman's "The Little Foxes." It's based on the play "The Rattlers" by Rumanian playwright Al Kiritescu.

Whether stinging wasps or venemous rattlesnakes, the three elderly sisters at the hub of this tale set in the 1930s are a meanspirited lot. One of them, a peasant who has inherited her husband's wealth, controls the family pursestrings with a tight hand. Two sons are similarly avaricious, and when they drive their troubled sister to suicide they turn her funeral into a celebration.

The film has been described as a satire, but the clan is so despicable it's hard to find anything to laugh about. The problem may lie in poor subtitles. Rumanian-speaking members of the audience at screening caught frequently laughed heartily at lines which offered little humor in translation.

Horea Popescu's direction is uneven, marred by many rough transitions. Washed-out color in several scenes is sub-professional. Pic's top virtue is the fine, natural acting by the large Rumanian cast.

In the U.S., "Wasps' Nest" is suitable only for arthouses in metropolitan centers. —*Rees.*

CANNES COMPETING

Miles From Home

A Cinecom Entertainment Group production and release in association with J&M Entertainment. Produced by Frederick Zollo, Paul Kurta. Executive producers, Amir J. Malin, Ira Deutchman. Directed by Gary Sinise. Screenplay, Chris Gerolmo; camera (color), Elliot Davis; editor, Jane Schwartz Jaffe; music, Robert Folk; production design, David Gropman; art direction, Nicholas Romanac; set decoration, Karen Schulz; costumes, Shay Cunliffe; sound (Dolby), Kim Ornitz; assistant director, James A. Chory; associate producers, Randy Finch, Russ Smith; casting, Bonnie Timmermann. Reviewed at Cannes Film Festival (competing), May 18, 1988. Running time: **112 MIN.**

Frank Roberts Sr. .... Brian Dennehy
Young Frank .... Jason Campbell
Young Terry .... Austin Bamgarner
Nikita Khrushcher .... Larry Poling
Frank Roberts Jr. .... Richard Gere
Terry Roberts .... Kevin Anderson
Mark .... Terry Kinney
Sally .... Penelope Ann Miller
Jennifer .... Helen Hunt
Frank's Girl .... Moira Harris
Barry Maxwell .... John Malkovich

Cannes — "Miles From Home" tackles the worthy subject of family farm foreclosures — addressed in several other pics of late — but suffers from an excessively maudlin approach. Told with unrelieved intensity, this version is devoid of any light moments.

Even those with the greatest sympathies for farmers' plight may find pic too burdensome. Thus, audience prospects at home and abroad appear slim.

Richard Gere is characteristically somber, remote and troubled as the key figure of Frank Roberts Jr., who inherits corn acreage after his celebrated father dies. Frank Sr. (Brian Dennehy) had been Farmer of the Year in 1963 — four years after his Iowa farm was visited by

Nikita Khrushchev (Larry Poling).

Frank and younger brother Terry (Kevin Anderson) fall prey to heavy bills and overdue bank loans. Latter appears more level-headed from the start — portrayed with excellent reserve by Anderson — but Frank leads the pair down a bitter road of retribution. They begin by burning their house, barn and cornfields to spite the bank and purchaser.

On the run from police, they quickly become celebrated by a local newspaper, which calls their action "desperately eloquent." With the die cast, Frank is determined to remain on the run, particularly since there's no home to which they can return.

Script by Chris Gerolmo delivers an ironic twist as the brothers stop by the Farmers Home Administration and steal a Mercedes. Next stop is a low-rent bar where they're befriended and somehow put in touch with a Rolling Stone reporter, nicely portrayed by the versatile John Malkovich. Interview is one of the strongest scenes as Frank verbalizes bitter frustrations about farm business' high costs and low returns.

In a savage commentary on media hype, the Robertses are paid thousands for a cover story labeling them "Outlaws For The '80s." Replete with a cocky photo of them in cowboy hats and draped on a T-bird, article later prompts Frank to conclude they're just like the Old West James brothers.

Flush with cash, pair are joined at a county fair by femmes seen earlier in a weak subplot. A drunken Frank causes a scene but they're

deemed folk heroes by some and get help escaping police. "They really like me," says Frank, who's enamored of the notoriety.

Terry is increasingly alarmed and friction boils over when Frank decides to pull an armed robbery at the bank responsible for the foreclosure.

Chaotic resolution can't help but build empathy despite Frank's psychotic behavior.

In spite of script's weaknesses, first-time feature director Gary Sinise's work is commendable. As for Dennehy and Poling, screen time is limited to a nonspeaking sequence depicted as a news coverage-style flashback. —*Tege.*

Welcome To Germany
(WEST GERMAN-COLOR/B&W)

A Metroplis (Munich) presentation of a Von-Vietinghoff-Film/George Reinhardt (Zurich/Road Movies (Berlin) production in association with Zweites Deutsches Fernsehen (Christoph Holch) and Film Four Intl. Produced by Joachim von Vietinghoff and George Reinhardt. Directed by Thomas Brasch. Screenplay, Brasch, Jurek Becker; camera (color/black & white), Axel Block; editor, Tanja Schmidbauer; music, Gunther Fischer; art direction, Albrecht Konrad; costumes, Marlies von Soden; sound, Axel Arft; production manager, Gerhard Czepe. Reviewed at Cannes Film Festival (competing), May 17, 1988. Running time: **102 MIN.**

Cornfield .... Tony Curtis
Körner .... Matthias Habich
Sofie .... Katarina Thalbach
Mrs. Cornfield .... Alexandra Stewart
Donelly .... Michael Morris
Silbermann .... Charles Regnier
The Rabbi .... George Tabori
Danner .... Guntbert Warns
Rosa .... Ursula Andermatt
KZ Commandant .... Irm Herrmann
Also with: Karin Baal, Fritz Marquardt, Birul Unel, Gedeon Burkhard, Harry Baer.

Cannes — "Welcome To Germany" (released in Germany as "Der Passagier") by Thomas Brasch, who returned to Cannes with his second competition entry, is yet another exploration of Holocaust guilt. This time the guilt is perceived as weighing as heavily on Jewish as on German minds.

The picture is spectacular to look at and has Tony Curtis performing strongly in the lead, but it also is a tortured intellectual exercise built around a mystery with too many red herrings and no straight clues or answers. Its international future would look dim even with awards.

Did Cornfield, an American television director about to shoot his first major feature in Berlin from a nonexisting screenplay actually kill a fellow concentration camp prisoner to get of Germany in 1942? And is he now doing his film as psychotherapy instead of seeing a psychiatrist?

Cornfield has sets built and assembles actors, who find their film will be about events tied to the shooting of another film, done in 1942 by a German director, Körner, who had Nazis' blessing to promise 13 Jews from a camp free passage to

Switzerland if they acted in Körner's opus about a village Shylock and his evil deeds.

While the two films gradually merge, the characters and the actors playing them also somehow melt into each other. Everybody is suspicious of the American director who is suspicious of himself. He is especially preoccupied with finding a way to explain how two of the Jewish actors engineered an escape, while the eventual return to the camp of all 13 prisoner-actors was to be a matter of official record.

We never find out, and Cornfield finally gives up and drops the project.

"Welcome To Germany" looks gorgeous in sequences alternately in color and b&w, a lucid specimen of philosophical mystification. Brash's collaboration with cinematographer Axel Block deserves high praise, and the acting is strong and nuanced throughout. —Kell.

L'enfance de l'Art
(Childhood Of Art)
(FRENCH)

A Partner's Prod., Films A2 presentation of a Partner's production. Produced by Ariel Zeitoun. Directed by Francis Girod. Screenplay, Girod, Yves Dangerfield (Vincent Vallier); camera (color), Dominique Chapuis; editor, Geneviève Winding; music, Romano Musumara; sound, André Hervée, Claude Villand; art direction, Sylvain Chauvelot. Reviewed at Cannes Film Festival (competing), May 22, 1988. Running time: **107 MIN.**
Marie ....Clotilde de Bayser
Simon ....Michel Bompoil
Régine ....Anne-Marie Philipe
Jean-Paul ....Yves Lambrecht
Ludivine ....Marie-Armelle Deguy
Martine..................Régine Cendre
Samuel ....Bruno Wolkowitch
Lucas ....Etienne Pommeret
Philippe ....Vincent Vallier
Juliette ....Hélène Alexandridis
Ferrand..................Dussollier
Also with: Laurence Masliah, Pierre Gérard, Olivia Brunaux, Patricia Varnay, Azize Kabouche, Nelle Alard, Philippe Brizard, William Cagnard, Daniel Chevalier, Henri Colpi.

Cannes — The last film in the Cannes competition this year was one of the most disappointing. A Gallic version of "Fame," it lacks the vitality, talent and imagination which distinguished Alan Parker's picture, and most certainly lacks its pace.

Focusing on a class of drama students at the Paris Conservatory, the script, by director Francis Girod with novelist Vincent Vallier, a drama student who plays a small part in the film, drags in the most hackneyed clichés, indulges in soap opera sentimentality and offers a bunch of hysterical, hardly credible characters who pretend to be insecure about their calling. Given their performance here, they certainly have real reasons to worry.

There's a film within the film, which André Dussollier, the only name star in the picture, is supposed to direct; it is difficult to understand how anybody could treat it serious-ly. At best, it looks to be an exotic potboiler about a Western woman fascinated by the desert. But as this is a highly artistic achievement selected to represent France at the Venice Film Festival, it's an insult both to the intelligence of the audience and the professional capacity of the Venice selectors.

Director Girod, who teaches at the Paris Conservatory, started from the idea of using only Conservatory students in this picture, a legitimate intention which fails because none of them makes the transition from amateur to professional performance. As for Dussollier, he looks highly apologetic as the philandering director.

Production level is higher than the artistic one, all technical credits being above average. But it is difficult to understand what determined the inclusion of this film in the competition. — Edna.

Krótki film o zabijaniu
(A Short Film About Killing)
(POLISH)

A Film Unit Tor production. Production manager, Ryszard Chutkowski. Directed by Krzysztof Kieslowski. Screenplay, Krzysztof Piesiewicz, Kieslowski; camera (color), Slawomir Idziak; editor, Ewa Smal; art direction, Halina Dobrowolska; music, Zbigniew Preisner; sound, Malgorzata Jaworska. Reviewed at Cannes Film Festival (competing), May 16, 1988. Running time: **84 MIN.**
Yatzek ....Miroslaw Baka
Lawyer ....Krzysztof Globisz
Taxi driver ....Jan Tesarz

Cannes — Krzysztof Kieslowski, one of Poland's aces, comes through with another intense, original work of cinema whose moral force is rivaled only by its technical bravura. "A Short Film About Killing" comes out of Kieslowski's mammoth tv project of filming the Ten Commandments one by one. This is based on Thou Shalt Not Kill, and is about as far from Cecil B. DeMille as you can get. A fest hit, it drew a great deal of interest from quality-film programmers who know their audiences.

Film is summarized in the two opening shots of a dead rat and a hanged cat, images which seem excessive till film's irresistible forces of evil start their portentous march toward tragedy. From sinister camera angles and cutting to disquieting details and music (score by Zbigniew Preisner), pic keeps tension rising and viewers in knots. If Hitchcock had filmed Dostoevsky, this would be the result.

Three characters are introduced one dismal Warsaw morning. Their destinies are certainly linked, but part of the game is guessing how. Yatzek (Miroslaw Baka), a 20-year-old drifter with a delinquent's face, ranges aimlessly around town. An idealistic young lawyer (Krzysztof Globisz) passes his bar exam and celebrates with his girlfriend. A hateful cabbie (Jan Tesarz) spitefully leaves passengers stranded. In simply introducing them, Kieslowski shows he's a master of suspense, to rivet attention to the screen with the classic query, what will happen next?

Answer is the boy Yatzek's senseless murder of the malicious cabbie in a protracted scene of stomach-churning violence. No explanation is offered, no extenuating circumstances given, and the attack goes on and on until the stocky taxi driver finally dies.

In a flash we are in a courtroom; the young lawyer has just lost the case; Yatzek is condemned to death. Unwilling to accept the verdict, the lawyer attends the execution and, almost by chance, hears the boy tell how his sister got run over by a tractor when he was drunk. Then the guards come and, step by step, the hanging follows its course, even more unbearable than the cabbie's murder because of its socially sanctioned banality.

Tersely edited, film is a powerful moral indictment of capital punishment, but its moral scope has a far greater and more disturbing range. The performances could not be better.

Even the putrid green hues of Orwocolor contribute their murky bit to the chilling, godless atmosphere of crime paid by crime. — Yung.

Os Canibais
(The Cannibals)
(FRENCH-PORTUGUESE)

A Paolo Branco (Lisbon) presentation of a Filmargem (Lisbon), Gemini Films (Paris) production, in association with AB Cinema (Rome), Light Night (Geneva), Pandora Films (Frankfurt), Portuguese Film Institute, Portuguese Radio & Television Co. and Calouste Gulbenkian Foundation. Produced by Paolo Branto. Directed by Manoel de Oliveira. Screenplay, De Oliveira, adapted from story by Alvaro Carvalhal; music & book (libretto), João Paes; camera (Eastmancolor), Mario Barroso; editor, de Oliviera, Sabine Franel; art direction, Luis Montero; costume design, Jasmin de Matos; sound, Joaquim Pinto; assistant director, Jaime Silva; production manager, Danielle Beraha, Graca de Almeida. Reviewed at Cannes Film Festival (competing), May 20, 1988. Running time: **98 MIN.**
The Viscount ....Luis Miguel Cintra
His singing voice ....Vaz de Carvalho
Marguerite ....Leonor Silveira
Her singing voice ....Filomena Amaro
Don Joao ....Diogo Doria
His singing voice ....Carlos Guilherme
Also with: actors Pedro da Silva, Joel Costa, Rogerio Samora, Rogerio Vieira, Antonio Loja Neves, singers Antonio Silva, Carlos Fonseca, Luis Madureira and actor-singer Oliveira Lopes plus Gloria de Matos with the Women's Choir of the Gulbenkian Orchestra.

Cannes — "The Cannibals" by Manoel de Oliveira, Portugal's grand old master of stylized cinema, is an opera film with a difference. From the outset and well into an hour of its running time, item is pretty tame and traditional for its genre. Then follow a final 30 minutes of grotesque fun that should help the picture achieve a limited distribution in those situations that cater to opera buffs.

The music and libretto are by former Lisbon Opera House manager and composer João Paes, who has done works on commission for Oliveira before. The music mixes 19th century harmonics with contemporary strains. It will require repeated listening to evaluate its potential, but it certainly has no kind of 11 o'clock aria to follow you to the door.

Things move along rather heavily as a host-narrator takes us into an 18th century mansion where a ball is held after the wedding of beautiful Marguerite and the Viscount d'Aveleda, who are madly in love with each other even if the groom appears a mite gloomy. In the background or out in the garden lurks the classical Don João/Juan/Giovanni, who hates to see Marguerite pass him by.

When the married couple is sent upstairs to the nuptial bed, the languid mood is shattered as the Viscount discloses that all his limbs are artificial. He takes them off and leaves Marguerite to decide whether she still loves him. She swoons and falls out the window, and the Viscount hurls what is left of himself into the flames of the fireplace.

The grotesqueries continue as the bride's father, on finding the nuptial bed untouched, invites his two sons to partake in the roast he has found in the fireplace. After that, cannibalism escalates and is soon rampant, with everybody spouting fangs around the old estate. Everybody dies but somehow keeps on dancing and singing (all actors have singing doubles).

There is more than a touch of morbid Buñuelian satire about Oliveira's listing of the less than discreet aristocratic charms. The acting is rather wooden, but "The Cannibals" looks good. Had picture's first two-thirds been a bit more tongue-in-cheek, the entire proceedings would have been more thoroughly enjoyable. —Kell.

For Queen & Country
(BRITISH)

An Atlantic Releasing release (U.S.) of a Zenith presentation of a Working Title production. Produced by Tim Bevan. Directed by Martin Stellman. Screenplay, Stellman, Trix Worrell; camera (Eastmancolor), Richard Greatrex; editor, Stephen Singleton; music, Michael Kamen; production design, Andrew McAlpine; art direction, Charmian Adams; sound, Mike Turner; production manager, Sarah Cellan-Jones; assistant director, Peter Bennett; casting, Leo Davis; stunts, Gareth Milne. Reviewed at Cannes Film Festival (market), May 17, 1988. Running time: **105 MIN.**

Reuben James . . . . Denzel Washington
Fish . . . . Dorian Healey
Stacey . . . . Amanda Redman
Kilcoyne . . . . George Baker
Colin . . . . Bruce Payne
Bob Harper . . . . Sean Chapman
Lynford . . . . Geff Francis
Debbie . . . . Stella Gonet

Cannes — First-time director Martin Stellman, who scripted the political thriller "Defense Of The Realm" two years ago, has come up with a violent, devastating thriller about a black ex-paratrooper trying to adjust to civilian life in strife-torn inner-city London. A powerful central performance from Denzel Washington and a script in which the screws are turned slowly on the beleaguered hero will offset the downbeat climax of the film. Solid returns can be expected.

Washington, with a convincing cockney accent, is Reuben James, born on the West Indies island of St. Lucia, living in Britain since he was a child. After getting into trouble as a youth, he joined the British army and became a paratrooper, seeing action in the Falklands War where his best friend Fish (Dorian Healey) lost a leg. Now Reuben is trying to adjust to civilian life, but finds jobs are scarce and the inner-suburb where he lives a morass of desperate people, drug pushers and racist, violent cops.

Reuben wants to go straight. He rejects a lucrative offer of employment from a drug-pusher friend (Bruce Payne), actively seeks work, and has a romance with widowed Stacey (Amanda Redman); but when he applies to have his passport renewed so he and Stacey can go to Paris for a weekend, he's refused. Despite the fact that he's served Queen and country in a brutal war, he's no longer a British citizen under the terms of the 1981 British Nationality Act.

Director Stellman builds the tension gradually until the final reel which erupts into bloody violence and a downbeat ending suggesting that in Britain today it's impossible to overcome the racism of the trigger-happy cops or the poverty brought about by mass unemployment created by the policies of the present government. Film can be compared to Stephen Frears' "Sammy And Rosie Get Laid" in its depiction of the streets of London as a war zone: it's a grim picture of a disintegrating, violent society.

Pic may be too violent for some, and the London accents may at first be hard to decipher for non-British auds. (Some relooping may be necessary to overcome this problem.) Stellman has done a mostly fine job of direction first time out, but there are a couple of confusing bits that could have been handled with greater clarity. The opening sequence is not defined clearly as to time and place, and the irony of the final scene may not be immediately appreciated by audiences, unless they have very sharp eyes.

No doubt, though, that "For Queen & Country" is an impressive picture, with solid performances and first-rate technical credits. Music is a bit insistent in spots. —*Strat.*

Silent Night
(WEST GERMAN)

A TAT Filmproduction/Silent Night production. Produced by Ernst R. von Theumer. Written and directed by Monica Teuber, from story idea by Friedel Schnitzler. Camera (Agfa color), Armando Nannuzzi; editor, Stefan Arnsten; music, Cliff Eidelman; sound (Dolby), Michael Etz, Hajo von Zundt; production design, Gianni Quaranta; assistant director, Carlo Quinterio; casting, Bob Marones. Reviewed at Cannes Film Festival (market), May 19, 1988. Running time: **113 MIN.**

Father Joseph Mohr . . . . Steve Bond
Magdalena . . . . Nastassja Kinski
Baron Von Seidl . . . . David Warner
Prior . . . . Günter Meisner
Franz Guber . . . . Cyrus Elias
Helga . . . . Katharina Böhm
Janza . . . . Franco Nero
Father Nossler . . . . Anthony Quayle
Archbishop . . . . Ferdy Mayne
Rudolf . . . . William Carr Hickey
Anna . . . . Janet Agren
Robert . . . . Max Tidof
Elisabeth . . . . Karina Szulc
(Original English soundtrack)

Cannes — "Silent Night" is a well-mounted, romantic costumer that recounts the dramatic and historical events in 1818 that backdropped the writing of the Christmas hymn of the title. Old-fashioned approach will find more interest overseas than Stateside, despite the highly professional English dialog track.

Set in Oberndorf (near Salzburg) story concerns a new priest in town, Father Mohr (U.S. thesp Steve Bond), who's staying with the family of teacher and composer Guber (Cyrus Elias). A local baron (David Warner) is persecuting everyone in sight, including his own family (he won't let his lovely daughter Helga (Katharina Böhm) marry Guber's son Robert (Max Tidof).

Key subplot has B-girl at the local inn Magdalena (Nastassja Kinski) falling in love with Mohr, who obviously can't reciprocate. Meanwhile, rebel Janza (Franco Nero) is on the warpath, trying to get a revolution going.

Film suffers from having several false endings, as action keeps climaxing and then leading to an even more bizarre development. Idealized approach is fun, almost amounting to a fable, as ultimately even baddie Warner repents and gives the peasants back their land. Another arch-villain, Günter Meisner (as a continually plotting prior) is aghast at Warner's change of heart, but he, too, finally bears his soul and asks God for forgiveness.

Given the script's emphasis on thematic and religious significance, the decision to shoot in English (for international markets) hurts the pic's credibility. Time and again characters intone about their era's repressiveness and the need to bring people back to religion by praying "in our own language." Yet when Bond and Elias team up to add lyrics to a waltz theme of Elias' (switched to 4/4 time), it turns out that English is "our language." It ain't Latin, but it doesn't ring true.

With beautiful lighting by ace Italian lenser Armando Nannuzzi and a bountiful symphonic score by Cliff Eidelman, pic is impressive. Filmmaker Monica Teuber's eschewing of humor makes it oppressive, however.

Kinski is fresh and moving as the heroine, but Bond is inexpressive as the valiant priest-hero, miscast due to his modern demeanor. Supporting cast is fine, with Böhm an attractive new face, Agren getting a character part (instead of glamorous decoration) as the housekeeper for a change and Warner generating surprising sympathy in a blackguard role. Meisner's lipsmacking, snake-hiss readings are delightfully campy, though not on the same wavelength as the other players. —*Lor.*

Heart Of Midnight

A Samuel Goldwyn Co. release. Produced by Andrew Gaty. Written and directed by Matthew Chapman. Camera (color), Ray Rivas; editor, Penelope Shaw; music, Yanni; production design, Gene Rudolf; art direction, Christa Munro; set decoration, Stephanie Waldron; costumes, Linda Fisher; sound, Alan Selk; assistant director, Richard Feury; casting, Donna Jacobson. Reviewed at Cannes Film Festival (market), May 15, 1988. Running time: **101 MIN.**

Carol Rivers . . . . Jennifer Jason Leigh
Sharpe/Larry . . . . Peter Coyote
Sonny . . . . Gale Mayron
Fletcher . . . . Sam Schact
Mariana . . . . Denise Dummont
Ledray . . . . Frank Stallone
Richard . . . . James Rebhorn
Tom . . . . Nick Love
Eddy . . . . Steve Buscemi
Betty . . . . Brenda Vaccaro

Cannes — "Heart Of Midnight" is a twisted little sadomasochistic outing that does have some cinematic merits and intense proceedings, but is hardly worth the time. Pic may find a small audience and even support in some critical quarters but prospects in all territories are slim.

Plot centers on Carol Rivers (Jennifer Jason Leigh), a young woman with psychological problems. When her uncle Fletcher (Sam Schact) dies of AIDS, she inherits property being transformed into the "Midnight" club.

Against the wishes of her mother Betty (Brenda Vaccaro), Carol moves to the building, only to find a bizarre series of rooms upstairs. They suggest Fletcher was hosting sex parties for people of various persuasions.

Shockingly bright colors capture the intensity of this house of horrors and swiftly Carol is plunged into her own hell as a couple of workmen try to rape her. A cop (Frank Stallone) is suspicious of her story since she has a history of mental trouble and substance abuse.

If the assault wasn't problem enough, signs appear that someone else is on the premises. Such presence, as well as the repeated sexual overtones are signaled effectively with various uses of the Biblical sign of temptation — an apple.

Police detective Sharpe is to follow up on the rape attempt investigation and when an unknown man (Peter Coyote) shows up, she assumes it's Sharpe. Surrealistic interpretations escalate as Coyote turns out to be a fake cop and surreptitiously drugs Carol. Her wounded psyche now reels out of control, with strong and threatening images commingling with the actual mischief of the unseen intruder.

Her suspicions of being taunted are reinforced by rape crisis worker Mariana (Denise Dummont), who is the rock of stabilty — with a cross conspicuously hanging from her neck — in this small world of madness.

Events proceed to particularly sadistic circumstances, in which the Coyote character's linkage as an ex-business partner of Fletcher is revealed. Reason for Carol's years of torment and her relationship to her late uncle also come to light.

Performances are strong all around, particularly by Leigh and Vaccaro. Coyote is not up to his usual level. However, their work and that of director Matthew Chapman can hardly rise above the low starting point of Chapman's script. —*Tege.*

A Night In Havana: Dizzy Gillespie In Cuba
(DOCU)

A Jane Balfour Films (London) presentation of a Chisma (N.Y.) production for Cubana Bop Partners. Produced by Nim Polanetska. Directed by John Holland; camera (color), William Megalos; editor, Vincent Stenerson; interviewer, Alan Honigberg; sound, Larry Provost. Reviewed at Cannes

Film Festival (market), May 18, 1988. Running time: **84 MIN.**

Cannes — Writer-interviewer Alan Honigberg and docu director John Holland followed bebop trumpeter Dizzy Gillespie and his small group to the Fifth Intl. Jazz Festival in Havana. Their "A Night In Havana: Dizzy Gillespie In Cuba" will work largely as tv fare, though very specialized situations featuring music items may want to present the great man cavorting and conversing with Fidel Castro and Cubans of lesser rank.

Gillespie, when not blowing "A Night In Tunisia," "Cubana Bop" or other favorites, speaks in his rough, melodious voice (and with vocal phrasings rather like those of Louis Armstrong) about his South Carolina background and his strong musical ties to both Afro-Cuban rhythms and the harmonics of more European inspiration.

The encounter with Castro is brief and their conversation conventional; Gillespie obviously has more fun with Cuban dancers and musicians. The interviews that alternate with musical performances have no structure and lead largely nowhere beyond amicable banter. — *Kell.*

Track 29
(BRITISH)

An Island Pictures release of a Handmade Films production. Produced by Rick McCallum. Executive producers, George Harrison, Denis O'Brien. Directed by Nicolas Roeg. Screenplay, Dennis Potter; camera (Technicolor), Alex Thomson; editor, Tony Lawson; music, Stanley Myers; art direction, David Brockhurst. Reviewed at Cannes Film Festival (market), May 15, 1988. MPAA Rating: R. Running time: **86 MIN.**
Linda . . . . Theresa Russell
Martin . . . . Gary Oldman
Nurse Stein . . . . Sandra Bernhard
Henry . . . . Christopher Lloyd
Also with: Colleen Camp (Alanda), Seymour Cassel.

Cannes — This Nicolas Roeg film, made by Handmade last year and never released in the U.S., turned up in the Cannes market, in some ways a peculiarly appropriate place for it.

Though clearly of above-average quality in direction, psychology and Theresa Russell's 3-D performance as a childless housewife with a dark secret in the closet, "Track 29" is connected closely to the classic American smalltown horror film. Its playoff possibilities lie more in thriller markets than arthouses.

Dennis Potter's screenplay is set in a Southern town where strange things happen every day. Linda (Russell) and husband Henry (Christopher Lloyd) are at odds over Linda's burning desire for a child and Henry's preference for his model trains. He also enjoys being spanked by Nurse Stein (Sandra Bernhard) in the nursing home where he is a negligent doctor.

Into this world of normal absurdity arrives a stranger. Young Martin (Gary Oldman) has trouble making himself understood with his pronounced British accent and odd ways. He convinces Linda he's her baby boy born out of wedlock and taken from her at birth, but viewer begins to have doubts that the appearing-disappearing weirdo isn't a figment of her imagination.

Perverse humor is the keynote of the Oedipal complexed duo, who spend a long day going to bars, exchanging unplatonic caresses, and acting out their traumas. Russell and Oldman are consummate thesps able to reach the edge of frenzy (and beyond) while remaining fun and original.

Roeg turns an ironic, at times disgusted eye on film's All-American scene — for example, when Henry, president of the model train association, rouses a hall full of hobbyists to a fever pitch like a revivalist preacher. Costume is cruelly realistic (Russell plays a whole scene in a hideous bathing cap), so are the characters, like the fairgrounds worker who seduces her as a teenager, and who later comes back as a trucker with "Mother" tattooed on his arm.

If the coincidences with which film abounds (Martin hitching a ride with the trucker who may be his father) seem like tongue-in-cheek "Twilight Zone," the frustrated housewife's invisible son and unchained unconscious read like armchair Freud. It may not be Roeg's most profound or intriguing film, but "Track 29" is full of wry humor and enjoyable cinema.

The cool, low-key finale is something of a letdown, though. Good technical work throughout.
— *Yung.*

Foxtrot
(ICELANDIC)

A Viking Film/Filmeffekt (Norway) presentation of a Frost Film (Reykjavik) production. Produced by Hlynur Oscarsson. Executive producer, Dag Alveberg. Directed by Jon Tryggvason. Screenplay, Svainbjorn L. Baldvinsson; camera (Eastmancolor), Karl Oskarsson; editor, Russel Lloyd; music, Erik Gunvaldsen, Stein B. Svendsen; sound, Gunnar Hermannsson; art direction, Geir Ottar; associate producers, Oskarsson, Asgeir Bjarnarson. Reviewed at Cannes Film Festival (market), May 17, 1988. Running time: **97 MIN.**
Kiddi . . . . Vladimar Orn Flygenning
Tommy . . . . Steinarr Olafsson
Lisa . . . . Maria Ellingsen
Also with: Eyvindur Erlendsson, Jon Sigurbjörnsson, Gudrun Gisladottir, Halldora Björnsdottir.

Cannes — Shot from the start with English dialog, firsttime helmer Jon Tryggvason's "Foxtrot" is a thriller that works on all levels. It should post some pickups outside its Iceland base.

Iceland's fiery rivers rushing down from snowclad volcanic mountains and 2-lane blacktops stretching across immense plains, serve as striking backdrop to a story told with clipped dialog, precise editing, camera movements alert to the action, and thesping by fine young U.S.-trained actors.

Half-brothers Tommy, young and starry-eyed, and Kiddi, a bit older and corrupted by misfortune in marriage and a sports career, are hired to drive a van full of money to the other end of Iceland. En route, they are waylaid by Lisa, a pretty blond hitchhiker.

Lisa taunts Kiddi and charms young Tommy. The enraged Kiddi tries to rape her. She escapes, steals the car, but is shot by Kiddi and left for dead in an abandoned mountain camp. Violence follows and leads to a surprise ending.

Suspense rises from the start and never lags. Plot is believable and logical. Violence is shown to be the natural consequence of ordinary human frustration. Sveinbjörn Baldvinsson's screenplay and Russel Lloyd's editing serve the director with total empathy — *Kell.*

Buy And Cell

An Empire Films presentation of an Altar production. Produced by Frank Yablans. Executive producer, Charles Band. Directed by Robert Boris. Screenplay, Ken Krauss, Merrin Holt; camera (color), Daniele Nannuzzi; editor, Bert Glatstein; music, Mark Shreeve; production design, Giovanni Natalucci; associate producers, Louis Perano, Debra Dion; production manager, Stefano Priori; assistant director, Gianni Cozzo. Reviewed at Cannes Film Festival (market), May 15, 1988. Running time: **91 MIN.**
Herbie Altman . . . . Robert Carradine
Sly . . . . Michael Winslow
Warden Tennant . . . . . Malcolm McDowell
Dr. Ellen Scott . . . . Lise Cutter
Wolf . . . . Randall (Tex) Cobb
Shaka . . . . Ben Vereen
Also with: Imogene Coca, Fred Travalena, Roddy Piper, Tony Plana, Michael Goodwin.

Cannes — A limp comedy from Empire Films, "Buy And Cell" is a prison pic about convicts who play the stock market and win. Basic problem here is a flaccid and rarely amusing screenplay.

Robert Carradine is the nerdy Herbie Altman who takes the rap for his boss' corporate fraud and winds up serving 13 years in the pen. Before long, he's organized his fellow cons to play the market, with incredible success, and a multi-million-dollar company, Con Inc., is established.

If the above doesn't sound like the basis for a laugh riot, it isn't. Only real pleasure, and it's a minor one, comes from a blond Malcolm McDowell, camping it up as the prison warden who has a sign, "It's Fun To Be On The Winning Side," hanging on his wall next to the President's portrait.

The rest of the cast struggles gamely against a losing battle with the script, though Lise Cutter emerges as a charmer. Imogene Coca is in a nothing part.

As with most Empire productions, the production design is handsome and quite elaborate, but that won't help this clinker find an audience.
— *Strat.*

People Of The Forest
(DOCU)

A National Geographic Society production. Executive producer, Dennis B. Kane. Produced and directed by Hugo Van Lawick. Narration written by Nancy LeBrun, based on research by Jane Goodall; camera (color), Van Lawick; editor, David Dickie, Revel Fox; music, Jennie Muskett; sound (Dolby), Peter Marler, Van Lawick, Anthony Walker, Len Gillard; postproduction consultant, David O'Dell; narrator, Helen Mirren. Reviewed on vidcassette, N.Y., May 4, 1988. (In Cannes Film Festival Market). No MPAA Rating. Running time: **103 MIN.**

"People Of The Forest" is a deceptively simple, quite moving documentary relating the everyday life of a group of chimpanzees living in Africa, their forest habitat threatened by man's encroachment.

Aimed at theatrical release by National Geographic Society, feature should play well in specialized situations and have a long life in ancillary and educational markets.

Filmmaker Hugo Van Lawick photographed the chimps over a 20-year period in their natural, protected locale in Tanzania. The feature telescopes this footage effectively into a disarmingly natural, almost cinéma vérité look at their lifestyle, given a fictional, dramatic and anthropomorphic structure via effective narration written by Nancy LeBrun.

The story that unfolds in mainly flashback is that of Fifi, a chimp observed from age five through 25. She becomes attached to her infant brother Flint and eventually inherits the mothering role for her clan following the death of her mom, the matriarch Flo. Common, everyday occurrences and behavior are contrasted with extreme traumas (e.g., the death of Flo, fights among the chimps and the effects of a polio epidemic which kills several chimps including a newborn infant as well as paralyzing Fifi's brother Faben).

With Helen Mirren reading the narration in quite touching fashion, film easily builds to the mood of a fable, resembling the mythic narratives of the late novelist George R. Stewart, particularly his sci-fi novel "Earth Abides." The kinship of these primates to man is unmistakable and their collective fate, as the final freezeframe suggests the horror of their forest being cut down by man, is provocative. Jenny Muskett's spare, dreamy musical score is most effective.

Chimps that Van Lawick filmed were those studied by Jane Goodall in her groundbreaking work and the intimacy and naturalness achieved is a remarkable achievement.—*Lor.*

Mortuary Academy

A Taurus Entertainment release of a Landmark Films production. (Sales, Skouras Pictures.) Produced by Dennis Winfrey, Chip Miller. Executive producer, Kim Jorgensen. Directed by Michael Schroeder. Screenplay, William Kelman; camera (Monaco and Foto-Kem color), Roy H. Wagner; editor, Ellen Keneshea; music, David Spear; sound (Ultra-Stereo), Trevor Black; production design, Jon Rothschild; art direction, Gary New; production manager, Alain Silver; additional music, Brian Mann; additional camera, Ron Vidor. Reviewed at Cannes Film Festival (market), May 18, 1988. MPAA Rating: R. Running time: **85 MIN.**

Dr. Paul Truscott	Paul Bartel
Mary Purcell	Mary Woronov
Sam Grimm	Perry Lang
Dickson	Tracey Walter
Max Grimm	Christopher Atkins
Valerie	Lynn Danielson
James Dandridge	Stoney Jackson
Abbott Smith	Anthony James
Bernie Berkowitz	Wolfman Jack
Captain	Cesar Romero
Corpse	Cheryl Starbuck

Cannes — "Mortuary Academy" is a genuinely amusing feature, getting a lot of laughs from black humor involving necrophilia. Specialized nature of this poor taste material naturally will limit audience saturation, but pic works very well on its own terms.

The "Eating Raoul" acting team of Paul Bartel and Mary Woronov adapts quite comfortably to similar roles as the manager and top lecturer at Grimm Mortuary and Academy, which has just been inherited by brothers Sam and Max Grimm (Perry Lang, Christopher Atkins) on the condition they graduate as morticians.

Rambunctious group of oddball students gets up to antics that would do the "Carry On" team proud, climaxing in the mechanical whiz in their midst (deadpan Tracey Walter) reanimating a dead heavy metal band to perform one last gig with the aid of animatronics, and thereby earn enough money to save the academy, which Bartel has bled dry.

Hilarious running gag has Bartel falling in love with a young cheerleader who choked on popcorn at a drive-in movie (corpse played by Cheryl Starbuck). This love affair goes far beyond the reaches of bad taste, but is a hoot, climaxing with an indescribable scene of the students using Tracey's mechanics to blackmail Bartel as he makes love to Starbuck. Coda has Bartel and his corpse honeymooning on a cruise ship with grotesque results and a tag line homage to "Some Like It Hot."

Aided by a very funny romantic score by David Spear, director Michael Schroeder and writer William Kelman deliver fresh, uncensored material. Pacing is just right and Bartel's unctuous delivery (à la Vincent Price) hits just the right note of campiness without exaggeration.

Woronov's arch delivery again is the perfect foil for Bartel, supported by a solid ensemble. Of special note is the familiar saturnine-faced Anthony James, getting maximum laughs out of some of the script's best lines in his role as a parolee on a rehab program at the academy.
— *Lor.*

Se Lo Scopre Gargiulo
(What If Gargiulo Finds Out?)
(ITALIAN)

A Titanus Prod./AMA Film coproduction, in association with Reteitalia. Produced by Gianni Minervini. Written and directed by Elvio Porta. Camera (Telecolor, color by Luciano Vittori), Alfio Contini; editor, Mario Morra; music, Pino Daniele; art direction, Elena Ricci Poccetto. Reviewed at Cannes Film Festival (market), May 15, 1988. Running time: **108 MIN.**

Teresa	Giuliana De Sio
Ferdinando	Richard Anconina
Friariello	Nicola Di Pinto

Also with: Mario Scarpetta, Marzio C. Honorato, Enzo Cannavale.

Cannes — "What If Gargiulo Finds Out?" is a comic Neapolitan actioner, centered around the night-long adventures of a middle-class wife in search of $1,000. Scriptwriter Elvio Porta makes his directorial bow without much fanfare or technique, but with enough intuition to locate the pulse of a broad local audience.

In spirit, if not quality, it is related to producer Gianni Minervini's hit "Piccone Sent Me." Offshore looks like rough sailing for markets not in tune with ethnic product.

Nervous redhead Giuliana De Sio holds centerstage as Teresa Gargiulo, the downtrodden, super-exploited wife of a lazy bum who sleeps with his mother instead of with her. As a nurse in the Gargiulo wing of the hospital (named for her illustrious father-in-law), Teresa brings home the bacon while hubby and mama give themselves airs.

After an overlong, overdone buildup showing how Teresa needs the money to save her dad, pic finally takes off. Teresa meets the enigmatic, roguish Richard Anconina and spends the next hour resisting his charm (audience will find it harder). With Ferdinando's pal Friariello (Nicola Di Pinto), a good soul with a fatal drug habit, Teresa goes through many comic adventures in the Naples underworld: dog races, dope pushing, a gambling bordello where she is auctioned off at a bingo game. Naturally she comes through it all with scarcely a run in her stockings.

Teresa makes her money, but Ferdinando loses his, when some tough customers steal his truck and dough. A pair of well-choreographed chase scenes later, Ferdinando blows up his truck and recovers the cash. Battered but happy, the three friends meet in the hospital, where Teresa gives her evil relations their comeuppance.

De Sio's broad nonstop acting oft runs out of control, but costar Anconina effortlessly chalks up sympathy just by playing it cool and flashing a seductive smile. Film tends toward caricature anyway — witness De Sio's low-cut dress à la Loren or Lollobrigida. Setting is full of local color. — *Yung.*

Maniac Cop

A Shapiro Glickenhaus Entertainment release. Executive producer, James Glickenhaus. Produced by Larry Cohen. Coproducer, Jef Richard. Directed by William Lustig. Screenplay, Cohen; camera (Foto-Kem color, Medallion prints), Vincent J. Rabe; editor, David Kern; music, Jay Chattaway; sound (Ultra-Stereo), Craig Felburg; art direction, Jonathon Hodges; assistant director-production manager, Sanford Hampton; casting, Geno Havens. Reviewed at Criterion 2 theater, N.Y., May 23, 1988. (In Cannes Film Festival Market.) MPAA Rating: R. Running time: **85 MIN.**

Lt. McCrae	Tom Atkins
Jack Forrest	Bruce Campbell
Theresa Mallory	Laurene Landon
Commissioner Pike	Richard Roundtree
Capt. Ripley	William Smith
Sally Noland	Sheree North
Matt Cordell	Robert Zdar

"Maniac Cop" is a disappointing thriller that wastes an oddball premise and offbeat point-of-view regarding the current cycle of police actioners.

Writer-producer Larry Cohen's gimmicky approach has the novelty of all leading characters (male and female) working for the police force. A maniac dressed in police blues is terrorizing New Yorkers and the investigator on the case Lt. McCrae (no-nonsense Tom Atkins) is convinced the killer is really a cop or an ex-cop, not an imposter as is the prevailing view.

A fellow cop with marital problems Jack Forrest (Bruce Campbell of the "Evil Dead" films) is framed by the killer, but after McCrae is murdered, Forrest takes over the investigation to try to clear himself, aided by his girlfriend, undercover vice cop Theresa (Laurene Landon).

Director William Lustig, who helmed the violent horror thriller "Maniac" in 1980, keeps the killer's face offscreen or bathed in shadows, but it's the massively built, angular featured Robert Zdar who's on the rampage, avenging his being bounced from the force and sent to Sing Sing 20 years ago. Besides its violent murders, pic overtly moves into the horror genre by emphasizing Zdar's unkillable aspects (à la the human monsters in the "Halloween" and "Friday The 13th" series) leading to an unsatisfying, open ending.

Acting is deadpan and straight-ahead, but pic quickly is overwhelmed by black humor, making it unbelievable. Sheree North has an interesting character role as a hobbling, crippled girlfriend to the maniac, combining bitterness and pathos. —*Lor.*

The Wash

A Skouras Pictures release of an American Playhouse Theatrical Films presentation of a Lumiere production. Produced by Calvin Skaggs. Executive producer, Lindsay Law. Directed by Michael Toshiyuki Uno. Screenplay, Philip Kan Gotanda; camera (color), Walt Lloyd; editor, Jay Freund; music, John Morris; sound, Agamemnon Andrianos; production design, David Wasco. Reviewed at Cannes Film Festival (market), May 16, 1988. Running time: **93 MIN.**

Nobu	Mako
Masi	Nobu McCarthy
Marsha	Patti Yasutake
Judy	Marian Yue
Sadao	Sab Shimono

Cannes — A touching drama which should appeal to general audiences, "The Wash" probably is too slow moving for broad commercial release. Although it explores the special concerns of people raised in a traditional ethnic environment with values which seem outmoded in contemporary California, this adds depth but does not limit its effect. The personal interaction has implications which are universal.

Masi and Nobu, a Japanese couple, have been married almost 40 years. The marriage is disintegrating and it seems impossible for them to have even a single interchange without it turning into a fight. Masi confronts Nobu directly about their lack of sexual intimacy.

Masi moves into her own flat and soon has a suitor, Sadao, a tender widower who courts her on fishing outings. She thrives in a relationship which supplies the nurturing absent in her marriage. Nobu begins to date a sweet, but unsophisticated woman, but he is not content.

The title refers to the laundry that Masi continues to do each week for Nobu, a symbol of the reluctance she feels at abandoning him. The effect of the parents' separation on their daughters is sensitively explored. The love scenes between Masi and Sadao and she and Nobu when briefly reunited, are completely natural, rather remarkable since few films have the courage to deal with the sexuality of elderly people.

Because of the balanced script and excellent acting by Nobu McCarthy and Mako, neither Masi nor Nobu are villains. Although Nobu's main concern when he is told about Masi's affair is to preserve his honor in the eyes of the community, he is seen as sympathetic because of his attempts to regain his wife's love. The film was made with the support of American Playhouse and one has a sense of watching a filmed play since almost all action takes place in interiors and the camerawork is very conventional.
— *Sam.*

The Wizard Of Speed And Time

A Richard Kay presentation of a Jittlov/Kay Prods. and Rochambeau Prods. picture, in association with Shapiro Glickenhaus Entertainment. Produced by Richard Kaye and Deven Chierighino. Executive producer, Don Rochambeau. Written, directed and edited by Mike Jittlov. Camera (color), Russ Carpenter; music, John Massari; sound, Steve

Mann. Reviewed at Cannes Film Festival (market), May 13, 1988. MPAA Rating: PG. Running time: **95 MIN.**

With: Jittlov, Kaye, Lucky Straecker, Paige Moor, Brian Lucas, Philip Michael Thomas.

Cannes — Ostensibly a solo effort to showcase the special effects talents of Mike Jittlov in a feature film format — to date he's concentrated on shorts — "The Wizard Of Speed And Time" is a sometimes trite, but ultimately good-natured offering that could well appeal to a younger homevideo audience.

Pic, however, doesn't sport the whiz-bang effects audiences have become used to, or enough of its occasional good moments to sustain a theatrical release.

A film within a flm, "Wizard" chronicles the travails of struggling special effects creator Jittlov, playing himself, on his first proper commission: an effects sequence for a tv show saluting same.

There's an obligatory baddie — one of the producers making the show tries to thwart Jittlov's efforts in order to win a bet — and a tentative romance. Focus though is on Jittlov and his disparate bunch of friends, as they prepare and make the sequence.

It's mainly stop-motion work, and there are some fine moments, as well as some nice touches generally, such as the gadget-filled house of Jittlov and some of the effects sequences worked within the film itself. Actual 3-minute special effects sequence (which film's distribs claim qualified for Academy Award nomination) is okay, but disappointing as the pic's climax.

Overall plot becomes somewhat tiresome and convoluted, but there's enough pace and color to sustain a young teen audience's interest. Thesping is suitably lightweight, music of bubblegum standard. *—Doch.*

Prime Evil

A Crown Intl. Pictures release of a Reeltime Distributing Corp. Production. Produced by Walter E. Sear. Directed by Roberta Findlay. Screenplay, Ed Kelleher, Harriette Vidal; camera (color), Findlay; music, Sear; special effects, Ed French. Reviewed at Cannes Film Festival (market), May 14, 1988. MPAA Rating: R. Running time: **85 MIN.**
Thomas Seaton . . . . .William Beckwith
Alexandra Parkman . . . . .Christine Moore
Bill King .Tim Gail
George Parkman . . . . .Max Jacobs
Sister Angela . . . . .Mavis Harris
Detective Dan Carr . . . . .Gary Warner

Cannes — Here's another supernatural thriller built around satanic goings-on that offers nothing to distinguish it from other low-budget occult pics.

Indeed, "Prime Evil" hasn't the chills or gore to recommend it to fans of this genre. Consign it to the seemingly bottomless, nondiscerning B-grade homevid market.

In a plot with no twists, "Prime Evil" is about a satanic sect harking

back to 14th century England that maintains immortality via pacts with the devil through the sacrifice of blood relations. Led by William Beckwith, fallen priest brought over to the dark side, sect now is working in New York; George Parkman, rapidly running out of relations to keep him from growing old, decides to sacrifice granddaughter Christine Moore.

While her associates and boyfriend and mother are either killed or nabbed by the sect, saintly Sister Angela (Mavis Harris), who had a brush with the sect as a child, infiltrates the group with an eye to destroying it.

In a thoroughly unsatisfying and confusing climax built around the leadup to Moore's ritual sacrifice, Harris effortlessly wastes the apparently ancient demon the group is built around — it's lobster red, salivating, and not the stuff of nightmares — with a knife, only to watch Beckwith escape with a twirl of his cape avowing he'll return.

For the splatter scenes and nubile titillation aficionados of this genre might seek, "Prime Evil" fails to deliver; as for old-fashioned thrills and chills, look elsewhere. *—Doch.*

Prisoner Of Rio
(SWISS)

A Multi Media AG-Samba Corp. production. Produced by Juliusz Kossakowski, Mark Slater. Executive producers, Klaus Pagh, Michael Lunderskoff. Directed by Lech Majewski. Screenplay, Majewski, Ronald Biggs, Julia Frankel; camera (Rank color), George Mooradian; editor, Darren Kloomok; music, Luis Bonfa, Hans Zimmer; production design, Oscar Ramos; associate producers, Roberto Mann, Julia Frankel; sound, Marc Van Der Willigen; production manager, Peter Price; assistant director, Jessel Buss; casting, Celestia Fox. Reviewed at Cannes Film Festival (market), May 12, 1988. Running time: **104 MIN.**
Jack McFarland . . . . .Steven Berkoff
Ronald Biggs . . . . .Paul Freeman
Clive Ingram . . . . .Peter Firth
Stella . . . . .Florinda Bolkan
Police Commissioner . .Desmond Llewellyn
Salo . . . . .Jose Wilker
Rita. . . . . .Zeze Motta
Gil . . . . .Breno Moroni
Mickey . . . . .Ronald Biggs
(Original English soundtrack)

Cannes — The real-life story of socalled Great Train Robber Ronald Biggs, breathlessly covered in the first five minutes of "Prisoner Of Rio," is much more exciting than this flashy, anticlimactic piece of fiction.

Despite vivid Rio locations, and a couple of solid performances, pic lacks the punch it needs to lift it successfully into the theatrical market. A video career looms as more promising.

Biggs, an amiable, publicity-conscious character, was kidnaped from his Brazilian hideaway by Scotland Yard agents in 1981, since he was still wanted in Britain for his part in the spectacular $5,000,000 1964 train robbery, and for escaping

from prison. Biggs collaborated on the screenplay of "Prisoner Of Rio," which presents a fictional tale of another bungled attempt to return him to British justice.

Steven Berkoff plays McFarland, a fanatical Scotland Yard officer, who comes to Rio aiming to grab Biggs, then get him aboard a British naval ship. McFarland's ally is the effete Clive Ingram (Peter Firth), son of police commissioner Desmond Llewellyn (whose brief appearance at the beginning of the film evokes his Q character from the James Bond films).

Given Biggs' role as co-screenwriter, it's no wonder the exile, as played by Paul Freeman, is a charming rogue who loves his small son and only wants to be left alone; he's the film's hero opposed to Berkoff's violent, scheming cop. Plot basically involves getting into Biggs' confidence and then luring him to a seaside villa from which he can be shipped to a naval vessel, but things quickly go wrong thanks partly to Biggs' resourcefulness and partly to Ingram's deviousness. At any rate, it leaves a big anticlimax at the end of the pic, which just peters out in familiar scenes of carnival revels.

Polish expatriate Lech Majewski does a flashy job of direction, favoring extreme closeups, odd angles and often ugly compositions. There's much naked flesh in nightclub and carnival scenes, much of it thrust into the camera lens; device may enthrall voyeurs, but doesn't advance the plot.

Rio is, as always, a sumptuous film location and the city's streets and landmarks are well used. Berkoff and Freeman give efficient performances, but the disappointingly bland screenplay lets them down. *— Strat.*

Out Of The Body
(AUSTRALIAN)

A Premiere Film Marketing-Medusa Communications presentation of a David Hannay production. (Intl. sales: The Movie House Sales Co.) Produced by David Hannay, Charles Hannay. Executive producer, Tom Broadbridge. Line producer, Lynn Barker. Directed by Brian Trenchard-Smith. Screenplay, Kenneth A. Ross; camera (Eastmancolor), Kevan Lind; editor, Allen Woodruff; music, Peter Westheimer; special makeup, Deryck de Niese; production design, Darrell Lass; sound, Timm Lloyd; production manager, Barbi Taylor; assistant director, Jake Atkinson. Reviewed at Cannes Film Festival (market), May 14, 1988. Running time: **89 MIN.**
David Gaze . . . . .Mark Hembrow
Neva St. Clair . . . . .Tessa Humphries
Dr. Lydia Langton . . . . .Carrie Zivetz
Carla Dupre . . . . .Linda Newton
Det. -Sgt. Whitaker . . . . .John Clayton
Sgt. Delgano . . . . .John Ley
Barbara . . . . .Helen O'Connor
Marry Mason . . . . .Mary Regan
Maggie . . . . .Margi Gerard
Also with: Shane Briant, David Hannay.

Cannes — A slick addition to the psychic horror stakes, "Out Of The Body" should easily reach its in-

tended market, which is in the horror section on video shelves. Pic isn't especially original, but keeps the audience guessing, even after the fadeout.

Women, all professional and successful, are being horribly murdered in Sydney, their bodies discovered minus their eyes. Composer David Gaze (Mark Hembrow) discovers to his dismay that he can foresee the murders, but each time he tries to warn a victim he's brushed off.

Finale reveals no human was responsible for the killings, but that a creature from inside Hembrow, invisible and all-powerful, has been the monster. That's not before a half-dozen femmes have bitten the dust and Hembrow's lissome girl (Tessa Humphries) had narrowly escaped.

Director Brian Trenchard-Smith is an old hand at this kind of thing, and pulls off the requisite number of shocks per minute while downplaying the actual killings (which may inhibit buyer interest in territories where more graphic mayhem is preferred). Performances mostly are up to scratch, with John Clayton and John Ley amusing as the cops in charge of the case. Occasional witticisms ("Men are a health hazard!") in the screenplay keep the viewer alert between the numerous scenes of gore.

Technically tops, with good makeup effects. *—Strat.*

A Soldier's Tale
(NEW ZEALAND)

An Atlantic Releasing release of a Mirage Entertainment and Atlantic Entertainment Group production. Executive producer, Don Reynolds. Produced and directed by Larry Parr. Screenplay, Grant Hinden Miller, Parr, from novel by M.K. Joseph; camera (Eastmancolor), Alun Bollinger; editor, Michael Horton; music, John Charles; production design, Ivan Maussion; line producers, Dominique Antoine, Finola Dwyer; sound, Mike Westgate; production manager, Paul Giovanni; assistant director, Jean-Luc Olivier. Reviewed at Cannes Film Festival (market), May 16, 1988. Running time: **97 MIN.**
Saul . . . . .Gabriel Byrne
Belle . . . . .Marianne Basler
Charlie . . . . .Paul Wyett
The Yank . . . . .Judge Reinhold

Cannes — Not a war story, as the title might imply, this is a touching wartime love story set in Normandy in 1944. Thanks to a lovely central performance from Marianne Basler as a lonely French girl who falls in love with a British sergeant (Gabriel Byrne), the film could have theatrical potential, and certainly will have a long residual life.

Though this is a Kiwi film, it has nothing of New Zealand in it (except a passing reference). Characters are British, French and American, and the setting is entirely French. Saul (Byrne) is having a breather from the war when he stumbles across the beautiful Belle (Basler) who lives alone in a farmhouse. With lust on his mind, Saul decides to protect her against

French resistance fighters who want to execute her for collaboration with the enemy. She professes her innocence, though admits to sleeping with a German officer.

After a period in which she naturally resents Saul's presence, and is disgusted when he virtually rapes her, a love affair grows between the two, an affair which ends in tragedy when it becomes obvious Saul won't be able to save her from the vengeful French. Director Larry Parr handles all this with delicacy and feeling, though his pacing is on the slow side. There are a few annoying errors (in uniform and weapon details) but these should only upset pedants. The love story's the thing, and it works.

It's something of a surprise to see Judge Reinhold, fourth billed, playing a tiny cameo in the film. He's a Yank soldier who also covets the girl, but is held at bay by Saul.

Alun Bollinger's camerawork captures both the beauty of the French setting and of the film's leading lady. Other technical credits are pro down the line. — *Strat.*

Call Me

A Vestron Pictures release, in association with Great American Films, of a Martel Media Enterprises production. Produced by John Quill, Kenneth Martel. Executive producers, Mitchell Cannold, Steve Reuther, Ruth Vitale. Line producers, Richard Gelfand, Mary Kane. Directed by Sollace Mitchell. Screenplay, Karyn Kay, from story by Kay, Mitchell; camera (Duart color), Zoltan David; editor, Paul Fried; music, David Frank; sound (Dolby), Tom Nelson; production design, Steven McCabe; assistant director, Gary Marcus; additional camera, Terry Hopkins, Tim Houser; casting, Lynn Kressel. Reviewed at Cannes Film Festival (market), May 16, 1988. MPAA Rating: R. Running time: **93 MIN.**
Anna . . . . Patricia Charbonneau
Jellybean . . . . Steven McHattie
Bill . . . . Boyd Gaines
Alex . . . . Sam Freed
Switchblade . . . . Steve Buscemi
Cori . . . . Patti D'Arbanville

Cannes — "Call Me" is an unusual melodrama that boasts solid performances, but is too farfetched to fly. Cult possibilities loom for this Gotham-lensed Vestron release.

Initial series of plot devices are the toughest to swallow; Anna (Patricia Charbonneau), a beautiful journalist for a Village Voice-type periodical receives an obscene phone call that turns her on. She mistakenly believes it's her boyfriend Alex and agrees to meet him at a bar she's just written about.

At the bar a strange but alluring man (Steven McHattie) comes on to her, but all hell breaks loose when she witnesses the murder of a transvestite in the ladies' room by a corrupt cop involved in a drug case.

The dirty phone calls continue and she now assumes (erroneously) they're from McHattie. Actually, McHattie is searching for her, since he was a principal in the drug deal.

Topical subject of phone sex is the hook for this contrived thriller,

with a bland acquaintance of Anna's (whom she eventually and improbably sleeps with) turning out to be the mystery caller. Climax where all the cast principals happen to show up at a warehouse for a violent confrontation rings false.

Cementing the loose ends together is a strong performance by Charbonneau. The pic's sexy centerpiece is her masturbation scene following instructions from the caller, photographed tastefully as the camera circles around her loft several times. McHattie is suitably creepy, but ambiguous enough to generate sympathy as the lead heavy, with his hophead partner Switchblade (Steve Buscemi) turning in a scene-stealing job. Styled as a platinum blond, Patti D'Arbanville adds warmth as Anna's best friend.

Pic is shot with a very hard-edged, gritty look that avoids the glamor of recent romantic thrillers in favor of generating a mean city streets/film noir mood. —*Lor.*

Phoenix The Warrior

An Action Intl. Pictures release. Produced by Peter Yuval. Executive producers, David Winters, Bruce Lewin, Don Crowell Jr. Directed by Robert Hayes. Screenplay, Hayes, Dan Rotblatt; camera (color), Paul Maibaum; editor, Brian Evans; production design, Rotblatt; associate producers, Jon Mercedes 3d, Persis Khambatta; production manager, Michael Bogert. Reviewed at Cannes Film Festival (market), May 18, 1988. Running time: **86 MIN.**
With: Persis Khambatta, Kathleen Kinmont, Peggy Sands, James Emery, Sheila Howard.

Cannes — "Phoenix The Warrior" is a truly awful offering about a post-apocalyptic future populated solely by slim, long-legged women boasting leather-clad thighs and skimpy animal skins.

An extended male fantasy more than any serious attempt at general fantasy, pic is destined to be the unavoidable inclusion at the tail end of a cheap homevideo package.

Thanks to the never explained genetic manipuliating of this feminine future by an evil high priestess, only winsome women now populate the earth. One of them (Peggy Sands) has been impregnated from the priestess' sperm bank so a male boy can be born, which, again inexplicably, will boost the priestess' dark powers upon its death.

Sands escapes and is saved by the nomadic Phoenix (Kathleen Kinmont), a "sand hopper," whatever that is. After having her baby, Sands and her warrior companion are pursued relentlessly by the priestess' sadistic henchwoman (she collects ears for a hobby) Cobalt (Persis Khambatta) and her never changing team of beautiful bruisers. Along the way, duo happens to find the only man left on earth (James Emery), who, rather lackadaisically for someone who hasn't seen a woman for years, romantically tan-

gles with Sands.

There are numerous excuses for various forms of combat, cheap titillation, captures, rescues and chases in some tatty "Mad Max" type dune buggies; this is topped off by a particularly silly and none-too-clear ending.

Prize for inanity though goes to the dreaded Eluz, bubble-faced mutants who occupy the "badlands" and capture the fleeing group; they're surrounded by old armchairs, televisions and TV Guides, and prepare to release their captives' "souls to the airwaves," all the while chanting such things as " 'Sesame Street,' " " 'Lives Of The Rich And Famous' " and "Nielsen, Nielsen..." It's a particularly torrid moment.

Tech values are adequate enough, but sets, props and design are woeful. Thesping is what could be expected under the circumstances, and it can't be denied Kinmont is a real looker, but that's not going to save "Phoenix The Warrior" from complete anonymity. —*Doch.*

Catacombs

An Empire Pictures presentation of a Charles Band and David Schmoeller production produced by Hope Parello. Executive producer, Charles Band. Directed by Schmoeller. Screenplay, Giovanni Natalucci, R. Barker Price; camera (color), Sergio Salvati; editor, Tom Meshelski; music, Pino Donaggio; production design, Giovanni Natalucci; associate producer, Debra Dion. Reviewed at Cannes Film Festival (market), May 14, 1988. Running time: **85 MIN.**
With: Timothy Van Patten, Laura Schaefer, Jeremy West, Ian Abercrombie.

Cannes — Good production credits and fine lensing aren't enough to keep interest from flagging in this mostly bland pic set in an old monastery in Italy.

With little violence and no sex, item boils down to a succession of haphazard and unexplained mystifications; none leading anywhere.

Prelude is set in the early 16th century and chronicles the last torments of a satanic character chained in the catacombs of the monastery who swears to wreak unholy revenge on his tormenters. Jump forward to modern times. A young American girl turns up to visit the monks and beds down for a spell.

Soon the special effects crew gets swinging with arcane oddities while one of the younger monks develops a crush on the Yank visitor. There's also a peasant girl who can foretell when a death will occur in the abbey (which inevitably it does), and a crazed knife-wielding priest who tries to do in the young Yank.

Pic should be suitable for ancillary markets, but doesn't have enough teeth to make a bite in the theatrical sector. —*Besa.*

Tommy Tricker And The Stamp Traveller
(CANADIAN)

A Cinéma Plus/Cinénove release (Canada) of a Les Prods. La Fête production. Produced by Rock Demers. Line producer, Ann Burke. Written and directed by Michael Rubbo. Camera (Bellevue Pathé Quebec & Sonofilm color), Andreas Poulsson; editor, André Corriveau; art direction, Vianney Gauthier; music, Kate, Anna & Jane McGarrigle; sound, Yvon Benoit; animation director, Bernard Lajoie; casting, Lois Siegel. Reviewed at Cannes Film Festival (market), May 20, 1988. Running time: **105 MIN.**
Ralph . . . . Lucas Evans
Tommy . . . . Anthony Rogers
Nancy . . . . Jill Stanley
Albert . . . . Andrew Whitehead
Cass . . . . Paul Popowich
Also with: Chen Yun Tao, Catherine Wright, Han Yun, Cree Rubbo, Rufus Wainwright.

Cannes — "Tommy Tricker And The Stamp Traveller" is a delightful children's fantasy which tackles the unusual screen topic of stamp collecting. The seventh entry in producer Rock Demers' "Tales For All" film series will entertain and edify smallfry and have some interest for older philatelists as well.

Writer-director Michael Rubbo has peppered the feature with concise and accurate descriptions of stamp terminology as well as collecting methods and interests. This educational material is interwoven painlessly with the fictional story.

Tommy Tricker (nicely essayed by Anthony Rogers) is a young prankster who finagles a rare stamp variety worth several hundred dollars from his friend Ralph, taken from Ralph's dad's collection. Ralph (Lucas Evans) and his sister Nancy (Jill Stanley) try to get it back from the local stamp store where Tommy sold it, but end up with a 1928 collection instead.

Inside the 1928 album they find a little boy's letter and magical rhymes to be chanted that will reduce the sender to miniature size, in order to travel around the world on the stamps on letters. A rare collection is said to await the sender at an address in Australia.

Ralph undertakes the mission and has colorful and atmospheric adventures shot on location in China and Sydney. Pic carefully demonstrates the romance of philately by using fantasy to concretely depict the sublimated travel to faraway lands.

The kids are cute and tech credits first-rate. Rubbo stages a novel and amusing foot chase in a mall midway through the film and keeps the action moving. Animated effects and rotoscoping for the process of miniaturization and return to normal size are nicely done. — *Lor.*

American Roulette
(BRITISH)

A Film Four Intl.-British Screen presentation in association with the Mandemar Group of a Roulette production. Produced by Graham Easton. Executive producer, Verity Lambert. Written and directed by Maurice Hatton. Camera (Fujicolor), Tony Imi; editor, Barry Peters; music, Michael Gibbs; production design, Austen Spriggs; sound, David Crozier; production manager, Laura Julian; assistant director, Gino Marotta; casting, Sheila Trezise. Reviewed at Cannes Film Festival (market), May 18, 1988. Running time: **102 MIN.**

Carlos Quintas	Andy Garcia
Kate	Kitty Aldridge
Screech	Robert Stephens
Morrissey	Al Matthews
Ramon	Andrew Michelson
Susannah York	Herself

Cannes — When, in the opening scene of a film, a voiceover narrator calls attention to the absurdity of the basic situation, you know you're in trouble. That's the case with "American Roulette," a clumsy attempt at a Hitchcockian romantic-drama about a Latin American head of state on the run from assassins in London and falling for a possibly treacherous blond. Maurice Hatton's film is never very exciting or romantic, and returns are likely to be negligible.

Andy Garcia is the hunted politico, head of a government-in-exile following a military coup. Sought by a death squad, he's variously helped and hindered by a British secret service type, a CIA man and a couple of ludicrously comic Russians. Garcia rushes about London, survives an assassination attempt, is kidnaped and rescued from his country's embassy — but all this is achieved in the most listless style.

Sometimes it seems director Hatton, who's done good work in the past, knows how preposterous and clichéd it all is and is quietly sending it up; but the overall tone is so uncertain the viewer is never really sure how to take lines like "Without love, what are we fighting for?"

Andy Garcia walks through his role, and though Kitty Aldridge has an attractive presence, she's unable to make her character come alive. Tony Imi's camerawork, on a variety of London locations, deserves a nod, but overall this is a picture that falls wide of the mark, whatever mark might have been intended.
—*Strat.*

Lethal Pursuit

A Shapiro Glickenhaus Entertainment release. Produced by Gary Gibbs. Executive producer, Alan Solomon. Directed by Don Jones. Screenplay, Roger Stone; camera (color), Stuart Asbjornson; editor, Doug Jackson; music, Richard Hieronymous; production design, Yoram Barillai; costumes, Karen Patch; associate producer, Jerry Landesman. Reviewed at Cannes Film Festival (market), May 12, 1988. Running time: **92 MIN.**

Debra J	Mitzi Kapture
Warren	Blake Bahner
Andy	John Stuart Wildman
Lennie	Stephanie Johnson

Also with: Blake Gibbons, William Kerr, Thom Adcox.

Cannes — Shapiro Glickenhaus has "Lethal Pursuit" in the Cannes market, but buyers will discover its market value is limited.

Ironically, the feature that limits its market potential also is the film's sole saving grace. There is little of the overt sexual behavior or violent scenes one might expect from an action picture starring someone named Mitzi Kapture.

In fact, most of the sex and violence takes place off screen. A problem, since the dwindling drive-in audience won't go far for a bloodless pic and video stores can make better use of shelf space selling product with a discernible target audience.

Kapture plays a rock star returning home to show her new boyfriend her smalltown roots. They go straight to the abandoned cabin she once called home and discover a wounded teenager seeking refuge from a gang of car thieves. The gang already has murdered his two friends and completes the job when the rock star takes the boy to a local hospital.

Turns out the gangleader is the rock star's first love and he wants to turn back the clock. When he sees there is no interest on her part, he commits rape. Her boyfriend stops by the cabin but when he sees the gangleader's car decides to leave. The next morning he sees her in the light of day and decides to get even but endangers both their lives when he overhears the gang discussing the murders.

The title of the pic is accurate enough, but although there are several chase scenes, most are executed so poorly that the pic never generates the kind of pace an actioner requires. Pic could have used a name actor in a major role.
—*Cadd.*

Konitz
(CANADIAN-DOCU)

A Films du Crépuscule (Montreal) release of a Robert Daudelin production, in association with the Canada Exploration Program and the National Film Board's Independent Film Help Program. Produced and directed by Daudelin. Camera (Eastmancolor, 16m), Jacques Leduc; music, Lee Konitz in live performances of own and other compositions; sound, Claude Beaugrand. Reviewed at Cannes Film Festival (market), May 12, 1988. Running time: **83 MIN.**

Cannes — "Konitz" is a no-frills closeup of U.S. jazz alto saxophonist Lee Konitz in performances with touring partner/pianist Harold Danko, in Montreal's Palais des Arts; lecturing music students in that city's Concordia U.; and talking about his music and its influences to producer-director Robert Daudelin.

Film and Konitz come to the point in words and cinematically well-framed music with ease and precision and a sense of fun, too. Film will open in New York in September and should easily fit into specialized slots wherever jazz is spoken.

Konitz, in his mid-60s, looks like a stern but friendly vicar or college dean. Little personal beyond his musical tastes and convictions is learned here.

For many, Konitz, a white musician who found fame as a top cool jazz artist in the late 1940s, still is in full command of his legato tone and fluency with intricate harmonics, but today he may be understood better as the essentially hot player he has been from the beginning.

Konitz talks about his lifelong inspiration from Louis Armstrong. We hear him try — then admit defeat — to emulate on his saxophone what Armstrong did with quarter notes on his trumpet on a 1930 recording of "Struttin' With Some Barbecue."

After playing six numbers, Konitz kids around with his instrument, making it sound like a Barbie Doll vocalizing, while Danko plays rhythm guitar on the piano strings. Konitz' humor permeates the film, quite in accordance with his opening statement: "I play the sax, and I have no ax to grind." —*Kell.*

Under The Boardwalk

A New World Pictures release of a Chanin/Blackwell production. Produced by Gregory S. Blackwell, Steven H. Chanin. Executive producer, David Saunders. Directed by Fritz Kiersch. Screenplay, Robert King, from story by Matthew Irmas, King; camera (Foto-Kem color; Technicolor prints), Don Burgess; editor, Daniel Gross; music, David Kitay; sound (Ultra-Stereo), Stephan von Hase-Mihalik; production design, Maxine Shepard; assistant director, Scott Javine; additional camera, Steve Grass; second unit camera, George Billinger 3d; coproducer, Irmas; casting, Cathy Henderson. Reviewed at Cannes Film Festival (market), May 18, 1988. MPAA Rating: R. Running time: **100 MIN.**

Andy	Keith Coogan
Allie	Danielle von Zerneck
Nick Rainwood	Richard Joseph Paul
Reef	Steve Monarque
Gitch	Roxana Zal
Backwash	Wally Ward
Mrs. Yorpin	Greta Blackburn
Midas	Hunter von Leer

Also with: Stuart Fratkin, Tracey Walter, Dick Miller, Sonny Bono, Corky Carroll, Elizabeth Kaitan, Tawny Fere.

Cannes — "Under The Boardwalk," known during production as "Wipeout," is a would-be surfing epic that sinks under the weight of endless clichés. Pic should attract some teen business this summer, but its impenetrable surfer jargon and odd point of view will keep adults away.

Film limns a weekend in the life of California surfers competing for an annual prize. The guys (and one talented femme, Gitch, played by precocious Roxana Zal), are warring amongst themselves as well, in the territorial manner of gangs.

Cornball romantic subplots have Allie (cute Danielle von Zerneck) having a crush on surf whiz Nick Rainwood (Richard Joseph Paul, a Michael Paré type), while her possessive brother Reef (Steve Monarque) objects since Nick is a Valley guy. Nick's cousin Andy (Keith Coogan) is visiting but considered a pariah due to his nerd behavior; he falls for Gitch who reciprocates.

Under the influence of his mentor Midas (Hunter von Leer), Nick ultimately sees the light and drops out of the 1-to-1 competition with Reef at the last wave, with Gitch predictably winning over the men. Awkward structure has Andy 20 years in the future telling the tale of Nick to fellow, younger surf nuts. The dialog is so extreme it sounds like Anthony Burgess' made-up language of the future for "A Clockwork Orange."

Director Fritz Kiersch crowds the frame with so many representatives of differing contemporary lifestyles and stereotypes (particularly in a messy nightclub scene) that it is difficult to assimilate the action, language notwithstanding. There are some good gags, particularly the casting of Sonny Bono as an ancient surfer given to waxing nostalgically about the good old days.

Biggest mistake is the inclusion of extremely rough language on the soundtrack, thereby earning an R rating. There isn't a drive-in audience alive that wouldn't trade several dozen mentions of the f-word for a couple of good nude scenes, latter wholly absent from "Boardwalk."

Acting and tech credits are okay, but the surfing footage is unexciting. —*Lor.*

Pasodoble
(Two-Step)
(SPANISH)

A Tesauro production. Produced by Hervé Hachuel. Associate producer, Tadeo Villalba. Directed by José Luis García Sánchez. Screenplay, Rafael Azcona, Manuel Gómez Pereira, García Sánchez; camera (Eastmancolor), Fernando Arribas; editor, Pablo G. del Amo; sets, Rafael Palmero; sound, Daniel Goldstein, Ricardo Steinberg; music, Carmelo Bernaola. Reviewed at Cannes Film Festival (market), May 17, 1988. Running time: **93 MIN.**

Don Nuño	Fernando Rey
Juan Luis	Juan Diego
Montoya	Antonio Resines
Macarena	Caroline Grimm

Also with: Cassen, Mari Carmen Ramirez, Kiti Manver, Eva León, Miguel Rellán, Antonio Gamero, Luis Ciges, Pedro Reyes, Maria Galiana, Manuel Caro, Juan Luis Galiardo, Antoñita Colomé.

Cannes — This is a local farce bearing the hallmark of scripter Rafael Azcona (usual collaborator of García Berlanga), with the usual zany ingredients, loquacity and touches of black humor typical of the scripter. The silly shenanigans may provoke an occasional laugh in Spain's domestic market, but aren't liable to make a ripple anywhere farther afield.

Yarn concerns a pretty French girl who arrives in Córdoba seeking her putative father, Don Nuño, who lives with his son, Juan Luis. Meanwhile, a bedraggled family of outcasts decides to squat in one of the city's small museums when its curators leave temporarily.

When two bumbling cops and Don Nuño try to oust them, the squatters threaten to destroy the valuable artifacts in the building. Elements of incest, sacrilege and adultery are treated whimsically as Don Nuño's son falls for the pretty French miss and one of the cops is convinced to join the squatters. Pic ends with the squatters and their opponents dancing a 2-step, as a SWAT team starts to assault the museum. —*Besa.*

Mad About You

A Pinnacle Entertainment production. (Sales, August Entertainment.) Executive producer, Eleo. Produced, written and directed by Lorenzo Doumani. Camera (CFI color), Cliff Ralke; editor, Mark Harrah; music, John England; sound (Ultra-Stereo), Blake Wilcox, Dean Gilmore; assistant director, David Cobb. Reviewed at Cannes Film Festival (market), May 19, 1988. Running time: 90 MIN.

Casey Harris	Claudia Christian
Edward Harris	Adam West
Joey	Joseph Gian
Renee	Shari Shattuck
Randolph	James Daughton
Jeff Clark	Wolf Larson
Wally	Steve Donmyer
Gee	David Gee
Mogul	Alan Lee
Darlene	Lola Falana

Cannes — "Mad About You" is a misguided effort to reinvent 1930s style romantic comedy, only without the wit and originality typical of the Golden Age studio films. It's destined for undemanding audiences, perhaps in tv syndication.

Claudia Christian plays Casey Harris, the beautiful but thoroughly unlikable L.A. rich girl who has to choose between boyfriends: a dull preppy (James Daughton), handsome jock (Wolf Larson) and an engaging waiter who wants to become a rock singer (Joseph Gian). Corny antics play like a teen comedy in need of Geritol, with plenty of well-done musical interludes (Gian does his own soundtrack singing) to pad out the running time.

Lorenzo Doumani's direction is adequate, but his script lacks the snappy repartee necessary for this lightweight genre. Christian has the classic movie star features of a Linda Darnell but her acting comes off as smug and severely limited. Adam West is fun as her square daddy; luscious Shari Shattuck steals the spotlight as her sexy best pal. Gian is engaging as the hero, but David Gee as his roommate overdoes the hokey impressions of Jack Nicholson, Bruce Springsteen, etc. Lola Falana pops up pointlessly in a minor role as a secretary. —*Lor.*

It Couldn't Happen Here
(BRITISH)

A Liberty Film release. Executive producer, Martin Haxby. Produced and directed by Jack Bond. Screenplay, Bond, from a story by him and James Dillon. Camera (Rank color), Simon Archer; editor, Rodney Holland; art direction, James Dillon; costume design, Leah Archer; sound (Dolby), Paul Le Mare; assistant directors, Peter Price, Roger Pomphrey. Reviewed at Lorimar Telepictures screening room, L.A., May 16, 1988. (Also in Cannes Film Festival Market.) No MPAA Rating. Running time: 90 MIN.

With: Neil Tennant, Chris Lowe, Joss Ackland, Neil Dickson, Gareth Hunt, Barbara Windsor.

Hollywood — What defines a feature film in no way relates to "It Couldn't Happen Here," a musical road trip with English rockers The Pet Shop Boys. This is one long rock music video made with much pretense and self-indulgence and no coherent narrative, which if cut into 4-minute vignettes would be perfect for MTV. Theatrical outlook looks paltry.

Jack Bond, who produced, directed and cowrote with James Dillon, makes a vain attempt at surrealism, though the result seems more like Monty Python without the humor. Having Pet Shop Boys Neil Tennant and Chris Lowe meet up with English eccentrics who talk weird but aren't funny on their journey through parts of England does not necessarily constitute engaging cinema without some intelligible dialog to pull it together as a story.

The "film" actually would have been better as strictly a rock music picture if there were no speaking parts. A good portion of it is visually arresting, especially the opening sequence shot at a seaside resort. Simon Archer's fine camerawork catches singer Neil Tennant riding his bike along the causeway and any frame would make a beautiful still.

If filmmakers were trying to say something — there's a long, rambling monolog where a biplane pilot talks about the meaning of time — it's unclear what it is.

There's a bit about politicians and a completely off-the-wall scene where Joss Ackland, playing a vicar, rails into a rainstorm while a cross is being hoisted by a group of very wet clerics.

Ackland shows up later, that is after Tennant has sung another hit or two, hitching a ride from the rockers where he sharpens a knife in the back seat while Lowe continues to drive on nonchalantly.

Lyrics of the Boys' songs don't sync with disjointed travelog either. Discoish "West End Girls" plus "What Have I Done To Deserve This," a duet with Dusty Springfield, or even the crooner tune "Always On My Mind" are more mainstream than the images being put to them would suggest.

"It Couldn't Happen Here" is just another example of what most rock singers should do — stick to singing.—*Brit.*

Crusoe

An Island Pictures and Virgin Vision release. Produced by Andrew Braunsberg. Directed by Caleb Deschanel. Screenplay, Walon Green, Christopher Logue, from Daniel Defoe's novel "Robinson Crusoe;" camera (color), Tom Pinter; music conducted by Michael Kamen; production design, Velco Despotovic; art direction, Nemanja Petrovic; set decoration, Vladislav Tomanovic, Ivan Ujevic; costumes, Nada Perovic; associate producer, Peter Sobajic; casting, Susie Figgis, Noel Davis. Reviewed at Cannes Film Festival (market), May 17, 1988. Running time: 91 MIN.

Crusoe	Aidan Quinn
The Warrior	Ade Sapara
Runaway Slave	Elvis Payne
Colcol	Richard Sharp
Clerk	Colin Bruce
Auctioneer	William Hootkins
Mr. Mather	Shane Rimmer

Cannes — "Crusoe" is a gentle, beautiful variation of the classic Daniel Defoe novel. Updated somewhat, Caleb Deschanel film warmly evokes transformation of Robinson Crusoe from slave trader to guardian of one's individual human dignity. If carefully positioned, pic should find selective audience appreciation in global markets.

Story opens at an early 19th century Virginia slave auction where Crusoe (Aidan Quinn) is as ruthless as the next white slave dealer. He wins the backing of a rich merchant for another voyage to kidnap more blacks for the lucrative marketplace.

Shipwreck on the high seas maroons Crusoe on an island alone except for the vessel's mascot dog. Close bond develops as the canine provides Crusoe the companionship needed to persevere.

Deschanel's helming shines from the start. Early effectiveness is clear in the conveyance of the soulful alliance between Crusoe and the dog, which is vital to Crusoe's mental and physical survival. Quinn pulls it off with aplomb as there's little in the way of verbal communication — save for that endearing type of contact that great pets can generate.

Crusoe's exploitive nature, however, remains intact as he happens upon natives from another island who are engaging in a sacrificial ceremony. He fires a shot and one of the prospective victims escapes. But not for long.

Capturing the man himself, Crusoe is bent on forming a master-slave arrangement. When this hostage escapes from a leg iron and is killed, Crusoe himself is ensnared by a native "warrior." Played with grace by Ade Sapara, this warrior exerts his will upon Crusoe and the pair establishes a grudging friendship that leads Crusoe to personal enlightenment.

By the time a white slave ship arrives, Crusoe's salvation — and that of the warrior — is assured. Story really amounts to a fable, one that seems especially poignant in the context of worldwide pressure concerning apartheid.

Tech credits here abound, with particular kudos due d.p. Tom Pinter, production designer Velco Despotovic and music conductor Michael Kamen. —*Tege.*

Brennende Betten
(Burning Beds)
(WEST GERMAN)

An Impuls-Film release (West Germany). (Sales, Exportfilm, Bischoff & Co.) Produced by Pia Frankenberg, in cooperation with Bayerischer Rundfunk, funded by Hamburg Filmförderung and Hamburg Filmbüro. Executive producer, Jan-Michael Brandt. Directed by Frankenberg. Camera (color), Raoul Coutard; editor, Bettina Bohler; music, Horst Muhlbradt, songs, Frankenberg, Ian Dury; sound, Wolfgang Schukrafft; set decoration, Christian Bussmann; costumes, Sabine Jesse, makeup, Rolf Baumann; special effects, Harry Wiesenhaan. Reviewed at Cannes Film Festival (market), May 16, 1988. Running time: 86 MIN.

Gina	Pia Frankenberg
Harry	Ian Dury
Karl	Gerhard Gabers

Cannes — The second feature of Pia Frankenberg, who also plays the lead, is an off-beat romantic comedy that should appeal to audiences who have developed a taste for the low-key humor of independent productions rather than the sometimes predictable plots of mainstream movies. The presence of rock star Ian Dury should be a draw for the younger set.

Gina (Frankenberg) is rebelling against the indifference of the typical German male who prefers lavishing his attention on his automobile rather than his lady. She leaves her boyfriend Karl and continues working as an automobile inspector by day and prowls the bars at night, looking for companions.

When Gina meets an eccentric kettledrummer Harry (Dury) and asks, "How do I know you're okay?" Harry replies smugly, "I'm British, my dear." She retorts, "So was Jack the Ripper!" This verbal sparring sets the tone for their relationship. Gina takes Harry in as a roommate but makes it clear their arrangement is strictly pragmatic. In a curious role reversal, she explains she is free to indulge in sexual experimentation but insists he refrain from bringing any female guests home.

While Gina is involved in passionate encounters with an endless stream of lovers, Harry causes his own conflagrations. He has a penchant for creating explosions when he is not meditating. He inadvertently sets the table on fire while eat-'ing crepes suzettes at an exclusive French restaurant and burns up the kitchen curtains while boiling water for tea.

Gina has more tolerance for these clumsy bunglings than she does for the intrusion of the female violinist he eventually beds. When she becomes livid and accuses him of breaking their agreement, he counters by calling her a "sexual junkie" and telling her he is moving out.

The score features pleasant pop rock with a smattering of Marlene Dietrich and classical music thrown in. The blossoming of the romance between a most unlikely pair is laced with sly comment on sexual politics. Gina's hip cynicism can be abrasive but is mellowed by her growing realization that uncommitted sex may be more limiting than liberating. —*Sam.*

Zombie Brigade
(AUSTRALIAN)

A Smart Egg Pictures-Cinema Enterprises Australia presentation of a CM Films production. Produced, written and directed by Carmelo Musca, Barrie Pattison. Camera (color), Alex McPhee; editor, Tan Thien Tai; music, John Charles, Todd Hunter; production design, Julieanne Mills; sound, Hugo Cleverly; production manager, Frances Walker; assistant director, Gerard Letts. Reviewed at Cannes Film Festival (market), May 15, 1988. Running time: **95 MIN.**

Jimmy	John Moore
Yoshie	Khym Lam
Mayor Ransom	Geoff Gibbs
Kinoshita	Adam A. Wong
Madam Rita	Maggie Wilde West
Wild	Bob Faggetter
Constable Bill Jackson	Leslie Wright
Uncle Charlie	Michael Fuller

Cannes — A tongue-in-cheek zombie pic aiming at cult status, this Aussie offering has a few laughs, but not enough pace or gore to compete with Yank efforts along similar lines (e.g., the "Living Dead" series). Video prospects loom more brightly than theatrical.

Longtime film buff and writer on violence in the cinema in both Britain and Australia, Barrie Pattison gets his first credit as feature film director on this one (credits on the print caught list Pattison, along with Carmelo Musca, as joint writer-producer-director, but handouts at the fest list Musca only as producer with Pattison as sole writer-director).

Setting is the small West Australian township of Lizard Gulley where the conniving mayor (Geoff Gibbs) has solved the current rural depression by selling land to a Japanese company to build a theme park based on cartoon character Robotman. Problem: right in the middle of the land is a memorial to Vietnam vets. No problem: the mayor orders the memorial's destruction.

First 30 minutes establish, quite amusingly, relations between the xenophobic Aussies and their Japanese guests, a smooth businessman (Adam A. Wong) and his interpreter-mistress (Khym Lam); the locals put on plenty of local color for the visitors, including kangaroos, sheep and a drab social function in the town hall, attended by local prostie Madam Rita and her girls.

Needless to say, the destruction of the memorial awakes the corpses of the vets who emerge with fanged teeth and lust for blood. As the locals are decimated, a hero comes to the fore: John Moore plays Jimmy, an aborigine, who's able to call on tribal elder Uncle Charlie to help defeat the zombies. It's the first time an Aussie action pic has featured an aborigine as hero (and, incidentally, an Asian heroine) and that's a plus in itself.

Unfortunately, "Zombie Brigage" doesn't, in the end, deliver. Pacing is too slow and, crucially, scenes of carnage are too tame. Also, many of the supporting actors are amateurish. Still, buffs may well seek this one out at midnight screenings or on the video shelf. —*Strat.*

Little Sweetheart
(BRITISH)

A Nelson Entertainment presentation of a BBC/West One Film production. Produced by Louis Marks. Written and directed by Anthony Simmons, from novel "The Naughty Girls" by Arthur Wise. Camera (color), John Hooper; editor, John Stothart; music, Lalo Schifrin; production design, Gerry Scott; casting, Meg Simon, Fran Cumin. Reviewed at Cannes Film Festival (market), May 16, 1988. Running time: **102 MIN.**

Robert	John Hurt
Dorothea	Karen Young
Thelma	Cassie Barasch
Elizabeth	Ellie Raab
Mom	Barbara Bosson
Uncle David	John McMartin
Sheriff	Guy Boyd
Richard	Jamie Waterston
Also with: Jack Gilpin, Ann McDonough.	

Cannes — "Little Sweetheart" is an amoral modern version of the "Bad Seed" school of precocious kid melodrama. First BBC production aimed at theatrical release faces a tough sell, due to rather brittle treatment of the material.

Atmospherically lensed in Florida, adaptation of Arthur Wise's novel "The Naughty Girls" concerns 9-year-old terror Thelma (hissably played straight by Cassie Barasch, baby fat and all), who teams up with her new neighbor Elizabeth (Ellie Raab) to nose into all the adults' business in their rural location. Chief victims are an odd couple (John Hurt and Karen Young), on the lam from Hurt's bank where he's just embezzled some bonds and left his wife.

Thelma's pestering of the couple results in Hurt trying to buy her off with a camera as a birthday present, which she proceeds to use to photograph them making love and blackmail them.

Plot complications multiply rapidly, as the brats break into Hurt's residence, photograph evidence of his embezzlement, blackmail him further and, significantly, Thelma steals his gun. Improbably, she shoots little Elizabeth during an argument and Hurt is framed for the youngster's abduction and murder. Climax is tragic with an effective final twist tinged in acid irony.

The trouble is that writer-director Anthony Simmons (known for sensitive work such as tv's "On Giant's Shoulders") gets some very shrill and unbelievable performances from his supporting cast, especially Karen Young and Jamie Waterston as Thelma's older brother. Wild plot developments, particularly Thelma's ice-cold demeanor, require exceptional versimilitude to be accepted and it just isn't there. Major theme is that tv and other

stimuli from the adult world have corrupted Thelma, but it is hammered home unsubtly.

Hurt acquits himself well in the tailor-made fall guy role (which he fit to a T in "10 Rillington Place") and Barasch is memorably evil. Lalo Schifrin's jaunty, jazzy score is quite a treat. —*Lor.*

Sonhos de Menina Moça
(Best Wishes)
(BRAZILIAN)

. An Embrafilme production and release. Produced by Tereza Trautman, Herbert Richers Jr. Written and directed by Trautman. Camera (color), Jean Benoit Crepon; music, Guto Graça Melo; art direction, Silvana Gontijo. Reviewed at Cannes Film Festival (market), May 21, 1988. Running time: **93 MIN.**

With: Tonia Carrero, Louise Cardoso, Marieta Severo, Zeze Motta, Xuxa Lopes, Jofre Soares, Herbert Richers Jr.

Cannes — "Best Wishes" is a nice, unpretentious incursion on women's souls through a story set in a family's mansion during one night. A good location and a fine cast (mostly women) make the film appealing.

Director Tereza Trautman has been involved mostly in film and tv projects; this is only her second full length film. First, "Os Homens Que Eu Tive," was released 15 years ago. As with her new work, it dealt basically with women's ambitions, passions and frustrations.

It is evident Trautman, still in her 30s, has grown in her vision of cinema and life. "Best Wishes" is not revolutionary, but rather a quite conventional film marked by simplicity.

There is only one location and the whole story takes place in one night, precisely the last night of a family in a mansion in which they have lived for 40 years and which is to be destroyed. A farewell party is held, and three generations of women suddenly get together. They find themselves involved with their deepest dreams and frustrations.

If plot is not original, it is very much helped by one of the finest female casts that a filmmaker can find in Brazil. The performances, especially by Toni Carrero, Louise Cardoso and Marieta Severo, are convincing. The location — a beautiful mansion downtown Rio — becomes more stimulating for the eyes through the cinematography by French-born Jean Benoit Crepon. Other senses also are stimulated as love scenes are not with great sensuality and good taste.

Good taste is indeed a constant in the film, not intellectually demanding but fluent, easy to follow and equally appealing to most audiences, especially, of course, women. — *Hoin.*

Blood Relations
(CANADIAN)

A Miramax Films release of an SC Entertainment production and release. Produced by Nicolas Stilliadis. Executive producers, Syd Cappe, George Flak. Directed by Graeme Campbell. Screenplay, Stephen Saylor; camera (color), Rhett Morita; editor, Michael McMahon. Reviewed at Cannes Film Festival (market), May 20, 1988. Running time: **90 MIN.**

Dr. Andrea Wells	Jan Rubes
Marie DeSette	Lydie Dernier
Thomas Wells	Kevin Hicks
Sharon Hamilton	Lynne Adams
Yuri	
Jack Kaplan	Stephen Saylor
Diane Morgan	Carrie Leigh
Charles MacLeod	Ray Walston

Cannes — "Blood Relations'" distribs compare the film to some top pics but it really doesn't bear much resemblance to any of the listed films. The boast might have served its purpose, however, since the producers' presales are surprisingly high. It's doubtful the final product will add greatly to the marketing total.

It stars Jan Rubes as a surgeon who grieves for his wife three years after her death. His son blames him for the car accident in which she was killed and has returned home to make him pay for driving drunk that night.

At least that's what he tells the girlfriend who has accompanied him to the family mansion. She thinks she's there to help him cause his father's death by heart attack so the son can claim the millions to be left to father and son when his mother's rich father dies. She begins to think there might be other plans afoot, however, when she learns about the brain transplants taking place in the basement.

Suspense films only work when the audience cares about characters who are endangered. It is difficult to care about a character who voluntarily involves herself in a murder plot. When there's no one to worry about — and none of the characters in "Blood Relations" is interesting enough to inspire concern — the outcome of the film becomes irrelevant. —*Cadd.*

Gemini: The Twin Stars
(SWISS)

A Primwest (Los Angeles) presentation of Jaques Sandoz (Geneva) production with Zoe Zahm (N.Y.) and Strada Films (Geneva) Produced and directed by Sandoz. Screenplay, Jean-Bernhad Billeter, based on story by Sandoz; camera (Eastmancolor), Timothy Eaton; editor, Peter Lile; art direction, Alex Ghassem; music, Nigel Holton, Louis Crelier; title song composed and performed by Fantuzzi & The Flexible Band; costumes, Ricardo Delgado; costumes, Ricardo Delgado; production manager, Philippe Guerdat/Television Suisse Romande. Reviewed at Cannes Film Festival (market), May 21, 1988. Running time: **96 MIN.**

Mrs. Buffington	Aurore Clément
Matthew McLaren	Gene Patrick
Thomas Fässler	Thomas Nock
Also with: Dennis Moynahan, Mark Folger, John Petrella, Lorenz Hugener, Tessie Tellmann, Nadia Nock, Mikos Kouros,	

Jango Edwards.
(Original English Soundtrack)

Cannes — No slots can be firmly predicted for Jaques Sandoz' English (American) language youth feature "Gemini: The Twin Stars," since it features boys in bed with mature women along with more innocuous, it not downright childish, entertainment.

Handsome and health-looking Matthew (Gene Patrick) escapes a New York drug bust in which his friend gets killed. Matthew has money only for a 1-way ticket to Switzerland, where he aims to hide out, but luckily he runs into a Swiss Mrs. Robinson a.k.a. Buffington (Aurore Clément), who is looking for some fun and excitement while her U.S. senator husband is in Washington, D.C.

In Switzerland, escape of another kind becomes necessary for Matthew, who now finds refuge with a farmer family. Thomas (Thomas Fassler), the grownup son, takes the American under his wing, teaching him mountain climbing and eagle-scouting.

When Matthew is seen kissing Thomas' sister, he has outstayed his Swiss welcome. In Lugano, he rejoins both Mrs. Buffington and Thomas, who has decided to leave home. They all proceed to the Greek island of Mykenos, and not until new trouble develops there, does writer-director Sandoz get around to exploring the title's theme of a mental twin relationship between the two youngsters, but by this time, both plot and boys are literally waterlogged.

All production credits are of a fine order and so is most of the acting. There is plenty of music from rock to "Edelweiss" to fill out the holes in the story. —*Kell.*

Kalamazoo
(CANADIAN)

A Malofilm Distribution release. Produced by Jean Dansereau, Louise Gendron. Directed by Marc-Andre Forcier. Screenplay, Forcier, Jacques Marcotte; camera (color) Alain Dostie; editor, François Gill; music, Joel Bienvenue; production design, Michel Proulx; costumes, François Laplante; assistant director, Pierre Plante; associate producer, Yvon Provost. Reviewed at Cannes Film Festival (market), May 15, 1988. Running time: **88 MIN.**
Mermaid/Helena Montana . . . . Marie Tifo
Cotnoir . . . . Remy Girard
Globensky . . . . Tony Nardi
Wilfrid . . . . Gaston Lepage
Jacques De La
Durantay . . . . Jacques Marcotte
Werther . . . . Daniel Briere
J.D. Bellow . . . . Terence Labrosse
Jerome . . . . Christian Vidosa
Marcel . . . . Jean Guilda

Cannes — The only market bait in this fishy fantasy about a mermaid is costars Remy Girard and Marie Tifo.

Girard toplined the successful Quebec film "The Decline Of The American Empire" while Tifo starred in two films that did well outside of Quebec: "Pouvoir Intime" and "Maria Chapdelaine."

That probably won't be enough to get "Kalamazoo" a wide international release since the story is a dud. Girard is Felix Cotnoir, an aging virgin who falls for the photo of a writer on the back of a hardcover novel called "Kalamazoo." Enchanted, he sets off with her former lover to bring her back to Montreal from the French island of St. Pierre.

The film breaks down completely when he misses the boat to the islands and fantasizes she has turned into a mermaid. He brings the mermaid back to Montreal and is so convinced she's real, his friends also are convinced. The fantasy becomes a reality to everyone he meets, leading to suspect there is no real difference between the two if one "believes."

This idea has been around a while and no new ground is broken in "Kalamazoo." Girard works hard, but he was better in the ensemble cast of "Decline." The character is too lightweight to carry a film on its own, particularly one that carries little comedy value in its Marc-Andre Forcier-Jacques Marcotte screenplay. Tifo is wasted in the duel rule of mermaid/author.
—*Cadd.*

Boulevard Of Broken Dreams
(AUSTRALIAN)

A Hoyts (Australia) release of Boulevard Films production. (World Sales: Overview Films). Executive producer, Peter Boyle. Produced by Frank Howson. Executive producer, Peter Boyle. Directed by Pino Amenta. Screenplay, Howson; camera (Eastmancolor), David Connell; editor, Phil Reid; music, John Capek; production design, Tel Stolfo; sound, Andrew Ramage; associate producer, Barbi Taylor; production manager, John Suhr; assistant director, John Powditch; casting, Greg Apps. Reviewed at Cannes Film Festival (market), May 17, 1988. Running time: **95 MIN.**

Tom Garfield . . . . John Waters
Helen Garfield . . . . Penelope Stewart
Suzy Daniels . . . . Nicki Paull
Ian McKenzie . . . . Kym Gyngell
Geoff Borman . . . . Kevin Miles
Jonathan Lovell . . . . . . Andrew McFarlane
Cameron Wright . . . . Ross Thompson

Cannes — A cliché-ridden tear-jerker about a famous Australian writer who sacrificed his family for his career in the U.S. and now returns to Melbourne dying of cancer, "Boulevard Of Broken Dreams" is almost saved by a sterling performance by John Waters, but still looms as a tough sell.

Waters rejects a busy career in L.A. to try to get together again with his ex-wife (Penelope Stewart) and daughter, but the wife's now living with another man, so Waters spends his time in a hotel room, or wandering the dank streets of Melbourne (not Australia's most photogenic city). For a while it looks as though he might establish a relationship with ambitious actress Nicki Paull, who plays the femme lead in his new play, but nothing eventuates. Final bittersweet ending comes across as contrived and sentimental.

A fine actor, Waters, almost brings off his self-pitying character, but his best emotional scene is undercut by the inappropriate intrusion of a Tom Waits song. Lines like "We behaved badly in the Garden of Eden" don't help.

As in "Backstage," cowritten by this film's writer-producer Frank Howson, depiction of Melbourne's theater world is bizarre: here, too, is a ridiculously caricatured stage producer, horribly overacted by Kevin Miles. If comedy was intended, it falls flat.

Moody use of the Buddy Holly standard "True Love Ways" (heard twice) provides pic's most effective moments. Black and white flashbacks involving Waters in a long wig are unintentionally funny.

Femme players don't register much, but Kym Gyngell is good as Waters' struggling writer-buddy. This is what used to be termed a woman's picture, but in today's market it looks to be a hard nut to crack. As usual in Aussie pics, it's technically superb. —*Strat.*

The Dreaming
(AUSTRALIAN)

An FGH presentation of an Intl. Film Management-Genesis Film production. Produced by Craig Lahiff, Wayne Groom. Executive producer, Antony I. Ginnane. Directed by Mario Andreacchio. Screenplay, Rob George, Stephanie McCarthy, John Emery, from an idea by Lahiff and Groom; camera (color), David Foreman; editor, Suresh Ayyar; music, Frank Strangio; production design, Michael Ralph; sound, Rob Cutcher; production manager, Ron Stigwood; assistant director, Gus Howard. Reviewed at Cannes Film Festival (market), May 13, 1988. Running time: **88 MIN.**
Prof. Bernard Thornton . . . Arthur Dignam
Dr. Cathy Thornton . . . . Penny Cook
Geoff Douglas . . . . Gary Sweet
Najira . . . . Laurence Clifford
Warindji . . . . Kristina Nehm

Cannes — A tired, lame mystic thriller, "The Dreaming" is likely to put audiences to sleep. Theatrical chances are nil, but with a new title and come-on packaging, video fans may be suckered in, though they'll be in for a dull time.

Set in and around Adelaide, tale centers on a woman doctor (Penny Cook) who treats a dying aboriginal girl (Kristina Nehm) who's been wounded while robbing a museum of an aboriginal artifact discovered by Cook's scientist father (Arthur Dignam) in a remote island cave. Not only does Cook develop strange marks on her wrist (never explained), she also keeps seeing a vision of an attack by frenzied whalers on an aboriginal encampment, something that supposedly happened 200 years ago. In these dreams, Cook sees Nehm as a rape victim and her father, heavily bearded, as the harpoon-wielding leader of the invaders.

Almost all of what passes for action, until the final reel, occurs in the dreams, repeated ad nauseam; screenplay thus offers minimal suspense and almost no excitement. Matters aren't helped by the wan performances of the leads, with Penny Cook walking listlessly through her heroine role and Arthur Dignam dull as the unfeeling scientist and positively ludicrous as the 200-year-old villain.

Director Mario Andreacchio, perhaps understandably, brings far less interest to this feeble screenplay than he did to his first film, "Fair Game," which also dealt with a woman threatened by violent rape. Technical credits are so-so, with production design notably poor: the secret cave obviously is made of plastic bags, and Cook's apartment is one of the strangest domiciles imaginable. Only plusses are the sweeping helicopter shots of the coastline which open and close the film, and an uncharacteristically inventive moment when an X-ray of Nehm's skull, being examined by Cook, suddenly becomes animated. It's about the only lively moment in the pic. —*Strat.*

Ghosts Of The Civil Dead
(AUSTRALIAN)

A Correctional Services Film Prods.-Outlaw Values production. Produced by Evan English. Directed by John Hillcoat. Screenplay, Nick Cave, Gene Conkie, English, Hillcoat; camera (Eastmancolor), Paul Goldman; editor, Stewart Young; music, Cave; production design, Chris Kennedy; sound, Bronwyn Murphy; production manager, Denise Patience; assistant director, Phil Jones; casting, Lucy Maclaren. Reviewed at Cannes Film Festival (market), May 18, 1988. Running time: **92 MIN.**
Wenzil . . . . Dave Field
Hale . . . . Mike Bishop
Greschner . . . . Chris de Rose
Maynard . . . . Nick Cave
Ruben . . . . Vincent Gil
Waychek . . . . Bogdan Koca
Glover . . . . Kevin Mackey
Jack . . . . Ian Mortimer

Cannes — The problem of overcrowded prisons and the fact that they often serve as breeding grounds for even tougher criminals, are the concerns of "Ghosts Of The Civil Dead," an ambitious, confronting first feature from John Hillcoat.

With ruggedly explicit language and violence, the film will be tough for audiences and certainly not a relaxing evening's entertainment. If the pic gets critical support, it may do art house business, with a video life indicated.

Setting is a correctional institution of the near future (exterior of the facility was filmed in Nevada) film traces the events leading up to a riot and "lockdown." Drama centers around the arrival of new-comer Dave Field, who discovers a nightmare world where drugtaking and gay sex are ignored by guards and where violence is the order of the day.

Film concludes that the authorities encourage violence in the prison system to crack down further, and that hardened cons are being deliberately bred to go into the outside world to create havoc; the film's chilling final image sums this notion up to perfection.

Cast includes rock performers Nick Cave, Chris de Rose and Dave Mason, a handful of pro actors (Vincent Gil, Bogdan Koca) and a large number of nonpros, some of them actual ex-cons. Production design is striking, the music score interesting, and the ideas important and challenging.

But the barrage of nonstop 4-letter dialog, plus some really rugged scenes of violence, will make the film a very hard sell. Fests, especially those on the lookout for originally conceived first features, could help in getting the reputation of this one spread abroad.—Strat.

Man Eaters
(U.S.-FRENCH)

A Bel Air Pictures and R.T. Prods. presentation. Produced by Patrice Martineau, Marc-André Grynbaum. Directed by Daniel Colas. Screenplay, Colas, based on his play; camera (color), Jean Orgollet; editor, Pierre Didier; music, Aldo Frank; set design, Eric Martineau; post-synchronization director, Allan Wenger. Reviewed at Cannes Film Festival (market), May 17, 1988. Running time: **87 MIN.**

Deborah	Catriona MacColl
Elizabeth	Roberta Weiss
Audrey	Coralie Seyrig
Hubert	Daniel Colas

Also with: Mark Sinden, Ray Lonnen, Yves Renier, Daniel Russo.

Cannes — The oddball black comedy "Man Eaters" provides some okay slapstick, but a little goes a long way. Shot on scenic Sierra Leone locations, this 1-joke comedy will fare best in video.

Encumbered with far too much and not very witty voiceover narration, story has anthropologist Hubert (played by pic's director Daniel Colas) shipwrecked on an island with a pal who is soon eaten by three beautiful cannibal women. They keep him alive as a sexual plaything until hunger pangs strike again.

Predictable sight gags and black humor arising from the cannibalism premise wear thin and aren't helped by Colas' less than inspired gag setups. Midway through the picture an awkward 15-minute flashback is inserted showing how the gals degenerated to eating human flesh; it's just a banal runthrough of "The Admirable Crichton" and adds nothing to the film.

Skimpily dressed actresses Roberta Weiss, Catriona MacColl (a fave from Italian horror pics) and Coralie Seyrig add pulchritude), but their postsynched English dialog is done crudely. —Lor.

Sons Of Steel
(AUSTRALIAN)

A Jet Films production. Produced by James Michael Vernon. Executive producers, Charles Waterstreet, Klaus Sellinger. Written and directed by Gary L. Keady. Camera (color), Joe Pickering; editor, Amanda Robson; music director, Keady; production design, Graham (Grace) Walker; sound, Paul Radcliffe; production manager, Brigitte Zeisig; assistant director, Peter Fitzgerald; casting, Big Island. Reviewed at Cannes Film Festival (market), May 16, 1988. Running time: **104 MIN.**

Black Alice	Rob Hartley
Hope	Roz Wason
Secta	Jeff Duff
Honor	Dasha Blahova
Mal	Mark Hembrow
Djard	Elizabeth Richmond
Karzoff	Ralph Cotterill
Ex	Wayne Snell

Cannes — "Sons Of Steel" is aimed at a very narrow and specific audience: fans of heavy metal rock. It also has sci-fi trappings and a freaky sense of humor, plus outstanding production design, all of which should appeal to rock video fans, provided they want to see a 104-minute videoclip. Good business within the music fringe is to be expected, with little or no crossover biz.

Pic is set in "Oceana" (Australia) sometime in the near future. Most of the action takes place in tunnels under the city. The hero is hulking, pate-shaven Black Alice (Rob Hartley) who's rough and tough and socks over a mean lyric. Frequently acknowledging the camera, with nods and winks, Hartley creates an amusingly ugly character.

Plot is a time-travel yarn which climaxes in a race to prevent a nuclear accident in Sydney Harbor. Narrative clarity isn't the strong point of the film, and when someone says, "Will you tell me what's going on?" many in the audience will sympathize. The plot is not as important here as the look and sound the filmmakers, led by first-time writer-director Gary L. Keady, were striving for. Music is loud and plentiful and the film is visually impressive, with fluid camerawork and inventive lighting. Graham (Grace) Walker's production design is fun.

Above all, the film has energy to spare. Even if the viewer seldom knows exactly what's happened, you can sit back and enjoy the sounds and images — and offbeat sense of humor — provided here. There also are jokey editing wipes, and occasional titles like "200 Hours Later," all adding to the enjoyment.

A possible cult movie here.
—Strat.

Walking After Midnight
(CANADIAN)

A Kay Film production. Executive producers, William Schaffer, Christopher K. Shaffer. Produced, written and directed by Jonathon Kay. Camera (color), Peter Mettler, Baird Bryant, Geza Synkovics; editor, Harvey Zlatarits; music, Mychael Dana. Reviewed at Cannes Film Festival (market), May 19, 1988. Running time: **92 MIN.**

With: Helen Shaver, Rae Dawn Chong, Catherine Oxenberg, Martin Sheen, James Coburn, Willie Nelson, Dennis Weaver, Donovan, K.D. Lang and the Reclines, Ringo Starr, the Dalai Lama.

Cannes — If Shirley MacLaine can sell thousands of copies of her autobiographical books on reincarnation, it should follow that a documentary featuring several stars recalling experiences in past lives would have some market value.

Among the stars profiled are Martin Sheen, Willie Nelson, Catherine Oxenberg and Canadian country singer K.D. Lang who considers herself the reincarnation of country star Patsy Cline, killed in a 1962 plane crash a few months before Lang's birth. Sheen recalls being drawn towards a "mysterious" force while suffering a heart attack during the filming of "Apocalypse Now;" Nelson sings some songs about reincarnated cowboys and Oxenberg goes under a hypnotic spell to dredge up past lives.

"Walking After Midnight" suffers in comparison with Diane Keaton's "Heaven." While "Heaven" leaned on comedy, "Walking After Midnight" takes itself far too seriously. To be fair, it does make good use of its musical score but we spend far too much time listening to the meandering analysis of Sheen, who offsets the upbeat tone of songs by Lang, George Harrison and Donovan with his ponderous observations. — Cadd.

Another Chance

A Womanizers Anonymous production. (Sales, Shining Armour Communications.) Produced by Roger Camras. Written and directed by Jesse Vint, from story by Vint, Camras. Camera (CFI color), Richard C. Glouner; editor, N. Mario di Gregorio; music, Ron Bloom; sound (Ultra-Stereo), Frank Meadows; art direction, Woodie Willis; assistant director, Mike Snyder. Reviewed at Cannes Film Festival (market), May 19, 1988. Running time: **96 MIN.**

John Ripley	Bruce Greenwood
Jacky	Vanessa Angel
Russ Wilder	Frank Annese
Harlan	Jeff East
Mickey Pinio	Robert Sacchi
St. Peter	Bernard Behrens
R.J.	Allan Rich
Temptress	Barbara Edwards
Sandy	Brenda Bakke
Kenneth Rosicka	Jesse Vint
Landlady	Anne Ramsey

Cannes — "Another Chance" is a sex comedy with enough laughs (both intentional and otherwise) to find an audience in today's crowded market. Unfortunately, it tries to cram in too much contrasting material, resulting in wide swings in tone

and tastefulness that keep it out of the first rank.

Bruce Greenwood is fresh and appealing as antihero John Ripley, a womanizer who stars in a tv soap. Though all women are his targets (and the film piles on a nonstop parade of California beauties), he soon focuses on British model Jacky (voluptuous Vanessa Angel), and their romance is progressing smashingly until she catches him with fantasy temptress Barbara Edwards (former Playboy magazine model).

As hinted by an opening nightmare scene of Ripley facing judgment in heaven before St. Peter for his misdeeds, pic is a fantasy, recalling the cautionary Cecil B. DeMille pageants of sin and redemption. Actor turned director Jesse Vint lays it on a bit too thick in contrasting the good side of Ripley's nature (idyllic visits to his cornpone family's farm) and the sleazy lifestyle that not only he but also his vulgar agent (Frank Annese in a well-tuned performance) and seemingly all of Hollywood epitomize. Pic errs in trying to simultaneously portray sexist attitudes (with the usual exploitation of femme bodies and their depiction as airheads) combined with a criticism of same.

Some outlandish scenes, particularly in the escalating final reels, stand out, as Robert Sacchi carefully satirizes his typecasting by portraying a psychotic Bogart imitator, with the switch that he picks fights with people rather than the other way around; down and out after breaking up with Jacky, destitute Ripley is reduced to hiring on as an imitator of himself and in one of the film's more acid scenes has to put up with stinging criticism from a lowlife agent.

To pic's detriment, Vint also includes spurious material, such as a disconnected scene of Ripley's beautiful white German shepherd getting killed (so it can figure sentimentally later on) and overreliance on dream sequences, which render the underlying fantasy elements confusing.

Angel (previously in "Spies Like Us") is a real find in the lead role and supporting cast is solid. Rocky the dog certainly is an able scene stealer. In a single scene as the landlady, Anne Ramsey virtually duplicates her recent Oscar-nominated "Throw Momma" persona. —Lor.

Petos
(The Betrayal)
(FINNISH)

A Finnkino release, Natiol-Filmi foreign sales and production. Produced by Marko Röhr. Written and directed by Taavi Kassila, from novel by Jussi Kylätasku. Camera (Eastmancolor), Henrik Paersch; editor, Olli Soinio; music, Upi Sorvali; sound, Oskari Viskari. Reviewed at Cannes Film Festival (market), May 14, 1988. Running time: **100 MIN.**

Hilarius Ruokonen	Paavo Pentikäinen
Dynamite Lahti	Harri Hyttinen
Aila Kantola	Eeva Litmanen
Police Chief	Martti Tschokkinen
Suti	Pekka Räty

Also with: Liisa-Maija Laaksonen, Jarkko Rantanen, Errko Saarela.

Cannes — A 1950 Helsinki post office robbery is used by writer-director Taavi Kassila in "The Betrayal," his third feature film, as takeoff point for a chase thriller with a difference.

Often verging on comedy, picture has elements of "Bonnie & Clyde," but everybody involved is totally unglamorous. Instead, characters evoke sympathy primarily by looking like plain folks. An occasional offshore theatrical sale might precede a safe haven in tv.

The quartet of robbers led petty bourgeois lives before, involved in shady affairs on the side. They get away with 4,000,000 Finnmarks, but betraying each other in various ways, they are soon caught.

Their leader, balding, middle-aged Hilarius Ruokonen (a tense, witty performance by Paavo Pentikäinen), is an escape artist, too. By ruthlessly yet charmingly using his friends inside and outside prison, he and a stumpy sidekick lead the police a merry chase across-Finland.

Everything is told with flash and funny asides that never detract from the suspense. There is plenty of period atmosphere, served up with authenticity. When Ruokonen finally kills himself, audiences will feel quite good about the fact that he doesn't surrender the money, too. In reality, it has never been found.
—Kell.

Now I Know
(U.S.-IRISH)

A Now I Know Partners production, in association with Strongbow Prods. (Sales, J&M Entertainment.) Produced by Michael W. Taylor, Lelia D. Pappas. Executive producer, F. Leslie Dollinger. Written and directed by Robert Kane Pappas. Camera (Duart color), Jack Conroy; editor, Paul Ziller; music, Stan Beard; sound, Thomas Cosgrove (U.S.), Liam Saurin (Ireland); production design, Guy Tuttle (U.S.), Annie Siggins (Ireland); assistant director, Eric Mofford (U.S.), Des Martin (Ireland); line producers, Robert Baron (U.S.), Arthur Lappin (Ireland); coproducers, David Collins, Robert K. Pappas; John Kelleher; casting, Debra Aquilla (U.S.), Nualla Moselle (Ireland). Reviewed at Cannes Film Festival (market), May 18, 1988. Running time: **88 MIN.**

Jim	Matt Mulhern
Maggie	Maeve Germaine
Steve	Robert Sedgewick
Siobhan	Alice Farrell
Patti	Patience Moore
Maggie's dad	Oliver Maguire

Cannes — A languid, uneventful romance, "Now I Know" fails to whip up any dramatic conflict or involvement for an audience. Commercial prospects are poor.

Slight story has fledgling tv commercials director Jim (Matt Mulhern) falling in love with an Irish girl Maggie (Maeve Germaine). She has to return to Ireland for exams; they eventually vow to marry despite her parents' objections and ultimately drift apart.

That's it, with a laborious subplot concerning her virginity (she sleeps with him, but won't have sex for the first half of the film) and a lame twist of him cheating with an old flame the same night he proposes over the transatlantic phone. With banal dialog, little detailing and characters who have no aspirations beyond the immediate romance, film is a complete bore. Due to lack of dramatic opportunities, acting is flat as well.

Lensing on Irish and Atlanta (poorly subbing for New York setting) locations is perfunctory.
—Lor.

Martha, Ruth & Edie
(CANADIAN)

A Simcom (Canada) release of a Sunrise Films production. Produced by Deepa Mehta Saltzman, Rossie Grosse. Directed by Norma Bailey, Deepa Mehta Saltzman and Danièle J. Suissa. Screenplay, Anna Sandor, Barbara O'Kelly, Janet Maclean; camera (color), Doug Koch; editor, Lara Mazur; art direction, Tom Doherty; music, Alexina Louie, Alex Pauk; sound, Bryan Day, David Appleby; sound editing, Tony Currie, Anke Bakker, Wink Martin. Reviewed at Cannes Film Festival (market), May 17, 1988. Running time: **91 MIN.**

Martha	Jennifer Dale
Ruth	Andrea Martin
Edie	Lois Maxwell
Young Edie	Margaret Langrick
Mrs. Peebles	Kate Trotter
Mario	Chuck Shamata

Cannes — The hidden gem among the new Canadian releases being shown in the Cannes film market was "Martha, Ruth & Edie," a film about three Toronto women attending a self-help conference. Simcom Releasing plans to play it at the Toronto, Montreal and Vancouver festivals to give a national profile in Canada and then try a broad release in urban markets.

It should do well in the cities, particularly with women, given it is a refreshingly intelligent tale that manages to shatter some myths about the needs of women in relationships. There is also a distinctly Canadian tone to the film. Every character is patient, almost stoic, portrayals that fit the Canadian profile.

The film is divided into separate vignettes, each of the title characters given a chance to tell her story about important relationships. Edie's is of how she met her husband of 40 years; Ruth's centers on her slow recovery from the death of her mother; and Martha's is a recounting of her marital breakup.

None of the stories is as predictable as might be expected. Edie's begins with her confession that she only fantasized about one man — a barnstormer named C.W. She would sit at the top of her driveway waiting for the mailman to drop off a letter from him. The mailman thought she was waiting for him to ask for a date and, even though she was married to the mailman for 40 years, to the day he died she never let on she was waiting for a letter from another man.

Ruth recounts a story about the visit of her maiden aunts to her mother's funeral. Their independent natures had led them to leave smalltown Ontario for the bright lights of Hollywood; even though neither ever became a star, they had always represented an ideal of sorts to Ruth, who had stayed in the small town to look after her mother while working in a local library, but had lived life vicariously through letters from her aunts.

Martha was dumped by her husband of 17 years and chose to work as a teacher in a medium-security prison in order to support her three children. Her husband wants to send her to a psychiatrist because he thinks she has taken the job because his leaving has caused a nervous breakdown.

The three vignettes were written and directed by different individuals, but there is a similarity to the screenplays that allows the stories to fit into the same film. As a result, they work far better together than they would apart. The performances are nicely underplayed, with the lead actresses all making the portrayals look easy. *—Cadd.*

Daniya, Jardin del Harem
(Daniya, Garden Of The Harem)
(SPANISH)

An Imatco production, in collaboration with Televisió de Catalunya, FR 3-TV, La Sept and Moroccan TV. Executive producer, Pere Roca. Producer, Carlos Jover Ricart. Written and directed by Carles Mira. Camera (Eastmancolor, Agfacolor, Fujicolor), Tomás Pladavall; editor, Emilio Rodriguez; sets, Isidre Prunés, Montserrat Amenós; music, Enric Murillo; production manager, Modesto Pérez Redondo. Reviewed at Cine Azul, Madrid, May 5, 1988. (In Cannes Film Festival market.) Running time: **95 MIN.**

Bernat	Ramón Madaula
Laila	Laura del Sol
Conde Berenguer	Paco Guijar

Also with: Marie-Christine Barrault, Paco Casares, Rafael Diaz, Fermi Reixach, Fernando Bilbao, Imelda Biajakue, Conchita Oko, Alfred Lucchetti, Montserrat Salvador, Noel Samson.

Madrid — The relationship between the sophisticated Arab world in 12th century Spain and that of its medieval Christian neighbors, former based in Daniya, latter in Barcelona, thus far has been little explored by filmmakers here, and would seem to offer fascinating potential for an ambitious film.

Unfortunately, Carles Mira's treatment of the subject misses the target on every count. Direction is slow and disjointed, editing sloppy, story virtually nonexistent, camerawork amateurish and thesping stilted. Laura del Sol performs a few Moorish dances, but they lack the fire and flair that made her performance in "Carmen" memorable.

Pic lacks drama, action and a believable historical backdrop; most of it seems to have been shot in interiors. As for the harem, seldom has a filmmaker selected such a homely lot of girls; there is not the faintest suggestion of anything erotic in the film, and the contrast in the Moorish and Christian cultures never comes across. *—Besa.*

Breaking Loose
(AUSTRALIAN)

An Avalon Films production. Produced by Phillip Avalon. Executive producers, Eric Jury, James M. Vernon. Written and directed by Rod Hay. Camera (color), Richard Michalak; editor, Ted Otton; music, Jan Preston; production design, Andrew Paul; sound, Bob Clayton; production manager, Andrew W. Morse; assistant director, Carolynne Cunningham. Reviewed at Color-film screening room, Sydney, April 22, 1988. (In Cannes Film Festival Market.) Running time: **87 MIN.**

Ross Cameron	Peter Phelps
Robbie Woods	Vince Martin
Helen	Abigail
Davie	David Ngoobumjarra
Williams	John Clayton
Bill	Gary Waddell
Samson	Shane Connor
Caroline Dixon	Sandra Lee Patterson
Rick Dixon	Tom Richards
Girlfriend	Angela Kennedy

Also with: Christopher Greaves, Dee Krainz, Sharon Tamlyn, Kate Grusovin.

Sydney — In 1977, Phillip Avalon wrote, produced and acted in "Summer City," a low-budget surf pic about four friends who leave the city to drive up the coast for a surfing weekend. One of them, Boo, played by Steve Bisley, seduces a local girl, Caroline (Debbie Forman) and is killed by her father. The pic was notable mainly for introing Mel Gibson as one of the four, but though it achieved cult status among the surf set, crossover biz was negligible (pic was never reviewed in *Variety*).

"Breaking Loose," a belated sequel, takes up the story 20 years later (earlier film was set in the '60s). Central character is Ross (Peter Phelps), offspring of Boo and Caroline, who's been living in the city with his mother and stuffy stepfather. Life gets too much when he falls afoul of a biker gang, one of whom is fatally injured in a drag race with Ross.

Ross heads north for the oceanside township of Wundarra to look up his father's old pal Robbie (the character played by producer Avalon in the first film, and here by Vince Martin). Robbie lives in a shack on the beach with an aboriginal friend Davie (David Ngoobumjarra) and spends most of his time surfing.

Ross also becomes involved with Helen (Abigail, a holdover from the first film), her brutal husband (John Clayton) and willing daughter. Eventually, the bikers, who've kidnaped Ross' city girlfriend, track him down for a violent confrontation.

Rod Hay's screenplay is peopled with stock characters and clichéd situations (such as a "Wild Angels"-inspired scene in which the bike gang grab the body of their dead mate from the hospital and give him a viking-style funeral). Subplots are left dangling, while the climax is over all too quickly and easily.

Peter Phelps does his own surfing, but seems too old to play the teen hero, and has fared better in other films, especially the Kiwi pic "Starlight Hotel." The usually reliable John Clayton overacts as Abigail's drunken spouse, and minor characters are ordinary.

Hay's direction is as mechanical as his screenplay, and the pic's technical credits are only average. Even the music score, which might have contributed a lot, has little to recommend it.

Pic will have a tough time in mainstream venues, but could have a life on video. —*Strat.*

Boundaries Of The Heart
(AUSTRALIAN)

An Intl. Film Management-Tra La La Films-FGH Films production. Produced by Patric Juillet. Executive producer, Antony I. Ginnane. Directed by Lex Marinos. Screenplay, Peter Yeldham; camera (Eastmancolor), David Sanderson, Geoff Simpson; editor, Philip Howe; music, Sharon Calcraft; production design, Melody Cooper; sound, Ken Hammond; line producer, Tim Read; associate producers, Wendy Hughes, Norman Kaye; production manager, Michael Fuller; assistant director, Robert Kewley. Reviewed at Cannes Film Festival (market), May 20, 1988. Running time: **99 MIN.**
Stella Marsden . . . . Wendy Hughes
Andy Ford . . . . John Hargreaves
W.H. (Billy) Marsden . . . . . . Norman Kaye
June Thompson . . . . Julie Nihill
Blanco White . . . . Max Cullen
Arthur Pearson . . . . Michael Siberry
Riley (Cop) . . . . John Clayton
Ted Mason . . . . Robert Faggater
Freda . . . . Vivienne Garrett
Millie . . . . Beverley Shaw

Cannes — A top Aussie cast, all of whom have done work of distinction, flounder in this theatrical, predictable drama set in a remote country town. Beautifully made, but empty, pic looks to be facing an uphill battle to recoup costs.

The setting is Olwyn's Boundary, population 49, a township in the vast Western Australian desert (film actually was lensed at Coolgardie, W.A.). Stella (Wendy Hughes), unmarried and nearing 40, lives and works at the hotel and bar owned by her father, Billy (Norman Kaye), once a famous cricketer whose career was destroyed over a sex scandal.

Over the years, Stella has relieved her frustrations via fleeting relationships with a number of men, of which the first was rodeo rider Andy Ford (John Hargreaves) who comes to Olwyn's Boundary every

New Year's hoping she'll marry him. This particular year he's come to try one last time.

There are two other strangers in town: June (Julie Nihill), who's just been booted out of her job as nanny at a nearby estate when she was caught in bed with her boss, and Arthur (Michael Siberry), a city man passing through on vacation who stays over when his car breaks down.

Arthur and Stella spend the night together, which she initiates; and he can't wait to get out of town as soon as possible afterwards. The meaningless affair kills forever Stella's chances with the adoring Andy. Meanwhile, her father decides to marry June, and the townsfolk celebrate, while making dirty jokes about the bride-to-be's racy background.

There's a lot of sex going on in Olwyn's Boundary, but none of it on screen. A potentially interesting and painful romantic drama, set against the stifling heat of the Christmas-New Year period, is shot down by Peter Yeldham's very conventional screenplay. Yeldham writes as if this were a '50s stage production, not a film. Director Lex Marinos tries to make the drama more cinematic, but his pacing is very slow and the events unfold sans surprises.

Nor is the film saved by the performances. None of the three principals seem relaxed in their roles, and Hargreaves adopts a slow drawl which might be authentic but which makes the stagy dialog he has to speak seem even stagier. Best thesping comes from Julie Nihill as the father's new flame and Max Cullen as the local store/garage owner, who spends most of his time sleeping off a hangover.

Visually, the film is fine and makes the most of its remote location, but it lacks the individuality and energy sorely needed in so many Aussie productions at the moment.
—*Strat.*

Hotel Terminus: Klaus Barbie, His Life And Times
(DOCU)

A Samuel Goldwyn Co. release (20th Century Fox in France) of a Memory Pictures production. Executive producers, John S. Friedman, Hamilton Fish, Peter Kovler. Produced and directed by Marcel Ophuls. Camera (color), Michael Davis, Pierre Boffety, Ruben Aaronson, Wilhelm Rosing, Lionel Legros, Daniel Chabert, Paul Gonon; sound, Michael Busch, Judy Karp, Bernard Bats, Yves Zlotnicka, Francisco Adrienszen, Alain Champoleier, Paul Bertolt (mixing); editors, Albert Jurgenson and Catherine Zins; sound editors, Michel Trouillard, Anne Weil; associate producer and production manager, Bernard Farrel, assistant directors, Dieter Reifarth (Germany), Sophie Brunet (France), Christopher Simpson (U.S.); documentarians, Christopher Simpson, Beatriz Glover. Reviewed at the Cannon-France screening room, Paris, May 9, 1988. (In Cannes Film Festival, Un Certain Regard.) Running time: **267 MIN.**

Paris — "Hotel Terminus" is Marcel Ophuls' latest, compelling inquiry into the nightmare of Nazism and its horrors, centering on Nazi war criminal Klaus Barbie, whose sadism earned him the title "The Butcher Of Lyons," where during the German Occupation he headed the local Gestapo. Located in Bolivia and extradited to France in 1983, Barbie was sentenced to life imprisonment. Ophuls, whose "The Sorrow And The Pity" was an immediate landmark in documentary film art, whittled down 120 hours of material to 4½ hours of rigorously structured and edited film. In this era of "Shoah," it cannot be said to be too long.

Ophuls has ruthlessly avoided a stupid "banality of evil" essay. Relying less than before on newsreel and library footage, he has traced Barbie's life and career as seen or related by those who crossed his barbarous path: childhood friends and apologists, tortured resistance fighters, alleged collaborators, Gestapo officers, victims, former CIA agents, business contacts, former Bolivian politicos, Nazi hunters, lawyers, as well as a host of more detached commentators (including "Shoah" director Claude Lanzmann).

It's not so much a dark chronicle of one man's evil action as an epic (and frequently black comedy) of reaction to evil. With his fierce, often sarcastic moral concern, Ophuls pries and probes and pushes, and has assembled his material with scalpel-like editorial precision.

Among the many sequences that will no doubt provoke much comment and controversy are those concerning the shameful role of American intelligence services in the recruiting of Barbie after the war as an undercover agent in anti-Communist activities in a defeated Ger-

many. Ophuls' quite frank conversations with a number of former secret agents who hired and hobnobbed with Barbie is an extraordinary exposure of moral vacuity.

Ophuls treats the Barbie trial by questioning some of its major witnesses, but especially in confronting the attorney general of Lyons and Jacques Vergès, Barbie's smug, disturbingly ambiguous French lawyer, who's quite a show in himself.

It's worth noting that no French funding could be found for the making of this film, despite various attempts by Ophuls and his producers. Apparently little has changed since the Swiss-produced "Sorrow And The Pity" had to wait 12 years before French television would deign to broadcast it in 1981. ("Memory Of Justice" and "A Sense Of Loss," Ophuls docu on Northern Ireland, still remain to be seen here.) Not surprising then that "Hotel Terminus" will be distributed in France — by 20th Century Fox. Samuel Goldwyn Co. is releasing Stateside, and Orion Pictures internationally.

After ignoring Claude Lanzmann's epochal "Shoah" in 1985, the Cannes Film Festival tapped "Hotel Terminus" for this year's official selection, but buried it in the non competitive Un Certain Regard section. —*Len.*

Directed By Andrei Tarkovsky
(SWEDISH-DOCU)

A Swedish Film Institute presentation of an SFI production. Produced by Lisbet Gabrielsson. Written and directed by Michal Leszczylowski. Camera (Eastmancolor), Arne Carlsson; editor, Leszczylowski, Lasse Summanen; sound, Lars Ulander; literary material, Andrei Tarkovsky's book "Sculpting In Time;" reading voice, Erland Josephson; voiceover narrator, Brian Cox. Reviewed at Cannes Film Festival (Un Certain Regard), May 21, 1988. Running time: **101 MIN.**

Cannes — "Directed By Andrei Tarkovsky" has been patched together by the late Soviet director's co-editor on "The Sacrifice," Poland's Michal Leszczylowski, who used rejected footage and snippets from assistant cinematographer Arne Carlsson's many film shots of Tarkovsky in action, along with clips from tv interviews granted by the exiled Russian in his final years.

It all comes together as a fluent, consistently captivating docu that will be a natural in worldwide tv distribution. It also will be a must in film education situations.

Tarkovsky is seen as a man of a short, lithe body, who moves energetically and rhythmically all over his place of work. Out of his deeply lined face with its cropped black hair and mustache emerges Russian speech always ready for print. He understood English perfectly but never used the language beyond an occasional "thank you."

"The Sacrifice" grew out of two screenplays, "The Witch" and "The Offering," done while Tarkovsky was still in Moscow, but his widow, a handsome, statuesque blond, claims the two originals had little likeness to what was to become her husband's last film. She seems to have understood his artistic needs and aims perfectly.

When, during the shooting of the crucial scene of the burning house, one of Sven Nykvist's two cameras jammed, Tarkovsky was so crushed that he called for his wife to fly up to the Gotland island location at once even though she was busy settling down in Italy, where she had just arrived from Moscow with their children.

The Swedish crew did a phenomenal rebuilding of the house in just three days and the reshooting was successful, Tarkovsky kissed Nykvist's forehead. He was never afraid of physical expression.

Always ready to hold forth on art and life, professionalism, dreams and fear of physical punishment, his favorite subjects, Tarkovsky also says death did not worry him: "I once dreamed that I was dead, and it was a wonderful feeling of lightness and freedom." He then adds: "Maybe I will feel different about it when I really have to face it."

Mrs. Tarkovsky does not think so: "Honestly," she says, "Andrei believed himself to be literally immortal." He died in Paris in 1986 of cancer.—Kell.

Die Venusfälle
(The Venus Trap)
(WEST GERMAN)

A Futura Filmverlag der Autoren presentation of a Robert van Ackeren production in association with M&B Film and Project Film (Munich). Produced and directed by Van Ackeren. Executive producer, Martin Moszkowicz. Screenplay, Van Ackeren, Catharina Zwerenz; camera (Eastmancolor), Jürgen Jürges; no editor's credit; music, Peer Raben; production manager, Kirsten Hager; casting, Catharina Zwerenz. Reviewed at Cannes Film Festival (Directors Fortnight), May 19, 1988. Running time: **107 MIN.**
Marie . . . . .Myriem Roussel
Max . . . . .Horst Günther Marx
Coco . . . . .Sonja Kirschberger
Also with: Rolf Zacher, Hanns Zischler.

Cannes — With "A Woman In Flames," West Germany's Robert van Ackeren achieved worldwide attention four years ago. "The Venus Trap," Van Ackeren's new feature, is likely to travel well and to meet divided response.

Like an adolescent, Max, a young doctor, strolls around in a Berlin world full of nubile, willing women. Is he dreaming? Is this really happening? Never mind. It is depicted in cleanly composed frames and by

actors of fairly little facial expression. Some of the women Max lies down with, others he passes by. One is his wife Coco, jealous and sexually voracious, another is Marie, the cooler dreamgirl.

There is much disrobing and the sexual practices are of the kind supposedly still illegal in some nations. Languid jazz or quotes from the classics float in the air in interiors of either strained modernist taste or outright kitsch.

Max' wanderings are mostly nocturnal, and what the various women offer him always has a tinge of the less than traditional, the forbidden. If the wanderings lead to anything, the point of Max' arrival is as disguised as the yearning for virtue in a brothel. All acting in the three leads is expressed mostly in body language. The dialog is sophomoric chitchat or snide taunting.

Whatever "The Venus Trap" is, however, it has been produced with expertise and care. — Kell.

Rouge Of The North
(TAIWANESE)

A Hsu Shin-chi, Liu Bin Sun presentation of a Central Motion Picture Co. production. Produced by Lin Tung-fei, Chen Cun-sung. Executive producer, James Y. Liu. Written and directed by Fred Tan, based on novel by Eileen Chang. Camera (color), Yang Wei-han; editor, Chen Po-wen; music, Peter Chang; sound, Duh Duu-jy; production design, Chow Chi-liang; costumes, Lu Shi-chi. Reviewed at Cannes Film Festival (Un Certain Regard), May 22, 1988. Running time: **112 MIN.**
Ying-ti . . . . .Hsia Wen-shi
Mr. 3 . . . . .Hsu Ming
Mr. 2 .Kao Chieh
Chi-sho . . . . .Emily Chang
Mrs. Pu . . . . .Shirley Chen
Mrs. Yao .Kwan-yi
Also with: Hu Shian-ping, Ting Yeh-tieh, Wu-yien, Li-ying, Chang Yu-ling.

Cannes — **Based on a novel by a respected and highly mysterious Chinese writer living in the States, this portrait of a Chinese woman's life in Shanghai between 1910-35 starts as a melodrama and ends as a cruel tale of vengeance against the world. Without being feminist, it is a grim and critical image of a woman's desolate lot in traditional Chinese society.**

Ying-ti, the protagonist, starts as a young orphan living with her brother and sister-in-law. They won't let her marry the poor druggist across the road, but arrange a marriage with the second son of a rich family, who turns out to be blind, hunchbacked and asthmatic. She is terrorized by her spouse's tyrannical mother and hated by her two sisters-in-law. She manages to get impregnated by her crippled husband before he dies and bears him a son, but is doomed to live her life alone, her brief attempt at romance with the husband's younger brother failing piteously.

When the family inheritance is distributed, she gets the short end, but still has the means to afford a

comfortable life. She grows more bitter and spiteful with every passing year. When her son reaches marriage age, she forces him into the same kind of relationship she had to accept, and, when the homely bride turns out to have tuberculosis as well, the son is married for a second time with a healthy maid, who continues to function as a servant after the ceremony, as mother and son retreat gradually into the fantasy world of opium hallucination.

Shot on three different sets, marking the three stages of Ying-ti's life, scenery and costumes are crucial to the narrative and indicate the social position of each character. Fred Tan, who studied filmmaking at UCLA, manages to convey a claustrophobic effect of the woman's life, practically never allowed outside into open air.

While Tan does a great job directing the camera and setting the shots, he seems less comfortable with his actors, who are sometimes allowed to indulge in some heavy hamming, particularly Kao Chieh as the crippled husband. He gets a nicely restrained performance from Hong Kong star Hsia Wen-shi in the lead, who is almost constantly on screen.

Much was made in the press conference following the first screening of the film about Tan's political difficulties at home and the unwillingness of the authorities to have his film represent Taiwan. Now, that it is out, it seems likely he will follow in the tracks of better known compatriots like Hou Hsiao-hsien and Edward Yang and become a favorite of the fest circuit.—Edna.

Romance da Empregada
(The Story Of Fausta)
(BRAZILIAN)

An Embrafilme release (Brazil) of an L.C. Barreto production. Produced by Lucy and Luis Carlos Barreto. Executive producer, Marisa Leao. Directed by Bruno Barreto. Screenplay, Naum Alves De Sousa; camera (color), Jose Medeiros, Jose Tadeu Ribeiro; editor, Isabelle Rathery; music, Rubén Blades; art direction, Paulo Flaksman; costume design, Rita Murtinho. Reviewed at Cannes Film Festival (Directors Fortnight), May 21, 1988. Running time: **100 MIN.**
With: Betty Faria, Daniel Filho, Brandao Filho, Cristina Pereira, Antonio Pedro.

Cannes — **"The Story Of Fausta" is the story of an average working class Brazilian woman and the way in which economic difficulties determine moral values. Strong and well narrated, it is Bruno Barreto's best work since "Dona Flor And Her Two Husbands."**

Fausta is a poor Brazilian woman in her 40s living in a slum on the outskirts of Rio de Janeiro and working as a maid in middle class homes to survive. Like thousands of other women in her condition, she does not count with any protection in her job. Fausta is exploited, hu-

miliated, despised. Her husband drives a truck but is most of the time unemployed. He is an alcoholic, as is their teenage son. Their house is in a constant danger of collapsing under the frequent floods.

Their disastrous life, not different from many others, result only in the deteriorating of their moral values. Fausta meets an old man — still poor, but with money enough to buy Fausta small gifts — and they start a cruel relationship. This trajectory is conveyed sensitively by director Barreto who centers on three characters — Fausta, the husband and the lover — a much wider portrait of an unfair society.

Story may suffer from some screenplay problems (Laura's obsession in taking the old man's money is repeated to exhaustion) but is strong, realistic and often emotional. Baretto focuses on several aspects of Fausta's life. She victimizes people around as she herself is a victim of circumstances.

Performances by Betty Faria, Daniel Filho and Brandao Filho are convincing and the sets by Paulo Flaksman reveal in detail life in a Rio slum. Deliberately, there is no romanticism, no samba, no lovely dreams for the future. There is no future in the characters' lives and this straight narrative leaves no question about it. — Hoin.

L'Autre nuit
(The Other Night)
(FRENCH)

A Lasa Films (Paris) production and release. Directed by Jean-Pierre Limosin. Screenplay, Limosin, Emmanuelle Bernheim; camera (Eastmancolor), Acacio de Almeida; editor, Denise de Casablanca; music, Eric Tabuchi; sound, Nicolas Lefebre, Gérard Rousseau. Reviewed at Cannes Film Festival (Perspectives on French Cinema), May 21, 1988. Running time: **90 MIN.**
With: Julie Delpy (Marie), Sylvain Jamois, Luc Thuillier, Roger Zabel, Catherine Belkodja, Albert Delpy, Nicolas Silberg, Thierry Rey.

Cannes — **"The Other Night" is publicized as adult fare, but writer-director Jean-Pierre Limosin should consider himself lucky if his third feature makes it into tv youth slots here and there.**

Even then, it will take very gullible youngsters to swallow his preposterously contrived story of an 18-year-old girl's attempts at revenging her parents' death in a car crash on the young driver who survived after having caused the fatal accident.

Not being able to tell her 12-year-old kid brother Eric that their parents are no longer alive, Marie takes the boy along on the holiday trip that was planned anyway. When their money is stolen, she promptly turns thief herself. She soon finds the young survivor, who is both a thug and an amateur boxer.

While the kid brother still thinks everything is all right, he bounces around with a stubborn cuteness that is offset by Marie's determined behavior. Marie starts carrying a pair of scissors around in her purse, and in the end she uses them.

By that time, all action and narration has become so rigged it kills the suspense. All thesps read their lines as if they were performers in a school play. Only Julie Delpy, also starring in Bertrand Tavernier's ''Beatrice,'' moves with a certain grace and a demure mien through a picture that has production credits of an okay professional standard.
—*Kell.*

Les portes tournantes
(Revolving Doors)
(CANADIAN-FRENCH)

A UGC (France) release of a Malofilm/-UGC/Canal Plus coproduciton with the collaboration of the Office National du Film du Canada and ACPAV. Produced by René Malo, Francyne Morin. Executive producers, Lyse Lafontaine, Jacques-Eric Strauss, Monique Letourneau. Directed by Francis Mankiewicz. Screenplay, Jacques Savoie, Mankiewicz; camera (color), Thomas Vamos; editor, André Corriveau; music, François Dompierre; sound, Bernard Aubouy, Hans-Peter Strobl; art direction, Abe Lee; assistant director, Jacques Benoit, Lise Abastado. Reviewed at CNC, Paris, April 26, 1988. (In Cannes Film Festival, Un Certain Regard.) Running time: **100 MIN.**
Céleste Beaumont . . . . . . Monique Spaziani
Blaudelle . . . . Gabriel Arcand
Lauda . . . . Miou-Miou
Pierre Blaudelle . . . . Jacques Penot
Antoine . . . . François Méthé
Simone Blaudelle . . . . . . François Faucher

Paris — ''Les portes tournantes'' is a disappointingly superficial drama from Canada's Francis Mankiewicz, of whom one has come to expect more psychological density and stylistic flavor. Shown at Cannes in the Un Certain Regard program, the Canadian-French coprod has surface polish, an appealing central performance and some poignancy, but leaves one unsatisfied.

Jacques Savoie's patchy script chronicles the life of a young woman with musical talents and big hopes (Monique Spaziani). As a teen in provincial Quebec in the 1920s she lands a job as a pianist for silent movies, but suddenly finds herself unemployed when talkies arrive.

Courted by a young man of good family (Jacques Penot), Spaziani lets herself drift into an unhappy marriage. When her husband is killed in the war and their child virtually appropriated by her stuffy in-laws, she drifts to New York where she ends up living with a black musician and playing in a jazz club.

This last section is perhaps what's most interesting in the story, but it's never dramatized. Film is cast as a flashback via a diary Spaziani sends to the son she never knew (Gabriel Arcand), an artist with a broken marriage of his own (to French-woman Miou-Miou) and a young son (François Méthé). The child, deprived of a motherly presence like his dad, happens upon the diary and

runs away to New York to find her grandmother. The film ends on their first contact.

Mankiewicz has packaged the story with conventional skill, though what emotion pic generates comes primarily from the versatile Spaziani. Other performances are adequate and tech credits are slick.
—*Len.*

Testament
(BRITISH)

A Black Audio Film Collective production. Produced by Lina Gopaul, Avril Johnson. Written and directed by John Akomfrah. Camera (color), D. Scott; editor, B. Thumim; music, T. Mathison. Reviewed at Cannes Film Fest (Intl. Critics Week), May 16, 1988. Running time: **80 MIN.**
With: T. Rogers.

Cannes — ''Testament'' is a small-scale drama made by a black collective and filmed in Ghana. It's a modest item of rather specialized interest.

The story centers around Abena, a British tv presenter who left her native Ghana in 1966 after a coup. Now, 22 years later, she returns ostensibly to cover the filming of Werner Herzog's ''Cobra Verde,'' but actually to seek out old friends and old memories.

Via a series of rather statically filmed encounters, contemporary life in Ghana is evoked, heavily weighed down by memories of past political upheavals.

Students of Africa and its politics will find much of interest in this film which, nonetheless, addresses itself to a limited audience. Given an obviously meager budget, it's technically good. — *Strat.*

Natal da Portela
(One-Armed Natal)
(BRAZILIAN-FRENCH)

An Embrafilme relase of a Cout du Coeur Films (Paris)/Sant'Anna/CFPA/Embrafilme (Rio de Janeiro) coproduction. Written and directed by Paulo Cesar Saraceni. Camera (color) Mario Carneiro; editor, Dominique Roy; music, Paulo da Portela, Almir Guineto, Monarco and other composers from School of Samba Portela; art direction, Ferdy Carneiro; sound, Philippe Lioret. Reviewed at Cannes Film Festival (Directors Fortnight), May 18, 1988. Running time: **100 MIN.**
Natal . . . . Milton Goncalves
Paulo da Portela . . . . Almir Guineto
Natal's father . . . . Grande Otelo
Maria Eliza . . . . Zeze Motta
Dona Lota . . . . Adele Fatima
Also with: Ana Maria Nascimento Silva, Paulo Cesar Pereio, Joao Nogueira, Monarco da Portela, Jamelao.

Cannes — Paulo Cesar Saraceni's film on the life of famous School of Samba leader Natal is faithful to the facts and to director's style. It heavily relies on fine characterization by Milton Goncalves, though sometimes the plot may be confusing for non-Brazilian audiences.

The modern story of the School of Samba is connected with the socalled ''Jogo do Bicho,'' and illegal gambling nevertheless widely practiced in Brazil and controlled by ''Bicho'' bankers, a kind of local Mafia. Over the last three decades, Bicho bankers managed to control also the School of Samba due to their high production budgets. Unlike the cold professionalism of ''Jogo do Bicho,'' though, bankers' commitment to their Schools of Samba is affectionate and passionate.

Natal was a fine example of such character. Born in a poor environment, he worked in a railroad until being mutilated in an accident. In order to survive, he started working with a Bicho banker and shortly became a banker himself. But his greatest love was the School of Samba Portela, which he financially supported several years.

Director Saraceni was, in the '60s, one of the founders of ''Cinema Novo,'' especially with ''O Desafio.'' One of his films of the period, ''Capitu,'' was shown at Cannes Directors Fortnight nine years ago. Over this period, a lot changed in the Brazilian film industry, but Saraceni's vision is still that of a crafty artist.

Saraceni manages to humanize his character, and is ably helped by a highly emotional performance by Goncalves portrays his character with a strong emphasis on his own relationship with the Brazilian culture. At times, however, Saraceni fails to shoot action sequences or to provide information that could help foreign audiences to understand Natal's environment.

Yet, pic succeeds as an intimist musical not too much concerned with spectacular dance sequences but with the roots of the samba itself. Composers Monarco and Joao Nogueira appear as characters, as well as several other leading School of Samba composers. Veteran actor Grande Otelo is strong in a small supporting role, and among high technical credits is cinematography by Mario Carneiro. He conveys the director's idea of not making a touristy set of sequences about Brazilian samba but an intellectually oriented approach to the deep relationship between samba, misery and organized crime. — *Hoin.*

Une Touche de bleue
(A Touch Of Blue)
(FRENCH)

A CFPA (Paris) production. Written and directed by Claude Timon Gaignaire. Camera (color), Marcel Combes; editor, Martine Bouquin; music, Robert Cohen-Solal. Reviewed at Cannes Film Festival (Perspectives on French Cinema), May 18, 1988. Running time: **90 MIN.**
With: Jean-Claude Frissung, Lolette Miniana-Gregogna, Jean-Michel Yoyotte, Moni Grego.

Cannes — ''A Touch Of Blue'' is

a first feature by Claude Timon Gaignaire, who chose his native Sète, an industrial port city near Lyon, as the locale for a low-key story about a policeman's encounter with a double-talking population.

He is looking for a certain Fanfan, who may be a murderer, but nobody seems inclined to help him. Not aiming at fashioning anything like a straight thriller, Gaignaire will hardly establish contact with larger audiences, but he is a talent to watch nonetheless.

Da Costa, the policeman, is a dour and lean man who suffers from many things, mostly a lack of cooperation, but also a very bad cough. He has no clues in his search for Fanfan other than a videotape of a fairly young guy with a receding hairline who moves in and out of dives in the docks and caves on the shore.

Da Costa looks up Fanfan's acquaintances; all talk willingly but don't really say a thing of use.

Camera tracks the quays and warehouses and enters restaurants and homes with an eye for detail, while we hear empty chatter delivered in what would appear to be impromptu dialog.

When the writer-director has delivered a portrait of the city, he takes pity on the suffering policeman and has him shot after Fanfan has been found drowned and shot. It takes a long time to get that far. If the portrait of Sète is correct, ''A Touch Of Blue'' will not draw many tourists. In the role of Da Costa, Jean-Claude Frissung is a fine updated version of Simenon's Maigret. Too bad Da Costa had to be bumped off so soon. —*Kell.*

Vréme Razdelno
(Time Of Violence)
(BULGARIAN)

A Boyana Studio production. Directed by Ludmil Staikov. Screenplay, Staikov, Radoslav Spassov, Gueorgui Danailov, Mikhail Kirkov, based on a novel by Anton Donchev; camera (Cinemascope, color), Radoslav Spassov; art direction, Georgi Todorov; editor, Violeta Tochkova; music, Georgi Genkov. Reviewed at Cannes Film Festival (Un Certain Regard), May 16, 1988. Running time: **160 MIN.**
Karaibrahim . . . . Yossif Surchadjiev
Monal . . . . Ivan Krustev
Venetian . . . . Walter Toschi
Sevda . . . . Ania Pencheva
Elitza . . . . Kalina Stefanova
Momchil . . . . Momchil Karamitev
Priest . . . . Roussi Chanev
Also with: Vassil Mikhailov.

Cannes — Ludmil Staikov, one of Bulgaria's leading directors and head of the national film organization Bulgariafilm, has made a sweeping, costly spectacular telling of the forced Islamization of a Bulgarian valley in the Rhodopes during the 17th century. Released domestically as two films with a total running time of 4½ hours, ''Time Of Violence'' has been seen by a third of all Bulgarians in its

first month, making it a record-breaker onshore.

It was ably cut to an almost seamless 160 minutes for its Cannes screening. Packed with top production values, widescreen action, a cast of hundreds, substantial violence and an absorbing story, this historical blockbuster should have takers in many lands.

Outside of Turkey, that is: many Turkish viewers at Cannes rebelled against film's portrait of the Ottoman invaders as leering cutthroats and torturers. Though film has a positive Turkish character, and concludes with a plea for reasoned coexistence between Christians and Moslems, it is not likely to do much for the two countries' historically bad relations.

Film's grand scale and epic sweep are evident from the first shots, as the sultan's army crosses mountain ranges on horseback in Cinemascope. Women run screaming and peasants tremble at the approach of Karaibrahim (a nuance villain as played by Yossif Surchadjiev). Even the liberal local ruler, Suleyman Aga, shudders before his merciless cruelty and corpses-or-converts policy. At that time a hated practice was taking Christian boys of 10 off to become "janissaries," soldiers in the sultan's personal army. It's not too much of a surprise to learn the ruthless Karaibrahim is one of them — born in the very village he's intent on razing.

"Time Of Violence" sweeps mightily along from cold-blooded murder to the resistance, headed by super-shepherd Manol (Ivan Krustev in the familiar role of the little giant who won't give in, leading his people to death rather than capitulation). Rounded up at Manol's lavish wedding, the resisters are faced with rape or torture, unless they renounce Christianity and embrace Islam. Nobody does. The men are beheaded, impaled, and drawn and quartered with grisly realism; at least the women are ravaged offscreen.

Point film is trying to make, which is there but a bit subtle, is that it isn't just a question of religion but of national identity. This message, however, is certainly secondary to the often dazzling, wide-screen spectacular, whose classic craftsmanship could give a lesson to a lot of Western epics.

— *Yung.*

Tabataba
(MADAGASCAR-FRENCH)

A Films du Volcan presentation of a Minazara, Madagascar, Films du Volcan, Paris, production. Produced by Jacques Le Glou. Written and directed by Raymond Rajaonarivelo. Camera (color), Bruno Privat; editor, Suzanne Koch; music, Eddy Louis; sound, Jean-Pierre Houel. Reviewed at Cannes Film Festival (Directors Fortnight). May 19, 1988. Running time: **85 MIN.**
With: Philippe Nahoun, François Botozandry, Lucien Dakadisi, Soatody, Soavelo.

Cannes — The main interest of this item is its country of origin, the island of Madagascar off the east African coast, hardly known for film production. Director Raymond Rajaonarivelo was born on the island, studied cinema in France and, in his first feature film, relies heavily on technical assistance and know-how from the French coproducers.

Unfolding an episode of the national struggle for independence, and focusing on the repressions of the French against the slightest separatist initiatives in the villages, the film has a thin plot line, which barely keeps it going, a slow pace and each detail elaborated way beyond necessity.

On the other hand, the rural landscape is breathtaking, the local characters are portrayed sympathetically while the French, as expected, tend to be caricatured. Eddy Louis supplies an imaginative musical soundtrack, which takes over quite often, the film functioning more as a picturesque travelog than as a drama about the systematic destruction of village society. —*Edna.*

Mon cher sujet
(My Dear Subject)
(SWISS-FRENCH)

A Metropolis Films presentation. Produced by CNC, La Cinq, Les Films du Jeudi, JLG Films, Xanadu Films, RTSR, DFI. Written and directed by Anne-Marie Mieville. Camera (color), Jean-Paul Rosa da Costa, Jean-Bernard Menoud, Daniel Barrau, Martin Gressman, Denis Jutzeler, Patrick Schickel, Philippe Chazal, Michel Gabbay, Alain Mugnier, Jean-Marc Fabre, Christian Thurot; editor, Mieville; music, Fauré, Mozart, Gluck, Schubert, Mahler, Sebastian Santamaria; sound, Pierre Camus, Raoul Fruhauf; sets, Yvan Niclass, Fanny Gagliardini. Reviewed at the Cannes Film Festival (Intl. Critics Week), May 18, 1988. Running time: **96 MIN.**
Angèle..................Gaele le Roi
Agnès..................Anny Romand
Odile..................Helene Roussel
Also with: Yves Neff, Bernard Woringer, Hanns Zischler, Marc Darnault, Anne Michel, Jonathan Kerr, Michel Ferrer.

Cannes — A close associate of Jean-Luc Godard and a cosignatory in different capacities of all his films since 1973, Anne-Marie Mieville signs her first solo feature and as expected is strongly influenced by her experience in the last 15 years.

While she is much less adventurous than her tutor in breaking new ground for film grammar, the subject and its treatment will be familiar to Godard aficionados. The picture is a portrait of three women — daughter, mother and grandmother — each with a different mentality and way of tackling personal problems. Mieville's "My Dear Subject" includes all the basic ingredients in a woman's life — birth, death (the film starts with a funeral), and all the social and emotional levels of a woman's life.

The 20-year-old daughter Angèle, studying to become a soprano, must decide whether to have a child and keep alive her relationship with the father, who isn't enthusiastic about the timing. The mother, Agnès, 40, an intellectual who has never married, still cannot make up her mind what should be the nature of her relations with the men in her life. Grandmother Odile, working for a car salesman, belongs to a family tradition on its way out, at the age when independence is becoming a burden.

The experimental aspects of the films are relatively limited, like disassociating sound and image and indulging in some of the controversial abrupt editing techniques employed in early Godard films. Militant in everything concerning the female condition, and portraying men at all ages as hopeless egotists who cannot perceive and fully satisfy a woman's needs, Mieville stops short of extreme feminist propaganda and displays a degree of sympathy for her characters, except a caricature here and there, which soften considerably the stentorian tone of the message.

Men, in any case, take the back seat here, focus being exclusively on the women, whose personalities, professions and responses reflect the changes which have taken place in the later generations.

Photography is amazingly homogenous, sharp and crisp, considering the number of different cameramen credited; sound has been worked out creatively in detail; opera buffs will love a sequence in which Gaele le Roi is tutored through a Gluck aria, then delivers Mozart's "Queen Of The Night" lament; all performances are uniformly sympathetic.

Traditional plot line is mostly ignored in favor of separate statements made by each scene. The film could find a niche on art circuits, where Mieville already has an established reputation.—*Edna.*

Mapantsula
(SOUTH AFRICAN-AUSTRALIAN-BRITISH)

A Haverbeam and David Hannay presentation of a Max Montocchio production. Produced by Montocchio. Executive producers, Hannay, Keith Rosenbaum. Directed by Oliver Schmitz. Screenplay, Schmitz, Thomas Mogotlane; camera (Irene color), Rod Stewart; editor, Mark Baard; music, The Ouens; art direction, Robyn Hofmmeyr. Reviewed at Cannes Film Festival (Un Certain Regard), May 21, 1988. Running time: **105 MIN.**
Panic..............Thomas Mogotlane
Stander............Marcel Van Heerden
Pat....................Thembi Mtshali
Ma Mobise.............Dolly Rathebe
Duma..................Peter Sephuma
Sam..................Eugene Majola

Cannes — That "Mapantsula," a blunt attack on apartheid made by South Africans in South Africa, exists at all is rather more fascinating than the film itself. The tale of a smalltime black hoodlum who only with great difficulty becomes conscious of political, as opposed to personal, realities, pic presents a vivid panorama of the diversity of black life within a bitterly divided country, but is too poorly paced and written to engage undivided interest.

To get it made, filmmakers submitted to local authorities an apolitical gangster script with the same characters and locations, then secretly shot their explicitly political drama under officials' noses in Johannesburg and Soweto. "Mapantsula" thus is virtually unprecedented as an example of anti-government guerrilla cinama created by blacks and whites together within South Africa, as opposed to anti-apartheid films produced elsewhere.

Unfortunately, the script by director Oliver Schmitz and main actor Thomas Mogotlane constructs serious barriers to viewer involvement at the outset in that the anti-hero lead, nicknamed Panic, is an extremely arrogant, unlikable thug whose status at the lower levels of an oppressive society does nothing to alleviate the fact that he would be an undesirable menace to any community.

Screenwriters fashion a parallel structure in which Panic's arrest, imprisonment and interrogation by the authorities is set alongside his assorted sordid activities which lead to his capture.

It is these latter events that create most of the aggravation; ironically, if the pulp, gangsterish elements had been more engagingly handled, pic might have had considerably more impact. As it is, Panic makes his alternately dull and abrasive rounds involving confrontations with his colleagues, landlady, girlfriend, girlfriend's boss, girlfriend's possible new suitor and crime victims, who invariably are white.

Although the film's politics are quite clear from the start, it takes altogether too long for the drama to develop its apt analysis of how the operative system uses and manipulates the uneducated, unaware and criminal elements within the black population to keep other blacks down. Along the way, however, an admirable portrait evolves of blacks on multiple levels of South African society, notably within the police force, something "Cry Freedom" deceptively avoided.

Potent ending stresses how defiance of the regime can result in possible progress, and is hopeful in its presentation of movement from a self-absorbed mentality to a socially conscious one by even the lowliest of citizens.

Pic looks and sounds decent, and would require subtitles in any country due to its mix of heavily accented English and Afrikaans. —*Cart.*

Big

A 20th Century Fox Film release. Produced by James L. Brooks, Robert Greenhut. Co-produced by Anne Spielberg, Gary Ross. Directed by Penny Marshall. Screenplay, Ross, Spielberg; camera (Duart color, Deluxe prints), Barry Sonnenfeld; editor, Barry Malkin; music, Howard Shore; sound (Dolby), Les Lazarowitz; production design, Santo Loquasto; art direction, Tom Warren, Speed Hopkins; costume design, Julianna Makovsky; Ornstein; casting, Juliet Taylor, Paula Herald. Reviewed at Avco Center theater, L.A., May 26, 1988. MPAA Rating: PG. Running time: **102 MIN.**

Josh . . . . .Tom Hanks
Susan . . . . .Elizabeth Perkins
Paul .John Heard
Billy . . . . .Jared Rushton
MacMillan . . . . .Robert Loggia
Young Josh . . . . .David Moscow

Hollywood — No fewer than four role reversal-themed films have been released in the past year, and "Big," the latest, is the most charming of the lot. While the others were more for kids, this has the kind of sophisticated humor that adults will enjoy and a large part of its appeal stems from the performance of the completely engaging Tom Hanks. Fox has a winner.

From almost the opening scene, there's a feeling that this picture will unspool with genuineness and ingenuity — and it does on both accounts — even though the situation is pure fantasy.

This time around it's a 13-year-old junior high kid Josh (David Moscow) who is transformed into a 35-year-old's body (Tom Hanks) by a carnival wishing machine — all because he so desperately wanted to grow "big" and be as tall as the cute, blond classmate he secretly pines for.

Immediate dilemma, since going back to school is not an option and his Mom thinks he's an intruder and doesn't buy into the explanation that he's changed into a man, is to escape to anonymous New York City and hide out in a seedy hotel.

Play pal Billy (Jared Rushton) hangs out with him initially and the two of them indulge in all kinds of boyhood silliness that begins with a junk food binge after which they both pretend to get sick and squirt shaving cream at each other.

Pretty soon, the viewer forgets that what's happening on screen has no basis in reality. The characters are having too much fun enjoying life away from responsibility, which begs the question why adults get so serious when there is fun to be had in almost any situation.

It's clear scripters (and coproducers) Anne Spielberg and Gary Rose speak to the child wanting to come out in everyone, though credit goes to director Penny Marshall for pulling it off so smoothly on screen.

Story could have reached a plateau and become tired soon if scripters continued to rely upon sight gags, but they went far beyond that.

Hanks plays chopsticks on a walking piano at F.A.O. Schwarz with a man turns out to be his boss (Robert Loggia) and as a result of this freespirited behavior is promoted way beyond his expectations, but it's what he does with all his new-found self-worth that propels this "dramedy."

Greatest growth comes from his involvement with coworker Elizabeth Perkins, though by no means is he the only one getting an education.

She moves quickly to get this up-and-coming toy wizard to seduce her and instead is seduced by the fact he's so unslick, unsmooth and unaggressive — unlike all the other rising young execs she's latched herself on to up to now.

What she takes at first to be his hands-off policy as a sign of disinterest in her as a sex object, turns out to be more than just his unknowing virginal way — and that's what really becomes his most attractive quality. He doesn't want to attack her; he just likes hanging around together.

Perkins plays a good 1980s neurotic career female-type and Hanks accomplishes with her what most men couldn't — he makes her feel good about herself even as she learns she really can never have him for keeps.

The dialog they have is priceless and their first overnight stay where he insists upon being "on top" — as in, top of the bunk bed — and then gives her a glowing moonstone ring as a sign of affection instead of a kiss is pretty cute stuff indeed.

Context of other encounters, especially at the office, puts into perspective how people can be so unappealing when ambition and greed get in the way, though this message is cloaked in such a way to be humorous, not heavy.

Will success spoil big Josh for little Josh? In a way, yes.

No more nights playing pinball and shooting hoops with Rushton in that loft apartment crammed with expensive toys and a trampoline. Now, it's more and more work with timeouts for fondling Perkins.

Fortunately, goopy final few minutes of the film can't begin to take away all that was delightful in the preceding hour-plus. —*Brit.*

Funny Farm

A Warner Bros. Pictures release. Produced by Robert L. Crawford. Executive producers, Patrick Kelley, Bruce Bodner. Directed by George Roy Hill. Screenplay, Jeffrey Boam, based on book by Jay Cronley; camera (Technicolor), Miroslav Ondricek; editor, Alan Heim; music, Elmer Bernstein; sound (Dolby), Clark King; production design, Henry Bumstead; set design, Judy Cammer; costume design, Ann Roth; assistant director, Jim Van Wyck; assistant camera, Gary Muller; second unit director, Mickey Moore; casting, Marion Dougherty. Reviewed at the Burbank Studios, Calif., May 25, 1988. MPAA Rating: PG. Running time: **101 MIN.**

Andy Farmer . . . . .Chevy Chase
Elizabeth Farmer . . . . .Madolyn Smith
Sheriff . . . . .Kevin O'Morrison

Hollywood — Chevy Chase is mellowing. The comedian tones down his goofy shtick, moves to the country with wife Madolyn Smith and has an occasional humorous encounter or two with the locals in "Funny Farm." As pleasant yuppie comedies go, this is about par, which is to say b.o. should be fair.

Plot is something of a rehash of so many other city-slickers-take-on-rural-life situations, making most of the setups are predictable.

Weightless material gets some good handling by professional All-American Boy Chase and his gorgeous costar Smith — leaving audiences feeling good though few will remember what happened a half-hour out of the theater.

This time around, Chase is a sportswriter with ambitions as a novelist. The wife is a schoolteacher with no other apparent ambitions, except initially to make the clapboard home cozy with chintz and antiques from the local shop of nearby Redbud and to get ready for the family they both want. Of all the names in the name book, wouldn't you know theirs are Andy and Elizabeth Farmer.

Redbud is populated with eccentrics, like the sheriff who's had his driver's license revoked, the softball umpire in a body cast and the postman who screeches by in his exhaust-spewing truck to throw, not deliver, the mail to those on his route, including these two.

Along with the fact that Chase suffers from writers block and then when he does manage to crank it out, his wife lets him know it's awful, none of the townsfolk are even friendly. This really goads him and he takes to the bottle. Meanwhile, she writes a terrific children's story based on his antics with him disguised in the book as a squirrel.

During his many idle moments, Chase has a field day playing games with whatever distractions comes his way, be it with the irritatingly chirping bird outside his study or the maniacal postman.

Director George Roy Hill shows little distinction with this material, but then again, the material here isn't very distinctive.

Some of the setups work better than others, though most are of the sitcom variety that just as easily will be enjoyed at home via videotape.

About the only truly inventive scene comes at the end when Chase and Smith are ready to divorce — he's jealous of her writing talents and she's mad about his slovenliness — so they seek cooperation from the townsfolk to parade around as Norman Rockwell types for an evening while trying to hype Redbud to a couple interested in buying their house.

It's worth a few chuckles to see generally unattractive locals come out in force to lay on the thick, fake smalltown charm dressed up in Christmas colors signing carols ad infinitum.

Smith has a natural comedic way about her and is a good choice to pair with Chase, who can overdo it given the opportunity.

Tech credits are all fine and production designer Henry Bumstead certainly has a feel for creating a yuppie's vision of the perfect country cottage — complete with a duck pond and view of rolling green hills. —*Brit.*

Picasso Trigger

A Malibu Bay Films release. Produced by Arlene Sidaris. Executive producer, Michael Donohew. Written and directed by Andy Sidaris. Camera (United color), Howard Wexler; editor, Michael Haight; music, Gary Stockdale; sound, Neil Wolfson; production design, Peter Munneke; art direction, Mark Haskins; assistant director, M.M. Freedman; karate choreography, Harold Diamond; costumes, Fionn; second unit camera, Harmon Lougher; casting, Tom Stockfisch. Reviewed at Magno preview 4 screening room, N.Y., May 25, 1988. MPAA Rating: R. Running time: **99 MIN.**

Travis Abilene . . . . .Steve Bond
Donna . . . . .Dona Speir
Taryn . . . . .Hope Marie Carlton
Jade . . . . .Harold Diamond
Picasso Trigger . . . . .John Aprea
Pantera . . . . .Roberta Vasquez
L.G. Abilene . . . . .Guich Koock

Also with: Rodrigo Obregon, Cynthia Brimhall, Bruce Penhall, Dennis Alexio, John Brown, Kym Malin, Patty Dufek, Liv Lindeland, Wolf Larson, Rustam Branaman, Richard LePore.

"Picasso Trigger" is a campy action picture jampacked with beautiful women and musclebound hunks. In regional release since February, pic is likely to arouse considerable interest in ancillary markets.

Filmmakers Andy and Arlene Sidaris' gimmick is that all seven "Picasso" leading ladies are former Playboy magazine models. Dona Speir and Hope Marie Carlton encore from the previous opus from the Sidarises, "Hard Ticket To Hawaii," as two government agents stationed in Molokai. They're called in to join the international team to stop Salazar, a.k.a. Picasso Trigger (John Aprea), who's sent his henchmen to assassinate the agents who got his brother.

Organized by L.G. Abilene (Guich Koock), who is one of the marked men, team is headed by Travis Abilene (former soap star Steve Bond) and includes a motley group of fighting experts (including Harold Diamond, another "Hard Ticket" alumnus) and bombshells (Cynthia Brimhall, Kym Malin, Patty Duffek). Also on board is the voluptuous but suspicious-looking foreign agent Pantera (Roberta Vasquez), who coincidentally was Travis' sweetheart in college.

With many cute gadgets, including toy plane, car and dynamite-laden boomerang, injected into the action, film plays firmly tongue-in-cheek as a comic strip approach to international intrigue. All the characters and thesps are larger than life, with silly bon mots peppering the dialog. Episodic format, with too much time addressed to side issues or rounding up the team, is a drawback.

Acting is variable, with most of the cast used to posing rather than reading lines. Bond, recently miscast in a West German period piece "Silent Night," is convincing as the hero who can't shoot straight, allowing his lovely costars to assert themselves in the killing and self-defense departments. Speir and Carlton are enthusiastic, uninhibited heroines with newcomer Vasquez making a strong impression as the villainess.

Playboy fans will be glad to see Liv Lindeland again, looking great and delivering a couple of funny lines (her film career peaked with a character role in "Save The Tiger" 15 years back).

Tech credits including numerous explosions are fine, with atmospheric location photography in Hawaii, Texas and Louisiana. —*Lor.*

CANNES REVIEWS

Manifesto

A Cannon Group release and production. Executive producers, Michael J. Kagan, Tom Luddy. Produced by Menahem Golan, Yoram Globus. Written and directed by Dusan Makavejev, inspired by "For A Night Of Love" by Emile Zola. Camera (Rank color), Tomislav Pinter; editor, Tony Lawson; music, Nicola Piovani; production design, Veljko Despotovic; sound, Drew Kunin; costumes, Marit Allen; associate producer/casting, Bojana Marijan; production managers, Peter Cotton, Gorjan Tuzija; assistant director, Dejan Karaklajic; stunts, Ivo Kristof. Reviewed at Ambassades theater, Cannes, May 20, 1988. Running time: **94 MIN.**

Svetlana	Camilla Søeberg
Avanti	Alfred Molina
Hunt	Simon Callow
Christopher	Eric Stoltz
Lily Sachor	Lindsay Duncan
Emile	Rade Serbedzija
Rudi	Svetozar Cvetkovic
Wango	Chris Haywood
Dr. Lombrosow	Patrick Godfrey
Stella	Linda Marlowe
Tina	Gabrielle Anwar
The King	Enver Petrovci

Also with: Ronald Lacey (Conductor), Tanja Boskovic (Olympia), Zeljko Duvnjak (Martin), Danko Ljustina (Baker).

Cannes — Privately sneaked during Cannes (not as part of the fest market), Dusan Makavejev's latest, **"Manifesto," turns out to be a chirpy, quirky, erotic and visually lush charmer. Mellow in tone, it contains many of this director's most characteristic ideas about sex and revolution, and though not as tough as his very best work, still looms as a good arthouse bet.**

Makavejev's previous films were made in Australia, Sweden and Canada, but the setting of his new one is his native Yugoslavia, specifically the glorious picture-postcard village of Skofja Loka in Slovenia, named Waldheim in the picture, which is set in 1920 in an unnamed central European country.

As an opening title has it, the new governments that appeared after the fall of the great empires took themselves very seriously, and "life became hard for revolutionaries; however, ice-cream was sold and enjoyed..." Film centers around a half-hearted attempt to assassinate the country's king, but both the would-be assassins and the secret police seem more interested in matters of the flesh.

Makavejev has found another of his typical, beauteous heroines in Danish actress Camilla Søeberg ("Twist And Shout"); she plays Svetlana, an ingenue returning to her home town after a spell in the city and concealing, in her frilly knickers, a gun with which the king will be killed. Svetlana is welcomed by her widowed mother (Linda Marlowe) and a shy young postal worker (Eric Stoltz) who has loved her from afar for years.

Less pleasant, initially, is the interruption of her evening bath by the arrival of Emile (Rade Serbedzija), a macho servant in the family house who had seduced her as a young girl; Svetlana's loathing for this brute is matched by her lust for him, resulting in the first of several spirited coupling scenes in the film.

Also in town is Avanti (Alfred Molina), head of the secret police, who leads a band of comic cops trying to root out subversives. Avanti is more interested in pursuing pretty women, whether middle-aged, like Svetlana's mother, or very young, like the nymphet (Gabrielle Anwar) who sells ice-cream in the town square.

Other characters include Aussie actor Chris Haywood as a crazy photographer who performs complicated sexual acts with his pretty model; Simon Callow as the incompetent chief of police; Lindsay Duncan, a highly moral schoolteacher who winds up an ardent revolutionary; and Svetozar Cvetkovic as the would-be asssassin who's been arrested and placed in the Bergman Sanitorium, run by doctor Patrick Godfrey.

Makavejev throws all these characters into a melting pot that contains plenty of sex and nudity, quite a few sly jokes, and occasional sharp barbs at revolutionaries and corrupt officialdom. Wide-eyed children and animals are frequent witnesses to all the mayhem, with a clutch of tiny puppies incongruously present when Emile gets accidentally killed and wrapped in a carpet, whereupon people keep politely stepping over him.

With or without her clothes, Camilla Søeberg is a charming heroine, and indeed all the players are good, with Alfred Molina (in complete contrast to his role in "Prick Up Your Ears") a standout. Tomislav Pinter's camerawork perfectly captures the beauty of the small-town setting and the unclad femmes.

Feminists may balk at some scenes, but Makavejev's films have always been filled with sex-loving characters, and this one is too. There may be disappointment that the ruthless political satire of the director's early work is absent, as it has been from his last few films, or that the plot (based on an Emile Zola story filmed several times before) is so often shunted aside in favor of more cavortings.

There's a perky music score from Nicola Piovani, fine production dress, and delightful animated credits at the start and end of this charming, gently amusing and very typical Makavejev film. No doubt it will compete at a major fest later this summer. —*Strat.*

The Suitors

An Ebra Films production. Produced, written and directed by Ghasem Ebrahimian. Camera (color), Manfred Reiff; editor, Ebrahimian; sound, Amir Naderi; sound, Tommy Louie; music, Nicholas Kean, F. Shabazian, A. Veseghi. Reviewed at Cannes Film Festival (Directors Fortnight), May 22, 1988. Running time: **106 MIN.**

With: Pouran Esrafily, Ali Azizian, Shahab Navab, Assurbanipal Babila, Bahman Maghsoudlou, Manuchehr Harsini.

Cannes — "The Suitors" is an off-beat, sometimes intriguing pic about a group of Iranians in New York who, by trying to maintain tradition, trigger a series of tragic events. Item, largely spoken in Farsi, could find a select audience in arthouse circuits as an oddity.

A group of Iranians decide to sacrifice a sheep in an apartment, but their harmless idea is misinterpreted by the police, who mistake the group for terrorists. A SWAT team is dispatched to handle the situation, and some of the Iranians are killed in the action.

The widow of one of those killed aspires to break away from the strict veil-wearing confines of her life. After knifing one of her new suitors, she urges a second to take her along with him to Europe. After being refused passage at the airport due to her not having a passport, the pretty widow convinces her suitor to pack her into a suitcase and ship her off as luggage, but at the last moment the widow thinks better of it and slips out.

Low-budget pic shows some promise, and its esoteric story and underground milieu are sure to find some enthusiasts on the fest circuit. —*Besa.*

Dolunay
(Full Moon)
(TURKISH)

An Art Film production and release. Written and directed by Şahin Kaygun, based on the novel "Calypso" by Guseli Inal. Camera (color), Salih Dikisci; art direction, Mihri Nur; music, Server Acim. Reviewed at the Istanbul Film Festival, April 15, 1988. (In Cannes Film Festival Intl. Critics Week.) Running time: **100 MIN.**

Girl	Asli Altan
Ömer	Macit Koper
Ahmet	Kenan Bal

Istanbul — A delicate, poetic film about a young woman painter unable to overcome a creative block, "Full Moon" points up director Şahin Kaygun, a well-known photographer on his second feature, as a newcomer to be watched in Turkey. Film's strong visual sense and stately musical rhythm should encourage art house programmers looking for quality from faraway places.

There's noting particularly Turkish about the tale, though setting, on a magnificent island in the Aegean, is one of the film's attractions. Asli Altan is a young painter who hasn't set brush to canvas in two years, prey to a mysterious psychological malaise. Her husband of four years, Kenan Bal, is already forgetting wedding anniversaries and shows no sympathy for his wife's melancholic languishing.

The arrival of the husband's bosom buddy Ömer (Turkey's most versatile thesp, Macit Koper, in a double role) sets emotions going. In a series of flashbacks — no more than strictly necessary — the girl remembers her mad uncle, Ömer's lookalike, who taught her to paint. His candlelit cellar studio appears over and over again, evoked by the woman's contact with Ömer, now her lover. With Freudian recall, she relives her attraction to her uncle, who paints her lips red, rages against the world of human beings, and dies mad.

Excellent lighting and lensing highlight the breathtaking seascape and fine art direction. Score by Server Acim is a brief, moving theme, unfortunately repeated too often. Altan is not an actress of great range, but her moody contemporary beauty and low voice fit pic to a tee; her inexpressiveness masking tragic passion reads as the outward sign of her inward block. Ending in a murder is a disappointingly facile way to conclude a story that seems more complex. — *Yung.*

The Fruit Machine
(BRITISH)

A Vestron Pictures release of a Granada Films, Ideal Communications production. Produced by Steve Morrison. Coproducer, Robbie Douet. Directed by Philip Saville. Screenplay, Frank Clarke; camera (color), Dick Pope; editor, Richard Bedford; music, Hans Zimmer; production designer, David

Brockhurst. Reviewed at Cannes Film Festival (market), May 20, 1988. Running time: **102 MIN.**

Eddie . . . . Emile Charles
Michael . . . . Tony Forsyth
Opera singer . . . . Robert Stephens
Manager . . . . Clare Higgins
Killer . . . . Bruce Payne
Annabelle . . . . Robbie Coltrane

Cannes — This insouciant, adolescent gay romance is bound to appeal to specialized audiences who might brush up on Liverpudlian dialect or otherwise face some difficulty following the dialog.

Film starts on a light tone, halfheartedly attempting to develop in its second half some serious pretensions, vindicated by the downbeat ending.

Eddie and Michael are two homosexual teenagers who decide to elope together. Eddie is the shy, innocent, girlish type, Michael, the hustler making a living on the streets.

Together they stumble into a gay nightclub and accidentally witness the murder of its owner at the hand of a pro killer with a machete. Once he discovers their presence, he sets out to silence them permanently.

They escape and manage to find temporary shelter with an aging opera singer, with whom they drive from Liverpool to Brighton. The killer finally catches up with them, at the Marine Wonderland, among the dolphins with whom Eddie has identified time and again in his dreams.

Fastpaced and efficiently written, plot moves along briskly without quite deciding what direction to embark upon. Hesitating between love story and thriller, satire and ecological militancy, the picture wavers in between and never fully commits itself.

Its strength lies, however, in the lively performances of Charles and Forsyth, highly polished photography by Dick Pope and impeccable production by British tv giant Granada, in another one of its attempts to break into theatrical distribution. —*Edna.*

Hell Hunters
(WEST GERMAN)

A Cinevest/Cinevision presentation of a TAT/Heart Of Darkness production. Executive producers, Roman S. Von Rupp, Lou Paciocco. Produced and directed by Ernst R. von Theumer. Screenplay, James D'Alessandro, Louis Russo 2d; camera (color), Mario De Leo; editor, David Blewitt; associate producer, Monica Teuber. Reviewed at Cannes Film Festival (market), May 20, 1988. Running time: **98 MIN.**

Dr. Martin Hoffman . . . . . Stewart Granger
Heinrich . . . . George Lazenby
Amanda . . . . Maud Adams
Karl . . . . William Berger
El Pasado . . . . Eduardo Conde
Ally . . . . Candice Daly
Tonio . . . . Romulo Arantes
Kong . . . . Russ McCubbin
Nelia . . . . Nelia Cozza

Cannes — Stewart Granger must've been thinking about something else when he signed on for this one. "Hell Hunters" is an in-

credulous actioner with about as much depth as a kiddie's pool and just as exciting; formula action element, however, and Granger's moniker, will no doubt propel it onto homevideo shelves and the small screen.

Scheming surviving Nazi Martin Hoffman (Granger) has developed a serum from a jungle spider venom that, inexplicably, makes people open to fascist doctrine; he plans to introduce it into L.A.'s water supply as a test run, but is found by beautiful Nazi hunter Amanda (Maud Adams), who's married Hoffman's nephew (William Berger) just so she can get into the doctor's compound, hidden in the jungles of Paraguay.

She in turn is found out and killed by the doctor's sadistic henchman, El Pasado (Eduardo Conde); daughter Ally (Candice Daly) finds out and becomes embroiled in the search for her mother's diaries, which pinpoint the doctor's secret location, aided by macho Tonio (Romulo Arantes), who knew her mother. From there it's stock seek out and destroy, coupled with the addition of gung ho helpers Kong (Russ McCubbin) and Nelia (Nelia Cozza), who naturally get together at pic's end, as of course do Ally and Tonio despite the initial coolness between them.

All of them, strangely, can shoot and fight par excellence, and never get hurt, although lots of villains do. Thesping is uninspiring, particularly the wooden scenes between Arantes and Daly. Granger isn't the slightest bit sinister. Suspense is nil. Tech credits, though, are good. —*Doch.*

Herseye Ragman
(Despite Everything)
(TURKISH)

A Mine Film production and release. Directed by Orhan Oguz. Screenplay, Nuray Oguz; camera (color), Orhan Oguz; editor, Eral Sahin; music, Cahit Berkay. Reviewed at Cannes Film Festival (Directors Fortnight), May 18, 1988. Running time: **96 MIN.**

With: Talat Bulut (Hasan), Serif Sezer, Bulent Oran, Hakan Ciraci.

Cannes — "Despite Everything" is a delicate first film by Orhan Oguz, a prizewining director of photography. Simple tale about a lonely hearse-driver is a touching story that seeks to go deep inside the character's psyche.

Result is almost a minimalist, 3-character film with a real feel for Turkish life. Shot in a square tv format, it should interest cultural channels abroad as well as fest playoffs.

Hasan (Talat Bulut) has been the victim of a bad childhood. Film opens when he gets out of prison, an introverted, alienated man unable to communicate with others. His sister's death leaves him all alone in the world. He reluctantly takes a job as the hearse driver for a Protestant

church and survives in a depressing 1-room apartment, where he has nightmares about being trapped in his hearse by a woman's giant breasts.

Though sentiments are delicate, Oguz is heavy-handed with the funeral music that too obviously underlines Hasan's inconsolable sadness. Then he meets Ayse, a young widow with a son. Hasan feels more attracted by the boy than the woman, whose loose morals are signaled by the fact she smokes and drinks beer. After she moves in on Hasan, she also prostitutes herself. Hasan's faint hope for a normal married life evaporates, but despite everything, at least he has the little boy around to cheer him up.

Film builds great sympathy for its unhappy hero, though mediocre lensing and technical quality somewhat undercut the film's virtues. — *Yung.*

Deadly Addiction

A JJV Motion Pictures production. Executive producer, John James. Written and directed by Jack Vacek. Camera (color), Tony Syslo; music, John Cascella; production manager, Jeffrey Davis; designer, Ron Morris; associate producer, Michael Brennan. Reviewed at Cannes Film Festival (market), May 21, 1988. Runing time: **97 MIN.**

With: Joseph Jennings, Michael Robbin, Alan Shearer, Trice Shubert, Jack Vacek.

Cannes — A stock shoot 'em up police actioner, "Deadly Addiction" is a hardly memorable addition to the genre, with the exception of one or two car stunts. It's an item strictly for cable and lowerend homevideo.

John Turner (Joseph Jennings) is a cop hell bent on sweeping the streets of Hollywood clean of drug-dealers following the death of his wife. He sets his sights on one particular drug ring following a run-in, and the rest of the film sees him tracking down the syndicate's big guns.

It's peppered with car chases — one has a spectacular ending — and innumerable gun battles, but the sum total — and there's a lot of chasing, shooting and blasting away gong on — is a yawn. Jennings and his romantic interest Trice Schubert, playing a freelance photographer doing a piece on kids involved in drug crime, are pretty wooden and, annoyingly, virtually indestructible given the number of bullets aimed their way.

Although formula-driven, pic has solid tech credits. — *Doch.*

Hawks
(BRITISH)

A Skouras Pictures release of a Barry Gibb/David English presentation, in association with Producer Representative Organization. (Sales, Manson Intl.) Produced by Steve Lanning, Keith Cavele. Executive producers, Morrie Eisenman, Richard Beck-

er. Directed by Robert Ellis Miller. Screenplay, Roy Clarke; camera (Rank color), Doug Milsome; editor, Malcolm Cooke; music, Barry Gibb; production design, Peter Howitt; costumes, Cathy Cooke; sound, Brian Simmons; assistant director, David Tringham; casting, Mary Selway. Reviewed at Cannes Film Festival (market), May 20, 1988. Running time: **107 MIN.**

Bancroft . . . . Timothy Dalton
Decker . . . . Anthony Edwards
Hazel . . . . Janet McTeer
Maureen . . . . Camille Coduri
Nurse Jarvis . . . . Connie Booth
Sister . . . . Julie T. Wallace
Walter . . . . Robert Lang
Vivian . . . . Jill Bennett
Byron . . . . Bruce Boa
Millie . . . . Pat Starr
Carol . . . . Caroline Langrishe
Regina . . . . Sheila Hancock

Cannes — This black comedy about terminal cancer patients escaping for one last fling stares death in the face and laughs, but takes too long to get to the punch line.

Quirky performance by Timothy Dalton post-James Bond should spark some interest in a limited release, but overall returns loom brighter offshore.

From the start, it's clear that director Robert Ellis Miller is using Roy Clarke's script about men facing an early death to examine how people deal with their fears and how they try or fail to disguise it from others. In this instance, terminal bone cancer pits lawyer Bancroft (Timothy Dalton) and ex-football pro Decker (Anthony Edwards) together in a team effort to thwart their disease (and the ward nurses) with laughs, grit and a last pilgrimage to a Dutch bordello.

Edwards as the jock initially is suicidal as his body betrays him, while Bancroft, whose cancer is less debilitating and slower to progress, urges his ward-mate to fight the good fight with humor and determination not to lie down and take it. Bancroft despises his fate as much as Decker does, but he's determined to go out screaming and kicking, savoring every last bit life has to offer.

This includes crashing Bancroft's ex-flame's wedding on their way to Holland in a stolen ambulance, at which point the duo's moods reverse — Decker's outlook turns optimistic, with prospect of scoring, while Bancroft broods about the g.f. who left him to deal solo with his fate. His mood fails to improve when they're sidetracked by Hazel (Janet McTeer) and Maureen (Camille Coduri), two English girls with car trouble on their way to visit Hazel's Dutch boyfriend.

That's because Decker and perky blond Maureen take an instant liking to each other, while the now-sullen Bancroft considers the plain, gawky Hazel an unpleasant interruption on their sojourn. Neither side knows the others' secret — that the men are terminally ill or that Hazel is pregnant, and initialy it stays that way.

Comic misinterpretation ensues

as girls aim to surprise their new friends at "Hotel Paradise," in fact a 4-story whorehouse, allowing director Miller to engage in kinky voyeurism from p.o.v. of the inexperienced (but more than curious) Hazel. Denouement comes when both sides learn what the other's hiding, leading to a tenderly funny love scene between Hazel and Bancroft in which he lets down his callous facade in response to Hazel's lustful (if clumsy) sincerity.

But death won't wait any longer, and reality of their situation quickly becomes evident, leading to a tear-jerker death scene virtually sans dialog that displays Miller's deft touch and Dalton's and Edwards' acting ability. Epilog, however, ends pic on truly upbeat note — too bad it takes so long to get there.

Dalton goes a bit overboard as Bancroft, occasionally stretching believability. Edwards plays it straight as the Yank jock, but brings out the laconic ladies' man in his character despite being nonambulatory much of the time.

Standout thesping is turned in by Janet McTeer, the clumsy, unsure Hazel. Her anxious bedroom turn with Dalton is memorable (as are her giraffe-length legs), and overall perf is on the mark.

Editing is iffy, with choppy transitions throughout. Other tech credits are okay. Barry Gibb's music was unobtrusive until end credits. —*Mich.*

Dangerous Game
(AUSTRALIAN)

A Quantum Films presentation of a Virgo Prods. picture (international sales, MCEG Intl.). Produced by Judith West and Basil Appleby. Executive producer, Robert Mercieca. Directed by Stephen Hopkins. Screenplay, Peter West; camera (color), Peter Levy; editor, Tim Wellburn, production design, Igor Nay; music, Les Gock, Steve Ball. Reviewed at Cannes Film Festival (market), May 16, 1988. Running time: **98 MIN.**
David Forrest . . . . Miles Buchanan
Jack Hayward . . . . Marcus Graham
Patrick Murphy . . . . Steven Grives
Ziggy . . . . Sandie Lillingston
Kathryn . . . . Kathryn Walker
Tony . . . . John Polson

Cannes — "Dangerous Game" is the latest in a series of thrillers to come out of Oz over the past year, and it's a compelling contribution to the genre, while marking a winning feature debut for helmer **Stephen Hopkins.** Theatrical playoff potential would seem to be good, if pic is aimed at a teen to mid-20s audience.

Somewhat implausible, ponderous beginning is a fault, but that's forgotten as the pic's scenario, plausible or not, neatly gathers momentum.

Jack Hayward (Marcus Graham) is being harassed by obsessive cop Patrick Murphy (Steven Grives) because he believes Hayward's now-deceased father, once Murphy's superior, is responsible for his poor police record.

Harassment goes too far when Murphy smashes his motorcycle — it's a superb stunt sequence — in pursuit of Hayward for allegedly speeding. He's suspended, which worsens his near psychotic state.

Meanwhile, wisemouth computer whiz David Forrest (Miles Buchanan), in a bet with Hayward, taps into the computer system of a large city department store to trigger the opening of a security door. Duo, with girlfriends Ziggy (Sandie Lillingston) and Kathryn (Kathryn Walker) and friend Tony (John Polson) naturally go and check to see if the door opens on cue.

It does, and curiosity spurs them to enter, only to be followed by Murphy, who locks the door. Thus begins a game of cat and mouse, at first with intentions to scare, not harm, on Murphy's part, until Tony is killed accidentally by Murphy, who then snaps and rounds the group up one by one. Tense climax and twist ending are highly satisfactory.

It's hardly cerebral, but Hopkins artfully builds pace and tension, particularly for Murphy's initial scare tactics. Likewise, he more than provides a fair share of well orchestrated action, topped off by some spectacular stunt work.

Five young actors — most making their feature debut — credibly display their fear and horror. High praise must go to pic's editors and production designers; shop interior, complete with elevators, is the largest indoor set yet constructed in Oz, and it's most effective.

It's no secret "Dangerous Game" is a thriller that sparks off action rather than a twist-filled plot, and that, combined with the ages portrayed (all are young university students) in the terrorized group, would indicate healthy potential in the youth market. —*Doch.*

Bad Taste
(NEW ZEALAND)

A Wingnut Films production. Produced, written and directed by Peter Jackson. Consultant producer, Tony Hiles. Additional script, Tony Hiles, Ken Hammon; camera (color), Jackson, postproduction supervisor, Jamie Selkirk; music, Michelle Scullion. Reviewed at Odeon Theater, Palmerston North, N.Z., April 11, 1988. (In Cannes Film Festival Market.) Running time: **92 MIN.**
Derek . . . . Peter Jackson
Frank . . . . Mike Minett
Barry . . . . Pete O'Herne
Ozzie . . . . Terry Potter
Giles . . . . Craig Smith
Crumb . . . . Doug Wren

Palmerston North, N.Z. — Boy's Own Fodder Horror comes closest to describing "Bad Taste," an outstandingly awful, at times awfully brilliant, first feature from Peter Jackson. Its faults are many, from badly setup opening and some inept playing through to over-extended scenes that shriek for the scissors. Yet, at fade out, a bravura registers, causing a smile not a smirk, that an-

nounces the arrival of a new and considerable talent to the small band in the Kiwi film industry.

Made on the proverbial shoestring over 4½ years by dedicated writer-director-producer (Jackson also plays a lead role and takes credit for cinematography, special effects and makeup), "Bad Taste" generally belies its lengthy, haphazard birth.

Derek (Jackson) and his gang of not-so-merry men from the Alien Investigation and Defense Service are on a search and destroy mission. A small town has been depopulated by aliens planning to promote homo sapiens as low-calorie delicacies on their intergalactic fastfood chain.

Derek is a casualty (almost) in the early stages of the bloody, entrails-ripping battle, while an unwitting charity collector Giles (Craig Smith) penetrates alien headquarters only to be clobbered and marinated for the invaders' victory feast.

All is not lost. In a big showdown, a stunning array of weapons decimates the aliens with Derek finally wreaking terrible personal vengeance — in space — upon the sinister Lord Crumb (Doug Wren).

While the gristle and gore are enough to turn the strongest stomach, there are moments that twist the grotesque to sudden delight.

Such occurs when the head of an alien, like a football, is neatly booted out a window, to the line: "The old magic's still there!"

With so much blood spilled, spurted and occasionally slurped, it would seem in keeping with the ironic, anarchic energy of the film that Derek's boys should be employees of an organization, the initials of which spell out AIDS.

Jackson, Smith and Wren (marvelously voiced-over as Lord Crumb by Peter Vere-Jones) are the best thesps on view.

"Bad Taste's" unevenness and tendency towards jokiness of particular Kiwi taste and sound may make it difficult to market theatrically overseas. What the film certainly does, however, is serve notice that Jackson's next picture will be one to look out for. —*Nic.*

Living Dreams

A Rough Beast production. (Sales, Films Around the World.) Executive producer, Victor Sher. Produced, written and directed by Alan Greenberg. Camera (Duart color), Orson Ochoa; editor, Sheryl Riley; music, Andrew Rosen, Raul Murciano, John Salton; sound, Dick Bomser, Lenny Hirshtritt; production manager-coproducer, Stan Bickman; codirector, Sher; associate producer, Stephen Levien. Reviewed at Cannes Film Festival (market), May 19, 1988. Running time: **91 MIN.**
Martica . . . . Martica
Fred . . . . Gary Keats
Victor Sher . . . . Victor Sher
Nick Jamster . . . . Nick Amster
Numero Uno . . . . Xavier Orosz
T. Valentine . . . . Steve Zimmerman
Jill . . . . Jill Kahn
Lucille . . . . Donna Day

Fidel Castro . . . . Ramses Naser
T.V.'s sister . . . . Cherry Doctor

Cannes — "Living Dreams" is an off-the-wall, underground comedy that serves more as an audition feature for helmer Alan Greenberg (a scripter for Werner Herzog with one previous docu to his credit) than a fully realized film. Commercial prospects are for cult viewers only.

Miami-set yarn concerns a bunch of oddballs who hang out at the Numero Uno nightclub. They all have pipe dreams: club owner Numero Uno (Xavier Orosz) hopes to invade Cuba, using as a Mata Hari to get to Castro his featured singer Martica. Victor Sher plays himself, a European emigré making a movie (he's exec producer of "Living Dreams" and addresses the viewer directly from time to time). Gary Keats gives the best performance as a gay Vietnam vet who segues into Flannery O'Connor's "Wise Blood" when he suddenly forms the Church Of God Without God.

Episodic format doesn't hold together well and the acting (particularly by the women) is rough and ready. Steve Zimmerman and Nick Amster provide welcome comedy routines as respectively a rap singer from Brooklyn and a hipster record promoter. Tech credits are low-budget. — *Lor.*

Noujoum A'Nahar
(Daytime Stars)
(SYRIAN)

An Organisme National du Cinema (Damascus) production. Written and directed by Oussama Mohammad. Camera (color), Abdel Kader Charbaji; editor, Antoinette Azaria; music, traditional; sound, Emile Saade, H. Salem, A. Kaook. Reviewed at Cannes Film Fest (Directors Fortnight), May 23, 1988. Running time: **105 MIN.**
With: Abdellatif Abdelhamid, Zouher Ramadan, Zouher Abdel-Karim, Mana Al Saleh, Saba Al Salem, Saddin Bakdounes.

Cannes — Drama of life in a small Syrian village, structured around a lengthy wedding celebration, Oussama Mohammad's first feature, "Daytime Stars," is best described as a worthy effort.

Impact of modernization on village life is indicated, as well as the dense set of sometimes bitter rivalries that erupt into violence.

Print shown in Cannes had an appallingly scratched and battered first reel, and looked murky throughout. Additionally, subtitles were often almost illegible. Strictly for those interested in developments in Arab cinema.—*Strat.*

Frankenstein General Hospital
(COLOR/B&W)

A New Star Entertainment production and release. Produced by Dimitri Villard. Executive producer, Robby Wald. Directed by Deborah Roberts. Screenplay, Michael Kelly, Robert Deel, from novel "Frankenstein" by Mary Shelley; camera (color, b&w), Tom Fraser; editor, Ed Lotter; music, John Ross; sound, Izak Ben-Meir; production design, Don Day; assistant director, Michael Grossman; production manager, Whitney Hunter; makeup effects, Doug White; stunt coordinator, Bud Graves; second unit director, Villard; postproduction supervisor, Gardner Monks; casting, Kevin Alber. Reviewed on New Star vidcassette, N.Y., May 27, 1988. (In Cannes Film Festival Market.) MPAA Rating: R. Running time: **92 MIN.**

Dr. Bob Frankenstein	Mark Blankfield
Iggy	Leslie Jordan
Dr. Frank Reutger	Jonathan Farwell
Dr. Alice Singleton	Kathy Shower
Monster	Irwin Keyes
Dr. Andrew Dixon	Hamilton Mitchell
Dr. Saperstein	Lou Cutell
Nurse Verna	Katie Caple

Also with: Dorothy Patterson, Bobby (Boris) Pickett.

"Frankenstein General Hospital" is a rather flat sendup of horror films, closer to aping "Young Doctors In Love" than Mel Brooks' classic "Young Frankenstein." In regional release since March, it's headed for homevideo.

Mark Blankfield, who unsuccessfully sent up another genre classic in Paramount's flop "Jekyll & Hyde … Together Again," toplines as Dr. Bob Frankenstein, great-great-grandson of the legendary scientist, who's busy experimenting on the creation of a perfect human in the basement of General Hospital where he works. Gag of all the downstairs scenes being in black & white offers a pleasant visual variation.

Saddled with dumb puns and lots of running gags that don't work, nearly plotless film proceeds by fits and starts, with an occasional, brief topless scene by former Playboy magazine model Kathy Shower (cast unconvincingly as the hospital shrink) or voluptuous nurse Katie Caple to liven things up. Blankfield is hamstrung by the weak material; ditto his diminutive assistant Iggy, played unfunnily by Leslie Jordan.

In casting reminiscent of the 1940s films of Rondo Hatton, distorted-featured Irwin Keyes plays the monster with little makeup required; it works for a while, but Keyes is far too normal looking and unscary to support the latter reels when he's supposedly on the rampage upstairs in the hospital and everyone screams at the sight of him.

Tech credits are acceptable.
—*Lor.*

P.S. Sista sommaren
(P.S. Last Summer)
(SWEDISH)

A Sonet Film release of an Omega Film production in association with the Swedish Film Institute, Sandrews, Four Seasons Venture Capital and Sonet Media. Produced by Mats Arehn, Peter Kropénin. Written and directed by Thomas Samuelsson, based on the novel by Bo Green Jensen. Camera (Fujicolor), Mischa Gaurjusjov; editor, Susanne Lindmann; music, Ola Hakansson, Tim Norell, others; art direction, Martin Jonsson.

Reviewed at Cannes Film Festival (market), May 19, 1988. Running time: **97 MIN.**

Lisa	Lena Nilsson
Matte	Patrick Stenman
Kranken	Roberto Jelinek

Cannes — "P.S. Last Summer," the feature bow of Sweden's Thomas Samuelsson, has made a mint at home. A youth film with a minuscule thriller element, it's airy and light as a summer wind and may well blow into a few offshore pickups.

Three kids in their late teens — Matte, Kranken and the girl Lisa — spend their holiday camping on a Baltic Sea island. Lisa sleeps with one, then the other, so the idyll is threatened.

She says nobody owns her. The idyll is restored, then threatened in various ways. A couple of middle-aged campers try to lure the kids into their private den of vice. Kranken is sought by the police, but there's no charge. At the end, a gang of hoodlums attack the sleeping kids and Lisa is saved from being raped by Kranken, who gets knifed.

What's important is the interplay among the three youths, who speak and act with natural ease. There is plenty of international quality Swedish rock. Only the rough stuff seems pasted on, which it is, since there was none of it in the book on which Samuelsson based his screenplay. — *Kell.*

Kyoshu
(Remembrance)
(JAPANESE)

A Project A production. (World Sales: Shibata Organization.) Produced by Hiroshi Ishikawa, Tetsuo Konda, Shinsuke Achida. Executive producers, Shunji Oki, Yoshinori Takazawa. Written and directed by Takehiro Nakajima. Camera (color), Junichiro Hayashi; music, Toshinoori Kondo. Reviewed at Cannes Film Festival (market), May 20, 1988. Running time: **115 MIN.**

With: Hiroshi Nishikawa, Sairi Komaki, Kazuko Yoshiyuki, Masahiro Tsugawa, Kirin Kiki, Takaaki Enomoto, Cacy Takamine, Arase.

Cannes — "Remembrance" is a beautiful and very assured first feature in which writer-director Takehiro Nakajima looks back at his childhood in a fishing village in the early '50s. Tender tale breathes fresh life into the autobiog genre.

Central character is Sumio, a 15-year-old who lives with his sister Yasuko and his mother. They're struggling to make ends meet since Sumio's father, a painter, left his family to live with his mistress, a restaurant owner, in a neighboring town.

For much of the film, Sumio is a silent observer of the fate of his older sister, who falls in love with a schoolteacher. Her mother won't let them marry, purely for financial reasons. The teacher marries someone else, and Yasuko is reduced to

working in a bar, where she meets various men, some of whom she sleeps with. Eventually, she leaves for the city and an uncertain future.

Sumio, meanwhile, struggles with his schoolwork, becomes tentatively friendly with the son of his father's mistress, and experiences sex for the first time with a willing girl. But he has major lessons to learn, and the departure of his beloved sister is a terrible blow.

The film is made up of dozens of minor incidents reflecting life in this backwater town (pic was filmed in the same village where Nakajima spent his youth). There is the communal bathhouse, where the boys spy on the girls and sing rude songs; the bars and the cinema; also the tramp woman who'll expose herself to eager schoolboys in return for some food. Sumio's best friend dies from a fit, and he gets beaten up when he accompanies a couple of schoolfriends on a trip outside the village.

From the start, with images of the father's paintings seen through the ripples of a stream into which they've fallen, the film is a visually rich experience.

"Remembrance" already has played the Honolulu, Rotterdam and Hong Kong fests, and deserves further exposure. Arthouses also could take a look at this very lovely film. —*Strat.*

The Decline Of Western Civilization Part II: The Metal Years
(DOCU)

A New Line Cinema release of an I.R.S. World Media production. Produced by Jonathan Dayton, Valerie Faris. Executive producers, Miles Copeland 3d, Paul Colichman. Directed by Penelope Spheeris. Camera (Foto-kem color), Jeff Zimmerman; editor, Earl Ghaffari; sound, Mark Hanes; associate producer, Guy Louthan. Reviewed at Filmland Screening Room, Culver City, Calif., May 23, 1988. (In Cannes Film Festival Market.) MPAA Rating: R. Running time: **90 MIN.**

With: Joe Perry, Steven Tyler of Aerosmith; Alice Cooper; Gene Simmons and Paul Stanley of Kiss; Lemmy of Motorhead; Ozzy Osbourne, Chris Holmes, Tawn Mastrey, Bill Gazzarri.

Hollywood — In "The Decline Of Western Civilization Part II: The Metal Years," documentarian director Penelope Spheeris takes a hard-edged look at heavy-metal rock and stuff like that. To her credit, she tries to tackle a mindless subject with intelligence and stuff like that. There's little appeal here beyond the bunch who say stuff like that about stuff like that. Boxoffice will likely just be stuffed.

Certainly, "Metal" displays enough music and musicians, cursing and craziness to satisfy basic fans, which is presumably the producers' intent. The film never really tries — even if it were possible — to distinguish heavy-metal

rock from any other kind and the outrageousness of the practitioners seems no different now than ever.

As one fellow defines it, "If the parents hate it, it's rock 'n' roll." Thus it ever has been.

No harm, though, when the beat is good. Spheeris and crew do an excellent job of capturing that in various clubs around L.A., but her interviews wander pointlessly and repetitively, rarely accomplishing any communication beyond the Cromagnon and self-consciously cute.

The conceit, of course, is that there's something shockingly new in all of this. Except for the age group aimed for, the struggles, frustrations and excess energy of this subculture is just the same old showbiz story told anew.

Spheeris can't be faulted for an obviously sincere effort to douse drug use. Over and over, most of her subjects decry the devastating effects. As usual, though, these warnings come within the inevitable message that sex, drugs and rock 'n' roll still are the anthem for the next generation seeking fun.

There is one brutally effective interview with rocker Chris Holmes, floating drunkenly and fully dressed in his swimming pool, opening quarts of vodka he splashed down his gullet. "I'm a piece of crap and a full-blown alcoholic," Holmes boasts, adding he's not looking forward to a long life enjoying gold records. As Holmes concedes, "I don't like being the person I am," Spheeris gently pans to a closeup on his mother sitting poolside. It's a hauntingly sad look on mom's face.

Other scenes seem contrived by comparison. She interviews handsome Paul Stanley of Kiss on a bed being stroked by three beautiful scantily clad girls. If this is a real scene, Spheeris might have taken the opportunity to talk to the girls themselves about their life style, which she doesn't.

Here and there are cogent observations on the scene from the likes of Gene Simmons, Ozzy Osbourne and Alice Cooper. Even they are parroting superstar statements made many times before. In the end, nobody in heavy metal is going to rise any higher or die any deader than legions who've gone before.
—*Har.*

Big Business

A Buena Vista release of a Touchstone Pictures presentation, in association with Silver Screen Partners III. Produced by Steve Tisch, Michael Peyser. Directed by Jim Abrahams. Screenplay, Dori Pierson, Marc Rubel; camera (color), Dean Cundey; editor, Harry Keramidas; music, Lee Holdridge; sound (Dolby), Thomas Causey; production design, William Sandell; set decoration, Richard C. Goddard; costume design, Michael Kaplan; production manager, William S. Beasley; assistant director, Bruce A. Humphrey; second unit director, Peyser; special visual effects, Dream Quest Images; associate producer, Bonnie Bruckheimer-Martell; casting, Howard Feuer. Reviewed at Cinerama Dome, L.A., June 6, 1988. MPAA Rating: PG. Running time: 97 MIN.

Sadie & Sadie	Bette Midler
Rose & Rose	Lily Tomlin
Roone Dimmick	Fred Ward
Graham Serbourne	Edward Herrmann
Fabio Alberici	Michele Placido
Chuck	Daniel Gerroll
Michael	Barry Primus
Dr. Marshall	Michael Gross
Binky Shelton	Deborah Rush
Hunt Shelton	Nicolas Coster
Iona Ratliff	Patricia Gaul
Garth Ratliff	J.C. Quinn
Nanny Lewis	Norma Macmillan
Desk clerk	Joe Grifasi
Hotel manager	John Vickery
Chauffeur	John Hancock
Judy	Mary Gross
Jason	Seth Green

Hollywood — "Big Business" is a shrill, unattractive comedy with just enough laughs and punchy hipness to put it over as another Touchstone b.o. hit. Stars Bette Midler and Lily Tomlin, who play two sets of twins mixed up at birth, have distinctly different comic styles, with the former's loud brashness generally dominating the latter's sly skittishness. The pleasure of seeing Midler strut her stuff as a ruthless business tycoon will probably be enough in itself to satisfy summer general audiences.

A mishap at a rural hospital pairs off the daughters of a hick couple with the sprigs of a major industrialist and his society wife. Jump to New York today, where dynamic Moramax Corp. board chairman Sadie Shelton (Midler) is forced to tolerate her scatterbrained, sentimental sister Rose (Tomlin) while trying to push through the sale of a subsidiary firm in their birthplace of Jupiter Hollow to an Italian, who intends to stripmine the bucolic community.

To try to thwart the sale at a stockholders' meeting, another Sadie and Rose, of the Ratcliff clan, leave Jupiter Hollow for the big city. As soon as they arrive at the airport, the complications begin, as they are swept into the Moramax limousine by the smooth Italian executive and check into the Plaza Hotel, where they are assumed to be the powerful Shelton sisters.

The mistaken identity gambit is played for all it's worth for nearly 90 minutes, with several men assuming they are romancing one lady when they are actually with the baffled but sometimes not unwilling lookalike. These scenes, and similar business-related misunderstandings, are as laborious as often as they are amusing, but the antics of the cast keep things tolerably afloat from a lowbrow comedy p.o.v.

Of the four performances by the two leads, the one easiest to enjoy is Midler's as venal corporate boss. Dressed to the nines and sporting a mincing but utterly determined walk, Midler tosses off her waspish 1-liners with malevolent glee, stomping on everyone in her path.

There are moments of delight as well in her other characterization as a country bumpkin who has always yearned for the material pleasures of Babylon, and Midler's eyes light up as big as saucers as they focus upon the windows of Cartier and Tiffany.

Tomlin has her moments, too as she hisses out a serpentine warning to interlopers and shakes her bracelet like a rattler, but her two sweetly flakey, nay-saying characters for a while seem so similar that they are differentiated only with difficulty.

Supporting cast offers some fine character turns, notably by Joe Grifasi, Edward Herrmann, Daniel Gerroll, Deborah Rush and Michele Placido.

When all four women finally meet up, with apologies to "Duck Soup," it's a massive freakout, followed by a rushed wrapup that is best not dwelled upon, given the implausibility of the various male-female matchups.

Good use is made of a massive Plaza Hotel interior set, but lensing and editing are unappealing, making pic look garish and a bit cheap. Director Jim Abrahams, in his solo debut after his successful career with the Zucker brothers, catches the obvious laughs in Dori Pierson and Marc Rubel's screenplay, but misses others through unsteady timing. —Cart.

Killer Klowns From Outer Space

A Trans World Entertainment release of a Sarlui/Diamant presentation of a Chiodo Bros. production. Produced by Edward Chiodo, Stephen Chiodo, Charles Chiodo. Executive producers, Paul Mason, Helen Sarlui-Tucker. Directed by Stephen Chiodo. Screenplay, Charles Chiodo, Stephen Chiodo; camera (color), Alfred Taylor; editor, Chris Roth; music, John Massari; sound (Dolby), Patrick Moriarity; production design, Charles Chiodo; art direction, Philip Dean Foreman; costume design, Darcee Olson; special visual effects, Fantasy II Film Effects; assistant director, Fred Wardell; clown design, Charles Chiodo. Reviewed at the Egyptian 3 Theater, L.A., June 3, 1988. MPAA Rating: PG-13. Running time: 88 MIN.

Mike	Grant Cramer
Debbie	Suzanne Snyder
Officer Dave Hanson	John Allen Nelson
Farmer Green	Royal Dano
Officer Mooney	John Vernon
Rich	Michael Siegel
Paul	Peter Licassi

Hollywood — This week's theatrical preview of an imminent homevideo release is "Killer Klowns From Outer Space," a klutzy teen scifier that will be better remembered for its title than anything in the picture itself. Tiny opening day matinee audience on Hollywood Boulevard appeared to consist almost entirely of people who worked on the film, which sums up its b.o. potential.

Familiar 1950s format has a small town terrorized by invading aliens for the latter's nutritional benefit. Instead of zombies, giant insects or beings of superior intelligence, creatures this time are outsized clowns who shoot people down with popcorn-spewing guns, pelt them with acid-filled pies and spin their captives into cotton candy cocoons.

With a premise this exciting, it's a wonder brothers Edward, Stephen and Charles Chiodo, who in assorted capacities are responsible for this concoction, couldn't sell Steven Spielberg or one of the major studios on it. As it stands, the viewer is treated to some of the chintziest sets and special effects seen since the waning days of Monogram Studios, the quality of which is obscured only partially by the murky photography.

To give credit where credit is due, the clown face creations by Charles Chiodo are nicely malevolent and expressively pliable, and it will hardly be spoiling the suspense for anyone to reveal that the clowns' Achilles heel lies in the big red noses smack in the middle of their awful-looking faces.

Except for the juicy expressions of nastiness and contempt from cynical cop John Vernon, the performances are strictly amateur night, the film seemingly interminable. If sci-fi has come to this, it's time for a break. —Cart.

Trading Hearts

A Cineworld Enterprises release of a Vista Organization production. Produced by Herb Jaffe, Mort Engelberg. Executive producer, Josi W. Konski. Directed by Neil Leifer. Screenplay, Frank Deford; camera (Deluxe color), Karen Grossman; editor, Rick Shaine; music, Stanley Myers; sound, Henri Lopez; production design, George Goodridge; art direction, James R. Bilz; assistant director, Jim Bigham; casting, Nina Axelrod. Reviewed at Aidikoff Screening Room, Hollywood, May 18, 1988. MPAA Rating: PG. Running time: 88 MIN.

Vinnie	Raul Julia
Donna	Beverly D'Angelo
Yvonne	Jenny Lewis
Robert	Parris Buckner
Ducky	Robert Gwaltney
Pepe	Ruben Rabasa
Ralph	Mark Harris

Hollywood — "Trading Hearts" poses one question of whether the characters played by talented Raul Julia and Beverly D'Angelo will get together by the end and live happily ever after. It also raises a second question of why Julia and D'Angelo ever got together on such a pointless project in the first place.

The lame, predictable and unexciting story definitely is the problem. This first feature penned by veteran sportswriter Frank Deford must have had something there on paper in the first place to attract its stars. Director Neil Leifer extracts a charm and energy from his cast, but that doesn't compensate for what was missing to begin with or he lost along the way.

Whatever its weaknesses, "Hearts" is a sassy showcase for little Jenny Lewis. As an 11-year-old tomboy trying to get mother D'Angelo hitched to Julia, Lewis brings the picture most of its fun.

Mother and daughter live in a seedy trailer next to a cheap Florida motel while D'Angelo pursues her dreams of becoming a nightclub singer, fighting off the lounge lizards along the way. One other major plus of the picture is D'Angelo's dandy vocals.

Julia is a major league pitcher who's lost his good stuff and has been cut loose in spring training. When he stops overnight at the motel, Lewis matches him to her collection of baseball cards and decides he's just the dad she needs. Naturally, however, he and D'Angelo have had a misunderstanding at a bar the night before and do not initially share the little girl's hopes.

The setup is fine and all three performers seem ready and able to take the story somewhere. Yet all that happens is a clumsy threat from Lewis' father, Parris Buckner, to take Lewis out of this environment to his wealthy home, which he in some vague way has the legal right to do. This device mainly serves to throw the adults together to protect the girl, ignite their romance, and transfer the runaway trio to an out-of-the-way minor league training camp where Julia becomes determined to have one more go at his former profession.

That subplot quickly fizzles and eventually Buckner gets his daughter. With little difficulty, however, the loving couple soon get her back. Thanks to the little girl's larcenous talent for forging names, they also get away with $10,000 from dad's bank account to start anew.

Since dad never comes across as anything but a reasonably nice guy with best intentions for his daughter, this is hardly a morally uplifting solution to the problems. In any case, with their new fortune, the likable reunited family finances a new life running a hall of fame for alligators. —Har.

Nikutai No Mon
(The Gates Of Flesh)
(JAPANESE)

A Toei release. Produced by Kazuto Amano, Toshio Zushi. Directed by Hideo Gosha. Screenplay, Kazuo Kasahara, based on novel by Sojiro Tamura; camera (color), Fujiro Morita; editor, Osamu Ichida; music, Mochifumi Izumimori; sound, Yoshio

Horiike; art direction, Yoshinobu Nishioka; planning, Goro Hikebe, Masao Satoh. Reviewed a Toei Grand, Tokyo, May 13, 1988.
Running time: 111 MIN.

Sen Asada	Rino Katase
Maya Suge	Miyuki Kano
Hanae Yasui	Chisato Yamabuki
Mino Inui	Naomi Hase
Mitsuyo	Yoshimi Ashikawa
Sachiko Shibata	Chie Matsuoka
Machiko Kikuma	Mineko Nishikawa
Shintaro Ibuki	Tsunehiko Watase
Yoshio Kotoda	Jimpachi Nezu
Osumi	Yuko Natori
Horizumi	Shinsuke Ashida

Tokyo — Hideo Gosha has received many awards as a director of films about women who are not above selling their charms. The heroines of Gosha's latest, "Nikutai No Mon," are once again *filles de joie*, but it's doubtful that this film will earn the director any prizes.

This is the fifth filmed version of Sojiro Tamura's bestselling novel and looks it, suggesting a remake than a retread. Its lack of visual and dramatic distinction is especially puzzling given that Gosha has been assisted by many of the same "Yokiro" staffers, including cinematographer Fujiro Morita and art director Yoshinobu Nishioka, who made that award-winning film such a pleasurable experience.

Heavy hang many a metaphor over the story of prostitutes in Occupation-era Yurakucho who vow to split their hard-earned yen equally, to concentrate on work to the exclusion of love and to use one-third of their profits one day to build a dance hall called Paradise. Here we have the formula for Japan's amazing postwar socio-economic success: equitable distribution of income, devotion to the work ethic and the determination to construct a paradise on the smoldering ruins of a nation that has been through hell.

Before the dream can become a reality, there must be a complete break with the past. Inside the charred building where the prostitutes live and work is an unexploded bomb, referred to by the ladies as their *go-honzon,* a term used in Japan when explaining to whom a temple is dedicated. Since it carries all the weighty import of a loaded gun placed on the mantlepiece during the first act of a 3-act play, it is absolutely certain that this device be detonated prior to the final curtain, finally destroying the crumbling remnants of the old order.

As if to distract attention from the sound of symbols clashing, Gosha offers several of the melodramatic, confrontational set pieces for which he is famous, including one in which a prostitute, immediately after saving another from the depredations of a U.S. serviceman, jitterbugs with the grateful woman to the strains of "Take The A Train." These bravura moments don't come often enough to save this truly uninvolving film. — *Bail.*

Enkel resa
(One Way Ticket)
(SWEDISH)

A Sonet Film release of Spice/Omega Film production, in association with KB Enkel Resa, Viking Line, Sonet Media, PR Produktion. Produced by Peter Hald. Executive producers, Mats Arehn, Peter Kropénin. Written and directed by Hans Iveberg. Camera (Eastmancolor), Mischa Gavrjusjov; editor, Susanne Lindmann; music, Ola Hakonson, Tim Norell, performed by Lili & Susie, Inger Lise Rypdal; costumes, Hedvig Ander. Reviewed at Sandrews 1-2-3, Malmö, Sweden, May 26, 1988. Running time: **95 MIN.**

Johannes	Sven Wollter
Jagetoft	Sten Ake Cederhök
Birgit	Inger Lise Rypdal
Pekka	Asko Sarkola
Astrid	Siv Ruud
Manuel	Jarl Borssén
Body	Dan Ekborg
Carlo	Gösta Engström

Also with: Jahn Teigen, Sten Ljunggren, Svante Grundberg, Peter Harryson.

Malmö, Sweden — Once again Hans Iveberg, the screenwriter, has defeated Hans Iveberg, the director. The screenplay of "One Way Ticket," a diamond heist caper farce, serves up embarrassingly contrived drafts of intended volleys of sight & sound gags, all devoid of logic, and the helmer proceeds to press the trigger earnestly with an unbroken line of either duds or misses as the result.

Iveberg made boxoffice waves in 1981 with the similarly inane "Clear The Canal," and he may do so again, at least on home territory where the facial contortions he provokes from established thesp talent will be of some built-in appeal. Even though some of the participating actors are recruited from Finland and Norway, the item probably will be turned away from the borders of these Scandinavian sister nations.

The story has a reformed swindler (Sven Wollter, internationally known via a major role in Andrei Tarkovsky's "The Sacrifice") don a cardinal's robes in order to carry through the caper that is to free him forever from a mobster chieftain's grip. Involved are a set of czarist jewels en route on a tourist boat from Helsinki to Stockholm plus various mugs dressed up as a nun, a monk and a priest. Another one is dressed down to appear as a corpse, unlikely to be searched for the treasure the gang of clerics aim to hide in his coffin.

Before you can say disrobe, the cardinal is spotted in hot embrace with the nun, now wearing briefs only; the monk is seen in his cups at the bar; and the corpse is on public display as it dashes in and out of staterooms and galleys with its shroud waving like a banner. The police lieutenant meant to maintain security gets himself locked up in the ship's liquor store overnight.

Nothing wrong with any of the above action except that it contains not an iota of the common human denominator that even the Marx Bros. gave priority. Film's tech credits are okay, and Wollter strives mightily to give character substance to his role. Sif Ruud, Jarl Borssén and Finland's Asko Sarkola (as the corpse) do likewise, but eventually they all are hopelessly at sea. —*Kell.*

CANNES REVIEWS

Salaam Bombay
(Hello Bombay)
(INDIAN)

A Jane Balfour presentation of a Mirabai production. Coproduced by National Development Co. (Bombay), Channel Four (London), Cadrage (Paris). Produced and directed by Mira Nair. Screenplay, Sooni Taraporevala; based on original story by Nair, Taraporevala; camera (color), Sandi Sissel; editor, Barry Alexander Brown; music, L. Subramaniam; sound, Juan Rodriguez. Reviewed at Cannes Film Festival (Directors Fortnight), May 20, 1988. Running time: **113 MIN.**

Krishna	Shafik Syed
Koyla	Sarfuddin Qurassi
Keera	Raju Barnad
Chillum	Raghubir Yadav
Baba	Nana Patekar
Rekha	Aneeta Kanwar

Also with: Hansa Vithal, Mohanraj Babu, Chandrashekhar Naidu, Shaukat Azmi, Dinshaw Daji, Alfred Anthony, Ramesh Deshavani, Anjan Srivastava.

Cannes — A kind of Indian "Pixote" about kids living on the sidewalks of Bombay utilizing their wits, this picture has raised considerble controversy between its supporters, who appreciate the polished, Western style of docu-drama, and detractors, who seem to think it looks too much like cinema and not enough like real life. "Salaam Bombay" won the Camera d'Or, as best first feature in Cannes 1988.

The story evolves around a young boy, Krishna, who leaves his home village, kicked out by his family who suspects him unjustly of stealing money. He comes to the big city, hoping to make quickly the 500 rupees which would permit him to return home. Carrying tea in a Bombay slum for pimps and prostitutes, sleeping on a pile of rubble and learning the ways of the street and the means to survive, innocence gradually is beaten out of him by the circumstances.

He is left alone by the end of the picture, deprived of the company of the few persons to whom he had ever felt close: a juvenile drug pusher who dies of an overdose, an adolescent girl of the north kidnaped and nursed carefully into prostitution and a call girl who rejects her pimp and tries to get her daughter back from a government shelter.

Director Mira Nair, trained in America, is very much in control of her material, tells her story efficiently and has most of the cast, none of them real professionals, under total control. She indulges in some melodramatic explorations, however, dangerously verging on a romanticized Oriental tearjerker mood.

Superior camerawork and editing, which keep the story moving along briskly, certainly will make this picture easier to take for large audiences than the grittier, darker portraits of society's underbelly.
—*Edna.*

Camomille
(FRENCH)

A K.G. production and release. Produced by Michèle Ray-Gavras. Written and directed by Mehdi Charef. Camera (Eastmancolor), Patrick Blossier; editor, Luc Barnier; art direction, Philippe Chiffre; sound, Pierre Gamet, Bernard Leroux; music, Tony Coe. Reviewed at the Gaumont Ambassade cinema, Paris, May 10, 1988. (In Cannes Film Festival Market.) Running time: **82 MIN.**

Camille	Philippine Leroy-Beaulieu
Martin	Rémi Martin
Mother	Monique Chaumette

Also with: Guy Saint Jean, Albert Delpy, Michel Peyrelon, Solenn Jarniou, Geneviève Lallemang.

Paris — Mehdi Charef, who made a spectacular leap from factory worker to prizewinning filmmaker with his 1985 debut feature "Tea In The Harem," checks in discreetly with his third feature, "Camomille," which opened here on the eve of the Cannes fest where it was passed up in all official selections.

An unjust omission, since "Camomille" confirms Charef's growing assurances with the medium, even if the screenplay (written before Charef's helming debut) doesn't quite click.

Pic injects an upbeat note in Charef's bleak vision of society's misfits (helmer's previous "Miss Mona" seemed to touch the bottom in despair). "Camomille" has been described as being a fairytale.

But sordid details abound in this story of a cowered, stuttering young baker's assistant with a passion for cars and cats who takes in attractive young jetset junkie, sequesters her in his garret and impregnates her. His act succeeds in saving the girl from despair and himself from the grips of a dour, manipulative mother (Monique Chaumette).

With its echoes of "The Collector" and Jacques Doillon's early intimate features, "Camomille" benefits from Charef's furtive direction, Patrick Blossier's striking camerawork and the performances by Rémi Martin (one of the youths of "Tea In The Harem") and the appealing Philippine Leroy-Beaulieu.

Yet the story is insufficiently developed and some of the symbolism is pat (Martin is constructing an automobile in his garret, from which it can never be removed). Still, Charef remains one of the few new talents of recent years worth following. —*Len.*

Vampires

A Len Anthony Studios production. Executive producer, Heather Scala. Produced and directed by Anthony. Screenplay, James Harrigan, Anthony, from story by Anthony; camera (Studio Film color), Ernest Dickerson, Larry Revene; editor, Damian Begley, Anthony; music, Chris Burke; art direction, Cosmo Vinyl; special visual effects, Arnold Gargullio. Reviewed at Cannes Film Festival (market), May 12, 1988. Running time: **92 MIN.**
Dr. Charles Harmon . . . . Duane Jones
Madeline Abadon . . . . Jackie James
Ione . . . . Orly Benair
Deborah . . . . Robin Michaels
Mike . . . . John Bly

Cannes — "Vampires," previously titled "Abadon," is a low-budget horror film with a frustratingly unfinished look about it. Interest will be limited to extreme cultists.

Fragmentary story unfolds at Abadon, a private school in Connecticut presided over by old-fashioned villainess Madeline (Jackie James). Using a machine (very cheap designwork) created by her late scientist husband, she has achieved immortality by stealing the energy of her students.

Dr. Harmon (Duane Jones, star of "Night Of The Living Dead") is an occultist who fills us in on the pic's scientific background with mumbo-jumbo dialog. Amidst several stalker-type murder scenes, pointless cutaway shots to closeups of tarot cards or gargoyles on the building's facade, filmmaker Len Anthony inserts numerous phoned-in scenes or voiceover during pointless filler footage. Key scenes, such as the fate of heroine coed Ione (played by attractive Orly Benair) or a flashback concerning the surprise parentage of fellow student Deborah (Robin Michaels) are missing.

Anthony has some occasionally striking shots by cameraman Ernest Dickerson and Larry Revene, but the acting is awkward.—*Lor.*

Kadaicha
(AUSTRALIAN)

A Premiere Film Marketing-Medusa Communications production. Produced by David Hannay, Charles Hannah. Executive producer, Tom Broadbridge. Directed by James Bogle. Screenplay, Ian Coughlan; camera (Eastmancolor), Stephen F. Windon; editor, Andrew Aristedes; music, Peter Westheimer; special makeup, Deryzk de Niese; line producer, Lynn Barker; production manager, Julia Ritchie; sound, Pam Dunne; assistant director, Deuel Droogan; casting, Carrie Zivetz. Reviewed at Cannes Film Festival (market), May 15, 1988. Running time: **88 MIN.**
Gail Sorensen . . . . Zoe Carides
Matt . . . . Tom Jennings
Alex Sorensen . . . . Eric Oldfield
Tracey . . . . Natalie McCurry
Fizz . . . . Fiona Gauntlett
Mr. Fitzgerald . . . . Sean Scully
Also with: Kerry McKay, Steve Dodd, Deborah Kennedy.

Cannes — Aboriginal legends and

curses are the in thing this year for Aussie horror pics; with "The Dreaming" and now "Kadaicha" the message is the same: aboriginal curses will kill unwary whites. Despite the awkward title, and basically familiar plot, "Kadaicha" chills up enough scares to ensure a life on video.

Setting is a wealthy Sydney suburb where highschool kids (all of them sexually active, natch) are being mysteriously killed. First, they dream of an aborigine in a cave who hands them a mysterious crystal; then they wake up to find the crystal, or kadaicha, on their pillow. From then on it's just a matter of time.

One girl's done in by a savage hound, a boy by a lethal spider, while another youngster is savaged by an unseen, eel-like thing when she's swimming. Cause of the trouble stems from the fact that heroine Zoe Carides' developer father (Eric Oldfield) knowingly built houses and a shopping mall atop an aboriginal sacred site (cf., "Poltergeist"). Attractive teen actors play the threatened youngsters, and there's a sharp, if too brief, cameo from Sean Scully as headmaster of the school whose pupils are being decimated mysteriously.

Pic is a bit too low-key for the most hardened fans of this genre; it's technically okay, though never very scary. —*Strat.*

Sredi Sreyrk Kamney
(Among The Grey Stones)
(SOVIET)

A Sovexportfilm release of a Ukrainian Filmmakers Union production. Written and directed by Kira Muratova, based on novel by V. Korolenko. Camera (color), Alexei Rodionov; editor, Valentin Olienik; art direction, Valentin Ghidoulianov. Reviewed at Cannes Film Festival (Un Certain Regard), May 21, 1988. Running time: **88 MIN.**
With: Igor Chaparov, Oksana Schlapak, Roman Levtchenko, S. Popov, S. Govorouhin.

Cannes — This picture was made five years ago, mutilated out of recognition and allowed out only recently, after director Kira Muratova became a sensation for her earlier films as well as for her tormented career.

As it is now, film at most is an indication of her talent to handle actors and camera as well as her rich visual imagination, but otherwise remains an inconclusive series of separate sketches.

A weird community of destitute hobos, each pretending to a glorious past, lives under a disaffected church, after an unspecified world-shattering event which deprived them of all their possessions. Nearby, a powerful judge is disconsolate after the loss of his beloved wife. He neglects his children, particularly his son, who roams about the neighborhood, discovers the hobo colony and befriends them.

The contact between those who have and those who haven't, the gap between the adult world bridged to a certain extent by the innocence of childhood, and the heavy memories separating adults (while hope rests only with those who are too young to have memories) are the themes at work, but in its present condition, it is difficult to make heads or tails of the plot, as separate scenes hardly relate to each other.

Muratova, who had picked the original Korolenko story believing it to be her passport to legitimacy (since Korolenko is an accepted author by the Soviet regime), was criticized at home for too pessimistic a picture. It also is possible more significance was read into the sympathetic portrayal of hobos, who could have been the victims of the October revolution, hidden by the church. One would require lots of imagination to find any clear political or ideological messages beyond the humanistic recommendation to love one's neighbor.

Director herself concedes this isn't quite the picture she made. It can only serve as a museum piece, to be displayed next to the more accomplished work of this talented director. — *Edna.*

Buckeye And Blue

A.J.C. Prods. picture. (Sales, Overseas Filmgroup.) Produced by John Cushingham, Nicholas Wentworth. Executive producer, David Grossberg. Written and directed by J.C. Compton. Camera (color), Mark Irwin; editor, Wentworth; music, Bruno Nicolai. Reviewed at Cannes Film Festival (market), May 18, 1988. Running time: **92 MIN.**
With: Robyn Lively, Jeffrey Osterhage, Rick Gibbs, Will Hannah, Kenneth Jensen, Patrick Johnston, Stuart Rogers, Michael Horse.

Cannes — "Buckeye And Blue" is a cutesy, sugar sweet Western that's nowhere near gritty enough to attract oater aficionados and too cloying for anyone over 14. Hitch this one to a young homevid audience still supervised by parents, market in which it could have okay prospects.

Cute, dimpled Robyn Lively takes the lead as Baby Lou; she's waiting for the return of handsome Jeff Osterhage — inexplicably named Blue Duck — who has promised to return after the Civil War when Baby Lou has "growed up," as she puts it in her torturous Southern accent.

He doesn't, and it becomes clear why when his photo appears on wanted posters. Baby Lou one day stumbles on a bumbling group of ex-soldiers who say they've ridden with Blue Duck, so she plans to run away with them to track her beau down. While waiting for the gang to get her later that night she falls asleep, to be aroused by a clumsy arrival; off she rides into the night, discarding her name for her horse's,

Buckeye, perhaps because she's now grown up.

She soon takes charge of the inept gang, partakes in the usual Western goings on — saloon brawls, stagecoach holdups — meets up finally with Blue Duck, who steals her idea to rob a bank and is caught; she naturally succeeds, but loses her gang, rescues Blue Duck, and rides off an independent woman, well and truly grown up, sans the man.

It is, of course, all a dream; instead of riding off with the gang, she offers them work on her father's farm, forgetting entirely about Blue Duck.

It's corny stuff and will require an undemanding audience. Some awkward thesping on Lively's part reflects that. Technically, pic comes across okay, but overall there's not much there when you scrape off the syrup. —*Doch.*

Stealing Heaven
(BRITISH-YUGOSLAV)

A Film Dallas Pictures presentation of an Amy Intl./Jadran Films production. Produced by Simon MacCorkindale, Andros Epaminondas. Executive producer, Susan George. Directed by Clive Donner. Screenplay, Chris Bryant, based on novel by Marion Meade; camera (color), Mikael Salomon; editor, Michael Ellis; music, Nick Bicât; production design, Voytek; costume design, Phyllis Dalton; visual consultant, Jocelyn Rickards. Reviewed at Cannes Film Festival (market), May 20, 1988. Running time: **110 MIN.**
Abélard . . . . Derek de Lint
Héloïse . . . . Kim Thomson
Fulbert . . . . Denholm Elliott
Bishop . . . . Bernard Hepton
Suger . . . . Kenneth Cranham
Agnes . . . . Patsy Bryne
Jourdain . . . . Mark Jax
François . . . . Tim Watson
Prioress . . . . Rachel Kempson
Sister Cecilia . . . . Angela Pleasence
Also with: Cassie Stuart, Philip Locke, Victoria Burgoyne, Antonia Cutic, Andrew McLean, Thomnas Lockyer, Mark Audley, Kai Dominic, Slavica Maras, Miki Hewitt, Yvonne Bryceland, Vjenceslav Kapural, Ivo Husnjak, Jeremy Hawk, Moniek Kramer, Drago Mitrovic.

Cannes — This handsome historical pageant attempts to tell the "true story" behind one of history's most famous romances, that of 12th century French philospher Pierre Abélard and his beloved Héloïse, which has survived through the ages in the exchange of letters between them, each of them shut off from the world in another convent.

Chris Bryant's script, based on Marion Meade's novel, originally commissioned by Tri-Star and at one time projected to star Susan George and Simon MacCorkindale, was taken over by the two British actors who preferred to remain on the other side of the camera, as producers.

For quite a while, Bryant's script and Clive Donner's direction pull toward a sharp and witty, anticlerical, feminist tract. Abélard shuns emotional commitments as dangerous to his intellectual capacities; Fulbert, Héloïse's uncle, is a mercenary bigot who looks for the best deal on his niece; and Héloise is the smart, intelligent and unconventional girl with the courage to assume responsibility for her feelings. The question of whether love is a blessing or a source of eternal guilt generates several quick-witted dialog exchanges, supported by an equally effective score.

As the plot inevitably follows the historical indications and Fulbert's minions castrate Abélard, who couldn't resist his passion any more and made love to Héloise, script and direction begin to falter towards pure melodrama.

Donner uses the Serbian landscape, untouched by time, to great advantage, and all technical credits are superior, with kudos to production designer Voytek, the costumes of Phyllis Dalton and excellent camerawork by Denmark's Mikael Salomon.

Kim Thomson's fresh performance augurs well for this newcomer and Derek de Lint's handsome presence certainly will delight the romantically inclined. Denholm Elliott heads a cast of thorough British pros in the supporting parts.

With production values as high as they are here, and with the fame of an eternal love story, as well known as Romeo & Juliet or Tristan & Isolde, the picture may have a solid theatrical career, but some of the love scenes may have to be abridged for tv use. —*Edna*.

Kamilla And The Thief
(NORWEGIAN-BRITISH)

A Penelope Film (Kristiansand, Norway, and London, England) production. Produced by Odd Hynnekleiv. Directed by Grete Salomonsen. Screenplay, Salomonsen, based on novel by Kari Vinje; camera (color), Odd Hynnekleiv; editor, Howard Lanning, Geraldine Creed; music, Ragnar Bjerkreim, Benny Borg; sound, Fred Sharp., Kristine Bjorvatn; art direction, Sven Wickman; costumes, Magda Stallamo, Ann Rasmussen; production manager, Dagfinn Löken, Jarl Erik Finland. Reviewed at Cannes Film Festival (market), May 12, 1988. Running time: **94 MIN.**

Kamilla . . . . Veronica Flaat
Sebastian . . . . Dennis Storhöi
Sofia . . . . Agnete Haaland
Joakim Jensen . . . . Kaare Kroppan
Christoffer . . . . Morten Harket
Also with: Helge Nygaard, Maria Del Mar Del Castillo, Normann Liene, Alf Nordvang, Trine Liene, Brith Munthe, Björn Furuborg, Gwynn Overland.

Cannes — Shot simultaneously, the Norwegian version of Grete Salamonsen's Disneyesque "Kamilla And The Thief" did record box-office in Norway as a UIP pickup. The English version of fun and thrills with a freckled 8-year-old boasts less than super-sophistication, but should do well with adults and tots in tow almost everywhere.

The little girl is whirled into danger and adventure when her stepparents send her off to live with an older sister who lives alone in a remote rural mountain community. Saved

from juvenile muggers by blond, blue-eyed young Sebastian, Kamilla is the last to find out the boy is a thief on the run.

Actually it was a miscarriage of justice that led Sebastian to steal. He and Kamilla get themselves into various messes until Sebastian decides to face the music. He surrenders to the police, but leaves her a message on a kite saying he will come back.

Sure enough, "Kamilla & Her Friends" is promised audiences while they watch end credits through misty eyes. The producer-director team has a thorough film schooling in England and it shows in the technical and narrative areas.

The acting by adult professionals and kiddie amateurs, including Veronica Flaat as Kamilla, is seasoned with strong doses of the burlesque, but it generally works neatly with the period (1913) dress.

Dennis Storhöi oozes charm without becoming sticky as Sebastian. Morten Harket of the a-ha pop group is squeezed into a cameo with little to do. Music is nicely supportive. —*Kell*.

The Wizard Of Loneliness

A Skouras Pictures release of a Virgin Vision, American Playhouse Theatrical Films presentation. (Sales, Gavin Films.) Produced by Thom Tyson, Philip Porcella. Directed by Jenny Bowen. Screenplay, Nancy Larson, based on John Nichols' novel; camera (color), Richard Bowen; editor, Lisa Day; music, Michel Colombier; sound, Doug Axtell; production design, Jeffrey Beecroft; costume design, Stephanie Maslansky; assistant director, Chuck Alfred; production manager, Helen Pollak; associate producers, Mary Cooper, Shanley Heffelfinger. Reviewed at Cannes Film Festival (market), May 20, 1988. MPAA Rating: PG-13. Running time: **110 MIN.**

Wendall . . . . Lukas Haas
Sybil . . . . Lea Thompson
John . . . . Lance Guest
Doc . . . . John Randolph
Duffy . . . . Dylan Baker
Cornelia . . . . Anne Pitoniak

Cannes — This is another piece of World War II nostalgia, seen through the eyes of a bright but spoiled L.A. brat, whose mother dies and whose father joins the army to ease his personal sorrow.

The 12-year-old Wendall is packed off to his grandparents, living in a small Vermont town, and for a while, his only concern is to lay his hands on enough money to pay for his trip back to California. As time goes by, the sunny disposition of his grandparents and his increasing involvement in the lives of his new acquaintances relieve his homesickness and introduce him to aspects of pain and suffering he had known nothing about.

Most of all, he is affected by his uncle John, who is rejected by the army because of his physical disability and feels he has let everybody down, while John's sister, Sybil, gives birth to an illegitimate child whose real father is a deserter suffering from war traumas.

As everything is filtered through Wendall's personality in the script, there is a considerable loss of dramatic impact, as if the entire story is told second-hand, a personal but not terribly involving souvenir from days gone by.

John Nichols, lately associated with the Sundance Institute and Robert Redford, wrote the original antiwar novel in 1966, and has left his mark on Nancy Larson's script. Director Jenny Bowen, also associated in the past with the Sundance Institute and better known for "Street Music," does a reliable but unexceptional job. It's a pedestrian rendition, efficiently told but devoid of magic or imagination.

Lukas Haas as Wendall is very much in control, almost too smooth for his part, with Lea Thompson and Lance Guest providing solid assistance in the background.

All technical credits are satisfactory but final result seems destined mainly for a small-screen career. —*Edna*.

Proc
(Why)
(CZECH)

A Filmexport Prag release of a Barrandov Studios production. Directed by Karel Smyczek. Screenplay, Smyczek, Radek John; camera (color), Jaroslav Brabek; editor, Jan Svoboda; music, Michael Pavlicek; art direction, Boris Halmi. Reviewed at Cannes Film Festival (Un Certain Regard), May 20, 1988. Running time: **90 MIN.**
With: Jiri Langmajer, Jan Potmesil, Pavlina Murkova, Martin Dejdar, Pavle Zvaric, Marketa Zmozkova.

Cannes — A formally ambitious but thematically shallow attempt to exploit the recent explosions of violence among young European soccer afficionados as a symptom of juvenile unrest, this Czech picture is equally unsympathetic to parents and their offspring.

It shows society to be impotent to do anything beyond enforcing the law, which is like cutting off the arm instead of healing the wound.

Teenage fans of a leading soccer team, Sparta, are arrested for vandalizing a passenger car on a train while returning from a championship match outside town. The film moves back and forth between the trial, the personal background of the accused and the events which took place on the fateful trip, in a documentary-like research of the case.

What this research uncovers is that all the culprits are profoundly frustrated by conditions at home, their excessive drinking and brutal acts of violence the result of an almost physical need to release their pent-up anger. Soccer is only an excuse to let their fury explode and the picture allows no hope they might outgrow their conduct.

All the parents are insensitive egotists who have only themselves to blame for bringing up their chil-

dren the way they did, and the social system seems to have no way to channel this excessive energy into something more productive, or to supply the youngsters with some interest beyond fanatical allegiance to a soccer team, beer, sex and vandalism. While it is not implied directly, the image frighteningly suggests an ideal breeding ground for a new brand of fascism.

Since the film does not attempt to go beyond standard dramatic justification, this looks more like the exasperated reaction of an older person trying to attempt to understand what is happening.

The large cast in most cases does a reliable job, even if it is not allowed much depth in developing characters. Nervous, effective editing moves the story from one level to another, displaying remarkable control over the material. —*Edna*.

Bull Durham

An Orion Pictures release of a Mount Co. production. Produced by Thom Mount, Mark Burg. Executive producer, David V. Lester. Written and directed by Ron Shelton. Camera (Deluxe color), Bobby Byrne; editor, Robert Leighton, Adam Weiss; music, Michael Convertino; sound (Dolby), Kirk Francis; production design, Armin Ganz; art direction, David Lubin; set decoration, Kris Boxell; costume design, Louise Frogley; assistant director, Richard J. Kidney; associate producer, Charles Hirschhorn; casting, Bonnie Timmerman. Reviewed at Samuel Goldwyn theater, L.A., June 7, 1988. MPAA Rating: R. Running time: **108 MIN.**

Crash Davis	Kevin Costner
Annie Savoy	Susan Sarandon
Nuke Laloosh	Tim Robbins
Skip	Trey Wilson
Larry	Robert Wuhl
Millie	Jenny Robertson
Max Patkin	Himself
Jimmy	William O'Leary

Hollywood — "Bull Durham" is a fanciful and funny bush league sports story where the only foul ball is its overuse of locker-room dialog. Even so, both boys and girls of summer can't fail to be thoroughly entertained by Kevin Costner as the quintessential American male who loves romance, but loves baseball even more. Orion will homer with this one.

Forget most of the previous filmed sports stories like "The Natural" that idolize the star athlete and consider his grassy environment as so sacrosanct to be next to godliness. This is not the majors; this is a satire of the minors, at least initially.

Specifically, the Durham Bulls of North Carolina dream of getting called up to be "in the show" as they endure another season of riding town to town on the team bus and suffering the dubious distinction of being one of the losingest clubs in Carolina league history.

Sent over from another "A" farm team to instruct, insult and inspire the Bulls' bullet-fast pitcher Ebby Calvin (Nuke) Laloosh (Tim Robbins) is embittered veteran catcher Crash Davis (Kevin Costner). His job is to get the cocky kid's arm on target by game time. Otherwise, Costner opts to sit in the bullpen when it comes to Robbins' off-the-field playing involving a certain crass-talking Bulls groupie (Susan Sarandon) who also has a very uninhibited manner when it comes to dispensing advice — be it on baseball or bedtime pleasures.

Director-writer Ron Shelton has a virtual field day with the script, which takes shots at sports management, the intelligence quotient of professional athletes, the libido factor of same (and what they can get away with), the gullible sports press and many more alleged truisms of what it's like to get up close and personal with some of the unsung heroes of America's favorite pastime.

Costner is a natural as the dyed-in-the-wool ballplayer. His best lines are when he's philosophizing, like on being an All-American male who hates anything by Susan Sontag and an all-American athlete who supports a Constitutional Amendment to ban Astroturf and the designated hitter. Though there are more warts than beauty marks in this depiction of down-on-their-luck athletes, their seedy clubhouses and smallminded managers, it's umpired with the most comical hand.

Aficionados will revel in all the baseball talk that takes place mostly while Costner is behind the plate and Robbins on the mound — their signaling, the bad calls, the plays, the sneaky little maneuvers that are managed so well with voiceovers. There is a scene here to satisfy every armchair jock in America.

Action outside the team's activities is a lot of stuff and nonsense, mostly playful fantasy and all of it involving Sarandon's character. She is never believable as a community college English lit teacher who, at the start of every season, latches on to the most promising rookie — in this case Robbins — with whom she takes particular pleasure in tying to the bed post as she educates him by reading the poetry of Walt Whitman as a tease for more exciting lessons planned for later on. Her role is a throwback more to a pre-feminist than pre-AIDS mentality.

Somewhere halfway into the action, Shelton gets serious with the material and has his players come to terms with their worth as it relates to baseball. Everyone matures in a very short time.

So much tension has built up to get Sarandon and the ever-standoffish Costner together finally — after she spends 90% of the film in bed with the wrong guy — the whole mood of the story moves from light comedy to melodrama.

Robbins is as good as a hick ballplayer as he is a slick, cliché-spewing Jim McMahon clone later on. There are a couple of weak attempts at creating interesting or funny side characters, Jimmy the Jesus freak teammate (William O'Leary) and Millie, his not so virginal bride (Jenny Robertson), as the sorriest examples, though others like baseball clown Max Patkin are nicely done.

Overall, "Bull Durham" is a heck of a lot more involving than the average baseball game and wins out on sheer watchability and for its no-losers ending. *—Brit.*

Body Count

A Poor Robert production. (Sales, Manson Intl.) Produced and directed by Paul Leder. Screenplay, Leder, from story by William W. Norton Sr.; camera (color), Francis Gruman; editor, Leder; music, Bob Summers; sound, Scott Smith; set design, Elpedio Vasquez; assistant director, Richard Hernandez; production manager, Paul Bagley; associate producer, Bob Cook; casting, Geraldine Leder. Reviewed on Forum Home Video videcassette, N.Y. May 25, 1988. No MPAA Rating. Running time: **93 MIN.**

Robert Knight	Bernie White
Joanne Knight	Marilyn Hassett
Charles Knight	Dick Sargent
Ralph Duris	Greg Mullavey
Lt. Chernoff	Thomas Ryan
Kim	Haunani Minn
Tom Leary	Steven Ford
Deborah	Lauren Woodland

Also with: James Avery, Julia Campbell, Oceana Marr, Jennifer Rhodes, Richard Stanley.

"Body Count," a.k.a. "The 11th Commandment," is a ho-hum suspense feature, direct-to-video.

Cast is okay, but a little more effort in scripting would have been in order to qualify as either a theatrical feature or network telefilm.

Bernie White portrays hapless Robert Knight, committed to a mental institution by his greedy relatives. He escapes in order to avenge himself, leaving a trail of bodies in his wake.

Chief gimmick here is that our hero has been wronged, yet is *really* crazy and a bona fide killer, so audience sympathies are bound to be mixed. Villains are rather soft, chiefly Dick Sargent as his uncle, while erstwhile ingenue Marilyn Hassett proves to be impressive as a sexy, ruthless baddie.

Paul Leder's direction and all technical contributions are functional but uninspired. — *Lor.*

Red Heat

A Tri-Star Pictures release of a Mario Kassar and Andrew Vajna presentation of a Carolco/Lone Wolf/Oak production. Produced by Walter Hill, Gordon Carroll. Executive producers, Kassar, Vajna. Directed by Hill. Screenplay, Harry Kleiner, Hill, Troy Kennedy Martin, story by Hill; camera (Technicolor), Matthew F. Leonetti; editor, Freeman Davies, Carmel Davies, Donn Aron; music, James Horner; sound (Dolby), Richard Bryce Goodman; production design, John Vallone; art direction, Michael Corenblith; set design, Nick Navarro; set decoration, Ernie Bishop; associate producer, Mae Woods; assistant director, James R. Dyer; second unit director-stunt coordinator, Bennie Dobbins. Reviewed at the Coronet theater, L.A., June 10, 1988. MPAA Rating: R. Running time: **103 MIN.**

Ivan Danko	Arnold Schwarzenegger
Art Ridzik	James Belushi
Lou Donnelly	Peter Boyle
Viktor Rostavili	Ed O'Ross
Lt. Stobbs	Larry Fishburne
Cat Manzetti	Gina Gershon
Sgt. Gallagher	Richard Bright
Abdul Elijah	Brent Jennings
Gregor Moussorsky	Savely Kramarov
Consul Stephanovich	Gene Scherer
Night clerk	Pruitt Taylor Vince
Salim	J.W. Smith
Hooker	Gretchen Palmer

Hollywood — Hot on the heels of "Rambo III," the good folks over at Carolco have come up with their contribution to *glasnost* in "Red Heat," a picture dedicated to illustrating how much more effective ruthless Russian techniques are in dealing with murderous drug dealers than are namby-pamby American methods.

Walter Hill has essentially remade "48 HRS." with Arnold Schwarzenegger substituting for Eddie Murphy, and while Schwarzenegger isn't quite as funny as Murphy, he's a lot tougher, and his manhandling of the bad guys here will give his fans enough to hoot and holler about to make this heavy actioner into a summer winner.

Regardless of its merits, "Red Heat" has earned a place in the history books as the first entirely American-produced film to have been permitted to lens in the USSR, and it is admittedly a thrill to see Red Square and other landmarks in such a context, even if location work was essentially limited to establishing shots.

Given the setting, violent opening sequence seems all the more bizarre, almost like something out of Visconti's "The Damned," as a horde of nearly naked, strapping men (and a few voluptuous women) work and hang out in a dungeon-like gym of steamy decadence.

Entire early Moscow section (shot mostly in Budapest) established the notion that one of the prices the East will pay for opening up is an increase in the Western disease of drug dealing. A particularly loathesome practitioner in the field named Viktor (Ed O'Ross) manages to slip through the fingers of the Red Army's top enforcer (guess who) and heads for Chicago, where he joins up with two other Russian emigrés enjoying the criminal fruits of the free society.

In full uniform, Schwarzenegger arrives at O'Hare Airport, where he is greeted by two working stiffs from the Chicago Police Dept., James Belushi and Richard Bright. Belushi is assigned to keep tabs on the terminator as the latter tracks down Viktor, which sets up a comic team that may not be the most hilarious ever invented, but still embodies enough amusing oppositions to keep the viewer diverted.

Despite a generally irreverent attitude, Belushi at least pretends respect for the rights of the accused and attempts to instruct his guest on the niceties of the Miranda decision. Schwarzenegger's reaction to this is even more derisive than Dirty Harry's and is turned into a running gag that will delight knee-jerk right-wingers everywhere.

Like those of Dirty Harry (of whom Schwarzenegger's Ivan Danko has pointedly never heard), the Russian's methods are of a fascistic law-and-order variety, but they get the job done where all else fails and are therefore mightily satisfying to mass audiences.

Although it could arouse ire in some quarters, one particularly potent scene, due to its pointed dialog and fine acting of Brent Jennings, has a black Islamic druglord explaining to Schwarzenegger from his prison base how the Russians are failed revolutionaries, and how he, the only true Marxist in the room, hopes to afflict as many whites as possible worldwide with destructive drug addiction.

Hill's storytelling falls down in a few places, notably in the ambiguous role played by the only woman of note in the cast, a go-between figure essayed by Gina Gershon, and in the action climax, a bus chase that comes off as just gruesomely destructive.

The attitudinizing quips, tongue-in-cheek repartee of the two leads, snappy pace and (sometimes literally) black-and-white stand-offs between good and evil keep things reasonably entertaining on an undemanding cartoon level.

Schwarzenegger, who, when he dons a green suit, is dubbed "Gumby" by Belushi, is right on target with his characterization of the iron-willed soldier, and Belushi proves a quicksilver foil.

As usual on Hill's pictures, production values are very high across the board, although lenser Matthew F. Leonetti's compositions tend to group the objects of their focus toward the center of the frame, as if with eventual vidcassette and tv showings in mind.

Pic is dedicated to second unit director-stunt coordinator Bennie Dobbins, who died during production. —Cart.

Glashjertet
(The Glass Heart)
(DANISH)

An SFC release of a Filmforsyningen production in association with the Danish Film Institute and DR/TV. Written and directed by Elisabeth Rygaard. Camera (Eastmancolor), Jesper Bech Sörensen; art direction, Sös Brysch, Elisabeth Holst; editor, assistant director, Lizzi Weischenfeldt; sound, Hans Packert, Iben Haahr Andersen; music, Pernille Utzon Ravn. Reviewed at the Grand, Copenhagen, May 9, 1988. Running time: 62 MIN.
Maja ....Louise Helner
Peter..............Troels Hagen Findsen
The Mother..................Ilse Rande
The Father................Kurt Ravn
The Grandmother ....Birgit Brüel
The Girlfriend ....Susanne Lundberg

Copenhagen — "The Glass Heart" has no real action and consists of closeups of a family in and immediately after a breakup.

The camera and writer-director Elisabeth Rygaard reserve most of their sympathy for the two children of the divorcing couple. Film is soft-spoken, low-keyed and has handsome cinematography, a natural narrative flow and fine acting in all roles. Although given a theatrical release on home territory, item's natural window, also because of its brief length, is television.

The breakup of the young married couple is depicted without excess of hysterics; both parents remain moderately sympathetic throughout. It is what the breakup causes the children in heartbreak, anger and other suffering that holds attention through the no-plot action. A puppet theater and a glass heart trinket plus visits with a

youthful grandmother help the kids come through their trial period with unbroken spirits.—Kell.

Poltergeist III

An MGM/UA Distribution Co. release of an MGM production. Produced by Barry Bernardi. Executive producer, Gary Sherman. Directed by Sherman. Screenplay, Sherman, Brian Taggert; camera (Astro color, Technicolor prints), Alex Nepomniaschy; editor, Ross Albert; music, Joe Renzetti; sound (Dolby), Glenn Williams; production design, Paul Erads; special makeup design, John Caglione Jr., Doug Drexler; special makeup consultant, Dick Smith; special visual effects design, Sherman; casting, Jane Alderman, Shelley Andreas. Reviewed at Filmland, Culver City, Calif., June 9, 1988. MPAA Rating: PG-13. Running time: 97 MIN.
Bruce Gardner ....Tom Skerritt
Patricia Gardner ....Nancy Allen
Carol Anne ....Heather O'Rourke
Tangina ....Zelda Rubinstein
Donna ....Lara Flynn Boyle
Dr. Seaton ....Richard Fire
Scott ....Kip Wentz
Kane ....Nathan Davis

Hollywood — True to the first two, "Poltergeist III" features a lot of people running around believing everything will be just fine if they can make it to the light. They're right. Eventually, the film's over and the light comes on, ending all the horror.

As the third chapter unfolds, poor little Carol Anne (the late Heather O'Rourke) has had to move again. As those who've followed her previous real-estate adventures may recall, the young girl has an unfortunate tendency to get pulled into the framework of her domiciles by poltergeists. Once in the walls, the idea is she can help the demons get out or something like that; it's never been too clear.

For whatever reason, her parents (played by Craig T. Nelson and JoBeth Williams before) have had enough of such annoyance and shipped Carol Anne off to live with her aunt and uncle (Nancy Allen and Tom Skerritt) in a brand-new Chicago high-rise.

It's a good thing uncle manages the building and didn't ask for references because no sooner does Carol Anne move in than the mirrors start to crack and icebergs begin to form, not to mention the noise in her bedroom and the smoke that follows her down the hallway.

The family relationships are somewhat confused, but there's a teenage daughter (Lara Flynn Boyle) and her boyfriend (Kip Wentz) who get dragged into the basement floor with Carol Anne and a know-it-all school psychiatrist (Richard Fire), who may or may not have been dropped down the elevator shaft. If anybody expects to find out by the end what happens to all of these people, or why, that is far too much to anticipate.

Oh, yes, Zelda Rubinstein is back as Tangina, the friendly psychic who knows more about the inside of walls than a carpenter. It's best not

to try to figure out how she fits into the picture, either.

Following the pattern set by his "Poltergeist" predecessors, director-cowriter Gary Sherman demonstrates absolutely no interest in whether this film ever has a modicum of meaning as he rushes from one special effect to another. Even there, Sherman arrives too late. Though done well, the effex here have pretty much become standard, up to and including the usual bursting bodies.

Finally, good old Tangina takes the chief poltergeist preacher off into the air-conditioning ducts and somewhere he'll be happy and Auntie Allen is sorry she ever regretted asking her niece to move in with them, saving Carole Anne from a long life in the streets. Good thing: the homeless have enough trouble already. —Har.

The Presidio

A Paramount Pictures release of a D. Constantine Conte production. Produced by Conte. Executive producer, Jonathan A. Zimbert. Directed by Peter Hyams. Screenplay, Larry Ferguson; camera (Panavision, Technicolor), Hyams; editor, James Mitchell; music, Bruce Boughton; sound (Dolby), Gene S. Cantamessa; production design, Albert Brenner; art direction, Kandy Stern, set design, Roland E. Hill Jr., Harold L. Fuhrman, Bernard P. Cutler; set decoration, Marvin March; special effects coordinator, Philip C. Cory; stunt coordinator, Glenn Wilder; coproducer, Fred Caruso; assistant director, Alan B. Curtiss; casting, Janet Hirshenson, Jane Jenkins. Reviewed at Samuel Goldwyn theater, L.A., June 8, 1988. MPAA Rating: R. Running time: 97 MIN.
Lt. Col. Caldwell ....Sean Connery
Jay Austin ....Mark Harmon
Donna Caldwell ....Meg Ryan
Sgt. Maj. Maclure..........Jack Warden
Arthur Peale ....Mark Blum
Col. Lawrence ....Dana Gladstone
Patti Jean Lynch ....Jenette Goldstein

Hollywood — Sure to be talked about for its vivid chase scenes and worthy performances, "The Presidio" is nonetheless an elaborate distraction built around a slight crime story. Likely to capture the public's curiosity but not its imagination, pic should rank high in initial 1,100-screen release, then quickly lose stripes.

Sean Connery and Mark Harmon go head to head as an Army provost marshal and a San Francisco cop who clash jurisdictions and styles in the investigation of an M.P.'s murder.

Naturally, there's a backstory — they'd locked horns earlier when Connery was Harmon's c.o. in the military — and a complication — Harmon gets involved with Connery's frisky and equally willful daughter, Meg Ryan.

Tug of war for dominance among the trio provides the interest in an otherwise ordinary crime story, as Harmon and Connery end up working to piece together clues in a convoluted smuggling caper.

Along the way there are three

very splashy action sequences — a car chase through the army base and the streets of S.F., a footrace through crowded Chinatown and the final, treacherous shootout in a water bottling plant that becomes as hairy as the swamps of 'Nam.

Editor Jim Mitchell, sound mixer Gene Cantamessa, composer Bruce Broughton and production designer Albert Brenner deserve kudos for the taut, explosive texture of these vivid scenes.

Director-cinematographer Peter Hyams brings off a punchy, fast-paced and well-rounded film, giving plenty of weight to relationship scenes as well, but writer Larry Ferguson's ambitious attempts at character development don't quite go over. Dialog is often over-obvious and not too original. Story is entertaining and well-produced, but unconvincing, with a professional, made-to-order feel.

Location filming doesn't seem to matter much to the story, which has little to say about the Army or the 212-year-old Presidio army base.

While Ferguson has skillfully woven its locations, such as the museum and the cemetery, into the fabric of the story, this pic is even less about the Presidio than "The Big Easy" was about New Orleans.

Hyams, a skilled visual stylist, uses its canvas to advantage in carefully composed shots. Cinematography throughout has a spacious, fluid look and artful lighting creates interest even in interiors as drab as army quarters.

Connery is the most compelling of the stars as the topflight old officer with the lingering Scottish burr, his contradictions glimmering just beneath the surface of a tough hide.

Harmon, meanwhile, creates a character of such brickheaded intensity that he definitely holds his own with Connery, as well as with Ryan. He also does many of his own stunts, including a grueling steeplechase over the tops of cars in the Chinatown scene.

Ryan, playing a femme whose raison d'être is to cause tension between men, makes a fetchingly impulsive, if inconsequential, foil.

Story goes the distance with Connery, including a cemetery scene at the end where he sheds tears, and a drunk scene where he opens up to his pal. Yet the script lets him down — it's disappointing that when a guy like him lets down his guard, he doesn't have something more interesting to say.

While Ferguson (who also penned "Beverly Hills Cop II") sets up a skillful back-and-forth struggle between the two leads, the crime caper that's supposedly at the core of this vehicle isn't very interesting, and the murder of the M.P. seems to matter only on principle.

Jack Warden does a sympathetic turn as Connery's war-hero pal, while Mark Blum and the excellent

Dana Gladstone in minor roles add texture and credibility to the cast.
— *Daws.*

Sensations

A Platinum Pictures production. Produced and directed by Chuck Vincent. Screenplay, Craig Horrall, based on story by Vincent; camera (color), Larry Revene; music, Joey Mennonna; sound, Dale Whitman, production design, Faizool Husain, Mark Hammond; costumes, Jeff Wallach, associate producer, Jeremiah Hawkins. Reviewed at Cannes Film Festival (market), May 14, 1988. MPAA Rating: R. Running time: **91 MIN.**

Jenny Hunter	Rebecca Lynn
Brian Ingles	Blake Bahner
Della Randall	Jennifer Delora
Dave Salt	Rick Savage
Harold Nichols	Frank Stewart
Beatrice Cox	Loretta Palma
Tippy	Jane Hamilton
Duke	W.P. Dremak
Mr. Sikes	Scott Baker
Baxter	Harvey Siegel

Cannes — The once hardcore and now softcore helmer Chuck Vincent has always distinguished his work with a keen sense of plot as well as a sensuous way of handling sex scenes. With "Sensations," Vincent seems to have lot his touch.

Watching this mostly tedious item about the love life of a male stripper and female hustler, the thought occurs that the pic is unredeemable except for the sexual content. Unfortunately, the erotica comes too late and too little.

Vincent dotes here on all the things in which he's weakest: acting, production values, music, photography, etc. It doesn't help matters that Craig Horrall's screenplay is silly, an inexplicable turn of events for a Vincent pic (script is based on director's story).

Principal character as played by Rebecca Lynn (a.k.a. porn star Krista Lane) is a shrill prostie who accidentally meets a chiseled gigolo-male stripper (Blake Bahner). The two take such an exaggerated dislike to one another it's inevitable they'll wind up in various romantic situations.

Before getting there, there's some silliness about winning the lottery, a forced marriage and various other encounters too silly to go into. Enough said, the script forces these largely unformed performers into performances of various shades of unpleasantness.

By the time the sex scenes arrive — nudity is tastefully handled although a tad beyond the usual R pic — "Sensations" is irretrievably lost. Single nice acting turn is contributed by Jane Hamilton (former hardcore heroine under the name Veronica Hart), as a strip club proprietress. All else is yawns. — *Sege.*

Blanc de chine
(Chinese White)
(FRENCH)

An AMLF release of an Adelaide Prods./ CFC/Ciné Cinq coproduction. Produced by Marjorie Israel, Marc Chayette. Directed by Denys Granier-Deferre. Screenplay, Granier-Deferre, Yves Stavrides; camera (color), Raoul Coutard; editor, Sophie Cornu; music, Romano Musumara; sound, Dominique Levert, Gérard Lamps; art direction, Jean-Marc Kerdelhue; assistant director, Olivier Peray; production manager, Hugues Nonn. Reviewed at the Gaumont Ambassade cinema, Paris, May 3, 1988. (In Cannes Film Festival Market.) Running time: **85 MIN.**

Mathieu	Robin Renucci
Batz	Michel Piccoli
Jay	Marguerite Tran
Jason Hunt	Denys Hawthorne
Malcolm	Don Henderson
Mayotte	J.C. Quinn
Sang	Ham Chau Luong
Bastien	Antoine Dulery
Rinaldi	Claude Faraldo

Paris — Third feature film by Denys Granier-Deferre, son of veteran helmer Pierre Granier-Deferre, is a routine thriller with international locations, typically convoluted plotting and assorted killings.

Like his dad, helmer has no personal style and is only as good as his screenplay, which in this case is not much.

Tale, by director and Yves Stavrides, jumps between Hong Kong and Paris and musters up some fearful questions about a series of murders in Paris' Asiatic community, where Chinese and Vietnamese are slaughtering each other.

Soon it becomes clear that much of the ado concerns a lovely young Vietnamese orphan (Marguerite Tran), who was whisked out of Vietnam during the fall of Saigon in 1975.

Her savior was Robin Renucci, the son of Corsican plantation owners, who had to marry the girl (then only seven) in order to get her out. Now, some 10 years later, Renucci is pressed into service by the government to help resolve the mystery.

Up to this point, the script and direction have some flavor and promise, but it soon becomes disappointingly clear that all the spilled blood is a smokescreen for a settling of accounts between two characters once involved in a CIA plot, during the Vietnam War. This sets up an odd climactic scene in which Renucci and his two antagonists sit down to a mortal game of Russian roulette, Chinese style.

Michel Piccoli was recruited for a little added relief as a vulgar secret service boss, though his scenes are superfluous.

Tech credits are okay. Ace lenser Raoul Coutard seems to have relaxed his talents on this one, turning in a merely workmanlike job. —*Len.*

Gaspard et Fils
(Gaspard And Son)
(CANADIAN)

A Cinema Plus release of a Films Vision 4 production. Produced by Suzanne Henault, Claude Bonin. Directed by François Labonte. Screenplay, Monique Proulx; camera (color), Michel Caron; editor, Jean Guy Montpetit; music, Denis Larochelle; art direction, Jean Baptiste Tard; costumes, Denis Sperdouklis; sound, Dominique Chartrand; sound editing, Marcel Pothier. Reviewed at Cannes Film Festival (market), May 13, 1988. Running time: **91 MIN.**

Gaspard Chuinard	Jacques Godin
Claude Chuinard	Gaston Lepage
Aunt Evelyn	Monique Miller
Maxime	Yves Desgagnes
Venezuelan girl	Monica Verge
Also with Julien Poulin, Mimi Destee.

Cannes — "Gaspard et Fils" is being shown on large screens at the film market, but seems destined for video and tv sales.

Highlight is lead performances by Quebec star Jacques Godin and Gaston Lepage, but it's unlikely a dubbed version could accurately interpret the relationship between father and son.

Pic probably will stay in Quebec with possible French video action. Gaspard Chuinard assumes his 40-year-old son Claude is a 1-dimensional bookworm when the reality is Claude sits in his office pretending to be different characters from various plays. Claude assumes his father just sits around the house they share burping and making a mess. Instead, Gaspard spends his days reading the books in his son's extensive library.

They continue the charade to please one another and to create a distance that has been particularly pronounced since the death of Madame Chuinard 11 years earlier. They are given an opportunity to close the gap when Gaspard realizes a winning lottery ticket is missing. The search for the ticket takes them into the streets of Montreal, where Gaspard has not set foot since his wife died, to New York City and eventually Venezuela. The gap grows even greater, however, with neither showing a sign of lessening his dislike for the other.

"Gaspard et Fils" is not particularly good, but in lesser hands it could have been a nightmare. Writer Monique Proulx doesn't give either character much of interest to say in the early going, so director François Labonte gives the actors a lot of room to move. The actors do their best, but the lack of a strong script almost overwhelms the fine acting. —*Cadd.*

The Unnamable

A K.P. Prods. presentation of a Yankee Classic Pictures production. Produced by Dean Ramser, Jean-Paul Ouellette. Executive producer, Paul White. Line producer, Terry L. Benedict. Directed by Ouellette. Screenplay, Ouellette, from H.P. Lovecraft's story; camera (Foto-Kem color), Tom Fraser; editor, Wendy J. Plump; music, David Bergeaud; sound, Stuart Fox; production design, Gene Abel; art direction, Tim Keating; set decoration, Ann Job; special makeup effects, R. Christopher Biggs; production manager-associate producer, Michael Haney; casting, Paul McKenna. Reviewed on Vidmark Entertainment vidcassette, N.Y., June 9, 1988. MPAA Rating: R. Running time: **87 MIN.**

Howard Damon	Charles King
Randolph Carter	Mark Kinsey Stephenson
Tanya	Alexandra Durrell
Wendy	Laura Albert
Alyda Winthrop	Katrin Alexandre
Bruce	Eben Ham
John Babcock	Blane Wheatley
Joel Manton	Mark Parra

"The Unnamable" is an unsuccessful attempt to adapt one of H.P. Lovecraft's early short stories (circa "Herbert West: Re-Animator") to the screen. Feature is being released direct-to-video.

Lovecraft's brief tale "The Unnamable" was written in 1923 and presents the author's trademark description of indescribable dread, monsters too horrible to contemplate. In the opening reel, filmmaker Jean-Paul Ouellette faithfully presents Lovecraft's notions of imagination vs. pedestrian reality, but the remainder of the film is a tedious trek through a spooky house by teen college students from Miskatonic U., firmly in the vein of trite fraternity/sorority hazing adventures.

Whereas Lovecraft drew horror from suggestion and innuendo, film tries to concretely depict the unnamable, and fails. There is considerable graphic bloodletting on view but nothing scary. The monster from the attic room turns out to be a female harpy, very well played in mime and heavy makeup by Katrin Alexandre.

Although the effects are acceptable, pic suffers from a low budget, with weak detailing, e.g., a prolog with a couple of early 18th century guys sporting modern haircuts. Quickie happy ending with a jokey tagline doesn't fit at all. — *Lor.*

Red Nights

A Trans World Entertainment presentation, in association with Gad Lesham, Amnon Lesham. Produced by Ron Wolotsky. Executive producers, Moshe Diamant, Gad Lesham, Amnon Lesham. Line producer, Rafael Eisenman. Written and directed by Izhak Hanooka. Camera (color), Jacob Eleasari; editor, David Lloyd; music, Tangerine Dream; sound, Ami Ron, Robert Janiger; production design, Rina Binyamini; set decoration, Myron Emery; associate producer, Lisa Yesko; casting, Gary Adams, Bob Gould. Reviewed on TWE vidcassette, N.Y., June 3, 1988. MPAA Rating: R. Running time: **89 MIN.**

Randy	Christopher Parker
David	Brian Matthews
Bruce	Tom Badal
Betty	Patti Bauer
Uncle Solly	Jack Carter
Jeff	James Mayberry
Phillip	William Smith
Peter	Ivan E. Roth
Helen	Tawny Capriccio
Stripper	Anna Louise

"Red Nights" is a rather tame entry in the Hollywood exposé genre, chronicling the disillusionment and tragedy of a would-be movie actor struggling in tinseltown. Pic has predictably gone the direct-to-video route.

Innocent-looking Christopher Parker portrays Randy, a kid from New Hampshire who once had a role in a locally lensed tv movie, who arrives in Hollywood with hopes of a career in Westerns. His best buddy David (Brian Matthews) already has fallen into the drug scene, with evil Bruce (Tom Badal) putting the screws on him to push the stuff.

Randy falls in love with a cute blond, Betty (Patti Bauer) whom he meets at a party, but is crushed when he finds out this aspiring actress makes ends meet by acting in porno films, produced by of all people Jack Carter, the comic cast here as a sleazeball.

Hero's downward spiral accelerates as he doesn't show up for work at a novelty shop run by William Smith, quits his acting workshop and holes up in his shabby apartment. Climax occurs as he goes after Bruce for deadly revenge after the drug kingpin has David killed; unnecessary flashback structure tells the whole story from the point at which Randy is under siege by the police.

Filmmaker Izhak Hanooka gets convincing performances but his story is one long cliché, shedding no new light on the tawdry image of the film capital. Final irony of a reporter asking Randy: "I hear you're an actor?" as the police hustle him to the hoosegow — cut to a closeup of Randy on the tv screen newscast, featured at last, is cornball.

Parker and Matthews are effective, with Badal as the heavy with a weird laugh adding an unusual wrinkle to the proceedings. Tangerine Dream's trademark pulsating score punches up the action. — *Lor.*

Who Framed Roger Rabbit
(LIVE/ANIMATED)

A Buena Vista release of a Touchstone Pictures and Amblin Entertainment presentation, in association with Silver Screen Partners III. Executive producers, Steven Spielberg, Kathleen Kennedy. Produced by Robert Watts, Frank Marshall. Directed by Robert Zemeckis. Screenplay, Jeffrey Price, Peter S. Seaman, from Gary K. Wolf's book "Who Censored Roger Rabbit?" Camera (Rank color, Metrocolor and Deluxe prints), Dean Cundey; editor, Arthur Schmidt; music, Alan Silvestri; sound (Dolby), Tony Dawe (U.K.), Michael Evje (U.S.); animation director, Richard Williams; production design, Elliot Scott, Roger Cain; special visual effects, Industrial Light & Magic, supervisor, Ken Ralston; mechanical effects supervisor, George Gibbs; costume design, Joanna Johnston; production managers, Patricia Carr (U.K.), Jack Frost Sanders (U.S.); assistant director, Michael Murray (U.K.), David McGiffert (U.S.); second unit directors, Ian Sharp and Frank Marshall (U.K.), Max Kleven (U.S.); art direction, Stephen Scott (U.K.), William McAllister (U.S.); set decoration, Peter Howitt (U.K.), Robert R. Benton (U.S.); additional camera, Paul Beeson; supervising animators, Andreas Deja, Russell Hall, Phil Nibbelink, Simon Wells; animation effects supervisor, Christopher Knott; matte and rotoscope supervisor, Annie Elvin; animation camera supervisor, John Leatherbarrow; additional animation — supervising animator, Dale L. Baer; animation consultants, Walt Stanchfield, Stan Green, Chuck Jones; post-production supervisor, Martin Cohen; associate producers, Don Hahn, Steve Starkey; casting, Priscilla John (U.K.), Reuben Cannon & Associates (U.S.). Reviewed at Disney Studios, Burbank, Calif., June 13, 1988. MPAA Rating: PG. Running time: **103 MIN.**

Eddie Valiant	Bob Hoskins
Judge Doom	Christopher Lloyd
Dolores	Joanna Cassidy
Marvin Acme	Stubby Kaye
R.K. Maroon	Alan Tilvern
Lt. Santino	Richard Le Parmentier
Raoul Raoul	Joel Silver
Jessica performance model	Betsy Brantley

Voices of:

Roger Rabbit, Benny the Cab, etc.	Charles Fleischer
Jessica	Kathleen Turner (speaking), Amy Irving (singing)
Baby Herman	Lou Hirsch
Daffy Duck, Bugs Bunny, Tweety Bird, Sylvester, Porky Pig	Mel Blanc
Gorilla	Morgan Deare
Betty Boop	Mae Questel
Donald Duck	Tony Anselmo
Yosemite Sam	Joe Alakey
Wheezy, Lena Hyena	June Foray
Droopy	Richard Williams
Mickey Mouse	Wayne Allwine
Minnie Mouse	Russi Taylor
Goofy	Tony Pope
Woody Woodpecker	Cherry Davis
Pinocchio	Peter Westy
Singing Sword	Frank Sinatra

Hollywood — Years in the planning and making, "Who Framed Roger Rabbit" is an unparalleled technical achievement where animation is brilliantly integrated into live action. Yet, for the obvious effort and expense it took to pull this off visually, the story it's set to amounts to little more than inspired silliness about the filmmaking biz where cartoon characters face off against cartoonish humans.

Combination of the curiosity factor, a great trailer and a PG rating likely will turn this into another moneymaker for the studio.

Announcement that Gary Wolf's book "Who Censored Roger Rabbit?" would be made into an animated feature for Walt Disney Prods. was first made in 1981. During the turmoil at the studio, project was developed slowly but didn't go into production until 1986 when it evolved into a live-action/animated feature done in association with Steven Spielberg's Amblin Entertainment and shot primarily in London. It subsequently became a Touchstone Pictures release (in association with Amblin) as studio execs figured some suggestive scenes featuring a buxom lounge singer who figures prominently in the film were not Disney material.

Given all this background, it is interesting to see how the energies of a lot of talented visual effects types — animators and others — was spent (about 300 people are listed in the 7-minute credit crawl at the end of the film).

Pic opens appropriately enough with a cartoon, a hilarious, overblown, calamitous scene where Roger Rabbit, a famous contract Toon player (as in ca*rtoon*) for Maroon Studios, is failing in his attempt to keep Baby Herman (voice by Lou Hirsch) from the cookie jar. Roger (voice by the amazing Charles Fleischer) gets electrified, slips on a soap bar, is crushed under the weight of a refrigerator and so on and in characteristic cartoon fashion comes through a little worse for wear but very much "alive."

From here, the camera backs up from the set where we find Roger getting yelled at by the director (a cameo role for producer Joel Silver) because when he gets conked in the head, he sees dumb birds instead of stars. Things aren't going well for poor Roger. Ever since he became estranged from his voluptuous human character Toon wife Jessica (sultry, uncredited voice courtesy of Kathleen Turner) he just can't act.

This is the context from which scripters Jeffrey Price and Peter S. Seaman, in adapting Wolf's story, try to work up a Raymond Chandler-style suspenser where Roger becomes an innocent murder suspect, with a disheveled, alcoholic private eye (Bob Hoskins) being his only hope to help him beat the rap.

The reaches they go to achieve a tongue-in-cheek parody of a 1940s meller are commendable, except that the results fall somewhere short of expectations.

The fact that this is fantasy doesn't excuse some basic flaws in character development — most notably Roger himself, an obnoxious, irritating rabbit with no discernible charm to have such a super vixen for a wife. (She says later she loves him for his sense of humor.)

Hoskins compensates somewhat by having the good sense to throttle the wired hare given any opportunity — and there are many — as he goes about solving who murdered whom and why Roger is being set up.

Inside jokes about Hollywood abound, though they probably won't be lost on the audience, while others on the history and development of Los Angeles (destruction of the Red Car system to make way for freeways) are clearly funnier to local filmgoers.

Triumphing over the material, which loses freshness and oomph as it goes along, is the filmmaking itself.

Robert Zemeckis, whose sole film project since the 1985 blockbuster "Back To The Future" has been "Who Framed Roger Rabbit," has a good sense of pacing for the live-action scenes, though it is hard to separate them out for distinctive direction when nearly all of them contain animated figures superimposed later.

The real stars are the animators, under British animation director Richard Williams, who have pulled off a technically amazing feat of having humans and Toons seem to be interacting with one another. It is clear from how well the imagery syncs that a lot of painstaking work went into this production — and clearly a lot of money.

Arguably the funniest moment in the film is when Hoskins gets his first introduction to Jessica as she steps down from the stage during her lounge act at the Ink and Paint Club — bust thrust forward and tiny waist pinched in by a slinky strapless gown — to sexily cozy up to him and gag king Marvin Acme (Stubby Kaye) as they stare drooling while she moves closer.

Visual impact of her on screen never lessens and she remains sexy and alluring throughout, more than can be said for real-life love interest of Hoskins, Joanna Cassidy, a warmhearted bar owner whose personality is found somewhere between Mae West and Goodie Two Shoes.

Other major human performances are played by Christopher Lloyd, crazy-eyed evil but not on par with his looney "Back To The Future" role, and Alan Tilvern as the cigar-chompin' movie mogul R.K. Maroon.

Many recognizable Disney and Warner Bros. cartoon characters, who here are residents of Toonville, take turns either thwarting or abetting Hoskins.

Great jazzy background music by Alan Silvestri gives atmosphere to the production. Production designers Elliott Scott and Roger Cain did an equally terrific job recreating a seedy Sam Spade office for Hoskins and okay railway bar — *Brit.*

De laatste reis
(The Last Voyage)
(DUTCH)

A Netherlands Filmmuseum release of a Rolf Orthel/Frans van de Staak production. Directed by Kees Hin. Screenplay, Hin, Otto Ketting; camera (color, 16m), Mat van Hensbergen; editor, Van de Staak, Hin; music, Matthijs Vermeulen, orchestrated by Ketting;

sound, Piotr van Dijk; set decoration, Ruben Schwarz; production manager, Dick van den Heuvel, Carol Bloom, Marieke Willekens. Reviewed at Rialto theater, Amsterdam, May 28, 1988. Running time: **100 MIN.**

Matthijs Vermeulen .... Hans Hoes
Annie/Thea .... Judy Doorman
Brother .... Michel van Rooij
Archivist . . Diederik de Groot van Embden

Amsterdam — Finely crafted with imagination and intelligence, "The Last Voyage" is a biopic about Matthijs Vermeulen (1888-1967), the son of poor Catholics who studied to be a missionary, but instead became one of Holland's most influential and controversial music critics.

He was a talented composer as well, but the antagonism of Willem Mengelberg, the undisputed czar of the Dutch music world (until his disgrace after World War II as a Nazi collaborator) effectively prevented Vermeulen from having his work performed anywhere.

Director Kees Hin, a prolific filmmaker who has worked in documentaries, industrial films and features with the same abiding sense of eccentric curiosity, dramatizes the decisive moments of a life in brief sequences, capturing the essence of a man living in, through and for his music.

There is a skillful blend of realism and fantasy, with the Soldier of Rupert Brooke's famous Great War poem (which Vermeulen set to music) making periodic apperances, as does the legendary Flying Dutchman, and a young man in formal dress with white gloves, who acts as a kind of guide for the protagonist and the audience. Despite the use of nonrealistic elements, there is never a feeling of preciosity or artiness.

Despite a mere $55,000 budget, Hin and his collaborators have fashioned a technically outstanding production which proves an art film about an artist can be engrossing and entertaining.

Special mention is due to Otto Ketting for his orchestration and conducting of Vermeulen's music. Acting, notably Hans Hoes in the central role, is uniformly good.
— *Wall.*

The Great Outdoors

A Universal Pictures release of a Hughes Entertainment production. Produced by Arne L. Schmidt. Executive producers, John Hughes, Tom Jacobson. Directed by Howard Deutch. Screenplay, Hughes; camera (CFI color), Ric Waite; editor, Tom Rolf, William Gordean, Seth Flaum; music, Thomas Newman; production design, John W. Corso; set design, Sharon Busse; sound (Dolby), Darin Knight; choreographer, Kenny Ortega; stunt coordinator, Walter Scott; associate producers, Stephen Lim, Ellen Spiotta; assistant director, Lim; second unit director, Scott; second unit camera, Robert Thomas; casting, Judith Weiner. Reviewed at Directors Guild theater, L.A., June 15, 1988. MPAA Rating: PG. Running time: **90 MIN.**

Roman .... Dan Aykroyd
Chet .... John Candy
Connie .... Stephanie Faracy
Kate .... Annette Bening
Buck .... Chris Young
Ben .... Ian Giatti
Cara .... Hilary Gordon
Mara .... Rebecca Gordon
Wally .... Robert Prosky
Cammie .... Lucy Deakins

Hollywood — John Hughes comes nearly full circle with his 10th film and arrives the poorer for ideas. Like his first, "National Lampoon's Vacation," this is a family summer vacation sendup with a "Saturday Night Live" graduate (Dan Aykroyd) at the helm, but the scattered plot shows signs of stress.

Hughes should have vacationed before he wrote this one. Bright package and gag-laden trailer should make this a popular weekend destination in wide release to start, but theaters soon should have plenty of vacancies.

John Candy stars as a sweet, slightly dopey family man who wagoneers his happy brood up from Chicago for a big-pines getaway. No sooner do they unpack than obnoxious brother-in-law Aykroyd and his maladjusted family blast in uninvited to spend the week.

Aykroyd is offensive in every way available to the modern American male — rude, crude, abrasive, aggressive, obsessed with financial 1-upmanship. His pampered wife (Annette Bening) eggs him on, while his spooky kids (twins Hilary and Rebecca Gordon) never say a word.

Hughes conjures up a romance between Candy's teenage son (Chris Young) and a local girl (Lucy Deakins), but that proves the film's biggest letdown. The man who wrote "Sixteen Candles" and "Breakfast Club" suddenly can't think of a thing for teens to say to each other. Deakins' initial tough-talking persona (she has one good line: "I'm not a tourist attraction") flies out the window almost instantly, leaving her putty in the hands of this wordless goon from Chicago.

Last third of the film is a real mess, as filmmakers try to whip up a crisis that will unite the family, with the redheaded twins getting lost in a mineshaft during a wild rainstorm. While Aykroyd rescues them, composer Thomas Newman tries to pump up this unscary scene with an overwrought score à la "Star Wars."

Conversely, the next scene, which is supposed to be funny, is actually scary, as a 1,400-pound grizzly bear chases Candy through the woods and into the house.

Just as in "Planes, Trains & Automobiles," there's also a very shaky third act transition scene: in this case, the much-abused Candy, for an unconvincing reason, lends his creep brother-in-law all the money he has. Then the creep, unconvincingly, becomes conscious-stricken and gives it back.

Despite all this, the Aykroyd-Candy pairing is charmed, with both creating a convincing sense of family despite their wide differences. Aykroyd's performance is aggressive, mental and verbally inventive, his rapidfire timing right on; while Candy is all emotion and reaction. Best scene is their stand-off, when Candy kicks Aykroyd out.

Stephanie Faracy is excellent as Candy's sweet, happy wife, and Bening is also savvy in her role. Ian Giatti makes a good impression as Candy's 10-year-old son. Robert Prosky has limited success in a comic role as the innkeeper.

Pic teams director Howard Deutch with writer-executive producer Hughes for the third time, while Ric Waite lenses, and all tech credits are just fine. — *Daws.*

Taffin
(BRITISH/U.S.)

An MGM/UA Communications release of a United British Artists/Rafford Films/MGM production. Produced by Peter Shaw. Executive producer, Allan Scott. Directed by Francis Megahy. Screenplay, David Ambrose, based Lyndon Mallet's book; camera (Technicolor), Paul Beeson; editor, Peter Tanner; music, Stanley Myers, Hans Zimmer; production design, William Alexander; associate producer, John Davis; casting, Ros and John Hubbard. Reviewed on MGM/UA vidcassette, N.Y., June 16, 1988. MPAA Rating: R. Running time: **96 MIN.**

Taffin .... Pierce Brosnan
O'Rourke .... Ray McAnally
Charlotte .... Alison Doody
Martin .... Jeremy Child
Mrs. Martin .... Dearbhla Molloy
Conway .... Jim Bartley
Sprawley .... Alan Stanford
Ed .... Gerald McSorley
Mo Taffin .... Patrick Bergin
Mrs. Taffin .... Britta Smith
Also with: Jonathan Ryan, Liz Lloyd, Ronan Wilmot, Liam O'Callaghan, Frank Kelley, Catherine Byrne.

Credit MGM/UA for accurately assessing this shaggy action/adventure's narrow theatrical potential, and moving it quickly after a brief Texas run in February into the homevid market. "Taffin" is a minor vehicle for primetime tv star Pierce Brosnan, and his name doesn't seem strong enough to realize more than minor ancillary returns.

Brosnan is Mark Taffin, a raffish Irish lad who has never left his hometown and is on good terms with his family. He's a black sheep who dropped out of the seminary and became a freelance debt collector.

He's only in it for the money until big city developers threaten the local athletic field. Using his smarts, Brosnan succeeds in getting the project (a chemical plant) moved to an adjacent empty lot, but when the developers' hired thugs go too far, the hero ultimately becomes an Irish "Equalizer."

Technicolor pic's characters and issues are strictly black and white. The heavies, comprised of the icy thugs, their greedy boss and corrupt solons, are too heavy. The good guys, led by self-righteous Ray McAnally, spout clichés on environmental destruction.

Taffin occupies the grey area for much of the pic while his family, fellow citizens and girlfiend (Alison Doody) nag him into Doing The Right Thing. Until his commitment, culminating in a Western-style shootout with the executive villain, the Brosnan character's contradictions are more confusing than enriching.

His studious traits — "The brain is more powerful than muscle," he says — are rendered implausible when Taffin, like his adversaries, uses plenty of muscle.

Resulting action and violence makes "Taffin" tailor-made for the male audience. Females, however drawn they are to Brosnan's charisma, will be turned off by the pic's stock femme characters.

Pic seems too tame for its R rating. Technical contributions are adequate and apparently rendered with the small screen in mind.
— *Binn.*

Going Undercover
(BRITISH)

A Miramax Films release of a Jefferson Colegate-Stone presentation of a Norfolk Intl. production. Produced by John D. Schofield, Colegate-Stone. Executive producers, Sean Redmayne, Barry Plumley. Written and directed by James Kenelm Clarke. Camera (Technicolor), John Coquillon; editor, Eric Boyd-Perkins, Danny Retz; music, Alan Hawkshaw; art direction, Jim Dultz; costume design, Moss Mabry; sound (Dolby), Billy Kaplan; assistant director, Andy Armstrong; second unit director, Stanzi Stokes; second unit camera, Bjorn Blixt; associate producer, Paul Jordan. Reviewed at the AMC Century 14, L.A., June 17, 1988. MPAA Rating: PG-13. Running time: **88 MIN.**

Henry Brilliant .... Chris Lemmon
Maxine De La Hunt .... Jean Simmons
Marigold De La Hunt ..... Lea Thompson
Billy O'Shea .... Mills Watson
Mrs. Bellinger .... Viveca Lindfors
Stephanie .... Nancy Cartwright
Gary .... Joe Michael Terry
Peaches .... Jewel Shepard

Hollywood — That the world is not breathlessly awaiting a lame-brained, unfunny mystery spoof such as "Going Undercover" is borne out by the fact that the picture has been on the shelf for four years. Lensed under the title "Yellow Pages," this hodgepodge of artificial, overworked devices represents an example of a film made with no imaginable audience in mind.

Miramax is going through the motions of a theatrical release, with current solo booking in Los Angeles, and homevid fans won't have to wait long for this one.

Exhibiting many of father Jack's mannerisms, Chris Lemmon stars as a rich boy whose idea of striking out on his own is to emulate Sam Spade and Philip Marlowe by working as a private dick out of the shabbiest office in L.A. Unfortunately, he has none of his idols' cool, and makes his way in life tracking down stray dogs and cats for a few bucks a shot.

As seems to happen with such fellows, however, the entrance of an elegant, mysterious woman through their doors casts everything in a new light, and so it is with Lemmon's Henry Brilliant when Jean Simmons turns up on the other side of his desk. This Beverly Hills matron volunteers to pay $2,000 for the young man to keep an eye on her sexy stepdaughter Lea Thompson on the latter's trip to Europe, the best offer Mr. Brilliant has ever heard.

Little Lea turns out to be quite a little bitch, but her contemptuous attitude toward her chaperone seems justified, as Brilliant repeatedly proves himself an unsophisticated, wimpy nudge, putting a damper on every occasion with his badgering.

The daughter of an eminent scientist, Lea ultimately is kidnaped in Copenhagen, upon which the aspiring detective must swing into action and prove his mettle against sinister but hardly overwhelming foes.

Climax is set in a giant amusement park at night, the better to pay tired homage to Orson Welles via a "Lady From Shanghai" hall of mirrors shootout, and to Alfred Hitchcock for "Strangers On A Train," and what transpires on board the giant rollercoaster is far from convincing.

Only vaguely amusing conceit in writer-director James Kenelm Clarke's screenplay is a similar film buff vein: when Lemmon jumps in a taxi and demands that the driver speed away to elude some pursuers, the cabbie complies and then proceeds to reel off all the great car chases in film history, complete with directors' names, year of release and studio.

If one closes one's eyes to just listen to his line readings, one could easily mistake Chris Lemmon for father Jack's younger self. His protestations, nervous laugh and expressions of anxiety are also remarkably similar. He'll need to bring everything down several notches, however, to make peace with the viewer. Other cast members have almost invariably been seen to better advantage in previous outings.

Visual quality is cheesy, and Alan Hawkshaw's loud and overactive score vainly tries to distract attention from the deficiencies parading about onscreen.—*Cart.*

Mamba
(Fair Game)
(ITALIAN)

An Eidoscope/Reteitalia coproduction. Produced and directed by Mario Orfini. Screenplay, Orfini, Lidia Ravera; camera (Cinecittà color), Dante Spinotti; editor, Claudio Cutry; music, Giorgio Moroder; art direction, Ferdinando Scarfiotti, Osvaldo Desideri; costume consultant, Milena Canonero. Reviewed at Cinecittà, Rome,

May 4, 1988. Running time: **85 MIN.**
Eva . . . . Trudie Styler
Gene . . . . Gregg Henry
Frank . . . . Bill Mosley

Rome — Producer-director Mario Orfini has gone all out in making an American-look production in "Mamba" (also called "Fair Game"), story of a snake and a girl locked in an apartment together. Story concept, setting, and thesping all show a happy marriage of quality Italo technical work and Yank taste. Half-character study, half-thriller, film is a natural pickup for offshore markets.

Pic opens in a very American desert, where Bill Mosley is a reclusive, hippie snake dealer. The steely-eyed, 3-piece-suited Gene (Gregg Henry) knows just what he wants: a deadly little number capable of bumping off his estranged wife. The motive is sheer maliciousness, though there's a strong hint Gene has some ego problems that make female rejection unbearable. He gets the handler to up the hormone count in the mamba's body to make it more feisty; then he tries the nasty critter out on the unsuspecting dealer. It works.

Next step is introducing the snake into the dazzling artistic scenery of wife Eva's loft, a converted warehouse on a hill outside L.A. Trudie Styler plays Eva as a kooky, extroverted sculptress, light years away from her husband's robot-like rigidity. It takes her over half an hour to realize the danger she's in, giving plenty of time to build comical near misses while the mamba forlornly tries to sink his teeth into Eva's temptingly naked legs. Outside, Gene follows the action on a monitor in his car.

When Eva finally notices there's a hyped-up poisonous snake in the house, she gives way first to panic, then switches to comical combat tactics. The final winner isn't hard to deduce, but there are screams anyway strewn through the script. Too schematized to be serious, "Mamba" strikes an entertaining balance between tension and humor.

Styler, known heretofore as Sting's great and good friend, is fine as the elf-like woman who won't give up; Henry a heavy it's a pleasure to hate. The snake is appealing, too, with plenty of p.o.v. shots of its own. Ferdinando Scarfiotti has designed a fantasy loft only the Italians could imagine, while Giorgio Moroder keeps the pace fast with a nervous score. Dante Spinotti's camera is mobile and professional. — *Yung.*

Aurelia
(ITALIAN)

A BIM release of a Telecentauro Films/-Antea coproduction. Produced by Chantal Bergman, Giovanni Marina. Written and directed by Giorgio Molteni. Camera (Technicolor, 16m), Raffaele Martes; editor, Carlo Fontana; music, Paolo Conte. Reviewed at

Fiamma Cinema, Rome, June 8, 1988. Running time: **85 MIN.**
Giuditta . . . . Maddalena Crippa
Tommaso . . . . Fabio Sartor
Also with: Bruno Carandini, Nicola Pistoia, Carlo Monini.

Rome — "Aurelia" is an Italian road movie, penned and shot on a shoestring by Giorgio Molteni. The concept is fresh enough and pair of lead thesps manages to hold interest in a film built around character, not incident.

End result is an offbeat effort that should be neither damned nor praised, but has the merit of trying to do something original.

Tommaso (Fabio Sartor), a young scientist who is getting married in a few days, decides he will hitchhike from Rome to the Ligurian coastal town where his girlfriend lives as a kind of rite of passage from one life to another. While he is unsuccessfully waiting for a ride, a mysterious girl, Giuditta (Maddalena Crippa), appears out of nowhere and becomes his traveling companion. They sleep together in a single sleeping bag and soon are hooked on each other.

Tommaso impulsively says he'll skip the wedding, but the girl rationally argues they have to take life as it comes. Passion rises and cools, and they part without trauma on the morning of Tommaso's wedding.

With cropped, bleached hair and aggressively feminine attire, Maddalena Crippa holds center stage throughout. At one point she suddenly turns up driving an antique MG, wearing a cowboy hat — never explained. Next to her anybody would be dull, but Fabio Sartor provides a good foil as a moody, straight guy. Technically, film is a little grainy but okay. Music by Paolo Conte is fine, but repeated far too often. — *Yung.*

El Tunel
(The Tunnel)
(SPANISH)

A Santiago Cinematográfica production. (Sales, Interaccess Film Distribution.) Produced by Arturo Feliu. Executive producer, Lynn Jones. Directed by Antonio Drove. Screenplay, Carlos A. Cornejo, José A. Mahieu, Drove, based on novel by Ernesto Sábato; camera (Eastmancolor), Giberto Azevedo; editor, Pilar Soto; music, Augusto Alguero Jr., sets, Francisco Prosper, Ercilia Alonso; set design, Elizabeth Menz; production managers, Francisco Ariza, Antonio Ottone. Reviewed at Cine Conde Duque, Madrid, May 6, 1988. Running time: **112 MIN.**
Maria Iribarne . . . . Jane Seymour
Juan Pablo Castel . . . . Peter Weller
Allende . . . . Fernando Rey
Also with: Victoria Zinni, Marga Herrera, Oscar San Juan, Yelena Samarina, Tomás Saez, Anne Henry, Jaime Toja.
(Original English soundtrack)

Madrid — This tale of an obsessive love affair set in Buenos Aires in the 1940s borders on the ludicrously melodramatic and is never quite believable, partly because the characters are too sketchily presented.

Juan Pablo, a successful painter, is fascinated by a beautiful woman who seems absorbed in one of his most "intimate" canvases during an art show. The artist hurries over to accost her, but she has vanished. Obsessively, he seeks her in the streets of Buenos Aires, meets and loses her twice again, until he finally corners her.

Temperamental, alternately suspicious and groveling, the painter now spends every hour with his obsessive infatuation for Maria, who, he gradually learns, comes from a wealthy family and is married to an elderly intellectual. The fiery relationship ends with the painter stabbing his lover to death. However, since yarn is told as one long flashback, we know what is coming from the start.

Never explained is what makes either of the characters tick, nor what their backgrounds are, nor how they have come to be in the situation they are in. Each exists in a vacuum, as though only for the purpose of the story.

Pic uses a very few locations in Buenos Aires, but most of pic is shot in interiors, and could just as well have been set in modern Spain or Argentina. There is a kind of antiquated, almost pastiche look to the film. The manic-depressive vagaries of the painter become tiresome, though both Peter Weller and Jane Seymour put in fine performances as the ill-fated lovers. Music is obtrusive; other credits are okay.

Commercial prospects are decidedly dim in all territories, though pic might be suitable for ancillary markets, especially since it is shot in English. —*Besa.*

Night Friend
(CANADIAN)

A Cineplex Odeon Films release, in association with Film Arts and the Film House Group. Produced by Patricia Gerretsen. Executive producer, Don Haig. Written and directed by Peter Gerretsen. Camera (color), Douglas Koch; editor, Michael Todd; music, Heather Conkie, Rory Cummings; production manager, Patricia Gerretsen; set decoration, Alexa Anthony; assistant director, Roman Buchok; casting, Richard Conkie. Reviewed at Cineplex Odeon Eaton Center, Toronto, June 17, 1988. Running time: **100 MIN.**
Jack . . . . Chuck Shamata
Lindsay . . . . Heather Kjollesdal
Lenny . . . . Daniel MacIvor
Myles . . . . Real Andrews
Maggie . . . . Cynthia Belliveau
Monsignor O'Brien . . . . Art Carney
Rita the Bag Lady . . . . Jayne Eastwood
Father Bill . . . . John Blackwood

Toronto — "Night Friend" (previously titled "A Cry From The Heart") is a well-meaning effort that tries to circumvent the usual exploitative elements of teen prostitution films. Pic's theatrical life will be very brief, however, because it's mired in good intentions with little dramatic resonance.

Writer-director Peter Gerretsen's predictable script finds Reverend

Jack (Chuck Shamata) as a do-gooder priest who meets a 14-year-old hooker while driving around midtown one rainy night. After a brief conversation he's inspired to embark on a personal crusade to save Lindsay (Heather Kjollesdal) from the streets. He has to defend his extra time and money spent on this mission to a very dour Art Carney as Monsignor O'Brien, who disapproves of the attention given to someone who should be placed in a shelter.

It turns out Lindsay has escaped an incestuous relationship at home with her father, which resulted in pregnancy. She's turning tricks each night to help her would-be rock musician boyfriend Lenny (Daniel Mac-Ivor) to buy tires for his car so they can get to L.A. Lenny forces Lindsay to make her $350 per night quota so he can escape the evil machinations of her pimp.

Shamata wears earnestness on his sleeve and plays the priest as a 1-note crusader. While Kjollesdal is not as jaded or made up as her street colleagues, she doesn't inspire sympathy because she's just too dumb.

The only hint of sex portrayed on the screen involves young hookers getting in and out of cars and then relating stories about their kinky encounters.

Gerretsen could have aimed for more realism and tension here but instead took the purposefully conventional — and tiresome — route. —*Devo.*

Coming To America

A Paramount Pictures release. Produced by George Folsey Jr., Robert D. Wachs. Executive producers, Mark Lipsky, Leslie Belzberg. Directed by John Landis. Screenplay, David Sheffield, Barry W. Blaustein, from story by Eddie Murphy; camera (Technicolor), Woody Omens; editor, Malcolm Campbell, George Folsey Jr.; music, Nile Rodgers; sound (Dolby), William B. Kaplan; production design, Richard MacDonald; assistant director-associate producer, David Sosna; art direction, Richard B. Lewis; special makeup, Rick Baker; costumes, Deborah Nadoolman; choreography, Paula Abdul; casting, Jackie Burch. Reviewed at the Academy of Motion Picture Arts & Sciences, L.A., June 21, 1988. MPAA Rating: R. Running time: 116 MIN.

Prince Akeem, others . . . . . . Eddie Murphy
Semmi, others . . . . Arsenio Hall
Cleo McDowell . . . . John Amos
King Jaffe Joffer . . . . James Earl Jones
Lisa McDowell . . . . Shari Headley
Queen Aoleon . . . . Madge Sinclair
Darryl . . . . Eriq LaSalle
Patrice McDowell . . . . Allison Dean
Oha . . . . Paul Bates
Maurice . . . . Louie Anderson
Sweets . . . . Clint Smith
Imani Izzi . . . . Vanessa Bell

Also with: Don Ameche, Ralph Bellamy.

Hollywood — "Coming To America" starts on a bathroom joke, quickly followed by a gag about private parts, then wanders in search of something equally original for Eddie Murphy to do for another couple of hours. It's a true test for loyal fans.

Aside from a need for fresher material, the main problem pops up immediately: the undeniably talented Murphy works best when a story thrusts him hip, slick and cool among the sleek, stiff and perturbable where he can create proper havoc. Though probably "high concept" on paper, "America" struggles slavishly to shove Murphy in the opposite direction.

Murphy has no difficulty creating a pampered young prince of Zamunda who would like a chance to live a little real life and select his own bride instead of being forced into a royal marriage of convenience. Murphy even makes the prince sympathetic and genuine, complete to his stilted English. When he and courtly sidekick Arsenio Hall venture to Queens to find a queen, however, the pair are instantly on the wrong end of Murphy's successful formula.

Working their way through the streets, most of the time Murphy and Hall can do little but react. Ironically, the very best moments of the film are those when Murphy and Hall are out among other characters played by themselves. These are done so artfully it's sometimes hard to tell which one of them is playing whom, if at all. The contrast, unfortunately, only underscores how empty the central players are.

The plot's no help since it's just one more variation on an ancient fairytale (and Murphy should be ashamed for copping a story credit). Longing for someone to love him for himself, Murphy discovers

beautiful Shari Headley and goes to work mopping floors in father John Amos' hamburger emporium to be near her.

She, no surprise, already has a well-to-do, insufferable boyfriend (Eriq LaSalle) that dad is anxious for her to marry. How does a janitor capture the heart of such a maiden? Well, he just has to be a super-swell guy and never let her know for a moment he's the one sending the $500,000 ruby earrings in secret.

If an American woman discovers he's fabulously rich, handsome and all-powerful, she won't love him, Murphy believes. This, of course, is his first visit to America.

Just when the scheme is progressing nicely, King James Earl Jones and Queen Madge Sinclair show up to complicate their son's secret. Everything works out eventually (and a bit abruptly), to nobody's surprise. It should be noted that Murphy and Headley actually manage to concoct a rather sweet little romance out of all this sappiness, at least enough to hope they do live happily ever after.

Throughout the opulent picture, the prince shows no concern for how much anything costs, tossing money and expensive items in all directions in pursuit of his limited achievements. Much the same can be said for director John Landis. —*Har.*

Sukeban Deka — Kazama Sanshimai No Gyakushu
(Girl Cops — Counterattack Of The Three Sisters)
(JAPANESE)

A Toei release. Produced by Masaharu Nakasone, Osamu Tezuka, Asao Tsunoda, Maya Kawai, Takashi Ishihara. Directed by Hideo Tanaka. Screenplay, Izo Hashimoto, story by, Shinji Wada; camera (color), Kensaku Ikeda; lighting, Fusao Kobayashi; editor, Nobuya Tadano; music, Ichiro Natti; art direction, Maruo Yasui, sound, Kiyohiko Kakinuma; assistant director, Noboru Matsui; planning, Kazuya Maeda, Masaharu Ueda. Reviewed at Toei screening room, Tokyo, May 11, 1988. Running time: 90 MIN.

With: Yui Asaka, Kika Onishi, Yumi Nakamura, Masaki Kyomoto, Kosuke Toyohara, Minako Fujio, Koji Tanaka.

Tokyo — "Sukeban Deka — Kazama Sanshimai No Gyakushu" is the third in a successful series of adventures involving three distaff members of a special high school student detective squad with a mandate to root out juvenile crime, which, this time around, involves setting off explosives at a jam-packed rock concert.

Like hall monitors with licenses to kill, the young ladies are equipped with specially designed yo-yos that sprout blades and can do as much damage as any weapon in a ninja's extensive armory. One of the heroines even uses hers to bring down a light aircraft, a feat even more spectacular than "walking the

dog."

The film, like so many others in Japan, is based on a popular comic strip, and therein lies an intriguing irony. Comic strips, according to those who've studied the subject, owe much of their popularity to clever use of cinematic techniques — the closeup, zoom in, zoom out, tracking shot, et al. Now, cinema must depend on comic strips to capture the teen moviegoer. The "Sukeban Deka" strip, before being turned by Toei into a film series, was a popular early evening program on Fuji-TV.

The three principal girl cops probably are not going to make any Western viewers forget the stereotype of Oriental women as shy and retiring types. Although supposed to be pretty tough cookies, they talk slangily in mousey voices not likely to frighten a jaywalker, much less a mad bomber. Even more unbelievable, given how unthreatening they look and act, is their use of the *jingi*, or formal greeting, favored by Japan's yakuza, or gangsters. In a stylistic filip not uncommon to Japanese films, the three principal actresses have the same first names as the characters they portray. —*Bail.*

Hey, Maestro!
(SOVIET)

A Gruziafilm production. Directed by Nodar Managadze. Screenplay, Erlom Achvlediani, Managadze, Davi Giavachischvili; camera (color), Levan Paataschvili; music, Nodar Mamissachvili. Reviewed at San Remo Film Festival, March 20, 1988. Running time: 85 MIN.

With: Tenghiz Ameridze, Dali Ctaladze, Makvala Gonaschvili.

San Remo — "Hey Maestro!" is the second film of Nodar Managadze to appear on the fest scene this year ("Living Legends" screened at Cannes). This sensitive, curious mood piece is a natural fest choice.

Story of a pianist-outsider and his loves strongly recalls the plot of "Five Easy Pieces" to the Western viewer, a coincidence that offers a reference point in a stylistically complicated film.

Arcil (Tenghiz Ameridze) had a brilliant career predicted for him when he studied music in the Conservatory. For reasons never spelled out, he has become a common piano tuner, traveling around Georgia to find instruments to tune and sleeping in his beatup old car.

Introverted to an almost pathological degree, Arcil silently and humbly performs his task in the homes of the nouveau riche (posh interiors and squandered wealth are a constant, unvoiced social criticism in the film). Bored housewives try to seduce the sympathetic lad, to no avail. Fat husbands subject him to body searches to see if he's made off with any of the silver, disgruntled rival tuners beat him within an inch of his life, and in a moment of folly

Arcil abandons his car in the river. A chance encounter with a young girl may foretell an upward swing in this loser's life, but don't bet on it.

Director Managadze is as sensitive and gentle as his hero (who, when he finally gets in the mood, plays up a storm on an antique piano). Camerawork by Levan Paataschvili is moody and expressive, ditto Ameridze's low-key performance as the pianist-wanderer at odds with painful existential problems. Film won the special jury prize at San Remo. — *Yung.*

Crystalstone

A TMS Pictures release. Produced by John Williams. Executive producer, Jose Carredano. Coproduced by Britt Lomond. Written and directed by Antonio Pelaez. Camera (Fotofilm, color), John Stephens; editor, Arnold Baker; music, Fernando Uribe; production design, George Costello; art direction, Mario Caso; costume design, Julia Sanchez; sound, Charles L. King 3d; assistant director, Yousaf Bokhari; associate producer, Jorge Gonzalez; casting, Eleanor Cooke (U.K.), Pedro Sopena (Spain). Reviewed at Hollywood Egyptian theater, L.A., June 24, 1988. MPAA Rating: PG. Running time: **103 MIN.**

Pablo	Kamlesh Gupta
Maria	Laura Jane Goodwin
Captain	Frank Grimes
Hook	Edward Kelsey
Old man	Sydney Bromley
Policeman	Terence Bayler

Hollywood — "Crystalstone" is **a time-passer for tots aged 5-9 and most assuredly is destined for the children's shelf at the local vid store.**

Director-scripter Antonio Pelaez makes an earnest attempt to create a magical fable where a coveted piece of quartz — the crystalstone — becomes the sought-after treasure for a couple of orphaned Spanish kids, 9-ish older brother Pablo (Kamlesh Gupta) and 5-ish Maria (Laura Jane Goodwin).

Story doesn't amount to much as the kids fend off a hook-handed renegade murderer, sponge a couple of meals off the local fat-and-happy femme innkeeper and take up with a drunk sailor-type who helps them in their quest to solve the clues to finding the crystalstone.

We never learn what's so great about this crystalstone and why it's worth all the trouble to locate, besides which the medieval plotting isn't adapted well into the early 20th Century setting where trains already are a fixture and cars emerging ones.

Confusing matters, setting is coastal Spain, yet nearly all the actors have thick British accents, especially Goodwin, the little girl who looks way too Anglo with her big blue watery eyes and long blond hair to be playing the younger sister to her black hair and eyed bro.

Given the rather banal dialog that positively drips with sentimentality, both Gupta and Goodwin manage to hold hands and cry and cuddle together while seldom looking self-conscious. This is a plus, given they are in nearly every scene in the film.

The same can't be said for the rest of the cast whose acting abilities are limited to characterizations. As the hook-handed pirate type, Edward Kelsey might well be out of "Peter Pan," while Sydney Bromley as the sorcerer, or whatever he's supposed to be, jumps out of the book illustrations of Rasputin.

It's possible Terence Bayler as the hapless town policeman is trying to parody John Cleese.

Topping all performances is that by Frank Grimes as the kids' long lost dad. One minute he's remorseful about his drinking and the next, joyful unto the heavens to discover these two are his progeny — cinematic moments that are worthy of operatic scoring.

Production values are mediocre, though that is to be expected for what is surely a low-budget effort. Mostly, scenes are lensed at nighttime or in dimly lit areas, which presumably is supposed to add intrigue and suspense, though it probably is for the better it doesn't since it will be small children who might be afraid to sit through this — if anyone does at all. — *Brit.*

Coverup: Behind The Iran Contra Affair
(DOCU)

An Empowerment Project (theatrical, educational) and MPI (video) release of an Empowerment Project production. Produced by Barbara Trent, Gary Meyer, David Kasper. Directed by Trent. Written by Eve Goldberg; camera (color), Meyer; editor, Kasper, Goldberg; music, Richard Elliott. Reviewed on MPI videocassette, L.A., June 23, 1988, 1988. No MPAA Rating. Running time: **75 MIN.**

Hollywood — **All the long-circulated charges and theories concerning CIA involvement in drug running, arms dealing and other illicit activities in support of the Nicaraguan contras and assorted right-wing causes are given full voice in this potentially controversial documentary. Politically potent content probably will play only to the already converted, but filmmakers are taking a novel route in an attempt to reach a many viewers as possible.**

World premiered in L.A. June 24, pic will play a handful of theatrical engagements in some major markets, then quickly be released on vidcassette July 13. Vid distributor MPI is the same company that sold 50,000 copies of Oliver North's testimony last year.

Docu's thesis is that the 13-week Congressional hearings on the Iran-Contra affair operated on the principle of "damage control," that the line of questioning pursued stopped well short of eliciting the full story; promo materials proclaim "'Coverup' starts where the hearings left off!"

All the charges are of a highly explosive nature and, it must be said, are laid out in such a way to provide maximum embarrassment to George Bush during his quest for the presidency.

In question are such allegations as: the Regan-Bush campaign's "secret deal" with the Khomeini regime to delay release of U.S. hostages until after the 1980 election; the existence of a "shadow government" that conducts illegal foreign policy; the longterm involvement, from Laos and Vietnam during the war there until Central America today, of the CIA and former CIA operatives in drug running; CIA involvement in an attempt on the life of the Nicaraguan political figure Eden Pastora, which killed an American journalist and wounded many more, and a Reagan-Bush plot, masterminded by Oliver North, to suspend the Constitution as a way to deal with political enemies.

If any of these assertions could be proved true, there would obviously result a scandal of considerable proportions, and the Christic Institute, which participated heavily in this film, is attempting to press the issues in a current lawsuit. Virtually all the information and evidence provided by "Coverup" has been aired extensively in print over the past year, however, as can be seen here by the succession of visuals featuring newspaper articles.

Therefore, the docu succeeds only in consolidating all the conspiracy theories and seemingly extreme allegations formulated to date, and certainly doesn't prove anything. In the waning days of the Reagan administration, when the attention of the press is turning to the upcoming election and other matters, "Coverup" keeps the pressure on regarding a very murky area, insisting that considerably more digging remains to be done. —*Cart.*

A Summer Story
(U.S.-BRITISH)

An Atlantic Entertainment Group release of an ITC Entertainment Group production. Produced by Danton Rissner. Directed by Piers Haggard. Screenplay, Penelope Mortimer, from John Galsworthy's story "The Apple Tree; "camera (Agfa-Gevaert color by Rank), Kenneth MacMillan; editor, Ralph Sheldon; music, Georges Delerue; sound (Dolby), David Hildyard; production design, Leo Austin; costume design, Jenny Beavan; assistant director, Chris Hall; production manager, Joanna Gollins; casting, Celestia Fox. Reviewed at Broadway screening room, N.Y., June 20, 1988. MPAA Rating: PG-13. Running time: **95 MIN.**

Megan	Imogen Stubbs
Ashton	James Wilby
Jim	Kenneth Colley
Stella	Sophie Ward
Mrs. Narracombe	Susannah York
Joe	Jerome Flynn
Bank clerk	John Savident

"A Summer Story" is a beautifully made pastoral romance, skillfully adapted by Penelope Mortimer from a John Galsworthy story. Picture is a natural for class audiences (pun intended) **currently hankering for British literary efforts.**

Best known for "The Forsyte Saga," whose PBS broadcast version two decades ago virtually opened the U.S. market for British drama, Galsworthy in his story "The Apple Tree" was comfortably writing in the rustic vein associated with such stalwarts as A.E. Coppard and H.E. Bates. Screen version is set in Devon in 1902, portraying the ill-fated romance one summer between weak-willed young barrister Ashton (James Wilby, perfectly cast) and a lovely country lass Megan (newcomer Imogen Stubbs).

Holed up at a country farm on holiday due to a sprained ankle, Ashton procrastinates, delaying his departure due to a crush on Megan. Shortly after they consummate the relationship, he heads for home via the resort at Torquay and procrastinates again, lolling with a beautiful sister (Sophie Ward) of an old school chum he meets there rather than returning quickly to fetch Megan as promised. Tragic note is introduced when the lovestruck girl pursues him to Torquay and the weak Ashton hides rather than meeting her, thereby breaking her heart and spirit.

Helmer Piers Haggard, whose previous work encompasses horror and sic-fi as well as the formidable Bob Hoskins tv series "Pennies From Heaven," directs with pinpoint control, keeping the simple story suspenseful as well as true to its romantic roots. A flashback structure, in which Ashton returns to the farm 20 years later to try and make his peace, gains poignancy through the sterling acting of Kenneth Colley, portraying the farm's caretaker.

Stage actress Stubbs is a real find as the heartbroken heroine, bringing a modern strength to the period role, while Wilby follows up "Maurice" and the current "A Handful Of Dust" with another sympathetic version of the archetypal weak young aristocrat. Supporting cast of Ward, Susannah York and, as Megan's farm beau, Jerome Flynn, is solid.

Kenneth MacMillan's razor-sharp lensing captures the beauty of the authentic locations without resorting to any soft-focus gimmickry, abetted by Georges Delerue's unobtrusive score. —*Lor.*

The Underachievers

A Lightning Pictures presentation of a PMS Filmworks production. Executive producers, Lawrence Kasanoff, Ellen Steloff. Produced and directed by Jackie Kong. Coproducer, Jimmy Maslon. Creative consultant, Mr. (William) Osco. Screenplay, Kong, Tony Rosato, Gary Thompson, from story by Rosato; camera (color), Chuck Colwell; editor, Tom Mesheiski; music, Don Preston; sound, Vic Carpenter; production design, Jay Burkhardt; art direction, Woodward Romine Jr.; set decoration, Jay Kaiwai; associate producer, Tikki Goldberg; casting, Bengston/-

Cohn & Associates. Reviewed on Vestron vidcassette, N.Y., May 30, 1988. MPAA Rating: R. Running time: **90 MIN.**

Danny Warren	Edward Albert
Katherine	Barbara Carrera
Murphy	Michael Pataki
Mrs. Grant	Susan Tyrrell
Kline	Mark Blankfield
Dummont	Garrett Morris
Coach	Vic Tayback
Carlos	Jesse Aragon

Also with: Jewel Shepard, Lee Arenberg, Fox Harris, Judd Omen, Burton Gilliam, Roslyn Kind, Monte Landis.

"The Underachievers," which carries a 1987 copyright, was filmed under the title **"Night School,"** and indeed that institution passes for the setting of the hijinx. New title, however, more accurately reflects the work here of some not inestimable talents. Nonsensical comedy has gone to homevid sans theatrical release.

Edward Albert (with blond hair) plays a failed Single A shortstop who somehow gets requisitioned to act as a "narc on spec" at a night school suspected of harboring drug dealers. He's promised $10,000 per arrest, but soon forgets his mission when he lays eyes on faculty member Barbara Carrera, who's gung ho to maintain the reputedly high academic standards at the school. Her foil (Susan Tyrrell) is in on some shady dealings with the corrupt administration.

Pic is a nonstop barrage of overaged "students" — many of them convicts placed there as a sort of rehabilitation — having fights, throwing things, practicing wine tasting, taking backstroke lessons from a nubile instructor. Scenes jump haphazardly and script seems nonexistent.

Comic highlight for some may be an extended brawl between the cool and lovely Carrera and the hysterical Tyrrell. Though it matters not one whit, tech credits are decent. — *Gerz.*

Bumaznij Patefon
(The Paper Gramophone)
(SOVIET)

A Lenfilm production. Directed by Dmitri Dolinin. Screenplay, Aleksandr Chervinski, based on his play "My Happiness;" camera (color), Lev Kolganov; music, Z. Shorochova; music, Gennadi Banshchikov; sound, Boris Andreev; art direction, Vladimir Kostin; costumes, N. Lev. Reviewed at Pesaro Film Festival, June 15, 1988. Running time; **87 MIN.**

Vika	Angelika Nevolina
Senia	Gleb Soshnikov
Lidia Ivanova	Elizaveta Nikishchichina

Also with: Nikolai Pastuchov.

Pesaro— Acclaimed cameraman Dmitri Dolinin tries his hand at directing for the third time with "The Paper Gramophone," a curious story of a free-thinking girl in 1947 determined to have a baby. Film was made for tv as "Viktoria," then released theatrically.

"Gramophone" is a refined work with some intriguing glimpses of Stalinism. Overall effect is a little flat, however, maybe due to its stage origins which are more intellectual than emotionally involving. Film is worth a look for art circuits in quest of recent developments in Soviet cinema.

Heart and soul of the film is Vika, admirably limned as a fragile but determined young girl by Angelika Nevolina. After Vika's father was arrested, presumably for political reasons, she is taken under the wing of a school principal, Lidia Ivanova (Elizaveta Nikishchichina), a Stalinist fanatic with a heart of gold. In her lonely new life as the live-in school janitor, Vika has won the affection of an old teacher and, for reasons not clear, married him, though they live apart. Her desire for a baby (as an excuse for the marriage) leads her to boldy lure a straight-arrow young marine, Senia (Gleb Soshnikov), into her lair and seduce him.

Besides its explicit criticism of Stalinism, "Gramophone" also touches on the previously taboo theme of religious persecution — Senia's diplomatic career is in difficulty because his father is a churchgoing "Baptist." Without undue emphasis, these elements create the atmosphere in which the fleeting love story between Senia and Vika takes place. Last act is a bitter postscript on the betrayal of friendship and love, when Vika, now six months pregnant, realizes Senia will marry the girl who denounced her to the authorities.

Lensed in a square tv format, film's beautifully constructed sets suffer from greenish film stock. — *Yung.*

La rosa bianca
(The White Rose)
(ITALIAN)

A Telimmagini Cooperative production. Produced, written and directed by Francesca Romana Leonardi. Camera (Cinecittà color), Bruno Di Virgilio; music, CAM; art direction, Annabruna Gola. Reviewed at the San Remo Film Festival, March 29, 1988. Running time: **85 MIN.**

Lilli	Valeria D'Obici
Giorgio	Michele Mirabella

Also with Nadia Ferrero (Gloria), Ivano Errera (gypsy).

San Remo — Young helmer Francesca Romana Leonardi makes her feature film bow with a graceful, introverted film about a lonely woman, "The White Rose." Pic's merits lie in the delicate balance in which elements hang together on a thin thread of story.

Kudos go to Valeria D'Obici (best actress award at San Remo) for a 1-woman tour de force. Pic would be a top choice for a women's (or other) fest.

D'Obici plays Lilli, a 40-year-old housewife whose husband has been working abroad for four years. She receives news he will come home briefly at the same time as the editor of a publishing house she works for saddles her with writing the last chapter of a women's novel in a weekend.

"The White Rose" is a small film filled with a woman's feelings — Lilli's relationship to her empty apartment, her photos of happy days spent with the missing husband, everyday objects. While she writes and rewrites the novel's finale (will the heroine go back to her old love, or run off with the passionate gypsy?), Lilli is forced to reassess her marriage and grounds for her own happiness. Film ends with her subtle shift of attitude and a big decision.

Leonardi shows good control of mood that keeps Lilli's quiet mental odyssey engrossing. Musical bits (including the Trio Lescano from the 1930s) are well picked. — *Yung.*

Bingo, Bridesmaids
And Braces
(AUSTRALIAN-DOCU)

A Film Australia-The Big Picture Co. production. Produced by Gillian Armstrong, Tristram Miall. Directed by Armstrong. Camera (color), Steve Arnold, Malcolm Richards; editor, Nicholas Beauman; music, Mark Moffat; sound, Toivo Lember; production manager, Ian Adkins; additional camera, Tom Cowan, Kerry Brown; additional sound, Rod Pascoe, Laurie Fitzgerald. Reviewed at the Sydney Film Festival, June 11, 1988. Running time: **92 MIN.**

Sydney — Before Gillian Armstrong made her successful first feature "My Brilliant Career" (1979) she visited the South Australian city of Adelaide to make a short docu, "Smokes And Lollies," a study of three 14-year-old girls. That was 1977, and in 1981 she returned to make a further study of the trio, "14's Good, 18's Better." Now, after three successful feature films, Armstrong has come up with a further look at her three working class heroines in "Bingo, Bridesmaids And Braces."

The three, all from similar backgrounds, are Diana, Josie and Kerry. Armstrong cuts between footage filmed for her previous films and new material featuring the young women now aged 26. Diana at 14 felt she was fat and ugly; at 18, she was married and pregnant, her young husband up on an assault charge. Against the odds, she's still married at 26, and coping with the fact that her husband is often out of work. They have a premature child, but a seemingly stable relationship, though Diana, far more attractive than she once was, is starting to show signs of independence.

Josie, at 15, was an unmarried mother. She subsequently married, then divorced, but has a good relationship with her 11-year-old daughter, and is about to marry again.

Kerry is the most conservative of the three, who's lived till now with her mother and delightful old grandfather. Her very elaborate wedding climaxes the film.

Childhood obsessions with boys, and fear of pregnancy, naturally now have given way to a more balanced outlook on the world for the three. Youthful high spirits and disdain for authority have been replaced by a sense of responsibility. The three, with whom Armstrong evidently has a close rapport, are lively and tough characters, and the film is plenty of fun. Issues such as abortion are raised, and handled tactfully.

Pic is a bit confusing at times, since Diana radically changed her appearance over the years and consequently there are moments that lack clarity. Comparisons will be made to Michael Apted's "28 Up," British docu along similar lines; but Armstrong's range is concentrated on one social group, where Apted went for a wider impression of a whole generation.

Pic goes out theatrically in Australia in September, and should attract audiences. Overseas, fests are indicated, with tv exposure definitely a prospect. Pic is technically fine, given time-gaps between the different stages of its production. — *Strat.*

Silent Assassins

An Action Bros. production, in association with Panache Prods. Produced by Jun Chong, Phillip Rhee. Executive producers, Peter E. Strauss, Irwin Jaeger. Directed by Lee Doo-yong; codirector, Scott Thomas. Screenplay, Will Gates, Ada Lim, from story by James Bruner; camera (Foto-Kem color), Son Hyun-Chae; editor, William Hoy; music, Paul Gilman; sound, Scott Smith; art direction, John Nakayama; fight choreography, Chong, Rhee; second unit director-stunt coordinator, Kim Kahama; production manager, Martin Wiley; associate producer, David Chong; casting, Chris Trainor & Associates. Reviewed on Forum Home Video vidcassette, N.Y., June 10, 1988. No MPAA Rating. Running time: **92 MIN.**

Sam	Sam J. Jones
Sara	Linda Blair
Jun Kim	Jun Chong
Bernard	Phillip Rhee
Dr. London	Bill Erwin
Kendrick	Gustav Vintas
Dyama	Mako
Amy	Rebecca Ferrati

Also with: Peter Looney, Elise Briesette, Stuart Damon, Bill (Superfoot) Wallace.

Bearing the novelty of being a U.S. action film made by transplanted South Korean filmmakers, "Silent Assassins" is an okay timekiller that has gone the direct-to-video route.

Sam Jones (he gets his J. middle initial back in the end credits) stars as an L.A. cop out to avenge the death of his partner at the hands of an ex-CIA operative Kendrick (Gustav Vintas). To get to the villain, he teams up with a Korean (Jun Chong) whose niece was kidnaped in the incident and a kendo expert (Phillip Rhee). Kendrick also has kidnaped a scientist trying to get a secret formula that would threaten the world with deadly chemical-biological war.

Pic boasts good plot progressions and action scenes, resulting in a sinister open ending. One problem is that costar Linda Blair, cast as Jones' tough girlfriend, has little to do. More impressive here is former Playboy magazine model Rebecca Ferrati, as a statuesque villainess. Costars Chong and Rhee also produced the film and handled the fight scenes. — *Lor.*

Makom Le'yad Hayam
(A Place By The Sea)
(ISRAELI)

A Gelfand Films presentation of an Arfilm production. Produced by Sylvain Assouline. Written and directed by Rafael Rebibo. Camera (color), Jean Boffety; editor, Danny Shik; music, Dov Seltzer; sound, David Liss; art direction, Rami Shai. Reviewed in Tel Aviv, June 1, 1988. Running time: **93 MIN.**
With: Alon Aboutboul, Anath Zahor, Shlomo Tarshish, Arie Moscona, Alexis Sellam, David Menahem, Yoel Liba, Yaakov Banai, Liora Grossman.

Tel Aviv — Based in Switzerland but making his second film in Israel, Rafael Rebibo seems bent on tales of desperation, his heroes squashed by some kind of system which is beyond their powers to defeat.

A former convict and his girlfriend, who walked the streets while he was in jail, seek to start life again. They restore an old building by the sea, far away from the unpleasant memories of the past, but the girl's pimp wants her back, loan sharks demand payment and the spark of hope is extinguished before it has a chance to blossom.

A naïve Mediterranean melodrama with sketchy characters, paperthin script and amateurish acting (but sporting lots of nudity and dedicating considerable footage to landscape), film displays some nice sunrises and sunsets shot by French cameraman Jean Boffety. Other technical credits, particularly cutting which tends to shrink the hours of the day in a strange fashion, are less commendable. —*Edna.*

License To Drive

A 20th Century Fox release of a Davis Entertainment Co.-Licht/Mueller Film Corp. production. Produced by Jeffery A. Mueller, Andrew Licht. Executive producer, John Davis. Directed by Greg Beeman. Screenplay, Neil Tolkin; camera (Deluxe color), Bruce Surtees; editor, Wendy Greene Bricmont; music, Jay Ferguson; production design, Lawrence G. Paull; set design, Greg Papalia; set decoration, Jeff Haley; sound (Dolby), Art Rochester; stunt coordinator, Joe Dunne; associate producer-production manager, Mack Bing; assistant director, Mike Kusley; casting, Penny Perry. Reviewed at AMC Century 14 theater, L.A., June 30, 1988. MPAA Rating: PG-13. Running time: **88 MIN.**
Les ....Corey Haim
Dean ....Corey Feldman
Mom.......................Carol Kane
Dad ....Richard Masur
Mercedes ....Heather Graham
Chales ....Michael Manasseti
Professor................Harvey Miller
Paolo ....................M.A. Nickles

Hollywood — Shallow as a puddle of motor oil and just as slick, "License To Drive" is a lightweight teen fantasy-adventure that picks up speed as it goes along. Fan magfave stars and radio-ready soundtrack should make it diverting for unexceptional teens, but current blockbuster b.o. competition will soon send it cruising toward the Dept. of Mundane Videos.

Though the concept at first seems completely unpromising, story actually begins to move under Greg Beeman's revved-up direction. Corey Haim plays Les, a teen who's about to take his driver's test — and pass through the magical gateway from Mom-dependent adolescent to free, mobile, rubber-burning adolescent. Too bad he fails the test.

With his underage pals depending on him to change their social horizons and a dishy dream girl waiting at home for the Saturday night date he's bluffed his way into, Les decides to fake it.

He sneaks the car — his grandfather's pristine powder-blue 1972 Cadillac — out of the garage for his first night on the town while his parents are sleeping.

Once that happens, there's no way out for Les, and as the threats to the car's impeccable paint job and Les' formerly secure family standing pile up, the pic becomes pretty good fun.

First of all, the girl (Heather Graham) turns out to be a reckless drunk who dances on the car-hood in high heels and instructs him to park it in a tow-away zone from which it gets towed. Then there's his pushy pal Dean (Corey Feldman), who wants to smoke cigars inside it, take flash pictures in Les' face while he's driving, and hijack the car out to Archie's Astro Burger drive-in, a real cruiser's paradise.

Then there's the gang of rabid, pissed-off thugs who want to race him in the streets, then attack his paint job with their bare hands.

Beeman, in his first time behind the wheel of a feature, should get much of the credit for giving this vehicle some horsepower. At every opportunity he pushes the comic potential of stunts or characterizations to the limit. Every car stunt is dramatic; every minor character, from DMV officials to tow-truck drivers, some kind of overwrought maniac. Results at first seem overly broad but build up to an engaging comic momentum.

Neil Tolkin's script contains holes big enough to drive a school bus through and operates on a level roughly comparable to a car commercial, promoting shallow, materialistic values throughout. Even its imaginative opening dream sequence, which shows Les chained inside a hellishly hot schoolbus while outside, the dream girl beckons from a convertible, plays like an advertising scenario.

Corey Haim, 16, still plays a few years too young on screen for this role, but is fairly engaging in the everyday kid characterization. Feldman does what he's supposed to do as the brash, self-assured best friend, but it's been done so many times before. Graham is lovely to look at but has a tiresomely vapid role as the love object.

Carol Kane, as the Les' pregnant mom, is a breath of fresh air as the only genuine kook in a movie full of fake kooks and Richard Masur does a good job as the bearish, confounded suburban dad.

The Cadillac, of course, is excellent as are the well-chosen L.A. locales.

Bruce Surtees' glossy, colorful cinematography is well-suited to Beeman's directorial style, and production values are high for the genre.—*Daws.*

Arizona Heat

A Spectrum Entertainment presentation of an Arizona Heat production. (Sales, Overseas Filmgroup.) Executive producer, Michael A.P. Scording. Produced and directed by John G. Thomas. Screenplay, Daniel M. Colmerauer; camera (United color), Howard Wexler; editor, Thomas; music, Gary Stockdale; sound, Marty Kasparian; art direction, Brian Densmore; assistant director, Liam O'Brien; production manager, Chris Rogers; stunt coordinator, Spanky Spangler; associate producer, Ken Hulbert; casting, Danny Travis; additional camera, Chris Pidgeon. Reviewed on Republic Pictures Home Video vidcassette, N.Y., June 4, 1988. MPAA Rating: R. Running time: **91 MIN.**
Larry Kapinski............Michael Parks
Jill Andrews..............Denise Crosby
Capt. Samuels..........Hugh Farrington
Toad ....Ron Briskman
Paul Murphy..........Dennis O'Sullivan
Lisa.....................Renata Lee

In the midst of a trend of mismatched cop pics and tv shows, "Arizona Heat" presents a novel variation on the theme. Like filmmaker John Thomas' previous feature "Banzai Runner," this 1986 production is going direct-to-video Stateside, though both films mark him as ready for the big show.

Michael Parks toplines as Kapinski, an Arizona cop with a "maniac" reputation due to the level of violence generated on his cases. His boss teams him up with female detective Jill Andrews (Denise Crosby) who's pretty but a tough cookie, and duo sets out to find the killer of a string of cops.

Key plot peg is that Jill turns out to be a lesbian, with Kapinski reacting predictably. What's unpredictable is that he goes to bed with her lovely, live-in girlfriend and the already battling partners are really at each other's throats when Jill finds out. Of course, a crisis unites them in the end.

Mystery plot isn't very interesting and the killer's identity is telegraphed from the outset, but Thomas displays a wry sense of humor and enough odd details to keep the film interesting. Parks and Crosby team effectively, while the Phoenix and Scottsdale locations offer some novelty from the usual screen police beats. Music also helps, with pic atmospherically opening à la "Easy Rider" with Hoyt Axton's "The Pusher" performed by Steppenwolf and closing with Gary Stockdale's excellent out-theme "Caught In the Heat." — *Lor.*

Short Circuit 2

A Tri-Star Pictures release of a Turman-Foster Co. production. Produced by David Foster, Lawrence Turman. Executive producer, Michael MacDonald. Directed by Kenneth Johnson. Screenplay, S.S. Wilson, Brent Maddock, based on characters created by them; camera (Medallion color; Technicolor prints), John McPherson; editor, Conrad Buff; music, Charles Fox; production design, Bill Brodie; art direction, Alicia Keywan; set decoration, Steve Shewchuk; costume design, Larry Wells; sound (Dolby), Douglas Canton; associate producer-robotics supervisor, Eric Allard; assistant directors, Donald Baton, Tony Lucibello; second unit director, Michael MacDonald; casting, Stuart Aikins (Toronto), Stuart Howard Associates (N.Y.), Kathy Rowe (L.A.). Reviewed at the Plaza theater, L.A., June 28, 1988. MPAA Rating: PG. Running time: **110 MIN.**
Ben Jahrvi ....Fisher Stevens
Fred Ritter ....Michael McLean
Sandy Banatoni...........Cynthia Gibb
Oscar Baldwin ....Jack Weston
Saunders ....Dee McCafferty
Jones..................David Hemblen
Voice of Johnny Five.........Tim Blaney

Hollywood — Mild and meek, "Short Circuit 2" has an uncomplicated sweetnesss that will put it over as a successful followup to the original robot kiddie comedy. First entry earned a nice $17,000,000 in domestic film rentals, but its status as a top vidcassette seller last year may have had even more to do with decision to proceed with a sequel.

Minus original cohorts Ally Sheedy (whose voice appears briefly on the soundtrack) and Steve Guttenberg, jerry-rigged genius "Johnny Five" makes his way to the Big City, where protector Fisher Stevens struggles to make ends meet hawking toy models of his mechanical wonder on the street.

Cutie-pie department store employee Cynthia Gibb needs to bring a novel item to her shelves, and sends Stevens and self-styled entrepreneur Michael McKean into instant action by ordering 1,000 of the little buggers for the Christmas season. Underhanded banker Jack Weston has some other ideas for the tireless automaton, scheming to kidnap it and press it into service stealing some priceless jewels from a safe deposit box.

It's not much as stories go and, at 110 minutes, at least 15 minutes too long in the telling. What amusement there is stems from the ceaseless stream of malapropisms flowing from the mouth of Stevens ("We are manufacturing them like gangbangers," "You're hitting the nail right between the eyes," etc.), and the lively rap continuously delivered by the bright, cheerful Number Five.

Although derivative, the robot, made up of all manner of spare electronic parts, remains charming, and kids will undoubtedly find delightful scenes in which Number Five jumps around from place to place and sails through the air amid the skyscrapers of Toronto.

Speaking of the location, the film is set in a generic U.S. metropolis, complete with American flags and a citizenship swearing-in ceremony. However, as the vast majority of the picture was shot on downtown city streets, the city is constantly recognizable as Toronto to anyone who has ever been there. One can speculate on when a city becomes sufficiently well-known for its own sake to become unusuable as anything but itself — would New York, San Francisco, Los Angeles or Chicago ever so boldly be passed off as anything but themselves? —*Cart.*

Slaughterhouse

An American Artists production, in association with Slaughterhouse Associates. (Sales, Manson Intl.). Produced by Ron Matonak. Executive producer, Jerry Encoe. Written and directed by Rick Roessler. Camera (Cinema color, United prints), Richard Benda; editor, Sergio Uribe; music, Joseph Garrison; songs, Vantage Point; sound (Ultra-Stereo), Joe Thompson Jr.; producton design, Michael Scaglione; special effects makeup, Barney Burman, Mark Lane; assistant director, Andrew Jones; production manager, Mike Shanin; stunt coordinator, Mike Sharkey. Reviewed on Charter Entertainment vidcassette, N.Y., June 22, 1988. MPAA Rating: R. Running time: **85 MIN.**
Liz Borden . . . . Sherry Bendorf
Lester Bacon . . . . Don Barrett
Sheriff Borden . . . . William Houck
Buddy . . . . Joe Barton
Annie . . . . Jane Higginson
Skip . . . . Eric Schwartz
Buzz . . . . Jeff Grossi

"Slaughterhouse," not to be confused with recent release "Slaughterhouse Rock," is a standard horror pic released regionally last year and currently in homevideo distribution, reviewed here for the record.

Rather uninspired premise has various teens due for a slaughtering when they visit a local pig slaughterhouse as a whim during a long weekend of partying for a "Pig-Out" event sponsored by a radio station. Slaughterhouse owner Lester Bacon (Don Barrett) and his retarded, oversize son Buddy (Joe Barton) are on the rampage, brutally murdering their perceived enemies due to site being auctioned off for back taxes, as well as knocking off teens for good measure.

Film emphasizes dumb puns and black humor, boasting okay makeup effects but never capturing the intended quirky mood of its obvious model, "The Texas Chainsaw Massacre." Sudden freeze-frame ending is supposed to be a switch on happy endings, but doesn't come off. —*Lor.*

Illusory Thoughts

Produced, written, directed and choreographed by Patrick Chu. Camera (color, 16m), Paul Gibson, Mark Trottenberg; editor, Tom Agnello, Philip Rucci; music, Janet Lund; sound, Lund; production design, Dale Chan. Reviewed at Asian American Intl. Film Festival, N.Y., June 24, 1988. Running time: **72 MIN.**
With: Patrick Chu.

Patrick Chu, a Hong Kong-born New Yorker in his mid-30s, conceived and created "Illusory Thoughts" and is also its principal actor and dancer, appearing in most scenes. This is a highly personal and idiosyncratic film, following the subjective internalized ruminations of a New York choreographer, played by Chu, as he ponders the untidy mess called life.

There is almost no story, thus conventional critiques don't apply. Scenes and tableaux take place on a beach, as five dancers perform; in a dance studio during rehearsal; in a bedroom or two; at tea; in a garden restaurant; elsewhere. Chu is a dynamic screen presence but with little discernible dramatic action. He is passionately into his role, but with little purpose that is apparent.

Chu's divided affections for two attractive Chinese artists are part of the slim plot. We hear his troubled thoughts as well as theirs. Thoughts are in the title and they abound on the soundtrack in voice-over narration and in conversations, thoughts on art and religion and relationships. These are incomplete thoughts expressed as tantalizing fragments, thoughts as aphorisms turned sideways, thoughts variously illusory, elusive, allusive.

Rich music and sounds combine with dance and motion and stylized gestures, also Chu in extraordinary makeup, an amalgam of western modern with traditional Chinese sensibility. Parallel to the slight conflict of the double affair is Chu's dilemma about identity and lifepurpose. —*Hitch.*

Coo-ee
(AUSTRALIAN-DOCU)

A Film Australia production. Produced by Geoff Barnes. Directed and edited by Graham Chase. Camera (color), John Hosking; music, Ludwig van Beethoven; sound, Rodney Simmons. Reviewed at Mosman screening room, Sydney, May 31, 1988. (In Sydney Film Festival.) Running time: **93 MIN.**

Sydney — In 1915, men from the New South Wales outback town of Gilgandra set out on a spontaneous march to Sydney, nearly 500 miles away, to recruit men to fight in World War I and also to protest the apparent lack of concern city folk had for country people.

In this bicentennial year of 1988, the people of Gilgandra decided to restage the socalled (because of the rallying cry of the marchers) "Cooee" march, and their 22-day hike, mostly in wet weather, has been recorded in this documentary.

Director Graham Chase, whose previous docu was the excellent "Democracy," record of a political campaign, doesn't make his new subject very interesting. He observes the eccentric antics of dogged rural types with a mixture of sympathy and patronization, but can't sustain the subject matter over such a lengthy film. Far more editing was called for, since, as it is now the viewer slogs along with the marching men seemingly endlessly.

Best moments come as the marchers near Sydney, passing homes where recent immigrants to the country watch, wide-eyed, at the strange goings-on. Pic is technically very good, and could play successfully on tv in Oz, but it's doubtful it will spark much overseas interest. —*Strat.*

La Meridienne
(The Lounge Chair)
(SWISS-FRENCH)

A Cout de Coeur release of a Cab Prods. (Lausanne)/Télévision Suisse Romande/AO Prods. (Paris) coproduction. Executive producer, Jean-Louis Porchet. Directed by Jean-François Amiguet. Screenplay, Jean-François Goyet, Anne Gonthier; camera (Eastmancolor), Emmanuel Machuel; editor, Elisabeth Waelchli; music, Gaspard Glaus, Antoine Auberson; sound, Laurent Barbey; art direction, Yanko Hodjis; assistant director, Dominique Guerrier; production manager, Gérard Ruey; associate producer, Marie-Pascale Osterrieth. Reviewed at the UGC Biarritz cinema, Paris, June 20, 1988. Running time: **78 MIN.**
With: Jérôme Angé, Kristin Scott-Thomas, Sylvie Orcier, Patrice Kerbrat, Michel Voita, Judith Godrèche.

Paris — A comedy of mild manners in the ironic mode of Eric Rohmer, this Swiss feature (screened in Cannes in the Un Certain Regard section) might have had some gossamer charm and finesse in Rohmer's hands. Unfortunately, Swiss helmer Jean-François Amiguet (in his second theatrical feature effort) gives a languid reading to an inconsequential and often precious script by Jean-François Goyet and Anne Gonthier.

Dull tale chastely relates the dilemma of a young cinema projectionist (Jérôme Angé) who decides he wants to get married but is not sure who's to be the (lucky?) lady.

The most likely candidates are the two apparently platonic girl friends he's been sharing a house with for some 10 years (Kristin Scott-Thomas and Sylvie Orcier). He seems in fact manifestly in favor of former (who lounges about most of the day on the chair of the title).

Angé's oddball plan to help him make up his mind is to ask Scott-Thomas to hire a private detective (Patrice Kerbrat) to trail him and report on his extramural romances, in the hope that the flatfoot's reports will provide the key to his future.

Angé dallies so long that Scott-Thomas and the detective fall in love with one another and marry, leaving the goofball romantic free to pursue other potential Dulcineas.
—*Len.*

Une Nuit a l'Assemblée nationale
(A Night At The National Assembly)
(FRENCH)

A Bac Film release of a Cinémax/Koala Films coproduction. Produced by Andre Djaoui. Directed by Jean-Pierre Mocky. Screenplay, Mocky, Patrick Rambaud; camera (Kodak-Pathé color), Marcel Combes; editor, Mocky; music, Gabriel Yared; art direction, Jean-Michel Hugon; sound, Bernard Rochut; production manager, Patrick Delauneux. Reviewed at the Georges V cinema, Paris, June 27, 1988. Running time: **92 MIN.**
Walter Arbeit . . . . Michel Blanc
Octave Leroi . . . . Jean Poiret
Henriette Brulard . . . . . Jacqueline Maillan
Kayzer . . . . Darry Cowl
Olympe . . . . Sophie Moyse
Agnello . . . . Roland Blanche
Marcel . . . . Jean Benguigui
Madam Dugland . . . . Bernadette Lafont
A journalist . . . . Josiane Balasko

Paris — "A Night At The National Assembly" is a vulgar, feeble political farce from local enfant terrible Jean-Pierre Mocky, who has been overcranking in recent months (this is his third feature in the past year!).

Mocky obviously timed his comedy for current national elections, but his satiric targets bear little rapport with current themes in French politics.

Script by Mocky and Patrick Rambaud is a gross, witless mishmash concerning a nudist colony leader (Michel Blanc) who thinks he's been decorated with the Legion of Honor for his ecological exploits only to learn that he's been suckered into a black market on official honors. With the aid of raging leftwing militant (Jacqueline Maillan), Blanc tries unsuccessfully to stir up a scandal against a royalist (Jean Poiret) who's a big wheel in the decorations trafficking.

A saving grace of Mocky's previous bad-taste comedies has often been his actors, but here neither the tart gusto of Maillan nor the suave knavishness of Poiret are of use.

Michel Blanc, the bald, puny funnyman who has been biding his screen time since winning Cannes honors in 1986 for Bertrand Blier's "Menage," is left in the raw by the script both figuratively and literally. Sporting a hairpiece, a beard and a pair of shoes, he spends most of the film in the altogether. (It's interesting to note how full frontal male nudity has become commonplace these days in local pics.)

Film had a poor start at local wickets (in a large 45-screen Paris booking) and seems even to have embarrassed Mocky's usual hardcore buff following, whose hallelujah chorus has for once lost its voice. —*Len.*

Pickles Make Me Cry
(HONG KONG-U.S.)

An International Projection Enterprise, Hong Kong and N.Y., production. Executive Producer, Riki Ishak. Produced and directed by Peter Chow. Screenplay, Chow, Joseph Chow; camera (color), Larry Banks; editor, Peter Cheung, Marcus Chun, Joseph Chiang; music, Tan Dun; art direction, Bing Lee. Reviewed at Asian American Intl. Film Festival, N.Y., June 24, 1988. Running time: 85 MIN.

With: Thomas Hsiung (William), Karen Lee (Jeannie), Bill Wong (Uncle Sen), Stephen Chen (Uncle Charlie), Asie Laos (George).

Pickles are a ridiculous fruit or vegetable or whatever they are. They don't make a lot of sense but we like them. Used in a film title, pickles suggest a certain tasty sour humor, misshapen but enjoyable. "Pickles Make Me Cry," which takes place in New York, is such a comedy-thriller. It could succeed in selected venues with proper handling.

The two Chinese lovers in "Pickles" eat kosher pickles in bed after lovemaking. He is William (Thomas Hsiung), a nice guy fresh from Hong Kong and eager to make a big score. She is Jeannie (Karen Lee), Chinese-American dancer learning to combine classical ballet with kung fu gymnastics. They're in a pickle because a nasty Chinatown gang shoots William and blacks his eye. The gang is muscling in on a protection racket, extorting a heavy fee from a Chinatown laundry owned by kindly Uncle Sen (Bill Wong). In retaliation, mean Uncle Charlie (Stephen Chen) mobilizes a counter-team to stamp out the incoming marauders.

The stage is set for a Chinatown showdown and shoot-out. It's all settled off-screen when the top brass sends orders down to cool it. Thus "Pickles" keeps its emphasis on William's on/off/on romance with Jeannie and his friendship with former Hong Kong pal George (Asie Laos), dreamer and loser. George can't hold a job, wastes time with aborted schemes, and is henpecked by his adulterous wife. For George, the U.S. is a fraud, he just can't

succeed here, so he flies back to Hong Kong, his tail between his legs. For William, the U.S. is his youthful dream come true, now with his loving Jeannie and the promise of a job as stunt coordinator for low-budget movies.

Accordingly, "Pickles" illustrates the ambivalence of the foreigner's experience of America — one nation, divisible, with riches for some and failure for the others. Films that deal with this dubious duality, as incoming aliens test themselves within our system, are rather common. The U.S. is bitter disillusionment for those who cannot make it here, but it is bliss for those who can. It's a crapgame. If "Pickles" enters the U.S. distribution mainstream, the success/failure, hit-or-bust mentality of our foreign residents may come as a big surprise to American audiences. —*Hitch.*

Arthur 2 On The Rocks

A Warner Bros. release of a Havlin-Robert Shapiro production. Produced by Shapiro. Executive producer, Dudley Moore. Directed by Bud Yorkin. Screenplay, Andy Breckman, based on characters created by Steve Gordon; camera (Technicolor), Stephen H. Burum; editor, Michael Kahn; music, Burt Bacharach; production design, Gene Callahan; art direction, Hub Braden; set decoration, Lee Poll; set design, P. Michael Johnstone; costume design, Anna Hill Johnston; sound (Dolby), Jim Tannenbaum; assistant director, Bob Girolami; casting, Mike Fenton, Jane Feinberg, Valorie Massalas. Reviewed at Samuel Goldwyn theater, Beverly Hills, Calif., June 27, 1988. MPAA Rating: PG. Running time: 113 MIN.
Arthur .... Dudley Moore
Linda .... Liza Minnelli
Martha .... Geraldine Fitzgerald
Fairchild .... Paul Benedict
Hobson .... John Gielgud
Mrs. Canby .... Kathy Bates
Susan .... Cynthia Sikes
Burt Johnson .... Stephen Elliott
Ralph .... Barney Martin
Super .... Jack Gilford

Hollywood — Overly long by 15 minutes and very contrived, "Arthur 2 On The Rocks" is not as classy a farce as the original, but still manages to be an amusing romp for most of its length. Audiences who found Dudley Moore a most charming, irresponsible rich drunk in the first chapter most likely will enjoy more of his antics here as he tries to sober up — resulting in a nice summer hit for Warner Bros.

Absent for much of the film is Arthur's (Moore) sarcastic and now-deceased butler, John Gielgud, who was the foil for many of the setups in "Arthur," and in this followup comes in late in the show as an admonishing ghost only when his former charge is experiencing the d.t.s.

To fill the void, scripter Andy Breckman replaces their funny symbiotic relationship with a series of anxiety-causing conflicts that make Arthur drink himself — literally — into a homeless state.

Five years into their marriage and

living the enviable Park Avenue lifestyle with the kind of digs photographed by Architectural Digest (production designer Gene Callaghan deserves special recognition for his lavish, tasteful sets), wife Linda (Liza Minnelli) finds she's unable to conceive and goes about adopting a baby.

While Minnelli is gung ho to expand the fold, Arthur's ex-girlfriend's father (Stephen Elliott) seeks to break it apart. Vindictive over having his love-struck daughter stood up at the altar by Arthur last time around, he works up a legal trick to take away the wastrel's $750,000,000 fortune and force him to marry his daughter after all.

Penniless, unskilled and not exactly ambitious, Arthur — still drinking — tries to find work but is thwarted at every turn at the same time his wife all-too-easily adapts to waitressing at a diner to make ends meet.

Some of the drinking gags are reworked or expanded to adapt to this scenario versus the simpler plotting of Arthur's prior dilemma to marry or not to marry the WASP g.f. (Cynthia Sikes this time).

Though not critical to the pleasures of watching Moore in one of his best screen roles, it does undermine his performance when he has lesser personalities to tease. New butler Fairchild (Paul Benedict) is a bit of a dull tool as compared to the pricelessly dry Gielgud, and Sikes is as pretty but not nearly as humorously airheaded as was Jill Eikenberry in the same role. Back again to speak a few vulgarities is Geraldine Fitzgerald as the family matriarch.

Minnelli loses some of her working class sassiness as the downtown-gone-uptown-gone-downtown wife trying to put her house in order, though credit is due her for carrying plot's best scenes.

When the playful protagonist's excessive drinking (some would say alcoholism) puts him in the streets and in the company of winos, the plot goes sour.

Pic concludes in a great, messy heap with too much tied up too easily. We can assume that if Arthur finally sobers up for good, he won't be funny enough for another chapter.

Production values, for the most part, are terrific. Gotham — also repped by studio shooting in Burbank — photographed at Christmastime (which is kind of odd for a summer release), looks lovely under Stephen H. Burum's lensing, though Michael Kahn's editing is occasionally choppy. Scoring by Burt Bacharach is strangely nondescript.

Pic is dedicated to "Arthur" director and scripter Steve Gordon, who died following the release of the first film. — *Brit.*

West Is West

A Rathod production. Written, produced and directed by David Rathod. Coproducer-art direction, Cristi Janaki Rathod; camera (color), Christopher Tufty; music, Sheila Chandra, Jai Uttal; sound, Andy Wiskes. Reviewed at Asian American Intl. Film Festival, N.Y., June 24, 1988. No MPAA Rating. Running time: 80 MIN.

With: Ashotosh Gowariker (Vikram), Heidi Carpenter (Sue), Pearl Padamsee (Mrs. Shah).

Rudyard Kipling was wrong — east is east, west is west, but the twain can meet when love triumphs over the U.S. Bureau Of Immigration and Naturalization. "West Is West" is an entertaining international romantic comedy, with musical interludes, taking place in San Francisco and in India.

Like so many films seen at the Asian American Intl. Film Festival this year and in the past, the central figure is a naive alien who arrives in the U.S. with extravagantly illogical expectations of achieving fame, wealth and love as a new American citizen. Naturally, he or she is bitterly disappointed. It's a good premise on which to build story complications and audience interest, both as comedy and as drama.

Vikram (Indian actor Ashotosh Gowariker), handsome would-be immigrant from Bombay, arrives at the San Francisco airport with three suitcases of enthusiasm but runs smack into stonewall U.S. Customs officers. As Pres. Reagan's portrait on the wall behind them smiles down genially, the government officers trim Vikram's tourist visa from six months to one. When Vikram arrives at his sponsor's house in the suburbs, he finds it abandoned. Further, he is rejected for matriculation by the University of California. His visa expiring, forbidden to work or to enroll as a student, Vikram faces a peck of plot convolutions. Only way out is to propose marriage to sweet Sue (Heidi Carpenter), a punk-rock swinger who vends popcorn in a late-night horror-flick moviehouse.

While dodging Immigration cops threatening to deport him, Vikram encounters sundry colorful characters, most colorful being Mrs. Shah (Pearl Padamsee, actress and director of Bombay's avant-garde theater). Mrs. Shah is proprietress of a seedy hotel who befriends Vikram. Padamsee is plainly a top pro.

Producer-director David Rathod's background in U.S. commercials and music videos is evident in "West" and lends itself to a clever satire of the musical numbers common in Indian films. —*Hitch.*

The Perfect Murder
(BRITISH-INDIAN)

A Merchant Ivory production. Executive producer, Ismail Merchant. Produced by Wahid Chowhan. Directed by Zafar Hai. Screenplay, Hai, H.R.F. Keating, based on Keating's novel; camera (color), Walter Lassally; editor, Charles Rees; music, Richard Robbins; production design, Kiran Patki, Sartaj Noorani; art direction, Ram Yedekar; costumes, Sally Turner. Reviewed at Crown Preview theater, London, June 21, 1988. Running time: 93 MIN.

Inspector Ghote	Naseeruddin Shah
Dilap Lal	Dalip Tahil
Mrs. Lal	Madhur Jaffrey
Axel Svenson	Stellen Skarsgard
Lala Heera Lal	Amjad Khan
Neena Lal	Sakeena Jaffrey
Minister	Vinod Nagpal
Mr. Perfect	Dinshaw Daji
Miss Twinkle	Archana Puran Singh
Mrs. Ghote	Ratna Pathak Shah

London — The color, heat and atmosphere of Bombay are captured perfectly in "The Perfect Murder," fascinating combination of traditional Indian filmmaking and the sharper international awareness of the Merchant Ivory production house.

With producer Ismail Merchant taking executive producer credit, music by Richard Robbins and veteran cinematographer Walter Lassally, the talent is certainly there, but whether pic can make an impact offshore seems doubtful. Need for careful handling, with strong pitch to immigrant Indian communities, is obvious.

Essentially, "Perfect Murder" is a traditional Western detective story transplanted to Bombay, with a few red herrings, chases and some slapstick along the way until Naseeruddin Shah as a police inspector solves the various mysteries.

Shah is teamed with a visiting police officer, a bumbling Swede played by Stellen Skarsgard, who proceed to wander around Bombay getting into trouble but eventually becoming the best of buddies.

Shah is faced with the prospect of solving a number of crimes — diamond smuggling, the theft of a ring and the "perfect" murder, which actually turns out to be just an attack on a man named Mr. Perfect. Shah and Skarsgard seem to spend the film hunting for various witnesses and getting involved with plenty of eccentric characters, with Shah finally unraveling the crimes almost as an afterthought.

In line with Indian cinema tradition, everything is brightly colored, and Lassally brings out the best of Bombay, giving it an appealingly cheerful appearance. An opening chase through a film poster painting yard is amusing and the expected Indian song and dance, by Archana Puran Singh as Miss Twinkle, also is appealing.

While some of the actors happily go over the top, best work is by Shah as the harrassed policeman, and Dalip Tahil as a huge millionaire who speaks in a singsong.

Family connections feature strongly in the production, with Shah's wife, Ratna Pathak Shah, playing his screen spouse (their scenes together have amusing appeal) while mother and daughter Madhur Jaffrey and Sakeena Jaffrey appear together for the first time, also as mother and daughter.

"The Perfect Murder" is pleasantly old-fashioned in both story and direction. Pic warrants a look, even if only for the exquisite camerawork of Lassally. —*Adam.*

ARCHIVE REVIEWS

Michel Strogoff
(FRENCH-B&W-TINTED-1925-26)

A Cinémathèque Française restoration of a Ciné-France-Film (Consortium Westi/-Films de France (Société des Cinéromans) production (1925-26). Produced by Noë Bloch. Directed by Vyacheslav Tourjansky. Screenplay, Tourjansky, Ivan Mosjoukine, Boris de Fast, from the Jules Verne novel; camera (b&w), Léonce-Henri Burel, Nicolas Toporkoff, Fedote Bourgassoff; sets, Alexandre Lochakoff, Pierre Schildknecht, Edouard Gosch, César Lacca, Vladimir Meingart; costumes, Leon Zack; makeup, Vladimir Kvanin, Boris de Fast; production administrator, Simon Schiffrin; restoration editor, Renée Lichtig. First released in Paris, Dec. 3, 1926 by Pathé-Consortium-Cinéma. Reviewed at Cinémathèque Française, Paris, April 29, 1988. Length: 12,200 ft. Running time (at 20 f/s): 163 MIN.

Michel Strogoff	Ivan Mosjoukine
Nadia Fedoroff	Nathalie Kovanko
Ivan Ogareff	Acho Chakatouny
Harry Blount	Henri Debain
Alcide Jolivet	Gabriel de Gravonne
Marfa Strogoff	Jeanne Brindeau
Czar Alexandre 2d/ Jules Verne	Eugène Gaidaroff
Feofar Khan	Boris de Fast
Zingara	Tina de Izarduy

Paris — Jules Verne's beloved tale of the Czarist courier Michel Strogoff has inspired numerous films, but none has ever surpassed this 1925 French production for fidelity, style and spectacle. Recently restored by the Cinémathèque Française from a deteriorating original negative, it is a fine candidate for live-orchestral revival, especially after the recent international success of the reconstituted 1926 extravaganza "Casanova," made by the same group of filmmakers.

"Michel Strogoff" gains relief and excitement in having been produced by the extraordinary émigré Russian film colony which revitalized the ailing French film industry in the 1920s with its artistry and showmanship. Even moreso than in "Casanova" (shot only months later), "Strogoff" provided these uprooted Slavs with the chance to conjure up a fantasy image of the homeland they had fled in 1919-20.

It was in fact largely shot on location in Latvia, where the army provided manpower and resources for its vivid recreation of the Russian Empire in the shadow of Tatar revolt, while the brilliant set designer Alexander Lochakoff and his team erected magnificent interiors in the Parisian studios. It proved to have such large-scale sweep that star Ivan Mosjoukine and director Vyacheslav Tourjansky were soon lured to Hollywood with major contracts (which proved unhappy and brief experience for both).

Film's superiority over subsequent German, American, French and Italian remarks also was due to the fact that its makers never tried to apologize for the story's naiveté and improbabilities, which they understood to be part of its enduring charm.

Mosjoukine and Tourjansky pulled most of their setpieces right off the page and transferred them to the screen with brio and imagination. Mosjoukine-Strogoff makes his way across rivers, steppes, towns and mountains to help quell Tatar revolt in the Siberian provinces, it often appears as if the famous illustrations & engravings of the novel's original editions had suddenly come to 3-dimensional life.

To their credit, the filmmakers notably played it straight with the blinding of Strogoff with a red-hot saber by the arch-villain Ivan Ogareff and the miraculous recovery of his eyesight. Subsequent adaptors seemed to blush at Verne's poetical pirouette about the hero's tears (provoked by the sight of his dear mother) protecting his eyes from definitive damage, and they bent over backwards to invent another solution — invariably that the excutioner was bribed to fake it!

Though Tourjansky's direction tends to drag in quieter scenes, he's at his best with movement and spectacle, which often bear the strong influence of Abel Gance. And no wonder: Tourjansky began "Strogoff" after having assisted Gance in the early shooting of "Napoleon," and both films lensed side by side at Billancourt Studios.

One of the film's most magnificent sequences is the parallel opening section of the Czar's ball and the uprising in the provinces. As troubled reports arrive and the monarch begins to imagine the invading hordes, the director intercuts rampaging Tatars and ballroom dancers, climaxing in royal headache in which the Czar confuses barbaric horsemen and civilized Moscovites both rushing headlong towards the camera in a dizzying whirl of rapid-montage.

Mosjoukine embodies Verne's hero with a panache that made him one of Europe's most popular silent screen idols. He's so much the part that one can today forgive him some histrionic excesses and self-indulgence (notable a bizarre dream sequence that is an embarrassing intrusion).

Film's chief fault in fact is that it's too long, running 2¾ hours at appropriate silent speed (20 f/s — running it at sound speed will solve nothing and ruin the action scenes in particular). A rousingly good musical score can easily help modern audiences over the bumps in narrative and acting.

Cinémathèque intends to restore film with its original tints and stencil-colored effects, which provide a filip to the film's best setpieces. — *Len.*

For The Term Of His Natural Life
(AUSTRALIAN-B&W-1926-27)

A National Film and Sound Archive restoration of Union Master World Picture, an Australasian Films production. Produced, written and directed by Norman Dawn, from the novel by Marcus Clarke. Camera (b&w), Len Roos, William Trerise, Bert Cross; editor, Dawn, Katherine Dawn, Mona Donaldson; titles, Dawn, Gayne Dexter; art direction, Dorothy Gordon, Dawn. Running time (at sound speed): 100 MIN.

Rufus Dawes/John Rex	George Fisher
Sylvia Vickers	Eva Novak
Maurice Frere	Dunstan Webb
Sarah Purfoy	Jessica Harcourt
Gabbett	Arthur McLaglen
Mrs. Vickers	Katherine Dawn
Warden Troke	Arthur Tauchert

Sydney — The most daunting project of restoration ever undertaken by Australia's National Film Archive was "For The Term Of His Natural Life," the most lavish of all Aussie silent films. This melodramatic drama of convict life and mistaken identity was produced in 1926-7 at the then princely figure of £60,000 and was shot on locations in southern Tasmania where a notorious convict prison actually stood.

Originally, pic was to have been directed by Australia's foremost silent director, Raymond Longford ("The Sentimental Bloke") but a late decision by the production company was made to import an American, Norman Dawn, with scant directorial experience (there is an apocryphal story that a cable was sent ot Allan Dwan, then riding high, but got scrambled and was received by Dawn instead, who accepted).

Pictorially, the film is magnificent, the use of locations impressive, and special effects, including a convincing story at sea, rousing. The plotting is very much Victorian melodrama (twin brothers, one sent into penal servitude for the other's crime), but there are elements here that were daring in their day, such as the emphasis on cannibalism among a band of convicts who manage to escape from their ghastly prison.

It was hoped that the film would crack the U.S. market but, unfortunately for the producers, its completion coincided with the arrival of talkies, and though it was hugely successful in Australia, it had scant bookings in America (it opened at the Stanley in New York in June,

1929, in a cut version).

When the Archive received a copy of the film, in 1960, four of its ten reels were missing. The picture was painstakingly restored over the years, partly with hitherto "lost" footage found in the U.S., and the restored version preemed at the 1981 Sydney film festival with one of its stars, Jessica Harcourt, in attendance. — *Strat.*

Saigon Commandos

A Concorde Pictures presentation. Produced by John Schouweiler, Isabel Sumayao. Directed by Clark Henderson. Screenplay, Thomas McKelvey Cleaver, from Jonathan Cain's novel "Saigon Commandos — Mad Minute;" camera (Motion Picture color), Juanito Pereira, Conrado Baltazar; editor, Pacifico Sanchez; music, Samuel Asuncion, Noli Aurillo; sound, Gavino Maximo; production design, Mariles Gonzales; assistant director, Hernan Robles; second unit director, Allan Noble; casting, Barbara Remsen & Associates, Ann Remsen. Reviewed on Media Home Entertainment vidcassette, N.Y., May 24, 1988. MPAA Rating: R. Running time: **83 MIN.**

Sgt. Mark Stryker	Richard Young
Jean Lassiter	P.J. Soles
Tim Bryant	John Allen Nelson
Will Thomas	Jimi B. Jr.
Jon Toi	Spanky Manikan
Nguyen Huu Tri	Joonee Gamboa
Capt. Daniels	Fred Bailey

A serviceable action picture which has gone the direct-to-video route, "Saigon Commandos" is of interest for its similarity to the recent Fox release "Off Limits" (starring Willem Dafoe and Gregory Hines). Both films utilize the same offbeat premise, though "Commandos" was shot a year earlier, in the Philippines.

Pic is set in Saigon in 1970, concerning the activities of tough military police stationed there (referred to sarcastically by the troops in country as "Saigon commandos") and their conflict with various South Vietnamese officers and officials.

Main nemesis is a politician Tri (Joonee Gamboa) who is riling up the population against the Yanks. Hero Sgt. Stryker (Richard Young playing it tough guy-style) is investigating the socalled hollowpoint killer, who's been offing drug dealers. The baddies frame Stryker for the murders, but he is able to solve the case on his own. P.J. Soles is along for the ride as a pretty Associated Press correspondent initially assigned to tag along with Stryker.

Though a subplot involving a gung ho soldier who becomes a vengeful sniper doesn't work, film is okay. It lacks the sensationalism of "Off Limits" and ends up being merely routine. Tech credits are acceptable.—*Lor.*

Last Man Standing
(CANADIAN)

A Rose and Ruby presentation of a Busted Up II production. Produced by David Mitchell, Damian Lee; line producer, John Ryan. Executive producers, Lawrence Nesis, Steve Ippolito, Andrew Ippolito. Directed by Lee. Screenplay, Mitchell, Lee; camera (Filmhouse color), Ludvik Bogner; editor, Gary Zubeck; music, Charles Barnett; sound, Chaim Gillad; art direction, Ron Dickie; assistant director, Rob Malenfant; stunt coordinator, T.J. Scott; casting, Lucinda Sills. Reviewed on Academy Entertainment vidcassette, N.Y., June 22, 1988. Running time: **88 MIN.**

Roo	Vernon Wells
Casper	William Sanderson
Napoleon	Michael Copeman
Batty	Franco Columbu
Charlie	Sonja Belliveau
Tenney	Frank Moore
Razor	Real Andrews
Gus	Danny Burns

Being released direct-to-video, "Last Man Standing" is an effective Canadian pic covering similar ground to Walter Hill's classic Charles Bronson-starrer "Hard Times."

Aussie thesp Vernon Wells (memorable as the oversize nemesis in "The Road Warrior") is well cast as Roo, a streetfighter in what are dubbed "circle fights," bareknuckled boxing inside a steel cage. He works for gym owner Casper (William Sanderson), but there is all sorts of corruption involved, led by club owner Napoleon (Michael Copeman) and crooked cop Tenney (Frank Moore).

Roo is tormented by memories of eight years in an insane asylum and the shock treatment he received there, but in genre's time-honored tradition he comes back to fight a new star, and then battles Napoleon's cocky pro talent Razor (Real Andrews).

Except for an unconvincing, tacked-on happy ending shot, film plays well, with standard dramatics, okay fight scenes and a most unusual romance between Roo and offbeat leading lady Sonja Belliveau, who works as a mechanic and is big and strong enough to beat up most of the cast. Wells and Sanderson are sympathetic, the villains ordinary. Same production team earlier made another fight film, "Busted Up," toplining Paul Coufos and Irene Cara. — *Lor.*

Letniaia Poezdka k Moriu
(A Trip To The Sea)
(SOVIET)

A Lenfilm production. Directed by Semën Aranovich. Screenplay, Yuris Klepikov; camera (color), V. Ilin; editor, R. Izakson; music, O. Karavaichuk; art direction, G. Mekinian. Reviewed at Pesaro Film Festival, June 15, 1988. Running time: **105 MIN.**

With: N. Skorobogatov, A. Gorin, I. Fokin, A. Kurennoi, A. Zotov, V. Porskurin, I. Matveev; D. Zarubin, V. Boltov.

Pesaro — Veteran helmer Semën Aranovich, director of the all-action war film "Torpedo Bombers," **made a curious variation on the war film genre in 1978 called "A Trip To The Sea."**

The all-male cast is a group of boys (orphans?), taken to a remote island in the Arctic Ocean in the summer of 1942 to collect bird eggs. Nazis attack the island. This drama for stout-hearted sportsmen has its engaging moments, with spectacular scenes set in the splendid natural landscape. Foreign audiences look to be limited.

Wartime or not, it's hard to believe young boys would be used so casually in the dangerous business of climbing down cliff faces, attached to a rope held without great care by equally frail companions. Conditions on the island are spartan in the extreme: water comes from the next island, food and medicine from a ship.

Here toughness is the rule and the boys don't complain, or show homesickness for Leningrad under fire or their families. They get by on their own wits, under the sympathetic guidance of a kindly old sailor, only adult on the expedition.

Action scenes are plentiful and well choreographed: a Nazi plane strafes the island and is shot down in a dogfight; the supply ship is torpedoed to smithereens and the survivors brutally murdered; finally Nazis invade the island and destroy the carefully gathered crates of eggs.

Youthful thesps are diversified, sound performers. The island's millions of birds clinging to the cliffs and soaring in flight are unforgettable. —*Yung.*

Der Joker
(Lethal Obsession)
(WEST GERMAN)

A Vidmark Entertainment presentation of a Lisa/CTV 72/KS Film production. Directed by Peter Patzak. Screenplay, Jonathan Carroll, Patsak, from story by Mortimer Ellis; camera (color), Igor Luther, Dietrich Lohmann; editor, Michou Hutter; music, Tony Carey, Frank Diez, Carl Carlton, Peter Maffay; sound, Milan Bor; set design, Claus Kottman. Reviewed on Vidmark vidcassette, N.Y., June 12, 1988. MPAA Rating: R. Running time: **96 MIN.**

Jon Bogdan	Peter Maffay
Daniela Santini	Tahnee Welch
Serge Gart	Elliott Gould
Toni Black	Massimo Ghini
Henry Black	Karl Merkatz
Axel	Armin Mueller-Stahl
Dr. Proper	Michael York

Also with: Joachim D. Mues, Marquard Bohm, Werner Pochath, Uwe Hacker, Monica Bliebtreu, Bernhard Freyd.

(Dubbed English soundtrack)

"Lethal Obsession" is a glum, European-made *film noir* featuring name talent including Tahnee Welch, Elliott Gould and Michael York. Their efforts go for little in attempting to redeem an impenetrable storyline, directed by Peter Patzak with far too many musicvideo and "Miami Vice" riffs.

Direct-to-video release toplines Peter Maffay (unconvincingly dubbed with a neutral American accent) as a tough cop partnered with Massimo Ghini who are both in love with Welch. Baddies kill Welch's restaurateur dad with a bomb, which also leaves Maffay paralyzed from the waist down. He goes on a quest for vengeance against the criminal mastermind The Ace, dubbing himself The Joker (pic's original title is "Der Joker").

Novelty of Maffay rolling around town in a wheelchair strong-arming folks wears off when he suddenly recuperates and can walk again, but pretends to be still paralyzed to give himself an edge against the heavies. Cynical ending is downbeat, sudden and pointless.

A sullen nonperformance by Maffay (who also contributed to the musical score) renders the film lifeless. Welch is okay, as is guest star York as a surprisingly friendly hitman, but Gould has nothing to do but deliver expository dialog in a tacked-on small role. — *Lor.*

Die Hard

A 20th Century Fox release of a Gordon Co./Silver Pictures production. Produced by Lawrence Gordon, Joel Silver. Executive producer, Charles Gordon. Directed by John McTiernan. Screenplay, Jeb Stuart, Steven E. de Souza, based on novel "Nothing Lasts Forever" by Roderick Thorpe; camera (Panavision, Deluxe color), Jan De Bont; editor, Frank J. Urioste, John F. Link; music, Michael Kamen; production design, Jackson DeGovia; art direction, John R. Jensen; set design, E.C. Chen, Roland Hill; set decoration, Phil M. Leonard; costume design, Marilyn Vance-Straker; sound (Dolby), Al Overton; visual effects, Richard Edlund; stunt coordinator, Charles Picerni; associate producer-second unit director; Beau E.L. Marks; assistant director, Benjamin Rosenberg; casting, Jackie Burch. Reviewed at the Samuel Goldwyn theater, Beverly Hills, Calif., July 7, 1988. MPAA Rating: R. Running time: **131 MIN.**

John McClane	Bruce Willis
Hans Gruber	Alan Rickman
Holly Gennaro McClane	Bonnie Bedelia
Karl	Alexander Godunov
Sgt. Al Powell	Reginald Veljohnson
Dwayne T. Robinson	Paul Gleason
Argyle	De'voreaux White
Thornburg	William Atherton
Ellis	Hart Bochner
Takagi	James Shigeta
Big Johnson	Robert Davi
Little Johnson	Grand L. Bush
Theo	Clarence Gilyard Jr.

Hollywood — "Die Hard" is as high tech, rock hard and souped up as an action film can be, which will win it high marks in some people's books and demerits in others.

A suspenser pitting a lone wolf cop against a group of terrorists that has taken over a highrise office tower, richly produced drama delivers more than enough goods to satisfy mainstream audiences, so only doubts concerning its ultimate b.o. reach must stem from the genre, as the summer's two male-oriented actioners to date, "Rambo III" and "Red Heat," have been commercial disappointments.

While set in the recognizably real world populated by nothing but human beings, pic plays like a reworked version of Fox' "Aliens," with terror lurking in the bowels of an enormous man-made structure and striking from any angle at any time. Director John McTiernan does not often play for outright shock, but atmosphere of claustrophobia and ever-present threat is eerily similar.

Bruce Willis plays John McClane, an overworked New York policeman who flies into Los Angeles at Christmas to visit his two daughters and estranged wife Holly (Bonnie Bedelia), who since their separation has done exceptionally well as an executive at a Japanese-owned company.

Planning a rather different holiday agenda are the terrorists led by Hans Gruber (Alan Rickman). The dastardly dozen invade the plush 30th floor offices of the Nakatomi Corp. during its Christmas party, murder the boss and then hold the employees hostage as a computer whiz goes about the hours-long process of cracking a code that will put the mainly German bad boys in possession of $600,000,000 in negotiable bonds.

Slipping out of the party in the nick of time with nothing but his handgun, Willis is the fly in the ointment of the criminals' plans, picking off one, then two more of the scouts sent on pest control missions. Willis seemingly spends half the picture hoisting himself up and down elevator shafts, bounding up back stairways, crawling through heating ducts and dodging bullets in vacant office space, getting bloodier and sweatier with each scene.

Action shifts out of the highrise on occasion thanks to Willis' CB communication with L.A. cop Reginald Veljohnson, who is the first of what ultimately becomes a batallion-sized police and FBI contingent outside the skyscraper.

Even at an overlong 131 minutes, pic is never dull, but it often becomes so overwrought that it feels faintly ridiculous, particularly where the terrorists are concerned. One waits patiently to find out what these guys really want, only to discover that they are rebels without a cause.

Beefed up considerably for his role, Willis is amiable enough in the opening stretch, but overdoes the grimacing and heavy emoting later on. The cooler and more humorous he is the better, and his one attempt at a heavy emotional scene, in which he pours out his feelings about his wife, is embarrassing enough to warn him off similar material in the near future.

Alan Rickman has a giddy good time but sometimes goes over the top as the henchman, and meets a stunning fate lifted from Hitchcock's "Saboteur." Most notable supporting turns come from Veljohnson, and De'voreaux White, who has a high time waiting out the seige in a stretch limo.

Technical aspects are top drawer Hollywood all the way, with Jan De Bont's sulfurous lensing, Richard Edlund's visual effects, Charles Picerni's stunt contributions and Jacson DeGovia's chic production design taking special bows. McTiernan dissipates in the tension of several scenes, notably the final battle between Willis and thug Alexander Godunov, by too much intercutting, and resolution proves patly predictable. —*Cart.*

Sad Zhlani
(The Garden Of Desire)
(SOVIET)

A Mosfilm Studio production. Directed by Ali Khamraev. Screenplay, Sergei Lazutkin; camera (color), Vladimir Klimov; art direction, Parviz Teimurov, Viktor Zenkov. Reviewed at Tashkent Film Festival (market), May 26, 1988. Running time: **90 MIN.**
Asya	Marianna Velezheva

Also with: Olga Zarkhina, Irina Shustaieva, Galina Makarova.

Tashkent — After several conflicts with the authorities over film projects, Uzbek director Ali Khamraev agreed to shoot Sergei Lazutkin's script "The Garden Of Desire" for Mosfilm Studio. Result is a storyless, almost wordless allegory likely to disappoint Khamraev fans used to more personal fare.

A concept film that is all atmosphere, "Garden" soon grows weedy. Three pretty, adolescent girls romp through the woods in pic's first half. They represent innocence and nature, and spend an idyllic summer vacation at grandma's swinging from tree boughs and playing around white sheets. Prettiest of them is Asya (Marianna Velezheva), whose budding feminine beauty is the object of much admiration. The sensual interest is clear, but film stops at nude backs.

Amid dark forebodings of war (noisy cars, a man arrested), Asya experiences the pangs of first love. It is never to be realized, because enemy planes bomb the village and kill every living thing. Last shot is an overgrown cemetery with organ music playing and two blond kinds skipping through it — optimism after tragedy.

Lensing is atmospheric, but print screened was very dark. — *Yung.*

A Fish Called Wanda

An MGM/UA Distribution Co. release of an MGM production. Produced by Michael Shamberg. Executive producers, Steve Abbott, John Cleese. Directed by Charles Crichton. Screenplay, John Cleese, from story by Cleese, Crichton; camera (Technicolor), Alan Hume; editor, John Jympson; music, John Du Prez; production design, Roger Murray-Leach; art direction, John Wood; set decoration, Stephanie McMillan; costume design, Hazel Pethig; sound, Gerry Humphreys; associate producer, John Comfort; assistant director; Johnathan Benson; casting, Priscilla John. Reviewed at MGM, Culver City, Calif., July 8, 1988. MPAA Rating: R. Running time: **108 MIN.**
Archie Leach	John Cleese
Wanda	Jamie Lee Curtis
Otto	Kevin Kline
Ken	Michael Palin
Wendy	Maria Aitken
George	Tom Georgeson
Mrs. Coady	Patricia Hayes

Hollywood — In a "A Fish Called Wanda," Monty Pythoners John Cleese and Michael Palin get caught up in a double-crossing crime caper with a mismatched and hilarious pair of scheming Yanks, Jamie Lee Curtis and Kevin Kline.

Though it is less tasteless, irreverent and satirical than the Python pics, film still is wacky and occasionally outrageous in its own, distinctly British way. While avid Python fans may be disappointed with the watered-down humor, adding a couple of Americans to the formula might interest a whole new kind of audience. MGM should get a good catch at the b.o.

This has the stamp of executive producer and scripter John Cleese written all over it. He is Archie Leach (which was Cary Grant's real name —*Ed.*), an uptight, respected barrister who becomes unglued when Wanda (Jamie Lee Curtis), the girlfriend of a crook he's defending, comes on to him for no apparent reason. Curtis fakes it as an American law student looking to learn about English law when really she just wants to get information out of Cleese about some diamonds she's recently heisted with his client George (Tom Georgeson) and two others — her "brother" Otto (Kevin Kline), who's really no relation and a stuttering animal rights freak Ken (Michael Palin), the proud owner of a fish tank and a fish named Wanda.

Curtis plays them off against each other and is a lover to three of them, hoping to confuse things well enough so she can escape with the booty all to herself. To further complicate matters, Kline tries to cover up for his overt moves on Curtis by hitting on Palin, too, causing the helpless, heterosexual bloke consideration consternation.

Where the story runs thin and setups become a bit repetitive, characterization becomes everything and mostly it's very well managed by the entire troupe. Kevin Kline is particularly funny in his first screen comedy as an ersatz Italian stallion/sinister type who's about as threatening as Wanda ... the fish.

As in past Python outings, Cleese takes an opportunity to poke fun at something ripe for riducule — this time, the love-hate rivalry between the Brits and the Yanks, casting the former as typically repressed and aching to break out of type and their counterparts as hyperactive, boisterous and crass. It's funny without being mean, since both sides get their due.

Curtis steals the show with her keen sense of comic timing and sneaky little grins and asides.

Palin has too limited a role: either he's trying to spit out words, which is funny in a cruel way, or trying to carry out a mission to kill an old lady when he ends up squashing her three beloved pooches instead.

Humiliation seems to be the ultimate fate of nearly everyone in this romp, except Curtis who remains cool through to the end.

From the looks of it, everyone involved seemed to enjoy themselves mightily making this picture.

Music by John Du Prez is loud and indistinctive, otherwise production credits are fine. —*Brit.*

Hanussen
(HUNGARIAN-W. GERMAN)

A Columbia Pictures presentation (U.S.) of a Hungarofilm presentation of an Objektiv, Mafilm, CCC Filmkunst, ZDF, Hungarofilm, Mokep production. Produced by Artur Brauner. Coproduction manager, Judit Sugar. Directed by Istvan Szabo. Screenplay, Szabo, Peter Dobrai; camera (Eastmancolor), Lajos Koltai; editor, Zsuzsa Csakany; music, Gyorgy Vukan; sound, Gyorgy Fek; art direc-

tion, Jozsef Romvari; costumes, Nelly Vago. Reviewed at Cannes Film Festival (competing), May 21, 1988. Running time: **140 MIN.**
Hanussen . . . . Klaus Maria Brandauer
Dr. Bettelheim . . . . Erland Josephson
Sister Betty . . . . Ildiko Bansagi
Propaganda minister . . Walter Schmidinger
Nowotny . . . . Karoly Eperjes
Valery . . . . Grazina Szapolowska
Dagma . . . . Colette Pilz-Warren
Wally . . . . Adriana Biedrzynska
Trantow-Waldbach . . . . . Gyorgy Cserhalmi

Cannes — Istvan Szabo's third foray into the split personality of the Central European soul between the two World Wars, is the least spectacular and the most introverted to date.

Dealing again with a person who sacrifices his ethics for what he believes to be his higher calling, Szabo sticks closer than ever to his hero, most of the film consisting of long, searing closeups of Klaus Maria Brandauer, leaving the rest of the characters and events in the background.

Based on the life of a real character who became a celebrity in German-speaking countries of Europe in the 20s and early 30s, "Hanussen" starts as a corporal in the Austrian Army during World War I, incurs a head injury and is sent to a hospital. While he heals physically, he suffers from acute migraines and disturbing vision.

Dr. Bettelheim, a surgeon who does psychoanalytic research, helps Hanussen to discover his gifts for hypnotism. By the end of the war he even entertains his fellow soldiers with a performance of magic tricks and soothsaying.

Once the war is over, he develops an act and under the management of a former officer, starts touring the Austro-Hungarian territories.

He catches the fancy of a German counselor, later the Berlin Minister of Propaganda in the pre-Nazi period, who invites him to Berlin. Though staying away from politics, he allows himself to be goaded into guessing the results of the forthcoming elections.

Once he points to Hitler as the winner, he becomes the darling of the National Socialist movement, a position he accepts willingly in spite of his personal misgivings concerning the party, daily reconfirmed by their acts. His hour of glory, however, is short-lived, for once he predicts the burning of the Reichstag and indicates who the real culprits are, he becomes the type of nuisance that has to be eliminated quickly, before he causes any more embarrassment.

Mystifying public performances, in which the audience is left to guess the extent of sham put over by the consummate showman, brief encounters which supply the relevant political information and several romantic adventures never detract the camera's attention from Hanussen himself.

Klaus Maria Brandauer, in his third time around with Szabo, is

practically on screen for the entire film. He tones down his performance to subtler shades. The rest of the cast is dependable, including Erland Josephson, as the man who revealed Hanussen to himself, and also Ildiko Bansagi, Grazina Szapolowska and Adriana Biedrzynska, as the three women in his life. Lajos Koltai's camera again does wonders supplying Szabo with that special blue mood he favors in these films and other technical credits are superior.

More difficult to take than either "Mephisto" or "Colonel Redl," this pic reduces the theme to its bare essentials. —*Edna.*

Phantasm II

A Universal Pictures release. Produced by Roberto A. Quezada. Executive producer, Dac Coscarelli. Written and directed by Don Coscarelli. Camera (Foto-Kem color), Daryn Okada; editor, Peter Teschner; music, Fred Myrow with Christopher L. Stone; production design, Philip J. C. Duffin; art direction, Byrnadette di Santo; set decoration, Dominic Wymark; costume design, Carla Gibbons; sound (Dolby), Izak Ben-Meir; special makeup, Mark Shostrum; special effects, Wayne Beauchamp; special visual effects, Dream Quest Images; associate producer, Robert Del Valle; assistant director, Alan Brent Connell; casting, Elizabeth Miller Fels. Reviewed at Universal Studios, Universal City, Calif., July 6, 1988. MPAA Rating: R. Running time: **90 MIN.**
Mike . . . . James Le Gros
Reggie . . . . Reggie Bannister
The Tall Man . . . . Angus Scrimm
Liz . . . . Paula Irvine
Alchemy . . . . Samantha Phillips
Father Meyers . . . . Kenneth Tigar

Hollywood — For no apparent reason, "Phantasm" has ruptured its way out of the past after nine years to take the form of this utterly unredeeming, full-gore sequel. Mercifully, this one can be expected to slither out of theaters almost as soon as it appears.

The special effects horrors that originated in "Alien" have run amok here, with slimy, hissing apparitions constantly erupting from the bodies of the afflicted.

After a brief, clumsy recap of the original, story involves the morbid obsessions of two psychically connected teens, Mike (James Le Gros) and Liz (Paula Irvine). The pair are tortured in their dreams by the Tall Man (Angus Scrimm, reprising the role), a ghoulish mortician who wreaks evil via flying spheres that carve up people's faces.

Working out of his Morningside Mortuary, the Tall Man robs graves and hauls away corpses via a band of dwarves whose costumes look suspiciously like those of the Jawas in "Star Wars."

All of this might be a hoot if molded in the right spirit, but in writer-director Don Coscarelli's hands it's incredibly morbid and meaningless.

As in "Aliens," hero Mike decides to seek and destroy the evil from which he once escaped, but in this case there's no redeeming met-

aphor, no sense of universal struggle.

Muddily written story takes the form of a gloomy, obsessive foray into mausoleums, crematoriums and the graveyards of the Northwest, told with brooding voiceover and filmed in sparse, Gothic style.

Pic gives real meaning to the term low-budget, with nary an extra in sight, and dialog, such as it is, consists mainly of characters flatly stating what the viewer already has figured out.

Whatever budget there was seems to have gone into creating the revolting, derivative special effects which, like the production design, incorporate a remarkable number of styles.

About two-thirds of the way through, pic veers completely out of control, as dialog grows intentionally ludicrous, and a wild hitchhiker (Samantha Phillips) seduces Mike's buddy Reg (Reggie Bannister) in a graphic scene that gets the pic an R rating, cutting out the young teen audience.

Poor direction and artless editing complete the list of crimes. This one's for sickos and the utterly bored.—*Daws.*

Les Predateurs de la nuit
(Faceless)
(FRENCH)

An ATC 3000/Films de la Rochelle release of a René Chateau production. Directed by Jesus Franco. Screenplay, Fred Castle, Michel Lebrun, Jean Mazarin, Pierre Ripert; camera (Fujicolor), Maurice Fellous; editor, Christine Pansu; music, Romano Musumurra; sound, Jean-Louis Ducarme; art direction, Bernard Ciberot; special effects, Jacques Gastineau. Reviewed at the Georges V cinema, Paris, June 26, 1988. Running time: **98 MIN.**
With: Helmut Berger (Dr. Flamand), Brigitte Lahaie (Nathalie), Chris Mitchum (Sam Morgan), Telly Savalas (Hallen), Anton Diffring (Karl Heinz Moser), Caroline Munro (Barbara Hallen), Christiane Jean (Ingrid), Howard Vernon (Orloff), Gérard Zalcberg (Gordon), Stéphane Audran, Thilda Thamar, Florence Guérin.

Paris — A routine gore-and-soft-core shocker obviously geared more for homevid than theatrical, "Faceless" is not a remake of Georges Franju's horror classic, "Les Yeux sans visage" (1960), according to pic's producer (and local homevid distrib) René Chateau.

Yet the plot similarities between the two thrillers are striking: a brilliant plastic surgeon resorts to the kidnaping of young women in order to graft a new face onto that of a disfigured loved one (the doctor's daughter in Franju's pic, his sister in this new item). In both films the doctor also has a female assistant who's in charge of finding the guineau pigs.

The resemblances pretty much stop there since "Faceless" scripter Fred Castle and his collaborators proceed to spice up the basic premise with lots of genre clichés, including a chainsaw-and-power-tool-

slinging psychosexual goon, assorted other murders, a filip of rape and incest, and even a touch of Edgar Allan Poe.

There's also a brilliant ex-Nazi doctor brought out of exile to perform the delicate grafting operation he perfected in the good old days of Nazi death camps, when medical morality was at a premium.

A name international cast has been enlisted for this tediously unterrifying dual-lingo production (reviewed here in its French version): Helmut Berger is the plastic surgeon and local softcore star Brigitte Lahaie is his perverse, vicious associate.

Small guest role has been devised for Telly Savalas as a New York businessman who hires private eye (and Vietnam vet) Chris Mitchum to find his missing top model daughter (Caroline Munro), who has been kidnaped by Berger and Lahaie. The Nazi doctor is Anton Diffring (of course), and Howard Vernon is also on hand as a former Diffring colleague.

Special gore effects are par for the course. The director, Jesus Franco, a specialist of porn and horror films, seems to have directed with his eyes closed. —*Len.*

The Sisterhood

A Concorde Pictures release of a Santa Fe production. Produced and directed by Cirio H. Santiago. Associate directors, Bobby Santiago, Joe Mari Avellana. Screenplay, Thomas McKelvey Cleaver; camera (color), Ricardo Remias; editor, Edgar Viner; musical director, Jun Latonio; sound, Vicente Dona, Do Bolutano; art direction, Ronnie Cruz; production design, Avellana; assistant director, Jose Torres; production manager, Honorato Perez Jr.. Reviewed on Media Home Entertainment vidscassette, N.Y., June 25, 1988. MPAA Rating: R. Running time: **76 MIN.**
Alee . . . . Rebecca Holden
Mikal . . . . Chuck Wagner
Marya . . . . Lynn-Holly Johnson
Vera . . . . Barbara Hooper
Jon . . . . Henry Strzalkowski
Lord Barah . . . . Robert Dryer
Also with: David Light, Jim Moss, Anthony East, Tom McNeeley.

"The Sisterhood" is a recently released futuristic sci-fi actioner, now available on vidcassette. It breaks no new ground but includes diverting material drawn from the "Mad Max" cookbook.

Title refers to female warriors who each bear magical powers and have banded together against the male-dominated post-nuclear war society. Marya (Lynn-Holly Johnson) is a hot prospect for the team, with her ability to communicate with her trained hawk. Eventually she's adopted into the clan by its leaders Alee (Rebecca Holden) and Vera (Barbara Hooper) as they trek across the Filipino countryside amidst numerous captures and escapes.

Various mutations (not scary due to cheap makeup effects) lurk in the forbidden zone they must cross, eventually ending up in a city to free their imprisoned sisters.

Pic has many a similarity to other genre films, with the Sisterhood having mystical reverend mothers (à la "Dune"). A villain who's basically a good guy (he has a grudge against the Sisterhood for stealing his sister away) is played by Chuck Wagner, who previously starred in Cannon's very similar 1986 pic "America 3000," one scene of which, when the gals discover a military command center with modern weapons in a cave, is mirrored here.

Rebecca Holden casts a dashing figure (styled to resemble Wonder Woman) in the leading role, with okay support from Johnson and Hooper. Helmer Cirio H. Santiago does all right, except for the very wimpy ending.—*Lor.*

La Donna della Luna
(Woman In The Moon)
(ITALIAN)

A DMV release of a Gierre Film production, in association with Reteitalia. Produced by Grazia Volpi. Directed by Vito Zagarrio. Screenplay, Lucio Mandarà, Zagarrio, Emanuela Martini; camera (color), Luigi Verga; editor, Roberto Perpignani; music, Franco Piersanti; art direction, Gianni Sbarra; costumes, Anne Marie Heinreich. Reviewed at the Pesaro Film Festival, June 18, 1988. Running time: **90 MIN.**
Angela . . . . Greta Scacchi
Salvo . . . . Luca Orlandini
Steve . . . . Tim Finn
Also with: Miko Magistro (Toti Mazza), Marcello Perracchi (Joe Lacagnina), Pasquale Spadola (Zazà Valenza).

Pesaro — **"Woman In The Moon" is a low-budget Italo indie, dominated by the presence of Greta Scacchi in the role of an Italo-American girl on her way to her father's funeral in Sicily.**

Lensed with top professionals, "Woman" is a respectable offering that never quite gets off the ground. Local chances will hinge on Scacchi's popularity as a drawing card; elsewhere, interest looks slim.

Angela (Scacchi) is a blasé New Yorker not too interested in making friends with a teenage boy who pushes himself into her car on the ferry to Sicily. Salvo (played by spunky newcomer Luca Orlandini) claims he's in trouble with some big-time drug dealers, a story that isn't true and which Angela sometimes believes and sometimes doesn't. After many miles on the road, the girl's hostility slowly melts while the boy's libido warms up. Angela's flirtation with a Yank stationed at the NATO base brings out Salvo's jealousy.

At last the odd couple Angela-Salvo go to bed together in a soft initiation scene without much power. Next thing you know, Salvo gets gunned down accidentally on his way to buy milk, and the love story is over.

With his film lover's background and a good technical staff to back

him up, Zagarrio concentrates on nuance in a yarn that lacks meat. Scacchi holds the screen with eye-catching good looks, but is underpowered in the loose story. Orlandini contributes most of the dynamism as Salvo, though he comes over too much as an exasperating brat and his heavily underlined Southernness tends toward stereotype. Generous glimpses of Sicilian color are an armchair traveler's treat. —*Yung.*

Bez Bebek
(Cloth Doll)
(TURKISH)

A Varlik Film production and release. Written and directed by Engin Ayca. Camera (color), Erdogan Engin; editor, Celal Köse; music, Melih Kibar, Gülsen Tuncer; art direction. Deniz Özen. Reviewed at Istanbul Film Festival, April 14, 1988. Running time: **110 MIN.**
Melek . . . . Hülya Kocyigit
Ahmet . . . . Hakan Balamir
Recep . . . . Mehmet Akan
Also with: Kemal Toraman, Kenan Bal, Tufan Balamir, Begüm Örnek, Sener Gezgen, Oktar Durukan, Savas Ustay.

Istanbul — **"Cloth Doll" is one Turkish film that works both as a drama and a penetrating, unsentimental view of the hard, lonely life of a woman in the country.**

The heroine's attraction to a bricklayer and the crime of passion that follows is told with great naturalness by Engin Ayca, a first-time helmer who worked in tv and was an assistant to Yilmaz Güney. Film is worth a look for off-shore programmers interested in quality Turkish product.

Story unfolds from Melek's p.o.v. (played by fine thesp Hülya Kocyigit), a woman living in a small country house with her young daughter. Her husband is about to be released from prison, and Melek's brother-in-law arranges to have the house fixed up in preparation for his return.

The growing attraction between Melek and the muscular mason Ahmet (Hakan Balamir) is shown in subtle erotic details — glimpses of him sweating, her without her headscarf, etc. When they finally make love in a scene that is almost rape, the sense of rigid social codes of conduct being shattered comes as a shock. The husband's return can't quell the illicit passions that have been aroused, and Ahmet murders him without regret while Melek watches passively. The police begin an investigation, a witness tries to blackmail them and another murder is committed.

What sounds like the plot of a Western *film noir* takes place in the sunny, domestic confines of the simply little house and garden, bringing the drama back to a social problematic; namely, the superhuman asexuality demanded of the woman and the uncontrollable consequences that result from infringing on the rules. Technically accept-

able, film owes much to low-key acting of principals and direction.—*Yung.*

The Dead Pool

A Warner Bros. release of a Malpaso production. Produced by David Valdes. Directed by Buddy Van Horn. Screenplay, Steve Sharon, from story by Sharon, Durk Pearson, Sandy Shaw, based on characters created by Harry Julian Fink, R.M. Fink; camera (Technicolor), Jack N. Green; supervising editor, Joel Cox; editor, Ron Spang; music, Lalo Schifrin; sound (Dolby), Richard S. Church; production design, Edward C. Carfagno; assistant director, L. Dean Jones Jr.; stunt coordinator, Richard (Diamond) Farnsworth; casting, Phyllis Huffman. Reviewed at The Burbank Studios, Calif., July 7, 1988. MPAA Rating: R. Running time: **91 MIN.**
Harry Callahan . . . . .Clint Eastwood
Samantha Walker . . . . . .Patricia Clarkson
Al Quan . . . . .Evan C. Kim
Peter Swan . . . . .Liam Neeson
Harlan Rook . . . . .David Hunt
Capt. Donnelly . . . . .Michael Currie
Lt. Ackerman . . . . .Michael Goodwin
Patrick Snow . . . . .Darwin Gillett
Lou Janero . . . . .Anthony Charnota

Hollywood — **Dirty Harry Callahan isn't the best and brightest of cops but you can't kill him with cannon, mace and chain. "The Dead Pool" isn't the best and brightest of the Dirty Harry films, either, but just as invincible.**

It's possible that Clint Eastwood and crew are just enjoying a bit of self-mockery with this one. If not, and any one of them took this thing seriously for a moment, then the failure is monumental.

From the original on, Harry has always been a fantasy character but his stories have been involving. Here, he remains absurdly separated from reality in an exceedingly lame yarn that lurches from one shootout to the next.

Out for a drive, Harry's set upon by a gang with Uzis who put holes through every inch of his sedan without hitting him once. Out for a walk, he comes across a robbery in a Chinese restaurant that's demolished by gunfire that never comes near the hero. Out for an elevator ride with lady friend Patricia Clarkson, he's ambushed by more gangsters with machine guns who level the lift without scratching the couple.

Conversely, the evildoers always are obliging, invariably pausing in their dastardly deeds just long enough for Harry to unholster his .44, get it out from under his jacket, smile wickedly, say something cute and finally kill them. Quite often, these scenes play as if director Buddy Van Horn had to remind Eastwood he's supposed to shoot someone and the extra in question seems to be thinking if this goes on long enough, he may get overtime.

The plot has something to do with a crime lord whom Harry has dispatched to San Quentin and a psychotic film fan out to eliminate local celebrities, which include the cop and Clarkson, in the current cliché

role of the peppery newscaster. In the background is a low-budget film company boringly run by Liam Neeson, a suspect who's never remotely suspicious for a moment.

There are chuckles here and there and a wildly preposterous car chase up and down the hills of Frisco. This time, though, it's a teeny little toy car in pursuit of the policemen, intending to overtake them with a bomb.

Improbably, the model finally overtakes Harry and partner Al Quan (Evan C. Kim), who doesn't grasp that when the bomb finally rolls under their car, Harry won't think to jump out because he can never die. This is costly for Quan.

Eventually, everybody who should be dead is dead and somebody says, "Whatever they're paying you, Harry, it couldn't be enough." Considering what the picture cost and how much it's probably going to take in, it's more than enough. —*Har.*

Dedé Mamata
(BRAZILIAN)

A United International Pictures release of a Cininvest production. Executive producer, Renata Almeida Magalhaes. Produced by Carlos Diegues, Paulo Cesar Ferreira. Directed by Rodolfo Brandão. Screenplay, Antonio Calmon, Vinicius Vianna, based on novel "Dedé Mamata," by Vianna; camera (color), Jose Tadeu Ribeiro; editor, Marta Luz; music, Caetano Veloso; art direction, Lia Renha; sound, Jorge Saldanha; associate producers, Multiplic, CDK, Elipse. Reviewed at Gramado Film Festival, June 23, 1988. Running time: **95 MIN.**
Dedé . . . . .Guilherme Fontes
Lena . . . . .Malu Mader
Alpino . . . . .Marcos Palmeira
Cumpade . . . . . .Luis Fernando Guimarães
Jacques . . . . .Tunico Pereira
Also with: Guará Rodrigues, Lidia Mattos, Flavio Sao Thiago, Daniel Fontoura, Natalia Thimberg, Paulo Betti, Antonio Pitanga, Geraldo Del Rey, Thais Campos, Paulo Porto.

Gramado, Brazil — **Debut feature by director Rodolfo Brandão, "Dedé Mamata" was the unexpected surprise at the 16th Gramado Film Festival. Funny and sensitive, it boasts outstanding performances and promises enjoyment for a wide variety of international audiences.**

Dedé is a middle-class teenager raised and educated by his grandparents, a couple of anarchists also involved with the Brazilian Communist party. By the early '70s, grandmother is dead and grandfather is very ill, unable to walk or speak, so the leaders of the illegal Communist party ask Dedé to take over the political tradition of the family.

Such is not among Dedé's dreams. He is being introduced to another illegal activity: the consumption of cocaine, introduced to him by his best friend, Alpino.

Dedé's trajectory is a youngster's search for his own way in a universe in which political leaders lack credibility and drugs look like the ultimate truth.

Original book by Vinicius Vianna, published two years ago, was not very successful in Brazil. Vianna, along with Antonio Calmon, turned the novel into a brilliant screenplay, which Rodolfo Brandão carefully directed to achieve one of the best Brazilian films of this year. For a debuting film, ''Dedé Mamata'' shows an impressive maturity both in the narrative and in the development of characters.

Outstanding performances are turned in by Guilherme Fontes as Dedé, Luis Fernando Guimarães as drug dealer Cumpade and especially Marcos Palmeira as Alpino. Music is by Caetano Veloso, greatest living poet of the Portuguese language and also a filmmaker.—*Hoin.*

Hayallerim, Askim ve Sen
(My Dreams, My Love And You)
(TURKISH)

An Odak Film production and release. Produced by Cengiz Ergun. Directed by Atif Yilmaz. Screenplay, Ümit Ünal; camera (color), Cetin Tunca; editor, Mevlüt Kocak; music, Esin Engin. Reviewed at Istanbul Film Festival, April 20, 1988. Running time: **100 MIN.**
Derya Altinay . . . . Türkan Soray
Coskun . . . . Oguz Tunc
Scriptwriter . . . . Müsfik Kenter

Istanbul — Atif Yilmaz' ''My Dreams, My Love And You'' is a film about the cinema peppered with bits of imaginative business and jokes. A local hit like most of Yilmaz' films, ''My Dreams'' has enough charm to get some offshore play in the right situations.

Coskun (Oguz Tunc) is an enthusiastic, naive youngster who aspires to become a screenwriter. He is literally haunted by the presence of two comic ''ghosts'' — Nuran and Melek, characters made famous by the star Derya Altinay when she was young. Now aged and carping, Nuran and Melek wander around Coskun's apartment in the heart of old Istanbul, bickering and giving him advice.

Chance allows Coskun to meet his favorite actress (all three roles are played by Türkan Soray, a real star of Turkish cinema and a versatile comedienne). Sensually mature and a bit on the tacky side, Derya resembles a local version of Joan Collins. She shows the boy's script, written just for her, to her producer and lo and behold, the film is made. Nuran and Melek grow old with jealousy and lose their voices.

When Coskun sees the finished film, he is crushed to find it has become exactly the kind of commercial stereotype he hates.

This spirited salute to the B-movie gains from being filmed by a helmer without pretensions who has no doubt churned out quite a few bread and butter works himself. Music and lensing are solidly commercial, on a par with the message that the best thing to do is resign yourself to being entertained by a master. —*Yung.*

Dead Man Walking

A Metropolis Pictures and Hit Films presentation of a Gernert/Brown production. Executive producer, Walter Gernert. Produced and directed by Gregory Brown. Screenplay, John Weidner, Rick Marx; camera (United color), Paul Desatoff; editor, uncredited; music, Claude (Coffee) Cave; sound, Mark Hanes, Steve Hawk; production design, Rick Wiggington; assistant director, Joseph Sassone; production manager, Craig T. Suttle; stunt coordinator, Brian Smrz; coproducers, Desatoff, Suttle; casting, Linda Phillips Palo. Reviewed on Republic Pictures Home Video vidcassette, N.Y., June 25, 1988. MPAA Rating: R. Running time: **90 MIN.**
John Luger . . . . Wings Hauser
Dekker . . . . Brion James
Lelia . . . . Pamela Ludwig
Snake . . . . Sy Richardson
Nomad farmer . . . . Leland Crooke
Chaz . . . . Jeffrey Combs
Gordon . . . . Joseph d'Angerio
Rika . . . . Tasia Vallenza
Also with: John Walter Davis, Penelope Sudrow, John Petlock, Nancy Locke.

A direct-to-video feature film, ''Dead Man Walking'' is a tongue-in-cheek sci-fi adventure that lays on the satire a bit much. It marks the mainstream film debut for filmmakers Gregory Brown and Walter Gernert, previously working in documentaries and as The Dark Bros. in the adult film and video field.

Story is set in 2004, 10 years after a plague virus annihilated half the U.S. population. (Repeated references make it clear the AIDS epidemic is being treated metaphorically here.) Wings Hauser, well cast, starts as devil-may-care John Luger, one of the zero men, who has only one or two years left to live due to the plague.

He is hired by Chaz (Jeffrey Combs, star of ''Re-Animator'') to trek after a trio of nutty prison escapees (Brion James with orange hair, Sy Richardson and Joseph d'Angerio) who've kidnaped young Lelia (Pamela Ludwig), daughter of Chaz' boss. Enemy of the piece is the new world power Unitus, which is working on creating housing projects in which to quarantine the contaminated people.

Scripters John Weidner and Rick Marx have trouble keeping the pot boiling in film's road movie format that features too many confrontations, but satirical dialog (often delivered in the form of update tv newscasts) is effective. Acting, especially by Hauser and James, is fine. Rushed happy ending, which phones in Hauser's fate, doesn't satisfy. —*Lor.*

Solomennie Kolokoka
(Straw Bells)
(SOVIET)

A Kiev Film Studios production. Written and directed by Yuri Ilienko. Camera (color), Ilienko; art direction, Alexander Denilenko, Alexander Sheremet; songs, Nina Matvienko. Reviewed at Tashkent Film Festival (market), May 28, 1988. Running time: **146 MIN.**
With: Sergei Podgorni, Mikhail Golubovich, Les Serdiuk, Ludmila Yefimenko, Natalia Sumskaia.

Tashkent — Ukrainian helmer Yuri Ilienko comes up with a wartime shocker in ''Straw Bells.'' This tale of atrocities is horrifying but enthralling, capable of keeping an audience in knots for its 2½-hour duration. Film is a sure bet for fests and programmers looking for quality Russian work.

It takes some concentration to keep the large cast of characters separate as they come and go. Story is split between the German massacre in 1943 and the present day, in which several key characters survive to take vengeance on each other. Pivot is Vilgota, an irascible old man whose son, a traitor working with the German police, was killed during the war. The present-day action unfolds unhurriedly in the sleepy village full of old rancor and hatred, until the villain Vilgota finally is flushed out and killed.

The striking part of ''Bells'' takes place in the past. One nightmarish episode follows another. The horror is all the more harrowing for being psychological and not Grand Guignol.

Climax arrives in a tense, extended sequence showing the Germans opening fire on the villagers and burning the place down, with details like infants thrown into the fire and running kids shot at as if they were game. Nor does the horror stop after the war: a little boy gets his leg blown off by a mine, and the heartless Vilgota makes him hobble on crutches through misery-filled trains and beg.

In contrast to all this wretchedness is Ilienko's lyrical sense of cinema (he also is the cameraman) and expressive, non-naturalistic technique. More than performances, thesps contribute moving faces.
— *Yung.*

Biri Vo Digerleri
(One And The Others)
(TURKISH)

A Magnum Film production and release. Written and directed by Tunc Basaran. Camera (color), Aytekin Cakmakoi; editor, Basaran; music, Süheyl Denizci. Reviewed at Istanbul Film Festival, April 17, 1988. Running time: **90 MIN.**
With: Aytac Arman, Meral Oguz, Sharon Sinclair, Mücap Ofluoglu, Füsun Demirel, Savas Yurttas.

Istanbul — Winner of the national film prize at the last Istanbul festival for reasons unknown, ''One And The Others'' is a fable about two nameless people who meet in a bar. Despite its laurels, film has slim chance of interesting locals or offshore viewers.

Pretentious, unbelievable and static in the extreme, film is the pet project of Tunc Basaran, helmer of over 40 feature films, now into advertising.

All the merits, and demerits, of ''One'' lie in the concept. Whole film is shot inside a fancy bar one night, where regulars come and go: a young couple, an old couple, some Mafia types, some good-time girls, an actor down on his luck, etc. A clean-cut, spacy young man (Aytac Arman) is in search of something abstract like happiness.

He fantasizes about a buxom blond lover while he chats up a pretty, lonely woman. In the end he says his name is Peace, she says her name is Hope, and they part friends.

Thesps are more cyphers than even the director intended. Musical score is irritating, the cutting is heavily symbolic and dialog is talky deadweight. —*Yung.*

Rented Lips

A Cineworld release of a Vista Organization presentation. Produced by Mort Engelberg. Executive producer, Martin Mull. Line producer, Mel Howard. Directed by Robert Downey. Screenplay, Mull; camera (Deluxe color), Robert D. Yeoman; editor, Christopher Greenbury; additional editing, Brian Berdan, Jay Ignaszewski; production design, George Costello; costume design, Lisa Jensen; sound (Ultra-Stereo), David Brownlow; assistant director, Anthony Brand; associate producer, Greenbury; casting, Nina Axelrod. Reviewed at the Aidikoff screening room, L.A., June 21, 1988. MPAA Rating: R. Running time: **80 MIN.**
Archie Powell . . . . Martin Mull
Charlie Slater . . . . Dick Shawn
Mona Lisa . . . . Jennifer Tilly
Heather Darling . . . . Edy Williams
Wolf Dangler . . . . Robert Downey Jr.
Archie's mother . . . . June Lockhart
Reverend Farrell . . . . Kenneth Mars
Bill Slotnik . . . . Shelley Berman
Milo . . . . Mel Welles
Herb the auditor . . . . Jack Riley
Winky . . . . Pat McCormick
Hotel desk clerk . . . . Eileen Brennan
Bobby Leaping Mouse . . . . . Michael Horse
Tyrell . . . . Tony Cox
Farrell's goons . . . . . . Eric Bruskotter, Karl Bruskotter

Hollywood — The shadow of Mel Brooks' ''The Producers'' looms heavily over ''Rented Lips,'' a singularly feeble and unfunny showbiz comedy about a virginal documentary filmmaker who is pushed into making a porno epic.

Astonishingly out of touch with the targets of its alleged satire as well as any imaginable audience, pic will need to have rented viewers if distrib Cineworld hopes to find anyone in theaters for this one.

Embarrassingly out-of-date concept has self-serious documentarian Martin Mull (who also penned the inept screenplay) dragged into directing ''an art film about sexual practices in Nazi Germany'' in exchange for the chance to realize his dream docu project, ''Indian Farming Techniques.''

This naturally throws the naive 40-year-old in with the seedy sexpo cast, which is filled with leather-clad practitioners of s&m, bondage and the like, all quite mildly represented herein. Also in the unsavory stew is Mull's bimbo discovery, Jennifer Tilly, over whom he exerts considerable energy hiding the true nature of the picture they're making, "Halloween At The Bunker."

Eventually, the picture itself is transformed into some sort of ludicrous farm musical, and after the startling revelations that a PBS executive finances sex pics under the table and that a rampaging evangelical preacher actually is a former porno filmmaker and Tilly's papa to boot, it just sort of ends.

Mull and director Robert Downey miss even their easy marks by quite a long way, and the easy jokes about sexual hypocrites, porno spectaculars and cinematic purity seem about 15 years old and probably wouldn't have been funny even then. To say the least, Mull's script is a structural mess, and obvious patch-up work in postproduction hasn't helped.

Cast is full of people who have inspired hilarity on other occasions, including "Producers" veterans Kenneth Mars and the late Dick Shawn. Half of them are virtually unrecognizable in their getups here, for which they may be grateful. The rest just have to brave it out while wondering, along with the viewer, what they're doing there. — *Cart.*

Chelovek S Bulvara Kapushinov
(The Man From Boulevard Des Capucines)
(SOVIET)

A Mosfilm Studio production. Directed by Alla Surikova. Screenplay, Eduard Akopov; camera (color), Grigori Belenki; music, Gennadi Gladkov, art direction, Yevgeni Markovich. Reviewed at Tashkent Film Festival (market), May 25, 1988. Running time: **90 MIN.**
With: Andrei Mironov, Alexandra Assmae, Mikahil Boyarkski, Oleg Tabakov, Nikolai Karachentsov.

Tashkent — A surprise from Mosfilm Studio, "The Man From Boulevard Des Capucines" is a tongue in cheek, but amazingly convincing, Western from femme helmer Alla Surikova.

Complete with stagecoaches attacked by Indians and slapstick barroom brawls, "Boulevard" comes close to being a top-notch sendup. As it stands, it earns many a smile, and not just for the kick of seeing Monument Valley done on the steppes. Film won first prize at last year's Women's Film Fest in L.A.

Mr. Fest, the soft-spoken hero, arrives in the Wild West town of Santa Carolina one day reading "The History Of World Cinema." He has come to bring civilization to the drunk, tough cowboys with his film projector and seemingly inexhaustible supply of silent 1-reelers, from the Lumiére Bros. on.

The blond chorus girl Diana (who sings ballads in Russian, naturally) loses her heart to the peace-loving stranger, and the cowboys, enthralled by the new medium, give up booze and fighting and start drinking milk. The bawdy chorus girls switch to a sophisticated romantic show, the town bully sings in the church choir, and hardened criminals are reproved with, "Johnson! Where are your manners, entering after the third shot?" Even the Indians hang up their tomahawks to see the show.

When Mr. Fest leaves town, however, evil interests (the saloon proprietor and lascivious minister in cahoots) bring in zombie pictures to turn customers back into hard drinkers. Can the cinema change the world? For good and evil, says "Boulevard."

Lots of action scenes and special effects keep the film hopping. Lensing is marred by some zoom madness, and thesping remains on the primitive side. The ladies have strong roles. —*Yung.*

Feliz Año Velho
(Happy Old Year)
(BRAZILIAN)

An Embrafilme release of a Tatu Filmes production. Executive producers, Boby Costa, and Suzana Villas Boas. Produced by Claudio Kahns. Directed by Roberto Gervitz. Screenplay, Gervitz, based on Marcelo Rubens Paiva's novel; camera (color), Cesar Charlone; editor, Galileu Garcia Jr.; music, Luiz Henrique Xavier; art direction, Clovis Bueno; choreography, J.C. Viola; sound, Jose Luiz Sasso. Reviewed at Gramado Film Festival, June 19, 1988. Running time: **100 MIN.**
Mario .... Marcos Breda
Ana/Angela .... Malu Mader
Lucia .... Eva Wilma
Gisela .... Isabel Ribeiro
Beto .... Marco Nanini
Klaus .... Carlos Loffler
Carlos .... Odilon Wagner
Soninha .... Betty Gofman
Arnaldo .... Alfredo Damiano
Edu .... Augusto Pompeo
Gorda .... Julio Levy
Salvador .... Flavio Sao Thiago

Gramado, Brazil — Based on a bestselling autobigoraphical novel, "Felz Año Velho" tells the story of a young student who becomes handicapped after an accident, and his struggle to face a new life.

Familial ties with a political activist drives the young man's thoughts to a broader comprehension of Brazilian political facts. Neither this process nor the victim's suffering, though, is quite convincing, despite the technical qualities of the production.

Marcelo Rubens Paiva was a student in his early 20s when an accident robbed him of the use of his legs and arms. By that time he already was involved in student political movements, and committed to the fate of his father, a political activist kidnaped and killed by Brazilian military forces in the late 70s. Two years after the accident, Marcelo published "Feliz Año Velho," where he reviewed his life, dreams, the relation to his father and the political activity and his struggle to get accustomed to his new life. Book immediately became a bestseller.

Director Roberto Gervitz, 30, with one only previous credit (a short about a workers' strike in São Paulo in 1978), dramatically changes the structure of Paiva's written narrative. He keeps its worst elements, especially the self-indulgence and the predictable immaturity of the political approach. Good technical standard of the Claudio Kahns production is not sufficient to raise much interest in the student's drama.

Independent elements of the production are mainly superior to the whole, including the music by Luiz Henrique Xavier and the acting, where Marcos Breda is technically correct even if failing to bring emotion to his inconsistent central character.

Yet, film may be appealing to undemanding audiences, as the book has been for some hundred of thousands of readers. Paiva's real drama unquestionably is touching and the technical efforts result in a clean rather than sophisticated narrative. —*Hoin.*

Midnight Run

A Universal Pictures release of a City Lights production. Executive producer, William S. Gilmore. Produced and directed by Martin Brest. Screenplay, George Gallo; camera (Astro Color, Metrocolor), Donald Thorin; editor, Billy Weber, Chris Lebenzon, Michael Tronick; music, Danny Elfman; production design, Angelo Graham; art direction, James J. Murakami; set decoration, George R. Nelson; set design, Peter J. Kelly; costume design, Gloria Gresham; sound (Dolby), Jim Alexander; second unit director - stunt coordinator, Glenn H. Randall Jr.; assistant directors, Bill Elvin, Jerry Ziesmer; second unit camera, John M. Stephens; associate producer, Dan York; casting, Michael Chinich, Bonnie Timmerman. Reviewed at the Cineplex Odeon Century City theater, L.A., July 13, 1988. MPAA Rating: R. Running time: **122 MIN.**
Jack Walsh .... Robert De Niro
Jonathan Mardukas ...... Charles Grodin
Alonzo Mosely .... Yaphet Kotto
Marvin Dorfler .... John Ashton
Jimmy Serrano .... Dennis Farina
Eddie Moscone .... Joe Pantoliano
Tony Darvo .... Richard Foronjy
Joey .... Robert Miranda
Jerry .... Jack Kehoe

Hollywood — "Midnight Run" shows that Robert De Niro can be as wonderful in a comic role as he is in a serious one. Pair him, a gruff ex-cop and bounty hunter, with straight man Charles Grodin, his captive, and the result is one of the most entertaining, best executed, original road pictures *ever*. It looks like a winner for Universal.

It's De Niro's boyish charm that works for him every time and here especially as the scruffy bounty hunter ready to do his last job in a low-life occupation. He's to nab a philanthropically minded accountant hiding out in Gotham (Grodin) who embezzled $15,000,000 from a heroin dealer/Las Vegas mobster and return him to Los Angeles in time to collect a $100,000 fee by midnight Friday.

Kidnaping Grodin is the easy part; getting him back to the west coast turns out to be anything but easy.

Plot is structured along the lines of John Hughes' "Planes, Trains & Automobiles" where two guys who can't stand each other are stuck together for the duration of a journey neither particularly wants to be on. "Midnight Run" is more than a string of well-done gags peppered by verbal sparring between a reluctant twosome; it is a terrifically developed script by George Gallo full of inventive, humorous twists made even funnier by wonderfully realized secondary characters.

Needless to say, De Niro and Grodin don't take the fast route from New York to California. What very preliminarily starts out as a simple nonstop first-class airplane trip from A to B quickly becomes a low-budget zigzag adventure via Amtrak, bus, donated car, stolen truck, commercial jet and so on through the back roads of America while trying to maneuver around the FBI, another bounty hunter, a couple of inept hit men, and occasionally a slew of cops.

Martin Brest directs here with an easier, more relaxed hand than he showed in "Beverly Hills Cop," letting the actors come to their own sense of comic timing without having to be so frenetic about getting to the laughs. Film does end up being about 15 minutes too long due to this lighter handling, but it's a minor flaw given that most of the 122 minutes contain worthwhile moments.

Every other word is some version of the F word, none of it particularly offensive given that it fits De Niro's chain-smoking, nervous, disheveled personality and that of a majority of his adversaries as well.

What is precious about him is the way he responds to Grodin, a man of completely the opposite constitution — though it works the other way around just as well. They are in nearly every scene together playing oneupmanship. De Niro's personal habits gross-out Grodin, who isn't shy about lecturing him on them, while Grodin's stiff, holier-than-thou rationale for stealing money and giving it to charity — never mind that it's from a mobster — gets beautifully taken apart by De Niro. Most of the time, the helplessly handcuffed Grodin has a real puppy dog expression. When he's free of them, though, he goes momentarily wacko in what turns out to be the film's most inventive and hilarious scenes.

Coming at them from all sides is the bumbling pair of mafia-type heavies (Richard Foronjy, Robert Miranda), sent by Dennis Farina, who are as funny as Laurel & Hardy. John Ashton, who was the dumb sergeant in "Beverly Hills Cop," is a dumb competing bounty hunter here, never quite able to wrest Grodin from De Niro.

Joe Pantoliano is a perfectly cast bail bondsman and Jack Kehoe an equally good choice for his stupid assistant. For his part Yaphet Kotto, whose identity as Alonzo Mosely is ridiculously mangled and misused by De Niro, is one of the better grey-suited incompetents ever to be cast as an FBI lead man — managing to keep just this side of losing complete control of the situation.

Lensing by Donald Thorin is exemplary — just the right balance of close-in shots framing De Niro and Grodin with long ones showing various settings in train stations, then out in nowhere America and against the stunning copper-and-red monuments of Arizona.—*Brit.*

Cherry 2000

An Orion Pictures release of an ERP production. Executive producer, Lloyd Fonville. Produced by Edward R. Pressman, Caldecot Chubb. Directed by Steve de Jarnatt. Screenplay, Michael Almereyda, from a story by Fonvielle; camera (Deluxe color), Jacques Haitkin; editor, Edward Abroms, Duwayne Dunham; music, Basil Poledouris; production design, John J. Moore; costumes, Julie Wass;

casting, Jane Jenkins; coproducer-production manager, Elliot Schick; assistant director, Jerry G. Grandey. Reviewed on RCA/Columbia vidcassette, Sydney, July 8, 1988. (In U.S., MPAA Rating: PG-13.) Running time: **93 MIN.**

E. Johnson . . . . Melanie Griffith
Sam Treadwell . . . . David Andrews
Six Finger Jake . . . . Ben Johnson
Lester . . . . Tim Thomerson
Stacy . . . . Brion James
Cherry . . . . Pamela Gidley
Snappy Tom . . . . Harry Carey Jr.
Also with: Cameron Milzer (Ginger), Michael C. Gwynne (Slim); Jennifer Mayo (Randa), Marshall Bell (Bill), Jeff Levine (Marty), Howard Swaim (Skeet).

Sydney — A tongue-in-cheek sci-fi action pic which owes a considerable debt to the "Mad Max" movies, "Cherry 2000's" greatest asset is topbilled Melanie Griffith, who lifts the material whenever she's on screen. Actress hasn't helped pic's commercial chances, though, and it's gone fast to video after the briefest of theatrical outings.

Griffith plays E. Johnson, a tracker who lives at the edge of a desert known as The Zone. The year is 2017, and white-collar yuppie Sam Treadwell (David Andrews), who hails from Anaheim, seeks Johnson's help in replacing his beloved Cherry 2000 (Pamela Gidley), a robot sex-object who suffered internal meltdown when Treadwell unwisely tried to make love to her in soapsuds.

For obscure reasons, replacement Cherry clones are stored far out in the Zone, which is ruled over by the psychotic Lester (Tim Thomerson) and his gang. Bulk of the film consists of efforts of Johnson and Treadwell to avoid capture by Lester and reach the robot warehouse (located in what was once Las Vegas).

Along the way they meet Ben Johnson as a philosophical old-timer and Harry Carey Jr. as a treacherous gas-station owner. There's a modicum of action, none of it very exciting, and lots of rather tired in-jokes (characters with names like Snappy Tom and Man Ray).

That the film works at all is entirely due to Melanie Griffith, who deserves far better material than this. She sails through the pic looking delightful and unflappable, and seizing every opportunity to have fun with her character.

Technically, pic is quite lavish and the Nevada locations suitably rugged. Production design by John J. Moore is a major plus. —*Strat.*

Mr. North

A Samuel Goldwyn Co. release of a Skip Steloff/Steven Haft production from Heritage Entertainment. Produced by Haft, Steloff. Executive producer, John Huston. Coproducer, Tom Shaw. Directed by Danny Huston. Screenplay, Janet Roach, John Huston, James Costigan, based on the novel "Theophilus North" by Thornton Wilder. Camera (Metrocolor), Robin Vidgeon; editor, Roberto Silvi; music, David McHugh; production design, Eugene Lee; set decoration, Sandra Nathanson; costume design, Rita Riggs; sound (Ultra-Stereo), William Randall;

associate producers, David R. Ames, Sandra Birnhak Ames; assistant director, Anthony J. Cerbone; casting, Risa Bramon, Billy Hopkins. Reviewed at Filmland screening room, Culver City, Calif., July 6, 1988. MPAA Rating: PG. Running time: **92 MIN.**

Theophilus North . . . . . . Anthony Edwards
James McHenry
Bosworth . . . . Robert Mitchum
Mrs. Amelia Cranston . . . . . Lauren Bacall
Henry Simmons . . . . . Harry Dean Stanton
Persis Bosworth-
Tennyson . . . . Anjelica Huston
Elspeth Skeel . . . . . Mary Stuart Masterson
Sally Boffin . . . . Virginia Madsen
Sarah Baily-Lewis . . . . Tammy Grimes
Dr. Angus McPherson . . . . David Warner
Galloper Skeel . . . . Hunter Carson
YMCA clerk . . . . Christopher Durang
George Harkness Skeel . . . . . Mark Metcalf
Mary Skeel . . . . Katharine Houghton

Hollywood — By cowriting and serving as executive producer, the late John Huston could be said to have passed the baton to son Danny Huston on "Mr. North." Unfortunately, Danny has not only dropped the stick but tripped over his own feet in his feature film debut, a woefully flat affair which even a stellar cast cannot bring to life. Commercial prospects look dim.

Even under the best of circumstances, the 1973 novel by Thornton Wilder represents the sort of whimsy that could be successfully dramatized only when the chemistry is just right and Lady Luck bestows her blessing. A resolutely old-fashioned tale about an unusually gifted young man who stirs things up among the rich folk in Newport, R.I., circa 1926, this pic, or a story like it, might have been pulled off by a Frank Capra, Gregory La Cava or Preston Sturges, in their primes, with a young James Stewart as its star.

But while the script, on which the elder Huston worked along with Janet Roach and James Costigan, offers up perfectly plausible, playable scenes, they are simply recorded onscreen here, with every comma, pause and period intact and in an utterly inexpressive, unimaginative manner. The issue of style never even raises its head, and the film just sits there, moribund, as a result.

Wilder's fanciful yarn has Theophilus North, a bright Yale graduate, arriving in the seaside bastion of old money and extravagance and making his way in society by magically curing the rich of what ails them, and charming them to boot. Endowed with mysterious electrical powers, as well as a talent for foreign languages and jujitsu, North liberates an old man from the imprisonment of his mansion by mending the latter's bladder problem, frees a young lady from torment by obliterating her chronic headaches and shows another comely lass how she can win back her great love.

All of this gains North a reputation as something of a savior, but doesn't go down too well with the pillar of the local medical community, who drags the shining fellow

into court. Virtue prevails in the end, however, and all's well in Richtown by final fadeout.

What the viewer is supposed to take away from this odd little fable is anyone's guess, especially in this colorless telling, in which even simple sequences are bungled by clumsy staging and awkward editing. Pic never gets to first base in forcing a suspension of disbelief, and thus can never proceed to the weightier matters of creating emotions, developing themes and so forth.

Anthony Edwards gives it a reasonable try in the leading role, his matter-of-factness in the face of extraordinary accomplishments proving rather appealing, but he can't singlehandedly rescue this waterlogged vessel.

Two performances make one sit up and take notice. Although her screen time is very brief, Mary Stuart Masterson, heretofore best remembered for her tough tomboy/punk roles in "Heaven Help Us" and "Some Kind Of Wonderful," is exceptionally good here in a much softer, more vulnerable role. It also is quite amusing to observe Harry Dean Stanton, normally known for his tough Western characters, assume an English accent to portray a gentleman's valet.

The many other pros in the cast, including Lauren Bacall, Anjelica Huston, Tammy Grimes, Davis Warner and Virginia Madsen, certainly are watchable, but do nothing of particular interest. Robert Mitchum looks healthy as a horse in the part of the sickly philanthropist, which he took on at the last minute when John Huston became too ill to do it (Huston died in the middle of production).

Picture was lensed on the actual opulent locations, but the best possible use has not been made of them, as the film leaves a lot to be desired visually. —*Cart.*

Emmanuelle 6
(FRENCH)

An ASP production and release. Produced by Alain Siritzky, in association with George Korda and SGGC. Directed by Bruno Zincone. Screenplay, Jean Rollin, from story idea by Emmanuelle Arsan; camera (Eastmancolor), Max Montheillet, Serge Godet; editor, Michel Crivallero; music, Olivier Day; sound, Antoine Rodet; makeup, Eric Pierre; stills, Otto Weisser; theme song lyrics, Sylvie Koechlin; production manager, Jose Berger. Reviewed at the Georges V cinema, Paris, July 11, 1988. Running time: **77 MIN.**

With: Nathalie Uher (Emmanuelle), Jean-René Gossart, Gustavo Rodriguez, Tamira, Thomas Ozermuller.

Paris — It's more of the same — or rather less of the same — for France's celluloid sex queen, Emmanuelle, in her sixth softcore screen turn. Curiosity about yet another new face in the title role may help business on this one, but Emmanuelle faithfuls should be noticing that the skein has been getting more cheapjack and indigent with each new film.

This could be the low point of the series, though it has stiff competition from last year's "Emmanuelle 5," made by the once-illustrious Walerian Borowczyk at the nadir of his career.

Austrian newcomer Nathalie Uher is third in line as successor to Sylvia Kristel, but is likely to join previous candidates Mia Nygren and Monique Gabrielle, both dumped after one film each, in the Emmanuelle Rejects Club.

Film 6 rates zero on story, direction and erotics, and even is a bust as travelog (pic in part was purportedly lensed in Venezuela, though the jungle scenes have no more exoticism than a Paris suburban woodland).

Section of the film takes place aboard a Mediterranean luxury liner where Emmanuelle and some colleagues are modeling a new line of jewelry. Girls and gems are kidnaped by white slave traders and placed in a jungle auction room, where they are saved by a band of friendly headhunters.

Copulations are few and far between and tend to give way to lesbian gropings. Emmanuelle, who comes out of the adventure with temporary amnesia, is rather passive, in the end preferring herself to a playmate.

Script and direction are credited respectively to Jean Rollin (a local purveyor of quickie horror films) and Bruno Zincone. Tech credits, including the atrocious dubbing, are beneath series standards.

Producer Alain Siritzky is still promising a primetime tv spinoff.
—Len.

The Rejuvenator

An SVS Films release of a Jewel production. Produced by Steven Mackler. Line producer, Robert Zimmerman. Directed by Brian Thomas Jones. Screenplay, Simon Nuchtern, Jones, from story by Nuchtern; camera (Technicolor), James McCalmont; editor, Brian O'Hara; music, Larry Juris; sound, Pawel Wdowczak, Mark Weingarten; production design, Susan Bolles; art direction, Lynn Nigro; special makeup effects, Edward French; assistant director, Denis Hann; associate producer, Bernard E. Goldberg; casting, Lisa Gladstone. Reviewed at Cine 1 theater, N.Y., July 15, 1988. MPAA Rating: R. Running time: **86 MIN.**

Elizabeth Warren/monster . . Vivian Lanko
Dr. Gregory Ashton . . . . John MacKay
Wilhelm . . . . James Hogue
Dr. Stella Stone . . . . Katell Pleven
Dr. Germaine . . . . Marcus Powell
Ruth Warren . . . . Jessica Dublin
Hunter . . . . Roy MacArthur
Tony . . . . Louis F. Homyak
Poison Dollys . . . . Themselves

"The Rejuvenator" is a pleasantly old-fashioned horror film, while still integrating today's requisite dose of elaborate makeup effects and gore. It is variously known as "Rejuvenatrix" (title displayed on print) and for foreign markets, "Juvenatrix."

Premise is the old reliable one of

---

a woman seeking to regain her youth: former movie star Ruth Warren (Jessica Dublin), who funds the research of Dr. Gregory Ashton (John MacKay). He discovers the part of the brain controlling aging, and via lab experiments with rats, comes up with a serum to reverse the aging process.

Warren eagerly volunteers to act as human guinea pig and is turned into her younger self (actress Vivian Lanko taking over the role in second reel), dubbing herself Elizabeth Warren, her own fictitious niece. Problem is that she turns into a hideous monster, requiring increasing dosages of the serum to be brought back to normal youth.

Ashton breaks the law in acquiring numerous cadavers to prepare the serum, derived from human brains. In her monstrous state, Warren takes to killing innocents in order to survive, ultimately discovering how to get the same rejuvenation effect directly from a victim's brain (for lunch) without resorting to the doc's serum. He eventually develops a synthetic serum but by then it is too late.

Low-budgeter works because it is played absolutely straight, with campy elements, such as the obvious references to "Sunset Boulevard" (Warren even has a Stroheim-like butler from the old days), allowed to blossom unforced. Adroit casting has Jessica Dublin and Vivian Lanko physically matched in the central role, each playing it in appropriately florid and bitch manner. John MacKay and the Sandy Dennis-like Katell Pleven as his assistant are utterly earnest and believable as the scientists, while James Hogue plays Warren's butler/former lover with panache.

Highlight of the production is Edward French's elaborate makeup effects, moving from the routine expanding bladders under the skin to an original design of Medusa-like proportions as her head expands to monster scale. Tightly directed by Brian Thomas Jones, pic is designed to appeal to B-movie connoisseurs who can tolerate the explicit violence of contemporary horror efforts. —Lor.

Death Chase

An Action Intl. Pictures production. Produced by Peter Yuval. Executive producers, David Winters, Don Crowell Jr. Directed by David A. Prior. Screenplay, James L. Hennessy Jr., Craig L. Hyde, Prior; camera (United color), Keith Holland; editor, Brian Evans; music, Tim James, Steve McClintick, Mark Mancina; sound, Paul Howard; art direction, Leigh Nicolai; production manager, Steve Blue; assistant director and second unit director, Tom Baldwin; stunt coordinator, Fritz Matthews; coproducer, Yakov Bentsvi; associate producers, Bruce Lewin, John Mercedes 3d. Reviewed on New Star vidcassette, N.Y., July 14, 1988. No MPAA Rating. Running time: **88 MIN.**

Steele . . . . Paul Smith
Lt. MacGrew . . . . Jack Starrett
Steven Chase . . . . William Zipp

Diana Lewis . . . . Bainbridge Scott
Eddie . . . . Reggie DeMorton
Sgt. Boone . . . . Paul Bruno
Chairman . . . . C.T. Collins
Also with: Christine Crowell, Mike Hickam, Susanne Tegman, Francine Lapense, Brian O'Connor, Andria Savio.

"Death Chase" is an underchieving action picture, released last month domestically direct-to-video. It's too close to an amateur effort for comfort.

William Zipp toplines as Steven Chase ("Chase" was pic's shooting moniker), an innocent bystander out jogging with his sister (Christine Crowell) when she's killed by stray gunfire. A dying man gives Chase his gun, declares "You're it," and the chase begins.

It seems an evil corporation head known as the chairman (C.T. Collins) is staging the dry run of an elaborate, lethal game in which various teams hunt each other in an urban landscape, with burly Paul Smith as gamemaster. Premise resembles John Brunner's sci-fi novel "The Squares Of The City" (in which real-life people and events are manipulated by higherups like chess pieces), but without the sci-fi.

Pic plays as one long chase, with Smith popping up constantly as *deus ex machina*. The gun Chase receives is the key to the mystery, but the trick ending is merely confusing.

Helmer David A. Prior overdoes the gimmick of exploding blood-packs on victims and action footage is on the cheapjack side. Extremely poor post-synching of the dialog makes it tough to watch, and pretty much sabotages the performances, particularly that of the pretty heroine Bainbridge Scott. Action helmer Jack Starrett dons his actor's cap to costar as a corrupt cop. —Lor.

It Takes Two

An MGM/UA Distribution release from United Artists. Produced by Robert Lawrence. Executive producer, Steve Nicolaides. Directed by David Beaird. Screenplay, Richard Christian Matheson, Thomas Szollosi; camera (color), Peter Deming; editor, David Garfield; music supervision, Peter Afterman; music, Carter Burwell; production design, Richard Hoover; art direction, Mark Billerman, Gregory Bolton, Michael Okowita; set decoration, Suzette Sheets; costume design, Reve Richards; sound (Dolby), Walter B. Martin Jr.; special effects, Greg Hull, William Purcell; assistant director, Christopher Griffin; second unit camera, Anthony Gaudioz; casting, Paul Bengston, David Cohn. Reviewed at Mann's Westwood theater, L.A., July 11, 1988. MPAA Rating: PG-13. Running time: **81 MIN.**

Travis Rogers . . . . George Newbern
Stephi Lawrence . . . . Leslie Hope
Jonni Tigersmith . . . . Kimberly Foster
George Lawrence . . . . Barry Corbin
Wheel . . . . Anthony Geary
Joyce Rogers . . . . Frances Lee McCain
Dee Dee . . . . Patrika Darbo
Dave Chapman . . . . Marco Perella
Judd Rogers . . . . Bill Bolender

Hollywood — "It Takes Two" twists the elements of the tired teen genre — dream cars and sex fantasies — into a fresh, charming and stylish surprise of a film.

Quirky enough to confound marketers — current print and tv campaigns don't quite capture it — pic has a strong potential audience but will need word of mouth to sell tickets. B.o. looks mild; careers promising.

This is essentially a picture about a guy getting married and buying a car, but it's much more interesting than that. George Newbern plays Travis Rogers, a 20-year-old Texan whose impending marriage to his lifelong sweetie (Leslie Hope) is making him feel as crazy and pent-up as a wild horse in a rodeo chute.

Days before the wedding, he bolts the ranch for Dallas to spend his oilfield savings on a car we assume will at least partly slake his high-style disco fantasies — a hellfire-red Lamborghini clone called a Trovare. Along with it he gets a saleslady Jonni Tigersmith (Kim Foster); sexy enough to make him forget the girl at home having her wedding dress fitted.

He gets caught up in troubles so wild — including a high-speed chase and an exploding car dealership — that he almost forgets the church full of people waiting for him to attend his own wedding.

Jonni, after giving him the night of his life in her Dallas penthouse, wants to take him to California.

Though there's never any real doubt which way Travis will point the Trovare, director David Beaird, in his first outing with major studio backing, makes this a fast and funny spin.

Comedy is high-style and inventive — particularly a dream scene inside Travis' stomach while he tries not to barf up a Torpedo Burrito — and videogame-style driving scenes add up-to-the-minute edge.

Casting is hyper-interesting and pic is loaded with shining character turns, particularly Anthony Geary as a Zen-spouting mechanic with a conscience (in a far more effective variation on his "Pass The Ammo" role).

Newbern is excellent and versatile as Travis, and Hope is particularly good as his sparkling, self-confident bride-to-be, managing to create a convincing relationship even though she must play her critical scenes via phone or from a distance.

Scripters, who have long tv credits, provide clever framework, but Beaird should get the real credit for an adroit balancing act that blends something fresh from unlikely elements. Pic is better on every count than his "Pass The Ammo."

Carter Burwell contributes a rich, bouyant score, and musical content includes Buckwheat Zydeco performing in the hot Dallas Alley club district in a scene that sums up what makes this pic sophisticated.

Peter Deming's camerawork includes both sparkling, immaculate visuals of the Dallas skyline and idyllic pastoral views of the North Texas ranch where Travis lives.

Production design by Richard Hoover, from the wedding preparation scenes to the high-tech neon Emerald Motors Auto-Plex in Dallas, is firstrate. —*Daws.*

Malinkaiya Vera
(Little Vera)
(SOVIET)

A Mosfilm production. Directed by Vassili Pitchul. Screenplay, Maria Khmelik; music, Vladimir Matietski; art direction, Vladimir Pasternak. In color. (No further credits available.) Reviewed at Tashkent Film Festival (market), May 29, 1988. Running time: **130 MIN.**

Vera	Natalia Niegoda
Sergei	Andrei Sokolov
Father	Yuri Nazarov
Mother	Ludmila Zaisova
Viktor	Alexander Niegreva

Tashkent — "Little Vera" is that rare work that looks like a classic on first viewing. Two hour-plus tale of what might be termed in the West working class life is as compulsively watchable as it is strikingly realistic.

With the immediate impact of a Czech film of the '60s, "Vera" has already attracted the attention of several fests and buyers. It is being held up for release domestically and internationally for unspecified reasons, but in the current Soviet climate it's doubtful it can be kept out of circulation long.

Story is set in "an industrial city in Russia." Vera, played by wonderfully shaggy newcomer Natalia Niegoda, looks like a bleached blond, gum-chewing teen from the Bronx. She likes rock concerts, short skirts and oversize sunglasses. Her parents are always bugging her because she quit school, smokes, and hangs out with a fast crowd. In short, Vera is one of the most hip and understandable characters to appear in Soviet film for a long time.

At an outdoor dance raided by the cops, Vera meets a good-looking hunk named Sergei (Andrei Sokolov). Pretty soon they're in bed together in what looks like his dorm room. The bedroom scene is cool, natural, and very tame by Western standards (breasts on view only), but has caused waves locally.

Life proceeds through a series of semi-comic family feuds in which Vera is mercilessly picked on and the father is always drunk. Vera and a girlfriend with 2-tone hair get smashed a lot, too. Eventually Vera gets pregnant and Sergei moves in with her family, causing more tension. One night the father unexpectedly stabs Sergei, who's rushed to the hospital. The family applies pressure on Vera not to tell the police. Tough as Vera is, she breaks down in this hellish life.

Although there are slow-downs in this long pic, it basically wins out with sheer originality and freshness. Filmer Vassili Pitchul (making his feature debut) is full of ideas and good at developing scenes. Whole cast is fine. Lensing gains confidence as the pic goes along.
— *Yung.*

Miss Milionersha
(Miss Million)
(SOVIET)

A Lenfilm production. Directed by S. Rogozhkin. Screenplay, Anatoli Usov; camera (color), Ivan Bagaiev; music, Vladislav Panchenko; art direction, Alexandr Zagoskin. Reviewed at Pesaro Film Festival, June 18, 1988. Running time: **136 MIN.**

Koval	Nikolai Karachensov
Nina	Tatiana Mikhalevkina

Pesaro — "Miss Million" is a Lenfilm satire on perestroika that strongly recalls the caustic view of tv journalism in "Broadcast News." In the Russian film, tampering with the videotaped truth gets the reporter fired in disgrace, and even badder guys win in the network.

An uneven film with a tendency to repeat itself and drag, even to sermonize, "Miss Million" looks slated to interest mainly specialists. It is directed with enough liveliness, however, to be worth a look.

Popular stage and screen thesp Nikolai Karachensov lends a roguish charm to the hero Koval, who has assured his place in the town tv station by courting the boss' daughter; she's rich (sports car) if not pretty.

When the city officially reaches 1,000,000 inhabitants, it will automatically get boosted into a higher administrative class. Koval does a splashy interview with the mother about to give birth to No. 1,000,000. Only during the followup does he realize poor Nina (unpretentiously limned by Tatiana Mikhalevkina) is an unstable, unwed mother, and the man she's named as her husband doesn't even know her — he's just pretending, to get hold of a promised 3-room apartment. Koval proceeds to make things look good for his audience.

So far, so good, but the climax never comes. The baby dies of neglect and its funeral casts a chill note. Koval risks all for naught, going on the air live to plead for better child care. His girlfriend finds someone better, and Koval gets canned. He drives moodily to the country, realizing the fat cats are on top again.

Lensing is adequate. — *Yung.*

Exquisite Corpses

An ASA Communications release of an Upfront Films presentation. (Sales, Double Helix Films.) Executive producers, David Mazor, Glenn Dubin. Produced and directed by Temistocles Lopez. Coproducer, Ken Schwenker. Screenplay, Lopez; camera (Studiolab color, 16m), Steve McNutt; editor, John Murray; music, Gary Knox; sound, Joe McGirr; art direction, Carlos de Villamil; costume design, Alfredo Villoria, Frederico Macquhae; additional photography, Carolyn Chen, Tom Sigel. Reviewed at Mark Goodson theater, N.Y., June 23, 1988. No MPAA Rating. Running time: **99 MIN.**

Belinda	Zoë Tamerlaine Lund
Tim	Gary Knox
Joe	Daniel Chapman
Sue	Ruth Collins
Lou	Frank Roccio
Pat	Chuck Perley
Ginny	Lucy Re
Rock singer	David Ilku
Club owner	Robert Lund

"Exquisite Corpses" is an offbeat, New York-made black comedy that will be of interest to followers of the indie scene, both locally and in Europe. Pic debuted at the Cannes film market in May. Currently in 16m, feature is due for a 35m blowup before release.

Pic has a cult hook in casting of Zoë Tamerlaine Lund (formerly Zoë Tamerlis), who first scored in Abel Ferrara's thriller "Ms. 45." She portrays Belinda, a mysterious femme fatale who ultimately spells curtains for the hapless hero Tim (musician Gary Knox in his film acting debut).

In a pastiche on "Midnight Cowboy," Tim is a cowboy from Oklahoma who arrives in the Big Apple with high hopes of stardom. After the usual mistreatment by the cruel bit city denizens, he lands a gig as singer/dancer/trombonist in a cabaret. His undoing is getting mixed up in a murder triangle involving Belinda and her weak husband.

Stylized with the sort of pastel lighting associated with Amos Poe's "Subway Riders" (which was lensed by "Sugarbaby's" Johanna Heer), "Corpses" is best in its scenes of wacky humor and decadent cabaret routines, benefiting at times from Knox' uneven musical score which veers from lyrical to gauche.

Final reel attempts to create a tough guy, film noir feel, but is too talky, burdened with unconvincing plot twists (regarding how the murder actually was committed) and a failed attempt at whipping up some international intrigue regarding a communist agent. Frank Roccio contributes an effective supporting role as Tim's aggressively homosexual talent agent.

In the leads, Lund is suitably exotic and has a very strange musical production number to boot. Knox is better at the naive early scenes than his fey transition to successful cabaret star. Likewise, debuting filmmaker Temistocles Lopez, a Venezuelan transplant to New York with stage experience, shows promise but produces here a film of extreme highs and lows.

Picture is dedicated to the late film historian Carlos Clarens, who was set for a supporting role but died before production commenced.
— *Lor.*

Cocktail

A Buena Vista release of a Touchstone presentation in association with Silver Screen Partners III of an Interscope Communications production. Produced by Ted Field, Robert W. Cort. Directed by Roger Donaldson. Screenplay, Heywood Gould, based on his book; camera (Metrocolor), Dean Semler; edited by Neil Travis; editor, Barbara Dunning; music, J. Peter Robinson; sound (Dolby), Richard Lightstone, Tod Maitland (N.Y., Jamaica); production design, Mel Bourne; art direction, Dan Davis; decorator, Milton Rosemarin, set decoration, Leslie Bloom (N.Y.); costume design, Ellen Mirojnick; assistant directors, Rob Cowan, Michael Tadross (N.Y.); casting, Donna Isaacson, John Lyons, Stuart Aldins Casting (Toronto). Reviewed at Crest theater, L.A., July 25, 1988. MPAA Rating: R. Running time: **104 MIN.**

Brian Flanagan	Tom Cruise
Doug Coughlin	Bryan Brown
Jordan Mooney	Elisabeth Shue
Bonnie	Lisa Banes
Mr. Mooney	Laurence Luckinbill
Kerry Coughlin	Kelly Lynch
Coral	Gina Gershon
Uncle Pat	Ron Dean
Eleanor	Ellen Foley

Hollywood — Blatantly designed as a star vehicle for Tom Cruise, "Cocktail" shouldn't disappoint the young actor's legion of female admirers, as Cruise struts, smiles, shakes and sweettalks his way to the top of the Third Avenue bar scene.

With just a wisp of a story on which to hang a string of sexy incidents, pic delivers the flashy moves expected of this sort of young-man-on-the-rise entertainment, and should pay off accordingly.

Heywood Gould's script, based upon his book inspired by some years as a New York bartender, contains nary a surprise, as Cruise hits Manhattan after a hitch in the Army and immediately catches on as the hottest thing the uptown girls have seen in a saloon in years.

Under the tutelage of old pro Bryan Brown, Cruise learns every trick in the book, and the pair soon move to the club scene downtown, where Cruise becomes poetaster to the too-hip crowd in addition to taking his pick of trendy ladies.

After the two fellows fall out over a woman, Cruise moves his act down to Jamaica to regroup for his assault on the big time back in Gotham. Lo and behold, who should show up on the beach but Brown, now the dissolute husband of a filthy rich girl. Brown goads his buddy into setting his sights on one of the many women with big bucks who patronize the resort, which gets Cruise into trouble with the girl he's becoming sweet on, Elisabeth Shue.

Once the action shifts back to New York, story takes a heavy melodramatic turn, as Cruise is given a crash course in the lessons of life. Anxious to win Shue back after spurning her in the tropics, he's forced to grow up and make all the right moral decisions, which he does with a correctness even the late Louis B. Mayer would have applauded.

Under Roger Donaldson's impeccably slick direction, film continually plays on Cruise's attractiveness, as women make goo-goo eyes at him throughout as he does his juggling act with liquor bottles, serves up drinks like a disco dancer and charms his way through every situation. To his credit, though, the actor brings plenty of energy and winning riffs to his performance, and easily puts the film over on the strength of his personality.

Bryan Brown comfortably slides through as the seen-it-all, know-it-all barkeep with an attitude and aphorism for every occasion, while Elisabeth Shue's nice girl characterization is on the bland side.

Hyperactive soundtrack is crammed full of rock tunes, and all tech contributions are precision tooled to the nth degree. —Cart.

Hell Comes To Frogtown

A New World Pictures release of a Donald G. Jackson production. Produced by Jackson, Randall Frakes. Line producer, William W. Edwards. Directed by R.J. Kizer, Jackson. Screenplay, Frakes, from story by Jackson, Frakes; camera (Foto-Kem color, Technicolor prints), Jackson, Enrico Picard; editor, Kizer, James Matheny; music, David Shapiro; sound, Robert Janiger; production design, Dins Danielsen; art direction-set decoration, Suzette Sheets; special makeup effects, Steve Wang; assistant director, Gary M. Bettman; production manager, Cheryl Hayes; stunt coordinator, Bobby Bragg; casting, Randy Stone Associates, Shana Landsburg. Reviewed on New World vidcassette, N.Y., July 9, 1988. MPAA Rating: R. Running time: 86 MIN.
Sam Hell . . . . Roddy Piper
Spangle . . . . Sandahl Bergman
Centinella . . . . Cec Verrell
Capt. Devlin/Count
  Sodom . . . . William Smith
Looney Tunes . . . . Rory Calhoun
Bull . . . . Nicholas Worth
Arabella . . . . Kristi Somers

Wacky in the extreme, "Hell Comes To Frogtown" is a futuristic sci-fi film with appeal for fanciers of the tongue-in-cheek wing of the genre. After brief theatrical play in Texas in January, it has been released in video stores.

Sam Hell, or Hellman (Roddy Piper), is grabbed by the government 10 years after World War III (a nuclear exchange that lasted only 10 days but rendered most of the human race sterile). He's a sexually potent male, assigned to go on a mission with two Amazonian babes (Sandahl Bergman, Cec Verrell) to rescue fertile females from Frogtown and then impregnate them.

Frogtown, complete with its "Star Wars" cantina of strange folk, is deep in mutant territory, where nuclear survivors have elaborate frog heads (nice makeup effects by Steve Wang in "Planet Of The Apes" vein) and humanoid bodies. Helped by scruffy old pal Looney Tunes (Rory Calhoun), Hell & Co. ultimately escape with the femmes after numerous battles with the greenies.

Childish but not aimed at children, pic operates on the level of

cute jokes in bad taste. With endless wisecracks about his sexual prowess, Piper plays most of his scenes outfitted with an ECR, an electronic codpiece armed with an electric stinger which gives him a painful jolt if he tries to run away from the mission commander played by Bergman. She and Verrell keep seducing him, though he's supposed to service only fertile women to help the government's repopulation and war effort.

It's amusing, thanks to the pleasant personality of ex-wrestler Rowdy Roddy Piper in his second film role (after "Body Slam"). Casting of Bergman and Verrell is a coup, since they are both tough cookies and beauties, Bergman specifically mocking her terping talents background when forced to do the "dance of the three snakes" for evil Frogtown major domo Commander Toty.

A marked improvement on Donald G. Jackson's previous New World feature "Rollerblade," pic also features effective action scenes, in which a heavily armed Piper smoothly arrives in the muscular action hero pantheon with his cry of "Eat lead, froggies!" Film is dedicated to top serial directors such as Ford Beebe, Frederick Stephani and Ray Taylor. —Lor.

Caddyshack II

A Warner Bros. release of a Guber-Peters production. Produced by Neil Canton, Jon Peters, Peter Guber. Directed by Allan Arkush. Screenplay, Harold Ramis, Peter Torokvei; camera (Technicolor), Harry Stradling; editor, Bernard Gribble; music, Ira Newborn; production design, Bill Matthews; costume design, May Routh, set decoration, Dawn Snyder, Carroll B. Johnston; sound (Dolby), Gene S. Cantamessa; assistant director, Marty P. Ewing; casting, Glen Daniels. Reviewed at Pacific's Paramount theater, L.A., July 22, 1988. MPAA rating: PG. Running time: 93 MIN.
Jack Hartounian . . . . Jackie Mason
Elizabeth Pearce . . . . Dyan Cannon
Chandler Young . . . . Robert Stack
Cynthia Young . . . . Dina Merrill
Ty Webb . . . . Chevy Chase
Capt. Tom Everett . . . . Dan Aykroyd
Peter Blunt . . . . Randy Quaid
Kate Hartounian . . . . Jessica Lundy
Harry . . . . Jonathan Silverman
Miffy Young . . . . Chynna Phillips
Todd Young . . . . Brian McNamara

Hollywood — Warner Bros. scores a double bogey with "Caddyshack II," thanks largely to a loose grip and weak follow-through.

Eight years after the original, comedy's harder to come by at the Bushwood Country Club. This one probably saw most of its green during lensing.

Scripters Harold Ramis and Peter Torokvei have sent a weak plot onto the links saddled with a gag-bag full of tire irons. Energetic slicing and whacking by director Allan Arkush only digs things deeper into the sandtrap.

Chevy Chase injects some bumbling flair in a supporting role as

millionarie zen golfer Ty Webb, but Dan Aykroyd fares poorly as an inept, deranged special tactics war vet.

In the populist tradition of "Police Academy," "Back To School," ad infinitum, "Caddyshack II" casts everyman comic Jackie Mason as an excuse for bringing lowbrow mayhem to plague the snob set at an exclusive golf club.

Mason, a wealthy contractor with blue-collar manners, wants to join the club to please his daughter (Jessica Lundy), who's obsessed with moving up in the world.

Trouble is, filmmakers want her to be likable at the same time that she's vapid, insensitive and wishy-washy. It doesn't make good sense or a good story hook.

Daughter sits passively by while Mason goes through various humiliations in his attempt to fit in. He's being sued by the club president (Robert Stack) over a land-use dispute; meanwhile daughter is blithely befriending Stack's daughter (Chynna Phillips, daughter of Michelle) and dating his son (Brian McNamara).

It would all be pretty tough on Mason if not for Dyan Cannon as a free-thinking club member who cuddles up to him as if he were Tom Selleck.

But one can't expect reality from a pic that keeps cutting to shots of an animated gopher doll (a holdover from the first film) who steals junk food and guzzles it down in his lair.

At one point, Mason, after being denied membership, buys the majority of club's stock and turns it into a garish, roadside-tacky golf amusement park, so that "everyone can enjoy the privileges you people have," or something to that effect.

But the thoroughly nonplussed members continue to play golf there as if robotically rooted to the spot.

It finally comes down to a "Scotch twosome" golf match pitting the upper class, Stack and McNamara, against the middle class, Mason and a caddy (Jonathan Silverman) who's romancing his daughter.

The only suspense comes from wondering how Aykroyd, who's stuck out in the woods on a sabotage mission doing a half-hearted Bobcat Goldthwait imitation, will get through his part.

After gags too numerous to mention, pic wraps in a predictable manner, ends neatly tied in a throwaway bundle.

And with Bushwood in middle-class hands, it's safe to assume there won't be another sequel, unless the club falls prey to a takeover. That would be ill-advised.

Randy Quaid has an initially engaging role as a sassy lawyer with a rabid, Hunter Thompsonesque edge, but like the pic in general, the role soon degenerates into excess.

Production designer Bill Matthews comes up with some pretty

amazing ideas for the wacky golf course, including a "firetrap trap" inspired by the work of Red Grooms. Other than that, tech work is just okay. —Daws.

Contrainte par corps
(Bodily Restraint)
(FRENCH)

A GPFI/Canal Plus Productions coproduction. Produced by Jean-Claude Fleury. Line producers, Patrick Delauneux, Antonio da Cunha Telles. Directed by Serge Leroy. Screenplay, Leroy, François Chevallier, from story by Loula Ioanne; camera (color), André Domage; editor, François Ceppi; music, Olivier Meston; sound, Eric Vaucher, Paul Bertault; art direction, Jean-Louis Poveda; assistant directors, Elisabeth Parnière, Jorge Paixao Costa; production manager, Antonia Sebra. Reviewed at Marignan-Concorde cinema, Paris, July 7, 1988. Running time: 95 MIN.
Claire . . . . Marianne Basler
Kasta . . . . Vittorio Mezzogiorno
Lola . . . . Catherine Wilkening
Josette . . . . Tanya Lopert
Emilie . . . . Caroline Sihol
Vicky . . . . Anne Jousset
Helga . . . . Lisette Malidor
Rula . . . . Maria Blanco
Mother . . . . Annick Blancheteau

Paris — An unenthralling melodrama about a young Frenchwoman persecuted by a perverse, macho policeman on a Mediterranean island, "Contrainte par corps" devotes most screen time to former's incarceration in a women's prison.

Marianne Basler, a tawny good-looker, is the hapless protagonist vacationing on an isle where a cop, Vittorio Mezzogiorno, spies on her necking (topless) with a boyfriend on an empty beach.

Mezzogiorno has her arrested on an immorality charge, and then, failing to get a signed confession, frames her for drug trafficking and has her packed off to an island prison.

Basic premise of apparently unmotivated harrassment then gives way to predictable prison events in which the innocent Basler must cope with fellow inmates (a motley array of drug-fiends, lesbians, hookers and child-killers) before earning their solidarity for a climactic showdown with Mezzogiorno, who is not so pure as he wants to have others think and gets a proper comeuppance.

Serge Leroy, who coscripted and directed, commendably generally avoids the voyeuristic and salacious aspects of the material, but doesn't bring credibility, style or excitement to mostly familiar dramatic situations.

Basler is fair as a modern but unpromiscuous woman whose sun-kissed vacation turns into nightmare, while the brutish-looking Mezzogiorno is monolithic and inscrutable as the destructively puritanical policeman. Others include Catherine Wilkening as a junkie inmate, and Amazonian ex-Folies Bergères star Lisette Malidor as a lesbian jailbird.

Lensed on location in Portugal, pic's credits are professional.

— *Len.*

Big Top Pee-wee

A Paramount Pictures release. Produced by Paul Reubens and Debra Hill. Executive producers, William E. McEuen, Richard Gilbert Abramson. Directed by Randal Kleiser. Screenplay, Paul Reubens and George McGrath; camera (Technicolor), Steven Poster; editor, Jeff Gourson; music, Danny Elfman; sound (Dolby), Kirk Francis; production design, Stephen Marsh; visual effects, Richard Edlund; art direction, Beala B. Neel; assistant director, Roger Joseph Pugliese; costumes, Robert Turturice; casting, Victoria Thomas. Reviewed at Paramount Studios, L.A., July 20, 1988. MPAA Rating: PG. Running time: **86 MIN.**

Pee-wee Herman . . Himself (Paul Reubens)
Mace Montana . . . . Kris Kristofferson
Gina . . . . Valeria Golino
Winnie . . . . Penelope Ann Miller
Midge . . . . Susan Tyrrell
Mr. Ryan . . . . Albert Henderson
Otis . . . . Jack Murdock
Deke . . . . David Byrd
Mrs. Dill . . . . Mary Jackson
Mrs. Haynes . . . . Frances Bay
Andy . . . . Mihaly (Michu) Meszaros

Hollywood — "Big Top Pee-wee" again demonstrates that Pee-wee Herman is one very strange screen personality; he previously scored with his 1985 feature debut, "Pee-wee's Big Adventure." He could repeat. Maybe he won't.

"Big Top" is probably funny in its own weird way. At least, it seems funny at the time without knowing why later. There are certainly sufficient sight gags to appeal to the silliness in all ages. And Herman noodles around nicely with nonsensical nostalgia.

Surrounded by animals as strange as himself, Herman pursues a career in agricultural extravagance with the help of his goggled talking pig Vincent (amusingly voiced by Wayne White). Together, they grow outsized vegetables and a hot dog tree while wanly romancing pretty Penelope Ann Miller, hoping passion will propel them past her egg salad sandwiches.

A storm brings a broken-down circus to Herman's farm, adding a menagerie of freakish animals and people to his already curious collection. Kris Kristofferson oversees the visitors and keeps them rallied with hearty circus sayings, along with explanations of how he came to marry his miniature wife (Susan Tyrrell) whom he carries around in his pocket.

"They said the marriage wouldn't work, but they were wrong," Kristofferson assures Herman, who seems to accept that as normal enough.

Herman might have been more curious, except for his own virginal condition which will soon be corrected. (After his asexual debut in "Adventure," anticipation of Herman's introduction to manhood created an advance stir for this film, which hopefully is satisfied within

the PG, Hitchcockian symbolism of a train, a tunnel and fireworks.)

Alas, love brings Herman into a triangle with Miller and adorable circus star Valeria Golino. If romance weren't dangerous enough, Herman also tries to master some talent that will make him a circus star, too.

Very little of this is interesting or amusing on paper, which must have been a real challenge to director Randal Kleiser, who ably keeps all the surrounding players in tune to whatever it is that Herman's up to at any given moment.

The final word has to be charming with a chuckle. No, the final word is Herman, just Herman.

— *Har.*

Monkey Shines

An Orion Pictures release. Produced by Charles Evans. Executive producers, Peter Grunwald and Gerald S. Paonessa. Written and directed by George A. Romero, based on the novel by Michael Stewart. Camera (Deluxe color), James A. Contner; editor, Pasquale Buba; sound (Dolby, Spectral Recording), John Sutton; music, David Shire; production design, Cletus Anderson; art direction, J. Mark Harrington, Jim Feng; assistant director, Nick Mastandrea; associate producer, Peter McIntosh; casting, Dianne Crittenden. Reviewed at Coronet theater, L.A., July 19, 1988. MPAA Rating: R. Running time: **115 MIN.**

Allan Mann . . . . Jason Beghe
Geoffrey Fisher . . . . John Pankow
Kate McNeil . . . . Melanie Parker
Dorothy Mann . . . . Joyce Van Patten
Maryanne Hodges . . . . Christine Forrest
Dean Burbage . . . . Stephen Root
Dr. Wiseman . . . . Stanley Tucci
Linda . . . . Janine Turner
Doc Williams . . . . William Newman

Hollywood — "Monkey Shines" is a befuddled story about a man constrained from the neck down told by a director confused from the neck up.

If not, it's the bewildering story of drug abuse among laboratory animals and the men who feed their needs. In either case, just say no.

There's a disclaimer at the end which assures that nothing like this yarn really ever happened in the 10-year history of the Helping Hands Project in Boston. That's good to know because Helping Hands is truly an inspired program which has trained monkeys to serve the manual (and emotional) needs of those who are paralyzed.

In dealing with that, in fact, director George Romero has a fairly involving film going the first third of the way. Jason Beghe starts out as a very virile, able-bodied young man with everything going for him, an up-and-coming physical specimen much desired by his girlfriend, Janine Turner, and fawned over by mother Joyce Van Patten.

An accident robs Beghe of all physical ability below his jawline, leaving him despondently dependent on an array of technology. It also leaves him vulnerable to the faithlessness of Turner, who literal-

ly adds insult to injury by running off with his doctor (played with proper sleaze by Stanley Tucci). For added indignity, he has to be bathed naked in a bathtub sling by Van Patten, who shows indecent enthusiasm for the duty, and suffer the indifferent care of his nurse (Christine Forrest) and her beastly bird.

As melodrama, this is all pretty good stuff and could have continued to a convincing conclusion. But by contract, inclination and reputation (not to mention the book the film's based on), Romero is a horror-film director.

So here comes Beghe's best friend John Pankow, a yuppie mad scientist busy at the nearby university slicing up the brain of a dead Jane Doe and injecting the hormones into monkeys to make them smarter. To add additional hours to his work week, Pankow also injects himself with energizers.

To help his friend, Pankow volunteers one of his highly intelligent, chemically dependent capuchins to be trained by Melanie Parker to serve as Beghe's companion and helper. For a while, this all works beautifully. Until something dreadful happens. What it was that happened, however, is never quite clear.

Back at the lab Pankow is shooting up and singing ditties designed to further science. But he's obviously lost all track of what he set out to do and so has Romero. Everything begins to go wrong and the monkeys rebel. (There's another disclaimer that no monkey was injured in the filming, but it does not say whether any of them was ever required to read the script. That could explain the rebellion.)

Up to this point, Romero has telegraphed everything that's coming, so the finish is just a matter of remembering. (For example, when Parker sets out to shave Beghe's beard, she chooses to use a straight razor. Now, there may be a lot of modern young ladies who know how to use a straight razor and would choose to have one handy. If not, then it's a safe bet that same menacing razor is going to show up in the film again under different circumstances.)

And is it possible — do we dare hope — that Beghe might actually walk again if he could just show some ability to move one muscle? There's been oodles of dialog to that effect. Could a capuchin gone crazy make him do it?

The answer is enough to make a person think Darwin was wrong; evolution must be working the other way. After all, you don't see monkeys making movies like this one. — *Har.*

Notturno
(Love Has Lied)
(FRENCH)

A Teamfilm and Star Prod. presentation in association with ORF, ZDF, SRG and La Sept. Produced by René Letzgus. Written and directed by Fritz Lehner. Camera (Eastmancolor), Gernot Roll; editors, Helga Wagner, Juno Silva Englander; music, Franz Schubert; set decoration, Allan Starski, Anna Prankl. Reviewed at Barcelona Film Festival (competing), July 3, 1988. Running time: **104 MIN.**

Schubert . . . . Udo Samel
Schober . . . . Daniel Olbrychski
Kajetan . . . . Wojtek Psoniak
Also with: Daniel Barrilly, Mireille Geisler, Dagmar Schwarz, Michaela Widhalm.

(Original German soundtrack)

Barcelona — Superb cinematography, topnotch production values and fine thesping mark this distinguished, albeit rambling episode in the life of composer Franz Schubert that should prove a prestigious vehicle for tv rather than theatrical release.

Story, set in 1823, Vienna, is handled with subtlety and innuendo by Fritz Lehner, who prefers meaningful glances, gestures and camera movements to superfluous dialog. Pic has an element of intimacy to it, a suggestive mood that may put off some viewers, but will be appreciated by discriminating audiences.

There is little action; the rambling episodes and esthetic fondling of details are sensitively limned.

Story starts with Schubert's release from a kind of hospital-asylum where he apparently has been treated for a venereal disease; he has lost much of his hair and is despondent. However, he tries to pick up the strands of his life. He seeks out his martinet father as well as other members of his family, then takes up with freewheeling, wealthy friend Schober, who invites him to his house in the country for a merry romp.

Schubert is disoriented, lonely, embarrassed and seemingly friendless. However, at end of pic he forms a blood pact with Schober and in one long camera shot we are transported from Schober's window, through the teeming street, up to Schubert's spartan apartment, with the enigmatic title "Love Has Lied" appearing on the screen.

Though some of Schubert's music is used as a backdrop, and the protagonist does play a bit during a reception, item concentrates on this downbeat episode of the composer's life, rather than being a vehicle for his music. Samel and Olbrychski are superb, as is Psoniak as a crippled beggar who gets to know Schubert in the hospital and then follows him about to all parts. —*Besa.*

The New Adventures Of Pippi Longstocking

A Columbia release of an Adham/Moshay/Mehlman production, coproduced by Svensk Filmindustri. Produced by Gary Mehlman, Walter Moshay. Executive producer,

Mishaal Kamal Adham. Directed, written and coproduced by Ken Annakin, based on the books by Astrid Lindgren. Camera (Deluxe color), Roland (Ozzie) Smith; editor, Ken Zemke; music, Misha Segal; songs, Harriet Schock, Segal; sound (Dolby), David Relson; production design, Jack Senter; art direction, Stephen M. Berger; set decoration, Frederick C. Weiler; costume design, Jacqueline Saint Anne; special effects chief designer, Richard Parker; associate producer, Robin Clark; assistant directors, Tom Connors, James Turley. Reviewed at AMC Century 14, L.A., July 23, 1988. MPAA Rating: G. Running time: **100 MIN.**

Pippi	Tami Erin
Miss Bannister	Eileen Brennan
Mr. Settigren	Dennis Dugan
Mrs. Settigren	Dianne Hull
Mr. Blackhart	George Di Cenzo
Captain Efraim	John Schuck
Glue Man	Dick Van Patten
Tommy	David Seaman Jr.
Annika	Cory Crow
Rype	J.D. Dickinson
Rancid	Chub Bailly

Hollywood — "The New Adventures Of Pippi Longstocking" is a competently made kidpic that nevertheless proves all but insufferable from an adult perspective.

Moppets under 10, who will no doubt be unaware that there were ever any old Pippi Longstocking adventures, may enjoy it well enough, but this is definitely a picture for the pintsized crowd only.

Several Swedish-West German pics based upon Astrid Lindgren's internationally popular children's book series were made beginning in 1969, but received only marginal playoff in the U.S. This, too, may enjoy greater acceptance in foreign territories, where the title character is better known.

Heroine's appeal stems from her anything-goes attitude, sense of fun and adventure, and avoidance of all responsibility, except taking care of her pet monkey and horse. She also is endowed with some vaguely magical physical powers, enabling her to vault great distances, lift objects many times her weight and spin around in place so fast she can stand in for the rotor blades of a helicopter.

Here, in what would appear to be the 1940s, Pippi becomes separated from her seafaring father in a storm, washes up in a small Florida town and takes up residence in a large cobweb-ridden house across the street from Tommy and Annika, who, to their father's distress, instantly fall in with Pippi's wild ways.

The newcomer's favorite antics, including food fights with ice cream and pancakes, usually leave a disagreeable mess behind, but occasionally Pippi comes up with brighter ideas, such as concocting her own flying machine to spirit away Tommy and Annika, or tightrope walking into a burning orphange to save some wee ones.

In any event, Pippi prevails wherever she goes and with whomever she meets, including the officious Miss Bannister, who is determined to curb the girl's carefree existence and stick her in the home for way-

ward youth. Pippi's allure, finally, is akin to Peter Pan's — the avoidance of domesticity, school walls and adulthood, the embrace of unfettered adverturousness as a way of life.

Unfortunately, Tami Erin is so overbearing in the leading role that one longs for a little peace and quiet. Especially toward the beginning, she is constantly making unattractive faces and sporting an obnoxious know-it-all attitude, and she never betrays any humanity or dimension. With her green eyes, freckles and red pigtails, she looks just right, but putting up with her charmlessness for 100 minutes is a tall order.

Eileen Brennan applies all the comic twists she can muster to her spinster schoolmarm, Dianne Hull is appealing as the kids' sympathetic mother, and John Schuck is all bluster and warmth as Pippi's elusive pa.

Despite major gaps in some of the staging, Ken Annakin's production is presentable enough for what's needed here. —Cart.

Dun-Huang
(JAPANESE)

A Toho release of a Dun-Huang Project Committee production. Produced by Atsushi Takeda, Yuzo Irie. Executive producers, Yasuyoshi Tokuma, Gohei Kogure, Kazuo Haruna. Directed by Junya Sato. Screenplay, Sato, Tsuyoshi Yoshida, from the novel by Yasushi Inoue; camera (color), Akira Shizuka; music, Masaru Sato; editor, Akira Suzuki; lighting, Shigeru Umetani; sound, Yasuo Hashimoto; art direction, Hiroshi Tokuda; assistant producers, Yo Yamamoto, Shigeru Mori, Shingo Mori; special producers, Yoshihiro Yuki, Ma Wang Liang, Masahiro Sato. Reviewed at Shinjuku Musashinokan, Tokyo, July 15, 1988. Running time: **143 MIN.**

Zhao Xingte	Koichi Satoh
Zhu Wangli	Toshiyuki Nishida
Weichi Kuang	Daijiro Harada
Li Yuanhao	Tsunehiko Watase
Princess Tsurpia	Anna Nakagawa

Tokyo — "Dun-Huang" owes whatever notoriety it has almost solely to its pricetag. Costing a reported 4.5-billion yen (about $33,000,000), this period feature is the most expensive Japanese film ever made. If this record is broken, "Dun-Huang" quickly will lose the attention of filmgoers.

Because it so quickly follows the Oscars sweep of "The Last Emperor," the temptation may be great to compare how well each film took advantage of much-coveted permission to shoot in China. This temptation should be resisted, unless one is searching for a way to make Bernardo Bertolucci's epic, which cost approximately one-third less than "Dun-Huang," look even more gorgeously expensive than it already does.

"Dun-Huang," based on a prizewinning novel by Yasushi Inoue, is the name of a walled city in northwestern China that was a military outpost on the Silk Road and attracted the attention of scholars

when a cache of Buddhist sutras and manuscripts, hidden for some 900 years, was discovered in nearby caves.

Inoue, mixing historical fact with informed speculation, offered a fictional account of events leading, over a period of about 10 years in the early 10th century, to the concealment of those writings.

Zhao Xingte (Koichi Satoh), an unsuccessful candidate for a civil service examination, is inspired by a Xixia woman he sees being sold in a marketplace. Because of this encounter, he serves as a soldier and participates in many battles; works for over a year editing a Xixia-Chinese dictionary; falls in love with a princess (Anna Nakagawa) who later commits suicide to demonstrate her faithfulness to him; becomes interested for the first time in his life in religion, and commences copying Buddhist sutras of the sort. he eventually hides in the caves from the destruction that results when a headstrong warrior, Zhu Wangli (Toshiyuki Nishida), leads a revolt against the Xixia ruler (Tsunehiko Watase).

The film succeeds all too well in duplicating the novel's major failing, an overreliance on uninvolving and frequently confusing military actions, while capturing few of its virtues.

Although presenting itself as a production worthy of international attention, "Dun-Huang" has lessened its chances of success abroad by focusing on a purely domestic consideration. The film is what is referred to here as a "mombusho sentei saku," or an Education Ministry-selected work, a designation many local studios see as almost invariably stimulating ticket sales in this education-oriented country.

Although Inoue's hero has only two encounters with women in the novel, both of them of brief duration yet lasting impact, neither of them salacious, they've been bowdlerized so that parents who bring their kids to this film won't have to explain anything embarrassing. In the book, the woman being auctioned is naked and is having the tips of her fingers sliced off by the auctioneer; in the film she is a completely clothed Yoshiko Mita, making a cameo appearance, and slices her own cheek with the auctioneer's knife so that no one will want to buy her.

Similarly, Zhao's night with the princess is reduced to some clenching and kissing. Nor does she refer to him, as she does in the novel, as the reincarnation of her late finance, thereby reassuring the audience that she's not the sort of girl who fooled around before Mr. Right came along.

Changes made in order to transform Inoue's novel into an "acceptable" film not only fail to give "offense," they turn Zhao into a hero

more appealing to young viewers. Inoue made Zhao 32 years old and took him well into middle age. Scenarists Sato and Yoshida, undoubtedly anticipating the school-kids-on-summer-holiday audience, have turned an adventure of the mind into a boy's adventure of the mind, with an anachronistically well-tanned Koichi Satoh playing Zhao as a seemingly ageless youth.

Though apparently serious about its responsibility to be educational, this pedantic film fails not only to make clear the importance of "Dun-Huang, but to use this story to explain why China, never successfully invaded from the south, for generations has been especially sensitive about its northern borders, across which have galloped a host of invaders. If the film teaches anything, it is that entertainment, not to mention education, is too important to be dictated by educators.—Bail.

Uninvited

An Amazing Movies presentation of a Heritage Entertainment production. Executive producer, Douglas C. Witkins. Produced and directed by Greydon Clark. Screenplay, Clark; camera (color), Nicholas Von Sternberg; editor, Travis Clark; music, Dan Slider; sound, Al Ramirez; production design, Peter Paul Raubertas; set decoration, Greg Maher; assistant director-production manager, Whitney Hunter; associate producer, Robert Steloff; casting, Wendy Kurtzman. Reviewed on New Star vidcassette, N.Y., July 2, 1988. MPAA Rating: PG-13. Running time: **89 MIN.**

Mike Harvey	George Kennedy
Walter Graham	Alex Cord
Albert	Clu Gulager
Rachel	Toni Hudson
Martin	Eric Larson
Bobbie	Clare Carey
Corey	Rob Estes
Suzanne	Shari Shattuck

Also with: Beau Dremann, Austin Stoker, Greydon Clark.

"Uninvited" is a preposterous horror film that lamely tries to pep up a tired-blood thriller set aboard a yacht with the appearance of a murderous tabby cat. A good cast is wasted in this drivel, which bypassed U.S. theatrical release for a video store destination.

Alex Cord portrays an unscrupulous Wall Street wizard who, with his henchmen George Kennedy and Clu Gulager, has to leave Fort Lauderdale and get to his Cayman Islands bank pronto to put over a vast deal. Unbelievably, he arranges for some teens, in town for Spring Break, to come along with them on his yacht as "cover."

Unbeknownst to everyone, including the yacht's underage skipper Rachel (played by the perky but miscast Toni Hudson), the cute orange cat the teens bring aboard is an escapee from a genetics lab and has been exposed to radiation, making it mucho dangerous (director Greydon Clark cameos as the lab doctor in the opening scene).

It's never explained why or how, but the cat opens its mouth occasionally to emit a huge, rodent-like puppet that violently attacks people. As sci-fi goes, film makes no sense whatsoever, but is merely an excuse for goopy makeup effects of the bulging-bladders-under-the-skin variety.

Trapped on the yacht, the humans' behavior becomes increasingly phony, as film devolves into the usual study of greed vs. heroism in a crisis format. Extremely poor post-synching of the sound in several scenes destroys any remaining credibility.

Best acting is contributed by Cord, who gives a feel for how the Oscar-laureled Michael Douglas character Gecko of "Wall Street" might behave in such cramped quarters. As the two bimbos on board, Clare Carey and Shari Shattuck provide alluring visual diversion sans nudity. George Kennedy is overkill casting in the stock role of a henchman who writhes around a lot in pain after the puppet bites his ankle.—Lor.

Dark Age
(AUSTRALIAN-U.S.)

An RKO Pictures-FGH presentation. Executive producer, Antony I. Ginnane. Produced by Basil Appleby. Directed by Arch Nicholson. Screenplay, Sonia Borg, from Grahame Webb's novel "Numunwari;" camera (Panavision, Eastmancolor), Andrew Lesnie; editor-second unit director, Adrian Carr; music, Danny Beckerman; sound (Dolby), Garry Wilkins; production design, David Copping; assistant director, Barry Hall; production manager, Renate Wilson; casting, Faith Martin. Reviewed on Charter Entertainment vidcassette, N.Y., July 4, 1988. MPAA Rating: R. Running time: 90 MIN.
Steve . . . . John Jarratt
Cathy . . . . Nikki Coghill
John . . . . Max Phipps
Oondabund . . . . Burnam Burnam
Adjaral . . . . David Gulpilil
Rex . . . . Ray Meagher
Mac . . . . Jeff Ashby
Jackson . . . . Paul Bertram

Australia's answer to "Jaws," "Dark Age" is a competently made horror film about a legendary large croc on the rampage. It's not a strong enough title on its own and got lost in the distribution pipeline before its current homevideo release.

Local color (atmospherically filmed in far north Queensland and Northern Territory) highlights this tall tale of Numunwari, a 25-foot long crocodile held sacred by the aborigines. Storms cause the beastie to head down river and start eating humans.

John Jarratt plays a government ranger who's fighting poachers and trying to save crocs from extinction. Ironically, he's assigned by his government superior to hunt down the big beast, while every amateur hunter in sight uses the emergency as an excuse to declare open season on all crocs.

Aboriginal folklore gives "Dark Age" its own flavor, but too many scenes and plot devices directly ape "Jaws" to cornball effect. The issue of protecting local interests against the adverse publicity of recurring croc attacks, the ultimate 3-man trek (Jarratt and two aborigines) after the beast and a very familiar scene of kids swimming peacefully in a harbor when the croc arrives to attack lack originality.

Jarratt is an appealing hero, with the lovely Nikki Coghill effective as an anthropologist and romantic interest. Burnam Burnam is solid as the aborigine elder, supported ably by David Gulpilil.

Director Arch Nicholson (of HBO's Rachel Ward-starrer "Fortress") has a topflight technical team, but the killer croc's fake look doesn't help to generate scares or suspense. —Lor.

Juillet en septembre
(July In September)
(FRENCH)

An AAA release of a Compagnie Française Cinématographique/TF1 Films coproduction Produced by Cyril Bourbon de Rouvre. Written and directed by Sébastien Japrisot. Camera (Eastmancolor). Edmond Richard; editor, Hélène Plemmianikov; music, Eric Demarsan; makeup, Josée de Luca; art direction, Etienne Mery; assistant director, Patrick Jaquillard; production manager, Alain Darbon. Reviewed at Marignan-Concorde cinema, Paris, July 5, 1988. Running time: 95 MIN.
Juillet . . . . Laetitia Gabrielli
Marie . . . . Anne Parillaud
Jacques . . . . Eric Damain
Marbas . . . . Daniel Desmars
Mme. Dewacker . . . . Giselle Pascal
Mr. Challe . . . . Jean Gaven
Domino . . . . Pascale Pellegrin
Dottie . . . . France Dougnac

Paris — Sébastien Japrisot's second feature is not likely to advance his career as a filmmaker. His script falls between two stools, being at once a comedy about a pretty young orphan in search of her mother, and a drama about a psychotic killer of attractive young women.

Japrisot sets things up so that their paths will finally cross, anticlimactically as it turns out. They have one thing in common — their loneliness. The meeting is of consequence for both (she gives up the search for mom and decides to live for the future; he hangs himself), but it's trivial for the spectator.

Japrisot banks only marginally on suspense or terror, since he portrays the killer (Daniel Desmars) as a chronically timid neurotic who sees red when he encounters a manifestly happy young couple. Apart from his sanguinary hobby, he's not a bad sort.

Understandably more screen time is spent on the girl (played by pretty, wide-eyed young newcomer Laetitia Gabrielli), who has returned to the coastal resort town where she began life as a foundling. Unable to find any trace of her real mother, she expends much of her energy comically trying to befriend a yuppie couple next door (Anne Parillaud and Eric Damain) who eventually attract the murderous eye of the peripatetic Desmars.

From the poor handling of story and character, one would hardly guess "July" was the work of a successful mastermind of print thrillers, Japrisot's most recent success turned into a top grossing film being "One Deadly Summer." (He flirted with filmmaking with a couple of shorts in 1961 and a feature in 1976, directed under his real name, Jean-Baptiste Rossi). Direction betrays a lack of understanding for cinematic essentials. Tech credits are okay. —Len.

Happy End
(SWISS)

A Challenger Films production in association with Television Suisse Romande. Produced by Jean-Luc Metzker. Directed by Marcel Schüpbach. Screenplay, Schüpbach, Jean-Gabriel Zufferey; camera (Eastmancolor), Hugues Ryffel; editor, Maya Schmid; music, Léon Francioli; sound, Laurent Barbey. Reviewed at Barcelona Film Festival, June 30, 1988. Running time: 95 MIN.
Jean . . . . Carlo Brandt
Alex . . . . Marie-Luce Felber
Also with: Arnold Walter, Michel Voita, Jean-François Panet, Jacques Roman, Jean-Louis Feuz, Fabienne Guelpa, Geoffrey Dyson.

Barcelona — "Happy End" is a road film which leads nowhere; its two leading characters are about as unattractive a couple as one could come up with, and the little action there is, barring the denouement, is rambling and pointless.

A Swiss shoplifter and a stockbroker who have little in common drive off in the latter's snazzy BMW to France and England ad-libbing their relationship as they pile up the miles. He's more attracted to her than vice versa, and for over an hour they doodle about, talk, have sex, drift apart and then together again in a sequence of filmic vagaries.

Film concludes in an orgy of violence, with the demise of both characters, but most viewers will not lament their loss. Commercial chances seem dim for this futile, plotless exercise in tedium whose title is a misnomer.—Besa.

Scenes From The Goldmine

A Hemdale release. Executive producers, John Daly, Derek Gibson. Produced by Danny Eisenberg. Coproducers, Marc Rocco, Pierre David. Directed by Rocco. Screenplay, Rocco, John Norvet, Eisenberg; camera (Foto-Kem color), Cliff Ralke; editor, Russell Livingstone; music, Steve Delacy, Rocco, Eisenberg; songs, Bobby Woods, Bryan Adams & Jim Vallance, Melissa Etheridge, Timothy B. Schmit, James House, others; sound (Ultra-Stereo), David Kelson; production design, Matthew Jacobs; art direction, Pola Schreiber; set decoration, Scott Mulvaney; assistant director, Betsy Pollock; casting, Jane Feinberg, Mike Fenton. Reviewed on Charter Entertainment vidcassette, N.Y., July 6, 1988. MPAA Rating: R. Running time: 105 MIN.
Debi DiAngelo . . . Catherine Mary Stewart
Niles Dresden . . . . Cameron Dye
Harry . . . . Steve Railsback
Manny . . . . Joe Pantoliano
Kenny Bond . . . . John Ford Coley

Dennis . . . . Timothy B. Schmit
Dana . . . . Jewel Shepard
Ian Weymouth . . . . Lee Ving
Nathan DiAngelo . . . . Alex Rocco
Stephanie . . . . Pamela Springsteen
Kerry DiAngelo . . . . Mark Michaels
Also with: Lotus Weinstock, Lisa Blake Richards, Nick Gilder, Lesley-Anne Down, Bobby Woods.

"Scenes From The Goldmine" is a diverting drama about success and disillusionment on the rock music scene. Familiar storyline is punched up by an excellent song track, good performances and tight direction.

Currently in homevideo distribution, pic's theatrical release was minimal, following an unveiling at last year's Houston Film Festival with a brief run in Cleveland.

Pic limns the hard-luck tale of Debi DiAngelo (Catherine Mary Stewart), lovely keyboard player-vocalist-composer who gets a gig with up-and-coming rock group Niles Dresden & The Pieces.

Dresden (Cameron Dye) becomes romantically involved with her, but as the group's big break comes in signing with a record label, it doesn't take much coercing from evil Rush Records magnate Manny (Joe Pantoliano) to get Dresden to take credit for her songs and ease her out of the big time. As directed by Marc Rocco, who also contributed to the screenplay and background music, "Scenes" credibly depicts the real-world problem of receiving accurate credit (and remuneration) for one's creative efforts and doesn't pull any punches.

Highlighted by that song "Lonely Dancer," penned by Melissa Etheridge, as well as other strong numbers by Bobby Woods ("Every Good Girl Falls") and the team of Bryan Adams & Jim Vallance ("Play To Win," alternate moniker for the film), pic benefits greatly from having the lead thesps handle their own on-screen singing. Catherine Mary Stewart is feisty and affecting in the lead role of Debi, while Cameron Dye is properly glamorous and evil as Dresden, luring her along; both vocalize ably.

Joe Pantoliano scores as the venal Manny, making the stereotypical character come alive, Jewel Shepard essays some dramatic moments well as Debi's best friend who faces the problem of unwed pregnancy and real-life performers John Ford Coley and Timothy B. Schmit bring credibility to the band and milieu. — Lor.

An Uns Glaubt Gott Nicht Mehr
(God Does Not Believe In Us Anymore)
(AUSTRIAN-B&W-16m)

A Roxie Releasing release. Produced by Kurt Kodal for ORF, ZDF and SRG. Directed by Axel Corti. Screenplay, Georg Stefan Troller; camera (black & white), Wolfgang Treu; editors, Ulrike Pahl, Helga Wagner; sound, Herbert Koller. Reviewed at Film Forum, N.Y., July 13, 1988. Running time: 110 MIN.

Ferry Tobler . . . . Johannes Silberschneider
Gandhi . . . . Armin Mueller-Stahl
Alena . . . . Barbara Petritsch
Mehlig . . . . Fritz Mulier
Kron . . . . Georg Corten
Dr. Fein . . . . Eric Schildkraut
(Original German soundtrack)

"God Does Not Believe In Us Anymore" is Part One of the Axel Corti trilogy "To Where And Back." Film traces the escape of a teenage Viennese Jew from the Nazis, from November 1938 to late 1940, after the fall of France.

The film is strong and relentless, never relaxing tension, as the teenager and other refugees struggle to stay ahead of the Nazis and their eager-to-oblige collaborators. It's clearly one of the best films of its genre, the World War II escape and survival film.

Film opens in Vienna as Ferry Tobler mourns the death of his father at the hands of Nazi thugs. The family garment shop is "Aryanized," assigned to new Gentile owners, as the Tobler apartment is looted by neighbors.

With great difficulty and risk, Ferry crosses the Austrian border and in Prague joins thousands of refugees of many nationalities who seek passports, visas, residence papers, real or forged, desperately exchanging news and rumors, sleeping 10 to a room.

Meanwhile, the film intercuts Nazi newsreels and radio broadcasts of Hitler's impending annexation of the Sudetenland. A refugee-committee worker, Alena (Barbara Petritsch), makes a special effort to save Ferry. Together they reach Paris as the Nazis attack Poland.

They befriend a big gentle anti-Nazi German (Armin Mueller Stahl), who has escaped from Dachau, where fellow prisoners had nicknamed him Gandhi because of his humanistic idealism. He and Alena become lovers.

The French police, anti-Semitic and deeply suspicious of this unwanted avalanche of refugees from Central Europe, conducts sudden raids. Ferry, Alena and Gandhi are caught.

Imprisoned in a French government camp as the Nazis break into France in May 1940, Ferry and Gandhi stand aside to watch Jewish prisoners pray. As Gandhi dons a yarmulke and joins them, he explains to Ferry: "No, I'm not religious, but you mustn't feel that fate will make you an exception; you must remain concerned."

Ferry asks: "Why do they hate us so, those others?" Gandhi replies: "They hate you because of the atrocities that they have committed against you." Soon Gandhi is caught, doomed to return to Dachau.

Corti uses black & white to assure the feel of wartime newsreels,

which with newspaper headlines and radio newscasts are intercut throughout the fictional scenes, skillfully achieving seamless transitions. In all, Corti maintains superb control of a huge canvas.—*Hitch.*

Santa Fe
(AUSTRIAN-B&W-16m)

A Roxie Releasing release. Produced by Matthias Barl for Thalia Film, with ORF, ZDF and SRG. Directed by Axel Corti. Screenplay, Corti, Georg Stefan Troller; camera (black & white), Gernot Roll; editors, Claudia Rieneck, Tamara Euller; sound, Rolf Schmidt-Gentner, Walter Amann. Reviewed at Film Forum, N.Y., July 13, 1988. Running time: 110 MIN.

Ferry Tobler . . . . Johannes Silberschneider
Freddy (Alfred) Wolff . . . . . Gabriel Barylli
Feldheim (Johnny Field) . Ernst Stankovsky
Popper Shapiro . . . . Gideon Singer
Dr. Treuman . . . . Peter Luhr
Lissa . . . . Doris Buchrucker
Frau Marmorek . . . . Dagmar Schwarz
(Original German soundtrack)

"Sante Fe," Part Two of the Axel Corti trilogy "To Where And Back," continues the saga of Jewish refugees fleeing the war in Europe.

The centerpiece film of the trilogy, "Santa Fe" is less urgent and forceful than the films that precede and follow. Like the refugees newly arrived in New York, the film has a shaky sense of place and no clear direction.

It is late 1941, but pre-Pearl Harbor, as the refugees arrive by ship in New York (the scene was shot in Trieste and lacks a New York look). They are now safe from the Nazi grasp but still face enormous problems of language, unemployment, alienation.

Ferry (Johannes Silberschneider), the teenage hero of Part One, is drowned in the first minutes of "Santa Fe" while rescuing a mute survivor of the Nazi camp at Ravensbruck. Ferry is succeeded as protagonist by Freddy (Gabriel Barylli), whose background as a young Viennese Jew is very similar (Freddy continues into Part Three, "Welcome In Vienna").

Freddy remains in New York with the emigre community but longs to go west to Santa Fe, perhaps to become a cowboy. He becomes involved with other refugees. One is a writer, dreaming of improving the world; another is an actor dreaming of Hollywood; some become opportunistic and cynical. Ethics suffer, as Freddy's lover Lissa (Doris Buchrucker) observes: "Over there, we were ourselves, despite the anti-Semitism. But here we are cheaters, down to our very souls."

Freddy buys and carries around a train ticket to Santa Fe. He, too, has a dream deferred. He never uses the ticket and instead joins the U.S. Army. We last see him in uniform, atop a Manhattan skyscraper, shredding the New York German-language newspaper Aufbau and throwing it to the winds.

"Santa Fe" has a dozen clumsy

anachronisms and unlikely incidents, but these are minor complaints that do not diminish Corti's extraordinary accomplishment.
—*Hitch.*

Tucker: The Man And His Dream

A Paramount Pictures release of a Lucasfilm Ltd. production from Zoetrope Studios. Produced by Fred Roos, Fred Fuchs. Executive producer, George Lucas. Directed by Francis Ford Coppola. Screenplay, Arnold Schulman, David Seidler; camera (Technovision, Technicolor), Vittorio Storaro; editor, Priscilla Nedd; music, Joe Jackson; additional music, Carmine Coppola; sound (Dolby), Michael Evje; production design, Dean Tavoularis; art direction, Alex Tavoularis; set design, Bob Goldstein, Jim Pohl; set decoration, Armin Ganz; costume design, Milena Canonero; sound design, Richard Beggs; associate producer, Teri Fettis; assistant director, H. Gordon Boos; stunt coordinator-second unit director, Buddy Joe Hooker; casting, Janet Hirshenson, Jane Jenkins. Reviewed at Paramount Studios, L.A., July 29, 1988. MPAA Rating: PG. Running time: 111 MIN.

Preston Tucker . . . . Jeff Bridges
Vera Tucker . . . . Joan Allen
Abe Karatz . . . . Martin Landau
Eddie Dean . . . . Frederic Forrest
Jimmy Sakuyama . . . . Mako
Howard Hughes . . . . Dean Stockwell
Sen. Homer Ferguson . . . . . . Lloyd Bridges
Alex Tremulis . . . . Elias Koteas
Marilyn Lee Tucker . . . . . Nina Siemaszko
Preston Tucker Jr. . . . . Christian Slater
Noble Tucker . . . . Corky Nemec
Johnny Tucker . . . . Anders Johnson
Frank . . . . : . . . . Marshall Bell
Stan . . . . Don Novello
Kirby . . . . Jay O. Sanders
Kerner . . . . Peter Donat
Bennington . . . . Dean Goodman
Millie . . . . Patti Austin

■ Hollywood — The true story of a great American visionary who was thwarted, if not destroyed, by the established order, "Tucker: The Man And His Dream" represents the sunniest imaginable telling of an at least partly tragic episode in recent history.

Like a glittering, briskly moving big brass band, splashy film parades the life of revolutionary automobile designer Preston Tucker across the screen so as to make it resemble a noisy, colorful, rambunctious public spectacle. Approach leaves little room for depth, emotion or a rewarding human dimension, but the upbeat tempo and attitude carry the viewer right along through an irresistibly engaging tale, one that should activate a fair measure of interest at the boxoffice.

Francis Ford Coppola is on record to the effect that this "Tucker" is considerably different, less bitter and more optimistic, than the film he originally envisioned years ago, and one only has to recall the dark, brooding qualities of the "Godfather" epics and "Apocalypse Now" to imagine what "Tucker" might have been like had the director tackled it back in the 1970s.

Film that has emerged represents the first artistic collaboration between Coppola and George Lucas, with one of them as director, since the similarly car-obsessed "American Graffiti" in 1973, and one might confidently guess that Lucas had more than a little to do with determining the rosy, positive attitude toward life's vicissitudes on view here.

On the other hand, Tucker's life and career present so many parallels to Coppola's own it is easy to see why he has coveted this project for so long. Industryites will nod in recognition of this story of a self-styled genius up against business interests hostile to his innovative ideas, but also will note the accepting, unbelligerent stance adopted toward the terms of the struggle.

In a mild echo of "Citizen Kane," this exquisitely produced picture opens with a facsimile of an in-house promotional film about Tucker's activities up through World War II, showing how his speedy combat vehicle proved impractical for the Army but how his design for machine-gun turrets won wide acceptance.

After World War II, seemingly on the strength of his enthusiasm alone, Tucker got a small core of collaborators to work on his dream project, which he called "the first completely new car in 50 years" and was sold as "The car of tomorrow — today." Boasting a striking, streamlined look, the Tucker promised such advanced features as a rear engine, disc brakes, fuel injection, a center headlight, seat belts and a pop-out windshield, and would sell for less than $2,500.

With a factory in Chicago, Tucker managed to turn out 50 of his beauties, but vested interests in Detroit and Washington dragged him into court on fraud charges, shutting him down and effectively ending his automobile career. As his moneyman tells him, "You build the car too good."

It's a classically American tale of the maverick trying to buck the system, and Coppola presents it all as if his stage were a 3-ring circus, a place where introspection, analysis and second thoughts are not allowed. Rare is the scene with only two people in it, and Coppola does give a strong impression of what it's like to create something ambitious under enormous private pressure and public scrutiny.

Everything about Coppola's bright rendition of Arnold Schulman and David Seidler's peppy script expresses a winning, can-do attitude, and the pros and cons of this approach are perfectly exemplified in Jeff Bridges' performance in the leading role. Flashing his charming smile and oozing cocky confidence, his Tucker is inspiring because he won't be depressed or defeated by anything. At the same time, however, the viewer can't claim to know him at all, for nothing resembling a 3-dimensional human being ever emerges.

In fact, virtually everyone in the film makes a vivid, appealing impression, but is restricted similarly by the 1-note, let's-put-on-a-show angle. However, Martin Landau manages to break thorugh with a

highly sympathetic, sometimes moving portrayal of Tucker's financial manager, and Dean Stockwell, as Howard Hughes, effectively presides over an eerie scene, brilliantly staged in the Spruce Goose hangar, in which two iconoclastic, beleaguered industrialists briefly meet.

Technically, the film is a dream. Shooting in the San Francisco Bay Area, production designer Dean Tavoularis, costume designer Milena Canonero and cinematographer Vittorio Storaro have conjured up a splashy, slightly stylized vision of the late 1940s that bears some resemblance to magazine photography of the period. Score by pop music figure Joe Jackson consists of propulsively uptempo big band material. And then there are the cars themselves, a constant pleasure to behold.

Rousing approach to Tucker's life here takes the view that it was the man's dreams, and his inspiring attempt to make them come true, that remain important, not the fact that he lost when the final buzzer sounded. This may make the picture more accessible to the general public than it might have been otherwise, but it also flattens out the ironies, complexities and richness inherent in the story itself. —Cart.

Married To The Mob

An Orion Pictures release of a Mysterious Arts/Demme production. Produced by Kenneth Utt, Edward Saxon. Executive producers, Joel Simon, Bill Todman Jr. Directed by Jonathan Demme. Screenplay, Barry Strugatz, Mark R. Burns; camera (Duart color; Deluxe prints), Tak Fujimoto; editor, Craig McKay; music, David Byrne; sound (Dolby), Christopher Newman; production design, Kristi Zea; art direction, Maher Ahmad; set decoration, Nina Ramsey, Don Ivey (Florida); costume design, Colleen Atwood; associate producer; assistant director, Ron Bozman; casting, Howard Feuer. Reviewed at Coronet theater, L.A., July 26, 1988. MPAA Rating: R. Running time: 103 MIN.
Angela De Marco	Michelle Pfeiffer
Mike Downey	Matthew Modine
Tony Russo	Dean Stockwell
Connie Russo	Mercedes Ruehl
Frank De Marco	Alec Baldwin
Regional Director Franklin	Trey Wilson
Rose	Joan Cusack
Ed Benitez	Oliver Platt
Tommy	Paul Lazar
Rita Harcourt	(Sister) Carol East
Theresa	Ellen Foley
The Clown	Chris Isaak
Phyllis	O'Lan Jones
Angela's hairdresser	Charles Napier
Joey De Marco	Anthony J. Nici
Karen Lutnick	Nancy Travis
The Priest	David Johansen
Uncle Joe Russo	Al Lewis
Vinnie the Slug	Frank Ferrara
Nick the Snake	Frank Gio
Al the Worm	Gary Klar

■ Hollywood — Fresh, colorful and inventive, "Married To The Mob" is another offbeat entertainment from Jonathan Demme.

Due both to the relatively cartoonish approach and the essential implausibility of the central relationship, stylistically ambitious picture plays mostly on the level of sur-

face pleasures, and odd mix of tones automatically pitches it toward hip and sophisticated, rather than general, audiences. Underworld setting, broad comedy and Michelle Pfeiffer's vulnerable but resourceful lead character hold enough wide appeal to promise a decent b.o. reception.

Storyline's basic trajectory has unhappy suburban housewife Pfeiffer taking the opportunity presented by the sudden death of her husband, who happens to have been a middle-level gangster, to escape the limitations of her past and forge a new life for herself and her son in New York City.

But the real interests of Demme and writers Barry Strugatz and Mark R. Burns lie in applying up-to-the-minute comic topspin to genre expectations and stock characters, and in cross-culturalizing this star-crossed romance of a WASP and an Italian-American to the point that it blossoms as a veritable Third World bouquet.

Opening with a hit on a commuter train and following with some murdurous bedroom shenanigans, film establishes itself as a suburban gangster comedy. Demme and his enthusiastic collection of actors take evident delight in sending up the gauche excesses of these particular nouveau riches, as the men strut about in their pinstripes and polyester and the women spend their time at the salon getting their hair teased.

When local kingpin Tony (The Tiger) Russo (Dean Stockwell) does in (Cucumber) Frank De Marco (Alec Baldwin) for dallying with his girlfriend, it would appear to be the perfect moment for the Cucumber's beautiful wife Angela (Pfeiffer) to sever her connections with the mob and start over again elsewhere.

Unfortunately, Tony the Tiger has the hots for Angela and quickly locates her after she and her son move into a filthy tenement apartment on the Lower East Side. At the same time, Angela meets Mike (Matthew Modine), an apparent neighbor who actually is an FBI agent eager to nail Tony.

Only after Mike and Angela enter **into a tentative romance is the young man forced to reveal his true identity, and it all ends up in Miami,** with both the FBI and an insanely jealous wife out to take the Tiger by the tail.

Throughout, the filmmakers delight in creating as many unexpected oppositions and goofy juxtapositions as possible, placing criminals in tract housing, making a tiny white kid a three card monte ace, giving Pfeiffer a job at a Jamaican hairdressing salon, making a fast-food restaurant clown a hitman, and in general overlaying the action with an imaginative selection of ethnically diverse pop music.

Demme aims high here in his attempt to fuse multiple styles, guid-

ing his performers through manic but deadpan comic work while cooking up a visual stew so bright and exaggerated it approaches the cartoon-like.

But as pleasing and amusing as all these qualities may be, there is little supporting them to supply any deeper satisfaction. As in his "Something Wild," Demme throws a very straight professional man together with a volatile, unpredictable young woman, but the basis for his appeal to her remains questionable, and the ending stands as a tribute to Demme's incurable romanticism, regardless of believability. The style becomes the substance of the picture, which is an impressive achievement, but renders it a diversion, little more.

The enormous cast is a total delight, starting with Pfeiffer, who, with hair dyed dark, a New York accent and a continuously nervous edge, has never been better than in showing this very different portrait of a mobster's wife than she displayed in "Scarface."

Modine proves winning as the seemingly inept FBI functionary who grows into his job, and Stockwell is a hoot as the unflappable gangland boss, slime under silk and a fedora.

Lenser Tak Fujimoto, production designer Kristi Zea and costume designer Colleen Atwood have combined to create a look so vibrant the film virtually pops off the screen, and the long final credit sequence is particularly fascinating, as it features alternate takes and scenes to those actually used in the foregoing picture, thereby constituting a mini-lesson in the filmmaking process and the innumerable choices it entails. —Cart.

The Blob

A Tri-Star Pictures release. Produced by Jack H. Harris, Elliott Kastner. Executive producer, Andre Blay. Line producer, Rupert Harvey. Directed by Chuck Russell. Screenplay, Russell, Frank Darabont; camera (Technicolor), Mark Irwin; editor, Terry Stokes, Tod Feuerman; music, Michael Hoenig; production design, Craig Stearns; art direction, Jeff Ginn; set design, Randy Moore, Gary Steele, Sally A. Thornton; set decoration, Anne Ahrens; costume design, Joseph Porro; sound (Ultra-Stereo), Robert J. Anderson Jr.; visual effects supervisor, Hoyt Yeatman; special visual effects, Dream Quest Images; creature effects design and creation, Lyle Conway; makeup effects design and creation, Tony Gardner; additional creature effects design and supervision, Stuart Ziff; assistant director, Josh McLaglen; casting, Johanna Ray. Reviewed at Tri-Star screening room, L.A., Aug. 1, 1988. MPAA Rating: R. Running time: 92 MIN.
Meg Penny	Shawnee Smith
Brian Flagg	Kevin Dillon
Paul Taylor	Donovan Leitch
Sheriff Herb Geller	Jeffrey DeMunn
Fran Hewitt	Candy Clark
Mr. Penny	Art La Fleur
Mrs. Penny	Sharon Spelman
Rev. Meeker	Del Close
Scott Jeskey	Ricky Paull Goldin
Deputy Briggs	Paul McCrane
Can Man	Billy Beck

Dr. Meddows . . . . Joe Seneca
Kevin Penny . . . . Michael Kenworthy

■ **Hollywood — Some 30 years after the campy, low-budget original
became a cult fave, the Blob is back
with a vengeance. Updated with
awesome, no-expense-spared special
effects and a feisty female hero,
horrific outing should prove thoroughly satisfying for fans of the
genre.**

(A comedy sequel was directed by
Larry Hagman in the early
1970s.—*Ed.*)

A great B-movie with an A-pic
budget, "Blob" will have to stick
fast to envelop as much cash at the
boxoffice as it devoured during
lensing. Theatrical and video
careers combined should yield a
globful of dollars.

Thanks to the special effects
work of Hoyt Yeatman, Lyle Conway and a host of others, the

Original Film

A Paramount release of a Jack H. Harris
production. Stars Steven McQueen; costars
Aneta Corseaut, Earl Rowe. Directed by Ir-
vin S. Yeaworth Jr. Screenplay, Theodore
Simonson and Kate Phillips, from idea by Ir-
vine H. Millgate; camera (Deluxe color),
Thomas Spalding; music, Jean Yeaworth;
song, Burt Bacharach, Mack David; editor,
Alfred Hillmann, Tradeshown in N.Y., Sept.
4, 1958. Running time: **85 MIN.**
Steve . . . . Steven McQueen
Judy . . . . Aneta Corseaut
Police Lieut. . . . . Earl Rowe
Old Man . . . . Olin Howlin

malevolent plasma is clearly the star
of this familiar layout. Starting life
as an aggressive glueball that creeps
out of a fallen meteor and attacks a
vagrant in the woods, it grows to
raging, ferocious proportions, gobbling unlucky locals and carrying
their blood and body parts along
with it. Glutinous glutton has only
one weakness — ice — and that's
hard to come by in this warm, wea-
ther-blighted ski town.

Blob itself packs less visual punch
than the way it attacks its victims,
dropping a gluey, viscuous blanket
over them and thrashing them from
inside and out. Effects take up
where "Aliens" left off, and should
draw hoots of admiration in theaters.

Director Chuck Russell ("A
Nightmare On Elm Street 3") builds
suspense slowly and carefully,
devoting 30 minutes to establishing
apple-pie normalcy before the first
grisly strike. Likewise, suspense in
third-act crisis scenes is pumped for
all it's worth.

Formulaic, by-the-numbers script
leaves little room for misinterpretation. Weakest moments involve the
creaky sci-fi explanation for Blob's
presence, which is part of a germ
warfare experiment run amok. Joe
Seneca has the thankless role of the
mad scientist, part of a government
team in goofy spacesuits who allegedly come to save the town, but
end up turning on the teen heroes.

Perfs by Kevin Dillon as an out-

law kid who ends up battling the
blob and Shawnee Smith as a cheerleader who turns into a machinegun
toting she-devil to save her town are
adequate for the genre, with Dillon's the more resonant.

Far from being seamless, pic has
all the gaps and gapes of the genre,
with contrast between its ambitious,
airy, eerie opening images and
goofy, tacked-on ending suggesting
a breakdown between goal and finished product.

The blow that kills the Blob,
pulled off by Smith, is clumsily
staged. By that time, any denouement is a relief. The magnificent
monster, of course, is not all gone:
the ending sets up its return. It's a
good bet it'll be back.

Jack H. Harris, who coproduced
with Elliott Kastner, also produced
the original.—*Daws.*

Les Pyramides bleues
(The Blue Pyramids)
(FRENCH-MEXICAN)

An Artedis release of a Sofracima/FR3
Films/Mexico INC coproduction, in associ-
ation with the French Ministry of Culture,
SLAV 1 and Lorimar Home Video. Produced
by Catherine Winter. Directed by Arielle
Dombasle. Screenplay, Dombasle, Winter,
Nelson E. Breen; camera (color), Renan
Polles; editors, Françoise Coispeau, Michel
Lewin; music, Francis Lai; sound, Yves Bez-
er; art direction, Michèle Susini, Jean-Pierre
Kohut-Svelko, Omero Espinoza; artistic ad-
visers, Eric Rohmer, Chris Marker; assistant
directors, Christian Garreau, Alfonso Cua-
ron; production managers, Yves Marin, Hugo
Green, Alain Guadalpi. Reviewed at Tri-
omphe cinema, Paris, July 5, 1988. Running
time: **97 MIN.**
Alex . . . . Omar Sharif
Elise . . . . Arielle Dombasle
Marc . . . . Hippolyte Girardot
Perez-Valdez . . . . Pedro Armendariz Jr.
Noah . . . . Pierre Vaneck
Mother Superior . . . . Françoise Christophe
Woman in bar . . . . Martine Kelly
Charles . . . . Pascal Greggory

■ **Paris — "Les Pyramides bleues"
is an oddball melodrama about a
young woman who leaves a rich elder lover to prepare for a religious
vocation in a convent.**

Cowritten and directed by and
starring actress Arielle Dombasle,
pic has a comic strip naiveté, but not
enough humor or stylistic control to
make it entertaining kitsch. Lorimar
Home Video helped finance this
French coprod with Mexico, titled
in English "Paradise Calling."

Dombasle, known to arthouse
audiences from her roles in the films
of Eric Rohmer (who's billed alongside Chris Marker as "artistic advisers") plays a young French beauty
in Mexico who lives a life of luxury
and ease in the home of a powerful
magnate who dotes on her (Omar
Sharif).

Sharif discovers he has an even
more powerful rival — Jesus Christ.
Dombasle's religious preoccupations get the upper hand of her love
for Sharif, and she decides to enter
a convent in France where her lover
cannot find her.

Sharif does track her down and

pays agents to lure her back to him.
Among them is the corrupt leader of
a religious sect (Pierre Vaneck) who
uses a young disciple (Hippolyte
Girardot) to bring the newly reborn
Dombasle into his fold where she
finds herself part of a delegation —
for Mexico.

Plans go awry because Girardot
in fact is a muckraking journalist
doing a reportage on sects. He plays
along but falls in love with Dombasle. By the time she's back within Sharif's reach, the novice has
sworn her life to her new lover.

Dombasle, who spent part of her
childhood in Mexico, makes the
most of the picturesque locations,
but fares poorly with herself and
fellow thesps. Absurd plotting collapses into the ridiculous in final
section with a protracted chase sequence, which ends anticlimactically when Sharif unexpectedly gives
up Dombasle to his younger rival.
Tech credits are slick.—*Len.*

L'Amor Es Estrany
(Love Is Strange)
(SPANISH)

A Diafragma/Catalonia Films production.
Produced and directed by Carlos Balagué.
Screenplay, Balagué, Marcos Ordoñez;
camera (color), Josep Gusi; editor, Marisa
Aguinaga; music, Emili Baleriola, Coque
Vázquez; set decoration, Marcelo Grande;
production manager, Mónica Borrull.
Reviewed at Barcelona Film Festival, July 4,
1988. Running time: **100 MIN.**
Victor . . . . Mario Gas
Carlota . . . . Eulalia Ramón
Silvia . . . . Muntsa Alcañiz
Emilio . . . . Pep Munné
Alberto . . . . Fernando Guillén
Also with: Ana Maria Mauri, Margarita
Minguillón, Carles Sales, Constantino
Romero, Teresa Manresa.
(Original Catalan soundtrack)

■ **Barcelona — "Love Is Strange,"
is a tawdry, cliché-ridden yarn partly set against Barcelona's underworld of pimps and hookers, concerning the intermingling of an executive and his liaisons with various
women.**

Carlos Balagué spends a good
part of the film in bedroom scenes,
and another chunk in the violent second half. Item might chalk up
some sales for Third World territories, or form part of a homevid
package, the kind which is sold by
weight rather than content.

On all levels pic is clumsy and unconvincing, as the clean-cut protagonist becomes involved in sex
and mayhem, latter involving cutting up a corpse with a chainsaw
and preservation of a servered head
in the fridge. The tasteless shenanigans, when not laughable, are simply jejune. —*Besa.*

Kingsajz
(King Size)
(POLISH)

A Zespoly Filmowe, Kadr Studio production, through Film Polski. Produced by
Andrzej Soltysik. Directed by Juliusz Machulski. Screenplay, Machulski, Jolanta Hartwig;

camera (color), Jerzy Debski; editor, Miros-
lav Garlicka, music, Krzesimir Debski; art
direction, Janusz Sosnowski. Reviewed at
Karlovy Vary Film Festival, July 8, 1988.
Running time: **105 MIN.**
Adam . . . . Jarek Chmielnik
Big Eater . . . . Jerzy Stuhr
Ala . . . . Katarzyna Figura
Also with: Grzegorz Herominski, Joachin
Lamza, Maciej Kozlowski, Jan Machulski,
Leonard Pietraszak, Liza Machulska, Witold
Pirkosz.

■ **Karlovy Vary — Director Juliusz
Machulski, who had some commercial success with "Sex Mission,"
this time has chosen a fairytale format to tell what will, coming from
Poland, inevitably have political
parallels.**

It's a comedy detailing the adventures of a young scientist in the contemporary world, who actually has
come from a world of dwarves,
thanks to a magic potion, held by
the Big Eater, ruler of the dwarves.

This dwarf kingdom, Shuflandia,
exists in the cellar of a library, and
only the most obedient get the
chance to grow to king size and inhabit the larger world. Once there
nobody wants to return to Shuflandia, where disobeying the Big Eater
leads to assemblyline work. Another drawback to Shuflandia is that
there are no women — in the director's previous film the world was inhabited only by women.

Machulski and coscripter Jolanta
Hartwig, who worked together on
"Sex Mission" again have come up
with a novel concept, which can be
taken on a number of levels. It is not
a fairytale for children, and unfortunately the broad humor means its
possible audience in the West, expecting either a biting satire or a social comedy, are likely to be disappointed.

Some may object to the treatment
of women, with Katarzyna Figura
playing the scatterbrained blond to
the full.

Film does have a major asset in
the special effects carried out at the
Czech Barandov studios, but even
they can't overcome the old-fashioned, blundering tone of the pic.
Other technical aspects are well
done. — *Cain.*

Luna de Lobos
(Wolves' Moon)
(SPANISH)

A Brezal production. Produced by José
Luis Olaizola. Directed by Julio Sánchez
Valdés. Screenplay, Sánchez Valdés, Julio
Llamayares based on Llamayares' novel;
camera (Agfa color), Juan Molina; editor,
Teresa Font; music, Luis Mendo, Bernardo
Fuster; sets decoration, Juan José Carrillo;
production manager, Rafael Diaz-Salgado.
Reviewed at Karlovy Vary Film Festival (non-
competing), July 18, 1988. Running time: **105
MIN.**
Ramiro . . . . Santiago Ramos
Angel . . . . Antonio Resines
Gildo . . . . Alvaro de Luna
Also with: Kiti Manver, Fernando Vivan-
co, César Varona, Cristina Collado.

■ **Karlovy Vary — "Wolves'
Moon" is a politically neutral account of a group of Republican**

soldiers in northern Spain who hide in the hills for years after the Civil War has ended.

Activities of such "quinquis" provide a minor, but curious footnote to Spanish history. Despite a good many shootouts with Civil Guards and a subplot concerning the relationship between the sister of one of the hunted and a guard, item is too plodding as one after another of the group is caught or shot.

Helming, thesping and production values are okay, but Spanish audiences have wearied of the Civil War as a subject. Pic flopped on its commercial release in Spain.

Director Julio Sánchez Valdés tries to keep audience sympathy for the outlaws as they kidnap a wealthy villager, hold up a bus and raid shops to obtain food, but we know their efforts are doomed.

Rather than end on a downbeat note, script has the last of the survivors making his escape in a train, though we're left to guess whether he'll make it. —Besa.

La Maison assassinée
(The Murdered House)
(FRENCH)

A Gaumont production and release. Produced by Alain Poire. Directed by Georges Lautner. Screenplay, Lautner, Jacky Cukier, Didier Cauwelaert, from the novel by Pierre Magnan; camera (color), Yves Rodallec; editor, Michelle David; music, Philippe Sarde; art direction, Jacques Dugied; sound, Alain Lachassagne, Jean-Paul Loublier; assistant director, Dominique Brunner; production managers, Marc Goldstaub, Guy Azzi. Reviewed at Studio 28, Paris, June 22, 1988. Running time: **110 MIN.**
Seraphin Monge . . . . Patrick Bruel
Marie Dormeur . . . . Sophie Brochet
Rose Pujol . . . . Agnes Blanchot
Charmaine Dupin . . . . Ingrid Held
Patrice Dupin . . . . Yann Collette
Celestat Dormeur . . . . . Jean-Pierre Sentier
Zorme. . . . . Roger Zendly

■ Paris — "La Maison assassinée" is a rural period whodunit with an interesting sociological backdrop that unfortunately is blotted out by an overly convoluted and unsatisfactory plot.

Veteran director Georges Lautner has directed with a modicum of professionalism but no imagination.

Story relates the homecoming of a young World War I veteran whose entire family was murdered when he was a baby. Learning of his dark heritage, and uncovering the identities of the apparent criminals (all local notables), he sets out for revenge, but his targets all die mysteriously before he can get to them.

Script makes interesting overtures to dramatizing some of the effects of the Great War on a small southern French village whose young male population has been decimated, but the hokey melodramatics prevail.

An interesting secondary character is that of a young "gueule cass-

ée," a veteran with a hideously battered skull, but the writers contrive quickly to reduce his importance by finding him a pretty young fiancée not bothered by his deformity.

That leaves Patrick Bruel at centerstage as the would be avenger of his slaughtered family, but he is inexpressively inadequate as a hero. Among a supporting cast largely and ineffectually recruited from the theater, only vivacious screen newcomer Sophie Brochet provides authentic life amidst the artificial story contortions as Bruel's principal love interest.—Len.

The Last Temptation
Of Christ

A Universal Pictures release of a Universal and Cineplex Odeon Films presentation. Produced by Barbara De Fina. Executive producer, Harry Ufland. Directed by Martin Scorsese. Screenplay, Pual Schrader, based on novel by Nikos Kazantzakis; camera (Technicolor), Michael Ballhaus; editor, Thelma Schoonmaker; music, Peter Gabriel; production design, John Beard; art direction, Andrew Sanders; set decoration, Giorgio Desideri; costume design, Jean-Pierre Delifer; sound (Dolby), Amelio Verona; assistant director, Joseph Reidy; casting, Cis Corman. Reviewed at Universal Studios, Universal City, Calif., Aug. 6, 1988. MPAA Rating: R. Running time: **164 MIN.**
Jesus . . . . Willem Dafoe
Judas . . . . Harvey Keitel
Mary Magdalene . . . . Barbara Hershey
Saul/Paul . . . . Harry Dean Stanton
Pontius Pilate . . . . David Bowie
Mary Mother of Jesus . . . . . Verna Bloom
John the Baptist . . . . André Gregory
Girl Angel . . . . Juliette Caton
Aged Master . . . . Roberts Blossom
Zebedee . . . . Irvin Kershner
Andrew Apostle . . . . Gary Basrada
Peter Apostle . . . . Victor Argo
John Apostle . . . . Michael Been
Phillip Apostle . . . . Paul Herman
James Apostle . . . . John Lurie
Nathaniel Apostle . . . . Leo Burmester
Thomas Apostle . . . . Alan Rosenberg
Lazarus . . . . Thomas Arana
Rabbi . . . . Nehemiah Persoff
Jeroboam . . . . Barry Miller

■ Hollywood — A film of challenging ideas, and not salacious provocations, "The Last Temptation Of Christ" is a powerful and very modern reinterpretation of Jesus as a man wracked with anguish and doubt concerning his appointed role in life.

Intensely acted and made with tremendous cinematic skill and resourcefulness, this deeply felt work has become a notorious event before reaching the public due to exaggerations of the picture's content and a total, perhaps even willful misunderstanding of what it is saying. Unfortunately, climate generated by the hysteria, which has prompted Universal to rush the film into release Aug. 12, will prove unconducive to rational discussion of its many virtues and some central flaws.

From a b.o. point of view, controversy clearly has stirred up interest that wouldn't have existed otherwise, but there will be fear among some prospective patrons as well. At heart, this is a serious American art film, and any crossover business it does will be due, in large degree, to the protests and their coverage.

As a written prolog simply states, "Last Temptation" aims to be a "fictional exploration of the eternal spiritual conflict," "the battle between the spirit and the flesh," as Nikos Kazantzakis summarized the theme of his novel. As with "Amadeus," "Last Temptation" — book and film — will put some people's noses out of joint because of its fresh, unorthodox approach to conventionally accepted wisdom. What matters, then, is the strength and creativity with which the new argu-

ments are put forth, not their ultimate verifiability.

Virtually every Hollywood treatment of the life of Christ has taken a reverential approach, usually characterized by inspirational readings of scripture, grandiose spectacle and swelling music. Most have proved less than satisfactory. From the opening scene here, there is no question director Martin Scorsese and screenwriter Paul Schrader are tackling the subject from a very different angle.

Seized with convulsive headaches, this Jesus writhes in the agony of indecisiveness, uncertain whether the voices he hears come from God or Satan, and charged by his closest friend, Judas, with being a collaborator for using his skills as a carpenter to build crosses for use by the Romans in crucifixions.

After rescuing Mary Magdalene from the stone-throwers, Jesus tentatively launches his career as religious leader, preaching the gospel of love. But his fear and doubt overcome him, and it is only after his return from the desert and his hallucinatory exposure to representations of good and evil, that he is transformed into a warrior against Satan, performing miracles and finally convinced he is the son of God.

The combative relationship between Jesus and Judas receives dramatic emphasis here, and one of the most provocative aspects of the screenplay has Jesus commanding his most loyal supporter to betray him, to the latter's distress.

Staged so as to intensely convey the suffering involved, Jesus finally is put on the cross, whereupon the profound struggle between the spirit and the flesh reasserts itself in a long dream sequence that both contains the source of film's controversy and is the linchpin of Scorsese, Schrader and Kazantzakis' thematic investigation.

In this serene, carefully cadenced flight of fancy, Jesus finds himself approached on the cross by a guardian angel in the guise of an exquisite young girl. He accepts her offer to rescue him and experiences great relief that he is no longer required to be the Messiah.

As the dream continues, Jesus projects what might have been his "normal" life as a mere mortal man. He marries Mary Magdalene and, in the couple of shots from which the most vehement accusations of blasphemy stem, makes love to her. Surrounded by family and friends, Jesus grows old, and calls the evangelist Paul a liar for claiming Jesus died on the cross and was resurrected.

As Jesus lies dying, the everangry Judas reappears, shouts, "Traitor! Your place was on the cross!" and proceeds to demonstrate that his friend had abandoned his holy responsibility, that the lovely guardian angel actually was Satan in disguise. Accepting his fate once and for all, Jesus agrees to "die like a man" and makes his way back to the cross.

To a filmwise viewer, the cumulative effect of all this resembles nothing so much as an inverted variation on Frank Capra's "It's A Wonderful Life." Jesus is made to see that it is only by dying that his life will make a difference, that he cannot forsake his Father and future supporters because of his own acknowledged selfishness and unfaithfulness.

To answer the film's theological critics, most of whom, when they made their accusations, at least, had not seen it, "Last Temptation" follows its own dark and skeptical road to a final embrace of Jesus' uniqueness and divinity.

On the other hand, what this telling gains in making Jesus a dimensional human being, it loses by not supplying a convincing portrait of his spiritual leadership. Partly because of his self-doubts, and also because many of his famous speeches and lessons have been rendered in a very prosaic, flattened-out English, it is difficult to believe this man did enough to distinguish himself from the would-be prophets and saviors running around at the same time, much less that he would change the world.

In general, Scorsese's presentation, as it always has been, is so visceral that the spiritual aspects, and the balance they would provide, are missed. Although the film remains engrossing throughout, some scenes bog down a bit in too much talk, and there are occasional jarring colloquialisms.

Blondish and blue-eyed in the Anglo-Saxon physical tradition of Jesus, Willem Dafoe offers an utterly compelling reading of his character as conceived here, holding the screen with authority at all times. Harvey Keitel puts across Judas' fierceness and loyalty, and only occasionally lets a New York accent and mannered modernism detract from total believability.

Barbara Hershey, adorned with tattoos, is an extremely physical, impassioned Mary Magdalene, Juliette Caton makes a striking impression as the guardian angel, and one could have used more of David Bowie's subdued, rational Pontius Pilate. Others, including Harry Dean Stanton as Paul, André Gregory as John the Baptist and Verna Bloom as Mary, are all of a piece with the director's highly energetic style.

Working on Moroccan locations with a highly restrictive $6,500,000 budget, Scorsese has turned out a terrifically impressive looking film. Pic looks spare but rich, rough yet elegant, with lenser Michael Ballhaus, production designer John Beard, costume designer Jean-Pierre Delifer and editor Thelma Schoonmaker making critical contributions.

Special note must also be made of Peter Gabriel's exceptionally imaginative score, which uses North African and Middle Eastern musical motifs as its major inspirations and heavily strengthens the impact of the picture. — *Cart.*

Clean And Sober

A Warner Bros. release. Produced by Tony Ganz and Deborah Blum. Executive producer, Ron Howard. Directed by Glenn Gordon Caron. Screenplay, Tod Carroll; camera (Technicolor), Jan Kiesser; editor, Richard Chew; music, Gabriel Yared; sound (Dolby), Ron Judkins; production design, Joel Schiller; art direction, Eric W. Orbom; assistant director, James Simons; coproducer, Jay Daniel; casting, Marion Dougherty, Glenn Daniels. Reviewed at The Burbank Studios, Calif, July 27, 1988. MPAA Rating: R. Running time: 124 MIN.

Daryl Poynter .... Michael Keaton
Charlie Standers .... Kathy Baker
Craig .... Morgan Freeman
Richard .... M. Emmet Walsh
Martin .... Brian Benben
Lenny .... Luca Bercovici
Donald .... Tate Donovan
Xavier .... Henry Judd Baker
Iris .... Claudia Christian
Tiller .... J. David Krassner
Bob .... Dakin Matthews
Cheryl Ann .... Mary Catherine Martin
June .... Pat Quinn

■ Since Hollywood certainly did its best at one time to glamorize drug use, it's about time a film like "Clean And Sober" comes along to deal with the mess left behind. Too bad the easy sell in the fun of going up beats the grim message in coming down.

Covering the first 30 days of attempted recovery by middle-class cocaine addict Michael Keaton, "Sober" is sobering indeed, perhaps too grim. Aside from its unnecessary length, the film's worst failing is its incessantly bleak sentiments. As many recovering addicts and alcoholics know, often it's the laughs at the shared insanity that help them through, one day at a time.

Still, as the story of one group of addicts in one rehab hospital, "Sober" fairly reflects the underlying reality: even those most desirous and most dedicated to recovery aren't likely to make it. As Keaton realistically demonstrates, the lucky few often succeed against their own best efforts to fail.

By necessity, writer Tod Carroll and director Glenn Gordon Caron skim over the mysterious questions of why some people make it and some don't. Except in the skimpiest way, "Sober" avoids the complexities inherent in the fact that the only successful treatment known for chemical abuse is one abuser helping another.

Understandably, writer and director were out to make a drama, not a documentary. Yet for a film about recovery, Keaton's reefer-madness antics consume too much of the running time with old news, adding nothing to what every school kid already has been told about the dangers of addiction. Common sense dictates that anybody who makes it into a recovery program has paid for his chair out in the streets, but what happens next?

"Sober's" fresh challenge was to tackle that — and the challenge is only half met. That's not to say this one story could not be true, but there are so many equally interesting, and far more inspiring, real dramas that could have been drawn upon.

Keaton carries his heavy load well enough, on screen a vast majority of time as a hotshot real estate executive whose cocaine use has gotten him $92,000 into hock on embezzled company money and into bed with a young girl dying of an overdose.

On the run, Keaton decides to hide out in a recovery hospital, attracted more by its policies of strict confidentiality than any desire for rehabilitation. There, he falls under the strict supervision of ex-junkie Morgan Freeman, which will do him good, but also develops a romantic interest in fellow recovering addict Kathy Baker, which won't.

"Sober" chooses to focus on the couple's shared attraction for each other (and cocaine), follows them to a predictable end without making it plain such a liaison between two freshly recovering addicts would have been actively discouraged by everyone around who had more time. It's precisely that kind of omission, where the fundamentals of recovery are sacrificed for dramatic development, which haunts the picture too often.

There's some suspense in whether both of them will make it. Hopefully, the answer might encourage someone in the audience to give recovery a chance. As they say in the programs, "it takes what it takes to get you here" and if "Clean And Sober" saves just one, it will be a worthwhile undertaking whatever the budget and boxoffice. —*Har.*

The Rescue

A Buena Vista release of a Touchstone Pictures presentation, in association with Silver Screen Partners III. Produced by Laura Ziskin. Coproduced by Jim Thomas, John Thomas. Directed by Ferdinand Fairfax. Screenplay, Jim Thomas, John Thomas; camera (color), Russell Boyd; editor, David Holden, Carroll Timothy O'Meara; music, Bruce Broughton; sound (Dolby), Michael Hilkene; production design, Maurice Cain; art direction, Robin Tarsnane; set decoration, Thomas L. Roysden; assistant director, Mark Egerton; second unit director, Max Kleven; aerial unit supervisor, Phil Pastuhov; special effects coordinator, Nick Allder; underwater camera, Ron Taylor; casting, Mary Gail Artz, L.A., Todd M. Thaler, N.Y., Diana Rowan, New Zealand, Norman Ng, Hong Kong. Reviewed at the Avco Center theater, L.A., Aug. 1, 1988. MPAA Rating: PG. Running time: 98 MIN.

J.J. Merrill .... Kevin Dillon
Adrian Phillips .... Christina Harnos
Max Rothman .... Marc Price
Shawn Howard .... Ned Vaughn
Bobby Howard .... Ian Giatti
Commander Howard .... Charles Haid
Commander Merrill .... Edward Albert

■ Hollywood — Comic book characters played by Sylvester Stallone, Chuck Norris and Arnold Schwarzenegger get competition from a group of teens in "The Rescue," a dubious effort from Touchstone/Disney where the kids, sophisticated beyond their years, blow away a whole bunch of Commies without ever exhibiting an ounce of remorse.

One yearns for the Disney of yore upon coming to the closing credits of "The Rescue," an offensive actioner for the impressionable teenage boys who will make up the film's limited b.o. audience. Film should be rated R, like other exploitation pics of the genre.

Where is the spirit of fun, the refreshing inquisitiveness that characters of the less-slick age once used without having to resort to high-tech gadgetry to get them out of sticky situations? If a new age has dawned in juvenile adventure entertainment — as evidenced here — it means imagination and inventiveness has been put aside in favor of quick, facile solutions of questionable morality.

Kevin Dillon, Christina Harnos, Marc Price, Ned Vaughn and Ian Giatti teen children of SEALS (Navy sea, air, land specialists) based in South Korea who steal a power boat and an amazing array of armaments to incredibly maneuver their way behind enemy lines to free their dads from prison in North Korea.

The dads (Charles Haid, Edward Albert among them) get pulled from international waters by a chopper full of North Korean airmen while on a mission to destory an American sub containing top-secret info before the enemy can get their hands on it.

Under the guise of a conflict pitting the SEALS' commander, who wants to rescue his men, against the State Dept., which doesn't want to stir up tensions between the divided Koreas and the U.S. peace-keeping forces, is this handful of vigilante-minded progeny who defy authority and all plausible odds to achieve their aim — not unlike the kinds of feats Norris accomplishes in his "Missing In Action" films.

In the beginning, the kids appear earnest and wholesome enough and scripters Jim Thomas & John Thomas devote about three minutes of screen time to each of them by which we learn that Dillon, for instance, walks around with a chip on his shoulder and Price, the commander's son, is an electronics whiz.

They're plucky — and practically super-human, we soon find out.

The group dodges machinegun fire and rocket launchings in foiling its enemy attackers. Then, this handful of Anglos in a sea of Asians make it to the prison compound unspotted where they handle explosives and brandish firearms like trained killers.

For instance, Dillon, 22 in real life and portrayed younger in the film, holds a pistol like Clint Eastwood — except here there's no attempt to make him act particularly distressed when he kills his first faceless Commie before moving on with his pals to knock a few score more in one great, bloody finale.

This is one production not to remember Ferdinand Fairfax by. The British director of such BBC miniseries as "Winston Churchill — The Wilderness Years" and "Danger: UXB" could have used a more worthy premise than this waste of such beautiful New Zealand, Hong Kong and Macau shoots. —*Brit.*

Stealing Home

A Warner Bros. release of a Mount Co. production. Produced by Thom Mount, Hank Moonjean. Written and directed by Steven Kampmann, Will Aldis. Camera (Technicolor), Bobby Byrne; editor, Anthony Gibbs; music, David Foster; art direction, Vaughan Edwards; set decoration, Robert Franco. Reviewed at the Burbank Studios, Calif., Aug. 2, 1988. MPAA Rating: PG-13. Running time: **98 MIN.**
Billy Wyatt (adult) . . . . Mark Harmon
Ginny Wyatt . . . . Blair Brown
Katie Chandler . . . . Jodie Foster
Alan Appleby (teen) . . Jonathan Silverman
Alan Appleby (adult) . . . . . . Harold Ramis
Sam Wyatt . . . . John Shea
Billy Wyatt (teen) . . . . William McNamara

■ Hollywood — For all the sadness and loss in "Stealing Home," the story of how a privileged boy's love for playing baseball is gone with the sudden death of his father, the film remains too remote emotionally to elicit more than a sigh of relief at its conclusion.

To make the summer of a WASPy preppie more than just a retread of "Summer Of '42," filmmakers needed to create characters that rise above the cliche-ridden characteristics of burying their feelings so way down there appears little reason to care for them — or cry for them. "Stealing Home" won't turn many turnstiles for WB.

There's a loving family living out the dreamy country-club existence in suburban Philadelphia of big homes and summer beach houses where most of the kids are all-American like Billy Wyatt (played at 10, teenage and 38 by Thacher Goodwin, William McNamara and Mark Harmon respectively) and his pal Alan Appleby (Jonathan Silverman, Harol Ramis as teenager and adult). Around for temptation and valuable lessons on how to grow up fast is the wayward and rebellious Katie (Jodie Foster), the family friends' daughter and the irresponsible babysitter that becomes for Billy a mentor, lover and tragic figure.

During their prep school time, everything's a lark to these teenage boys — school, discovering girls, learning to look suave smoking and drinking — except that for Billy, baseball takes priority. It's something he breathes for and something he cherishes sharing with his equally-fanatical baseball-loving dad (John Shea).

Using flashbacks and even flashbacks within flashbacks, we are introduced to Billy (Harmon) as a slovenly, wasted guy cohabiting with a cocktail waitress at a seedy beachside motel when he gets a call from mom (Blair Brown) that Katie has killed herself and he has been named in the will to dispose of her ashes.

For all the pain one would feel for a close friend who meant so much to an individual's emotional makeup — even personality — Harmon remains strangely aloof and detached.

To have the actor (whose image is deservedly clean cut) unshaven and smoking incessantly, appear so unappealing does little to dispel the notion that he is merely in a temporary state before rediscovering his Main Line roots.

What pathos and anxiety that isn't getting through his stoicism as he sits and stares out the window on the long ride home presumably comes from his bittersweet reminiscences. Being nostalgic doesn't necessarily translate to much more than just retelling of a too familiar tale — as these are.

Much of the screen time is given over to Billy as a teenager (McNamara, who bears an uncanny resemblance to a young Ricky Nelson, Harmon's late real-life brother-in-law), as he learns about love through his parents, sex through a loose g.f. and camaraderie through his buddy. Rather than conjuring up a swell of feelings, it's as if a third person standing off to the side were taking a home movie of the goings-on. Nothing is particularly telling or interesting about these visits with an average boy of well-off parents of the late-1950s, early 1960s.

The acceptance of death does not come easily to too many people — even for WASPs, as "Ordinary People" so beautifully explored — though here Billy learns of a second untimely death, by the greater tragedy of suicide, and copes with it by reverting to his adolescence.

Foster's complex and confused character would have been the better choice upon which to center this melodrama. The actress is perfect for the part and, along with Ramis' warm and funny short screen time as the adult Alan, brought whatever emotional energy there was to the proceedings.

Castings of Shea and Brown are quintessentially correct in the upper-crust roles and McNamara, in looks for sure, also perfect as their preppie son.

Script by codirectors Steven Kampmann, Will Aldis is well-structured if predictable in all its plot points, though the dialog is too stilted.

Technically, production is fine all around and Bobby Byrne's lensing on location in Pennsylvania and New Jersey gives the appropriate bleached-wood and/or Chippendale wash to everything. — *Brit.*

Hero And The Terror

A Cannon Films release. Produced by Raymond Wagner. Executive producers, Menahem Golan, Yoram Globus. Directed by William Tannen. Screenplay, Dennis Shryack, Michael Blodgett, based on Blodgett's novel; camera (TVC color), Eric Van Haren Noman; editor, Christian Adam Wagner; music, David Frank; sound, Kim Ornitz; production design, Holger Gross; art direction, Douglas Dick, Mark Haskins; assistant director, Frank Bueno; associate producer, John Zane; casting, Caroline Zelder. Reviewed at Cannon Films, L.A., Aug. 1, 1988. MPAA Rating: R. Running time: **96 MIN.**
O'Brien . . . . Chuck Norris
Kay . . . . Brynn Thayer
Robinson . . . . Steve James
Simon Moon . . . . Jack O'Halloran
Dwight . . . . Jeffrey Kramer
Mayor . . . . Ron O'Neal
Theater manager . . . . Murphy Dunne

■ Hollywood — Trying to broaden his audience appeal, "Hero And The Terror" takes Chuck Norris on a detailed and deliberate tour of the refurbished Wiltern Theater in Los Angeles, which should delight any historical preservation group interested in urban renewal. Norris' usual kung-fu fans may be disappointed, however.

As a career departure, "Hero" is actually harmless enough. When not whirling and whopping, Norris has always shown a pleasant screen personality. He's no great dramatic force, of course, but he can handle the role of a human being believably.

Thus, Norris gets to enjoy a romantic interest in Brynn Thayer and the impending birth of their child, which allows him to practice portraying love and tenderness. What's more, policeman Norris lives in fear of meeting up again with The Terror (Jack O'Halloran), which allows him to practice portraying emotional frailty.

It's his search of the crooks and crannies of the Wiltern (and a few other points of historical interest on the Santa Monica pier) that consume an immense amount of the picture's running time. With flashlight and pistol at the ready, Norris proves to be quite an accomplished searcher, poking here, probing there, looking into one opening after another and finding nothing. Weighed as he is by his humanly concerns, it's exciting stuff.

Yet you have to give The Terror credit, too. For someone 6'6" and weighing several jillion pounds, O'Halloran is a terrific hider. Even when he's wandering around with a body over his shoulder, nobody ever seems to notice him.

Norris has good reason to fear The Terror because he's encountered him once before, storing dead girls at the pier. They had a terrible fight then and Norris got all the credit as a hero for his single-handed arrest. Deep inside Norris knows The Terror actually knocked himself out falling down a ladder with the cop atop him.

That's no big problem, though, so long as the killer is safely locked up. As it's easy to tell from his evil, ugly teeth, The Terror has been saving his dental floss for something else and, sure enough, while the guards aren't looking he flosses through the iron bars and escapes.

Unfortunately, while getting away, The Terror drives the truck off a cliff and into the river, where his body is never discovered.

Sure enough, The Terror ha washed ashore somehow in midtown Los Angeles and taken up residence at the Wiltern, where it suddenly becomes unsafe for ladies to use the restroom. Meanwhile, Norris has been cuddling and showing concern for Thayer and whether she will marry him once the baby arrives.

The Hero needn't have wasted all that fear on meeting up with The Terror again. In a fight scene that's hardly worth the seeking, Norris quickly teaches that big bully a thing or two. With a wince and a limp, it's back to the hospital for a reunion with the little woman and the baby.

Everything finishes on a freeze frame, a sure sign of a happy, humanly ending.—*Har.*

Mauri
(NEW ZEALAND)

An Awatea Films presentation. Produced and directed by Merata Mita. Screenplay, Mita; camera (color), Graeme Cowley; editor, Nicholas Beauman; music, Hirini Melbourne; production design, Ralph Hotere; sound, Gethin Creagh. Reviewed at Wellington Film Festival, Embassy theater, Wellington, N.Z., July 21, 1988. Running time: **99 MIN.**
Rewi Rapana . . . . Anzac Wallace
Kara . . . . Eva Rickard
Steve . . . . James Heyward
Ramari . . . . Susan D. Ramari Paul
Hemi . . . . Sonny Waru
Awatea . . . . Rangimarie Delamere
Willie Rapana . . . . Willie Raana
Mr. Semmens . . . . Geoff Murphy

■ Wellington — Merata Mita's first feature, "Mauri," is a brave attempt to fuse film genres into an epic story with recurring themes of birth, life and death.

Set in a small New Zealand community of the late 1950s, the pic is superbly mounted (lensing by Graeme Cowley) but lacks that clarity of storyline and convincing character motivation/interplay necessary to achieve its ambitions.

A confused focus, and some inexperienced acting, ultimately undermine a powerful universal tale.

At one level "Mauri" is suspense. Rewi (Anzac Wallace), on the run from prison, finds refuge in a Maori community. His presence is mysterious and ambiguous, even though he professes kin connections. An old woman, Kara (Eva Rickard), befriends him without too many questions, and Ramari (Susan Paul) falls in love with him even though she is determined to marry a European, Steve (James Heyward).

On another level "Mauri" is about a rural Maori community under pressure, facing the threat of loss of land and the impact of its young people migrating to the cities.

The most profound intent of "Mauri," which means life force, is to evoke the ebb and flow of a community, and the individual lives that comprise it, through the eyes of a young girl Awatea (Rangimarie Delamere) who lives with Kara.

Juggling these elements of thriller, love story, psychological drama and epic documentary, the story ends with the recapture (but personal redemption) of Rewi, the death of Kara and new awareness for Awatea.

The greatest strengths of "Mauri" lie in its visuals. Cowley's camera tracks the coastal landscape of the setting and delivers big gestures — the sudden pulling of a blind, the swoop of a heron — often with stunning effect. It is not enough.

What the film lacks is a sure, creative center. In its telling, the story proves too disconnected and diffuse with the love triangle involving Rewi, Ramari and Steve underwritten and unconvincing.

While there are flares of inspiration and delight in the performances of Delamere, as Awatea, and Willie Raana, a natural, as Uncle Willy, such moments are rare.

Neither Rickard, as Kara, nor Geoff Murphy, overplaying outrageously as the redneck European, Mr. Semmens, convincingly bear the necessary weight-of-age to make these important characters credible.

"Mauri" will not be easy to market theatrically, outside festival appearances. —Nic.

Vibes

A Columbia Pictures release of an Imagine Entertainment production. Produced by Deborah Blum, Tony Ganz. Executive producer, Ron Howard. Directed by Ken Kwapis. Screenplay, Lowell Ganz, Babaloo Mandel; story, Blum, Lowell Ganz, Mandel; camera (Panavision, color), John Bailey; editor, Carol Littleton; music, James Horner; sound (Dolby), Richard Bryce Goodman; production design, Richard Sawyer; costume design, Ruth Myers; visual effects, Richard Edlund; casting, Carrie Frazier, Shani Ginsburg; coproducer, Ray Hartwick; associate producers, Kate Long, David Wolff. Reviewed at the Directors Guild of America, L.A., July 29, 1988. MPAA Rating: PG. Running time: **99 MIN.**
Sylvia Pickel . . . . Cyndi Lauper
Nick Deezy . . . . Jeff Goldblum
Dr. Harrison Steele . . . . Julian Sands
Ingo Swedlin . . . . Googy Gress
Harry Buscafusco . . . . Peter Falk
Burt Wilder . . . . Michael Lerner
Eli Diamond . . . . Ramon Bieri
Consuela . . . . Elizabeth Peña
Carl . . . . Ronald G. Joseph

■ Hollywood — "Vibes" is another case of an extremely viable premise — two bizarre characters with psychic abilities unwittingly recruited to help in the search for a lost city — that bumps its head badly due to lowbrow execution.

Despite a few engaging moments thanks to its principals, if Columbia had the gift of foreseeing the future they'd have spared themselves from releasing this destined boxoffice migraine.

Cut from the same cloth as "Romancing The Stone," "Vibes" seeks to strike the same balance between playful romantic humor, exotic locales and, in this case, even some firstrate pyrotechnics from effects whiz Richard Edlund. The result should be a big boost for Ecuador tourism and a minor setback to the careers of most of those involved.

The lone exception in that regard may be singer Cyndi Lauper, who in her first starring vehicle — and this doubtless betrays some initial bias — isn't nearly as irritating as one might expect. She actually exhibits some comedic flair, though the Betty Boop speaking voice will likely preclude more serious roles.

Beyond that, unfortunately the surprises all go the other direction, with "Splash" scribes Lowell Ganz and Babaloo Mandell churning out a remarkably pedestrian screenplay of inane innuendoes and 1-liners that sour even in the mouths of Jeff Goldblum and Peter Falk.

Lauper and Goldblum play two standout psychics who meet amid a pool of six assembled by a Dr. Steele (Julian Sands) to test their mental powers. He has the ability to see events relating to objects by touching them, while she has a spirit contact who provides her with limited ability to predict the future.

Falk recruits them originally to help find his lost son, only to later reveal (neither could sense he was lying?) he actually wants their help in locating a "city of gold" that, legend has it, sits deep in the mountains.

The city, however, is actually a bastion of psychic power, and the trio is pursued by a rival group — fronted by another one of the psychics (Googy Gress) — that will stop at nothing to beat them to the site.

It's all rather interesting at the outset — particularly when we're introduced to Goldblum's ability, as he discovers his girlfriend's infidelity by touching her panties.

Still, the plane soon touches down in Ecuador and the movie crashes, struggling through a series of rather lame episodes as the inevitable romantic bond is forged between Goldblum and Lauper.

The biggest shame is how the film squanders Goldblum, whose neurotic eyes and twitching manner make him a perfect choice for someone gifted/cursed with second sight. The problem is that the script has him dashing off snappy, James Bond-esque 1-liners in moments of crisis that prove completely incongruous and serve to undermine any sympathy one might feel for him. The same goes to an even larger extent for Falk's character, who, like a bad greeting card, has a stupid line for every occasion.

Peripheral characters, under the guidance of director Ken Kwapis, are generally undistinguished. Elizabeth Peña is a nice cameo as a vamp who tries to seduce and then kill Goldblum, while Gress has an odd accent/speech impediment that draws an initial chuckle and, like most everything else here, ultimately proves annoying due to overexposure.

Technical side is generally okay, with a few breathtaking settings and a nifty, lighthearted score by James Horner. Still, the thinly veiled pitch for a potential sequel at pic's end suggests no one picked up any vibes from a sure-to-be-underwhelmed public during filming. — Bril.

Door
(JAPANESE)

A Joy Pack Film release of an Agent 21-Directors Co. coproduction. Produced by Fumio Takahashi. Planning by Satoshi Watanabe. Directed by Banmei Takahashi. Screenplay, Takahashi, Naka Nogawa; camera (color), Yahsushi Sasakihara; lighting, Yutaka Iwasaki; sound, Shin Fukuda; art, Terumi Hosoishi; editor, Junichi Kikuchi; music, Moritsune Tsuno; special makeup, Tomoo Harughuchi; associate producer, Kosuke Hisasato. Reviewed at Shinjuku Toei Palace 2, Tokyo, June 23, 1988. Running time: **95 MIN.**
Haruko Honda . . . . Keiko Takahashi
Yamakawa the salesman . Daijiro Tsutsumi
Satoshi Honda . . . . Shiro Shimomoto
Takuto Honda . . . . Takuto Maizu

■ Tokyo — "Door" is an understated but very effective horror feature that eschews reliance on special effects and concentrates, for the most part, on psychological suspense.

Keiko Takahashi (the actress previously known as Keiko Sekine) is a housewife terrorized by a door-to-door salesman, Daijoro Tsutsumi, after she slams her front door on his hand.

For director Banmei Takahashi, offscreen husband of Keiko and coauthor of the screenplay with Naka Nogawa, doors swing both ways, not only protecting those inside from a society's minor dysfunctions (an unseen individual who deposits a trashbag on the doorstep, persistent salesmen, obscene phone callers), but also serving to isolate, to forestall any sense of community in what is putatively a group-oriented culture.

Human relationships are compartmentalized, defined almost solely in terms of whom doors are opened and closed to. Those doors can be either literal or figurative, as in the case of the unsympathetic policeman who speaks to the housewife literally face-to-face but figuratively as through a door, his voice electronically altered on the soundtrack to suggest his distance from the woman.

Technically, this tale of a knife-wielding maniac works because the director understands the most important cutting does not take place in front of the camera.

He is perhaps too intent on paying homage to "The Shining," both with an early traveling shot of an apartment building's corridors that recalls the Steadicam roaming through the hotel in Stanley Kubrick's earlier film, as well as with the salesman's chainsaw assault on a locked bathroom door that is an imitation of Nicholson's mad axing. Yet during most of its 95 minutes, Takahashi's exercise in edge-of-the-seat entertainment succeeds very well indeed. —Bail.

La Lumiere du Lac
(The Light Of The Lake)
(FRENCH)

An Erato Films/Canal Plus production in association with Sofintergie and Sofica Creations. Produced by Daniel Toscan du Plantier. Written and directed by Francesca Comencini. Camera (color), Denis Lenoir; editor, Agnes Guillemot. Reviewed at Barcelona Film Festival (competing), July 2, 1988. Running time: **90 MIN.**
With: Nicole Garcia, Wadeck Stanczak, Francesca Romana Prandi, Jean-Louis Barrault, Madeleine Renaud.

■ Barcelona — Can a reclusive, poetic, highbrow femme novelist living alone in a sequestered lakeside cabin find True Love with a city slicker-gigolo on the lam? Francesca Comencini in this improbable and moody study in solitude seems to think she can, though most audiences will see the absurdity of the misalliance from the start.

"The Light Of The Lake" dwells upon the interrelations between the novelist and the gigolo and former's relationship with a neighboring mixed up girl, also desperately unhappy. Latter in turn cares for an old man (Jean-Louis Barrault), also unhappy, with an obsession for sunflowers, which he moons over as a symbol of unrequited love.

Slowmoving, sentimental, at times poetic, pic fails to adequately explain the motivations of the principals; nor does it explore their passivity. This is the sort of film made by esthetes for others of their ilk, where Victor Hugo is quoted and sex is antiseptic.

The predictable denouement (the gigolo is shot by the mafiosi) is as deadpan as most of what precedes it. The light on the lake never illuminates, it only flickers feebly on the sad and unhappy losers living out their cowed despair. —Besa.

Die Schauspielerin
(The Actress)
(EAST GERMAN)

A DEFA production and release. Directed by Siegfried Kuhn. Screenplay, Regine Kuhn.

from the novel "Arrangement With Death" by Hedda Zinner; camera (Orwocolor), Peter Ziesche; editor, Brigitte Krex; music, Stephan Carow; sound, Klaus Heidemann; costumes, Katrine Cremer; assistant director, Roland Helia; camera assistant, Frank Bredow. Reviewed at Karlovy Vary Film Festival, July 9, 1988. Running time: **89 MIN.**

Maria Rheine	Corinna Harfouch
Mark Lowenthal	Andre Hennicke
Mario Montegasso	Michael Gwisdek

Also with: Blanche Kommerell, Jurgen Watzke, Martin Brand and Steffie Spira.

■ **Karlovy Vary — Director Siegfried Kuhn has used a novel by Hedda Zinner as the basis for his film about the love between two actors who work at a small German theater before the war. She is Maria Rheine, a striking blond; he, Mark Lowenthal, dark and Jewish.**

Film traces their relationship during an increasingly difficult time as Nazism got itself into gear. The advent of the Nuremberg Laws forbidding interracial marriages causes Maria to face up to a choice between her love for the theater with the increasingly larger roles she is obtaining and her love for Mark who has gone to work for a Jewish theater in Berlin.

The theme is nothing new in cinema, of course, with "Mephisto" being a notable recent example, as well as the Austrian film " '38." In East Germany itself, Kurt Maetzig's "Marriage In The Shadows" took the same theme.

Corinna Harfouch provides the main reason for seeing this version and deservedly picked up the best actress award at Karlovy Vary, giving a good performance as the budding actress, moving confidently into her "theatrical" roles on stage. Not so convincing is her escape and transformation into a dark-haired Jewish woman; narrative logic leaves the film at times, and we are not spared some Jewish cliches that make one wonder about the author's intentions.

Film lacks the power and sweep of say "Mephisto" and the limited budget shows in the outdoor scenes which have an underfed look to them.

Other technical credits are up to standard. —*Cain.*

Color escondido
(Hidden Color)
(ARGENTINE)

A Distrifilms release. Produced and directed by Raúl de la Torre. Screenplay, De la Torre "with the collaboration of" Diana Nikutowski; camera (color), Enrique Medina; music, a collage of tunes assembled by De la Torre, Edgardo Rudnitzky, Victor Melillo, Daniel Fainzilber; sets, Abel Facello. Reviewed at Distrifilms screening room, Buenos Aires, May 23, 1988. (Rating in Argentina: forbidden for under 18s.) Running time: **92 MIN.**

Helena	Carola Reyna
Mario	Gastón Carvallo
Three Graces	Rosario Blefari, Vanessa Miller, Virginia Innocenti
Boss	Silvia Dabove
Marta	Maria Socas
Ex-husband	Carlos Evaristo
Mother	Regina Lamm

Father	Juan Alberto Croce

■ **Buenos Aires — Exceptionally beautiful color photography is the hallmark of this probe into a young woman's psyche — particularly her grappling with an Elektra complex — by one of Argentina's leading helmers, Raúl de la Torre.**

De la Torre's prior films almost invariably have delved into the psychological makeup of young women, sometimes also emphasizing their social circumstances.

The difference is that while on previous occasions he peeled their minds open through the skillful use of dialog, here De la Torre advances the story almost wordlessly, through his heroine's actions, reveries, recollections and imaginings.

Beginning with a scene in which Helena, on her way home from work, imagines that three boisterous youths who barge into her train carriage are raping her, we follow her real and mental encounters with a former husband who betrayed her, her current and true love, her disapproving boss and other threatening figures, a mysterious man who peeps at her, etc. All the while three female characters (described in the pressbook as three Graces) act as a kind of wordless chorus.

There is much nudity and sex, and Helena disrobes so often it may become tiresome.

The film has the look of a glossy commercial. "Hidden Color" probably would have made a splendid visual poem at around 45 minutes, but film distribution demands no feature be significantly shorter than twice that. Helena's problems are resolved neatly at the end, but by that time she may have overstayed her welcome. —*Olas.*

Sussi
(CHILEAN)

An Area production in association with ZDF (Germany) and Anabasse Films (France). Executive producer, Alberto Celery. Directed by Gonzalo Justiniano. Screenplay, Justiniano and Gustavo Frias; camera (color), Jorge Roth; editor, Claudio Martinez; music, Tomás Lefever, Claudio Lefever, Mará José Levin, Sebastián Piga; sound, Eugenio Gutierrez; costumes, Kaioia Sota, Estela Fernandez. Reviewed at Rex II, Santiago, Chile, July 19, 1988. Running time: **111 MIN.**

With: Marcela Osorio (Sussi), Bastián Bodenhofer, Jaime Celedón, Malucha Pinto, Miriam Palacios, Cristián Campos, Maria Corvinos, Patricia Rivadeneira, Javier Maldonado, Luis Alarcon, Alberto Chacon, Pablo Lavin, Pola Monbano.

■ **Santiago — Gonzalo Justiniano's second film "Sussi" stands a fair chance of becoming one of the year's top 10 in its home market, but is unlikely to obtain similar results abroad, largely due to an uneven screenplay and an inconclusive nonending.**

Story deals with Sussi, the little country girl who comes to the big city (Santiago), landing in a small boardinghouse with two well-meaning but rather ridiculous older women, plus an eccentric (if not outright dotty) student she falls in love with. Employment at a hospital doesn't work out because everyone makes passes at her.

A job at a sleazy nightclub leads to modeling plus an intimate relationship with the head of an influential advertising agency, thanks to which she is chosen as the symbol of Chilean women in a large but unidentified campaign. At this stage pregnancy is revealed. Her employers want her to abort and continue her modeling work. She wants her student who has disappeared without trace from the boardinghouse and that's that.

The film fails to head in a specific direction and becomes an accumulation of episodes, some quite amusing in themselves, but without either a unifying style or some sort of kaleidoscopic dimension. There is little attempt at directing the actors and each just does his own thing; in some cases, like Jaime Celedón, that's not at all bad. Marcela Osorio's Sussi, buffeted in first one direction, then another, with little chance to develop a personality of her own, shows off her good looks but not her talent. The use of local types and in-jokes may be part of the explanation of the pic's local success. Technical credits are adequate. —*Amig.*

Terminal Entry

A United Film Distribution Co. release (in 1987) of an Intercontinental Releasing presentation, in association with TBA Film A/S. Executive producers, Sandy Cobe, Tom Jenssen. Produced by Sharyon Reis Cobe. Directed by John Kincade. Screenplay, Mark Sobel, David Mickey Evans, from story by Sobel; camera (Foto-Kem color), James L. Carter; editor, Dean Goodhill; music, Gene Hobson; sound, David Waelder; art direction, Alexandra Kicenik; set decoration, Pamela Clouse; production manager-associate producer, Ronnie Hadar; assistant director, Stefani N. Deoul; stunt coordinator, John Michael Stewart; associate producer, Paul Smith; casting, Bresler & Associates. Reviewed on Celebrity Home Entertainment vidcassette, July 13, 1988. MPAA Rating: R. Running time: **98 MIN.**

Capt. Danny Jackson	Eddie Albert
Col. Styles	Yaphet Kotto
Stewart	Paul Smith
Chris	Heidi Helmer
Bob	Patrick Labyorteaux
Dominique	Tracy Brooks Swope

Also with: Yvette Nipar, Rob Stone, Sam Temeles, Jill Terashita, Kabir Bedi, Kavi Raz, Mrzhar Khan, Barbara Edwards.

■ **"Terminal Entry" is an imaginative action feature pumping new life into the video games genre previously spotlighted in such films as "Tron" and "WarGames."**

Pic had brief theatrical exposure last fall ahead of its current video-cassette status. It promises to have a busy afterlife among genre fans.

Topical element deals with Middle East terrorism coming home to roost in the U.S. as Kabir Bedi leads a large group of arab fanatics infiltrating our nation over the Mexican border. Edward Albert is the squad leader and Yaphet Kotto his military boss, both in undermanned positions on the border patrol, and catching hell from their superior, a White House security adviser essayed by Paul Smith (doubling as an associate producer on the film). Things are heating up since a U.N. peace meeting is taking place shortly on the president's California ranch.

Simultaneously, a group of six young computer hackers are spending a weekend at a remote house and tap into a difficult-to-access computer program called Terminal Entry, which they think is a new form of interactive computer fiction (game). Actually it is Bedi's command program for ordering and coordinating acts of assassination and terrorism by his farflung troops.

The premise of the screenplay by Mark Sobel (who previously made the computer-themed film "Access Code") and David Mickey Evans is more ingenious than its predecessor "WarGames" in that the film's action and complications are predicated on the kids not knowing that the game they're playing is the real thing. They blithely order assassinations (carried out on real people) and in a cute twist, hacker Patrick Labyorteaux gets into the true spirit of the competition by assuming the terrorists' point-of-view and making himself and the other five youngsters a target. This leads to a well-staged climax of Albert, Kotto & Co. to the rescue when terrorists attack the kids' house.

Briskly paced (except for some romantic interludes with the kids), film is well-enacted by the adults plus convincing gung-ho computer whips played by Labyorteaux, Rob Stone and Heidi Helmer. Director John Kincade's balance of action and gamesmanship at the computer terminal is solid as are tech credits.

Finale is overly cynical, however, as the kids don't even get their wrists slapped (even though they "ordered" several killings) and Labyorteaux' voiceover during the end credits implies a form of megalomania rather than having learned a lesson.—*Lor.*

Haitian Corner
(GERMAN-FRENCH-U.S.)

A Journal Film, ZDF, Film News Now Foundation presentation of a Klaus Vokenborn (Journal Film), Andreas Schreitmüller (ZDF) production. Produced by Christine Choy, Renee Tajima. Written and directed by Raoul Peck. Camera (color, 16m), Michael Chin; editor, Ailo Auguste-Judith; music, Mino Cinélu; art direction, Kirsten Bates. Reviewed at Locarno Film Festival (competing), Aug. 5, 1988. Running time: **98 MIN.**

Joseph	Patrick Rameau
Sarah	Ailo Auguste-Judith
Hegel	George Wilson

Also with: Emile St. Lot, Jean-Claude Michel, Toto Bissainthe, Jean-Claude Eugene.

■ **Locarno** — **Haitian Raoul Peck, now working in West Germany, applies a familiar formula in dealing with the trauma of a former Tonton Macoute victim, who spent seven years in a Haitian jail and later emigrated to New York.**

His attempts to return to a normal life are shattered when he thinks he recognizes his torturer on the street, and is prepared to sacrifice everything in order to wreak vengeance on him.

While plotwise, the script is simple and unfolds along predictable lines, most of the interest is in the almost documentary fashion Peck uses to describe the life of Haitain refugees in New York, and the inevitable conflict between those who have not left their country of origin (emotionally) and the rest, who are trying to adapt and start a new life in Gotham. Other observations, almost obligatory for the subject, involve the victim's profound sense of shame for having let himself be victimized and the pacts that have to be struck sometimes with the perpetrators of such crimes in order to save other potential victims.

Shot in 16m on a miniature budget in a New York which looks strangely unfamiliar (the way refugees see it), and avoiding, except for one sequence, any explicit violence or brutality, Peck concentrates on what happens in the head of his hero Joseph as he gradually severs all of his relations, obsessed only with revenge.

Acting is rough, spontaneous and sometimes amateurish, but with Haiti back on the front pages after another military coup, it is no wonder this film is doing the festival rounds. —*Edna.*

Filou
(SWISS)

A Christa Saredi presentation of a Dschount Ventschr, Videoladen Zurich production. Directed by Samir. Screenplay, Samir, Martin Witz; camera (color, 16m), Lukas Strebel; editor, Katrin Pluss; music, Ruth Schnydrig, Werner Haltinner, Urs Heistand, Florian Eidenbenz; sound, Florian Eidenbenz; art direction, May Wegmüller, Rolli Altermatt. Reviewed at Locarno Film Festival (competing), Aug. 7, 1988. Running time: **91 MIN.**

Max	Werner Haltinner
Lizzy	Marianne Schmid
Jiri	Stanislav Oriesek

Also with: Hakima Bannwarth, Hans-Ruedi Twerenbold, Michel Hüttner, Luc Schaedler, Markus Kenner, Lorenz Wütrich, Susan Zahnd, Franco Cren.

■ **Locarno** — **A disorganized picture about marginals, with some delightful inventions and some very trite ones, this is the type of rebellious film in the '60s, whose inspiration stems mostly from commercials, with a touch of fashionable anarchy.**

Max, the main character referred to in the title nickname, is an unemployed young man, sharing an apartment with a prostitute who dreams of getting a stand in a spa, and Jiri, a Czech refugee who believes life is over for him and everyone else as well.

Max drifts from one shady deal to another, pushing a little drugs, stealing bicycles or keeping an eye on Lizzy, the prostitute, as she services her clients. He warns her of vicious pimps who do not appreciate the competition. He has his scuffles with the police and the pushers, while searching around for the deal of his life that will make him rich. He also aspires to build a flying machine.

Jumping from one miniplot to another, piling up references and winks to the audience, tributes to other filmmakers and settling his accounts with the tv, by constantly dropping sets from upper floors to the sidewalk all through the film, director Samir keeps the picture moving along diligently, but not always very effectively. The performers lend themselves merrily to this game, and technical quality is remarkable in spite of the low budget and the original Super 16m stock used.

An energetic film debut, it is most likely to find its audiences among the younger set who can sympathize with the spirit of the characters and the unruly pace of the proceedings. — *Edna.*

Zimmer 36
(Room 36)
(SWISS-B&W/COLOR)

A Boa Filmproduction presentation of a Boa/ZDF/Condor Films production. Produced and directed by Markus Fischer. Screenplay, Fischer, Rosemarie Fendel; camera (b&w, color), Jorg Schmidt-Reitwein; editor, Lilo Gerber; music, Alberto Ginastera, Heitor Villa Lobos, Vincenzo Bellini; art direction, Hans Mader, Regula Wetter. Reviewed at Locarno Film Festival (Swiss section), Aug. 6, 1988. Running time: **90 MIN.**

Widow	Babett Arens
Journalist	Peter Cieslinski
Widow's mother	Anne-Marie Blanc

Also with: Volker Prechtel, Christiane Krüger, Horst Warning, Eva Scheurer.

■ **Locarno** — **A neat and visually polished psychological thriller about a journalist investigating the suicide of a man in a hotel that rents rooms by the hour, Markus Fischer's new film is a clear tribute to** *film noir.*

The journalist's enquiry leads him to the dead man's wife, who plays the harp, to her over-possessive and slightly deranged mother, and also to a strange guy by the name of Becker, who keeps a room at the hotel where the suicide was committed.

Pic's mannered direction tends to take the unnatural for the stylish. The story, freely manipulated by Fischer, fits in with established clichés complete with the obligatory nightmare and flashback scenes. It takes place mostly at night and the plot moves arbitrarily, while the actors give forced performances.

Technical credits, however, are superior, the black & white camerawork exemplary, and orchestral music chosen outside the mainstream repertory functions well to preserve moods. Sought after by several festivals, the film will be featured later this month in the Montreal competition. — *Edna.*

La Donna Spezzata
(A Woman Destroyed)
(ITALIAN)

A Sacis presentation of a Fidoscope Intl., RAI 2 production. Produced by Mario Orfini. Directed by Marco Leto. Screenplay, Lucia Drubi Demby, Leto, Léa Massari, based on story by Simone de Beauvoir; camera (color), Aiace Parolin; editor, Giuseppe Giacobino; music, Egisto Macchi; sound, Goffredo Salvatori; art direction, Giancarlo Bartolini Salimbeni; costumes, Claudio Cordaro. Reviewed at Locarno Film Festival (noncompeting), Aug. 6, 1988. Running time: **103 MIN.**

Virginia	Léa Massari
Maurizio	Erland Josephson
Silvano	Jean-Luc Bideau

Also with: Marisa Mantovani, Consuelo Ferrara, Marisa Bartoli, Carla Bizzarri, Francesca Neri, Agnes Blanchot.

■ **Locarno** — **Many critics remember Marco Leto fondly for his 1973 first feature "La Villeggiatura," a debut whose promise was never quite kept by his subsequent work.**

Based on a short story by Simone de Beauvoir, "A Woman Destroyed" describes the case of a woman who falls apart when she discovers, after 25 years of what she believes was a perfect marriage, that her husband has betrayed her. It's a tearjerker, and Leto can't completely overcome all the emotional pitfalls.

Léa Massari is perfect as the lead, beautiful, mature, self-composed and possessing that serenity the film constantly refers to. Whether or not she was long involved with the script, hers is the only solid, well-rounded character in the picture.

Massari's Virginia stands out even more next to a dubbed Erland Josephson as the husband. He looks preposterous with unlikely dark hair and a tan applied by the makeup department, illfitting clothes and a distinctly uncomfortable demeanor. No wonder, since the part is of one note; he is never more than the selfish cad victimizing his wife for no good reason.

There's an attempt to create a comfortable upper-middle-class ambience, but pic succeeds instead in lending the scenery the intimacy of an expensive furniture shop. The editing, which resorts to countless fadeouts, and an over-dramatic score, pull the entire picture straight back into tv-type melodrama.

This may be intentional, since there already is a 3-hour version ready for the small screen.

All other parts are sketchy or parodical, including Jean-Luc Bideau's stint as Virginia's longtime admirer who also is a virtuoso cellist, the two daughters on whom the mother leans in her moments of crisis and the runaway teenager Virginia picks one day on the highway and tries unsuccessfully to help.

Massari announced her decision to retire after this picture; she should try for a better finale.

—*Edna.*

PULA FEST REVIEWS

Za Sada Bez Dobrog Naslova
(Still Lacking A Good Title)
(YUGOSLAV)

A Yugoslavia Film presentation of a Beograd Films, Centar Films production. Written and directed by Srdjan Karanovic. Camera (Fujicolor), Bozidar Nikolic; editor, Branislava Ceperac; music, Zoran Simjanovic; art direction, Aleksandar Denic; costumes, Sasa Kuljaca. Reviewed at Pula Film Festival (competing), July 28, 1988. Running time: **89 MIN.**
Director . . . . Meto Jovanovski
Actress . . . . Mira Furlan
Nadira . . . . Sonja Jacevska
Miloljub . . . . Cedo Orobabic
Also with: Boro Begovic, Vlastimir Djuza Stojiljkovic, Mira Banjac, Mica Tomic, Eva Ras, Abdurahman Salja, Mladen Andrejevic.

■ **Pula — A complex and multileveled satire, rushing at breakneck speed to cover several types of ground at once, ''Still Lacking A Good Title'' is one of the most intriguing and sophisticated pics in Pula this year.**
A film director collects material for a documentary about an incident which took place in Kosovo, the Yugoslav region next to the Albanian border. There the Moslem-Albanian population gradually is forcing the Serbs, already a minority there, to depart. A Young Serb, Miloljub, has fallen in love with an Albanian, Nadira, against the wish of both families. They are about to elope together when the country Romeo is captured by unknowns and emasculated.

The case itself, and the political situation in Kosovo (now a regular front page item in Yugoslavia), are one level of the story. The second is the film within the film, the director's efforts to convince a production house to finance it, in spite of the fact it is not the comedy he had promised them, and the tortuous bureaucratic and financial labyrinths he has to go through. On a third level, there is his tentative romance with a film actress, who at one point is considered for the role of Nadira in a fictional rendering of the story. There is a fourth plot, involving the ethics of such a documentary which evidently exploits two already victimized people and denies them their privacy.

Srdjan Karanovic mixes video footage with film, and forces the viewer to be constantly on his toes. The ironic approach spares nobody, neither the ill-starred lovers, nor Yugoslav law enforcement, scientific pretensions and not the local film industry, a subject on which he is particularly virulent.

First and foremost a virtuoso piece for Karanovic, pic features a tense, sympathetic performance from Meto Jankovski as the director, and simple, touching ones from Sonja Jacevska and Cedo Odobabic as the two lovers. Rest of the cast,

a combination of professionals and amateurs, is beyond reproach. Photography is not always exemplary, but video footage is well integrated. Pulsating score sustain the fast pace, and exemplary editing avoids mixing the issues.

Not an easy picture to assimilate away from its home ground, it is however a natural for arthouses and festivals, with Montreal and London already having picked it up for their next editions. —Edna.

Kuca Pored Pruge
(The House By The Railway Tracks)
(YUGOSLAV)

A Yugoslavija Film release of an Avala Films production. Written and directed by Zarko Dragojevic. Camera (color), Milos Spasojevic; editor, Snezana Ivanovic; music, Vojkan Borisavljevic; sound, Milan Davidovic, Marko Rodic; art direction, Vladislav Lasic; costumes, Olgica Pavlovic. Reviewed at Pula Film Festival (competing), July 28, 1988. Running time: **107 MIN.**
Stanisha . . . . Ljubisha Samardzic
Mitar . . . . Slobodan Bestic
Kosovka . . . . Andelka Milivojevic
Bozidar . . . . Meto Jovanovski
Also with: Dusica Zegarac, Zaim Muzaferija, Dubravko Jovanovic.

■ **Pula — ''Kuca Pored Pruge'' is another topical drama about the ethnic troubles in Kosovo, on the Albanian border, a part of Yugoslavia which has a strong separatist movement of the Albanian population, Moslems who are now the vast majority there.**
A Serbian family, forced to leave Kosovo and go north into Serbia, finds it extremely difficult to adjust to the people and the place in their new home, particularly since nobody seems very keen to welcome them. Starting with a squabble over the right to build on the land between two houses, and ending with a message of hope in the midst of tragedy, if offers in between a timid romance for the daughter, the parents' hopeless trip back to Kosovo in search of a healer for the mother's emotional breakdown, and the son's attempt to make some badly needed easy money by stealing dynamite and selling it on the black market.

The picture painted is not a pretty one. The family fled Kosovo after the daughter was raped by Moslems in front of her mother; the law didn't do a thing to punish the perpetrators. The family tombs they left behind were desecrated, their fear of the new environment is reciprocated by the animosity of their neighbors, and discrimination, poverty and ignorance threaten to deal them a deadly blow at any minute. The downbeat image is relieved to a great extent by the sympathy

for the characters which transcends the miserableness of their conditions.

This is best exemplified by Meto Jovanovski's refreshing performance as a friend of the family, a bus driver who left Kosovo 15 years before and feels protective towards his newly arrived friends. Ljubisha Samardzic, a familiar face on the local screens as the father, Slobodan Bestic and Andelka Milivojevic as his offspring give creditable performances. Director Zarko Dragojevic adds touches of political satire, the best being the moment when the police are afraid to tear down a wall, because a picture of Tito and a Yugoslav flag had been hung on it.

Photography has the rough edge to be expected in this type of gritty realism, and locations are carefully chosen to avoid any trace of glamor and stick to the general mood of the picture. The trip to Kosovo, however, unveils a corner of the country not often seen on the screen, a strange combination of Western and Islamic influences.

Inscribing itself in the line of humane political films Yugoslavia has a reputation for, this is a promising debut for Dragojevic, whose previous experience was limited to short subjects and documentaries.
—Edna.

Buster
(BRITISH)

A Tri-Star Pictures release from Hemdale of The Movie Group presentation of an NFH production. Produced by Norma Heyman. Executive producers, Frank Giustra, Peter Strauss. Directed by David Green. Screenplay, David Shindler; camera (color), Tony Imi; editor, Lesley Walker; music, Anne Dudley; production design, Simon Holland; art direction, Clinton Cavers; set dresser, Crispian Sallis; costume design, Evangeline Harrison; sound, Ken Weston; associate producer, Redmond Morris; casting, Debbie McWilliams. Reviewed at Bijou Preview theater, London, Aug. 15, 1988. Running time: **103 MIN.**
Buster . . . . Phil Collins
June . . . . Julie Walters
Bruce . . . . Larry Lamb
Franny . . . . Stephanie Lawrence
Nicky . . . . Ellen Beaven
Harry . . . . Michael Attwell
Ronnie . . . . Ralph Brown
George . . . . Christopher Ellison
Mrs. Kothery . . . . Sheila Hancock
Inspector Mitchell . . . . Martin Jarvis
Sgt. Chalmers . . . . Clive Wood
Sir James McDowell . . . . . Anthony Quayle

■ **London — ''Buster'' is part romantic comedy, part crime thriller and part moral tale, but more importantly it features a charismatic big screen bow by popster Phil Collins in the title role. Pic could click offshore if handled properly.**

Though archetypically British in many ways, the film may travel more easily because of the Collins name and his voice on the soundtrack. His natural charm and exuberance are given full rein to the extent that his normally spirited costar Julie Walters gives an unusually restrained performance.

Pic opens in London of 1963 with self-proclaimed smalltime ''lucky thief'' Phil Collins stealing clothes from a showroom dummy for a funeral and raiding a children's shop to get items for his family's new baby. He and Walters are blissfully happy, but she dreams of buying a house so they don't have to hide behind the sofa every time the rent man comes around.

Collins gets involved in a scheme to rob a Royal Mail train of £2,600,000, and when the gang pulls off the raid, hailed as The Great Train Robbery, they find themselves regarded as folk heroes.

Collins, wife Walters and daughter Ellen Beaven go into hiding, but police pressure mounts and the family is forced to go on the run to Switzerland and finally Acapulco. In Mexico, the Collins-Walters marriage is stretched as the two try and adjust to a totally alien environment.

Walters eventually leaves for England and Collins follows, despite the fact that he knows he will be caught and sent to jail. Pic ends with Collins, now out of jail, selling flowers by the River Thames in contempo London.

''Buster'' can't seem to make up its mind what sort of film it is. It plays as a romantic comedy to begin with, then switches to a caper pic before ending with domestic drama.

Helmer David Green directs all aspects well, adding nice insights into the characters, especially when in Mexico, but there is an overall feeling that the pic is slightly disjointed.

"Buster" is full of little comic gems, mainly from Collins, who plays Buster Edwards with impish charm, but the script is a little heavy-handed when it comes to regular references to the couple's "dream," whether it be getting to Mexico or stealing the money.

The train robbery scenes are excellently handled, with fine work by cinematographer Tony Imi, and most amusing is the sight of the xenophobic Brits Collins and Walters taking to the Mexican beaches still dressed as if for London in spring.

Singer/songwriter Collins, who acted in an episode of "Miami Vice" and as a youngster performed in the musical "Oliver" in the West End, seems totally at home in front of the camera, but then his role as a jokey Londoner is not far from his real character. Walters is much more restrained, but still more than holds her own in the acting stakes.

An excellent supporting cast gives the pic strength in depth, with nice cameo performances turned in by Sheila Hancock as Walters' mother and Anthony Quayle as a government official who manipulates harsh prison sentences for the train robbers.

The end of the pic sees an older Collins talking directly to the camera, a ploy that tries to recapture the lighter side of the film. "Buster" is essentially a love story with that favorite old message that crime just doesn't pay. —*Adam.*

Gost
(The Visitor)
(SOVIET-B&W)

A Sovexportfilm presentation of a Mosfilm/Lenfilm production. Directed by Aleksandr Kaidanovski. Screenplay, Kaidanovski, inspired by "St. Mark's Passion" and "The Betrayal Of Judas" by Jorge Luis Borges; camera (b&w), Y. Rezditski; art direction, Marina Assisjan; costumes, Elena Ostrogorskaya. Reviewed at Locarno Film Festival, Aug. 8, 1988. Running time: **88 MIN.**
With: N. Ispoulatous (the visitor), L. Abachidze, L. Pilmani, N. Koundoukhov, S. Panfilova.

■ Locarno — A former Andrei Tarkovsky actor and obviously a spiritual disciple to judge by this film, Aleksandr Kaidanovski's first effort is a mystical exploration of the Christian myth, which could eventually be also read as a grim satire of narrow-minded religious or political dogmatism.

Inspired by two Jorge Luis Borges novels, the script places this new version of the Passion in a remote, isolated mansion. A 33-year-old intellectual comes to visit and is left in charge of the place, with three servants to take care of him, a father, his son and his daughter, all of them primitives who barely know the use of language, communicating mostly by incomprehensible grunts.

While attempting to produce a personal interpretation for Judas' treason and Christ's sacrifice, the intellectual acquaints his caretakers with civilization through the Holy Book, reading to them the story of the crucifixion as a parable of Christ's sacrifice for mankind's redemption. His audience takes the text literally, seeing in the visitor a new incarnation of the Son of Man and they subject him to the same treatment, possibly to be redeemed by his death.

Almost a companion piece to Martin Scorsese's "The Last Temptation Of Christ" (Kaidanovski also has his Messianic protagonist make love to the daughter), this can be taken in the spirit of Dostoievski who argued that had Christ returned to Earth he would have been recrucified. It can also be a metaphor on blind faith, be it religious or political, and its deadly results.

Replete with moody scenes and significant, over-amplified heavy breathing, pic is shot in black and white which can be one moment strikingly luminous and the next fuzzily somber. It has long passages of gloomy introspection, building up elaborate atmosphere at the expense of plot.

As a first effort, it shows visual imagination and an original approach but is too self-indulgent and not sufficiently coherent. —*Edna.*

A Nightmare On Elm Street 4: The Dream Master

A New Line Cinema release of a New Line Cinema, Heron Communications and Smart Egg Pictures presentation of a Robert Shaye production. Produced by Shaye, Rachel Talalay. Executive producers, Sara Risher, Stephen Diener. Directed by Renny Harlin. Screenplay, Brian Helgeland, Scott Pierce, from story by William Kotzwinkle, Helgeland, based on characters created by Wes Craven; camera (Metrocolor), Steven Fierberg; editor, Michael N. Knue, Chuck Weiss; music, Craig Safan; production design, Mick Strawn, C.J. Strawn; art direction, Thomas A. O'Conor; makeup effects, Steve Johnson, Magical Media Industries, Screaming Mad George, R. Christopher Biggs; Freddy Krueger makeup, Kevin Yagher; mechanical special effects, Image Engineering; special visual effects, Dream Quest Images; associate producer-production manager, Karen Koch; assistant director, Mary Ellen Woods; second unit directors, Peter Chesney, T.G. Vujovich; casting, Annette Benson; in Dolby stereo. Reviewed at Mark Goodson theater, N.Y., Aug. 12, 1988. MPAA Rating: R. Running time: **93 MIN.**

Freddy Krueger	Robert Englund
Alice	Lisa Wilcox
Joey	Rodney Eastman
Danny	Danny Hassel
Rick	Andras Jones
Kristen Parker	Tuesday Knight
Sheila	Toy Newkirk
Kincaid	Ken Sagoes
Debbie	Brooke Theiss
Elaine Parker	Brooke Bundy

Also with: Jeff Levine, Nicolas Mele, Hope Marie Carlton, Robert Shaye, Linnea Quigley.

■ **Imaginative special effects highlight the fourth entry in the "Nightmare On Elm Street" series, giving indie distrib New Line a crowd-pleasing pic fully capable of competing with major distrib releases as a leading boxoffice draw.**

Extending a winning formula, streamlined approach here emphasizes the elaborate physical, visual and makeup effects (credited scene by scene in well-annotated end titles) plus the black humor of monster Freddy Krueger's funny 1-liners. Modest storyline picks up from the end of Part 3, with three surviving youngsters afraid to sleep since undead Freddy literally tries to kill them in their dreams.

As before, he's out for revenge on the kids of Elm Street for their parents' having murdered him after he killed several children in the first place. Freddy's conjured up in the kids' nightmares and a clever plot has him rapidly (and unexpectedly) dispensing with the surviving kids, only to extend his mayhem to their friends, starting with Alice (Lisa Wilcox).

Spectacular climax, in which the trapped bodies (representing souls) of Freddy's victims squirm out of an oversize model of his torso, seemingly dispenses with the baddie forever, but a tag scene fully indicates he'll be brought back again for Part 5.

Wilcox in the lead role resembles a teen Blair Brown and gives a solid performance ranging from vulnerable to resourceful, as she gains strength from her departed friends to do battle with Freddy. Casting brings back several thesps from Part 3 (Rodney Eastman, Ken Sagoes, Brooke Bundy) while substituting dissimilar Tuesday Knight in Patricia Arquette's role.

Robert Englund, receiving star billing for the first time, is delightful in his frequent incarnations as Freddy, delivering his gag lines with relish and making the grisly proceedings funny.

Finnish director Renny Harlin, who previously helmed "Prison" and "Born American," does an excellent job maintaining a brisk pace that succeeds in allaying disbelief. He's aided by the fluid camerawork, including novel overhead shots, of Steven Fierberg and atmospheric design by Mick and C.J. Strawn.

The effects artists contribute arresting set pieces, ranging from Freddy turning victim Brooke Theiss into an insect trapped in a Roach Motel to asthmatic Toy Newkirk literally having the life sucked out of her by his kiss.

— *Lor.*

Young Guns

A 20th Century Fox release of a James G. Robinson and Joe Roth presentation of a Morgan Creek production. Produced by Roth, Christopher Cain. Coproducers, Irby Smith, Paul Schiff. Executive producers, John Fusco, Robinson. Directed by Cain. Screenplay, Fusco; camera (Deluxe color), Dean Semler; editor, Jack Hofstra; music, Anthony Marinelli, Brian Banks; production design, Jane Musky; art direction, Harold Thrasher; set decoration, Robert Kracik; costume design, Richard Hornung; sound (Dolby), Carey Lindley; sound design, supervision, Mike Minkler, Wylie Stateman; assistant director, Myers; casting, Penny Perry. Reviewed at UA Coronet, L.A., Aug. 10, 1988. MPAA Rating: R. Running time: **107 MIN.**

William H. Bonney	Emilio Estevez
Doc Scurlock	Kiefer Sutherland
Chavez Y Chavez	Lou Diamond Phillips
Dick Brewer	Charlie Sheen
Dirty Stephens	Dermot Mulroney
Charley Bowdre	Casey Siemaszko
John Tunstall	Terence Stamp
L.G. Murphy	Jack Palance
Alex McSween	Terry O'Quinn
Susan McSween	Sharon Thomas
J. McCloskey	Geoffrey Blake
Yen Sun	Alice Carter
Buckshot Roberts	Brian Keith
Texas Joe Grant	Tom Callaway
Pat Garrett	Patrick Wayne

■ **Hollywood — "Young Guns" is a lame attempt at a brat pack "Wild Bunch." Executed without style or feel for the genre and, for the most part, colorlessly populated by some of the more fashionable new actors of the moment, pic will do nothing to help restore the reputability or popularity of the Western. A short ride at the b.o. seems in store.**

Meager efforts at offbeat characterization are made at the outset, as British gang ringleader Terence Stamp seeks to better the lot of his renegade boys by encouraging them to read and call each other "gentlemen."

Stamp's early murder by town bigshots prompts quick retaliation by the trigger-happy kids, who are briefly deputized but whose irresponsibility and inclination toward gunplay brands them as outlaws and sets in motion an irreversible chain of violence that inevitably leads to a fateful confrontation.

Attitude of the picture faintly echoes the revisionist Westerns of the late 1960s and early 1970s, with the protagonists positioned as romantic antiheroes who justify their belligerent behavior as the most appropriate response to a corrupt society.

In charting the emergence of Billy the Kid, John Fusco's unshapely script recapitulates the notion of an outlaw fascinated by his own publicity, and treatment of the countless killings is handled in a casual way that invites a lighthearted response.

In the final shootout, "Young Guns" wallows in violence in a way that, again, limply recalls some of the memorable climaxes of two decades ago, such as those to "The Wild Bunch" and "Bonnie And Clyde." Slow-motion technique also provides a cover for some utterly implausible actions and escapes in the face of overpowering odds.

What this film has that few, if any, Westerns ever have had before is a hard rock score. Music's every appearance on the scene throws one right out of the scene and serves to remind that this is a high-tech artifact of the late 1980s.

As Billy, Emilio Estevez is the nominal star here, but no one really shines. Dean Semler's lensing gives the film a measure of visual distinction, but Christopher Cain's undynamic direction never finds a groove that even allows the conventions of the genre and the actors' posing to carry things along. —*Cart.*

Mac And Me

An Orion Pictures release of an R.J. Louis production. Produced by Louis. Executive producers, Mark Damon, William B. Kerr. Directed by Stewart Raffill. Screenplay, Raffill, Steve Feke; camera (CFI color; Deluxe prints), Nick McLean; editor, Tom Walls; music, Alan Silvestri; production design, W. Stewart Campbell; set decoration, John Anderson; sound (Dolby), Darren Enight; alien effects, Martin J. Becker; alien design, Ruben Aquino, Christopher Swift; assistant director, Clifford C. Coleman; casting, Caro Jones. Reviewed at Egyptian theater, L.A., Aug. 12, 1988. MPAA Rating: PG. Running time: **93 MIN.**

Janet	Christine Ebersole
Michael	Jonathan Ward
Courtney	Katrina Caspary
Debbie	Lauren Stanley
Eric	Jade Calegory

■ **Hollywood** — **The only surprise surrounding ''Mac And Me,'' a modest little fantasy about a cute creature from outer space stranded in the wilds of suburban Los Angeles, is that it is not being distributed by Columbia, since the alien's family is revived from near-death by a quick jolt of Coca-Cola.**

In all other respects, this is a benign but pointless replay of motifs from ''E.T.,'' and biz should be just okay on the kiddie circuit. Adults need not apply.

Tantalizing pre-credits sequence has an unmanned American spacecraft landing on arid terrain that would seem to belong to a moon of Saturn, and being inspected by a curious family of four humanoids, who look as though they come from just the next moon over from that of E.T., since they've got leathery skin, long limbs and fingers, and sensitive, inquiring eyes.

The foursome gets vacuumed into the ship and returned to earth, whereupon little Mac becomes separated from his folks and sibling and ends up in a house that, once again, looks to be around the corner from E.T. Drive and Poltergeist Street, and is just becoming occupied by Christine Ebersole and her two sons from Chicago.

One of the kids, Eric, is confined to a wheelchair, and it is he and a neighbor girl who begins seeing evidence of the elusive creature. Unfortunately, it takes an unnecessarily long 40 minutes for Mac and the kids to finally confront each other openly and join forces against the authorities, who undoubtedly would

do something awful to the harmless alien, who only wants to be reunited with its family.

Last half of the pic is devoted to the neighborhood youngsters spiriting Mac to the desert, where Ma and Pa are waiting. Time out is taken for an elaborately choreographed musical number at the local McDonald's, which reps just one of several prominent product plugs in the picture. (The fast-food chain is involved with the film, with a share of proceeds going to charity. — *Ed.*)

Jade Calegory in the leading role of Eric is spunk and upbeat, and cast overall gives a cheery account of themselves, but agreeable mood can't overcome the tedium provoked by the incredible familiarity of events. Similarly, the execution of the aliens is appealing enough, but the specter of their famous ancestor looms over everything.

— *Cart.*

Betrayed

An MGM/UA release of an Irwin Winkler production for United Artists. Produced by Winkler. Executive producers, Joe Eszterhas, Hal W. Polarie. Directed by Constantin Costa-Gavras. Screenplay, Eszterhas; camera (Alpha Cine and Astro color), Patrick, Blossier; editor, Joële Van Effenterre; music, Bill Conti; production design, Patrizia Von Brandenstein; art direction, Stephen Geaghan; set decoration, Jim Erickson; costume design, Joe I. Thompkins; sound (Dolby), Pierre Gamet, Claude Villand (Chicago); assistant director, Rob Cowan; casting, Mary Goldberg, Lynne Carrow (Canada), Jane Alderman, Shelly Andreas (Chicago). Reviewed at Raleigh Studios, L.A., Aug. 16, 1988. MPAA Rating: R. Running time: **127 MIN.**

Katie Phillips/Cathy	Debra Winger
Gary Simmons	Tom Berenger
Michael Carnes	John Heard
Gladys Simmons	Betsy Blair
Shorty	John Mahoney
Wes	Ted Levine
Flynn	Jeffrey DeMunn
Al Sanders	Albert Hall
Jack Carpenter	David Clennon
Dean	Robert Swan
Sam Kraus	Richard Libertini
Rachel Simmons	Maria Valdez
Joey Simmons	Brian Bosak

■ **Hollywood** — **''Betrayed'' is a political thriller that is more political than thrilling. Never less than absorbing due to the combustible subject matter, that of the white supremacist movement, and the sympathetic central presence of Debra Winger, Costa-Gavras' latest film suffers from erratic pacing, considerable implausibility and lack of dramatic tension.**

A measure of strong critical support could put this over initially in limited urban runs, but pic isn't exciting or convincing enough to make it with mainstream audiences.

Clearly inspired by the murder of Denver radio talk show host Alan Berg, opening scene has abrasive Chicago broadcaster Richard Libertini followed home and gunned down by assailants who identify themselves only by spraying the letters ''ZOG'' on the victim's car.

Cut to the endless wheat fields of the rural Midwest, where Winger has come up from Texas as a ''combine girl.'' Local farmer Tom Berenger, whose wife has left him, leaving him to raise their two kids, quickly takes a shine to the new gal in town, while she responds to the warmth of his family life.

Costa-Gavras and scenarist Joe Eszterhas tip their hand a half-hour in, when Winger hops back to Chicago to brief her superiors at the FBI on her progress in infiltrating the group suspected of perpetrating Libertini's murder.

Before long, Winger's first undercover assignment presents her with more than she bargained for, as Berenger drags her along for a little night ''hunting,'' which turns out to be a sick version of ''The Most Dangerous Game'' in which a black man is let out into the woods with a gun and 10 bullets, then pursued by a bunch of dogs and heavily armed men. It's not too tough to guess who wins.

Like Ingrid Bergman in ''Notori-

ous,'' Winger is pushed even further in her masquerade by her chief government contact, John Heard, who from all appearances is in love with her himself. Unlike the heroine of the Hitchcock classic, however, Winger develops a strong romantic bond with the man she's supposed to turn in, although it remains impossible to believe that these emotions could overwhelm or even match the revulsion she feels toward her lover's attitudes and activities.

Promised a ''camping'' vacation, Winger is led to a white supremacist compound, complete with white-hooded revelers, cross burnings and Nazi flags. Children are taught to hate blacks and Jews, and political candidates promise the return of an America for ''real Americans.'' ''ZOG,'' it turns out, stands for the Zionist Occupation Government in Washington, D.C.

Suspected by at least one man of being an infiltrator, Winger is forced into a Patty Hearst-like participation in a bank robbery and finally shoots two people in the course of her duties. All this keeps her very precariously walking the fence for nearly the entire running time, but despite her responsive, dominant performance, one is never swept into the action as the filmmakers no doubt intended, mainly because of the dramatic liabilities of the storytelling.

Many of the cuts, especially in the early-going, seem very abrupt, jolting one out of the scene-setting. The willingness of Berenger and the others to allow a stranger as untested as Winger to join their nocturnal hunt is more than a bit much, and Winger's increasingly frantic and frequent phone calls back to her bosses, and the suspicious reactions they provoke, border on the laughable.

Despite the undoubted existence and hatefulness of all that Costa-Gavras and Eszterhas seek to expose, there is also a sense of exaggerated alarm and pessimism permeating the creative attitude here. The government is bad, the home-grown citizens are bad and, once again, a couple of warped Vietnam vets, determined not to lose this war, are responsible for much of the mayhem. A postscript designed to demonstrate the devastating aftereffects of Winger's assignment is promisingly probing, but ultimately inconclusive.

Berenger proves forceful and properly unpredictable in his vulnerable macho role, entire cast is nicely low-keyed, and tech contributions, with the exception of some noticeably post-synched sound, are fine.

Provocative as the material may be, the director has blended human and political concerns much more effectively on previous occasions, most recently in ''Missing.'' —*Cart.*

Dzusovy Roman
(A Juicy Romance)
(CZECH)

A Ceskoslovensky Filmexport presentation of a Barrandov Film Studios production. Written and directed by Fero Fenic. Camera (color), Jaroslav Brabec; music, Miky Jelinek. Reviewed at Locarno Film Festival, Aug. 10, 1988. Running time: **76 MIN.**

With: Alena Mihulova, Laura Kurovska, Josef Vaidis, Ladislav Balous, Ludmila Bastincova, Iveta Kopecka.

■ **Locarno** — **A first film which attempts to recapture the ironic, semi-documentary tone of the Czech school of the '60s, Fero Fenic's "A Juicy Romance' falls short of the original because the characters he uses lack the richness and the versatility once put on the screen by his elders.**

The story of young girl, Alena, who decides to work in a factory away from home in spite of her mother's urging, and her one night stand with a body builder who leaves her pregnant, the film is first and foremost a portrait of working class conditions in Czechoslovakia, and a far from flattering one.

All the obligatory scenes are there, from the factory activities and the workers' unwillingness to invest too much effort in them, to the clumsy organized social life (instead of taking the workers to a musical, as promised, they are sent to a body building competition) and to their excessive drinking.

Alena is the only character with any kind of depth, a quiet, introspective girl, usually hiding under the authority of a more assertive friend.

Done in an almost documentary style with handheld camera constantly on the move, this is the type of film which appears lively but only skims the surface of the world it presents. —*Edna.*

Beginnelse på en historie
(The Beginning Of A Story)
(NORWEGIAN)

A KF release of Norsk Film production. Produced by Ola Solum, Lasse Glomm. Written and directed by Margrete Robsahm. Camera (Eastmancolor), Rolv Haahn; editor, Edith Toreg, Inge-Lise Langfeldt; music, Christian Eggen; production design, Harald Egede-Nissen; costumes, Katherine Tholo; sound, Sturla Einarson; assistant director, Inge-Lise Langfeldt; production management, Wenche Solum. Reviewed at Norwegian Film Festival, Haugesund, Norway, Aug. 15, 1988. Running time: **83 MIN.**

Marin	Linda Pedersen
Her mother	Linn Stokke
Aunt Ally	Wenche Foss
The Padre	Frode Rasmussen

Also with: Liv Thorsen, Jan Frode Lunde, Morten Loge, Jan Aagre, Gretelil Henden, Christian Steinsland, Ove Birkeli Pettersen.

■ **Haugesund, Norway** — **"The Beginning Of A Story" is told in cliché dialog with cardboard adults and stiffly moving children, providing neither narrative rhythm nor camera imagery to take it out of its cinematic doldrums.**

Margrete Robsahm makes her feature film helmer bow with a recounting of one summer in her own life. She has Linda Pedersen, a pretty blond of seven (and of sweetly sad visage) to play her protagonist Marin, who says goodbye to an uneasy life with her mother and her siblings on a rock island before entering what we are given to understand is the prison of a Catholic boarding school in Oslo.

Pedersen plays her role well, now demure, now stoically sad, but with sudden flashes of genuine and moving temperament. Why she has to enter a Catholic school in otherwise Protestant Norway is never enlarged upon. The crudely moralistic padre and a school seen only at night (and at angles to suggest a dungeon) are clearly nothing but symbols of the writer-director's objects for hate.

The action takes place in 1947, and it is indicated that Marin's father serves a jail term for wartime collaboration with the Germans. This theme is left totally floating, too.

Marin's mother waxes alternately hot and cold in her relation to her children, Marin especially. The mother is goodlooking and has many friends. She drinks red wine while doing her housework, but again a possible theme, alcoholism, is not enlarged upon. Since Marin's older brother is allowed to stay home, we never hear why Marin has to leave her affluent family to enter the convent school.

Often, Marin seeks refuge with an elderly aunt, who is all Granny sweetness and light. The subteen girls and boys of the neighborhood are mostly nasty towards her, but they are paraded across the screen only as puppets. Neat little insights in the psychology of a rather lonely child relieve the boredom, but that is not enough to redeem the utter monotony of a picture that never even begins to resemble a story. — *Kell.*

Crossing Delancey

A Warner Bros. release. Produced by Michael Nozik. Executive producer, Raphael Silver. Directed by Joan Micklin Silver. Screenplay, Susan Sandler, based on her play; camera (Duart color), Theo Van de Sande; editor, Rick Shaine; music, Paul Chihara; additional music, The Roches; production design, Dan Leigh; art direction, Leslie E. Rollins; set decoration, Daniel Boxer; costume design, Rita Ryack; sound (Dolby), Danny Michael; assistant director, Louis D'Esposito; casting, Meg Simon, Fran Kumin. Reviewed at the Burbank Studios, Burbank, Calif., Aug. 16, 1988. MPAA Rating: PG. Running time: **97 MIN.**

Isabelle Grossman	Amy Irving
Bubbie Kantor	Reizl Bozyk
Sam Posner	Peter Riegert
Anton Maes	Jeroen Krabbé
Hannah Mandelbaum	Sylvia Miles
Marilyn	Suzzy Roche
Lionel	George Martin
Nick	John Bedford Lloyd
Cecilia Monk	Claudia Silver
Mark	David Pierce
Pauline Swift	Rosemary Harris
Ricki	Amy Wright
Candyce	Faye Grant
Karen	Deborah Offner
Myla Bondy	Kathleen Wilhoite

■ **Hollywood** — **In an unexpectedly enjoyable way, "Crossing Delancey" addresses one of the great societal issues of our day — the dilemma of how the 30ish, attractive, successful, intelligent and unmarried female finds a mate she can be happy with.**

Even if perhaps a little too old-fashioned and ethnic for some, still there's enough pathos and warmth to draw more of an interest than from single femmes trying to placate their frustrated mothers (and grandmothers). B.o. will be limited, but has potential to be a vidcassette hit.

Off-off-Broadway fans may remember the title from playwright Susan Sandler's semi-autobiographical 1985 comedy about how her loving, old-worldly and slightly overbearing Lower East Side N.Y. Jewish grandmother engages the services of a matchmaker to find her a suitable marriage partner.

Amy Irving is the dutiful granddaughter who works in a pretentious Manhattan bookstore by day, keeps her own apartment and is reasonably happy with a small circle of similarly situated friends but always finds time to make frequent visits to her precious *Bubbie* (Yiddish actress Reizl Bozyk). Presumably, like many of her contemporaries around the country, Irving finds herself, at 33, explaining repeatedly to those of previous generation how she could possibly be content and still be single.

Irving's situation is not one too many women can relate to — Jewish or not — where a matchmaker (Sylvia Miles) brings her together with an unlikely candidate, pickle maker Sam Posner (Peter Riegert). Their ultimate union, however, is secondary to the fairly obvious message that life is more meaningful shared than lived solitary.

Under Joan Micklin Silver's easygoing direction, "Crossing Delancey" builds slowly to capture its audience. It is easy to see how the subject worked so well in theater: the characters are clearly defined, the settings limited and the humor derived from the Jewish experience that is so much a part of New York City.

To draw in those not familiar with this upbringing, Sandler, in adapting her own play to the screen, incorporates several images that women of all ethnicity can relate to — done in such a fashion whereby Irving is persuaded to give Riegert a second, third and fourth look.

Subtlety is not the operative word here. The major set-ups focus on Irving's torn affections between the rakish, smooth-talking charm of pulp novelist Anton Maes (Jeroen Krabbé), who gives good readings on rainy days at the bookstore, and earnest, straight-forward, vulnerable Riegert, who unabashedly holds his heart in his hand for her.

To the credit of most of the actors, the sentimentality doesn't sink the story. Keeping things at all times light and entertaining is Bozyk, a real find as the spirited, good-hearted, nosy Jewish grandmother who alternately one would want to strangle and later give a squeeze of affection. Riegert is also excellent, as naturally relaxed in his role here as he was in "Local Hero." Only Miles as the loud, vulgar yenta Hannah Mandelbaum plays too much to type.

For a "small" picture, much good use is made of establishing exterior shots for the set-ups, covering ground from Boyzk's visit to the open-air produce markets of the Lower East Side to the tony, old-worldly New Day bookstore on the Upper West Side. Dutch cinematographer Theo Van de Sande personalizes impersonal Manhattan by filming the characters at a normal conversational distance, a good strategy for getting the flavor of the city without being dwarfed by it.

Music by the Roches, an all-femme band, is a good choice for background and Suzzy Roche, making her film debut as Irving's girlfriend Marilyn, is humorously good-natured given that she was hopeful to date Riegert when Irving was on the fence about him. —*Brit.*

Honneponnetje
(Honeybunch)
(DUTCH)

A Cannon Tuschinski release of a Trapper Film production. Produced by Jos van der Linden, Ruud van Hemert for Twoclip (Amsterdam), Multimedia (Brussels). Executive producer, Van der Linden. Written and directed by Ruud van Hemert. Camera (Eastman color, prints by Cineco), Willy Stassen; editor, Willem Hoogeboom; music, Peter Schon, Van Hemert; sound, Peter Flamman; art direction, Hubert Pouille; production manager, Tina Weemaes; stunt coordinator, Tip Tipping; casting, Hans Kemna. Reviewed at City Theater, Amsterdam, July 7, 1988. Running time: **93 MIN.**

Honneponnetje	Nada van Nie
Harry	Marc Hazewinkel

Also with: Nora Kretz, Jet van der Meij, Coen Flink, Juda Bar-Noor, Marijke Merckems, Hans Man in't Veld.

■ **Amsterdam** — **The fast, funny comic strip-like lunacy of writer-director Ruud Van Hemert's first two features ("Darlings" and "Mama Is Mad!") is deficient in "Honeybunch." Flabby and tepid, it's a string of compromises, neither flesh nor fowl (maybe just a turkey).**

Though "Darlings" drew one out of every 10 Dutchmen to theaters, this Cannon pic is doing only fair business after unanimously negative reviews.

Story concerns a girl named Honeybunch, whose rich parents are having her brought up in an extremely strict orthodox convent, where temptation nonetheless makes an entrance in the form of a lurid romantic novel.

Eager to check out the real world, she flees the nunnery on her 16th birthday in miniskirt and copious makeup (and with her considerable savings) and gets involved in a series of madcap adventures, while parents, convent and police act on the wild conclusion she's been kidnaped. Plot twists and turns with lecherous leering, car chases, and an ever innocent and naive heroine.

Gags are programmed around types such as nuns, stupid bureaucrats, a winking male figure on a cross and a lesbian cabbie. Some of programming connects, but most of the time the comedy short-circuits.

Among a mostly perfunctory cast, newcomer Nada van Nie is relentlessly cute, but the main acting charms are generated by Marc Hazewinkel, who has relaxed good humor and charm as a poor student who helps out Honeybunch. Ironically, Hazewinkel was an emergency substitute for the original cast thesp, who suffered an accident during production. After a debut like this one, he won't have to wait in line for a role next time. —*Wall.*

Nissuim Fiktivi'im
(Fictive Marriage)
(ISRAELI)

A Nachshon Films presentation of a Tom Films production. Produced by Micha Sharf-shtein. Directed by Haim Buzaglo. Screenplay, Buzaglo, Yossi Savaya, based on idea by Buzaglo; camera (color, 16m), Amnon Salomon; editor, Tova Asher; music, Itzhak Klepter, theme song, Shmuel Kraus, Yaakov Rotblith; sound, Yaakov Sarig; art direction, Yehuda Eko, Karol Yanoshvinsky. Reviewed at United Studios screening room, Tel Aviv, July 20, 1988. Running time: **100 MIN.**
Eldad . . . . Shlomo Bar-Abba
Reception clerk . . . . Irith Sheleg
Eldad's wife . . . . Ofra Weingarten
Painter . . . . Idith Tepersohn
Inspector . . . . Yossi Savaya
Bashir . . . . Eli Yatzpan
Kamel . . . . Adiv Gehshan

■ **Tel Aviv** — Haim Buzaglo's directorial debut is a blend of pungent social satire and vulgar comedy, precariously juggled between these two extremes, sometimes losing its equilibrium, but coming out in the end on the credit side.

Plot concerns Eldad, a Jerusalem school techer who is supposed to fly to New York. Instead, once he reaches the airport, he leaves his luggage lying around, creating immediate havoc with the security officers, then goes by taxi to Tel Aviv and takes a room in a cheap hotel, pretending to be an Israeli resident of New York on a short visit home.

From this point, Buzaglo proceeds with three different plots. The airport security inspector investigates the strange disappearance and goes to visit Eldad's wife and children. At the same time, in Tel Aviv, Eldad returns every evening to his hotel, to play the Israeli who has made it abroad, for the benefit of the admiring reception clerk

whose dream is to find a man to take her to America. Finally, during the day, Eldad impersonates a poor, dumb Arab worker, the dumb act necessary in order to hide his imperfect accent in this language.

Buzaglo covers a lot of ground in his film: the uneasy relations between Israelis and Arabs, and the American dream nursed by many Israelis who believe they can fulfill themselves only there.

. However, lacking the experience that would have allowed better control of this material, Buzaglo confuses punch with lewdness. He bends over backwards to paint an idyllic picture of Arab society, in contrast with a more disturbed and far more critical picture of the Israelis.

Shot in 16m on a low budget and then blown up to 35m, the images have the rough quality of the humor. Performances vary from a solid, underplayed one by Shlomo Bar-Abba in the lead, to an exaggerated one by Yossi Savaya as the inspector, while dialog switches constantly from sharp to blunt to gross.
— *Edna.*

Macao
(SWISS-WEST GERMAN)

A Christa Saredi presentation of an Ombra-Film, Pandora-Film production, coproduced with ZDF and SRG. Produced by Reinhard Brundig, Klaus Baumgartner, Roger Garcia, Ge Grumbach. Directed by Clemens Klopfenstein. Screenplay, Klopfenstein; Wolfram Groddeck, Felix Tissi; camera (color), Klopfenstein; editor, Fee Lichti, Mirjam Krakenberger; music, Christine Lautenburg, Res Margot, Susanne Jaberg, Thomas Keller, Esther Müller-Jaberg, Christoph Kuhn, Hanspeter Kuhn, Daniel Krieg, Shirley Wong, David Ma, Tommy Ho, Michael Lam; sound, Ivan Seifert; art direction, Serena Kiefer. Reviewed at Locarno Film Festival, Aug. 10, 1988. Running time: **90 MIN.**
Mark . . . . Max Rüdlinger
Alice . . . . Christine Lautenburg
Pilot . . . . Hans-Dieter Jendreyko
Also with: Hans-Rudolf Twerenbold, Paul Spahn, Che Tin Hong, Jeong Sio Heng, Chan Yuen Shi, Chok Ka Cheng, Che Pui San, Wong Pui San, Shirley Wong.

■ **Locarno** — This fantasy on life and death is an unusually exotic entry for the Swiss cinema even if not quite a satisfactory one.

Mark, a Swiss etymologist, flies from Zurich to Stockholm, his plane blows up over the Baltic Sea and he finds himself swimming to the shore of Macao, on the opposite side of the planet. Or at least so it seems, since the place he reaches is a mysterious floating island with friendly inhabitants looking Chinese and speaking no language other than their own. There is no way off of this island and no possibility of communicating with the rest of the world.

Mark and the plane's pilot who reached the same destination, try to find an escape route out of this peaceful haven only to realize after some time passes, they are dead and the island is a sort of paradise, or purgatory or transitory stage be-

tween life and eternity.

That is as far as director Clemens Klopfenstein develops his idea, which is insufficient to support a full-length feature film. The fantasy which requires the audience to relate Mark's new existence in Macao with the Danish Coast Guard searching for survivors of the accident in the Baltic is on the heavy-handed side. So are several attempts at humor and irony.

The production spreads over thousands of miles, from Switzerland through Denmark to the real Macao. Klopfenstein enjoys shooting landscapes and does it well: all technical credits are satisfactory and the actors fit in with the requirements. With a script like this, Klopfenstein could have turned out a brilliant short. Insisting on feature length was a tactical mistake.
—*Edna.*

Sama
(The Trace)
(TUNISIAN-BELGIAN-
WEST GERMAN)

A No Money production. Written and directed by Nedjia Ben Mabrouk. Camera (color, 16m), Marc-André Batigne; editor, Moufida Tlatli; music, François Gaudard; sound, Faouzi Thabet. Reviewed at Locarno Film Festival, Aug. 9, 1988. Running time: **90 MIN.**
With: Fatma Khemiri (Sabra), Basma Tadjin (Sabra as young girl), Mouna Noureddine (Sabra's mother), Othman Khemili (Sabra's father).

■ **Locarno** — The name of the production company (No Money) and the time it took to shoot this film, started in 1982 and finished only in May 1988, indicate the hardships femme helmer Nedjia Ben Mabrouk had to surmount for her feature film debut, and explain to a certain degree some of its shortcomings.

A typical portrait of a woman's condition in a male-dominated society, in this case a Tunisian village, it shows a young woman trying for an academic degree. She's discriminated against to such an extent that her only way out is to take flight from her homeland and wipe out every trace she might have left behind her.

Sabra is a young woman who in spite of her family's poverty, her father's resistance and the general opposition offered by everyone around her, sticks to her studies. She spends sleepless nights by a burning candle trying to prepare for her exams, rejects brutal macho advances and refuses to comply with either traditions or age-old superstitions ruling the people surrounding her.

. She is the true portrait of a stubborn feminist surviving under impossible conditions. Flashbacks indicate she was already rebelling when she was 10, at least partially encouraged by her mother, who is still enslaved to the old ways, but is

at the same time conscious of a woman's lot in Moslem society and dearly wishes to spare her daughter a similar fate.

Much more a statement of facts than a conventional drama, pic is shot grittily in locations which look perfectly authentic, skimping on lighting to the point where it is sometimes difficult to distinguish between details on the screen. Actors appear to be amateurs and this is first and foremost a militant tract. Final result is bound to attract the attention of ethnographers and socio-political activists. —*Edna.*

Folk og røvere i
Kardemomme By
(Folks And Robbers Of
Cardamom City)
(SWEDISH-NORWEGIAN)

A KF (Oslo) release of a Marcusfilm production, with Sandrew Film (Sweden) and the Swedish Film Institute. Executive producer, Svein H. Toreg. Produced and directed by Bente Erichsen. Screenplay, Bente Erichsen, Rolv Haan, based on Torbjörn Egner's novel and play; camera (Eastmancolor), Rolv Haan; editor, Björn Breigutu; music and production design, Torbjörn Egner; costumes, Egner, with Wenche Petersen; sound, Svein Hovde, Svein Kalvö; musical arrangements, Egil Monn-Iversen; choreography, Runar Borge; associate producer, Katinka Farago; production management, Binne Thoresen. Reviewed at Norwegian Film Festival, Haugesund, Norway, Aug. 13, 1988. Running time: **96 MIN.**
Police Chief Bastian . . . Brasse Brännström
Aunt Sofie . . . . Kjersti Dövigen
Old Tobias . . . . Henki Kolstad
Kaspar . . . . Sverre Anker Ousdal
Jesper . . . . Oivind Blunck
Jonatan . . . . Jon Eikemo
The Barber . . . . Sven-Bertil Taube
Mrs. Bastian . . . . Grynet Molvig
Also with: Lasse Aberg, Jon Skolmen, Karl Sundbye, Arve Opsahl, Kaja Glomm, Marius Rypdal, Sive Böe, Reidar Sörensen, Jacob Holmbroe.

■ **Haugesund, Norway** — Torbjörn Egner's bestselling 1955 burlesque novel-to-be-read-aloud "Folks And Robbers Of Cardamom City," later a musical play, becomes a motion picture that should please Scandinavians of all ages.

Modern audiences' demands on the musical form may slow down the entertainment's further traveling, however.

"Cardamom" has always worked, and still does, on its appeal to innocent oddity. In this repsect it bears a clear resemblance to Hugh Lofting's "Dr. Doolittle," "Cardamom" has Police Chief Bastian reigning benevolently in his never-never land toy city, where only spinsterish Aunt Sofie adds a sour note by denying her small niece leave to go to the annual city festival.

The order of things is threatened only by a trio of robbers, Kaspar, Jesper and Jonatan, who steal what they need in way of foodstuffs, but otherwise live peacefully and blissfully unscrubbed outside the city with a tame but dutifully growling lion as their only companion.

The police chief avoids trouble at

all costs. When the robbers, having dreamed wistfully of a woman's cooking, abduct Sophie, they promptly send her back home when the price she asks for her services is that they literally (with soap and water) clean up their act.

Every now and again the characters, alone or in ensemble, break into song & dance, the tunes very catchy, the dance routines modest. Soon the robbers are turned into model citizens, and the lion lands a circus job.

Director Bente Erichsen has adhered (by contractual obligation) only too faithfully to the literal words and original stage directions of Torbjörn Egner, preventing her film from becoming cinematically airborne.

In a cast of fine actors, all performing aimiably, only Sweden's Brasse Brännström as Police Chief Bastian succeeds in emerging as a truly engaging individual character. A sunny mood and warm charm permeate the proceedings throughout, and helmer-adapter Erichsen has diligently avoided the pitfalls of adult sneering at the material at hand. —*Kell.*

La Travestie
(The Transvestite)
(FRENCH)

An AAA release of a Sara Films production. Executive producer, Alaine Sarde. Produced by Philippe Guez. Written and directed by Yves Boisset, from the novel by Alain Roger. Camera (Eastmancolor), Yves Dahan; editor, Laurence Leininger; music, Philippe Sarde; sound, Jean-Charles Ruault; art direction, Claude Bouvard; makeup, Eric Muller; assistant director, Antoine Lorenzi; production manager, Catherine Maziéres. Reviewed at Les Images cinema, Paris, Aug. 14, 1988. Running time: **107 MIN.**

Nicole Armingault	Zabou
Myriam	Anna Galiena
Anne-Marie	Valérie Steffen
Alain	Yves Afonso
Christine	Christine Pascal

■ Paris — Action film specialist Yves Boisset has wasted a good story idea in "La Travestie," drama of an emotionally and professionally frustrated young woman who decides to pose as a man in order to gain control of her life.

Helmer betrays his material with poor scripting and haphazard direction.

Zabou is a young provincial lawyer fed up with masculine hypocrisy. Embezzling funds from her firm, she heads for Paris where she tries to pass as an effeminate-looking but strong-willed young man.

Her hunger for a lasting emotional bond leads her to two lesbian relationships (including a hooker for whom she also serves as pimp) and an affair with a man who is not interested in a serious involvement. The guy however pays the price for Zabou's series of disappointments by being gunned down by her.

This tale of obsessive role-playing and loneliness that leads to murder and schizophrenia is treated for surface effects by Boisset, who misses the nuances and pathos of the theme. Cast as a result fails to provide credibility to the proceedings. —*Len.*

Remote Control
(COLOR/B&W)

A Vista Organization production. Produced by Scott Rosenfelt, Mark Levinson. Executive producers, Herb Jaffe, Mort Engelberg. Written and directed by Jeff Lieberman. Camera (Deluxe color, b&w), Timothy Suhrstedt; editor, Scott Wallace; music, Peter Bernstein; sound (Ultra-Stereo), Jan Brodin, Sunny Meyer; production design, Curtis Schnell; set decoration, Douglas Mowat; costume design, Daniel Paredes; assistant directiro, Michael Kennedy; production manager, Rosenfelt; stunt coordinator, William Lane; additional camera, Robert New; casting, Nina Axelrod. Reviewed on Intl. Video Entertainment vidcassette, N.Y., Aug. 9, 1988. MPAA Rating: R. Running time: **88 MIN.**

Cosmo	Kevin Dillon
Belinda	Deborah Goodrich
Georgie	Christopher Wynne
Victor	Frank Beddor
Allegra	Jennifer Tilly
Patricia	Kaaren Lee
Bill Denver	Bert Remsen

■ "Remote Control" is an unsuccessful attempt to use the homevideo phenomenon as a plot peg for science fiction. Given the subject matter, pic appropriately has been released direct to videostores, bypassing the originally intended theatrical release step.

Kevin Dillon, Matt's bro (starring here before he toplined "The Rescue" and "The Blob"), energetically portrays a clerk at a videostore who unwittingly becomes the chief suspect, along with his boss Christopher Wynne, in a murder case when a neighbor spots them at the crime scene.

Farfetched premise has aliens from Outer Space fabricating a film on video, a black & white feature purporting to be a sci-fi made in the '50s, which causes the viewer to see himself acting *within* the film and turns him into a homicidal maniac. Dillon's mission, on the lam with Wynne and his dream girl Deborah Goodrich, is to destroy all copies of the video and its manufacturing plant, run by Bert Remsen.

Helmer Jeff Lieberman, whose horror pic "Squirm" was an effective 1970s B title, does well with the b&w film-within-a-film footage (also titled "Remote Control"), but claustrophobic approach fails to elaborate on the basic storyline. Though opening title sets the action on "Earth 1987," Daniel Paredes' fanciful costumes create something of a parallel-world atmosphere. Various details ring false, particularly Dillon's memorizing the *English-dubbed* dialog from a video of François Truffaut's "Stolen Kisses" in order to impress (which he succeeds in doing) Goodrich, a fan of that Antoine Doinel feature.

Cast, particularly Jennifer Tilly in a supporting role (with kookie hairdo and voice) as Dillon's new wave girlfriend, is peppy. Remsen previously was featured in a dissimilar sci-fi film about aliens invading via tv, "Terrorvision." —*Lor.*

Mirazhi Ljubvi
(Mirages Of Love)
(SOVIET-SYRIAN)

A Kirghizfilm-Tadzhikfilm (USSR), Ganem Film (Syria) production. Directed by Tolomush Okeyev. Screenplay, Okeyev, Timur Zulfikarov; camera (Sovcolor), Nurtai Borbiyev; music, Rumil Vildanov; production design, Rustam Odinayev, Sergei Romankulov. Reviewed at Mandolin theater, Sydney, July 12, 1988. Running time: **95 MIN.**

With: Fakhridin Makhamatdinov, Asel Eshimbayeva, Farkhad Mirzoyev.

■ Sydney — This exotic biopic of the early life of Kirghiz artist Mani was such a success at a Soviet film week in Australia early this year that it's back now for a theatrical outing.

Pic, dated 1986, boasts spectacular locations in the Soviet Central Asian cities of Samarkand and Bukhara, as well as scenes shot in Damascus. It adds up to a familiar story boosted by rarely seen settings.

Drama spans more than two decades, beginning with Mani's father whose wives have so far not given him the son he craves. He takes a slave girl from the market and, though she hates her master, she bears a son. However, on the night of his birth, she commits suicide by jumping into a swollen river.

When the boy, Mani, is 12 years old his talent as an artist is already evident, but enemies of his father break the boy's right hand. He is sent far away, and many years later has become famous. He decides to return home to see his father (not knowing the old man has died) but along the way spies a beautiful woman bathing naked in Lake Issyk-Kul; although he knows she is married, he's determined to have her for himself.

This retelling of ancient legends proceeds at a stately pace, with the pale colors of the print under review a handicap given that the locations are so impressive. Music is majestic, but the dubbing of Russian over the original, presumably Kirghiz, dialog is a distraction.

An old-fashioned affair, it's beautiful but rather empty. —*Strat.*

Fu-Zung Cen
(Hibiscus Town)
(CHINESE)

A Shanghai Film Studio production. Directed by Xie Jin. Screenplay, Jin, Ah Cheng; camera (color), Lu Junfu; music, Ge Yan; art direction, Jin Qifen. Reviewed at Karlovy Vary Film Festival (competing), July 17, 1988. Running time: **150 MIN.**

Hu Yuyin	Liu Xiaoqing
Qin Shutian	Jiang Wen
Gu Yanshan	Zheng Zaishi
Li Guoxiang	Xu Songzi
Wang Qiushe	Zhu Shibin
Li Mangeng	Zhang Guangbei
Li Guigui	Liu Linian
Wu Zhaola	Xu Ning

■ Karlovy Vary — The well-deserved blue ribbon winner of the Karlovy Vary Festival was Xie Jin's splendid "Hibiscus Town," already briefly released in London and certainly deserving playoff in specialized situations wherever Chinese films are shown.

This riveting, often astonishing and very moving account of the dramatic hardships endured by ordinary people under the "four purges" and subsequent Cultural Revolution can't be beat for acting, comprehensibility and impact. It comes close to being a contemporary masterpiece in veteran helmer Xie Jin's distinguished filmography.

Although pic took the Grand Prix at Karlovy, it was probably not screened in its full-length version, which is reputed to be nearly three hours long and to contain some amazingly frank — and comic — love-making scenes between two of the villains, party leaders in the small Hibiscus Town. Fest catalog advertised 110 minutes, but 2½ hours were actually shown, indicating that multiple versions exist.

Heroine is Hu Yuyin (played skillfully by Liu Xiaoqing), making a modest living when film opens with her husband Guigui. Their little sidewalk restaurant allows them to save up to build a house — which they do, lugging stones uphill on their own backs and constructing it themselves.

All is well till a dogmatic party woman arrives and begins the first purge. Hu Yuyin's pretty face, as much as her nice new house, excites the leader's envy, and the couple is publicly denounced as enemies of the people. Hu flees, their house and money are confiscated and her weak husband commits suicide. When she returns to the village, she is ignominiously put to work sweeping streets, along with an intellectual, Qin Shutian (the very appealing Jiang Wen).

Film relentlessly uncovers the bigotry and horror of the times (the bad guys always coming out on top), the people's fear and unhappiness. A moment of joy appears when Hu and Qin fall in love; their street sweeping and daily humiliation as village pariahs draw them together in several romantic, touching scenes.

When Hu gets pregnant, however, Qin gets a 10-year sentence in a labor camp and Hu is made to repair roads. Her son is born during a stormy winter night. Film ends on an upbeat note, with Qin coming home after Party changes make for a more moderate society, and he launches a warning against any more turnarounds.

Lensing by Lu Junfu is of top international quality. —*Yung.*

Zaboravljeni
(The Forgotten Ones)
(YUGOSLAV)

A Yugoslavija Film release of an Avala Film, Belgrade TV production. Directed by Darko Bajic. Screenplay, Gordan Mihic; camera (color), Boris Gortinski; editor, Branislav Milosevic; music, Vlatko Stefanovski; sound, Branco Dordevic; art direction, Vlasta Gavrik; costumes, Emilija Kovacevic. Reviewed at Pula Film Festival (competing), July 27, 1988. Running time: **103 MIN.**

With: Srdan Todorovic, Mirjana Jokovic, Boris Milivojevic, Mustafa Nadarevic, Vera Cukic, Olivera Markovic.

■ **Pula — The result of long, detailed research by director Darko Bajic and veteran scripter Gordan Mihic into the causes of juvenile delinquency, which produced a tv series "Grey Home," film uses characters and situations developed on the small screen in a different, more concise context.**

Three teenagers (two boys and a girl) are focused upon; each one's alienation is described in detail. One of them has chosen to live with his mother when his parents divorced, and when he attempts later to go back to his father he is brutally rejected, time after time. The mother of the other boy is in Germany, incapable emotionally of taking care of herself, much less of her son.

The girl was adopted by a wealthy couple, but when they divorced she was left without a home.

The three huddle together for companionship and love. Every time one of them is hurt, the others help him work out his frustrations, wreaking vengeance on the indifferent world around them by gratuitous acts of vandalism and destruction. Society has a difficult time dealing with them, neither jail nor mental hospitals being the kind of treatment capable of solving their problems, which finally lead to their own destruction.

A grim portrait of abandoned, misguided youth, placing the blame squarely on the parents and other uncomprehending adults who are supposed to deal with this tragedy, the picture sympathetically follows the anarchic despondency of its three protagonists.

Diligent performances by Srdan Todorovic, Mirjana Jokovic and Borij Milivojevic as the three forgotten heroes help the film, which deals with a recurrent theme in an honest and earnest fashion, but doesn't really offer any new insights. —*Edna.*

Dum Pro Dva
(A House For Two)
(CZECH)

A Barrandov Studios production. Directed by Milos Zábransky. Screenplay, Rudolf Raz; music, Jan Paukert, Pavel Drazan; in color; art direction, Zbynek Hloch. Reviewed at Karlovy Vary Film Festival (competing), July 18, 1988. Running time: **78 MIN.**
Dan .... Ondrej Vetchy
Bóza .... Jiri Schmitzer
Magda .... Ivana Velichova
Mother .... Jirina Trebicka
Also with: Miloslav Marsalek, Zdena Sajfertová, Jaroslav Mares, Milan Tahotny.

■ **Karlovy Vary — The official Czech entry at the Karlovy Vary fest from Barrandov Studios, "House For Two" is a Bressonian exercise in style and spirituality destined to make an impression on Czech cinema.**

Tale of a saintly older brother who redeems his kid brother's misbehaving, even marrying the girl he gets pregnant, will be of interest to fest directors and specialized programmers abroad. It is Milos Zábransky's third feature.

Bóza (an austere Czech version of Harry Dean Stanton, played with mournful fatalism by Jiri Schmitzer) is a hard-working printer who loves his aging mother and is concerned about his wild kid brother Dan (Ondrej Vetchy), a boozing, sardonic joker who works in the same plant. Despite all his defects, Dan gets the girls, his mother's love and audience sympathy.

When a pretty new girl turns up at work, Bóza falls hard for her; out of sheer malice, Dan seduces and abandons her. With nobility not of this world, the older brother visits the girl's family and offers to marry her. Dan returns from the Army, as fun-loving as ever, to find Bóza and Magda (Ivana Velichova) have an apartment and two kids. Dan seduces Magda again. Bóza is killed crossing the street. Dan is chastized and haunted by Bóza's ghost.

More than the improbable story, film is out to put across a moral message, underlined by the strangely unmotivated behavior of Bóza and Magda. Dan, the wayward brother, is the most fleshed out character, and the one on whom all the heavy responsibility falls.

It's a novel approach, and gives the film its personality. Some sophistication is lost through too-obvious Christian symbols (Bóza dies with outstretched arms, as though on a cross) and other symbols (the mysterious white horse Bóza keeps seeing, running down the street). —*Yung.*

VENICE FEST REVIEWS

Encore (Once More)
(FRENCH)

A UGC release of a Diagonale/La Sept co-production. Produced, written and directed by Paul Vecchiali. Camera (color), Georges Strouve; editor, Vecchiali, Franck Mathieu; music, Roland Vincent; song lyrics, Vecchiali; art direction, Jean-Jacques Cernolle; sound, Antoine Bonfanti; assistant director, Didier Albert; production manager, Nicole Flipo. Reviewed at the UGC screening room, Neuilly, France, Aug. 18, 1988. (In Venice Film Festival — competing. Also in Montreal Film Festival — noncompeting.) Running time: **87 MIN.**

With: Jean-Louis Rolland (Louis), Florence Giorgetti (Sybele), Pascale Rogard (Anne-Marie), Nicolas Silberg (Yvan), Patrick Raynal (Frantz), Severine Vincent (Immondice), Michel Gautier (Michel), Catherine Becker (Cathy), Albert Dupontel (Alain), André Sallée (André), Marc Briones (Marcel), Anne Richard (Marthe), Dora Doll (the mother).

■ **Paris — "Encore (Once More)" is a stylistically eccentric, but strangely affecting drama about a man's decision to renounce his stagnant marital life and family to explore his homosexual inclinations.**

Film will undoubtedly cause discussion for the wrong reasons (the hero finally dies of AIDS), for essentially this is an unsensational, generally restrained exploration of love and solitude in contemporary society. Film is competing at Venice and should get around specialized circuits easily.

Producer-writer-director Paul Vecchiali has not given up his disconcerting penchants for movieland conventions, buff references and technical virtuosities. They're all present here, but his profound sincerity is what cements the often disparate elements into a dramatic whole.

Central technical exploit is that it was shot in 10 days, one sequence filmed each day. Each scene represents one day or moment per year from 1978 to 1988, generally corresponding to the birthday of the protagonist's daughter. Though Vecchiali has performed similar virtuoso shoots in the past (his 1985 "Trous de memoire" was lensed in six hours!), this formal arrangement gives the succession of scenes a growing intensity and sense of changes without sacrificing character development or plot consistency.

First scene, for example, takes place in the bedroom of the protagonist (sensitively played by newcomer Jean-Louis Rolland, who has a slight resemblance to Vecchiali himself). Staged like an act in trite marital legit comedy, Vecchiali deliberately plays on clichés of situation and dialog to underline the man's breakup with his wife, Florence Giorgetti.

Subsequent scenes follow Rolland's discovery of homosexual love, a first disastrous liaison that lends to a suicide attempt and a disillusioned turn as a gay prostitute. Rolland finally finds a deeper relationship with a man who remains with him even after he learns he's contracted AIDS. The final scene, in 1988, at Rolland's hospital deathbed with his lover at his side is remarkably restrained and moving.

Vecchiali's script also describes Rolland's changing relationship with his ex-wife and his adoring daughter, nicely played by Pascale Rocard. There are as well a couple of seedy characters (Nicolas Silberg and Severine Vincent) who all too clearly represent Fate and seem like rejects from a 1930s French film (which Vecchiali adores and has used as inspiration in previous pics, with less success).

To top off the film's formal oddities, its hero even breaks out suddenly into song on a couple of occasions, notably at the wedding party of his daughter where he sings the film's life affirming (and Claude Lelouch-like) theme song, with the entire cast climactically joining in. It's a high-wire moment that Vecchiali keeps from plunging into sheer puerility.

Despite the self-imposed production schedule, there's no feeling of technical inadequacy, thanks especially to the virtuoso work of lenser Georges Strouve and his camera crew.

"Encore" is sure to divide critical and public opinion but there's little doubt that Vecchiali has made one of his most personal films to date. — *Len.*

Obsessed
(CANADIAN)

A New Star Entertainment release (U.S.) of a Telescene Films production. Executive producers, Neil J.P. Leger, Paul E. Painter. Produced by Robin Spry, Jamie Brown. Directed by Spry. Screenplay, Douglas Bowie, from a story by Bowie, Spry, suggested by the book "Hit And Run" by Tom Alderman; camera (color), Ron Stannett; editor, Diann Ilnicki; music, Jean-Alain Roussel; production design, Claude Paré; production manager, Peter Bray; assistant director, Mireille Goulet; casting, Vera Miller. Reviewed on Palace Entertainment vidcassette, Sydney, Aug. 8, 1988. (MPAA Rating in U.S.: PG-13.) Running time: **103 MIN.**
Dinah Middleton .... Kerrie Keane
Max Middleton .... Daniel Pilon
Owen Hughes .... Saul Rubinek
Karen Hughes .... Lynne Griffin
Françoise Boyer .... Mireille Deyglun
Det. Sgt. Sullivan .... Ken Pogue
Phil Grande .... Vlasta Vrana
The Judge .... Colleen Dewhurst
Conrad Vaughan .... Alan Thicke
Alex Middleton .... Leif Anderson
Also with: Jacob Tierney (David Hughes), Mathew Mahay (Tony), Jeremy Spry (Scott).

■ **Sydney — In 1969, Canadian Robin Spry's feature "Prologue," about the Chicago Democratic Convention riots of 1968, was a hit at** the Venice fest; now Spry's back in Venice (in the "Venice Night" section) with his latest, a modest, very well-acted drama about a hit-and-run driver and the bereaved parents of a dead child.

Pic, previously titled "Hitting Home," should get critical kudos, and be a natural for video and the tube, while a bit slight for theatrical release.

Interestingly, Spry again deals with Canadian-U.S. relations. The accident occurs on a Montreal side street when a rental car driven by New York businessman Owen Hughes (Saul Rubinek) hits 12-year-old Alex (Leif Anderson), skateboarding sprig of divorced couple Dinah (Kerrie Keane) and Max (Daniel Pilon). After lingering awhile in hospital, the lad expires.

The hit-and-runner is tracked down, but under the terms of the existing U.S.-Canada treaty, he can't be extradited to face Canadian law on such a supposedly minor charge. Egged on by his lawyer, Hughes refuses to return to Montreal to face the music.

A case of manslaughter is brought against him but, despite an obviously sympathetic judge (a lovely cameo from Colleen Dewhurst) is thrown out of court on legal technicalities. The distraught Dinah then goes beyond the law in her search for justice, though the film never gets close to becoming a simple revenge movie; its concerns lie in other directions.

The point being made here, and made forcefully, is that such an accident is all too easy to occur when a driver is lost in a strange city, and that anyone could react the way Hughes does. That running away is cowardly and reprehensible is never in doubt, but it's also all-too-human, and Rubinek's fine performance brings out all the complexities of his character. As the tormented mother, Kerrie Keane is also tops.

Via this vehicle, director Spry explores the love-hate relationship many Canadians have for Yanks, and does so with subtlety. Less subtle, and often outright destructive, is the film's over-insistent music score that often crassly and needlessly underlines the points the film is making. Otherwise, credits are tops.

Packing quite an emotional charge, "Obsessed" will move many people, but looms as too slight for the chancey theatrical market. On video and the tube it should hit home, and the Venice exposure will help spark international attention. It shows that Spry is still one of English Canada's top talents.
—*Strat.*

MONTREAL REVIEWS

The Deceivers
(BRITISH-INDIAN)

A Cinecom Pictures release of a Merchant Ivory Prods./Michael White production, in association with Cinecom and Film Four Intl. Produced by Ismail Merchant. Executive producer, Michael White. Coproducer, Tim Van Rellim. Directed by Nicholas Meyer. Screenplay, Michael Hirst, based on novel by John Masters; camera (Technicolor), Walter Lassally; editor, Richard Trevor; music, John Scott; production design, Ken Adam; costumes, Jenny Beavan, John Bright; sound (Dolby), Claude Hitchcock; associate producer, Leon Falk; art direction, Gianfranco Fumagalli, Ram Yedekar; casting, Celestia Fox (U.K.); Jennifer Jaffrey (India). Reviewed at Columbia Pictures screening room, N.Y., July 26, 1988. MPAA Rating: PG-13. Running time: 112 MIN.

William Savage	Pierce Brosnan
Hussein	Saeed Jaffrey
Chandra Singh	Shashi Kapoor
Sarah Wilson	Helena Michell
Col. Wilson	Keith Michell
George Angelsmith	David Robb
Feringeea	Tario Yunis
Nawab	Jalal Agha
Lt. Maunsell	Gary Cady

■ Those accustomed to the genteel cinema of manners recently perfected by Merchant Ivory Prods. may be startled by the mayhem of this sumptuously produced historical action adventure tale, set in pre-Raj India circa 1825.

"The Deceivers" falls short of fully developing its most interesting theme — the struggle of the rational Western psyche with the supernatural seductions of the East — but its exotic locations, briskly paced narrative and MIP cachet present hit-hungry Cinecom with an opportunity for a theatrical success in selective release.

Pierce Brosnan is William Savage, a "resident collector" for the British East India Co., which blazed the trail for England's colonialization of the Indian subcontinent. The India of "The Deceivers" is an untamed land of barbaric customs, in which British control is tenuous and extends only to certain districts. Omnipresent danger strikes in a tingling setup sequence in which a Company patrol is mysteriously ambushed and murdered in the dead of night.

When Brosnan discovers the bodies in a gruesome mass grave, the fearless, straight-arrow officer is outraged. A rising Company star who has married the commander's daughter (Helena Michell), he risks his career by setting out to prove the murders are part of a horrifying conspiracy. Brosnan's father-in-law Colonel Wilson (Keith Michell, real-life dad of Helena) wants to focus on Company business as usual, and relieves the zealous Brosnan of his post for rounding up Indian suspects from outside the British district.

One of these suspects, however, is so terrified by Brosnan's interrogation technique that he confesses all. According to Hussein (Saeed Jaffrey), the murders are the work of the Thuggees — a centuries-old, pan-Indian brotherhood of evildoers who worship Kali, the goddess of destruction. Their modus operandi is to deceive travelers by posing as harmless merchants, attach themselves to their victims' caravans, then rob and murder them by night in a ritual of neck-cracking strangulation and disfigurement. Paradoxically repulsed and intrigued, Brosnan goes native in makeup and mufti with the hapless Jaffrey on an undercover mission to expose the killer cult.

Adapting John Masters' fact-derived novel, director Nicholas Meyer makes the most of an opportunity for hommage to Alexander Korda adventure movies. Brosnan's otherworldly hegira on the Thuggees' trail leads through wild landscapes, timeless villages, and a fateful initiation into the religious and fraternal ceremonies of the cult.

As psychological drama, Meyer's effort to depict Brosnan's spiritual struggle with the dark forces unleashed by Kai-worship is undermined by the actor's limited range. Brosnan plays the disguised officer behind an intense but inarticulate facade, which makes the extent of his interiorized transformation a matter of guesswork. Brosnan and Meyer are not helped by an elliptical screenplay which fails to exploit the complex possibilities inherent in the cross-cultural confrontation.

Brosnan's dissolution accelerates when he is compelled to bloody his hands participating in a Thuggee ambush. In one scene of indelible power, the undercover man joins his comrades in a wild orgy and grapples for his identity through a hypnotic haze of drugged, erotic abandon. Brosnan is nearly lost in a maze of deception and counter-deception when he's discovered by the Thuggees' extensive network of spies and forced to flee for his life.

The cavalry-to-the-rescue resolution of "The Deceivers" would seem disappointingly conventional for an MIP film were it not for a crucial climactic gesture. Irrevocably changed by his descent into the nightmarish world of the Thuggees, the bitter Brosnan rejects all that he previously held sacred by tossing his Christian's cross into the Indian dust.

This closes "The Deceivers" with a haunting resonance not evident throughout the film, although

Walter Lassally's stunning cinematography is riveting even when there's less on screen than meets the eye. —*Rich.*

Shag
(BRITISH)

A Tri-Star Pictures release of a Hemdale Film Corp. presentation of a Palace production. Produced by Stephen Woolley, Julia Chasman. Executive producers, John Daly, Derek Gibson, Nik Powell. Directed by Zelda Barron. Screenplay, Robin Swicord, Lanier Laney, Terry Sweeney, from story by Laney, Sweeney; camera (color), Peter MacDonald; editor, Laurence Mery Clark; music, various; art direction, Jon Hutman; production design, Buddy Cone; set decoration, Kara Lindstrom; costume design, Mary E. Vogt; choreography, Kenny Ortega; associate producer, Kerry Boyle; casting, Elisabeth Leustig. Reviewed at Cannon Haymarket, London, Aug. 8, 1988. (In Montreal Film Festival — Cinema of Today and Tomorrow section.) Running time: 100 MIN.

Carson McBride	Phoebe Cates
Chip Guillyard	Scott Coffey
Melaina Buller	Bridget Fonda
Pudge Carmichael	Annabeth Gish
Luanne Clatterbuck	Page Hannah
Buzz Ravenel	Robert Rusler
Harley Ralston	Tyrone Power 3d
Jimmy Valentine	Jeff Yagher

■ London — As a dance flick, "Shag" suffers from an unexciting dance-style and so-so choreography but compensates with a fine young cast and likable story. Ambiguous title could be a drawback but pic may find a "Dirty Dancing"-type market.

Lines like "You don't happen to shag, do you?" will raise an unintended snigger from some audiences (title has a sexual meaning, at least to British and Australian ears) and may detract from a charming, almost old-fashioned, pic replete with the usual period iconography.

The well-worn format of a group of girls heading to the beach to meet boys could easily have degenerated into soft porn and banal dialog, but, to helmer Zelda Barron's credit, she instills the film with warmth and compassion and gives "Shag" a dignity that so many of its genre lack.

Pic is set in South Carolina in 1963 and opens with three girls, Page Hannah, Annabeth Gish and Bridget Fonda, picking up pal Phoebe Cates for her last summer fling with the girls before she marries dull Tyrone Power 3d.

They head for Myrtle Beach and the Sun Fun Festival, full of boys, beer, a beauty parade and shagging — the current dance craze. Within hours of their arrival Cates becomes fascinated by hunky Robert Rusler and plump Gish falls for preppy Scott Coffey.

What follows is a traditional foray into teenage love; with Cates fighting, but eventually falling for, Rusler and his belief in "free love;" Gish teaching the awkward Coffey how to shag and fall in love; Hannah and Power discovering they were made for each other when he comes looking for Cates, and Fonda — who wants to get to Hollywood — seducing the manager of the local teen idol. In all, it's a happy ending.

The four female leads are excellent, though it is Fonda who exudes confidence and star quality and looks destined for great things. Of the guys, Scott Coffey's character is the only one with any depth; the rest seem to play hunks, wimps or louts.

Acting-family connections are strong in "Shag," including Bridget Fonda (daughter of Peter), Page Hannah (sister of Daryl) and Tyrone Power 3d (billed as "Junior" but son of star Tyrone Power and grandson of Tyrone Power Sr.), though Annabeth Gish is no relation to the thesp sisters.

Choreography is by the ubiquitous Kenny Ortega, fresh from "Dirty Dancing" and "Salsa." As a dance-step, though, "Shag" is pedestrian compared to Ortega's previous efforts and the dancing itself is not a high priority in the pic.

Barron ably directs her young cast, who all seem to enjoy themselves, and keeps "Shag" fun, breezy and in many ways the perfect summer movie. Standout is the exceptional soundtrack which includes tracks performed by the Voltage Bros. — *Adam.*

Clandestinos
(Living Dangerously)
(CUBAN)

A Cuban Institute of Cinematographic Arts and Industries (Icaic) production. Produced by Santiago Llapur. Directed by Fernando Pérez. Screenplay, Jesús Díaz; camera (color), Adriano Moreno; editor, Jorge Abello; sound, Ricardo Istueta. Reviewed at Festival Latino, N.Y., July 28, 1988. (Also in Montreal Film Festival — Latin American Cinema section.) Running time: **98 MIN.**
Ernesto Ardeniz . . . . . . Luis Alberto García
Nereida . . . . Isabel Santos
Carmen . . . . Susana Pérez
Pino . . . . Jorge Luis Sánchez

■ **Based on real events and dedicated to those who died in combat, the Cuban pic "Clandestinos" (Living Dangerously, a.k.a. Underground) depicts the terrorist activities of a group of revolutionaries during the turbulent period just before the Cuban revolution. Film picked up best first work and best actress nods at the ninth Havana Film Festival.**

Although technically well made and at times gripping, pic appears to be aimed at strictly local b.o. since it does not give a larger context for those unfamiliar with the Cuban revolution. Our small band of terrorists works independently, and is not shown as part of a widespread dissent.

Domestically, pic is important

because it recognizes that there were independents in 1958 working outside of Fidel's July 26th Movement, which has traditionally taken full credit for the downfall of the Batista regime.

Plot begins with mild protests: the males interrupt a baseball game while their femme counterparts wreck havoc at a "Queen For A Day" broadcast. Not content with banners and slogans, the revolutionaries escalate activities to shootouts with the police, armed robbery, planting bombs and inciting civil disobedience. They then move from hideout to hideout with the vigilant police in hot pursuit. Betrayal also breaks out in the ranks, which brings about pic's final battle.

Photography is sharp and film is distinguished by a loving attention to detail, with an almost nostalgic recreation of Havana in the 1950s. Taking predominance are ubiquitous advertisements for U.S. products, stressing Cuba's former economic domination by transnational (i.e., American) business interests.

At the film's core is a love story, bearing a classic notion of lovers doomed by history and circumstance. While acting by the principals is strong, there is little the actors can do with skimpy roles stressing only doom and the purity of fighting for a cause. In this, director Fernando Pérez treats his subjects with the reverence of a hagiographer chronicling Christian martyrdom. —*Lent.*

Berlin Blues
(SPANISH)

An Emiliano Piedra production, with participation of Spanish TV. Written and directed by Ricardo Franco. Screenplay adaptation, Lawrence Dworet; camera (Eastmancolor), Teo Escamilla; editor, Teresa Font; music, Lalo Schifrin; songs, Schifrin, Matt Mueller; sets, Gerardo Vera; sound, Carlos Faruolo; makeup, Cristóbal Cristo; choreography, Giorgio Aresu; sound effects, Luis Castro; production manager, Emiliano Otegui. Reviewed at Cinearte screening room, Madrid, July 12, 1988. (In Montreal Film Festival, competing.) Running time: **102 MIN.**
Lola . . . . Julia Migenes
Prof. Huessler . . . . Keith Baxter
David . . . . José Coronado
Also with: Javier Gurruchaga, Gerardo Vera, Jesús López Cobos, Mereia Ross, José Maria Pon, Maximilian Reuthelein.
(English soundtrack)

■ **Madrid — Incorporating elements of "The Blue Angel" and "Cabaret," this pic, with modern Berlin as a backdrop, has some fine music written by Lalo Schifrin and a topnotch performance by Julia Migenes.**

Difficult to categorize in any particular genre, since both the music and the story form integral parts of pic, item could appeal to a wide spectrum of audiences.

Migenes is cast as an expatriate Yank making a tough living belting out songs in a Berlin nitery. She becomes embroiled in an affair with an East German concert pianist visiting the West on tour. The budding romance is interrupted by the conductor of the East German orchestra, a vitriolic, lonely taskmaster utterly dedicated to his art.

When David, the young pianist, is forced to return to the East, the professor stays on and himself becomes embroiled with the flighty singer. When the girl loses her job due to the club being shuttered by the police after a Yank serviceman is mortally stabbed during a row, the middle-aged conductor gives her a helping hand, and even tries to get her a job in the opera. His efforts are rewarded in bed. End of pic is left hanging, but eschews any touch of tragedy, as each of the three protagonists returns to his own niche in life.

British thesp Keith Baxter puts in a fine performance as the aging conductor having his fling with the young songstress. Production values are good, especially recording of the score, which includes some catchy numbers. — *Besa.*

Zivot sa Stricem
(My Uncle's Legacy)
(YUGOSLAV)

A Yugoslavija Film release of a Kinematografi, Zagreb presentation of a Urania Film (Zagreb), Avala Film (Belgrade), Stassen Prods. (L.A.) production. Produced by Tomica Milanovski, Branko Baletic, Ben Stassen. Directed by Krsto Papic. Screenplay, Ivan Aralica, Papic, based on Aralica's novel "Framework For Hatred;" camera (color), Boris Turkovic; editor, Robert Lisjak; music, Branislaw Zivkovic; art direction, Tihomir Piletic; costumes, Jasna Novak. Reviewed at Pula Film Festival, July 27, 1988. (Also in Montreal Film Festival, competing.) Running time: **108 MIN.**

With: Davor Janjic, Alma Prica, Miodrag Krivokapic, Branislaw Lecic, Anica Dobra, Ivo Gregurevic, Filip Sovagovic, Nenad Srdelic, Ilija Zovko, Dejan Acimovic, Perica Martinovic, Fabijan Sovagovic.

■ **Pula — Veteran director Krsto Papic deals with the political turmoils and confusion which rocked the country in the early '50s, following Tito's decision to sever his ties with Moscow.**

This particular script was considered too subversive and the director had to appeal to the courts in order to get clearance to shoot it.

The plot concerns a group of students, some of peasant stock, others of urban proletarian origins, all of whom are studying to become teachers. The central figure is Martin, a bright boy with an uncanny talent for caricatures satirizing the everyday events in school.

Living with his grandfather since the death of his own father, Martin feels particularly close to an uncle who is a high party dignitary, and

who is trying to persuade the grandfather to give up his land to the agricultural collective in the village and join in as a member.

The old man, set in his ways, who had worked all his life for this land, refuses and becomes a thorn in his own son's political conscience. At the same time, Martin and his friends from the country are victimized at school by the corrupt principal who can't stand having his authority questioned nor his favorite student, (a girl who sleeps with him) ridiculed in public. As long as the powerful uncle extends his protection, Martin is relatively safe, but when that is withdrawn, he becomes an easy prey to political manipulations intended to kick him out.

Using a healthy dose of humor in the portrayal of school climate, Papic shows solid craftsmanship.

Martin is accidentally emasculated by the fault of that uncle, who, on his death bed, asks him, as a last wish, to arrange for him a Christian burial, something no self-respecting communist, let alone an important leader, would dream of doing. There could be no plainer indication of the moral bankruptcy of the system.

Carefully produced and visually rewarding, the film could stand some additional pruning in the middle, but otherwise is one of the more satisfying items. —*Edna.*

La Lectrice
(The Reader)
(FRENCH)

An AAA release of an Eléfilm/AAA Prods./TSF Prods./Ciné-5 coproduction. Directed by Michel Deville. Produced and written by Michel and Rosalinde Deville, based on the books "La Lectrice" and "Un Fantasme de Bella B. et autre récits" by Raymond Jean; camera (Eastmancolor), Dominique Le Rigoleur; editor, Raymonde Guyot; music, Beethoven; art direction, Thierry Leproust; costumes, Cecile Balme; sound, Philippe Lioret; makeup, Joel Lavau; production manager, Franz Damamme. Reviewed at the Marignan Concorde cinema, Paris, Aug. 21, 1988. (In Montreal Film Festival — competing.) Running time: **100 MIN.**

With: Miou-Miou (Constance/Marie), Christian Ruché (Jean/Philippe), Maria Casarès (the General's widow), Patrick Chesnais (business executive), Marianne Denicourt (Bella), Pierre Dux (magistrate), Sylvie Laporte (Francoise), Brigitte Catillon, Michel Raskine, Christian Blanc, Regis Royer, Simon Eine, André Wilms, Clotilde de Bayser, Bérangère Bonvoisin, Jean-Luc Boutté.

■ **Paris — A stylish frothy "light read" of a film, "La Lectrice" recounts the adventures of a young woman who rents her services as a professional reader to bourgeois clients ill-disposed to doing their own page-turning.**

After the hollow theatrical conceits of his last feature, "Le Paltoquet," writer-producer-director Michel Deville has fashioned an elegant entertainment with humor, irony, eroticism. Pic is shaping up as a "bestseller" at local wickets and could translate into foreign art house salons.

Miou-Miou is the engaging heroine, a young woman of Arles who enjoys reading, has an attractive voice and obviously enjoys meeting people. Upon a friend's suggestion she places an ad in a local paper to offer reading services.

Naturally, the clientele is varied and usually have ulterior motives other than love of literature, though she responds with good-humored indulgence to their various vagaries, which often tend to the sexual.

Miou-Miou reads Guy de Maupassant to a young cripple aroused by the view of her casually uncovered thigh, goes through Karl Marx and Tolstoy for the widow of an Eastern European general (Maria Casarès) and beleaguers a neurotic inhibited business exec (Patrick Chesnais) with Marguerite Duras while they hop into bed together.

She finally decides to turn the final page on her little metier when an aging local magistrate (Pierre Dux) asks her to read some salacious prose from the Marquis de Sade for a round table of fellow notables.

Deville has composed this playful little opus with a deluxe production that makes every scene a pleasure for the eye, from Thierry Leproust's witty production design to Cecile Balme's colorful costume schemes, bound with finesse by Dominique Le Rigoleur's color lensing.

Picturesque exteriors of winding streets and alleyways in the old quarter of Arles puncuate the film's glossy look.

Miou-Miou, who is at her most appealing in this relaxed comic role, is perfectly supported by Casarès, Dux and a host of lesser known thesps. —Len.

Sokol Ga Nije Volio
(The Stallion Didn't Like Him)
(YUGOSLAV)

A Yugoslavija Film release of a Zagreb Films production. Directed by Branko Smit. Screenplay, Smit, Fabijan Sovagovic; camera (color), Goran Trbuljak; music, Zoran Mulic; art direction, Stanko Dobrina; costumes, Vjera Ivankovic. Reviewed at Pula Film Festival (competing), July 24, 1988. (Also in Montreal Film Festival — Yugoslavian Cinema of Today section.) Running time: 86 MIN.
With: Fabijan Sovagovic, Filip Sovagovic.

■ Pula — A first film displaying a considerable political courage, but in need of tighter script editing, this WWII picture shows its sympathies for the helpless rural population victimized first by the fascists, then by the communists.

Sime, a shrewd peasant with land of his own, hopes that by playing along with both sides, the *ustashi* who are hand in hand with the Nazis, and the partisans, who are fighting to throw them out, he will

keep his family and his property intact. His son is drafted by the fascists into the military, but when he comes home on leave, Sime prevents him from going back and hides him in the attic. At the same time, he offers shelter to the resistance, without having too much sympathy for them. None of his calculations work out, for the events are much stronger than he.

Director Branko Smit adds to the story of Sime and his family episodes concerning the other villagers, who face similar plights. Film starts with the fascists deporting Jews and gypsies, and ends it with the communists deporting their political opponents, the equation being perfectly obvious. So is his attitude towards functionaries on both sides, representing arbitrary and inhuman power crushing the individual.

The stallion of the title is a magnificent black one in Sime's possession, never quite tamed by his master, who symbolically takes out on it all the frustations that he has no way of protesting against in another manner.

Fabijan Sovagovic, who shares writing credits, gives a solid performance in the lead role, but his is the only part with any depth in it, the rest of the cast having to deal with sketchy, 1-dimensional characters.

Well shot, using handsome locations but with a script that lacks breadth in developing dramatic situations, the film wears its good intentions on its sleeve. It will have problems scoring with audiences who are not deeply concerned with this specific historical moment.
—*Edna*.

A Sega Nakude
(Where Do We Go From Here?)
(BULGARIAN)

A Bulgariafilm production. Directed by Rangel Vulchanov. Screenplay, Vulchanov, Georgi Danailov; camera (color), Radoslav Spassov; music, Kiril Donchev; sound (Dolby), Ivan Ventcheslavov; art direction, Irina Stoicheva. Reviewed at Karlovy Vary Film Festival (competing), July 12, 1988. (Also in Montreal Film Festival — Cinema of Today and Tomorrow section.) Running time: 92 MIN.

With: Ani Vulchanova, Albena Stavreva, Antoineta Stancheva, Darina Georgieva, Elena Arsova, Irina Doichinova, Krasimira Miteva, Stefka Yordanova, Teodora Voinova.

■ Karlovy Vary — Dean of Bulgarian cinema Rangel Vulchanov presents a tour-de-force in "Where Do We Go From Here?"

Title is confusingly similar to his previous comedy "Where Are You Going?" but film is a distinct offering from an ever-inventive director. The battle of 26 would-be actors before an invisible jury to be accepted into drama academy is an allegory between Kafka and "A Chorus

Line." For those philosphically inclined, "Where Do We Go From Here?" presents a thought-provoking metaphor for society in microcosm, with an ending to be puzzled out.

On an entertainment level, film is a colorful array of youthful rivals scrambling for a shot at the big time. Large cast (composed of real acting students) quickly gets sorted out into types: the femme fatale banking on her looks, the country boy, the cocky braggart, the nice fat girl, etc. Dialog (by Vulchanov and Georgi Danailov) keeps pic moving along at a fast clip.

Aspirants get their instructions from a disembodied, mocking microphone, which they obey blindly until 'the inevitable rebellion — quelled as, one by one, they dribble back to take more senseless tests before a panel of hidden judges. Their consciences are put on trial when one boy is eliminated for being politically suspect.

Most determined of all is a girl who comes late and is locked outside the theater. Her struggle to get inside brings her into contact with a handsome mute boy, but she opts for the stage over romance, sacrificing all for her profession.

A well-balanced and diversified work from a master entertainer, film is boosted by fine technical work all around. —*Yung*.

Moj Ata, Socialisticni Kulak
(My Dad, The Socialist Kulak)
(YUGOSLAV)

A Yugoslavia Film release of a Viba Film production. Directed by Matjaz Klopcic. Screenplay, Tone Partljic, based on his novel and play; camera (color), Zivko Zalar; editor, Darinka Persin-Andromako; music, Joze Privsek; sound, Matjaz Janezic; art direction, Niko Matul; costumes, Alenka Bartl; make-up, Mirko Mackic. Reviewed at Pula Film Festival (competing), July 29, 1988. (Also in Montreal Film Festival — Yugoslavian Cinema of Today section.) Running time: 122 MIN.
Father ....Polde Bibic
Mother ....Milena Zupancic
Olga ....Urska Hlebek
Tincek ....Matjaz Partlic
Also with: Ivo Ban (Vanc), Ivan Godnic (policeman), Anton Petje (priest).

■ Pula — A black comedy reminiscent of the Czech cinema of the '60s, this is a humorous attempt to describe communist indoctrination in a small village.

The simple people are trying to maneuver between revolution and tradition, ideological fashions and their basic aspirations, such as getting some meat with their potatoes, or obtaining a piece of land of their own.

(Film won grand prize at the Pula fest. — *Ed*.)

Starting immediately after WWII, pic depicts the government promising a golden future and the party

making sure nobody dares doubt it aloud, but the villagers are still dependent on the local kulak (landowner) for work and a place to live.

Film focuses on a typical family and how it experiences the bliss of socialism, imaginatively described by the young son as "the purgatory before the Paradise of Communism."

For some reason Matjaz Klopcic, a veteran director with mostly dramatic experience, finds it necessary to use an over-romanticized visual style hinting at some kind of fantasy the script does not substantiate. The material, by now pretty familiar from many other films on the same period, suffers from plodding presentation.

Impeccably shot and featuring some broad comic performances, the film has its entertaining moments, but drags on, wearying the watcher long before the end.
— *Edna*.

Sweetwater
(NORWEGIAN)

A KF release of Marcusfilm production, in association with Kodak Norway and the Swedish Film Institute. Produced by Bente Erichsen. Directed by Lasse Glomm. Screenplay, Glomm, based on Knut Falbakken novels; camera (Panavision, Eastmancolor), Philip Oegaard; editor and sound, Peter Ekvall, Mats Kruger; music, Stefan Nilsson; production design, Anders Barreus; costumes, Kjell Torheim; production management, Jeanette Sundby; Italian production assistance, Fracesca Boesch, Adriana Cortese de Bosis; British production assistance, Terry Bamber; stunts, Terry Cape, 'Paul Heatman, Franck Henderson, Benito Stefanelli. Reviewed at Norwegian Film Festival, Haugesund, Norway, Aug. 17, 1988. (Also in Montreal Film Festival — competing.) Running time: 120 MIN.
Allan ....Bentein Baardson
Lisa ....Petronella Barker
Mary Diamond .....Alphonsia Emmanuel
Smiley ....Per Jansen
Doc ....Sven Wollter
Boy ....Martin Disch
Run-Run ....Sverre Anker Ousdal
Felix ....Björn Sundquist
Also with: Tom Tellefsen, Elsa Lystad, Morten Faldaas, Terjse Strömdahl.

■ Haugesund (Norway) — "Sweetwater," a competition pick for the upcoming Montreal film festival, was seen in its world preem by a hushed audience, familiar with and respectful of the Knut Falbakken visionary scare novels on which writer-helmer Lasse Glomm has based his austere work.

Hushed? Well, maybe also asleep, since Glomm has put all his and cinematographer Philip Oegaard's care and artistic invention in the composing, lighting and shooting of spectacular Panavision frames, in which all characters move either like sonambulists or Olympic runners, that is when they are not copulating or beating madly away at dead animals or at each other.

Whatever happens (and everything is told with loose ends flying around to clutter any idea of a storyline), austerity beyond the point of self-indulgency reigns as Allan and Lisa and their small son Boy flee the horror of some war-devastated city (called Sweetwater) to seek some kind of peaceful survival in the desert wastes of the municipal dump (actually that of Rome' where most of the location shooting was done).

Here, sour-faced Allan sees to it that Lisa gets pregnant in a hurry, signifying, supposedly, that life must go on. He soon chooses to sleep with Mary Diamond, a black prostitute, instead. Her pimp is a brute who spouts improbable wisdom. Soon, a little group of survival-seekers, some looking like graduates of Beckett dramas, others like takeoffs of Sergio Leone Western characters, begin to live uneasily together. A huge deaf-mute protects the boy called Boy, a doctor who once made a career of abortions, helps bring Lisa's baby girl into the world.

By and by (the film runs a mortifying 120 minutes), Sergio Leone gets the upper hand of Samuel Beckett in the fragmented narration which is all to the good since the dialog removes itself more and more from even comic book literacy.

The ending has Allan trading his wife for a gun and leading the group back into Sweetwater. Since they cannot escape violence, they might as well face it wholesale. At least, that could be one way of interpreting things.

To look at "Sweetwater" is nothing less than stunning. With the actors mostly left to their own devices, the rest is just plain numbing.
— *Kell.*

The Lair Of The White Worm
(BRITISH)

A Vestron Pictures release of a White Lair Prods. production. Executive producers, William J. Quigley, Dan Ireland. Line producer, Ronaldo Vasconcellos. Produced and directed by Ken Russell. Screenplay, Russell, from Bram Stoker's novel; camera (Technicolor), Dick Bush; editor, Peter Davies; music, Stanislas Syrewicz; sound (Dolby), Ray Beckett; set design, Anne Tilby; costume design, Michael Jeffrey; choreography, Imogen Claire; special makeup effects, Image Animation; additional camera, Robin Browne; stunt coordinator, Stuart St. Paul; production manager, Laura Julian; assistant director, Chris Hall; casting, Gail Stevens. Reviewed at Montreal World Film Festival (noncompeting), Aug. 29, 1988. (Also in Toronto and Boston film festivals.) MPAA Rating: R. Running time: **93 MIN.**

Lady Silvia Marsh .... Amanda Donohoe
Lord James D'Ampton ...... Hugh Grant
Eve Trent .... Catherine Oxenberg
Mary Trent .... Sammi Davis
Angus Flint .... Peter Capaldi
Peters .... Stratford Johns
P.C. Erny .... Paul Brooke
Dorothy Trent .... Imogen Claire
  Also with: Chris Pitt, Gina McKee, Christopher Gable, Lloyd Peters, Miranda Coe, Linzi Drew, Caron Anne Kelly, Fiona O'Conner, Caroline Pope, Elisha Scott, Tina Shaw.

■ **Montreal — Those who hated "Gothic" (and there was good reason to) are strongly urged to give Ken Russell another chance and consider this rollicking, terrifying, post-psychedelic headtrip, "The Lair Of The White Worm." Vestron Pictures should gear up to exploit the huge cult hit potential of an original, fun-filled nightmare.**

Adapted from a tale by Bram Stoker, creator of Dracula, "Lair" features a fangy vampiress of unmatched erotic allure. Lady Sylvia Marsh, as she goes by in her Jaguar-tooling civilian existence, lives in a sprawling mansion not far from the state-of-the-art castle inhabited by Lord James D'Ampton.

Hugh Grant ("Maurice") essays Lord James as a kind of post-Prince Charles democratic nobleman, insufferably in command but eager to rub shoulders with the hoi poloi. Lord James even throws open his castle for a wild party, inving all and sundry. Among the guests are Lord James' tenants, Eve and Mary Trent and Mary's new boyfriend, Angus Flint.

Eve and Mary have been running their parents' country inn since mon and dad disappeared one night on a walk through the woods. Angus is an archeology student who's been digging in their front yard. On the day of the big party, just before nightfall, Angus finds a bizarre, unclassifiable skull.

The castle party is celebrating Lord James' inheritance of the estate as well as a family holiday commemorating a legendary ancestor said to have slain a dragon. In the Lampton clan mythology, the dragon is represented as an overblown, jawsy white worm, a model of which is ceremonially slain at the festivities.

In a bit of class-system byplay probably best appreciated by U.K. audiences, the uppercrust Brit noble ("Scotch is a drink") scholar engage in some mano-a-mano intellectual sparring, and come away admiring each other's erudition. They agree that the whole dragon-snake-worm business can be traced back to pagan religions that flourished in Olde England when the Romans ruled.

All this unfolds with a jittery energy that suggests something is definitely out of kilter in this neighborhood's collective reality. It might have something to do with Lady Sylvia who has moved back to her ancestral manse at just about the time of Lord James' return.

Soon the duke and the digger divine an eerie connection between the mysteriously burgled skull, the white worm legend and cases of snakebite plus more strange disappearances close by the Lady's mansion. Then things start to get scary.

Russell dips into his "Altered States" cornucopia of transdimensional visual effects, creating startling tableaux of 3-D palpability, no specs needed. He also succeeds in evoking a shocking sensuality from gore-splashed scenes.

Amanda Donohoe as the vampire seductress projects a beguiling sexuality that should suck the resistance out of all but the most cold-blooded critics. She is also hilarious, a virtue shared by everyone and everything in "The Lair Of The White Worm."

Does Lord James act in time to save the beautiful Eve (Catherine Oxenberg) from the human sacrifices reserved for virgins? Does Angus marry Mary or has he bitten off more than he can chew? How does one really kill a vampiress? It's possible that many will return for a second viewing even after they know the answers. — *Rich.*

I Yineka Pou Evlepe ta Onira
(The Woman Who Dreamed)
(GREEK)

A Greek Film Center presentation of a GFT, ET-1, Nikos Panayatopoulos production. Directed by Panayatopoulos. Screenplay, Panayatopoulos, Christos Vakalopoulos; camera (color), Aris Stavrou; sound, Marinos Athanassopoulos; art direction, Dyonissis Fotopoulos; costumes, Mariana Spanoudaki. Reviewed at Locarno Film Festival (noncompeting), Aug. 12, 1988. Running time: **105 MIN.**
With: Myrto Paraschi, Yannis Bezos.

■ **Locarno — Ten years after being awarded a Golden Leopard on the Piazza Grande for his best known film to date, "Idlers Of The Fertile Valley," Greek helmer Nikos Panayatopoulos is back, this time out of competition, with another allegory of modern alienation.**

Film concerns a lawyer's wife who insists on sharing her strange dreams with her husband. At first receptive or at least polite, the spouse, involved in a complex and mystifying murder trial, finally is exasperated by her double life and refuses to listen any more.

Offended because she feels a part of her personality is rejected, the wife drifts away from her husband, who suspects she has found somebody else to whom she can confide, hires a detective to shadow her and almost destroys what was until then a happy marriage.

Panayatopoulos seems concerned mainly with the man's rejection of his wife and the private world she offers to share with him. Hubby's lack of imagination and his capacity to grasp only the real, threaten to be his downfall, as his egotism leaves no room for married life.

The script, however, doesn't take the trouble to flesh out and integrate either the dreams or the trial perturbing the man's peace of mind, into the main theme, leaving it all on a metaphorical level.

While very well shot and technically polished, the film lacks sufficient dramatic material to keep an audience alert. Myrto Paraschi; in the title role, doesn't seem to take her dreams too seriously either and Yannis Bezos as her husband is particularly stolid. —*Edna.*

Eight Men Out

An Orion Pictures release of a Sanford/-Pillsbury production. Produced by Sarah Pillsbury, Midge Sanford. Coproducer, Peggy Rajski. Executive producers, Barbara Boyle, Jerry Offsay. Directed, written by John Sayles, based on the book by Eliot Asinof; camera (Duart color), Robert Richardson; editor, John Tintori; music, Mason Daring; production design, Nora Chavooshian; art direction, Dan Bishop; set decoration, Lynn Wolverton; costume design, Cynthia Flynt; sound, David Brownlow; assistant director, Gary Marcus; casting, Barbara Shapiro (N.Y.), Carrie Frazier (L.A.), Shani Ginsbert, Avy Kaufman (location); second unit camera, Marc Reshovsky. Reviewed at the Orion screening room, L.A., Aug. 5, 1988. MPAA Rating: PG. Running time: **119 MIN.**

Buck Weaver .... John Cusack
Charles Comiskey .... Clifton James
Arnold Rothstein .... Michael Lerner
Bill Burns .... Christopher Lloyd
Kid Gleason .... John Mahoney
Hap Felsch .... Charlie Sheen
Eddie Cicotte .... David Strathairn
Shoeless Joe Jackson .... D.B. Sweeney
Swede Risberg .... Don Harvey
Chick Gandil .... Michael Rooker
Fred McMullin .... Perry Lang
Lefty Williams .... James Read
Dickie Kerr .... Jace Alexander
Ray Schalk .... Gordan Clapp
Billy Maharg .... Richard Edson
Eddie Collins .... Bill Irwin
Abe Attell .... Michael Mantell
Sport Sullivan .... Kevin Tighe
Hugh Fullerton .... Studs Terkel
Judge Kenesaw Mountain
  Landis .... John Anderson
Ring Lardner .... John Sayles
Kate Jackson .... Wendy Makkena
Rose Cicotte .... Maggie Renzi

■ **Hollywood — Perhaps the saddest chapter in the annals of professional American sports is recounted in absorbing fashion in "Eight Men Out."**

Story of how the 1919 Chicago White Sox threw the World Series in cahoots with professional gamblers, in what became known as the Black Sox Scandal, stands as a worthy companion piece to writer-director John Sayles' last film, "Matewan," in its depiction of owner exploitation of the little guy in post-World War I America.

Strong reviews and interest in the innately fascinating episode should make for solid business in upscale urban markets, but dryness and the inevitable air of disenchantment hanging over the tale will make breakout to the general public difficult.

Frequently announced by various filmmakers over the years, this project fortunately ended up in the hands of Sayles, who effectively presents an amazing amount of information and a vast array of colorful characters at an only moderate sacrifice of depth.

Based on Eliot Asinof's 1963 best-seller, Sayles' densely packed screenplay lays out how eight players for the White Sox, who were considered shoo-ins to beat the Cincinnati Reds in the World Series, committed an unthinkable betrayal of the national pastime by conspiring to lose the Fall Classic.

One by one, and seemingly a bit too easily in this telling, the players fall in line. While the justifications for abandoning their pride and principles appear vague in some instances, they are all crystalized in Sayles' view by the case of aging star pitcher Eddie Cicotte. At a time when player salaries on the team fell in the $2,500-5,000 range, Cicotte had been promised a $10,000 bonus if he won 30 games. When ultra-cheap owner Charles Comiskey refuses any reward because he only won 29, Cicotte decides to throw in with the schemers, thereby setting up Sayles' central themes of class exploitation and the economic imperative.

While the plan is backed at the highest level by underworld bigshot Arnold Rothstein, it is carried out on a practical level by an astonishing collection of smalltime hustlers and deadbeats. On the other side are sports writers Ring Lardner and Hugh Fullerton, who are so suspicious of the Sox' bad play as the series progresses that they are able to begin piecing together the outlines of the conspiracy.

Some of the characters here are the stuff of baseball legend, notably the all-time great Shoeless Joe Jackson, who was the target of the immortal line, uttered by a disbelieving kid, "Say it ain't so, Joe. Say it ain't so."

The most compelling figures here are Cicotte, a man nearing the end of his career who feels the twin needs to insure a financial future for his family and take revenge on his boss, and Buck Weaver, an innocent enthusiast who took no cash for the fix but, like the others, was forever banned from baseball due to his participation in the scheme.

The limitation of telling a yarn so loaded with characters and history lies in the lack of time to deeply characterize and motivate the key players. This is complemented by a certain aridity and possibly necessary jumpiness of style.

On balance, however, Sayles has done an outstanding job in getting so much content and production value up on the screen, and he has shrewdly assembled a cast able to bring their characters vividly to life despite limited screen time.

Taciturn and brooding, his feelings buried deep, David Strathairn is a fantastic Cicotte. Entirely contrasting is John Cusack's youthful, brimming Weaver, a man who vainly spent the rest of his life trying to clear his name, as did Jackson, splendidly embodied by D.B. Sweeney.

The other young actors playing the White Sox mesh wonderfully as an ensemble, from Charlie Sheen's hustling center fielder to Gordon Clapp's hot-tempered catcher. Michael Lerner makes a perfect, businesslike Rothstein, Clifton James a smugly self-assured Comiskey, and John Mahoney a quintessential manager, both tough and compassionate. As the two key sportscribes, Studs Terkel and John Sayles almost have the makings of a comedy team, the former short and feisty, the latter a reedy piece of timber.

As a director, Sayles made a major stride on the visual level working with cinematographer Haskell Wexler on "Matewan," and he has held the same ground in collaboration with Robert Richardson ("Salvador," "Platoon") here.

The work of production designer Nora Chavooshian, costume designer Cynthia Flynt and the many hands who helped recreate the milieu of major league baseball, circa 1919, under the resourceful guidance of producers Sarah Pillsbury and Midge Sanford and coproducer Peggy Rajski, cannot be overpraised, for it is all captivating and convincing. Music by Mason Daring is also a strong plus. — *Cart.*

Biglal Hamilkhama Hahi
(Because Of That War)
(ISRAELI-DOCU)

An Israeli Film Service presentation of a Manor production. Produced by Shmuel Altman, David Schitz. Written and directed by Orna Ben Dor-Niv. Camera (color, 16m), Oren Schmukler; editor, Rachel Yagil; music, Yehuda Poliker. Reviewed at United Studios screening room, Tel Aviv, July 2, 1988. Running time: **90 MIN.**

■ Tel Aviv — A rare Israeli theatrical documentary, this has been produced by the Israeli government film service, mostly with tv distribution in mind, but initial reception was so enthusiastic, distributors and exhibitors have been competing to handle it theatrically.

Triggered by a record album entitled "Ashes And Dust" and dedicated exclusively to one subject, the Holocaust, Orna Ben Dor-Niv's film focuses on singer-composer Yehuda Poliker and lyricist-producer Yaakov Gil'ad, who created the album together.

Poliker's father and Gil'ad's mother are former Auschwitz inmates, and have raised their children in the shadow of the terrible memories they carried with them. Poliker Sr. lost all his family — a wife and children — in the extermination camp and almost committed suicide after the war. He chose to come to Israel, where he started a new family but could never rid himself of the past.

Gil'ad's mother, Halina Birnbaum, born in Poland, is a writer and poet who dedicates her life exclusively to the publication of works by artists killed in the camps, and to lectures to high school students.

The film is a series of conversations, first with the artists, then with the parents, and later having all of them meet together. The film's strength lies in its unpretentiousness, allowing each one of these four to unload their painful personal experiences in a straightforward manner and hardly pushing them along the way. Always edifying, often moving and sometimes wrenching, the film is a powerful document on the effect of the Holocaust on the second generation, born after the war and yet still living under its terrifying impact.

Several sequences won't be easily forgotten, whether it is Poliker Sr. remembering the journey to Auschwitz and breaking down in the middle, or Halina Birnbaum talking to high schoolers who start by being rather passive to a topic they think they know only too well, but gradually becoming horribly fascinated as the speaker relives her past in front of them.

Shot in eight days and assembled carefully, the film has that peculiar quality of life caught in the raw. Already invited to the Berlin Forum, its emotional intensity is likely to get it a lot of dates in the next few months. It even stands a good chance to reach young audiences at home as well, who will be first attracted by the identity of the two stars, and only through them reach the subject itself. Sequences of recording sessions for the last album, as well as copious excerpts from the songs, will make the bitter pill easier to swallow. —*Edna.*

El camino del sur
(The Road South)
(ARGENTINE-YUGOSLAV)

A Jorge Estrada Mora Producciones presentation of a Jorge Estrada Mora Producciones (Argentina) and Art Film 80 (Yugoslavia) coproduction. Producer, Jorge Estrada Mora. Directed by Juan Bautista Stagnaro. Screenplay, Stagnaro, Elida Ceccone, based on plot idea by Stagnaro, Beda Docampo Feijoó; camera (color), Karpo Godina; editor, Enrique Muzio; music, Zoran Simjanovic; sets, Santiago Elder, Nikola Lazarevsky; costumes, Beatriz Di Benedetto, Evelyn Bendjeskov. Reviewed at Vigo screening room, Buenos Aires, June 15, 1988. (Rating in Argentina: forbidden for under 16s.) Running time: **104 MIN.**

Máximo Brockman	Adrián Ghio
Jana	Mira Joković
Rufino	Osvaldo Santoro
Moritz	Žarko Laušević

Also with: Mira Furlan, Marla Fiorentino, Mauricio Dayub, Eva Ras, Joaquín Mónaco, Milan Erak.

■ Buenos Aires — A mixed Argentine-Yugoslav cuisine, "The Road South" provides a potent if somewhat uneven dish. It could find a market wherever the immigrant experience in the Americas strikes a responsive chord; wherever a special sidelight on the Jewish experience, in particular, is of interest, and wherever strong melodrama is appreciated.

The starting-off point for the story is the generally acknowledged fact that, among the numerous Jewish immigrants who arrived in Argentina at the beginning of the century, though perhaps the most significant contingents headed for agrarian colonies in the interior of the country, a certain percentage turned to brothel keeping and white slaving.

Antihero of "The Road South" is Brockman, already a longtime resident of Argentina, who turns up in his automobile in a Jewish village in Yugoslavia to pick himself a wife. Enter the heroine, Jana; he later tells her he chose her because she has the look of a virgin. Actress Mira Joković is nuance-perfect in a display of fresh but just slightly petulant appeal.

Best part of the film shows the wife selection process, the wedding, the genuinely moving goodbye, etc., in the old country (this part was shot on location in Macedonia).

The tone of the relations between man and wife changes on the boat coming over, and soon it is obvious, even to Jana, that Brockman is a white slaver in Buenos Aires. However, he hasn't simply collected her on false pretenses to dump her in a brothel and forget all about her save for her earnings. Though he makes her work as a prostitute, he actually does keep her as his wife.

Life in Buenos Aires develops in a picturesque neighborhood, but the area is also low-lying, which cues in a major set-piece flood.

Thereafter, events become ever more melodramatic, as Jana begins to be courted by an honest bloke, her son risks life and limb on a rooftop, her husband uses the son to blackmail her emotionally, and a brother (by trade a butcher) she left behind in the old country turns up in the hope of avenging her honor.

Believability and impact are choppier here, but do not disappear. The overall balance: somewhat formulaic but vigorous and vivid.
— *Olas.*

Running On Empty

A Warner Bros. release of a Lorimar Film Entertainment presentation of a Double Play production. Produced by Amy Robinson, Griffin Dunne. Executive producers, Naomi Foner, Burtt Harris. Directed by Sidney Lumet. Screenplay, Foner; camera (Technicolor, Metrocolor prints), Gerry Fisher; editor, Andrew Mondshein; music, Tony Mottola; sound, James Sabat; production design, Philip Rosenberg; art direction, Robert Guerra; set decoration, Philip Smith; costume design, Anna Hill Johnstone; assistant director, Burtt Harris; casting, Todd M. Thaler. Reviewed at The Burbank Studios, Burbank, Calif., Aug. 25, 1988. MPAA Rating: R. Running time: **116 MIN.**

Annie Pope	Christine Lahti
Danny Pope	River Phoenix
Arthur Pope	Judd Hirsch
Lorna Phillips	Martha Plimpton
Harry Pope	Jonas Arby
Mr. Phillips	Ed Crowley
Gus Winant	L.M. Kit Carson
Mr. Patterson	Steven Hill
Mrs. Patterson	Augusta Dabney
Dr. Jonah Reiff	David Margulies

■ **Hollywood** — The continuing shock waves emitted by the cataclysmic events of the 1960s are dramatized in fresh and powerful ways in "Running On Empty." On the surface a tough picture to market, it could build into a solid, steady performer in more upscale areas if it receives the reviews and develops the cachet it deserves.

A complex, turbulent tale told with admirable simplicity, film successfully operates on several levels — as study of the primacy of the family unit, an anguished teen romance, a coming-of-age story and a look at what happened to some political radicals a generation later.

The two central adult characters are Weathermen-like urban bombers who have been living underground since 1971.

Arthur and Annie Pope (Judd Hirsch and Christine Lahti) have been on the FBI's Most Wanted list since bombing a university defense research installation, an act that blinded a janitor. Their life since then has required them to be as unobtrusively middle-class as possible, and to be able to pick up and leave for a new destination on a moment's notice.

At the outset, the Popes elude surveillance in Florida and settle down again in New Jersey, where the parents take routine jobs and the kids try to fit in at yet another school. Danny (River Phoenix), now 17, is quickly recognized by the local music teacher as an exceptionally promising pianist, and is nudged along toward an eventual audition for Juilliard.

At the same time, Danny slowly commences an edgy but potent first love with the teacher's daughter Lorna (Martha Plimpton). The scenes between the two highly attractive kids are so well written and performed, and ring so true, that they stand as a bracing rebuke to a decade's worth of mindless teen sex comedies.

Although the Popes live under constant threat of exposure, imminent danger enters their lives in the person of Gus (L.M. Kit Carson), a former colleague and obvious loser who tries to get them to help rob a bank.

In fact, the only valid defense for these self-made exiles in their own world is the strength of the family, which in itself represents an ironic outgrowth of the radical political experience. Despite its tensions, the Popes' marriage feels legitimate and enduring, and a splendid birthday party scene for Mom, at which Danny introduces his girlfriend to his parents, surges with mutual love and undercurrents of burgeoning romance.

Instead of climaxing melodramatically with a shootout, capture, trial or something of the sort, Naomi Foner's superior screenplay keeps the focus intimate, forcing the head of the family to face the prospect of the family's breakup so that his son can pursue his own talents and interests. The numerous key scenes are emotionally wrenching and always intelligent and well judged.

Director Sidney Lumet has gotten full value out of Foner's script, mainly by keeping things simple and concentrating on the performances, which are almost uniformly superb. Lahti and Hirsch are in top form, and Phoenix and Plimpton simply put on the most convincing display of initial attraction developing into inevitable love in recent memory. Only gratingly written and acted character is that of Carson, whose emotional and political provocations seem presumptuous and almost out of another picture.

Tech contributions are all quietly supportive of the film's more obvious strengths. — *Cart.*

Rocket Gibraltar

A Columbia Pictures release of an Ulick Mayo Weiss production. Produced by Jeff Weiss. Coproducer, Marcus Viscidi. Executive producers, Michael Ulick, Geoffrey Mayo, Robert Fisher. Directed by Daniel Petrie. Screenplay, Amos Poe; camera (Duart color, Deluxe prints), Jost Vacano; editor, Melody London; music, Andrew Powell; production design, Bill Groom; set decoration, Betsy Klompus; costume design, Nord Haggerty; sound, Bill Daly; assistant director, Matthew Carlisle; casting, Donna Isaacson, John Lyons. Reviewed at The Burbank Studios, Burbank, Calif., Aug. 3, 1988. MPA Rating: PG. Running time: **100 MIN.**

Levi Rockwell	Burt Lancaster
Aggie Rockwell	Suzy Amis
Rose Black	Patricia Clarkson
Ruby Hanson	Frances Conroy
Amanda (Billi) Rockwell	Sinead Cusack
Rolo Rockwell	John Glover
Crow Black	Bill Pullman
Dwayne Hanson	Kevin Spacey
Orson Rockwell	John Bell
Max Hanson	Nicky Bronson
Kane Rockwell	Dan Corkill
Cy Blue Black	Macaulay Culkin
Dawn Black	Angela Goethals
Flora Rockwell	Sara Goethals
Emily Rockwell	Emily Poe
Jessica Hanson	Sara Rue
Dr. Bonacker	George Martin

■ **Hollywood** — Neither a sci-fi epic nor a mountain climbing adventure, "Rocket Gibraltar" is rather a thin domestic drama about three generations of an affluent east coast family.

The ever-imposing Burt Lancaster stands as the centerpiece and only real point of interest in this small-scale, David Puttnam-era Columbia picture, which would have seemed more at home on the tube. As it is, b.o. prospects loom as very limited.

Amos Poe's skin-deep screenplay has Lancaster's son, daughter-in-law, three daughters, two sons-in-law and eight grandchildren converging on his Long Island estate to celebrate his 77th birthday. Script's tactic for differentiating these folks, who as a whole are almost impossibly good-looking, is to give each of them a single, self-absorbed characteristic and then hammer away at it over and over.

So that we understand that the old man's only single daughter, Suzy Amis, is a nympho, she wears a perpetual leering grin along with her miniskirts and invites a different guy to her bed every night. Lancaster's son, John Glover, is a hyper studio executive whose portable phone may as well be implanted on his ear, and sons-in-law Bill Pullman and Kevin Spacey are identified exclusively by their professions, those of baseball pitcher with control problems and a comedian bereft of funny jokes, respectively. Unfortunately, the characterizations never go any further than these superficial traits.

No one on the screen today plays old men of emotional and intellectual gravity more appealingly or convincingly than Lancaster — he's been doing it periodically ever since "Birdman Of Alcatraz" and "The Leopard" in the early 1960s, even though he was still in his 40s at the time. His role here as a revered pater familias would seem tailormade for his talents, but the part, as written, just isn't up to the actor.

Lancaster's Levi Rockwell takes an only casual interest in his offspring. Claiming that, "My life is 90% memory, past," he spends much of his time in thoughtful reveries, reading, dreaming, napping in his hammock, listening to Billie Holiday records. This is all fine and dandy for him, but pretty dull for the audience.

Perhaps halfway into the film, it is stated that Lancaster was a blacklisted writer, poet and teacher, raising hopes that the film will begin to bore into his soul and feelings about his life. Instead, nothing more is made of it, and one never learns what the man wrote, the nature of his political and moral principles, his satisfactions and regrets, in other words, all the things that would bring him to life. Even the revela-

tion that he is suffering from a terminal illness fails to elicit the expected poignancy, simply because the viewer hasn't been invited to closely know the man.

What passes for the major action of the picture has the grandchildren, led by the adorable little blond boy played by Macaulay Culkin, who enjoys a psychic connection with his grandpa, building a special boat so that Lancaster can have a Viking funeral when the time comes. A lovely gesture, to be sure, but, again, hardly the stuff of potent cinema.

Daniel Petrie, who took over from Poe after a week or two of lensing, directed in a pleasant, unemphatic manner, but can't lift the picture above the limitations of the screenplay, which is lacking the major emotional scenes it needs. Tech contributions are okay. —*Cart.*

Envoyez les violons
(Bring On The Violins)
(FRENCH)

An AMLF release of a Films de l'Alma/-FR3 Films/Planète et Cie./Nina Prods./-GPFI coproduction. Produced by Jean-Claude Fleury. Directed by Roger Andrieux. Screenplay, Michael Elias, Roger Andrieux, from story idea by Elias, Eve Babitz; camera (Eastmancolor, Agfa-Gevaert color), Dominique Brenguier; editor, Kénout Peltier; music, William Sheller, Mozart, Bach; art direction, Patrice Mercier; sound, Jean-Bernard Thomasson, François Groult; assistant director, François Vantrou; production managers, Aude Girard, François Nesa. Reviewed at Marignan-Concorde cinema, Paris, Aug. 7, 1988. Running time: **90 MIN.**

Fred Segal	Richard Anconina
Isabelle	Anémone
Pizzoli	Michel Galabru
Franck	Martin Lamotte
Lise	Fabienne Perineau
Gérard	Bernard Freyd

■ **Paris** — An innocuous romantic item that should do okay as summer fare domestically, "Envoyez les violons" pairs local thesps Anémone and Richard Anconina in a banal, hesitation waltz love affair.

Background interest is that the stars are in fact an off-screen couple as well, though not yet of sufficient media interest to fuel boxoffice.

Anconina is a hyperactive director of commercials whose marriage is on the rocks. Rather than see a shrink he opts for music therapy and decides to learn to play the flute. His teacher is Anémone, a talented soloist whose music soothes Anconina's marital pains while more insidiously awakening new romantic feelings. It takes both characters nearly 90 minutes to realize they're in love.

Both deserve better material than this programmed comic hearttugger, as does Roger Andrieux, who coscripted and directed without distinction. Tech credits are good.
—*Len.*

Eternamente Pagu
(Pagu Forever)
(BRAZILIAN)

An Embrafilme release of a Flai Comunicações production. Executive producer, Agostinho Janequine. Directed by Norma Bengell. Screenplay, Bengell, Marcia de Almeida, Geraldo Carvalho; camera (color), Antonio Luiz Mendes; editor, Dominique Paris; music, Turibio Santos, Roberto Gnatalli; art direction, Alexandre Meyer; costumes, Carlos Prieto; associate producers, Sky Light, Maksoud Plaza. Reviewed at Gramado Film Festival, June 21, 1988. Running time: **95 MIN.**

Pagu . . . . Carla Camuratti
Sideria . . . . Nina de Padua
Oswald de Andrade . . . . Antonio Fagundes
Tarsila do Amaral . . . . Esther Goes
Geraldo Ferraz . . . . Octavio Augusto
Also with: Norma Bengell, Paulo Villaça, Antonio Pitanga, Brena Moroni, Kito Junqueira, Suzana Faini, Eduardo Lago, Marcello Picchi, Marla Silvia, Carlos Gregório, Ariel Coelho, Beth Goulart.

■ Gramado, Brazil — Debut feature film by actress Norma Bengell, "Pagu Forever" is based on the life of a Brazilian avant-garde intellectual of the '20s. Local cultural environment is carefully recreated, though narrative may seem slow to audiences demanding some action.

Pagu was a revolutionary before she was 20. When she met writer Oswald de Andrade, leader of the Modernist movement, she was immediately raised to a top position in Brazilian cultural life, whose exponents included De Andrade and painter Tarsila do Amaral, all committed to the subversion of bourgeois values, though living in bourgeois luxury.

Pagu's trajectory is followed by Bengell in an almost didactic narrative, not much concerned with creativity. For those who would like to get acquainted with the Brazilian Modernist movement of the '20s, "Pagu" may be a good starting point. Acting is convincing and tech credits are okay.—*Hoin.*

Doc's Kingdom
(FRENCH)

A Garance, Filmargem production. Executive producers, Dominique Vignet, Paulo Branco. Written and directed by Robert Kramer. Camera (color), Robert Machover; editor, Sandrine Cavafian, Christine Aya; music, Barre Phillips; sound, Olivier Schwob. Reviewed at Locarno Film Festival (noncompeting), Aug. 10, 1988. Running time: **90 MIN.**

Doc . . . . Paul McIsaac
Jimmy . . . . Vincent Gallo
Senor Ruy . . . . Ruy Furtado
Cesar . . . . Cesar Monteiro
Rozzie . . . . Roslyn Payne

■ Locarno — Expatriate American director Robert Kramer obviously invested much of himself in this picture about a former Weatherman who switched from killing to healing, became a doctor, and chose to live at "the edge of the European Continent" in self-imposed exile.

Kramer, once a luminary of the N.Y. underground scene in the '60s, takes some time elaborating on the doctor's past, on his alcoholism and his loneliness resulting from his decision to withdraw from a world he couldn't change and help his fellow men to the extent of his own capacity, of whose limitation he is reminded daily in his work at hospital. At the same time, Kramer inserts into this portrait images of an angry young man sitting by the bed of his dying mother, who discovers after her death that his father is still alive somewhere in Europe and goes to look for him.

The second part of the film is taken up by the father and son meeting, a series of moving, perceptive scenes which finally emerge into something similar to the "lost generation" syndrome of the 1920s.

A modest production shot entirely in Portugal, focusing on the persuasive performance of Paul McIsaac, (who looks very much like director Kramer), the picture is mainly concerned with transmitting emotions rather than plot, with man's solitude facing death as the main theme.

Vincent Gallo is effective as the son crushed by his mother's death and the discovery of a father whose existence he didn't even expect. Kramer takes it all at a leisurely pace, creates an intimate mood, as the self-destructive tendencies of the hero, Doc, who suffers from a mysterious disease contracted in Africa, are established by intelligent use of the camera roaming around the desolate locations and effective direction of actors.

Produced in 1987, this is, by its very nature, just the right stuff for art houses and film festivals.
—*Edna.*

Fengslende dager for Christina Berg
(The Captivating Days Of Christina Berg
(NORWEGIAN)

A Telko-Film release of Telko Film with Filmgruppe 84 production. Produced by Hans Otto Nicolayssen. Written and directed by Egil Kolstö. Camera (Fujicolor), Rolv Haan; sound, Jacob Trier. No further credits available. Reviewed at Saga-5, Oslo, Aug. 21, 1988. Running time: **105 MIN.**

With: Marit Oestby (Christina Berg), Gro Solemdal (Bibbi), Janne Kokkin (Elin), Trude Birkelund.

■ Oslo — "The Captivating Days Of Christina Berg" by veteran writer-helmer Egil Kolstö is a female prison tragi-comedy that opts more for psychological probing than for the action fireworks otherwise inherent to the genre.

The production is modest and at times technically faltering, but item is doing well on the Norwegian exhibition circuit and should at least see some easy offshore tv sales.

Christina Berg is a personally wealthy social worker who arrives at a small rural prison to serve 30 days for drunk driving. She is assigned a cell that looks more like a summer camp cottage. Her fellow prisoners here are Elin, a demurely pretty and nearly mute graduate of public window-smashing and robust Bibbi, serving time for vagrancy and general lack of social adaptability.

The threesome soon settle down to a routine of various easy work chores. Gregarious Bibbi smuggles alcohol into the room (it never looks like a cell) and exudes a lot of animal gusto and naive goodness. Elin keeps to herself. She tries to commit suicide, but is saved by the two other women.

Christine Berg tries her level best to be nice all around, but the point of the story is that the social worker does not even begin to understand the drives or blockings of Bibbi and Elin. When she has served her time, she is picked up by a car and leaves in style although clearly shattered by having been roundly cursed by Bibbi.

Chubby Gro Solemdal was deservedly nominated for a Best Actress Award in this year's Norwegian Amanda sweepstakes. She performs with lusty intensity and a fine sense of humor. The other actresses are fine, too, but they don't really have much to do. Rolv Haan's cinematography works neatly within the narrow confines. —*Kell.*

Fréquence meurtre
(FM — Frequency Murder)
(FRENCH)

An AAA release of a La Guéville/-Capac/AAA/Films A2 coproduction. Produced by Danièle Delorme and Yves Robert. Associate producers, Xavier Gélin and Paul Claudon. Directed by Elisabeth Rappeneau. Screenplay, Rappeneau, Jacques Audiard, from the novel "When Dark Man Calls" by Stuart Kaminsky; camera (color), William Lubtchansky; editor, Martine Barraqué; music, Philippe Gall; art direction, Peter Gompertz; sound, Jean-Pierre Ruh, Dominique Hennequin; production manager, Michel Propper; assistant director, Dominique Tabuteau. Reviewed at George V cinema, Paris, June 7, 1988. Running time: **100 MIN.**

Jeanne Quester . . . . Catherine Deneuve
Frank Quester . . . . André Dussollier
Simon Lieberman . . . . Martin Lamotte
Roger . . . . Etienne Chicot
Pauline . . . . Ines Claye
Faber . . . . Philippe Lehembre
Ida Faber . . . . Madeleine Marie

■ Paris — Slickly made but routine suspenser, "Fréquence meurtre" casts Catherine Deneuve as a psychiatrist with a radio call-in show who begins receiving ominous on-the-air calls.

Presumed caller is a lunatic who was the convicted murderer of Deneuve's parents (when she was a child). Deneuve learns the man recently has been released from a mental institution and may be the mysterious intruder who's been leaving some terrifying traces in her apartment.

Script, adapted from an American suspense novel by Stuart Kaminsky, evolves along the familiar genre lines as Deneuve is hounded and harassed by the mysterious caller, who of course turns out not to be the most likely suspect. Climactic surprise twist, capped by a last-minute rescue, will be predictable pretty early on in the action by attentive filmgoers.

Elisabeth Rappeneau, veteran scriptgirl and screenwriter (notably to her brother, director Jean-Paul Rappeneau) co-authored and directed in her first effort, which is skillful. William Lubtchansky's lensing creates a mood of anxiety.

Acting helps maintain audience interest in an otherwise strained plot. Deneuve is good but André Dussollier is better as her brother, a high-ranking cop who promises her round-the-clock protection. —*Len.*

Bonjour l'angoisse
(Hello Anxiety)
(FRENCH)

An AMLF release of a T. Films/Films A2/Messine Prod. coproduction. Produced by Alain Terzian. Directed by Pierre Tchernia. Screenplay, Tchernia, Marcel Gotlieb; camera (Eastmancolor, Agfa-Gavaert, Pyral color), Jean Tournier; editor, Françoise Javet; sound, Paul Lainé, Jean-Paul Loublier; art direction, Serge Douy; assistant director, Valérie Othnin-Girard; production managers, Philippe Lièvre, Françoise Galfré. Reviewed at the UGC Biarritz cinema, Paris, Aug. 22, 1988. Running time: **95 MIN.**

Michaud . . . . Michel Serrault
Jacqueline Michaud . . . Geneviève Fontanel
Aymeric . . . . Pierre Arditi
Desfontaines . . . . Jean-Paul Bacri
Lambert . . . . Guy Marchand
Mr. Robert . . . . Hubert Deschamps
Commissioner Marechal . . Bernard Fresson
Baudu . . . . Henri Corseaux
Waiter . . . . Bernard Haller

■ Paris — "Bonjour l'angoisse" is a routine, but agreeable variation on the Walter Mitty formla comedy, designed as a vehicle for actor Michel Serrault. It should do nicely at home, with some commercial possibilities in territories where its star has some drawing power.

Pierre Tchernia, popular French tv film gameshow producer host and occasional filmmaker (this is his third feature), took a sabbatical from pubcaster Antenne-2 to write (with Marcel Gotlieb) and direct this Alain Terzian production, in which Serrault is given solid support from a good backup cast including Pierre Arditi, Guy Marchand, and Jean-Pierre Bacri. Serrault is funny, but it's not a solo-show because Tchernia also attends to other comic roles.

Serrault plays a timorous but inventive senior technician in a security system manufacturing firm who suffes from chronic anxiety, indecision, the jibes of colleagues and the contempt of his Other Self, who taunts and insults him from the other side of the looking glass.

Escaping occasionally into daydreams (including an opening fantasy sendup of "The Untouchables"), Serrault is put to the test when he's unwittingly involved in the holdup of a bank which has been wired by his firm. Slowly learning that a crooked fellow exec has masterminded the job, Serrault comes out of his cocoon and sets a trap for the robbers.

This is hardly innovative comedy, but some snappy dialog and perky rhythm carry the film through its good-natured antics. —*Len.*

Der Wilde Mann
(The Wild Man)
(SWISS)

A Xanadu Films presentation of a Xanadu Films, ZDF production. Written and directed by Matthias Zschokke. Camera (color, 16m), Adrian Zschokke; editor, Maya Schmid; sound, Felix Singer; art direction, Dani Schneider-Wessling; costumes, Monica Schmid. Reviewed at Locarno Film Festival (special screening), Aug. 13, 1988. Running time: **69 MIN.**

With: Dieter Laser (salesman), Beatrice Kessler (waitress), Ingrid Kaiser (actress), Hainer Walti (projectionist), Joseph J. Arnold (filmmaker), Hans-Rudolf Twerenbold (doctor).

■ Locarno — **This is a fierce, pitiless satire of the Swiss, portrayed as simple-minded, unimaginative, complacent, provincial, lonely people who constantly invade each other's privacy but never escape their solitude.**

The allegorical plot follows a former German nobleman reduced to selling sex appliances, who reaches a small Swiss village and takes a room at the local inn, "The Wild Man," hoping to convince the owners to install a vending machine for his merchandise in the lobby. He stays there for one night only, a ghoulish experience which drains the life out of him.

To begin with, nobody wants his products, his tentative homosexual advances to a rugged country boy are bluntly rejected and he rents a room for the night only to have everyone step in and out of it at one time or another. The local band rehearses downstairs and won't let him sleep.

Director Matthias Zschokke spends quite a bit of time on exposition, but once he gets going he piles up insults and offenses addressed at his fellow countrymen without missing a beat.

A short feature, almost a sketch, its dry humor is faithfully transmitted by a cast capable of keeping a straight face even in the most ridiculous situations.

Shot in 16m at night, even the pretty Alpine scenery won't sweeten this bitterly sarcastic pill. —*Edna.*

Nakhoda Khorshid
(Captain Khorshid)
(IRANIAN)

A Farabi Cinema Foundation presentation of a Pakhishiran Corp., Peiman Film Group production. Directed and edited by Naser Taghvai. Screenplay, Taghvai, freely adapted from Ernest Hemingway's "To Have And Have Not;" camera (color), Mehrdad Fakhimi; music, F. Naseri; sound, Roubik Mansouri; art direction, Shahim-Dokht Behzadi. Reviewed at Locarno Film Festival (competing), Aug. 13, 1988. Running time: **117 MIN.**

With: Ali Nassirian (Cpt. Khorshid), Darioush Arjmand, Parvaneh Massoumi.

■ Locarno — **This very free adaptation of the Hemingway novel, previously filmed in classic fashion by Howard Hawks, is one of the rare Iranian products emerging on the international scene.**

The story has been moved from the Caribbean to the Persian Gulf and main character is Captain Khorshid, a tough, 1-armed smuggler operating his own boat, who has invested his life's savings in a cigaret shipment. The local crime baron, a cripple specializing in pearls, would not allow such an independent venture to take place without his participation and informs the customs officials, who grab the whole shipment and burn it in public.

Left with no choice, Khorshid agrees to help political refugees escape the country, and later, when police threaten to impound his boat, he decides on a final fling, carrying a group of exiled criminals across the Gulf to Dubai.

All the characters are familiar from the Western pattern of crime pictures, from the strong, silent hero, through the manipulator, the brutal killers, the evil crime shark, the sympathetic barman and the human flotsam drifting around a harbor. To helmer Nasser Taghvai's credit, he has given them strong local roots. With a keen eye for the locations, he indeed manages to impart the feeling this is the end of the world, desolate, falling to pieces, a place one dreams to leave as soon as he arrives. The story is efficiently (if at times rather elaborately) told, local color is rich, and the morality tale is perfectly clear.

What is much less clear are the political implications. The entire event is left hanging in the air, it isn't quite clear who are the exiles and why they are there, what was the essence of their crimes and what they intend to do about it.

With Ali Nassirian giving a solid performance in the title role and the rest of the cast looking natural enough, this picture seems closely related to the Iranian school flourishing before the Fundamentalist Revolution. Taghvai was formed by that school and has had to bide his time since then, working for tv. —*Edna.*

Suéltate el Pelo
(Let Down Your Hair)
(SPANISH)

A Manuel Summers, Hombres G, Paco Lara and Ricardo de la Morena production. Executive producer, Paco Lara Polop. Directed by Manuel Summers. Screenplay, Paco, Tomás and Manuel Summers; camera (color), Tote Trenas; editor, Maria Elena Sainz de Roxas; music, David Summers, Angel Muñoz; direct sound, Richard Steinberg. Reviewed at Cine Coliseo, July 27, 1988. Running time: **90 MIN.**

With: David Summers, Daniel Mezquita, Javier Molina and Rafael Gutierrez (Hombres G group), Paloma San Millán, Tomás Zori, Vicente Bartual, Toni Cantó, Tatiana, Ana Summers, Paco Martin, Cristina Galbó, Chumy Chúmez, Miguel Chicharro, Antonio Mingote.

■ Madrid — **The popular "Hombres G" rock group scores again in a fast-moving, melodic and amusing film with special appeal to the 12-16-year-old distaff moppet audiences who will squeal in glee at the antics of the four performers.**

In this their second feature, fans will be treated to plenty of the G-Men's songs, some set in recording studio backgrounds, others at live concerts in Madrid and Acapulco. But the Summers boys have kept pacing lively by throwing in a plot in which a young fan of the group follows them to Acapulco and back to Madrid.

The girl's infatuation becomes ammunition for a scandal photographer and his cronies, who blackmail David, the leader of the rock group. Helmer Manuel Summers keeps the dialog snappy and slangy, with plenty of wisecracks. A lot of it will be hard to catch by those not plugged into the latest Madrid jargon. Yet enough of the jokes are visual to keep audiences anywhere amused.

Pic should be a natural in all Hispano markets where the Hombres G are already popular as a group. Some sales might be racked up in other territories as well, conditioned by the popularity of the Hombres G in each country. —*Besa.*

Incident At Raven's Gate
(AUSTRALIAN)

A Hemdale release of an FGH-Intl. Film Marketing presentation of an Acquabay production. Produced by Marc Rosenberg, Rolf de Heer. Executive producer, Antony I. Ginnane. Directed by De Heer. Screenplay, Rosenberg, De Heer, from an original screenplay by James Michael Vernon; camera (Super 35m, color), Richard Michalak; editor, Suresh Ayyar; music, Graham Tardif, Roman Kronen; sound, Rob Cutcher; production design, Judith Russell; special effects, Jon Armstrong; production manager, Ron Stigwood; assistant director, Carolynne Cunningham. Reviewed at Film Australia screening room, Sydney, Aug. 13, 1988. Running time: **93 MIN.**

Eddie Cleary	Steven Vidler
Rachel Cleary	Celine Griffin
Richard Cleary	Ritchie Singer
Felix Skinner	Vincent Gil
Annie	Saturday Rosenberg
Dr. Hemmings	Terry Camilleri
Sgt. Taylor	Max Cullen

■ Sydney — **This modestly budgeted sci-fi action thriller turns out to be the finest suspense pic made in Australia since the last "Mad Max" outing.**

Owing something to "Blood Simple" in its hallucinating use of sights and sounds, pic should score at wickets the world over and attract attention at sci-fi fests.

Shot in South Australia at a small farm known as Raven's Gate, the pic deals with phenomena that play havoc with electrical equipment, causing motors to stop and start

and wells to run dry. The unknown things (presumably aliens, though, for once, they're never seen) also are causing normally sober citizens to go berserk.

Eddie (Steven Vidler) is out on parole in custody of his farmer brother Richard (Ritchie Singer) after spending time in prison for stealing a cop car. Richard's bored wife Rachel (Celine Griffin) is attracted to Eddie, but initially he's more interested in Annie (Saturday Rosenberg), a voluptuous barmaid he meets, and beds, in the nearby town. The town cop, Felix Skinner (Vincent Gil), a manic opera buff, also lusts after Annie.

As the aliens make themselves felt, Felix goes over the top and kills Annie when she refuses to accompany him on a trip to the Sydney Opera House; he's last glimpsed sitting alone in an opera box, enjoying the performance.

Meanwhile Richard, suspecting that Eddie and Rachel have commenced a love affair, also goes bonkers. Drama reaches its climax with the destruction of the farmhouse and the escape of the lovers.

One of the film's strengths is that it leaves the audience to imagine the destructive forces; nothing's seen and nothing's explained. The pic's final image is, in its own way, as haunting as the fadeout of Andrei Tarkovsky's "Solaris."

Rolf de Heer's second feature (after the charming "Tail Of The Tiger" in 1984) is inventive and classy. The screenplay, by De Heer and producer Marc Rosenberg, is witty and the characters more than usually interesting. Performances are good, with Vincent Gil a standout as the cop with an opera fixation.

Use of sound is excellent, and the Super 35 widescreen camerawork, with its use of extreme blacks and whites, also is outstanding, with full credit going to director of photography Richard Michalak.

Filled with standout scenes (the sky raining dead birds, a friendly dog that suddenly attacks Eddie, the abrupt death of Annie, the ghosts of an elderly couple half-glimpsed in the dark), "Incident At Raven's Gate" packs a wallop. Given the right kind of distribution, cult and crossover status seem assured.—*Strat.*

Kholodnoe Leto Piatdesiat Tretiego
(Cold Summer Of 1953)
(SOVIET)

A Mosfilm Studio production. Directed by Alexander Prochkin. Screenplay, Edgar Dubrovski; camera (color), Boris Brozhovsky; music, Vladimir Martinov; art direction, Valeri Filipov. Reviewed at the Tashkent Film Festival (market), May 29, 1988. Running time: **103 MIN.**

Luzga	Valeri Priyemikhov
Kopalich	Anatoli Papanov

Also with: Viktor Stepanov, Nina Usatova, Zoya Buriak.

■ **Tashkent — "The Cold Summer Of 1953" is one of the most interesting entries in the current Sovexportfilm catalog, with appeal for theatrical programmers of Russian product as well as specialized settings.**

Film falls into that curious local genre of arty pics set in places where nothing ever happens until a gang of ruthless gangsters turns up and the shooting starts. "Cold Summer" has gangsters, an anti-hero, a certain amount of political daring and enough experimental lensing to be of interest from a technical point of view. It's a pleasing work that should find audiences abroad.

In a small Siberian village, two political prisoners, unjustly sent into exile, live their said lives. Luzga (Valeri Priyemikhov) is the silent, moody hero, an ex-Army scout who casts smoldering glances at Stalin's detested portrait. Kopalich is an ex-archaeologist (last role of famed thesp Anatoli Papanov).

A gang of criminals stumbles across the village and terrorizes the inhabitants. Luzga and Kopalich, the exiles, lead the fight against the besiegers, winning the day with guerilla warfare. It is also the year of Stalin's death, and a more liberal political climate that allows Luzga to return to Moscow.

Noteworthy is the extremely realistic portrait of the remote town and its ragged inhabitants of poor boatmen, a handicapped mother, etc. The crooks reflect the ferocious cruelty of the time; they are depicted as unsentimentally as Luzga's revenge for Kopalich's death.

Lensing is adequate, though there are a lot of repetitive shots, and the shoot-out in particular runs very long. The two principals are ruggedly convincing. —*Yung.*

Cérémonie d'amour
(Rites Of Love)
(FRENCH)

A Sara Films production and release. Executive producer, Alain Sarde. Produced by Philippe Guez. Written and directed by Walerian Borowczyk, from the novel, "Tout disparaitra" by André Pieyre de Mandiargues. Camera (Fujicolor), Gérard Monceau; music, Bach; sound, Thierry Godard, Alain Muslin; assistant director, Gérard Gregory; production manager, Catherine Mezières. Reviewed at Forum Orient Express cinema, Paris, Aug. 10, 1988. Runnng time: **98 MIN.**
With: Marina Pierro (Miriam Gwen), Mathieu Carrière (Hugo Arnold), Josy Bernard (Meriem), Isabelle Tinard (Nora Nix).

■ **Paris — Walerian Borowczyk, defrocked high priest of European art film erotica, officiated over this sad attempt to regain some of his former prestige. Despite a reunion with one of his erstwhile literary muses, it's not likely to do much for anyone involved.**

Film, originally titled "Tout disparaitra" (Everything Must Go), is drawn from a tale by André Pieyre de Mandiargues, a Gallic purveyor of pretentious literary erotomania, which has inspired the helmer in previous efforts. Pseudopoetic monologs and dialogs plus minimal sexual activity make this a poor softcore market product outside homevid.

Tale involves the meeting between a hedonistic young aesthete (Mathieu Carrière) and an attractive actress (Marina Pierro) moonlighting as hooker in the Paris subway.

After much preliminary literary foreplay in the subway station, a church and the streets of Saint-Germain-des-Près, she brings him to a borrowed apartment for the promised sexual favors, but he finds himself humiliated in a symbolic emasculation scene.

Wandering dazed afterwards on the river banks, he encounters another young woman emerging from a dip in the Seine, who promptly pulls out a knife and stabs herself. The hapless Carrière is arrested for murder.

Film's lack of genuine sensuality and long gab sequences are aggravated by story's underlying misogyny, apparently inherent in the source material. The two performers recite their verbose texts like unenthusiastic candidates at an audition. —*Len.*

Corps Z'a Corps
(Body-To-Body)
(FRENCH)

An ATC 3000/Films de la Rochelle release of an ATC 3000/TF1 Films coproduction. Produced by Benjamin Simon. Directed by André Halimi. Screenplay, Halimi, Christian Watton, Jacques Vilfrid; camera (Eastmancolor), Francois About; editor, Eva Zora; music, Vladimir Cosma; assistant director, Christophe Vassort; production manager, Léone Jaffin; casting, Béatrice Halimi. Reviewed at the Georges V cinema, Paris, June 27, 1988. Running time: **83 MIN.**
Jean Chabert . . . . Philippe Khorsand
Edna Chabert . . . . Stéphane Audran
Press boss . . . . Jean-Pierre Kalfon
Françoise . . . . Véronique Moest
Gilberte . . . . Kathleen Johnsen
Also with: Xavier Saint-Macary, Jean-Luc Bideau, Christophe Bourseiller, Jean Rougerie, Jacques Legras, Fabrice Josso, Hubert Deschamps.

■ **Paris — This routine Gallic sex comedy marks the feature filmmaking debut of André Halimi, journalist, tv producer and cofounder-director of the Deauville American Film Festival.**

Halimi says he used some of his own press experience for his original story, developed with veteran scripters Jacques Vilfrid and Christian Watton, though there are too many predictable farce turns and stereotypes to make it fresh and personal.

Tale follows the tribulations of a veteran newspaper editor (Philippe Khorsand) who is assigned to revamp a failing girlie magazine.

Plot involves him up to his ears in uninhibited secretaries and collaborators, horny readers and marital problems that finally drive him to refuge in a monastery.

Halimi has enough tv experience to make his move to feature films without technical hitches, and the seasoned cast is at least adequate (veteran screen lechers Jean-Pierre Kalfon and Jean-Luc Bideau do their thing) so that comedy is somewhat less tasteless and vulgar than other efforts of this sort. It only lacks imagination and body. —*Len.*

No Hagas Planes con Marga
(Don't Make Plans With Marga)
(SPANISH)

A Rafael Alcázar production. Written and directed by Alcázar. Camera (Fujicolor), Tote Trenas; editor, Miguel González Sinde; music, Bernardo Bonezzi; production manager, Jaime Fernández Cid; set decoration, Victor Alarcón; sound, D. Goldstein and R. Steinberg. Reviewed at Barcelona Film Festival, June 30, 1988. Running time: **90 MIN.**
Andrés . . . . Miguel Molina
Marga . . . . Nina Ferrer
Lolo . . . . Angel de Andrés López
Esteban . . . . Juan Echanove
Also with: Antonio Dechent, Laura Cepeda, Aitana Sánchez Gijón, Eufemia Román, Enrique Pérez Simón.

■ **Barcelona — Using mostly Madrid-by-night locations, but also shooting scenes in London and Santiago de Compostela, neophyte helmer Miguel Molina limns a youth-oriented love story which has its gripping moments.**

Though there's not much of a plot, "Don't Make Plans With Marga" manages to hold interest. Some timeshifts and an occasional dream sequence may confuse viewers.

Andrés, a hep young madrileño, is obsessed with a pretty young girl, Marga, who eludes him over the years. Though he has other girlfriends, it is Marga he has his romantic eyes set upon. At one point he catches up with her, and she reveals in flashback part of her sordid and unhappy past as a lush, unfaithful wife.

But Andrés remains undeterred, despite sneers and down-to-earth advice from his best friend. Finally, Andrés succeeds in tracking down Marga again and living a brief idyll with her, but what the final outcome will be remains unclear.

Item is well thesped, dialog is lively and production vlaues are good. However, story is rather too anemic for pic to have much going for it commercially. It may be okay for the domestic market. —*Besa.*

Kamu Onna
(A Woman Who Bites)
(JAPANESE)

A Cine Ropponica release. Produced by Kota Yamada. Directed by Tatsumi Kumashiro. Screenplay Haruhiko Arai, from story by Masahiro Ketsujo; camera (color), Noboru Shinoda; lighting, Haruo Kawasima; editor, Ko Suzuki; music, Reijiro Koroku; sound, Fujio Sato; art, Fusae Kikukawa; assistant director, Toshihiro Sato. Reviewed at Shinbashi Ropponica, Tokyo, July 14, 1988. Running time: **103 MIN.**
Chikako Koga . . . . Kaori Momoi
Yuichi Koga . . . . Toshiyuki Nagashima
Kotaro Yamazaki . . . . Mitsuru Hirata
Sanae Ebino . . . . Kimiko Amari
Yohei Tsunoda . . . . Yoshihiro Katoh
Fumie . . . . Kaoru Kusuda
Tsunoda . . . . Maiko Maekawa

■ **Tokyo — In "Kamu Onna" (A Woman Who Bites), the "A" picture on Cine Ropponica's (formerly Nikkatsu) first non-porno double bill, the "hero" is a producer of softcore videos who, when not viewing his handiwork on the company VCR, is cheating on his wife with a variety of tootsies.**

The playboy producer is subject to bouts of sexual dysfunction and eventually comes to a very bad, very violent end.

The film should perhaps be viewed as corporate psychodramma, in which a studio struggles to come to terms with its identity, both acknowledging and attempting to kill off the past, while displaying uncertainty about the future. Just as softcore has benefited Nikkatsu/Cine Ropponica, so its benefits for the producer are apparent in his spacious home, tasteful furnishings and two cars. Just as the studio best known for softcore alienated the very important female sector of the market, so the softcore producer is alienated from the woman who eventually seals his fate. Finally, "Kamu Onna" concludes on a note of unease, much as, one suspects, Cine Ropponica commences its quest for a new audience.

Should that quest eventually fail, it won't be due to screenplays lacking in subtext. This chilling portrait of a self-deluding family *in extremis,* beset by an obsessive and vengeful former fling of the producer's, is no less riveting for having borrowed quite blatantly from "Fatal Attraction."

"Kamu Onna" is midway between an apologia and a final binge before going on the wagon, a feverishly performed medley of everything from the sado-masochistic content of so much of the defunct Nikkatsu's *roman poruno* (the producer responds sexually when his blood is drawn) to its frequent anti-feminine bias (the producer's violent end is brought about by a conspiracy between two women).

Should Cine Ropponica's quest for a new audience eventually fail, it won't be due to a yenny-pinching reluctance to hire the best: Toshiyuki Nagashima is the producer, Kaori Momoi his wife, Mitsuru Hirata his best friend. Nagashima, whose list of impressive screen performances is so long it comes as a surprise to realize he's only 31, is anti-heroic without resorting to mustache twirling. Momoi is subdued here, suggesting a wealth of secrets behind a Gioconda smile. The success of "Kamata Koshinkyoku'' probably ensured Hirata's employment for the rest of his professional life as a sidekick, a situation which, thankfully, has not dampened his enthusiasm. —*Bail.*

Poutnici
(Pilgrims)
(CZECH)

A Gottwaldov Studio production. Directed by Zdenek Zaoral. Screenplay, Zaoral, Ondrej Pavelka, Eva Paskova; camera (color), Michal Kulic; music, Václav Hálek; production manager, Vojtěch Kunclk. Reviewed at the Karlovy Vary Film Festival, July 17, 1988. Running time: **90 MIN.**
Pavel . . . . Ondrej Pavelka
Honda . . . . Karel Habl
Vanda . . . . Eva Salzmannová
Also with: Lubos Vesely (Jirno), Hana Srsnová (Zuzana), Petra Lustigová (Petra), Alena Mihulová (Radka).

■ **Karlovy Vary** — Film critic turned helmer Zdenek Zaoral's second feature "Pilgrims," departs from his first work's shock-corridor realism to show a young people's theatrical company traveling around country towns.

While its youth appeal is clear, pic isn't especially topical for the foreign viewer, and tends to drag at times.

Made at Gottwaldov children's studio on a shoestring, "Pilgrims" is sufficiently outside mainstream Czech cinema to be of interest. A cast of mainly non-pros plays the amateur thesps with spontaneity and candor. Four girls and a boy are directed by temperamental Pavel (Ondrej Pavelka, who helped pen the script), a moody but sensitive tyrant intent on squeezing the maximum out of his players. They perform at country fairs, before soldiers, and so on. In their spare time they cut up, quarrel, and camp out in the splendid natural setting of Southern Bohemia.

Biggest obstacle for foreigners is the untranslatable poetry used both in the play the group performs and in scattered references throughout the pic. —*Yung.*

Armon
(While Leaving, Stay)
(SOVIET)

An Uzbekfilm Studio production. Directed by Malis Abzalov. Screenplay, Rihsiwoi Muhamedianov, Vladimir Sokolov; music, Vildanov Rumil; art direction, Abdul Salamov Shavkat; In color. Reviewed at the Tashkent Film Festival (competing), May 25, 1988. Running time: **111 MIN.**
With: Aibarchin Bakirova, Dilorom Egamberdyeva, Bakhtiar Zakirov.

■ **Tashkent** — Uzbek history lusciously unfolds in Malis Abzalov's "Armon," a costume pic that is watchable and original. Film is of interest particularly in shows highlighting new cinema from the Soviet republics.

Colorful widescreen images show the difficult period of adjustment in the years after Uzbekistan came under Soviet power. The new government has given land to peasant farmers, but no seeds. They are forced to take seed from the stores of an aristocratic lady resembling Silvana Mangano. In the end she generously concedes. Her foreman, bent on vendetta, kills the farmers' leader and the lady kills her foreman — it turns out the farmer is the secret father of her son.

In the 1940s, the village has turned into a smoothly oiled collective farm. The son returns a grown man, there is romance and gaiety, and then the war breaks out. All the men are mobilized and the noble lady, now reduced to pauperdom, donates a treasure chest of gems to the war effort.

There is so much picturesque color in "Armon" (translated, not literally, as "While Leaving, Stay") it almost looks false. Yet Abzalov's realistic low-key approach to dramatic events is never rhetorical or simple-mindedly patriotic. Film conveys a strong love of the land and the inhabitants in a natural, entertaining format. —*Yung.*

Cavka
(Blackbird)
(YUGOSLAV)

A Yugoslavia Film release of a TRZ Film i Ton (Belgrade), Croatia Film (Zagreb), Smart Egg (London) production. Directed by Milos Radivojevic. Screenplay, Radivojevic, Svetozar Vlajkovic; camera (color), Radoslav Vladic; music, Kornelije Kovac; art direction, Nemanja Petrovic; costumes, Nada Perovic. Reviewed at Pula Film Festival (competing), July 25, 1988. Running time: **92 MIN.**
With: Mirko Ratic, Slobodan Negic, Milena Dravic, Aleksandar Bercek, Sonja Savic, Dragan Nikolic, Rada Zivkovic, Branislav Lecic, Lidija Pletl, Bogdan Diklic.

■ **Pula** — "Blackbird" is a well-acted satire about Profa, a sharp-witted, nearsighted son of an important executive who has divorced his wife and remarried and Tchavka (or Cavka), whose mother is dead and whose father is in jail. They strike up a strange friendship in spite of their different backgrounds.

Profa's sheltered family life is in sharp contrast with Tchavka's total lack of means, but the two have in common a need for affection and attention that is not readily available for them at home or in school.

With characters and events manipulated at times in an arbitrary fashion, the film relies mainly on the soulful performances of the two kids, Mirko Ratic and Slobodan Negic, and on cameos by veteran stars Milena Dravic, as a nervous, insecure teacher who drinks in secret and dreams of being a prima ballerina, and Bogdan Diklic as the school principal, a martinet easily scared by anyone of political influence.

The other characters, such as Profa's separated parents or Tchavka's father, are largely stereotypes, or, in the case of the school psychiatrist, sheer caricatures.

Not quite the social satire it attempts to be, or a serious discussion on broken homes, the picture probably will appeal mostly to younger audiences . — *Edna.*

Hot To Trot

A Warner Bros. release. Produced by Steve Tisch. Directed by Michael Dinner. Screenplay, Stephen Neigher, Hugh Gilbert, Charlie Peters, from story by Neigher, Gilbert; camera (Technicolor), Victor Kemper; editor, Frank Morriss; music, Danny Elfman; production design, William Matthews; set decoration, Mickey S. Michaels; set design, Judy Cammer; sound (Dolby), Glen Anderson; assistant director, Joseph Moore; coproducer, Wendy Finerman; casting, Melissa Skoff. Reviewed at Mann National Theater, L.A. Aug. 26, 1988. MPAA Rating: PG. Running time: **83 MIN.**
Fred P. Chaney . . . . Bob Goldthwait
Walter Sawyer . . . . Dabney Coleman
Voice Of Don . . . . John Candy
Allison Rowe . . . . Virginia Madsen
Boyd Osborne . . . . Jim Metzler
Victoria Peyton . . . . Cindy Pickett

■ **Hollywood** — For a talking horse story, "Hot To Trot" is dog food. B.o. should be nil.

Comedian Bob (formerly billed as Bobcat) Goldthwait plays a guy dumber than his costar horse (voice by John Candy), an amiable beast that turns stock tips overheard at the stables into a small fortune for his owner.

Dabney Coleman is Goldthwait's philandering stepfather with silly fake buck teeth that any successful broker would have had the money to fix.

The two men are at odds sharing the partnership at the family brokerage house in a setup where neither of them is funny or, for that matter, intelligible.

Goldthwait has a strange, high-pitched voice that always seems to be on the verge of cracking and Coleman, with those teeth, makes Bugs Bunny sound good. The horse wins out for clarity of speech.

Candy does a fine job giving a human dimension to Don, the horse. That is, the horse might as well have been a regular horny, upwardly mobile male who talks like a stud but otherwise has very little of interest to say.

Horse and owner get along like brothers. They share pizza and Tab while being couch potatoes in front of the tv, and on weekends take time to visit the horse's folks (also talkers) out in the country. On one such visit, the talking horse Dad expires after lecturing his son on producing an heir. Dad later comes back as a horsefly.

The horse is too clear-headed and Goldwait stupid, not having the comic resources to make something out of his ridiculous situation.

There is one good laugh to be had on Don's name when he races for the El Segundo stakes at San Gabriel Valley Park (really, Hollywood Park). The joke is beaten to death and surely not worth sitting through the picture. Mr. Ed remains king of the genre.

Horse trainers Glenn and Corky Randall are worth mentioning for teaching Don to move his lips at the same time — sort of — as the voice track.
—*Brit.*

Eden Miseria
(FRENCH)

A Paulo Branco presentation of a Paulo Branco, FPC production. Executive producer, Paolo de Souza. Directed by Christine Laurent. Screenplay, Philippe Arnaud, Laurent, based on Isabelle Eberhardt's "Journals;" camera (color), Thierry Arbogast; editor, Francine Sandberg; music, A.Z. Dyne, J.S. Bach; sound, Nicolas Lefevre, Antoine Rodet; art direction, Isabel Branco. Reviewed at Locarno Film Festival (competing), Aug. 13, 1988. Running time: **102 MIN.**
Isabelle Eberhardt . . . . Danuta Zarazik
Herbst . . . . Philippe Clevenot
Slimene . . . . Abdallah Badis
Stella . . . . Ines de Medeiros
Also with: Stephane Jobert (Henri), Philippe Landoulsi (Charles), Kader Boukhanef (Idir), Mostafa Djadjam (Tahar), Sotigui Kouyate (Samst).

■ **Locarno** — It is very tempting to draw parallels between the physical aspects of the desert and its mysteries and the emotional life of its protagonists. This was doubtless the intention of filmmaker Christine Laurent, a former painter and set designer whose rich visual imagination make this film a striking pictorial achievement.

What's more, Laurent's choice of Isabelle Eberhardt, a young woman who fell in love with the desert at the turn of the century, traveled extensively across it and found her death there at the age of 27, offers a portrait of a modern, liberated woman before its time. She goes around in a man's disguise and assumes male responsibilities which do not diminish her devotion for the Moslem husband who patiently waits for her to come back home. Laurent uses Eberhardt's diaries as an inspiration and Eberhardt herself as the main character.

A painter capable of creating powerful images, Laurent is less successful telling Eberhardt's story, or at least not very consistent in her choice of a style. Asking her actors for declamatory speeches directly to the camera and indulging in poetic speculations which look ostentatious, one has the feeling the cast was performing instructions without really perceiving the reasons behind them.

The outcome is an overwhelming picture of Nature at its most imposingly majestical, with brilliant use of camera and decor to establish atmosphere. The visual beauty is the main thing and realism is denied to the point where characters parade in colorful costumes usually donned only for festivities and photo sessions, never in real life. It is only when these perfect pictures start to move that arguments about their validity will arise.

Thierry Arbogast's camera works magic on the African landscapes of Cape Verde and the insistent flute improvisations on the soundtrack combined with a Bach Fugue reflect the cultural clash referred to by the film. The image of the desert and its people is very persuasive to the eye and it is quite possible that had she been content to cram less significance into every scene, Laurent would have come out with a better film. —*Edna.*

Nablyudatel
(Birdwatcher)
(SOVIET)

A Sovexportfilm release of a Talinfilm production. Directed by Arvo Ikho. Screenplay, Marina Septunovova; camera (color), Tatyana Loginova. Reviewed at Karlovy Vary Film Festival, July 8, 1988. Running time: 83 MIN.
With: Svetlana Tormakhova, Erik Ruus.

■ **Karlovy Vary — First time Estonian director Arvo Ikho brings off a sharply observed film which manages to deal with a range of topics within an essentially chamber drama.**

This is a compelling drama which touches on ecological and national problems as delineated by the use of Russian and Estonian languages. As personal drama it is an example of new realism in Soviet cinema, with implied incest and frank but natural nudity of both sexes.

It's set in the virgin nature reserve on an island in the far north of Estonia, where Sasha, a woman in her 40s, has been living and working as a forester. She is joined for the summer by a young Estonian student of ornithology, Peter, to study the bird population. The age gap creates difficulties between the two, compounded by their different attitudes toward nature. Despite this, they become lovers until they discover Sasha's long ago lover is Peter's father. This leads to further tensions and a tragic conclusion.

Director Ikho was a cameraman and his direct style creates something of a documentary feel to the sequences of the young man photographing birds and adapting to the tough terrain and climate. He is well served by lensing director Tatyana Loginova. Marina Septunovova, with her fourth film script, has welded together a number of themes skillfully.

Svetlana Tormakhova plays the tough woman who at first mocks her young guest, but is later confused by rekindled sexual feelings, while Erik Ruus complements her as

the young man confident of his modern views about ecology until personal feelings interfere. Film deservedly picked up the Fipresci prize for best first film at Karlovy Vary.—*Cain.*

Azra
(YUGOSLAV)

A Jugoslavija Film presentation of a Forum Film, Sarajevo TV production. Produced by Mirza Pasic. Directed by Mirza Idrizovic. Screenplay, Zlata Kurt; camera (color), Danijal Sukalo; editor, Andrija Zafranovic, Vesna Kreber; music, Esad Arnautalic; sound, Ljubomir Petek; art direction, Kenal Hrustanovic; costumes, Vanja Popovic. Reviewed at Pula Film Festival (competing), July 25, 1988. Running time: 100 MIN.
With: Dara Dzokic (Azra), Mladen Nelevic (Hamo), Semka Sokolovic, Zvonko Lepetic, Senad Basic, Snjezana Martinovic, Boris Kozic, Faruk Begoli.

■ **Pula — A feminist tale on a Moslem background, "Azra" is a portrait of Sarajevo and its way of life, immediately after World War II.**

Azra is a liberated woman, a major in the Army who returns to her native city after participating actively in its liberation. She has a solid relationship with her husband, Hamo, a high-ranking officer just like her, and both are involved deeply in the effort to wipe out the last vestiges of fascism and introduce a new socialist, egalitarian society.

While the couple seems to stand united in their goals, Moslem mentality turns out to be stronger than political indoctrination, equality between sexes being impossible to achieve overnight. The son Azra has left behind to join the Resistance barely knows her and deeply mistrusts her, while her husband has an affair with a local courtesan, suspected of collaboration with the enemy.

The plot concerning Azra herself is a slender one, more time being dedicated to episodes of violence, the disparity between sexes and the tragedy of families torn apart by war, one brother fighting with the partisans and the other with the Germans.

Acting and technical credits are adequate, but film's appeal is mostly local, designed to address audiences familiar and emotionally involved with these issues. — *Edna.*

Fairytale For 17-Year-Olds
(VIETNAMESE-B&W)

Distributed by Film Department, Ministry of Culture. Produced by Vietnam Feature Film Studios. Directed by Nguyen Xuan Son. Screenplay, Trinh Thanh Nha. No other credits available. Reviewed at Asian American Intl. Film Festival, N.Y., June 24, 1988. Running time: 77 MIN.

■ **This film from Vietnam, directed**

by a woman, deals with the 30-year war against, first, the French, then the Americans, followed by prolonged frontier fighting against the Chinese.

Predictably, the film is noble and patriotic, but with a difference — it concentrates on the homefront and on the brave Vietnamese women who stoically await the return of sons and husbands.

An, a schoolgirl of 17, is virtuous, studious, obedient to elders and content with simple, innocent pleasures. She's cheerful even in her austere Hanoi suburb, as U.S. bombs fall in the distance. Her father, on leave, is recalled into service.

She visits an attractive war widow whose son is away fighting. His framed photograph fortifies the mother and fascinates An, who becomes strangely drawn to him, writing him, loving him although they never meet. An creates chaste fantasies of their idyllic courtship, the fairytale of the title. He is killed, of course, leaving her a legacy of immaculate passion.

The film ends as the day of victory over the Americans is being celebrated — yet the war continues, as the Vietnamese turn north to fight the Chinese, who encroach across the border.

The tone of the film, written by a recent graduate of Vietnam's film academy, plainly favors An, who is nonpolitical and who becomes, in effect, an antiwar symbol, despite what we know of the hard-line government that controls the Vietnamese film industry. — *Hitch.*

Sadovnik
(The Gardener)
(SOVIET)

A Lenfilm Studio production. Directed by Viktor Buturlin. Screenplay, Valeri Zolotucha; camera (color), Vladimir Vasilev; editor, R. Lisova; music, Algirdas Paulavicus; sound, Alexander Gruzdev; art direction, Alexander Zagoskin; costumes, G. Antipina. Reviewed at Pesaro Film Festival, June 16, 1988. Running time: 103 MIN.
Liosha Glazov .... Oleg Borisov
Kolia Staklov .... Lev Borisov
Tanya .... E. Smolianinova
Also with: Kostia Yuchov (Sanka), V. Shabalina (Aunt Irka), I. Rakshina (Raika), V. Bichkov (Vitek), P. Drockoi (Lesha's son), C. Cepaev.

■ **Pesaro — "The Gardener" could be classed an ecology film of the glasnost period. To its conservationist message against a bureaucratic order to destroy an ancient apple orchard, film adds sensuous lensing of a paradisical natural setting.**

This second feature by Lenfilm's up and coming Viktor Buturlin (prized nationally for his "Applause, Applause") looks like a fest item of potential interest for Soviet film programmers.

Aging hero Liosha (finely played by Oleg Borisov) has been the gar-

dener of the orchard, named after his father, since the old gardener died. As green as Eden, the old trees go back many years (flashbacks to peasant celebrations before the war). People write to Liosha from all over the country for seedlings, which he sends at his own expense (this lands him in trouble with the local authorities, but he is vindicated).

Liosha's fanaticism about the garden loses him his wife and best friend and turned him into a a hermit. When a commission comes up with a plan to raze the garden and put a chicken farm in its place, he defends his beloved trees and wins a victory against the bureaucracy.

Buturlin shows a strong flair for realistic lensing. With the help of cameraman Vladimir Vasilev's expressive use of color, he carefully captures the atmosphere of the garden, the interiors of houses, objects and individual characters. From foggy rivers to cool green groves, "Gardener" is a visual treat. Evocative power makes up for some slowdowns in the storytelling.

—*Yung.*

Braca Po Materi
(Half-Brothers)
(YUGOSLAV)

A Jugoslavija Film presentation of a Beograd Films production. Directed by Zdravko Sotra. Screenplay, Sotra, Jovan Radulovic, based on Radulovic's novel; camera (color), Radoslav Vladic; editor, Ljiljana Vukobratovic; music, Dusan Karuovic; art direction, Borislav Njezic; costumes, Mira Cohadzic. Reviewed at Pula Film Festival (competing), July 24, 1988. Running time: 105 MIN.
Braco .... Zarko Lausevic
Veselin .... Slavko Stimac
Vranka .... Mira Furlan
Also with: Sonja Savic, Drago Cuma, Slobodan Ninkovic, Drago Cuma, Petar Bozovic, Dragan Bjeolgrlic, Vesna Trivalic.

■ **Pula — The story of two half-brothers who have never met, the older one, Braco, self-exiled in Austria and the younger, Veselin, in a Yugoslav jail, this is as much a personal drama as it is an allegory of the frictions between brother nations within this federal republic, a much discussed topic in Yugoslavia.**

The two brothers communicate by recorded cassettes, in which they recount the story of their lives and implicitly of their mother, Vranka. A Serbian orphaned girl looking for work before the war, she married a Croatian peasant, who was drafted into the insurgent Croatian army, fighting for separation from Serbia. After he is killed during the war, she is chased away with her son by the other Croatian villagers who consider her a Serb, wanders into a Serbian village, and once again finds a man who takes her in and later marries her.

Her son goes on carrying the Croatian stigma because of his father. When he grows up he is cheated out of having the girl he loves, who is forced instead to accept the brutal chief of police, and disgustedly decides to leave the country.

The second husband hangs himself when the law comes looking for him, leaving the mother once again on her own, to raise the second son born from this marriage. She does it valiantly without anybody's help, but years later, when the Croatian neighbors revive their nationalist movement, she once again is suspected, this time by the Serbs for having been married once to an enemy.

All this emerges from the twin recorded tales, allowing a script construction which moves back and explained events and characters better. Prettifying the image by using costumes and objects which look as if they have just come off the store shelf doesn't help much either.

Zarko Lausevic and Slavko Stimac do a creditable job as the brothers but Mira Furlan, a top local star, tries too hard to look the submissive, martyr mother on whom age has no effect whatsoever, while many of the supporting parts, particularly the policeman and his unwilling bride who becomes an alcoholic, just ham it up.—*Edna.*

Ingen kan älska som vi
(There Is No Love Like Ours)
(SWEDISH)

A Svensk Filmindustri release of Filmen Kompisar production with Sparbankarna, Finansfsstet, Wendros. Produced by Christer Hagström. Written and directed by Staffan Hildebrand. Camera (Eastmancolor), Istvan Borbas; editor, Anders Oehrn; music, Grace (Chris Lancelot, Erik Holmberg, Mikael Lundgren, Jan Person, Claus Bergwall, Drutten Hansson; singer, Tina Moe); sound, Kell Landin, Per Sundström; costumes, Gabriella Koesen, Nina Carlsson; co-author on screenplay and assistant director, Joakim Schröder; production management, Rune Hjelm, Ola Björnemyr, Marianne Broddesson, Magnus Theorin. Reviewed at the Spegeln, Stockholm, Aug. 28, 1988. Running time: **98 MIN.**
Annelie . . . . Izabella Scorupco
Her mother . . . . Anki Lidén
Her father . . . . Stig Engström
Jonny . . . . Hakon Engström
His father . . . . Marten Thomasson
Boardinghouse matron . . . . . Kim Anderzon
Mackan . . . . Markus Trapp
Raffe . . . . Ulf Granquist
Also with: Dominic Henzel, Andrej Anderzon-Möller, Patrik Ehrman, Thea Oestling.

■ **Stockholm** — There is an endearing innocence to writer-helmer **Staffan Hildebrand's "There Is No Love Like Ours,"** but naiveté and a too-loose narrative structure ultimately drain his second youth meller (the first was the highly successful **"G"** from 1983) of dramatic punch.

If Hildebrand's picture is to cross borders, it will be because of its peculiar moral tone, novel to the genre. Amidst explosions of rock music in and around discos, the youngsters bed down and neck seriously, but only to the solid old limits of ultimate nonconsummation.

Not that sexual abstinence is talked about, but Hildebrand makes his protagonists seem absolutely happy with it. Otherwise, he displays fine insights in mid-teen behavior patterns and a near-obsession with the sounds and sights of rock which has combined to make "There Is No Love Like Ours" a neat b.o. grosser at home.

Too bad the dramatic potential inherent in the story remains almost totally unexplored. Annelie (sweetly demure Izabella Scorupco) defeats her mother by going to the remote north of Sweden to see her father, estranged from the family for 10 years.

When father and daughter don't hit it off immediately, Annelie goes into a deep-freeze sulk that also threatens to kill the romance that was developing between her and Jonny (Hakon Lindberg), an overly cleancut local boy of her own age.

In between clashes and reconciliations between the two youngsters and Annelie's final leavetaking of her father (behind doors closed to the cinema audience), Hildebrand indulges heartily in large doses of either lyrical contemplation of rural landscapes or of rock musicians and dancers in action. The singer Tina Moe and the rock group Grace perform with gusto and talent. —*Kell.*

Schlaflose Nächte
(Sleepless Nights)
(SWISS-WEST GERMAN)

A Cactus Films presentation of a Kyros Films, Vulcano Films production, coproduced with WDR, Köln, SRG, Zurich. Produced by Frank Hofer. Directed by Marcel Gisler. Screenplay, Gisler, Rudolf Nadler; camera (color, 16m), Patrick Lindenmaier; editor, Catherine Steghens; music, Charlie Mingus, Beethoven String Quartets; art direction, Kirsten Johannsen. Reviewed at Locarno Film Festival (competing), Aug. 12, 1988. Running time: **100 MIN.**
With: Rudolf Nadler (Ludwig), Anne Knaak (Anna), Cordula Stepanek, Andreas Herder, Matthias Tiefenbacher, Dina Leipzig, Christoph Krix.

■ **Locarno** — **This is the type of film which emerges once every few years, one more exploration of youth alienation, the portrait of a generation lost in the incertitude of its own aspirations and dreams.**

Marcel Gisler has already done something similar, on a smaller scale, three years ago, in "Tagediebe," also shot entirely in Berlin, and now he seems to have elaborated and widened the scope

Around the character of Ludwig (an assistant director who quits an unfulfilling job and reaches a state of crisis in his affair with Anna, a photographer who has a brief infatuation for one of her young male models), Gisler draws the image of an entire class of young Berlinese, all of them drifting aimlessly. They try unsuccessfully to establish deeper emotional commitments, and all of them fail, precisely because they do not know exactly what they need and how far they are prepared to invest themselves in order to obtain it.

Gisler looks at them all with a sympathetic eye, he gives an accurate portrait of their confusion, and treats all these "on again, off again" affairs with a gentle and tender approach. What he lacks is the impetuosity which would make these proceedings compelling and lend some urgency to the different crises he describes. One of his characters is quite correct when he defines the main problem in the picture as a lack of necessity on the part of everybody involved to do something or get somewhere, either on a romantic or economic level.

The quality of the image is quite polished considering its 16m origin. The direction and the editing create the fluid feeling of the old New Wave and acting is simple and natural. While experienced film buffs will certainly have a feeling of déjà vu at the sight of this film, younger audiences, of social background similar to that referred to in the picture, may find it easier to identify with the protagonists and their problems. —*Edna.*

Stesso Sangue
(The Same Blood)
(ITALIAN)

A Libra Films presentation of a Libra Films production, with RAI and the Ministry of Tourism and Spectacles. Produced by Francesca Noe. Written and directed by Egidio Eronico, Sandro Cecca. Camera (color), Roberto Meddi; editor, Anna Napoli; music, Penguin Café Orchestra, This Mortal Coil; sound, Andrea Petrucci; art direction, Giuseppe Gaudino; costumes, Alessandra Montagna. Reviewed at Locarno Film Festival (competing), Aug. 12, 1988. Running time: **100 MIN.**
Bruno . . . . Daniele Nuccetelli
Irene . . . . Alessandra Monti
Walter . . . . Rick Hutton
Also with: Enrico Salvatore, Maria Fiore, Gianfranco Amoroso, Paolo Agosti, Egidio Eronico.

■ **Locarno** — **This road movie follows the hapless, clumsy attempts of a brother and a sister to survive on their own wits after their parents' death, in a kind of fruitless Bonnie and Clyde flight across the Italian countryside.**

Bruno, a 24-year-old terminal diabetic, refuses to entrust his 14-year-old sister Irene to a state agency once they become orphans. Instead, the two run away together and are soon forced into a career of petty crimes, the only way they know how to provide for their essential needs. On the way, they meet a lecherous patron who tries to lay hands on Irene: a British blues singer, Walter, who joins them for a while on their career of crime, and a cupid peasant woman who hates all town folk without distinction.

Irene is the lucid half of this improbable tandem, who fully realizes the hopelessness of their venture but sticks with it for the sake of her brother. Bruno loses contact with reality as he gets sicker and drifts into mystical, impractical fantasies, such as going to Egypt and being reborn there. The script offers precious little to sustain this type of adventure, and the acting looks totally insecure, of the type that copies faithfully directing instructions without trying to make any sense of them.

Egidio Eronico and Sandro Cecca are much better at directing the camera than the actors, and their use of locations displays definite visual imagination. It is the film's main achievement, by far more convincing than its theme or the treatment of its characters. —*Edna.*

Moon Over Parador

A Universal Pictures release. Produced and directed by Paul Mazursky. Coproducers, Pato Guzman, Geoffrey Taylor. Screenplay, Leon Capetanos, Mazursky, based on a story by Charles G. Booth; camera (Deluxe color), Donald McAlpine; editor, Stuart Pappé; music, Maurice Jarre; sound (Dolby), Jim Webb; production design, Guzman; art direction, Markos Flaksman; set decoration, Alexandre Meyer; costume design, Albert Wolsky; assistant director, Irby Smith; production manager, John Broderick, Jose Joaquim Salles (Brazil); second unit director-stunt coordinator, Bill Catching; associate producers, Lindsay Flickinger, Gary Shusett; casting, Ellen Chenoweth. Reviewed at Universal screening room, N.Y., Aug. 24, 1988. (In Montreal World Film Festival, noncompeting.) MPAA Rating: PG-13. Running time: 105 MIN.
Jack Noah . . . . Richard Dreyfuss
Roberto Strausmann . . . . Raul Julia
Madonna . . . . Sonia Braga
Ralph . . . . Jonathan Winters
Alejandro . . . . Fernando Rey
Sammy Davis Jr. . . . . Himself
Clint . . . . Michael Greene
Midge . . . . Polly Holliday
Carlo . . . . Milton Gonçalves
Madame Loop . . . . Charo
Magda . . . . Marianne Sagebrecht
Gunther . . . . René Kolldehoff
Mama . . . . Paul Mazursky
Also with: Richard Russell Ramos, Jose Lewgoy, Dann Florek, Roger Aaron Brown, Dana Delany, Dick Cavett, Ike Pappas, Edward Asner.

■ Paul Mazursky's elaborate farce about the actor as imposter (here posing as dictator of the mythical Latin nation Parador) has moments of true hilarity emerging only fitfully from a ponderous production. Reteaming of director with star Richard Dreyfuss looks to fall far short of prior ''Down And Out In Beverly Hills'' hit status at the box-office.

Cutely bookended with location footage at Joe Papp's Public Theater in Greenwich Village, pic has Dreyfuss well-cast as a fairly successful stage and film actor on a location shoot in the English-speaking Parador. He's given an offer he can't refuse by police chief Raul Julia to impersonate the just-deceased dictator.

Physically resembling the late major domo, Dreyfuss reluctantly adopts the role, at first chafing at the ''results-oriented'' superficiality of his impromptu performance, but soon taking on the new persona in earnest after being coached by the dictator's sexy mistress Madonna (Sonia Braga in a flamboyant, delicious turn).

Ruse comes to a climax when Dreyfuss starts instituting reforms inimical to Julia and other powerful interests, and tiring of his role manages to escape in a faked assassination utilizing special effects expertise learned on a movie set.

Encouraging wild overplaying by the principals that pushes the film over into Mel Brooks territory at times, Mazursky's mix of satire and namedropping in-jokes lacks the sharp comedy writing needed to maintain its gag momentum. Unfortunately, a very interesting international cast ends up playing second fiddle to setpieces utilizing thousands of extras on location in Brazil. Sumptuously photographed by Aussie ace Donald McAlpine, pic too frequently halts to admire its handiwork.

Dreyfuss' panache in playing an actor's actor carries the film most of the way, ably played off Braga's lusty and glamorous character. Julia is very convincing as the stern local despot and Jonathan Winters makes the most of his transparent Ugly American role as our CIA man in Parador. Supporting cast members, eccentrically ranging from Charo to Marianne Sagebrecht (of ''Sugarbaby'') on the palace staff, get very little screen time. Quick laughs are provided by cameos such as Sammy Davis Jr. doing virtually an SCTV Sammy Maudlin satire of himself and Ed Asner playing himself as a ''visiting American liberal.''

Scripters Leon Capetanos and Mazursky overemphasize the 1-gag premise of Germanic influence upon their fictional Parador, while endless namedropping strikes out more often than scoring (latter in a highlight reference to Mandy Patinkin). Mazursky himself shows up uncredited in drag in the role of the dictator's dowager mother.

Besides McAlpine's lensing, all other tech credits are tops for this big budgeter, including Albert Wolsky's eye-catching costumes.
— Lor.

Quest For Love
(SOUTH AFRICAN)

A Filmtrust release (U.S.) of an Elegant Film Prod. Ltd. production. Produced by Shan Moodley. Directed by Helen Nogueira. Screenplay, Helen Nogueira, based on ''Q.E.D.'' by Gertrude Stein; camera (color), Roy McGregor; editor, Helen Nogueira; music, Tony Rudner; set design, Adrianne Grabman; sound, Owen Keyser; costumes, Leigh van der Merwe. Reviewed at Montreal World Film Festival (Cinema of Today and Tomorrow), Aug. 25, 1988. Running time: 93 MIN.
Alex . . . . Jana Cilliers
Dorothy . . . . Sandra Prinsloo
Mabel . . . . Joanna Weinberg
Michael . . . . Wayne Bowman

■ Montreal — Audiences still hungry for films about South African journalists in peril probably will give ''Quest For Love'' a try. However, they will come away disappointed if they try to compare it to ''Cry Freedom'' or ''A World Apart.'' This low-budget film has neither the natural drama of the latter nor the strong characterizations of the former.

Instead, Helen Nogueira presents a film with no real sense of purpose.

Ostensibly a film about a journalist's inability to commit to relationships or revolution, it wanders too much to be interesting.

Alex loves Dorothy, a gay woman who lives in an independent African island nation, but doesn't want to end up like Dorothy's fawning lover Mabel. She thinks she could love an activist named Michael, but she isn't sure if it's love or admiration for the cause. She also thinks she could have a cause of her own but she finds it hard to ''love'' the Africans she has gone to jail to ''save.''

Alex is well played by Jana Cilliers, but the writing is not strong enough to carry all the notions and attitudes that Alex appears to possess. Alex is a writer, but we never really see any reason for her to have that profession. She is blind to almost everything that occurs around her.

Perhaps Nogueira made Alex a journalist in an attempt to capture the market created by ''Cry Freedom'' and sustained by ''A World Apart.'' Whatever the reason, it is hard to imagine devotees of those films spending too much time with this pic. Distribs might be better off going straight to specialty vidstores.
—Cadd.

Powwow Highway
(BRITISH-U.S.)

A Handmade Films presentation. Produced by Jan Wieringa. Executive producers, George Harrison, Denis O'Brien. Directed by Jonathan Wacks. Screenplay, Janet Heany, Jean Stawarz, based on the novel by David Seals; camera (color), Toyomichi Kurita; editor, James Austin Stewart; music, Barry Goldberg; production design, Cynthia Sowder; costumes, Isis Mussenden; casting, Junie Lowry; associate producer, Carl Kraines. Reviewed at the Montreal World Film Festival (Cinema of Today and Tomorrow), Aug. 25, 1988. MPAA Rating: R. Running time: 91 MIN.
Buddy Red Bow . . . . A Martinez
Philbert Bono . . . . Gary Farmer
Rabbit Layton . . . . Amanda Wyss
Bonnie Red Bow . . . . Joanelle Nadine Romero
Chief Joseph . . . . Sam Vlahos
Wolf Tooth . . . . Wayne Waterman
Imogene . . . . Margo Kane
Sandy Youngblood . . . . Geoff Rivas
Agent Jack Novall . . . . Roscoe Born

■ Montreal — A buddy picture with an independent spirit, ''Powwow Highway'' follows two contemporary American Indians on an offbeat journey to self-realization. Modern reservation life and the perpetuation of native Americans' underclass existence are too seldom explored on film, and ''Powwow Highway'' presents this world vividly.

Although a little rough around the edges, its curious blend of bitter social commentary, bent humor and mythical fancy could find a selective audience.

On the Northern Cheyenne Reservation in Montana, Buddy Red Bow (A Martinez) is a hot-tempered firebrand activist, a veteran of Vietnam and the Wounded Knee protests, fighting a hopeless rear-guard battle against the encroachments of giant mining companies on Indian lands. His childhood pal Philbert (Gary Farmer), is an overweight, passive dreamer who fantasizes about the days when red men of awesome physical and spiritual powers ruled the land as great and wise warriors.

The sinister mining company, in league with ''The Feds'' decides to squeeze Buddy by acting against his sweet-natured sister in far away Santa Fe. With the connivance of the local police there, sister Bonnie is framed on a drug charge and jailed. Buddy and Philbert ride off to the rescue in a decrepit jalopy.

There are lapses of continuity and plot logic in ''Powwow Highway,'' as if a written script had been severely truncated for shooting. Why Buddy gets a call to aid a sister he hasn't been seen in 10 years and what separated them in the first place is never clearly explained. Most Indians, even those who try to assimilate, lead tough lives, the scenario suggests, but tribal roots rule when real trouble comes down.

Buddy and Philbert's fevered ride becomes a journey into the enigma of Indian identity. On the way to Santa Fe they detour through South Dakota to a sacred Indian ground in the Black Hills. They pass through Indian communities where the accents and jargon are all-American, but the situation, as Buddy notes ruefully, is ''Third World.'' The differences between the hot-tempered rebel and his placid, daydreaming traditionalist pal are played out with a subtle balance of tension and affection in two nice performances.

The main drawback to ''Powwow Highway'' is its depiction of all non-Indians as unfeeling racist exploiters — a polemic generalization that the film seems to extend to any Indian who steps off the reservation. Less critical is the picture's failure to develop further the psychological dimension in which its characters are clearly under siege from within as well as without.

At its best moments ''Powwow Highway'' offers an unusual sense of the American west as a special place where the parallel world of Indian life is fenced-in on a vanishing primal landscape. Songs by Robbie Robertson, formerly of The Band, give the road scenes emotional drive. — Rich.

Not Since Casanova

Produced by Bradford Owen and Brett Thompson. Written and directed by Brett

Thompson. Camera (color), Andreas Kossak-editor, Arthur Farkus, Thompson; music, John Debney; sound, David John West; design, Doug Miller; costumes, Robyn Reichek; animation, David Cutler. Reviewed at the Montreal World Film Festival (Cinema Of Today And Tomorrow), Aug. 26, 1988. Running time: **80 MIN.**

Prepski Morris . . . . .Charles Solomon
Gina .Diana Frank
Tommi . . . . .Tomi Griffin
Laurie . . . . .Leslie Mitts
Denise . . . . .Lucy Winn
Serina . . . . .Karen Smith
Hilary . . . . .Kare N. Marcus
Lorna Doom . . . . .Robin Reichek
Jeff . . . . .Erol Landis
Also with: Dr. Klaus Hoppe, Trevor Lapresle.

■ **Montreal** — Torn from today's headlines — in trendy newspaper "lifestyle" sections and in glossy women's magazines — "Not Since Casanova" is a better than sophomoric but basically lightweight look at the phenomenon of over-30 men who "won't grow up."

Brett Thompson's comic essay on the so-called Peter Pan or Casanova complex features a likeable airhead hero who can't chose between the "seven beauties" in his life. The concept is good, but the film addresses it with a grabbag of contemporary clichés and very ordinary performances that shouldn't stand up in theatrical release.

Prepski Morris has the magic combo of hunky athleticism and ingenuous charm that ladies love — and he loves them. His life story — from a broken home in L.A. suburbia to the uneasy bliss of perpetual bachelorhood — is related in a series of voguishly cartoonish, skit-like episodes strung together with intertitles and a few flashes of narrative ingenuity.

Making sure no one misses the point, flashbacks show Prepski's abandoned mom cavorting with her love and joy dressed up in a Peter Pan outfit. When he gets older, phallic stud Prepski likes rockets and rugby balls, and the girls like him. Prepski's life is one long weekend fraternity party that doesn't end with college.

The spice of his life comes in a variety of feminine flavors: Gina, a paradigm existing in his fantasies; Tommi, a sexually voracious aerobics ace; Denise, a spoilt rich right-wing prepette; Serina, his childhood love; Hilary, a hippie earth-momma, and Lorna Doom, a desperate young spinster. Then along comes Ms. Right, Laurie, and Prepski must think the unthinkable: marriage!

Predictably, the screenplay touches on such familiar themes as sexual reformation in the age of AIDS, narcissism, commitment vs. boredom and the impossible quest for perfection in human relations. Charles Solomon as Prepski bears a passing resemblance to Jeff Daniels in looks and endearing naif mannerisms, but plays the character as a caricature.

The pic is touched up with some film school filigree, including a cute animation sequence and a false ending. —*Rich.*

Fever
(AUSTRALIAN)

A Norstar Releasing release (in Canada) of a J.C. Williamson production. Produced by Terry Jennings. Directed by Craig Lahiff. Screenplay, John Emery; camera (Eastmancolor), David Foreman; editor, Denise Harazis; music, Frank Strangio; production manager, Elspeth Baird; art direction, Derel Mills; sound, Rob Cutcher; wardrobe, Ruth De La Lande; makeup, Leanne White; executive producers, Ron Saunders, Lahiff. Reviewed at Montreal World Film Festival (noncompeting), Aug. 27, 1988. Running time: **92 MIN.**

Jack Welles . . . . .Bill Hunter
Jeff . . . . .Gary Sweet
Leanne Welles . . . . .Mary Regan
Morris .Jim Hay

■ **Montreal** — "Fever," the story of a string of doublecrosses in a small South Australian town, will probably get a Canada-wide release by Norstar Releasing but does not look to have the sales potential of Australian predecessors.

Its likely venue in most markets is video stores, given that it does not have the cinematic scope of successful Aussie theatrical releases like "Gallipoli" and "Breaker Morant."

It does have "Gallipoli" costar Bill Hunter, who plays local lawman Jack Welles, an honest cop who turns bad when he comes across thousands of dollars in drug money. He sees it as an opportunity to give his young wife all the things he promised her but never delivered. That changes when he finds her with another man but, before he can get away with the money himself, the couple render him unconscious and leave him for dead in an abandoned mine.

"Fever" offers a number of plot twists, some of which should help to keep audience interest in the absence of new ideas. Writer John Emery uses the twists to spice up what is essentially a run-of-the-mill chase film. His dialog is predictable and the performances lack enthusiasm.

North American audiences, spoiled by high-caliber Australian outdoor films won't break into a sweat over "Fever," which doesn't use either its Southern Australian backdrop or talented lead to great effect. —*Cadd.*

The Carpenter
(CANADIAN)

A Cinepix (Canada), Capstone Film Co. (U.S.) release of a Goldgems Canada production. Produced by Pierre Grisé. Directed by David Wellington. Screenplay, Doug Taylor; camera (color), David Franco; editor, Roland Pollack; music, Pierre Bundock; sound, Juan Gutierrez; set design, Sylvain Gendron. Reviewed at Montreal World Film Festival (Panorama Canada), Aug. 27, 1988. Running time: **87 MIN.**

Ed .Wings Hauser
Alice .Lynn Adams
Martin . . . . .Pierre Lenoir
Rachel . . . . .Barbara Jones

■ **Montreal** — Most small Canadian films eventually find their way to public or private Canadian tv networks looking to boost Canadian content. "The Carpenter," which looks like a made-for-tv film, is probably too violent to qualify for tv programming.

Perhaps Cinepix will try a limited release with the Canadian theater chain Famous Players, with whom they just signed an agreement for exhibition of Canadian-made product.

Whether this black comedy will attract paying customers is another question. The story of a woman who falls for the ghost of an executed mass murder, it is filled with violent depictions of the severing of limbs, all done tongue-in-cheek. The ghost appears in the human form of a carpenter returning to the house he was in the process of building when he was executed. He wants to finish the job and he won't let anyone, including the carpenters hired by the woman's husband, get in his way.

Director David Wellington is a university film school graduate making his first film. That makes sense since this is an almost experimental pic of little substance. Every time Wellington runs out of ideas he throws in another grisly murder, done in a humorous manner but grisly nonetheless.

The script is confusing and the actors never seem to know if the scene calls for drama or comedy. The result is a mess that appears unsuitable for any market and doesn't even appear to have cutrate video potential. — *Cadd.*

Marusa No Onna II
(A Taxing Woman's Return)
(JAPANESE)

An Itami Prods. production. Produced by Yasushi Tamaoki, Seigo Hosoge. Written and directed by Juzo Itami. Camera (color), Yonezo Maeda; editor, Akira Suzuki; music, Toshiyuki Honda. Reviewed at the Montreal World Film Festival (noncompeting), Aug. 28, 1988. Running time: **127 MIN.**

Yuoko Itakura . . . . .Nobuko Miyamoto
Also with: Rentaro Mikuni, Masahiko Tsugawa.

■ **Montreal** — Juzo Itami's 1987 "A Taxing Woman" was the third largest b.o. smash in Japan. American audiences familiar with Itami's bizarre satirical arthouse success "Tampopo" and the first "Taxing Woman" should return in equal numbers for a followup that's funnier and more corrosive than the original.

Doughty, zealous freckle-faced Ryoko (Nobuko Miyamoto, wife of Itami), the only woman investigator in her tax collection bureau, is on the track of a greedy and corrupt cabal of politicians, land speculators and mobsters who are intent on gobbling up every square meter of Tokyo and making billions at it. Still gutsier and smarter than her male bosses and coworkers, Ryoko remains an inveterate snoop, obsessed this time with ferreting out the secret machinations of a big bank, a wealthy realtor and a powerful pol.

This amoral and dangeorus bunch has its eyes on a residential lot it wants to clear for a skyscraper. When a few tenants refuse payments to move, they are blackmailed and threatened with all sorts of mayhem to change their minds. Okinazawa, the realty boss, sets up a phony cult religion, hoping to cover his tracks by claiming tax-exempt status. This works until Ryoko comes on the case.

In the formal and meticulous world of bureaucratized Japanese society, however, the tax department, must make an airtight case, backed up with material evidence. Determined to get her men, this very taxing woman is not above bending a few rules.

Her new adventure gives Itami another opportunity to remorselessly skewer the covetous sanctimony underpinning public morality in Japan. Among Itami's targets are entreprenurial spirituality, sexual exploitation and the exalted status of Tokyo University.

The real focus, though, is on the blurry distinctions between legitimate and illegitimate power in Japan. Money, "a living thing" from the realtor's perspective, is the nexus of everything. As it turns out, the power of money and the ruthless inexorability of power are too much even for Ryoko.

This suggests that the taxing woman could return again, not necessarily a bad thing if Itami can manage to make a slightly more concise film the next time Ryoko hits the streets. — *Rich.*

High-Frequency
(Aquarium)
(ITALIAN)

A Medusa Distribuzione release of a Cinecittà production. Produced by Gianfranco Piccioli, Giorgio Leopardi. Directed by Faliero Rosati. Screenplay, Rosati, Franco Ferrini, Vincenzo Cerami; camera (Eastmancolor), Pasqualino De Santis; editor, Anna Napoli; music, Pino Donaggio; sound, Remo Ugolinelli; set design, Giantito Burchiellard; costumes, Maurizio Millenotti. Reviewed at Montreal World Film Festival (noncompeting), Aug. 25, 1988. Running time: **105 MIN.**

Peter .Vincent Spano
Danny . . . . .Oliver Benny
Sylvie . . . . .Anne Canovas
Anna Sweder . . . . .Isabelle Pasco
Spy .David Brandon
(English soundtrack)

■ **Montreal** — It was inevitable that someone would take a high-tech Hitchcock to the marketplace to cash in, but it's unlikely this Italian production will make much noise in U.S. theatrical release.

"High-Frequency" (a.k.a. "A-quarium") could have legs on video since it has some youth appeal with its spy vs. spy theme, but it is too unsophisticated for adult tastes.

Vincent Spano stars as Peter, a satellite relay station attendant assigned to Mont Blanc and Oliver Benny debuts as Danny, the 11-year-old Main ham operator he befriends. While watching a boxing match Peter sees a murder being committed on a satellite monitor. From that moment on, he and Danny try to piece together the mystery and save a young woman who appears to be the next victim of the murderer.

Director Faliero Rosati has taken the premise of "Rear Window" and propelled it into the present without preserving any of the strong characterizations of the original.

Spano is all right as the station attendant but newcomer Benny adds nothing to the crucial role of the child caught in the middle of a great adventure. There is no intensity to his performance, and the wide-eyed portrayal reminds one more of old Disney pics than Hitchcock.

It might work with kids hooked to the Disney channel but it won't impress many adults looking for a theatrical pic that takes the best of a classic and polishes it. — *Cadd.*

Yen Family
(JAPANESE)

A Herald Ace and Nippon Herald Films release of a Fuji TV production, in cooperation with Melies. Produced by Shuji Miyajima, Shinya Kawai. Executive producer, Koichi Murakami. Directed by Yojiro Takita. Screenplay, Nobuyuki Isshiki, from story by Toshihiko Tani; camera (color), Yoichi Shiga; editor, Isso Tomita; music, Katsuo Ohne; art direction, Katsumi Nakazawa; sound, Hisayuki Miyamoto. Reviewed at the Montreal World Film Festival, noncompeting. Aug. 25, 1988. Running time: **113 MIN.**
Hajime Kimura . . . . Takeshi Kaga
Noriko Kimura . . . . Kaori Momoi
Terumi Kimura . . . . Hiromi Iwasaki
Taro Kimura . . . . Mitsunori Isaki
Shinichi Amamiya . . . . Midori Kiuchi
Mitsu Amamiya . . . . Akiko Kazami
Masashi Takakura . . . . . . Hiroyuki Konishi
Sayaka Takakura . . . . Michiko Shimizu
Ken Takakura . . . . Maketo Nakano
Tokijuro . . . . Yoshi Kato

■ **Montreal — The success of the Japanese comedy "Tampopo" in the U.S. release has lead to a small invasion by Japanese filmmakers. The latest to try his luck with the U.S. market is 32-year-old Yojiro Takita, who brought "Yen Family" to the Montreal Film Festival with hopes for limited release Stateside.**

Although the film is not as innovative as "Tampopo," it might have some success in urban centers, if only because it reinforces stereotypes of Japanese culture.

The pic stars Takeshi Kaga as a money-loving father of two who organizes his family into a small corporation. Despite holding down a regular job, he oversees a variety of family businesses, including a news-paper delivery service, a catering company and a taxi service. His daughter has organized her school pals into a corporate entity and his wife runs a telephone sex service.

The only family member who feels out of place is 10-year-old Taro, who apologizes to an uncle when his father forces him to present the uncle a bill for massage services and lies to his parents when bullies steal the pennies he has earned. When his uncle gives him a Bible he starts to dwell on the passages about greed and begins to question his family's values.

The first 20 minutes of "Yen Family" are funny and augur well. Takita whets our appetite, but he never quite fills the order. The one joke — the family's passion for moolah — gets old quickly and isn't able to offer plot or characters interesting enough to care about.

The morality play that follows our introduction to the family is destructive to the comedy. The family's pleasure in making money is replaced by a self-examination that has no whimsy to it. The aunt and uncle, who are completely joyless, are allowed to determine the direction of the family's moral fortunes somewhere around the midpoint of film and, even though the script allows the Kimuras a more rational and upbeat coming-to-terms, the damage to the comedic momentum is extensive.

Even when the family's struggle with its need for money is resolved, the messages leave the viewer unsatisfied. The comedy is forgotten by the time the curtain comes down on "Yen Family," and that could hurt the film's chances in single-theater urban distribution where word-of-mouth is of such importance. —*Cadd.*

The Stick
(SOUTH AFRICAN)

An Artistic Film Production Co. production. Produced by Anant Singh. Directed by Darrell Roodt. Screenplay, Roodt, Carole Shore; camera (color), Paul Witte; editor, Lee Percy, David Heitner; music Dana Kaproff; sound, Robin Harris; design, David Barkham; costumes, Sue Steel, Lisa Perry. Reviewed at Montreal World Film Festival (competing), Aug. 24, 1988. Running time: **98 MIN.**
Cooper . . . . Sean Taylor
O'Grady . . . . Greg Latter
Lieutenant . . . . Frantz Dobrowsky
Witchdoctor . . . . Winston Ntshona
Also with: Gys De Villiers.

■ **Montreal — Darrell Roodt's "The Stick," banned in his native South Africa, is a sincere, violent and intermittently interesting anti-war film with political overtones, patently derivative of "Platoon" but not in the same company as Oliver Stone's Oscar-winner.**

Commercial prospects seem limited, but an adventurous U.S. distributor could market the film as a timely item too hot to handle in its homeland.

Cooper, the film's cynical and embittered narrator, relates in voice-over his horrific experiences as a South African infantryman engaged "in a war with no rules" against black guerrillas in the jungles and plains. When yet another patrol is ambushed and wiped out, a "stick" of eight men is broken off from Cooper's platoon and transported across the border by helicopter to engage in a Vietnam-style "search and destroy" mission. The retrospective narrative device as used by the filmmaker consistently works against suspense by telegraphing plot developments. It's apparent from the outset that nothing good will come of this mission.

The patrol of seven white men and a black "tracker" is perpetually wracked by fatigue and fear. These combat veterans are already over the edge of hysteria, but Roodt never shows how they got that way. Similarly, intense personality conflicts within the group are presented, rather than developed. Chief antagonist is O'Grady, an off-the-wall maniac who enjoys the blood lust opportunities of war. There are plenty of these, as the soldiers proceed to kill a young cowherd, a troublesome witchdoctor and then slaughter an entire village in an orgy of panic and frustrated rage at their inability to find the enemy.

Roodt toys with the mystical theme of shamanism and the supernatural, but does so incoherently in a jumble of totemic imagery and disconnected episodes. The witchdoctor, it seems, is able to cast his spells from beyond the grave. Soon the patrol members are killing off one another — an appropriate, but obvious metaphor for South Africa as a country in the throes of self-destruction.

The screenplay tends to be either aphoristic or naturalistically profane. There are some very good production values, however, including evocative cinematography, an appropriately folkloric score and excellent sound recording that buzzes with the cacaphony of the fecund jungle. — *Rich.*

La Rusa
(Code Name: The Russian)
(SPANISH)

A Pedro Maso production. Directed by Mario Camus. Screenplay, Juan Luis Cebrian, based on his novel; camera (color), Hans Burmann; editor, Jose Maria Burrun; music, design, Rafael Palmero; music, Anton Garcia Abril; design, Rafael Patero, sound, Bernardo Menz. Reviewed at Montreal World Film Festival (competing), Aug. 25, 1988. Running time: **122 MIN.**
Begoña . . . . Angeli Van Os
Juan Altamirano . . . . Didier Flamand
Eva . . . . Muntsa Alcañiz
Minister . . . . Eusebio Lazaro
Pedro . . . . Fernando Guillen
Jon . . . . Luis Hostalot
Hurtado . . . . Jose Pedro Carrion
Hernando . . . . Jacques François

■ **Montreal — A lethargic love story about a bourgeois politician and his radical mistress set in Spain during the post-Franco transition to democracy, "La Rusa" is too portentous, passionless and rambling for American audiences who don't have a special interest in the period.**

Even those who do are apt to find the latest effort by Mario Camus a curiously disappointing exercise in the Costa-Gavras style of romantic political thriller.

Juan lives a comfortable family life and serves as an advisor to the Spanish government. He's cynical about the capacity of politics to effect change, but drawn to the energy of an emerging radical movement. At a left-wing rally he meets a younger woman, Begoña, a radical law professor with a striking head of red hair and mile-long legs. He pursues her ardently and after an initial rebuff she surrenders. Their affair develops in an escalating string of sneak-away dalliances during which barbed political-philosophical debates, like an aphrodisiac formality, invariably precede their lovemaking.

A bigshot government minister with compromising photos of Juan and Begona informs the hero that she is a KGB agent codenamed "La Rusa." Juan is effectively blackmailed into volunteering for a secret mission to initiate negotiations with Basque terrorists operating out of Brussels and Paris. When his Basque contact is assassinated, Juan realizes he's been duped by revanchist forces at work somewhere within the military or the police.

Slowly, Juan tries to rouse himself from a lifetime of political compromise and emotional vacillation. Unsure whether his girlfriend is or is not a Soviet spy, he's prepared to sacrifice everything for love. Begoña, meanwhile, has become more and more attracted to her pensive lover's limousine lifestyle and philosophy of disengagement. For fear of losing her commitment to the cause, she flees to Cuba.

Didier Flamand and Angeli Van Os are believable enough in the lead roles, but the actors and the filmmaker do not succeed in making the couple particularly sympathetic until melodramatics are brought in at the end. The message that political dedication is futile in a world of complex and clashing interests is neither particularly original nor delivered with stunning force.—*Rich.*

Geteilte Liebe
(Maneuvers)
(WEST GERMAN-COLOR/B&W)

A Helma Sanders-Brahms/Metropolis Films production. Produced, written and directed by Helma Sanders-Brahms. Camera (color), Claus Deubel; editor, Regine Heuser; music, Jurgen Knieper; costumes, Inge Stiborski; design, Andrea Fritsch. Reviewed at

Montreal World Film Festival (competing), Aug. 28, 1988. Running time: **100 MIN.**

Elly Wackornagel	Adriana Altaras
Lt. Max Klett	Johannes Herrschmann
Col. Dinklage	Alfred Edel
Frau Dinklage	Elizabeth Zundel

■ **Montreal** — Helma Sanders-Brahms brings a wry comic perspective to post-WW II German history in this absurdist tale of a bungling East German spy "infiltrating" West Germany at the height of the cold war.

Given the recent solid arthouse runs of highbrow comedies by new wave German filmmakers such as Dorris Dörrie and Percy Adlon, foreign film specialty companies might gamble on releasing "Geteilte Liebe."

Shy, gangly Max Klett, a lieutenant in the East German army, is getting ready in 1959 for a top secret mission with intensive training in tango dancing and etiquette. His assignment: cross into West Germany, then find and seduce Elly Wackernagel, the secretary and anxious spinster mistress of Colonel Dinklage, a pompous conniver with access to military secrets.

Col. Dinklage lives in the country with his henpecking wife and pesty daughter, but contrives to spend most of his time at his office in Bonn, where he's been carrying on a 3-year affair with Wackernagel. Now the mistress wants to be the Colonel's wife, and Dinklage's unwillingness to get a divorce sets the stage for the unlikely Casanova, Klett.

A series of comic misadventures surrounding Klett's attempt to pry secrets from Wackernagel is used by Sanders-Brahms as a platform for lampooning German militarism and materialism. The filmmaker makes coherent and amusing use of inter-cut newsreel footage in aiming her satirical barbs at the nation's historical tendency to line up behind leaders and causes of the moment.

The funny ensemble parts are distinctive and actors Adriana Altaras (Wackernagel), Johannes Herrschmann (Klett), Alfred Edel (Col. Dinklage) and Elizabeth Kundel (Frau Dinklage) do a good job in preventing the silliness from getting out of hand. The film's resolution is a bit slight, but its whimsical spirit disguises the more serious subtext on the nature of German national character, which Sanders-Brahms suggests is undivided in spite of itself. —*Rich.*

Tiger Warsaw

A Sony Pictures release of a Continental Film Group production. Executive producer, Navin Desai. Produced and directed by Amin Q. Chaudhri. Screenplay, Roy London; camera (color), Robert Draper; editor, Brian Smedley-Aston; music, Ernest Troost; production design, Tom Targownik; set decoration, Chris O'Neal; costume design, Sheila Kehoe; sound, Abe Nejad; assistant director, Bob Hurrie; associate producers, Gay Mayer, Watson C. Warriner Jr.; casting, Deborah Aquila. Reviewed at Magno Review 2 screening room, N.Y., Aug. 22, 1988. (In Toronto Film Festival.) MPAA rating: R. Running time: **92 MIN.**

Chuck (Tiger) Warsaw	Patrick Swayze
Frances Warsaw	Piper Laurie
Mitchell Warsaw	Lee Richardson
Paula Warsaw	Mary McDonnell
Karen	Barbara Williams
Tony	Bobby DiCicco
Val	Jenny Chrisinger
Roger	James Patrick Gillis

Also with: Michelle Glaven (Emily), Kevin Bayer (Robin), Beeson Carroll (Uncle Gene), Sally-Jane Heit (Aunt Barbara), Kaye Ballard (Aunt Thelma), Thomas Mills Wood (Lt. Fontana), Cynthia Lammel (Paula's secretary).

■ **More an ensemble than a star vehicle for Patrick Swayze, "Tiger Warsaw" is an emotional exploration of a middle class family's collapse and reconciliation. Characters threaten violence, but never upset the pic's sweet disposition. Sweetness, however, generally doesn't sell a lot of tickets and whether Swayze will here is iffy.**

Picked up for domestic distribution by Sony's newborn theatrical distrib arm, modestly budgeted pic was filmed in western Pennsylvania just before Swayze's "Dirty Dancing" clicked at the boxoffice. Advertising art for Sony's debut release duly puts the young actor's name above the title.

Swayze fans may flock to "Tiger Warsaw" initially, but it's debatable whether they'll swoon over this incarnation of their dancing hero. A former drug addict tormented by past mistakes, Swayze's "Tiger" registers plenty of sympathy, but his scruffy and dishevelled looks belie star material. His unkempt hair often shines from pomade or rain.

Upsetting the well-manicured order of Sharon, Pa., Tiger Warsaw (his high school basketball team was the Tigers) returns 15 years after he shot and injured his father during a quarrel. Played by Lee Richardson, Dad has lived in a numbed daze ever since.

Mother Warsaw (Piper Laurie, in a nice turn), Tiger's highschool sweetheart (Barbara Williams) and buddy (Bobby DiCicco) support the prodigal son in his attempt to resolve the past, but his sister (Mary McDonnell), her fiance (James Patrick Gillis) and assorted relatives strive to sabotage his comeback.

In a partially successful effort to maintain interest, screenplay makes a mystery out of why father and son fought so nastily, but the dark flashbacks and character recollections offer conflicting evidence. Was teenage Tiger ransacking the house for drug money? Did his sister let dad think his kids had an incestuous relationship? Or did Tiger just get caught eavesdropping on his sister as she changed clothes?

Ultimately, forgiveness and love win out in this 2- or 3-hankie drama. Symbolizing, none too originally, the revived family, pic ends with the McDonnell-Gillis nuptials, and a strong hint that Swayze and Williams also will live happily ever after.

Technical contributions are adequate, as are the performances. —*Binn.*

Bravestarr
(ANIMATED)

A Taurus Entertainment release of a Filmation production. Produced by Lou Scheimer. Directed by Tom Tataranowicz. Screenplay, Bob Forward, Steve Hayes; camera supervisor (CFI color), F.T. Ziegler; editor, Ludmilla Saskova; music, Frank W. Becker; in Dolby stereo; art direction, John Grusd; special effects animation supervisor, Brett Hisey. Reviewed at Criterion 5 theater, N.Y., Sept. 3, 1988. MPAA Rating: PG. Running time: **91 MIN.**

Voices of: Charlie Adler, Susan Blu, Pat Fraley.

■ **"Bravestarr" is a disappointing animated feature applying the Western format directly to an Outer Space saga. Pretty backgrounds and explosions do not adequately cover for lackluster characters, given limited animation movements.**

Title character (on screen it reads "Bravestarr The Legend," but "Bravestarr The Movie" in ads) is an indistinctive looking American Indian-styled cowboy destined to save the planet of New Texas from various monster meanies, led by Stampede (a huge dragonlike steer) and Tex Hex (a reanimated, skeletal cowboy). The ancient Shaman gives Bravestarr his orders and magical powers, largely calling upon the strength of the Bear constellation (a repetitious device).

Though its occasional attempts at comic relief fall flat, film plays off foolishly with its 1-joke premise of a planet with modern technology but styled after all the corny clichés of a Western movie. Critters are robots, except for the Prairie People, cutesy little burrowing humanoids forced to work as slaves in mining operations.

Opposite the bland Bravestarr, heroine J.B., who's the local judge, is nondescript, as is her mustachioed dad McBride, given a Scottish brogue right out of James Doohan in "Star Trek."

Much running time is given to introing each of Tex Hex' henchmen, but they have nothing to do or say in the film, wasting at least one unusual creation, the exotic Vipra, villainess riding a vast serpent.

Characters mainly pose, with very mechanical movement of the limited sort familiar from tv. Toddlers may overlook this thanks to okay action scenes involving flying vehicles and well-executed battle explosions.

Frank Becker's tinny musical score is a big letdown when it attempts to ape Western motifs on synthesized keyboards. —*Lor.*

La Recompensa
(The Reward)
(COLOMBIAN)

A Focine release of a Copelco production. Produced by Néstor Barrantes. Directed by Manuel Franco Posse. Screenplay, Elsa Vásquez; camera (color, 16m), Jorge Pinto; editor, Rafael Umana; sound, Lina Uribe. Reviewed at Festival Latino, N.Y., Aug. 6, 1988. Running time: **60 MIN.**

Tobias Bolivar	Rafael Maldonado
Maria Luis Bolivar	Lucy Martinez
Roberto Aldana	Juan Pablo Franco

Also with: Jaime Osorio, Antonio Aparicio, Alfredo Bolaños, Elsa Paez, Gabriel de los Rios.

■ **The Colombian pic "La Recompensa" (The Reward) is an ironic moral tale that puts to practice Oscar Wilde's famous dictum that no good deed goes unpunished. Its 1-hour length will limit international pickup possibilities.**

Directed by Manuel Franco Posse, who boasts a respectable career on Colombian tv, film fuses notions of honesty with naiveté, noting conversely that dishonesty is savvy.

Satisfying and straightforward narrative concerns hard-working petty official Tobias (Rafael Maldonado), who discovers a suitcase containing $80,000, neatly packed in bundles of crisp $100 bills.

Tobias does the unexpected. He brings the suitcase to lost & found, which sparks a media blitz of human interest stories on "the last honest man in Colombia." He is alternately referred to as a saint or fool by those close to him: his boss basks in the notoriety while his wife refuses to sleep with him. The crooks are furious and deliver demands. In short, his whole life changes.

Film has the sensibility and texture of a Guy de Maupassant story. Characters present various personifications of self-interest and greed within Colombian society, and ride the narrow edge of satire. Acting and tech credits are okay. — *Lent.*

Freeway

A New World Pictures release of a Gower Street production. Produced by Peter S. Davis, William Panzer. Executive producer, Guy Collins. Directed by Francis Delia. Screenplay, Darrell Fetty, Delia, based on novel by Deanne Barkley; camera (color), Frank Byers; editor, Philip J. Sgriccia; music, Joe Delia; sound, Brian Bidder; production design, Douglas Metrov; assistant directors, Tony Perez, Marty Schwartz; associate producer, Steve Beswick; art direction, Shane Nelson; casting, Janet Cunningham. Reviewed at New World Pictures, L.A., Aug. 30, 1988. MPAA Rating: R. Running time: **91 MIN.**

Sunny Harper . . . . Darlanne Fluegel
Frank Quinn . . . . James Russo
Edward Heller . . . . Billy Drago
Dr. David Lazarus . . . . Richard Belzer
Lt. Boyle . . . . Michael Callan
Gomez . . . . Joey Palese
Ronnie . . . . Clint Howard

■ Hollywood — **If the filmmakers had trusted the actors and story they started with, ''Freeway'' might have emerged as an above-average thriller. Unfortunately, all are too soon sacrificed for mindless action and car crashes, insuring no worry about traffic jams on the way home from this one.**

Tattered if not torn from the headlines, ''Freeway'' focuses on the terror taking place on the interstates when a mad gunman amuses himself by pulling alongside fellow travelers to demonstrate how well he can steer with one hand and shoot with the other.

Pretty widow Darlanne Fluegel is among the first to lose her handsome doctor husband to the killer and she remains obsessed at the lack of progress by Lt. Michael Callan's police department. Grieving constantly, she wanders about her Hollywood apartment in undies and less, listening to the traffic on the freeway below.

Somewhere out there, crazy ex-priest Billy Drago cruises along picking victims and chatting with radio psychologist Richard Belzer.

Just because real life was (is?) scary enough when one or more of these nuts was loose in L.A. and other cities, director Francis Delia enjoys a lot of audience involvement going in. Fluegel, Belzer, Callan and Drago do their best to build believability.

Then, unfortunately, James Russo shows up with the wallet.

Exactly how Russo comes into possession of Fluegel's billfold is somewhat unclear, but everything about Russo's character as a bounty-hunting ex-cop is confusing, made more so by his meandering method acting.—*Har.*

Perfect Victims

A Vertigo Pictures production. Produced by Jonathon Braun. Executive producers, Deborah Shelton, H.S. Flor. Directed by Shuki Levy. Screenplay, Levy, Joe Hailey, Bob Barron; camera (CFI color), Frank Byers, Michael Mathews; editor, Braun; music, Levy; sound design (Ultra-Stereo), Clive Mizumoto; art direction, Shane Nelson; set decoration, Ann Banks; assistant director, Worth Keeter; production manager-associate producer, Steven Beswick; second unit camera, R. Michael Stringer; stunt coordinator, Eric Cord; casting, Billy Damota. Reviewed on Academy Entertainment vidcassette, N.Y., Aug. 24, 1988. MPAA Rating: R. Running time: **100 MIN.**
Liz Winters . . . . Deborah Shelton
Steven Hack . . . . Lyman Ward
Brandon Poole . . . . Tom Dugan
Lt. Kevin White . . . . . Clarence Williams 3d
Melissa Cody . . . . Nikolette Scorsese
Carrie Marks . . . . Jackie Swanson
Also with: Phil Roberson, Geoffrey Rivas, John Agar.

■ ''Perfect Victims,'' a.k.a. ''Hidden Rage,'' is a standard-issue thriller for video release that sports the dubious novelty of a maniacal killer on the loose who has AIDS.

Deborah Shelton, of Brian DePalma's ''Body Double,'' toplines for hubbie-director Shuki Levy, cast here as a high-powered models' agent who becomes the target of violent nutcase Brandon (Tom Dugan). First Brandon uses his modus operandi of a veterinary drug to knock out two of Shelton's pretty clients (Nikolette Scorsese and Jackie Swanson) before raping Swanson.

In the third reel, cop Clarence Williams 3d announces solemnly the results of a blood test: ''the killer has AIDS.'' This topical touch certainly grabs one's attention, but proves to be irrelevant to the action. Dugan plays the heinous murderer well, but character's lifelong resentment against women is ably and typically expressed in killings. As demonstrated in a clumsy voiceover ending, pic would play identically without the AIDS gimmick.

Shelton and supporting cast are effective, with director Levy's self-penned orchestral music score a plus. What's lacking is the visual bravura of the master, Hitchcock, or his pupil, DePalma. — *Lor.*

Senior Week

An Upfront Films, Stuart Goldman Prods. and Matt Ferro presentation. Produced by Ken Schwenker, Matt Ferro. Directed by Stuart Goldman. Screenplay, Jan Kubicki; additional material, Goldman, Stacey Lynn Fravel; camera (Technicolor), John A. Corso; editor, Richard Dama; music, Ken Mazur; Russ Landau; sound, Carl Carden; production design, John Lawless; assistant director, Gil Stose (Florida), James Miner (New Jersey); second unit director, Corso; postproduction supervisor, Simon Nuchtern; associate producer, Barry E. Rosenthal; casting, Leonard Finger. Reviewed on Vestron vidcassette, N.Y., Aug. 31, 1988. No MPAA Rating. Running time: **98 MIN.**
Everett . . . . Michael St. Gerard
Jody . . . . Gary Kerr
Jamie . . . . George Klek
Tracy . . . . Jennifer Gorey
Stacy . . . . Leesa Bryte
Kevin . . . . Alan Naggar
Miss Bagley . . . . Barbara Gruen
Also with: Devon Skye, Jaynie Poteet, Gordon MacDonald.

■ ''Senior Week'' is a ho-hum video release in the overworked teen comedy genre. It adds little more to the field than documenting the shift of Florida spring break from Fort Lauderdale to Daytona Beach.

Michael St. Gerard leads a quartet of New Jersey students at Nixon High School who head to the Sunshine State on the week before graduation. Overworked and uninteresting plot hook has him forcing classmate Gary Kerr to write his term paper, required by a mean teacher (Barbara Gruen, overacting horrendously), or our hero won't graduate.

In the wake of ''Porky's'' and scores of imitations, the antics here are very tame, padded out by extraneous dream sequences featuring girls going topless. Complications engendered when teach and the guys' girlfriends pursue the quartet to Florida are strictly mechanical.

Cast handles the script's stereotypes (nerd, fatso, etc.) with enthusiasm. Biggest letdown is that hero's extremely beautiful dream girl (Jaynie Poteet) is given nothing to do and minimal screen time. Tech credits are okay. — *Lor.*

VENICE REVIEWS

Madame Sousatzka
(BRITISH)

A Universal Pictures release of a Cineplex Odeon presentation of a Sousatzka production. Produced by Robin Dalton. Directed by John Schlesinger. Screenplay, Ruth Prawer Jhabvala, Schlesinger, from novel by Bernice Rubens; additional material, Peter Morgan, Mark Wadlow; camera (Rank color), Nat Crosby; editor, Peter Honess; music, Gerald Gouriet; production design, Luciana Arrighi; art direction, Ian Whittaker, Stephen Scott; sound (Dolby), Simon Kaye; costumes, Amy Roberts; musical supervisor, Yonty Solomon; associate producer, Simon Bosanquet; production manager, Mary Richards; assistant director, Chris Rose; casting, Noel Davis, Jeremy Zimmerman. Reviewed at Venice Film Festival (competing), Sept. 4, 1988. MPAA Rating: PG-13. Running time: **122 MIN.**
Mme. Irina Sousatzka . . . Shirley MacLaine
Manek Sen . . . . Navin Chowdhry
Lady Emily . . . . Peggy Ashcroft
Jenny . . . . Twiggy
Sushila . . . . Shabana Azmi
Ronnie Blum . . . . Leigh Lawson
Mr. Cordle . . . . Geoffrey Bayldon
Vincent Pick . . . . Lee Montague
Leo Milev . . . . Robert Rietty
Woodford . . . . Jeremy Sinden
Lefranc . . . . Roger Hammond
Conductor . . . . Christopher Adey
Pianist at Portman Hall . . . . Barry Douglas

■ Venice — **Although essentially a rather old-fashioned British pic, and definitely overlong, ''Madame Sousatzka'' is filled with pleasures, not the least of them being Shirley MacLaine's effervescent performance. For music lovers, and MacLaine fans, Universal and Cineplex Odeon should have a prestige success on their hands.**

Setting is London where middle-aged Mme. Sousatzka, of Russian parentage but raised in New York, teaches piano to only the most gifted students. She insists her pupils not only learn to play, but also to live the kind of traditional cultured lifestyle which she herself does: which means dressing correctly, reading the right books, drinking the right wine, and so on.

Her strict routine, and lack of interest in the commercial end result of perfecting piano technique, led an earlier student to depart, a betrayal she hasn't forgiven. Her latest protégé is a 15-year-old Indian youth, Manek, or Mani for short (Navin Chowdhry) whose mother (Shabana Azmi) left Calcutta years before to get away from her husband. The mother supports them by selling home-cooked Indian food to a swank food store.

Madame Sousatzka lives in a crumbling house owned by old Lady Emily (Peggy Ashcroft). One by one the other houses in the street are being sold and developed, and Lady Emily, too, would like to move out of the city and into the country. Besides Madame Sousatzka, her tenants include a model and would-be pop singer (delightfully played by Twiggy) who looks much younger than she is; and a middle-aged gay osteopath (Geoffrey Bayldon).

The singer's married lover (Leigh Lawson) is a music agent who hears Mani play and offers the boy the chance to play at a swank sponsored concert, something strenuously opposed by his teacher. When his mother loses her job (hairs are found in her food) Mani decides to take the money, and reluctantly leaves his music teacher, who'd become almost a second mother to him. Now the last remaining tenant in the house, Madame Sousatzka is left to greet her next pupil.

The film is based on a screenplay by Schlesinger and Ruth Prawer Jhabvala, adapted from a novel by Bernice Rubens; the writing is lovely, but further editing might have been advisable to contract the characters and keep the running time down. The gay osteopath, though well acted, is one character that could have been dropped easily.

In some ways, Schlesinger is trying to cram too much into the film. The story of young Mani's education, the lives of the other tenants in Lady Emily's house, the relationship between the girl and the music agent, and the lifestyle of Mani's mother are all given considerable weight, and it's a bit too much.

Crucial, though, is the central relationship between MacLaine, who's seldom been better than she is here, and the youngster, warmly played by Navin Chowdry. All their scenes have great charm, with the piano playing effectively handled. The climactic concert, part of a sponsored arts festival, is beautifully handled with a stand-out cameo from real-life conductor Christopher Adey.

First-time producer Robin Dalton has come up with a classy up-market pic, well directed and very well acted. Good to very good runs may be expected in quality situations, with word-of-mouth for the MacLaine performance a factor. The pic's humor and uplifting sentiments will also weigh in its favor. Audiences who don't go for lengthy slabs of classical music will be bored, however.

Pic is technically fine, with excellent sound recording. A special nod for production designer Luciana Arrighi, whose art direction of the Sousatzka apartment adds to the viewer's sum of knowledge of the character. Apart from the film's length, only other flaw are some misjudged flashbacks to Sousatzka's youth, which are unintentionally comic. — *Strat.*

Tempos Dificeis
(Hard Times)
(PORTUGUESE-B&W)

A João Botelho production, in association with Artificial Eye Film Prods.; Executive producer, Manuel Guanilho. Written and directed by João Botalho, based on Charles Dickens' novel. Camera (b&w), Elso Roque; editor, Botelho; music, Antonio Pinho Vargas; sound, Joaquim Pinto. Reviewed at Venice Film Festival (competing), Aug. 30, 1988. (Also in Toronto and New York fests.) Running time: **90 MIN.**
Mr. Bounderby . . . . Henrique Viana
Stephen Blackpool . . . . . Joaquim Mendes
Louisa Gradgrind . . . . Julia Britton
Thomas Gradgrind . . . . Ruy Furtado
   Also with: Eunice Muñoz, Isabel de Castro, Isabel Ruth, Lia Gama, Ines Medeiros, Luis Estrela, Pedro Cabrita Reis, Maria Alicia Pereira, Pedro Hestnes, Maria José Oliveira, Beatriz Moreno.

■ **Venice — Offbeat, updated adaptation of the Dickens novel ''Hard Times'' is purposely filmed in a mannered, stilted style in which lines are recited rather than acted.**

As a curiosity, item might attract some art circuits, but most audiences will be prone to slumber through this experiment in stylized cinema which strives to use some of the techniques of early cinema.

Action of story has been set in a modern, grimy industrial village in Portugal known as Poço do Mundo (World's End). Plot more or less follows the Dickens story and involves a martinet schoolmaster, a bullying self-made man of wealth, a waif whose father has deserted her, a distraught laborer with a drunken wife plus a gallery of minor parts.

Story of how the rich man marries the waif, hounds the laborer and intrigues with the schoolmaster is well-enough known. There is nothing of the spirit, humor or grace of Dickens. —*Besa.*

Things Change

A Columbia Pictures release of a Filmhaus production. Produced by Michael Hausman. Directed by David Mamet. Screenplay, Mamet, Shel Silverstein; camera (color), Juan Ruiz-Anchia; editor, Trudy Ship; music, Alaric Jans; production design, Michael Merritt; sound, John Pritchett; production manager, Hausman; assistant director-associate producer, Ned Dowd; casting, Cyrena Hausman. Reviewed at Venice Film Festival (competing), Aug. 31, 1988. MPAA Rating: PG. Running time: **100 MIN.**
Gino . . . . Don Ameche
Jerry . . . . Joe Mantegna
Joseph Vincent . . . . Robert Prosky
Frankie . . . . J.J. Johnston
Mr. Silver . . . . Ricky Jay
Mr. Green . . . . Mike Nussbaum
Repair Shop Owner . . . . Jack Wallace

Butler . . . . Dan Conway
   Also with: Willo Varsi Hausman (Miss Bates), Gail Silver (Housemaid), Len Hodera (Ramone), Josh Conescu (Bellenza), Merrill Holtzman (No Pals), Adam Bitterman (Marcotti), W.H. Macy (Billy Drake), Steve Goldstein (Randy), Sarah Ekhardt (Cherry), Karen Kohlhaas (Grace).

■ **Venice — Following the prestige success of his first feature as director, the ingenious ''House Of Games,'' David Mamet proves that was no fluke with ''Things Change,'' a dry, funny and extremely intelligent comedy about an innocent mistaken for a Mafia don.**

With critical support, pic should do extremely well on exclusive runs, with wider chances depending on favorable word of mouth. Don Ameche's sublime performance also will be a factor.

Pic opens in Chicago as the elderly Gino (Ameche), a shoeshine boy, is "invited" to meet a Mafia boss whom he physically resembles. The boss has killed a man and there were witnesses: he wants Gino to confess to the murder and take the rap (two or three years is suggested), and as a reward he can have his heart's desire, which turns out to be owning a fishing boat back home in Sicily.

After initial hesitation, Gino agrees, and is handed over to Jerry (Joe Mantegna), a very junior member of the Mafia clan, on probation and reduced to dishwashing for the boss after some unspecified foulup. All Jerry has to do is coach Gino in his story for two days, then deliver him to the law. Instead, Jerry decides to give the oldster a final fling, and takes him to Lake Tahoe where, unknown to him, a Mafia convention is about to take place.

Gino is instantly mistaken for a senior Don and given royal treatment: lavish hotel suite, unlimited credit, girls, limo. He's also invited to meet the local Mafia kingpin (Robert Prosky) with whom he instantly strikes up a close rapport, while Jerry sees himself getting into deeper and deeper trouble.

This comedy of mistaken identity centers around a beautifully modulated starring performance from Ameche as the poor but painfully upright and honest Gino. As the dimwitted Jerry, Mantegna is consistently funny and touching. Indeed, the entire film is beautifully cast with every character making an impact; notable are W.H. Macy and Steve Goldstein as Tahoe yesmen.

Apart from a scene in which two lookers share a sunken bath with Ameche and Mantegna, pic is without significant female presence. This is a classic buddy/odd couple movie, given plenty of new twists in the very witty screenplay by Shel Silverstein and Mamet.

Mamet has become a strikingly good director, whose timing and structure, allied to precise camera movement and direction of actors, are all impressive. The film's final

joke will send audiences home happy.

No doubt ''Things Change'' (a rather prosaic title) won't have broad appeal in the hinterlands, but in urban centers it should perform and will certainly bring kudos to all concerned. It has to be in line for a Venice prize, possibly for Ameche's exemplary performance.—*Strat.*

High Hopes
(BRITISH)

A Film Four-British Screen presentation of a Portman Films production. Produced by Victor Glynn, Simon Channing-Williams. Executive producer, Tom Donald. Written and directed by Mike Leigh. Camera (Eastmancolor), Roger Pratt; editor, Jon Gregory; music, Andrew Dixon; production design, Diana Charnley; costumes, Lindy Hemming; sound, Billy McCarthy; production manager, Caroline Hill; assistant director, Howard Arundel; casting, Sue Whatmough. Reviewed at Venice Film Festival (Critics Week), Aug. 29, 1988. (Also in New York fest.) Running time: **112 MIN.**
Cyril . . . . Philip Davis
Shirley . . . . Ruth Sheen
Mrs. Bender . . . . Edna Dore
Martin . . . . Philip Jackson
Valerie . . . . Heather Tobias
Laetitia Booth-Braine . . . . . Leslie Manville
Rupert Booth-Braine . . . . . . David Bamber
Wayne . . . . Jason Watkins
Suzi . . . . Judith Scott

■ **Venice — Mike Leigh has been a major figure in British tv over a number of years. ''High Hopes'' is only his second theatrical feature (after ''Bleak Moments'' in 1971), and though it has some interesting characters and provocative ideas, it comes across as an uneven effort.**

It's unlikely to achieve the same international theatrical success as other recent British pics.

Basic idea is a good one. In the working-class London suburb of Kings Cross, yuppies are moving into old houses, restoring them, and driving out the locals who've lived there for ages; it's a pattern repeated all over the world. Old Mrs. Bender, a widow, lives in one house; her neighbors are the fearfully uppercrust Booth-Braines (he's in the wine business) and they treat the old lady with ill-disguised contempt when she seeks help after locking herself out of her home.

Mrs. Bender's two children are an ill-assorted pair. Cyril, with long hair and beard, works as a courier, lives with his down-to-earth girl-friend Shirley, and despises the British establishment (he says he'll shave his hair and wear a tie the day they assassinate the Royal Family). Cyril and Shirl worship at the grave of Karl Marx and keep a gigantic cactus they call Thatcher (because it's a pain in the butt).

Daughter Valerie, on the other hand, is a would-be yuppie, married to a crass used car dealer, and living in a garishly over-decorated home. She's completely self-centered and insensitive to her elderly mother's needs.

Around these characters, Leigh builds a slight story intended to be a microcosm of today's London. Unfortunately, the director has a tendency to caricature the people he obviously despises, and as a result Valerie and the Booth-Braines come across as rather ludicrous figures who seem to have strayed from a tv sitcom. Valerie, as played by Heather Tobias, with her ugly clothes and huge spectacles, looks like a clone of the Barry Humphries character Edna Everage.

In contrast, Cyril and Shirl, attractively played by Philip Davis and Ruth Sheen, are more recognizable types, leftovers from the more idealistic '60s, while Edna Dore gives a lovely performance as poor old Mrs. Bender.

Technical credits are good, but the film's overstatement of an undoubtedly tragic and not uncommon situation may well put off audiences who expect a more subtle approach to Britain's ongoing class divisions.—*Strat.*

Une Affaire de femmes
(Women's Affair)
(FRENCH)

An MK2 production and release. Coproducers, Film A2, Films du Camélia, La Sept. Produced by Marin Karmitz. Directed by Claude Chabrol. Screenplay, Chabrol, Colo Tavernier O'Hagan, freely inspired by the book by Francis Szpiner; camera (Eastmancolor), Jean Rabier; editor, Monique Fardoulis; music, Mathieu Chabrol; sound, Jean-Bernard Thomasson, Maurice Gilbert; art direction, Françoise Benoit-Fresco; costumes, Corinne Jorry; assistant directors, Alain Wermus, Michel Dupuy; production manager, Yvonn Crenn. Reviewed at Club 13, Paris, Aug. 29, 1988. (In Venice Film Festival, competing. Also in Toronto Film Festival.) Running time: **108 MIN.**
Marie . . . . Isabelle Huppert
Paul . . . . François Cluzet
Lucie . . . . Marie Trintignant
Lucien . . . . Nils Tavernier
   Also with: Lolita Chammah, Aurore Gauvin, Guillaume Foutrier, Nicolas Foutrier, Marie Bunel, Dominique Blanc.

■ **Paris — Though his direction lacks the imaginative flair of his best earlier work, Claude Chabrol is in good form otherwise in ''Une Affaire de femmes,'' arguably his most accomplished film since ''Violette Nozières'' (1978).**

Fascinating story, substantial script and especially Chabrol's reunion with Isabelle Huppert (who portrayed ''Violette'') should give director good chances to recover erstwhile admirers disappointed by his recent string of trivial melodramas and thrillers.

Like ''Violette,'' Chabrol's new film is inspired by a cause célèbre: the story of the last woman to receive capital punishment in France. The time was 1943 and the condemned person was a provincial housewife tried as an abortionist and sent to the guillotine by a Vichy tribunal in 1943.

Screenplay by Chabrol and Colo Tavernier O'Hagan (who scripted ''La Passion Béatrice'' for ex-hubby

Bertrand Tavernier) is a free dramatization of the case through which Chabrol composes a dispassionate and forceful portrait of provincial amorality and hypocrisy (a Chabrol specialty). Of the many pictures in recent years devoted to France under the German Occupation, ''Une Affaire de femmes'' perhaps best captures the ambiguities and realities of daily experiences.

After several years abroad, Huppert makes an excellent homecoming in the main role, limning a smalltown mother of two who discovers that providing abortion services to fellow wives (especially those with husbands who have been carted off to forced labor in Germany) is the answer to the drab privations of the Occupation.

Soon Huppert's affairs are flourishing so well that she can move to a new house where she has the space to rent a room to a hooker girlfriend (Marie Trintignant).

Her upwardly mobile opportunism finally is denounced — by her husband, François Cluzet, pathetically fine as a demobilized soldier stymied by his family's sudden prosperity and frustrated by Huppert's lack of affection. When Huppert takes a lover, the previously passive, weak-willed hubby composes an anonymous letter to the police, leading to Huppert's arrest, trial and severe sentence as an ''example'' in a defeated country promoting the hypocritical motto ''Work, Family, Homeland.''

Chabrol wisely keeps the final scenes of trial and punishment streamlined and elliptical, though he could have done without some demonstrative scenes designed to underline the moral bankruptcy of Maréchal Petain's puppet government. Another intrusion is the late introduction of a voiceover (spoken by Chabrol) repping Huppert's son. (What happens to Cluzet after he squeals on his wife is never referred to.)

Production, Chabrol's fourth for Marin Karmitz' MK2 outfit, has solid credits guaranteed by helmer's usual collaborators, including the faithful Jean Rabier at the camera and Monique Fardoulis in the cutting room. Music by Mathieu Chabrol, helmer's son, is discreet. —Len.

La Leggenda del santo bevitore
(The Legend Of The Holy Drinker) (ITALIAN)

A Columbia Pictures Italia release of an Aura Film/Cecchi Gori Group Tiger Cinematografica/RAI-TV Channel 1 coproduction. Produced by Roberto Cicutto, Vincenzo De Leo. Directed by Ermanno Olmi. Screenplay, Olmi, Tullio Kezich, based on story by Joseph Roth; camera (Cinecittà color), Dante Spinotti; editor, Olmi; music, Igor Stravinsky; art direction, Gianni Quaranta. Reviewed at Venice Film Festival (competing), Sept. 1, 1988. Running time: **125 MIN.**

Andreas . . . . Rutger Hauer
Gentleman . . . . Anthony Quayle
Gabby . . . . Sandrine Dumas
Woitech . . . . Dominique Pinon
Also with: Sophie Segalen (Karoline), Jean-Maurice Chanet (Kaniak), Cecile Paoli, Joseph De Medina, Franco Aldigheri.
(English soundtrack)

■ Venice — Joseph's Roth's story ''The Legend Of The Holy Drinker,'' a small gem set in 1920s Paris, provides the framework for a stirring, curious film about miracles worked on a drunkard who sleeps under bridges.

Read as a religious parable, ''Drinker'' comes across strong thanks to director Ermanno Olmi's quiet conviction and graceful lensing. Its entertainment quotient is lower, due to an excessive running time of 2-hours-plus that makes the tale's fable-like repetitions numbingly heavy.

Overall, pic is likely to be admired for uniqueness and sincerity, but passed over lightly at the boxoffice.

Considering shot in English (with some basic French mixed in for flavor) and given the extra-territorial appeal of cast topper Rutger Hauer, pic ought to line up limited playoffs abroad for discerning audiences.

Deliberately blurring time references, film takes place in an indefinable date between the 1920s and our day. Andreas (Hauer), a Polish immigrant, is reduced to leading a bum's life. Once a coal miner, he lost his job after accidentally killing a pal whose beguiling wife (Sophie Segalen) he craved. The unexpected appearance of a distinguished gentleman in a homburg (Anthony Quayle) who presents him with 200 francs is a real miracle in Andreas' penurious existence. He vows to pay the sum back to the gentleman's patron saint, Theresa of Lisieux, after mass on Sunday.

This is only the first miracle for gentle Andreas: washed and shaven, work falls into his lap, old buddies turn up with presents, money suddenly appears every time he needs it. Yet every Sunday, some obstacle arises that prevents him from repaying the debt to the saint.

Women are his main source of temptation (along with the wine bottle). The fleeting return of the woman who ruined him makes it impossible to reach church on Sunday; next week, a light romance with coquette Sandrine Dumas delays him. On the third Sunday Andreas dies a light and easy death (from drink) with his eyes fixed on little St. Theresa.

Rutger Hauer plays the hero as a weak, naive, generous character of noble intentions but weak flesh; only jarring note is his out-of-place American accent that keeps breaking through the sparse dialog. Entirely believable is Anthony Quayle as Andreas' mysterious benefactor; supporting players are well cast.

Stravinsky's music makes an excellent soundtrack, in keeping with the

pic's timeless flavor. Dante Spinotti's camerawork is unobtrusively atmospheric.

''Drinker's'' real problem boils down to its excess length, requiring saintly patience from the audience to get through to a finale that seems like it will never come. A stiff trim would greatly help the second half. — *Yung.*

Niezwylka Podroz Balthazara Kobera
(The Tribulations Of Balthazar Kobera) (POLISH-FRENCH)

A Film Polski (Warsaw)/Jock Film/La Sept (Paris) coproduction. Directed by Wojciech J. Has. Screenplay, Has, from the novel by Frederick Tristan; camera (Agfacolor), Grzegorz Kedzierski; editor, Wanda Zeman; music, Zdislaw Szostak; production design, Wojciech Jaworski, Albina Baranska; sound, Janusz Rosol; costumes, Magdalena Biernawska, Maria Nowotny; production managers, Pawel Rakowski, Jean Lefevre. Reviewed at Venice Film Festival (competing), Aug. 29, 1988. Running time: **115 MIN.**
Balthazar Kober . . . . Rafal Wieczynski
Cammerschulze . . . . Michael Lonsdale
Rosa . . . . Adrianna Biedrzynska
Gertrud . . . . Gabriela Kownacka
Mother . . . . Emmanuele Riva
Rector . . . . Daniel Emilfork

■ Venice — The dreamlike odyssey of a young man across plague-ridden 16th century Germany yields a pic that's often extremely beautiful, but it's too remote and lethargic to command full audience attention. It looms as an elegant failure.

Director Wojciech J. Has is best known for ''The Saragossa Manuscript'' (1965), and there are occasional elements of that haunting pic in this stolid adaptation of a novel by French author Frederick Tristan. Central character is a visionary youth, the eponymous Balthazar, an orphan with a vivid imagination. He can conjure up an image of the angel Gabriel, complete with wings and sword, who shows him how to walk through fire; he also can ''see'' his dead parents and other visions of heaven and hell.

Despite all this, Balthazar finds it hard to communicate because of a severe stutter. Nevertheless, he's taken in hand by a wise man (played with style by Michaël Lonsdale) who philosophizes about God and Knowledge.

As the teenage hero, Rafal Wieczynski gives a monotonous performance. More interesting is Emmanuele Riva, briefly seen as his long-dead mother. There are reminders here of ''The Seventh Seal,'' via the plague-ridden landscape across which the hero wanders, and the dreamlike visions. ''Tribulations'' is a much softer film, and great patience is demanded of audiences during this overlong journey.

Most disappointingly, the magic to be found in ''The Saragossa Manuscript'' and in another famous Has film, ''The Sandglass'' (1973), is largely absent here; attempts at

humor are only fitfully successful.

Outside of Polish film weeks, international chances look to be very difficult.—*Strat.*

Luces y Sombras
(Lights And Shadows) (SPANISH)

A Tibidabo Films production. Produced and directed by Jaime Camino. Screenplay, Camino, José Sanchis Sinisterra; camera (Eastmancolor), José Maria Civit; editor, Emilio Rodriguez; music, Xavier Monsalvatge; production manager, Juan Torres Martori; art direction, Eduardo Arranz Bravo; costumes, Pep Duran; casting, Consol Tura; sound, Joan Quilis. Reviewed at Venice Film Festival (competing), Sept. 3, 1988. Running time: **105 MIN.**
Diego de Velázquez . . . . . José Luis Gómez
Teo . . . . Jack Shepherd
Charo . . . . Angela Molina
King Felipe IV . . . . Fermi Reixach
Also with: Marti Galindo, Victor Rubio, Noel Samson, Iñaki Aierra, Victoria Peña, Maria Mercader, Montserrat Anda, Elisenda Nogue.

■ Venice — Velázquez' famous painting in the Prado, ''Las Meninas,'' depicting the court of Philip IV and the painter himself are the basis of a film fantasy which is too meandering and undramatic to appeal to audiences in or out of Spain.

Jaime Camino mixed reality and fantasy as a young boy actually enters the canvas and comes out at the court of the Spanish king. In order to return home, he must somehow convince Velázquez to paint his renowned picture.

Story skips back and forth between the court (a few interiors are all we see) and the making of a film about Velázquez. The director of this film, whose marriage is on the rocks, has a lover the mother of the young girl playing the Infanta. He is confused, undecided what to shoot, unwilling to tell a story, make a point or even define what the purpose of the film within a film is.

Unfortunately the film itself is equally vague. Though Camino has used some top Spanish thesps such as Angela Molina and José Luis Gómez, there's nothing for them to get their teeth into. Pic doesn't attempt to delve into the character of Velázquez or the king, while the problems of the irascible director are as commonplace as Catalan custard.

An added impediment in the Venice version is that half of the dialog is in Catalan, the other half in Castilian, presumably as a concession to the regional government which subsidized the film. Commercial prospects are decidedly dim. —*Besa.*

Codice Privato
(Secret Access) (ITALIAN)

A Filmauro release of a Filmauro production, in association with RAI-TV Channel 1. Produced by Luigi and Aurelio De Laurentiis. Executive producers, Maurizio Amati, Roberta Cadringher. Written and directed by Francesco Maselli. Camera (Technicolor), Luigi Kuveiller; editor, Alessanda Perpignani; music, Giovanna Marini Salviucci; general organizer, Pietro Innocenzi; art direction, Marco Dentici. Reviewed at Venice Film Festival (Special Events), Aug. 30, 1988. Running time: **90 MIN.**

Anna . . . . .Ornella Muti

───────

■ **Venice** — Ornella Muti fans at home and abroad will be happily surprised to find the engaging actress tackling a demanding role for a change and carrying off a 1-woman-show with intriguing aplomb.

Vet helmer Francesco Maselli may repeat his success of last season, "Love Story" (launching tyro Valeria Golino), with the offbeat thriller "Secret Access."

Muti plays a poor girl in love with a rich and famous writer, with both heart and a head on her shoulders. The only thesp in the entire film, she communicates with the outside world via telephone and computer. Playing a major role, however, is film's astonishing set (a creation of art director Marco Dentici), a huge fantasy apartment around which the camera roams restlessly after Muti.

These anything but humble digs are the reflection of the personality of Emilio Flora, a writer in line for a Nobel prize, with whom Anna (Muti) has lived for the last three years. As pic opens he has just left her without telling her why. Anna feverishly searches through Emilio's pretentious, overwhelming flat for the reason their affair ended. She thinks she has found it inside Emilio's sophisticated computer, after she stumbles onto a secret access code that lets her into its private parts.

The premise is ingenious and, in the beginning, it seems as though film is going to pull it off. Computer graphics skillfully alternate with Anna's anxious thirst to know the truth, and keep viewer curious. Anna's tense phone calls to friends provide half-clues to the mystery of her abandonment.

Then film runs out of cleverness, and finds no better way to end than with a twist that makes all answers moot.

Before that disappointing finale, however, a lot gets told about the character of Anna and her missing lover. Emilio got off on being Pygmalion to poor Anna, a girl he educated by having her reorder his 13,000-volume library. He's bored when his protegé becomes a mature, independent woman.

At best, Maselli uses an entertaining format to unveil his characters. Technically it's very good, especially Luigi Kuveiller's quality lensing. *—Yung.*

───────

Topio Stin Omihli
(Landscape In The Mist)
(GREEK-FRENCH-ITALIAN)

───────

A Greek Film Center-ET-1 (Athens)-Paradis Film (Paris)-RAI 2 (Rome) coproduction. Produced and directed by Theo Angelopoulos. Screenplay, Angelopoulos, Tonino Guerra, Thanassis Valtinos; camera (color), Giorgos Arvanitis; editor, Yannis Tsitsopoulos; music, Eleni Karaindrou; production design, Mikes Karapiperis; sound, Marinos Athanassopoulos; production manager, Emilios Konitsiotis. Reviewed at Venice Film Festival (competing), Aug. 31, 1988. Running time: **127 MIN.**

Alexandros . . . . .Michalis Zeke
Voula . . . . .Iania Palaiologou
Oreste . . . . .Stratos Tzortzoglou
Also with: Eva Kotmanidou, Aliki Georgouli, Vassilis Kolovos, Vassilis Bouyouklakis, Ilias Logothetis, Vangelis Kazan.

───────

■ **Venice** — Greece's foremost director, Theo Angelopoulos, has come up with another ravishingly beautiful and haunting film with "Landscape In The Mist," tale of two children searching for the father they've never seen.

Admirers of the director will find this one well up to his high standard, while those not on his wavelength probably will find the pic overlong and slow.

Story begins in Athens as 11-year-old Voula and her 5-year-old brother Alexandros decide to go to Germany in search of their father. The sprigs apparently are illegitimate; their mother is never seen.

They're thrown off a train because they don't have a ticket. The police take them to an uncle who wants nothing to do with them. When the police momentarily are distracted by a sudden snowstorm (a scene filled with that special kind of magic only Angelopoulos can provide) they slip away to continue their journey.

Along the way they meet some sympathetic characters, including a kindly youth who turns out to be gay, but they're given a ride by a lecherous truck driver who, in a scene all the grimmer for its extreme reticence, takes little Voula into the back of his truck and rapes her.

Eventually, the children reach "the border" (though Greece has no border with Germany) and some kind of mystical experience which ends the film on a note of exceptional beauty.

Since "The Traveling Players" (1975), all of Angelopoulos' films have centered around journeys across the Greek landscape. This one takes in familiar territory — roadside cafes, small towns, deserted beaches — and breathes new life into them. The traveling players from the earlier film even reappear, still wandering in a vain search for a theater in which they can perform.

No Angelopoulos film would be complete without the breathtaking photography of the immensely gifted Giorgos Arvanitis, undoubtedly one of the world's prominent cameramen. Scene after scene in "Landscape In The Mist" takes the breath away. The score by Eleni Karaindrou also is memorable.

Actors are part of the landscape rather than center stage. The young-

sters are fine, and Stratos Tzortzoglou is sympathetic as the youth. A scene where he teaches Voula to dance on a beach is one of many memorable moments. There's also a nod to Fellini in a strange moment in which a helicopter winches a giant stone hand from beneath the sea, as the children look on, amazed. *—Strat.*

───────

Caro Gorbaciov
(Dear Gorbachev)
(ITALIAN)

───────

A UIP release of an RPA Intl. production, in association with RAI-TV Channel 2. Produced by Filiberto Bandini. Directed by Carlo Lizzani. Screenplay, Lizzani, Augusto Zucchi; camera (Widescreen, color), Roberto Benvenuti; editor, Angela Cipriani; music, Luis Bacalov; art direction, Luciano Sagoni; costumes, Adriana Berselli. Reviewed at Venice Film Festival (competing), Aug. 28, 1988. Running time: **85 MIN.**

Nikolai Bukharin . . . . .Harvey Keitel
Anna Larina Bukharin . . .Flaminia Lizzani
Anna as a child . . . . .Francesca Lucidi
Yuri Bukharin . . . . .Gianluca Favilla
(English soundtrack)

───────

■ **Venice** — "Dear Gorbachev" can find little to do with its timely idea — a film version of the last night Russian revolutionary Nikolai Bukharin spends at home with his young wife Anna, before Stalin has him arrested and shot.

Director Carlo Lizzani bases his story on a magazine account by Anna Larina Bukharin, whose desire to rehabilitate her husband's name happily coincided with Soviet Secretary Mikhail Gorbachev's wishes — hence the catchy title, which otherwise has little to do with the film.

With Harvey Keitel in the role of the doomed Bolshevik, and lensed in English, pic might turn up some offshore play in spite of glaring dramatic weaknesses. Most interest so far has been from the Russians, who are anxious to screen it in the USSR.

Theoretically all the action takes place in the Bukharins' apartment in the Kremlin, and film idea began with intention to make a stage play. Film opens with a big interview with the press in which the aged Anna Larina recounts her dramatic last night with her husband. Why this framing device is used is a puzzle, since continual cross-cutting to the press meet undermines involvement in the main story.

In 1939 Bukharin, sensing the precariousness of his position with the Communist Party controlled by Joseph Stalin, makes his wife memorize a long testament to future generations during a long sleepless night. The docile Anna (played as a naive, hero-worshipping girl by the director's daughter Flaminia Lizzani) for once rebels against her husband's wishes, inwardly resisting the idea the letter is his farewell to the world. As the night wears on and her endless attempts to memorize the words reach grating depths, Anna comes to learn more of Stalin's evil

deeds. Finally she learns the darn thing.

Scripters have had to take certain liberties with historical fact in an attempt to make the couple's last night more filmically dramatic. Oddly, drama is just what's missing in the end product, while emotional involvement with Anna and Nikolai's plight is virtually nil. Film unfolds slowly and repetitively.

There is much in the subject of inherent interest, and producer Filiberto Bandini could hardly have chosen a better time to lens the project — Bukharin received full political rehabilitation in the USSR while pic was in postproduction. Yet, despite the human and social drama of his case (in many of his liberalizing ideas he preceeded current thinking in the Gorbachev era), script chooses to leave the moments of high drama offscreen: the firing squad, Anna's arrest and decades of exile, her separation from her son. Result is often stagey and lifeless.

Keitel makes a convincing physical double for Bukharin, but his pronounced American accent (as well as Flaminia's) and aggressive thesping are incongruous. The talky script makes the use of English in a Bolshevik household a bit parodistic. *—Yung.*

───────

A Corps Perdu
(Straight To The Heart)
(CANADIAN-SWISS-COLOR/B&W)

───────

A Les Films Téléscène (Montreal)-Xanadu Film (Geneva) coproduction, in collaboration with Telefilm Canada, SOGIC, Swiss Federal Cultural Affairs and TV Suisse. (World sales, Films Transit, Canada.) Produced by Denise Robert, Robin Spry. Coproduced by Ruth Waldburger. Directed by Léa Pool. Screenplay, Pool, Marcel Beaulieu, from the novel, "Kurwenal," by Yves Navarre; camera (color, b&w), Pierre Mignot; editor, Michel Arcand; music, Osvaldo Montes; production design, Vianney Gauthier; sound, Luc Yersin, Marcel Pothier; line producers, Jamie Brown, George Reinhart. Reviewed at Venice Film Festival (competing), Sept. 3, 1988. Running time: **92 MIN.**

Pierre Kurwenal . . . . .Matthias Habich
Sarah . . . . .Johanne-Marie Tremblay
David .Michel Voita
Quentin . . . . .Jean François Pichette
Noémie . . . . .Kim Yaroshevskaya
Mother . . . . .Jacqueline Bertrand

───────

■ **Venice** — A potentially familiar tale in mid-life crisis after the breakup of a menage à trois in which he's lived for 10 years, "Straight To The Heart" becomes a haunting experience thanks to the extremely skillful direction of Léa Pool and the luminous photography of Pierre Mignot.

With careful handling, an international art house career is indicated.

Pic opens in Nicaragua (filmed in Cuba) where Pierre (Matthias Habich) is working as a photo-journalist, witnessing seemingly random killings. He returns to Montreal to find both the woman, Sarah (Johanne-Marie Tremblay) and man,

David (Michel Voita) with whom he's lived have left him. While he broods (in black and white flashbacks) over past happiness, Pierre becomes obsessed to know why he's been abandoned.

At the same time he launches into a project of photographing the city of Montreal, seeing it sans rosecolored glasses, and as if for the first time. After brief and frustrating encounters with both of his former lovers, he tentatively begins a new relationship, with Quentin (Jean-François Pichette), a young deaf-mute.

Habich gives a strong performance as the distraught protagonist, but the film's strengths lie in the direction and camerawork, which are precise, detailed and perfectly in tune with the drama. Another major plus is the film's beautiful music score by Osvaldo Montes.

Pierre's bisexuality is handled without comment, and flashbacks of the three lovers sharing shower and bed together are tactfully handled. This charting of a man's inward journey could have proved awesomely dull if not for the talents behind and before the camera.

Getting such a film across to the public obviously won't be an easy matter, but could be worth the effort. The English title, though, is a poor one: "Heart And Soul" might be a more effective, and punchy, translation of the original. —*Strait.*

Nachsaison
(Off Season)
(AUSTRIAN-W. GERMAN)

A Marwo Film (Vienna)-Voiss Film (Munich) coproduction, with participation of OFF, ORF, BMI and Bavarian Rundfunks. Produced by Monika Maruschko. Coproduced by Peter Voiss. Directed by Wolfram Paulus. Screenplay, Paulus, Uli Neulinger; camera (Eastmancolor), Christian Berger; editor, Paulus; music, Bert Breit; production design, Christoph Kanter; sound, Fritz Baumann; production manager, Monika Maruschko; assistant director, Uli Neulinger. Reviewed at Venice Film Festival (Critics

Week), Sept. 3, 1988. Running time: **88 MIN.**
Lenz . . . . Albert Paulus
Fussek . . . . Günther Maria Halmer
Lisbeth . . . . Daniela Obermeir
The Dancer . . . . Mercedes Echerer
Roth . . . . Claus Homschak
Walter . . . . Michael Reiter
David . . . . Simon Paulus
Wally . . . . Marika Green

■ **Venice** — Here's a mood piece set in one of those vast, once elegant old hotels which used to cater to the very wealthy in small mountain resorts. Now, the old place is a white elephant, and symbolizes the fading hopes of the film's protagonist, a young husband and father driven to petty crime to make ends meet.

Lenz is a masseur whose clients are mostly plump old ladies. He earns little from the job and debts mount up alarmingly. A friend persuades him to break the law, stealing furniture and selling it (or using it to furnish his apartment).

Meanwhile, Lisbeth, his wife, is becoming slowly affected by Lenz' behavior, and matters are complicated by a fetching young dancer, one of the few guests in the hotel, whose feet he massages daily, and who eventually takes him to bed.

In his second feature, Wolfram Paulus takes a familiar theme about modern angst and gives it added life via the grand, decaying setting: a thundering waterfall alongside the old hotel seems to contain all the force and power lacking in the life of the increasingly desperate Lenz.

The film's pacing is slow, the routine of this off-season life is placidly depicted and dramatic moments (such as the moment Lenz finally goes to bed with the dancer, or when his car is stopped by police) are quickly over and done with. There are puzzling plot points, and the film's somber mood won't be to everyone's taste, but thanks especially to Christian Berger's crisp camerawork, "Off Season" is always watchable.—*Strat.*

TORONTO REVIEWS

Dead Ringers
(CANADIAN)

A 20th Century Fox release (U.S.), Astral Films release (Canada) of a Mantle Clinic II production, presented by James C. Robinson, Joe Roth. Executive producers, Carol Baum, Silvio Tabet. Produced by David Cronenberg, Marc Boyman. Directed by Cronenberg. Screenplay, Cronenberg, Norman Snider, based on the book "Twins" by Bari Wood, Jack Geasland; camera (color), Peter Suschitzky; editor, Ronald Sanders; music, Howard Shore; production design, Carol Spier; costumes, Denise Cronenberg; art direction, James McAteer; sound, Bryan Day; special effects design, Gordon Smith; mechanical design, Walter Klassen; associate producer, John Board. Reviewed at Cumberland theater, Toronto, Sept. 1, 1988. In the Toronto Festival of Festivals. Running time: **115 MIN.**
Beverly & Elliot Mantle . . . . . Jeremy Irons
Claire Niveau . . . . Genevieve Bujold

Cary . . . . Heidi Von Palleske
Danuta . . . . Barbara Gordon
Laura . . . . Shirley Douglas
Anders Wolleck . . . . Stephen Lack

■ **Toronto** — "Dead Ringers" is David Cronenberg's most serious and least bloody major work to date.

Intense, multi-layered and expertly done, it is certain of mainstream attention but whether to the level of Cronenberg's last feature, "The Fly," remains a question.

"Dead Ringers," filmed under the title of "Twins," is about identical twin gynecologists, both expertly played by Jeremy Irons, whose intense bond is fatally sliced when they both fall in love with the same internationally known actress.

The doctors are renowned, work and live together in a fashionable apartment, interchangeably take on the same patients and make public appearances, with no one guessing who's who.

Yet they are different as Irons, seamlessly playing both roles with only different hair combing and variation of clothing, demonstrates. One is outgoing, a smooth talker and a ladies man, and the other, more dependent and less sociable.

The neurotic, pill-popping actress, portrayed stylishly by Genevieve Bujold, is in town filming a tv miniseries and visits their clinic for a diagnosis.

First, the outgoing twin beds her and then so does the next one. She senses a difference, learns they are twins from a friend, elegantly played by Shirley Douglas in a winning cameo, and angrily confronts them.

Bujold chooses the shy twin, for reasons not explained in the otherwise gripping script by Cronenberg and Norman Snider. From that point, disintegration of the twins bond and their careers sets in.

Promising to return, the actress leaves for filming elsewhere. The reclusive twin comes apart, separated from her and growing apart from his brother who has made plans to leave the clinic and teach.

Left alone, the shy twin gets heavily into drugs and is barred from hospital privileges after trying to use sculptured instruments of torture and being too drugged to operate. The actress returns but too late to reverse the situation.

The outgoing twin realizes his dependency on his deteriorating brother and the two begin a drug binge that ends with the reclusive twin carving him up in a bloody death in their apartment which is a shambles. Pic ends with the living twin holding his dead brother, in a scene lit and photographed like a religious painting.

Along the way, scripters Cronenberg and Snider show sly wit about acting with Bujold telling her agent to accept a film she hates because, "I need the humiliation and the work." The scripters presage the unfolding plot with Irons telling Bujold early on, "Pain is distortion."

Director Cronenberg handles his usual fondness for gore in muted style; a brief scene has the shy twin dreaming of biting apart the skin joining Siamese twins; and the final operation, though bloody, is not lingered over.

His direction is its usual top class, but in this one he works in a more measured pace to strong effect. Irons turns in dynamic performances. Bujold is firstrate.

Striking Heidi Von Palleske does an attention-making turn, frolicking with the outgoing twin, but her precise place in the medical fraternity and in their lives is left unclear.

Peter Suschitzky's camerawork is excellent. So are Carol Spier's production design, Denise Cronenberg's upmarket costuming, James McAteer's art direction and Howard Shore's glove-fitting music.

Some tightening is required because action flags a bit just after the actress leaves and also in some later scenes. —*Adil.*

Birds Of Prey
(FILIPINO)

A Global Film production. Produced by Jarold Sole, Gil Portes. Executive producers, Federico Macaranas, Rene Mapua. Directed by Portes. Screenplay, C. del Mundo Jr., H. del Mundo, Ricardo Lee, Portes; camera (color) Ely Cruz; editor, Edgardo Vinarao; art direction, Marshall Factora. Reviewed at Bloor Cinema, Toronto; (in Toronto Festival of Festivals), (Also in Montreal Film Festival. Running time: **106 MIN.**
With: Gina Alajar, Edward Swan, Susan Africa.

■ **Toronto** — Director Gil Portes examines life in the Philippines of Cory Aquino in "Birds Of Prey," a film that is as absorbing in its contemporary political observations as it is shaky in its main character development.

Outside of fest circuit and home territory, theatrical prospects are iffy.

Cecilia (Gina Alajar) is a Filipino actress who's been living in New York City for 13 years. At her performance in an avant-garde political play, she meets Steve (Edward Swan), a photojournalist who is doing a magazine piece on Filipinos living in New York.

When Cecilia gets word from home that her ex-husband, Buddy, a dissident leader, has been killed by the Aquino government's military, she feels she must return to Manila to find their daughter Layla, who she left behind. Steve, head over heels in love with Cecilia after one date and under the guise of good journalistic research, accompanies her to Manila and stays on in her parents' fancy digs.

Cecilia's friend Nona (Susan Africa), a comrade of Buddy's, helps her search for the truth about Buddy's murder and to find Layla.

While the script is stilted and flowery, and the romance between Cecilia and Steve almost inconceivable, the pic excels when the trio travels from squatters' homes to military stations to orphanages and to the mountains in quest of Layla.

The differences in modern Filipino life between the time of Marcos and the reign of Cory is integral to the story. Even the most general social chitchat is steeped in political overtones.

Alajar is a wonderful actress, who brings warmth and commitment to a role that takes her on an extensive journey not only for her daughter but for her lost country and, ultimately, her self.

Portes grabs the flavor and sensibility of contempo Filipino life with texture and verve. —*Devo*.

Milk And Honey
(CANADIAN-BRITISH)

A Cinema Plus release of an Independent Pictures/Zenith Prods. Ltd. production. Produced by Peter O'Brian. Directed by Rebecca Yates, Glen Salzman. Screenplay, Trevor Rhone, Salzman; camera (color), Guy Defaux; editor, Bruce Nyznik; music, Micky Erbe, Maribeth Solomon; art direction, Francois Sequin; sound, Bruce Nyznik. Reviewed at Bloor Cinema, Toronto (in Toronto Festival of Festivals), Aug. 29, 1988. Running time: **89 MIN.**
Johanna . . . . Josette Simon
Adam . . . . Lyman Ward
David . . . . Richard Mills
Del . . . . Djanet Sears
Gordon . . . . Errol Slue
Also with: Leonie Forbes, Fiona Reid, Tom Butler.

■ Toronto — **"Milk And Honey" can boast a radiant performance by Josette Simon, but it falls way short of expectations for a gripping social drama about a Jamaican immigrant's experiences in embracing her new homeland, Canada.**

While it's a story that needs to be told, pic's midpoint slide into sentimentalism makes it a tough sell commercially.

Story centers on Johanna (Josette Simon), who leaves her young son and family in the poverty of her native Jamaica to emigrate to Toronto to take a supposedly well-paying nanny job. She works for an ambitious 2-career yuppie couple and quickly attaches herself lovingly to their children.

She networks with other nannies in the park, who complain about low pay for foreign domestics and the difficulties in getting landed immigrant status.

Jo misses her son David terribly and flies him up for Christmas va-cation. Encouraged by her buddies to keep him in Canada illegally, she succumbs to the inflated promises of Gordon, the black immigration "Mr. Fixit," who can phony up the boy's documents and keep him in school.

David's school principal (Lyman Ward), a former night-school English prof of Jo's who once tried to seduce her — and on whom she pulled a knife — participates in the scam by ignoring the false papers and warning Jo that he'll be feigning ignorance if the authorities crop up.

Rest of pic follows Jo's dodging of immigration officers after a friend rats on her. Ultimately Jo and David are deported, but not before the principal befriends them and boards them in his home.

Climax is too ridiculously contrived, with the principal moving down to Jamaica to join Jo after he's arrested for aiding and abetting.

First-time feature directors Rebecca Yates and Glen Salzman (a husband-wife team) extract some fine performances, in addition to topliner Simon, from Djanet Sears as an upwardly mobile ex-nanny and Erroll Slue as the flashy extortion expert.

Screenplay touches on some arresting issues, but soon backslides from its original plucky tone. Filmed on location in Toronto and Jamaica, pic has a fine sense of place, but there's a too-static camera technique in interior shots.

Toronto's burgeoning immigrant population — over one-third of the residents don't count English as their first language — does indeed make it a land of milk and honey, but a richer, grittier story is here for the telling. — *Devo*.

MONTREAL REVIEWS

To Kill A Priest
(Le Complot)
(FRENCH)

A Columbia Pictures release (U.S.), Impéria-AMLF (France), release of a J.P. Prods./FR3 Films coproduction. Executive producer, Jean-Pierre Alessandri. Production supervisor, Timothy Burill. Directed by Agnieszka Holland. Screenplay, Holland, Jean-Yves Pitoun; camera (Panavision, color), Adam Holender; editor, Hervé de Luze; music, Georges Delerue; additional music, Zbigniew Preisner, Verdi; theme song "The Crimes Of Cain" written and performed by Joan Baez; art direction, Emile Ghigo; sound, Daniel Brisseau, Gérard Lamps; costumes, Anna Sheppard, Mic Cheminal; assistant director, Michel Cheyko; production manager, Gérard Molto; associate producers, Marie-Christine Lefèbvre, Michael Cooper; casting, Margot Capelier, Priscilla John. Reviewed at the AMLF screening room, Paris, Aug. 24, 1988. (In Montreal World Film Festival, competing.) Running time: **116 MIN.**
Father Alec . . . . Christophe Lambert
Stefan . . . . Ed Harris
Anna . . . . Joanne Whalley
The Colonel . . . . Joss Ackland
The Bishop . . . . David Suchet
Felix . . . . Tim Roth
Joseph . . . . Peter Postlethwaite
Also with: Cherie Lunghi, Gregor Fisher, Charles Condou, André Chaumeau, Vincent Grass, Matlock Gibbs, Nicolas Serreau, Brian Glover, Paul Crauchet, Janine Darcey, Wojtek Pszoniak.
(English soundtrack version)

■ Paris — **Polish by subject and director, French by official production and shooting locations, American by soundtrack and partial financing, and transatlantic in casting, "To Kill A Priest" is an ambitious political thriller emptied of substance by its heterogeneous components and hybrid dramaturgy.**

Backed by Columbia under the brief Puttnam regime, this fictional recreation of the murder of Polish priest Jerzy Popieluszko by security police in 1984 will be a tough sell for the Yank major in both mainstream and art house sectors.

Exiled Polish helmer Agnieszka Holland (whose German-made "Bitter Harvest" was an Oscar nominee for best foreign language film in 1985) has not found her way through the labyrinth of international coprods with her erstwhile sense of observation and control.

Though the theme and background are obviously intensely close to her, Holland's recreation on French soil of her homeland under the banner of Solidarity and the boot of martial law lacks a sense of time and place, a socio-political density to give the action and characters credible cultural and psychological identity.

Film's lack of texture is only partially a problem of art direction — Philip Kaufman and an imaginative technical crew destroyed some preconceived notions in "The Unbearable Lightness Of Being." Holland and her production designer Emile Chigo, and Polish-born lenser Adam Holender have found urban sights around France that could pass for sections of Polish cityscapes, but the production's very glossiness fights the tonally gloomy theme.

Central weakness is the casting of France's linguistically versatile Christophe Lambert, playing a rather bland "charismatic" priest and Solidarity apostle, and America's Ed Harris, not quite the right stuff as the Polish militia officer who engineers and executes the plot to assassinate him.

Ironically, though Lambert is film's major selling point, Holland has chosen Harris as the protagonist of her drama. Her script tries to probe the near-psychotic motivations and initiatives of this privileged Communist security officer and family man, repulsed by what Lambert represents, yet at moments hypnotized by the man. The Cain and Abel theme is spelled out literally in Joan Baez' bookending theme song (the score is by Georges Delerue).

Lambert, poor fellow, is martyrized for the second time in a year, though less absurdly than as the neo-Hollywoodian outlaw hero of Michael Cimino's "The Sicilian." He has little to do here other than preach nonviolent resistance and ooze a quiet, secular saintliness. Some auxiliary scenes meant to fill out the man are mostly superfluous.

As political suspenser à la Costa-Gavras, film picks up some steam and dramatic interest in the second half, though by this time one's empathy or antipathy for the principals of the story has been severely tried.

Maybe Holland, too close to the material to treat it with dramatic efficiency under the esthetic compromises of the international production, would have done better to push the stylization in fictionalizing the country (as Costa-Gavras did with success in his greatest triumph "Z.") —*Len*.

Some Girls

An MGM/UA Communications release from MGM Pictures of an Oxford Film Co. production. Produced by Rick Stevenson. Directed by Michael Hoffman. Screenplay, Rupert Walters; camera (color), Ueli Steiger; editor, David Spiers. Reviewed at Montreal World Film Festival (noncompeting), Sept. 2, 1988. MPAA Rating: R. Running time: **94 MIN.**
Michael . . . . Patrick Dempsey
Gabby . . . . Jennifer Connelly
Irenka . . . . Sheila Kelly
Father . . . . André Gregory
Also with: Ashley Greenfield, Florinda Bolkan, Lila Kedrova.

■ Montreal — **A cross-cultural teen sex farce with some good moments, "Some Girls" (a.k.a. "Sisters"), may not be consistently funny enough for a long-distance theatrical run in the U.S., but has a better chance to become a hit in Canada due to its made-in-Quebec milieu.**

MGM will be faced with a marketing and distribution challenge in coaxing audiences to sample the film, then will have to depend on word-of-mouth to break it.

"Some Girls" hinges on the deadpan comic timing of Patrick Dempsey, who plays Michael, an American student invited by his college sweetheart Gabby (Jennifer Connelly) to spend Christmas with her family in Quebec City. The architecturally stately city is presented as a snow-covered fairyland in the eyes of the Yank visitor, an impression that's reinforced when he arrives at the castle-like home of Gabby's family.

Shortly after an effusive greeting, Gabby informs Michael that she doesn't love him anymore and that sleeping arrangements will be separate. This condition of Michael's visit is assiduously enforced by Gabby's mother and just as determinedly contested by Michael, whose randiness is the movie's central running gag.

Fortunately for Michael, Gabby has two fetching sisters who each show more than a passing interest in Gabby's well-intentioned, slightly wimpoid ex. Eccentric spice is provided by the girls' father, a head-in-the-clouds scholar with a proclivity for working in the nude, portrayed by André Gregory in a little gem of a performance. There's also a sweet, batty grandmother, who's consistently running away from the hospital and who's convinced that Michael is her long-dead husband, also named Michael.

Director Michael Hoffman and screenwriter Rupert Walters have fun mixing and mismatching these comic elements and succeed in springing a few flashes of wacky hilarity. A bittersweet touch is added with the grandmother's impending death, but to their credit the filmmakers rein in the sentimentality of the situation and use it to their advantage with a supernatural flourish. — *Rich.*

Wildfire

A Zupnik Cinema Group release of a Jerry Tokofsky-Stanley R. Zupnik production. Produced by Jerry Tokofsky. Executive producers, Stanley R. Zupnik, Irvin Kershner. Coproducer, Hunt Lowry. Directed by Zalman King. Screenplay, Matthew Bright, King, from a story by Bright; camera (color), Bill Butler; editor, Caroline Biggerstaff; music, Maurice Jarre; production design, Geoffrey Kirkland. Reviewed at Montreal World Film Festival (competing), Sept. 2, 1988. MPAA Rating: PG. Running time: **98 MIN.**
Frank . . . . Steven Bauer
Kay . . . . Linda Fiorentino
Mike . . . . Will Patton
Lewis . . . . Marshall Bell
Also with: Sandra Seacat, Richard Bradford, Alisha Byrd-Pena, Jonah Ellers-Issacs, Michelle Mayberry, William Hall, Sarah Luck Pearson, Jack Spratt, Tony Amendola, Calvin Collins, O-Lan Jones, Marc Siegler, Nancy Fish.

■ **Montreal** — **A dubious exercise in ersatz melodrama, this dismal tale of ill-fated love is almost as difficult to watch as its cloying Maurice Jarre score is to listen to. Boxoffice prospects are virtually nil, but the presence of attractive costars Steven Bauer and Linda Fiorentino qualify "Wildfire" as fodder for the video/cable maw.**

Pic opens with a weepy Fiorentino walking by the seaside and declaiming in voiceover about a bitter fate brought on by "too much love." This gives way to a sappy flashback montage in which little Kay (Fiorentino) and little Frank (Bauer) are thrown together in an institution for orphans and unwanted kids. In a jiffy the couple is post-pubescent and running away to have their child and start a dream life together.

There's a little problem about money, which Bauer plans to solve by knocking over a country bank. Not surprisingly, the stickup is foiled, and Bauer is shot and jailed. Fiorentino (inconceivably full-bloomed for an ostensible 16-year-old) is adopted by kindly folks who live in a picture-perfect California town. Mike (Will Patton), the handsome, hardworking boy next door, immediately takes a shine to the leggy, raven-haired knockout.

Director Zalman King then flash-forwards to the present (eight years later), with Fiorentino and Patton living out the yuppie dream, complete with House Beautiful Home, two button-cute kids, a wise black housekeeper and a Mercedes Benz. High school dropout Fiorentino passes her spare time refining her rough edges by learning French.

Everything is hunky dory — until Bauer gets out of jail and tracks down the love of his life. Fiorentino wants no part of handsome Mr. Trouble, but Bauer is a charming and persistent sort, who keeps harping on their old ties. Finally, when Patton is away on a business trip,

the ex-lovers have several meetings, which are strictly platonic.

Fiorentino's doting hubby is predictably jealous and refuses to believe the meetings were innocent. This sets events careening on an improbable narrative spiral, as the two ex-lovers run away together with Patton in hot pursuit. Also tagging along is Lewis (Marshall Bell), Frank's buddy from the joint, whose function is to deliver expository speeches to the effect that Frank has turned himself around in jail. Bauer, in fact, is heading to San Diego for a job restoring antique cars. He begs Fiorentino to just come along for the ride.

On the way they make a meaningless detour to track down Fiorentino's real mom — a floozy working as a barmaid in a dive in Stockton ("Fat City"), Calif. When Patton catches up with the wayward couple in San Diego, violence erupts, Bauer loses his head and Fiorentino impulsively goes off with him to Mexico.

This happens to be the location of the opening seaside scene where unfortunate viewers came in. It's a good bet some will walk out without waiting for the ridiculous, flaming conclusion of "Wildfire."

The principal actors are serviceable enough, but the script is embarrassing. "I didn't mean for it to go this way," Bauer's character says at one point — a line that also could serve as a suitable copout for the makers of this movie. — *Rich.*

Lonely Child —
The Imaginary World Of
Claude Vivier
(CANADIAN-DOCU)

A Cinema Libre release of a Silverfilm production. Produced by Johnny Silver, Michael Nacina. Directed by Silver. Screenplay, Owen Burges; camera (color), Dennis Pike; editor, Silver, Marguerite Cleinge; music, Claude Vivier; sound, David Millar. Reviewed at Montreal World Film Festival (Panorama Canada), Aug. 29, 1988. Running time: **75 MIN.**
Claude Vivier at 34 . . . . . . Germain Houde
Claude Vivier at 26 . . . . Denis Forest
Claude Vivier at 16 . . . . Ivan Beaulieu
(In French and English soundtrack version.)

■ **Montreal** — **Like British playwright Joe Orton, Quebec composer Claude Vivier was killed by a homosexual lover. Yet while Stephen Frears' film about Orton — "Prick Up Your Ears" — had international distribution, Johnny Silver's "Lonely Child" probably won't fare well outside French Canada and France, the two areas in which Vivier was best known.**

This is essentially a tv documentary that uses actors to portray Vivier at three stages of his life. Conversations with various friends and colleagues are integrated into the film to comment on his compositions and the lifestyle that eventually led, in 1983, to his death at the hands of a young homosexual in the streets of Paris.

The film begins with Vivier at 16,

proceeds to 26 and then to his final year in Paris at the age of 34. Several of Vivier's erotic dance pieces are included as are his compositions — including the title piece — "Lonely Child." The film works best during these stretches and is weakest when Silver turns to fiction since he doesn't allow any of his three performers an opportunity to add much to our understanding of Vivier.

Perhaps the film would have a better chance for distribution as a straight documentary, but as is, should go directly to Radio Canada's tv archives, with some chance of video or university distribution in France. — *Cadd.*

Big Time
(DOCU)

An Island Pictures release of an Island Visual Arts production. Executive producer, Chris Blackwell. Produced by Luc Roeg. Directed by Chris Blum. Written by Tom Waits, Kathleen Brennan, Blum; camera (color), Daniel Hainey; editor, Glenn Scatlebury; music, Waits, Brennan; sound, Biff Dawes; design, Sterling Storm, Blum; costumes, Hank Ford. Reviewed at Montreal World Film Festival (Cinema of Today and Tomorrow), Aug. 31, 1988. MPAA Rating: PG. Running time: **90 MIN.**
With: Tom Waits, Michael Blair, Ralph Carney, Greg Cohen, Marc Ribot, Willie Schwarz.

■ **Montreal** — **"Big Time" is a chromatically splashy concert performance film featuring Tom Waits, the rubber-faced, gravel-voiced, post-beat blues bard of low life.**

Waits (who has acted in "Down By Law" and "Ironweed") is an acquired musical taste, and although this film offers an absorbing journey into Waits' demimonde, the recent boxoffice fizzles of concert pics featuring Prince ("Sign O' The Times") and Sting ("Bring On The Night") present Island with a clear challenge in attracting audiences who are not already converts.

Director Chris Blum and cinematographer Daniel Hainey dress up "Big Time" with a hot, candy-coated palette, an eye-riveting hook abetted by hip design and costumes. In the vogue of recent concert pics, Blum attempts to provide some "narrative" connection between generous-segments of skillfully intercut sequences from different Waits concerts. The non-musical linkage consists of vertiginous snippets of hero Tom waking or sleeping in some idealized postmodern hotel room, sort of a dive for those who've hit the big time.

Black & white tv static provides another (if not entirely original) stylistic leitmotif. All of this is interspersed with a hallucinatory repetitiveness reminiscent of surrealist Raul Ruiz.

Any concert performance pic, naturally, is made or broken by the music and the performance — and Waits delivers the goods. His

refractive approach to the blues is shot through with open homage to Satchmo and is tattooed with a gumbo of influences, including Dylan, gospel and New Orleans voodoo funk. Waits also slouches in the tradition of sardonic raconteur spawned by Lenny Bruce, and his scathingly funny patter provides stiletto counterpoint to scenes of emotionally feral musical expressionism. — *Rich.*

The Dawning
(BRITISH)

A TVS Entertainment presentation in association with the Vista Organization. Produced by Sarah Lawson. Directed by Robert Knights. Screenplay, Noira Williams, based on novel "The Old Jest" by Jennifer Johnston; camera (color), Shaun O'Dell; music, Simon May; sound, Ivan Sharrock; art direction, Diana Charnley; makeup, Tommie Manderson; assistant director, Andrew Montgomery. Reviewed at Bijou Preview theater, London, Aug. 23, 1988. (In Montreal Film Festival, competing). Running time: **97 MIN.**
Cassius . . . . Anthony Hopkins
Nancy . . . . Rebecca Pidgeon
Aunt Mary . . . . Jean Simmons
Grandfather . . . . Trevor Howard
Maeve . . . . Tara MacGowran
Harry . . . . Hugh Grant
Bridie . . . . Ronnie Masterson
Joe Mulhare . . . . Mark O'Regan

■ **London** — **Anthony Hopkins displays why he is one of his generation's ace actors with an excellent performance in "The Dawning," which also offers the late Trevor Howard's last screen role.**

"The Dawning" is a lyrical and intelligent film that is both politically tough and disarmingly gentle at the same time. Strong acting from a fine cast combines with elegant direction and cinematography to produce a "small" film to relish.

Pic is set in 1920 in Southern Ireland where orphan Rebecca Pidgeon lives with grandfather Trevor Howard and aunt Jean Simmons. She is a naive, romantic teenager and when she meets a stranger (Anthony Hopkins) hiding in her beach hut she innocently trusts him (after naming him Cassius) even though he carries a pistol.

Pidgeon agrees to take a message for him to Dublin where she befriends her young contact Mark O'Regan. Only when she witnesses the shooting of 12 British officers does she realize what the message was.

Despite her shock at the killings she stays loyal to Hopkins and rushes to the beach late at night to warn him about an army search. At the beach she sees him shot down by the patrol.

A winning performance by Pidgeon (in her first major screen role) as the young Nancy and the refined, powerful playing by Hopkins gives "The Dawning" its strength. Hopkins appears in relatively few scenes but manages to project his mark on the whole picture.

Howard, as a doddery old army officer and though obviously old in reality, still delivers his lines with gusto. He is nicely complemented by an elegant Jean Simmons while Hugh Grant ably plays the typical English stuffed shirt.

There is little explanation of the political background and offshore audience may be a little bemused about the goings-on. Though pic shows acts of violence by both the British army and the Irish Republican forces, it leans towards the Republican side.

Helmer Robert Knights slightly overplays the beautiful sunset/daybreak shots and the opening few minutes seem slightly awkward, but overall direction is fine, aided by sharp lensing by Shaun O'Dell. Other technical credits are fine.
—*Adam.*

Determinations
(CANADIAN-DOCU-COLOR/B&W)

A Hockenhull Releasing release of a Luminous Eye production. Produced and directed by Oliver Hockenhull. Screenplay, Hockenhull; camera (color, b&w), Hockenhull; editor, Hockenhull; music, Dennis Burke; set design, Keith Groat. Reviewed at Montreal World Film Festival (Panorama Canada), Aug. 28, 1988. Running time: **75 MIN.**

With: Louise Ross, Doug Chomyn, Andrew McIlroy, Derek Neen, Karen Sawatsky, Carolyn McCluskie, Fumiko Kiyooka, Judy Radul, Jamie Parker, Lisa Adams.

■ **Montreal** — **Oliver Hockenhull's personal philosophy limits his film's market potential considerably. His attempt at presenting the "whole" argument is as biased as any rightwing diatribe and won't appeal to target markets outside of the loony left.**

Hockenhull addresses the arrest and trial of a radical British Columbia group called "The Squamish Five," using documentary footage, newsreels, theater, animation and poetic narration to compare the crimes of the "Five" — the bombing of video stores and hydro substations and plots against a Canadian air force base — with the actions of various governments.

"Determinations" is an assault on the senses with all manner of objectionable audio and visual forces combining to deter the viewer from thinking positive thoughts of these new revolutionaries. This is a joyless, passionless work that might have had some potential within university communities had there been an ounce of objectivity included in its simplistic message.—*Cadd.*

Distant Thunder
(CANADIAN-U.S.)

A Paramount Pictures release of a Paramount Canada Ltd. production. Produced by Robert Schaffel. Executive producer, Richard L. O'Connor. Directed by Rick Rosenthal. Screenplay, Robert Stitzel, from story by Stitzel, Deedee Wehle; camera (Technicolor), Ralf D. Bode; editor, Dennis Virkler; music, Maurice Jarre; artistic consultant, Robert Cowan; production manager, Warren Carr; cos-

tume design, Tish Monaghan; casting, Lynn Stalmaster & Associates. Reviewed at Montreal World Film Festival (noncompeting), Sept. 2, 1988. MPAA Rating: R. Running time: **114 MIN.**

Mark Lambert	John Lithgow
Jack Lambert	Ralph Macchio
Char	Kerrie Keane
Harvey Nitz	Reb Brown
Barbara Lambert	Janet Margolin
Larry	Dennis Arndt
Moss	Jamey Sheridan
Louis	Tom Bower

Also with: John Kelly, Michael Currie, Hilary Strang, Robyn Stevan, David Longworth, Gordon Currie, Walter Marsh.

■ **Montreal** — **If "Distant Thunder" is any indication of the kind of product that will be produced by Canadians and Americans working more closely together under the Free Trade agreement, both countries should seriously reconsider the alliance.**

The film is billed here as a Canadian-American coproduction, and was filmed in British Columbia — doubling as the state of Washington — with Canadian crews and a mostly Canadian cast. The subject is pure Americana — vets coping with memories of the war in Vietnam — and the toppers are U.S. actors John Lithgow and Ralph Macchio.

Lithgow plays vet Mark Lambert, who headed for the hills after his tour of duty was complete, and Macchio is his son Jack, abandoned by his father when he was three. Against the wishes of his mother, Jack leaves his suburban Chicago home on his 18th birthday to find his father. The trip to Washington was precipitated by a letter from dad — the first father-son correspondence in 15 years.

When young Lambert arrives in Washington he discovers his father has left his lumber mill job to flee back into the woods after a fight with a friend's jealous boyfriend. The friend and Jack decide to venture into the woods to bring his father back, but first have to cope with a bunch of middle-aged crazies for whom the war is still very real.

Even more real is this film's marketing problems. Pic starts out with some nice moments, but degenerates into a soapy mess.

As a depiction of the current state of Viet vets, pic may have some early theatrical legs, thanks to the popularity of recent war movies. However, Lithgow — who shuffles sullenly across the screen like Sasquatch in "Harry And The Hendersons" — and his fellow onscreen "vets" Reb Brown and Larry Arndt set the veteran image back 10 years with their hard-to-believe performances.

"Distant Thunder" probably will go to video and cable quickly. Since the only international star that fares well here is the impressive backdrop of the British Columbia mountains, it will have even less appeal on the small screen. —*Cadd.*

Adada
(SOUTH KOREAN)

A Hwa Chun Trading Co. production. Produced by Park Chong-Chan. Directed by Im Kwon-t'aek. Screenplay, Yun Sam-Yook; camera (color), Chung Il-Sung. Reviewed at Montreal World Film Festival (competing), Sept. 1, 1988. Running time: **120 MIN.**

Adada	Shin Hye-Soo

Also with: Han Ji-Il, Lee Kyung-Young.

■ **Montreal** — **"Adada" is beautifully photographed and skillfully produced, but its overlong descent into extreme pathos will be alien to audiences in the West.**

The film's eponymous heroine is a sweet-natured, deaf-mute Korean country girl given in marriage by her poor but noble family to a nice young man whose corruption by wealth precipitates tragic changes in her life.

The opening hour of "Adada" is rich with anthropological nuggets as it examines the feudal customs and work ethic of Korean farmers under Japanese rule sometime around the 1920s. Indeed, the timelessness of Adada's way of life makes it hard to get a period-fix on the film until town scenes show men in early 20th century suits and a phonograph is introduced. The record player, in fact, signals the onset of the heroine's tragedy — it's a gift to her mother-in-law from her husband's second wife.

After several years of poor but happy pastoral marriage, Adada's husband gets restless down on the farm, goes drinking and whoring in town and then abruptly goes abroad. He returns rich, westernized and with a fashionable new spouse.

Adada makes a courageous effort to hold her ground, but her handicap and the powerlessness of women in this culture conspire against her. Although sympathetic, her in-laws cannot control Adada's husband when he expels her from the house. Her tragedy is compounded when her own family — according to custom — refuses to take her back for fear of disgrace. Adada finally finds hope with a poor but loving peasant from her own village — but then he too becomes interested in money. The consequences are fatal.

Shin Hye-Soo gives a moving performance in the mute title role and is surrounded by a good supporting cast. The film may well be a major hankerchief-soaker in Seoul and elsewhere in the region. —*Rich.*

Sasek a Kralovna
(The Jester And The Queen)
(CZECH)

Produced by Barrandov Film Studios, Prague. Directed by Vera Chytilová. Screenplay, Boleslav Polivka, Chytilová, based on theater piece by Polivka; camera (color), Jan Malir; music, Jiri Bulis; set design, Dusan Zdimal. Reviewed at Montreal World Film Festival (competing), Sept. 1, 1988. Running time: **116 MIN.**

Slach, the Jester	Boleslav Polivka
The Queen, Regina	Chantal Poulainova
The King, Mr. Konig	Jiri Kodet
Vaclav	Vlastimil Brodsky

■ **Montreal** — **Vera Chytilová has hit paydirt with a bold and striking adaptation of Czech mime Boleslav Polivka's 2-person theater piece "The Jester And The Queen."**

Her greatly expanded version is a comedy-fantasy-reality game, open to multilevel interpretations, between a Czech peasant, Slach, who fancies himself a medieval jester, a German tourist, Mr. Konig, who arrives in a white Mercedes to visit an old Bohemian castle, and his haughty fiance Regina, who is French. (The national metaphors are not lost.)

Both Polivka, an exceptional mime from Moravia's Brno theater and strikingly beautiful Chantal Poulainova, French theater actress now working in Czechoslovakia, play out a parable of power and humiliation in which each manipulates the other in parallel stories that interweave Slach's present sense of reality, and his imagined past.

As caretaker of an abandoned castle, he prepares to welcome the two well-to-do foreigners, in for a bit of hunting in the splendid deer park and surrounding forests. As befits the role of jester, Slach is both sycophant and philosopher, who inevitably must entertain the irascible and imperious queen while being drawn ever closer by fear and fascination to her cruel beauty. Chytilová's camera expertly conveys his fluctuating "deja vu" experience in the medieval court with the mundane reality of his comic turns in the village pub where locals humor him as the town dolt for his wild fabrications.

The mutual attraction/revulsion between jester and queen reach erotic planes which don't quite materialize while in reality there is promise of deeper involvement with Regina, and dawning recognition from the jealous Konig that Slach is not just another tour guide.

As the queen's demands become crazier and more sadistic and roles are exchanged, it is the jester who takes over and presides at revels featuring horsey games.

When the fairy-tale queen orders a beheading, Slach's hallucinatory reveries come down to earth and the sharp relaity of the queen as a cripple is touchingly revealed.

Performances are tops in all departments and technical credits good. Polivka is outstanding in his mime bits, which belie the theater performance origins of the script.

Film is suitable for general audiences as a universal fairy-tale that presents a now-fashionable darker side of the use of enchantment. Film had played for more than three months in Czechoslovakia since release first of the year. First North-American exposure here indicates a possible wide art-house bet, festivals and cultural tv. —*Milg.*

Miracle Mile

A Tri-Star Pictures release of a Hemdale Film Corp. production. Produced by John Daly, Derek Gibson. Written and directed by Steve de Jarnatt. Camera (color), Theo Van de Sande; editor, Stephen Semel, Kathie Weaver; music, Tangerine Dream; sound, Ken Hall; design, Claire Gaul, Jerry Casillas; costumes, Shay Cunliffe. Reviewed at Montreal World Film Festival (noncompeting), Sept. 3, 1988. MPAA Rating: R. Running time: **87 MIN.**
Harry . . . . Anthony Edwards
Julie . . . . Mare Winningham
Also with: John Agar, Lou Hancock, Mykel T. Williamson, Kelly Minter, Kurt Fuller.

■ **Montreal — Steve De Jarnatt (whose first feature "Cherry 2000" was never released by Orion), displays unmistakable filmmaking talent in this cautionary, depressing tale of two lovers who meet in the hours before a nuclear war.**

"Miracle Mile" has the tingling stylistic ingredients of a notable cult film, but its uncompromising ending, guaranteed to send audiences wobbling to the exits, may deter all but the most committed distributors from handling it.

In a nicely crafted credits and set-up sequence Harry (Anthony Edwards) a shy, traveling jazz musician meets Julie (Mare Winningham) an equally shy waitress, at a museum near Los Angeles' La Brea Tar Pits. This setting allows Harry to deliver a voiceover soliloquy on the wondrous millennia of life's evolution on Earth. The love-at-first-sight couple agree to meet at Julie's 24-hour diner when her shift ends at midnight. Harry oversleeps at his hotel and scrambles to the diner far too late to find the broken-hearted girl.

Standing around at a loss, Harry impulsively picks up the ringing phone in the booth outside the diner. During this punchy plot-point sequence a panic-stricken voice on the other end of the line warns Harry of an impending nuclear war within the hour. The voice belongs to a soldier in a missle silo who meant to call his father in Orange County (area code 714) but dialed the diner phone booth (area code 213) instead. A dumbfounded Harry listens as the missile man is cut off by gunshots. He's then told by an official sounding voice to "forget everything you've ever heard and go back to sleep."

To his credit, De Jarnatt manages to control his film as the rest of Harry's night spins precipitously out of control. The musician embarks on a desperate, obsessed search for Julie, while a small group he's managed to convince of the rapidly approaching apocalypse makes plans to load a helicopter and get away. Though ridiculous on the surface, the film's bizarre logic makes this Darwinian race for survival believable in spite of its total improbability. After a nightmarish string of increasingly violent and crazed events, Harry and Julie are reunited but their love story has no happy ending.

Anthony Edwards gives a bravura performance as the musician transformed by events into a resolute survivalist. Mare Winningham and others populate the picture with convincing supporting performances. De Jarnatt, who evokes an edgy suspense reminiscent of classic '50s tv fare such as "The Twilight Zone" and "Panic," is abetted by fine camerawork and design, plus a Tangerine Dream score of ominous ethereality. —*Rich.*

Bu-Su
(JAPANESE)

A Toho Pictures production. Produced by Hitoshi Ogura. Directed by Jun Ichikawa. Screenplay, Makiko Uchidate; camera (color), Tatsuhiko Kobayashi; editor, Yoshihiko Okuhara; music, Bun Itakura; sound, Hisayuki Miyamoto; design, Katsumi Kaneda; costumes, Eiji Konno, Kumiko Miyagoshi. Reviewed at Montreal World Film Festival (competing), Aug. 27, 1988. Running time: **95 MIN.**
Mugiko . . . . Yasuko Tomita
Also with: Michiyo Okusa, Minako Fujishiro, Mitsuko Oka.

■ **Montreal — This story of a girl torn between the night-and-day worlds of geisha life and high school — and alienated from both — is essentially a classy Japanese telefilm. Commercial prospects in the west are zero, but "Bu-Su" is well suited for locked-run series or festival sidebars on contemporary Japanese cinema.**

"Bu-Su" is the Japanese word for "wretched," an appropriate term for the inner state of taciturn Mugiko, an 18-year-old who tries to escape her unhappiness with village life by coming to Tokyo to live and work in the geisha house run by her aunt. The daughter of a once-great geisha, Mugiko is entitled by blood to train in the geishas' ancient art of classical Japanese song and dance.

Contrary to common Western belief the geishas are primarily entertainers — but they can be prostituted for a high enough price. This reality lends a subtle tension to "Bu-Su," as Mugiko shuttles between the world of her clique-ish superficial schoolmates and the strict hierarchical subculture of the geisha house.

In Japan, where individualism is discouraged and conformity a virtue, separation from the group is a type of purgatory, and Mugiko's self-perpetuated isolation from the two major groups in her life is designed to compound the poignancy of her story for Japanese viewers. Westerners, however, will probably be bored by the film's quotidian episodic structure in which nothing very exciting happens to the pretty, impassive girl.

There are some unusual glimpses into geisha life, and the hard lot of its trainees. In a feudal gesture of obeisance, Mugiko is compelled to run behind her aunt's rickshaw every night.

While it's by no means a blackboard jungle, Mugiko's high school is a rowdy departure from the stereotypical depiction of Japanese high as a pressure-cooker environment preparing students for life-determining college entrance exams. The major preoccupation at Mugiko's school is its centennial celebration. Mugiko makes no effort to hide her geisha life from her curious schoolmates, and when plans for the celebratory talent show begin to fizzle, she reluctantly agrees to perform a classic geisha dance about a young girl whose unhappiness caused her to burn down her village.

This ends disastrously, but Mugiko is redeemed by the attentions of another loner, a student boxer who admires her spunk. Hope is held out for their future as a couple ("society's smallest unit," as Mugiko's best friend says), but the film is more pessimistic about the fate of traditional Japanese culture under the onslaught of western-style pop-junk values.

Razor-sharp cinematography complements cinematic stunts involving blip-like flashbacks and freeze-frames freely employed in "Bu-Su." There's also a blatant MTV-type sequence obviously designed for the home market.
—*Rich.*

Savannah (La Ballade)
(FRENCH)

An Impéria-AMLF release of a JP Prods./FR3 Films coproduction. Produced by Jean-Pierre Alessandri. Written and directed by Marco Pico, based on the screenplay "Savannah Smiles" by Mark Miller. Camera (Eastmancolor), François Lartigue; sound, Michel Brethez; art direction, Anne Violet; editor, Marco Pico; music, Jean-Claude Petit; theme song, Jacques Higelin; production manager, Vincent Darrasse. Reviewed at Gaumont Halles cinema, Paris, Sept. 6, 1988. Running time: **100 MIN.**
Colin . . . . Jacques Higelin
Mailland . . . . Daniel Martin
Savannah . . . . Elodie Gautier
Geneviève . . . . Sylvie Granotier
Fabien . . . . René Féret
Coplan . . . . Marcel Bozzuffi
Jeanne . . . . Dominique Blanc
Gas station attendant . . . . . . Benoit Regent
Policeman . . . . Jacques Nolot

■ **Paris — At a time when Hollywood more than ever is snatching Gallic boxoffice babies for domestic retread, along comes a French remake of a Stateside picture.**

Frenchman Marco Pico has recast 1982 indie feature "Savannah Smiles" in a local provincial context. Original, scripted by Mark Miller and helmed by Pierre de Moro, never was seen here. The redo already has come and gone locally, though it's not as bad as all that, merely a skillful execution of a formula heart-tugger.

Pico seems to have changed little of the original plotline, in which

Original Film: Savannah Smiles

A Gold Coast Film release (subsequently released by Embassy Pictures) of a Mark Miller-Don Williams production. Produced by Clark L. Paylow. Directed by Pierre DeMoro. Story, screenplay, Mark Miller; camera (CFI color), Stephen W. Gray; editor, Eva Ruggiero; music, Ken Sutherland; production design, Charles Stewart; art direction, Allen Terry; sound, Ken King; associate producer, Laurette DeMoro Gafferi; assistant director, Dennis White; second unit director, David Kass. Reviewed at The Burbank Studios, Burbank, May 12, 1982. MPAA Rating: PG. Running time: **107 MIN.**
Alvie . . . . Mark Miller
Boots . . . . Donovan Scott
Savannah . . . . Bridgette Andersen
Harland Dobbs . . . . Peter Graves
Richard Driscoll . . . . Chris Robinson
Lt. Savage . . . . Michael Parks
Joan Driscoll . . . . Barbara Stanger
Father O'Hara . . . . Pat Morita
Chief Pruitt . . . . Philip Abbott
Farmer Wilma . . . . Fran Ryan
Grocery Clerk . . . . John Fiedler
Mr. Greenblatt . . . . Ray Anzalone
Doreen . . . . Carol Wayne

two small-time hoods on the lam find themselves saddled with a 7-year-old runaway. Naturally, parents and police assume it's a kidnaping and give chase to the hapless outlaws with shoot-to-kill resolution, though little Savannah finds a moment of happiness and friendship with her not-so-tough toughs.

To his credit, Pico avoids the saccharine pitfalls of the story with a modicum of taste, firm technical control and notably some nice low-key performances from principals and subsidiary cast.

The two hoods are played engagingly by Jacques Higelin, best known as a pop singer-composer, who has a natural screen presence as the harder-hearted of the pair, and Daniel Martin, a fine stage actor, as the more sensitive buddy who's the first to succumb to Savannah's charms. Title role is embodied by blond cupcake Elodie Gautier, who's endearing without being cloying.

Supporting cast includes filmmaker René Féret as Savannah's hypocritical politician dad, and the late Marcel Bozzuffi, in his final screen role as the overly self-confident veteran cop in charge of bagging the "kidnapers."

Pico makes fine use of the vast natural mountain-scapes of the Aude region. Tech credits are smart. —*Len.*

Waxwork

A Vestron Pictures release of a Staffan Ahrenberg/Mario Sotela production. Produced by Ahrenberg. Executive producer, Sotela. Executive producers/Vestron, William J. Quigley, Dan Ireland. Written and directed by Anthony Hickox. Camera (Foto-Kem color), Gerry Lively; editor, Christopher Cibelli; music, Roger Bellon; production design, Gianni Quaranta; art direction, Peter Marangoni; costume design, Leonard Pollock; sound (Dolby), T.A. Moore Jr., Mark Ettl, Jeff Gomillion; special effects, Bob Keen; assistant director, Gary Bettman; second unit director, Keen; second unit camera, John Schuerborn; associate producer, Eyal Rimmon; casting, Caro Jones. Reviewed at Raleigh Studios, L.A., Sept. 8, 1988. MPAA Rating: R. Running time: 97 MIN.
Mark .Zach Galligan
Sarah . . . . .Deborah Foreman
China . . . . .Michelle Johnson
Mr. Lincoln . . . . .David Warner
Tony . . . . .Dana Ashbrook
Sir Wilfred . . . .'. . .Patrick Macnee
Det. Roberts . . . . .Charles McCaughin
Marquis De Sade . . . .J. Kenneth Campbell
Count Dracula . . . . .Miles O'Keeffe
Anton Weber . . . . .John Rhys-Davies

■ Hollywood — "Waxwork," fittingly, is much like its subject — a handsomely turned-out but lifeless recreation of a horror film. Recycled smorgasbord approach offers gore galore and a greatest-hits-of-the-genre lineup of monsters and effects, but script lacks a heartbeat and pace is dreary.

After mining fringe interest, b.o. should be inert.

British director Anthony Hickox (great-grandson of U.K. film industry kingpin J. Arthur Rank) brings a flip approach and nasty tone to the tale of college kids trapped in a museum where the monsters come to life and claim them as victims.

Hickox, who's already scripted a sequel for Vestron, draws heavily on what's come before in both British and Stateside horror films, but "Waxwork" is ostensibly original, not a remake of the 1924 Paul Leni film "Waxworks."

Hickox has penned an elaborate plot, and premise does offer some intrigue — the unwitting victims

travel back in time and struggle against figures like Count Dracula and the Marquis De Sade — but he consistently fails to set things up in a way that is either convincing or truly frightening.

Direction and writing are uneven throughout, with attempts at humor falling flat and some principal characters abruptly switching tone from flip and nasty to earnest and sympathetic.

Zach Galligan ("Gremlins") starts out as a jaded rich kid and evolves into a stalwart type eager to do the right thing. He's engaging in both roles, in the latter providing the shred of humanity that carries the film to its ending.

Of the considerable production talent pressed into the service of Hickox' shaky vision, Gianni Quaranta offers striking, diverse sets and Leonard Pollock creates rich, handsome costumes, particularly in the Marquis De Sade scene.

Pic never builds suspense, and free-for-all ending is merely goofy. More uninspired recycled cinema is just what the film world doesn't need. —*Daws.*

Defense Play

A Trans World Entertainment release of a Kodiak Films presentation. Produced by Wolf Schmidt. Directed by Monte Markham. Screenplay, Aubrey Solomon, Steven, Greenberg, from story by Schmidt, Stan Krantman; camera (Foto-Kem color), Timothy Galfas; supervising editor-associate producer, James Ruxin; music, Arthur B. Rubinstein; production design, Petko Kadiev; art direction, Michael Clausen; set decoration, Greg P. Oehla; sound (Ultra-Stereo), Peter Chaikin; costume design, Marjorie Bowers; special effects, Pete Slagle; assistant director, Bradley M. Gross; casting, Carol Dudley. Reviewed at Vine theater, L.A., Sept. 9, 1988. MPAA Rating: PG. Running time: 93 MIN.
Scott Denton . . . . .David Oliver
Karen Vandemeer . . . . .Susan Ursitti
Col. Mark Denton . . . . . .Monte Markham
Starkey . . . . .Eric Gilliom
Gen. Philips . . . . .William Frankfather
Norm Beltzer . . . . .Jamie McMurray
Eddie Dietz . . . .'. . . .Jack Esformes
Chief Gill . . . . .Tom Rosqui
Anton . . . . .Milos Kirek
Ann Denton . . . . .Patch Mackenzie
Prof. James Vandemeer . . .Terrance Cooper
Mrs. Vandemeer . . . . .Rutanya Alda

■Hollywood — "Defense Play" is a great picture if you enjoy looking at a computer video screen for the better part of 90 minutes.

Probably the closest thing yet to a dramatized video war game, this limp thriller about teens who become mixed up with a rocket launch, Russian spies and remote control fighting helicopters is making a quick stop in theaters before landing in its rightful home at video shops.

Gobs of stock footage of military jets and a NASA launch pad sets the stage for an SDI test flight that some Soviet spies would like to sabotage. To this end, the commies have established headquarters on a trawler offshore and enlisted one local student as an infiltrator.

Key to the Russkies' plans are several DART helicopters, 3-foot buzzflies outfitted with laser cannons that can outwit F-16s and infiltrate restricted airspace. A professor at the university physics department is in charge of the prototypes, which is how all the kids get involved in the caper.

The better part of the film truly does seem to be taken up with watching people watch computer screens, type in codes, fly a teeny chopper by remote control and so forth. Even fanatics for such things could hardly find this very entertaining, since one likes to be in charge, not just observe others playing with these serious toys.

Screenplay clearly was concocted by people who know how to compose computer commands better than they can write dialog. Monte Markham, who also plays the largest adult role, has directed to no particular effect, and entire production looks about as substantial as the little flying machines that are the objects of so much fascination here. Pic overall is as farfetched as it is dull. — *Cart.*

Karma
(SOUTH KOREAN)

A Tae Hung Production. Directed by Lee Doo-yong. Screenplay, Yun Sam-Yuk, Lee Doo-yong; camera (color) Son Hyon-Chae; editor, Lee Kyong-Ja; music, Choe Chang-Gwon; sound, Lee Jae-Woong; set design, Do Yong-U; costumes, Kwon Yu-Jin. Reviewed at Montreal World Film Festival (noncompeting), Sept. 2, 1988. Running time: 106 MIN.
With: Nam-Gung Won, Kang Soo Yeon, Kim Yong Chol, Kim Yun-Gyong, Min Bok-Ki, Tae II.

■ Montreal — Biggest selling point of this South Korean production is the look of the film. Pic's set design, costumes and photography all suggest theatrical release potential.

Look would be lost on video and the story itself could be a little too absurdist for most video markets.

Plot has a district Mandarin punishing a superstitious man who is making phalluses that are reputed to have the power of chasing spirits away from houses where they hang. The Mandarin — caught in the midst of an epidemic that is killing thousands of Koreans every day — decides to do battle with superstitions, despite the fact that he himself thinks he might have met the phallus peddler's wife in another life.

Pic has some intriguing early moments, particularly when the Mandarin is questioning his beliefs. Unfortunately, the film loses its charm during a violent emasculation scene that will hurt its potential with urban arthouses. The ending is overwrought and unsatisfying, leaving little chance that viewers outside of pic's home country will aid attendance with word-of-mouth promo. —*Cadd.*

Ghoulies II

An Empire Pictures presentation of a Charles Band production. Executive producer, Charles Band. Produced and directed by Albert Band. Screenplay, Dennis Paoli, from story by Charlie Dolan; camera (Technicolor), Sergio Salvati; editor, Barry Zetlin; music, Fuzzbee Morse; sound (Ultra-Stereo), Primiano Muratori; production design, Giovanni Natalucci; creatures design, John Buechler; stop-motion animation, David Allen Prods.; assistant director, Mauro Sacripanti; ghoulies' voices, Hal Rayle; associate producer, Frank Hildebrand; casting, Anthony Barnao. Reviewed on Vestron vidcassette, N.Y., Aug. 28, 1988. MPAA Rating: PG-13. Running time: 90 MIN.
Larry . . . . .Damon Martin
Uncle Ned . . . . .Royal Dano
Sir Nigel . . . . .Phil Fondacaro
P. Hardin . . . . .J. Downing
Nicole . . . . .Kerry Remsen
Also with: Dale Wyatt, Jon Maynard Pennell, Sasha Jenson, Starr Andreeff, William Butler, Mickey Knox, Anthony Dawson.

■ Assemblyline filmmaking (in this case, Charles Band's former stamping ground Empire Studios in Rome) is the curse of "Ghoulies II," a lame followup belatedly debuting this fall in videostores.

First pic, a shameless "Gremlins" imitation that emerged as Empire Pictures' top b.o. attraction, was a west coast-lensed horror comedy spotlighting cutesy John Buechler hand puppets. Sequel features a few more puppets and is set in the Carolinas, but lensed on gaudy sets in Rome with a nondescript cast.

A priest (British thesp Anthony Dawson) tries to destroy the little title demons, but they escape, holing up in a failing carnival show run by Royal Dano and his nephew Damon Martin. Presence of the supernatural critters perks up attendance, staving off the foreclosure efforts of meanie J. Downing, but the ghoulies start killing people, a no-no even for a Grand Guignol attraction.

Preposterous climax has the good guys conjuring up an oversize monster (it doesn't look much better than its pintsized ghoulies) to knock off the beasties.

Albert Band (father of defunct Empire's major domo Charles) directs with apparent disinterest, just cranking out another title in a production slate. These doll-like figures just aren't scary and the attempted black humor falls flat. The inherent contradiction of producing fantasy films without imagination is evident in bold relief.

Technical team, largely Italian, delivers competence within a creative vacuum. Dwarf actor Phil Fondacaro sticks out as way too talented for this material. —*Lor.*

La Maitre de Musique
(The Music Teacher)
(BELGIAN)

Produced by ATBF and K2 One (Belgian tv, Brussels). Executive producer, Jacqueline Pierreux. Directed by Gerard Corbiau. Screenplay, Corbiau, Andree Corbiau, Patrick Iratni, Christine Watton, Pierreux; camera (Fujicolor), Walther Vanden Ende;

music, Mahler, Verdi, Bellini, Mozart, Offenbach, Schubert, Schumann (extracts); voices, Jose Van Dam, Dinah Bryant, Jerome Pruett; musical interpretation by Nouvel Orchestra Symphonique of ATBF, directed by Ronald Zollman; sound, Andre Defossez; set design, Zouc Lanc; costumes, Catherine Frognier. Reviewed at Montreal World Film Festival (noncompeting), Aug. 29, 1988. Running time: 95 MIN.

With: Jose Van Dam (Joachim Dalyrac), Anne Roussel (Sophie), Philippe Volter (Jean), Sylvie Fennec (Estelle), Johan Leysen (François), Patrick Bauchau (Prince Scotti).

■ Montreal — Music, song, opera and cinema blend naturally into a totality for the screen that captivated audiences here, as the film had done on home grounds in Belgium (where it did boffo business earlier this year).

As a genuine sleeper at the Montreal fest, first-time feature-length film director Gerard Corbiau's story about an opera star who quits the stage at the height of his career, to groom a pupil of promise, is a sure winner for special arthouse audiences that eat up high culture at modest prices.

Film is a seldom-seen balance of narrative, image and music that spells class.

Corbiau centers his action during the banquet years of the European concert hall just before World War I. A famous Belgian baritone (Jose Van Dam), his voice beginning to crack, announces to disappointed fans he's leaving the stage forever, to devote his tutelage to a single pupill (Anne Roussel) with a marvelous voice.

On the way to his chateau, the celebrated master encounters a charming scoundrel (Philippe Volter) at the village market whose voice also captivates him. He also invites him to the chateau for a bit of professional polish. The trying apprenticeship for both students leaves little time for dalliance and lots of time for the audience to hear great music and appreciate the countryside as seasons pass.

A true professional, the music teacher prides discipline and concentration over psychological twists in Corbiau's storyline. The place is a perfect setting for romantic passion (which audience waits for but which never develops, despite long coach rides through woods and rain).

There will be a great singspiel at the prince's manor. The master will send his two wards into the musical ring against the protégé of the prince, a fabuously rich patron of the arts who nurses a fierce hatred for the master.

The song contest leaves the outcome in suspension (participants wear masks) until master's pupils triumph while Van Dam bows out of the story via heart crisis in a fitting but sad and beautiful ending to this escapist confection made for "Amadeus"-type audiences.

Technical credits are of high standard, dubbing of Roussel and Volter's voices undetectable. Van Dam, who does his own voice, is also an accomplished actor, having appeared most notably in role of Leporello in Joseph Losey's "Don Giovanni." —Milg.

A gauche en sortant de l'ascenseur
(Door On The Left As You Leave The Elevator)
(FRENCH)

An AMLF release of a Renn Prod./Fideline/Orly Films coproduction. Executive producer, Claude Berri. Produced by Pierre Grunstein. Directed by Edouard Molinaro. Screenplay, Gérard Lauzier, based on his play "L'Amuse gueule;" camera (Canavision, Agfa-Gavaert Eastmancolor), Robert Fraisse; editor, Nicole Gauduchon; music and songs, Murray Head; art direction, Jacques Bufnoir; sound, Daniel Brisseau, Gérard Lamps; assistant director, Catherine Molinaro; production manager, Michel Choquet. Reviewed at the Gaumont Ambassade cinema, Paris, Sept. 5, 1988. Running time: 80 MIN.

Yann . . . . Pierre Richard
Boris . . . . Richard Bohringer
Eva . . . . Emmanuelle Béart
Florence . . . . Fanny Cottençon
André . . . . Pierre Vernier
Jean-Yves . . . . Jean-Michel Dupuis
Marilda . . . . Martine Maximin
Natasha . . . . Aina Walle
First cop . . . . Michel Creton
Second cop . . . . Eric Blanc
Motorist . . . . Albert Simono

■ Paris — Bargain basement romantic farce adapted by cartoonist-screenwriter Gérard Lauzier from his own legit success of a few seasons ago, "A gauche en sortant de l'ascenseur" is fast but unfunny, wasting a talented cast on a gag machine that doesn't work.

Edouard Molinaro has fashioned a good-looking package for this mostly 1-set boulevard fluff about a successful painter (Pierre Richard) whose attempts to seduce a married woman (Fanny Cottençon) in his atelier apartment are frenetically complicated by his nextdoor neighbors, a violently jealous ne'er-do-well artist and his provocatively lovely wife (Richard Bohringer and Emmanuelle Béart).

Players do their professional best to spice up their puppet roles, but the farce mechanisms of Lauzier's plot are rusty and ill-mounted.

Sorriest waste in the cast is the promising and beautiful Béart, who has done only one film ("Date With An Angel" in America) since her César-winning (yet unconvincing) title role in Claude Berri's "Manon des sources," but still awaits the film that will put her talents to a genuine test.

Among other players Eric Blanc, a fast-rising black comic, does a quietly funny cameo as a cop trying to assess a quid pro quo situation. —Len.

Report On Pollution At The Women's Kingdom
(CHINESE)

A China Film Export & Import Corp. release of a Beijing Film Studio production. Directed by Wang Yan, Yang Lanru. Screenplay, Qian Gongle, Ye Shisheng; camera (color), Zhang Zhongping; editor, Yan; music, Gu De; set design, Shi Jiangdu. Reviewed at Montreal World Film Festival (noncompeting), Sept. 1, 1988. Running time: 102 MIN.

With: Shen Danping, Ma Congle, Tan Tianqiang, Cao Cuifen.

■ Montreal — "Report On Pollution At The Women's Kingdom" bears a theme — a woman is harassed by local villagers who are jealous of her moneymaking abilities — that is simple and would appear to have potential in urban markets.

This film, while well-made, is hardly competitive with big-budget releases like "Red Sorghum" and "King Of Children," both of which competed at Cannes.

The film's greatest asset is codirectors Wang Yan and Yang Lanru's ability to make one care for the characters. The film is as predictable as it is simplistic, but the characters are neither heroes nor villains. They are ordinary people who cannot comprehend that their idle gossip has the potential to destroy lives.

The pic should appeal to the groups with large Chinese populations and even to the Anglo-American festival and art house markets. —Cadd.

Regeneration
(CANADIAN)

A Thomas Howe & Associates release of an Intl. Heliotrope production. Produced by Tony Dean. Directed by Russel Stephens. Screenplay, Stephens; camera (color), Tobias Schliessler; editor, Shirley Claydon; set desing, Keith Groat; costumes, Jori Woodman. Reviewed at Montreal World Film Festival (Panorama Canada), Aug. 31, 1988. Running time: 87 MIN.

With: John Anderson, Marek Cieszewski, Suzanne Ristic, Dermot Hennelly, Dennis Shooter, Michael Grandley.

■ Montreal — Had writer, director Russel Stephens made "Regeneration" as a second or third film, this story of a professor who brings people back to life using only photographs could have been a marketable film with some repertory theater potential.

The plotline even includes a piece of perfect timing — someone pleading with the professor to use his computerized system to bring back Elvis Presley.

Unfortunately, Stephens came to this film straight from university film and and it's all too obvious. Pic has some well-written scenes but they are lost to hamfisted editing and poor voice synchronization. The acting, particulary by lead John Anderson, is abysmal, and almost every technical aspect of the film leads to disaster. —Cadd.

Purgatory
(AUSTRIAN-B&W)

An EPO-Film release and production. Produced by Dieter Pochlato. Directed by Wili Hengstler. Screenplay, Hengstler, Jack Unterberger; camera (b&w), Jiri Stibr; editor, Eliska Stibrova; music, Karl-Heinz Miklin; sound, Walter Fiklocki; set design, Andrea Jaufer; costumes, Renee Diamand. Reviewed at Montreal World Film Festival (Cinema of Today and Tomorrow), Sept. 2, 1988. Running time: 90 MIN.

With: Jurgen Goslar, Bobby Prem, Jeanette Muhlmann, Kathi Wressnig, Ingrid Ettelmayer, Hartmut Nolte, Peter Uray, Ute Radkohl, Gigi Tapella.

■ Montreal — "Purgatory" would appear to have some European potential in theatrical release but pic looks to be too gritty for most American arthouses. Some American video action is possible but only in specialty venues.

Pic is the true story of Austrian lifer Jack Unterberger, who wrote a book about his criminal past while serving his time in prison. The story is hardly original, touching all the hard-luck bases. Unterberger was abandoned by his prostitute mother who appears to have been molested by her father, who then gets to raise Jack in his own image.

From there he goes on to be a ward of the state, spending time in foster homes and prisons, eventually ending up with a life sentence for assaulting a woman. Although we've seen all this before director Wili Hengstler does some interesting things with black and white film. The hopelessness of Unterberger's life is graphically articulated by the style if not by the rather weak screenplay.

That style won't help arouse viewer empathy. The Unterberger character comes across as mean-spirited rather than as a victim of social coincidence. While it might add to the critical appreciation it probably won't do much for audiences looking to find some sympathy for Unterberger, particularly within the urban-liberal arthouse market. —Cadd.

Noi Vivi
(We The Living)
(ITALIAN-B&W)

An Angelika Films release of a Scalera Films (Rome) production. Restored version by Duncan Scott Prods., in association with Henry Mark Holzer, Erika Holzer. Directed by Goffredo Alessandrini. Screenplay, Anton Giulio Majano, based on novel by Ayn Rand; adaptation by Corrado Alvaro, Orio Vergani; camera (b&w), Giuseppe Caracciolo; editor, Eraldo Da Roma; music, Renzo Rossellini; art direction, Andrea Beloborodoff, Giorgio Abkhasi, Amleto Bonetti; costumes Rosi Gori; sound, Piero Cavazzuti, Tullo Parmegiani; assistant director, Giorgio Cristallini. Reviewed at USA Cinemas screening room, Aug. 30, 1988. (In the Boston Film Festival.) Running time: 170 MIN.

Kira Argounova . . . . Alida Valli
Leo Kovalensky . . . . Rossano Brazzi
Andrei Taganov . . . . Fosco Giachetti
Tishenko . . . . Giovanni Grasso
Pavel Syerov . . . . Emilio Cigoli
Comrade Sonia . . . . Cesarina Gheraldi
Victor Dunaev . . . . Mario Pisu

■ **Boston — Shot in 1942 in Fascist Italy, this adaptation of Ayn Rand's anticommunist novel "We The Living" turns out to be grand and lavish entertainment, with some real commercial possibilities on the art/specialty circuit.**

Once the viewer gets over the anomaly of screen Russians saying things like "bueno sera" and "prego," it is difficult not to get caught up in the intense romantic triangle at the center of the story.

The film concerns Kira Argounova, played by a 21-year-old Alida Valli whose looks impress as much as her already apparent acting skills. Kira and her family return to Petrograd in the early 1920s, with Kira entering school to pursue a career as an engineer. She becomes involved with Leo Kovalensky (26-year-old Rossano Brazzi), the son of an aristocrat who is trying to escape questioning from the GPU, the secret police.

As the story unfolds, Kira becomes Leo's mistress in the approved Rand style, making her own choices freely rather than merely being seduced. When Leo comes down with TB and is denied proper treatment because he is not a Communist Party member, Kira raises the money by having an affair with Andrei Taganov (Fosco Giachetti), a GPU leader who is at the university. Film builds to climactic confrontation when Andrei must arrest Leo for black market operations

and learns about Kira's real feelings.

Director Goffredo Alessandrini works equally well in intimate scenes, such as when Kira and Leo are discovered together in bed trying to flee the country, and in the large moments such as the parties and a scene, seeming somewhat odd given the context, in a nightclub.

His only annoying tic is a repeated taste for cutesy transitions, such as showing one character stubbing out a cigaret in an ashtray, then cutting to another character removing a cigar from a different ashtray.

Film was a big-budget production for Scalera Films in the midst of the war, and it received the Volpi Cup at the 1942 Venice Film Festival. Fascist authorities quickly got wise that the film's anti-authoritarian message directed at the communists could just as easily be meant for them, and it was suppressed five months after its release.

"We The Living" was rediscovered 20 years ago when Erika and Henry Mark Holzer, Ayn Rand's attorneys, began a search for the film at her request. Although made without her legal permission, she apparently liked the film when she finally saw it.

Unlike the 1949 Hollywood version of "The Fountainhead," "We The Living" holds up well, and must be considered an important rediscovery. —*Kimm.*

VENICE REVIEWS

Haunted Summer

A Cannon Group release and production. Executive producers, Menahem Golan, Yoram Globus. Produced by Martin Poll. Directed by Ivan Passer. Screenplay, Lewis John Carlino, from novel by Anne Edwards; camera (Telecolor), Giuseppe Rotunno; editor, Cesare D'Amico, Richard Fields; music, Christopher Young; production design, Stephen Grimes; costumes, Gabrielle Pescucci; sound, Drew Kunin; associate producers, John Thompson, Mario Cotone; production manager, Attilio Viti; assistant directors, Carlos Quintero, Mauro Sacripanti; casting, Jose Villaverde. Reviewed at Venice Film Festival (competing), Sept. 5, 1988. MPAA Rating: R. Running time: **115 MIN.**
Lord Byron . . . . Philip Anglim
Claire Clairmont . . . . Laura Dern
Mary Wollstonecraft Godwin . . Alice Krige
Percy Shelley . . . . Eric Stoltz
Dr. Polidori . . . . Alex Winter

■ **Venice — Given that Ken Russell's all-too-recent "Gothic" didn't set any boxoffice records, it's really puzzling that producer Martin Poll, director Ivan Passer and the Cannon Group should have decided to remake the pic so soon, and to so little effect.**

Langorous tale of a group of exiled English intellectuals of the early 19th century involved in drug-induced sex games in a lakeside chateau was handled in livelier fashion by Russell, and the new version

looks to face a dim boxoffice future.

What's fatally lacking here is any feeling of passion or eroticism, and that's crucial to this tale of scandalous relationships. The poet Shelley was, after all, involved simultaneously with half-sisters Mary and Claire, and the latter had also been the mistress of the bisexual Lord Byron, whose present lover, a broodingly jealous doctor, is also in residence. Yet given this combustible material, all Passer can come up with are a couple of excessively long and conventionally filmed love scenes notable only for their lack of excitement.

Part of the trouble may lie in the casting, and it seems odd indeed to give such quintessentially English roles to American actors, given the wealth of thesping talent in Britain right now. The one exception is South African-born Alice Krige, who gives a delicate performance as Mary, but standout in the acting stakes is Laura Dern, giving another beautiful performance as the pregnant Claire. Alex Winter has moments as Polidori, forever being humiliated by his lover Byron, but both Philip Anglim as Byron and Eric Stoltz as Shelley seem insuffi-

ciently charismatic for their romantic roles.

Film is a visual treat, thanks to Giuseppe Rotunno's camerawork and the production design of Stephen Grimes, but in the end pretty pictures are no substitute for drama, and here the film is sadly lacking. A more forthright approach to the sexual relationships might have given the film a stronger center, but after an early scene in which Eric Stoltz gambols full-frontally in a stream, nudity and eroticism are avoided.

Nor are the opium-induced nightmares that eventually inspired Mary, as Mary Shelley, to write "Frankenstein," very excitingly handled: Ken Russell was much more adept than Passer at bringing the nightmares to life.

Lewis John Carlino's screenplay, based on a novel by Anne Edwards, was apparently much admired by the late John Huston, who had wanted to film this project before illness forced him to withdraw. However, the screenplay is another of the film's major problems, being a mixture of impossibly "poetic" dialog of the National Theater variety, and banal anachronisms. The actors can be forgiven for having trouble with some of these lines.

There is yet another version of this story in the pipeline coming this time from Spain, but meanwhile the best film about the inspiration for "Frankenstein" remains the brief prolog to James Whale's "Bride Of Frankenstein" (1935) in which Elsa Lanchester was so memorable as Mary Shelley. —*Strat.*

Burning Secret
(BRITISH-U.S.- WEST GERMANY)

A Vestron Pictures release of a NFH Ltd. and CLG Films production, in association with BA Produktion. Executive producers, William J. Quigley, M.J. Peckos. Produced by Norma Heyman, Eberhard Junkersdorf, Carol Lynn Greene. Directed by Andrew Birkin. Screenplay, Birkin, from short story "Brennendes Geheimnis" by Stefan Zweig; camera (color), Ernest Day; editor, Paul Green; music, Hans Zimmer; production design, Bernd Lepel; costumes, Barbara Baum, Monica Jacobs; Vestron supervising producer, Ron Carr, sound, Chris Price; production managers, Wolfram Kohtz, Jan Kadlec; assistant director, Vladimir Michalek; casting, Mary Selway, Bridget Gilbert, Miroslav Vostiar. Reviewed at Venice Film Festival, (competing), Sept. 7, 1988. Running time: **106 MIN.**
Sonya . . . . Faye Dunaway
The Baron . . . . Klaus Maria Brandauer
Edmund . . . . David Eberts
The Father . . . . Ian Richardson

■ **Venice — With its intriguing story of a mother's near-adultery as seen through the impressionable eyes of her 12-year-old son, coupled with the elegant setting of post-World War I Austria in winter, "Burning Secret" should find class audiences in quality theaters the world over.**

First-time director Andrew Birkin (brother of France-based actress

Jane Birkin) has adapted a Stefan Zweig short story set in 1919 and previously filmed in Germany in 1933 by Robert Siodmak. Drama has some of the same elements

Original Film: Brennendes Geheimnis
(GERMAN-B&W)

A Tonal-Universal production. Directed by Robert Siodmak. Screenplay, Friedrich Kohner, based on Stefan Zweig's story; camera (b&w), Baberske and Angst. Featuring Willi Forst, Hilde Wagener, Ernst Joachim Schaufus, Hans Richter, Alfred Beierle, Ernest Dumske. Reviewed in Berlin, March 29, 1933.

found in Zweig's more famous story, "Letter From An Unknown Woman," sublimely filmed in Hollywood in 1948 by Max Ophüls: a woman jeopardizes her marriage and her position in society — and even the health and well-being of her son — in the pursuit of a reckless love affair.

In this case the woman is Sonya (Dunaway), elegant wife of a stuffy diplomat (Ian Richardson) far older than she. When their young son, who suffers severely from asthma, is sent for treatment at a sanitorium in the mountains, the mother accompanies him and the pair check in at a luxury resort hotel (paralleling Louis Malle's "Murmur Of The Heart").

On the first morning, the son meets Baron Alexander Maria von Hauenschild (Brandauer), a charming veteran of the war, still nursing a bayonet wound which has made part of his body symbolically insensitive. The impressionable boy is instantly drawn to this man who is able to talk to him in the way his aloof father never has. It's a while before he realizes the Baron is using him to get closer to his mother.

Sonya, whose loveless life is plain to see, is quite willing to seize the opportunity of a passionate love affair which is only constrained by the constant presence of her innocent, inquisitive son. Drama reaches its climax on New Year's Eve when the boy discovers his mother and the Baron together and is jolted into awareness of the real situation.

Although the material is a little slight by today's standards, the drama works thanks to the flawless performances. Faye Dunaway is coolly stylish and yet passionate — and loving towards her son — as the woman on the brink of a love affair. Brandauer brings a touch of menace to his charming character to great effect. Young David Eberts (son of former Goldcrest exec Jake Eberts) is a find as the trusting youngster whose trust is betrayed.

The production was filmed entirely in Czechoslovakia, on locations in Prague (doubling for Vienna) and Marienbad. Ernest Day's camerawork and Bernd Lepel's production design make for a lush background to the drama, and the splendid old Hotel Esplanade, retitled the Winter Garden for the film, is a star in itself.

This is an old-fashioned romantic melodrama of the type once referred to as "a woman's picture." Vestron will have to tap into that kind of audience, predominately middle-aged and older, to get the best results. —*Strat.*

Trena Di Panna
(Milk Train)
(ITALIAN)

A Medusa Distribuzione release of an Azzurra Film-Reteitalia production. Produced by Claudia Mori, Luciano Luna. Directed by Andrea De Carlo. Screenplay, De Carlo; camera (color), Alfio Contini; editor, Ugo De Rossi; music, Ludovico Einaudi; sound, Graziano Ruzzeddu; production managers, Angelo Zemella, Stefano Rolla; assistant director, Luca Lachin. reviewed at Venice Film Festival (Horizons), Sept. 7, 1988. Running time: **114 MIN.**

Giovanni	Sergio Rubini
Marsha Mellows	Carol Alt
Jill	Christina Marsillach
Rada	Rosalinda
Tina	Irene Grazioli
Ron	Maurizio Faulisi

■ **Venice** — "Milk Train" is simple comedy based on the "Crocodile Dundee" formula: take a naive character out of his element and plunk him down in New York City. Result in this case is a witless affair which is unconvincingly in almost every detail.

Giovanni is an Italian musician who arrives in the Big Apple with only his electric guitar, which is soon stolen by a couple of muggers. He manages to get a job as waiter in a bizarre Italian restaurant and, later, a better job as an Italian teacher in a language school, somewhat surprising since his command of English remains tenuous.

This is a New York known only to naive Italian filmmakers, a city where most people speak Italian (even the black desk clerk at a scrungy Times Square hotel) or, if they don't, they speak a foul-mouthed English conjured up only by a screenwriter with the most limited vocabulary.

In the leading role, Sergio Rubini is another in a seemingly endless line of gormless Italian comics, some of whom are funny and charming. Unfortunately, on the strength of this effort, Rubini is neither.

Pic has remote international possibilities despite presence of superstar model Carol Alt in the cast, but deserves full marks for speed of production: in one scene the hero walks past a cinema advertising the opening of "Big" on June 4.
—*Strat.*

Il Bacio Di Giuda
(The Kiss Of Judas)
(ITALIAN)

An Istituto Luce release of a Cooperativa Alfea Cinematografica production, in association with RAI 3. Produced and directed by Paolo Benvenuti. Screenplay, Benvenuti,

Marcella Niccolini, Gianni Menon; camera (Afgacolor), Aldo Di Marcantonio; editor, Mario Benvenuti; music, Stefano Bambini, Andrea Di Sacco; costumes, Marcella Niccolini, Damiano Sini; consultant, Roberto Filippini. Reviewed at Venice Film Festival (Critics Week), Sept. 5, 1988. Running time: **87 MIN.**

The Nazarene	Carlo Bachi
Judas Iscariot	Gorgio Algranti
Nicodemuś	Emidio Simini
Mary Magdalene	Marina Barsotti
Simon Peter	Pio Gianelli
John	Nicola Checchi

■ **Venice** — As if one controversial film about Jesus Christ in a year wasn't enough, here's another. This micro-budgeted Italian variation on the Gospel story is controversial in that it justifies the betrayal by Judas, seen as Christ's closest friend, on the grounds that it was indispensable for the salvation of the human race.

Pros and cons in Italy may be a local factor, but stolidly made pic is unlikely to travel.

The film opens with the infamous kiss and betrayal itself, then moves back in time to cover the last few days of Christ's life on earth, culminating in the Last Supper. No crucifixion scene here.

Film is slowly paced, and the minimal score leaves for long passages of silence. Camerawork is murky, especially in interiors. Acting is reverential.

A key scene has Judas searching through the scriptures to find the prophesies about the death and resurrection of the Messiah. Point here is that Christ *wills* his friend to perform the act of betrayal, making Judas the only one of the 12 to understand that the Master *had* to die to fulfill his destiny.

Production is minimal, but effective on its restricted level. However, recollections of Pier Paolo Pasolini's Christ film "The Gospel According To St. Matthew" (1964) confirm that Pasolini came closer than anyone in successfully "modernizing" the Gospel story. "The Kiss Of Judas" looks like ending up merely as a footnote. —*Strat.*

Let's Get Lost
(DOCU-B&W)

A Little Bear Inc. production. Executive producer, Nan Bush. Produced and directed by Bruce Weber. Camera (b&w), Jeff Preiss; editor, Angelo Corrao; music, Chet Baker; associate producers, Itaka Schlubach-Hicks, Steven Cohen. Reviewed at Venice Film Festival (Critics Week), Sept. 7, 1988. Running time: **119 MIN.**

With: Chet Baker, Carol Baker, Vera Baker, Paul Baker, Dean Baker, Missy Baker, William Claxton, Ruth Young, Diane Vavra.

■ **Venice** — Jazz fans, and lovers of the sublime musical artistry of the late Chet Baker, who died in May after a fall from an Amsterdam hotel room, will be disappointed, even angered, by this "tribute."

Bruce Weber's film is more interested in exploring Baker's tangled personal life than in his music.

This documentary centers on a

lengthy interview Baker gave the film crew a few months before his death. His slurred, hesitant speech suggests he was under the influence of drugs during the interview, and he admits his preference for a cocaine/heroin mixture. Other interviewees include his mother, wife Carol, children and two mistresses, Diane Vavra and Ruth Young.

All too frequently, extremely personal questions are put to the participants, who plead to be allowed not to answer, or that their reply not be used. Baker's mother is asked if he was a disappointment as a son, and after much hesitation admits he was; his wife is quizzed about the other women in his life, and reluctantly replies, requesting to be off the record.

Baker himself is disarmingly frank about his relationships, and about his Italian prison sentence in the early '60s. Apart from the interview, he's seen during a recording session and at the 1987 Cannes Film Festival, where he gives a haunting rendition of "Almost Blue" to a hushed audience.

Vintage footage shows the young Baker, looking strikingly like James Dean, in a '50s tv show and, later, on a Steve Allen program from 1968. He's also glimpsed in a Columbia quickie, "Hell's Horizon," and in a couple of Italian films. A scene from Metro's "All The Fine Young Cannibals," in which Robert Wagner played a jazz trumpeter inspired by Baker, also is included.

All too often the music is insensitively handled. Just as Baker begins to play "My Funny Valentine," a voiceover interrupts, and this happens time and again through the film. It's as if the filmmakers didn't care at all about Baker's music.

It adds up to a sad study of a gifted and instinctive young musician who died too young after living life in a very fast lane. Chet Baker deserves a more sensitive tribute than Bruce Weber provides in "Let's Get Lost."

Film's production company Little Bear Inc. should not be confused with French director Bertrand Tavernier's production company of the same name.—*Strat.*

Asik Kerib
(SOVIET)

A Gruzia Film production. Directed by Sergei Paradjanov, David Abashidze. Screenplay, Georgi Badridze; camera (color), Albert Javurian; music, Zhavanshir Kuliev, art direction, Shota Gogolashvili, Georgi Meschishvili, Nikolas Zandukeli. Reviewed at Venice Film Festival (Special Events), Aug. 29, 1988. Running time: **90 MIN.**

With: Yuri Mgoian, Veronique Matonidze, Levan Natroshvili, Sofico Chaureli.

■ **Venice** — The new film by Armenian director Sergei Paradjanov (co-direction credit to David Abashidze) carries on the sophisticated folklore for which the director is known

("The Color Of Pomegranates," "The Legend Of Suram Fortress") in a haunting love story.

Stylistically very close to "Suram Fortress," though using a little more camera movement than its predecessor, "Asik Kerib" should delight Paradjanov fans, who are grouped around the more discerning arthouses.

Story, based on a Lermontov tale, describes the love of a handsome young wandering minstrel, or "ashug," for the daughter of a rich Turkish merchant. Asik Kerib, the hero, is poor but can sing and play the saaz (Turkish balaika) wonderfully. When the girl's father angrily snubs his gift of rose petals, he embarks on seven years of roaming the Caucasian countryside to seek his fortune.

His wondrous adventures, recounted in Paradjanov's inimitable style of motionless tableaux figures in ritual poses, include playing at weddings of the blind and the deaf, visiting a profaned convent, and being aided by St. George on his white horse and two guardian angels. In the end, he returns home and embraces his blind mother and fiancée.

The moving camera brings still and almost-still images to life, creating a magical, exotic world in which every gesture, look, and detail in makeup and costume vibrates with significance. Even if the viewer often can't grasp the meaning of surrounding details, film sweeps along on a magic carpet ride of wondrous nights.

Unforgettable are the fabulous clothes and objects used in the film; what isn't an authentic museum piece is reconstructed with maniacal precision. The hero, with his shaven head and heavily made-up eyes, is an enigmatic figure with hypnotic charm. Lensed with more free-wheeling fantasy than cash, pic has a basic richness and sumptuousness that few Western megaproductions can boast.

This fable was shot in all three of the Trans-Caucasian republics — Georgia, Armenia and Azerbaijan. The one jarring note is the Georgian voiceover that offers essential explanation to supplement the dialog in Armenian dialect.

Music by Zhavanshir Kuliev is an elaborate, at times obsessive complement to the visuals. —*Yung.*

Eldorado
(The Midas Touch)
(HUNGARIAN)

A Hunnia Film Studio, Mafilm, production. Directed by Géza Beremenyi. Screenplay, Beremenyi; camera (Eastmancolor), Sandor Kardos; editor, Teri Losonci; music, Ferenc Darvas; production design, Gyula Pauer; sound, Istvan Sipos; production manager, Andras Ozorai. Reviewed at Venice Film Festival (competing), Sept. 1, 1988. Running time: **110 MIN.**

Monori	Karoly Eperjes
Berci	Peter Andorai
Mrs. Monori	Judit Pogany

Marika . . . . Eniko Eszenyi
Also with: Pal Sztarenki, Geza Balkay, Barnabas Toth, Andras Papcsik, Lili Monori, Peter Gothar.

■ **Venice** — Spanning the decade between the end of World War II and the uprising of 1956, "The Midas Touch" centers on a rugged individual involved in the black market and in the illegal hoarding of gold. Writer-director Géza Bereményi creates a powerful central character, but stylistic overkill too often swamps the production.

Fest kudos are a possibility, with theatrical chances iffy.

Tale is set in Budapest's Teleki Square, site of a large market where, after the war, Monori (powerfully played by Karoly Eperjes) is a leading force. Almost oblivious to the political changes taking place, he hoards gold which, he is convinced, will solve all problems. Indeed, anything can be bought and sold in the market, including women and even a killer on the run.

Monori is devoted to his grandson, but despises the husband of his daughter, and pays him to go away. Under the new Communist regime, secret police come to search for the hidden gold, even planting dollars in order to trap Monori who, however, is too smart for them. When the child is taken ill during a diptheria epidemic (startling scenes of vast numbers of corpses laid out in an ill-equipped hospital), Monori's gold does, in fact, buy his grandson's life.

During the Soviet invasion that followed the 1956 uprising, however, Monori's attempts to escape with the gold and his grandson come to a tragic conclusion.

There's a strong story here, but it's all too often swamped by the frenetic direction and camerawork. Too many scenes involve vertigo-inducing images shot at odd angles by a hand-held camera, sometimes at ground level. The point, presumably, is to present the chaos of life in the market and its environs, but it's an ugly and audience-alienating device, especially when allied to a noisy soundtrack.

When Bereményi keeps his camera still and lets his fine actors carry the film, the impact is far greater than in the selfconsciously clever material he seems to prefer.

This cinematic overkill apart, the film has considerable qualities and several finely staged scenes, such as an encounter between Monori and his second son-in-law amid huge snowdrifts. Some scenes, such as the abrupt suicide of a man after listening to a sentimental song, pack a punch, but a particularly nasty sequence in which Monori brutalizes a horse for no apparent reason should be excised.

Sense of period seems imprecise at times, but the film comes into its own in the final third with newsreel footage of the savage fighting in the streets of Budapest in 1956 intercut with the personal story of Monori, stricken with severe appendicitis, trying to escape with his gold and his grandson. —*Strat.*

Komitas
(WEST GERMAN)

A Margarita Woskanjan Filmproduktion, in collaboration with WDR, SFB, Channel 4, and the Alex Manoogian Cultural Fund. Produced by Margarita Woskanjan. Directed by Dan Askarian. Screenplay, Askarian; camera (color), Giorgos Arvanitis, Martin Gressman; editor, René Perraudin, Marlon Regentrop; music, Komitas, Donizetti, Teyra; production design, Jürgen Kiebach, Michael Poladian; costumes, Bernhard Mühl; sound, Michael Bootz; production manaager, Bessie Voudoury. Reviewed at Venice Film Festival (noncompeting), Sept. 5, 1988. Running time: **96 MIN.**
Komitas . . . . Samuel Ovasapian
Terlomesian . . . . Onig Saadetian
Pupil . . . . Margarita Woskanjan
Katholikos . . . . . , . Rev. Yegishe Mangikian
Armenian
  Monk . . . . Rev. Gegham Khatcherian
Nurse . . . . Sybille Vogelsang
Also with: Mohammad Tahmasebi, Eskander Abadil, Kaweh Jaryani, Sonja Askarian.

(In Armenian)

■ **Venice** — **Though made in West Germany, this Armenian film is inspired by the life of a famous monk and musician, Komitas (1869-1935), who was so profoundly affected by the 1915 massacres in his homeland that he spent the last 20 years of his life in mental hospitals.**

Film is a poetic hymn to Armenian culture, and of a very specialized nature.

This isn't a straight biography of Komitas. The inspiration seems to be the work of Armenian-born Soviet lenser Sergei Paradjanov, whose visual style writer-director Dan Askarian emulates. This means ultra-slow pacing, as the camera pans across landscapes or walls or paintings, or people, often in middle-distance, in traditional costume involved in religious or cultural rituals.

Much of this is exceedingly lovely, and the appeal for exiled Armenians the world over will be significant; other audiences, outside a limited arthouse crowd, will find the film too obscure and too lacking in conventional narrative. It should have a loyal following.

Underlying drama is the tragedy of the massacres, still officially denied by Turkey, in which 75% of the Armenian population of Asia Minor were slaughtered.

Frequent use is made here of original music by Komitas, who's seen at first as a teacher and later as a man broken by the knowledge of the fate suffered by his people.

Armenian dialog is very sparely used. Pic makes for a beautiful, sad and rather remote experience. —*Strat.*

Appuntamento A Liverpool
(Appointment In Liverpool)
(ITALIAN)

An Istituto Luce Italnoleggio Cinematografica release of a Numero Uno Intl. production. Produced by Claudio Bonivento. Directed by Marco Tullio Giordana. Screenplay, Giordana, Leone Colonna, Luciano Manuzzi; camera (Telecolor), Roberto Forges Davanzati; editor, Claudio Di Mauro; music, Carlo Crivelli; production design, Carlo Gervasi; sound, Gianni Zampagni; production manager, Roberto Onorati. Reviewed at Venice Film Festival (Horizons), Sept. 2, 1988. Running time: **97 MIN.**
Caterina . . . . Isabella Ferrari
British Police Inspector . . . . . . John Steiner
Mother . . . . Valeria Ciangottini
The Hooligan . . . . Nigel Court
Tiziana . . . . Roberta Lena
The Asian . . . . Marne Maitland
The Mechanic . . . . Ugo Conti
Italian Commissioner . . Vittorio Amandola
Hooligans . . . . Laurence Flaherty,
James Edward Sampson

■ **Venice** — **A self-important but dramatically fuzzy revenge pic, "Appointment In Liverpool" concerns Catarina, a teenage girl who was a witness when her beloved father was one of the Italian football fans killed at a stadium in Brussels in 1985 when British supporters of the Liverpool soccer club rioted.**

Catarina is haunted by a nightmare in which she sees her father's killer strike the fatal blow.

She's visited by a Liverpool police inspector (who, incredibly, speaks perfect Italian, one of the film's many gaping flaws) and among the photos he shows her, she recognizes the man from her dream.

So, she chucks in her job and drives her father's car to Liverpool seeking revenge.

What follows will be almost farcical for anyone expecting a realistic treatment of the young Italian girl's experiences in the northern British city, once home to The Beatles. Details such as a hotel which from the outside looks tiny but which inside has giant — but filthy — rooms will cause British audiences, at least, to scoff. Also weird is a Spanish maid who joins Caterina during the night claiming the hotel's West Indian manager is always having sex with her; the monosyllabic Asian (vet actor Marne Maitland) from whom Caterina buys a gun; and the character of the English cop, with his appalling dress sense and his totally un-English style and persona.

Maybe the film was intended as a fantasy, but even so it trivializes the tragedy of the football riot with its inane revenge plot. Climax, with Catarina facing her father's killer, gun in hand, only to discover that he's the father of a cute little girl, adds the final banal touch.

Isabella Ferrari sleepwalks through her role as the breaved heroine and Valeria Ciangottini fails to convince as the mother who seems to be well-heeled yet is willing to join her daughter in a Liverpool hotel room so sordid that the health department would have long since closed the place down. —*Strat.*

TORONTO REVIEWS

Spike Of Bensonhurst

A Film Dallas Pictures release. Produced by David Weisman, Nelson Lyon. Executive producer, Sam Grogg. Coproducer, Mark Silverman. Directed by Paul Morrissey. Screenplay, Alan Bowne, Morrissey; camera (color), Steven Fierberg; editor, Stan Salfas; music, Coati Mundi; costumes, Barbara Dente; production design, Stephen McCabe; casting, Leonard Finger. Reviewed at Toronto Festival of Festivals, Sept. 8, 1988. MPAA Rating: R. Running time: **101 MIN.**
Spike Fumo . . . . Sasha Mitchell
Baldo Cacetti . . . . Ernest Borgnine
Sylvia Cacetti . . . . Anne DeSalvo
Congresswoman . . . . Sylvia Miles
Helen Fumo . . . . Geraldine Smith
Bandana's Mother . . . . Antonia Rey
Bandana . . . . Rick Aviles
Angel . . . . Maria Patillo
India . . . . Talisa Soto
Also with: Chris Anthony Young, Mario Todisco, Rodney Harvey, Frank Adonis, Frankie Gio, Robert Compono, Tony Goodstone, Justin Lazard.

■ **Toronto** — **Paul Morrissey's absurdist comedy about a headstrong young rebel amongst Brooklyn mafiosi will inevitably court comparisons to Jonathan Demme's "Married To The Mob" — and they deserve to be favorable.**

Morrissey's foray into the commercial mainstream does go sporadically *fazool*, but his simpatico with the passions of Gotham's ethnically circumscribed tribes enables him to floridly distort the conventions of mob, boxing and turf-war pics for some quick laughs.

Whether or not Film Dallas will be able to muster the marketing muscle to invade the boxoffice territory Orion took with Demme's widely overpraised sleight-of-hand, and whether critics will be as tolerant of Morrissey's blunders and excesses as they were with "Married To The Mob" will determine the fate of "Spike Of Bensonhurst."

Spike Fumo (Sasha Mitchell) doesn't want to end up like his father, a loser-at-life mafia soldier who's taking a rap in Sing-Sing for Bensonhurst nabe mob boss Baldo Cacetti (Ernest Borgnine). The tough, good-looking kid aspires to boxing glory, and he's willing to occasionally throw a club fight to Puerto Rican pugilists from Red Hook when Borgnine's boys deem that it's not his night.

Borgnine, a stand-up guy, is supporting Spike's foulmouthed lesbian mother and the rest of the Fumo family while dad does his time in the pen. Borgnine has fatherly affection for Spike until the boxer gets romantically involved with Angel (Maria Patillo) the don's feisty blond princess of a daughter.

Like all respectable middle-class fathers, the mafioso wants his daughter to marry a college grad with a future. Spike's future, as Borgnine sees it, is in numbers running and leg-breaking to ensure smooth running of his various enterprises.

These include bootleg videostores and drug dealing, under the protection of a clownish, coke-snorting congresswoman (Sylvia Miles) whose son's bar mitzvah Borgnine dutifully attends. When Spike won't break off with the don's daughter he's banished from Bensonhurst and moves to Red Hook to live and train with Puerto Rican boxer Bandana (Rick Aviles), his wacky-wise mother (Antonia Ray) and beautiful sister India (Talisa Soto).

Soon Spike is the pending poppa of two babies in two neighborhoods. The hero works out of his jam only by making the most unlikely of career moves.

Morrissey works this turf for both broad gags and dart-like lampooning of the mobsters' bourgeois inclinations. The Brooklyn of "Spike Of Bensonhurst" veers between a romanticized ideal of the Italian conclave as a haven of self-regulated order (where teens do old-country folk dances to new wave music outdoors at the pizza parlor) and a gritty, naturalistic portrayal of a squalid, anarchic Puerto Rican barrio.

Sasha Mitchell's marble-mouthed rendering of the swaggering hero makes Spike a believable bridge between these two worlds, and Borgnine turns in one of his best recent turns as the soft-hearted mobster losing a farcical fight to keep his own house in order. The speech rhythms and mannerisms are unerringly on target and provide most of the film's best laughs.

Morrissey fails to rein in some of his caricatures and tends to pile the ethnic gags pretty high on the plate. An incessant soundtrack by the pop group Coati Mundi is irritatingly overused, as if the producers lacked full confidence in the strength of the narrative. Cinematography lends an air of playful splashiness appropriate to the carryings on.—*Rich.*

Hellbound: Hellraiser II
(BRITISH-U.S.)

A New World Pictures release of a Film Futures production. Produced by Christopher Figg. Executive producers, Christopher Webster, Clive Barker. Directed by Tony Randel. Screenplay Peter Atkins, based on story by Barker; camera (color), Robin Vidgeon; music, Christopher Young; production design, Mike Buchanan; sound, John Midgley. Reviewed at Toronto Festival of Festivals, Sept. 9, 1988. Running time: **96 MIN.**

With: Clare Higgins, Ashley Laurence, Ken Cranham, Imogen Boorman, William Hope,

Doug Bradley.

■ **Toronto** — "Hellbound: Hellraiser II" is a campy, gore-soaked horror tale with technically first-rate effects sufficiently shocking to pose censorship problems in those international markets that have low tolerance for the outer limits of slash 'n' gash fare.

It should go over as a specialty item in the North American bloodbath market and is suited to after-midnight "event" screenings, which was its context at the Toronto Festival of Festivals.

With marginal action and scattershot storytelling technique, helmer Tony Randel returns to the off-the-wall tale of a psychotic psychiatrist's long struggle to get the better of something called the Lament Configuration, a kind of demonic, silver-filigreed Rubik's Cube whose solution opens the transdimensional doors into a parallel world of sinful pleasure and unspeakably hellish pain.

This fiendish shrink takes a special interest in a new patient, Kristy, whose family was massacred in appropriately gruesome fashion by box-sprung flesh-eating ghouls called Cenobites. The demented sawbones has a whole cellar full of demento patients whom he feeds to these very hungry hellraisers.

As Kristy and the shrink head toward the big showdown in Hades, the movie unfolds with a tableau of can-you-top-this gross-outs revolting enough to provoke walkouts even by the strong of stomach. "Hellraiser II" is a maggotty carnival of mayhem, mutation and dismemberment, awash in blood and recommended only for those who thrive on such junk. —*Rich.*

Earth Girls Are Easy
(BRITISH)

A Vestron Pictures release (in U.S.) of an Earth Girls Are Easy production. Produced by Tony Garnett. Directed by Julien Temple. Screenplay, Julie Brown, Charlie Coffey, Terrence E. McNally; camera (color), Oliver Stapleton; editor, Richard Halsey; music, Nile Rodgers; production design, Dennis Gasner; sound, Anna Behlmer. Reviewed at Toronto Festival of Festivals, Sept. 9, 1988. MPAA Rating: PG. Running time: **100 MIN.**

Julie	Geena Davis
Mac	Jeff Goldblum
Candy	Julie Brown
Wibok	Jim Carrey
Zeebo	Damon Wayans
Ted	Charles Rocket
Pool boy	Michael McKean

■ **Toronto** — "Earth Girls Are Easy," a dizzy, glitzy fish-out-of-water farce about three horny aliens on the make in L.A., figures to avoid the dismal boxoffice fate of Julien Temple's underappreciated new wave musical about England's hip '50s underground scene, "Absolute Beginners."

Temple's splashy new entertainment is not as affecting as that ambitious 1985 film and lacks its serious socio-political subtext, but its

reckless escapism and bawdy energy are a good bet to fill seats and introduce new audiences to an inventive filmmaker.

Originally made for De Laurentiis Entertainment Group, film is being released by Vestron Pictures instead.

Julie (Geena Davis), a gorgeous Valley Girl, works as a manicurist in a high-tech beauty salon operated by Candy (Julie Brown) a Val-Queen supreme who likes good times and good sex. Julie is not getting much of the latter because her philandering live-in physician fiancé Ted (Charles Rocket), is too busy playing "Dr. Love" with other gals.

Meanwhile in outer space, three aliens who look like tie-dyed werewolves are wandering around our solar system going bonkers with randiness. In keeping with the film's hot-pastel, contempo-trash design motif, their spacecraft looks like the inside of a pinball machine. When it lands in Julie's swimming pool, the broken-hearted girl who's just broken off with her nogoodnik lover takes it for an oversized hair dryer.

Julie brings this gruesome threesome to Candy's beauty parlor for a complete "makeover." They emerge as three hairless hunky dudes: the captain, Jeff Goldblum and two flaked-out crewman, Jim Carrey and Damon ("he turned out black") Wayans. The two val-gals and their alien "dates" take off for a weekend of L.A. nightlife, where the visitors' smooth adaptation to Coast culture is intended by Temple and his screenwriters to affectionately skewer Tinseltown lifestyles and L.A.'s pre-fab urban landscape.

The aliens, employing a time-honored sci-fi stunt, learn English via instant mimickry and spout tv junk-jargon at every opportunity. They also are quick studies in disco dancing and piano playing, but have a tougher time learning how to drive a stick shift.

These extraterrestrial party animals also are physiologically suited for earth girls, indeed are blessed with some out-of-this-world endowments. For self-defense, the aliens are equipped with a kind of instant love-touch, that renders antagonists blissfully helpless and also does wonders for Goldblum when he finally beds Davis.

Temple's talent for staging musical production numbers, spawned effortlessly from narrative twists, is in full play here and as accomplished as it was in "Absolute Beginners." Funk-meister Nile Rodgers infuses the picture with a juicy, sexy musical momentum. In one of the movie's best song-and-action sequences, Davis tosses unfaithful Rocket out the door and proceeds to trash her entire house of his memory in a skillfully built emotional plot-bridge to her first confrontation with the spaceguys.

Davis, who's onscreen constantly, is fortunately good to look at, blessed with a self-effacing comic sensibility. Julie Brown, who cowrote the script, is ideal as her tightly wrapped airhead buddy who appreciates interesting dudes when she meets them. The male leads also are funny, as is Michael McKean playing a brain-burnt surfer poolboy who helps the visitors get their spacecraft ready for takeoff.

"Earth Girls Are Easy" can be tabbed as cinematic cotton candy, but, like a good sweet snack, it's energizing and feels good going down.—*Rich.*

Lightning Over Braddock: A Rustbowl Fantasy
(DOCU)

A Tony Buba production. Produced and directed by Buba. Camera (color, 16m), Brady Lewis; editor, Buba; music, Stephen Pellegrino. Reviewed on vidcassette (at Toronto Festival of Festivals), Sept. 6, 1988. Running time: **80 MIN.**

With: Sal Caru, Stephen Pellegrino, Natalka Voslakov, J. Roy.

■ **Toronto** — Tony Buba, native son of Braddock, Pa., again records life in his dying steel mill town, with crusading journalistic style and self-ingratiating humor.

His first feature-length film after 15 short docus about the town percolates with working-class life.

It's an offbeat, absorbing autobiographical mix, from his reportage of striking mill workers protesting against their bosses who elect to close the mill, to clips from his own films and the disruptive a. ¹s of a former numbers man whom he featured in one of the docus and who insists he made the career of filmmaker Buba.

Docu should make its mark at fests and, with some words bleeped, on public tv. —*Adil.*

Growing Up In America
(CANADIAN-DOCU-B&W/COLOR)

A Morley Markson and Associates Ltd. production. Executive producer, Don Haig. Produced and directed by Morley Markson. Camera (b&w, color, 16m) & editor, Markson; sound, Tom Burger, Anthony Hall, James Plaxton. Reviewed on vidcassette (at the Toronto Festival of Festivals), Sept. 2, 1988. Running time: **90 MIN.**

With: Abbie Hoffman, Jerry Rubin, Allen Ginsberg, Timothy Leary, William Kunstler, John Sinclair, Don Cox, Fred Hampton Jr., Deborah Russell.

■ **Toronto** — Lacking a proper narrative framework, this documentary looks at leading U.S. rebels of the 1960s via newsreel clips and updates them today, sometimes laughing at themselves then and going about their now-calmer lives.

Participants do not reflect on what they hoped to accomplish — producer-director Morley Markson lets the clips speak for themselves — and do not express any disappointment.

Only Abbie Hoffman, still an activist but on environmental matters, laughingly sums up his 1960s action: "the arrogance of youth." Activist lawyer William Kunstler says if he had his life to live over he would take the same route.

Today's comments need sharper editing and Markson assumes too much is remembered about the Yippie uproar at the 1968 Democratic Convention and the Black Panthers. Docu is clearly for tv or specialized fests. —*Adil.*

Far North

An Alive Enterprises release of an Alive Films production with Nelson Entertainment, in association with Circle JS Prods. Produced by Carolyn Pfeiffer, Malcolm Harding. Executive producer, Shep Gordon. Written and directed by Sam Shepard. Camera (color), Robbie Greenberg; editor, Bill Yahraus; music, the Red Clay Ramblers; production design, Peter Jamison; costumes, Rita Salazar; associate producer, James Kelley. Reviewed at Toronto Festival of Festivals, Sept. 9, 1988. MPAA Rating: PG-13. Running time: **90 MIN.**
Kate . . . . Jessica Lange
Bertrum . . . . Charles Durning
Rita . . . . Tess Harper
Uncle Dane . . . . Donald Moffat
Amy . . . . Ann Wedgeworth
Jilly . . . . Patricia Arquette
Gramma . . . . Nina Draxten

■ Toronto — In his film directing debut, Sam Shepard forsakes the fevered elliptical prose flights of his plays, and films such as "Paris, Texas" for a straightforward approach of surprising flatness and sentimentality that never gets airborne.

Commercial prospects are dim for this conventional tale of a Minnesota farm family coming to terms with its past and present in a time of accelerating change.

Bertrum (Charles Durning), a veteran of two wars and the railroad, is thrown from a cart by his rebellious runaway horse, and lands in the hospital obsessed with exacting revenge from the nag. His citified, unmarried pregnant daughter Kate (Jessica Lange) flies out from New York to comfort the curmudgeon in his crisis, but he greets her gruffly and makes her promise that she will shoot the beast for him.

In what's meant to be taken as a profound gesture of filial obeisance, Lange reluctantly agrees to assassinate the horse. This mystifies Lange's slightly dotty mom (Ann Wedgeworth) and outrages her fiery farm-bound sister Rita (Tess Harper).

Adding to the emotional fireworks in this world without men (a motif that Shepard hammers to death) is the post-pubescent defiance of Harper's daughter Jilly (Patricia Arquette), who plays fast and loose with the local boys for amusement in this nowhere town.

Shepard also introduces a 100-year-old grandmother and an alcoholic uncle (Donald Moffat) who's

conveniently checked himself into the same hospital, where he plays a kind of north woods Ed Norton to Durning's Minnesota fat Ralph Kramden. The two men bemoan the passing of days when men would marry the women they "knocked up" and women wouldn't dream of raising kids alone or going off to Gotham for business careers.

This loving but fractious little family is intended by Shepard to represent the dislocation of fundamental American values in the socially vertiginous '80s. Although the screenplay is not without moments of ironic humor, the family, the horse and the writer quite literally get lost in the woods pursuing the scenario's deeper meanings.

Professional performances all around — and bracing outdoorsy Minnesota locations — are nice, but do not obviate the film's pat dramaturgy and unbroken blandness. —*Rich.*

Strangers In A Strange Land: The Adventures Of A Canadian Film Crew In China
(CANADIAN-DOCU)

A McKeown/McGee Films production. Produced and directed by Bob McKeown. Written by McKeown; camera (color, 16m), Michael Boland; editor, Michael Morningstar; music, Terence McKeown; sound, Axo Loo, Terence McKeown; narrator, David Fox. Reviewed on vidcassette (at the Toronto Festival of Festivals), Sept. 3, 1988. Running time: **83 MIN.**

■ Toronto — Multiple problems on the still-uncompleted, $16,000,000 Canada-China coproduction feature "Bethune: The Making Of A Hero" are recorded dryly and objectively in this documentary.

The feature's director Phillip Borsos looks constantly exasperated and finally blames the producers, Montreal's Filmline Intl., for not doing enough homework about the difficulties of filming in China.

The Canadian crew argues with the Chinese crew and stages a work stoppage over no fresh water, no location toilets and lack of proper food — the last quickly improved.

Topliner Donald Sutherland, playing the late Dr. Norman Bethune (a Canadian medical advisor to Mao's troops and a hero in China), and scripter Ted Allan are shown at serious odds with each other. They are filmed separately.

Producers Pieter Kroonenburg and Nicholas Claremont blame the lack of services promised by Beijing's August 1 Studio.

Documentary, obviously for tv, is instructional on what can go wrong in an undertaking of this size, filmed in remote villages of China.

No mention is made that the production has been suspended for one year, that the China portion remains only 80% completed, that script problems remain, or that

further filming is set for Spain and Montreal. —*Adil.*

Wherever You Are
(BRITISH-POLISH-
W. GERMAN)

A Gerhard Schmidt Filmproduktion/-Filmpolski production. Produced by Enzo Peri, Marie Francoise Mascaro, Ludi Beoken. Executive producer, Mark Forstater. Written and directed by Krzysztof Zanussi. Camera (color), Swavomir Idziak; editor, Mark Denys; music, Wojciech Kilar; art direction, Jausz Sosnowski. Reviewed at Toronto Festival Of Festivals, Sept. 8, 1988. Running time: **109 MIN.**
Julian . . . . Julian Sands
Nina . . . . Renée Soutendijk
   Also with: Maciej Robakiewicz, Tadeusz Bradecki, Joachim Krol.
   (English soundtrack)

■ Toronto — Polish film maker Krzysztof Zanussi revisits his country's traumatic experience of World War II in "Wherever You Are," a picture more ambitiously produced and better performed than "The Year Of The Quiet Sun," but just as depressing.

The casting coup pairing of Julian Sands ("A Room With A View") and Renée Soutendijk ("The Fourth Man") might lure arthouse patrons, but this unrelievedly dark historical-psychosexual melodrama will be a tough sell for any specialty distributor bold enough to take it on.

Told almost entirely in flashback on VE Day is the story of newlyweds Julian (Sands) and Nina (Soutendijk) who travel from Uruguay to Poland on the eve of the war. He's a diplomat of mixed Uruguayan-German-British blood, who doubles as a businessman running German-owned machine factories in Poland. In the manner of prewar ladies of good breeding, she's a dutiful professional wife, although somewhat frigid when the couple are alone. This turns their boudoir into a battlefield in which Sands must frequently outflank his spouse from the rear.

The couple are guests at the lavish estate of a wealthy Pole whose son works as Sands' chief foreman. Although war clouds are thickening on the horizon, virtually no one wants to acknowledge the possibility, least of all Sands, who is intent on savoring wedded bliss and doing good business.

One day Soutendijk suffers a serious riding accident and seems near death until a charismatic nun's prayers miraculously revive her. She is tragically transformed by the experience, however, experiencing clairvoyant future-flashes of the coming holocaust and the onset of incurable schizophrenia.

Sands, meanwhile, discovers that the Germans have been using his factory as a front for smuggling arms into Poland. When his foreman tries to alert the police, he's murdered by Nazi sympathizers, and Sands feel personally responsi-

ble.

The situation degenerates as the Nazis take power and Soutendijk descends into padded-cell insanity. Sands slowly and painfully arrives at a deeper understanding of himself, his wife and the world around him, but these hard-won insights are too little too late. Selfishly, he returns to Uruguay one step ahead of the blitzkrieg, leaving his mad wife in the care of a clinic. When the film's flashback comes full circle and Sands returns to a ruined postwar Poland, he learns she was slaughtered in a Nazi execution of "lunatics," a scene disturbingly recreated by Zanussi in a haunting sequence.

Zanussi unfolds this bleak tale in somber, shadowy textures and with an incisive feel for the rigid manners of the upper classes in prewar Poland. The period mood is enhanced by impeccable production design. The couple's tormented relationship and its anguished disintegration is rendered with unrelenting force by the actors and the director. The effect of watching this story of doomed love in a doomed world is akin to that of reliving a very bad dream, which undoubtedly was Zanussi's intention. —*Rich.*

Witnesses
(CANADIAN-DOCU)

A Stornoway Production by Daivd Ostriker. Directed by Martyn Burke. Written by Burke; camera, (color, 16m), Francis Granger, Pascal Manoukian; editor, Darla Milne; art direction, Nina Beveridge; sound, Chris Barton. Reviewed on vidcassette at the Toronto Festival of Festivals, Sept. 3, 1988 Running time: **90 MIN.**

■ Toronto — Canadian producer-director Martyn Burke gets off another of his well-researched, hard-hitting journalistic documentaries in "Witnesses," which shows the Afghanistan-Soviet war from the Afghan side.

The witnesses are western observers who include a tv cameraman, a news reporter, a nurse and a human rights worker. Footage shot by Burke and his crew on the scene flesh out the ravages of war on the Afghans, who live in a harsh environment and lack goods regarded as normal in many other countries.

Intricacies of the war and who is who are carefully explained by Burke's polished narration. Docu will best travel to tv in most countries. —*Adil.*

Macho Dancer
(FILIPINO)

A Special People Prods. production. Produced by Boy C. de Guia. Directed by Lino Brocka. Screenplay, Ricardo Lee; camera (color), Joe Tutanes; production design, Benjie de Guzman; sound, Johnny Mendoza. Reviewed at Toronto Festival of Festivals, Sept. 7, 1988. Running time: **125 MIN.**
   With: Allan Paole, William Lorenzo, Daniel Fernando, Jaclyn Jose, Princess Pun-

zalan, Bobby Samo, Joel Lamangan, Lucita Soriano, Charlie Catalla, Anthony Taylor, Johnny Vicar.

■ **Toronto — Lino Brocka's homoerotic proclivity nearly overwhelms "Macho Dancer," but this project dear to the heart of the noted Filipino filmmaker transcends its worst excesses with a vivid depiction of teenage prostitution and its underworld subculture in Manila.**

At its finest, "Macho Dancer" is a unique contemporary Third World youth film with a daring political perspective, but Brocka's lubricious celebration of gay eros will limit the film's Western exposure to only adventurous arthouses and cinémathèques.

When his American G.I. lover's tour of duty is over, Paul, a goodhearted kid from the countryside, is compelled to go to Manila to try his luck. Brocka opens the film with an X-ish gay love scene between the two, immediately serving notice that "Macho Dancer" is not for the prudish.

A sense of total economic depression pervades the lives of Paul, his family and friends, and Brocka's achievement lies in convincing us his actions run against the boy's true nature.

Paul's heroism is his readiness to do anything simply to survive in a political-economic system that consigns most of its citizens laissez-faire to the human scrapheap.

Paul becomes a barroom "macho dancer," one of many lissome, babyfaced boys who pour into the city to become homosexual entertainers and prostitutes. Brocka portrays Paul and his "call-boy" friends with great sympathy, implying that a part of them remains innocent in spite of the extraordinary sordidness of their exploited existences. Paul's pay is something like $1.50 per day, so he and his roommate Noel try to find sidelines.

They learn that all illegitimate businesses in their barrio are controlled by a corrupt cop called The Kid. To cross this mobster/policeman is dangerous.

Paul and Noel withhold some drug deal profits from The Kid, hoping to use funds to find and rescue Noel's sister from slavery in a brothel. Along the way, Paul falls in love with Bambi, a spunky and beautiful call girl, and their first night together provides the film's only heterosexual highlight.

Bambi rescues Paul from a beating by The Kid, an event which sets in motion of chain of bloody events in which Paul loses a friend but gets the grim satisfaction of revenge.

The action in "Macho Dancer," however, is incidental to its milieu, a neon-colored netherworld of lust, cruelty and fear, moving to a dizzy soundtrack of bad rock and disco appropriate to the cheap setting.

There are frequent and generous dancing routines featuring total nudity and bump 'n' grind gay foreplay, overplayed to the point of tiring non-gay viewers.

Nevertheless, the macho dancers emerge as real personalities, none of whom seem overtly gay, most of whom coexist with a give-and-take camaraderie. The bleached-out cinematography is probably not intentional but enhances the mood of a tawdry fringeworld of outcasts, which Brocka evokes with an unerring eye. —*Rich.*

Tougher Than Leather

A New Line Cinema release of a Def American Picture. Produced by Vincent Giordano. Executive producers, Russell Simmons, Rick Rubin. Directed by Rick Rubin. Screenplay, Ric Menello, Rubin, based on a story by Bill Adler, Lyor Cohen, Ric Menello; camera (color), Feliks Parnell; editor, Steven Brown. Reviewed at Loews Astor Plaza, N.Y., Sept. 16, 1988. MPAA Rating: R. Running time: 92 MIN.
Run . . . . Joseph Simmons
DMC . . . . Darryl McDaniels
Jam Master Jay . . . . Jason Mizell
Bernie . . . . Richard Edson
Pam . . . . Jenny Lumet
Vic . . . . Rick Rubin
Charlotte . . . . Lois Ayer
Nathan . . . . George Godfrey
Russell . . . . Russell Simmons
Arthur . . . . Ric Menello
Runny Ray . . . . Raymond White
Marty . . . . Mickey Rubin
   Also with: Francesca Hodge, Daniel Simmons, Vic Noto, Nick D'Avolio, Carl Jordan, Russ Keehl, Larry Kase, Tim Summer, Will Rokos, Wayne Carisi.

■ **Produced independently by Run-DMC and its management, "Tougher Than Leather," is part home movie, part homage to Clint Eastwood and part concert pic that should attract a sizable portion of the No. 1 rap group's record/concert audiences as long as they don't mind pic's tyro lensing, acting and stunts.**

Leading off the pic's mixed bag of styles is a jocular opening sequence lifted directly from an Eastwood Spaghetti Western as tight closeups of the three singers alternate with long shots of stark landscape. Joseph Simmons (Run) has just been released from jail on an assault charge.

After this isolated scene, the trio proceeds to New York and a homecoming party enlivened with "Tougher Than Leather." Run-DMC and the Beastie Boys are signed to their first deals by sleazy booking agents played by Richard Edson, Ric Menello and, stepping out from behind the camera, Rick Rubin.

Rubin, who uses Strut Prods. to launder drug money, fatally shoots an employee (Mickey Rubin) who's had his hand in the till. Runny Ray (Raymond White), a friend and roadie for Run-DMC, also is shot when he stumbles into the gruesome killing, which is made to look like a crack deal gone sour.

Adapting a "Dirty Harry" approach to crimefighting (you have to break a few rotten eggs to make the omelet of justice), the three singers set out to solve their friend's murder, which the police are satisfied was drug-related.

Along the way they enlist the help of Strut's secretary (Jenny Lumet) and the Rubin character's girlfriend (Lois Ayres, the porn actress spelling her surname "Ayer" in this pic), and, in a warehouse, Rubin is dispatched à la Eastwood.

Comedy in "Tougher Than Leather" derives from Run, DMC and Jam Master Jay's unflappable approach to the battles between the sexes, blacks and cops, musicians and corrupt music industry types. The Beastie Boys' well-known penchant for raunch and sloppiness also was intended to elicit guffaws.

Unhappy with its sanitized motion picture debut in Warner Bros.' "Krush Groove," Run-DMC presents "Tougher Than Leather" as a more accurate description of their image and rap culture. Their goal is best realized when the music, including appearances by the Beastie Boys, Slick Rick, Junkyard Band and other rap groups, dominates the action.

Off-camera is where the pic's problems emerge. Although fans will find Run-DMC's charisma intact, it looks like director Rubin used the first take at every turn of each supporting actor. Stunts involving brawls generally look illcoordinated, and much of the action is unconvincing. —*Binn.*

Messenger Of Death

A Cannon Group release of a Golan-Globus production. Produced by Pancho Kohner. Executive producers, Menahem Golan, Yoram Globus. Directed by J. Lee-Thompson. Screenplay, Paul Jarrico, based on the novel "The Avenging Angel" by Rex Burns; camera (TVC color), Gideon Porath; editor, Peter Lee-Thompson; music, Robert O. Ragland; art direction, W. Brooke Wheeler; set decoration, Susan Carsello-Smith; costume design, Shelley Komarov; sound (UltraStereo), Craig Felburg; associate producer, Patricia G. Payre; assistant director, Robert C. Ortwin Jr.; additional camera, Tom Neuwirth. Reviewed at the Paramount Theater, L.A., Sept. 16, 1938. MPAA Rating: R. Running time: **90 MIN.**
Garret Smith . . . . Charles Bronson
Jastra Watson . . . . Trish Van Devere
Homer Foxx . . . . Laurence Luckinbill
Chief Barney Doyle . . . . . Daniel Benzali
Joephine Fabrizio . . . . Marilyn Hassett
Orville Beecham . . . . Jeff Corey
Zenas Beecham . . . . John Ireland
Trudy Pike . . . . Penny Peyser
Junior Assassin . . . . Gene Davis
Senior Assassin . . . . John Solari
Saul . . . . Jon Cedar
Wiley . . . . Tom Everett
Lieutenant Scully . . . . Duncan Gamble

■ **Hollywood — There's plenty of killing going on in "Messenger Of Death," but for once, Charles Bronson isn't responsible for any of it. In the old days, this would have been regarded as a routine programmer, but in these days of mindless mayhem and random plotting, Paul Jarrico's script at least offers some substance.**

Pic is being sold just like any other Cannon fodder, so b.o. results are likely to be unexceptional.

Rex Burns' novel of detection is set in an interesting milieu, that of renegade Mormons who have broken with the "Salt Lake theocracy." Shocking opening has an unidentifiable gunman blow away three women and six children at the isolated mountain home of one of the flock, Orville Beecham.

After writing up the slaughter for the Denver Tribune, old-pro crime reporter Bronson begins sizing up the suspects, who most prominently include Beecham's fanatical preacher father (Jeff Corey) and the preacher's estranged brother Zenas (John Ireland), who are playing out some sort of Cain and Abel game mixed up with elements from the Hatfields and the McCoys.

Whoever was responsible, the motive for the murders appears to have something to do with the concept of an "avenging angel," which holds that the killers are doing the victims a favor by knocking them off. A perfectly understandable notion to the religious elite, of course, but one that mere "gentiles" cannot hope to understand.

It takes the sleuthing Bronson a reasonably engaging 90 minutes to put all the pieces together, and he manages to do so without shooting anybody, even though the baddies try to get him out of the way any number of times.

Jarrico's script is a few notches above the usual intelligence level for a mass audience actioner, although this counts more as a mystery than a typical shoot-'em-up. J. Lee-Thompson's direction is perfunctory but sensible, while fine Colorado locations could have looked more impressive than they do through Gideon Porath's chalky lensing. Thesping is proficient. —Cart.

Sweet Hearts Dance

A Tri-Star Picture release of a Chestnut Hill Production. Produced by Jeffrey Lurie. Executive producer, Robert Greenwald. Directed by Greenwald. Screenplay, Ernest Thompson; camera (Technicolor), Tak Fujimoto; editor, Robert Florio; original music, Richard Gibbs; music supervision, Debbie Gold; production design, James Allen; set decoration, R. Lynn Smart; costumes, Bobbie Read; sound (Dolby), Mark F. Ulano; associate producer, Bruce Pustin; assistant director, Allan Nicholls; second unit camera, Dyanna Taylor; casting, Lora Kennedy. Reviewed at Tri-Star screening room, L.A., Sept. 12, 1988. MPAA Rating: R. Running time: 101 MIN.
Wiley Boon . . . . Don Johnson
Sandra Boon . . . . Susan Sarandon
Sam Manners . . . . Jeff Daniels
Adie Nims . . . . Elizabeth Perkins
Pearne Manners . . . . Kate Reid
Kyle Boon . . . . Justin Henry
Debs Boon . . . . Hollyw Marie Combs
BJ Boon . . . . Heather Coleman

■ Hollywood — Maturing baby boomers might find something they need in this pic's core conflict — a gritty, heartening look at a couple with children struggling to save a 15-year-old marriage gone stale.

With no hint of that in the marketing, and with story emphasis on male bonding between unlikely best pals Don Johnson and Jeff Daniels, boxoffice prospects look mild, and film's scattered, offbeat virtues are likely to fall by the wayside.

Johnson plays construction boss Wiley Boon and Daniels high school principal Sam Manners who've grown up together in a tightly bound Vermont community. Johnson, married to Sandy (Susan Sarandon) with three kids, is realiz-

ing he's fallen out of love just as bachelor buddy Daniels meets a new teacher (Elizabeth Perkins) and grows marriage-minded.

Ernest Thompson ("On Golden Pond") has scripted a slow-motion smalltown saga that evolves as part meandering mood piece, part buddy film, part family drama. Though pic generates some genuine emotional pull by third reel, situations and dialog often seem aimless and clunky, and under Robert Greenwald's uncertain direction, actors flounder through their roles before hitting their strides about halfway through.

Johnson, although well-suited to his role, relies mostly on a cantankerous-young-man act, and is unconvincing in a close relationship with either Daniels or Sarandon. Perkins, as a flinty young woman not sure she needs anyone, makes a good counterpart to mild, peacemaking Daniels, but it is Sarandon who makes the most significant contribution as a vulnerable but tough woman determined not to let her life collapse even though its core, Wiley, is spinning out of control. Her final struggles with Wiley over their marriage are pic's bravest and most affecting scenes.

Much of the film is dreamy reverie about the texture of smalltown life, with such offbeat but resonant scenes as men and boys singing "California Girls" in a tent during a snowbound camping trip. Amusingly, community is so tight that even a vacation getaway to the Caribbean is done en masse, with mom, neighbors and friends in adjoining hotel rooms.

Unfortunately, director Greenwald's results often seem out of sync with his intentions, as in an awkward ice-skating scene in which Wiley weeps over his marriage.

Other production aspects are in capable hands, with handsome production design by James Allen and giddy, nostalgic music by Richard Gibbs. —Daws.

Seven Hours To Judgment

A Trans World Entertainment release. Produced by Mort Abrahams. Executive producers, Paul Mason, Helen Sarlui-Tucker. Directed by Beau Bridges. Screenplay, Walter Davis, Elliot Stephens, from story by Davis; Camera (Deluxe color), Hanania Baer; editor, Bill Butler; music, John Debney; production design, Phedon Papmichael; set decorator, Geraldine Hofstatter; costume design, Larry Lefler; sound (Ultra-Stereo), Jim Pilcher; postproduction supervisor, Fima Noveck; casting, Alana H. Lambros. Reviewed at the Hollywood Egyptian theater, L.A., Sept. 16, 1988. MPAA Rating: R. Running time: 88 MIN.
John Eden . . . . Beau Bridges
David Reardon . . . . Ron Leibman
Lisa Eden . . . . Julianne Phillips
Ira . . . . Tiny Ron Taylor
Chino . . . . Reggie Johnson
Danny Larwin . . . . Al Freeman Jr.

■ Hollywood — "Seven Hours To Judgment" has about seven minutes of plot, but director-actor Beau

Bridges manages to pull off a fairly entertaining low-budget suspenser through taut editing and location switches.

Boxoffice might be minimal, but Trans World Entertainment has a good vid hit on its hands.

Justice is not being served by the nightmare-ridden Judge John Eden (Beau Bridges) when he has to dismiss for lack of evidence a handful of gang members he knows are guilty of viciously attacking the wife of an electronics retailer (Ron Leibman).

Leibman quickly becomes a vengeful psychotic. First he kidnaps the wife (Julianne Phillips), then Bridges, whom he forces to get the evidence to convict the killer within seven hours or Phillips is history.

This basic story line has been shot a million times and a million ways.

Instead of resorting to vigilantism — the Chuck Norris-Charles Bronson-Sylvester Stallone method — Bridges accomplishes his mission within the confines of what's legal. He may have lost his Harvard Law School ring to some Latino hustlers, but not his sense of morality.

Bridges' puppy-dog face and earnest wide-eyed expressions give his character the pathos to make his predicament one worth caring about.

With such a stock situation, scripters Walter Davis and Elliot Stephens redeem themselves somewhat by keeping things moving along from short scene to short scene — never stopping long enough for viewers to realize there isn't much going on other than movement, noise, music and shots of Bridge's panic-stricken face.

Leibman plays a good crazed electronics nerd, coming up with a convoluted computer-controlled method of trapping and intimidating Bridges with security cameras, videotape and an omnipresent multispeaker sound system set up in his downtown warehouse.

Why it always has to be creepy-looking 1-dimensionally drawn blacks and Latinos as gang members is indicitive of unimaginative scripting, but not unexpected for this genre.

Phillips doesn't get to act much, given that she's drugged or gagged and bound for much of the picture. Wearing only a silky slip throughout, she manages to emote through her eyes, though it's likely her fans will be looking elsewhere.

Worst characterization is of Ira, played by 7-foot former U. of California basketball player Tiny Ron Taylor.

Most of the action takes place in the scummy areas of the city or in the subway, giving the appropriately seedy, uncomfortable overcast look to the proceedings.

Production notes say this is supposed to be New York, though exteriors look at all times like Seattle, where it was lensed. —Brit.

Homeboy

A Capital-Cinéma (France) release of a Redbury Ltd. production. Produced by Alan Marshall, Elliott Kastner. Directed by Michael Seresin. Screenplay, Eddie Cook, from story by Mickey Rourke; camera (Technicolor), Gale Tattersall; editor, Ray Lovejoy; music, Eric Clapton, Michael Kamen; art direction, Brian Morris; costumes, Richard Schisser; assistant director, Lewis Gould; production manager, Clayton Townsend; associate producer, Jayne Kachmer; casting, Mary Colquhoun. Reviewed at UGC Normandie cinema, Paris, Sept. 10, 1988. Running time: 112 MIN.
Johnny Walker . . . . Mickey Rourke
Wesley Pendergrass . . Christopher Walken
Ruby . . . . Debra Feuer
Lou . . . . Thomas Quinn
Grazziano . . . . Kevin Conway
Ray . . . . Anthony Alda
Mac Fingers . . . . Jon Polito

■ Paris — Hollywood's latest celebration of American Sleaze is "Homeboy," actor Mickey Rourke's decade-old pet project about a battered, burnt-out small-time boxer. A sort of "Raging Bull" without horns, pic wallows dully in the clichés of movieland gutter romanticism.

Film has had its world premiere in France, where Rourke has a strong following, though it doesn't seem destined to longterm boxoffice. With no match set Stateside, odds on a real commercial release are against it.

Though nominally written by Eddie Cook and directed by Alan Parker's habitual lenser Michael Seresin in his helming debut, this in fact is all Rourke's show, as he's made it bluntly clear in local interviews, and he's refused himself nothing — except a good screenplay and direction.

Rourke's tale is a purported homage to a boxer he idolized in his youth when he himself trained to be a fighter. Here called Johnny Walker, Rourke's hero is just another inarticulate All-American lowlife, providing another Grungier-Than-Thou opportunity for Rourke.

Adopting a neo-Neanderthal expression and cowboy duds, Rourke is first seen slouching into an Atlantic coastal town for a fight engagement.

Coming from "nowhere" and apparently headed nowhere, character is a seedy silhouette which Rourke doesn't bother to delineate with any valid psychological or biographical detail. Rourke seems less to have fashioned a free biopic about a figure he once admired than to have masochistically fantasized his own future as a boxer. (He explained in interviews that the cowboy garb was a personal choice drawn from his own teen sartorial tastes.)

His zombie-like condition doesn't prevent him from being befriended by Christopher Walken, who steals the show with a colorful portrayal of a narcissistic 2-bit hoodlum. Walken tries to sucker Rourke into taking part in a jewelry shop hold-up he long has been dreaming of.

Rourke demurs, even though Walken reveals that the boxer has a fractured temple bone and that another blow in the right place could provide the coup de grâce.

But Rourke decides to go back into the ring for the love of a young fairground operator (Debra Feuer, the ex-Mrs. Rourke), whose business is failing.

Script is made up of poorly rewoven conventions, dutifully packaged by Seresin with some gimmickry optical and soundtrack distortions (to translate Rourke's physical deterioration) and glossy photography by Gale Tattersall.

Eric Clapton-Michael Kamen score strums agreeably throughout, even when breaking down into a blues variation of "Dixie."—*Len.*

Twisted Nightmare
(HORROR-COLOR)

A United Filmmakers production and release. Produced by Sandy Horowitz. Executive producer, T. Beauclerc Rogers 4th. Written and directed by Paul Hunt. Camera (Astral Bellevue Pathé color), Hunt, Gary Graver; editor, Allen Persselin; special effects, Cleve Hall; associate producers, Frederic Leslie, Robert Goldman. Reviewed at 42d St. Liberty theater, N.Y., Sept. 14, 1988. MPAA Rating: R. Running time: **94 MIN.**
With: Rhonda Gray, Cleve Hall, Brad Bartrum, Robert Padillo, Heather Sullivan, Scott King, Juliet Martin.

■ "Twisted Nightmare" is a perfunctory horror film bringing back to null effect rather corny genre themes. Ongoing theatrical release is unwarranted compared to many direct-to-video titles, though pic has a catchy moniker.

Main mystery stems from pic's origins; print caught had a 1982 copyright (in Roman numerals) onscreen, yet ad materials and date of MPAA rating imply film actually was made in 1987. Pic probably is fresh, but plays like the lookalike films made at the beginning of the decade when horror boomed.

A group of young people are summoned to Camp Paradise, where they camped regularly until two years ago when Mathew, the brother of pretty brunet Laura (Rhonda Gray), died mysteriously in flames. Confused storyline blames the subsequent 1-by-1 murders of the cast members on those old standbys: (1) ancient revenge against the white man (plus a black couple for good measure) for desecrating Indian burial grounds, the site of the camp, and for massacring local Indians (only survivor was a medicine man, whose grandson is the sinister farmhand-type resident of the camp); and (2) unbalanced Laura's obviously telegraphed need to avenge bro's death.

Gory killings are standard for horror flicks, while Paul Hunt's execution of a "Friday The 13th" or "The Outing" type screenplay is relentlessly dull. Cast is attractive but the acting is flat. Big, hairy monster (mainly shown in silhouette) is disappointing.—*Lor.*

The Beast

A Columbia Pictures release of an A&M Films production. Produced by John Fiedler. Executive producers, Gil Friesen, Dale Pollock. Directed by Kevin Reynolds. Screenplay, William Mastrosimone, based on his play "Nanawatai;" camera (Rank color), Douglas Milsome; editor, Peter Boyle; music, Mark Isham; production design, Kuli Sander; art direction, Richard James; costumes, Ilene Starger; sound (Dolby), David Crozier; stunt coordinator, Paul Weston; associate producer, Christopher Dalton; assistant director, Robert Roe; production manager, Dalton; second unit director, Mark Illsley; second unit camera, Dana Christiaansen; casting, Ilene Starger. Reviewed at Directors Guild of America, L.A., Sept. 9, 1988. MPAA Rating: R. Running time: **109 MIN.**
Daskal . . . . George Dzundza
Koverchenko . . . . Jason Patric
Taj . . . . Steven Bauer
Golikov . . . . Stephen Baldwin
Kaminski . . . . Don Harvey
Akbar . . . . Kabir Bedi
Samad . . . . Erick Avari
Moustafa . . . . Shosh Marciano

■ **Hollywood** — **A harrowing, tightly focused war film that becomes a moving, near-Biblical allegory, "The Beast" represents a stellar achievement for all involved but a potential tough sell.**

Talented but little-known cast and challenging approach to a foreign war with no U.S. involvement means pic, which could easily appeal to a wide audience, will depend on critics and word of mouth to earn its well-deserved b.o. reward.

Based on William Mastrosimone's play "Nanawatai," which debuted at the Los Angeles Theater Center, pic explores a single fictional incident set in 1981, the second year of the Russian occupation of Afghanistan.

A Russian tank gets trapped in a no-exit valley after its brutal decimation of a nearby Afghan village, and the surviving villagers, who've recovered a weapon capable of destroying the tank, decide to track it down for revenge.

From pic's harrowing opening scene to its beautiful, meditative final stroke, director Kevin Reynolds ("Fandango") displays remarkably mature and effective storytelling skills.

Mastrosimone's typically intense scripting makes this a kind of "Das Boot" of the desert, as the crew of the deteriorating tank races for survival.

"The Beast" is the tank, a formidably efficient war machine that becomes the center of the pic. Among its crew are Daskal (George Dzundza), a vicious, paranoid commander capable of killing his own crewmen, and Koverchenko (Jason Patric), a conscience-stricken former philosophy student who begins to explore the ways of the Afghans.

The Afghans, who see the war in religious terms, include a young man (Steven Bauer) struggling to attain a leadership role that includes making moral decisions. "Allah, I am a stone in your sling," he declares upon setting out after the tank.

Performances, many of them repeated from the stage version, are remarkably evocative, particularly from the Afghans, who speak in subtitled dialect (the Russians speak English). Patric gives a resonant portrayal of the questioning Russian.

While its action scenes are cuttingly visceral and admirably authentic, pic also achieves a powerful spiritual dimension as Patric and the Afghans confront each other.

Mastrosimone's Biblical references to David and Goliath are effectively and unblushingly built in.

Photography of Douglas Milsome ("Full Metal Jacket") in Israeli desert locales is striking. Mark Isham's eerie, moody score adds to the suspense.—*Daws.*

TORONTO REVIEWS

Gorillas In The Mist

A Universal Pictures (U.S.) and Warner Bros. (foreign) release of a Guber-Peters production, in association with Arnold Glimcher. Produced by Glimcher, Terence Clegg. Executive producers, Peter Guber, Jon Peters. Coproducers, Robert Nixon, Judy Kessler. Directed by Michael Apted. Screenplay, Anna Hamilton Phelan, story by Phelan, Tab Murphy, based on the work by Dian Fossey and the article by Harold T.P. Hayes; camera (Technicolor), John Seale; editor, Stuart Baird; music, Maurice Jarre; production design, John Graysmark; art direction, Ken Court; set decoration, Simon Wakefield; costume design, Catherine Leterrier; sound (Dolby), Peter Handford; associate producer-special makeup effects, Rick Baker; assistant directors, Chris Brock, Tim Lewis, Robert Mugemana; casting, Marion Dougherty, Mary Selway; second unit director-camera, Simon Trevor; special gorilla photography (Zaire), Alan Root. Reviewed at Samuel Goldwyn theater, Beverly Hills, Calif., Sept. 14, 1988. (In Toronto Festival Of Festivals.) MPAA Rating: PG-13. Running time: **129 MIN.**
Dian Fossey . . . . Sigourney Weaver
Bob Campbell . . . . Bryan Brown
Roz Carr . . . . Julie Harris
Sembagare . . . . John Omirah Miluwi
Dr. Louis Leakey . . . . Iain Cuthbertson
Van Vecten . . . . Constantin Alexandrov
Mukara . . . . Waigwa Wachira
Brendan . . . . Iain Glen
Larry . . . . David Lansbury
Kim . . . . Maggie O'Neill

■ **Hollywood** — **The life story of the late anthropologist Dian Fossey posed considerable challenges to the filmmakers tackling it, and they have been met in admirable fashion in "Gorillas In The Mist."**

Fossey focused world attention on the plight of the endangered mountain gorillas of central Africa, and the picture predictably, if rightly, frames the tale with optimism about how the animals would have been extinct by now had it now been for Fossey's obsessive dedication.

Yet many of the events depicted, and the questions they raise, are profoundly disturbing, and one emerges from the film in a state of sober depression.

Solid acclaim will greet Sigourney Weaver's fierce central performance and the film's faithful adherence to Fossey's principles, which should translate into good b.o. in markets receptive to intelligent, serious fare. Warner Bros./Universal coproduction was premiered last week at the Toronto Festival of Festivals.

Fossey devoted nearly 20 years to observing, and trying to protect, the gorillas who live in a small area in the Virunga mountain range, which extends into Rwanda, where Fossey established her Karisoke Research Center. Thanks to National Geographic and films made by Bob Campbell, her work became internationally known, but she alienated a number of people, and was murdered in 1985. (Although her research assistant was convicted in absentia, many feel guilt lies elsewhere.)

Telling here starts out on the dry side, as Fossey leaves Louisville, Ky., and her fiance to do a census of the primates for Dr. Louis Leakey. Quite a bit of exposition is covered in narrated passages of letters, encouraging polite interest in the material, but little more.

After a while, just as Fossey began making unprecedented physical contact with these imposing animals, Weaver seems to establish an exceptional familiarity and rapport with the jungle inhabitants. The intense bond makes the later scenes relating to the gorilla slaughter by poachers all the more powerful.

Campbell, played by Bryan Brown, turns up unannounced to photograph her activities and, after initial resistance, Fossey not only welcomes his presence but takes the married man as her lover. Despite Campbell's divorce of his wife and willingness to marry Fossey, she banishes him for presuming to pursue his work elsewhere for a while, considering this a betrayal of the gorillas and her mission.

Fossey becomes more distrustful, generally with good reason, especially after the hideous murder of her favorite gorilla Digit. Gradually, her job is transformed from naturalist into warrior. She forces confessions from little kids and stages mock executions of poachers, playing her locally perceived role of foreign witch to the hilt.

Weaver is utterly believable and riveting in the role. Her scenes with the apes are captivating, not just in the "cute" way of Hollywood animal pictures, but through undeniable connections established on film. Her unmistakable intelligence, physicality and guts are also essential to her outstanding characterization of a woman who paid a heavy price for her commitment.

Brown lends a nice lilt to his sympathetic interloper, and John Omirah Miluwi was a fine choice as Fossey's stalwart African tracker, although his character inexplicably recedes into a wordless background once Brown arrives.

Lensed high in the mountains of Rwanda, the production looks impressive but is not glossy or overproduced. Anna Hamilton Phelan's smart, informative script hits the key aspects surrounding the existence of wild animals in the face of perceived higher priorities in the Third World, even as the film seems to want to soft-pedal the circumstances of Fossey's death; her murder carries not nearly the impact of Digit's.

A documentarian from the beginning of his career, director Michael Apted ("28 Up") keeps the focus intimate and the extended story in control.

Presence of Rick Baker as associate producer and creator of special makeup effects is a tipoff that not all of the gorillas are for real. Knowing this, one can make educated guesses as to the authenticity of the apes, but in fact, they are all completely convincing, the ultimate tribute to Baker's work. General audiences never will suspect there's a ringer in bunch.—*Cart.*

Palais Royale
(CANADIAN)

A Spectrafilm release of a Metaphor Prods. production. Produced by David Daniels, Lawrence Zack. Executive producers, Steven Levitan, Daniels, Zack. Directed by Martin Lavut. Screenplay, Hugh Graham, Daniels, Zack, Jo Ann Mcintyre; camera (color), Brenton Spencer; editor, Susan Martin music, Jonathon Goldsmith; art direction, Ruben Freed; sound, Bruce Nyznik. Reviewed at Toronto Festival of Festivals, Sept. 10, 1988. Running time: **100 MIN.**
Odessa . . . . .Kim Cattrall
Gerald . . . . .Matt Craven
Tony .Kim Coates
Dattalico . . . . .Dean Stockwell
Gus .Brian George
Sgt. Leonard . . . . .Michael Hogan
Also with: Jan Rubes.

■ **Toronto — "Palais Royale" is an excruciatingly bad attempt at a Toronto-set film noir that shoots itself in the foot conceptually and stylistically.**

Pic wouldn't last a week in U.S. theaters, but its local genesis may help in Canada in spite of the pic's embarrassment to indigenous filmmaking aspirations.

Surprisingly, "Palais Royale" starts off with some promise as a '50s period fantasy. Gerald (Matt Craven), an ambitious farm boy, works as a bookkeeper for a Toron-

---

to advertising agency and daydreams about creating unforgettable ad campaigns. The shy, hawk-faced hero is haunted and inspired by a beautiful model on a billboard outside his window. Had the filmmakers turned their misdirected attempts at satire to making a Canadian "Putney Swope"-style comedy about mass mind-conditioning, the results may have been a little better than what actually transpires.

By chance, natch, Gerald meets his dream face, Odessa (Kim Cattrall) and trails her to a sinister nightclub, the Palais Royale. He immediately gets involved with the sultry beauty and the bungling mobsters who run her life. These gangsters are trying to keep their noses clean with legit businesses, a not-so-funny plot premise that spawns lame satirical in-jokes about "Toronto The Good," meaningless to non-Canadian audiences and even now old-fashioned in Toronto itself.

Wooden banality fo the dialog and the rigor mortis of the film's narrative cannot be disguised by its pretentious neon-glo art direction and cinematography. A good performance by Dean Stockwell as the mob boss who would rather go straight in squeaky-clean Toronto only raises questions about how he got involved in the project. Everyone and everything else in "Palais Royale" becomes unbearably tiresome long before its pointless conclusion. —*Rich.*

We Think The World Of You
(BRITISH)

A Cinecom Pictures release (U.S.), Norstar Entertainment release (Canada) of a Cinecom Entertainment Group presentation of a Gold Screen production. Produced by Tommaso Jandelli, Paul Cowan. Directed by Colin Gregg. Screenplay, Hugh Stoddart, from the novel by Joseph R. Ackerley; camera (Technicolor), Mike Garfath; editor, Peter Delfgon; music, Julian Jacobson; production design, Jamie Leonard; costumes, Doreen Watkinson; sound, Tony Dawe; production manager, Fran Triefus; casting, Simone Reynolds. Reviewed at Toronto Festival of Festivals, Sept. 16, 1988. Running time: **94 MIN.**
Frank Meadows . . . . .Alan Bates
Johnnie . . . . .Gary Oldman
Tom . . . . .Max Wall
Millie .Liz Smith
Megan . . . . .Frances Barber
Margaret . . . . .Sheila Ballantine

■ **Toronto — Followers of the quirkier side of British film production may respond to this shaggy dog story in which a middle-aged homosexual in postwar Britain settles for life with a beautiful German shepherd bitch when he can't have the man he loves.**

Well-acted comedy holds plenty of small pleasures, but on the whole looms as rather too slight for successful theatrical release. The tube and video look to be safer bets.

Alan Bates is in top form as Frank Meadows, a smart office worker still harboring a yen for Johnnie (Gary Oldman), son of

---

Frank's former charwoman. Johnnie, however, has married the ever-pregnant Megan (Frances Barber), a tenacious Welsh girl Frank can't stand.

When Johnnie's sentenced to a year in prison on a stealing charge, Frank's frustrations mount, as he's denied even visiting rights, and Johnnie communicates with him only via the hated Megan. However, he regularly visits Johnnie's parents, Millie and Tom (Liz Smith, Max Wall), who are caring for the latest baby and also for Johnnie's beloved dog, Evie.

Observing that the dog is rarely exercised, Frank starts taking her for walks, and becomes more and more attached to the lovely, boisterous animal. This provokes a row with Millie when Frank has the dog stay overnight in his apartment.

Eventually, after Johnnie's release, Frank buys Evie from him. By now the dog completely dominates his life, sharing his bed, coming to the office with him, disrupting his social engagements. In a rueful final encounter with Johnnie, Megan and their growing brood of offspring, Johnnie's wry comment to Frank that "You had the best of the bargain" rings all too true.

All this is done in the very best of taste. There are no gay scenes, apart from a couple of chaste embraces, and certainly no hint of bestiality. The mood of the film is light and very British. Indeed, some of the accents are strong and the print caught had muffled sound, making it hard to pick up all the dialog.

Colin Gregg ("Lamb") directs in straightforward style, but is unable to lift this from its telemovie origins. Drab colors and production design undoubtedly reflect the grimness of Britain in the early '50s, but also make for a visually dull film.

The actors are all in top form, with Bates giving one of his most subtle performances as the respectable man who hides his sexual preferences all too well. Scenes between him, Smith and Wall, in which his real interest in their son never is mentioned openly, are beautifully written and handled.

For all its qualities, though, this remains a modest cinema experience, so Cinecom and Norstar will have to handle it carefully to attract even those regular supporters of British cinema. The presence of Bates and Oldman (in a relatively small role) certainly will help. The dog is extremely beautiful. —*Strat.*

Issue de Secours
(BELGIAN)

A Les Films de la Passerelle/RTBF/Unifilm production. Executive producer, Christine Pireaux. Written and directed by Thierry Michel. Camera (color), Jean-Claude Neckelbrouck; editor, Emmanuelle Dupuis; music, Marc Herouet; sound, Jean Claude Boulanger. Reviewed at Toronto Festival of Festivals, Sept. 13, 1988. Running time: **90 MIN.**

With: Philippe Volter.

■ **Toronto — Succeeding more as a docu on Moroccan life than as a fictional search for self, "Issue de Secours" is a tiresome, self-indulgent exercise. Commercial prospects are very slim.**

Thierry Michel's story centers on Alain (Philippe Volter), a Belgian man who, after the suicide of his lover Leila, travels to Morocco to search out her past and the reasons for her drastic gesture.

Alain's narration serves as background music to the action, which consists largely of the hero taking buses and walking across parched deserts, ostensibly to look for Leila's sister and grandfather, but ultimately to uncover his own secret passions and sexual desires, as well as making peace with his ex-wife and daughter.

He checks in and out of grungy hotels; parties with locals; beds a young girl and, later, a boy; and walks through the markets and slums on his personal journey.

Except for the lovely, sunburned cinematography and docu aspects of examining faces and street life in Casablanca and small towns in Morocco, pic is an entirely dry as dust affair. —*Devo.*

Paperhouse
(BRITISH)

A Vestron Pictures release of a Working Title production. Executive producers, MJ Peckos, Dan Ireland. Produced by Sarah Radclyffe, Tim Bevan. Directed by Bernard Rose. Screenplay, Mathew Jacobs, from novel by Catherine Starr; camera (Technicolor), Mike Southon; editor, Dan Rae; music, Hans Zimmer, Stanley Myers; production design, Frank Walsh, Ann Tilby; sound, Peter Glossop; sound composition, Nigel Holland; assistant director, Waldo Roeg; casting, Ros Hubbard. Reviewed at Toronto Festival of Festivals, Sept. 10, 1988. MPAA Rating: PG-13. Running time: 92 MIN.
Anna Madden . . . . .Charlotte Burke
Father . . . . .Ben Cross
Mother . . . . .Glenne Headly
Mark . . . . .Elliott Spears
Dr. Sarah Nicholls . . . . .Gemma Jones

■ **Toronto — "Paperhouse" is the thinking person's "A Nightmare On Elm Street." A riveting fantasy film, centering on the vivid dreams and nightmares of an 11-year-old girl, it heralds a new director of talent in Bernard Rose.**

Pic will need very special handling if it's to find the audience which will really appreciate its beauty and strangeness, a real marketing challenge.

The premise here is that Anna (Charlotte Burke), psychologically disturbed, perhaps because of the frequent long absences from home of her beloved father (Ben Cross), has become a discipline problem at school via her bossy, unappealing ways. While undergoing minor punishment, she faints and finds herself by a strange house on a cliff-top, a house similar to one she'd earlier drawn on paper.

Gradually, she discovers that as she embellishes the drawing, she can enter the house in her dreams, and after drawing a face at an upper window, she discovers a boy her own age who's alone and unable to walk. Anna draws a picture of her father intending him to help the children, but the dreams become nightmares as the father becomes a chilling, threatening figure from whom the youngsters must somehow escape.

Between her dreams, Anna discovers her kindly doctor (Gemma Jones) is treating a dying boy who seems to be identical to the boy in the house. It all adds to the mystery and intrigue.

First-time director Bernard Rose has done a great job, creating genuine suspense and magic from the most basic materials. He could have taken the easy route and made a standard horror pic, but he's opted for something far more difficult and exciting; there's no violence in this film, but there's considerable suspense and tension. The Toronto fest audience responded most enthusiastically to the approach.

Crucial to the film's success is a superb soundtrack, with a strong music score, but also heightened sound effects of great impact. Camerawork (Mike Southon) is also outstanding, helping to make this dream world very strange indeed, and the production designers also deserve kudos for their clever matching of studio material with locations (filmed in North Devon).

Young Charlotte Burke isn't a looker, but is aptly cast as the girl, while Glenne Headly makes a considerable impact as her sympathetic mother. Other members of the small cast are all good.

From the start, Rose creates an edgy mood, and is to be commended for keeping the suspense boiling through to the end even after a point (just over an hour into the pic) when it seems the story might be coming to a premature conclusion. Pic is very imaginative and technically seamless. —*Strat.*

BOSTON FEST REVIEWS

Flesh Eating Mothers

A Panorama Entertainment release. A Miljan Peter Ilich and James Aviles Martin presentation. Executive producers, Fred Martin, Peter Lewnes. Produced by Ilich, James Aviles Martin. Directed by James Aviles Martin. Screenplay, James Martin, Zev Shlasinger; camera (color), Harry Eisenstein; editor, Eisenstein, James Martin; music, Minerva; sound, Chris Lowbardozzi; special effects, Carl Sorensen; art direction, Michael Veasey; animation, Lee Corey. Reviewed at Boston Film Festival, Sept. 16, 1988. No MPAA Rating. Running time: **88 MIN.**

With: Robert Lee Oliver, Donatella Hecht, Neal Rosen, Valorie Hubbard, Terry Hayes, Katherine Mayfield, Suzanee Ehrlich, Louis Howtak, Ken Eaton.

■ Boston — **This low-budget horror item appeared at a midnight showing at the Boston Film Festival, but it is in no way a festival film. Except for filling out the bottom of a horror bill at a drive-in, it's difficult to see that this movie has anywhere to go.**

Thin plot has to do with a suburban town where a philandering husband is spreading a virus that turns women who have had children into cannibals. Mothers of the title go on rampage, à la "Night Of The Living Dead," and their teen kids have to unite with the town coroner to get their moms back to normal.

Problem is that film is so woodenly acted and scripted that gore scenes are laughable rather than frightening. Conversely, intentional humor falls flat, preventing pic from achieving some sort of cult status as did "Street Trash," which played last year's festival.

Humor is on the order of teens complaining they are "fed up" with cannibal moms, or that they will get "chewed out." This wears thin very quickly.

Pic might have some success on video, strictly on the basis of its lurid title. —*Kimm.*

An African Dream
(BRITISH)

A Hemdale release of a Jonoma presentation. Produced and written by John Smallcombe, Nodi Murphy. Directed by John Smallcombe. Camera (color), Paul Beeson, editor, Murphy; sound, Allan Morrison; production design, Johan Engels. Reviewed at USA Cinemas screening room, Boston, Sept. 9, 1988. (In Boston Film Festival.) MPAA Rating: PG. Running time: **93 MIN.**
Katherine Hastings . . . . Kitty Aldridge
Khatena . . . . John Kani
Reginald Hastings . . . . . . Dominic Jephcott
Harry Endicott . . . . John Carson
Sgt. Briscoe . . . . Richard Haines
Enid Endicott . . . . Joy Stewart Spence
George Bailey . . . . Kenneth Hendel
Agnes Cartwright . . . . Lyn Hooker

■ Boston — **"An African Dream" is another one of those films about how beastly colonial rule was for Africa — especially for the white liberals who had to stand by and watch. Modestly budgeted film has little hope at the boxoffice, but might attract some small notice on video.**

Story centers on Katherine (Kitty Aldridge) who arrives in the Cape Colony, Africa, in 1906 to marry Reginald Hastings (Dominic Jephcott). They're very much in love, as syrupy music and swirling camerawork make clear. She has little interest in joining other colonial wives in the "Daughters Of The Empire," a bunch of gossiping biddies who seem to have come from a road company of "The Music Man."

Instead she agonizes about how poorly native blacks are treated, although she seems perfectly comfortable with her house full of servants. One day Katherine meets Khatena (John Kani), an English-educated black African who runs a school on the Xhosa reservation, and whose father was killed in a battle with the colonials 10 years before. His entrance is greeted with such a dramatic surge of music we know he's in for trouble.

A schoolteacher before she arrived in Africa, Katherine begins teaching at Khatena's school. While her husband allows it, even welcoming Khatena into his home, it is clear Katherine has gone beyond what polite colonial society finds acceptable. Only eccentric Harry Endicott (John Carson) can't understand what all the fuss is about.

Climax involves an attack on Khatena and his school while the loyal British subjects are enjoying a minstrel show imported from the U.S. Result is death and destruction, with the redeeming fact — as an end title informs us — that Katherine was inspired to continue teaching African children.

Script is clichéd from start to finish, with local scenery being the main draw. While several shots seem reminiscent of "Out Of Africa," one scene, with badly matted-in night sky, seems more like a low-budget horror film. Performances are adequate if unmemorable, and will probably look better on the small screen. —*Kimm.*

Vampire's Kiss

A John Daly and Derek Gibson presentation for Hemdale Film Corp. of a Magellan Pictures production. Produced by Barry Shils, Barbara Zitwer. Directed by Robert Bierman. Screenplay, Joseph Minion; camera (Duart color), Stefan Czapsky; editor, Angus Newton; music, Colin Towns; production design, Christopher Nowak; art direction, Ruth Ammon; casting, Marcia Shulman. Reviewed at USA Cinemas screening room, Sept. 7, 1988. (In Boston Film Festival.) MPAA Rating: R. Running time: **103 MIN.**
Peter Loew . . . . Nicolas Cage
Alva Restrepo . . . . Maria Conchita Alonso
Rachel . . . . Jennifer Beals
Dr. Dorothy Glaser . . . . . . Elizabeth Ashley
Jackie . . . . Kasi Lemmons
Emilio . . . . Bob Lujan
Sharon . . . . Jessica Lundy

■ Boston — **Hemdale is having a hard time getting a distribution deal on "Vampire's Kiss" and it's not difficult to see why. Other than as a cult item at midnight, confused pic has limited commercial possibilities, due to muddled script and another eccentric performance from Nicolas Cage.**

Cage is Peter Loew, a New York literary agent who works hard and plays hard, especially with the various young women he picks up at local niteries. Only indication that all is not O.K. are his sessions with his shrink (Elizabeth Ashley).

One night his latest pickup (Jennifer Beals) exposes her fangs which she quickly sinks into his neck. Instead of killing him, she keeps him alive so that she may continue to feed. As a result he starts getting the urge for blood himself, becoming even more manic at work and taking it out on his beleaguered secretary (Maria Conchita Alonso).

So far the tone has been serio-comic, suggesting a story that seems as if Jay McInerney has rewritten "Dracula." Call it "Bright Lights, Big Teeth." The film takes a major U-turn, suddenly getting deadly serious as it appears that Loew is not turning into a vampire at all, but is becoming a full-blown psychotic. Latter portion of the film shows him raping, murdering and pleading with people to kill him.

Problem is that Cage's over-the-top performance generates little sympathy for the character, so it's tough to be interested in him as his personality disorder worsens. Additionally, since this development comes out of left field and subverts much of what has been seen in the first part of the film, audiences are likely to become confused about the character's predicament.

Cage always has been at his best when surrounded by other characters who are larger than life, as in "Raising Arizona" or "Moonstruck." Here, as in "Peggy Sue Got Married," his acting seems out of sync with the rest of the film, making his performance rather than his character the center of attention.

The supporting cast is given little to work with, as Alonso mostly cowers and Beals mostly bites Cage. Ashley fares best as the psychiatrist, particularly in a fantasy sequence at the end, in which she tells Cage's character what he wants to hear.

Pic might have worked as a horror comedy or as a case study psychological drama. This hybrid is unlikely to please fans of either genre.—*Kimm.*

Heartbreak Hotel

A Buena Vista release of a Touchstone Pictures presentation, in association with Silver Screen Partners III of a Hill/Obst production. Produced by Linda Obst, Debra Hill. Supervising producer, Stephanie Austin. Directed by Chris Columbus. Screenplay, Columbus; camera (Metrocolor), Stephen Dobson; editor, Raja Gosnell; music, Georges Delerue; production design, John Muto; art direction, Dan Webster; set decoration, Anne Kuljian; costume design, Nord Haggerty; sound (Dolby), Donald B. Summer; choreographer, Monica Devereux; associate producer, Stacey Sher; production managers, Robin Clark, Timothy Silver; assistant director, Mark Radcliffe; casting, Todd M. Thaler. Reviewed at the National Theater, Westwood, Calif., Sept. 26, 1988. MPAA Rating: PG-13. Running time: 93 MIN.

Elvis Presley . . . . David Keith
Marie Wolfe . . . . Tuesday Weld
Johnny Wolfe . . . . Charlie Schlatter
Pam Wolfe . . . . Angela Goethals
Rosie Pantangellio . . . Jacque Lynn Colton
Steve Ayres . . . . Chris Mulkey
Irene . . . . Karen Landry

■ Hollywood — Even Elvis never made a picture this bad. Writer-director Chris Columbus' weakly conceived fantasy makes the ultimate mockery of the late idol. After initial sampling, b.o. should be nil.

Charlie Schlatter plays a small-town teen who kidnaps Elvis Presley after a 1972 concert appearance and brings him home to cheer up his ditzy mom (Tuesday Weld), who's been roughed up by her latest rotten boyfriend (Chris Mulkey).

Seems family life hasn't been too good since Dad left, and the only thing that makes Mom smile is memories of Elvis, who apparently resembles Dad (and who, incidentally, Weld played opposite in "Wild In The Country" in 1961).

Once he arrives out in Nowheresville, Elvis (David Keith) offers some token resistance, then settles right into the family for a few days, soothing bedtime traumas for little sister and lonely mama alike. He also garishly redecorates the old hotel the family lives in, gives junior some pointers on rock 'n' roll and women, and performs with junior's hand at the high school talent contest.

In short, whatever Elvis might have been, here he serves as all things to all people, and having him around makes everything better.

In the end, he flies off in a big airplane after letting each member of the family know how swell they are and that he'd stay if he could.

Even goony nonsense like this might have achieved some degree of charm in the right hands, but here, it's worse than it sounds.

Columbus seems at a loss to decide what his story's about or convey a consistent tone or message. One minute he makes a monkey out of Elvis, the next he takes a cornball stab at making him a hero.

Schlatter's character spends half the time in sneering confrontations with Elvis about how he's given up and lost touch with his roots. Supposedly, this little jolt of reality serves to turn "The King" around.

So what if history says different.

Dialog for the most part is dreadful. Rapport between Elvis and the kid consists of them calling each other "man" a lot.

Weld's role is vacuous; she does what she can with it. Keith is credible enough as Elvis under the dismal circumstances, and occasionally gets the Southern charm across, though he's not exactly a dead ringer. He's mighty trim for 1972.

Predictably, what passes for rock 'n' roll in this pic is the sanitized Disneyland variety.

It's hard to believe anyone from the Presley Estate could have further diluted Presley's oversold image by lending it to this farce. One feels sorry for the few children who will be exposed to it.

Tech credits are okay; Georges Delerue's confused score, with its schmaltzy romantic music, is a bust.
—Daws.

Night Of The Demons

An Intl. Film Marketing release of a Meridian Pictures presentation of a Paragon Arts Intl. production. Produced by Joe Augustyn. Executive producer, Walter Josten. Directed by Kevin S. Tenney. Screenplay, Augustyn; camera (color), David Lewis; editor, Daniel Duncan; music, Dennis Michael Tenney; art direction, Ken Aichele; set decoration, Sally Nicolav; costumes, Donna Reynolds; sound (Ultra-Stereo), Bo Harwood; special make-up effects, Steve Johnson; stunt coordinator, John Stuart; supervising producer, Jeff Geoffray; line producer, Don Robinson; associate producers, Michael Josten, Rene Torres, Patricia Bando Josten; assistant director, Kelly Schroeder. Reviewed at AMC Northland 2, Southfield, Mich., Sept. 10, 1988. MPAA Rating: R. Running time: 89 MIN.

Jay . . . . Lance Fenton
Judy . . . . Cathy Podewell
Roger . . . . Alvin Alexis
Stooge . . . . Hal Havins
Angela . . . . Mimi Kinkade
Suzanne . . . . Linnea Quigley
Max . . . . Phillip Tanzini
Fran . . . . Jill Terashita
Helen . . . . Allison Barron
Sal . . . . William Gallo
Billy . . . . Donnie Jeffcoat

■ Detroit — "Night Of The Demons" combines high energy, fine production values, effective special effects, credible acting and sprightly script to turn out one of the better it's-Halloween-so-let's-blow-away-some-teenagers films.

Although the plot is threadbare by now, a good dose of humor and a funhouse approach make this a pleaser for fans of this type of film. Limited release, however, and a modest campaign could conspire to exorcise "Demons" at the box-office.

We've been here before. It's Halloween — this time demons are allowed to be AWOL from hell for a little R&R at our expense.

A group of teens plan a party at what used to be a funeral parlor, before the head of the house wasted his family and himself. Since then, the place has been rumored to be possessed.

It's the perfect place to get down,

say Angela and Suzanne, a pair of attractive albeit weird teens who plan to scare the bejesus out of some classmates.

Trouble is, during a makeshift seance they get down a little too far, all the way to hell, and unknowingly release a demon, who possesses the spooky pair.

Once it's clear Angela and Suzanne mean business, the rest of the pic is filled trying to get out of the house, or at least make it until dawn, when Halloween is over and the demons must retreat.

"Demons" comes from the same people who presented the dreary "Witchboard." Thanks to some hip writing from Joe Augustyn and earnest directing by Kevin S. Tenney, "Demons" is a fanciful romp through the funeral parlor funhouse.

Teen lust, burned out 1960s parents and the myriad teen slaying pics are all parodied here, with a nod to such genre staples as "Evil Dead" and "The Exorcist."

You know from the minute one of the teenager says "maybe we should get out of here" that most of them aren't going to make it to dawn. The fun is trying to guess who will. In this respect, "Demons" offers a few surprises, including a hip and satisfying conclusion. *—Advo.*

Il Giovane Toscanini
(Young Toscanini)
(ITALIAN-FRENCH)

A Carthago Films (Paris)/Canal Plus/-FR3/La Sept/Italian Intl. Pictures (Rome)/-RAI-TV Channel 1 coproduction. Produced by Fulvio Lucisano, Tarak Ben Ammar. Directed by Franco Zeffirelli. Screenplay, William H. Stadiem; camera (Technicolor, Eclair color), Daniele Nannuzzi; editor, Jim Clark, Brian Oats, Franca Silvi, Amadeo Giomini; art direction, Andrea Crisanti, Enrico Fiorentini, Angelo Santucci; costumes, Tom Rand; associate producer, Giuseppe Pisciotto. Reviewed at Venice Film Festival (Special Events), Sept. 5, 1988. Running time: 120 MIN.

Arturo Toscanini . . . . . . C. Thomas Howell
Nadina Bulichoff . . . . Elizabeth Taylor
Margherita . . . . Sophie Ward
Mother Allegri . . . . Pat Heywood
Claudio Rossi . . . . John Rhys-Davies
Dom Pedro II . . . . Philippe Noiret
Also with: Franco Nero (Claudio Toscanini), Nicholas Chagrin, Irma Capece Minutolo (Mantelli), Leon Lissek, Carlo Bergonzi, Giovanna Stella La Nocita, Simon Gregor, Elsa Agalbato.

■ Venice — Franco Zeffirelli's $14,000,000-plus biopic "Young Toscanini," featuring C. Thomas Howell and Elizabeth Taylor, was met at Venice with derogatory guffaws from a hostile press indisposed to the popular Italo director after his remarks on "The Last Temptation Of Christ."

Part of the hilarity, however, arises from the film itself, a pompous comic strip rendition of the first bloomings of artistic genius amid costly overdressed sets, Liz in blackface singing "Aida," and a Mother Cabrini nursing Brazilian

slaves. Excess is the order of the day in "Young Toscanini," and film perversely won supporters for its very kitsch.

Some of pic's gems may be toned down by the director, who wants to trim 10 minutes from the version screened in Venice in the interest of subtlety. It would be a pity, as well as unavailing.

For the charms of "Toscanini" lie exclusively in its brazen extravagance and anti-historical overstatement. Obviously directed at the kind of audience who used to get its kicks at the Colosseum, pic revels in its triteness and spares not even Taylor, who looks fabulous but does nothing to turn opera star Nadina Bulichoff into a serious role. Still without U.S. distribution at press time, pic is likely to get plenty of exposure on the world's small screens.

Tone is set from opening scene at La Scala (1883) where the 18-year-old Arturo Toscanini (the flashing-eyed C. Thomas Howell, an able performer) auditions to a disinterested selection committee. He bangs his cello case shut and tells them off, losing the job but earning the respect of impresario Claudio Rossi (jolly John Rhys-Davies). He leaps at a tour with Rossi's orchestra to South America.

Some of pic's finest moments occur aboard ship. Arturo takes the initiative to severely rehearse the company's singers, winning the attention of Sister Margherita (Sophie Ward, an angelic thesp who despite all sticks in the mind). This blond from a rich Milanese family wants to dedicate her life to missionary work, at the side of Mother Allegri (the high-spirited Pat Heywood, in pic's one real performance).

Though attracted to the passionate young musician with Socialist ideals, Margherita keeps her doe-like eyes fixed on her hapless patients, when their ills don't turn her delicate stomach. Arturo consoles himself during a fearful tempest, directing the waves with fiery zeal while bathed by the driving storm.

The orchestra debarks in Rio and Arturo is given his toughest assignment: to get the diva Bulichoff to rehearsals. Taylor, glimpsed in her Aida get-up in a flashback, now reappears with a simple tan in her jungle mansion, whose excesses of decor stun even the hero. Arturo is rebuffed on his first attempt, but will come back later and convince Bulichoff the world needs her voice.

Between visits to Margherita's hospital for slave children, tempestuous orchestra rehearsals and telling off the prima donna for keeping one of her slaves chained to a Gone With The Wind tree outside the house, Arturo reaches opening night. He is still a cellist, but when Rossi loses his incompetent orchestra director he raises the cry, "Call Toscanini!"

The young genius puts on a show the audience will never forget (including Philippe Noiret as a strangely subdued Emperor of Brazil (who is Bulichoff's lover and has been told off by Toscanini for running a country with slaves). The high point, however, belongs to Liz, who steps forward in the middle of the opera gripping the hands of two crawling black extras and launches a plea for the abolition of slavery.

This ludicrous scene — taken from history, yet — ends the film on the note it began, and occasions, for the third time, the line, "There are things more important in life than music."

Visually it's lusher than even Zeffirelli's "La Traviata." Bits of "Aida" are pleasant. —*Yung.*

Memories Of Me

An MGM/UA release of an MGM Pictures presentation of an Odyssey Entertainment production. Produced by Alan King, Billy Crystal, Michael Hertzberg. Executive producers, Gabe Sumner, J. David Marks. Directed by Henry Winkler. Screenplay, Eric Roth, Crystal; camera (color), Andrew Dintenfass; editor, Peter E. Berger; music, Georges Delerue; production design, William J. Cassidy; casting, Mike Fenton, Jane Feinberg, Judy Taylor. Reviewed at Toronto Festival of Festivals, Sept. 13, 1988. MPAA Rating: PG-13. Running time: **105 MIN.**

Abbie	Billy Crystal
Abe	Alan King
Lisa	JoBeth Williams
Sean Connery	Himself
Dorothy Davis	Janet Carroll
First assistant director	David Ackroyd

Also with: Phil Fondacaro, Robert Pastorelli, Mark L. Taylor, Peter Elbling, Larry Cedar, Sheryl Bernstein, Joe Shea, Jay (Flash) Riley, Billy Beck, Margarito Mendoza, Noni White, Zachary Benjamin.

■ **Toronto — A conventional father-and-child reunion pic that's not as funny as it should have been, "Memories Of Me" qualifies for only a perfunctory theatrical release prior to video playoff, the ideal medium for a tv movie.**

Personality-driven performances by Billy Crystal as a lightly neurotic surgeon and Alan King as his insensitive Hollywood bit-player father should attract fans of the two to this by-the-book directing debut by Henry Winkler.

When wisecracking, trumpet-playing Dr. Abbie Polin (Crystal) has a heart attack in the operating room, his ex-girlfriend and colleague Lisa (JoBeth Williams) rallies to his side. The illness forces Crystal to reexamine his relationship with the lovely fellow doc and with the Hollywood father he hasn't seen in years.

Crystal flies from New York to L.A. where he immediately begins to replay past squabbles with King, a man who's been an extra in scores of big movies and is on first-name terms with stars like Sean Connery (who cameos) but has "never had my name in *Variety.*" King, however, has convinced himself that he's had a boffo career ("there's an art to being incidental") and a good life in spite of divorce and a distant relationship with his son.

Slowly and predictably, old Abe and young Abbie heal old wounds in a script that never deviates from story-conferenced norms. This rote scenario includes a plot-pointed "surprise" arrival in L.A. by Williams, who provides some lovely and impartial triangulation to this whole business of coming to terms.

Unfortunately, the filmmakers jettison the satirical/black humorous possibilities of their story in favor of some passingly amusing injoke commentary on showbiz and a cloyingly maudlin resolution that sadly underestimates the sophistication of contemporary audiences. Byplay concerning Crystal-Williams' Jewish-Gentile pairing is another element totally lacking in originality. —*Rich.*

Daffy Duck's Quackbusters
(ANIMATED)

A Warner Bros. release. Produced by Steven S. Greene. Coproduced by Kathleen Helppie-Shipley. Directed and story by Greg Ford, Terry Lennon. Sequences directed by Chuck Jones, Friz Freleng, Robert McKimson. Camera (Technicolor), Nick Vasu Inc.; music, Carl Stalling, Milt Franklyn, Bill Lava; animators, Brenda Banks, Nancy Beiman, Daniel Haskett, Mark Kausler, Norm McCabe, Rebecca Rees, Darrell Van Citters, Frans Vischer; production manager, Bill Exter; postproduction supervisor, Jim Champin; production design, Robert Givens. Reviewed at 23d St. West 3 theater, N.Y., Sept. 24, 1988. MPAA Rating: G. Running time: **80 MIN.**

Voices: Mel Blanc, Mel Tormé, Roy Firestone, B.J. Ward.

■ **The fifth of WB's animated compilation films to be released this decade, "Daffy Duck's Quackbusters" is an entertaining effort. Effect wears thin on the big screen but pic will make noise in ancillary markets.**

Overall concept and new footage directed by Greg Ford and Terry Lennon has Daffy Duck inheriting a fortune from J.P. Cubish, but is haunted by the skinflint's ghost. Our hero forms an exorcising company, Ghosts 'R' Us, hiring pals Porky Pig and Bugs Bunny as assistants, and within this framework 11 WB cartoons dealing vaguely with the supernatural are packaged.

Most of the shorts were directed by Chuck Jones, with his trademark chases and falls on view, with Sylvester and Tweety Pie also featured. Transitions to new footage are okay, although the stalwart Mel Blanc's voice changes slightly for Porky Pig and Daffy, and the color varies detectably.

Ford and Lennon's structuring of the material works except for several "commercial breaks" of Daffy hawking his wares on tv which accentuate the episodic format.

Besides the classic cartoons, including Chuck Jones' "The Abominable Snow Rabbit" (with its monster parodying Lenny in "Of Mice And Men") plus Friz Freleng's "Hyde And Go Tweet" (riff on "Dr. Jekyll") and Robert McKim-

son's "Prize Pest," film is highlighted by inclusion of Ford and Lennon's 1987 "The Duxorcist," a funny and hip parody in which Mel Blanc is well supported by B.J. Ward in the vocal department.

Feature's prolog consists of stand-alone new short "The Night Of The Living Duck" (in which Mel Tormé provides Daffy with a nightclub singing voice), also directed by Ford and Lennon. —*Lor.*

John Huston
(DOCU-COLOR/B&W)

A Point Blank presentation. Produced by Joni Levin. Executive producers, David Ganz, Judith Ganz. Directed by Frank Martin. Written by Martin and Charles Beagelman; camera (color), Harry Dawson; editor, Robert L. Sinise; production design, Thomas A. Walsh; art direction, Jane Osmann; music, Steven Goldstein. Reviewed at USA Cinemas Copley Place, Boston, Sept. 19, 1988. (In Boston Film Festival.) No MPAA Rating. Running time: **126 MIN.**

With: Robert Mitchum (narrator), Paul Newman, Lauren Bacall, Evelyn Keyes, Arthur Miller, Michael Caine, Anjelica Huston, Danny Huston, Oswald Morris, Burgess Meredith.

■ **Boston — "John Huston" offers filmgoers a chance to revel in the life and career of the late director, and it's hard to see anyone walking away disappointed by anything except the length. Even at over two hours, it still leaves you hungry for more.**

Filmmakers Frank Martin and Joni Levin combine film clips, home movies and interviews to trace Huston's life, with narrator Robert Mitchum as a guide. Mitchum appears on an attic set filled with Huston memorabilia and props connected to his various films.

Perhaps the most interesting material, even beyond such things as color home movies on the set of "Beat The Devil," are the dozen or so interviews Huston gave over the years, pulled together for the first time. They allow Huston to remain an active participant in his life story, commenting on everything from how generous Warner Bros. was to let him direct "The Maltese Falcon" to how his love of James Joyce led to his making "The Dead."

The recent interviews, with stars, colleagues and family, provide several amusing anecdotes, especially from cinematographer Oswald Morris, a frequent Huston collaborator. Morris recalls shooting "Moulin Rouge" and how Huston ended up telling off the people from Technicolor who didn't like the smoky look he was using for the film. Of the interview subjects, only Arthur Miller seems to overstay his welcome, popping up on subjects where he seems no more than a distant observer.

Michael Caine also provides an interesting look at Huston on what was supposed to have been his death bed a decade ago. After bidding him and "The Man Who Would Be

King" costar Sean Connery a final farewell, Huston wouldn't see Caine again for several years, by which time, Caine notes, Huston had made four more films.

Pic's length is an asset in an unexpected way. Rough cut apparently ran some 3½ hours; cutting to two has given short shrift to his later career, with "Wise Blood" and "Victory" not even mentioned. While film might be shortened a few minutes more for commercial run, it also can be expanded for tv and vid markets, where greater length might make film seem more like an "event." —*Kimm.*

Imagine: John Lennon
(DOCU)

A Warner Bros. release of a David L. Wolper production. Produced by Wolper, Andrew Solt. Coproducer, Sam Egan. Directed by Solt. Written by Egan and Solt; camera (color), uncredited; supervising film editor, Bud Friedgen; editor, Bert Lovitt; additional editing, David Gaines; sound, John Bolz; Beatles songs remixed by George Martin, John Lennon songs remixed by Rob Stevens; editorial consultant, Frank Palmieri. Reviewed at Warner Bros. studios, Burbank, Calif., Sept. 22, 1988. MPAA Rating: R. Running time: **103 MIN.**

■ **Hollywood — Even in a world saturated with images of pop-culture icons, "Imagine: John Lennon" stands as a remarkably vital and valuable document of one of the most influential creative spirits of this century.**

Boxoffice looks promising and video prospects should be long-range, as this filmed portrait should hold interest as lasting as the music's.

Filmmakers, blessed with the extraordinary good fortune of Lennon's exhaustive archives, have delivered an honest, nearly naked telling that includes much fresh footage that speaks volumes about a man and an era.

Lennon's widow Yoko Ono reportedly opened the 200 hours of film and video footage in the archives to producer David Wolper because she wanted someone "tough," who she couldn't "push around," to make the definitive film on Lennon. Reportedly, she had no approvals at any point or any say in the final picture.

Resulting film is two-thirds about the Beatles, one-third about John's activities with Yoko, and while much that is unflattering is left out, there is enough balance, including segments of unguarded confrontation between the couple and their critics, to give it dimension well beyond a mere "tribute."

Lennon's energy, sense of involvement with the world, and constant growth all speak for themselves — the story is extremely engaging.

Pic begins with John's boyhood traumas and moves into formation of the Beatles, capturing the hysteria and discovery of the global phenomenon that resulted in swift and telling style. Last third focuses on Lennon's work as a conceptual artist and peace activist with Ono.

Despite a chronicle of events familiar to most everyone over 25, there is much in "Imagine" that is fresh and revealing. Lennon's life apparently was one of the best documented ever lived; there always was a camera running.

In one segment, Lennon discovers a bedraggled young disciple lurking on the grounds of his estate in Ascot, England, and gives him a paternal lecture on not taking the music too personally. The young man, overwhelmed by the meeting and embarrassed by the camera, actually quotes lyrics he thinks were written specifically for him. Lennon determinedly sets him straight, then invites him in for dinner.

Another unexpected scene is a confrontation between the Lennons and cartoonist Al Capp during their Montreal Bed-In, in which Capp is extremely insulting and critical. The cameras roll and roll while the couple tries to respond.

There are intimate scenes shot in the Lennons' bedroom two weeks before John's death, and photos taken of him emerging from a limo instants before he was shot.

The murder is particularly well handled with a montage as though Lennon's life is passing before his eyes, and filmmakers wisely refrain from any mention or image of Lennon's assassin. The slo-mo shot of Lennon-like spectacles shattering seems a bit too stagy.

Footage of the candlelight vigils and outpouring of sorrow that followed in December 1980 is extremely moving.

Much of the film actually is narrated by Lennon — through sound bites snipped from interviews. There also are recent interviews with his first wife Cynthia, sons Sean and Julian, producer George Martin, Lennon's Aunt Mimi, who raised him, friend Elliiot Mintz and others. Beatles Paul McCartney, George Harrison and Ringo Starr, interestingly, are not interviewed.

It all comes out at a time when Albert Goldman's unflattering biography has laid Lennon's life bare — and raised controversy that will no doubt benefit "Imagine" at the b.o. —Daws.

Dolly, Lotte und Maria
(WEST GERMAN-DOCU)

A Film by Rosa von Praunheim. Produced (in association with NDR-TV) and directed by Von Praunheim. Camera (color), Jeff Preiss; editor, Mike Shepard, Von Praunheim; sound, Shepard; collaboration, Claudia Steinberg. Reviewed at Collective for Living Cinema, N.Y., Sept. 7, 1988. Running time: 60 MIN.

With: Dolly Haas, Lotte Goslar, Maria Piscator.

■ German director Rosa von Praunheim continues his fascination with the stars and stories of Berlin's golden time between the wars. This time he tracks down three surviving female personalities of the 1920s.

Each had successful careers in Germany and Europe before emigrating to the U.S. a kick step ahead of the Nazis. It's the three grand dames telling their own stories that lift this docu above the routine.

They all began their careers as dancers, and though non-Jews, they fled Germany's growing social and political unrest, ultimately settling in Hollywood and New York. They remained in the U.S. after the war and continued their careers with varying degrees of success. All three currently reside in the New York area.

Clown dancer Lotte Goslar is still active with her company, and a couple of seasons back made her stage acting debut in Martha Clarke's "Vienna Lusthaus." Early in her career she worked with modern dance pioneer Mary Wigman, and after arriving in the U.S. choreographed for fellow expatriate Bertolt Brecht.

Dolly Haas, now married to New York Times caricaturist Al Hirschfeld, starred in films in Germany and England, including the 1936 remake of D.W. Griffith's "Broken Blossoms." Arriving in Hollywood with a studio contract, she was never cast. Eventually she appeared on the New York stage in the late 1940s.

Maria Piscator, the third subject chronicled by Von Praunheim, began as a specialty dancer performing internationally. She choreographed for Max Reinhardt, and later married legendary theater director Erwin Piscator. Together they founded the influential Dramatic Workshop at the New School. She remains active at 90, recently opening the Dramatic Workshop II.

Von Praunheim's straightforward approach takes things pretty much as the ladies wish themselves presented. As a bouquet to their longevity and talent, Von Praunheim has crafted a fitting tribute. Camerawork and editing are adequate but the film's low budget shows. —Owl.

Dream Demon
(BRITISH)

A Palace Pictures production and release (Spectrafilm in North America). Executive producers, Jonathan Olsberg, Nik Powell, Peter Watson-Wood, Timothy Woolford. Produced by Paul Webster. Directed by Harley Cokliss. Screenplay, Christopher Wicking, Cokliss; camera (color), Ian Wilson; editor, Ian Crafford. David Martin; music, Bill Nelson; production design, Hugo Luczyc-Wyhowski; coproducer, David A. Barber; production supervisor, David Brown; sound editor, Ron Davis; special makeup effects, Animated Extras; makeup supervisor, Daniel Parker. Reviewed at the Bijou Theater, London, Sept. 20, 1988. Running time: 89 MIN.

Jenny	Kathleen Wilhoite
Diana	Jemma Redgrave
Paul	Jimmy Nail
Peck	Tim Spall
Little girl	Annabelle Lanyon
Oliver	Mark Greenstreet
Deborah	Susan Fleetwood
Jenny's father	Nickolas Grace
Minister	Robert Warner

■ London — A rare British entry in the psychological thriller/horror stakes. "Dream Demon" is an uneven blend of truly dazzling special effects, nonsensical plot and truly awful dialog.

A fist punching clean through a human head, a maggot bursting through a doll's eye, a bridegroom who loses his head — literally — at the altar, and other ghoulish tricks likely will turn off more people than are turned on.

That, and the absence of marquee names, probably will limit its theatrical life to hardcore devotees of the genre, but it's ideal fare for the more easily satisfied homevid consumers. Script by London-based Yank director Harley Cokliss and Christopher Wicking visits terrible things upon naive English socialite Diana Markham (Jemma Redgrave) when she sleeps. As she appears to suffer from narcolepsy, that's often.

Actually, her waking moments aren't much fun either. A press photographer and reporter (Tim Spall and Jimmy Nail), the kind who give much of Fleet Street a deservedly bad name, hound her because they're unaccountably curious about her impending marriage. Her fiance, Oliver (Mark Greenstreet) an airman who was a hero of the Falklands war, is a priggish stuffed shirt who clearly does not love her.

Only explanation offered for her nightmares is some textbook gibberish quoted by her doctor friend to the effect that as a virgin she's scared stiff of the marital bed. To add to her woes, Diana is befriended by Kathleen Wilhoite as a hip, streetwise Los Angelino who's come to London to discover the secrets of her upbringing there, of which she conveniently has no memory.

For both girls, nightmares and reality converge, as the demons of their past and present assail them. Cokliss springs plenty of surprises thanks to his expert special effects team but his efforts to build tension to what could have been a potent climax are sabotaged by scenes that are too silly to be scary, and patches of dumb dialog.

In this kind of production, makeup and other effects are primary, and the acting secondary. Redgrave (daughter of Corin, of that esteemed thesping family) in her film debut, is not required to do much more than register terror and scream. Wilhoite brings more presence to her role as the Yank punk whose childhood comes back to haunt her. Greenstreet as the hugely unlikable fiance has the most thankless task and is saddled with

nearly all of the film's worst lines.

Bill Nelson's thunderous, overwrought music might have been more effective if the visuals merited such heavyweight treatment.
—Dogo.

Punchline

A Columbia Pictures release. Produced by Daniel Melnick, Michael Rachmil. Written and directed by David Seltzer. Camera (Deluxe color), Reynaldo Villalobos; editor, Bruce Green; music, Charles Gross; production design, Jack DeGovia; art direction, John Jensen; set decoration, Peg Cummings; set design, Joe Hubbard, Pete Smith; sound (Dolby), Robert Grieve; assistant director, Jim Van Wyck; casting, Jackie Burch. Reviewed at the Burbank Studios, Calif., Sept. 14, 1988. MPAA Rating: R. Running time: 128 MIN.

Lilah Krytsick	Sally Field
Steven Gold	Tom Hanks
John Krytsick	John Goodman
Romeo	Mark Rydell

Also with comics: Pam Matteson, George Michael McGrath, Taylor Negron, Barry Neikrug, Angel Salazar, Damon Wayans, Joycee Katz, Mac Robbins, Max Alexander, Paul Kozlowski, Barry Sobel, Marty Pollio.

■ Hollywood — Despite its title, "Punchline" is not a comedy. It's an uneven melodrama where Tom Hanks exhibits flashes of brilliance as a caustically tongued stand-up comic in a strange, undefinable romance with protege Sally Field.

Hanks is the real reason to see the film and those who enjoyed watching him in "Big" will find a different, more realized comedian in "Punchline."

"Punchline" opens up the unfunny backstage world of stand-up comics by zeroing in on the lives and motivations of two very different people — Hanks as a failing medical student who derives his humor from his experiences with cadavers and other things and Sally Field, a Jersey housefrau and achingly bad novice comic with an unfulfilled desire to make people laugh.

Writer/director David Seltzer has tapped into one of the more intriguing subcultures of the entertainment world, here a place called the Gas Station in Manhattan where club owner Mark Rydell gives almost anyone a break.

In-between some Felliniesque routines by such real-life comics like George Michael McGrath, a singing nun, Max Alexander, a pathetically unfunny 1-liner-type comic and Mac Robbins, who plays a sad has-been, is the consistently hilarious Hanks.

There's a dark side to his character, which makes his time on stage more than superficially entertaining. We learn of his unbridled ambition through his interaction with fellow comics, his self-loathing for abandoning the family profession of medicine and his irresponsible behavior when it comes to paying the rent.

Field supposedly brings out his soft side, playing the most unlikely of romantic interests — a styleless 40ish Mom of two kids. At first, she is embarrassingly bad at telling dirty Polish jokes and then, after some instruction by Hanks to find her voice through her own suburban experiences, develops a kind of goofy, MOR routine.

How she manages to escape her claustrophobic existence playing wife to a traditionally minded insurance salesman husband (John Goodman) to try her schtick with the other wanna-bes is never quite believable. Even less convincing is why Hanks would find her attractive and so desirable that he makes a failing attempt to convince her to leave her family behind and marry him.

Domestic scenes where she tries to juggle her clandestine outings to the Gas Station with throwing together dinners for hubby and clients or explaining to her daughters how mommy really needs to perform are cornball indeed.

Sentimentality in scenes like these cuts into the edge that Seltzer establishes so well in the beginning to the point where it would have been better to leave her completely out of the story and focus solely on Hanks, or perhaps have him be with a woman of a more compelling stripe.

The production overall manages to keep its audience off-center with surprisingly unpredictable moments — notably when Rydell is on the scene trying to keep things or his comics together. His watching Hanks falling apart on stage is disturbing, poignant and memorable cinema. It would be great to see director Rydell before the cameras more frequently.

Lensing by cinematographer Reynaldo Villalobos and scoring by Charles Gross are exemplary.

—*Brit.*

War Party

A Tri-Star Pictures release of a Hemdale production. Executive producers, Chris Chesser, Franc Roddam. Produced by John Daly, Derek Gibson, Bernard Williams. Directed by Franc Roddam. Screenplay, Spencer Eastman; camera (CFI color), Brian Tufano; editor, Sean Barton; production design, Michael Bingham; sound, Ed White; production manager, Bernard Williams; assistant director, Pete Guiliano; casting, Lora Kennedy. Reviewed at Toronto Festival of Festivals, Sept. 17, 1988. Running time: **99 MIN.**
Sonny ....Billy Wirth
Skitty ....Kevin Dillon
Warren...................Tim Sampson
Jay ....Jimmy Ray Wales
Calvin.............Kevin M. Howard
Detweiler.............M. Emmet Walsh
Lindquist ....Cameron Thor
Sheriff ....Jerry Hardin

■Toronto — A lethal contemporary game of Cowboys and Indians is played out in this revisionist western whose thesis is that, deep down, old hatreds never die. British director Franc Roddam comes down firmly on the side of the Native Americans in this downbeat

action pic which looks to do average biz.

Opening scene is the aftermath of a massacre that took place 100 years ago: a camera pan, following runaway horses, brings us, without a cut, to present-day Montana and a small town with a large Indian population. The (white) Mayor has planned, as a Labor Day tourist attraction, a re-enactment of that old battle; but racial hatreds run deep, and a drunken white boy takes the game too seriously, shooting and killing an Indian youth whose pals quickly avenge him.

Pic then develops into a manhunt as five Indian youths take off on horseback, soon reduced to three when one is shot, another scalped by an unofficial posse of racist whites. As the situation gets out of control, the Governor calls in the National Guard and the escaping Indians, now reduced to two, are forced to make a final stand against overwhelming odds.

It's to the credit of Roddam, and the late screenwriter Spencer Eastman (to whom pic is dedicated) that the present-day world of the West's Indians is so thoughtfully and seriously presented. Yet as the film progresses, credulity is stretched as a well-aimed Indian arrow downs a light aircraft, or the officer in charge of National Guard troops manages to make the most unlikely decisions.

Billy Wirth and Kevin Dillon impress as the two young Indian leaders, and Tim Sampson, who looks a lot like his late father, Will, has a moving, if unduly protracted, death scene.

Despite its interesting depiction of modern Indian life, "War Party" is basically just another pursuit movie, no better or worse than the average. Technical credits are all good, but pic will probably have a longer life on video shelves than in the theatrical market. —*Strat.*

Criminal Law

A Tri-Star Pictures release of a Hemdale presentation of a Northwood production. Executive producers, John Daly, Derek Gibson. Produced by Robert Maclean, Hilary Heath. Directed by Martin Campbell. Screenplay, Mark Kasdan; camera (color), Philip Meheux; editor, Christopher Wimble; music, Jerry Goldsmith; production design, Curtis Schnell; sound, Peter Shewchuk; coproducer, Ken Cord; casting, Vera Miller. Reviewed at Toronto Festival Of Festivals, Sept. 15, 1988. MPAA Rating: R. Running time: **117 MIN.**
Ben Chase ....Gary Oldman
Martin Thiel ....Kevin Bacon
Ellen Faulkner ....Karen Young
Detective Mesel..........Joe Don Baker
Det. Stillwell ....Tess Harper
Gary Hull ....Ron Lea
Claudia Curwen ....Karen Woolridge
Dr. Thiel ....Elizabeth Sheppard
Prof. Clemens .....Michael Sinelnicoff
Also with: Terrence Labrosse, Jennie Walker, Rob Boy, Tyrone Benskin.

■Toronto — A very good actor plays a good lawyer in a badly written and directed crime drama and loses the case for suspenseful film-

making in "Criminal Law."

Gary Oldman's trouper turn as a hotshot attorney who ditches his ethics to trap a serial killer he's just had acquitted won't save this picture in the boxoffice court of public opinion. Tri-Star should move for early ancillary release on this disappointing treatment of a promising concept.

Director Martin Campbell (BBC's "Edge Of Darkness") opens his feature with police in Boston (played by Montreal) discovering a mutilated rape victim in a rain-soaked tableau of blackish-blue gloom, a mood/color motif that's recycled throughout the movie. Action then fast-forwards to a courtroom where cocky lawyer Ben Chase, rendered with superb American accent and mannerisms by British Oldman, pulls a sly trick out of his hat to demolish an eyewitness and free his wealthy, self-absorbed client Martin Thiel (Kevin Bacon).

No sooner is Bacon back on the streets, however, than the killer strikes again. Oldman realizes he's unleashed a monster, and is reminded of this constantly by two detectives (Joe Don Baker and Tess Harper).

The stage is set for a clumsily plotted psychological cat-and-mouse game between Oldman and Bacon. The bored rich-kid killer admires the streetwise lawyer and hopes to toy with him as an alter ego. The lawyer is intrigued and appalled by his amoral, sick client, and after overheated tumble-drying of his conscience, Oldman determines to bring Bacon to justice.

Oldman's resolve permits screenwriter Mark Kasdan to unleash upon the viewer a string of air-blown incoherent speeches on justice and morality that collapse under the weight of their cliched pomposity. A former law professor of Oldman's (played by Michael Sinelnicoff) is introduced only to provide a sounding board for these philosophical posturings.

As the narrative moves through some inconceivable plot twists to its never-in-doubt denouement, Campbell and Kasdan keep the red-herring pot boiling with blatant "say BOO!" quick-scare gimmicks that are unintentionally laughable. Along the way it's revealed that Bacon has chosen to become a self-styled "avenger" of unborn fetuses done in by his frosty abortionist mother Dr. Thiel (Elizabeth Sheppard). Seems that all of his victims were patients at the abortion clinic where mom works.

Oldman discovers this with the help of Ellen Faulkner (Karen Young), a comely blond who initially despises him but eventually winds up in the lawyer's bed in what may be the first cinematic sequence ever to intercut a violent, solo 4-wall squash set with a violent, sweaty lovemaking scene. This may be intended to establish Young's phys-

ical toughness when she has to fight off Bacon in a scene that unfortunately doesn't bring the movie to a climax.

Although Bacon is convincing as the icy, deranged killer, his character's menace is undermined by the story's ill-defined pretensions as an essay on the American legal system and a herky-jerky continuity that's fatiguing instead of tingling.

—*Rich.*

Full Moon In Blue Water

A Trans World Entertainment release of a Turman-Foster Co. production. Executive producers, Moshe Diamant, Eduard Sarlui. Produced by Lawrence Turman, David Foster, John Turman. Directed by Peter Masterson. Screenplay, Bill Bozzone; camera (Panavision, Technicolor), Fred Murphy; editor, Jill Savitt; music, Phil Marshall; casting; Ed Mitchell, Ed Johnston; costumes, Rondi Davis. Reviewed at USA Cinemas screening room, Sept. 20, 1988. (In the Boston Film Festival.) MPAA Rating: R. Running time: **94 MIN.**
Floyd....................Gene Hackman
Louise ....Teri Garr
The General ....Burgess Meredith
Jimmy....................Elias Koteas
Charlie.................Kevin Cooney
Virgil....................David Doty
Baytch ....Gil Glasgow

■Boston — An interesting cast is stranded in this utterly ordinary film about a man who thinks he has nothing to live for being saved by the woman who loves him. Cast and a strong advertising push might invite some sampling, but it's unlikely to have any staying power.

Story centers around Floyd (Gene Hackman), the proprietor of the Blue Water Grille, a run-down Texas saloon that has seen better days. Floyd spends his time watching home movies of his wife Dorothy, who disappeared the year before and is presumed dead. He has so lost the will to live that he can't even gather up the strength to demand payment from the few patrons he does have.

The main people in his life are the wheelchair-bound General (Burgess Meredith); Jimmy (Elias Koteas), the mentally disturbed young man who looks after the General; and Louise (Teri Garr), a school bus driver who, inexplicably, carries a torch for Floyd. Main drive to the plot is a plan to cheat Floyd out of his property by not letting him know that land values are about to rise due to the construction of a bridge to the mainland.

Pic is very stagebound, with most of the action taking place at the Blue Water, and twists of the plot largely seem created to give the characters something to do. Floyd and Louise have a major argument which ends with them hurling vicious insults at one another, yet suddenly they are reconciled after she tells him about the land fraud.

Another plot twist concerns Jimmy's fear that he has accidentally killed the General. He then holds Floyd and company hostage until he can figure out how to escape. This not particularly amusing situation gets dragged out until someone can finally outmaneuver him.

Cast does what they can with material, but principals are largely stuck with barely developed characters. Koteas has a nice turn as Jimmy, struggling to figure out how he can avoid being sent back to an institution, and Gil Glasgow draws a chuckle or two as a dim local sheriff. For the most part, though, the plot and characters are strictly by the numbers.

Tech credits are OK, but it does seem odd that a film where everyone keeps talking about the full moon of the title seems to take place mostly in daylight. —*Kimm.*

Elvira, Mistress Of The Dark

A New World Pictures release of an NBC production. Produced by Eric Gardner, Mark Pierson. Executive producer, Michael Rachmil. Directed by James Signorelli. Screenplay, Sam Egan, John Paragon, Cassandra Peterson; camera (CFI color), Hanania Baer; editor, Battle David; music, James Campbell; production design, John De Cuir Jr.; set design, Beverli Eagan; set decoration, Bruce A. Gibeson; costume design, Betsy Heimann; assistant director, Paul Moen; second unit director, Arthur Anderson; casting, Dennis Erdman; in Dolby stereo. Reviewed at Mann Chinese theater, Hollywood, Sept. 22, 1988. MPAA Rating: PG-13. Running time: **96 MIN.**

Elvira	Cassandra Peterson
Chastity Pariah	Edie McClurg
Mrs. Meeker	Pat Crawford Brown
Mr. Meeker	William Duell
Patty	Susan Kellermann
Bob Redding	Daniel Greene
Uncle	W.W. Morgan Sheppard

■ **Hollywood** — Elvira vamps shamelessly in "Elvira, Mistress Of The Dark," a film distinguished by the fact that the actress' face competes with her cleavage for screen time. Sophomoric and fun, pic should play well and generate some needed cash for New World.

This is a comedy where much of the humor is derived from jokes about the horror picture tv hostess' milky-white bosom that precariously stays inside her slinky trademark black floor-length dress for all but the last four minutes of the film — when she does a Vegas bit that showcases her particular anatomical talents.

After minor film roles ranging from Stephanie Rothman's "The Working Girls" to "Allan Quatermain," Cassandra Peterson as cult queen Elvira finds herself out of her tv hosting job just about the time she's notified to appear for the reading of her great aunt's will in the small Massachusetts town of Fallwell.

Elvira arrives in her fake leopard upholstered T-bird at the backlot of this cheesy-looking production and turns nearly every repressed puritan into slobbering sex-obsessed maniacs, the young boys especially.

Instead of money she so desperately needs to stage her comeback on the Vegas strip, Elvira is willed a seedy Victorian mansion, really a not-so-haunted house, a yapping poodle which she punks out with pink and blue paint (one of the film's funnier moments) and a cookbook that contains precious recipes her evil-eyed great uncle (W.W. Morgan Sheppard) covets.

Peterson, along with coscripters Sam Egan and John Paragon, puts herself in position to flaunt her form in every scene, spicing up the visuals with more double entendres than Mae West spoke in a lifetime.

PG-13 rating is right on target for most of the setups which are staged to mildly titillate the audience, skirting the rude and crude most of the time.

Under the guise of a story about witchcraft, filmmakers manage to have a good time ripping off memorable moments from a number of popular pictures, notably "The Wizard Of Oz" — referring to Kansas on her cross-country trip as "The Land Of Ahhs." About the only uncomfortably hilarious scene is watching her and her dinner date try and kill a squishy green "Alien"-type creature by shoving it in the garbage disposal.

Playing off her in good form as the town's horny old maid is Edie McClurg as Chastity Pariah, and long-suffering, henpecked William Duell whose wife (Pat Crawford Brown) takes the nasty part à la the late Anne Ramsey.

Smaller, equally silly roles, are well done by Susan Kellermann, Elvira's rival for chest size, and Daniel Greene, the dumb jock who runs the local theater.

Low-budget production quality is fitting for the level of humor; sometimes things are in focus and sometimes not. In any event, it's almost irrelevant since the two objects mostly photographed aren't often stationary. —*Brit.*

Night Wars

An SVS Films release of an Action Intl. Pictures production. Produced by Fritz Matthews. Executive producers, David Winters, Marc Winters. Directed by David A. Prior. Screenplay, Prior, from story by Prior, Ted Prior, William Zipp; camera (United color), Stephen Ashley Blake; editor, Reinhard Schreiner; music, Tim James, Steve McClintock, Mark Mancina; sound, Ken Segar; art direction, Ted Prior; assistant director, Richard Wright; production manager, Thomas Baldwin; special effects, Chuck Whitton; stunt coordinator, Bob Ivy; associate producer, Bruce Lewin; casting, William Zipp. Reviewed at 42d St. Selwyn theater, N.Y., Sept. 25, 1988. MPAA Rating: R. Running time: **88 MIN.**

Sgt. Trent Matthews	Brian O'Connor
Dr. Campbell	Dan Haggerty
Jim	Cameron Smith
McGregor	Steve Horton
Johnny	Chet Hood
Susan	Jill Foor

■ "Night Wars" presents an extremely goofy approach to the familiar theme of Vietnam War vets' malaise, treated in supernatural terms. Pic is a standard-issue quickie, more for video than theatrical fans.

Brian O'Connor and Cameron Smith are the vets who have nightmares and hallucinations relating to their leaving behind platoonmate Chet Hood back in Vietnam. Problem is that the nightmares are for real, with wounds inflicted while sleeping still there upon wakeup and even Hood's severed finger materializing for real.

Another war buddy, Dan Haggerty, is now a shrink who rather laughably doesn't believe the heroes' tales of their predicament and gives them a sedative instead of keeping them awake. When machinegun fire from the Great Beyond kills Matthews' pretty wife Jill Foor, Haggerty is a believer.

Silliest scene has O'Connor and Smith putting on camouflage makeup and outfits, arming themselves to the teeth and lying down on a bed together to sleep — they're to do battle with their renegade nemesis Steve Horton, but visually it's campy.

Prior's action scenes are perfunctory, but the acting is okay, except for a very hammy turn by Horton. The supernatural content linking dreams with reality is unconvincing, used in "anything goes" fashion. —*Lor.*

De Wording
(Genesis)
(DUTCH-DOCU)

An RVD release of a Rasker Groep production. Produced by Frans Rasker. Directed by Cherry Duyns. Camera (color), Marc Felperlaan; editor, Ot Louw; sound, Menno Euwe. Reviewed at Tuschinski Theater, Amsterdam, Sept. 1, 1988. Running time: **60 MIN.**

With: Hans van Manen, Carel Visser, Reinbert de Leeuw, Armando, Ida Gerhardt.

■ **Amsterdam** — Conceived as a gift from the Dutch government to Queen Beatrix on her 50th birthday, film has been prepared in English, Spanish and French versions, and will cater to fests, art school programs and culture tv slots.

Pic follows five artists in their creation of a work, from conception to execution. Artists are choreographer Hans van Manen, sculptor Carel Visser, composer-conductor Reinbert de Leeuw, painter Armando and poet Ida Gerhardt.

Cherry Duyns, journalist, author, tv exec and occasional actor, has directed with the same integrity and sense of detail that characterized his previous docu work (notably a recent 3-part tv docu on a hospital cancer ward).

Duyns' camera scrutinizes his subjects, unobtrusively. The editing creates links among them, underlining what they all share: the intense concentration, the urge to translate what's in their head into paint or metal, movement, music or words.

Individual peculiarities are captured: Visser's grunts and chats with his mongrel Moses; Armando's melodious round-lipped whistle; van Manen's grimaces when his feet fall behind his imagination, etc.

"Genesis" captures a fascinating blend of imaginative artistry and disciplined craftsmanship. Docu's excellent tech credits reflect that mastery of craft. —*Wall.*

War

A Troma release of a Lloyd Kaufman/Michael Herz production. Produced by Kaufman, Herz. Directed by Herz, "Samuel Weil" (Kaufman). Screenplay, Mitchell Dana, with Eric Hattler, Thomas Martinek, Kaufman; camera (color), James London; music, Christopher De Marco; production manager, Jeffrey W. Sass; stunt coordinator, Scott Leva; postproduction supervisor, Brian Sternkopf; special effects cordinators, William Jennings, Pericles Lewnes; associate producers, Sass, Ryan Richards. Reviewed at Adams theater, Detroit, Sept. 23, 1988. No MPAA Rating. Running time: **99 MIN.**

Lydia	Carolyn Beauchamp
Taylor	Sean Bowen
Parker	Michael Ryder
Kirkland	Patrick Weathers
Dottie	Jessica Dublin
Marshall	Steven Crossley
Hardwick	Charles Kay Hune
Maria	Lorayn Lane DeLuca
Cooney	Ara Romanoff
Kim	Brenda Brock

■ **Detroit** — "War" is Troma's latest splatterfest and a worthy companion to such other totally unredeeming efforts as "Bloodsucking Freaks," "The Toxic Avenger" and "Surf Nazis Must Die."

Whether this will be the guilty pleasure of enough filmgoers to keep it turning boxoffice stiles very long is unlikely. "War" mixes enough slow-motion murder and campy puns to satisfy fans and guarantee a healthy homevideo reincarnation.

The plot, such as it is, finds a planeload of Tromaville residents crashlanding on what they believe to be a deserted island.

The passengers immediately start giving the only surviving member of the crew a hard time, wanting to now how he is going to get them home on time and demanding to see the captain.

The captain, like most of the plane, is over here, and over there and over there.

As this motley crew of yuppies, used car salesmen, housewives and Jewish grandmothers starts to regroup, they discover the island is overrun with terrorists hatching a diabolical plot to invade the U.S.

The Tromavillians are the only ones who can save America. They rise to the challenge in a way that would make even Oliver North stand up and salute.

Once the terrorists are dispatched again and again, the tourists-turned-commandos attack the headquarters in a final fight scene that makes "Rambo III" look like "Lassie Come Home." —*Advo.*

Dark Before Dawn

A PSM Entertainment release of an E.K. Gaylord 2d presentation of a Lazy "E" production, in association with Kingpin Prods. Produced by Ben Miller. Executive producer, Gaylord. Directed by Robert Totten. Screenplay, Reparata Mazzola; camera (Panavision, color), Steve M. McWilliams; editor, Ron Hanthaner, Tom Boutross; music, Ken Sutherland; art direction, Richard Carver; associate producer, Rex Linn; casting, Becky Grantham. Reviewed at Seville Square Cinema, Kansas City, Mo., Sept. 20, 1988. MPAA Rating: PG-13. Running time: **95 MIN.**

Jeff Parker	Sonny Gibson
James Kirkland	Doug McClure
Jessica Stanton	Reparata Mazzola
Sheriff	Ben Johnson
Cabalistas Leader	Billy Drago
Glen Logan	Rance Howard
J. B. Watson	Morgan Woodward
Charlie Stevens	Buck Henry
Roger Crandall	Paul Newsom
Andy Peterson	Jeff Osterhage
Hal Porter	Red Steagall
Sen. Henry Vance	John L. Martin
Don Haleys	Rex Linn

■ **Kansas City** — "Dark Before Dawn" delves into agri-business as focused on the wheat fields of southwestern Kansas seeking to become a "Farmgate" of the farm crisis that is ruining the small farmer.

It has all the ingredients in the do-it-right young farmers, the scheming, unscrupulous grain conglomerate, investigative network reporters and a faithful farm country locale. The script by author-actress Reparata Mazzola seeks to cover the subject in a broad spectrum, but final result (disowned in release version by Mazzola and costar Sonny Gibson) jostles formula characters in episodic fashion. Direction by Robert Totten never ties it all together.

Morgan Woodward heads Farmco, the international cartel which would manipulate the wheat market to make a cool billion, even though it will bring the price of bread on the table in the farm home to $6 per loaf. Paul Newsom as the reporter out of Washington puts on tape his findings about suspicious moves of Farmco at its grain elevator in fictitious Milo, Kan. (pop. 1;972) and sends it off to Mazzola at the bureau in Washington.

She goes to Milo to investigate his "accidental" death and to follow the leads of Farmco maneuvers he has left to her on the tape. She gets some help from the farmer group led by Gibson and newspaperman Buck Henry, and from another angle, Doug McClure, a member of the Farmco board who recants about his part in the international swindle because he can't stomach the idea of $6 per loaf of bread.

When government grain inspector Gary Johnson gets too nosy, he is simply shot on Woodward's order to Rance Howard, the Farmco representative at the Milo elevator. That is too simple when Farmco decides it must eliminate Mazzola. She is called to a meeting at night, drugged with ether (plainly labeled on the bottle with a felt marker and shown in a close-up by at least three takes), then bound and gagged and dumped in the wheatfield where the huge harvester already is cutting swaths.

She is saved by Gibson and his brother, who spot her body from their private plane. Woodward and board members are indicted, on the basis of her findings, in Senate hearings held by John Martin. It's all formula and too ludicrous to be amusing.

In a few sequences the film veers toward the documentary with some fine camerawork on the waving fields of wheat ready for the harvest, fields of sunflowers ready to give up their tasty seeds and grain loading from trucks at the huge grain elevator. Music by Ken Sutherland has some rousing moments underscoring wheatfields set ablaze by Farmco and more subtle phrasing behind the shots of the spacious fields.

The producers had generous assistance from the Kansas Film Commission in finding the location sites near Hugoton in southwestern Kansas. There may be some regional interest on that basis, but outside the farm belt it's a "so what?" for most moviegoers.

Film had a premiere in Hugoton in late August and opened wide in the Midwest Sept. 16. A showcase of seven screens in K.C. turned in but a minimal gross.—*Quin.*

Spellbinder

An MGM/UA Communications release of an MGM/Indian Neck Entertainment presentation of a Wizan Film Properties production. Produced by Joe Wizan, Brian Russell. Executive producers, Howard Baldwin, Richard Cohen. Coproducers, Todd Black, Kate Benton, Mickey Borofsky, Steve Berman. Directed by Janet Greek. Screenplay, Tracey Tormé; camera (color), Adam Greenberg; editor, Steve Mirkovich; music, Basil Poledouris; production design, Rodger Maus; set design, Roland Hill; set decoration, Tom Bugenhagen; sound, Joe Kenworthy; associate producers, Bob Doudell, Tracey Tormé; assistant director, Craig R. West; casting, Ellen Myer, Sally Stiner. Reviewed at the Lorimar-Telepictures Studios, Culver City, Sept. 19, 1988. MPAA Rating: R. Running time: **98 MIN.**

Jeff Mills	Timothy Daly
Miranda Reed	Kelly Preston
Derek Clayton	Rick Rossovich
Mrs. White	Audra Lindley
Aldys	Anthony Crivello
Grace Woods	Diana Bellamy
Lt. Lee	Cary-Hiroyuki Tagawa
Tim Weatherly	James Louis Watkins
Herbie Green	Kyle Heffner
Ed Kennerle	Roderick Cook

■ **Hollywood** — Just when it was apparent that the world might be able to survive indefinitely without any new occult devil worship pictures, along comes "Spellbinder" to ruin the experiment.

Maybe this one's lack of b.o. success, which is all but guaranteed, will forestall any others for some years to come.

For the first couple of reels, it appears that Tracey Torme's tale has the makings of a nicely anxiety-ridden naturalistic thriller. One night, fellow lawyers Timothy Daly and Rick Rossovich rescue beautiful Kelly Preston from a beating being administered by evil-looking, knife-yielding Anthony Crivello in a parking lot.

Daly offers the vulnerable young lady the protection of his home for the night and, to his astonishment, she not only sleeps with him, but becomes his girlfriend.

Clearly, the menacing Crivello is not the sort to take this insult lying down, but his method of retribution does take unexpected forms, such as levitating, then torching Daly's car by aiming his fingertips at it.

Preston finally reveals that she's long been a member of a cult of Satan worshippers, and enlists Daly's help in trying to escape from the group's tight grasp. He falls for this hook, line and sinker, and ends up paying a heavy price for having been stupid enough to enter the ring with Lucifer.

Unfortunately, a viewer pays with 98 minutes of precious life by sitting through this hokum, which grows progressively unpleasant and unrewarding the more explicitly it reveals its true subject. As proficient a director as Janet Greek may be (she has episodes of "L.A. Law," "St. Elsewhere" and "Max Headroom" to her credit), one can only puzzle at her decision to take on such ludicrous material for her feature debut.

Performances are okay and behind-the-scenes contributions are very sharp, but to no avail.—*Cart.*

Kansas

A Trans World Entertainment release. Produced by George Litto. Executive producers, Moshe Diamant, Chris Chesser. Directed by David Stevens. Screenplay, Spencer Eastman; camera (DeLuxe color), David Eggby; editor, Robert Barrere; music, Pino Donaggio, Natale Massara; production design, Matthew Jacobs; set decoration, Stewart K. McGuire; costume design, Nancy G. Fox; sound (Dolby), Jacob Goldstein; associate producer, Vic Ramos; casting, Ed Mitchell, Rosalie Joseph. Reviewed at Cary Grant theater, Culver City, Calif., Sept. 15, 1988. MPAA Rating: R. Running time: **106 MIN.**

Doyle Kennedy	Matt Dillon
Wade Corey	Andrew McCarthy
Lori Bayles	Leslie Hope
Buckshot	Brent Jennings

■ **Hollywood** — If ever there was a case to be made for an entire state to petition to have its name removed from a film, "Kansas" is it. Midwestern farmers would find three years of drought less disastrous to live through than this.

For everyone else, it belongs on the compost heap. B.o. looks barren.

Whatever compelled anyone to put energies into this silly good boy-bad boy (Andrew McCarthy, Matt Dillon, respectively) suspense meller, where the material floats on about a '50s naivete level of sophistication, is a question for the ages (about 13 years max).

"Kansas" is kind of a bad "Two Rebels Without A Cause." Dillon and McCarthy meet up while freight-train-hopping somewhere in the middle of nowhere Kansas. Both broke, Dillon gets McCarthy to help him rob a bank. With the police hot on their trail, the two are forced to separate and it's McCarthy who ends up with the loot, which he stashes under a bridge just at the moment a car with the governor's daughter plunges into the river below.

Remembering he's on the lam, McCarthy has to split the minute he brings the little girl to the surface, but not before the local newshound takes his Pieta-inspired picture carrying her out of the water and puts it on the cover of the newspaper. Meanwhile, Dillon gets a job at the midway. "One will become a criminal, one will become a hero," or so the ads for "Kansas" promised. How hokey can you get?

Middle-class values are played out here in wholesome, bucolic splendor (cinematographer David Eggby gets some credit for catching the nuances of the wheat field). Some 15 minutes into the picture, however, one wonders if the late scripter Spencer Eastman had any respect for Midwesterners at all since it makes them out to be gosh-golly types.

Dillon plays a fairly convincing renegade who would be Donna Reed's nightmare. He smokes, he drinks, he rolls up the sleeves of his T-shirt.

Conversely, McCarthy appears as if he took his get-straight lesson from "Less Than Zero" a little too much to heart. If he were any more "earnest," he could double for Eddie Haskell. Hope, in her first starring role, manages to kiss and ride a horse simultaneously pretty well.

To add a sense of excitement to the proceedings when none exists (most of the film), the filmmakers engaged the services of Italian scorers Pino Donaggio and Natale Massara to fill in the gaps with some Spaghetti Western music.

The "People from the Great State of Kansas" are thanked in the end credits. They ought to be begged for forgiveness. —*Brit.*

VENICE REVIEWS

Un Señor Muy Viejo Con Unas Alas Enormes
(A Very Old Man with Enormous Wings)
(CUBAN-ITALIAN-SPANISH)

An El Instituto Cubano del Arte e Industria Cinematograficos/El Laboratorio de Poeticas Cinematograficas De Fernando Birri/Te'evision Espanola production, in association with the Fundacion del Nuevo Cine Latinoamericano. Executive producers, Camiio Vives, Settimio Presutto, Luis Reneses. Directed by Fernando Birri. Screenplay, Birri, with Gabriel Garcia Marquez, based on Marquez' story. Camera (color), Raul Perez Ureta; music, Jose Maria Vitier, Gianni Nocenzi, Pablo Milanés; production manager, Miguel Mendoza; art direction, Raul Oliva; costumes, Jesus Ruiz. Reviewed at Venice Film Festival (competing), Sept. 7, 1988. (Also in Toronto Film Festival.) Running time: **90 MIN.**
Elisenda . . . . Daisy Granados
Old Man . . . . Fernando Birri
Pelayo . . . . Asdrúbal Meléndez
Father Gonzaga . . . . Luis Alberto Ramiréz
Also with: Adolfo Llaurado (Lucky the Caribbean), Marcia Barreto, Silvia Planas, Parmenia Silva, Maria Luisa Mayor, Marabu, Rene Martinez, Rodrigo Utria.

■ **Venice** — Gabriel Garcia Marquez' story "A Very Old Man With Enormous Wings" springs to life in the colorful, gently sardonic hands of Argentine helmer Fernando Birri, revered as a founder of Latin American cinema.

The director himself appears in the mute title role. A fable, but above all an entertaining tale about a beat-up old angel who falls to earth one night during a tropical storm, "Old Man" should appeal to specialized venues looking for imaginative folklore with an authentically South American flavor.

Marquez, who has a minor script credit, never called the old man an angel; nor does the film. He lands in the Caribbean sea behind the shack of Elisenda (Daisy Granados) and Pelayo (Asdrúbal Meléndez). Seeing his battered plumes, the couple can think of nothing better to do with him than put him in the chicken coop.

Soon word spreads that an angel has landed in New Old Town. First locals (including hyper-excitable priest Luis Alberto Ramírez, determined to damn the creature), then a whole stream of pilgrims appear to gawk at the bedraggled old man in the chicken coop. Elisenda and Pelayo see their chance and start charging admission. Finally Lucky the Caribbean arrives with his pitiful sideshow circus featuring a Spider Woman he copulates with during the show.

For a fable, film doesn't try to hide the violence, ugliness and exploitation of its characters. Unexpectedly, no miracle is worked by the old man — the most that happens is his wings catch fire and he looks even more decrepit than before.

Six years pass and people lose interest in the angel (or Martian, or albino vampire...) Pelayo and Elisenda have a new house filled with consumer trash; their angel is reduced to the level of a mistreated household pet. One day the old man silently finishes sewing new feathers into his wings. While Elisenda weeps (but maybe it's just from peeling onions), he takes off and soars into the heavens.

Birri builds his film around opposites: the cruelty of everyone against the gentle helplessness of the old man (Birri's drooping gray hair and sad eyes are expressive without words); explosive colors and merry music (soundtrack is by Jose Maria Vitier and Gianni Nocenzi, with a memorable song by Pablo Milanés) in contrast to the squalor and pettiness of men. Lensing is lively and serviceable. — *Yung.*

Une Histoire de Vent
(A History Of Wind)
(FRENCH)

A CAPI Films/La Sept coproduction, with the participation of the Ministry of Culture. Executive producer, Marceline Loridan. Written and directed by Joris Ivens, Loridan. Camera (color), Thierry Arbogast, Jacques Loiseleux; editor, Geneviéve Louveau; music, Michel Portal. Reviewed at Venice Film Festival (Special Events), Sept. 8, 1988. Running time: **78 MIN.**
With: Joris Ivens, Han Zenxiang, Wang Delong, Liu Zhuang, Wang Hong, Fu Dalin, Liu Guillian, Chen Zhijian, Zou Quaoyu, Paul Sergent.

■ **Venice** — Screened in honor of Joris Ivens, who picked up the career achievement award at the Venice Film Festival just days before his 90th birthday, "A History Of Wind" is a winning docu-fantasy by this great documaker.

With Ivens himself in the main "role" of an old filmer short of breath who goes to China to make a film about wind, pic is a backward look at a long and glorious career, a salute to China and to the cinema. It should charm audiences wherever magical filmmaking is appreciated.

From the opening shot of a plane soaring through heavens of blue clouds, to the final surprise of another plane appearing to roll down railroad tracks while patient Chinese commuters wait for it to pass, "A History Of Wind" lets loose the fearsome imagination of Ivens and codirector Marceline Loridan. Wandering from very real images to figments of imagination, "Wind" has an appeal that goes far beyond the merely documentary.

Ivens appears as a watery-eyed old man, his long white hair hanging like a mane as he gazes out at mute sand dunes. The locale is the Gobi desert in China, and he and his film crew are waiting for the wind to rise. Comically, the radio reports tempests and tidal waves everywhere but in China. Ivens falls off his chair and is rushed to the hospital, where a magical creature has his dream of the Méliès film "A Trip To The Moon." Suddenly the moon opens its mouth and Ivens emerges to chat with a bored Chinese lady.

Back on earth, an aged martial arts teacher talks to Ivens about the importance of good breathing. (Ivens has had asthma all his life, and has to be carried to the farther desert sets in a litter.)

One of the pic's highlights is the scene where Ivens spends days negotiating with bureaucrats over shooting 7,000 giant figures of soldiers guarding the emperor's tomb. In a clever sleight of hand, pic makes the figures (which in the end Ivens has to buy from vendors to fake the shot) spring to life and march.

The wind, China and the cinema are the heroes of this metaphysical, dreamlike film. In the end, the Dutch filmmaker has to give up his immodest aim of taming the wind, and content himself with filming its wildness, which makes quite an impressive sequence. Even more impressive, though, is the way the work sums up a career that spans the 20th century. — *Yung.*

Fiori di Zucca
(Zucchini Flowers)
(ITALIAN)

A Nicon Intl. release of a PLB Film production. Executive producers. Nicolo Pomilia, Luciano Caproni. Written and directed by Stefano Pomilia. Camera (Telecolor), Gianfranco Maioletti; editor, Luigi Zita; music, Piero Montanari; art direction, Andrea Fantacci. Reviewed at Venice Film Festival (Horizons), Sept. 8, 1988. Running time: **97 MIN.**
Giulia . . . . Marina Suma
Sergio . . . . Massimo Ciavarro
Pietro . . . . Enzo Decaro
Clelia . . . . Isa Barzizza
Enzo . . . . Silvio Vannucci
Also with: Manuela Gatti, Sandro Ghiani, Ilary Blasi, Jinny Steffan.

■ **Venice** — "Zucchini Flowers" is an inane title for an amateurish first film by tyro Stefano Pomilia. Tale of three pals in their 30s who never grew up is trite and unfunny; lensing uncertain.

An audience for this effort is going to be hard to scare up. Yet, film's premise is on target: the generation of Italo males in their 30s missed the excitement of '68 and the comforts of yuppiedom, and have remained immature and directionless. All that's missing for an engrossing film is thesping, lensing and a script.

The babyish trio is composed of Enzo (Silvio Vanucci), back in Rome after 10 years in Brazil with his nasty wife Giulia (played unpleasantly by a down-at-the-heels Marina Suma), Sergio (teen idol Massimo Ciavarro), an unwed father more of a baby than his offspring Ilary Blasi, and Pietro (Enzo Decaro in the most convincing role of the three), a drug addict and male prostitute with hound-dog eyes.

Meeting by chance, they organize an illfated party at Enzo's parents' house, which is intended as funny but draws nary a laugh. An attempt to organize a soccer match fails miserably, and the trio part ways again in three pathetic finales.

Of no help to the misfired script is a banal score and amateurish lensing. The original intention behind "Zucchini Flowers" may have been serious; results are not. — *Yung.*

I Cammelli
(The Camels)
(ITALIAN)

A Medusa release of a Dania Film/Colorado Film/National Cinematografica coproduction, in association with Reteitalia. Produced by Luciano Martino, Maurizio Totti. Directed by Giuseppe Bertolucci. Screenplay, Vincenzo Cerami, Bertolucci; camera (color), Fabio Cianchetti; editor, Nino Baragli; art direction, Paolo Biagetti; music, Nicola Piovani. Reviewed at Venice Film Festival (Venice Night), Sept. 6, 1988. Running time: **100 MIN.**
Ferruccio Ferri . . . . Paolo Rossi
Camillo . . . . Diego Abatantuono
Anna . . . . Giulio Boschi
Anna's father . . . . Giancarlo Sbragia
Also with: Sabina Guzzanti, Laura Betti (Anna's mother), Ennio Fantastichini, Maurizio Solda, Fiorenzo Serra.

■ **Venice** — Helmer Giuseppe Bertolucci snaps back to the idiosyncratic, offbeat charm of his best efforts ("An Italian Woman," "Secrets, Secrets") in "The Camels."

Film is animated by delectable comic performances from an eccentric cast and a script set in helmer's native Po Valley, which really is about, among other things, camels. Sparkling dialog is going to be tough to translate.

Hip youth audiences onshore are assured. Offshore markets will get less out of pic, and will probably be more disturbed by its odd structure that seems to divide it into two separate parts.

Pintsize hero of the tale is Ferruccio Ferri (played by Paolo Rossi, a comedian growing in popularity as his film roles increase). He knows everything about camels, and has been the unbeatable champion on a tv quiz show. As his shot at winning the jackpot approaches, Ferruccio is dragged around by small-time showman Camillo (the ever-inventive Diego Abatantuono) on an absurd promotional tour through the Po Valley, riding a camel.

Camillo's pathetic troupe (including the hilariously bad singer Sabina Guzzanti) resembles something out of an early Fellini film, with wackier situations. They steal some of the thunder from the Paolo Rossi character, with the result that when the film becomes entirely his in the second half, it looks like a separate skit.

Having lost the jackpot on the quiz, Ferruccio boards a train for home. There he is induced by a beautiful girl, Anna (played by Giulia Boschi, a serious thesp with Marilyn Monroe sex appeal) to pretend he's her secret lover and father of her unborn child. Object is to get rid of a boring fiance in front of mama Laura Betti and dad Giancarlo Sbragia. Sequence is a little strung out, but works as film cabaret where thesping's the thing.

Technical work is as sophisticated as the rest, from Fabio Cianchetti's ironic camerawork to Nicola Piovani's Arabic tunes. — *Yung.*

Mortu Nega
(GUINEA BISSAU)

An Instituo Nacional do Cinema production. Directed by Flora Gomes. Screenplay, Gomes, Manuel Rambault Barcellos, David Lang; camera (color), Dominique Gentil; editor, Christiane Lack; music, Sidonio Pais Quaresma, Djanun Dabò; sound, Jose Da Silva. Reviewed at Venice Film Festival (Critics Week), Aug. 29, 1988. Running time: **85 MIN.**
Diminga . . . . Bya Gomes
Sako . . . . Tunu Eugenio Almada
Sanabaio . . . . Mamadu Uri Balde
Also with: M'Male Nhasse, Pedro Da Silva, Homna Nalete.

■ Venice — Flora Gomes' "Mortu Nega," the first feature produced by the small West African country of Guinea Bissau, is a sweeping historical panorama of the nation's history from the war of independence with Portugal to the present day.

Title means "he who death passes over" and refers to babies who survive birth. Pic introduces a promising new talent to the African scene in Gomes, a former documaker whose project for "Mortu Nega" won a Swedish Film Institute prize back in 1983. It is sure to interest specialists and could jump over to limited playoffs with the right promo.

Story is told in three blocks and centers on a strong woman character, Diminga (played with natural grace by Bya Gomes). In 1973, in the 10th year of the war with Portugal, Diminga braves a trek along mined jungle paths to reach her husband Sako (Tunu Eugenio Almada) at the front. The toll in human lives and the destruction of the savannah don't dampen the partisans' will to fight. Action scenes, lensed on a shoestring but effective dramatically, bring the war home, while Gomes ably sketches in a number of characters. Also well used is a soundtrack mixing tribal music with whistling missiles and sounds of war.

Midsection shows Diminga returning to her village to live the first days of peace amid high hopes, gleeful kids and neighbors full of solidarity who help her till her field.

In 1977, Sako has returned home crippled from an old war wound. A terrible drought destroys the crops,

and the nation — shown ruled by a benevolent left-wing government — is no longer united. Diminga leads a vast crowd in a traditional "ceremony of the living and dead" to pray for rain from their ancestors. It rains.

Though the historical sense of "Mortu Nega" predominates, it sidesteps sociology and ethnology for a human perspective on events. The love story between Diminga and Sako is touchingly real, the war and its after-effects dramatically defined. Cast is credible; final scene uses 3,000 extras.

Mixed French and Guinean crew do a good job on the technical side. — *Yung.*

Nosferatu a Venezia
(Nosferatu In Venice)
(ITALIAN)

A Medusa Film release of a Scena Film Prod./Reteitalia coproduction. Executive producer, Carlo Alberto Alfieri. Produced, written and directed by Augusto Caminito. Camera (color), Tonino Nardi; editor, Claudio Cutry; music, Luigi Ceccarelli, with songs from Vangelis; art direction, Joseph Teichner, Luca Antonucci; costumes, Vera Cozzolino. Reviewed at Venice Film Festival (Venice Night), Sept. 9, 1988. Running time: **96 MIN.**
Nosferatu . . . . Klaus Kinski
Helietta Canins . . . . Barbara De Rossi
Giuseppe Barnabo . . . . Yorgo Voyagis
Don Alvise . . . . Donald Pleasence
Paris Catalano . . . . . Christopher Plummer
Maria . . . . Anne Knecht
Also with: Elvire Audray, Giuseppe Mannajuolo, Maria Cumani Quasimodo.

■ Venice — Klaus Kinski, vampire king of Werner Herzog's remake of "Nosferatu," is back with the elongated dentures in "Nosferatu In Venice," his 17th century look blending in nicely with Carnevale.

Producer-director Augusto Caminito assembles a very respectable cast and crew for this quality production, more kitsch than horror but with enough chills to ring up some boxoffice. With fascinating location work in Venice, and name actors, this ghoul shouldn't be stopped by national boundaries.

Script follows the classic route, mainly inventing a maze of new rules about vampire hunting. Helietta Canins (Barbara De Rossi), starts the ball rolling by calling in vampirebuster Christopher Plummer, played with the sad resignation of a character doomed from the start. It seems there's a legend in her ancient aristocratic family that the coffin in the basement, 30 feet under the Grand Canal, is Nosferatu.

Actually it's just her vampire ancestor and lookalike Letitia, while Nosferatu is boring himself amid a band of gypsies off the Bay of Biscayne.

Drawn to Venice by Helietta's call at a seance, the monster begins by getting 100-year-old Princess Maria Cumani Quasimodo to jump

out a window and impale herself in the picturesque courtyard below. Exorcist priest Donald Pleasence is wholly ineffectual, since this vampire doesn't respond to crosses in the slightest. Helietta lets herself be carried off by Nosferatu, and Plummer jumps into a canal in defeat.

The only remedy, we know, is for Nosferatu to have sex with a virgin, thus becoming mortal. Maria (Anne Knecht), Helietta's younger sister but of little family resemblance (being black or of Brazilian aspect) volunteers. She follows the Prince of Darkness to a sinister island, where she makes love to him so he might die (after all these centuries, he's willing).

Just a second too soon, Helietta's boyfriend Yorgo Voyagis bursts in on the busy couple and fires at them

with an elephant gun, fatally wounding Maria and enraging Nosferatu. The dying Maria begs to be vampirized so she can live on with him, but final cut is unclear whether this actually happens. Nosferatu is last seen stalking the canals with his naked love in his arms.

Tonino Nardi's moody lensing creates a ghostly city of great beauty, not to mention the interiors in some splendid Venetian palaces. Cast plays their roles straight, and Kinski is particularly memorable for his melancholy portrayal of yesteryear's Elephant Man. More than the Prince of Evil, he resembles a ferocious beast tired of fighting priests and vampirologists. Soundtrack full of shrieking female voices contains excerpts by Vangelis.
— *Yung.*

TORONTO REVIEWS

Comic Book Confidential
(CANADIAN-DOCU)

A Cineplex Odeon release (in Canada) of a Sphinx production. Produced by Martin Harbury, Don Haig, Ron Mann. Written and directed by Ron Mann, Charles Lippincott. Camera (color), Robert Fresco, Joan Churchill; editor, Mann, Robert Kennedy; music, Dr. John, Shadowey Men on a Shadowey Planet, Keith Elliot, Gerard Leckey, Nicholas Stirling of Strange Nursery; art direction, Gerlinde Scharinger; sound, Steve Munro. Reviewed at Toronto Festival of Festivals, Sept. 13, 1988. Running time: **90 MIN.**
With: Lynda Barry, Robert Crumb, Will Eisner, William M. Gaines, Jack Kirby, Harvey Pekar, Art Spiegelman.

■ Toronto — Following up on a jazz docu ("Imagine The Sound") and poetry-as-performance art pic ("Poetry In Motion"), Toronto docu filmmaker Ron Mann continues his North American cultural chronicle with "Comic Book Confidential," a lively, enthusiastic look at this once-maligned art form.

Not strictly for the comic groupies who flock to conventions to trade issues of "Tales From The Crypt," pic is a fest natural, already skedded for Berlin next year. It also should be showcased in specialty houses, where word of mouth will ensure longevity.

Mann intercuts interviews with more than 20 of the seminal comic book artists with some obscure newsreel footage of the U.S. Senate subcommittee on juvenile delinquency in the 1950s, which linked rowdy teenage behavior with that vulgar habit, comic book reading.

Artists such as William Gaines — founder of MAD, who attributes to his father the invention of the first comic book, Famous Funnies, in 1934 — get the chance to reminisce and inject sociological comments about the history of the genre.

Veteran Will Eisner (The Spirit) discusses the development of comics as a literary form. Mann's talking

heads outline the chronology of comics, from the early war efforts to the resurgence of the superheroes.

Among the celebs given the floor: Marvel Comics' Stan Lee, who opted for a more realistic superhero; Robert Crumb, who led off the underground comics with Fritz the Cat and Mr. Natural, which he admits inventing while on LSD; and Harvey Kurtzman (MAD), who even satirized the McCarthy hearings. Other undergrounders Spain ("Trashman") and Gilbert Shelton (Fabulous Furry Freak Brothers) read from their own strips, and Shary Flenniken gives the feminist view of her Trots And Bonnie.

Dan O'Neill recounts the Disney lawsuit he was involved in for misrepresenting Mickey Mouse in his "Air Pirates" strip, Bill Griffith discusses Zippy the Pinhead's philosophy, and Art Spiegelman ("Maus") explains his strip as a family history.

"Comic Book Confidential" is not the definitive comic book retrospective, — newspaper strips and animated features (from which comic books have been made) are not included. It serves as a primer for the skeptical who perceive comic books as throwaway art and junk culture.

Mann uses state-of-the-art video techniques to "animate" the still comics, and employs a spirited soundtrack. There are quick takes of identifiable and esoteric comic covers, from "Weird Science" to "Millie The Model."

Mann's thesis is that comic book art has matured and flourished as more skilled artists and writers enter the field. He injects a touching tagline, with Eisner stating that when he started out in the 1940s he fantasized about working in a permanent art form. —*Devo.*

Driving Me Crazy
(BRITISH-DOCU)

A Virgin Vision/VCL Communications/Telemunchen production. Produced by Andrew Braunsberg. Directed by Nick Broomfield. Camera (color), Robert Levi; editor, John Mister; sound, Broomfield. Reviewed at Toronto Festival of Festivals, Sept. 10, 1988. Running time: **85 MIN.**
With: Andre Heller and the cast of "Body And Soul."

■ Toronto — Nick Broomfield was hired to do a film on the making of European impresario Andre Heller's multimillion-dollar black musical extravaganza "Body And Soul," to be mounted at the Munich Opera House. "Driving Me Crazy" is his hilarious and rich chronicle of the catastrophes of the production.

As a disaster-on-the-set pic, it's a surefire bet for fest circuits, but with proper handling could find a place in specialized houses.

Broomfield was asked to make another "Fame" by producer Andrew Braunsberg ("Being There"). As he pulls up to a rehearsal hall in New York City in his white limo, director Andre Heller says he envisions "Body And Soul" as the biggest theatrical event in the history of the world. Right away, however, the budget is cut from $1,600,000 to $300,000.

Broomfield's deadpan voiceover highlights what is to come and he films each mishap in action. He's reduced to a crew of two. The producer envisions a fictional character in the docu, but the writer, Joe, a master of pretentious, cryptic double-talk, disagrees profoundly.

One of the three choreographers has dropped out and is replaced by Mercedes Ellington, Duke's granddaughter, who is hit on the head with a camera while working on a dance number.

The black choreographer George and assistant director Howard are the most honest and witty characters on board. They plead into the camera, "Give us some money." Howard gets angry with Broomfield for taking up the callback dancers' time in getting footage for his docu when the finances for the real stage show in Munich are precarious. Andre's solution to calm down disgruntled cast members is to send flowers.

Broomfield films the discussions in hotels and on telephones between the producer and the investors — VCL, Virgin Vision and Telemunchen — and shows the rapid deterioration of the funding.

The lighting crew blows the fuses in the rehearsal hall. A German production coordinator says on camera that he hates black people except for rappers and blues singers. Joe the writer is furious his rewrites aren't being used. George the choreographer sighs that some of his dancers are "total idiots."

Broomfield does get great gospel music, breakdancing, blues numbers and jazz routines on film. Yet the docu soars in recording the ego clashes and esthetic control power struggles. Its intrusive style angers the staff, but at the same time they're all hams who want to be on camera.

The director's ambiguous narration is always amusing, and by simply recounting the events as they unfold he's able to create a textured record of an untoward film shoot.
—*Devo*.

Voices Of Sarafina!
(DOCU)

A Lincoln Center/Noble Enterprises production. Executive producers, Gregory Mosher, Bernard Gerstein. Produced by Bernard Gerstein, Nigel Noble. Directed by Noble. Camera (color), John Hazzard; editor, Joan Morris. Reviewed at Toronto Festival of Festivals, Sept. 13, 1988. Running time: **90 MIN.**
With: cast of the Broadway production of "Sarafina!" and Miriam Makeba.

■ Toronto — Nigel Noble delivers a stirring docu by interspersing rousing excerpts from Lincoln Center's production of "Sarafina!" with stark comments from the youthful South African cast about their troubled homeland.

Though eager to return home, the performers talk openly about the destructive force of apartheid and the misery of the black townships. The show's writer-director, Mbongeni Ngema, explains that with South Africa newspapers outlawed from reporting much of the daily news theater has become a vital outlet of such communication.

He also is seen advising his cast on giving media interviews without making them targets of government action back home. Backstage and gathering in hotel rooms, the high-adrenalin performers match their energy on stage.

In a near-end scene unlikely to leave a dry eye, they meet their heroine, singer Miriam Makeba who has been banned from South Africa — with everyone, including her, in tears. She praises their efforts in bringing their story to the world and leads them in song and that's where the pic should end. It continues with yet more interviews filmed beforehand.

Despite its strong message and its smashing effect, theatrical release will be limited. There's a good life ahead on tv and at fests. —*Adil*.

Krik? Krak!
Tales Of A Nightmare
(HAITIAN-U.S.-CANADIAN)

A Mountain Top Films production. Executive producer, Camilo Vives. Produced and directed by Jac Avila, Vanyoska Gee. Screenplay, Gee; camera (color), Michael Anderson; editor, Avila, Gee; music, Jean-Claude Martineau, Juan Marquez; sound, Gregory Heller, Gee. Reviewed at Toronto Festival of Festivals, Sept. 10, 1988. Running time: **82 MIN.**

■ Toronto — A bold but inflated look into Haiti's politics and spirituality, "Krik? Krak! Tales Of A Nightmare" is a difficult pic to peg.

It's a hybrid docu which uses a half-cooked narrative of a peasant woman's entrapment into a voodoo priest's spell as well as news clippings and statistics to transmit its message. Jac Avila and Vanyoska Gee will find their first feature a better bet on public tv than in theatrical release.

It's a disjointed mix as the woman's voiceover tells how she was manipulated by a houngon (voodoo priest). She talks of "these days of our nightmare" and claims her ancestors would die if they knew the Duvaliers made millions selling out to Dominican plantations. Yet she relishes her cultural memories and makes reference to them throughout the pic.

A voodoo priest speaks of white and black magic and the power he has over people in the government. Even Papa and Baby Doc hired people who believed in voodoo. Two men talk about the risks of joining a boat of compatriots to the U.S., and this is juxtaposed with footage of boat people washed up on the shores of Miami.

Maimings and killings by the Duvalier government are constantly interspersed. Filmmakers go to Fort Dimanche, ostensibly the most inhumane prison in the world, to get their story, and show mangled corpses and the living dead in their cells.

Pic is technically shaky, with unsure camerawork, although the shots of Haitian topography and daily life tasks are fascinating.

Avila and Gee bombard the screen with too many simultaneous images to make sense of the corrupt post-Duvalier politics and the collective unconscious of the Haitian people. There's a barrage of gripping docu footage that leaves the viewer numb, and considering the appalling state of politics of Haiti, maybe that's not so bad. —*Devo*.

Break Of Dawn

A Cinewest production. Produced by Jude Pauline Eberhard. Written and directed by Isaac Artenstein. Camera (color), Stephen Lighthill; editor, John Nutt; music, Mark Adler; art direction, Celeste Lee; sound, Anne Evans. Reviewed at Toronto Festival of Festivals, Sept. 12, 1988. Running time: **105 MIN.**
Pedro J. González . . . . Oscar Chavez
Wife . . . . Maria Rojo
Cousin . . . . Pepe Serna
Also with: Tony Plana, Peter Henry Schroeder, Socorro Valdez, Kamala Lopez, Harry Woolf.

■ Toronto — Good intentions are roughly served in this wooden biopic about one Pedro J. González, a Mexican-American who was a veteran of Pancho Villa's campaign, an immigrant laborer, a Spanish radio announcer and popular composer-singer, a political activist and ultimately a minor martyr in California during the '30s.

Isaac Artenstein's debut feature brings a heavy-handed touch to this story, squeezing it dry of drama and momentum. Boxoffice and video prospects are poor, although the pic could be sold to Hispanic outlets here and abroad.

Artenstein follows the progress of González (capably played by Oscar Chavez) from his entry into the U.S. with his wife (Maria Rojo) until his jailing (and eventual release and deportation) on a rape charge trumped up by racist politicians intent on framing him.

Along the way, the enterprising and quietly rugged hero becomes the first Spanish-language radio personality in the U.S. González' heartfelt *canciones*, richly rendered by Chavez, are the best thing about "Break Of Dawn," but the filmmaker overdoes the music, just as he clumsily overdoes other key elements.

The film consistently red-flags its sympathies with clichéd character confrontations and banal set pieces (there are too many sequences panning to Mexican-Americans huddled around the radio), artlessly hammering home a dialectical history lesson about the deep prejudices confronted by Mexicans in California. Appropriately there are the villainous, manipulative district attorney and an Uncle Tomaso Mexican-American cop who learns too late about the treachery of Anglo power-brokers.

Most of the acting is directed to play like high-toned soap melodrama and is totally unaffecting. Technically, the film unfolds in muted sepia tones that only abet the dragging narrative's lugubrious pace. Artenstein does make some interesting use of apparently colorized newsreel footage and is not afraid to employ subtitles for the sake of preserving the film's sense of ethnic authenticity.

Unfortunately, it takes more than just discovering a potentially interesting American story to make an engaging film. Ultimately, "Break Of Dawn" fails to engender deep identification with the aspirations of its protagonist. —*Rich*.

Snuff Bottle
(HONG KONG)

A Southern Film Corp. presentation of a New Kwun Lun film. Written and directed by Li Han-xiang. Camera (color), Zhao Le-tian; music, Wang Xian. No other credits supplied. Reviewed at Toronto Festival of Festivals, Sept. 12, 1988. Running time: **100 MIN.**
With: Wang Xi-shan, Cheng Dao-ming, Li Dian-xiang.

■ Toronto — A visually rich (but dramatically wobbly) melodrama about a famous Chinese artist whose delicate paintings on tiny snuff bottles are now collector's items, "Snuff Bottle" should find favor on the fest circuit.

The film opens with a prolog in which veteran director Li Han-xiang and an aide tour museums in Paris and London looking at snuff bottles. The film proper begins with a flourish as the principal characters are introed: a veteran artist, as proud as he is talented; his student; and his daughter, who loves the student. There's also a Lord, for whom the artist has traditionally worked, and whose desire for new, Japanese-influenced, styles creates an impossible situation for the old man.

Just about every image in the film is breathtakingly beautiful, with fine camera direction and sense of pacing and movement. Unfortunately, the narrative is extremely hard to follow, not least because of sloppily spelled and ungrammatical subtitles. Even allowing for these annoyances, there does seem to be a basic problem with the way the story is told.

The film has a feminist slant to it, via a woman who breaks a taboo by invading hitherto all-male territory, a bathhouse; and there's also the tragedy of a woman raped. The period setting is sumptuous, with rich sets and costumes. —*Strat.*

Jin
(The Well)
(CHINESE)

A China Film presentation of an E'mei Film Studio production. Directed by Li Yalin. Screenplay, Zhang Xian, from novel by Lu Wenfu; camera (color), Li Baoqi, Pan Jing; music, Tang Qingshi; production manager, Cheng Lu'an. Reviewed at Toronto Festival of Festivals, Sept. 16, 1988. Running time: **98 MIN.**
With: Xu Lisha, Pan Hong, Li Zhiyu.

■ **Toronto** — **Audiences interested in the role of women in today's China should take a look at "The Well," which is not to be confused with last year's Tokyo fest prizewinner, "The Old Well."**

The central character in this drama, which spans over 20 years ending in the present, is an intelligent, attractive young woman who refuses to accept the stereotype of "a woman's role." She has a better job than her rather dull husband, and isn't interested in doing household chores. She also decides, arbitrarily, to have an abortion rather than interrupt her career with motherhood.

At every turn, she's frustrated by the old moralities, as expressed by her bitchy mother-in-law and the gossips who live in her neighborhood. After she has fallen out of love with her husband, she still has to submit to him in what is virtual rape.

Brief happiness comes via another man she meets at work, but the film takes a rather ambivalent stance in its portrait of a career woman. At the end the heroine is abandoned by her lover and locked out by her husband. She's last seen sitting alone on a street corner.

A fine performance by Xu Lisha is central to this thought-provoking pic which is ably, if not spectacularly, directed by newcomer Li Yalin. —*Strat.*

Clara's Heart

A Warner Bros. release of an MTM production. Produced by Martin Elfand. Executive producer, Marianne Moloney. Directed by Robert Mulligan. Screenplay, Mark Medoff, from Joseph Olshan's novel; camera (Technicolor prints), Freddie Francis; editor, Sidney Levin; music, Dave Grusin; sound (Dolby), Bill Nelson; production design, Jeffrey Howard; art direction, Stephen Walker; set decoration, Anne H. Ahrens; costume design, Bambi Breakstone; assistant director, David McGiffert; production managers, Albert J. Salzer, Daniel T. Franklin; associate producers, McGiffert, Salzer, Franklin; casting, Ken Carlson. Reviewed at Coronet theater, N.Y., Sept. 29, 1988. MPAA Rating: PG-13. Running time: **108 MIN.**
Clara Mayfield . . . . Whoopi Goldberg
Bill Hart . . . . Michael Ontkean
Leona Hart . . . . Kathleen Quinlan
David Hart . . . . Neil Patrick Harris
Peter Epstein . . . . Spalding Gray
Dora . . . . Beverly Todd
Blanche Loudon . . . . Hattie Winston
Also with: Jason Downs, Caitlin Thompson, Maria Broom, Wandachristine, Maryce Carter, Angel Harper, Mark Medoff.

■ **Buoyed by a beautifully measured star turn by Whoopi Goldberg and a smashing screen debut for young Neil Patrick Harris, "Clara's Heart" is a powerful, unabashedly sentimental drama that should win over class audiences everywhere.**

Adaptation by Mark Medoff of Joseph Olshan's novel pays attention to the values of a well-wrought character study of a noble Jamaican servant (Goldberg) and the young rich kid (Harris) she guides through adolescent rites of passage. Pic marks a strong return to the screen (after the 1982 flop "Kiss Me Goodbye") of director Robert Mulligan, projecting the qualities of his best work, including "To Kill A Mockingbird" and "Summer Of '42."

Goldberg enters Harris' spoiled, uppercrust world in a family mansion outside Baltimore in a roundabout fashion: Harris' weepy mom (Kathleen Quinlan) is vacationing in Jamaica with hubbie (Michael Ontkean), tormented by the death of her infant daughter, when the hotel maid Clara, played by Goldberg, brings her back to life with doses of folk wisdom. Young Harris has a conniption fit when his parents return home with the Jamaican nanny to lord over him and serve as Quinlan's live-in companion/housekeeper.

Second-act plot twists involve the breakup of Quinlan's marriage, occasioned by Ontkean's philandering and her taking up with a self-help seminar guru, Dr. Epstein (Spalding Gray). Broken-home theatrics drive the boy into Goldberg's arms, providing irresistible, folksy good humor as the precocious young thesp mimics her Jamaican accent and begins to fit in with Blanche (Hattie Winston) and Goldberg's other Jamaican friends living in Baltimore.

Fly in the ointment comes with Goldberg's old-time foe from the Islands, Dora (Beverly Todd), who goads Harris to find out his nanny's deep, dark secret by rifling the red suitcase she keeps hidden uner her bed.

Third-act verbal revelation scene tastefully addresses such strong topics as rape and incest with care; less effective is film's climax in which the disillusioned boy hurls a racial slur at Goldberg when he feels abandoned by her. Harris plays the scene well and there can be no questioning of the filmmakers' motives, but it still hurts the mood of an otherwise tightly honed production. Reunion coda is a bit distended, but ends pic on an upbeat note of closure and inspiration.

Captured in lush autumnal hues by ace British lenser Freddie Francis, "Clara's Heart" is a beauty to behold, buttressed by a moving, wistful Dave Grusin score. Goldberg's control and strength, including an unwavering Jamaican accent, build cumulatively to deep emotional impact, while costar Harris is a real find, making the most of Medoff's bon mots and never striking a false note. Together they provide an honest '80s version of the 3-hankie picture of yore, with some of the surefire dramatic appeal of classics like Carol Reed's "The Fallen Idol."

In fact, though contemporary in setting and jargon, "Heart" plays like the films of 25 years ago and this return to traditional screen values could occasion sleeper success against the grain, à la "On Golden Pond." However, pic will need special handling to avoid the potential catcalls of those critics and audiences who currently view sentimentality with a jaded eye.

Support roles are ably filled including the required callousness of Quinlan's and Ontkean's characters. Sole sore thumb here is Spalding Gray, whose guru might just as well be a real estate salesman, given the false reading.

All tech credits are tops, with Francis and others likely to be singled out for recognition come awards time. —*Lor.*

Nightfall

A Concorde Pictures release of a New Horizons production. Produced by Julie Corman. Directed by Paul Mayersberg. Screenplay, Mayersberg, from Isaac Asimov's story; camera (Foto-Kem color), Dariusz Wolski; editor, Brent Schoenfeld; music, Frank Serafine; additional music, Steve Dancz; sound, Craig Felburg; production design, Craig Hodgetts; art direction, Carol Bosselman; costume design, Stephen Chudej; production manager, Reid Shane; assistant director, Richard Strickland; visual effects consultant, Chuck Comisky; associate producer, Lynn Whitney; casting, Al Guarino. Reviewed at Eastside theater, N.Y., Oct. 1, 1988. MPAA Rating: PG-13. Running time: **82 MIN.**
Aton . . . . David Birney
Roa . . . . Sarah Douglas
Sor . . . . Alexis Kanner
Ana . . . . Andra Millian
Bet . . . . Starr Andreeff
Kin . . . . Charles Hayward
Architect . . . . Jonathan Emerson
Boffin . . . . Susie Lindeman

Zol . . . . Russell Wiggins

■ **Paul Mayersberg's film of "Nightfall" takes Isaac Asimov's classic sci-fi story of nearly five decades ago and turns it into a dull, pretentious and fragmented exercise of major disappointment to genre fans.**

Pic has been a regional release since April, reviewed here for the record.

Project, lensed last year, actually dates back 10 years for Mayersberg and Julie and Roger Corman (then with their New World banner), following Mayersberg's successful sci-fi script adaptation for Nicolas Roeg, "The Man Who Fell To Earth." As his second feature direction, it shares the coldness and remoteness of his debut "Captive" but lacks that British film's visual beauty.

Asimov's story speculates on the behavior and spiritual beliefs of people inhabiting a planet orbiting a 3-sun-system, in which the daily (for us) phenomenon of nightfall only occurs about every 1,000 years. The awe of such an event brings chaos, forcing civilization to rebuild each time.

With the ninth nightfall in recorded history approaching, two camps prepare: one led by astronomer Aton (David Birney) plans to hide underground in a keep and ride out the unknown catastrophe; another cult led by blind prophet Sor (Alexis Kanner) uses a braille holy book and ritualistic blinding ceremonies (eyes pecked out by birds) for converts to get ready for apocalypse.

Key subplot has a sexy mystery woman from the desert (Andra Millian) who claims to be a snake princess seducing both Aton and his son-in-law Kin (Charles Hayward).

Shredded editing renders the film virtually unwatchable for general audiences as Mayersberg's alienation effects prove wholly unsuitable to the material. Asimov's mood and spirit are lost; a naturalistic approach involving invisible editing and camerawork but strong performances would have maximized viewer empathy. Acting styles don't match either, ranging from the ultra-serious readings of Birney to villain Kanner's almost campy, mannered thesping, resembling Roddy McDowall in a toga epic.

Andra Millian is quite alluring as the temptress, with her topless sex scenes pressuring the limits of the pic's liberal PG-13 rating. Starr Andreeff also makes a good impression as Birney's beautiful daughter, cast in the Amanda Pays mold.

Interesting Arizona locations utilizing Paolo Soleri's communities of Arcosanti and Cosanti do not make up for lack of budget to suggest other-worldliness; also, Birney's shoulder-length hair contrasts with some other male characters' incongruous '50s/'80s greasy looks.

Final matte shot of the stars coming out is about all that Asimov fans can take home from this one.
—*Lor.*

Alien Nation

A 20th Century Fox release. Produced by Gale Anne Hurd, Richard Kobritz. Directed by Graham Baker. Screenplay, Rockne S. O'Bannon; camera (DeLuxe color), Adam Greenberg; editor, Kent Beyda, Curt Sobel; production design, Jack T. Collis; art direction, Joseph Nemec 3d, set decoration, Jim Duffy; costume design, Erica Phillips; aliens creators (Stan Winston Studios), Alec Gillis, Shane Mahan, John Rosengrant, Tom Woodruff Jr., Shannon Shea; makeup, Zoltan, John Elliott; sound (Dolby), David MacMillan, Charles Wilborn; assistant directors, Herb Adelman, Newton D. Arnold; second unit director/stunt coordinator, Conrad E. Palmisano; second unit camera, Frank Holgate; casting, Joan Bradshaw. Reviewed at Fox Studios, L.A., Sept. 31, 1988. MPAA Rating: R. Running time: **94 MIN.**
Sykes . . . . .James Cann
Sam Francisco . . . . .Mandy Patinkin
William Harcort . . . . .Terence Stamp
Kipling . . . . .Kevin Major Howard
Cassandra . . . . .Leslie Bevins

■ **Hollywood — Despite its buddy-cop formula structuring, "Alien Nation" is still an engrossing new chapter from sci-fi producers Gale Anne Hurd ("The Terminator," "Aliens") and Richard Kobritz ("Christine").**

Solid performances by leads James Caan and his humanoid partner Mandy Patinkin move this production beyond special effects, clever alien makeup and car chases. Fans of the genre undoubtedly will return to view more aliens in action, meaning Fox has a solid fall hit on its hands.

A whole culture of aliens, called "newcomers," land in the Mojave desert in the 1990s and are allowed refuge by the U.S. government as if they were Salvadorans or Vietnamese Boat People. Some are good, decent, upstanding citizen types, others just the opposite.

Racism is the underlying theme in "Alien Nation," though it's played out in actioner fashion. The "newcomers," an exploited humanoid race, find America a land of ideological confusion. Americans speak of equality yet aren't consistent when it comes to acting on those beliefs.

Pic is handled by British director Graham Baker on a slightly more serious than comic book level. There's a lot of violence and noise in a futuristic adaptation of a drug pusher story, but also a compelling human-humanoid drama.

"Newcomer" detective Patinkin, a thoughtful, soft-spoken family man, gets paired with the bitter, alcoholic Caan after Caan chooses him to help solve a murder/conspiracy case that some "newcomers" are behind.

"Alien Nation" has all the elements that have come to characterize the genre, cleverly disguised by creating "newcomers" who look other-worldly, with their blotchy, reptilian skin-heads that distinguish them physically, while they also exhibit certain human emotional frailties.

Realistic-looking makeup of the humanoids, crafted by Stan Winston Studios creators Alec Gillis, Tom Woodruff, John Rosengrant Shannon Shea and Shane Mahan, is integral to carrying this off. The rubber prosthetics that cover the aliens' heads appear seamless, allowing them the ability to emote through facial expressions.

Caan is nicely suited to his role. He's mellower and sadder, realistically taking on a part where he is supposed to have matured without losing some of that jaded, irresponsible side that he's so well conveyed before. What is the saving grace for his relationship with Patinkin is how his attitude of working just inside the law influences his laconic partner.

Just when things begin to wind down to a violent, dull pace, Patinkin springs life into the production by metamorphosing from a by-the-books type to a man who acts on his sense of moral outrage. Catalyst is "newcomer" Terence Stamp, assimilated to the top of Los Angeles society, scheming to control his fellow "newcomers" with a drug that woos them into indentured servitude.

Pic doesn't quite sustain a heart-pounding, eerie tone throughout. Perhaps because so much effort is made humanizing the aliens, the car chase sequences and gory ending seems less potent. That's also true for some of the most exotic of scenes, notably when the tantalizing "newcomer" nightclub dancer Cassandra (Leslie Bevins) comes on to Caan — and it doesn't look as weird as it should. —*Brit.*

Jacob
(RUMANIAN)

A Rumaniafilm and Artexim production. Directed by Mircea Daneliuc. Screenplay, Daneliuc, from stories of Geo Bogza; camera (color), Florin Mihailescu; editor, Maria Neag; sound, Horia Murgu; art direction, Magdalena Marasescu; costume design, Svetlana Mihailescu. Reviewed at N.Y. Film Festival, Sept. 30, 1988. Running time: **117 MIN.**
With: Dorel Visan, Cecilia Birbora, Ion Fiscuteanu, Maria Seles, Livia Baba, Dinu Apetrei.

■ **A film of complex psychological and social meaning, "Jacob" concerns oppressed miners and their families who are caught in an ugly system that is, at least to some extent, of their own creation, and derives from man's nature.**

Dorel Visan in the title role is extraordinary, especially as he is alone (without words) for the last 20 minutes of the film.

Jacob is a tall husky miner who has married the widow of a suicide and lives with her, her mother and four small children in a small house. Work in the local goldmine is so dangerous and pays so little that some miners risk terrible punishment to steal gold ore, hiding it on their persons as they leave the mine. Inspectors and militia guards are vigilant, however, and suspected miners betrayed by informers are stripped naked for searches, sometimes even forced to take powerful laxatives, so the search becomes doubly thorough and humiliating.

Jacob raves against the brutal authority of the mine operators, backed by military government. Who are these authorities? The story is based upon a Geo Bogza work published in 1942, concerning conditions in the 1930s, when Rumania was a corrupt monarchy with a working class in semi-slavery. It would be easy to locate the time and atmosphere of the film accordingly, within an unjust capitalist system. Yet director Mircea Daneliuc invites the audience to find its own meanings.

We may equally place the time of the film within modern Communist Rumania, providing a totally different political context. The film is meant as a fable to have universal and timeless relevance, quite apart from transient regimes that come and go.

Jacob as a Rumanian miner is the vessel for a kind of Everyman. An admirable, passionate man, he also is devious, lecherous, abusive to his wife & children, and a thief of gold ore. Jacob asserts his fallible humanity so forcefully that we love the man even as we fear for him.
—*Hitch.*

In Dangerous Company

A Sandstar release of a Preuss Entertainment Group presentation of a Zuban production. Produced by Ruben Preuss, Robert Newell. Coproducers, John Herman Shaner, Mitch Brown. Directed by Preuss. Screenplay, Brown; camera (Foto-Kem color), James Carter; editor, W.O. Garrett; music, Berington Van Campen; production design, Mark Simon; costume design, Maria Metivier; sound, Scott Smith; assistant director, Matt Hinkley. Reviewed at Raleigh Studios, Hollywood, Sept. 30, 1988. MPAA Rating: R. Running time: **96 MIN.**
Blake . . . . .Cliff DeYoung
Evelyn . . . . .Tracy Scoggins
Ryerson . . . . .Steven Keats
Chris . . . . .Chris Mulkey
Alex Aguilar . . . . .Henry Darrow
Peggy . . . . .Catherine Ai
Troung . . . . .Dana Lee
Richie . . . . .Michael Shaner

■ **Hollywood — "In Dangerous Company" is a paper-thin attempt at a *film noir* thriller that's neither suspenseful nor stylish. Currently booked at a single Panorama City hardtop, this low-budgeter is headed straight for video, where it'll be lucky if it recoups costs.**

Mitch Brown's script mixes jaded Vietnam vets who hang out in L.A.'s Little Saigon with wealthy pretenders to the world of fine art.

His characters' background as vets and their friendship with some Vietnam natives is supposed to lend depth to the story; it doesn't. The whole thing plays like daytime tv.

Cliff DeYoung is Blake, a vet and former hitman who becomes a fool for Tracy Scoggins as Evelyn, a game-playing gal with zero integrity and a Barbie Doll body who claims she needs his help.

She's the playmate of a rich art collector (Steven Keats) who's involved with forgers; he's also a pervert, or as she puts it, "a reptile." Meanwhile, she's gotten involved with his teenage chauffeur, a wild-eyed idiot (Michael Shaner) who now wants to kill her.

Blake, who's unable to keep his hands off her anytime they're alone, is just the patsy she needs to pull off an elaborate scheme that even by the end makes no particular sense.

Minus believability, menace or a reason to care, pic never comes close to its mark. Sex scenes are perhaps its only drawing card; they're barely within R boundaries.

DeYoung doesn't work as the hitman who lives in a fleabag downtown hotel. His face and voice suggest a Westside softie better suited to an episode of "thirtysomething." Scoggins is out of bounds straying beyond tv soaps.

Pic is the U.S. feature debut of director Ruben Preuss, a former U.K. commercial director who here relies on glittery helicopter shots of L.A. at night to establish the style missing in script or cast.

Production design and lighting are flat, though production did have the use of some high-tone locales. The same establishing shot of a Hollywood Hills manse is used at least six times. Editing is abrupt while the score is mediocre.
—*Daws.*

Quelques jours avec moi
(A Few Days With Me)
(FRENCH)

A UGC release (Galaxy Intl. release in U.S.) of a Sara Films/Cinéa/Films A2 coproduction. Produced by Alain Sarde, Philippe Carcassonne. Directed by Claude Sautet. Screenplay, Sautet, Jérôme Tonnerre, Jacques Fieschi, from novel by François Robin; editor, Jacqueline Thiedot; music, Philippe Sarde; art direction, Carlos Conti; costumes, Olga Berlutti; sound, Pierre Lenoir, Jean-Paul Loublier; assistant director, Yvon Rouve, production manager, Gérard Gaultier. Reviewed at UGC Biarritz cinema, Paris, Sept. 10, 1988. (In Montreal Film Festival, non-competing.) Also in Toronto fest. Running time: **131 MIN.**

Martial . . . . .Daniel Auteuil
Francine . . . . .Sandrine Bonnaire
Fonfrin . . . . .Jean-Pierre Marielle
Madame Fonfrin . . . .Dominique Lavanant
Fernand . . . . .Vincent Lindon
Régine . . . . .Thérèse Liotard
Mme. Pasquier . . . . .Danièlle Darrieux
Also with: Gérard Ismael, Philippe Laudenbach, Tanya Lopert, Dominique Blanc, Jean-Pierre Castaldi, Jean-Louis Richard, François Chaumette.

■ **Paris — After a 5-year absence ("Garcon!" with Yves Montand in 1983), Claude Sautet is back with a new look at the discreet anxieties of the bourgeoisie.**

Despite excessive running time and some disjointed and strained plotting, "Quelques jours avec moi" boasts fine portraiture, first-rate actors and effective comedy-drama. It should do well locally and be a strong export item.

Though the decor often remains unchanged from Sautet's earlier middle-class tales, the protagonists are younger. Accordingly Sautet has sought out a new generation of screenwriter to adapt a novel about a disconnected young bourgeois trying to reemerge into life's mainstream. Coauthors are a couple of critics turned scripters, Jérôme Tonnerre and Jacques Fieschi, who hold promise in France's leaky pool of writing talent. (Film's coproducer Philippe Carcassonne also is a former critic-colleague of Tonnerre and Fieschi.)

Still, Sautet and his collaborators have left some knots untied in this story of a supermarket empire heir (Daniel Auteuil) who sets off on a tour of provincial stores after internment in a mental hospital.

Auteuil's first stop is his last stop, Limoges, where he notes some discrepancies in the account books held by local manager Jean-Pierre Marielle. Auteuil is ready to overlook the matter and head out of the stifling provincial atmosphere, but changes his mind when he notices Marielle's housemaid, Sandrine Bonnaire, whose insolent, independent manner attracts and fascinates him.

Auteuil rents an expensive apartment, wines and dines Bonnaire and invites her to spend a few days with him. For the working girl the occasion is something of a lark and a chance to take revenge on her small-minded former employees. For the rich, abnormally introverted Auteuil, the liaison is a quietly desperate groping for an emotional contact that continues to short-circuit.

Sautet is in perfect control of his story and characters in the first half, replete with colorful encounters, two disparate principals superbly rendered by a radiant Bonnaire and a subtly riveting Auteuil, backed up a gallery of gently caricatured social types. Among film's best comic set pieces is the party Auteuil and Bonnaire throw for their local acquaintances.

When the plot wheels begin to turn, the direction wobbles. Disturbed by his erratic spendthrift behavior, Auteuil's business-minded mother (an ever-perfect Danièlle Darrieux) lures him back to Paris, while Bonnaire, thinking the interlude over, decides to leave her loser boyfriend (a touchingly pathetic Vincent Lindon) to shack up with a brutish cafe-owner. Auteuil returns

to town in time to anticipate an impending drama.

Film has trouble getting to its moving conclusion, with Sautet suddenly lumping secondary characters into a cumbersome chorus led by Marielle, and resorting unexpectedly to a narrator to bridge narrative jumps and evacuate certain characters before the lump-in-the-throat finale.

Despite it's narrative weaknesses, "Quelques jours avec moi" ranks well in current production.

Tech credits are up to the (high) Sautet standards. —*Len.*

L'Etudiante
(The Student)
(FRENCH-ITALIAN)

A Gaumont release of a Gaumont/Gaumont Prod./TF1 Films Prod./Cecchi Gori Group/Tiger Cinematografica coproduction. Produced by Alain Poiré. Directed by Claude Pinoteau. Screenplay, Danièle Thompson, Pinoteau; camera (color), Yves Rodallec; editor, Marie-Josephe Yoyotte; music, Vladimir Cosma; theme song lyrics, Jeff Jordan; song performed by Karoline Kruger; sound, Bernard Bats; art direction, Jacques Dugied; costumes, Catherine Leterrier; makeup, Michel Deruelle; assistant director, Francis de Gueltzl; production managers, Marc Goldstaub, Guy Azzi; casting, Françoise Menidrey. Reviewed at the Club Gaumont Matignon, Paris, Sept. 21, 1988. Running time: **104 MIN.**

Valentine . . . . .Sophie Marceau
Edouard . . . . .Vincent Lindon
Céline . . . . .Elisabeth Vitali
Charly . . . . .Jean-Claude Leguay
Also with: Elena Pompei, Roberto Attias, Brigitte Chamarande, Christian Pereira, Beppe Chierici, Nathalie Mann, Elie Chouraqui.

■ **Paris — Director Claude Pinoteau, scripter Danièle Thompson and actress Sophie Marceau of hit "La Boum" and its 1982 sequel have been called back to active service for a new youth product that will probably score on home ground, though this latest confection is a mostly trite boy-meets-girl romance.**

Chief appeal is provided by Marceau, who was 13 when she made her screen debut in "La Boum" and is now a physically ripe and pretty 21, and Vincent Lindon, whose gauche, cuddly charm appealingly complements Marceau's snooty collegiate demeanor.

"L'Etudiante" is not strictly speaking a followup to "La Boum," in which Marceau was a budding teen from a comfy bourgeois family, but the film's commercial formula is in the same vein.

No longer a virgin, Marceau's personage is a plucky, outspoken Sorbonne hopeful with no ostensible family background. Teaching part-time to pay for her way and sharing an apartment with others, she has no time for romance as she feverishly prepares for her degree exams.

It's bad timing when she meets Lindon, an aspiring composer who plays with an itinerant rock band, and with whom she has little in

common.

Script by Thompson and Pinoteau spins a series of mechanical variations on the situation of lovers with conflicting time schedules (and opposing views on love).

Only scene that stands out is the climactic oral exam in a Sorbonne amphitheater, where Marceau turns a dry dissertation on the responsibilities of love in Molière's The Misanthrope" into a passionate analysis of her own relationship with Lindon, who is in the room.

Pinoteau has packaged the material with the same sense of taste and professionalism that he applied to his previous films. Tech credits are fine.—*Len.*

Camp de Thiaroye
(Camp Thiaroye)
(SENEGALESE-TUNISIAN-ALGERIAN)

A Sidec (Dakar), Istituto Luce (Italy), release of a SNPC (Dakar)/Satpec (Tunis)/Enaproc (Algiers) coproduction, in association with the Ministries of the Armed Forces, Communications and the Interior of Senegal. Written and directed by Ousmane Sembène, Thierno Faty Sow. Camera (color), Ismail Lakhdar Hamina; editor, Kahena Attia, Riveill; music, Ismaila Lo. Reviewed at Venice Film Festival (competing), Sept. 6, 1988. Running time: **150 MIN.**

Aloise Diatta . . . . .Ibrahima Sane
Pays . . . . .Sijiri Bakaba
Capt. Raymond . . . . . . .Jean-Daniel Simon
Also with: Gustave Sorgho, Camara Dansogho Mohamed, Gabriel Zahon, Casimir Zoba, Mohamed Camara, Pierre Orma.

■ **Venice — "Camp Thiaroye" will go down in the history of African cinema as one of the most powerful indictments of colonialism on the continent. Its depiction of a massacre ordered by the French Army against black veterans returning from World War II opens a practically unknown page of history and shows the war's effects on shaping the future of Africa.**

Lensed in a spare, classic style like an American war film of the '40s, directed by Senegal's premier helmer Ousmane Sembène (with Thierno Faty Sow codirecting), "Camp Thiaroye" should range wide on fest and arthouse circuits. France, the major European market for African films, could balk at the subject matter (it is of note that the film was turned down by the Cannes fest this year).

In Senegal, 1944, African infantry troops disembark and prepare to make their way home after four years in the French army. They have seen Europe in flames, the collapse of the French army, the Occupation — and for them, the myth of the white man's superiority is over.

The transit camp where they are to get their pay and be demobilized consists of a few quickly constructed barracks. Though their white captain (Jean-Daniel Simon) is liberal and supportive, the other officers are racist to the core, and it isn't hard to see trouble is brewing.

The tragedy occurs when the French commanders try to give the infantrymen only half of their back pay. With their new self-awareness, the soldiers spontaneously rebel, and take the French general hostage for a few hours. The general promises to pay up, but that night he surrounds the camp with tanks and razes it to the ground, blasting the unarmed infantrymen to pieces.

The final massacre is lensed without the thrilling special effects of a Western-made film, and without using many camera setups, yet its impact is chilling. Equally important are the two hours-plus that precede it, in which Sembène and Faty Sow depict characters and relationships. Sergeant Major Aloise Diatta is an unforgettable portrait of an African intellectual, played with ironic wit by Ibrahima Sane. Multilingual, a lover of classical music and refined literature, Diatta infuriates the bigoted officers with his cultural superiority (and his white wife waiting for him in Paris).

Care is taken to individualize many of the soldiers, who come from all over Africa, converse in the lingua franca French, are Moslems, Catholics, animists. One puzzling thing is pic's large number of historically inaccurate details: from anachronistic books and records to concentration camps, errors are so glaring they seem deliberate.

— *Yung.*

Invasion Earth:
The Aliens Are Here
(COLOR/B&W)

A New World Pictures presentation of a New World and Rearguard Prods. production. Produced by Max J. Rosenberg. Executive producers, Robert L. Fenton, William H. Lange. Directed by George Maitland. Screenplay, Miller Drake; camera (Foto-Kem color), Austin McKinney; editor, Drake, William B. Black; music, Anthony R. Jones; sound, Lee Strosnider; production design, Michael Novotny; visual effects supervisor, Dennis Skotak; creature creator, Michael McCracken; assistant director, John Vomero; production manager, Mel Welles; second unit director, Pat McClung; alien voices, Corey Burton, Tony Pope; associate producer, Julie G. Moldo; casting, Debra Neathery. Reviewed on NW cassette, N.Y., Sept. 11, 1988. No MPAA Rating. Running time: 83 MIN.
Joanie ....Janice Fabian
Billy ....Christian Lee
Tim ....Larry Bagby 3d
Mike ....Dana Young
Mr. Davar ....Mel Welles

■ Part fiction, part compilation, "Invasion Earth: The Aliens Are Here" is a subpar nostalgia piece for monster movie fans. Lightweight effort bypassed theatrical release and currently is in videostores.

Premise is similar to an earlier effort (also unreleased theatrically) "Midnight Movie Massacre:" Aliens from Outer Space invade a small town where a motley audience is watching sci-fi pictures. Pic is set at the Gem Theater (actually filmed at the Warner Grand in San Pedro,

Calif.), and its audience stereotypes lack the humor which highlighted "Massacre."

Four youngsters unite to fight the invaders, who in a nod to Don Siegel's classic "Invasion Of The Body Snatchers" are using pods to take over the bodies of audience members after first numbing their brains with endless sci-fi features and trailers.

Unfortunately, this film, credited to George Maitland but with special effects expert Bob Skotak announced as director during production, also is numbing with its endless clips from very familiar pictures, mostly from the 1950s. A very young or novice sci-fi fan probably will enjoy the excerpts, but pic's target audience has seen them all many times over, complete. Unimaginative use of vintage movie theater material also is a letdown, consisting mainly of a "Let's All Go To The Lobby" animated intermission film.

Insect-styled humanoid monsters created by Michael McCracken are okay but not scary. Casting of Mel Welles, erstwhile Mr. Mushnick from "The Little Shop Of Horrors," as the theater manager is a cute touch; he also doubles as pic's production manager.

Producer Max J. Rosenberg coproduced the unrelated "Dr. Who" film with a similar moniker: "Invasion Earth: 2150 A.D." —*Lor.*

Filu
(SWISS)

A Dschojnt Ventschur/Videoladen Zurich/DRS production. Directed by Samir Jamal Aldin. Screenplay, Jamal Aldin, Martin Witz; camera (color), Lukas Strebel; editor, Kathrin Pluess; sound, Florian Edenbenz. Reviewed at Toronto Festival of Festivals, Sept. 16, 1988. Running time: 85 MIN.
Max Huber ....Werner Haltiner
Lizzi ....Marianne Schmied
Jiri ....Andreas Loeffel
Also with: Wolfi Berger, Stanislav Oriscek.

■ Toronto — A cinematic spit in the eye of conformity from that most conformist of countries, Switzerland, Samir Jamal Aldin's "Filu" uses a hot mix of film and video razzle-dazzle to relate the bizarre adventures of a young Swiss-Italian social outsider and his friends in Zurich.

Decidedly uncommercial, "Filu" is alive with daredevil creativity and an off-center spirit that should make it a must for any program or festival of new wave cinema.

Max (Werner Haltiner), a middle-class dropout, lives in a loft in Zurich's Italian district. His room and his life adjoins those of Lizzi (Marianne Schmied), a hooker who's dreaming of running her own hotel, and Jiri (Andreas Loeffel), a Czech emigré who dreams of violin glory.

Max is the greatest dreamer of them all, avoiding honest work for penny-ante drug dealing, hapless

thievery, cafe life and a consuming fantasy of designing a bigger and better Zeppelin, powered by photoelectric cells. He loves American soul music, and filmmaker Jamal Aldin peppers his soundtrack with song fragments by James Brown and other r&b artists.

Style is substance, as the director goes for every trick his budget can buy: time-lapse photography, film/video fusions, hand-held loopiness and overlapping dialog tracks, to name a few. The influence of Wim Wenders is apparent and it hasn't been a bad one in this case.

"Filu" skewers targets such as modern media overload and Swiss social complacency, and also has a zoological motif suggesting that animals' lives are in ways superior to those of humans. Meanwhile, Max, played with ingratiating charm by Haltiner, and Lizzi get involved with dangerous gangsters, international spies and some nasty local police. The hero's schemes blow up in his face and he sees love turn to tragedy, but Max ends up with his head properly in the clouds — an apt perspective for considering this unconventional, dizzying film. —*Rich.*

Zärtliche Chaoten II
(Three Crazy Jerks II)
(WEST GERMAN)

A Tivoli Filmverleigh release of a K.S. Film/Roxy Film and Co. KG production. Directed by Holm Dressler. Screenplay, Thomas Gottschalk; camera (color), Atze Glanert; editor, Ute Albrecht-Lovell; sound, Peter Hummel; set design, Smart Design; lighting, Klaus Emberger, Helmut Klee, Peter Kunze. Reviewed at the Arsenal Kino, Hamburg, Sept. 29, 1988. Running time: 96 MIN.
Ronny ....Michael Winslow
Frank ....Thomas Gottschalk
Xaver ....Helmut Fischer
Sandy ....Deborah Shelton

■ Hamburg — West Germany's top-rated tv game show host, Thomas Gottschalk, has paired up with a top tv gameshow content editor, 38-year-old Holm Dressler, to come up with a sequel that tops last year's German summer hit.

As with the first film, however, prospects are bleak in America for this lightweight spoof on "Back To The Future." Pic could travel to more exotic locales as a feature or video release due to Dressler's directing and Gottschalk penning his own lines.

Otherwise the only major change is the casting of "Dallas" thesp Deborah Shelton as the woman who has the three male cast members literally tripping over themselves to get at her. They think she's destined to be the mother of the guy who's their hated boss 50 years from now, and take bumbling steps to change that.

Top billing deservedly goes to Michael Winslow, 1-man sound effects generator and "Police Academy" regular. As he did before, he carries this film. Gottschalk's

screenplay parcels out good lines to all, including Austrian actor Helmut Fischer, a cop show thesp with little comic ability.

Location shooting in the Canary Islands and a Top 40 mix soundtrack lend to film's holiday mood.
— *Gill.*

Labedzi Spiew
(Swan's Song)
(POLISH)

A Polish Film Corp. "Kadr" Unit production. Directed by Robert Glinski. Screenplay, Boleslaw Michalek; camera (color), Andrzej Jaroszewicz; editor, Alina Faflik; music, Henryk Kuzniak; art direction, Jacek Turewicz; production manager, Urszula Orczykowska, Jacek Gwizdala. Reviewed at Gdynia Film Festival, Sept. 16, 1988. Running time: 90 MIN.
Stefan Dziedzic ....Jan Peszek
Ewa ....Grazyna Barszczewska
Girl ....Jolanta Pietek-Gorecka
Director ....Tomasz Zygadlo
Also with: Magdalena Zawadzka. Bronislaw Pawlik, Leon Niemczyk, Maria Probosz, Boguslaw Sobczuk.

■ Gydnia — "Swan's Song," as title by newcomer Robert Glinski is translated, is a wacky spoof on the film industry. This behind the scenes, cinema-as-circus comedy had local audiences in stitches at the Polish Film Festival, but jokes didn't come across as clearly to offshore viewers.

Fans of helmer's hour-long "Sunday Pranks" may decide to put the director on hold till next time around.

The genre is familiar to anyone who has seen a Fellini film. Stefan, a well-known scriptwriter (droll performance by Jan Peszek) trying to find a subject for his next screenplay, is tormented by the stupid ideas of producers, actors and his wife. His dentist wants a fortune to fix his teeth and the car needs overhauling. Wife Ewa (Grazyna Barszczewska) has turned their apartment into a cactus ranch while she waits for an acting part.

In the chaos, Stefan fantasizes about films that could be made — a gangster film, love story, musical, porn flick. Female nudity is abundant. The spoofs probably work best on audiences familiar with bad Polish films, though a send-up of Gene Kelly's "Singin' In The Rain" number, set in a grimy Warsaw back alley, is a romp that can be universally appreciated.

Glinski has a good sense of comic timing, and "Song" could be one of the year's top grossers in Poland.
— *Yung.*

Traxx

A DEG production in association with De Laurentiis Film Partners L.P. Produced by Gary DeVore. Coproducer, Richard McWhorter. Directed by Jerome Gary. Screenplay, DeVore; camera (Technicolor), Giuseppe Macarri; editor, Michael Kahane; music, Jay Gruska; production design, Jack Poplin; art direction, Dennis Bradford; set decoration, Joseph Stone; sound, Bud Alper; assistant director, Donald Roberts; costumes, Clifford Lapone; casting, Marilyn Black (North Carolina, Fincannon & Associates). Reviewed on HBO Video vidcassette, N.Y., Sept. 10, 1988. MPAA Rating: R. Running time: **84 MIN.**

Traxx	Shadoe Stevens
Mayor Alexandria Gray	Priscilla Barnes
Deeter	Willard E. Pugh
Chief Emmett Decker	John Hancock
Commissioner R.B. Davis	Hugh Gillin
Mayhew	Michael Kirk
Tibbs	Raymond O'Connor
Aldo Palucci	Robert Davi

Also with: Hershal Sparber, Jonathan Lutz, Lucius Houghton, Darrow Igus, Arlene Lorre, Wally (Famous) Amos.

■ **"Traxx,"** boasting deejay/"Hollywood Squares" performer Shadoe Stevens' feature debut, is a comic strip actioner made by DEG and caught up in the company's financial malaise. Whatever the reasons it's been kept out of theaters, it's unlikely the healthiest distrib would have released it. Implausible pic has hit the video trail.

Sporting a muscled physique, long, blown-dry blond locks and a persistent gleaming smile, Stevens plays it for (infrequent) laughs as a Texas state trooper turned mercenary Rambo-type who shoots up rebels in El Salvador, then the Mideast, then Nicaragua. He wants to give up the wild life, however, to join in another battle — the cookie war.

Traxx returns to Hadleyville, Texas, to concoct his strange crab cookies, tuna cookies, laxative & cough drop cookies, ad nauseum, but he needs cash to capitalize his business, and so hires himself out to the burg's police chief (John Hancock) and mayor (Priscilla Barnes) as a "town tamer." Thus, he's brandishing his weaponry again, this time against the nogoodniks of this impossibly chaotic town. (Shot at DEG's North Carolina studios, phony-looking cross between New Orleans and New York succeeds as looking like No Street, U.S.A.)

Pic does manage a few decent jokes, chiefly involving a suspicious and nihilistic mob boss (Robert Davi). Barnes looks sharp as the stuck-up mayor who, natch, comes unglued at the mere sight of the glorious Traxx, but the sex-themed lines she's given don't quite make it as double entendres.

Stevens gives it a game try, but apparently has been given little direction other than to shoot fast, tilt his head back and smile. (Note his trademark long hair tucked up under his state trooper hat — no Method-man he.) Things otherwise are helped along by Davi and several other good character actors.

Despite the sometimes set-bound look, film is okay technically, with a jumpy score that hints at the lighthearted tone the filmmakers had hoped to achieve. — *Gerz.*

Ada dans la jungle
(Ada In The Jungle)
(FRENCH-IVORY COAST)

An AAA release of a FIT Prod./La Sept/Générale d'Images/Ministry of Information, Culture, Youth and Sports (Ivory Coast) coproduction. Executive producer, Jean-Pierre Ramsay Levi. Produced by Alain Depardieu. Directed by Gérard Zingg. Screenplay, Zingg, Francesco Altan, based on Altan's comic strip album; camera (Eastmancolor), Renato Berta; editor, Luc Barnier; sound, Michel Vionnet, François Groult; costumes, Mara Chaves; makeup, Susan Robertson, Diane Duchesne; art direction, Jean-Pierre Kohut-Svelko; assistant director, Jean-François Chaintron; caste, Mamade. Reviewed at Club de L'Etoile, Paris, Sept. 24, 1988. Running time: **90 MIN.**

Pilic	Richard Bohringer
Bumbo	Isaach de Bankolé
Carmen	Victoria Abril
Ada	Marie Louisa
Collins	Bernard Blier
Rudi	Philippe Léotard
Nancy	Charley Boorman

■ **Paris** — A live-action screen adaptation of a popular French comic strip album by Francesco Altan, "Ada In The Jungle" fails like most previous efforts in the genre.

Despite having a generally well-chosen cast, Gérard Zingg, who co-adapted the 1982 cartoon with its author and directed, finds no cinematic equivalent for the elliptical, zany humor of the strip's grotesques.

Shot in the Ivory Coast, story follows the odyssey of nubile young Ada, niece and heiress to a dying British lord, whose final wish is that she find the son he deliberately lost in the African jungle some 20 years earlier.

Set in 1942, Altan's convoluted 'toon gets the heroine entangled with Germans, a disinherited cousin set on stopping her (Charley Boorman) and a homosexual couple living off tomatoes and elephant tusks (Bernard Blier and Philippe Léotard).

There are also a Serbo-Croatian Spanish Civil War veteran (Richard Bohringer) who has the hots for Ada's fickle Spanish maid (Victoria Abril) and a handsome young native (Isaach de Bankolé) who turns out to be her romantic savior, not to mention the illegitimate son of her dear, dead artisocratic uncle.

All turns out well for Ada (played by a charming but inexperienced Venezuelan model, Marie Louisa), but it's the spectator who's left in the quicksand of a poorly articulated script, witless dialog and unimaginative direction.

Tech credits, notably Renato Berta's pop color lensing, are nonetheless professional. — *Len.*

Schodami W Gore, Schodami W Dol
(Upstairs, Downstairs)
(POLISH)

A Polish Film Corp. "Dom" Unit production. Directed by Andrzej Domalik. Screenplay, Wladyslaw Terlecki, based on the novel by Michal Choromanski; camera (color), Dariusz Kuc; editor, Malgorzata Domalik; music, Jerzy Satanowski; art direction, Malgorzata Wloch; production manager, Iwona Ziulkowska. Reviewed at Gdynia Film Festival, Sept. 13, 1988. Running time: **120 MIN.**

Painter	Jan Nowicki
Karol	Maciej Robakiewicz
Baroness	Anna Dymna
Hypnotist	Jan Peszek
Wife	Maria Pakulnis

Also with: Adrianna Biedrzynska (Maryjka), Krzysztof Gosztyla.

■ **Gdynia** — After Andrzej Domalik's feature film bow with his prize-winning "Siegfried," his second effort, "Upstairs, Downstairs," comes as a let-down. Again concerned wiith the inner life of artists, film describes an aspiring young painter who idolizes Stanislaw Ignacy Witkiewicz (a.k.a. Witkacy).

Though the main character is the youth and Witkacy is never called by name, it's the portrait of the famous artist that disappoints. Atmosphere is lush, music rich, but film's focus is blurred and uninvolving. It will have a difficult time traveling abroad.

Setting is Zakopane, famed artists' community of prewar Poland. Amid breathtaking mountain scenery and opulent sets, Domalik stresses the decadence of a world coming to an end. Witkacy, called simply the Painter, is played by Jan Nowicki as an ironic Marlon Brando figure in his panama hat and scarf. When starry-eyed tyro painter Karol (Maciej Robakiewicz) first visits his swank studio, he's tustling with a willing model and throws the boy out.

Karol starts painting on his own and takes a role in an amateur production of one of Witkacy's plays. Story slides into a series of light love affairs for Karol, drugged evenings for the Painter and his fashionable Bohemian pals. The round of parties, drugs, alcohol and erotics comes to an abrupt end in September 1939. The body of a Don Juan doctor is dragged behind a German army car, the Painter disappers (Witkacy committed suicide), and the young artist is left setting up his lonely canvas in a field.

Film is a merry-go-round of images and sensations, with a classy cast and technical crew. Its recreation of the Bohemian community, personal as it is, is stuffed with familiar ideas about decadent artists that does little justice to the historical figure involved. — *Yung.*

La petite amie
(The Girlfriend)
(FRENCH)

An AMLF release of a T. Films/FR3 Films/Messine Prod. coproduction. Produced by Alain Terzian. Directed by Luc Béraud. Screenplay, Béraud, Bernard Stora, from story idea by Bertrand Javal; camera (Fujicolor), Dominique Chapuis; editor, Armand Psenny; art direction, Dominique André; sound, Paul Lainé, Jean-Paul Loublier; assistant director, Michel Thibaud; production managers, Claude Parnet, François Galfré. Reviewed at Marignan-Concorde cinema, Paris, Sept. 14, 1988. Running time: **91 MIN.**

Guillaume Bertin	Jacques Villeret
Martin Morel	Jean Poiret
Agnès	Agnès Blanchot
Beatrice Morel	Eva Darlan
Benoit	Jacques Sereys
Odile	Catherine Hiegel
Charles	Jacques Boudet
Anne-Sophie	Catherine Arditi
Picard	Claude Evrard

■ **Paris** — This poorly plotted romantic comedy casts Jacques Villeret as an importuning architect who accepts philandering public works exec Jean Poiret's proposal to pose as his teen mistress' husband during an Alpine ski holiday at Poiret's family chalet.

Situations revolve around Poiret's unsuccessful attempts to spend some time alone with his girlfriend, and Villeret's strained rapport with her. Things turn out morally hunky-dory as Villeret and the phony wife develop a true romance while Poiret's indulgent mate (Eva Darlan) forgives him his extramarital adventures.

Script is mechanical, commercial hash from Bernard Stora and Luc Béraud, who have seen better days with more personal subjects, notably in the films they made with director Claude Miller.

Béraud directed in his first helming assignment in seven years. What a way to end a long and undeserving hiatus! — *Len.*

Fábula de la Bella Palomera
(Fable Of The Beautiful Pigeon Fancier)
(SPANISH)

An Intl. Network Group/Televisión Española/New Latin American Film Foundation production. Produced by João Alfredo Viegas. Executive producer, Max Marambio. Directed by Ruy Guerra. Screenplay, Guerra, Gabriel García Márquez, from story by García Márquez; camera (color), Edgar Moura; editor, Mair Tavares; music, Egberto Gismonti; sound, Antonio Carlos da Silva. Reviewed at Toronto Festival of Festivals, Sept. 12, 1988. Running time: **82 MIN.**

Don Orestes	Ney Latorraca
Fulvia	Claudia Ohana

Also with: Tonia Carrero, Dina Sfat, Chico Díaz, Cecil Thire, Ruy Rezende, Julio Levy, Ataide.

■ **Toronto** — Brazilian Ruy Guerra returns for inspiration to the prose of Columbia author Gabriel García Márquez in "The Fable Of The Beautiful Pigeon Fancier," a dreamy sliver of a film that does not approach the haunting hallucinatory power of their 1983 collaboration "Erendira."

Based on a fragment from García Márquez' latest novel "Love In The Time Of Cholera," Guerra's new film is best suited for special programs on Latin American cinema.

This is a fable about obsessive love set in the late 19th century Brazil and filmed on stunningly beautiful locations. Don Orestes, a fastidious, imperious rum baron, lives with his strong-willed mother and pines away waiting for a great and true love to enter his life. His mother, in keeping with the García Márquez esthetic of magical realism, simply dreams up a dreamgirl for him. She's Fulvia (Claudia Ohana, the star of "Erendira"), the pigeon-keeping wife of a local musician.

They have a brief incendiary affair that changes both of them permanently. She's murdered by her husband. He's tormented for the rest of his life — which lasts well into the middle of the 20th century.

The small pleasures of this film are the sonorous richness of García Márquez' Spanish, a brief but indelible celebration of erotic fulfillment and meticulously framed cinematic images. The narrative, however, is too slight to fully support the fable's grim moral implications about the price life can exact for the realization of its rarest moments.
— *Rich.*

Qiwang
(Chess King)
(CHINESE)

A Xi'an Studio production. Directed by Teng Wenji. Screenplay, Wenji, Zhang Xinxin, based on the novel by Zhong Acheng; camera (Widescreen, color), Wang Xinsheng; editor, Li Jingzhong; art direction, Cao Wenping; music, Guo Wenjing; production manager, Lui Chengshun. Reviewed at Venice Film Festival (competing), Sept. 8, 1988. Running time: **91 MIN.**
Wang Yisheng . . . . Xie Yuan
Azhong. . . . . Li Hui
Ying . . . . Duan Xiu
Ni Bin . . . . Ren Ming
Tiehan . . . . Shao Liang
Party secretary . . . . Niu Ben

■ **Venice — Lensed by a director of entertainment films, Teng Wenji, "Chess King" is the curious story of a poor chess buff in the Chinese provinces who takes on nine opponents at once and defeats them all.**

Film builds cleverly to the final sequence, which plays like an intellectual version of Rocky in the ring, or a martial arts finale with one man against impossible odds. This surprisingly extroverted film, more collective farm than solitary thinker, has a winning freshness that should earn it a place at the year's fests and at better art houses.

"Chess King" is the second book in a trilogy by Zhong Acheng, which includes "The King Of Children" (screened at Cannes). Once more the setting is the collective farms where intellectuals (and hundreds of thousands of young Chinese) were sent during the Cultural Revolution (time is 1968) to work and learn from the peasants. Among them are four friends including Wang who is on the lam from the Red Guards in Beijing as a politically suspect element.

Wang, the cropped-hair hero with serious eyes (Xie Yuan), is poor and uneducated, but has a genius for chess. He has been taught by an old Taoist rag-seller, whose metaphysical approach to the game obviously pays off. In the country, he often leaves the farm to wander from village to village in search of worthy opponents.

He easily beats a rich boy with a Ming chess set, sent to work in the fields like everyone else but still able to pull strings. A good loser, he trades his chess set to a local bigwig to get Wang a place at a provincial tournament, but Wang is still kept out. He challenges the winners, among whom is Li "the Nail," so-called for his habit of nailing his General (the Chinese version of king) to the board and never moving it. In pic's key sequence, as tense as a boxing match and as Chinese as egg rolls, Wang takes on nine opponents simultaneously, playing all the games in his head without a chessboard. Naturally he emerges the new champion, defeating even The Nail.

Very nicely handled are the scenes of life on the farms, which present a striking picture of the hard labor and even hunger involved (when the girls scatter at the sight of a snake, the boys leap on it as dinner). Lensing is first-rate and colorful, pace snappy, cast lively and entertaining.
— *Yung.*

Gli Invisibili
(The Invisibles)
(ITALIAN)

An Artisti Associati Intl. release of a Vidi production. Directed by Pasquale Squitieri. Screenplay Nanni Balestrini, Italo Moscati, Squitieri, based on novel by Balestrini; camera (Luciano Vittori color), Giuseppe Tinelli; editor, Mauro Bonanni; music, Renato Serio; art direction, Franco Velchi. Reviewed at Venice Film Festival (competing), Sept. 4, 1988. Running time: **100 MIN.**
Sirio . . . . Alfredo Rotella
Apache . . . . Igor Zalewsky
China . . . . Giulia Fossa
Maurizio. . . . . Victor Cavallo
Also with: Lorenzo Piani, Paola Rinaldi, Alessandro Zama, Daniela Igliozzi, Patrick Cristaldi.

■ **Venice — The generation of political radicals who, in the late '70s, found themselves caught between a system they considered repressive and armed terrorism makes an intriguing subject for what is probably Pasquale Squitieri's most thought-provoking film.**

"The Invisibles," based on a novel by Nanni Balestrini, a famous member of the '77 movement who was incriminated for terrorism and subsequently absolved, is of chief interest to Italo audiences who have lived through the newspaper headlines. Curious viewers offshore probably will have to hunt up a local screening, as Squitieri's tv-closeup lensing doesn't lend itself much to fest screenings.

Yet "The Invisibles" distinguishes itself for at least two reasons: it is the first Italo picture to deal directly and convincingly with the movement known as Autonomy (depicted rigorously but sympathetically); and the first to show prison riots, in scenes that would have created a furor 10 years ago.

Sirio (newcomer Alfredo Rotella in a lowkey, functional performance) is 20, an ex-student rebel involved in a political radio station. He angrily opposes friends like Apache (Igor Zalewsky, a strong new face) who have splintered off into terrorist groups.

Arrested only because he's present at Apache's arrest, Sirio initially finds prison not the horrible place he heard it was. He shares a cell with buddies from the movement and meets The Professor (obviously meant to represent political theorist Toni Negri), all of whose books he's read.

Squitieri depicts prison life — which makes up most of the film — with an eye to accuracy (relations with the guards, with common criminals, etc.) more than elegant lensing. Close shots and a banal night club music score are in odd contrast with the breadth of the subject. Best sequence showing helmer's skill as an action director is the long, anguishing Trani prison revolt (a real event), which climaxes in masked guards beating the defeated rioters with trudgeons and iron bars.

Rhythm of the film is curiously flat, in spite of Sirio's evolution from idealistic innocent to desperate, forgotten prisoner, destroyed by a Kafkaesque legal sytem that has kept him in prison for years, the failure of the movement (his girlfriend China has become a model) and the death in prison of Apache.

This reflection on the Italian movement of '77 makes a darkly serious film, often disquieting and tense, but rarely entertaining. Its importance would have been great had it been made earlier. — *Yung.*

CINETEX REVIEWS

BAT 21

A Tri-Star Pictures release of a Tri-Star/Vision P.D.G. presentation of an Eagle Films production. Produced by David Fisher, Gary A. Neill, Michael Balson. Executive producer, Jerry Reed. Coproducers, David Saunders, Mark Damon. Line producer, Evzen W. Kolar. Directed by Peter Markle. Screenplay, William C. Anderson, George Gordon, based on book by Anderson; camera (Deluxe color), Mark Irwin; editor, Stephen E. Rivkin; music, Christopher Young; production design, Vincent Cresciman; art direction, Art Riddle, Terry Weldon; costume design, Audrey Bansmer; sound (Dolby), Itzhak Ike Magal; assistant director, Craig Huston; second unit director, Everett Creach; second unit camera, Philip Holahan; casting, Nancy Banks. Reviewed at the Cinetex Film Festival, Las Vegas, Sept. 28, 1988. MPAA Rating: R. Running time: **105 MIN.**
Lt. Col. Iceal Hambleton . . Gene Hackman
Capt. (Bird-Dog) Clark . . . . . Danny Glover
Col. George Walker . . . . Jerry Reed
Ross Carver . . . . David Marshall Grant
Sgt. Harley Rumbaugh . . . Clayton Rohner
Major Jake Scott . . . . Erich Anderson
Col. Douglass . . . . Joe Dorsey

■ **Las Vegas — "BAT 21" represents the flip side of "Rambo." The true story of an officer forced to parachute into enemy-infested jungle during the Vietnam War and survive on his own until a rescue can be attempted, this is a straightforward, surprisingly somber picture that sticks to the facts and does not hype up the action in the usual Hollywood fashion.**

General audiences would probably appreciate this intimate war yarn if they saw it, but meaningless title and paucity of the sort of action normally expected in combat films present an uphill marketing battle for Tri-Star, which will begin a platform release Oct. 21.

Produced independently on location in Sabahn, Borneo, with the cooperation of the Malaysian military, this $10,000,000 venture recounts the exceptional efforts of a reconnaissance flyer nicknamed Bird-Dog to keep tabs on the downed missile intelligence expert, Lt. Col. Iceal Hambleton, who has never before seen actual combat or come face-to-face with the enemy.

After bailing out when his bomber is hit by a missile, Hambleton, played by Gene Hackman, is quickly spotted by Danny Glover's Capt. Bird-Dog Clark.

Only Glover's personal initiative and daring gives Hackman any chance of escaping before the jungle is napalmed to smithereens.

In the meantime, Hackman, with no training or experience in tropical survival tactics, is obliged to live by his wits. Several times, he comes within inches of being spotted by VC patrols.

Equipped with a radio to keep Glover posted on his whereabouts, Hackman can't be too explicit in his messages for fear of being intercepted, so he brightly adapts golf course terminology to inform Glover of his movements.

All this makes for a good real-life tale with a strong wrap-up, but as told here, it lacks the heightened storytelling qualities of first-rate fiction. Hackman's Hambleton is essentially a passive character merely trying to stay out of harm's way until he is saved and, as such, the actor doesn't have many real dramatic opportunities to display his considerable gifts.

Weight of the picture, then, falls more on Glover, who does most of the talking during their radio communications, squares off on occasion with his superior, nicely etched by Jerry Reed (who was also exec producer) and enjoys the benefit of being at the joystick for the snazzy flying scenes. Glover turns in a solid job and is engaging company but, as with Hackman, he remains 1-dimensional, as the viewer learns nothing much about his background, aspirations or deep concerns.

As with Bruce Willis and the cop in "Die Hard," "BAT 21" has a white man in jeopardy on the inside being helped by a black man he's never met on the outside. An unusual bond grows between them in the course of their parallel struggles but, once they are finally united, they have little to say to one another. On all counts, pic lacks the extra dimension that would have lifted it from a straight recounting of incidents to the level of a grand story of courage and individual will.

Few films in memory have spent so much time physically up in the air, so fans of flight photography will definitely want to catch it. Cinematographer Mark Irwin is also credited with aerial lensing, so major kudos must go to him. Peter Markle's direction is dramatically sound and visually crisp, and Christopher Young's score is a plus.

End credits leave a very bad taste behind, as they inform the viewer what happened to Hambleton afterward, but not what became of Bird-Dog Clark. Since the story is at least as much the black man's as the white's, this omission has unavoidable racial overtones and definitely ought to be corrected before release.—Cart.

Without A Clue

An Orion Pictures release of an ITC Entertainment Group presentation of an Eberhardt-Stirdivant production. Produced by Marc Stirdivant. Directed by Thom Eberhardt. Screenplay, Gary Murphy, Larry Strawther; camera (Rank color, CFI prints), Alan Hume; editor, Peter Tanner; music, Henry Mancini; production design, Brian Ackland-Snow; art direction, Terry Ackland-Snow, Robin Tarsnane; set decoration, Peter James, Ian Whittaker; costume design, Judy Moorcroft; sound, David Hildyard; assistant director, Don French; associate producers, Diana Buckhantz, Ben Moses; casting, Noel Davis, Jeremy Zimmerman, Nancy Foy (L.A.). Reviewed at Orion screening room, L.A., Sept. 22, 1988. MPAA Rating: PG. Running time: **106 MIN.**
Sherlock Holmes . . . . Michael Caine
Dr. Watson . . . . Ben Kingsley
Inspector Lestrade . . . . Jeffrey Jones
Fake Leslie . . . . Lysette Anthony
Prof. Moriarty . . . . Paul Freeman
Lord Smithwick . . . . Nigel Davenport
Mrs. Hudson . . . . Pat Keen
Greenbough . . . . Peter Cook
Sebastian . . . . Tim Killick
Wiggins . . . . Matthew Savage

■ **Hollywood — It's Sherlock Holmes who hasn't got a clue in "Without A Clue," another revisionist look at the celebrated sleuth. Twist here is that Dr. Watson is the brilliant one.**

Holmes is just a third-rate actor hired to impersonate the leading character of Watson's hugely popular stories of detection.

This novel approach generates a few laughs and smiles, but of a markedly mild nature and with most of them provoked by the shrewdly judged antics of the two stars, Michael Caine and Ben Kingsley. Domestic b.o. outlook looks fair.

Casting of Caine as the legendary crime solver would seem irregular under normal circumstances, but it works here, as he is actually playing one Reginald Kincaid, an unemployable thespian whose ego has grown in direct proportion to the fame of his greatest role.

After cracking, at the outset, yet another case, Watson simply can no longer abide the undeserving, overweening Kincaid/Holmes, or the media attention he receives, and kicks him out of the house.

His publisher is not the least interested in stories featuring, "John Watson, The Crime Doctor," and when an inspector and the Chancellor of the Exchequer demand to meet with Holmes about an urgent case Watson is forced to patch things up with his cohort.

The case in question involves the theft from the Royal Mint of the plates used to print five-pound notes, and sends the pair to the Scottish Lake District to pursue some errant leads. To be sure, the evil hand of Prof. Moriarty is to be found behind it all, and this Holmes is put to his supreme-test when Watson, his prompter, teacher, adviser and role model in all things, disappears, leaving him on his own to foil the culprits and save the empire.

Die-hard Holmes fans may not particularly enjoy seeing their idol cut down so thoroughly in size and stature, for the effect is that of watching the infantilization of a genius. Many of his pranks border on the buffoonish, but Caine, as always, is able to pull the character off with style.

Kingsley's sharp-witted but perpetually frustrated and exasperated Watson is a much-needed antidote to the broadly conceived Holmes, and the actor gets good comic mileage out of his pained reactions to his partner's ineptitude and to the unending insults and rudeness heaped upon him by others.

Unfortunately, writers Gary Murphy and Larry Strawther fail to generate much interest in the details of the mystery, with the result that the pic sags rather badly during the middle stretch. Things pick up again at the climax, which allows Kincaid/Holmes the opportunity to melodramatically resume his place on the theatrical stage.

Due mainly to his two leads, director Thom Eberhardt is able to deliver most of the amusement potential inherent in the limited material. Film looks fine, and Henry Mancini's spritely score helps keep matters bouncing along. —Cart.

Bum Rap
(COLOR/B&W)

A Millennium production. Executive producers, Jon Kilik, Mindy Schneider, Eric Seidman. Line producer, Christopher Quinn. Produced, written and directed by Daniel Irom. Camera (Technicolor, b&w), Kevin A. Lombard; editor, Michael Borenbaum; music, Robert Kessler, Ethan Neuburg; art direction, Lyn Pinezich; costume design, Beatrix Aruna Pasztor; assistant director, Hugh Rawson; casting, Robin Monroe. Reviewed at Cinetex Film Festival, Las Vegas, Sept. 26, 1988. No MPAA Rating. Running time: **117 MIN.**

Paul Colson . . . . Craig Wasson
Lisa DuSoir . . . . Blanche Baker
Mr. Wolfstadt . . . . Al Lewis
Drunk Woman . . . . Anita Gillette
Phyllis . . . . Frances Fisher
Grace . . . . Anne Carlisle
Joe Franklin . . . . Himself
Dr. Stanton . . . . Ron Parady
Man in Tuxedo . . . . Stephen De Fluiter
Steg . . . . Jim Downey
Tommy . . . . Irving Metzman
Sammy . . . . Eddie Mekka
Fred . . . . Les Shenkel
Dad . . . . Barton Heyman
Mom . . . . Augusta Dabney
Pizza Girl . . . . Brooke Alexander

■ **Las Vegas — A good idea is overcooked and served with too bland a sauce in "Bum Rap." Craig Wasson stars as an ordinary Joe suddenly informed that he has only three days left to live.**

While the premise and aspects of the execution are strong enough to sustain interest, both the lead character and the picture are too soft and muddle-headed to satisfyingly fulfill the theme's potential. An indie distributor looking for a challenge might consider taking this on, but it would be an uphill struggle.

Handsomely and professionally made first feature by Daniel Iron focuses upon hapless aspiring actor Paul Colson (Wasson), who divides his time between driving a cab and making the rounds to fruitless auditions. Although just turning 30, he looks, with his shaggy hair and unkempt beard, like a refugee from the heyday of hippiedom, he lives in the shabbiest of apartments, and appears to have no meaningful relationships.

Haunted by the not entirely inappropriate tag of "spineless jellyfish" hung on him in childhood by a nasty neighbor, this affable loser has the grave misfortune to be informed by a doctor that he is only the 18th recorded victim of a rare form of lymphoma and has precisely 72 hours to live.

Once this sinks in, Paul gets drunk, then heads for the beach, where he rants to God about his fate and soliloquizes on the subject of "What did I do with my life?" before passing out.

When he awakes from his stupor, the film, for which the first half-hour has been in rather flat black-and-white, suddenly shifts into color, aptly but somewhat pretentiously stressing how Paul now sees life with a new intensity.

Director Irom clearly knows his stuff where film technique is concerned, as pic looks sharp on a low budget. Yet he has not been sufficiently tough-minded with inherently profound material, and his indulgences with Wasson's actorish recitations and meanderings result in a far too protracted wind-up. Some cutting from the 2-hour running time would help.

Wasson makes his character intensely believable, although the character's ability to virtually will away his initial depression and continue to behave like the same good old Paul is a bit hard to swallow. Blanche Baker is good as the lady of the pavement, and Brooke Alexander is eye-popping gorgeous as the unlikeliest of pizza delivery girls.
—Cart.

Apartment Zero
(BRITISH)

A Summit Co. Ltd. presentation of a Stephen J. Cole production. Produced by Martin Donovan, David Koepp. Executive producer, Cole. Coproducer, Brian Allman. Directed by Donovan. Screenplay, Donovan, Koepp, story by Donovan; camera (CFI color), Miguel Rodriguez; editor, Conrad M. Gonzalez; music, Elia Cmiral; production design, Miguel Angel Lumaldo; costume design, Angelica Fuentes; assistant director, Fernando Altschul; associate producers, Ezequiel Donovan, Brian Reynolds. Reviewed at Cinetex Film Festival, Las Vegas, Sept. 30, 1988. Running time: **124 MIN.**
Adrian LeDuc . . . . Colin Firth
Jack Carney . . . . Hart Bochner
Margaret McKinney . . . . Dora Bryan
Mary Louise McKinney . . . . Liz Smith
Carlos . . . . Fabrizio Bentivoglio
Vanessa . . . . James Telfer
Laura Werpachowsky . . . Mirella D'Angelo
Alberto Werpachowsky . . . . Juan Vitali
Mrs. Treniev . . . . Cipe Lincovsky
Claudia . . . . Francesca d'Aloja
Mr. Palma . . . . Miguel Ligero
Adrian's Mother . . . . Elvia Andreoli
Tango Singer . . . . Marikena Monti

■ **Las Vegas — The hybrid international production represented by "Apartment Zero" emerges as a genuinely creepy, disturbing and gripping psychological piece.**

Confidently probing touchy sexual, moral and political themes, pic is decidedly not for everyone, but will find devotees among buffs internationally and is a possibility as an offbeat, specialized item domestically.

The lead character runs a dying revival cinema, knows every arcane detail of film history and has covered his apartment with elegantly framed movie star portraits. Clearly, director Martin Donovan, who was born and raised in Argentina but lived for many years in the U.K., qualifies as a major buff himself, and his film is suffused with references to earlier pictures that fortunately have more to do with mood and setting than inside jokes.

With its aberrant sexuality, gradual merging of characters, political context, violent eruptions and disquieting sense of dislocation, picture reminds of "The Tenant" and "Kiss Of The Spider Woman," with flashes of "The American Friend," "Psycho" and Jim Thompson's novel "The Killer Inside Me," among others.

Story's fundamental opposition is between Colin Firth, the nervously repressed, emotionally constipated British cinephile, and Hart Bochner, a charming, loose, Yankee rascal whom Firth takes into his lovely flat as a boarder when finances demand it.

Firth, who has photographs of Montgomery Clift and Charles Laughton prominently positioned in his living room, clearly is both attracted to and threatened by Bochner's confident animal appeal, and kowtows to the American in an attempt to win his friendship. For a while, Firth's starchy humorlessness and frantic fastidiousness are nearly insufferable, but Donovan includes considerable amusement around the edges, and the ship gradually rights itself as the two become increasingly implicated in each other's lives.

Periodically, there are reports of serial murders taking place throughout Buenos Aires, and suggestions that mercenary foreigners who came to Argentina in the employ of the Death Squads may still be active. Suspicion grows that the enigmatic Bochner may not be what he claims, and the drama's principal fascination lies in fathoming who these characters really are and what they want.

Both actors are excellent, with Firth expressing and transcending the irritating emotional constriction of a non-participant in life, and Bochner displaying hitherto unrevealed talent portraying a profoundly split personality.

Donovan has populated the stylish old apartment building where much of the action unfolds with lively, colorful types — a pair of birdlike English spinsters, an alluring woman whose husband is often gone, a transvestite and others. Pic also gets out of the house for long stretches to paint a fascinating, ominous portrait of Buenos Aires as a modern city full of living ghosts.

At more than two hours, film does run a bit long for its own good, but each scene is important and overall work has been paced so carefully that one would be hard-pressed to suggest anything specific to cut. Even as it becomes gruesome in its final couple of reels, film is shot through with boisterous absurdist comedy, a daring stroke that Donovan manages to pull off.

Indie production looks impressive, and is immeasurably helped by an outstanding, unusual score by Elia Cmiral.—*Cart.*

Aida
(SWEDISH)

An Isis Film/Swedish Film Institute/Swedish Television TV2/Filmhuset production. (Intl. sales, Visionventures, Intl. Ltd.) Produced by Staffan Ryden. Executive producers, Klas Olofsson, Katinka Farago. Directed by Claes Fellbom. Revised text, screenplay by Fellbom; camera (color), Jorgen Persson; music, Giuseppe Verdi; original libretto, Antonio Ghislanzoni; art direction, Lotta Melanton; costume design, Inger Persson; choreography, Anne-Charlotte Lindstrom; makeup, hair stylist, Janne Kindhal. Reviewed at Cinetex Film Festival, Las Vegas, Sept. 27, 1988. Running time: **116 MIN.**

Amneris	Ingrid Tobiasson
Radames	Niklas Ek
Radames' voice	Robert Grundin
Amneris	Ingrid Tobirasson
Amonasro	Jan Van Der Schaaf
Ramfis	Alf Haggstam
Pharaoh's spokesman	Staffan Ryden
High Priestess	Françoise Drapier
High Priestess' voice	Mirianne Myrsten
The Messenger	Lennart Hakansson
The Messenger's voice	Thomas Annmo
Aide Of Pharoah	Manuel Corujo Martin
Aida (as child)	Diana Vinoly Umpierrez
Her sisters	Nereida Barrera, Agar Barrera

■ **Las Vegas — Regardless of its assorted artistic merits, this Swedish opera film is destined to be forever known as the topless "Aida," as virtually every woman in the cast, including the title character, goes about her business in an almost continual state of severe undress.**

This is merely the most immediately apparent reflection of director Claes Fellbom's attempt to render Verdi's late 19th century romantic opera more Egyptian than is usually the case. The effort is certainly interesting, sometimes bracing and always beautiful, but as opera buffs represent the only real audience for it, video represents a more promising market than does theatrical release.

Impassioned tale recounts the love between Aida, an Ethiopian princess reduced to a slave girl by the Egyptians who captured her, and Radames, an Egyptian warrior who will soon lead an invasion of Aida's country. Aida serves Princess Amneris, who also is in love with Radames, and much of the unfolding drama concerns Amneris' jealous vengeance upon her rival, and Radames' torn allegiance between his nation and the woman he loves.

Based upon Fellbom's successful stage production with the Swedish Folkopera, of which he is artistic director, $1,800,000 picture was shot entirely on stark, volcanic Lanzarote in the Canary Islands, and is distinguished by several striking visual aspects. Rugged natural landscapes have been dotted with oases of exceptional beauty and serenity, with considerable action taking place in or around assorted bodies of water (original version actually had a swimming pool built onstage). A vast, sculpted temple set is imposing yet simple. Costumes and props have been designed with an eye to exotic verisimilitude based on impressions derived from original Egyptian paintings, succeeding in evoking an elegant primitivism.

The opera does sound a bit odd being sung in Swedish rather than Italian, and specialists will have to judge the vocal qualities of the individual performances (all the leading roles were sung by the performers who appear onscreen except for Radames). Characters and emotions emerge vividly in this unusual but entirely reverent rendition.

The voluptuous, darkly colored Margareta Ridderstedt throws herself into the role of the tragic heroine with great physical abandon and etches a strong impression throughout. Ingrid Tobiasson's bald, imposing Amneris is loaded with authority and treachery, but Niklas Ek's Radames is pretty much a stick figure.

Some of the set pieces featuring processions and dancing girls become boring in their static presentation, but the piling up of the severed hands of slaughtered Ethiopians possesses brute force, and the finale, in which the reunited lovers proceed into a mysterious underworld, is hauntingly beautiful as filmed in a natural cave.

The sight of Aida delivering arias with virtually nothing on and romping ecstatically in the sand with her lover will prove a bit much for some, and will provide distraction for others. Fellbom's approach is undeniably novel and well thought-out, not just a stunt, and works rather nicely. .—*Cart.*

The Laser Man

A Peter Wang Films/Hong Kong Film Workshop production. Produced, written and directed by Peter Wang. Camera (color), Ernest Dickerson; editor, Grahame Weinbren; music, Mason Daring; theme song, Ryuichi Sakamoto; production design, Lester Cohen; art direction, Daniel Talpes; costume design, Barbara Weis; assistant director, Lisa Zimble; second unit camera, Larry Banks. Reviewed at the Cinetex Film Festival, Las Vegas, Sept. 25, 1988. Running time: **92 MIN.**

Arthur Weiss	Marc Hayashi
Janet Cosby	Maryann Urbano
Joey Chung	Tony Ka-Fei Leung
Lt. Lu	Peter Wang
Ruth Weiss	Joan Copeland
Hanson	George Bartenieff
Jimmy Weiss	David Chang
Susu	Sally Yeh
Martha Weiss Chung	Neva Small

■ **Las Vegas — "The Laser Man" is a quirky, cross-cultural, high-tech comedy about serious matters from Peter Wang, who made an impression two years ago with "A Great Wall."**

Oddball, self-consciously implausible story concerning the manipulation of a laser expert by big business serves as a pegboard on which Wang hangs any number of amusing observation about The Melting Pot, 1988, particularly where Chinese-Americans are concerned.

Appealingly idiosyncratic film would certainly garner enough good reviews to warrant thorough release on the specialized circuit, with good prospects lying down the road in ancillary markets.

Wang, who appears periodically throughout the picture as a New York police investigator, sets a light-hearted tone at the outset, so much so that one can't really be sure that laser researcher Arthur Weiss (Marc Hayashi) really does accidentally kill a colleague in an experiment.

Yet he did, and is instantly rendered so unemployable that he is forced to sign on with a suspicious firm involved in space age weaponry and arms smuggling. In the meantime, the viewer is introduced to the ethnically goofy collection of family and friends surrounding Weiss, who is so named because he has a Jewish mother who happens to believe she has a Chinese soul and persists in cooking perfectly dreadful Chinese meals.

Also in the picture are Joey Chung, Arthur's best friend, who is married to a Jewish woman and reveals that he has never slept with a Chinese, never, that is, until he meets Susu, a stunning, newly arrived immigrant who lives and works in a massage parlor and dreams of going to Las Vegas, where she would undoubtedly fit in just fine.

Last, but certainly not least, there is Janet, a Caucasian woman obsessed with things Oriental, who, to Arthur's distinct frustration, would rather meditate than make love, the better to eventually achieve her dream of reaching climax without any physical activity.

Wang weaves his cultural concerns into the narrative with deft and continual dexterity, but it is the narrative that presents problems. Weiss' creation of a spiffy, portable laser gun for his baddie bosses is so hokey that one often imagines it was intended facetiously. At the same time, however, Wang obviously has weighty themes on his mind relating to the responsibilities of apolitical, by-contract weapons inventors and the morality of their work.

Unfortunately, the plotting is not always hospitable to engagingly flippant tone Wang mostly maintains, especially when one of the major characters becomes the victim of the fancy gun, only to be casually resurrected later on.

Perhaps because they are incidental to the plot mechanics, scenes with the women are invariably the most human, humorous and resonant in the film, with each one, particularly Maryann Urbano as the Eastern worshipper, registering a nifty, individualistic characterization. Hayashi makes for a very affable lead, and everyone hits the right notes for Wang's desired comic effects.

Behind-the-scenes contributions are outstanding, notably Ernest Dickinson's richly hued lensing, Lester Cohen's resourceful production design and Mason Daring's inventive score. —*Cart.*

SAN SEBASTIAN REVIEWS

La Amiga
(The Girlfriend)
(ARGENTINE-WEST GERMAN)

A Journal Film Klaus Volkenborn (Berlin), Jorge Estrada Mora Prods. (Buenos Aires) and Alma Film production. Associate producers, Jeffrey Steiner, Hans-Gerhard Stahl. Directed by Jeanine Meerapfel. Screenplay, Meerapfel, Alcides Chiesa, in collaboration with Osvaldo Bayer, Agnieszka Holland; camera (color), Axel Block; editor, Juliane Lorenz; music, José Luis Castiñeira de Dios; production design, Jorge Marchegiani, Rainer Schaper; sound, Dante Amoroso, Günther Kortwich. Reviewed at San Sebastian Film Festival, Sept. 21, 1988. Running time: **108 MIN.**
María . . . . Liv Ullmann
Raquel . . . . .Cipe Lincovsky
Pancho . . . . Federico Luppi
Diego . . . . Victor Laplace
Also with: Harry Baer, Lito Cruz, Greger Hansen, Nicolás Frei, Cristina Murta, Amancay Espindola.

■ San Sebastian — "La Amiga" is a well-intentioned but overfamiliar pic about Argentina's "missing" and the Mothers of the Plaza de Mayo's struggles to first find what has happened to their lost ones, and then, as the years go by, to keep alive their own hopes.

Film uses the story of the friendship between one of these mothers and a famous actress to unfold the yarn, but despite some excellent touches, pic remains distant.

Item starts in the early 1980s during the military dictatorship in Argentina, when thugs roamed the streets of Buenos Aires, people were arrested (often indiscriminately) and terror ruled the country. Maria is the mother of one of those kidnaped and, despite her husband's opposition, joins the periodic protests in front of the Casa Rosada.

Her bosom buddy, Raquel (a successful actress) flees to West Berlin and lives there for a number of years as an exile. Even after the military government has been ousted, María carries on her campaign, refusing to admit that her son has been killed. On several occasions she even accuses her girlfriend of copping out and being a coward.

At the end, the girlfriend returns to Argentina from Berlin, and despite the slights from María, maintains her friendship. Acting by Liv Ullmann, Cipe Lincovsky, Federico Luppi and Victor Laplace is fine, but early part of the film is too familiar, and latter part too slim to generate much in the way of sales. Ullmann's name may draw some attention to the pic. —*Besa.*

Krótki Film O Milosci
(A Short Film About Love)
(POLISH)

A Polish Film Corp. "Tor" Unit production. Directed by Krzysztof Kieslowski. Screenplay, Kieslowski, Krzysztof Piesiewicz; camera (color), Witold Adamek; editor, Ewa Smal; music, Zbigniew Preisner; art direction, Halina Dobrowolska; production manager, Ryszard Chutkowski. Reviewed at Gdynia Film Festival, Sept. 12, 1988. (Also in San Sebastian Film Festival, competing.) Running time: **86 MIN.**
Tomek . . . . .Olaf Lubaszenko
Magda . . . . Grazyna Szapolowska
Landlady . . . . Stefania Iwinska
Roman . . . . Piotr Machalica

■ Gdynia — An extraordinary work by any standard, "Love's" light dims only a little beside the fist in the stomach quality of Krzysztof Kieslowski's "Thou Shalt Not Kill," but is certain to be Poland's top fest and art house entry this year.

Having won top honors at the national fest in Gdynia, it also copped three awards at the San Sebastian festival.

Story utilizes the same stark, pared down approach Kieslowski is known for. The secularized religious touch — never obvious, a moral dilemma for viewer as much as the characters — shows once again an astonishing ability to reach the heart of complex ethical questions with a minimum of script.

Tomek (played by newcomer Olaf Lubaszenko with tender delicacy) is 19 and in love with his neighbor Magda (sex symbol Grazyna Szapolowska, winner of Gdynia's best actress laurels). He knows her only by sight — he spies on her every night through a telescope in his room. He does other terrible things like holding back her mail (he works at the Post Office) and making anonymous phone calls.

Magda, a sexually liberated woman bitter about men's love, ridicules the peeping tom, stages a provocative performance in the bedroom for his benefit, then has her boyfriend go and beat him up.

Most viewers will be on Magda's side up to this point, but the moral telescope abruptly swings around when Magda insensitively tries to seduce Tomek, maybe to rid him of his infatuation and prove love doesn't exist. He slits his wrists and disappears into a hospital. In an ambiguous climax, Magda repents of her cynicism and goes to visit him. Her attention is drawn, "Rear Window" style, to the telescope and its magical-cinematical view on her apartment and her life.

Kieslowski ably keeps pace moving and curiosity aroused from start to finish. Touches of humor lace pic in points where the spiritual meets the utterly banal — Miss Poland on tv, or a gas co. emergency staged by jealous Tomek to keep Magda's lover at bay. This is not terribly emotional filmmaking, but it has a strong cerebral grip that will win the cool-headed director new fans.

Lensing by Witold Adamek is top-notch. —*Yung.*

Remando al Viento
(Rowing With The Wind)
(SPANISH)

A Ditirambo Films production, in association with Viking Films (Norway) for Cia. Iberoamericana de TV. Executive producer, Andrés Vicente Gómez. Directed by Gonzalo Suárez. Screenplay, Suárez; camera (color), Carlos Suárez; editor, José Salcedo; music, Alejandro Masso; sets, Wolfgang Burman; production manager, José Jacoste; costumes, Yvonne Blake; special effects, Reyes Abades; sound, Daniel Goldstein, Ricardo Steinberg. Reviewed at San Sebastian Film Festival, Sept. 19, 1988. Running time: **96 MIN.**
Lord Byron . . . . Hugh Grant
Mary Shelley . . . . Lizzy McInnerny
Shelley . . . . Valentine Pelka
Claire Clairmont . . . . Elizabeth Hurley
Polidori . . . . José Luis Gómez
Also with: Virginia Mataix, Ronan Vibert, José Carlos Rivas, Kate McKenzie, Jolyon Baker, Terry Taplin, Karen Westwood, Bibi Andersen.

(Original English language soundtrack)

■ San Sebastian — This distinguished and handsome production, shot in English, of the famous encounter of Lord Byron with Mary and Percy Bysshe Shelley in Switzerland and Italy in the early 19th century, should appeal to discriminating audiences around the world.

However, pic is subtle and literary, and will require special handling in prestige locations and word of mouth promotion.

Following on the heels of two other films dealing with the same subject, director Gonzalo Suárez has nonetheless given some special twists to the story. He eschews the scenes of orgy and concentrates alternately on the wry comments and bon mots of Byron. He also introduces the Frankenstein monster, created in fiction by Mary Shelley, which haunts the lives and forecasts the doom of most of the principals taking part in the drama, as was the case historically.

This gives the film a special dimension and a kind of inner logic which was lacking in the events themselves as they occurred. Story is told as one long flashback as Mary, writing aboard a ship creaking through the frozen wastes near the North Pole, recalls the tragic events.

Plot pretty well follows the facts: Byron's extravagances and biting wit, the uncertainties of Byron's personal physician Polidori, the death of Shelley's children and the relationship between the two poets. Shelley's inability to swim, Byron's plans to fight for freedom in Greece and Mary's growing obsession that it has been her creation of the monster which is causing the string of tragedies in her life all are part of the story and are buoyed to brilliance by Suárez' ebullient and witty script.

Thesping is superb, with outstanding performances by Hugh Grant, Lizzy McInnerny, Valentine Pelka and José Luis Gómez. Last-named puts in a wonderful performance as the pathetic Polidori. Production values are excellent: Carlos Suárez' lensing is breathtaking, Yvonne Blake's costumes are perfect and all other credits topnotch.

Audiences here felt that some of the dialog was a bit stilted, and pacing occasionally slackens, but on the whole, pic is a visual delight and one of the best to come out of Spain in a long time. —*Besa.*

Cartas del Parque
(Letters From The Park)
(CUBAN)

An Intl. Network Group and Television Española production in association with the Cuban Film Institute (ICAIC). Executive producer, Max Marambio; associate producer, Luis Reneses. Directed by Tomás Gutiérrez Alea. Screenplay, Eliseo Alberto Diego, Gutiérrez Alea, Gabriel García Márquez, based on Marquez' story; camera (color), Mario García Joya; editor, Miriam Talavera; music, Gonzalo Rubalcaba; production manager, Santiago Llapur; sound, Germinal Hernández; sets, Fernando O'Reilly; costumes, Miriam Dueñas. Reviewed at San Sebastian Film Festival, Sept. 17, 1988. Running time: **93 MIN.**
Pedro . . . . Victor Laplace
María . . . . Ivonne López
Juan . . . . Miguel Paneque
Also with: Mirta Ibarra, Adolfo Llaurado, Elio Mesa, Paula Ali, Amelita Pita, Dagoberto Gainza, José Pelayo.

■ San Sebastian — Sensitively crafted and steeped in the Hispanic literary traditions of the past century, this charming, albeit slow-paced vignette may prove a delight to those versed in poetry but will be deemed rather too literary for broader audiences.

Set in Matanzas City in 1913, pic's narrator tell us this is a simple story about Pedro, María and Juan. It is divided into four parts named after the seasons of the year. Story, indeed, is simple, poetic and winsome. It concerns a middle-aged scribe (a widower) who scrapes out a living by setting up a table in the street and writing letters for those who don't know how to turn a phrase.

Two new clients arrive, the first a boy working in a pharmacy who is fascinated by balloons and air travel, the second a young girl, María. Pedro, the scribe, who has largely withdrawn to the world of books (though he occasionally makes an escapade to the local brothel), pens the love missives for both of the young sweethearts, who, by chance, happen to be writing to each other.

The youngsters' romance seems to be progressing nicely, but then the boy's interest in aviation eclipses his romantic involvement and he ceases to see the girl. The scribe tries to keep the romance alive and sends the girl postcards from around the world, signing the boy's name. At the end she realizes the deception and switches her affection to the author of the wonderfully poetic letters.

Nice production values recreating old Cuba, occasional touches of wry humor, an appealing performance by Victor Laplace as the scribe and good direction make this well-made film a charming experience, though the extensive quoting of passages of poetry and literary references will limit non-Hispanic audiences. Commercially it's more suited to tv than theaters. —*Besa.*

Muhsin Bey
(Mr. Muhsin)
(TURKISH)

An Umut Film presentation. Executive producer, Abdurrahman Keskiner. Written and directed by Yavuz Turgul. Camera (color), Aytekin Çakmakçi; music, Attila Özdemiroglu. Reviewed at San Sebastian Film Festival, Sept. 15, 1988. Running time: **102 MIN.**
    With: Şener Şen, Ugur Yücel, Sermin Hürmeric, Osmun Carci.

■ San Sebastian — Despite its technical flaws and excessive running time, this Turkish entry comes across as a touching, sincere film that could find its way in art circuits. Story is universal, and touches of humor in the character studies lighten a poignant and appealing yarn.

Story revolves around a dour, middle-aged café owner, an aging bachelor who maintains his conservative habits, still drives an old car, talks to his plants and he waters them, and listens to old 78 rpm records.

Into his stolid life suddenly erupt several people, first a new neighbor, a flashy divorcee nightclub singer with a child, who clearly has designs on him. Next appears a pathetic bumpkin who seeks out Muhsin in the café and introduces himself as a friend of a friend. He announces he has come to Istanbul to break into the "big time" as a folk singer.

Rest of the story is built around this odd threesome, as the cautious Muhsin is gradually drawn into foolish adventures in which, after sheltering his protegé in his house, he manages to get him entered into a song contest and later even finances the recording of a tape for the singer.

After naive efforts to launch the seemingly untalented neophyte singer, Muhsin decides to organize his own song contest, but the droll efforts ultimately land him in jail. All ends on an upbeat note as he and the flirtatious neighbor settle into domestic contentment.

Using as background the everyday life of lower-middle class Istanbul, director Yavuz Turgul deftly develops the alternately comic and touching relationship of his characters, all of them believable as human beings. Niceties of the Arab music, which is a part of the story, will be lost on non-Moslem viewers, but pic nonetheless is broad enough in its appeal to please discerning audiences on both sides of the Atlantic. —*Besa.*

Baton Rouge
(SPANISH)

A Modigil presentation. Executive producers, Eduardo Campoy, Edmundo Gil; associate producer, Antonio Llorens. Directed by Rafael Moleón. Screenplay, Agustin Diaz Yanes, Moleón; camera (color), Angel Luis Fernández; editor, José Salcedo; music, Bernardo Bonezzi; sets, Javier Fernández; sound, Goldstein and Steinberg S.A. Reviewed at San Sebastian Film Festival, Sept. 19, 1988. Running time: **94 MIN.**
Isabel Harris . . . . Carmen Maura
Antonio . . . . Antonio Banderas
Ana Alonso . . . . Victoria Abril
    Also with: Angel de Andrés López, Laura Cepeda, Noel Molina, Rafael Diaz, Aldo Grilo, Paco Guijar, Pedro Diaz del Corral.

■ San Sebastian — This tale of intrigue, sex and murder, well-produced and thesped, lacks believability, but has enough going for it to spark possible interest in secondary markets outside Spain.

Many of the story's loose ends are left untied in an ambiguous finale, but that shouldn't prevent less critical audiences from enjoying the yarn.

Antonio, a beefy gigolo, thrusts himself upon a wealthy, middle-aged woman in the toilet of a cafe and thereafter moves into her fancy apartment. The lady pampers him, buys him fancy clothes, and tells him she is separated from her husband. Isabel, though her sexual needs are sated by Antonio, suffers nightmares in which she dreams she is being raped.

The couple consult with a pretty lady psychiatrist, and soon a plot is hatched whereby Antonio and the shrink (whom he seduces) decide to murder Isabel's husband, cash in on the fortune and put the blame on Isabel. The gigolo's great dream is to take a trip through the States with his kid brother and visit Baton Rouge in Louisiana.

The plot thickens as the naive scheme backfires, each of the trio tries to doublecross the others and unsuspected twists are introduced once the police start investigating the murder.

Carmen Maura, Antonio Banderas and Victoria Abril are okay in their parts, but much of the contrived story can be guessed before it happens. Some of the sex scenes may prove a come-on for some spectators. —*Besa.*

Malaventura
(Misadventure)
(SPANISH)

A Luis Megino production, in association with Televisión Española and Productora Andaluza de Programas. Directed by Manuel Gutiérrez Aragón. Screenplay, Gutiérrez Aragón, Megino; camera (Eastmancolor), José Luis Alcaine; editor, José Salcedo; sound, R. Steinberg and D. Goldstein; production manager, José Lacoste; production design, Antonio Cortes; sets, José Luis Cerezo. Reviewed at San Sebastian Film Festival, Sept. 16, 1988. Running time: **90 MIN.**
Manuel . . . . Miguel Molina
John . . . . Richard Lintern
Rocio . . . . Iciar Bollain
Alcántara . . . . José Luis Borau
    Also with: Francisco Merino, Cristina Higueras, Daniel Martin, Manuel de Blas.

■ San Sebastian — The title of Manuel Gutiérrez Aragón's latest pic, "Misadventure," pretty well sums up this embarrassingly awkward film which was received by stamping and boos both during its press and evening screenings here.

Though helmer/scripter again throws in a few cabalistic leads, most of pic is straightforward and tries to tell a story, but loses control and direction almost from the first frame.

Set in Seville, and told as one long flashback of a first-person story, pic is partly a promotional vehicle for the city of Seville (though the seamy side is also reflected on occasion). Main character is a young man who suddenly, over his dinner plate, feels depressed. It is never made clear whether it is because of unrequited love, a bad meal, a toothache or general *weltschmertz.*

While sitting in a dentist's chair he happens to witness a murder, in which a man throws a girl off an apartment house terrace. Manuel, the witness, does not utter a word. In fact, he doesn't say a word for about half the film, but mopes about, gets mugged, meets a judge who happens to be the father of the girl that jilted him, and encounters the estranged husband and murderer of the girl who's been jettisoned from the terrace. Latter is a Briton who's been living in Seville for a year.

When Miguel does finally speak, he doesn't have much to say, and mumbles in a virtually unintelligible Andalusian accent. Pic concludes with the Englishman, who's also sweet on the girl, slashing Manuel's face, and then getting caught by the cops. Jump to the year 2003 when Manuel has settled into domestic bliss with his future wife and the kiddies; cut and end.

Gutiérrez Aragón has avoided using some of his usual mystifications but even here he cannot resist dwelling upon an old notebook belonging to the girl with a sort of Masonic sketch inserted into it, the hint of collusion between the police chief and the Englishman, plus a few other leads which never go anywhere.

Thesping is mostly awkward and clumsy, never believable, and even José Luis Alcaine's photography cannot help the film from having a flat and mundane look to it. Commercial prospects would seem to be nil, even in Spain. —*Besa.*

El Aire de Un Crimen
(The Hint Of A Crime)
(SPANISH)

An Isasi Prods. Cinematograficas film, in collaboration with Televisió de Catalunya. Executive producer, Antonio Isasi Jr. Directed by Antonio Isasi-Isasmendi. Screenplay, Isasi-Isasmendi, Gabriel Castro, and the collaboration of Jorge R. del Alamo, based on novel by Juan Benet; camera (Agfacolor), Juan Gelpi; editor, Amat Carreras; music, Francisco Aguarod, Luis Fatas; sets, Ramiro Gómez; sound, Joan Quilis; special effects, Reyes Abades. Reviewed at San Sebastian Film Festival, Sept. 21, 1988. Running time: **124 MIN.**
Col. Olvera . . . . Paco Rabal
Capt. Medina . . . . José María Mazo
Amaro . . . . Germán Cobos
Chiqui . . . . Maribel Verdú
    Also with: María José Moreno, Miguel Rellán, Ovidi Montllor, Alfred Luchetti, Rafaela Aparicio, Agustin González, Terele Pavez, Pep Corominas, Ramoncín, Fernando Rey.

■ San Sebastian — The first 10 minutes of this pic are engaging enough, presenting the mystery of a double crime in a Spanish village in 1956, but the succeeding two hours never deliver, as the script wanders confusingly and the mystery turns heavy-handedly into tedium.

Pic jumps back three months to relate a convoluted tale concerning a detachment of soldiers, the intrigues of land speculators, a house of prostitution outside the village, the doings of a smuggler with a retarded daughter and a hidalgo (played by Fernando Rey) who sojourns in the village a while, chatting up the locals.

Before film is halfway through, most audiences will have ceased to care about this murky rural drama in a very minor key. Continuity is often clumsy; the music builds up in certain scenes for no particular reason, then nothing happens; scenes constantly fade in and out; and the script meanders, instead of building up. There is never any real suspense.

Commercial prospects are remote, even in Spain, that is if the film even gets picked up for distribution.—*Besa.*

Mignon é Partita
(Mignon Has Left)
(ITALIAN-FRENCH)

An Ellepi Film (Rome) and Chrysalide Film (Paris) coproduction, with RAI Radiotelevisione Italiana RAI-3. Produced by Leo Pescarolo, Guido de Laurentiis. Directed by Francesca Archibugi. Screenplay, Archibugi, Gloria Malatesta, Claudia Sbarigia; camera (Eastmancolor), Luigi Verga; editor, Alfredo Muschietti; music, Roberto Gatto and Battista Lena; sound, Claudio Raini; sets, Luca Gobbi. Reviewed at San Sebastian Film Festival, Sept. 23, 1988. Running time: **94 MIN.**
Mama . . . . Stefania Sandrelli

Federico . . . . .Jean-Pierre Duriez
Aldo . . . . .Massimo Dapporto
Mignon . . . . .Celine Beauvallet
Prof. Girelli . . . . .Micheline Presle
Giorgio . . . . .Leonardo Ruta
Also with: Francesca Antonelli, Daniele Zaccaria, Eleonore Sambiagio, Flavio Chiappalone, Lorenzo de Pasqua, Giuseppe Giordani, Giulio Marcello, Valentina Cervi, Roberto Berini.

———

■ **San Sebastian — This is an altogether delightful and refreshing comedy with a core of realism about a prissy 16-year-old Parisian who visits her down-to-earth relatives in Rome. Humor and pathos make this one of the most attractive films to come out of Italy this year.**

It could prove a crowd-pleaser in art circuits in the U.S. and perhaps in broader releases in other countries.

A scintillating script, in which the 14-year-old Giorgio recounts the half-year visit of his pretty cousin Mignon, covers not only the boy's infatuation with the aloof girl, but also his mother's solitude and brief amorous fling with her brother-in-law, as well as the boy's relationship with his ailing Latin teacher.

There are some wonderful touches of realism, even tragedy, but they always are tempered with tender humor. The unapproachable intruder from Paris, after first trying to flee from what she considers the vulgarity of her poorer cousins, settles into the family, though she is never really integrated into it.

From the start, Giorgio is enamored of the girl, but on one propitious and crucial occasion, is afraid to kiss her. Mignon, meanwhile, takes up for a while with an older boy she meets in the street, to Giorgio's chagrin. The father, who runs a bookshop, meanwhile is carrying on with an employee.

Mignon is brought down to earth through her daily life with the Roman family, but also because she learns that in Paris her father has been sentenced to a jail term for using faulty construction materials in a building.

Pic ends with Mignon returning to Paris, but bonds of friendship have been established between her and her poorer relatives. Thesping is excellent all around, but especially memorable is Stefania Sandrelli as the long-suffering, but cheerful mama.—*Besa.*

———

Zhen Nu
(Two Virtuous Women)
(CHINESE)

———

A Beijing Film Studio production. Directed by Huang Jianzhong. Screenplay, Gu Hua; camera (color), Chen Youqun; music, Shi Wanchun; art direction, Yu Fengmin. Reviewed at San Sebastian Film Festival, Sept. 17, 1988. Running time: **110 MIN.**
Guihua . . . . .Gu Yan
Qingyu . . . . .Fu Yiwei
Che Ganzi . . . . .He Wei
Wu Laoda . . . . .Li Baotian

———

■ **San Sebastian — "Zhen Nu" is a slow-paced, stylized pic telling two**

parallel stories, one set in modern times, the other during the Qing dynasty; both make a plea for women's rights and decry the traditionally oppressive social inhibitions of life in China.

It could garner some attention riding on the current wave of interest in new Chinese cinema, but story is rather too sketchy.

Familiar subject of village taboos and sexual repression has Guihua, the wife of an impotent innkeeper in the contemporary yarn, becoming a widow and trying to find a release for her pent-up sexual frustrations.

In olden times, Qingyu, only 18, is also widowed and vows to forsake the pleasures of this world. She pines away reading scriptures and longing for love.

Pic skips back and forth from one story to the other, underlining their parallels, which occasionally makes for some confusion. Production values are pretty basic.
—*Besa.*

———

Sti Skia Tou Fovou
(In The Shadow Of Fear)
(GREEK)

———

A Greek Film Center/ET-1/Giorgos Karipidis production. Executive producer, Pavlos Philipou Ltd. Written and directed by Giorgos Karipidis. Camera (color), Giorgos Arvanitis; editor, Yannis Tsitsopoulos; music, Dimitris Papadimitriou; sets, Anastasia Arseni; sound, Giorgos Michaloudis. Reviewed at San Sebastian Film Festival, Sept. 20, 1988. Running time: **92 MIN.**
With: Giorgos Constas, Antonis Katsaris, Nikos Papakonstantinou, Christos Simardanis, Evangelia Secha, Lambros Tsangas.

———

■ **San Sebastian — Sales prospects seem nil for this pretentious, muddled film with a Kafkaesque plot about a composer fleeing from "the present."**

Deucalion, a composer, mixes up dreams and reality, spouts philosophical banalities and succeeds only in exasperating those trying to make sense out of his adventures.

Film is chock full of unexplained riddles: a woman who faints while waiting on a line in front of a bank teller, who then suddenly turns up on line again and denies anything has happened; a priest in a church who is being talked to by the composer, and then suddenly is not there; a police inspector who interrogates the composer, accused him of passing counterfeit bills, and who then similarly vanishes, and so on.

The persecuted composer is unable to grasp "reality," while audiences will be unable to grasp why the film was made or what it is clumsily trying to say. —*Besa.*

———

La Boca del Lobo
(The Lion's Den)
(PERUVIAN-SPANISH)

———

An Inca Films (Peru) and Tornasol Films (Spain) coproduction. Produced by Gerardo Herrero, Francisco Jose Lombardi. Directed by Lombardi. Screenplay, Augusto Cabada,

Giovanna Pollarolo, Herrero; camera (color), José Luis López Linares; editor, Jan San Mateo; music, Bernardo Bonezzi; associate producers, Javier López Blanco, Felipe de Gregori; sets, Marta Méndez; sound, Daniel Padilla. Reviewed at San Sebastian Film Festival, Sept. 20, 1988. Running time: **122 MIN.**
Lieutenant Iván Roca . . . . .Gustavo Bueno
Vitín Luna . . . . .Toño Vega
Gallardo . . . . .José Tejada
Sgt. Moncada . . . . .Gilberto Torres
Also with: Berta Pagaza, Antero Sánchez, Aristoteles Picho, Fernando Vasquez, Luis Saavedra, Lucio Yabar, Walter Florián.

———

■ **San Sebastian — Set against the terrorist activities of the Shining Path movement in rural Peru, "Lion's Den" tells the story of a detachment of soldiers isolated in a remote village in a mostly gripping fashion that should generate sales for specialized release.**

Dramatic situation builds up effectively as the detachment arrives in the "lion's den," or hotbed of the insurgents. One night the Peruvian flag over the soldiers' headquarters has been replaced by a terrorist flag; another day the detachment's commanding officer is ambushed and massacred as he tries to communicate with a nearby town.

A new commander is sent, who is ruthless and ambitious. However we never see the terrorists, only the results of their actions, which weakens the film and makes is seem overlong. Most action is offstage. Tension meanwhile builds up between the peasants and the intrusive soldiers, ending in a massacre of the former.

The sergeant, one of the career soldiers and a minority of others are horrified by the wanton massacre. Final scences of the pic are a Russian roulette duel between the macho officer and the young objector.

Though the Russian roulette scene is gripping, it is rather too familiar to audiences to be fully effective. Pic ends somewhat unconvincingly with the young soldier simply wandering off into the communist-infested hills.

Item is well thesped and directed, but a trifle too long and slow, lacking the full dramatic impact of director Francisco Lombardi's previous film, "The City And The Dogs." —*Besa.*

———

Land der Väter,
Land der Söhne
(Land Of Fathers, Land Of Sons)
(WEST GERMAN-COLOR/B&W)

———

A B.A. Film Munich and Nico Hoffmann Film Prod. film for the Southwest German Broadcasting Corp. and the Bavarian Broadcasting Corp. Written and directed by Nico Hoffmann. Camera (color, b&w), Laszlo Kadar; editor, Clara Fabry; music, Peter Zwetkoff; sound, Winfried Leyh. Reviewed at San Sebastian Film Festival, Sept. 23, 1988. Running time: **96 MIN.**
Thomas and Eberhard
Kleinert . . . . .Karl-Heinz Liebezeit
Dorothea (young) . . . .Katharina Meinecke
Dorothea (old) . . . . .Lieselotte Rau
Trainer Machacheck . . . . .Adolf Laimböck
Also with: Karin Schroeder, Thomas Ott,

Wolfgang Preiss, Eva Kotthaus, Wolf-Dietrich Sprenger, Günther Ziessler.

———

■ **San Sebastian — The story of a young German delving into his late father's activities during the Second World War is by now a fairly familiar theme, and Nico Hoffmann, rather than adding some new twist, only succeeds in limning a boring tale which will lose most audiences before it's halfway through.**

Commercial prospects, other perhaps than tv, seem nil.

To make the turgid story less dramatic, pic jumps back and forth throughout its length between present times (in color) and the events of 1943 (shot in black and white), but with the same actor playing father and son.

A young journalist becomes intrigued with his father's activities in Poland during the war. The father committed suicide in 1972, a fact concealed from the son. Also, he had run a factory in Germany which went bankrupt, and during the war ran a factory in Poland, for which labor was used which was then sent to concentration camps.

The son travels to the site of the Polish factory and starts trying to discover the facts of his father's activities. Naturally, they are unsavory and ultimately led to his suicide when it seemed they would be published in postwar Germany. The tale unfolds in such a slothful, anticlimactic manner that most viewers will cease to care what the outcome will be. —*Besa.*

Another Woman

An Orion Pictures release of a Jack Rollins and Charles H. Joffe production. Produced by Robert Greenhut. Executive producers, Rollins, Joffe. Directed by Woody Allen. Screenplay, Allen; camera (Duart color), Sven Nykvist; editor, Susan E. Morse; sound, James Sabat; production design, Santo Loquasto; art direction, Speed Hopkins; set decoration, George De Titta Jr., costume design, Jeffrey Kurland; production manager, Joseph Hartwick; associate producers, Thomas Reilly, Helen Robin; assistant director, Reilly; casting, Juliet Taylor. Reviewed at Orion screening room, L.A., Oct. 7, 1988. MPAA Rating: PG. Running time: **84 MIN.**

Marion	Gena Rowlands
Hope	Mia Farrow
Ken	Ian Holm
Lydia	Blythe Danner
Larry	Gene Hackman
Kathy	Betty Buckley
Laura	Martha Plimpton
Marion's dad	John Houseman
Claire	Sandy Dennis
Young Marion's dad	David Ogden Stiers
Sam	Philip Bosco
Paul	Harris Yulin
Lynn	Frances Conroy

■ Hollywood — Woody Allen once again explores the human condition via the inner turmoil of gifted New Yorkers, this time with more optimism and considerably more success than in "September."

Cast, all new to Allen pics except Mia Farrow, issues resonant performances across the board, most notably a luminous and absorbing turn by Gena Rowlands in the lead. Probing, illuminating and sometimes slyly funny, with a plot that unfolds with a touch of mystery, pic should do steady business in limited release.

Interestingly given what Allen may have experienced after his roundly disliked previous pic, story deals with a very successful, often idolized character who discovers around the time of her 50th birthday that she has made many mistakes, but people have been more or less too deferential to confront her.

Rowlands plays Marion Post, head of a graduate philosophy department, married to a doctor, the kind of person whose former students approach her at restaurants to tell her that she inspired them and changed their lives.

An off-color anecdote from another couple at a party, about how their landlord surprised them making love on the living room floor, gets under her skin.

Then she takes an apartment downtown in which to write a book, and begins overhearing analysis sessions from the psychiatrist's office next door. At first she's annoyed, then gets hooked as a patient (Farrow) tells of her unsettling conviction that her marriage has begun to disintegrate.

Before long Post, who's at first so focused that she brushes off a relative who's an hour late for an appointment, is wandering the streets in a haze in search of a clue to what's troubling her.

Soon, she's reliving some of the turning points in her life, through dreams, flashbacks and chance encounters with family and friends. Throughout, she's haunted by the memory of a man (Gene Hackman) who once loved her passionately, with whom she declined to get involved.

At its best, pic peels away polished surfaces via characters who say the unexpected. Scene in which Betty Buckley, as a wronged ex-wife, barges into a highbrow birthday party for Post and sets the record straight, is priceless. Sandy Dennis also has a ripe moment in a similar setup.

There are fine, rich currents of theme and character at work throughout, guided by the interior thoughts of Rowlands, via voice-over. Ian Holm gives a measured, exactly right performance as Post's husband, John Houseman is moving as her father, a domineering man grown weak with age, and Martha Plimpton is fresh and straight-across as Holm's teenage daughter.

Rowlands plays an extremely capable woman who's come to rely on control as a means of avoiding emotional difficulty. What's interesting is the consistency of the character study in which, upon becoming aware of her problems, she squarely faces them.

Film that emerges is brave, in many ways fascinating, and in all respects of a caliber rarely seen.

Shot by Sven Nykvist on Manhattan locations last fall, pic maintains an insulated look that explores a comfortable, textured, well-bred world. Outdoor shots are tight; there are no extras. Score contributes much to the atmosphere, selections both melancholy and wistful by Brecht, Satie, Cole Porter, Hammerstein & Kern, and Bach.—*Daws.*

The Bell Of Chernobyl
(SOVIET-DOCU)

A Sovexportfilm presentation, produced by Central Studio of Documentary Film, Moscow. Directed by Rollan Serghienko. Written by Serghienko, Vladimir Sinelnikov; camera (color), K. Durnov, I. Dvoinokhov, V. Frolenko. (No other credits available.) Reviewed at Margaret Mead Film Festival, N.Y., Sept. 14, 1988. Running time: **84 MIN.**

■ Overlong and somewhat clumsy, "The Bell Of Chernobyl" is nevertheless a valuable document on film, the official Soviet read-out on the Chernobyl disaster of April 1986.

The film surveys the nuclear reactor accident and records the furious reactions of Chernobyl citizens who demand harsh punishments, including the death penalty, for Chernobyl's bungling bosses. Curiously, the film also is turned into propaganda against the U.S.-USSR arms race.

Immediately following the Cher-nobyl disaster, Kiev tv aired a report and a second quickly followed on the heroic specialists who voluntarily risked their lives (some died) to contain the damage. "Bell," more reflective than those reports, was shot May 23-June 26, weeks after the explosion. It chronicles the efforts of a few men to seal the damaged reactor within a container of concrete, called its tomb.

The town of Chernobyl, ex-population 45,000, is now evacuated, an eerie sight as traveling shots glide past tall housing complexes along streets empty of all life. At the hospital, families mourn the dead and dying. Farmers fear that radiation in the soil will travel via plants into birds, fowls and livestock, then to humans.

American observers praise the daring of Soviet workers wearing protective gear who hose and dig in the smouldering ruins. We see clean-up volunteers living in improvised tent cities, even newlyweds.

People within the film, reinforced by the insistent English narration, state that governments must shake off medieval suspicions of one another that lead to the arms race.

The film is a natural for public tv, especially if accompanied by up-to-date supplementary information. It may need new narration, however, as the present job is stiff and colorless, reciting all voices monotonously. —*Hitch.*

Young Einstein
(AUSTRALIAN)

A Warner Bros. release (Greater Union Distribs in Australia) of A Serious Film production. Executive producers, Graham Burke, Ray Beattie. Produced by Yahoo Serious, Warwick Ross, David Roach. Directed by Yahoo Serious. Screenplay, Roach, Serious; camera (color), Jeff Darling; editor, Serious; music, William Motzing, Martin Armiger, Tommy Tycho; production design, Steve Marr, Laurie Faen, Colin Gibson, Ron Highfield; sound, Geoff Grist; choreography, Aku Kadogo; associate producer, Lulu Pinkus; production manager, Antonia Barnard; assistant director, Keith Heygate; casting, Michael Lynch; stunts, Serious. Reviewed at Hoyts 6, Sydney, Sept. 21, 1988. Running time: **89 MIN.**

Albert Einstein	Yahoo Serious
Marie Curie	Odile Le Clezio
Preston Preston	John Howard
Mr. Einstein	Pee Wee Wilson
Mrs. Einstein	Su Cruickshank
Charles Darwin	Basil Clarke
Wilbur Wright	Esben Storm

Also with: Lulu Pinkus (The Blonde), Kaa-rin Fairfax (The Brunette), Jonathan Coleman (Wolfgang Bavarian), Roger Ward (Cat Pie Cook), Max Meldrum (Mr. Curie), Rose Jackson (Mrs. Curie), Adam Bowen (Marconi), Tim McKew (Sigmund Freud), Phillipa Baker (Freud's mother), Geoff Aldridge, Hugh Wayland (Lumiere Brothers), Ian James Tait (Thomas Edison).

■ Sydney — This wild, cheerful, off-the-wall comedy showcases the many talents of Australian satirist Yahoo Serious, who not only directed and plays the leading role, but also co-wrote (from his own original story), coproduced, edited and handled the stunts. Quite a lot to take on for a first-time filmmaker.

Purporting to be "the untold saga" of the early life of "the most brilliant, enigmatic and eccentric individual of the 20th century," pic posits young Einstein as the only son of eccentric apple farmers from Australia's southern island, Tasmania. He has a fertile mind, and is forever discovering things: it's not his fault that, by 1905 when the film's set, gravity has already been discovered by someone else.

Einstein's Dad (engagingly played by former pop singer Pee Wee Wilson) is a cheerful anti-conservationist, while corpulent Mum (Su Cruickshank) just handles the household chores.

According to the film, Einstein discovers accidentally how to split the atom while experimenting methods of injecting bubbles into home-brewed beer. He sets off for mainland Australia (a comically lengthy journey) to patent his invention, and meets French genius Marie Curie (Odile Le Clezio) on a train; he also meets villain and patents stealer Preston Preston (John Howard), scion of a family of Perth entrepreneurs.

After various misadventures, including being ejected from Sydney University and spending time in a lunatic asylum, Einstein winds up in France for the 1906 Science Academy Awards (attended by Darwin, Marconi, Edison and other brains of the day) where the lad's latest invention is revealed: rock 'n' roll! He returns in triumph to Tasmania, a rock star as well as a scientist.

The entire production rests on the shoulders of its director/star, and success or failure of the film will depend on audience reaction to this gangly, long-haired clown. Fortunately Serious (born Greg Pead) exhibits a brash and confident sense of humor, and endearing personality, and a fondness for sight gags which should have audiences, especially teens, chuckling.

Surrounding Serious and his jokes is a lush production, with rich camerawork from Jeff Darling and superbly detailed production design. Pic is almost *too* good looking, its visual splendors sometimes distracting attention from the comedy itself.

"Young Einstein" has had a lengthy postproduction history. Originally completed mid-1986, it was submitted and screened in the Australian Film Awards that year, receiving nominations for screenplay, music, sound and cinematography, and winning for music. Subsequently, a decision was made to re-edit and re-shoot, and, via Roadshow Distributors, Warner Bros. came in as international distrib. Main changes are to be found in the second half of the film, which now has a much more upbeat ending than heretofore.

Ironically, given that two years ago the film was prized for its music, there's a lot of new music now, including tracks from rock groups such as Mental As Anything.

"Young Einstein" has a Christmas booking down under, indicating distrib and exhib confidence. Undoubtedly the film's zany comedy and endearingly naive hero will have considerable appeal, so it's quite possible all concerned have a hit on their hands, with young audiences likely to be particularly receptive to Serious and his madcap character. Older viewers will smile at lines like: "If you can't trust the governments of the world, who *can* you trust?"—*Strat.*

Platoon Leader

A Cannon release of a Breton Film Prods. Ltd. production. Produced by Harry Alan Towers. Executive producer, Avi Lerner. Directed by Aaron Norris. Screenplay, Rick Marx, Andrew Deutsch, David Walker, adapted by "Peter Welbeck" (Towers) from James R. McDonough's book; camera (Rank color), Arthur Wooster; editor, Michael J. Duthie; music, George S. Clinton; art direction, John Rosewarne; set decoration, Emilia Roux; costume design, Kady Dover; sound (Ultra-Stereo), Paul Le Mare; stunt coordinator, Jannie Weinand; assistant directors, Miguel Gil, Steve Fillis; second unit camera, Dennis Kington; casting, Marquoula Tsongas. Reviewed at Cannon Pictures, L.A., Oct. 3, 1988. MPAA Rating: R. Running time: **100 MIN.**
Jeff Knight . . . . Michael Dudikoff
Michael McNamara . . . . . . Robert F. Lyons
Raymond Bacera . . . . Michael De Lorenzo
Robert Hayes . . . . Rich Fitts
Joshua Parker . . . . Jesse Dabson

■ **Hollywood — Cannon has reached its nadir with "Platoon Leader," the latest of its exploitation pictures that is set in Vietnam, shot in South Africa and is largely a bloody, pointless genre retread that rips off the title from the Oscar-winning "Platoon" but has little else to commend it.**

When "Platoon" is out of stock at the vidstore, confused patrons might pick this up.

Director Aaron Norris, Chuck's brother, has worked on better Vietnam actioners, including "Braddock: Missing In Action III" starring his brother and also a Cannon release.

Lt. Jeff Knight (Michael Dudikoff) leads about two handfuls of men in the 103d Airborne on daily forays into the jungle outside their heavily barricaded compound isolated deep in V.C. territory to kill as many of the enemy as possible. The odds are tremendous, so it's no suprise that with every patrol, another buddy is mortally wounded.

In a few days time — how long it is, is never made clear — Dudikoff and his No. 1 soldier Sgt. McNamara (Robert F. Lyons) are just about all that remains of the original bunch, perhaps a little more

scarred than they'd like, but more determined than ever to squash their foe.

Gratuitous violence is a by-product of these films, and this one offers up its own variation of the most expedient way to fell the enemy.

Armored choppers, MiGs, grenades and machine guns are the firepower that here are practically equaled in effectiveness by the dead-accurate aim of one of Knight's more determined troopers, who likes to pick off the enemy one by one with a rifle he has to reload after every shot.

Our boys even partake in a little friendly fire. When Lyons discovers druggie pfc Bacera (Michael De Lorenzo) dead from an overdose, he yanks out the needle, removes the rubber hose and riddles his body with bullets, explaining to the others it's better this way 'cause Lorenzo's Mom will think her son died a hero.

Considering the material, Dudikoff, Lyons, Lorenzo and Jesse Dabson, as the frightened radioman who gets too little screen time, are quite good in their limited roles.

The 11 actors who represent the hundred or so VC who are blown away during the course of the fighting sequences deserve special mention, not for their acting particularly, but for the fact that by their simply wearing helmets throughout the film, the audience is never quite sure whether any of them could be identified as having already been killed.

South Africa doubles well enough for Vietnam, even if it looks a bit on the dusty side. (Cannon lists only "Africa" in the press materials.)

George S. Clinton's score is effective and above par for a low-budgeter. Otherwise, production credits are average. —*Brit.*

Yvette Chauviré: Une etoile pour l'ememple
(Yvette Chauviré: A Star For Example)
(FRENCH-DOCU)

A Films du Prieuré production and release. Coproduced by La Sept, Lieurac Prod., AROP, the Cinémathèque de la Danse. Directed by Dominique Delouche. Camera (color), Daniel Vogel; editor, Isabelle Dedieu; sound, Philippe Lioret. Reviewed at Vendome Opera cinema, Paris, Sept. 14, 1988. Running time: **80 MIN.**
With Yvette Chauviré, dancers of the Paris Opera Ballet: Florence Clerc, Isabelle Guérin, Sylvie Guillem and Monique Loudières, and Marie Claude Pietragalla, Elisabeth Maurin, Dominique Khalfouni, Rudolf Nureyev, Henri Sauguet.

■ **Paris — a must for ballet buffs, this portrait of French ballet star Yvette Chauviré is an okay docu feature for educational and tv exposure.**

Lost amid the celluloid jungle of Cannes last May, it's currently enjoying a 1-screen theatrical release in a theater aptly just a few steps

from the Paris Opera, where most footage was shot.

There's little to say about Dominique Delouche's direction other than it doesn't strain for any cinematic embroidering, praise enough in this kind of film.

At an astonishingly youthful and ever gracious 70, Chauviré is radiant as she reminisces about her career and triumphs (notably with Serge Lifar), and guides several of the Paris Opera's new generation of star dancers in rehearsals of several of her greatest roles.

There are some (rather poor quality) film documents of her dancing, notably her 1972 Paris Opera farewell performance of "Giselle," but unhappily not a frame of her luminous dramatic film debut in Jean Benoit Levy and Marie Epstein's "La Mort du cygne" (1937), which due to currently insoluble rights problems can no longer be shown anywhere.

Among film's highlights is Chauviré's moving visit to the aged composer Henri Sauguet, who tells her: "I hear my music in your movements." On the other hand, an interview with Rudolf Nureyev is disappointingly bland. —*Len.*

The Kiss

A Tri-Star Pictures release of a Tri-Star and Astral Film Enterprises presentation of a Trilogy Film production. Produced by Pen Densham, John Watson. Executive producer, Richard B. Lewis. Directed by Densham. Screenplay, Stephen Volk, Tom Ropelewski, from story by Volk; camera (Bellevue Pathé color), François Protat; editor, Stan Cole; music, J. Peter Robinson; production design, Roy Forge Smith; art direction, Suzanna Smith; costume design, Renee April; makeup, creature effects, Chris Walas Inc.; special effects supervisor, Louis Craig; sound (Dolby), Austin Grimaldi, Dino Pigat, Keith Elliott; assistant director, Henry Bronchtein; casting, Pennie DuPont (U.S.), Rosina Bucci (Canada). Reviewed at Lorimar screening room, L.A., Oct. 5, 1988. MPAA Rating: R. Running time: **101 MIN.**
Jack . . . . Nicholas Kilbertus
Felice . . . . Joanna Pacula
Amy . . . . Meredith Salenger
Brenda . . . . Mimi Kuzyk

■ **Hollywood — In a sense, "The Kiss" is a horror picture. It's horrible. Tri-Star can kiss this one off in all markets.**

The filmmakers have created a kind of unpalatable horror stew by throwing in every scary trick in the cinematic book but coming up instead with a muddled concoction that never is terrorizing or even slightly tantalizing.

There was a kernel of a decent story, that of an evil woman (Joanna Pacula) who passes on her powers via a kiss, but it's never fleshed out in the script or compensated in any way in the filming.

If the setups were hokier, they might have been funny. Unfortunately, this is not the case.

As just one example, to create a

sense of eerieness, there's a scene where a pool sweep snakes its way through the water while ominous music plays. Nothing happens and then the camera cuts to somewhere else.

Film is destined from the beginning to never build to anything as the credits seem to take up at least the first 10 minutes, and are flashed up between location captions like "Belgian Congo 1963."

There's a chilling enough moment when the first devastating kiss is bestowed on the younger version of Pacula (Pricilla Mouzakiotis), but when the action moves to present-day suburia in the backyard barbecue of the Hallorans who are celebrating daughter Amy's (Meredith Salenger) confirmation, whatever suspense is foretold dissipates quickly.

There are vew connectives to link the elements of the plot. What kind of sorceress is Pacula — if, in fact, that's what she is — and why is Catholicism played up so highly when the practice of it doesn't give Salenger any protection against Pacula's powers?

To add to the goulash, there's a shrieking little monster that attacks Pacula's victims, howling winds, mysteriously opened winows and other formula attempts to prop up this weak effort.

Of the cast, Mimi Kuzyk is the one saving grace of this production as the Hallorans' neighbor Brenda. The fact she keeps a straight face as she discusses with Salenger the trauma of losing one's virginity is a testament to her ability.

Tech credits, including the special effects, are okay though they seem cheesy in this context. —*Brit.*

Drums Of Winter
(DOCU)

An Alaska Native Heritage Film Project, U. of Alaska Museum, Fairbanks. Produced, written and directed by Sarah Elder, Leonard Kamerling; camera (color, 16m), Kamerling; sound, Elder; editor, Elder, Ray Karpicki; consultant, Inupiaq language and culture, Walkie Charles. Funded by National Endowment for The Arts, Alaska State Council on The Arts, Institute for Alaska Native Arts, the Rock Foundation. Reviewed at Margaret Mead Film Festival, N.Y., Sept. 14, 1988. Running time: **90 MIN.**

■ **"Drums Of Winter" explores in fascinating detail the ancient music and dance of an Eskimo people, the Yup'ik of Emmonak, who live in the Yukon Delta on the Bering Sea.**

Although their music and other traditions have undergone changes due to a century of repressive policies from the Church, their music remains the heart of the Yup'ik social and spiritual life. Narration based on old diaries and letters of missionaries, plus archival photos and footage, provides the film's historical background.

Drums are the principal instrument used in the long potlatch ceremony of winter, when villagers gather for their celebration of renewal. Each movement of the dance, often quite frenzied, contributes to a story or saga, lasting up to 25 minutes. Songs are handed down for generations, although new music is created to reflect complex modern life.

A Jesuit priest, working among the Yup'ik for 30 years, deplores the former policy of the Church in forbidding so-called pagan ceremonies. He says their dancing is very personal, an expression of their spirituality.

In a dance-off with visitors from another village, the hosts shower gifts of clothing and food on their guests. Repeatedly the film emphasizes giftgiving even to strangers, because "Our spirits live by giving, things we give will return in larger amounts, because the wilderness has enough for all." Yet the wilderness is changing — huge tanks and oil derricks are visible in the background. —*Hitch.*

ZEN — Zona Espansione Nord
(ZEN — Zone Of Expansion North)
(ITALIAN)

A Medusa Cinematografica release of a San Francisco Film/RAI-TV Channel 3 co-production. Produced by Giovanni Bertolucci. Written and directed by Gian Vittorio Baldi. Camera (color), Claudio Meloni; editor, Baldi; music, Laura Fisher. Reviewed at Venice Film Festival (Horizons), Aug. 30, 1988. Running time: **100 MIN.**
Sister Chiara . . . . Consuelo Lupo
Don Luigi . . . . Franco Scaldati
  Also with: Serena Barone, Valentina Barresi, Luigi Maria Burruano, Domenico Ciaramitaro, Gabriella De Fina, Sabina De Pasquale, Massimo Pupella, Claudio Russo, Laura Viviano.

■ Venice — **"ZEN — Zone Of Expansion North" may sound like an exotic remake of "Alphaville," but is actually an incisive docudrama about one of Italy's most ill-famed slums. The hellish Palermo ghetto is depicted in all its violence and horror with a compassionate Christian eye by helmer Gian Vittorio Baldi.**

The reconstructed episodes of ghetto life are fascinating in their everyday horror, though not all Baldi's actors are pros capable of carrying off their roles and some stretches of the film need a good trimming. Most likely market is cultural-documentary tv.

ZEN 2, as the neighborhood is called, was constructed only 3 years ago but is already in a state of total unlivability. Occupied by homeless families (population 25,000), it has no drinkable water, open sewers, electricity stolen from nearby power lines. Kids play in the street, sick from the air and water. The slum boasts the highest rate of drug dealing in Sicily and main source of income comes from violent crime,

prostitution, purse snatching and robbery.

Authorities refuse to enter the area and police wouldn't escort Baldi's crew inside. Only two people in ZEN work to offer local youngsters an alternative to a life of crime: a priest and a nun. Don Luigi (bearish thesp Franco Scaldati) and Sister Chiara (the very fine actress Cunsuelo Lupo, who seems to be the real nun playing herself until the final credits) tirelessly take the kids on trips, show them films, urge them to play sports instead of selling heroin and snatching bags, but the impression is much of their labor will bear little fruit.

"ZEN" loses altitude when it attempts to dramatize a drunk's violence or an addict's hell — acting and direction simply aren't up to the task, and results are amateurish. Film is at its best in simple sequences that show local life without exaggeration; here reality speaks for itself. The prefab church and its survival-level work recalls South American churches of liberation, while suggesting religious as well as civil officialdom has turned their back on a problem too ugly to look at. —*Yung.*

Blackout

An Ambient Light Entertainment presentation. Produced by Doug Adams, Joseph Stefano. Line producer, Herman Grigsby. Directed by Adams. Screenplay, Stefano, based on an original screenplay by Adams, Laura Ferguson, Cynthia Williams; camera (color), Arledge Armenaki; editor-associate producer, Zach Staenberg; music, Don Davis; production design, Peter Kanter; set decoration, Effie Rosen; costume design, Trudy Kapner; sound (Ultra-Stereo), Gerald Wolfe; assistant director, D.K. Miller; casting, Penny Perry, Meagan Branman. Reviewed at Cinetex Film Festival, Las Vegas, Sept. 27, 1988. No MPAA Rating. Running time: **91 MIN.**
Mother . . . . Carol Lynley
Caroline Boyle . . . . Gail O'Grady
Uncle Alan . . . . Michael Keys Hall
Luke . . . . Joseph Gian
Angela . . . . Deena Freeman
Eleanor Carpenter . . . . Joanna Miles

■ Las Vegas — **"Blackout" poses the question of whether long-dead Daddy is in the attic, and coming from the pen of "Psycho" author Joseph Stefano, the question is a creepy one.**

A combination of old-style scare melodrama and new-fangled gory shock, first feature by Doug Adams is well-mounted hokum that might be exploited for its violent disturbed-young-woman angle to modest profits.

Beautiful, demure Caroline Boyle returns to her small Northern California hometown upon receiving a note from her father, who mysteriously disappeared seven years earlier, when the girl was 14. Her mother is none too happy to see her, as her daughter reminds her of the man she so despises, but local boy Luke is delighted, and picks up courting Caroline where he left off

before she left several years earlier.

Caroline hears weird noises coming from upstairs and experiences jarring memory flashes of a long-suppressed incident from her childhood, which mother, in an attempt to get rid of the kid, finally explains stem from her having been molested by dad, then killing him.

The favored weapon in this bedevilled clan is a screwdriver, which Luke discovers to his misfortune when he tries to put the make on the comely Caroline. Two neighbors meet undeserved ends in the course of her investigation into what really happened to dear old dad, which unavoidably throws suspicion upon Uncle Alan, mother's housemate of longstanding.

Plotting is sometimes farfetched and presentation of the heavily expository material is exceedingly deliberate. Shock cuts of graphic violence work like sudden jolts of electricity — they're crude, but they do the job.

Gail O'Grady, who could just about pass for Greta Scacchi's sister, makes for an unusually quiet, retreating leading character, but she maintains a steady resolve in the face of all the adverse occurrences. Carol Lynley as the mother is a hard, sultry babe whose concern for her daughter is buried very deep, and Joseph Gian proves quite likeable as Caroline's undying admirer. Try as he might to play it straight, Michael Keys Hall can't help but be weird as Uncle Alan.

Director Adams displays elegant touches of style to go along with some of the more plodding moments, and shows some promise, as does lenser Arledge Armenaki. Don Davis' music, quite effective in its more melodious sections, comes on too strong in the horrific scenes. —*Cart.*

Mystic Pizza

A Samuel Goldwyn Co. release. Executive producer, Samuel Goldwyn Jr. Produced by Mark Levinson, Scott Rosenfelt. Line producer, Susan Vogelfang. Directed by Donald Petrie. Screenplay, Amy Jones, Perry Howze, Randy Howze, Alfred Uhry, from story by Jones; camera (Duart color), Tim Suhrstedt; editor, Marion Rothman, Don Brochu; music, David McHugh; production design, Davi Chapman; art direction, Mark Haack, set decoration, Haack; costume design, Jennifer Von Mayrhauser; sound (Ultra-Stereo), Russel Fager; assistant director, Mark Radcliffe; production manager, Rosenfelt. Reviewed at Lorimar screening room, L.A., Sept. 19, 1988. MPAA Rating: R. Running time: **104 MIN.**
Daisy Araujo . . . . Julia Roberts
Kat Araujo . . . . Annabeth Gish
Jojo Barboza . . . . Lili Taylor
Bill Montijo . . . . Vincent D'Onofrio
Tim Travers . . . . William R. Moses
Charlie Winsor . . . . Adam Storke
Leona Valsouano . . . . Conchata Ferrell
Margaret . . . . Joanna Merlin

■ Hollywood — **"Mystic Pizza" is the kind of small-scale, big-impact film that rarely gets made and rare-**

ly gets made this well. A deftly told coming-of-age story about three young femmes as they explore their different destinies, mostly through romance, it's genuine and moving, with enough edge to impress contemporary audiences.

With the Goldwyn Co. pumping in hefty marketing support, pic stands a good chance of becoming a hit. Only drawback is the R rating, which could turn away young teens who'd be particularly taken with it.

Title refers to a pizza parlor in the heavily Portuguese fishing town of Mystic, Conn., where three best friends, two of them sisters, are working the summer after high school graduation, all on the verge of pursuing different directions in life.

Jojo (Lili Taylor) apparently is headed for marriage to high school sweetheart Bill (Vincent D'Onofrio), but the idea terrifies her, while he's all for it. In a twist, she's eager to "go all the way" but he's holding out for a commitment.

Of the two sisters, Daisy (Julia Roberts) is a vamp who's after the good life and knows how to use her looks, while Kat (Annabeth Gish) is the "perfect" one — intelligent, focused, hardworking and headed for college on an astronomy scholarship. Unlike her sister, she's not too savvy about men, and falls for the married man (William Moses) she babysits for, with painful results.

Script, which evolved through four writers and came out first-rate, is remarkably mature in its dealings with teens. Characters are funny and vulnerable but capable of shaping their lives, and script artfully weaves in themes of class, destiny and friendship.

Donald Petrie, in his feature debut, demonstrates a strong feel for the material. Some scenes are uneven, but more often the direction shines, particularly in the well-modulated performances from the young cast.

Taylor, in particular, brings high-voltage comedic charm to her role, while both Roberts and Gish are remarkably well cast (though they don't look like sisters).

D'Onofrio (who played a much different role as the fat psychotic in "Full Metal Jacket") is extremely good as frustrated Bill — he could find himself becoming a teen idol after this turn.

Oft-mentioned in the pic is the "secret ingredient" that makes Mystic Pizza the best around; this pic seems to have a secret ingredient of its own working for it. Leave it to the marketing folks to discover what it is.

Where tie-ins are concerned, franchises take note — one sure feels like eating a slice of pizza after this pic. —*Daws.*

Georgia
(AUSTRALIAN)

A Generation Films production. Produced by Bob Weis. Directed by Ben Lewin. Screenplay, Lewin, Joanna Murray-Smith, Weis; camera (color), Yuri Sokol; editor, Edward McQueen-Mason; music, Paul Grabowsky; production design, John Dowding; sound, John Phillips. Reviewed at Bloor Cinema, Toronto, Sept. 6, 1988. (In Toronto Festival of Festivals, Contemporary World Cinema.) Running time: **90 MIN.**

Nina/Georgia	Judy Davis
William Karlin	John Bach
Elizabeth	Julia Blake
Laszlo	Alex Menglet
Frank LeMat	Marshall Napier

■Toronto — "Georgia" is a stylishly lensed, only slightly intriguing thriller, all of whose elements don't quite coalesce. It's graced with a vibrant central performance by the luminous Judy Davis, whose box-office appeal will be the big draw for any commercial sparks.

There are some initial chilling components in this Melbourne-set yarn, where Davis plays Nina Bailey, a tax fraud investigator. At a photography gallery opening, she's drawn to a b&w shot of a blond woman holding a baby. The next day she asks her mother Elizabeth (Julia Blake) to accompany her to the exhibit to point out a photo of her, too.

Mom spills the beans and curtly tells Nina the blond woman in the photograph was her real mother, the photographer Georgia White, and that Elizabeth adopted Nina after her natural mother died in a mysterious accident. This is a big admission for the audience — and for Nina — to take, but Davis handles it with aplomb.

Understandably overwhelmed by the news, Nina goes on a personal quest to unveil the circumstances of Georgia's death by drowning at a party given by Elizabeth and her then-husband William Karlin, a money launderer and shady real estate dealer. Also in attendance were Elizabeth's current lover Laszlo and now-retired, embittered ex-cop Frank LeMat (Marshall Napier).

Nina is stalked throughout the pic by Georgia's would-be killer, complete with rubber mask and razor, and manages to outrun him on two occasions, even knocking him out with her mother's camera, which Laszlo gave to her before he had to skip town.

Director Ben Lewin slickly weaves the action with flashbacks to the fateful party where Georgia died running off the pier, using different people's memories and retellings to embellish the story. Davis gets to play her mother Georgia as well, giving the thesp a chance to have fun with an impetuous, volatile character as well as the level-headed government worker, Nina.

After so many of the same accounts, the tale gradually becomes eroded and the chilling aspects were flattened. Pic looks right and feels right, thanks to Yuri Sokol's outstanding cinematography and Paul Grabowsky's haunting music, but the script is a letdown.

Lewis has a polished style and gets uniformly strong performances from the tight ensemble cast, but is ill-served by a basically unfulfilled whodunnit. —*Devo.*

Turnabout
(CANADIAN)

A Zebra Films production. Produced, written and directed by Don Owen. Camera (color), John Hertzog, Doug Koch; editor, Michael Todd; sound, Christopher Leech. Reviewed at Toronto Festival of Festivals, Sept. 16, 1988. Running time: **70 MIN.**

Alexandra	Judith Gault
Crystal	Jane Gibson

■Toronto — Two Toronto women, one rich and one poor, meet again after 20 years and trade their unhappy existences without fulfillment in "Turnabout." A modest little film that makes its point with low-key drollery and without pretense, "Turnabout" is suited for independent festivals or, if trimmed down to an hour, for public tv.

Alexandra, a good-hearted, bored-stiff, upper middle class housewife (Judith Gault), and Crystal, a cynical, tough, unhappy hooker (Jane Gibson), offer their perspectives on the story via documentary-style talking head confessions and narrative flashback. When Alexandra sees Crystal shoplifting in a neighborhood market, she recognizes an old friend from good times in Montreal two decades past.

She persuades Crystal to visit her snazzy home, and the poor woman is abashed by the vast difference in their material circumstances. Both women, however, are deeply distressed with their lives and their men — a hotshot advertising art director (Alexandra's husband) and a freeloading, unemployed bar bouncer (Crystal's live-in). After a considerable test of wills in an emotional tug of war, the two form an uneasy friendship and finally swap lives.

Crystal moves into Alexandra's home, where she's treated passionately by her friend's husband. Alexandra takes over Crystal's housing project flat and gets some hot love from from the free and easy bouncer. Once the novelty wears off, however, neither woman is able to shake her existential depression.

Making sure audiences don't miss the point, filmmaker Don Owen hits us over the head with the fable's moral, a quote from Oscar Wilde to the effect that the two great tragedies in life are not getting what you want — or getting it. Performances from both actresses are first-rate and keep the film afloat. —*Rich.*

Cellar Dweller

An Empire Pictures presentation of a Dove production. Produced by Bob Wynn. Directed by John Carl Buechler. Screenplay, Kit DuBois; camera (Technicolor), Sergio Salvati; editor, Barry Zetlin; music, Carl Dante; sound (Ultra-Stereo), Primiano Muratori, Jan Brodin (U.S.); art direction, Angelo Santucci; second unit camera, Tom Callaway; special creature effects, Buechler; casting, Anthony Barnao. Reviewed on New World videocassette, N.Y., Sept. 15, 1988. No MPAA Rating. Running time: **77 MIN.**

Whitney Taylor	Debrah Mulrowney
Philip	Brian Robbins
Meshelski	Vince Edwards
Lisa	Cheryl-Ann Wilson
Colin Childress	Jeffrey Combs
Amanda	Pamela Bellwood
Mrs. Briggs	Yvonne De Carlo
Cellar Dweller	Michael S. Deak

■A stillborn entry from the late Empire Pictures, "Cellar Dweller" is a claustrophobic cheapie which fails to breathe life into the genre using cartoonists as a subject (best repped by Alain Jessua's "Jeu de Massacre").

After a prolog featuring Jeffrey Combs (star of Empire's hit "Re-Animator"), pic bogs down in an underdeveloped tale of pretty Debrah Mulrowney arriving at Yvonne De Carlo's Throckmorton Art Institute, where she wants to follow in Combs' artistic footsteps. Combs years earlier created a classic horror comic, "Cellar Dweller," serving as her inspiration.

Underpopulated film consists of a few American actors ensconced at Empire's Rome studio. Guest stars have brief assignments: Vince Edwards as a would-be hardboiled mystery writer who likes to act out his ideas, and Pamela Bellwood as a video specialist who goes around taping everything.

The cellar is off limits, so naturally Mulrowney visits it, finds Combs' book of legendary curses and brings the title monster to life. As handled by Michael S. Deak in a furry suit, it's not scary, just an overgrown counterpart to filmmaker John Buechler's "Ghoulies" creatures.

Plot premise that what Mulroney draws in a cartoon then happens in real life is cornball and the climax is threadbare: the monster is destroyed by pouring white-off on the cartoon! Audiences post-"Roger Rabbit" won't sit still for that kind of cheapness, and pic has gone direct to video via Empire's output deal with New World Video.

Cheryl-Ann Wilson contributes some pulchritude to the film, including a sexy shower scene. Buechler showed more promise as a director in a subsequent assignment, Paramount's "Friday The 13th Part VII — The New Blood." —*Lor.*

The Storms Of August
(WELSH)

A Gaucho Cyf production. Produced by Pauline Williams. Directed by Endaf Emlyn. Screenplay, Emlyn and W.S. Jones; camera (Agfacolor), Richard Branczik; editor, Martin Sage; sets, Hayden Pearce. Reviewed at Vevey Film Festival, Switzerland, Aug. 25, 1988. Running time: **104 MIN.**

Penri	Arwel Gruffydd
Miss Edwardes	Judith Humphreys
Catrina	Alaw Bennet Jones
Margaret	Helen Griffiths

Also with: Robert E. Roberts, Ifan Williams, Trefor Selway, Clive Roberts, Dyfan Roberts, Owen Garmon, Iola Gregory, Stewart Jones.

(Welsh soundtrack)

■Vevey — Set in 1957 in a small Welsh village, "The Storms Of August" is a nostalgia piece about the coming of age of a boy at about the same time the arrival of tv starts to revolutionize local customs.

Helmer Endaf Emlyn underlines the traditional Welsh values and language, which vainly try to stave off the incursions of the outside world. Pic has its tender and touching moments, but the Welsh lingo soundtrack is sure to limit sales.

A generational confrontation provides the background of the yarn, as militant and hypocritical conservatives in the village try to stymie the tastes for rock music, tv and sexual experiences craved by some of the youths of the Welsh village. Penri, the son of the local newspaper editor, has a crush on his music teacher, takes up sex lessons from the hashslinger at the village cafe, and plays tricks on the stuffy elders of the town.

The editor, in a 1-man crusade, horrified at the dehumanization brought by tv, decides to jam the sond of tv programs from a transmitter hidden in his car. His son, Penri, fascinated by rock music and tv, meanwhile gets a job installing tv antennas on the tops of houses, which also enables him to observe the liaisons occurring between his schoolmaster and his piano teacher.

Pic ends with the son dutifully returning to the print shop and running the linotype. Thesping by femme leads is more convincing than that of the elders, who lack flair and conviction. Pic is a decidedly minor effort, retelling a familiar story, but is well paced and winsome.

Item could generate some interest in audiences looking for nostalgia, but story is too bland; the confrontations are never followed through with any sense of the dramatic. —*Besa.*

Arder eta Yul
(Arder And Yul)
(SPANISH)

An Igeldo Zine production, in collaboration with the Culture and Tourism Dept. of the Basque Government and Spanish TV. Produced by Angel Amigo. Directed by Ana Diez. Screenplay, Diez, Amigo; camera (color), Gonzalo F. Berridi; editor, Ivan Aledo; music, Amaya Zubiria; Pascal Gaigne; sets, Iñaki Eizaguirre; sound, Aurelio Martinez. Reviewed at San Sebastian Film Festival, Sept. 18, 1988. Running time: **90 MIN.**

Ander	Miguel Munarriz
Yul	Isidoro Fernández
Sara	Carmen Pardo

Also with: Joseba Apaolaza, Ramón Barea, Ramón Agirre, Aitzpea Goenaga, Eneko Olasagasti, Mikel Garmendia, Carlos Zabala.

■ San Sebastian — Using a soundtrack mostly in euskera (the Basque language), newcomer Ana Diez limns a film the first 90% of which seems to be sympathetic to the Basque terrorist organization ETA, but which turns around at the very end as condemnation of the separatists.

From a dramatic standpoint, item has plenty of weaknesses, but might arouse some interest from those concerned with the Basque problem.

Ander is an ex-ETA member who has turned to pushing narcotics. After release from jail, where he has done a stint, he heads back to his hometown of Rentería, takes up with a girl on the loose, latches on to the drug-traffickers in the street and eventually meets an old pal from the ETA, Yul. He renews his contact with Yul, coincidentally witnessing the ETA member shooting down a man in the street.

The police (who are consistently depicted in an unfavorable light) question Ander and eventually track down the terrorists, who have started executing drug pushers to show that they (the terrorists) are also concerned with the well-being of the population. Among those on the list is Ander, and Yul is the one who guns him down remorselessly.

Excepting the end, pic is rather talky and rambling, unlikely to appeal to any but regional audiences.
—*Besa.*

Horses In Winter
(CANADIAN)

A Raxlen Prods. release of a Raxlen production. Produced by Rick Raxlen. Directed by Raxlen, Patrick Vallely. Screenplay, Raxlen; camera (color), Steven Reizes; editor, Raxlen, Vallely; music, Fred Torak; sound, Glen Hodgins; art direction, costumes and set decoration, Kathy Horner, Deborah Creamer. Reviewed at Montreal World Film Festival (Panorama Canada), Sept. 2, 1988. Running time: **90 MIN.**

Ben Waxman at 9	Jacob Tierney
Ben Waxman as adult	Rick Raxlen
Mrs. Waxman	Vicki Barkoff
Dr. Waxman	Jacques Mizne
David Waxman	Colin Kish
Ruby Waxman	Erin Whitaker
Mrs. Arthur	Leni Parker
Mr. Arthur	Lou Israel
Fran Waxman	Elizabeth Balim

■ Montreal — The best thing about "Horses In Winter" is the photography of Steven Reizes. Unfortunately, this low-budget film has little theatrical release potential and will probably end up on the small screen via video and tv venues.

That will limit appreciation of Reizes' outdoor images, some of which recall the best camerawork in "On Golden Pond."

This film, too, is about cottage life. Its setting is the rural Quebec lake on which the narrator spent his summer vacations. The particular year chosen for the story is 1953, which the narrator-producer-director-writer Rick Raxlen tells us was the most idyllic of his life.

"Horses" is a very personal film. A thinly disguised autobiography, pic might have fared better with more money and better timing. Raxlen could have written the screenplay and had it produced and directed by people with fewer ties to the subject matter, thereby allowing some market potential. However, pic in any event is a nostalgia piece produced in what appears to be the dog days of that trend. —*Cadd.*

Prisonnières
(Women In Prison)
(FRENCH)

A Capital Cinéma release of an Apple Film/TF1 Films Prod./Capitol Cinéma coproduction. Produced by Roger Andrieux. Written and directed by Charlotte Silvera. Camera (Eastmancolor), Bernard Lutic; editor, Danielle Fillios; music, Michel Portal; art direction, Gérard Viard; sound, Alix Comte, Dominique Dalmasso; costumes, Christian Gasc; assistant director, Jean-Jacques Albert; makeup, Antoine Garabedian; production manager, Francis Peltier. Reviewed at Ariane Screening room, Paris, Aug. 24, 1988. (In Montreal World Film Festival, noncompeting.) Running time: **100 MIN.**

Nicole	Agnès Soral
Marthe	Annie Girardot
Nelly	Bernadette Lafont
Lucie	Milva
Brigitte	Fanny Bastien
Sabien	Corinne Touzet
Mme. Dessombes	Marie-Christine Barrault

■ Paris — Charlotte Silvera, whose debut feature "Louise, l'insoumise" won the Georges Sadoul prize in 1984, moves away from the autobiographical mode in her second feature, a women-in-prison drama.

Silvera skillfully avoids sensationalism and melodrama in her treatment, but her script fails to probe beyond surfaces, making this an interesting but unsatisfactory reworking of familiar genre motifs.

Star casting of such veterans as Bernadette Lafont and Annie Girardot alongside a younger generation of rising actresses tends to unbalance audience attention, which already is off-kilter in the screenplay. Silvera reveals little of these female offenders' pasts, opting instead for a present-tense cross-section view of a special universe (seen in a different, more sensational male light in the recent "Contrainte par corps" by action director Serge Leroy).

Aided by Bernard Lutic's effectively muted lensing, Silvera smoothly introduces the viewer into the confines of the prison (shot in fact in several former monasteries). Pre-credit scene of a group of handcuffed women being escorted aboard a train in a Paris station sets the tone adroitly.

Camera initially singles out Agnès Soral, a young woman sentenced for infanticide, but pretty much abandons her as a protagonist once she's gone through the humiliating registration procedures.

Focus shifts to tensions and alliances among several other inmates, notably Girardot, a domineering murderess who enjoys special privileges from the warden (Marie-Christine Barrault), and the independent-minded Lafont, who is framed for possession of drugs and sent to solitary confinement.

In another subplot, young Corinne Touzet, imprisoned for armed robbery, develops a lesbian attachments to the older, more reserved Milva, whose release is imminent.

Overall, Silvera's cinematic control is a major improvement over the somewhat amateurish though sincere gropings of her first film, but "Prisonnières" rarely breaks the shackles of its conventions.
—*Len.*

Tango: Baile Nuestro
(Tango: Our Dance)
(ARGENTINE-DOCU-COLOR/ B&W)

A Condor Films production. Produced by Jorge Zanada. Directed by Jorge Zanada. Camera (color, b&w), Gabriel Perosino, Marcelo Camorino, Juan C. Lenardi, Carlos Torlaschi, Yito Blanc, Andres Silvart, Juan Ferro; choreography, Marcel Bo, Maria Audisio, Jorge Zanada, Gustavo Mollajoli, Vladimir Vassiliev, Julio Lopez; music, Daniel Binelli; sound, Jose Luis Dias, Jorge Ventura; costumes, Mary Tapia. Reviewed at Montreal World Film Festival (Latin American Cinema), Aug. 30, 1988. Running time: **69 MIN.**

With: Oscar Martinez, Arturo Bonin, Emiliano Guerrero, Pablo Macnado, Patricia Mariscotti, Jorge Torres, Jorge Marrone.

■ Montreal — Thus Far, Argentina's "Tango: Our Dance" has no international distributor, but its popularity with Spanish audiences at the Montreal World Film Festival suggests it eventually should make some noise in Latin countries and with North America's Latin communities.

That probably could be best accomplished through video sales since pic fits video dimensions. Its 69-minute length and small-screen look also might make good for ethnic tv.

The film blends staged dancing vignettes with interviews and documentary footage, all intended to give an understanding of the role of the tango in Argentine life. Producer-director Jorge Zanada tries to link the aspects of the dance to the persona of Argentines. His amateur dancers are particularly representative, each adding a personal touch to the interpretation of the dance.

That makes for better viewing than the segments of the film in which the dances are performed by professionals. The amateur classes and the amateur renditions also should have more appeal to the marketplace since they allow tango dancers a sense of identification, a good selling tool for any documentary about a cultural institution.
—*Cadd.*

The Accused

A Paramount Pictures release of a Jaffe/-Lansing production. Produced by Stanley R. Jaffe, Sherry Lansing. Directed by Jonathan Kaplan. Screenplay, Tom Topor; camera (Alpha Cine Services color; Technicolor prints), Ralf Bode; editor, Jerry Greenberg, O. Nicholas Brown; music, Brad Fiedel; production design, Richard Kent Wilcox; design consultant, Mel Bourne; art direction, Sheila Haley; set decoration, Barry W. Brolly; costume design, Trish Keating; sound (Dolby), Rob Young; assistant director, David W. Rose; associate producer, Jack Roe; casting, Julie Selzer, Sally Dennison, Michelle Allen (Canada). Reviewed at the National theater, L.A., Oct. 4, 1988. MPAA Rating: R. Running time: **110 MIN.**
Kathryn Murphy . . . . Kelly McGillis
Sarah Tobias . . . . Jodie Foster
Ken Joyce . . . . Bernie Coulson
Cliff (Scorpion) Albrecht . . . . Leo Rossi
Sally Fraser . . . . Ann Hearn
D.A. Paul Rudolph . . . Carmen Argenziano
Bob Joiner . . . . Steve Antin
Larry . . . . Tom O'Brien
Attorney Paulsen . . . . . . Peter Van Norden
Danny Rudkin . . . . Woody Brown
Asst. D.A. Al Massi . . . . Allan Lysell

■ Hollywood — Last year it was "Fatal Attraction," and this fall's anti-sex story from Jaffe/Lansing Prods. is "The Accused," a dry case study of a rape incident whose only impact comes from the sobering crime itself, not the dramatic treatment.

Journalistic subject matter and presale approach to it would have seemed more suitable for the home screen, where pic would be right at home except for the profanities and rough violation scene itself. B.o. prospects look iffy in the long run.

Inspired by, but not based upon the 1983 barroom pooltable gang rape in New Bedford, Mass., Tom Topor's screenplay is designed to pose questions about the thin line between sexual provocation and assault, seduction and force, and observation of and participation in a crime. Issues here are certainly sufficiently volatile to hold the interest, and Jodie Foster's lower class character is an interesting choice for the focus of such an inquiry, but all other roles are drawn boldly in but one dimension, and storytelling is highly elementary.

Pic begins with a bloodied, dishevelled Foster stumbling out of a roadhouse. A young patron calls the police to report an incident, and in short order three mean plead guilty to the reduced charge of reckless endangerment (the film's original title) rather than rape.

All this takes place without the participation of the victim, who becomes furious with her lawyer, Kelly McGillis, when she learns via television of the legal deal, since it is not on record that the rape actually occurred. So just when it looks like the case, as well as the story, is closed, McGillis abruptly decides to pursue the matter much further by, in an unprecedented move, prosecuting some of the onlookers in the bar for criminal solicitation, legalese for encouraging and cheering the rapists on.

Based on the testimony of the kid who phoned the cops, the audience finally gets to see the crime, which has been withheld, a la "In Cold Blood," for a long stretch. Low-living Foster has just had a beef with her boyfriend and heads to the bar for a couple of beers with a ladyfriend.

Dressed invitingly to say the least, she eyes a guy at the bar and is quickly dancing with him very, very close. Pushed further by the young man, she ends up on a pinball machine and, in a harrowing sequence, the guy and two others jump her one after another.

Unfortunately, the film provokes no emotion other than disgust over the crime, an easy accomplishment under the circumstances. In a sense, the picture is preaching to the converted, since no one is going to side with the rapists, and the outrage that is justifiably aroused by the way the justice system can treat crime victims is assuaged by story's end.

Foster is edgy and spunky in by far her most impressive adult performance to date, but McGillis' role, as conceived, is a joke, since she exists only as a stick figure with no psychology or background offered up over the course of nearly two hours. The severe limitation prevents the relationship between these two women from amounting to anything, which in turn renders all but the courtroom scenes hopelessly flat and unpersuasive.

With British Columbia standing in for Washington State, pic looks only okay, and Brad Fiedel's pounding synthesized score is an irritant. —*Cart.*

Cohen And Tate

A Tri-Star Pictures release of a Nelson Entertainment presentation. Produced by Antony Rufus Isaacs, Jeff Young. Written and directed by Eric Red. Camera (Eastman color), Victor J. Kemper; editor, Ed Abroms; music, Bill Conti; production design, Davis Haber; production manager, Andy Howard; sound, Bob Waller, Tim Hines; casting, Sally Denison, Jilie Selzer, Patrick Rush. Reviewed at Sitges Film Festival, Spain, Oct. 12, 1988. MPAA Rating: R. Running time: **85 MIN.**
Cohen . . . . Roy Scheider
Tate . . . . Adam Baldwin
Travis . . . . Harley Cross
Also with: Cooper Huckabee, Suzanne Savoy.

■ Sitges — Despite tight scripting, occasional violence and some tense scenes, this pic about two mobsters driving a kidnaped boy from Oklahoma to Houston is too much of a 1-situation story to hold interest to the end.

Halfway through, pic becomes a uphill struggle to come up with new twists for the 3-in-a-car setting and story often becomes familiar and predictable.

Audience reaction at Sitges fest was mixed, suggesting item could garner a moderate success in international release, but probably less than filmmaker Eric Red's scripted "The Hitcher" (which was helmed by Robert Harmon).

Cohen and Tate are professional killers, one a psychopath, who have been told to bring back a 12-year-old boy to Houston for questioning, a 675-mile drive. After killing two FBI agents and gunning down the boy's parents in their remote prairie house, the hit men pack the kid into a car and start their long drive.

Along the way various twists occur, as the boy tries to set the two killers against each other, escapes and is caught again, tries to tip off police and a gas station attendant, and to do anything to outwit his captors.

The two mobsters rather unconvincingly crash police roadblocks and eventually confront each other in an oil field. By then the plot has run thin and pic resorts to some of the threadworn tricks of the genre, like the "body in the trunk."

There's fine thesping by the boy, Harley Cross. Roy Scheider is excellent as the old pro Cohen, but perhaps a trifle too unmenacing. Adam Baldwin's performance as a psychopath is convincing, even though at times it borders on caricature of the type.

Technical credits are good, and the atmosphere of the lonely vastness of Texas is nicely caught.
—*Besa.*

Un Pasaje de Ida
(A One-Way Ticket)
(DOMINICAN REPUBLIC)

A Prod. Testimonio production. Produced and directed by Agliberto Meléndez. Screenplay, Meléndez, Adelso Cass, Danilo Taveras; camera (Eastman color, super 16m), Pedro Guzmán Cordero; editor, Pericles Mela; music, Rafael Solano; sound, Miguel Heded; art direction, Orlando Menicucci. Reviewed at San Juan Film Festival, Puerto Rico, Oct. 1, 1988. Running time: **92 MIN.**
René . . . . Angel Muñiz
Isidro . . . . Carlos Alfredo
Payano . . . . Horacio Veloz
Turin . . . . Miguel Bucarelly
Also with: Rafael Villalona, Víctor Checo, María Castillo, Giovanny Cruz, Teresita Basilis, Angel Haché.

■ San Juan — Dominican director Agliberto Meléndez makes a firm entry into feature filmmaking with "Un Pasaje de Ida" (A One-Way Ticket) which, if handled right, could make modest in-roads at select sites, besides interest generated by Hispanic audiences.

Film picked up top honors at the San Juan Film Festival, besides receiving kudos at Biarritz and Cartagena.

Film narrates real events that took place in 1981 aboard the ship Regina Express bound for Puerto Rico. A group of about 40 Dominicans, en route illegally to the United States, were drowned under tragic circumstances.

Theme captures concerns voiced by many Latins suffering economic hardships in their native lands and enticed by the American dream to travel north in search of a better life. Their desperation makes them easy prey to unscrupulous types, who rake in high fees for their guarantees of illegal passage.

Realistic script avoids sentimentality and despite a couple of exceptions, tries to provide shades of grey to characters who could easily be depicted by black-hat/white-hat roles. Ensemble blend of pro and amateur thesps works well to provide fresh exchange for naturalistic dialog.

So-so lensing, amplified from super 16m, tends toward the dark side, while cross-cutting during final dramatic moments is effective.

Given pic's topical nature, with parallel stories of Mexican illegal aliens found dead in sealed Texas boxcars, pic goes beyond journalistic docudrama and demonstrates that some people will risk everything for a chance to escape misery back home. — *Lent.*

Zabitaya Melodia dlia Fleiti
(A Forgotten Tune For The Flute)
(SOVIET)

A Fries Entertainment release of a Sovexportfilm presentation. Directed by Eldar Ryazanov. Screenplay, Ryazanov, Emil Bra|gansky; camera (color), Vadim Alisov; music, Andrei Petrov; lyrics for chorale, Evgeny Yevtushenko; art direction, Alexander Borisov. Reviewed at Magno Review 2 screening room, N.Y., Oct. 3, 1988. Running time: **131 MIN.**
Leonid . . . . Leonid Filatov
Lida . . . . Tatyana Dogileva
Elena . . . . Irina Kupchenko

■ This delightful Soviet sex comedy gleefully attacks the bloated bureaucracy and its privileged parasites. The two key words of Gorbachev's reform program — glasnost and perestroika — are frequently uttered throughout the film, uttered with fear and loathing by the beleaguered bureaucrats and with hope and enthusiasm by common citizens.

The film abounds in delicious political satire yet is packaged within a triangle love story that alternates joyous and sad moments. One is surprised by the brio and bold self-confidence of the film, which can catch on with American audiences.

The feature opens with snappy music and lyrics that sharply satirize the bureaucracy for its hypocrisy, sloth, stupidity, greed and opportunistic careerism. That tone doesn't moderate during the story that follows, illustrating the satiric prolog. The ridicule is so strong that the governmental system must be more corrupt and discredited than we here may have realized.

Performances are excellent, from the leads to minor characters who are cleverly individualized. Leonid (Leonid Filatov) is a likable middle-aged bureaucrat within the commissariat of culture and entertainment. He is near the top but his advancement is blocked by an ancient Stalinist holdover.

Leonid's marriage soured long ago; his daughter is grown and gone away; while his wife Elena (Irina Kupchenko) is preoccupied with her own scholarly career. Her papa is high in government, and his political clout assures Leonid's career.

Although Elena and Leonid are estranged, she is aroused to jealous fury when Leonid begins a torrid affair with a stunning and vivacious nurse Lida (Tatyana Dogileva) half his age.

Leonid formerly was an idealistic musician, a serious flutist aiming for concert fame. He had compromised for security and instead had entered the culture bureaucracy, promoted by Elena's papa. Leonid now sits with cynical colleagues in bored judgment of avant-garde theatrical troupes, chorales, painters and poets, variously dispensing approval, denial, subsidy or oblivion. Leonid enjoys his power and its emoluments.

Now all that authority and comfort is threatened. Lida makes him search his closet for this old flute, dust it off and play her a lovely tune while she dances, a tune that he had long ago forgotten — hence the film's title.

It is at this critical moment of his newly emerging selfhood that Leonid's old mossback chief is forcibly retired by perestroika — "democracy has broken out!" Leonid must make a moral decision: he can choose the flute and Lida, resignation from the bureaucracy, on the one hand; or he can choose resumption of a stale marriage with Elena, and promotion to culture czar, on the other.

These alternatives facing Leonid are amusingly illustrated in the film by his occasional dreams and fantasies. In one we see former government officials begging in the streets with signs around their necks — "unemployed bureaucrats." Leonid fears that, so he must ponder carefully as he makes his choice.
— *Hitch.*

Pumpkinhead

An MGM/UA Distribution Co. release from United Artists of a Lion Films production. Produced by Richard C. Weinman, Howard Smith. Directed by Stan Winston. Screenplay, Mark Patrick Carducci, Gary Gerani; from story by Carducci, Winston, Weinman; camera (Technicolor), Bojan Bazelli; editor, Marcus Manton; music, Richard Stone; special effects director, Alec Gillis; casting, Bob Morones. Reviewed at Point of View screening room, Southfield, Mich., Oct. 6, 1988. MPAA Ratiing: R. Run-

ning time: **86 MIN.**
Ed Harley . . . . Lance Henriksen
Chris . . . . Jeff East
Joel . . . . John DiAquino
Kim . . . . Kimberly Ross
Steve . . . . Joel Hoffman
Tracy . . . . Cynthia Bain
Maggie . . . . Kerry Remsen

■ **Southfield, Mich. — "Pumpkin-head" is a story of a man's revenge on a band of teenagers who accidentally kill his son.**

The fact that it's opening — after a year at De Laurentiis Entertainment Group before being bought by MGM/UA — around Halloween won't hurt, and word of mouth should help bring this a respectable b.o. and a spritely life in the home-vid hereafter.

It's a nasty little horror pic that borrows liberally from several films of this genre. Despite its derivative nature, however, picture works for a variety of reasons, including its quick pacing, believable special effects and well intentioned, albeit confusing, moral.

Director Stan Winston — whose makeup and special effects credits include "Aliens" and "The Autobiography Of Miss Jane Pittman" — and scripters Mark Patrick Carducci and Gary Gerani portray Harley and his son Billy as a poor but loving father and son who have little but their warm relationship.

Without warning, a half-dozen youths out for a weekend of dirt biking enter their lives: When Billy wanders too close to their reckless driving, he's run over and killed by one youth.

Enraged, Harley seeks out "an old woman with powers" who looks like Freddy Krueger's older sister and who he believes can bring Billy back to life. She can't. But she can summon Pumpkinhead, a grotesque demon strikingly akin to "Alien," who can revenge Billy's senseless murder by killing the youths responsible.

Harley agrees, and Pumpkinhead (so named because when not on retainer he lies buried in the pumpkin graveyard out in the woods) begins to stalk the teens, violently gashing their faces, twisting their heads and shoving them through glass windows. Harley comes to regret ever summoning Pumpkinhead, but can't stop him.

On the level of horror stories similar to ones told around campfires on cold fall nights in the woods, "Pumpkinhead" works fine. Pic ultimately remains unapproachable by failing to give the audience anyone to emphatize with.

As the body count piles up, the moral becomes clear; there is no forgiveness — a truly scary, and ultimately nasty, concept. —*Advo.*

Shadowman
(DUTCH)

A Hungry Eye Pictures distribution of a Riverside Pictures production, an Otger Merckelbach, Robert Swaab, Gys Versluys presentation. Executive producer, Remmelt Remmelts. Produced by Gys Versluys. Written and directed by Piotr Andreyev. Camera (color), Wit Dabal; editor, Ton Ruys; sound, Marcel de Hoogd, Gusta van Eljk; art direction, Ban van Os, Jan Roelfs. Reviewed at Cinema Intl., Amsterdam, Sept. 13, 1988. Running time: **93 MIN.**
Theo . . . . Jeroen Krabbé
Shadowman . . . . Tom Hulce
Monique . . . . Manouk van der Meulen
Mrs. Wisse . . . . Trudy Labij
Fuchs . . . . Thom Hoffman
Also with: Hans Hoes, Hans Dagelet, Karin Bloemen.
(Original English soundtrack)

■ **Amsterdam — Refugee Polish filmmaker Piotr Andreyev falls flat on his face in his Dutch feature debut. Unbelievable story, lensing that mistakens dark images for art, good actors valiantly struggling to add a third dimension to their cardboard roles all add up to a wasted effort.**

Events obviously take place in Amsterdam during World War II, though the film coyly situates the story during "a" war, which is a cost-cutting alibi to not use authentic uniforms, automobiles or precise production design.

A Polish Jew on the run (Tom Hulce) is directed to a Dutch profiteer for help, but it turned away when latter (Jeroen Krabbé) learns he has no money. The frightened Jew however refuses to leave, and the profiteer (who on a previous occasion revealed some soft spots) finally takes him in as he would a stray dog, feeding him, protecting him and even in the end sacrificing his life for him. The deed is heroic, the climax, like much of that precedes it, is quite ridiculous.

Everyone in the film speaks English, even the Dutch among themselves (except when they suddenly and inexplicably burst into their real tongue).

Except for the title and the credits, Hulce's refugee is never called Shadowman in the film, and there's no reason he should be. We last see him swimming for his life in an Amsterdam canal under a hail of police bullets. Subsequently he sends a letter from America. Some swimmer. —*Wall.*

Dangerous Love

A Concorde Pictures release of Motion Picture Corp. of America production. Produced by Brad Krevoy, Steven Stabler. Written and directed by Marty Ollstein. Camera (color), Nicholas von Sternberg; editor, Tony Lanza; sound, Clifford Gynn; production design, Michael Clousen; art direction, Greg Maher; set decoration, Chava Danielson; costumer, Brian Cotton; assistant director, Matt Hinkley; production manager/second unit director, Philip Marcus; second unit camera, Josh Morton; casting, Lee Daniels. Reviewed at Forest Park Theaters, Chicago, Oct. 6, 1988. MPAA Rating: R. Running time: **94 MIN.**
Gabe . . . . Lawrence Monoson

Chris . . . . Brenda Bakke
Jay . . . . Peter Marc
Rick . . . . Elliott Gould
Mickey . . . . Anthony Geary
Also with: Sal Landi, Angelyne, Eloise Broady, Teri Austin, Robin Klein, Bernie Pock.

■ **Chicago — Obviously an earnest, low-budget effort to create a serious suspense thriller with a romantic subplot, "Dangerous Love" nonetheless falls short of the mark on all counts. B.o. potential is zilch, but name cast and modest t&a factor could make pic a candidate for late-night cable viewing or $1 video rental.**

Thoroughly improbably plot of this tepid whodunit (better labeled a who-cares-whodunit) involves Gabe, a nebbishy computer exec who joins a video dating club just about the time the video dream-date girls begin to be offed by a psycho with a video camera, who gets his kicks by taping the proceedings.

Naturally, suspicion quickly falls on Gabe. Detective assigned to the case (Elliott Gould) makes no secret of the fact that he has reserved a room for him in the local slammer, pending sufficient evidence to clinch the case. The detective's lovely partner/paramour (Brenda Bakke) has different ideas, falling in love with Gabe for no reason whatsoever and believing in his innocence despite appalling amount of evidence that piles up against him as the pictures wears on.

On an idealistic plane, writer-director Marty Ollstein can be credited for trying to take the high road with his material, drawing on sources as wide-ranging as Hitchcock's "The Wrong Man" and Michael Powell's "Peeping Tom," and eschewing the cheap thrills of explicit sex and violence. In actuality, substance of "Dangerous Love" simply doesn't hold interest and pic's lack of exploitative elements, save for some tame disrobing and lingerie modeling by the various victims, keeps it from being even mildly diverting.

Tech credits are fair except for the editing, which is choppy at best and downright confusing at times. Acting is unnoteworthy save former soap opera topliner Anthony Geary's strangely believable turn as the sleazy operator of the video dating service. Gould's presence lends a touch of class to the project, but he ultimately seems lost and a bit sad in this role that is so far below the level he achieved in his heyday.
— *Brin.*

Het oog boven de put
(The Eye Above The Well)
(DUTCH-DOCU)

Produced by Noshka van der Lely and Johan Van der Keuken. Written and directed by Van der Keuken. Camera (color, 16m), Van der Keuken; editor, Jan Dop, Van der Keuken; sound, Van der Lely. Reviewed at Dutch

Film Days, City theater, Utrecht, Netherlands, Sept. 25, 1988. Running time: **94 MIN.**

■ Amsterdam — Johan van der Keuken's "The Eye Above The Well" may have future classic status, but it's difficult to describe. Reportage? Film essay? Cinematic poem? It is all three at once.

Contrary to much of Van der Keuken's previous non-fiction work, this film, shot in Kerala, India, has no commentary. Political or social comment, philosophical musings take a back seat. Van der Keuken here looks about in a country not his own, searching for the thoughts and feelings which form the basis of this people's existence.

Van der Keuken films landscapes of fascinatingly serene beauty, bustling city streets, a family at their dinner table, students lapping up tradition by imitating their teachers.

Two sequences in particular are unforgettable; a remarkably made-up actor mimes an ape's slow painful acceptance of death; a singing teacher does vocal exercises with three girls, then bursts into a energetic, buoyant song, full of pleasure and life. As Van der Keuken puts it: "the film is a journey into one's head."

Van der Keuken took his camera everywhere, shooting when it seemed worthwhile, unaware if the take would be long or short. The editing, and the sound work by his wife Noshka van der Lely, are painstakingly vivid, giving the impression of life caught in full flight.

Van der Keuken's work is well-known internationally. This Indian-lensed film has the universal appeal to travel far. —*Wall*.

Tender Hooks
(AUSTRALIAN)

A, Tru Vu Picture. Produced by Chris Oliver. Directed by Mary Callaghan. Screenplay, Callaghan; camera (color), Ray Argall; editor, Tony Stevens; music, Graham Bidstrup; production design, Kerri Brown; sound, Pat Fiske; production manager-associate producer, Anna Grieve; assistant director, Ian Page. Reviewed at Chauval theater, Paddington, Sydney, Aug. 11, 1988. Running time: **95 MIN.**
Mitch . . . . .Jo Kennedy
Rex Reeson . . . . .Nique Needles
Gaye .Anna Phillips
Yawn . . . . .Robert Menzies
Tony .John Polson
Vic . . . . .Ian Mortimer
Lorraine . . . . .Toni Scanlon
Connie . . . . .Kim Deacon
Wayne . . . . .Shane Conner

■ Sydney — Mary Callaghan's first feature is a downbeat and frustratingly uninvolving love story set in the seedy inner-Sydney district of Kings Cross. Low-budget production tries to make its young lovers charming, but finding audiences willing to be charmed will be tough indeed.

Pic will need special handling and positive reviews to find any success at home, while offshore chances look slim.

Central character is Mitch (Jo Kennedy), a sloppy red-headed hairdresser who lives in an untidy 1-room apartment with her pet tortoise. Mitch is supposed to be a lively, optimistic character, but though the actress tries hard, she fails to make her a very interesting or likeable protagonist. It's not Kennedy's fault; the screenplay just takes too much for granted and asks too much of the audience.

Mitch is a winner, though, when compared to her love interest, Rex (Nique Needles), a drifter involved in petty crime. Needles is getting to be an irritating actor, whose mannerisms become more familiar and less appealing with each new role. His attempts to make his character charming in this film are resistible, and thus the love affair, supposed to take center-stage, never sparks because obviously Mitch deserves better than this no-hoper.

Other characters include Robert Menzies as a monosyllabic druggie (a very disappointing performance after his lead role in the Paul Cox film "Cactus"); Anna Phillips as a wan little prostie; and John Polson as her lover/pimp. Kim Deacon is briefly effective as Needles' ex, but has too little screen time.

Film's set pieces include stealing meat from a butcher's shop to take to a barbecue hosted by a friendly policeman; and robbing the apartment of a rich doctor with a collection of porn videos.

Eventually, Needles is arrested and jailed. Kennedy visits him in prison, until he and a friend break out. After a desultory scene involving the trio plus a couple of girls the friend has picked up, the film simply ends on one of those increasingly irritating freeze-frame images, indicating that the screenplay really has no satisfactory ending.

Production is a low-budget effort, and looks to have been shot entirely on location. Editing is jarring at times, to no purpose. Music, though, is a plus factor.

Director Callaghan previously scored with a prize-winning featurette, "Greetings From Wollongong," but her first feature lacks the originality and spark that might have made it an art house bet at home and abroad. Final impressions are of a fuzzy, familiar and drab affair. — *Strat*.

Ein Schweizer namens Nötzli
(A Swiss Named Nötzli)
(SWISS-W. GERMAN)

An Elite-Film Zurich release of an Erwin C. Dietrich/Freddy Burger/Walter Roderer and Ascot-Film West German-Swiss coproduction. Exective producer, Dietrich. Directed by Gustav Ehmck. Screenplay, Ralph Engler, Roderer, based on a play "Mit besten Empfehlungen" by Hans Schubert and its Swiss stage adaptation "Buchhalter Nötzli;" camera (color), Peter Baumgartner; music, Walter Baumgartner; title song "Triebjagd" written by Udo Jürgens and Michael Kunze, performed by Jürgens; assistant director, Birgitta Trommler; production manager, Piet Lessnick. Reviewed at Capitol 1, Zurich, Sept. 24, 1988. Running time: **97 MIN.**
Josef Nötzli . . . . .Walter Roderer
Hilde Hartmann . . . . .Ursela Monn
Alfred Neubauer . . . . .Jochen Schroeder
Arribert Müller .Friedrich Georg Beckhaus
Eva Brock . . . . .Julia Biedermann
Dr. Karl Brock . . . . .Heinz Theo Branding
Juliane Kahr . . . . .Ruth Jecklin
Frau Brock . . . . .Eva Astor
Fau Stehberger . . . . .Dagmar Altrichter
Herr Stehberger . . . . . .Joachim Tennstedt
President Fonsheim . . . . .Ludwig Rembold
Also with: Simone Diane Brahmann, Andread Grothusen, Tamio Ichimura, Fukimo Matsuyama, Raimund Salewski, Cornelia Scholkmann, Charly Anelone.

■ Zurich — One of German Switzerland's most popular vet stage comedians, Walter Roderer, in his first film role since 1975, based on a stage comedy in which he starred in over 900 sellout performances, should guarantee a boxoffice hit, at least in his native Switzerland.

Whether "A Swiss Named Nötzli" will catch on to the same degree in West Germany, where release is set for Feb. 23, and Austria, where Roderer is not as popular, depends on word of mouth and advance touting. The latter, judging by the heavy Swiss promotion campaign, should be no problem.

At a time when comedies with established personalities such as Otto Waalkes ("Otto — Der Film," "Otto — Der neue Film"), Loriot ("Ödipussi") and Gerhart Polt ("Man spricht Deutsh") are climbing to boxoffice heights in German-speaking territories, "Nötzli" seems right in the trend. It's the classic story of the reliable, conscientious, but timid little underdog who has missed all his chances in 26 years as a bookkeeper at a chemical plant in West Berlin.

One day, a letter of recommendation from a high-echelon minister to the plant's general manager (a clear case of nepotism) is applied, by a case of mistaken identity, to Nötzli. He is catapulted up the career ladder to a top director's post. His, until then, suppressed or sneered-at capacities and ideas now flourish, spelling financial success for the firm as well.

When one day the misunderstanding comes to light, Nötzli is kicked back to his former modest post. Since this is a farce, not social drama, all ends happily with honest little Nötzli winning out over big-boss arrogance and nepotism.

Much of the humor derives from the lead character's heavy Swiss accent and his clumsy, cautious and slow-moving behavior associated in Germany with "the Swiss prototype." Roderer is the perfect incarnation of the type, to which he owes his immense popularity in his native land for 30 years. His stage successes (he's his own indie producer), include such perennials as "Model Husband" and "Charley's Aunt."

Direction by Gustav Ehmck is routine, and camerawork by Peter Baumgartner, while less than inspired, is a pro job. The same can be said of supporting players among which Jochen Schroeder stands out as Nötzli's sympathetic young office pla. Ursela Monn as Nötzli's secret office love, cannot pump much life into a colorless, distinctly underwritten part. Other credits are all pro. — *Mezo*.

Mullaway
(AUSTRALIAN)

A Hemdale Film Corp. release of an Intl. Film Management-Ukiyo Films production. Executive producer, Antony I. Ginnane. Produced by D. Howard Grigsby. Directed by Don McLennan. Screenplay, Jon Stephens, from the novel by Bron Nicholls; camera (Eastmancolor) & editor, Zbigniew Friedrich; music, Trevor Lucas, Michael Atkinson; sound, Lloyd Carrick; production design, Patrick Reardon; costumes, Jeannie Cameron; production manager, Andrew Wiseman; assistant director, Bob Donaldson; casting, Greg Apps, Liz Mullinar. Reviewed at Chauvel theater, Sydney, July 27, 1988. Running time: **90 MIN.**
Phoebe Mullens . . . . .Nadine Garner
Mr. Mullens . . . . .Bill Hunter
Mrs. Mullens . . . . .Sue Jones
Steve Mullens . . . . .Craig Morrison
Alan Mullens . . . . .Bradley Kilpatrick
Jodie Mullens . . . . .Kymara Stowers
Jim . . . . .Dominic Sweeney
Guido .Juno Roxas
Helen . . . . .Mary Coustas

■ Sydney — A fine central performance from teenage actress Nadine Garner is the peg on which hangs a grimly realistic, but prosaically handled, drama about a Melbourne family with more than its fair share of problems.

Critical support is essential for this one to succeed in any territory, and a change of title would also be of help.

Setting is the St. Kilda district of Melbourne, a beachside suburb of limited charm. The Mullens family, Dad (a security guard and Born Again Christian), sickly Mum and four children live in a working-class weatherboard house with minimal facilities. When Mum is stricken with a terminal illness during the mid-summer Christmas celebration, it's up to 17-year-old Phoebe (Garner) to drop out of school and look after everyone.

Phoebe, called "Mull" by just about everyone, has to grow up fast. Her father (Bill Hunter) works nights and takes his religion very seriously; the two younger children are also true believers, though Mull and her older brother, Steve (Craig Morrison) remained unconvinced. Mull has less and less time for best friend Helen (a beautiful performance from Mary Coustas) as she has to cook and wash and clean for her ungrateful family. Matters get worse as the mother's health declines and Mull discovers that Steve is (a) taking heroin and (b) involved in a gay relationship with Guido (Juno Roxas), a would-be rock singer.

This is a kitchen-sink drama that desparately needs a poetic element missing from Don McLennan's front-on direction. Despite Garner's immensely appealing performance, most viewers will remain unmoved by a film that never reaches the emotional heights of really successful drama. Some scenes (Helen's wedding; Guido and Mull finding a baby penguin under the rocks on the beach) are charming, but overall result is a well-intentioned, well-acted piece which has more the feeling of a tv pic than a theatrical film.

Visually, the film is rather ordinary; Zbignew Friedrich's camerawork might have given the film the lift it needed, and his editing is sometimes a fraction off. Though the film runs a tight 90 minutes, it seems longer.

The title (also the title of the book on which the film is based) is needlessly obscure, and nowhere in the film is it explained. Since the pic won't be an easy commercial sell, every effort should be made to make it as palatable to audiences as possible, and a title change would certainly help.

Pic ends on a note of resignation, with its plucky heroine facing an uncertain future. Viewers are likely to come away with the memory of Nadine Garner's performance the main asset of this curiously sterile offering. That would seem validated by Garner recently picking up this year's Aussie Film Institute Award for fest actress. Pic itself took onto the AFI's Members' award for excellence. —Strat.

Borderline
(AUSTRIAN)

An EPO Film production. Executive producer, Michel König. Written and directed by Houchang Allahyari. Camera (color), Horst Hubbauer; editor, Chrlotte Mullner, Angela Kauf; music, Guido Mancusi; sound, Harald Hennicke. Reviewed at Toronto Festival of Festivals, Sept. 16, 1988. Running time: 120 MIN.
Thomas Lindner . . . . Michael Lakner
Also with: Robert Hauer-Riedl, Sibylle Kos, Lieselotte Plauensteiner, Trude Marlen, Verena Angst, Ronald Seboth, Cecilia Brantley.

■ Toronto — Iranian-Austrian filmmaker Houchang Allahyari's background in psychiatry sheds a little light on the psychological motifs in "Borderline," a crime and self-punishment story about a brilliant young pianist whose shaky inner state compells him to confess to a murder he did not commit.

The film contains some dazzling, geometrically framed imagery, but its convoluted, time-shifting narrative style and plodding pace make it an unlikely candidate for North American arthouse distribution.

Thomas Lindner (played strongly by Michael Lakner) returns to the home of his wheelchair-bound piano teacher, following a recital, to find him murdered and the place swarming with cops. Panicked, he runs, is apprehended and charged with the murder.

The story unfolds along Kafkaesque lines as the brutal and homophobic police (the teacher was gay, Lindner is not) subject him to beatings and psychological torture, finally extracting a confession. After fierce resistance, the pianist's confession is so all-embracing that neither he nor the viewer can be certain whodunit.

Comic relief is provided by the pianist's grandmother, a feisty, artsy grande damme who is determined to prove her grandson's innocence, relentlessly testing the implacability of the Viennese police bureaucracy. Meanwhile the imprisoned Lindner descends ever deeper into a disturbed inner world of fantasy and tortured recollection over the death of his father.

Unlike grandma, the pianist's mother is a cold Teutonic type who's all too ready to wash her hands of her son and his trouble. Grandmother finally carries the day, but not until a great deal of psychobabble sound and fury passes all too slowly on screen. —Rich.

The Outside Chance Of Maximilian Glick
(CANADIAN)

A Northern Lights Media Corp. production, with the assistance of the National Film Board of Canada, Telefilm Canada and the Canadian Broadcasting Corp.. Produced by Stephen Foster, Richard Davis. Directed by Allan E. Goldstein. Screenplay, Phil Savath, from novel by Morley Torgov; camera (color), Ian Elkin; editor, Richard Martin; production design, Kim Steer; sound, Leon Johnson. Reviewed at Toronto Festival of Festivals, Sept. 16, 1988. Running time: 97 MIN.
Maximilian Glick . . . . Noam Zylberman
Celia Brzjinski . . . . Fairuza Balk
Rabbi Teitelbaum . . . . Saul Rubinek
Also with: Jan Rubes, Susan Rubes, Aaron Schwarz, Sharon Corder, Nigel Bennett.

■ Toronto — Stereotypes never get out of the box in this slight small-town comedy about a 12-year-old Jewish boy who dreams of being a classical pianist and his Hassidic rabbi who yearns to be a standup comic.

Pic boasts a bright screenplay by Phil Savath, and there's a strong, steady performance by a handsome, freckle-faced screen newcomer Noam Zylberman in the title role of a boy always able to encapsulate situations with wise quips far beyond his years.

His grandparents boss both him and his parents; a patient piano teacher guides him; and his rabbi, new to the town and out of place, becomes a buddy and they confess their secret yearnings to each other.

Saul Rubinek waltzes through the rabbi's role and gets out of town. The other performers don't.

Director Allan E. Goldstein in his first feature seems incapable of keeping others in the cast from stereotypical mugging and he doesn't sustain the action. Production values are limited.

Theatrical potential is dim. It maybe okay as a tv entry in Canada. —Adil.

Calling The Shots
(CANADIAN-DOCU)

A World Artists (Cineplex Odeon Films in Canada) release of a Women in Cinema production. Produced, written and directed by Janis Cole, Holly Dale. Camera (color), John Walker, Sandi Sissel, Judy Irola; editor, Cole; sound, Aerlyn Weissman, Alan Barker; music, Lauri Conger. Reviewed at Bloor Cinema, Toronto, Sept. 2, 1988. (In Toronto Festival of Festivals, Perspective Canada.) Running time: 118 MIN.

■ Toronto — Toronto filmmakers Janis Cole and Holly Dale are to be commended for their accomplished and detailed documentary on the struggles of women directors, screenwriters, and producers in "Calling The Shots."

Duo displayed their slick interviewing skills and editing techniques in "Hookers On Davie" and "PW4: Prison for Women," and carried them through smoothly to this pic.

It's a must for fest circuits, and with proper handling should find specialized playoffs. While it may seem like the same old story to cinephiles, mainstream film audiences will be intrigued to hear these difficult, funny and creative memoirs of female filmmakers in an industry that has been a bit unyielding to them.

With interviews from filmmakers as divergent as Lizzie Borden and Jeanne Moreau, pic taps into their personal ordeals and victories. Susan Seidelman recalls the battles she had convincing the studio to cast Madonna in "Desperately Seeking Susan;" Sandy Wilson ("My American Cousin") remembers "dining for dollars" to raise capital for her film; Claudio Weill ("Girlfriends") admits that docu filmmaking was her passport to the field; Martha Coolidge ("Valley Girl") states that every success that has happened to women directors has affected other women directors. Yet the flops made by women are held against them as well as all women directors.

Talks with Randa Haines, Ann Hui, Mai Zetterling, Karen Arthur, Donna Deitch, Joan Tewkesbury, Margarethe von Trotta, Joan Micklin Silver, Agnès Varda, Amy Heckerling, Lee Grant and Léa Pool provide an international and historical chronicle.

There's footage of these directors in action on their sets and clips from the films under discussion. Culled

from innumerable hours of interviews, the results on screen are pungent, probing, and witty.

Cole and Dale have used talking heads shots almost exclusively without any narration and that works in creating an intimacy with the subjects. —Devo.

The Place In The Sun
(SOUTH KOREAN)

A New Bird production. Produced by Young Y. Jin, Ann Jin. Executive producer, John Song. Written and directed by Young Y. Jin. Camera (color), Shin Ouk Hyun; editor, Lee Kyoug Ja; music, Kim Soo Chul; art direction, Na Han Ho; sound, Kim Kyng Il. Reviewed at Toronto Festival of Festivals, Sept. 10, 1988. Running time: 90 MIN.
With: Chun Ho Jin, You Dong Kun, Yun Il Bong, Jung Hye Sun, Yun Yang Ha, Kim Hyung Ja, Kim Boo Sun.

■ Toronto — Young Y. Jin's feature debut is an assured and culturally enlightening effort that is a bit bogged down by blatant symbolism.

Although a more somber film, "A Place In The Sun" may find the same audiences who appreciated the nuances and flavor of Juzo Itami's "The Funeral," but in this outing it's the Korean mix of Christian and native religious practices that is considered.

Film kicks off with a clip from the 1987 Reagan-Gorbachev summit, celebrating the nations' reconciliation, then proceeds with the narrative.

Man Ji is a student living in Los Angeles who is summoned home to Seoul to visit his sick father in the hospital, but arrives to late. The rich industrialist left him and his mother behind, as well as an illegitimate son, Min Woo.

Man Ji, as chief mourner, must organize the funeral, greet the mourners, accept their condolences and arrange the burial. The funeral rites of Korea are open for illumination as well as satire, and the universal family conflicts come to the forefront.

The deceased company president was the rival of his brother-in-law, who during the mourning craftily announces his own plans to redevelop the business. Man Ji tries to make his older brother (a garage mechanic) the chief mourner, but since Min Woo has taken his mother's name and has had a lifetime of bitterness since his father abandoned him, he refuses.

Man Ji's high school mates come by to pay their respects and are hilariously inexperienced in funeral etiquette. We see mourners paying condolence money at the door. The dead father's mistress shows up at the mourner's hall and everyone acknowledges this as another fact of the deceased's life.

Family life, friendships and business associations are all dissected and rearranged here. Tech credits are first-rate, with crisp camerawork and nicely paced editing.

Young Y. Jin has elicited fine performances from his cast, full of subtlety and sharp humor. His script could have ended with the touching reconciliation between the two brothers, instead of continuing with them assisting a pregnant lady give birth after they return from their father's funeral.

It's not only a sibling truce but a North and South Korea reunion that is the heavy-handed subtext here. —*Devo.*

The Search For
The Kidnappers
(BRITISH-DOCU)

A Central Independent TV, (U.K.), coproduction with Mario Arruda, Vincente Rios and the Universidade Catolica de Goias. Produced by Roger James. Directed by Adrian Cowell. Camera (color, 16m), Chris Cox, Pasco MacFarlane, Rios, Jimmy Dribling; editor, Terence Twigg; sound, Albert Bailey, Godfrey Kirby, Vandorlei de Castro, Clive Pendry; narration written and spoken by Cowell. Previewed at Margaret Mead Film Festival, N.Y., Sept. 14, 1988. Running time: **75 MIN.**

■ "The Search For The Kidnappers" is the first of four films within the award-winning British tv series, "The Decade Of Destruction," tracing the commercial exploitation of the Brazilian rain forest, which will be 80% destroyed before the turn of the century.

Producer Adrian Cowell, who has spent more than 10 years in Brazil, has achieved an intelligent, austere but moving account of how greed and ignorance combine to obliterate vast tracts of virgin jungle.

"Kidnappers" is part thriller, as a search party sets out to rescue 7-year-old Fabio, kidnaped by Indians. Fabio and his two older brothers were sons of the Prestes family, one of the impoverished families from Brazil's rural south who are being resettled in the Amazon basin as the government burns and bulldozes the jungle, clearing the land for highways and for farming.

Dispossessed Indians nearby, their sources of game and fish vanished, retaliate with rains of arrows against the poor frontier farmers plowing their new land. The two teenage Prestes brothers are killed, while Fabio is seized. A search party, including Cowell and his cameras, sets out, trying not to provoke the Indians.

Thus "Kidnappers" is partly the trek to retrieve Fabio, and partly a report on the ecological disaster taking place within the enormous Amazonian subcontinent. For the nomadic Indians, who were decimated by the white man's smallpox, further resistance seems a lost cause. Bullets and bulldozers, dredges and power-saws, shatter the Indian way of life. Disease and drunkenness

await those Indians who approach out of the trees to join the white man in his rough frontier towns.

Ironically, the government's energetic but clumsy program of colonization is in vain, as the Amazonian soil is too thin and arid to support farming. Even the vast coffee plantations fail, and abandoned, eroded fields with forlorn stumps are left.

In time, the Prestes family and other farmers are forced to become sharecroppers to survive. We learn Fabio's fate — the Indian kidnapers, who had intended to raise him as their own, killed the little boy on the trail because he cried too much and couldn't keep up. There are tears aplenty in this sad tale of misguided colonialization. —*Hitch.*

Further And Particular
(BRITISH)

A Spectre Prods./La Maison de la Culture du Havre/Channel 4 production. Produced by Simon Hartog. Written and directed by Stephen Dwoskin. Camera (color), Dwoskin; editor, Anthea Kennedy, Dwoskin; music, Schaun Tozer; sound, Stan Phillips. Reviewed at Toronto Festival of Festivals, Sept. 14 1988. Running time: **110 MIN.**

With: Richard Butler, Bruce Cooper, Jean Fennell, Irene Marot, Julia Righton, Nicola Warren, Carola Regnier.

■ Toronto — **Avant-garde artist and filmmaker Stephen Dwoskin experiments with camera-eye reflections on the mutability of memory in a difficult counter-realistic work, "Further And Particular." This piece, intended for only the most rarefied sensibilities, should be high on the list of avant-garde programmers.**

Dwoskin plunges into the murky waters of recollected psychosexual pain in a non-linear narrative concerning a tormented intellectual's memories of his domineering, hedonistic mother, her younger lesbian lover and the nymphet she procured for her son's own initiation into the mysteries of pleasure. Dwoskin's people are addicted to an idealized, interiorized concept of love, struggling for its attainment with great torment from which there is no apparent relief.

Using an ensemble of highly skilled actors, Dwoskin permits his camera to linger for long interludes on faces distorted with a complex play of soul-stretching emotions. The filmmaker shows considerable imagination in choreographing sexual fantasy sequences, and a penchant for dark humor in rambling monologs that come across in postmodernized Shakespearean cadences.

Dwoskin's characters inhabit a hermetic world where cerebral and sensual passions intersect in a dreamscape that's alternately repelling and fascinating. —*Rich.*

Romance
(BRAZILIAN)

A Brazilian Film Foundation release of an S.B. Producoes Cinematograficas-Embrafilm production. Directed by Sergio Bianchi. Screenplay, Fernando Coni Campos, Mario Carneiro, Caio Fernando de Abreu; camera (color), Marcelo Coutinho; editor, Marilla Alvim; music, Chance. Reviewed at Bloor Cinema, Toronto, Sept. 2, 1988. (In Toronto Festival of Festivals). Running time: **103 MIN.**

With: Rodrigo Santiago, Imara Reis, Hugo Della Santa, Isa Kopelma.

■ Toronto — **First-time feature director Sergio Bianchi has journeyed into corrosive political territory in "Romance," a hard-edged Brazilian entry about the repercussions of a left-wing intellectual's death.**

Pic could be of interest to Spanish-speaking territories, but it'll be a rough pitch to mainstream audiences.

When artist and intellectual Antonio Cesar dies in the middle of writing a scathing book exposing local politicians responsible for the release of pesticides in the country and the sale of adulterated drugs, three people are specifically affected. His girlfriend Fernanda tries to live out Cesar's liberal social philosophy, believing the collective dreams are the source of collective revolution. She parties wildly and freely and winds up going mad.

Journalist Regina is convinced that Cesar's death and the disappearance of his book was engineered by the people he was denouncing, and goes to friends and relatives for answers. She ingratiates herself to the local minister, and after his henchmen try to run her over with a car, she sells out and works for the bureaucrats in the name of Cesar.

Andre, Cesar's homosexual roommate, is overcome by the loss of his friend, and has anonymous sexual encounters to alleviate his depression.

Bianchi intercuts footage of Cesar's political speeches with segments of the three characters' disenchanted personal journeys. Cesar rages about the retention of the wealth in the hands of the few, that the model of the U.S. seems to have taken over Brazil's senses and that the country operates on the level of incompetence. The director gives these scenes the proper sense of urgency.

The principals are involved in compelling yet depressing struggles. Performances are mostly fine, with just a bit too much histrionics from Fernanda. Music is used dramatically to good effect, too.

Some disjointed filmmaking sequences and explicit gay sexual encounters are troublesome, but the writing is sharp and hard-hitting.

Film's premise of disillusioned

political stances in Brazil today is ultimately so bleak that when Fernanda jumps off her apartment ledge, much of the audience wants to join her. —*Devo.*

Shadow Dancing
(CANADIAN)

A Shapiro Glickenhaus Entertainment release of a Source Prods. production. Produced by Kay Bachman. Executive producers, Robert Phillips, Don Haig. Directed by Lewis Furey. Screenplay, Christine Foster; camera (color), Rene Ohashi; music, Jay Gruska; sound editor, Michael Dandy; production design, Barbra Matis; choreography, Timothy Spain; casting, Lucinda Sill. Reviewed at Filmhouse screening room, Toronto (in-Toronto Festival of Festivals), Aug. 29, 1988. Running time: **105 MIN.**

Jessica/Lili . . . . .Nadine Van der Velde
Edmund Beaumont . Christopher Plummer
Paul .James Kee
Philip Crest . . . . .Gregory Osborne
Anthony Podopolis . . . . .John Colicos
Grace Meyerhoff . . . . .Charmion King
Sophie Beaumont . . . . .Kay Tremblay
Nicole . . . . .Shirley Douglas
Alexei Karnov . . . . .Brent Carver

■ Toronto — **Even a principal dancer from the National Ballet of Canada and a flock of vet Canadian thesps can't remedy "Shadow Dancing" 's only marginally interesting choreography and fatuous script.**

Aside from the peripheral "Flashdance" associations in the plot, this Lewis Furey ("Night Magic") directorial effort will make a quick dash to the video shelves.

Ostensibly a mystery set in the world of contempo dance, story centers on ambitious young hoofer Jessica (Nadine Van der Velde), who must have attended the Jennifer Beals school of acting. By default she nabs a role as company member in the Philip Crest (National Ballet's Gregory Osborne) dance troupe, which is hoping to revive the old, ornate Edmund Beaumont theater with a vital new work. Seems that 50 years ago Beaumont (Christopher Plummer) was in love with the dynamic dancer Lili La Nuit, who mysteriously died during a performance of "Medusa."

Beaumont now lives in the dilapidated theater, haunted by memories of his old flame. Jessica, however, gradually taps into the ghostly vibrations of Lili, dons her lace shawls and Medusa masks, encounters Lili's ex-lover Karnov (Brent Carver) and, once totally taken over by her spirit, re-creates Lili's final dance on the altar.

Furey makes sure the music swells to ominous tones to preface any "danger" that might lurk behind a diaphanous curtain. There's little subtlety in Christine Foster's screenplay, so any possibility of a mystical revelation is evaporated quickly.

There are some interesting techniques touched on in the way cinematographer Rene Ohashi covers dance and movement via slo-mo leaps and mirroring images, but that can't mask the lackluster choreography.

Spare efforts are made by Canadian vets who play mostly thankless roles: Charmion King as a wealthy arts patron who still pines for Beaumont; Shirley Douglas as a hard-edged assistant and lover of the young dance director; Brent Carver as Lili's brooding Russian lover; John Colicos as a curious theater critic; and Kay Tremblay as a dotty sister.

Plummer tries to create a pale Edwardian oddity in his Beaumont, but isn't helped by his lines. Osborne is strong on charisma but short on vocal skills to carry off his role as the difficult director.

"Shadow Dancing" will leap quickly off the screen without a trace. — *Devo*.

Student Affairs

A Platinum Pictures production. Produced and directed by Chuck Vincent. Screenplay, Craig Horrall, Vincent, from story idea by John Weidner; camera (color), Larry Revene; editor, Marc Ubell (Vincent), James Davalos, Chip Lambert; music, Flash Cadillac & the Continental Kids; sound, Peter Penguin, Alexandra Baltarzuk; art direction, D. Gary Phelps; assistant director, Andrew E. Kristie; production manager, Buck Westminster; associate producers, Bill Slobodian, Jeanne O'Grady; casting, John Amero. Reviewed on Vestron vidcassette, N.Y., Aug. 27, 1988. MPAA Rating: R. Running time: **94 MIN.**
Louie Balducci . . . . Louie Bonanno
Andy Armstrong. . . . . .Jim Abele
Kelly . . . . .Deborah Blaisdell
Alexis . . . . Beth Broderick
Devon Wheeler . . . . Alan Fisler
Veronica Harper . . . . .Jane Hamilton
Rudy . . . . .Richard Parnes
B.C. . . . . .Ron Sullivan
Also with: Janice Doskey, W.P. Dremak, John Fasano, Jeanne Marie, Andy Nichols, Molly O'Mara, David F. Friedman, Eddie Prevot, Adam Fried.

■ **The notion of doing a behind-the-scenes "Day For Night"-type treatment of high school comedies delivers very little in "Student Affairs," a 1986 production debuting on video.**

Prolific filmmaker Chuck Vincent rounds up his usual complement of adult film performers (Tracey Adams, Veronica Hart, billed as Deborah Blaisdell, Jane Hamilton) plus mainstream thesps to portray actors and crew shooting a '50s teenpic, "Oakwood High," in New Jersey.

Film-within-a film is utterly banal, as are the tribulations of an uppity actor on set (Jim Abele), the centerfold beauty trying to prove her acting mettle (all-too-true role for Adams/Blaisdell) and a disgruntled screenwriter interfering with the shoot (Andy Nichols).

Concept of watching thesps in three separate personas (auditioning to impress, in film roles and "real life") turns out to be synthetic. Only coup is the very believable thesping by Ron Sullivan as the

"Oakwood" pic director; he's the prolific adult film helmer usually credited as Henri Pachard.

Credit Vincent for trying something different, but without many laughs it's hard to watch as a "Porky's" carbon. —*Lor*.

Ballhaus Barmbek
(Let's Kiss And Say Goodbye)
(WEST GERMAN)

A Roxy-Film-Filmverlag der Autoren production. Produced by Luggi Waldleitner. Written and directed by Christel Buschmann. Camera (color), Mike Gast; editor, Nani Schumann; art direction, Heidrun Brandt; sound, Willi Krollpfeifer. Reviewed at Toronto Festival of Festivals, Sept. 16, 1988. Running time: **80 MIN.**
With: Jorg Pfenningwerth, Ulrich Tukur, Kiev Stingl, Eva-Maria Hagen, Jutta Jenthe, Rocko Schamoni, Joey Buschmann, Zazie de Paris, Nico.

■ **Toronto — Director Christel Buschmann was so enthralled with Hamburg's Ballhaus Barmbek, the setting for her segment of the 4-femme-helmed "Felix," that she decided to film a feature there. "Let's Kiss And Say Goodbye" studies the alienated souls that frequent the dance hall in an unconventional, unstructured way, which makes it a tough sell outside of art and specialty houses.**

With echoes of Ettore Scola's "Le Bal," the pic loosely travels from one patron to another, all of whom are society's fringe members. An obese Elvis groupie sets up a shrine to the King, while an Elvis impersonator confesses that in Elvis he found everything he ever needed. The house stud, a.k.a. the Swinging Axel, has to satisfy all the sexually starved matrons by seductively dancing with them and listening to their marital woes. An old bald man rails out poetry about destruction.

The ballroom has telephones at each table as a social convenience to speed up the mating process. A black American guitarist sings the blues, while two single girls get up the nerve to phone a guy at a nearby table.

The soundtrack is filled with nonstop German and English songs about lost love, loneliness, and death, with quick bits of conversation peppered above the lyrics.

Each actor — both professional and amateur — gets a chance to either sing or lip-synch an appropriately wrenching song. Camerawork is haunting and the music score is the key to highlight these wandering misfits.

Buschmann's script, such as it is, is injected with humor as well as compassion. Audiences have a chance to be voyeurs in this fringe landscape. While it worked for 20 minutes in "Felix," Buschmann's effort doesn't successfully support a feature-length evening at the ballhaus. —*Devo*.

Alias Will James
(CANADIAN-DOCU)

A National Film Board release of a National Film Board production. Produced by Eric Michel. Written and directed by Jacques Godbout. Camera (color), Jean-Pierre Lachapelle; editor, Monique Fortier; music, Robert M. Lepage; sound effects, Vital Millette; location sound, Richard Besse; assistant director, Serge Lafortune; animation camera, Raymond Dumas. Reviewed at Montreal World Film Festival (noncompeting), Aug. 30, 1988. Running time: **83 MIN.**

■ **Montreal — "Alias Will James" is an ambitious National Film Board picture that should get some attention from international distributors for its light approach to the subject of French Canada's identity complex.**

The story centers on cowboy writer Will James, whose books about the West were considered the genuine article in the 1920s and '30s. Several were turned into Western films, helping to perpetuate the myth of the stoic Western hero.

Although Will James knew the West as well as any rodeo cowboy of his time, he was born and raised in Quebec of French Canadian parents. As the film shows, his autobiography never acknowledged that background and, in interviews with relatives of James — real name: Ernest Dufault — director Jacques Godbout reveals that James wrote letters to his family pleading that they never tell the truth about his identity.

Godbout's film would have been interesting enough had he stopped there, but the pic gets better when Godbout shows that French Canadian cowboys haven't changed too much since James' time. Through interviews and brief tours with rodeo cowboys Daniel David and Michel Benard, he demonstrates they too would rather just slip into an American identity.

The point he makes is that the French Canadian — like his English counterpart — measures success by the degree of acceptance in the American marketplace. For a French Canadian, slipping out of the cultural and linguistic conditioning is far more difficult and uncomfortable.

By using the extraordinary example of James, and by mixing in two modern French Canadians as reinforcement, the director has fashioned a thesis that is entertaining and certainly has far greater market potential than other strident documentaries about the problems of North America's French Canadian minority.—*Cadd*.

Tales From The Gimli Hospital
(CANADIAN-B&W)

A Winnipeg Film Group release of an Extra Large production. Produced, written,

directed, edited and camera (b&w), by Guy Maddin. Assistant director, Kyle McCulloch; art direction, Jeff Solylo; story consultant, George Toles. Reviewed at Montreal World Film Festival (Panorama Canada), Aug. 31, 1988. Running time: **72 MIN.**
Einar, the lonely . . . . .Kyle McCulloch
Gunnar . . . . .Michael Gottli
Snjofridur . . . . .Angela Heck
Amma . . . . .Margaret Anne McLeod
Elfa Egilsdottir . . . . .Caroline Bonner

■ **Montreal — Guy Maddin's innovative "Gimli Hospital" is a brave first feature that has built-in market limitations. The story of two men who share a hospital room during a turn-of-the-century smallpox epidemic, it is shot in black and white to simulate silent films.**

There is some dubbed sound but the process has the feel of the era in which it is set. That will appeal to academic institutions but probably won't give it legs in theatrical release.

Its video potential might also be limited, if not by the process then by the violent hospital scenes. Although the blood is in black, there is a sense of revulsion that comes with scenes that could turn off distributors looking for some family video release for what would otherwise be acceptable family viewing, considering that the premise is a children's tale. —*Cadd*.

Urinal
(CANADIAN)

A John Greyson production. Produced, written and directed by Greyson. Camera (color), Adam Swica (film), Almerinda Trassavos, Greyson (video); editor, David McIntosh (film), Greyson (video); music, Glenn Schellenberg; sound, Bill Lasovich, Marg Moores. Reviewed at Toronto Festival of Festivals, Sept. 9, 1988. Running time: **100 MIN.**
With: Pauline Carey, Paul Bettis, Mark Gomes, Keltie Creed, Olivia Rojas, David Gonzales, Karl Beveridge, Clive Robertson, Lance Eng.

■ **Toronto — "Urinal" is an overproduced, funny, sociologically jolting first feature by Toronto video artist John Greyson, whose excesses make much of the film vexing.**

While the subject matter — an examination of the official harassment of men who have gay sex in public washrooms — makes it a must-see on the gay fest circuit, it will have an uphill battle for mainstream audiences.

Greyson assembles a group of prominent deceased gay and lesbian artists in a Toronto garden to accept a mission in 1987 to discover why there is so much widespread persecution against the gays in present-day Ontario and the thrust behind the arrests of gay men who are having sex in public facilities.

At the home of sculptor Florence Wyle are gathered fictional Dorian Gray, director Sergei Eisenstein, writer Yukio Mishima, poet Langston Hughes, Mexican painter Frida Kahlo, and sculptor Frances Loring.

Dorian Gray infiltrates the police force, while the rest do their research and make presentations on such topics as the history of the toilet seat, the first public bathrooms, and variations on theme of gay sex. There are bios of each of the principals and quotes from their diaries, elucidating details about gay and lesbian history.

Greyson includes tours of Toronto's most famous "tearooms," with descriptions of arrests by undercover cops, confessions of men (in elaborate masks and disguises) who have washroom sex, and admission by a man arrested for gross indecency. One guy admits AIDS seems to have taken some of the fun out of washroom sex, but there are ways to compensate.

Pic is the work of the ultimate video artist, with washes of experimental video techniques punctuating each still, alternated with docu bits, interviews and voiceover narration. There are fictional interviews with the artists as well as real discussions with gay activists and victims of the police raids.

Greyson suffuses the film with so much information and imagery that much of the message is weakened. The acting is stilted and awkward, but the effect of the ensemble is high camp.

While pic is overly ambitious it makes its points by blending humor with facts about pervasive homosexual discrimination. Because the issue of the repeal of Ontario's gross indecency law in 1988 and the ramifications of public washroom sex are so compelling, "Urinal" may have worked better as a "straight" documentary. —Devo.

Finding Mary March
(CANADIAN)

A Malofilm Group release of a Red Ochre Prods. production. Produced, written and directed by Ken Pittman. Camera, (color) Michael Jones; editor, Derek Norman; music, Paul Steffler, Pam Morgan; set design, Pam Hall; sound, Jim Rillie; costumes, Peggy Hogan; assistant director, Paul Pops. Reviewed at Montreal World Film Festival (Panorama Canada), Aug. 31, 1988. Running time: **90 MIN.**
Nancy George . . . . Andrée Pelletier
Ted Buchans . . . . Rick Boland
Bernadette Buchans . . . . Tara Manual
Micmac Boy . . . . Yvon Joe
Mary March . . . . Jacinta Cormier

■ **Montreal — Newfoundland's "Finding Mary March" might do well with some theatrical dates in its home province but probably won't buck the tradition of poor results for Canadian historical films.**

To its credit, it takes a slightly different approch to history — telling the fictional story of a modern search for the graves of the last living members of the Beothuk tribe of Indians, wiped out in the early 1800s by Europeans who hunted the natives down for sport.

That could give pic enough modern appeal to convince some foreign distribs its story is universal, since most countries have some interest in reviving the lore of its indigenous peoples. However, "Finding Mary March" spends a lot of time examining the relationship between its two chief protagonists. One is a native guide searching for his Micmac wife, lost while looking for the grave of the last Beothuk, Mary March — to whom she believes she was related.

The other is a photographer who also is looking for Beothuk graves but thinks they may give her insight into her own native ancestry. Stilted telling of their stories limits the personal history, the history of the Beothuks and probably any foreign or Canadian distribution potential. *Cadd.*

Tabu
(Taboo)
(POLISH)

A Polish Film Corp. "Oko" Unit production. Directed by Andrzej Baranski. Screenplay, Baranski, based on the novel by Timo Mukki; camera (color), Krzysztof Ptak; editor, Marek Denys; music, Zygmunt Konieczny; art direction, Boleslaw Kamykowski; production manager, Kostanty Lewkowicz. Reviewed at the Gdynia Film Festival, Sept. 14, 1988. Running time: **105 MIN.**
Mother . . . . Grazyna Szapolowska
Milka . . . . . Bernadett Machala-Krzeminska
Krystian . . . . Krzysztof Gosztyla
Organist . . . . Bronislaw Pawlik
Also with: Zofia Merle, Olaf Lubaszenko (Stefek).

■ **Gdynia — After "Woman From The Provinces," Andrzej Baranski tackles another tale of tragic female relations in "Taboo." Beautifully lensed, sensitively shot, slow but ultimately touching, "Taboo" should be of special interest to fest and art house programers looking for solid craftsmanship over flash.**

Story comes from a Finnish novel (already lensed in Finland) about the tragic love triangle that develops among a mother, daughter and farmhand. Baranski takes the story back to the last century and sets it entirely in sweeping fields and simple interiors.

Grazyna Szapolowska is a good-looking widow, living alone on the farm her husband left her with teenage daughter Milka (Bernadette Machala-Krzeminska). Her sunny disposition improves whenever their neighbor Krystian (Krzysztof Gosztyla) comes around to help in the fields. He would probably marry her if the restless daughter didn't decide to seduce him at all costs.

Krystian gives in to Milka's provocation and becomes the girl's secret lover (as well as the mother's). When the scene gets too hot, he runs away, leaving the mother shattered and the daughter pregnant.

The mother loses her mind with grief. The daughter, a more practical spirit, marries an ugly old organist who had been courting her mother and works out a fairly happy life. In a poetic finale, the mother burns herself inside Krystian's abandoned cottage.

Slow pace will put off some, but patient viewers will appreciate scenes constructed with reverent care. Psychology of the three comes out little by little, without false moralizing, and minimum dialog.

Cinematographer by Krzysztof Ptak is execeptional and greatly contributes to film's atmosphere of languid tragedy, which may not be tragedy as much as the natural order of things. Cast is first-rate, particularly Szapolowska as the mother and bewitching newcomer Machala-Kreminska as seductive Milka.

A simple 3-note melody by Zygmunt Konieczny effectively accompanies scenes with its eerie tune. —*Yung.*

Pericles In America
(DOCU)

Produced, directed, camera (color, 16m), and edited by John Cohen. Assistant camera, Rufus Cohen; sound, Rufus Cohen, Dena Schutzer, Connie Kieltyka, Bob Bielecki; associate editor, Schutzer; liaison, Epirot community and Greek government, Ethyl Raim and Martin Koenig of Ethnic Folk Center; translators, Leslie Ergli, Takis Petrakos; voiceover, Petrakos. Produced with assistance of Greek Ministry of Culture and N.Y. Epirot Society. Reviewed at Margaret Mead Film Festival, Sept. 14, 1988. Running time: **70 MIN.**

■ **The Pericles of this film is not the great statesman of ancient Greece but Pericles Halkias, elderly Greek-American clarinetist who, with several hundred thousand other Greek-Americans, lives in Astoria, Queens.**

The film traces the Halkias clan, with its seven generations of musicians, also examining other Greek-Americans, to whom Greek tradition remains very strong. This is a likable, entertaining film with lots of colorful, even eccentric Greek mountain folk who love to play music, sing and dance. A drop of Ouzo washes the film down very nicely.

Pericles Halkias has been given a National Heritage Award from the National Endowment for the Arts, in recognition of his musical excellence and efforts to preserve traditional Epirot music. In the film, he is pessimistic because most young Greeks and Greek-Americans today prefer modern rhythms and instrumentation, neglecting their musical roots.

Part of "Pericles" is devoted to George Rabos, handsome young hard-working Greek-American who longs for the native village of his childhood. His intense patriotism for his homeland, especially the northwest province of Epirus, adjacent to hostile Albania, is one motif of the film — once a Greek, always a Greek. Yet the "Greekness" of these Greek-Americans does not diminish their Americanized allegiances and attributes. These people are not halved, but doubled. After George returns to his parents' village to choose a bride, Athena, and after the Greek Orthodox ceremony and the old-fashioned wedding feast, he brings her back to the U.S., to the Immigration office, to be naturalized.

Sung in Greek, translated with English subtitles, songs often concern love, work, family, long-ago wars, and the pain of farewell as young people leave the village to migrate abroad. —*Hitch.*

Okhota Na Lis
(Foxhunting)
(SOVIET)

A Mosfilm production. Directed by Vadim Abdrashitov. Screenplay, Alexander Mindadze; camera (Sovcolor), Yuri Nevsky; music, Eduard Artemiev; production design, Vladimir Korovin. Reviewed at Toronto Festival of Festivals, Sept. 11, 1988. Running time: **95 MIN.**
With: Vladimir Gostukhin, Irina Muravieva, Igor Nefyodof, Andrei Turkov, D. Kharatian.

■ **Toronto — "Foxhunting" is an incisive drama in which a victim of a mugging identifies to the police his assailant, who's duly arrested and imprisoned.**

Belov (the victim of the attack) then starts to visit Vladimir (his attacker) in the clink to try to find out why the youth turned to crime, and to help with his redemption and eventual return to become a useful member of society.

It's hard to see why this 1980 production suffered a delayed release, unless it was as a result of the image of youthful drifters and petty criminals seen in the strikingly filmed opening sequence as a police patrol drives through a wood at night, its spotlight falling on numerous groups of sullen and disrespectvul youngsters.

Director Vadim Abdrashitov is best known for his 1984 pic "Planets On Parade," which toured the international fest circuit a couple of years ago. —*Strat.*

Painted Faces
(HONG KONG)

A Golden Harvest-Shaw Brothers production. Executive producers, Leonard Ho, Mona Fong. Produced by Mabel Cheung, Alex Law. Directed by Law. Screenplay, Yeung Ting; camera (color), David Chung; editor, Timothy Yu; music, Lowell Lo; production design, Yank Wong. Reviewed at Toronto Festival of Festivals, Sept. 17, 1988. Running time: **100 MIN.**
With: Sammo Hung, Kam-bo, Chang Pei-pei, Lam Ching-ying, John Sham.

■ **Toronto** — "Painted Faces" is an affectionate tribute to the Peking Opera School, now closed down but, in the '60s, training ground for such popular Hong Kong stars as Jackie Chan and Sammo Hung.

Hung plays the school's director and, apparently, only instructor, a man devoutly dedicated to a dying art of traditional training for Chinese actors.

The film opens in 1962 with the enrollment of an eager 9-year-old by his mother, who signs a contract agreeing the boy will train for 10 years. The film then follows the rigorous training procedures, early (not successful) attempts at putting on a show, and the way the teacher copes with discipline problems. There's even romance as the boys mix with students of a girls' academy.

The boys are delightful, and Hung, in a role different from his usual over-the-top characterizations, is excellent as the kindly, dedicated, tenacious teacher. This is the first film directed by Alex Law (Law Kai-yui) and he demonstrates a talent for observation and detail that should result in an interesting career. —*Strat.*

Tadpole And The Whale
(CANADIAN)

A New World Mutual release (in Canada) of a Prods. La Fête production. Produced by Rock Demers. Directed by Jean-Claude Lord. Screenplay, Jacques Bobet, André Melançon, from original idea by Bobet; camera (color), Tom Burstyn; editor, Helene Girard; music, Guy Trepanier, Normand Dubé; costumes, Hugette Gagne; art direction, Dominique Ricard; sound, Serge Beauchemin. Reviewed at Toronto Festival of Festivals, Sept. 17, 1988. Running time: **92 MIN.**

Daphne . . . . Fanny Lauzier
Michael . . . . Denis Forest
Julie . . . . Marina Orsini
Alex . . . . Félix-Antoine Leroux
Ann . . . . Lise Thouin
Daphne's mother . . . . Louise Richer
Daphne's father . . . . Thomas Donohue
Grandpa Hector . . . . Roland Laroche

■ **Toronto** — "Tadpole And The Whale," the sixth family pic from Montreal's Prods. La Fête is a winsome adventure of a young girl and her affection for a dolphin and whales and vice versa.

Fanny Lauzier, a young freckle-faced charmer, makes a bright screen debut playing wih the dolphin at her family's summer tourist resort and enlisting a friendly tourist couple in her adventures. Along the way, she helps rescue a trapped whale and is herself rescued underwater by her pal the dolphin. She also prevents grandpa from selling the resort. Her nickname is tadpole.

Director Jean-Claude Lord keeps the action brisk and the script by Jacques Bobet and André Melançon is believable. English dubbing of the Quebec French-track pic is good, as are production values. So is the cuddly, kissable dolphin. The adult

cast turns in efficient performances.
Kids at home and abroad should like this one and international tv sales also should be splashy.
—*Adil.*

Glembajevi
(The Glembays)
(YUGOSLAV)

A Jugoslavija Film presentation of a Jadran Film, Zagreb TV production. Directed by Antun Vrdoljak. Screenplay, Vrodljak, based on play and novel by Miroslav Krleza; camera (Eastmancolor), Vjekoslav Vrdoljak; editor, Damir German; music, Arsen Dedic; sound, Jurica Breges; art direction, Zeljko Senecic; costumes, Ika Skomrlj; makeup, Berta Meglic; production manager, Ljubo Sikic. Reviewed at Pula Film Festival (competing), July 29, 1988. Running time: **119 MIN.**

Leon Glembay . . . . Mustafa Nadarevic
Baroness Castelli . . . . Ena Begovic
Ignazio Glembay . . . . Tonko Lonza
Angelica . . . . Bernarda Oman
Also with: Matko Raguz (priest), Zarko Potocnjak (lawyer), Zvonimir Strmac (uncle), Zvonimir Zoricic (butler).

■ **Pula** — An adaptation of a famous play which never manages to depart from its stage origins, this sumptuous drama looks very much like a tv product. Indeed, there is already a 3-hour version prepared for the small screen.

Alternating between long shots (to show off the excellent production values) and closeups (the one and only angle the actors are allowed to perform in), this is a heavy-handed affair, overburdened by lengthy dialogue passages transposed to the screen in a conventional manner.

The portrait of a self-destructive banking family in Zagreb on the eve of World War I, it leads to the family's annihilation when Leon, the only surviving son from the banker's previous marriage, a painter living abroad, comes home for a brief visit and reveals to his father the treacherous nature of his young wife, a supposed baroness. He's out to revenge the death of his mother, brother and sister, who all committed suicide.

All the performances are theatrically top-heavy, an attitude possibly resulting from excessive respect for author Miroslav Krleza, a leading literary figure. The only liberties director Antun Vrdoljak allows himself are brief flashbacks to substantiate Leon's consuming passions, and imaginary conversations he holds with his dead mother, but even these are presented stagily.

The film is highly polished and response of local Pula audience was enthusiastic. —*Edna.*

Burning Snow
(TAIWANESE)

A Hasua-pu production. Produced by Chian Mei-teng. Directed by Patrick Tam. Screenplay, Tam, Ming-Long Lai; camera

(color), no credit supplied; editor, Teh-yiang Cho; production design, Tam. Reviewed at Toronto Festival of Festivals, Sept. 10, 1988. Running time: **84 MIN.**

With: Erh-liu Wong, Ta-wah Jen, Lin Pai, Hou-si, Chin-cheng Yeh.

■ **Toronto** — Stylishly directed by Hong Kong director Patrick Tam, this melodramatic tale of sex and violence should do well on Asian cinema circuits, but internationally its appeal will be limited to Asian film buffs, since its unsubtle acting style is inferior to that seen in the work of the best Taiwanese directors.

Plot is similar to that of James M. Cain's "The Postman Always Rings Twice." A pretty young girl is forced to marry a much older man who runs a roadside bar. He's a drunken brute who regularly rapes her.

Then along comes a young man on the run from the police and wanted for murder. The wife hides him and they become passionate lovers. The husband finds out and betrays the youth to the cops, who gun him down; the wife stabs her husband to death.

Acting is unrestrained, but Tam does have an interesting visual style. The film is usually striking to watch, even when the plot mechanics get more and more out of control.
—*Strat.*

The Majorettes

A Major Films presentation of a Ross & Hinzman production. Produced by John Russo. Executive producer, J.C. Ross. Directed by Bill Hinzman. Screenplay, Russo, based on his novel; camera (WRS color), Paul McCollough; editor, Hinzman, McCollough; music, McCollough; sound, Eric Baca; special effects & makeup, Gerald Gergely; casting, Cassandra Ross, Tom Madden, Raymond Laine. Reviewed on Vestron vidcassette, N.Y., Aug. 20, 1988. MPAA Rating: R. Running time: **92 MIN.**

Jeff . . . . Kevin Kindlin
Vicky . . . . Terrie Godfrey
Sheriff Braden . . . . Mark V. Jevicky
Judy . . . . Sueanne Seamens
Helga . . . . Denise Huot
Roland . . . . Carl Hetrick
Also with: Mary Jo Limpert, Harold K. Keller, Tom E. Desrocher, Jacqueline Bowman, Colin Martin, Russ Streiner, John Russo, Bill Hinzman.

■ **Several alumni of George A. Romero's "Night Of The Living Dead"** made the strictly ordinary stalker horror film "The Majorettes," just released direct-to-video.

The cheerleaders for a high school football team are being knocked off by a hooded maniac. Effective plot revolves around greedy nurse Helga (Denise Huot) plotting to use the killings as a cover for her disposing of her rich employer and pretty granddaughter Vicky (Terrie Godfrey) in order to grab a $500,000 inheritance.

John Russo's screenplay contains several interesting twists, particularly the involvement of the local sheriff in the deaths, and an amoral con-

clusion. Unfortunately, execution by helmer Bill Hinzman is routine and the acting is poor, often amateurish. Production values are likewise weak. —*Lor.*

I skugga Hrafnsina
(In The Shadow Of The Raven)
(ICELANDIC-SWEDISH)

A Sandrews (Sweden) release of Cinema Art (Sweden) production with the Icelandic Film Fund, FILM (Reykjavik), the Swedish Film Institute, Sandrews, Filmhuset, SVT TV1, 88 KB and Film Teknik. Produced by Christer Abrahamsen. Executive producers, Katinka Farago, Klas Olofsson. Written and directed by Hrafn Gunnlaugsson. Camera (Fujicolor), Esa Vuorinen; editor, Edda Kristjansdottir; music, Hans-Erik Philip; production design, Karl Juliusson; interiors, Bo Lindgren; sound, Gunnar Smari Helgasson; production management, Gisela Bergquist, Kristjan Hrafnsson; assistant director, Daniel Bergman. Reviewed at Film Teknik screening room, Stockholm, Oct. 7, 1988. Running time: **118 MIN.**

Trausti . . . . Reine Brynolfsson
Isold . . . . Tinna Gunnlaugsdottir
Hjörleif . . . . Egil Olafsson
The Bishop . . . . Sune Mangs
Sigrid . . . . Kristbjörg Kjeld
Sol . . . . Klara Iris Vigfusdottir
Grim . . . . Helgi Skulason
Leonardo . . . . Johann Neumann
Edda . . . . Helga Backman
Egil . . . . Sigurdur Sigurjonsson
Also with: Sveinn Meidsson, Flosi Olafsson, Gudmunda Eliasdottir, Rurik Haraldsson.

■ **Stockholm** — With "In The Shadow Of The Raven," an independent sequel to his 1984 "The Raven Flies," Hrafn Gunnlaugsson has what surely will keep worldwide audiences with hands clasped at guts, hearts and throats for most of this Viking-era actioner-love story-morality tale.

Maybe Gunnlaugsson should have split his story into two or even three films. Packing so much dynamite into almost every frame not only takes your breath away, it also threatens to deafen and blind you while piling on plots and subplots that tend to confuse and, occasionally, leave you numb.

In the story's opening bloody fight, farmers of young Trausti's tribe and the warriors of rich chieftain Erik battle over a huge whale stranded on the beach of the barren island. One of Trausti's men kills Erik, whose daughter swears vengeance. Her name is Isolde, and Trausti is Icelandic for Tristan.

You can forget Wagner and the classic chivalry tragedy. In all the fighting, plotting, betraying, loving and killing that follows, Gunnlaugsson's (he wrote as well as directed) Isolde especially is far from the traditional blushing maiden. As played by Tinna Gunnlaugsdottir, a Reykjavik stage actress, she is a cunning, scheming, ruthless power-player, who also happens to be blond and pretty.

It takes much feuding between Trausti's tribe, the forces of the late Erik and Iceland's mighty landowning bishop, whose son is a candidate for Isolde's hand, before Trausti and Isolde can get on any kind of intimate terms. Actually, their first meeting is in a church where he, a newly converted Christian, kneels in prayer, while she tries to knife him from behind.

As a Christian, Trausti cannot take arms but must preach peace among the violence-prone Icelandic heathens, while the ravens, scouts of the ancient god Odin, remind him of his real heritage.

At long last, Trausti is forced to meet violence with violence, and at film's end, he chops off his worst enemy's head with one hand as he leads Isolde's daughter to the alter with the other to teach her the gospel of love.

Apart from Tinna Gunnlaugsdottir's Isolde, some of the acting is genuinely strong (the women especially), some just typed but forcefully so. As the wavering Trausti, Reine Brynolfsson is suitably Hamletish, although he can look distracting like an absent-minded owl.

Iceland's natural scenery supplies a rock arch, a huge waterfall, a steaming geyser. Esa Vuorinen's camera moves in rhythm with the action, never wobbling for a moment, and Hans-Erik Philips score is similarly to the point.

Hrafn Gunnlaugsson reportedly has promised his producer to cut some good-sized slices from the export version of "The Shadow Of The Raven." By doing away with the expendable matter, he will have won his battle to come up with a truly great film.—*Kell.*

El Sada El Regal
(Gentlemen)
(EGYPTIAN)

An Adel El-Mihi production. Written and directed by Raafat El-Mihi. Camera (color), Samir Farag; editor, Said El-Cheikh; music, Mohamed Helal. Reviewed at Vevey Film Festival, Switzerland, Aug. 23, 1988. Running time: **125 MIN.**
With: Mahmoud Abdel-Aziz, Maali Uayed, Hela Fouad.

■ **Vevey — An amusing but obvious local comedy, ''Gentlemen'' revolves about a change of sex in an Egyptian wife and office worker, which gives rise to many droll situations.**

Women's lib overtones and digs at Egyptian machismo could spark some interest in femme audiences, but otherwise pic is too simplistic for wider appeal.

Story concerns a married couple with a small child. The wife is fed up with her husband and while he is away on a business trip, she decides to have a change of sex operation, despite opposition from the doctors. The operation is a success and the new she/he returns to her job at a bank, while hubby raves, rants, punches the doctor in the eye, and takes charge of bringing up baby.

The situation becomes further complicated when the husband falls for the wife's girlfriend and colleague at the bank. All of the humor is kept in a light vein and the criticism is limited to good-humored kidding, though criticism of Egyptian establishment values has made pic a hit in its own country. Production values, thesping and direction are basic. Commercial outlook is probably limited to the Arab market. —*Besa.*

Cherni Monakh
(The Black Monk)
(SOVIET-COLOR/B&W)

A Mosfilm Studio production. Directed by Ivan Dikovichni. Screenplay, Dikovichni, Sergei Soloviov, based on a story by Anton Chekhov; camera (color, b&w), Vadim Jusov; editor, E. Praksina; music, Teimuraz Bakuradze; art direction, Liudmila Kusakova. Reviewed at Venice Film Festival (competing), Sept. 5, 1988. Running time: **90 MIN.**
Kovrin . . . . Stanislav Liubshin
Tania . . . . Tatiana Drubich
Tania's father . . . . Petr Fomenko

■ **Venice — ''The Black Monk'' is a first feature by Ivan Dikovichni. This film version of Chekhov's story about a man haunted by a ghost uses such an ethereal approach that action and characters dissolve, and the meaning of it all remains murky.**

Visuals are of a staggering beauty, though, in Vadim Jusov's masterful cinematography, creating a soulful atmosphere for the hero's spiritual crisis. It probably will be seen in more fests and a few daring art houses.

Top Russian thesp Stanislav Liubshin plays Kovrin, a gentle, sensitive soul, a man out of the ordinary. He is obsessed with the legend of a black monk who roams the world and, one day, he sees the ghost and talks to him. Maybe he's just conversing with a part of himself, an impression heightened by the frustrating way the "ghost" is never shown.

At least the spook has some wisdom to import, reassuring Kovrin he hasn't gone mad and that he should live life to the hilt.

The country manor where Kovrin is staying is owned by a nutty old man who dearly loves his garden. His charming daughter Tania (fine actress Tatiana Drubich) is eager to marry Kovrin. At first their union is happy, but when father and daughter notice Kovrin talks to himself, they demand he seek treatment.

The doctors succeed too well — they turn the patient into a "normal man." Feeling he has lost what made him unique, Kovrin turns irritable and violent, and leaves Tania and her father's garden forever, to lead a dissipated and unhappy life.

The idyllic beauty of the Russian landscape and of the two lovers makes their final destruction melancholy, indeed. Lack of drama, however, makes pic seem long and draggy. The director's devotion to the late director Andrei Tarkovsky is evident in pic's reverence for man and nature (as well as the overly languorous pace). As in the master's tradition, Dikovichni concentrates his attention on the first languishing, then cantankerous figure of the hero, leaving Tatiana Drubich as little more than female decoration as Tania — certainly a disservice to Chekhov.

Most striking thing about ''The Black Monk'' is its Gorbachev-era assertion of the importance of individuality, seen as an inalienable human right whose straitjacketing within conventional norms leads to disaster. —*Yung.*

Diario de Invierno
(Winter Diary)
(SPANISH)

A Castor Films presentation. Produced by Angel Somolinos. Directed by Francisco Regueiro. Screenplay, Regueiro, Angel Fernandez Santos; camera (Fujicolor), Juan Amorós; editor, Pedro del Rey; production manager, Enrique Bellot; sets, Gumersindo de Andrés; sound, Carlos Faruolo. Reviewed at San Sebastian Film Festival, Sept. 18, 1988. Running time: **104 MIN.**
León . . . . Eusebio Poncela
Father . . . . Fernando Rey
Snake-Catcher . . . . Francisco Algora

■ **San Sebastian — This turgid, self-indulgent exercise in incomprehensibility left most spectators and critics here nonplussed; even the director's press conference failed to shed any light on what the film is supposed to convey.**

"Cain wanted to kill God but instead murdered his brother Abel," the press notes tell us. Supposedly this is Cain's story seen from the "hellish world of a police station, the chaos of a split-up family, on a mystical journey through childhood."

Yet Francisco Regueiro's film is so inaccessible that the images succeed each other without any seeming connection. There may be something about a cop seeking his own identity, a snake-charmer who is being held in a cell, a father who died in a fire and practiced euthanasia, plus a mother who is a cross between a saint and a slut. All of it is presented in such a disjointed and confusing way that anyone's guess on what this film is "about" will be valid.—*Besa.*

Hector
(BELGIAN)

A Movie DA/MC4 (France) release of a Multimedia/Linden Film coproduction. Produced by Erwin Provoost. Directed by Stijn Coninx. Screenplay, Urbanus, Coninx; camera (color), Willy Stassen; editor, Kees Linthorst; music, Jan de Wilde; art direction, Jean Block, Els Rastelli; sound, Peter Flamman; assistant director, Frank Van Mechelen. Reviewed at Forum Arc-en-ciel cinema, Paris,

Sept. 5, 1988. Running time: **90 MIN.**
Hector . . . . Urbanus
Ella . . . . Sylvia Millecam
Achiel . . . . Frank Aendenboom
Jos . . . . Mar Van Eeghem

■ **Paris — Yet another variation on the boy-in-a-man's-body comedy formula, ''Hector'' is a Belgian boxoffice smash that's had 'em rolling in Flanders Field and Holland.**

This innocuous vehicle for Flemish funnyman Urbanus won Grand Prize at France's Chamrousse Humor Festival and has opened theatrically in Paris (without apparent success). It doesn't appear likely to be a sleeper discovery in the vein of "The Gods Must Be Crazy" and other UFFO (Unidentified Flying Film Objects).

''Hector'' is the film debut for Urbanus (who's succeeded on stage, tv and records) as well as for his director, Stijn Coninx, with whom he wrote the poorly contrived script.

Falling back on a long tradition of gentle, bemused, ill-attired innocents from Harry Langdon to Jacques Tati's M. Hulot, Urbanus casts himself as a somewhat retarded 35-year-old who's been abandoned in a Flemish orphanage, until the day his pretty aunt (Dutch actress Sylvia Millecam) comes to claim him as auxiliary help in her husband's bakery.

The bearded, shleppy Urbanus doesn't realize he's being exploited by his uncle (Frank Aendenboom) who wants to free his athletic son to train for an upcoming bicycle meet.

Auntie too entertains a pipe dream about becoming a film star and going to Hollywood. The scripters indulge her in an unlikely plot turn when a top film director comes out to the sticks to see her in an amateur stage production (in which Urbanus becomes the unexpected highlight).

The weaknesses of the script are capped when Millecam miraculously lands a movie contract anyway, but in the final scene amazingly decides to chuck it all to the winds and rejoin the man of her life — Urbanus! (Hubby has conveniently expired of a heart attack during the climactic play.)

Home success of ''Hector'' now promises ''Hector II,'' with the same director. An inventive scriptwriter with a few ideas about how to mold Urbanus' screen image wouldn't hurt its chances for outside markets. —*Len.*

Zockerexpress
(Gambling Express)
(WEST GERMAN)

A H.S. Film release of an H.S. Film, Tao Film, Champion Film coproduction. Produced by Hanno Schilf. Directed by Klaus Lemke. Screenplay, Lemke, Schilf; camera (color), Lothar Stickelbrucks. Reviewed at Dutch Film Days, City Theater, Utrecht, Netherlands, Sept. 26, 1988. Running time: **81**

MIN.
Danny .... Huub Stapel
Barry .... Hanno Poschl
Winni .... Dolly Dollar
   Also with: Sabrina Diehl, Jasamin Zadeh, Ivan Desny.

■ **Utrecht — The story of Danny (Huub Stapel), a compulsive gambler and conman, is told with knowhow despite its limited budget.**

Danny runs a disco in a German town with an American garrison, and operates a prostitution business as well. While business is good, Danny can't stop gambling and owes the bank and some unpleasant Mafia types.

He outwits the Mafiosi, which really isn't a smart thing to do because they burn down his disco and take away the three girls as partial payment. Two of the girls opt for the riches, though they keep yearning for Danny.

The third girl sticks with him as he starts a mobile gambling parlor disguised as a traveling library. Life is fine until Danny gambles away all his money. Dastardly Danny dies under the wheels of a car. Serves him right. This is a moral tale.

Acting is good all around, and technical credits are okay. Pic should travel abroad.

There is quite a lot of sex and violence in the screenplay, but viewers are left to use their imagination.
— *Wall.*

El Misterio Eva Peron
(The Eva Peron Mystery)
(ARGENTINE-DOCU-COLOR/B&W)

A Profilms 21 production. Directed by Tulio Demicheli. Written by Demicheli, Emilio Villalba Welsh; camera (color, b&w), Antonio Merayo, Luis Vechione, Jose Pizzi, Rodolfo Albonico, Juan Carlos Bello, Andres Silvart, Antonio Parodi, Emilio Walfisch; editor, Federico Parrilla; music, Oscar Cardozo Ocampo; sound, Osvaldo Vaca. Reviewed at Montreal World Film Festival (Latin American Cinema), Aug. 31, 1988. Running time: **118 MIN.**
With: Mauri Rubistein, Pascual Pelliciotta, Marcos Zucker, Tulio Demicheli, Manuel Ferradas Campos, Julio Alcaraz, Padre Hernan Benitez, Ernesto Sabato, Jose Maria Castiñeira De Dios, Dr. Roman Cereijo, Cipriano Reyes, Delia Parodi, Fermin Chavez, Ricardo Vittani, Pablo Vicente, Francisco Manrique, Jorge Daniel Paladino, Prof. Dr. Raul Matera, Hector Cabanillas, Prof. Domingo Tellechea.

■ **Montreal** — Who was Eva Duarte Peron? This exhaustive blend of documentary and docudrama endeavors to peel back the mystique of the demi-goddess who held a nation in her thrall and cast the charm of political invincibility on the chameleon-like populist movement that bore the name of her husband, Argentine dictator Juan Peron.

The answers provided here are enlightening but inconclusive, and should be of primary interest to students of Latin American history and documentary buffs.

Documentarist Tulio Demicheli

---

was assistant director on "La Pródiga," the only film in which Eva the actress played a leading role. Drawing upon extensive interviews with people who knew the uncrowned queen of Argentina during various stages of her life, his docu traces her evolution from an unhappy adolescence as a poor, illegitimate child in a small town, to her days as a struggling actress in Buenos Aires, to her breakthrough into the artistic and political high society of the capital and on to her ascension as the woman behind one of the century's most charismatic politicians.

The documentary hammers home the theme that Eva's popularity did not diminish with her death more than 30 years ago. This is addressed by a long inquisition into the fate of her corpse, which was moved by Peron's enemies for fear that a permanent grave would become a perpetual shrine for the contentious forces that have made political instability a way of life in Argentina.

Although the mystery of her corpse's disappearance is "solved" in this documentary, her power to mesmerize a turbulent nation in life and in death remains an ineluctable phenomenon, likened by one observer to "a great force of nature."

The docudrama touches, which serve to link the archival footage and the interviews, are not especially compelling. — *Rich.*

Huller i suppen
(Holes In The Soup)
(DANISH)

A Kärne Film release of Per Holst Filmproduktion production. Produced by Per Holst. Conceived, written and directed by Povl Erik Carstensen, Morten Lorentzen; camera (Eastmancolor), Jan Friis; editor, Peter Engleson; music, Frans Bak; production management, Gitte Sindlev, Preben Seltoft; sound, Ole Lyd Rasmussen. Reviewed at the Palads, Copenhagen, Sept. 26, 1988. Running time: **67 MIN.**
With: Povl Erik Carstensen, Morten Lorentzen, Arne Siemsen.

■ **Copenhagen** — With "Holes In The Soup," producer Per Holst relaxes after his Cannes Golden Palm winner "Pelle The Conqueror" with some kind of a Candid Camera carbon copy of the South African hit in Denmark, "Funny People."

Like all such duplication, "Holes" is shot through with all the inherent flaws: blurry outlines and a muddy stamp of non-authenticity.

"Holes In The Soup" is conceived, outlined, directed by and starring local stage and television pranksters Morten Lorentzen and Povl Erik Carstensen. They are seen as a couple of tv show anchormen who fumble desperately with their lines as well as with glasses of water while they verbally preface the shot-on-the-sly episodes rigged by themselves.

Lorentzen and Carstensen plus professional actor Arne Siemsen are also seen in a multitude of disguises as the straight-faced characters who put various lures like phony money, phony dog turds, phony corpses and phony phone calls in the way of people on and off the city streets and innocent of being watched by the hidden camera.

Unfortunately, most everybody smells the lures a mile off, forcing the fun to break off before it has really begun. Lorentzen and Carstensen are either inept at carrying through their designs, or they are just too nice to be as tactless and vicious as candid camera fun really requires.

Test run of "Holes" for invited audiences reportedly had 'em rolling in the aisles. Seeing is sometimes disbelieving. — *Kell.*

Spoorloos
(The Vanishing)
(DUTCH)

A Hungry Eye Pictures release of a Golden Egg Films production. Produced by Anne Lordon, George Sluizer. Directed by Sluizer. Screenplay, Tim Krabbe; camera (color), Toni Kuhn; editor, Sluizer; music, Henny Vrienten; sound, Piotr van Dijk; set design, Santiago Isidro Pin; costumes, Sophie Dussaud. Reviewed at Montreal World Film Festival (Cinema of Today and Tomorrow), Aug. 29, 1988. Running time: **107 MIN.**
Rex .... Gene Bervoets
Saskia .... Johanna Ter Steege
Mr. Lemorne .... Bernard-Pierredonnadieu
   Also with: Gwen Exkhaus.

■ **Montreal** — This slick psychodrama should get international play before going to Dutch video counters. It is the ultimate tribute to Alfred Hitchcock, daring to offer up an ending that goes beyond even the master's memorable climaxes.

The film examines one man's obsession with going beyond the limit. He's an average man named Lemorne who decides to kidnap a woman, any woman, just to test his ability to go a step over the line. The woman he finally entices into his car is a young Dutch woman, in France with her boyfriend for the Tour de France.

When she disappears, her boyfriend spends the next three years searching for her and trying to find the man who is taunting him with postcards and letters.

Director George Sluizer has fashioned an unpredictable film that takes three normal people and puts them into a situation over which none has complete control. His villain, Mr. Lemorne, appears from the beginning to be an inoffensive man with some irregular attitudes toward women. Instead he is a psychological terrorist playing a frightening game of cat and mouse with the Dutch tourists.

Should Sluizer decide to issue a dubbed version of the film, it might find a large audience in the U.S. It

---

has all the ingredients of the best American suspense films and could do well. Its ending, while a little bleak and not for all tastes, is a sensible choice that is almost a signature for the film. —*Cadd.*

El Embajador de la India
(The Ambassador From India)
(COLOMBIAN)

A Focine production. Executive producer, Abeldardo Quintero López. Directed by Mario Ribero. Screenplay, Gilberto Valderrama, based on the play "The Inspector General," by Nikolai Gogol; camera (color), Mario González; editor, Agustin Pinto, Ribero; sound, Eduardo Castro; art direction, Victor Sánchez; music, Jorge Villamil. Reviewed at Festival Latino, N.Y., Aug. 10, 1988. Running time: **85 MIN.**
Jaime Flores (Ambassador) .. Hugo Gomez
   Also with: Manuel Currea, Manuel Rachón, Julio Roberto Gómez, Lucero Gómez, Diego Camacho, Roberto Franco, Pilar Ruiz.

■ **Colombia's "The Ambassador From India," by Mario Ribero, is a hilarious south-of-the-border take-off on Nikolai Gogol's "The Inspector General." If handled right, pic has good international b.o. potential.**

Film not only affirms P.T. Barnum's observation that there's a sucker born every minute, but it goes further to say that people want to be fooled. They will reject the truth, even when it stares them full in the face. On the other hand, lies foster illusion, which the filmmaker finds much more satisfying dramatically than real life because it elevates daily experience.

An off-screen narrator opens the film, introducing viewers to the country, town and cast of characters. Tongue-in-cheek delivery sets the ironic tone for the fable to follow.

Story converns inveterate liar Jaime Flores (Hugo Gómez), who tells two fellow bus passengers that he is an ambassador from India traveling incognito, to see the country. Speaking a mixture of English and bad Spanish, Jaime's practical joke soon gets out of hand. When they arrive at a small Colombian town, word of the ambassador's visit spreads quickly and Flores is installed at the best hotel in town receiving official state visits by the governor, mayor and the crème de la crème of local society.

Helmer Ribero has a good feel for detail and invention and manages to inject a plethora of suprises into the basic 1-joke premise. The townsfolk go out of their way to please their distinguished guest, trying to make him feel at home. Much humor comes from their confused impressions of India, which sometimes lie between Turkey and Tangiers. In one example, a radio tribute to Indian music consists of "Hava Nagilah."

Decision to relocate the story from pre-revolutionary Russia to

Latin America is a logical one because of the formality and conceits still retained in many Latin countries. Local functionaries are particularly vulnerable to light-hearted lampooning.

Pic's pace is brisk. Acting and tech credits are up to par in this fun romp through Latin American self-satire, where no one is spared a jab or two. —*Lent.*

Aloa — Praznik Kurvi
(Aloa — The Whores' Feast)
(YUGOSLAV)

A Jugoslavija Film presentation of a Jadran Films, Zagreb TV production. Directed by Lordan Zafranovic. Screenplay, Veljko Barbieri, Zafranovic, based on Barbieri's novel; camera (Eastmancolor), Andrija Pivcevic; editor, Andrija Zafranovic; music, Igor Savin; sound, Mladen Pervan, Josip Laca, Mladen Prebil; art direction, Ivica Sporcic; costume design, Lada Gamulin; makeup, Jasna Crnobrnja. Reviewed at Pula Film Festival (competing), July 26, 1988. Running time: **101 MIN.**
With: Neda Arneric, Ranko Zidaric, Stevo Zigon, Dusica Zegarac.

■ **Pula** — A familiar figure on the international festival circuit, with several visually striking historical dramas to his credit, Lordan Zafranovic unsuccessfully attempts this time an intimate piece with obvious allegorical intentions, using mythological references to reinforce his theme.

A German archeologist and his young Yugoslav wife take rooms for the summer on the Dalmatian coast with a widow and her son. The encounter between the older intellectual past his prime, his unsatisfied wife looking for sexual relief, the angry but appetizing young man who likes to dive in the nude, and the mature, lonely mother, deprived of male companionship, ignites the expected fireworks.

Instant infatuation of the wife for the young man leads to torrid lovemaking the husband can do nothing about, and reaches a violent climax when the lover rebels against being used and discarded. The conflict is both personal and national, a clash between the decadent West and the primal emotions of a less developed nature.

Among several mythological references, there is one ancient Greek rite, about prostitutes being blindfolded and sent to look for ceramic phalluses, the quality of the next year depending on their capacity to find same. Hecuba and the King of Troy figure in it too, as well as film quotes from Richard Thorpe's "Champagne For Caesar" and Carl Th. Dreyer's classic "Gertrud." There also is a masked ball, a black dog and a sudden thunderstorm added to the collection of symbols attempting to add significance to the subject.

Unhappily this does not work

out, because the script is altogether too self-evident and the direction surprisingly heavy-handed. Several revealing sex scenes and abundant nudity may lend the picture commercial appeal, but the smoldering passions behind it all look manipulated and false. Wooden, unsympathetic performances by Ranko Zidaric and Neda Arneric don't help put the story across.

Technical credits are high class with Zafranovic displaying his usual flair for sumptuous visuals. —*Edna.*

Koragashi Ryota — Gekitotsu! Monster Bus
(Ryota Korogashi — Crash! Monster Bus)
(JAPANESE)

A Cine Ropponica release of a Nikkatsu production. Produced by Naoya Narita. Directed by Naosuke Kurosawa. Screenplay, Toshimichi Okawa, based on the cartoon by Hiroyuki Murata; camera (color), Hiroshi Munakata; lighting, Kazuo Yabe; editor, Yoshiyuki Okuhara; music producer, Yoko Tensho; art direction, Yuji Maruyama; sound, Nobushige Fukushima; assistant director, Yasuyuki Otani. Reviewed at Tokyo Gas Hall, July 30, 1988. Running time: **97 MIN.**
Ryota . . . . Riki Takeuchi
Reiko . . . . Naomi Akimoto
Takashi . . . . Kazutaka Komai
Tajima . . . . Kenji Kasai
Yoshimoto . . . . Shuji Kato
Tetsuji . . . . Gao Ginji

■ **Tokyo** — Live and animated films based on popular *magna* (comics) have been commonplace in Japan for years, but few have managed to capture what made the original so popular in the first place. An exception is this new release from Cine Ropponica, which combines the look of a comic strip with the anarchic exuberance of a cartoon.

With each frame of the film, director Naosuke Kurosawa recreates, as nearly as possible, panels in the strip drawn by Hiroyuki Murata. There is the same quick shifting from closeup to medium shot to full shot, the same restless changing of camera angles which comic strip artists can manage so cheaply and easily and most budget-constrained filmmakers don't even attempt.

There are inspired uses of fast motion, and the post-synchronized dialog seems always to emanate from the foreground of the frames, just as dialog balloons almost invariably appear in the foreground of panels.

The actors in this fast-paced story of a comically irresponsible bus driver and his battles with a host of baddies of varying degrees of fearsomeness are enjoyably and appropriately unreal, like amalgams of pen-and-ink and flesh-and-blood.

Riki Takeuchi, who plays the bus driver Ryota Korogashi, is normally an impossibly handsome leading man, but here, his good looks toned down by a tight permanent and a

goofily happy expression, he is a marvelously effective physical comedian.

As the sultry femme fatale Ryota falls for, Naomi Akimoto exudes the mind-bending sensuality that used to be the trademark of Atsuko Asano before she became connected with the popular "Abunai Deka" tv and movie series. As does Takeuchi, Akimoto looks as if she stepped out of a cartoon, albeit one drawn by Antonio Vargas. — *Bail.*

Krajina S Nabytkem
(Landscape With Furniture)
(CZECH)

A Barrandov Film Studio production. Directed by Karel Smyczek. Screenplay, Milan Lezak, based on book by Zdenek Rozenbaum; camera (color), Jiri Macak; music, Emil Viklicky; sets, Jiri Matolin. Reviewed at Vevey Film Festival, Switzerland, Aug. 24, 1988. Running time: **92 MIN.**
Zdeněk . . . . Vladimir Javorský
Eva . . . . Yvetta Kornová
František . . . . Michal Suchánek
Mother . . . . Marcela Martinková

■ **Vevey** — This tale of a gawky country bumpkin whom all the pretty girls in the village fall for starts with meandering heavyhandedness and never manages to quicken its pace.

A tiresome exercise in the obvious, with nary a new or original idea in its predictable plot, pic is doomed to speedy burial.

Slim plot involves a music student who works one summer as a postman in a rural village. There he encounters several girls as well as a landscape painter who seems to commit suicide, though it is not clear why.

In the fall, the bumpkin is approached by one of the girls he romanced, who tells him she's pregnant. After delivering her offspring, she dumps the kid on Zdeněk, who starts caring for it, even though he later learns it is not his child.

Vladimir Javorský looks so hickish, seems so inept and characterless, that his presence on screen is an ordeal to watch; as a bumpkin he is certainly convincing, but not as a music student or an admirer of art. Pic is intended to have its comical side (which is why it was in the Vevey fest), but a suicide, a distraught unmarried mother and an abandoned baby in this case don't tickle any funnybones. —*Besa.*

Gwiazda Piolun
(The Star Wormwood)
(POLISH)

A Polish Film Corp. "Rondo" Unit production. Directed by Henryk Kluba. Screenplay, Wladyslaw L. Terlecki; camera (color), Jaroslaw Szoda; editor, Jerzy Pekalski; music, Andrzej Trzaskowski; art direction, Andrzej Plocki; production manager, Marek Depczynski. Reviewed at Gdynia Film Festival, Sept. 14, 1988. Running time: **105 MIN.**
Man . . . . Tadeusz Huk

Woman . . . . Katarzyna Bargielowska
Also with: Zofia Rysiowna, Zygmunt Bielawski, Ignacy Machowski.

■ **Gdynia** — Avant-garde artist and playwright Stanislaw Ignacy Witkiewicz, a.k.a.in art Witkacy, is enjoying a vogue at the moment, with two films made about him this year, "The Star Wormwood" by Henryk Kluba is the more direct attempt to get close to the historical figure.

Lensed in a disconnected, oniric style (meant, no doubt, to recall the artist's creations), "Wormwood" is a sometimes fascinating, mostly incoherent, filmic journey. It will be quite obscure for those not armed with foreknowledge, and a hard sell abroad.

Film refrains from mentioning the hero by name, referring to him simply as "the Man" (sensitive, vibrant Tadeusz Huk), and to his fetching female companion (the hypnotic Katarzyna Bargielowska) as "the Woman." This coy usage is in awkward contrast with the two, very concrete central characters, whom Huk and Bargielowski manage to make touchingly real, despite all the lensing and editing fireworks.

Time is 1939, the war had started, and the Man and Woman are rich, privileged observers of the catastrophe taking shape around them. They ride past legions of fleeing refugees in German cars, even though they detest the Germans. The Woman wants to escape, the Man to swallow the vial of poison he always carries with him.

Film uses the technique of interior monolog to show what the Man is thinking — mostly dark thoughts about a grim future. Amid mass evacuation of the countryside, he declaims apocalyptic verses. There are ominous flashes to the front (newsreel?) and tender bedroom scenes between the doomed couple. They are almost torn to pieces by some peasants outraged by their German connections.

With timing that is to make him an underground hero, the Man takes his life on Sept. 18, 1939, date of the Russian invasion of Poland. His grieving lover watches him die.

Pic's eerie atmosphere owes much to Jaroslaw Szoda's brilliant camerawork, which really comes close to Witkacy's distorted artwork.— *Yung.*

El Placer de Matar
(The Pleasure Of Killing)
(SPANISH)

A Laurenfilm/Errota (Barcelona) production. Produced by Antonio Llorens, in cooperation with the Ministry of Culture. Directed by Felix Rotoeta. Screenplay, Rotoeta, Domingo Sanchez, Mario Gas, Angel Faccio, based on novel "Las Pistolas" by Rotoeta; camera (color), Acacio d'Almeida; music, Carlos Miranda; set design, Javier Fernandez Gutierrez. Reviewed at Montreal World Film Festival (Cinema of Today and

Tomorrow), Aug. 26, 1988. Running time: **100 MIN.**

With: Antonio Banderas, Mathieu Carrière, Victoria Abril, Berta Riaza, Walter Vidarte, Victoria Pena, Mario Gas.

■ **Montreal** — Breaking taboos in Spanish cinema has a long tradition, but this first feature by Felix Rotoeta turns out to be not much fun at all. Interest lies in a quartet of secondary characters in a fast-paced story having little heart or psychological finesse.

Dyspeptic 30-year-old bachelor/match teacher Mathieu Carrière from an upper-class family and sometime drug pusher/punk Antonio Banderas happen to meet by chance over an assignment to dispatch several marked victims at a country estate near Madrid. Killings are engineered by an old firing range instructor in the military with ambiguous police connections.

The pair soon become strange bedfellows in a mounting rhythm of shootings, always accomplished by a bloodless zap with silencers between the eyebrows. After more than dozen corpses, baffled police assign a man to the case.

Suspense in the story collapses halfway through film, however, when it turns out Carrière and Banderas are neither psychopaths, closet terrorists nor in the pay of police but kill simply because of the asocial pleasure of aiming through gunsight crosshairs (the hunt is a pervasive Spanish film theme).

Story fails to exploit Victoria Abril's talents as Banderas' girlfriend nor plumbs the psychological nuances of the relationship between upper bourgeois Carrière and subprole Banderas, though social observation of Spanish high society on the Carrière side of the story provides some amusement.

Production credits are technically good. Offshore chances are for cable tv and the exploitation market. Film opens in October in Madrid. —*Milg.*

Making Opera
(CANADIAN-DOCU)

A Films Transit release of a Cineroutes Prods. production. Produced, written and directed by Anthony Azzopardi. Camera (color), Ron Stannett; editor, Jack Morbin; music (adapted), Giuseppe Verdi; sound, Stuart French, John Thomson, Patrick Rowan. Reviewed at Montreal World Film Festival (Panorama Canada), Aug. 31, 1988. Running time: **88 MIN.**

■ **Montreal** — There always is a market for musical films that give the movie audience the feel of being inside the production. This documentary does a good job of putting the viewer backstage and then transporting him into the audience for the grand finale.

That could earn foreign tv rights should the distributors decide to go that route.

They have investment from a Canadian tv network — the Canadian Broadcasting Corp. — and from the government-run Ontario educational network. This is both an educational exercise and an entertainment experience.

The education comes with the approach to the Giuseppe Verdi opera "La Forza del Destino." Non-opera fans can look at the passion and color and see the grandness of opera, thus taking some of the fear out of the musical and vocal aspects.

However, the documentary works just as well when it concentrates on entertaining. Particularly easy to watch is Canadian Opera director John Copley, who is part-comic, part-enlightened despot, but always in control. The backstage shenanigans don't fit traditional images of opera and they allow one to get closer to the people involved and to get the feel of the show itself.

"Making Opera" is an ambitious undertaking that should be seen in both schools and on the small screen. It could also get some urban play in a theatrical release. —*Cadd.*

I Will Not Make Any More Boring Art
(CANADIAN-DOCU)

A Picture Plant production. Produced by Terry Greenlaw. Directed by William D. MacGillivray. Camera (color), Lionel Simmons; editor Angela Baker, MacGillivray; sound, Alex Salter; music, CCMC; research, David Craig. Reviewed at Toronto Festival of Festivals, Sept. 17, 1988. Running time: **82 MIN.**

With: Garry Neill Kennedy, Martha Wilson, Michael Snow, Robert Frank, Les Levine, Dan Graham, Dara Birnbaum, Krzysztof Wodiczko, June Leaf, David Askevold.

■ **Toronto** — For a few years in the '70s, the small Halifax-based Nova Scotia College of Art and Design (NSCAD) became one of the world's centers of post-modern art. This docu looks at the college and some of the people who generated its reputation.

First among them is Garry Kennedy, appointed NSCAD's director in 1967, and generally credited with its renaissance. Director Bill MacGillivray, whose feature film "Life Classes" sparked interest earlier this year in Berlin, takes a non-reverential approach to the artists who worked at NSCAD, most of whom, when interviewed, prove to be remarkably inarticulate. Much of their work, as seen on video or film, seems dated too.

This docu will be of interest to tv programmers or fests with slots to fill on modern art, and has the immense advantage of not taking itself too seriously.

In the program catalog of the Festival of Festivals, and in the fest's schedules, pic was consistently mistitled as "I Will Make No More Boring Art." —*Strat.*

La Boite à Soleil
(The Box Of Sun)
(CANADIAN)

A Cinak Ltd. production. Produced and directed by Jean-Pierre Lefebvre. Screenplay, Lefebvre; camera (color), Lionel Simmons; editor, Barbara Easto; music, Lefebvre; sound, Michel Charron; assistant director, Louis Ricard. Reviewed at Toronto Festival of Festivals, Sept. 12, 1988. Running time: **73 MIN.**

With: Joseph Champagne, Arsinee Khanjian, Simon Esterez, Barbara Easto, Atom Egoyan, Jerome Sabourin.

■ **Toronto** — "The Box Of Sun" is an abstract pic, completely lacking dialog, which will find its release limited to specialized venues and fests. It harks back to the experimental cinema of two decades ago.

Quebec director Jean-Pierre Lefebvre started out making such films more than 20 years ago, then graduated to a series of often impressive mainstream dramas (such as "Wild Flowers," made in 1982); now, it seems, his career has come full circle.

Pic centers on an old man who sits on a chair in the woods in winter; he seems to be a filmmaker, maybe willing events to happen. Children clip bright images from women's magazines, which are then animated: Lipstick tubes become missiles, photos of pretty models are distorted. The youngsters then go off on a trek in the woods.

There's a city woman in blond wig who seems to have lost her lover, maybe through death. In addition, a woman veiled in black pushes a baby carriage through deserted streets.

The old man gives the children gifts of boxes painted black. The lonely woman somehow goes one and opens it: Her lover (played by film director Atom Egoyan) then appears for a joyful coupling. The veiled woman reaches the sea, and removes her veil. The surviving children also rejoice in the sun's rays.

The idea of a gloomy world just waiting for sunlight is a positive one, but the film, despite its many visual and aural qualities, is all too often maddeningly obscure as to its meaning. No doubt it will spark debate, but it seems a step backwards for one of Canada's most interesting, if wayward, directors. —*Strat.*

Yuan Ni Zan Zeng De Nian Dai
(Far Removed From The War)
(CHINESE)

An August 1 Film Studio (Beijing) production. Directed by Hu Mei. Screenplay, Li Bao Lin; camera (color), Zhang Li; editor, Huang Zongluo, Wang Xuegi; art direction, Fan Xuzhi. Reviewed at the Tashkent Film Festival (competing), May 28, 1988. Running time: **88 MIN.**

Grandfather . . . . Huang Zonglo
Son . . . . Wang Xuen Jin
Wife . . . . Zu Ling

■ **Tashkent** — China's Hu Mei, a young femme helmer who has already received international attention, lenses a multi-layer tale of disintegrating family tradition as modern life advances in China in "Far Removed From The War."

Title is deceiving, as film deals with an old man who runs away from his son and daughter-in-law, too busy with their own lives to pay any attention to him. It is an evocative, often poetic film that deserves playoff in special situations offshore.

The view of contemporary Beijing may come as a shock to fans of exotica: the large family apartment is being redecorated in tasteful Western style, the neighborhood is modern, the young couple a Chinese version of successful yuppies. He (Wang Xuen Jin) teaches a course entitled "Hostilities of the Future" to Army officers; she (Zu Ling) is an opera singer (though too slender and attractive to be convincing) rehearsing "Madame Butterfly." Their son gets shunted off to school.

Most dignified member of the family is grandpa (Huang Zonglo). Perhaps feeling the end is near, he tries to communicate his memories of youth to his son, but is frustrated time and again. Finally he disappears, taking a train to a distant province to look up the nurse he fell in love with during the war. She's dead but the search itself stirs the old man's memories.

Constant flashbacks and cross-cutting get to be a bit much. Lensing, however, is sensitive, full of evocative images and camerawork.
—*Yung.*

Dotknieci
(The Afflicted)
(POLISH)

A Karol Irzykowski Film Studio production. Directed by Wieslaw Saniewski. Screenplay, Saniewski, based on a story by Andrzej Kijowski; camera (color), Witold Adamek; editor, Irena Chorynska; music, Przemyslaw Gintrowski; art direction, Allan Starski; production manager, Barbara Pec-Slesicka. Reviewed at Gdynia Film Festival, Sept. 15, 1988. Running time: **118 MIN.**

Jan . . . . .Piotr Franczewski
Wife . . . . .Ewa Wisniewska
Wanda . . . . .Joanna Irzepiecinska
Kramer . . . . .Olgierd Lukaszewicz
    Also with: Ewa Blaszczyk, Aleksander Bardini.

■ **Gdynia** — Fans of helmer Wieslaw Saniewski ("Custody") will find a different approach used in "The Afflicted," tale of how the family of a mentally ill woman falls apart.

A talky picture constructed around dialog between the unhappy family members and good and evil doctors, "The Afflicted" quickly veers off into melodrama — classy but over the top.

Though not hard to watch, film is so gabby it will have trouble reaching beyond Polish film weeks abroad. Its principal importance is local — it's the first Polish film to go inside the doors of the psychiatric hospitals.

Hero is Jan (Piotr Franczewski), a mousey college teacher soon to be fired for being too distracted. His problem is wife Joanna (Ewa Wisniewska), an attractive older woman who has been in and out of mental hospitals all her life. After a last attempt to bring her home, Joanna takes a bottle of pills in a fit of depression and dies.

For Jan and his teenage kids, it's the end of a nightmare. Then, a new doctor at the hospital (Olgierd Lukaszewicz, who plays the villain with sadistic glee) accuses him of causing his wife's death. Jan goes on trial, having lost the respect of his children, the affection of his mistress, and everything else, and confesses his moral responsibility. He voluntarily becomes a patient in the evil doctor's mental ward, where he is tortured with electroshock in "Cuckoo's Nest" fashion. Only his son's selfish fears for his pregnant girlfriend bring Jan home again.

Camerawork by Witold Adamek is elegant and evenly paced. Cast is professional. — *Yung.*

Técnicas de Duelo
(Dueling Techniques)
(COLOMBIAN-CUBAN)

A Focine-Fotograma-Icaic production. Directed by Sergio Cabrera. Screenplay, Humberto Dorado; camera (color), José Madeiros; editor, Justo Vega; music, Juan Márquez; art direction, Enrique Linero; sound, Heriberto Garcia. Reviewed at San Juan Film Festival, Puerto Rico, Oct. 4, 1988. Running time: **97 MIN.**

Teacher . . . . Frank Ramírez
Butcher . . . . Humberto Dorado
Miriam . . . . Florina Lemaitre
Also with: Vicky Hernández, Edgardo Román, Fausto Cabrera, Manuel Pachón, Kepa Amuchástegui, Luis Chiappe, Angelo Javier Lozano, Antonio Aparicio, Elio Meza.

■ **San Juan, Puerto Rico — Colombian feature "Técnicas de Duelo" (Dueling Techniques) is a subtle comedy of manners, which should stand a fair chance in the international dueling arena. As a satire of Latin life, director Sergio Cabrera's marksmanship is right on the mark.**

Set in a small Andean town, pic begins with preparations for a duel between two former best friends, the schoolmaster (Frank Ramírez) and the town butcher (Humberto Dorado). Although the duel's raison d'être is never given, film revolves around each man's actions as **the fatal hour approaches and death seems imminent.**

Duel becomes the town event with chief of police and mayor placing bets on the eventual outcome. The men make their own preparations: ordering coffins, paying off

---

debts, bidding final goodbyes, etc.

Latin society and attitudes are aptly taken to task: honor, machismo, government bureaucracy, religious duty and self-important petty officials all receive their share of stabs.

Photography is lush and imaginative, dialog crisp and thesping is first rate. "Dueling Techniques" scores direct hits all around. — *Lent.*

Reisen ins Landesinnere
(Voyage Inside The Country)
(SWISS-DOCU)

A Look Now presentation. Produced, written and directed by Matthias von Guten. Camera (color, 16m), Pio Corradi; editor, Bernhard Lehner; sound, Felix Singer, Martin Witz. Reviewed at Locarno Film Festival (special program), Aug. 6, 1988. Running time: **94 MIN.**

■ **Locarno — The story of five persons and one place, this documentary moves along parallel lines, managing in an almost dry but highly effective manner to draw an incisive portrait of the Swiss nation today.**

Helmer Matthias von Gunten has carefully chosen his objects, each one remarkable on its own, which together fashion a composite picture of the people in his country. Pic never attempts to be symbolic or preachy.

His survey includes an old spinster (the last of her family) who refuses to leave the house in which she was born, representing the old traditions of frugality and protestant thriftiness; a successful Zurich fashion designer who dropped out in his mid-50s to live alone in the mountains; and an Italian who lives across the border but is responsible, to a great extent, for the maintenance of a miniaturized tourist exhibition of Swiss landscapes.

Also covered are a specialist employed by the government to record the national artistic treasures and preserve these records, and as much of the art objects as possible, in special antinuclear shelters prepared by the Swiss; and a lady coordinator of the Swiss tv news service, whose office is constantly invaded by images of the world at large, the only one of the five people selected by Von Gunten whose horizons go beyond the Alps.

Finally, in a spot just beyond the landing strip of an airport, a new breed of ornithologists watch planes instead of birds, typical of those who always dream of faraway places but never leave home.

Each of these separate cases is exposed systematically and intelligently to offer pertinent observations on the anxieties and the utter solitude of the Swiss, on foreign labor, on old age, on perfect order and even on the Swiss sense of humor.

Film is often inadvertently funny, but never less than serious, a rele-

---

vant image of the late '80s to be kept after its exhibition in the Swiss vaults to be reviewed by the historians of the next millennium.

With shooting spread over a period of several months in order to observe the same persons in different conditions, Von Gunten's picture should be a natural for film fests and specialized houses. The Berlin Forum has already secured it for its next winter's program. — *Edna.*

Cannot Run Away
(DUTCH-DOCU)

A Cinemien release of a Molenwiek production. Produced and directed by Hillie Molenaar, Joop van Wijk. Camera (color, 16m), Eugène van den Bosch; editor-sound, Hens van Rooy; music, Patricio Wang; interviews, Adul de Leon. Reviewed at Desmet Theater, Amsterdam, Aug. 29, 1988. Running time: **63 MIN.**

■ **Amsterdam — Hillie Molenaar found backing from a Dutch tv station and feminist organizations in the Netherlands and the Philippines for this sober, probing and often moving documentary on the trade in women, both on local and international scenes.**

Technically well made, it's fine fest fare, a must for feminist organizations and events, and has good tv prospects.

Molenaar and her collaborators managed to get not only some of the girls to talk frankly before the camera, but also cornered policemen, lawyers, local girl traders, and even Dutch doctors with unconvincing answers to questions about their roles in certain cases of forced prostitution.

Women are promised good jobs abroad and receive an advance in travel money from white benefactors. Upon arrival, the girls find themselves in a brothel, where they are relieved of passports and papers and — an apparently standard procedure — raped. If they refuse to work, they are beaten and locked up. Amid strangers, and unfamiliar with local language, they usually give in.

About one hundred such cases are recorded each year in the Netherlands, double that in Germany. Japanese brothels are estimated to have some 50,000 girls from the Philippines.

Main section of the film deals with Nena and Alma, two Philippine girls who in 1981 were hoodwinked by a Dutch trader and found themselves stranded on a isolated "sex farm" in the Dutch countryside, bordello catering to a motorized "respectable" clientele.

The story of these two girls catalyzed Molenaar's documentary project. After securing financing she flew to the Philippines and found the trader in question, who was finally arrested, tried and convicted — seven years after the deed.
— *Wall.*

Beach Balls

A Concorde Pictures release of a New Classics presentation. Produced by Matt Leipzig. Directed by Joe Ritter. Screenplay, David Rocklin; camera (Foto-Kem color), Anthony Cobbs; editor, Carol Oblath; music, Mark Governor; sound, David Kelson; production design, Stephen Greenberg; assistant director, Randy Pope; production manager, Susan Stremple; second unit director, Kristine Peterson; second unit camera, Sandra Chandler; casting, Al Guarino. Reviewed on Media Home Entertainment vidcassette, N.Y., Oct. 5, 1988. MPAA Rating: R. Running time: **77 MIN.**

Charlie Harrison . . . . Phillip Paley
Wendy . . . . Heidi Helmer
Toni . . . . Amanda Goodwin
Scully . . . . Steven Tash
Doug . . . . Tod Bryant
Keith . . . . Douglas R. Starr
Kathleen . . . . Leslie Danon
Dick . . . . Morgan Englund
Babcock . . . . Charles Gilleran
Gina . . . . Tami Smith

■ **"Beach Balls," previously titled "Summertime Fun," is a routine teen comedy briefly released last May and currently in homevideo distribution.**

Familiar format deals with young unrequited romances, intertwined as follows: hero Charlie (Phillip Paley) has the hots for beautiful beach girl Wendy (Heidi Helmer), while Charlie's older sister Kathleen (Leslie Danon) dreams only about lifeguard Doug (Tod Bryant), who just happens to be Wendy's protective brother.

Proper pairings take nearly the whole film to accomplish, while Douglas R. Starr sings some okay rock numbers and an unfunny Erich von Zipper gang of hooligans led by Charles Gilleran make trouble. Genre hasn't progressed much in over two decades with its stereotyped depictions of parents.

Director Joe Ritter doesn't get many laughs from these teen antics and the sexual sequence of whether beautiful but timid Danon will get it on with Bryant is dragged out in very corny fashion. Windup is in the very dated "my life was saved by rock 'n' roll" vein. —*Lor.*

Agosto
(August)
(PORTUGUESE-FRENCH)

A Filmargem (Lisbon), Arion Prods. and La Sept (Paris) coproduction. Executive producer, Paolo Branco. Directed by Jorge Silva Melo. Screenplay, Silva Melo, Philippe Arnaud; camera (color), Acacio de Almeida; editor, Claire Simon; music, José Mario Branco. Reviewed at San Sebastian Film Festival, Sept. 24, 1988. Running time: **97 MIN.**

With: Christian Patey, Olivier Cruveiller, Marie Carré, Pedro Hestnes Ferreira, Manuela de Freitas, José Nascimento, Fernando Mora Ramos, Glincinia Quartin, Rita Blanco.

■ **San Sebastian — This clumsy, amateurish and mortally dull film *looks* like it was shot in one week, with actors making up the lines as they went along.**

Pic has not one saving grace, for direction, thesping, editing, camerawork and music are all on an amateurish level.

Set in August of 1964, the non-story concerns a violin teacher who spends a month in the country with a childhood friend and a married couple. Most of the pic consists of static shots of talking heads using dialog that is so banal it's almost funny. —Besa.

People's Hero
(HONG KONG)

A Maverick Films production. Produced by John Sham. Executive producers, Wang Ying-hsiang, John Sham. Directed by Yee Tung-shing. Screenplay, Yee, Li Pak-ling; camera (color), Wilson Chan; editor, John Ma; music, Lowell Lo; art direction, Wong Yan-kwai. Reviewed at Toronto Festival of Festivals, Sept. 15, 1988. Running time: **82 MIN.**

Sunny Koo .... Ti Lung
Ah Sai .... Tony Leung
Boney .... Ronald Wong
With: Leung Kar-fai, Elaine Jin, Paul Chun.

■ **Toronto** — "People's Hero" is more a meditation on the layers of the criminal mind than an exercise in violence. Yee Tung-shing's second directorial effort is basically a Hong Kong version of "Dog Day Afternoon," focusing on psychological revelations of the gangsters and marked with wit and sympathy.

Slick criminal Sunny Koo (Ti Lung) is about to rob a Hong Kong bank minutes before closing time when his plan is foiled by two rank amateurs with the same intentions. Young Boney and Ah Sai bungle their attempt when Boney has a sudden epileptic fit in the midst of the burglary. When they take the remaining tellers and customers hostage, Koo, gun in hand, emerges on the scene and takes over the operation.

Gradually Sunny's personality unfolds to reveal a caring, moralistic person. He evokes more sympathy than the hostages, who are enraptured by the cachet of being held by a famous criminal.

He allows his captives to call home and tell their loved ones they might be late for dinner. He gives a wounded Pakistani guard enough money to open up a curry shop. He lectures a teenage girl about showing respect for her mother and empathizes with the bank teller whose girlfriend has just ditched him.

Yee sets up each character in economically complete ways and develops their relationships naturally. Personal histories are revealed and weaknesses come to the fore. Tension is punctuated by humorous turns and Yee keeps the pace snappy.

Tech credits are fine throughout and acting is solid. Despite the violent ending, there's probably not enough blood in the pic to satisfy voracious Hong Kong audiences. Theatrical prospects for other territories are iffy. —Devo.

Rojet e Mjegulles — Cuvari Magle
(Guardians Of The Fog)
(YUGOSLAV)

A Yugoslavia Film release of a Kosovafilm production. Directed by Isa Qosja. Screenplay, Fadil Hysaj, Qosja; camera (color), Menduh Nushi; music, Gjon Gjevelekaj; art direction, Nazim Sadiku; costumes, Nuredin Loxha. Reviewed at Pula Film Festival (competing), July 26, 1988. Running time: **104 MIN.**

With: Xhevat Qoraj, Qun Lajqi, Enver Petrovci, Ismajl Ymeri, Florije Siarina.

■ **Pula** — An avant-garde attempt to relate a writer's experiences under a totalitarian regime, using figments of his imagination and his fiction to enlarge the scope, this is a valiant but confusing effort to develop a personal film language and make a courageous political statement.

It's about a writer whose artistic freedom is a thorn in the flesh of the law enforcers, who are trying to find evidence of subversive activities to justify his arrest and punishment.

To do so they capture a tailor (the writer's friend) whose wife is in the grip of the police chief, and put him in the hands of an asthmatic torturer who is supposed to obtain from him an incriminating confession.

All this could be only theoretical, part of the writer's fantasies, but it could also be fact, a detail the picture does not elucidate.

Film is full of wildly violent spectacles, including a burning horse, which sets fire to the crops, and the same horse stuck up to its neck in mud. A woman is raped by a miller in exchange for the flour he gives her, then is murdered by a gang of kids — an ear is bitten off in closeup.

For most of the picture all this could be the image of any reign of terror, but by the end of the script makes it clear that it refers to socialism as it is now.

Dark images, an overdose of symbolism and plenty of gratuitous pretensions raise expectations that are never fulfilled, while a loud, exotic soundtrack sustains the somber mood. Of limited appeal for general audiences, this film may however find a niche in arthouses. —Edna.

Rödtotterne og Tyrannos
(The Redtops Meet Tyrannos)
(DANISH)

A Karne Film release of Per Holst Film production. Produced by Per Holst. Directed by Svend Johansen. Screenplay, Marie Louise Lefèvre; camera (Eastmancolor), Manuel Sellner; editor, Anders Sorensen; music, Anders Koppel; sound, Hans Packert, Per Streit Jansen; production design, Soren Skjar; costumes, casting, Jette Termann; production management, Thomas Lydholm, Henrik Moller Sorensen, Ditte Christiansen, Allan Ohlsson; assistant director, Marie Louise Lauridsen. Reviewed at the Dagmar, Copenhagen, Oct. 11, 1988. Running time: **73 MIN.**

Rune .... Sune Carlsson Kolster
Mina .... Sara Danielle Arentsen
Martin .... Michel Belli
Janne .... Line Kruse
Jonas .... Michael Kastberg
Helen .... Helle Fagralid
Kristine .... Trine Vildbak Hansen
Also with: Karen-Lise Mynster (Karen), Kirsten Lehfeldt, Peter Hesse Overgaard, Kirsten Olesen, Peter Schröder, Lisbeth Dahl, Nils Vest, Henrik Kofoed, Pernille Hansen, Nina Rosenmeir, Mette Sorensen, Mogens Eckert, Sören Skjär, Dag Hollerup, Jytte Strandberg.

■ **Copenhagen** — Helmer Svend Johansen upholds the Nordic tradition for clean, swift and bright cinematic storytelling for preteens with "The Redtops Meet Tyrannos." Item is sure to find plenty of tv sales and a few theatrical and homevideo offshore deals are likely.

Marie Louise Lefèvre's original screenplay draws its inspiration from "The Seven Samurai" without being too serious about it. Seven school kids forget about a variety of grievances to join a very human fairy queen in thwarting an evil real-estate developer's scheme to turn their beloved neck of the woods into a housing project.

Magic mingles with happenstance and the kids' natural ingenuity to carry proceedings through both hokum and mild suspense to a pretty contrived ending. En route, Johansen has coached alert performances out of a bunch of 12-year-olds and succeeds in not making the adults look more foolish than necessary. —Kell.

Fogo e Paixão
(Fire And Passion)
(BRAZILIAN)

A WKW Filmes production. Executive producer, Angelo Gastal. Written and directed by Isay Weinfeld, Marcio Kogan. Camera (color), Pedro Farkas; editor, Mauro Alice; music, Servulo Augusto, Gil Reyes; sets, Felippe Crescenti, Weinfeld, Kogan; associate producer, Sergio Ajzemberg. Reviewed at Vevey Film Festival, Switzerland, Aug. 24, 1988. Running time: **90 MIN.**

Accordian teacher .... Mira Haar
English teacher .... Cristina Mutarelli
Duke .... Carlos Moreno
Guide .... Mariana Suza
Stockbroker .... Fernando Amaral
Also with: Riva Nimitz, Iara Jamra, Kenichi Kaneko, Yvonne Buckingham, Edwin Stanton, Julio Levy, Cassiano Ricardo, Virginia Punko, Norival Rizzo.

■ **Vevey** — This spoof on tourists in Brazil on a sightseeing bus relies mostly on caricaturing each nationality and providing non-stop sight gags. The clowning becomes repetitious and ultimately tedious as the broad farce turns to ennui.

Main characters in the international busload are two middle-aged, homely Brazilian woman teachers out for an "adventure." They eye their companions on the bus, each one repping a popular cliché. There is the smiling, camera-toting Japanese, a characterless American couple, a Brazilian leftwing intellectual, a French girl whose only utterance is "merde," et al.

As the two overweight Brazilians imagine the private lives, tragedies and backgrounds of each of the characters, we are presented comical skits to illustrate the episodes. Interspersed (and quite irrelevant) are dozens of sight gags which cease to be funny after a quarter of an hour. Even the most simpleminded audience will know that when the camera pulls back from a closeup they're in for yet another gag.

The gags and fun-poking are kept at a lively clip. Pic might appeal to less discerning audiences, but most spectators will find the pastiche laid on a bit thick. —Besa.

Himmel og Helvede
(Heaven And Hell)
(DANISH)

A Warner and Metronome Film release of Metronome Film production. Produced by Bent Fabricius-Bjerre. Executive producers, Mads Egmont Christensen, Tivi Magnusson. Directed by Morten Arnfred. Screenplay, Morten Arnfred and Jörgen Ljungdahl, based on Kirsten Thorup's novel; camera (Fujicolor), Dirk Brüel; editor, Lizzy Weischenfeldt; music, Ole Arnfred and excerpts from Max Bruch's Violin Concerto, Bach's Concerto For Two Violins; musical supervision, Kim Sjögren; production design, Palle Arestrup; costumes, Manon Rasmussen; sound (Dolby), Niels Arild; second unit directors, Niels Vest, Anders Refn, Birger Larsen, Mads Egmont Christensen; second unit camera, Dan Lausten; production management, Michael Christensen, Sanne Arnt Torp; Danish Film Institute producer-consultants, Claes Kastholm Hansen, Peter Poulsen, Kirsten Bonnen Rask. Reviewed at the Dagmar, Copenhagen, Oct. 3, 1988. Running time: **120 MIN.**

Maria .... Karina Skands
Jonny .... Ole Lemmeke
Miss Andersen .... Lise Ringheim
Jasmin .... Harriet Andersson
Bols .... Erik Mörk
Also with: Waage Sandö, Kim Sjögren, Peter Schröder, Veli Dastan, Anne Marie Helger, Judy Gringer, Pernille Höjmark, Dorte Hojsted, Vibeke Hastrup, Leif Monsted, Nikolaj Steen, Michael Christensen, Stig Moller, Soren Schou.

■ **Copenhagen** — "Heaven And Hell" is a drama about a young girl emerging into womanhood. The somber hues overshadow the joyous colors, but Morten Arnfred has created yet another feature about the ultimate victory of a young heart.

He has done so within the self-imposed confines of a kind of cinematic chamber music. The result is likely to satisfy discriminating adult hearts and minds wherever the international fest circuit and selective theatrical exhibition may lead it.

Kirsten Thorup's bestselling and widely translated 1982 novel about Copenhagen's semi-slums is a sprawling panorama of characters, oddball and ordinary, revolving around 18-year-old Maria. The girl is a violin prodigy and a late bloomer into womanhood an independence. Amidst poverty and cruelty, she lives a sheltered life.

Arnfred has cut Thorup's cast of characters, plot and action to the bone, which is well enough. Like Thorup, he steers clear of maudlin socio-political sentiment, and nobody is ever exposed to ridicule.

Karina Skands is fine as the darkly luminous Maria, who knows nothing about her own beauty. She has submitted quietly to the tyranny of over-protection as exerted by her father, who is culturally ambitious on her behalf. She gets no support from her mother, who has a suppressed gypsy soul.

In what is essentially a fairytale love story with its own particular twist (boyfriend Jonny is a closet homosexual) and with a touch of magical realism, Maria plunges headlong into the enjoyment of feeling her blooming body and soul.

When their relationship proves doomed, there is genuine heartbreak for both of them when Maria leaves Jonny. She picks up her long-abandoned violin again, and plays it while finding herself on the street surrounded by a swirl of political demonstrators and riot police.

The simultaneous liberation of her parents' lodger (Lise Ringheim) and of her mother (Sweden's Harriet Andersson) is sketched in. Along with Ole Lemmeke, like Skands a film first-timer, and Erik Mörk (Maria's father), all actors put in restrained yet expressive performances.

Cinematographer Dirk Brüel displays virtuosity under total artistic control.

Lizzy Weischenfeldt's editing melts everything into a pattern of perfect story development. Music is unobtrusive yet always to the point. —*Kell.*

Hakaitz Shel Avia
(Avia's Summer)
(ISRAELI)

A Shapira Films presentation. Produced by Gila Almagor, Eitan Even. Directed by Eli Cohen. Screenplay, Cohen, Almagor, Haim Buzaglo, based on Almagor's novel and play; camera (color), David Gurfinkel; editor, Tova Neeman; music, Shemtov Levi; art direction, Yoram Sheier; costumes, Rona Doron. Reviewed at United Studios screening room, Tel Aviv, July 1, 1988. Running time: **98 MIN.**

Henia .... Gila Almagor
Avia .... Kaipu Cohen
Ganz .... Eli Cohen
Also with: Avital Dikkar, Rami Baruch, Marina Rosetti, Dina Avrech, Yossi Kanz, Yaakov Eyali, Ariela Rabinovitz, Sandra Sadeh.

■Tel Aviv — **Israeli stage and film star Gila Almagor has already scored with this story, first as a novel and then as a solo stage show, before deciding to go for a film adaptation. Using some of her own personal memories and experiences, she tells the story of one summer in the life of Avia (in Hebrew the name means "her father"), retold by Avia herself, as an adult, on the**

soundtrack.

The action takes place in 1951, shortly after Israel became an sovereign state. Henia, Avia's mother, is a Holocaust survivor, who has fought with the partisans, was caught and sent to Auschwitz and lost her husband there. Emotionally unstable, she is in and out of mental hospitals, but for one summer she takes her daughter out of boarding school to her suburban house, where she is making a living washing and ironing for the neighbors.

That summer, Avia attempts to convince herself and the others that her father is not really dead. She clashes with the other children and has a frustrating relationship with a young music and ballet teacher, who for a while is charmed by Avia's imagination but then rejects her.

Little Kaipu Cohen, in the title role, gives the least affected and most natural performance. Historical reconstruction is only approximate, but otherwise technical credits are okay and the film might find a receptive audience because of its theme. —*Edna.*

Sarikat Sayfeya
(Summer Thefts)
(EGYPTIAN)

An MISR Intl. Films production. Produced, written and directed by Yousry Nasrallah. Camera (color), Ramses Marzoek; editor, Rahma Montasser; music, Omar Khayrat; sound, Gerard Rousseau. Reviewed at Bloor Cinema, Toronto (in Toronto Festival of Festivals, Contemporary World Cinema), Sept. 6, 1988. Running time: **102 MIN.**

With: Ahmad M. Ahmad, Hani Hussein, Menha Batraoui, Mona Zakareya, Abla Kamel, Chawki Chamekh.

■Toronto — **A nostalgic first feature, "Summer Thefts" is an appealing chronicle of life in Egypt in the summer of 1961, based on director Yousry Nasrallah's own childhood memories upon his return to Egypt after a 20-year self-imposed exile.**

Fests surely will be interested in this effort, but commercial success will be modest.

Nasrallah's script centers on Yasser, the film's young hero, who lives a comfortable upper-middle-class existence in the town of Kayed, a tranquil domain in the midst of Nasser's social upheaval. His mother and father are getting divorced. When he and his Granny use paper cups and string to snoop on his mother's conversation with her sister Mona, he thinks his mother is saying they have no money.

He and his siblings commiserate on their fate, and Yasser is convinced he should steal from the rich, like Robin Hood, to save his family. He befriends Leil, a peasant boy, with whom he develops a mischievous yet close kinship.

Yasser's Aunt Mona is being

wooed by an aide of Nasser's and his educated cousin Dahlia returns home, where she has to end a romantic liaison with an army man because he is low-class. The whole family — dotty aunts, opinionated uncles and bratty cousins — gathers around the radio to hear Nasser announce new procedures to revolutionize production and reform land, and the family thinks the government has expropriated them.

Tech credits are quite fine. The camera preserves the innocence of the child's point of view. Some of the scenes have the intimacy of a home movie. There are relaxed performances from an interesting cast.

Nasrallah, like his colleague Youssef Chahine (with whom he worked on "Memory" and "Adieu, Bonaparte"), has recounted an absorbing time in Egypt's history and has juxtaposed it with the ingenuousness of childhood pleasures. Pic marks the arrival of a sensitive director. —*Devo.*

Dogodilo se na Daneanji Dan
(It Happened On This Very Day)
(YUGOSLAV)

A Jugoslavia Film presentation of a CFS Avala Film production. Produced by Branko Baletic, Jasmine Vladic. Directed by Miroslav Lekic. Screenplay, Deana Leskover; camera (color), Radoslav Vladic; set design, Aleksandra Gligorijevic. Reviewed at Montreal World Film Festival (Yugoslavian Cinema of Today), Aug. 31, 1988. Running time: **98 MIN.**

With: Olja Bekovic, Marica Vuletic, Zarko Lausevic, Zoran Cvijanovic, Srdan Topalovic, Milena Dravic.

■Montreal — **An old corner of Belgrade is the setting for this unpretentious but slight neo-realistic comedy about teenagers during the repressive early '60s seen from a late-'80s perspective by a promising new-generation Yugoslav director.**

For the new '80s Yugo generation, the hammer-and-sickle is an empty symbol, a floppy and deflated balloon in the "Youth Day" parade opening this irreverent second feature film by 34-year-old Miroslav Lekic.

The time is 1963, in a side-street courtyard of a Belgrade worker's suburb. Until a heart-tug at the end, the viewer is easily carried along through the daily round of teen cares, from evading the social worker who wants to reclaim a truant from a broken home to writing the school essay homework assignment. In the social microcosm of the film, a half-dozen high-school age kids and a few moppets are encircled in their own hermetic backdoor of the courtyard, with only occasional intervention from surrounding adults.

One kid is a scalper at soccer games; none of them seem to take high school very seriously. Puppy-

love crushes blossom at school dances, while neighborhood bullies disrupt the milk route of a likable protagonist.

What is unusual in this Yugoslavian film is a fresh celebration of the ordinary for a change, sans political message, melodrama and high hysterics, with a well-cast panoply of unpretentious new faces exhibiting sincere friendship for one another within their milieu.

By virtue of direction, casting and script — though hardly any plot — this summer of '63 has rewarding charm, which all comes to an abrupt fade as the circle breaks, with two of the central kids leaving, never to return.

Technical credits good. Prospects are mainly seen as festival fare, Yugo Weeks abroad, limited art house exposure and cable tv.
—*Milg.*

Memorias y Olvidos
(Things Forgotten And Not)
(ARGENTINE)

An Instituto Nacional de Cinematografía Argentina (Inca) release of a Producciones Gerardo Arazi production. Written and directed by Simón Feldman. Camera (color), Esteban Pablo Courtalón; music, Rodolfo Mederos; art direction, Ponchi Morpurgo; sound, Enrique Zalcman. Reviewed at Festival Latino, N.Y., Aug. 14, 1988. Running time: **94 MIN.**

With: Arturo Maly, Juan Leyrado, Lorenzo Quinteros, Harry Havilio, Elvira Vicario, Marcela Casabella, Pablo Napoli, Adolfo Yanneli, Sergio Corona, Silvia Moldován, Ana Masi, Sebastián Miranda, Carlos Kaufman.

■**Argentina's "Memorias y Olividos" (Things Forgotten And Not, a.k.a. Our Memory Is Short) is a botched attempt to explain what has gone wrong in the southern zone. But, the real question here is "What has gone wrong with this film?"**

At pic's heart is a docu, which filmmaker Simón Feldman tries desperately to avoid. Instead he emerges with a fictionalized open grabbag that is talky, static, stagey and just plain doesn't work.

Pic's premise deals with a tv producer (Arturo Maly), who wants to make an all-encompassing docu that will explain to the world why Argentina has never lived up to the potential of a first-world nation. To accomplish this, he assigns three separate docu projects to two national journalists (one male and one female) and a Swiss historian. He hopes that all three works might be fused to yield satisfying results.

At film's end the trio present their disparate versions, which are hotly critiqued by all involved. This debate is, supposedly, the message of the film. Docus include real historical footage, stills, newspaper headlines and authentic man-on-the-street interviews conducted all over the republic.

Much of the material collected

could be used to make a fascinating docu, but the fictional treatment is stilted and confusing. There are forced love conflicts that go nowhere and hints at characterizations that are never developed. Lensing is consistently dark throughout. Potentially interesting docu material is presented tediously via closeups of tv monitors, while soundtrack consists of arguments about what is presented.

The final word on the subject is that in Argentina, history repeats itself endlessly without advancing. The final word on the film is that it mirrors Argentina's history. —*Lent.*

ARCHIVE REVIEWS

Ajantrik
(Pathetic Fallacy)
(INDIAN-B&W)

An L&M Films Intl. production. Produced by Pramod Lahiri. Written and directed by Ritwik Ghatak, from a story by Subodh Ghosh, Camera (b&w), Dinen Gupta; editor, Ramesh Joshi; music, Ali Akbar Khan; sound, Mrinal Guha Thakurta, Satyen Chatterjee; art direction, Ravi Chatterjee. Reviewed at the Berlin Film Festival (Forum), Feb. 20, 1988. Running time: **102 MIN.**
Bimal . . . . .Kali Bannerjee
Also with: Ganesh Mukherjee, Satindra Bhattacharya, Gangapada Basu.
(In Bengali)

■ **Berlin — Reviewed for the record, "Ajantrik" (1958) is the third feature made by the great Indian director Ritwik Ghatak. Its producer called it "a total flop" when it came out, but foreign critics like Georges Sadoul and Henri Langlois hailed it as a landmark work.**

Ghatak is said to have been agonized over the public's rejection and began his long, destructive relation to alcohol while making it. Seen today the b&w tale of a poor man's love for his taxi, which he treats as human, is a tragicomic gem suitable for art house revival.

Bimal (played effectively by Kali Bannerjee) is the driver of an old jalopy he calls Jagoddal which he bought, significantly, the day his mother died. It's the oldest taxi in his small Bengali town, despised because of its age and sorry state of repair, but grudgingly admired for still running smoothly.

The fact is, Jagoddal is alive: it moves its headlights like eyes, throws temper tantrums, and returns Bimal's affection by running on almost no gas.

"Ajantrik" moves through a series of farcical situations where comedy melts into a disturbing reflection on man's need to love. Bimal tolerates no insults to his fiercely beloved vehicle, and is likely to throw out his passengers in the middle of a ride for a disparaging word. In one anguishing scene, some little boys hurl mud at the car in play; Bimal throws himself against Jagoddal and takes the mudballs himself, as if they were bullets.

The undoing of this passionate romance between man and machine is a girl. Bimal meets her eloping with a man who soon leaves her alone and desperate. Jagoddal is so jealous of Bimal's tenderness towards the girl it refuses to drive him to the train station to catch up with her. Instead it stops beside a valley where a strange tribal rite is taking place that distracts Bimal till morning.

In anger he turns against the car; one kick is enough to make it break down completely. Their tragic reentry into town typically combines film's humor and pathos, reflected in the villagers' cruel hilarity at the sight of the limping Jagoddal. When Bimal at last sells his beloved to the junkman for a handful of coins, he laughs with tears in his eyes to hear the only surviving part, the horn, croaking its petulant grief. grief.

Both charming and complex, "Ajantrik" offers a foretaste of a great filmmaker's tormented spirit, his feeling for his people and sensibility to their troubles. Film is lensed with striking care and intimately mated to its score, which ranges from local music to a disquieting drumbeat. — *Yung.*

Blue Scar
(BRITISH-B&W)

A British Lion release (in 1949) of an Outlook Films production. Produced by William MacQuitty. Written and directed by Jill Craigie. Camera (b&w), Jo Jago; editor, Kenneth Hume; music, Grace Williams. Reviewed at Museum of Modern Art (print from National Film Archive, London), N.Y., Sept. 26, 1988. Running time: **92 MIN.**
Tom Thomas . . . . .Emrys Jones
Olwen Williams . . . . . . .Gwyneth Vaughan
Gweneth Williams . . . . .Rachel Thomas
Alfred Collins . . . . .Anthony Pendrell
Ted Williams. . . . . .Prysor Williams
Granny . . . . .Madoline Thomas
Dai Morgan . . . . .Jack James
Thomas Williams . . . . . . .Kenneth Griffith

■ **Virtually unknown in the U.S., "Blue Scar" is an unusual 1949 British picture telling the familiar story of the hardships of Welsh coal miners in a combination of militant realism and a contrasting romanticism.**

Central story concerns the attempt of beautiful Olwen (Gwyneth Vaughan) to escape from the stultifying environment of her small mining village of Abergwyfni by becoming an opera singer in London. Her boyfriend Tom (Emrys Jones), like her family, is a miner, but she wants him to quit and get a "collar and tie job."

Set in 1946-47, most of the first portion of the picture deals with the miners' grievances and problems under postwar nationalization of the industry, which does not live up to its promise of improving their lot. With unsafe conditions in the mine depicted as well as the tragic fate of Olwen's dad, film builds to a confrontation where the miners are ready to walk out in support of their mate who has had a run-in with a nasty new supervisor (Jack James).

Abruptly, a compromise is struck and story backs off from its militant stand to a more typical "making do" payoff.

Olwen's rosy views of the rich life in London are humorously debunked in a blistering scene of the shallow, snooty cafe society there. Film's heart is with the rugged Welsh landscape, beautifully photographed by Jo Jago, who later worked on second unit for such major films as "The Cruel Sea."

Unusual credit card at opening states: "This film is written and directed by Jill Craigie," a documentary filmmaker who was one of the few women postwar feature directors in England, followed soon after by Muriel Box and Wendy Toye. Her work here is uneven but shows promise, apparently never realized with another fiction feature.

Welsh cast is adequate, notably including as Olwen's layabout brother Kenneth Griffith, later seen in many screen comedies. — *Lor.*

Pechki Lavochki
(Stones And Benches)
(SOVIET-B&W)

A Maxim Gorky Studio production. Written and directed by Vasily Shukshin. Camera (Widescreen, black & white), Anatoli Zabolotsky; music, Pavel Chekalov; production design, Igor Bakhmetyev; sound, A. Matvememko. Reviewed at Toronto Festival of Festivals, Sept. 16, 1988. Running time: **99 MIN.**
With: Vasily Shukshin, Lydia Fedoseyeva, Vsevolod Sanayev, Georgy Burkov.

■ **Toronto — Made in 1972, this Vasily Shukshin film is a disarming comedy centered around a long train journey undertaken by a Siberian tractor driver (played by the writer-director) and his wife who leave their village for a trip to the seaside.**

Charming opening scenes in the village give way to amusing scenes on the train as the innocents abroad run into a variety of characters, including a conman and a collector of folk songs.

The film's structure is very loose (it is said to have run for over five hours in roughcut) but it's all the more charming for that.

As the country couple coming up against the city slickers, Shukshin and Lydia Fedoseyeva are tremendously warmhearted and funny.
—*Strat.*

Zabitá nedéle
(A Wasted Sunday)
(CZECH-B&W)

A Barrandov Studio production (1969). Produced by Richard Nemec. Directed by Drahomíra Vihanová. Screenplay, Vihanová, Jiri Krenek, based on Krenek's novel; camera (b&w), Peter Volf; editor, Miros Lahásek; music, Jiri Sust; art direction, Vladimir Labsky. Reviewed at Karlovy Vary Film Festival, July 14, 1988. Running time: **80 MIN.**
Arnost .Ivan Paluch
Waitress . . . . .Mila Myslíková

■ **Karlovy Vary — Drahomira Vihanová's remarkable 1969 feature "A Wasted Sunday" was her first and last feature. Kept out of circulation since it was made by authorities leery of its relentless portrait of nihilism and the futility of Army life, film received its first public screening (though unannounced) at the women directors' show within the Karlovy Vary fest.**

Though film's stylization and b&w lensing are signs of the time when it was made, it still has the freshness and snap of an unfettered work, bound to be of keen interest to fests and specialized programmers.

Arnost (Ivan Paluch) is a youthful Army officer, c.o. of an unmanned barracks in some remote town. Peter Volf's fluid, continually moving camera depicts him awkwardly trying to make breakfast on Sunday morning. The good-looking soldier is revealed as a cynical, macho type infatuated with his uniform and his revolver (he likes to test his nerves at Russian roulette in front of the mirror).

A few incidents bring out the fellow's repulsive character. He has disturbing, though apparently harmless conversations with a little neighbor girl. A pair of giggling teenage girls are arrested for sunbathing topless and brought before the severe c.o., but they scorn him so much he can't manage to type out a report. Some nude scenes recall to Arnost's mind memories of wild nights. He shoots rats for sport.

Although there's little more to the story than these few scenes suggest, "A Wasted Sunday" succeeds in riveting the attentive viewer with the limpid beauty of its black and white lensing. Paluch plays the main role with understated antipathy. Sets are minimal in the extreme.

Originally, pic was skedded for shooting in August 1968, but the events in Prague made it possible only to lens the exteriors before the next year. Drahomira was allowed to finish the film, but it was at once put on the shelf on the grounds, per the director, "it doesn't correspond to the conditions under which we live." The director was inactive for the next seven years, after which she began a successful documentary career. — *Yung*.

Kommunist
(The Communist)
(SOVIET-B&W)

A Mosfilm production. Directed by Yuli Raizman. Screenplay, Yevgeny Gabrilovich; camera (b&w), Alexander Shelenkov, Chen Yu-lan music, Rodion Shchedrin; production design, Mikhail Bogdanov, Gennady Myasnikov; sound, S. Minervin. Reviewed at Toronto Festival of Festivals (Soviet Retrospective), Sept. 10, 1988. Running time: **115 MIN.**

Vassili Gubanov.......Yevgeny Urbansky
Anyuta...................Sofia Pavlova
With: Sergei Yakovlev, Boris Smirnov, Yevgeny Shutov.

■ **Toronto — Made in 1957, when the so-called Krushchev thaw launched a new spirt in Soviet cinema (that included such classics as "The Cranes Are Flying"), "The Communist" is much better than its didactic title would suggest.**

Set in 1918, when the post-revolutionary Civil War was still raging, its outcome uncertain, pic centers on a young firebrand, Gubanov, sent to manage the supply depot at a power plant under construction in the countryside near Moscow. He discovers a place where food and sugar are worth more than money, where lodging must be shared, and at a price, and where a great many people are waiting for the Whites to regain power so a few scores can be settled.

Basic necessities, like nails with which to build the plant, are not to be found, and Gubanov travels to Moscow and actually gets in to see Lenin, who stops a meeting to make a few phone calls to track down a source of supply. It may sound silly, but it's handled with such skill that it humanizes Lenin in a rather charming way.

To complicate matters, Gubanov falls heavily in love with the pretty wife of an anti-Communist. "Will there be love under communism?" he asks a colleague.

Director Yuli Raizman, whose career started in the '20s, and who was still directing in the 1980s, has captured the chaotic and uncertain mood of the period with skill and humor, aided by fluid camerawork and robust performances. "The Communist" can now be seen as one of the films which helped breathe new life into the reverential Soviet cinema of the period. —*Strat*.

Obyasnenie V Lubvi
(Declaration Of Love)
(SOVIET)

A Lenfilm production. Directed by Ilya Averbach. Screenplay, Pavel Finn, based on "Four Quarters" by Yevgeni Gabrilovich; camera (Sovcolor), D. Dolinin; music, Bach, Vivaldi, Mahler; sound, B. Andreyev; production design, V. Svetozarov. Reviewed at Toronto Festival of Festivals, Sept. 14, 1988.

Running time: **130 MIN.**

Philipok................Yuri Bogatyriov
Zina................Ewa Szykulska
Gladishev................Kirill Lavrov
Old Woman................A. Stepanova
Old Man................Bruno Freindlikh
Girl................Dasha Mikhailova
Boy................Nikita Sergeyev

■ **Toronto — An elegiac, romantic pic with a very hard center, "Declaration Of Live," (also known as "To My Beloved") was made in 1977 and based on a book by Yevgeni Gabrilovich which told a personal story against the background of political events in the Soviet Union in the post-revolutionary era.**

The film begins with an old man visiting his wife in a nursing home; he presents her with a book he's just had published, but she seems unimpressed. Flashbacks tell their story.

Philipok (Yuri Bogatyriov) is an anarchist frequently harassed by the communists when he meets Zina (Ewa Szykulska), an unconventional unwed mother. They become lovers and later marry, but his work as a journalist often takes him away from home. He's a witness of a police raid on an allegedly criminal house and also observes and writes about the collectivization program. On one of his trips, he returns home to find his wife has a lover.

Story encompasses the war years as well as subjects that must still have been touchy in the mid-'70s, but the love story dominates, suggesting that our personal problems linger in the memory more persistently than great political upheavals.

In addition, and like Bernstein in "Citizen Kane," Philipok is haunted by a youthful memory: a beautiful girl in a white dress he saw on the deck of a steamer one sunny day many years ago.

Despite its controversial themes, "Declaration Of Love" was never suppressed by the Soviet authorities; on the contrary, it was scheduled to compete at the Berlin fest in 1979, but was withdrawn to protest the inclusion in that year's program of Michael Cimino's "The Deer Hunter." — *Strat*.

Nebo Nashevo Detstva
(The Sky Of Our Childhood)
(SOVIET-B&W)

A Kirghizfilm Studio production. Directed by Tolomush Okeyev. Screenplay, Okeyev, O. Omerkulov; camera (widescreen, b&w), Kadyrzhan Kydyraliyev; music, T. Yermatov; production design, S. Ishyenov. Reviewed at Toronto Festival of Festivals, Sept. 11, 1988. Running time: **78 MIN.**

With: M. Ryskulov.

■ **Toronto — The year 1967 must have been an extremely sensitive one for Soviet film bureaucrats: not only were Alexander Askoldov's "Commissar" and Andrei Konchalovsky's "Asya's Happiness" banned that year, but also this poetic first feature of Kirghiz director Tolomush Okeyev. Now, at last, it's free to be seen.**

Film is set in remote mountain country where a traditional way of life tentatively survives. A young boy flies by helicopter from school in the city to spend a vacation with his parents, who live in a tent along with other families. They raise horses, as they and their ancestors always have.

Inevitably this remote, traditional, religious world is changing. Not only are the children receiving city educations, after which most opt to stay on in the city, but a highway is being constructed through the area, and the herdsmen have to move on to new pastures.

Probably it was the filmmaker's innate sympathy for the fate of these people that found disfavor with the Moscow authorities. Certainly they seem ill-treated by the road construction team, and are not even officially informed they will have to leave their traditional homes. One amazing moment has a mob of horses inadvertently driven into an area where blasting is taking place; the herd stampedes as a sudden series of explosions occur right in their path.

Pic is beautifully shot in widescreen and black & white, and it's a quietly moving plea for the future of these Asian people. It packs more emotional impact than such later Okeyev films as "The Fierce One" (1974) or "The Descendant Of The Snow Leopard" (1985). —*Strat*.

Sedmoi Sputnik
(The Seventh Satellite)
(SOVIET-B&W)

A Lenfilm Studio production. Directed by Alexei Gherman, Grigori Aronov. Screenplay, Yuri Klepikov, Edgar Dubrovski, based on a story by Boris Lavrenev; camera (b&w), Eduard Rozovski; editor, R. Izakson; music, I. Shvarc; sound, B. Antonov; art direction, I. Vuskovich; costumes, V. Rachmatulina. Reviewed at Pesaro Film Festival, June 15, 1988. Running time: **89 MIN.**

Adamov..................Andrei Popov
Also with: A. Anisimov, G. Shtil, P. Chernov, V. Osenev, V. Abramov, S. Giacintova, V. Erenberg, V. Michailov, G. Shpigel, P. Kudlai, G. Yumatov.

■ **Pesaro — Leningrad helmer Alexei Gherman's first feature (codirected with Grigori Aronov in 1968), is a little-seen b&w curiosity item of sure interest for retros and homages.**

After a static and unpromising opening, film gets down to business and tells how the honest Russian intellectual Adamov (a fine performance by veteran Andrei Popov), an old Czarist general and law prof, joins the revolution and dies a hero fighting for Soviet power. As rhetorical as it sounds, story is actually quite subtle and spiced with historical irony.

Time is late 1918, when counter-revolutionaries are on the offensive. Adamov is rounded up along with all kinds of old Czarist supporters. Accused of treason, he is tried by a Soviet military tribunal and, to his own surprise, found innocent. He has nowhere to go, since his spacious apartment has been requisitioned and divvied up among numerous families; his old bourgeois friends won't help him out. He asks the Soviet commissar to be taken on as a laundry boy, but is soon sent out on missions. On one he is shot and killed in a poetic shot of a snowy field.

Title derives from Adamov's explanation of why he joined the revolution: "When a big planet passes by, smaller bodies are drawn into its orbit." The hero's doubts and contractions foreshadow the theme of Gherman's later work — the blurring of ideological certainties and the complexity of real life. —*Yung*.

Vash Syn I Brat
(Your Son And Brother)
(SOVIET-B&W)

A Maxim Gorky Studio production. Written and directed by Vasily Shukshin. Camera (black & white), Valeri Ginsberg; music, Pavel Bachmetiv; production design, Igor Bachmetiv. Reviewed at Toronto Festival of Festivals, Sept. 16, 1988. Running time: **92 MIN.**

Father..................Vsevolod Saneyev
Mother..................A. Filipova
Stepan..................Leonid Kuravlev
Vera..................M. Grakhova
Ignaty..................A. Vanin
Maxim..................I. Reutov
Vassily..................V. Shakhov

■ **Toronto — An early (1966) film by Siberian actor-writer-director Vasily Shukshin, whose premature death in 1975 robbed Soviet cinema of one of its great talents, this poetic tale of family life in a small Siberian village evokes the work of John Ford via its genuine sentiment and feeling for family ties.**

Pic begins one spring morning with lovely images of ice melting and life returning to normal after the winter. A youth returns home, after serving a spell in prison, and is greeted by members of his family in scenes that inevitably recall Ford's "The Grapes Of Wrath." Stepan has escaped from prison, feeling that his inevitable capture is worth it if he can only see his parents and deaf-mute sister, Vera, again. During family celebrations, he's re-arrested.

This is the first of three short stories linked together in the film. In the other two, the old couple's city-based sons try to locate some snake venom liniment for their mother's lumbago, but are frustrated at every turn, eventually restorting to under-the-counter dealing to procure the medicine.

The final segment has Ignaty, one of the city boys, bringing his new wife home to meet his disapproving parents.

Shukshin, who often acted in his films but didn't in this one, was a great lyrical filmmaker. There's little dialog here, but a look is made to speak volumes. Valeri Ginsberg's camerawork is a joy. It's a shame Shukshin's work is so little known in the west. —*Strat.*

Wigilia
(Christmas Eve)
(POLISH-B&W)

A Karol Irzykowski Film Studio production. Written and directed by Leszek Wosiewicz. Camera (b&w), Krzysztof Ptak; editor, Jadwiga Lesniewicz; music, Krzysztof Konieczny; art direction, Wojciech Mierzwiak; production manager, Krzysztof Was. Reviewed at Gdynia Film Festival, Sept. 14, 1988. Running time: **60 MIN.**
Grandmother Paulina . . . Zofia Mrozowska
Maria . . . . Barbara Wrzesinska
Ania . . . . Ewa Blaszczyk

■ Gdynia — "Christmas Eve" should be just about the last shelved Polish film from the martial law period (it was shot in 1982) to receive official release and fest showcasing.

In graphic black and white, film recreates the tension of a holiday shared by three tense women whose man is missing — presumably on the lam from authorities (or arrested) for his connection to the outlawed trade union Solidarity.

Director Leszek Wosiewicz deliberately tries to tone down events and focus on psychological drama, but result is a 1-note situation without dramatic impetus. It could find takers on the fest circuit and, of course, in Polish film weeks.

Date is Dec. 24, 1981; place, a big, run-down apartment. Ania (Ewa Blaszczyk) and grandma Paulina (the fine actress Zofia Mrozowska, controlled and very human) worry about Ania's husband Witek, who has been missing for 10 days. Maria (Barbara Wrzesinska), Witek's young mother, is on the brink of hysteria, helpless (she can't get the Christmas tree up) and uncertain.

Constructed like a stage drama, film mostly unfolds during a tense, unpleasant dinner. Ania's parents make an awkward appearance; one of Witek's friends, also in hiding, briefly appears; a priest comes and offers some reassuring prayers. Witek, however, never shows, leaving the women in a state of anguished uncertainty.

Atmosphere has an authentic feel, making the story a test of nerves for the audience, too. B&w lensing gives pic a bleak starkness which, like the rather overdone soundtrack of plucked strings, appeals at first but ends up as overkill. Cast is professional, but directed like stage actors (only grandmother Mrozowska is able to play down her role and seem natural).

Yet in spite of its shortcomings, "Christmas Eve" is an impressive document of the times — not surprisingly, since Wosiewicz began shooting in January '82. His subsequent short subject, "The Case Of Herman The Stoker," won several prizes, including Oberhausen in 1987. — *Yung.*

MILL VALLEY REVIEWS

From Hollywood
To Deadwood

A Nightfilm production. Executive producer, Bill Byrne. Produced by Jo Peterson. Written and directed by Rex Pickett. Camera (Duart color), Peter Deming; editor, Steven Adrianson, Robert Erickson; music, Alex Gibson, Gregory Kuehn; sound, Patrick Moriarty; art direction, Tori Hourafchan; costumes, Meg Goodwin. Reviewed at the Mill Valley Film Festival, Calif., Oct. 8, 1988. No MPAA Rating. Running time: **102 MIN.**
Raymond Savage . . . . Scott Paulin
Jack Haines . . . . Jim Haynie
Lana Dark . . . . Barbara Schock
Steve Reese . . . . Jurgen Doeres
Nick Detroit . . . . Chris Mulkey
Ernie November . . . . Mike Genovese
Peter Mueller . . . . Norbert Weisser
Ted Field . . . . Tom Dahlgren
Bobby . . . . Campbell Scott

■ Mill Valley — An early favorite in its preem at the Mill Valley Film Festival, "From Hollywood To Deadwood" puts its feet up and relaxes with an amusing, engaging piece of pulp detective fiction, proving anew that story and dialog can still be more effective than special effects.

There are only two gunshots fired

in writer-director Rex Pickett's melodramatic murder mystery, but no more are needed. Even better, as Pickett's pair of off-beat private eyes follow the clues, their aging auto is never tempted into a single car chase, lucky enough to keep air in its tires and water in its hoses.

Even when the corpse appears, it's charmingly dainty, reposed in a minimum of blood on the pillow case, a shotgun by its head. To Pickett's credit, he sees no need to excite his audience with the obvious reality that a shotgun in such a situation would have left no head.

As the dubious detective team, Scott Paulin and Jim Haynie are terrific, comfortably and familiarly playing off each other as if it were the sixth year of a series. The thoughtful intellectual, Paulin has a lowkey Clint Eastwood quality which Pickett deftly contrasts with Haynie's boozing, knuckle-dusting approach to any problem.

Down and out and in desperate need of funds — as gumshoes always are in these outings — Paulin and Haynie are hired by a semi-

sleazy Hollywood film company to find its star, Barbara Schock, who has taken a powder in the midst of production.

Nothing that happens after that is ever radically original, but it's fun, nonetheless, to follow the detectives on the trail. Moreso, it's fun to listen to them talk. Sample: "Does that girl look crazy to you?" Paulin asks. "You never know 'till you buy them a drink," Haynie answers.

Watching her old movies for a hint to her motives, Paulin develops a crush on Schock, convincing himself she must be an innocent victim of whatever's going on, a conclusion that naturally upsets Haynie's hopes of getting the reward money quickly without complication.

For just a moment, "Deadwood" almost dissolves in the dramatics of Paulin's obsession, never quite believable at best and a drain on the dialog at worst. The pair quickly pull themselves back together and get on with solving the case.

Supporting cast is excellent, including some highly competent efforts by Schock, Jurgen Doeres as a producer and Mike Genovese as another private eye. Tech credits are yeoman within the low budget. —*Har.*

Una Casa in Bilico
(Tottering Lives/A House
On A Limb)
(ITALIAN)

A Positive Vision release. Produced and directed by Antonietta de Lillo, Giorgio Magliulo. Screenplay, Guiditta Rinaldi, De Lillo, Magliulo; camera (Kodak color), Magliulo; editor, Mirco Garrone; music, Franco Pieranti. Reviewed at the Mill Valley Film Festival, Calif., Oct. 11, 1988. No MPAA rating. Running time: **90 MIN.**
Maria . . . . Marina Vlady
Giovanni . . . . Riccardo Cucciolla
Teo . . . . Luigi Pistilli

■ Mill Valley — U.S. distributor Positive Vision has tentatively retitled this release "Tottering Lives" for the Mill Valley Film Festival, but the major problem with the picture is not that it totters, but that it slumps.

Essentially sweet story features a trio of oldsters attempting to adjust to one another after moving into an apartment together in Rome. The interplay is nice and all three performers are quite good, but nothing much happens. When it does, the problems are either quickly and neatly resolved or beyond solution.

Exuberant Riccardo Cucciolla has inherited the apartment and invited Marina Vlady, a lovely Russian immigrant, and Luigi Pistilli, his fastidious, timid friend from college days, to share it with him.

Producer-directors and cowriters Antonietta de Lillo and Giorgio Magliulo given plenty of hints that there's much more to these char-

acters beyond the surface, but rarely get beyond the surface.

One subplot concerns Vlady's desire to get Pistilli to marry a young Russian friend of hers so the subsequent Italian citizenship can then grease the girl's way to get to the U.S., but it's resolved too quickly. Ditto some confusion over whether Cucciolla really owns the apartment.

Even worse, nothing that goes before quite sets up the bittersweet ending. On balance, consequently, picture is nothing to hate, nothing to be particularly bored by, but nothing to bother with, either. —*Har.*

Journey To Spirit Island

A Pal Prods.-Seven Wonders Entertainment film. Produced by Bruce Clark. Executive producers, Rodger Spero, Laszlo Pal, Clark. Directed by Laszlo Pal. Screenplay, Crane Webster; camera (Alpha Cine color), Vilmos Zsigmond; editor, Bonnie Koehler; music, Fred Myrow; sound, Robert Marts; production design, Bruce Jackman; coproducer, Robert Spero; associate producer, Bruce Dwiggins; casting, April Webster, Patti Kallas. Reviewed at the Mill Valley Film Festival, Calif., (Also in Chicago Film Festival.) Oct. 9, 1988. No MPAA Rating. Running time: **93 MIN.**
Maria . . . . Bettina
Jimmy Jim . . . . . Marie Antoinette Rodgers
Michael . . . . Brandon Douglas
Willie . . . . Gabriel Damon
Klim . . . . Tarek McCarthy
Hawk . . . . Tony Acierto
Tom . . . . Nick Ramus
Phil . . . . Attila Gombacsi

■ Mill Valley — Cinematographer Vilmos Zsigmond makes a virtual postcard out of "Journey To Spirit Island" while director Laszlo Pal and an able cast of youngsters composes the kind of family adventure film that once could find easy markets. Only question is whether those family markets still exist.

Lensed on the Olympic Peninsula and San Juan Islands of the Pacific Northwest, the picture simply couldn't be prettier, nature supplying the perfect backdrop for a modern spiritual fable of American Indians.

Living on a reservation, teenage Bettina is caught between miniskirted, pop music peer pressure and the old ways of grandmother Marie Antoinette Rodgers, herself making a last stand against the development of tribal burial island into a resort.

In troubled dreams, Bettina seems to be beckoned to the island by an ancestral spirit. It's no wonder she eventually ends up shipwrecked there when a kayak springs a leak while on an outing with her younger brother, Tarek McCarthy, and two city friends from Chicago, Brandon Douglas and Gabriel Damon.

Grandmother's tribal opponent, Tony Acierto, and henchman Attila Gombacsi show up to further their plot to sell out to the developers and are surprised to learn the youngsters have witnessed their misdeeds. They corner the kids in a cave and seal it off, leaving them to their doom.

This is all standard family adventure stuff but the youngsters are likeable and their trials and eventual triumph over the villains stay well within the believable, given the mystical spiritual assistance Bettina receives from great-great-granddad.

Rodgers and Acierto are both good as generational opponents and Nick Ramus adds solid support as Bettina's father, admiring both his mother's tradition and his daughter's independence. —*Har.*

Final Season
(DOCU)

A Halcyon Days production. Produced by Mike Tollin and Fredric Golding. Directed by Mike Tollin. Camera (color), Charles S. Cohen; editor, Susan Crutcher; music, Jim Jacobsen. Reviewed at the Mill Valley Film Festival, Calif., Oct. 9, 1988. No MPAA Rating. Running time: **100 MIN.**

■ Mill Valley — **After the fact of Tampa Bay Bandits' owner John Bassett's death, documentarian Mike Tollin strives to make ''Final Season'' something more than a locker room visit. Only the hardiest of pro football fans could find much appeal in the time spent with a herd of inarticulate, second-rate players.**

Bassett himself was a cornerstone of the now defunct U.S. Football League and for a while his Bandits were among the most promising teams. In the midst of the struggle to keep team and league alive in 1985, Bassett developed two fatal brain tumors and died a few months after the last game.

No doubt, Bassett was a forceful personality and Tollin captures a glimpse of why. That still comes across as an afterthought to Tollin's interest in the players, the coaches and the games — none of which is particularly inspiring or unique.

Though efforts ahead of time at the Mill Valley Film Festival attempted to elevate ''Final Season'' to some kind of celebration of the human spirit, giveaway comes in the semi-prurient opening titles as two cheerleader bimbos writhe around the muscular body of a ball-player. This may be human, but it ain't quite spiritual.

With only a few exceptional moments, ''Season'' remains content to listen to the usual macho mouthings about pain, pride, team spirit, kicking A, gluttonous eating and women, some of whom are shown to be equally empty-headed as they prepare for their participation as cheerleaders.

For both players and coaches, the locker-room mentality of football seems set at the junior-high level and never changes, except for the salaries. With a few exceptions, even the salaries weren't that great in the U.S. League and Tollin does outline some of the career panic that haunts the players, most barely semipros who may soon be selling cars if this chance doesn't work out.

On the field, the Bandits may have had their moments and, off the field, many on the squad were doubtlessly devoted to Bassett and affected by his unfortunate illness. Except for loyal fans, however, there's little in ''Final Season'' to make anybody care whether it was their last hurrah or not. —*Har.*

L'Ours
(The Bear)
(FRENCH-70M)

An AMLF release of a Renn production. Executive producer, Claude Berri. Produced by Pierre Grunstein. Directed by Jean-Jacques Annaud. Screenplay, Gérard Brach, based on novel, ''The Grizzly King'' by James Oliver Curwood; camera (70m Panavision, Eastmancolor), Philippe Rousselot; editor, Noëlle Boisson; music, Philippe Sarde; sound, Laurent Quaglio; art direction, Toni Ludi; animation, Bretislav Pojar; special effects, Jim Henson's Creature Shop; animal adviser, Jean-Philippe Varin; second unit and assistant director, Xavier Castano; production manager, Léonard Cmuer. Reviewed at Gaumont Ambassade theater, Paris, Oct. 19, 1988. Running time: 95 MIN.
With: the cub bear La Douce; the kodiak bear brothers Bart, Doc, Griz, Bianca; the puma Check-Up; and Tcheky Karyo, Jack Wallace, André Lacombe (the hunters).

■ Paris — **Jean-Jacques Annaud's $20,000,000 shaggy bear saga is good family fare whose principal weakness is that it's a lot less fascinating than its long preproduction and production history.**

Discrepancy between the time, effort and cost of the Claude Berri (Renn Prod.) picture and the finished film about an orphaned bear cub and a deadly kodiak on the run from hunters in 19th century British Columbia may provide ammunition to critics and industryites eager to take potshots at the successful producer and director, though general audiences probably won't take notice. Film has opened to long-toothed business in France and should migrate easily to other box-office climes.

Annaud and screenwriter Gérard Brach, freely adapting a backwoods literary yarn by James Oliver Curwood, bank on the familiar schemas of physical danger and survival, cuddly sentiment and ecological sentimentality (''live and let live'').

Annaud has sufficient taste and control to avoid most excesses, though he and Brach are presumptuous enough to offer us some ursine dream sequences that are a rip in the film's texture.

These scenes, few and brief, were executed by Czech puppet animation master Bretislav Pojar and are remarkable in themselves. One senses that Annaud had second thoughts about their place in the film, but was obliged to keep a minimum in the final cut to justify the investment.

Otherwise this visually lush film follows the adventures of a bear cub (dubbed Youk in press materials) who loses her mother in a landslide and falls into the (unlikely) company of a no-nonsense adult grizzly bear, Kaar.

They have little time for bear hugs because a couple of determined hunters are literally after Kaar's hide. A series of pursuits and encounters follow, climaxing in a terrifying face-to-face meeting between Kaar and one of the pursuers.

Cornering the human, Kaar scares the living daylights out of him, but mysteriously, and anticlimactically, spares him. The hunter, transformed, returns the favor by not shooting the retreating beast and by freeing the cub (whom in the meantime they had captured).

Annaud, shooting for six months largely in the spectacular high altitudes of the Italian and Austrian Dolomites, has conceived his direction in unabashedly academic terms, which at times bridle the intended excitement.

Helmer's real achievement is to have fashioned a coherent, seamless dramatic film with volatile (and highly dangerous) beasts whose ill-humor could easily have sabotaged the best-laid plans of its human entrepreneurs.

Backed by highly skilled technical collaborators and animal specialists and trainers, Annaud manages to conceal most of the artifices and special effects, which include mechanical animal doubles for particularly difficult shots (specially contrived by Jim Henson's Creature Shop).

Film's young cub star, identified as La Douce, is a sweet little ball of fur whose whimpering antics will endear him to millions, as he whines over the carcass of his crushed mother, bounds puppy-like after a frog, looks bored and miserable while his kodiak protector connects with a hot-to-trot female, or is caught between a hungry puma and a dangerous torrent.

Two Kodiak brothers, Bert and Doc, trained for four years to enact the demands of the elaborately storyboarded script, play the predatory adult bear, whose killing instincts are redeemekd by his climactic ''human'' gesture.

France's Tcheky Karyo and Yank thesp Jack Wallace are the human hunters, and parcel out the film's rare (English) dialog. They are soon joined by a third, André Lacombe, who has no visible role other than bringing a pack of hunting dogs for the chase. Karyo, who has the right rugged look but an oddly phony accent, goes beyond the usual call of thespian duty in the ostensibly unfaked eyeball-to-eye-ball encounter with his prey.

Annaud also owns much to the superb Panavision compositions of lenser Philippe Rousselot, and the patient professionalism of editor Noëlle Boisson, who with Annaud whittled down a mountain of rushes to a crisp 95 minutes. Other tech credits are slick. —*Len.*

Tesoro
(Treasure)
(PUERTO RICAN)

A Taleski Studios release. Produced by Donald Myerston, Camilo Vives, Efrén Santiago. Directed by Diego de la Texera. Screenplay, De la Texera, Claribel Medina, Myerston, Emilio Rodríguez; camera (color), Julio (Pavo) Valdés; music, Gilberto Márquez.

Reviewed at San Juan Film Festival, Puerto Rico, Oct. 7, 1988. Running time: **96 MIN.** With: Maya Oloe, Xavier Serbiá.

■ San Juan — "Tesoro" (Treasure), by Puerto Rican helmer Diego de la Texera, is a good example of why films featuring extended scenes shot in caves should be seriously avoided. Even a detailed treasure map won't help pic's discovery at Latino locations.

Even though Puerto Rican locations are bathed in light, more than half the pic is shrouded in darkness. At times, visibility is reduced to counting weak flashlight beams move across the screen.

Plot is just as murky, as it attempts to bring together various disparate genres: a kidpic, a ghost tale, an adventure story and a socially relevant probe into the plight of illegal Haitian refugees. That four separate names are cited for the pithy plot shows a serious lack of individual talent.

Pic's dubious selling point is Xavier Serbiá, former member of the rock quintet Menudo, whose acting here consists of a few pouts. His presence here best illustrates the wisdom in retiring Menudo members at age 13, as film probably will dispel even the most die-hard Menudo fan. — *Lent.*

Halloween 4: The Return Of Michael Myers

A Galaxy Intl. Releasing release of a Trancas Intl. Films production. Executive producer, Moustapha Akkad. Produced by Paul Freeman. Directed by Dwight H. Little. Screenplay, Alan B. McElroy, from story by Dhani Lipsius, Larry Rattner, Benjamin Ruffner, McElroy; camera (color), Peter Lyons Collister; editor, Curtiss Clayton; music, Alan Howarth; Halloween theme music, John Carpenter; sound (Ultra-Stereo), Mark McNabb; art direction, Roger S. Crandall; set decoration, Nickle Lauritzen; special makeup effects, Magical Media Industries, designer, John Buechler; assistant director, Denis Stewart; production manager, S. Michael Formica; special effects coordinator, Larry Fioritto; stunt coordinator, Fred Lerner; associate producer, M. Sanousi; casting, David Cohn, Paul Bengston. Reviewed at 23d Street West 3 theater, N.Y., Oct. 22, 1988. MPAA Rating: R. Running time: **88 MIN.**

Dr. Loomis	Donald Pleasence
Rachel	Ellie Cornell
Jamie	Danielle Harris
Michael Myers	George P. Wilbur
Dr. Hoffman	Michael Pataki
Sheriff Meeker	Beau Starr
Kelly	Kathleen Kinmont
Brady	Sasha Jenson
Earl	Gene Ross
Jack Sayer	Carmen Filpi

■ Fourth entry in the "Haloween" horror series is a no-frills, workmanlike picture, due to grab fast business over the holiday and then exit. Planned obsolescence has a fifth entry already in preparation.

Designed as a direct sequel to John Carpenter's 1978 hit, with no reference to the events chronicled in parts 2 and 3, pic resurrects monster Michael Myers (preivously referred to mainly as The Shape), who escapes from a hospital to return home and wreak havoc, with the vague notion of getting to his niece Jamie (Danielle Harris). Typical of film's in-jokes, her late mom Jamie Lee Curtis is featured here only in repeated shots of family photos.

His face scarred from an earlier altercation with the monster, Donald Pleasence reprises his role as Dr. Loomis, now hell-bent on destroying the obviously unkillable Myers. Pic's main subplot concerns Harris' foster sister and babysitter Ellie Cornell, who is having romantic troubles with boyfriend Sasha Jenson. Statuesque Kathleen Kinmont plays the other woman (and sheriff's daughter), caught dallying with Jenson and later becoming the pic's most spectacular victim.

Uninteresting screenplay doesn't generate much interest until the final reel, when the young leads are left barricaded in the sheriff's house with Myers inside with them. At this point helmer Dwight Little tightens the screws and generates some genuine fright, leading to an okay twist ending.

John Buechler's makeup effects are good, while explicit gore is deemphasized in this edition. Cornell is a rather bland herone but the rest of the cast, including cute little Harris is effective. Peter Lyons Collister's mainly-at-night photography is quite helpful in creating the horror atmosphere. —*Lor.*

Shadows In The Storm

A Vidmark Intl. release (foreign) of a Mediacom Filmworks production. Produced by Strath Hamilton, J. Daniel Dusek. Written and directed by Terrell Tannen. Camera (color), John Connor; editor, Marcy Hamilton; music, Sasha Matson; art direction, Elizabeth Moore; sets, Regina Puksar; costume design, Lesley Nikolson; special effects, Tom Ryba; casting, Paul Ventura. Reviewed at Sitges Film Festival, Spain, Oct. 13, 1988. Running time: **81 MIN.**

Thelo	Ned Beatty
Melanie	Mia Sara
Earl	Michael Madsen

Also with: Donna Mitchell, James Widdoes, Joe Dorsey, William Bumiller.

■ Sitges — Even audiences that aren't very bright will be a step or two ahead of the plot of this totally transparent thriller about a middle-aged librarian who quotes John Donne and seeks an idyll of youthful beauty.

Suspense never builds up, nor does the plot. Pic's release seems limited to homevid and tv.

A dreamy librarian (Ned Beatty) gets fired from his job for hitting the bottle too often and, with his severance pay, decides to drive into the woods to write poetry modeled after Donne. He still dreams of his ideal of feminine pulchritude, imagines he sees her, and then finally meets her face to face. He sees her being mistreated in one of the other cabins in the woods that are part of the vacant motel he is staying in.

Next day he timidly approaches the girl; she complains of how she is being terrorized, and meets him at night by the river. All the librarian's dreams seem to come true as she rather precipitously gives herself to him in the rain on the riverbank. Their lovemaking is interrupted by the girl's companion, who, however, is quickly dispatched and dumped into the river.

The couple decide to escape, but are contacted by a blackmailer who supposedly has seen the crime. Audiences will not be terribly surprised to learn that the shots fired were blanks, and that the girl is in cahoots with the motel-owner.

Beatty is fine as the bumbling librarian, though at times he strains credibility even as a romantic-minded drunk. Mia Sara is convincing as the young temptress, and all technical credits are up to crack. The not-very-catchy title is from a poem of Donne's. — *Besa.*

Caribe
(CANADIAN)

A Miramax Films release of an SC Entertainment production, in association with Global Television Network. Executive producer, Syd Cappe. Produced by Nicolas Stiliadis. Directed by Michael Kennedy. Screenplay, Paul Donovan; camera (Agfa color), Ludek Bogner; editor, Michael McMahon; music, Michael Danna; sound, Chaim Gilad; assistant director, Roman Buchok; production manager, Paco Alvarez; stunt coordinator, T.J. Scott; second unit camera, Angel Gonzalez; postproduction coordinator, Stan Cole; casting, Adriana Grampa-Michel. Reviewed at 42d St. Cine 42 theater #1, N.Y., Oct. 17, 1988. MPAA Rating: R. Running time: **89 MIN.**

Jeff Richardson	John Savage
Helen Williams	Kara Glover
Whitehale	Stephen McHattie
Roy Forbes	Sam Malkin
Capt. Burdoch	Maury Chaykin
Tommy Goff	Zack Nesis
Mercenary	Paul Koslo

■ "Caribe" is a picturesque but dull actioner, vaguely reminiscent of the exotic programmers of yesteryear while lacking their energy.

John Savage toplines as a laid-back agent for British Intelligence, whose mission is to abort an illegal sale of explosives in Belize. Stephen McHattie is an ex-CIA agent who's masterminding the operation, using as dupes two Yanks, Sam Malkin and Kara Glover, who are attempting to raise $500,000 to cover an embezzlement from their munitions company.

Pic's main switch is that Glover, exhibiting fashion model beauty in even the most primitive of jungle locations, handles most of the rough stuff while Savage contents himself with calling the shots. There's some okay stuntwork and speedboat chases, but action tends to be languorous as we gaze at lovely Belize scenery (previously spotlighted in "The Mosquito Coast").

Glover and Savage make a comfortable team, immediately encoring together as leads of Vestron's "The Beat." Zack Nesis has a showy role as a mystical hippy left over from the '60s ethos, who aids the duo at crucial moments.

— *Lor.*

Dakota

A Miramax Films release of a Kuntz Bros. production. Produced by Darryl J. Kuntz, Frank J. Kuntz. Directed by Fred Holmes. Screenplay, Lynn and Darryl Kuntz; camera (color), Jim Wrenn; editor, Leon Seith; music, Chris Christian; art direction, Pat O'Neill; costume design, Rondi Hillstrom Davis; sound, Darrell Henke; associate producer, Lou Diamond Phillips; assistant director, John Colwell; second unit camera, Lito White. Reviewed at Metropolitan Theaters screening room, L.A., Oct. 18, 1988. MPAA Rating: PG-13. Running time: **97 MIN.**

Dakota	Lou Diamond Phillips
Walt	Eli Cummins
Molly	DeeDee Norton
Casey	Jordan Burton
Bo	Steven Ruge
Rooster	John Hawkes
Rob	Tom Campitelli
Aunt Zard	Herta Ware
Diamond	Lawrence Montaigne

■ Hollywood — Lou Diamond Phillips did this picture before "La Bamba" and "Stand And Deliver" made him a b.o. draw. Now the Texas indie company that produced it in 1987 is launching its first nationwide release on his starpower, with his blessing.

Though production values and pace fall well below minimum standards, pic has sure moral values and sufficient moving moments to keep younger fans entertained, plus plenty of footage of Phillips doing ranch work in tight jeans and sleeveless T's. Pic stands a fair chance of recouping its minimal investment.

Low-key is the operative word here, as pic ambles through the tale of a youth, John Dakota (Phillips), on the run from his troubled past who winds up working on a Texas horse ranch to pay off a debt.

There, he gets involved three ways — as the slowly developing love interest of the rancher's daughter, Molly (DeeDee Norton); as the encouraging big brother to the rancher's handicapped son Casey (Jordan Burton); and as the key mechanic preparing an antique car for a cross-country race that serves to tie the story together.

When his involvement starts to get deep, Dakota wants to bail out, afraid he'll wind up hurting everyone again as he did in the past.

In spite of its general lack of tension and laconic, almost inert dialog, pic has some emotional moments of surprising punch, as when Dakota performs a kind of anguished ballet of destruction in the barn as he's torn between wanting to move forward and succumbing to his doubts and fears.

Phillips has no trouble with the emoting chores and easily carries the film, though it's often a wobbly platform.

Little Jordan Burton also ably

anchors down his spot as the gritty, matter-of-fact kid who's lost a leg to bone cancer.

General tone of the story falls in line with religious proselytizing films that don't usually find their way into wide release — not surprising, since director Fred Holmes has spent years making films for the church market. Though he's got a flair for touching moments, nothing else here suggests a crossover into the big arena.

Though there are a few nice-looking segments, pic is marred by abruptly ended scenes, too many lingering establishing shots of signs, etc., and amateurish supporting players.

Pic's messages of courage and responsibility probably will do audiences some good, and even if ending is contrived, at least it's not cloying. PG-13 ratings comes out of nowhere — this one's as harmless as "Bambi." — *Daws.*

Illegally Yours

An MGM/UA Communications release from United Artists of a De Laurentiis Entertainment Group presentation of a Crescent Moon production. Executive producers, Peggy Robertson, William Peiffer. Produced and directed by Peter Bogdanovich. Screenplay, M.A. Stewart, Max Dickens; camera (Technicolor), Dante Spinotti; editor, Richard Fields; music, Phil Marshall; sound, Art Rochester; production design, Jane Musky; second unit director-stunt coordinator, Greg Walker; assistant director, Jerry Ziesmer; associate producer, Steve Foley; coproducer, George Morfogen; casting, Jane Jenkins, Janet Hirshenson. Reviewed on CBS/Fox vidcassette, N.Y., Oct. 22, 1988. MPAA Rating: PG. Running time: 102 MIN.
Richard Dice . . . . Rob Lowe
Molly Gilbert . . . . Colleen Camp
Hal Keeler . . . . Kenneth Mars
Wally . . . . Harry Carey Jr.
Suzanne Keeler . . . . Kim Myers
Donald Cleary . . . . Marshall Colt
Ruth . . . . Linda MacEwen
Freddie Boneflecker . . . . Rick Jason
Mrs. Dice . . . . Jessica James
Andrew Dice . . . . Andrew Heiden
Judge . . . . George Morfogen
Konrat . . . . Tony Longo
Harry . . . . Howard Hirdler
Sharon . . . . L.B. Straten

■ "Illegally Yours" is an embarrassingly unfunny attempt at screwball comedy, marking a career nadir for producer-director Peter Bogdanovich and his miscast star Rob Lowe.

They inadvertently lucked out as the financial woes of De Laurentiis Entertainment Group and skinflint "release" (1-week booking last May in San Francisco/San Jose only) by foster distrib MGM/UA has kept this misfire from public scrutiny.

Pic resembles in format Bogdanovich's hit "What's Up, Doc?" and Colin Higgins' "Foul Play" in harking back to '30s comedies but it remains stillborn. Script was credited to Michael Kaplan, John Levenstein and Ken Finkleman during production, but screen credits go mercifully to the presumably fictitious M.A. Stewart and Max Dick-

ens. (Exec producers were listed during production as Gareth Wigan and Paula Weinstein.)

Hectic pre-credits sequence, loaded with telltale, expository voiceover by Lowe, crudely sets up an uninteresting story of a blackmailer's murder, witnessed by young Kim Myers and her friend L.B. Straten, in which innocent Colleen Camp is arrested as the fall guy. An audiotape recording of the murder is the item everyone is trying to get their hands on.

Lowe is cast, with unbecoming glasses throughout, as a college dropout trying to get his life in order back home in St. Augustine, Fla. Between endless pratfalls (even Harold Lloyd would have trouble pulling off this nonsensical role) Lowe finds himself on jury duty in Camp's case. He lies, telling the court he's never met her when in fact in first grade he began having a lifelong crush on the attractive sixth grader.

With dialog delivered at Howard Hawks speed, Bogdanovich mechanically runs through elements of farce with an eccentric yet uninteresting gallery of stereotyped characters. Rick Jason, who costarred with Vic Morrow on tv's "Combat" series, is virtually unrecognizable as the cop dating Lowe's mom, Jessica James; Kenneth Mars is wasted as Myers' rich dad (both he and Myers were being blackmailed separately); and in a nothing role that repitiously mocks her Canadian roots, L.B. Straten (*sic*), younger sister of slain model/-actress Dorothy R. Stratten, debuts as Myers' very tall, but bland friend.

En route to sorting out the boring mystery of what became of the kidnaper's corpse, Lowe is thoroughly out of his element, even adopting a silly voice for a dumb drag scene. Colleen Camp is given little to do and no chemistry develops between the mismatched stars. Script's corny high point occurs in the final reel when Camp predictably removes Lowe's spectacles and comments on how handsome he is without them.

Johnny Cash warbles several nothing songs (cowritten by Bogdanovich) over the action. Tech credits are good in a losing cause. —*Lor.*

Leave To Remain
(BRITISH)

A Film Four Intl. presentation of a Spellbound production. Produced by Irving Teitelbaum. Directed by Les Blair. Screenplay, Rob Ritchie, Iraj Jannatais; camera (Metrocolor), Ivan Strasburg; editor, Ian Gregory; music, Simon Brint, Rowland Rivron; coproducer, Paul Harris. Reviewed at Mill Valley (Calif.) Film Festival, Oct. 13, 1988. Running time: 107 MIN.
Shabin Mohamedi . . . . Meda Kidem
James Johnstone . . . . Jonathan Phillips
Also with: Karuko Nahki, Nasser Nemar-

zia, Sahand Mashoot.

■ Mill Valley — In "Leave To Remain," Meda Kidem stoically struggles between her desire to enjoy life as a Westernized woman studying in England and the pull of revolutionary politics in her Iranian homeland. Unfortunately, Kidem's dilemma doesn't drive the picture with the energy it should have.

Kidem is so low-keyed that none of her many problems ever seems any more important to her than another. By the finish, director Les Blair has evolved her from politically uninvolved to committed, but the transition is gratingly gradual and muddily motivated. There's no real sense that whatever was reached by the end couldn't just as well have been true at the beginning.

Plainly, Kidem believes there's more to life than endless political upheaval back home. That's one reason she remained in England when her fiance chose to return to Iran as a revolutionary. Secondly, she has enjoyed her privilege as the daughter of a wealthy Iranian family abroad and shares no desire for the drab, secondary station of her countrywomen.

Now, however, Kidem's school funds have been intercepted by the Ayatollah government, apparently for political reasons she's not privy to. She hasn't heard from her family or her fiance for months.

Having lost her student status, her only hope for remaining in England is an arranged marriage. Hired as a husband, Jonathan Phillips comes off the streets a cut above Cockney but still well below her in class and education. He shows a genuine interest in Kidem and her country's problems, which annoys her. Even worse, he wants to make a real marriage out of the situation, which annoys her more.

Though it's unclear why, Kidem socializes almost exclusively with fellow Iranians, most of whom are revolutionaries suspected by the Ayatollah's minions in England. Even though she resists their blatant efforts to involve her in the struggle, it seems apparent that her associations are part of her problems with the government.

Eventually, her concern for the plight of her former fiance, who has been captured, sinks the sham marriage with Phillips and draws her into the fight. Phillips, who has emerged a rather likable fellow confused by his situation, ends up tossed into the cold, forgotten by her and director Blair as well.

All of this may be more gripping for an audience closer to the situations. From a distance, however, the picture offers more reason to leave than to remain. — *Har.*

Snack Bar Budapest
(ITALIAN)

A Medusa release of a San Francisco Film/Metro Film/Reteitalia coproduction. Produced by Giovanni Bertolucci, Galliano Juso. Directed by Giovanni Tinto Brass. Screenplay, Brass, based on a novel by Marco Lodol, Silvia Dre; camera (Telecolor, Eastmancolor), Alessio Gelsini; editor, Brass; music Zucchero; art direction, Paolo Biagetti. Reviewed at Metropolitan Cinema, Rome, Oct. 11, 1988. Running time: 98 MIN.
The lawyer . . . . Giancarlo Giannini
Partner . . . . Philippe Léotard
Molleco . . . . François Negret
Also with: Raffaella Baracchi, Silvie Orcier, Carlo Monni.

■ Rome — "Snack Bar Budapest" was supposed to mark an interlude for Giovanni Tinto Brass from the likes of "The Key" and "Miranda," but here, too, reeling with softcore fantasies, the director indulges to the full his prurient interest in the uncovered female anatomy.

Cinematographer Alessio Gelsini whips up a storm of hazy, backlighted special effects to give pic atmosphere. This is about all the glue it has to keep its endless gallery of below-the-belt shots together. The boredom quotient runs high on this effort, and star faces Giancarlo Giannini and Philippe Léotard merely looks like they opened the wrong stage door at Cinecittà and stumbled onto somebody else's film.

Looking seedier and more burned out than in all his Wertmüller films put together, Giannini plays "the Lawyer," an ex-legal eagle who maladroitly wound up in the clinker and is now collecting debts for boss Léotard. In a windswept seaside town, he drops his girlfriend (or Léotard's?) off at the local hospital to have an overnight abortion and proceeds to meet teenage crime master Molleco (François Negret), out to build a city Mafia-style.

Giannini becomes Molleco's man for one heady night, terrorizing a surreal hotel called the Snack Bar Budapest to force the owners out. The plan backfires, Giannini kills one of Molleco's punks, and has a whole army of drunken, undressed women shooting at him and Léotard.

Suspense isn't the thing in "Budapest." Brass creates little tension, and the gang's bursts of violence remain limp. Only reason for watching this dull picture is to ogle femmes in see-through dresses. Camera does the rest with off-the-floor lensing and obsessive views of backsides.

Seamy characters, lurid neon-lit sets, and merchandised sex combine to keep the sleaze rolling.

All things considered, it is surprising how Giannini manages to inject moments of acting into the lawyer's perpetual air of bored resignation, and in combo with Léotard even gets an exchange of clownish dialog going. —*Yung.*

Vampire At Midnight

A Skouras Pictures release. Produced by Jason Williams, Tom Friedman. Directed by Gregory McClatchy. Screenplay, Dulhany Ross Clements, from story by Williams, Friedman; camera (United color), Daniel Yarussi; editor, Kaye Davis; music, Robert Etoll; sound, Vic Carpenter; art direction, Beau Peterson; special makeup effects, Mecki Heussen; assistant director, Darcy Brown; production manager, Todd King; second unit director, Williams. Reviewed on Key Video vidcassette, N.Y., Oct. 20, 1988. MPAA Rating: R. Running time: **93 MIN.**

Det. Roger Sutter	Jason Williams
Victor Radkoff	Gustav Vintas
Jenny Carlon	Lesley Milne
Amalia	Jeanie Moore
Lucia	Esther Alise
Capt. Takato	Ted Hamaguchi
Childress	Robert Random
Lee	Jonny Solomon

Also with: Barbara Hammond, Eddie Jr., Christina Whitaker.

■ "Vampire At Midnight" is an above-average sexy horror thriller marking a departure for Skouras Pictures, which elected to give it a domestic theatrical release alongside distrib's artier fare.

What makes this sexploitation film work is a respect for various genre needs: okay bloodsucking thrills plus a bevy of undraped beauties in the cast. That spells decent prospects in the homevideo/paycable market.

Jason Williams (erstwhile star of the campy "Flesh Gordon") toplines as a police detective in L.A. on the trail of a serial killer dubbed a vampire since the victims are found with the blood drained from their body.

Audience is clued early on that balding Gustav Vintas is the villain, a hypnotherapist whose gaze has a mesmerizing effect on folks (particularly women), whom he kills for their blood. Some of his victims become drones, providing regular sups but left alive to do his bidding.

Though film is played straight and receives solidly atmospheric lensing and scoring, there is a tongue-in-cheek element in the systematic topless footage accorded to the femme cast. Even Williams' policewoman friend, played by Esther Alise, handcuffs him to the bed one night and removes her black lace undies for a sex scene which is definitely not strict police procedure.

Director Gregory McClatchy keeps matters tightly controlled, eliciting a nicely shaded turn from baddie Vintas. Beautiful heroine Lesley Milne is given a fine showcase here. Moody finale reveals that story's supernatural overtones were a red herring. —Lor.

Grotesque

A Concorde Pictures release of a United Filmmakers Group production. Executive producers, Maurice Smith, Ray Sterling. Produced by Mike Lane, Chris Morrell. Directed by Joe Tornatore. Screenplay, Mikel Angel, from characters and concept by Tornatore; camera (Foto-Kem color), Bill Dickson; music, Bill Loose, Jack Cookerly; sound, Craig Felburg; art direction, Richard McGuire; special effects makeup, John Naulin; assistant director-stunt coordinator, Eddie Donno; production manager, Sanford Hampton; associate producers, Linda Blair, Lincoln Tate. Reviewed on Media Home Entertainment vidcassette, N.Y., Oct. 10, 1988. MPAA Rating: R. Running time: **79 MIN.**

Lisa	Linda Blair
Rod	Tab Hunter
Kathy	Donna Wilkes
Scratch	Brad Wilson
Gibbs	Nels Van Patten
Orville Kruger	Guy Stockwell

Also with: Sharon Hughes, Michelle Bensoussan, Charles Dierkop, Chuck Morrell, Lincoln Tate, Luana Patten, Robert Zdar, Billy Frank, Bunki Z, John Goff, Mikel Angel, Stacy Alden, Mike Lane.

■ Various low-budget filmmakers team up for the forgettable "Grotesque," a horror exercise aimed primarily at the video trade.

Awkward structure has Linda Blair fronting for the first few reels, driving home for a family reunion, accompanied by pal Donna Wilkes. Her dad Guy Stockwell is a super makeup effects expert, treated to a dose of gore when a gang of punkers (who've had a run-in with Blair on the road) invade the house and start killing everyone.

Blair escapes in the snow and is saved when an overgrown, retarded relative is set free from his secret room by the punkers and goes on the rampage. Cops led by Charles Dierkop (of tv's "Police Woman" series) believe the punkers' story blaming the relative for all the trouble.

Though surviving and hospitalized, Blair is written out of the film at this point, with Tab Hunter taking over lead role as her plastic surgeon uncle. He takes the law into his own hands and predictably avenges his family's massacre by surgically mutilating the punkers' faces in yucky fashion.

Makeup effects here are unimpressive. Credits include many familiar names from indie pics, ranging from composer Bill Loose to "The Love Butcher" codirector Mikel Angel. Luana Patten, absent from the big screen for two decades, has a small role as a gothic old lady in an opening film-within-a-film segment.

Hunter attacks his unsympathetic role with some relish, but Blair, who previously toiled for helmer Joe Tornatore in reshoots on "Nightforce," has little to sink her teeth into.—Lor.

The Good Mother

A Buena Vista release of a Touchstone presentation in association with Silver Screen Partners IV of an Arnold Glimcher production. Produced by Glimcher. Directed by Leonard Nimoy. Screenplay, Michael Bortman, based on novel by Sue Miller; camera (Metrocolor prints), David Watkin; editor, Peter Berger; music, Elmer Bernstein; production design, Stan Jolley; art direction, Richard Harrison, Hilton Rosemarin; set decoration, Anthony Greco; costume design, Susan Becker; sound (Dolby), Richard Lightstone, David Lee; assistant directors, Tony Lucibello, Daniel Jason Heffner; casting, Barbara Shapiro, Stuart Aikins (Toronto), Collinge Pickman (Boston). Reviewed at Avco Cinema, L.A., Oct. 27, 1988. MPAA Rating: R. Running time: **103 MIN.**

Anna Dunlap	Diane Keaton
Leo Cutter	Liam Neeson
'Muth	Jason Robards
Grandfather	Ralph Bellamy
Grandmother	Teresa Wright
Brian Dunlap	James Naughton
Molly Dunlap	Asia Vieira
Frank Williams	Joe Morton
Ursula	Katey Sagal
Babe	Tracy Griffith

■ Hollywood — The traumatic subject matter of a child custody fight is handled with restraint and intelligence in "The Good Mother."

Superbly acted by an imaginatively chosen cast, adaptation of Sue Miller's 1986 bestseller goes so far to avoid tear-jerking pathos the result may have come out a little drier than anticipated. But this is absorbing adult drama, and likely to be appreciated by audiences looking for same.

Culturally, the film is about and will play best to people in their 30s and 40s sensitive to the warp and contradictions between 1960s liberalism and 1980s pragmatism and moral scrutiny. The issues presented here are real, complex and not easily resolved by applying one point of view or another, so the picture is likely to provoke discussion.

After a 10-minute prolog illustrating how little Anna was inspired during her childhood lakeside summers by her adventurous young aunt Babe, Michael Bortman's well-judged script presents Anna Dunlap (Diane Keaton) as the recently divorced mother of Molly, an enthusiastic child of six. Living in the Boston area, working parttime in a lab and teaching piano, Anna is committed to her daughter above all else.

Skittish and insecure where men are concerned, she nevertheless allows herself to be seduced by Leo (Liam Neeson), an iconoclastic, thoroughly charming Irish sculptor who awakens her to an exciting sex life. Before long, Leo, who also wins over Molly, is staying at Anna's most of the time and, in a critical scene, is making love to Anna when the little girl enters the bedroom and pulls up next to her mother to sleep, apparently oblivious to what has been going on.

Shortly, the boom is lowered. Anna's cold ex-husband Brian (James Naughton), an attorney now remarried, slaps a custody suit on her, announcing that Molly has informed him that Leo in some way molested her sexually and that she will henceforth be staying with her father.

The legal proceedings that follow reveal that in the relaxed, perhaps permissive atmosphere that prevailed in Anna's home, the adults felt it was all right to go about in the nude in Molly's presence. One time, when Anna was absent, Molly asked Leo, who was emerging from the shower, if she could touch his genitals. Responding, he says, to her inherent curiosity, he said yes. That was it as far as any contact went, but enough to possibly prevent Anna from ever again having custody of her daughter.

In the legal crunch, Brian and his attorney (Joe Morton) have the easier job, to show, in this conservative era, that Anna's bohemian, live-in lifestyle, casual moral stance and negligent attitude toward her boyfriend's behavior with Molly represent a clear danger to the child.

So shaky is the ground under Anna's feet that her lawyer (Jason Robards) urges her to admit that Leo did the wrong thing, and to promise that she will give him up if necessary in order to keep Molly.

Everything is weighted entirely in favor of Anna and Leo, a fact abetted by the enormous appeal of Keaton and Neeson. A rawer, more open version of the episode would have included more of the frank sexuality the couple is being forced to defend themselves against; as played by Keaton, Anna is so sensitive about sex that it's a bit hard to believe that — her idol Babe notwithstanding — she would be that casual about it around the house.

Despite the moderate dramatic reserve, which partly stems from director Leonard Nimoy's predominant use of medium-shots, this is compelling stuff, and the performances are uniformly first-rate. High-strung and defensive over not having achieved a significant career, Anna takes her place among Keaton's memorable characterizations.

The film unquestionably will put Irish actor Liam Neeson on the map as a major romantic leading man, very much because he's so different from the norm. With shaggy brown hair, brilliant blue eyes and brogue intact, he's effortlessly winning onscreen, the quintessential offbeat artist.

Asia Vieira is a charmer as Molly. Ralph Bellamy and Teresa Wright are delights as Anna's grandparents (some explanation as to her parents' whereabouts would have been helpful), and Robards and Morton etch sharp impressions. Tracy Griffith also is vivid as the impulsive Babe.

Expanding impressively from the safe confections of two "Star Trek" films and "Three Men And A Baby," Nimoy has directed carefully and well, aided greatly by David

Watkin's exquisitely clean, light-bathed lensing. Other contributions, notably Elmer Bernstein's lovely score, are nicely understated.

—*Cart.*

U2 Rattle And Hum
(DOCU-B&W/COLOR)

A Paramount Pictures release of a Midnight Films production. Executive producer, Paul McGuinness. Produced by Michael Hamlyn. Directed by Phil Joanou. Camera, (Duart b&w), Robert Brinkmann, (Deluxe color), Jordan Cronenweth; editor, Joanou; supervising sound editor (Dolby), Scott A. Hecker; music produced by Jimmy Iovine; music re-recording mixer, Chris Jenkins; production manager-assistant director-associate producer, Gregg Fienberg. Reviewed at Paramount studios, L.A., Oct. 26, 1988. MPAA Rating: PG-13. Running time: **99 MIN.**

■ Hollywood — Visionary Irish rock band U2 has not sold itself short with "U2 Rattle And Hum," a deeply felt cinematic treatment of band's music and concerns infused with striking visual style and electric momentum.

Pic should stand at least a fighting chance of recouping reported $5,000,000 production cost given U2's huge worldwide popularity.

Pic opens in concert, with U2 performing an electrifying version of the Beatles' "Helter Skelter," then segues to the moving grace of band's own "Van Demien's Land," with guitarist the Edge doing a rare lead vocal while camera sweeps over Irish landscape and waters.

Docu captures U2 during a period of exploration of American music and culture following the blockbuster commercial and critical success of its seventh album, "The Joshua Tree."

Sense of awareness and discovery adds dimension, as film follows the band throughout the landscape of American-roots music, encountering street musicians in Harlem, collaborating with a gospel choir for a rousing new twist on No. 1 hit "I Still Haven't Found What I'm Looking for," performing with bluesmaster B.B. King on the brassy r&b "Love Comes To Town," penned in his honor; and recording "Angel Of Harlem," a poignant re-memberance of Billie Holiday at Sun Studios in Memphis.

There also is plenty of homage paid to the '60s, with covers of Bob Dylan, the Beatles and Jimi Hendrix. None of it takes away from riveting performances of U2's own music, captured mostly at concert venues in Denver, Ft. Worth and Arizona.

Director Phil Joanou films mostly in black & white, save one color concert sequence, using grainy blowups of 16m footage to create a gritty texture for the "street" segs and a startling mixture of silhouette and shadow for the concert footage.

Joanou's strobelight-style editing during some of the intense concert segments makes the band appear like flashing spirits dancing in front of the electric cacophany of the music.

It's during the color segment that the momentum drops and the previously strong visual approach gets diffused. Live color centerpiece was filmed at Sun Devil Stadium in Tempe, Ariz., and marks the place where the band finally kicks into a solid live set of its own music. Despite the talents of cinematographer Jordan Cronenweth ("Stop Making Sense") and a dozen camera operators, version of "Where The Streets Have No Name" falls below potential, as does followup "MLK."

Just when it seems pic will never find the higher ground needed to make this final segment climactic, it switches back to black & white and pulls way ahead for a blazing, cathartic ending on anthems like "Sunday Bloody Sunday" and "Pride (In The Name Of Love)."

Climax of pic's visual line is achieved when lead singer Bono picks up a spotlight and shines it on guitarist the Edge; the lights, which along with fog and shadow have enhanced the film's look, are at last part of the performance.

Throughout, camerawork and direction are beautifully expressive of band's themes and music.

The one misstep is when the band visits Elvis Presley's Graceland mansion. Footage of the gawking behind the velvet ropes is awkward; the material goods on display offer no sense of connection, but, rather, create distance.

More than anything, U2 seems to offer a message of awareness of the currents of history and world politics, as well as the power of love. "U2 Rattle And Hum" captures the dirve to merge those concerns with their music in resonant cinematic style.

For anyone who's fallen out of touch, this remarkable concert documentary is exhilarating evidence that rock 'n' roll is vitally alive, informed and bursting with relevance; for longtime fans who couldn't get tix to band's last sold-out tour, this is rich compensation. —*Daws.*

A Cry In The Dark

A Warner Bros. release of a Cannon Entertainment/Golan-Globus production, in association with Cinema Verity Ltd. Executive producers, Menahem Golan, Yoram Globus. Produced by Verity Lambert. Line producer, Roy Stevens. Directed by Fred Schepisi. Screenplay, Robert Caswell, Schepisi, based on book "Evil Angels" by John Bryson; camera (Panavision, color), Ian Baker; editor, Jill Bilcock, music, Bruce Smeaton; production design, Wendy Dickson, George Liddle; art direction, Dale Duguid, Brian Edmonds; costume design, Bruce Finlayson; sound (Dolby), Gary Wilkins; assistant director, Steve Andrews; casting, Rhonda Schepisi, Forcast. Reviewed at Warner Hollywood Studios, L.A., Oct. 13, 1988. MPAA Rating: PG-13. Running time: **121 MIN.**

Lindy Chamberlain . . . . Meryl Streep
Michael Chamberlain . . . . Sam Neill
Barker . . . . Bruce Myles
Justice Muirhead . . . . Charles Tingwell
Charlwood . . . . Nick Tate
Phillips . . . . Neil Fitzpatrick
Barritt . . . . Maurie Fields
Tipple . . . . Lewis Fitz-gerald

■ Hollywood — One of the oddest and most illogical murder cases of modern times is recounted in intimate, incredible detail in the classy, disturbing drama "A Cry In The Dark."

The saga of Lindy Chamberlain's harassment, trial and imprisonment for having allegedly murdered her baby daughter, when there was literally no evidence against her, has been the biggest news story in Australia for the past eight years.

It is difficult to guess whether that fascination will transfer to filmgoers around the rest of the world, including those in the U.S., but this film should draw serious-minded viewers on the basis of Meryl Streep's name.

The particulars of the case, as well as the participants, are simultaneously banal and exceptionally peculiar, creating something a fiction writer would never dream up in a million years. As handled by director Fred Schepisi, this is docudrama of the highest order, prose written by a fine novelist.

Opening section is deliberately uneventful, as meaningless small talk and everyday chit-chat impressionistically sketches the quality of life of the Chamberlain family, which consists of Michael, a Seventh Day Adventist pastor, his drab, humorless wife Lindy, their two young sons and 9-week-old daughter Azaria. Yank audiences whose only exposure to Aussie accents have been in the "Crocodile Dundees" may encounter a little trouble penetrating the conversation during this stretch.

In 1980, the Chamberlains visit Australia's most popular tourist attraction, the monumental Ayers Rock in the outback. With the baby put to sleep in a tent, the family begins enjoying a nighttime barbeque when a cry is heard. Checking the tent, Lindy briefly glimpses a dingo slipping out of it and then, to her horror, finds Azaria missing from her bed.

No trace of the infant is found, and the conclusion appears to be that the dingo made off with her as it would a rabbit or baby sheep.

Astonishingly, however, sentiment begins to grow throughout the country to the effect that Lindy killed her daughter.

From there, the press can't let the story die, and begins spreading no end of rumor, exaggeration and innuendo about the disappearance that help lead, after two contradictory inquests, to Lindy being charged with murder and Michael being named as accessory after the fact.

Lindy is found guilty and sentenced to life imprisonment at hard labor. She delivers another child while incarcerated and serves time while a groundswell of support, growing from the perceived injustices, takes shape. Released "on compassionate grounds," Lindy finally was cleared of all charges in September of this year.

The case itself holds its own bizarre fascination, and Schepisi's rigorous but unemphatic method of relating it possesses a deceptive, lingering power. The choreography of events and people here — there are some 350 speaking parts and thousands of extras — is all the more impressive for its unshowy naturalism, and the attack on elements in the legal system, the media and human nature that made all this possible is discreet but devastating.

If one didn't know who Meryl Streep is, one could easily guess Lindy was played by a fine, unknown Australian actress. Bravura in the sense that she mastered yet another difficult accent and assumed one more socio-cultural mindset, Streep still achieves the effect of a highly self-effacing performance.

Sam Neill, who here looks remarkably like the real Michael Chamberlain, well conveys the tentative strengths and very real weaknesses of a man thrust into an unimaginable situation.

Decision to shoot in widescreen Panavision is indicative of Schepisi's and cinematographer Ian Baker's desire to achieve a grand, heightened realism, something they and the huge cast and crew, working on diverse locations, have utterly succeeded in doing. —*Cart.*

Akatanikitoi Erastes
(Invincible Lovers)
(GREEK)

A Greek Film Center/Stavros Tsiolis/Alekos Papageorgiou production. Written and directed by Stavros Tsiolis. Camera (color), Vassilis Kapsouros; sound, Costas Poulantzas. Reviewed at Greek Film Festival, Thessaloniki (competing), Oct. 7, 1988. Running time: **81 MIN.**

Vassilis . . . . Tassos Miliotis
Woman with car . . . . Olia Lazaridou
Also with: Konstantinos Tzoumas, Maria Panoutsou, Dimitra Voulgaridi.

■ Thessaloniki — "Invincible Lovers" is a slow-moving odyssey of two loners, an orphan and a young woman, who drive around looking for the house of the boy's grandmother. Handsomely lensed by Vassilis Kapsouros, the Greek Peloponnese scenery is striking but little depth is given to the lead characterizations.

Vassilis runs away from the orphanage to find his grandmother. He wanders around Athens and hops a train to Tripolis, a large town in the south of mainland Greece. While hiking through the mountainous countryside, he comes upon a young woman whose car has stalled. After he fixes it, they pair up and drive around during the summer, looking for his grandmother's house. Fleeting glimpses of village celebrations or sequences with folk songs played on a guitar, give a brief sketch of the flavor of rural life.

Young Tassos Miliotis is shyly appealing as Vassilis in his ever-present straw hat and is impressively enterprising, making his bread and butter through odd jobs. Dialog is sparse and we learn little about him or his life before this time. Heroine Olia Lazaridou is more verbal but rarely alters her pouty expression. The breakdown of barriers between them is indicated by the playfulness that develops as they go swimming and sit by a campfire at night.

Much of the action and interaction of "Invincible Lovers," which shared the prizes for best film and best director at its Thessaloniki debut, are seemingly directionless. Fest audience reaction was mixed.
—*Sam.*

Everybody's All-American

A Warner Bros. release of a New Visions production. Executive producer, Stuart Benjamin. Produced by Taylor Hackford, Laura Ziskin, Ian Sander. Coproducer, Alan C. Blomquist. Directed by Hackford. Screenplay, Tom Rickman, based on book by Frank Deford; camera (Technicolor), Stephen Goldblatt; editor, Don Zimmerman; music, James Newton Howard; production design, Joe Alves; art direction, George Jenson; set design, Sig Tingloff; set decoration, Rosemary Brandenburg; costume design, Theadora Van Runkle; sound (Dolby), Jeff Wexler; special makeup design, Dick Smith; assistant director, Jerry Ballew; casting, Nancy Klopper. Reviewed at Raleigh Studios, L.A., Oct. 28, 1988. MPAA Rating: R. Running time: 127 MIN.
Babs Rogers Grey . . . . Jessica Lange
Gavin Grey . . . . Dennis Quaid
Donnie "Cake" . . . . Timothy Hutton
Lawrence . . . . John Goodman
Narvel Blue . . . . Carl Lumbly
Bolling Kiely . . . . Ray Baker
Darlene Kiely . . . Savannah Smith Boucher
Leslie Stone . . . . Patricia Clarkson

■ Hollywood — "Everybody's All-American" is a pop culture vision of beautiful Southern kids who have it all when they're young and then have to face living the rest of their lives.

Drama has its moments, particularly as regards the residue of the sporting life, and remains watchable due to its two attractive leads, but is too predictable and not nearly incisive enough to achieve the exalted synthesis of sociological and domestic observation to which it clearly aspired. Boxoffice outlook appears moderate.

The world of Baton Rouge in the mid-1950s was made for the likes of Gavin and Babs. Dashing, easy-going and likable, Gavin is "The Grey Ghost," the running back who leads his school to triumph in the Sugar Bowl. Gorgeous blond Southern belle Babs represents everyone's dream girl but yearns only to become Mrs. Gavin Grey.

Nothing stands in the way of this dream and, with Gavin excelling as a pro with the Redskins, the couple moves comfortably into the expected environs of suburbia, a steady flow of babies, sports-themed restaurant ownership and the like.

However, in the legitimate but very conventional terms of the film, the innocence of youth and the '50s inevitably yield to the turmoil and doubt of the '60s. Against the backdrop of racial conflict, gangland murder, increased corporatism and changing values of all kinds, the Greys get wiped out financially and then see Gavin's star fall as his playing career winds down, just as Babs belatedly starts coming into her own.

It's an archetypal view of life, from both the intimate and epic perspectives, that urgently needs a sharp edge if the picture is to move beyond the level of primary colors and pop tunes in its evocation of emotional reality. Tom Rickman's screenplay holds Gavin and Babs squarely centerscreen throughout, so that the ebbs and flows of their relationship cannot help but be examined closely and with concern.

Unfortunately, every other person and element in their lives, except for football, seems to skim across them like a stone over water. Most notably, there is Donnie "Cake," a scholar who admires his uncle Gavin but secretly lusts after Babs. "Cake" pops up every so often to provide a sounding board for the two principals, but serves virtually no dramatic function.

Consigned to a life as a player's wife, Babs has no women friends, neither her nor Gavin's parents are even mentioned, and Gavin's only pal is his gregarious former blocker who now runs his restaurant. Even as students in the 1950s, everyone here is cool enough to visit the other side of the tracks to share beer and ribs with black folks. Southern racism existed, of course, prompting the tiny subplot tracing the evolution of Narvel Blue from athlete to black activist to entrepreneur in the New South, but none of the characters can possibly be tainted by it.

A viewer could do a lot worse than have to watch Jessica Lange and Dennis Quaid for two hours, and they definitely get far into their parts here. After just getting by posing as 21-year-olds, both age through the years convincingly, with Quaid becoming a picture of the middle-aged jock alcoholic as he is trotted out to sing the praises of artificial turf and recount his moments of glory one more time.

The basic superficialty of director Taylor Hackford's approach can't help but affect them too, so scenes of domestic happiness and strife come and go with little real feeling settling in, and Gavin and Babs come across as believable but not 3-dimensional. Still, this is far better than anyone else can do, notably Timothy Hutton, who not only has no role to play but looks about 10 years younger than his friends even when sporting some unbecoming whiskers.

What comes off right is sports. The football scenes were filmed with full verisimilitude during actual games in full stadiums, and it shows. Better, one gets a strong sense of how former stars, famous especially for one heroic moment, are prisoners of their illustrious pasts and have slim hopes of equaling their youthful achievements in any other field.

Behind-the-scenes staff had a tall order in illustrating the gradual passing of 25 years in numerous locales, and production designer Joe Alves and costume designer Theadora Van Runkle have led the way in contributing strong work on this score. —*Cart.*

Destroyer

A Moviestore Entertainment release of a Back East Money production, in association with Wind River Prods. Executive producer, Joseph Ignat. Produced by Peter Garrity, Rex Hauck. Directed by Robert Kirk. Screenplay, Garrity, Hauck; camera (Foto-Kem color), Chuy Elizondo; editor, Mark Rosenbaum; music, Patrick O'Hearn; sound (Ultra-Stereo), Robert Abbott; production design, Paul Staheli; art direction, Randy Holland; special makeup effects, Patrick Ryan Denver, Rex L. Whitney; assistant director, Robert King; production manager, Hauck; stunt coordinator, Brian Veatch; second unit camera, Len Aitken; casting, Cecily Adams. Reviewed on Virgin Vision vidcassette, N.Y., Oct. 26, 1988. MPAA Rating: R. Running time: 94 MIN.
Susan Malone . . . . Deborah Foreman
David Harris . . . . Clayton Rohner
Ivan Moser . . . . Lyle Alzado
Director Edwards . . . . Anthony Perkins
Russell . . . . Tobias Andersen
Sharon Fox . . . . Lannie Garrett
Rewire . . . . Jim Turner
Warden . . . . Pat Mahoney
Fingers . . . . David Kristin

■ "Destroyer," previously titled "Shadow Of Death," combines two recent horror genres to tiresome effect and very little in the way of novelty.

Former football star Lyle Alzado is well-cast as a man-mountain convict on death row for murdering 24 people. Odd touch in electric chair opening scene has prison filled with tv monitors showing a gameshow while Alzado fries.

Not surprisingly, Alzado is not so easily dispensed with, coming back to kill folks one by one when a locationing film crew lenses at the prison for a women-in-stir epic some 18 months after a riot closed down the facility.

This combo of such recent fright pics' premises as "Prison" and "Return To Horror High" provides few thrills as Alzado digs peeping at the filming of the requisite shower scene for "Death House Dolls," but is busier offing the cast in gory fashion. Anthony Perkins, Clayton Rohner and Deborah Foreman as the film-within-a-film's director, screenwriter and stuntwoman respectively, have perfunctory assignments.

Just prior to a disappointing, inconclusive ending, pic reaches its nadir of silliness when a burned-up and blown-up Alzado confronts Foreman one more time and calmly pulls off what's left of his ear and eats it. This may have been intended as a horror movie gross-out effect, but it comes off as macho posturing carried to the extreme.
—*Lor.*

Feds

A Warner Bros. release. Executive producer, Ivan Reitman. Produced by Ilona Herzberg, Len Blum. Directed by Dan Goldberg. Screenplay, Blum, Goldberg; camera (CFI color, Technicolor prints), Timothy Suhrstedt; editor, Don Cambern; music, Randy Edelman; production design, Randy Ser; art direction, Phil Dagort; set decoration, Julie Kaye Towery; set design, Sally Thornton; costume design, Isabella B. Van Soest; sound (Dolby), David Brownlow; associate producers, Kool Marder, Robert E. Lee; assistant director, Betsy Pollock; assistant camera, Mark Karen; casting, Stanzi Stokes. Reviewed at Mann Chinese theater, L.A., Oct. 28, 1988. MPAA Rating: PG-13. Running time: 91 MIN.
DeWitt . . . . Rebecca DeMornay
Zuckerman . . . . Mary Gross
Brent . . . . Ken Marshall
Belecki . . . . Fred Dalton Thompson
Butz . . . . Larry Cedar

■ Hollywood — Should the FBI ever need to discourage women from joining up, a revival of "Feds" ought to do the trick. Besides that, it's hard to think of a redeeming social purpose for this hapless compendium of female-bonding gags.

Rebecca DeMornay and Mary Gross are FBI academy trainees in a buddy picture that plays more like a biddy picture. There isn't a fresh idea or a new 1-liner in all of Len Blum and Dan Goldberg's script, an anthology of inert retreads from the "Police Academy" series and "Private Benjamin."

DeMornay as the spunky athletic one and Gross as the uptight, studious one go up against the boys in pizza contests, chin-up exercises and constitutional law classes. They ultimately graduate at the head of the class but not before undergoing considerable humiliation.

Sexual equality is the supposed theme, and maybe the filmmakers have at least succeeded in managing to bring the level of humor for both sexes down to an equally low common denominator.

There are a few quasi-vulgar jokes (pic is rated PG-13) while the other ones attempted fall at a level that wouldn't make a 10-year-old laugh. Gross trying to some some bank robbers by making a stick-'em-up gesture with her finger and later garbling her recitation of the Miranda rights to some poor extras cast in this film is groaner material.

This is a case where it's nearly impossible to fault the actors since they are expected to save face through some pretty embarrassing scenes that provide no room for inventiveness, spontaneity or even a chance to mug for the cameras. Dan Goldberg's leaden direction pretty much takes care of that.—*Brit.*

Party Line

A SVS Films release of a Westwood production. Produced by Tom Byrnes, Kurt Anderson, William Webb. Coproduced by Monica Webb. Directed by William Webb. Screenplay, Richard Brandes, from story by Tom Byrnes; camera (color), John Huneck; editor, Paul Koval; music, Sam Winans; art direction, Mark Simon; sound, Glen Berkovitz; stunt supervisor, Jeff Smoleck. Reviewed at the AMC Americana 8, Southfield, Mich. MPAA Rating: R. Running time: **91 MIN.**

Dan . . . . Richard Hatch
Stacy . . . . Shawn Weatherly
Seth . . . . Leif Garrett
Angelina . . . . Greta Blackburn
Capt. Barnes . . . . Richard Roundtree
Henry . . . . James O'Sullivan
Simmons . . . . Terrence McGovern
Mrs. Simmons . . . . Shelli Place
Alice . . . . Tara Hutchins
Butch . . . . Marty Dudek

■ **Southfield, Mich. — "Party Line" is a grim and predictable film whose mediocre acting fails to raise it above tv fare. A lengthy theatrical run seems unlikely, and little spark can be expected in the homevideo market.**

The film tries to exploit the current party-line fad — multiple phone lines for a fee that enable you to talk to several strangers at the same time — with a conventional killer-on-the-loose theme.

The killers are Leif Garrett (Seth) and Greta Blackburn (Angelina), a nutso brother and sister pair pushed over the edge by their mother's suicide and an abusive father. Never fully recovering from the former and having snuffed out the latter, Seth and Angelina continue to murder, finding their victims through the Party Line.

Their method is generally the same, Angelina lures the men to her boudoir and Seth rips their heads off with his father's straight razor.

Richard Hatch is the good but unconventional cop (Dan). Former Miss Universe Shawn Weatherly is the pretty but inexperienced deputy district attorney (Stacy). Richard Roundtree turns in a forgettable appearance as the captain with a soft spot for the rogue cop.

There's the leering D.A., a stable of smarmy middle-aged victims, a host of gratuitous murders and a wide-eyed performance by Garrett as the poor little rich kid with an Oedipus complex.

All the pic's elements reek with age, and none of them work. Because Seth slashes the first victim within minutes of the film's opening, we know who the murderers are and why they love to kill.

Suspense never builds, and the 1-dimensional characters are in-

capable of generating any sympathy. —*Advo.*

Australian Daze
(AUSTRALIAN-DOCU)

A Velate Holdings P/L production. Produced by Pat Fiske, Graeme Isaac. Directed by Fiske. Segment directors, Karin Altmann, Mario Andreacchio, Graham Chase, Sharon Connolly, Sue Cornwell, Ruth Cullen, Bernice Daly, Jack Davis, Jim Everett, Jen Feray, Pat Fiske, Trevet Graham, Martin Goddard, John Hughes, Tony Jones, Jeni Kendell, Ned Lander, Dick Marks, Dennis O'Rourke, Christine Sammers, Carole Sklan, Tony Steinbrecker, Paul Tait, Gordon Taylor, Jeni Thornley, Nick Torrens, Madelon Wilkins. Camera (color), Erika Addis, Ray Argall, Jaems Grant, David Noakes, Dennis O'Rourke, others; editor, Denise Haslan; Tim Litchfield; muisc, Davood Tabrizi; sound, Max Bowering, Pat Fiske, Gary Kildea, Stephen Vaughan, others; associate producers, O'Rourke, Anna Grieve. Reviewed at Mosman screening room, Sydney, Oct. 17, 1988. Running time: **75 MIN.**

■ **Sydney — "Australian Daze" looms to become the principal record of Australia's 1988 bicentennial celebrations. On Australia Day, Jan. 26, 1988, 24 film crews across the country filmed from dawn till midnight, and their work has been edited into an invigorating and often thought-provoking whole.**

Some of the country's most prominent documentary directors participated. Dennis O'Rourke ("Half Life") filmed at Alice Springs in the country's Red Center; Graham Chase ("Democracy") covered the celebrations at the tiny mining town of Paraburdoo in Western Australia; Jeni Thornley ("For Love Or Money") was at a maternity hospital; Ned Lander ("Dirt Cheap") was at famous Bondi Beach in Sydney; Mario Andreacchio (helmer of the features "Fair Game" and "The Dreaming") was in the streets of Adelaide; Sue Cornwell ("Kids In Trouble") was on Sydney Harbor. All captured evocative footage of vastly differing celebrations.

Main focus is on Sydney, where a fleet of tall ships, recreating the original First Fleet of 1788, sailed into the majestic Harbor. Here, the rich celebrate with champagne on board their yachts or in harborside mansions. A short distance away, a mass demonstration of aborigines, who were cruelly dispossessed of their traditional land by the Europeans, mass in protest with their white supporters.

Pat Fiske, credited as overall director, has done a great job, together with editors Denise Haslam and Tim Litchfield, in lucidly assembling what was evidently a vast mass of material. Film presents a sweeping panorama of a vast country gripped by communal celebrations, and newscasts (including a royal speech from Prince Charles and comments from Prime Minister Bob Hawke) flesh out the picture.

Apart from the glorious vistas on Sydney Harbor, the viewer brings

away from the film the pride and conviction of the arboriginal leaders, and, on a less inspiring level, the casual racism directed against them and Vietnamese refugees (seen in Adelaide). At a celebration in a small country town, one man blandly asserts that "90% of aborigines are useless," while on the other hand, a stockman professes admiration for Australia's original inhabitants, pointing out that they fed themselves and managed the land for thousands of years with great skill.

"Australian Daze" will have a long life in Australia, with theatrical release initially indicated, and then plenty of tv and video success.
—*Strat.*

They Live

A Universal Pictures release of an Alive Films presentation of a Larry Franco production. Produced by Franco. Executive producers, Shep Gordon, Andre Blay. Directed by John Carpenter. Screenplay, Frank Armitage, based on short story "Eight O'Clock In The Morning" by Ray Nelson; camera (Panavision, Deluxe color), Gary B. Kibbe; editor, Gib Jaffe, Frank E. Jimenez; music, Carpenter, Alan Howarth; art direction, William J. Durrell Jr., Daniel Lomino; set decoration, Marvin March; makeup, Frank Carrisosa; sound (Dolby), Ron Judkins; assistant director, Franco; associate producer, Sandy King. Reviewed at Universal Studios, Universal City, Calif., Nov. 2, 1988. MPAA Rating: R. Running time: **93 MIN.**

Nada . . . . Roddy Piper
Frank . . . . Keith David
Holly . . . . Meg Foster
Drifter . . . . George (Buck) Flower
Gilbert . . . . Peter Jason
Street Preacher . . . . . Raymond St. Jacques

■ **Hollywood — Conceived on 1950s B movie sci-fi terms, "They Live" is a fantastically subversive film, a nifty little confection pitting us vs. them, the haves vs. the have-nots.**

Viewers responsive to the enormously clever basic premise — that those in control of the global economic power structure are secretly other-worldly aliens — won't mind the deficiencies in dramatic, acting and budget areas, and pic is sufficiently fresh and provocative to develop a cult following and decent b.o. returns.

Whatever John Carpenter has sacrificed budget-wise under his 4-picture deal with Alive Films, which traded off distribution to Universal, he has more than made up for this time out in freedom to choose material.

Screenplay by Frank Armitage (presumably another Carpenter pseudonym as was "Martin Quatermass" for his previous script "Prince Of Darkness"), based on a Ray Nelson short story, evokes any number of vintage fantasies and sci-fiers, most notably "Invasion Of The Body Snatchers," in its plausible paranoia, socially minded outrage, political urgency and revolutionary zeal.

His leading character, pretentiously named Nada (Roddy Piper), is a heavily muscled working Joe, a wanderer who pulls into Los Angeles, lands a construction job and makes his way to Justiceville, a shantytown settlement for the homeless in the shadows of downtown's skyscrapers.

After considerable footage devoted to the circumstances of society's rejects, Nada happens upon some sunglasses which, when worn, reveal a whole alternate existence, a black and white world in which signs and magazines issue such edicts as "Obey," "Stay Asleep" and "No Independent Thought," and in which certain individuals — the ruling class — are instantly recognizable due to their hideously decomposed, skeletal faces.

Nada catches on immediately to what's going on and becomes an outlaw, picking off aliens wherever he can. The odds clearly are stacked against him and he naturally seeks an accomplice, first in Meg Foster, who unwillingly rescues him from the police, and then in black coworker Keith David, another body builder whom he has to fight seemingly forever before getting him to try on the glasses.

Carpenter takes his time setting up the situation, and the same expository information could have been conveyed in considerably less time. The guided tour Piper and David are given of the establishment's broadcasting compound, from which its power emanates, is pretty hokey and farfetched, present all to clearly to rush the story to its climax. Some of the tough-guy throwaway lines come off as bargain-basement posturing.

Carpenter draws the lines for the revolution very clearly — you're either on one side or the other, and it's very easy to choose. The situation proves amusing as well as ominous, at least to anyone who has thought about such issues as subliminal advertising, multinational corporate power, the zombie-ization of the public by tv, the secret agenda of the right wing and so forth.

Pro wrestler Piper comes across quite adequately as the blue collar Everyman, and remainder of the cast is okay, although Meg Foster is a bothersome enigma as a woman who performs contradictory acts throughout the story. Tech credits are fine on what clearly was a limited budget. —Cart.

Ghost Town

A Trans World Entertainment release of an Empire Pictures production. Executive producer, Charles Band. Produced by Timothy D. Tennant. Directed by Richard Governor. Screenplay, Duke Sandefur, from story by David Schmoeller; camera (Foto-Kem color), Mac Ahlberg; editor, Peter Teschner, King Wilder; music, Harvey R. Cohen; sound (Ultra-Stereo), Bill Fiege, Margaret Duke; production design, Don De Fina; art direction, Rick Brown; special makeup effects, MMI — John Carl Buechler; assistant director, Jim Avery; production manager, Amanda DiGiulio; stunt coordinator, Kane Hodder; second unit director, Lamar Carroll; special mechanical effects, Etan Enterprises, design, Eddie Surkin; additional camera, Stephen W. Gray; casting, Anthony Barnao. Reviewed on New World vidcassette, N.Y., Oct. 30, 1988. MPAA Rating: R. Running time: **85 MIN.**
Langley ....Franc Luz
Kate ....Catherine Hickland
Devilin ....Jimmie F. Skaggs
Grace ....Penelope Windust
Dealer ....Bruce Glover
Blacksmith ....Zitto Kazann
Harper .:................Blake Conway
Etta ....Laura Schaefer
Bubba ....Michael Aldredge
Ned ....:................Ken Kolb
Billy ....Will Hannah

■ **The supernatural thriller "Ghost Town" is a better-than-usual fright pic from Empire Pictures, earning a theatrical release this month from** TWE ahead of homevideo availability via New World.

Atmospheric lensing by Empire stalwart Mac Ahlberg on Tucson locations offers a pleasant relief from recent studiobound (in Rome) product from the late fantasy outfit.

Odd variation on familiar suspense format has pretty blond Catherine Hickland driving her Mercedes on a remote road out West when she has a flat tire and is suddenly whisked away by a phantom rider coming out of a dust cloud.

Deputy sheriff Franc Luz investigates and finds a literal ghost town whose inhabitants are undead, condemned to remain same by a dying sheriff's curse. Luz is given the old sheriff's badge and appointed to end the curse by destroying the lead baddie Devlin (Jimmie F. Skaggs) and saving Hickland from the villains' clutches.

Convincing makeup effects by John Buechler enhance Richard Governor's tight direction, which wisely grounds the fantasy in verisimilitude. Stunt director Kane Hodder later played Jason for Buechler in the most recent "Friday The 13th" feature. —Lor.

The Chocolate War

A Management Co. Entertainment Group production and release. Produced by Jonathan D. Krane. Coproducer, Simon R. Lewis. Directed by Keith Gordon. Screenplay, Gordon, based on book by Robert Cormier; camera (color), Tom Richmond; editor, Jeff Wishengrad; production design, David Ensley; set decoration, Melissa Matthies; costume design, Elizabeth Kaye; sound, Mary Jo Devenney; associate producer, Susan I. Spivak; assistant director, Michelle Solotar; assistant camera, Richard Miller; casting, Susan Dixon. Reviewed at Chicago Intl. Film Festival (competing), Oct. 20, 1988. MPAA Rating: R. Running time: **100 MIN.**
Brother Leon ....John Glover
Jerry ....Ilan Mitchell-Smith
Archie ....Wally Ward
Obie ....Doug Hutchison
Carter ....Adam Baldwin
Emille ....Brent Fraser
Brother Jacques ....Bud Cort

■ **Chicago — Too dismal for popular acceptance, "The Chocolate War" is nonetheless a serious, well-crafted film that could find favor among those who enjoy elaborate social allegories that offer not a shred of hope. Arthouses should take note.**

Pic could be a companion piece to Peter Brook's "Lord Of The Flies." Whereas that film examined a group of schoolboys marooned on an island to detail the disintegration of civilized society, "The Chocolate War" uses schoolboys in their natural habitat to illustrate society's inescapable power — particularly the pressures it brings to bear on the individual to conform.

Based on the popular novel by Robert Cormier, "The Chocolate War" follows young Jerry Renault (Ilan Mitchell-Smith) through his freshman term at St. Trinity school for boys, an institution more rife with intrigue, corruption and treachery than the court of Richard III.

Jerry makes an initial bid to fit in at Trinity by trying out for the school football team, but soon runs afoul of the forces that control life at the school: ambitious Brother Leon (John Glover) and Machiavellian Archie (Wally Ward), a leader of secret school gang, the Vigils.

Brother Leon, hoping to become headmaster, has doubled the quota of chocolates to be sold by each student during the school's annual candy sale/fundraiser, browbeating the boys into accepting the supposedly voluntary assignment. Archie, in charge of handing out the Vigils' hazing assignments to freshmen, gives Jerry the task of publicly refusing to sell the chocolates for 10 days.

At first, Jerry complies, earning the wrath of Brother Leon and the admiration of his fellow students, who consider him a rebel. Then, ashamed of his weakness, he truly rebels and refuses to sell the chocolates beyond the 10-day limit, making himself an enemy of both Brother Leon and the Vigils.

A lesser story would have turned this decision into a moral victory for Jerry, allowing him to triumph against the odds. "The Chocolate War" is remarkable because it does just the opposite. Brother Leon and the Vigils, employing propaganda, intimidation and brute force, transform Jerry from a hero into a pariah and finally make him an instrument of the system.

Picture is an impressive, technically assured debut for director Keith Gordon (heretofore an actor) and is boosted throughout by vivid performances, especially from Glover as the near-psychotic Brother Leon and Ward as gloomy, hyper-cynical Archie.

Yet it's difficult to imagine a more bleak worldview than the one on display here. Death, weakness and despair are exhibited at every turn — relieved only by a very brief but welcome comic cameo by Bud Cort — making the final result interesting but almost overwhelmingly dreary. —Brin.

The In Crowd

An Orion Pictures release of a Force Ten production. Executive producers, John F. Roach, Jeff Franklin. Produced by Lawrence Konner, Keith Rubinstein. Directed by Mark Rosenthal. Screenplay, Rosenthal, Konner; camera (Deluxe color), Anthony Richmond; editor, Jeffrey Wolf; music, Mark Snow; sound (Dolby), Russell Williams 2d, Steve Rodgers; production design, Joseph T. Garrity; art direction, Patrick Tagliaferro; set decoration, Jerie Kelter; costume design, Peter Mitchell; choreography, Jerry Evans; additional choreography, Lynne Taylor-Corbett; assistant director, Fred Baron; production manager, Bridget Murphy; visual consultant, Dan Perri; additional camera, Jeff Jur; coproducers, Karen Essex, Jeffrey Hornaday; associate producers, Ken Golden, Patricia Whitcher; casting, Lynn Stalmaster & Associates, David Rubin. Reviewed on Orion vidcassette, N.Y., Oct. 15, 1988. MPAA Rating: PG. Running time: **95 MIN.**
Del Green ....Donovan Leitch
Perry Parker ....Joe Pantoliano
Vicky...................Jennifer Runyon
Gail ....Wendy Gazelle
Popeye ....Sean Gregory Sullivan
Norris ....Bruno Kirby
Lydia ....Page Hannah
Dugan ....Scott Plank
Also with: Charlotte D'Amboise, Mark Soper, Peter Boyle.

■ **Barely released last February in a test booking on its home turf in Philadelphia, "The In Crowd," a.k.a. "Dance Party," is an unsuccessful nostalgia film from Orion about the tv dance shows of the sort popularized by Dick Clark.**

Though Clark is mentioned several times on screen as an icon, pic rather pointlessly is about a fictional tv host Perry Parker (ably played with high energy by Joe Pantoliano) on Philly tv in 1965 whose goal is to fill Clark's shoes now that the "American Bandstand" pioneer has gone Hollywood.

While there is obvious interest out there in the story of Clark's early career, given the myriad rock stars he helped launch, screenwriters Mark Rosenthal and Lawrence Konner ("The Jewel Of The Nile") have concocted a weak and uneventful narrative for this fictional pastiche.

Donovan Leitch (handsome son of singer Donovan) plays Del, a high schooler who crashes Parker's "Dance Party" show and becomes an instant teen rave, paired with show's blond beauty Vicky (Jennifer Runyon). While Pantoliano maneuvers to hype his ratings, Leitch plays good samaritan, fronting for Runyon's bad boyfriend (Scott Plank), enabling the duo to ultimately elope against parents' wishes.

Not much else happens in this excuse for some okay dance numbers plus a mediocre selection of circa 1965 songs (of which Vince Guaraldi's instrumental "Cast Your Fate To The Wind" is repeated ad nauseam). As hinted by the title, theme of peer pressure and the pain of not being "in" is brought up, but treated superficially.

Absence of humor is another drawback, though the inherent silliness of the dialog and situations in later reels is campy. John Waters' "Hairspray," filmed a year later, has the social satire and panache wholly missing here.

Only Pantoliano's performance is of interest, taking a stereotype and breathing life into it, as a gung ho host who even dances energetically beside his young protégés. Rest of cast is bland. Tech credits, particularly British lenser Anthony Richmond's richly hued visuals, are top-notch. —Lor.

The Brain
(CANADIAN)

A Shapiro Glickenhaus Entertainment presentation; a Brightstar Films (in Canada) release of a Brightstar Films production. Produced by Anthony Kramreither. Executive producer, Don Haig. Directed by Edward Hunt. Screenplay, Barry Pearson; camera (color), Gilles Corbeil; music, Paul Zara; art direction, Byron Patchette; editor, David Nicholson; special effects, Mark Williams; stunt coordinator, Gary Brown. Reviewed at Cineplex Odeon screening room, Toronto, Nov. 3, 1988. MPAA Rating: R. Running time: 85 MINS.

Jim	Tom Breznahan
Janet	Cyndy Preston
Dr. Blake	David Gale

Also with: George Buza, Brett Pearson.

■ Toronto — "The Brain" emerges as a cliché-ridden effort, with little comic or ironic relief to put a spin on its sci-fi banalities.

The tale of middle-America residents hypnotized by the evil machinations of a tv psychologist must have seemed like a potential powderkeg idea for a horror film to producer Tony Kramreither and director Edward Hunt.

Strictly for homevideo shelves, pic's ambition to comment on the power of tv and the gullibility of its viewers vanishes quickly.

Set in Meadowvale, U.S.A. (actually Toronto subbing for a bland American city), script finds a rash of townspeople being murdered after watching Dr. Blake's broadcasts from the Psychological Research Institute. When Jim, an upstart high schooler, is reprimanded for pulling one too many pranks, his principal sends him to PRI to be reconditioned. It is there Jim discovers a huge brain that Dr. Blake has developed for transmitting special waves over tv lines to control the thoughts of the world.

Jim and his virginal girlfriend Janet set out to stop the ever-growing mass of brain tissue from taking over the universe and to get the goods on Dr. Blake.

Barry Pearson's screenplay is loaded with classic twists of the genre, but they don't work here. The special effects are negligible, as the pulsing red tentacles of the monster brain try to strangle various victims.

There are a few unintentionally hilarious lines here. Mom informs her son Jim, "Dr. Blake wouldn't be on tv if he wasn't good." There are endless chase sequences down the corridors of PRI that do nothing to propel any tension, and the hallucination scenes are witless, too.

Cast is caught in a clunker of a film that even their best thesp intentions can't save. —Devo.

Child's Play

An MGM/UA Communications release from United Artists. Executive producer, Barrie M. Osborne. Produced by David Kirschner. Directed by Tom Holland. Screenplay, Don Mancini, John Lafia, Holland, from story by Mancini; camera (Astro color and Technicolor; Technicolor prints), Bill Butler; editor, Edward Warschilka, Roy E. Peterson; music, Joe Renzetti; sound (Dolby), James E. Webb Jr.; production design, Daniel A. Lomino; set decoration, Cloudia; costume design, April Ferry; assistant director, Michael Green; production managers, Robert Latham Brown, Carl Olsen; Chucky doll creator, Kirschner, design, Kevin Yagher; visual effects, Apogee Inc., supervisor, Peter Donen; additional editor, Scott Wallace; special effects supervisor, Richard O. Helmer; second unit director; Bud Davis; associate producer, Laura Moskowitz; casting, Richard Pagano, Sharon Bialy, Chicago: Jane Alderman, Shelley Andreas. Reviewed at Todd-AO screening room, N.Y., Oct. 18, 1988. MPAA Rating: R. Running time: 87 MIN.

Karen Barclay	Catherine Hicks
Det. Mike Norris	Chris Sarandon
Andy Barclay	Alex Vincent
Charles Lee Ray	Brad Dourif
Maggie Peterson	Dinah Manoff
Jack Santos	Tommy Swerdlow
Dr. Ardmore	Jack Colvin

■ "Child's Play" is a near-miss at providing horrific thrills in a tale of a doll come to murderous life, told with a knowing tongue-in-cheek attitude. Fun withers in stretching the thin material to feature length.

Pic's immediate forebear is the final "Amelia" segment of Dan Curtis' tv classic "Trilogy Of Terror," in which Karen Black was tormented by a Zuni spirit-doll that scooted along the floor at lightning speed.

Tom Holland summons impressive technical skill in charting the preposterous story of a nutcase (Brad Dourif) who climaxes a fatal shootout in a Chicago toystore with cop Chris Sarandon by chanting a voodoo incantation and (unbeknownst to reality-prone Sarandon) passing his spirit into a cute, red-headed doll.

Next plot device also is hard to swallow as nice mom Catherine Hicks makes a last-minute buy of the doll from a grubby street peddler for her cute son Alex Vincent. The possessed doll, named Chucky, kills Alex' babysitter Dinah Manoff and who else but Sarandon is the detective on the case.

Violence and paranoia escalate as Alex naturally is blamed for what happens until finally Chucky comes out of the closet and becomes a tangible killer in Hicks' eyes and eventually to Sarandon as well. Film's fun is based on viewer knowing what's going on and enjoying the characters' predicament in not figuring out the cause of their ills until Chucky literally pounces on them.

Both Hicks and Sarandon commendably keep straight faces during these outlandish proceedings, and little Vincent is an effective innocent foil for the doll. Top technical contributions milk the doll gimmick for all its worth, switching from minimal effects in the opening reels to grotesque facial distortions (and cute simulation of walking movements) as the doll transforms.

Problem is that the novelty is not buttressed by an interesting story to go along with the gimmick. Three leads' roles merely exist in order to play off the doll so we don't care much about them. —Lor.

Paramedics

A Vestron Pictures release of a Ruddy-Morgan production, in association with Crow Prods. Produced by Leslie Greif. Line producer, Alan P. Horowitz. Directed by Stuart Margolin. Screenplay, Barry Bardo, Richard Kriegsman; camera (color), Michael Watkins; editor, Allan A. Moore; music, Murray MacLeod; music supervision, Jim Messina; sound (Dolby), Skip Frazee, production design, Jack Marty; production manager, Kathleen Caton; second unit director-stunt coordinator, Randy Fife; second unit camera, Michael Shea; associate producer, Dennis Bishop; casting, Shari Rhodes. Reviewed on Vestron videocassette, N.Y., Oct. 23, 1988. MPAA Rating: PG-13. Running time: 91 MIN.

Uptown	George Newbern
Mad Mike	Christopher McDonald
Bennie	Javier Grajeda
Blade Runner	Lawrence-Hilton Jacobs
Savannah	Elaine Wilkes
Lisette	Lydie Denier
Capt. Prescott	John P. Ryan
Chief Wilkens	James Noble
Danger girl	Karen Witter
Dr. Lido	John Pleshette
First patient	Ray Walston

■ A formula comedy in the worn-out "service" vein mined successfully in many features following the success of "Stripes" and "Police Academy," "Paramedics" has little to offer beyond technical expertise and an above average song score spotlighting Jim Messina.

George Newbern and Christopher McDonald are the peppy leads in this episodic exercise, sent to work by their mean boss John P. Ryan to South Central in the tough part of town (nicely lensed in Dallas). Pic posits them as heroic rule-breakers, in this instance foiling a gang of cardboard meanies who are trafficking illicitly in human organs.

Though earning a PG-13 rating, pic has the same quota of titillating sex comedy and topless footage of the genre's R entries. Main emphasis is on chasing around in the paramedics' ambulance vehicles, with an awards ceremony finale right out of the "Police Academy" textbook.

Actor-turned-director Stuart Margolin gets some laughs with some well-timed gags but audiences are tired of these lookalike comedy efforts. —Lor.

Twice Dead

A Concorde Pictures release. Produced by Guy J. Louthan, Robert McDonnell. Directed by Bert Dragin. Screenplay, Dragin, McDonnell; camera (Foto-Kem color), Zoran Hochstatter; editor, Patrick Rand; music, David Bergeaud; sound, William Fiege; special makeup effects, Michael Burnett; assistant director, Kelly Shroeder; stunt coordinator, John Branagan; casting, Kevin Alber. Reviewed at Technicolor screening room, N.Y., Nov. 2, 1988. MPAA Rating: R. Running time: 85 MIN.

Scott	Tom Breznahan
Robin/Myrna	Jill Whitlow
Crip/Tyler	Jonathan Chapin
Silk	Christopher Burgard
Harry	Sam Melville
Sylvia	Brooke Bundy
Candy	Joleen Lutz
Petie	Todd Bridges

Also with: Ray Garcia, Travis McKenna, Shawn Player.

■ Though competently enacted, "Twice Dead" is a supernatural horror film suffering from tired blood, as helmer Bert Dragin adds little to the haunted mansion genre.

The Cates family moves into the ancestral home in L.A., a rundown manse known as the Tyler place after a movie star who hanged himself there. A feud breaks out immediately between the Cates and some local punkers who view this as an invasion of their turf.

It seems Tyler's spirit is haunting the joint, with his apparition appearing in mirrors and causing objects to move invisibly. Twist is that Tyler proves not to be malevolent but rather aids the Cateses in their bloody war against the punks.

Corny script contrivance has Ma & Pa Cates (Sam Melville, Brooke Bundy) exiting early on to leave their kids in charge. Tom Breznahan and Jill Whitlow as the offspring resourcefully use artistic and makeup effects abilities to scare the devil out of the punkers, before Tyler sends them to their just reward.

First problem here is that the punkers are cast as wimps, not the threatening grotesques intended. One (Jonathan Chapin), who keeps trying to ravish lovely heroine Whitlow, in fact plays a dual role, portraying Tyler in flashback and ghost guise. The punks' moll, Joleen Lutz, is far too sympathetic, even reforming at film's end and becoming the kid's friendly schoolmate. None of this is conducive to terror creation.

Michael Burnett's makeup effects do the job, with an interesting contrast between the homemade, crude effects essayed by the kids and the "real" gore shown later. Well-lit, film otherwise looks like a cheapie. —Lor.

Fear

A Cinetel Films release. Executive producer, Paul Hertzberg. Produced by Lisa M. Hansen. Directed by Robert A. Ferretti. Screenplay, Rick Scarry, Kathryn Connell, story by Ferretti. Camera (Foto-Kem color), Dana Christiaansen; editor, Michael Eliot; music, Alfi Kabiljo; art direction, Fernando Altschul; set decoration, Trevor Norris; costume design, Jan Rowton; sound, Thomas E. Allen Sr.; assistant director, Richard Oswald. Reviewed at Egyptian theater, L.A., Nov. 4, 1988. MPAA Rating: R. Running time: 96 MIN.

Don Haden	Cliff DeYoung
Sharon Haden	Kay Lenz
Jack Gracie	Robert Factor
Brian Haden	Scott Schwartz
Jennifer Haden	Geri Betzler
Robert Armitage	Frank Stallone
Cy Canelle	Charles Meshack
Mitch Barnett	Michael Watson
Lenny	Eddit Banker

■ Hollywood — There's nothing like being taken hostage by a bunch of escaped convicts to draw an unhappy family closer together. Such is the moral of "Fear," which presents viewers with yet another deranged Vietnam vet compelled to enact the war one more time before he dies.

Robert A. Ferretti's debut feature is far from the worst low-budget suspenser ever made, but is still pointless as a theatrical release, as indicated by its current token Los Angeles run in advance of its Nov. 16 appearance in videostores via Virgin Vision.

Lensed as "Honor Betrayed," pic has the Haden family heading out in a van to Uncle Billy's cabin in the mountains to try to patch up their numerous problems. Along the way they run into four escaped cons, a swell bunch made up of two certified killers, a desperately scared kid and the vet who, living in flashback, believes every moving thing is a commie to be blown away.

Story follows a tiresomely predictable course, with tensions among the felons unsurprisingly thinning their ranks, and clever makeshift tactics by the Hadens eventually tipping the balance in their favor once they reach the cabin.

Happily for them, Pa Haden also is a Vietnam vet and knows a thing or two about setting jungle boobytraps, but he still can't hold a candle to his teenage daughter, who has the presence of mind to incapacitate a would-be rapist with a mousetrap.

Cliff DeYoung and Kay Lenz do the best they can as the Haden parents, and acting by those playing the cons (Robert Factor, Frank Stallone, Charles Meshack, Michael Watson) is nothing if not intense. Ferretti does an okay job at the helm on an obviously small budget, but to no avail, as this is a film with no apparent audience. —Cart.

Otstupnik
(The Apostate)
(SOVIET)

A Belarusfilm Studios production with participation of Sovinfilm, V. Myich K.G. Studio Hamburg (W. Germany) and Klinkartfilm (Austria). Written and directed by Valery Rubinchik; based on a novel by P. Bagryak. Camera (color), Yuri Yalkhov; production design, Alexander Chertovich. No other credits available. Reviewed at Sitges Film Festival, Spain, Oct. 14, 1988. Running time: 163 MIN.
With: Grigury Gladily, Nikolai Yeremenko, Andrei Kashker, Larisa Belogurova, Valentina Shendrikova.

■ Sitges — This long, intricate and complexly structured film doubtless will appeal to a sector of highbrow critics, but most filmgoers will find it hopelessly incomprehensible.

A wealth of striking imagery and moody intrigue may make it palatable to specialized art-circuit audiences who will be able to argue for hours about film's "meaning." Pic is essentially the director's personal trip into his past and the world he lives in.

Item is supposedly set in "some imperialist country," though this is not apparent in the film. A still photographer, after lensing a scientist who has committed suicide, suddenly sees the same man in the street. Story is about two clones, attempts by a general to seize the invention for producing matrix molds capable of reproducing any living thing, the personal lives and views of the cloned scientist, and a bevy of intrigues involving the cloning of the president of the country.

All the foregoing is more easily understood from the sparse synopsis provided the press than from the film. Latter jumps from seemingly unrelated sequence to sequence, some of them very striking, but lacking any kind of story continuity or coherence.

Technically, print shown here was filled with flaws; the color was often so faded as to seem almost monochrome, and music track splicing was also faulty. —Besa.

Drôle d'endroit pour une rencontre
(A Strange Place For An Encounter)
(FRENCH)

A UGC release of a Hachette Première/DD Prod./Deneuve S.A./Orly Films/Les Editions Sidonie/Hachette Prods./Films A2 coproduction. Executive producer, René Cleitman. Directed by François Dupeyron. Screenplay, Dupeyron, Dominque Faysse; camera (Eastmancolor), Charlie Van Damme; sound, Pierre Gamet, Jean-Paul Loublier; art direction, Carlos Conti; makeup, Renaldo Ribeiro de Abreu; costumes, Caroline de Vivaise, Gil Noir; assistant director, Xavier Castano; production manager, Patrick Bordier; casting, Romain Romain Bremond. Reviewed at UGC, Neuilly, Sept. 28, 1988. Running time: 97 MIN.
France . . . . Catherine Deneuve
Charles . . . . Gérard Depardieu
Sylvie . . . . Nathalie Cardone
Georges . . . . André Wilms
Pierrot . . . . Jean-Pierre Sentier

■ Paris — "Drôle d'endroit pour une rencontre" is an off-the-road movie by newcomer François Dupeyron, who gives a stylish lift to a theatrically unprepossessing premise.

Stars Catherine Deneuve and Gérard Depardieu were eager enough about the screenplay to accept not only to appear in a first feature but also to share the risk as coproducers. Not bad for a firsttimer.

Screenplay is basically a 2-hander with several subsidiary characters skillfully placed throughout the action to set off the principal relationship. In itself idea is not much of a turn-on, but performances, dialog and direction provide a dynamism to an essentially static situation.

The stars meet one cold night on a highway rest-stop. Deneuve, who has been traveling with her husband, is unceremoniously ejected by hubby after a heated argument. Distraught and confused, she meets Depardieu, who has spent two nights trying to fix his car motor, which he has taken apart but is unable to reassemble.

What follows is a predictable close encounter of two different kinds. Dupeyron (who coscripted with wife Dominique Faysse) has style enough and a way with dialog to steer clear of triteness and formula scenes.

Dupeyron owes a great deal to his actors, notably Depardieu. Without any biographical material supplied to the viewer (all we know is that he's a doctor), Depardieu creates a sharp portrait of a man clearly burned by life and wary of dependency (symbolized, rather patly, by his tenacious desire to fix his car alone).

Deneuve, who has accepted a string of feeble roles of late, finally has something to sink her teeth into. She fares well as the abandoned bourgeois wife who refuses to accept the obvious reality (which the gradually lovesick Depardieu instinctively understands) that this time her mate will not be coming back.

Action, which moves from the rest stop to a truckstop area and roadside cafeteria, is well blocked out within a 48-hour period, and the sundry scenes with subsidiary characters, including a waitress and some truck drivers, are freshly imagined and visualized.

Dupeyron, 38, a graduate of the IDHEC film school, has directed a handful of prizewinning fiction and docu shorts. Though "Rencontre" is only doing modestly at local wickets, it should have international mileage on the strength of its names.

Tech credits, topped by Charlie Van Damme's superb nocturnal photography, are smooth down the line. —Len.

Ernest Saves Christmas

A Buena Vista release of a Touchstone Pictures production in association with Silver Screen Partners III. Executive producers, Martin Erlichman, Joseph L. Akerman, Jr. Produced by Stacy Williams, Doug Claybourne. Directed by John Cherry. Screenplay, B. Kline, Ed Turner, based on a story by Turner; camera (Continental color; Metrocolor prints), Peter Stein; music, Mark Snow; art direction, Ian Thomas; set decoration, Chris August; costume design, Peter Mitchell; sound (Dolby) Rich Schirmer; coproducers, Justis Green, Coke Sams; associate producer, Turner; visual effects supervisor, Tim McHugh; assistant director, Patrice Leung; second unit director, Sams; casting, Kathleen Letterie. Reviewed at Mann's Hollywood Theater, Hollywood, Nov. 11, 1988. MPAA Rating: PG. Running time: 89 MIN.
Ernest P. Worrell . . . . Jim Varney
Santa . . . . Douglas Seale
Joe Carruthers . . . . Oliver Clark
Harmony . . . . Noelle Parker
Marty . . . . Robert Lesser
Chuck . . . . Gailard Sartain
Mary Morrissey . . . . Billie Bird
Bobby . . . . Bill Byrge
Pyramus . . . . Buddy Douglas
Thisbe . . . . Patty Maloney

■ Hollywood — Ernest saves Christmas, and word-of-mouth might save Ernest, if parents discover the charms of this Touchstone release.

Delightful holiday comedy pits well-meaning disaster Ernest P. Worrell and a sweet-spirited but aging Santa Claus against a cynical, disbelieving world. Without getting syrupy, it captures the meaning and magic of the season. Youngsters will be enchanted and parents well-entertained. Early release is wise, as pic could show some legs.

Santa Claus (Douglas Seale) arrives via airplane in Orlando, Fla., dressed in a business suit. At 151 years old, his magic powers are dimming and he's come to pass the torch on to a kindly but down-on-his-luck children's tv host (Oliver Clark) whose show has just been canceled.

But when Santa gets into a cab driven by disaster-prone Ernest, his plan begins to unravel, and with only so many hours till Christmas, it's a real scramble to pull it off.

Naturally, Ernest gets involved every step of the way, as does another passenger in the cab, teenage runaway Harmony (Noelle Parker), who embodies the half-grown, half-child element that can't quite decide what to think about Christmas.

Great chemistry and some very astute characterizations rank as the chief charms of this second feature-length "Ernest" adventure, along with the often clever script by Ed Turner and the mysterious "B. Kline."

Director John Cherry, the ad exec who created and developed the lucrative loud-mouthed tv pitchman, segues nimbly from the sweetness of the pic's Spielbergian magic touches (like when all the kids at the airport secretly recognize Santa) to the raucous hijinks and broad gags associated with Ernest.

Jim Varney gets to show off a good chunk of his comic range in varied get-ups as he resourcefully outwits the authorities, and Seale, with his clipped British accent and twinkly eyes, makes a gentle and elegant Santa Claus.

Noelle Parker is beguiling and multidimensional as the coy, tough-talking teen who falls into step quite charmingly with Ernest.

As it turns out, Santa's protégé (Oliver Clark) has to choose between the old man's unlikely pitch and an offer to play the lead in a Christmas slasher pic.

Pic sets up a tug-of-war for adult viewers between what we want to believe in and what experience has taught us to succumb to. Christmas season, it suggests, is the time to believe once again in magic and hope.

Casting by Kathleen Letterie is remarkably thoughtful, and sets and costumes, including Ian Thomas' design for Ernest's tacky Florida cottage, make a keen contribution. —*Daws.*

Split Decisions

A New Century/Vista release of a Wizan Film Properties production. Produced by Joe Wizan. Coproducers, Mickey Borofsky, Todd Black. Directed by David Drury. Screenplay, David Fallon; camera (CFI color), Timothy Suhrstedt; editors, John W. Wheeler, Jeff Freeman, Thomas Stanford; music, Basil Poledouris; visual consultant, Alfred Brenner; art direction, Michael Z. Hanan; set decoration, Kathe Klopp, Carol Nast (N.Y.); costume design, Hilary Cochran; sound (Ultra-Stereo), Steve Nelson, Larry Loewinger (N.Y.); fights staged by Paul Stader; associate producers, Jean Higgins, Rachel Singer; assistant director, Michale Daves; casting, Lynn Stalmaster & Associates, Mall Finn. Reviewed at Hollywood Pacific theater, L.A., Nov. 11, 1988. MPAA Rating: R. Running time: **95 MIN.**

Eddie McGuinn	Craig Sheffer
Ray McGuinn	Jeff Fahey
Dan McGuinn	Gene Hackman
Pop McGuinn	John McLiam
Barbara Uribe	Jennifer Beals
Julian 'Snake' Pedroza	Eddie Velez
Lou Rubia	Carmine Caridi
Benny Platone	James Tolkan

■ Hollywood — "Split Decisions" merits a split decision of its own. On one hand, the film is a reasonably involving drama about three generations in a family of Irish working-class boxers. On the other, it increasingly threatens to reduce itself to the level of another "Rocky" clone, finally capitulating in its far-fetched climax in the ring.

A cut above the usual non-press-screened indie fodder, this still looks destined for quick theatrical playoff on the road to video release.

With its gritty Hell's Kitchen atmosphere and ripe family tensions, first American feature from David Drury ("Defense Of The Realm") draws the viewer in almost immediately and maintains considerable promise for some time. Young Eddie McGuinn (Craig Sheffer) is a promising amateur boxer with a real chance for gold at the Olympics, but he's smart enough to have been ac-

cepted at a good college and to know that an education is more important than momentary athletic glory.

By contrast, his brother Ray (Jeff Fahey), also a fine boxer, is an arrogant punk who has alienated his father Dan (Gene Hackman) by taking up with the slimiest element of the old fight game. At the same time, Ray has dumped his local girlfriend Barbara (Jennifer Beals), who is consoled by Eddie.

After Ray signs to battle the fearsome "Snake" Pedroza (Eddie Velez), with the winner promised a title shot, he is stunned when informed that he is expected to throw the fight. In due course, he refuses, and is summarily beaten and killed by the underworld thugs who control the action and by Pedroza himself.

What has heretofore been a fairly realistic, if familiar, drama now becomes implausible fairytale, as an enraged Eddie decides to forego his Olympic dream by turning pro and attempting to avenge Ray's death by taking his brother's place in the ring opposite Pedroza. His father, himself a failed fighter and now a smalltime manager and corner man, reacts furiously at first, but finally comes around and joins his father (John McLiam), also an ex-pugilist, **in training the kid for what he announces will be his only pro fight.**

The bout itself is hyped-up wish fulfillment, and quite unsatisfying from the p.o.v. of a fight fan. The rounds, as staged and cut, go by much too quickly, only lasting about 15 seconds, and camera coverage is excessively tight, as if to hide the inability of the actors to punch and defend convincingly. Without giving it all away, suffice it to say that it just doesn't happen like this.

Up to the third act, however, there are numerous well-written scenes from first-time screenwriter David Fallon, solid acting from the ensemble, and an agreeable evocation of the blue collar, mixed-ethnic world of club boxing and low-level professionals. This pain·in these pent-up Irish souls, so common in dramas of decades past, feels relatively fresh on the screen today, but is washed away by modern contrivance and the pointedly rousing Basil Poledouris score, making for a film of decidedly contradictory ambitions.—*Cart.*

Iron Eagle II
(CANADIAN-ISRAELI)

A Tri-Star Pictures release of an Alliance Entertainment production, in association with Harkot Prods. Executive producer, Andras Hamori. Produced by Jacob Kotzky, Sharon Herel, John Kemeny. Directed by Sidney J. Furie. Screenplay, Kevin Elders, Furie; camera (Bellevue Pathé color), Alain Dostie; editor, Rit Wallis; music, Amin Bhatia; art direction, Ariel Roshko; costume design, Sylvie Krasker; set decoration, Giora Porter; sound (Ultra-Stereo), David Lis; air-to-air photog-

raphy, Clay Lacy; aerial camera, David Nowell; stunt coordinator, Terry Leonard; associate producers, Stephanie Reichel, Asher Cat; assistant director, Michael Zenon; production manager, Doron Mizrachi; casting, Clare Walker. Reviewed at Tri-Star screening room, Century City, Calif., Nov. 9, 1988. MPAA Rating: PG. Running time: **105 MIN.**

Chappy	Louis Gossett Jr.
Cooper	Mark Humphrey
Stillmore	Stuart Margolin
Varkovsky	Alan Scarfe
Valeri	Sharon H. Brandon
Downs	Maury Chaykin
Yuri	Colm Feore
Graves	Clark Johnson
Hickman	Jason Blicker
Bush	Jesse Collins
Balyonev	Mark Ivanir
Koshkin	Uri Gavriel

■ Hollywood — **A lot's changed since the first "Iron Eagle" stormed the boxoffice almost three years ago — and sequel nervily tries to update the formula. Plot meanders and fails to really fire its engines until deep into the story. Boxoffice should be middling.**

Now that "Top Gun" has set the obvious, if empty, standard for airborne entertainment, the "Iron Eagle II" producers fold that pic's trademarks into the mix as well. Neither the visuals nor the soundtrack of this lower-budget effort can compare, meaning audiences are likely to be underwhelmed.

Puppyfaced rock 'n' roll fighter pilots, including Tom Cruise-lookalike Mark Humphrey, accidentally stray into Soviet airspace and one gets shot down. The survivor, Cooper (Humphrey), starts nursing a big grudge against Soviets.

Next thing you know he's recruited for a secret mission led by Louis Gossett Jr. (reprising his role as Chappy) who's been given a general's star as incentive to lead U.S. and Soviet pilots on a joint mission to destroy a nuclear weapons base in an unnamed Mideast country that is a threat to them both.

Setting causes endless conflict, since the American team members are shown as prejudiced slobs given to pranks, insults and dirty tricks, always on the verge of a punch-out with their Soviet counterparts.

To make things worse for Cooper, one of his new Soviet teammates, Vardovsky (Alan Scarfe), was part of the squadron that gunned down his buddy, and also keeps a jealous eye on an alluring female Soviet pilot, Valeri Zuyeniko (Sharon H. Brandon), whom Cooper wastes no time strutting for.

Pic's chief weakness is that for much of the screentime, the "joint mission" seems like just a weak premise to bring together both sides for lowbrow "Police Academy"-style antics and infighting.

On the plus side, the goons slowly and grudgingly develop a bond and understanding that proves to be the pic's crowning glory. Filmmakers are determined to make their point, quite blatantly at times, that war has no winners. Planted in an action film, followed with the requisite bombs-and-fireworks ending,

it's a pretty shaky maneuver.

Third act provides plenty of fireworks, as the odds against the attackers look impossible, and the hostile missile base, once hit, is shown destructing from inside. By never identifying the men they're blowing up and setting on fire, filmmakers skirt the implications of this particular violence. (They may be trying to have it both ways, but it's still a hopeful sign when war pics end as diplomatically as this one does.)

Aside from the final segment, production values are okay. Aerial photography and stunts are good, with some nerve-rattling segments and nice flourishes, but skies are often bleak and visuals lack the "Top Gun" dazzle.

Gossett gives a gritty performance in a role he's played before, and Humphreys is appealing as the lower-rung Tom Cruise. —*Daws.*

Oliver & Company
(ANIMATED)

A Buena Vista release of a Walt Disney Pictures presentation, produced in association with Silver Screen Partners III. Directed by George Scribner. Animation screenplay, Jim Cox, Timothy J. Disney, James Mangold; story, Vance Gerry, Mike Gabriel, Roger Allers, Joe Ranft, Gary Trousdale, Jim Mitchell, Kevin Lima, Chris Bailey, Michael Cedeno, Kirk Wise, Pete Young, Dave Michener, Leon Joosen; additional story material, Gerrit Graham, Samuel Graham, Chris Hubbell, Steve Hulet, Danny Mann; inspired by Charles Dickens' novel "Oliver Twist;" camera (Deluxe color; Metrocolor prints), various; editor, Jim Melton, Mark Hester; sound (Dolby), Sandy Berman; music, J.A.C. Redford; songs, Barry Mann & Howard Ashman, Tom Snow & Dean Pitchford, Ron Rocha & Robert Minkoff, Dan Hartman & Charlie Midnight, Barry Manilow, Jack Feldman & Bruce Sussman, Rocky Pedilla, Michael Eckhart & Jon St. James, Rubén Blades; supervising animators, Mike Gabriel, Hendel Butoy, Glen Keane, Mark Henn, Ruben A. Aquino, Doug Krohn; art direction, Dan Hansen; casting, Mary V. Buck, Susan Edelman; special optical printing, Chris B. Bushman. Reviewed at Guild 50th St. theater, N.Y., Nov. 9, 1988. MPAA Rating G. Running time: **72 MIN.**

Voices of:

Oliver	Joey Lawrence
Dodger	Billy Joel
Tito	Richard (Cheech) Marin
Georgette	Bette Midler
Fagin	Dom DeLuise
Francis	Roscoe Lee Browne
Einstein	Richard Mulligan
Rita	Sheryl Lee Ralph
Jenny	Natalie Gregory
Sykes	Robert Loggia
Roscoe	Taurean Blacque
Desoto	Carl Weintraub
Winston	William Glover

■ **Disney's "Oliver & Company" is an extremely entertaining cartoon that gives the venerable animation company's approach an update into hip, '80s music and manners.**

Boxoffice outlook is clouded by the unusually cutthroat competition in which pic bows the same day as ex-Disney animator Don Bluth's "The Land Before Time" from Universal, both films aimed at the same audience.

Once the initial theatrical bloodletting is over, Disney will have a perennial favorite that owes only its premise to Charles Dickens. In this loose adaptation, Oliver is an irresistibly cute orange kitten (ably voiced by Joey Lawrence), taken in by a gang of dogs by streetwise hound Billy Joel. A derelict human Fagin (bearing no resemblance to previous incarnations of the Dickens character), voiced by Dom DeLuise, takes care of the pooches.

Fagin has been given three days to come up with money owed to gangster/loan shark human Sykes (the ubiquitous Robert Loggia) and the dogs and kitten help out. Oliver meanwhile is taken in by a rich youngster human Jenny (Natalie Gregory) and pic climaxes in a showdown with Sykes who kidnaps Jenny for ransom.

Pic boasts several terrific songs, particularly "Why Should I Worry" spotlighting Joel and a full-scale production number, "Perfect Isn't Easy," sung by Jenny's poodle as voiced by Bette Midler. Doing a sort of takeoff on Gloria Swanson in "Sunset Boulevard," Midler is consistently delightful and helps set the film's tone of animals vs. humans with her highly affected "Bark! Bark!" pronouncements when speaking to humans (animals converse in English amongst themselves here).

As a peppy Chihuahua, Cheech Marin provides terrific comic relief, managing to slip in contemporary argot and sexual innuendo without threatening the film's G rating. Roscoe Lee Browne as a British bulldog also is impressive.

Pic's visual background is closer to Ralph Bakshi than traditional Disney in its evocation of contemporary Manhattan, but the anthropomorphic character work is on-target with warm and winning creations.

Director George Scribner peppers the slim (72-minute) feature with eventful action sequences and his vast team of animators capture different moods well, including pathos of Oliver as an abandoned kitty in the rain at film's outset (accompanied by a contrasting cheerful song sung by Huey Lewis) or his lyrical romp with Jenny in Central Park. —Lor.

Mon ami le traitre
(My Friend The Traitor)
(FRENCH)

An AMLF release of a Sara Films/TF1 Films coproduction. Produced by Alain Sarde. Directed by Jose Giovanni. Screenplay, Claude Sautet, Alphonse Boudard, Jose Giovanni, from Giovanni's novel; camera (color), Jean François Gondre; editor, Jacqueline Thiédot; art direction, Roland Deville; music, Jean Marie Senia; sound, Pierre Lenoir; costumes, Olga Berluti; makeup, Josée de Luca; assistant director, Raphael Blanc; production manager, Christine Gozlan. Reviewed at Marignan-Concorde theater, Paris, Nov. 7, 1988. Running time: **120 MIN.**
Georges .... Thierry Fremont

Rove .... André Dussollier
Louise .... Valérie Kaprisky
Also with: Jean-Jacques Moreau, Jean-Pierre Sentier, Philippe Dormoy, Michel Peyleron, Yves Kerboul, Steve Kalfa, Jean-Pierre Bernard, Jean-Michel Noiret, Frédéric Rate.

■ **Paris** — Novelist-filmmaker Jose Giovanni contributes to the current run of wartime dramas of Occupied France with this adaptation of his own novel about a young hood's attempts to redeem his erstwhile activity as a collaborator.

Coscripting by director Claude Sautet and novelist-scripter Alphonse Boudard (both past masters of the suspense genre) no doubt accounts for the sober tone of the story. Like many previous Giovanni pics, "Mon ami le traitre" is weakened seriously by its underlying sentimentality about "thieve's honor." Giovanni also lacks subtlety in his depiction of moral hypocrisy toward the end of the war, when the French began hunting and punishing Nazis and countrymen who had betrayed the homeland.

Pic, based on a true story, is set during these post-D-Day purgings and dramatizes the fate of a Marseilles delinquent who offers to help French intelligence nab war criminals in exchange for developing "amnesia" of his own activities.

Giovanni keeps a lively pace with much conventional movieland gunplay and pursuits, but plotting eventually bogs down in a simple-minded exposure of the double standards of Liberation judges and executioners, who demand full justice for small-time collaborators but allow bigger Nazi game to be recruited by the Americans for anticommunist witch-hunting.

Giovanni's best move is his casting. Thierry Fremont, the unloved backward child of a rape victim in Marion Hansel's "Les Noces barbares" and the mild-mannered movie buff of Jean-Charles Tacchella's "Travelling avant," musters up previously untapped dynamism as the repentant young hoodlum, and André Dussollier lends his quiet, thoughtful dignity to the role of the intelligence officer who grooms him as a stool pigeon.

Valérie Kaprisky, however, gets the wrong end of the star credits as the young bourgeois woman whose love gives Fremont the desire for a new life. It's a character Giovanni fails to bring to credible life.

Tech credits are good. —Len.

Trois places pour le 26
(Three Seats For The 26th)
(FRENCH)

An AMLF release of a Claude Berri-Renn production. Produced by Pierre Grunstein. Written and directed by Jacques Demy. Camera (Eastmancolor), Jean Penzer; editor, Sabine Mamou; music, Michel Legrand; art direction, Bernard Evein; sound, Andrée Hervé; costumes, Rosalie Varda; makeup, Eliane Marcus; choreography, Michael Peters; assistant director, Denis Epstein;

production manager, Michel Choquet; associate producer, Jacques Tronel; casting, Romain Brémond. Reviewed at Max Linder Panorama theater, Paris, Nov. 4, 1988. Running time: **103 MIN.**
Yves Montand .... Himself
Marion .... Mathilda May
Mylène .... Françoise Fabian
Toni Fontaine .... Patrick Fierry
Betty Miller .... Catriona MacColl
Max Leehman .... Paul Guers
Alice .... Catherine Varda
Nicole .... Marie-Dominique Aumont
Librarian .... Hélène Surgère

■ **Paris** — Yves Montand plays himself in this new musical by Jacques Demy, produced by Claude Berri. Though the actor-singer's international popularity should guarantee wide exposure, film is far from a highpoint in anybody's career.

It tritely rehashes conventions of musical comedy in general and Demy's style of musical in particular.

It's at once an homage to Montand's flamboyant career and Demy's self-conscious harking back to his earlier successes, such as "Lola" and "The Umbrellas Of Cherbourg."

The setting is no longer the Cherbourg or Nantes of Demy's childhood, but the Marseille of Montand's youth, another port city where dreams of departure and first love resurface in the typical singsong jargon that Demy has made his own. Marseille, however, apparently inspires Demy less than its Normandy counterparts.

Demy's languid scenario brings Montand back home to star in an autobiographical musical, which evokes his docker days, Edith Piaf, Simone Signoret and his first American movie contract in 1960 ("Let's Make Love"). Oddly, the show seems to end with last-named event, though story clearly is set in the late 1980s.

Demy and Michel Legrand have composed new songs for the Montand retrospective, which are okay, though one vainly entertains hopes of some genuine Montand standards. Choreographer Michael Peters (famed for his work with Michael Jackson) stages the dance numbers, but Montand remains a relatively stationary figure against a teeming background of extras and dancers. Set design, both on stage and off, by Demy's longtime collaborator Bernard Evein is stylish and colorful.

Several numbers are placed outside the literal theatrical setting, but the framing story is mechanically contrived and in surprisingly poor taste.

The show is threatened when Montand's leading lady, portraying his first lost love from Marseille, drops out of the show just weeks before opening night.

In one of the hoariest clichés of the genre, a charming young local hopeful (Mathilda May) just happens to be there when crisis breaks. Desperately shunted into the vacant role she triumphs as a new variety

light, and also makes her way into Montand's bed.

What Montand doesn't know is that May in fact, is the daughter of the old flame (Françoise Fabian), whom the debutant is portraying. This leads to implied incest (Fabian having told Montand that he is the real father of her daughter), though this dubious plot device turns out to be unfounded. (Besides May is 22 in the film; the fictional Montand-Fabian romance dates back some 40 years!)

Among such embarrassing insinuations about his backstage romancing, it's no wonder that when he's not singing, Montand seems ill at ease and stiff playing himself. By contract, May is fresh, radiant and gracious — a perfect Demy type. —Len.

Profundo
(Deep)
(VENEZUELAN-COLOMBIAN)

A Focine-Doble Ele C.A. (Venezuela)-Ulrika Cine (Colombia) production. Produced by Reinaldo de los Llanos. Directed by Antonio Llerendi. Screenplay, José Ignacio Cabrujas; camera (color), Livio Delgado; editor, Alberto Torija; music, Miguel Angel Fuster; art direction, Valentina Herz, Gonzalo Denis, Ricardo Fuenmayor. Reviewed at San Juan Film Festival, Puerto Rico, Oct. 1, 1988. Running time: **97 MIN.**
Büey .... Carlos Muñoz
Magra .... Hilda Vera
Mangazón .... Orlando Urdaneta
Lucrecia .... Tania Sarabia
Asunción .... Rafael Briceño

■ **San Juan** — Firmly planted in the Latin American tradition of magic realism, the Venezuelan-Colombian coprod "Profundo" is an amusing mix of unexpected surrealistic and fantastic scenes within the everyday lives of one Venezuelan family. Cult status is a possibility on the international arthouse circuit.

Drama is sparked by a dream of a mitered bishop leading herds of pigs. A witch (Rafael Briceño) is called in, who interprets this vision as a harbinger of riches to be found at the site. Ensuing efforts to purify the house and its inhabitants brings out the different relationships of the family members.

Humorous script was penned by Venezuelan playwright José Ignacio Cabrujas, capturing the comic quirks and personality conflicts of the various characters as they strive for purity. Family patriarch Büey (Carlos Muñoz) has the lion's share when it comes to purification since he must come to terms with his lustful past and establish legitimacy for his various children scattered around the country.

Helmer Antonio Llerendi manages to strike the right balance between fantasy and reality in this no-holds-barred effort. Rich lensing helps to highlight magical moments, charging the scenes with bright colors. — Lent.

Lethargy
(SOVIET)

A Mosfilm Studio production and release. Directed by Valery Lonskoy. Screenplay, Vladimir Zheleznikov; camera (color), Anatoly Ivanov. Reviewed at Denver Intl. Film Festival, Oct. 16, 1988. Running time: **99 MIN.**

With: Andrei Myagkov, Natalya Sayko, Valentina Panina, Rimma Korosteleva.

■ **Denver** — This film, which had its premiere at the Denver Intl. Film Festival, deals with a Russian bureaucrat made apathetic by a chronic inability to relate to life.

He is unable to find a way to deal with his younger wife's announcement of her pregnancy anymore than with his teenage daughter he can barely recall. His reluctance to get involved is partially a result of the futility he feels in carrying out his bureaucratic duties.

Fortunately this lassitude is not reflected dramatically in a film which is terse in exploring the relationships. The writing is convincing and the film takes place in a real world rather than the often sterile world of many Russian features.

The melodrama which comes rushing into his life is horrifying but altogether believable. The hooligans who figure in a key scene are surely the element which withheld this 1983 film from timely release. This brutal sense of a world out of joint gives the film immediate relevance with reference to matters in the headlines the world over.

Lead actor Andrei Myagkov's cool surface is underlaid by fears and frustrations which indicate the desperation of his condition. The applause tape which he plays after he has entertained himself with some guitar playing is certainly indication of this. The film is smooth technically, and ably directed by Valery Lonskoy.

It is an impressive example of glasnost at work in the arts.
—*Alyo.*

Bloodspell

An MCEG and Vista Street Prods. presentation of a Feifer/Miller production. Executive producers, Jerry Feifer, Tony Miller. Produced by Jessica Rains. Directed by Deryn Warren. Screenplay, Gerry Daly; camera (color), Ronn Schmidt; editor, Miller; music, Randy Miller; sound, Michael Draghi; production design, Peter Kanter; special effects makeup, Wade Daily; production manager-associate producer, Chris Munson; assistant director, Richard Kanter; second unit director, Schmidt. Reviewed on Forum Home Video vidcassette, N.Y., Nov. 5, 1988. MPAA Rating: R. Running time: **88 MIN.**

Daniel . . . . Anthony Jenkins
Charlie . . . . Aaron Teich
Debbie . . . . Alexandra Kennedy
Luther . . . . John Reno
Also with: Edward Dloughy, Jacque J. Coon, Kimble Jemison, Heather Green, Christopher G. Venuti, Susan Buchanan, Douglas Vale, Tia Lachelle.

■ **The gory horror pic "Blood-**

spell" is another nightmarish genre title going out direct to video, reminiscent of last April's Fox release "Bad Dreams."

Anthony Jenkins plays Daniel, a teen with telekinetic powers sent to St. Boniface, a holding center for the evaluation of troubled students, run by Alexandra Kennedy. He's there for his own protection, since his dad (John Reno), the villain of the piece, is after him. It turns out, however, that Jenkins is a menace, killing the fellow students one by one for petty annoyances.

Everyone thinks these gruesome murders are accidents rather than supernaturally caused. Finally dad shows up, a monster (via weak facial makeup effects) who seeks to use his son to further his own rejuvenation.

Young cast is okay (though encouraged to overact) and pic is generally an improvement over same production team's earlier "Mirror Of Death." However, it's still a long road (and budget increase) to bridge the gap between this level of filmmaking and the popular theatrical releases in the "Elm Street" and "Halloween" series. —*Lor.*

Apsaras
(FRENCH-DOCU)

An Atelier Prisme 9, La Sept, FR3, CNRS AUdiovisuel, du CNC, du Ministere des Affaires Etrangeres production. Written and directed by Jacques Kebadian. Camera (color, 16m), Jerome Blumberg; editor, François Prenant; sound, Francois Didio; made in collaboration with Le Ballet Classique Khmer de Paris, l'Ecole de Danse du Camp de Refugies, Site B. Reviewed at Nyon Intl. Film Festival, Switzerland, Oct. 23, 1988. Running time: **90 MIN.**

■ **Nyon** — "Apsaras" depicts the heroic efforts of a few survivors of the Khmer Rouge in Cambodia terror, when 300 dancers perished, to rebuild in Paris an exiled cultural tradition that was almost exterminated.

Princess Bopha Devi, daughter of Cambodia's former monarch, Prince Norodom Sihanouk, directs L'Ecole de Danse du Camp du Refugies du Site B. The Ballet Classique Khmer de Paris is directed by Princess Norodom Vacheara. Set design is by the famed sculptor Ipousteguy, subject of an earlier documentary by Jacques Kebadian, director of "Apsaras."

Scenes include the private lives of the adult dancers and their moonlighting jobs as waiters and nightclub singers. Most enchanting are scenes of the selection and training of Cambodian children for the company. Photos and memories describe the decimation of whole families by the Khmer Rouge. Dancers were special targets because they were associated with decadent royal patronage and class privilege.
—*Hitch.*

Alien From L.A.

A Cannon release of a Golan-Globus production. Executive producer, Avi Lerner. Produced by Menahem Golan, Yoram Globus. Line producer, Tom Karnowski. Directed by Albert Pyun. Screenplay, Debra Ricci, Regina Davis, Pyun; camera (TVC color), Tom Fraser; editor, Daniel Loewenthal; music, James Saad, Tony Riparetti, Simon LeGassick, Jim Andron; sound (Ultra-Stereo), Dane Davis; production design, Pamela Warner; costume design, Birgitta Bjerke; visual effects, Fantasy II; special effects supervisor, John Hartigan; assistant director, Scott Cameron; production manager, Michael Games; stunt coordinator, Solly Marx; second unit camera, Roy MacGregor; casting, Nicola van der Walt, Julie Pyken, Nancy Lara, Lindy Blythe. Reviewed on Media Home Entertainment vidcassette, Oct. 29, 1988. MPAA Rating: PG. Running time: **87 MIN.**

Wanda . . . . Kathy Ireland
Charmin . . . . Thom Mathews
Robbie . . . . Don Michael Paul
Auntie Pearl/Freki . . . . . . Linda Kerridge
Father . . . . Richard Haines
Gus . . . . William R. Moses
Gen. Rykov/Shank . . . . . . Janie du Plessis
Loki . . . . Russel Savadier
Crassus/Mailman . . . . Simon Poland
Professor . . . . Lochner de Kock
Mambino . . . . Deep Roy

■ **"Alien From L.A."** originally titled **"Odeon,"** is a laughably awful attempt at high-tech (but low-budget) fantasy that proves to be a most embarrassing film starring debut for supermodel Kathy Ireland.

She toplines as a bespectacled, timid Valley Girl who prays to God that something will happen to change her life after her boyfriend callously dumps her for being a stick-in-the-mud. Next thing you know her explorer father falls down a bottomless pit in Africa, Ireland is summoned there and she falls too (Alice In Wonderland-style), ending up in the lost city of Atlantis in the middle of the earth.

Her relentlessly pointless and unimaginative adventures in an Orwellian-styled society of Atlantis have a heavily stylized but inappropriate punk noir look favored by filmmaker Albert Pyun in his previous flop "Radioactive Dreams." The whole exercise seems like a lame attempt to amortize the sets of Canon's costly and as yet unreleased (after over two years on the shelf) "Journey To The Center Of The Earth" remake with lensing once again in the Zimbabwe/South African region.

Running gag, repeated ad nauseam, is that Ireland's whiny, little-girl voice gives every character a headache, and unfortunately that includes the audience. The inhabitants of Atlantis, supposedly from Outer Space originally, sport British Empire accents leaning towards Aussie, while Aussie thesp Linda Kerridge in a dual role does a poor attempt at a Southern accent. Ambiguous premise that it's all a dream apes "The Wizard Of Oz" right down to many characters playing multiple roles.

Despite the misguided attempt here, it's impossible to make the beauteous Ireland look mousey and

plain, so her predictable transformation midway into a covergirl knockout has no impact. Supporting cast is very weak. —*Lor.*

Baby Doll
(DANISH)

A Warner & Metronome Film release of Crone Film production. Produced by Nina Crone. Directed by Jon Bang Carlsen. Screenplay, Bang Carlsen, Lisbeth Gad, based on story by Gad; camera (Eastmancolor), Björn Blixt; editor, Grete Moldrup; music Gunnar Möller Pedersen; sound, Henrik Langkilde, Iben Haar Andersen, Thomas Krag; production design, Sören Krag Sorensen; Danish Film Institute consultant producer, Kirsten Bonnen Rask. Reviewed at the Dagmar, Copenhagen, Nov. 2, 1988. Running time: **85 MIN.**

Eva . . . . Mette Munk Plum
Her grandmother . . . . Bodil Udsen
Her mother . . . . Birgit Sadolin
Her father . . . . John Hahn Petersen
Also with: Lone Kellermann, Lone Helmer, Benedikte Hansen, Ricki Kildeskov Olsen, Katharina Lindevig Kjöge, Morten Thulin, Jacob Mynster Blundikow.

■ **Copenhagen** — High on psycho-medical case history detail and low on old-fashioned shock, Jon Bang Carlsen follows an American outing ("Time Out") with a beautifully produced "Baby Doll." The inspiration owes a lot to Roman Polanski chillers, nothing to Elia Kazan's 1956 title namesake.

Eva (looking uncannily like Mia Farrow) is spooked by the past when she chooses to spend her maternity leave with her newborn child on an isolated Jutland North Sea coastal farm.

No reference is made to the baby's father, but Eva obviously wants to exorcise the fear put into her during childhood years spent on the farm, where a tough and unpleasant grandmother spun scary tales with a moralistic point.

Not really up to her role as a first-time mother, Eva soon is unnerved by the baby's crying and refusal to eat. Grandmother, from her portrait on the wall, is a stern onlooker who almost literally steps out of her frame to do a now-you-see-me now-you-don't act. Eva seeks solace by more or less returning to childhood.

A life-size doll in the attic becomes the real object of Eva's affection rather than her real baby, who is reprimanded with retellings of Granny's old tales of the big sea monster that comes to punish wicked kids.

Bang Carlsen's picture has a tragic ending that is more convincing than the shocks he rigs en route. He keeps one alert rather than in suspense, however, with richly observed detail in the psychology of hysteria.

"Baby Doll" is also impressive for its production craftsmanship. The cinematography of Björn Blixt has dazzle and daring; it expands on the narrative without interfering with it.

Merete Munk Plum is the only member of the cast, apart from the baby and the doll, really to take center stage. She does so quite coolly, as if wary of aiming for anybody's true compassion. As the ghost grandmother, Bodil Udsen is far too discreet ever to become truly menacing. —Kell.

Sexpot

A Platinum Pictures production. Produced, directed and conceived by Chuck Vincent. Screenplay, Craig Horrall, based on 1974 film "Mrs. Barrington," written by James Vidos, Vincent; camera (color), Larry Revene; editor-production manager, James Davalos; music, Joey Mennonna; sound, Larry Provost; art direction, Edmond Ramage; assistant director-casting, Chip Lambert. Reviewed on Academy Entertainment vidcassette, N.Y., Nov. 3, 1988. MPAA Rating: R. Running time: 93 MIN.

Ivy Barrington	Ruth Collins
Boopsie	Joyce Lyons
Jackson	Frank Stewart
Damon	Gregory Patrick
Beth	Jane Hamilton
Barbara	Jennifer Delora
Betty	Christina Veronica
Phillip	Troy Donahue
Cal Farnsworth	Jack Carter
Gorilla	Scott Bergold

■ Filmmaker Chuck Vincent repeats himself with "Sexpot," a trite sex comedy based on his 1974 Kim Pope-starrer "Mrs. Barrington," which still plays occasionally on cable tv. Laughs seem forced this time around.

Ruth Collins adopts a convincing Marilyn Monroe breathy voice and look as 8-times-widowed Ivy Barrington, a specialist in the art of marrying rich old guys and bumping them off in what appear to be accidents. Her foes are the three disinherited daughters (Jane Hamil-

Mrs. Barrington

A Monarch Releasing Corp. release of an Allan Shackleton production. Produced by Shackleton. Directed by Chuck Vincent. Screenplay, Vincent and James Vidos; camera (Cineffects color), Stephen Colwell; editor, Marc Ubell; score, Richard Billay; sound, William W. Meredith; mixer, Aaron Nathanson; costumes, Robert Pusilo; production manager, Norman C. Berns. Reviewed at Preview Screening Room, N.Y., May 4, 1974. Self-applied X Rating. Running time: 86 MIN.

Mrs. Barrington	Kim Pope
Eloise	Ida Klein
Roberto	David Hausman
Ralph or James	Marlow Ferguson

Also with: David Kirk, Jack Sylva, Jennifer Welles, Jeffrey Hurst, Rebecca Brooke, Guy Thomas, Chris Jordan, Eric Edwards, Steve Tucker, Joseph Corral, Paul Giacobbe.

ton, Jennifer Delora, Christina Veronica) of one of her victims.

Pic retains a Brechtian device of the original, whereby various characters speak directly to the viewer in lengthy asides: Collins, to explain her behavior; her black companion/servant Joyce Lyons telling us about a screenplay she's writing; and butler Frank Stewart,

an aspiring actor. Goonish humor involving monosyllabic Gorilla (played by Scott Bergold) falls flat.

Collins displays some comedy talent while Vincent's favorite actress, Jane Hamilton, has fun with the Bryn Mawr accent. Unfortunately, the consistent overplaying gets to be a drag. Ironic black humor in the final reel is unsuccessful. —Lor.

Obrazy Stareho Sveta
(Pictures Of The Old World)
(CZECHOSLOVAKIAN-DOCU-B&W)

A Slovenska Filmova, Bratislava production, distributed by Ceskoslovensky Filmexport, Prague. Written and directed by Dusan Hanak. Camera (b&w), Alojz Hanusek; editor, Alfred Bencic; music, Handel, Vaclav Halek, Josef Malovec. Reviewed at Nyon Intl. Film Festival, Switzerland, Oct. 20, 1988. Running time: 74 MIN.
(In Slovak, with English subtitles)

■ Nyon — This 1972 b&w documentary was suppressed for 16 years by censors in Slovakia because it dares to suggest that Czechoslovak society is imperfect, especially for old folks living in poverty in mountain villages. Film won Nyon's grand prix plus awards from two other juries.

Filmmaker Dusan Hanak announced at Nyon that the praise of Soviet critics, who had seen the film privately, helped to obtain this world premiere at Nyon, the first time Hanak had seen it with an audience. Film now goes to the Berlin festival, along with Hanak's suppressed fiction feature, "I Love, You Love."

Despite their hardships and poor diet, these toothless old men, formerly farmers and shepherds, try uncomplainingly to keep up appearances. Replying to questions from the unseen filmmaker, they thoughtfully search for life's meanings and settle on love, family, health and work close to nature. Because each of these brave old men lives alone and forsaken by society (within a proletarian paradise dedicated to social services for its honorable senior citizens) the film is ironic and deeply sad.

This sensitive, poetic film concerns human dignity and worth among *les misérables* — their faith, nonpolitical patriotism and simple wisdom. Hanak went after the essentials of our humanity, and he got them. —Hitch.

Guldregn
(Showers Of Gold)
(DANISH)

A Warner & Metronome release of a Metronome Film production. Produced by Bent Fabricius-Bjerre. Executive producer, Tivi Magnusson. Directed by Sören Kragh-Jacobsen. Screenplay, Kragh-Jacob-

sen, based on tv series by Anders Bodelsen; camera (Eastmancolor), Dan Lausten; editor, Leif Axel Kjeldsen; music, Jacob Groth; sound, Niels Arnt Torp, Lars Lund; costumes, Jette Termann; production design, Gunilla Allard; production management, Marianne Christensen, Henrik Möller-Sörensen; assistant director, Birger Larsen. Reviewed at Dagmar, Copenhagen, Oct. 19, 1988. Running time: 96 MIN.

Jorn	Ricki Rasmussen
Lasse	Ken Vedsegaard
Karen	Tania Frydenberg
Nanna	Nanna Böndergaard
Sunshade	Torben Jensen

Also with: Sören Oestergaard, Helle Merete Sörensen, Ulla Gottlieb, Kirsten Cenius, Kamilla Kämpe, Hans Henrik Clemmensen, Jens Okking.

■ Copenhagen — With "Showers Of Gold," director Sören Kragh-Jacobsen essays a crime thriller taking the point of view of a group of young teenagers. The kids are brought violently out of their game-playing fantasy world when they find themselves with a boxful of very hot money.

At first, the kids are jubilant about the hidden treasure they have unearthed and they decide to keep the money, at least until they can be assured of getting a reward for returning it. Here, they actually move into their own borderland of crime, and this makes the further spinning of the yarn (based on an original tv manuscript by novelist Anders Bodelsen) interesting far beyond the thriller element.

When the kids soon have to face both their parents and the real robbers, their wits, guts and consciences are put to a test from which they emerge victorious, yet not about to brag about it. Some genuine chills have passed through them and through audiences as well.

Kragh-Jacobsen knows the art of making young amateurs act naturally and with no touch of the coy or cloying. He leaves the adults of his cast mostly to their own professional devices but at least they are given, in the writing, more nuance that the genre usually bestows.

"Showers Of Gold" is actually edited down from the director's highly praised (and widely sold) 1986 kidvid miniseries. In item's cleaner and tighter shape, helped by Jacob Groth's both sinewy and lissom score, a bright future in both domestic and offshore cinemas seems likely. —Kell.

One Day A War Could Start
(BRITISH-DOCU)

Produced and distributed by National Film & TV School, Beaconsfield, U.K. Directed by George Drion. Camera (color, 16m) & editor, Drion; sound, Alan James, Anne Connan. Reviewed at Nyon Intl. Film Festival, Switzerland, Oct. 20, 1988. Running time: 81 MIN.
(In German and French)

■ Nyon — This is a film about Al-

sace, reflecting on the transience of nationhood and the confusions of citizenship.

During World War II, after the lightning Nazi victory over France in June 1944, Alsace and Lorraine were annexed formally to Germany, which had lost the border provinces to France per the Versailles Treaty following World War I. Prior to that, they had been German.

After the German surrender in May 1945, the provinces again reverted to France. Stock footage and reminiscences of veterans describe the period and divided loyalties.

Final scenes of the film concern French youths from shepherds' families being conscripted into the French Army and shipped off to camp for training. In their final night in their hometown, they engage in bragging, roughhouse, street dancing and copious drinking. The film asks if these young soldiers are any different from their ancestors. Can the concrete bunkers of World War II be fitted out as shelters for a nuclear war? What have we learned?

The film is produced by a young Alsatian, George Drion, who attended the National Film & TV School in England for three years and now resides there. —Hitch.

Azul
(DOCU)

An Azul production (N.Y.). Produced and directed by Roland Legiardi-Laura. Coproducers, Joanna Kiernan, Katy Martin. Camera (color, 16m), Mark Daniels, Emilio Rodriguez, Anthony Forma, Frank Pineda; editor, Kiernan; music, Russell Curie; sound, T. J. Takagi; translations, Sarah Arvio. Reviewed at Nyon Intl. Film Festival, Switzerland. Oct. 17, 1988. Running time: 105 MIN.

■ Nyon — Two dozen poems by Nicaraguans are excerpted in "Azul" in English translation, dealing with love, nature, family, social idealism and everyday events.

Some poems make direct political comment, such as Leonal Rugama's "The Earth Is A Satellite Of The Moon," concerning the enormously expensive Apollo moonshots. Rugama's poem states that such costs deny food to generations of starving peasants.

Nicaraguan soldiers guarding frontiers against the contras also are poets. "Chuck Norris" is a red-haired, fair-skinned combat vet, young and confident, who reads his poetry about a soldier's night-time ruminations.

Several Nicaraguan poets and journalists complain openly to the camera that Sandinista cultural czars ride herd on artists, compelling a form of socialist realism. Such complaints aside, "Azul" is largely a celebration of poetry's benign, nonpolitical place within Nicaraguan life. Many poems are happy and playful; many are written by women, blacks and the poor, all eager and able to express themselves in verse.

Regarding the Sandinista vs. Contras controversy, "Azul" has bias, but it is not offensively dogmatic. The poems favor peace, but are prepared for war. The film engages the viewer, is informative, often amusing and affirms poetry for itself.—*Hitch.*

The Bengali Night
(FRENCH)

A Gaumont release of a Films Plaint Chant/CFC/Films A2 coproduction, with participation of Canal Plus, George Reinhart Production (Zurich), the CNC, La Sept, Investimage, Sofimage. Produced by Philippe Diaz. Written and directed by Nicolas Klotz, from the novel "La Nuit bengali" by Mircea Eliade. Script collaborator, Jean-Claude Carrière; camera (Fujicolor), Emmanuel Machuel; editor, Jean-François Naudon; music, Brij Narayan, Michel Portal, Steve Potts; art direction, Alexandre Trauner, Didier Naert; sound, Jean-Paul Machuel, Dominique Hennequin; costumes, Catherine Gorne; production manager, Jean-Louis Monthieux. Reviewed at Gaumont Ambassade theater, Paris, Nov. 4, 1988. Running time: 111 MIN.
Allan . . . . Hugh Grant
Lucien Metz . . . . John Hurt
Indira Sen . . . . Shabana Azmi
Gayatri . . . . Supriya Pathak
Narendra Sen . . . . Soumitra Chatterjee
Guertic . . . . Anne Brochet
Harold . . . . Pierre-Loup Rajot
Khokha . . . . Anjan Dutt
Norinne . . . . Elisabeth Perceval
(English language soundtrack)

■ Paris — **An ambitious but muddled cross-culture romance set in Calcutta of the 1930s, "The Bengali Night" is an overreaching enterprise for neophyte helmer Nicolas Klotz.**

It's a logistically complex English-lingo adaptation of an autobiographical novel by renowned Rumanian-born author and essayist Mircea Eliade.

Thanks to one of France's most enterprising new producers, Philippe Diaz, Klotz rounded up an ample 22,000,000-franc budget, an Anglo-Indian-French cast and top collaborators (including designer Alexandre Trauner).

Klotz fails to limn his characters with fresh psycho-cultural perception and glosses over his central theme of East-West attraction and discord.

Hugh Grant is bland as a young European engineer in Calcutta welcomed into the home of his Bengali employer and benefactor Soumitra Chatterjee to convalesce from an illness.

At Chatterjee's country residence outside Calcutta, Grant finds himself drawn into a romantic liaison with former's enchanting teenage daughter, Supriya Pathak, thinking his host and his wife, played by Indian screen star Shabana Azmi, are in favor of an East-West marriage.

Grant's tragic naiveté sparks a domestic crisis when the affair comes to light. The European is unceremoniously expelled from the traditionalist Bengali household and returns broken and bewildered to a Calcutta boarding house where he'd previously lived with other Westerners.

Limited to this basic dramatic situation and treated with more rigor and insight, film might have gained in poignancy and scope. Klotz burdens the action with a long, poorly articulated opening section that provides a hammy preamble for John Hurt as a superstitious Life magazine photojournalist who's come to Calcutta from an assignment in China.

A former acquaintance of Grant's, he accompanies the young man on a visit to his Indian hosts. A series of minor accidents convinces Hurt that India has nothing but bad luck in store. He hurriedly exits the country — and the film.

Pic suffers throughout by bumpy editing that leaves huge plot holes and glaring continuity errors.

More serious are the fuzzy circumstances of Grant's life in Calcutta and his sudden employment by Chatterjee — why is Grant shabbily dressed for his appointment with the Indian, and why does the meeting take place in a bookshop? The miniseries probably answers these and other questions, but the cinema spectator has to settle for disconcerting abridgements.

For all his clumsiness, Klotz does exhibit some visual flair and works charm in individual scenes between Grant and Pathak. He also communicates his fascination with India vividly through Emmanuel Machuel's excellent photography and the meticulous production design by Trauner and Didier Naert.
—*Len.*

Fakelos Polk Ston Aera
(Polk File On The Air)
(GREEK-COLOR/B&W)

A Greek Film Center/Cinegroup/ET-1 Greek TV production. Written and directed by Dionysis Gregoratos. Camera (color, b&w), Prokopes Dafnos; editor, Vangelis Gousias; music, Costas Mylonas; art direction, Alekos Pennas; sets-costumes, Dora Leloudas. Reviewed at Greek Film Festival, Thessaloniki (competing), Oct. 4, 1988. Running time: 153 MIN.
Grigoris in 1948 . . . . Costas Hazoudis
George Polk . . . . Nikos Hytas
Also with: Agape Manoura, Michael Cosmides, Vangelis Kazan, Katerina Karayanni, Pavlos Kontoyannidis, Alkis Panayotidis, Tassos Polychronopoulos, Dimitris Poulikakos, Constantine Tzoumas, Christos Tsangas, Panos Hadzicoutselis.

■ Thessaloniki — **This psychological thriller, based on the still-unsolved murder of CBS news correspondent George Polk in northern Greece in 1948, is laden with atmosphere. But the plot unfolds in a confused fashion and takes a back seat to technical effects.**

A young couple working on a contemporary radio program begin an investigation into the details of the Polk case, supposedly to draw a parallel between the climate of hysteria set off by Polk's murder and that engendered by recent acts of terrorism in Greece.

Polk had been covering the Civil War in Greece. Before he disappeared, he had made contacts for an interview with the leader of the guerrillas in order to file a more objective report. His body turned up on a beach outside Thessaloniki some days later.

A superior thriller based on the Polk case, Dimosthenis Theos' "Kierion," was made in 1968 but not released in Greece until after the fall of the junta in 1974.

Present-day scenes are in color while flashbacks are in b&w. The luminescent lensing of the recreation of the post war hotels and nightclubs, which got a special award for Prokopes Dafnos, and the excellent costumes by Dora Leloudas, which won her an award at the fest, make the flashbacks more compelling than the contemporary scenes.

It is sometimes difficult to follow the reconstruction of the events that led up to the murder and the arrest of his colleague Griogoris Staktopoulos, the Reuters correspondent who was one of his go-betweens. Although the editing is polished, the transitions are numerous and the device of shifting back and forth from color to b&w becomes distracting.

Agape Manoura plays several roles, including the wife of Polk and the actress working for the radio station, which adds to the confusion.

Good acting by Costas Hadzoudis (cast as Staktopoulos in 1948) and a number of notable actors cast in minor roles, is not enough to hold one's attention. The movie clocks in at 2½ hours, so a bit of trimming might be in order. —*Sam.*

Return Of The Killer Tomatoes

A New World Pictures release of a Four Square production. Produced by J. Stephen Peace, Lowell D. Blank. Directed by John DeBello. Screenplay, DeBello, Peace, Constantine Dillon; editor, DeBello, Stephen F. Andrich; music, Rick Patterson, Neal Fox; sound, Paul Fabbrini; production design, Dillon; art direction, Roger Ambrose; assistant director, Thomas Owens; casting, Samuel Warren & Associates. Reviewed on New World vidcassette, N.Y., Nov. 7, 1988. MPAA Rating: PG. Running time: 98 MIN.
Chad . . . . Anthony Starke
Matt . . . . George Clooney
Tara . . . . Karen Mistal
Igor . . . . Steve Lundquist
Prof. Gangrene . . . . John Astin
Also with: Charlie Jones, Rock Peace, Frank Davis, C.J. Dillon, Teri Weigel.

■ Same team that made the 1977 release "Attack Of The Killer Tomatoes" returns with a somewhat different helping in this entertaining sequel. Pic had some midnight bookings last spring but is mainly a video title.

The original film was shown widely and attained a footnote in film history because of its catchy title and considerable unintentional humor from its shlockiness. New pic is a bit more calculated but fun nonetheless.

Premise, illustrated by some footage from "Attack ...," is that Earth won the war against monstrous tomatoes, yet the normal versions of the fruit still strike fear in humans. Anthony Starke is a pizza (made from boysenberry and other goofy non-tomato sauces) delivery boy who gets a crush on evil scientist John Astin's beautiful assistant Tara (Karen Mistal), but is shocked to find out she is really a tomato converted into a woman by Astin's gene-splicing experiments.

Loosely structured pic is built around the format of being shown on a tv phone-in movie show, with frequent, cute self-references, as when director John DeBello yells cut and interrupts the film with the news that the budget has run out. Film restarts after someone has the bright idea of using product placement for funding, cueing some sharp satire of plugola as pic's subsequent *raison d'etre*.

Examples of pic's wideranging lampooning include emphasis on a "Win a date with Rob Lowe" contest and Tara's cute little furry tomato pet named F.T. Cast is enthusiastic and includes a real find in Karen Mistal, a very sexy young actress. Musical score by Rick Patterson and Neal Fox is a plus. —*Lor.*

Sleepaway Camp 2: Unhappy Campers

A Double Helix Films production. Executive producer, Stan Wakefield. Produced by Jerry Silva, Michael A. Simpson. Directed by Simpson. Screenplay, Fritz Gordon, from story idea by Robert Hiltzik; camera (Cinefilm color), Bill Mills; editor, John David Allen; music, James Oliverio; sound, Mary Ellis; art direction, Frank Galline; assistant director, Jerry Pece; production manager-associate producer, Bob Phillips; special makeup effects, Bill Johnson; stunt coordinator, Lonnie Smith; casting, Shay Griffin. Reviewed on Nelson Entertainment vidcassette, N.Y., Oct. 19, 1988. MPAA Rating: R. Running time: 80 MIN.
Angela Baker . . . . Pamela Springsteen
T.C. . . . . Brian Patrick Clarke
Molly . . . . Renée Estevez
Uncle John . . . . Walter Gotell
Mare . . . . Susan Marie Snyder
Phoebe . . . . Heather Binion
Also with: Tony Higgins, Terry Hobbs, Kendall Bean, Valerie Hartman, Julie Murphy, Carol Chambers, Amy Fields.

■ A rather outré exercise in slasher horror as black humor, this belated followup to the 1983 release stands a decent chance to build a word-of-mouth following in the homevideo market.

In her biggest screen role to date,

Pamela Springsteen (Bruce's younger sister) is quite convincing as a deceptively calm but crazy camp counselor who systematically murders her young charges in outrageously gory fashion, pretending she's simply sent the kids home one by one for misbehavior.

As a quick recap (in form of a tall tale around the campfire) informs us early on, the transvestite murderer from the original film has survived and had a sex change operation to continue his antisocial behavior as a she.

Filmmaker Michael Simpson, working for the producers of the first film, tries to pack in too many elements, ranging from "Meatballs" genre comedy hijinks to explicit spoofs of the "Friday The 13th" films. Pic works nonetheless thanks to Springsteen's always sincere performance, no matter how exaggerated the tastelessness of her murders. Renée Estevez, another sibling in the second-generation Sheen clan, is appealing as the heroine, while rest of the femme cast fulfills t&a assignments.

Pic finishes on an open-ended note, leading to a third film that was shot back-to-back with this episode. —Lor.

Zan Boko
(BURKINA FASO)

An Atria Film (Paris) release. Produced, written and directed by Gaston Kaboré. Camera (color), Sekou Ouegraogo; editor, Andre Davanture; music, Georges Ouedraogo; art direction, Joseph Kpobly. Reviewed at Carthage Film Festival (competing), Tunis, Oct. 28, 1988. Running time: **102 MIN.**

Tinga	Joseph Nikiema
Nopoko	Colette Kaboré
Yabre	Celestin Zongo

Also with: Hyppolyte Wangrawa (gardener), Simone Tapsoba (Tiraogo's wife), Gady Pafadnam (Tiraogo).

■ Tunis — "Zan Boko," winner of the Silver Tanit at the Carthage fest, is a surprisingly direct attack on a government policy of forced urbanization of villagers and media censorship in Burkina Faso.

Conceived many years ago by director-scripter Gaston Kaboré, one of Burkina Faso's foremost helmers, and financed by the very institutions (like the Ministry of Information) it cuffs, "Zan Boko" remains a forceful critique of custom in a very real, concretely named African country. Cinematography is a major plus. Though pace is slow, film is likely to attract aficionados of Africana.

Film opens with idyllic scenes of village life — workers in the fields, women carrying water gourds on their heads, a child being born. The women chat together and men gather around a fire each evening, until one day surveyors from the city arrive and assign all the pretty mud brick huts harsh white numerals. While the villagers get nervous, an official squashes a reporter's story on housing conditions.

Tinga (Joseph Nikiema) and his wife Nopoko (Colette Kaboré) move to a concrete blockhouse in Ouagadougou, overlooking the backyard of a rich couple. They want Tinga to sell them his land in the country (now the city's outskirts) so they can build a swimming pool. He steadfastly refuses, but they outmaneuver him with political contacts.

The reporter, now a tv host, goes on the air with a live debate on forced urbanization, with Tinga as his guest. A few minutes later the program is censored.

The pictorial quality of "Zan Boko" is exceptional, with clean, sharp images and precise framing. There is a moral lesson in each shot of the gentle, nonviolent folk full of humor and principle who are faced with the corruption of the city.

—Yung.

Body Beat
(Dance Academy)
(ITALIAN-U.S.)

A Vidmark Entertainment release of an RAI-1/Together Prods. Intl. production. Executive producers, Guido De Angelis, Maurizio De Angelis, Giuseppe Giacchi. Produced by Jef Richard, Aldo U. Passalàcqua. Directed by Ted Mather. Screenplay, Mather, from story by Mather, Guido De Angelis; camera (Alpha Cine color), Dennis Peters; editor, Rebecca Ross; music, Guido and Maurizio De Angelis; songs, Guido and Maurizio De Angelis, Mather, Chuck Francour; sound (Dolby), Michael Moore; art direction, Gene Abel, Francesco Cuppini (Italy); choreography, Dennon Rawles, Saymber Rawles; assistant director, Sanford Hampton, Maurizio Casa (Italy); production manager, Joan Weidman; stunt coordinator, Greg Gault. Reviewed on Vidmark vidcassette, N.Y., Nov. 1, 1988. MPAA Rating: PG. Running time: **96 MIN.**

Moon	Tony Dean Fields
Jana	Galyn Görg
Tommy	Scott Grossman
Patrizia	Eliska Krupka
Vince	Steve La Chance
Paula	Paula Nichols
Miss McKenzie	Julie Newmar

Also with: Serge Rodnunsky, Michelle Rudy, Read Scot, Virgil Frye, Leonora Leal, Patricia Zanetti, Timothy Brown.

■ This pleasant teen dancing film was shot in 1986 prior to the influential release of "Dirty Dancing" and harks back to "Fame" for inspiration. It bears the moniker "Body Beat" for U.S. release and originally was titled "Dance Academy" in Europe.

Tony Dean Fields portrays David Bronson, a.k.a. Moon, a wise guy sent to shake up Julie Newmar's classical ballet dance academy with some modern jazz technique. Pic limns the professional struggles and romantic entanglements of the students, notably proletarian hero Steve La Chance, sexy flashdancer Galyn Görg and talented singer Paula Nichols.

Similar to "Staying Alive," helmer Ted Mather climaxes the feature with an overdone, glitzy production number on stage for a big talent showcase, but otherwise the choreography of Dennon and Saymber Rawles is naturalistic. Attractive young cast makes a good impression, particularly Nichols (who doesn't dance, but sings and plays keyboards), La Chance and Görg.

Plot is weak as are the songs, mainly by brothers Guido and Maurizio De Angelis, known for their Italian film soundtracks and backers of this Italian/U.S. coproduction. Production values in both L.A. and Rome are fine. —Lor.

Take Two

A TBJ Films presentation of a Ronnie Hadar production. Executive producers, Tom Jenssen, Carol M. Rossi. Produced by Hadar. Directed by Peter Rowe. Screenplay, Moshe Hadar; camera (Foto-Kem color), James Mathers; editor, Terry Chiappe; music, Donald Hulette; sound (Ultra-Stereo), John Lifavi; assistant director, Jonathan Tzachor; production manager-second unit director, Meir Sharony; casting, Adriana Giampa-Michel. Reviewed on Academy Enertainment vidcassette, N.Y., Nov. 2, 1988. MPAA Rating: R. Running time: **100 MIN.**

Barry/Frank	Grant Goodeve
Susan Bentley	Robin Mattson
Ted Marvin	Frank Stallone
Betty Griffith	Nita Talbot
Apartment manager	Warren Berlinger
Det. Stratton	Mickey Morton
Gun dealer	Darwyn Swalve
Sherrie	Suzee M. Slater
Dorothy	Karen Mayo-Chandler

■ Fans of the traditional B-film probably will enjoy "Take Two," which contains today's requisite R-rated nude scenes but otherwise is a pleasant throwback to the plot-twisty pics of yore.

Grant Goodeve plays identical twins, parted at birth by mom Nita Talbot who secretly kept Barry (the good one) for herself and delivered Frank (the baddie) to the surrogate father who paid for her mothering services. She tells grownup Barry the tall tale on her deathbed and encourages him to head to L.A. and get his just share of an inheritance from rich Frank.

Frank is a businessman who has no time to listen to Barry's odd story on the phone, but the have-not brother (via mistaken identity) finagles his way into Frank's life, even going to bed with Frank's wife Robin Mattson. Since Frank is mistreating her, it isn't long before Mattson teams up with Barry to plan Frank's murder.

Fly in the ointment is Mattson's possessive boyfriend, a rock singer played by Frank Stallone, but many twists later almost everyone is dead.

Helmer Peter Rowe and scripter Moshe Hadar keep the viewer guessing, with only drawback being a bit of padding (now Bs run 100 minutes instead of 70). Goodeve does a fine job of differentiating the twins (with enough ambiguity to keep the pot boiling) and Mattson is impressive in an earthy portrayal. She also contributes three (count 'em) nude shower scenes, with statuesque Suzee M. Slater as Frank's secretary/mistress also adding to film's pulchritude content. —Lor.

One Minute To Midnight

A Curtin Intl. Prods. release. Executive producer, Lawrence Curtin. Produced by Dara Murphy. Directed by Robert Michael Ingria. Screenplay, Curtin; camera (Continental color), Ingria; editor, Curtin, Murphy; sound, Paul Speck; assistant director-production manager-casting, Murphy. Reviewed on Curtin Intl. vidcassette, N.Y., Oct. 8, 1988. No MPAA Rating. Running time: **103 MIN.**

David Lawrence	Lawrence Curtin
Bo	Diane Coyne
Brock	Rob Fuller
Mike	Nelson Brungart
First wife	Sydney Messett

■ In "One Minute To Midnight" debuting filmmaker Lawrence Curtin exorcises some personal demons but fails to connect his autobiographical story with the viewer. Pic played breifly on its home turf in Florida last January.

Curtin's fictionalized life story revolves around his marital predicaments: first wife, portrayed here largely offscreen (yet cryptically she is the occasional narrator, giving film an inverted point-of-view), supposedly took him for all his money and keeps hounding him unscrupulously for child support he's already paid.

In Florida, Curtin goes on a secret government drug enforcement mission to Colombia and ends up with a job selling outdoor advertising. He romances and weds Bo (Diane Coyne), but by film's end she's suing him for divorce after catching him with another woman.

Bo's family are religious fanatics, and though Curtin satirizes this sort of behavior he also posits a spiritual revival as saving him from the abyss, represented rather clumsily in a clock-ticking finale of himself about to shoot a bullet in his brain with one minute till the witching hour.

Crammed with too many incidents for a low-low-budgeter, film is fitfully interesting but overstays its welcome. In filmmaking debut, Curtin, brother of actress Jane Curtin, falls into the common trap of trying to cram everything into the stewpot. Climax of him dragged off to a mental hospital for three days (purportedly, his threat of a lawsuit brought the film end money from the hospital, enabling picture to be completed!) lacks force due to distended presentation of earlier subplots.

As his own leading man, Curtin displays an ingenuous, flippant attitude giving the tortured film a blessedly light tone. Supporting cast is adequate, as is direction by Robert Michael Ingria, who previously helmed the dissimilar wrestling film "Hammerhead Jones." Curtin's script treats most sitsolutions like tv sketches, with quick and dirty technical credits to match.

—Lor.

Mord i Paradis
(Murder In Paradise)
(NORWEGIAN)

A Nordisk Film Distribution release of Nordisk Film production. Produced by Bo Christensen. Directed by Sune Lund-Sörensen. Screenplay, Erik Balling, Henning Bahs, Lund-Sörensen, based on novel by Dan Turell; camera (Eastmancolor), Claus Loof, Jesper Find; editor, Leif Axel Kjeldsen, Karen Margrethe Nielsen; music, Pete Repete; "Ulrich" theme, Michael Falch; production design & special effects, Sören Skjär; sound, Bjarne Risbjerg, Michael Dela, others; costumes, Annelise Hauberg; production management, Lene Nielsen, others; assistant director, Karen Bentzon. Reviewed at the Imperial, Copenhagen, Oct. 12, 1988. Running time: **94 MIN.**
The Reporter . . . . Michael Falch
Gitte . . . . Susanne Breuning
The Receptionist . . . . Kirsten Lehfeldt
Chief-of-Police . . . . Björn Puggaard-Müller
Ulrich . . . . Lars H.U.G.
Ehlers . . . . Ole Ernst
Kasparsen . . . . Hans Henrik Voetman
Otzen . . . . Morten Grunwald
Also with: Hans Henrik Krause, Michael Hasselflug, Lone Helmer, Charlotte Sieling, Pia Koch, John Martinus, Johnny Hedegaard, Peter Schröder, Peter Larsen, Lise-Lotte Norup, Deni J. Kjurcijev, Ahmed Rahmani, Gunnar Obel, Jan Hertz.

■ **Copenhagen — Danish helmer Sune Lund-Sörensen had a good thing going with "Murder In The Dark" (1986), but the wit and suspense peter out in this followup in spite of much macho energy spent on each action sequence.**

Michael Falch once again performs with morose charm and weary energy as the nameless crime reporter who replaces Philip Marlowe in Dan Turell's homage books to Raymond Chandler. This time around he moves from his preferred big city mean streets to bang and bash his sturdy head against a neat provincial town's shiny surfaces that hide, of course, all the usual vicious crime and high-level corruption.

The Paradise of the title is found to be a brothel. Our elegantly seedy hero beds down en route with a female defense attorney (Susanne Breuning, a musical stage star who moves and talks stiffly), who had started out hating him. Reason: the rag he works for once pinned her down nude and then up for the world to see.

There are lovers' quarrels to overcome before reporter and lawyer join forces in exposing an international drug ring covered up for by the local chief of police, whose musician son (played convincingly by rock star Lars H.U.G.) is hooked on heroin. The Mr. Big behind it all is never seen and supposedly escapes justice to serve in yet another Turell-based picture.

Lund-Sörensen is deft with all technical credits beyond the writing of the screenplay, in which he took part himself. In roles and situations like set pieces, several good actors cannot help appearing slightly somnolent.

A jazz-inspired score is used to fine effect. —*Kell.*

A'rab
(Arab)
(TUNISIAN)

An Apollo release of an Intl. Monastir Film/Collectif du Nouveau Film/Carthago Film coproduction. Directed by Fadhel Jaziri, Fadhel Jaibi. Screenplay, Le Nouveau Theater; camera (color), Belgacem Jelliti; editor, Moufida Tlatli; art direction, Jaziri Jaibi; production manager, Radhi Trimèche. Reviewed at Carthage Film Festival (competing), Tunis, Oct. 21, 1988. Running time: **100 MIN.**
Houria . . . . Jalila Baccar
Kuraich . . . . Lamine Nahdi
Khalil . . . . Fadhel Jaziri
Mannubi . . . . Fethi Haddaoui
Arbia . . . . Zahira Ben Ammar
Asfour . . . . Fatma Ben Saidane

■ **Tunis — Adapted from their hit stage play by the 20-year-old Tunisian stage company Le Nouveau Theater, "A'rab" is Tunisia's most ambitious film of the year.**

Co-helmers Fahdel Jaziri and Fahdel Jaibi aim at summarizing and commenting on nothing less than the history of the Arab world. While undoubtedly an important work that few Middle East watchers will want to miss, the film version makes for difficult viewing for those without a firm grasp of history.

Film won the Bronze Tanit at the Carthage Festival and opened wide in Tunisia the following day.

Lensed at the vast church of St. Louis in Carthage, "A'rab" retains a strong stage flavor. A flight attendant who just has left war-torn Beirut arrives at the church (never precisely located, a symbol for Western civilization) in search of her lost lover, and finds herself in a besieged fortress.

Leader of the motley group of guerrillas, is Kuraich, a hero gone mad who takes out his wrath and disappointment on Mannubi (Fethi Haddaoui) in scenes of stomach-churning violence.

Keeping to himself, lost in his dreams, is Khalil (played by codirector Fahdel Jaziri, whose face is familiar from "Les Traversees"). There are also two women, one the unbeatable, half-mystic Arab woman Arbia (Zahira Ben Ammar), the other, cowed little Asfour (Fatma Ben Saidane, with an unforgettable face and birdlike scurrying). Their interaction provides film with its motor.

The dialog-ridden, intellectual film demands attentive viewing, but rewards the patient. Precision lensing by Belgacem Jelliti is a pleasure to watch, and cast, all of which participated in writing script and dialog, is universally fine. — *Yung.*

La nuit avec Hortense
(The Night With Hortense)
(CANADIAN)

A Famous Players release (in Canada) of a Les Ateliers Audio-Visuels du Quebec production. Produced by Nicole Lamothe. Written and directed by Jean Chabot. Camera (color), Daniel Jobin; editor, Claude Beaugrand; music, Richard Desjardins. Reviewed at Intl. Festival of New Cinema and Video, Montreal, Oct. 24, 1988. Running time: **90 MIN.**

With: Carole Laure, Lothaire Bluteau, Paul Herbert, Denis Bouchard.

■ **Montreal — Lust with a stranger on a wet steamy night was a hot subject in the 1970s but this less-than-stimulating attempt is 10 years too late.**

Even as recently as two years ago, a debate about graphically sexual movies raged around the question "is it pornography or eroticism?" Director Jean Chabot said his film is not "erotic" but "passionate." "The Night With Hortense" (Carole Laure is Hortense) is none of the above.

The film is an excuse to bare Laure's breasts, something this Quebec actress became renowned for as early as 1973 in Gilles Carle's "Les Corps Celestes." Even Laure's most devoted fans will have difficulty digesting this one.

A well-preserved Laure meets Lothaire Bluteau during what seems to be an adolescent crisis. They spend a sometimes mildly masochistic night rolling about in wet leaves beside a cold and gloomy river, fumbling with each's clothing and avoiding the neighbor's dog. Once inside an abandoned house, they don't even bother to remove their underclothing before going at it again.

A strong orchestral soundtrack carries the film. At best, it will fare well during "adult" hours on late-night pay tv, with or without an English translation. —*Suze.*

Cheerleader Camp
(Bloody Pom Poms)

An Atlantic Releasing release of a Quinn/Prettyman production in association with Prism Entertainment and Daiei Co. Ltd. Produced by Jeffrey Prettyman, John Quinn. Directed by Quinn. Screenplay, David Lee Fein, R.L. O'Keefe; camera (Foto-Kem color), Bryan England; editor, Jeffrey Reiner; music, Murielle Hodler-Hamilton, Joel Hamilton; production design, Keith Barrett; costume design, Gini Kramer; makeup, Ramona; production manager, Joan Weideman; assistant director, Matt Hinkley; choreography, Lucinda Dickey; casting, Geno Havers, Marcia Karr. Reviewed on Prism Entertainment videcassette, N.Y., Oct. 12, 1988. MPAA Rating: R. Running time: **88 MIN.**
Alison Wentworth . . . . Betsy Russell
Brent Hoover . . . . Leif Garrett
Cory Foster . . . . Lucinda Dickey
Bonnie Reed . . . . Lorie Griffin
Pop . . . . Buck Flower
Timmy Moser . . . . Travis McKenna
Pam Bently . . . . Teri Weigel
Theresa Salazar . . . . Rebecca Ferratti
Miss Tipton . . . . Vickie Benson
Also with: Jeff Prettyman, Krista Pflanzer, Craig Piligian, William Johnson Sr., Kathryn Litton.

■ **"Cheerleader Camp" is a mundane thriller in the decadent youth-slaughter genre. Pic played theatrically for about a week earlier this year via Atlantic Releasing, under the title "Bloody Pom Poms," before reaching video shelves. Topcast looker Betsy Russell isn't enough to put this one over.**

Paper-thin plot involves a group of six cheerleaders and their mascot who travel to a rural camp to participate in a regional cheering competition. Russell, we're shown in an early dream sequence, is a troubled young woman who imagines violent scenes and apparently suffers from periodic blackouts. Her cheerleader boyfriend (Leif Garrett) is inexplicably unattentive to the insecure girl's need for affection; he'd rather make time with a voluptuous competing cheerleader (Krista Pflanzer) or with teammate Teri Weigel.

When members of the group and other camp personnel begin to drop violently, all signs point to the psychologically unsettled Russell, though filmmakers throw in some over-obvious heavies to confuse matters a bit. Denouement has an unsuspected villain emerging, adding a nice, if improbable, twist.

The largely attractive cast does well with sparse material, particularly Russell and Dickey, who is too pretty to be believable as the looked-down-upon lowly mascot.

Interesting note is the obvious overdubbing of profanity and the scissoring of what appear to have been nude scenes. Japanese coproducer Daiei may have had something to do with toning down the sex, but has consented to several gruesome effects.

Pic, shot in Sequoia National Forest and Bakersfield, Calif., has a pretty look. Other tech credits are adequate.—*Gerz.*

Deadly Dreams

A Concorde Pictures release of a New Classics presentation. Executive producer, Victor Simpkins. Produced by Matt Leipzig. Directed by Kristine Peterson. Screenplay, Thom Babbes; camera (Foto-Kem color), Zoran Hochstatter; editor, Bernard Caputo; music, Todd Boekelheide; sound, Lloyd Nelson; production design, Stephen Greenberg; special makeup effects, Deborah Zoeller; assistant director, Randy Pope; production manager, Susan Stremple; postproduction supervisor, Steve Barnett; second unit director, Melitta Fitzer; second unit camera, Phedon Papamichael; casting, Al Guarino. Reviewed on Virgin Vision videcassette, N.Y., Nov. 4, 1988. MPAA Rating: R. Running time: **79 MIN.**
Alex . . . . Mitchell Anderson
Maggie . . . . Juliette Cummins
Jack . . . . Xander Berkeley
Danny . . . . Thom Babbes
Young Alex . . . . Timothy Austin
Also with: Beach Dickerson.

■ **An interesting low-budget horror pic, "Deadly Dreams" provides an okay switch on the genre's morbid family in-fighting theme. It was released direct-to-video around Halloween time.**

Mitchell Anderson's parents were killed on Christmas Eve 10 years ago by a hunter wearing an animal mask, who turned out to be an embittered ex-business partner who then committed suicide. Grown up, Anderson is plagued with recurring nightmares involving the hunter.

With adequate hints planted by

screenwriter Thom Babbes (who costars as Anderson's best friend), story paints a deadly conspiracy working against our hero, involving his older brother and girlfriend. Final plot twists are morbid enough to qualify the pic as film noir, resulting in a cold, vengeful finale.

Helmer Kristine Peterson, previously handling second unit work on Roger Corman pics, does a good job of maintaining the downbeat mood of the piece and even includes a somewhat daring sex scene that is relevant to the storyline. No-name cast is effective, including a cameo by one of Corman's '50s regulars, Beach Dickerson. —Lor.

Captive Rage

The Movie Group presentation in association with OKA Film Prods. (ancillary markets, Moviestore Entertainment). Executive producer, Avi Lerner. Produced by Harry Alan Towers. Directed by Cedric Sundström. Screenplay, Rick Marx, Sundström, from story by "Peter Welbeck" (Towers); camera (color), George Bartels; editor, Allan Morrison; music, Mark Mitchell, Mick Hope Bailie; sound, John Bergman; production design, George Canes; assistant director-associate producer, John Stodel; production manager, Danny Lerner; coproducers, Barry Wood, Ketih Rosenbaum; stunt coordinator, Ed Anders. Reviewed on Forum Home Video vidcassette, N.Y., Oct. 18, 1988. MPAA Rating: R. Running time: **92 MIN.**
Gen. Belmondo . . . . Oliver Reed
Edward Delacorte . . . . Robert Vaughn
Chiga . . . . Claudia Udy
Lucy Delacorte . . . . Lisa Rinna
Also with: Maureen Kedes, Sharon Schaffer, Diana Tilden-Davis, Deon Stewardson, Trish Downing, Frank Notaro.

■ Producer-out-of-a-suitcase Harry Alan Towers comes up with one of his wackier efforts in "Captive Rage," an actioner set in the mythical South American nation of Parador (Paul Mazursky, please note) but lensed unconvincingly in Africa.

Pic, variously named "Fighting Fire With Fire" and "Fair Trade," stars an enthusiastic Oliver Reed as renegade Gen. Belmondo, hiding in the remote veldt of Parador with his troops. He's hopping mad when U.S. Drug Enforcement Agency topper Robert Vaughn has his son arrested as a drug kingpin. Reed retaliates by having a planeful of coeds, including Vaughn's daughter Lisa Rinna, hijacked and diverted to his camp.

The women are tortured as Reed demands his son be freed within 72 hours or 10 femmes will bite the dust. People get fed to piranhas, Rinna and her pals escape and villainess Claudia Udy (usually cast as a vulnerable victim in pics like these) torments a few girls until an angry Rinna returns and gives Reed what-for.

Among the pic's sillier elements is the instant transition of girls from Loyola Marymount into dead-eye shots accomplished with automatic weaponry, mowing down Reed's soldiers with ease.

Formula of women in bondage

clearly is still in vogue, but "Captive Rage" has little to offer in the way of novelty once its oddball setting is established. Tech credits are fine. —Lor.

Aufrecht Gehen
(WEST GERMAN-DOCU-B&W/COLOR)

A Journal Film (West Berlin) production. Directed by Helga Reidemeister. Camera (color, 16m), Lars Barthel, Judith Kaufmann, Hartmut Lange, Fritz Pappenberg; editor, Petra Heymann. Reviewed at Nyon Intl. Film Festival, Switzerland, Oct. 16, 1988. Running time: **78 MIN.**

■ Nyon — "Aufrecht gehen" translates as "walk straight ahead," which fits a memorial documentary about charismatic student revolutionary Rudi (the Red) Dutschke.

Mortally wounded by a right-wing assassin in 1968, Dutschke remains a hero within the liberal circles of West German politics. Although his name is little remembered in the U.S., Dutschke was a counterpart of Abbie Hoffman, Tom Hayden and other "Chicago Seven" radicals.

Film is an amalgam of b&w newsreels with contemporary color interviews of Dutschke's American wife, their son and former colleagues. His brothers and father in East Germany discuss their memories of the strong-willed boy who grew up to become the terror of West Germany's conservative politicians. The father is quite frail but comes alive when proudly showing the camera around the farm where Rudi played and worked as a boy.

Stock footage shows Dutschke as a street orator and includes vicious fighting as troopers attempt to subdue students. Film is both a reverential tribute to a departed political icon and also a partisan commentary on West German society, its unrest and uncertain identity since World War II. —Hitch.

El Compromiso
(The Compromise)
(VENEZUELAN)

A Foncine release of a Trova Cinematográfica-U. de los Andes (ULA) production. Directed by Roberto Siso. Screenplay, Elizabeth Baralt, Edgar Larrazbal; camera (color), César Jawovski; editor, Siso; music, Waldemar de Lima; art direction, Rubén Siso. Reviewed at San Juan Film Festival, Puerto Rico, Oct. 3, 1988. Running time: **91 MIN.**
With: Alejo Felipe, Carmen Julia Alvarez, Irene Arcila, Leonardo Acosta.

■ San Juan — A more able director might have been capable of breathing some life into the Venezuelan feature "El Compromiso" (The Compromise), but its current rambling and uninspired state seems destined for a no-win at international wickets.

Plot concerns an intellectual (Alejo Felipe), who is promised an

international diplomatic post in return for his support in the presidential elections. As an intellectual, our hero is none too bright. It takes him well over an hour to understand what the audience perceives from the very first encounter: he has been duped.

He sells his home and ends up living in the street while endlessly waiting for the position to materialize. It never does. Neither does any tension as the storyline unwinds in plodding fashion.

Photography is flat and the dialog clumsy. Length could easily be chopped by half. —Lent.

Affetti Speciali
(Special Affections)
(ITALIAN)

A Techno Image Prod. release of an Orango Film production. Produced by Alessandro Verdecchi. Directed by Felice Farina. Screenplay, Giovanni di Gregorio, Farina, Luciano Manzalini, Eraldo Turra; camera (Luciano Vittori color), Roberto Meddi; editor, Domenico Varone; music, Lambero Macchi; art direction, Giancarlo Aymerich. Reviewed in Rome, Sept. 15, 1988. Running time: **90 MIN.**
Ivano . . . . Luciano Manzalini
Cris . . . . Eraldo Turra
Marzia . . . . Anita Zagaria
Anna . . . . Sabina Guzzanti
Mother . . . . Emilia Della Rocca
Dr. Sacchetti, truck driver . . . . Peiro Natoli
Also with: Felice Farina (Prof. Perrier), Rosa Di Brigida, Elisabetta Sanino, Claudio Spadaro, Osvaldo Alzari.

■ Rome — "Special Affections" is an offbeat comedy heading into black humor and personal drama. Lensed by newcomer Felice Farina with savvy and originality, film revolves around the improbable attempts of two brothers to keep their comatose mother alive artificially.

This weird mixture of gags is still awaiting release in Italy; mean-

while, it might tempt young-cinema fests.

Cris (Eraldo Turra) and Ivano (Luciano Manzalini) are the ill-matched frères, played by a comedy team ironically called the Ruggeri Twins, but resembling each other as much as Laurel does Hardy. Cris, the fat one, is a dynamic, successful guy with a flashy car and a passion for chasing women, who adore him. Ivano is the skinny one who drinks and whose job consists of raising a useless bar in the middle of a road when trucks pass by.

The brothers live with their doting mother (Emilia Della Rocca) in the fairytale happiness of a big house full of friends, until one day mom goes into a coma.

Rest of "Special Affections" shows how the brothers try to keep her alive in the basement with the diabolical machine of a greedy scientist, played by Farina. The family falls apart, Cris falls in love, Ivano gets beaten up and nothing is as good as it used to be.

Farina has a deft hand with his actors and a penchant for unusual locations — here, the unrecognizable outskirts of Rome. The gags sometimes strike a repetitive note, made worse by collegial humor.

Cris' cavalier, on-the-spot seductions and abuse of dumb girls deadens the Don Juan yucks considerably. Nevertheless, pic achieves a unique balance between absurdity and the horrors of real life, in an intelligent and mostly entertaining parade of deformed emotions.

Film reaffirms Farina (who debuted in 1986 with "He Looks Dead ... But He's Only Fainted") as an original talent to be watched.
—Yung.

ARCHIVE REVIEWS

Die Wunderbare Lüge der Nina Petrowna
(GERMAN-B&W)

A Radiotelevisione della Svizzera Italiano (RTSI)/Bayerisher Rundfunk presentation of an Erich Pommer production for UFA. Directed by Hanns Schwarz. Screenplay, Hans Székely; camera (b&w), Carl Hoffmann; sets, Robert Herlth, Walter Rohrig; costumes, René Hubert; artistic supervisor, Alexandre Arnstam; music (1929), Maurice Jaubert; orchestration and additional music (1987), Paul Glass; tv version produced by Carlo Piccardi. First released by UFA in Berlin, April 1929. Restored print by the National Film Archive (London). Reviewed on U-Matic vidcassette, Paris, Oct. 15, 1988. Length: 8.330 feet. Running time (at sound speed): **92 MIN.**
Nina Petrowna . . . . Brigitte Helm
Lt. Rostoff . . . . Franz (Francis) Lederer
The colonel . . . . Warwick Ward

■ Paris — Swiss-language Italian pubcaster RTSI, under the impetus of music programmer Carlo Piccardi, revived this unjustly forgot-

ten little gem as part of its excellent program of silent film resurrections with original period scores, often unheard since pic's premiere.

For "Die Wunderbare Lüge der Nina Petrowna," Piccardi made a momentous musical reconstruction of the 1929 Paris first-run orchestral score by Maurice Jaubert, whose music for early French talkies earned him a lofty place in the pantheon of great screen musicians.

Jaubert composed an unusually subtle and complex score for "Nina Petrowna," one of the last silent flourishes of the great German film company UFA. The coming of sound condemned the film to a brief (but critically appreciated) career. A few years later it was replaced by a vastly inferior sound version, made in France with Isa Miranda and Fernand Gravey, under the direction of Russian émigré director Viatcheslav (Victor) Tourjansky.

The UFA film preserves its freshness, warmth and poignancy. Hanns Schwarz, an UFA director, executed Hans Székely's original script with vivid cinematic imagination and sympathy.

Story itself is essentially familiar material, a romantic triangle melodrama set in military czarist Russia, where codes of honor conflict tragically with personal gratification.

Brigitte Helm, the undulating robot temptress of Fritz Lang's "Metropolis," found her most subtly sympathic role as Nina Petrowna, the mistress of a colonel in the Imperial Guard, played by an American specialist in screen cads, Warwick Ward.

Greatly attached to material comforts of a kept woman, Helm nonetheless finds true love and heartbreak when she meets a handsome and naive young lieutenant, portrayed with ingratiating boyish appeal by Franz (later Francis) Lederer.

Abandoning her powerful protector, her luxury apartment and clothes, Helm shacks up with Lederer in wretched living conditions. Ashamed of his poverty, the desperate young officer is lured into a card game by Ward at their club and is caught cheating. Ward makes him sign a confession and uses it to force Helm's return to him.

To save Lederer's honor and career, Helm tells him she's fed up with the material deprivation (the last and the most tragic of her "lies" in the course of the story) and returns, shattered, to her posh quarters.

In the superb final scene, Ward arrives the next morning with a conciliatory bouquet of flowers, which he begins gallantly to scatter across Helm's inert, outstretched body. Suddenly he notices the telltale empty vial near her hand. The camera slowly pans down Helm's lifeless body to stop on a closeup of her cheap shoes, Lederer's touching gift.

Prepared for tv, the music-and-film reconstruction deserves large-screen, live orchestral presentation to give full body to film's splendid UFA-styled pictorial attractions and the dense lyricism of Jaubert's score.

Next year's centenary salute at the Berlin Film Festival to pic's producer Erich Pommer would be a good place to start. —*Len.*

Michaël
(GERMAN-B&W)

A Danish Film Museum presentation of a Decla Bioscop production in association with UFA (1924). Produced by Erich Pommer. Directed by Carl Theodor Dreyer. Screenplay, Thea von Harbou, Dreyer, from the novel "Mikael" by Herman Bang; camera (Agfa b&w), Karl Freund, Rudolph Maté (exteriors); set design, Hugo Haring. First released by UFA in Berlin, 1924. Reviewed at Danish Film Museum, Copenhagen, May 30, 1988. Length: 6,478 ft. Running time (at 18 frames per second): 96 MIN.

With: Benjamin Christensen (Claude Zoret), Walter Slezak (Michael), Nora Gregor (Princess Lucia), Robert Garrison (Switt), Grete Mosheim (Mrs. Adelskjold), Max Auzinger (butler), Didier Aslan (the Duke), Alexander Murski (Mr. Adelskjold), Karl Freund (Leblanc), Wilhemine Sandrock (Dowager Duchess).

■ **Copenhagen — The dynamic German producer Erich Pommer (whose centenary will be celebrated by the Berlin Film Festival next year) called Denmark's Carl Theodor Dreyer to the German capital in 1924 to direct "Michaël."**

Pic is based on a favorite novel of Pommer's by Danish author Herman Bang, already filmed in Sweden in 1917 by Mauritz Stiller ("Wings" — of which an incomplete print was discovered recently in Norway).

"Michaël" itself was considered lost until it was unearthed in the East Berlin archives in 1958, 34 years after its premiere, and turned over for restoration to the Danish Film Museum.

"Michaël" is a melodrama with a late 19th century setting and many of the inherent clichés of gesture and characterization.

Dreyer subsequently never considered it one of his major works, but he told the story with superior skill and technical mastery: the interplay of light and shadow remains extraordinary (lensing by two masters, Karl Freund and the up-and-coming genius, Rudolph Maté); and the performances coached from a fine cast confer unexpected contrasts and depth to the story.

Plot centers on a parental-filial relationship between an artist and his disciple, colored (in both book and film) by flimsily concealed homosexual overtones.

Dreyer's fellow Danish filmmaker Benjamin Christensen plays the protagonist, a celebrated painter and sculptor based on Auguste Rodin, whose pupil and model Michael (played by a young, angelic Walter Slezak) finally "betrays" his master with a lover while the artist lies on his deathbed. Latter has willed his protégé everything and declares that death has no sting since he has witnessed "love at its greatest."

Central theme and subsidiary developments are heightened by some lively portraiture, least conventional of which is Robert Garrison's art critic, at first a vicious caricature that deepens in Dreyer's hands into a more subtle characterization vulnerable to pain yet capable of generosity.

While Christensen's artist is supposed to be an uncontested genius, it's curious to note the mediocrity of the painted works that are displayed in Hugo Häring's main set of the large studio apartment. Dreyer would later claim that these samplings were imposed by pic's producer and designer. —*Kell.*

Harakiri
(GERMAN-B&W)

A Decla Film-Ces. Holz & Co. production (1919), preserved by the Bundesarchiv Filmarchiv (Coblenz). Directed by Fritz Lang. Screenplay, Max Jungk, based on the John Luther Long and David Belasco play "Madame Butterfly;" camera (b&w, tinted), Max Fassbaender; sets, Heinrich Umlauf, with the collaboration of the I.F.G. Museum Umlauff of Hamburg. First presented in Berlin Dec. 19, 1919. Reviewed at Pordenone (Italy) Silent Film Festival, Oct. 6, 1988. Length (restored print): 5,538 ft. Running time (at 18 frames per second): 82 MIN.

With: Lil Dagover (O-Take-San), Paul Bienfelt (Daimyo Tokuyawa), Georg John (the bonze), Meinhard Maur (Prince Matahari), Käte Küster (Hanake), Niels Prien (Olaf J. Anderson), Herta Hedem (Eva).

■ **Pordenone — "Harakiri" is nothing other than "Madame Butterfly," with a cast of Germans playing mincing Orientals in this 1919 production, which followed by four years the Hollywood version with Mary Pickford.**

Preserved by Germany's Bundesarchiv from an original, handsomely tinted nitrate print found at the Dutch Film Museum, film would go down as merely a quaint curiosity if it had not been directed by Fritz Lang.

It's probably a measure of Lang's budding talents that "Harakiri," 70 years later, is not ridiculous and has a certain charm. Though it would be outrageous to call this an early Lang masterpiece (as is being done in European critical circles), film nonetheless reveals the director's future concern for stylized performance and art direction.

Lang tells the famous tearjerker straight, and future German screen star Lil Dagover takes her first dainty steps as O-Take-San, a pure young thing persecuted by a wicked bonze, who wants to add her to his collection of temple geishas.

The love of a Danish navy officer forestalls the evil design, but Dagover eventually finds herself alone with a child fathered by the Dane. The lover returns to Japan (accompanied by his wife) though not in time to save the despairing Dagover from ritual suicide.

Though the mannered performances leave today's viewer indifferent at best, film has pictorial appeal in Lang's meticulous recreation of Japanese decor and ritual, which are heightened by the often-lovely tints. Lang's future taste for striking setpieces are here evident in such sequences as an autumn festival, complete with lantern-garlanded boats on shimmering lakes.—*Len.*

Cocoon: The Return

A 20th Century Fox release of a Zanuck/-Brown Co. production. Produced by Richard D. Zanuck, David Brown, Lili Fini Zanuck. Directed by Daniel Petrie. Screenplay, Stephen McPherson, from a story by Petrie, Elizabeth Bradley; camera (Deluxe color), Tak Fujimoto; editor, Mark Roy Warner; music, James Horner; production design, Lawrence G. Paull; set decoration, Frederick C. Weiler, Jim Poynter; costume design, Jay Hurley; cocoon designer, Robert Short; visual effects, Industrial Light & Magic; special effects coordinator, J.B. Jones; sound, Hank Garfield; associate producer, Gary Daigler; assistant director, Katterli Frauenfelder; casting, Beverly McDermott. Reviewed at Avco Center Theater, L.A., Nov. 17, 1988. MPAA Rating: PG. Running time: 116 MIN.

Art Selwyn	Don Ameche
Ben Luckett	Wilford Brimley
Joe Finley	Hume Cronyn
Bernie Lefkowitz	Jack Gilford
Jack Bonner	Steve Guttenberg
Mary Luckett	Maureen Stapleton
Alma Finley	Jessica Tandy
Bess McCarthy	Gwen Verdon
Ruby	Elaine Stritch
Sara	Courtney Cox

■ **Hollywood — Not altogether charmless, "Cocoon: The Return" still is far less enjoyable a senior folks' fantasy than "Cocoon." An overdose of bathos weighs down the sprightliness of the characters, resulting in a more maudlin than magic effort.**

If "Cocoon: The Return" falls into the successful pattern of sequels of other hit films, however, b.o. should be good.

Back in fine form are all the characters from the original "Cocoon." For the senior set, "Cocoon" and now "Cocoon: The Return" is a dream adventure for those too old to believe in such fantastic possibilities as being given the choice of living in a world where there is "no illness, no poverty, no wars" — and no aging — or remain on earth to suffer joy and pain as mortals.

Quandary here begins with the return to St. Petersburg, Fla., of this plucky group lead by the twinkle-eyed Don Ameche for a 4-day visit from the utopian extra-terrestrial world of Antarea. Upon being reunited with family and friends, each questions his own choice for leaving in the first place and, at the end of the picture, the rationale for either returning to space or remaining on terra firma.

Jack Gilford as irascible widower Bernie Lefkowitz and Steve Guttenberg as Jack, the glass-bottom boat tour guide cum shlocky seashell merchandise salesman, keep this overly sappy production afloat.

While most of the others wallow in self-doubt and do too much moralizing about their unique predicament, particularly the Jessica Tandy-Hume Cronyn duo — who do a sort of death role reversal end scene that's akin to high opera — Gilford manages to brighten the screen every time the camera is on him. He emotes, he complains, he sits at his beloved wife's gravestone and laments — always humorous as his cranky character becomes less kvetchy and more lovable. The realization that he finds his situation as the original stay-at-home man not so bad after all, with a sassy woman (Elaine Stritch) as the great incentive to stick around, is the one truly delightful aspect of this film.

Guttenberg, on the other hand, is just goofy, but it's a role he's taken to with a certain panache. Sight gags not withstanding — and he has most of them — the actor has developed a kind of flair for always being the winsome unsophisticate. How he gets the girls (Tahnee Welch, Courtney Cox) is a wonder.

Stephen McPherson's script unfolds like an ensemble piece with each couple getting their time in the sun, a framework that works better in tv than here. Trying to work in a subplot about a captured cocoon that is slowly dying in the hands of experiment-happy scientists (lead by the sympathetic Cox) takes the focus away from the real comedy/drama playing out in the lives of three main couples back in town.

There's tension enough with everyone worrying about what disease of theirs is going to recur or how wonderfully ridiculous it will be watching Gwen Verdon manage motherhood at her advanced age without this plot device.

Ameche, Verdon and occasionally Cronyn want to play funny and loose but are restrained by Daniel Petrie's direction, which too often is unfocused. Pic needs more long shots, such as the aged boys playing basketball against some local toughs, in the kind of breaking-out-of-type behavior seen in "Cocoon." But here the principals discuss what a drag it is to be physically worn down when the mind and heart are still youthful.

To give a sense of unfailing optimism to the proceedings when situations go awry, like when Tandy gets hit by a car, or the dialog drippy (emphasis on the latter third of the film), is James Horner's great, jazzy swing score complemented by a track of standards, including one vocal by Frank Sinatra, "You Make Me Feel So Young."

The music makes the 116 minutes go by a lot more quickly, as do many of the visuals that take the viewer underwater to swim with porpoises, to "Miami Vice" color-washed motels and through the special effects scenes where Industrial Light & Magic transforms humans into ethereal, ghostly cocoons and the night sky over the ocean into an unreal sci-fi set complete with a flying saucer. —Brit.

Asa Branca - Um Sonho Brasiliero
(Asa Branca - A Brazilian Dream) (BRAZILIAN)

An Embrafilme release of a Cinema do Seculo XXI production. Written and direct-

ed by Djalma Limongi Batista. Camera (color), Gualter Limongi Batista; editor, Jose Motta; music, Mario Valerio Zaccaro; set design, Jefferson Albuquerque Jr., Felipe Crescenti; costumes, Tania Magaldi, Crescenti. Reviewed at Sorrento Intl. Encounter, Oct. 26, 1988. Running time: **111 MIN.**
With: Edson Celulari, Eva Wilma, Walmor Chagas, Geraldo d'El Rey, Gianfranco Guarnieri, Rita Cadilac, Ruth Rachou, Mira Haar.

■ Sorrento — "Asa Branca" is a vacuous realization of the teenage dream to reach soccer stardom. A wholesome, provincial, adolescent jock strong-arms his way to fame through endless sacrifice and moral corruption.

In this dripping saga, Antonio Dos Reis (Edson Celulari) switches his name to Asa Branca (white wings) and abandons home and friends to fulfill the role of angel at dismal local carnivals. He sells his soul to a succession of corrupt soccer club owners and intolerant, servile coaches.

Lonely and confused, he heads to the big city to have his innocence tempted and (mildly) tarnished. The happy ending is a kitschy special effects ascension to immortality.

This wholly predictable pic is tiresome and mediocre at best. Acting is improbable even to teen idol worshipers or sport fans. Shoddy soccer footage and poor lensing and soundtrack further decrease audience chances. —Chin.

1969

An Atlantic Entertainment Group release. Produced by Daniel Grodnik, Bill Badalato. Executive producer, Thomas Coleman. Written and directed by Ernest Thompson. Camera (color), Jules Brenner; editor, William Anderson; music supervisor, Jolene Cherry; original music, Michael Small; production design, Marcia Hinds; art direction, Bo Johnson; set decoration, Jan K. Bergstrom; costume design, Julie Weiss; sound (Ultra-Stereo), Donald F. Johnson; associate producer, Ariel Bagdadi; assistant director, David Householter; associate editor, Armen Minasian; casting, Mike Fenton, Jan Feinberg, Valerie Massais. Reviewed at Raleigh Studios, Hollywood, Nov. 17, 1988. MPAA Rating: R. Running time: **90 MIN.**
Ralph . . . . Robert Downey Jr.
Scott . . . . Kiefer Sutherland
Cliff . . . . Bruce Dern
Jessie . . . . Mariette Hartley
Beth . . . . Winona Ryder
Ev . . . . Joanna Cassidy
Alden . . . . Christopher Wynne
Marsha . . . . Keller Kuhn

■ Hollywood — Affecting memories and good intentions don't always add up to good screen stories, and such is the case in "1969," one of the murkiest reflections on the Vietnam War era yet.

Notwithstanding good performances all around and bright packaging of Kiefer Sutherland and Robert Downey Jr. in the leads, pic faces a struggle at the boxoffice.

Director-screenwriter Ernest Thompson ("On Golden Pond") has a wonderful feel for the texture of relationships, and as a result, first third of pic is loaded with pungent moments and subtle promise. It's only when it comes time to de-

liver a screen-size story that things go goofy.

Protagonists, college students and best pals Scott (Sutherland) and Ralph (Downey) have adopted a lifestyle and scruffy mode of dress in sharp contrast to the buttoned-down mores of their families in a small Maryland town 83 miles away.

When they hitchhike home, there's conflict, particularly between Scott and his older brother Alden (Christopher Wynne in an extremely sympathetic turn), who's shipping out for the war.

But that's over quickly, and pic never recovers the same edge.

Trouble is, beyond having fun and following the youthful inclination to be radical, Scott and Ralph don't seem to really believe in anything beyond avoiding the draft and maintaining their own safety and comfort.

As a result, story is not exactly gripping. Instead, it's a mild trip down memory lane as the two hit the road in a psychedelic van to taste America in their last "summer of innocence."

Some of the episodes are truly a hoot — though perhaps not intentionally — as when Ralph overdoses on LSD during a high-school graduation and goes dancing around in his underwear.

Even the road adventures don't develop far, as Ralph, who's grown increasingly negative and morose after flunking out of college, decides to come home and rip off his file from the draft board — a stunt that, unbelievably, lands him in jail.

Meanwhile, Scott's brother has been reported missing in action — which Scott callously insists must mean he is dead.

Both these scenes are clumsily handled, and even when confronting the issues, Thompson's stand slides along the surface.

Conclusion that the war in Vietnam was not a good one and therefore deserved resistance is soft indeed. Pic's final scene might have had resonance in 1969; in 1988, it's too late too late.

On the other hand, Sutherland gives one of his best and most natural performances as Scott, and Downey is very good in a role that's similar to his "Less Than Zero" junkie, but gives him less to work with.

Joanna Cassidy gives a topnotch supporting performance as Ralph's spunky, effervescent and slightly liberal mother, and Winona Ryder is a scene-stealer as younger sister Beth, who's the only one with any ideas, even if painfully naive. Mariette Hartley is quite affecting as Scott's mother, who's been frozen out of her marriage to uptight Bruce Dern (whose performance seems a tad overwrought).

Production designer Marcia Hinds does well with both the trendy elements and the well-reserved

small-town appearances, and the soundtrack is a fine collection of some of the most affecting sounds of the '60s. —Daws.

Flamengo Paixão
(Flamenco Passion) (BRAZILIAN-DOCU)

A Moderna Producão da Arte production. Produced by Carlos Moletta, Joachim Vaz de Carvalho. Directed by David Neves. Written by Vaz de Carvalho; camera (color), Fernando Duarte; editor, Marco Antonio Cury; sound, Carlos Moletta. Reviewed at Sorrento Intl. Encounter, Oct. 26, 1988. Running time: **110 MIN.**

■ Sorrento — "Flamenco Passion" is a rousing feature-length documentary on glories of the Rio soccer team and its fans' adulation.

Soccer and "saudade" (nostalgia, love), common Brazilian fixations, are coupled in this worship of immense proportions. Via period newsreels and recent on-field footage, traces the 50-year history of club-supplied national idols (Zizhino, Pele, Zico, among others) and the mass fan support that has accompanied them.

Syncopated with the mounting rhythm of heartbeats, sambas, team songs and slogans, the intensity of this national passion also is captivating as a sociological report on mass hysteria.

Occasional low-budget technical frailties do not disturb film's communication of its theme. —Chin.

Scrooged

A Paramount Pictures release of an Art Linson production in association with Mirage Prods. Executive producer, Steve Roth. Produced by Richard Donner, Linson. Coproducer, Ray Hartwick. Directed by Donner. Screenplay, Mitch Glazer, Michael O'Donoghue; camera (Technicolor), Michael Chapman; editors, Fredric Steinkamp, William Steinkamp; music, Danny Elfman; production design, J. Michael Riva; art direction, Virginia L. Randolph; Thomas Warren (N.Y.); set design, William J. Teegarden, Nancy Patton, Dianne Wager; set decoration, Linda DeScenna; John Alan Hicks (N.Y.); costume design, Wayne Finkelman; sound (Dolby), Willie Burton; Al Mian (N.Y.); special makeup effects, Thomas R. Burman, Bari Breiband-Burman; associate producer, Jennie Lew-Tugend; assistant director, Chris Soldo; additional camera, Peter Norman; casting, David Rubin. Reviewed at National Theater, L.A., Nov. 15, 1988. MPAA Rating: PG-13. Running time: **101 MIN.**
Frank Cross . . . . Bill Murray
Claire Phillips . . . . Karen Allen
Lew Hayward . . . . John Forsythe
Brice Cummings . . . . John Glover
Eliot Loudermilk . . . . . . Bobcat Goldthwait
Ghost of Christmas Past . . David Johansen
Ghost of Christmas Present . . . Carol Kane
Preston Rhinelander . . . . . Robert Mitchum
Calvin Cooley . . . . Nicholas Phillips
Herman . . . . Michael J. Pollard
Grace Cooley . . . . Alfre Woodard
Gramma . . . . Mabel King
James Cross . . . . John Murray
Jacob Marley . . . . Jamie Farr
Robert Goulet . . . . Himself
Scrooge . . . . Buddy Hackett
John Houseman . . . . Himself
Lee Majors . . . . Himself
Ghost of Christmas
Present (TV) . . . . Pat McCormick
Earl Cross . . . . Brian Doyle Murray
Mary Lou Retton . . . . Herself

■ **"Scrooged" is an appallingly unfunny comedy, and a vivid illustration of the fact that money can't buy you laughs.**

Its stocking spilling with big names and production values galore, this updating of Dickens' "A Christmas Carol" into the world of cutthroat network television is, one episode apart, able to generate only a few mild chuckles here and there, falling flat a great majority of the time.

Nevertheless, Bill Murray's name atop his first comedy since "Ghostbusters" four years ago will guarantee a smash holiday season for this broad-based Paramount release. Beyond that, audiences will have to decide whether to heed soft word-of-mouth or, as in the case of Eddie Murphy and "The Golden Child," ignore it.

Idea behind Mitch Glazer and Michael O'Donoghue's screenplay wasn't necessarily a bad one. Scrooge here is an utterly venal network chief whose taste runs beneath the lowest common denominator, has no friends, sacks any underlings who dare to disagree with him and possesses a personal history based entirely upon having watched tv since infancy.

Unfortunately for the film, things ring false from the start because boss Frank Cross' cruelty seems very arbitrary, unfunny and ultimately unconvincing, so much so that one deduces that, despite the project having been built around him, Bill Murray is fundamentally miscast in this role. His patented attitude of cutting insincerity doesn't jibe with much of what he's called upon to do here, throwing the thrust of the story off.

Murray's network IBC is preparing to broadcast a live version of "A Christmas Carol" (with, in a good bit, Buddy Hackett as Scrooge), so it is against this backdrop that Murray's own journey through his past and toward his personal salvation takes place.

Lunatic taxi driver David Johansen spirits Murray back to his deprived childhood in 1955, when little Billy is seen watching "Howdy Doody" and being abused by his nasty father. By 1968, Murray is a nerdy hippie working as an office boy at the network when he bumps into the idealistic Karen Allen and takes up with her.

Within three years, however, the love of his life has left, and so starts Murray's ascent from portraying a dog on a kiddies' show into the top executive suite at the company, and his descent into ruthless, unfeeling selfishness.

Pic's comic highlight unquestionably is Carol Kane's appearance as the Ghost of Christmas Present. With the look and bearing of the Good Witch of the North, Kane dispenses verbal and physical punishment on her victim with sadistic glee, occasionally generating the only bellylaughs to be found in the film.

But it then takes a quick talespin, as special effects monsters terrify Murray into confronting his mortality, softening him up in a way bleeding-heart Karen Allen, who now runs a shelter for the homeless, was never quite able to do. It all ends unbelievably, with the main story and "A Christmas Carol" predictably converging as Murray expounds upon his newfound feeling of love and generosity in an impromptu address to a live tv audience.

Aside from Carol Kane and Bobcat Goldthwait, who sparks a few laughs as the most mistreated of Murray's employees, all members of the illustrious cast have been seen to decidedly better advantage on previous occasions. The late John Houseman appears as the Alistair Cooke-like host of the live "Carol" and is made fun of by Murray, while a few other performers put in ho-hum cameos as themselves.

Level of inspiration throughout runs low, and it remains to be seen if the public will go for so much inside trade humor, for which the tv network setting provides a springboard. Without doubt the most tasteless joke comes when Murray throws ice water on a restaurant waiter whose *flambée* dish has ignited him as well and then says, "I'm sorry, I thought you were Richard Pryor."

Every set, costume and special effect is of the most lavish variety, screaming out how much they cost. By contrast, Danny Elfman's score is appealingly bright and sparkly.
—*Cart.*

Blücher
(NORWEGIAN)

A KF release of Norsk Film production. Produced by Elin Erichsen. Directed by Oddvar Bull Tuhus. Screenplay, Tuhus, Sverre Arness; camera (Eastmancolor), Harald Paalgard; editor, Malte Wadman; music, Lillebjörn Nilsen, Arild Andersen; sound, Svein Hovde; production design, Tone Skjelfjord, Viggo Jönsberg; costumes, Anne Hamre; assistant director, David Wingate. Reviewed at Frogner theater, Oslow, Nov. 12, 1988. Running time: **91 MIN.**
Vidar Vestheim . . . . Helge Jordal
Linda Welder . . . . Hege Schöyen
Bernt Dez . . . . Frank Krog
Leif Welder . . . . Finn Kvalem
Olaf Böe . . . . Jack Fjeldstad
    Also with: Reidar Sörensen, Mike Sean Right, Björn Floberg, Geir Börresen.

■ **Oslo — "Blücher" has now been doubly victimized. As a German battleship, the "Blücher" was sunk by Norwegian cannons April 9, 1940, when the Nazis invaded Norway. As an action thriller with political overtones, "Blücher" displays even more fatal holes.**

The costly item may have been doomed from the start, being a salvage job performed on a different project altogether.

Originally conceived under the title of "Haltenbanken" as a thriller about events on a North Sea oil rig, "Blücher" carries the load of various production ingredients forced upon producer Elin Erichsen. The transition also made writer-director Oddvar Bull Tuhus team up with cinematographer Harald Paalgard in spite of obvious differences between the two men.

Tuhus opted for the slick, slam-bang actioner, Paalgard for the sophisticated thriller in which the lopsided rear-mirror image of an object hurled into a black pool lit only by a pale moon carried a world of meaning. Their combined efforts leave one confused about both plot and action.

Only the publicity synopsis offers clues to the story of two maverick divers who defeat authorities, police and assorted hired thugs to bring forth from the sunken battleship (never yet explored in real life) secrets that brand present-day Norwegian bigwigs as traitors back in 1940.

Current business shenanigans to supplant nuclear power installations with excessive exploitation of North Sea natural gas deposits gives pic high moralistic airs, while men get beaten or kill themselves or just flex their muscles to impress a nosy blond newshen.

Helge Jordal puts on his best wry mien of skepticism as one of the divers. Hege Schöyen, Norway's answer to Goldie Hawn, overacts as the journalist, while everyone else in the cast performs with stolid conviction, bordering on parody, in their cliché roles as more or less corrupt members of the Establishment.

From opening shot to last, "Blücher" is a series of false starts, blurry narrative dead-ends and out-of-whack editing. The underwater cinematography is technically impressive but never carries forward the action. —*Kell.*

Fresh Horses

A Weintraub Entertainment Group release through Columbia Pictures of a Dick Berg production. Executive producer, Allan Marcil. Produced by Berg. Directed by David Anspaugh. Screenplay, Larry Ketron, based on his play; camera (CFI color; Film House prints), Fred Murphy; editor, David Rosenbloom; music, David Foster, Patrick Williams; production design, Paul Sylbert; set decoration, Ken Turek; costume design, Colleen Atwood; sound (Dolby), Hank Garfield; associate producer, John G. Wilson; assistant director, Peter Giuliano; casting, Amanda Mackey. Reviewed at Hollywood Pacific Theater, L.A., Nov. 18, 1988. MPAA Rating: PG-13. Running time: **105 MIN.**
Jewel . . . . Molly Ringwald
Matt Larkin . . . . Andrew McCarthy
Jean . . . . Patti D'Arbanville
Tipton . . . . Ben Stiller
Larkin's Dad . . . . Leon Russom
Ellen . . . . Molly Hagan
Green . . . . Viggo Mortensen
Sproles . . . . Doug Hutchison
Alice . . . . Chiara Peacock
Maureen . . . . Marita Geraghty
Bobo . . . . Rachel Jones
Christy . . . . Welker White
Laurel . . . . Christy Budig

■ **Hollywood — An offbeat, wrong-side-of-the-tracks romance receives a muted, conventional treatment in "French Horses." Giving appealing performances in unusually serious roles, Molly Ringwald and Andrew McCarthy represent the total b.o. hope for this first in-house Weintraub Entertainment Group production to see release.**

But pic will have to do most of its business over its first two weekends, as it has no chance of standing up against the Christmas biggies lurking just around the corner.

Larry Ketron's play of the same name received considerable favorable notice when it opened off-Broadway in 1986. Critics made note of its occasionally explosive humor, something entirely missing from this dour, very sober look at a difficult, obsessive love story.

One senses that other things are missing as well, for as many potentially potent and interesting scenes have been pointedly omitted from this fundamentally involving tale as have been included.

Engaged to a very proper monied girl, straight, industrious Matt (McCarthy), a senior in engineering in Cincinnati, is lured by a buddy out to a somewhat shabby house in the country where wild parties and shady people are supposed to be the order of the day.

Matt turns up on what must be an off-day, for all he finds is Jewel (Ringwald) folding the laundry. But that's enough for him, and on his third visit the two launch head-first into a very unexpected, passionate romance that offers each of them something entirely new.

Jewel is an uneducated country girl who makes allusions to her mistreatment by an unseen stepfather. She is, in her own way, more guarded than the naturally cautious Matt, who dumps his fiancée and lets all other aspects of his life slide in favor of following his heart.

But the town will talk, and Matt is told by others that Jewel may be only 16, rather than 20, as she says, and that she is married. The former point remains a mystery, while her unconvincing, defensive explanations for the latter situation open the door of doubt in Matt's mind about his choices, and inevitably lead to a traumatic confrontation with Jewel's mean-spirited, gun-crazy husband.

Story has poignant, older-but-wiser conclusion, but one senses it could have amounted to something more than another recapitulation of the sadness of first love. The dark, wet, barren look of Ohio and Kentucky in early winter, as sensitively captured by lenser Fred Murphy, endows the film with a powerful visual atmosphere throughout, and sets a firm tone for a somber romance. Ketron's ear for dialog is very good, and his sense of what moments of the couple's relationship to show, and which should be withheld, is intriguing.

But for a story centered upon such intense emotions and risk-taking, the picture emerges as too placid, lacking in edge and danger. Point of view is conventionally weighted to illustrate the coming of age of a sensitive young man, yet the viewer is left with no strong feeling as to how he might have been changed by the powerful experience.

The film could have been considerably more effective with a more unusual, turbulent score. Music here plays right into all the softest, easiest-to-identify emotional aspects of the scenes, pushing the tone toward routine sentimentality instead of complex tension, which seems to be what Ketron is going for.

Director David Anspaugh, fresh from "Hoosiers," elicits fine work from McCarthy and particularly Ringwald. At times evoking the young Marilyn Monroe and Tuesday Weld, she toughly plays a child-woman who already has been kicked around too much by life, but still maintains a touching degree of hope and innocence. McCarthy must cope with many ambiguous shifts of Matt's mind, but is solid nonetheless as a conservative guy on a reckless journey.

All supporting work and tech contributions are very good.

—*Cart.*

Last Rites

An MGM/UA Communications release of an MGM presentation. Produced by Donald P. Bellisario, Patrick McCormick. Written and directed by Bellisario. Camera (Deluxe color), David Watkin; editor, Pembroke J. Herring; music, Bruce Broughton; production design, Peter Larkin; art direction, Victor Kempster, Fernando Ramirez (Mexico); set decoration, Steven Jordan; costume design, Joseph G. Aulisi; sound (Dolby), Les Lazarowitz, David Moshlak; assistant directors, Joe Napolitano, Jesus Marin (Mexico); second unit directors, David Jones, Napolitano; additional camera, Michael Stone; casting, Joy Todd. Reviewed at Lorimar Telepictures Studios, Culver City, Calif., Nov. 10, 1988. MPAA Rating: R. Running time: 103 MIN.
Father Michael Pace . . . . Tom Berenger
Angela . . . . Daphne Zuniga
Nuzo . . . . Chick Vennera
Zena Pace . . . . Anne Twomey
Carlo Pace . . . . Dane Clark
Father Freddie . . . . Paul Dooley
Tio . . . . Vassili Lambrinos

◾ **Hollywood — "Last Rites"** **holds a certain interest but also often borders on the ludicrous, accommodating all the ripest themes that can be derived from the dilemma of being an Italian-American Catholic priest and son of a top Mafioso.**

Legal vs. religious responsibility, abstinence, family loyalty, the sanctity of the confessional — all this and more are rolled into the melodrama. Given the shortcoming of this effort, which had to be outstanding if it were to draw any attention, commercial prospects look dim.

A rather unlikely Tom Berenger stars as Father Michael Pace, a young priest at St. Patrick's Catholic Cathedral in New York who runs around in hip civilian clothes most of the time and has a close relationship with the cops thanks to this old friend on the force, Nuzo (Chick Vennera).

Startling opening scene has an elegant woman stride, pistol in hand, into a ritzy hotel suite and gun down a mobster while he is making love to a woman. The woman, a Mexican named Angela, escapes and eventually comes under the protection of Pace in his quarters at the church.

The rugged holy man finds himself having erotic dreams about the saucy young thing in his bed, and finally spirits her south of the border to shed her of her pursuers and himself of his priestly responsibilities.

Along the way, it is revealed that Pace is the estranged son of a Mafia kingpin and the brother of Zena, the woman who shot the hood and is now after Angela. Once again, Pace can't live down his family roots and is forced to choose from among his earthly passion, family loyalty and religious convictions.

Donald P. Bellisario, longtime tv writer and producer who co-created "Magnum, P.I.," stages much of the action vividly, but it's just not very convincing. The basic situation is too loaded, some of the scenes seem farfetched and the acting doesn't carry the conviction needed to put it all over.

One can spend the entire running time trying to decide whether to accept Berenger as a streetwise priest who has not before dealt with such a challenge to his vows of abstinence. His casting was an interesting idea, but probably a mistake. Similarly Daphne Zuniga has divided impact as the femme fatale, as she sends out the proper mixed signals as to her intentions but sports a highly variable Spanish accent.

Dane Clark smoothly plays the Mafia chieftain, Anne Twomey has the right chilled impact as his daughter, but Vennera and Paul Dooley, as a stuttering priest, overdo things in their roles.

Production values are very strong across the board. —*Cart.*

The Land Before Time
(ANIMATED)

A Universal release of a Sullivan-Bluth Studios production in association with Amblin Entertainment. Executive producers, Steven Spielberg, George Lucas. Co-executive producers, Frank Marshall, Kathleen Kennedy. Produced by Don Bluth, Gary Goldman, John Pomeroy. Directed by Don Bluth. Screenplay by Stu Krieger, based on a story by Judy Freudberg, Tony Geiss; music, James Horner; editor, Dan Molina, John K. Carr; sound editor (Dolby stereo), Kevin Brazier; Ian Fuller; production design, Bluth; storyboard, Bluth, Larry Leker, Dan Kuenster; assistant directors, Russell Boland, G. Sue Shakespeare, David Steinberg; directing animators, John Pomeroy, Linda Miller,

Ralph Zondag, Kuenster, Lorna Pomeroy, Dick Zondag; production camera (Technicolor), Jim Mann; layout supervisor, David Goetz; background stylist, Don Moore; associate producer, Deborah Jelin Newmyer; casting, Nancy Mayor. Reviewed at Universal's Alfred Hitchcock Theater, Universal City, Calif., Nov. 12, 1988. MPAA Rating: G. Running time: 66 MIN.
Narrator/Rooter . . . . Pat Hingle
Littlefoot . . . . Gabriel Damon
Littlefoot's mother . . . . Helen Shaver
Cera . . . . Candice Houston
Ducky . . . . Judith Barsi
Petrie . . . . Will Ryan
Daddy Topps . . . . Burke Barnes

◾ **Hollywood — Same team that drew up "An American Tail," creating the mouse that roared in holiday boxoffice two years ago, delves into the dinosaur era to deliver "The Land Before Time," indeed, one of the slowest hours ever to crawl across a screen.**

Animation quality is fine, but 2-dimensional story will try the patience of about all but the tiniest viewers. Steven Spielberg-George Lucas aegis should lure initial business, but pic faces extinction soon after.

Sure, kids like dinosaurs, but beyond that premise doesn't find far to go. Following the "American Tail" pattern, story is about Littlefoot (Gabriel Damon), in innocent dinosaur tyke who gets separated from his family and after a perilous journey finds them again in a new land.

In this case it's a journey from a dried-up part of the land to another, known as the Great Valley, where the herds frolic in abundant greenery.

After Littlefoot's mother dies, he has to make the journey alone, dodging hazards like earthquakes, volcanoes and a predatory carnivore named Sharptooth. Along the way, he pulls together a band of other little dinosaurs of different species who've been brought up not to associate with each other.

Idea develops that surviving in a changing environment depends on achieving unity among the species.

Put forth in a gentle fashion probably suited to under-10 viewers, idea isn't strong enough to carry the tale. Imagination shouldn't be the missing ingredient in a venture of this kind, but that's precisely the case.

For the most part, pic is about as engaging as what's found on Saturday morning tv.

Animated characters, blended from cuteness and desire for authenticity, are fine to watch, while background paintings of prehistoric terrain are sometimes striking.

Music by James Horner and theme song sung by Diana Ross are okay, but not as rousing as the Oscar-nominated "Tail" anthem.

Pat Hingle's kindly, growly approach to narration is an asset, while some of the other voices come off too sugary, strident or clichéd.

—*Daws.*

Howling IV …
The Original Nightmare
(BRITISH)

An Allied Entertainment presentation. Executive producers, Edward Simons, Avi Lerner, Steven Lane, Robert Pringle. Produced by Harry Alan Towers. Directed by John Hough. Screenplay, Clive Turner, Freddie Rowe, from story by Turner, based on novels by Gary Brandner; camera (color), Godfrey Godar; editor, Claudia Finkle, Malcolm Burns-Errington; music, David George; additional music, Barrie Guard; sound, Colin McFarlane; special effects, Steve Johnson's XFX Inc.; production manager, Danny Lerner; assistant director-2d unit director, Cedric Sundström; stunt coordinator, Reo Ruiters; coproducer, Turner; casting, Don Pemrick, Gianna Pisanello & Associates. Reviewed on IVE videcassette, N.Y., Nov. 12, 1988. MPAA Rating: R. Running time: 92 MIN.
Marie . . . . Romy Windsor
Richard . . . . Michael T. Weiss
Tom . . . . Antony Hamilton
Janice . . . . Susanne Severeid
Eleanor . . . . Lamya Derval
Sheriff . . . . Norman Anstey
Mrs. Orstead . . . . Kate Edwards
Tow truck driver . . . . Clive Turner

◾ **After a creative comeback in Part 3, this werewolf horror series hits a snag with "Howling IV," a poorly executed, uninvolving programmer.**

Though set in California, pic was lensed (as are so many other recent Harry Alan Towers productions) in South Africa, giving the four "Howling" films the odd touch of each having been shot on a different continent. Romy Windsor portrays a bestselling novelist who's emotionally unstable and takes her doctor's advice to get away from it all.

Staying at remote Wilderness Cottage near the town of Drago, she's beset by nightmares and hallucinations, involving howling in the woods and a beast on the prowl. Teaming up with an ex-nun (Susanne Severeid) searching for the reason behind a fellow nun's death in the vicinity, Windsor uncovers a plot to hide the presence of werewolves. Pic climaxes at a bell tower, containing a 16th century bell from Rumania, linked to the curse.

Disconcerting post-synched dialog has supporting cast dubbed with neutral or southern U.S. accents, while leads handle their own voicings, including Antony Hamilton and his Aussie inflection in a small role as Windsor's literary agent.

Helmer John Hough previously has done a fine job with supernatural material, e.g., "Legend Of Hell House," but strikes out with unconvincing makeup effects this time. Climax of Windsor's husband (Michael T. Weiss) disintegrating with gloppy effects out of "The Devil's Rain" literally brings the film to a halt and is inappropriate. Werewolf puppet is shown only fleetingly in quick cuts.

Cast is unexceptional, though Lamya Derval displays an imposing figure as a villainous neighbor who, natch, seduces Weiss. An invigorating theme song (played twice),

"Something Evil, Something Dangerous" sung by the Moody Blues' Justin Hayward, is pic's classiest element. —*Lor.*

Jungfruresan
(Maiden Voyage) (SWEDISH)

An SF release of an SF (Svensk Filmindustri) production, with the Swedish Film Institute. Produced by Waldemar Bergendal, Jan Marnell. Written and directed by Reidar Jönsson. Camera (Eastmancolor), Roland Lundin; editor, Leon Flamhole, Jan Persson; music, Björn Isfält; sound, Bo Persson, Owe Svensson; production design, Bengt Fröderberg; costumes, Inger Pehrsson; production manager, Jutta Ekman; assistant director, Daniel Alfredson; casting, Hakan Bjerking. Reviewed at the Downtown, Malmö, Sweden, Nov. 16, 1988. Running time: **103 MIN.**

Leif	Peter Andersson
Lindquist	Philip Zanden
Helmer	Lars Väringer
Burken	Nils Moritz
Staffan	Fredrik Stahlne
Mette	Eva Mutvei
Gittan	Elisabeth Nordkvist
Helena	Lena Raeder
Anna	Ewa Maria Björkström
Anette	Suzanne Reuter

Also with: Percy Brandt, Else Marie Brandt, Christian Törnquist, Amanda Cremer, Kajsa Ejemyr, Greta Lundborg.

■ Malmö, Sweden — Novelist and sometime tv director Reider Jönsson, whose "My Life As A Dog" became a Lasse Hallström film hit, has his feature writer-helmer bow with "Maiden Voyage." It's a dog of a different fur, dripping wet all over, including at the domestic Swedish boxoffice.

"Maiden Voyage" tells of a group of middle-class suburbanites who sell their houses to foot the costs of building a small yacht that will take them to some never-never-land of ease and idleness.

When the men make a wreck of their ship before it is launched, they lie to their womenfolk about it. After some skirmishes, amorous and otherwise, they steal another ship to replace the wreck.

The picture itself runs aground almost from the outset. Neither plot, subplots nor character delineations hold water. Every gag or pun floats as forlornly as debris on stagnant water.

The superb actor Philip Zandén strives to make a Woody Allenesque character come to life but he, like the rest of the cast, is working in a vacuum. Since not a single sequence is allowed to come to a natural conclusion, one wonders why the editor allowed the no-fun to run as long as a tedious 103 minutes. —*Kell.*

High Spirits
(BRITISH-U.S.)

A Tri-Star release of a Vision p.d.g. presentation of a Palace production. Executive producers, Mark Damon, Moshe Diamant, Eduard Sarlui. Produced by Stephen Woolley, David Saunders, Nik Powell, Selwyn Roberts. Written and directed by Neil Jordan. Camera (Rank color), Alex Thomson; editor, Michael Bradsell; editorial consultant, Lynzee Klingman; music, George Fenton; production design, Anton Furst; supervising art director, Les Tomkins; art direction, Nigel Phelps, Alan Tomkins (Ireland); set decoration, Barbara Drake; costume design, Emma Porteous; sound (Dolby), David John; special visual effects, Derek Meddings; associate producer, Jon Turtle; assistant director, Patrick Clayton; second unit director, Meddings; second unit visual effects and camera, Paul Wilson; casting, Janet Hirshenson, Jane Jenkins (U.S.), Susie Figgis (U.K.). Reviewed at Cineplex Odeon Century Plaza, L.A., Nov. 16, 1988. MPAA Rating: PG-13. Running time: **97 MIN.**

Mary Plunkett	Daryl Hannah
Peter Plunkett	Peter O'Toole
Jack	Steve Guttenberg
Sharon	Beverly D'Angelo
Miranda	Jennifer Tilly
Brother Tony	Peter Gallagher
Martin Brogan	Liam Neeson
Malcolm	Martin Ferrero
Plunkett Senior	Ray McAnally
Marge	Connie Booth
Eamon	Donal McCann
Mrs. Plunkett	Liz Smith
Katie	Mary Coughlan

■ Hollywood — "High Spirits" is a piece of supernatural Irish whimsy with a few appealingly dark underpinnings, but it still rises and falls constantly on the basis of its moment-to-moment inspirations.

Intermittently amusing comic ghost tale holds mild entertainment value for general audiences, but undoubtedly will disappoint the most fervent admirers of writer-director Neil Jordan's earlier films, "Angel," "The Company Of Wolves" and "Mona Lisa." Boxoffice potential looks light.

Elaborate physical production is set almost entirely at Castle Plunkett, a rundown Irish edifice that proprietor Peter O'Toole opens as a tourist hotel in order to meet the mortgage payments. With the American market in mind, O'Toole bills the place as a haunted castle, to this end having his staff dress up like ghouls of various persuasions, installing spinning beds, sending apparitions flying by occupants' windows and overall concocting a raucous supernatural show for his guests' edification.

The exhausting lengths to which the local help will go to try to please the American visitors proves rather depressing, and contributes to the somewhat laborious, overly lengthy opening section. At the same time, however, it sets up what could be the hidden, real theme of the film, which relates to the contortions a filmmaker from a small country must go through in order to make international (read American-slanted) motion pictures.

Be that as it may, it comes as little surprise that the castle turns out to be actually haunted. Steve Guttenberg, who is not getting along with wife Beverly D'Angelo, comes to meet ghost Daryl Hannah, who was killed on the premises years ago on her wedding night by Liam Neeson, who takes a fancy to D'Angelo.

Hannah and Neeson repeat their murderous ritual regularly until Halloween night, when they briefly return to human form and have the chance to save themselves and rendezvous with new mates. This sort of ghostly temptation, with Hannah pining that Guttenberg will join her in a transcendent permanent love and Neeson simply trying to seduce the manic D'Angelo, creates the only tension, such as it is, in the story, but also results in some nice, sensual visual effects between solid bodies and transparent ones.

In stabs at broad physical comedy, the cast gets soaked with water and blown through the air on numerous occasions, and vast pieces of the castle come loose variously to threaten and transport the besieged guests during their eventful stay on the Emerald Isle. After a while, the sheer extent of clamorous destruction taking place becomes a bit tiresome.

The challenge of such fanciful material is to keep it afloat at all times. Jordan falls off the high wire many times, but gamely climbs back up for more, and finally comes through with a partially successful fantasy that improves after the beginning, but then goes on too long for its own good.

O'Toole spins through the action in impresario-like fashion, Hannah and Guttenberg are okay as destiny's lovers, and D'Angelo and Neeson play their exaggerated roles with relish. With her aggressively determined attitude contrasting amusingly with her bimbo-ish voice, Jennifer Tilly registers well as she attempts to win handsome novitiate Peter Gallagher before he takes his vows, and Liz Smith has fun as O'Toole's mother.

Special effects overseen by Derek Meddings have an appealingly homemade, non-high tech quality. Anton Furst designed the impressively multifaceted castle set, Alex Thomson's lensing and Emma Porteous' costumes are attractive, and George Fenton's active score helps keep things moving. —*Cart.*

Day Of The Panther
(AUSTRALIAN)

A Virgo Prods., TVM Studios presentation, in association with the Mandemar Group. Executive producers, Judith West, Grahame Jennings. Produced by Damien Parer. Directed by Brian Trenchard-Smith. Screenplay, Peter West, from story by West, David Groom; additional dialog, Trenchard-Smith; camera (Atlab color), Simon Akkerman; editor, David Jaeger, Kerry Regan; music, Gary Hardman, Brian Beamish; sound, David Glasser; assistant director-second unit director, Stuart Wood; production manager, Deb Copland; fight coordinators, Edward John Stazak, Jim Richards; stunt coordinators, Guy Norris, Rocky McDonald. Reviewed on Celebrity Home Entertainment vidcassette, N.Y., Nov. 5, 1988. Running time: **84 MIN.**

Jason Blade	Edward John Stazak
William Anderson	John Stanton
Jim Baxter	Jim Richards
Gemma Anderson	Paris Jefferson
Damien Zukor	Michael Carman
Colin	Zale Daniel
The constable	Matthew Quartermaine
Linda Anderson	Linda Megier

■ The Aussie-made action pic "Day Of The Panther" is standard issue martial arts material, well executed but strictly ho-hum.

Edward John Stazak is physically right as Jason Blade, trained by Chinese cult the Panthers, who heads from Hong Kong to Perth on a secret mission against local druglord Zukor (Michael Carman). His teammate Linda (Linda Megier) is killed and Blade teams up with her cousin Gemma (Paris Jefferson).

The local cops tolerate Blade's activities, later encouraging him when they finally see through his cover story as a mercenary killer and identify his mission. In typical genre format, pic builds to a bloody annual gladiatorial tournament held by Zukor, but oddly omits same, instead staging a climax of Blade 1-on-1 against Zukor's chief henchman Baxter (Jim Richards).

Fight scenes, staged by thesps Stanzak and Richards, are effective and Jefferson makes a beautiful redheaded leading lady. Otherwise pic is perfunctory and ends abruptly with announcement of its sequel "Strike Of The Panther," which was filmed back-to-back with this installment. —*Lor.*

Evil Laugh

A Cinevest release of a Wildfire production. Executive producers, Arthur Schweitzer, Krisha Shah. Produced by Dominick Brascia, Steven Baio. Supervising producer, Dominick Brascia Sr. Directed by Dominick Brascia. Screenplay, Baio, Brascia; camera (color), Stephen Sealy; editor, Brian McIntosh, Michael Scott; music, David Shapiro; sound, Stephen Doster; art direciton, Jeffrey Diamond; special makeup effects, David Cohen; assistant director, Eric Brown; production manager, David Windham; second unit director, Sealy; casting, Johnny Venocur. Reviewed on Celebrity Home Entertainment vidcassette, N.Y., Nov. 12, 1988. MPAA Rating: R. Running time: **87 MIN.**

Johnny	Steven Baio
Connie	Kim McKamy
Sammy	Tony Griffin
Tina	Jody Gibson
Freddy	Johnny Venocur
Barney	Jerold Pearson

Also with: Myles O'Brien, Susan Grant, Howard Weiss, Karyn O'Bryan, Gary Hays.

■ "Evil Laugh" is a rather self-conscious horror film in the slasher vein, in regional theatrical release since last March prior to video availability.

Title refers to the cackle of a masked killer, preying on a bevy of young med students and interns who spend the weekend at an abandoned orphanage. Kids are there to fix up the place for Jerry (Gary Hays), who's planning to buy it and refurbish the facility, but he's killed in the first reel.

While the youngsters party, the killer picks them off. Identity of the fiend is linked to a murderous event there 10 years ago. Attempts at black humor, including unwitting cannibalism, are ineffectual as filmmakers Dominick Brascia and Steven Baio emphasize a wiseguy character (Jerold Pearson), who keeps commenting on events resembling things happening in ''Friday The 13th'' or ''Halloween'' films. Most viewers will be well aware of the genre clichés without prompting.

Gore effects emphasize plenty of hemoglobin. Finale, involving heroine Kim McCamy, is rather silly. —Lor.

Il Piccolo Diavolo
(The Little Devil)
(ITALIAN)

A Columbia Pictures Italia release of a Yarno Cinematografica/Cecchi Gori Group/Tiger Cinematografica coproduction. Produced by Mauro Berardi, Mario and Vittorio Cecchi Gori. Directed by Roberto Benigni. Screenplay, Vincenzo Cerami, Benigni; camera (Eastmancolor, Luciano Vittori prints), Robby Müller; editor, Nino Baragli; music, Evan Lurie; art direction, Antonio Annichiarico. Reviewed at Columbia screening room, Rome, Nov. 15, 1988. Running time: **110 MIN.**

(English soundtrack)

Giuditta	Roberto Benigni
Maurice	Walter Matthau
Nina	Nicoletta Braschi
Cusatelli	John Lurie
Patrizia	Stefania Sandrelli

Also with: Paolo Baroni, Franco Fabrizi, Giacomo Piperno, Flavio Bonacci, Annabella Schiavone, John Karlsen, Mirella Falco.

■ **Rome — As effervescent and off-beat as director-comic Roberto Benigni (though lacking the deadpan hilarity of Jim Jarmusch's ''Down By Law,'' which introduced the clown to American viewers, ''The Little Devil'' stars odd couple Benigni and Walter Matthau.**

Despite being of two different comic stripes, the duo generate plenty of fun onscreen.

Pic has topped the Italo boxoffice with whopping admissions. Gags are off-beat but not off-color; even though main characters are a priest with a girlfriend and a devil with a sexual obsession, film has the mild taste of a Mr. Hulot comedy.

Father Maurice (Matthau) exorcizes a demon from a fat, middle-aged lady who has inexplicably begun singing ''Tom Dooley,'' in English, in a deep, masculine voice. Out pops Giuditta (or Judith — played by Benigni), clothing his nakedness in the fat lady's fur coat. A funny little devil prone to admiring himself in mirrors and repeating nonsense phrases (with a delightful Italo accent), Giuditta attaches himself to the gruff priest and wreaks havoc in his life.

Later Giuditta hops a train north and falls for Nina (Nicoletta Braschi), a freewheeling gambler with an aversion to wearing shoes and underwear. Maurice arrives in search of his distraught love, Stefania Sandrelli (looking matronly in a chaste cameo). When Maurice discovers Nina (as well as poker-faced Germanologist John Lurie) are two

devils sent to reclaim Giuditta, he tries to warn him. Too late: the little devil is happily possessed — literally — by his lady love, and cheerfully exits the scene.

Benigni, famous as a pungent, tongue-twisting standup comic, is forced back on visual comedy here of the mildest sort. He still does a better job perverting his lines than does Matthau, yet both appeal with facial and body humor. Braschi and Lurie are comic-book characters without depth, good only as foils.

Lensing by Robby Müller is unobtrusively in the service of the jokes. Evan Lurie's circus score is catchy fun. —Yung.

Aduéfuè
(Les Guerisseurs/
The Lords Of The Streets)
(IVORY COAST-FRENCH)

An Afriki Projection production. Produced by Ayala Bakaba. Written and directed by Sijiri Bakaba. Camera (color), Mohamed Soudani; editor, Olivier Morel; music, Serge Franklin; art direction, Alama Kanate. Reviewed at Carthage Film Festival (competing), Tunis, Oct. 25, 1988. (Also in Chicago Film Festival.) Running time: **89 MIN.**

Kadjo	Georges T. Benson
Tony	Pierre-Loup Rajot
El Hadj Diakite	Mory Traore
The president	Sijiri Bakaba

Also with: Alpha Blondy (Tcholo), Nayanka Bell (Sally), Loukou Yao (Attila), Salif Keita, Madoussou Diakite.

■ **Tunis — Known best as black Africa's biggest star, Sijiri (formerly Sidiki) Bakaba turns his hand to directing in ''Les Guerisseurs'' (English title: ''Lords Of The Streets'') with the same style and freshness that distinguishes him in front of the camera.**

His portrait of the Ivory Coast capital where money is king (referred to respectfully as an imaginary ''Kata-Kata,'' but obviously meant to be Abidjan) is devastating, while the Western-style script and fast-moving, professional lensing make for easy viewing.

A colorful, aggressive and bitterly critical film, ''Lords'' ought to do especially well in Paris and other sites with a high African concentration. It is one of the most successful attempts so far to adapt the gangster genre to a sub-Saharan locale.

Kadjo (nice guy Georges T. Benson) has just come home after two years in France with tastes well above his means. In the bright, hip city of nightclubs, girls and easy cash, Kadjo falls in with some tough guys (particularly Pierre-Loup Rajot), forgetting he's the son of a ''king.'' They move from prostitution to a not too convincing holdup of a bank truck.

During the robbery Attila, a popular circus strongman, is gunned down by the white boss, and Kadjo runs for his life, belonging neither to family nor the flashy new generation of entrepreneurs and crooks.

Offbeat and amusing, ''Lords''

boasts some very good performances, not least from the director himself. Few fans will recognize Bakaba as the drunken, obscene ''President,'' a tour-de-force role of abject degradation. Several fancy nightclub numbers pad out the entertainment quotient. Technical work is high quality throughout.

It is noteworthy that the Ivory Coast government chipped in 11% on the production.—Yung.

La Maison de jade
(House Of Jade)
(FRENCH)

An AAA release of a Sara Films/Ciné Cinq coproduction. Produced by Alain Sarde. Directed by Nadine Trintignant. Screenplay, Trintignant, Madeleine Chapsal, from Chapsal's novel; camera (Eastmancolor), William Lubtchansky; editor, Joëlle Van Effenterre; music, Philippe Sarde; sound, Pierre Gamet; art direction, Michèle Abbe; production manager, Christine Gozlan. Reviewed at Images cinema, Paris, Nov. 3, 1988. Running time: **99 MIN.**

Jane Lambert	Jacqueline Bisset
Bernard	Vincent Perez
Cermaine	Véronique Silver
Ignace	Yves Lambrecht

■ **Paris — Jacqueline Bisset's first French film since 1973 (when she appeared in both François Truffaut's ''Day For Night'' and Philippe de Broca's ''Le Magnifique'') is a disappointing romantic drama about a middle-aged woman's ill-fated love affair with a younger man.**

Story was adapted by filmmaker Nadine Trintignant from a recent autobiographical bestseller by Madeleine Chapsal, who collaborated on the screenplay.

Bisset plays a Franco-British novelist who is swept off her feet by an ambitious young businessman who is pushing 30 when they meet. Despite an unhappy marriage (which stumbled because of her infertility) Bisset throws away caution and career to live her imprudent passion.

After months of youthful bliss, her lover's ardor begins to cool suspiciously until the day he reveals that he has been seeing someone else and is frustrated by their relationship because he wants children.

Bisset tries to hang on to him, even attempting suicide. But she finds a life buoy by exorcizing her love and heartbreak in a novel.

Trintignant, whose earlier films revealed a talent for playing the heartstrings adroitly, is missing a good score here.

She brings no insight or interior perspective to a trite romantic situation. Trintignant fails to make her lovers sympathetic.

Bisset is open to a flattering criticism. She may be the right age for the role, but she cannot help looking and acting like someone 10 years younger — even without makeup. That factor fudges the basic dramatic point about the discrepancy in age and experience, though we learn little about her private past. All we

know about her lover is that he was a foundling and probably looks to Bisset as a mother figure.

The man is played by Vincent Perez, a new face in films but not in theater. His character is obnoxious, never deepening beyond a certain juvenile impetuosity that turns to sullen, self-centered indifference and vague disgust. Anyone who'd want to throw over the lovely Bisset can't be all that sensitive and intelligent.

—Len.

Nuovo Cinema Paradiso
(New Paradise Cinema)
(ITALIAN-FRENCH)

A Titanus release of a Cristaldi Film (Rome)/Films Ariane (Paris) coproduction, in association with RAI-TV Channel 3, Forum Picture. Produced by Franco Cristaldi. Written and directed by Giuseppe Tornatore. Camera (Eastmancolor), Blasco Giurato; editor, Mario Morra; music, Ennio Morricone; art direction, Andrea Crisanti. Reviewed at Anica, Rome, Nov. 3, 1988. Running time: **155 MIN.**

Salvatore as a boy	Salvatore Cascio
Salvatore as a youth	Marco Leonardi
Salvatore as a man	Jacques Perrin
Alfredo	Philippe Noiret
Young Elena	Agnese Nano
Elena	Brigitte Fossey

Also with: Pupella Maggio (old mother), Antonella Attili (young mother), Enzo Cannavale (Spaccafico), Isa Danieli (Anna), Leo Gullotta, Leopoldo Trieste (priest), Tano Cimarosa, Nicola Di Pinto (madman), Roberta Lena, Nino Terzo.

■ **Rome — ''New Paradise Cinema'' is a colorful, sentimental trip through the happy days when the Italo film biz wasn't in a perennial ''crisis'' and when every seat in the local bijou was filled.**

This ''Amarcord'' about a marvelous Sicilian hardtop and a boy who loves the movies boasts eye-catching technical work and a solid cast. Young helmer Giuseppe Tornatore (''The Professor'') is an able storyteller who knows the value of cute kids and easy emotion. Beneath the schmaltz lie buried a lot of good ideas.

Clocking in at an overlong 2½ hours (cut from three), ''New Paradise Cinema'' may be expected to fall victim to the same audience disinterest it poignantly denounces, followed by a very satisfactory run on tv, where its larger-than-life emotions will be right at home.

Film divides into three parts, corresponding to the three ages of cineaste-hero Salvatore. As an adorable 10-year-old moppet (first-timer Salvatore Cascio is child acting discovery of the year), the boy sneaks into the parochial Paradise Cinema to watch priest Leopoldo Trieste snip out all the kissing scenes. He worms his way into the heart of crusty peasant projectionist Alfredo (a well-balanced Philippe Noiret) who speaks in film dialog.

With Alfredo the cinema is magic — like the night he regales patrons unable to get into a Totò comedy with a free show beamed on a wall in the piazza. Mid-show, the old nitrate film catches fire and destroys the theater.

The youngster miraculously drags the unconcious projectionist downstairs and saves his life, but Alfredo is blinded, and the boy, clambering up on a stool, becomes the projectionist of the rebuilt New Paradise.

Second part shows Salvatore as a teenager in love with a blond banker's daughter, Agnese Nano. Naturally her parents are against the match, and painful circumstances end the kisses in the rain and passion in the projection booth.

Last, and least satisfying, is Salvatore as white-haired Jacques Perrin, now a famous (what else?) film director. He returns to Sicily for Alfredo's funeral and finds his long lost love, now played by Brigitte Fossey. Amid many tears, Salvatore learns it was his blind friend who broke up this one, true romance of his life.

His only consolation (and viewer's, after this weepy nostalgia) is film: he has spliced together all the censored kisses of his youth and created a great homage to celluloid love. If Perrin had kept the tears out of his eyes, it would also be moving.

Topnotch lensing by Blasco Giurato and sets by Andrea Crisanti (the cinema itself is a small masterpiece) create a strong atmosphere.

Ennio Morricone's score reinforces the sugary sentiment that defaces the film. Stage thesp Pupella Maggio has a wonderful cameo as the old mother. —*Yung.*

Ahlam Hind wa Camilia
(Dreams Of Hind And Camelia)
(EGYPTIAN)

An El Alamia for TV and Cinema release of an Egyptian Film Center production. Produced by Hussein Kalla. Written and directed by Mohammed Khan. Camera (color), Mohsen Nasr; editor, Nadia Chukri; music, Ammar Shevai; art direction, Onsy Aluseif. Reviewed at Carthage Film Festival, Tunis, Oct. 26, 1988. Running time: **109 MIN.**

Camelia .Nagla Fathi
Hind .Aida Riyadh
Eid . . . . .Ahmed Zaki
Also with: Hassan Adl, Osman Abdelmunim.

■ **Tunis** — "Dreams Of Hind And Camelia" by Mohammed Khan is the delicate, convincing story of the friendship between two chambermaids.

Subject held it back at the domestic boxoffice, but film has moved successfully through the fest circuit and ranks among the best Egyptian films of this year.

Camelia (played with popular feminism by Nagla Fathi) is an independent-minded girl who prefers to live on her wages cleaning houses than lose her freedom by marrying. Hind (the gentle Aida Riyadh) is a timid country girl in love with handsome rascal Eid (played by the ir-

resistible Ahmed Zaki).

Camelia dreams of getting a house with Hind; but Hind dreams of marrying Eid. When she gets pregnant, Camelia bosses Eid into tying the knot. Camelia herself is forced by her brother to marry a brute, but soon runs away from him.

Cairo's lower depths are explored with convincing realism and without condescension. The girls get by on their work and their wits (especially Camelia's) and their friendship is attractive and credible. Eid keeps going to jail for petty crimes, and the two women lean on each other for support. Ending skirts tragedy to reaffirm the value of just being alive.

"Dreams" is well lensed and acted. —*Yung.*

La Couleur du vent
(The Color Of The Wind)
(FRENCH)

A Bac Films release of a Paradis Films/Ciné Cinq/Générale d'Images coproduction. Produced by Eric Heumann, Stephane Sorlat. Directed by Pierre Granier-Deferre. Screenplay, Jean-Marc Roberts, Granier-Deferre, from an original scenario by Brigitte Fiore; camera (Eastmancolor), Pascal Lebegue; editor, Jean Ravel; music, Philippe Sarde; art direction, Jacques Saulnier; sound, Alex Comte, Claude Villand; production manager, Dominique Toussaint. Reviewed at Marignan-Concorde cinema, Paris, Nov. 2, 1988. Running time: **79 MIN.**

Louise Rivière . . . . .Elizabeth Bourgine
Serge . . . . .Philippe Léotard
Pierre . . . . .Fabrice Luchini
Decourt . . . . .Jean-Pierre Léaud
Colbert . . . . .Jean-Pierre Bisson
Norma . . . . .Anna Massey
Also with: Caroline Chaniolleau, Pascal Greggory, Lucienne Hamon, Christine Pascal, Marcel Bozonnet.

■ **Paris** — "La Couleur du vent" dramatizes the passion of a romantic young publishing house employee who falls in love with a submitted manuscript, then with its mysterious author, an American.

Their professional correspondence soon takes a personal turn that upsets the French woman's psychological equilibrium.

Scripted by director Pierre Granier-Deferre and novelist-screenwriter Jean-Marc Roberts, from a scenario by one Brigitte Fiore, drama is keen and involving in its first half, establishing attractive Elizabeth Bourgine in her personal and professional rapports.

Tone shifts to suspense and mystery when Bourgine, breaking off her relationship with her caring printer-boyfriend (Philippe Léotard) by admitting her love for a man she knows only through his writings, leaves for New York on a wild goose chase that has a nasty, macabre surprise in store for her. Strain in the script, with its touch of the psychopathic thriller, is fatal to the film.

Cast generally is good, with special mention to Léotard, who strikes the most pathetic notes as the reject-

ed lover. Various types at the Paris publishing house where protagonist works are well silhouetted by Jean-Pierre Bisson and Fabrice Luchini. Too bad Granier-Deferre and Roberts (who uses his own experience as a prize winning novelist to detail certain scenes) didn't keep the story in a mundane setting.

Special guest star Anna Massey just gets by in the sticky role as the mother of the mysterious American novelist, who welcomes Bourgine to her isolated snowbound Vermont home to await her son's supposed homecoming. Maybe the (Norman) Bates Motel is just down the road. —*Len.*

La Boda del Acordeonista
(The Accordionist's Wedding)
(COLOMBIAN)

A Focine release of a Grupo Cine-Taller production. Executive producer, Fernando Riaño. Written and directed by Luis Fernando Bottia. Camera (color, 16m), Riaño; editor, Agustín Pinot; music, Adolfo Pacheco, Maestre, Luis Pulido; sound, Osmar Chávez; art direction, Camilo Sandino. Reviewed at San Juan Film Festival, Puerto Rico, Oct. 5, 1988. Running time: **94 MIN.**

With: Orangel (Pangue) Maestre, Iris Oyola, Natalia Caballero, Rosalba Goenaga, Lucy Mendoza, Rafael Caneva, Rebeca Lopez, Grace Molina.

■ **San Juan** — Working from an interesting premise, "La Boda del Acordeonista" (The Accordionist's Wedding) by Colombian director Luis Fernando Bottia is a technically and artistically confused venture that unsuccessfully weds a local folk legend to a contemporary love story.

Outside of a few special-interest locales, b.o. prospects appear slim.

Blown up from 16m, pic lacks visual texture in its retelling of the tale of Mohana, Caribbean goddess of the waters, who carries off a fisherman/accordionist on his wedding night. Editing is quirky and acting uneven.

Colombian folklore and traditional music prove to be the only highlights of this missed venture. Pic grabbed best music prize at the 1986 Nantes fest, along with best first film at the eighth Havana Film Fest. — *Lent.*

The Naked Gun

A Paramount Pictures release. Executive producers, Jerry Zucker, Jim Abrahams, David Zucker. Produced by Robert K. Weiss. Directed by David Zucker. Screenplay, Jerry Zucker, Abrahams, David Zucker, Pat Proft; camera (Technicolor), Robert Stevens, editor, Michael Jablow; music, Ira Newborn; production design, John J. Lloyd; art direction, Donald B. Woodruff; set decoration, Rick T. Gentz; costume design, Mary E. Vogt; sound, Thomas D. Causey, Ronald Judkins; associate producers, John D. Schofield, Kevin M. Marcy; assistant director, John T. Kretchmer; casting, Fern Champion, Pamela Basker. Reviewed at Mann Bruin Theater, L.A., Nov. 22, 1988. MPAA Rating: PG-13. Running time: **85 MIN.**

Frank Drebin . . . . .Leslie Nielsen
Ed Hocken . . . . .George Kennedy
Jane Spencer . . . . .Priscilla Presley
Vincent Ludwig . . . . . .Ricardo Montalban
Nordberg . . . . .O.J. Simpson
Mayor . . . . .Nancy Marchand

■ **Hollywood** — "Naked Gun" is **crass, broad, irreverent, wacky fun — and absolutely hilarious from beginning to end. It's a surefire laugh riot from the "Airplane!" team and no doubt will be a killer at the b.o., leveling the holiday competition through the Christmas season and probably beyond.**

Subtitled "From The Files Of 'Police Squad,' " based on illfated too-hip-for-tv series a few seasons back, comedy from the crazed Jerry Zucker, Jim Abrahams, David Zucker yock factory is chockablock with so many sight gags, it's doubtful audiences will catch every joke from chortling so hard.

This brand of humor isn't for everyone (pic's PG-13 rating is a bit of a stretch), but "ZAZ" — as scripters like to be called — and co-writer Pat Proft have managed to equal the energy level of "Airplane!" and surpass it in the degree of silly celebrity turns.

Leslie Nielsen is the clumsy detective reprising his tv role (including the running gag used in all six episodes where he is contantly driving his car into things) and George Kennedy his straight sidekick who wreaks havoc in the streets of L.A. trying to connect shipping magnate and socialite Ricardo Montalban with heroin smuggling.

Scintilla of a plot weaves in an inspired bit of nonsense with Queen Elizabeth II lookalike Jeannette Charles as the target for assassination at a California Angels' baseball game, where she stands up and does the wave like any other foolish-looking fan, plus a May-December romance between Nielsen and vapid-acting Priscilla Presley whose exchanges of alternatingly drippy or suggestive dialog would make great material for a soap parody.

There are many, many "Three Stooges"-inspired conceits. O.J. Simpson as Nielsen's illfated partner is in the best of them as the temporarily mute hospital-bedridden victim, though mania on the ballfield between the Angels and the Seattle Mariners with Nielsen as the umpire doing a kind of homoerotic weapons check of each player comes a close second.

For all the inspired extremes taken to achieve the greatest comic effect, it is nevertheless something of a feat that nearly every setup is funny, even the overdone few like the wrong-way car chase with driving instructor John Houseman that seemed to be the only unoriginal bit in the entire film.

Tight editing by Michael Jablow intensifies the pace, beginning with the opening sequence where the major terrorist jerks of the world — Khomeini, Khadafi, Amin — are plotting their next target with so-called peaceniks Gorbachev and Arafat in a scene that ends so ludicrously, one only wishes it could come true.

Title sequence alone is brilliant and is vintage ZAZ. Ira Newborn's jazzy score complements the tone of the "ride."

The unsung heroes are casting directors Fern Champion and Pamela Basker who managed to get the best possible performers. In addition to the infatigible Kennedy, the smarmy Montalban and perfectly proper Nancy Marchand as the mayor are perfectly selected stand-ins for famous faces.

Cameos are terrific, especially lineup of sportscasters led by Curt Gowdy who calls the baseball game which is a hoot. Weird Al Yankovic, Dr. Joyce Brothers and radio personalities Ken (Minyard) & Bob (Arthur) go by almost too fast to be fully appreciated for their fees, though producers get their money's worth from showman Reggie Jackson.

Production is firstrate, down to the little details like the takeoff *Daily Variety* headline that flashes across the screen along with a number of other newspaper frontpages showing a photograph of Nielsen and the Queen in a compromising position.

Bathroom humor is kept to a minimum while sex jokes are played up. People offended by this most likely aren't the target audience anyway. —*Brit.*

La Peau et les os
(Skin And Bones)
(CANADIAN-DOCU)

A Canadian National Film Board production. Executive producer, Monique Létourneau. Produced by Louise Gendron. Directed by Johanne Prégent. Camera (color), Jacques Leduc; editor, Pierre Bérnier; sound, Richard Besse. Reviewed at Intl. Festival of New Cinema and Video, Montreal, Oct. 19, 1988. Running time: **90 MIN.**
With: Hélène Bélanger, Sylvie-Catherine Beaudoin, Louise Turcot, Hubert Gagnon, Sophie Faucher.

■ **Montreal — Johanne Prégent's first feature film is a thorough yet somewhat confused attempt to both fictionalize and document the problem of self-inflicted starvation,** anorexia.

There are three different stories being told simultaneously, and even though they're all compelling tales about anorexia victims, two stories in fiction format and one in docu style make for awkward continuity.

The first fiction story revolves around a convent where one of the sisters (Sylvie-Catherine Beaudoin) starves herself to death "to understand the poor and gain love" from God. Filming and music attempt an "Agnes Of God" intensity fairly successfully, but it is never clear if this scenario is intended to explain the roots of anorexia or its significance to the other two stories in the film.

The second fiction story concerns the family problems of a teenager, Andréanne, who develops anorexia to prove she can control her life and gain her father's love. Hélène Bélanger's interpretation is overshadowed by a *real* anorexia victim, Eisha, the natural star of the docu segments.

Footage of Eisha when she was barely more than a skeleton, elegantly mixed with scenes of her talking about the affliction in retrospect, provide the chilling shock value the whole feature clearly was intended to achieve.

Feature is best suited to family tv and fest venues. —*Suze.*

Mississippi Burning

An Orion Pictures release. Produced by Frederick Zollo and Robert F. Colesberry. Directed by Alan Parker. Screenplay, Chris Gerolmo. Camera (color), Peter Biziou; editor, Gerry Hambling; music, Trevor Jones; production design, Philip Harrison, Geoffrey Kirkland; art direction, John Willett; set decoration, Jim Erickson; costume design, Aude Bronson Howard; supervising sound editor, Bill Phillips; assistant director, Aldric La'Auli Porter. Reviewed at Orion Pictures screening room, Los Angeles, Nov. 22, 1988. MPAA Rating: R. Running time: **125 MIN.**
Anderson	Gene Hackman
Ward	Willem Dafoe
Mrs. Pell	Frances McDormand
Deputy Pell	Brad Dourif
Mayor Tilman	R. Lee Ermey
Sheriff Stuckey	Gailard Sartain
Townley	Stephen Tobolowsky
Frank Bailey	Michael Rooker
Lester Cowens	Pruitt Taylor Vince
Agent Monk	Badja Djolm
Agent Bird	Kevin Dunn

■ **Hollywood — Though its credibility is undermined by a fanciful ending, "Mississippi Burning" ranks as one of the most potent and insightful views of racial turmoil yet produced. Approach is fictional, but Chris Gerolmo's script captures much of the truth in its telling of the impact of a 1964 FBI probe into the murders of three civil rights workers.**

Director Alan Parker does some of his best work yet, and boxoffice return should be strong.

Story follows the FBI men (Gene Hackman and Willem Dafoe) who've been sent down to Jessup, Miss., to investigate the disappearance of three voter activists, one black and two white Jews.

Dafoe is a straightforward, humorless Harvard man who's put in charge though he knows little of the South; his straightforward tactics quickly prove dangerous. Hackman, a former Mississippi sheriff himself, is a deceptively easygoing jokester who knows now to sidle around people.

The two run into resistance from both the guilty parties and the blacks, who've been terrorized into silence. It's the fearless Dafoe who wears a hole through the wall and Hackman who knows what to do on the other side.

Dafoe gives a disciplined and noteworthy portrayal of Ward, who squelches his emotions as his moral indignation burns, and whose few bitten-off words are direct and searing. But it's Hackman who steals the picture as Anderson, a messily sympathetic man who connects keenly but briefly with the people, and feels generally powerless to change things.

Glowing performance of Frances McDormand as the deputy's wife who's drawn to Hackman is an asset both to his role and the picture.

Parker pushes the picture along at a fervent clip, with the character scenes back-to-back with chases or violence. The burnings, bombings and lynchings are so frequent that they grow wearisome, but if they are what it takes to reach the resonance of the scene in which the black preacher cries "I have no more love to give," then the filmmaker did the right thing.

Film is richly and authentically decorated and beautifully photographed and conceived. Parker finds images that stay with the eye, such as the line of black-suited FBI men slogging into a swamp behind a stolid Indian, or the blacks holding a service in the ruins of their burned-out church.

Pic's entertainment value is assured by its yahoo-style ending, but real value is in its reminder that change is never easily won.

Trevor Jones' original music and understated score of spirituals and honky-tonk tunes are just right — inspirational and simple. —*Daws.*

Tequila Sunrise

A Warner Bros. release of a Mount Co. production. Produced by Thom Mount. Executive producer, Tom Shaw. Written and directed by Robert Towne. Camera (Deluxe color), Conrad L. Hall; editor, Claire Simpson; music supervisor, Danny Bramson; music, David Grusin; production design, Richard Sylbert; art direction, Peter Lansdown Smith; costume design, Julie Weiss; sound (Dolby stereo), Bruce Bisenz; assistant directors, David Anderson, Albert Shapiro; second unit director, Dave Cass; second unit camera, Robert E. Seaman; casting, Bonnie Timmerman. Reviewed at Warner Bros. studios, L.A., Nov. 22, 1988. MPAA Rating: R. Running time: **116 MIN.**
Dale McKussic	Mel Gibson
Nick Frescia	Kurt Russell
Jo Ann Vallenari	Michelle Pfeiffer
Escalante	Raul Julia
Maguire	J.T. Walsh
Gregg Lindroff	Arliss Howard
Shaleen	Ann Magnuson
Andy Leonard	Arye Gross
Cody McKussic	Gabriel Damon

■ **Hollywood — There's not much kick in this cocktail, despite its mix of quality ingredients. Casually glamorous South Bay is the setting for a story of little substance as writer-director Robert Towne attempts a study of friendship and trust but gets lost in a clutter of drug dealings and police operations.**

Mel Gibson plays Dale (Mac) McKussic, a former bigtime drug operator who's attempting to go straight just about the time his high school pal, cop Nick Frescia (Kurt Russell), is required to bust him. Frescia tries to dodge the duty by pressuring his friend to get out, but Mac owes one last favor to an old friend who's a Mexican cocaine dealer (Raul Julia).

Russell and Gibson are pushed into a cat-and-mouse game, complicated by their attraction to high-class restaurant owner Jo Ann Vallenari (Michelle Pfeiffer).

Frescia moves right in on her, figuring he'll use her to keep track of Mac, who's a regular customer. Mac takes the long road in a campaign to convince her he's worth getting involved with.

Pfeiffer quickly tumbles for Frescia, until she discovers she's being used. When Mac finally tips his hand, she falls for his sincerity. But by then, Mac's Mexican drug connection has arrived and the police are dragging in their surveillance net.

Ending piles up contrivance and cliché amid fireworks and gunfire. Story has chased off in so many directions that all of its goals elude it.

Characters may be true to life for a certain milieu, but never are particularly compelling. Scenes set in Jo Ann's restaurant have a nighttime soap quality that doesn't help.

Gibson projects control skating atop paranoia, and is appealing as a man you'd want to trust. Russell is fine as the slick cop who's confused by his own shifting values, and Pfeiffer achieves a rather touching quality with her gun-shy girl beneath the polished professional.

Dave Grusin's predictable light jazz soundtrack emphasizes the clichés and slickness of the story, and the sense that it's directed at a yuppie consumer market. —*Daws.*

Yoom Helw...Yoom Mor
(Sweet Days, Bitter Days)
(EGYPT)

An El Alamia for TV & Cinema production and release. Produced by Hussein Kalla.

Directed by Khairy Bishara. Screenplay, Bishara, Fayez Ghali; camera, Tarek El'Telmessani; art direction, Ounsi Abou Seif. Reviewed at Carthage Film Festival (competing), Tunis, Oct. 23, 1988. Running time: 125 MIN.
Aicha ....Faten Hamama
Orabi ....Mohamed Mounir
Souad ....Abla Kamel
Sanaa ....Hanan Yousef
Also with: Simone.

■ **Tunis — Popular thesp Faten Hamama won best actress kudos at the Carthage fest for her Mother Courage role in "Sweet Days, Bitter Days" by quality helmer Khairy Bishara.**

Though some found her performance unnervingly above the lines, Hamama is the center of this melodrama from the backstreets of Cairo. Place and time are never specified, though, and story has a generality that leaves it empty in the middle. Its easy watchability is a virtue that should help at the box-office and get it screened in Egyptian film weeks.

Aicha (Hamama) is an enterprising, sly, domineering widow who always manages to stay one step ahead of catastrophe. In an attempt to keep body and soul together, her four daughters honest and her young son a breadwinner, Aicha loses all — though there's consolation at the end to dry the tears.

Film is strong on atmosphere, but the poor neighborhood where the family lives seems too picturesque to be authentic. The daughters conduct miserable lives, working out marriage contracts with bounders like Mohamed Mounir, who marries one daughter and seduces another. The little boy is the most convincing actor of the lot; taken out of school to work at 10, he runs away from Mama to become a street urchin.

Technical work is professional.
— Yung.

Book Of Days
(COLOR/B&W)

A Tatge-Lasseur Prods. (N.Y.)/Foundation for the Arts/La Sept production in association with Alive From Off Center. Produced by Catherine Tatge, Dominique Lasseur. Written and directed by Meredith Monk. Camera (color, b&w), Jerry Pantzer; editor, Girish Bhargava; music, Monk; production design, Jean Vincent Puzos; associate producer, Amy Schatz. Reviewed at Intl. Festival of New Cinema & Video, Montreal, Oct. 31, 1988. Running time: 73 MIN.
With: Gerd Wameling, Lucas Hoving, Rob McBrien, Gail Turner, Greger Hansen, Meredith Monk.

■ **Montreal — Meredith Monk's first feature is everything one would expect from an awardwinning performance artist living in New York city. It's theatrical, intense and refreshing.**

With a flair for dramatics, Monk's story is a blast to the past as she subtly parallels the joys and fears of the everyday man living in the Middle Ages versus a modern metropolis.

The film begins with modern construction workers dynamiting a brick wall, effectively "blasting" one into the tranquility of the 13th century.

Monk employs a unique technique to exaggerate the similarities and differences between these centuries: she interviews people from the 13th century with contemporary equipment. This black and white footage is occasionally intercut with color flashes to the present where life is frantic and speechless.

Monk herself appears in the ancient footage as the town's crazy woman who can see into the future. She also aids a young girl to decipher her own futuristic flashes.

The foreboding visual mood of ancient times — including references to famine, war and disease — is delicately balanced with a script suggesting life was fine when expectations were simple and there was no definition for the word stress. However, "Book Of Days" — a title indicative of the Dear Diary format — carefully avoids a romantic vision of simpler days.

Then-current fears of leprosy are offered as a parallel against today's fear of AIDS and the origins of modern genocide are inherent in Monk's depiction of ancient massacres.

A minimalist soundtrack complements this poetic presentation featuring a cast of theater veterans, which is sure to appeal to lovers of theater, performance art and sophisticated experimental cinema.

Ultimately, "Book Of Days" is a hopeful vision which prophesizes that things haven't really changed.
— Suze.

Elvis Hansen — en samfundshjälper
(Elvis Hansen — A Pillar Of Society) (DANISH)

A Regnar Grasten Film release of Regnar Grasten Film with Nordisk Film production. Produced by Sven Methling. Directed by Jan Hertz. Screenplay, Ole Boje, based on story by Grasten; camera (Eastmancolor), Peter Roos; editor, Maj Soya; music, Michael Hardinger, Jörgen Thorup; sound, Leif Jensen; costumes, Annelise Hauberg; associate producer, Jesper Boas Smith. Reviewed at Palads, Copenhagen, Nov. 23, 1988. Running time: 75 MIN.
Elvis Hansen ....Steen Springborg
Herdis, his wife ....Lone Helmer
Brian, their son ....Jörn Lendorph
Alex von Porter ....Poul Bundgaard
Putte, his wife ....Kirsten Rolffes
Ingrid, their daughter ...Britta Michaelsen
Also with: Ove Sprogöe, Jesper Klein, Ulf Pilgaard, Leif Skouby, Eva Karitz, Ulla Jessen, Birthe Backhausen, Vera Gebuhr.

■ **Copenhagen — "Elvis Hansen — A Pillar Of Society" gives no credit to the fact that it is strikingly similar to Dick Maas' 1986 Dutch farce "Flodder," which was distributed in Europe outside Holland by UIP to limited success.**

If "Elvis Hansen" makes it at all, it will be on Danish home turf where mere appearance of popular thesps in incongruous situations usually rates a laugh.

As in "Flodder," title character is a vulgar lout who, with his family, is relocated from his condemned slum dwelling to a minor mansion in a plush neighborhood. The Hansens wreak havoc on the respectability and property of their rich neighbors.

What Danish writer Ole Boje and director Jan Hertz have failed to transfer convincingly from the original Dutch pic is that the lout and his thieving family are lovable characters, and that they possess folksy wisdom that eventually endears them to their neighbors.

As played by Steen Springborg, Elvis is just loud, so loud his own huge laughs drown out whatever witticisms he may have spouted. Joining him in overacting is Lone Helmer as his wife and Kirsten Rolffes as the next-door society lady. Trying not to look too embarrassed, stellar actors Ove Sprogöe and Jesper Klein add shine to their cameos, while Poul Bundgaard and Ulf Pilgaard seem to shrink within themselves as they go dutifully about earning paychecks in rather major roles.

A lack of narrative, directorial and editing techniques is seen throughout. A note about the title: a Pillar of Society is colloquial Danish for beer bottle opener. — Kell.

Stormquest
(ARGENTINE)

An Aries Film production, in association with Benlox Investment. Executive producer, Ed Garland. Produced by Hector Olivera. Directed by Alex Sessa. Screenplay, Charles Saunders, from story by Sessa; camera (Citeco color), Leonard Solis; editor, Ed Lowe; music, Cardozo Ocampo; sound, George Stavropoulos; production design, Albert T. Naxi; assistant director, Albert Leech; production manager, Ralph Smoker; second unit camera, Oscar Onzal; associate producer, Frank K. Isaac Jr.; casting, Geno Havens, Leech. Reviewed on Media Home Entertainment vidcassette, N.Y., Nov. 16, 1988. Running time: 89 MIN.
Zar ....Brent Huff
Ara ....Kai Baker
Tani ....Monica Gonzaga
Sulan ....Rocky Giordani
Stormqueen ....Linda Lutz
Kinya ....Dudizile Mkhize
Asha ....Christina Whitaker
Girda ....Anne Marie Ricci
Also with: Nilda Raggi, Pia Uribel, Annie Larronde, Marc Woinski, George Chernoff.

■ **"Stormquest" is an enjoyable fantasy feature lensed in Argentina that Philip Wylie might have enjoyed: the women battling the men.**

Unlike Wylie's classic novel (yet to be filmed) "The Disappearance," in which men and women are split off in separate societies, here momism is carried to the nth degree as women have subjugated men. In the kingdom of Ishtan, men are either studs or drones, while neighboring kingdom Kimbia has dispensed with men altogether (the femmes go hunting elsewhere for an unwary male when procreation requires a sperm donation).

Statuesque Kai Baker stars as a woman of Kimbia condemned to death when she rescues her sister Christina Whitaker from execution for having romanced and protected a man. Duo and their black sorceress pal Dudizile Mkhize team up with he-man Brent Huff and help him in his male revolt for equality in Ishtan.

Pic sports good action scenes and its trump card is extensive footage of vast waterfalls located in Argentina. Black humor and comic relief (some of it in rather poor taste) is provided energetically by Linda Lutz as Ishtan's chubby, kinky Stormqueen, who is revealed to be something else again at pic's climax.

Huff, convincing in these roles ever since "Perils Of Gwendoline," and the beauteous babes acquit themselves well and supporting cast is adequately dubbed into English. Pic fits neatly as a companion piece to helmer Alex (Alejandro) Sessa's previous effort "Amazons" with a village set familiar from earlier Aries and Concorde fantasies shot in Argentina. — Lor.

To Magiko Yiali
(The Magic Glass) (GREEK)

Produced and directed by Maria Gavala. Screenplay, Gavala, Thodoros Soumas; camera (color), Phillipos Koutsaftis; editor, Ioanna Spiliopoulou; music, Mozart, Schubert, Dizzy Gillespie and a children's song; costumes, Amalia Michailidou; sound, Argiris Lazaridis. Reviewed at Greek Film Festival, Thessaloniki (competing), Oct. 7, 1988. Running time: 103 MIN.
Nikoletta ....Noni Ioannidou
Markos ....Akis Sakellariou
Also with: Smaragda Diamantidou, Bonita Papastathi, Lelouda Petrou, Babis Hatzidakis.

■ **Thessaloniki — "The Magic Glass" is a lightweight romantic drama about a suspicious wife who suspects her husband is up to hanky-panky. Initially it is developed entertainingly if overly cutely, but the various plot threads are never woven into a cohesive whole and the pic fizzles midway through.**

Nikoletta returns to Athens after a sojourn to an island. Her husband Markos eagerly awaits her and has prepared a special meal which is apparently unpalatable. She is curious when Markos keeps going to the bathroom.

Upon investigating, she looks through their bathroom window and spies a curvaceous neighbor massaging her breasts with cream. Nikoletta decides this must be the object of her husband's lust and becomes concerned with her own sex appeal and discusses this with a friend.

Markos meets a woman with a dog who shows him her box with a "magic glass" in which one can see anything one wants, in any color. Oddly, the significance of this "magic glass" of the title is never explored nor is it seen again.

Although Nikoletta is described as a "girl of contemporary Athens," she seems surprisingly conventional in her relationship with her husband and her close friend. The humorous touches, although developed without finesse, are welcome and quite a rarity in the often overly somber Greek films.

Noni Ioannidou as the wife is gorgeous and shows promise, as does Akis Sakellariou whose demeanor and comic timing are reminiscent of Gérard Depardieu.
—Sam.

New York — Batavia
(DUTCH-DOCU-COLOR/B&W)

A Meatball Stichting Werkgroep Video, The Hague production for VPRO TV. Distributed by NIS, The Hague. Written and directed by Rien Hagen. Camera (color), Jan Blom; editor, Hagen, Cesar Messmaker; music consultant, Fred Smits; sound, Max Mollinger, P. Calicher; decor, Messmaker. Produced with assistance from Dutch Filmfund. Reviewed at Nyon Intl. Film Festival, Switzerland, Oct. 17, 1988. Running time: 130 MIN.

Voices of Joanna Stevens, Harry Barrowslough.

■ **Nyon** — "New York — Batavia" **is a docudrama reconstruction of events that occurred more than 40 years ago in New York City and in Batavia (in the former Dutch East Indies; it is now renamed Jakarta, capital of Indonesia).**

The letters of a devoted wife and husband, separated by the war, cover two years and provide voiceover commentary in English. The film transcends their family predicaments and reverberates toward the entire Southeast Asia upheaval — World War II, Japanese occupation and liberation by British troops, culminating in the independence of those native peoples, who won and founded the modern state of Indonesia after 350 years of Dutch rule.

Fortunately, the film uses a minimum of dramatic reenactments, which are clumsy, and instead concentrates on rare b&w footage from the National Archives, BBC, Polygoon (Netherlands Newsreel) and other sources.

The husband is a dutiful Dutch civil servant who returns to Batavia as the war is ending, when the Dutch government sought to refurbish its once profitable Southeast Asian empire. The days of empires had passed, as he recognizes, as the Indonesian nationalists take heart, having seen the white man beaten by non-whites, the Japanese. The film catches that historic turnaround. —Hitch.

Quebec, Une Ville
(CANADIAN-DOCU)

A Les Prods. Dix-Huit and Films François Brault, Montreal production. Distributed by Cinema Plus, Montreal. Written and directed by Gilles Carle. Camera (color, 16m), Brault; music, François Guy; editor, Christian Marcotte; music numbers performed by Chloe Sainte-Marie. Reviewed at Nyon Intl. Film Festival, Switzerland, Oct. 20, 1988. Running time: 84 MIN.

■ **Nyon** — Gilles Carle, dean of French Candian documentary, portrays Quebec City's special qualities, adding humor, history and interviews with Quebec experts. The film is entertaining and informative.

The old French vs. British rivalry in Canada, Quebecois patriotism and the controversial separatist movement are parts of this film, documented by stock footage, artifacts, drawings and military memorabilia. The emphasis is on modern Quebec.

Satiric commentary comes via Chloe Sainte-Marie, chanteuse and magician who looks like a Hollywood starlet in Central Casting Navajo costuming, with electric guitar backup from a quartet of young men wearing Indian headfeathers.
—Hitch.

H Fanella Me To Ennia
(Striker With The No. 9)
(GREEK)

A Greek Film Center/ET-1/Pantelis Voulgaris production. Directed by Voulgaris. Screenplay, Vangelis Raptopoulos, based on novel by Menis Koumandareas; camera (color), Alexis Grivas; editor, Takis Yannopoulos; music, Stamatis Spanoudakis; sets-costumes, Julia Stavridou; sound, Andreas Achladis. Reviewed at Greek Film Festival, Thessaloniki (competing), Oct. 5, 1988. Running time: 121 MIN.

Bill . . . . Stratos Tzortzoglou
Bartender . . . . Themis Bazaka
Also with: Nikos Bousdoukos, Stamatis Tzelepis, Nikos Tsachiridis, Costas Kleftoyannis, Stavros Kalaroglou, Zanno Danias, Yannis Hadziyannis, Vassilis Vlachos, Katia Sperelaki, Anna Avgoula, Thanassis Mylonas.

■ **Thessaloniki** — Pantelis Voulgaris has made a fast-paced, visually appealing action-drama, "Striker With The No. 9," which should appeal to broad audiences in Europe in theatrical, video and tv releases. Enough footage was shot to make a 4-hour miniseries.

"Striker" is a profile of Vassilis, or "Bill," who is a restless football (soccer) forward. He wanders from bar to bar and woman to woman while yearning to be a sports star. Bill's dream comes true but his triumph is short-lived when he becomes entangled in the wheelings and dealings that underlie professional sports and that seem to take precedence over the well-being of the players.

The excellent lensing by Alexis Grivas is especially adept at capturing the action on the field. Stamatis Spanoudakis' score, which ranges from simple folk instruments to powerful synthesizers, provides a driving rhythm which accents Bill's exhiliration when he scores the winning goal and the crowd goes wild.

Stratos Tzortzoglou is appealing as the young athlete and Themis Bazaka distinguishes her role as the sympathetic bartender who has a soft spot for Bill. Supporting thesping includes a polished performance by Yannis Hadziyannis, one in a series of Bill's chainsmoking coaches who promises Bill an interview with a first-division coach if he "throws" a game.

Action scenes on the field are balanced by amorous interludes and nighttime escapades, including one realistic outing to an earthy nightclub at which Bill dances a cocky zeybekiko while his companions break plates.

"Striker" was largely overlooked in the major awards at Thessaloniki, receiving only two minor prizes. Although it doesn't have the emotional depth of helmer's 1985 "Stone Years" or the touching intimacy of Voulgaris' "The Engagement Of Anna" (1972) it's nevertheless an audience pleaser with solid commercial appeal. —Sam.

Kaftane El Hob
(Caftan Of Love)
(MOROCCAN-FRENCH)

An Agence Universelle Cine Theater (Morocco) release of an Imago Film (Morocco)/Cine Magma (Paris) coproduction. Executive producer, Frank Cabot. Directed by Moumen Smihi. Screenplay, Gavin Lambert, Smihi; camera (color), Jean-Michel Humeau; editor, Martine Giordano; music, Jorge Arriagada. Reviewed at Carthage Film Festival (competing), Tunis, Oct. 24, 1988. Running time: 90 MIN.

Khalil . . . . Mohamed Mehdi
Rachida . . . . Nathalie Roche
Also with: Nezha Regragui, Larbi Doghmi, Touria Jebrane, Chaibia Adraoui.

■ **Tunis** — "Caftan Of Love," second in a series of films about helmer Moumen Smihi's native Tangiers, is a fable that starts out better than it finishes.

Smihi loads pic with references to psychoanalysis and film classics, and builds on intriguing situation of a man married to a narcissistic murderess.

Somewhere between the thriller and the Scheherazade tale, however, "Caftan" loses its way, mainly because neither of the principals comes across sympathetically. Outings for this rather ambitious film probably will be Moroccan film weeks.

Khalil, played with expressionless hauteur by shaggy-haired Mohamed Mehdi, is a rich young bachelor who prefers farming at his family's country house to city life. He dreams about a beautiful girl named Rachida (kittenish Nathalie Roche), and the next day meets her on the street in flesh and blue jeans.

Despite his parent's displeasure at the girl's merchant class origins, Khalil marries her. At first their life is happy, though Rachida is hooked on staring at her lovely reflection in the mirror for hours on end. When a son is born, her mirror image coaxes her to kill the child, starting a cycle of split-personality murders. Khalil consults a shrink, but the film ends mystically, with Khalil living with his dead love in his dreams.

In the midst of these convolutions, the modernity of the couple comes as a comic surprise. Tech credits are okay. —Yung.

Rattornas vinter
(Rat Winter)
(SWEDISH)

A Vestron Pictures release of a Filmstallet production for Exat & CoKb. Produced by Anders Birkeland. Written and directed by Thomas Hellberg, based on novel by Erik Eriksson. Camera (color), Peter Mokrosinski; editor, Thomas Holéwa; music, Bengt Anre Wallin, Nils Landgren; sound (Dolby), Bosse Persson, Lasse Ulander; production design, Anders Barrús; costumes Lena Mari Wallström; production manager, Stefan Lundberg, Johann Zollitsch. Reviewed at the Camera, Malmö, Sweden, Nov. 22, 1988. Running time: 78 MIN.

Walter Olsson . . . . Kent Andersson
Maria/Lilly . . . . Ulrika Hansson
Carina . . . . EvaBritt Strandberg
John B. Svensson . . . . Peder Falk
Stellan . . . . Stig Engström
Anita . . . . Helena Bergström
Susanne . . . . Eva Carlström
Leo . . . . Dan Lindhe
Also with: Johan Sörberg, Mia Benson, Lasse Petterson, Björn Kjellman, Lena Nilsson, Fredrik Ohlson, Anita Ekström, Peter Alvérus, Torsten Wahlund, Göran Boberg.

■ **Malmö, Sweden** — Thomas Hellberg, an accomplished stage/screen actor, bows as writer-helmer with "Rat Winter," a murky symbol-laden actioner about an elderly loner one day faced with a 13-year-old-girl forced into drug addiction and prostitution by a gang of crooks.

The loner (a subdued performance by Kent Andersson) has spent most of his life on the high seas with an occasional detour into amateur boxing. We are given no clue why his indignation at seeing Maria (played forcefully by Ulrika Hansson) ply her trade under her nom de guèrre Lilly makes him kill the gang's two leaders.

The point is made, however, that the old man is frustrated by the laxity of local authorities in dealing with child prostitution. In hunting down his targets, he is aided by Carina (EvaBritt Strandberg), a veteran prostitute with, quite obviously, the requisite heart of gold. Without her, the ex-sailor probably would have been killed himself.

Hellberg never bothers to explain his characters; they simply serve as symbols.

Peter Mokrosinski's camera depicts Stockholm's hellish side with artistry and expertise, presenting impressionistic portraits of squalor. This detracts from any suspense in the story, and while the characters gradually develop into phantoms of the underworld, the film dies from lack of real psychological and artistic depth. —*Kell.*

La Citadelle
(The Citadel)
(ALGERIAN)

A CAAIC production and release. Written and directed by Mohamed Chouikh. Camera (Eastmancolor), Allel Yahiaoui; editor, Yamina Chouikh; music, Jawad Fasla; production manager, Mohamed Tahar Harhoura. Reviewed at Carthage Film Festival, Tunis, Oct. 29, 1988. Running time: **95 MIN.**
Kaddour . . . . Khaied Barkat
Sidi . . . . Djillali Ain-Tedeles
Helima . . . . Fettouma Ousliha
Aissa . . . . Momo
Nedjma . . . . Fatima Belhadj
Also with: Boumedienne Sirat, Nawel Zaatar, Hamid Habati, Ourdia, Sissani, Mohamed Bouamari, Mohamed Haimour, Asmaa.

■ **Tunis — Perhaps Algeria's best all-around entry of the year, "The Citadel" is a moving, compelling tale of a young man forced to marry.**

Switching the roles around, director Mohamed Chouikh presents a powerful indictment of patriarchal Arab society, with its polygamy, wife-beating and contempt for sensitivity. Although asked for by fests in Montreal, Venice, Karlovy Vary and Carthage, film has been plagued by misfortune and has never competed anywhere except at the local Algerian fest in Annaba, where it won first prize.

In a rugged little village, life is divided into male and female society. The men have as many wives as they can afford. The women have as many babies as they can (they also do all the cooking and weave cloth all day). The men have a good time joking and hustling each other; the women wear head-to-foot veils, etc.

Old Sidi has three oppressed wives (one on the verge of depressive suicide) and wants another. He beats his adoptive son Kaddour (expressive Khaied Barkat) for mooning romantically over a married woman; then slips into the same woman's house and seduces her. Poor Kaddour, meanwhile, performs penance and magic rites dictated by a charlatan guru to win the girl's affection.

Sidi vows to marry Kaddour off in one day or repudiate his wives. In order to keep his vow he has the eager boy go through an elaborate wedding ceremony (stunningly lensed), only to find the bride beneath the veil is a wooden store dummy. Kaddour throws himself and his "bride" off a cliff in front of the laughing village.

Chouikh fills out this grim Tale of Hoffmann with a great sense of humanity, witty dialog and poignant portraits of the victims of religious-cultural excess. Film knows how to balance its tears with laughter.

Cast is first-rate, though Barkat stands out in the memory as the unforgettable little-man hero. —*Yung.*

Bikutsi Water Blues
(L'Eau de misère)
(CAMEROONIAN)

A COE release of a Les Films du Raphia production. Produced, written and directed by Jean Marie Teno. Camera (color), Joseph Guerin; editor, Noun Serra; music, Zanzibar and the Têtes Brulées. Reviewed at Carthage Film Festival (competing), Tunis, Oct. 25, 1988. Running time: **104 MIN.**
Boy . . . . Alphonse
Teacher . . . . Marie Philomene Mga
Sanitation director . . . . Tadie Tuene
Also with: Zanzibar & the Têtes Brulées, Tabi Abossolo, Marthe Ewane, Essindi Mindja, Ngonga Ignace.

■ **Tunis — Jean Marie Teno's "Bikutsi Water Blues" puts a timid fictional frame around a documentary on sanitation problems in Cameroon. Film gives the impression being made for local educational purposes, with a lot of sugar on the pill.**

Structure is not the pic's strong point. It begins with a scene of a schoolboy breaking a water jug filled with bad water. That night he explains what he learned in school to his family and neighbors. At school, a dynamic new teacher (Marie Philomene Mga) introduces her class to a sanitation engineer (Tadie Tuene) who recalls his first day at work. For some reason, wild and wooly rock band Zanzibar & the Têtes Brulées is in the classroom, performing.

Just when all these parentheses seem ready to close, "Bikutsi" turns into a series of interviews with locals who explain that, though the Cameroon is full of water, little of it is drinkable. Two illnesses out of three are caused by contaminated water.

This curious effort cries out for logical editing; it is definitely too long to be entertaining. What it does do well is show scenes of everyday African life with powerful simplicity and raw directness. —*Yung.*

Bab Sama Maftouh
(A Door On Heaven)
(MOROCCAN-TUNISIAN-FRENCH)

A France Media (Paris)/CCM (Morocco)/Satpec (Tunis) production. Executive producer, Hassan Daldoul. Written and directed by Farida Benlyazid. Camera (color), Georges Barski; editor, Moufida Tlati; music, Anouar Braham; art direction, Khadija Lahman, Latifa Amor. Reviewed at Carthage Film Festival (competing), Tunis, Oct. 24, 1988. Running time: **105 MIN.**
Nadia . . . . Zakia Tahiri Gomperiz
Kirana . . . . Chaibia Adraoui
Leila . . . . Eva St. Paul
Also with: Soumaya Akaaboun, Bachir Skirej, Baygua, Mourad Gamra.

■ **Tunis — "A Door On Heaven" describes the dawning of spirituality in a rich Moroccan girl used to being a material girl in Paris.**

On a production plane, "A Door On Heaven" distinguishes itself for two reasons: It is the first Moroccan-Tunisian coprod and it is the first Moroccan feature directed by a woman.

An eye-catching film, "Door" could find offshore audiences at women's meets. Others may find the heroine's illumination through liberally interpreted Islam a hard tale to swallow, however glittering the surroundings.

Nadia, seductively limned by Zakia Tahiri Gomperiz, arrives in her native Fez to see her dying father, a Westernized patriarch who used to go around in tailored suits and a bowler hat. With her black minidress and red & blue tinted hair, Nadia feels out of place in the family mansion, a superb old house imbued with tradition. There is even a ghost who puts her on the right path.

At her father's funeral, Nadia is enthralled by the rhythm and words of the Islamic chants. She dons Arab robes and soon founds a retreat for women in the empty house. She fills it with holy women, runaways and battered wives. Nadia leaves the thriving colony with a young man who shares her sensitive, individualistic approach to spiritual life.

Helmer Farida Benlyazid shows a gift for stretching a small budget into a rich-looking film. Lensing has a pro look full of color and gorgeous natural sets. In the main role, Gomperiz goes from punk-aggressive in her Paris phase to enlightened wisdom and gentleness. If the tone veers dangerously into Hari Krishna territory, Benlyazid opens a door to a side of Arab women rarely viewed, working within a potentially commercial framework.
—*Yung.*

A Dama Do Cine Shanghai
(The Lady From The Shanghai Cinema)
(BRAZILIAN)

An Embrafilme release of a Star/Raiz production. Written and directed by Guilherme de Almeida Prado. Camera (color), Jose Roberto Eliezer; editor, Jair Duarte; music, Hermelino Nader; set design, Chico Andrade; costumes, Luis Fernando Pereira. Reviewed at Sorrento Intl. Encounter (official selection), Oct. 28, 1988. Running time: **115 MIN.**
With: Antonio Fagundes, Maitê Proença, Paulo Villaça, José Lewgoy.

■ **Sorrento — This purposely artificial cinephile's delight, a diligent and complex parody of '40s B-grade gangster pics, takes a lusty, job-weary employee on flights of imagination into a celluloid world that seesaws action between fact and fiction. It succeeds as a cult film.**

Lucas (Antonio Fagundes), ex-boxer and unmotivated real estate hireling, ducks into a movie house one night in his gaudy metropolis, where a gangster film is playing.

In the shadowy atmosphere of the near-empty theater, his attention is lured to a fascinating lady, lookalike to the onscreen heroine. This seemingly coincidental encounter is the springboard which launches Lucas, led by wily Suzana (Maitê Proença) through a maze of dangerous and suspenseful crimes and a world of tacky violence.

Tongue-in-cheek antics both on- and off-screen rely on deceptive pranks full of Bogart-style 1-liners.

Careful attention to detail, control of acting, adept imitation of atmosphere, plus toned-down tempo with period-influenced soundtrack make this sharp exercise an enjoyable, if exasperating jaunt. The self-indulgent story manipulation could tire a general audience. —*Chin.*

Bakayaroo! (Watakushi, Okotteimasu)
(You Bloody Fool! I'm Angry)
(JAPANESE)

A Shochiku release of a Kowa Intl. production. Produced by Hideji Miyajima, Kazuko Misawa. Directed by Eriko Watanabe, Tetsuya Nakajima, Takahito Hara, Yukihiko Tsutsumi. Screenplay, Yoshimitsu Morita; camera (color), Koichi Kawakami, Yuichi Osada; editor, Isao Tomita; sound, Hisayuki Miyamoto; music, Masanori Sasaji, Atsushi Nakao, Tomohiko Kira, Kiyohiko Sanba. Reviewed at Shochiku screening room, Tokyo, Oct. 3, 1988. Running time: **93 MIN.**
Shizuka Atsugi . . . . Haruko Sagara
Kazuki Numayama . . . . Tsuyoshi Ihara
Sae Karuma . . . . Narumi Yasuda
Mamoru Oishi . . . . Hiroshi Isobe
Tamako Shiraishi . . . . Maeko Ogawa
Masahisa Masako . . . . Yasuo Daiichi
Tokuko Muraoka . . . . Keiko Saito
Shigeru Sakisaka . . . . Kaoru Kobayashi
Nanako . . . . Shigeru Muroi

■ **Tokyo — "Bakayaroo! (Watakushi, Okotteimasu)" is an omnibus feature of four stories, thematically linked and written by Yoshimitsu Morita.**

Part 2, directed by Tetsuya Nakajima, more than redeems the pic's slow first segment by winningly dealing with a fact of social life in the big city that is seldom, if ever, touched upon in films. Because office lady Narumi Yasuda lives so far away from the capital city's "date spots" and must rely on public transportation, which ceases operation shortly after midnight, her relationship with Hiroshi Isobe deteriorates to the point that he finds a new lover.

A story of a cabdriver precedes the requisite big finish provided by Part 4, directed by Yukihiko Tsutsumi. Kaoru Kobayashi, who tries to master English before a job transfer to Chicago, comes into contact with a number of resident foreigners, not one of them sympathetic. Morita builds up to a punch line with that exquisite sense of timing characterizing the best of his work, such as "Family Game" in 1984. —*Bail.*

Les Tisserands du Pouvoir
(Mills Of Power, Part I)
(CANADIAN-FRENCH)

Produced by René Malo, Marie-José Raymond. Directed by Claude Fournier. Screenplay, Monique Champagne; camera (color), John Berrie; editor, Yurij Luhovy, Fournier; music, Martin Fournier. Reviewed in Montreal, Oct. 20, 1988. Running time: **116 MIN.**
With: Gratien Gélinas, Juliette Huot, Michel Forget, Aurélien Recoing, Paul Hébert, Pierre Chagnon, Donald Pilon, John Wildman, Rémy Girard, Denis Bouchard, Dominique Michel, Andrée Pelletier, Francis Reddy, Anne Létourneau, Gérard Paradis, Corinne Dacla, Vlasta Vrana, Dennis O'Connor, Jean Desailly, Francis Lemaire.

■ Montreal — Politics, power, war, money, romance — all elements essential to a tv miniseries — dominate this feature about Quebecers who migrate to the Eastern U.S. at the turn of the century to find employment from French industrialists.

The fact that this film is part one of two separate features — as well as a kick-off to an epic 6-part miniseries of the same name — is blatant. Helmer Claude Fournier is clearly trying to direct and edit too many stories at the same time. It lacks the action-adventure elements crucial for the big screen.

An enormous cast of well-known Quebecois and French faces are painstakingly established alloting almost equal screentime to each star, which slackens the pace to the speed of a pricey American tv soap.

Endearingly told as a flashback story by an old French-speaking Quebecois man (Gratien Gélinas) living in Rhode Island today, this chapter colorfully contrasts the industrialist era from 1907-1920 to the technological world of 1988.

Gélinas delivers a performance so superb that his apparent insanity in modern times is justified by the end of the film. However, so much time is spent setting his story up, that just when it seems to get rolling, the film ends.

Enter part two which will premiere in Quebec at the end of November. While producing two features to tell one story is somewhat of a revolutionary concept, the miniseries style would be better left to the small screen where you can tune in next week instead of next month. —*Suze.*

Gombrowicz o La Seducción
(Gombrowicz)
(ARGENTINE)

An Instituto Nacional de Cinematografia Argentina (Inca)-Centro Cultural San Martin production. Directed by Alberto Fischerman. Screenplay, Rodolfo Rabanal, Fischerman; camera (color, 16m), Salvador Melita; editor, Rolando Santos; music, Adrian Russovich; art direction, Coca Oderigo; sound, Jorge Longo. Reviewed at Festival Latino, Public theater, N.Y., Aug. 16, 1988. Running time: **110 MIN.**
With: Mariano Betelú, Jorge Di Paola, Juan Carlos Gómez, Alejandro Russovich, Jorge Calvetti, Adolfo de Obieta, Alicia Giangrande, Halina Grodzicka, Maria Switczewska.

■ Argentine feature "Gombrowicz o La Seducción" is an experimental look at Polish writer and dramatist Witold Gombrowicz (1904-1969) and will probably draw comparisons with "My Dinner With Andre" as a talky, albeit entertaining vehicle.

Film lies somewhere between docu and scripted tribute, and is not always successful in its conceits. At the core of the picture is a filmed discussion of the master, who lived in Argentina from 1939-63, by four intelligent and charming "disciples." The audience's role here is as an eavesdropper into Argentine cafe life, the conversations, arguments and above all the friendships and bonds these four men formed with their mentor, a one time Nobel Prize candidate.

Spanish title links the film to Gombrowicz' play "The Seduction." A subtitle notes that this work here is "Played by His Disciples." Through these devices pic attempts to be a cinematic entry into Gombrowicz' oeuvre through style and content, yet this is also the movie's undoing.

The static but fascinating conversations and interactions are crosscut with individual interviews with each of the men, talking-head anecdotes with friends and colleagues from the Polish expatriate community. There are also some obvious and extraneous grating images — such as a little girl repeating a short Gombrowicz poem in Polish over and over to the point of ridiculousness — that interrupt pic's overall texture.

In short, the film is interesting but uneven, which can also be said about the tech credits. Its nearly 2-hour length makes it unwieldy. A tight 1-hour version focusing on the four would give it more direction. —*Lent.*

...Lipotaktis
(...Deserter)
(GREEK)

A Greek Film Center/Giorgos Korras/Christos Voupouras and ET-1 TV production. Written, directed and edited by Giorgos Korras, Christos Voupouras. Camera (color), Andreas Bellis; music, Eleni Karaindrou; sets-costume design, Damianos Zarifis; sound, Nikos Achladis. Reviewed at Greek Film Festival, Thessaloniki (competing), Oct. 8, 1988. Running time: **118 MIN.**
With Stelios Mainas, Toula Stathopoulou, Leonidas Nomikos, Stelios Pavlou, Cinda Stefanopoulou, Giorgos Yannopoulos, Stelios Reppas, Yannis Christoyannis, Magda Tsangani, Tassos Pantzartzis, Panayotis Stamatopoulos.

■ Thessaloniki — "...Deserter" highlights the ambivalent friendship between two young Greeks while they are together in a village. Although beautifully lensed by Andreas Bellis with an evocative string score with haunting bouzouki solos composed by Eleni Karaindrou, film's plot is too weak to sustain interest for two hours.

The first glimpse of Christos, an intense young Athenian and his friend Manolis, a rebel who has been in prison after going AWOL from the army three times, is on a ferry on their way to Manolis' village. Christos has a hard time accepting Manolis' hard drinking and irresponsible behavior. He also views Manolis as his alter ego, a free spirit who follows his impulses for better or worse.

Toula Stathopoulou won the best supporting actress award here for her expressive portrayal of the mother who is caring but exhausted by her constant struggle to make ends meet.

The interiors of village houses authentically recreated, "...Deserter" touches on issues facing contemporary Greece such as the corruption of traditional life by the influx of tourism. Manolis' friends spend long afternoons lolling in a cafe, drinking imported liquor and bragging about their conquests of foreign women.

Pic tries to inject sociological commentary about Manolis and his attempt to adjust to "the harsh society" of the village through voiceover comments representing the thoughts of Christos. More interest is generated by the strong homosexual undercurrent of the excessive male bonding, which is never resolved. —*Sam.*

I Zoe Me Ton Alki
(Life With Alkis)
(GREEK)

A Greek Film Center/Dimitris Collatos production. Written and directed by Dimitris Collatos. Camera (color), Spyros Nounessis; editor, Babis Alepis, Chronis Theocharis; music, Michalis Grigoriou; sets, Lia Kariotou; costumes, Dimitra Sotiropoulou; sound, Athanasios Gagaloudis. Reviewed at Greek Film Festival, Thessaloniki, Oct. 4, 1988. Running time: **101 MIN.**
Father . . . . Dimitris Collatos
Mother . . . . Dora Sitzani
Alkis . . . . Alexandros Collatos
Also with: Costas Bozonis, Katy Kritsotaki, Costas Laos, Panos Nikolaidis, Angelos Georgiadis, Alekos Petrides, Olga Avlonitou, Giorgos Saltoglou.

■ Thessaloniki — "Life With Alkis," a well-intentioned but 1-dimensional autobiographical drama about a father's struggle to maintain custody of his autistic child, will have a hard time attracting a broad general audience but could score well at specialty fests.

The 11-year-old Alkis (Alexandros Collatos) has a high IQ, but shuts himself off from the world. His father (Dimitris Collatos) tries with the aid of a sympathetic psychologist to communicate with his son through games and songs.

His French mother Claudine (Dora Sitzani) is unable to accept her son's condition and goes first to France, then to a Greek island. When she returns, she listens to the advice of a psychiatrist friend. She starts a court case to have Alkis placed in an institution. The father and psychologist wage a battle to keep Alkis at home.

Alexandros Collatos, the real-life Alkis, gives a remarkably sensitive performance which won him an honorable mention from the festival. The elder Collatos, who doubles as helmer and actor, is sympathetic and believable as the father. Instead of being characterized as superhuman, he admits that the strain of devoting his life to nurturing his son alone has taken its toll and he is simply exhausted.

The psychiatrist is portrayed as an unfeeling martinet who adds some unintentional humor when he becomes frustrated with his interaction with Alkis and sheds his clothes as he joins the boy in ripping up a phonebook.

Despite a faint haze to the film in places, technical credits are adequate.

"Alkis" might have served its purpose better if it had been made as a straight docu delving further into the mysterious and much-debated autistic condition. The opening and closing segments featuring the orchestra of the Aegina Autistic Children's Camp add a nice touch and whet one's appetite for more info on this and similar programs.

—*Sam.*

Thelonius Monk: Straight, No Chaser
(DOCU-COLOR/B&W)

A Warner Bros. release of a Malpaso production in association with the Michael Blackwood Co. Executive producer, Clint Eastwood. Produced by Charlotte Zwerin, Bruce Ricker. Production executive, David Valdes. Directed by Zwerin. Camera (Duart color/-b&w), Christian Blackwood, Joan Churchill, Stuart Math; narrator, Samuel E. Wright. Reviewed at The Burbank Studios, Burbank, Calif., Nov. 23, 1988 (also at London Film Festival). Running time: **89 MIN.**

With: Charlie Rouse, Harry Colomby, Barry Harris, Tommy Flanagan, Thelonious Monk Jr., Bob Jones, voice of the Baroness Nica de Koenigswarter.

■ Hollywood — **Usually considered one of the most enigmatic and eccentric of the jazz greats, the late Thelonious Monk gets his image and reputation focused and fortified in this engaging new documentary.**

Based to a great extent upon 14 hours of mostly unseen footage shot in the late 1960s, pic brings this idiosyncratic, innovative figure to life in a way never before possible on film, and fans of his music will have plenty to enjoy.

World premiered at the London Film Festival, pic will be distributed theatrically by Warner Bros., but greater potential lies down the road in vidcassette release.

Although some first-rate material here derives from Monk's handful of American and European tv appearances and a few other sources, film essentially is built around a selection from 14 hours of footage shot by Christian Blackwood over a 6-month period in 1967-68. At the time, Blackwood cut his film down to a 1-hour documentary that was shown once on German tv and was then shelved, as were his outtakes.

Blackwood, Bruce Ricker and Charlotte Zwerin began plotting a use of the latter in the early 1980s, and in 1987 Clint Eastwood, then in the midst of preparing "Bird," saw Ricker's jazz docu "The Last Of The Blue Devils." Eastwood presented that film as a Warner Bros. release in France and Italy, and arranged to finance the completion of the Monk project.

Zwerin and company make a perfunctory stab at conventional biography, quickly runing through his upbringing in San Juan Hill in New York City and his early traditional experience before ushering in the bebop era in the 1940s.

Although top Monk tunes are laced throughout, film really digs in with footage of the pianist at a recording session with Teo Marcero. Monk's seriousness and sense of humor come through strongly here, and heavy interest is maintained through the sections dealing with his erratic behavior, drastic mood swings and especially the major European tour so candidly documented by Blackwood.

The composer is glimpsed getting ready for the trip with his wife Nellie, in the plane, coping with insufficiently briefed and underrehearsed musicians in London, trying to order from room service, and soaking up tumultuous receptions in Paris and Copenhagen, among other stops. Once back in New York, Monk is seen backstage at the Village Vanguard with the Baroness Nica de Koenigswarter, who took him under her wing as she previously had Charlie Parker.

Because Blackwood's footage constitutes the film's great treasure trove, docu possesses a perhaps unavoidably awkward structure, beginning and ending rather abruptly. Filmmakers clearly have opted to include as much of the real man and his music as possible, but still might have slipped in a few more facts.

All those interviewed, notably manager Harry Colomby and Monk's son, contribute worthwhile points of view, but no one ever says, in so many words, what Art Blakey once proclaimed: "Monk is the guy who started it all; he came before Parker and Gillespie."

Similarly, the end of Monk's career is skated over. It seems odd that no footage from his Giants of Jazz tours in the early 1970s is present, and no explanations for the fade-out of his musical career shortly thereafter are offered other than the vague "something happened."

Nevertheless, this is a constantly entertaining, occasionally funny, sometimes bracing look at an insufficiently understood jazz genius, a lovely gift to jazz fans worldwide. —*Cart.*

Antarjali Yatra
(Voyage Beyond)
(INDIAN)

A National Film Development Corp. production. Executive producers, Ravi Malik, Debashish Majumdar. Directed by Goutam Ghose. Screenplay, Ghose, with additional dialog by Sunil Gongopadhaya, from a story by Kamal Kumar Majumdar, camera (Eastmancolor), Ghose; editor, Moloy Banerjae; music, Ghose; production design, Dilipo Banerjee; art direction, Ashoke Bose; set design, Joyti Chatterjee, Anup Mukherjee; costumes, Neelanjana Ghosh. Reviewed at London Film Festival, Nov. 19, 1988. Running time: **118 MIN.**

Baiju	Shatrughan Sinha
Sitaram	Promode Ganguly
Yashobati	Shampa Ghosh

Also with: Basanta Chowdhury, Robi Ghosh, Sajal Roychoudhury, Mohan Agashe, Kalyan Chatterji, Rathin Lahiri.

■ London — **Set in a crucial and complicated period of Indian history, the 1830s, "Voyage Beyond" makes a strong statement about the clash between outmoded conventions and irrepressible human passions.**

Rather than relying on a huge historical canvas to make its points, however, it reduces a complicated story of love and death to its barest bones.

By and large it succeeds, though only a limited arthouse audience will respond to a film so minimalist in its approach that the main action is waiting for a man on a stretcher to die, and where the heroine hardly utters a word, and the only locale is a beachfront along the Ganges.

The dying man is of course a symbol of the Brahmin value system, under particular threat in the period from modern western ideas and practices. Before his funeral pyre is set alight, however, his friends and relatives decide the best way to protect themselves — and profit from their piety — is to procure him a bride. The hapless young woman is expected to defy the new ruling of the colonial government by allowing herself to be burned along with her husband, honoring, that is, the ancient practise of "suttee."

To complicate things, the newly-wed bride is alternately encouraged to be brave by her father (who will inherit the dying man's wealth), and urged to rebel by an Untouchable. However, film is not rational in the sense that characters debate issues: the Untouchable mostly rants and raves; the heroine mostly weeps; the dying man comes to life at the oddest moments, displaying wonderfully funny capacity for jealousy and petulance.

In one powerful scene the heroine demonstrates the bond she feels for her "lord" by saving him from drowning and then wallows in the mud with the Untouchable in an embrace which can only be a prelude to her own doom.

Assured camerawork, disciplined performances and subtle comic touches make this film worth the effort. —*Guid.*

Just Ask For Diamond
(BRITISH)

A Coverstop Film Finances/British Screen/Zenith/Children's Film & Television Foundation/Red Rooster/20th Century Fox production. Produced by Linda James. Directed by Stephen Bayly. Screenplay, Anthony Horowitz, from his novel "The Falcon's Malteser;" camera (Eastmancolor), Billy Williams; editor, Scott Thomas; production design, Peter Murton; art direction, Cliff Robinson; music, Trevor Jones; sound, David Crozier; costumes, Maria Price; special effects, Alan Whibley. Reviewed at London Film Festival, Nov. 20, 1988. Running time: **94 MIN.**

Tim Diamond	Dursley McLinden
Nick Diamond	Colin Dale
Lauren Bacardi	Susannah York
Brenda von Falkenberg	Patricia Hodge
Jack Splendide	Roy Kinnear
The Professor	Michael Medwin
Gott	Peter Eyre
Himmell	Nickolas Grace
Chief Insp. Snape	Bill Paterson
Boyle	Jimmy Nail
Mr. Patel	Saeed Jaffrey

■ London — **"Just Ask For Diamond" is an affectionate homage to the film noir private eye genre, but aimed squarely at the youth audience. Script and direction are witty and refined with an impressive supporting cast giving pic a look of class.**

Film originally was called "The Falcon's Malteser," but an injunction from the Dashiell Hammett estate (which has rights on his novel "The Maltese Falcon") led to the title change. Plot revolves around a box of candies (called Maltesers in the U.K., malted milk balls in the U.S.), hence the original title's pun, which is slightly lost on the new version.

"Just Ask For Diamond" is set in contempo London, but shot with a noir edge and tongue firmly in cheek. Helmer Stephen Bayly — whose only other feature is the Welsh-language "Coming Up Roses" — directs confidently, making good use of offbeat London locales and stylish camera angles.

Pic opens with an attractively drawn credits sequence with a foot-tapping theme song by local band the Wee Papa Girl Rappers and is a lighthearted scene-setter for the pic.

Inept private eye Colin Dale (Nick Diamond) and his young brother Dursley McLinden (Tim Diamond) are paid £200 to look after a box of Maltesers by South American midget Rene Ruiz.

A suitably complicated plot sees them pursued by various villainous types including a skeletal Fat Man (Michael Robbins), bungling German hit man, slinky femme fatale and obligatory hard-nosed cops.

When Dale gets thrown in jail it is up to young McLinden to solve the mystery, which he does in fine style despite being variously bound and gagged, shot at and half buried in cement.

The fine supporting cast seem to relish their roles, with Jimmy Nail (especially) as the brutal policeman Boyle and Susannah York as singer Lauren Bacardi virtually stealing the pic. Youngster McLinden performs manfully though is sometimes unable to give the lines the irony they deserve.

Nice setpieces include a shootout in the Selfridges' Christmas grotto where Father Christmas clone Uncle Holly is shot. Technical credits are all excellent and special notice should go to Anthony Horowitz' amusing adaptation of his popular book. —*Adam.*

Wild Things
(BRITISH)

A BBC Television production. Produced by

David M. Thompson. Directed by Rob Walker. Screenplay, David Pirie; camera (Eastmancolor), John Hooper; editor, Bill Wright; production design, Paul Joel; music, Richard Hartley; sound, Dick Manton; costumes, Dinah Collin; assistant director, Peter Kondal. Reviewed at London Film Festival, Nov. 13, 1988. Running time: **78 MIN.**

Jane	Karen Young
Andrew	Stuart Wilson
Laura	Willow Grylls
Will	Ben Robb
Sarah	Tusse Silberg
Brigadier Buchanan	Donald Churchill
Sophie Buchanan	Janet Henfrey
Felicity Buchanan	Joanna Joseph
Mal Redfern	Aaron Swartz

■ **London — Television pic "Wild Things" proved its cinematic worth in a big-screen showing at the London Film Festival, with fine acting, excellent script, nice direction and impressive Cornish locations.**

Helmer Rob Walker and scripter David Pirie have combined to produce an intelligent, amusing and gripping family drama set in a grand Gothic wave-lashed hotel at Christmas. Stuart Wilson is perfect as the father while young Willow Grylls is excellent as his willful daughter.

Two youngsters — Grylls and Ben Robb — are taken to the hotel for Christmas by their father (Wilson) to meet his new girlfriend Karen Young, an American he plans to marry.

The two start to wage a guerrilla conflict against Young through the meandering corridors of the hotel, finally getting her to admit on video that she doesn't love Wilson. But though the two may have won a battle, the war of "divorce" hangs over them, and the ending, with their mother at hand, is suitably enigmatic.

Scripter Pirie gives the youngsters troubled outlooks — Grylls constantly listens to Eddie Cochran on her headset while Robb stalks the hotel looking for ghosts — as they struggle to come to terms with their parents' separation.

The Cornish locations, though, are the real winners. The stately Newquay hotel stands on a windswept rocky outcrop, leading to some impressive footage and backgrounds. Walker employs unusual camera angles, adroitly handles his young leads and is aided by a strong performance by the underrated Stuart Wilson.

American thesp Young handles her schizophrenic role with aplomb, especially in the closing scenes when faced with video proof of her false affection. Other technical credits are fine. —*Adam.*

Blue elettrico
(Electric Blue)
(ITALIAN)

A Solaris Cinematografica production with RAI-1. Executive producer, Aldo U. Passalacquia. Produced by Adriano Arie. Written and directed by Elfriede Gaeng. Camera (color), Gianfranco Transunto; editor, Claudio Di Mauro; music, Stelvio Cipriani; production design, Davide Bassan; art direction,

Valeria Paoloni; sound, Gianni Zampagni; costumes, Blanche Cardinale. Reviewed at London Film Festival, Nov. 16, 1988. Running time: **86 MIN.**

Tata	Claudia Cardinale
Ale	Sara Triulzi
Bibo	Matteo Mobilia
Silvia	Athina Cenci
Giorgio	William Berger

■ **London — Italo pic "Electric Blue" has an undeniably charming and beguiling quality, with standout performances by the two young leads and a graceful turn by the always elegant Claudia Cardinale.**

Enigmatic ending may not be everyone's choice, but local prospects could be okay; offshore hopes are not too promising.

Pic is a classy affair — crisp photography and direction, excellent locations, proficient cast and an intelligent screenplay combine to offer a sharp child's vision of life, love and death, though the film dips close to the esoteric on occasion.

Brother and sister Ale and Bibo live in a grand mansion, replete with servants and high-tech toys but inattentive parents. The pair make up for their parents' absence with their vivid imaginations, and when a new nanny (Cardinale) arrives she appears to be everything they have been wishing for.

After a funeral, Cardinale explains heaven to the children as lying among the stars full of light and love. With children's logic the two start killing small animals, then gazing at the stars in the hope of seeing the animals on the secret path to heaven.

Ending is either a copout or a clever twist, depending on how you look at it — the children decide to kill themselves to find the route to heaven, but it transpires they were imagining all their adventures while waiting for a new nanny to arrive (who actually turns out to be Cardinale).

First-time director Elfriede Gaeng helms confidently, though her screenplay is a little naive with the overall theme of the film leaning towards pretentiousness. Acting by youngsters Sara Triulzi and Matteo Mobilia is fine, while Cardinale is required to do little more than smile and look serene. —*Adam.*

Dustforough
(The Peddler)
(IRANIAN)

An Arts Bureau of the Organization for the Propagation of Islamic Thought production. Directed by Mohsen Makhmalbaf. Screenplay, Makhmalbaf, from story by Alberto Moravia (first episode); camera (color) (first episode) Homayun Payvar, (second episode) Mehrdad Fahkimi, (third episode) Ali R. Zarindast; editor, Makhmalbaf; music, Majid Antezami. Reviewed at London Film Festival, Nov. 15, 1988. Running time: **95 MIN.**

With: Zohreh Saramadi, Esmail Saramadian, Behzad Behzadpour, Faridkashan Fallah, Morteza Zarrabi.

■ **London — Iranian pic "The Peddler" is made up of three episodes looking at the underbelly of life in**

contempo Iran. Helmer Mohsen Makhmalbaf has crafted a colorful and insightful pic destined for the festival circuit where Iranian movies are few and far between.

First of the three deals with a poverty-stricken couple trying to find someone to adopt their new daughter, but constantly worried about who will take the child. The second features the misadventures of a mentally unstable man looking after his elderly mother.

The third section deals with the peddler of the title. He has witnessed a gangland killing and constantly imagines his own execution by the gang until ultimately he is assassinated.

Despite their dour-sounding subject matter, all three episodes have gentle humor and lush color. Makhmalbaf lapses into pretension occasionally but displays fine skills, especially in the final section where the shootouts almost have a mainstream U.S. gangster-pic feel.

—*Adam.*

Kacamak
(Impromptu)
(TURKISH)

An Arzu/Erler Film production. Produced by Ertem Egilmez, Turker Inanoglu. Written and directed by Basar Sabuncu. Camera (Fujicolor), Erdal Kahraman; editor, Ismail Kalkan; production design, Annie G. Pertan; music, Atilla Ozdemiroglu; sound, Gokhan Siraci; costumes, Annie G. Pertan. Reviewed at London Film Festival, Nov. 15, 1988. Running time: **106 MIN.**

Suna	Mujde Ar
Orhan	Cetin Tekindor
Nermin	Hale Akinli
Ekrem	Engin Senkan
Naciye	Nezihe Becerikli
Remzi	Nezih Tuncay
Guller	Bercis Fesci

■ **London — "Impromptu" has a gentle charm and attractive lead performances by Mujde Ar and Cetin Tekindor, but though intriguing to begin with it rather outstays its welcome and turns repetitive.**

Pic proves, though, that sophisticated cinema does exist in Turkey as it ranges middle-class life and moralities. "Impromptu" takes on the form of a rondo though the ending proves slightly unsatisfactory.

Tekindor and Ar meet at a mortuary identifying the bodies of their spouses — clandestine lovers — both killed in a car crash. They start a series of encounters in flats, restaurants and offices as they come to terms with their losses.

They take on roles of enemies, courting couple and even act like a married pair, but are never really sure how they should be reacting. The end sees them at the scene of the original crash acknowledging they can never really be together. These encounters provide the film's gentle humor, with Basar Sabuncu's fluid direction giving the film a stylish quality. —*Adam.*

Das Kalte Paradies
(Frosty Paradise)
(SWISS)

A Bernard Safarik Filmproduktion/SRG/-Istvan Akos production. Executive producers, Dionys Hunziker, Heidi Kopfer. Produced and directed by Bernard Safarik. Screenplay, Safarik, Jaroslav Vejvoda; camera (color), Widigo von Schultzendorff, Tomi Streiff, Pavel Schnabel; editor, Zuzana Brejcha; art direction, Catherine Walthard-Lutz; music, Gerald Karfiol; sound, Hanspeter Giuliani; costumes, Catherine Warlthard-Lutz, Monika Vogt. Reviewed at London Film Festival, Nov. 14, 1988. Running time: **97 MIN.**

Elba Morales	Nohemi Dragonne
Jan Lipawski	Julius Effenberger
Ruth Egli	Berta Alig
Andreas Wehrli	Istvan Akos
Rosemarie Egger	Verena Keller
Friend of Jan	Wladyslaw Slebodzinski

■ **London — The harsh underbelly of seemingly perfect Switzerland is seen in Bernard Safarik's "Frosty Paradise," dealing with the trials and tribulations of two political refugees hoping to settle in the country. Commercial prospects, though, look nil.**

Safarik's pic was triggered by a newspaper report of a couple of refugees who wanted to marry in Switzerland, were not allowed to and despite having a child the father still was expelled.

That, in essence is the story, though the performances of Julius Effenberger and especially Nohemi Dragonne give the pic a more rounded feel, especially when it comes to their final separation.

Pic opens with the two meeting at a Swiss center for political refugees and follows their attempts to carve out a new life despite numerous bureaucratic setbacks. Safarik shoots in an almost documentary style. —*Adam.*

Utekajme, uz ide!
(Hurry, He's Coming)
(CZECHOSLOVAKIAN)

A Slovenska filmova tvorba production. Produced by Jan Tomaskovic. Directed by Dusan Rapos. Screenplay, Jozef Hariban, Jozef Slovak, Rapos; camera (Orwo color), Vladimir Jesina; editor, Maximilian Remen; production design, Roman Rjachovsky; art direction, Vladimir Matus; music, Jozef Slovak, Rapos; sound, Pavol Sasik; costumes, Tatiana Balkovicova. Reviewed at London Film Festival, Nov. 16, 1988. Running time: **84 MIN.**

Sysel	Marian Zednikovic
Syslova	Zuzana Bydzovska
Dr. Mahm	Milan Lasica
Hadzi	Andrej Hyrc
Andrejka	Slavka Sabova
Dodo	Tomas Zednikovic

■ **London — Czechoslovakia's "Hurry, He's Coming" is a genuine comedy delight, with touches of social commentary and an underlying wry and sometimes hilarious sense of humor. Film proves Czech comedy, on the back of Jiri Menzel's "My Sweet Little Village," is alive and well.**

Helmer-cowriter Dusan Rapos displays a fine eye for comic detail and is well served by an excellent cast who certainly rise to the occasion.

Pic opens with Sysel (Marian Zednikovic), his wife and two children struggling to live in their 1-room flat. Slight envy sets in when single magician Dr. Mahm (Milan Lasica) moves into the larger next-door flat.

In an effort to improve himself, Zednikovic takes up karate, but while practicing kicks a hole in the wall. When the family discover how luxurious their neighbor's flat is they take to staying there while he is out of town.

Comic misadventures abound as Zednikovic is mistaken for the magician, his wife proves her skill as a snake dancer and the children get to enjoy the life of luxury.

Zednikovic as the lugubrious Sysel (replete with Slavic mustache) is excellent, looking suitably bemused. Slavka Sabova as his young daughter is a beautiful delight, while Andrej Hyṛc as Indian magician Hadzi takes "Hurry, He's Coming" away from the parochial feel of some Czech pics. —Adam.

Cheap Shots
(U.S.)

A Twin Swans Corp./Twin Swans Film Associates production. Executive producer, William Coppard. Produced, written and directed by Jeff Ureles and Jerry Stoeffhaas. Camera (Duart color), Thom Marini; editors, Ken McIlwaine, Andrew Praskai; production design, Carl Zollo; art direction, Anne La Lopa; music, Jeff Beal; sound, Dirk Large; costumes, Lana Momano. Reviewed at London Film Festival, Nov. 20, 1988. Running time: **92 MIN.**
Louie Constantine . . . . Louis Zorich
Arnold Posner . . . . David Patrick Kelly
Dotty Constantine . . . Marie Louise Wilson
Jack . . . . Michael Twaine
Franklin . . . . Clarke Gordon
The blond . . . . Patience Moore
Paul . . . . John Galateo

ARCHIVE REVIEWS

Oktyabar
(October)
(SOVIET-B&W)

A British Film Institute Distribution presentation in association with the London Film Festival and Contemporary Films Ltd. of a Sovkino production (1927-28). Written and directed by Sergei M. Eisenstein. Assistant director, Grigory Alexandrov; camera (b&w), Edouard Tisse; art direction, Vassily Kovrigin; assistant directors, Maxim Straukh, Mikhail Gomorov, Ilya Trauberg; music (1928), Edmund Meisel, restored and conducted by Alan Fearon. First released in Moscow, March 14, 1928. Reviewed at London Film Festival, Nov. 13, 1988. Length: 9,540 feet. Running time (at 22 frames per second): **115 MIN.**
With: Vasily Nikandrov (Lenin), N. Popov (Kerensky), Boris Livanov (Tereschenko), Edouard Tisse (a German).

■ **London — Fifty years after its premiere, when it was received with bemusement, Sergei Eisenstein's classic evocation of the Bolshevik Revolution, "October," stormed**

Biker . . . . Judson Camp

■ **London — "Cheap Tricks" is a quirky U.S. indie comedy offering chuckles rather than guffaws. Pic is an obvious shoestring affair but features inventive direction by first-time cohelmers Jeff Ureles and Jerry Stoeffhaas and a lead performance to be treasured by Louis Zorich.**

The codirectors (who also coproduced and cowrote) self-consciously use as many plot devices as possible (voyeurism, murder, blackmail) which gives the pic a slightly contrived feel, but their offbeat filming style gives "Cheap Shots" a distinctly un-American edge that more than compensates.

Pic is set in a rundown motel owned by Louie (Zorich), whose major preoccupation along with buddy Arnold (David Patrick Kelly) is observing a beautiful blond and her boyfriend staying at the motel.

The two acquire a video camcorder, hide it in the lovers' room and take to watching their sex sessions. When they accidentally record the lovers' murder the bungling duo find themselves involved with police investigations and mob killers.

All seems to end in a shootout with the mob, but final scene sees the duo licking their wounds poolside at a tacky resort with a few injuries, but several thousand dollars richer.

Zorich and Kelly (more often seen in demented-killer roles) are excellent as the oddball pair and there is some nice character playing by Marie Louise Wilson and Michael Twaine.

Ureles and Stoeffhaas direct fluidly, using some sweeping camera movements to give "Cheap Shots" a different look. —Adam.

the London Film Festival, this time to no uncertain enthusiasm.

Epic filmmaking that shows Eisenstein's strengths and weaknesses, this Soviet superproduction, familiar mostly to cinematheque audiences (usually in unsubtitled Russian prints) could become a big festival crowdpleaser and a tv buff-slot package.

London screening, timed to the 90th anni celebrations of Eisenstein's birth, also saw the revival of the original 1928 German orchestral score by Edmund Meisel, restored and conducted by Alain Fearon, who last year performed Meisel's highly innovative music for "Potemkin." The "October" score, apparently unheard since the 1930s, provides rousing percussive support to Eisenstein's tumultous epic.

Eisenstein himself considered

"October" a failure, and abandoned to posterity no less than four divergent versions (not including the sundry watered-down export copies invariably released as "Ten Days That Shook The World.")

Commissioned for the 10th anni festivities of the 1917 Revolution, "October" was held up for release for months while Eisenstein, under orders from Stalin, cut out the many episodes of his film concerning Leon Trotsky, who was expelled from the Communist Party as film was being completed.

London fest printed thus is not a reconstitution of Eisenstein's original montage, but a composite of two variant prints dictated by Meisel's extant sheet music. Pic now runs nearly two hours and seems as satisfactory a whole as one can expect for contemporary commercial purposes.

Film traditionally has been criticized for its lack of clarity and often idiosyncratic interpretation of the major events leading from the deposition of the czar in the February Revolution to the Bolshevik seizure of power eight months later.

For all its incoherence, "October" carries the spectator on a tidal wave of stunning imagery, with such high points as the tragically dispersed workers' demonstration in Petrograd and the climactic brilliantly sustained siege of the Winter Palace (said to be much more spectacular than the original event).

Of course, no praise of Eisenstein's visual masters can be complete without mention of his inventive chief cameraman Edouard Tisse.

Eisenstein's often playful experiments in intellectual montage have long occupied film scholars and theoreticians, but they are not always his forte here. Though the famous satiric passage on Prime Minister Kerensky's symbolic rise to power in the Provincial Government still is cinematically sharp, other sequences are longwinded and hermetic.

An apposite footnote: "October" shared festival program with another silent masterwork, D.W. Griffith's "Intolerance," a film that Eisenstein is said to studied extensively before making his film debut. Seeing both back to back was quite a lesson in early film history, esthetics and technique. —Len.

Dom na Trubnoi
(The House On Trubnaya Square)
(SOVIET-B&W)

A Mezhrabpom-Russ production (1928), preserved by Cosmofilmofond film archives (USSR). Directed by Boris Bafnett. Screenplay, Boris Zorich, Anatoly Marienhof, Vadim Shershenevich, Victor Shklovsky, Nikolai Erdman; camera (b&w), Yevgeny Alexeyev; art direction, Sergey Kozlovsky; assistant directors, V. Nemolayev, A. Joutayev. First released in Moscow, Sept. 4, 1928. Reviewed at Royal Belgian Film Archive, Brussels, Nov. 18, 1988. (Also at London Film Festival.)

Length: 5,425 feet. Running time (at 18 frames per second): **81 MIN.**
With: Vera Maretskaya (Parasha Pitounova), Vladimir Fogel (Golikov), Yelena Tyapkina (Mrs. Golikova), Vladimir Batalov (Semyen Byvalov), Anna Sudakevitch (Marina), Sergey Komarov (Lyadov).

■ **Brussels — Filmgoers whose knowledge of the classic Soviet cinema is limited to the confirmed greats such as Eisenstein, Pudovkin and Dovzhenko owe it to themselves to get acquainted with the comedies of Boris Barnett (1902-1964), whose best films are marvelous blends of American slapstick, the French touch à la René Clair, and the satiric gaiety of the experimental Soviet FEKS group.**

"The House Of Trubnaya Square" is first-class early Barnett comedy, shown at the London Film Festival as an homage to the late Jacques Ledoux, longtime curator of the Royal Belgian Film Archives, whose extensive exchanges with the Soviet archives enriched the Brussels cinematheque with the richest collection of Russian and Soviet film in Europe.

This 1928 silent film — it was Barnett's third production, his second as solo helmer — is an exhilarating blast of good humor, satire and parody, following the misadventures of a naive peasant girl who comes to Moscow and finds employment as the exploited servant of an unscrupulous barber and his wife in a crowded tenement.

Barnett, a former boxer and actor, places his comic punches with extraordinary timing and pacing, shifting tone and narrative directions with deft sleight-of-camera virtuosity. Opening expository scenes of the apartment block (seen in a cut-away set of the stairwell) gradually coming to vivid early morning life is alone a masterpiece of farce direction.

The energy and fun never flag, even when the script (upon which no less than five writers slaved) seems to meander in search of a focal point. Some vagueness undoubtedly is due to apparently missing footage, but it's evident Barnett is no disciple of tidy harmonious storytelling. He is translating into boisterous comic terms the turbulence of city life in the USSR, circa 1928, with its housing crisis, labor unions, its amateur agit-prop plays and workers' parades, all of which the sweetfaced heroine (played by the delicious Vera Maretskaya) experiences with bemused big-heartedness.

The vagaries of film distribution (and Sovexport) until recently have kept from western audiences a rich part of the Soviet film heritage. If glasnost is the real thing, then Boris Barnett should become the posthumous ambassador of Slavic screen humor. His sly contagious laughter blows away the Iron Curtain of official culture. —Len.

Twins

A Universal Pictures release. Executive producers, Joe Medjuck, Michael C. Gross. Produced and directed by Ivan Reitman. Screenplay, William Davies & William Osborne, Timothy Harris & Herschel Weingrod; camera (Deluxe color), Andrzej Bartkowiak; editors, Sheldon Kahn, Donn Cambern; music, Georges Delerue; sound (Dolby Stereo), Gene Cantamessa; additional music, Randy Edelman; production design, James D. Bissell; art direction, Chris Burian-Mohr; set design, Nancy Patton, William James Teegarden, Edward S. Verreaux; set decoration, John T. Walker; costumes, Gloria Gresham; associate producers, Kahn, Gordon Webb; assistant director, Peter Giuliano; second unit camera, Craig De Nault; casting Michael Chinich. Reviewed at Samuel Goldwyn Theater, L.A., Nov. 30, 1988. MPAA Rating: PG. Running time: **112 MIN.**

Julius Benedict . . . Arnold Schwarzenegger
Vincent Benedict . . . . Danny DeVito
Marnie Mason . . . . Kelly Preston
Linda Mason . . . . Chloe Webb
Mary Ann Benedict . . . . Bonnie Bartlett
Webster . . . . Marshall Bell
Beetroot McKinley . . . . Trey Wilson

■Director Ivan Reitman more than delivers on the wacky promise of Universal's high-profile ad campaign for "Twins" in this nutty, storybook tale of siblings separated at birth and reunited at age 35.

Inspired pairing of Arnold Schwarzenegger and Danny DeVito and story's bathetic affirmation of family ties should push buttons with a wide audience, making for a merry Christmas at MCA.

Schwarzenegger plays Julius Benedict, a perfect specimen of a man in both body and soul, raised as an orphan in pristine innocence on a tropical isle. As pic begins, his scientist guardian tells him the truth about his origins — that he was created in a genetic experiment and he has a twin brother on the mainland. Lionhearted Julius, filled with familial longing, rushes off to L.A. to search for bro — only to discover he'd have found him faster by looking under rocks.

DeVito's Vincent Benedict is a major creep, a guy you wouldn't mind seeing get hit by a car. Actually, he steals them for a living — and he's got a gang of thugs on his tail trying to settle some scores. Does this guy care about family? To him, Julius is a dopey nut who makes a good bodyguard.

Julius, too innocent to size Vincent up, persists in his quest to make him believe in the bonds of brotherhood between them. They finally set out to locate their mother, but Vincent still is on his incorrigible path.

Pic gets near-perfect execution in Reitman's hands, with a lively mix of sight gags and fresh, topical jokes supported by a solid emotional through-line. Camera and all design and casting elements come together to create a 2-D cartoonish look for the picture that supports its wacky tone.

Schwarzenegger is a delightful surprise in this perfect transitional role to comedy. (He's still playing a kind of fantasy character — this time a well-bred superman who's opposed to violence but has to crack a lot of heads anyway.)

So strongly does he project the tenderness, nobility and puppy-dog devotion that make Julius tick that one is nearly hypnotized into suspending disbelief.

Chloe Webb ("Sid & Nancy") holds up the other end of the love-blanket that warms this romp, playing DeVito's adoring girlfriend. Both she and Schwarzenegger have to convince us they could be devoted to this creep and still have their marbles, and they manage quite charmingly.

DeVito is a blaze of energy and body language as Vince, articulating the part as though he'd written it himself.

Least effective character is the Mom, as played by Bonnie Bartlett, a kind of idealized, pastel-colored notion of womanhood who resides at a colony of artists. She's perfect, but unlike Julius, she's not funny (not even when she punches out a scientist), so pic definitely sags in her corner. Unfocused final scene is a bit much for even Reitman to pull off.

True comedy core of "Twins" are the sight gags pairing pintsized greaseball DeVito and golden-haired Adonis Schwarzenegger as twins. Without going overboard, Reitman has a lot of fun with it, achieving best laughs when Vince tries to teach Julius how to strut down the street.

Able script, created by two teams of writers, also trades heavily on "Crocodile Dundee"-style humor about the initiation of a rube (Julius) into the urban milieu, with this time L.A. yielding material for topical amusement rather than New York.

Kudos to costume designer Gloria Gresham, whose choices — particularly Schwarzenegger's funny shorts — add much to the characters and the "twins" concept; and to casting director Michael Chinich, who presumably found Marshall Bell to play Webster and Trey Wilson to play Beetroot McKinley.

Buoyant, whimsical score by Georges Delerue and Randy Edelman is firstrate. —*Daws.*

Torch Song Trilogy

A New Line Cinema release of a Howard Gottfried/Ronald K. Fierstein production. Produced by Gottfried. Executive producer, Fierstein. Directed by Paul Bogart. Screenplay, Harvey Fierstein, based on his play; camera (Metrocolor), Mikael Salomon; editor, Nicholas C. Smith; music adapted by Peter Matz; production design, Richard Hoover; art direction, Okowita, Marcie Dale; set decoration, Michael Warga, Marlene Marta (N.Y.); costume design, Coleen Atwood; sound (Dolby), Steve Nelson, Gary Rich (N.Y.); choreography, Scott Salmon; associate producer, Marie Cantin; assistant directors, Dennis Maguire, Peter Bogart; casting, Gail Lovin, Lauren Lloyd. Reviewed at Lorimar Screening Room, Culver City, Calif., Dec. 1, 1988. MPAA Rating: R. Running time: **117 MIN.**

Ma . . . . Anne Bancroft
Alan . . . . Matthew Broderick
Arnold Beckoff . . . . Harvey Fierstein
Ed . . . . Brian Kerwin
Laurel . . . . Karen Young
David . . . . Eddie Castrodad
Murray . . . . Ken Page
Bertha Venation . . . . Charles Pierce
Marina Del Rey . . . . Axel Vera

■One of the major theatrical events of the 1980s, "Torch Song Trilogy" has been diminished in its belated transfer to the big screen, but some of its sympathetic, likable qualities nevertheless remain intact.

Broadly played by a talented cast, pic clearly is pitched (comedically and emotionally) to appeal to a mainstream public, but it remains questionable whether the film can cross over to general na-

Original Play

The Glines presentation of three 1-act comedies by Harvey Fierstein. "The International Stud," "Fugue In A Nursery" and "Widows And Children First!" Staged by Peter Pope; settings, Leon Munier; costumes, Mardi Phillips; lighting, Scott Pinkney; music, Ada Janik; musical direction, Ned Levy; general manager, Lawrence Lane; publicity, Fred Nathan Assocs. Opened Jan. 15, 1982, at the Actors Playhouse; N.Y.; $15 top weeknights, $18.50 weekends.

Cast: Harvey Fierstein, Court Miller, Matthew Broderick, Estelle Getty, Payl Joynt, Diane Tarleton.

tional audiences the way the play was able to attract a cross-section of theatergoers in New York and other urban centers.

Harvey Fierstein repeats his Tony Award-winning performance as Arnold Beckoff, a flamboyant drag queen looking for love and respect. Originated as separately staged 1-acts, the play, when finally mounted as a unified work in 1982, proved bracing in its frank depiction of gay sex life, both promiscuous and committed, and won over even the blue-rinse matinee ladies with its riotous humor and warm presentation of familiar family problems.

At the time, play seemed like one of the rich flowerings of the gay pride movement, arriving shortly before an awareness of AIDS took hold. In the course of boiling his more than 3-hour epic down to two hours, Fierstein essentially has been forced to make it a period piece, assigning the rampant bed-romping to the 10-year period between 1971-81 so that his characters could play out their lives as originally conceived, unencumbered by the tragic specter of the decimating disease.

Highly theatrical as a live show, "Torch Song" retains heavy vestiges of its origins. After a brief prolog showing Brooklyn boy Arnold trying on his mother's clothes and makeup, pic introduces the grownup version in his dressing room at his drag club, ruminating directly to the camera about life and love.

Nervous, mannered, gravelly voiced, overly sensitive, campy and with a taste for eyerolling rivaled only by Groucho Marx in modern showbiz annals, Arnold appears a bit gun-shy of romance, but allows himself to be picked up in a gay bar by Ed (Brian Kerwin), a good-looking, straight-seeming fellow who openly announces his bisexuality.

This doesn't stop Arnold from falling head over heels for his Middle American catch, but causes him endless pain when he discovers Ed with a young woman, Laurel (Karen Young). Forever fretting and panicking about every twist and turn in his life, Arnold cannot fathom this perceived betrayal and goes into a prolonged funk.

In what is effectively Act Two, Arnold meets Alan (Matthew Broderick), to him an impossibly good-looking kid who used to be a hustler and actively seeks out Arnold for his human, as opposed to superficial, qualities. Alan clearly is the love of Arnold's life, although classic sex farce complications intervene when Ed and Laurel invite them to their country farm for the weekend and Ed and Alan head off to the barn together.

Alan meets a tragic, poignant end, and Act Three, the most conventional of the sections, is given over to Arnold's efforts to handle an adopted teenage son and sort out his strained relations with his mother (Anne Bancroft).

Due to the normalization of the behavior here away from the stylization of the stage piece, the antic humor has been diminished from the original, although the clever waspishness of Fierstein's lines provides sustained amusement. Conversely, the unrestrained performances create a sense of theatricality that distances the viewer from direct response to emotional material.

All the same, Fierstein's accomplishment in forging such a strong statement about the gay experience, and doing so with such abundant humor, remains a substantial one.

Sounding like Popeye when he sings, Fierstein wins one over through sheer force of personality, although he does get carried away at times. Bancroft goes through the roof with her typical and/or definitive Jewish mother turn, flailing away and yelling at deafening volume. Kerwin is fine as the simple, sometimes oafish heartthrob, and Broderick, who played the adopted adolescent onstage, makes a good stab at playing the aggressively gay mate with results that are often appealing but perhaps not uniformly convincing.

Paul Bogart directed in straightforward, unremarkable fashion, and tech credits are acceptable, with special attention having been paid to the drag club numbers.
—*Cart.*

... And I Was Such A Lovely Baby
(BRITISH-DOCU-16m)

A National Film & Television School production. Produced and directed by Bob Hartley. Production coordinator, Margaret Allison. Camera (16m Fujicolor), Wayne Derrick; editor, Martin Collins, Bob Hartley; music, Alistair, Jonathan, Sarah (end title), Elaine Streeter, arranged by Peter Miller; sound, Hartley. Reviewed at London Film Festival, Nov. 25, 1988. Running time: **100 MIN.**

■ **This charming and moving film follows the lives of children at the Mulberry Bush School for emotionally disturbed and deprived children, not looking at them through rose-colored glasses but with genuine compassion and care.**

The troubled children battle among themselves and with the staff, often as a plea for attention or an act of desperation. The staff are firmly gentle and despite the many blue moods of the youngsters, aged 5-12, relentlessly patient.

Hartley's camera follows the youngsters from waking up until going to sleep and through their varied moods and traumas. He gently interviews them with his main question: "If you had one wish, what would it be?" Almost all wish they could be with their parents.

The children interviewed and overheard are remarkably articu-

late about why they are at the school and many seem quite aware of their own shortcomings as well as their parents' problems.

"... And I Was Such A Lovely Baby" makes quite compelling viewing thanks to Bob Hartley's dedicated and determined filming. He doesn't make judgements but lets his film speak for itself. —*Lor.*

Talk Radio

A Universal Pictures release of a Cineplex Odeon Films presentation of an Edward R. Pressman production in association with Ten Four Prods. Executive producers, Greg Strangis, Sam Strangis. Produced by Pressman, A. Kitman Ho. Directed by Oliver Stone. Screenplay, Eric Bogosian, Stone, based on the play "Talk Radio" created by Bogosian, Tad Savinar, written by Bogosian, and the book "Talked To Death: The Life And Murder Of Alan Berg" by Stephen Singular; camera (Deluxe color; the Film House Group prints), Robert Richardson; editor, David Brenner; coeditor, Joe Hutshing; music, Stewart Copeland; sound (Dolby), Tod A. Maitland; production design, Bruno Rubeo; art direction, Milo; set decoration, Derek R. Hill; costume design, Ellen Mirojnick; associate producers, Diane Schneier, Neal Weisman; assistant director, Joseph Reidy; casting, Risa Bramon, Billy Hopkins. Reviewed at Carolco Screening Room, L.A., Nov. 21, 1988. MPAA Rating: R. Running time: **110 MIN.**

Barry Champlain	Eric Bogosian
Dan	Alec Baldwin
Ellen	Ellen Greene
Laura	Leslie Hope
Stu	John C. McGinley
Chuck Dietz	John Pankow
Kent	Michael Wincott
Sid Greenberg	Zach Grenier
Woman at basketball game	Anna Levine
Jeffrey Fisher	Robert Trebor
Sheila Fleming	Linda Atkinson
Vince	Allan Corduner

■ **"Talk Radio" casts a spotlight on the unpalatable underside of American public opinion, and turns up an unlimited supply of anger, hatred and resentment in the process.**

Superbly directed by Oliver Stone and pungently performed by Eric Bogosian, author of the original play of the same name, this will primarily appeal to serious, upscale filmgoers interested in Stone and the issues in question, but could break out to a wider audience due to the current fascination for confrontational media programs — the format that provides the context for the picture.

Known in theatrical circles as a monologist and performance artist, Bogosian debuted the initial incarnation of "Talk Radio" in Portland, Ore., in 1985, and last year starred in a well-received expanded version at the Public Theater in New York. For the screenplay, he and Stone worked in material relating to Alan Berg, the Denver talkshow host mur-

dered by neo-Nazis in 1984, and also created a flashback to illuminate their antihero's personal background and beginnings in the radio game.

Most of the film, however, unfolds in the modern studio of KGAB, a Dallas station from which the infamous Barry Champlain holds forth. Young, caustic, rude, insulting, grand-

---

Original Play

N.Y. Shakespeare Festival/Joseph Papp presentation of a play in one act by Eric Bogosian, based on an idea by Ted Savinar. Staged by Frederick Zollo. Settings, David Jenkins; visual graphics, Ted Savinar; costumes, Pilar Limosner; lighting, Jan Kroeze; associate producer, Jason Steven Cohen; stage managers, Alan R. Traynor, Pat Sosnow; general managers, Laurel Ann Wilson, Robert MacDonald; publicity, Richard Kornberg. Opened May 28, 1987 at the Public/Martinson Hall, N.Y., $25 top.
Cast: Linda Atkinson, Eric Bogosian, William DeAcutis, Susan Gabriel, Zach Grenier, Michaele M. Mariana, John C. McGinley, Mark Metcalf, Peter Onorati, Robyn Peterson, Michael Wincott.

---

standing, flippant and mercilessly cruel, the talkshow host spews vitriol impartially on those of all races, colors and creeds, spares the feelings of no one and specializes in quickly identfying and then picking up on people's vulnerabilities and handicaps.

Partly because he attracts the afflicted, Champlain draws out the nighttime's seamiest denizens from under their rocks, fringe characters whose access to the airwaves gives them a platform for their loony views and who collectively constitute a disturbing portrait of the American mentality.

For their trouble, of course, the callers absorb a torrent of abuse from Champlain, but the public also takes advantage of his appearance at a local basketball game to turn the tables, booing him so vociferously he must beat a hasty retreat.

A dramatic structure has been imposed on the proceedings by the arrival of a radio syndicator who wants to take Champlain's show nationwide. Instead of greeting this news happily, however, the host takes extra bottles of acid off his shelf and showers everyone with it, so distrustful is he of this potential new overload.

At the same time, Champlain's ex-wife Ellen (Ellen Greene) arrives in town, which occasions a look back at the man's origins in the clothing business, his immediate success on the air when invited on as a guest, his change to a non-Jewish name, and the destruction of his marriage due to

his infidelity and mean thoughtlessness.

Ellen's presence also allows for the most probing exploration into the astonishing depth of Champlain's anger and self-loathing, but this attempt at creating a psychological portrait of the man falls rather short of truly explaining the roots of his aggressive behavior.

Along the way, the most prominent recurring motif relates to racism and, more specifically, anti-Semitism. Redneck callers complain about Jews and persistently threaten Champlain over his religion. It is against his instincts to take these crackpots seriously, but any viewer familiar with the Alan Berg case will be able to feel a tragic end lying in wait for Champlain.

Although the work began with and still belongs to Bogosian, "Talk Radio" in some ways makes for an interesting companion piece to Stone's "Salvador" in its portrait of a driven, self-destructive maverick media figure. Both Champlain and James Woods' journalist in the earlier film bridle at all authority, go too far when restraint might not be in order and seem to will themselves into dangerous situations.

In his attitudes and treatments of all those around him, Champlain is far from sympathetic or likable, but Bogosian commands attention in a patented tour-de-force. At times hard to take because he's clearly in love with the sound of his own voice, he has an undeniable inner demon that compels him ever forward, and Bogosian is utterly convincing as he takes on the world.

Supporting performances are all vividly realized, notably Greene's understanding, all-too-human spouse, John C. McGinley's ever-faithful engineer, Alec Baldwin's harried station manager, Leslie Hope's strained assistant/girlfriend and, in a scene-stealing turn, Michael Wincott's drug-crazed Champlain fan invited to the studio for a tête-à-tête with the host.

Abetted once again by ever-inventive lenser Robert Richardson, Stone has created a beautifully fluid, visually stimulating film out of what started as a 1-set piece. Keyed around Stewart Copeland's score as well as some pop tunes, soundtrack is sharp and the sound mix in general is very creatively multilayered. —*Cart.*

My Stepmother Is An Alien

A Columbia Pictures release of a Weintraub Entertainment Group film. Executive producers, Laurence Mark, Art Levinson. Produced by Ronald Parker, Franklin R. Levy. Directed by Richard Benjamin. Screenplay, Jerico Weingrod, Herschel Weingrod, Timothy Harris, Jonathan Reynolds; camera (Deluxe color), Richard H. Kline editor, Jacqueline Cambas; music, Alan Silvestri; sound, Jerry Jost; production design, Charles Rosen; set decoration, Don Remacle; costumes, Aggie Guerard Rodgers, special effects, John Dykstra, Apogee Prods.; assistant director Alan Curtiss; casting, Nancy Foy. Reviewed at AMC Century City 14, L.A., Dec. 1, 1988. MPAA Rating: PG-13. Running time: 108 MIN.

Dr. Steve Mills	Dan Aykroyd
Celeste	Kim Basinger
Ron Mills	Jon Lovitz
Jessie Mills	Alyson Hannigan
Dr. Lucas Budlong	Joseph Maher
Voice of Purse	Ann Prentiss

■ "My Stepmother Is An Alien" is a failed attempt to mix many of the film genres associated with the "alien" idea into a sprightly romp.

A hokey-looking cyclops snake as the not-so-evil alien and some obvious continuity flaws reduce this high-concept romantic comedy to a lower order film when it appears the filmmakers tried desperately to work this into something better by having Dan Aykroyd and Kim Basinger in the leads. The b.o. books less than stellar for Weintraub Entertainment Group.

Title sequence, with multicolored laser lights swirling against a starry sky with goofy, sci-fi-ish sounding score in the background, makes it seem as if this will be a spoof.

But it's the jittery p.o.v. camera work in the opening sequence that is what really sets the tone for what follows — a succession of what would better be described as a series of disjointed sketches, than a fully realized story, though some scenes could stand alone as inspired comic bits akin to those once seen on "Saturday Night Live."

Aykroyd, as a rumpled, overweight, widower scientist, foils one of his own experiments using lightning and a high-powered satellite dish which results in a signal reaching beyond our galaxy to a planet in peril.

Soon afterwards, a flying saucer lands on a Southern California beach and two aliens alight. They come in the form of quintessential American beauty Kim Basinger in a slinky red sheath dress with an alien-buddy-mentor (the aforementioned snake, voice courtesy of Ann Prentiss) hiding in her purse.

Their mission is to get Aykroyd to repeat his experiment, which will save their planet.

It is the lengths to which Basinger is expected to go wending her way into Aykroyd's otherwise nerdy suburban lifestyle that is supposed to levitate this fish-out-of-water story to comedic heights.

It seems that only an alien would go for a shlumpy guy like Aykroyd, so there is a certain humorous satisfaction seeing a sexy blond — who is programmed to go for anything Aykroyd suggests — make a complete fool out of herself to accomplish her assignment.

Watching her watch a compilation of great Hollywood screen kisses and later a porno flick to learn how humans make love, as the awestruck Aykroyd reacts in disbelief, is silly and hilarious (also somewhat titillating).

There are several other such shameless situations that Basinger carries off with aplomb, even as the freshness she brings to her role is diminished by having to act credibly through too skittish a plot.

Script is sophomoric in its realization, which may be the fault of the wrtiers for trying to cover all the emotional ground it takes for Basinger to become "human" — her motherly attitude towards Aykroyd's teenager daughter (Alyson Hannigan) is ridiculously sentimental — but may also be the failing of director Richard Benjamin to know when to exorcise lines of dialog or situations that don't further the jokes.

Because it's never made clear if a parody is being attempted, one wonders if it was intentional that there are some jarring continuity flaws, like how Basinger has straight hair one minute and kinky hair the next (this happens at least twice), or why all the aliens look and talk like humans, except for the fake snake (which speaks with a New York accent).

Still, some terrific performances survive through this muddled mess, especially that of Aykroyd's horny playboy brother, played wonderfully smarmily by Jon Lovitz.

Tech credits are alternatingly great or awful. John Dykstra's special effects get kudos for the eerie, glowing spaceship, while the laser and lightning stuff looks amateurish. —Brit.

Zwei Deutsche — Jahrgang 1928
(EAST GERMAN-DOCU-B&W/COLOR)

A Defa-Studios fur Dokumentar Filme, Gruppe Effekt (East Berlin) production. Directed by Gitta Nickel. Written by Nickel, Wolfgang Schwarze; camera (color), Niko Pawloff. Reviewed at Nyon Intl. Film Festival, Switzerland, Oct. 19, 1988. Running time: 94 MIN.

■ "Zwei Deutsche" traces the military services of Hans-Georg Henke and Wilhelm Hubner, 16-year-old German soldiers in the final months of World War II, using stock footage and color interviews.

Film contributes to the historical record of World War II, as there were quite a few teen warriors in Nazi service, known as kindersoldaten.

These two became rather famous when their photographs were publicized throughout Nazi Germany as morale propaganda. Hubner was among a small group of young soldiers personally honored by Hitler in his Berlin bunker during a photo opportunity. Henke at 16 served on the Eastern front.

Henke today describes his war experiences, his return to his district, which became East Germany, his conversion to communism and his rise through party ranks to become the party-appointed manager of a hospital.

"Zwei Deutsche" probably is the first East German docu to be shown in West Germany. It is plainly a film tailored for both Germanys but will need trimming if it surfaces Stateside on public tv.
—Hitch.

Rain Man

An MGM/UA Communications release from United Artists of a Guber-Peters Co. production. Executive producers, Peter Guber, Jon Peters. Produced by Mark Johnson. Co-producer, Gerald R. Molen. Directed by Barry Levinson. Screenplay, Ronald Bass, Barry Morrow, based on a story by Morrow; camera (Deluxe color), John Seale; editor, Stu Linder, music, Hans Zimmer; production design, Ida Random; art direction, William A. Elliott; set decoration, Linda DeScenna; costume design, Bernie Pollack; sound (Dolby), Richard Goodman; associate producers, Gail Mutrux, David McGiffert; assistant director, McGiffert; casting, Louis DiGiaimo. Reviewed at Samuel Goldwyn theater, L.A., Dec. 8, 1988. MPAA Rating: R. Running time: 140 MIN.

Raymond Babbitt	Dustin Hoffman
Charlie Babbitt	Tom Cruise
Susanna	Valeria Golino
Dr. Bruner	Jerry Molen
John Mooney	Jack Murdock
Vern	Michael D. Roberts
Lenny	Ralph Seymour
Iris	Lucinda Jenney

■ One of the year's most intriguing film premises — a callow young hustler (Tom Cruise) must gain the confidence of his autistic brother (Dustin Hoffman) in order to pry away from him an enormous inheritance — is given uneven, slightly off-target treatment in UA's "Rain Man."

Casting of Cruise and various other aspects suggest an attempt to broaden audience appeal rather than deepen the story. Even so, pic should do very well as a quality alternative in a holiday box-office dominated by comedies.

Hoffman's character Raymond Babbitt is an autistic savant, a person extremely limited in some mental areas and extremely gifted in others. His younger brother, hard-driving luxury car dealer Charlie Babbitt (Cruise), has his limitations too — mostly in the areas of kindness and understanding.

Unaware of Raymond's existence (he'd been institutionalized when Charlie was very young) until his estranged father dies, Charlie is brought up short when he learns the old man's entire $3-million fortune has been willed to his brother.

After a trip to the east coast institution where Raymond resides, Charlie shanghais him, without regard for his welfare, into a cross-country trip to L.A., dangling a Dodger game as bait. Meanwhile, he threatens Raymond's guardian, the bland Dr. Bruner (Jerry Molen), with a custody battle unless he hands over half the fortune.

Director Barry Levinson ("Diner," "Good Morning, Vietnam,") lingers long on the road trip segment, building the relationship between the brothers degree by degree and decorating it with spectacular, if self-conscious, landscapes shot through tinted lenses. Result is lightly engrossing, buoyed here and there by emergence of Raymond's unique abilities (for example, he can memorize half a telephone book in an evening and also can perform extravagant multiplications in a flash).

Along the way, Charlie, whose talents seem at first confined to barking orders and being inconsiderate, is getting his edges buffed by Raymond's ingratiating eccentricities and attachment to routine.

Then Charlie learns by phone, in Tucumcari, N.M., that he's just lost $80,000 in a business deal, and pic's placid surface erupts in a bombast of music and camera tricks as he takes Raymond to the Las Vegas gaming tables to exploit his mathematical genius. Needless to say, it's a very successful idea. Raymond even learns a little about women, and in a charming scene with Cruise, learns how to dance.

For most of its longish 140 minutes, "Rain Man" is limited by its subject — it's about getting to know a guy (Raymond) who can't respond or change except by the slightest degrees. Road segment often feels hastily, loosely written, with much extraneous screen time. By the last third, pic becomes quite moving as these two very isolated beings discover a common history and deep attachment.

If an actor with more range than Cruise had been cast, pic might have gone over the top in its final scenes. As is, it stops a little short. It's a mature assignment for Cruise and he's at his best in the darker scenes. When the executor of the will shields information from him, the actor displays an utterly grim, brickheaded determination that is frightening.

Hoffman achieves an exacting physical characterization of Raymond, from his constant nervous movements to his rigid, hunched shoulders and childish gait. Though he can neither look anyone in the eye nor engage in real conversation, Raymond certainly can be funny, with his well-timed offhand responses to Charlie's hammering questions. (Cruise: Raymond, am I using you? Hoffman: Yeah.)

Italian actress Valeria Golino strikes just the right chord as Charlie's sensitive, long-suf-

fering girlfriend.

Though it never builds a great deal of momentum, "Rain Man" does offer some delightful scenes of droll comedy in running gags between the two brothers, built around such daily trivia as maple syrup and boxer shorts.

Locations, costumes and tech contributions are good, particularly considering pic was lensed in a rushed nine weeks of location work.

Music by Hans Zimmer is fresh and provocative. —Daws.

Retracing Steps: American Dance Since Postmodernism
(W. GERMAN-U.S.-DOCU)

A Michael Blackwood release of a Westdeutscher Rundfunk and Michael Blackwood Prods., N.Y. coprod. Executive producer, Manfred Grater. Produced and directed by Blackwood. Writer and consultant, Sally Banes; associate producer, Kelley Forsyth; associate directors, Mead Hunt, Julie Sloane; camera (color, 16m), Hunt; editor, Sloane; sound, Stephen Plumlee. Reviewed at Film Forum, N.Y., Dec. 1, 1988. Running time: **88 MIN.**

With: Stephen Petronio, Mollissa Fenley, Diane Martel, Wendy Perron, Blondell Cummings, Jim Self, Johanna Boyce, Bill T. Jones, Arnie Zane.

■ "Retracing Steps" is an apt title for this splendid documentary surveying the work of nine young American post-Postmodernist choreographers.

Steps are retraced in the sense that traditional dance is reexamined, admired but judged inadequate for the creative purposes of each of the nine. Also, each choreographer retraces her or his particular steps in an autobiographical sketch. Most impressive is their emphasis on struggle, liberty and individualism.

To the credit of filmmaker Michael Blackwood, he rejects the temptation to provide narration or to people it with dance scholars and critics who categorize and pontificate.

These choreographers accept the unpleasant aspects of their profession as part of their duty — the competition, even intriguing, for foundation support; the scrounging for materials and space, often breaking fire laws; the disappointments and uncertainties as well as their distance from the mainstream dance audience.

Because "Retracing Steps" may be the only in-depth feature documentary on this topic, it may get theatrical exhibition in certain venues. Schools and public tv are a natural.—Hitch.

Dirty Rotten Scoundrels

An Orion Pictures release. Produced by Bernard Williams. Executive producers, Dale Launer, Charles Hirschhorn. Directed by Frank Oz. Screenplay, Launer, Stanley Shapiro, Paul Henning, based (uncredited) on 1964 film "Bedtime Story," written by Shapiro, Henning; camera (Deluxe color), Michael Ballhaus; editor, Stephen A. Rotter, William Scharf; music, Miles Goodman; production design, Roy Walker; art direction, Steve Spence, Damien Lanfranchi; set decoration, Rosalind Shingleton; costume design, Marit Allen; sound (Dolby), Ivan Sharrock; assistant directors, Bernard Williams, David Tringham; casting, Donna Isaacson, John Lyons (U.S.), François Combadiere (Paris), Caroline Mazuric (Nice), Debbie McWilliams (London). Reviewed at Samuel Goldwyn theater, Beverly Hills, Calif., Dec. 6, 1988. MPAA Rating: PG. Running time: **110 MIN.**

Freddy Benson	Steve Martin
Lawrence Jamieson	Michael Caine
Janet Colgate	Glenne Headly
Inspector Andre	Anton Rodgers
Fanny Eubanks	Barbara Harris
Arthur	Ian McDiarmid
Mrs. Reed	Dana Ivey

■ "Dirty Rotten Scoundrels" is a wonderfully crafted, absolutely charming remake of the 1964 film "Bedtime Story." Orion won't have to pull any fast ones here to draw in the crowds.

In this classy version, Steve Martin and Michael Caine play the competing French Riviera con men trying to outscheme each other in consistently amusing and surprising setups.

This is a seemingly custom-made script for Steve Martin, who takes the crass American role played in the Universal Pictures film by Marlon Brando, and Michael Caine, who pays homage to the role's equally stylish predecessor, David Niven, by

ORIGINAL FILM:
Bedtime Story

Universal release of Stanley Shapiro production. Stars Marlon Brando, David Niven, Shirley Jones. Directed by Ralph Levy. Screenplay, Shapiro, Paul Henning; camera (Eastman), Clifford Stine; editor, Milton Garruth; music, Hans J. Salter; asst. director, Joseph E. Kenny. Reviewed at Grauman's Chinese, May 12, 1964. Running time, **99 MIN.**

Freddy	Marlon Brando
Lawrence	David Niven
Janet	Shirley Jones
Fanny Eubank	Dody Goodman
Andre	Aram Stephan
Col. Williams	Parley Baer
Mrs. Sutton	Marie Windsor
Miss Trumble	Rebecca Sand

sporting a thin mustache, slicked back hair and double-breasted blue blazer in a sort of 1930s British yachtsman look.

Though Martin takes to his role as the wildly gesturing loud mouth — some would say "ugly American" — and nearly always plays it broad, Caine's even, consistently cool balancing act gives this come-

dy a sustained air of sophistication. It doesn't hurt that the setups all occur against the most beautiful, ritzy and colorful of locations on the Côte d'Azur, with Nice standing in for the fictional seaside town of Beaumont-sur-Mer.

Every element in the film works splendidly, which is no surprise with a script by a current master of comedic-twist writing, Dale Launer ("Ruthless People"), with Stanley Shapiro and Paul Henning (original "Bedtime Story" scripters) deftly working in jokes.

Caine, ensconced in a seaside mansion, comes upon small-time con artist Martin in a train dining car ordering water instead of a meal while telling some poor doe-eyed French woman a sob story about how he has to save money for his sick grandmother. The knowing Caine is at first amused: his own m.o. is to take on much bigger bait at the casinos, where he poses as a prince to unsuspecting rich and impressionable women from the Midwest, pleading to them to support his various causes "for the homeland" like funneling money to "freedom fighters" and other bogus nonsense.

Beaumont-sur-Mer, where Martin suddenly turns up, is not big enough for two men to go after the same bait, a situation that irritates Caine to the point he challenges Martin to a $50,000 wager: The first one to extract that sum from the next unsuspecting fool gets to stay.

Things get very sticky when the femme, a "soap queen" (Glenne Headly) from Cleveland, becomes the object of the bet. Headly doesn't look the part of the innocent abroad, but she plays it well enough.

There is much that leads up to this encounter that sets the tone for the increasingly complicated double-crossing, of which a good part is given over for Martin's mock posturings as various sympathetic characters, including his funniest as Caine's bizarre "brother" Ruprecht, a slobbering, idiotic nerd. There is a good deal of Martin's brand of physical humor — from the clumsy, imitative bit he does of Caine's suave routine to his familiar outstretched arms "I'm a wild and crazy guy" swagger.

Caine's posturing as a Swiss psychiatrist with a Prussian accent is particularly engaging, as are his plottings with Beaumont-sur-Mer's corrupt police chief Andre (Anton Rodgers, sporting a great, overdone French accent), who takes the Claude Rains part from "Casablanca."

Director Frank Oz clearly has fun with his subjects, as much here as he seemed to have in "Little Shop Of Horrors," helped out in good part by clever cutting by Stephen Rotter and William Scharf that moves things along at a clip and a great, imitative '30s jazzy score by Miles Goodman.

Production designer Roy Walker beautifully captured the essence and elegance of the settings, which included the fabulous Grand Hotel du Cap Ferrat, with equally luxurious interiors — furnishings, flowers, vases, antiques — down to the last detail. —*Brit.*

Working Girl

A 20th Century Fox Film release. Produced by Douglas Wick. Executive producers, Robert Greenhut, Laurence Mark. Directed by Mike Nichols. Screenplay, Kevin Wade; camera (Duart color, Deluxe prints), Michael Ballhaus; editor, Sam O'Steen; music, Carly Simon; production design, Patrizia Von Brandenstein; art direction, Doug Kraner; set decoration, George DeTitta; costume design, Ann Roth; sound (Dolby), Les Lazarowitz; assistant director, Nathalie Vadim; production manager, Greenhut; casting, Juliet Taylor. Reviewed at the Darryl Zanuck theater, L.A., Dec. 7, 1988. MPAA Rating: R. Running time: 113 MIN.
Tess McGill . . . . Melanie Griffith
Jack Trainer . . . . Harrison Ford
Katherine Parker . . . . . . Sigourney Weaver
Cyn . . . . Joan Cusack
Mick Dugan . . . . Alec Baldwin
Oren Trask . . . . Philip Bosco
Ginny . . . . Nora Dunn
Lutz . . . . Oliver Platt
Turkel . . . . James Lally
Bob Speck . . . . Kevin Spacey
Armbrister . . . . Robert Easton
Personnel director . . . . . . Olympia Dukakis

■ "Working Girl" is enjoyable largely due to the fun of watching scrappy, sexy, unpredictable Melanie Griffith rise from Staten Island secretary to Wall Street whiz. Pic should earn some nice coin for Fox.

Essentially, "Working Girl" lacks the biting social satire of Mike Nichols' previous films "The Graduate," "Carnal Knowledge" and "Heartburn" or the unsettling truths as dramatized in "Silkwood."

It is, rather, a sweet, quixotic, oftentimes amusing feminized Ragged Dick tale that tracks the improbable transformation of Griffith to an uptown girl, the kind with an eye for stock figures — the numeral kind and the real kind (Harrison Ford).

Carly Simon's catchy title song establishes the frenetic pacing that characterizes the daily grind of one handful of workaday commuting secretaries, in and out of Manhat-

tan on the ferry with off times spent with their equally workaday-minded boyfriends who are more comfortable employed near home.

Physical appearance of the girls, zeroing in on Griffith and close g.f. Joan Cusack mostly, is what sets them off from the white-collar male-dominated milieu of their environs, the high-volume trading houses of lower Manhattan. Bouffant hairdos, chunky jewelry and gobs of rainbow eyeshadow brand them unsophisticates visually, which is further emphasized when they open their mouths to speak in that exaggerated New Yawk squawk.

Griffith stands apart, both for her eagerness to break out of her clerical rut and her tenacity dealing with whomever seems to be thwarting her, at first a lecherous brokerage house exec, whom she very cleverly and humorously exposes, and then a much more formidable and disarming opponent, femme boss Sigourney Weaver.

Just because they're both "girls" trying to make their way amidst a sea of men doesn't, however, make them friends, as it becomes especially apparent when each's romantic interest turns out to be the same guy.

Weaver is cast as a haughty, male-dressed-as-a-female professional piranha. Character may be a little too 1-dimensional, but is a good foil for Griffith in that she enhances sympathy for latter.

Griffith's ability to take over Weaver's management position as a savvy mergers-and-acquisitions specialist while the latter is laid up because of a skiing accident is the stuff of fable. It never really seems believable, given the relatively short timeframe, that she could also do a snow job on a major player of a competing brokerage house, the slightly mystified Ford.

New York seems a strange, frenetic city of contrasts and opportunities — all wrapped up in Griffith's feisty character.

With Weaver conveniently out of town, Griffith gets to play Cinderella to Ford's Prince Charming. She takes over her boss' elegant Upper East Side digs, borrows liberally from her designer-gown stuffed closets and, with the exception of a couple pangs of guilt, is brazen enough to sub for Weaver at social functions where she can meet those oh-so-important business contacts. Her tenacity, as expected, pays off in some fairly predictable ways.

Romance between Griffith and

Ford doesn't generate much fire, perhaps because it stems more from a business liaison than some other, more sexually ripe situation.

Probably unintentionally, there's more electricity in her relationship with the slightly roguish boat-driving beau back across New York Harbor, played winningly by Alec Baldwin.

Scene switching contrasts to good effect all the upscale interiors — the brightly-lit, VDT-blinking Petty-Marsh trading floor and darkly wooded corporate headquarters of takeover company Trask Industries — with the warm worn, Staten Island sites. Production designer Patrizia Von Brandenstein also does wonders creating the tackiest Caribbean wedding set that could possibly go up within the confines of such a high-brow (fictional) private Union club (really, the Convent of the Sacred Heart off Fifth Avenue).

Seemless editing by Sam O'-Steen and the well-distanced p.o.v. at conversational distance established by cinematographer Michael Ballhaus contribute to the overall very personal feel of the production.

This is not a laugh-out-loud film, though there is a lighthearted tone that runs consistently throughout, Griffith's innocent, breathy voice being a major factor.

Joan Cusack is better here as the outlandishly outfitted office compatriot than she was in "Broadcast News," a sure sign the actress is on the rise as a future comedic star. —*Brit.*

Dangerous Liaisons

Hollywood   A Warner Bros. release of an NFH Limited production from Lorimar Film Entertainment. Produced by Norma Heyman, Hank Moonjean. Coproducer, Christopher Hampton. Directed by Stephen Frears. Screenplay, Hampton, based on his play and the novel "Les Liaisons Dangereuses" by Choderlos de Laclos; camera (color), Philippe Rousselot; editor, Mick Audsley; music, George Fenton; production design, Stuart Craig; art direction, Gerard Viard, Gavin Bocquet; set decoration, Gerard James; costume design, James Acheson; sound (Dolby), Peter Handford; assistant director, Bernard Seitz; casting, Juliet Taylor, Howard Feuer. Reviewed at Glen Glenn Sound, L.A., Dec. 6, 1988. MPAA Rating: R. Running time: 120 MIN.
Marquise de Merteuil . . . . .Glenn Close
Vicomte de Valmont . . . . .John Malkovich
Madame de Tourvel . . . . Michelle Pfeiffer
Madame de Volanges . . . . . . Swoosie Kurtz
Chevalier Danceny . . . . Keanu Reeves
Madame de Rosemonde . . Mildred Natwick
Cecile de Volanges . . . . .Uma Thurman

■ A scandalous, often censored literary sensation for two centuries and a highbrow international theatrical hit for the last two years, "Les Liaisons Dangereuses" has been turned into a good but incompletely realized film.

Being released as "Dangerous Liaisons," this incisive study of sex as an arena for manipulative

STAGE PRODUCTION:

Les Liaisons Dangereuses

James M. Nederlander, The Shubert Organization, Jerome Minskoff, Elizabeth I. McCann and Stephen Graham, in association with Jonathan Farkas, presentation of a Royal Shakespeare Co. production of a play in two acts by Christopher Hampton, adapted from the novel by Choderlos de Laclos. Staged by Howard Davies; setting and costumes, Bob Crowley; lighting, Chris Parry, Beverly Emmons; sound, Otts Munderloh, John A. Leonard; music, Ilona Sekacz; fight staging, Malcolm Ransom; stage managers, Susie Cordon, Jane Tamlyn; associate producer, Sylvia Brennick; general management, Mary Nealon, David Musselman; publicity, Josh Ellis. Opened April 30, 1987, at the Music Box Theater, N.Y.
Major-domo . . . . .Barry Heins
La Marquise de Merteuil . .Lindsay Duncan
Mme. de Volanges . . . . . .Kristin Milward
Cecile de Volanges . . . . .Beatie Edney
Le Vicomte de Valmont . . . .Alan Rickman
Azolan . . . . .Hugh Simon
Mme. de Rosemonde . . . . . .Jean Anderson
Le Presidente de Tourvel . .Suzanne Burden
Emile . . . . .Lucy Aston
Le Chevalier Danceny . . . . . .Hilton McRae

power games boasts a basic intelligence and the inherent fascination of aristocratic decadence, but takes too long to catch fire and suffers from a deficient central performance. Boxoffice prospects look promising in urban, upscale markets, but top reviews and other accolades would be needed for crossover to general audiences.

Choderlos de Laclos' 1782 epistolary novel expertly chronicled the cunning, cold-blooded sexual calculations of the French pre-revolutionary upper class as represented by two of its idle, brilliant members, the Marquise de Merteuil and the Vicomte de Valmont. Former lovers, these two ideally matched players hatch schemes of deceit, revenge and debauchery.

The classic rake, Valmont (John Malkovich) at the outset is challenged by Merteuil (Glenn Close) to deflower a 16-year-old virgin, Cecile de Volanges (Uma Thurman), before Merteuil's former lover can go through with his marriage to the exquisite adolescent.

Valmont considers this too easy, however, and instead proposes to seduce Madame de Tourvel (Michelle Pfeiffer), a virtuous, highly moral married woman. Succeeding with her would represent Valmont's greatest victory, and Merteuil agrees to reward her friend with a night in the sack should he land his prey.

Tale is a classic battle of the sexes played to the limit that, with only slight modifications, would seem right at home on "Dallas" or "Dynasty" and did, in fact, serve as the basis of Roger Vadim's contemporary 1959 film. In evaluating Christopher Hampton's stage piece, many made the equation between the bankrupt values of the 1780s and the 1980s, although its ending was designed to illustrate the imminent collapse of the aristocracy in the French Revolution.

Stephen Frears has directed some of the most sexually subversive and politically corrosive films of the last several years, and might have been expected to bring a caustic, socially conscious edge to his analysis of the depraved shenanigans depicted herein. Surprisingly, he and Hampton have entirely eliminated any reference to the historical or social context; rarely has there been a period film with so detached an attitude from the well-known events of its time and place.

Due to this approach and the casting of American, rather than British, actors in the leading roles, the strategy was plainly to make the material as directly accessible and relevant as possible, to cause viewers to feel the action could as easily happen now as then. This places greater responsibility on the quality of the performers, and it is here that the film surprisingly falters.

Glenn Close is admirably cast as the proud, malevolent Merteuil, and has found an ideal way of speaking that conveys an aristocratic bearing without employing conventional British snootiness. Close clearly relishes

the role and handles it adroitly, even if one is left feeling Merteuil hasn't been squeezed for all she is worth.

The real problem is Malkovich's Valmont. This sly actor knows the effects he is going for, and by all means conveys the character's snaky, premeditated Don Juanism. But he lacks the devilish charm and seductiveness one senses Valmont would need to carry off all his conquests (although, paradoxically, Malkovich is particularly good in the actual bed scenes with Thurman and Pfeiffer). He has annoyingly made no attempt to modify his blatant American accent, and this, along with his slovenly posture and sloppy manners, makes him unconvincing as an aristocratic gentleman.

Pfeiffer makes a fragile, touching Madame de Tourvel, as her suffering under Valmont's incessant pressure becomes palpable. The ravishing Thurman is everything the broken, then awakened Cecile should be, and Mildred Natwick, Swoosie Kurtz and Keanu Reeves are effective and sometimes amusing in the key supporting parts.

The strong melodrama generated by the sexual machinations sustains engaged interest, but the Americanized, deformalized performances serve to dilute delectation of material's delicious decadence.

All the same, the physical trappings are properly splendid. Philippe Rousselot's lustrous camerawork captures the opulent production design of Stuart Craig and the numerous locations used. James Acheson does all he can to try to equal his costuming triumph on "The Last Emperor," and much is made of the putting on and taking off of clothing and makeup. George Fenton's score elaborately combines original composition with classical motifs. —Cart.

The Boost

Hollywood   A Hemdale release of a John Daly and Derek Gibson presentation of a Becker/Blatt/Ponicsan production. Produced by Daniel H. Blatt. Executive producers, Daly, Gibson. Coproducer, Mel Howard. Directed by Harold Becker. Screenplay, Darryl Ponicsan, based on the book "Ludes" by Benjamin Stein; camera (color), Howard Atherton; editor, Maury Winetrobe; music, Stanley Myers; production design, Waldemar Kalinowski; art direction, Ken Hardy; set decoration, Cindy Carr; costume design, Susan Becker; sound, Walter Hoylman; associate producer-assistant director, Tom Mack; casting, Ilene Starger. Reviewed at Carolco screening room, L.A., Nov. 22, 1988. MPAA Rating R. Running time: **95 MIN.**

Lenny Brown . . . . James Woods

Linda Brown . . . . Sean Young
Joel . . . . John Kapelos
Max . . . . Steven Hill
Rochelle . . . . Kelle Kerr
Ned Lewis . . . . John Rothman
Barbara . . . . Amanda Blake
Sheryl . . . . Grace Zabriskie
Also with: Scott McGinnis, Zina Bethune.

■ **For all the talent that has gone into "The Boost," there is no escaping the film's overly familiar dramatic trajectory, nor the feeling that the story arrives on the screen a bit out of time sociologically.**

Most easily described as a "Days Of Wine And Roses" for the cocaine generation, pic is powerfully acted and convincingly told, but contains virtually no surprises due to the inevitable patterns dictated by the ebbs and flows of drug addiction. Commercial prospects look chancy for this Hemdale release.

Based on Benjamin Stein's book "Ludes," Darryl Ponicsan's well-wrought screenplay is a cautionary tale about a couple involved in a mutually destructive, coke-dominated lifestyle.

Young and very much in love, Lenny and Linda Brown (James Woods and Sean Young) are still struggling to make ends meet in New York City when Lenny, a born hustler with financial smarts, receives an extraordinary opportunity from businessman Steven Hill to make his fortune by moving to Los Angeles and selling tax shelters.

Woods has so strong a personality it is unbelievable a man his age wouldn't have found an angle by this time. Woods is riveting throughout, but he's just too old to express the sort of youthful, unspoiled optimism he's called upon to play in the initial scenes.

Fat L.A. cats with money on their hands nearly climb over one another to invest in Lenny's real estate schemes.

His expanding balloon is popped by word that Congress proposes to close the tax loopholes through which he and his clients are benefiting. In a panic, Lenny steals $20,000 from his boss, is dismissed, and suddenly finds himself deep in the hole financially, as well as hooked on the cocaine he started taking only as a "boost" to get him through rough times.

The couple retreats to the simple life in Santa Cruz to dry out and readjust. It's just self-delusion, as a visit from their main connection and his bimbo gets them hooked again and hurls them much further down the hellhole.

For the film to work at all, the love story between Lenny and Linda must feel as overpowering as it is meant to, and Woods and Young put this over with miles to spare. Both actors are live wires, so the passion, care and commitment the characters have for one another is palpable at all times.

Unfortunately, the characters' easy, unthinking acceptance of cocaine into their lives feels like an outdated concept at the end of 1988. Although a lot of people clearly are still using it, on this level of society, coke is no longer the chic, ever-present social drug it is depicted here as being, which throws the picture out of whack and makes it seem like a true-life tale of five years ago, perhaps, but not so much of today.

Pic has been well produced with high attention to visual details in settings, costumes and locations, meriting special attention to production designer Waldemar Kalinowski and Howard Atherton for his evocative lensing in many diverse spots. —Cart.

Black mic-mac 2
(Black Hanky Panky 2)
(FRENCH)

Paris   An AMLF release of a Chrysalide Prod./Ciné-Cinq coproduction. Produced by Monique Pauly. Directed by Marco Pauly. Screenplay, Albert Kantof, Marco Pauly; camera (Eastmancolor), Yves Dahan; editor, Christiane Leherissey; music, Jean-Yves D'Angelo, Manu Kathe, Kamil Rustam; art direction, Yan Arlaud; sound, Dominique Lovert, William Flageollet; production manager, Francoise Leherrissey; assistant director, Philippe Berenger. Reviewed at Georges V cinema, Paris, Nov. 29, 1988. Running time: **79 MIN.**

Felix . . . . Eric Blanc
Gabriel . . . . Marc Citti
Taxi Brousse . . . . Félicité Wouassi
Kennedy . . . . Diana Bienvenu
Innocence . . . . Laurentine Milebo
Commissioner . . . . Jean-Claude Dreyfus
Mme. Sauret . . . . Liliane Rovere

■ **The law of sequels applies to "Black mic-mac 2," producer Monique Annaud's followup to her blithe 1986 comedy hit: it's vastly inferior to the prototype.**

Cut from a similar pattern — a white man's tribulations among African immigrant Parisians — it has high spirits but a poor script and undistinguished direction by Marco Pauly.

Original story by Albert Kantof imagines a white police inspector's wild goose chase for a missing jacket with a winning lottery ticket (shades of René Clair). His frantic investigation is complicated by a black journalist and a big African mamma who has the hots for the young white man.

Film showcases Eric Blanc, a rising young black comic who specializes in impersonations of white personalities, but with nothing to lean on, his brashness is wasted. —*Len.*

The Accidental Tourist

Hollywood A Warner Bros. release. Executive producers, Phyllis Carlyle, John Malkovich. Produced by Lawrence Kasdan, Charles Okun, Michael Grillo. Directed by Kasdan. Screenplay, Frank Galati, Kasdan, based on the novel by Anne Tyler; camera (Panavision, Technicolor), John Bailey; editor, Carol Littleton; music, John Williams; sound (Dolby), David MacMillan; production design, Bo Welch; art direction, Tom Duffield; set decoration, Cricket Rowland; set design, Paul Sonski, Nick Navarro, Ann Harris; costume design, Ruth Myers; assistant director, Michael Grillo; casting, Wallis Nicita. Reviewed at Warner Hollywood screening room, L.A., Dec. 5, 1988. MPAA Rating: PG. Running time: 121 MIN.
```
Macon . . . . . . . . . . . . . . . William Hurt
Sarah . . . . . . . . . . . . . . Kathleen Turner
Muriel . . . . . . . . . . . . . . . Geena Davis
Rose . . . . . . . . . . . . . . . . Amy Wright
Julian . . . . . . . . . . . . . . . Bill Pullman
Alexander . . . . . . . . . . . . Robert Gorman
Porter . . . . . . . . . . . . David Ogden Stiers
Charles . . . . . . . . . . . . . . Ed Begley Jr.
```

■ "The Accidental Tourist" is a slow, sonorous and largely satisfying adaptation of Anne Tyler's bestseller of one man's intensely self-contained passage from a state of grief to one of newfound love.

With William Hurt and Kathleen Turner in the title roles and Lawrence Kasdan directing, this should earn some early coin from film buffs and may, with additional acclaim from literary circles, do well in limited release at upscale houses.

Anne Tyler's novel about an uptight, travel book writer (Hurt) from the slightly eccentric, financially comfortable Leary family of unmarried middle-aged siblings won the National Book Critics Circle Award. An essentially simple narrative story told in Tyler's witty, inventive style, it is awash in warmth and wisdom about the emotional human animal.

Kasdan and coscripter Frank Galati have made an earnest attempt to stick to the outline of the tome — the chronology and settings are changed only slightly for dramatic emphasis — and much dialog seems to have been lifted right off the pages. Although they succeeded in closely approximating the sensitivity of Tyler's prose, this film version lacks Tyler's humor.

"The Accidental Tourist" still stands on its own as a film that packs an emotional, if restrained, wallop. Weighty tone is set from

the opening scene where Turner, having just made tea for Hurt upon his return from a travel-writing excursion, calmly informs him she's moving out. The murder of their 12-year-old son the previous year at summer camp has dampened her spirit and enthusiasm to interact with other people — and especially with Hurt, her laconic, stoic and seemingly emotionally vacant spouse.

Then, in a series of strange, unpredictable and out-of-character encounters with his unruly dog's trainer (Geena Davis), Hurt finds himself in another, vastly different, relationship.

Davis is unabashedly forward, poor, openly vulnerable; a flamboyant dresser and most importantly, has a sickly son (Robert Gorman) who fills the parental void in Hurt's life.

Kasdan takes his time with the characters, especially Hurt, who is in every scene in the film, so it isn't until halfway through that the scenario begins to jell as the closed, routine-oriented, thin-lipped personalities of the Leary family (Amy Wright, David Ogden Stiers, Ed Begley Jr.) work to move Hurt towards the warm and open Davis.

That Hurt remains expressionless and speaks in a monotone, except at the very end, puts a damper on the hopefulness of his changing situation.

Filmmakers overuse close head shots, which may have been an attempt to expose some of Hurt's feelings by zeroing in on the actor's blank looks. This becomes a wearisome technique, effectively weighing the material down unnecessarily.

Davis is the constant, upbeat force in the proceedings, although her verbal hits at Hurt to force his hand come too much from left field. Turner is equally compelling and sympathetic throughout, never crying and trying valiantly to maintain some dignity through considerable humility.

The sepia-washed look to this production, from the dark paneled interiors of the Leary house to the somewhat seedy, overdecorated tenement flat Davis has on the other side of the tracks, effectively juxtaposes stifling orderliness with chaos and warmth. Bo Welch gets credit for creating the settings that match the brown and gold look of an eastern fall.

Visual strategies aside, development is not as well realized in the one secondary relationship, that between Hurt's painfully desperate sister (beautifully played by Amy

Wright) and his book publisher, Julian (Bill Pullman), whose nice looks and relative youth make him an unlikely match for such a plain wallflower as Wright.

Set to a constant and uncharacteristically restrained score by John Williams, pic gradually builds to its inevitable conclusion where Hurt literally places his baggage on a Paris sidestreet, signaling a break with the past.

As unintentionally serious as pic turned out to be, it still is a cathartic film experience which should touch many. —*Brit.*

Onno 23
(DUTCH)

Amsterdam A Frans Van de Staak production. Written and directed by Bea Reese. Camera (color, 16m), Reinhard Köcher; editor, Rob Klinkert, Menno Boerema; sound, Erik Langhout. Reviewed at the Dutch Film Museum, Amsterdam, Sept. 12, 1988. Running time: 73 MIN.
With: Inna van der Molen, Wally Tax, Har Smeets, Ad Fernhout, Huub van der Lubbe, Jannke Dekker, Merel van Neerbos, Filip Bolluyt, Jack Montan.

■ A first film that obeys the theatrical unities of time, place and action, "Onno 23" offers some slickly choreographed camerawork to expand writer-director Bea Reese's birthday party premise, which examines the inexorable boredom of the Me Generation.

Reese pokes her camera around the apartment where friends are gathering for the 23d birthday of title character, Onno. Helmer displays sophisticated cinematic ability but the material remains more suited for the stage where its gabby goings-on have a more apt frame. —*Wall.*

Beaches

Hollywood A Buena Vista release of a Touchstone Pictures presentation in association with Silver Screen Partners IV of the Bruckheimer/South-All Girl production. Produced by Bonnie Bruckheimer-Martell, Bette Midler, Margaret Jennings South. Executive producer, Teri Schwartz. Coproducer, Nick Abdo. Directed by Garry Marshall. Screenplay, Mary Agnes Donoghue, based on the novel by Iris Rainer Dart; camera (Metrocolor), Dante Spinotti; editor, Richard Halsey; music, Georges Delerue; production design, Albert Brenner; art direction, Frank Richwood; set design, Harold L. Fuhrman; set decoration, Garrett Liews; costume design, Robert de Mora; sound (Dolby), Jim Webb; assistant director, Benjamin Rosenberg; second unit director, Nick Abdo; casting, Mike Fenton, Judy Taylor. Reviewed at the Avco Cinema, L.A., Dec. 7, 1988. MPAA Rating: PG-13. Running time: 123 MIN.
```
CC Bloom . . . . . . . . . . . . . . Bette Midler
Hillary Whitney Essex . . . Barbara Hershey
John Pierce . . . . . . . . . . . . . John Heard
Dr. Richard Milstein . . . . . . Spalding Gray
Leona Bloom . . . . . . . . . . . . Lainie Kazan
```

```
Michael Essex . . . . . . . . . . . . James Read
Victoria Essex . . . . . . . . . Grace Johnston
CC (age 11) . . . . . . . . . . . . Mayim Bialik
Hillary (age 11) . . . . . . . . . Marcie Leeds
```

■ Although it is a pulpy concoction that approaches deep concerns in a superficial way, "Beaches" still functions effectively as an engaging tearjerker for mass audiences.

In her most multi-dimensional role since "The Rose," one closely patterned on the popular idea of her own personality, Bette Midler dominates the proceedings as usual with a dynamic performance. Pic is a significant one for Touchstone, in that it features one of its top comedy stars leading viewers into more serious territory, but the transition should prove a simple one and no damper to b.o. prospects.

Story is one of a profound friendship, from childhood to beyond the grave, between two wildly mismatched women, a lower-class Jew from the Bronx whose every breath is showbiz, and a San Francisco blueblood destined for a pampered but troubled life. Men, marriages and career vicissitudes come and go, but their bond ultimately cuts through it all.

Concept is firmly grounded in soap opera but, to the credit of writer Mary Agnes Donoghue and director Garry Marshall, things never become overtly schmaltzy or embarrassingly sentimental, as the 30-year emotional epic is handled with reasonable taste and intelligence. At the same time, it is almost never credible and gets by as entertainment only through a thorough suspension of disbelief.

CC Bloom, from New York and Californian Hillary Whitney meet by chance as 11-year-olds in Atlantic City and have enough fun together to keep corresponding over the years. This frolicsome, sun-bathed section proves enjoyable mainly due to the extraordinary girl, Mayim Bialik, who was found to portray the young Bette Midler. She can sing, she can dance, and she seems amazingly like the carrot-topped star as she brazenly bulldozes her way through a musical routine and most real-life situations.

Jump to the late 1960s, when Hillary, played by Barbara Hershey, turns up in New York and moves into the Alphabet City apartment occupied by CC, now a struggling singer. Attempting to break with her privileged upbringing, Hillary goes to work as an attorney for the ACLU, while CC begins breaking through with an avant-garde theater company run by John Heard.

The pair's friendship turns to enmity once they marry, Hillary to a rich San Francisco lawyer and CC to Heard. After these more transitory unions break up, the women grow back together, mutually realizing the rarity of what they share.

Final section has the ebullient CC, by now a Tony-winning star and bestselling recording artist, nursing Hillary through a grave illness and growing close to the latter's little daughter. Tragic climax and its uplifting follow-up will have many viewers in tears, and in boxoffice terms will probably demonstrate once again that a good cry can be as profitable as a good laugh.

Which is not to say that there aren't a fair share of yocks herein. Midler's strutting, egotistical, self-aware character gets off any number of zingers, but all in the context of a vulnerable woman who seems to accept, finally, that certain things in life, notably happiness in romance and family, are probably unreachable for her. Nothing can stand in the way of CC's professional ambition, which contributes to the touching nature of the choice she makes on behalf of her closest friend.

Midler is winning all the way, and manages to work in numerous musical numbers that help chart her way up the ladder from Off-Broadway actress to revue singer to big-time Broadway star.

By way of needed contrast, Hershey plays her more emotionally untouchable part with an almost severe gravity. Hillary seems to have no real center, which in Hershey's interpretation could be part of the point, as nothing really works out for this woman who has everything — looks, intelligence, money — going for her. Audiences will note that Hershey looks quite different here, with notably fuller lips and a more mature bearing overall, and the effect is a bit disconcerting at first.

Noticeably slimmed down, Heard is appealing as the man who comes between the women for awhile, while Lainie Kazan scores in a perfect casting coup as Midler's mother and Spalding Gray has a nice bit as the one potential prospect in Midler's later period.

Loaded with music and attractively varied settings, pic has been well produced from top to bottom.
— *Cart.*

Sirppi ja Kitara
(From Russia With Rock)
(FINNISH-DOCU)

London A Villealfa Filmproductions production. Executive producer, Aki Kaurismäki. Produced by Pauli Pentti. Directed by Marjaana Mykkänen. Camera (color), Keikki Ortamo, Christian Valdes, Olli Varja; editor, Veikko Aaltonen; sound, Antti Ortamo, Ilgis Sharafutdinov, Mikael Sievers; assistant director, Pauliina Kaarakka. Reviewed at London Film Festival, Nov. 18, 1988. Running time: **108 MIN.**

With: Nautilus Pompilius, Brigada S. Billy Bragg and Aquarium, Boris Grebentsykov, Mister Twister. Avia, Nuance. Va Bank. Cruise, Uriah Heep, Televizor.

■ **Directed by Finnish tv helmer Marjaana Mykkänen, "From Russia With Rock" is the rock docu format at its best, offering a fascinating view of the vibrant world of contempo Soviet sounds. It should prove a draw on tv and the fest circuit.**

The 108-minute pic also provides a unique window on modern Russia as it struggles with the tensions created by perestroika and glasnost. Particularly intriguing is how an authoritarian state copes with a potentially subversive art form when it begins to loosen the chains.

Mykkänen was the only Westerner permitted to film Rockpanorama, a 7-day 50-band event billed as the first rock festival to take place in Russia. For the first time, unofficial bands were allowed to perform alongside sanctioned groups.

There is some remarkable behind-the-scenes footage of the underground Moscow rock circuit. Russian rockers speak with great eloquence (in English) about the significance of rock 'n' roll in their lives and their commitment is reminiscent of a previous generation of Western artists.

On the evidence here, Russian rock is thriving. The groups on show run from heavy metal to futuristic punk and mostly create accessible (often original) sounds. They also seem to have a natural grasp of rock as visual theater.

Pic is considerably enhanced by a sense of suspense surrounding one of the key groups appearing at the fest, Nautilus Pompilius. Hailing from the unlikely environs of Siberia, Nautilus is the fest revelation and faces a classic pop dilemma — to sell out (which in Russian terms means signing on as a state-controlled group) or to continue the "indie" route.

Camera and sound work are top quality in what is overall a rich and satisfying film. — *Coop.*

I'm Gonna Git You Sucka

Chicago An MGM/UA Communications release from United Artists of an Ivory Way production, in association with Raymond Katz Prods. and Front Films. Produced by Peter McCarthy, Carl Craig. Coproducers, Eric Barrett, Tamara Rawitt. Executive producers, Raymond Katz, Eric L. Gold. Written and directed by Keenen Ivory Wayans. Camera (Deluxe color), Tom Richmond; editor, Michael R. Miller; music, David Michael Frank; production design, Melba Farquhar, Catherine Hardwicke; set decoration, Kathryn Peters-Hollingsworth; costume design, Ruth E. Carter; sound (Ultra-Stereo), Oliver L. Moss; assistant directors, Elliot Lewis Rosenblatt, Scott White; casting, Jaki Brown, Robi Reed. Reviewed at Chestnut Station theater, Chicago, Dec. 7, 1988. MPAA Rating: R. Running time: **87 MIN.**

Jack Spade	Keenen Ivory Wayans
John Slade	Bernie Casey
Flyguy	Antonio Fargas
Kung Fu Joe	Steve James
Hammer	Isaac Hayes
Slammer	Jim Brown
Ma Bell	Ja'net DuBois
Cheryl	Dawnn Lewis
Mr. Big	John Vernon

■ **This one's a natural. It's hard to imagine a genre more ripe for parody than the blaxploitation films of the '70s and "I'm Gonna Git You Sucka" milks the opportunity for all it's worth, which should be quite a lot, yielding a sure-fire winner for United Artists.**

Pic is an impressive directorial debut for Keenen Ivory Wayans, who manages to capture the spirit of films like "Shaft," "The Mack" and "Three The Hard Way," while he's making fun of them.

"I'm Gonna Git You Sucka" isn't based on ridicule; it has more to do with good-natured kidding and that protects the integrity of Wayans' story and his characters. Audience can laugh throughout the film at former ghetto crimebuster turned community worker John Slade (Bernie Casey), but when he comes out of retirement for one final effort to clean up the streets and strides, radiating machismo, into a tight closeup to the theme from "Shaft," they scream with appreciation.

Set in "Any Ghetto USA," story opens with discovery of the body of Junebug Spade, who has OG'd (died of an overdose of gold chains) in a dismal parking lot, leaving behind his wife, Cheryl (Dawnn Lewis) and mother, Ma Bell (Ja'net DuBois). Two goons sent by Mr. Big, the sleazy white crime lord, inform the ladies that Junebug died owing $5,000 to the boss and the only way to repay the debt is for Cheryl to join his stable of prostitutes.

Jack Spade (Wayans), Junebug's big brother, returns home from the army just as Ma Bell is

tossing the two goons down the stairs and vows to make Mr. Big pay for his crimes. He enlists the aid of neighborhood bad dudes Slade, Hammer (Isaac Hayes), Slammer (Jim Brown), Flyguy (Antonio Fargas) and Kung Fu Joe (Steve James), and proceeds to kick Big's butt.

Casting is near perfect all the way down the line. Most of the principals have played this sort of thing straight in numerous pics and obviously relish the chance to do it for laughs.

Damon Wayans and Kadeem Hardison are hilarious in supporting roles as the two hapless thugs who end every encounter with the forces of good by tumbling down the nearest staircase. Wayans himself is likable in the lead and quite funny at times, particularly when demonstrating his "combat training" while dancing around in a hail of gunfire. Chris Rock turns a walk-on into a standout as a cheap rib-joint customer who risks severe bodily harm by irking proprietor Hammer.

Wayans' script is tightly written and he uses it to advantage as director, moving things along at a fast clip and throwing in enough sight gags to make a second viewing worthwhile (such as the "10 Most Ugly" wanted poster on the wall in police headquarters). From beginning to end, pic is fast-paced, inventive and, above all very funny. In short, "I'm Gonna Git You Sucka" gits down. — *Brin.*

Inuksuk
(FINNISH)

Lübeck A Gaudeamus release of a Gironfilmi production, with SVT (Lulea) and Inuit Broadcasting Corporation (Canada). Directed by Markku Lehmuskallio. Screenplay, Lehmuskallio, Niilo Hyttinen; camera (color), Pekka Martevo, Bjarne Lönnros; editor, Juho Gartz; music, Mikael Segerström, Hans Sandin; production design, Matti Taponen; sound, Antero Honkanen, Arto Jokisuu, Tom Forsström. Reviewed as official entry in Nordic Film Days, Lübeck. W. Germany, Nov. 6, 1988. Running time: **93 MIN.**

Kaarle Berg	Per Olof Grape
Canadian scientist	Eva Janikova
Eskimo guide	Rasmus Thygesen
Saara Berg	Liisi Tandefeldt

■ **"Inuksuk" is a bleak look at a scientist's life one winter and early spring in Canada's Arctic wastes.**

There is sincerity and a measure of somber poetry in writer-helmer Markku Lehmuskallio's approach to his man-versus-nature subject matter, but it would take audiences accustomed to watching icicles take shape to sit through it.

Loosely based on the diaries of scientist Kaarle Anton Berg, "Inuksuk'' offers the sparse conversation between the researcher of polar bear life and his Eskimo (Inuit is the native word) guide while they sit in their hut or make forays in search of the actual animals.

One day a Canadian scientist joins them. She is a researcher of buffalo life. We never see any buffaloes either, but this Czechoslovakian-born woman at least adds a bit of fun to life in the neighboring huts by teaching the men to draw and serving them Czech doughballs for dinner.

Returning from an expedition, the men find the woman dead, killed (ostensibly) by a polar bear. Now they get into a fight about what kind of burial, European or Inuit, the woman should be given. The guide leaves the hut, while the scientist goes outside to do a little dance of either despair or general craziness.

In doing his dance, the man emulates an Inuksuk, which is a pile of stones put up to look at a distance like a human form. It will come as no surprise at this point to learn that no such Inuksuk is actually seen in the film. —Kell.

Crime Zone

Chicago   A Concorde Pictures release of a Concorde-New Horizons production. Produced and directed by Luis Llosa. Executive producer, Roger Corman. Screenplay, Daryl Haney; camera (color), Cusi Barrio; editor, William Flicker; music, Rick Conrad; art direction, Angel Valdez, Jose Troncojo, Susana Aragon, Adrian Arias; costume design, Patricia Maguill; special effects, Fernando Vasquez de Velasco; sound, Edgar Lostanau; assistant director, Jorgo Garcia Bustamante; casting, Al Guarino, Sandra Wiese. Reviewed at Wood theater, Chicago, Dec. 12, 1988. MPAA Rating: R. Running time: 93 MIN.
Jason . . . . David Carradine
Bone . . . . Peter Nelson
Helen . . . . Sherilyn Fenn
Creon . . . . Michael Shaner
Alexi . . . . Orlando Sacha
J.D. . . . . Don Manor
Cruz . . . . Alfredo Calder
Hector . . . . Jorgo Bustamante

■Roger Corman's latest opus is a competent sci-fi actioner that exceeds its expectations due to producer-director Luis Llosa's stylish handling of the somewhat familiar material. Pic's drawing power is limited by lack of an enticing hook, but it's nonetheless a quality product that should satisfy anyone who strays into the theater.

Script is fuzzy on details and unoriginal in setting, but the plot is interesting. Taking place in some sort of vague, postwar, postplague, futuristic society divided into rigidly defined strata, "Crime Zone" concerns the adventures of

Helen and Bone, a couple of "subgrades" who turn to a life of crime when Jason (David Carradine), a "first tier" bigshot, offers to help them escape from their bleak surroundings in "the dead zone" if they'll pull off a robbery.

Jason turns out to be a traitor, a government operative who recruits criminals to give the police something to do. Helen and Bone, however, turn out to be better-than-average outlaws, something of a post-holocaust Bonnie and Clyde, who elude the cops, go on a real crime spree and finally make a break for freedom. Picture concludes with a twist ending which, while it doesn't come as a complete surprise, adds a nice touch of irony.

"Crime Zone" fills out its screen time with a lot of miscellaneous and oft-seen sci-fi elements, such as a cryogenic hibernation garden for wealthy citizens.

Performances are strong throughout. Sherilyn Fenn and Peter Nelson turn in credible portrayals as the young renegade lovers, despite costume and makeup's apparent intention to turn them into, respectively, copies of Madonna in her like-a-virgin phase, and Michael Biehn, as he appears in "The Terminator."

Michael Shaner is a standout as Creon, the vengeful, half-psycho member of the gang Bone leaves behind. Carradine offers his usual, effectively low-key performance as the completely amoral government agent.

Greatest credit must go to Llosa, who has lensed "Crime Zone" in an energetic style that makes it consistently watchable and entertaining, and provided pic with character that outscripts its relatively meager premise. —Brin.

The Purple People Eater

Hollywood   A Concorde Pictures release of a Motion Picture Corp. of America production. Produced by Brad Krevoy, Steve Stabler. Written and directed by Linda Shayne, based on the song by Sheb Wooley; camera (Foto-Kem color), Peter Deming; editor, Cari Ellen Coughlin; music, various artists; production design, Stephen Greenberg; costume design, Terry Dresbach; choreographer, Ted Lin; sound, Ike Magal; second unit director, Jack Behr; casting, Linda Shayne. Reviewed at Royal theater, L.A., Dec. 10, 1988. MPAA Rating: PG. Running time: 92 MIN.
Grandpa . . . . : . . . . . Ned Beatty
Billy Johnson . . . . Neil Patrick Harris
Rita . . . . Shelley Winters
Mom . . . . Peggy Lipton
Dad . . . . James Houghton
Molly Johnson . . . . Thora Birch
Mr. Noodle . . . . John Brumfield
Mayor . . . . Little Richard
Singer . . . . Chubby Checker

■"The Purple People Eater" film is about on the level of sophistication of the 1958 Sheb Wooley song it's based upon, but what was silly and juvenile 30 years ago seems even more so today.

Hence the virtues of this filmed version most likely won't be sung by anyone older than five. Concorde Pictures has opened it in limited runs at selected sites.

Pic would have had a G rating except for the use of one fairly innocuous expletive. Director-scripter Linda Shayne expands upon the lyrics of Wooley's song about a 1-eyed purple alien creature that drops to earth when a 12-year-old daydreaming boy (Neil Patrick Harris of "Clara's Heart") plays one of his folks' old '50s tunes on a turntable long since put away.

Purple (various voices) looks a little like Cousin It on tv's "The Addams Family" with a shaggy acrylic coat of a particularly garish color, only he has a unicorn horn on his head that lights up and emits musical notes when he's happy and in the mood to be musical with his newfound pal, budding musician Harris.

The duo get together a garage band comprised of neighborhood kids and find themselves instant pop celebrities via the radio waves. When Harris' grandpa (Ned Beatty) and neighbor (Shelley Winters) are threatened with eviction from their bungalow complex by greedy landlord Mr. Noodle (John Brumfield), the Purple People Eaters come to the rescue and hold a benefit concert where Little Richard shows up in his role as the mayor — thereby saving the day and preventing any effort to oust the seniors so that their homes are okayed for condo conversion.

This is the simplist of stories told in a lively enough fashion for tots, who can very easily follow the linear plot and well understand the central dilemma of how Purple and his earthly friends beat out their unpopular foe just by being enthusiastic and energetic kids and joining forces to oppose him.

Musical cameo appearance by Chubby Checker at the lead singer at a Purple People Eater concert is surprisingly well choreographed but the other numbers staged by the group come off strangely since it's fairly obvious that Harris' lounge singer type voice doesn't match his prepubescent speaking one.

For a low-budgeter, pic doesn't

flag any egregious production flaws, even as it at all times seems as if it were lensed within about a 2-block radius of a suburban Southern California neighborhood.—Brit.

Watchers
(CANADIAN)

San Francisco   A Universal Pictures release of a Concorde and Centaur Films presentation of a Rose & Ruby production in association with Canadian Entertainment Investors No. 2 and Company Ltd. Partnership. Executive producer, Roger Corman. Produced by Damian Lee, David Mitchell. Coproducer, Mary Eilts. Directed by Jon Hess. Screenplay, Bill Freed, Lee, based on the novel by Dean R. Koontz; camera (Filmhouse color), Richard Leiterman; editor, Bill Freda, Carolle Alain; music, Joel Goldsmith; production design, Richard Wilcox; art direction, Tom Duquette; set decoration, Marti Wright; costume design, Monique Stranan; sound, Frank Griffiths; assistant director, Lee Knippelberg; sound unit director, Lee; additional camera, Curtis Petersen; casting, Trish Robinson. Reviewed at Kabuki Theater, San Francisco, Dec. 6, 1988. MPAA Rating: R. Running time: 92 MIN.
Travis . . . . Corey Haim
Nora . . . . Barbara Williams
Lem . . . . Michael Ironside
Tracey . . . . Lala
Sheriff Gaines . . . . Duncan Fraser
Cliff . . . . Blu Mankuma
Deputy Porter . . . . Colleen Winton
Hockney . . . . Norman Browning

■It's never very clear here who the watchers are, what they are watching or why, but it's quickly certain nobody will be watching the "Watchers" for long.

Once again, Something Has Gone Wrong in one of those secret government laboratories and the result is a dog that types and plays Scrabble and a hairy orange monster who hates him.

The monster's name is Oxcom, which has to be one of the worst names for a monster in years. Oxcom and the dog were part of a brilliant government scheme for the next war. The plan was to pair these lovable, brilliant dogs with the deadly predators and set them loose on the foe. Once the dog ingratiated itself with the enemy camp, Oxcom would follow up and kill them all.

On the lam, the dog takes up with Corey Haim and his mom Barbara Williams, while Oxcom trails along behind biting the heads off various folks in one of those small horror-film towns where the disappearance of the citizenry never seems to make a whole lot of difference.

Tracking the runaways and those who harbor them, Michael Ironside is a villainous government agent who will stop at nothing to get the animals back. Little do we know, or care, that Ironside himself is the subject of a scientific experiment, trained to kill without conscience.

After much growling and thrashing and blood splashing, in which lenser Richard Leiterman obviously has been instructed never to allow a clear look at Oxcom, everybody ends up at the cabin in the woods.

There's a battle in which Ironside gets his; Haim gets stabbed in the leg; Williams and Haim's girlfriend (Lala), get hysterical; and the dog gets dizzy. —*Har.*

Moonwalker

London   A Warner Bros. release of a Lorimar film. Executive producers, Michael Jackson, Frank Dileo. "Smooth Criminal" segment produced by Dennis Jones. Directed by Colin Chilvers. Written by David Newman, based on a story by Michael Jackson; camera (color), John Hora; editor, David E. Blewitt; original music, Bruce Broughton; production design, Michael Ploog; costumes, Betty Madden; choreography, Vince Paterson, Michael Jackson; visual effects, Hoyt Yeatman. **Anthology Segments:** Produced by Jerry Kramer, Dennis Jones. Directed by Kramer. Co-directors, Will Vinton, Jim Blashfield. Camera (color), Fred Elmes, Crescenzo Notarille; original music, Bruce Broughton; production design, Bryan Jones, John Walker; costumes, Betty Madden; choreography, Russell Clark, Vince Paterson; special effects, Eric Brevig. Reviewed at Warner Bros. preview theater, London, Dec. 7, 1988. Running time: **93 MIN.**
Michael . . . . .Michael Jackson
Sean .Sean Lennon
Katie . . . . .Kellie Parker
Zeke (Baby Bad) Michael . .Brandon Ames
Mr. Big .Joe Pesci

■ **As a hodgepodge of Michael Jackson music videos and lightweight exploration of his thoughts and feelings "Moonwalker" is quite compulsive, but as a theatrical film it is a nonstarter.**

Pic is — understandably — going straight to video in the U.S., but gets a theatrical release in some territories to cash in on Jackson-mania following his recent sellout tours.

What is clear is that Michael Jackson is an entertainment phenomenon, though what also shines through are his many contradictions and quirks. Jackson the mature man seems to be emerging from that naive, childlike Peter Pan figure that has for so long been the Michael Jackson image and those two aspects seem to be not yet reconciled.

"Moonwalker" — also the title of a recent Jackson autobiography — seems unsure of what it was supposed to be. At the center of the pic is the "Smooth Criminal" segment, a musical/dramatic piece full of dancing, schmaltzy kids, sci-fi effects and blazing machine guns. Around it are really just numerous Jackson music videos with little or no linkage. Although quite enjoyable the whole affair does not make for a structured or professional movie.

Pic opens with hi-tech concert footage of "Man In The Mirror" and then quickly switches into a rather indulgent retrospective of Michael Jackson's career featuring clips of old songs, shows and videos.

Next up is a re-shot version of Jackson's "Bad" video, this time featuring 8 to 10-year-old children dancing and miming the song, with Brandon Ames playing the Jackson part. Amusing to begin with, the section becomes rather unsettling as the children pretend to be adults, with pelvic thrusts, fake stubble, et al.

Next segment is "Speed Demon" with Jackson disguised as a rabbit chased by fans. Skillful blend of live-action and animation make it quite fun, but again indulgent. Next up is the song "Leave Me Alone," the most fascinating section, featuring comments about Jackson from the tabloids accompanied by expert animation by Jim Blashfield. Section shows Jackson can take the jokes and also features a guest appearance by his monkey Bubbles.

The "Smooth Criminal" section is the cornerstone of "Moonwalker" featuring Michael and his kiddie pals (including Sean Lennon) chased by gun-toting, black-garbed baddies. The 11-minute music and dance sequence is genuinely fine.

"Smooth Criminal" blends into a live performance of Jackson singing the Beatles' song "Come Together," and over the credits Ladysmith Black Mambazo perform "The Moon Is Walking."

In many ways "Moonwalker" is the ultimate home movie with Jackson getting the chance to indulge in his fantasies. His manager Frank Dileo gets featured (in-joke is that the Mr. Big baddie in "Smooth Criminal" is also based on him) and undoubtedly it was fun making for all concerned. Jackson fans will love "Moonwalker," but great music and sharp dancing do not a good movie make. —*Adam.*

Never Say Die
(NEW ZEALAND)

Auckland   An Everard Films production in association with the N.Z. Film Commission. (Intl. sales except N.Z., Kings Road Intl.) Produced by Geoff Murphy, Murray Newey. Executive producer, Barrie Everard. Written and directed by Geoff Murphy. Camera (color), Rory O'Shea; editor, Scott Conrad; music, Billy Kristian, Sam Negri; production design, Bill Gruar; sound, Mike Westgate. Reviewed at St. James Theater, Auckland, N.Z., Dec. 9, 1988. Running time: **103 MIN.**
Alf . . . . .Temuera Morrison
Melissa . . . . .Lisa Eilbacher
Inspector Evans . . . . .Tony Barry
Witten . . . . .George Wendt
    Also with: John Clarke, Martyn Sanderson, Phillip Gordon, Judith Fyfe, Jay Laga'aia, Paul Murphy, Peter Tait, Geoff Murphy.

■ **"Never Say Die" is an upmarket version of Geoff Murphy's 1981 road movie "Goodbye Pork Pie" and confirms his reputation as New Zealand's foremost and most tantalizing director.**

Admittedly shot on a tight timetable and budget earlier this year, this sometime spoof of the James Bond genre ignites here and there but never quite fires. On this evidence, the promise still lies just out of reach.

Newspaper reporter Alf (Temuera Morrison) returns to New Zealand having just survived O.E. (Overseas Experience). He is in a highly agitated state.

He is welcomed back by his American love, Melissa (Lisa Eilbacher), who diagnoses paranoia until Alf convinces her that their love nest in Auckland's inner city Ponsonby was not blown up as a result of leaking gas.

She recalls a sinister conversation overheard at an L.A. airport when she was traveling to New Zealand. Neither now is sure who is the target and who is out to get whom. Neither, it seems, is Inspector Evans (Tony Barry).

While hiding out on an island, the couple shoot an intruder who might or might not be pursuing them. Soon the entire police force is after them, as well as the "enemy," as they attempt to solve the mystery on the run.

"Never Say Die" is long on stunts and car chases and short on cohesive story flow that would help capture and hold audience attention.

Some set pieces delight. A notable sequence involves Melissa holding out against a helicopter attack while an old disk of "Ghost Riders In The Sky" bumps around a battered turntable. There are also moments of groaning parody that work well — a love scene intercut with the shiny barrel of a hunting rifle being unzipped from its case.

While leads Morrison and Eilbacher are not helped by a thin script, they perform creditably. Eilbacher lights up the screen whenever given the chance. Morrison, less experienced and lacking a tad in old-fashioned smoulder, projects a wry, laid-back quality and shows a talent for comedy. Tony Barry, a carryover from "Goodbye Pork Pie," is reliable and there is juicy playing from Judith Fyfe and Martyn Sanderson as a couple of Kiwi gothics.

Standout moments come from comedian John Clarke in a cameo role as a used car salesman with a palate for antipodean patter.

Murphy is a filmmaker of serious concerns who often seems overpowered by his delight in (technical) incendiary effects.

"Never Say Die" should do well on the home market where it is being given wide release over Christmas and New Year's. Off-shore, it may need more careful handling. —*Nic.*

Fright Night Part 2

Sydney A New Century/Vista release (Tri-Star in Australia), of a Vista Organization film. Produced by Herb Jaffe, Mort Engelberg. Directed by Tommy Lee Wallace. Screenplay, Tim Metcalfe, Miguel Tejada-Flores, Wallace, based on characters created by Tom Holland; camera (color), Mark Irwin; editor, Jay Lash Cassidy; music, Brad Fiedel; production design, Dean Tschetter; costume design, Joseph Porro; visual effects coordinator, Gene Warren Jr.; special effects, Rick Josephson. Reviewed at Fox Columbia screening room, Sydney, Sept. 27, 1988. MPAA Rating: R. Running time: **101 MIN.**

Peter Vincent	Roddy McDowall
Charley Brewster	William Ragsdale
Alex	Traci Lin
Regine	Julie Carmen
Belle	Russell Clark
Bozworth	Brian Thompson
Louie	Jonathan Grieg
Dr. Harrison	Ernie Sabella
Ritchie	Merritt Butrick

■ **"Fright Night Part 2" begins with scenes from 1985's original, and continues in the same vein. Pic has played off modestly in Australia, and though its camp humor and goopy effects are familiar, it's better than the average shlocker.**

At the outset, young Charley (William Ragsdale) has completed therapy and is cautiously certain he just imagined that vampire neighbor in Part 1. Before long a quartet of sinister types have come to live in the old apartment where Charley's friend, tv horror host Peter Vincent (Roddy McDowall) resides, and the mayhem starts all over again.

This time, the vampires are led by a slinky femme fatale (Julie Carmen) and include an androgynous black, a leather-jacketed hood and a muscle-bound, silent type. Vincent and Charley face the usual assortment of terrors before the creatures are vanquished.

Helmer Tommy Lee Wallace brings freshness to the proceedings via inventive use of the wide screen (destined to be lost when the pic makes a swift transition to video) and a ghoulish sense of humor, such as introing the character of a shrink who keeps on behaving like a shrink even after he's been vampirized.

Special effects are very good, and pic delivers just as many thrills and chuckles as its predecessor; as a sequel, it's about on a par with the original, and far more up-market than most items of this genre. In this one, the pretty college girl (Traci Lin) asks Charley for a date — not to a disco or to a rock gig, but to a Mahler concert!
—*Strat.*

Pulse

New York A Columbia Pictures release of an Aspen Film Society production. Executive producer, William E. McEuen. Produced by Patricia A. Stallone. Written and directed by Paul Golding. Camera (Deluxe color). Peter Lyons Collister; editor, Gib Jaffe; music, Jay Ferguson; sound (Dolby), Susumu Tokunow; production design, Holger Gross; art direction, Maxine Shepard; set decoration, Greta Grigorian; assistant director, Mike Topoozian; production manager, Charlie Skouras; macro photography, Oxford Scientific Films; additional camera, James R. Tynes; second unit camera, Gary Wagner; additional editor, Norman Buckley; stunt coordinator, Mike Cassidy; associate producer, Robert C. Edwards; casting, Meg Liberman. Reviewed on RCA/Columbia Home Video vidcassette, N.Y., Dec. 3, 1988. MPAA Rating: PG-13. Running time: **91 MIN.**

Bill	Cliff DeYoung
Ellen	Roxanne Hart
David	Joey Lawrence
Stevie	Matthew Lawrence
Old man	Charles Tyner
Pete	Dennis Redfield
Paul	Robert Romanus
Howard	Myron D. Healey

■ **"Pulse" is a superior sci-fi thriller that finds horror in the context of everyday electrical appliances gone amuck.**

Pic received only a token theatrical release last March by Columbia, duly protested by the filmmakers, but will find an appreciative audience on the rebound (now in homevideo release) among genre buffs.

Opening scenes are most disquieting, as the man next door to happy suburban couple Cliff DeYoung and Roxanne Hart goes crazy one night and destroys his home, with all the neighbors watching helplessly. DeYoung's son Joey Lawrence comes to L.A. from his mom's place in Colorado to spend the summer and understandably is apprehensive as stepmom Hart shows him the house's protective devices, including prison-like bars which snap shut in front of the living room's picture window.

Paranoia, described here as merely "heightened awareness," soon takes hold of the kid as writer-director Paul Golding carefully develops a host of small details into a convincing pattern of technology gone haywire. Tantalizing (but left ambiguous to spur the viewer's imagination) sci-fi explanation is that sudden pulses of electricity have altered the appliances in several homes as if some alien force were communicating destructive messages to the Earthly machinery. An old coot (ably played by Charles Tyner) tells the boy this tale and gradually it seems credible.

Surefire format of "boy who cried wolf," as no one believes Joey's fears, extends well to Hart finally coming around (but put out of commission in a scalding shower scene) and then dad DeYoung joining up with Joey to fight the "possessed" house in a harrowing finale. It's scary and easy to identify with, especially Golding's plot point that consumers (and repairmen alike) know little of the workings of faulty equipment and are a bit uneasy at those mysterious noises emitted at night by furnaces, refrigerators, etc.

Cast, especially young Joey Lawrence, is quite effective in making one believe in the far-fetched. Pic is extremely well photographed, with kudos to Peter Lyons Collister and others, plus eerie macro photography of circuit boards with solder bubbling and other extreme closeup work by Oxford Scientific Films (ace lenser Haskell Wexler gets a thank you credit as well). —*Lor.*

Sans peur et sans reproche
(Without Fear Or Blame)
(FRENCH)

Paris An AMLF release of a CPFI/Arturo Prods./TF1 Films coproduction. Produced by Jean-Claude Fleury. Directed by Gérard Jugnot. Screenplay, Jugnot, Christian Biegalski, Jean-Bernard Pouy; camera (color), Gérard de Battista; editor, Catherine Kelber; music, Yves de Bujadoux; art direction, Jean-Louis Poveda; costumes, Christine Guegan; sound, Guillaume Sciama, Claude Villand, Bernard Le Roux; makeup, Catherine Demesmaeker; assistant director, Laurent Laubier; production manager, Charlotte Fraisse. Reviewed at Marignan-Concorde theater, Paris, Dec. 15, 1988. Running time: **98 MIN.**

Bellabre	Gérard Jugnot
Bayard	Rémi Martin
Jacques de Mailles	Gérard Darmon
Blanche de Savoie	Anne-Gisel Glass
Mignard de Parthode	Ticky Holgado
Charles VIII	Patrick Timsit
Sottomayor	Roland Giraud
François de Paule	Romain Bouteille
Jeanne	Victoria Abril
Louis XII	Martin Lamotte

Also with: Gérard Klein, Bruno Carette, Alain Doutey, Jean-Louis Foulquier, Anémone, Michel Blanc, Josiane Balasko, Carol Brenner, Jacques Delaporte.

■ **A spirited but only sporadically funny historical pastiche, "Sans peur et sans reproche" is funnyman Gérard Jugnot's third foray behind (and in front of) the camera.**

A product of the Parisian cafe-theater milieu, he continues to work in a brash, often sophomoric style of comedy that may be basically for local tastes.

Script by Jugnot, Christian Biegalski and Jean-Bernard Pouy starts from a genuine medieval legend about a low-born squire (Rémi Martin) who, out of a frustrated passion for a noblewoman (Anne-Gisel Glass), joins King Charles XIII's campaign to reconquer the kingdom of Naples at the end of the 15th century and becomes a hero.

Jugnot casts himself as a conceited army captain interested in forging his own legend but gradually obliged to groom Martin as a successor of sorts. Latter, after defying the newly enthroned King Louis XII (Martin Lamotte) and a sadistic Spanish marquis (Roland Giraud), wins the woman and returns to an anonymous life.

Action, which begins with a farcical tournament, jostles with sight gags, anachronistic dialog and parody to mixed results, which often recall the gruesome lunacy of "Monty Python And The Holy Grail," minus the savage, anarchistic inspiration. Jugnot thumbs his nose at taste and it's in flash visual gags that he raises some of the most raucous laughs.

Jugnot, sporting a wig and hook hand, is ably supported by comic troupers who include some of his old cafe-theater cronies (with Anémone, Michel Blanc and Josiane Balasko in cameo appearances). Actor-director shows fair ability in handling a costume production much more elaborate than his two previous, modern-dress comedies.

Tech credits are good. Film was lensed in Portugal. —*Len.*

Vicious
(AUSTRALIAN)

New York An SVS Films release of a Premiere Film Marketing Ltd. presentation, in association with Medusa Communications Ltd., of a David Hannay production. Executive producer, Tom Broadbridge. Produced by David Hannay, Charles Hannah. Line producer, Lynn Barker. Directed by Karl Zwicky. Screenplay, Paul J. Hogan, Zwicky, from Hogan's original idea; camera (Atlab color), John Stokes; editor, Roy Mason; music, Robert Scott, John Sleith; sound, David Glasser; art direction, Marc Ryan, Diana Reynolds; production manager, Barbi Taylor; assistant director, Bob Howard; special makeup effects, Deryck De Neise; stunt coordinator, Bernie Ledger. Reviewed at West Side Cinema 1, N.Y., Dec. 24, 1988. No MPAA Rating. Running time: **88 MIN.**

Damon Kennedy	Tamblyn Lord
Terry	Craig Pearce
Sondra Price	Tiffiny Dowe
Felix	John Godden
Benny	Kelly Dingwall
Claire	Leather
Diane Kennedy	Joanna Lockwood
Gerry	Frank McNamara
Professor	Ralph Cotterill

■ **"Vicious" is an obnoxious**

Australian exploitation film that's unlikely to arouse much interest following its inappropriate holiday-season booking in Manhattan.

Sony sent director Karl Zwicky's previous pic, a supernatural horror opus titled "Contagion," direct to video Stateside and that would seem to have been the appropriate course for this violent cheapie.

Tamblyn Lord gives an earnest performance as Damon Kennedy, a rich young kid who's turned into a ruthless killer after falling in with a trio of juvenile delinquents in the environs of Harvest Bay and Sydney. At first he enjoys the "liberating" aspects of their amoral lifestyle, but learns the hard way when they take his mention of a rich businessman acquaintance as an excuse to rob his house and coldbloodedly kill his family.

Vulgar screenplay by Zwicky and Paul J. Hogan (emphatically not the "Crocodile Dundee" star) relies upon too many coincidences to be credible and becomes ludicrous when striving to ape Sam Peckinpah's "Straw Dogs" in the theme of an innocent put to the test by mindless violence. In fact, cynical ending has Damon not triumphing over baser instincts but rather accommodating them, as an act of revenge supposedly equips him for today's business world where one has to have a "killer" mentality.

Tech credits are subpar for an Aussie offering, particularly the sound mix which has plenty of dead spots.—*Lor.*

Lodz Ghetto
(DOCU-B&W/COLOR)

Florence Produced by the Jewish Heritage Project with a grant from the National Endowment for the Humanities and the Corp. for Public Broadcasting. Produced by Alan Adelson. Executive producer, Stephen Samuels. Directed by Kathryn Taverna, Adelson. Screenplay, Adelson; camera (b&w, color), Jazef Piwkowski, Eugene Squires; editor, Taverna; music editor, Taverna; original score, Wendy Blackstone; still photography, Gary Becker, Taverna. Voice of Mordechai Chaim Rumkowski: Jerzy Kosinski. Reviewed at the Festival dei Popoli, Florence, Italy, Dec. 3, 1988. Running time: **103 MIN.**

■The powerful impact of "Lodz Ghetto," where Polish and later Czech Jews were used as slave labor by the Nazis from 1940 to their extermination camps in 1944, owes much to its unusual blend of scrupulously reconstructed historical documents (photos, diaries, even color cinematography) and a fiction-like dramatic structure.

Alan Adelson and Kathryn Taverna have collected a stunning array of images that speak for themselves, creating a chilling emotional impact.

Lodz (pronounced Wudge in Polish, Ludge in the film) was occupied by the Germans in September 1939 to the welcoming "Heil Hitlers" of German-Poles. In March, all the city's Jews were locked in the rundown ghetto or shot. With the arrival of over 1,000 Czechs after the "de-Jewing" of Prague, the ghetto's population touched 200,000. Only 800 survived till liberation.

Film tells the ghetto's story with amazing immediacy, using 1,000 still photographs made at great risk by ghetto dwellers, color slides taken by an unknown German photographer, and six minutes of authentic filmed images made in the ghetto by the Nazis. Cleverly blended in is footage of today's ghetto. The whole is smooth, narrated by voices taken from diaries and writings.

While the Jewish community becomes a labor camp for the Nazis, struggling to keep alive on ever-dwindling rations, the Nazi-appointed ghetto leader Mordechai Chaim Rumkowski (played with bleating insistence by novelist Jerzy Kosinski, who lost his family in the Lodz ghetto) goads them to work harder, keep quiet and obey the Germans. At one point the Germans demanded 20,000 child victims under 10, and Rumkowski, weeping, urges parents to turn them over to "save the ghetto." Though many believed Rumkowski would protect the ghetto from being liquidated, in the end he is put on a train with the rest of them and deported to a death camp. Demoralized, near starvation, the last of the community boards the trains. Only a few frightened resisters hide out in the cellars and survive.

Words cannot express the horror of the Lodz story, but Adelson and Taverna come close in this chillingly narrated and illustrated photo-documentary. Cinematography is crisp and clear, sound imaginatively used. —*Yung.*

The Girl In A Swing
(BRITISH-U.S.)

Copenhagen A Nordisk Film release (in Denmark) of a Panorama Film Intl. production. (Intl. sales, J&M Entertainment.) Produced by Just Betzer, Benni Korzen. Directed by Gordon Hessler. Screenplay, Hessler, based on Richard Adams' novel; camera (Eastmancolor), Claus Loof; editor, Robert Gordon; music, Carl Davis; sound, Preben Mortensen; production design, Rob Schilling; casting, Marilyn Johnsson, Simone Reynolds (England), Myers-Tesschner (U.S.); costumes, Betina Betzer, Marjorie Lavelly; production management, Sally Pardo, Michael Obel; assistant directors, John Hilbard, Tony Dyer; associate producer, Pernille Siesbye. Reviewed at Palads, Copenhagen, Dec. 13, 1988. Running time: **117 MIN.**
Karin . . . . Meg Tilly
Alan . . . . Rupert Frazer
The Vicar . . . . Nicholas Le Prevost
Mrs. Dresland . . . . Elspet Gray
Flick . . . . Lorna Heilbron
Angela . . . . Claire Shepherd
Mrs. Taswell . . . . Jean Boht
Deidre . . . . Sophie Thursfield
Barbara . . . . Lynsey Baxter
 Also with: Klaus Pagh, Hanne Borchsenius, Axel Strölye, Ebbe Langberg, Jan Petersen, Helen Cherry, Patrick Godfrey, June Ellis, Hilary Minster, Leonard McCuire, Oliver Ford Davis.

■British writer-director Gordon Hessler has turned Richard Adams' 1980 psycho-chiller novel "The Girl In A Swing" into a smooth, fine-looking piece of romantic-erotic entertainment with many a fine Hitchcockian touch and a rather special star turn by Meg Tilly.

Item is a J&M world sales pickup outside the U.S. and looms as a small but solid winner in general exhibition.

In Adams' novel, the story is wordy and obscure, but Hessler has clarified matters considerably, to the point of introducing a direct cause-and-effect explanation of heroine Karin Föster's death wish. This keeps her from finding lasting happiness with Alan (Rupert Frazer), a shy British ceramics dealer.

During their brief Florida honeymoon Karin's feelings of guilt and Alan's premonitions of disaster mount. They seek solace in their joy of sex. Karin also joins Alan in his hunt for ceramic treasures. When she succeeds in finding, and buying for next to nothing, a third example of the porcelain rarity "The Girl In The Swing" (the others reside in London's Victoria & Albert Museum and in Boston's Museum of Fine Arts), they are assured of instant wealth, and Karin tries to take Holy Communion from a vicar friend to make a clean break with the past.

Instead of absolution, Karin finds fear and guilt taking full possession of her, while Alan indulges her. It becomes more and more obvious that Karin must have killed the baby that came before the one she is now pregnant with.

The recurring theme of guilt, atonement and punishment is gently explored during the development of suspense, while the time taken out for sexual relief is accounted for rather ploddingly in sequences that are unlikely to raise anyone's pulse. None of the many secondary actors are allowed to do much more than stand around feeding cue lines, while Tilly and Frazer are in practically every frame.

Frazer displays deep-rooted emotion under a surface of cleancut reserve. Tilly, on the contrary, runs the gamut of manners and moods. She is, in spite of a contrived Teutonic accent combined with a (supposedly coquettish?) lisp, wholly convincing whether expressing sexual abandon, poetic frailty or fear-stricken despair.

All production credits, including cinematography by Claus Loof and music by Carl Davis, are first-rate while the 117 minutes' running time could stand some pruning. —*Kell.*

INDEX

A

B

Bab Sama Maftouh (A Door on Heaven) 11-30-88
Babette's gastebud (Babette's Feast) 5-6-87
Baby Boom 9-23-87
Baby Doll 11-16-88
Bach & Broccoli 3-25-87
Bachelor Girl 11-18-87
Bacio Di Giuda, Il (The Kiss of Judas) 9-14-88
Back to the Beach 8-12-87
Backfire 5-20-87
Backstage 4-20-88
Bad Dreams 4-6-88
Bad Taste 6-1-88
Baixo Gavea (Gavea Girls) 4-22-87
Baja Oklahoma 2-24-88
Bakayarool (Watakushi, Okotteimasu) (You Bloody Fool! I'm Angry)
    11-30-88
Balada Da Praia Dos Caes (The Ballad of Dogs' Beach) 9-23-87
Ballhaus Barmbek (Let's Kiss & Say Goodbye) 10-19-88
Bamba, La 5-20-87
Bantsuma-Bando Tsumasaburo no Shogai (Bantsuma-The Life of
    Tsumasaburo Bando) 3-30-88
Banzai Runner 6-24-87
Bar-cel-ona 4-22-87
Barbablu Barbablu (Bluebeard Bluebeard) 10-7-87
Barbarians, The 5-20-87
Barenhauter, Der (Bear-Skinned Man) 5-6-87
Barfly 5-13-87
Bari, Al (The Innocent) 4-13-88
BAT 21 10-5-88
Baton Rouge 10-5-88
Batteries Not Included 12-16-87
Beach Balls 10-19-88
Beaches 12-21-88
Beaks (Birds of Prey) 12-2-87
Beast, The 9-21-88
Beat Generation, The - An American Dream 3-18-87
Beat, The 5-20-87
Beauf, Le 2-11-87
Beauty & the Beast 5-27-87
Bedroom Window, The 1-7-87
Beetlejuice 3-30-88
Beginnelse pa en historie (The Beginning of a Story) 8-24-88
Beirut: The Last Home Movie 11-25-87
Bejalai (To Go on a Journey) 5-6-87
Believers, The 6-10-87
Belinda 5-20-87
Bell Diamond 4-8-87
Bell of Chernobyl 10-12-88
Bellman & True 12-2-87
Belly of an Architect, The 5-6-87
Bengali Night, The 11-16-88
Benji the Hunted 6-17-87
Berlin Blues 8-24-88
Bernadette 2-17-88
Berserker 5-27-87
Besame Mucho (Kiss Me Tight) 9-2-87
Besokarna (The Visitor) 5-25-88
Best Seller 9-23-87
Betrayed 8-24-88
Better Tomorrow II, A 2-17-88
Betzilo Shel Helem Krav (China Ranch) 4-27-88
Beverly Hills Cop II 5-20-87
Beyond the Rising Moon 5-18-88
Bez Bebek (Cloth Doll) 7-13-88
Big 6-1-88

Big Bad Mama II 10-14-87
Big Bang, The 8-5-87
Big Blue, The 2-24-88
Big Business 6-8-88
Big Shots 9-23-87
Big Time 9-7-88
Big Top Pee-wee 7-27-88
Big Town, The 9-16-87
Biglal Hamilkhama Hahi (Because of That War) 8-31-88
Bikini Shop, The (The Malibu Bikini Shop) 2-18-87
Bikutsi Water Blues (L'Eau de misere) 11-30-88
Biloxi Blues 3-23-88
Bingo, Bridesmaids & Braces 6-29-88
Bird 5-18-88
Birds of Prey 9-7-88
Biri Vo Digerleri (One & the Others) 7-13-88
Bit Part, The 11-4-87
Black mic-mac 2 (Black Hanky Panky 2) 12-21-88
Black Widow 2-4-87
Blackout 10-12-88
Blanc de chine (Chinese White) 6-15-88
Blind Date 4-1-87
Blindside 9-2-87
Blob, The 7-27-88
Blond Dolly 4-8-87
Blood Diner 9-2-87
Blood Money 5-18-88
Blood Relations 5-25-88
Blood Sisters 6-17-87
Bloodspell 11-16-88
Bloodsport 3-2-88
Bloody New Year 5-27-87
Bloody Wednesday 11-11-87
Blucher 11-23-88
Blue City Slammers 5-4-88
Blue elettrico (Electric Blue) 11-30-88
Blue Iguana, The 4-20-88
Blue Monkey 10-7-87
Blue Movies 2-10-88
Blue Scar 10-19-88
Blueberry Hill 5-18-88
Blues LaHofesh HaGadol (Late Summer Blues) 8-26-87
Boca del Lobo, La (The Lion's Den) 10-5-88
Boda del Acordeonista, La (The Accordionist's Wedding) 11-23-88
Body Beat (Dance Academy) 11-16-88
Body Count 6-15-88
Body Slam 5-20-87
Bohater Roku (Hero of the Year) 4-29-87
Boheme, La 2-24-88
Boite a Soleil, La (The Box of Sun) 10-19-88
Bol'se Sveta! (More Light!) 3-30-88
Bonjour l'angoisse (Hello Anxiety) 8-31-88
Bony a Klid (Big Money) 4-27-88
Book of Days 11-30-88
Boost, The 12-21-88
Border 2-3-88
Border Radio 11-25-87
Borderline 10-19-88
Born Again: Life in a Fundamentalist Baptist Church 9-23-87
Born in East L.A. 8-26-87
Born of Fire 10-28-87
Born to Race 2-10-88
Bosque Animado, El (The Enchanted Forest) 10-7-87
Bouba 1-6-88
Boulevard of Broken Dreams 5-25-88
Boundaries of the Heart 5-25-88
Braca Po Matieri (Half-Brothers) 8-31-88
Braddock: Missing in Action III 1-27-88
Brain Damage 4-20-88
Brain, The 11-9-88
Brand New Day 12-23-87
Brave Little Toaster, The 7-15-87
Bravestarr 9-7-88
Break of Dawn 9-28-88

Dolghyie Provod (The Long Goodbye) 4-8-87
Dolls 4-22-87
Dolly, Lotte & Maria 9-28-88
Dolunay (Full Moon) 6-1-88
Dom na Trubnoi (The House on Trubnaya Square) 11-30-88
Domani Accadra (It'll Happen Tomorrow) 5-11-88
Dominick & Eugene 3-16-88
Donna della Luna, La (Woman in the Moon) 7-13-88
Donna Donna! 4-27-88
Donna Spezzata (A Woman Destroyed) 8-10-88
Doom Asylum 2-17-88
Door 8-10-88
Dorado, El 5-11-88
Dorst (Thirst) 5-4-88
Dotknieci (The Afflicted) 10-19-88
Down Twisted 3-18-87
Doxobus 2-10-88
Dr. Sun Yatsen 4-8-87
Drachenfutter (Dragon Food) 9-23-87
Dragnet 7-1-87
Dragonard 5-27-87
Dream Demon 9-28-88
Dreamaniac 2-25-87
Dreaming, The 5-25-88
Dreckschleuder, Die (The Muckrakers) 4-22-87
Drehort Berlin (Set in Berlin) 3-25-87
Dressmaker, The 5-11-88
Drifter, The 3-16-88
Driving Me Crazy 9-28-88
Drole d'endroit pour une recontre (A Strange Place for an Encounter) 11-9-88
Drowning by Numbers 5-11-88
Drums of Winter 10-12-88
Du Mich Auch 3-11-87
Dudes 9-23-87
Dueno del Sol, El 7-22-87
Duenos del Silencio, Los (The Owners of Silence) 5-6-87
Dum Pro Dva (A House for Two) 8-24-88
Duma Vez Por Todas (Play...Boy) 5-6-87
Dun-Huang 7-27-88
Dustforough (The Peddler) 11-30-88
Dutch Treat 3-18-87
Dzusovy Roman (A Juicy Romance) 8-17-88

E

Earth Girls Are Easy 9-14-88
Eastern Condors 9-2-87
Eat the Rich 9-30-87
Eau/Ganga (Water/Ganges) 4-22-87
Eden Miseria 8-31-88
Edge of Hell, The (Rock 'n' Roll Nightmare) 7-8-87
Een maand later (A Month Later) 9-23-87
Ei (Egg) 5-18-88
Eiga Joyu (Actress) 9-2-87
Eight Men Out 8-31-88
Eighteen Again 3-16-88
Eighty-seven Days + Eleven 10-28-87
Einstweilen Wirdes Mittag (Meantime, It's Already Noon) 4-27-88
Ekti Jiban (Portrait of a Life) 3-2-88
El Sada El Regal (Gentlemen) 10-19-88
Eldorado (The Midas Touch) 9-14-88
Ele, o Boto (He, the Dolphin) 8-5-87
Elvira, Mistress of the Dark 9-28-88
Elvis Hansen - en samfundshjalper (Elvis Hansen - A Pillar of Society) 11-30-88
Elvis-Kissan Jaljilla (On the Trail of Elvis the Cat) 9-2-87
Emanon 2-3-88
Embajador de la India, El (The Ambassador from India) 10-19-88

Emmanuelle 5 1-21-87
Emmanuelle 6 7-20-88
Emperor's New Clothes, The 5-27-87
Empire of the Sun 12-2-87
Empire State 4-8-87
En Dernier Recours (In the Last Resort) 9-2-87
En el Humo de Esta Epoca (The Houses Are Full of Smoke) 9-23-87
En el Nobre de Dios (In the Name of God) 6-24-87
En el nombre del hijo (In the Name of the Son) 12-2-87
En is jartam Isonzonal (I Too Was at the Isonzo Battle) 4-15-87
En Retirada (In Retirement) 8-12-87
En toute innocence (No Harm Intended) 3-30-88
Encore (Once More) 8-24-88
End of the Line 2-24-88
Enemy Territory 5-20-87
Enfance de l'Art, L' (Childhood of Art) 5-25-88
Enigma 3-2-88
Enkel resa (One Way Ticket) 6-8-88
Ennemis intimes (Intimate Enemies) 1-13-88
Entre Compadres Te Veas (Dirty Dealings Between Buddies) 4-6-88
Entre Ficheras Anda el Diablo (The Devil Lurks among Bar Girls) 9-2-87
Envoyez les violons (Bring on the Violins) 8-31-88
Epidemic 4-29-87
Equalizer 2000 6-24-87
Ernest Goes to Camp 5-20-87
Ernest Saves Christmas 11-16-88
Erzekeny Buscu A Fejedelemtol (A Fond Farewell to the Prince) 4-29-87
Es Cosa Con Plumas (With Feathers) 4-13-88
Escuadron de la Muerte (Death Squad) 5-6-87
Esperame en el Cielo (Wait for Me in Heaven) 3-23-88
Esperando la Carroza (Waiting for the Pallbearers) 9-2-87
Estacion Del Regreso, La (The Season of Our Return) 12-2-87
Et Dieu...Crea La Femme 3-9-88
Etat de grace, L' (State of Grace) 1-7-87
Ete dernier a Tanger, L' (Last Summer in Tangiers) 4-29-87
Ete en pente douce, L' (Summer on a Soft Slope) 7-29-87
Eternal Evil 5-4-88
Eternamente Pagu (Pay Forever) 8-31-88
Etter Rubicon (After Rubicon) 8-26-87
Etudiante, L' (The Student) 10-5-88
Eu (Me, Myself & I) 5-13-87
Eulalia 9-2-87
Eva Guerrillera 10-14-87
Everlasting Secret Family, The 3-9-88
Everybody's All-American 11-2-88
Evil Dead 2 3-18-87
Evil Laugh 11-23-88
Evil Spawn 10-7-87
Evil Town 12-2-87
Extrano Hijo del Sheriff, El (The Sheriff's Strange Son) 1-7-87
Extreme Prejudice 4-29-87
Eye of the Eagle 1-6-88

F

F...ing Fernand 11-25-87
Fabula de la Bella Palomera (Fable of the Beautiful Pigeon Fancier) 10-5-88
Fakelos Polk Ston Aera (Polk File on the Air) 11-16-88
Falsch 5-20-87
Falsche Wort, Das (The False Word) 12-2-87
Famiglia, La (The Family) 2-25-87
Family Viewing 9-23-87
Far North 9-14-88
Farm, The 5-20-87
Fat Guy Goes Nutzoid 4-15-87
Fatal Attraction 9-16-87

G

H

H Fanella Me To Ennia (Striker with the No. 9) 11-30-88
Ha'Instalator (The Plumber) 5-6-87
Hairspray 1-27-88
Haitian Corner 8-10-88
Haizi Wang (King of the Children) 5-18-88
Hajnali Haztetok (Roofs at Dawn) 5-6-87
Hakaitz Shel Avia (Avia's Summer) 10-19-88
Halloween 4: The Return of Michael Myers 10-26-88
Halodhia Choraye Baodhan Khai (The Catastrophe) 2-17-88
Hamburger Hill 8-12-87
Hamlet Liikemaailmassa (Hamlet Goes Into Business) 3-23-88
Hammerhead Jones 5-20-87
Handful of Dust, A 5-11-88
Hangmen 5-27-87
Hanna's War 4-27-88
Hanoi Hilton, The 3-25-87
Hansel & Gretel 5-27-87
Hanussen 7-13-88
Happy Bigamist 6-17-87
Happy End 7-27-88
Happy Hour 5-27-87
Happy New Year 8-12-87
Harakiri 11-16-88
Hard Rock Zombies 1-13-88
Hard Ticket to Hawaii 6-10-87
Harry & the Hendersons 5-27-87
Haunted Summer 9-14-88
Haunting of Hamilton High, The 5-27-87
Havinck 11-25-87
Hawaiian Rainbow 11-4-87
Hawks 6-1-88
Hay Que Deshacer La Casa (We Must Undo the House) 2-25-87
Hayallerim, Askim ve Sen (My Dreams, My Love & You) 7-13-88
He's My Girl 9-16-87
Heart 11-4-87
Heart of Midnight 5-25-88
Heartbeat 100 7-8-87
Heartbreak Hotel 9-28-88
Hearts of Fire 11-4-87
Heartstrings: Peter, Paul & Mary in Central America 4-29-87
Heat & Sunlight 9-30-87
Heat 3-11-87
Heaven 4-1-87
Hector 10-19-88
Hei Pao Shi Jian (The Black Cannon Incident) 4-8-87
Hell Comes to Frogrown 7-27-88
Hell Hunters 6-1-88
Hellbound: Hellraiser II 9-14-88
Hello Actors Studio 11-25-87
Hello Again 11-11-87
Hellraiser 5-20-87
Helsinki Napoli All Night Long 5-18-88
Henri Storck, Eyewitness 11-25-87
Her Name Is Lisa 2-11-87
Herencia de Valientes (Legacy of the Brave) 6-17-87
Hero & the Terror 8-10-88
Heroic Pioneers 4-1-87
Herseye Ragman (Despite Everything) 6-1-88
Het oog boven de put (The Eye above the Well) 10-12-88
Hey, Maestro! 6-29-88
Hi-Fi 7-29-87
Hidden City 5-27-87
Hidden, The 10-28-87
Hiding Out 11-4-87
High Hopes 9-7-88
High Season 6-3-87
High Spirits 11-23-88
High Tide 5-20-87
High-Frequency (Aquarium) 8-31-88
Higher Education 5-27-87
Hijo de Piedro Navajas, El (The Son of Pedro Navajas) 5-6-87
Hikaru Anna (Luminous Woman) 10-7-87

Himmel og Helvede (Heaven & Hell) 10-19-88
Himmel Uber Berlin, Der (The Sky over Berlin) (Wings of Desire) 5-20-87
Himmo, Melech Yerushalayim (Himmo, King of Jerusalem) 12-23-87
Hip, Hip, Hurra! (Hip, Hip, Hurray!) 9-2-87
His Girl Friday 3-2-88
Histoire de Vent, Une (A History of Wind) 9-28-88
Hol Volt, Hol Nem Volt (A Hungarian Fairy Tale) 4-29-87
Hollywood Chainsaw Hookers 3-30-88
Hollywood Cop 2-17-88
Hollywood Shuffle 3-18-87
Holy Terror 11-25-87
Hombre de Exito, Un (A Successful Man) 1-21-87
Hombre de la Deuda Externa, El (The Man of the Foreign Debt) 5-6-87
Hombre Desnudo, El (The Naked Man) 9-23-87
Home Is Where the Hart Is 12-9-87
Home Remedy 12-23-87
Homeboy 9-21-88
Homme amoureux, Un (A Man in Love) 5-13-87
Homme Voile, L' (The Veiled Man) 10-14-87
Hong Gaoliang (Red Sorghum) 2-24-88
Honneponnetje (Honeybunch) 8-24-88
Hope & Glory 7-15-87
Horsenschimmen (Mind Shadows) 2-24-88
Horses in Winter 10-12-88
Hostage 11-4-87
Hot Child in the City 8-12-87
Hot Pursuit 5-13-87
Hot to Trot 8-31-88
Hotarugawa (River of Fireflies) 9-2-87
Hotel Colonial 1-21-87
Hotel de France 5-20-87
Hotel du Paradis 5-20-87
Hotel St. Pauli 5-18-88
Hotel Terminus: Klaus Barbie, His Life & Times 5-25-88
Hotet/Uhkkadus (The Threat) 4-22-87
Hotreal (Damn Real) 3-2-88
Hotshot 2-11-87
Hour of the Assassin 4-8-87
House 6-24-87
House II: The Second Story 5-20-87
House of Games 9-9-87
House on Carroll Street, The 3-2-88
Housekeeping 10-7-87
Howling IV...The Original Nightmare 11-23-88
Hoxsey: The Quack Who Cured Cancer 9-30-87
Hudodelci (The Felons) 5-4-88
Huller i suppen (Holes in the Soup) 10-19-88
Hungry Feeling, A: The Life And Death Of Brendan Behan 5-11-88
Hunk 3-11-87
Hunter's Blood 5-27-87

I

I Cammelli (The Camels) 9-28-88
I Kekarmeni (Shaved Heads) 4-15-87
I Love N.Y. 5-20-87
I Married a Vampire 4-27-88
I Miei Primi Quarant'Anni (My First Forty Years) 11-25-87
I morgen er det slut (Tomorrow It Is Over) 2-17-88
I skugga Hrafnsina (In the Shadow of the Raven) 10-19-88
I Was a Teenage Zombie 7-8-87
I Will Not Make Any More Boring Art 10-19-88
I Yineka Pou Evlepe ta Onira (The Woman Who Dreamed) 8-31-88
I Zoe Me Ton Alki (Life with Alkis) 11-30-88
I'm Gonna Git You Sucka 12-21-88
I've Heard the Mermaids Singing 5-20-87
Ibunda (Mother) 6-24-87
Idegenlegiosok (Mercenaries) 5-6-87

If Looks Could Kill 12-30-87

Igry Dlja Detej Skol'nogo Vozrasta (Games for Schoolchildren)
  3-11-87

Iguana 5-18-88

Il est genial Papy! (Gramps Is a Great Guy!) 12-23-87

Illegally Yours 10-26-88

Illusory Thoughts 7-6-88

Illustrious Energy 4-20-88

Imagen Latente (Latent Image) 1-27-88

Imagens do inconsciente (Pictures from the Unconscious) 5-4-88

Imagine: John Lennon 9-28-88

In a Shallow Grave 4-27-88

In Crowd, The 11-9-88

In Dangerous Company 10-5-88

In der Wuste (In the Wilderness) 10-14-87

In Georgian (In Georgia) 2-24-88

Incident at Raven's Gate 8-31-88

Indian Summer 5-27-87

Indianer, Der (The Red Indian) 4-13-88

Ingen kan alska som vi (There Is No Love Like Ours) 8-31-88

Initiation 5-27-87

Innerspace 6-24-87

Innocents, Les (The Innocents) 2-3-88

Inquiesta, L' (The Investigation) 3-25-87

Inseln Der Illusion (Isles of Illusion) 5-4-88

Instant Justice (Marine Issue) 4-1-87

Interventsia 8-19-87

Inuksuk 12-21-88

Invasion Earth: The Aliens Are Here 10-5-88

Invisible Kid, The 4-6-88

Io e Mia Sorella (Me & My Sister) 1-13-88

Ira, You'll Get into Trouble 7-1-87

Irgendwie Power Machen (Get Your Finger Out) 5-4-88

Iris 5-27-87

Iron Eagle II 11-16-88

Iron Warrior 3-25-87

Ironweed 12-16-87

Is-Slottet 2-24-88

Ishtar 5-13-87

Issue de Secours 9-21-88

Isten Veletek, Barataim (Farewell to You) 4-27-88

It Couldn't Happen Here 5-25-88

It Takes Two 7-20-88

Itazu (Forest of Little Bear) 9-2-87

J

Jaahyvaiset Presidentille (Goodbye, Mr. President) 2-25-87

Jack's Back 5-4-88

Jacob 10-5-88

Jakob Hinter Der Blauen Tur (Jacob Behind the Blue Door) 5-4-88

Jane & the Lost City 4-8-87

Jane B. par Agnes V. (Jane B. by Agnes V.) 2-24-88

Jarrapellejos 4-27-88

Jaws - The Revenge 7-22-87

Jeg elsker dig (I Love You) 2-25-87

Jenatsch 5-20-87

Jeux d'artifices (Games of Artifice) 8-5-87

Jilted 11-4-87

Jim & Piraterna Blom (Jim & the Priates) 4-22-87

Jin (The Well) 9-28-88

Jocks 1-28-87

John & the Missus 2-11-87

John Huston & the Dubliners 8-26-87

John Huston 9-28-88

Johnny Be Good 3-23-88

Johnny Flash 4-15-87

Johnny Monroe 9-23-87

Joker, Der (Lethal Obsession) 7-6-88

Joshua, Joshua 3-30-88

Journal d'un fou, Le (The Diary of a Madman) 11-4-87

Journey to Spirit Island 10-19-88

Journey, The 3-25-87

Juana la Cantinera (Juana the Saloon Keeper) 6-24-87

Judgment in Berlin 5-4-88

Juego Mas Divertido, El (The Most Amusing Game) 2-24-88

Juillet en septembre (July in September) 7-27-88

Julia & Julia 9-9-87

Julia's geheim (Juliet's Secret) 10-7-87

Jumpin' Night in the Garden of Eden, A 3-2-88

Junge Mit Dem Grossen Schwartzen Hund, Der (The Boy with the Big
  Black Dog) 4-15-87

Jungfruresan (Maiden Voyage) 10-23-88

Juntos (Together) 8-5-87

Jupon rouge, Le (The Red Skirt) 9-23-87

Just Ask for Diamond 11-30-88

Just Like America 10-14-87

K

Kacamak (Impromptu) 11-30-88

Kadaicha 6-8-88

Kaftane El Hob (Caftan of Love) 11-30-88

Kalamazoo 5-25-88

Kalte Paradies, Das (Frosty Paradise) 11-30-88

Kamilla & the Thief 6-8-88

Kampen om den rode ko (The Fight for the Red Cow) 12-30-87

Kamu Onna (A Woman Who Bites) 8-31-88

Kandyland 1-13-88

Kansas 9-28-88

Kapax del Amazonas (Kapax, The Man from the Amazon) 1-21-87

Karhozat (Damnation) 2-24-88

Karma 9-14-88

Kataku No Hito (House on Fire) 11-11-87

Katinka 5-18-88

Katze, Die (The Cat) 2-10-88

Ke Dyo Avga Tourkias (And Two Eggs from Turkey) 12-2-87

Keeping Track 6-24-87

Kelvin & His Friends 12-2-87

Keresztuton (On the Crossroad) 3-11-87

Keufs, Les (The Flatfoots) 2-3-88

Kholodni Mart (Cold March) 5-18-88

Kholodnoe Leto Piatdesiat Tretiego (Cold Summer of 1953) 8-31-88

Kiattas es Kialtas (Cry & Cry Again) 3-30-88

Kid Brother, The 9-2-87

Kidnapped 5-20-87

Killer Klowns from Outer Space 6-8-88

Killer Workout 4-15-87

Killer's Nocturne 6-3-87

Killing Affair, A 4-27-88

Killing Time, The 10-28-87

Kindred, The 1-21-87

King James Version 4-6-88

King Lear 9-2-87

Kingsajz (King Size) 8-3-88

Kiss Daddy Good Night 11-25-87

Kiss the Night 4-20-88

Kiss, The 10-12-88

Kitchen Toto, The 5-13-87

Kleine Staatsanwalt, Der (The Little Prosecutor) 3-11-87

Kol Ahavotai (All My Loving) 1-21-87

Komissar (Comissar) 8-5-87

Komitas 9-14-88

Kommunist (The Communist) 10-19-88

Komplizinnen (Accomplices) 5-4-88

Konbu Finze (The Terrorizers) 3-11-87

Konitz 5-25-88

Konzert fur die Rechte Hand (Concerto for the Right Hand) 3-11-87

Madonna Mann, Der (The Madonna Man) 2-24-88
Madrid 7-29-87
Magdalena Viraga 10-7-87
Magic Snowman, The 1-6-88
Magic Sticks 9-2-87
Magic-Queen in Hungary 3-11-87
Magino-Mura Monogatari (Tales from the Magino Village) 5-6-87
Magnat (The Magnate) 10-7-87
Magnificent Warriors 5-27-87
Magyar Stories 4-6-88
Maid to Order 7-29-87
Maison assassinee (The Murdered House) 8-3-88
Maison de jade, La (House of Jade) 11-23-88
Maison de Jeanne, La (Jeanne's House) 2-24-88
Maitre de Musique, La (The Music Teacher) 9-14-88
Majorettes, The 10-19-88
Making Mr. Right 3-25-87
Making Opera 10-19-88
Makom Le'yad Hayam (A Place by the Sea) 6-29-88
Mal d'aimer, Le (The Malady of Love) 1-21-87
Maladie d'amour (Malady of Love) 11-25-87
Malarpirater (Pirates of the Lake) 11-25-87
Malaventura (Misadventure) 10-5-88
Maldeniye Simion (Simion of Maldeniye) 2-25-87
Malinkaiya Vera (Little Vera) 7-20-88
Malom a Pokolban (Mills of Hell) 3-11-87
Malone 5-13-87
Mamba (Fair Game) 6-22-88
Man Eaters 5-25-88
Man on Fire 9-9-87
Man Outside 1-13-88
Man Spricht Deutsch 4-27-88
Man Who Mistook His Wife for a Hat, The 5-4-88
Man with Three Coffins, The 10-7-87
Maniac Cop 5-25-88
Manifesto 6-1-88
Mankillers 11-4-87
Mannequin 2-11-87
Mapantsula 5-25-88
Maramao 11-4-87
Marauders 10-7-87
Mariana, Mariana 2-3-88
Marie S'en Va-T-En Ville (Marie in the City) 2-24-88
Marilyn Monroe: Beyond the Legend 12-9-87
Maroc, Corps et ames (Morocco, Bodies & Souls) 3-30-88
Married to the Mob 7-27-88
Marsupials, The: The Howling III 5-20-87
Martha, Ruth & Edie 5-25-88
Marusa No Omna II (A Taxing Woman's Return) 8-31-88
Marusa No Onna (A Taxing Woman) 9-16-87
Mas Alla del Silencio (Beyond Silence) 10-14-87
Mas Buenas quel el Pan (Better Than Bread) 2-25-87
Mas Vale Pajaro en Mano...(A Bird in the Hand Is Worth...) 7-22-87
Mascara 5-20-87
Maschenka 5-20-87
Maschera, La (The Mask) 5-18-88
Masik Ember, A (The Other Person) 3-2-88
Masquerade 3-16-88
Masques (Masks) 3-4-87
Massacre in Dinosaur Valley 1-21-87
Masterblaster 7-8-87
Masters of the Universe 8-12-87
Matar o Morir (Kill or Die) 6-17-87
Matewan 5-20-87
Matka Krowlow (The Mother of Kings) 10-7-87
Mauri 8-10-88
Maurice 8-26-87
Means & Ends 4-8-87
Meatballs III 5-20-87
Meier 3-11-87
Memoire des apparences: la vie est un songe (Life Is a Dream) 12-2-87
Memorias y Olvidos (Things Forgotten & Not) 10-19-88
Memories of Me 9-21-88
Mendiants, Les 8-19-87

Mer om oss barn i Bullerby (More about the Children of Bullerby Village) 9-23-87
Mercenary Fighters 3-30-88
Meridienne, La (The Lounge Chair) 7-6-88
Messalina, Messalina 7-29-87
Messenger of Death 9-21-88
Messenger, The 4-29-87
Method, The 5-20-87
Mi General (My General) 6-17-87
Mi Nombre Es Gatillo (My Name Is Gatillo) 7-8-87
Michael 11-16-88
Michel Strogoff 7-6-88
Michelangelo, Self-Portrait 9-23-87
Midnight 7-8-87
Midnight Crossing 5-11-88
Midnight Movie Massacre 5-18-88
Midnight Run 7-20-88
Mientras Haya Luz (While There Is Light) 10-7-87
Mignon e Partita (Mignon Has Left) 10-5-88
Mikroscop, Das (The Microscope) 3-30-88
Milagro Beanfield War, The 3-9-88
Miles from Home 5-25-88
Milk & Honey 9-7-88
Million Dollar Mystery 6-17-87
Mind Killer 12-2-87
Mio in the Land of Faraway 8-26-87
Miracle Mile 9-7-88
Miracles 5-6-87
Miracule, Le 3-4-87
Mirage 5-27-87
Mirazhi Ljubvi (Mirages of Love) 8-24-88
Mirch Masala (A Touch of Spice) 8-5-87
Miss Arizona 3-23-88
Miss Millionersha (Miss Million) 7-20-88
Miss Mona 4-15-87
Miss...Or Myth? 7-1-87
Missile 3-30-88
Mississippi Burning 11-30-88
Misterio Eva Peron, El (The Eva Peron Mystery) 10-19-88
Moa 2-11-87
Moderns, The 4-13-88
Mofles y los Mecanicos, El (Mofles & the Mechanics) 4-1-87
Moine et La Sorciere, La (Sorceress) 9-23-87
Mois d'avril sont meurtriers, Los (April Is A Deadly Month) 8-5-87
Moj Ata, Socialisticni Kulak (My Dad, the Socialist Kulak) 8-24-88
Moloka'i Solo 5-4-88
Momo 3-18-87
Mon ami le traitre (My Friend the Traitor) 11-16-88
Mon bel amour, ma dechirure (My True Love, My Wound) 7-8-87
Mon cher sujet (My Dear Subject) 5-25-88
Mondo New York 4-20-88
Monkey Shines 7-27-88
Monster Squad, The 8-12-87
Monte Napoleone 4-1-87
Montecarlo Gran Casino 1-13-88
Month in the Country, A 5-13-87
Moon in Scorpio 2-24-88
Moon over Parador 8-31-88
Moonstruck 12-16-87
Moonwalker 12-28-88
Mord i Paradis (Murder in Paradise) 11-16-88
Morgan Stewart's Coming Home 2-18-87
Morning Man, The 4-15-87
Moros y Cristianos (Moors & Christians) 12-2-87
Mortu Nega 9-28-88
Mortuary Academy 5-25-88
Mosca Addio (Moscow Farewell) 4-1-87
Moustachu, Le (The Field Agent) 5-27-87
Movidas del Mofles, Las (Mofles' Escapades) 1-6-88
Moving 3-9-88
Moziklip (Movie Clip) 5-4-88
Mr. Nice Guy 5-27-87
Mr. North 7-20-88
Mr. Universe 3-2-88

N

O

P

Q

R

S

T

Tel Aviv-Berlin 8-26-87
Telephone, The 1-27-88
Teljes nap, Egy (A Full Day) 3-2-88
Tempos Dificeis (Hard Times) 9-7-88
Tender Hooks 10-12-88
Tenebrae 2-18-87
Tenku no shiro Laputa (Laputa) 12-2-87
Tequila Sunrise 11-30-88
Tequiman 2-3-88
Teresa 12-23-87
Terirem 2-3-88
Terminal Entry 8-10-88
Terminus 3-18-87
Terre etrangere/Das Weite Land (Unknown Country) 5-20-87
Terre Para Rose (Land for Rose) 1-27-88
Terror Squad 4-27-88
Terug naar Oegstgeest (Return to Oegstgeest) 5-20-87
Tesoro (Treasure) 10-26-88
Testament 5-25-88
Testament d'un poete juif assassine (Testament of a Murdered Jewish
    Poet) 5-27-87
Testet (The Test) 5-20-87
Testimony 12-23-87
Texas Comedy Massacre, The 1-6-68
Thanatos 1-7-87
The Year My Voice Broke 8-19-87
Thelonius Monk: Straight, No Chaser 11-30-88
Theofilos 11-18-87
They Live 11-9-88
They Still Call Me Bruce 6-3-87
Thin Blue Line, The 3-23-88
Things Change 9-7-88
Thinkin' Big 4-27-88
Thirty Million Rush, The 7-29-87
This Is Not Our Destination 11-4-87
This Is Our Home, It Is Not for Sale 12-2-87
Thorny Way to the Stars, The 12-2-87
Those Dear Departed 8-19-87
Thou Shalt Not Kill...Except 9-30-87
Three Bewildered People in the Night 8-19-87
Three by Three 4-1-87
Three for the Road 4-8-87
Three Kinds of Heat 5-20-87
Three Men & a Baby 11-25-87
Three O'Clock High 9-2-87
Three to Get Ready 5-4-88
Thrill Kill 1-13-88
Throw Momma from the Train 12-16-87
Thunder Warrior 2 6-24-87
Thy Kingdom Come...Thy Will Be Done 2-3-88
Ti Presento Un'Amica (Quite by Chance) 3-30-88
Ticket 10-14-87
Tierra de Valientes (Land of the Brave) 12-2-87
Tiger Warsaw 9-7-88
Tiger's Tale, A 8-26-87
Tilinteko (The Final Arrangement) 2-24-88
Time Guardian, The 11-25-87
Time of Destiny, A 4-13-88
Time Out 2-3-88
Tin Men 3-11-87
Tisserands du Pouvoir, Les (Mills of Power, Part I) 11-30-88
To Hurt & to Heal 7-1-87
To Kill a Priest (Le Complot) 9-7-88
To Magiko Yiali (The Magic Glass) 11-30-88
To Mend the World 9-2-87
Tod des Empedokles, Der (The Death of Empedocles) 3-4-87
Toda la Vida (All Life Long) 5-6-87
Tokyo Pop 4-13-88
Tommy Tricker & the Stamp Traveller 5-25-88
Too Much 9-16-87
Too Outrageous! 9-9-87
Topio Stin Omihli (Landscape in the Mist) 9-7-88
Torch Song Trilogy 12-7-88
Tot Oder Lebendig (Dead or Alive) 2-24-88

Touche de bleue, Une 5-25-88
Tough Guys Don't Dance 5-20-87
Tougher than Leather 9-21-88
Track 29 5-25-88
Trading Hearts 6-8-88
Trage des Anderen Last, Einer (Bear Ye One Another's Burdens) 3-2-88
Tragico Terremoto en Mexico (Tragic Earthquake in Mexico) 12-23-87
Traigo...Muertas, Las (I Do 'Em In) 4-1-87
Train of Dreams 9-2-87
Traum Vom Elch, Der (I Dreamed of My Elk) 2-18-87
Travelling avant (Dolly In) 8-26-87
Travelling North 1-21-87
Travestie, La (The Transvestite) 8-24-88
Traxx 10-5-88
Treasure of the Moon Goddess 5-27-87
Treibhaus, Das (The Hothouse) 5-6-87
Trein naar Holland (Train to Holland) 6-17-87
Trem Para as Estrelas, Um (A Train for the Stars) 5-20-87
Trena Di Panna (Milk Train) 9-14-88
Trente-deux Dicembre (The 32d of December) 4-13-88
Trente-Six Fillette (Size 36 Girls) 5-18-88
Tres menos eu (Three Minus Me) 5-4-88
Trespasses 8-26-87
Tribunal, Das - Mord am Bullenhuser Damm (The Tribunal - The
    Murders on Bullenhuser Street) 3-11-87
Trinajstata Godenica Na Princa (The Thirteenth Bride of the Prince)
    4-22-87
Triumph Der Gerechten (Triumph of the Just) 3-18-87
Trois places pour le 26 (Three Seats for the 26th) 11-16-88
Trouble with Spies, The 12-9-87
True Colors 2-18-87
Tucker: The Man & His Dream 8-3-88
Tuesday Wednesday 9-2-87
Tunel, El (The Tunnel) 6-22-88
Turnabout 10-12-88
Tuske A Korom Alatt (A Thorn under the Fingernail) 3-23-88
Twice Dead 11-9-88
Twins 12-7-88
Twisted Nightmare 9-21-88
Two Dollars & a Dream 12-2-87
Two Hundred Thirty-Five million 4-27-88
Two Moon Junction 5-4-88

U

U ime naroda (In the Name of the People) 7-29-87
U2 Rattle & Hum 11-2-88
Uhoho Tankentai (The Hours of Wedlock) 5-6-87
Ultimo Momento (Last Moment) 12-2-87
Umbruch (Marble in Pieces) 11-25-87
Una Pura y Dos con Sal (One Straight & Two with Salt) 5-6-87
Unbearable Lightness of Being, The 2-3-88
Under Cover 6-10-87
Under the Boardwalk 5-25-88
Underachievers, The 6-27-88
Unfinished Business... 3-11-87
Unholy, The 4-27-88
Uni To Dokuyaku 3-11-87
Uninvited 7-27-88
Unnamable, The 6-15-88
Unsichtbare, Der (The Invisible Man) 12-23-87
Untouchables, The 6-3-87
Uppu (Salt) 3-30-88
Urgences (Emergencies) 5-4-88
Urinal 10-19-88
Ursula 4-1-87
Usodni Telefon (The Fatal Telephone) 7-29-87
Utekajme, uz ide! (Hurry, He's Coming) 11-30-88
Uvek spremne zene (Woman's Day) 7-29-87

V

Va de Nuez (Once Again) 10-14-87
Valahol Magyarorszagon (Rear-Guard) 3-2-88
Valdei Stalin (Stalin's Children) 1-13-88
Valet Girls 5-6-87
Vallee fantome, La (The Ghost Valley) 9-2-87
Vampire at Midnight 10-26-88
Vampire's Kiss 9-21-88
Vampires 6-8-88
Van geluk gesproken (Count Your Blessings) 1-13-88
Vargenstid (Age of the Wolf) 4-27-88
Varjoja paratiisissa (Shadows in Paradise) 2-25-87
Vash Syn I Brat (Your Son & Brother) 10-19-88
Veneno para las Hadas (Poison for Fairies) 1-21-87
Venner for altid 2-25-87
Vent De L'illa, El (The Island Wind) 4-27-88
Venusfalle, Die 5-25-88
Veo Videno (Deja Vu) 7-29-87
Vera 3-4-87
Verbieten Verboten (Forbidden to Forbid) 5-4-88
Vergessen Sie's (Just Forget It) 3-2-88
Verliebten, Die 3-4-87
Verlockung, Die (The Temptation) 3-2-88
Vermischte Nachrichten (Odds & Ends) 3-11-87
Verne Miller 9-2-87
Vernehmung der Zeugen (Interrogation Of The Witness) 1-13-88
Versteckte Liebe (Secret Love) 4-1-87
Viaje al Paraiso (Trip to Paradise) 7-22-87
Vibes 8-10-88
Vice Versa 3-2-88
Vicious 12-28-88
Video Dead, The 11-25-87
Vie del Signore Sono Finite, Le (The Ways of the Lord Are Finite)
    1-6-88
Vie dissolue de Gerard Floque, La (The Debauched Life of Gerard Floque)
    2-18-87
Vie est Belle, La (Life Is Rosy) 5-27-87
Vie est un long fleuve tranquille (Life Is a Long Quiet River) 2-24-88
Vie Platinee, La (Treichville Story) 10-14-87
Ville etrangere (Foreign City) 5-11-88
Vincent - The Life of Vincent Van Gogh 5-20-87
Violins Came with the Americans, The 4-8-87
Vios Ke Politia (Living Dangerously) 11-18-87
Viper 5-18-88
Viragaya (The Way of the Lotus) 8-12-87
Virgin Queen of St. Francis High, The 12-9-87
Vision, The 1-6-88
Visione del Sabba, La (The Witches' Sabbath) 3-23-88
Vlci Bouda (Wolf's Lair) 3-4-87
Voices of Sarafina! 9-28-88
Volpone, Il (The Big Fox) 3-23-88
Voyage of the Rock Aliens 2-10-88
Vreme Razdelno (Time of Violence) 5-25-88
Vroeger Is Dood (What's Past Is Dead) 2-25-87
Vroom 5-11-88
Vzlomshik (Burglar) 7-1-87

W

W Starym Dworku (In an Old Manor House) 5-6-87
W zawieszeniu (Suspended) 10-7-87
Walk Like a Man 4-15-87

Walk on the Moon, A 2-11-87
Walker 12-2-87
Walking After Midnight 5-25-88
Wall Street 12-9-87
Wann, Wenn Nicht Jetzt (When, If Not Now?) 5-4-88
Wannseekonferenz, Die (The Wannsee Conference) 3-4-87
Wanted: Dead or Alive 1-21-87
War 9-28-88
War Party 9-28-88
Warm Nights on a Slow Moving Train 5-20-87
Warrior Queen 2-4-87
Warriors of the Apocalypse 10-7-87
Wash, The 5-25-88
Watashi o Ski Ni Tsuretette (Take Me Out to the Snowland) 12-2-87
Watchers 12-21-88
Water Also Burns 5-6-87
Waxwork 9-14-88
Way Upstream 12-23-87
We Think the World of You 9-21-88
Weapons of the Spirit 4-8-87
Weave of Time, A 4-22-87
Weeds 10-28-87
Welcome Maria 12-9-87
Welcome to Germany 5-25-88
Werwolf von W., Der (TheWerewolf of W.) 4-6-88
West Is West 7-6-88
Whales of August, The 5-13-87
What's Love 5-27-87
Wheels of Terror 2-11-87
When the Wind Blows 2-11-87
Where the Heart Roams 5-27-87
Wherever You Are 9-14-88
White Mischief 12-2-87
White Monkey, The 12-2-87
White Phantom 10-14-87
White Water Summer 12-30-87
White Whales 5-27-87
White Winter Heat 11-25-87
Whites of the Eye 5-20-87
Who Framed Roger Rabbit 6-22-88
Who Killed Vincent Chin? 3-9-88
Who's That Girl 8-12-87
Wielki Bieg (The Big Race) 6-17-87
Wierna rzeka (The Faithful River) 10-14-87
Wigilia (Christmas Eve) 10-19-88
Wild Pair, The 12-23-87
Wild Thing 4-22-87
Wild Things 11-30-88
Wilde Mann, Der (The Wild Man) 8-31-88
Wildfire 9-7-88
Willow 5-18-88
Wimps 11-25-87
Wind, The 11-25-87
Winners Take All 6-17-87
Winter Tan, A 9-23-87
Wisdom 1-7-87
Wish You Were Here 5-13-87
Witch Hunt 6-24-87
Witchboard 1-21-87
Witches of Eastwick, The 6-10-87
With Love to the Person Next to Me 8-19-87
With Time to Kill 2-17-88
Withnail & I 2-11-87
Without a Clue 10-5-88
Witness to a Killing 10-14-87
Witnesses 9-14-88
Wizard of Loneliness, The 6-8-88
Wizard of Speed & Time, The 5-25-88
Wo-te ai (This Love of Mine) 3-30-88
Wohin? (Where to Go?) 5-4-88
Women's Club, The 5-27-87
Wonder Women 11-25-87
Wording, De (Genesis) 9-28-88
Working Girl 12-14-88